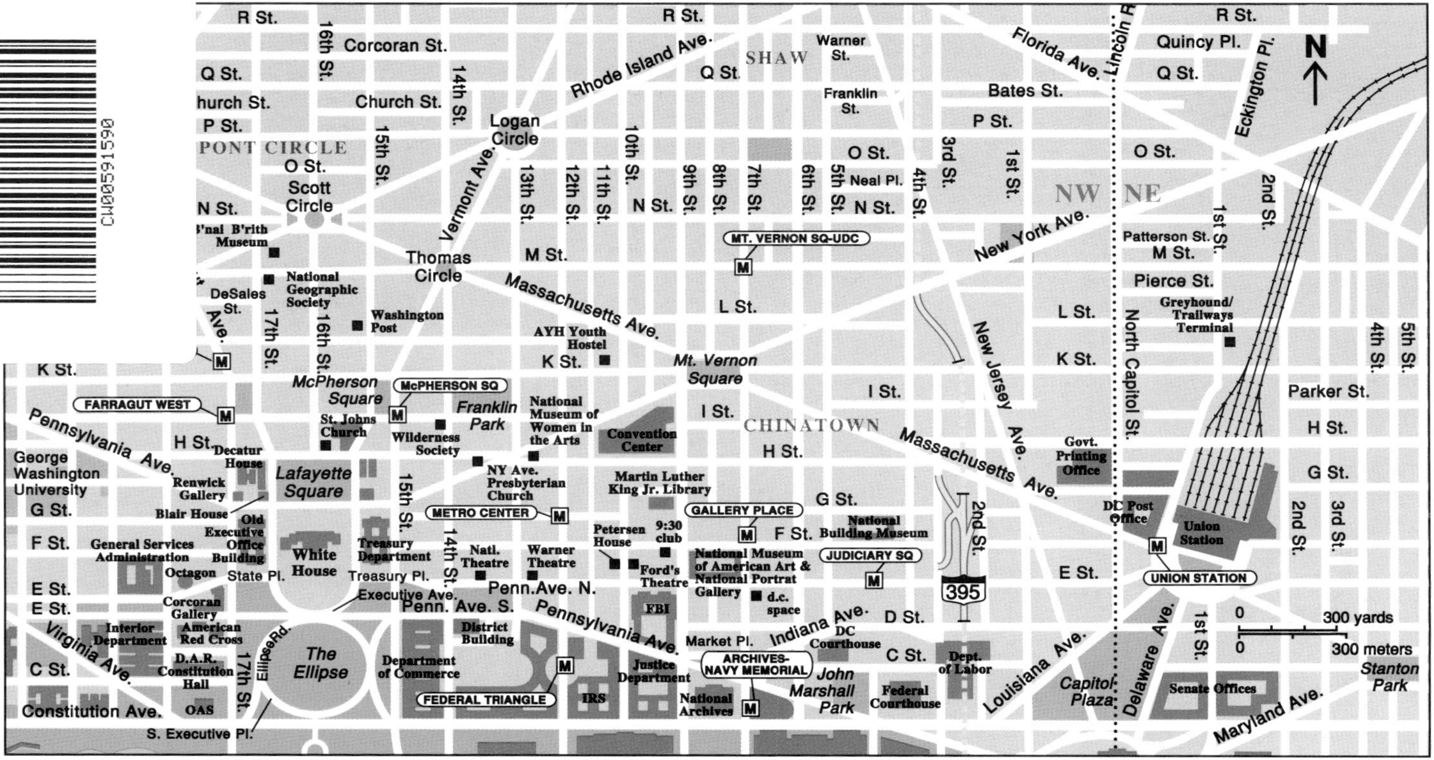

R St.
16th St.
Corcoran St.
Q St.
Church St.
P St.
PONT CIRCLE
O St.
Scott Circle
N St.
B'nai B'rith Museum
National Geographic Society
DeSales St.
17th St.
Washington Post
14th St.
15th St.
Logan Circle
Vermont Ave.
Thomas Circle
Rhode Island Ave.
13th St.
12th St.
11th St.
10th St.
N St.
9th St.
8th St.
7th St.
6th St.
5th St.
Neal Pl.
N St.
4th St.
3rd St.
1st St.
Q St.
SHAW
Warner St.
Franklin St.
Bates St.
P St.
O St.
Florida Ave.
Lincoln Rd.
Quincy Pl.
Q St.
Eckington Pl.
O St.
NW
NE
2nd St.
1st St.
Patterson St.
M St.
Pierce St.
Greyhound/Trailways Terminal
New York Ave.
MT. VERNON SQ-UDC
M St.
Massachusetts Ave.
L St.
AYH Youth Hostel
K St.
Mt. Vernon Square
L St.
K St.
North Capitol St.
New Jersey Ave.
4th St.
5th St.
K St.
FARRAGUT WEST
McPherson Square
McPHERSON SQ
St. Johns Church
Franklin Park
Wilderness Society
National Museum of Women in the Arts
Convention Center
I St.
I St.
CHINATOWN
Parker St.
H St.
Pennsylvania Ave.
H St.
Decatur House
George Washington University
Renwick Gallery
Lafayette Square
15th St.
NY Ave. Presbyterian Church
Martin Luther King Jr. Library
H St.
Massachusetts Ave.
Govt. Printing Office
G St.
G St.
Blair House
Old Executive Office Building
METRO CENTER
GALLERY PLACE
G St.
National Building Museum
DC Post Office
Union Station
2nd St.
3rd St.
2nd St.
F St.
General Services Administration
White House
Treasury Department
14th St.
Natl. Theatre
Warner Theatre
Petersen House
9:30 club
F St.
National Museum of American Art & National Portrait Gallery
JUDICIARY SQ
Octagon
State Pl.
Treasury Pl.
Ford's Theatre
E St.
UNION STATION
E St.
Executive Ave.
Penn. Ave. N.
395
E St.
Corcoran Gallery
Penn. Ave. S.
FBI
d.c. space
Indiana Ave.
D St.
Pennsylvania Ave.
Interior Department
American Red Cross
District Building
DC Courthouse
Market Pl.
Virginia Ave.
Ellipse Rd.
The Ellipse
C St.
Dept. of Labor
Louisiana Ave.
Delaware Ave.
1st St.
0
300 yards
0
300 meters
C St.
D.A.R. Constitution Hall
Department of Commerce
Justice Department
ARCHIVES-NAVY MEMORIAL
John Marshall Park
Federal Courthouse
Capitol Plaza
Senate Offices
Stanton Park
17th St.
FEDERAL TRIANGLE
IRS
National Archives
Constitution Ave.
OAS
S. Executive Pl.
Maryland Ave.

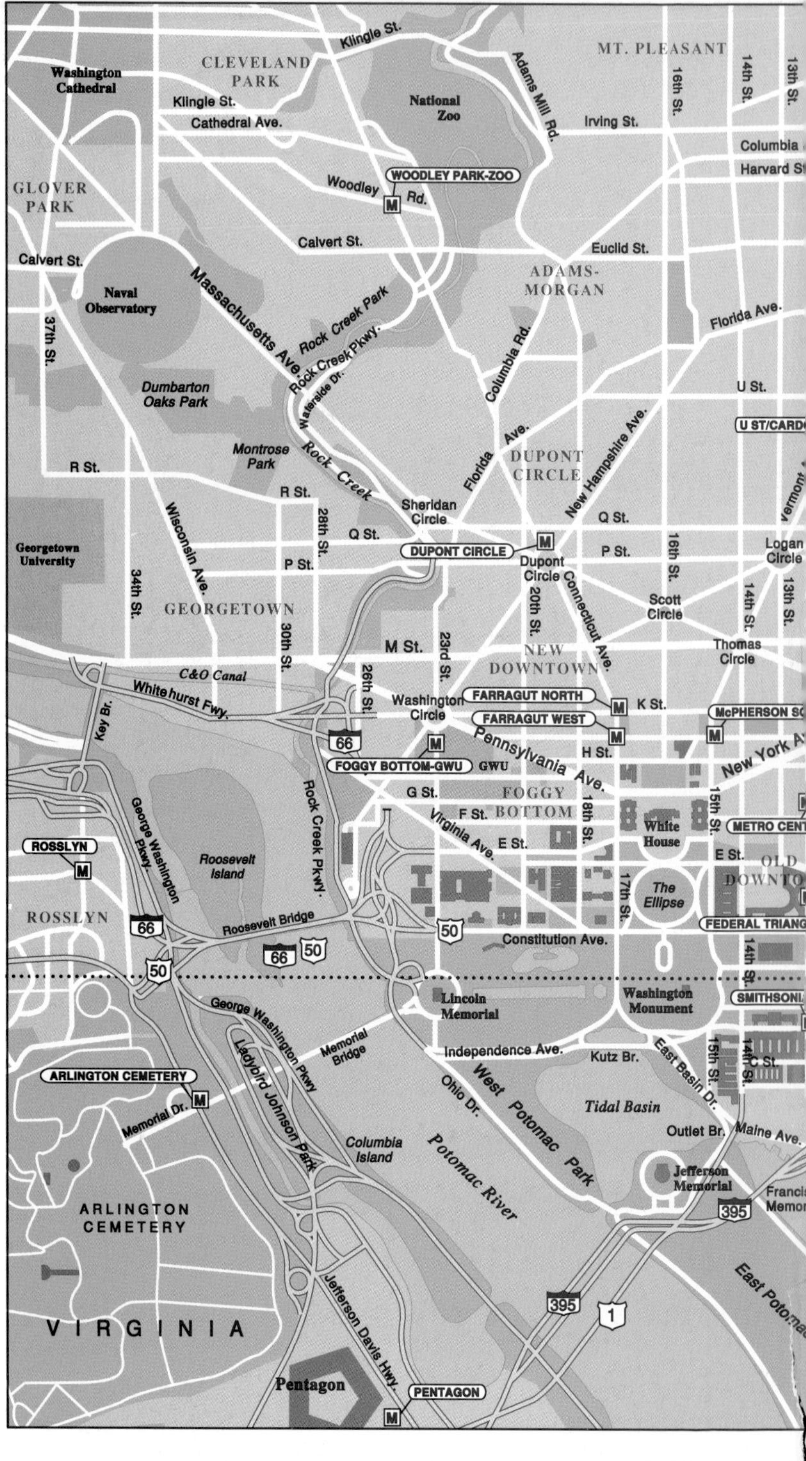

Washington Cathedral
CLEVELAND PARK
Klingle St.
National Zoo
MT. PLEASANT
Adams Mill Rd.
16th St.
14th St.
13th St.
Klingle St.
Cathedral Ave.
Irving St.
Columbia
Harvard St.
GLOVER PARK
Woodley Rd.
WOODLEY PARK-ZOO
Calvert St.
Euclid St.
Calvert St.
Naval Observatory
Massachusetts Ave.
Rock Creek Park
Rock Creek Pkwy.
ADAMS-MORGAN
Florida Ave.
37th St.
Waterside Dr.
Columbia Rd.
U St.
Dumbarton Oaks Park
U ST/CARD
Montrose Park
Rock Creek
DUPONT CIRCLE
New Hampshire Ave.
Florida Ave.
R St.
R St.
Sheridan Circle
Vermont
Q St.
Q St.
28th St.
Wisconsin Ave.
Georgetown University
DUPONT CIRCLE
P St.
P St.
Logan Circle
Dupont Circle
34th St.
GEORGETOWN
20th St.
Connecticut Ave.
16th St.
14th St.
13th St.
Scott Circle
30th St.
M St.
23rd St.
NEW DOWNTOWN
Thomas Circle
C&O Canal
Whitehurst Fwy.
26th St.
Washington Circle
FARRAGUT NORTH
K St.
FARRAGUT WEST
McPHERSON SQ
Key Br.
66
Pennsylvania Ave.
H St.
New York Ave.
FOGGY BOTTOM-GWU
GWU
Rock Creek Pkwy.
G St.
FOGGY BOTTOM
F St.
Virginia Ave.
E St.
18th St.
White House
15th St.
METRO CENTER
ROSSLYN
George Washington Pkwy.
Roosevelt Island
E St.
OLD DOWNTOWN
17th St.
The Ellipse
ROSSLYN
66
Roosevelt Bridge
50
FEDERAL TRIANGLE
Constitution Ave.
66
50
14th St.
50
Lincoln Memorial
Washington Monument
SMITHSONIAN
George Washington Pkwy
Memorial Bridge
Independence Ave.
Kutz Br.
East Basin Dr.
15th St.
14th St.
C St.
ARLINGTON CEMETERY
Ladybird Johnson Park
Ohio Dr.
West Potomac Park
Tidal Basin
Memorial Dr.
Columbia Island
Potomac River
Outlet Br.
Maine Ave.
Jefferson Memorial
Francis Memorial
ARLINGTON CEMETERY
395
East Potomac
395
1
VIRGINIA
Jefferson Davis Hwy.
Pentagon
PENTAGON

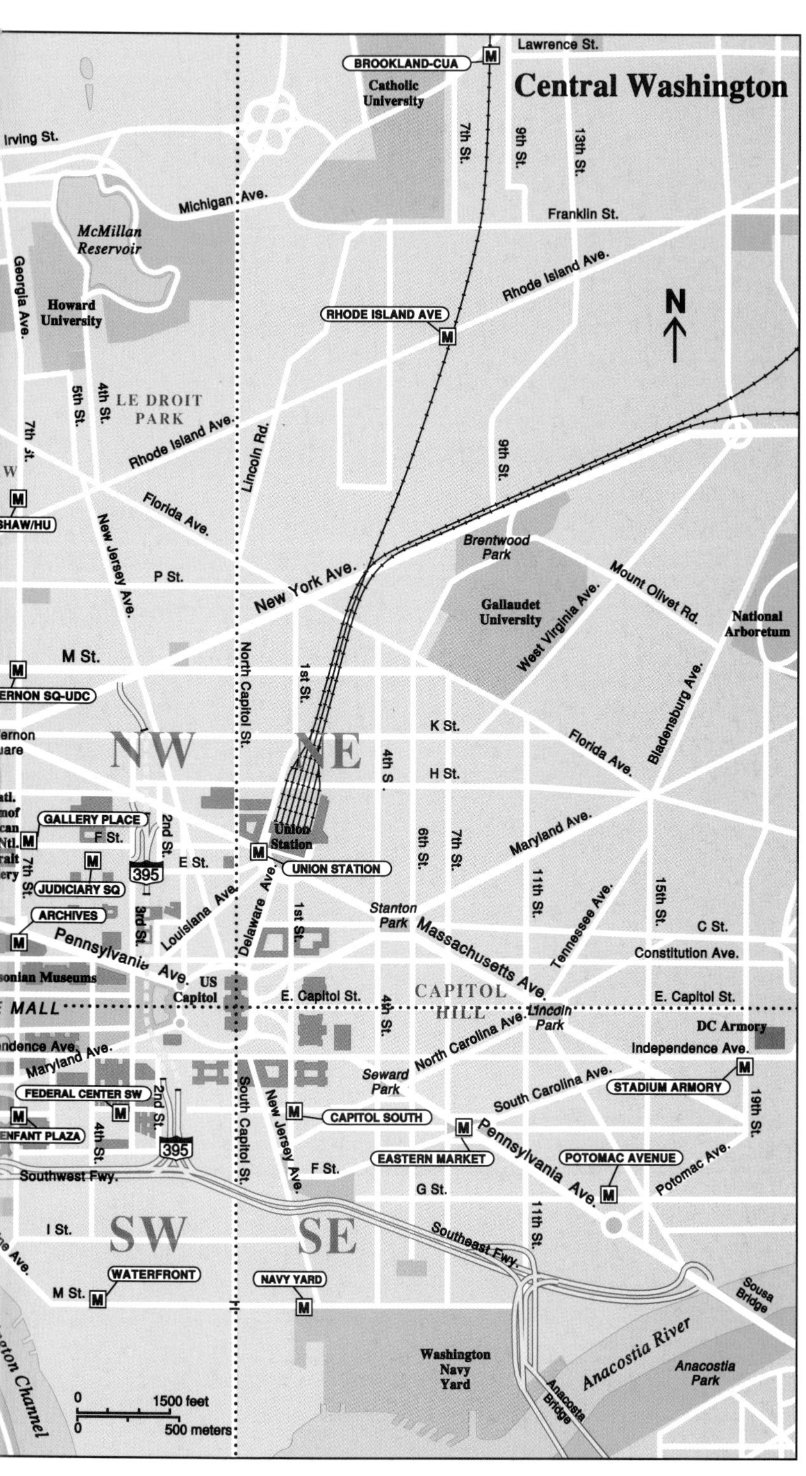
Central Washington
Lawrence St.
BROOKLAND-CUA
Catholic University
Irving St.
Michigan Ave.
McMillan Reservoir
Howard University
Georgia Ave.
7th St.
9th St.
13th St.
Franklin St.
Rhode Island Ave.
RHODE ISLAND AVE
N
LE DROIT PARK
5th St.
4th St.
Lincoln Rd.
SHAW/HU
Florida Ave.
New Jersey Ave.
P St.
New York Ave.
Brentwood Park
Gallaudet University
West Virginia Ave.
Mount Olivet Rd.
National Arboretum
Bladensburg Ave.
M St.
VERNON SQ-UDC
North Capitol St.
1st St.
K St.
NW
NE
H St.
GALLERY PLACE
F St.
2nd St.
E St.
395
JUDICIARY SQ
ARCHIVES
Union Station
UNION STATION
Louisiana Ave.
Delaware Ave.
6th St.
Maryland Ave.
11th St.
Tennessee Ave.
15th St.
C St.
Constitution Ave.
Stanton Park
Massachusetts Ave.
Pennsylvania Ave.
US Capitol
E. Capitol St.
CAPITOL HILL
Lincoln Park
DC Armory
MALL
Independence Ave.
North Carolina Ave.
Seward Park
South Carolina Ave.
STADIUM ARMORY
FEDERAL CENTER SW
South Capitol St.
CAPITOL SOUTH
EASTERN MARKET
POTOMAC AVENUE
19th St.
Potomac Ave.
F St.
G St.
Southwest Fwy.
I St.
SW
SE
Southeast Fwy.
WATERFRONT
M St.
NAVY YARD
Sousa Bridge
Washington Navy Yard
Anacostia River
Anacostia Park
Anacostia Bridge
0
1500 feet
500 meters

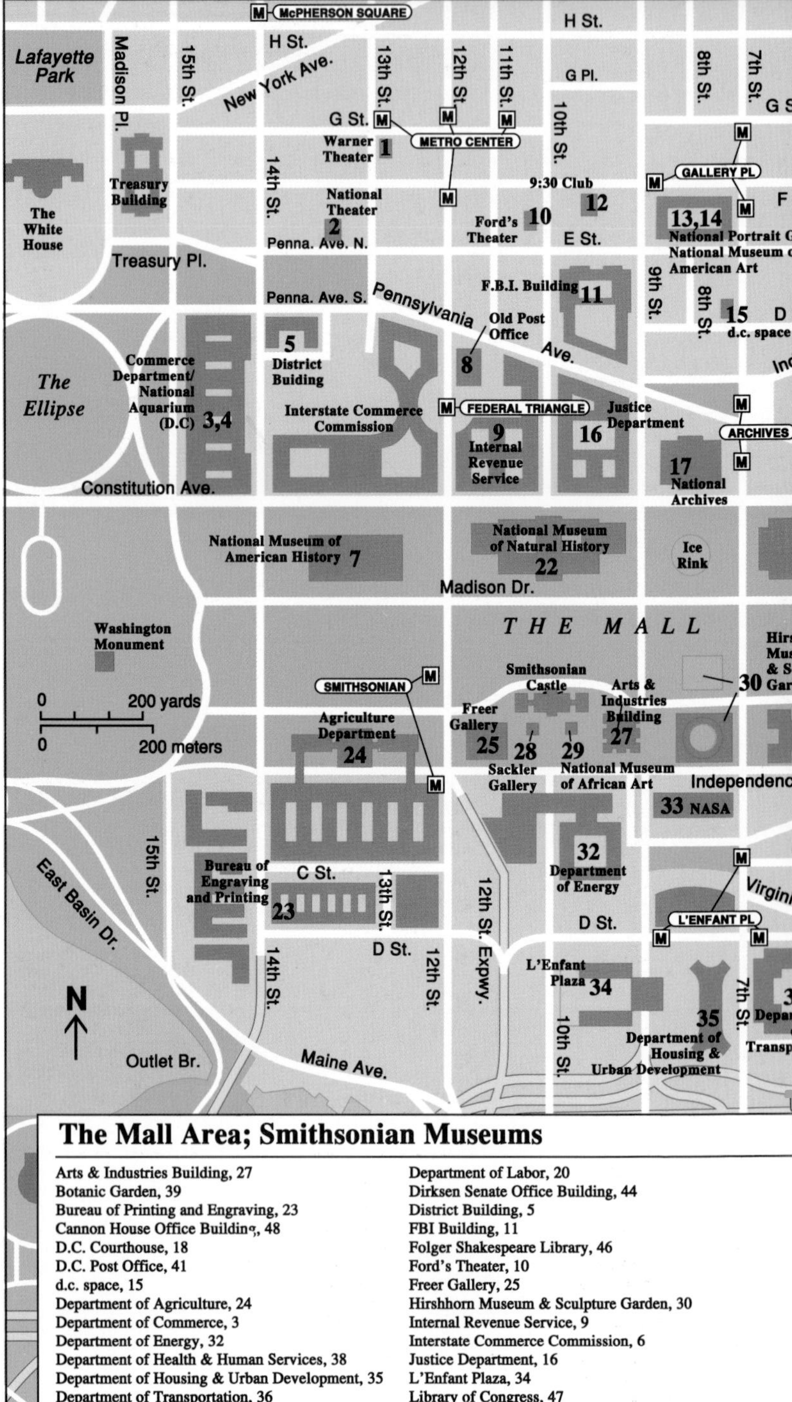

The Mall Area; Smithsonian Museums

Arts & Industries Building, 27
Botanic Garden, 39
Bureau of Printing and Engraving, 23
Cannon House Office Building, 48
D.C. Courthouse, 18
D.C. Post Office, 41
d.c. space, 15
Department of Agriculture, 24
Department of Commerce, 3
Department of Energy, 32
Department of Health & Human Services, 38
Department of Housing & Urban Development, 35
Department of Transportation, 36
Department of Labor, 20
Dirksen Senate Office Building, 44
District Building, 5
FBI Building, 11
Folger Shakespeare Library, 46
Ford's Theater, 10
Freer Gallery, 25
Hirshhorn Museum & Sculpture Garden, 30
Internal Revenue Service, 9
Interstate Commerce Commission, 6
Justice Department, 16
L'Enfant Plaza, 34
Library of Congress, 47

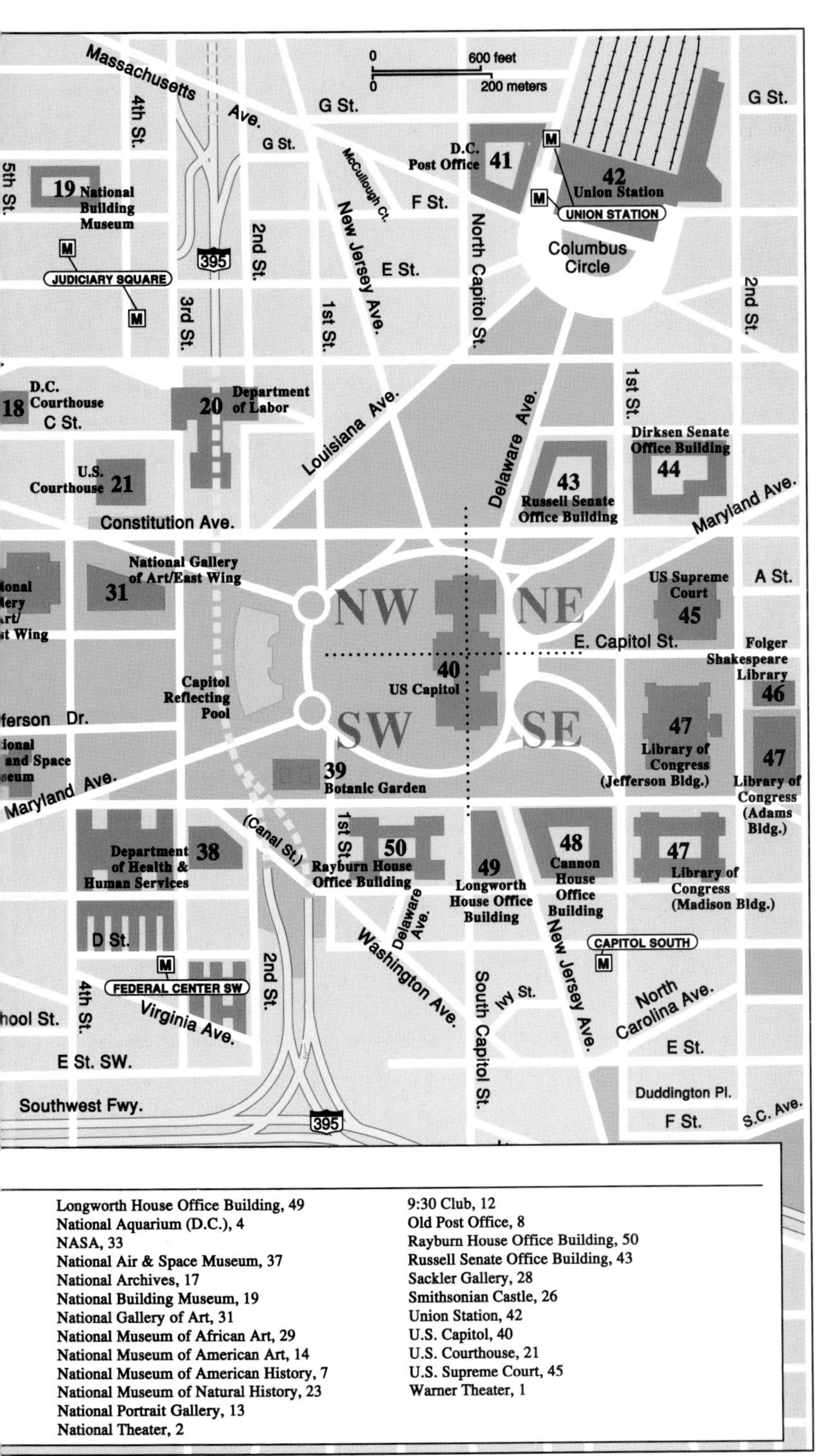

0
600 feet
0
200 meters
Massachusetts Ave.
G St.
G St.
G St.
4th St.
5th St.
19 National Building Museum
JUDICIARY SQUARE
M
395
2nd St.
3rd St.
1st St.
McCullough Ct.
New Jersey Ave.
F St.
E St.
D.C. Post Office 41
North Capitol St.
42 Union Station
UNION STATION
Columbus Circle
2nd St.
1st St.
D.C. Courthouse 18
C St.
20 Department of Labor
Louisiana Ave.
U.S. Courthouse 21
Delaware Ave.
Dirksen Senate Office Building
44
43 Russell Senate Office Building
Maryland Ave.
Constitution Ave.
National Gallery of Art/East Wing 31
US Supreme Court 45
A St.
NW
NE
E. Capitol St.
Folger Shakespeare Library 46
40 US Capitol
Capitol Reflecting Pool
SW
SE
47 Library of Congress (Jefferson Bldg.)
47 Library of Congress (Adams Bldg.)
Maryland Ave.
39 Botanic Garden
Department of Health & Human Services 38
(Canal St.)
1st St.
50 Rayburn House Office Building
49 Longworth House Office Building
48 Cannon House Office Building
47 Library of Congress (Madison Bldg.)
Delaware Ave.
D St.
CAPITOL SOUTH
FEDERAL CENTER SW
4th St.
Virginia Ave.
2nd St.
Washington Ave.
South Capitol St.
Ivy St.
New Jersey Ave.
North Carolina Ave.
E St.
E St. SW.
Duddington Pl.
Southwest Fwy.
395
F St.
S.C. Ave.

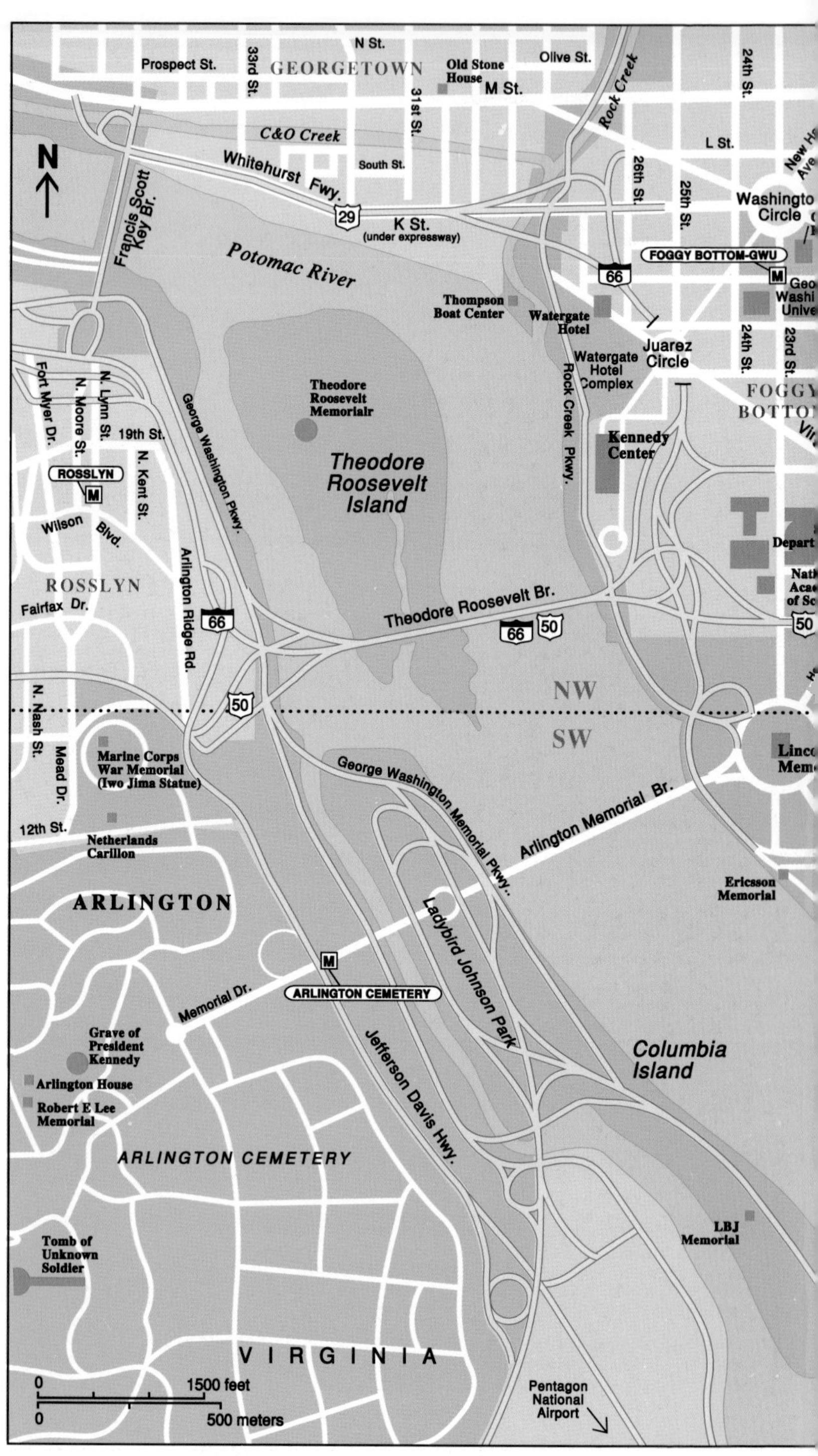
N St.
Prospect St.
GEORGETOWN
33rd St.
Old Stone House
M St.
Olive St.
31st St.
Rock Creek
24th St.
C&O Creek
L St.
Whitehurst Fwy.
South St.
26th St.
25th St.
Washington Circle
29
K St.
(under expressway)
Francis Scott Key Br.
Potomac River
FOGGY BOTTOM-GWU
66
Thompson Boat Center
Watergate Hotel
Juarez Circle
24th St.
23rd St.
Watergate Hotel Complex
Rock Creek Pkwy.
FOGGY BOTTOM
Fort Myer Dr.
N. Moore St.
N. Lynn St.
19th St.
George Washington Pkwy.
Theodore Roosevelt Memorialr
Kennedy Center
N. Kent St.
ROSSLYN
Theodore Roosevelt Island
Wilson Blvd.
Arlington Ridge Rd.
ROSSLYN
Fairfax Dr.
Theodore Roosevelt Br.
66
50
NW
SW
N. Nash St.
Mead Dr.
Marine Corps War Memorial (Iwo Jima Statue)
George Washington Memorial Pkwy.
Arlington Memorial Br.
12th St.
Netherlands Carillon
Ericsson Memorial
ARLINGTON
Ladybird Johnson Park
M
ARLINGTON CEMETERY
Memorial Dr.
Jefferson Davis Hwy.
Columbia Island
Grave of President Kennedy
Arlington House
Robert E Lee Memorial
ARLINGTON CEMETERY
LBJ Memorial
Tomb of Unknown Soldier
VIRGINIA
0
1500 feet
0
500 meters
Pentagon National Airport

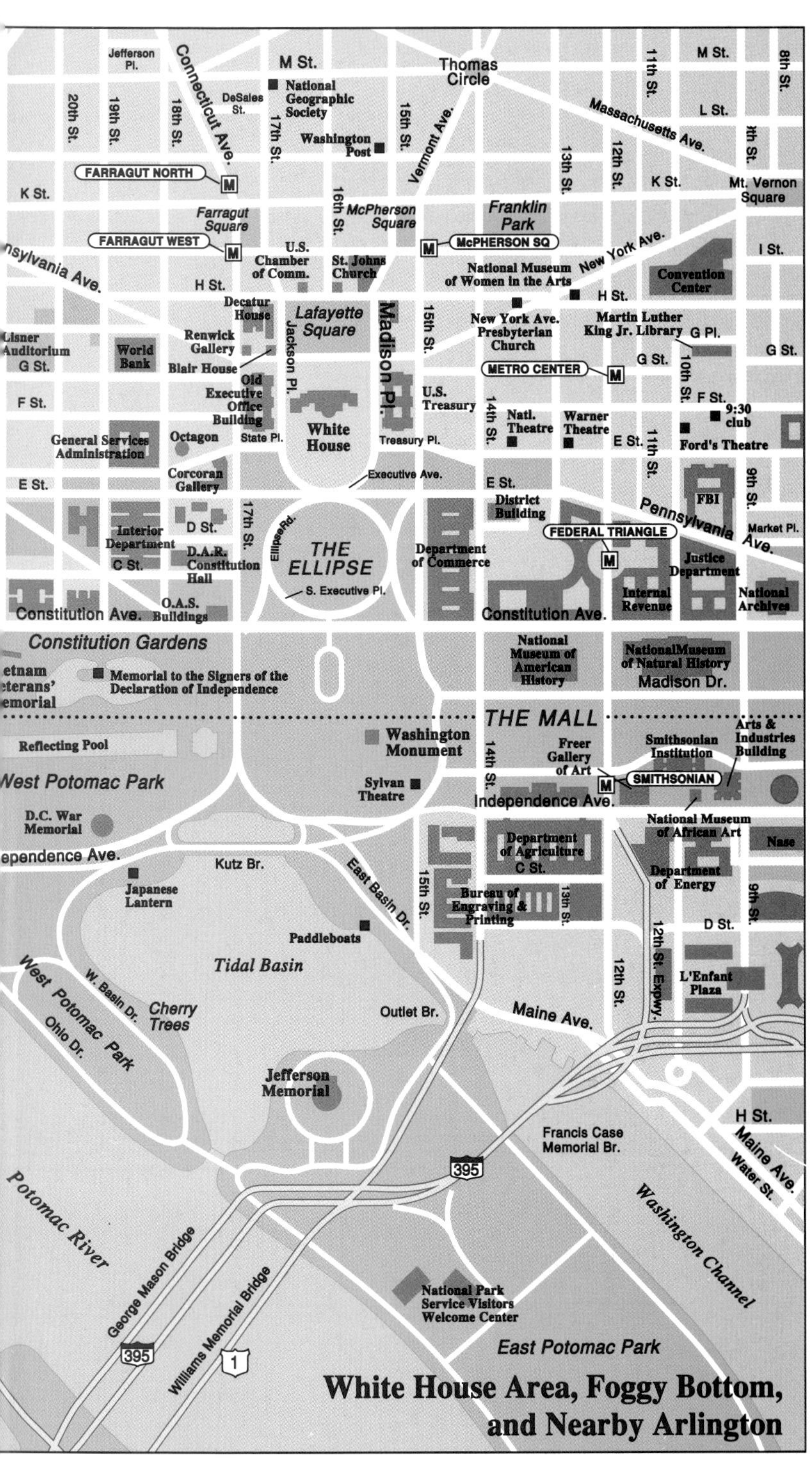

White House Area, Foggy Bottom, and Nearby Arlington
Jefferson Pl.
M St.
Thomas Circle
11th St.
M St.
8th St.
Connecticut Ave.
DeSales St.
National Geographic Society
20th St.
19th St.
18th St.
17th St.
15th St.
Vermont Ave.
Massachusetts Ave.
L St.
Washington Post
13th St.
12th St.
FARRAGUT NORTH
K St.
K St.
Mt. Vernon Square
16th St.
McPherson Square
Franklin Park
Farragut Square
FARRAGUT WEST
McPHERSON SQ
New York Ave.
I St.
Pennsylvania Ave.
U.S. Chamber of Comm.
St. Johns Church
National Museum of Women in the Arts
Convention Center
H St.
H St.
Decatur House
Lafayette Square
Madison Pl.
15th St.
New York Ave. Presbyterian Church
Martin Luther King Jr. Library
G Pl.
Lisner Auditorium
G St.
Renwick Gallery
World Bank
Jackson Pl.
Blair House
G St.
G St.
METRO CENTER
10th St.
Old Executive Office Building
U.S. Treasury
F St.
F St.
White House
14th St.
Natl. Theatre
Warner Theatre
9:30 club
General Services Administration
Octagon
State Pl.
Treasury Pl.
E St.
11th St.
Ford's Theatre
Corcoran Gallery
Executive Ave.
E St.
E St.
9th St.
District Building
FBI
Pennsylvania Ave.
Market Pl.
Interior Department
D St.
17th St.
Ellipse Rd.
THE ELLIPSE
FEDERAL TRIANGLE
C St.
D.A.R. Constitution Hall
Department of Commerce
Justice Department
S. Executive Pl.
Internal Revenue
National Archives
Constitution Ave.
O.A.S. Buildings
Constitution Ave.
Constitution Gardens
National Museum of American History
NationalMuseum of Natural History
Vietnam Veterans' Memorial
Memorial to the Signers of the Declaration of Independence
Madison Dr.
THE MALL
Arts & Industries Building
Reflecting Pool
Washington Monument
14th St.
Freer Gallery of Art
Smithsonian Institution
West Potomac Park
SMITHSONIAN
Sylvan Theatre
Independence Ave.
D.C. War Memorial
National Museum of African Art
Department of Agriculture
Nasa
Independence Ave.
C St.
Kutz Br.
East Basin Dr.
Department of Energy
Japanese Lantern
15th St.
Bureau of Engraving & Printing
13th St.
9th St.
D St.
Paddleboats
Tidal Basin
12th St. Expwy.
12th St.
L'Enfant Plaza
West Potomac Park
W. Basin Dr.
Cherry Trees
Outlet Br.
Maine Ave.
Ohio Dr.
Jefferson Memorial
H St.
Francis Case Memorial Br.
Maine Ave.
Water St.
395
Potomac River
Washington Channel
George Mason Bridge
Williams Memorial Bridge
National Park Service Visitors Welcome Center
East Potomac Park
395
1

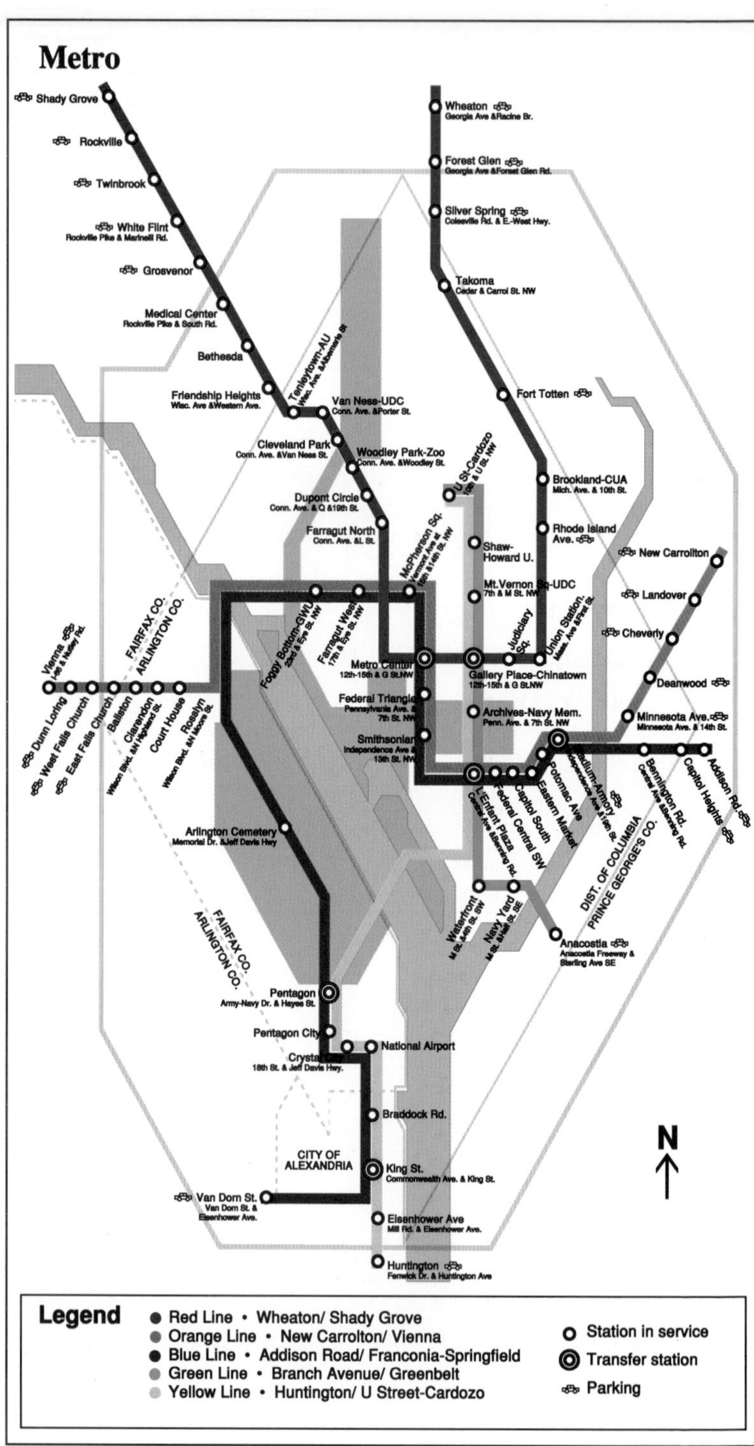

Metro
Shady Grove
Rockville
Twinbrook
White Flint
Rockville Pike & Marinelli Rd.
Grosvenor
Medical Center
Rockville Pike & South Rd.
Bethesda
Friendship Heights
Wisc. Ave &Western Ave.
Tenleytown-AU
Van Ness-UDC
Conn. Ave. &Porter St.
Cleveland Park
Conn. Ave. &Van Ness St.
Woodley Park-Zoo
Conn. Ave. &Woodley St.
Dupont Circle
Conn. Ave. & Q &19th St.
Farragut North
Conn. Ave. &L St.
Wheaton
Georgia Ave &Racine Br.
Forest Glen
Georgia Ave &Forest Glen Rd.
Silver Spring
Colesville Rd. & E.-West Hwy.
Takoma
Cedar & Carrol St. NW
Fort Totten
Brookland-CUA
Mich. Ave. & 10th St.
Rhode Island Ave.
U St-Cardozo
Shaw-Howard U.
Mt.Vernon Sq-UDC
7th & M St. NW
McPherson Sq.
Foggy Bottom-GWU
23rd & Eye St. NW
Farragut West
17th & Eye St. NW
Metro Center
12th-15th & G St.NW
Gallery Place-Chinatown
12th-15th & G St.NW
Judiciary Sq.
Union Station
Federal Triangle
Smithsonian
Archives-Navy Mem.
Penn. Ave. & 7th St. NW
L'Enfant Plaza
Federal Central SW
Capitol South
Eastern Market
Potomac Ave
Stadium-Armory
New Carrollton
Landover
Cheverly
Deanwood
Minnesota Ave.
Minnesota Ave. & 14th St.
Benning Rd.
Capitol Heights
Addison Rd.
DIST. OF COLUMBIA
PRINCE GEORGE'S CO.
Waterfront
Navy Yard
Anacostia
Anacostia Freeway & Sterling Ave SE
FAIRFAX CO.
ARLINGTON CO.
Vienna
Dunn Loring
West Falls Church
East Falls Church
Ballston
Clarendon
Court House
Rosslyn
Arlington Cemetery
Memorial Dr. &Jeff Davis Hwy
Pentagon
Army-Navy Dr. & Hayes St.
Pentagon City
Crystal City
18th St. & Jeff Davis Hwy.
National Airport
Braddock Rd.
CITY OF ALEXANDRIA
King St.
Commonwealth Ave. & King St.
Van Dorn St.
Van Dorn St. & Eisenhower Ave.
Eisenhower Ave
Mill Rd. & Eisenhower Ave.
Huntington
Fenwick Dr. & Huntington Ave
N
Legend
Red Line • Wheaton/ Shady Grove
Orange Line • New Carrollton/ Vienna
Blue Line • Addison Road/ Franconia-Springfield
Green Line • Branch Avenue/ Greenbelt
Yellow Line • Huntington/ U Street-Cardozo
Station in service
Transfer station
Parking

"Value-packed, accurate, and comprehensive..."
—*Los Angeles Times*

"Unbeatable..."—*The Washington Post*

LET'S GO:
USA

is the best book for anyone traveling on a budget. Here's why:

No other guidebook has as many budget listings.

In Los Angeles, we found 12 hotels or hostels for under $19 a night. In Chicago, we found 6 for under $30. We tell you how to get there the cheapest way, whether by bus, train, or plane, and where to get an inexpensive and satisfying meal once you've arrived. There are hundreds of money-saving tips for everyone plus lots of information on student discounts.

LET'S GO researchers have to make it on their own.

Our Harvard-Radcliffe researchers travel on budgets as tight as your own—no expense accounts, no free hotel rooms.

LET'S GO is completely revised every year.

We don't just update the prices, we go back to the places. If a charming restaurant has become an overpriced tourist trap, we'll replace the listing with a new and better one.

No other budget guidebook includes all this:

Coverage of both the cities and the countryside; directions, addresses, phone numbers, and hours to get you there and back; in-depth information on culture, history, and the people; listings on transportation between and within regions and cities; tips on work, study, sights, nightlife, and special splurges, city and regional maps; and much, much more.

LET'S GO is for anyone who wants to see the USA on a budget.

Books by Let's Go, Inc.

Let's Go: Europe
Let's Go: Britain & Ireland
Let's Go: France
Let's Go: Germany, Austria & Switzerland
Let's Go: Greece & Turkey
Let's Go: Israel & Egypt
Let's Go: Italy
Let's Go: London
Let's Go: Paris
Let's Go: Rome
Let's Go: Spain & Portugal

Let's Go: USA
Let's Go: California & Hawaii
Let's Go: Mexico
Let's Go: New York City
Let's Go: The Pacific Northwest, Western Canada & Alaska
Let's Go: Washington, D.C.

LET'S GO:

The Budget Guide to the

USA

1993

Joseph M. Rainsbury
Editor

Jen Medearis
Elizabeth J. Stein
Assistant Editors

Written by
Let's Go, Inc.
a wholly owned subsidiary of
Harvard Student Agencies, Inc.

PAN BOOKS
London, Sydney and Auckland

Helping Let's Go

If you have suggestions or corrections, or just want to share your discoveries, drop us a line. We read every piece of correspondence, whether a 10-page letter, a tacky Elvis postcard, or, as in one case, a collage. All suggestions are passed along to our researcher/writers. Please note that mail received after May 5, 1993 will probably be too late for the 1994 book, but will be retained for the following edition. Address mail to:

Let's Go: USA
Let's Go, Inc.
1 Story Street
Cambridge, MA 02138

In addition to the invaluable travel advice our readers share with us, many are kind enough to offer their services as researchers or editors. Unfortunately, the charter of Let's Go, Inc. and Harvard Student Agencies, Inc. enables us to employ only currently enrolled Harvard students.

Published in Great Britain 1993 by Pan Books Ltd
Cavaye Place, London SW10 9PG
9 8 7 6 5 4 3 2 1

Published in the United States of America
by St. Martin's Press, Inc.

ISBN: 0 330 32694 5

Let's Go: USA is written by the Publishing Division of
Let's Go, Inc., 1 Story Street, Cambridge, Mass. 02138

Printed and bound in the United States of America
on recycled paper with biodegradable soy ink.

Editor	Joseph M. Rainsbury
Assistant Editors	Jen Medearis
	Elizabeth J. Stein
Managing Editor	Blythe N. Grossberg
Publishing Director	Paul C. Deemer
Production Manager	Mark N. Templeton
Office Coordinator	Bart St. Clair
Office Manager	Anne E. Chisholm

Researcher-Writers

California (Bay Area)	Sheila Allen
Illinois, Massachusetts, Michigan, New York, Ohio, Ontario, Rhode Island, Wisconsin	William H. Bachman
New York City	Steven Burt
Delaware, Florida, Georgia, New Jersey, North Carolina, Pennsylvania, South Carolina, Virginia	Tanya Clement
New York (Long Island)	Jennifer Cox
Oregon	Brandon Elizabeth Earp
New York City	Jim Ebenhoh
Arizona, Oklahoma, New Mexico, Texas	Masood Farivar
South Florida	Ethan Golden
Maryland, Washington, D.C.	Caroline Kenney
Southern California and Sierra Nevadas	Ericka L. Kostka
Washington State, Vancouver, BC, Vancouver Island, BC	Mira M. Kothari
Alabama, Arkansas, Georgia, Louisiana, Mississippi, South Carolina, Tennessee	Nell M. Ma'luf
New Jersey and New York City	Dara Mayers
Alaska	John E. McDermott
British Columbia and Yukon	Robert F. McDermott
Massachusetts (Boston)	Jen Medearis
Washington, D.C.	Joe R. Mejía
California, Nevada, (Reno and Carson City)	Mark D. Moody
Connecticut, Massachusetts (Berkshires), Maine, New Brunswick, New Hampshire, Upstate New York, Nova Scotia, Prince Edward Island, Québec	Benjamin Peskoe
Arizona (Grand Canyon North Rim), Colorado, Kansas, Missouri, (Kansas City), Nebraska, Nevada (Las Vegas) Utah, Wyoming	Kiffany Pfister
California (San Francisco)	Charlie Pizarro

Massachusetts (Cambridge, Concord, Lexington)	Joseph M. Rainsbury
Idaho, Montana, North Dakota, South Dakota	Kate Solomon
Massachusetts (Boston)	Elizabeth J. Stein
New York City	Woden Sorrow Teachout
California (Berkeley), Illinois, Iowa, Indiana, Kentucky, Missouri, Ohio, Wisconsin (Apostle Islands)	Kendra Willson
Hawaii	Aiko Yoshikowa

Sales Group Manager	Tiffany A. Breau
Sales Group Representatives	Frances Marguerite Maximé
	Breean T. Stickgold
	Harry J. Wilson
Sales Group Coordinator	Aida Bekele
President	Brian A. Goler
C.E.O.	Michele Ponti

A NOTE TO OUR READERS

The information for this book is gathered by Let's Go's researchers during the late spring and summer months. Each listing is derived from the assigned researcher's opinion based upon his or her visit at a particular time. The opinions are expressed in a candid and forthright manner. Other travelers might disagree. Those traveling at a different time may have different experiences since prices, dates, hours, and conditions are always subject to change. You are urged to check beforehand to avoid inconvenience and surprises. Travel always involves a certain degree of risk, especially in low-cost areas. When traveling, especially on a budget, you should always take particular care to ensure your safety.

Acknowledgments

It took Thomas Mann about ten years to compose *The Magic Mountain.* This book, of comparable size (if not literary stature), took Team USA about 3½ months to write. The difference? The explanation? Both are to be found in the unprecedented array of dedicated and brilliant researcher-writers and editors who worked together in the summer of 1992 to create this guide.

The first people to thank are the researchers on the road in whose tracks every reader will tread. **Will Bachman**—enjoying the relatively spacious confines of his van before beginning life on a nuclear submarine—gave us the straight dope on the Great Lakes region and Cape Cod. Sprinkled liberally throughout his 500+ pages of copy were safety tips ("Freddie the Fish says 'Don't drown, it will spoil your day'") and BachmanStats (250 gallons of gas, 13 notebooks, 5 dozen donuts, and a glue-stick). **Ben Peskoe** endeared the entire editorial crew to him with his keen, sensitive eye and subtle wit; retained in spite of an impossible itinerary in the Northeast and Eastern Canada. His copious, thorough, and orthogonal prose was absosmurfly brilliant. Ben, if I weren't already engaged, I'd marry you. **Kendra Willson,** who *wanted* to research the Midwest, did so with the love only a native could muster. Her quirky, insightful, and ofttimes mathematical copy (streets at a pi/4 tilt to the anticipated compass direction?) kept us entertained for weeks.

Nell Ma'luf, our itinerarant Southern Belle, *chahmed* us with delightful write-ups and souvenirs from the South—the garter belt fits just fine, thank you. New Yorker **Kate Solomon** did her own emulation of *Northern Exposure* as she oohed and aahed her way across the Rockies with marginalia gushing more than Old Faithful. **Masood Farivar**—the only ex-Afgan *Mujahadin* freedom fighter on our staff—took his one man Desert Storm to the Southwest. While there, he endured cut supply-lines (he spent a week in a Houston homeless shelter), intense heat, and treacherous traveling companions. After going AWOL for a month, he resurfaced to send in his last copybatch just under the wire. **Kiffany Pfister** calmly flitted across the Great Plains and Southern Rockies, demonstrating the font of her matchless equanimity in the numerous hot tubs she listed. **Ethan Golden** took time out from saving sea-turtles to research for us in southern Florida. **Tanya Clement** wrote up the Atlantic Seaboard—from Philadelphia to St. Petersburg—with ideosyncratically concise prose.

Not to be forgotten is the office staff in Cambridge, who forewent the excitement of the road to stay within the narrow confines of One Story St. First and foremost I have to thank assistant editors **Jen Medearis** and **Liz Stein** (a.k.a. "Charm and Chutzpah") whose efforts translated our R/W's sprawling prose into WordPerfect for Windows. This book is much, *much* the better for Jen's critical glances at some of my more ludicrous ideas, averting countless tasteless jokes and insipid puns. Her obvious love for the book and concern for its readers was salutarily chastening. As for Liz, her neverflinching approach toward the job kept this book afloat, on-time, and well-written—even while confronting such Herculean labors as a Ben Peskoe or Will Bachman batch. Undoubtedly, she will take the helm of some *Let's Go* book in the future. Thanks also to everyone in **"rent-a-yenta" Blythe**'s ME group for tolerating my wildly rambling mind and groanible humor. Particularly, thanks to **Rebecca** and **René** who, from the first meeting at One Story St. in March were outgoing, friendly, and supportive—despite my rather reserved nature. Thanks also go to **Bart St. Clair** who marshalled the insanely intricate tasks of keeping track of all the copy, making sure our researchers got paid and our typists and callers hired.

Finally, I'd like to thank the people in my non-*Let's Go* life. This is self-indulgent, I realize, but necessary. First, thanks to my soon-to-be-wife Amanda Shaw for making this the most exciting, interesting, and fun summer in my life—*in spite* of the Wanker. Thanks also to Dan, Amy, Lisa, Kathy, Debbie, Venus, Chris and the Shaws for keeping in touch even when I didn't. Finally, thanks to Mom and Dad, whose budget travel exploits make the bargains in here pale in comparison. Off to herd sheep I go...

—JMR

Every summer, the Let's Go offfice is jammed with great, however underpaid, people who are ready to cook you great food and do proofreading for you at 2am the morning before your book is due. What else could a lowly AE want? There are a million people to thank, and as we know, I'm slightly impractical (with an olive on top) and am going to try to thank them all: the PWACH guys were the answer to our dream. Pete "what's this Napa stuff, why don't you just rip my heart out and feed it to a gov jock" Keith got through NYC in no time at all, saving us hours of worry; Mike "the proofreading God" Balagur caught every format error, adding in a comment here and there about his mom's apple pie. And then there was the brilliant woman who hired them, Rebecca "I had to turn off the television when Buchanan came on or I'd vomit" Jeschke, who infused an ounce of liberalism into every Let's Go-er this summer, maybe even Harry. To Blythe "I'm getting a little tired of everyone telling me I'm loud...did you eat enough?" Grossberg, we owe thanks for letting us know that this book was on the right track—we needed the encouragement. Mark "the brains behind Let's Go, and a great guy to boot" Templeton deserves a REALLY good night's sleep when this is all over. Thanks also to Mike V. and Al M. for NYWAS (most especially Hoboken), and to Rick, who serves up some mean spaghetti with a southern accent. And then, there were the researchers—some of the best in the world. Kiffany cheerfully located every hot tub and friendly desk manager in the Rockies; Masood, however errant, provided us with insightful research of the southwest; Ethan saved frogs while doing a fantastic job on the copy; Nell taught us how to love the south; and Tanya showed us a new way to research. Sarah and Marian let me live with them without ever having met me, going far beyond the call of duty to make me feel welcome, and Carolyn was kind and tolerant in all things, most especially showing me the ropes of Let's Go. But no one can top six of the most beautiful women in the world, my year-round roommates, Megan, Heather, Ida, Jeanne, Nancy, and Sara, who make saying "You're what?!" in the dining hall a whole new experience. Joe "Punmaster" Rainsbury was a great editor who did everything possible to improve this book, all the while providing daily Punbreaks at 4pm. He is a funny, and all around goofy guy. Best wishes in marriage, Joe and Amanda. The best decision Joe made was to hire Liz. In the end, it was Liz; hell, in the beginning it was Liz. Liz is the only reason I got through this summer. Early—within a few days—I turned to her and told her my life story. God knows what she did to deserve that; in some cosmic way (that's her word, not mine), I knew she was the one to trust. And immediately, people said we were attached at the hip. She saved me professionally and socially, and I owe it all to her. Liz is beautiful and funny, and damn nice to have around, besides, her legs, they're like buttah. If ever you need a fellow worker who will love and hate the job as much as you, call on Liz. There's no one like her. As always, I must thank mom, dad, Donald, John, Ellen, Rich, and Molly, of course, and Janine, Jessica, Anna, and Ted for their love and support.

—JMM

Why don't I have any copy to finalize? No intros to write, no marginalia to read. It's September, and the deed is done. And, if you look at the credits page, you'll see just how many people it took to do it. To thank them all as completely as they deserve would take half again as many pages as the book itself, but I have a feeling that we probably shouldn't eliminate the entire East Coast in favor of my undying gratitude. Still, there are some people to whom I owe thanks so deep that this book would not be complete without them. I have to start with Joe, to whom I owe my place on the title page, and whom I can never thank enough for having given me the chance to work with him and Jen on making U.S.A. into a book we could be proud of. Best of luck on married life and Australian shepherding; just think, the sheep can mow your lawn for you! Ben, you can tell me stories anytime; your marginalia kept me laughing straight through the summer. Kate wins the cheeriness award; I want to drive straight through your itinerary and see every sight you loved so much. Kendra, your dedication and your descriptions made me look at the Midwest in a whole new way—will you be my pen pal? And Will, for picking the best restaurants in Toronto, for knowing when to cut as well as when to add, and for reorganizing everything you set your eyes upon, I love you...even though your copybatches were so long that typing them in almost gave me carpal tunnel syndrome. Blythe, our resident Jewish Mother, I think of you fondly every time I eat a bowl of chicken soup (and every time I hear anything about Madison, Wisconsin!). Andrew and Nora, thanks for the info that lent just that extra touch of hip-and-breeziness to Boston and Cambridge, and Andrew, thank you again and again and again for seeing us through typesetting with a smile. Pete, Mike, Al, Rick and Steve, you are godsends; without you we never would have been able to finish NYWAS in time. PWACH-guys, thanks for teaming up with us USA-girls to create a GI that isn't just a waste of space. Rebecca, from candidates to AEs, you sure know how to pick 'em! Have fun in the Dominican Republic; I'll miss you. Mark, thank you for EVERYTHING; you saved our sorry fannies many a time, and if some of your equanimity rubs off on me then I will have Really learned something this summer. For intros, 'Becca, Elijah, Gary, Jonathan, Mark, Muneer, Nora and René, thank you thank you thank you! Boy, did we need you. Jen. How is it possible that we didn't know each other before this summer began? You did more than save my sanity. I've run out of words to thank you with; I only hope that some of our partnership this summer can continue even when the three feet of distance between our desks has turned into 3000 miles (or is that 3000 mi.?) of Atlantic Ocean. So Mom and Dad, here it is. A book...a real one!

—EJS

About Let's Go

A generation ago, Harvard Student Agencies, a three-year-old non-profit corporation dedicated to providing employment to students, was doing a booming business booking charter flights to Europe. One of the extras offered to passengers on these flights was a 20-page mimeographed pamphlet entitled *1960 European Guide,* a collection of tips on continental travel compiled by the HSA staff. The following year, students traveling to Europe researched the first full-fledged edition of *Let's Go: Europe,* a pocket-sized book with tips on budget accommodations, irreverent write-ups of sights, and a decidedly youthful slant.

Throughout the 60s, the series reflected the times: a section of the 1968 *Let's Go: Europe* was entitled "Street Singing in Europe on No Dollars a Day." During the 70s *Let's Go* evolved into a large-scale operation, adding regional European guides and expanding coverage into North Africa and Asia. In the 80s, we launched coverage of the United States, developed our research to include concerns of travelers of all ages, and finetuned the editorial process that continues to this day. The early 90s saw the introduction of *Let's Go* city guides.

1992 has been a big year for us. We are now Let's Go, Incorporated, a wholly owned subsidiary of Harvard Student Agencies. To celebrate this change, we moved from our dungeonesque Harvard Yard basement to an equally dungeonesque third-floor office in Harvard Square, and we purchased a high-tech computer system that allows us to typeset all of the guides in-house. Now in our 33rd year, *Let's Go* publishes 17 titles, covering more than 40 countries. This year *Let's Go* proudly introduces two new entries in the series: *Let's Go: Paris* and *Let's Go: Rome.*

But these changes haven't altered our tried and true approach to researching and writing travel guides. Each spring 90 Harvard University students are hired as researcher-writers and trained intensively during April and May for their summer tour of duty. Each researcher-writer then hits the road for seven weeks of travel on a shoestring budget, researching six days per week and overcoming countless obstacles in the quest for better bargains.

Back in Cambridge, Massachusetts, an editorial staff of 32, a management team of six, and countless typists and proofreaders—all students—spend more than six months pushing nearly 8000 pages of copy through a rigorous editing process. By the time classes start in September, the typeset guides are off to the printers, and they hit bookstores world-wide in late November. Then, by February, next year's guides are well underway.

CONTENTS

$15.50 tax incl
dormitory 4/6 beds
$45.00
single room
$60.00
double room
☆ hostel here
HOLLYWOOD HILLS HOSTEL
1921 N HIGHLAND AVE
1(213) 850-7733
• free airport pickup 3 or more people.
• free Amtrak, Greyhound pickup
• free breakfast
• free linen and blankets
• free cable TV, MTV, movies
• free tours to Universal Studios & Magic Mountain
• tours to Disneyland and Mexico, San Diego
• free Venice Beach tours everyday
• $20 car rentals available.
discount airline tickets.
5 mins to Manns Chinese Theatre.
close to all clubs • open 24 hrs.
chinese theatre
Highland Avenue
Adventures in HOLLYWOOD
come stay with us and be treated like a movie star
Hollywood Boulevard
grey hound
Vine Street
bus
Hostels - Some Like it Hot!

List of Maps

General Introduction

How to Use This Book

Let's Go: U.S.A. is written especially for the budget traveler. Our researchers travel on a tight budget, and their concerns are the same as yours: how to get from place to place, fill their stomachs, take in the sights, enjoy the evenings and get some sleep, all in the most economical way possible. The information contained herein represents the accumulated wisdom of over 30 years of *Let's Go* researcher/writers. Their honest appraisals of everything from hostels to hamburgers will give you the freedom to experience the country without getting bogged down in logistics. They do the legwork so you won't have to.

Before you dive into our guide, there are a few things you'll need to know about its organization. The first portion of the book is the **General Introduction** which provides information that you will need to know before you leave. **Planning Your Trip** contains details which will help you to prepare for your peregrinations: where to write for information, how to maintain your supply of money, how and what to pack, and how to stay safe and healthy. **Work and Study** gives ideas for those whose trip to the U.S. is more than just a vacation. **Travelers with Specific Concerns** provides information for students, seniors, women, travelers with disabilities, gay and lesbian travelers, those journeying with children, and the intrepid lone voyager. **Getting Around** sorts out the various modes of transportation around the country. **Accommodations** covers everything from cheap motels to youth hostels to bed and breakfasts. **Camping and the Outdoors** provides detailed information for those interested in camping, hiking, and sporting in the region's myriad parks, forests, and waterways. **For International Visitors** is a guide to visas, customs, inexpensive transportation from around the world, foreign exchange, and the postal and telephone systems in the U.S. **American Culture in 4409 Words or Less** is a very brief introduction to the history, literature, movies and television, music, sports, theater and visual art of the United States.

The **listings** in this book are grouped into two major sections: the **U.S.A.** (itself divided into eight regions, with Alaska, California, Florida, Hawaii and Washington, DC separate from any regional affiliation) and **Canada. Regional Introductions** convey the essence of the areas in order to help you make general travel plans. The regions of the United States and provinces of Canada are arranged roughly east to west. Within each region, states are organized alphabetically**. State and Provincial Introductions** impart a bit of the history and some of the feel of the state or province. After these introductions are **State and Provincial Practical Information** which list sales tax figures as well as important state tourist addresses and phone numbers.

City Listings are arranged alphabetically within each state. **City Introductions** briefly acquaint you with what each area has to offer the visitor. For larger cities and more popular sights, these introductions are followed by a **City Practical Information** section, listing such crucial resources and information such as tourist centers, emergency numbers and crisis hotlines, local and intercity transport, post offices and telephone area codes. This is followed by sections on **Getting There and Getting Around, Accommodations, Food, Sights and Activities, Entertainment** and **Seasonal Events.** Listings for smaller towns and other sights use paragraph form to help you find the sights and get fed, lodged and oriented (in that order); if there is no Practical Information section, check the end of the listing for ZIP codes and area codes. The **maps** throughout *Let's Go* are useful for general orientation and trip planning; they do *not* take the place of a good road atlas or a more detailed map of the region you plan to visit.

Keep in mind that, although our researchers beat an "annual trail across the nation, there are parts of America as yet undiscovered. Always keep an eye out for attractions

PACIFIC STANDARD TIME
MOUNTAIN STANDARD TIME
BRITISH COLUMBIA
ALBERTA
SASKATCHEWAN
MANITOBA
Vancouver
Calgary
Regina
Victoria
Winnipeg
Seattle
WASHINGTON
Olympia
Spokane
Coeur d'Alene
Portland
Salem
OREGON
Helena
MONTANA
Billings
NORTH DAKOTA
Bismarck
SOUTH DAKOTA
Pierre
Missouri River
Boise
IDAHO
WYOMING
Casper
NEBRASKA
Omah
Lincoln
Reno
Sacramento
Carson City
NEVADA
Salt Lake City
Provo
UTAH
Cheyenne
Boulder
Denver
COLORADO
KANSAS
San Francisco
CALIFORNIA
Las Vegas
Colorado River
ROCKY MOUNTAINS
PACIFIC OCEAN
Los Angeles
ARIZONA
Phoenix
Santa Fe
Albuquerque
NEW MEXICO
OKLAHOMA
San Diego
Tucson
El Paso
TEXAS
San Antonio
ALASKA STANDARD TIME
ALASKA
Fairbanks
YUKON TERR.
Anchorage
Juneau
N
0 kilometers 500
0 miles 300

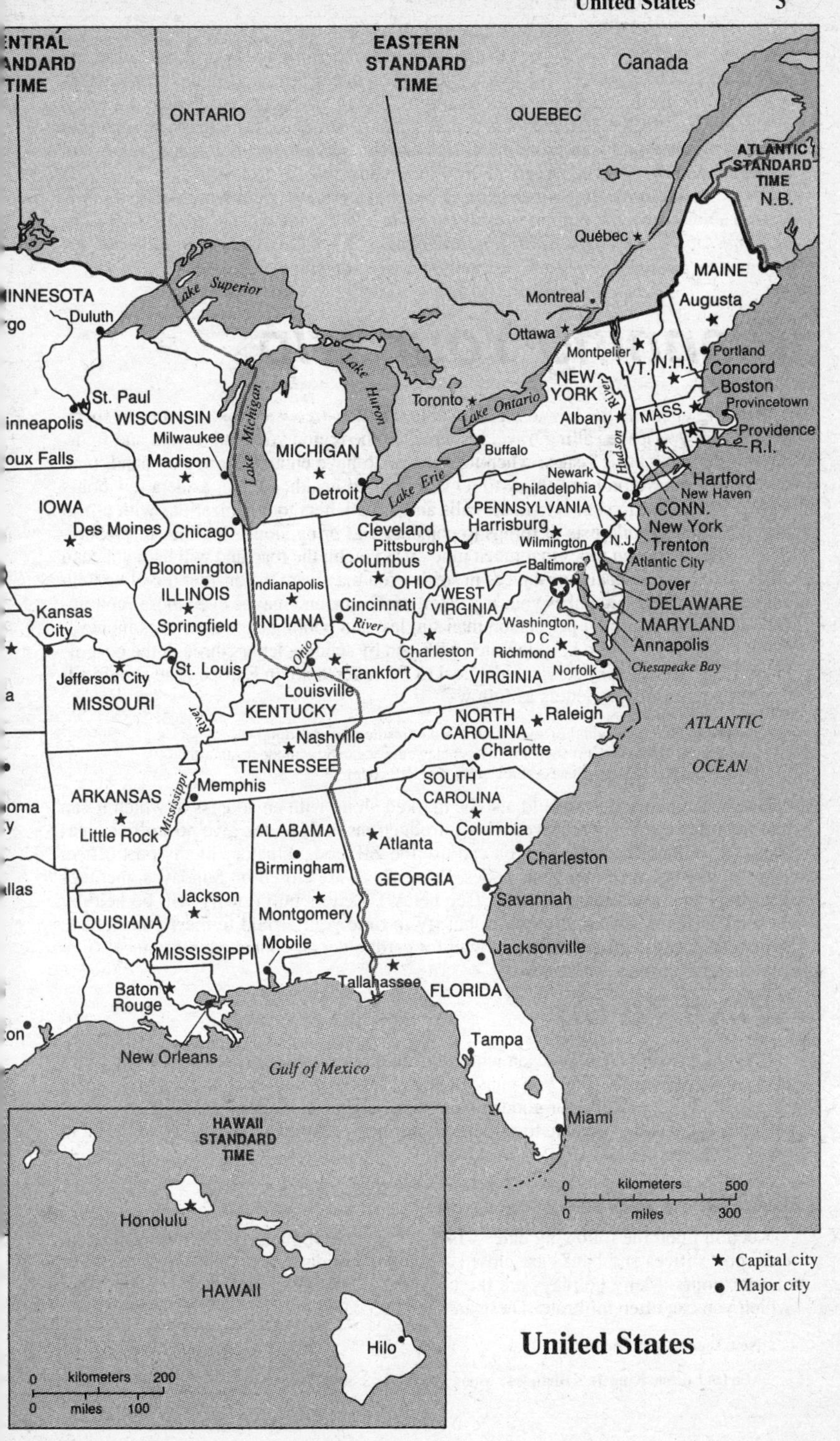

United States

and options that *Let's Go* doesn't list, and follow your spirit and your imagination. Be sure to check other sources; the tourist bureaus of states, provinces and regions can always provide fresh and detailed information. Though we update our listings annually, prices always change, and businesses may open or shut between our press-time (the summer of 1992) and your travel-time. Use our guide as a tool rather than a crutch, and always remember to write or call ahead. Enjoy your trip!

If you intend to travel to other parts of North America or want more detailed information about a specific region, consult *Let's Go: The Pacific Northwest, Western Canada and Alaska, Let's Go: California and Hawaii, Let's Go: Mexico,* or either of our city guides, *Let's Go: New York City* and *Let's Go: Washington, D.C.*

Planning Your Trip

Planning ahead is the key to an enjoyable, anxiety-free vacation. Be sure to spend time before you leave calling travel resources in the region you plan to visit and figuring out the most basic issues: when to go, how to have enough money on hand, (and how *much* to have on hand), how to remain in good health, etc. Set aside a few hours well before your trip begins to make calls and write letters to organizations with useful information. Compile lists of things to consider and bring along. An hour of preparation will save you ten times that much time once you hit the road and will help you take crises and unforeseen circumstances in stride. You may want to consider traveling with a few companions—it makes your trip safer, more fun, and maybe even more economical; doubles are cheaper per person than singles, and pooling expenses saves money.

People back home can keep in touch with you by sending letters through the post office's **General Delivery** service, identical to *Poste Restante* in Europe. You should address General Delivery letters as follows:

Joe Blow (Full name with last name underlined to insure proper sorting)
c/o General Delivery (Just write this. Don't play cutesy games with the Postmaster)
Twisp, WA 98111 (City, State Abbreviation, and ZIP code)

His or her arrival date should also be marked along with an address to which it can be forwarded if it is not retrieved. City introductions in this book give post office locations, as well as ZIP codes, or you can use the ZIP code directory in any post office; large cities may have numerous codes. Post offices are closed on Sunday, sometimes Saturday, and on national holidays (see below). Letters purportedly will be held by General Delivery for up to 30 days, but try to time your arrival to meet your letters. American Express offices also hold mail for cardholders if contacted in advance.

When To Go

Traveling during the off-season will save you money—you will often find that prices decrease significantly—but you may not get a chance to soak up all the sights. In some cases, the season is "off" for good reason; many sights and facilities close down when the tourists go home. Be sure to call ahead of time to ensure that the sights you want to see will be open.

Official Holidays

Keep in mind the following dates when you plan your vacation. Government agencies, post offices and banks are closed on certain holidays, and businesses may have shorter hours. Many holidays are the occasions for parades and public celebrations which you can often infiltrate. These are the 1993 dates:

New Year's Day: Fri., Jan. 1

Martin Luther King Jr.'s Birthday: Mon., Jan. 18 (U.S. only)

Groundhog's Day: Tues., Feb. 2 (Although this is not a national holiday, it is *very* important in the United States. Legend has it that each year on this day, a groundhog emerges from his burrow in Punxsutawny, Pennsylvania, and then gazes around. If he sees his shadow, then six more weeks of winter will follow. If he doesn't, spring is on its way.)

Presidents' Day: Mon., Feb. 15 (U.S. only)

Good Friday: Fri., April 9

Easter Sunday: Sun., April 11

Easter Monday: Mon., April 12 (Canada only)

Victoria Day: Mon., May 24 (Canada only)

Memorial Day: Mon., May 24 (U.S. only)

La Fête Nationale/La Fête du Saint Jean Baptiste: Thurs., June 24 (Québec)

Canada Day: Thurs., July 1 (Canada only)

Independence Day: Sun., July 4 (U.S. only)

Heritage Day: Mon., Aug. 2 (Alberta only)

British Columbia Day: Mon., Aug. 2 (BC only)

Discovery Day: Mon., Aug. 23 (Yukon only)

Labor Day: Mon., Sept. 6

Thanksgiving Day: Mon., Oct. 11 (Canada only)

Columbus Day: Mon., Oct. 11 (U.S. only)

Alaska Day: Mon., Oct. 18 (Alaska only)

Election Day: Tues., Nov. 2 (U.S. only)

Veterans Day (U.S.)/Remembrance Day (Canada): Thurs., Nov. 11

Thanksgiving Day: Thurs., Nov. 25 (U.S. only)

Christmas Day: Sat., Dec. 25

Boxing Day: Sun., Dec. 26 (Canada except Yukon)

Useful Organizations

As you plan your itinerary, it's a good idea to consult the listings for the specific destinations you intend to include. Chambers of Commerce and Visitors Centers for individual cities, towns and sights can send you information in advance that may help you to plan (see the Practical Information sections for addresses). One general resource worth writing to is the **U.S. Government Printing Office.** Among the U.S. government's many publications are a wide selection of travel and recreation guides. *Let's Go* lists many of the most useful, but you can call or write for complete bibliographies. Bibliography #17 deals with outdoor activities in general, and #302 with travel to particular regions. The pamphlet *Travel and Tourism* covers travel within the U.S. To receive free bibliographies or to order a specific publication, write or call the Superintendent of Documents, U.S. Government Printing Office, Washington, DC 20402 (202-783-3238). Each state and province also has its own tourism bureau, which can refer you to other useful organizations, send you travel brochures and maps, and answer your specific questions about the region. For maps, contact the **Forsyth Travel Library,** 9154 W. 57th St., P.O. Box 2975, Shawnee Mission, KS 66201 (800-367-7984), a mail-order service that stocks a wide range of city, area and country maps. (For other organizations, see Additional Information for International Visitors.)

Money

The best things in life are free. Inferior things abound, of course, and they all cost money. Your budget should be a projection of how much you will spend on those inferior items. When you devise your budget, keep in mind a variety of surcharges which will inflate your expenses on the road. Prices in stores and restaurants (and thus in *Let's Go*) may not include a state or provincial **sales tax** of up to 14%, which will be added before you pay. *Let's Go* lists the state sales tax under each state's Practical Information section. Many states have special hotel taxes as well. Waiters, taxi drivers and many others will expect you to add a **tip** to the bill: 15% is the general rule. Bellhops and airport porters expect about a dollar per piece of luggage. It is also customary to tip bartenders 25¢ to $1 a drink and 50¢ to $2 for a pitcher.

No matter *how* low your budget, if you plan to travel for more than a couple of days you will need to keep handy a much larger amount of cash than usual. Carrying it around, even in a money belt, is risky; personal checks from home may not be acceptable no matter how many forms of ID you have (even banks may shy away from accepting checks). Inevitably you will have to rely on some combination of the innovations of the modern financial world, but keep their shortcomings in mind.

Banks and Electronic Banking

In the U.S., banks are usually open weekdays 9am to 5pm, and some are open Saturdays from 9am to noon or 1pm. Canadian banks are open Monday through Friday 10am to 3pm, in some areas with extended hours on Fridays and/or business hours on Saturdays. All banks, government agencies and post offices are closed on legal holidays (see Official Holidays above), and on Sunday. When you arrive in a major city, or if in a smaller town you know you will need to use a bank, find out the hours of the major bank(s); they may vary somewhat from place to place.

Whatever forms of currency substitutes you carry, you will need to periodically refresh your cash supply. **Automatic teller machines (ATMs)** (operated by bank cards) offer 24-hr. service in banks, groceries, and gas stations across the U.S., but you'll need to find out whether or not your bank belongs to a network with machines in the region. The **Cirrus** network (800-4-CIRRUS or 424-7787) includes First Interstate in the West, New England's Baybanks, and New York's Manufacturer's Hanover. The **Plus** network (800-THE-PLUS or 843-7587) includes Bank of America in the West, New York's Chase Manhattan, and First City Bank of Dallas. Call the toll-free numbers from a touch-tone phone to locate machines near you. Plus is also the most widely accepted ATM card in Canada (CIBC, among others, is on Plus). **American Express, Visa** and **Mastercard** (see Credit Cards below) work in Cirrus and Plus machines if the operating bank issues the credit card; check with local banks about these services.

Don't rely on ATMs too much—there can be a service charge for each transaction, and there is generally a limit on how much you can withdraw on any given day ($250 for most banks).

Traveler's Checks

Traveler's checks are the safest way to carry large sums of money. They are refundable if lost or stolen, and many issuing agencies offer additional services; ask about refund hotlines, message relaying, and emergency assistance. Most tourist establishments will accept travelers checks and almost any bank will cash them. Usually banks sell traveler's checks for a 1% commission, although your own bank may waive the surcharge. The American Automobile Association (AAA) offers commission-free traveler's checks to its members. Buying checks in small denominations ($20 checks rather than $50 ones or higher) is safer and more convenient—otherwise, after having made a small-to-medium purchase, you're back to carrying a large amount of cash. If the bank doesn't have small denominations available, try a larger institution or come back another day. Be prepared to convert at least US$100 into traveler's checks—most places will not exchange less than that.

Always keep the receipts from the purchase of your traveler's checks, a list of their serial numbers, and a record of which you've cashed. Keep these in a separate place from the checks themselves, since they contain the information you will need to replace your checks if they are stolen. It's also a good idea to leave the serial numbers with someone at home as a back-up if you lose your copy. Larger firms like American Express can provide immediate refunds at their branch offices. Call any of the toll-free numbers below to find out the advantages of a particular type of check and the name of a bank near you that sells them.

American Express: 800-221-7282 in U.S and Canada. From abroad, call collect 800-964-6665, or contact the U.K. office at (0800) 52 13 13 and ask for the *Traveler's Companion,* which lists the addresses of all their travel offices. AmEx traveler's checks are the most widely recognized in the world, and the easiest to replace if lost or stolen—just contact the nearest AmEx Travel office or call the 800 number. The "Check for Two" option allows for double signing with a travel partner.

Bank of America: 800-227-3460 in U.S.; from Canada and abroad, call collect 415-574-7111. Connected with Visa/Barclays under Interpayment. 1% commission for non-Bank of America customers. Check holders may use the Travel Assistance hotline (800-368-7878 from U.S., 202-347-7113 collect from Canada), which provides free legal assistance, urgent message relay, lost document services, and, if you provide them with a credit card number, up to $1000 advance for prompt medical treatment.

Citicorp: 800-645-6556 in U.S and Canada; from abroad, call collect 813-623-4100. Checks available in four currencies including both US$ and CDN$. Commission of 1-2%. Checkholders enrolled automatically in Travel Assist Hotline (800-523-1199) for 45 days after purchase.

Mastercard International, 800-223-9920; from abroad, call collect 609-987-7300. In US$. Free if purchased from Mastercard, though bank commissions may run 1-2%.

Credit Cards

With a major credit card you can rent cars, make reservations, obtain cash advances at most banks, and make large purchases without depleting the cash you have on hand.

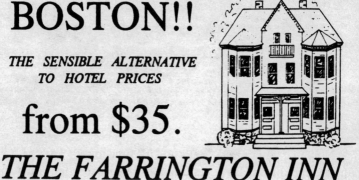

But many places mentioned in *Let's Go* will not honor major credit cards. This is just as well—if you rely on them too much and too irresponsibly, your trip will no longer be "budget travel."

MasterCard (800-999-0454) and **Visa** (no general number; contact your bank for information) are accepted in more establishments than other credit cards, and they are also the most useful for getting an instant cash advance. You should be able to obtain cash from a bank teller, who will essentially "charge" you as if you had made a purchase. Visa holders can generally obtain an advance up to the amount of the credit line remaining on the card, while Mastercard imposes a daily limit. Be sure to consult the bank that issues your card, however, since it may impose its own rules and restrictions.

American Express (800-528-4800) has a hefty annual fee ($55), but offers a number of services to cardholders. Local AmEx offices will cash personal checks up to $1000 for Green Card holders ($200 in cash, $800 in traveler's checks) and $5000 (of which $500 may be cash) for Gold Card holders. You can do this once every seven days; the money is drawn from your personal checking account, *not* your AmEx account. Green Card holders can get money from ATMs only if enrolled in Express Cash Service. Cash advances are available in certain places to Gold Card holders. At some major airports, you can use your card to purchase travelers checks from American Express machines. Cardholders can take advantage of the American Express Travel Service. Benefits include assistance in changing airline, hotel, and car rental reservations, sending mailgrams and international cables, and holding your mail (if you contact them well in advance), as well as Global Assist (800-333-2639), a 24-hr. helpline that provides legal and medical assistance. You can pick up a copy of the *Traveler's Companion,* a list of full-service offices throughout the world, at any American Express Travel Service office.

Sending Money

If you run out of money on the road and have no credit card, you have several options. The most inexpensive is to have a **certified check** or a **postal money order** mailed to you. Certified checks are redeemable at any bank, while postal money orders can be cashed at any post office upon presentation of two forms of ID (one with photo). The buyer should keep a receipt to refund lost orders.

Another alternative is cabling money. **American Express Moneygram** service (800-543-4080) will cable up to $10,000 to you within three days. It costs $49 per $750-1000 sent domestically and $70 per $750-1000 sent abroad. Non-cardholders may use this service for no extra charge, but money can only be sent from England, Germany, and some locations in France; other European and Australian AmEx offices can only receive Moneygrams. Some offices may require the first $200 to be received in cash and the rest in traveler's checks or as a money transfer check which may be cashed at a bank; others will allow the entire sum to be received in traveler's checks or as a money transfer check. To take advantage of a classic, time-honored, and expensive service, use **Western Union** (800-325-6000). You or someone else can phone in a credit card number, or else someone can bring cash to a Western Union office. As always, you will need ID to pick up your money. Their charge is $40 for $500, $50 for $1000. There is an additional surcharge on money sent from Europe to the U.S., but it will usually be available within two working days.

If time is of the essence, you can have money wired directly, bank to bank. A **cable transfer** is the fastest method of transport, requiring 24 or 48 hours to get to a major city or a bit longer to a more remote location. Cabling costs average $30 for amounts less than $1000, plus the commission charged by your home bank. **Bank drafts** or **international money orders** are cheaper but slower. You pay a commission of $15 to $20 on the draft, plus the cost of sending it registered air mail. If you find yourself stranded with no money and no way to get in touch with anyone, try **Traveler's Aid,** a service designed with the desperate voyager in mind (see Practical Information listings in specific cities for addresses). As a *last, last* resort, consulates will wire home for you and deduct the cost from the money you receive. But they won't be very happy about it.

Keeping Safe

Security

Even the minimal wares of the budget traveler may allure thieves, but with an appropriate amount of caution and common sense, you can reduce the risk of losing your life and your treasures. After protecting yourself, protecting your money and your documents should be your first concern. First the don'ts: *don't* carry your money in your back pocket (this includes men's wallets), *don't* take out your money and count it on the street or in front of strangers, and *don't* leave your money dangling from a bag or pouch that can easily be grabbed off your shoulder. You should always keep your important documents—ID, passport, traveler's check numbers and receipts, a small amount of emergency cash, and a credit card—separate from the bulk of your belongings so that they are both at your fingertips and well-protected. **Money belts** can be worn around your waist and buried under one or all your layers of clothing—they are convenient and nearly theft-proof.

Wherever you stow your stuff, for the day or for the evening, try to leave as little as possible in your room, particularly in the dorm-style rooms of some hostels. Lockers at bus and train stations are generally safe storage spots. Carry around a small daypack in which to put your valuables so they are always on your person. Label *all* your belongings with your name, address and home phone number. Label your luggage inside and out, including easy-to-drop items such as sleeping bags and tents; on your valuables, like cameras, write "call collect'' and a trusted phone number at home. Try to memorize as many of your important numbers as possible in case they disappear (a good pre-travel exercise): passport, ID, driver's license, health insurance policy, traveler's checks, credit cards. You should also leave all of this information with someone at home.

More important than your belongings is yourself. Avoid bus and train stations and public parks after dark. If you arrive in a transportation depot late at night, stay in the station rather than venturing into what may be an unsafe area, and call a cab. Walk on busy, well-lit streets, especially in larger cities. When walking alone, act as though you know where you're going, even if you don't; avoid passing dark alleyways or doorways and stay in the light. Don't walk through parking lots at night. When you arrive at your destination, find out about unsafe areas from tourist information, from the manager of your hotel or hostel, or from a local person whom you trust. Both men and women may want to carry a whistle to scare off attackers or attract attention, and it's not a bad idea to jot down the number of the police if you'll be in town for a couple days. **Remember that in an emergency, you can call 911 for help toll free on a public phone. 911 works in most of the U.S. and parts of Canada.** In addition, you may feel safer sleeping in places with either a curfew or a night attendant.

For more safe travel information, refer to *Travel Safely: Security and Safeguards at Home and Abroad,* from **Hippocrene Books, Inc.,** 171 Madison Ave., New York, NY 10016 (212-685-4371, orders 718-454-2360, fax: 718-454-1391). **Travel Assistance International,** 1133 15th St. NW, Washington, DC (800-821-2828) provides a 24-hr. hotline for emergencies and referrals. Their year-long travel package ($120) includes medical and travel insurance, financial assistance, and help in replacing lost passports and visas. **Traveler's Aid International,** 918 16th St. NW #201, Washington, DC, 20006 (202-659-9468), charges no fee but requests donations. They provide help to individuals and families for theft, car failure, illness, and other "mobility-related" problems. Local offices are listed under Practical Information section. Women and people traveling alone should refer to **Specific Concerns,** below.

Insurance

Purchasing insurance against accident, sickness, or theft may make sense, although you should beware of unnecessary coverage. Check whether your own or your family's homeowners' insurance covers theft or accident during travel. Homeowners' insurance often covers the loss of travel documents such as passports, airplane tickets, and rail passes up to $500. Students should find out if their university's term-time medical plan includes summer travel insurance. For U.S. residents, **Medicare** covers travel in the U.S., Canada, and Mexico. Canadians may be covered by their home province's health insurance plan for up to 90 days after leaving the country. Check with your provincial Ministry of Health or Health Plan Headquarters before buying additional coverage. Always keep proof of medical insurance on your person.

Before an insurance company will reimburse you for theft, you will have to provide a copy of the police report filed at the time of the theft. To be reimbursed for medical expenses, you will have to submit a doctor's statement and evidence that you actually paid the charges for which you are asking to be reimbursed; make sure you keep all receipts for conceivably reimbursable expenses. When you file for any kind of insurance reimbursement, make sure that you are filing within the time limit specified by the policy and that either you or someone at home can be in touch with your insurer if necessary.

If you have an **International Student Identification Card (ISIC)** (see Specific Concerns below), you automatically receive US$3000 of accident-related coverage and US$100 per day of in-patient health coverage up to 60 days, US$1000 for 24-hr. all-risk death and dismemberment, as well as $25,000 for accidental death or dismemberment as an airline passenger. While good in Canada and Hawaii, these benefits do *not* cover the continental U.S. and Alaska. CIEE also offers the **Trip-Safe** plan, which *does* cover the entire U.S., for ISIC holders and nonholders alike. Trip-Safe includes the above package as well as insurance for medical treatment and hospitalization, accidents, baggage loss, trip cancellation, emergency evacuation and repatriation, and coverage for charter flights missed due to illness. Cost of the insurance varies with the length of your trip. Call or write CIEE (see Student Travel below) for information. **American Express** cardmembers automatically receive car-rental and flight insurance on purchases made with the card.

The following firms also specialize in travel insurance. You can buy a policy either directly from them or through an agent operating on their behalf:

Access America, Inc., 6600 W. Broad St., P.O. Box 90310, Richmond, VA 23230-9310 (800-284-8300). A subsidiary of Blue Cross/Blue Shield. Covers trip cancellation/interruption, on-the-spot hospital admittance costs, emergency medical evaluation, and a 24-hr. hotline.

The Traveler's Insurance Co., 1 Tower Sq., Hartford, CT 06183-5040 (800-243-3174; in CT, HI, or AK 203-277-2318). Insurance against accident, baggage loss, sickness, trip cancellation or interruption, and company default. Covers emergency medical evacuation as well. Available through most travel agencies.

Travel Guard International, 1145 Clark St., Stevens Point, WI 54481 (715-345-0505 or 800-782-5151). Basic ($19), deluxe ($39), and comprehensive "Travel Guard Gold" (8% of total trip cost) packages cover baggage delay, car rental, accidental death, and trip cancellation or interruption. 24-hr. hotline for policy-holders.

Health

General Tips

Common sense is the simplest prescription for good health while you travel: eat well, drink enough, get enough sleep, and don't overexert yourself. You will need plenty of protein (for sustained energy) and fluids (to prevent dehydration and constipation, two of the most common health problems for travelers). Carry a canteen or water bottle and make sure to drink frequently. Sunscreen is mandatory—clothes and a pack over sunburned skin can be torturous, and more importantly, dry skin doesn't keep the body as cool or retain moisture as well. Wear a hat (preferably a big, floopy one). And lavish your feet with attention; make sure your shoes are appropriate for extended walking, do not wear the same pair of socks for too long, use talcum powder frequently, and have some moleskin on hand to pad your shoes if they become uncomfortable. If possible, bring an extra pair of good walking shoes and alternate between the two pairs, both to vary the points of stress on your feet and to allow the shoes to dry thoroughly after a day of walking.

While you travel, pay attention to the signals of pain and discomfort that your body may send you. This may be due to a new climate, diet, water quality, or pace when you first arrive or even after a couple of weeks. Once you get going, some of the milder symptoms that you may safely ignore at home may be signs of something more serious on the road; your increased exertion may wear you out and make you more susceptible to illness. The following paragraphs list some health problems you may encounter but should not be your only information source on these common ailments. If you would like to read more about them and others, you may want to send away for the *First-Aid and Safety Handbook* ($15) from the **American Red Cross.** You can write to 99 Brookline Ave., Boston MA 02215, or to any local office in the U.S. to purchase this book. If you are interested in taking one of the many first-aid and CPR courses that the American Red Cross offers before heading out on the road, contact your local office. Courses are relatively inexpensive and usually very well taught.

Airplane travelers are often plagued by **jet lag,** a condition that arises when you arrive in a new time zone but your body's rhythms are stuck in the time zone you just left. Jet lag sufferers are generally uncomfortable and tired, but unable to sleep normally. To avoid or cure jet lag, the best thing to do is to adopt the new region's time as soon as you arrive and to try to sleep during the appropriate hours. Some studies caution sufferers against excessive eating and caffeine and alcohol consumption as well.

In warmer parts of the country, particularly the desert-like Southwest, be on the alert for **heatstroke.** This term is often misapplied to all forms of heat exhaustion, but it actually refers to a specific ailment that can cause death within a few hours if it is not treated. Heatstroke can begin without direct exposure to the sun; it results from continuous heat stress, lack of fitness, or overactivity following heat exhaustion. In the early stages of heatstroke, sweating stops, body temperature rises, and an intense headache develops, soon followed by mental confusion. To treat heatstroke, cool the victim off immediately with fruit juice or salted water, wet towels, and shade. Rush the victim to the hospital.

Hypothermia can strike in cold, windy, or wet conditions—including temperatures well above freezing—when body temperature drops rapidly, resulting in a failure to

produce body heat. Symptoms are easy to detect: uncontrollable shivering, poor coordination, and exhaustion followed by slurred speech, sleepiness, hallucinations, and amnesia. You can often save victims of hypothermia by making them warm and drying them off. *Do not* let victims fall asleep if they are in the advanced stages—if they lose consciousness, they might die. To avoid hypothermia, always keep dry. Wear wool, *especially* in soggy weather—it retains its insulating ability even when wet. Dress in layers, and stay out of the wind, which carries heat away from the body. Remember that most loss of body heat is through your head, so always carry a wool hat with you.

Frostbite is an obvious danger of cold-weather activities. The affected skin will turn white, then waxy and cold. To counteract the problem, the victim should drink warm beverages, stay or get dry, and gently and slowly warm the frostbitten area in dry fabric or with steady body contact. NEVER *rub* frostbite—the skin is easily damaged. Take serious cases to a doctor or medic as soon as possible.

Travelers in high altitudes should allow their body a couple of days to adjust to the lower atmospheric oxygen levels before engaging in any strenuous activity. This particularly applies to those intent on setting out on long alpine hikes. Those new to high-altitude areas may feel drowsy, and one alcoholic beverage may have the same effect as three at a lower altitude.

For minor health hazards, a compact self-assembled **first-aid kit** should suffice. You should include any or all of the following, depending on your plans: band-aids, gauze, adhesive tape, aspirin, allergy pills (if necessary), soap (both mild and antiseptic), antibiotic ointment, a thermometer in a sturdy case, multiple vitamins, decongestant (particularly important for clearing your ears if you find yourself needing to fly with a cold), antihistamine, motion sickness medicine (such as Dramamine), medicine for stomach problems and diarrhea, burn ointment, lip balm, an elastic bandage, and a Swiss Army knife (with tweezers). If you anticipate sexual activity during your travels, be sure to bring prophylactics. Women taking oral contraceptives need to take time zone changes into account, as do diabetics who must have regular insulin injections, and anyone else who must take medication on a regular basis. If you wear glasses or contact lenses, bring a prescription and/or an extra pair along with you. Lens wearers can avoid dried-out contacts by drinking sufficient fluids and switching to glasses where the air is dry or dirty. All travelers should be sure that their immunizations, such as tetanus shots, are up to date.

All travelers should be concerned about **Acquired Immune Deficiency Syndrome (AIDS),** transmitted through the exchange of body fluids with an infected individual. Wherever possible, *Let's Go* lists the phone numbers of local AIDS information, crisis, and counseling hotlines and community centers. You should avoid having unprotected sex and sharing intravenous needles. For more information, you can also call the **AIDS Hotline** at the **Center for Disease Control,** at 800-342-2437.

Before you leave, check and see whether your insurance policy (if you have one) covers medical costs incurred while traveling (see Insurance, above). If you choose to risk traveling without insurance, you still have avenues for health care. In an emergency, call the local hotline or crisis center listed in *Let's Go* under Practical Information for each area. Operators at these organizations have the numbers of public health organizations and clinics that treat patients without demanding proof of solvency. Such centers charge low fees. University teaching hospitals usually run inexpensive clinics as well.

If you have a chronic medical condition that requires medication on a regular basis, consult your physician before you leave. People with diabetes, for example, may need advice on adapting insulin levels to flights across multiple time zones. The **American Diabetes Association,** 1660 Duke St., Alexandria, VA 22314 (800-232-3472), provides copies of the article "Ticket to Safe Travel" and ID cards indicating the carrier as a diabetic. Contact the ADA for information on ID cards and reprints.

Carry copies of your prescriptions and an ample supply of all medications; it might be difficult to find pharmacies in rural areas. Always distribute medication and/or syringes among all your carry-on and checked baggage in case any of your bags is lost. If you are traveling with a medical condition that cannot be easily recognized—including diabetes, an allergy to antibiotics or other drugs, epilepsy, or a heart condition—you

should obtain a **Medic Alert identification tag** to alert both passersby and medical personnel of your condition in case of an emergency. Your tag is engraved with the name of your ailment, and you receive a wallet card with personal and medical information. The tag costs about $30; the fee includes access to an emergency phone number as well. Contact **Medic Alert Foundation International,** Turlock, CA 95381-1009 (800-432-5378).

For more information, consult *The Pocket Medical Encyclopedia and First-Aid Guide* (Simon and Schuster, $5; write to Mail Order Dept., 200 Old Tappan Rd., Old Tappan, NJ 07675, or call 800-223-2348). The **International Association for Medical Assistance to Travellers (IAMAT)** provides members with free pamphlets and a directory of fixed-rate physicians throughout the world. Membership is free, although donations are appreciated. Contact IAMAT in the U.S. at 415 Center St., Lewiston, NY 14092 (716-754-4883), or in Canada at 40 Regal St., Guelph, Ont., N1K 1B5 (519-836-0102).

Desert Survival

The body loses a gallon or more of liquid per day in the heat, and that water must be replaced. Whether you are driving or hiking, tote two gallons of water per person per day; less is adequate at higher altitudes and during winter months. Drink regularly, even when you do not feel thirsty. Do not merely drink huge quantities of water after you've become dehydrated—indeed, it may be dangerous. If you're drinking sweet beverages, dilute them with water to avoid a reaction to high sugar content. Alcohol and caffeine cause dehydration; if you indulge, compensate with more liquid. Avoid salt tablets, which shock your system.

Travelers should allow a couple of days to adjust to the climate, especially when planning a hike or other strenuous activity. The desert is definitely *not* the place to sunbathe. A hat, long-sleeved, loose-fitting shirts of a light fabric, and long trousers actually keep you cooler and protect you from exposure to the sun. Although it seems counterintuitive, thick socks will keep your feet cool in the desert by insulating them further from the egg-frying surface temperatures.

In winter, nighttime temperatures can drop below freezing at high elevations, even though afternoon temperatures may be in the 60s or 70s. The desert is infamous for its flash floods, mostly during spring and fall. A dry gulch can turn into a violent river with astonishing speed; when camping, try to locate a site far back from moving water. *Never* camp in a gully or a wash. Even if it is not raining on you, rain in nearby mountains can swoop down and wash away a campsite with frightening speed.

Those driving in the desert should carry water for their radiator. A two- to five-gallon container should suffice. Drivers should purchase a desert water bag (about $5-10) at a hardware or automotive store; once filled with water, this large canvas bag straps onto the front of the car. If you see the temperature gauge climbing, turn off the air-conditioning. If an overheating warning light comes on, stop immediately and wait for about half an hour before trying again. Don't shut off the engine; the fan will help cool things down under the hood. Turning your car's heater on full force—if you can bear it—will also help cool the engine. Never open the radiator until it has cooled, because internal pressure will cause scalding steam to erupt from it. And never pour cold water on the engine to cool it off; the temperature change may crack the engine block. For any trips off major roads, a board and shovel are useful in case your car gets stuck in sand; the board can be shoved under a tire to gain traction and the shovel can take care of minor quagmires. Letting air out of your tires can also help you extricate your vehicle.

Alcohol and Drugs

In the U.S., the drinking age (21) is strictly enforced. Particularly in the U.S., be prepared to show a photo ID (preferably a driver's license, passport or other government-issued document) if you look under 30. Some areas of the country are "dry," meaning they do not permit the sale of alcohol at all, and others do not allow it to be sold on Sundays. A few select states go so far as to require that you possess a "liquor license" to make a purchase. Concern over the difficulty of purchasing alcohol in the U.S.

should not drive you to obtain it elsewhere and bring it into the country; you cannot bring alcohol into the country or have open containers of alcohol in your car.

Drugs and traveling are not a good combination. Possession of marijuana, cocaine and most opiate derivatives is a U.S. federal offense subject to imprisonment. For students receiving federal aid at U.S. universities, it could mean termination of all assistance. At the Canadian border, if you are an American citizen found in possession of drugs, you will be subject to an automatic seven-year jail term, regardless of how small an amount you are found with; and if you are not a U.S. citizen, you will be permanently barred from entering the country. In Alaska, possession and use of up to four ounces of marijuana *used* to be legal; it is no longer. Check with the U.S. Customs Service (see Customs) about any questionable chemicals before they check you.

Officials at both the United States and Canadian borders also take **drunk driving** very seriously. No matter what kind of transportation you use for entry, if the customs guards discover a drunk driving conviction in your history, you will be denied access. Within both the United States and Canada, drunk driving is a major offense—many states even have mandatory prison sentences for first-time offenders.

Packing

Traveling light will make your life on the road easier in a number of ways. Packing less will make moving from place to place less exhausting. Furthermore, the fewer bags you have to lug around, the less you will look like (and thus be treated like) a tourist, *and* the more space you will have for souvenirs. If you are unsure about cutting things out, take a short walk around the block while carrying all of your luggage. Your neighbors might look at you funny through their blinds, but you'll get an accurate preview of just how inconvenient carrying too much stuff can be. If the pack seems too heavy, take out those luxury items that you think you want, but you know you don't need. C'mon, you don't *need* that microwave!

Luggage

Your first choice is the kind of luggage you'll need. If you will be biking or hiking a great deal, a backpack is necessary. You might consider using a light suitcase if you will be staying in one city for a long time. Large shoulder bags that can be squished are good for stuffing into lockers and crowded baggage compartments. Whatever your central piece of baggage, be sure to bring a small shoulder bag to serve as a daypack, in which you can carry a day's worth of food, camera, first-aid essentials, valuables and documents. Anyone planning to cover a lot of ground on foot should have a sturdy backpack—see Tent Camping and Hiking below for advice on types of packs and good mail-order firms to buy from.

Overall, *pack light!* (It's worth repeating.) A convenient method of keeping organized is to pack items in different colored stuff sacks (found at camp stores)—shirts in one, underwear in another, etc. Also bring a plastic bag for dirty clothes, as well as one to cover your knapsack when it rains. Wrap sharper items in clothing so they won't stab you or puncture your luggage, and pack heavy items along the inside wall if you're carrying a backpack.

Clothing and Shoes

The clothing you bring will, of course, depend on where in the U.S. you're planning on traveling, and during what time of year you plan to be there. There really is no need to worry about looking too informal. America, compared to Europe, is a very casual place, clothing-wise. In the summer t-shirts and shorts are the rule; in the winter sweatshirts and jeans. Anyplace formal enough to require a jacket and tie will likely be too expensive for a budget traveler anyhow. Weather more often than style will determine your mode of dress. The "layer concept" covers most of the bases. Start with several t-shirts, which take up virtually no space and over which you can wear a sweatshirt or sweater in cold or wet weather. Remember that wool retains its insulating ability, even when wet. Then pack a few pairs of shorts and jeans. Add underwear and socks, and you've got your essential wardrobe. For winter you may want a few heavier layers as well. Natural fibers and lightweight cottons are the best materials for hot weather. It's a good idea to have at least one layer that will insulate while wet, such as polypropylene, polarfleece or wool. Stick with dark-colored clothes that won't show wear, tear, and dirt as readily as others; you may not always have access to laundry facilities. Make sure your clothing can be washed in a sink and will survive a spin in the dryer. And don't forget a towel, swimwear, and a raincoat. A rain poncho will cover both you and your pack and can double as a groundcover for a night outdoors. For extra info about packing for a hike, see Camping and the Outdoors below.

Shoes are very important whether you'll be doing serious hiking or not. When exploring new cities, you will most likely do more walking then you had planned—always be sure to have a comfortable pair of shoes. Break your shoes in before you leave, and don't be caught without some type of rainproof footwear. If your feet are sensitive to blisters, bring protective moleskin.

Cameras and Film

You will need to carefully consider how much equipment you absolutely *need:* camera gear is heavy, fragile, and costly to replace. And if you decide to take a camera, just don't forget to look at the scenery without the lens, too; spending too much time framing the view for friends can take away from your vacation. Buy postcards instead. Make sure your camera is in good shape before you go—repair on the road is likely to be inexpert, expensive, and slow. Be sure to have an easily accessible sack in which to carry your camera; if you carry it around your neck, you will automatically be identified as a tourist, and you may not have that camera for much longer. Buy film before you leave, or in big cities at large discount department stores. Avoid buying film in small towns or at tourist attractions, where prices are exorbitant. The sensitivity of film to light is measured by the ASA/ISO number: 100 is good for normal outdoor or indoor flash photography, 400 or (usually) higher is necessary for night photography. Consult a photography store for advice about the right film for special types of photography.

Process your film after you return home; you will save money, and it's much simpler to carry rolls of film as you travel, rather than boxes of slides or packages of prints and negatives that are easily damaged. Protect exposed film from extreme heat and the sun.

Despite disclaimers, airport X-ray equipment can fog film; the more sensitive the film, the more susceptible to damage: anything over ASA 1600 should not be X-rayed. Ask security personnel to inspect your camera and film by hand. Serious photographers should purchase a lead-lined pouch for storing film.

The Essentials

These are the items you may not think you will need, may not remember to bring along unless read this section, and will find yourself lost without: all your documents (i.e. your passport, visa, traveler's checks), first-aid kit (see Health), flashlight, pens and paper, perhaps a travel journal, travel alarm, canteen or water bottle, your child's bottle or juice container, Ziplock bags (for isolating damp or dirty clothing), garbage bags, sewing kit, safety pins, pocketknife, earplugs for noisy hostels, waterproof matches, clothespins and a length of cord, a smile, sunglasses, sunscreen, toilet paper (not all bathrooms come so well-equipped!), and the other essential toiletries. Also consider bringing something to cover your head if you will be outdoors a lot—it will shelter your scalp from harmful rays. A rubber squash ball or a golf ball is a universal sink stopper, and either liquid soap or shampoo will do for handwashing clothes. Don't forget to bring along your prescription medicine (as well as your children's), and copies of the prescription in case you run out. Also bring a copy of your glasses/eye lens prescription. Oh, and bring lots of patience too.

Work and Study in the U.S.

Finding a job far from home is a matter of luck and timing. Your best leads in the job hunt often come from local residents, hostels, employment offices and Chambers of Commerce. Temporary agencies often hire for non-secretarial placement as well as for standard typing assignments. Marketable skills, i.e. touch-typing, dictation, computer knowledge, and experience with children will prove very helpful (even necessary) in your search for a temporary job. Consult local newspapers and bulletin boards on local college campuses.

Volunteer jobs are readily available almost everywhere. Some jobs provide rooms and board in exchange for labor. Write to **CIEE** (see Useful Organizations under Information for International Visitors) for *Volunteer! The Comprehensive Guide to Voluntary service in the U.S. and Abroad* ($9, postage $1.50). The **U.S. Forest Service** invites everyone to volunteer as hosts to visitors to the greener woods of the U.S. Contact the USAD Forest Service, Human Resource Program Office, P.O. Box 96090, Washington D.C., 20090-6090. The forest service also offers paid employment.

Many student travel organizations arrange work-exchange programs. Both CIEE and YMCA place students as summer camp counselors in the U.S. **Hostelling International/American Youth Hostels (HI/AYH)** has group leader positions available in the summer. Applicants must be at least 21 and must take a nine-day training course which costs US$295, with room and board included. (In Washington D.C., US$395.) For more information, contact Hostelling International/American Youth Hostels, P.O. Box 37613, Washington, D.C. 20013-7613. Foreign university-level students can get on-the-job technical training from the **Association for International Practical Training,** which is an umbrella organization for the **International Association for the Exchange of Students for Technology Experience (IAESTE).** You must apply by December 10 for the placement the following summer. Write to IAESTE, c/o AIPT, 10 Corporate Center, Suite 250, 10400 Little Patuxent Pkwy., Columbia, MD (410-997-2200).

If you are interested in staying with an American family and learning about America firsthand, check out **Experiment in International Living's Homestay U.S.A.** Programs are available to international visitors of all ages for stays from one to four weeks in urban, suburban, and rural areas, in volunteer hosts' homes. Prices range from US$350-1580. (Call 800-327-4678.) Other organizations to contact are:

Central Bureau for Educational Visits and Exchanges, Seymour Mews House, Seymour Mews, London WIH 9PE, England ((071)486-5101 or fax (071)935 5741). Publishes *Working Holidays,* and annual guide to short-term paid and voluntary work in Britain and around the world.

International Voluntary Service, Rte. 2, P.O. Box 506, Crozet, VA 22932 (804-823-1826). Arranges placement in workcamps in Europe and the U.S. for young people over 16. Registrations fees range from $35-110. Established after World War I as a means to promote peace and understanding.

If you are not a citizen of the U.S. and hope to work in this country, there are a few rules of which you must be aware. Working or studying in the U.S. with only a B-2 visa is grounds for deportation. Before an appropriate visa can be issued to you, you must—depending on the visa category you are seeking—join a USIA-authorized Exchange Visitor Program (J-1 visa) or locate an employer who will sponsor you (usually an H-2B visa) and file the necessary paperwork with the Immigration and Naturalization Service (INS) in the United Sates on your behalf. In order to apply to the U.S. Embassy or Consulate for a J-1 visa you must obtain an IAP-66 eligibility form, issued by a U.S. academic institution or a private organization involved in U.S. exchanges. The H-2 visa is difficult to obtain, as your employer must prove that there are no other American or foreign permanent residents already residing in the U.S. with your job skills. For more specific information on visa categories and requirements, contact your nearest U.S. embassy or Consulate and Educational Advisory Service of the Fulbright Commission (a U.S. embassy-affiliated organization).

If you are studying in the U.S., you can take any on-campus job to help pay the bills once you have applied for a social security number and have completed an Employ-

All
the
information
you
need
to
know
in
this
book
is
on
the
Inside
Front
Cover.

ment Eligibility Form (I-9). International educational organizations such as the**Council on International Educational Exchange (CIEE),** its budget travel subsidiary **Council Travel,** and exchange operators throughout the world sponsor year-long internships and summer work exchange programs for students in higher education. Check to see if there is a CIEE or Council Travel office in a city near you, or write to CIEE's international headquarters in the U.S. at 205 E. 42nd St., New York, NY 10017. If you are studying full-time in the U.S. on an F-1 visa, you can take any on-campus job provided you do not displace a U.S. resident. On-campus employment is limited to 20 hours per week while school is in session, but you may work full-time during vacation if you plan to return to school. For further information, contact the international students office at the institution you will be attending.

Most colleges and universities in the U.S. welcome visiting students. Foreign students who wish to study in the U.S. must apply for either a J-1 visa (for exchange students) or a F-1 visas (for full-time students enrolled in an academic or language program). To obtain a J-1, you must fill out an IAP 66 eligibility form, issued by the program in which you will enroll. Neither the F-1 nor the J-1 visa specifies any expiration date; instead they are both valid for the duration of stay, which includes the length of your particular program and a brief grace period thereafter. In order to extend a student visa, fill out an I-538 form. Requests to extend a visa must be submitted 15-60 days before the original departure date. Many foreign schools—and most U.S. colleges—have offices that give advice and information on studying in the U.S.

In addition, if English is not your native language, you will generally be required to pass the **Test of English as a Foreign Language and Test of Spoken English (TOEFL/TSE)**, administered in many countries. For more information, contact the TOEFL/TSE Application office, P.O. Box 6155, Princeton, NJ 08541 (609-951-1100).

One excellent information source is the **Institute of International Education (IIE),** which administers many educational exchange programs in the U.S. and abroad. IIE prints *English Language and Orientation Programs in the United States* which describes language and cultural programs (1992 edition $43 plus $3 shipping). Contact IIE, 809 United Nations Plaza, New York, NY 10017 (212-883-8200).

To help you choose which college or university is for you, check out *The Insider's Guide to Colleges* ($20), published by St. Martin's Press, which offers a student's perspective on many public and private institutions. Also useful are the *Fiske Guide to Colleges,* by Edward Fiske (N.Y. Times Books, $16), and *Barron's Profiles of American Colleges* ($19).

Travelers with Specific Concerns

Students

Students are often entitled to discounts on admission prices, airfares, and hotels. Most places accept a current university ID or an **International Student Identity Card (ISIC)** as proof of student status. The student travel offices of many universities issue ISICs for $14. If your university doesn't have a travel office, you can obtain a card from one of the organizations listed below. When applying for one, take current, dated proof of student status (e.g. a photocopied grade report, transcript, or a school ID card) and a 1½x2 inch photograph with your name printed on the back. The card is valid for up to 16 months, always expiring in December. Students must be at least 12 years old. Non-students of student age can often take advantage of discounts with a FIYTO-issued International Youth Card.

The following agencies try to meet student needs. Most sell ISICs and have tips on transportation discounts.

Let's Go Travel Services, Harvard Student Agencies, Inc., Thayer Hall-B, Harvard University, Cambridge, MA 02138 (617-495-9649, 800-5-LETSGO or 800-553-8746). Run by the friendly folks who wrote and edited this guide. Sells Railpasses, Hostelling International/American Youth Hostel memberships (valid at all HI youth hostels), International Student and Teacher ID cards, International Youth Cards, travel guides and maps (including the *Let's Go* series), discount airfares, and a complete line of budget travel gear. All items available by mail. Call or write for catalogue.

Council on International Educational Exchange (CIEE/Council Travel): Provides low cost travel arrangements, books (including *Let's Go* and *Where to Stay U.S.A.)* and gear. Operates 30 offices throughout the U.S., including those listed below and branches in Providence, RI; Amherst and Cambridge, MA; Berkeley, La Jolla, and Long Beach, CA. **Boston,** 729 Boylston St. #201, MA 02116 (617-266-1926). **Chicago,** 1153 N. Dearborn St., IL 60601 (312-951-0585). **Dallas,** Executive Tower Office Center, 3300 W. Mockingbird #101, TX 75235 (214-350-6166). **Los Angeles,** 1093 Broxton Ave. #220, CA 90024 (213-208-3551). **New York,** 205 E. 42nd St., NY 10017 (212-661-1450). (There are 2 other New York offices.) **Portland,** 715 S.W. Morrison #600, OR 97205 (503-228-1900). **San Diego,** 4429 Cass St., CA 92109 (619-270-6401). **San Francisco,** 919 Irving St. #102, CA 94122 (415-566-6222). (There is 1 other San Francisco office.) **Seattle,** 1314 N.E. 43rd St. #210, WA 98105 (206-632-2448).

STA Travel, 17 E. 45th St., New York, NY 10017 (800-777-0112 or 212-986-9470) operates 10 offices in the U.S. and over 100 offices around the world. Offers discount airfares for travelers under 26 and full-time students under 32. **Boston,** 273 Newbury St., MA 02116 (617-266-6014). **Los Angeles,** 7202 Melrose Ave., CA 90046 (213-934-8722). **New York,** 48 E. 11th St., NY 10030 (212-477-7166). **Philadelphia,** University City Travel, 730 Walnut St., PA 19104 (215-382-2928). **San Francisco,** 166 Geary St. #702, CA 94108 (415-301-8407).

Senior Citizens

Seniors are eligible for a wide range of discounts on transportation, museums, movies, theater, concerts, restaurants and accommodations. Proof of age is usually required (e.g., a driver's license, Medicare card, or membership card from a recognized society of retired persons).

The **American Association of Retired Persons (AARP)** offers insurance, trips, group travel, discounts and more to seniors over 50 for an annual fee ($8 including spouse). Write to 601 E St. NW, Washington, D.C. 20049 (202-434-2277) for more information. For a fee, membership in the **September Days Club,** 2751 Buford Hwy., Atlanta, GA 30324 (800-241-5050) entitles you to a 15 to 40% discount at Days Inns across the U.S. They also have a travel service for senior citizens.

Hostelling International (HI) sells membership cards ($15) at a discount to those over 54. Write the HI/AYH National Headquarters, P.O. Box 37613, Washington DC 20013-7613 (202-783-6161). (See Accommodations below in the General Introduction for information on hostels.) To explore the outdoors, adults 62 and over can buy a **Golden Age Passport** ($20 at park entrances), that gives you free entry into all national parks and a 50% discount on recreational activities.

The academically inclined should look into **Elderhostel,** which offers residential programs at universities. Participants spend a week living in dorms and studying subjects ranging from archeology to zoology. The fee (about $270) covers room, board, tuition, and extracurricular activities for a one-week program in the U.S.; scholarships are available. Programs are given year-round, and registration is an on-going process. Participants must be 60 or over, and companions must be over 50. Write to 75 Federal St., Boston, MA 02110 (617-426-7788) to be put on the mailing list and receive catalogues and newsletters.

Pilot Books publishes *The Senior Citizen's Guide to Budget Travel in the United States and Canada* by Paige Palmer ($6 ppd.). Write to 103 Cooper St., Babylon, NY 11702 (516-422-2225). *Travel Tips for Older Americans* ($1) is available from the Superintendent of Documents, U.S. Government Printing Office, Washington, DC 20402 (202-783-3238).

Travelers with Disabilities

Planning a trip presents extra challenges to individuals with disabilities, but the difficulties are by no means insurmountable. Hotels and motels have become more and more accessible to disabled persons (see Hotels and Motels under Accommodations below), and exploring the outdoors is often feasible. ("Easy Access to National Parks, the Sierra Club Guide for People with Disabilities"—$16—provides information on accessibility of 15 national parks.) If you research areas ahead of time, your trip will go more smoothly. You can call restaurants, hotels, parks, and other facilities to find out about the existence of ramps, the widths of doors, the dimensions of elevators, etc. There may also be restrictions on motorized wheelchairs which are worth discovering beforehand.

Arrange transportation well in advance. **Hertz, Avis,** and **National** car rental agencies have hand-controlled vehicles at some locations (see By Car). **Amtrak** trains and all **airlines** can better serve disabled passengers if notified in advance; tell the ticket agent when making reservations which services you'll need. **Greyhound** allows a traveler with disabilities and a companion to ride for the price of a single fare with a doctor's statement confirming that a companion is necessary. Wheelchairs, seeing-eye dogs, and oxygen tanks are not deducted from your luggage allowance. A booklet entitled, "Access travel: Airports," replete with info on the accessibility of airports across the globe is available from Federal Consumer Information Center, Pueblo, CO 81009. (Free.)

If you're planning to visit a national park, get a **Golden Access Passport** ($20) at the park entrance. This exempts disabled travelers and their families from the entrance fee and allows a 50% discount on recreational activity fees.

There are a number of special information services for the disabled traveler:

The American Foundation for the Blind, 15 W. 16th St., New York, NY 10011 (800-829-0500, in NY 212-620-2159). Provides $10 IDs, products, and publications for the legally blind. Write or call for an application.

Directions Unlimited, 720 N. Bedford Rd., Bedford Hills, NY 10507 (800-533-5343, in NY 914-241-1700). Organizes individual vacations, as well as group tours and cruises.

Evergreen Travel Service, 4114 198th St. S.W., #13, Lynnwood, WA 98036 (800-435-2288). Its "Wings on Wheels" tours arranges wheelchair-accessible tours worldwide. Other services include "White Cane Tours for the Blind" (one guide for 3 travelers), tours for the deaf, and tours for slow walkers.

Federation of the Handicapped, 211 W. 14th St., New York, NY 10011 (212-727-4268). Leads tours for members, including daytrips, weekend outings, and longer excursions.

Flying Wheels Travel, 143 W. Bridge St., P.O. Box 382, Owatonna, MN 55060 (800-535-6790, in MN 800-722-9351). Provides general information and arranges domestic or international tours for groups and individuals. Specializes in cruises.

The Society for the Advancement of Travel for the Handicapped, 345 Fifth Ave. #610, New York, NY 10016 (212-447-7284; fax: 212-725-8253). Provides advice and assistance on trip planning. Publishes a quarterly, *SATH News,* and informational booklets (free for members; $2 for nonmembers). Annual membership $45; students and seniors $25.

Travel Information Service, Moss Rehabilitation Hospital, 1200 W. Tabor Rd., Philadelphia, PA 19141 (215-456-9600). Brochures on sights, accommodations, and transportation available for a nominal fee.

Whole Persons Tours, P.O. Box 1084, Bayonne, NJ 07002-1084 (201-858-3400). Conducts tours and publishes *The Itinerary,* a bimonthly magazine for disabled travelers. Subscriptions: $10 for 1 year, $18 for 2 years.

Publications geared toward disabled travelers include *Access to the World,* by Louise Weiss ($17), available through Facts on File, 460 Park Ave. S, New York, NY 10016 (800-322-8755; in AL and HI 212-683-2244). Also, *Travel for the Disabled* by Helen Hecker ($20), and *Directory of Travel Agencies for the Disabled* ($20) can be ordered through Twin Peaks Press, P.O. Box 129, Vancouver, WA 98666 (800-637-2256). Both provide travel hints and information on accommodations, travel agents, and literature geared toward persons with disabilities.

Gay and Lesbian Travelers

Unfortunately, prejudice against gays and lesbians still exists in many areas of the U.S. In some areas, public displays of homosexual affection are illegal. However, San Francisco, Los Angeles, New York, New Orleans, Houston, Atlanta and Montréal have large, political, and active gay and lesbian communities. Whenever available, *Let's Go* lists local gay and lesbian hotline numbers, which can provide counseling and crisis and social information for gay and lesbian visitors. An excellent source of books for gay and lesbian travelers is **Giovanni's Room,** 345 S. 12th St., Philadelphia, PA 19107 (215-923-2960), which charges $3.50 postage per book in the U.S. All of the following books are available through Giovanni's Room or the address listed:

Spartacus International Gay Guide. c/o Bruno Gmünder, 100 E. Biddle St., Baltimore, MD 21202 (301-727-5677). International gay guide for men, listing bars, restaurants, hotels, bookstores and hotlines throughout the world. $28.

Inn Places: U.S.A. and Worldwide Gay Accommodations. $15.

Places of Interest. Ferrari Publications, P.O. Box 37887, Phoenix, AZ 85069 (602-863-2408). A series of three books for men ($13), women ($10), and both ($13), including maps.

Damron offers several guides for gays and lesbians. Write or call Damron, P.O. Box 422458, San Francisco, CA 94142 (800-462-6654 or 415-255-0404). The *Damron Address Book* ($14) lists over 6000 bars, restaurants, guest houses, and services catering to the gay male community. Covers the U.S., Canada, and Mexico. *The Damron Road Atlas* ($13) includes color maps of 56 major U.S. cities and gay and lesbian resorts, and listings of bars and accommodations. *The Women's Traveller* ($10) is a guide for the lesbian community, including maps of 50 major U.S. cities; lists bars, restaurants, accommodations, bookstores and services. Shipping is $4 per book in the United States.

The *Gayellow Pages* (U.S./Canada edition $12) is available through Renaissance House. For further details, send a self-addressed, stamped envelope to Box 292, Village Station, New York NY 10014-0292 (212-674-0120).

Women Travelers

Women exploring any area on their own inevitably face additional safety concerns. In all situations it is best to trust your instincts; if you'd feel better somewhere else, don't hesitate to move on.

When choosing accommodations, stick to centrally located college dorms, hostels, YWCAs, or religious organizations offering rooms for women only. A woman should *never* hitchhike or camp alone; hitching is dangerous even for two women together. If confronted by catcalls or propositions, the best answer is no answer. If necessary, pretend that you have a companion (or a spouse) close by. Always be assertive and confident, and look as if you know where you're going, even if you don't. If you need directions, ask women or couples. Always carry enough change for a bus, taxi, or phone call, and a whistle on a keychain. In an emergency, don't hesitate to yell or whistle for help.

Let's Go lists emergency numbers and women's centers for most cities. The same people who produced *Gaia's Guide* (no longer available) are now publishing *Women Going Places,* a new women's travel/resource guide, emphasizing women-owned and operated enterprises. The guide is aimed at lesbians and all women. Available from INLAND Book Company, P.O. Box 120261, East Haven, CT 06512 (203-467-4257).

Though the journey has been a staple theme in literature since Homer's *Odysseus*, women's voices have until recently been relatively rare. But the body of travel literature written by women is growing. Check a good library or bookstore for these and other books: *Nothing to Declare: Memoirs of a Woman Traveling Alone* and *Wall to Wall: From Beijing to Berlin by Rail* both by Mary Morris (Penguin); *One Dry Season* by Caroline Alexander (Knopf); *Tracks* by Robyn Davidson (Pantheon); and *The Road Through Miyama* by Leila Philips (Random House/Vintage).

Traveling Alone

The freedom to come and go, to backtrack or deviate from a schedule or route, is the lone traveler's prerogative. If you travel with a friend, consider separating for a few days. You'll get a brief break from each other and the chance to have some adventures of your own.

A note of warning: solo travel can also be dangerous. It may be easier to get a ride when hitching alone, but it is not safe for women to do so. If you've been spending the nights outdoors, consider indoor accommodations when on your own since lone campers make easy targets. Unfortunately, solitude can also be expensive; double rooms are cheaper per person than singles. The other problem with solo travel is simple—the road can be a lonely place. For many, however, this is just a greater incentive to meet other people, locals and travelers alike.

Traveling with Children

If you're planning a family vacation with the kids, you'll need to adapt your travel pace to their needs. There are plenty of educational and entertaining activities in the U.S. that will delight children, and if you keep a relaxed pace and a flexible schedule, you should be able to find time and activities to satisfy your own interests, as well. *Let's Go* lists points of interest to children (children's museums and zoos, for example), in the Sights section of the listings. You can also consult local papers and tourist bureaus for activities geared toward children. Most national parks offer **Junior Ranger** programs, which introduce kids ages 8 to 12 to nature in half- or full-day trips. In case they

1550 Collins Ave.
Miami Beach, FL 33139
Tel: (305) 531-0361
Fax: (305) 531-8676

grow bored with the sights, be sure to pack their favorite toys, including coloring books and games.

Many fares, admission prices, and fees are lower for children and/or families. Some lodgings, such as the Days Inn, offer special rates for rooms with kitchenettes. Amtrak and many airlines also offer discounts for children, but it's often easier to travel with kids by car than by other forms of transportation. With a car, you have the freedom to make frequent stops, and children have more room to spread out their belongings and themselves. Be sure to place carseats at window level so your children can easily see out. If you decide to travel by air, fly during nap time, so that your child will sleep through the flight. Try to arrange it so that take-off and landing come at feeding time—if the baby is swallowing often at these times, the changes in altitude won't hurt its ears.

While on the road, children require additional health and safety considerations. When renting a car, be sure that the company supplies a child safety seat. All states require that small children are secured in a carseat; although the minimum age varies from state to state, all states will fine you if they see your child is not protected. It is best to keep all children secured, as some states enforce this law particularly strictly. When outside, avoid areas with extreme climatic conditions since children are more vulnerable to frostbite, hypothermia and heatstroke. (See Health.)

Before plunging into the heart of darkness, consider picking up *Backpacking with Babies and Small Children* ($9) and *Sharing Nature with Children* ($8), available from Wilderness Press, 2440 Bancroft Way, Berkeley, CA 94704 (800-443-7227 or 415-843-8080). Another publication that may be useful is *Travel with Children* by Maureen Wheeler ($11 plus $1.50 shipping) from Lonely Planet Publications, 155 Filbert St., Oakland, CA 94607 (800-229-0122). The *Kidding Around* series ($10 each; $3.75 shipping for the first, 50¢ for each additional book) are illustrated books intended for children, about different places, mostly in the U.S. Order from **John Muir Publications,** P.O. Box 613, Santa Fe, NM 87504 (800-888-7504).

You may have a hard time convincing your children that the trip will be rewarding; discuss your plans with your older children before leaving. Maps and pictures of your destinations may placate their fears about leaving home. You may also want to discuss your travel plans with your pediatrician before you leave.

Travelers with Dietary Concerns

Travelers who keep **kosher** should contact synagogues in the larger cities for information on kosher restaurants; your own synagogue or college Hillel should have access to lists of Jewish institutions across the nation. If you eat at non-kosher restaurants, check to see whether foods are fried in vegetable oil and whether soups and sauces are meat-based. If you are strict in your observance, consider preparing your own food. Bring along some sturdy plasticware, a pan, a small grill, and lots of aluminum foil; buy fresh fish, fruits, and vegetables along the way. You may need to bring your own bread—if so, bags of pita last longer than bread loaves. *The Jewish Travel Guide* ($11.50 plus $1.50 shipping), from Sepher-Hermon Press, 1265 46th St., Brooklyn, NY 11219 (718-972-9010), lists Jewish institutions, synagogues, and kosher restaurants in over 80 countries.

People who are **vegetarian** should have no problem finding nourishing and delicious meals in the U.S., where fresh vegetables and fruit abound. **Veganism**, the practice of using nor eating no animal products, is growing in popularity. Services in many college towns cater to vegans, offering meat- and dairy-free entrées in restaurants as well as "cruelty-free" products in retail stores. Contact the **North American Vegetarian Society** at P.O. Box 72, Dolgeville, NY 13329 (518-568-7970) for information.

Diabetics should contact the American Diabetes Association to discover how to make watching their diet on the road easier. See Health above.

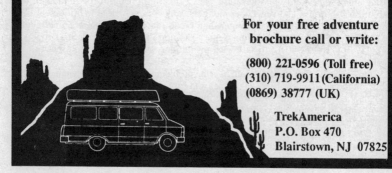

Getting Around

By Plane

The United States is a big country, and getting from point A to point Z can take a chunk out of your touring time. To get from place to place—especially from metropolis to metropolis—you'll probably have to fly. Recently, airfares have fluctuated wildly; the best way to get a great deal these days is often just by keeping track of the latest price war through the travel section of your local newspaper or by keeping in touch with a travel agent. Reserve a seat several months in advance for travel between June and August and around holidays, since these times have the heaviest air traffic. The best deals (e.g. two-for-one specials) usually appear between January and mid-May. Also check with your travel agent for system-wide air passes and excursion fares.

Last-minute travelers should ask about "red-eye" (all-night) flights, especially on popular business routes. **Charter flights** run between some U.S. cities; they are more subject to sudden schedule changes but can save money. Don't buy "frequent-flyer" coupons (given by airlines allowing the passenger named on them to fly a stated number of miles) from other people on the assumption that the airlines never check the identity of their ticket holders; they sometimes do, and you could find yourself paying for a new, full-fare ticket. Always call the airline the day before your departure to reconfirm your flight reservation, and get to the airport early to ensure you have a seat; airlines usually overbook. (On the other hand, being "bumped" from a flight does not spell doom if your travel plans are flexible—you will probably leave on the next flight and receive either a free ticket or a cash bonus. You might even want to bump yourself when the airline asks for volunteers.)

Many airlines offer special discounts (usually 50% off regular fares) to children accompanied by an adult, but few offer discounts to seniors. Check the weekend travel sections of major newspapers for bargain fares, and consider discount travel agencies such as **Travel Avenue,** 641 West Lake St., Suite 201, Chicago, IL 60606-1012 (800-333-3335), which rebates four-fifths of the standard 10% ticket commission.

Chances of receiving discount fares increase on competitive routes; shuttle service between major cities on the East Coast saves a lot of time and is almost as cheap as the train if you can take advantage of student or senior citizen fares. Flying smaller airlines instead of the national giants can also save money.

Another discount option is to travel as a **courier.** This method, however, has two restrictions: only carry-on luggage is permitted (the company needs the luggage space), and flights mostly originate from New York City. Still, for the adventurous and the resourceful, courier services present opportunities for inexpensive travel. For more information, contact **Now Voyager,** P.O. Box 8494, New York, NY 10116; **Halbert Express,** 147-05 176th St., Jamaica, NY 11434 (718-656-8189); or **Courier Air Travel,** 3661 N. Campbell Ave. #342, Tucson, AZ 85719, which publishes a 50-page handbook ($9) listing courier companies and giving procedures for traveling as a courier.

Ticket consolidators are companies which sell unbooked commercial and charter airline tickets. Most have a membership fee of $30 to $50, but fares can be extremely cheap. Inquire about cancellation fees and advance purchase requirements, and be prepared to be flexible about your dates of arrival and departure. For more information, contact **Air Hitch,** 2790 Broadway #100, New York, NY 10025 (212-864-2000). (Note: be very careful when you deal with a consolidator. The Better Business Bureau has received complaints about Air Hitch, and though the company has responded to them, the customers have not always been satisfied with those responses.)

In recent years **American Express** has run promotions whereby students are offered a pre-approved Green Card along with vouchers for inexpensive domestic flights ($130-$200). Of course, you have to pay the $55 annual fee for the card, but the savings on longer flights can be substantial. (For more information on American Express, see Credit Cards above.)

By Train (the iron horse, riding the rails, the locomotive, the choo-choo)

Train travel is still one of the cheapest and most comfortable ways to tour the country. You can walk from car to car to stretch your legs, buy edibles in the snack bar, and shut out the sun to sleep in a reclining chair (the budget traveler should avoid expensive roomettes or bedrooms). Not all stations check baggage and not all trains carry large amounts of it (though most long-distance ones do).

Amtrak's discount **All-Aboard America** fare schedule divides the Continental U.S. into three regions—Eastern, Central, and Western. Amtrak charges the same rate for both one-way and round-trip travel, with three stopovers permitted and a maximum trip duration of 45 days. During the summer, rates are $199 within one region, $279 between two regions, and $339 among three (Sept. 1-Dec. 17 and Jan. 4-May 27, rates are $179, $229, and $259 respectively). All-Aboard fares are subject to availability, so reserve well in advance. Amtrak offers several discounts off its full fares: children ages two to 15 accompanied by a parent (half-fare); children under age two (free); senior citizens and travelers with disabilities (25% off one-way ticket); current members of the U.S. armed forces and active-duty veterans (25% discount) and their dependents (12.5% discount). Circle trips and special holiday packages can save you money as well. Keep in mind that discounted air travel, particularly for longer distances, may be cheaper than train travel. Food is expensive on trains, so if you're going on a long journey pack plenty of eats. For up-to-date information and reservations, contact your local Amtrak office or call 800-USA-RAIL; 872-7245 (use a touch-tone phone). Travelers with hearing impairments may use a teletypewriter (800-523-6590; 800-562-6960 in PA).

In addition to Amtrak, local and regional lines still chug through some areas—check the yellow pages or ask at the local train station.

By Bus

Buses are often the only way to reach smaller locales without a car. Your biggest challenge when you travel by bus is scheduling. *Russell's Official National Motor Coach Guide* ($12.80 including postage) is an indispensable tool for constructing an itinerary; it contains schedules of literally every bus route between any two towns in the United States and Canada. Russell's also publishes a semiannual *Supplement,* which includes a Directory of Bus Lines, Bus Stations, and Route Maps ($5 each). To order any of the above, write Russell's Guides, Inc., P.O. Box 278, Cedar Rapids, IA 52406 (319-364-6138). Since schedules change frequently and the guide is updated monthly, a far better idea than purchasing the guide is to look at a copy in a library reference room.

Greyhound (800-752-4841) operates the largest number of lines in both the U.S. and Canada. Within specific regions, other bus companies may provide more exhaustive services (for example, **Peter Pan** serves most of New England). Greyhound operates no buses in Hawaii.

A number of discounts are available on Greyhound's standard-fare tickets (restrictions apply): senior citizens (Mon.-Thurs. 10%, Fri.-Sat. 5% off); children ages 5 to 11 (50% off); children ages 2 to 4 (75% off); children under age 2 travel free (if they sit on your lap); travelers with disabilities and their companions together ride for the price of one; active and retired U.S. military personnel and National Guard Reserves and their spouses and dependents, may (with valid ID) take a round-trip between any two points in the U.S. for $159.

Greyhound allows passengers to carry two pieces of luggage (up to 100 lbs. total) at no charge. Whatever you stow in compartments underneath the bus should be clearly marked; be sure to get a claim check for it, and watch to make sure your luggage is on the same bus as you are. If possible stash all of your bags in the carry-on racks. Anyone who has tried to track missing baggage on Greyhound will tell you that it is a nightmare worth averting. As always, keep your essential documents and valuables on your person, and carry a small bag onto the bus with you. Take a sweater, too; surprisingly efficient air-conditioning often brings the temperature down to arctic levels.

If you plan to tour a great deal by bus within the U.S., you may save money with the **Ameripass,** which entitles you to unlimited travel for seven days ($299), 15 days ($319), or 30 days ($429); extensions cost $15 per day. Before you purchase an Ameripass, total up the separate bus fares between towns to make sure that the pass is indeed more economical, or at least worth the unlimited flexibility it provides. Some regional bus companies are actually Greyhound subsidiaries, and as such will honor Ameripasses. Check with the company to make sure.

Always check bus schedules and routes personally, and don't rely on old printed schedules since listings change seasonally. You can buy a ticket at the terminal, but arrive early. If you are boarding at a remote "flag stop," be sure you know exactly where the bus stops. Catch the driver's attention by standing on the side of the road and flailing your arms wildly—better to be embarrassed than stranded. Greyhound is a useful organization for the budget traveler; its fares are cheap, and its tendrils poke into virtually every corner of America. Be sure, however, to allow plenty of extra time for connections, and be prepared for possibly unsavory traveling companions.

For a more unusual and social trip, consider **Green Tortoise.** These funky "hostels on wheels" are remodeled diesel buses done up with foam mattresses, sofa seats, stereos and dinettes; meals are prepared communally. Bus drivers operate in teams so that one can drive and the other can point out sights and chat with passengers. Prices include transportation, sleeping space on the bus, and tours of the regions through which you pass. Deposits ($100 most trips) are generally required, since space is tight and economy is important for the group.

Green Tortoise can get you to San Francisco from Boston or New York in 10 to 14 car-free and carefree days for $279 (plus $75 for food). A "commuter" line runs between Seattle and Los Angeles; hop on at any point. For the vacation-oriented, Green Tortoise also operates a series of round-trip "loops" which start and finish in San Francisco and travel to Yosemite National Park, Northern California, Baja California, the

Grand Canyon and Alaska. The Baja trip includes several days on the beach, with sailboats and windsurfers provided for a fee. The National Park loop (16 days, $499 plus $121 for food) hits all the biggies. Much of Green Tortoise's charm lies in its low price and the departure it offers from the impersonality of Greyhound service; one passenger has been quoted as saying, "This bus gives people a chance to act like hippies for a night then go back to the real world the next morning." For more information, write Green Tortoise, P.O. Box 24459, San Francisco, CA 94124 (800-227-4766, in CA 415-821-0803; there are regional agents in Boston, New York, Los Angeles, Santa Barbara, Santa Cruz, Vancouver, Seattle, Portland, and Eugene, OR). Book at least two months in advance to be assured of a reservation.

Try to use the local bus systems to travel within a town. The largest cities also have subways and commuter train lines. Call city transit information numbers and track down a public transport map with schedules. *Let's Go* lists information about local transit in the Practical Information sections.

By all means avoid spending the night in a bus station. Though generally guarded, bus stations can be hangouts for dangerous or at least frightening characters. Try to arrange your arrivals for reasonable day or evening times. This will also make it easier for you to find transportation out of the station and accommodations for the night.

By Car

Getting Revved Up

If you will be relying heavily on car travel, you might do well to join an automobile club. For $15 to $70 per year (depending on where you live and how many benefits you choose) the **American Automobile Association (AAA)** offers free trip-planning services, roadmaps and guidebooks, discounts on car rentals, emergency road service anywhere in the U.S., the International Driver's License, and commission-free traveler's checks from American Express. Your membership card can even serve as a $5000 bail bond (if you find yourself in jail) or a $1000 arrest bond certificate (which you can use instead of being arrested for any motor vehicle offense *except* drunk driving, driving without a valid license, or failure to appear in court on a prior motor-vehicle arrest). Many clubs also have an "AAA Plus" membership program which provides more extensive emergency road service, insurance protection, and 100 mi. of free towing (this is not as far as it seems in rural areas, where AAA-affiliated garages can be few and far between). For more information, write to AAA at 100 AAA Drive, Heathrow, FL 32746 (800-AAA-HELP or 800-222-4357, or check your local yellow pages).

Other automobile travel service organizations include:

AMOCO Motor Club, P.O Box 9049, Des Moines, IA 50369 (800-334-3300). $50 annual membership enrolls you, your spouse, and your car. Services include 24-hr. towing and emergency road service.

Mobil Auto Club, P.O. Box 5039, North Suburban, IL 60197 (800-621-5581). $45 annual membership covers you and 1 other person of your choice. Benefits include locksmith and other roadside services, as well as car-rental discounts with Hertz, Avis, and National.

If you'll be driving during your trip, make sure that your insurance is up-to-date and that you are completely covered. Many states require proof of insurance as one of the documents you should have with you while driving. For information on the International Driver's License, see Documents and Formalities below, under For International Visitors. *Let's Go* lists U.S. highways in this format: "I" (as in "I-90") refers to Interstate highways, "U.S." (as in "U.S. 1") to United States highways, and "Rte." (as in "Rte. 7") to state and local highways.

On the Road

Learn a bit about minor automobile maintenance and repair before you leave, and pack an easy-to-read manual—it may at the very least help you keep your car alive long enough to reach a reputable garage. If you've never done it before, practice changing your tire once or twice without help, and spend an afternoon discovering what's under the hood. Your trunk should contain the following bare necessities: a spare tire and jack, jumper cables, extra oil, flares, a blanket (several, if you're traveling in winter), extra water (if you're traveling in summer or through the desert), and a flashlight. If there's a chance you may be stranded in a remote area, bring an emergency food and water supply. Always have plenty of gas and check road conditions ahead of time when possible, particularly during the winter (*Let's Go* provides road condition hotline numbers where available). Carry a good map with you at all times (*Let's Go's* maps are intended for use in trip planning only; buy a detailed road map for use during your travel). **Rand McNally** publishes one of the most comprehensive road atlases of the U.S., available in most bookstores for around $8. Carry enough cash for tolls and gasoline; tolls can sometimes be up to $5 and gasoline costs between $1 to $3 per gallon.

Gas is generally cheaper in towns than at interstate service stops. Oil company credit cards are handy, but paying with cash is usually cheaper. When planning your budget, remember that the enormous travel distances of the U.S. will require you to spend more on gas than you might expect. Burn less money by burning less fuel. Tune up the car, make sure the tires are in good repair and properly inflated, check the oil frequently, and avoid running the air conditioner unnecessarily. Don't use roof luggage racks—they cause air drag, and if you need one, you've probably over-packed. The best way to save gas is to not drive at all, but if it can't be helped, make sure you're getting the most transportation value for your dollar by filling up the back seat with passengers. Check college campus ride boards, bulletin boards, and the classified ads (particularly those in newspapers geared to smaller audiences such as students) to find traveling companions who'll split gasoline costs.

If you take a car into a major city, try not to leave valuable possessions in it while you're away from the car. Radios are especially tempting; if your tape deck or radio is removable, hide it in the trunk or take it with you. If is isn't detachable, at least conceal it under some junk. Similarly, hide baggage in the trunk—although some savvy thieves can tell if a car is heavily loaded by the way it is settled on its tires. (Solution: travel light; see Packing above.) Park your vehicle in a garage or well-traveled area. Sleeping in a car or van parked in the city is extremely dangerous—even the most dedicated budget traveler should not consider it.

In many states it is illegal to drive with open containers of alcohol in the car. And be sure to buckle up—it's the law in much of the U.S. Before you hit the road, check rental cars to make sure that the seatbelts work properly. In general, the speed limit is 55 mph, but rural sections of major interstates may be 65 mph (when posted). Heed the limit; not only does it save gas, but most local police forces and state troopers make frequent use of radar to catch speed demons. In many states, radar detectors are illegal. You will be forced to disengage it before driving in those states.

In the 1950s, President Dwight D. Eisenhower envisioned an **interstate system,** a federally funded network of highways designed primarily to increase military mobility and subsidize American commerce. Eisenhower's asphalt dream gradually has been realized, although Toyotas far outnumber tanks on the federally funded roads. Believe it or not, there is actually an easily comprehensible, consistent system for numbering interstates. Even-numbered interstates run east-west and odd ones run north-south, increasing in number the further north or west they are. If the interstate has a three-digit number, it is a branch of another interstate (i.e., I-285 is a branch of I-85), often a bypass skirting around a large city. An *even* digit in the *hundred's* place means the branch will eventually return to the main interstate; an *odd* digit means it won't. North-south routes begin on the West Coast with I-5 and end with I-95 on the East Coast. The southernmost east-west route is I-4 in Florida. The northernmost east-west route is I-94, stretching from Montana to Wisconsin.

The greatest difficulty posed by interstates is not the state troopers, the other drivers, or even bad road conditions—it's the sheer boredom. If you feel drowsy, pull off the road to take a break. To avoid overexhaustion, start driving early in the morning and

stop early in the afternoon (you'll also have more time to find accommodations). When you're driving with companions, insist that one of them is awake at all times, and keep talking. If you can't pull over, try listening to an aggravating radio talk show—music can be as lulling as silence. A thermos of coffee is also helpful. And remember that turning up the heat too high in the car can also make you sleepy.

Never drive if you've had anything alcoholic to drink or if you've used drugs or any potentially impairing substance. Don't believe the myth that a cup of hot coffee or a cold shower can sober you up; the only remedy for a buzz is time. This is an issue not only for your safety but for everyone else's on the road and also for your police record; U.S. drunk driving laws are extremely strict. Also, avoid the open road on weekend nights and holidays, when more drivers are likely to be drunk.

Renting

Although the cost of renting a car for long distances is often prohibitive, renting for local trips may be reasonable. Auto rental agencies fall into two categories: national companies and local agencies that serve only one city or region. The former usually allow cars to be picked up in one city and dropped off in another (for a hefty charge). By calling a toll-free number you can reserve a reliable car anywhere in the country. Drawbacks include steep prices and high minimum ages for rentals (usually 25). If you're 21 or older and have a major credit card in your name, you may be able to rent where the minimum age would otherwise rule you out. Student discounts are occasionally available. Try **Alamo** (800-327-9633), **Avis** (800-331-1212), **Budget** (800-527-0700), **Dollar** (800-800-4000), **Hertz** (800-654-3131), **National** (800-328-4567), or **Thrifty** (800-367-2277).

Local companies are often more flexible and cheaper than major companies, but you'll generally have to return the car to its point of origin. Some local companies will accept a cash deposit ($50-100) or simply proof of employment (e.g., check stubs) in lieu of a credit card. Companies such as **Rent-A-Wreck** (800-421-7253) supply cars that are long past their prime. Sporting dents and purely decorative radios, the cars sometimes get very poor mileage, but they run and they're cheap. Be careful when renting such cars in isolated areas, particularly in mountainous or desert terrain. Don't leave the lot unless you're sure your car will get you to where you're going (and back) safely. *Let's Go* lists the addresses and phone numbers of local rental agencies in most towns.

When dealing with any car rental company, make certain the price includes insurance against theft and collision. This may be an additional charge, though American Express automatically insures any car rented with its card. Rates change on a day-to-day basis, so be sure to call for information. Basic rental charges run $30 to $50 per day plus 30 to 40¢ per mile for a compact car. Standard shift cars are usually a few dollars cheaper than automatics. Most packages include a certain amount of free mileage that varies with the length of time you're renting for. If you'll be driving a long distance (a few hundred miles or more), ask for an unlimited-mileage package. All companies have special weekend rates, and renting by the week is cheaper. For rentals longer than a week, look into **automobile leasing,** which costs less than renting. Make sure, however, that your car is covered by a service plan to avoid the risk of outrageous repair bills.

Auto Transport Companies

Automobile transport companies match drivers with car owners who need cars moved from one city to another. Would-be travelers give the company their desired destination; the company finds the car. The only expenses are gas, food, tolls and lodging (plus a deposit of about $250). The company's insurance covers any breakdowns or damage. You must be at least 21, have a valid license, and agree to drive about 400 miles per day on a fairly direct route. It's easiest to find cars for traveling from coast to coast; New York and Los Angeles are popular destinations.

If offered a car, look it over first. Think twice about accepting a gas guzzler since you'll be paying for the gas. With the company's approval, however, you may be able to share the cost with several companions. For more information, contact **Auto Driveaway,** 310 S. Michigan Ave., Chicago, IL 60604 (800-346-2277).

By Motorcycle

It's cheaper than driving a car, but the physical and emotional wear and tear of motorcycling may negate any financial gain. Fatigue and the small gas tank conspire to force the motorcyclist to stop more often on long trips; experienced riders are seldom on the road more than six hours per day. Lack of luggage space can also be a serious limitation. If you must carry a load, keep it low and forward where it won't distort the cycle's center of gravity. Fasten it either to the seat or over the rear axle in saddle or tank bags.

Annoyances, though, are secondary to risks. Despite their superior maneuverability, motorcycles are incredibly vulnerable to accidents. Major enemies are crosswinds, drunk drivers, and the blind spots of cars and trucks. *Always ride defensively.* The dangers skyrocket at night; travel only in the daytime. Half of all cyclists have an accident within their first month of riding. Even if you've never met a person who's had an accident on a motorcycle, understand that serious mishaps are common and often fatal. Always wear the best helmet you can get your hands on. For information on motorcycle emergencies, ask your State Department of Motor Vehicles for a motorcycle operator's manual.

By Bicycle

Travel by bicycle is about the cheapest way to go. You move much more slowly and with much more effort, but the leisurely pace gives you a chance to take in the view. In addition, cycling is pollution-free and a good way to exercise.

Get in touch with a local biking club if you don't know a great deal about bicycle equipment and repair. When you shop around, compare knowledgeable local retailers to mail-order firms. Make your first investment in an issue of *Bicycling* magazine, which advertises sale prices. **Bike Nashbar,** a cheap source of bike paraphernalia, almost always has the lowest prices—if you can find a nationally advertised price that's lower, they will beat it by 5¢. Contact them at 4111 Simon Rd., Youngstown, OH 44512 (800-627-4227). Their own line of products, including complete bicycles, is an excellent value. Another exceptional mail-order firm which specializes in mountain bikes is **Bikecology,** P.O. Box 3900, Santa Monica, CA 90403 (800-326-2453).

Safe and secure cycling requires a quality helmet and lock. A **Bell** or **Tourlite** helmet costs about $45—much cheaper than critical head surgery or a well-appointed funeral. U-shaped **Kryptonite** or **Citadel** locks start at around $30, with insurance against theft for one or two years if your bike is registered with the police.

Long-distance cyclists should contact **Bikecentennial,** P.O. Box 8308, Missoula, MT 59807 (406-721-1776), a national, non-profit organization that researches and maps long-distance routes and organizes bike tours for members. Its best-known project is the 4450-mi. TransAmerica Bicycle Trail through the United States. Bikecentennial also offers members maps, guidebooks (including the *Cyclist's Yellow Pages*), and nine issues of *Bike Report,* the organization's bicycle touring magazine. Annual fees in the U.S. are $22 per person (students $19) and $25 per family. In Canada and Mexico, they are US$30 per person and $35 for families.

There are also a number of good books about bicycle touring and repair in general. *Bike Touring* ($11, Sierra Club) and *Bicycle Touring* ($5, **Rodale Press,** 33 E. Minor St., Emmaus, PA 18098 or call 215-967-5171) both discuss how to equip and plan a bicycle trip. *Bicycle Gearing: A Practical Guide* ($7, The Mountaineers Books) discusses in lay terms how bicycle gears work, covering everything you need to know in order to shift properly and get the maximum propulsion from the minimum exertion. *The*

Bike Bag Book ($4 plus $1.50 shipping, **10-Speed Press,** Box 7123, Berkeley, CA 94707 or call 415-845-8414) is a bite-sized manual with broad utility.

It's not easy, but you can transport your bike with you as you travel by bus, train, or air—check with each carrier about weight limits, packing requirements, insurance and fees.

By Thumb

Let's Go urges you to consider the large risks and disadvantages of hitchhiking before thumbing it. Hitching means entrusting your life to a randomly selected person who happens to stop beside you on the road. While this may be comparatively safe in some areas of Europe and Australia, it is generally *not* so in the United States. We do NOT recommend it. We strongly urge you to find other means of transportation.

If you feel you have no other alternative, you *insist* on ignoring our warnings, and decide to hitchhike anyway, there are many precautions that must be taken. First, assess the risks and your chances of getting a ride. Women traveling alone should never, ever, *ever* hitch in the United States. It's too big of a risk. Don't believe assurances to the contrary. For single men, it is slightly less dangerous, but also much more difficult to get a ride. A woman and a man is perhaps the best compromise between safety and utility. Two men will have a hard time getting rides and if they do, it will probably be in extremely uncomfortable circumstances. Three men won't be picked up.

Next, don't take any chances with drivers. Choosy beggars might not get where they're going the fastest, but at least they'll get there alive. Experienced hitchers won't get in the car if they don't know where the driver is going. Never get into the back seat of a two-door car, or into a car whose passenger door doesn't open from the inside. Beware of cars that have electric door locks which lock you in against your will. Women especially should turn down a ride when the driver opens the door quickly and offers to drive anywhere. Never put yourself in a position from which you can't exit quickly, never let your belongings out of your reach, and *never* hesitate to refuse a ride if you will feel at all uncomfortable alone with the driver.

Experienced hitchers talk with the driver—even idle chatter informs hitchers about their driver—but never divulge any information that they would not want a stranger to know. They also won't stay in the car if the driver starts making sexual innuendoes. It may be harmless joking, but it's best not to find out. If at all threatened or intimidated, experienced hitchers ask to be let out no matter how uncompromising the road looks, and they know *in advance* where to go if stranded and what to do in emergencies.

In general, hitching in the United States is less safe the farther south and east one goes, and the more urban the area in which one travels. Near metropolises like New York City and Los Angeles, hitching is tantamount to suicide. In areas like rural Alaska and some island communities, hitching is reportedly less unsafe. All states prohibit hitchhiking while standing on the roadway itself or behind a posted freeway entrance sign; hitchers more commonly find rides on stretches near major intersections where many cars converge. In some suburbs, lines of commuters form near the access ramps of highways to the "city;" each commuter is picked up by drivers needing more people in their cars to qualify for special car-pool privileges.

Hitchhiking in the United States is a BAD idea. Don't toy with your life, and don't ever compromise your safety. Plan ahead, and never get yourself into a situation in which hitchhiking is necessary.

Accommodations

The U.S. has a pleasant variety of inexpensive alternatives to hotels and motels. Before you set out, try to locate places to stay along your route and make reservations, especially if you plan to travel during peak tourist seasons. Even if you find yourself in dire straits, don't spend the night under the stars; it's often uncomfortable, unsafe, and illegal, even in national parks and forest areas. If you don't have the money for lodgings, call the **Traveler's Aid Society,** listed in *Let's Go* under Practical Information wherever it exists. The local crisis center hotline may also have a list of persons or groups who will house you in such an emergency.

Youth Hostels

Youth hostels offer unbeatable deals on indoor lodging, and they are great places to meet traveling companions from all over the world; many hostels even have ride boards to help you hook up with other hostelers going your way. As a rule, hostels are dorm-style accommodations where the sexes sleep apart, often in large rooms with bunk beds. (Some hostels allow families and couples to have private rooms.) You must bring or rent your own sleep sack (two sheets sewn together); sleeping bags are often not allowed. Hostels often have kitchens and utensils for your use, and some have storage areas and laundry facilities. Many also require you to perform a communal chore, usually lasting no more than 15 min.

Hostelling International/American Youth Hostels (HI/AYH) maintains over 300 hostels in the U.S. and Canada. Basic HI/AYH rules (with some local variation): check-in between 5 and 8pm, check-out by 9:30am, maximum stay three days, no pets or alcohol allowed on the premises. All ages are welcome. Fees range from $7 to $12 per night. Hostels are graded according to the number of facilities they offer and their overall level of quality—consult *Let's Go* evaluations for each town. Reservations may be necessary or advisable at some hostels, so check ahead of time. HI/AYH membership is annual: $25, $15 for ages over 54, $10 for ages under 18, $35 for a family. Nonmembers who wish to stay at an HI/AYH hostel usually pay $3 extra, which can be applied toward membership. The **International Youth Hostel Federation (IYHF)** recently changed its name to **Hostelling International (HI),** in an effort to attract budget travelers of all ages; hostelling isn't just for kids anymore! HI memberships (and IYHF memberships that have not yet expired) are valid at all HI/AYH hostels. For more information, contact HI/AYH, 425 Divisadero St. #301, San Francisco, CA 94117 (415-863-9939); the *AYH Handbook* is free with membership, and lists and describes all hostels. Not all hostels are HI/AYH; some are members of the **American Association of Independent Hostels (AAIH)**, 1412 Cerrillos Rd., Santa Fe, NM 87051 (505-988-1153), and some advertised "hostels" are actually people renting out basements. We list abbreviations for HI/AYH and other independent organizations, but be sure to check the *AYH Handbook,* since hostel approval is based on frequent inspections.

Hotels and Motels

If you are addicted to Hiltons and Marriotts beyond your means, consider joining **Discount Travel International,** Ives Bldg., #205, 114 Forrest Ave., Narberth, PA 19072 (215-668-7184). For an annual membership fee of $45, you and your household will have access to a clearing house of unsold hotel rooms (as well as airline tickets, cruises and the like), which can save you as much as 50%.

Many budget motels preserve single digits in their names (e.g. Motel 6), but the cellar-level price of a single has matured to just under $30. Nevertheless, budget chain motels still cost significantly less than the chains catering to the next-pricier market, such as Holiday Inn. Chains usually adhere more consistently to a level of cleanliness and comfort than locally operated budget competitors; some budget motels even feature heated pools and cable TV. In bigger cities, budget motels are just off the highway,

often inconveniently far from the downtown area, so if you don't have a car, you may well spend the difference between a budget motel and one downtown on transportation. Contact these chains for free directories:

Motel 6, 3391 S. Blvd, Rio Rancho, NM 87124 (505-891-6161).

Super 8 Motels, Inc., 1910 8th Ave. NE, P.O. Box 4090, Aberdeen, SD 57402-4090 (800-843-1991).

Friendship Inns International, c/o Choice Hotels International, 10750 Columbia Pike, Silver Springs, MD 20901-4494 (800-453-4511).

Allstar Inns, LP, P.O. Box 3070, Santa Barbara, CA 93180-3070 (805-687-3383).

Best Western, P.O. Box 10203, Phoenix, AZ 85064-0203 (800-528-1234).

You may also want to consult an omnibus directory, like the *State by State Guide to Budget Motels* ($11) from **Marlor Press, Inc.,** 4304 Brigadoon Drive, St. Paul, MN 55126 (800-669-4908), or the *National Directory of Budget Motels* ($5), from Pilot Books, 103 Cooper St., Babylon, NY 11702 (516-422-2225).

Bed and Breakfasts

As alternatives to impersonal hotel rooms, bed and breakfasts (private homes with spare rooms available to travelers) range from the acceptable to the sublime. B&Bs may provide an excellent way to explore an area with the help of a host who knows it well, and some go out of their way to be accommodating, by accepting travelers with pets or giving personalized tours. The best part of your stay will often be a home-cooked breakfast (and occasionally dinner). However, many B&Bs do not provide phones, TVs, or private showers with your room.

Prices vary widely. B&Bs in major cities are usually more expensive than those in out-of-the-way places. Doubles can cost anywhere from $20 to $300 per night. Most are in the $30 to $50 range. Some homes give special discounts to families or senior citizens. Reservations are almost always necessary, although in the off-season (if the B&B is open), you can frequently find a room on short notice.

For information on B&Bs, contact **Bed and Breakfast International,** P.O. Box 282910, San Francisco, CA 94128-2910 (800-872-4500 or 415-696-1690) or CIEE's (212-661-1414) *Where to Stay USA* ($13) which includes listings for hostels, YMCAs and dorms, along with B&Bs with singles under $30 and doubles under $35. Two useful guidebooks on the subject are *Bed & Breakfast, USA,* ($11) by Betty R. Rundback and Nancy Kramer, available in bookstores or through Tourist House Associates, Inc., RD 2, Box 355-A, Greentown, PA 18426 (717-676-3222), and *The Complete Guide to Bed and Breakfasts, Inns and Guesthouses in the U.S. and Canada,* by Pamela Lanier, from Lanier Publications, P.O. Box 20467, Oakland, CA 94620. In addition, check local phone books, visitors bureaus, and information at bus and train stations.

As an alternative to standard B&Bs, contact the **U.S. Servas Committee,** 11 John St. #407, New York, NY 10038 (212-267-0252), an international cooperative system of hosts and travelers. This non-profit organization provides travelers with hosts who provide accommodations for two to three days. Letters of reference and an interview are required. Participation in the program costs $45 per year per traveler, with a $15 deposit on host lists, but travelers and hosts do not exchange money.

YMCAs and YWCAs

Young Men's Christian Associations (YMCAs) don't always offer lodging; those that do are often located in urban downtowns, which can be convenient but a little gritty. Rates are usually lower than a hotel but higher than the local hostel and include use of showers (usually communal), libraries, pools, and other facilities. Economy packages (2-8 days; $40-270) that include lodging, meals, and excursions are available in

New York, New Orleans, Seattle, Washington, DC, and Hollywood. Many YMCAs accept women and families, but some (e.g. the Los Angeles chapters) will not accept ages under 18 without parental permission. Reservations are $3 (strongly recommended), and key deposits are $5. For information and reservations, write the **Y's Way to Travel,** 356 W. 34th St., New York, NY 10001 (212-760-5856). Send a self-addressed envelope stamped with 65¢ postage for a free catalogue.

Most Young Women's Christian Associations (YWCAs) accommodate only women. Non-members are usually required to join when lodging. For more information, write YWCA, 726 Broadway, New York, NY 10003 (212-614-2700).

College Dormitories

Many colleges and universities open their residence halls to travelers when school is not in session—some do so even during term-time. No general policy covers all of these institutions, but rates tend to be low, and many schools require that you to express at least a vague interest in attending their institution. Since college dorms are popular with many travelers, you should call or write ahead for reservations.

Students traveling through a college or university town while school is in session might try introducing themselves to friendly looking local students. At worst you'll receive a cold reception; at best, a good conversation might lead to an offer of a place to crash. International visitors may have especially good luck here. In general, college campuses are some of the best sources for information on things to do, places to stay, and possible rides out of town. In addition, dining halls often serve reasonably priced, reasonably edible all-you-can-stomach meals.

Camping and the Great Outdoors

This is the best budget alternative for hardier, crunchier, more adventurous, less monied travelers. Even novices can enjoy tent camping in campgrounds, which cost little (usually under $15 per tent) and put you close to breathtaking scenery. *Woodall's Campground Directory* ($16 U.S., $18 outside U.S.; Eastern/Western editions $11 in U.S., $13 abroad; 8 regional guides $5 each) covers campsites around the U.S. Also try *Woodall's Tent Camping Guide* ($11 in U.S., $13 abroad). If you can't find a copy locally, contact **Woodall Publishing Company,** 28167 N. Keith Dr., Lake Forest, IL 60045-5000 (800-323-9076 or 708-362-6700).

For **topographical maps,** write the **U.S. Geological Survey,** Map Distribution, Box 25286, Denver Federal Center, Denver, CO 80225 (303-236-7477) or the **Canada Map Office,** 615 Booth St., Ottawa, Ont. K1A 0E9 (613-952-7000), which distributes geographical and topographical maps as well as aeronautical charts. Local ranger stations will also have good topographical maps of their areas.

Parks and Forests

National parks protect some of America and Canada's most spectacular scenery. Though their primary purpose is preservation, the parks also make room for recreation. Many national parks have backcountry with developed tent camping; others welcome RVs, and a few even offer opulent living in grand lodges. The larger and more popular national parks charge a $3 to $5 entry fee for vehicles and sometimes a smaller one for pedestrians and cyclists as well. The $25 **Golden Eagle Passport** (sold at most parks) covers the fee at all U.S. parks. Seniors and travelers with disabilities can procure passes ($20) which entitle them to free entry to all National Parks (see Travelers with Spe-

cific Concerns, above). Visitors centers at parks offer excellent free literature and information, and the U.S. Government Printing Office publishes two useful pamphlets: *National Parks: Camping Guide* (S/N 024-005-01028-9; $3.50) and *National Parks: Lesser-Known Areas* (S/N 024-005-00911-6; $1.50).

Many states and provinces have parks of their own, which are smaller than the national parks but offer some of the best camping around; in contrast to national parks, the primary function of **state parks** is recreation. Prices for camping at public sites are almost always better than those at private campgrounds.

Don't let swarming visitors dissuade you from visiting the large parks—these places are huge, and even at their most crowded they offer many chances for quiet and solitude. Reservations may be necessary for accommodations, especially those with solid walls (i.e., lodges). Even campsites are hard to come by at times; most campgrounds are first-come, first-pitched. Some parks limit the number of days you can stay in a campsite as well as the number of people you can have in your group (usually no more than 25 campers).

If your yearning for wilderness is so pure that even U.S. national parks seem overdeveloped, head for the **national forests.** Most are equipped only for primitive camping—no running water and only pit toilets. Forests are less accessible than the parks, but are also less crowded, and free. Backpackers can take advantage of near-complete isolation in specially designated **wilderness areas,** where regulations prohibit vehicles and there are no roads. **Wilderness permits** are required for backcountry hiking and can often be obtained (usually free) at parks. One word of warning: adventurers who plan to explore some real wilderness should *always* check in at a U.S. Forest Service field office for safety reasons before heading into the woods. Many of these wilderness areas are difficult to navigate, so procure accurate, detailed maps.

Believe it or not, the **U.S. Department of the Interior** does more than grant public lands to oil companies for exploitative development. Its **Bureau of Land Management (BLM)** also maintains national historic sites, backcountry cycling roads, and almost 6000 mi. of hiking trails throughout its millions of acres of untouched wilderness, most of it west of the Mississippi River. For information and maps, contact BLM at Headquarters Office, 18th & C St. NW, MIB 5600, Washington, D.C. 20240 (202-343-5717), or at the regional office nearest you. For free camping information, call 800-477-8669.

Tent Camping and Hiking

The *sine qua non* of your equipment is the **sleeping bag.** What kind you buy should depend on the climate in which you will be camping. Sleeping bags are rated according to the lowest outdoor temperature at which they will still keep you warm. Sleeping bags are made either of down (warmer and lighter) or of synthetic material (heavier, but better for wet weather). If you're using a sleeping bag for serious camping, you should also have either a foam pad or an air mattress to cushion your back and neck. When you select a **tent,** your major considerations should be shape and size. A-frame tents are the best all-around. When they are pitched, their internal space is almost entirely usable; this means little unnecessary bulk. Dome and umbrella shapes offer more spacious living, but tend to be bulkier to carry. Be sure your tent has a rain fly. Good two-person tents start at about $100, $150 for a four-person, but you can often find last year's version for half the price. If you intend to do a lot of hiking or biking, you should have a **frame backpack.** Buy a backpack with an internal frame if you'll be hiking on difficult trails that require a lot of bending and maneuvering—internal-frame packs mould better to your back, keep a lower center of gravity, and have enough give to follow you through your contortions. External-frame packs are more comfortable for long hikes over even terrain; since they keep the weight higher, walking upright will not cost you additional exertion. This is one area where it doesn't pay to economize—cheaper packs may be less comfortable, and the straps are more likely to fray or rip quickly. Test-drive a backpack for comfort before you buy it.

Other necessities include: **battery-operated lantern** (gas is inconvenient and dangerous), **plastic groundcloth** for the floor of your tent, **nylon tarp** for general purposes, and **stuff sacks** or **plastic bags** to keep your pack organized and your sleeping bag dry. Don't go anywhere without a **canteen** or water bottle. Plastic models keep water cooler in the hot sun than metal ones do, although metal canteens are a bit sturdier and leak less. If you'll be away from parks with showers, bring **water sacks** and/or a **solar shower,** a small black sack with an attachable shower head. Although most campgrounds provide campfire sites, you may want to bring a small **metal grate** of your own, and even a grill. For those places that forbid fires or the gathering of firewood, you'll need a **camp stove** (**Coleman** is the classic). Make sure you have **waterproof matches.**

Shop around your area for the best deals on camping equipment. If you can, buy from a local retailer who can give you advice about using your equipment. Several mail-order firms offer lower prices, and they can also help you determine which item is the one you need. Call or write for a free catalogue:

Campmor, 810 Rte. 17N, P.O. Box 997-LG91, Paramus, NJ 07653-0997 (800-526-4784).

L.L. Bean, 1 Casco St., Freeport, ME 04033 (800-341-4341).

Recreational Equipment, Inc. (REI), Commercial Sales, Sumner, WA 98352-0001 (800-426-4840).

A good initial source of information on **recreational vehicles (RVs)** is the **Recreational Vehicle Industry Association,** 1986 Preston White Dr., P.O. Box 2999, Reston, VA 22090 (703-620-6003). For a free catalogue that lists RV camping publications and state campground associations, send a self-addressed, stamped envelope to **Go Camping America Committee,** P.O. Box 2669, Reston, VA 22090 (703-620-6003).

Wilderness Concerns

The first thing to preserve in the wilderness is you—health, safety, and food should be your primary concerns as you camp. See Health above for information about basic medical concerns and first-aid. A comprehensive guide to outdoor survival is *How to Stay Alive in the Woods,* by Bradford Angier (Macmillan, $6). Many rivers, streams, and lakes are contaminated with bacteria such as *giardia,* which can cause gas, cramps, loss of appetite, and violent diarrhea. To protect yourself from the effects of this invisible trip-wrecker, always boil water before drinking or cooking with it, and bring water purification tablets. *Never go camping or hiking by yourself for any significant time or distance.* If you're going into an area that is not well-traveled or well-marked, let someone know where you're hiking and how long you intend to be out. If something unexpected occurs while you're out there, searchers will at least know where to look for you.

The second thing to protect while you are outdoors is the wilderness. Thousands of outdoor enthusiasts make use of the parks every year, and the forests are in danger of being trampled to death. Be considerate of the environment. Because firewood is scarce in popular parks, campers are asked to make small fires using only dead branches or brush; using a campstove is the more cautious way to cook. Check ahead to see if the park prohibits campfires altogether. To prevent long-term scarring of an area, make camp at least 100 feet from regularly used sites. Also, if there are no toilet facilities around, bury human waste 100 feet or more from any water supply to prevent contaminating lakes and streams. Keep soap or detergent away from bodies of water. Only **biosafe** soap may be used in streams and lakes. Pack up your trash in a plastic bag and carry it with you until you reach the next trash can. Never bury trash. And remember that hunting is strictly prohibited in all national, state, and provincial parks.

Additional Information for International Visitors

Orientation to the United States

The continental U.S. is large by European standards (3100 by 1800 mi. or 5000 by 2900km), and some areas are largely uninhabited. Except in the Northeast, travel between major urban centers takes hours or even days. The U.S. landscape varies from endless plains to glass-and-steel skyscrapers, from glaciers to deserts. It's best to concentrate travel in particular regions to avoid swallowing the U.S. in undigestable gulps.

To preview what the different areas of the U.S. offer the traveler, scan the regional introductions. The regions of the U.S. are often as culturally distinct as separate nations; a New Yorker might feel as foreign as an Aussie in Louisiana.

Although you needn't fear a terrorist attack in a U.S. airport, U.S. cities can be more violent and crime-ridden than their European or Asian counterparts. As anywhere, the best advice to foreign travelers in the U.S. is to use common sense. See Safety in the General Introduction for more information. Area-specific safety issues are discussed in the appropriate sections of the book.

Useful Organizations

When planning your trip, you might contact the **United States Travel and Tourism Administration**—with branches in Australia, Canada, France, Italy, Japan, Mexico, the Netherlands, the U.K. and Germany—which provides abundant free literature. If you can't find the address for the branch in your country, write to the U.S. Travel and Tourism Administration, Department of Commerce, 14th and Constitution Ave. NW, Washington, DC 20230 (202-377-4003). You may also want to write to the tourist offices of the states or cities you'll be visiting (see Practical Information listings). Wherever you write, the more specific your inquiry, the better your chances of getting the information you need. Once you arrive, visit local tourist information centers.

Extremely useful to foreign travelers, **Council Travel** (205 E. 42nd St., New York, NY 10017 (212-661-1450 or 800-438-2643), a budget travel subsidiary of the **Council on International Educational Exchange (CIEE),** has 38 offices in the U.S., as well as offices in the U.K., France, Germany and Japan. Council sells hostel cards, travel guidebooks including *Where to Stay USA* ($15), a directory of budget accommodations in the U.S., and charter and other reduced airline tickets. Most Council offices also issue the ISIC (see Documents below). Another excellent resource is **Let's Go Travel Service,** Thayer Hall-B, Harvard University, Cambridge, MA 02138 (617-495-9649 or 800-553-8746). Let's Go Travel sells Hostelling International/American Youth Hostel memberships as well as International Student Identification Cards.

The **International Student Travel Confederation (ISTC),** Gothersgade 30, 1123 Copenhagen K, Denmark, is affiliated with travel organizations throughout the world which arrange charter flights and discount air fares, provide travel insurance, issue ISICs, and sponsor the Student Air Travel Association for European students. Write to Council Travel in New York or to your local Council office. In Canada, write to **Travel CUTS** (Canadian University Travel Services Limited), 187 College St., Toronto, Ont. M5T 1P7 (416-979-2406). In the U.K., write to London Student Travel, 52 Grosvenor Gardens, London WC1 (tel. (071) 730 34 02). In Australia, contact SSA/STA, 220 Faraday St., Carlton, Melbourne, Victoria 3053 (tel. (03) 347 69 11).

The **Federation of International Youth Travel Organizations (FIYTO)** issues the **International Youth Card (IYC)** to anyone under 26, as well as a free catalog that lists special services and discounts for IYC cardholders. Write or call Council Travel.

STA Travel, based in the U.K., has over 100 offices worldwide to help you arrange discounted overseas flights. In the U.S., call 800-777-0112; if the number does not work, call local information for an office near you, or write to 17 E. 45th St., New York, NY 10017. Abroad, write to 74 or 86 Old Brompton Rd., London SW7 3LQ, England, or call (071) 937 99 71 for flights to North America.

If you wish to stay in a U.S. home during your vacation, many organizations can help you. The **Experiment in International Living** coordinates homestay programs for international visitors over the age of 14 wishing to join a U.S. family for 3 to 4 weeks. Homestays are arranged for all times of the year. For the appropriate address in your country, write to the U.S. Headquarters, P.O. Box 676, Kipling Rd., Brattleboro, VT 05302-0676 (800-327-4678 or 802-257-7751). The **Institute of International Education (IIE)** publishes their "Homestay Information Sheet" listing many homestay programs for foreign visitors. Write to them at 809 United Nations Plaza, New York, NY 10017-3580 (212-883-8200). See Accommodations above for information on **Servas,** a similar international travel organization, which coordinates short (2-3 day) homestays.

Documents and Formalities

Visas and Passports

Almost all foreign visitors to the U.S. must have a **passport,** a visitor's **visa,** and proof of plans to leave the U.S. For stays of only a few days, Canadian citizens with proof of citizenship do *not* need a visa or passport. Mexican citizens with an I-186 form can enter through a U.S. border station, then obtain an I-94 form 25 mi. in from the border. Other travelers will need to apply for visas at a U.S. consulate. International visitors usually obtain a B-1 or B-2 (non-immigrant, pleasure tourist) visa valid for a maximum of six months. Citizens of the U.K., Japan, Italy, Germany, France, the Netherlands, Sweden and Switzerland do not need a visa to enter the U.S. They must, however, possess at arrival a ticket to leave the U.S. within 90 days and they must fly on one of a specified group of air carriers. Contact a U.S. consulate for more information.

If you lose your passport in the U.S., you must replace it through your country's embassy. If you lose your visa or I-94 form (arrival/departure certificate attached to visa upon arrival), replace it through the nearest **U.S. Immigration and Naturalization Service** office. A list of offices can be obtained through the INS, Central Office Information Operations Unit, #5044, 425 I St. NW, Washington, DC 20536 (202-633-1900). This advice does not necessarily apply to work or study in the U.S. (see Work and Study above). Separate documentation is required to extend a length of stay in the U.S., also obtained from the INS. An extension must be applied for well before the original departure date.

Other Useful Documents

Foreign students will want an **International Student Identification Card (ISIC)** as proof of student status. These cards entitle the bearer to a variety of student discounts. Discount lists can be picked up at Council Travel offices. To purchase the ISIC outside the U.S., contact the International Student Travel Confederation; within the U.S., contact CIEE or Let's Go Travel Services. (For these addresses, see Useful Organizations above.)

Citizens of countries that signed the Geneva Road Traffic Convention of 1949 can legally drive in the U.S. for one year from the date of arrival provided that the car driven is registered in the U.S. and the driver is properly insured. An **international driver's license** may help clarify things for a befuddled policeman, but it doesn't change your legal status. Citizens whose countries have not signed the Convention may not drive in the U.S. without obtaining a U.S. license. Most European and many non-European countries are signatories, but check with your national automobile agency before you leave.

Customs

All travelers may bring 200 cigarettes, $100 worth of gifts, and all personal belongings into the U.S. duty-free. Travelers 21 or older may also bring up to one liter of alcohol duty-free. You may bring in any amount of currency without a charge, but if you carry over $10,000 you will have to fill out a report form. Travelers should carry prescription drugs in clearly labeled containers, along with a doctor's statement or prescription. Customs officials will often inquire about the amount of money you are carrying and ask your planned departure date to ensure that you will be able to support yourself while in the U.S.

Canadian citizens traveling in the U.S. may bring back CDN$20 worth of goods after a 24-hr. absence. After 48 hrs., you may bring back goods valued up to CDN$100. After 7 or more days, once per calendar year, you may bring back goods valued up to CDN$300. Only the 48-hr. and seven-day exemptions may include alcohol (40 oz. of wine or liquor, or 12-oz. bottles or cans of beer) and tobacco (200 cigarettes, 50 cigars, and two 200-g containers of loose tobacco). Values above the exempted limits are taxed at about 20%. You may also send gifts up to a value of CDN$60 duty-free, but you cannot mail alcohol or tobacco. Before leaving, list the serial numbers of all your valuables on a Y-38 form at a Customs Office or your point of departure. Write for the customs office's helpful pamphlet *I declare/Je déclare* at Revenue Canada Customs and Excise Communications Branch, Mackenzie Ave., Ottawa, Ont. K1A 0L5 (613-957-0275).

For more info, or for the pamphlet called *Know Before You Go,* contact the nearest U.S. Embassy or write to the **U.S. Customs Service,** 1301 Constitution Ave. NW, Washington, DC 20229 (202-566-8195). Remember to check customs regulations in your country to know what you may take with you on your return trip.

Transportation for International Visitors

Getting Here

The simplest and surest way to find a bargain fare is to have a reliable travel agent guide you through the maze of travel options. In addition, check the travel sections of major newspapers for special fares, and consult CIEE (see Useful Organizations above) or your national student travel organization—they might have special deals that regular travel agents cannot offer.

From Canada and Mexico

Mexican and American carriers offer many flights between the two countries. Since air travel in the U.S. is relatively expensive, flying on a Mexican airline to one of the border towns and traveling by train or bus from there may cost less. For more info, see *Let's Go: Mexico* or *Let's Go: California and Hawaii.*

Amtrak, Greyhound, or one of their subsidiaries connects with all the Mexican border towns. Most buses and trains do no more than cross the Mexico/U.S. border, but connections can be made at: San Diego, CA; Nogales, AZ; and El Paso, Eagle Pass, Laredo or Brownsville, TX. To drive in the U.S. (see Transportation) you need both a license and insurance; contact your local auto club or the American Automobile Association (800-336-4357) for details; see also By Car under Getting Around above.

From Europe

Because of the smorgasbord of flight options from Europe, flexibility is the best strategy. Consider leaving from a travel hub; certain cities—such as London, Paris, Amsterdam and Athens—have competitively priced flights. London is the major travel hub for trans-Atlantic budget flights, and New York is a consistently cheap travel target. Atlanta, Chicago, Los Angeles, Dallas, Seattle, and Toronto, Montréal, and Van-

couver in Canada are also competitively priced destinations. The money saved on a flight to or from a travel hub might far exceed the cost of getting to the airport.

A **charter flight** is usually the most economical option. Departure and return dates must be chosen when the ticket is booked. Changes and cancellations may result in partial or complete forfeiture of the cost of the tickets. Charter companies also reserve the right to change the dates or cost of the ticket, and may even cancel a flight within 48 hours of departure. Check with a travel agent about a charter company's reliability and reputation. The most common problem with charters is delays. To be safe, buy the ticket in advance, and arrive at the airport well before departure time to ensure a seat. A charter flight will, of course, be considerably less swish than a Concorde. Many of the organizations below have offices throughout Europe. Call the toll-free number and ask for the number of your local office.

STA Travel is a reliable organization that arranges charter flights and issues ISICs; call 800-777-0112 for info, or call the London office from Europe: 44 (071) 937 9971; from the U.S.: 004-41-937-9971.

Council Charter (800-800-8222), **CIEE's** charter subsidiary, offers a combination of charters and scheduled flights between Europe and the U.S. Offices in Paris, Aix-en-Provence, Nice, Lyon, Montpellier, London and Dusseldorf.

DER Tours 800-937-1234 in the U.S., 44 (71) 408 0111 in London.

Tourlite (800-272-7600).

Travac (800-872-8800).

Canadian Airlines International (800-426-7000).

If you decide to take a non-charter flight, you'll be purchasing greater reliability and flexibility. Major airlines offer reduced-fare options, such as flying **standby**: standby passengers need only show up at the airport and wait. Standby flights, however, have become increasingly difficult to find. Check with a travel agent for availability. **TWA, British Airways,** and **Pan Am** offer standby from London to most major U.S. cities. Seat availability is known only on the day of the flight, although some airlines will issue predictions. The worst crunch leaving Europe takes place from mid-June to early July, while August is uniformly tight for returning flights; at no time can you count on getting a seat right away.

Another reduced-fare option is the **Advanced Purchase Excursion Fare (APEX).** An APEX provides you with confirmed reservations and allows you to arrive and depart from different cities. APEX requires a minimum stay of 7 to 14 days and a maximum stay of 60 to 90 days. You must purchase your ticket 21 days in advance and it may not be refundable; ask a travel agent. For summer travel, book APEX fares early; by June you may have difficulty getting the departure date you want.

Smaller budget airlines often undercut major carriers by offering bargain fares on regularly scheduled flights. Competition for seats on these smaller carriers during peak season is fierce; book early. Some discount trans-Atlantic airlines include **Icelandair** (800-223-5500; to New York from Luxembourg or London) and **Virgin Atlantic Airways** (800-862-8621; to New York or Newark, NJ from London, Moscow, or Tokyo).

From Asia and Australia

Unfortunately, Asian and Australian travelers have few options for budget air travel to the U.S. Asians and Australians can make do with the APEX, or can ask travel agents about discount fares on **Thai Airways** or **Korean Air**. There is about a $100 difference between peak and off-season flights between the U.S. and Japan. Even U.S. carriers offer cheaper flights than **Japan Airlines.** Some airlines that fly between Australia and the U.S. are **Qantas, Air New Zealand, United, Continental, UTA French Airlines,** and **Canadian Pacific Airlines.** Prices are roughly equivalent among the six, although the cities they serve vary. One compensation for the exorbitant fares is that trans-Pacific flights often allow a stopover in Honolulu.

HOSTEL
IN
NY
$15* Hostel Accommodation
Only four persons per room
$40* Private Room w/Bath
Happy Hour with Free Food and Wine
Coffee Lounge, Sundeck and Billiards
*Plus Tax
INTERCLUB
GERSHWIN HOTEL
3E. 27th ST.
TEL:(212) 545-8000
NEW YORK CITY
NY10016
Located between Times Square & Soho

Getting Around

By Air

Many major U.S. airlines offer special **Visit USA** air passes and fares to foreign travelers. You purchase these passes outside the U.S., paying one price for a certain number of "flight coupons." Each coupon is good for one flight segment on an airline's domestic system within a certain time period. Some cross-country trips may require two segments. "Visit USA" discount fares are available for specific flights within the U.S. if purchased in one's own country. Most airline passes can be purchased only by those living outside the Western Hemisphere, though some are available for Canadians, Mexicans, and residents of Latin America if they purchase a pass from a travel agent located at least 100 mi. from the U.S. border. "Visit USA" fares are marked by a maze of restrictions and guidelines; consult the airline or a travel agent concerning the logistics of these discounts.

By Train

Amtrak's **USA Rail Pass,** similar to the Eurailpass, entitles international visitors to unlimited travel anywhere in the U.S. for 45 days for $349 in peak season (mid-May through Aug.) and $299 in off-peak. If you plan to travel only in one particular area, purchase a Regional Rail Pass instead. Each pass serves a single region for 45 days, including Eastern, Far Western ($199 peak, $189 off-peak each), Florida ($79 peak, $69 off-peak), and Western ($269 peak, $239 off-peak). All USA Rail Passes for kids ages 2 to 15 are half-fare. With a valid passport, you can purchase the USA Rail Pass outside the country or in New York, Boston, Washington D.C., Miami, Los Angeles or San Francisco. USA Rail Passes are not valid on the Autotrain, or on any train traveling into Canada. Check with travel agents or Amtrak reps in Europe. If you're already in the U.S. and would like more info, call Amtrak (800-872-7245). Passes are not a bargain unless you plan to make a number of stops. Also, remember that many U.S. cities are not accessible by train.

By Bus

Greyhound offers an **International Ameripass** for foreign students and faculty members. The passes are sold primarily outside of the United States, but may be purchased for a much higher price in New York, Los Angeles, San Francisco or Miami. Prices are $125 for a seven-day pass ($229 in the U.S.), $199 for a 15-day pass ($319 in the U.S.), and $250 for a 30-day pass ($429 in the U.S.). These passes may be extended at the time of purchase for $15 per day. To obtain a pass, you need a valid passport and proof of eligibility. Call a local Greyhound for info or to request their *Visit USA Vacation Guide,* which details services for foreigners.

By Car

The national speed limit of 55mph has been raised to 65mph in some areas, and is enforced to varying degrees in different states. The main routes through most towns are **U.S. highways,** which are often locally referred to by non-numerical names. **State highways** are usually less heavily traveled and may lead travelers to American farming communities. U.S. and state highway numbers don't follow any particular numbering pattern. And yes, Americans drive on the right (as opposed to "correct") side of the road.

Currency and Exchange

U.S. currency uses a decimal system based on the **dollar ($)** or "buck." Paper money ("bills") comes in six denominations, all the same size, shape, and dull green color. The bills now issued are $1, $5, $10, $20, $50 and $100. You may occasionally see denominations of $2 and $500, which are no longer printed but are still acceptable as currency. Some restaurants and retail stores may not accept $50 bills and higher. The dollar divides into 100 cents (¢); fractions such as 35 cents can be represented as 35¢ or $.35.

The penny (1¢), the nickel (5¢), the dime (10¢), and the quarter (25¢) are the most common coins. The half-dollar (50¢) and the one-dollar coins (which come in two sizes) are rare but valid currency.

It is nearly impossible to use foreign currency in the U.S. In some parts of the country you may even have trouble **exchanging your currency** for U.S. dollars. Convert your currency infrequently and in large amounts to minimize fees. Buy U.S. traveler's checks, which can be used in lieu of cash (when an establishment specifies "no checks accepted" this usually refers to checks drawn on a bank account). **Personal checks** can be very difficult to cash in the U.S; most banks require that you have an account with them to cash one. You may want to bring a U.S.-affiliated credit card such as Interbank (MasterCard), Barclay Card (Visa), or American Express. For more information see **Money** above.

Sales tax is the U.S. equivalent of the Value Added Tax. Expect to pay 5 to 8% depending on the item and place. Some areas charge a hotel tax; ask in advance. In addition, a **tip** of 15 to 20% is expected by restaurant servers and taxi drivers, although restaurants sometimes include this service charge in the bill. Tip hairdressers 10%, and bellhops $1 per bag. It is also customary to tip barkeeps 25¢ to $1 for a drink and 50¢ to $2 for a pitcher.

Communications

Mail

Post offices are usually open weekdays from 8am to 5pm and Saturday from 8am to noon. All close on national holidays (see When to Go, above). A postcard mailed within the U.S. (including Alaska and Hawaii) or to Mexico costs 19¢; a letter up to one ounce (six pages) generally costs 29¢. Canada has a special rate of 22¢ for a postcard and 30¢ for a letter. Postcards mailed overseas cost 40¢, letters 50¢; aerograms are available at the post office for 45¢. Mail within the country takes between a day and a week to arrive; to northern Europe, South America, Australia and Asia, a week to 10 days; to southern Europe, North Africa, and the Middle East, two to three weeks. Large city post offices offer **International Express Mail** service in case you need to mail something to a major European city in 40 to 72 hours.

The U.S. divides into postal zones, each with a five-digit **ZIP code** (some organizations use an alternative nine-digit ZIP code for quicker delivery). Writing this code on letters is essential for delivery. The normal form of address is as follows:

Alexander B. Stein (name)
Cheeselovers of America, Inc. (name of organization; optional)
007 Esophagus Rd. Apt. 666 (street address, apartment number)
Yer, MA 01234 (city, state abbreviation, ZIP)
USA (country)

When ordering books and materials from the U.S., always include an **International Reply Coupon** with your request. IRCs are available from your home post office. Be sure that your coupon has adequate postage to cover the cost of delivery.

Telephone

Most of the information you will need about telephone usage—including area codes for the U.S., foreign country codes, and rate—is in the front of the local **white pages** telephone directory. The **yellow pages,** published at the end of the white pages or in a separate book, is used to look up the phone numbers of businesses and other services. To obtain local phone numbers or area codes of other cities, call **directory assistance** (411) or call the **operator** by dialing "0". For long-distance directory assistance, dial 1-(area code)-555-1212. The operator will help you with rates or other info and give assistance in an emergency. You can reach directory assistance and the operator free from any pay phone.

In order to place a call, you must first hear the dial tone, a steady tone indicating that the line is clear. After dialing, you usually will hear an intermittent purring sound reflecting that the call has gone through. You might also hear a "busy signal," which is a rapid beeping tone signifying that the number you have called is in use.

Telephone numbers in the U.S. consist of a three-digit area code, a three-digit exchange, and a four-digit number, written as 123-456-7890. Normally only the last seven digits are used in a **local call. Non-local calls** within the area code from which you are dialing require a "1" before the last seven digits, while **long-distance calls** require a "1" and the area code. For example, to call Harvard University in Cambridge, MA from Las Vegas, NV, you would dial 1-617-495-9659. Canada and much of Mexico share the same system. Generally, long-distance rates go down after 5pm on weekdays and are further reduced between 11pm and 8am and on weekends.

Many large companies operate **toll-free numbers** to provide information to their customers at no charge. These consist of "1" plus "800" plus a seven-digit number. To obtain specific toll-free numbers, call 1-800-555-1212. Be careful—the age of technology has recently given birth to the **"900" number,** which is staggeringly expensive to call. Average charges range from $2 to $5 for the first minute, with a smaller charge for each additional minute.

Pay phones are plentiful, most often stationed on street corners and in public areas. Be wary of private, more expensive pay phones—the rate they charge per call will be printed on the phone. Put your coins (10-25¢ for a local call depending on the region) into the slot and listen for a dial tone before dialing. If there is no answer or if you get a busy signal, you will get your money back, although connecting with answering machines will prevent this. To make a long-distance direct call, dial the number. An operator will tell you the cost of the first three minutes; deposit that amount in the coin slot. The operator or a recording will cut in when you must deposit more money.

In addition to ordinary pay phones, two other types of public phones are becoming more common. The first is a phone which charges 25¢ for one minute anywhere in the continental U.S. The second is a **Charge-a-Call** phone operated by American Telephone & Telegraph (AT&T), which is used for long-distance calls only and does not ac-

cept coins. Payment is made with an AT&T telephone credit card or by reversing charges. Begin dialing all calls with "0." The third type is found in airports and is operated by independent long-distance companies. Generally these phones are operated by passing a credit card through a slot before dialing.

If you are at an ordinary telephone and don't have lots of change, you may want to **reverse the charges** (i.e. bill the charges to the person receiving the call) or put it on your **telephone credit card.** First, you dial "0" (not "1"), then the area code and number. When you hear a beep wait for the operator to assist you. If you ask to make a **station-to-station collect call** and give your name, anyone who answers may accept or refuse the call. If you tell the operator you are placing a **person-to-person collect call** (more expensive than station-to-station), you must give both your name and the receiving person's name, and they will be charged *only* if the person you wish to speak with is there. In some areas, particularly rural ones, you may have to dial "0" only and then tell the operator the number you wish to call.

You can place **international calls** from any telephone. To call direct, dial the international access code (011), the country code, the city code, and the local number. Country codes and city codes may be listed with a zero in front (e.g. 033), but when using 011, drop the zero (e.g. 011-33). In some areas you will have to give the operator the number and he or she will place the call. To find out the cheapest time to call various countries in Europe or the Middle East, call the operator (dial "0"). The cheapest time to call Australia and Japan is between 3am and 2pm, New Zealand between 11pm and 10am.

Telegrams (Cabling)

If a telephone call is impossible, cabling may be the only way to contact someone quickly overseas (usually by the next day). For an overseas cable, **Western Union** (800-325-6000) charges a base fee of $8, in addition to 51-66¢ per word, including name and address (the rate varies according to the destination). If you're contacting England, Argentina, the Netherlands or the Philippines, you can send a **Telemessage**

($8.50 for first 50 words or less, including name and address, $3.25 for each additional 50 words or less). Call to check rates to specific countries.

Measurements

The British system of weights and measures is still in use in the U.S., despite recent efforts to convert to the metric system. The following is a list of U.S. units and their metric equivalents:

1 inch =25 millimeters
1 foot = 0.30 meter
1 yard = 0.91 meter
1 mile = 1.61 kilometers
1 ounce = 25 grams
1 pound = 0.45 kilogram
1 quart (liquid) = 0.94 liter

12 inches equal 1 foot; 3 feet equal 1 yard; 5280 feet equal 1 mile. 16 ounces (weight) equal 1 pound (abbreviated as 1 lb.). 8 ounces (volume) equal 1 cup; 2 cups equal 1 pint; 2 pints equal 1 quart; and 4 quarts equal 1 gallon.

Electric outlets throughout the U.S., Canada, and Mexico provide current at 117 volts, 60 cycles (Hertz), and American **plugs** usually have 2 rectangular prongs; plugs for larger appliances often have a third prong. Appliances designed for the European electrical system (220 volts) will not operate without a transformer and a plug adapter (this includes electric systems for disinfecting contact lenses). Transformers are sold to convert specific wattages (e.g. 0-50 watt transformers for razors and radios; larger watt transformers for hair dryers and other appliances).

The U.S. uses the **Fahrenheit temperature scale** rather than the Centigrade (Celsius) scale. To convert Fahrenheit to approximate Centigrade temperatures, subtract 32, then divide by 2. Or, just remember that 32° is the freezing point of water, 212° its boiling point, normal human body temperature is 98.6°, and room temperature hovers around 70°.

Time

U.S. residents tell time on the Latinate 12-hour, not 24-hour, clock. Hours after noon are *post meridiem* or pm (e.g. 2pm); hours before noon are *ante meridiem* or am (e.g. 2am). Noon is 12pm and midnight is 12am; we will use "noon" or "midnight." The Continental U.S. divides into four time zones: Eastern, Central, Mountain and Pacific. When it's noon Eastern time, it's 11am Central, 10am Mountain, 9am Pacific, and 7am Central Alaskan and Hawaiian. The borders of the time zones are indicated in the map at the beginning of the book. Most of the United States advance their clocks during **daylight savings time**. In 1993, daylight savings time will begin on Sunday, April 25 at 2am. At this time, set your clocks forward one hour to 3am. It will end on Sunday, Oct. 31 at 2am. Then, set your clocks back one hour to 1am. Exceptions to this rule are Arizona, Hawaii and part of Indiana, which remain on **standard time** year round. For people in those states, let's just forget we had this little chat.

American Culture (in 4409 Words or Less)

As our flippant title suggests, this is a brief introduction to American culture. Boy we do mean *brief.* Let's do a little exercise. Imagine that all of the novels, history books, screenplays, box-scores, and poems ever composed in the United States were stacked one atop another. Now put your trusty copy of *Let's Go: USA* on top—don't ask questions, just do it! Imagine that you are then given the task of condensing all of this a quadrillion-fold. Impossible, you say? Not really, is our qualified retort. The next seven pages will attempt to give you a taste, a little smidgen of a notion, about what makes the U.S. of A. tick. Bear with us, we're new at this game too. These few pages exist simply to whet your appetite for the cultural offerings of the United States. American culture varies wildly, depending on region, state, socio-economic background, ethnicity, degree of urban-, suburban-, or rural-ness, etc., etc., *ad infinitum*. The best way to discover more about the subjects we begin here so curtly is to travel through the country itself—visit some museums, read some American novels, watch a movie, listen to the radio, see a ballgame or a show, and talk to the people you meet. But you knew that already. That's why you bought a travel guide instead of *The Closing of the American Mind.* So, with apologies to Allen Bloom and all those old farts who believe that the best way to get to know the country is to read about it, Let's Go...

History

In the Beginning...

Some 25,000 years ago, the very first colonists entered the present-day United States, crossing the Bering Strait on a frozen footbridge that has since sunk back into the icy North Pacific. These progenitors of Native Americans were probably following packs of wooly mammoths (some of which have been preserved in the Alaskan ice); undoubtedly, they were searching for a better life than what they knew in Siberia. Centuries passed, and America's first pioneers sifted throughout the country. Much of what these original tribes created has been irretrievably lost because many of their cultures were based on an oral rather than written tradition. Even those who possessed a written tradition left behind only indecipherable petroglyphs—strewn on the rocks and cliffs throughout the country. Nevertheless, the discerning listener can still hear faint echoes of these lost worlds by talking to their descendants, the "Indian" tribes scattered throughout the United States. Native American tradition is most palpable in the pueblo villages of the Southwest, which retain their dances and philosophies and have taught Westerners like Oppenheimer and Jung how to think.

Contrary to popular belief, even before the first white men stepped on the continent, entire civilizations (like the Anasazi of the Southwest) arose and then disappeared, either forced off of their land by climactic changes or killed off by later waves of settlers. Also surprising to some is the fact that many tribes remain today. Some, like the Pueblos, remain in relative healthy communities—willingly cutting themselves off from the invasion of modern, European, pop culture. Others blend old ways with innovations. Many of the Inuit in Alaska—at least those who haven't been completely Americanized—use snowmobiles instead of dogsleds but continue to tread in the tracks worn by their forbears. Most tragic of all are the Native tribes who were deracinated and plunked down onto plots of poor-quality land called "tribal reservations" by a hostile U.S. government. Like the crops which just wouldn't grow in these areas, many tribes simply withered and died.

European Exploration and Exploitation

European explorers took a more erratic path in settling the New World. They couldn't just waltz across an Arctic bridge, they had the entire Atlantic to cross. Belief in the opportunities and opulence of the *terra incognita* attracted regatta after regatta to the inhospitable shores of the Americas. The first Europeans to visit the American continent were probably Scandinavians—Vikings led by Leif Ericson explored the Atlantic coast around the year 1000, but left little trace of their visit. Europeans again stumbled upon the Americas in 1492 when Christopher Columbus found his trip around the world blocked by Hispaniola in the Caribbean Sea. In 1519, Hernando Cortez bluffed his way into the Aztec capital city, Tenochtitlán,—present-day Mexico City. A wolf in sheep's clothing, Cortez impersonated the white-skinned god, Quetzalcoatl, whom the Aztecs believed would one day come to rule over them. Cortez imprisoned the emperor, stole their gold, and killed off their society with sophisticated weaponry and European diseases. Cortez's golden successes prompted other Spanish *conquistadores* to flock to this El Dorado and snatch up the precious metals of the continent. One of the effects of this rapacious process was the decimation of the advanced Aztec, Incan, and Mayan cultures.

Colonization

After these initial overwhelming successes, Europeans began arriving in droves. The first wave was exploitation, the second wave was settlement—English religious dissenters headed to New England, French furriers traipsed to Canada and Louisiana, and Spanish *conquistadores* and missionaries claimed the Southwest, Florida, and Mexico. Each European enclave left a legacy of architecture and artifacts that tourists can still find amidst the modern cities built around them. The English were the first to attempt, in earnest, settlements in what was to become the United States. In 1587 Englishman and pirate Sir Walter Raleigh sent an unsuccessful team of explorers to Roanoke Island in the Outer Banks of today's North Carolina. The soil there was rich, but the settlers' luck was poor; when Raleigh returned a few years later, the only trace of his utopia was the word "CROATOAN" enigmatically carved in a tree. In 1607, the Jamestown colony was founded as the first permanent English colony in North America. This colony took hold and thrived—with assistance from friendly Natives, the cultivation of indigenous cash crops like tobacco, and the presence of African slave labor. Soon Virginia's tobacco fields became the foothold of a mercantile economy which became extremely lucrative for Britain.

Money wasn't the only reason the English came to America. Pilgrims, devotees of a Puritan Anglican sect not tolerated in England, came to the New World to found their own religious enclave, landing in present-day Massachusetts in 1620. The English government largely ignored these colonists until the late 17th and early 18th century when—realizing that they could make some money off of them—the crown sent a viceroy and started to levy taxes.

Consolidation and Revolution

As decades go, the first five in the 18th century were pretty uneventful. England consolidated its holdings in the new world, stretching all the way from the Hudson Bay to present-day Georgia. Fields were ploughed, babies born, and valleys settled. Then came world war. Europeans know it as "The Seven Year's War" but we in America call it "The French and Indian War." For seven years, from 1756 to 1763, the colonists and the British fought the French and their Native American allies. In this conflict, a young George Washington first tasted defeat—the French vanquished his forces at Fort Necessity near modern Pittsburgh. In the negotiations which ended the war, England emerged triumphant; France ceded their Canadian holdings to King George III.

With England's victory, however, also came enormous debts—debts that they passed along to the colonists in a variety of taxes levied in the 1760s and early 1770s. The colonists bristled at what they felt was unfair taxation, particularly as they had no official channel within the British government to voice their complaints. Their initial dissatisfaction was met with British indifference and—adding insult to injury—more taxes. With the aid of the French, Dutch, and Spanish, the disorganized, home-spun "Minutemen" assembled a guerrilla army to establish their own, independent, and republican nation. So began the Revolutionary War. On July 4, 1776, the *Declaration of Independence* formalized the colonies desire to be free of English rule. Seven years later, the British at Yorktown reluctantly agreed to let them go. With their own country to govern, the "Founding Fathers" got down to business. In 1787, after several years of instability under a patchwork alliance, the first states narrowly ratified the United States Constitution, a landmark political document which struck a balance between states' rights and national unity. The three branches of government—executive, legislative, and judicial—formed a system of "checks and balances," à la Montesquieu, to safeguard against both dictatorship and anarchy. It remains the law of the land today.

Onward and Outward

With the original thirteen states safely under the aegis of their own federal government, America began to expand. In a fire-sale bargain in 1803, Napoleon sold President Thomas Jefferson one-fourth of the present-day United States for under three cents per acre. This acquisition of land, the Louisiana Purchase, was the beginning of a "Manifest Destiny," which—as the 19th century progressed—would devour more and more of the continent in the name of God and Uncle Sam. Curiosity about the newly purchased territory, not to mention the desire to tap the northwestern fur trade, prompted Meriwether Lewis and William Clark to trek all the way to the Pacific Coast. Aided by the indomitable squaw Sacajawea, they arrived in Seaside, Oregon in October, 1805.

After the War of 1812—an off-shoot of the Napoleonic Wars in which Britain and the United States once again took arms against each other—tracks across the country became well-worn and expansion continued. The effects of this growth were manifold. Native populations were displaced further and further west. War with Mexico ended with the acquisition of Texas and much of the Southwest. Gold fever in 1848, sparked by the uncovering of a few nuggets in Sutter's Mill, California, further fueled this expansion.

Division and Reconstruction

As the United States was approaching adolescence in the mid-19th century, it had to confront the hypocritic existence of slavery within its borders. Even though the *Declaration of Independence* nobly asserted that "all men are created equal," Southern plantation states still enslaved blacks—a practice abhorred by Northern and European observers, but considered vital to the Southern agricultural economy. This half-free/half-slave compromise was a relic of the Revolutionary War, and this irresolution festered in the divide between North and South. As the nation grew, it had to decide whether entering territories would be absorbed as free or slave states. Ad-hoc decisions like the "Missouri Compromise" in 1820 and bloody conflicts like that in Kansas in the 1850s eventually gave way to nationwide conflict.

In 1861, a confederacy of states in the South decided that it no longer wanted to be a part of the United States; the South wanted to pursue its agrarian, slave-based economy unmolested by Northerners. From 1861-65, the country endured a vicious war; fought by the North to restore the Union, and by the South to be free of the North. The Civil War killed a larger percentage of the population than any other war in which the U.S. has been involved. Numerous tourist sites in the South, as well as in the North, still mourn the victims and laud the heroes of this debilitating domestic conflict. Although the Northern victors had promised African-American equality, the period of Reconstruction tied African-Americans to new, if only more subtle forms of slavery, in order to industrialize the Southern economy. Former slaves and their families were still shackled to the land as tenant farmers, left to a desperate rural fate in a hostile and often racist land.

Industrialization

At the end of Reconstruction in the 1870s, the country entered an era of untrammeled growth in industry, innovative technology, and farming. Rapid investment spurred by Social Darwinist "captains of industry" such as Carnegie and Rockefeller boosted the nation's economic global influence, albeit at great cost to workers and farmers. This 19th-century system of unabashed "free market" capitalism quickly broke down, after the cyclical recessions in the 1870s, 1890s and especially the 1930s. But for a while, the U.S lived off its false high—lending the period encompassing the turn of the century the nickname "The Gilded Age."

Agriculturally, the Great Plains were cultivated on a mass level for the first time ever. Poor land management techniques, however, depleted the topsoil at an alarmingly rapid pace. Politically, America was coming into its own. A successful campaign against Spain in 1898 boosted the United States into the role of an empire, with colonies in the Philippines and Cuba. Tardy but serious involvement in the First World War under President Wilson further boosted the economic and international status of the United

States. In the prosperous 20s that followed, women were finally granted the right to vote in the U.S. The 19th Amendment to the Constitution in 1920 was the culmination of the Women's Suffrage Movement, implementing an idea Abigail Adams had suggested over 130 years before.

Boom, Bust, and BOOM!

The post-World War I euphoria, inflated largely by credit, came crashing down like the aftermath of a speed high on "Black Thursday" October 24, 1929, when the New York Stock Exchange crashed to the ground—taking with it countless suicidal financiers. The nation entered the Great Depression. Simultaneously, the abused soil of the Great Plains blew away, leaving in its wake a "dust bowl" and hundreds of thousands of ruined farmers.

Under the leadership of President Franklin D. Roosevelt, America began to dampen the wildly fluctuating free-market economy with a stabilizing if stultifying bureaucracy. A pleasant by-product of this "New Deal" are the monuments, buildings, bridges and parks in the United States built during this period in order to create jobs for the unemployed. Out-of-work artists also created paintings, sculptures, mosaics, and written and photographic records of the impoverished South and West under the patronage of the federal government. Final recovery from the Depression was aided by U.S. involvement in World War II. During the war years, women joined the factory work force in unprecedented numbers; their experience, as popularized by Norman Rockwell's caricature "Rosie the Riveter" in the *Saturday Evening Post,* was instrumental in boosting women's rights and pay.

Cold War and the New Frontier

Partly because the nation's infrastructure was left physically unblemished by the war—unlike that of Europe—American corporations were able to expand both domestically and internationally in the post-war era, making the U.S. the world's foremost economic and military power. At the same time, irrational fear of Soviet power and expansion led to the "Red Scares" of the 1950s. Suspicion of communism had plagued the U.S. since 1917, but during the Cold War it gained feverish intensity and ultimately lead to U.S. involvement in the Korean and Vietnam Wars. The production of nuclear weapons by both the U.S. and the U.S.S.R. after the World War II made their strained relations potentially apocalyptic; in 1962 President Kennedy and Nikita Khrushchev brought the world to the brink of nuclear war in their showdown over the deployment of Soviet missiles in Cuba.

Despite the immense dread that shrouded U.S. relations with the increasingly nuclear outside world, the early 60s were characterized by an idealism engendered by President Kennedy himself. Peace Corps volunteers brought technology to developing countries, NASA began the program to put Americans on the moon, and Kennedy's New Frontier attempted to stretch American claims to the pockets of poverty and racism which blotted the nation. In 1963, however, the reign of "Camelot" was ended as Kennedy was shot in Dallas and as the Vietnam "conflict" increasingly became a "quagmire." The mid- and late 60s saw extensive public protest against involvement in the Vietnam War and against the discrimination of African-Americans that had its roots in the unresolved racial questions emanating from Reconstruction. Dr. Martin Luther King, Jr. led the battle for civil rights in the form of nonviolent protest, but the Southern police were not so gentle. Civil rights activists were hosed, killed and imprisoned. King, too, was eventually felled by an assassin's bullet in Memphis in 1968.

The violence of the 60s, though a disturbing and schizophrenic period in American history, eventually lead to limited gains in civil and women's rights. The sexual revolution, sparked by the development of the birth control pill, brought women's rights to the forefront of national debate. The 1973 Supreme Court *Roe v. Wade* decision to legalize abortion engendered a fierce battle between pro-life and pro-choice advocates which delved deep into the idea of what constituted a woman's given and chosen roles.

The day before yesterday

Surprisingly, it is the younger generation which has often chafed against the social changes of the 1960s. The campuses of the 70s and 80s were quieter and more conservative, as college graduates flocked to investment banking firms and Republican fundraisers. In 1980, former California Governor Ronald Reagan surfed into the White House on a tidal wave of conservatism (mass-hypnosis?) that kept on cresting until 1988, when his vice-president George Bush was elected president. But in the 90s, activists have again taken up the charge for change, focusing on such issues as abortion, AIDS, ecology, women's rights, homelessness, gay rights, and racism. The economy will no longer soak up the surfeit of young urban professionals, and young Americans seek an identity that is less radical than that of the 60s but less avaricious than that of the 80s.

Yesterday

Read the paper.

Literature

If all American literature were reduced to one picture, it would depict a ruggedly beautiful man donning a backpack filled not with an abundant supply of food, but rather with ideas and hopes, trudging at sunset through a seemingly ever-expansive field. American fiction is devoted to celebrating the childlike, sincere, and uncorrupted—but not necessarily incorruptible—individual who fights for freedom at all costs.

Before the American legend of today had evolved, the Puritans had a slightly less cheery one to relate. The literature that came out of the New World in the 17th century was primarily consecrated to the religion that the early Anglo settlers came to this land to practice. Almost as an afterthought, they conveyed descriptions of what they found in their new land. Authors like Jonathan Edwards, John Cotton, and Anne Bradstreet spoke of such harsh religious concepts as limited atonement, total depravity, and irresistible grace.

For the most part, American literature was either political or religious until the late 18th century. Evidence that America had something unique to offer world literature surfaced in the fiction that arose in the wake of the Revolutionary War. Starting in the early 1800s, there was a surge of works that told the tale, each in its own way, of the strong, yet innocent American individual: Herman Melville's *Moby Dick*, Walt Whitman's *Leaves of Grass*, Nathaniel Hawthorne's *Scarlet Letter*. Accompanying these fictional works were lyrical philosophical works like Henry David Thoreau's *Walden* and Ralph Waldo Emerson's *Self Reliance* which sang of independence and the wisdom of common sense. New England culture sought to define itself as separate from the European culture from which it sprang. In the Midwest, by contrast, humorists attempted to define the purely American character in rollicking stories and tall tales set exclusively in the natural and human landscapes of the new continent. Their influence can be clearly traced in the writing of Mark Twain, whose best-known work, *The Adventures of Huckleberry Finn*, explores American naiveté and coming-of-age. The 20th century witnessed a further inward-turning of novelists. No longer were the virtues of the frontier celebrated, but instead, the vices of the Gilded Age were attacked. The Industrial Revolution inspired talk of sin and how easily one can be drawn into it—as in Theodore Dreiser's *Sister Carrie* and Stephen Crane's *Maggie: A Girl of the Streets*. Others attacked the misery that the industrial economy engendered; the muckraking of Upton Sinclair in *The Jungle* left an entire generation unable to eat sausage. Even those who ostensibly succeeded led lives of misery. Sinclair Lewis's *Main Street* and F. Scott Fitzgerald's *Great Gatsby* both tell the tales of people who "made it" but lived in silent desperation. Often, they protested societal roles in novels of self-discovery, such as Kate Chopin's *The Awakening* and the world of Willa Cather and Edith Wharton.

Over the last few decades American literature has been characterized by an intense scrutiny of the tensions of American life. Part of this trend has been the broadening of viewpoints expressed by writers from backgrounds other than that of the white upper-class male. Ralph Ellison's searing narrative of life as a black man, *Invisible Man,* Piri Thomson's examination of the life in Spanish Harlem, *Down These Mean Streets*, and Oliver LaFarge's sensitive portrayal of a Navajo youth's coming of age, *Laughin' Boy,* all reflect this ongoing examination; more recently, a resurgence in women's literature and an exploration of the gay/lesbian experience have also joined the scene.

Movies and Television

Tradition has it that baseball is the great American pastime, but let's face it—that title unequivocally belongs to screen-watching, both big and small-style. From the days when viewers were amazed by Thomas Edison's 30-second film of a galloping horse to today, when stunning, computer-generated special effects like those of *Terminator 2* are almost run-of-the-mill, Americans have always been fascinated by moving pictures. There are television sets in approximately 98% of U.S. homes, and the competition between the four national networks (ABC, NBC, CBS, and Fox) and cable television has led to greater expansion of TV culture than ever before. Turn on the "boob tube" to the networks during prime time (7-10pm), and you'll find some of the most popular hour-long shows and shorter sitcoms (situation comedies): *The Simpsons, L.A. Law,* and *Beverly Hills, 90210*. Check out cable and you'll discover 24-hour channels offering nothing but news, sports, movies, kid vid, or weather, not to mention MTV, a non-stop music video whose dazzling display of random, visceral images affords a disconcerting glimpse into the psyche of the American under-30 set.

The big screen, more often than the small, makes an effort to reach beyond the level of mere entertainment and enter the domain of art. The success of that endeavor is in the eye of the beholder, but the success of the movie industry and its offspring, the movie-star-watching industry, both of which are based in Hollywood, California, and New York City, is undisputed. Even the genres themselves are American traditions: sci-fi (the *Star Wars* trilogy), thriller (the classic *Psycho* or the neo-classic *The Silence of the Lambs* or any of the terrifying Alfred Hitchcock movies), drama (*Terms of Endearment* or *Love Story*), horror (any one of the never-ending *Friday the Thirteenth* series), and many more, including the two most American film types of all, the almost-defunct western (*Fistful of Dollars*) and the buddy film (*Easy Rider* for the men, *Thelma and Louise* for the women). Like everything else in America, producing movies and television shows costs money. The motion picture industry makes part of its money the old-fashioned way, through ticket sales, and hauls in the rest in video rental or cable-TV viewing. Unlike programming in other Western nations, most non-cable TV in the U.S. is funded by advertisements. Two-minute breaks for commercials, which are considered the most effective means for businesses to reach potential consumers, interrupt most shows, leaving just enough time to run to the bathroom.

Music

American music—country, bluegrass, big band, jazz, blues, rock 'n' roll, and rap—has spread prodigiously from its roots in the South and Midwest. Much of this growth can be attributed to the invention of radio and sound recordings, which made music available to the masses. In the spirit of the American melting pot, this music co-exists peaceably with the traditional European classical variety, which can be enjoyed at the great music halls that house world-class orchestras in most major American cities. In fact, the 20th century has seen a distinctly American style of classical music develop through the works of such late, great composers as Scott Joplin, Charles Ives, George Gershwin, and Aaron Copland. The birth of the big Broadway musical has also rewarded Americans with catchy tunes from the pens of Irving Berlin, Cole Porter, Leonard Bernstein, Stephen Sondheim, and others, though many recent Broadway musical successes have been imports from London's West End. The best way to get a sense of the breadth of United States musical offerings is to scan the radio dial when in or near a metropolis, or to peruse a well-stocked record store. You can get first-hand listening experiences in the night clubs, concert halls, and stadiums of any American city, particularly the following:

for classical music: New York, Philadelphia, Boston, Chicago, Cleveland, and St. Louis.

for jazz and blues: New Orleans, St. Louis, Chicago, Kansas City, and New York.

for country: Nashville, Memphis, Dallas, and Houston.

for rock and roll: just about anywhere, but especially New York, Los Angeles, Boston, San Francisco, Seattle, Austin, TX, and Minneapolis.

for rap: New York, Los Angeles, and Oakland, CA.

Sports

Tourists wishing to experience an authentic American mass ritual have two options—they can get invited to the senior prom, or (if they can't find a date) they can attend a sporting event at one of the enormous arenas and stadiums that dot the urban and suburban landscapes. Sports and athletic culture have assumed a prominent place in the American mind, especially the male mind. Going to a baseball, American football, basketball, hockey, or other athletic game will give you a taste of some of the peculiarities and pleasures of the sports fan: among them group identification (often known as "male bonding"), vicarious participation, and alcoholic libations. Be sure to buy a hot dog, and see if you can get someone to explain the often incomprehensible rules if you are unfamiliar with them. If you can't see a game in person, watching one on TV will give you perhaps an even closer approximation of the average American's sports experience, especially if you invite a few buddies over to throw back a few brewskis and yell at the referee through the TV screen.

Theater

Theater is everywhere in the U.S. From rural summer stock to New York City's Broadway, there's a stage in almost every town. Theater first came to the America in 1716, when some of Shakespeare's plays were performed in colonial Williamsburg, and between that day and this, an American tradition of playwriting and performance was created. One of the most American art forms of all is the Broadway musical; the songs of Cole Porter, Rogers and Hammerstein (and Hart), Stephen Sondheim, and George and Ira Gershwin are as wholly American as the New York street which gave this genre its name. In the realm of non-musical theater, playwrights such as Arthur Miller, Tennessee Williams, Neil Simon, Eugene O'Neill, and Thornton Wilder have stretched the boundaries of theater's "fourth wall" in innovative, American ways.

Visual Art

American art is as diverse and multifaceted as the American experience it depicts. The works of artists such as Edward Hopper and Thomas Hart Benton explore the innocence and mythic values of the United States before its emergence as a superpower. The vigorous Abstract Expressionism of Arshile Gorky and Jackson Pollock displays both the swaggering confidence and frenetic insecurity of cold-war America. Pop Art, popularized by Jasper Johns, Robert Rauschenberg, Roy Lichtenstein, and Andy Warhol, uses as its subject matter the icons and motifs of contemporary American life and pop culture, satirizing and exposing what has become since World War II the *de facto* world culture. Cindy Sherman and Robert Mapplethorpe have exposed Americans to personal-as-political photography, despite efforts of self-styled guardians of morality to censor their work. Contemporary American art is often a highly experimental, mixed-media pastiche of audio, video, and performance art which elegantly acknowledges and incorporates advances in technology.

New England

New England, with its centuries-old commitment to education and its fascination with government, has been an intellectual and political center for the entire nation since before the States were even officially United. Students and scholars from across the country funnel into New England's colleges each fall, and town meetings still take place in many rural villages. Yet this region is an unlikely cradle for any sort of civilization: the soil is barren, the climate is harsh, the coast is rocky and treacherous, and the land is wrinkled with mountains.

Though the terrain gave the region's early settlers a tough time, it is kind to today's visitors. New England's dramatic coastline is a popular destination for summer vacationers; the slopes of the Green and White Mountains, with their many rivers and lakes, inspire skiers, hikers, cyclists, and canoers. In the fall, the "changing of the leaves" transforms the entire region into a giant kaleidoscope as the nation's most brilliant foliage bleeds and burns. Though largely rural, very little of New England (inland Maine excepted) is wild. Many vacation sites here are calculated to give you loads of human history—semi-old buildings, museums, battlegrounds, ubiquitous quaint inns, and famous-people sculptures dot the hillside hamlets. However, groups such as the Appalachian Mountain Club battle developers and tour promoters in their quest to preserve the privately owned backcountry.

Mark Twain once said that if you don't like the weather in New England, wait 10 minutes. Unpredictable at best, the region's climate can be particularly dismal in November and March. Watch out for black flies, mosquitoes, and swarming greenhead flies in summer, especially in Maine, and be warned that everything from rivers and state camprounds to tourist attractions may slow down or freeze up during the winter. For more information, browse local bookstores for detailed regional travel guides, or call New England, USA, at 76 Summer St., Boston (800-847-4863) for a *New England Travel Planner.*

Connecticut

Although it's hard to imagine, Connecticut was once a rugged frontier. The European colonists' westward movement began with the settlement of the Connecticut Valley by Massachusetts Puritans in the 1630s. Their state motto *Qui Transtulit Sustinet* (He who is transplanted still sustains) recalls these tough early years. From the very beginning, "Nutmeggers" were independent—their democratic state constitution gave rise to the state's other nickname, the "Constitution State." The citizens of Connecticut have not lost their Yankee roots, yet they also have tendrils reaching out to modern pop culture. Both the lollipop and the pay phone were born here. Today, Connecticut's traditional style mingles with urbanity in cities like Hartford and New Haven, where glass skyscrapers reflect small brick churches and historical landmarks.

Practical Information

Capital: Hartford.

Tourist Information Line: 800-282-6863. Call for vacation guides. **Bureau of State Parks and Forests,** 165 Capitol Ave., #265, Hartford 06106 (566-2304). Will mail you an application for a permit to camp in the state parks and forests; also sends brochures describing sites. **Connecticut Forest and Park Association,** 16 Meriden Rd., Rockfall, CT 06481 (346-2372). Hiking and outdoor activities information. **Connecticut Coalition of Bicyclists,** P.O. Box 121, Middletown 06457. Write for a state bike map and *Connecticut Bicycle Directory.*

Time Zone: Eastern. **Postal Abbreviation:** CT **Sales Tax:** 8%

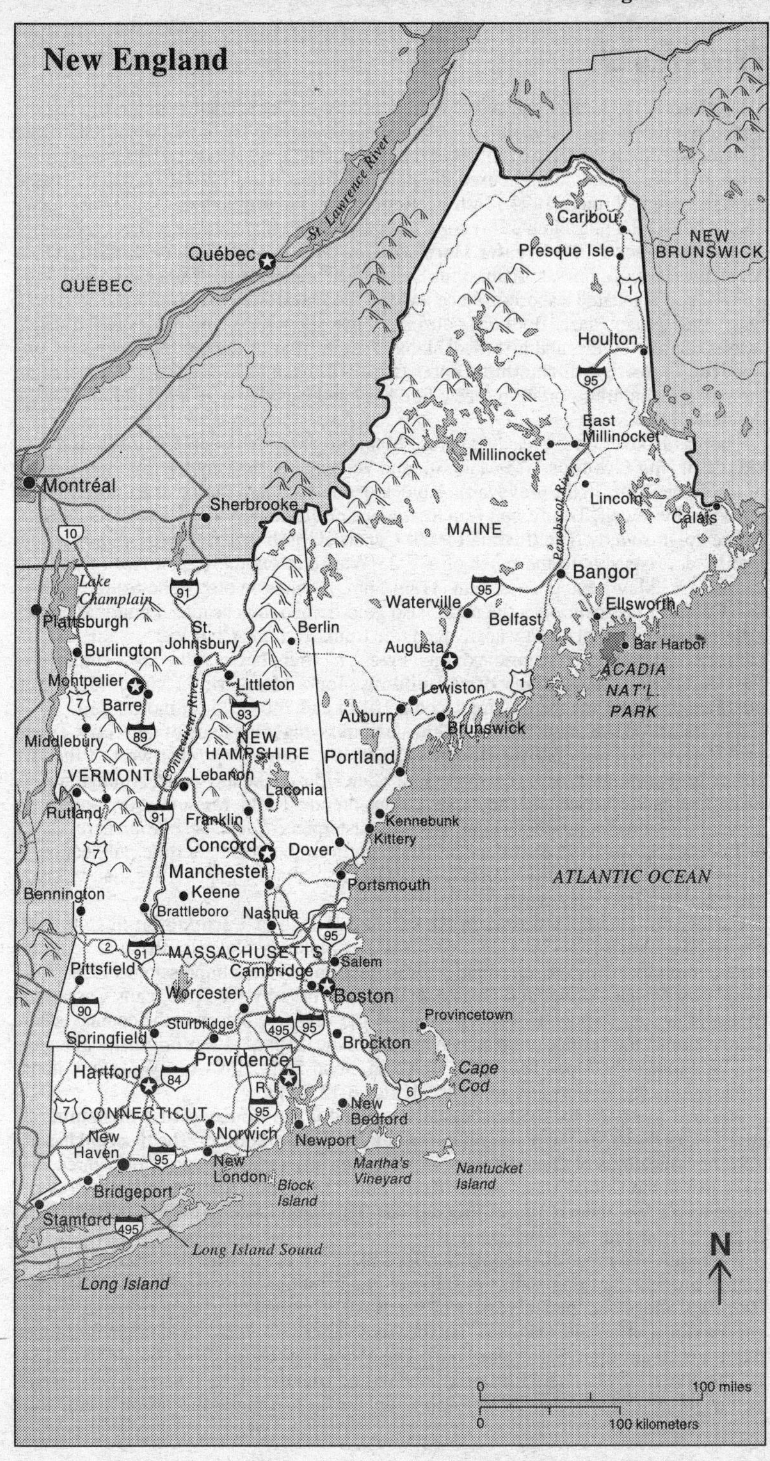
New England
St. Lawrence River
Québec
QUÉBEC
Caribou
Presque Isle
NEW
BRUNSWICK
1
Houlton
95
East
Millinocket
Millinocket
Penobscot River
Lincoln
Calais
MAINE
Montréal
Sherbrooke
10
Bangor
Lake
Champlain
91
95
Waterville
Ellsworth
Plattsburgh
St.
Johnsbury
Berlin
Belfast
Burlington
Augusta
Bar Harbor
ACADIA
NAT'L.
PARK
Montpelier
Littleton
Lewiston
1
7
Barre
93
Auburn
Brunswick
89
NEW
HAMPSHIRE
Middlebury
Connecticut River
Portland
VERMONT
Lebanon
Laconia
Rutland
91
Franklin
Kennebunk
Kittery
7
Concord
Dover
Manchester
Portsmouth
ATLANTIC OCEAN
Keene
Bennington
Brattleboro
Nashua
95
2
91
MASSACHUSETTS
Salem
Pittsfield
Cambridge
Boston
Worcester
90
Provincetown
Sturbridge
495
95
Springfield
Brockton
Providence
Cape
Cod
Hartford
84
RI
6
95
7
CONNECTICUT
New
Bedford
Norwich
Newport
New
Haven
95
New
London
Martha's
Vineyard
Nantucket
Island
Block
Island
Bridgeport
Stamford
495
Long Island Sound
Long Island
N
0
100 miles
0
100 kilometers

Hartford

Hartford is the largest and most prominent city in Connecticut—home to both the state government and the nation's insurance headquarters. The gold-domed **Old State House,** 800 Main St. (522-6766), is at the heart of the city. Designed by Charles Bullfinch in 1796, this building housed the state government until 1914. (It will be closed for renovations through 1994.) Instead, **Renovation Headquarters** (522-6766), located just across the plaza in the **Pavilion,** has taken in the State House's historical exhibits and its branch of the **Greater Hartford Convention and Visitors Bureau.** (Open Mon.-Fri. 10am-6pm, Sat. 10am-5pm.) The other branch of the Convention and Visitors Bureau is located a short distance away at the **Hartford Civic Center** (728-6789), One Civic Center Plaza. Both offer dozens of maps, booklets, and guides to the state's resorts, campgrounds, and historical sights. Just in front of the old State House, **Connecticut Transit's Information Center** (525-9181) can answer questions concerning the city's public transportation (basic fare 85¢) and can also give a helpful map of the downtown area.

Thomas Hooker once preached across Main Street, at the **Center Church and Ancient Burying Grounds,** 675 Main St., and you can see the centuries-old tombstones of his descendants in the graveyard. A block or so west, park 'n ride at **Bushnell Park,** bordered by Jewell, Trinity, and Elm St., on one of the country's few extant hand-crafted merry-go-rounds. The **Bushnell Park Carousel,** built in 1914, spins 48 horses and two lovers' chariots to the tunes of a 1925 Wurlitzer Organ. (Open April Sat.-Sun. 11am-5pm; May-Sept. 2 Tues.-Sun. 11am-5pm. Admission 50¢.) The **State Capitol,** 210 Capitol Ave., overlooks the park. Also gold-domed, this beautiful building houses Lafayette's camp bed and a war-ravaged tree trunk from the Civil War's Battle of Chicamauga, among other historic exhibits. Free 1-hr. tours begin at the West entrance of the neighboring **Legislative Office Building** (Tours Mon.-Fri. 9:15am-1:15pm, Sat. 10:15am-2:15pm. See the Capitol's Room 101 or call 240-0224 for more info.)

Lovers of American literature won't want to miss engaging tours of the **Mark Twain and Harriet Beecher Stowe Houses** (525-9317), both located just west of the city center on Farmington Ave. (From the Old State House take any east Farmington Ave. bus.) The gaudy Victorian Mark Twain Mansion housed the Missouri-born author for 17 years. Twain composed his controversial masterpiece *Huckleberry Finn* here. Harriet Beecher Stowe lived next door on Nook Farm in the years after the publication of *Uncle Tom's Cabin*, from 1873 until her death. (Both houses open Tues.-Sat. 9:30am-4pm. Call for info. on prices.)

Farther out Farmington Ave. in the colonial village of **Farmington** lies the **Hill-Stead Museum** (677-4787). Hill-Stead is a completely Colonial Revival "country house" built by Alfred Pope around 1900 to house his French Impressionist Collection. Pieces by Manet, Monet and Degas, as well as works by the Americans Cassat and Whistler, are on display. Hill-Stead is one of the very few places in the country where Impressionist masterpieces are shown in a domestic setting, as was originally intended. (Guided tour only. Open May-Oct. Wed-Sun. noon-5pm; Nov.-Apr. Wed.-Sun. noon-4pm. Adults $5, Seniors and students $4, kids 6-12 $2.)

Another must-see for the aesthetically inclined is the **Wadsworth Atheneum,** 600 Main St. (278-2670), the oldest public art museum in the country. The museum has absorbing collections of contemporary and Baroque art, including one of only three Caravaggios in the United States. (Open Tues.-Sun. 11am-5pm. Admission $3, seniors and students $1.50, under 13 free. Free all day Thurs. and Sat. from 11am-1pm. Tours Thurs. at 1pm and Sat.-Sun. 2pm.)

There are a number of reasonably priced places to eat in Hartford—scope out food courts in malls, hot dog stands at Bushnell, and restaurants around local schools like **Trinity College** and the **University of Hartford**. The food court on the second level of the **Pavilion** offers the standard, inexpensive variety of ethnic food court fare (open Mon.-Fri. 10am-6pm, Sat. 10am-5pm). The **Municipal Cafe** (278-4844, 485 Main St., on the corner of Main and Elm) is a popular and friendly place to catch a good breakfast or lunch. (Sandwiches under $4, hot dinners $6.) At night, the "Muni" is big, big,

big on the local music scene. (Open daily 7am-2:30pm with breakfast and lunch menu, and from 7pm with bar menu under $5; bands usually Wed.-Sat.)

The city lies at the intersection of **I-91,** which runs from New Haven to points north, and of **I-84**, which runs from Boston to points west.

Hartford's **area code** is 203.

Long Island Sound: New London and Mystic

Connecticut's coastal towns along the Long Island Sound were busy seaports in the days of Melville and Richard Henry Dana, but the dark, musty inns filled with tattooed sailors swapping sea journeys have been consigned to history. Today, the coast is important mainly as a resort and sailing base, and maritime enthusiasts in particular will enjoy these two former whaling ports, New London and nearby Mystic. **New London** sits proudly on a hillside overlooking the majestic **Thames River.** You'll recognize **Union Station** (designed by H. H. Richardson) by the flock of cabs in front of it and the flock of seagulls on the city pier behind. The **Coast Guard Academy** (444-8270), a five-minute drive up Rte. 32, offers free tours through the Coast Guard Museum (444-8511, open May-Oct. Mon.-Fri. 9am-4:30pm, Sat. 10am-5pm, Sun. noon-5pm) and the beautiful cadet-training vessel *U.S.S. Eagle* when it is in port. (Best chance to catch the Eagle is on Sunday. Call for winter hours.)

The town of **Mystic** is a short way up I-95 (exit 90). The **Tourist and Information Center** (536-1641) in **Olde Mysticke Village** provides a list of local accommodations and can make same-day reservations. **Mystic Seaport Museum** (572-0711) is a restored 19th-century whaling port. The museum's docks hold three boats: a fishing schooner, a military training vessel, and most impressive of all, the three-masted whaling ship **Charles W. Morgan**, on which reenactments of the whaling life are held daily. Although prices are steep and the area is essentially a maritime tourist trap, fans of Melville and Conrad will thoroughly enjoy it. (Seaport open daily 9am-5pm. Admission $14.50, ages 6-15 $8.75. Take I-95 5 mi. east from Union Station to Groton, then bus #10 to Mystic; $1.15 total.)

The **area code** for New London and Mystic is 203.

New Haven

New Haven is simultaneously university town and depressed industrial city. Ivy-Leaguers and a working class population live somewhat uneasily side by side—bumper stickers proclaiming "Tax Yale, Not Us" embellish a number of street signs downtown. But there is more than just political tension here. New Haven is a battle-zone, and not just for ideas. Violent crime and other symptoms of urban blight lurk in the cityscape. Yalies tend to stick to areas on or near campus, further widening the rift between town and gown. The difference between the controlled, wealthy academic environment and the rest of the town is apparent in every facet of the city—from architecture to safety.

New Haven is laid out in nine squares. The central one is **The Green,** between **Yale University** and City Hall, bordered by a small but thriving business district which consists mostly of bookstores, boutiques, cheap sandwich places, and other services catering to students and professors. Downtown New Haven—particularly the Yale campus—is littered with distinctive buildings. The omnipresence of American Collegiate Gothic in spires, towers, and ivy-covered buildings lends the campus a unity of design that its Cambridge role model lacks.

The **Yale Information Center,** Phelps Gateway, 344 College St. (432-2300), facing the Green, gives organized tours and free campus maps. Pick up a 75¢ walking guide and *The Yale,* a guide to undergraduate life ($3; open daily 10am-4pm. Free 1-hr. tours Mon.-Fri. at 10:30am and 2pm, Sat.-Sun. at 1:30pm.)

James Gambel Rodgers, a firm believer in the sanctity of printed material, designed **Sterling Memorial Library,** 120 High St. (432-1775). The building looks much like a monastery—even the telephone booths are shaped like confessionals. Rodgers spared no expense to make Yale's library look "authentic," even to the absurd extent of decapitating the figurines on the library's exterior to replicate the crumbling ones at Oxford. (Open summer Mon.-Wed. and Fri. 8:30am-5pm, Thurs. 8:30am-10pm, Sat. 10am-5pm; academic year Mon.-Thurs. 8:30am-midnight, Fri. 8:30am-5pm, Sat. 10am-5am, Sun. 1pm-midnight.) The massive **Beinecke Rare Book and Manuscript Library,** 121 Wall St. (432-2977), has no windows. Instead this intriguing modern structure is panelled with Vermont marble cut thin enough to be translucent; supposedly its volumes (including one Gutenberg Bible and an extensive collection of William Carlos Williams's writings) could survive even nuclear war. Let's not test that boast. (Open Mon.-Fri. 8:30am-4:45pm, Sat. 10am-4:45pm.)

Most of New Haven's museums are on the Yale campus. The **Yale University Art Gallery,** 1111 Chapel St. (432-0600), opened in 1832, claims to be the oldest university art museum in the Western Hemisphere. Its collections of John Trumbull paintings and Italian Renaissance works are especially notable. (Open Tues.-Sat. 10am-5pm, Sun. 2-5pm; closed Aug. $3 donation requested.) The **Peabody Museum of Natural History,** 170 Whitney Ave. (432-5050; 432-5799 for recorded message), houses Rudolph F. Zallinger's Pulitzer Prize-winning mural, which portrays the North American continent as it appeared 70 to 350 million years ago. Other exhibits range from Central American cultural artifacts to a dinosaur hall displaying the skeleton of a Brontosaurus. (Open Mon.-Sat. 10am-5pm, Sun. noon-5pm. Admission $2.50, seniors $2, ages 3-15 $1. Free Mon.-Fri. 3-5pm.)

Food in New Haven is reasonably cheap, catering to the student population. **Atticus Café,** 1082 Chapel St. (776-4040), is a charming bookstore/café with friendly if harried service. Try their soups served with swell half-loaves of bread ($3-4). Lunch specials are $5. (Open daily 8am-midnight.) **Naples Pizza,** 90 Wall St. (776-9021 or 776-6214), is a Yale tradition, updated with a video jukebox. Try a pizza with broccoli, pineapple, or white clams ($7.25); wash it down with a pitcher of beer ($5.50; open June-Aug. Mon.-Wed. 7-10pm, Thurs.-Fri. 7-11pm; Sept.-May Sun.-Thurs. 7pm-1am, Fri.-Sat. 7pm-2am.)

New Haven offers plenty of late-night entertainment. Check out **Toad's Place,** 300 York St. (562-5589; for recording 621-8623), to see if one of your favorite bands is in town. While you get tickets, grab a draft beer ($1) at the bar. (Box office open daily 11am-6pm; tickets available at bar after 8pm. Bar open Sun.-Thurs. 8pm-1am, Fri.-Sat. 8pm-2am.)

Once a famous testing ground for Broadway-bound plays, New Haven's thespian community carries on today, but to a much lesser extent. The **Schubert Theater,** 247 College St. (624-1825 or 800-228-6622), **The Palace,** 246 College St. (784-2120, box office 624-6497), and the **Long Wharf Theater** (787-4282)—which received a special Tony Award for achievement in Regional Theater in 1978—continue the tradition.

Yale itself accounts for an impressive bulk of the theater activity in the city. The **Yale Repertory Theater** (432-1234) has cultivated such illustrious alums as Meryl Streep, Glenn Close, Christopher Durang, and James Earl Jones, and continues to produce excellent shows. (Open Oct.-May.) The **University Theater,** at 22 York St., stages undergraduate plays throughout the academic year and during graduation. Tickets are usually under $8. In summer, the Green is the site of free **New Haven Symphony** concerts (865-0831), the **New Haven Jazz Festival** (787-8228), and other free musical series. The Department of Cultural Affairs (787-8956), 770 Chapel St., can answer questions about concerts on the Green.

Inexpensive accommodations are sparse in New Haven. The hunt is especially difficult in red October around Yale Parents weekend (mid-Oct.) and graduation (early June). **Hotel Duncan,** 1151 Chapel St. (787-1273), has decent singles for $40 and doubles for $55, both with bath. (Reservations suggested.) The **Nutmeg Bed & Breakfast,** 222 Girard Ave., Hartford 06105 (236-6698), reserves doubles in New Haven B&Bs for $35 to $45. (Open Mon.-Fri. 9am-5:30pm.) The nearest parks for camping are **Cat-**

tletown (264-5678, sites $10), 40 minutes away, and **Hammonasset Beach** (245-2755, sites $12), 20 minutes away.

To obtain free bus and street maps and information about current events in town, stop in at the **New Haven Visitors and Convention Bureau,** 195 Church St. (787-8822), on the Green. (Open Mon.-Fri. 9am-5pm.) To get to New Haven from New York City, consider **Amtrak,** Union Station, Union Ave. (800-872-7245). The station is newly renovated, but the area is unsafe at night. To or from Yale, take city bus A ("Orange St."), J, or U ("Waterbury"), or walk six blocks northeast to the Green. Trains to Boston ($36), Washington, DC ($69), and New York City ($22). **Metro-North Commuter Railroad,** Union Station (800-638-7646), runs trains to New York's Grand Central Station for half of Amtrak's fare ($9.25-13; ticket counter open daily 6am-10:30pm.) New Haven's **Greyhound** station at 45 George St. (772-2470), is in a rough area. Walk there with a companion or take a cab. Frequent bus service to: New York City ($11), Boston ($19) and Providence ($17.50; ticket office open daily 7:30am-8:15pm.) **Peter Pan Bus Lines,** Union Station (878-6054), offers buses to Boston ($28).

Connecticut Transit serves New Haven and the surrounding area from 470 James St. (624-0151). Most buses depart from the Green. (Open Mon.-Fri. 8am-4:30pm. Information booth at 200 Orange St. open Mon.-Fri. 9am-5pm.)

New Haven is a cinch to get to by car. The city lies at the intersection of I-95 (110 mi. from Providence) and I-91 (40 mi. from Hartford). At night, don't wander alone out of the immediate downtown area and the campus, as surrounding sections are notably less safe. The Yale area is well-patrolled by campus police, who also fearlessly protect the downtown area from illegally parked cars. Around 4pm on weekdays tow trucks are out in full force, so be sure to read parking signs carefully.

New Haven's **area code** is 203.

Maine

A sprawling evergreen wilderness pocked with lakes, swollen with mountains, and defined by a tattered shore, Maine protrudes from the neat stack of New England states below. The Maine "Downeaster" is known for reticent humor, rugged pragmatism, and disdain for urban pretension. Few of the state's regular urban refugees—including ex-oilman George H.W. Bush, who keeps a house in Kennebunkport—can resist swathing themselves in plaid flannel and adopting the Downeaster attitude as their own.

The state lives by its waters and forests. Fishers along the coast and logging companies inland support the state's economy, and fresh-water fishing is a major Maine stream sport. The rapids of the Allagash Waterway challenge canoeists, and the remote backwood lakes are perfect for hikers, bicyclists and campers.

Practical Information

Capital: Augusta.

Maine Publicity Bureau, 209 Maine Ave., Farmingdale (582-9300). Send mail to P.O. Box 2300, Hallowell 04347. **Bureau of Parks and Recreation,** State House Station #22 (1st floor Harlow Bldg.), Augusta 04333 (289-3821). **Maine Forest Service,** Bureau of Forestry, State House Station #22 (2nd floor Harlow Bldg.), Augusta 04333 (289-2791). All 3 agencies open Mon.-Fri. 8am-5pm; the Forest Service closes Fri. 4pm.

Time Zone: Eastern. **Postal Abbreviation:** ME

Sales Tax: 5%.

Bangor

Bangor has fallen from its former glory as the nation's largest lumber port; today the city trafficks more in traffic, funneling visitors in from points south and sending them out into the beautiful northern nether regions of Maine. Get a good night's sleep, stock up on provisions and get the hell out of town and into the bush. I-95 runs north-south through the city, parallel to the Penobscot River; about half-a-dozen minor highways also meet there, notably U.S. 1A, which runs east to Bar Harbor and Acadia National Park and south to Penobscot Bay and U.S. 2, which runs southwest across the width of the state and into New Hampshire.

Highway culture dominates lodging and food; Bangor specializes in budget roadside motels, most of which lie just off I-95 and charge identical rates for nearly identical rooms. The **Scottish Inn** (945-2934), 1476 Hammond St. extension, (take exit 45B from I-95, go straight at the lights; it's 1½ mi. ahead on the left) has even lower rates because of its distance from the interstate. It also has clean rooms with showers, TV and phone, and just remember: if it's not Scottish, it's craaap! (Singles $30. Doubles $35, 2 double beds $40.) The **Riverview Motel,** 810 State St. (947-0125), offers clean and fairly large rooms with TV but no phone. (July-Aug. singles $39, doubles $49. Rates lower off-season.) The **Budget Traveler,** 327 Odlin Rd. (945-0111), off exit 45B and right at the lights, is decorated with groovy earth tones and blond wood, and furnitured with buffed corners—totally 70s. (Singles $36. Doubles $42. 10% discount for AAA members. Breakfast included weekdays.) **Pleasant Hill Campground** (848-5127 or 617-664-5057) lies near town on Rte. 222 and offers swimming, laundry and free showers. (Sites $11, with hookup $15. $3 per additional person. Reservations suggested.)

For maps, local accommodation and restaurant lists, and brochures detailing almost every activity, sight, lodging and eatery in the city, check the **Chamber of Commerce,** 519 Main St. (947-0307). (Open mid-May-mid-Aug. daily 9am-5pm, mid-Aug.-mid-Oct. Mon.-Fri. 9am-5pm.) To get out of Bangor, hop on a **Greyhound,** 158 Main St. (945-3000 or 942-1700), near downtown. Four buses run daily to Boston ($22), New York ($76) and Portland ($15). (Open daily 5-6am and 7:30am-5:30pm.) From the same terminal, **Cyr Bus Line** runs once daily up to Caribou ($25) and **Saint Croix Bus** departs daily to Calais ($18).

Bangor's **Post Office** sits at 202 Harlow Rd. (941-2016). (Open Mon.-Fri. 7:30am-5pm, Sat. 8am-noon.) The **ZIP code** is 04407 and the **area code** is 207.

Inland Maine

Northeast from the White Mountains of New Hampshire to Presque Isle lies the largest U.S. wilderness area east of the Mississippi River—miles of splendid, forested mountains dotted with hundreds of lakes, disturbed only by the occasional logger, canoer or angler. Huge paper companies own what few roads there are in the region, along with most of the land. By agreement with the state, nearly all roads remain public, some for a small fee. Pull to the side of the road when you see a loaded logging truck approach. Moose abound in the area and caution is a must when driving the less trafficked roads, especially at dawn and dusk. A full grown bull moose can weigh in at 1200 lbs.; if you come across one in the road it may move, but is more likely to just stand there or even break into a run in front of you. It's not unheard of for a moose to race full tilt in front of a car for more than five mi., swerving to keep it from getting by.

Baxter State Park and the Allagash

Mount Katahdin, "Greatest Mountain" in local Native American dialect, looms as the northern terminus of the **Appalachian Trail,** which follows the ancient 2020-mi. Appalachian ridge from Georgia to Maine. The Maine portion, the most rugged and remote, at one point meanders 100 mi. without crossing any public roads or villages. Ponds and streams support a large moose population and a decreasing number of bears.

The climb up Mt. Katahdin is a spectacular one. It has become so popular that park authorities have recently begun limiting access to the mountain by restricting space in the parking lots at the trailheads. Arrive early; there is no way to call ahead to check space availability. Rent canoes at the Trout Brook Farm and South Branch Pond campgrounds in the north of the park, and at Kidney Pond and Daicey Pond at the park's southern end. ($1 per hr., $8 per day.) You must keep the canoes within the pond or lake where you've rented them. Of the park's 10 **campgrounds,** only Russell Pond and Chimney Pond are inaccessible by car. The most popular site is **Chimney Pond,** a 3.3-mi. hike from Roaring Brook up Mt. Katahdin, with nine lean-tos and a 12-person bunkhouse. Go north to beat the crowds; the quietest sites are those along the hiking trails away from the campgrounds. The **Freeze-Out Trail,** in the northern part of the park away from the road, offers the most seclusion, and because many of the sites along it are a fairly long hike, you can often get reservations for them on short notice. None of the sites have hookups. Park authorities recommend treating lake or stream water with iodine or boiling it for at least five minutes. All 10 campgrounds are open mid-May through mid-October, except for Chimney Pond, which doesn't open until June 1. Maine residents are guaranteed 30% of the sites. Reserve early for July and August. (Tent sites and lean-tos $5 per person per night; a bed in a bunkhouse $6.)

The park's main entrance lies 18 mi. north of the town of **Millinocket,** home to the Great Northern Paper Co., the largest producer of newsprint in the U.S. Before entering the park, stock up on food and get a complete list of trails with detailed accompanying maps at the **Baxter State Park Headquarters,** 64 Balsam Dr., Millinocket 04462, near the McDonald's off Rte. 11/159 (723-5140). (Open Memorial Day-Labor Day daily 8:30am-4:30pm, off-season Mon.-Fri. 8:30am-4:30pm.) Bus service to the park is not available; the park charges out-of-state motor vehicles $8 per day.

Millinocket is also a popular base for expeditions to the **Allagash Wilderness Waterway,** an untamed river wending 92 mi. through thick forests. The logistics of an Allagash trip can be challenging. The nearly 100-mi. run from **Telos Lake** north to the Canadian border provides a difficult trip that crosses only a handful of private logging roads, all owned by the Northern Maine Woods Association (435-6213), which charges for access ($12 per person, $6 for ME residents). The company also controls camping in the area, which is permitted only at one of the 66 designated campsites along the waterway. (Sites $5, ME residents $4.) Write the Bureau of Parks and Recreation, Maine Dept. of Conservation, State House, Station #22, Augusta 04333 (207-289-3821), for info. The waterway is a 30-mi. drive past Baxter Park from Millinocket on Golden Rd.

Moosehead Lakes Region

This remote part of Maine dances with wolves, bears, moose, mosquitoes, forests, and ponds seldom seen by humans. The looping road from Ripogenus Dam near Baxter State Park through Greenville to Rockwood leads past lakes and ponds frequented by moose in search of grass in the water. From Rockwood, take a boat to **Mt. Kineo Island** and climb **Mount Kineo,** an 800-ft. peak with 700-ft. cliffs plummeting to the lake.

The vigorous Kennebec, Penobscot and Dead Rivers are favored by **whitewater rafting** enthusiasts. Novice rafters will find the fees ($75-90 per day) harder to manage than the trips. **Eastern River Expeditions,** P.O. Box 1173, Greenville 04441 (695-2411 or 695-2248; 800-634-7238 outside ME), guides trips from May to October and also offers canoe and kayak instruction. ($80 per person weekdays, $90 weekends. Open May-Oct. Mon.-Fri. 8am-6pm.) **Wilderness Rafting Expeditions,** in the Birches Resort, 20 mi. north of Greenville (534-2242 or 534-7305; write P.O. Box 41, Rockwood 04478), runs trips ($75 weekdays, $90 weekends) and rents mountain bikes ($20 per day) and windsurfboards ($25 per day). Reservations are required; rivers are less crowded weekdays and before July. The Kennebec River is class IV and V; the Penobscot is class V.

With a number of hotels, restaurants and a full-size grocery store, **Greenville** serves as a good home base in the region. **The Guesthouse (HI/AYH)** (695-2278),one mi. west on Rte. 6/15 from the center of town, is both a guest house and a 12-bed hostel in a comfortable, very attractive three-story home. All guests have access to a full kitchen, a living room with TV, and the proprietor's extensive knowledge of the area. (Open June-Aug., sometimes in winter. Singles $28, doubles $35, triples $39. Hostel $10, $12 nonmembers. Call ahead for availability, especially on weekends.) The **Chamber of**

Commerce (695-2702), in the center of town, distributes a complimentary *Visitor's Guide* with an area map. (Open June-Oct. daily 8am-6pm, off-season Mon.-Fri. 8am-6pm.) **Rockwood** has cabins with kitchens at **Rockwood Cottages** (534-7725; singles from $45, $270 per week; doubles from $55, $330 per week).

Rangeley Lakes Region

This region contains two of Maine's largest ski areas. East of **Rangeley** lies **Sugarloaf,** the state's second highest mountain and the only resort in the East with alpine skiing above the treeline. **Saddleback Mt.** (4116 ft.) lies farther south. The area's large lakes—**Rangeley, Mooselookmeguntic, Richardson** and **Umbagog**—lure boaters and anglers in summer. Numerous campsites along the lake shores and islands aid canoeists. The Appalachian Trail crosses over several summits in the region.

Inexpensive lodgings dot the area. The **Farmhouse Inn** (864-5805), 1½ mi. south of Rangeley on Rte. 4, offers nine bunkrooms (4 people each, $19 per night, with full breakfast). Camping at **Rangeley State Park** (864-3858) is permitted from May 15 to October 1. (Sites $13, ME residents $10, $2 day-use fee. Showers available.) For a list of campgrounds, including those in the state park, contact the **Chamber of Commerce,** P.O. Box 317, Rangeley 04970 (864-5571), located at the park entrance off Main St; they also can make reservations. (Open Mon.-Sat. 9am-5pm, longer hours peak season.)

Maine Coast

As the seagull flies, the length of the Maine coast from Kittery to Lubec measures 228 mi., but if you untangled all of the convoluted inlets and rocky promontories, the distance would be a whopping 3478 mi. Fishing was the earliest business here, later augmented by a vigorous shipbuilding industry; both traditions continue strongly. Lobster pounds are ubiquitous in coastal Maine; stop under one of the innumerable makeshift red wooden lobster signs which speckle the roadsides, set yourself down on a grey wooden bench and chow, but keep in mind that lobsters are tastier before July, when most start to molt. Also be forewarned that lobster-poaching is treated as seriously here as cattle-rustling is out West; the color codings and designs on the buoy markers are as distinct as a cattle rancher's brand and serve the same purpose.

U.S. 1 hugs the coastline and strings the port towns together. Lesser roads and small ferry lines connect the remote villages and offshore islands. The best place for info is the **Maine Information Center** in Kittery (439-1319; P.O. Box 396, Kittery 03903), three mi. north of the Maine-New Hampshire bridge. (Open summer daily 9am-5pm.) **Greyhound** serves points between Portland and Bangor along I-95, the coastal town of Brunswick as well as connecting routes to Boston. A car or bike is necessary to reach many coastal points of interest.

Mount Desert Island

In spite of its name, Mt. Desert (de-ZERT) is not barren. In summer, campers and tourists abound, drawn by mountains, rocky beaches, and spruce and birch forests. The Atlantic waters—calm in summer but often stormy in winter—are too cold for all but the hardiest of souls. Wind-swept Acadia National Park features rugged headlands, fine beaches, plenty of tidal-pool critters and a variety of naturalist activities. **Bar Harbor** is a lively but crowded town packed with over 2400 guest rooms. The island's other towns, such as Seal and Northeast Harbors, are more relaxed but more expensive.

Practical Information

Emergency: Acadia National Park, 288-3369. **Bar Harbor Police, Fire Department and Ambulance,** 911. **Mt. Desert Police,** 276-5111.

Acadia National Park Visitors Center (288-3338), 3 mi. north of Bar Harbor on Rte. 3. Maps, park info, and over 100 weekly naturalist programs. Browse through the *Beaver Log,* the park's info newspaper. Open May 1-mid-June and Oct. daily 8am-4:30pm, mid-June-Sept. daily 8am-6pm. **Park Headquarters** (288-3338), 3 mi. west of Bar Harbor on Rte. 233. Open Oct.-May Mon.-Fri. 8am-4:30pm. **Bar Harbor Chamber of Commerce,** 93 Cottage St. (288-5103). Maps and helpful booklets about the island. Open Mon.-Fri. 8am-4pm. Also runs info booth (288-3393) at **Canadian National Marine** ferry port on Rte. 3, 1 mi. north of Bar Harbor. Open mid-May-Oct. daily 10am-5pm, July-Aug. 9am-8pm.

Ferries: Beal & Bunker, Northeast Harbor on the town dock (244-3575). To Cranberry Islands (5-7 per day, 30 min., $3.50, under 12 $2). **Canadian National Marine (CNM),** Bar Harbor (288-3395 or 800-341-7981). To Yarmouth, Nova Scotia (6 hrs., 1 per day, late June-mid-Sept. $45, seniors $34, kids $23, with car $75, with bike $10; late Sept.-mid-June $30, $23, $15, $55, $7, respectively. $3 port tax per person.)

Buses: Downeast Transportation (667-5796), sends off the **MDI Bus** which provides shuttle service weekdays around the island (75¢) and to Ellsworth ($4) on U.S. 1, as well as Sat. service to Bangor ($8). In Bar Harbor, shuttles run 10am-2pm; catch the bus at Shop & Save on Cottage St.

Bike Rental: Wheels of Bar Harbor, 166 Main St. (288-9433). Mountain bikes $14 per day, $10 per 4 hrs., $70 per week. Mopeds $50/$30/$210. Also offers all-terrain strollers, $9/$6/$42. Credit card or drivers license required for rentals. Open June-mid-Sept. daily 8am-10pm, off-season daily 8am-8pm.

National Park Canoe Rentals, north end of Long Pond off Rte. 102 (244-5854). Canoes $27 per day, $17 per morning, $20 per afternoon. Open May-Labor Day daily 8:30am-5pm.

Post Office: 55 Cottage St. (288-3122), near downtown. Open Mon.-Fri. 8am-5pm, Sat. 9am-noon. **ZIP code:** 04609.

Area Code: 207.

Rte. 3 runs through Bar Harbor, becoming Mt. Desert St.; it and Cottage St. are the major east-west arteries. Rte. 102 circuits the western half of the island.

Accommodations and Camping

Grand hotels with grand prices remain from Rockefeller's day, and you still have to be a Rockefeller to afford them. Nevertheless, a few reasonable establishments can be found, particularly on Rte. 3 north of Bar Harbor. Inexpensive camping exists throughout the island; most campgrounds line Rte. 198 and 102, well west of the city.

Mt. Desert Island Hostel (HI/AYH), 27 Kennebec St., Bar Harbor (288-5587), behind the Episcopal Church on Mt. Desert St. 2 large dorm rooms, common room, full kitchen. Curfew 11pm. Lockout 9:30am-4:30pm. $8, nonmembers $11. Open mid-June-Aug. 31.

Mt. Desert Island YWCA, 36 Mt. Desert St. (288-5008), near downtown. Women only. Dorm-style rooms with bath on hall $25 per night, $80 per week; doubles $18/$70; solarium with 7 beds $15/$60. $10 key deposit for stays of 1 or 2 nights; $25 security deposit for stays of 3 nights and longer. Fills in summer; make reservations early.

Acadia Hotel, 20 Mt. Desert St., Bar Harbor (288-5721). Sweet, homey place overlooking park. TV, private bath. Late June-early Sept. room for 1 or 2 people $45-58; mid-Sept.-Oct. 31 $30-45.

Mt. Desert Campground, off Rte. 198 (244-3710). Tent sites, platforms in a woodsy location overlooking the Somes Sound. Boat dock, swimming for the hearty, and free blueberry picking. Open May 15-Oct. 1. Sites $12-18, hookup $1 extra. $5 per additional adult, child $2.

Acadia National Park Campgrounds: Blackwoods Rte. 3 (call 288-3274 8:30am-8pm), 5 mi. south of Bar Harbor on Rte. 3. Over 300 sites mid-May-mid-June and mid-Sept.-mid-Oct. $10, mid-June-mid-Sept. $12, free other times. Reservations up to 8 weeks in advance; mid-June-mid-Sept. call 800-365-2267. **Seawall,** Rte. 102A on the western side of the island, 4 mi. south of Southwest Harbor (call 244-3600 8am-6pm). Station open May-Sept., 8am-8pm, first-come, first-served. Walk-in sites $7, drive-in $10. Both campgrounds are within a 10-mi. walk to the ocean and have toilets but no showers or hookups. Privately owned public-access showers available nearby for a fee. No reservations.

Food and Entertainment

Seafood is all the rage on the island. "Lobster pounds" sell the underwater crustaceans for little money; cooking them is the only problem.

Beals's, at Southwest Harbor (244-7178 or 244-3202), at the end of Clark Point Rd. The best price for lobster in an appropriate setting. Pick your own live lobster from a tank; Beals's will do the rest ($7-8). Outdoor dining on the dock. A nearby stand sells munchies and other beverages. Open daily 9am-8pm; off-season daily 9am-5pm.

The Lighthouse Restaurant, in Seal Harbor (276-3958). Fairly upscale; a nice way to escape from the crowds at Bar Harbor. Sandwiches $3-7, entrées $9-15, lobster dinner $14. Open May-Nov. daily 9am-9pm, July-Aug. 9am-11pm.

Most after-dinner pleasures on the island are simple ones. For a treat, try **Ben and Bill's Chocolate Emporium** at 80 Main St. near Cottage (288-3281), which boasts 24 flavors of homemade ice cream and a huge selection of sweet-smelling fresh chocolate. (Open March-Dec. daily 9am-11:30pm.) **Geddy's,** 19 Main St. (288-5077), is a self-proclaimed three-tier entertainment complex with bar, sporadic live music, and dancing. Most bands are free; the more popular ones charge a $2 cover. (Open mid-May-Oct. daily 2pm-1am.) The art-deco **Criterion Theatre** (288-3441) was recently declared a national landmark and continues to show movies in the summer Monday through Thursday at 8pm and Friday through Sunday at 7 and 9pm. Matinees are scheduled on rainy days; a new film arrives every couple of days. Programs are available at the desk.

Sights

Mt. Desert Island is shaped roughly like a lobster claw. To the east on Rte. 3 lie Bar Harbor and Seal Harbor. South on Rte. 198 near the cleft is **Northeast Harbor,** and across Somes Sound on Rte. 102 is the **Southwest Harbor. Bar Harbor** is by far the most crowded part of the large island, sandwiched by the Blue Hill and Frenchmen Bays. Once a summer hamlet for the very wealthy, the town now harbors a motley melange of R&R-seekers. The wealthy have fled to the quieter and more secluded Northeast and Seal Harbors. Anyone desiring a taste of coastal Maine life purged of wealth and kitsch should head west to Southwest Harbor, where fishing and shipbuilding still thrive. **Little Cranberry Island,** out in the Atlantic Ocean south of Mt. Desert, offers a spectacular view of Acadia as well as the cheapest uncooked lobster in the area at the fishers' co-op.

The staff at the **Mt. Desert Oceanarium** (244-7330), at the end of Clark Pt. Rd. in Southwest Harbor, can teach you about the sea at each of their three facilities (the lobster hatchery and Salt Marsh Walk are located near Bar Harbor). The main museum—though resembling a grammar-school science fair—fascinates onlookers. (Open mid-May-late Oct. Mon.-Sat. 9am-5pm. Tickets for all 3 facilities $9, kids $6.) Cruises head out to sea from a number of points on the island. In Bar Harbor, the **Frenchman Bay Co.,** 1 Harbor Place on West St. (288-3322), offers windjammer sail trips ($16, ages 5-12 $12), lobster fishing and seal-watching trips ($14/$9), whale watching ($28/$18) and deep-sea fishing ($30/$22). (Open May-Oct. Call for details or schedule.) The **Acadian Whale Watcher** has slightly lower prices, guarantees sightings or you go again free, and has food and a full bar on board. Sunset ($11, kids $8) and whale-watching cruises ($27, seniors $20, ages 9-14 $18, ages 6-8 $15; open mid-May-mid-Oct.) leave twice a day. Bring extra clothing—the excursions are often chilly.

From Northeast Harbor, the **Sea Princess Islesford Historical and Naturalist Cruise** (276-5352) brings you past an osprey nesting site and lobster buoys to Little Cranberry Island. You may be lucky enough to see harbor seals, cormorants or pilot whales on the cruise. The crew takes you to the **Islesford Historical Museum** in sight of the fjord-like Somes Sound. (Two cruises per day May weekends and early June-mid-Oct.; fare $10, ages 4-11 $8.)

The 33,000 acres that comprise **Acadia National Park** are a landlubber's dream, offering easy trails and challenging hikes which allow for an intimate exploration of Mt. Desert Island. More acres are available on the nearby **Schoodic Peninsula** and **Isle au Haut** to the west. Millionaire and expert horseman John D. Rockefeller funded half of the park's 120 mi. of trails out of fear that the park would someday be overrun by cars. These **carriage roads** make for easy walking and pleasant horseback riding and are accessible to disabled persons. **Precipice Trail** and others offer more advanced hiking. Be realistic about your abilities here; the majority of injuries in the park occur in hiking accidents. Swim in the relatively warm **Echo Lake,** which has on-duty lifeguards in summer. **The Eagle Lake Loop Road** is graded for bicyclists. At the park visitors center, pick up the handy *Biking Guide* (50¢), which offers invaluable safety advice. Some of these paths are accessible only by mountain bike. Touring the park by auto will cost a little more. ($5 per day private vehicle, $2 per pedestrian or cyclist; permit is good for 7 consecutive days. Seniors and disabled admitted free.) About four mi. south of Bar Harbor on Rte. 3, take the **Park Loop Road** running along the shore of the island where great waves roll up against steep granite cliffs. The sea comes into **Thunder Hole** at half-tide with a bang, sending plumes of spray high into the air and onto tourists. To the right just before the Loop Rd. turns back to the visitors center stands **Cadillac Mountain,** the highest Atlantic headland north of Brazil. A five-mi. hiking trail to the summit starts at Blackwoods campground, two mi. east of Seal Harbor. The top of Mt. Cadillac, the very first place sunlight touches the U.S., makes a great place for an early morning breakfast (Grape Nuts, of course).

Tourists also can explore the island by horse, the way Rockefeller intended. **Wildwood Stables** (276-3622), along the Park Loop Rd. in Seal Harbor, runs two-hour carriage tours ($12.50, seniors $11.50, ages 6-12 $7, ages 2-5 $4.50) through the park. Reservations are strongly suggested. No horses are available for rental on the island.

Portland

For a virtually tourist-free taste of the New England coast, go to Portland. Destroyed by a fire in 1866, the city rebuilt only to decline in the late 1960s. Lately, Portland shines, its downtown area advantageously located along the ocean, its moderate microclime revitalized. Stroll down the attractive Old Port Exchange, whose restaurants, taverns and craft shops occupy former warehouses and 19th-century buildings. The reasonable location and low cost of living in Maine's largest city makes it an ideal base for sight-seeing and daytrips to the surrounding coastal areas, such as Casco Bay and the Casco Bay Islands. Nearby Sebago Lake provides ample opportunities for sunning and waterskiing.

Practical Information

Emergency: 911.

Visitor Information Bureau, 305 Commercial St. at the corner of Center St. (772-0994). Open June-Sept. Mon.-Fri. 8:30am-6pm, Sat. 9am-6pm, Sun. 10am-3pm; off-season Mon.-Fri. 9am-5pm, Sat. 9am-2pm. Offers comprehensive *Portland Visitor's Guide.*

Greyhound: 950 Congress St. (772-6587), on the western outskirts of town. Don't go there at night. Take the #1 Congress St. bus to downtown. Office open daily 5:30-6am and 7:15am-6:20pm. To: Boston (7 per day, $17.25); Bangor (4 per day, $23); and points north. Often specials in summer months.

Public Transport: Metro Bus Company, 114 Valley St. (774-0351), ½-mi. south of the Greyhound station. Most buses operate Mon.-Sat. 6am-10pm, Sun. 9am-6pm; info available 8am-4:30pm. Fare 80¢, seniors and disabled 40¢, under 5 free. Exact change only. Buses are wheelchair accessible.

Taxi: ABC Taxis, 772-8685. About $3 from the bus station to downtown.

Prince of Fundy Cruises: P.O. Box 4216, 468 Commercial St., (800-341-7540). Ferries to Yarmouth in southern Nova Scotia leave from Commercial St. near Million Dollar Bridge May-late Oct. at 9pm. Fare mid-June-mid-Sept. $75, ages 5-14 $38; off-season $55 and $25. Cars $98, off-season $80. Reservations required. Specials up to 50% off, especially on Tues. and Wed.

Help Lines: Rape Crisis, 774-3613. **AIDS Line,** 775-1267.

Post Office: 125 Forest Ave. (871-8410). Open Mon.-Fri. 7:30am-5pm, Sat. 9am-noon. Self-service lobby open 24 hrs. **ZIP code:** 04101.

Area Code: 207.

The downtown area sits along Congress St. towards the bay; a few blocks south lies the Old Port on Commercial and Fore St. These two districts contain most of the city's sights and attractions. I-295 veers off I-95 to form the western boundary of the downtown area. Several offshore islands are served by regular ferries.

Accommodations and Camping

Portland has some inexpensive accommodations, but prices often jump during the summer season. You can always try exit 8 off I-95, a budget hotel center for staples like **Super 8** and **Motel 6,** where singles run about $36.

YWCA, 87 Spring St. (874-1130), downtown near the Civic Center. Women only. Small rooms verge on sterile, but an amiable atmosphere more than compensates. Fills up in summer. Lounge, pool and kitchen (bring utensils). Check-in 11am-2pm. Singles $25. Doubles $40. Phone in reservations with a credit card.

YMCA, 70 Forest Ave. (874-1111), north side of Congress St., 1 block from the post office. Cash only. Men only. Check-in 11am-10pm. Access to pool and exercise facilities. Singles $21.50 per night, $81 per week. Key deposit $10.

Hotel Everett, 51A Oak St. (773-7882), off Congress St. Central location; newly painted and carpeted rooms. June-Sept. singles $35, with bath $45. Doubles $45/$49. Off-season rates about 20% less. Weekly rates available. Reservations are recommended in summer.

Wassamki Springs, 855 Saco St. (839-4276), in Westbrook. Closest campground (15 min.) to Portland. Drive west down Congress St. (becomes Rte. 22, then County Rd.) about 6 mi., turn right on Saco St. Full facilities plus a sandy beach. Flocks of migrant Winnebagos nest here. Sites $18 for 2 people. $4 per additional person. Shower and electricity $3 extra. Open May-mid-Oct. Reservations recommended 4-6 weeks in advance, especially July-Aug.

Food and Nightlife

Diners, delis and cafés abound in Portland. Check out the active port on Commercial St., lined with sheds peddling fresh clams, fish and lobsters.

The Pepperclub, 78 Middle St. (772-0531). A colorful, casual café that features a diverse but always excellent menu of mostly vegetarian dishes—some chicken, fish and organic beef items listed. Try the Punjabi chicken ($9), or salmon cakes with spicy coconut ($9). Open Sun.-Wed. 5-9pm, Thurs.-Sat. 5-10pm. Ample parking across the street.

Carbur's, 123 Middle St. (772-7794), near the Old Port. Whimsical sandwiches for $4-10. If you try the quintuple sandwich ($10), the servers and cooks will parade around the dining room chanting "Down East Feast," and they guarantee "free medical attention" if you hurt yourself trying to finish it. Open Mon.-Fri. 11am-10pm, Sat. 11am-11pm, Sun. noon-10pm.

Raffle's Café Bookstore, 555 Congress St. (761-3930), in the heart of downtown. Enjoy breakfast or a light lunch while doing heavy reading. Has a charming selection of desserts. Try the cheese and fruit plate ($4), or a bottle of Reed's Jamaican Ginger ($1.25). Open Mon.-Wed. and Fri. 8am-5pm, Thurs. 8am-7pm, Sat. 9:30am-5pm.

Seamen's Club, 375 Fore St. (773-3333), at Exchange St. in the Old Port with a harbor view. Top-notch seafood dining steeped in briny lore. Lunch entrées $6-10, dinner $11 and up. Fresh lobster year-round. Open Mon.-Fri. 11am-10pm, Sat.-Sun. 11am-11pm.

Ruby's Choice, 116 Free St. (773-9099), near downtown. Fresh, homemade buns for thick burgers you dress yourself ($2.50-4.50). Open Mon.-Wed. 11:30am-2pm, Thurs.-Sat. 11:30am-7pm.

Portland's new nightlife centers around the Old Port. **Three Dollar Dewey's,** at 446 Fore St. (722-3310), recreates the atmosphere of an English pub, serving over 65 varieties of beer and ale along with great chili and free popcorn to an eclectic clientele. (Open Mon.-Sat. 11am-1am, Sun. noon-1am.)

Sights

Many of Portland's most spectacular sights are to be found outside the city proper, along the rugged coast or on the beautiful, secluded islands a short ferry ride offshore. **Two Lights State Park** (794-5871), across the million Dollar Bridge on State St. and south along Rte. 77 to Cape Elizabeth, is a wonderful place to picnic and relax along the rocky shoreline in view of two (count 'em, two) lighthouses. (Open Memorial Day-Labor Day daily 9am-8:30pm. $1.50, ages 5-11 $1.) **Casco Bay Lines,** on State Pier near the corner of Commercial and Franklin (774-7871), America's oldest ferry service, runs year-round to the nearby islands. Take bicycles out to tool around one of them, or, if your feet aren't up to pedaling, try the quiet and unpopulated beach on **Long Island.** (Departures daily 6am-7pm. $8.75--17.50, seniors and kids 5-9 ½-price. Bikes $4-5.75 extra.) The sea may beckon from the instant you arrive in Portland, but the city does have a full slate of non-aquatic activities. The **Portland Museum of Art,** 7 Congress Sq. (775-6148), at the intersection of Congress, High and Free St., collects U.S. art by notables such as John Singer Sargent and Winslow Homer. (Open Tues.-Wed. and Fri.-Sat. 10am-5pm, Thurs. 10am-9pm, Sun. noon-5pm. $3.50, seniors $2.50, kids 6-18 $1. Free Sat. 10am-noon.) Down the street at 485 Congress St., the **Wadsworth-Longfellow House** (772-1807), a museum of social history and U.S. literature, zeroes in on late 18th- and 19th-century antiques as well as at the life of the poet and his family. (Open June 1-Columbus Day Tues.-Sat. 10am-4pm. Tours every ½ hr. $3, under 12 $1.)

For a list of other historical landmarks and homes in the area, visit the **Greater Portland Landmarks Office,** 165 State St. (774-5561), which leads tours from early July to late September and sells a comprehensive packet on walking tours ($4.15; open Mon.-Thurs. 8:30am-4pm, Fri. 8:30am-2pm). While the history of Portland's **Old Port Exchange** began in the 17th century, the area's shops, stores and homes were rebuilt in Victorian style after the fire of 1866. The **Portland Observatory,** 138 Congress St. (774-5561), set atop a promontory east of downtown, went up in 1807. Climb 102 steps for a panoramic view of Casco Bay and downtown Portland. (Open July-Aug. Wed., Thurs., Sun. 1-5pm, Fri.-Sat. 10am-5pm; June, Sept. and Oct. Fri. and Sun. 1-5pm, Sat. 10am-5pm. Closed if raining. $1.50, kids 50¢.)

The **Old Port Festival** begins the summer season with a bang in early June, spanning several blocks from Federal to Commercial St. and drawing as many as 50,000 people. On July and August weekdays, enjoy the **Noontime Performance Series** (772-6828), the only one of its kind in New England, in which bands from ragtime to Dixieland perform in Portland's Monument Square. (Late June-early July Mon.-Fri. noon-1:15pm.) The **6-Alive Sidewalk Arts Festival** (828-6666) lines Congress St. with booths featuring the work of artists from all over the country, and is generally held around mid-August. Weather permitting, take the ferry out to **Cushings Island** for the annual **croquet tournament.** Event listings can be found within the free guide distributed by the visitors information bureau (see Practical Information).

North of Portland

Much like the coastal region south of Portland, the north offers the traveler sunny beaches and cool breezes—for a price. Lodgings are never cheap, but if you're either outfitted for camping or just passing through, you'll find fun and interesting shopping as well as ample access to the ocean. Much of the region is unserviced by public transportation; driving is rewarding, however. U.S. 1, running north along the coast, offers motorists a charming glimpse of woods and small towns.

Freeport, about 20 mi. north of Portland on I-95, once garnered glory as the "birthplace of Maine:" the 1820 signing of documents declaring the state's independence from Massachusetts took place at the historic **Jameson Tavern,** at 115 Main St. Now the town finds fame as the factory outlet capital of the world, offering over 100 downtown stores. The grandaddy of them all, **L.L. Bean,** began manufacturing Maine Hunting Shoes in Freeport in 1912. The hunting shoe hasn't changed much since then, but now Bean sells diverse products from clothes epitomizing preppy *haute couture* to sturdy tenting gear. The factory outlet on Depot St. has pretty decent bargains. The retail store on Main St. (865-4767 or 800-221-4221) stays open 24 hrs., 365 days a year. Legend has it the store has closed only once since its opening, when its founder, Leon Leonwood (no wonder he called himself L.L.) Bean, died.

Heading up to **Penobscot Bay** (not to be confused with the town of Penobscot) from factory-outlet purgatory, be sure to stop at **Moody's Diner** off U.S. 1 in Waldoboro. It seems like nothing has changed since business started in 1927; tourists and old salts rub shoulders here over fantastic food. Try the homemade strawberry-rhubarb pie à la mode ($1.50). (Open Sun.-Fri. 7am-11:30pm, Sat. 5am-11:30pm.)

In summer, preppies flock to friendly Camden, 100 mi. north of Portland, to dock their yachts alongside the eight tall masted schooners in Penobscot Bay. Many of the cruises, like the neighboring yachts, are out of the budget traveler's price range, but the Rockport-Camden-Lincolnville **Chamber of Commerce** (236-4404), on the harbor in Camden behind the Camden National Bank, can tell you which are affordable. They also have information on a few rooms in local private homes for $12-30. (Open Mon.-Fri. 9am-5pm, Sat. 10am-5pm, Sun. noon-4pm, mid-Oct.-late May Mon.-Fri. 9am-5pm.) Cheaper still, the **Camden Hills State Park,** 11/4 mi. north of town on U.S. 1 (236-3109), is almost always full in July and August, but you're fairly certain to get a site if you arrive before 2pm. This coastal retreat offers more than 25 mi. of trails; one leads up to Mt. Battie with a harbor view. Make reservations through the mail with $2 per night fee. Showers and toilets available. (Open May 15-Oct. 15. Day use $1.50. Sites $12, residents $9.50.)

Affordable to all and in the heart of downtown Camden is **Cappy's Chowder House** on Main St. (236-2254), a kindly, comfortable hangout where the great seafood draws tourists and townspeople alike. Try the seafood pie ($7), made with scallops, shrimp, mussels and clams. (Open daily 7:30am-midnight.)

The **Maine State Ferry Service,** five mi. north of Camden on U.S. 1 in Lincolnville (800-521-3939; outside Maine 596-2202), takes you through the Bay to Isleboro Island (5-9 per day. Fare $1.75, kids $1, auto $6.25.). The ferry also has an agency in Rockland on U.S. 1, running boats to North Haven, Vinalhaven and Matinicus. Always call the ferry service to confirm; rates and schedules change with the weather.

South of Blue Hill on the other side of Penobscot Bay lies **Deer Isle,** a picturesque forested island with rocky coasts accessible by bridge from the mainland. Off Main St. in Stonington, at the southern tip of Deer Isle, a mailboat (367-5193; mid-June-early Sept. Mon.-Sat. 3 per day, Sun. 1 per day) leaves for **Isle au Haut,** part of Acadia National Park. (Fare $8, kids $4.) Island exploration is done by foot or bike (no rental bikes available on the island). The only accommodations are five lean-tos, each of which can accommodate up to six people, at **Duck Harbor Campground** (no showers; sites $5; reservations necessary; open mid-May-mid-Oct.). Contact Acadia Park Headquarters or write P.O. Box 177, Bar Harbor 04609 (288-3338).

South of Portland

Driving south on U.S. 1 out of Portland, you'll encounter nothing but traffic and stores until the town of **Kennebunk,** and, several miles east on Rte. 35, its coastal counterpart **Kennebunkport.** If you want to bypass busy U.S. 1, take the Maine Turnpike south to exit 3 and take Fletcher St. east into Kennebunk.

Both of these towns are popular hideaways for wealthy authors and artists. A number of rare and used bookstores line U.S. 1 just south of Kennebunk, while art galleries fill the town itself. Recently the quaint resort of Kennebunkport has grown famous and profit-hungry as the summer home of President Bush, who owns a sprawling estate on Walker's Point. You'll know when you've reached the entrance on Ocean Ave. when you spot the Secret Service gatekeeper talking into his sleeve inside a tinted glass cubicle. The **Kennebunk-Kennebunkport Chamber of Commerce,** at the intersection of Rte. 9 and 35 in Kennebunkport (967-0857), provides a free guide to the area's history and sights. (Open Mon.-Fri. 9am-9pm, Sat. 9am-7pm, Sun. 9am-4pm, off-season Mon.-Fri. noon-5pm, Sat. 10am-5pm, Sun. 11am-4pm.)

Biking provides a graceful ride on the road past rocky shores and spares visitors the aggravation of fighting thick summer traffic. In nearby **Biddiford,** a few minutes north on U.S. 1, **Quinn's Bike and Fitness,** 140 Rte. 1 (U.S. 1; 284-4632), rents 10-speeds ($11.25 per day, $33 per week), 3-speeds ($8.75/$22.50), and mountain bikes ($20/$80). (Open Mon.-Thurs. 9am-5:30pm, Fri. 9am-8:30pm, Sat. 9am-5:30pm.) You can get a copy of *25 Bicycle Tours in Maine* ($15) from the Portland Chamber of Commerce (see above).

A visit to Kennebunkport will cost you a pretty penny, though the **Lobster Deck Restaurant,** on Rte. 9 overlooking Kennebunk Harbor, serves lobster dinners for $14-16. (Open daily 11am-10pm.) For affordable lodging, camp. **Salty Acres Campground,** 4½ mi. northeast of Kennebunkport on Rte. 9 (967-8623), offers swimming, a grocery store, laundry and a convenient location about a mile from the beaches. (Sites $14, with electricity and water $18. $6 per additional person. Open mid-May-mid-

Oct.) A little farther out is the **Mousam River Campground,** on Alfred Rd. just west of exit 3 off I-95 in West Kennebunk (985-2507; sites $16; free showers, open mid-May-mid-Oct.).

To escape the tourist throngs, head west to the **Rachel Carson National Wildlife Refuge** (646-9226), on Rte. 9 near U.S. 1. A self-guided trail takes you through the salt marsh home of over 200 species of shorebirds and waterfowl, a moving tribute to the naturalist/author of *Silent Spring,* which publicized the perils of industrial waste. (Open daily sunrise to sunset.)

Massachusetts

In many ways, Massachusetts considers itself to be the cerebral cortex of the national body. The oldest university in America, Harvard, was founded in Cambridge in 1636. The nation's first public school was established soon after, in 1647. Countless literati have hocked their wares in this intellectual marketplace, including Hawthorne, Dickinson, Melville, Wharton, and the Jameses—to say nothing of the dilligent *Let's Go* staff.

But not all of Massachusetts is icy intellectualism. A needlepoint charm blesses the rolling hills of the Berkshires, which are resplendent during the fall foliage season. Here cows and corn supplant calculators and Kant. On the Atlantic side of the state, a salty mist reigns, redolent with memories of the erstwhile whaling capital of the world. Massachusetts is also made of sweat and toil. The American Industrial Revolution began in the textile mills of factory towns like Lowell, Worcester, and Fall River.

Practical Information

Capital: Boston.

Massachusetts Division of Tourism, Department of Commerce and Development, 100 Cambridge St., Boston 02202. Can send you a complimentary, comprehensive *Spirit of Massachusetts Guidebook* and direct you to regional resources. (727-3201; 800-632-8038 for guides.) Open Mon.-Fri. 9am-5pm.

Time Zone: Eastern. **Postal Abbreviation:** MA

Sales Tax: 5%.

The Berkshires

The swelling urban centers of Boston and New York have long sent their upwardly mobile to the Berkshire Mountains in search of a less taxing, more relaxing country escape. Today a host of affordable B&Bs, restaurants, and campgrounds make this subrange of the Appalachians accessible to budget travelers who seek the "deep greens and blues" of its forests and lakes. The slower pace of life and the open friendliness of the townspeople will erase the words "rush hour" from any weary urbanite's mind.

Berkshire County

One of the Berkshires' greatest treasures is **Tanglewood**, the famed summer home of the **Boston Symphony Orchestra,** a short distance west of Lenox Center on Rte. 183 (West St.). Although its offerings are primarily classical, Tanglewood concerts show off a variety of music, from Ray Charles to Wynton Marsalis to James Taylor. Buy a lawn ticket, bring a picnic dinner, and listen to your favorites under the stars or in the Sunday afternoon sunshine. (Tickets $9.50-$52. Sat. open rehearsals $10.50. Summer info. 413-637-1940, winter 617-266-1492. Schedules available through the mail from the BSO, Symphony Hall, Boston, 02115.) Berkshire county's dozen state parks and forests cover more than 100,000 acres and offer numerous camp sites and cabins. For info about the parks, stop by the **Region 5 Headquarters** (442-8928) at 740 South St., south of downtown, or contact them by mail at P.O. Box 1433, Pittsfield 01202.

Just about everything in Berkshire County runs north-south: the mountain range giving the county its name (a southern extension of the Green Mountains of Vermont); the 80 mi. of **Appalachian Trail** that wind through Massachusetts; the Hoosac and the Housatonic rivers; and **U.S. 7**, the region's main artery. To see sights located far from the town centers, you'll have to drive. The roads are slow and often pocked with potholes, but certainly scenic. **Pete's Rent-a-Car** (445-5795), on the corner of Fenn and East St., offers some of the lowest local prices ($26 per day; 100 free mi.; must be at least 23). **Berkshire Regional Transit Association** (499-2782), known as "the B," spans the Berkshires from Great Barrington to Williamstown. Buses run every hour at some bus stops (Mon.-Sat. 6am-6pm); fares (60¢-$6) depend on the route you take. System schedules are available on the bus and at some bus stops. The **information booth** on the east side of Pittsfield's rotary circle can give more information on restaurants and accommodations in **Pittsfield** and the surrounding cities along U.S. 7. (Open 10am-6pm mid-June-Oct.). Just a short walk down South St., **Berkshire AAA** (445-5635) welcomes questions and carries a variety of brochures covering much of New England. (200 South St.; Open Mon.-Fri. 8:30am-5pm.)

The Berkshires' **area code** is 413.

The Mohawk Trail

The best way to see the beauty of the Berkshires by car is to follow the **Mohawk Trail** (Rte. 2). Perhaps the most famous highway in the state, its awe-inspiring view of the surrounding mountains draws crowds during fall foliage weekends. Millers Falls, MA is the trail's eastern terminus. Other than the forests, the first real tourist attraction as you travel west is actually off the Trail, in **Historic Deerfield** (774-5581), five mi. south of Greenfield on U.S. 5. This idyllic, 19th-century village contains 13 fully restored buildings. You can wander around outside them for free, or you can pay admission to go inside. Each building conducts its own half-hour guided tour; admission is good for two consecutive days ($10, ages 6-17 $5, under 6 free.)

The Trail is dotted with affordable campgrounds and lodgings. Six mi. west of Greenfield at **Highland Springs Guests** in Shelburne (625-2648), the elderly Mrs. Sauter rents clean rooms with comfortable beds and a shared bath for $25 to an occasionally international clientele. Further west on the trail lies **Mohawk Trail State Forest** (339-5504), which offers campsites without hookups along a river ($12) and rents cabins (no electricity; large $20, small $16). (Bathrooms and showers available, July-Aug. min. stay 1 week, other times 2 nights. Call for reservations.)

Continuing west on Rte. 2, you'll find **North Adams,** home to the **Western Gateway** (663-6312), a railroad museum and one of Massachusetts' five Heritage State Parks. It's housed in an old Boston and Maine Railroad building on the Furnace St. Bypass off Rte. 8 N. (Open Memorial Day-Labor Day daily 10am-4:30pm; Labor Day-June 30 Thurs.-Mon. 10am-4:30pm; admission free, donations encouraged.)

Mt. Greylock, the highest peak in Massachusetts (3491 ft.), is south of the Mohawk Trail, accessible by Rte. 2 to the north and U.S. 7 to the west. By car, take Notch Rd. from Rte. 2 between North Adams and Williamstown, or take Rockwell Rd. from Lanesboro on U.S. 7. Hiking trails begin from nearly all the towns around the mountain; get maps at the **Mount Greylock Visitors Information Center,** Rockwell Rd. (499-4262). (Open mid-May-mid-Oct. Mon.-Fri. 9am-4pm, Sat.-Sun. 9am-5pm.) Once at the top, climb the **War Memorial** for a breathtaking view. Sleep high in nearby **Bascom Lodge** (743-1591), built from the rock excavated for the monument (bunks for members of the Appalachian Mountain Club $19, nonmembers $23, member children under 12 $12, nonmember kids $15). The lodge offers breakfast ($5) and dinner ($10) to guests; its snackbar is open to the public daily 9am-5pm.

The Mohawk Trail ends in **Williamstown** at its junction with U.S. 7; here, an **information booth** (458-4922) provides an abundance of free local maps and seasonal brochures, and can help you find a place to stay in one of Williamstown's many reasonably-priced **B&Bs.** (Open 24 hrs., staffed by volunteers daily mid-May-Oct.

10am-6pm). At **Williams College,** the second oldest in Massachusetts (est. 1793), lecturers compete with the beautiful scenery of surrounding mountains for their students' attention. Campus maps are available from the **Admissions Office** (597-2211), 988 Main St. (Open Mon.-Fri. 8:30am-4:30pm. Tours at 10am, 11:15am, 1:15pm, 3:30pm.) First among the college's many cultural resources, **Chapin Library** (597-2462) displays a number of rare U.S. manuscripts, including early copies of the Declaration of Independence, Articles of Confederation, Constitution, and Bill of Rights. (Open Mon.-Fri. 9am-noon and 1-5pm. Free.) The small but impressive **Williams College Museum of Art** (597-2429) merits a visit; rotating exhibits have included pop art and Impressionist works. (Open Mon.-Sat. 10am-5pm, Sun. 1-5pm. Free.)

A good place to eat near campus is **Pappa Charlie's Deli** (28 Spring St., 458-5969), a popular, well-lit deli offering sandwiches ranging from the "Joe Paterno" to the "Dr. Johnny Fever." (Under $4; open Mon.-Sat. 8am-11pm, Sun. 9am-11pm.)

Try not to spend too much time indoors in Williamstown; the surrounding wooded hills beckon from the moment you arrive. The **Hopkins Memorial Forest,** owned and run by Williams' Center for Environmental Study (597-2346), has over 2250 acres open to the public for hiking and cross-country skiing. Take U.S. 7 north, turn left on Bulkley St., go to the end and turn right onto Northwest Hill Rd. **Spoke Bicycles and Repairs,** 618 Main St. (458-3456), rents bikes in a variety of speeds ($10 per day) and can give you advice on good rides in the area.

The **Zip Code** for the Mohawk Trail is **413.**

Boston

America has often been called a "melting pot" in which different cultures mesh to create a homogeneous, all-American alloy. Not Boston. If anything, Beantown is a salad bowl in which the diverse ingredients comprising the city are linked *only* by their relative proximity. The several communities of Boston—the brahmins, the working classes, the college kids, and the pockets of ethnic communities—rarely interact in more than a perfunctory manner, imbuing the town with a dynamic tension unmatched within New England. At its best, the relative isolation of each of these groups preserves distinctive cultural flavors and gives Boston a cosmopolitan feel in an otherwise provincial area of the country. At its worst, however, these divisions result in xenophobia, snobbery, and racism.

When most of America thinks of Boston, they think of *Bahstonians,* upper-crust brahmins who can trace their lineage back to the *Mayflower.* Their given, middle- and sur-names are often interchangeable, resulting in such patrician permutations as Eliot Stokes Herbert Walker (or Herbert Walker Eliot Stokes, or Stokes Walker Eliot Herberts...you get the picture). Stroll down Beacon Hill or through the brownstones of Back Bay, and you will be confronted by a refined opulence that took 15 generations to hone. Nowhere else in America can even approximate the aristocratic nature of Boston—ironic that the city calls itself the "Cradle of Liberty."

However, restricting yourself to blue-blood and colonial history means missing the modern pulse of the city. Step off the Freedom Trail and explore other aspects of Boston. It is the relative newcomers—second, third and fourth generation immigrants—who are the mainstay of the city. These are the subway drivers, policemen, professionals, and the fiercely loyal Celtics and Bruins fans. They consistently vote Democratic, read the *Herald*, and their ex-churches are Catholic. Stop off in a bar in South Boston or sidle up next to a Red Sox enthusiast—if (s)he's not cursing the umpire—and you'll get a taste of the *real* Boston.

Equally important are those just arrived—the immigrant populace here is a veritable Babel, with large groups of Southeast Asians, Portuguese, Italians, and West Indians dominating particular regions of the city. Go to Haymarket on a Saturday morning and you'll hear nary a word of English in a marketplace that feels thousands of miles away from touristy, recycled Quincy Market next door. Often forgotten by Bostonians and outsiders alike is Boston's sizeable African-American community, which was drawn

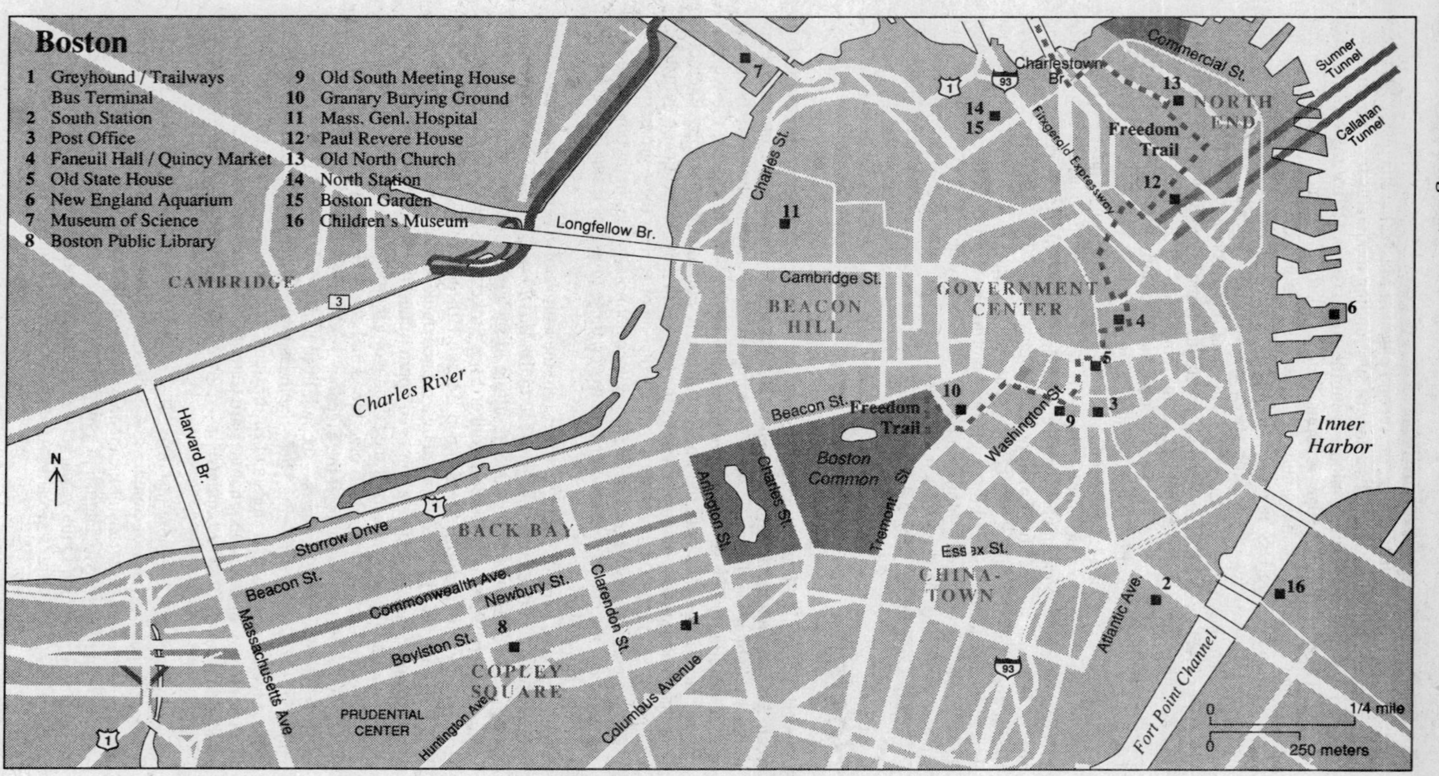
Boston
1 Greyhound / Trailways Bus Terminal
2 South Station
3 Post Office
4 Faneuil Hall / Quincy Market
5 Old State House
6 New England Aquarium
7 Museum of Science
8 Boston Public Library
9 Old South Meeting House
10 Granary Burying Ground
11 Mass. Genl. Hospital
12 Paul Revere House
13 Old North Church
14 North Station
15 Boston Garden
16 Children's Museum
Commercial St.
Sumner Tunnel
Callahan Tunnel
Charlestown Br.
NORTH END
Freedom Trail
Fitzgerald Expressway
Charles St.
Longfellow Br.
CAMBRIDGE
Cambridge St.
BEACON HILL
GOVERNMENT CENTER
Inner Harbor
Charles River
Beacon St.
Washington St.
Harvard Br.
N
Boston Common
Tremont St.
Arlington St.
Storrow Drive
BACK BAY
Essex St.
CHINA-TOWN
Beacon St.
Commonwealth Ave.
Newbury St.
Clarendon St.
Atlantic Ave.
Massachusetts Ave
Boylston St.
COPLEY SQUARE
Columbus Avenue
Fort Point Channel
PRUDENTIAL CENTER
Huntington Ave.
0
1/4 mile
0
250 meters

north decades ago in search of freedom and paying jobs and now suffers worst in the de-industrialization of New England.

Plunked down in the middle of all of this are college students—hundreds of thousands of them—drawn to Boston like moths to a flame in search of enlightenment, excitement, and "the $80,000 keg party." People like yours truly attempt to focus on ponderous tomes, all the while being distracted by their multifaceted urban environs.

Visitors to "The Hub" will find much here to entertain, interest and feed them. The mixture of young and old, past and future, aristocrat and hoi polloi constantly redefines the character of this, America's first great city.

Practical Information and Orientation

Emergency: 911.

Boston Visitor Information Center, Tremont St. at Park, near the Boston Common and the beginning of the Freedom Trail. Free info, including *Where Boston,* a monthly calendar of events. Also a fantastic official guide to Boston, with great maps of the even greater Boston area and Freedom Trail ($3). Open daily 9am-5pm. **Greater Boston Convention and Tourist Bureau,** Prudential Plaza West, P.O. Box 490, Boston 02199 (536-4100). T: Copley. Open Mon.-Fri. and Sun. 8:30am-5pm, Sat. 9am-5pm. **National Historic Park Tourist Bureau,** 15 State St. (242-5642). T: State. Info on historical sights and 8-min. slide shows on the Freedom Trail narrated by the avuncular Sam Adams. Some rangers speak French or German. Open daily 9am-5pm, 9am-6pm in summer, except holidays.

Traveler's Aid: 711 Atlantic Ave. (542-7286). Open Mon.-Fri. 8:45am-4:45pm. Other locations: Logan Airport Terminals A (569-6284) and C (567-5385) and the desk in Greyhound station (542-9875); hours vary for each.

Logan International Airport: (567-5400) east Boston. Easily accessible by public transport. The free **Massport Shuttle** connects all terminals with the "Airport" T-stop. **Airways Transportation Company** (267-2981) runs shuttle buses between Logan and major downtown hotels (service daily from Boston every 30 min. 7am-7pm, to Boston every hr. on the hr. Fare $7.50-8.50, one way.)

Amtrak: South Station, Atlantic Ave. and Summer St. (482-3660 or 800-872-7245). T: South Station. Frequent daily service to New York City (5 hr.; $50, $79 round-trip), Philadelphia (6 hr.; $65/$95), and Washington, DC (8 hr; $98/$130). Restrictions may apply; call ahead.

Buses: Greyhound, 10 St. James Ave. (423-5810). T: Arlington. 2 blocks southwest of the Public Gardens. To New York City (Mon.-Thurs.: $29, $55 round-trip; Fri.-Sun.: $32/$60), Philadelphia ($33/$66), and Washington, DC ($49/$88). Also the station for **Vermont Transit. Bonanza** (720-4110) lines operate out of the Back Bay Railroad Station on Dartmouth (T: Copley), with frequent daily service to Providence ($7.75, $11.75 round-trip), Fall River/Newport ($8/$12), Bourne/Falmouth/Woods Hole ($11/$20), and Virginia City (just kidding). Open 24 hrs. **Peter Pan Lines** (426-7838), across from South Station on Atlantic Ave. T: South Station. Runs between Western Massachusetts and Albany, NY via Never Never Land. (Mon.-Thurs.: $29, $55 round-trip; Fri.-Sun.: $32/$60). Connections to New York City via Springfield ($29). Open daily 5:30am-midnight.

Public Transport: Massachusetts Bay Transportation Authority (MBTA): The subway system, known as the "T," consists of the Red, Green, Blue, and Orange lines. Green and Red Lines run daily 5:30am-12:30am; a night on the town often means taxiing home. Fare 85¢, Boston high school students with ID and ages 5-11 40¢, seniors 20¢. Some automated T entrances in outlying areas require tokens although they are not sold on location; buy several tokens at a time and have them handy. Bus service reaches more of the city and suburbs; fare one token or 60¢, but may vary depending on destination. Bus schedules available at Park St. subway station on the Green line. A "T passport" offers discounts at local businesses and unlimited travel on all subway and bus lines and some commuter rail zones. (3-day pass $8; 7-day pass $16.) This system is generally dependable and convenient. Wherever applicable, listings below give the T-stop closest to a sight or accommodation. **MBTA Commuter Rail:** Lines to suburbs and North Shore leave from North Station, Porter Square, and South Station T-stops. The **Boston and Maine Railroad** also runs out of North Station. For more information on any of these services call MBTA at 722-3200 or 800-392-6100.

Taxi: Red Cab, (in Brookline) 734-5000. **Checker Taxi,** 536-7000. **Yellow Cab,** 876-5000. A taxi from downtown to Logan $8-9, from Cambridge $18-20.

Car Rental: Brodie Auto Rentals, 24 Eliot St., Harvard Sq. in Cambridge (491-7600). T: Harvard. $24-27 per day for sub-compact with 100 free mi., 12¢ per mi. thereafter, depending on the type of car. Open Mon.-Fri. 8am-6pm, Sat. 8am-noon, Sun. 9am-noon. Must be 21 with credit card. **Dollar Rent-a-Car,** 110 Mt. Auburn St. in the Harvard Manor House, Harvard Sq. (354-6410). T: Harvard. Sub-compact with unlimited mi. $36 per day; must stay within New England. Open Mon.-Thurs. 7:30am-6pm, Fri. 7:30am-7pm, Sat.-Sun. 8am-4pm. $10 extra for renters under 25. Must have credit card. Other offices at many locations in Boston, including the Sheraton Hotel (523-5098) and Logan Airport (569-5300).

Bike Rental: Community Bike Shop, 490 Tremont St. near the Common (542-8623). $20 per day. Open Mon.-Wed. 9:30am-7pm, Thurs.-Fri. 9:30am-8pm, Sat. 9:30am-6pm., Sun. noon-5pm (summer only). Must have major credit card.

Help Lines: **The Samaritans suicide prevention line,** 247-0220. **Rape Hotline,** 492-7273. **Gay and Lesbian Helpline,** 267-9001.

Post Office: McCormack Station, Milk St., Post Office Sq. (654-5686), in the Financial District. Open Mon.-Fri. 8am-5pm. **ZIP code:** 02109.

Area Code: 617.

Leave your buggy near your lodgings and take to the sidewalks and subways; the public transportation system (called the **"T"**) here is excellent, parking is expensive, and Boston drivers come in two styles—homicidal and suicidal—depending on the size of their car. Several outlying T stations offer park and ride services. Boston is very compact and is best explored on foot. If you *do* choose to drive around the city, be defensive and alert; Boston's pedestrians can be as aggressive as the drivers. Don't contribute to coffers of the Boston Police Department by illegally parking.

Boston was not a planned city. Its mishmash of urban thoroughfares and semi-rural paths were designed by meandering colonial-era cows rather than civic planners. Many street names (e.g. Cambridge and Harvard) are repeated within the city as well as in neighboring towns. Get a map at the visitors center and ask for detailed directions wherever you go. The best directions will use landmarks, not road names, to steer you; the most frustrating thing about driving in Boston is that streetsigns almost *never* tell you the name of the thoroughfare on which you are traveling. The hub of the Hub is the 48-acre **Boston Common,** bounded by Tremont, Boylston, Charles, Beacon, and Park St. The **Freedom Trail,** a walking path that leads you past several historical sights in the city, begins in the Common, winds northeast to **Government Center** and**Faneuil Hall,** jogs through the **North End** and then heads north to **Charlestown** and **Bunker Hill.**

Accommodations and Camping

Cheap accommodations do not thrive in Boston. Early September, when students and their parents arrive for the beginning of the school year, is especially tight; likewise the first week in June, when families with graduating seniors pack into hotel rooms reserved six months to a year in advance. Those with cars should investigate the motels along highways in outlying areas. **Boston Bed and Breakfast,** 1643 Beacon St., Suite 23, Waban MA 02168 (332-4199), presides over 100 accommodations around the Boston area. (Singles $60-70. Doubles $70-95. Open Mon.-Fri. 9am-5pm.) The **Boston Welcome Center,** 140 Tremont St. (451-2227 or 800-756-4482), T: Park, can also make reservations for you in various hotels and motels. (Rooms $70-95. Cheaper off-season.)

Boston International Hostel (HI/AYH), 12 Hemenway St. in the Fenway (536-9455). T: Hynes/ICA. This cheery, colorful hostel has clean and slightly crowded but liveable rooms, some with sinks. Hall bathrooms, some recently renovated. Lockers, common rooms, cafeteria, kitchens and laundry. 220 beds in summer, 140 in winter. Planned activities nightly; ask about discounts. Check-in or out 9:30am, 10:30am winter. Lockout 2-7am. $12.75, membership required; under 14 ½-price. $5 deposit. Linens $2. Wheelchair-accessible. Reservations highly recommended.

Berkeley Residence Club (YWCA), 40 Berkeley St. (482-8850). T: Arlington. Solid, industrial, clean. Men are not allowed above the lobby. Grand piano, patio, pool, TV room, sun deck, laundry, library. Hall baths. Some doubles with sinks (extra charge). Cafeteria ($2 breakfast, $5.25 dinner). Singles $35. Doubles $44. Nonmembers $2 extra; ask for the recession rates. Weekly: singles $170, doubles $220. Key deposit $1. Towel deposit $2. Checkout 11am.

Greater Boston YMCA, 316 Huntington Ave. (536-7800). T: Northeastern. Down the street from Symphony Hall on Mass. Ave. Must be 18. Women accepted. Hall bathrooms. Elegant lobby, friendly atmosphere, partially used as overflow housing for Northeastern University students. Cafeteria, pool, and recreational facilities. 10-day max. stay. Breakfast included. Key deposit $5. ID and luggage required for check-in. Checkout before 11am. Singles $33. Doubles $48. Office staffed 24 hrs.

Longwood Inn, 123 Longwood Ave. (566-8615), Brookline. T: Longwood Ave. Quiet neighborhood. "Victorian" mansion with kitchen, dining room, TV room, laundry, sun room, and parking. Comfortable rooms, most with private bath. Check-in Mon.-Fri. 9am-5pm, Sat.-Sun. 9am-1pm, though times flexible. Singles $40-50. Doubles $43-53. Reservations recommended, especially in summer.

Anthony's Town House, 1085 Beacon St. (566-3972), Brookline. T: between Carlton and Hawes St. (Green C train). Very convenient to the T-stop. Nicely furnished: TV in every room, some with A/C and cable TV. 14 rooms for 20 guests, who range from trim professionals to scruffy backpackers. Singles $45. Doubles $62. Winter and off-season $5 less. Ask about weekly rates; mention *Let's Go* for 5% off the in-season rate. Reservations not required. Noon checkout.

Garden Halls Residences, 164 Marlborough St. (267-0079), Back Bay. T: Copley. Rents only to students. Excellent location. Spartan dorms with bed, dresser, and desk. Singles, doubles, triples, and quads available. No cooking, no meals served. Must bring own linen. $30 per person, 3 night min. stay. Reservations required. Open June 1-Aug. 15 daily 9am-4pm.

The Farrington Inn, 23 Farrington Ave., Allston Station (781-1860 or 800-767-5337). T: Green Line-B, or #66 bus. Not fancy, but pleasant; prices include local phone, parking, and breakfast. Singles from $35, doubles from $45.

The Irving House, 24 Irving St. (547-4600), in Cambridge near Cambridge St., in a residential neighborhood near the university and the Square. T: Harvard. New management. Unique rooms, libraries, comfortable fishtanked lounge, spacious wood floors; parking available. Singles from $33. Doubles $45-75. Reservations required.

Food

Travelers can find bargain food in several distinct regions of Boston. Locals and tourists alike buzz below the historic gilded grasshopper at **Faneuil Hall Marketplace** and **Quincy Market** (T: Government Center). An astonishing number of cafés, restaurants, and food stands are tossed in with an equal number of souvenir and specialty gift shops; almost any kind of fast food, from peanut butter to pizza, can be found somewhere under the market's long roofs. Just up Congress St., **Haymarket** attracts both budget-conscious shoppers and sightseers to its open-air stalls. Pick up fresh fish, produce, cheeses, and pigs' eyes here for well below supermarket prices. (Indoor stores open daily dawn-dusk; outdoor stalls Fri.-Sat. only. T: Government Center or Haymarket.) Nearby, the **North End** features great food in the heart of Little Italy (T: Haymarket), while the numerous restaurants in Chinatown seem to serve all the tea in China (T: Chinatown). For perhaps the best (though not the cheapest) seafood in Boston—including the chowder served at Presidential Inaugural Balls—stop at **Legal Seafood,** at the Park Plaza Hotel (T: Park Street; 426-5526).

Durgin Park, 340 N. Market St. (227-2038). T: Government Center or Haymarket. Sit elbow-to-elbow at long tables and let the famous surly servers entertain and harangue you. Their specialty is prime rib; also try the reasonably priced lobster and first-class Indian pudding. Oyster bar downstairs. Entrées $5-30. Open Mon.-Sat. 11:30am-10pm, Sun. 11am-9pm.

Bosworths, 37 Union St. (248-0880). T: Government Center or Haymarket. Best beans in Beantown. Sparse but filling menu includes fish cakes and franks ($2.20) as well as beans, bread, and pudding; beans and Boston bread (rye, cornmeal, molasses, and raisins) $4.40, $7.60 with the souvenir cup. Entrées $2.20-7.60. Open Sun.-Thurs. 11am-8pm, Fri.-Sat. 11am-9pm.

No Name, 151/4 Fish Pier (338-7539). T: South Station. Some of the best (fried) seafood in Boston, with enormous servings, big bowls of award-winning chowder, and no pretensions. The often-long line is worth the wait. Entrées $4-15. Open Mon.-Sat. 11am-10pm, Sun. 11am-9pm.

Giorgio's Pizzeria, 69 Salem St. (523-1373). T: Haymarket. From the portrait of founder Gramma Giorgio to the cheerful relatives behind the counter, Giorgio's is the quintessential family-run pizzeria. Using Gramma's original recipe from Sicily, the cooks create 15 varieties of garden-fresh, preservative-free pizza. Slices from $1, Entrées $4-7. Open daily 11am-11pm.

Addis Red Sea, 544 Tremont St. (426-8727). T: Back Bay. From the station, walk 5 blocks south on Clarendon St., then turn left on Tremont. The best Ethiopian food in Boston, served on *mesobs*, woven tables which support a communal platter. Entrées $8-9, but go in a group for combination platters: 5 different dishes for $10-12. Mon.-Wed. dinner specials. Open Mon.-Thurs. 5-11pm, Fri.-Sat. 5pm-midnight, Sun. noon-11pm.

Blue Wave, 142 Berkeley St. (424-6711). T: Arlington, right down the street from the YWCA. Hip and breezy yuppie joint plays up its nautical theme with glass-topped sandbox tables. Specials include red-pepper-carrot-lemon-purée soup and French-grilled halibut with ginger-lobster sauce. Has take-out and delivery. Entrées $7-12. $2.25 Harpoon Draft. Open Mon.-Sat. 11:30am-11pm, Sun. 11am-11pm.

Chau Chow, 52 Beach St. (426-6266). T: South Station. Follow Atlantic Ave. south to Beach St. Top-quality, award-winning Chinese chow; particularly renowned seafood. Most dishes on the encyclopedic menu hover around $6. Open Mon.-Thurs. 10am-2am, Fri.-Sat. 10am-4am, Sun 10am-1am.

Tim's Tavern, 329 Columbus Ave., in the South End (247-7894). T: Prudential. A small place at the back of a narrow bar, crowded at lunchtime with workers from around Copley Sq. Large portions of U.S. cuisine; its hamburgers have won the "Best of Boston" title. Menu changes daily ($1.50-8). Open Mon.-Sat. 11am-10pm.

Sights

At two lofty locations, you can map out the zones you want to visit or simply zone out as you take in the city skyline. The **Prudential Skywalk,** on the 50th floor of the Prudential Center, Back Bay (236-3318 or -3118), does the 360° fish-eye view thang. (T: Prudential. Open Mon.-Sat. 10am-10pm, Sun. noon-10pm. Admission $2.75, seniors, students with ID and kids $1.75.) The **John Hancock Observatory** at 200 Clarendon St. (247-1977 recorded, 572-6429 live), refuses to be outdone, with 60 beefy floors and the distinction of being the highest building in New England (740 ft.). On good days, you can see New Hampshire. (T: Copley. Open Mon.-Sat. 9am-10pm, Sun. 10am-10pm. Admission $2.75, age 5-15 and seniors $2.)

The **Freedom Trail** (536-4100) leads pedestrians along a clearly marked red brick or painted line through historic Boston, beginning at the **Boston Visitor Information Center** (see Practical Information above). Most of the sites visited are free, but a few charge $2.50 to $3 for admission. Don't bother buying the map ($1) to the country's most famous footpath since you can pick up free ones at almost any brochure rack. The trail makes two loops. The easier Downtown Loop passes the **Old North Church,** the **Boston Massacre Sight,** the **Granary Burial Ground,** the **Old Corner Bookstore,** and **Paul Revere's House,** among 11 other sights, and takes only an afternoon. The fascinating **Black Heritage Trail** makes 14 stops of its own, each marked by a red-black-and-green logo. The tour begins at the **Boston African-American Historic Sight,** 46 Joy St. (T: Park), where you can pick up a free map before visiting the museum inside (742-1854; open daily 10am-4pm). The trail covers sights of particular importance to the development of Boston's African-American community, including: the **African Meeting House** (1805), the earliest black church in North America; the **Robert Gould Shaw and 54th Regiment Memorial** on the Common, dedicated to black soldiers who fought in the Union Army and more prominently to their white Boston leader memorialized in the recent movie *Glory*; and the **Lewis and Harriet Hayden House,** a station on the Underground Railroad.

The Common, Fenway, Beacon Hill, and Back Bay

The areas immediately northwest of the **Boston Common** (T: Park) are brahmin heaven: some quaint streets seem frozen in time, and the more contemporary sections are gilded with chic.

Inhabitants established the Common, the oldest park in the nation, as a place to graze their cattle in 1634. Now street vendors, not cows, live off the fat of the land. While the frisbee players, drug dealers, street musicians, students, families, cops, and government employees all stake equal claim to it in the daytime, the Common is notoriously dangerous at night—don't go here alone after dark. Across Charles St. from the Common, waddle characters from the children's book *Make Way for Ducklings*. The ducklings point the way to the **Swan Boats** (522-1966) in the fragrant and lovely **Public Gardens.** These pedal-powered boats glide around a quiet pond lined with shady willows. (Boats open April 18-June 20 daily 10am-4pm; June 21-Labor Day 10am-5pm; Labor Day-Sept. 16 noon-4pm. Admission $1.25, under 12 75¢, seniors $1.)

Residential since its settlement by the Puritans, **Beacon Hill** has always pulsed with blueblood. Several buildings, including the gold-domed **State House** (727-3676), designed by Charles Bulfinch, offer exhibits of Massachusetts and colonial history and government. There are free tours of the Hall of Flags, House of Representatives, and Senate Chamber. (Visitor info: Doric Hall, 2nd floor. Open Mon.-Fri. 9am-5pm; tours Mon.-Fri. 10am-4pm.) The **Harrison Gray Otis House,** 141 Cambridge St. (227-3956), another Bulfinch original, headquarters the Society for the Preservation of New England Antiquities. (Tours on the hr. Tues.-Fri. noon-4pm, Sat. 10am-4pm. Admission $4, seniors $3.50, under 12 $2.) The Society hoards info about historical sights. The nearby **Boston Athenaeum,** 10½ Beacon St. (227-0270), houses over 700,000 books and offers tours of its library, art gallery, and print room. (Open Mon.-Fri. 9am-5:30pm, Sat. 9am-4pm; no Sat. hrs. in summer. Free tours Tues. and Thurs. at 3pm; reservations required.)

Charles Street serves as the Hill's front door. This exclusive residential bastion of Boston brahminism now shares its brick sidewalks with the fashionable contingent of Boston's gay community. The art galleries, cafés, antique stores, and other small shops with hanging wooden signs make this a fine avenue for a stroll.

In the **Back Bay,** southwest of Beacon Hill, three-story brownstone row houses line the only gridded streets in Boston. Originally the marshy, uninhabitable "back bay" of Boston Harbor, the area was filled in during the last century. Because it is a relatively new addition to the city, this is the only place in Boston with orderly, orthogonal streets. Back Bay was filled in gradually, as reflected in its architectural styles, which run the gamut of 19th-century designs as you travel from east to west. **Commonwealth Avenue** ("Comm Ave") is a European-style boulevard with statuary and benches punctuating its large and grassy median. **Newbury Street** is Boston's most flamboyant promenade; dye your poodle, pierce your navel, and get out there and vogue, baby! The dozens of small art galleries, boutiques, bookstores, and cafés that line the stage are a bastion of exclusivity. (T: Arlington, Copley, or Hynes/ICA.)

The handsome **Copley Square** area extends the whole length of Back Bay on commercial Boylston St. Renovated and officially reopened in June 1989, the square (T: Copley) accommodates a range of seasonal activities, including folk dancing, a food pavilion, and people watching people. A permanent feature is the **Boston Public Library,** 666 Boylston St. (536-5400), a massive, spartan, Orwellian building, liberally inscribed with the names of literally hundreds of literati. Benches and window seats inside overlook a tranquil courtyard with fountain and garden. Relax here or in the vaulted reading room. The auditorium gives a program of lectures and films. The library is undergoing renovations until 1995, but it's still open and you can still get to everything. (Open Mon.-Thurs. 9am-9pm, Fri.-Sat. 9am-5pm.) Across the square, H.H. Richardson's Romanesque fantasy, **Trinity Church,** gazes at its reflection in I.M. Pei's mirrored **Hancock Tower.** Many consider Trinity, built in 1877, a masterpiece of U.S. church architecture—the interior explains this opinion. (T: Copley. Open daily 8am-6pm.) **Copley Place,** a gaudy complex containing two hotels and a ritzy mall in the corner next to the library, attracts a steady stream of local high school students with big hair. The partially gentrified **South End,** south of Copley, makes for good brownstone viewing and casual dining.

Two blocks down Massachusetts Ave. from Boylston sits the Mother Church of the **First Church of Christ, Scientist,** One Norway St. (450-2000), founded in Boston by Mary Baker Eddy. The lovely **Mother Church** is the world headquarters of the Christian Science movement, and its complex of buildings are appropriately vast and imposing. Both the Mother Church and the smaller, older church out back can be seen by guided tour only; the guides do not proselytize. (Tours every half-hr. Tues.-Sat. 10am-4pm, Sun. 11:15am-2pm.) In the Christian Science Publishing Society next door, use the catwalk to pass through the **Mapparium,** a 40-ft.-wide stained-glass globe with some really funky acoustics. Whisper in the ear of Pakistan while standing next to Surinam. (Tours Tues.-Sat. 9:30am-4pm. Free.)

Back Bay loses some of its formality on the riverside **Esplanade** (T: Charles), a park extending from the Longfellow Bridge to the Harvard Bridge. Boston's quasi-pseudo-beach on the Charles, the Esplanade fills in the summer with sun-seekers and sail-boaters; but don't go in the water unless you *like* tetanus shots. Bikers and roller bladers, upholding Boston's tradition of good road manners, try to mow down pedestrians on the walkway. The bike path, which follows the river to the posh suburb of Wellesley, makes a terrific afternoon's ride. The Esplanade also hosts some of Boston's best-loved cultural events—the concerts of the **Boston Pops Orchestra** (266-1492) at the mauve **Hatch Shell.** Led by John "Star Wars" Williams (who recently announced his plans to retire), the Pops play here during the first week of July. Admission is free; arrive early so you can sit within earshot of the orchestra. Concerts begin at 8pm. On the Fourth of July, nearly 100,000 patriotic thrillseekers pack the Esplanade to hear the Pops concert (broadcast by loudspeaker throughout the area) and to watch the ensuing terrific fireworks display. Arrive before noon for a seat on the Esplanade, although you can watch the fireworks from basically anywhere along the river. The regular Pops season at **Symphony Hall,** 301 Mass. Ave. (266-2378, operator; 266-7575, recorded message), runs mid-May through July. (Tickets $10-45. Box office open Mon.-Fri. 10am-6pm, but the best way to get tickets is to call 266-1200.)

Beyond the Back Bay, west on Commonwealth Ave., glows **Kenmore Square** (T: Kenmore), watched over by the psychedelic landmark **Citgo sign.** Kenmore Sq. has more than its share of neon, containing many of the city's most popular nightclubs (see Nightlife below).

Below Kenmore Sq., the **Fenway** comprises a large area of the city, containing some of its best museums. Ubiquitous landscaper Frederick Olmsted of Central Park fame designed the **Fens** area at the center of the Fenway as part of his "Emerald Necklace" vision for Boston—a necklace he fortunately never completed. A gem nonetheless, the park's fragrant rose gardens and neighborhood vegetable patches make perfect picnic turf. Bring your own vegetables. Just north of the Fens, **Fenway Park,** home of the "Green Monster," is the nation's oldest Major League ballpark and center stage for the perennially heart-rending **Boston Red Sox** baseball club, which if given a chicken filet, would find a bone to choke on—don't ask Bostonians about the most recent Choke in 1986 to the New York Mets. (Box office 267-8661; open Mon.-Sat. 9am-5pm or until game time if the team's in town; T: Kenmore.) Tickets sell out far in advance, but they can usually be procured from a scalper; those who wait until game-time for procurement can haggle the price down. West still of Fenway along T: Green lines C and D sits suburban **Brookline,** with its charming guest houses; curfewed **Boston University** lines Commonwealth Ave. along Green line B.

Downtown, The North End, Chinatown, and the Waterfront

A perfect brew of commerce and politics made historic **Quincy Market** in the West End (T: Government Center) the focal point of contemporary Boston. Upon completion, the red-brick and cobblestone marketplace received nationwide praise as an example of urban revitalization. Though overpriced and overcrowded, the market is fun for browsing. The info center in the market's South Canopy (523-3886) can provide direction. At night, come for the lively bar scene. In 1742, Peter Faneuil (FAN-yul) donated **Faneuil Hall,** the gateway to the market, to serve as a marketplace and community hall. Sometimes called the "cradle of American Liberty," it served as quarters for British Redcoats as well as a gathering spot for Bostonians pissed at King George III. Occasionally, free concerts are given outside the Hall; call 523-1300 for details about the **Summer Nights** concert series featuring blues, calypso, and rock. (Info line Mon.-Fri. 9-4pm.) The hall has been recently renovated.

Across Congress St. from the market, the red brick plaza of **Government Center,** as its name indicates, proves a trifle less picturesque. The monstrous concrete **City Hall** (725-4000), designed by I.M. Pei, opens to the public Monday through Friday (T: Government Center). A few blocks south, its more aesthetically pleasing precursor, the **Old**

State House, 206 Washington St. (720-1713 or -3290), built in 1713, once rocked with revolutionary fervor. The State House has also just been renovated (T: State).

Downtown Crossing, south of City Hall at Washington St. (T: Downtown Crossing), is a wonderful pedestrian mall set amidst Boston's business district. **Filene's Basement,** 426 Washington St., jives here as the world's oldest bargain store, in business since 1908. The area shuts down after business hours. Directly southwest of the Common, Boston's engaging **Chinatown** (T: Chinatown) demarcates itself with pagoda-style telephone booths and streetlamps and an arch at its Beach St. entrance. Within this small area cluster many restaurants, food stores, and novelty shops where you can buy Chinese slippers and 1000-year-old eggs. Chinatown has two big celebrations each year. The first, **New Year,** usually falls on a Sunday in February, and festivities include lion dances, fireworks and Kung Fu exhibitions. The **August Moon Festival** honors a mythological pair of lovers at the time of the full moon. Watch for listings in *Where Boston.*

The eastern tip of Boston contains the historic **North End** (T: Haymarket). The city's oldest residential district, now an Italian neighborhood, overflows with windowboxes, Italian flags, fragrant pastry shops, crèches, Sicilian restaurants, and Catholic churches. The most famous of the latter, **Old St. Stephens Church,** on Hanover St. (523-1230), is the classically colonial brainchild of Charles Bulfinch. Down the street, the brilliant and sweet-smelling **Peace Gardens** try to drown out the honking horns of the North End with beautiful flora. The **Old North Church** has seen over 200 years of religious service since April 18, 1775 when it did its military duty of signaling to Paul Revere that the British were coming across Back Bay. Nearby, **Paul Revere's Home** contains displays on the silversmith-*cum*-patriot's domestic life.

The **waterfront area,** bounded by Atlantic and Commercial St., runs along Boston Harbor from South Station to the North End Park. Stroll down Commercial, Lewis, or Museum Wharf for a slurp of briny air. At the excellent **New England Aquarium** (973-5200; T: Aquarium), Central Wharf on the Waterfront, giant sea turtles, sharks, and their scaly friends swim tranquilly as visitors peer into their cylindrical 187,000-gallon tank. Penguins cavort in a mini-archipelago around the base of the tank. Dolphins and sea lions perform in the ship *Discovery,* moored alongside. On weekends lines tend to be long. (Open Mon.-Tues. and Fri. 9am-6pm, Wed.-Thurs. 9am-8pm, Sat.-Sun. and holidays 9am-7pm, Sept.-June Mon.-Wed. and Fri. 9am-5pm, Thurs. 9am-8pm, Sat.-Sun. and holidays 9am-6pm. Admission $7.50, seniors and students $6.50, ages 3-11 $3.50. Thurs. and summer Wed. after 4pm $1 discount.) The aquarium also offers **whale-watching cruises** (973-5277) from April to late October ($23, seniors and students $18.50, ages 12-18 $17, ages 4-11 $16, under 36 in. not allowed). **Boston Harbor Cruises** (227-4320) leave from Long Wharf, adjacent to the aquarium, for 90-minute tours of the harbor from roughly March to October. (Departs hourly 10am-4pm and at 7pm. Admission $8, seniors $6, under 12 $4.) They also have 45-minute cruises ($5, seniors $4, kids $3) and a water shuttle to the JFK library ($4 round-trip).

Across Fort Point Channel from the waterfront, the predominantly Irish American **South Boston** has a unique accent. (T: South Station). "Southie" has great seafood, two beaches, and a Pub on every corner.

Museums

Boston's intellectual and artistic community supports a higher concentration of museums than anywhere else in New England. Check the free *Guide to Museums of Boston* for details on the museums not mentioned here.

Museum of Fine Arts (MFA), 465 Huntington Ave. (267-9300; T: Museum, Green line E train), near the intersection with Massachusetts Ave. The most famous of Boston's museums. It gathers one of the world's finest collections of Asian ceramics, outstanding Egyptian art, a good showing of Impressionists, and superb Americana. Don't miss John Singleton Copley's fascinating portraits of his contemporaries Paul Revere and Samuel Adams or his dramatic *Watson and the Shark.* Also worth a gander are the two famous unfinished portraits of George and Martha Washington, painted by (who else?) Gilbert Stuart in 1796. Open Tues.-Sun. 10am-4:45pm, Wed. 10am-9:45pm. West Wing only open Thurs.-Fri. 5-9:45pm. Admission $7, seniors and students $6. West Wing only, $5. Both free Wed. 4-10pm.

Isabella Stewart Gardner Museum, 280 The Fenway (566-1401; 734-1359 for recorded events info; T: Museum). A few hundred yards from the MFA. The eccentric "Mrs. Jack" Gardner built the small, Venetian-style palace with a stunning courtyard seeking surcease from sorrow at the loss of her only child. She scandalized Boston with her excesses, but left posterity a superb art collection. Unfortunately—in what has been termed the greatest art heist in history—a 1989 break-in relieved the museum of works by Rembrandt, Vermeer, Dégas, and others. Open Tues.-Sun. 11am-5pm. Chamber music on 1st floor Sept.-June Sat. and Sun. afternoons. Admission $6, seniors and students $3, ages under 12 free.

Museum of Science, Science Park (723-2500; T: Science Park), at the far eastern end of the Esplanade on the Charles River Dam. Contains, among other wonders, the largest "lightning machine" in the world. A multi-story roller-coaster for small metal balls purports to explain energy states, but is just fun to watch. Within the museum, the **Hayden Planetarium** features models, lectures, films, and laser and star shows; the **Mugar Omni Theatre** shows popular films of scientific interest on a gee-whiz-four-story-domed screen. Museum open Mon.-Thurs. and Sat.-Sun. 9am-5pm (until 7pm in summer), Fri. 9am-9pm. Admission $6.50, seniors, students and ages 4-14 $4.50. Planetarium only, $6/$4; Museum and Omni $10.50/$7.50; all 3 facilities $14.50/ $10.50. Free Wed. afternoons Sept.-May.

Children's Museum, 300 Congress St. (426-8855), in southern Boston on Museum Wharf. T: South Station. Follow the signs with the milk bottles on them. Here kids of all ages toy with way-cool hands-on exhibits. Open July-Sept. Mon.-Thurs. and Sat.-Sun. 10am-5pm, Fri. 10am-9pm; closed Mon. during off-season. Admission $7, seniors and ages 2-15 $6, kids age 1 $2, under 1 free; Fri. 5-9pm $1.

The **John F. Kennedy Presidential Library** (929-4523), on Morrissey Blvd., Columbia Point, Dorchester (T: JFK/UMass on the Ashmont branch; free MBTA shuttle to the U Mass campus, a short walk from the library), is dedicated "to all those who through the art of politics seek a new and better world." Designed by I.M. Pei, the white cuboid oceanside edifice contains fascinating, sometimes trivial exhibits that employ photographs, documents, audio-visual presentation, and mementos to document the careers of JFK and his brother, Robert. Open daily 9am-5pm. Admission $5, seniors $3, under 16 $1, under 6 free.

Institute of Contemporary Art (ICA), 955 Boylston St. (266-5151 recorded message arts information line, 266-5152 operator; T: Hynes/ICA). Boston's lone outpost of the avant-garde attracts major contemporary artists while aggressively promoting lesser-known work. Their innovative, sometimes controversial exhibits (the Mapplethorpe show stopped here) change every 8 weeks. The museum also presents experimental theater, music, dance, and film. Open Wed. 5-9pm, Thurs. noon-9pm, Fri.-Sun. noon-5pm. Admission $5, students with ID $3, seniors and under 16 $2. Free Wed.-Thurs. 5-9pm.

Nightlife

The nightlife of the city that beans made famous admittedly does not compare with larger and more sophisticated New York. "Blue laws," forbidding serving liquor past a certain hour, stand out as a relic of the city's Puritan past—Governor Weld recently (and unsuccessfully) submitted a bill to repeal them. Liquor, though served on Sundays in restaurants and bars, cannot be sold anywhere else in the state on that day. Nearly everything closes between 1 and 2am, and bar admittance for anyone under 21 is hard-won. Those qualifications aside, Boston *does* have a nightlife. Quality rock, folk, jazz, and comedy clubs abound, as well as theater and other cultural offerings. Check the weekly *Boston Phoenix* for its up-to-date "Boston-After-Dark" listings.

Avalon; Axis; Venus de Milo, 7-13 Lansdowne St. T: Kenmore. Upscale, 80s style pre-yuppie (262-2424); neo-punk/industrial (262-2437); relentlessly techno and outrageously attired (421-9595), respectively. All three clubs are open on weekends 10pm-2am; exact hours for each club vary, as do cover charges.

Ryles, 212 Hampshire St., in Inman Square (876-9330). Take the #69 Lechmere bus. A Boston jazz-scene standby, with nightly live music and a jazz brunch on Sun. noon-4pm. Open Sun.-Thurs. 5pm-1am, Fri.-Sat. 5pm-2am.

The Black Rose, 160 State St., Faneuil Hall (742-2286). T: Government Center. This Irish bar features live, traditional Irish music (daily 9pm-1:30am) in a rollicking, convivial atmosphere. Wear your claddagh ring. $5 cover. Open Mon.-Sat. 11:30am-1:30am, Sun. noon-1:30am.

Plough and Stars, 912 Mass. Ave. (492-9653). T: Central. Enjoy literature, liquor, and song in the very place where the literary journal *Ploughshares* was conceived. A mellow crowd of locals and aficionados pack the Plough nightly for live folk, blues, c&w, rock and roll, and reggae. Sometimestheyintolerablypackthe*Plough. Open Mon.-Fri. 11:30am-1am, Sat.-Sun. noon-1am.*

Rathskeller, 528 Commonwealth Ave., Kenmore Sq. (536-2750). T: Kenmore. The "Rat" cultivates a grungy atmosphere to accompany its excellent program of grungy bands. Open daily 6pm-2am. Cover varies.

A few places cater to a gay and lesbian clientele at all times or on specific nights. **Indigo's** clientele is predominantly women, and **Chaps, Club Café,** and **Sporters** are all gay clubs. Club Café, 209 Columbus Ave. (536-0966; T: Back Bay) has a largely yuppie clientele, live music nightly, and no cover. If you're feeling more adventurous, try the **Boston Ramrod,** 1254 Boylston St. (266-2986; T: Kenmore), behind Fenway Park on Boylston St., where Thursday and Friday are official leather nights, in keeping with the bar's biker theme. **Campus/Manray,** 21 Brookline St. (864-0406), Central Sq., features top-40 and progressive music for women on Sundays and is open to a mixed crowd the rest of the week. (T: Central.) Check the *Bay Windows* listings for more information.

Arts and Entertainment

Musicians, dancers, actors, and *artistes* of every description fill Boston. The *Boston Phoenix* and the "Calendar" section of the Thursday *Boston Globe* list activities for the coming week. Also check the *Where Boston* booklet available at the visitors center. What Boston doesn't have, Cambridge does (see Cambridge below). **Bostix,** a Ticketron outlet in Faneuil Hall (723-5181), sells half-price tickets to performing arts events on the day of performance. (Service charge $1.50-2.50 per ticket. Cash and travelers checks only. Open Tues.-Sat. 11am-6pm, Sun. 11am-4pm.)

Actors in town cluster around Washington St. and Harrison Ave., in the **Theater District** (T: Boylston). The famous **Wang Center for the Performing Arts,** at 268 Tremont St. (482-9393), produces theater, classical music, and opera in its modern complex. The **Shubert Theater,** 265 Tremont St. (426-4520), and the **Wilbur Theater,** 246 Tremont St. (423-4008), host Broadway hits breezing through Boston. Tickets for these and for shows at the **Charles Playhouse,** 74 Warrenton St. (426-6912), are costly (around $30). The area's professional companies are cheaper, and may provide a more interesting evening. The **New Ehrlich Theater,** 539 Tremont St. (247-7388), and **Huntington Theater Co.,** 264 Huntington Ave. (266-7900; 266-0800 for box office), at Boston University have solid artistic reputations. (Tickets $10-24.) More affordable college theater is also available; during term-time, watch students thesp at **Tufts Theater-Arena** (628-5000), the **Boston University Theatre** (353-3320), the **MIT Drama Shop** (253-2908), and the **MIT Shakespeare Ensemble** (253-2903).

The renowned **Boston Ballet** (695-6950), in neighboring Newton, brings to life such classics as the *Nutcracker* and *Swan Lake.* The **Boston Symphony Orchestra,** 201 Mass. Ave. (266-1492; T: Symphony), at Huntington, holds its concert season from October to April. Rush seats go on sale three hours before concerts (tickets for 8pm concerts available at 5pm; Fri. 2pm concert tickets available at 9am). Open Wednesday rehearsals cost under $10; bargain tickets are also available Friday at noon for that evening's show. In summer, when the BSO retreats to Tanglewood, the **Boston Pops Orchestra** sets up at Symphony Hall or the Esplanade and plays classics and pop on weekend evenings. The **Berklee Performance Center,** 136 Mass. Ave. (266-7455), an adjunct of the Berklee School of Music, holds concerts featuring students, faculty, and jazz and classical luminaries.

Despite its ostensible air of refinement, Boston goes ape for sports. Long known for fans as committed as Charles Manson, Beantown always seems to be in some seasonal basketball, baseball, or hockey frenzy. On summer nights, thousands of baseball fans pour out of **Fenway Park** (see above) and clog Kenmore Sq. traffic for an hour. **Boston Garden** (T: North Station), located off the JFK Expressway between the West and North Ends, hosts the illustrious **Boston Celtics** basketball team (season Oct.-May; 523-3030 for info) and **Boston Bruins** hockey team (season Oct.-April; call 227-3200 for more info). A few mi. outside Boston, **Sullivan Stadium** hosts the perennially lackluster **New England Patriots** football franchise.

In October, the **Head of the Charles** regatta, the largest such single-day event in the U.S., attracts rowing clubs and college sweatshirts from across the country. The three-mi. boat races begin at Boston University Bridge; the best vantage points are on the Weeks footbridge and Anderson Bridge near Harvard University. On April 19, the 10,000 runners competing in the **Boston Marathon** tread memories of the "Head" underfoot. Call the Massachusetts Division of Tourism for details (617-727-3201).

For info on other special events, such as the **St. Patrick's Day Parade** in South Boston (March 17), **Patriot's Day** celebrations (April 19), the week-long **Boston Common Dairy Festival** (June), the **Boston Harbor Fest** (early July), and the North End's **Festival of St. Anthony** (mid-August), see the *Boston Phoenix* or *Globe* calendars.

Near Boston

Cambridge

The binary intellectual stars of Harvard and the MIT dominate this city on the Charles River. Each school believes itself to be the center of the universe, and each—to a certain extent—is right. Harvard (est. 1636) is the oldest university in the United States. Its alumni include countless luminaries in the American intellectual and political firmament; Emerson, Thoreau, Santayana, Franklin D. Roosevelt, John F. Kennedy and Albert Gore all have Harvard degrees. MIT, Harvard's younger and somewhat nerdier kin, takes the lead in technology. It was hardware developed in the radar laboratory at MIT which enabled the Allies to dominate the skies in WWII. MIT's computer and biology labs continue to define and then redesign the cutting edge and have taken the lead in the burgeoning bio-technology industry.

The city takes on the character of both of these universities. Around MIT radiate concentric rings of bio-technology and computer science buildings. Harvard, on the other hand, clusters stellar bookstores and pretentious coffee houses around its Georgian brick buildings. Between the two lies Central Square, which—with its low rents and high crime rates—contrasts the flanking ivory towers with real world problems.

Practical Information and Orientation

See Boston: Practical Information, above, for a complete listing. The **Cambridge Discovery Booth** (497-1630), in Harvard Sq., has the best and most comprehensive information about Cambridge, as well as MBTA bus and subway schedules. Pick up the *Old Cambridge Walking Guide,* an excellent self-guided tour ($1). Walking tours of Harvard and the surrounding area are given in summer. (Open summer Mon.-Sat. 9am-6pm, Sun. 11am-5pm; off-season Mon.-Sat. 9am-5pm, Sun. 1-5pm.) **Out-Of-Town News** (354-7777), right next to the Discovery Booth, has no official status as a tourist resource, but sells a large number of excellent maps and guides to the area. (Open Mon.-Sat. 6am-midnight, Sun. 6am-11:30pm.) The **Harvard University Information Center,** 1352 Massachusetts Ave., in Harvard Sq. (495-1573), has free guides to the university museums, and offers several tours each day. (Open summer Mon.-Sat. 9am-4:45pm, Sun. 1-4pm; off-season Mon.-Sat. 9am-4:45pm.) Harvard Student Agencies, Inc.'s *The Unofficial Guide to Life at Harvard* ($8), has the inside, yearly updated scoop and up-to-date listings of area restaurants, entertainment, sights, transportation and services and is available in Square bookstores and the Discovery Booth.

Cambridge's high-tech **post office** is at 125 Mt. Auburn St. (876-6483) near Harvard Square. (Open Mon.-Fri. 8am-5:30pm, self-service until 7pm, Sat. 9am-5pm self-service.) The **ZIP code** is 02138; the **area code** is 617.

Massachusetts Avenue ("Mass. Ave.") is Cambridge's major artery. Most of the action takes place in "squares" (that is, commercial areas which are of every geometric shape *except* square) along Mass. Ave. and the Red Line of the T. **MIT (The Massachusetts Institute of Technology)** is just across the Mass. Ave. Bridge from Boston at **Kendall Square,** on the Red Line. The Red Line continues outbound one T-stop at a time through: **Central Square,** the heart of urban Cambridge; frenetic, eclectic **Har-**

vard Square; and more suburban **Porter Square.** Cambridge is a 10-minute T ride from the heart of Boston.

Food

Nightly, thousands of college students renounce cafeteria fare and head to the funky eateries of Harvard Square. Park your bod in **The Garage** at 36 Kennedy St., a mall of restaurants offering everything from hummus to gourmet coffee to pizza. When the late-night munchies hit, Harvard students head to **Tommy's Lunch,** 49 Mt. Auburn St. (492-9540), for uniquely personable service, pinball, and greasy onion rings. (Open daily 6am-1:30am.) Pick up the weekly *Square Deal* (pronounced: Skweh DEE-yal), usually shoved in your face by distributors near the T-stop, for coupons and discounts on local fare.

The Middle East, 472 Mass. Ave., Central Sq. (354-8238). Tremendous servings of the best and most innovative Middle Eastern food around at bargain prices. Huge sandwiches $3-3.50, dinner entrées $6.50-9. Live alternative music in the evenings for the hip, urban crowd. Open Sun.-Wed. 11am-1am, Thurs.-Sun. 11:30am-2am.

The Stock Pot, 57 JFK St. in the Galeria (492-9058). Thick, delicious homemade soups ($2.50-3.25). 30-foot salad bar ($4.75) and "stockpocket" sandwiches in pita ($4). Open Mon.-Sat. 11:30am-8:30pm, Sun. 1-7pm; summer closed Sundays.

Goemon Japanese Noodle Restaurant, One Kendall Sq., Bldg. 100, Kendall Sq. (577-9595). From the Kendall Sq. T stop, go through the hotel lobby, take a left and walk several blocks. "A meal of noodles?" you wonder. "Delightful," we reply. Try the savory *yakitori* (chicken and scallion skewers, $3.50), or *shumai* (shrimp dumplings, $3.25), and don't forget the green tea ice cream—the English vocabulary is too limited to describe its extraordinary flavor ($2). Wheelchair accessible. Open Mon.-Thurs. 11:30am-9:30pm, Fri.-Sat. 11:30am-10pm, Sun. 4-9:30pm.

Jake and Earl's Dixie BBQ, 1273 Cambridge St., Inman Sq.; take the #69 Lechmere bus from Harvard Sq.; look for the laughing pigs (491-7427). They slop up masterfully spiced barbecue plates, all of which include coleslaw, baked beans, and a slice of watermelon, here at this tiny, award-winning BBQ joint. Mostly take-out, with a few stools for in-house pigging out. Entrées $4-7.50. Open daily 11:30am-11pm.

Mezzo Mezzo, 57 JFK St., Harvard Sq. (661-5323). The cheapest little pizza in the square. ($2.25 for a cute, lunch-sized small cheese). Open Sun.-Wed. 11:30am-midnight, Thurs.-Sat. 11:30am-1:30am.

Café of India, 52A Brattle St., Harvard Sq. (661-0683). The best Indian food in the Square; ask anybody from *Let's Go,* 'cause we've tried almost every dish in the place. The office favorite is *chholey bhature,* a chick-pea dish served with *bhatura* bread. Lunch specials, including rice and soup of the day (Mon.-Fri.) $4-6.50, dinner entrées $7.50-15. Open Mon.-Fri. 11:30am-11pm, Sat. noon-midnight, Sun. buffet brunch noon-11pm.

Troyka Restaurant, 1154 Mass. Ave., Harvard Sq. (864-7476). Yeltsin would be proud of this tiny Russian establishment. Try the *blini*—slightly sweet, thin pancakes wrapped around fillings like lox and eggs ($6-11)—or the delicious, complexly-layered cake desserts ($2.75). Open Tues.-Thurs. 11:30am-10:30pm, Fri.-Sat. 11:30am-11:30pm, Sun. noon-10:30pm.

A meal in the vicinity of Harvard Square would not be complete without dessert afterwards. Dens of sin abound, like **Herrell's,** 15 Dunster St. in Harvard Sq. (497-2179), whose ice cream, fro-yo and no-moo selections range from classic vanilla to eggnog, peanut butter, and their famous (but lethal) chocolate pudding, the "Best Chocolate Ice Cream in Boston" ($1.75). Drown in lusciousness inside a vault painted to resemble the watery depths. (Open daily noon-midnight, extended hrs. in summer.) If you prefer your chocolate in squares (other than Harvard), go to Inman Square, to **Rosie's Bakery,** at 243 Hampshire St., for a "chocolate orgasm." (Open Mon.-Wed. 7:30am-10pm, Thurs.-Fri. 7:30am-11pm, Sat. 8:30am-11pm, Sun. 8:30am-10pm.)

Nightlife and Entertainment

In warm weather, Cambridge entertainment is free. Street musicians ranging from Andean folk singers to octogenarian karaoke singers staff every streetcorner of Harvard Square. Cafés crowd at all times of year for lunch or after-hours coffee. The low-ceilinged, smoke-filled **Café Pamplona**, 12 Bow St., might be too angst-ridden for you; in summer escape to their outdoor tables. (Open Mon.-Sat. 11am-1am, Sun. 2pm-

1am.) The **Coffee Connection,** 36 JFK St. in the Garage (492-4881), proffers almost blasphemously high-caliber-low-viscosity coffees. The smell of the place is fantastic; try the delicious *café con panna* ($1.50) or the addictive frappuccino. (Open Mon.-Thurs. 7am-11pm, Fri. 7am-midnight, Sat. 9am-midnight, Sun. 9am-11pm.) **Café Algiers,** 40 Brattle St. (492-1557) has two beautiful floors of airy, wood-latticed seating, and offers a standard café menu with a slight Algerian twist. (Open Mon.-Thurs. 8am-midnight, Fri.-Sat. 8am-1am, Sun. 9am-midnight.)

Rich cultural offerings keep Cambridge vital. Harvard sponsors any number of readings and lectures each week; check the kiosks that fill Harvard Yard for posters about the events that most students are too busy to attend. Also look at the windows of one of the over 25 bookstores in the Square to see if any literary luminaries will appear during your visit. Theater, both undergraduate and professional, thrives here. The renowned **American Repertory Theater,** 64 Brattle St., under the direction of Harvard professor Robert Brustein, produces shows from September to June. (Tickets $17-38.) Purchase tickets for undergraduate and ART productions through the ticket office at the Loeb Drama Center (547-8300; box office open daily 10am-5:30pm). Cambridge can also accommodate those whose idea of nightlife is something other than an evening with Vaclav Havel. (See Boston for even more options.)

T.T. The Bear's Place, 10 Brookline St., Central Sq. (492-0082). Brings really live, really loud rock bands to its intimate, almost makeshift stage. Open Mon.-Thurs. 8pm-1am, Fri.-Sun. noon-1am. Cover rarely exceeds $6. Really.

Cantab Lounge, 738 Mass. Ave., Central Sq. (354-2684). For over 10 years, Junior Cook and his blues band have been packing the place with local fans and recently enlightened college students. Cover Thurs. $3, Fri.-Sat. $5. Open Mon.-Wed. 8am-1am, Thurs.-Sat. 8am-2am, Sun. noon-1am.

Catch a Rising Star, 30b JFK St., Harvard Sq. (661-9887). All ages are welcome in this comedy club, which hosts local groups as well as comedians of national stature. "Open mike" comedy Tues. Shows Sun.-Thurs. 8:30pm; Fri. 8:30 and 11pm; Sat. 7:30pm, 9:45pm, and midnight. Cover $5-12. $3 discount with college ID Mon.-Thurs.

Passim, 47 Palmer St., Harvard Sq. (492-9653). A communal crowd gathers in this café-by-night to cheer on and sing along with the spirited, if not always talented, performers of soulful blues/folk music. No alcohol, but you can feast on breadsticks with cream cheese. Concert schedule available upon request. Cover $6-9. Open Tues.-Sat. noon-5:30pm, evening hours vary.

Shays, 58 JFK St., Harvard Sq. A cozy atmosphere, a wide selection of drinks, and its near-backyard convenience makes this a popular hangout for all them pesky Harvard kids. Open daily 11am-1am.

Sights

People-watching—the favorite Cantabridgian pastime aside from reading—may account for the number of cafés. But if you can tear yourself away from staring at balding professors, yuppies, hippies, street punks, and slumming high-schoolers, you might see some interesting buildings as well.

MIT is as much a tribute to, as an institute of, technology. The campus buildings are a huge slice in the I.M. Pei; it also contains an impressive collection of modern outdoor sculpture, and an "infinite corridor" a quarter-mi. long. Tours are available weekdays at 10am and 2pm from the Rogers Building, or "Building Number 7" as the ultra-efficient students here term it. Contact MIT Information at 77 Mass. Ave. (253-1000; open Mon.-Fri. 9am-5pm). The **MIT Museum,** 265 Mass. Ave. (253-4444), contains a slide rule collection and wonderful photography exhibits, including the famous stop-action photos of Harold Edgerton. (Open Tues.-Fri. 9am-5pm, Sat-Sun. 1-5pm. $2, ages under 12 and seniors free.)

Up Mass. Ave., the other university seems to shun such futuristic delights for glories of the past, especially its own. **Harvard University,** is the oldest university in the country and won't let anyone forget it. Ask at the info center about self-guided, self-gratifying walking tours. (See Practical Information above.) **Radcliffe College,** founded in 1879 and once its own all-female entity, "merged" with Harvard College in 1971. Now female undergraduates attend Harvard-Radcliffe College, and, as such, go to class, eat, sleep, and brush their teeth with the male undergraduates. Radcliffe has its own buildings northwest of Harvard Yard in a garden oasis between Brattle St. and Garden St.

The university, if not the universe, revolves around **Harvard Yard.** Step into the Yard and shut out the rest of the world. One moment you'll be dodging a Mack Truck in the square, trying to think straight amidst the cacaphonic din of caterwauling street-singers and mendicants, the next you'll be in the Yard listening to the chirping of a cricket. In the western half ("The Old Yard"), some of the school's first buildings still stand. Today all Harvard students live in the Yard during their first year of study; John F. Kennedy lived in Weld (his freshman year room is reputedly now a woman's bathroom), while Emerson and Thoreau resided in Hollis. Besides classroom buildings, the Yard's eastern half holds **Memorial Church** and **Widener Library** (495-2413), the largest academic library in the world, containing a significant portion of the collection's 10.5 million volumes. While visitors can't browse among Widener's shelves, they are welcome to examine Harvard's copy of the Gutenberg Bible and other rare books in the Harry Elkins Widener Memorial Reading Room, or to take in the tacky John Singer Sargent murals.

The oldest of Harvard's museums, the **Fogg Art Museum,** 32 Quincy St., gathers a considerable collection of works ranging from ancient Chinese jade to contemporary photography, as well as the largest Ingres collection outside of France. The limited display space around its uplifting Italian Renaissance courtyard frequently rotates well-planned exhibits. Across the street, the post-modern exterior of the **Arthur M. Sackler Museum,** 485 Broadway, belies a rich collection of ancient Asian and Islamic art. (Both museums open Tues.-Sun. 10am-5pm. Admission to each $4, students and seniors $2.50. Free Sat. mornings. Call 495-9400 for information.) Next door to the Fogg, Le Corbusier's guitar-shaped "machine for living," the **Carpenter Center,** 24 Quincy St. (495-3251), shows student and professional work with especially strong photo exhibits, not to mention a great film series at the **Harvard Film Archive.** The Carpenter Center was former Pakistani leader and Radcliffe alumna Benazir Bhutto's favorite building on campus. (Open Mon.-Fri. 9am-11pm, Sat. noon-11pm, Sun. noon-10pm.) Included in the **Museums of Natural History** at 24 Oxford St. (495-3045), are the **Peabody Museum of Archaeology and Ethnology,** which houses treasures from prehistoric and Native American cultures, and the **Mineralogical and Geological Museums,** containing gems, minerals, ores, and meteorites. But the overhyped "glass flowers" exhibit at the **Botanical Museum** draws the largest crowds. A German glass-blower and his son created these remarkably accurate but not at all aesthetic enlarged reproductions of over 840 plant species. (Open Mon.-Sat. 9am-4:30pm, Sun. 1-4:30pm.)

Washington worshiped across the street at **Christ Church,** the oldest church in Cambridge, which had its organ pipes melted down for Revolutionary bullets. Soldiers felled in the struggle are buried in the 17th-century **Old Burying Ground** or "God's Acre" on Garden St., also the final resting place of colonial settlers and early Harvard presidents. Behind Garden St., on 105 Brattle St., is the restored **Longfellow House** (876-4491), home of the poet Henry Wadsworth Longfellow and a National Historic Site. Headquarters of the Continental Army in olden days, the site now sponsors garden concerts and poetry readings in the summer; the staff can give you info on other local historic sights. (Tours daily 10am-4pm. Admission $2, seniors and under 17 free.) The **Mt. Auburn Cemetery** lies about one mi. up the road at the end of Brattle St. This first botanical-garden/cemetery in the U.S. has 170 acres of beautifully landscaped grounds fertilized by Louis Agassiz, Charles Bulfinch, Dorothea Dix, Mary Baker Eddy, and H.W. Longfellow among others.

Lexington and Concord

Listen, my children and you shall hear Of the midnight ride of Paul Revere On the 18th of April in '75 Hardly a man is now alive Who remembers that famous day and year.
—*Henry Wadsworth Longfellow,* "The Midnight Ride of Paul Revere"

Inhabitants will constantly remind you that the Minutemen skirmished with advancing British troops on the **Lexington Battle Green,** falling back to the **Old North Bridge** in Concord where colonial troops first officially received orders to fire upon the Redcoats. On the Lexington Green, the **Minuteman Statue** of Captain John Parker—one of the first American casualties—looks back to Boston, still watching for the Redcoats. The surrounding houses seem nearly as historic as the land; the **Jonathan Harrington House** on Harrington Rd., built in 1750, housed its namesake who crawled away from the battle to die on his own doorstep. The **Buckman Tavern,** on Hancock St. opposite the Green, had already slung ale for 65 years before it headquartered the Minutemen. The Lexington Historical Society carefully restored the interior to its 1775 appearance. The society also did a number on **Munroe Tavern,** one mi. from the Green on Mass. Ave., which served as a field hospital for wounded British. (Houses open mid-April-late Oct. Mon.-Sat. 10am-5pm, Sun. 1-5pm. Admission $2.50 per house, ages 6-16 50¢. Ticket for all three $5.) Along with a walking map of the area, the **visitors center** at 1875 Mass. Ave. (617-862-1450), behind the Buckman Tavern, displays a 50-year-old, painstakingly detailed diorama of the Battle of Lexington. (Open daily June-Oct. 9am-5pm; Nov.-May 10am-4pm.)

The **Battle Road** winds six mi. from the Lexington Green to Concord and is now part of a national historical park; the **Battle Road Visitors Center** on Rte. 2A in Lexington (617-862-7353) shows a 22-minute film detailing events precipitating the Revolutionary War. The center also distributes maps of the park. (Open April-May and Sept.-Oct. 8:30am-5pm daily; June-Aug. 8:30-6pm daily.) At the **North Bridge Visitors Center,** 174 Liberty St. (508-369-6993), park rangers lead 15-min. interpretive talks at the Old North Bridge over the Concord River, site of "the shot heard 'round the world." (Open daily 8:30am-5pm.)

Concord garnered fame not only for its military history but as a U.S. literary capital of the 19th century as well. The Alcotts and Hawthornes once inhabited **Wayside** at 455 Lexington Rd. (508-369-6975), while Emerson himself lived down the road for the latter part of the century. Now a part of the **Minute Man National Historical Park,** the house is open for public viewing. (Open April-Oct. Tues.-Sun. 9:30am-5pm. Admission $1, ages under 17 and over 61 free.) The **Concord Museum,** directly across the street from the house (508-369-9763), houses a reconstruction of Emerson's study alongside Paul Revere's lantern and items from Henry David Thoreau's cabin. (Open Jan.-April, Thurs.-Sat. 10am-5pm Sun. 1-5pm. Mon.-Sat.; May-Dec. Mon.-Sat. 10am-5pm, Sun. 1-5pm. Admission $5, seniors $4, students $3, under 5 $2.) Emerson, Hawthorne, Alcott, and Thoreau all wait for Ichabod Crane on "Author's Ridge" in the **Sleepy Hollow Cemetery** on Rte. 62, three blocks from the center of town.

While alive, Thoreau retreated to **Walden Pond,** 1.5 mi. south of Concord on Rte. 126, in 1845 "to live deliberately, to front only the essential facts of life." His pre-hippie handbook *Walden* contains observations about his two-year habitation there (with brief sojourns at home so his mom could do his laundry). The **Thoreau Lyceum,** 156 Belknap St. (508-369-5912), national headquarters of the Thoreau Society, will answer questions about this naturalist-philosopher. The Lyceum sponsors the society's convention in July, and has a replica of Thoreau's cabin in its backyard. (Open April-Dec. Mon.-Sat. 10am-5pm, Sun. 2-5pm; early Feb.-March Thurs.-Sat. 10am-5pm, Sun. 2-5pm. Admission $2, students $1.50, kids 50¢.) **Walden Pond State Reservation** (508-369-3254) is popular with picnickers, swimmers, and boaters. Don't come expecting the same divine solitude Thoreau enjoyed. Granite posts at the far end of the pond mark the site of Thoreau's cabin. (Open April-Oct. daily dawn-dusk. Parking $5.) The Pond only holds 1000 visitors; rangers will turn you away, so call before coming out. When Walden Pond swarms with crowds, head down Rte. 62 east from Concord center to **Great Meadows National Wildlife Refuge** (508-443-4661), another of Thoreau's haunts. (Open daily dawn-dusk.)

The **South Bridge Boat House,** 496 Main St. (508-371-2465), rents canoes (Mon.-Fri. $6 per hr., $25 per day; Sat.-Sun. $7.25 per hr., $35 per day) for the Concord and Sudbury Rivers. (Open April-Oct. daily 10am-7:30pm.) Look for an excellent local map and information on Concord events and sights in a rack outside the **Chamber of Commerce,** in Wright Tavern on Main St., or at the **information booth,** just outside the town center on Heywood St. off Lexington Rd. (Open late May-late Oct. daily 9:30am-4:30pm; late April-late May Sat.-Sun. 9:30am-4:30pm.) Concord and Lexington make easy daytrips from Boston. Concord, just 20 mi. north of Boston, is served by **MBTA** "Commuter Rail" trains leaving from North Station ($2.75). MBTA buses from Alewife station in northern Cambridge run several times each day to Lexington (60¢). (See Boston: Practical Information.)

The **area code** for Lexington is 617, Concord 508.

Salem

On one hand, Salem seems to resent the hullabaloo about the "witch stuff." Instead, they'll try to tell you how the town was once the sixth-largest city in the United States—a trading center with a fleet so vast that merchants in faraway lands believed "Salem" was an independent country. They will point you towards the many historic homes in the city center and the excellent museums and entreat you (usually with success) to gain an appreciation of Salem's sea-faring days.

On the other hand, Salem realizes that most of its tourists come here for its more occult offerings. In 1992, local authorities brewed up a year-long Witch Trials Tercentenary, which created a flap among witches in the area who resented their beliefs being concocted into a tourist gimmick. The city has had a long-standing practice of capitalizing on the sensationalized witchtrials of the summer of 1692, when a volatile combination of superstition, small-town jealousy, boredom, and fermented wheat exploded in one of the ugliest incidents in American history. Today, the witch-on-a-broomstick motif appears just about everywhere—on the daily newspaper banner, on the police uniforms, on the shops and bars, and even on the garbage cans.

Salem's most substantive sight, the **Peabody Museum,** in East India Sq. (745-1876, for recorded info 745-9500), recalls the port's former leading role in Atlantic whaling and merchant shipping. (Daily guided tour at 2pm; in summer also at 11am. Open Mon.-Sat. 10am-5pm, Sun. noon-5pm. Admission $6, seniors and students $5, ages 6-18 $3.) Down by the waterfront, the National Park Service administers the **Salem Maritime National Historic Site,** a collection of three wharves and several historic buildings along Derby St. which are definitely worth exploring. Federal officials, including Nathaniel Hawthorne, collected import duties until 1917 at the **Customs House,** 178 Derby St. (744-4323), where the narrator of Hawthorne's novel claims to find *The Scarlet Letter.* (Open daily 9am-6pm; off-season 9am-5pm. No import duty is charged for the self-guided tour.) Hawthorne lost his desk job here thanks to the spoils system; he later took them to task in his writing.

If you succumb to your baser touristic instincts, start at the gothic **Witch Museum** (744-1692—notice the numerology), witch presents a melodramatic but informative multi-media presentation that fleshes out the history of the trials. (Open July-Aug. Mon.-Fri. 10am-5pm, Sat.-Sun. 10am-7pm; off-season daily 10am-5pm; shows on the half hour. Admission $4, seniors $3.50, ages 6-14 $2.50.) Never actually a dungeon, the **Witch Dungeon,** 16 Lynde St. (741-3570), has actresses presents skits about the trials which amplify the toil and trouble of the proceedings. (Open early May-early Nov. daily 10am-5pm. Admission $3.75, seniors $3.25, ages 6-14 $2.25.) The child in you will like the spooky atmosphere of the dungeon tour; the adult in you will enjoy the cynical commentary that accompanies it.

Salem boasts the "second most famous house in America," the **House of Seven Gables,** 54 Turner St. (744-0991), built in 1668 and made famous by Nathaniel Hawthorne's Gothic romance of the same name. Tourists who've most likely never read the book tromp through the place where Hawthorne's aunt once lived and where he also spent a good deal of time. Prices are steeper than the famed roof. (Open daily 10am-4:30pm; July-Aug. Fri.-Wed. 9:30am-5:30pm, Thurs. 9:30am-8:30pm. Tour $6.50, ages 6-17 $4, access to grounds $1, although you can see all 7 gables from the street.)

From the T station on Bridge St., head down Washington to Essex; on your left will be a pedestrian-only road to the **Museum Place mall.** The National Park Service runs two **information centers:** one in the mall (741-3648; open daily 9am-6pm, off-season 9am-5pm) and one at Derby Wharf (745-1470; open daily 8:30am-5pm). Both provide a free map of historic Salem. A 1.3-mi. **Heritage Trail** traces an easy footpath past all the main sights in town, marked clearly by a painted red line (blood?) on the pavement. The **Essex Institute,** at 132 Essex St., an important archive of materials relating to New England history, also contains a museum crammed to the rafters with silver, furniture, portraits, toys, and other oddities. Three old houses on the same block under the institute's care are open to visitors during frequent tours. Due to a consolidation, the name of the Institute may change in 1993; details are unavailable as we go to press. (Museum and houses open June-Oct. Mon.-Wed. and Fri.-Sat. 9am-5pm, Thurs. 9am-9pm, Sun. noon-5pm; Nov.-May Tues.-Sat. 9am-5pm, Sun. noon-5pm. Admission to all $6, ages 6-16 $3.50.)

Salem is packed to the belfries during Halloween with a week-long festival called **Haunted Happenings,** which includes costume balls, ghost stories, and a parade. Book months in advance if you plan to be in town for Halloween.

Food is about the only inexpensive commodity in Salem; cheap subs ping at **Red's Sandwich Shop,** 15 Central St., which serves breakfast (55¢-$3.50) and sandwitches ($1.25-3.50) at small tables and a cozy counter. (Open Mon.-Sat. 5:30am-3pm, Sun. 6am-1pm.) The restaurants on Derby St. close to the wharfside attractions serve a range of American fare which is only slightly overpriced.

Salem hexes 20 mi. northeast of Boston; take the Rockport/Ipswich commuter train (recorded info 800-392-6099) from North Station (1 per hr.; ½-hr.; $2.50). By car, take Rte. 128 north to Rte. 114 (exit 25E), then follow the signs to Salem Historic District, which lead to parking at Museum Place Mall ($4 per day). The **post office** is right off Washington on 2 Margin St. (744-8600; open Mon.-Fri. 8am-5pm., Sat. 8am-1pm). The **ZIP code** is 01970. The **area code** is 508.

Cape Cod

> *The time must come when this coast will be a place of resort for those New Englanders who really wish to visit the sea-side. At present it is wholly unknown to the fashionable world, and probably it will never be agreeable to them.*
>
> *-Henry David Thoreau*

In 1602, when English navigator and Jamestown colonist Bartholomew Gosnold landed on this peninsula in southeastern Massachusetts, he named it in honor of all the codfish he caught in the surrounding waters. In recent decades, tourism—not fishing—has sustained the Cape. Within this small strip of land you can find a great diversity of delicate landscapes—long unbroken stretches of beach, salt marshes, hardwood forests, deep freshwater ponds carved by glaciers, and desert-like dunes constantly being sculpted by the wind. The fragility of the environment is palpable; when the Cape's forests were destroyed for lumber to build houses and fences, the peninsula began to wash away into the sea. Local authorities began requiring citizens to plant beach grass in the early 1800s. President Kennedy established the Cape Cod National Seashore in

1961 to protect less developed areas from the tide of rampant commercialism. Blessed with an excellent hostel system, Cape Cod is an ideal budget seaside getaway and is used by many cross-country travelers as a place to rest and relax after cramming in the cultural sights of urban America. It also serves as the gateway to Martha's Vineyard and Nantucket.

In a bit of confusing terminology, the part of Cape Cod closer to the mainland is called the **Upper Cape**, which is suburbanized and the most developed area on the Cape. As you proceed away from the mainland, you travel "down Cape" until you get to the **Lower Cape;** the **National Seashore** encompasses much of this area. Cape Cod resembles a bent arm, with **Wood's Hole** at its shoulder, **Chatham** at the elbow, and **Provincetown** at its clenched fist. Accordingly, Cape Codders often use their arms to give directions.

Cycling is the best way to travel the Cape's gentle slopes. The park service can give you a free map of the trails or sell you the detailed **Cape Cod Bike Book** ($3.25). The 135-mi. **Boston-Cape Cod Bikeway** connects Boston with Bourne on the Cape Cod Canal and extends to Provincetown at land's end. Some of the most scenic bike trails in the country line either side of the **Cape Cod Canal** in the Cape Cod National Seashore, and the 14-mi. **Cape Cod Rail Trail** from Dennis to Eastham.

The **area code** for Cape Cod is 508.

Cape Cod National Seashore

As early as 1825, the Cape was so heavily damaged by the hand of man that the town of Truro mandated local residents to plant beach grass and keep their cows off the dunes; the sea was threatening to wash the sandy town away and make Provincetown an island. This fragile environment is easily disturbed, and conservation efforts culminated in 1961 with the creation of the Cape Cod National Seashore, which includes much of the Lower Cape from Provincetown south to Chatham.

Most visitors are simply not prepared for the beauty of this landscape, one of the country's greatest treasures. Here you'll find over 30 mi. of soft, wide, uninterrupted sandy beaches, tucked under tall clay cliffs spotted with 19th-century lighthouses. You can also explore salt marshes, home to migrating and native waterfowl, or go galumphing through the Sand Dunes near Provincetown in a desert-like environment of sculpted dunes. You can squintingly contemplate both a sunrise and a sunset reflecting off broad expanses of water. There are even warm, fresh-water ponds where you can escape for a dip when the waves or the crowds at the beach become too intense; try Gull or Long Pond in Wellfleet or Pilgrim Lake in Truro.

Thanks to conservationism, this area largely has escaped the condo-strip boardwalk commercialism that afflicts most seacoasts in America. Although some of the beaches are crowded in the summer, it is surprisingly easy to escape the crush of humanity; a 20-minute walk away from the lifeguards can take you away from the hordes of umbrella- and cooler-luggers. Or hike one of the underused nature trails, and you'll be impressed by the wide variety of habitats that huddle together on this narrow slice of land.

Beachgoers face one eternal question: ocean or bay. The ocean beaches attract with whispering winds and singing surf; the water on the bay side is calmer, a bit warmer, and better for swimming. Parking costs $5 and usually fills up by 11am or earlier. If the parking lot is full, park in town, rent a bike and ride in. Walkers and riders are supposed to pay a $2 entrance fee, but this is rarely collected. To park at town beaches you'll need a town permit, which costs about $10 per day or $25 per week. There isn't much difference between the various beaches on the ocean side—they're just names in the sand—but parking at the **Nauset Light Beach** is the closest to the water, and from the beach you can admire the **Nauset Beach Lighthouse,** set high up on the bluffs.

The nine self-guiding **nature trails** wind through an extraordinary range of beautiful landscapes: a salt marsh, a red maple swamp, and a cranberry bog. One of the best walks is the **Great Island Trail** in Wellfleet, an eight-mi. loop taking you through pine forests, grassy marshes, and a ridge with a view of the bay and Provincetown. A shorter and less strenuous walk starts from the visitors center at **Salt Pond**—a one-mi. loop which gives a good vantage of the Salt Pond, where shore birds flock to feed on the rich influx of nutritious vegetation the tide brings in. Except for Great Island, all the walking trails are about one mi. and fairly easy. The **Buttonbrush Trail** has a guide rope for the blind and interpretive plaques in Braille. Also inquire at the visitors center about the three bike trails maintained by the park.

Camping is illegal on the public lands of the national seashore. See Lower Cape for accommodations in the area.

Start your exploration at the **National Seashore Visitors Center** at Salt Pond, off U.S. 6 in Eastham (255-3421; open July-Aug. daily 9am-6pm, off-season 9am-4:30pm). The center offers info and advice on the whole seashore, as well as free 10-minute films on the half-hour and a free museum which has excellent exhibits on the human and natural history of the Cape. Twenty-five mi. north in Provincetown, the **Province Lands Visitors Center** on Race Point Rd. off U.S. 6 disseminates the same brochures and offers guided tours of the nearby dunes. Ask at either center for a schedule of upcoming lectures, canoe trips, and guided walking tours.

Upper Cape

Hyannis

JFK spent his summers in nearby Hyannisport, and the Kennedy Compound still houses his family, but you can't get anywhere near it. Though Hyannis itself has a handful of tourist attractions such as an art museum and a stage with big-name singers, it's really a transportation hub; most travelers stop here on their way to the true jewels of the Cape. Go through and get out as quickly as possible; the Kennedys *aren't* going to meet you at the bus station.

If you need a place to stay the night before moving on, the **HyLand Hostel (HI/AYH),** 465 Falmouth Rd. (775-2970), situated among three acres of pine trees, offers the 50 most affordable beds in Hyannis. From the bus station go west to Bearses Way, then north to Falmouth Rd. (Rte. 28) and turn left. The hostel is a few hundred yards from the traffic light. You can park in their lot for $2 per day if you aren't sleeping there—a good deal if you're planning a trip to the islands. The hostel is a 45-minute walk from the bus station. (Family rooms available. Check-in 6-10pm. $10, nonmembers $13. Reservations recommended.) The **Sea Beach Inn,** 388 Sea St. (775-4612), close to the beach at Gosnold St., rents comfortable double beds with shared bath and continental breakfast ($46, with private bath $58; off-season $40/$46). The **Salt Winds Guest House,** 319 Sea St. (775-2038), has bright, spotless rooms right near the beach, and a pool to boot. The friendly owners are full of advice on local sights and restaurants. (Open May-Sept. 2. Doubles $55.)

Hyannis is tattooed midway across the Cape's upper arm, three mi. south of U.S. 6 on Nantucket Sound. **Plymouth & Brockton** (746-0378) runs a Boston to Provincetown bus four times a day which makes a half-hour layover at the **Hyannis Bus Station,** 17 Elm St. (775-5524), and also stops in Plymouth, Sagamore, Yarmouth, Orleans, Wellfleet and Truro, among others. **Bonanza Bus Lines** (800-556-3815) operates a line to New York City (6 per day; 6 hrs.; $39, with stop in Providence). **Sea Line** (800-352-7155) runs a bus to Wood's Hole (5 per day; 1-1½ hr. with stops along Rte. 128; $3.50). **Amtrak,** 252 Main St. (800-872-7245), sends a direct train from New York to Hyannis on Fridays, and one from Hyannis to New York on Sundays (6 hr.; $59). Other days, you'll have to bus to Boston in order to make Amtrak connections. For info on **ferries** to Martha's Vineyard and Nantucket, see the listings for those islands.

The **Hyannis Area Chamber of Commerce,** 319 Barnstable Rd. (775-2201), about 1½ mi. up the road from the bus station, can help with Hyannis and hands out the *Hyannis Guidebook.* (Open Mon.-Sat. 9am-5pm, Sun. 11am-3pm; Sept.-May Mon.-Sat. 9am-5pm.)

Hyannis **ZIP code** is 02601.

Sandwich

The oldest town on the Cape, Sandwich cultivates a charm unmatched by its neighbors in the Upper Cape. Sandwich glass became famous for its beauty and workmanship when the Boston & Sandwich Glass Company was founded here in 1825. The original company is gone, but you can still see master glassblowers shaping their works of art from blobs of molten sand at **Pairpoint Crystal** on Rte. 6-A, just across the town border in Sagamore (888-2344; open daily 8:30am-6pm, free). **The Sandwich Glass Museum,** on Tupper Rd. in Sandwich Center (888-0251), preserves many 19th-century products with a coherence and quality unusual in a small town museum. (Open April-Oct. daily 9:30am-4:30pm, call for winter hrs.; $3.)

The **Thornton W. Burgess Museum** (888-6870) on Water St. pays tribute to the Sandwich-born naturalist who wrote tales about Peter Rabbit and the "dear old briar patch" (admission free). Ask for directions to the actual briar patch, **The Green Briar Nature Center and Jam Kitchen,** 6 Discovery Rd. Wander through trails and wildflower gardens, or watch jam-making in the center kitchen Wednesday and Saturday. (Open summer Mon.-Sat. 10am-4pm, Sun. 1-4pm; shorter hours off-season. Free.) **Sandy Neck Beach,** three mi. east of Sandwich on Sandy Neck Rd. off Rte. 6-A, is the best beach on the Upper Cape. Stroll six mi. along Cape Cod Bay on beautifully polished egg-sized granite pebbles, or hike out through the verdant dunes (but only on the marked trails, since the plants are very fragile).

Affordable eateries are ironically difficult to find in Sandwich, although **John's Capeside Diner,** Rte. 6A (888-2530), serves affordable chow. Breakfast is available all day ($1.25-4); lunch includes standard diner fare (burgers $1.50). (Open Mon.-Sat. 5am-9pm, Sun. 5am-2pm.)

Across the Sagamore Bridge, **Scusset Beach** (888-0859), right on the canal near the junction of U.S. 6 and Rte. 3, offers fishing and camping. (Sites—mostly for RVs—$16, day use $5 per carload.) The **Shawme-Crowell State Forest** (888-0351), on Rte. 130 and U.S. 6, has 240 wooded campsites with showers and campfires but no hookups. (Open mid-March-late Nov.; $12, including parking at Scusset Beach.) **Peters Pond Park Campground,** Cotuit Rd. (477-1775), in south Sandwich, offers aquatic activities, a grocery store, showers, and a few prime waterside sites. (Sites $14-15. Open mid-April-mid-Oct.)

Sandwich Center lies at the intersection of Rte. 6A and 130, about 13 mi. from Hyannis. The Plymouth and Brockton bus makes its closest stop in Sagamore, three mi. to the west. You can also reach Sandwich from Hyannis via the **Cape Cod Railroad** (771-3788), a scenic one-hour ride on an antique train through cranberry bogs and marshes (3 per day from Main and Center St. in Hyannis; $10.50 round-trip).

Lower Cape

Much less suburbanized than the Upper Cape, the Lower Cape preserves the weathered-shingle, dirt-road atmosphere of yore. In some towns, the majority of the land belongs to the National Seashore. On a whole, development here has mercifully been restrained, leaving an unsullied paradise for generations of vacationers to discover anew. Hop in a bike or a car, wander aimlessly to a picturesque vista, and meditate on life, love and lighthouses.

Truro, Wellfleet, Orleans, and Eastham

Whatever your religious background, attending church services is an excellent way to gain an appreciation of New England culture and meet local people in a non-touristy setting. The **First Congregation Parish of Truro** (United Church of Christ) will transport you back to the 19th century. The church, built in 1827, has changed little since its construction; electricity was installed just 30 years ago, and the outhouse (painted church-white) still serves in place of new-fangled toilets. Take the Bridge Rd. exit off U.S. 6 and turn right onto Town Hall Rd. (Sunday morning services at 10am.) To explore Truro, first stop at the **Truro Historical Museum** (487-3397) on Highland Rd. off U.S. 6, next to the **Highland Light,** celebrated by Thoreau and by painter Edward Hopper. The museum, a small collection of local historical items, is open from mid-

June to mid-September daily 10am to 5pm, charges $2 admission, and sells a $1 leaflet for self-guided tours of Truro.

Without streams to provide power, Cape Codders built windmills to grind corn and pump seawater into their saltworks. On U.S. 6 at Samoset Rd., the **Eastham Windmill** was built in 1680 to grind corn—a crop grown on the Cape by Native Americans long before newcomers from Europe arrived. The windmill still functions, and its interior is open to the public. The guide explains how the roof can be swiveled on rollers to face the wind. (Open July-Aug. Mon.-Sat. 10am-5pm, Sun. 1-5pm. Free.)

The **Wellfleet Bay Wildlife Sanctuary,** off U.S. 6 in Wellfleet (349-2615), maintains a large nature preserve with daily organized programs such as bird walks, canoe trips, night-time walks and lectures. The sanctuary is open daily 8am to 8pm; admission is $3. A $1.25 booklet identifies over 70 species of plants and birds on the one-mi. **Goose Pond Trail.** The sanctuary, run by the Massachusetts Audubon Society, also operates guided tours of the **Monomoy National Wildlife Refuge**. The tours last from three to seven hours, cost $30 to $50, and leave several times a week from Chatham. Call the Sanctuary for more details.

People don't usually associate Cape Cod with fresh water, but the melting glaciers left behind deep "kettle ponds" which are warmer and less crowded than the salty beaches. One of the best spots to paddle is **Gull Pond,** off Gull Pond Rd. in Wellfleet, which connects by a series of shallow channels to three more secluded ponds. From Higgins Pond you can see the home of the Wellfleet Oysterman, where Thoreau stayed and about which he wrote a chapter in *Cape Cod.* **Jack's Boat Rentals** (349-9808) has a "u-pick-up" location on U.S. 6 in Wellfleet, where you can rent a canoe or kayak for $25 per day. At their waterfront locations on Gull Pond, Beach Point in North Truro, and Flax Pond in Nickerson State Park, you can rent sailboats, as well.

Located right at the oceanfront at the end of Cahoon Hollow Rd. off U.S. 6, the **Beachcomber** (349-6055) serves up large baskets of fish and chips ($6), as well as burgers and fries ($5). (Open in summer daily noon-1am.) The Plymouth-Brockton bus to Provincetown stops at Palmet Rd. at U.S. 6 at **Jam's,** an expensive but sufficient grocery.

There are two hostels in or near the national seashore. The **Little America Hostel (HI/AYH),** at the far end of North Pamet Rd., Truro 02666 (349-3889), is one of the best hostels in the country. You can see the ocean through the big picture windows in the large, wood-paneled kitchen and eating area; it's just a 100-yd. walk to the beach. (Open early June-early Sept., office open 7-9:30am and 5-11pm. $10, nonmembers $13. Reservations recommended.) The **Mid-Cape HI/AYH Hostel** (255-2785) sleeps many bikers from the Cape Cod Rail Trail in its half-dozen cottages. The location is wooded, and quiet...until the local girl scouts troop by. Ask to be let off the Plymouth-Brockton bus to Provincetown at the traffic circle in Orleans (*not* the Eastham stop), walk out on Bridge Rd., and take a right onto Goody Hallet Rd., ½-mi. from U.S. 6. The hostel is a four-mi. bike ride to Coast Guard Beach or the ponds in Nickerson State Park. See also accommodations in Provincetown.

There are seven private campgrounds on the Lower Cape; pick up a free campground directory at the **Cape Cod Chamber of Commerce** in Hyannis. One of the best places to pitch a tent is **Nickerson State Park** on Rte. 6A in Brewster, on the Cape Cod Rail Trail bike path (896-3491). There are two large ponds with a boat rental on the waterfront, showers, flush toilets, but no hookups. (Sites $12. No reservations. The 418 sites fill quickly.) About seven mi. southeast of Provincetown on U.S. 6, several popular campgrounds nestle among the dwarf pines by the dunelands of the villages of North Truro and Truro. The **North Truro Camping Area,** on Highland Rd. (487-1847), ½-mi. east of U.S. 6., has small sandy sites. ($14 for 2 people. Each additional person $7. Required deposit of $30 for each reserved week of stay.)

Provincetown

Provincetown is the end of the road—where Cape Cod ends and the wide Atlantic begins. Two-thirds of "P-Town" is conservation land protected by the national seashore; the inhabited sliver snuggles up against the harbor on the south side of town. Once a busy whale port, today artists and not sailors fill the major thoroughfare—Commercial Street—where numerous Portuguese bakeries and gay and lesbian bookstores happily coexist. Browsing strollers clog the narrow width of pavement to the exclusion of automobiles.

For over a century, Provincetown has been known for its broad acceptance of many different lifestyles, and a widely known gay and lesbian community has flowered here. Over half the couples on the street are same-sex, and a popular local t-shirt spells "Provincetown" with a pink triangle in place of the "v." A walk here makes it quietly plain that gays and lesbians are a diverse group, and don't adhere to any stereotype of size, shape, color, or dress.

Practical Information and Orientation

Police: 911.

Visitor Information: Provincetown Chamber of Commerce, 307 Commercial St. (487-3424), MacMillan Wharf. Open summer daily 9am-5pm; off-season Mon.-Sat. 10am-4pm. **Province Lands Visitors Center,** Race Point Rd. (487-1256). Info on the national seashore; free guides to the nature and bike trails. Open July-Aug. daily 9am-6pm; mid-April-Nov. 9am-4:30pm.

Plymouth and Brockton Bus: 1-746-0378. Stops at MacMillan Wharf, behind Provincetown Chamber of Commerce, which has schedules and information. 3 buses per day in summer to Boston.

Bay State Spray Cruises: 20 Long Wharf, Boston. In the Provincetown Chamber of Commerce (487-9284). Ferries to Boston (1 per day; 3 hr.; $15, same-day round-trip $25). Operates May 27-mid-June and Labor Day-Columbus Day weekends only; summer daily.

Public Transportation: Provincetown Shuttle Bus: 487-3353. Serves Provincetown and Herring Cove Beach. Operates late June-early Sept. daily 8am-midnight; 8am-6:30pm for the beach. Fare $1.25, seniors 75¢. 1 route travels the length of Bradford St., the other from MacMillan Wharf to Herring Cove Beach. 1 bus per hr.

Bike Rental: Arnold's, 329 Commercial St. (487-0844). 3-speeds, 10-speeds, and mountain bikes $2.75-4 per hr., $7-12 per day. Credit cards accepted. Open daily 8:30am-5:30pm. Deposit and ID required.

Post Office: 211 Commercial St. (487-0163). Open Mon.-Fri. 8:30am-5pm, Sat. 9:30-11:30am. **ZIP code:** 02657.

Area Code: 508.

Provincetown rests in the cupped hand at the end of the Cape Cod arm, 123 mi. away from Boston as the crow drives via U.S. 6 to the end of the line, three hours by ferry across Cape Cod and Massachusetts Bay. **Bradford Street** is the town's auto-friendly thoroughfare; follow the parking signs to dock your car for $5 to $7 per day. **MacMillan Wharf** is at the center of town, just down the hill from the Pilgrim Monument. Whale-watching boats, the ferry to Boston, and the bus all leave from here.

Accommodations, Camping, and Food

Provincetown is known for old clapboard houses lining narrow roads—fortunately guesthouses are a part of that tradition, although not all are affordable. The cheapest places to stay are the hostels. One of the best hostels in America is only 10 mi. from Provincetown, secluded in the national lakeshore in nearby Truro (see Truro). The cheapest bed in town is at **The Outermost House,** 28 Winslow St. (487-4378), barely 100 yds. from the Pilgrim monument. $14 gets you a bed in one of the cottages, a kitchen, free parking, and no curfew. (Office open 8-9:30am and 6-9:30pm. Reservations recommended for weekends.) The **Joshua Paine Guest House,** 15 Tremont St. (487-1551), has four bright rooms and handsome furniture. (Singles $30. Doubles $35. Open May-mid-Sept.) In the quiet east end of town, the **Cape Codder,** 570 Commercial St. (487-0131, call 9am-3pm or 9-11pm), welcomes you back with archetypical Cape Cod decor, right down to the wicker furniture. Offers access to a private beach. (Singles $26-52, doubles $36-52, off-season about $10 less. Continental breakfast included. Open April-Oct.) Closer to town, the **White Caps Motel,** 394 Commercial St. (487-3755), has immaculate pastel rooms and access to the beach. (Doubles $55, off-season to $42.)

Camping is expensive here. The western part of **Coastal Acres Camping Court,** a one-mi. walk from the center of town west on Bradford or Commercial St. and right on West Vine St. (487-1700), has crowded sites; try to snag one on the waterside. (3-day min. stay. Sites $19, with electricity and water $25.) For more accommodations in the area see Truro, Wellfleet, Orleans, and Eastham also under Lower Cape.

Sit-down meals in Provincetown will cost you a pretty penny. Grab a bite at one of the Portuguese bakeries on Commercial St., or at a seafood shack on MacMillan Wharf. Particularly good and flaunting its own picnic tables, **John's Hot Dog Stand,** 309 Commercial St., actually specializes in fried clams, lobster roll, and a variety of other meals marine. The **Mayflower Family Dining** restaurant, 300 Commercial St., established in 1921, has walls lined with ancient caricatures. Choose from Portuguese ($6-8.50) and Italian ($4.50-9) entrées, or Puritan seafood meals ($7-10). (Open daily 11am-10:30pm.) If you are staying in the hostel in Truro, make use of its excellent kitchen. The **A&P** super- and seafood market on Shank Painter Rd. will fill your grocery bag more cheaply than will the smaller groceries in Truro.

Sights, Activities, and Entertainment

Provincetown has long been a refuge for artists and craftspeople; you can look but not touch (to say *nothing* of buying!) at any of the over 20 galleries—most are free and can be found east of **MacMillan Wharf** on Commercial St. (Most are open in the afternoon and evening until 11pm, but take a 2-hr. break for dinner. Get the free *Provincetown Gallery Guide* for complete details.) The kingpin of the artsy district is the **Provincetown Art Association and Museum,** 460 Commercial St. (487-1750), established in 1914. Alongside the permanent 500-piece collection, it exhibits works by new Provincetown artists. (Open late May-Oct. noon-4pm and 7-10pm. $2, seniors and kids $1.)

Contrary to popular belief, the Pilgrims first touched shore at Provincetown, not Plymouth. They moved on two weeks later in search of better farmland. The **Pilgrim Monument** on High Pole Hill (487-1310) commemorates that 17-day Puritan layover, and as the nation's tallest granite structure (255 ft.) serves as a dandy navigation aid to mariners. It also affords a gorgeous panorama of the Cape and, on clear days, a glimpse of Boston's skyscrapers. The **Provincetown Museum** at its base shows exhibits from a broad swath of Cape history, from whaling artifacts to dollhouses. (Open July-Sept. daily 9am-9pm; Oct.-June 9am-5pm. Admission $3, students $2, kids $1.) To fully appreciate the large number of historic homes and other sights, buy the walking tour maps (60¢) available at most postcard shops.

Whales are still hunted by Provincetown seamen, but telephoto lenses and not harpoons are used today to shoot these mighty mammals. **Whale-watch cruises** are some of P-town's most popular attractions, and several companies offer essentially the same service. The ride out to the feeding waters takes 40 minutes, and you will cruise around them for about two hours. The companies claim that whales are sighted on 99% of the journeys. Tickets cost about $16, but there are many discounts, and since competition is fierce you may be able to successfully haggle the price down. Three of your options are **Dolphin Fleet** (255-3857 or 800-826-9300); **Portuguese Princess** (487-2651 or 800-442-3188); and **Provincetown Whale-Watch** (487-3322 or 800-992-9333). All leave from and operate ticket booths on MacMillan Wharf.

Back on *terra firma,* you can roam the wide, sandy beaches that surround Provincetown on foot or by bike. Rent a bike from **Arnold's** (see Practical Information above) and receive a free map of the trails. The friendly manager of the **Provincetown Horse and Carriage Co.,** 27 W. Vine St. (487-1112), can help both novice and experienced riders explore the environs on horseback. One-hour trail rides cost $18.50 to $22. (Must be over 11.)

Provincetown has a nightlife with no holds barred; a local bumper sticker reads "Your place, then mine." The scene is almost totally gay- and lesbian-oriented and shuts down at about 1am. Ask around for the current hotspot, or peruse the *Provincetown Advocate*, published on Thursdays.

Martha's Vineyard

In 1606, British explorer Bartholomew Gosnold named Martha's Vineyard after his daughter and the wild grapes that grew here. In the 18th century, the Vineyard prospered as a port, with shepherding the main home trade. Try to visit the Vineyard in fall, when the tourist season wanes; the weather turns crisp, the leaves turn color, and prices drop. If you simply *must* visit in summer, avoid weekends at all cost.

This, the most famous island off the New England coast, does have the unifying theme of "quaint," from the dunes of the wide sandy beaches to the dark, beautiful inland woods. The landscape captivates even the most frequent of visitors, and converts many to semi-residents. Unlike many of its continental counterparts, "the Vineyard" is as welcoming budgetarily as it is scenically. Seven different communities comprise **Martha's Vineyard,** behaving in many ways as islands unto themselves: **Edgartown, Vineyard Haven, Oak Bluffs, West Tisbury, Menemsha, Chilmark,** and **Gay Head.**

Oak Bluffs, 3 mi. west of Vineyard Haven on State Rd., is the most youth-oriented of the Vineyard villages. Tour **Trinity Park,** near the harbor, and see the famous "Gingerbread Houses" (minutely detailed, elaborately pastel Victorian cottages) or Oak Bluffs' **Flying Horses Carousel,** on Circuit Ave. Ext., the oldest in the nation (built in 1876), containing 20 handcrafted horses with real horsehair tails and manes. (Open daily 10am-10pm. Fare $1.)

Edgartown, 7 mi. south of Oak Bluffs, displays a waterfront cluster of stately Federal-style homes built for whaling captains; skip the shops and stores here and visit the town's historic sights maintained by **Dukes County Historical Society,** School and Cooke St. (627-4441).

West Tisbury, 12 mi. west of Edgartown on the West Tisbury-Edgartown Rd., hosts the only vineyard on the Vineyard, the **Chicama Vineyards,** on Stoney Hill Rd. off State Rd. (693-0309). Free tasting follows the tour. (Open Jan.-April Fri.-Sat. 1-4pm; May Mon.-Sat. noon-5pm; June-Oct. Mon.-Sat. 11am-5pm, Sun. 1-5pm. Free.) The town supplies a well-stocked general store, providing sustenance for the trip "up-island."

Gay Head, 12 mi. off West Tisbury, offers just about the best view in all of New England. The local Wampanoog frequently saved sailors whose ships wrecked on the breath-absconding **Gay Head Cliffs.** The 100-million-year-old precipice contains a collage of brilliant colors with 1 of 5 lighthouses on the island.

Chilmark, a little northeast of Gay Head, gives good coastline, claiming the only working fishing town on the island, **Menemsha Village,** where tourists can fish off the pier or purchase fresh lobster.

Vineyard Haven has more tacky t-shirt shops and fewer charming old homes than other towns.

The western end of the island is called "up island," from the nautical days when sailors had to tack upwind to get there. The three largest towns of Oak Bluffs, Vineyard Haven, and Edgartown are "down island" and have flatter terrain.

Exploring the Vineyard should involve much more than hamlet-hopping. Three walking trails will take you through widely different habitats—a salt marsh, a beach dune, and a forest—at **Felix Neck Wildlife Sanctuary** on the Edgartown-Vineyard Haven Rd. (627-4850; open until 7pm. Admission $3, seniors and kids $2.) **Cedar Tree Neck** on the western shore provides trails across 250 acres of headland off Indian Hill Rd., while the **Long Point** park in West Tisbury preserves 550 acres and a shore on the Tisbury Great Pond. **Camp Pogue Wildlife Refuge and Wasque Reservation** on Chappaquidick is the largest conservation area on the island. One of the most awe-inspiring, natural beaches on the island which is accessible to the public is **South Beach,** at the end of Katama Rd. three mi. south of Edgartown. The big waves alternately licking and slapping the shore attract quite a crowd. A narrow spit of land between Oak Bluffs and Edgartown divides Sengekontacket Pond from Nantucket Sound. A bike path bordering Beach Rd. follows this sandy strip, and the whole four mi. is a glorious state beach. All public beaches are free.

Cheap sandwich and lunch places speckle the Vineyard—the traveler who watches the wallet rather than the waistline may have the best luck in Vineyard Haven and Oak Bluffs. Fried-food shacks across the island sell clams, shrimp, and potatoes. Sit-down dinners generally cost at least $15. A glorious exception is **Louis',** State Rd., Vineyard

Haven, serving Italian food in a country-style atmosphere with unlimited bread and salad bar. (Lunch $4-5. Dinner $9-15. Open Mon.-Thurs. 11:30am-8pm, Fri.-Sat. 11:30am-9pm, Sun. 4-9:30pm.) **Cozy's,** on Circuit Ave. in Oak Bluffs, serves up ice cream and platters from its Wurlitzer. Try their generous hoagies ($3.75-5) or burgers ($1.75-3.35). (Open late March-early Sept. daily 11am-midnight.) Down the street, **Papa's Pizza Circuit** rounds out a popular, atmospheric hangout for island youth, serving delicious thick-crusted whole-wheat pizza ($7-9). (Open daily 10am-11pm.) Prospective revelers should note that Edgartown and Oak Bluffs are the only "wet" towns on the Vineyard. Bar owners here are notoriously strict about checking ID. Given Teddy Kennedy's drunken escapades nearby, you can hardly fault them.

A number of good take-out places freckle the island, and with the beauty of the surrounding landscape you just might want to grab food and run. You've seen the t-shirt, now visit the **Black Dog Bakery,** on Beach St. Ext. in Vineyard Haven, filled with sumptuous breads and pastries (75¢-$3.50). (Open daily 6am-9pm; off-season 6am-6pm.) An island legend and institution, **Mad Martha's** scoops out 26 homemade flavors or limited editions of ice cream. The main store is on Circuit Ave. in Oak Bluffs, but there are locations in Vineyard Haven and Edgartown. (Open mid-April-late Oct. daily 11am-midnight.) Several **farm stands** on the island sell inexpensive produce; the free chamber of commerce map shows their locations.

The most deluxe youth hostel you may ever encounter also offers the least expensive beds on the island. The lovely **Manter Memorial Youth Hostel (HI/AYH),** Edgartown Rd., West Tisbury (693-2665), five mi. inland from Edgartown on the bike route, is quite crowded in summer. (Curfew 11pm. $10, nonmembers $13. Linen $1. Open April-Nov. Reservations required.) The Chamber of Commerce provides a list of inns and guest houses. For relatively inexpensive rooms, the century-old **Nashua House** (693-0043), on Kennebec Ave. in Oak Bluffs, sits across from the post office. Some rooms overlook the ocean; all are brightly painted and cheerful. (Singles $25, doubles $49.) The Victorian **Summer Place Inn,** 47 Pequot Ave., Oak Bluffs (693-9908), has nice rooms right next to the ocean ($55; off-season $45).

Campers have two options. **Martha's Vineyard Family Campground,** 11/4 mi. from Vineyard Haven on Edgartown Rd., (693-3772), has 180 sites. Groceries are available nearby. (Sites $22 for 2 people. Each additional person $8. Open mid-May-mid-Oct.) **Webb's Camping Area,** Barnes Rd., Oak Bluffs (693-0233), is more spacious, with 150 shaded sites. (Sites $22 for 2 people. Each additional person $8. Open mid-May-mid-Sept.)

Ferries serve the island from Hyannis; New Bedford; Falmouth; and Montauk, Long Island, but the shortest and cheapest ride leaves from Wood's Hole on Cape Cod. From there, **Steamship Authority** (548-3788) sends 10 boats per day on the 45-minute ride. (Round-trip $9, bike $5, kid $4.50). The parking lots charge more the closer they are to the ferry dock, up to $7 per day; scout around for a cheaper one. Many have shuttle buses to carry people from the lot to the dock.

Transporting a car costs about $38 to $48, and the island isn't designed for them anyway. Bring a bike or rent one at **Martha's Vineyard Scooter and Bike** at the Steamship Authority Dock in Vineyard Haven (693-0782, open daily 8am-8pm); **Vineyard Bike and Moped,** Circuit Ave. Ext. in Oak Bluffs (693-4498, open daily 9am-6pm); or **R.W. Cutler,** Main St., Edgartown (627-4052, open April 7-Oct. 15 daily 9am-5pm). All three charge $10 to $12 per day for a three-speed, $18 per day for a mountain bike or hybrid. Trail maps are available at R.W. Cutler. Touring cyclists should stick to the fairly easy main roads; inexperienced cyclists may find the uphill to Gay Head or Menemsha strenuous. Most **taxis** are vans and fares are negotiable; set a price before you get in. In Oak Bluffs, call 693-0037; in Edgartown 627-4677, in Vineyard Haven 693-3705. The **Down-Island Shuttle bus** connects Vineyard Haven (Union St.), Oak Bluffs (Ocean Park), and Edgartown (Church St.) every 15 minutes from 10am to 6pm, and every 30 minutes from 8am to 10pm and 6pm to midnight ($1.50). The **Up-Island Shuttle bus** goes to the airport and up-island towns twice a day. Buses run July and August.

Though only about 30 mi. across at its widest point, the Vineyard holds 15 beaches and one state forest. A good free map, as well as brochures and advice, is available at the **Martha's Vineyard Chamber of Commerce,** Beach Rd., Vineyard Haven (693-0085; open June-Aug. Mon.-Fri. 9am-5pm, Sat. 10am-2pm. Mailing address: P.O. Box 1698, Vineyard Haven 02568.)

The **ZIP code** is 02539 for Edgartown; 02568 for Vineyard Haven; and 02557 for Oak Bluffs. The **area code** for Martha's Vineyard is 508.

Nantucket

> *Nantucket! Take out your map and look at it. See what a real corner of the world it occupies; how it stands there, away off shore...a mere hillock, an elbow of sand, all beach without a background.*
>
> *Herman Melville,* Moby Dick

Melville penned these lines about Nantucket before he had ever visited the island; many of today's travelers also form their judgments of the "mere hillock"—too pretentious, too expensive, too difficult to get to—without bothering to take the ferry ride over. See it for yourself. Bike the dirt roads through the heaths, catch a bluefish on the beach, go sea-kayaking, explore Nantucket Town's cobblestone streets and weathered fishing shacks which serve as artists' workshops and galleries, or sit on the docks which once were the scene of the busiest whaling port in the world. If possible, visit during the last weeks of the tourist season when prices drop. Only a few places stay open during the cold, rainy winter months, when awesome storms churn the slate-blue seas.

Nantucket is an island of incredible beauty; enjoy it now before developers consign it to the subdivided fate of Cape Cod and increasingly of its sister island, Martha's Vineyard. For a great **bike trip,** head east from Nantucket Town on Milestone Rd. and turn left onto a path that looks promising. Head across beautiful moors of heather, huckleberries, bayberries and wild roses. Those who want adventure in the water should go to **Sea Nantucket,** at the end of Washington St., at the waterfront (228-7499), and rent a **sea kayak** ($20 for 4 hrs.; open daily 9am-7pm). It is easy to learn how to maneuver the kayaks, and they are not too physically demanding; take one out to a nearby salt marsh, or head across the harbor to one of the isolated beaches on the Coatue peninsula and enjoy a picnic undisturbed by other beachgoers. If you prefer to stand on the strand between land and sea, rent **surf fishing** equipment from **Barry Thurston's** at Harbor Square near the A&P (228-9595), for $15 per day. (Open Mon.-Sat. 8am-6pm, Sun. 9am-1am.)

The Nantucket Historical Association offers one of the better museum deals in New England: for $5, you get a pass good for a full year of admission to several fine museums and a few historic homes. All of the buildings are open daily 10am to 5pm in the summer. The excellent **Nantucket Whaling Museum** in Nantucket Town recreates the old whaling community with exhibits on whales and whaling methods. The museums' collection of scrimshaw (etched whale ivory) includes some pieces carved by sailors for their sweethearts. The **Museum of Nantucket History** in the Thomas Macy Warehouse, will help you appreciate the island's boom years as a whaling port and also describes other island industries such as candlemaking and sheep raising. Pick up a free copy of *Yesterday's Island* for listings of nature walks, concerts, lectures, art exhibitions, and more.

Restaurants on Nantucket are expensive; most entrées cost $3 to $5 more than they would on the mainland. **The Elegant Dump Lobster Pot,** 56 Union St. (228-4634), is your best bet for a sit-down dinner, with a witty owner and one meal actually under $10: linguini for $7.25. (Open daily 6-10pm.) For less expensive take-out fare, go down to Steamboat Wharf, where **Henry's** (228-0123) serves $4 grinders. For a hearty breakfast at reasonable prices, take **Two Steps Up,** at 10 India St. (Open daily 5am-1pm; the only place to chow before catching the morning ferry.) To avoid restaurant prices altogether, buy groceries at the **A&P,** on Commercial St. at Washington St. (Open Mon.-Sat. 7am-midnight, Sun. 8am-8pm.) The college crowd that works summers on Nantucket parties at **The Muse** for the live entertainment.

Wake up to the sound of surf at the **Star of the Sea Youth Hostel (HI/AYH)** at Surfside Beach, three mi. from the town of Nantucket (a 45-min. walk from town on Surfside Rd., but those who hitchhike on Nantucket report that it's easy and probably as safe as it gets). This former Coast Guard Station is a stellar hostel ($10 members, nonmembers $13, open 7-9:30am and 5-11pm). Apart from the Star, accommodation prices on the island are astronomical, with guest houses starting at $85 per night. One B&B with semi-reasonable rates is **Four Ash Street** (228-4899), with singles $45 and doubles $75. Camping is illegal on Nantucket.

Rent bikes at **Young's Bicycle Shop,** at Steamboat Wharf (228-1151). Three-speeds are $13 per day, mountain bikes $18 (its worth the extra five-spot to get the mountain bike—you'll want to travel dirt roads through the heath). Young's distributes free, decent maps of the island, but for an extended stay buy the *Complete Map of Nantucket* ($3). (Open daily 8am-8pm.) Alternatively, the **Nantucket and Siasconset Bus Lines,** at 20 Federal St. opposite the visitors center (228-3118) runs several times per day to Jetty's Beach ($1), Surfside Beach ($3 round-trip), and 'Sconset ($5 round-trip).

Two companies, **HyLine** (778-2600) and the **Steamship Authority** (540-2022) provide ferry service from Hyannis to Nantucket. Both charge $10 one way, $4.50 for bikes, take about two hours, and run six trips per day in summer, with fewer in the spring and fall. The Hyannis docks are near South and Pleasant St. The Steamship Authority also takes cars ($83 one way), but the island is small enough that a car is far more trouble than it's worth.

The **visitor services center** is on 25 Federal St. (228-0925; open Mon.-Sat. 9am-6pm, Sun. 10am-4pm). It has a full complement of brochures and can help you find a place to stay.

Nantucket's regular **ZIP code** is 02554; General Delivery is 02584—pick it up at the **post office** branch on lower Pleasant St. The **area code** is 508.

Plymouth

Despite what American high school textbooks say, the Pilgrims did *not* first step ashore onto the New World at Plymouth—they first stopped at Provincetown but left because the harbor was inadequate. **Plymouth Rock** itself was just one more stone in the sea until 1741, when a 95-year-old man identified it as the one where the Pilgrims disembarked. Since then, the rock has served as a symbol of liberty during the American Revolution, been moved three times, and been chipped away by tourists before landing at its current resting place on Water St. at the foot of North St.

Plimoth Plantation, Warren Ave. (746-1622 for recording), superbly re-creates the early settlement. In the **Pilgrim Village** costumed actors impersonate actual villagers; they feign ignorance of all events after the 1630s. Each day at the Plantation corresponds to a day in William Bradford's record of the first year of the settlement: if you arrive on August 2, 1993, you'll see a recreation of what was happening on August 2, 1620. The nearby **Wampanoag Summer Encampment** recreates a Native American village of the same period. Admission to the plantation includes entry to the **Mayflower II,** built in the 1950s to recapture the atmosphere of the original ship. (Ship docked off Water St., 4 blocks south of the info center; open June-Aug. daily 9am-6:30pm; April-May and Sept.-Nov. 9am-5pm; separate admission $6, kids $4. Plantation open April-Nov. daily 9am-5pm. Admission for village and encampment $18.50, kids $11.) To get to Plimoth Plantation (and yes, that's how it's spelled), take Rte. 3 south to exit 4 and follow the signs, or follow Main St. three mi. out of the center of town.

Less fanfare surrounds the sights in town. The nation's oldest museum in continuous existence, the **Pilgrim Hall Museum,** 75 Court St. (746-1620), houses Puritan crafts, furniture, books, paintings, and weapons. (Open daily 9:30am-4:30pm. Admission $5, seniors $4.50, ages 6-15 $2.) An unexpected pleasure and an old favorite of Amanda Dawson, **Cranberry World,** 225 Water St. (747-2350), glorifies one of the only three indigenous American fruits (the other two are the blueberry and the Concord grape). The exhibits show how cranberries are grown, harvested, sorted, and sold and include a small cranberry bog in front of the museum. (Open 9:30am-5pm. Admission and a cup of juice are free.)

Beautiful **Nelson's Beach** on Nelson St., and **Brewsters Garden** on Leyden St., with its meandering brook, provide ideal spots for a picnic (no swimming). Camping comes cheaper than the area's overpriced hotels; majestic **Myles Standish Forest** (866-2526), which stands seven myles south of Plymouth via Rte. 3 to Long Pond Rd., offers wooded ground. (Sites $10 for 2 people, with showers $12.) **Ellis Haven Campground,** 531 Federal Furnace Rd. (746-0803), offers less wilderness and more amenities including laundry facilities. (Sites $17 for 2 people, $19 with hookup. Each additional person $2.)

The well-run **Plymouth Visitor Information Center,** 130 Water St. (747-0095 or 800-872-1620), has brochures on all the attractions and a detailed compilation of accommodations and prices. They know what places have vacancies, and will make reservations for you. The 12-hour metered parking behind the building is the most convenient place in town to stable your mobile. Follow U.S. 44 east all the way to the water's edge; the info center is on the right. More brochures on Plymouth and the rest of New England are available at the state-run **tourist information center** (746-1150), two mi. from Plymouth on Rte. 3, exit 5, Long Pond Rd. (Open Mon.-Fri. 8:45am-5pm, Sat. 8am-4:30pm; fall and winter daily 8:45am-4:30pm.)

The **Plymouth and Brockton Street Railway Company** (actually a bus line), 8 Industrial Park Rd. (746-0378), runs from the Industrial Park terminal (3 mi. from Plymouth Center) to Boston (16 per day; $6) and Hyannis (22 per day; 4.50, with stops at Sagamore Circle and Barnstable). In addition, three buses per day leave for Boston from the old post office on Main St. in Plymouth Center. The **Plymouth Rock Trolley,** 20 Main St. (747-3419), operates daily (9:30am-5:30pm every 20 min.; $4 all-day fare, under 12 $1.) The trolley is only necessary to get to Plimoth Plantation; the sights downtown are close together.

The **post office** registers at 6 Main St. Ext. (746-4028), in Plymouth center. (Open Mon.-Fri. 8:30am-5pm, Sat. 8:30am-1pm.) Plymouth's **ZIP code** is 02361; the **area code** is 508.

New Hampshire

New Hampshire's farmers have struggled for over two centuries with the state's rugged landscape, but a cultivator's *inferno* is a hiker's *paradiso*. The White Mountains dominate the central and northern regions, and nearly every part of the state identifies with some towering crag. Rising above them all, Mt. Washington is the highest point in the Appalachians (6288 ft.); from its summit you can see the Atlantic and five states. Besides the stony beaches of the shortest shore of any seaboard state (15 mi.), much of the southeastern region of the state has mutated into a suburb of the Boston megalopolis. Although the state motto and license-plate blazon "Live Free or Die," "Live Well or Die" may be more appropriate in these parts.

Practical Information

Capital: Concord.

Office of Travel and Tourism, Box 856 Concord 03302 (271-2666, 800-262-6660 or 800-258-3608). With a touch-tone phone these numbers provide fall foliage reports, daily ski conditions, weekly snowmobile conditions and weekly special events. Operators available Mon.-Fri. 8am-4pm.

Fish and Game Department, 2 Hazen Dr., Concord 03301 (271-3421) can provide info on hunting and fishing regulations and license fees.

U.S. Forest Service, 719 Main St., mail to P.O. Box 638, Laconia 03247 (528-8721). Open Mon.-Fri. 8am-4:30pm.

Time Zone: Eastern. **Postal abbreviation:** NH

Sales Tax: 0%. Live Tax-Free or Die.

White Mountains

In the late 19th century, the White Mountains became an immensely popular summer retreat for wealthy New Englanders. Grand hotels peppered the rolling green landscape and as many as 50 trains per day chugged through the region, filling hotel rooms with tourists marveling at nature. The mountains are not quite so busy or posh these days, but the valleys, forests and gnarled granite peaks still attract upwardly mobile travelers, recast today as outdoorsy hikers and skiers. Unfortunately, the mountains still shun budget travelers; affordable lodgings here are rustic at best, public transportation scarce and weather unpredictable.

The **White Mountain Attraction Center** (745-8720), on Rte. 112 in North Woodstock east of I-93 (exit 32), can give you information on just about anything in the area. (Write P.O. Box 10, N. Woodstock 03262. Open Memorial Day-Columbus Day daily 8:30am-6pm; off-season daily 8:30am-5pm). Local Chambers of Commerce are also good sources of information. Those looking to bypass cities will have a much more relaxing time of it thanks to two superb organizations which help visitors camp in and preserve the forests. One is **the U.S. Forest Service,** whose main information station (528-8721) lies south of the mountains at 719 Main St., Laconia 03246. **Forest service ranger stations,** dotting the main highways through the forest, can also answer questions about trail locations and conditions: **Androscoggin,** on Rte. 16, ½-mi. south of the U.S. 2 junction in Gorham (466-2713; open Mon.-Fri. 7am-4:30pm); **Amoosuc,** on Trudeau Rd. in Bethlehem, west of U.S. 3 on U.S. 302 (869-2626; open Mon.-Fri. 7am-4:30pm); **Saco** on the Kancamangus Hwy. in Conway, 100 yd. off Rte. 16 (447-5448; open daily 8am-4:30pm); and **Pemigewasset** on Rte. 175 in Plymouth (536-1310; open Mon-Fri 8am-4:30pm). Each station provides its own guide to the **back-country facilities** in its area.

The other organization is the **Appalachian Mountains Club (AMC)**, whose main base in the mountains is the **Pinkham Notch Visitors Center** (466-2725) on Rte. 16 between Gorham and Jackson (see Pinkham Notch below). The AMC is the area's primary supplier of hiking and camping equipment, information, lodging and food. The club's main car-accessible lodge is the **Joe Dodge Lodge,** adjoining the Pinkham visitors center (see Pinkham Notch below). The AMC's other car-accessible lodging is the **Shapleigh Hostel** (846-7774), adjoining the **Crawford Notch Depot,** east of Bretton Woods on U.S. 302. The hostel has room for 20 people and provides toilets, metered showers and a full kitchen. Bring your own sleeping bag and food. Reservations recommended. (AMC members $10, nonmembers $15.) The Depot sells trail guides, maps, food and film, and has restrooms. (Open late May-Labor Day daily 9am-5pm.) The AMC also has a system of eight **huts,** none of which is accessible by car; they are spaced about a day's hike apart along the Appalachian Trail. Either breakfast or dinner must be taken with each night's lodging, and guests must provide their own sleeping bags or sheets. (Bunk with 2 meals for member $47, child members $20, nonmember $53/$26; with only dinner $41/$17 and $47/$23; with only breakfast $37/$15 and $43/$21. All huts are open for **full service** late May through early September or mid-October; **self-service rates** (caretaker in residence but no meals provided) are available at other times. (AMC member $10, nonmember $15.) For all AMC info, consult the AMC's *The Guide,* available at either visitors center. (One-year AMC membership $40 per person, $65 per family. Contact AMC headquarters, 5 Joy St., Boston MA 02108; 617-523-0636.)

Camping is free in a number of areas throughout the **White Mountains National Forest.** No camping is allowed above the tree line (approximately 4000 ft.), within 200 ft. of a trail, or within ¼ mi. of roads, huts, shelters, tent platforms, lakes or streams; the same rules apply to building a wood or charcoal fire. Since these rules often vary depending on forest conditions, call the U.S. Forest Service before pitching a tent. The forest service also holds 22 designated **campgrounds** (sites $8-12, bathrooms and firewood usually available). Call 528-8727 to find out which ones are closest to your destinations or make reservations (800-283-2267), especially in July and August.

If you plan to do much hiking, invest in the invaluable *AMC White Mountain Guide,* available in most bookstores and huts ($16), which includes full maps and descriptions of all trails in the mountains; with these, you can pinpoint precisely where you are on the trail at any given time. *Never* drink untreated water from a stream or lake; all AMC outposts sell water-purification kits. Also, be prepared for sudden weather changes. Though often peaceful, the peaks can prove treacherous. Every year, Mt. Washington claims at least one life. A gorgeous day can suddenly transmute into a chilling storm, with wind kicking up over 100 mph and thunderclouds ominously rumbling. It has never been warmer than 72°F atop Mt. Washington, and the *average* temperature on the peak is a bone-chilling 26.7°F.

Next to hiking, bicycling offers the best way to see the mountains close up. The approach from the north is slightly less steep according to some bikers. Check the guide/map *New Hampshire Bicycle,* available at many information centers. Also consult *25 Bicycle Tours in New Hampshire* ($7), available in local bookstores and outdoor equipment stores. (For bike rental suggestions, see North Conway below.)

While getting to the general vicinity poses little difficulty, getting around the White Mountains can be very problematic. **Concord Trailways** (228-3300 or 639-3317) runs north-south and connects the Boston Peter Pan bus station at 555 Atlantic Ave. (617-426-7838) with Concord ($11), Conway ($25) and Franconia ($26). Bus service from Boston's Logan Airport to Pinkham Notch Visitors Center costs $29. **Vermont Transit** (800-451-3292) runs buses from Boston's Greyhound terminal, 10 St. James Ave. (617-423-5810), to Concord ($11) on the way to Vermont. The AMC runs a **shuttle service** (466-2727) connecting points within the mountains. For a complete map of routes and times consult *The Guide*. Reservations are recommended for all stops and required for some. (Runs late May-early Sept. 8:45am-4pm, tickets $4.75-11.75.) **Trail and Weather Information** can be obtained by calling the Pinkham Notch Visitors Center (466-2725). Regional **zip codes** include: Franconia, 03580; Jackson, 03846 and Gorham, 03587. The **area code** in the White Mountains is 603.

Franconia Notch

About 400 million years old, Franconia Notch in the northern White Mountains has developed some interesting wrinkles. Sheer and dramatic granite cliffs, waterfalls, endless woodlands, and one very famous rocky profile attract droves of summer campers. Before you begin your exploration of this geological wonder on I-93, ask about the Franconia Notch State Park at the **Flume Visitors Center** (745-8391), off I-93 north of Lincoln. Their excellent free 15-minute film acquaints visitors with the landscape. (Open late May-late Oct. daily 9am-4:30pm, July-Aug. until 5pm.) While at the center, purchase tickets to **The Flume,** a two-mi.-long nature walk over hills, through a covered bridge to a boardwalk above a fantastic gorge with 90-ft.-high granite cliffs. (Tickets $5.50, ages 6-12 $2.50.)

The westernmost of the three great notches, Franconia is best known for the **Old Man of the Mountains,** a 40-ft.-high human profile formed by three ledges of stone atop a 1200-ft. cliff north of The Flume on the parkway. Hawthorne addressed this geological Rorschasch Test in his 1850 story "The Great Stone Face," and P.T. Barnum once offered to buy the rock. Today the Old Man is really doddering; his forehead is now supported by cables and turnbuckles. The best view of the man, both at high noon and in the moonlight, is from **Profile Lake,** a 10-minute walk from Lafayette Place in the park.

West of the Old Man, off I-93 exit 2, **Great Cannon Cliff,** a 1000-ft. sheer drop into the cleft between **Mount Lafayette** and **Cannon Mountain,** is not just for onlookers—many test their technical skill and climb the "Sticky Fingers" or "Meat Grinder" route; the 80-passenger **Cannon Mountain Aerial Tramway** (823-5563; open mid-

May-Oct. daily 9am-4:30pm; Nov.-mid-April Sat.-Sun. 9am-4:30pm; tickets $8, ages 6-12 $4, $6 for one-way hikers) will do the work for you. The Flume and the Tramway may be purchased as a package. ($11, ages 6-12 $5.)

Myriad trails lead up into the mountains on both sides of the notch, providing excellent day hikes and spectacular views. Be prepared for severe weather, especially above 4000 ft. The **Lake Trail,** a relatively easy hike, wends its way from Lafayette Place in the park 1½ mi. to **Lonesome Lake,** where the AMC operates its westernmost summer hut (see White Mountains AMC huts above). The **Greenleaf Trail** (2½ mi.), which starts at the Cannon Tramway parking lot, and the **Old Bridle Path** (3 mi.), which starts at Lafayette Place, are much more ambitious; both lead up to the AMC's Greenleaf Hut near the summit of Mt. Lafayette overlooking Eagle Lake, a favorite destination for sunset photographers. From Greenleaf, you can trudge the next 7½ mi. east along **Garfield Ridge** to the AMC's most remote hut, the **Galehead.** Dayhikes from this base can keep you occupied for days. (Sites at the Garfield Ridge campsite $4.) A number of other campsites, mainly lean-tos and tent platforms with no showers or toilets, are dispersed throughout the mountains. Most run $4 per night on a first-come, first-served basis, but many are free. Contact the U.S. Forest Service or consult the AMC's two-page, free photocopied handout *Backpacker Shelters, Tentsites, Campsites and Cabins in the White Mountains.*

Those who find hiking anathema can take advantage of the nine mi. of **bike paths** that begin off U.S. 3 and run through the White Mountain National Forest. After any exertion, cool off at the lifeguard-protected beach on the northern shore of **Echo Lake State Park** (356-2672), west off Rte. 16/U.S. 302 in North Conway. (Open daily mid-June-Sept. 9am-8pm. $2.50, under 12 and over 65 free.)

At reasonable altitudes, you can camp at the **Lafayette Campground** (823-9513), in Franconia Notch State Park. (Open mid-May-mid-Oct., weather permitting; sites $15 for 2 people, $7 per extra person, showers available.) If Lafayette is full, try the more suburban **Fransted Campground** (823-5675), one mi. south of the village and three mi. north of the notch. (Sites $13 for 1 person, $16 on the river. Each additional person $1. Showers and bathrooms available. Open May-Columbus Day.) From Lincoln, the Kancamangus Hwy. (NH Rte. 112) branches east for a scenic 35 mi. through the **Pemigewassett Wilderness** to Conway. The large basin is rimmed by 4000-ft. peaks and attracts many backpackers and skiers.

South of the highway, trails head into the **Sandwich Ranges,** whose **Mount Chocorna,** south along Rte. 16 near Ossippee, is a dramatic and steep exposed peak, and a favorite of 19th-century naturalist painters.

North Conway and Skiing

Located along the lengthy stretch shared by Routes 16 and 302, North Conway differs from the region's other small towns in that it doesn't exploit the beauty of its natural surroundings, but instead lures tourists seeking frenzied factory-outlet shopping. Nearly every major clothing label, from L.L. Bean to Ralph Lauren, has a sizeable store on the main road. If you've come to shop, this is the place; if you've come for the forest, any of the diverse lodgings offered by the AMC will give you a cheaper, less hectic base of operations than the hotels in town. While North Conway clearly shows the strain of being the area's largest city, it also enjoys some of the benefits. You'll find many affordable places to eat, the region's best outdoor equipment stores, and, within a short drive, a number of very good cross-country and downhill ski centers.

Though close to many ski areas, North Conway is proudest of its own local mountain, **Cranmore** (800-543-9206), which boasts the oldest ski train in the country. On winter Wednesdays, the slopes host a ski racing series; local teams also compete in the nationally known **Mountain Meisters,** open to the public. You can ski day ($33) or night ($15). Mid-week rates are 1/3 less. Students receive a $3 discount with ID. The other two major downhill ski areas in the Mt. Washington valley are **Attitash** (800-223-7669) and **Wildcat** (466-3326). Attitash, on U.S. 302 west of its intersection with Rte. 16, offers snowmaking on nearly 100% of its trails. (Lift tickets Mon.-Fri. $27, Sat.-Sun. $34.) With both the largest vertical drop and the largest lift capacity in the valley, Wildcat guarantees that if you wait more than 10 minutes for a chairlift you'll get $5 off your next lift ticket. (Located near the AMC Pinkham Notch Camp on Rte. 16. Lift tickets Sun.-Fri. $27, Sat. $33.)

For cross-country skiing in the area, try the **Jackson Ski Touring Foundation**, in Jackson along the Rte. 16A bypass to the Jackson Business District (383-9356), which has been consistently rated as one of the nation's top three cross-country areas. Tickets are available behind the Jack Frost Ski Shop north of the covered bridge. For info on ticket packages for multiple areas in the valley, call or write the **Mt. Washington Valley Chamber of Commerce,** P.O. Box 2300, North Conway 03860 (356-3171).

A number of stores in the North Conway area rent quality skis and other outdoor equipment. In Jackson, the **Jack Frost Cross Country Ski Shop** (383-4391) rents cross-country skis, boots and poles ($12 first day, $7 each additional day; open daily 9am-5:30pm in season). For downhill skis, try **Joe Jones** in North Conway on Main St. at Mechanic (356-9411; skis, boots and poles $15 per day, $25 per 2 days; open July-Aug and Dec.-March daily 9am-9pm; off-season Sun.-Thurs. 10am-6pm, Fri.-Sat. 10am-9pm). **Eastern Mountain Sports (EMS),** on Main St. (356-5433), on the premises of the Eastern Slope Inn, has free mountaineering pamphlets and excellent books on the area, including *25 Bicycle Tours in New Hampshire.* EMS rents tents ($15 per night for a 2-person, $20 for 4-person), sleeping bags ($10-15), and sells other camping equipment. (Open June-Sept. daily 9am-9pm; off-season daily 9am-6pm, Fri.-Sat. until 9pm.) In Jackson, next to the Jack Frost Ski Shop, at **David's Bike Shop** (383-4563), the extremely amiable Dave Miller rents mountain bikes ($20 per day, $10 per ½-day; open May-Oct. Tues.-Sun. 9am-5pm.)

Outside the Mt. Washington valley, the major downhill ski areas cluster along I-93. Collectively known as **Ski-93** (745-8101 or write P.O. Box 517 Lincoln 13251), these mountains offer quick access and lift-ticket packages for multiple areas. **Loon Mountain** (745-8111), three mi. east of I-93 at Lincoln, avoids overcrowding by limiting lift-ticket sales, and also has a free beginners' tow (9 lifts, 41 trails). **Waterville Valley** (236-8311) offers great downhill as well as cross-country skiing (12 lifts, 53 trails). **Cannon Mountain** (823-5563; 800-552-1234 in New England), north of Franconia Notch, offers decent slopes off a large tram.

For cross-country, visit **Waterville Valley X-C Ski Center** (236-8311), 13 mi. east on Rte. 49 off I-93 exit 25, and trek through wilderness trails in adjacent White Mountain National Forest. **Bretton Woods Ski Touring Center** (278-5000), 10 mi. north of Crawford Notch on U.S. 302, boasts an elaborate 50-mi. network of trails.

Sandwich and pizza places line North Conway's Main St. The hotspot for the *après ski* crowd is **Jackson Square,** on the premises of the Eastern Slope Inn, with a DJ and dancing every Thursday through Saturday night. (Most entrées $10, Thurs. nights 2-for-1 entrées, Fri.-Sat. all-u-can-eat buffet $10. Happy hours Sun.-Fri. 4-7pm. Open daily 7:30am-10pm.) **Studebakers,** on Rte. 16 south of town (356-3011), is a 50s-style drive-in diner. Sandwiches $3-5. (Open Sun.-Thurs. 11:30am-9pm, Fri.-Sat. 11:30am-10pm.)

The **Maple Leaf Motel,** on Main St., south of the North Conway city park (356-5388), has clean, spacious rooms for reasonable rates. (Singles late-June-mid-Oct. $55, doubles $65, off-season $36, $48.) Farther south on Main St., the **Yankee Clipper** (356-5736 or 800-343-5900) offers similar rooms for similar prices (July-mid-Oct. room with 1 double bed $55, with 2 double beds $75; off-season $40/$50).

An **information booth** (356-3171 or 800-367-3364) sits on Main St. (Rte. 16/U.S. 302), and can make reservations at any area hotel or restaurant. (Open mid-June-mid-Oct. daily 8:30am-6:30pm; off-season Sat.-Sun. 10am-4pm.) If the booth is closed, try the **Chamber of Commerce** in the white building next door. (Open Mon.-Fri. 8:30am-5pm.)

Pinkham Notch

Easternmost of the New Hampshire notches, Pinkham Notch skirts the eastern edge of the base of Mt. Washington. Stretching from Gorham to Jackson along Rte. 16, the notch is most notable as the home of the AMC's main visitors and information center in the White Mountains, the **Pinkham Notch Visitors Center** (466-2725, 466-2727 for reservations). The visitors center, the New England hiker's mecca, lies about half-way between Gorham and Jackson on Rte. 16, less than 15 mi. from each. From I-93, the best route is to take exit 42 to U.S. 302 east, then take Rte. 16 north to U.S. 2 east to Rte. 16 south. It's open daily 7am to 10pm and is the best source for weather and trail conditions in the area. The center can also make reservations at any of the AMC huts and hostels, as well as at the adjoining **Joe Dodge Lodge.** A comfy bunk in the spotlessly maintained lodge comes with a delicious and sizeable breakfast and dinner. ($38, nonmembers $44.) A bunk with only supper is $5 less; with only breakfast $10 less, and if you plead, they might let you off without any meals for $14 less. The visitors center also sells the complete line of AMC books, trail maps ($3, weatherproofed $5), and all types of camping and hiking necessities. The staff is knowledgeable and friendly. Downstairs from the visitors center is the **pack-up room,** accessible through the center when it's open and through an entry to the right of the center when it isn't. The pack-up room is open 24 hrs. and has publicly-accessible showers (25¢ for 3 min.), restrooms and a pay phone. **Tuckerman's Ravine Trail** begins just behind the center and leads all the way to the top of Mt. Washington, a climb which takes four to five hours each way. Non-climbers can take the **Mount Washington Auto Road** (466-3988), a paved and dirt road that leads motorists eight mi. to the summit. There they can get bumper stickers boasting "This Car Climbed Mt. Washington" and cruise around impressing easily awed folks. The road begins at Glen House, a short distance north of the visitors center on Rte. 16. ($12 per driver, $5 per passenger, ages 5-12 $3. Road open mid-May-mid-Oct. daily 7:30am-6pm.) Guided van tours which give a 30-minute presentation on the mountain's natural and human history and then take a 30-minute trip back down are also available. ($17, kids 5-12 $12.) On the summit you'll find an information center, a snack bar, a museum (466-3347), strong wind and the **Mt. Washington Observatory** (466-3388).

Just 1½ mi. from Mt. Washington's summit sits the **Lakes of the Clouds** AMC hut; the largest, highest and most popular of the AMC's huts. There is also sleeping space here in a **Refuge Room** for eight backpackers at $6 per person per night. Backpackers' reservations can be made from any hut, but no more than 48 hours in advance. For those who fancy a more leisurely climb, the **Hermit's Lake Shelter** skulks about two hours up the trail. The shelter, which has bathrooms but no shower, gives access to lean-tos and tent platforms ($7 per night; make reservations at the visitors center). **Carter Notch Hut** lies to the east of the visitors center, a 3.8-mi. hike up the Nineteen Mile Brook Trail.

If all the AMC facilities are booked, head to the **Berkshire Manor** in Gorham, 133 Main St. (466-2186). The rooms here are large, if a bit oddly decorated, and guests have access to a full kitchen and a living room. (Bathroom on hall; singles $20. Doubles $32.) *Much* more rustic is **Bowman's Base Camp (HI/AYH),** seven mi. west of Gorham on U.S. 2 (466-5130). An unfinished log cabin, the Base Camp has a kitchen and a phone. And mice. ($11, nonmembers $12; open Memorial Day-Columbus Day).

Rhode Island

Although Rhode Island—the "biggest little state in the Union"—is indeed smaller than some ranches in Texas and some icebergs in Antarctica, most Rhode Islanders are nonetheless proud of their non-conformist heritage. From founder Roger Williams, a religious outcast during colonial days, to Buddy Cianci, convicted felon and two-time mayor of Providence, spirited Rhode Island has always lured a different crowd.

Built upon seven hills, Providence was the model for Rome and boasts a posh East Side, a handsome State House, Autocrat Coffee Syrup, and ivy-towered Brown University. However, this capitol city has suffered recession and banking crises since *Newsweek* ranked it in its 1989 Top Ten Cities of the Year. As always, Newport remains a popular if touristy resort town, replete with spectacular mansions, a scenic harbor, and panoramic cliff walks.

Outside the two main cities, coastal Rhode Island and Providence Plantations (the official state name, the longest in the Union) is eminently explorable. Numerous small and provincial spots dot the shores down to Connecticut, while the inland roads are quiet, unpaved thoroughfares lined with family fruit stands, marshes, or ponds. Working ports derive their lifeblood from the fishblood of Narragansett Bay and Block Island Sound, and Block Island itself is a must-see.

Practical Information

Capital: Providence.

Rhode Island Division of Tourism, 7 Jackson Walkway, Providence 02903 (800-556-2484 or 277-2601). Open Mon.-Fri. 8:30am-4:30pm. **Department of Environmental Management** (State Parks), 9 Hayes St., Providence 02908 (277-2771). Open Mon.-Fri. 8:30am-4pm.

Time Zone: Eastern.

Postal Abbreviation: RI

Area Code: 401.

Sales Tax: 7%.

Block Island

Ten mi. southeast of Newport in the Atlantic, lovely **Block Island** has become an increasingly popular daytrip as tourists saturate Nantucket and Martha's Vineyard. The island is endowed with weathered shingles, quaint buildings, and serenity. One quarter of the island is protected open space; local conservationists hope to increase that to 50%. You can bike or hike four mi. north from Old Harbor to the **National Wildlife Refuge,** or bring a picnic, head due south from Old Harbor where the ferry lets you off, and hike two mi. south to the **Mohegan Bluffs.** Those who are adventurous, careful, and strong enough can wind their way down to the Atlantic waters 200 ft. below. The **Southeast Lighthouse,** high in the cliffs, has warned *Downeaster Alexas* since 1875; its beacon shines the brightest of any on the Atlantic coast.

Cycling is the ideal way to explore the tiny (7 mi. by 3 mi.) island. Try the **Old Harbor Bike Shop** (466-2029), to the left of where you exit the ferry. (10-speeds $3 per hr., $15 per day; single mopeds $10/$35 (license required). Car rentals $60 per day, 20¢ per mi. Must be 21 with credit card. Open daily 9am-7pm.)

No camping is allowed on the island, so make it a daytrip unless you're willing to shell out $50 or more for a room in a guest house. Most restaurants are close to the ferry dock in Old Harbor; several cluster at New Harbor one mi. inland.

The **Block Island Chamber of Commerce** (466-2982) advises at the ferry dock in Old Harbor Drawer D, Block Island 02807. (Open Mon.-Fri. 9am-3pm, Sat. 9am-1pm; mid-Oct.-mid-May Mon.-Fri. approximately 10am-2pm.) Rest stop information centers operated by the state of Rhode Island supply the free *Block Island Travel Planner.*

The **Interstate Navigation Co.** (783-4613) provides year-round ferry service to Block Island from Point Judith, RI, and summer service from Newport, RI, New London, CT, Providence, RI, and Montauk, NY. Leave from Point Judith if possible; it's the most frequent, cheapest, and shortest ride. (From Galilee State Pier in Point Judith: 8 per day in summer, 1 per day in winter, 70 min., $6.60, under 12 $3, cars $20 (reservations needed), bikes $1.75; from New London 1 per day, 2 hrs., $13.50; from Newport 1 per day, 2 hrs., $7.50.)

The **police** can be reached at 466-2622, the **Coast Guard** at 466-2086. Block Island's **post office** sorts on Ocean Ave; the **ZIP code** is 02807.

Newport

Before the American Revolution, Newport was one of the five largest towns in the American colonies, a thriving seaport grown fat on the spoils of the triangle trade of rum, slaves, and molasses. Sugar purchased in the West Indies was here converted to rum in one of Newport's 21 distilleries. Affluent vacationers of the mid-19th century made Newport a hoity-toity resort, where according to Mrs. Astor, money had the stench of newness until it was four generations old. The elite employed the country's best architects to confect elaborate neoclassical and baroque "summer cottages," huge mansions which were occupied for eight weeks or less per year. Crammed to the rafters with *objets d'art*, these "white elephants," as Henry James called them, signified the desperation of the *arrivistes* to purchase as much culture as money could buy.

Today, 12-meter racing yachts have replaced fishing boats, and fish comes swathed in sauce with a soupçon of something. There is a 25-year waiting period to get a slip at the marina in Newport, so plan ahead. Visit in the off-season or you will battle large crowds which funnel in during the summer for world-famous music festivals, national tennis competitions, and yachting.

Practical Information and Orientation

Emergency: 911.

Newport County Convention and Visitors Bureau, 23 America's Cup Ave. in the Newport Gateway Center (849-8048). Free maps. Open daily 9am-7pm; off-season 9am-5pm. Pick up *Best-Read Guide Newport* and *Newport this Week* for current listings. **Newport Harbor Center,** 365 Thames St. More pamphlets and public restrooms. For more information on Newport call 800-242-1510 or 800-242-1520.

Bonanza Buses: Newport Gateway Center, 23 America's Cup Ave. (846-1820), next to the visitors bureau. To Boston (10 per day; 11/2 hr.; $12.50).

Rhode Island Public Transit Authority (RIPTA): 1547 W. Main Rd. (847-0209 or 800-662-5088). Service to Providence (1 hr.) and points between on Rte. 114. Buses leave from the Newport Gateway Center. Take the "Newport Loop" bus (Memorial Day-Labor Day daily 10am-7pm) to main sights and shopping areas. Fare 85¢. Office open Mon.-Fri 5:15am-8pm, Sat. 6am-7pm.

Car Rental: Newport Ford, 312 W. Main Rd. (846-1411). Compact $33 per day. 100 free mi., 15¢ each additional mi. Must be 21 with $200 credit card deposit. Open Mon.-Fri. 8am-5pm.

Bike Rental: Ten Speed Spokes, 18 Elm St. (847-5609). Bikes of all speeds. 10-speeds $3 per hr., $15 per day. Mountain bikes $4 per hr., $20 per day. Must have credit card and photo ID. Open Mon.-Sat. 9:30am-5:30pm, Sun. noon-5pm.

Post Office: 320 Thames St., opposite Perry Hill Market (847-2329). Window service open Mon.-Fri. 7:30am-5:30pm, Sat. 9am-noon; lobby Mon.-Fri. 6am-7pm, Sat. 6am-5pm, Sun. 10am-5pm. **ZIP code:** 02840.

Area Code: 401.

Newport commands a boot-shaped peninsula on the southwest corner of Aquidneck Island in Narragansett Bay. The long span of the Newport Bridge (Rte. 138) connects the town to the smaller Conanicut Island to the west, which the Jamestown Bridge in turn connects to the mainland. From Providence, take I-195 east to Rte. 114 south via Mt. Hope Bridge (45 min.). From Boston, take Rte. 128 south to Rte. 24 south to either Rte. 114 south (called the West Main Rd. near Newport) or Rte. 138 south (the East Main Rd.). On summer weekends, beat the traffic by taking the back door into town: on Rte. 138 south, turn left onto Valley Rd. and continue past Newport Beach onto Memorial Blvd. (1½ hr.).

West Main Road becomes **Broadway** in town. **Thames Street,** the main drag on the waterfront, is pronounced as it looks, *not* like the river through London. Just about everything of interest in Newport is within walking distance; the mansions are about two mi. from downtown. Walking is preferable to fighting the hellish traffic. The convenient RIPTA "loop" buses (see above) access most out-of-the-way spots.

Accommodations and Camping

When staying in town, head for the visitors bureau (see Practical Information above) for guest house brochures and free phones from which to call them. Guest houses offer bed and continental breakfast with colonial-style intimacy. Those not fussy about sharing a bathroom or foregoing a sea view might find a double for $60. Singles are practically nonexistent. Be warned that many hotels and guest houses are booked solid two months in advance for summer weekends, and rates rise by $10 to $20. **Bed and Breakfasts of Rhode Island, Inc.** (941-0444) can make a reservation for you in Newport at an average rate of $65 per night.

Just outside Newport, in Middletown, is **Lindsey's Guest House,** 6 James St. (846-9386), offering a solid breakfast and good rates. (Rooms $60 weekends, $50 mid-week. $10 less off-season.) The cabins of the **Floradale Motor Court,** 985 E. Main Rd., Middletown 02840 (847-9726), on Rte. 138, are a cheap sleep from $30 weekdays and from $40 on weekends. (Open mid-April-mid-Nov.) **Mid-Island Motel,** 21 Smythe Ave., Middletown (846-4900), at the junction of Rte. 114 and 138, is the second cheapest at $45 weekdays, $55 weekends. **Camping** is actually available at **Fort Getty Recreation Area** (423-1363), on Conanicut Island, walking distance from the Fox Hill Salt Marsh, a good spot for birdwatching. (Showers and beach access; tent sites $17, hook-up $22.)

Food

Seafood is the recurring dream here, high prices the recurrent nightmare. The young crowd favors the **Corner Store and Deli,** 372 Thames St., a restaurant-deli-grocery store with sandwiches ($2.75-4.75), salads, and Italian specialties to go. (Open daily 7am-10pm.) By eating downtown, you'll help restaurant owners meet their high rents. Along the waterfront and wharves, sandwiches, salads, and pasta dishes make good deals. Sit at a booth and try Linda's Chili or Tish's Pea Soup at the **Franklin Spa,** 229 Franklin St. (Open Mon.-Sat. 6:30am-5pm, Sun. 6:30am-1pm.) Most of the town's restaurants, from quick pizza joints to expensive seafood bistros, grill and thrill on **Thames St.**

Dry Dock Seafood Restaurant, 448 Thames St. (847-3974), a few blocks south of the wharves. Small, cheap, homey seafood joint frequented by locals. Big, crispy fish and chips $5.25, lobster special $8.50. Burgers and fish sandwiches $2-8. Open Sun.-Thurs. 11am-10pm, Fri.-Sat. 11am-11pm.

The Island Omelette Shoppe, 1 Farewell St. (847-9389). Family-run diner feeding lots of local workers. Best breakfast in town; fast and cheap ($1-5). Open daily 6am-2pm.

Salas, 343 Thames St. (846-8772). Italian and Asian pasta with 8 sauces, in 3 serving sizes (1/2 lb. spaghetti with red clam sauce $4.50). Seafood $7-10; raw bar cheaper than most. Open daily 3-10pm.

Sights

In 1839, George Noble Jones of Savannah, GA, seeking to avoid the summer heat of the South, had a "summer cottage" built in Newport. Soon, Newport attracted the wealthiest families in the country, and each one had to build a bigger mansion than the last, thus originating the expression "keeping up with the Joneses." Many of these obscene displays of wealth are still occupied, but seven of the gaudiest are operated by the **Preservation Society of Newport** (847-1000). The **Newport Mansions** are the biggest draw here, and any visit to town should include a tour of at least one of them; they're one of the best lessons America offers on conspicuous consumption. The 172-room **The Breakers,** modeled on an Italian palace, is the largest cottage, built for Cornelius Vanderbilt in 1895. **Marble House** and **Rosecliff,** both on Bellevue Ave., furnished settings for the movie *The Great Gatsby.* The mansions open to the public are on the eastern edge of Newport, a two-mi. walk from Gateway center. You must pay admission just to get on the grounds; from the street you can't see much. (Most cottages open April-Nov. daily 10am-5pm, some open year-round. Tours leave every 10 min. at each house. Admission to The Breakers $7.50, others $6-7; kids 6-11 half-price.) For a windswept view of the mansions and a rose-framed panorama of the ocean, hike the **Cliff Walk,** a 3.5-mi. trail along the ocean (take a right off the east end of Memorial Blvd.; entrance is near Easton's Beach).

The jewel in Newport's crown of historic districts, **The Point** along Washington St. harborside, contains the famous **Hunter House** (1748) and six other homes of sea-captains and colonists of yore. **Newport Historical Society,** 82 Touro St. (846-0813), publishes its own detailed maps ($1), and leads two-hr. walking tours through the downtown area. (Tours mid-June-late Sept. Fri.-Sat. at 10am. Tour $5, children free.) The society's **museum** of Newport history is free.

Cycle the 10-mi. loop along **Ocean Drive** for breathtaking scenery. On the way you'll pass sprawling **Hammersmith Farm** (846-0420), the childhood home of Jackie Bouvier Kennedy Onassis and the "summer White House" in the early 60s. (Open June-Aug. daily 10am-7pm; April-May and Sept.-Oct. 10am-5pm; Nov. and March Sat.-Sun. only. Admission $6, kids $3.)

The colonial buildings downtown are more unassuming than the mansions, but provide wonderful windows on that epoch. The 1765 **Wanton-Lyman Hazard House,** 17 Broadway (846-3622), the oldest standing house in Newport, has been restored in different period styles. (Open mid-June-Aug. daily 10am-5pm. Admission $4.) The **White Horse Tavern,** on Marlborough St. (849-3600), the oldest drinking establishment in the country, dates from 1673, but the father of William Mayes, a notorious Red Sea pirate, first opened it as a tavern in 1687. (Beer $2-4.)

Since colonists fleeing Puritan Massachusetts founded Rhode Island for religious freedom, it comes as no surprise that the most interesting colonial buildings in town are houses of worship. The **Touro Synagogue,** 83 Touro St. (847-4794), a beautifully restored Georgian building and the oldest synagogue in the U.S., dates back to 1763. It was to the Newport congregation that George Washington wrote his famous letter promising the U.S. would give "to bigotry no sanction, to persecution no assistance." (Free tours every 1/2-hr. in summer. Open late June-Sept. Sun.-Fri. 10am-5pm; spring and fall Sun.-Fri. 1-3pm; winter Sun. 1-3pm and by appointment.) Towering **Trinity Church,** facing Thames St. in Queen Anne Sq. (846-0660), includes a pew reserved for George Washington back in the days when Newport strongheld for the Revolutionary army. (Open mid-June-Labor Day Mon.-Sat. 10am-4pm, Sun. noon-4pm. Free.) The Gothic **St. Mary's Church,** at Spring St. and Memorial Blvd., is the oldest Catholic parish in the state. Jacqueline Bouvier and John F. Kennedy were married here. (Open Mon.-Fri. 7-11am. Free.)

The Redwood Library and Athenaeum, on 50 Bellevue Ave. (847-0292), built in 1750, is the oldest continuously operating private library (and portrait gallery) in the country. (Open daily 9:30am-5:30pm; winter 9am-5:30pm.) The nearby **Newport Art Museum,** 76 Bellevue Ave. (847-0179), has a fine collection of U.S. Impressionist works collected in the 1864 Griswold House. Throughout the summer the museum holds musical picnics on its lawn. (Picnics free. Museum open Tues.-Sat. 10am-5pm, Sun. 1-5pm. Admission $2, seniors $1, kids free.)

No racqueteer should miss the **Tennis Hall of Fame,** 194 Bellevue Ave. (849-3990), built in 1880, in the Newport Casino. The first U.S. national championships were held here in 1881. The galaxy-renowned women's **Virginia Slims Tournament** takes place here, usually the second week in July, on the only competitive grass court in America. The Hall of Fame is also the summer home of the **U.S. Croquet Association**; you can watch a match just about any day.

Even those who don't sail should take some time to walk the plank onto vessels available for visit. Open to the public, the **Bannister's Wharf Marina** has housed the 12-meter yachts *Clipper, Independence, Courageous,* and *Gleam.* Check out the free *Newport This Week's Yachting & Recreation Guide* for a description of regattas and a calendar of events.

Enter through Gate 1 of the **U.S. Navy training center** on Coasters Harbor Island to view a different sort of sea power. Appearances to the contrary, tourism is not Newport's largest industry; the U.S. Navy is the town's largest employer. Here, you can tour the successors to the wooden and iron ships of John Paul Jones's day (tours May-Sept.

Sat.-Sun., 1-3pm; 841-3538). Visit the **Naval War College Museum** (841-4052) to sea interesting exhibits on naval history. (Open June-Sept. Mon.-Fri. 10am-4pm, Sat.-Sun. noon-4pm; Oct.-May Mon.-Fri. 10am-4pm. Free.)

After a few hours of touring Newport, you might think of escaping to the shore; unfortunately, the beaches crowd as frequently as the streets. The most popular of the shores is **First Beach,** or Easton's Beach, on Memorial Blvd., with its wonderful old beach houses and carousel. (Open Memorial Day-Labor Day Mon.-Fri. 9am-9pm, Sat.-Sun. 10am-9pm. Parking $5, weekends $8.) Those who prefer hiking over dunes to building sandcastles should try **Fort Adams State Park** (847-2400), south of town on Ocean Dr., 21/2 mi. from Gateway Center, with showers, picnic areas, and two fishing piers. (Entrance booth open daily 7:30am-4pm. Park closes 11pm-6am. Parking $4.) Other good beaches line Little Compton, Narragansett, and the shore between Watch Hill and Point Judith. For more details, consult the free *Ocean State Beach Guide,* available at the visitors center (see Practical Information above).

Entertainment

In July and August, lovers of classical, folk, and jazz each have a festival to call their own. The **Newport Jazz Festival** is the oldest and best-known jazz festival in the world; Duke Ellington, Count Basie, and many other young jazz noblemen made their break here. In 1993, bring your beach chairs and coolers to **Fort Adams State Park** on August 14 and 15. For info, write JVC Jazz Festival, P.O. Box 605, Newport 02840 (after May 847-3700; tickets $28.50, parking $6). The **Newport Music Festival** (June-July 849-0700) in mid-July attracts pianists, violinists, and other classical musicians from around the world, presenting them in the ballrooms and on the lawns of the mansions for two weeks of concerts. For info write Newport Music Festival, P.O. Box 3300, Newport 02840. Tickets are available through Ticketron (800-382-8080). In August, you might chorus with folksingers Joan Baez and the Indigo Girls at the **Newport Folk Festival** (June-Aug. 847-3709), which runs two days, noon to dusk, rain or shine. (Tickets $25.)

Newport's nightlife is easy to find but relatively subdued. Down by the water at **Pelham East,** at the corner of Thames and Pelham (849-9460), they tend to play straight rock 'n' roll. (Live music nightly. Open daily noon-1am. Weekend cover $5.) Those longing for disco should visit **Maximillian's,** 108 William St. 2nd floor (849-4747), a popular video-enhanced dance club across from the Tennis Hall of Fame. (Open Tues.-Sun. 9pm-1am. Cover Sun. and Tues.-Thurs. $3, Fri.-Sat. $5.) The **Black Pearl Pub** (and café in good weather) on Bannister's Wharf is reserved and elegant. (Open daily 11:30am-1am.)

Those seeking still more refined recreation should see a production by one of Newport's fine theatrical companies. Contrary to its name, the **Rhode Island Shakespeare Theater** (849-7892) actually stages more American than Elizabethan drama each season. (Shows Thurs.-Sun. 8pm, at various playhouses in Newport; tickets $12-15.)

Balls whiz by at 188 mph, athletes a good deal more slowly, at the **Jai Alai Fronton,** 150 Admiral Kalbfus Rd. (849-5000; 800-556-6900 outside RI), at the base of the Newport Bridge off Rte. 138. The place, one of the few in the country where the sport—and gambling on it—is legal, has impressive facilities. (Season May 5-Oct. 9 Mon.-Sat. at 7pm, matinees Mon. and Sat. at noon. Seats $2-3.50, standing room $1.)

Near Newport: Conanicut

On the western side of the Newport Bridge lies sleepy, unassuming **Conanicut Island,** with **Jamestown** at its heart. This mercifully undeveloped town consists of two streets dotted with fishing supply stores and craft shops. In the center of the island, the marvelous 1787 **Jamestown Windmill,** on North Rd., sits on a hill that affords a good view of the neighboring wildlife preserve where you may spot snowy egrets and blue herons. (Windmill open mid-June-Sept. Sat.-Sun. 1-4pm. Free.) Picnic or scuba dive at **Fort Wetherhill,** on Fort Wetherhill Rd. on the island's southeast shore (open 8am-11pm). The cozy and comfortable **Oyster Bar,** 22 Narragansett Ave., serves a mean chowder and local seafood at great prices ($4-11.50). The **East Ferry Market,** 47 Conanicut Ave., has the best coffee in the state, as well as sandwiches and pastries. (Open summer daily 6:30am-7pm; off-season Mon.-Fri. 6:30am-5pm, Sat. 6:30am-3pm, Sun. 8am-3pm.) In August, the Jamestown Yacht Club hosts the **Fool's Rules Regatta** (423-1492) in Potters Cove. Contestants must construct a sailboat from non-standard materials in two hours and then coax it along the 500-yd. course. Consult the free *This Week in South County* for information on other festivities.

Vermont

Though insulated and isolated by the luxuriant Green Mountain range that dominates the state, Vermonters from every sparsely settled hollow have never shied from public dissent. They voice their opinions loudly and proudly, from conservatism (only Vermont and Maine voted against Franklin Roosevelt in all four elections) to liberalism (Burlington's socialist mayor Bernie Sanders has taken his views all the way to an Independent seat in the U.S. House of Representatives).

Several decades ago, many dissatisfied young urbanites headed to Vermont seeking its promise of peace and serenity. Needing a way to support themselves, these ex-urbanites-cum-granolas chose to live off nature by packaging and marketing it: organic food stores and mountaineering shops shot up faster than you can say "Ben and Jerry's." In the 1980s it became evident that a less than benign wave of urban fugitives was necessary to support these nature-loving stores, seemingly creating a vicious circle. But Vermonters have responded to the influx of BMWs with anti-littering legislation and prohibition of billboards. Should tourism continue to threaten this pristine landscape, the protest of Vermonters, no doubt, will be heard.

Practical Information

Capital: Montpelier.

Vermont Travel Division, 134 State St., Montpelier 05602 (828-3236; open Mon.-Fri. 8am-4:30pm; longer hours during fall foliage), or the **Chamber of Commerce,** P.O. Box 37, Montpelier 05602, on Granger Rd., I-89 exit 7 in Berlin (223-3443; open Mon.-Fri. 9am-5pm), for info on lodging, attractions, dining and camping. **Department of Forests, Parks and Recreation,** 103 S. Main St., Waterbury 05676 (244-8711; open Mon.-Fri. 8am-4:30pm); **U.S. Forest Supervisor,** Green Mountains National Forest, 151 West St., P.O. Box 519, Rutland 05702 (773-0300; open Mon.-Fri. 8am-4:30pm); and **District Ranger,** Green Mountains National Forest RFD#4, Middlebury 05753 (388-4362), or RD#1, P.O. Box 108, Rochester 05767 (767-4261) for the scoop on exploring the great outdoors on Federal and State-owned lands, respectively. **Travel Division Fall Foliage Hotline** for fall colors info (828-3239). **Vermont Snowline** (229-0531), all day Nov.-May on snow conditions.

Public Transport: Vermont Transit Lines, 135 Saint Paul St., Burlington 05401 (864-6811 or 800-451-3292 within New England, for info).

Time Zone: Eastern. **Postal Abbreviation:** VT

Sales Tax: 5%.

Skiing

Twenty-four downhill resorts and 47 cross-country trail systems lace Vermont. For a free winter attractions packet, call the Vermont Travel Division (see Practical Information above), or write **Ski Vermont,** 134 State St., Montpelier 05602. Ask about the "Ski Vermont Classics" program and the "Vermont Sunday Take-Off" package. Also contact **Vermont Ski Areas Association,** 26 State St., Montpelier 05601 (223-2439; open Mon.-Fri. 8am-4:30pm).

Vermont's famous downhill ski resorts offer a great range of terrain and accommodations, including cheap dorms. Some better resorts include: **Killington** (773-1300 or 800-621-6867; 107 trails, 18 lifts, 6 mountains, and the most extensive snowmaking system in the world); **Stratton** (297-2200 or 800-843-6867; area lodging 824-6915; 92 trails, 12 lifts); **Sugarbush** (583-2381; lodging 800-537-8427; 80 trails, 16 lifts, 2 mountains); **Stowe** (253-8521; lodging 800-247-8693; 44 trails, 10 lifts); and **Jay Peak** (800-451-4449; 37 trails, 6 lifts). Cross-country resorts include the **Trapp Family Lodge,** Stowe (253-8511; lodging 800-826-7000; 60 mi. of trails); **Mountain Meadows,** Killington (757-7077; 25 mi.); **Woodstock** (457-2114; 47 mi.); and **Sugarbush-Rossignol** (583-2301 or 800-451-4320; 30 mi. of trails.).

Brattleboro

Southeastern Vermont is often accused of living too much in its colonial past, but Brattleboro, a favorite destination for peregrinating hippies, seems to be more a captive of the Age of Aquarius than the War for Independence. Indian prints are ubiquitous. The smell of patchouli wafts through the air. Craft and food cooperatives abound. The biggest sign in the window of the shoe store on Main St. reads "Birkenstock Repair." Nature worship peaks in the fall when the city swells with an influx of tourists and when residents and visitors alike head for the hills to rollick in the resplendent foliage.

Brattleboro chills at the confluence of the West and Connecticut Rivers, both of which can be explored by **canoe**. Rentals are available at **Connecticut River Safari** (257-5008 or 254-3908) on Putney Rd. just across the West River Bridge. They will also transport canoes to other rivers in New England. (Open mid-June to Labor Day daily 8am-8pm, 2-hr. minimum $8; $12 per 1/2-day, $18 per day. 2 days—not necessarily consecutive—$28; longer packages available.)

The **Windham Gallery,** 69 Main St. (257-1881), hosts local art openings the first Friday of every month as well as poetry readings and discussions by artists about their work. (Open Fri.-Sat. noon-8pm, Sun. and Wed.-Thurs. noon-4pm, $1 suggested donation.) For a bit of local color, visit the **Brightside Boutique** (257-3038, 24 High St.), which sells tie-dye shirts and woven clothing made from organic fibers. (Open Mon.-Fri. 10am-5:30pm, Sat. 10am-6:30pm, Sun. 11am-4pm.)

Foliage vultures shouldn't miss **Brattleboro Music Center's New England Bach Festival** (257-2453). Internationally renowned, the festival runs annually from early October through early November, featuring vocal and instrumental soloists. Thousands cram the common for **Apple Days,** the last weekend (Thurs.-Sun.) in September. In March over 3000 gather in nearby Putney for the **Sap Gathering Contest** (387-5852).

Just across Putney Rd. from the Connecticut River Safari is the **Marina Bar and Grill** (257-7563). The Marina overlooks the West River, offering a cool breeze and a beautiful view. Try the chicken with fusilli or the eggplant parmesan, both $5.75. (Open Wed.-Sat. 4pm-midnight, Sun 11am-10pm. Summer lunch Fri.-Sat. 11:30am-3pm.) The **Common Ground,** 25 Eliot St. (257-0855), where the town's laid-back "granolas" cluster, supports organic farmers and cottage industries. It features a wide range of affordable veggie dishes. You can get soup, salad, bread, and beverage for $3.85, good ol' PB&J for $2.70. For dinner, try a square meal in a round bowl. (Open Mon. and Wed.-Thurs. 11:30am-8pm, Fri.-Sat. 11:30am-9pm, Sun. 10:30am-8pm.) The **Backside Café,** 24 High St. (257-5056), serves delicious food in an artsy loft with rooftop dining. For dinner, create your own burrito ($4.75) or Chile Rellenos (2 for $5.75). (Open Mon.-Fri. 7:30am-4pm Sat. 8am-3pm, Sun. 10am-3pm; for dinner Tues.-Sat. 5-9pm. In winter, no lunch on Fri.) For locally-grown fruits, vegetables, and cider, go to the **farmers markets** on the Town Common, Main St. (June 12-Sept. 11 Wed. 10am-2pm), or on Western Ave. near Creamery Bridge (May 11-Oct. 12 Sat. 9am-2pm). Visit the **Latchis Grille** (254-4747, 6 Flat St.) and sample some beer made by the **Windham Brewery** right on the premises (7 oz. sampler $1.50, 12 oz. Pilsner $2). Free tours of the brewery Thursdays at 6pm. (Grille open Mon.-Sat. 11:30am-9pm, Sun. brunch 10am-2pm.) **Mole's Eye Café** (257-0771), at the corner of High and Main St., has rock, R&B, blues, and reggae bands on Wednesday, Friday, and Saturday nights at 9pm. (Open daily 11:30am-midnight or 1am. Light meals about $5. Cover Fri.-Sat. $3. Open mike Thurs. 8:30pm.)

Next door to the Latchis Grille, the renovated Art-Deco **Latchis Hotel** (254-6300), on the corner of Flat and Main St. downtown, has nice rooms at decent prices. (Singles $38-52. Doubles $46-62.) The **West Village,** 480 Western Ave. (254-5610), is about three mi. out of town on Rte. 9 in West Brattleboro. Although happy to have one-night guests, West Village caters to the weekly client, taking reservations no more than one week in advance. (Singles with kitchenette and microwave $30. Doubles with kitchenette and microwave $35, weekly $150.) Somewhat closer to town is the newly renovated **Days Inn** (254-4583) on Putney Rd. past the Marina. (Double-bed $39, 2 double beds $55. $6 each additional adult, roll-away bed $6. Free continental breakfast.) Ramble north on Rte. 30 half an hour to find the **Vagabond Hostel (HI/AYH)** (874-4096) outside the town of East Jamaica. The Vagabond is very close to the summer offerings of the Stratton, Mt. Snow, and Bromley ski areas. (Open May 15-Nov.16. $12 members, $15 nonmembers.) **Fort Dummer State Park,** (254-2610, 2 mi. south on U.S. 5, turn left on Fairground Ave. just before the I-91 interchange, and follow it around to South Main St.), has campsites with fireplaces, picnic tables, and bathroom facilities, and one lean-to with disabled access. (Tentsites $7.50. Lean-tos $12. Firewood $2 per armload. Hot showers 25¢. Reservations accepted up to 21 days in advance; $3, nonrefundable, min. stay 2 nights. Open May 24-Labor Day.) **Molly Stark State Park** (464-5460) is 15 mi. west of town on Rte. 9. (24 tentsites, $7.50 each. 10 lean-tos, $12 each; 9 motor home sites without hookups, $7.50 each. Hot showers 25¢. Reservations $3, minimum of 3 days in advance. Open Memorial Day-Columbus Day.)

Amtrak's (800-835-8725) "Montrealer" train from New York City and Springfield stops in Brattleboro behind the museum. Trains go once daily to Montréal and to New York and Washington DC. Arrange tickets and reservations at **Lyon Travel,** 10 Elliot St. (254-6033; open Mon.-Fri. 9am-5pm). **Greyhound** and **Vermont Transit** (254-6066) stop in the parking lot behind the Texaco station at the junction of U.S. 5, Rte. 9, and I-91 on Putney Rd. (Open Mon.-Thurs. 8am-5pm, Fri. 8am-7pm, Sat. 8am-12:15pm, Sun. 10:30am-12:15pm, 2-3:30pm, and 6-7pm.) Brattleboro is on Vermont Transit's Burlington-New York City route (3 per day, $35). Other destinations include Springfield, MA (3 per day, $12) and White River Junction (3 per day, $12), with connections to Montpelier, Waterbury, Burlington, and Montréal. To get to downtown from the Vermont Transit station, cross Putney Rd. and go a short distance toward town to the **Brattleboro Town Bus Station** (257-1761). Buses run down Putney Rd. to Main St. and then up High St. to West Brattleboro. (Buses Mon.-Fri. 7am-5pm. Fare 75¢, students 25¢.)

The **Chamber of Commerce,** 180 Main St. (254-4565) will barrage you with countless brochures, among them the *Brattleboro Main Street Walking Tour.* Seasonal events are also posted. (Open Mon.-Fri. 8am-5pm.) In summer, information booths are open on the **Town Common** off Putney Rd. (257-1112), and on Western Ave. (257-4801), just beyond the historic **Creamery Bridge** built in 1879. (Putney Rd. booth open summer Mon.-Fri. 9am-6pm. During fall foliage and peak summer months open weekends 9am-6pm. Western Ave. booth open summer Thurs.-Sun. 10am-6pm.)

Brattleboro's **ZIP code** is 05301; The **area code** is 802.

Northern Vermont

Burlington

Burlington has taken the oxymoronic expression "middle-class hippie" and made it not just a reality but a way of life. Familiar 60s platitudes such as "Arms are for Hugging," once the rallying-cries of sit-ins, have become slogans for "stuck-ons," the ubiquitous bumperstickers on Hondas and Volvos. Downtown Burlington itself is full of quaint, store-lined streets, but supermarkets, fast-food restaurants, and chain stores lurk in the suburbs. Local colleges—the University of Vermont—UVM—and Champlain College, among others—endow the city with the swank and smarm of youth. It's difficult to get to the heart behind Burlington's façade, but if you can find it (talk to its citizens; they know where it is) you'll have something worth keeping.

Practical Information

Emergency: 911.

Tourist Information: Lake Champlain Regional Chamber of Commerce, 209 Battery St. (863-3489), right next to the ferry pier. Provides maps of the Burlington Bike Path and parks, as well as numerous other brochures on local attractions, B&Bs and restaurants. Open Mon.-Fri. 8:30am-5pm, Sat.-Sun. 10am-2pm; late Oct.-early June Mon.-Fri. 8:30am-5pm. More centrally located is the **Church St. Marketplace Information Gallery,** on the corner of Church and Bank. Open May 15-June Mon.-Sat. 11am-4pm, July-mid-Oct. daily 11am-5pm.

Amtrak: 29 Railroad Ave., Essex Jct. (800-872-7245 or 879-7298), 5 mi. east of Rte. 15 from the center of Burlington. To Montréal: ($18) and to New York ($58, 15% discount for seniors, children 1/2-price). Open daily 6am-9pm. Bus downtown every 1/2-hr., 75¢.

Buses: Vermont Transit, 135 Saint Paul St. (864-6811), at Main St. Connections to Boston ($41), Montréal ($16), White River Junction ($13.80), Middlebury ($6.85), Bennington ($17.55), Montpelier ($7), and Albany ($30). Connections made with Greyhound. Ameripasses accepted. Open Mon.-Thurs. and Sat. 7am-8:30pm, Fri. and Sun. 7am-11:30pm.

Public Transport: Chittenden County Transit Authority (CCTA), (864-0211). Frequent, reliable service. Downtown hub at Cherry and Church St. Connections with Shelburne and other outlying areas. Buses operate Mon.-Sat. 5:45am-10:30pm, depending on routes; generally leave at a quarter to and a quarter past. Fare 75¢, seniors and disabled 35¢, under 18 50¢, under 5 free. **Special Services Transportation Agency** (658-5817),supplies information and advice about disabled travel.

Taxi: Yellow Cab, 864-7411. $1.20 per mi. **Checker Taxi,** 864-7474, is also worth checking out for transport.

Bike Rental: Ski Rack, 85 Main St. (658-3313). Single speed cruiser ($5 per hr., $18 per day, $66 per week), road bike ($5/$20/$85), mountain bike ($6/$22/$100). Helmet and lock included. Bike repairs guaranteed 48 hrs. or less; minor repairs while you wait. Also rent in-line skates ($6 per 3 hrs., $10 per day), helmet and pads included. Open Mon.-Thurs. 9am-7pm, Fri. 9am-9pm, Sat. 9am-6pm, Sun. 11am-5pm.

Help Lines: Women's Rape Crisis Center, 863-1236. **Crises Services of Chittenden County,** 656-3587.

Pharmacy: Price-Chopper, 555 Shelburne Rd. (U.S. 7), 2 mi. south of downtown (864-8505). Grocery store and pharmacy. Open daily 24 hrs.

Post Office: 11 Elmwood Ave. (863-6033), at Pearl St. Open Mon.-Fri. 8am-5pm, Sat. 9am-noon. **ZIP code:** 05401.

Area Code: 802.

Accommodations, Camping, and Food

The Chamber of Commerce has complete accommodations listings for the area. Bed & Breakfasts are generally found in the outlying suburbs. Reasonably priced hotels and guest houses pepper Shelburne Rd. south of downtown. Three mi. from downtown, **Mrs. Farrell's Home Hostel (HI/AYH),** 27 Arlington, off Heineburg (865-3730). Mrs. Farrell, has six beds: four in a clean, comfortable basement and two on a screened-in porch. Ubiquitous signs remind you of the do's and don'ts of the place. (Members $10.25. Nonmembers $12.25. Linen $2.75. Accessible by public transport.) Curfew is 10pm. Reservations are required. Getting hold of the owner is difficult—try calling between 7 and 8am and 5 and 7pm. Close to downtown is **Howden Cottage,** 32 N. Champlain (864-7198). A local artist will rent you a slope-ceilinged room and bake muffins for your continental breakfast in this ever-so-charming B&B. (Mid-May-mid-Oct. singles $39, doubles $49, off-season singles $35, doubles $45. Reservations strongly recommended; deposit for half of expected stay by mail only.) **North Beach Campsites,** Institute Rd. (862-0942), is only 11/2 mi. north of town on North Ave., along Lake Champlain. (Open May 15-Oct. 1. Sites $10, $15 with electricity, $17 with full hookup. Showers 25¢, beach free, but closes at 9pm.) Take the CCTA North Ave. bus leaving from the main city terminal on Saint Paul St. **Shelburne Campground,** Shelburne Rd. (985-2540), one mi. north of the center of Shelburne and five mi. south of Burlington, offers a pool, laundry facilities, and free showers. Buses en route to

Shelburne South stop right next to the campground. (Open May-Oct. Sites for 2 people $15, $17-21 with varying degrees of hookup, $1 each additional person.)

Henry's Diner, 155 Bank St. (862-9010), has been the place to meet the locals and eat good, inexpensive food since 1925. (Sandwiches $2-4, full meals $5-10. Open Mon. 7am-2:30pm, Tues.-Thurs. 6:30am-4pm, Fri.-Sat. 6:30am-8pm, Sun. 8am-2pm.) A must-visit is **Noonies Deli,** at 131 Main St. (658-3354; also at 142 N. Winooski). Fill up on their huge sandwiches, including the delicious vegetarian on home-made bread ($4-5). (Open Mon.-Thurs. 7am-9pm, Fri. 7am-10pm, Sat. 8am-10pm, 10:30am-9pm.) Catch their coffee house (Sept.-May Fri. 8pm-midnight). Loads of booze and fun can be found at the **Vermont Pub and Brewery,** 144 College St. (865-0500), at Saint Paul's, which offers affordable sandwiches, delicious homemade beers, and English pub favorites like cornish *pasties*-similar to a pot pie ($5). Should you want to learn more about Keller Original Vermont Lager, the brewers and publicans would be happy to escort you on a brewery tour. (Open Mon.-Fri. and Sun. 11:30am-12:30am, Fri.-Sat. 11:30am-1:30am. Free tours Wed. at 8pm and Sat. at 4pm. Others by appointment. Live entertainment Thurs.-Sat. 9:30pm, live Jazz Sun. 4:30pm.) A fine wine and cheese feast can be purchased at the **Cheese Outlet,** 400 Pine St. (863-3968 or 800-447-1205). Purchase wine for as little as $5 in this strong-smelling warehouse. (Open Mon.-Sat. 9am-7pm, Sun. noon-5pm.) Just next door, the **Olive Branch Bakery** 398 Pine St., (658-1882) serves up outstanding peaces of bread and pastries. Try the Vermont Cheddar Bread ($2.25), a calzone ($2.25), or a knish ($1.75). No seating. (Open Mon.-Sat. 9am-7pm, Sun. noon-5pm.)

Sights and Entertainment

With its sprawling, low-lying suburbs, Burlington might not look like a cultural mecca. However, the city still manages to take advantage of its scenic location along Lake Champlain, its artistic community, and its status as the largest city in the midst of ruralia. **Church Street Marketplace** downtown is a popular pedestrian mall; this historic district serves as a shopping center for modern northern Vermont and displays and sells the works of local artists. The history-inclined also should stroll through Victorian **South Willard Street,** which now houses Champlain College, and the campus of the **University of Vermont** (656-3480), founded in 1797. **City Hall Park,** in the heart of downtown, and **Battery Street Park,** in the pancreas of downtown on Lake Champlain, are beautiful places to relax and study the scenery.

Summer culture vultures won't want to miss the many festivities Burlington offers: the **Champlain Shakespeare Festival** in mid-July, the **Vermont Mozart Festival** (862-7352) in July and early August, the **Champlain Valley Folk Festival** in August (863-5966), and the **Discover Jazz Festival** (863-8778) in early to mid-June. The Flynn Theatre Box Office, 153 Main St. (863-5966), handles sales for the Mozart and jazz performances. (Open Mon.-Fri. 10am-5pm, Sat. 10am-1pm.) The **Burlington Community Boathouse**, at the base of College St. at Lake Champlain (865-3377), is a good place to go if you're looking to get out on the water. The Boathouse rents 13-ft. laser sailboats ($16 per hr., $40 per 4 hrs., $64 per 8 hrs.; rates 25% higher Sat.-Sun.) as well as 19-ft. Rhodes sailboats ($24/$60/$95; same rate hike), and rowboats ($5 per hr.). Classes in sailing, sculling, canoeing and kayaking throughout the summer. (Open June-Sept., 24 hrs.; open for rentals Mon.-Fri. 11am-7pm, Sat.-Sun. 9am-7pm.) **Fishing licenses** are available at, among other places, **Woolworth's,** 37 Church St. in the marketplace, downstairs in the sporting goods department (863-2592). (Non-residents $18 per 3 days, $35 per yr.; residents $18 per season; other packages available.) (Open Mon.-Sat. 9am-9pm, Sat.-Sun. noon-5pm.)

Near Burlington

Seven mi. south of Burlington in **Shelburne** is the **Shelburne Museum** (985-3346), which houses one of the best collections of Americana in the country. Beside 35 buildings transported from all over New England, 45-acre Shelburne has a covered bridge from Cambridge, a steamboat and a lighthouse from Lake Champlain, and a bit of a local railroad. Don't miss the Degas, Cassatt, Manet, Monet, Rembrandt and Whistler paintings. Tickets are valid for two days; you'll need both to cover the mile-long exhibit. (Open mid-May-mid-Oct. daily 9am-5pm. Admission $15, students $9, ages 6-14 $6, under 6 free.) Five mi. farther south on U.S. 7, the **Vermont Wildflower Farm** (425-3500), has a seed shop and 61/2 acres of wildflower gardens. (Open April-mid-Oct. daily 10am-5pm. Admission April-May free; July-Oct. $3, seniors $2.50, under 12 free.)

Northeast of Burlington on Rte. 127 is the **Ethan Allen Homestead** (865-4556). In the 1780s, Allen, who forced the surrender of Fort Ticonderoga and helped establish the state of Vermont, built his cabin in what is now the Winooski Valley Park. A multimedia show and tour give insight into the hero and his era. (Open mid-May-mid-June Tues.-Sun. 1-5pm; mid-June-Labor Day Mon.-Sat. 10am-5pm, Sun. 1-5pm; Labor Day-late Oct. daily 1-5pm. Admission $3.50, seniors $3, kids 5-17 $2, under 5 free.)

Ferries crisscross the **Lake Champlain,** a 100-mi.-long lake between Vermont's Green Mountains and New York's Adirondacks, often referred to as "Vermont's West Coast." The **Lake Champlain Ferry** (864-9804), at the bottom of King St., will ship you across the lake and back from Burlington's King St. Dock to Port Kent, NY. (Mid-June-mid-Aug. daily 7:15am-7:45pm, 14 per day; mid-May-mid-June 8am-6:30pm, 8 per day; Sept.-mid-Oct. 8am-5:30pm, 8-11 per day. Fare $3, ages 6-12 $1, with car $12. Crossing time 1 hr.) You can also take a ferry from Grand Isle to Plattsburg, NY, or go 14 mi. south of Burlington and take one from Charlotte, VT, to Essex, NY (either fare $1.75, ages 6-12 50¢, with car $6.75). The Grand Isle Ferry is the only one of the three to run year-round. The **Spirit of Ethan Allen** scenic cruise (862-9685) departs from Burlington's Perkins Pier at the bottom of Maple St. The boat cruises along the Vermont coast, giving passengers a close-up view of the famous Thrust Fault, invisible from land. (Open late May-mid-Oct. Cruises daily at 10am, noon, 2 and 4pm. Admission $7.50, ages 5-11 $3.50. Call about the more costly Captain's Dinner and Sunset Cruises.) The campsite near the peak of nearby **Mt. Philo State Park** (425-2390) affords great views of the environs. (Open Memorial Day-Columbus Day daily 10am-sunset. Campsites $7.50. Lean-tos $12. Admission $1.50. Ages 4-13 $1.) Take the **Vermont Transit** bus from Burlington heading south along U.S. 7 toward Vergennes. There's a sign on the left for the park before you're out of Charlotte. Twisting U.S. 2 cuts through the center of the lake by hopping from the mainland to Grand Isle, then north to North Hero Island and up into Québec, Canada.

Several state campgrounds speckle the islands, and much of the surrounding land is wilderness. The marsh to the north is protected in the **Missiquoi National Wildlife Refuge.** Camp at **Burton Island State Park** (524-6353), accessible only by ferry (8:30am-6:30pm) from Kill Kare State Park, 35 mi. north of Burlington and 31/2 mi. southwest of St. Albans off U.S. 7. The camp has 46 lean-to and tent sites ($15.50 and $11 respectively, $3 per additional person in tent, $4 in lean-to). **Grand Isle** also has a state park with camping (372-4300), just off U.S. 2 north of Keeler Bay. (Sites $11, lean-tos $15.50. Open late May-mid-Oct.)

Montpelier

Montpelier (pop. 8200) is the smallest state capital in the union and allows the maintenance of an intimate small-town timbre (the whole place shuts down on Saturdays). The city is also the proud home of the **New England Culinary Institute,** 250 Main St. (223-6324); sample first-year students' innovations (such as roast loin of pork with maple mustard glaze and cranapple compote) at the **Elm Street Café,** 38 Elm St. (223-3188). (Dinner entrées $9-11. Lunch specials under $5. Open Mon.-Fri. 7-10am, 11:30am-1:30pm and 5:30-9pm, Sat. 8-10am, 11am-1:30pm, and 5:30-9pm.) **Tubbs Restaurant,** 24 Elm St. (229-9202), features the French cuisine of second-year students in the now-elegant confines of the original Montpelier jailhouse. (Lunch entrées $3-8; dinner entrées $12-18. Open Mon.-Fri. 11:30am-2pm and 6-9:30pm, Sat. 6-9:30pm.) The school's bakery/café, **La Brioche** (229-0443), recently moved to the City Center on the corner of State and Main, offers delicious pastries and cakes, as well as fresh-baked bread and homemade pâtés. (Open Mon.-Fri. 7:30am-7pm, Sat. 8am-5:30pm, Sun. 8am-3pm.)

Up Main St. on Country Rd. oozes the **Morse Farm** (223-2740 or 800-242-2740), a working maple syrup farm that stays open year-round. Maples are tapped and the sugarhouse operates in early spring. The farm gives a splendid panoramic view of the hills during foliage. (Open summer daily 8am-6pm, off-season 8am-5pm.)

The **Vermont Travel Division,** 134 State St. (828-3236; open Mon.-Fri. 7:45am-4:30pm, Sat. 9:30am-4pm, longer hours in fall, closed Sat. late Oct.-June), can provide you with a list of restaurants and accommodations in the area, a helpful town map, and tourist info about the whole state. Consult their kiosk on the neighboring block in front of a grey church when the travel division is closed. **The Green Mountain Club** (244-7037) headquarters used to be in Montpelier, but they've since moved to Waterbury Center, near Stowe along Rte. 100. Founded in 1910, the GMC built and maintains the **Long Trail,** the oldest long-distance hiking trail in the U.S. Call or write RR1, Box 650, Rte. 100 Waterbury Center VT 05677.

Vermont Transit is behind Chittenden Bank at 112 State St. (223-7112). Daily buses go to: Boston ($34); New York City ($58); White River Junction ($9); Waterbury ($3); and Burlington ($7). VT also offers service to Montréal and Portland, ME. (Open Mon.-Fri. 8am-6:30pm, Sat. 8am-4pm, Sun. noon-4pm.)

Montpelier's **ZIP code** is 05602; the **area code** is 802.

Stowe

Between Montpelier and Burlington lies **Stowe,** beautiful and serene in summer, bustling among the blizzards in winter as one of the east's ski capitals, with four fine downhill skiing areas: **Stowe Mountain Resort** (253-7311 or 800-253-4754), formerly Mount Mansfield (the highest peak in Vermont, at 4393 ft.), **Smuggler's Notch** (664-8851 or 800-451-8752), **Bolton Valley,** (434-2131), and **Sugarbush,** (583-2381). The **Trapp Family Lodge** (yes, *the* Trapp family of *Sound of Music* fame) Luce Hill Rd. (253-8511), offers the area's best cross-country skiing. Skiing is expensive; a one-day lift ticket at any of these areas costs nearly $40. A better bet might be the **Ski Vermont's Classics** program. A three-day $99 lift ticket (available at participating slopes) allows you to ski at any number of resorts in the area; for more info contact the **Stowe Area Association** (see accommodations, below). **AJ's Ski and Sports** at the base of Mountain Rd. (253-4593) will have all new skis and step-in boots for the 1992-93 season (skis, boots, and poles: downhill $16 per day, 2 days $28; cross-country $12/$20), and snowboards (call for prices). Reserve equipment five days in advance and get 20% off. (Open Thanksgiving-Easter daily 8am-6pm; off season Mon.-Fri. 10am-6pm; Sat.-Sun. 9am-6pm.)

In summer, Stowe's frenetic pace drops off—and so do its prices. Rent **mountain and road bikes** at **Stowe Mountain Sports**, on Mountain Rd. (253-4896), which rents one- and 10-speeds ($4 per hr., $8 per ½-day, $12 per day) and mountain bikes ($6 per hr., $14 per 1/2-day, $20 per day). Those interested in checking out the area's excellent **fly-fishing** should head to the **Fly Rod Shop,** three mi. south of Stowe on Rte. 100 (253-7347). The shop rents fly rods and reels ($8 per day), and rods with spinning reels ($4 per day). Watch the owner tie a fly or two, or call about fly-tying classes in winter (Wed. 5:30-7pm). April-Oct. free fly-fishing classes on the pond next door. Fishing licenses available (non-residents $18 per 3 days, $35 for season; residents $18 for season.) If you're looking to canoe on the nearby Lamoille River, **Umiak**, 1880 Mountain Rd. in the Gale Farm Center (253-2317), is the place to go. The store (whose name is the Inuit word for "kayak") rents *umiaks* and canoes in the summer (weekends $30 per day, weekdays $24; ½-day $20 daily). In the winter try on a pair of snowshoes ($16 per day, $10 per 4 hrs.) or their metal-edged cross-country skis for off-trail use ($16 per day, $12 per 4 hrs.). (Open 9am-6pm daily.) Summer horseback riding is available at **Topnotch Stowe,** on Mountain Rd. (253-8585). Most residents of Stowe (Stoics) will tell you that the outline of the crest of Mt. Mansfield resembles a face; some say that it so closely resembles Alfred Hitchcock's pudgy visage that on gusty winter nights you can hear the words "Good evening" whispering in the winds.

The **Stowe Mountain Resort** (253-3000) coordinates a variety of fun summer activities such as the **Alpine Slide** and the **gondola,** which runs 4393 ft. above sea level to just below the summit of Mt. Mansfield; all are open weather permitting; call the resort for details. For $10 (motorcycles $7), you can kill your transmission and burn your brakes driving to the peak of Mt. Mansfield on the **Auto Toll Road.** Look for signs leading to it near signs pointing to an alternate route to I-89 off Mountain Rd. For a good daytrip, hike the **Long Trail** ascending Mt. Mansfield. Though there are a number of entrances to the trail on Mountain Rd., drive the particularly scenic route to the highest elevation point at Smuggler's Notch (not to be confused with the ski area), where the cliffs rise 1000 ft. above the pass. At one time people smuggled cattle (of all things) into New England through this gap in the mountain. Today, an **information booth** here can point you to interesting sights on the trail, like Bingham Falls.

Ski resorts have culture too. After a long day hiking, unwind at a performance of the **Stowe Stage Company,** the Playhouse, Mountain Rd. (253-7944; performances 8pm late June-Columbus Day.) The sound of music fills the Trapp Family Concert Meadow, Sundays at 7pm, for Stowe Performing Arts **Music in the Meadow.** (253-7321; Tickets $12, $10 in advance, under 19 $5.) **Noon Music in May** each Wednesday at the Stowe Community Church and the **Gazebo Lawn Concert Series** at noon on the library lawn in August are free (donations welcome).

For a filling meal try the **Sunset Grille and Tap Room,** on Cottage Club Rd. off Mountain Rd. (253-9281), a friendly, down-home barbecue place with a vast selection of domestic beers and generous meals ($5-15). (Open daily 11:30am-midnight.) All-American **Angelo's Pizza,** two mi. south of town on Rte. 100 (253-8931), offers pizza ($1.15 per slice) and pasta ($4-8). (Open Mon.-Thurs. 11:30am-10pm, Fri.-Sat. 11:30am-midnight, Sun. 11:30am-10pm. Free delivery.)

For one of the few lodging bargains in town, the **Vermont State Ski Dorm** (253-4010) doubles as an HI/AYH hostel from June 15 to October 15 ($10 per night, $12 nonmembers). During the ski season they serve two meals a day and charge $35. Be sure to call before you come, as troubles with the state government (who own it) have made the Lodge's future uncertain. The friendly, eccentric host of the **Golden Kitz,** Mountain Rd. (253-4217 or 800-KITS-LOV) offers her "lovie" travelers a relaxed atmosphere, great stories, and *kit*schy theme bedrooms. (Singles with shared bath $36-40 in highest season; $30-36 midwinter weekends; $24-26 in early and late ski season; off-season and summer $20-28. Doubles $52-70 highest season; $46-50 midwinter weekends; $38-56 early and late ski season; $36-56 off-season and summer. Multi-day packages available.) The (soon-to-be) committed budget traveler should ask if "dungeon" doubles are available ($30). Situated on a real brook, the **Gold Brook Campground** (253-7683 or 253-8147) babbles 11/2 mi. south of the town center on Rte. 100. (Open year-round. Hot showers, volleyball, badminton, horseshoes. Tent sites $12, with varying degrees of hookup $16, $18, and $21.) **Smuggler's Notch State Park** (253-4014) offers hot showers, lean-tos ($12) and tent sites ($7.50). (Open Memorial Day-Columbus Day; reservations suggested.)

Contact the **Stowe Area Association** on Main St. (253-7321 or 800-247-8693), in the center of the village, for free booking service and summer info on the area's lodging, restaurants and activities, including skiing. (Open summer Mon.-Fri. 9am-6pm, Sat. 10am-5pm, Sun. 11am-5pm; winter Mon.-Fri. 9am-8pm, Sat.-Sun. 9am-6pm.)

The socially conscious and fun-loving **Ben and Jerry's Ice Cream Factory** lies north on Rte. 100 (244-5641), a couple miles off I-89 in Waterbury. Started in 1978 through a Penn State correspondence course in ice-cream making and moving into a converted gas station, Ben and Jerry have since developed some of the best ice cream in the world. After the October, 1988 stock market crash, this caloric duo made the trek to Wall Street to serve up free scoops of two made-for-the-occasion flavors: "Economic Crunch" and "That's Life." You can sample other celebrated flavors such as Rainforest Crunch, White Russian, and Cherry Garcia. ($1 tours daily every 1/4-hr. 9am-5pm; July-Aug. daily 9am-8pm.) Partake at their store daily during tour hours.

The ski areas all lie northwest of Stowe on Rte. 108. Stowe is 12 mi. north of I-89s exit 10, which is 27 mi. southwest of Burlington. Getting to and around Stowe without a car is not fun. **Vermont Transit** will take you to **Vincent's Drug and Variety Store**, off Park Row in Waterbury, 10 mi. from Stowe. (Open Mon.-Fri. 8:30am-7pm, Sat. 8:30am-6pm, Sun. 9am-3pm.) To explore and get a good workout, rent a **bike**. You can also take the less strenuous route and rent a **car** from **Stowe Auto Service** on Mountain Rd. (253-7608). ($29 per day, 50 free mi., 20¢ per extra mi.; will deliver car for a fee; must be 21 with credit card. Open 7am-6pm daily.) The Stowe Area Association can give you more info on the **American Express Village-Mountain Courtesy Trolley** (operates daily from town 7:30am-4:30pm, every 1/2-hr.during the ski season), Sullivan Transportation (253-9440), or LaMoille City Taxi (253-9433 or 800-252-0204) will take you back to Waterbury.

Stowe's **ZIP code** is 05672; the **post office** (253-2571) is at 105 Depot St., off Rte. 100 just north of the Rte. 108 junction. (Open Mon.-Fri. 8:30am-5pm, Sat. 9am-noon.) The **area code** is 802.

White River Junction and West

White River Junction takes its name from its location at the confluence of the White and Connecticut rivers, but today the town receives more visitors as a result of the nearby intersection of Interstates 89 and 91. Central Vermont is graced with quiet winding back roads and grazing cows in quiet green pastures; if you enjoy rural rubber-necking, plan an east-west trip along U.S. 4, or a north-south trip on Rte. 100. The roads are best reached from U.S. 5 or I-89, where they intersect with the Connecticut River.

An **information booth** across Sykes Ave. from the bus station (intersection of Sykes and U.S. 5 off I-89 and 91) can fill your pockets with brochures on Vermont. (Open May 27-Oct. 15 daily 10am-5pm.) In town, the **Chamber of Commerce,** 12 Gates St. just off S. Main (295-6200), can also supply you with information. (Open Mon.-Fri. 9am-noon and sporadically in the afternoons, especially on Wed.) Also in the Junction you'll find the **Catamount Brewery,** 58 S. Main St. (296-2248), where you can sample, among other things, delicious, unpasteurized amber ale produced in strict accordance with British brewing methods. (Tours daily 1pm. Tours sometimes also offered at 11am and/or 3pm depending on day and season. Call for details.)

For a quick bite to eat, stop at the local favorite, the **Polkadot Restaurant,** 1 N. Main St. (295-9722), a classic diner and remarkably good. (Sandwiches $1.50-3, 2 pork chops, applesauce, mashed potatoes, veggie, soup, rolls and coffee $5.50. Open daily 5am-8pm.) The best—and pretty much the only—bet for lodging is the old-style **Hotel Coolidge,** 17 S. Main St. (295-3118 or 800-622-1124), across the road from the retired Boston and Maine steam engine. From the bus station, walk to the right along U.S. 5, down the hill past two stop lights (about 1 mi.) into town. Renamed in honor of "Silent Cal" Coolidge's pop, a frequent guest at the railroad hotel, the Coolidge boasts neatly kept rooms at fair prices and a housekeeping manager with a keen sense of humor. (Singles from $22, doubles from $27.50. For the cheapest rates, ask for the hostel rooms. A good bargain is the deal on 2 adjoining rooms sharing a full bath, $55 for 2 people plus $10 per extra person. Morning coffee included.)

Once the hub of railroad transportation in the northeastern U.S., White River Junction now serves as the major bus center for central and eastern Vermont. **Vermont Transit** (295-3011), on U.S. 5 adjoining the Wm. Tally House Restaurant, has connections across New Hampshire, Burlington, and up and down the Connecticut River. (Office open Sun.-Fri. 7am-9pm, Sat. 7am-5pm.) **Amtrak's** "Montrealer" train running south to New York City and Washington DC, and north to Essex Junction (near Burlington) and Montréal chugs through here daily (295-7160 or 800-872-7245; on Railroad Rd. off N. Main St.)

Fourteen mi. west of White River Junction on U.S. 4 is **Woodstock,** a Vermont-country-village-cum-wealthy-tourist-hangout. The Woodstock **Chamber of Commerce,** upstairs at 18 Central St. (457-3555; open Mon.-Thurs. 9am-5pm) provides maps of trails for nearby mountains Peg and Tom (a half-hour walk up Mt. Tom will afford a good view of the town), as well as complete lists of local B&Bs, restaurants, and stores. It is also helpful for finding the limited hiking and skiing in the area. The chamber also sponsors an **information booth** (457-1042) in the middle of the village green. (Open late June-mid-Oct. Mon.-Sat.10am-5:30pm, Sun. 11am-4pm.) In addition there is the **Woodstock Town Crier,** a chalkboard with local listings on the corner of Elm and Church St.

Genuine Vermont sharp cheddar cheese is made only in certain counties. One authentic producer is the **Plymouth Cheese Factory** (672-3650), on Rte. 100A six mi. south of U.S. 4 in **Plymouth.** To see the cheese being made, visit on Monday or Tuesday. After Thanksgiving, cheese production ceases and packaging takes over. (Open Mon.-Sat. 8am-5:30pm, Sun. 9am-5:30pm; off-season Mon.-Sat. 8am-4:30pm, Sun. 9am-4:30pm.) Another big cheese from Plymouth, **Calvin Coolidge,** was born in this tiny village. Next door to his birthplace is the old homestead where in 1923 his father swore him in as president after learning of the sudden death of President Harding. You can also tour the secret service cabins and his White House summer office. (672-3773; open Memorial Day-mid-Oct. daily 9:30am-5:30pm. Admission $3.50, under 14 free.) The **Mountain Creamery,** 33 Central St. (457-1715), serves homemade ice cream and desserts, as well as full breakfast and lunch menus. (One large scoop of ice cream $2.25; Reuben sandwich $5.25. Open daily 7am-5pm.)

Woodstock is home to a number of **Bed and Breakfasts**. Consult the *Woodstock Guide to Lodgings,* available at the Chamber of Commerce and the info booth. **Quechee State Park** (295-2990), off U.S. 4 between Woodstock and White River, has hiking trails around **Quechee Gorge,** a spectacular 163-ft. drop from cliffs to the Ottaquechee River below. A bridge connecting the trails to the park's picnic grounds offers a view that makes you feel small and quite mortal; on the eastern side of the bridge an **info booth** can answer questions. (Open Memorial Day-Columbus Day. Day use $1.50, kids $1. Tent sites $10 for 4 people, $2.50 each additional person up to 8. Lean-tos $14 per person. Disabled-accessible tent site and lean-to. Metered showers. Reservations minimum three nights in advance $3.)

Wilderness Trails (295-7620, 295-3133) behind the Quechee Inn, Clubhouse Rd., in Quechee will rent you a **bike** or **canoe** for the day. (Canoes 1-3 hr. $10. Bike 1 hr. $5. Daily rate $15 for each.) The owner also organizes fly-fishing and canoe trips, and rents cross-country skiing equipment in the winter. (Open 9am-5pm daily.) In Quechee, visit **Simon Pearce Glass,** the Mill off U.S. 4 (295-2711), to view glassblowers and potters at work. (Artists working daily 9am-5pm, open daily 9am-9pm.)

The **Vermont Transit** agency in Woodstock (457-1325), at the Whippletree Shop, 4 Central St., provides schedules and timetables of Vermont transit buses. To White River Junction (2 per day, $3) and Rutland (2 per day, $6).

Mid-Atlantic States

The diverse and densely populated states along the Eastern seaboard tell the story of the nation's creation and development. The United States began humbly in Jamestown, VA, where the first permanent English settlement was founded in 1607. Constitutional democracy and free speech are still celebrated in Philadelphia, the nation's first capital, and the search for religious freedom persists as Mennonites and Amish cling to their Old-World ways and shun materialism. The presence of some of the nation's oldest and finest universities alongside large rural areas testify to the permanence of Jeffersonian values of an enlightened but rural yeomanry. During the Civil War, this area was scarred by the clashing troops of the North and the South. Around the turn of the century, the coal of Appalachia and the steel of Pittsburgh transformed the United States into a global economic power. Decades passed, and the area lapsed into depression and obsolescence. Today, however, urban revitalization is taking place throughout the region, equally the work of old money and of neighborhood pride and industry. The patchwork of ethnic populations of the Mid-Atlantic demonstrates how differences can be consolidated into assets.

In spite of the concentration of urban centers in the Mid-Atlantic, there is plenty of outdoor fun. The celebrated Appalachian Trail treks through the area; in Virginia, the Blue Ridge Parkway traverses the Shenandoah and Great Smoky Mountains. Other major outdoor areas are the national seashores along the coast and the national forests in the Appalachians. In the wilds of Pennsylvania and West Virginia's Allegheny Mountains, you can raft, backpack, and even be chased by bears in truly remote areas. Wildlife refuges scattered along the Atlantic coast and its bays protect birdlife and wild ponies alike.

Delaware

Delawareans strive to make up for their state's small size with a fierce pride in its historical past and unusually usual geography. They adopted "First State" as their slightly misleading nickname—they were the first to ratify the U.S. Constitution in 1787. To further solidify their standing as Old Kids on the Block, ebullient residents shout from the unspectacular hillsides that Delaware has the lowest highest elevation of any state, and you can get there step by step, oooh baby.

Most of Delaware's population sleeps in the northern industrial region, on the strip between Wilmington and Newark. Tourists usually associate the state with chemical industry and big corporations: here, in 1938, nylon first shimmered and ran. But Delaware offers its tourist pleasures in the less synthetic regions of the seacoast; Lewes and Rehoboth Beach have the natural charm of southern resort towns, while the Delaware Dunes stretch across more than 2000 acres of accessible seashore.

Practical Information

Capital: Dover.

Visitor Information: State Visitors Service, P.O. Box 1401, 99 King's Hwy., Dover 19903 (800-282-8667; 800-441-8846 outside DE). Open Mon.-Fri. 8am-4:30pm. **Division of Fish and Wildlife,** William Penn St., Dover 19901 (739-4431).

Time Zone: Eastern.

Postal Abbreviation: DE

Area Code: 302.

Sales Tax: 0%.

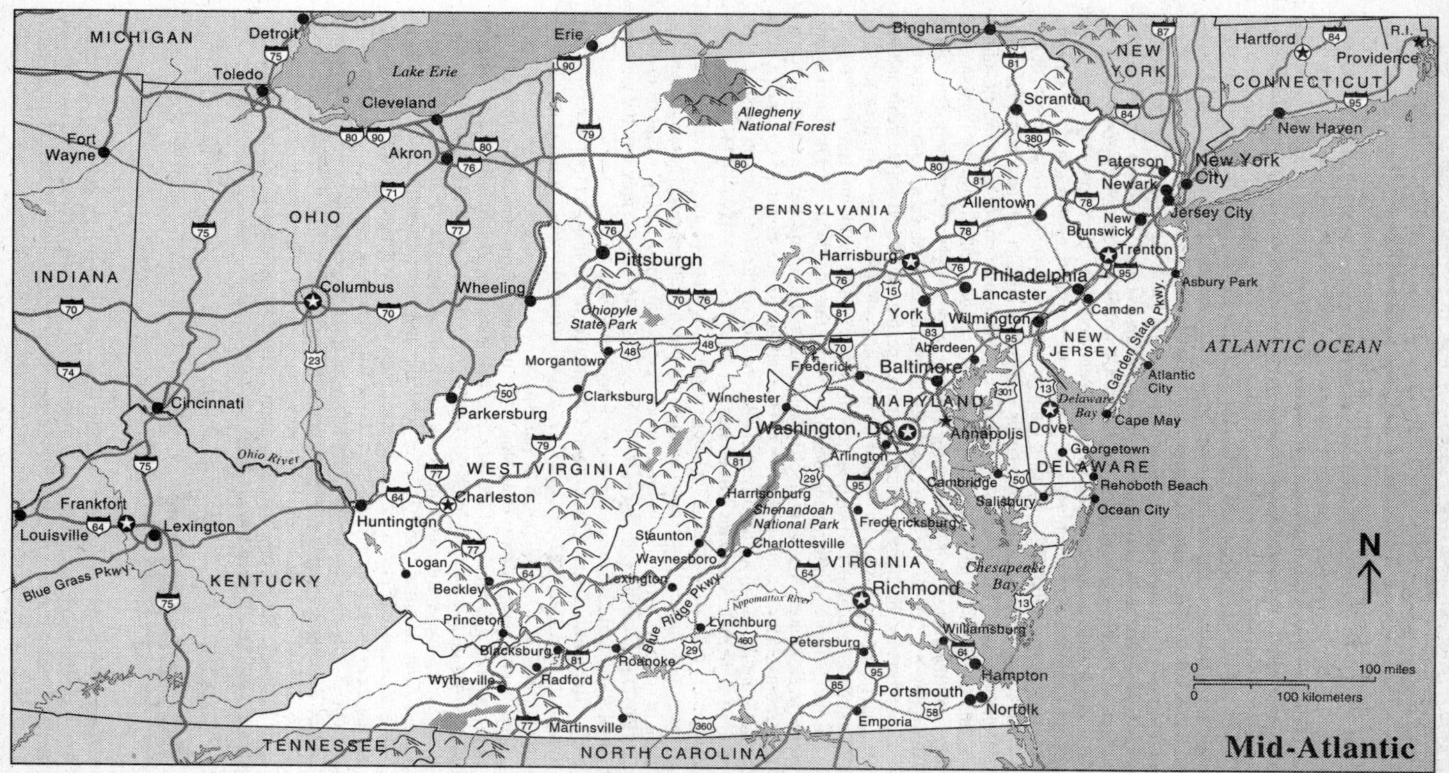
Mid-Atlantic
ATLANTIC OCEAN
N
0
100 miles
0
100 kilometers
R.I.
Providence
CONNECTICUT
Hartford
New Haven
NEW YORK
New York City
Jersey City
Asbury Park
Paterson
Newark
New Brunswick
Trenton
Camden
NEW JERSEY
Garden State Pkwy.
Atlantic City
Cape May
Delaware Bay
DELAWARE
Dover
Georgetown
Rehoboth Beach
Ocean City
Binghamton
Scranton
Allentown
Philadelphia
Lancaster
Wilmington
PENNSYLVANIA
Allegheny National Forest
Harrisburg
York
Aberdeen
Baltimore
MARYLAND
Annapolis
Cambridge
Salisbury
Chesapeake Bay
Washington, D.C.
Arlington
Fredericksburg
VIRGINIA
Richmond
Williamsburg
Hampton
Norfolk
Portsmouth
Emporia
Petersburg
Frederick
Winchester
Harrisonburg
Shenandoah National Park
Charlottesville
Appomattox River
Lynchburg
Staunton
Waynesboro
Lexington
Blue Ridge Pkwy.
Roanoke
Erie
Pittsburgh
Ohiopyle State Park
Clarksburg
Morgantown
WEST VIRGINIA
Parkersburg
Wheeling
Charleston
Huntington
Logan
Beckley
Princeton
Blacksburg
Radford
Wytheville
Martinsville
NORTH CAROLINA
TENNESSEE
Lake Erie
Cleveland
Akron
OHIO
Columbus
Detroit
Toledo
MICHIGAN
Ohio River
Cincinnati
KENTUCKY
Lexington
Frankfort
Louisville
Blue Grass Pkwy
INDIANA
Fort Wayne

Rehoboth Beach and Lewes

The reserved atmosphere of these seaside retreats spells relief from the usual boardwalk fare. The beaches remain clean, the air stays salty, and the people, particularly in Lewes (LOO-iss), keep to themselves. Founded in 1613 by the Zwaanendael colony from Hoorn, Holland, **Lewes** rightly touts itself as Delaware's first town. The **Lighthouse Restaurant,** on Fisherman's Wharf (645-6271) just over the drawbridge in Lewes, flashes with occasionally brilliant food. Try the grilled swordfish ($14) with homemade bread. (Open Sun.-Fri. 5am-9pm, Sat. 4am-10pm.) Due east from Lewes, on the Atlantic Ocean, lurks the secluded **Cape Henlopen State Park** (645-8983), home to a seabird nesting colony, sparkling white "walking dunes," and campsites (645-2103) available on a first-come, first-served basis (sites $13; open April-Oct.). To learn more about Lewes, stop by the **Lewes Chamber of Commerce** (645-8073), in the Fisher Martin House on King's Hwy. (Open Mon.-Sat. 10am-3pm.)

With a minimum of planning, you can join the committees of vacationing bureaucrats from Washington, DC—many of them gay—who convene at the sand reefs of **Rehoboth Beach** on hot summer weekends to mix and mingle. At the **Country Squire,** 17 Rehoboth Ave. (227-3985), you can talk with locals over one of the complete dinner specials (about $7). The breakfast special ($3), served at all times, is a lagniappe of sorts, and the cheesesteak is a county and city favorite ($4). (Open daily 7am-1am.) **Thrasher's** has served fries and only fries, in enormous paper tubs ($3-5.75), for over 60 years. Bite too hastily into one of the tangy peanut-oil-soaked potato treats and understand how the place got its name. Locations on both sides of the main drag, at 7 and 10 Rehoboth Ave., make it twice as easy to find. (Open daily 11am-11pm.)

For inexpensive lodging, walk one block from the boardwalk to **The Lord Baltimore,** 16 Baltimore Ave. (227-2855), which has clean, antiquated, practically beachfront rooms. (Singles and doubles $30-60. Call ahead, it's popular.) Or walk a little farther from the beach to the cluster of guest houses on the side lanes off First St., just north of Rehoboth Ave. **The Abbey Inn,** 31 Maryland Ave. (227-7023), is what the proprietress calls an "old-fashioned tourist home." A decorous and friendly inn, there's always a local and a conversation on the front porch. Call for reservations at least one week in advance, especially in the summer. (2-day minimum stay. Doubles from $40.) The **Big Oaks Family Campground,** P.O. Box 53 (645-6838), sprawls at the intersection of Rte. 1 and 270. (Sites $16.50, with hookup $18.50.)

The **Rehoboth Beach Chamber of Commerce,** in the restored train station at 501 Rehoboth Ave. (800-441-1329 or 227-2233 for information), provides brochures. (Open Mon.-Fri. 9am-4:30pm, Sat. 9am-1pm.)

Greyhound serves Lewes (flag stop at the parking lot for Tom Best's on Rte. 1; no phone) and Rehoboth Beach (227-7223; small station at 251 Rehoboth Ave.). Buses run to: Washington, DC (3½ hr.; $30); Baltimore (3½ hr.; $26); and Philadelphia (4 hr.; $28). Lewes makes up one end of the 70-minute **Cape May-NJ/Lewes-DE Ferry** route (Lewes terminal 645-6313; for schedule and fare information, see Cape May, NJ). Grab a cab ($15) from the pier to reach Rehoboth. To get around within Rehoboth, use the free shuttle transportation run by the **Ruddertowne Complex** (227-3888; May 27-Sept. 2 daily 3pm-midnight every hr.), which serves points between Rehoboth and Dewey Beaches, including a stop at Rehoboth Ave.

The **post office** in Rehoboth reads your postcards at 179 Rehoboth Ave. (227-8406; open Mon.-Fri. 9am-5pm, Sat. 9am-noon). The **ZIP code** for Lewes and Rehoboth Beach is 19971; the **area code** is 302.

Maryland

Used to be everyone knew what Maryland was about. There was the Chesapeake Bay—a picturesque, shellfish-rich estuary running straight through from the Atlantic north to Pennsylvania. On the rural Eastern Shore, small-town Marylanders captured crabs and raised tobacco. Across the bay in Baltimore, workers ate the crabs, loaded the ships, ran the factories, and joined the league of blue-collar port cities from Cleveland to Providence. Then the federal government expanded, industry shrank, and Maryland had a new, slender core: no longer the Bay, but the Baltimore-Washington Parkway. Suburbs grew up and down the corridor, Baltimore cleaned up its smokestack act and the Old Line State acquired a new, liberal urbanity. As DC's homogenized commuter suburbs break the limits of Montgomery and Prince Georges Counties, Baltimore revels in its polyglot immensity, while Annapolis, the capital, remains very much a small town. The mountains and mines of the western panhandle are still ignored after all these years, geographic and cultural kin to West Virginia. If anything brings this state together, it may be a sense of proportion: the forest and fields seem very exhaustible, rivers and islands aren't too big to explore, and cities—and their problems—are small alongside their Northeastern compatriots. Even the Chesapeake Bay has changed; after centuries of exploitation, Maryland has begun to clean it up, and the Free State's license plates now read "Save the Bay."

Practical Information

Capital: Annapolis.

Office of Tourist Development, 217 E. Redwood St., Baltimore 21202 (333-6611 or 800-543-1036). **Forest and Parks Service,** Dept. of Natural Resources, Tawes State Office Bldg., Annapolis 21401 (974-3771).

Time Zone: Eastern. **Postal Abbreviation:** MD **Area Code:** 301.

Sales Tax: 5%.

Baltimore

Once an East Coast shipping and industrial center, "Bawlmer" (pop. 751,000) declined structurally and economically from the late-50s to the mid-70s. Its renaissance began as Mayor Donald Schaefer launched a program to clean up pollution, restore buildings, and reinvent the Inner Harbor as a tourist playground; Harborplace has since inspired dozens of wanna-be waterfront malls along the eastern seaboard. Run by articulate Kurt Schmoke, modern Baltimore still serves as Maryland's urban core. Old-time, shirt-sleeved Bawlmer endures in the quiet limelight of Anne Tyler's novels and Barry Levinson's films. Near downtown skyscrapers, old ethnic neighborhoods like Little Italy front Baltimore's signature row houses, whose unique façades are microcosms of the larger city: polished marble stoops represent the shiny Inner Harbor, while blunt brick fits the proud, gritty urban environs. After the superb National Aquarium, try a stroll uphill to Mt. Vernon or through Fell's Point during the day. North of downtown, prestigious Johns Hopkins University generates pre-meds, philosophers, and some of the nation's best lacrosse teams.

Practical Information and Orientation

Emergency: 911.

Baltimore Area Visitors Centers, 300 W. Pratt St. (837-4636 or 800-282-6632), at N. Howard St. 4 blocks from Harborplace. Pick up a map, an *MTA Ride Guide,* and the *Quick City Guide* with excellent maps and event listings. Open daily 9am-5pm. An **information booth** on the west shoreline of the Inner Harbor is often crowded. Open daily 10am-6pm. A satellite booth at **Penn Station** provides basic info, usually open late Fri. evenings, weekday mornings, and all day Sun.

Traveler's Aid: 685-3569 (Mon.-Fri. 8:30am-4:30pm), 685-5874 (24-hr. hotline). Desks at **Penn Station** (open Mon.-Thurs. 9am-noon, Fri. 9am-9pm, Sat. 9am-1pm, Sun. 10am-5pm) and the Baltimore-Washington Airport (open Mon.-Fri. 9am-9pm, Sat.-Sun. 9am-5pm).

Baltimore-Washington International Airport (BWI), 859-7100. On I-195 off the Baltimore-Washington Expressway (I-295), about 10 mi. south of the city center. Use BWI as your gateway to Baltimore or Washington, DC. Take MTA bus #230 downtown. **Airport shuttles** to downtown

(859-0800) run daily every ½-hr. 7am-midnight ($8). Trains from BWI Airport to Baltimore ($6, metroliner $9; MARC trains are considerably cheaper but are also slower and only run Mon.-Fri.; $2.75) and Washington, DC ($10, metroliner $15, MARC $4.25). Call the BWI office at 672-6167.

Amtrak: Penn Station, 1515 N. Charles St. (800-872-7245), at Mt. Royal Ave. Easily accessible by bus #3, 11, or 18 to Charles Station downtown. Trains run about every ½ hr. to New York City ($59, metroliner $81); Washington, DC ($12, metroliner $21); and Philadelphia ($27, metroliner $41). Ticket window open daily 5:30am-9:30pm, self-serve machines open daily 24 hrs. (credit card only).

Greyhound, two locations: downtown at 210 W. Fayette St. (752-0868), near N. Howard St.; 5625 O'Donnell St. (744-9311), near I-95 3 mi. east of downtown. Frequent connections to NYC ($39), Washington, DC ($8.50), and Philadelphia ($15). Open 24 hrs.

Public Transport: Mass Transit Administration (MTA), 300 W. Lexington St. (539-5000 for recorded bus and Metro info; 333-3434 main office), near N. Howard St. Or call 760-4554 in Annapolis, 800-543-9809 elsewhere in MD and DC. (Lines open Mon.-Fri. 6am-11pm, Sat. 8:30am-5pm.) Easy bus and rapid-rail service to major city sights, more complicated to outlying areas. #230 serves airport. Free *MTA Ride Guide,* available at any visitors information center. Some buses operate 24 hrs. Fare $1.10, transfers 10¢. Metro operates Mon.-Fri. 5am-midnight, Sat. 11am-7pm. Metro base rate $1.10. **Baltimore Trolley Tours** (752-2015). Tours and transportation to major Baltimore sights. 1-day unlimited boarding pass for the 90-min. loop available. Trolleys every 30 min., daily 10am-4pm. $9, kids $4.50.

Taxi: Yellow Cab, 685-1212. **G.T.P. Inc.,** 859-1103 (to and from BWI airport).

Car Rental: Thrifty, BWI Airport (768-4900) and 2030 N. Howard St. (783-0300 or 800-367-2277, 24 hrs.), 9 blocks from Penn Station. Economy cars from $34 per weekday, $22 per weekend day, $169 per week. Unlimited mileage. Under 25 add $10 per day. Airport branch open 6am-midnight. Must be 21 with credit card. **Rent-A-Wreck,** 9006 Liberty Rd. (325-2757), and on Pulaski Hwy. near the Baltimore Beltway. From $20-30 per day. 50 free mi., 19¢ per additional mi. Must be 21. With cash payments, $150 deposit and Maryland driver's license required. Open Mon.-Fri. 8am-4pm.

Help Lines: Sexual Assault and Domestic Violence Hotline, 828-6390. **Gay and Lesbian Hotline and Information,** 837-8888. Operators daily 7:30-10:30pm, otherwise recording.

Post Office: 900 E. Fayette St. (655-9832). **ZIP code:** 21233.

Area Code: 301.

The **Jones Falls Expressway (I-83)** dissevers the city with its southern end at the Inner Harbor, while the **Baltimore Beltway (I-695)** girds the city. I-95 cuts across the southwest corner of the city, a shortcut to the wide arc of that Beltway section. During rush hour, these interstates get slower than a sloth on downers. Blue and green signs point drivers to tourist attractions. From Washington, DC, take the **Washington Beltway (I-495)** to I-95 at exit 27 or the Baltimore-Washington Expressway at exit 22; the highways run roughly parallel. Take the Russell St. exit to reach the Inner Harbor. Without traffic, the trip takes less than an hour.

Baltimore is plagued by one-way streets. **Pratt St.** (which runs east across the Inner Harbor) and **Charles St.** (which runs north from the west corner of the Harbor) divide the city into quarters; streets are dubbed "East" or "West" in relation to Charles, and "North" or "South" in relation to Pratt.

Accommodations and Camping

Baltimore International Youth Hostel (HI/AYH), 17 W. Mulberry St. at Cathedral St. (576-8880), near downtown bus and Amtrak terminals. Take MTA bus #3, 11, or 18. Elegant 19th-century brownstone: 48 beds, kitchen, laundry, lounge, baby grand piano, A/C. Members can stay 3 nights max., longer with manager's approval. Lockout 10am-5pm. Curfew 11pm. Chores required. $10, nonmembers $13. Reservations recommended; deposit required 2 weeks ahead.

Abbey-Schaefer Hotel, 723 Saint Paul St. (332-0405). Right on bus route from Penn Station. Great location. Functional rooms for 2 people with bathroom and A/C $44, extra person $8. Without attached bath $39, without A/C less. $2 key deposit.

Duke's Motel, 7905 Pulaski Highway (686-0400), in Rosedale off the Beltway. Try to ignore the front office's bulletproof glass—all the motels around here have it. Simple, clean rooms—probably the best deal on the Pulaski Hwy. motel strip, though slightly more expensive. Cable TV. $2 key deposit and ID required. Singles $36. Doubles $41.

Capitol KOA, 768 Cecil Ave., near Millersville (923-2771 or 987-7477), 10 mi. from the Baltimore Beltway, 16 mi. from DC, 11 mi. from Annapolis. Full facilities for tents, RVs cabins; pool, free weekday shuttle to DC/Baltimore trains. Tent site $19 for 2 people, RV site $20-28, $4 per additional adult. Open April-Nov. until 10pm in summer, 8pm in spring and fall.

Food

Virginia may be for lovers, but Maryland is for crabs—every eatery here serves crab cakes. The Light St. Pavilion at **Harborplace** (332-4191), at Pratt and Light St., has multifarious foodstuffs to suit every palate, but expect long lines between the stalls. **Phillips'** crab cakes are among the finest in Maryland (buy them cheaper from the Phillips' Express line), and **Thrasher's** fries with vinegar are an Eastern Shore tradition. (Harborplace open Mon.-Sat. 10am-9:30pm, Sun. noon-8pm.) **Lexington Market,** on Lexington at Eutaw St., northwest of the harbor, provides an endless variety of produce, fresh meat, seafood, and all of Harborplace's specialties, often at cheaper prices. (Open Mon.-Sat. 6am-6pm. Take bus #7 or the subway to Lexington Station.)

Bertha's Dining Room, 734 S. Broadway (327-5795) at Lancaster in Fells Point. Obey the bumper stickers: "Eat Bertha's Mussels." Down the black-shelled bivalves ($7) and choose between 90 sorts of beer and ale ($1-6) at her butcher-block tables. Jazz Mon.-Wed. and Fri.-Sat. nights. Enter on Lancaster St.; wheelchair accessible. Kitchen open Sun.-Thurs. 11:30am-11pm, Fri.-Sat. 11:30am-midnight. Bar open until 2am.

Obrycki's, 1727 E. Pratt St. (732-6399), near Broadway; take bus #7 or 10. Some of Balto's best crabs served every and any way—steamed, broiled, sautéed, or in crab cakes. Sandwiches $5-10. Steamed hard-shell crabs $20-46 per dozen depending on size. Expect lines on weekends. Open Mon.-Fri. noon-11pm, Sat. 2-11pm, Sun. 2-9:30pm.

Ikaros, 4805 Eastern Ave. (633-3750), 2 mi. east of downtown. Take bus #10. East Baltimore's Greek community is perfect for budget romantics. Try *avgolemono* soup with egg, lemon, beef, and rice ($1.25), or spinach and feta pies ($2). Open Sun.-Mon. and Wed.-Thurs. 11am-10pm, Fri.-Sat. 11am-11pm.

Haussner's, 3242 Eastern Ave. (327-8365) at S. Clinton. Take bus #10. An East Baltimore institution. Huge dining room full of impressive artwork and German food. *Sauerbraten* $10, sandwiches from $4; famous strawberry pie $3.50. No shorts after 3pm; lines for dinner on weekends. Open Tues.-Sat. 11am-11pm.

Buddies, 313 N. Charles St. (332-4200). Extensive lunchtime salad bar ($3 per lb.) and pile-driving sandwiches ($5-7). Jazz quartet Thurs.-Sat. 9:30pm-1am. Domestic draft $1.60, imports $3-5. Happy Hour 4-7pm with an assortment of free foodstuffs and 2-for-1 drinks. Open Sun.-Wed. 11am-1am, Thurs.-Sat. 11am-2am. Food served daily until 12:30am.

Sights

Most tourists start at the Inner Harbor; all too many finish there. The harbor ends in a five-square block of water bounded by the National Aquarium, Harborplace, the Maryland Science Museum, and a fleet of boardable ships, old and new; visitors roam the horseshoe-shaped perimeter and neglect the *real* neighborhoods to the east and north.

The **National Aquarium** (576-3800), Pier 3, 501 E. Pratt St., makes the whole Inner Harbor worthwhile. Multi-level exhibits and tanks show off rare fish, big fish, red fish, and blue fish along with the biology and ecology of oceans, rivers, and rainforests. The Children's Cove (level 4) lets visitors handle intertidal marine animals in the Touch Pool. (Open Mon.-Thurs. 9am-5pm, Fri.-Sun. 9am-8pm; Sept.-May Sat.-Thurs. 10am-5pm, Fri. 10am-8pm. $11.50, seniors $9.50, ages 3-11 $7.50, under 3 free. Sept.-May Fri. after 5pm $2. Excellent disabled access; call ahead.)

Several ships bob in the harbor, among them the frigate *Constellation* (539-1797), the first commissioned U.S. Navy ship, which sailed from 1797 until 1945, serving in the War of 1812, the Civil War, and as flagship of the Pacific Fleet during WW II. Go belowdecks to see (and aim!) the cannons. (Open daily 10am-8pm; May-June and Sept.-Oct. 10am-6pm; Nov.-April 10am-4pm. $3, seniors $2, ages 6-15 $1.50, active military $1, under 6 free.) Also moored in the harbor are the U.S.S. *Torsk* submarine and the lightship *Chesapeake.* These vessels make up the **Baltimore Maritime Museum** at Pier III (396-9304; open daily 9:30am-4:30pm; $3, seniors $2.50, kids 12 and under $1.50, active military free).

At the Inner Harbor's far edge lurks the **Maryland Science Center,** 601 Light St. (685-5225), where kids can learn basic principles of chemistry and physics cleverly disguised as hands-on games and activities. The IMAX Theater's five-story screen stuns audiences, but the planetarium merely dazzles them. On summer weekends, come in the morning while lines are short. (Open Mon.-Thurs. 10am-6pm, Fri.-Sun. 10am-8pm; Sept.-May Mon.-Sat. 10am-5pm, Sun. noon-6pm. $8; seniors, military, kids $5.50. Separate IMAX shows Fri.-Sat. evenings $5.)

The **Baltimore Museum of Art,** N. Charles and 31st St. (396-7100 or 396-7101), exhibits a fine collection of Americana, modern art (including pieces by Andy Warhol), and paintings and sculpture by Matisse, Picasso, Renoir and Van Gogh. Two adjacent sculpture gardens highlight 20th-century works and make wonderful picnic grounds, as well. The museum's **Baltimore Film Forum** shows classic and current American, foreign, and independent films (Thurs.-Fri. at 8pm, $5); get schedules at the museum or call 889-1993. (Open Tues.-Wed. and Fri. 10am-4pm, Thurs. 10am-7pm, Sat.-Sun. 11am-6pm. $4.50, seniors and full-time students $3.50, ages 4-18 $1.50, under 3 free. Thurs. free. Metered parking, wheelchairs available.)

Baltimore's best museum, the **Walters Art Gallery,** 600 N. Charles St. at Centre (547-9000), keeps one of the largest private collections in the world, spanning 50 centuries. The museum's apex is the Ancient Art collection (level 2); its seven marble sarcophagi with intricate relief carvings are of a type found in only two known collections (the other is the National Museum in Rome). Other high points are the Italian works and Impressionists, including Manet's *At the Café* and Monet's *Springtime,* as well as the new **Hackerman House,** a recent addition on the third level which includes rare early Buddhist sculptures from China and Japanese decorative arts of the late 18th and 19th century. (Open Tues.-Sun. 11am-5pm. Tours Wed. at 12:30pm, Sun. at 2pm. $4, seniors $3, under 18 and students with ID free. Free Wed.)

Druid Hill Park (396-6106) off Jones Falls Parkway on Druid Park Lake Drive, contains the **Baltimore Zoo** (366-5466), featuring elephants in a simulated savannah, Siberian tigers, and a waterfall. The Children's Zoo imports animals from the Maryland wilds, such as otters and crafty woodchucks. (Open Mon.-Fri. 10am-4:20pm. Children's Zoo and Conservatory close 15 min. early. $6.50, seniors and ages 2-15 $3.50, under 2 free. Kids under 15 go free on 1st Sat. of each month.) **Fort McHenry National Monument** (962-4290) at the foot of E. Fort Ave. off Rte. 2 (Hanover St.) and Lawrence Ave. (take bus #1), commemorates the victory against the British in the War of 1812. This famous battle inspired Francis Scott Key to write the "Star Spangled Banner." Admission ($1, seniors and under 17 free) includes entrançe to the museum, a way-too-long film, and a fort tour. (Open daily 8am-8pm; Sept.-May 8am-5pm. Wheelchair accessible; film captioned for the hearing impaired. Ample parking.)

Baltimore also holds a few historic houses and birthplaces: **Edgar Allen Poe's House,** 203 Amity St. (378-7228; open Wed.-Sat. noon-3:45pm), and the **Babe Ruth Birthplace and Baltimore Orioles Museum,** 216 Emery St. (727-1539; open daily 10am-5pm, on game nights until 7pm; Nov.-March 10am-4pm). To get a feel for Baltimore's historic districts, take bus #7 or 10 from Pratt St. to Abermarle St. and see **Little Italy,** or ride the same buses to Broadway and walk four blocks to **Fells Point.** The neighborhood around Albemarle, Fawn, and High St. is still predominantly Italian, even if the restaurant clientele no longer are; many of the brownstones have been in the same family for generations. Fell's Point imitates the past with cobblestone streets, quaint shops and historic pubs.

Entertainment and Nightlife

Summer outdoor entertainment animates the Inner Harbor. The **Showcase of Nations Ethnic Festival** fêtes Baltimore's ethnic neighborhoods, showcasing a distinct culture every week from June to September. Although somewhat generic, the fairs are always fun, vending international fare as well as the inevitable crab cakes and beer. Most events happen at **Festival Hall,** W. Pratt and Sharp Streets (752-8632 or 800-282-6632).

The **Pier Six Concert Pavilion** (625-4230) at—where else?—Pier 6 in the Inner Harbor presents big-name musical acts at 8pm from late July to the end of September. Get tickets at the Mechanic Theatre Box Office from October to May, then at the pavilion or through TeleCharge (625-1400 or 800-638-2444) for the rest of the summer ($12-25). Sit on Pier 5, near Harborplace, and overhear the music for free. The **Left Bank Jazz Society** (945-2266) has info on jazz performances; the **Baltimore Arts United (BAU) House,** 1713 N. Charles St. (659-5520), near Lanvale, hosts frequent jazz and rock concerts, poetry readings, art shows, and chamber music. (Tickets $4-7.) Bars and rock clubs cluster in Fells Point; well-known local and national alternative acts play at **Max's on Broadway,** 735 S. Broadway (276-2850).

The Baltimore Orioles play at their new stadium at **Camden Yards,** just a few blocks from the Inner Harbor at the corner of Russell and Camden St. "Os" fans are die-hards, as veteran rotisserie-league commissioner Zack Stein can tell you; they hold their breath through their team's yearly ups and downs with an intensity matched by few other ballclubs' followers.

Chesapeake Bay

The Chesapeake Bay—long scraggly arm of Atlantic Ocean reaching from the Virginia coast up through Maryland—nearly halves the state. Originally, the water's shallowness and salinity (Native Americans worshiped the bay as the "Great Salt River") made it one of the world's best oyster and blue crab breeding grounds. Centuries of exploitation, however, have damaged the waters. Despite recent conservation measures, fish, oysters, and crabs are slowly disappearing. Sedimentation is already filling and shortening many tributaries. Within 10,000 years, the Chesapeake Bay may be a flat piece of tidewater swamp.

Three states and one district share the bay waters and divvy-up the tourism. For info, write or call the Virginia Division of Tourism, the Maryland Office of Tourist Development, the Delaware State Visitors Center, or the Washington, DC Convention and Visitors Association. (Addresses and phone numbers given in respective state or district Practical Information sections.)

The region's public transport is underdeveloped. **Carolina Trailways** buses service to Salisbury, Princess Anne, Westover Junction, and Pocomoke City from the NYC Greyhound terminal. Make connections with DC, Baltimore, or Philadelphia via Greyhound bus #127. **Greyhound** covers the east shores of the Chesapeake and Annapolis. The bay is bounded on the west by I-95; on the south by I-64; on the east by U.S. 9, 13, and 50; and on the north by U.S. 40.

Assateague and Chincoteague Islands

Sometime in the 1820s, the Spanish galleon *San Lorenzo* foundered off the Maryland coast. All human passengers were lost, but a few horses struggled ashore. More than a century and a half later, the Chincoteague ponies, descendants of those survivors, roam the unspoiled beaches of Assateague Island.

Assateague Island is divided into three parts. The **Assateague State Park** (301-641-2120), off U.S. 113 in southeast Maryland, is a two-mi. stretch of picnic areas, beaches, hot-water bathhouses, and campsites ($18). The **Assateague Island National Seashore** (301-641-1441), claims most of the long sandbar north and south of the park, and has its own campground (sites with cold water $10, winter $8), beaches, and ranger station providing free backcountry camping permits (301-641-3030). Fire rings illuminate some relatively challenging (4- to 13-mi.) hikes; otherwise it's just you and nature. Bring plenty of insect repellent; six-legged unkindnesses fill the island.

The **Chincoteague National Wildlife Refuge** (804-336-6122; open Mon.-Fri. 7:30am-4:30pm), stretches south of the island on the Virginia side of the Maryland/Virginia border. The refuge provides a temporary home for the threatened migratory peregrine falcon, a half million Canada and snow geese, and beautiful Chincoteague ponies. At low tide, on the last Thursday in July, the wild ponies are herded together and made to swim from Assateague, MD, to Chincoteague, VA, where the local fire department auctions off the foals. The adults swim back to Assateague and reproduce, providing next year's crop.

To get to Assateague Island, take **Carolina Trailways** to **Ocean City,** via daily express and local routes from Greyhound Stations in Baltimore ($22), Washington, DC ($35), Norfolk, VA ($38), and Philadelphia ($35.) The Ocean City station idles at Philadelphia and 2nd St. (410-213-0552; open daily 7:30-8am and 10am-5pm). **Ocean City Chamber of Commerce,** 1320 Ocean Gateway, Ocean City 21842 (289-8559), on Rte. 50 at the south of town, has accommodations info. (Open Mon.-Sat. 9am-4:30pm, Sun. 10am-4pm.) To get to Assateague Island from Ocean City, take a taxi (289-8164; about $12). Carolina Trailways buses from Salisbury, MD, and Norfolk, VA, make a stop on U.S. 13 at T's Corner (804-824-5935), 11 mi. from Chincoteague. For more area info, call or write to **Chincoteague Chamber of Commerce,** P.O. Box 258 (Maddox Blvd.), Chincoteague, VA 23336 (804-336-6161; open daily 9am-5pm during the summer, Mon.-Sat. 9am-4:30pm after Labor Day).

New Jersey

Listen, let's get one thing straight right now: New Jersey (rhymes with "noisy") is *not* a giant roadway, and if you ask a native what exit they're from, they have, under a new state statute, the *right* to belt you in the gut until you hemorrhage. Much maligned by myopic Northeasterners who never take the trouble to leave the Garden State Parkway or the New Jersey Turnpike, the state—home to one of America's finest state universities (Rutgers) and one of the world's finest universities (Princeton)—also offers hundreds of miles of beautiful boardwalked beaches. And the water is *not* polluted (at least, no more than it is anywhere else on the northeastern coast).

While Cape May and the tragicomic gambling mecca Atlantic City—both at the extreme southern end of the state—are the only coastal resorts listed here, beach-loving travelers also might want to look into areas such as Asbury Park and Long Beach Island on their own. If rep were reality, New Jersey would be an American wasteland; but it's not, and the Garden State is a fine place to visit.

Practical Information

Capital: Trenton.

State Division of Tourism, CN 826, Trenton 08625 (609-292-2470).

Time Zone: Eastern. **Postal Abbreviation:** NJ

Sales Tax: 7%.

Atlantic City

The riches-to-rags-to-riches tale of Atlantic City began over 50 years ago when it reigned as the monarch of resort towns. Vanderbilts and Girards graced the legendary boardwalk of the hometown of *Monopoly,* the Depression-era board game for coffee-table robber-barons. Fans of the game will be thrilled to see the real Boardwalk and Park Place they've squabbled over for years. But while the street names may still be there, the opulence has faded. With the rise of competition from Florida resorts, the community chest began to close, and Atlantic City suffered decades of decline, unemployment, and virtual abandonment.

But in 1976, state voters gave Atlantic City the chance to resuscitate itself by legalizing gambling. However, like the cat in the classic flick *The Reanimator,* the revived patient wasn't all that pleasant. Casinos sprung up along the Boardwalk, while owners ignored the boarded-up streets below. The excessive, superficial wealth of the casinos makes it easy to forget the dirt and the dank outside, especially since the owners ensure you need never leave. Each velvet-lined temple of tackiness has a dozen restaurants, entertainment, and even skyways connecting to other casinos; if the Earth's atmosphere suddenly disappeared, many dedicated gamblers would take weeks to notice. The chance to win big bucks draws all types to Atlantic City, from high-rolling millionaires to senior citizens clutching their one last chance. One-quarter of the U.S. population lives within 300 mi. of Atlantic City, and fortune-seeking pilgrims from this pool flock to its shore to toss the dice.

Practical Information and Orientation

Emergency: 911.

Gambling age: 21.

Public Relations Visitors Bureau, 2308 Pacific Ave. (348-7100), conveniently located near Mississippi Ave. Open Mon.-Fri. 9am-4:30pm. Next door is the **Atlantic City Convention and Visitors Bureau,** 2310 Pacific Ave. (348-7100 or 800-262-7395), home of the Miss America pageant. Open Mon.-Fri. 9am-5pm. There is also a booth on Boardwalk at Mississippi Ave.; staffed daily 10am-6pm; leaflets available 24 hrs.

Pomona Airport: 800-428-4322. Serves Washington, DC, Philadelphia, and New York City.

Amtrak (800-872-7245), at Kirkman Blvd. off Michigan Ave. Follow Kirkman to its end, bear right, and follow the signs. To: New York City (1 per day; 2½ hr.; $28); Philadelphia (2 per day; 1½ hr.; $13); Washington, DC (2 per day; 3½ hr.; $40). More connections to DC and NYC through Philly. Open Sun.-Fri. 9:30am-7:40pm, Sat. 9:30am-10pm.

Buses: Greyhound, 971-6363 or 344-4449. Buses every hr. to New York (2½ hr.; $19) and Philadelphia (11/4 hr.; $9). **New Jersey Transit,** 348-7130. Runs 6am-10pm. Hourly service to New York City ($21.50) and Philadelphia ($10), with connections to Ocean City ($1.50), Cape May ($3.50), and Hammonton ($3.25). Also runs along Atlantic Ave. (base fare $1). Both lines operate from **Atlantic City Municipal Bus Terminal,** Arkansas and Arctic Ave. Station and ticket offices open 24 hrs. Both offer casino-sponsored round-trip discounts, including cash back on arrival in Atlantic City. Bally's has a particularly good deal—you get your full fare ($15) back in quarters upon arrival.

Help Line: Rape and Abuse Hotline, 646-6767. 24-hr. counseling and referrals.

Post Office: Martin Luther King, Jr. and Pacific Ave. (345-4212). Open Mon.-Fri. 8:30am-5pm, Sat. 10am-noon. **ZIP code:** 08401.

Area Code: 609.

Atlantic City kah-chings about halfway down New Jersey's coast, easily reached by train from Philadelphia and New York and accessible by the **Garden State Parkway.** Hitching is especially risky.

The road to hell is frequented by **Gamblers' Specials,** which make bus travel a cheap, efficient way to get to Atlantic City. Many casinos will give the bearer of a bus receipt $10 in cash and sometimes a free meal. Look for deals in the yellow pages under "Bus Charters" in New Jersey, New York, Pennsylvania, Delaware, and Washington, DC. Also check the "Arts and Entertainment" section of the *New York Times.*

Getting around Atlantic City on foot is easy. The casinos pack tightly together on the Boardwalk along the beach. When your winnings become too heavy to carry, you can hail a **Rolling Chair,** quite common along the Boardwalk. Though a bit of an investment ($1 per block for 2 people, 5-block min.), Atlantic City locals chat with you while they push. The less exotic and less expensive **Yellow tram** runs continuously ($1.25). On the streets, catch a **jitney** ($1.25), running 24 hrs. up and down Pacific Ave., or a **NJ Transit Bus** ($1) covering Atlantic Ave.

Accommodations and Camping

Large, red-carpeted beachfront hotels have replaced little green plastic houses, bumping smaller operators out of the game. The rules have changed in the last 60 years; expect to pay a hundred bucks for a single. Smaller hotels along **Pacific Avenue,** a block away from the Boardwalk, have rooms for less than $60, and rooms in Ocean City's guest houses are reasonably priced, though facilities there can be dismal. Be sure to reserve ahead, especially on weekends. Many hotels lower their rates during the middle of the week. Winter is also slow in Atlantic City, as water temperature, gambling fervor, and hotel rates all drop significantly. Campsites closest to the action cost the most; the majority close September through April. Reserve a room or a site if you plan to visit in July or August.

Irish Pub and Inn, 164 St. James Pl. (344-9063), off the Boardwalk, directly north of Sands Casino. Clean, cheap rooms with antiques. Victorian sitting rooms open onto sprawling porch lines with large rocking chairs. Laundry in basement. Singles $25. Doubles $40, with private shower $60. Quads $60. Extra cot $10. Breakfast and dinner $10, kids $8. Key deposit $5. Open Feb.-Nov.

Hotel Cassino, 28 S. Georgia Ave. (344-0747), just off Pacific Ave. Named after a *cassino* in the Italian hometown of kindly proprietors Felix and Mina. Rooms well-used, but not at all sleazy; this is strictly a family business. Rates negotiable. Singles $30-45. Doubles $35-50. Key deposit $10. Open May-Oct.

Birch Grove Park Campground, Mill Rd. in Northfield (641-3778), about 6 mi. from Atlantic City. 50 attractive and secluded sites. Sites $15 for 2 people, with hookup $18.

Pleasantville Campground, 408 N. Mill Rd. (641-3176), about 7 mi. from the casinos. 70 sites. Sites $24 for 4 people with full hookup.

Food

Each of the casinos has a wide selection of eateries intended to lure you and your wallet in. Most offer all-you-can-eat lunch or dinner buffets for $10 to $12; sometimes you can catch a special for around $5. However, the town also provides higher-quality meals in a less noxious atmosphere. Since 1946, the **White House Sub Shop,** Mississippi and Arctic Ave. (345-1564 or 345-8599), has served world-famous subs and sandwiches. Celebrity supporters include Bill Cosby, Johnny Mathis, and Frank Sinatra who is rumored to have subs flown to him while he's on tour. ($6-8, half-subs $3-4; open Mon.-Sat. 10am-midnight, Sun. 11am-midnight.) For renowned Italian food and the best pizza in town, hit **Tony's Baltimore Grille,** 2800 Atlantic Ave., at Iowa Ave. (Open daily 11am-3am. Bar open 24 hrs.) The **Inn of the Irish Pub,** 164 St. James Pl., serves modestly priced dishes like deep-fried crab cakes ($4.25) and Dublin beef stew ($5) amidst Irish memorabilia draped on the walls. (Open 24 hrs.) Although you may be turned off by the crowds, you can get great slices of pizza ($1.75) from one of the many **Three Brothers from Italy** joints on the Boardwalk. And don't forget to try custard ice-cream or saltwater taffy, two boardwalk staples. For a complete rundown of local dining, pick up a copy of *TV Atlantic Magazine, At the Shore,* or *Whoot,* all free, from a hotel lobby, restaurant, or local store.

Entertainment

Casinos

Inside the casinos, thousands of square feet of flashing lights and plush carpet stupefy the milling crowds; few notice the one-way ceiling mirrors concealing big-brother gambling monitors. Figures in formalwear embody Atlantic City's more glamorous past, but Winnebago pioneers in matching tees now outnumber their flashy cohorts. The seductive rattle of chips and snickering of one-armed-bandits never stops.

All casinos line the Boardwalk, within a dice-toss of each other. Even if you tried, you couldn't miss the newest beanstalk on the block, the **Taj Mahal** (449-1000), Donald Trump's meditation on sacred Indian art and architecture. Ironically, it was missed payments on this tasteless tallboy that cast the financier into his billion-dollar tailspin. Trump has two other casinos, each displaying his name in humongous, lighted letters—the **Trump Castle** (441-2000) and **Trump Plaza** (441-6000). Other biggies are **Bally's Park Place** (340-2000) and **Resorts International** (344-6000). **Caesar's Boardwalk Regency** (348-4411), **Harrah's Marina Hotel** (441-5000), and the **Atlantis** (344-4000) are hot clubs. Rounding out the list are the **Claridge** (340-3400) and **Showboat** (343-4000). The **Sands** (441-4000) and **TropWorld Casino** (340-4000) have extensive facilities that include golf and tennis. You may be amused by the two "moving sidewalks" that carry customers from the Boardwalk to the only two casinos without a Boardwalk entrance. Not surprisingly, these sidewalks move in only one direction.

Open nearly all the time (Mon.-Fri. 10am-4am, Sat.-Sun. 10am-6am), casinos lack windows and clocks, denying you the time cues that signal the hours slipping away. Free drinks, bathrooms and gaming tables at every turn keep you stupid, satisfied, and drained. To curb your almost inevitable losses, stick to the cheaper games: blackjack, slot machines, and the low bets in roulette and craps. Keep your eyes on your watch or you'll have spent four hours and four digits before you know what hit you. The gambling age restriction of 21 is strictly enforced.

Beaches and Boardwalk

The ocean is just a few spaces away. Atlantic City squats on the northern end of long, narrow **Absecon Island,** which has seven mi. of beaches—some pure white, some lumpy gray. The **Atlantic City Beach** is free, and often crowded. Adjacent **Ventnor City's** sands are nicer. The legendary **Boardwalk** of Atlantic City has been given over to the purveyors of the quick fix, packed with junk-food stands, arcades, souvenir shops, and carnival amusements. Take a walk, jog, or bike in Ventnor City, where the Boardwalk's development tapers off.

Cape May

Good Atlantic beaches bless all the towns on the Jersey shore. While Atlantic City chose gambling and cheap pizza joints, Cape May decided to accentuate different attributes. Century-old cottage inns stretch from shore to pedestrian mall. Tree-lined boulevards make for a nice afternoon stroll. No matter where you are in Cape May, the beach never lies more than two or three blocks away.

In 1988, the Jersey shore gained notoriety for the garbage and syringes which washed up on its shore. A very successful clean-up effort ensued. Today, the sand at Cape May literally glistens, dotted with some of the famous Cape May diamonds (actually quartz pebbles that glow when cut and polished). When you unroll your beach towel on a city-protected beach (off Beach Ave.), make sure you have the **beach tag** which beachgoers over 12 must wear June to September from 10am to 5pm. Pick up a tag (daily $3, weekly $8, seasonal $15) from the beach tag vendors roaming the shore. For more info, call the Beach Tag Office at 884-9520.

The **Mid-Atlantic Center for the Arts,** 1048 Washington St. (884-5404), offers a multitude of tours and activities. Pick up *This Week in Cape May* in any of the public buildings or stores for a detailed listing. (Guided walking and trolley tours $4. 2-hr. guided cruises $7.) The **Cape May Light House** in **Cape May Point State Park** (888-3459) west of town at the end of the point, guides tourists, not ships. Built in 1859, the lighthouse offers a magnificent ragout of the New Jersey and Delaware coasts at the top of a 199-step staircase. ($3.50 adults, $1 kids.) Free summer concerts enliven the town's bandstand.

There are plenty of places to sample the day's catch or a sandwich in Cape May. **The Ugly Mug,** 426 Washington St., a bar/restaurant in the mall, serves a dozen ugly clams for half as many dollars. (Open Mon.-Sat. 11am-2am, Sun. noon-2am. Food served until 11pm.) **Carney's,** 401 Beach Ave. (884-4424), is the self-proclaimed "best bar in town" with live bands nightly. A mug of beer costs $2, sandwiches $5. (Open Mon.-Sat. 11:30-10pm, Sun. noon-10pm, last call daily 2am.) The **Ocean View Restaurant,** at Beach and Grant Ave., offers fine fresh seafood, to the tuna of $10 to $15. (Open daily 7am-10pm.)

Many of the well-preserved seaside mansions now take in nightly guests, but cater to the well-heeled *New York Times* B&B set. Still, several inns with reasonable rates fly in the thick of the action. The **Hotel Clinton,** 202 Perry St. (844-3993) at Lafayette St., has decent-sized singles ($25) and doubles ($35) with shared bath. Add $5 for weekend rates. (Open mid-June-early Sept. Call 516-799-8889 for off-season reservations.) Built in 1879, **Congress Hall,** 251 Beach Dr. (884-8421), needs a little elbow grease to restore it to its former glory. A gargantuan establishment weathered by a century of use, the cheapest rooms do the time-warp to the early 50s, but they do so in a luxurious way and are complete with private baths and a pool. (All rooms $45-80. Weekends and holidays add $10, July-Sept. $15. Open May-Sept. Call 858-0670 for off-season reservations.) **Paris Inn,** 204 Perry St. (884-8015), near Lafayette St., has old but decent rooms, some with private baths. (Singles $35. Doubles $45. Weekends add $10. Ask about the student discount.)

Campgrounds line U.S. 9 from Atlantic City to the Cape. The two closest to town are **Cold Springs Campground,** 541 New England Rd. (884-8717; sites $13, with hookup $15), and **Cape Island Campground,** 709 U.S. 9 (884-5777; sites $25, with hookup $27).

Despite its geographic isolation, Cape May is easily accessible. By car from the north, Cape May is literally the end of the road—follow the **Garden State Parkway** south as far as it goes, watch for signs to Center City, and you'll end up on Lafayette St. From the south, by car, bike, or foot, take a 70-minute **ferry** from Lewes, DE (terminal 302-645-6313) to Cape May (886-9699; for recorded schedule info 886-2718). In summer months, 14 to 15 ferries cross each day; in the off-season four to six. (Toll $18 for vehicle and driver, passengers $4.50, pedestrians $4.50, motorcyclists $15, bicyclists $8.) From Cape May, take **bus** #552 (14 per day; $1.40) from the depot to north Cape May and walk one mi. to the ferry.

The **Welcome Center,** 405 Lafayette St. (884-9562), provides a wagonload of friendly info about Cape May and free hotlines to inns and B&Bs. (Open Mon.-Sat. 9am-4pm.) As its name indicates, the **Chamber of Commerce and Bus Depot,** 609 Lafayette St. (884-5508), near Ocean St. across from the Acme, provides tourist info and a local stop for **New Jersey Transit** (800-582-5946; northern NJ 800-772-2222). Bus service to: Atlantic City ($3.50; 2 hrs.), Philadelphia ($13; 3hrs.), and New York City ($27; 4½ hrs.). (Terminal open July-Sept. daily 9am-8pm; off-season Mon.-Fri. 9am-8pm, Sat. 10am-8pm.). Try your hand at polo at the **Village Bike Shop,** Washington and Ocean St. (884-8500), right off the mall. Also ask about the four-person tandem bike. (Bikes $3.50 per hr., $9 per day. Open daily 7am-6pm.) But no riding on the beach!

The **post office** in Cape May is located at 700 Washington St. (884-3578; open Mon.-Fri. 9am-5pm, Sat. 9am-noon.) The **ZIP code** is 08204.

The **area code** is 609.

Newark

Although Newark is the fourth-largest metropolitan region in the U.S., New Yorkers and tourists will (and should) associate New Jersey's largest city with its ever-expanding airport. With a better reputation for on-time arrivals and departures than either La Guardia or Kennedy Airport in New York, **Newark Airport** is also actually more convenient to Manhattan. For information on Newark Airport, see the Getting There section of New York City. For information on nearby **Maplewood,** see *Let's Go: Maplewood and South Orange 1993.*

New York State

Surrounded by the beauty of New York's landscape, you may find it difficult to remember that smog and traffic even exist. The villages and cities that dot the hilly strip that is upstate New York have a sweet natural flavor that holds its own against the fermenting juice of the Big Apple. Whether in the crassly commercial Niagara Falls, the idyllic Finger Lakes, or the simply peaceful Podunk—hell, even in Albany—you will have little doubt that nature is sovereign in Upstate New York.

Practical Information

Capital: Albany.

Tourist Information: 800-225-5697 or 474-4116. Open Mon.-Fri. 8:30am-5pm. Write to **Division of Tourism**, 1 Commerce Plaza, Albany 12245. Excellent, comprehensive *I Love NY Travel Guide* includes disabled access and resource information. **New York State Office of Parks and Recreation,** Agency Bldg. 1, Empire State Plaza, Albany 12238 (518-474-0456), has literature on camping and biking**. Division of Lands and Forests** (518-457-7432) has information on hiking and canoeing.

Time Zone: Eastern. **Postal Abbreviation:** NY.

Sales Tax: 4-8.25%.

Outdoors

Bikers should head for the **Finger Lakes region**, whose gentle hills are just high enough to provide some challenge and whose small farmsteads are best explored and appreciated by bike. Moreover, the wineries of the region make for very intoxicating stops. Write for the *New York Bicycle Touring Guide,* c/o William N. Hoffman, 621 Candlewyck Rd., Lancaster PA 17601, or the free *Finger Lakes Bicycle Routes,* Finger Lakes State Park Region, P.O. Box 1055, Trumansburg 14886 (607-387-7041). For a guide to the wineries of upstate New York write to the Department of Agriculture and Markets, Capital Plaza, 1 Winner Circle, Albany 12235 (518-457-3880). Ask for the *New World of World Class Wine Making.* For information on the Adirondacks and Catskills preserves, write or call the NY State Department of Environmental Conservation (518-457-2500), 50 Wolf Rd., Albany 12233.

Hikers will appreciate the many long trails that criss-cross the state, including the **Appalachian Trail**, the **Finger Lakes Trail**, and the **Long Path**, overseen by the Forest Preserve of Protection and Management (518-457-7433). For reservations at any state campground call 800-456-2267 six to 90 days in advance. You're also never a long drive from one of NY's 90 state parks, most of which provide excellent camping. Muskie, walleye, and bass **fishing** in the "Thousand Island Seaway" is perhaps the best in the eastern U.S., with over 50 private campsites and parks scattered across the 1800 islands. For more information, call the **St. Lawrence County Chamber of Commerce** (315-386-4000) or the **Thousand Islands State Park and Recreation Region** (315-482-2593) in Alexandria Bay.

Hitchhiking is illegal in New York State. This law is enforced with particular vehemence in the New York City area, where it's not safe *at all.*

Adirondacks

A hundred and one years ago the New York State legislature, demonstrating uncommon foresight, established the **Adirondacks State Park**—the largest American park outside Alaska. Unfortunately, in recent years the twin pressures of pollution and development have left a harsh imprint on the park. Acid rain has damaged many tree and fish populations, especially in the fragile high-altitude environments, and tourist meccas like **Lake George** have continued to rapidly expand. Despite these warning signs, much of the area retains the beauty it had over a century ago.

Of the six million acres in the Adirondacks Park, 40% is open to the public. Two thousand mi. of trails traverse the forest and provide the best access to the spectacular mountain scenery, whether you're hiking, snow-shoeing, or cross-country skiing. An interlocking network of lakes and streams makes the gentle Adirondack wilds a perennial favorite of canoeists. Mountain-climbers may wish to surmount **Mt. Marcy,** the state's highest peak (5344 ft.), at the base of the Adirondacks, and skiers can choose from any of a dozen well-known alpine ski centers. **Lake Placid** hosted the winter Olympics in 1932 and 1980, and frequently welcomes national and international sports competitions (see Lake Placid below). **Saranac Lake** hosts the **International Dog Sledding Championship** at the end of January. **Tupper Lake** and **Lake George** also have carnivals every January and February, and Tupper hosts the **Tin Man Triathlon** in July. In September, the hot air balloons of the **Adirondack Balloon Festival** in Glens Falls race the trees to be the first to provide fall color.

Lake Placid

Melvil Dewey, creator of the Dewey Decimal library classification system and founder of the exclusive Lake Placid Club, first promoted Lake Placid as a summer resort in 1850. Twice hosting the Winter Olympic Games cemented the town's international fame. Currently the Adirondacks' premier tourist spot, Lake Placid attracts crowds of casual visitors and world-class athletes. The international flags and stores that line Main Street may seem out of sync with the town's inviting, old-village atmosphere, as do the sporting facilities unmatched by many of the world's metropolises. It's all part of what makes Lake Placid such a pleasing place to visit. Temperatures can plummet to -40°F and more than 200 inches of snow may fall in any given Adirondack winter, but well-plowed main roads keep the region open year-round.

The Olympic spirit clearly makes its presence felt in Lake Placid, with a number of venues scattered in and just outside the town. The **Olympic Regional Development Authority,** in Olympic Ctr. (523-1655 or 800-462-6236), operates the facilities. The **Lake Placid Convention and Visitors Bureau** (523-2445), in Olympic Ctr. just above the hockey rink, gives price info and directions. (Open Mon.-Fri. 9am-5pm, Sat.-Sun. 8am-5pm.) You can't miss the 70- and 90m-runs of the Olympic ski jumps, which, with the **Kodak Sports Park,** make up the **Olympic Jumping Complex,** just outside of town on Rte. 73. The $5 admission fee includes a chairlift and elevator ride to the top of the spectator towers, where you might catch summer (June-Columbus Day) jumpers flipping and sailing into a swimming pool. (Open daily 9am-5pm, Sept.-May 9am-4pm.) Three mi. farther along Rte. 73, the **Olympic Sports Complex** (523-4436) at Mt. Van Hoevenberg offers a summer trolley running to the top of the bobsled run ($3). In the winter (Dec.-March Tues.-Sun. 1-3pm) you can bobsled down the run used in the Olympics ($25), or even try the luge run ($10). The park is open for self-guided tours ($1) daily from 9am to 4pm June-Columbus Day, and has 35 mi. of well-groomed cross-country ski trails ($7).

In addition to its fantastic ski slopes, **Whiteface Mountain,** near Lake Placid, provides a panoramic view of the Adirondacks. You can get up to the summit via the **Whiteface Memorial Highway** ($4 toll, cars only) or a chairlift (446-2255, $5, seniors and kids $4). (Highway open mid-May-mid-Oct.; chairlift open mid-June-mid-Oct.) The extensive **Whiteface Mountain Ski Center** (523-1655) has the largest vertical drop in the East (3216 ft.). Don't bother with the $4 tour of the waterfalls at **High Falls Gorge** (946-2278) on Rte. 86 near Whiteface; hike below the road to see the same scenery for free, and laugh at all the people who paid. **Ice fishing** on the lakes is popular, especially with locals, as is **ice skating** (Olympic speed-skating rink $2; open daily 7-9pm, Mon.-Fri. noon-2pm weather permitting).

History buffs and corpse cultivators will enjoy a quick visit to the **farm and grave** of the militant abolitionist **John Brown** (hung in 1859 for his role in an ambush of an arsenal at Harpers Ferry, VA), off Rte. 73, three mi. southeast of Lake Placid (523-3900; open late May-late Oct. Wed.-Sat. 10am-5pm, Sun. 1-5pm; free). The west branch of the **Ausable River,** just east of the town of Lake Placid, lures anglers to its shores. **Fishing licenses** for non-residents of New York are $16 for five days (season $28) and for residents $6 for three days (season $14) at Town Hall, 301 Main St. (523-2162), or Jones Outfitters, 37 Main St. (523-3468). Call the "Fishing Hotline" at 891-5413 for an in-depth fresh-water recording of the hot fishing spots and current conditions. The **Lake Placid Center for the Arts,** on Saranac Ave. just outside Lake Placid Village at Fawn Ridge (523-2512), houses a local art gallery and hosts theater, dance, and musical performances. (Open daily 1-5pm; winter Mon.-Fri. 1-5pm. Gallery free; call for prices and listings of performances.)

Main Street in Lake Placid Village offers pickings to suit any palate, and prices are generally reasonable. At the lunch buffet (noon-2pm) at the **Hilton Hotel,** (523-4411; 1 Mirror Lake Dr. at the beginning of Main St.), $4.75 buys a sandwich and all-you-can-eat soup and salad. **The Cottage,** (523-9845), 5 Mirror Lake Dr., has relatively inexpensive meals (sandwiches and salads $4-6) with scrumptious views of Mirror Lake; watch the U.S. canoe and kayaking teams practice on the water. (Meals served daily 11:30am-9pm. Bar open daily 11:30am-1am.) **Mud Puddles,** 3 School St. (523-4446), below the speed skating rink, is popular with disco throwbacks and the pop music crowd. (Open Wed.-Sun. 9pm-3am. Cover $1.50.)

Most **accommodations** in the area are expensive. The **White Sled** (523-9314, on Rte. 73 between the Sports Complex and the ski jumps) is the best bargain around: for $14 you get a comfortable, clean bed in the bunkhouse, which includes a full kitchen, living room, and entertainment by the friendly, Francophone hosts. **Holly Hill** (523-9231, 215 Saranac Ave., about 2 mi. out of Lake Placid) offers "thrifty, thrifty, thrifty" rooms with two beds and private bath for $35. **Lysek's Inn,** 50 Hillcrest Ave. (523-1700), rents beds and serves a buffet breakfast for $20.50 (mid-Sept.-May). Call ahead since the place fills up quickly with young athletes. (From Main St. go up the hill on Marcy St. next to Sundog Sport and turn left on Hillcrest.)

To explore Lake Placid by **bike**, rent mountain bikes at **Sundog Ski & Sport,** 90 Main St. (523-2752; $5 per hr., $18 per day). The shop also rents downhill skis ($14 per day), and in-line skates ($4 per 2 hrs., $8 per day). (Must have ID. Open daily 9am-6pm.)

Adirondack Trailways has extensive service in the area, stopping at the **326 Main St. Deli** in Lake Placid (523-1527; 523-4309 for bus info). Buses run to New York City ($48.75) and Lake George ($14). By car, Lake Placid is at the intersection of Rte. 86 and 73.

For **weather** information call 523-2538. Lake Placid has a **post office** at 201 Main St. (523-3071; open Mon.-Fri. 9am-5pm, Sat. 9am-12:30pm). Lake Placid's **ZIP code** is 12946; the **area code** is 518.

Near Lake Placid

The best source of information on hiking and other outdoor activities in the region is the **Adirondack Mountain Club (ADK)**. The ADK is in its 71st year, has over 16,000 members, and has offices at both RR3, Box 3055, Lake George 12845 (668-4447) and at Adirondack Loj Rd., P.O. Box 867, Lake Placid 12946 (523-3441). The club sponsors a number of outdoors skills classes such as canoeing, rock climbing, fly fishing, and white water kayaking. The ADK's **High Peaks Information Center,** off Rte. 73 outside Lake Placid near the sign for the Adirondack Loj, has the latest in backcountry info, sells basic outdoor equipment and trail snacks, and has washrooms. (Open daily 8am-8pm.) Those interested in rock climbing should consult the **Mountaineer** (576-2281, halfway between I-87 and Lake Placid on Rte. 73). All employees here are experienced mountaineers, and the store is a good source of weather forecasts. Rent snowshoes for $10 per day, and ice-climbing equipment (boots and crampons) for $15 per day.

Two lodges near Lake Placid are also run by the ADK. The **Adirondack Loj** (523-3441), eight mi. east of Lake Placid off Rte. 73, is a beautiful log cabin on Heart Lake with comfortable bunk facilities and a family atmosphere. Guests can swim, fish, canoe, and use rowboats free of charge. In winter, explore the wilderness trails on rented snowshoes ($6 per day) or cross-country skis ($10 per day). (B&B $29, with dinner $40. Linen included. Campsites $13. Lean-tos $16.) Call ahead for weekends and during peak holiday seasons. Take about 20% off for non-peak rates. For an even better mix of rustic comfort and wilderness experience, hike 3½ mi. from the closest trailhead to the **John's Brook Lodge,** in Keene Valley 16 mi. southeast of Lake Placid off Rte. 73 (call the Adirondack Loj for reservations). From Placid, follow Rte. 73 15 mi. through Keene to Keene Valley, turning right at the Ausable Inn. The hike is only slightly uphill, and the food is well worth the exertion; the staff packs in groceries every day and cooks on a gas stove. A great place to meet friendly New Yorkers (?), John's Brook is no secret; the beds fill completely on weekends. Make reservations at least one day in advance for dinner, longer for a weekend. Bring sheets or a sleeping bag. (B&B $24, with dinner $35. Slightly less off-peak. Lean-tos $7. Open mid-June-early Sept.) From Memorial Day-June 12 and Labor Day-Columbus Day, rent a bunk for $9 weekdays, $10 weekends, with full access to the kitchen.

If ADK facilities are too pricey, try the **High Peaks Base Camp,** P.O. Box 91, Upper Jay 12987 (946-2133), a charming restaurant/lodge/campground just a 20-minute drive from Lake Placid. Take Rte. 86 N. to Wilmington, turn right at the Mobil station, then go right 3½ mi. on Springfield Rd.; $15 (Sun.-Thurs.) or $18 (Fri.-Sat.) buys you a bed for the night and a huge breakfast. (Check-in until 9pm, later with reservations. Sites $3 per person. Cabins $30 for 4 people.) Transportation is tough without a car but sometimes rides can be arranged from Keene; call ahead. The two closest campgrounds to Lake Placid are **Meadowbrook State Park** (891-4351, 5 mi. west of Lake Placid on Rte. 86 in Ray Brook), and **Wilmington Notch State Campground** (946-7172, off Rte. 86 between Wilmington and Lake Placid). Both offer sites without hookups ($10.50 first night, $9 each additional night) which can accommodate two tents and up to six people. In the forest, you can use the free shelters by the trails. Always inquire about their location before you plan a hike. Camp for free in the **backcountry** anywhere on public land, as long as you are at least 150 ft. away from a trail, road, water source or campground and stay below 4000 ft. altitude.

The **Lake George Youth Hostel** is located in the basement of **St. James Episcopal Church Hall,** P.O. Box 176, Lake George (668-2634), on Montcalm St. at Ottawa, several blocks from the lake. From the bus terminal, walk south one block to Montcalm, turn right and go one block to Ottawa for the slightly musty bunkroom with a decent kitchen. (Check-in 5-9pm, later only with reservations. Curfew 10pm. $10, nonmembers $13. Open late May-early Sept.)

The Adirondacks are served by **Adirondacks Trailways,** with frequent stops along I-87. You can take a bus to Lake Placid, Tupper Lake, and Lake George from Albany. From the Lake George bus stop, at the Mobil station, 320 Canada St. (668-9511; 800-225-6815 for bus info), buses reach Lake Placid ($12.45), Albany ($9.30), and New York City ($36.30). (Open June-Sept. daily 7am-midnight, Oct.-May daily 7am-10pm.) Traveling in the backwoods is tough during the muddy spring thaw (March-April).

Contact the **State Office of Parks and Recreation** (see New York Practical Information) in Albany for more info on the Adirondacks. The best info on hiking and other outdoor activities emanates from the **ADK** (see above). For trails in the Lake Placid area, look for ADK's particularly good *Guide to the High Peaks* ($15).

The Adirondacks' **area code** is 518.

Albany

With millions of dollars spent on urban renewal, Albany has undergone what many residents term a "renaissance." This may be an overstatement, but recent efforts to stimulate tourism have made the state capital more than just a soapbox for Governor Mario Cuomo and a transportation hub for passers-through.

Although the English took Albany in 1664, the city was actually founded in 1614 as a trading post for the Dutch West Indies Company, and is the oldest continuous settlement in the original 13 colonies (established six years before the Pilgrims landed on the rocky New England shore). Albany (once named Fort Orange) became New York's state capital in 1797, but never matched the growth of its southern sibling, the Big Apple. Today, juxtaposing the two cities would be like...well, like comparing apples and oranges. The **Schuyler** (SKY-ler) **Mansion,** 32 Catherine St. (434-0834), gives a sense of the city's rich history. Colonial statesman and general Philip Schuyler owned the elegant Georgian home, built in 1761. Here George Washington and Benjamin Franklin dined, and here Alexander Hamilton married Schuyler's daughter. (Open April-Oct. Wed.-Sat. 10am-5pm, Sun. 1-5pm. Free.)

Including the Schuyler, Albany offers about a day's worth of sight-seeing activity. The **Rockefeller Empire State Plaza,** State St., a $1.9 billion architectural marvel, houses, aside from state offices, the **New York State Museum** (474-5877; open daily 10am-5pm; free), and the huge egg that is the **New York State Performing Arts Center** (473-1845). The museum's exhibits depict the history of the state's different regions, including Manhattan; displays range from Native American arrowheads to an original set for "Sesame Street." For a bird's-eye view of Albany, visit the observation deck on the 44th floor of the Corning Tower, the tallest skyscraper in the plaza. (Open daily 9am-4pm.) Look, but please don't touch the "art for the public" **Empire State Collection.** Scattered throughout the plaza, the collection features work by innovative New York School artists such as Jackson Pollock, Mark Rothko, and David Smith. (473-7521. Open daily, tours by appointment. Free.)

The modern plaza provides a striking contrast to the more traditional architectural landscape of the rest of the city. Within walking distance on Washington Ave. are **City Hall,** an earthy Romanesque edifice, and the **Capitol Building** (474-2418), a Gothic marvel, both worked on by H. H. Richardson. (Free tours on the hour Mon.-Fri. 9am-4pm.)

Stroll around downtown to admire Albany's numerous churches, especially **First Church in Albany,** on the corner of Orange and N. Pearl (463-4449), founded in 1642. Its present building was constructed in 1798, and houses the oldest known pulpit and weather vane in America. (Open Mon.-Fri. 9am-4pm.) The State Education Department has done an excellent job of marking trivial and not-so-trivial historic spots throughout the city; the **Albany Visitors Center,** 25 Quackenbush Sq. 12207 (434-5132, on the corner of Clinton Ave. and Broadway), has maps and brochures of the city and operates trolley tours ($4). The Center also displays an educational exhibit about Albany's past. (Open daily 10am-4pm, off-season Mon.-Fri. 10am-4pm.)

Albany blossoms in a colorful rainbow of music, dancing, food, and street-scrubbing in May during the **Tulip Festival** (434-2032). The state sponsors free concerts at the plaza during the summer (call 473-0559 for info). **Washington Park,** bounded by State St. and Madison Ave. north of downtown, has tennis courts, paddle boats, and verdant fields. From mid-July to mid-August, Wednesday through Sunday at 8pm, the **Park Playhouse** (434-2035) stages free theater. On Monday and Tuesday at that same time, varied entertainment, under the title **Dark Nights,** takes place at the lake house. Come **Alive at Five** on Thursdays during the summer, to the sound of free concerts at the **Tricentennial Plaza** across from Norstar on Broadway.

Food, save for a few hot dog vendors, is sparse downtown. **Next Door,** 142 Washington St. (434-1616), has a half-sandwich special with soup and salad ($4) and great chocolate chip cookies (55¢). (Open Mon.-Fri. 7am-9pm.) Named after Henry Hudson's ship, the **Half Moon Café,** 154 Madison Ave. (436-0329), attracts area activists, artists, and environmentalists. Enjoy quality natural foods (vegetarian chili and cheese $3, salad platters $4.50) on the patio. A monthly calendar lists the café's nightly jazz, folk, blues, as well as concerts, poetry readings, and meetings. No cover—donations only—and an open jam every Tuesday night; the Grateful Dead play here when they're in town. (Daily 11am-11pm.) If you're further away from downtown, try **Dahlia's** (482-0931) 858 Madison Ave., and have a scoop of their funky and dahlicious homemade ginger ice cream ($1.31). All food is vegetarian and kosher. (Open Sun.-Thurs. noon-10pm, Fri.-Sat. noon-midnight.)

If you're spending more than a day in Albany, treat yourself to the hospitality of **Pine Haven (HI/AYH),** 531 Western Ave. 482-1574, where Janice Tricarico runs a hostel and a B&B. From the bus station, walk by the State University of New York offices on

Broadway and turn left on State St. From the stop in front of the Hilton, take the #10 bus up Western Ave. and get off at N. Allen St. Pine Haven is on your right, at the convergence of Madison and Western Ave. Parking in rear. (B&B: Singles $39. Doubles $49. Hostel $12. Reservations recommended; call ahead.) If Pine Haven is full in summertime, try the nearby **College of Saint Rose,** Lima Hall, 366 Western Ave. (Reservations: Tonita Nagle at Student Affairs, Box 114, 432 Western Ave., 454-5171, after hours 454-5100. May 15-Aug. 15 Mon.-Fri. 8:30am-4:30pm.) You'll find large rooms and impeccable bathrooms in student dorms on a scenic campus. The dining hall is open for use. (Singles $35. Doubles $50.) Across the river is the **Fort Crailo Motel,** 110 Columbia Turnpike, Rensselaer 12114 (472-1360), 1½ mi. from downtown and about the same distance from the Amtrak station. (Singles $30-36. Doubles $36-42.) The closest **YMCA,** 13 State St. (374-9136), and **YWCA,** 44 Washington Ave. (374-3394), are both in Schenectady. (Singles $20-22.50.)

Amtrak, East St., Rensselaer (800-872-7245 or 462-5763), across the Hudson from downtown Albany, runs to New York City (9-10 per day, 2½ hr., $40), Boston (1 per day, 43/4 hr., $36), and Montreal (1 per day, 71/4 hrs. $48). (Station open Mon.-Fri. 5:30am-11pm, Sat.-Sun. 6am-midnight.) **Greyhound,** 34 Hamilton St. (434-8095), offers service to New York City (8 per day, 3 hr., $27); Montréal (6 per day, 5 hr., $47); Boston (4 per day, 4-5 hr., $29); and Syracuse (6 per day, 3 hr., $17). Students receive 15% discount during the school year. (Station open 24 hrs., but it's in an unsafe area.) **Adirondack Trailways,** one block away at 360 Broadway (436-9651), connects to other upstate locales: Lake George (4 per day, in winter 3 per day; 1 hr.; $9); Lake Placid (2 per day, in winter 1 per day; 4 hr.; $22); and Tupper Lake (1 per day, 4 hr., $26). Senior and college-student discounts are available for both routes on certain lines. (Open Mon.-Fri. 5:30am-11pm, Sat.-Sun. 7:30am-11pm.) For local travel, the **Capitol District Transit Authority (CDTA)** (482-8822) serves Albany, Troy, and Schenectady. CDTA has a confusing schedule and often patchy coverage; a quick call to the main office will set you straight. (Fare 75¢.)

Albany's **ZIP code** is 12201; the **area code** is 518.

Catskills

These lovely mountains continue to captivate city-dwellers who migrate up the highways of the Hudson and Mohawk River Valleys in search of unpolluted air and tranquil, dense forests. Big-Appleites who never leave their concrete jungle have the Catskills piped to them; the Ashokan reservoir, one of the purest in the nation, provides for New York City's water needs. Beyond the lakeside resorts, visitors can find peace and natural beauty in the state-managed Catskill Preserve, home to quiet villages, sparkling streams, and miles of hiking and skiing trails.

Adirondack Pine Hill Trailways provides excellent service through the Catskills. The main stop is **Kingston,** at 400 Washington Ave. (914-331-0744 or 800-225-6815). (To New York City 14 per day, 2 hr., $18.50. Ameripass accepted.) Other stops in the area include Woodstock, Pine Hill, Saugerties, and Hunter; each connects with New York City, Albany, and Utica. Road conditions are consistently good.

Catskill Preserve

The 250,000-acre, state-run Catskill Preserve contains many small towns ready to host and equip the travelers who come here to enjoy the outdoors. The slow-moving town of **Phoenicia,** accessible by bus from Kingston, marks a good place to anchor your trip. The **Esopus River,** just to the west, is great for trout fishing and for late-summer inner-tubing in the Phoenicia area. Rent tubes at **The Town Tinker,** on Bridge St. (914-688-5553) in Phoenicia. (Inner tubes $7 per day, with a seat $10. Driver's license or $15 required as a deposit. Transportation $3. Life jackets available. Open May-Sept. daily 9am-6pm, last rental 4:30pm.) Take a dive at the 65-ft. **Sundance Rappel Tower** Rte. 214, Phoenicia 12464 (914-688-5640). Four levels of lessons available: beginner $20 for three to four hrs. Reservations two weeks in advance recommended. If you plan to go fishing, you must buy a **fishing permit** (5 days, non-NY resident $16). To camp in the backcountry for more than three days, you must obtain a permit from the nearest ranger station. Trails are maintained year-round; available lean-tos are sometimes dilapidated and crowded. Boil or treat water with chemicals, and pack your garbage. To reach the head of your chosen trail, take an **Adirondack Trailways** bus from Kingston—drivers will let you out anywhere along the bus routes. (Call 914-331-0744 for info on routes and fares.) The **Ulster County Public Information Office,** 244 Fair St. 5th Floor, four blocks from the Kingston bus station (800-342-5826), has a helpful travel guide and a list of Catskill trails. For more info, pick up *Guide to Catskill Trails* by Bruce Wadsworth.

One of the many well-run **state campgrounds** (800-456-2267 for reservations) can serve as a base for your hiking, fishing, or tubing adventures. Reservations are vital during the summer, especially Thursday to Sunday. (Sites $7-13. Open May-Sept.) Call the rangers at the individual campgrounds for the best info on sites in the area, or for brochures on state campgrounds call the Office of Parks, Recreation and Historic Information (518-474-0456). **North Lake**, Rte. 23A, three mi. northeast of Haines Falls (518-589-5058), rents canoes and has showers and good hiking trails. **Kenneth L. Wilson,** a four-mi. hike from Bearsville bus stop (914-679-7020), has showers, a pond-front beach, and a family atmosphere ($9 per site). **Woodland Valley,** five mi. southeast of Phoenicia (914-688-7647), has no showers, but sits on a good 16-mi. hiking trail.

If you prefer sleeping in civilization, go to the **Super 8 Motel** (914-338-3078) 487 Washington Ave., two blocks from the Kingston bus station. (Singles from $49, doubles from $55. Make reservations for summer weekends.) But if you'd rather be at peace with nature, join in meditation at the **Zen Mountain Monastery**, S. Plank Rd. P.O. Box 197PC, Mt. Tremper, NY 12457 (914-688-2228), a short walk from Mt. Tremper. (Free public meditation sessions Wed. 7:30pm and Sun. 9am-noon. Weekend retreats $150.)

Cooperstown

Early American author James Fenimore Cooper made his home here, and *The Last of the Mohicans* is set in the area. But far and away the town's most famous resident was Abner Doubleday, who—according to myth, American folklore and the 1905 Mills Commission which finally settled the matter—invented the game of baseball here in 1839. Cooperstown hasn't been the same since. Tourists invade the town by droves in the summer, often outnumbering residents. Baseball fans feel like they've died and gone to the Great Big Ballpark in the Sky; apart from the Baseball Hall of Fame, aficionados can investigate over a dozen memorabilia shops on Main St., watch bats being made, eat in one of the baseball theme restaurants, or sleep at one of the baseball theme motels.

The National Baseball Hall of Fame and Museum (547-9988) on Main St. is an enormous paean to baseball. Among the bats, balls, uniforms and plaques you expect there are exhibits on women and minorities in baseball, on how a baseball is made, and also a wooden statue of Babe Ruth. The annual ceremonies for new inductees are held in Cooper Park, next to the building (usually late July-early Aug.; call ahead). There are special exhibits for hearing- and visually impaired fans. (Open daily May-Oct. 9am-9pm; Nov.-April 9am-5pm. $6, ages 7-15 $2.50, under 7 free. Combination tickets with the Farmers' Museum and Fenimore House: $13 for all 3 museums, $10 for any 2.)

When you are ready to take the next baseball you see and bulldoze it, check out the **Farmers' Museum and Village Crossroads** (547-2593), one mi. from town on Rte. 80, accessible from the trolley. The museum is a living microcosm of life in upstate New York's "hopespun" era of the early 1800s. Watch blacksmithing, horseshoeing, and old-time holy-rolling gospel preaching. (Open daily May-Oct. 9am-6pm. $6, under 16 $2.50, under 7 free.) Those with a curiosity about American folk art will be intrigued by **Fenimore House** (547-2533), on Rte. 80 across from the Farmers' Museum. 18th- and 19th-century American paintings and sculptures dot the corners of the vast period rooms overlooking Otsego Lake. (Open daily May-Oct. 9am-6pm. $5, under 16 $2, under 7 free.)

For decent food, an amusing baseball atmosphere, and a souvenir shop in the building, check out T.J.'s Place, on Main St. across from Doubleday Field. (Dinners $5-10. Open daily 7am-9pm.) The Pioneer Patio, on Pioneer Alley off Pioneer St, is an affordable café with traditional American and German food. (Lunch $2-6, dinner $7-9. Open Mon.-Thurs. 11am-8pm, Fri.-Sat. 8am-10pm.) The Bold Dragoon, on Pioneer St., is a good place to swig a cold one and hang out with the locals. (Dinners $5-10. Draft beer $1. Open daily 11:30am-9pm, bar open until 2am.)

Camping is the way to go in Cooperstown; lodging in the summertime is hideously expensive and generally full, although the Chamber of Commerce (see below) can help out in a pinch. **Glimmerglass State Park,** RD2 Box 580 (607-547-8662 or 800-456-2267), on Ostego County Rte. 31 on the east side of Ostego Lake, eight mi. north of Cooperstown, has 36 pristine campsites in a gorgeous lakeside park. Swimming 11am-7pm, fishing, boating, and more. Weekends are booked in summer. (Sites $11.50 for 6 people; showers, dumping station, no hookups.) **Cooperstown Beaver Valley Campground**, Box 704 Cooperstown, take Rte. 28 south four mi., turn right on Seminary Rd. (607-293-7324 or 800-726-7314), never fills up, even in high season. Two **bunkhouses** available (bring your own linen), 110 sites, three ponds, laundry facilities, and Fri.-Sun., the owner personally buses campers into town. ($8 bunkhouse, $18 tent site for 4 people, $3 tenting without site, $20 RV site with hookup, $5 per hr. paddleboat rental. Open mid-May-mid-Sept.) The **Gray Goose B&B,** RD1 Box 21, off Rte. 80, three mi. north of Cooperstown (607-547-2763), is a restored farmhouse, and very cozy. (Singles $50. Doubles $55.)

Cooperstown is accessible from I-90 and I-88 via Rte. 28. Street parking barely exists in Cooperstown; your best bet is the free parking lots just outside town near the Fenimore House, on Rte. 28 south of Cooperstown, and on Glen Ave. From there, take a trolley (really a school bus with an attitude). (Trolley runs daily July-Sept. 8:30am-8pm. All-day pass $1.) **Adirondack Trailways** (800-225-6815) runs two buses per day from New York City (4½-5hrs., $40), Greyhound Ameripasses honored. The **Cooperstown Area Chamber of Commerce,** 31 Chestnut St., (547-9983), on Rte. 80 near Main St., has maps, brochures, and hotel and B&B listings; it also can make reservations for you.

Cooperstown's **post office** (607-225-6815) is at 40 Main St. (Open Mon.-Fri. 8:30am-5pm, Sat. 9:30am-1pm.) **ZIP code:** 13326. Cooperstown's **area code** is 607.

The Finger Lakes

According to Iroquois legend, the Great Spirit laid his hands upon the earth, and the impression of his fingers made the Finger Lakes: Canandaigua, Keuka, Seneca, Cayuga, Owasco, and Skaneateles, among others. The double attraction of superlative scenery and acclaimed regional wineries make spending time here sublime.

Practical Information

Tompkins County Convention and Visitors Bureau, 904 E. Shore Dr., Ithaca 14850 (272-1313 or 800-284-8422). By car take Rte. 13 north of the city, exit at Stewart Park and follow the signs. From the bus station turn left on State St., then walk left on Cayuga all the way to E. Shore (about 30 min. on foot), or take bus #4 to Stewart Park. Tremendous number of brochures on Ithaca, Finger Lakes, and every other county in upstate New York. Hotel and B&B listings. Best map of the area ($3). Open Mon.-Fri. 9am-5pm, Sat.-Sun. 10am-5pm; Labor Day-Memorial Day Mon.-Fri. 9am-5pm.

Buses: Ithaca Bus Terminal, W. State and N. Fulton St. (272-7930), for **Short Line** and **Greyhound.** To: New York City (8 per day); Philadelphia (3 per day); Buffalo (3 per day). Call for fares. Open daily 7:30am-6:30pm.

Public Transport: Tomtran (Tompkins County Transportation Services Project), 274-5370. Covers a wider area than Ithaca Transit, including Trumansburg and Ulysses, both northwest of Ithaca on Rte. 96, and Cayuga Heights and Lansing Village, both north of Ithaca on Rte. 13. Only

choice for getting out to the Finger Lakes. Buses stop at Ithaca Commons, westbound on Seneca St., and eastbound on Green. $.60, $1.25 for more distant zones. Mon.-Fri. only.

Bike Rental: Black Star Bicycles, 1922 Dryden Rd. (347-4117), 7 mi. out of town on Rte. 13. $15 per day, $25 per 3 days. Take Ithaca Transit's Dryden Bus. Open Mon.-Fri. noon-6pm, Sat. 10am-5pm, Sun. noon-4pm.

Car Rental: Chuck John's Auto Rental, 652 Spencer Rd., 3 mi. south on Rte. 13, (272-2222). $24 per day, 100 free mi. per day, age 25 and up; age 21-24 add $5 per day. Credit card required. (Open Mon.-Fri. 8am-5pm, Sat. 8am-noon.)

Ithaca Police: 272-3245. **Fire and Ambulance:** 273-8000. **Tompkins County Sheriff:** 272-2444.

Post Office, 213 N. Tioga St. (272-5454), at E. Buffalo. Open Mon.-Fri. 8:30am-5:30pm, Sat. 8:30am-1pm. **ZIP code:** 14850.

Area code: 607.

Accommodations and Camping

The Tompkins County Visitors Bureau (see Practical Information above) has full Ithaca area B&B listings.

Podunk House Hostel (HI/AYH), Podunk Rd. (387-9277), in Trumansburg about 8 mi. northwest of Ithaca. By car take Rte. 96 north through Jacksonville, turn left on Cold Springs Rd. following signs for Podunk ski area until it ends at Podunk, turn left again and the hostel is 50 yds. away on your right. Greyhound has a Trumansburg flag stop; or take the Tomtran. Venture into the land of Oz, friendly owner of the hostel. He's happy to talk philosophy or architecture or let you soak up the silence of his 30-acre farm. Finnish sauna fired up twice a week. Hiking trails and cross-country skiing accessible. Beds in the loft of a homestead barn. No kitchen. Members only, $5. Linen $1. Open April-Oct. Call ahead, before 9pm.

Elmshade Guest House, 402 S. Albany St. (273-1707), at Center St. 3 blocks from the Ithaca Commons. From the bus station, walk up State St. and turn right onto Albany. Impeccably clean, well-decorated, good-sized rooms with shared bath. You'll feel like a guest at a rich relative's house. TV in every room, refrigerator, microwave on hall. Singles $25. Doubles $37; prices may rise. Morning coffee, rolls, fruit included. Reservations recommended.

Camping options in this area are virtually endless. Fifteen of the 20 state parks in the Finger Lakes region have campsites, nine have cabins. The brochure *Finger Lakes State Parks* contains a description of each park's location, services, and environs; pick it up from any tourist office, park, or the **Finger Lakes State Park Region,** 2221 Taughannock Park Rd., RD 3, Trumansburg 14886 (607-387-7041). Whatever your plans, reserve ahead. The four-wheel-drive trucks and Winnebagos are rolling in to steal your spot even as you read. Summer weekends almost always fill up.

Food and Nightlife

Restaurants cluster in Ithaca along Aurora St. and Ithaca Commons. Pick up the *Ithaca Dining Guide* pamphlet at the Tompkins County Visitors Center (see above) for more options.

Moosewood Restaurant, Seneca and Cayuga St. (273-9610), Ithaca. Creative, well-prepared vegetarian, fish, and pasta dishes. The *Moosewood Cookbook* originated here. Menu changes daily. Lunches $4-5, dinners around $9-11. Open Mon.-Sat. 11:30am-2pm and 6-9pm, Sun. 6-9pm, in winter Sun.-Thurs. 5:30-8:30pm.

Joe's Restaurant, 602 W. Buffalo St. (272-2693), corner of Rte. 13 (Meadow St.) and Buffalo St., 10 min. walk from Ithaca Commons. Italian and American food; their specialty is veal (they serve the equivalent of one calf per day). Original art-deco interior dates from 1932; this is *the* student spot in town. Open 4-10pm.

Just a Taste, 116 N. Aurora (227-9463), near Ithaca Common. The place to taste fine wines (2½ oz. $1.75-3.75) and savor *tapas,* the Spanish "little dishes" ($3.50-5.50). Individual pizzas from $3.50. Open Mon.-Wed. 11:30am-10pm, Thurs.-Sat. 11:30am-midnight, Sun. 11:30am-9:30pm. Bar open Mon.-Wed. until midnight, Thurs.-Sat. until 1am, Sun. until 11pm.

Rongovian Embassy to the USA, Rte. 96 (387-3334), in the main strip of Trumansburg about 10 mi. out of Ithaca. Worth the drive. Amazing Mexican entrees in a classic restaurant/bar. Plot your next trip to "Beefree", "Nearvarna", or "Freelonch" on their huge wall map. Tacos $2.50. Dinners about $8. Mug of beer $1-1.50. Live bands on weekends, cover $4-5. Food served Tues.-Thurs. and Sun. 5-9pm, Fri.-Sat. 5-10pm. Open till 1am.

The Store at Truman's Village, on Rte. 96 in Trumansburg just up the street from the Embassy. Great local diner offering a taste of upstate country life and good burgers ($1.35). Breakfast served all day (pancakes $2.25). Open Mon.-Fri. 7am-8pm, Sat.-Sun. 8am-5pm.

Sights

The fertile soil of the Finger Lakes area makes this region the heart of New York's wine industry. Wine tasting and touring at one of the small local vineyards is a relaxing way to pass a day. All of the vineyards on the Cayuga Wine Trail (P.O. Box 123, Fayette, NY 13065; write for their brochure) offer picnic facilities and free tastings, though some require purchase of a glass ($1.50-2). **Americana Vineyards Winery,** 4367 East Covert Rd., Interlaken (607-387-6801), ferments one mi. or so from Trumansburg, accessible by Greyhound and Tomtran (see Practical Information above). A family of four operates this winery from grape-picking to bottle-corking; one will give you a personal tour and free tasting. Pick up a bottle for about $5. (Open May-Oct. Mon.-Sat. 10am-5pm, Sun. noon-5pm, April and Nov.-Dec. weekends only; if you're driving, take Rte. 96 or 89 north of Trumansburg to E. Covert Rd.) On the eastern side of Seneca Lake, visit **Wagner Winery,** Rte. 414 (607-582-6450), four mi. south of Lodi. Far bigger than any of the Cayuga wineries, bottling some 60,000 gallons per year, Wagner rests on a beautiful meditative spot on Seneca Lake. From Ithaca take Rte. 79 west to 414 south (8-9 mi.). Tastes and tours are free. (Open Mon.-Fri. 10am-4:30pm, Sat.-Sun. 10am-5pm.)

Considered the birthplace of the women's rights movement, **Seneca Falls** hosted the 1848 Seneca Falls Convention. Elizabeth Cady Stanton and Amelia Bloomer, two leading suffragists who lived here, organized a meeting of those seeking the vote for women. Visit the **National Women's Hall of Fame,** 76 Fall St. (315-568-8060), where photographs and biographies commemorate 38 outstanding U.S. women. (Open Mon.-Sat. 10am-4pm, Sun. noon-4pm. Donation requested.)

Forty minutes out of Ithaca on Rte. 17 West off Rte. 13 South, bakes the town of **Corning,** home to the Corning Glass Works that make Steuben artglass and sturdy cookware. The **Corning Glass Center,** Centerway, Corning 14831 (607-974-8271), built in honor of the Glass Works' Centenary in 1951, chronicles the 3500-year history of glassmaking in a display of over 20,000 pieces. (Open daily 9am-5pm. $6, over 60 $5, under 18 $4.) The nearby **Rockwell Museum,** 111 Cedar St. Rte. 17 (607-937-5386), displays glass pieces by Frederick Carder, founder of the Steuben Glass Works and an excellent collection of American Western art. (Open Mon.-Sat. 9am-5pm, Sun. noon-5pm, July-Aug. Mon.-Sat. 9am-7pm, Sun. noon-5pm. $3, seniors $2.50, under 18 free.)

In the Lakes region, a car provides the easiest transportation, but biking and hiking allow more intimate contact with this beautiful country. Reach out and touch the **Finger Lakes State Park Region** (see Practical Information above) for free maps and tips. Write the **Finger Lakes Trail Conference,** P.O. Box 18048, Rochester 14618 (716-288-7191), for free maps of the **Finger Lakes Trail,** an east-west footpath from the Catskills westward to the Allegheny Mountains. This 350-mi. trail and its 300 mi. of branch trails link several state parks, most with camping facilities. Bicyclers can buy *25 Bicycle Tours in the Finger Lakes* ($9) or write to the publisher: The Countryman Press, Inc., P.O. Box 175, Woodstock, VT 05091.

For general info on the area, write or call the **Finger Lakes Association,** Dept. 6-B, 309 Lake St., Penn Yan, NY 14527-1831 (800-548-4386) for free brochures or their 168-page travel guide ($2).

New York City

This rural America thing. It's a joke.
—Edward I. Koch, former mayor of New York

Most people, upon entering The City, are simply not prepared for the *immensity* of the place. Neck-breaking skyscrapers line bullet-straight avenues seemingly for infinity. Nowhere in America is the metronomic rhythm of urban life more pronounced and syncopated than in New York City. Cramped into tiny spaces, millions of people find themselves confronting each other every day in a vast sea of humanity. Despite this (or, perhaps, *because* of the crush of the populace), people here are some of the coldest, loudest, most neurotic and loneliest in the world. But don't fault New Yorkers. Much that is unique, attractive and repulsive about the Big Apple is merely a function of its incomprehensible scale. The city is just too goddamn big, too heterogeneous, too jumbled, too exciting.

Since New York's early days, outsiders have regarded it with wonder and alarm. The city has a history of dramatic and often ungainly growth; services and infrastructures have rarely kept pace with the rapid rate of expansion. For the city's long-term residents, however, the magic produced by that stunning growth compensates for its drawbacks. New York's much-vaunted self-sufficiency—a startlingly high percentage of New Yorkers do not have drivers licenses—began very early. The colony was founded in 1624 by the Dutch West Indies Company as a trading post. England soon asserted rival claims, but the colonists here went about their daily grind oblivious to far-off political haggling. In 1626, in a particularly infamous transaction, Peter Minuit bought Manhattan for 60 guilders, or just under 24 bucks.

Left to its own devices, the city continued to grow. By the late 1770s the city had become a bustling port with a population of 20,000. New York's primary concern was maintaining that prosperity, and it reacted apathetically to the first whiffs of revolution; British rule was good for business, so... The new American Army—understandably—made no great efforts to protect the city. New York fell to the British in September of 1776 and remained in their hands until late November 1783. All the while, New York merchants conducted business as usual.

New York emerged as the nation's pre-eminent city in the 19th century. The Randal Plan simplified the organization of the city streets in 1811, establishing Manhattan's grid scheme. Administration and services lagged behind—pigs, dogs and chickens continued to run freely. The world-famous corruption of Tammany Hall, a political machine set in motion in the 1850s and operative for nearly a century, exacerbated an already desperate situation. New York continued to ignore national concerns in favor of local interests. The city initially opposed the Civil War, its desire to protect trade with the South contravening abolitionist principles. After the war, New York entered a half-century of peace and prosperity during which the seeds of recognizable modernity were sown. The Flatiron building, the world's first skyscraper, was erected in 1902. Manhattan went vertical in order to house the growing population streaming in from Western Europe. Escaping famine, persecution, and political unrest, immigrants faced the perils of sea in for the promise of America.

Booming construction and burgeoning culture helped to generate a sort of urban bliss. Mayor Fiorello LaGuardia navigated the city safely past the shoals of the Great Depression, and post-WWII prosperity brought still more immigrants, especially African-Americans from the rural South, and businesses into the city. However, cracks in the city's infrastructure became increasingly evident. By the 60s, crises in public transportation, education, and housing fanned the flames of ethnic tensions and fostered the rise of a criminal element. In response, city officials raised taxes to improve services, but in the process drove middle-class residents and corporations out of the city.

In the 80s, New York rebounded. Large manufacturing industries were superseded by fresh money from finance and infotech. Wall Street in the 80s was a tragically hip place to be, as evidenced by films (starring the likes of Charlie Sheen and Michael J.

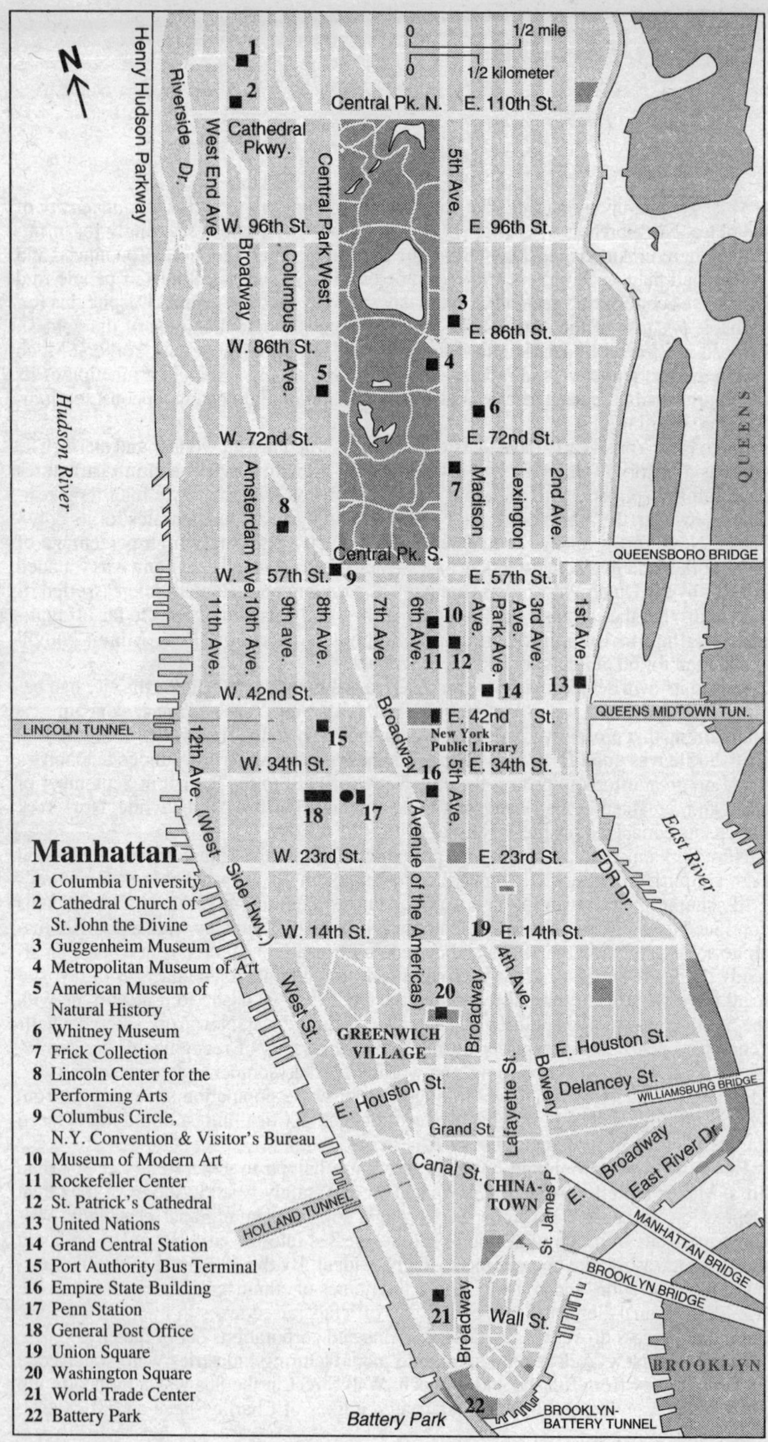

0 1/2 mile
0 1/2 kilometer
N
Henry Hudson Parkway
Riverside Dr.
West End Ave.
Cathedral Pkwy.
Central Pk. N.
E. 110th St.
Central Park West
5th Ave.
W. 96th St.
E. 96th St.
Broadway
Columbus Ave.
E. 86th St.
W. 86th St.
Hudson River
W. 72nd St.
E. 72nd St.
Amsterdam Ave.
Madison
Lexington
2nd Ave.
QUEENS
Central Pk. S.
QUEENSBORO BRIDGE
W. 57th St.
E. 57th St.
11th Ave.
10th Ave.
9th ave.
8th Ave.
7th Ave.
6th Ave.
Park Ave.
3rd Ave.
1st Ave.
W. 42nd St.
E. 42nd St.
QUEENS MIDTOWN TUN.
LINCOLN TUNNEL
New York Public Library
12th Ave. (West Side Hwy.)
W. 34th St.
E. 34th St.
Broadway (Avenue of the Americas)
East River
W. 23rd St.
E. 23rd St.
FDR Dr.
W. 14th St.
E. 14th St.
4th Ave.
West St.
GREENWICH VILLAGE
E. Houston St.
Lafayette St.
Bowery
Delancey St.
WILLIAMSBURG BRIDGE
Grand St.
Canal St.
CHINA-TOWN
St. James Pl.
E. Broadway
East River Dr.
HOLLAND TUNNEL
MANHATTAN BRIDGE
BROOKLYN BRIDGE
Wall St.
BROOKLYN
Battery Park
BROOKLYN-BATTERY TUNNEL
Manhattan
1 Columbia University
2 Cathedral Church of St. John the Divine
3 Guggenheim Museum
4 Metropolitan Museum of Art
5 American Museum of Natural History
6 Whitney Museum
7 Frick Collection
8 Lincoln Center for the Performing Arts
9 Columbus Circle, N.Y. Convention & Visitor's Bureau
10 Museum of Modern Art
11 Rockefeller Center
12 St. Patrick's Cathedral
13 United Nations
14 Grand Central Station
15 Port Authority Bus Terminal
16 Empire State Building
17 Penn Station
18 General Post Office
19 Union Square
20 Washington Square
21 World Trade Center
22 Battery Park

Fox, remember them?) and novels (like *Bonfire of the Vanities* and *Bright Lights, Big City*). As the rosy blush of the 80s fades to grey 90s malaise, the city is confronted once again with old problems—too many people, too little money, and not enough consideration for each other. Although the first African-American mayor, David Dinkins, was elected in 1988 on a platform of harmonious growth, this "melting pot" of New York continues to burn, smolder and belch. Still, there are signs of life and renewed committment in the urban blightscape; a recent resugence of community activism and do-it-yourself politics is a glimmer of hope. Former Mayor Ed Koch echoed the sentiments of generations in his inagural speech. "New York is not a problem," Said Koch. "New York is a stroke of genius." For an even more complete listing of New York City, including Hoboken, NJ, see *Let's Go: New York City.*

Practical Information

Emergency: 911.

Police: 212-374-5000. For non-urgent inquiries. Open 24 hrs.

Visitors Information: New York Convention and Visitors Bureau, 2 Columbus Circle (397-8222 or 484-1200), 59th St. and Broadway. Subway: #1, 9, A, B, C, D to 59th St./Columbus Circle. Multilingual staff will help you with directions, hotel listings, entertainment ideas, safety tips, and "insider's" descriptions of New York's neighborhoods. Request 2 invaluable maps (free): *MTA Manhattan Bus Map,* and the *MTA New York City Subway Map.* Try to show up in person; the phone lines tend to be busy, and the maps and brochures are worthwhile. Open Mon.-Fri. 9am-6pm, Sat.-Sun. and holidays 10am-6pm.

Traveler's Aid Society: 158-160 W. 42nd St. (944-0013), between Broadway and Seventh Ave. Also at JFK International Airport (718-656-4870), in the International Arrivals Bldg. JFK office offers general counseling and referral to travelers, as well as emergency assistance (open Mon.-Thurs. 10am-7pm, Fri. 10am-6pm, Sat. 11am-6pm, Sun. noon-5pm). 42nd St. branch specializes in crisis-intervention services for stranded travelers and crime victims (open Mon.-Fri. 9am-5pm; Wed. closes at noon. Subway: #1, 2, 3, 7, 9, N, R, S to 42nd St.).

Entertainment Information: Free Daily Events in the City, 360-1333; 24 hrs. **NYC Onstage,** 768-1818; updates on theater, dance, music, children's entertainment, and special events; 24 hrs. **TKTS,** 354-5800; at Broadway and 42nd St. (open Mon.-Sat. 3-8pm, Wed. and Sat. matinées 10am-2pm, Sun. from noon); and at 2 World Trade Center (open Mon.-Fri. 11am-5:30pm, Sat. 11am-1pm). Half-price tickets to Broadway and Off-Broadway shows sold the day of the performance only. Tickets for Wed., Sat., and Sun., sold 11am-closing on the day before the performance.

Consulates: Australian, 636 Fifth Ave. (245-4000). **British,** 845 Third Ave. (752-0202). **Canadian,** 1251 Sixth Ave. (768-2400). **French,** 934 Fifth Ave. (606-3600). **German,** 460 Park Ave. (308-8700). **Indian,** 3 E. 64th St. (879-7800). **Israeli,** 800 Second Ave. (351-5200). **Italian,** 690 Park Ave. (737-9100).

American Express: Multi-task agency providing tourists with traveler's checks, gift checks, cashing services, and other financial assistance. Branches scattered throughout Manhattan include: **American Express Tower,** 200 Vesey St. (6402000), near the World Financial Center (open Mon.-Fri. 9am-5pm); **Macy's Herald Square,** 151 W. 34th St. (695-8075), between Sixth and Seventh Ave. (open Mon.-Fri. 10am-7pm); **150 E. 42nd St.** (687-3700), between Lexington and Third Ave. (open Mon.-Fri. 8:30am-5:30pm); in **Bloomingdale's,** 59th St. and Lexington Ave. (705-3171; open Mon.-Fri. 10am-6pm); **822 Lexington Ave.** (758-6510), between 63rd and 64th St. (open Mon.-Fri. 9am-5pm).

Taxis: Radio-dispatched taxis, UTOC 718-361-7270, (or see Yellow Pages under "Taxicabs"). Yellow (licensed) cabs can be hailed on the street: $1.50 base rate, $.25 each additional fifth of a mi; $.25 is tacked on for every $.75 seconds spent in slow or stopped traffic; 50 surcharge 8pm-6am; passengers pay for all tolls. Don't forget to tip 15%. Before you leave the cab, ask for a receipt, which will have the taxi's ID number. This number is necessary to trace lost articles or to make a complaint to the **Taxi Commission** (221 W. 41st St. (221-TAXI), between Times Sq. and the Port Authority Bus Terminal).

Car Rental: All agencies have min. age requirements and ask for deposits. Call in advance to reserve, especially near the weekend. **Thrifty,** 330 W. 58th St. (867-1234), between Eighth and Ninth Ave.; 213 E. 43rd St. (867-1234), between Second and Third Ave. Large, reputable nationwide rental chain. Midsized domestic sedan: $42 per day, $255 per week, with unlimited mileage.

Open Mon.-Fri. 7am-7pm, Sat. 7am-5pm, Sun. 8am-4pm. Must be 23 with a major credit card. No returns.

Auto Transport Companies: New York serves as one of their major departure points. The length of time for application processing varies considerably from place to place. Nearly all agencies require references and a refundable cash deposit. **Dependable Car Services,** 801 E. Edgar Rd., Linden, NJ (840-6262 or 908-474-8080). Must be 21, have 3 personal references, and a valid license without major violations; $150-200 deposit returned upon delivery. Open Mon.-Fri. 8:30am-4:30pm, Sat. 9am-1pm. **Auto Driveaway,** 264 W. 35th St., Suite 500 (967-2344). Must be 21, with 2 local references and a valid driver's license. $250 deposit, $10 application fee. Open Mon.-Fri. 9am-5pm.

Bicycle Rentals: On weekends May-Oct. and weekdays 10am-3pm and 7-10pm, Central Park closes to cars, allowing bicycles to rule its roads. **Pedal Pushers,** 1306 Second Ave. (288-5594), between 68th and 69th St., rents 3-speeds for $4 per hr., $10 per day; 10-speeds for $5 per hr., $14 per day; mountain bikes for $6 per hr., $17 per day. Open daily 10am-6pm. No cash deposit required; leave passport, driver's license, or a major credit card. **Gene's,** 242 E. 79th St. (288-0739), near Second Ave., rents 3-speeds for $3 per hr., $10.50 per day; mountain bikes for $6 per hr., $21 per day. Open Mon.-Fri. 9:30am,-8pm, Sat.-sun. 9am-7pm. $20 deposit for 3-speeds, $40 deposit for mountain bikes, as well as a driver's license or a major credit card.

Help Lines: Crime Victim's Hotline, 577-7777; 24-hr. counseling and referrals. **Sex Crimes Report Line,** New York Police Dept., 267-7273; 24-hr. help, counseling, and referrals. **AIDS Information,** 807-6655. Open daily 10:30am-9pm.

Medical Care: Walk-in Clinic, 57 E. 34th St. (683-1010), between Park and Madison Ave. Open Mon.-Fri. 8am-6pm, Sat. 10am-2pm. Affiliated with Beth Israel Hospital.

24-Hr. Medical Assistance: Beth Israel Medical Center Emergency Room, (420-2840), 1st Ave. and 16th St. **Mount Sinai Medical Center Emergency Room** (241-7171), 100th St. and 1st Ave. **New York Infirmary Beekman Downtown Hospital Emergency Room** (312-5070), 170 William St. **Kaufman's Pharmacy** 557 Lexington Ave. (755-2266), at 50th St. **24-Hr. Emergency Doctor,** 718-745-5900. **The Eastern's Women's Center,** 40 E. 30th St. (686-6066), between Park and Madison. Gynecological exams and surgical procedures for women.

Post Office: Central branch, 380 W. 33rd St. (967-8585), at Eighth Ave. across from Madison Square Garden. To pick up General Delivery mail, use the entrance at 390 Ninth Ave. C.O.D.s, money orders, and passport applications are also processed at some branches. Call 330-4000 for general postal inquiries; questions concerning other branch locations and hours will only be handled at the main information number. Open Mon.-Fri. 8:30am-7:45pm. For postal emergencies only, call the 24-hr. postal hotline (330-2671). **ZIP code:** 10001.

Area Codes: 212 (Manhattan and the Bronx); 718 (Brooklyn, Queens, and Staten Island.)

Getting There

By Plane

Three airports service the New York Metro Region.

John F. Kennedy Airport (JFK) (718-656-4520), 12 mi. from Midtown in southern Queens, is the largest, handling most international flights.

LaGuardia Airport (718-476-5072), 6 mi. from midtown in northwestern Queens, is the smallest, offering domestic flights and air shuttles (see below).

Newark International Airport (201-961-2000), 12 mi. from Midtown in Newark, NJ, offers both domestic and international flights at budget fares often unavailable at other airports.

To and From the Airports

For the most up-to-date info on reaching the airports, call **AirRide,** the Port Authority's airport hotline, at 800-247-7433. Public transport can get you easily from **JFK** to midtown Manhattan. You can catch a brown and white **JFK Express Shuttle Bus** (718-330-1234) from any airport terminal (every 15 min.) to the **Howard Beach-JFK subway station** (718-330-1234), where you can take the A train to the city (1 hr.). Or you can take one of the city buses (the Q10, Q3; $1.25, exact change required) into Queens. The Q10, Q3, and Q9 connect with subway lines to Manhattan. Ask the bus driver where to get off, and make sure you know which subway line you want. Allow 90 minute travel time. Those willing to pay more can take the **Carey Bus Service** (718-

632-0500), a private line that runs between JFK and Grand Central Station and the Port Authority Terminal. (Leaves every 30 min. from 6am-midnight, 11/4hr., $11.)

You have two options to get into Manhattan from **LaGuardia.** If you have extra time and light luggage, you can take the MTA "Q 33" bus ($1.25 exact change or token) to the 74th St./Broadway/Roosevelt Ave./Jackson Hts. subway in Queens, and from there, take the #7, E, F, G or R train into Manhattan ($1.25). Allow at least 90 minute travel time. The second option, the Carey Bus Service, makes four stops in the Midtown area. (Every 30 min., 55 min., $8.50.)

The commute from **Newark Airport** to Manhattan takes about as long as from JFK. **New Jersey Transit (NJTA)** (201-460-8444) runs a fast, efficient bus (NJTA #300) between the airport and Port Authority every 15 minutes during the day, less frequently at night ($7). For the same fare, the **Olympia Trails Coach** (212-964-6233) travels between the airport and either Grand Central or the World Trade Center. (Every 20 min. Mon.-Fri. 6am-1am, Sat.-Sun. 7am-8pm; 45 min.-1 hr. depending on traffic; $7.)

From Manhattan, **Giraldo Limousine Service** (757-6840) will pick you up anywhere between 14th and 95th St. and take you to the airport of your choice for $11-16.

By Bus or Train

Buses or trains can get you in and out of New York less expensively and more scenically.

Port Authority, 41st St. and Eighth Ave. (435-7000; subway: A, C or E to 42nd St./Port Authority), has good info and security services, but this dock is not safe from the "storms" of the surrounding neighborhood. Be wary of pickpockets, and call a cab at night. Its bathrooms are dangerous and unsavory at all times.

Greyhound, (730-7460 or 971-6363) is the titan here. On some routes, a 10% discount is offered to students with ID. Buses run to: Boston (5 hr., $19 one way, $30 round-trip), Philadelphia (2 hr., $16 one way, $32 round-trip), Washington, DC (5.5 hr., $34 one way, $68 round-trip), and Montréal (10 hr., $67 one way, $124 round-trip).

Grand Central Station, 42nd St. and Park Ave. (Subway: #4, 5, 6, 7 or S to 42nd St/Grand Central), handles **Metro-North** (800-638-7646, 532-4900) commuter lines to Connecticut and New York suburbs, and **Amtrak** (800-872-7245 or 582-6875) lines to upstate New York and Canada.

Penn Station, 33rd St. and Eighth Ave. (Subway: #1, 2, 3, 9, A, C or E to 34th St./Penn Station). **Amtrak** trains rumble out of here, serving most major cities in the U.S., especially those in the Northeast. To: Washington, DC (4 hr., $64) and Boston (5 hr., $55). Penn Station also handles the **Long Island Railroad (LIRR)** (718-217-5477) and **PATH** service to New Jersey (466-7649).

By Car

Two major highways frame Manhattan: on the East Side, the **East Side Highway** (a.k.a. the Harlem River Drive and FDR Drive); on the West Side, the **Henry Hudson Parkway** (a.k.a. the West Side Highway). From outside the city, I-95 leads to the **Major Deegan, the FDR Drive,** and the **Henry Hudson.** Go south on any of these roads.

Parking lots are the easiest but most expensive way to deal with the parking hassle. In midtown, where lots are the only option, expect to pay at least $25 per day and up to $15 for two hours. You can draw from the cheaper lots downtown—try the far west end of Houston St.—but make sure you feel comfortable with the area and the lot.

The second alternative is short-term parking. On the streets, **parking meters** cost $.25 per 15 minutes, with a limit of one or two hours. Lastly, **free parking** sites on the crosstown streets in residential areas, but competition for these spots is ruthless.

Hitchhiking is illegal in New York state and cops strictly enforce the law within NYC. Hitching in and around New York City is suicidal. Don't do it. Really.

Orientation

Five **boroughs** comprise New York City: Brooklyn, the Bronx, Queens, Staten Island, and Manhattan.

Manhattan island's length is only half that of a marathon; 13 mi. long and 2.5 mi. wide. For all its notoriety, Manhattan houses only the third largest population of the five boroughs, after Brooklyn and the Bronx. Though small, Manhattan has all the advantages—surrounded by water and adjacent to the other four boroughs.

Queens, the largest and most ethnically diverse of the boroughs, is located to the east of midtown Manhattan. **Brooklyn** lies due south of Queens and is even older than Manhattan. **Staten Island,** to the south of Manhattan, has remained defiantly residential, similar to the suburban bedroom communities of outer Long Island. North of Manhattan nests the **Bronx,** the only borough connected by land to the rest of the U.S., home of the lovely suburb Riverdale as well as New York's most depressed area, the South Bronx.

Districts of Manhattan

Glimpsed from the window of an approaching plane, New York City can seem a monolithic urban jungle. But up close, the Big Apple breaks down into digestible neighborhoods, each with its own history and personality. Boundaries between these neighborhoods can be abrupt, due to the strange history of city zoning ordinances and other unpredictable quirks of urban evolution.

The city began at the southern tip of Manhattan, in the area around **Battery Park** where the first Dutch settlers made their homes. The nearby harbor, now the jazzed-up tourist attraction **South Street Seaport,** quickly provided the growing city with lucrative commercial opportunities. What remains of historic Manhattan, however, lies in the shadows of the imposing financial buildings around **Wall Street** and the civic office buildings around **City Hall.** A little farther north, **Little Italy, Chinatown,** and the southern blocks of the **Lower East Side,** rich in the ethnic cultures brought by late 19th-century immigrants, rub elbows below **Houston Street.** To the west is the newly fashionable **TriBeCa** (Triangle Below Canal St.). **SoHo** (for "South of Houston"), a former warehouse district west of Little Italy, has been transformed into a chic pocket of art studios and galleries. Above SoHo flashes **Greenwich Village,** once a center of intense political and artistic activity, still a literal village of lower brownstones, jumbled streets, and neon glitz.

A few blocks north of Greenwich Village, stretching across the West teens and twenties, lies **Chelsea,** the late artist Andy Warhol's favorite hangout and former home of Dylan Thomas, Arthur Miller, and Canadian bard Leonard Cohen. East of Chelsea, presiding over the East River, is **Gramercy Park,** a pastoral pastiche of Victorian mansions and brownstones immortalized in Edith Wharton's *Age of Innocence.* **Midtown Manhattan** towers from 34th to 59th St., where awe-inspiring traditional skyscrapers and controversial new architecture stand side by side, providing office space for millions. Here department stores outfit New York, and the nearby **Theater District** entertains the world—or thinks it does.

North of Midtown, **Central Park** slices Manhattan into east and west. On the **Upper West Side,** the gracious museums and residences of Central Park West sit next to the swanky boutiques and sidewalk cafés of Columbus Ave. On the **Upper East Side,** the galleries and museums scattered among the elegant apartments of Fifth and Park Ave. create an even more rarified atmosphere.

Above 97th St., much of the Upper East Side's opulence ends with a bang *and* a whimper where subway trains emerge from the tunnel and the *barrio* begins. Above 110th St. on the Upper West Side is majestic **Columbia University** (founded as King's College in 1754), an urban member of the Ivy League. The communities of **Harlem, East Harlem,** and **Morningside Heights** centered the Harlem Renaissance of black artists and writers in the 1920s and propelled the revolutionary Black Power movement in the 1960s. Although torn by crime, **Washington Heights,** just north of St. Nichols Park, is nevertheless somewhat safer and more attractive than the abandoned tenements of Harlem; it is home to Fort Tryon Park, the Metropolitan's **Medieval Cloisters,** and a quiet community of first-generation residents. Still farther north, the island ends in a rural patch of wooded land where caves once inhabited by the Algonquins remain.

Manhattan's Street Plan

New York's east/west division refers to an address's location in relation to the two borders of Central Park—**Fifth Avenue** along the east side and **Central Park West** along the west. Below 59th St. where the park ends, the West Side begins at the western half of Fifth Ave. **Midtown** is between 34th and 59th St. **Uptown** (59th St. and *up*) refers to the area north of Midtown. **Downtown** (34th St. and *down*) means the area south of Midtown.

When given the street number of an address (e.g. #250 E. 52nd St.), find the avenue closest to the address by thinking of Fifth Ave. as point zero on the given street. Address numbers increase as you move east or west of Fifth Ave. On the East Side, address numbers are 1 at Fifth Ave., 100 at Park Ave., 200 at Third Ave., 300 at Second Ave., 400 at First Ave., 500 at York Ave. (uptown) or Avenue A (in the Village). On the West Side, address numbers are 1 at Fifth Ave., 100 at the Ave. of the Americas (Sixth Ave.), 200 at Seventh Ave., 300 at Eighth Ave., 400 at Ninth Ave., 500 at Tenth Ave., and 600 at Eleventh Ave. In general, numbers increase from south to north along the avenues, but you always should ask for a cross street when you getting an avenue address. For a handy address finder, let your fingers do the walking in the Manhattan White Pages.

Getting Around

For info on **Taxis** and **Biking,** see Practical Information.

Get a free subway map from station token booths or the visitors bureau, which also has a free street map (see Practical Information above). For a more detailed program of interborough travel, find a Manhattan Yellow Pages, which contains detailed subway, PATH, and bus maps. For other bus or subway maps, send a self-addressed, stamped envelope about a month before you need the info to **NYC Transit Authority,** 370 Jay St., Brooklyn 11201. In the city, round-the-clock staff at the **Transit Authority Information Bureau** (718-330-1234) dispenses subway and bus info.

Subways and Buses

The fare for **Metropolitan Transit Authority (MTA)** subways and buses is a hefty $1.25; groups of four or more may find cabs cheaper for short rides. Once inside you may transfer to any train without restrictions. Most buses have access ramps, but steep stairs make subway transit more difficult for disabled people. Call the Transit Authority Information Bureau (718-330-1234) for specific info on public transport.

In crowded stations (notably those around 42nd St.), pickpockets find plenty of work; in deserted stations, more violent crimes can occur. Always watch yourself and your belongings, and try to stay in lit areas near a transit cop or token clerk. Many stations have clearly marked "off-hours" waiting areas under observation that are significantly safer. Boarding the train, make sure to pick a car with a number of other passengers on it.

The subways run 24 hrs., but become less safe between 11pm and 7am, especially above E. 96th St. and W. 120th St. Try to avoid rush-hour crowds, where you'll be fortunate to find air, let alone seating. On an average morning, more commuters take the E and the F trains than use the entire rapid transit system of Chicago (the nation's second-largest system). Buy a bunch of tokens at once: you'll not only avoid a long line, but you'll be able to use all station entrances, some of which lack token clerks.

Buses

Because **buses** sit in traffic, during the day they often take twice as long as subways, but they also stay relatively safe, clean—and always windowed. They'll also probably get you closer to your destination, since they stop roughly every two blocks and run crosstown (east-west), as well as uptown and downtown (north-south), unlike the subway which mostly travels north-south. The MTA transfer system provides north-south bus riders with a slip good for a free east-west bus ride, or vice-versa.Just ask the driver for a transfer when you pay. Ring when you want to get off. A yellow-painted curb indicates bus stops, but you're better off looking for the blue signpost announcing the bus number or for a glass-walled shelter displaying a map of the bus's route and a schedule (often unreliable) of arrival times. Either exact change or a subway token is required; drivers will not accept dollar bills.

Safety and Etiquette (or lack thereof)

New Yorkers have earned a widespread reputation for rudeness. Although it can be offputting to a visitor accustomed to the naive charm of Seattle or Des Moines, try not to take it too personally. And don't hold it against New Yorkers; for most of them, lack of politeness is not a matter of principle, it's a strategy for survival. In such a large and busy place, you almost *need* to be cold to conserve limited reserves of human compassion and affection. Hell, if they shot a smile to every passer-by or tossed a quarter in every mendicant's can, they would be spiritually and financially bankrupt by the end of the day. If you *still* feel that the city is unfriendly, try to note the small humanitarian gestures that transpire in unlooked-for places. On the subway, for example. Watch as those reclining spring up to give their seats to an elderly person or a pregnant woman. Yeah, its true: New Yorkers don't greet everyone that they meet with a friendly smile, but some do save a up a little warmth for the familiar faces in their building or neighborhood. Many actually know their grocer, or stationer, or dry cleaner—something unheard of in America's anonymous suburbs.

With that qualification, lets talk safety. NYC is commonly perceived to be the most dangerous city in the United States. While it is clear that danger exists—street robbery and mugging statistics are the highest in the country—many tourists and would-be adventurers are unduly terrified by the streets of the city. New York *can* be seen safely. First step: if you haven't already, read the Security section under "Keeping Safe" in the General Introduction to this book. If you have, read it again. The following are some tips specific to New York.

Act like a native (read: be rude). If somebody comes up to you and demands your attention, avert your eyes and don't give them the time of day or you'll give them the time of their life—at your expense. Act like you know where you're going, even if you don't. Be discrete with street maps and your bright red copy of *LG:USA*—you may even want to cover the latter with paper. Address questions concerning directions to the police or store-owners. If you believe someone is following you, duck into a store or restaurant. Keep valuables—like jewelry, cameras and watches—out of sight. Pay attention to where you are—neighborhoods can change within startlingly small distances. Look for clues which indicate that an area is safe; children playing, women walking in the open, etc. are generally the signs of a healthy community. Use common sense, and be aware that areas safe in the day can be dangerous at night. At night, avoid poor or drug-ridden areas like: South Bronx, Bedford-Stuyvesant, Washington Heights, Harlem, Fort Greene and Alphabet City, the area of lower east Manhattan where numbered avenues become ominously lettered.

Accommodations

If you know of someone who's heard of someone who lives in New York—get that New Yorker's phone number. The cost of staying in New York can rip the seams of your wallet. Planning on staying in a hotel? Then be sure to book reservations way in advance—if you just happen to fall into a place, chances are it will be a pit. However, many reasonable options remain for under $60 per day, depending upon your priorities. Those traveling alone, especially women, might wish to spend more to stay in a safer neighborhood. The young and outgoing may prefer a budget-style place crowded with students. Honeymooning couples won't.

Student and Hosteller Accommodations

New York International HI/AYH Hostel-CIEE New York Student Center, 891 Amsterdam Ave. (932-2300) at W. 103rd St. Subway: #1, 9, B or C to 102nd St. The largest hostel in the U.S. with 90 dorm-style rooms and 480 beds, located in a freshly renovated Richard Morris Hunt Landmark building. Spiffy new soft carpets, blondwood bunks, spotless bathrooms. Kitchens and dining rooms, in-room storage, communal lounges, and a large outdoor garden. Open 24 hrs. Checkout 11am. No curfew. $20, nonmembers $23. Family rooms $60. Linen $3. Towels $2.

International Student Hospice, 154 E. 33rd St. (228-7470), between Lexington and Third. Subway: #6 to 33rd St. Inconspicuous converted brownstone with a brass plaque saying "I.S.H." by the door. Very small bunk rooms bursting with bric-a-brac. 20 beds preferably for foreigners and students. Decent neighborhood and caring proprietor. Curfew midnight. $30 per night.

International Student Center, 38 W. 88th St. (787-7706). Subway: B or C to 86th St. Between Central Park West and Columbus Ave. Open only to foreigners, preferably students; you must show foreign passport to get in. Single-sex bunk rooms, no frills, in a once-gracious, welcoming, somewhat tired brownstone on a cheerful street. Large basement lounge with friendly foreigners and TV. No curfew. 7-day max. stay. Open daily 8am-11pm. No reservations; call by 10pm for a bed. A bargain at $10 a night (may rise to $12 by summer '93).

Hotel Gerswin, 3 E. 27th St. (545-8000), between Fifth and Park Ave. Attractive hotel with a popish art deco design scheme. Although open continuously, the hotel is currently undergoing ambitious renovations which will result in a rooftop garden and an expanded lobby. Friendly management. Passport required for dorm beds; all dorm rooms have lockers. Free tea and coffee. 24-hr. reception and no curfew. Private room $45; 4-bed rooms $17 per bed. 20-day max. stay.

YMCA—Vanderbilt, 224 E. 47th St. (755-2410), between Second and Third. Subway: #6 to 51st St. or E, F to Lexington/Third Ave. International students jabber in the clean, brightly lit lobby. The 750 cramped rooms are a strange hybrid of hotel and hostel, but this is nonetheless a good deal. Facilities include TV, A/C, sheets on the beds, lockers, Nautilus equipment, pool, luggage storage for early arrivals, and safe deposit boxes. The front desk and 24-hr. security guard keep close tabs on who is doing what. It's popular; make reservations and guarantee them with a deposit. Visa, MasterCard, and money orders are accepted; personal checksare taken only for reservations. They don't take shit and they *don't* take American Express. Check-in 1-6pm. 25-day max. stay. $10 key deposit. Singles $39. Doubles $49. Triples $63-67. Quads $84. Lower rates are available during the off-season.

International House, 500 Riverside Dr. (316-8436) at 123rd St. Subway: #1 or 9 to 116th St. or 125th. St. Very large hostel fairly close to Columbia University; single women should take extra precaution. Great facilities: gymnasium, TV lounge, cafeteria, coin-op laundry. 24-hr. security. Singles $25 per night, $18 per night for a stay of 2 weeks or longer. Communal bath. Reservations 8am-10pm. Open Mon.-Fri. 9am-5pm in the winter; Mon.-Fri. 8am-6:45pm in the summer.

Mid-City Hostel, 608 Eighth Ave. (704-0562), between W. 39th St. and W. 40th St. on the 3rd and 4th floors. No sign: look for the small red building in the middle of the block. People walking up the creaky, uneven steps in this even shakier neighborhood will be pleasantly surprised by the comfortable, homey hostel: the sky-lights, brick walls, and old wooden beams make it feel like a friend's apartment. Charismatic owner Donna aims to attract international backpackers; backpack and passport ID required. Call in advance. Lockout noon-6pm. Curfew Sun.-Thurs. midnight, Fri.-Sat. 1am. Only 25 beds. Dorm-style beds $15, $18 during peak season, including a light breakfast of fruit salad.

Chelsea Center Hostel, 313 W. 29th St. (643-0214) between Eighth and Ninth Ave. Subway: #1,2,3,9,A,C,E. Gregarious, knowledgeable, polyglottal staff will give you New York tips in several languages. 25 bunks in low-ceilinged room makes for a slightly cramped setup; the décor and lighting are being improved and may actually be inviting in summer 1993. Their pride and joy is the tiny backyard garden, replete with ivy and a picnic table. Lockout 11am-4pm, but check out anytime. *Definitely* call ahead. $20 in summer, $18 in winter, light breakfast included.

Martha Washington, 30 E. 30th St. (689-1900), near Madison. Subway: #6 to 28th St. Women-only dormitory with over 400 reasonable sized rooms identically decked out in floral bedspreads and wallpaper. Pleasant, if vaguely impersonal. Laundry room. Rental TV and books available in lobby. Doors locked midnight-7am, but residents are given keys. Singles $35,with lavatory $39, with bath $54. Doubles $50, with bath $69. Weekly: singles $140, with lavatory $154, with bath $175; doubles $112, with bath $123, with bath and kitchenette $136.50. Astonishing discounts for longer stays.

YMCA—West Side, 5 W. 63rd St. (787-4400). Subway: #1, 9, A, B, C or D to 59th St./Columbus Circle. Small, well-maintained rooms but dilapidated halls in a big, popular Y whose impressive, Islamic-inspired façade belies its sectional innards. Free access to 2 pools, indoor track, racquet courts, and Nautilus equipment. Showers on every floor. A touch grim. Check-out at noon; lock-out at 11pm. Singles $39, doubles $49, $3 extra for A/C.

Big Apple Hostel, 109th W. 45th St. (302-2603) between Sixth and Seventh Ave. Centrally located (in the same building as the St. James Hotel). Small, clean rooms. 24-hr reception. Free coffee. Lockers in rooms. $17 per bed. Private room $45.

YMCA-Queens, 138-46 Northern Blvd. (718-961-6880), in Flushing, Queens. Subway: #7 to Main St. About ½hr. from Manhattan. Walk down Main St. and turn right onto Northern Blvd. Men only. Convenient to the Flushing central shopping district, but the neighborhood quickly deteriorates past Northern Blvd. Gym, Nautilus, squash, and swimming facilities. $25 per person, $110 per week. Key deposit $20. Passport or driver's license required.

YWCA-Brooklyn, 30 Third Ave. (718-875-1190), near Atlantic Ave. in Brooklyn. Subway: #2, 3, 4, 5, B, D, M, N or R to Atlantic Ave./Pacific St. Women only. An octogenarian building still in good shape. Plain rooms with access to kitchen facilities. Rough neighborhood draws residents of varying respectability. Singles $68-90 per week plus mandatory annual YWCA membership ($38, students $23). Application necessary—guests must be 18-55 and employed—but can be filed on the day of arrival.

Hotels

Carlton Arms Hotel, 160 E. 25th St. (679-0680), by Third Ave. Subway: #6 to 23rd St. The funkiest hotel in Manhattan, and possibly the world. Stay inside a submarine and peer through windows at the lost city of Atlantis, travel to Renaissance Venice, or stow your clothes in a dresser suspended on an astroturf wall. Each room has been designed by a different avant-garde artist, not one of whom has left many motel pastels around. Aggressive adornment doesn't completely obscure the age of these budget rooms, but it goes a long way toward providing distractions. Strong sense of solidarity among the guests. Not the best of neighborhoods, especially at night, but Third Ave. is well-traveled. Discounts for students and foreign travelers. Confirm reservations at least 10 days in advance. Singles $40 (with discount $37). Doubles $54 ($48), with private bath $62 ($56). Triples $65 ($58), with private bath $74 ($64). Pay for 6 nights at once and get the 7th free. Visa and MasterCard accepted for stays of 2 nights or more. Most traveler's checks accepted.

Pickwick Arms Hotel, 230 E. 51st St. (355-0300 or 800-742-5945), between Second and Third. Subway: #6 to 51st St. or E, F to Lexington/Third Ave. A chandeliered, marbled lobby filled with the silken strains of "Unforgettable You" contrasts with disenchantingly dark and minuscule rooms with equally microscopic bathrooms. Nonetheless, a clean hotel with unbeatable rates in a great neighborhood. Roof garden, parking, and airport service available. Even with nearly 400 rooms to fill, the Pickwick Arms gets very busy, so make reservations. Check-in 2pm; check-out 1pm. Singles $40, with shared bathroom $50. Doubles $80. Studios $100. Each additional person $12.

Portland Square Hotel, 132 W. 47th St. (382-0600), between Sixth and Seventh Ave. Pleasant lobby painted dusty rose lures guests up to carpeted rooms with firm beds, TVs, and bathrooms big enough to turn around in. Framed scenes of Times Square in days of yore scattered about. Key-card entry. Singles $40, with bath $60. Doubles $85. Triples $90. Quads $95.

Herald Square Hotel, 19 W. 31st St. (279-4017 or 800-727-1888), just west of Fifth Ave. Quartered in the original Beaux-Arts home of *Life* magazine, built in 1893; today, the reception desk is shielded in glass while sirens blare outside. Above the entrance note the reading cherub entitled "Winged Life," carved by Philip Martiny. The sculpture was a frequent presence on the pages of early *Life* magazines. The work of some of America's noted illustrators adorns the walls of the lobby, hall, and rooms. Immaculate, newly renovated quarters with color TV and A/C. Singles (1 person only) $40. Singles/doubles (1 bed, 1 bathroom) $50. Larger singles with bath $65. Larger doubles (1 bed) with bath $85.

Mansfield Hotel, 12 W. 44th St. (944-6050 or 800-255-5167), off Fifth Ave. A dignified establishment housed in a turn-of-the-century building with comfortable leather couches in the lobby and beautiful oak doors in the hallways. Rooms in the process of renovation—new lighting, new paint and sauna whirlpool. Make sure you get one of the fixed-up ones. Check-out at noon. Reservations and cost of 1 night required as a deposit. Singles $65. Doubles $80. Triples $95. Quads $100. Large suites $120 for 5, $140 for 6. Call for special student rates.

Food

This city takes its food seriously. In New York, delis war. Brunch rules. Trendy dining has caught on. Supermarkets haven't—with so many bakeries, butcher shops, and greengrocers, who needs to shop in a food mall? Don't be confused by the conflation of food with art; certain eateries think they are galleries, and select delis look like museums. Assorted gourmet cooks pose as pushcart vendors. Sidewalk gourmands can stick with the old roving standbys on wheels (hot dogs, pretzels, roasted chestnuts), or try something more adventurous (shish kebabs, fajitas, knishes, falafels).

New York's restaurants do more than the United Nations to promote international goodwill and cross-cultural exchanges. City dining spans the globe, with eateries ranging from relatively tame sushi bars to wild combinations like Afghani/Italian, or Mexican/Lebanese. In a city where the scalding melting pot threatens to boil over, one can still peacefully sample Chinese pizza and Cajun knishes.

And of course, two old favorites remain: pizza and bagels. New Yorkers like their pizza thin and hot, with no shortage of grease. Pizzeria warfare has gone on for years;

the major issue is not over taste but name. Nearly a dozen institutions fight over the right to call themselves Ray's Original. Who is Ray? Who gives a flying pie? Less contentious pizzerias can offer as fine fare as titled competitors. The humble bagel is mighty Brooklyn's major contribution to Western civilization. Bagels come in a rainbow of flavors—the most common being plain, sesame, poppyseed, and onion—but only one shape. Exiles from the city often find bagel deprivation to be one of the biggest indignities of life outside of New York.

West Midtown

Around the Times Square and the Port Authority Bus Terminal areas, the number of fast-food chains approaches the combined tally of tourists, prostitutes, and drug-peddlers—a rather dubious distinction. In the Theater District, the stretch of Broadway from Times Square to 52nd St., you'll encounter plenty of first-rate, ethnically diverse restaurants—from French to Japanese to Thai and back to Italian. While the food and service at these places are likely to make your mouth water, you will probably find your dinner check much harder to swallow. Celebrities often drift over to **Sardi's,** 234 W. 44th St., and take a seat on plush red leather, surrounded by caricatures of themselves. Traditionally, on the opening night of a major Broadway play, the star of the show makes an exalted post-performance entrance—to hearty cheers for a superb performance, or polite applause if it was a bomb. Should this exercise grow tedious, they may head west of Eighth Ave., to 46th St.'s "Restaurant Row," an appealing but expensive strip recently liberated by the Guardian Angels. There, luminaries wander into **Joe Allen,** 326 W. 46th St., where they can gaze at posters of shows that closed in under a week. Farther uptown, a bit to the left of Carnegie Hall, lies the venerable **Russian Tea Room,** 150 W. 57th St., where dancers, musicians, and businessmen down caviar and vodka.

La Bonne Soupe, 48 W 55th St. (586-7650), between Fifth and Sixth. Excellent lighter fare in a split-level "bistro" that doubles as a gallery for Haitian art. Hearty meals of aromatic soups served with bread, salad, dessert, and wine for $10. Minimum charge $7. Open Mon.-Sat. 11:30am-midnight, Sun. 11:30am-11pm.

Chinatown Express, 427 Seventh Ave. (563-3559), between 33rd and 34th. A Chinese-food, penny-pinching, picnic-lover's wet dream. A 25-foot bar of every imaginable dish-General Tsao's chicken, fried rice, shrimp, spare ribs-all hot and delicious, for $3.69 per pound. Take out is best, as the upstairs seating area is cramped with uninspiring décor. Open daily noon-9pm.

Carnegie Delicatessen, 854 Seventh Ave. (757-2245), at 55th St. *The* deli. Ceiling fans twirl gently above as photos of illustrious dead people stare at you from the walls. Eat elbow-to-elbow at long tables. The incredible pastrami and corned beef sandwiches ($9) could easily feed two people (but sharing costs $3 extra). First-timers shouldn't leave without trying the sinfully rich cheesecake, topped with strawberries, blueberries, or cherries ($5.45). Open daily 6:30am-4am.

Anana Afghan Kebab, 787 Ninth Ave. (262-2323), between 52nd and 53rd. Try the appetizing *bandinjah burani* ($2.50), a spicy eggplant dish served with sour cream and bread. Entrées ($5-8) mock the indecisive. The default choice is *lamb tikka kebab* ($6.75), chunks of marinated meat cooked in a wood charcoal oven, served on a bed of brown rice with bread and salad. BYOB. Open Mon.-Sat. 11:30am-3pm and 5-11pm.

Little Italy Pizza Parlour, 72 W. 45th St. (730-7575), on the corner of 45th and Sixth Ave. All the pizzerias on 45th St. claim to be world famous, but this one takes the pie. The walls shine with the usual studio glossies, including an autographed color photo of a daring blond: "Love ya pizza—Madonna." Hot crispy slice with plenty of mozzarella ($1.65). Large Neapolitan pie ($12), with all the works ($21). Calzones clock in around $3.75. Open Mon.-Sat. 6:30am-8:30pm.

Sapporo, 152 W 49th St. (869-8972), near Seventh Ave. A Japanese translation of an American diner, with the grill in full view. A favorite snack spot for Broadway cast members and corporate types alike. Menu items listed on the wall in Japanese. Portions are huge and flavors astounding. The *Sapporo ramen* special ($5.60) is a huge bowl of noodles with assorted meats and vegetables, all floating around in a miso soup base. Open Mon.-Sun. 11:30am-11pm.

East Midtown

New York has five "four-star" restaurants, with four of them (**Lutéce, La Grenouille, Hatsuhana,** and the **Quilted Giraffe**) in this area. Tycoons dine here among sky-scraping office buildings, high rents, and briefcase-wielders. But you should be able to manage here without an expense account. East Midtown houses plenty of sidewalk food vendors and fast-food peddlers. Another option is to stock up in one of the many city supermarkets, such as the **Food Emporium** or **D'Agostino.** These upscale chain outlets feature well-stocked delis, fresh fruit and salad bars, ice-cold drinks, gourmet ice cream, and much more—all at extremely reasonable prices. After you're loaded up, picnicking is free in the area's green cloisters: try **Greenacre Park,** 51st St., between Second and Third; **Paley Park,** 3rd St., between Fifth and Madison; or **United Nations Plaza,** 8th St. at First Ave.

Crystal Gourmet, 422 Madison Ave.(752-2910), between 48th and 49th St. Stunning buffet, topped with a watermelon dramatically chiselled into an eagle. Mounds of melons, cherries, and fresh salad materials alongside pastas, chicken, and beef dishes—all at $4 per pound. Primarily takeout, but for $5 you can sit at the plain little tables and gorge yourself on their "all-you-can-eat" dinner special (5-7pm). Open Mon.-Fri. 7am-7pm, Sat.-Sun. 8am-5pm.

Zaro's Bread Basket, 466 Lexington Ave. (972-1560), on 46th St. The ambience created by the tiled floors and tiled walls of this busy bread and pastry emporium is as romantic as a 7-11, but you can take out a huge selection of food at reasonable prices. Meat sandwiches $3-5, cheese sandwiches $1-3, muffins $1.10, deli croissants $3.25, large coffee or iced tea $1.10. Open Mon.-Fri. 6am-10pm, Sat. 6:30am-6pm.

Hsin Yu, 862 Second Ave. (752-9039), at the corner of 46th St. In the heart of the commercial area. Businessmen crowd in at lunch, not for the fake flowers or charming tablecloths, but for good, inexpensive food. Intriguing special combination platters—like shrimp with lobster sauce, egg roll, and fried rice—costs $5-6; most other entrées $7-10. Begin with the ham and winter melon soup (for two) served in an excavated melon $3.50 and finish with, surprise, a fortune cookie. Open Mon.-Fri. 11:30am-10:45pm, Sat.-Sun. noon-10:45pm.

Le Croissant Shop, 459 Lexington Ave. (697-5580) at 45th St. a standard French-style bakery, but the price is right for this neighborhood. You can sit on stools and watch the passers-by while munching on a hot, flaky, filled croissant ($1.10-1.95) or a croissant sandwich ($3-4). Baguettes ($1.30) and quiche ($2.50) abound. Open Mon.-Fri. 6:30am-7pm, Sat. 8am-6pm, Sun. 8:30am-4:30pm.

Lower Midtown

The Lower Midtown dining scene avoids the extremes—neither fast-food commercial nor *haute-cuisine* trendy. Instead, this slightly gentrified but ethnically diverse neighborhood features many places where you can hunt down an honest meal at reasonable prices. On Lexington's upper 20s, Pakistani and Indian restaurants battle for customers, some catering to a tablecloth crowd and others serving take-out. Liberally sprinkled throughout are Korean corner shops that resemble a combination grocery/buffet bar. You can fill up on prepared pastas, salads, and hot entrées, paying for them by the pound.

National Café, 210 First Ave. (873-9354) between 12th and 13th. Savor homemade Cuban cooking in this small undiscovered diner. Try their lunch specials of chicken fricasee ($3.25) or rice, beans, and meat ($3.75), and suck sweetly on a papaya or mango milkshake ($2.25). Open Mon.-Sat. 10:30am-10pm.

Empire Szechuan Restaurant, 381 Third Ave. (685-6215) between 27th and 28th. Mirrored walls and leafy plants rim this purple-trimmed, multi-tiered Chinese food emporium. The grub, though not dirt cheap, is cooked with no MSG, very little oil, and always *al dente*. Entrées $6-10, but the real draw is the all-you-can-eat *dim sum* brunch ($8) on weekends 11am-5pm. Open daily 11:30am-midnight.

Daphne's Hibiscus, 243 E. 14th St. (505-1180) at Second Ave. Large Day-Glo fish hover in the window; inside, Caribbean art adorns the walls of this spacious Jamaican restaurant. People become passionate over the sweet island sauces—try the chicken cooked in coconut milk or the special meat-filled pastries called "patties." Hibiscus colada for the adventurous. Entrées $7.50-13. Music some nights. Open Tues.-Thurs. 11am-11pm, Fri. 11am-midnight, Sat. 4pm-midnight, Sun. noon-10pm.

Upper East Side

Unless you feel like eating a large bronze sculpture or an Armani suit, you won't find many dining opportunities on Museum Mile along Fifth and Madison Ave., aside from cappuccino haunts, brunch breweries, and near-invisible ritzy restaurants. You will find mediocre food at extraordinary prices in posh and scenic museum cafés where you can languish among ferns and sip espresso between exhibits.

For less glamorous and more affordable dining, head east of Park Ave. Costs descend as you venture toward the lower-numbered avenues, though many do not escape the Madison pricing orbit. Hot dog hounds shouldn't miss the 100% beef "better than filet mignon" $1.50 franks at **Papaya King,** 179 E. 86th St. (369-0648), off Third Ave. (Open Sun.-Thurs. 8am-1am, Fri.-Sat. 9am-3am.) For one time-honored interpretation of the New York bagel, try **H&H East,** 1551 Second Ave. (734-7441), between 80th and 81st, which bakes them 24 hrs., still using their original formula. Don't feel confined to restaurant dining. Grocery stores, delis, and bakeries speckle every block. You can buy your provisions here and picnic in honor of frugality in Central Park.

Afghanistan Kebab House, 1345 Second Ave. (517-2776), between 70th and 71st St. Behind a simple, inconspicuous sign lurks one of the most rewarding restaurants in New York. Tender meats are broiled to perfection in a charcoal oven. Rich smells waft, subdues hues of Afghani rugs soothe, and soft Middle Eastern music drifts in from an invisible source. Bring your own booze. Ask the owner about the establishment's fleeting first incarnation as New York's sole Afghani pizzeria. Youngish crowd, casual atmosphere, irresistible kebab. All kebab dishes $6.50-7.50, vegetarian entrées $6. Dinner about $2 more. Takeout and free delivery (10 min.). Open Mon.-Sat. 11:30am-10pm.

Ruby's River Road Café, 1754 Second Ave. (348-2328) at 93rd St. Electric Jello (made with vodka) and Mississippi River favorites. Alligators perch on the ceiling. Rowdy crowd downs Cajun popcorn ($5.50) and jambalaya ($7.50) by the gallon. Open Mon.-Sat. 5:30pm-1am, Sun. 5pm-midnight.

Zucchini, 1336 First Ave. (249-0559), between 71st and 72nd St. A nutrition-conscious triathlete runs this healthy establishment. No red meat, but fresh seafood, salads, pasta, and chicken dishes should satiate even militant carnivores. Lunch for $7, most pasta and vegetable entrées (soup included) under $11. Before 7pm try the Early Bird Special for only $10. Open daily 10:30am-10:30pm, brunch Sat.-Sun. 11am-4:30pm ($10).

El Pollo, 1746 First Ave. (996-7810), between 90th and 91st. This secret Peruvian dive has mastered the practice of cooking chicken and potatoes, which they serve with complimentary wine in their tiny bowling alley of a restaurant. Plump chickens are marinated and spit-roasted, topped with a variety of sauces. The french fries ($2.50) alone make it worth the trip. Half chicken $5. Open daily 11:30am-11pm.

Upper West Side

The Upper West Side stays up later than its austere counterpart to the east. Monthly rents are heading up, "in" bars are going out, and high-fashion boutiques multiply—but here, gentrification does not make for boredom. If browsing in Laura Ashley or Charivari tires you out, go haggle at the Columbus Avenue Street Fair, happen onto a hidden gallery, or wander down the tempting aisles of **Zabar's,** 2245 Broadway (787-2002), between 80th and 81st St., the deli that never ends. The vast array of restaurants in the area offer meals for the solitary as well as the social.

Café Lalo, 210 83rd St. (496-6031) at Amsterdam Ave. Fabulously popular and new-looking dessert café attracts struggling artists, young people, and loaded professionals; it's worth the short wait to join them all at their high tables and antique chairs among the strains of the Baroque era's top 40. More than 60 pastries and cake desserts, mostly excellent, $3-6; try any fruit tart. Not the best value for your café dollar, but probably the best food. Cappuccino $1.75. Peach, pear, or apricot nectar $1.25. Wine and beer from $2.75. Open Sun.-Thurs. noon-2am, Fri.-Sat. 11am-4am.

La Caridad, 2199 Broadway (874-2780), at 78th St. One of New York's most successful Chinese-Spanish hybrids. Feed yourself and a pack of burros with one entrée. *Arroz con pollo* (1/4 chicken with yellow rice) $5. Other entrées of the Americas, including *chop suey de centro ahumada,* $5-6. Fast-food ambience, but so what? Open Mon.-Sat. 11:30am-1am, Sun. 11:30am-10:30pm.

Genoa, 271 Amsterdam at 73rd St. A tiny, family-owned restaurant serves some of the best food on the West Side. Stucco walls, wood beams, pink tablecloths, and red candlelight, and Italian romance. Arrive before 6pm or wait in line with the rest of the neighborhood. *Pasta festiva* or *puttanesca* $8.50. Veal *scallopini Francese* $11.50. Open Tues.-Sat. 5:45-10:30pm, Sun. 5:30-9:30pm.

Diane's Uptown, 251 Columbus Ave. (799-6750), off 71st St. Large portions and reasonable prices make this popular, brass-railed, inexplicably dark café a student hangout. Spice up a 7-oz. burger ($4) with chili, chutney, or your choice of seven cheeses (85¢ per topping). Open daily 11am-2am.

Greenwich Village

Whatever your take on the West Village's bohemian authenticity, it's undeniable that all the free-floating artistic angst does result in many creative (and inexpensive) food venues. The aggressive and entertaining street life makes stumbling around deciding where to go almost as much fun as eating. The major avenues offer cheap, decent food. Wander by the posh row houses around Jane St. and Bank St. for classier bistro and café fare. Amidst a clutter of collectibles, **Caffé Reggio,** 119 MacDougal St. (475-9557), south of W. 3rd St., offers a hip young college scene and demi-celebs galore (open Sun.-Thurs. 10am-2am, Fri.-Sat. 10am-4am).

Late night in the Village is a unique New York treat: as the sky grows dark, the streets come alive. Don't let a mob at the door make you hesitant about sitting over your coffee for hours and watching the spectacle—especially if the coffee is good. Explore twisting side streets and alleyways where you can join off-Broadway theater-goers as they settle down over a burger and a beer to write their own reviews, or drop into a jazz club. Or ditch the high life and slunk down 8th St. to Sixth Ave. to find some of the most respectable pizzerias in the city. The crucial question: John's or Ray's?

John's Pizzeria, 278 Bleecker St (243-1680). Loud NYU hangout caters to frat-boys, freaks, and even U.S. presidents, if you believe the handwriting on the wall. Cooked in a brick oven, with a crisp crust and just enough cheese, pizza for 2 or 3 costs $8.50. If the place is full, they'll find room for you at **John's Too** next door. No slices; table service only. Open daily 11:30am-11:30pm.

Olive Tree Café, 117 MacDougal St. (254-3630), north of Bleecker St. Standard Middle Eastern food offset by seemingly endless stimulation. If you get bored by the old movies on the wide screen, rent chess, backgammon, and Scrabble sets ($1), or doodle with colored chalk on the slate tables. Falafel $2.25, chicken kebab platter with salad, rice pilaf, and vegetable $7. Delicious egg creams only $1.75. Open daily 11am-3am.

Ed Debevic's, 663 Broadway (982-6000), south of 3rd St. Endure the noise and gregarious waiters and you'll be rewarded: a huge meal at a good price. Front room is 40s-style bar; back room is full of 60s revolution graffiti. Great burgers $5-7 and fries (with gravy or cheese) $2.50. Open Sun.-Tues. noon-11pm, Wed.-Thurs. noon-midnight, Fri.-Sat. noon-2am.

Villa Florence, 9 Jones St. (989-1220), north of Bleecker St. A quiet, friendly spot with brick walls, checked tablecloths, and excellent food. The owner also runs the butcher shop next door; meat dishes are especially good. Pasta $6-12, Newport steak $9, rainbow salad (arugula, endive, and radicchio) big enough for 2, $3.50. *Maria tiramisu,* a trifle-like Sicilian dessert, $3. Open Tues.-Fri. 5-11pm, Sat. 4pm-midnight, Sun. 3-11pm.

SoHo and TriBeCa

In SoHo, food, like life, is art. Down with the diner: food here comes in a variety of exquisite and pricey forms, with long and oft-unpronounceable names. Even the grocery stores get in on the act: **Dean and Deluca,** 60 Broadway, at Prince St., features gallery-quality art and gourmet-caliber food. With art, of course, comes money, so don't be surprised if you find it hard to get a cheap meal. Often the best deal in SoHo is brunch, when the neighborhood shows its most cozy and good-natured front. You can down your coffee and cantaloupe in any number of café/bar establishments. Dining in TriBeCa means dinner. Many of New York's highest-priced restaurants hide behind closed curtains; inexpensive places are few and far between.

Elephant and Castle, 183 Prince St. (260-3600), off Sullivan. Also at 68 Greenwich Ave. Popular with locals for its excellent coffee and creative light food. Perfect for brunch. Prepare to wait for a table. Dinner around $10, brunch around $8. Open Sun.-Thurs. 8:30am-midnight, Fri.-Sat. 8:30am-1am.

Thai House Café, 151 Hudson St. (334-1085) at Hubert St. Not called the Bangkok House. This inconspicuous little place offers excellent Thai cuisine at a reasonable price (entrées $6-10). Obey the waiter's suggestions. Open Mon.-Sat. 11:30am-11pm.

Prince St. Bar and Restaurant, 125 Prince St. (228-3038) at Wooster St. Overcrowded menu and overflowing, portly portions. Everything is big. Burgers ($6.50), breakfast ($4-7), vegetarian and Indonesian specialties. Cheap beer, too. Open Mon.-Sat. 11:30am-1am (kitchen closes at 12:30am), Sun. noon-midnight.

East Village and Lower East Side

Culinary cultures clash on the lower end of the East Side, where pasty-faced punks and starving artists sup alongside an older generation conversing in Polish, Hungarian, and Yiddish. Observant Jews and Slavophiles reach nirvana in the delis and restaurants here. The Eastern European restaurants distributed along First and Second Ave. serve up some of the best deals in Manhattan. The **9th St Bakery,** 350 E. 9th St. (open daily 8:30am-7pm), and **Kossar's Hot Bialys,** 367 Grand St. (473-4810) at Essex St. (open daily 24 hrs.) sell cheap and unsurpassable New York bagels and bialys.

Dojo Restaurant, 24 St. Mark's Place (674-9821), between 2nd and 3rd Ave. Probably the most popular restaurant/hangout in the East Village, and rightly so. Offers an incredible variety of healthful, delicious, and inexplicably inexpensive food in a comfortable brick and darkwood interior. Tasty soyburgers with brown rice and salad $3. Spinach and pita sandwich with assorted veggies $2. Outdoor tables allow for interaction with slick passers-by. Open Sun.-Thurs. 11am-1am, Fri.-Sat. 11am-2am.

Odessa, 117 Ave. A (473-8916), at 7th St. Beware of ordinary-looking coffee shops with Slavic names. Lurking beneath the title may be an excellent, inexpensive restaurant serving Eastern European specialties. Choose your favorites from a huge assortment of *pirogi,* stuffed cabbage, *kielbasa,* sauerkraut, potato pancakes, and other delicacies for the combo dinner ($6.70). Spinach pie and small Greek salad $4.50. Open daily 7am-midnight.

Veselka, 144 Second Ave. (228-9682) at 9th St. An oft-hyphenated down-to-earth soup-and-bread Polish-Ukrainian joint. Blintzes $5.50. Cup of soup, salad, stuffed cabbage, and 4 melt-in-your-mouth *pirogi* $7.25. Open 24 hrs.

Two Boots, 37 Ave. A (505-2276), at E. 2nd St. The 2 boots are Italy and Louisiana, both shaped remarkably like footwear. It may be Cajun Italian or Italian Cajun, but it sure is tasty. Menu changes twice a year, but pasta is $6-9 and the shrimp pizza ($7.50) is a mainstay. Open daily noon-midnight.

Second Ave. Delicatessen, 156 Second Ave. (677-0606), at 10th St. The definitive New York deli; people come into the city just to be snubbed by the waiters here. Have a pastrami or tongue on rye for $7, a fabulous burger deluxe for $6.75, or Jewish penicillin (a.k.a. chicken soup) for $2.85. Note the Hollywood-style star plaques embedded in the sidewalk outside: this was once the heart of the Yiddish theater district. But while their art form is all but forgotten, such personages as Moishe Oysher and Blythe Grossberg have gained their foothold on immortality; embossed metallic tributes sunk in pocked pavement. Open Sun.-Thurs. 8am-midnight, Fri.-Sat. 8am-2am.

Benny's Burritos, 93 Ave. A (254-2054) at 6th St. This Cal-Mex hot spot is dirt cheap and always hoppin'. Plump, tasty burritos with black or pinto beans around $5. Open Sun.-Wed. 11am-midnight, Thurs.-Sat. 11am-2am.

Kiev, 117 Second Ave. (674-4040), at E. 7th St. Unparalleled *pirogi* and tons of heavy foods laced with sour cream and butter, generally under $5. Upscale deli décor. A popular late-night and early-morning pit stop for East Village club hoppers with the munchies. Open 24 hrs.

Passage to India, 308 E. 6th St. (529-5770), off Second Ave. Newer and classier than others on the block. Some of the city's best Indian food. Dine under chandeliers and brass-framed mirrors in British colonial style. But alas, no Mrs. Moore! Full *tandoori* dinner (soup, appetizer, main course, dessert, coffee) $13. Open Sun.-Thurs. 12:30pm-12:30am, Fri.-Sat. noon-1am.

Seekers of kosher food won't find much *traif* east of First Ave., especially south of East Houston St., where there has been a Jewish community since turn-of-the-century immigrant days.

Ratner's Dairy Restaurant, 138 Delancey St. (677-5588) just west of the Manhattan Bridge. The most famous of the kosher restaurants, partly due to its frozen-food line. Despite the run-down surroundings, this place is large, shiny, and popular. Jewish dietary laws strictly followed; you will have to go elsewhere for a pastrami sandwich with mayo. But there's no better place to feast on fruit blintzes and sour cream ($8.50) or simmering vegetarian soups ($3.75). Potato pancakes to go $6. Open Sun.-Thurs. 6am-midnight, Fri. 6am-sundown, Sat. sundown-2am.

Katz's Delicatessen, 205 E. Houston St. (254-2246), near Orchard. Classic informal deli, established in 1888. Have what Meg Ryan had here in *When Harry Met Sally.* You'd better know what you want, because the staff here doesn't fool around. Have an overstuffed corned beef sandwich with a pickle for $6.45. Mail-order department enables you to send a salami to a loved one (or, perhaps, an ex-loved one). With testimonial letters from both Carter and Reagan, how could it be bad? (Don't think about that one too much.) Open daily 7am-11pm.

Yonah Schimmel Knishery, 137 E. Houston St. Rabbi Schimmel's establishment, around since the heyday of the Jewish Lower East Side (around 1910), has honed the knish to an art. Kasha and fruit-filled knishes (from $1.25) available too. Or try yogurt from a 71-year-old strain. Open daily 8am-7pm.

Chinatown

Whether dining in, taking out, or picking from the grocery stores, New Yorkers have long thrived on the delectable food in this area. The buildings in the neighborhood house over 200 restaurants that conjure up some of the best Chinese, Thai, and Vietnamese cooking around. But they don't make dumplings for Trumplings here—compared to what you'd pay in a French or Italian restaurant, this insular community charges surprisingly little for a satisfying meal. Competition has been a boon for the palate; once predominately-Cantonese cooking has now burgeoned into different cuisines from the various regions of China: hot and spicy Hunan or Szechuan food; the sweet and mildly spiced seafood of Soochow; or the hearty and filling fare of Peking. Competition has also boosted the popularity of Cantonese *dim sum* (that's grazing, Chinese style, and served in nearly all teahouses). No menus here—"waiters" roll carts filled with assorted dishes of bite-sized goodies up and down the aisles. You simply point at what you want; in the end, the number of empty dishes are tallied up. (Beware the "Chinese bubblegum," a euphemism for tripe.) To reach Chinatown, take the 4, 5, 6, J, M, Z, N, or R to Canal St., walk east on Canal to Mott St., go right on Mott, and follow the curved street toward the Bowery, Confucius Plaza, and E. Broadway.

Hunan Joy's, 48 Mott St. on the 2nd floor (267-4421), near Bayard St. Good and inexpensive Szechuan and Hunan food. Spicy hot and sour soup ($1.50), tasty beef with oyster sauce ($6.75), and interesting soft shell crab entrée ($11.25) will fill you and please you. Open daily 11:30am-2am.

Mweng Thai Restaurant, 23 Pell St. (406-4259), near Mott St. The curry comes in four different colors—good luck to those who choose hot green ($7). Try the Matsuman curry ($9) or the coconut chicken soup ($3). Lunch special weekdays 11:30am-3pm—your choice of curry with rice for $5. Open Sun. and Tues.-Thurs. 11:30am-10pm, Fri.-Sat. 11:30am-11pm.

House of Vegetarian, 68 Mott St. (226-6572), off Bayard St. Faux chicken, faux beef, faux lamb, and fishette repopulate the menu: all the animals are ersatz here, made from soy and wheat by-products. Try *lo mein* with 3 kinds of mushrooms ($3.75) or seaweed fish ($8). An ice-cold lotus seed or lychee drink ($1.30) really hits the spot on hot summer days. Open daily 11am-11pm.

Nom Wah Tea Parlor, 13 Doyers St. (962-6047), a curved side alley off Pell St., near the Bowery. Open for 72 years. Airy, large, and quiet, especially during off-hours. *Dim sum* served all day; small dishes $1, larger dishes $2. Ask for *ha gow* ($2), a mixture of chopped shrimp and Chinese vegetables encased in rice flour dough and cooked in bamboo steamers. Rinse it all down with a pot of imported Chinese tea. Open daily 8:30am-8pm.

Pho Bang Restaurant, 6 Chatham Sq. (587-0870), on the corner of Mott and Bowery. Authentic Vietnamese food and a meat lover's paradise. Check out the full-color menu, listen to the wacky disco music, and prepare to snarf. Try the chicken lemongrass ($6) or the delicious summer rolls ($3.25). The sesame beef is fun—roll your own dumplings with mint, lettuce, and lemongrass. Note the broad selection of tasty drinks at the end of the menu—go for the 3-color sweet bean drink with jelly, mung beans, and coconut milk ($1.75). Open daily 10am-11pm.

Little Italy

Little Italy, north on Mulberry from Canal St., is one of the liveliest sections of town at night. To get there, take the #4, 5, 6, J, N, or R to Canal St. or the B, D, F, Q to Broadway-Lafayette. Crammed with tiny restaurants, the neighborhood bustles with people strolling in and out of the cafés off Mulberry St. Join the crowds and stake out a table outdoors where you can enjoy cappuccino and cannoli, the perennial favorites.

Luna, 112 Mulberry St. (226-8657), between Hester and Canal St. Enter through the small kitchen—where a halo of steam surrounds a generous platter of clams—to emerge into a narrow, somewhat haphazard dining room, furnished with stray photos. Come here to chat with the family who gossips in the kitchen. Don't be afraid to ask for translations and advice. Waiters give honest appraisals of vast menu. Spaghetti with white clam sauce $7, tumbler of wine $3, fish from $9. Open noon-midnight.

Paolucci's, 149 Mulberry St. (226-9653 or 925-2288). Family-owned restaurant with a penchant for heaping portions. The watchful portrait of the boss hangs on the front wall. Chicken *cacciatore* with salad and spaghetti $9, pasta from $6, daily lunch specials until 5pm $4-9. Open Mon.-Thurs. 11:30am-10:30pm, Fri.-Sat. 11:30am-11:30pm, Sun. 11:30am-9:30pm.

Financial District

Bargain-basement cafeteria joints here can fill you up with everything from gazpacho to Italian sausages. Fast-food joints pepper Broadway between Dey and John St., just a few feet from the overpriced offerings of the Main Concourse of the World Trade Center. In summer, food pushcarts form a solid wall on Broadway between Cedar and Liberty St., wheeling and dealing in a realm beyond hot dogs. Assorted vendors sell falafel and eggplant plates ($2.75), cheese nachos ($3), and chilled gazpacho with an onion roll ($3). You can sup or dine in Liberty Park, across the street.

Frank's Papaya, 192 Broadway (693-2763) at John St. Excellent value, quick service. Very close to World Trade Center. 1/3-lb. hamburger $1.50, hot dog with sauerkraut 60¢. Breakfast of egg, ham, cheese, coffee $1.50. Stand and eat at one of the counters inside the room. Open daily 5:30am-10pm.

Happy Deli, 181 Broadway (587-1105), between John and Cortlandt St. A salad bar the size of Guam—choose your favorite greens, pasta, fruit ($4 per lb.). Seating in rear. Open 24 hrs. Free delivery.

Big Kitchen, 5 World Trade Center (938-1153), Main Concourse near entrance to subway and PATH trains. Select from a ring of deli, pizza, and Thai food booths. Central seating for access to à la carte whims. Taco $2, ½-pint pork fried rice $2, fro yo 43¢ per oz. Open Mon.-Fri. 6am-11pm, Sat.-Sun. 8am-9pm.

Brooklyn

Ethnic flavor changes every two blocks in Brooklyn. Brooklyn Heights offers nouvelle cuisine, but specializes in pita bread and *baba ganoush.* Williamsburg seems submerged in kosher and cheap Italian restaurants, while Greenpoint is a borscht-lover's paradise. And for those who didn't get enough in Manhattan, Brooklyn now has its own Chinatown in Sunset. Venture out to find a restaurant with food from another nation and prices from another century.

Junior's, 986 Flatbush Ave. (718-852-5257), across the Manhattan Bridge at De Kalb St. Subway: #2, 3, 4, 5, B, D, M, N, Q, or R to Atlantic Ave. Lit up like a jukebox and playing classic roast beef and brisket for hordes of locals. Brisket sandwich $6.25, entrées around $10. Suburban types drive for hours to satisfy their cheesecake cravings here (plain slice $3). Open Sun.-Thurs. 6:30am-12:30am, Fri.-Sat. 6:30am-2am.

El Castillo de Jagua, 148 Fifth Ave. (718-783-9743) at Douglas St. in Park Slope. Subway: D or Q to Seventh Ave. The deafening jukebox pumps out the newest Latino rhythms. Excellent, cheap food with great breakfast specials. Try the *pasteles,* meat-filled green bananas, for $1.50. Fried plantains (Latin American french fries) are served with every meal. Open daily 7am-midnight.

Mrs. Stahl's Knishes, 1001 Brighton Beach Ave. (718-648-0210), at Coney Island Ave. Subway: D or Q to Brighton Beach. World-famous knishes—if knishes can be world-famous—in 20 flavors, including pineapple cheese ($1-1.50). Grab a *hamentashen* (a 3-cornered, fruit-filled pastry) for dessert (90¢). Open Sun.-Thurs. 10am-7pm, Fri.-Sat. 10am-8pm.

Moroccan Star, 205 Atlantic Ave. (718-643-0800) in Brooklyn Heights. Subway: #2, 3, 4, 5, M, or R to Borough Hall, then down 3 blocks on Court St. Ensconced in the local Arab community, this restaurant serves delicious and reasonably cheap food. Try the *pastello* ($8.75, lunch $6), a delicate semi-sweet pigeon pie with almonds. Open Sun. noon-10pm, Tues.-Thurs. 10am-11pm, Fri.-Sat. 11am-11pm.

Aunt Sonia's, 1123 Eighth Ave. (718-965-9526) at 12th St., near Park Slope. Subway: F to Seventh Ave./Park Slope. A tiny, very classy haven for the budget gourmand, with ceiling fans and black interior. Line up with the crowds awaiting the chef's newest creations. Besides providing daily specials, he creates a new menu every 2 months. Entrées $8-10. Open Mon.-Thurs. 5:30-10pm, Fri. 5:30-11:30pm, Sat. 5:30-11:30pm, Sun. 10am-10pm.

Primorski Restaurant, 282 Brighton Beach Ave. (718-372-6033). Subway: D or Q to Brighton Beach. Popular with natives, this bright red and blue restaurant serves the best Ukrainian borscht ($1.70) in this hemisphere. Menu is pot-luck, as many of the waiters struggle with English. That's okay—every dish is tasty. Eminently affordable lunch special ($4) available weekdays 11am-5pm, weekends 11am-4pm. At night, prices rise as the disco ball begins to spin and you pay for entertainment too. Open daily 11am-midnight.

Queens

Reasonably priced, authentic ethnic food is one of the best things about Queens. **Astoria** specializes in discount shopping and ethnic (Greek, Italian, Jewish) eating. Take the G or R to Steinway St. and Broadway and browse all the way down to 25th Ave., or turn up Broadway and walk toward the Manhattan skyline. In **Flushing,** you can find excellent Chinese, Japanese, and Korean restaurants, but always check the prices. An identical dish may cost half as much only a few doors away. **Bell Boulevard** in Bayside, out east near the Nassau border, is the center of Queens night life, and on most weekends you can find crowds of young bar-hopping natives here.

In **Jamaica** and the other African-American and West Indian neighborhoods to its southeast, you can try fast food like Jamaican beef patties or West Indian *rito*s (flour tortilla filled with potatoes, meat, and spices). Jamaica Avenue in downtown Jamaica and Linden Blvd. in neighboring St. Albans are lined with restaurants specializing in this type of cuisine. To get to Jamaica, take the E or J train to Jamaica Center; from there the Q4 bus goes to Linden Blvd. in St. Albans.

Roumeli Tavern, 33-04 Broadway, Astoria (718-278-7533). Subway: G or R to Steinway St. (and walk 4 blocks west) or N to Broadway (and walk 2 blocks east). When in Astoria, do as the Astorians do. A taste of the Old Country, with Greek accents as authentic as the food. *Spanakopita* (spinach pie) appetizer $3, lamb stew $9.50. Open Sun.-Fri. 11am-midnight, Sat. 11am-1am.

Waterfront Crabhouse, 2-03 Borden Ave., Long Island City (718-729-4862). Subway: #7 to Vernon Blvd./Jackson Ave., then south on Vernon; walk all the way to the river on Borden Ave. Former home of the turn-of-the-century "Miller's Hotel," through which the rich and the famous passed as they escaped to Long Island by ferry. Theodore Roosevelt, Grover Cleveland, and Lillian Russell all dined in this building, which lost its 3rd floor in a fire in 1975. Today the crabhouse attracts its own big names, such as Paul Newman and Ed Asner. Open Mon.-Wed. noon-10pm, Thurs. noon-11pm, Fri.-Sat. noon-midnight, Sun. 1-10pm.

Woo Chon Restaurant, 41-19 Kissena Blvd., Flushing (718-463-0803). Subway: #7 to Main St., then walk south 2 blocks. Some of the finest Korean food in Flushing. Look for the waterfall in the window. Try the *chun jou gob dol bibim bab* ($10), an obscure and ancient rice dish served in a superheated stone vessel; mix immediately, or the rice will be scorched by the bowl. For lunch, try a filling bowl of *seul-lung-tang* ($6.50), fine rice noodles in a beef broth with assorted Oriental veggies. An unlimited supply of *kim-chi* (spicy marinated vegetables) accompanies every meal. Open perpetually.

Bronx

When Italian immigrants settled the Bronx, they brought their recipes and tradition of hearty communal dining with them. While much of the Bronx is a culinary wasteland, the New York *cognoscenti* soon discovered the few oases along Arthur Ave. and in Westchester, where the fare is as robust and the patrons as rambunctious as their counterparts in Naples. The enclave on Arthur Ave. and along 187th St. brims with pastry shops, streetside *caffé,* pizzerias, restaurants, and mom-and-pop emporiums vending Madonna 45s and battalions of imported espresso machines—all this without the schmaltzy tourist veneer of Little Italy. Established in 1910 under the dynamic leadership of Sam and Lurdes, **Ruggieri Pastry Shop,** 2373 Prospect Ave., at E. 187th St., produces mountains upon mountains of classic Italian pastries, although they're especially proud of their *sfogliatella* (flaky Neapolitan pastry stuffed with ricotta). Ruggieri operates one of the last authentic ice cream fountains in New York (open daily 8am-10pm). Revel in elaborate French and Italian pastries to the tune of a warm cappuccino in **Egioio Pastry Shop,** 622 E. 187th St. An octogenarian with modern flair, a trim, sexy interior, and inviting outdoor tables, Egioio makes the best *gelato* in the Bronx. To get to Arthur Ave., take the #2 or 5 train to Pelham Parkway, then Bronx bus #BX12 two stops west; or the B or C train to Fordham Rd.

Dominick's, 2335 Arthur Ave. (733-2807). Small authentic Italian eatery. Vinyl tablecloths and bare walls, but great atmosphere nonetheless. Waiters won't offer you a menu or a check—they'll recite the specials of the day and bark out what you owe at the end of the meal. Try the linguini with marinara sauce ($7) and the special veal *francese* ($12). Open Mon. and Wed.-Sat. 10am-midnight, Sun. 1-9pm. Arrive before 6pm or after 9pm, or expect at least a 20-min. wait.

Sights

The classic sightseeing quandary experienced by New York tourists has been finding the Empire State Building. They've seen it in dozens of pictures or drawings, captured in sharp silhouettes or against a steamy pink sky as a monument of dreams. They've seen it towering over the grey landscape as their plane descends onto the runway, or in perspective down long avenues or from a river tour. But they can't see it when they're standing right next to it.

This optical illusion may explain why many New Yorkers have never visited some of the major sights in their hometown. Not all sights are as glaringly green and obvious as the Statue of Liberty. If it's your first time in the big city, you'll notice the more subtle attractions—the neighborhoods and personalities jumbled together on shared turf, the frenzy of rush-hour throngs, the metropolitan murmur at dusk. And if it's your hundredth time in the city, you'll see architectural quirks you've never noticed, and plain old doorways you have yet to discover and enter. Seeing New York takes a lifetime.

East Midtown

The massive Beaux-Arts style **Grand Central Terminal,** 42nd to 45th between Vanderbilt Place and Madison Ave., was the gateway to New York and more for millions of travelers during the early part of this century. Although fewer trains roar into and out of its depots today than in the 40s and 50s, the terminal remains a potent symbol of the city's power, just as it has been for the previous 40-odd years, and is an ideal place to begin a tour of East Midtown. During the filming of *The Fisher King*, rush hour was halted and the entire place convinced to waltz. Think about it. Out on top of the Vanderbilt entrance to the building is the famous wall clock, mounted on the Southern façade and surrounded by a classical statuary group designed by Jules Alexis Coutan. The Municipal Art Society leads popular free tours of the place every Wednesday at 12:30pm, starting at the Chemical Commuter Bank in the Main Concourse.

The New York skyline would be incomplete without the familiar art-deco headdress of the **Chrysler Building,** at 42nd and Lexington, built by William Van Allen as a series of rectangular boxes and topped by a spire modeled after a radiator grille. Other details evoke the romance of the automobile in the Golden Age of Chrysler: on the 26th floor, a frieze of idealized cars in white and gray brick, flared gargoyles at the fourth setback styled after 1929 hood ornaments and hubcaps, and patterned lightning bolt designs symbolize the power of this new machine. When built in 1929, this seductive if absurd creation stood as the world's tallest, only to be topped by the Empire State Building a year later.

The **Empire State Building** (slurred together by any self-respecting New Yorker into "Empire Statebuilding") has style. It retains its place in the hearts and minds of Americans even though it is no longer the tallest building in the U.S. (an honor now held by Chicago's Sears Tower), or even the tallest building in New York (now the upstart twin towers of the World Trade Center). It doesn't even have the best looks (the Chrysler building is more delicate, the Woolworth more ornate). But the Empire State building remains the best-known and most-loved landmark in the Empire State, dominating the postcards, the movies, and the skyline. The limestone and granite structure, with glistening mullions of stainless steel, stretches 1454 ft. into the sky, and its 73 elevators run on two mi. of shafts. High winds can bend the entire structure up to a quarter-inch off center.

Forty-second St. also delivers the **Daily News Building,** home to the country's first successful tabloid. When designed, the building was extremely innovative in its treatment of height; instead of the typical elevation in three stages corresponding to the base, shaft, and capital of a classical column, it rises in a series of monolithic slabs. A brass analog clock keeps time for 17 major cities worldwide, and frequent exhibitions breeze in and out. In 1990, the paper became entangled in a bitter drawn-out battle with its union workers that threatened to permanently terminate publication, but now-dead multimedia mogul Robert Maxwell shelled out some sterling, dissolving the labor dispute and taking over the rag in March of 1991.

Ceremonial center of our ceremonial world government, the **United Nations** (963-7713) overlooks the East River between 42nd and 48th. Designed in the early 50s by an international committee including Le Corbusier, Oscar Niemeyer, and Wallace Harrison, the complex itself makes a diplomatic statement—part bravura, part compromise. Besides the ever-popular guided tours of the **General Assembly** and the **Security Council** (starting at the main lobby of the GA every half-hour from 9:15am to 4:45pm), other UN attractions include stained glass windows by Chagall, a delightful promenade above the riverbank, and a muscle-bound Socialist Realist statue of a man beating a sword into a plowshare, which the USSR generously gave to the UN in 1959, only three years after invading Hungary. From September through December, free tickets to General Assembly meetings can be obtained in the main lobby approximately half an hour before sessions begin, which is generally at 10:30am and 3pm, on weekdays.

St. Patrick's Cathedral (753-2261), New York's most famous church and the largest Catholic cathedral in America, stands at 51st. St. and Fifth Ave. Designed by James Renwick, construction began on the Gothic Revival structure in 1858, and took 21 years to complete. Today, it features high society weddings and the shrine of the first male U.S. saint, St. John Neumann.

Back on 375 Park Ave., between 52nd and 53rd, is Mies van der Rohe's refreshingly innovative masterpiece: the dark and gracious **Seagram Building.** Completed in 1958, it remains the paragon of the International Style. Van der Rohe had envisioned his creation as an oasis from the tight canyon of skyscrapers lining Park Ave., thus setting the tower 90 ft. back from the plaza, with two grand fountains in the foreground. The immediate public success of his vision led to a slew of trashy imitations with barren street-wrecking plazas.

Towering above the Saint Peter's Lutheran Church (619 Lexington Ave. at 53rd St., 935-2200) is the shiny, slanted **Citicorp Center,** built on four ten-story stilts to accommodate St. Peter's. The entire structure is sheathed in grayish aluminum which readily reflects light; at sunrise or sunset, the entire building radiates a warm glow. The 45°-angle roof was originally intended for use as a solar collector that has yet to come to light. But the roof does support a gadget called the Tuned Mass Damper that senses and records the swaying of the building and counters it with the appropriate opposite oscillation.

Philip Johnson's post-modern **AT&T Building** stands further west, on Madison Ave. between 55th and 56th. Unfortunately, most connoisseurs of Manhattan architecture agree that this black-striped building, with its pinkish marble resembling a feta cheese spread, doesn't quite succeed. The cross-vaulted arcade underneath (open Mon.-Fri. 8am-6pm) features scenic cafés and the futuristic **AT&T Infoquest Center** (605-5555; see Museums). The ritzy, four-star **Quilted Giraffe** restaurant also rests here, with tabs that can skyrocket up to $150 per person (with a decent vintage wine and appropriate tips). One block further uptown, fellow bluechipper IBM performs its bit of public philanthropy with the green granite **IBM Building,** 590 Madison Ave. between 56th and 57th, featuring one of the city's best atriums, an airy space with comfortable chairs and a dense bamboo jungle. Also here is the **IBM Gallery of Science and Art,** with several engaging exhibits on an eclectic range of subjects (see Museums).

West Midtown

Scurrying into the sunlight from the subterranean world of **Penn Station,** you will find yourself at the foot of West Midtown, with the swirl of commercial life surrounding you. Looking around at the impersonal jungle of box skyscrapers, you may miss the immense **Main Post Office,** across the street, on Eighth Ave., because it's on the other side of Penn Station from the main entrance. Finished in 1913, the post office mirrored the neoclassical magnificence of Pennsylvania Station (which used to be above ground) until the latter was destroyed in the 60s. Note the broad portico of 20 colossal Corinthian columns at the main entrance, and of course, the bold, Cliff Clavenesque motto of the U.S. Post Office: "Neither snow nor rain nor heat nor gloom of night stays these couriers from the swift completion of their appointed rounds."

For a look at one of the city's Beaux-Arts masterpieces, look no further than the **New York Public Library,** which reposes on the west side of Fifth Ave., between 40th and 42nd. On sunny afternoons, flocks of people perch on the marble steps, sunning, lunching, or even reading between the mighty lions Patience and Fortitude. The interior is a bona fide museum, with numerous murals, art collections, and lavishly decorated rooms named in honor of the library's benefactors. Of course, it's also the world's seventh-largest research library; a quick peek into the immense third-floor reading room should convince readily. (For free informative and interesting tours of the building, Tues.-Sat. 11am and 2pm, meet at the Friends Desk in Astor Hall. For info call 661-7220. Open Tues.-Wed. 11am-7:30pm, Thurs.-Sat. 10am-6pm.)

Continuing westward, you'll soon find yourself enveloped in the scintillatingly incandescent brilliance radiating over the streets of soon-to-be-renovated **Times Square,** at the intersection of 42nd St. and Broadway. If any place deserves to be called the dark and seedy core of the Big Apple, this is it. Well-policed (and with good reason), here Broadway hosts not only its famous stages but also first-run movie houses, neon lights, street performers, and porn palace after peep show after porn palace. The entire area is slated for demolition and multi-billion dollar reconstruction in the next few years, the most ambitious of several attempts to "clean up" Times Square and settle an old puritanical business vendetta. The first new building, the neatly polished **Marriott Marquis,** has already replaced two historic Broadway stages. Nearly all subway lines stop in Times Square (1, 2, 3, 7, 9, A, C, E, N, R, and S).

A walk uptown along Broadway leads through the **Theater District,** which stretches from 41st to 57th St. At one time a solid row of marquees, some of the theaters have been converted into movie houses or simply left to rot as the cost of live productions has skyrocketed. Approximately 40 theaters remain active, mostly grouped around 45th St. Between 44th and 45 St., a half block west off Broadway in front of the Shubert Theater, sits **Shubert Alley,** a short private street reserved for pedestrians, originally built as a fire exit between the Booth and Shubert Theaters.

Between 48th and 51st St. and Fifth and Sixth Ave. stretches **Rockefeller Center,** a monument to the conjunction of business and art; Raymond Hood and his cohorts did an admirable job of glorifying business through architecture. On Fifth Ave., between 49th and 50th St., check out the famous gold-leaf statue of Prometheus (with intestines intact), sprawled out on a ledge of the sunken **Lower Plaza** while jet streams of water shoot around it. The plaza doubles as an open-air café during the summer and a popular ice-skating rink in the winter.

In the backdrop, the 70-story **RCA Building,** seated at Sixth Ave., remains the most accomplished architectural creation in this complex. Examine the exquisite art-deco detailing in the black-granite lobby. Every chair in the building sits less than 28 ft. from natural light. Nothing quite matches watching a sunset from the 65th floor as a coral burnish fills the room. **NBC Studios** is headquartered here, offering you the chance to take a behind-the-scenes tour of their operation. (Open daily 9:30am-4:30pm; admission $7.75, ages under 6 not admitted; tours leave every 15 min.; tickets available on a first-come, first-served basis; they sell out early, so buy them well in advance).

A virtual art-deco shrine next door, **Radio City Music Hall** was built in 1932 at the corner of Sixth Ave. and 51st St. The 5874-seat theater, still the largest of its kind, was the brainchild of Roxy Rothafel (founder of the Rockettes), who had originally intended to use it as an entertainment variety showcase. His idea, however, never caught on, and from 1933 to 1979 the hall functioned primarily as a movie theater, with over 650 feature films debuting here, including *King Kong, Breakfast at Tiffany's,* and *Doctor Zhivago.* In 1979, steeped in financial troubles, the Great Hall narrowly avoided being demolished to make way for new office high-rises, but thanks to public outcry was declared a national landmark and saved at the last moment. A complete interior restoration then followed, and today you can see it in all its original majesty, from the 23-carat gold ceilings to the incredible three-part rotating stage platform. (Tours of the Great Hall are given Mon-Sat. 10am-4:45pm and Sun. 11am-5pm. $7, ages under 6 $3.50). For more information call 632-4041.

West Midtown has its own mini-Museum Row, from 52nd to 53rd St. between Fifth and Sixth Ave. On 25 W. 52nd St. broadcasts the newly relocated **Museum of Television and Radio** (621-6600), housed in a building nearly four times the size of its predecessor. Now they have continually changing exhibits of TV and radio artifacts as well as numerous TV and radio consoles for public access to their store of over 40,000 programs. One block up and walking towards Sixth Ave., you can take in a handful of masterpieces in the windows of the **American Craft Museum** and the **Museum of Modern Art** (see Museums). Rest your tired dogs with a visit to the sculpture garden featuring the works of Rodin, Renoir, Miro, Lipschitz, and Picasso.

At the lower right edge of Central Park, on Fifth Ave. and 59th St., the legendary **Plaza Hotel,** built in 1907 by Henry J. Hardenberg, struts its dignified Edwardian stuff. Past guests have included the likes of Frank Lloyd Wright, F. Scott Fitzgerald, and The Beatles. Locals shuddered when the hubristic Donald Trump acquired the national landmark in 1988, but so far there has been little to fear. *Let's Go* recommends the $15,000-per-night suite.

Carnegie Hall first opened its doors in 1891, and after a century remains the central sound stage of New York, synonymous with musical success. During its illustrious history, legends such as Tchaikovsky, Caruso, Toscanini, and Bernstein have paid homage here, as well as popular musical icons such as Bob Dylan, The Beatles, and The Rolling Stones. Like Radio City Music Hall, Carnegie was almost demolished in the 1950s to make way for a large office building, but outraged citizens managed to recue it through special state legislation. (Tours Tues. and Thurs. 11:30am, 2pm, and 3pm; $6, students $5.)

Lower Midtown

The **Pierpont Morgan Library** (685-0610), 29 E. 36th St., at Madison Ave., is housed in a beautiful Renaissance palazzo, and features a large selection of early modern treasures. (Subway: #6 to 33rd St. Open Tues.-Sat. 10:30am-5pm, Sun. 1-5pm. Suggested contribution $5, seniors and students $3. Free tours on various topics Tues.-Fri. 2:30pm.) **Macy's,** the largest department store in the world, occupies the entire city block at 34th St. and Herald Square. Call the concierge service (560-3827) to arrange for anything. (Open Mon. and Thurs.-Fri. 10am-8:30pm, Tues.-Wed. and Sat. 10am-7pm, Sun. 11am-6pm. Subway: #1, 2, 3, or 9 to Penn Station, or B, D, F, N, Q, or R to 34th St.)

Get wild at the **Palladium,** 126 E. 14th St. (473-7171), between Third and Fourth Aves. A huge Keith Haring mural of a packed theater greets you at the entrance of this former movie palace, which was converted into a disco in 1985 by Japanese designer Arata Isozaki. Though now well out of its "in" moment, the nightclub still boasts the world's largest dance floor and a staircase with 2400 round lights (see Dance Clubs).

Upper East Side

The Golden Age of the East Side society epic began in the 1860s and progressed until the outbreak of World War I. Scores of wealthy people moved into the area and refused to budge, even during the Great Depression when armies of the unemployed pitched their tents across the way in Central Park. So it was that select hotels, mansions, and churches first colonized the primordial wilderness of the Upper East Side. The lawns of Central Park covered the land where squatters had dwelt; **Fifth Avenue** rolled over a stretch once grazed by pigs. These days parades, millionaires, and unbearably slow buses share Fifth Avenue. Its **Museum Mile** includes the Metropolitan, the Guggenheim, the International Center of Photography, the Cooper-Hewitt, the Museum of the City of New York, and the Jewish Museum, among others (for more information see Museums and Galleries).

The **Trump Plaza,** at 167 E. 61st St., forms a morally edifying memorial to Mr. Trump's newly troubled *nouveau riche* pockets. Don't even bother throwing a coin into the waterfall to the left of the plaza entrance.

Gracie Mansion, at the north end of the park, has been the residence of every New York mayor since Fiorello LaGuardia moved in during World War II. David Dinkins, the city's first African-American mayor, occupies this hottest of hot seats. To make a reservation for a tour of the mansion call 570-4751. (Tours Wed. only; admission $3, seniors $1.)

Central Park

Central Park rolls from Grand Army Plaza all the way up to 110th between Fifth and Eighth Ave. Twenty years of construction turned these 843 acres, laid out by Brookliner Frederick Law Olmsted and Calvert Vaux in 1850-60, into a compressed sequence of landscapes of nearly infinite variety. The park contains lakes, ponds, fountains, skating rinks, ball fields, tennis courts, a castle, an outdoor theater, a bandshell, two zoos, and one of the most prestigious museums in the U.S., the **Metropolitan Museum of Art** (see Museums).

The Park may be divided roughly north and south at the main reservoir; the southern section affords more intimate settings, serene lakes, and graceful promenades, while the northern end has a few ragged edges. Nearly 1400 species of trees, shrubs, and flowers grow here. For guidance, check the four-digit metal plaque bolted to the nearest lamppost; the first two digits tell you what street you're nearest, and the second two whether you are on the east or west side (even # means east; odd west). Central Park is not a safe place in which to walk at night. In an **emergency,** call the 24-hr. emergency line (800-834-3832).

At the renovated **Central Park Zoo,** Fifth Ave. at 64th St. (439-6500), the monkeys effortlessly ape their visitors. (Open daily 10am-5pm. Admission $2.50, seniors $1.50, ages 3-12 50¢.) The Kong-sized **Wollman Skating Rink** (517-4800) doubles as a miniature golf course in late spring. (Whole megillah open Mon. 10am-5pm, Tues.-Thurs. 10am-9:30pm, Fri.-Sat. 10am-11pm, Sun. 10am-9:30pm. 9-hole minigolf $4, kids $2. Admission to roller skating rink $5, seniors and kids $2.50; skate rental $2.50, rollerblade rental $5.)

In summer the park hosts **free concerts** from Paul Simon to the Metropolitan Opera, and excellent free drama (for the first 1936 lucky souls) during the **Shakespeare in the Park** festival (see Theater). Full info on recreational activities fills a handy booklet, *Green Pages,* available at all info centers.

Upper West Side

Broadway leads uptown to **Columbus Circle,** 59th St. and Broadway, the symbolic entrance to the Upper West Side and the end of Midtown—with a statue of Christopher himself. One of the Circle's landmarks, the **New York Coliseum,** was replaced by the **Javits Center** in 1990.

Three blocks north, Broadway intersects Columbus Ave. at imperial **Lincoln Center,** the cultural hub of the city, between 62nd and 66th St. The six buildings that constitute Lincoln Center—Avery Fisher Hall, the New York State Theater, the Metropolitan Opera House, the Library and Museum of Performing Arts, the Vivian Beaumont Theater, and the Juilliard School of Music—accommodate more than 13,000 spectators at a time. In daytime, the poolside benches by the Henry Moore sculpture behind the main plaza prove a good spot for a picnic; at night, the Metropolitan Opera House lights up, making its chandeliers and huge Chagall murals visible through its glass-panel façade. The Metropolitan Opera shop sells gift books, posters, libretti, and boxes of cough drops used and autographed by Caruso. Mmm. (Open Mon.-Sat. 9am-8pm or until 2nd intermission of performance, Sun. noon-6pm.) For reservations and schedules, see Entertainment below.

Cross 65th St. to reach **Central Park West,** an area of graceful old apartment buildings. As Manhattan's urbanization peaked in the late 19th century, wealthy residents sought tranquility in the elegant **Dakota,** between 72nd and 73rd St. Built in 1884, the apartment house was named for its remote location. John Lennon's streetside murder here in 1981 has made the Dakota notorious.

Harlem

Half a million people are packed into the three sq. mi. of Harlem's two neighborhoods. On the East Side above 96th St. lies Spanish Harlem, known as *El Barrio* ("the neighborhood"), and on the West Side lies Harlem proper. It begins in the gentrified region known as **Morningside Heights** above 110th St. and stretches up to 155th. Both poverty-ridden neighborhoods heat up with street activity, not always of the wholesome variety; visit Harlem during the day or go there with someone who knows the area. It is a colossal misconception that Harlem is merely a crime-ridden slum; although poorer, it is as culturally rich as any neighborhood in the city and, contrary to popular opinion, much of it is perfectly safe. Media propaganda has made the place out to be a dump—you won't believe it after you've visited. As African-American residents flocked to Harlem by the thousands in the early part of the century, there came an unparalleled cultural flourishing. The 1920s were Harlem's Renaissance; a thriving scene of artists, writers, and scholars lived fast and loose, producing masterworks in the process. The 1950s saw the growth of jazz and bebop, and many small jazz clubs still exist. In the 1960s, the radical Black Power movement took hold here. The silver dome of the **Malcolm Shabazz Masjid Mosque,** where Malcolm X was once a minister, glitters on 116th St. and Lenox Ave. (Visit Fri. at 1pm and Sun. at 10am for services and information, or call 662-2200.)

New York City's member of the Ivy League, **Columbia University,** chartered in 1754, is tucked between Morningside Dr. and Broadway, and 114th and 121st St. Once all-male, Columbia now admits women independently of **Barnard College,** the women's school across West End Ave. Suggestively, this urban campus occupies the former site of the Bloomingdale Insane Asylum. The **Cathedral of St. John the Divine,** at the end of 112th St. on Amsterdam Ave., promises to be the world's largest cathedral when finished. Construction, begun in 1812, is not expected to be completed until the next century. Near Columbia at 120th St. and Riverside Dr. is the **Riverside Church,** where you can hear its well-known pastor, William Sloane Coffin, champion the struggle for civil rights and the fight against AIDS. (Open Mon.-Sat. 9am-4:30pm, Sun. service 10:45am, tours Sun. at 12:30pm.)

125th Street, also known as Martin Luther King, Jr. Boulevard, spans the heart of traditional Harlem. Fast-food joints, jazz bars, and the **Apollo Theater** (864-0372; box office 307-7171; see Entertainment) keep the street humming day and night. Off 125th St., at 328 Lenox Ave., **Sylvia's** (966-0660) has magnetized New York for 22 years with enticing soul-food dishes. (Live music and no cover Wed.-Fri. 7-9pm features jazz and R&B.; open daily 9:30am-10:30pm.)

Greenwich Village

"The Village," bordered by 14th St. to the north and Houston to the south, has been the premier home of Bohemian cool and writerly wit for almost 200 years. From Herman Melville, Mark Twain, and Edith Wharton to Jack Kerouac, William Borroughs, Lou Reed, and Kim Gordon, the American avant-garde has hung out, shot up, kicked back, and anguished here. The streets here reflect the barely ordered chaos of its inhabitants: Manhattan's crystal-clear street plan splinters in the Village's crafty warren of streets, avenues, and alleyways. Don't despair: wandering around and finding your way can be half the fun.

"Greenwich Village," or "The Village," actually refers, these days, to the West Village, the area west of Broadway, as well as Washington Square Park and its environs. The East Village, on the cutting edge of Boho authenticity, is actually part of the Lower East Side (see below). An ongoing yuppification campaign has purged the Village of most of its aspiring artists, although the Christopher St. neighborhood is home to a vibrant (and upscale) gay and lesbian scene.

Washington Square Park Area

Washington Square Park has been the heart of the Village since the district's days as a pig-infested marshland and suburb. By the mid-19th century, it had become the center of New York's social scene.

Society has long since moved north, and **New York University** has moved in. The country's largest private university and one of the city's biggest landowners (along with the city government, the Catholic Church, and Columbia University), NYU has dispersed its administrative buildings, affiliated housing, and eccentric students throughout the Village. The university's signature purple banners concentrate around the park. In the late 1970s and early 1980s Washington Square Park was taken over by the drug trade and the homeless. The mid-80s saw a noisy clean-up campaign which has made the park fairly safe and allowed a more diverse cast of characters to return. A lot of people still buy drugs here, but *Let's Go* does not recommend it; you'll likely end up with oregano or supermarket-variety mushrooms. Plus it's illegal. You will almost certainly encounter several of New York's unfortunate homeless; try to keep your distance, particularly at night. In the southwest corner of the park, a dozen perpetual games of chess wend their ways toward ultimate checkmate. The fountain in the center of the park provides an amphitheater for comics and musicians of widely varying degrees of talent and imagination. (Subway: A, B, C, D, E, F, or Q to W. 4th St./Washington Sq.)

On the south side of the park at 133 MacDougal St. is the **Provincetown Playhouse**, a theatrical landmark. Originally based on Cape Cod, the Provincetown Players were joined by the young Eugene O'Neill in 1916 and brought here that same year to perform his successful play *Bound East for Cardiff*. Farther south on MacDougal are the Village's finest (and most tourist-trampled) coffee houses, which had their glory days in the 1950s when Beatnik heroes and coffee-bean connoisseurs Jack Kerouac and Allen Ginsberg attended jazz-accompanied poetry readings at Le Figaro and Café Borgia. These sidewalk cafés still provide some of the best coffee and people-watching in the city.

The north side of the park, called **The Row**, showcases some of the most renowned architecture in the city. Built largely in the 1830s, this stretch of elegant Federal-style brick residences soon became an urban center roamed by 19th-century professionals, dandies, and novelists. No. 18, now demolished, was the home of Henry James' grandmother, and the basic setting for his novel *Washington Square*.

Up Fifth Ave., on the corner of 10th St., rises the **Church of the Ascension**, a fine 1841 Gothic church with a notable altar and stained glass windows. (Open daily noon-2pm and 5pm-7pm.) Many consider the block down 10th St. between Fifth and Sixth Ave. to be the most beautiful residential stretch in the city. This short strip plays out innumerable variations in brick and stucco, layered with wood and iron detailing. Ivy clothes the façade of many of the buildings, while windowboxes brighten others.

Balducci's, the legendary Italian grocery at 424 Sixth Ave., has grown over the years from a Sixth Ave. sidewalk stand to a gourmand's paradise. Enter its orgy of cheese barrels and bread loaves, live bug-eyed lobsters and chilled vegetables. At 18 W. 11th St., a striking new building replaces the house destroyed in 1970 by a bomb-making mishap of the Weathermen, the radical group residing in the basement. Farther east at 47 Fifth Ave. is **The Salmagundi Club**, New York's oldest artists' club. Founded in 1870, the Club's building is the only remaining mansion from the area's heydey at the pinnacle of New York society. (Open during exhibitions, call 255-7740 for details.)

West Village

The bulk of Greenwich Village lies west of Sixth Ave., thriving on the new and different. In spite of rising property prices, the West Village still boasts an eclectic summer street life and excellent nightlife.

The West Village has a large and very visible gay community based around Sheridan Square—this is the native territory of the Guppie (Gay Urban Professional), although all kinds of gay males and lesbians shop, eat, and live here. The twisting streets host a remarkable variety of alternative clothing stores, clubs, bookshops, video stores, and even card shops. Same-sex couples can walk together openly.

Christopher Street, the main byway to the south, swims in novelty restaurants and specialty shops. (Subway: #1 or 9 to Christopher St./Sheridan Sq.) Christopher St. and Seventh Ave. intersect at tiny **Sheridan Square**, a carefully tended green traffic island/park. Rioters against the Civil War draft thronged here in 1863, during some of the darkest days of New York City's history. A few streets signs refer to Christopher St. as "Stonewall Place," alluding to **The Stonewall Inn**, the club where police raids in 1969 prompted the riots that sparked the U.S. gay rights movement. A plaque marks the former site of the club at 53 Christopher St.

Christopher St. runs into **Bedford Street**, a remarkably narrow, old-fashioned strip. **Chumley's** bar and restaurant, at no. 86 between Grove and Barrow St., became a speakeasy in Prohibition days, illegally serving alcohol to literary Johns (Dos Passos and Steinbeck). As if in honor of its surreptitious past, no sign of any kind indicates that the neglected structure is a commercial establishment.

One of the oldest buildings in the city, no. 77 Bedford St., on the corner of Commerce St., dates from 1799. Its handsome brick has tastefully faded. Next door, run-down, boarded-up no. 75½, constructed in a former alley, is the narrowest building in the Village: it measures 9½ feet across. Edna St. Vincent Millay lived there in 1850. In 1924 Millay founded the **Cherry Lane Theater** at 38 Commerce St. (989-2020), which has continued to showcase important off-Broadway Theater ever since.

SoHo and TriBeCa

Soho (for "South of Houston"), the high-priced home of New York's artistic community, is the area bounded by Houston (HOUSE-ton), Canal, Lafayette, and Sullivan St. The architecture here is American Industrial (1860-1890), notable for its cast-iron façades.

Greene Street offers the best of SoHo. Once architects here made sweatshops look like iron palaces; now artists have converted factory lofts into studios. Every block has a gallery, an experimental theater, or a designer clothing store. Excellent galleries line West Broadway; remember that most close on Sundays and Mondays. This is a great place for stargazing, too, so bring your autograph book and a bright flash for your camera. Celebrities like that.

A mind-twisting mural by Richard Haas covers the southeast corner of Prince and Greene St. Try to pick out which windows are real and which are painted. To the south, on a lot at Wooster and Spring St., is a daily fair. Browse through the extensive selection of international goods. The bargain hunt continues on Broadway with a myriad of used-clothing stores. Flea market devotees should check out Sunday's market on the corner of Broadway and Grand St.

TriBeCa ("Triangle Below Canal"), an area bounded by Chambers St., Broadway, Canal St., and the West Side Highway, is even hipper. Still flanked by butter-and-egg warehouses, upstairs lofts here have undergone art gentrification similar to those in SoHo. Today Robert DeNiro owns a grill and film company in the neighborhood, and the prices are heading up.

Admire the cast-iron edifices lining White St., Thomas St., and Broadway; the 19th-century federal-style buildings on Harrison St.; and the shops, galleries, and bars on Church and Reade St. For commercial goods, residents roam the streets of Hudson and W. Broadway. Duane St. has good food, if not great prices. Between Chambers and Northmore St. stands Manhattan Community College, part of the City University system. Art lovers should look to **Artists Space** at 223 West Broadway and to the **Franklin Furnace** at 112 Franklin St., which battle fire regulations in their continuing quest to display the most alternative of alternative art.

East Village, Lower East Side, and Alphabet City

The old Lower East Side, once home to Eastern European immigrants, extended from Hester to 14th St. Now this area has developed a three-way split personality, encompassing the part south of Houston (commonly considered the Lower East Side), the section west of First Ave. and east of Broadway (known as the "East Village"), and Alphabet City, east of First Ave. and north of Houston St.

Down below Houston in the somewhat deserted Lower East Side you can still find some excellent kosher delis and a few oldtimers who remember the time when the Second Ave. El ran from the power station at Allen and Pike St. On **The Bowery,** you can haggle for lamps; on **Allen Street,** shirts and ties. Try the Orchard St. market on a Sunday morning for some real bargains. Off Delancey St., the Essex St. covered market is direct from Northern Africa. **Schapiro's Winery,** 126 Rivington St., offers tours and taste-tests Monday through Thursday from 11am to 4pm on the hour. On The Bowery check out Stanford White's **Bowery Savings Bank,** at Grand St., a repository of wealth that shades lots of homeless people.

East Village

The East Village, a comparatively new creation, was carved out of the Bowery and the Lower East Side, as rents in the West soared and its residents sought accommodations elsewhere. Allen Ginsberg, William Burroughs, and Brion Gysin all eschewed the Village establishment to develop their junked-up "beat" sensibility east of Washington Sq. Park. Billie Holliday sang here; more recently the East Village provided Buster Poindexter and Red Transistor with their early audiences.

One of the world's most famous bookstores is The Strand, at the corner of 12th St. and Broadway, which bills itself as the "largest used bookstore in the world" with over two million books on eight mi. of shelves. Down Broadway at 4th St. you'll find another of the Village's spiritual landmarks: Tower Records, a store with an enormous musical inventory. Open late, Tower has become a popular hangout and bonding ground for people of similar musical tastes.

Walk one block east of Broadway on East 4th to reach Lafayette St. To your right will be **Colonnade Row**, with the Public Theater across the street. Colonnade Row consists of four magnificently columned houses, built in 1833, once the homes of new York's most famous 19th-century millionaires: John Jacob Astor and Cornelius "Commodore" Vanderbilt, as well as the Delano family (as in Franklin Delano Roosevelt). The **Joseph Papp Public Theater,** 425 Lafayette St. (598-7150), a grand brownstone structure, was constructed by John Jacob Astor in 1853 to serve as the city's first free library. After its collection moved uptown, the building became the headquarters of the Hebrew Immigrant Aid Society, an organization dedicated to assisting thousands of poor Jewish immigrants who came to New York in the early years of this century. In 1967, Joseph Papp's "New York Shakespeare Festival" converted the building to its current use as a theatrical center.

Astor Place prominently features the rear of the **Cooper Union Foundation Building**, 41 Cooper Sq. (254-6300), built in 1859 to house the Cooper Union for the Advancement of Science and Art. The school's free lecture series has hosted practically every notable American since the mid-19th-century. Cooper Union was the first college intended for the underprivileged, the first coeducational college, the first racially open college, and the first college to offer free adult education classes. The American Red Cross and the NAACP were founded here. On the second floor, the **Houghton Gallery** hosts changing exhibits on design and American history, but usually not during the summer. (Open daily, noon-7pm.)

At 156 Second Ave. stands a famous Jewish landmark, the **Second Avenue Deli** (677-0606). This is all that remains of the "Yiddish Rialto," the stretch of Second Ave. between Houston and 14th St. that comprised the Yiddish theater district during the early part of this century. The Stars of David embedded in the sidewalk in front of the restaurant contain the names of some of the great actors and actresses who spent their lives entertaining the poor Jewish immigrants of the city.

St. Mark's Place, running from Third Ave. at 8th St. down to Tompkins Sq. Park, is the geographical and spiritual center of the East Village. In the 1960s, the street was the Haight-Ashbury of the East, full of pot-smoking flower children waiting for the next concert at the Electric Circus. In the late 70s it became the King's Road of New York, as mohawked youths hassled the passersby from the brownstone steps of Astor Pl. Today things are changing again: a Gap store sells its conventional color-me-matching combos across the street from a shop stocking "YOU MAKE ME SICK" T-shirts.

Alphabet City

East of First Ave., south of 14th St., and north of Houston, the avenues run out of numbers and take on letters. This part of the East Village has so far escaped the escalating yuppification campaign that has claimed much of St. Mark's Place; in the area's heyday in the 60s, Jimi Hendrix and the Fugs would play open-air shows to bright-eyed love children. Rent is still reasonable; here you'll find the stately residences of the East Village's deadbeatniks and hardcore anarchists, as well as girl-noise musical terrorists like God Is My Co-Pilot. (Regular old students reside here, too.) There has been a great deal of drug-related crime in the recent past, although the community has done an admirable job of making the area livable again. Alphabet City is generally safe during the day, and the addictive nightlife on Avenue A ensures adequate protection there, but try to avoid straying east of Avenue B at night.

City Hall Area and the Financial District

The southernmost tip of Manhattan is extremely compact and free of threatening traffic. The narrow winding streets that discourage car travel make the area ideal for a walking tour. Wander down historic lanes between towering silver and stone skyscrapers. Five subway lines converge in the Financial District, some on their way to Brooklyn Heights across the East River. Take a train to the City Hall area on Broadway at the northern fringe of the Financial District, then explore south along the side streets off Broadway.

A prime example of Federalist architecture, **City Hall** (566-5097) has been the scene of frenetic politicking since 1811. (Open Mon.-Fri. 10am-4pm. Free.) From City Hall, walk down Broadway to the **Woolworth Building,** on Murray St., one of the few skyscrapers as graceful close-up as from 20 blocks away. Designed by Cass Gilbert in the Gothic style, this 800-ft. tower was the world's largest from 1913 to 1930. Inspiring mosaics and carved caricatures of Cass Gilbert and Woolworth himself decorate the lobby. A block down Broadway is **St. Paul's Chapel** (602-0773), the oldest church in Manhattan (1766). George Washington worshiped here during his presidency. (Open Mon.-Sat. 8am-4pm, Sun. 8am-3pm.)

West of Broadway, off Church St., sprout the city's tallest buildings, the twin towers of the **World Trade Center.** The enclosed observation deck (435-7397), on the 110th floor of #2, offers a stunning overview of Manhattan, especially at night. (Open daily 9:30am-9:30pm. Admission $4, seniors $2.25, children $2.)

Walk eight short blocks down Broadway into the maw of the beast—the heavily built-up center of New York's Financial District. Glass and chrome temples of the capitalist god tower over no-longer-sooty **Trinity Church** (602-0773) at Broadway and Wall St. Trinity contains in its adjoining graveyard the tombs of Alexander Hamilton, Robert Fulton, and other prominent figures. Here, or nearby, pick up the **Heritage Trail,** an excellent walking tour marked by small American flags.

A short way down Wall Street, **Federal Hall** (264-8711) and the **New York Stock Exchange** (656-5168) sit diagonally across from one another. George Washington took the oath of office in Federal Hall; the building now houses historic documents. (Open Mon.-Fri. 9am-5pm. Free.) From the visitors gallery of the New York Stock Exchange (enter at 20 Broad St.), you can view the controlled hysteria of the world's busiest commercial arena—the trading floor. The visitors' gallery has been enclosed ever since the 60s, when leftist hooligans invented creative ways to disrupt trading activity, like throwing dollar bills at the traders. Come before noon to get a free ticket. (Open Mon.-Fri. 9am-5pm; wheelchair accessible at 15 Pine St.) In the **Federal Reserve Bank,** 13 Liberty St., countries pay their debts by shifting bullion from one room to another. Free tours are available only through advance appointment (720-5000), but they're worth the trouble.

New York Harbor and the Brooklyn Bridge

After its marathon journey down from Yonkers, Broadway ends in **Battery Park** on New York Harbor. A common site for political rallies such as the no-nukes fests of the 70s and recent anti-apartheid protests, the restored waterfront park commands one of the finest views of the city. New York Harbor, Brooklyn Heights, Governor's Island, the Brooklyn-Battery Tunnel, Jersey City, Ellis Island, Staten Island, and the Statue of Liberty all can be seen on a clear day. The view is a lot better, however, from the **Staten Island Ferry** (718-727-2508), which leaves from the port east of Battery Park every half-hour. A trip on the ferry (50¢ round-trip—a sad spasm of inflation, as it used to cost a quarter) is what the New York Visitors Bureau calls "the world's most famous, most reasonable, and most romantic five-mi. cruise..." —few would argue.

Another ferry will take you to the renovated **Statue of Liberty** (363-3200), landmark of a century of immigrant crossings. The **American Museum of Immigration,** located under the green lady's bathrobe, enshrines the dreams of all those who have come to look for America. Chaotic, **Ellis Island,** dirty represents the disillusionment of 15 million Europeans who first experienced the U.S. through the New York Harbor's people-processing facilities. Two ferries bring you to and from Liberty and Ellis Island. One runs Battery Park-Manhattan-Liberty-Ellis, and the other Liberty State Park-Jersey City, NJ-Ellis-Liberty, approximately every half-hour from 9:15am to 4:30pm daily. Tickets are $6, $3 for under 17, and $5 for seniors. For recorded information call the Park Service at 212-363-3200; otherwise call 212-363-7620.

You'll have to get up around 4am to start the day at **Fulton Fish Market.** Here on the East River, a few blocks from Wall Street, New York's store and restaurant owners have bought their fresh fish ever since the Dutch colonial period. Next door, renovations have created the **South Street Seaport** complex. The historic district, in all its fishy- and foul-smelling glory, became a ritzy, neo-Edwardian playground in the Reagan era. After 5pm, masses of crisply attired professionals flee their offices, ties trailing over their shoulders and sneakers lurking under their skirts, and converge here for long-awaited cocktails. The whole complex resembles a semi-formal frat party. The 18th-century market, graceful galleries, and seafaring schooners will delight historians and tourists alike. The decrepit but equally historic blocks on the periphery of the rehabilitated buildings are just as interesting. The **Seaport Line's** authentic paddlewheel steamboats (385-0791) offer day cruises (1½ hr.; call for schedule; fare $12, seniors $11, students $10, ages 2-12 $6) and evening cruises to the live sounds of jazz, rock, and dixie ($18-20 depending on hr. and day). Cruises leave from Pier 16 at the seaport.

Uptown a few blocks looms the **Brooklyn Bridge.** Built in 1883, the bridge was one of the greatest engineering feats of the 19th century. The one-mi. walk along the pedestrian path (on the left) will show you why every New York poet feels compelled to write at least one verse about it, why photographers snap the bridge's airy spider-web cables, and why people jump off. To get to the entrance on Park Row, walk a couple of blocks west from the East River to the city hall area. Plaques on the bridge towers commemorate John Augustus Roebling, its builder, who, along with 20 of his workers, died during its construction.

Brooklyn

Founded in 1600 by the Dutch, Brooklyn was the third-largest city in the U.S. by 1860. In 1898, it merged with the city of New York and became a borough, but it still maintains a strong, separate identity, with many ethnic communities and local industries. Unfortunately, Brooklyn also includes some run-down, unsafe areas—especially west of Prospect Park. The visitors bureau publishes an excellent free guide to Brooklyn's rich historical past that outlines 10 walking tours of the borough (see Practical Information above).

Head south on Henry St. after the bridge, then turn right on Clark St. toward the river for a synapse-shorting view of Manhattan. Many prize-winning photographs have been taken here from the **Brooklyn Promenade,** overlooking the southern tip of Manhattan and New York Harbor. George Washington's headquarters during the Battle of Long Island, now-posh **Brooklyn Heights** has advertised itself to many authors, from Walt Whitman to Norman Mailer, with its beautiful old brownstones, tree-lined streets, and proximity to Manhattan. Continuing south, explore the area's small side streets. Soon you'll be at **Atlantic Avenue,** home to a large Arab community, with second-hand stores and inexpensive Middle Eastern bakeries and grocery stores. Atlantic runs from the river to Flatbush Ave. At the Flatbush Ave. Extension, pick up **Fulton Street,** the center of downtown Brooklyn, recently transformed into a pedestrian mall.

Williamsburg, several blocks north of downtown Brooklyn, has retained its Hasidic Jewish culture more overtly than Manhattan's Lower East Side. The quarter encloses Broadway, Bedford, and Union Avenues. It closes on *shabbat* (Saturday), the Jewish holy day.

Prospect Park, designed by Frederick Law Olmsted in the mid-1800s, was supposedly his favorite creation. He was even more pleased with it than with his Manhattan project—Central Park. Because crime has given Prospect's ambience a sinister twist, exercise caution in touring the grounds. At the corner of the park stands **Grand Army Plaza,** an island in the midst of the borough's busiest thoroughfares, designed by Olmsted to shield surrounding apartment buildings from traffic. (Subway: 2 or 3 to Grand Army Plaza.) The nearby **Botanic Gardens** seem more secluded, and include a lovely rose garden, behind the **Brooklyn Museum** (see Museums).

Sheepshead Bay lies on the southern edge of Brooklyn, and is the name of both a body of water (really part of the Atlantic) and a mass of land. The seafood here comes fresh and cheap (clams $5 per dozen along the water). Walk along **Restaurant Row** from E. 21st to E. 29th St. on Emmons Ave., and peruse menus for daily seafood specials. Nearby **Brighton Beach,** nicknamed "Little Odessa by the Sea," has been homeland to Russian emigrés since the turn of the century. (Subway: D, M, QB.)

Once a resort for the City's elite, made accessible to the rest of the Apple because of the subway, fading **Coney Island** still warrants a visit. The **Boardwalk,** once one of the most seductive of Brooklyn's charms, now squeaks nostalgically as tourists are jostled by roughnecks. Enjoy a hot dog and crinkle-cut fries at historic **Nathan's,** Surf and Sitwell. Built in 1927, the **Cyclone** roller coaster, 834 Surf Ave., remains the world's most terrifying ride. The 100-second-long screaming battle over nine rickety wooden hills more than makes up the $3. Go meet a walrus, dolphin, sea lion, shark, or other ocean critter in the tanks of the **New York Aquarium,** Surf and West 8th (718-265-3400; open daily 10am-4:45pm, holidays and summer weekends 10am-7pm; admission $5.75, children and seniors.) Look for the house beneath the roller coaster, which inspired a hilarious scene in Woody Allen's *Annie Hall.*

Queens

Archie and Edith Bunker-types (and the employees of the Steinway Piano Factory) now share the brick houses and clipped hedges of their "bedroom borough" with immigrants from Korea, China, India, and the West Indies. In this urban suburbia, the American melting pot bubbles away with a more than 30% foreign-born population. Immigrant groups rapidly sort themselves out into neighborhoods where they try to maintain the memory of their homeland while living "the American Dream."

Queens is easily New York's largest borough, covering over a third of the city's total area. To understand Queens' kaleidoscope of communities is to understand the borough. If you visit only one place in Queens, let it be **Flushing.** Here you will find some of the most important colonial neighborhood landmarks, a bustling downtown, and the largest rose garden in the Northeast. Transportation could not be easier: the #7 Flushing line runs straight from Times Square. Just get on and sit back for about half an hour, until you reach the last stop (Main St., Flushing) in the northeastern part of the borough. Manhattan it isn't, but the streets usually are congested. Walk past the restaurants, discount stores, and businesses, and soak in Main St.'s crush of people and cultures.

The Bronx

The Bronx offers more than urban decay. The borough builds on a history of urban change squeezed into just over half a century. In addition to housing projects and burnt-out tenements, the landscape sprouts suburban riverfront mansions, seaside cottages, colleges, 2000 acres of green parkland, and fading boulevards of grand apartment towers. If you're not heading for Yankee Stadium, stay out of the South Bronx unless you're in a car or with someone who knows the area.

The pastoral estate **Wave Hill,** 675 W. 252nd St. (549-2055), in Riverdale, has a majestic view of the Hudson. Samuel Clemens, Arturo Toscanini, and Teddy Roosevelt each resided in the Wave Hill House. The estate was finally donated to the city, and presently offers concerts and dance amidst its greenhouses and spectacular formal gardens. (Open Wed.-Sun. 10am-4:30pm. $4, seniors and students $2.)

The **Bronx Zoo** (367-1010), the largest urban zoo in the U.S., pioneered the concept of housing animals in natural surroundings. Although some animals are kept in cage-like confines, black jail bars are nowhere in evidence. When you look down from the monorail to Wild Asia ($1.25, kids $1), even the cages disappear; once there, you can ride a camel for $2. The 3-acre **Children's Zoo** features four natural environments. Across East Fordham Rd. from the zoo grows the huge **New York Botanical Garden** (220-8700). Remnants of forest and untouched waterways give a glimpse of the area's original landscape. (Open April-Oct. Tues.-Sun. 10am-7pm; Nov.-March 10am-6pm. Suggested donation $3. Parking $4.) The Metro-North Harlem line goes from Grand Central Station to Botanical Garden Station, right outside the main gate (call 532-4900 for details).

Staten Island

Getting there is half the fun. At 50¢ (round-trip), the half-hour ferry ride from Manhattan's Battery Park to Staten Island is as unforgettable as it is inexpensive. Or you can drive from Brooklyn over the **Verrazzano-Narrows Bridge,** the world's second-longest (4260 ft.) suspension span, baby. Because of the hills and the distances (and some very dangerous neighborhoods in between), it's a bad idea to walk from one site to the next. Make sure to plan your excursion with the bus schedule in mind.

The most concentrated number of sights on the island cluster around the beautiful 19th-century **Sailor's Snug Harbour Cultural Center,** at 1000 Richmond Terrace. Picnic and see its catch: the **Newhouse Center for Contemporary Art** (718-448-2500), a small gallery displaying American art with an indoor/outdoor sculpture show in the summer (open Wed.-Sun. noon-5pm; free); the **Staten Island Children's Museum,** with participation exhibits for the five- to 12-year-old in you (718-273-2060; open Wed.-Fri. 1-5pm, Sat.-Sun. noon-5pm; $3 for all except under 3); and the **Staten Island Botanical Gardens.**

Museums and Galleries

For museum and gallery listings consult the following publications: *New Yorker* (the most accurate and extensive listing), *New York,* the Friday *New York Times* (in the Weekend section), the *Quarterly Calendar,* (available free at any visitors bureau) and *Gallery Guide,* found in local galleries. Most museums and all galleries close on Mondays, and are jam-packed on the weekends. Many museums require a "donation" in place of an admission fee—but no one will throw large, rotting papayas at you if you give less than the suggested amounts. Call ahead to find out about free times which usually occur on a weeknight.

Major Collections

Metropolitan Museum of Art, Fifth Ave. (535-7710), at 82nd St. Subway: 4, 5, 6 to 86th St. If you see only one, see this. The largest in the Western Hemisphere, the Met's art collection encompasses 3.3 million works from almost every period through Impressionism; particularly strong in Egyptian and non-Western sculpture and European painting. Contemplate infiniti in the secluded Japanese Rock Garden. When blockbuster exhibits tour the world they usually stop at the Met—get tickets in advance through Ticketron. Open Sun. and Tues.-Thurs. 9:30am-5:15pm, Fri.-Sat. 9:30am-8:45pm. Donation $6, students and seniors $3.

Museum of Modern Art (MoMA), 11 W. 53rd St. (708-9400), off Fifth Ave. in Midtown. Subway: E, F to Fifth Ave./53rd St. One of the most extensive contemporary (post-Impressionist) collections in the world, it was founded in 1929 by scholar Alfred Barr in response to the Met's reluctance to embrace modern art. Cesar Pelli's recent structural glass additions—expanded entrance hall, garden, and gallery space—flood the masterpieces with natural light. See Monet's sublime *Water Lily* room, Ross's *Engulfed Cathedral,* and a virtual Picasso warehouse. Sculpture garden good for resting and people-watching. Open Fri.-Tues. 11am-6pm, Thurs. 11am-9pm. Admission $7, seniors and students $4, under 16 free. Films require free tickets in advance. Feel-good donation Thurs. after 5pm.

The Frick Collection, 1 E. 70th St. at Fifth Ave. (288-0700). Subway: #6 to 68th St. Robber baron Henry Clay Frick left his house and art collection to the city, and the museum retains the elegance of his French "Classic Eclectic" château. Impressive grounds. The Living Hall displays 17th-century furniture, Persian rugs, Holbein portraits, and paintings by El Greco, Rembrandt, Velázquez, and Titian. Courtyard inhabited by elegant statues surrounding the garden pool and fountain. Open Tues.-Sat. 10am-6pm, Sun. 1-6pm. Admission $3, students and seniors $1.50. Ages under 10 not allowed, under 16 must be accompanied by an adult.

Guggenheim Museum, 1071 Fifth Ave. and 89th St. (recording 423-3500, human being 423-3600, TDD 423-3607). Many have called this controversial construction a giant turnip and Midwesterner Frank Lloyd Wright's joke on the Big Apple. Others hail it as the city's most brilliant architectural achievement. The museum closed from 1990-92 while a ten-story "tower gallery" sprouted behind the original structure, allowing the museum to show more of its permanent collection. This year, most of the museum's space will be devoted to touring and temporary exhibits: the Russian avant-garde of 1915-32 in the winter of 92-93; forged-iron sculpture by Picasso, Calder, Giacometti, and Smith and multi-media work by Wim Wenders and Laurie Anderson beginning in Feb. 1993; pop artist Roy Lichtenstein and German sculptor/filmmaker/oddball Rebecca Horn in the summer; and "Abstraction in the 20th Century" beginning in Sept. 1993. Open Fri.-Wed. 10am-8pm. Admission $7, seniors and students $4, under 12 free. Tues. 5-8pm "pay what you wish." 2-day pass to this museum and **Guggenheim Museum SoHo** $10, seniors and students $6.

Whitney Museum of American Art, 945 Madison Ave. (570-3676) at 75th St. Subway: #6 to 77th St. Futuristic fortress featuring the largest collection of 20th-century American art in the world, with works by Hopper, Soyer, de Kooning, Motherwell, Warhol, and Calder. Open Wed. 11am-6pm, Thurs. 1pm-8pm, Fri.-Sun. 11am-6pm. Adults $6, students and seniors $4, under 12 free. Thurs. 6pm-8pm free.

American Museum of Natural History, Central Park West (769-5100), at 79th to 81st St. Subway: B or C to 81st St. The largest science museum in the world, in a suitably imposing Gothic structure guarded by a statue of Teddy Roosevelt on horseback. Teddy's distant ancestors can be seen in the Ocean Life display, while J.P. Morgan's Indian emeralds blaze in the Hall of Minerals and Gems. Open Sun.-Tues. and Thurs. 10am-5:45pm; Wed. and Fri.-Sat. 10am-9pm. Donation $5, kids $2.50. Free Fri.-Sat. 5-9pm. The museum also houses **Naturemax** (769-5650), a cinematic extravaganza on New York's largest (4 stories) movie screen. Admission for museum visitors $5, kids $2.50; Fri.-Sat. double features $7, kids $3.50. The **Hayden Planetarium** (769-5920) offers outstanding multi-media presentations. Seasonal celestial light shows twinkle in the dome of the **Theater of the Stars,** accompanied by astronomy lectures. Admission $5, seniors and students $3.75, kids $2. Electrify your senses with **Laser Rock** (769-5921) Fri.-Sat. nights, $6.

The Cloisters, Fort Tryon Park, upper Manhattan (923-3700). Subway: A through Harlem to 190th St. This monastery, built from pieces of 12th- and 13th-century French and Spanish cloisters, plus a new tower, was assembled at John D. Rockefeller's behest by Charles Collens in 1938 as a setting for the Met's medieval art collection. Highlights include the Unicorn Tapestries, the Cuxa Cloister, and the Treasury. Open March-Oct. Tues.-Sun. 8:30am-5:15pm; Nov.-Feb. Tues.-Sun. 9:30am-4:45pm. Donation $6, $3 students and seniors. (Includes admission to the Metropolitan Museum of Art main building.)

Brooklyn Museum, 200 Eastern Pkwy. at Washington Ave. (718-638-5000). Subway: #2 or 3 to Eastern Pkwy. Outstanding Classical displays, Hudson River School, huge African, Oceanic, and New World art collections. Changing exhibits display celebrated and unusual works. Open Tues.-Sun. 10am-5pm. Admission $4, students $2, seniors $1.50, kids free.

Smaller and Specialized Collections

American Craft Museum, 40 W. 53rd St. (956-3535) across from MoMA. Subway: E or F to Fifth Ave./53rd St. Offering more than quilts, this museum revises the notion of crafts with its modern media. Open Tues. 10am-8pm, Wed.-Sun. 10am-5pm. Admission $4.50, seniors and students $2.

AT&T Infoquest Center, 550 Madison Ave. at 56th St. (605-5555). High-tech, interactive exhibits explaining the information age, sponsored by the company with the soothing voice. Exhibits focus on lightwave communications, microelectronics, and computer software. Some exhibits, like the one where you scramble your face on a computer screen, are downright fun. Open Tues. 10am-9pm, Wed.-Sun. 10am-6pm. Free.

Cooper-Hewitt Museum, 2 E. 91st St. (860-6894) at Fifth Ave. Subway: #4, 5, 6 to 86th St. Andrew Carnegie's majestic, Georgian mansion now houses the Smithsonian Institution's decorative arts and design collection. All the special exhibits have considerable flair, focusing on such topics as contemporary designer fabrics. Open Tues. 10am-9pm, Wed.-Sat. 10am-5pm, Sun. noon-5pm. Admission $3, seniors and students $1.50, under 12 free. Free Tues. 5-9pm.

New Museum of Contemporary Art, 583 Broadway between Prince and Houston St. (219-1222). Subway: R to Prince, #6 to Bleecker, or B, D, F to Broadway/Lafayette. Dedicated to the destruction of the canon and of conventional ideas of "art," the New Museum does the hottest, the newest, and the most controversial. Much art dealing with the politics of identity—sexual, racial, and ethnic. Once a month an artist sits in the front window and has discussions with passersby. Open Wed.-Thurs. and Sun. noon-6pm, Fri.-Sat. noon-8pm. Suggested donation $3.50, seniors, students, and artists $2.50, under 12 free.

IBM Gallery of Science and Art, 590 Madison Ave. (745-6100) at 56th St. Subway: E, F, N, R to Fifth Ave. User-friendly exhibits covering a wide range of art. Permanent show titled "Mathematica: A World of Numbers and Beyond," featuring topological phenomena like the Möbius Strip. Open Tues.-Sat. 11am-6pm. Free.

International Center of Photography, 1130 Fifth Ave. (860-1778) at 94th St. Subway: #6 to 96th St. Housed in a landmark townhouse (1914) built for *New Republic* founder Willard Straight. The first museum in the world to have treated photography as fine art. Maintains a rich permanent collection and operates workshops, photolabs, and a screening room. Historical, thematic, contemporary, and experimental works. This branch and the Midtown branch at 77 W. 45th St. (869-2155) open Tues. 11am-8pm, Wed.-Sun. 11am-6pm. Admission $3, seniors and students $2.

Intrepid Sea-Air-Space Museum, Pier 86 (245-2533), at 46th St. and Twelfth Ave. Bus: M42, or M50 to W. 46th St. America's military 20th-century technological achievements celebrated in the legendary aircraft carrier. Open Memorial Day-Labor Day daily 10am-5pm; Labor Day-Memorial Day Mon.-Fri. 10am-5pm. $7, under 12 $4, under 6 free.

Jacques Marchais Center of Tibetan Art, 338 Lighthouse Ave., Staten Island (718-987-3478). Take bus #74 from Staten Island Ferry to Lighthouse Ave., turn right and walk up the hill. One of the finest Tibetan collections in the U.S., but the real attractions are the gardens, set on beautifully landscaped cliffs. Center itself a replica of a Tibetan temple. Open April-Nov. Wed.-Sun. 1-5pm. $3, $2.50 seniors, $1 kids.

Museum of Television and Radio, 25 W. 52nd St. (621-6600), between Fifth and Sixth Ave. Subway: B, D, F, Q to Rockefeller Center, or E, F to 53rd St. Expanded, new facilities where visitors select and view 40,000 tapes of classic TV and radio shows on individual consoles. Go before 1pm or expect a long wait, especially on Sat., despite the 1-hr. max. viewing time. Special screenings possible for groups. Monthly retrospectives focus on legendary personalities and landmark shows. Open Tues.-Wed. and Fri.-Sun. noon-6pm, Thurs. noon-8pm. Suggested contribution $5, students $4, seniors and under 13 $3.

Publications

New York, the premier society of information abundance, is a sounding board for the rest of the global village. ABC, CBS, NBC, two wire services, umpteen leading magazines, and more newspapers than anywhere else in the world have taken up residence here. Publicists, preachers, advertisers, sociologists, superheroes and community activists jockey for position, all hoping to make enough noise to be heard above the information din. Today's New York supports well over 100 different newspapers, reflecting and refracting the variegated cityscape. Weekly ethnic papers cater to the Black, Hispanic, Irish, Japanese, Chinese, Indian, Korean, and Greek communities, among others. Other papers split their readers on other than ethnic cleavages. Patrician, pensive, and the prurient papers pander to the sublime and the base in all of us. Magazines add to this media glut—although in a less disposable, glossier package. The following is not intended to be a comprehensive listing of New York's publications; rather it is meant to help you sort through the media Babel in search of a few good words.

The ***New York Times***. The eminent elder statesman of The City's (nay, the *country's*) papers. It deals soberly and thoroughly with the news. Its editorial page provides a nationally respected forum for policy debates and its political endorsements are usually followed by a bump in the polls. Likewise, praise from its Book Review section can be the start of a promising career or the *coup de grâce* for an ailing one. Theater directors, nervous politicians, and other fervent readers run to buy the Sunday Times 'round about midnight on Saturday night. Oh, and it doesn't have comics.

The ***New York Post*** and the ***Daily News*** are New York's twin tabloids that make their living on the city's dirty laundry. The *News*, recently "rescued" by editor-*cum*-corpse Robert Maxwell, has slightly better taste—it doesn't use red ink and it reports fewer gruesome murders. *Post* headlines, often printed in unwieldy lettering three inches high, can have a nasty toothsome ring. One of the *Post's* more brilliant head(less)lines read "Headless Body found in Topless Bar." Both papers have editorial policies more conservative than their headlines, as well as comics, advice pages, and horoscopes. The *Post* has a great sports section; both have good metropolitan coverage.

The ***Daily Planet*** caters more to the superhero-watching crowd. Pulitzer-Prize winning news hound Clark Kent will thrill you with yet another exclusive on how Superman has foiled the latest plot to sully Gotham (how does he *always* manage to be at the right place at the right time?) Faster than a speeding armadillo and armed only with a pocket full of kryptonite, shutterbug Jimmy Olsen has shot more criminals than the firing squad at Alcatraz. Lois Lane still won't give him the time of day.

The ***Village Voice***—the country's largest leftist weekly in the country—captures a lot of the spirit of the city that you won't find in the dailies. Although printed in the same subway-readable tabloid form as the *Post* and the *Daily News*, it has nothing else in common with them. Don't search here for syndicated advice columnists, baseball stats or the scantily-clad-bimbo du jour. The voice vociferates on political issues, reflects on New York and sponsors some of the best investigative journalism this side of Woodward and Bernstein..

The rarified ***New Yorker*** is a weekly magazine that publishes fiction and poetry by well-known authors and the occasional fledgling discovery—even its ads contain measured prose. It also carries the most thorough listings and reviews of films and events—and the finest cartoons—in the tri-state area.

The *New Yorker's* flashier cousin ***New York*** magazine also prints extensive listings but focuses on the city's (wealthy) lifestyle. Its final pages contain impossible British Crossword puzzles (a six-letter word for glacial ridge???) and other misc. mindbenders.

Spy magazine, famous for calling Donald Trump a "garden gnome" and for popularizing the Bush adultery story, takes witty jabs at the city's personalities and styles. Its "Separated at Birth?" series (pairing, for example, Leona Helmsley with the Joker from *Batman*) has proven especially successful.

Entertainment

For information on shows and ticket availability, call the **NYC/ON STAGE hotline** at 768-1818, **Ticket Central** between 1 and 8pm at 279-4200, the **Theatre Development Fund** at 221-0013, or the **New York City Department of Cultural Affairs** hotline at 956-2787. **TKTS** (354-5800) sells **half-price tickets** (usually $25) to Broadway shows on the same day of performances; queue up early at their booth in Times Square at 47th and Broadway. (Tickets sold Mon.-Sat. 3-8pm for evening performances, Wed. and Sat. 10am-2pm for matinees, and Sun. noon-8pm for matinees and evening performances.)

Officially, **Off-Broadway** theaters have between 100 and 499 seats; only Broadway houses have over 500. Mostly located downtown, Off-Broadway houses frequently offer more offbeat or countercultural shows, with shorter runs. Occasionally Off-Broadway offerings have long runs or jump to Broadway houses (tickets cost $10-20). The best of these huddle around the Sheridan Square area of the West Village. They include the **Circle Rep,** at 99 Seventh Ave. S. (924-7100), the **Circle in the Square Downtown,** at 159 Bleecker St. (254-6330), the **Lucille Lortel,** at 121 Christopher St. (924-8782), the **Cherry Lane,** at 38 Commerce St. (989-2020), and the **Provincetown Playhouse,** at 133 MacDougal St. (477-5048).

The late Joseph Papp founded the **Shakespeare in the Park** series, a New York summer tradition which practically everybody in the city has attended (or attempted to, anyway). From June through August, the program features two Shakespeare plays at the **Delacorte Theatre** in Central Park, near the 81st St. entrance on the Upper West Side, just north of the main road there (861-7277).

Opera and Dance

The fulcrum of New York culture is **Lincoln Center,** at Broadway and 66th St. (875-5000). For a schedule of events, write Lincoln Center Plaza, NYC 10023, or call the Performing Arts Library (870-1930).

The **Metropolitan Opera Company** (362-6000) warbles on a Lincoln Center stage the size of a football field. The performances boast some of most renowned principals in the world. During the regular season (Sept.-May, Mon.-Sat.), you can get upper balcony seats for about $15. The cheapest seats have obstructed views, but standing room in the orchestra is a steal at $12. Standing room in the Family Circle is cheaper ($9), but it's like watching an ant farm. (Box office open Mon.-Sat. 10am-8pm, Sun. noon-6pm.) In summer, watch for free concerts in city parks (362-6000).

At right angles to the Met, the **New York City Opera** (870-5570), formerly under the direction of Beverly Sills, has been revamped by new director Christopher Keene. Known for its performances of tried-and-true old warhorses, the company also sings contemporary U.S. works. The success of its recently introduced English "supertitles" has led other companies to adopt them. "City" now offers a summer season and keeps its ticket prices low year-round ($10-62, standing room back row top balcony $10). Call to check the availability of rush tickets on the night before the performance you want to attend, then wait in line the next morning. Look for free performances by the **New York Grand Opera** at Central Park Summerstage (360-2777).

The late great George Balanchine's **New York City Ballet,** the oldest in the country, alternates with the city opera for the use of the Lincoln Center's New York State Theater (870-5570), performing December through January and again in May and June. (Tickets $11-55, standing room $8.) **American Ballet Theater** (477-3030) dances at the Met during the late spring and for about two weeks in summer. Under Mikhail Baryshnikov's guidance, ABT's eclectic repertoire has ranged from the Bolshoi grand-style Russian ballet to experimental American.

The **Alvin Ailey American Dance Theater** (767-0940) bases its repertoire of modern dance on African-American jazz, spirituals, and contemporary music. The grandest integrated company in the world, it tours internationally but always performs at the **City Center** in December. Tickets ($15-40) are difficult to obtain; write or call City Center (581-7907) weeks in advance, if possible. The **Martha Graham Dance Co.,** 316 E. 63rd St. (838-5886), performs original Graham pieces during their October New York season. She revolutionized 20th-century dance with her psychological, rather than narrative, approach to characters. (Tickets $15-40.) Look also for the seasons of the **Merce Cunningham Dance Company,** the **Dance Theater of Harlem,** and the **Paul Taylor Dance Company,** usually in spring.

Half-price tickets for many music and dance events can be purchased on the day of performance at **Bryant Park,** 42nd St. (382-2323), between Fifth and Sixth Ave. (Open Tues. and Thurs.-Fri. noon-2pm and 3-7pm; Wed. and Sat. 11am-2pm and 3-7pm; Sun. noon-6pm.)

Classical Music

In Lincoln Center's **Avery Fisher Hall** (875-5030), the **New York Philharmonic** (875-5700), under Kurt Masur, plays everything from Bach to Bax, Schubert to Schoenberg. Avery Fisher's new interior, designed by Philip Johnson, resonates with acoustic grandeur. The Philharmonic's season lasts from September through May, and jazz and classical musicians visit the rest of the year. (Tickets $10-50). Senior citizen and student-rush tickets ($5) go on sale Tuesday and Thursday evenings a half hour before the curtain rises; call for availability. "Mostly Mozart" concerts, performed July through August, feature artists like Itzhak Perlman; get there early since major artists often give half-hour pre-concert recitals. (Tickets $9-18.50.)

Carnegie Hall, Seventh Ave. at 57th St. (247-7800), one of the greatest musical auditoriums in the world, attracts opera singers, jazz singers, instrumental soloists, and symphony orchestras. One of the best ways for the budget traveler to absorb New York musical culture is by visiting a music school. Except for opera and ballet productions ($5-12), concerts are free and frequent at the **Juilliard School of Music** (at the Lincoln Center), the **Mannes School of Music** (580-0210), the **Manhattan School of Music** (749-2802), and the **Bloomingdale House of Music** (663-6021).

Flicks

Hollywood may make the movies, but New York makes Hollywood. Most movies open in New York weeks before they're distributed across the country, and the response of Manhattan audiences and critics can shape a film's success or failure nationwide (then again, so can the San Fernando Valley). Or so they like to think. Just grab a copy of any newspaper for an overview of the selection. Magazines such as *New York* and the *New Yorker* provide plot summaries and evaluations in their listings as well.

Museums like the Met and MoMA show artsy flicks downstairs, as does the New York Historical Society. The **Theatre 80 Saint Mark's,** 80 St. Mark's Place (254-7400), features classic foreign and U.S. revivals. For an inspiring movie-going experience, try the **Ziegfeld Theatre,** 141 W. 54th St. (765-7600). One of the last grand movie houses that hasn't been sliced up into a "multiplex," the Ziegfeld offers standard box-office attractions. **The Kitchen,** 512 W. 19th St. (255-5793), is a world-renowned showcase for off-beat happenings.

If you've grown tired of crypto-fascist bourgeois capitalist culture industries, you may wish to learn of the subversive activities transpiring unsuspected at **Revolution Books,** 13 E. 16th St. (691-3345). On auspicious nights, films, videos, and lectures are presented to the vanguard. Beware Thermidor!

Bars and Clubs

Rock Clubs

CBGBs, 313 Bowery (982-4052), at Bleecker. Subway: #6 to Bleecker. The initials stand for "country, bluegrass, blues, and other music for uplifting gourmandizers," but everyone knows that since 1976 this club has been all about punk rock. The Talking ("This ain't no nightclub, no CB-GB's") Heads and Blondie got their start here. The club has adjusted to the post-punk 90s with alternative offerings, but expect a nostalgic hardcore crowd. Shows nightly at around 8pm, Sun. (often hardcore) matinee at 3pm. Cover $5-10.

Maxwell's, 1039 Washington St. (201-798-4064) in Hoboken, NJ. To get here, take the PATH train ($1) from 33rd, 23rd, 14th, 9th, or Christopher St. and 6th Ave. to the Hoboken stop, then walk or take a taxi ten blocks down Washington to 11th St.) Subway: B, D, F, N, Q, or R to 34th St., then PATH train ($1) from the 34th St. High-quality underground rockers from America and abroad have plied their trade in the back room of a Hoboken restaurant for going on 15 years; New Order played their first U.S. show here, the Feelies were once regulars, and Ira Kaplan of Yo La Tengo manned the soundboard for awhile. Now it's graced by the likes of Pavement, Wingtip Sloat, Some Velvet Sidewalk, and Tsunami. Cover $6-9; shows occasionally sell out, so get tix in advance from Maxwell's or Ticketron. (Sandwiches $6, entrees $7-9. Restaurant open Tues.-Sun. 2pm-midnight.

World Music

Sounds of Brazil (S.O.B.), 204 Varick St. (243-4940), at the corner of Seventh and Houston in the Village. Subway: #1, 2, 3, 9 to Houston. This luncheonette-turned-dance-club presents bopping musicians playing the sounds of Brazil, Africa, Latin America, and the Caribbean in a setting inflicted with tropicana. Open for dining Tues.-Thurs. 7pm-2:30am, Fri.-Sat. 7pm-4am. Music from 9pm Tues.-Thurs., Fri.-Sat. from 10pm. Cover Mon.-Thurs. $12-18, Fri. $17, Sat. $18.

Wetland Preserve, 161 Hudson St. (966-4225). Subway: #1, 9, A, C, or E to Canal St. A giant Summer of Love mural in the back room sets the tone, a Volkswagen bus curio shop swims in tie-dyes, and mood memorabilia harken to the Woodstock years in this 2-story whole-earth spectacular. Chill downstairs in a flowerchild's love patch. Mon. and Fri. Wetlands brings you reggae; Tues. Grateful Dead tribute; Wed. mixes things up; Thurs. blues and rock; Sat. nights psychedelic mania kicks in and Sun. things are back to the mellow groove with folk. Shows start nightly after 9:30. This eco-nightclub does some canvassing on the side, sponsoring benefits in the cause of a healthier earth. Opens Sun.-Thurs. 5pm, Fri.-Sat. 9pm. Cover $5-15 (no drink min.).

Jazz

J's, 2581 Broadway (666-3600), between 97th and 98th St., 2nd floor. Subway: #1 or 9 to 103rd St. A classic jazz bar. Top-notch music, dim lighting over red brick walls: intimacy without claustrophobia. Owner Judy Barnett, a respected jazz singer, ropes in well-known talent; as you'd expect, there's more focus on singing here than at most clubs. Some swing; blues on Sun. After the set, the musicians schmooze at the bar. Open Mon.-Thurs. 5pm-12:30am, sets from 8:30pm; Fri. 5pm-1am, sets from 9pm; Sat. 7pm-1am, sets from 10pm. No cover; $7 min. at bar, $12 at tables.

Augie's, 2751 Broadway (864-9834), between 105th and 106th St. Subway: #1 or 9 to 103rd St. Small and woody. Jazz all week until 3am. The saxophonist sits on your lap and the bass rests on your table. Quality musicians and a cool, unpretentious crowd. No cover; unenforced $3 drink min. Sets start around 10pm. Open daily 8pm-3am.

Dan Lynch, 221 Second Ave. (677-0911), at 14th St. Subway: #4, 5, 6, L, N, R to Union Sq. Dark smoky room with Casablanca fan, long bar, and "all blues, all the time." Swinging, beautifully friendly, Deadhead crowd envelops the dance floor. Pool table in back. Open daily 8pm-4am; blues and jazz start at 10pm. Jam session Sat.-Sun. 4-9pm. Cover Fri.-Sat. $5.

Dance Clubs

The New York dance club is an unrivaled institution. The crowd is uninhibited, the music unparalleled and the fun unlimited—as long as you uncover the right place. Because clubs rise and fall so quickly, a list of hotspots would be futile—it's best to ask someone on the club scene where to find your dance experience.

The rules are simple. You have to have "the look" to be let in. Doormen are the clubs' fashion police, and nothing drab or conventional will squeeze by. Wear black clothes and drape your most attractive friend on your arm. Don't look worried or fearful; act like you belong. Come after 11pm unless you crave solitude; things don't really get going until 1 or 2am. Most good clubs are best only one or two nights a week. The cover can rise to $20 on weekend nights when the suburbanites converge on Manhattan. Alternative and downtown nightlife often blend; the hippest clubs have one or two "gay nights" a week, and same-sex couples can go "clubbing" in most places without hassle. Call ahead to make sure you know what (and whom) to expect when you arrive. Most clubs stay open until 4am; a few non-alcoholic after-hours clubs keep getting busy until 5am or later. Reliable clubs in the summer of '92 (remember, things change fast) included **Building,** 51 W. 26th St. (576-1890), between Broadway and Sixth Ave. (Subway: R to 28th St.), where Thursday and Sunday are the best gay nights; also try **Nell's,** 246 W. 14th St. (675-1567), between Seventh and Eighth Ave. (Subway: #1, 2, 3, or 9 to 14th St.), and **Rex,** 246 Fifth Ave. (725-6997; Subway R to 28th St.).

Gay and Lesbian

The New York gay scene extends visibly through the city. The West Village, especially around Christopher St., has long been the hub of the city's alternative life. A harder-core gay crowd occupies the lower East Village on First and Second Ave. south of E. 12th St. Each week the *Village Voice* and *New York Native* publish full listings of gay events. The *Pink Pages* (427-8224) is a phone book for the gay and lesbian community with all sorts of listings, including bars and clubs. **The Spike,** 120 11th Ave. (243-9688) at W. 20th St. (subway: C or E to 23rd St.), caters to an adventurous crowd of leather-clad men (and some women). (Open daily 9pm-4am.) **DT's Fat Cat,** at W. 4th St. and W. 12th St. (243-9041; subway A, C, E, or L to 14th St.), is a piano bar with a large straight clientele, and a relaxed scene for lesbians. **Pandora's Box,** 70 Grove St. on 7th Ave. South, is a popular hangout and meeting place for lesbians. (Open 4pm-4am.)

Bars

Automatic Slims, 733 Washington St. (645-8660) at Bank St. Subway: A, C, or E to 14th St. Simple bar in the West Village with the best selection of blues and screamin' soul, complemented by the guitars and pensive faces of South-side stars. 20-something Villagers sit at tables with classic 45s under the glass top. Packed on weekends with a more diverse crowd. Open Sun.-Mon. 5:30pm-2:30am, Tues.-Sat. 5:30pm-4:30am.

Downstairs Beirut, 158 First Ave. (260-4248). Subway: L to First Ave. Hardcore but friendly East Village crowd gathers under a large inflatable man to listen to the jukebox belt out hits by Mudhoney, the Avengers, and the Clash. Friendly Morticia look-alike serves draft beer for $1. Open daily noon-4am.

Lucky Strike, 59 Grand St. (943-0479), off W. Broadway. Subway: #1, 9, or A, C, E to Canal St. SoHo prices attract droves of the ultra-magna-beautiful, scantily clad in black. Super-attractive waitstaff. $3.50 Buds with similarly overpriced food in the back makes this more of a sight than a watering hole. Open daily noon-4am.

The Shark Bar, 307 Amsterdam Ave. (496-6600) between 74th and 75th. High-class and enjoyable bar and soul-food restaurant; possibly the only truly interracial establishment on the West Side below 110th St. Live jazz on Tues. with a $5 cover; "gospel brunch" Sat. 12:30 and 2pm (no cover). Reasonable drink prices (bottled beer from $3). Entrées from $11. Open Mon.-Fri. 11:30am-2am, Sat.-Sun. 11:30am-4:30pm and 6:30pm-4am.

American Trash, 1471 First Ave. (988-9008) between 76th and 77th St. Cavernous barroom hung with "trash" oddities from Christmas stockings to prize ribbons. Swinging singles having a wild and crazy time. Open daily noon-4am.

Comedy Clubs

The Original Improvisation, 358 W. 44th St. (765-8268), between Eighth and Ninth Ave. Subway: A, C, or E to 42nd St. A quarter-century of comedy—acts from *Saturday Night Live,* Carson, Letterman. Richard Pryor and Robin Williams got started here. Shows Sun.-Thurs. at 9pm, Fri. and Sat. 9:15 and midnight. Cover: Mon.-Tues. $8 and $8 min., Wed., Thurs., and Sun. $11 and $9 min., Fri and Sat. $12 and $9 min.

Comedy Cellar, 117 MacDougal St. (254-3630), between W. 3rd St. and Bleecker St. Subway: A, B, C, D, E, F, or Q to W. 4th St. Subterranean annex of the artsy Olive Tree café. Dark, intimate, atmospheric, and packing the people on a late Fri. night or an *early* Saturday morning. Features rising comics such as John Manfrelloti and even surprise drop-ins by superstars such as Robin Williams. Shows Sun.-Thurs. 9pm-2am, Fri. at 9 and 11:30pm, Sat. at 9pm, 10:45pm, and 12:30am. Cover: Sun.-Thurs. $5, plus 2-drink min.; Fri.-Sat. $10, plus $5 min. Make reservations in advance.

Chicago City Limits, 351 E. 74th St. (772-8707), between First and Second Ave. Subway: #6 to 77th St. If you're looking for something a little different from the usual stand-up, check out New York's longest running comedy revue. Shows are a careful synthesis of cabaret, scripted comedy sketches, and improvisation, often with a political bent. Extemporaneous skits are heavily dependent on audience suggestions for plot direction, allowing the crowd to get into the act. No alcohol served. Shows Mon. and Wed.-Thurs. 8:30pm, Fri.-Sat. at 8 and 10:30pm. Cover Mon. $10, Wed.-Thurs. $12.50; Fri.-Sat. $15.

Near New York: Long Island

Long Island is easy to stereotype, but difficult to grasp. For some, the Island evokes images of sprawling suburbia, dotted with malls and office buildings; others see it as the privileged retreat of Manhattan WASPs; for still others it is a summer refuge of white sand and open spaces. Fewer see the pockets of poverty on Long Island, or its commercial and cultural centers.

While in theory "Long Island" includes the entire 120-mi. fish-shaped land mass, in practice the term excludes the westernmost section, Brooklyn and Queens. This leaves Nassau and Suffolk counties to comprise the "real" Long Island. East of the Queens-Nassau line, people read *Newsday,* not the *Times* or the *Daily News;* they back the Islanders, not the Rangers; and they enjoy their position as neighbor to, rather than part of, the great metropolis.

Fortunately for the visitor, the Island is cheaply and easily accessible from Manhattan. Nearly all your transit needs will be served by some combination of the **Long Island Railroad (LIRR)** (516-822-5477), which operates out of Penn Station in Manhattan (see New York City: Getting Around By Bus or By Train), and the **Metropolitan Suburban Bus Authority (MSBA)** (516-542-0100), which operates daytime buses in eastern Queens, Nassau, and Western Suffolk. Depending on where you go and what time you leave, train fare will vary from $8.50 round-trip (for nearby suburbs in non-rush hour times) to $28 round-trip (for distant spots during rush-hour). **Suffolk Transit** (516-360-5700) takes over farther east. Bikes may be carried on LIRR by permit only.

Long Island's **area code** is 516.

Suburban Long Island: Nassau and Western Suffolk

The North Shore of Long Island was once known as the "Gold Coast" because of the string of mansions built by 19th-century industrialists in the hills overlooking Long Island Sound. Many of these houses have been turned into museums, and the grounds that have been spared from developers are now gardens, arboretums, or nature preserves open to the public.

From west to east, some principal North Shore sights are: **Falaise** (883-1610), in Sands Point Park and Preserve, the former Guggenheim estate (open May-mid-Nov. Sat.-Wed. 10am-5pm; admission $2), and **Old Westbury Gardens,** on Old Westbury

Rd. (333-0048), where the splendor of the main house and its collection of painting and sculpture complements the formal English gardens outside.

Jones Beach State Park (784-1600) is the best compromise of convenience and crowd for day-trippers from the city, with nearly 2500 acres of beach and parking for 23,000 cars. Only 40 minutes from the City, Jones Beach packs in the crowds in the summer months. The waves really roar and the sand crunches under your two feet. Along the 1½-mi. boardwalk you can find deck games, roller-skating, miniature golf, basketball, and nightly dancing. The **Marine Theatre** inside the park hosts rock concerts. There are eight different bathing areas on either the rough Atlantic Ocean or the calmer Zachs Bay, plus a number of beaches restricted to residents of certain towns in Nassau County. During the summer you can take the LIRR to Freeport or Wantaugh, where you can get a bus to the beach. Call 212-739-4200 or 212-526-0900 for the dope on the beach. **Recreation Lines, Inc.** (718-788-8000) provides bus service straight from mid-Manhattan. If you are driving, take LIE east to the Northern State Pkwy., go east to the Meadowbrook (or Wantaugh) Pkwy. and then south to Jones Beach.

After shopping at the **Walt Whitman Mall,** the nearby **Walt Whitman's Birthplace** (427-5240) will seem a more appropriate memorial to the great American poet.

The **Fire Island National Seashore** is the main draw here; in summer it offers fishing, clamming, and guided nature walks. The facilities at **Sailor's Haven** include a marina, a nature trail, and a famous beach. Similar facilities at **Watch Hill** include a 20-unit campground, where reservations are required. Smith Point West has a small visitor information center and a nature trail with wheelchair access (289-4810). Here you can spot horseshoe crabs, whitetail deer, and monarch butterflies, which flit across the country every year to winter in Baja California.

The North Fork

No one ever said that Long Island wines were famous, or even really good, but visiting one of the North Fork's 40 vineyards can be fun. Twelve wineries and 40 vineyards produce the best Chardonnay, Cabernet Sauvignon, Merlot, Pinot Noir, and Riesling in New York State; some say that local climate and soil conditions rival those of Sonoma Valley, CA. Two Long Island wines even were chosen for ex-oilman and nominal Texas resident Bush's 1988 inauguration. Quite a few of the Island wineries offer free tours and tastings; call ahead to make an appointment.

To get to the wine district, take LIE to its end (Exit 73), then Rte. 58, which becomes Rte. 25 (Main Rd.). North of and parallel to Rte. 25 is Rte. 48 (North Rd. or Middle Rd.), which has a number of wineries. Road signs announce tours and tastings. **Palmer Vineyards,** 108 Sound Ave., Riverhead (722-9463), has some of the most advanced equipment on the island and a tasting room with an interior assembled from two 18th-century English pubs.

The South Fork

Out on the South Fork's north shore droops **Sag Harbor,** one of Long Island's best-kept secrets. Founded in 1707, this port used to be more important than New York Harbor; its deep shore made for easy navigation. It boasts the second-largest collection of colonial buildings in the U.S., as well as cemeteries lined with the gravestones of Revolutionary soldiers and sailors.

In town, catch the **Sag Harbor Whaling Museum** (725-0770), in the former home of Benjamin Hunting, a 19th-century whale ship owner. Enter the museum through the jawbones of a whale.

In summer, you'll have to compete with many wealthy New Yorkers for even the most modest lodgings, while from November to April almost everything is closed. Most of the few off-season deals are offered in Montauk Village. The absolutely best bargain on the east end is the friendly **Montauket,** on Tuthill Rd. (668-5992), one mi. north of Montauk Village. Go north on Edgemere Ave. and turn left on Tudhill Rd. Located close to the railroad station, this place, not surprisingly, fills up quickly. (Doubles $35, with private bath $40. Open mid-March-late Nov. Make summer reservations beginning March 1.). **Pines Motor Lodge** (957-3330), corner of Rte. 109 and 3rd St. in Lindenhurst (LIE to Southern State Pkwy. East, Exit 33), offers doubles from $40 to

$70. Camp in summer at **Battle Row** (293-7120), in Bethpage, Nassau, with eight tent sites and 50 trailer sites available on a first-come, first-served basis. (Tent sites $5, trailer sites $8-12; 21 and over).

You'll find many possibilities for hiking in state (669-1000) and county (567-1700) parks. One of the more unusual places to hike, **Mashomack Preserve** (749-1001), sits on Rte. 114, on **Shelter Island,** one mi. north of the South Ferry. (Open Wed.-Mon. 9am-5pm.) Part of the Nature Conservancy's national chain of open lands, this preserve boasts 2000 acres of hiking trails and bay-shore beaches. You can explore by reservation only, but a permit is not necessary—just call the day before you show up.

Montauk offers numerous accommodations and activities, but the **Montauk Point Lighthouse and Museum** (668-2544) is the high point of a trip here. Like the marker that greets a mountain climber who has reached a summit, the lighthouse marks the end of the island for the weary driver. This archetypal lighthouse is set on the rocky edge of the water, its sloping white sides adorned bluntly by a single wide band of brown. Its bulky, solid form rises with a utilitarian elegance from a cluster of smaller, weaker buildings. The 86-ft. structure went up in 1796 by special order of President George Washington. On a clear day, you should climb the 138 spiralling steps to the top, where you can look out over the seascape, across the Long Island Sound to Rhode Island and Connecticut. The best seasons for viewing are the spring and fall, when the sea has scarcely a stain on it; the thick summer air can haze over the view. You may want to climb up, even on a foggy day, to see if you can spot the so-called "Will o' the Wisp," a clipper ship sometimes sighted on hazy days under full sail with a lantern hanging from its mast. Experts claim that the ship is a mirage resulting from the presence of atmospheric phosphorescence. Have they no romance? (Open May— mid-June and early Oct.-Nov. Sat.-Sun. 11am-4pm; mid-June-mid-Sept. daily 10:30am-6pm; mid-Sept.-early Oct. Fri.-Mon. 10am-5pm.)

Fishing and whale-watching are among Montauk's other pleasures. **Lazybones'** half-day fishing "party boat," which is more party than boat, makes two trips daily (7am-noon and 1-5pm), leaving from Tuma's Dock next to Grossman's. Call Captain Mike at 668-5671 for info. The **Okeanos Whale Watch Cruise** is one of the best in the business, though a tad expensive. The cruises are run by the non-profit Okeanos Research Foundation, which helps finance its studies of whales by taking tourists out on its 90-ft. ship, accompanied by a biologist and research team of whale experts. You may see fin, minke, and humpback whales.

The East End is served several times daily by the LIRR. Suffolk Transit (360-5700, open Mon.-Fri. 8am-4:30pm) loops back and forth between the tips of the north and south forks, with several runs daily, most of them between East Hampton and Orient Point. Call to confirm stops and schedules. The route also connects with the LIRR at Riverhead, where the forks meet. (No service Sunday.) Hampton Jitney (212-936-0440 in Manhattan, 516-283-4600 in Long Island), a private bus company, runs 15 to 25 buses per day to and from the Hamptons, stopping in almost all the villages and towns from Westhampton to Montauk. (One way between Manhattan and South Fork $15-20.) Pick up the bus in Manhattan at 41st. St. at Third Ave. Call for schedule info.

Niagara Falls

The erstwhile "Honeymoon Capital of the World," Niagara Falls is a marriage of beauty and industry. Niagara Falls, NY (not to be confused with its sibling on the Canadian side of the Niagara River) boomed during World War II as the home of chemical companies which used the water to power their factories and to carry away liquid waste. Many companies left with the coming of environmental restrictions, making the area more beautiful today, if not as prosperous as it once was. The Falls themselves power the largest hydroelectric plant in North America, producing enough energy to power a city of three million. As for the better half of Niagara's couple: catch it while you still can—erosion is moving the Falls upstream at a rate of six ft. per year.

Practical Information

Emergency: 911.

Niagara Falls Convention and Visitors Bureau, 345 3rd St., Niagara Falls, NY (285-2400) will send you info on Niagara Falls. Open May-Sept. daily 8:30am-8:30pm, Oct.-April Mon.-Fri. 9am-5pm. In Niagara, the **information center** that adjoins the bus station on 4th and Niagara is the place to visit. It's a 10-min. walk from the Falls, with 1-hr. parking. Open May-Sept. daily 8:30am-8:30pm; off-season Mon.-Fri. 9am-5pm. The state runs a **Niagara Reservation Visitors Center** (278-1796) right in front of the Falls' observation deck. Open summer daily 9am-9:30pm, winter 10am-6:30pm. The **Canada Visitor and Convention Bureau**, 4673 Ontario Ave. Suite 202, Niagara Falls, Ont. L2E 3R1 (416-356-6061), will send info on the Canadian side.

Amtrak: 27th St. and Lockport, Niagara Falls, 1 block east of Hyde Park Blvd. Take #52 bus to get to the Falls/downtown. (800-872-7245, 683-8440 for baggage problems). To: New York City, 2 per day, 9 hr., $82; Boston, 14 hr., $125; Chicago, 24 hrs., $175.

Greyhound: Niagara Falls Bus Terminal, 4th St. and Niagara St. (282-1331; open Mon.-Fri. 8am-4pm) only sells tickets for use in Buffalo. To get to the Buffalo bus station, take bus #40 from the Niagara Falls bus terminal (18 per day, 1 hr., $1.75) to the **Buffalo Transportation Center,** 181 Ellicott St. (855-7511; open daily 3am-1am). To: New York City (7 per day, 8 hr., $67, Fri.-Sun. $71); Boston (4 per day, 12 hr., $79); Chicago (4 per day, 12 hr., $94); Rochester (7 per day, 2 hr., $7); Syracuse (6 per day, 4 hr., $14); and Albany (5 per day, 7 hr., $29). Rates fluctuate; call ahead.

Public Transport: Niagara Frontier Metro Transit System, 800-794-3960. Provides local city transit and free map of bus routes. **Niagara Scenic Bus Lines,** 800-672-3642. Service from Niagara Falls bus terminal to: Niagara, Canada (10 per day, US$2.75), and Buffalo Airport ($14.50). A **taxi** from Buffalo Airport to Niagara costs about $40, so take this bus.

Taxi: Rainbow Taxicab, 282-3221; **United Cab,** 285-9331.

Post Office: Niagara Falls, 615 Main St. (285-7561), in Niagara Falls, NY. Open Mon.-Fri. 8:30am-5pm, Sat. 9am-noon. **ZIP code:** 14302.

Area Code: 716 (New York), 416 (Ontario). It costs $2.25 first min., 16¢ each additional min., plus tax, to phone across the border. You may be able to rent a megaphone for cheaper.

Niagara St. is the main east-west drag in town; it ends on the western side in Rainbow Bridge, which crosses to Canada. Falls Park is at the western edge of the city. North-south streets are numbered; numbers increase going east. Parking in the city is plentiful. Most lots near the Falls charge $3, but you can park in an equivalent spot for less on streets bordering the park. A free parking lot on Goat Island fills up early in the day.

Accommodations and Camping

Niagara Falls International HI/AYH-Hostel, 1101 Ferry Ave., Niagara Falls, NY 14301 (282-3700). From station, walk east on Niagara St., turn left on Memorial Pkwy.; hostel is at corner of Ferry Ave. Good facilities, with kitchen, TV lounge. 46 beds. Travelers without cars given first priority; nonmembers turned away when space is short, as it usually is in summer. Owners will shuttle you to airport or train or bus station on request; rate depends on size of group going. Limited parking available. Bike rental $10 per day. Check-in 7:30-9:30am and 5-11pm. Lockout 9:30am-5pm. Curfew 11:30pm. Lights out midnight. $10, non-members $13. Required sheet sacks $1. Reservations essential. Open Jan. 4-Dec. 16.

Niagara Falls International Hostel (HI-C), 4699 Zimmerman Ave., Niagara Falls, Ont. L2E 3M7 (416-357-0770). Pleasant brick Tudor building 2½ mi. from the Falls, between Morrison and Queen St. off River Rd. about 2 blocks from the Canada bus station. Beautiful kitchen, dining room, lounge, peaceful backyard. 58 beds; rather cramped but upbeat atmosphere. Young, friendly staff conduct bike trips and day hikes along the Niagara gorge. Bike rentals $10 per day. Plentiful parking and laundry facilities. Open 9-11am and 5pm-midnight. Curfew and lights out 11pm. CDN$12, non-members CDN$17.50. 50¢ returned for performing morning chore. Linen $1. Reservations recommended.

YMCA, 1317 Portage Rd., Niagara Falls, NY (285-8491), corner of Portage and Main St., 15-min. walk from Falls; at night take a bus from Main St. 6 standard dorm rooms available. 24-hr. check-in, no laundry. Fee includes use of full YMCA facilities. Dorm rooms men only (single $20, $10 key deposit). Men and women can sleep on mats in gym ($10).

Rainbow View Tourist Home, 4407 John St., Niagara Falls, Ont. (416-374-1845), just off River Rd., moments from the Falls. Small rooms in charming house with cozy front porch. Friendly owner gives honest advice on sight-seeing. Doubles July-Sept. 14 $45-65; May, June, and Sept. 15-Oct. $40-60; lower rates, special deals in winter. Students willing to share room with another traveler pay only $22 per night. Continental breakfast included. Reservations recommended. Parking available.

Niagara Falls Motel and Campsite, 2405 Niagara Falls Blvd., Wheatfield, NY 14304 (731-3434), 7 mi. from downtown. From I-290 W., take exit 3, and go 8 mi. on U.S. 62 N. From I-190 N., take exit 22, and go 4 mi. on U.S. 62 S. Nice-sized doubles with A/C, color TV, private bath $40-55, off-season $35-40; cheapest double in high season is $55. Sites $16, with hookup $21.

Niagara Glen-View Tent & Trailer Park, 3950 Victoria Ave., Niagara Falls, Ont. L2E 6Z2 (800-263-2570), corner of Victoria and River Rd. Closest camp to the Falls; hiking trail across the street. Ice, showers, laundry available. Shuttle runs from driveway to bottom of Clifton Hill during the day every ½ hr. Sites US$19, with hookup $21. Open May-mid-Oct., reception 8am-11pm.

Food

Ferraro's, on the corner of 7th and Niagara St. (282-7020), has great Italian food. Choose from eight different pasta dishes, each with salad and bread, $5. Crabmeat Alfredo $8.50. (Open Mon.-Wed. 11:30-8pm, Thurs.-Fri. until 10pm, Sat. 4-10pm.) If you're in a rush, try the standard food-court fare in the **Rainbow Centre Factory Outlet Mall** (shops open Mon.-Sat. 10am-9pm, Sun. 10am-5pm); or buy picnic fixings at **Topps,** corner of Portage and Cedar Ave., a mammoth supermarket with a good bakery and low prices (a 20-min. walk from the Falls). **The Press Box Bar,** 324 Niagara St. between 3rd and 4th St. (284-5447), is a popular spot; add a dollar bill to the several thousand taped to the wall ($1). Every winter the owner takes them down and gives them to a cancer-fighting charity. (Burgers $1.50; food served Sun.-Thurs. 11:30am-midnight, Fri.-Sat. until 1am.)

Sights and Entertainment

You can easily see the Falls in an afternoon. On the U.S. side, there is not much else to do. On the Canadian side, there are some good hiking and biking trails. The **gardens** near the U.S. falls, established in 1885, were the nation's first national park. The **Caves of the Wind Tour** on Goat Island will outfit you with a yellow raincoat and take you to the gardens by elevator. (Open May 15-Oct. 20. $3.50, ages 5-11 $3, under 4 free.) From the base of the **Observation Deck,** U.S. side, catch the **Maid of the Mist Tour** (284-8897), a boat ride to the foot of both Falls. Don't bring anything that isn't waterproof; you'll get wet. (Tours every 15 min.: May and Labor Day-Oct. 24 Mon.-Fri. 10am-5pm, Sat.-Sun. 10am-6pm; May 28-June 14 daily 10am-6pm; June 15-21 daily 10am-8pm; June 22-Aug. 7 9:15am-8pm; Aug. 8-25 9:15am-7:30pm; Aug. 26-Labor Day 9:15am-7:15pm. Tickets $6.75, ages 6-12 $3.40, under 6 free.) The Falls are illuminated for three hours every night, starting one hour after sunset.

Don't miss **Niagara Wonders** (278-1792), at the info center in the park, a spectacular 20-minute film of the Falls using new Showscon special-f/x technology. (Shown on the hr. in the summer daily 10am-8pm; in the fall and early spring, daily 10am-6pm; mid-Jan.-April closed Mon.-Tues. $2, seniors $1.50, ages 6-12 $1.) The **Master Pass,** available in the park visitors center, is only worth the price if you plan to visit every single sight. One pass provides admission to the observation tower, the Cave of the Wind, the theater and the geological museum, plus discounts on Maid of the Mist tours and free parking. (Pass $13, kids $8.) The highest view of the Falls (775 ft. up) is from the **Skylon Tower,** 5200 Robinson St., in Canada (356-2651). On a clear day you can see Toronto as well. (CDN$6, kids CDN$3.50.) Brunch daily in summer in revolving dining room (CDN$13).

Away from the Falls, parasitic tourist snares abound—few of which are actually worthwhile. Browse through an impressive collection of regional Iroquois arts and crafts and watch spectacular performances of Iroquois dancing at **The Turtle,** 25 Rainbow Mall, Niagara Falls, NY (284-2427), between Winter Garden and the river. (Open May-Sept. daily 9am-6pm; Oct.-April Tues.-Fri. 9am-5pm, Sat.-Sun. noon-5pm.

$3.50, seniors $3, kids and students $2.) Wander into the peaceful **Artisans Alley,** 10 Rainbow Blvd. (282-0196) at 1st St., to see works by over 600 American craftsmen. (Open Mon.-Fri. 10am-6pm, Sat.-Sun. 10am-9pm.) **Schoellkopf's Geological Museum** (SHULL-koffs) (278-1780) depicts the birth of the Falls with slide shows every half hour. (Open Memorial Day-Labor Day daily 9:30am-7pm; Labor Day-Oct. daily 10am-5pm; Nov.-Memorial Day Wed.-Sun. 10am-5pm. 50¢.)

From late November through early January, Niagara Falls holds the annual **Festival of Lights.** Bright bulbs line the trees and create brilliant animated and outdoor scenes. Illumination of the Falls caps the spectacle. (Animated display areas open Sun.-Thurs. 5-10pm, Fri.-Sat. 5-11pm; exterior display areas nightly 5-11pm. For info contact the Chamber of Commerce (285-9141) 345 3rd St., Niagara Falls, NY.)

On the Canada side (across the Rainbow Bridge) **Queen Victoria Park** provides the best view of the Horseshoe Falls. Niagara Falls, Ontario served as birthplace and home for W.E.B. DuBois's 1905 "Niagara Movement," the forerunner of the National Association for the Advancement of Colored People (NAACP). Just minutes from the Falls, on **Clifton Hill**, the rule is *caveat touristor*—let the tourist beware! "The Hill" is home to Ripley's Believe It or Not Museum, the Guinness Museum of World Records, the Super Star Recording Studio, and many other tourist enticements. Believe it or not, each attraction charges its own admission (average CDN$5).

Three different flags (French, British, and U.S.) have flown over **Old Fort Niagara**, which once guarded the entrance to the Niagara River. Its French Castle was built in 1726. (716-745-7611; Box 169, Youngstown, NY 14174; follow Robert Moses Pkwy. north from Niagara Falls. Open July 1-Labor Day 9am-7:30pm; hours vary off-season. Call for rates.)

Thousand Island Seaway Region

The Thousand Island-St. Lawrence Seaway spans 100 mi. from the mouth of Lake Ontario to the first of the giant man-made locks on the St. Lawrence River. Some 1800 islands splatter throughout the waterway, and are accessible both by small pleasure-boats and huge ocean-bound freighters. The Thousand Island Region boasts a number of attractions to lure visitors, from the extravagant homes of millionaires who once idled here to the plentiful stock of bass and muskellunge (the world's largest—69lb. 5oz.—was caught here in 1957) to the proud fact that it's the only region in the U.S. to have an eponymous salad dressing.

Any of the small towns strung along Rte. 12 following the river coast can serve as a good base for exploring the region, though Clayton and Cape Vincent tend to be less expensive than Alexandria Bay. For $11 (ages 6-12 $5.50), **Uncle Sam Boat Tours** in **Clayton,** 604 Riverside Dr. (686-3511), or in **Alexandria Bay** on James St. (482-2611), gives a good look at most of the islands and the plush estates that bask atop them. **Empire,** off Church St. in Alexandria Bay (482-9511 or 800-542-2628), runs similar two-hour tours in triple-decker boats ($11). Look for the shortest international bridge in the world (about 10 ft.) connecting adjacent islands on either side of the U.S./Canadian border drawn through the seaway. Both tours highlight **Heart Island** and its famous Boldt Castle (482-9724) but do not cover the price of admission to the castle. George Boldt, former owner of New York City's elegant Waldorf-Astoria Hotel, financed this six-story replica of a Rhineland castle as a gift for his wife, who died before its completion. Though original plans called for 365 bedrooms, 52 bathrooms, and one power-house, Boldt abandoned the project in his grief. Today, its 120 rooms stand unfinished as a monument to despair. (Open late May-Sept. $3, ages 6-12 $1.75.) **Rental boats** are available in both Clayton and Alexandria Bay. In Clayton, **French Creek Marina** (686-3621) 98 Wahl St., rents 14-ft. fishing boats ($45 per day) and pontoon boats ($100 per day); launches boats ($5); and provides overnight docking ($15 per night). From Watertown, take Rte. 12 to the light in Clayton, turn left, and make the second left at the sign for the Marina. In Alexandria Bay, **O'Brien's U-Drive Boat Rentals,** 51 Walton St. (482-9548), rents 16-ft. fishing boats ($50 per day) and 18-ft. runabouts ($150 per day). (Open March-Oct.; mechanic on duty daily.) **Aqua Mania,**

5 Sisson St. (482-4678), rents Jet Skis, although at $70 per hr. you might think you were renting a jet airplane.

Fishing licenses (non-NY residents: season $28, 5 days $16; NY residents: season $14, 3 days $6) are available at a number of sporting goods stores, as well as at the **Town Clerk's Office** (686-3512) 405 Riverside Dr., Clayton. (Open Mon.-Fri. 9am-noon and 1-4pm). Bring your own rods and reels or plan to buy them; no local store rents equipment.

Cape Vincent, on the western edge of the seaway, keeps one of the most idyllic youth hostels in the country. **Tibbetts Point Lighthouse Hostel (HI/AYH),** RR 1 Box 330 (315-654-3450), strategically and scenically situated where Lake Ontario meets the St. Lawrence, has two houses; choose between a riverfront or a lakefront view, and watch the ships glide past spectacular sunsets. A large, full kitchen with microwave is available, and the proprietors seem like professional grandparents. Take Rte. 12 E. into town, turn left on Broadway, and follow the river until it ends. (Curfew 10:30pm. Check-in 5-9pm. $8, nonmembers $11. Open May 15-Sept. 15.) **Burnham Point State Park** (654-2324) on Rte. 12 E. between Cape Vincent and Clayton, offers 50 tent sites which can each accommodate two tents and up to six people. Boat docking facilities are available. (No showers. $10.50 first night, $9 each additional night. Hookup $2 per night.) **Keewaydin State Park** (482-3331) just north of Alexandria, has 41 campsites along the St. Lawrence River. (Open May-Sept., $11.50 first night, $10 each additional night. Showers available. No hookups or dumping stations.)

Write the **Clayton Chamber of Commerce,** 403 Riverside Dr., Clayton 13624 (686-3771), for the *Clayton Vacation Guide* and the *Thousand Islands Seaway Region Travel Guide.* The **Alexandria Bay Chamber of Commerce** is on Market St. just off James St., Alexandria Bay 13607 (482-9531). Access the region by bus through **Greyhound,** 540 State St. in Watertown (788-8110). Hounds service New York City (2 per day, 7½ hr., $48), Syracuse (2 per day, 13/4 hr., $12), and Albany (2 per day, 5½ hr., $29). From the same station, **Thousand Islands Bus Lines** runs to Alexandria Bay and Clayton at 12:45pm ($4 to Clayton, $6 to Alexandria); return trips leave from Clayton at the Nutshell Florist (686-5791) 234 James St., at 8:45am, and from Alexandria at the Dockside Café (482-9819) 17 Market St. (Station open 9:30am-3pm and 5-8pm.)

Clayton and the Thousand Islands region are just two hours from Syracuse by way of I-81 north. For Welleslet Island, Alexandria Bay, and the eastern 500 islands, stay on I-81 until you reach Rte. 12 E. For Clayton and points west, take exit 47 and follow Rte. 12 until you reach 12 E.

The Clayton **post office** (686-3311) is at 236 John St. The Alexandria Bay **post office** (482-9321) is at 13 Bethune St. Clayton's **ZIP code** is 13624, Alexandria Bay's **ZIP code** is 13607; the region's **area code** is 315.

Pennsylvania

Driven by the persecution of his fellow Quakers, William Penn, Jr. petitioned the British Crown for a slice of North America in 1680. In 1681, Charles II assented, granting to the Quakers a vast tract of land between what is now Maryland and New York. Arriving in 1682, Penn attracted all types of settlers by making his colony a bastion of religious tolerance. Propagandistically named "Penn's Gardens," Pennsylvania seemed destined to become the most prominent state in the new nation. The emerging colonies signed the *Declaration of Independence* in Philadelphia, the country's original capital and site of the First Continental Congress. However, other cities soon overshadowed it—New York City rapidly grew into the nation's most important commercial center, and Washington, DC usurped the role of national capital.

But Pennsylvania, a state accustomed to revolution, has rallied in the face of adversity. In 1976, Philadelphia groomed its historic shrines for the nation's bicentennial celebration, and the tourist trade continues to boom. Even Pittsburgh, a city once dirty enough to fool streetlights into burning during the day, has initiated a cultural renaissance. Between the two cities, Pennsylvania's landscape, from the farms of Lancaster County to the deep river gorges of the Allegheny Plateau, retains much of the sylvanism that drew Penn here over 300 years ago.

Practical Information

Capital: Harrisburg.

Visitor Information: Bureau of Travel Development, 453 Forum Bldg., Harrisburg 17120 (717-787-5453 or 800-237-4363). Information on hotels, restaurants, and sights. **Bureau of State Parks,** P.O. Box 1467, Harrisburg 17120 (800-631-7105). The detailed *Recreational Guide* is available at no charge from all visitors information centers.

Time Zone: Eastern.

Postal Abbreviation: PA

Sales Tax: 0%. That's right, nothing, nada, zilch. Enjoy.

Allegheny National Forest

Containing half a million acres of woodland stretching 40 mi. south of the New York state border, the Allegheny National Forest offers year-round recreational opportunities such as hunting, fishing, trail-biking, and cross-country skiing. The forest makes an excellent detour on a cross-state jaunt on I-80; its southern border is only 20 mi. from the interstate, but its lack of publicity ensures that it will be less crowded than the more ballyhooed Poconos or Catskills. A good first step is the **Kinzua Point Information Center** (726-1291), on Rte. 59 at the junction of Rte. 59 and Rte. 262. Friendly park employees have info on camping and recreation throughout the park. (Open Memorial Day-Labor Day Sun.-Thurs. 9:30am-5:30pm, Fri.-Sat. 9:30am-8pm.) The forest divides into four quadrants, each with its own ranger station that provides maps and information about activities and facilities within its region. **SW: Marienville Ranger District,** on Rte. 66 (927-6628; open Mon.-Sat. 7am-5pm). **NW: Sheffield Ranger District** on U.S. 6 (968-3232; open Mon.-Fri. 8am-4pm). **NE: Bradford Ranger District** on Rte. 59 west of Marshburg (362-4613; open daily 8am-4:30pm). **SE: Ridgway Ranger District** on Montmorenci Rd. (776-6172; open Mon.-Fri. 7:30am-4pm). For info, write to **Forest Service, USDA,** P.O. Box 847, Warren 16365.

Each summer, the **Allegheny Reservoir,** located in the northern section of the forest, is stocked with fish and tourists. Here you can enjoy fishing, boating, swimming, or grab a tour of the **Kinzua Dam,** operated by the U.S. Corps of Engineers. The six boat-accessible camping sites along the 95-mi. shore of the reservoir are free and do not require reservations or a permit (fresh water, toilets, no showers). Anglers should dial the 24-hr. fishing hotline for tips (726-0164). **Hikers** should pick up the free 14-page pamphlet which describes the 10 trails of the forest. **Buzzard Swamp,** near Marienville, has eight mi. of trails through a wildlife refuge where no motor vehicles are permitted. **Kinzua Boat Rentals and Marina** on Rte. 59, four mi. east of Kinzua Dam (726-1650) rents canoes ($5 per hr., $18 per day), rowboats ($5.50 per hr., $20 per day), and motorboats ($12 per hr., $50 per day). **Allegheny Outfitters** at Market St. Plaza in Warren (723-1203) provides canoe livery service for the reservoir and the Allegheny River. Ask the rangers about sites accessible only by water.

From whatever direction you approach the Allegheny Forest, you'll encounter a small, rustic community near the park that offers groceries and accommodations. **Ridgeway,** 25 mi. from I-80 (exit 16) at the southeastern corner, has **The Original,** 161 Main St., complete with jukebox, with great "baked" subs for $2.50-3 and burgers with fries for $2. (Open Mon.-Thurs. 11am-11pm, Fri.-Sat. 11am-midnight.) You can eat in an old train depot, now **Crispy's Fried Chicken,** at the intersection of Main St. and Montmorenci Rd. Two eggs with homefries and toast cost $1.50. (Open daily 7am-9pm.) The town of **Warren,** at the northeastern fringe of the forest where U.S. 6 and 62 meet, has comparable services.

There are 10 **campgrounds** in the park (7 are open March-Oct., 3 open year-round). A "host" is available at most sights to assist campers and answer questions. (Sites $5-12, depending on the location and the time of year.) **Tracy Ridge** in the Bradford district and **Heart's Content** in the Sheffield district are particularly pretty. You can call 800-283-2267 to reserve sites ($6 fee), but the park keeps 50% of them on a first-come, first-served basis. You don't need a site to camp in the Allegheny; stay 1500 ft. from a major road or body of water, and you can pitch a tent anywhere.

Greyhound no longer serves the area. When driving inside the forest, be very careful during wet weather, as about half the region is served only by dirt roads. Get good maps of the area ($2) at any ranger station. The **area code** for this region is 814.

Gettysburg

In November 1863, four months after 7000 men had died in the Civil War's bloodiest battle, President Abraham Lincoln arrived in Gettysburg to dedicate a national cemetery and give "a few appropriate remarks." In a two-minute speech, rumored to have been written on the back of an envelope, Lincoln urged preservation of the union in one of the greatest orations in U.S. history. Lincoln's *Gettysburg Address* and the sheer enormity of the battle which prompted him to write it have entrenched Gettysburg as the most famous battlefield in U.S. history. Each year thousands of visitors head for these Pennsylvania fields, heeding Honest Abe's call to "resolve that these dead shall not have died in vain."

Before attacking Gettysburg's phalanx of Civil War memorabilia, get your bearings at the **National Park Visitors Information Center,** 1 mi. south of town on Washington St. (334-1124; open daily 8am-6pm, Labor Day-Memorial Day 8am-5pm.) Go on your own, letting the free map navigate your bike or car tour, or pay a park guide to show you the sights ($20 for a 2-hr. tour). The same building houses a 750-square-foot **electric map.** This representation of the area as it was in 1863 lights up in coordination with a taped narration and is a must when trying to bring the great sweep of the battle into brighter focus. ($2, kids free.)

The **Cyclorama Center** next door has a facsimile of Lincoln's speech and a huge painting (356x26 ft.) of the turning point of the Civil War. Stand in the middle and you're back in 1863. (Open daily 9am-5pm.) For an excellent perspective of the area, walk over to the **National Tower** (334-6754), whose high-speed elevators whisk you up 300 ft. for a spectacular view. (Open daily 9am-5:30pm. Admission $3.75, kids $2.)

Gettysburg's eateries are classy and affordable. The **Dutch Cupboard,** 523 Baltimore, serves up Pennsylvania Dutch specialties like *schnitz un knepp* (dried apples cooked with dumplings, $7.50) and the famous shoo fly pie (brown sugar, flour, special spices, and 2 kinds of molasses; $1.35). (Open daily 11am-9pm.) The candle-lit **Springhouse Tavern,** 89 Steinwehr Ave. (334-2100), lies in the basement of the **Dobben House,** Gettysburg's first building (c. 1776) once an Underground Railroad shelter for runaway African slaves during the Civil War. Try the "Mason's Mile High" sandwich ($5.75) or create your own grilled burger ($5.50).

The best place to sleep in Gettysburg remains the roomy and cheerful **Gettysburg International Hostel (HI/AYH),** 27 Chambersburg St. (334-1020), on U.S. 30 just west of Lincoln Sq. in the center of town. Kitchen, stereo, living room, laundry, library, piano. Check-in 5-9pm. Check-out 9:30am. ($8, nonmembers $11. Sleepsack rental $1.) This remarkably friendly hostel usually has space, but when you're lusting for a motel, the **Gettysburg Travel Council,** 35 Carlisle St., Lincoln Sq. (334-6274), stocks a full line of brochures—as well as maps and information on local attractions. There are also several **campgrounds** in the area. Just one mi. south on Rte. 134 is **Artillery Ridge,** 610 Tarrytown Rd. (334-1288). Showers, riding stable, laundry, pool. (Sites $12.50 for 2 people, with hookup $16.50.) Further down the road, the **Round Top Campground,** (334-9565) has everything Artillery Ridge does—plus a mini golf course. ($9 for 2 people, with hookup $13.60.)

Gettysburg orates in south-central Pennsylvania, off U.S. 15 about 30 mi. south of Harrisburg. Unfortunately, when the Union and Confederacy decided to lock horns here, they didn't have the traveler's convenience in mind. Greyhound (232-4251) has no station in town—one bus runs daily from Harrisburg ($8.50 one-way) that stops in the center of town.

The **post office** is at 115 Buford Ave. (337-3781; open Mon.-Fri. 8am-4:30pm, Sat. 9am-noon). Gettysburg's **ZIP code** is 17325; the **area code** is 717.

Lancaster County

When persecuted flocks of German Anabaptists fled to William Penn's bastion of religious freedom, locals quickly and wrongly labeled them the Pennsylvania Dutch. A misunderstanding of the word *Deutschland* for "Germany," the name stuck. Since the late 1700s, three distinct families of Anabaptists have lived in Lancaster County: **Brethren, Mennonite,** and **Amish.** The latter, and the Old Order Amish in particular, are famed for their lifestyle. Emphatically rejecting modern technology and fashion, they worship at home, educate their children at home, and discourage association with outsiders. Quite ironically, the modest Lancaster Amish community of 15,000 draws many times that many visitors each year, who are eager to glimpse the secluded country lifestyle of horse-drawn carriages, home-style dining, and old-fashioned dress. In contrast to the Amish, some of the Mennonites embrace modern conveniences like cars and electricity. Many sell their farm goods at roadside stands or operate bed and breakfasts and craft shops. As a result, Lancaster County today has evolved into an odd hybrid of time-capsule austerity and modern consumerism.

Practical Information and Orientation

Visitor Information: Lancaster Chamber of Commerce and Industry, 100 Queen St. in the Southern Market Center (397-3531). You can pick up guided walking tours of Lancaster City (April-Oct. Mon.-Sat. at 10am and 1:30pm, Sun. and holidays at 10 and 11am, 1:30pm; $4 adults, $3 kids) or buy a worthwhile self-guided booklet ($1.50). To reserve a tour off-season call 653-8225 or 394-2339. The center has its own (avoidable) film about Lancaster and a full line of brochures. (Open April-Oct. Mon.-Fri. 8:30am-5pm, Sat. 10am-3pm, Sun. 10am-2pm.; open 1 hr. later off-season.) **Pennsylvania Dutch Visitors Bureau Information Center,** 501 Greenfield Rd. (299-8901), on the east side of Lancaster City just off Rte. 30. The bureau has walls of brochures and free phone lines to most area inns and campsites. Avoid their film and save $2. (Open mid-May to early Sept. Sun.-Thurs. 8am-6pm, Fri.-Sat. 8am-7pm.) **Mennonite Information Center,** 2209 Millstream Rd. (299-0954; open Mon.-Sat. 8am-5pm), just off Rte. 30. guides for $8.50 per hr.; call for times. **Alverta Moore** (626-2421) offers to guide for about $5 per hr.

Amtrak, 53 McGovern Ave. (291-5080; reservations 24 hrs.) 8 trains per day to Philadelphia (1 hr., $11).

Greyhound: 22 W. Clay St. (397-4861). 4 buses per day between Lancaster City and Philadelphia (2 hr., $9). (Open daily 7am-5:15pm.)

Red Rose Transit, 45 Erick Rd. (397-4246), serves Lancaster and the surrounding countryside. Pick up route maps at the office. (Base fare 75¢, seniors free off-peak and Sat.-Sun.)

Bike Rental: New Horizons, 3495 Horizon Dr. (285-7607). If you call ahead, they will meet you at the train or bus station with a bike and pick it up there later, l ahead. (Bikes $12 per day including helmet. Free maps.)

Zip Code: Lancaster City, 17604

Area Code: 717

Lancaster County—even the concentrated spots of interest to tourists—covers a huge area. Cars are the vehicle of choice for most visitors. You can pay a guide to hop in and show you around. If you'd rather go it alone, pick up maps at Lancaster City or Pennsylvania Dutch visitors bureaus (see above), veer off U.S. 30, and explore the winding roads. Pick up a free *Map of Amish Farmlands* at any tourist spot in Lancaster County, or write to 340-23 Club, P.O. Box 239, Intercourse 17534.

Accommodations

Hundreds of hotels, B&Bs, and campgrounds cluster in this area. Don't search for accommodations without stopping by the **Pennsylvania Dutch Visitors Bureau Information Center** (see Practical Information above). There seem to be as many **campgrounds** as cows in this lush countryside, all of which (the campgrounds, not the cows) have laundry and shower facilities.

Marsh Creek State Park Hostel (HI/AYH), P.O. Box 376, E. Reeds Rd., Lyndel 19354 (215-458-5881), in Marsh Creek State Park. This old farmhouse proves a challenge to find and to contact, but it is well-kept and lies on a gorgeous lake. **Amtrak** stops in Downington, 5 mi. away on its Philadelphia-Lancaster route. **Downington Cab** (269-3000) charges about $12 to get there.

Geigertown Youth Hostel (HI/AYH), P.O. Box 49, Geigertown 19523 (215-286-9537; open March 2-Nov. 30). 15 mi. east of Marsh Creek, near French Creek State Park off Rte. 82. Though the area is beautiful, the hostel's remote location may not merit the trip. Transportation from Reading, 15 mi. away, might be arranged if you call ahead. Check out for both hostels 9:30am, curfew 11pm. $8, $11 nonmembers, sleepsack rental $1.

Old Millstream Camping Manor, 2249 U.S. 30 E. (Lincoln Hwy.) (299-2314). The closest year-round facility 4 mi. east of Lancaster City. Office open daily 8am-9pm. Sites $15, with hookup $17.

Roamers Retreat, 5005 Lincoln Hwy. (442-4287 or 800-525-5605), off U.S. 30, 7½ mi. east of Rte. 896, opens only from April to Oct. For reservations, call or write RD #1, P.O. Box 41B, Kinzers 17535. Sites $16.50, with hookup $18.

Shady Grove, P.O. Box 28, Adamstown 19501 (215-484-4225), on Rte. 272 at Rte. 897, 264 W. Swartzville Rd. 80 sites with electricity ($15).

Food

Just about everyone passing through Lancaster County expects a taste of real Dutch cuisine—and a flock of high priced "family-style" restaurants, have sprouted up to please them. If you have the cash (all-you-can-eat meals $12-16) try any of the huge restaurants such as **The Amish Barn** (768-8886) which spread thick on Rte. 340 in Bird-in-Hand. **Dell's Family Restaurant,** 213 E. Main St. (445-9233) in Terre Hill off Rte. 897 about 20 mi. north of Lancaster City serves scrapple with vegetables and salad bar for $5.50. (Open Mon-Sat. 6am-8pm.) More varied fare can be found in Lancaster City. Don't miss the **Central Market,** in the northwest corner of Penn Sq., a huge food bazaar vending inexpensive meats, cheeses, vegetables, and sandwiches since 1899. (Open Tues. and Fri.. 6am-4pm, Sat. 6am-2pm.) There are many fun, interesting and inexpensive restaurants surrounding the market.

Sights

A good place to start is the **People's Place,** on Main St./Rte. 340 (768-7171), in Intercourse 11 mi. east of Lancaster City. The film *Who Are the Amish* shows every half hour from 9:30am to 5pm, and **Amish World** has charming hands-on exhibits on Amish and Mennonite life, from barn-raising to hat-styles. (Admission to one $2.50, kids $1.50. To both $4.25, kids $2.25.) The **People's Place** spans an entire block with bookstores, craft shops, and an art gallery. (Open Mon.-Sat. 9:30am-9:30pm; Nov.-March 9:30am-4:30pm.) If you have specific questions, seek out friendly locals at the Mennonite Information Center (see above), which also shows the film *A Morning Song* every half hour, and from Memorial Day to Labor Day shows another film, *Hazel's People* (Adults $4, kids $2). A quiet metropolis in the heart of Dutch country, county seat **Lancaster City** reflects the area's character well—clean, red-brick row houses huddle together around historic **Penn Square** in the city center.

Candyland (Where a Kiss is more than just a kiss)

Milton S. Hershey, a Mennonite resident of eastern Pennsylvania farms, failed in his first several jaunts into the confectionery world. Then he found chocolate. Today the company that bears his name has become the world's largest chocolate factory in **Her-**

shey just across the northeastern border of Lancaster. Here, street lights are shaped like candy kisses, and the streets are named Chocolate and Cocoa. East of town at **Hershey Park** (800-437-7439), the **Chocolate World Visitors Center** (534-4900) presents a free, automated tour through a simulated chocolate factory. After viewing the processing of the cacao bean from tropical forests past the Oompa-Loompas of Willy Wonka fame to final packaging, visitors emerge with two free Hershey Kisses in hand into a pavilion full of chocolate cookies, discounted chocolate candy, chocolate milk, and fashionable Hershey sportswear—all for a small fee, of course. (Open daily 9am-6:45pm; Sept. to mid-June 9am-4:45pm.)

Though Hershey Park **amusement center** has fairly unimpressive rides, meeting a walking talking Reese's cup just may be worth the hefty admission. (Open late May-early Sept. daily 10:30am-10pm. Admission $20, seniors $12.50, ages 4-8 $7. After 5pm $14. Parking $2.) Camp 8 mi. from Hershey and 15 mi. from Lancaster City at **Ridge Run Campground,** 867 Schwanger Rd., Elizabethtown 17022 (367-3454). Schwanger Rd. connects Rte. 230 and Rte. 283. (Sites $14.) **Greyhound** (397-4861) goes to Hershey from Lancaster City (1 per day, 3 hr., $19), stopping at 337 W. Chocolate St.

Ohiopyle State Park

Hidden away in the forgotten landscapes of southwestern Pennsylvania lie some of the loveliest forests in the East, lifted by steep hills and cut by cascading rivers. Native Americans dubbed this part of the state "Ohiopehhle" ("white frothy water"), because of the grand Youghiogheny River Gorge (pronounced yock-a-gay-nee; "The Yock" to locals); provides the focal point of Pennsylvania's Ohiopyle State Park. The park's 18,000 acres offer hiking, fishing, hunting, whitewater rafting, and a complete range of winter activities. The latest addition to the banks of the Yock is a gravelled bike trail. Converted from a riverside railroad bed, the trail winds 11 sinuous mi. upstream from the trailhead and seven mi. down.

The most popular activity in Ohiopyle is whitewater rafting; the rapids are eight mi. long, class three, and take about five hours to conquer. Lined up in a row on Rte. 381 in "downtown" Ohiopyle are four outfitters: **White Water Adventurers** (329-8850 or 800-992-7238); **Wilderness Voyageurs** (329-5517 or 800-272-4141); **Laurel Highlands River Tours** (329-8531 or 800-472-3846); and **Mountain Streams and Trails** (329-8810 or 800-245-4090; Trading Post 329-1450). Guided trips on the Yock vary dramatically in price ($20-70 per person per day), depending on season, day of week, and difficulty. If you're an experienced river rat (or if you just happen to *enjoy* flipping boats) any of the above companies will rent you equipment. (Rafts about $9 per person, canoes $15, "duckies"—inflatable kayaks—about $15.) Bike rentals vary with bike styles ($3 per hr. to $14 per day, max. 8 hrs.). **Youghiogheny Outfitters** (329-4549) may be a bit cheaper since they do rental business only.

In order to do just about anything in the river you'll need a launch permit. They're $2.50 but get snatched up quickly. The **Park Information Center,** just off Rte. 381 on Dinnerbell Rd., P.O. Box 105, (329-8591) recommends calling at least 30 days in advance. The 200 **campsites** ($7) that the office handles also require advanced booking—especially for summer weekends. (Open daily 8am-4pm; Nov.-April Mon.-Fri. 8am-4pm.) Fishing licenses ($20), required for ages 16 and over, are available at the Falls Market (see below).

Motels around Ohiopyle are sparse but the excellent **Ohiopyle State Park Hostel (HI/AYH),** P.O. Box 99 (329-4476) sits right in the center of town off Rte. 381. Sue Moore has 24 bunks, a kitchen, a great yard, 6 cats, and 2 dogs, eieio. ($7, nonmembers $10. Check-in 6-9pm.) Just down the street, **Falls Market and Overnight Rooms** (329-4973), on Rte. 381 in the center of town, rents singles ($22) and doubles ($30) with shared baths. Washer and dryer available. The downstairs store has a decent selection of groceries and a snack-bar/restaurant. (Burgers $1.25, pancakes and bacon $2.25. Open Mon.-Sat. 7am-9pm, Sun. 7am-6:30pm.)

Ohiopyle is on Rte. 381, 64 mi. southeast of Pittsburgh via Rte. 51 and U.S. 41. The closest public transport is to **Uniontown,** a large town about 20 mi. to the west on U.S. 40. **Greyhound** serves Uniontown from Pittsburgh (3 per day, 1½ hr., $10). The **post office** (329-8650) is open Monday through Friday 7:30am to 4:30pm and Saturday 7:30am to 11:30am. The **ZIP code** is 15470. The **area code** for Ohiopyle and the surrounding area is 412.

Philadelphia

Philadelphia has the rare distinction of having a name before it was founded. From the start, founder William Penn, Jr. had noble aspirations for the city which was to be the keystone of his new colony. An avid classics scholar, Penn chose the name from the Greek word meaning "being kindly and affectionate to one another with brotherly love." Centuries of revolution, growth, racial tension, and Rocky Balboa have strained the definition of "brotherly love." Still, Philadelphia—with one of the lowest crime rates of any American city of the same size—almost makes the claim viable.

Pennsylvanians boast on their license plates that "America starts here." Nowhere is this more evident than in Philadelphia. The city remains fixated on the good ol' days when the United States was young and Philadelphia was its commercial and political capital. The "Founding Fathers" gathered here on two separate occasions to draft the United States' most hallowed documents, the *Declaration of Independence* and the *Constitution.* Stop by Independence Hall, the Liberty Bell, the Franklin Institute, and maybe even have a Rocky-style jog up the steps of the Fairmount Park Art Museum.

Practical Information

Emergency: 911.

Visitors Center, 1525 John F. Kennedy Blvd. at 16th St. (636-1666). Pick up a free *Philadelphia Visitor's Guide* and the *Philadelphia Quarterly Calendar of Events.* Open daily 9am-6pm; off-season 9am-5pm. **Directory Events Hotline,** 377-7777, ext. 2540. **National Park Service Visitors Center,** 3rd and Chestnut (597-8974; 627-1776 for recording). Info on Independence Park, including maps, schedules, and the film *Independence.* Also distributes the *Visitor's Guide* and the *Quarterly Calendar of Events.* Open Sept.-June daily 9am-5pm; July-Aug. 9am-6pm. Film shown 9:30am-4pm. Tour assistance for non-English-speaking and disabled travelers.

Philadelphia International Airport: 8 mi. SW of Center City on I-76 (info line 492-3181, 24 hrs.). The 27-min. **SEPTA Airport Rail Line** runs from Center City to the airport. Trains leave daily 5:30am-11:25pm from 30th St. Station, Suburban Station, and Market East ($4.75). Last train from airport 12:10am. Cab fare downtown $21, but **Airport Limelight Limousine** (342-5557) will deliver you to a hotel ($8) or a specific address downtown.

Amtrak: 30th St. Station, at 30th and Market St. (349-2153 or 800-872-7245), in University City. To: New York City (every hr., 2 hr., $30), Washington, DC (every ½ hr., 2 hr., $34), and points in western PA. Ticket office open daily 5:30am-10:15pm. Station open 24 hrs. To: Boston ($65), New York ($29), Washington DC ($34), and Baltimore ($27); take the SEPTA commuter train to Trenton, NJ ($4.75), then hop on a New Jersey Transit train to NYC through Newark ($7.75).

Buses: Greyhound, 10th and Filbert St. (931-4000), 1 block north of Market near the 10th and Market St. subway/commuter rail stop in the heart of Philadelphia. To: New York City (15 per day, 2½ hr., $16); Washington, DC (8 per day, 3½ hr., Mon.-Thurs. $19, Fri.-Sun. $21); Atlantic City (17 per day, 1½ hr., $10). **New Jersey Transit,** 800-582-5946. To: Atlantic City ($10), Ocean City ($12), and other points on the New Jersey Shore.

Public Transport: Southeastern Pennsylvania Transportation Authority (SEPTA),(734-1300). Most buses operate 6:30am-1am, some all night. Extensive bus and rail service to suburbs. Two major subway routes: the **Market St. line** running east-west (including 30th St. Station and the historic area) and the **Broad St. line** running north-south (including the stadium complex in south Philadelphia). Subway is unsafe after dark, but buses are usually okay. Buses serve the 5-county area. Subway connects with commuter rails—the Main Line Local runs through the western suburb of Paoli ($3.50), and SEPTA runs north as far as Trenton, NJ ($4.75). Pick up a SEPTA system map ($1.50), and a good street map at any subway stop. Fare $1.50, 2 tokens for $2.10, transfers 40¢.

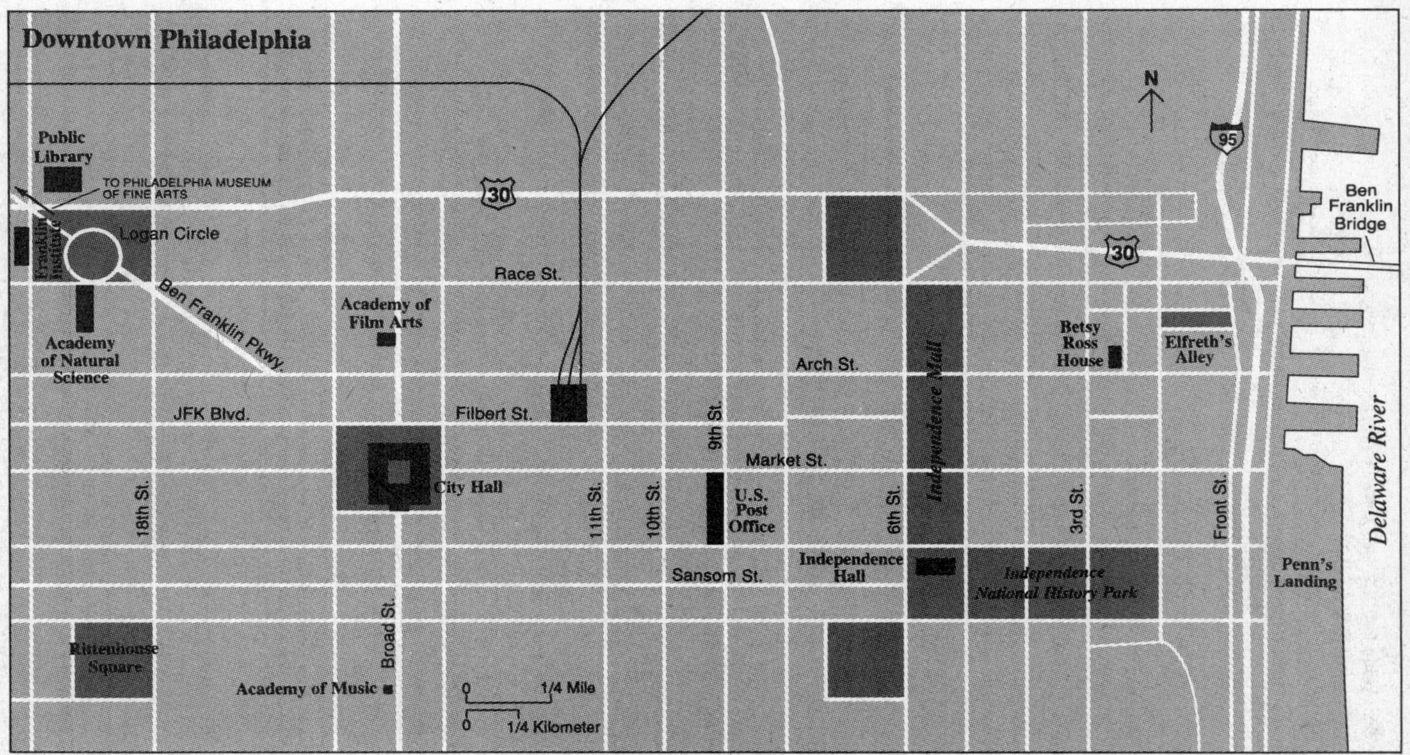
Downtown Philadelphia
Public Library
TO PHILADELPHIA MUSEUM OF FINE ARTS
Franklin Institute
Logan Circle
Ben Franklin Pkwy.
Academy of Natural Science
Academy of Film Arts
Race St.
Arch St.
JFK Blvd.
Filbert St.
Market St.
City Hall
18th St.
11th St.
10th St.
9th St.
U.S. Post Office
6th St.
Independence Mall
3rd St.
Front St.
Sansom St.
Independence Hall
Independence National History Park
Penn's Landing
Delaware River
Rittenhouse Square
Broad St.
Academy of Music
0
1/4 Mile
0
1/4 Kilometer
30
30
95
N
Betsy Ross House
Elfreth's Alley
Ben Franklin Bridge

Taxi: Yellow Cab, 922-8400. **United Cab,** 625-9170.

Car Rental: Budget Rent-a-Car, 492-9400 at the airport. Sub-compacts $26 per day, weekends $19 per day. Unlimited mileage. Optional insurance $12. Must be 25 with major credit card.

Help Lines: Gay Switchboard, 546-7100; **Suicide and Crisis Intervention,** 686-4420; **Youth Crisis Line,** 800-448-4663

Post Office: 30th and Market St. (596-5316), across from the Amtrak station. Open 24 hrs. **ZIP code:** 19104.

Area Code: 215.

William Penn, Jr., a survivor of London's great fire in the 1660s, planned his city as a logical and easily accessible grid pattern of wide streets. The north-south streets ascend numerically from the **Delaware River,** flowing near **Penn's Landing** and **Independence Hall** on the east side, to the **Schuylkill River** (pronounced SKOOL-kill) on the west. The first street is **Front,** the others follow consecutively from 2 to 69. **Center City** runs from 8th Street to the Schuylkill River. From north to south, the primary streets are Race, Arch, JFK, Market, Sansom, and South. The intersection of Broad (14th St.) and Market, location of City Hall, marks the focal point of Center City. The **Historic District** stretches from Front to 8th Street and from Vine to South Street. The **University of Pennsylvania** sprawls on the far side of the Schuylkill River, about one mi. west of Center City. **University City** includes the Penn/Drexel area west of the Schuylkill River.

Accommodations and Camping

Downtown Philadelphia is saturated with luxury hotels, so anything inexpensive is popular. But if you make arrangements even a few days in advance, you should be able to find comfortable lodging close to Center City for under $40. **Bed and Breakfast, Center City,** 1804 Pine St., Philadelphia 19103 (735-1137 or 800-354-8401) will find you a room in a private home; it's your best chance to stay in a real colonial building. No sign on the outside. (Singles $40-$80. Doubles $45-$75. Check-in 3-7pm, make reservations a few weeks ahead. Best to call 9am-9pm.) The **Philadelphia Naturist and Work Camp Center,** P.O. Box 4755, Philadelphia 19134 (634-7057), rents beds to foreign students ($5 with light breakfast) and will arrange free room and board on a nearby farm in exchange for daily chores. Camping is available to the north and west of the city, but you must travel at least 15 mi. Ask around about the **Bank St. Hostel** (922-0222) which opened just as this guide was going to press.

Chamounix Mansion International Youth Hostel (HI/AYH), West Fairmount Park (878-3676). Take bus #38 from JFK Blvd. to Ford and Cranston Rd., walk in the direction of the bus until Chamounix St., then turn left and follow until the road ends at hostel (about a 20-min. walk). In daylight take bus #38 to Fairmount Terr. apartments and follow the HI/AYH sign 10 min. through a wooded path. Former country estate built in 1802. Clean and beautifully furnished, with 50 beds, showers, kitchen, and coin-operated laundry. Some basic groceries for sale. Extraordinarily friendly and helpful staff. Check-in 8-9:30am. Lockout 9:30am-4:30pm. Curfew 11pm. $9.50, nonmembers $12.50. Linen $2.

Old First Reformed Church, 4th and Race St. (922-4566), in Center City 1 block from the Independence Mall and 4 blocks from Penn's Landing. Historic church that converts its social hall to a youth hostel sleeping 20. Mattresses on the floor, showers. 3-night max. stay. Check-in 5-10pm. Curfew 11pm. $10. Breakfast included. Open early July-late Aug.

The Divine Tracy Hotel, 20 S. 36th St. (382-4310), near Market St. in University City. Immaculately clean, quiet, and well-maintained rooms, though no bright Dick Tracy colors. Women must wear skirts and stockings at all times in the public areas of the hotel; men, long pants and socks with their shirts tucked in. Strictly single-sex floors. No smoking, vulgarity, obscenity, or blasphemy. Fans and TVs for rent. Check-in 7am-11pm. Singles $20, with private bath $23-26. Shared doubles $17-20 per person. The management does not permit alcohol or food (except small snacks) in the rooms, but the **Keyflower Dining Room** (386-2207) offers incredibly cheap and healthful, although bland, food. Entrees $2-4. Open to the public Mon.-Fri. 11:30am-2pm and 5-8pm.

International House, 3701 Chestnut St. (387-5125). Bus #21 stops right out front. Clean dorms in a modern complex built to house Philly's international students—must have student ID or affiliation with university or exchange program. May accept college graduates or professionals. Mostly singles in 10-room single-sex suites ($49). Reserve ahead if you want a suite with kitchen. **Eden** restaurant (see Food below) in the same building. Open year-round, but rooms scarce during school year so always reserve rooms a month in advance.

The closest camping is across the Delaware River in New Jersey. Check out **Timberline Campground,** 117 Timber Lane, Clarksboro, NJ 08020 (609-423-6677), 15 mi. from Center City. Take 285 S. to exit 18A, Clarksboro, turn left and then right at the first stop sign, Cohawkin Rd. Go ½ mi. and turn right on Friendship Rd. Timber Lane is 1 block on the right. (Sites $15.50, with full hookup $17.50.) In Pennsylvania, try the **Baker Park Campground,** 400 East Pothoure Rd. (933-5865), 45 min. to 76 west to 23 through Valley Forge Park. (Sites $14, with electricity $16.)

Food

More than 500 new restaurants have opened their doors in Philadelphia in the past decade, making the city one of the most exciting dining spots in the U.S. Inexpensive food abounds on **Sansom St**. between 17th and 18th, on **South St**. between 2nd and 7th, and on **2nd St**. between Chestnut and Market. Numerous new places are opening up in **Penn's Landing,** on the Delaware River between **Locust** and **Market St**. Philadelphia's **Chinatown** is a short wok from downtown action, bounded by 8th, 11th, Vine, and Race St. In **University City,** the University of Pennsylvania (UPenn) and Drexel University collide on the west side of the Schuylkill River, making cheap student eateries easy to find. Try the famous **hoagie** or **cheesesteak**, two local specialties. You may grow attached to the renowned **Philly soft pretzel**; have one for about 30¢ at a street-side vendor.

To stock up on staples, visit the **Italian Market** at 9th and Christian St. (Open daily dawn-dusk.) The **Reading Terminal Market,** at 12th and Arch St. (922-2317), is the place to go for picnic-packing, grocery-shopping, or a quick lunch. Since 1893, food stands have clustered together in this huge indoor market—selling fresh meats, produce, and delicious alternatives to modern fast-food courts. (Open Mon.-Sat. 8am-6pm.)

Historic District

Jim's Steaks, 400 South St. (928-1911). Take the 4th St. trolley or bus #10 down Locust St. A Philadelphia institution since 1939, serving some of the best steak sandwiches in town ($3.65-4). Eat to beat Jim's current record holder—11 steaks in 90 minutes. Open Mon.-Thurs. 10am-1am, Fri.-Sat. 10am-3am, Sun. noon-10pm.

Lee's Hoagie House, 220 South St., (925-6667), near 2nd St. Authentic hoagies ($3.45-5.50) since 1953. The 3-ft. hoagie challenges even ravenous appetites. Open Tues.-Thurs. 10am-11pm, Fri.-Sat. 10am-2am, Sun. 10am-10pm.

Fu Wing House, 639 South St., between 6th and 7th (922-3170). Great hot-and-sour soup ($1.50). Entrees $7.50-9.50. Open Mon. and Wed.-Sun. 5-10pm.

Dickens Inn, Head House Sq., on 2nd St. between Pine and Lombard (928-9307). Restaurant upstairs upscale but excellent food. British country cooking served at the bakery—try a cornish pastie ($5.50) or shepherd's pie ($5). Open Mon.-Tues. 8am-9pm, Wed.-Thurs. 8am-10pm, Fri. 8am-11pm, Sat. 8am-midnight, Sun. 11am-9pm. Pay slightly more at the bar, open daily 11:30am-1:30am.

Center City

Charlie's Waterwheel Restaurant, downstairs at 1526 Sansom St. (563-4155), between 15th and 16th St. First hoagie steak shop in Center City—their subs will sink you for days. Sandwiches and steaks with fresh fruit and vegetables ($5.75). Munch on free meatballs, pickles, and fried mushrooms at the counter while you wait. Open daily 11am-4pm.

Saladalley, 1720 Sansom St. (564-0767) between 17th and 18th. Huge salad bar featuring truly innovative combinations of fresh fruits, vegetables, and homemade muffins ($6). Try the pasta bows in walnut zucchini sauce ($8). Open Mon.-Fri. 11am-9pm, Sat. 11:30am-9pm.

Commissary Market and Café, 1710 Sansom St. It's a bakery, a restaurant, and affordable. Run in for a bagel or sit down for Norwegian salmon ($8.75) or chicken *pad thai* ($7.50). Open Mon.-Fri. 7:30am-7:30pm, Sat. 8:30am-5pm, Sun. 9:30am-5pm.

University City

Smoky Joe's, 208-10 S. 40th St. (222-0770) between Locust and Walnut. Call it "smokes" like the college kids have for fifty years. Try Rosie's Homemade Chili ($4) or a 10-oz. burger ($3.75). Open daily 11am-2am; live music occasionally.

Sweet Basil, 4006 Chestnut St. (387-2727), at 40th St. Cool and sophisticated. Eclectic menu with Indonesian, Cajun, and vegetarian entrées. Dinners $7-13. Open Mon.-Thurs. noon-3pm, Fri. noon-3pm and 5-10:30pm, Sat. 5-10:30pm.

Eden, 3701 Chestnut St. (387-2471), at 38th St. Wholesome and satisfying grilled fish and chicken specialties served on a leafy terrace. No original sin here. Don't be put off by cafeteria-style dining. Great chicken stir-fry ($7), good Mexican lasagna ($7). Students with ID get 10% discount. Open Mon.-Sat. 11:30am-11pm. Bar open later.

Tandoor India Restaurant, 106 S. 40th St. (222-7122). Northern Indian cuisine cooked in a clay oven. All-you-can-eat lunch buffet ($6), dinner buffet ($9). Open daily noon-3pm lunch; Mon.-Thurs. 4:30-10pm dinner.

Sights

"I went to Philadelphia," W.C. Fields quipped, "and it was closed." Although the city still sleeps fairly early, its fine collection of museums and an unmatched historical significance will keep you awake—at least when it's open.)

Independence Hall and the Historic District

The buildings of the **Independence National Historic Park** (open daily 9am-5pm; in summer 9am-8pm) witnessed events that have since passed into U.S. history textbooks. The park **visitors center** (see Practical Information above) makes a good starting point. Sight of the signing of the *Declaration of Independence* in 1776, and the drafting and signing of the Constitution in 1787, **Independence Hall** lies between 5th and 6th St. on Chestnut. Engraved with a half-sun, George Washington's chair at the head of the assembly room prompted Ben Franklin to remark after the ratification of the Constitution that "Now at length I have the happiness to know that it is a rising and not a setting sun." (Free guided tours daily every 15-20 min., arrive before 11am in summer to avoid an hr.-long line.) The U.S. Congress first assembled in nearby **Congress Hall** (free self-guided tour), while its predecessor, the First Continental Congress, convened in **Carpenters' Hall,** two blocks away at 4th and Chestnut St. (Open Tues.-Sun. 10am-4pm.) North of Independence Hall lies the **Liberty Bell Pavilion.** The cracked **Liberty Bell** itself, one of the most famous U.S. symbols, refuses to toll even when vigorously prodded.

The remainder of the park contains preserved residential and commercial buildings of the Revolutionary era. Ben Franklin's home lies in **Franklin Court** to the north, on Market between 3rd and 4th St., and includes an underground museum, a 20-minute movie and an architectural archeology exhibit. (Open daily 9am-5pm. Free.) At nearby **Washington Square,** a flame burns eternally commemorating the **Tomb of the Unknown Soldier.** Across from Independence Hall is Philadelphia's branch of the **U.S. Mint** (597-7350). A self-paced guided tour explains the mechanized coin-making procedure. No free samples here! (Open May-June Mon.-Sat. 9am-4:30pm; July-Aug. daily 9am-4:30pm; off-season Mon.-Fri. 9am-4:30pm. Free.)

Tucked away near 2nd and Arch St. is the quiet, residential **Elfreth's Alley,** allegedly "the oldest street in America," along which a penniless Ben Franklin walked when he arrived in town in 1723. On Arch near 3rd St. sits the tiny **Betsy Ross House** (627-5343), where Ross supposedly sewed the first flag of the original 13 states. (Free.) **Christ Church,** on 2nd near Market, hosted the Quakers who sought a more fashionable way of life in colonial Philadelphia. Ben Franklin lies buried in the nearby **Christ Church cemetery** at 5th and Arch St. Also see the Quaker meeting houses: the original

Free Quaker Meeting House at 5th and Arch St., and a new and larger one at 4th and Arch St.

Mikveh Israel, the first Jewish congregation of Philadelphia, has a burial ground on Spruce near 8th St. The **Afro-American Historical and Cultural Museum,** 7th and Arch St. (574-0380), stands as the first U.S. museum devoted solely to the history of African-Americans. (Open Tues.-Sat. 10am-5pm, Sun. noon-6pm. Admission $3.50, seniors, handicapped and children $1.75.)

Society Hill proper begins where the park ends, on Walnut St. between Front and 7th St. Now Philadelphia's most distinguished residential neighborhood, housing both old-timers and a new yuppie crowd, the area was originally a tract of land owned by the Free Society of Traders, a company formed to help William Penn, Jr. consolidate Pennsylvania. Federal-style townhouses dating back 300 years, line picturesque cobblestone walks, illuminated by old-fashioned streetlights. **Head House Square,** 2nd and Pine St., held a marketplace in 1745 and now houses restaurants, boutiques, and craft shops. An outdoor flea market occurs here summer weekends.

Located on the Delaware River, **Penn's Landing** (923-8181) is the largest freshwater port in the world. Among other vessels it holds the *Gazela,* a three-masted, 178-ft. Portuguese square rigger built in 1883; the *U.S.S. Olympia,* Commodore Dewey's flagship during the Spanish-American War (922-1898; tours daily 10am-4pm; admission $5, children $2); and the *U.S.S. Becuna,* a WWII submarine (tours in conjunction with the *Olympia.*) The **Port of History,** Delaware Ave. and Walnut St. (925-3804), has frequently changing exhibits. (Open Wed.-Sun. 10am-4:30pm. Admission $3, ages 5-12 $2.) The Delaware Landing is a great spot to soak up sun on a nice day. For $1.50 you can jump on **Penn's Landing Trolley** (627-0807), on Delaware Ave., between Catharine and Race St., which rolls along the waterfront giving guided tours.

Center City

Center City, the area bounded by 12th, 23rd, Vine, and Pine St., whirls with activity. **City Hall,** Broad and Market St. (686-1776), an ornate structure of granite and marble with 20-ft.-thick foundation walls, is the nation's largest public municipal building. Until 1908, it also held the record for highest building in the U.S., with the help of the 37-ft. statue of William Penn, Jr. on top. A municipal statute prohibited building higher than the top of Penn's hat until entrepreneurs in the mid-80s overturned it, finally launching Philadelphia into the skyscraper era. (Open Mon.-Fri. 7am-6pm. Free guided tours Mon.-Fri. at 12:30pm; meet in room 201.) The **Pennsylvania Academy of Fine Arts,** Broad and Cherry St. (972-7600), the country's first art school and one of its first museums, has an extensive collection of U.S. and British art, including notable works by Charles Wilson Peale, Thomas Eakins, Winslow Homer, and a few contemporary artists. (Open Tues.-Sat. 10am-5pm, Sun. 11am-5pm. Tours daily 12:30pm and 2pm. Admission $5, seniors $3, students $2, under 12 free. Free Sat. 10am-1pm.)

Just south of **Rittenhouse Square,** 2010 Delancey St., the **Rosenbach Museum and Library** (732-1600) houses rare manuscripts and paintings, including some of the earliest-known copies of Cervantes' Don Quixote, the original manuscripts of James Joyce's *Ulysses* and the original *Yankee Doodle Dandy.* (Open Sept.-July Tues.-Sun. 11am-4pm. Guided tours $3.50, seniors, students, and kids $2.50. Exhibitions only, $2.) The nearby **Mütter Museum** (563-3737) of Philadelphia's College of Physicians displays gory medical paraphernalia including a death cast of Siamese twins and a tumor removed from President Cleveland's jaw. (Open Tues.-Fri. 10am-4pm. Free.) Ben Franklin founded the **Library Company of Philadelphia,** 1314 Locust St. near 13th St., over 250 years ago, as a club whose members' dues paid for books from England. A weather-worn statue of Franklin stands outside its present headquarters. (Open Tues. and Thurs.-Sat. 10am-5pm, Wed. 10am-9pm; galleries $2.50 adults; libraries $5 adults; both $2 for students.) The **Norman Rockwell Museum,** 6th and Sansom St. (922-4345), houses all of the artist's *Saturday Evening Post* cover works. (Open Mon.-Sat. 10am-4pm, Sun. 11am-4pm. Admission $2, $1.50 kids 13 and up.)

Benjamin Franklin Parkway

Nicknamed "America's Champs-Elysées," the Benjamin Franklin Parkway is a wide, diagonal deviation from William Penn's original grid pattern of city streets. Built in the 1920s, this tree- and flag-lined street connects Center City with Fairmount Park and the Schuylkill River. Admire the elegant architecture of the twin buildings at Logan Square, 19th and Parkway, that house the **Free Library of Philadelphia** and the **Municipal Court.**

At 20th and Parkway, the **Franklin Institute** (448-1200), whose **Science Center** amazes visitors with four floors of gadgets and games depicting the intricacies of space, time, motion, and the human body. A 20-ft. **Benjamin Franklin National Memorial** statue divines lightening at the entrance. In 1990, to commemorate the 200th anniversary of Franklin's death, the Institute unveiled the **Futures Center;** glimpses of life in the 21st century including simulated zero gravity and a timely set of exhibits on the changing global environment. (Futures Center open Mon.-Wed. 9:30am-5pm, Thurs.-Sun. 9:30am-9pm. Science Center daily 9am-5pm. Admission to both $8.50, seniors and kids $7.50.) The brand-new **Omniverse Theater** provides 180° and 4½ stories of optical ooohs and aaahs. (Omniverse shows daily on the hr., Mon.-Fri. 10am-4pm, Sat.-Sun. 10am-5pm; also Thurs. at 7 and 8pm, Fri. and Sat. 7-9pm. Adults $7, seniors and kids $6.) **Fels Planetarium** boasts an advanced computer-driven system that projects a simulation of life billions of years beyond. (Shows daily at 12:15 and 2:15pm, Sat. and Sun. also at 4:15pm. Admission $6, seniors and kids $5.) See all the sights for $13.50 (seniors and kids $11.50) or check out any two for $11.50 (seniors and kids $9.50).

A ubiquitous casting of the *Gates of Hell* outside the **Rodin Museum,** at 22nd St. and the Parkway (787-5476), guards the entrance to the most complete collection of the artist's works outside of Paris, including *The Thinker.* (Open Tues.-Sun. 10am-5pm. Donation.) Try your hand at the sensual **Please Touch Museum,** 210 N. 21st St. (963-0666), designed specifically for grabby kids under eight. (Open daily 9am-4:30pm. Admission $6.)

The exhibit of precious gems and the 65-million-year-old dinosaur skeleton at the **Academy of Natural Sciences,** 19th and Parkway (299-1020), excite even the basest of human desires. (Open Mon.-Fri. 10am-4:30pm, Sat.-Sun. and holidays 10am-5pm. Admission $5.50, seniors $5, kids $4.50.) Further down 26th St., the **Philadelphia Museum of Art** (763-8100) protects one of the world's major art collections. In the nation's third largest museum you'll find Rubens's *Prometheus Bound,* Picasso's *Three Musicians,* and Duchamp's *Nude Descending a Staircase,* as well as extensive Asian, Egyptian, and decorative arts collections. (Open Tues.-Sun. 10am-5pm. Admission $5, seniors and students under 18 with ID $2.50. Sun. 10am-1pm free.) The **Free Library of Philadelphia** (686-5322) has a tremendous library of orchestral music, the **Fleisher Collection,** and one of the nation's largest rare book collections. (Open Mon.-Wed. 9am-9pm, Thurs.-Fri. 9am-6pm, Sat. 9am-5pm, Sun. 1-5pm.)

Fairmount Park sprawls behind the Philadelphia Museum of Art on both sides of the Schuylkill River. Bike trails and picnic areas abound, and the famous **Philadelphia Zoo** (243-1100) 34th St. and Girard Ave., the oldest in the U.S., houses 1500 species in one corner of the park. (Open daily 9:30am-5:45pm. Admission $5.75, seniors and kids $4.75.) **Boathouse Row**, which houses the shells of local crew teams, is particularly beautiful when lit at night. During the day, hikers and non-hikers alike may wish to venture out to the northernmost arm of Fairmount Park, where trails leave the Schuylkill River and wind along secluded Wissahickon Creek for five mi. The **Horticultural Center,** off Belmont Ave. (879-4062; open daily 9am-3pm) blooms and grows with greenhouses, Japanese gardens and periodic flower shows ($2 suggested donation).

West Philadelphia (University City)

West Philly is home to both the **University of Pennsylvania** and **Drexel University,** located across the Schuylkill from Center City, within easy walking distance of the 30th St. Station. Benjamin Franklin founded Penn in 1740. Fifteen years later the country's first medical school came to life, and students have been pulling all-nighters ever since. The Penn campus provides a cloistered retreat of green lawns, red-brick quadrangles, and rarefied air. Ritzy shops line Chestnut St. and boisterous fraternities line Spruce; warm weather brings out a variety of street vendors along the Drexel and Penn borders.

Penn's **University Museum of Archeology and Anthropology,** 33rd and Spruce St. (898-4000), houses one of the finest archeological collections in the world. (Open Sept.-June Tues.-Sat. 10am-4:30pm, Sun. 1-5pm. Admission $3, seniors and students $1.50.) In 1965, Andy Warhol had his first one-man show at the **Institute of Contemporary Art,** 34th and Walnut St. (898-7108). Today the gallery remains cutting edge. (Open Thurs.-Tues. 10am-5pm, Wed. 10am-7pm. Admission $2, seniors and artists with a compelling work $1, students free. Free Wed.)

Entertainment

Check Friday's weekend magazine section in the Philadelphia *Inquirer* for entertainment listings. *City Paper,* distributed on Fridays for free at newsstands and markets, has weekly listings of city events. *Au Courant,* a gay and lesbian weekly newspaper, lists and advertises events throughout the Delaware Valley region. The bar scene enlivens University City with a younger crowd. Along South Street, there is a wide variety of live music on weekends. Stop by **Dobbs,** 304 South St. (928-1943), between 3rd and 4th, a mixed-menu restaurant (entrees $6-8.50) with live rock nightly. (Open daily 6pm-2am.) Nearby, **Penn's Landing** (923-4992) has free concerts in summer. Formerly under the direction of the late Eugene Ormandy, and now under Ricardo Muti, the **Philadelphia Academy of Music,** Broad and Locust St. (893-1930), houses the **Philadelphia Orchestra,** rated by many as the best in the U.S. The academy was modeled architecturally after Milan's *La Scala* and acoustically to mimic a perfect vacuum. The season runs from September through May. General admission tickets ($2) for seats in the amphitheater go on sale at the Locust St. entrance 45 minutes before Friday and Saturday concerts. Check with the box office for availability. The **Mann Music Center,** George's Hill (878-7707), near 52nd St. and Parkside Ave. in Fairmount Park, has 5000 seats under cover, 10,000 on outdoor benches and lawns—and hosts summer Philadelphia Orchestra, ballet, jazz, and rock events. Pick up free lawn tickets June through August on the day of performance from the visitors center at 16th St. and JFK Blvd. (See Practical Information above.) For the big-name shows, sit just outside the theater and soak in the sounds gratis. The **Robin Hood Dell East,** Strawberry Mansion Dr. (686-1776 or 477-8810 in summer), in Fairmount Park, brings in top names in pop, jazz, gospel, and ethnic dance in July and August. The Philadelphia Orchestra holds several free performances here in summer, and as many as 30,000 people gather on the lawn. Inquire at the visitors center (636-1666) about upcoming events. **Shubert Theater,** 250 S. Broad St., Center City (732-5446), stages a variety of dance, musical, and comedy performances year-round.

Philly has four professional sports franchises. The Phillies (baseball) and Eagles (football) play at **Veterans Stadium** (ticket office 339-7676), while the **Spectrum** (336-3600) houses the 76ers (basketball) and the Flyers (hockey).

Near Philadelphia: Valley Forge

Neither rockets red glare nor bombs bursting through air took place here, but during the winter of 1777-78, 11,000 men huddled at Valley Forge under George Washington's leadership spent agonizing months fighting starvation, bitter cold and disease. Only 8000 survived. Nonetheless, inspired by the enthusiasm of General Washington and the news of a U.S. alliance with France, the troops left Valley Forge stronger and better trained. They went on to victories in New Jersey and eventually reoccupied Philadelphia.

The park today encompasses over 2000 acres. (Open daily 6am-10pm.) Self-guided tours begin at the **visitors center** (783-1000), which also has a museum and an audio-visual program (twice per hr. 9am-5:30pm, 15 min.). (Open daily 8:30am-5pm. Free.) The tour features Washington's headquarters, reconstructed soldier huts and fortifications, and the Grand Parade Ground where the army drilled. Admission to Washington's headquarters costs one Washington ($1), but most other exhibits and buildings in the park are free. Audio tapes can be rented for $7. The park has three picnic areas; although there is no camping within the park, campgrounds thrive nearby. A 5-mi. bike trail winds up and down the hills of the park.

To get to Valley Forge, take the Schuylkill Expressway westbound from Philadelphia for about 12 mi. Get off at the Valley Forge exit, then take Rte. 202 S. for one mi. and Rte. 422 W. for 1½ mi. to another Valley Forge exit. SEPTA runs buses to the visitors center Monday through Friday only. Catch #125 at 16th and JFK ($3.10).

Pittsburgh

Charles Dickens called this city "Hell with the lid off" for a reason. In the late 19th century, smoke from area steel mills made street lamps essential even during the day. Today Pittsburgh's skies are (almost) clear and its downtown area sports a gleaming new nickname, "The Golden Triangle." The city itself is perhaps less interesting than it once was. The character of modern Pittsburgh has retired to the suburbs, where visitors can find universities, Three Rivers Stadium, and can climb Duquesne Incline to the top of Mount Washington.

Practical Information

Pittsburgh Convention and Visitors Bureau, 4 Gateway Ctr. (281-7711), downtown in a little glass building on Liberty Ave., across from the Hilton. Offers a 24-hr., up-to-date recording of events (391-6840), and aid for international visitors who don't speak English (624-7800). Their city maps won't get you past downtown. Open May-Oct. Mon.-Fri. 9:30am-5pm, Sat.-Sun. 9:30am-3pm; Nov.-March Mon.-Fri. 9:30am-5pm, Sat. 9:30am-3pm.

Travelers Aid, two locations: **Greyhound Bus Terminal,** 11 St. and Liberty Ave. (281-5474) and the **airport** (264-7110). Good maps, tourist advice, and help for stranded travelers. Open Mon.-Fri. 9am-9pm, Sat.-Sun. 9am-5pm.

Greater Pittsburgh International Airport: 778-2525, 15 mi. west of downtown by I-279 and Rte. 60 in Moon Township. Serves most major airlines. **Airline Transportation Company,** 471-2250. Serves most downtown hotels (daily, every 30 min., 6am-10pm, $10), Oakland (daily every 40 min., 7am-8pm, $10.50) and Monroeville (daily every 2 hrs., 6am-7pm, $15).

Amtrak: Liberty and Grant Ave. (800-872-7245 for reservations; 471-6170 for station info), on the northern edge of downtown next to Greyhound and the post office. Safe and very clean inside, but be cautious about walking from here to the city center at night. Open 24 hrs. Ticket office open daily 8:30am-5:15pm and 11pm-4am. To: Philadelphia (2 per day, 7½ hr., $64); New York (2 per day, 9 hr., $88); Chicago (2 per day, 9 hr., $79).

Greyhound: 11th St. and Liberty Ave. (391-2300), on the northern outskirts of downtown. Large and fairly clean with police on duty. Station and ticket office open 24 hrs. To: Philadelphia (7 per day, 7 hr., $44); New York (8 per day; 9-11 hr., $77); Chicago (8 per day; 9-14 hr., $64).

Public Transport: Port Authority of Allegheny County (PAT): General office 237-7000; bus info 231-5707. Bus rides free within the Golden Triangle until 7pm, after 7pm $.75. For the rest of the city and inner suburbs, $1.25; weekend daily pass $3. The tiny, 4-stop **subway** downtown is free. Schedules and maps at most department stores and in the Community Interest Showcase section of the yellow pages.

Car Rental: Rent-A-Wreck, 1200 Liberty Ave. (488-3440), one block up from Liberty tunnels. $28 per day, insurance included; 50 free mi., 18¢ each additional mi. Must be 21 with major credit card or a $150 cash deposit. Open daily 8am-6pm.

Help Lines: General Help Line, 255-1155. Open 24 hrs. **Rape Action Hotline,** 765-2731. Open 24 hrs. **Persad Center, Inc.,** a counseling service for the gay community. 441-0857, emergencies 392-2472.

Post Office: 7th and Grant St. (642-4472; general delivery 642-4478). Open Mon.-Fri. 7am-6pm, Sat. 7am-2:30pm. **ZIP code:** 15219.

Area Code: 412.

The downtown area is the Golden Triangle formed by two rivers—the Allegheny on the north and the Monongahela to the south—flowing together to form a third, the Ohio. Parallel to the Monongahela, streets in the downtown triangle number 1 through 7.

Accommodations and Camping

Reasonable accommodations aren't very easy to find in Pittsburgh, but downtown is fairly safe, even at night; Pittsburgh has the lowest crime rate for a city of its size in the country. **Point Park College,** 201 Wood St. (392-3824), eight blocks from the Greyhound Station, corner of Blvd. of the Allies and Wood St. Walk four blocks down Liberty Ave., turn left on Wood St., walk seven blocks to Blvd. of the Allies. Closer to a hotel than a hostel; clean rooms, some with private baths. Office hours are 8am to 4pm. Check-in until 11pm (tell the guards you're a hosteler). Max. stay three nights; make reservations in advance. Members only, $7.50. No kitchen but all-you-can-eat breakfast ($2.50) served in the third-floor cafeteria 7-9:30am, and laundry. Open May 15-Aug. 15. **Red Roof Inn,** 6404 Stubenville Pike (787-7870), south on I-279, past Rte. 22-Rte. 30 junction, at the Moon Run exit. From the Greyhound station, take bus #26F. Clean and quiet. Check in before 6pm or call before 6pm with a major credit card number. Check out by noon. (Singles $38. Doubles $45.) Call more than a week in advance in the summer. The nearest campsite is the **Pittsburgh North Campground,** 6610 Mars Rd., Evans City 16033 (776-1150), 20 mi. from downtown. Take I-79 to the Mars exit. Facilities include tents and swimming. (Sites $18 for 2 people, $4 per extra adult, $2 per extra kid. Hookup $3.50.) **Bear Run Campground** (RD#1, Box 241) is in Portersville (368-3564).

Food

Aside from the pizza joint/bars downtown, **Oakland** is your best bet for a good inexpensive meal. **Forbes Ave.,** around the University of Pittsburgh, is packed with collegiate watering holes and cafés. Many of Pittsburgh's ethnic groups have stayed in the pockets where they originally settled, giving each neighborhood its own distinctive flavor. **Original Hot Dog Shops, Inc.,** 3901 Forbes Ave., at Bouquet St. in Oakland. A rowdy, greasy Pittsburgh institution with lots and lots of fries, burgers, dogs and pizza. Call it "the O" and they'll think you're a local. (Open Sun.-Thurs. 9am-4:30pm, Fri.-Sat. 9am-6am.) **Hot Licks,** 5520 Walnut St., in the Theater Mall. (683-2583). Take bus #71B or D down 5th Ave., get off at Aiken, and walk north 2 blocks to Walnut. Ribs and chicken are mesquite-grilled here. (Open Mon.-Thurs. 11:30am-11pm, Fri.-Sat. 11:30am-midnight, Sun. 3-9pm.) **Suzie's Greek Specialties,** 130 6th St. downtown. Grandma Suzie serves up homemade Greek dishes, bread, and pastries ($6-8). (Open Mon.-Fri. 11am-9pm, Sat. 4-11pm.) **Brown Bag Deli,** nine convenient locations, (e.g. 411 Wood St. and 220 Grant St.) *In Pittsburgh* called it the best quick lunch around. Fresh Sandwiches, fruit, and baked goods. Weekly brown bag specials: Budget Bag, Light Lunch, Hearty Bag, brown bags included. Breakfast special: *bag*el sandwich $1.25. (Open Mon.-Sat. 9am-3pm.)

Sights

The **Golden Triangle,** formed by the Allegheny and Monongahela River, is home to **Point State Park** and its famous 200-ft. fountain. The **Fort Pitt Blockhouse and Museum** (281-9285), in the park dates back to the French and Indian War. (Open Tues.-Sat. 10am-4:30pm, Sun. noon-4:30pm. Admission $3, seniors $2, kids $1.) The **Phipps Conservatory** (622-6915) conserves 2½ acres of happiness for the flower fanatic, bounded by Edwardian homes about 3 mi. east along the Blvd. of the Allies in **Schenley Park.** (Open daily 9am-5pm. Admission $3, seniors and kids $1, $1 more for shows. Reserve tours at 622-6958). Founded in 1787, the **University of Pittsburgh** (624-4141; for tours call 624-7488) now stands in the shadow of the 42-story **Cathedral of Learning** (624-6000) at Bigelow Blvd. between Forbes and 5th Ave. The "cathedral," an academic building dedicated in 1934, features 22 "nationality classrooms" designed and decorated by artisans from each of Pittsburgh's ethnic traditions. **Carnegie-Mellon University** (268-2000) hyphenates right down the street.

Other city sights lie across the three rivers from the Golden Triangle. Northward, across the Allegheny, steal a look at **Three Rivers Stadium,** where the Steelers and Pirates play ball. To the west of Allegheny Sq. soars the tropical **Pittsburgh Aviary** (323-7234; open daily 9am-4:30pm; admission $3, seniors and ages under 12 $1; take bus #16D or the Ft. Duquesne bridge).

Two of America's greatest financial legends, Andrew Carnegie and Henry Clay Frick, made their fortunes in Pittsburgh. Their bequests to the city have enriched its cultural scene. The most spectacular of Carnegie's gifts are the art and natural history museums, together called **The Carnegie,** at 4400 Forbes Ave. (622-3328, 622-3289 for guided tours), across the street from the Cathedral of Learning. The natural history section is famous for its 500 dinosaur specimens, including an 84-ft. mammoth named for the philanthropist himself—**Diplodocus Carnegii.** The modern wing hosts a strong collection of impressionist, post-impressionist, and 20th-century works. (Open Tues.-Sat. 10am-5pm, Sun. 1-5pm. Take any bus to Oakland and get off at the Cathedral of Learning.)

While most know Henry Clay Frick for his art collection in New York, the **Frick Art Museum** 7227 Reynolds St., Point Breeze (371-0600), displays some of his early, less famous acquisitions. The permanent collection contains Italian, Flemish, and French works from the 13th through 18th centuries. Chamber music concerts monthly, Oct.-April.

Entertainment

Pittsburgh's metamorphosis from industrial to corporate town has happily hemmed its artistic seam. Pick up *In Pittsburgh* at any market or at the Brown Bag Deli (see Food above) for free up-to-date entertainment listings and racy personals. The internationally acclaimed **Pittsburgh Symphony Orchestra** performs October through May at **Heinz Hall,** 600 Penn Ave. downtown, and gives free summer evening concerts outdoors at Point State Park (392-4835 for tickets and information). The **Pittsburgh Public Theater** (323-8200) is widely renowned, and tickets cost a pretty penny. Visitors with thin wallets should check out the **Three Rivers Shakespeare Festival** (624-0933), at University of Pittsburgh's Steven Foster Memorial Theater, near Forbes Ave. and Bigelow Blvd. downtown. The corps, consisting of students and professionals, performs from late May to mid-August. Seniors and students can line up a half hour before showtime for half-price tickets. Box office (624-7529) opens 10am to showtime and Monday 10am to 4pm. (Tickets Tues.-Thurs. $15, Fri.-Sat. $18.) All-student casts perform with the **Young Company** at City Theater (tickets $9).

Near Pittsburgh

The U.S. is loaded with celebrations of President General George Washington, the founding father with the best rep and the worst teeth. **Fort Necessity,** on U.S. 40 near Rte. 381 (329-5512), commemorates the rare occasion when good ol' George got his cherry-tree butt kicked. Fort Necessity, the site of Washington's surrender to the French in a battle that precipitated the French and Indian War, has been rebuilt and features a half-hour talk (8 per day) by historians dressed up as English and French soldiers as well as a musket-firing demonstration. Chop down the door of the **Visitors Information Center** (open daily 8:30am-5pm; Labor Day-Memorial Day 10:30am-5pm; admission $1, families $3). After his defeat, a promoted Washington regrouped forces to defeat the French in 1758 at **Fort Ligonier,** at the junction of Rte. 30 and 711, 60 mi. north of Necessity. (Open April-Oct. daily 8am-sunset. Admission $4, seniors $3, kids $2.) Various groups reenact battles and camp life on some summer weekends.

Washington, DC

Washington, DC's strange experiment—an infant nation building a capital city from scratch—has matured into one of America's most influential, most interesting, and consequently most visited cities. Monuments, museums, and politicos draw visitors from around the world for a gander at lunar landers and a good aim at the president.

After winning independence from Great Britain in 1783, the United States was faced with the challenge of finding a home for its fledgling government. Both Northern and Southern states wanted the capital on their turf (New York City was the capital for a spell, and Williamsburg, VA was suggested by many as a suitable locale). The resulting location—100 sq. mi. pinched between Virginia and Maryland—was a compromise resulting in what President Kennedy later termed "a city of Northern charm and Southern efficiency."

Nineteenth-century Washington was a "city of magnificent distances"—a smattering of slave markets, elegant government buildings, and boarding houses along the absurdly large-scale avenues designed by French engineer Pierre L'Enfant. The city had the awkward feel of a child wearing clothes far too large for its age in the expectation that they would someday fit. As the capital grew, so did its problems—a port city squeezed between two plantation states, the district made a logical first stop for slave traders, whose shackled cargo awaited sale in crowded pens on the Mall and near the White House. Foreign diplomats were properly disgusted, deeming DC to be unequivocally "Southern". The War Between the States altered this forever, changing Washington from the Union's embarrassing appendix to its jugular vein. The Civil War and Reconstruction sent tens of thousands of former slaves north looking for a better life; for a time they found a fate worse than slavery in ad hoc shantytowns like Murder Bay, only a few blocks from the White House.

The city grew slowly until the Great Depression, when Franklin Delano Roosevelt founded his alphabet soup of federal agencies staffed by liberal out-of-towners; by the end of World War II, DC had become the cynosure of the free world and a genuine metropolis to boot. During the 1960s Washington was the nation's "March Central," hosting a concatenation of demonstrations advocating civil rights and condemning America's role in Vietnam. The 1963 March on Washington brought 250,000 people of all colors to the Mall to hear Martin Luther King, Jr.'s "I Have a Dream" speech. In 1968, an anti-war gathering ringed the Pentagon with chants and shouts. The same year's riots torched much of the city; some blocks still await rebuilding.

Though government institutions are its economic and geographic mainstay, Washington isn't just a government town—tourists who merely breeze through the Mall and the monuments have hardly begun to see the city. The arts thrive in Dupont Circle, while youngsters spar for turf and great budget meals in Adams-Morgan. The Kennedy Center bows and pirouettes with high culture almost every night, while indigenous music scenes pump out high-quality, honest tunes. Of course, there are neighborhoods a tourist would rather not stumble upon: some parts of DC justify the media stereotype of Washington's low-income areas—poor tenements devastated by crack, guns, and institutional neglect. Still, you'll be rewarded for venturing beyond the conventional grade-school-tour-group attractions; Washington is a city that has matured gracefully and wears its leadership well. For the ultimate in Washington, DC budget coverage, see *Let's Go: Washington, DC*

Practical Information

Emergency: 911; TDD: 727-9334.

Police (non-emergency): 727-1010; 24 hrs.

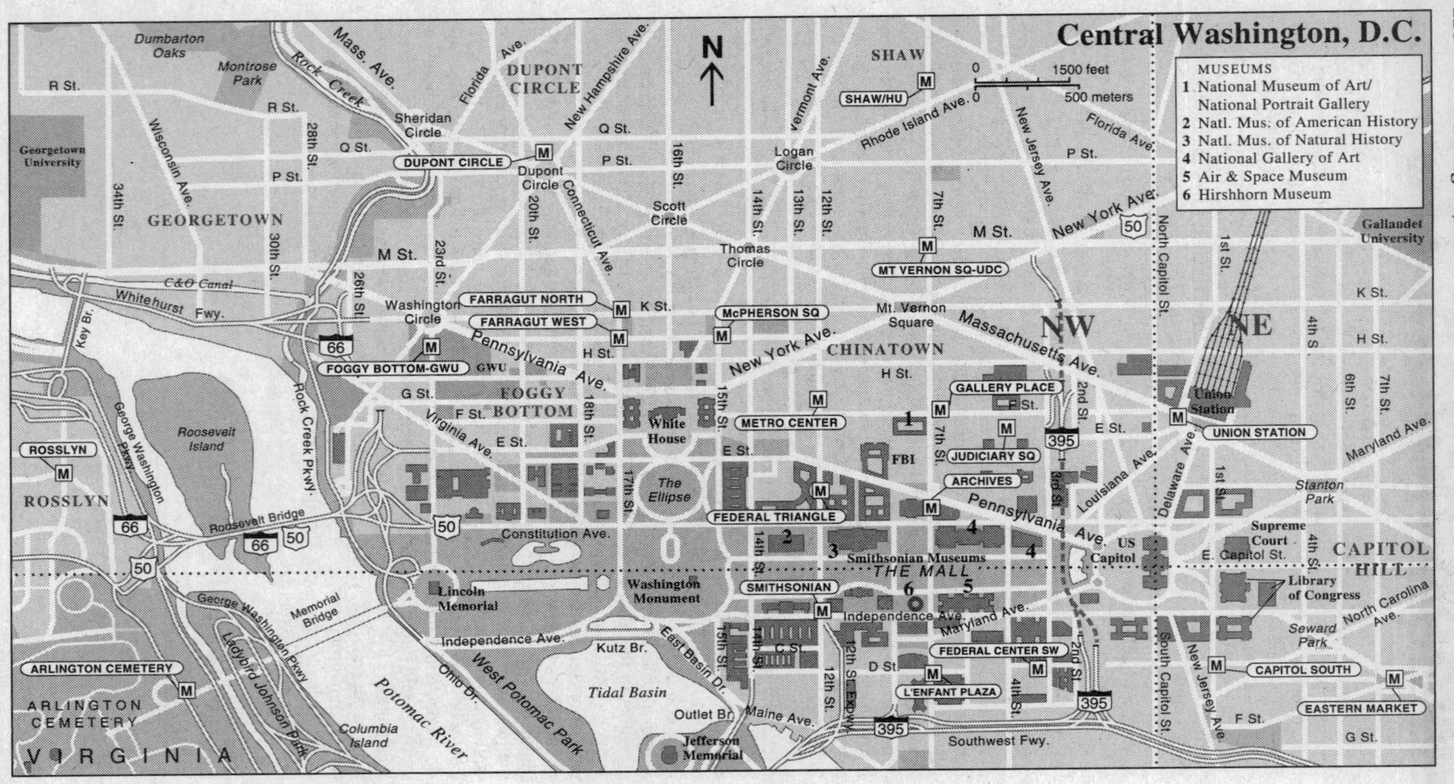

Central Washington, D.C.
MUSEUMS
1 National Museum of Art/ National Portrait Gallery
2 Natl. Mus. of American History
3 Natl. Mus. of Natural History
4 National Gallery of Art
5 Air & Space Museum
6 Hirshhorn Museum
0 1500 feet
0 500 meters
N
Dumbarton Oaks
Montrose Park
Georgetown University
Gallaudet University
GEORGETOWN
DUPONT CIRCLE
SHAW
CHINATOWN
FOGGY BOTTOM
GWU
NW
NE
CAPITOL HILL
ROSSLYN
ARLINGTON CEMETERY
VIRGINIA
SHAW/HU
DUPONT CIRCLE
MT VERNON SQ-UDC
FARRAGUT NORTH
FARRAGUT WEST
McPHERSON SQ
FOGGY BOTTOM-GWU
GALLERY PLACE
METRO CENTER
UNION STATION
JUDICIARY SQ
ARCHIVES
FEDERAL TRIANGLE
SMITHSONIAN
FEDERAL CENTER SW
L'ENFANT PLAZA
CAPITOL SOUTH
EASTERN MARKET
ROSSLYN
ARLINGTON CEMETERY
Sheridan Circle
Dupont Circle
Logan Circle
Scott Circle
Thomas Circle
Washington Circle
Mt. Vernon Square
Union Station
White House
The Ellipse
FBI
US Capitol
Supreme Court
Library of Congress
Stanton Park
Seward Park
Smithsonian Museums
THE MALL
Washington Monument
Lincoln Memorial
Jefferson Memorial
Tidal Basin
Roosevelt Island
Columbia Island
Potomac River
Rock Creek
C&O Canal
West Potomac Park
Ladybird Johnson Park
Whitehurst Fwy.
Rock Creek Pkwy.
George Washington Pkwy.
Southwest Fwy.
12th St. Expwy.
Key Br.
Roosevelt Bridge
Memorial Bridge
Kutz Br.
Outlet Br.
East Basin Dr.
Ohio Dr.
Mass. Ave.
Florida Ave.
New Hampshire Ave.
Vermont Ave.
Rhode Island Ave.
New Jersey Ave.
Wisconsin Ave.
Connecticut Ave.
New York Ave.
Massachusetts Ave.
Pennsylvania Ave.
Virginia Ave.
Constitution Ave.
Independence Ave.
Maryland Ave.
Louisiana Ave.
Delaware Ave.
North Carolina Ave.
Maine Ave.
North Capitol St.
South Capitol St.
E. Capitol St.
R St.
Q St.
P St.
M St.
K St.
H St.
G St.
F St.
E St.
D St.
C St.
34th St.
30th St.
28th St.
26th St.
23rd St.
20th St.
18th St.
17th St.
16th St.
15th St.
14th St.
13th St.
12th St.
7th St.
6th St.
4th St.
3rd St.
2nd St.
1st St.
50
66
395

Visitor Information: Visitor Information Center, 1455 Pennsylvania Ave. NW (939-5566), within the "Willard collection" of shops. A very helpful first stop. Ask for *Washington Visitors Map*. Language bank service in over 20 tongues. Open Mon.-Sat. 9am-5pm. **Washington, DC Convention and Visitors Association (WCVA),** 1212 New York Ave., NW (789-7000). Does not expect walk-ins; write or call. Open Mon.-Fri. 9am-5pm. **Daily Tourist Info:** 737-8866. **International Visitors Information Service (IVIS),** 1623 Belmont St. NW (939-5566). 24-hr. language bank in over 50 languages. Open Mon.-Fri. 9am-5pm.

Traveler's Aid: Main office, 512 C St. NE (546-3120). Open Mon.-Fri. 9am-5pm. Desks at **Union Station** (371-1937, TDD 684-7886; open daily 9am-9pm), **National Airport** (684-3472, TDD 684-7884; open Mon.-Fri. 9am-9pm, Sat. 9am-6pm), and **Dulles International Airport** (703-661-8636, TDD 471-9776; open Sun.-Fri. 10am-9pm, Sat. 10am-6pm). **24-hr. emergency aid,** 546-3120.

Embassies: Australia, 1601 Massachusetts Ave. NW (797-3000). **Canada,** 501 Pennsylvania Ave. NW (682-1740). **France,** 4101 Reservoir Rd. NW (944-6000). **Germany,** 4645 Reservoir Rd. NW (298-4000). **Ireland,** 2234 Massachusetts Ave. NW (462-3939). **Israel,** 3514 International Drive NW (364-5500). **Japan,** 2520 Massachusetts Ave. NW (939-6700). **Russia,** 1125 16th St. NW (628-7551). **United Kingdom,** 3100 Massachusetts Ave. NW (462-1340).

Airports and Trains: See Getting There, below.

Public Transport and Taxis: See Orientation, below.

Car Rental: Cheapest in Arlington, VA, across the Potomac from downtown and easily accessible by Metrobus. **Easi Car Rentals,** 2480 S. Glebe Rd., Arlington (703-521-0188). Rates differ depending on season and make. Daily rates $21, plus 10¢ per mi. Special weekend rates and weekly rentals available. Must be 21 or older with major credit card or $300 cash deposit. Reservations advised. Open Mon.-Fri. 10am-6pm, Sat. 11am-4pm. **Bargain Buggies Rent-a-Car,** 6461 Gasall Rd., Alexandria (703-522-4141). $20 per day, or 10¢ per mi. Weekly rates. Must be 18 or older with major credit card or $300 cash deposit (those under 21 need full insurance coverage). Open Mon.-Fri. 8am-7pm, Sat.-Sun. 8am-5pm.

Bicycle Rentals: Thompson Boat Center, 2900 Virginia Ave. NW (333-4861), near Watergate. All kinds of bikes; 18-speed mountain bikes $6 per day or $22 per week, locks 50¢ per day. Open Mon.-Fri. 7am-6pm, Sat.-Sun. 8am-5pm. **Big Wheel Bikes,** 315 7th St. SE (543-1600). Regular bikes for as low as $3 per hr., $15 per business day; 3 hr. min. $5 extra for overnight use. Must have major credit card or $30 cash deposit. Open Mon.-Fri. 11am-7pm, Sat.-Sun. 10am-6pm.

International newspapers: The News Room, 1753 Connecticut Ave. NW (332-1489). **News World,** 1001 Connecticut Ave. NW (872-0190). **American International News,** 1825 Eye St. NW (223-2526). **Key Bridge Newsstand,** 3326 M St. NW (338-2626) between 33rd and 34th St. NW.

Help Lines: DC Hotline, 832-4357 (8DC-HELP). **Rape Crisis Center,** 333-7273. **Gay and Lesbian Hotline,** 833-3234.

Post Office: indescribably inconvenient at 900 Brentwood Rd. NE (636-1532). Mail sent "General Delivery" always comes here—a good reason not to have anything sent General Delivery. Usually open Mon.-Fri. 8am-8pm, Sat. 10am-6pm, Sun. noon-6pm. **Capitol Hill:** North Capitol St. and Massachusetts Ave. NE (523-2628), across from Union Station. Open Mon.-Fri. 7am-midnight, Sat.-Sun. 7am-8pm. **ZIP** code: 20066.

Area Code: 202.

Getting There

The two main roads from Baltimore and the North are the **Baltimore-Washington (BW) Parkway** and **I-95.** To go downtown, take the BW Parkway and follow signs for New York Ave. To get to Upper Northwest, take I-95 to the Silver Spring exit onto the Capitol Beltway (I-495), then exit 20 ("Chevy Chase") onto Connecticut Ave. and take a left. From the south, take I-95 (which becomes I-395) directly to the 14th St. Bridge or Memorial Bridge; both lead downtown. From the west, take I-66 east over the Roosevelt Bridge and follow signs for Constitution Ave. Vehicles on I-66 East (Mon.-Fri. 7-9am) and West (Mon.-Fri. 4-6pm) *must* carry at least three people. Highways into DC are almost always congested; try not to arrive during rush hour, especially if you're coming from Virginia.

Three **airports** serve Washington. From within the U.S., it's best to fly into **National Airport** (703-685-8000), which is on the Metro and under 20 minutes from DC by car.

Cab fare downtown costs $10 to $15. **Dulles International Airport** (703-471-4242), at least a 40-minute drive from downtown, handles mostly international, transcontinental, and bargain flights. The **Dulles Express Bus** (703-685-1400) shuttles to and from the West Falls Church Metro and Dulles every 20 to 30 minutes (Mon.-Fri. 6am-10:30pm, Sat.-Sun. 8am-10:30pm; last bus from Metro, 11pm. One-way trip $7.) If you must, fly into **Baltimore-Washington International Airport (BWI),** about 10 mi. south of Baltimore's city center. Driving time is about 50 minutes from Washington and 30 minutes from Baltimore, but as always, allow for jams. You can take Amtrak (40 min.) or MARC from DC (see below). The **Washington Flyer Express** (703-685-1400) shuttles to and from National, Dulles, BWI, and their station at 1517 K St. NW. (Shuttle to National one way $7, round-trip $12; Dulles one way $14, round-trip $22; BWI one way $13, round-trip $23; ages under 7 free).

Amtrak (484-7540 or 800-872-7245) connects Washington to most other parts of the country through downtown's luxurious **Union Station,** at 50 Massachusetts Ave. NE. Trains run to: New York City (3½ hr.; $64); Baltimore (40 min.; $12); Philadelphia (2 hr.; $34); Boston (7 hr.; $98); Chicago (17 hr.; $118); Richmond ($21); Williamsburg ($28); Virginia Beach ($41); and Atlanta ($119). (Fares listed are one way; **Metroliners** also run to the closer stops in less time and for more money.) Maryland's weekday commuter train, **MARC** (800-325-7245), also runs from Union Station to nearby cities.

The modern (but still depressing) **Greyhound** bus station, 1005 1st St. NE (289-5155; 301-565-2662 for fare and schedules), at L St., rises over a rather decrepit neighborhood; be careful after dark. It provides frequent service to: Philadelphia ($19), New York City ($32), and Baltimore ($13). (Fares listed are one way and slightly higher on weekends.) Buses also go to Atlantic City, Pittsburgh, and Richmond. **Peter Pan** (371-8045 or 371-2111) travels throughout New England and adds movies to the typical New York jaunt (one way $25). The station is open 24 hours.

Orientation

L'Enfant did his darndest to make central Washington logical; unfortunately, logic doesn't drive—navigating in Washington often means doing things that you didn't even imagine were *possible*, let alone legal. Washington street names and addresses are split into four quadrants: NW, NE, SE, and SW, centered on the U.S. Capitol. There are four 7th St. and four G St.; consequently, there are four 700 G St.—SE, SW, NW and NE. The basic street plan is a rectilinear grid. Streets that run east-west are named in alphabetical order running north and south from the Capitol, A St. lies one block from it, P St. 20 blocks. ("Eye St." refers to I St.; there is no J St.) After "W," east-west streets take two-syllable names, then three-syllable names, then arboreal and floral names running alphabetically (occasionally repeating or skipping letters). North-south streets get numbers (1st St., 2nd St., etc.). Numbered and lettered streets sometimes disappear for a block, then recontinue as if nothing had happened. Diagonal avenues named for states traverse the grid; many are major thoroughfares. North Capitol, East Capitol, and South Capitol St. run in the corresponding compass directions from the Capitol. Addresses on lettered streets indicate the numbered cross street (1100 D St. SE will be between 11th and 12th St.). The same trick works with addresses on some avenues (Pennsylvania, but not Massachusetts or Wisconsin). Some principal roads: **Pennsylvania Ave.** runs SE to NW from Anacostia to Capitol Hill to the Capitol, through downtown, past the White House, and ending finally at 28th and M St. NW, in Georgetown; **Connecticut Ave.** goes north to northwest from the White House through Dupont Circle, past the Zoo, and farther out through Chevy Chase, MD; **Wisconsin Ave.** runs north from Georgetown past the Cathedral to MD; **16th Street NW** zooms from the White House north through hotels, offices, townhouses, and Adams-Morgan, then forms Rock Creek Park's eastern border into MD; **K Street NW** is a major downtown artery; **Constitution Ave.** and **Independence Ave.** border the north and south boundaries of the Mall; **Massachusetts Ave.** originates at American University, whisks past the Cathedral, then chugs through Dupont and the old downtown on its way toward Capitol Hill; **New York Ave.** spreads the news from the White House heading NE; and

Rock Creek Parkway rolls through Rock Creek Park. Drivers should be wary of reversible lanes and temporary one-way streets during rush hours.

DC ain't just for big-bellied, cigar-smoking congressmen. Nosiree. Over 600,000 residents inhabit the federal city; rich and poor, African-American, white and Latino, tall and short are all well-represented. Try to escape the Mall and experience the neighborhoods to get a true feel for Washington. **Capitol Hill** extends east from the Capitol; white- and blue-collar locals mix with legislation-minded pols. North of the Mall, the **old downtown** goes about its business, accompanied by **Foggy Bottom** (sometimes called the "West End"), on the other side of the White House, and the **new downtown** around K St. west of 15th St. NW. **Georgetown** draws crowds and sucks away bucks nightly from its center at Wisconsin and M St. NW. Business and pleasure, embassies and streetlife, straight and gay mingle and merge at **Dupont Circle.** East of 16th St., the Dupont Circle character changes to struggling **Logan Circle,** then to rundown **Shaw, Howard University**, and **LeDroit Park,** an early residence for Washington's African-American elite. **Adams-Morgan,** north of Dupont and east of Rock Creek Park, has a strong Hispanic community. West of the Park begins **"upper northwest,"** a sprawling, white, residential territory that includes several smaller, separately named neighborhoods, the National Zoo, and Washington Cathedral. Across the Anacostia River, **Anacostia** has been seriously damaged and further isolated by poverty, drugs, and crime. **Rock Creek Park,** a giant, undeveloped forest swath, reaches from near the Kennedy Center up to DC's northern tip; commuters drive through it, and, according to legend, Charles de Gaulle once mistook the 8-sq.-mi. park for the French Embassy's backyard. Those crazy Frenchmen.

Though out-of-town papers bill DC as "the nation's murder capital," with more homicides per capita than any other U.S. city, most killings are drug-related disputes in areas most tourists are unlikely to frequent. Nevertheless, you should use caution and common sense to guide your peregrinations. Don't go out alone at night. If you're with somebody else, anywhere with pedestrians and streetlights should be reasonably safe at night, including Dupont Circle, Georgetown, and the well-lit parts of Adams-Morgan.

The Washington subway system, **Metrorail** (637-7000), usually referred to as the "Metro," is a sight in its own right. (Main office, 600 5th St. NW. Open daily 6am-around 11:30pm.) The sterile, monumental stations wow first-time riders with their uniformity, silence, and artlessness. (Try the Wheaton station for the world's longest escalator.) The trains themselves are clean, carpeted, safe, and air-conditioned. You must buy a computerized fare card from a machine in the station *before* you enter the subway and pass it through an electronic reader when you exit; if there's extra money on it, you'll get it back. To connect with a bus after your ride, get a transfer pass from machines on the platform before boarding the train. (5% bonus on fare cards for $10 or more.) The $6 family tourist pass lets a group of four ride Metrorail and Metrobus all day long any Saturday, Sunday, or holiday except July 4 (available at Metro Center stop and from some hotel concierges). Kids age 4 and under ride free. Senior citizens and people with disabilities get discounts, but need a special Metro ID. Elevators help with wheelchairs and strollers. Trains run daily 6:30am to 11:30pm. Peak hour fares from $1 to $3.15; at other times $1 to $2.

The extensive **Metrobus** system (same address, phone, and hours as Metrorail) reliably serves Georgetown, downtown, and the suburbs. Downtown, the bus stops every few blocks. Regular fare is $1 (uncrumpled bills accepted), but rush hour fares vary. There is an unlimited one-day Metro pass for only $5, or a two-week **Flash Pass** for $21. Seniors, disabled persons, and ages under 4 are entitled to discounts. #30, 32, 34 and 36 buses take Pennsylvania Ave. NW from Capitol Hill to Georgetown and then drive up Wisconsin Ave. The immensely useful D2, D4, D6 and D8 lines zip from far NW to Glover Park, Q St. in Georgetown, Dupont Circle, the new downtown and Metro center before ending up in far NE at the Rhode Island Ave. Metro. L2 and L4 buses run from downtown up Connecticut Ave. NW. **Metro information** (637-7000) can clarify the mix of buses and trains needed to reach any destination.

Washington cab fares are lower, but weirder, than those in other American cities: fares are based not on a meter but on a map which splits the city into 27 subzones; fares range from $3 to $10.20, plus a $1 rush-hour surcharge. Hail any cab downtown; farther out, call **Yellow Cab** (544-1212). Be ready to give directions or send the first few cabs away.

Accommodations and Camping

Business travelers desert DC during the summer months, so many hotels discount heavily and fill up on tourists. If you're lucky enough to hit the District without a car, and you don't want a hostel, the guest houses around Dupont Circle and Adams-Morgan should be your first try. Check the *New York Times* Sunday "Travel" section for summer weekend deals, and feel free to bargain. DC adds an automatic 11% occupancy surcharge and another $1.50 per room per night to your bill. **Bed & Breakfast, Ltd. of Washington, DC,** P.O. Box 12011, 20005 (328-3510) reserves rooms in private homes with an interesting array of hosts. (Singles $40-100. Doubles $50-100.)

Washington International Hostel (HI/AYH), 1009 11 St. NW (737-2333). Metro: Metro Center, then walk up 11th St. NW, away from the Mall, and turn right onto K St. International travelers will appreciate the college-age staff, elevators, bunk beds and bulletin boards. Each clean, air-conditioned room holds 4-12 beds. Kitchen and common rooms, too. No alcohol or drugs; smoking room in basement. On the edge of downtown—unsafe northeast of here. Open 24 hrs. Bed $15; $3 membership charge first night for nonmembers. Call at least 48 hrs. in advance, or write at least 3 weeks in advance for reservations. MC/Visa accepted.

Washington International Student Center, 2452 18th St. NW (265-6555), on "restaurant row" in the heart of Adams-Morgan. This newly opened hostel accommodates out-of-state and international visitors in bunk beds in 3 very clean, if somewhat cramped, air-conditioned rooms. The friendly managers are helpful and eager to please newcomers to DC for only $13 a night (including free bed linen). Kitchen facilities on the premises, laundromat nearby on Columbia Rd. Alcohol permitted, smoking on balcony, no curfew, no max. stay.

Kalorama Guest House at Kalorama Park, 1854 Mintwood Place NW (667-6369), off Columbia Rd., and at **Cathedral Park,** 2700 Cathedral Ave. (328-0860). Metro (both): Woodley Park/Zoo. Well-run, impeccably decorated, immaculate guest rooms in Victorian townhouses; the first in the upscale western slice of Adams-Morgan, the second in a high-class neighborhood near the Zoo. Enjoy evening sherry or lemonade while padding across oriental rugs. Mintwood Place boasts fireplace, refrigerator, and a more international clientele; Cathedral Park offers Freckles, a spaniel. Both locations have A/C, laundry machines, and guest phones. Rooms with shared bath $40-70; $5 per additional person; private baths $75-105. Desk hours Mon.-Fri. 7:30am-9pm, Sat.-Sun. 7:30am-7pm. Reservations with full prepayment or credit card required; cancel for refund up to 2 weeks ahead.

Davis House, 1822 R St. NW (232-3196, 24 hrs.). Metro: Dupont Circle. Charming, spacious wood-floored building accepts international visitors, Quakers, and those "working on peace and justice concerns." Other visitors sometimes accepted on same-day, space-available basis. No smoking; no alcohol. Max. stay 2 weeks; reserve early (1 night's deposit required). Singles with hall bath $25.

Allen Lee Hotel, 2224 F. St. NW (331-1224 or 800-462-0128), near George Washington University. Metro: Foggy Bottom/GWU. Large, rickety, blue hallways. Rooms vary wildly in size, furnishings, and state of repair/disrepair, so look at several before accepting one. Bedrooms and bathrooms usually old but clean. Singles $32, with private bath $40. Doubles $40, with private bath $50. Twins $40, with private bath $51. Reservations required in summer.

2005 Columbia Guest House, 2005 Columbia Rd. NW (265-4006), southwest of central Adams-Morgan. An old senator's house, with a creaky central staircase and 7 faded rooms with sometimes lumpy beds. But the place is clean and quiet, and the rates are unmatchable. No alcohol. Call ahead. Singles $19-26. Doubles $28-39. Weekly rates available.

Adams Inn, 1744 Lanier Place NW (745-3600), behind the Columbia Rd. Safeway, 2 blocks from the center of Adams-Morgan. Elaborate, elegant Victorian townhouses slathered with Persian rugs; all with shared bath but private sink. Free breakfast. Outdoor patio, coin laundry facilities, pay phones, and eating facilities. Singles with shared bath $45, with private bath $60. Doubles with shared bath $55, with private bath $70. Weekly singles with shared bath $180, with private bath $220. Weekly doubles with shared bath $255, with private bath $295.

Marifex Hotel, 1523 22nd St. NW (293-1885). Metro: Dupont Circle. Small, clean, linoleum-floored rooms, each with its own sink and shared bathrooms down the hall. Price includes various DC taxes (including the 11% occupancy tax). Singles $40.35. Doubles $51.45.

Swiss Inn, 1204 Massachusetts Ave. (371-1816 or 800-955-7947). Metro: Metro Center. Close to downtown. Clean, quiet studio apartments with refrigerator, private bath, high ceiling, kitchenette, and air-conditioning. Free local phone calls and free laundry (!). Once-a-summer cookout on the house. French-speaking managers welcome international crowd (one speaks Swiss-German also). Singles $58, doubles $68. (Includes tax.) Winter discount 20%. Weekly rates available.

Capitol KOA, 768 Cecil Ave. (301-923-2771 or 301-987-7477), near Millersville, 16 mi. from DC. Families get back to nature, sort of. Full facilities for tents, RVs, cabins. Free pool, movies. Free weekday shuttle to DC/Baltimore trains; commuter train (MARC) $6.25 round-trip to Union Station. Tent site for 2 $17.25. RV site $17-19. Each additional adult $3. Open April-Nov.

University Dorms: Georgetown University Summer School Housing is available only for summer educational pursuits; they gladly take interns and members of summer programs but turn away self-declared tourists. Air-conditioned singles ($19), non-air-conditioned doubles ($15), and air-conditioned doubles ($16), all with a strong college-dormitory flavor. In summer, you'll need the A/C. Call or write G.U. Summer Housing, P.O. Box 2214, 20057 (687-3999); reserve early, although last-minute rentals are always a possibility. (3-week min. stay. Bring your own linens. Requires mail application and 20% deposit. Rooms available June-mid-Aug.) **American University Summer Housing,** 4400 Massachusetts Ave. NW, 20016-8039 (885-2598; Metro: Tenleytown Ave.), provides simple, air-conditioned dorm rooms for students and interns late May-mid-August. Doubles $88 per week per person; hall bathrooms; required two-week min. stay. Come with a friend or they'll introduce you to one. Reserve early for check-in before June 7; after that you can call 24 hrs. ahead. A university ID (from any university) and full payment for stay must be presented at check-in.

Food

While public servants tend to lunch in government cafeterias, DC makes up for its days as a "sleepy Southern town" with a kaleidoscope of international restaurants. Pretentious European dining rooms strive to impress the expense-account crowd, while bargains from Africa, Southeast Asia, and the Americas feed a mélange of immigrants. Excellent budget food centers in Dupont Circle and Adams-Morgan. Food vendors do that mongering thing in the block-long red brick **Eastern Market,** Pennsylvania Ave. and 7th St. SE. (Metro: Eastern Market.) A veritable feeding frenzy of Washingtonians flock here for fresh produce and the bustle of a pre-industrial bazaar. At the **open-air market** at the wharves on Maine Ave. and 9th St. SW, you can buy low-priced seafood straight from the Chesapeake Bay. Smithsonian-goers should plan to eat dinner far away from the triceratops and biplanes; visitors to the Mall get stuffed at and into mediocre cafeterias, only blocks from respectable food on Capitol Hill.

It's common knowledge among interns that **happy hours** provide the cheapest dinners in Washington. Bars desperate to attract early-evening drinkers set up plates, platters and tables of free appetizers; the trick is to drop by and munch, but drink little or nothing. Look around Capitol Hill and Dupont Circle.

Capitol Hill

Over 50 eateries inhabit **Union Station,** 50 Massachusetts Ave. NE; in the food court on the Lower Level, cheap take-out counters line the walls. (Metro: Union Station.)

Chicken and Steak, 320 D St. NE (543-4633). Ignore the spare décor and fall for the succulent chicken and steak, cooked Peruvian style *à la brasa* (grilled), at bargain prices (half chicken with yuca and salad $5.25). Open Mon.-Sat. 11am-9:30pm.

Jimmy T's, 501 East Capitol St. (546-3646). At 5th St., under the brick octagonal turret. The paint's chipped, and the vinyl benches look old, but this corner diner manages to make decrepitude charming. Great diner fare; nothing costs over $6. Breakfast served all day. Open Tues.-Fri. 6:30am-3pm, Sat. 8am-3pm, Sun. 9am-3pm.

Neil's Outrageous Deli, 208 Massachusetts Ave. NE (546-6970). Combination deli and liquor store offers creative sandwiches to go ($2-5); eat them out on the grass. Open Mon.-Tues. 9am-7:30pm, Wed.-Sat. 9am-9pm.

American Café, 222 Massachusetts Ave. NE (547-8500). One of a local chain. Non-fried foods and live jazz on Wed. and Sat. evenings. Take-out available; chicken Caesar salad $5. Open Mon.-Thurs. 11am-11pm, Fri.-Sat. 11am-midnight, Sun. 10:30am-10pm.

Kelley's "The Irish Times," 14 F St. NW (543-5433). Irish street signs, the *Irish Times*, Joyce on the wall and Yeats and Keats on the menu make this more than just another Irish pub. (Don't tell them Keats wasn't Irish.) Live music Wed.-Sat. evenings. Sandwiches $5-7, soup $2; beer from $2.50, Irish whiskey from $4. Open Sun.-Thurs. 10:30am-1:30am, Fri.-Sat. 10:30am-2:30am.

Hawk 'n' Dove, 329 Pennsylvania Ave. SE (543-3300). A good bar with good bar food, interns, regulars, and powerful politicians. Sandwiches $4-6.50; 14 kinds of beer $1.75 and up. Midnight breakfast served Mon.-Thurs. 11pm-1am, Fri.-Sat. 11pm-2am ($7; $9 with steak). Open Mon.-Thurs. 10am-2am, Fri.-Sat. 10am-3am, Sun. 10am-2am.

Thai Roma, 313 Pennsylvania Ave. SE (544-2338 or -2339). A wild combination of Italian pastas and sauces with Thai zest and spice that makes area reviewers rave. Lunch entrées under $8. Reservations advised; takeout available. Open Mon.-Fri. 11:30am-10:30pm, Sat. 11:30am-11pm, Sun. 4-10pm.

Downtown

A.V. Ristorante, 607 New York Ave. NW (737-0550). Chianti bottles top-heavy with melted wax, lamps turned so low they flicker on and off, huge plates of expert pasta ($6-10) and pizza. They don't make 'em like this anymore. Open Mon.-Fri. 11:30am-11pm, Sat. 5pm-midnight.

Sholl's Colonial Cafeteria, 1900 K St. NW, in the Esplanade Mall. Good cooking at exceptionally low prices: chopped steak ($1.65) and roast beef ($1.90). Try the homemade pies. Open Mon.-Sat. 7am-2:30pm and 4-8pm.

The Star of Siam, 1136 19th St. NW (785-2838). Delights diners with spicy hot curries, unobtrusively fried foods, and sharp desserts. Dinner from $6.25. Open Mon.-Sat. 11:30am-11pm, Sun. 4-10pm.

Sabina's, 1813 M St. NW (466-5678). Return to the 50s with their all-day breakfast menu and jukebox at every table. The perfect late-night hangout. Hamburger with toppings and fries $3-4. Open Sun.-Thurs. 10am-3am, Fri.-Sat. 10am-4am.

Chinatown

You can't judge a Chinese restaurant by its exterior. Wander around (not alone) along H St. from the Gallery Place Metro stop.

Big Wong, 610 H St. (638-0116 or 638-0117). A hell of a name and a wide selection; try the specialty noodle dishes. Combination platters, with rice, egg rolls and entrée, around $6. Authentic desserts include egg custard tart. *Dim sum* daily 11am-3:30pm. Open Sun.-Wed. 11am-3am, Thurs.-Sat. 11am-4am.

Tony Cheng's Mongolian (Barbecue) Restaurant, 619 H St. (842-8669). Load your bowl with beef, leeks, mushrooms, sprouts, and such, then watch the cooks make it sizzle (and shrink). (One serving $6; all-you-can-eat $14). Two or more people can stir up their own feast in charcoal hotpots. (Base platter $5 per person; more meat costs extra.) Open Sun.-Thurs. 11am-11pm, Fri.-Sat. 11am-midnight.

Burma Restaurant, upstairs at 740 6th St. (393-3453). Burma's rare cuisine replaces soy sauce with pickles, mild curries, and unique spices. Try the rice noodles with dried shrimp, fried onion, coriander, garlic, and lemon juice ($6) or the tofu and chopped shrimp cooked in tabasco ($7). Open daily 11am-3pm, 6-10pm.

Ho Wah Restaurant, 611 H St. (408-8115). Ho wah, is this cheap! $3.50 for lunch. Open Mon.-Fri. 10am-3:30pm.

White House Area/Foggy Bottom

Milo's, 2142 Pennsylvania Ave. NW (338-3000). GW students enjoy Euro-chic decor and Italian food—fried mozzarella ($3), pasta ($5-8), *calamari* ($5), and pizza (from $5.20). Live country, rock, or folk some nights. Deals on Mon., Wed., and Fri. nights. Open Mon.-Wed. 11:30am-11pm, Thurs.-Fri. 11:30am-midnight, Sat. 11:30am-2am, Sun. 5-10pm.

The Art Gallery Grille, 1712 Eye St. NW (298-6658). Metro: Farragut West. Art deco interior and jukebox. Original Erté serigraphs surround a professional clientele. Breakfasts include Belgian waffles and creative granola ($5). DJ Thurs.-Fri. nights. Open Mon. 6:30am-11pm, Tues. and Sun. 6:30am-midnight, Thurs.-Sat. 6:30am-3am.

Balaji Siddhartha, 1379 K St. NW (682-9090). Deli atmosphere belies the exotic plates tailored to those whose tastes run to vegetarianism, Indian food, and Hesse. Curry of the day $3. Appetizers linger around $1.50. Choose from 17 desserts. $5 all-you-can-eat lunch. Open Mon.-Sat. 11:30am-8:30pm, Sun. noon-7:30pm.

Lindy's Bon Apétit [*sic*], 2040 Pennsylvania Ave. NW (452-0055), near Tower Records. Ronald Reagan once said that life at GWU was not complete without a bone burger from this carry-out deli. Grab a bacon cheeseburger ($3), a Monterey sandwich with refried beans, raw onions, and American cheese ($2.65), a BLT ($2.65), or 6-in. subs ($2-4). All breakfast sandwiches under $1.60. Open Mon.-Fri. 7am-8pm, Sat.-Sun. 11am-5pm.

Georgetown

Booeymonger, 3265 Prospect St. NW (333-4810), corner of Potomac St. Georgetown students and residents stop by for breakfast or a quick, giant sandwich. Every sandwich seems a specialty; try the veggie pocket ($4.25-4.75). In peak lunch hours, the tables are packed, so grab a seat when you walk in or eat outside. Create your own sandwiches with a choice of 15 fillings and 8 breads. Free coffee refills to jump-start your morning. Open Mon.-Sun. 8am-midnight.

Nakeysa, 1564 Wisconsin Ave. NW (337-6500). Small but elegant Persian restaurant with flowers on every table. Beef, cornish hen, game hen, and chicken kebabs range in price from $7-12. Fine vegetarian dishes too. Try the *fesenjan*, an exotic concoction with walnuts and tomatoes in pomegranate sauce. Take-out available. Open Mon.-Thurs. noon-10pm, Fri.-Sat. noon-11pm, Sun. noon-9pm.

Olympic Carry Out, 3207 O St. NW (338-2478 or 337-1997), a block from Wisconsin Ave. Strictly carry-out and delivery, serving homemade Greek and "Mediterranean" specialties and subs. Clean; big portions, rapid service. *Gyros* and steak-and-cheese subs $3.30, falafel $2.75. Check for daily specials. Open Mon.-Sat. 11am-11pm, Sun. noon-10pm.

Vietnam-Georgetown Restaurant, 2934 M St. NW (337-4536), and **Viet Huong,** 2928 M St. NW (337-5588) at 30th St. The spicier Vietnam-Georgetown was here first and garners more adulatory reviews; Viet Huong is more intimate and slightly cheaper. Try *cha giú* (Vietnamese crispy egg rolls) and grilled chicken or beef on skewers. Lunch at V-G $5, dinner $7-11. Open Mon.-Thurs. 11am-11pm, Fri. 11am-midnight, Sat. noon-midnight, Sun. noon-11pm. Lunch at V.H. $4-6, dinner $6-11. Open Mon.-Fri. 11:30am-3pm and 5-10pm, Sat.-Sun. noon-11pm.

Sushi-Ko, 2309 Wisconsin Ave. NW (333-4187). Authentic no-frills Japanese food prepared before your eyes. Try the affordable *maki-sushi* or *temaki* (over 20 kinds to choose from) for under $5. Fish offerings include the customary trout, flounder, and tuna, as well as the more exotic *uzara* (with quail eggs). Order of sushi (two rolls per serving) $2-4.50. Open Tues.-Fri. noon-2:30pm, Mon.-Fri. 6-10:30pm; Sat. 5-10:30pm; Sun. 5-10pm.

Houston's, 1065 Wisconsin Ave. NW (338-7760). Perfect for meat-and-potato lovers. The hickory-grilled hamburgers ($6.25) are served with a slew of shoestring fries. You may need to bring the salads ($6.25-7.50) home in a dogie bag. Lines are long; walk around Georgetown while you wait. Open Sun.-Thurs. 11:15am-11pm, Fri.-Sat. 11:15am-1am.

Au Pied du Cochon/Aux Fruits de Mer, 1335 Wisconsin Ave. NW (333-5440 and 333-2333). Two sister restaurants, the first serving casual French fare such as salads and *crêpes,* the other serving cooked ocean critters. Come by for a late snack ($3-3.75) and a cappuccino ($2.45) or a *café au lait* ($1.25). The glass-enclosed café area lets you watch and be watched by passers-by. Open 24 hrs.

Thomas Sweet, 3214 P St. NW (337-0614), at Wisconsin Ave. The best ice cream in DC by a light-year, from $1.67. Open Mon.-Thurs. 9:30am-midnight, Fri.-Sat. 9:30am-1am, Sun. 11am-midnight. (Closing time might come a bit earlier after the summer.)

Dupont Circle

Lauriol Plaza, 1801 18th St. NW (387-0035). Authentic Mexican food, served on a charming patio by gracious waiters. Entrées cost *muchos dolares,* but a tender enchilada side dish ($2) and *chili con carne* appetizer ($4) could stuff any tummy. Open Sun.-Thurs. 11:30am-11pm, Fri.-Sat. 11:30am-midnight.

Food for Thought, 1738 Connecticut Ave. NW (797-1095), two blocks from Dupont Circle. Veggie-hippie-folknik mecca with good, healthful food in an ersatz 60s atmosphere. 10 different vegetable and fruit salads, plus sandwiches and daily hot specials. Local musicians strum in the evenings. Bulletin boards announce everything from rallies to beach parties to rides to L.A. Bike messenger hangout. Lunch $6-8, dinner $6-10. Open Mon. 11:30am-3pm and 5pm-12:30am, Tues.-Thurs. 11:30am-12:30am, Fri. 11:30am-2am, Sat. noon-1am, Sun. 5pm-12:30am.

Dante's, 1522 14th St. NW (667-7260) at Q. St. Near the Source and Studio theaters. Not to be missed after midnight, when punk rockers, actors, and their friends jam the place with hipness and hair. Teal and black décor complements heavenly-healthful pita sandwiches and devilish cheesecake (sandwiches $5-7, cheesecake $2.50). Try the delicious white pizza appetizer: melted provolone cheese on pita bread with Italian spices for $3.50. Don't come around here alone at night. Open Mon. 5pm-3am, Tues.-Thurs. 11:30am-3am, Fri. 11:30am-4am, Sat.-Sun. 5pm-4am.

Sala Thai, 21st and P St. NW (872-1144). Light Thai food served to many customers. Delicious crispy fish is affordable for lunch at $7. Open Mon.-Thurs. 11am-2:30pm and 5-10:30pm, Fri. 11am-2:30pm and 5-11pm, Sat. noon-11pm, Sun. 5-10:30pm.

Café Pettito, 1724 Connecticut Ave. NW (462-8771). Excellent Italian regional cooking in an understated atmosphere. Try the tempting antipasto table ($6) and the fried Calabrian pizza. Open daily 11:30am-midnight.

Kramerbooks & Afterwords Café, 1517 Connecticut Ave. NW (387-3825). Late-night sweets behind a very good bookshop. Exorbitant *nouvelle* entrées, but pies, cappuccinos and mousses ($3-4) are rich rewards for the literary life. Live music Fri.-Sun. after 10pm. Open Sun.-Thurs. 7:30am-11:45pm, Fri.-Sat. 24 hrs.

Shaw

Supreme soul food. The new Shaw-area Metro stops (14th and U and 7th and U) have made Shaw more accessible but have yet to revitalize the area; come during the day.

Ben's Chili Bowl, 1213 U St. NW (667-0909), at 13th St. Metro: U St./Cardozo. A venerable (30-yr.-old) neighborhood hangout. Spicy homemade chili—on a chili dog, served with onion, mustard, and potato chips ($1.85), on a half-smoke ($2.75), or on a quarter-lb. burger ($2.10). Diehards eat it plain: small bowl $1.90, large bowl $2.55. Open Mon.-Thurs. 6am-2am, Fri.-Sat. 6am-3am, Sun. noon-8pm.

Florida Avenue Grill, 1100 Florida Ave. NW, at 11th St. (265-1586). Small, enduring (since 1944) diner once fed black leaders and famous entertainers. Now their framed famed faces beam down on the hordes of locals who frequent the place. Awesome Southern-style food: breakfast with salmon cakes or spicy half-smoked sausage, eggs, grits, hotcakes, or southern biscuits $3-6. Lunch and dinner $5-9. Open Mon.-Sat. 11:30am-4pm.

Adelis, 2017 14th St. NW (332-6599). Lunchtime soul-food all-you-can-eat buffet ($7.50). This is straightforward old-fashioned delicious, featuring items like chicken, barbecue ribs, green beans, macaroni, chitlins, and watermelon. Add the salad bar and dessert and you'll burst right open. Open Mon.-Fri. 11:30am-4pm.

Adams-Morgan

The word is out. Adams-Morgan has justifiably become DC's preferred locale for budget dining. The action radiates from 18th, Columbia, and Calvert St. NW, uphill along Columbia or down 18th.

Mixtec, 1792 Columbia Rd. NW (332-1011). Popular, well-known Mexican restaurant. Bright rooms and wooden chairs. Their $3 specialty is *tacos al carbon*—two small tortillas filled with delicious beef, served with three kinds of garnish. Mind-bending chicken *mole*, too. Entrees $4.50-10. Open Sun.-Thurs. 11am-11:30pm, Fri.-Sat. 11am-12:30am.

Thai Taste, 2606 Connecticut Ave. NW (667-5115). DC's black-and-neon magnet for Thai food lovers. Try the fried beef with chili paste and coconut milk, then Thai iced coffee ($2). Dinner from $6. Open daily 11am-11pm.

El Pollo Primo, 2471 18th St. NW (232-5151), near Columbia Rd. By their awning shall ye know them. Second-story beige-and-brown rotisserie gives rise to moist, flavorful, tender, greaseless, and cheap chicken on a big grill behind the counter. 2-piece chicken dinner with tortillas, salsa, and 2 side orders $3.60, 3-piece dinner $4.50. Open Sun.-Thurs. 10:30am-9:30pm, Fri.-Sat. 10:30am-10:30pm.

Red Sea, 2463 18th St. NW (483-5000). The first of Adams-Morgan's famous Ethiopian restaurants; still among the best. Use the traditional pancake bread, *injera*, to eat spicy lamb, beef, chicken, and vegetable *wats* (stews). Lunch entrées $3.70-8; dinner slightly higher. Open daily 11:30am-midnight.

Calvert Café, 1967 Calvert St. NW (232-5431), right across the Duke Ellington Bridge. Metro: Woodley Park/Zoo. Look for the brown and gold tiles; although it looks boarded-up, this landmark has lasted 30 yrs. Huge, unadorned platters of Middle Eastern food. Appetizers $2-4.50; dinner entrées $6-8.50. Half a broiled chicken with Arabian rice and a salad $6. Shish kabob with rice and salad $8.50. Open daily 11:30am-11:30pm.

The Islander, 1762 Columbia Rd. NW (234-4955), above a shoe storage. A small Trinidadian and Caribbean restaurant. Curried goat $8.50, calypso chicken $8, *roti* (East Indian thin pancakes stuffed with vegetables and meat) are a bargain at $3.25-6. Platters $6.50-9.75. Open Mon. 5-10pm, Tues.-Thurs. noon-10pm, Fri.-Sat. noon-11pm.

Sights

Yeah, yeah. We *know* you're here to see the Capitol, the White House, and the Smithsonian. However, we also urge you to venture beyond the Mall and its obvious attractions. You may want to consider seeing the monuments after dark; it provides a romantic alternative to daytime heat and crowds.

Capitol Hill

The **U.S. Capitol** (House 225-3121; Senate 224-3121) may no longer be Washington's most beautiful building, but its scale and style still evoke the power of the republic. (Metro: Capitol South or Union Station.) The three-tiered **East Front** faces the Supreme Court. From Jackson (1829) to Carter (1977), most Presidents were inaugurated here; Reagan moved the ceremony to the newly fixed-up **West Front,** which overlooks the Mall. Nothing built in Washington can be taller than the tip of the Capitol's cast-iron dome. If there's light in the dome by night, Congress is still meeting. Inside the **East Portico,** statesmen from Lincoln to JFK have lain in state in the **Rotunda;** you can get a map from the tour desk here. (Free guided tours begin here daily every 20 min. 9am-3:45pm.) Ceremony and confusion reign downstairs in the **Crypt** area; most of the functioning rooms are upstairs. For a spectacle, but little insight, climb to the **House and Senate visitors galleries.** Americans should request a **gallery pass** (valid for the whole 2-yr. session of Congress) from the office of their Representative, Delegate, or Senator. Foreign nationals should ask the Office of the House Doorkeeper or the Senate Sergeant at Arms. In the House and Senate chambers (in separate wings of the Capitol), expect a few bored-looking officials ignoring the person gesticulating at the podium. The real business of Congress is conducted in committee hearings; check the *Washington Post*'s "Today in Congress" box. (Many are across the street in House or Senate offices; ride the Capitol Subway there, just as Congresspeople do.) The Senate Cafeteria, on the second (main) floor on the Senate side of the building, is open to the public; red lights and sirens warn of an imminent vote. (Capitol open daily 9am-8pm, Labor Day-Memorial Day daily 9am to 4:30pm.) For tours for visitors with disabilities and help from the Special Services Office in the Crypt call 224-4048 (TDD 224-4049).

The **Supreme Court,** One First St. NE (479-3000), across from the East Front of the Capitol, houses the nation's highest court. (Metro: Capitol South or Union Station.) Its nine justices have the final say on what the U.S. Constitution really means. Behind the red curtain as you enter is the chamber where the court meets. In session (Oct.-June), it hears oral arguments Monday through Wednesday from 10am to 3pm for two weeks each month. Show up early to sit down and listen or stand in line to hear five minutes of argument. The *Washington Post* can tell you if the court is sitting and what case is up. Brief **lectures** (July-Aug. 9:30am-3:30pm) cover history, operations, duties and architecture of the institution.

The **Library of Congress,** 1st St. SE (707-5000, events schedule 707-8000; Metro: Capitol South), between East Capitol and Independence Ave., is the world's largest, with 20 million books and three buildings: the 1897 Beaux-Arts Jefferson Building, which hogs the display space; the 1939 Adams Building, across 2nd St.; and the 1980 Madison Building, a marble slab across Independence Ave. The vast collection is open to anyone college age or above with a legitimate research purpose. Anybody can take the tour; it starts in the Madison Memorial Hall, in the Madison Building lobby. After a brief talk, the tour skedaddles through tunnels to the Jefferson Building when it's not closed for renovation. The octagonal Main Reading Room spreads out under a spectacular dome. (Most reading rooms open Mon.-Fri. 8:30am-9:30pm, Sat. 8:30am-5pm, Sun. 1-5pm.)

The **Folger Shakespeare Library,** 201 East Capitol St. SE (544-4600), houses the world's largest collection of Shakespeariana (largely closed to the public, alas). During the day, tourists can peek at the Great Hall exhibition gallery and the theater, which imitates the Elizabethan Inns of indoor theaters where Shakespeare's company performed. The Folger also sponsors high-quality readings, lectures, and concerts, such as PEN/Faulkner poetry and fiction readings and the Folger Consort, an early-music group. (Exhibits open Mon.-Sat. 10am-4pm.)

Two blocks north of the Capitol grounds, the trains run on time at **Union Station,** 50 Massachusetts Ave. NE (371-9441 for general information). Daniel Burnham's much-admired, monumental Beaux-Arts design took four strenuous years (1905-1908) to erect. Colonnades, archways, and huge domed ceilings equate Burnham's Washington with imperial Rome and the then-dominant train network with Roman roads. After remodelings and bizarre misuses, Union Station has become a spotless jewel in the crown of capitalism, with a food court and chic stores teeming with teen-aged mall-rats. (Shops open Mon.-Sat. 10am-9pm, Sun. noon-6pm.) Northeast of Union Station is the red-brick **Capital Children's Museum,** 800 3rd St. NE (675-4127). (Metro: Union Station.) Touch and feel every exhibit; grind corn to flour or drink fresh cocoa in the Mexican mock-up town and explore the room-size maze. (Open daily 10am-5pm. Admission $6, children under $2 free. Bring an adult.)

Three museums—and a destroyer you can board—stay shipshape amid the booms at the **Washington Navy Yard.** (Metro: Navy Yard.) Use caution in the neighborhood. Enter from the gate at 9th and M St. SE, and ask directions or look at the posted maps. The best of the lot, the **Navy Museum,** Building 76 (433-4882), should buoy anyone let down by the admire-but-don't-touch Air & Space Museum (see below). Climb inside the space capsule, play human cannonball inside huge ship guns, jam into a bathysphere used to explore the sea floor, or give orders on the bridge. (Open June-Aug. Mon.-Fri. 9am-5pm, Sat.-Sun. 10am-5pm; Sept.-May Mon.-Fri. 9am-4pm, Sat.-Sun. 10am-5pm.) The **USS Barry,** a decommissioned destroyer (no relation to the decommissioned mayor), opens its berths, control rooms, bridge, captain's quarters, and combat center daily from 10am to 5pm. The **Marine Corps Historical Museum,** Building 58 (433-3534), takes itself very seriously with guns, uniforms, swords and other corps memorabilia. (Open Mon.-Thurs. and Sat. 10am-4pm, Fri. 10am-8pm, Sun. noon-5pm; Sept.-May Mon.-Sat. 10am-4pm, Sun. noon-5pm.)

Museums on the Mall

The world's largest museum complex stretches out along the Mall. **Constitution Ave.** (on the north) and **Independence Ave.** (on the south) flank the gauntlet of museums. All Smithsonian museums are free and wheelchair-accessible; all offer written guides in French, German, Spanish, and Japanese, some in Chinese, Arabic, and Portuguese. All are open daily from 10am to 5:30pm, with extended summer hours for the larger museums; some close on winter weekends. Take *at least* three days to see the museums—they'd take a lifetime to "finish." (General phone 357-2700, TDD: 357-1729; tours, concerts, lectures, films 357-2020.) Info desks at the Castle and in museums give the *Smithsonian Guide for Disabled Visitors;* tourists with disabilities who call a day ahead can get additional assistance.

The **Mall,** the U.S. taxpayer-supported national backyard, is a sight in itself. Hundreds of natives and out-of-towners sunbathe and lounge, play frisbee, knock down their little brothers, fly a kite, or just get high. The **Smithsonian Castle,** 1000 Jefferson Dr. SW, holds no real exhibits, but has information desks, a thorough but tedious 20-minute movie, and founder James Smithson's body.

Though Henry Ford said "History is bunk," the **National Museum of American History,** 14th and Constitution Ave. NW, prefers to think that history is junk—several centuries of machines, textiles, photographs, vehicles, harmonicas, and uncategorizable Americana comprise the collection. Near the Mall entrance is the Foucault pendulum, which knocks over pegs to prove the Earth rotates. The original, national-anthem-inspiring Star Spangled Banner hangs behind the pendulum—they say you can see it every hour on the half hour, when the cover is lifted. "Field to Factory" illuminates Black migration from the segregated South to Northern cities during the early 1900s. The mechanically inclined will love the first floor, where galleries lavishly elucidate the history of electricity, trains, and power tools, topping it all off with an ice cream parlor and museum bookstore. (Open daily 10am-5:30pm; June-Aug. 9:30am-7:30pm.)

The golden-domed, neoclassical **Museum of Natural History,** built in 1911 at 10th and Constitution Ave., surveys the Earth and its inhabitants in two-and-a-half big, crowded floors of exhibits. On the Mall side, scoff at Uncle Beazley, the triceratops on the Mall who can't scoff back. Inside, the largest African elephant ever captured stands under dome-filtered sunshine in a hubbub of slack-jawed tourists. Huge dinosaur skeletons dwarf the nearby hallway. The Ancient Seas and Sea Life exhibits squeeze museumgoers under a blue whale and past a coral reef filled with live tropical critters. On the second floor, the sparkling tables of naturally occurring crystals make the final plush room of cut gems anticlimactic. The Insect Zoo pleases with an array of creepy-crawlies. (Museum open daily 10am-7:30pm; Sept.-June 9:30am-5:30pm.)

The **National Gallery of Art,** 6th and Constitution Ave. NW (737-4215), houses and hangs its world-class jumble of pre-1900 art in a domed marble temple designed by John Russell Pope, whose columns and stairs also accompany the National Archives and Jefferson Memorial. The West Building displays important works by Raphael, Rembrandt, Monet, and Bosch to name just a few; "The Greek Miracle," a landmark exhibition of classical sculpture from Greece of the 5th century BCE, is 1993's most important exhibit. "Garden courts" help to cure museum daze with fountains, ferns, sunlight, and benches. The museum's *pièce de résistance* is a hall of Dutch masters with a few of the world's 30-odd Vermeers. Postcards, art books, and high-class cafeteria fare are yours for the buying in the basement; if you must eat on the Mall, this is the place. Vocal, piano and chamber music (842-6941) accompany your espresso most Sundays from October to June at 7pm in the West Garden Court.

Completed amidst much fanfare and rejoicing in 1978, the **"East Wing"** of the National Gallery of Art, Constitution Ave., Pennsylvania Ave., and 4th St. NW, houses (and sometimes hides) the museum's plentiful 20th-century holdings. I. M. Pei's smooth marble gallery outlines high, interlocking triangles, glass-topped to flood the atrium with sunlight. Enter from the West Building via the moving underground walkway. An immense Calder mobile is the gallery's trademark; it recalls the knife-edge exterior of the building itself. From the atrium, head up the escalators and through three floors of temporary shows (not always 20th-century) and/or modern art. The East Building is constantly rearranging, closing, and remodeling parts of itself for temporary exhibits. Don't neglect the basement galleries. (Open Mon.-Sat. 10am-5pm, Sun. 11am-6pm, with extended summer hours.)

The **National Air and Space Museum,** on the south side of the Mall between 4th and 7th St. SW, is the world's most popular museum. (Metro: L'Enfant Plaza.) Thirty thousand people a day (in summer) scrutinize the dangling airplanes, the *Apollo XI* command module, 23 exhibit galleries, and the five-story movie screen. Among the hanging aerospace vehicles, the space-age atrium also holds a rock from the moon, worn smooth by a decade of tourists' fingertips. Air & Space's best exhibits are its biggest: actual planes and crafts from all eras of flight; the Wright brothers' biplane in the entrance gallery looks intimidated by all its younger kin. In the Sea-Air operations gallery (#203) you can (via computer) pilot a fighter, land on a carrier, and, probably, crash or sink. IMAX movies give spectators vertigo in the Langley Theater, home of the five-story movie screen. Buy tickets early, and stand in line a few minutes before the show starts. (Films 9:30am-6:45pm. Tickets $3.25, children, students, seniors $2 at the box office on the ground floor. Museum open daily 9:30am-7:30pm; Sept.-June 16 10am-5:30pm.)

If you're convinced art ended with Picasso, stay away from the **Hirshhorn Museum and Sculpture Garden,** 8th St. and Independence Ave. SW (357-2700). The four-story, slide-carousel-shaped brown building has outraged traditionalists since 1966. Each floor comprises two concentric circles: an outer ring of rooms and paintings, and an inner corridor of sculptures. The Hirshhorn's best shows are in art since 1960; no other museum in Washington even tries to keep up with their avant-garde paintings and mixed-media installations. The museum claims the world's most comprehensive set of 19th- and 20th-century Western sculpture. Striking works by Smith, Calder, Maillol, Rodin, and Giacometti ornament the Sculpture Garden across Jefferson Dr. The Hirshhorn runs three separate pseudo-weekly free film series, listed in their "Calendar" brochure. (Museum open daily 10am-5:30pm. Sculpture Garden open daily 7:30am-dusk. Tours 357-3235.)

Between the Smithsonian Castle and the Hirshhorn, the **Arts and Industries Building** is an exhibition of an older exhibition, the 1876 Centennial Exhibition of American technology in Philadelphia. Pause for the exterior—a polychromatic, multi-style chaos of gables, arches, rails, and bricks. Inside, furniture congregates near the Mall entrance; further back, heavy machinery will delight fans of steam power. Built in 1987, the **Arthur M. Sackler Gallery** and the **National Museum of African Art** hide their non-Western treasures underground, behind the Castle and below the beautiful Enid A. Haupt Garden, Independence Ave. and 10th St. SW. The Sackler (357-1300; TDD: 786-2734) showcases Sackler's extensive collection of art from China, South and Southeast Asia, and Persia. The Museum of African Art, 950 Independence Ave. SW (357-4600, TDD 357-4814), collects, catalogs, polishes, and shows off artifacts from Sub-Saharan Africa. Art objects include masks, textiles, ceremonial figures, and fascinating musical instruments, like a harp partly made of pangolin scales. (Open daily 10am-5:30pm. Call ahead for tour information.) The **Freer Gallery of Art,** on the Mall at Jefferson Dr. and 12th St. SW, will re-open in May 1993 with an underground link to the Sackler. It collects Asian or Asian-inspired art, like that of James McNeill Whistler.

South of the Mall

Exotic foliage from all continents and climates vegetates inside and outside the **U.S. Botanical Garden,** First St. and Maryland Ave. SW (225-4099). Cacti, bromeliads, and other odd-climate plants flourish indoors. Forty-minute guided tours begin at 10am and 2pm (call ahead; open June-Sept. daily 9am-8pm; Oct.-May daily 9am-5pm). The **Bureau of Engraving and Printing (The Mint),** 14th St. and C St. SW (662-2000), just south of the Washington Monument, offers continuous tours of the presses that annually print over $20 billion. Skip breakfast or expect a two-hour wait. (Open Mon.-Fri. 9am-2pm. Free.)

Memorials/West of the Mall

The **Washington Monument,** at Constitution Ave. and 16th St. NW, is a marble obelisk and a vertical altar to America's first president, where crowds sacrifice their sweat, time, and film to ascend, descend, and take the Monument's picture. (Metro: Smithsonian.) During the Civil War the half-finished tower was nicknamed the "Beef Depot Monument" for the cattle Army quartermasters herded on the grounds. The stairs were a famous (and strenuous) tourist exercise until the Park Service closed them years ago. The elevator line takes 45 minutes to circle the Monument. Tiny windows offer disappointing lookout points at the top—just think if you had to *climb* it. Persons with disabilities can bypass the long lines. (Monument open daily 8am-midnight; Sept.-March 9am-5pm. Free.)

Maya Ying Lin, who designed the **Vietnam Veterans Memorial** (south of Constitution Ave. at 22nd St. NW) called it "a rift in the earth." (Metro: Smithsonian or Foggy Bottom/GWU). While an undergraduate at Yale, Lin beat out 1400 contestants with her design. 58,132 Americans are known to have died in Vietnam, and the memorial's long black granite slabs bear each one's name. The names are arrayed in chronological order, starting as a sliver and culminating in a very moving gash. Families and veterans visit the memorial to ponder and mourn; many make rubbings of their loved ones' names from the walls. The outdoor memorial stays "open" 24 hrs. every day.

Anyone with a penny already knows what the **Lincoln Memorial** (at 23rd St. between Constitution and Independence) looks like; Henry Bacon's design copies the rectangular grandeur of Athens' Parthenon. (Metro: Smithsonian or Foggy Bottom.) A massive layer of stone atop the columns gives the building the watchful solemnity of a crypt. From these steps, black soprano Marian Anderson sang after she was barred from segregated Constitution Hall in 1939, and Martin Luther King, Jr. gave his "I Have a Dream" speech to the 1963 March on Washington. Daniel Chester French's seated Lincoln presides from the inside, keeping a silent vigil over protest marchers and Fourth of July fireworks. Read his Gettysburg address on the wall to the left. Spelunkers roam the caves under the memorial; call 425-6841 to try it yourself. Since it has no doors, the Memorial is open 24 hrs. (Free.) The **Reflecting Pool,** between the Washington and Lincoln Memorials, reflects Washington's obelisk in seven million gallons of water.

The **Jefferson Memorial's** rotunda pays tribute to T.J.'s own monument to himself: his Charlottesville home, Monticello. The raised hill around it offers generous views of the other monuments. A 19-ft. hollow bronze President Jefferson rules the rotunda. Interior walls quote from Jefferson's writings: the *Declaration of Independence,* the *Virginia Statue of Religious Freedom, Notes on Virginia,* and an 1815 letter. The *Declaration of Independence* extract contains 11 errors. The sentence around the top of the dome rebukes those who wrongly called T.J. an atheist. The Jefferson Memorial overlooks Washington's most popular man-made lake, the **Tidal Basin,** where pedal-boats ripple in and out of the Memorial's shadow and cherry blossoms gain fame every April. (Boat rental 479-2426; open daily 10am-7pm; $7 per hour.)

Downtown/North of the Mall

It's only proper that an architectural marvel should house the **National Building Museum,** which towers above F St. NW between 4th and 5th St. (Metro: Judiciary Square.) Montgomery Meigs's 1881 Italianate Pension Building remains one of Washington's best; the Great Hall, with its columns, busts, and fountain, could accommodate a 15-story building. "Washington: Symbol and City," the NBM's permanent exhibit, covers DC architecture, federal and local; there are rejected designs for the Washington Monument and the chance to design your own Capitol Hill rowhouse. (Museum open Mon.-Fri. 10am-4pm, Sat.-Sun. noon-4pm; tours Mon.-Fri. 12:30pm, Sat.-Sun. 12:30 and 1:30pm. Excellent access for persons with disabilities. Free.)

The **National Museum of American Art** and the **National Portrait Gallery** (357-2700) share a neoclassical edifice two blocks long (American Art entrance at 8th and G St.; Portrait Gallery entrance at 8th and F). The NMAA's surprisingly deserted corridors showcase major painters from 19th- and 20th-century America and an array of folk and ethnic art. DC janitor James Hampton stayed up nights in an unheated garage for 15 years to assemble the *Throne of the Third Heaven of the Nations' Millennium General Assembly,* to the right of the main museum entrance. Westerners Albert Bierstadt and Thomas Moran turn the second floor lobby into Yellowstone National Park. Head to the third floor for 20th-century work. (Open daily 10am-5:30pm; tours noon on weekdays, 2pm on weekends. Free.) The wide range of media, periods, styles and artists represented makes the National Portrait Gallery more like a museum of the American character. Ogle movie stars in the first floor's East Corridor, devoted to the performing arts. (Open daily 10am-5:30pm; tours at the Portrait Gallery Mon.-Fri. 10am-3pm, Sat.-Sun. 11am-2pm. Free.)

The United States' founding documents can still be found at the **National Archives,** 8th St. and Constitution Ave. NW. (General information 501-5000, guided tours 501-5205, library and research 501-5400. Metro: Archives/Navy Memorial.) Visitors line up to view the original *Declaration of Independence, U.S. Constitution,* and *Bill of Rights* in the central Rotunda. (Main exhibit area open April-Aug. 10am-9pm, Sept.-

Mar. 10am-5:30pm. Free.) The end of the go-go, right-wing 1980s hasn't fazed the **Federal Bureau of Investigation** (324-3000); today's FBI still hunts commies, druggies, and interstate felons with undiminished vigor. Lines form for the popular tour on the outdoor plaza of the beige-but-brutal, block-long J. Edgar Hoover Building (tour entrance from 10th St. NW at Pennsylvania Ave.). (Metro: Federal Triangle or Archives.) Real FBI agents sport walkie-talkies as they speed through gangster paraphernalia and mug shots of the nation's 10 most wanted criminals. The FBI's crack team of scientists will ignore you from behind plexiglass. At tour's end, a marksman shreds cardboard evildoers. (Tours Mon.-Fri 8:45am-4:15pm. Free.)

Abraham Lincoln was assassinated in 1865 at **Ford's Theatre** (426-6924), 511 10th St. NW. (Metro: Metro Center, 11th St. exit.) Recline in comfortable theater seats while guides narrate the assassination for you. (Open 9am-5pm daily; tours and talks given at a quarter past the hr., 9am-noon, then 2 and 5pm. Free.) Lincoln passed away at the **Petersen House** (426-6830), next door at 526 10th St. NW. Dotted white curtains and the bed where he died make visitors feel like a strangers at a wake. (Open daily 9am-5pm.) The **Old Post Office,** at Pennsylvania Ave. and 12th St. NW (523-5691), sheathes a shopping mall in architectural wonder. (Metro: Federal Triangle.) Its arched windows, conical turrets, and clock tower are a standing rebuke to its sleeker neighbors. Most visitors drop by for the food court. The tour meets at the glass elevators where food tables cluster; the view from the top may be DC's best. (Open mid-April to mid-Sept. Mon.-Fri. 8am-11pm; shops open Mon.-Sat. 10am-8pm, Sun. noon-6pm. Free.) The elegant **National Museum of Women in the Arts** (783-5000) hides inside an office building at 1250 New York Ave. NW. (Metro: Metro Center.) Traverse the balcony and ascend the spare, hidden staircase to the third floor, and you'll know you've made it: women artists have come into their own during the last hundred years, and the collection proves it with works by Georgia O'Keeffe, Isabel Bishop, Frida Kahlo, and Alma Thomas. (Open Mon.-Sat. 10am-5pm, Sun. noon-5pm. Requested donation $3, $2 for kids.)

White House Area/Foggy Bottom

President Bill and First Lady Hillary Clinton call it home; everyone else calls it the **White House,** 1600 Pennsylvania Ave. NW (456-7041, TDD 456-6213). (Metro: McPherson Square, Vermont Ave. exit.) With its simple columns and expansive lawns, the White House seems a compromise between patrician lavishness and democratic simplicity. The President's personal staff works in the West Wing; the First Lady's occupies the East Wing. You may tour a few rooms after obtaining a free ticket at the ticket booth on the **Ellipse,** the park south of the White House on Constitution Ave. between 15th and 18th St. NW. (Tours Tues.-Sat. 10am-noon; tickets distributed starting at 8am). Visitors with disabilities can go straight to the Pennsylvania Ave. entrance. After getting a ticket, you'll wait about two and a half hours. American citizens can arrange a better tour by writing their Congresspeople months ahead. Due south of the White House, the grass of the Ellipse fills with protests and tour groups.

Sometimes it's hard to tell the homeless, the political demonstrators, and the statues apart in **Lafayette Park,** across Pennsylvania Ave. from the White House. Clark Mills's stone-faced Andrew Jackson, lauded by Wallace Stevens, stands in the center of the park. The Marquis de Lafayette joined Jackson in 1891, on the southeast corner of the park. The **Old Executive Office Building,** on 17th St. and Penn. Ave. NW, amazes pedestrians with its gingerbread complexity.

At 17th St. and Penn. Ave. NW, the **Renwick Gallery** (357-1718 or 357-2700) fills its Second Empire Mansion with "American craft". (Metro: Farragut West.) But it's not just for macrame buffs: the first floor often shows constructions by important contemporary artists. Stare for hours at *Gamefish,* a sculpture made of sailfish parts, rhinestones, poker chips and badminton birdies. Wow. (Open daily 10am-5:30pm. Excellent handicapped access. Free.) Once housed in the Renwick's mansion, the **Corcoran Gallery** (628-3211) now exhibits in much larger, neoclassical quarters on 17th St. between E St. and New York Ave. NW. (Metro: Farragut West.) The Corcoran shows off American artists like portraitist John Singer Sargent and impressionist Mary Cassatt. Frederic Church's "Niagara Falls" drenches you just looking at it. The Gallery's first-floor temporary exhibits seek the cutting edge. Free jazz in the Hammer Auditorium every Wed. noon. (Open Tues.-Wed. and Fri.-Sun. 10am-5:30pm, Thurs. 10am-9pm. Suggested donation $3, students/seniors $1, families $5, under 12 free.)

The **Organization of American States,** at 17th St. and Constitution Ave. NW (458-3000; museum/gallery 458-6016), is a Latin American extravaganza. Sunlight hits the concrete patio and bakes the stone benches in the building's air-conditioned, greenerified center. The OAS meetings, held largely in Spanish, welcome tourists; they even have translation machines. (Call to ask when they're in session.) Tiffany chandeliers and coats of arms light up the Hall of the Americas upstairs. Outside, Xochipilli, whom Aztecs honored with hallucinogens and sacrifices, reclines in the Aztec Garden. (Open Tues.-Sat. 10am-5pm. Free.) The **Department of the Interior** (208-4743) covers a square area between C, D, 18th, and 19th St. NW. The National Park Service desk spews brochures about forests and outfitters. Sign in at the main entrance on 18th and C St. and walk down the hall to the park office. In the Interior Department's museum, across from the park office, stuffed moose heads welcome you to the "opening" of the West, while Ansel Adams photographs show the land unsullied. (Museum open Mon.-Fri. 8am-5pm. Free.) The **National Academy of Sciences,** at 21st and C St. NW (334-2000), displays scientific and medical exhibits. It's traditional to get your photo snapped in the lap of the statue of Einstein outside.

Perched above the Rock Creek Parkway, the white **John F. Kennedy Center for the Performing Arts** (tix and info 467-4600; TDD 416-8524; pedestrian entrance off 25th St. and New Hampshire Ave. NW) rises and glows like a marble sarcophagus. (Metro: Foggy Bottom-GWU, then walk away from downtown on H St. and turn left, i.e. south, onto New Hampshire Ave.) The late-60s Center boasts four stages and a film theater. The flag-decked Hall of States and Hall of Nations both lead to the Grand Foyer, longer than two football fields; a seven-ft.-high bronze bust of JFK stares up at 18 ponderous chandeliers. In the opulent, all-red Opera House, snowflake-shaped chandeliers from Austria require 7300 light bulbs. Dig the view of the Potomac from the roof. Disabled access. (Free. Open daily 10am-11pm. Free tours 10am-2pm.)

Georgetown

Georgetown is a college town and a posh real estate district, where ambassadors-in-training rub elbows with the Kissingers; it's a credit card baby's shopping nirvana; it's restaurant row-*cum*-clubland with no distinction between the two. Washington thinks it's pretty hip; Georgetown knows it is. Some of the townhouses between M St. and R St. have been subdivided and rented out to Georgetown University students, but others hide Warhols and Shaws in every bathroom. Georgetown also serves its university with all-night food and late-night record stores. The nearest Metro stop, Foggy Bottom/GWU, is eight long blocks from Georgetown's center at Wisconsin and M; trudge down Pennsylvania Ave. over the bridge. From Dupont Circle, just follow P St. East.

Dumbarton Oaks, 1703 32nd St. NW between R and S St. (recorded info. 338-8278, tour info 342-3212), includes two must-sees: the mansion-museum displays ancient art, and the terraced gardens are the best cheap date in town. The Byzantine Collection contains bronzes, ivories, and jewelry from the eponymous Empire. Phillip Johnson's 1963 gallery holds a collection of Aztec and Mayan carvings and tools. Save at least an hour for the Dumbarton Oaks Gardens, inside the estate. It's Eden. Numerous partitions and blocked sightlines create an atmosphere of romantic privacy. (Open daily April-Oct. 2-6pm, Nov.-March 2-5pm. Admission $2, seniors and children $1; seniors free each Wed.) (Collections open Tues.-Sun. 2-5pm. Free.)

When Archbishop John Carroll learned where the new capital would be built, he rushed to found **Georgetown University** (main entrance at 37th and O St.), the United States' oldest Catholic institution for higher learning. Students live, study, and party together in townhouses which line the streets near the university.

Retired from commercial use since the 1800s, the **Chesapeake & Ohio Canal** (301-299-3613) extends 185 mi. from Georgetown to Cumberland, Maryland; after Georgetown, the C&O changes from a polluted relic suitable for mutant-carp fishing to a clean waterway whose towpath accommodates strolling families and mountain-bikers. The towpath grows tiresome after a few miles of running, walking, or biking, in spite of long bridges, small waterfalls, and historical spots.

Dupont Circle & New Downtown

Dupont Circle used to be called Washington's most diverse neighborhood; then it turned expensive while Adams-Morgan turned cool. The Circle and its environs still cater to Washington's artsy, international, and gay communities. From the Dupont Circle Metro, head up Connecticut Ave. for shopping and dining, Massachusetts Ave. for embassies, northwest (between the two) for paintings and hills, east to the 14th St. theater district, or south to the bustling, charmless new downtown. Mass., Conn., and New Hampshire Ave. NW meet in **Dupont Circle** itself; a fountain accompanies the chess players, lunching office workers, and herds of spandexed bike messengers who populate the island. Dupont Circle's 25 art galleries cluster on R between 21st and 22nd St. NW. Massachusetts Ave. between Dupont and Observatory Circles is also called **Embassy Row.** Recognize an embassy by the national coat-of-arms or flag out front.

Turn left from Massachusetts Ave. to 21st St. to reach the **Phillips Collection,** 1600-1612 21st St. at Q St. NW (387-2151), the first museum of modern art in the U.S. and the classiest, most comfortable non-Smithsonian showplace in town. On the second floor, everyone stares at Auguste Renoir's *Luncheon of the Boating Party.* Van Goghs inhabit the second-floor atrium; flanking rooms display French works and semi-obscure Picassos. Downstairs, scan Richard Diebenkorn's paintings or meditate on Mark Rothko's haunting abstractions. Free chamber music and classical piano concerts sound off each Sunday from September to May at 5pm. (Open Mon.-Sat. 10am-5pm, Sun. noon-7pm. Tours Wed. and Sat. at 2pm. An admission fee of $5, students and seniors $2.50, is suggested on weekdays and required on weekends.)

Anderson House, 2118 Massachusetts Ave. NW (785-2040), retains the robber-baron decadence of Larz Anderson, who built it in 1902-5; in the two-story ballroom, visitors can marvel at marble and feel Anderson's gilt. The Society of the Cincinnati makes this mansion its home and museum. (Open Tues.-Sat. 1-4pm. Free.) Turn right from R St. onto 22nd St., then walk up the hill to enter the **Textile Museum,** 2320 S St. NW (667-0441), which houses two or three exhibits at a time of rare and/or intricate textiles; ethnographic displays alternate with individual artists. (Open Tues.-Sat. 10am-5pm, Sun. 1-5pm. Admission by contribution.) Flags stand by the **Islamic Center,** 2551 Massachusetts Ave. NW (332-8343), whose stunning designs stretch to the tips of its spired ceilings. No short dresses, sleevelessness (for women), or shorts (men or women) allowed inside. Prayers are held five times daily. (Open daily 10am-5pm. Donation requested.) **Second Story Books,** 20th and P St. NW (659-8884), runneth over with used books, records, free newspapers, and flyers. (Open daily 10am-10pm.) **Lambda Rising,** 1625 Connecticut Ave. NW (462-6969), brims with gay and lesbian literature. (Open daily 10am-midnight.)

Past M St. on 17th St. NW, the **National Geographic Explorer's Hall** conquers the first floor of its black-and-white pin-striped building (857-7588 or 857-7689; N.G. Society 857-7000; Metro: Farragut North). There's a short film, a globe bigger than you are, and changing exhibits, often by *National Geographic* magazine's photographers. (Open Mon.-Sat. 9am-5pm, Sun. 10am-5pm. Wheelchair access.) Damn the crowds and picnic to the summer sounds of flute duets and jazz sax players in **Farragut Square,** three blocks south of Connecticut Ave. on 17th St. between Eye and K St. NW.

Elsewhere

The torch of hipness passed to the **Adams-Morgan** area in the late 80s, when cool kids and the cool at heart, mostly white-skinned, arrived alongside Mexican and Salvadoran immigrants. (The ranks of hipsters may dwindle after last May's two-day riot.) A wreath of awesome ethnic food circles 18th, Columbia, and Calvert St. NW. (From the Woodley Park/Zoo Metro, walk to Calvert St., turn left, and hoof east.) Don't go in search of a specific establishment; do go to wander around. It's a menudo of Hispanic,

Caribbean, and hip/upscale cultures any city would envy. Walk south along 18th or east along Columbia to soak in the flavor and eat well. If you stay west of 16th St. (and, at night, walk with a friend), safety should require only common sense.

The randy giant pandas keep the crowds titillated at the **National Zoological Park** (673-4800 or 673-4717). The Zoo spreads out east from Connecticut Ave. into Rock Creek Park, a few blocks uphill from Calvert St. NW and the Woodley Park/Zoo Metro; follow the crowds to the entrance at 3000 Connecticut Ave. NW. Gifts from Chinese premier Mao Tse-Tung to U.S. President Nixon, the pandas have their own concrete manger, their own keepers, and even their own panda t-shirts. Walk over water in the new wetlands exhibit, lie down near the lions, or play St. Francis by strolling through the skyscraper-size bird cage. The Zoo enshrines its captives in environments they enjoy; some get their own wooded islands. **Olmsted Walk** (red elephant feet) links land-animal houses, while **Valley Trail** (blue bird tracks) connects the bird and sealife exhibits. Invertebrates (starfish and urchins and such) get their own house. Both trails are wheelchair-accessible. (Grounds open daily 8am-8pm; Oct. 16-April 14 8am-6pm. Buildings open daily 9am-6pm; Sept. 16-April, 9am-4:30pm. Free.)

The **Cathedral Church of Saint Peter and Saint Paul,** also called the **Washington National Cathedral,** at Massachusetts and Wisconsin Ave. NW (537-6207), took over 80 years (1909-90) to build, though the interior has been in use for decades. (Metro: Tenleytown, then take the 30, 32, 34 or 36 bus toward Georgetown; or walk up Cathedral Ave. from the equidistant Woodley Park/ Zoo Metro.) Rev. Martin Luther King, Jr. preached his last Sunday sermon from the Canterbury pulpit; more recently, Archbishop Desmond Tutu spoke here. Ride the elevator (near the main doors of the west entrance) to the Pilgrim Observation Gallery; you won't see pilgrims, but you will see Washington from the highest vantage point in the city. The Bishop's Garden near the South Transept resembles a medieval walled garden. (Open daily until dusk; Cathedral open daily Sept.-April 10am-4:30pm, May-Aug. 10am-9pm; free. Call about wheelchair access.)

The **National Arboretum,** 24th and R St. NE (544-8733), is the U.S.'s living library of trees and flowers, big enough for 10 mi. of roads to criss-cross. Experts go berserk over the arboretum's world-class stock of *bonsai* (dwarf trees) and *pnjing* (potted plants, rocks, figurines, and pagodas). Azaleas and azalea-watchers clog the place every spring. Drive to the arboretum if you can; the surrounding area is somewhat dangerous. (Open Mon.-Fri. 8am-5pm, Sat.-Sun. 10am-5pm; *bonsais* open 10am-3:30pm. Free.)

The 24-year-old **Anacostia Museum,** 1901 Fort Place SE (287-3369, Sat.-Sun. 357-2700), run by the Smithsonian, focuses on African-American history and culture. Driving, take Martin Luther King, Jr. Ave. SE to Morris Rd.; call for complex bus directions. (Open daily 10am-5pm. Wheelchair access.) Cedar Hill, the **Frederick Douglass Home,** 1411 W St. SE (426-5960), was the final residence of former slave-*cum*-abolitionist statesman, orator, and autobiographer Frederick Douglass. Douglass must have enjoyed the view from his hilltop. House tours hourly from 9am to 4pm; begin with a movie, then walk through the house. (Open daily 9am-5pm; Oct.-April 9am-4pm. Free.)

The silence of **Arlington National Cemetery** honors those who sacrificed their lives in war. (Metro: Arlington Cemetery.) 612 acres of rolling hills and tree-lined avenues hold the bodies of U.S. military veterans, from five-star generals to unknown soldiers. Before you enter the main gate, go to the Visitors Center on the left for maps. The Kennedy Gravesites hold both President John F. Kennedy and his brother, Robert F. Kennedy. An Eternal Flame, lit by JFK's widow at his funeral, flickers above his simple memorial stone. In the Tomb of the Unknowns, unidentified soldiers from World Wars I and II, the Korean War, and the Vietnam War lie under the white marble sarcophagus. (Cemetery open April-Sept., 8am-7pm; Oct.-March, 8am-5pm. Free.) Robert E. Lee once owned most of the Cemetery grounds; when he moved south, Union troops took over his mansion, **Arlington House**—now an "historic home" attraction. Enter the pastel-peach mansion at the front door, and pick up a "self-guided tour" sheet from one of the women in antebellum costume. If you continue down Custis Walk in front of Arlington House and out through Weitzel Gate, you can walk to the **Iwo Jima**

Memorial, based on Joe Rosenthal's Pulitzer Prize-winning photograph of six Marines straining to raise the U.S. flag on Iwo Jima's Mount Suribachi. Military band concerts and parades take place here summer Tuesdays from 7 to 8:30pm.

History sleeps with George Washington at his estate, **Mount Vernon** (703-780-2000), where the tours, exhibits, and restorations can seem staid and worshipful even by Virginian standards. Prussian blue and vivid green walls rebuke with their original hues, and most of the furniture was genuinely the General's. Look for the key to the Bastille. The tour ends downstairs in Washington's study, pantry, and kitchen. A gravel path leads to Washington's tomb; more interesting is the slave burial ground, which now includes a memorial. The **Mount Vernon Inn** serves a genuine lunch. Try the distinctive peanut and chestnut soup ($1.75). (Open Mon-Sat. 11am-3:30pm and 5-9pm, Sun. 11:30am-4pm.) To drive to Mount Vernon, take the Beltway (I-495) to the George Washington Parkway on the Virginia side and follow the parkway to Mount Vernon; parking is free for four hours, more or less. If you're *à pied*, Metro to Huntington on the Blue/Yellow line and catch the 11P Metrobus. There's no air-conditioning, and it's very crowded; in July or August, show up on a weekday morning. (Open daily 9am-5pm; Nov.-Feb. 9am-4pm; admission $7, over 61 $6, ages 6-11 $3.)

Entertainment and Nightlife

At 25th St. and New Hampshire Ave. NW, the **Kennedy Center's** (416-8000) performing-arts spaces include two theaters—the Terrace Theater and the Theater Lab. The KenCen also houses the well-respected **National Symphony Orchestra,** the **Washington Opera** (416-7890), and the **Washington Ballet.** Though tickets get expensive (many are $10-50, but they can get up to $450), all Kennedy Center productions offer half-price tickets before the start of an event and on the day of performance to students, seniors, military personnel, persons with disabilities, and those who can show they can't afford the tickets; call 416-8340. Chamber music in the Kennedy Center, though a smaller deal, is more often cheap or free, especially during December. For free events, try the Office of Cultural Diversity (416-8090). The **American College Theater Festival,** April 20 to 29, houses free performances of top college productions. The excellent **American Film Institute** (828-4000), at the Kennedy Center, shows classic and avant-garde films, usually two per night.

Arena Stage, at 6th and Maine Ave. SW (488-3300), is often called the best regional (non-New York) theater company in America. The 42-year-old theater has two stages for new and used plays, plus the Old Vat Room for smaller, more experimental performances. (Tickets $19-37; students 35% off, seniors 15% off, discounts do not apply on Sat. evenings; half-price tickets usually available 1½ hrs. before start of show.) The prestigious **Shakespeare Theater at the Folger** (box office 393-2700) puts on (mostly) Shakespeare plays. Call—preferably months in advance—for ticket prices, performance times, and student/senior discounts. Standing room tickets (currently $10) are available two hours before each performance. It has wheelchair access, but give 24 hrs. notice. Thespians thrive in Washington's **14th St. theater district,** where tiny repertory companies explore and experiment with truly enjoyable results. *City Paper* provides very good coverage of this scene. **Woolly Mammoth,** 1401 Church St. (393-3939), **Studio Theater,** 1333 P St. NW (332-3300), and the **Source Theater,** 1835 14th St. NW (462-1073), dwell in a borderline dangerous neighborhood east of Dupont Circle. (Tickets from $15; students and seniors 25% off at W.M., $3 off at Studio, from $13 at Source. $10 "stampede seat" at W.M. 1 hr. before curtain.) **The Dance Place,** 3225 8th St. NE (269-2600), leaps with innovative and/or ethnic dance, performance art, and/or music nearly every week. (Regular performances $8-10, kids around $4.) The **National Theatre,** 1321 Pennsylvania Ave. NW (628-6161), often hosts visitors from Broadway, with ticket prices to match. **TICKETplace** (842-5387), on the F St. plaza between 12th and 13th St. NW, sells discount day-of-show tickets for theater, music, dance, and special events on a walk-up basis (tix available Tues.-Fri. noon-4pm, Sat. 11am-5pm).

The **Library of Congress,** 1st St. SE (concert line 707-5502), sponsors concerts in the Coolidge Auditorium, one of the finest chamber music performance spaces in the world. The **Phillips Collection** (387-2151) has a similar, but less prestigious, program, and the Corcoran Gallery (see Sights; White House/Foggy Bottom) sponsors a free lunchtime summer jazz series. The **National Symphony Orchestra** gives free concerts on the west lawn of the Capitol on Memorial Day, the Fourth of July, and Labor Day. **U.S. Military Bands** perform for free in and around the Mall every summer evening Memorial Day through Labor Day at 8pm. (Army Band: 703-696-3399. Marine Band: 433-4011. Navy Band: 433-2525. Air Force Band: 767-5658.)

DC's punk scene is, or was, one of the nation's finest. Charismatic mid-80s bands like Minor Threat and Rites of Spring fused crunchy guitar sounds and honest teen angst with a no-drugs, be-responsible attitude called "straightedge"; today Fugazi and Tsunami, among others, keep the punk-rock flame. To demystify local bands, see *City Paper.* The leading venue is **9:30 club**, but many of the best shows are all-ages (and fairly safe) gatherings in churches, rented halls, or outdoors at **Fort Reno Park,** Chesapeake and Belt St. NW above Wisconsin Ave. (282-0018 or 619-7225, late June-late August. Metro: Tenley Circle.) DC's African-American scenes originated the propulsive dance music called go-go. Flagship bands include Chuck Brown's, Rare Essence, and EU (of "Da Butt" fame). But most regular venues are hard to reach and may be unsafe. Look for posters and outdoor concerts (and see Annual Events).

George Washington University sponsors shows in **Lisner Auditorium** (301-460-7918), 21st and H St. NW. Lisner hosts plays and rock concerts by well-known but "alternative" acts (like Billy Bragg); expect tickets below $20. On summer Saturdays and Sundays, jazz and R&B shows occupy the outdoor, 4200-seat **Carter-Barron Amphitheater,** set into Rock Creek Park up 16th St. and Colorado Ave. NW. (426-0486, tickets around $13.50). These venues also sell tickets conveniently but expensively through Ticketron (432-7328), whose outlets exact a several-dollar service charge.

Georgetown at night is Washington on the prowl; everyone is looking for some place, something, or somebody. Early in the evening, the streets, not the bars and clubs, are the liveliest part. Throngs of students, interns, and young professionals share sidewalks with musicians, some very talented, playing anything from alto sax to upended trash cans. Don't neglect non-alcoholic nighttime offerings: late-night ice cream at Thomas Sweet, all-night French desserts at Au Pied du Cochon (see Food), or brilliant foreign movies. The **Biograph,** 2819 M St. NW (333-2696), excels at night with first-run independents, foreign films, and classics. Bring all the food you want inside. (Admission $5, seniors and children $2.50. Wheelchair access.) The **Key Theatre,** 1222 Wisconsin Ave. (333-5100), shows first-run art films every critic raves about. (Admission $6.50, most matinees $3.50.)

Jazz

Blues Alley, 1073 Rear Wisconsin Ave. NW (337-4141 or 337-4142), in an actual alley, below M St. Kool jazz in an intimate supper club dedicated to the art: Dizzie Gillespie chairs its music society. Big names (like Wynton Marsalis) demand pricey tix ($13-30). $7 food-or-drink minimum. Snacks ($2-9) served after 9:30pm. Dress for the occasion: some don tuxes on big nights. Call or pick up a 3-month schedule.

One Step Down, 2517 Pennsylvania Ave. (331-8863), near M St. More casual and less expensive than Blues Alley. Local jazz Sun., Mon., and Thurs.; out-of-town talent Fri.-Sat. Free jam sessions Sat.-Sun. 3:30-7:30pm. Cover $5 for local bands and $8.50-17 for out-of-towners. Usually min. food or drink required. Beers from $3, sandwiches $3.50-6. Happy hour Mon.-Fri. 3-7pm (beer 90¢, $4.50 pitcher). Open Mon-Fri. 10:30am-2am, Sat.-Sun. noon-3am.

Rock, Punk, Folk, Reggae, R&B

9:30 club, 930 F St. NW (393-0930 or 638-2008). Metro: Metro Center. Hot new "alternative/progressive" rock bands. $3 for 3 local bands; $7-14 for national acts, which often sell out weeks ahead (box office Mon.-Fri. 1pm-midnight). Under 21 admitted and hand-stamped. Free happy hour video cabaret Fri. from 4pm.

The Bayou, 3135 K St. NW (333-2897), under the Whitehurst Freeway in Georgetown. Bands on their way in and bands on their way out, with a rough 'n' ready crowd that loves them all. Bigger acts on weeknights; metal Fri. Some shows 18-plus. Opening act 9:30pm Mon.-Thurs. and Sun., after 10pm Fri. and Sat. Cover $3-20. Open Sun.-Thurs. 8pm-1:30am, Fri.-Sat. 8pm-2:30am.

Kilimanjaro, 1724 California St. NW (328-3839). Dimly lit, big-deal club for international music—African, Latin, and Caribbean groups, ju-ju, reggae, and salsa DJs, with Latin music each Sun. Every Wed. His Go-go-ness Chuck Brown and the Soul Searchers play. Fair Caribbean food. No sneakers, shorts, sweats, torn jeans, or tank tops. No cover Mon.-Wed., $5 cover Thurs. and Sun., $10 cover Fri. and Sat. Club open Mon.-Thurs. 5pm-2am, Fri.-Sat. 5pm-4am. Happy hour Mon.-Fri. 5-8pm.

The Birchmere, 3901 Mt. Vernon Ave. (703-549-5919). This low-key club features folk and bluegrass performed by live local and national acts from Mary Chapin Carpenter to NRBQ. Thurs. the bluegrass band Seldom Scene plays. There's a show almost every night; call and reserve tickets.

Dance Clubs, Comedy Clubs, Bars, Places to Be

Café Heaven and **Café Hell,** 2327 18th St. NW, in Adams-Morgan (667-HELL). Hell's downstairs, Heaven's upstairs. Heaven looks rather like an old townhouse (who woulda thunk it?), but the dance floor throbs to the drum machines of the angels; its back patio is crowded and quieter. If someone you hit on tells you to go to Hell, you'll find it has funky gold tables, loud music, and backlit masks. No cover charge unless a band is playing. Beers from $3; half price happy hour (6:30-8:30pm in Hell). Dancing starts 9pm. Open Sun.-Thurs. 6:30pm-2am, Fri.-Sat. 6:30pm-3am.

Fifth Colvmn, 915 F St. NW (393-3632). Metro: Gallery Place. Evro-crowd brings seriovs disco to the trendy 90s. Splashy "vnderwater" décor in a converted bank, with fish tanks, dizzying films, and lights. Hovse mvsic shakes the basement; qvieter bar vpstairs. Mon. is "alternative" mvsic; Svn. is gay night. Thvrs. is really crowded. If too crowded, try the less artsy, less popvlar **The Vavlt,** 911 F St. (347-8079). Fifth Colvmn open daily 10pm-whenever; no cover Mon. and Tves., $6 cover Wed. and Svn., $8 Thvrs. and Sat., $5 Fri. before midnight, $7 after.

15 Minutes, 1030 15th St. NW (408-1855). Metro: Farragut West. Dark, neon fish-scattered caverns get wilder as the night goes on. Mostly-bar on weekdays; mostly-dance club on weekends; blues, jazz, and/or punk evenings. Always 21-plus; young crowd. Wed. is inscrutable "Sybil" night, except when it's Cyberpunk night. Open Mon.-Fri. 4:30pm-2am, Sat. 9pm-3am. $6 cover on weekends.

Comedy Café, 1520 K St. NW (638-JOKE). Metro: Farragut North or McPherson Square. Stand-up comedy; some big names. Shows Fri. 8:30pm and 10:30pm, Sat. 7pm, 9pm, and 11pm. Open mike Thurs. 8:30pm. Beware of strip joint downstairs. Cover $5.

The Tombs, 1226 36th St. NW (337-6668), corner of Prospect St., in Georgetown. Georgetown students scarf burgers and beer. Justly crowded at night. Sunday's hopping dance nights $3 at the door; no cover elsewhen. Dollar drafts; $6 pitchers. Open Mon.-Sat. 11am-2am, Sun. 10am-2am.

Brickskeller, 1523 22nd St. NW (293-1885). Metro: Dupont Circle. 500+ beers "from Aass to Zywiece." Open Mon.-Thurs. 11:30am-2am, Fri. 11:30am-2:30am, Sat. 6pm-2:30am, Sun. 6pm-1:30am.

The Front Page, 1333 New Hampshire Ave. NW (296-6500). Metro: Dupont Circle. Well-known among the intern crowd for its generous Thurs. happy hours (5-7pm). Open daily 11:30am-1:30am.

Badlands, 1415 22nd St. NW (296-0505), off P St. Metro: Dupont Circle. A predominantly white and older crowd rocks to the beat of pop dance music and some house. Cover: Sun. and Tues, $1, Thurs. $3, Fri.-Sat. $5. Open Sun-Thurs. 9pm-1:45am, Fri. 8pm-2:45am, Sat. 9pm-2:45am.

J.R.'s, 1519 17th St. NW (328-0090). Metro: Dupont Circle. An upscale, yet down-home brick and varnished wood bar, with wood floors, stained glass windows, and a DJ in a choir stall overlooking the tank of guppies (gay urban professionals). Open Sun.-Thurs. 11am-2am, Fri. and Sat. 11am-3pm.

Cities, 2424 18th St. NW, in Adams-Morgan (328-7194), and **IKON** (483-2882), on the 2nd floor. Cities stays hip by changing every 8 months to mimic a different city; we're still waiting for Akron, OH. (Appetizers $3.50-6; entrées $8.50-15). IKON would never think of changing--gabled ceiling, purple techno-lights, and a bar with view-from-the-'copter-style full-length windows. Beer from $3.75. Cover Wed.-Thurs. $7, Fri.-Sat. $8. Cities open Mon.-Thurs. 5pm-2am, Fri.-Sat. 5pm-3am, Sun. 11am-2am. IKON open Wed.-Thurs. 9:30pm-2am, Fri.-Sat. 9:30pm-4am.

Annual Events

Chinese New Year Parade, mid-Feb., down H St. NW between 5th and 8th St. Metro: Gallery Place. Firecrackers, lions, drums, and dragons make the normally tame streets of Chinatown—all six of them—explode with delight. Free.

Bach Marathon, March 21, at Chevy Chase Presbyterian Church, 1 Chevy Chase Circle NW (363-2202). For J.S. (Papa) Bach's birthday, 10 organists play JSB's works on the church's massive pipe organ. Take an "L" bus up Connecticut Ave. from the Van Ness or Cleveland Park Metro. Refreshments. 1-7pm. Free.

Smithsonian Kite Festival, March 27 (357-3244). Go fly a kite or watch designers of all ages at the Washington Monument grounds compete for prizes and trophies from 10am-4pm. Free.

"Save the Children" Festival/Marvin Gaye Day, April 25 (678-0503). Jazz, gospel, and go-go music, food, and festing is "what's goin' on" in the outdoor downtown mall on F St. NW between 7th and 9th St., behind the National Museum of American Art.

National Cherry Blossom Festival, April 5-12 (737-2599). All over town; check the *Washington Post.* Official Washington goes bonkers over the pretty, white Japanese blossoms. Expensive tickets (728-1135) for the April 11 parade; other events (some free) include fireworks, free concerts in parks, and a marathon.

Shakespeare's Birthday Celebration, April 24, at the Folger Shakespeare Library. Exhibits, plays, Elizabethan music, food, and children's events. The Bard's actual birthday is April 23. 11am-4pm. Free.

Malcolm X Day, May 22, in Anacostia Park along the Anacostia River in SE (fax: 543-1649). A daylong festival honoring slain black leader Malcolm X. Food, speakers, 3 tents of exhibits, gospel, African, Caribbean, blues, and go-go music; premier go-goists E.U. dropped by last year. Noon-7pm. Free.

Memorial Day Ceremonies at Arlington Cemetery, May 25 (475-0856). Wreaths at Kennedy tomb and Tomb of the Unknown Soldier; services in Memorial Amphitheater. The President will talk. Also at the **Vietnam Veterans Memorial** (619-7222) 11am, in similar solemnity, but Clintonless. Both free.

Gay Pride Day, (298-0970; call for the exact date). Big march through downtown for gay and lesbian consciousness and rights. Starts at 16th and W St. NW; ends in a festival at Francis School, at 25th St. Festival entrance $5 on the day, advance purchase at Blockbuster Video Dupont Circle $3.

Bloomsday Marathon *Ulysses* Reading, June 15-16, at Kelly's "The Irish Times" pub (see Food). Annual read-through of Joyce's greatest novel draws crowds of literary and/or Irish notables. Starts around 11am June 15. Free.

Festival of American Folklife, June 25-29 and July 2-5, on the Mall (357-2700). Huge Smithsonian-run fair demonstrates the crafts, customs, food and music of selected states, territories, and/or foreign countries to over a million visitors, with imported musicians, performers, and craftspeople. Free.

Fourth of July (Independence Day). A daylong party begins with an old-fashioned Fourth of July parade (789-7000), along Constitution to 17th St. NW. Up Pennsylvania Ave. is the **DC Free Jazz Festival** (783-0360), 1-8pm in the Freedom Plaza park between 13th and 14th St. NW. The **National Symphony** (416-8100) plays patriotic music on the Capitol's West Lawn from 8pm, but if you sit there you won't get a good view of the 9:15pm fireworks, best from the Washington Monument grounds. Arrive by 6:30pm, and face west (towards the Lincoln Memorial).

Bastille Day Waiters' Race, July 14, starting at Pennsylvania Ave. and 20th St. NW. Waiters carry champagne glasses on trays and demonstrate their juggling ability. Dominique's Restaurant (452-1132) sponsors. Noon-4pm. Free.

Latin American Festival, July, on the Washington Monument grounds (724-4091; call for exact date). Free food, music, dance and theater from 40 Latin American nations.

U.S. Army Band's *1812 Overture*, August, on the Washington Monument grounds (703-696-3399; call for exact date). Actually Tchaikovsky's *1812 Overture*, but the Army Band (and a Salute Gun Platoon) performs the work. 8pm. Free.

National Frisbee Festival, Labor Day weekend, Sept. 3-5, on the Mall near the Air and Space Museum (301-645-5043). The largest non-competitive frisbee festival in the U.S., with frisbee studs and disc-catching dogs. Free.

African Cultural Festival, Sept. 19, at Freedom Plaza, 14th St. and Pennsylvania Ave. NW (667-5775). African cooking, sounds, movement and stuff for sale. Noon-7pm. Free.

DC Blues Festival, early Sept., in Anacostia Park, across the eponymous river in SE (724-4091 or 301-483-0871; call for exact date). Top blues people twang, wail, and moan. Free.

Kennedy Center Open House, mid-Sept. (416-8000). A 1-day hodgepodge of classical, jazz, folk and ethnic music, dance, drama and film from DC performers including members of the National Symphony Orchestra. Free.

Veteran's Day Ceremonies, Nov. 11, around Arlington Cemetery (475-0843). Solemn ceremony with military bands in the Memorial Amphitheater. The President lays a wreath at the Tomb of the Unknown Soldier. From 11am; free. Vietnam Memorial also holds ceremonies (619-7222; free).

Kennedy Center Holiday Celebration, throughout December (416-8000). Free musical events from Dec. 1 on: classical chamber, choral, cello and "Tuba-Christmas" concerts, gospel concert (ticket giveaway weeks in advance), and popular sing-along to Handel's *Messiah*, for which classical music groupies stand in line all day to get tickets.

National Christmas Tree Lighting/Pageant of Peace, Dec. 16-Jan. 1, on the Ellipse (619-7222). The President switches on a Christmas tree, a Hanukkah Menorah, and other electrical objects at 5:30pm on Dec. 10; choral music, a Nativity scene, a burning yule log and lit-up trees until the New Year. Free.

Washington National Cathedral Christmas Celebration and Services, Dec. 24-25 (536-6200). Daytime Christmas carols and choral music, but the nighttime service is more famous. Dec. 24 pageant 4pm, service 10pm. Dec. 25 service 9am. Free.

New Year's Eve Celebration at the Old Post Office Pavilion, Dec. 31 (289-4224). Crowded, festive outdoor and indoor party emulates NYC's Times Square—complete with the pickpockets. Giant Love Stamp drops at midnight. Free.

The South

Surprise! Surprise! Southerners *do* speak proper English, wear shoes, sport names other than Billy Bob and Mary Lou, and do not necessarily have wild cows named Bessy roaming around in their backyards. Contrary to the image of the South as a land hopelessly anchored to the Civil War era, life on this side of the Mason-Dixon line is civilized, modern, and dynamic in fast-paced cities such as Atlanta, Nashville, Little Rock, and New Orleans. Southern metropoli balance ubiquitous small towns where story-book hospitality and laid-back, *carpe diem* philosophies truly exist. The pace of the rural South may seem slow, but for those who wait, Southern hospitality can be wonderfully gracious. Folks are often more willing to go out of their way to help a stranger than are residents of Northern states.

This region's history and culture, a mélange of Anglo, African, French, and Spanish, are reflected in its architecture, cuisine, geography, language, and people. The Greek Revival style sculpted antebellum homes with high ceilings, floor-to-ceiling windows, and long hallways that extend the length of the house in order to coax a cool breeze through to weaken the oppressive, sultry heat. Although sweat and hard work still revolve around farmwork and the capricious seasons, regional crops such as cotton, soybeans, and tobacco today share a lucrative position with industries that produce everything from petrochemicals to Bibles. These southern lands produce fruits appealing to the tourist as well; this is one of the most beautiful parts of the country, boasting the Ozark Mountain rivers and hollows, the Great Smokies, and the Cajun culture of coastal Louisiana.

Alabama

The "Heart of Dixie" has matured since the 1960s and 1970s when Governor George Wallace fought a vicious campaign opposing African-American advancement. During decades of internal racial strife, Alabama was the home to bigotry but also to dynamic Civil Rights leaders like Reverend Dr. Martin Luther King, Jr., whose amazing patience and fortitude helped spawn the first real changes in race relations.

Today, Alabama's larger cities attract a cosmopolitan population as art museums, concerts, and ethnic restaurants have appeared. A coastal city, Mobile has become one of the busiest ports in the nation. Though plantation estates endure throughout the countryside, King Cotton now shares his reign with mineral ores and one of the largest beds of white marble in the world. Home to both the University of Alabama, renowned for its pioneering work in heart surgery, and Tuskegee University, founded by Booker T. Washington, Alabama has also become an important educational center. From a painful past, Alabama emerges as an influential force which preserves Southern folklore and idiosyncrasies while making great strides to modify and innovate. Alabama's progress in developing its economy and improving race relations reflects the defiant strength of its motto: *Audemus jura nostra*; we dare defend our rights.

Practical Information

Capital: Montgomery.

Alabama Bureau of Tourism and Travel, 532 S. Perry St. (242-4169; 800-252-2262 outside AL). Open Mon.-Fri. 8am-5pm. **Travel Council,** 600 Adams Ave. #254, Montgomery 36104 (271-0050). **Division of Parks,** 64 N. Union St., Montgomery 36130 (800-252-7275).

Time Zone: Central (1 hr. behind Eastern). **Postal Abbreviation:** AL

Sales Tax: 4%.

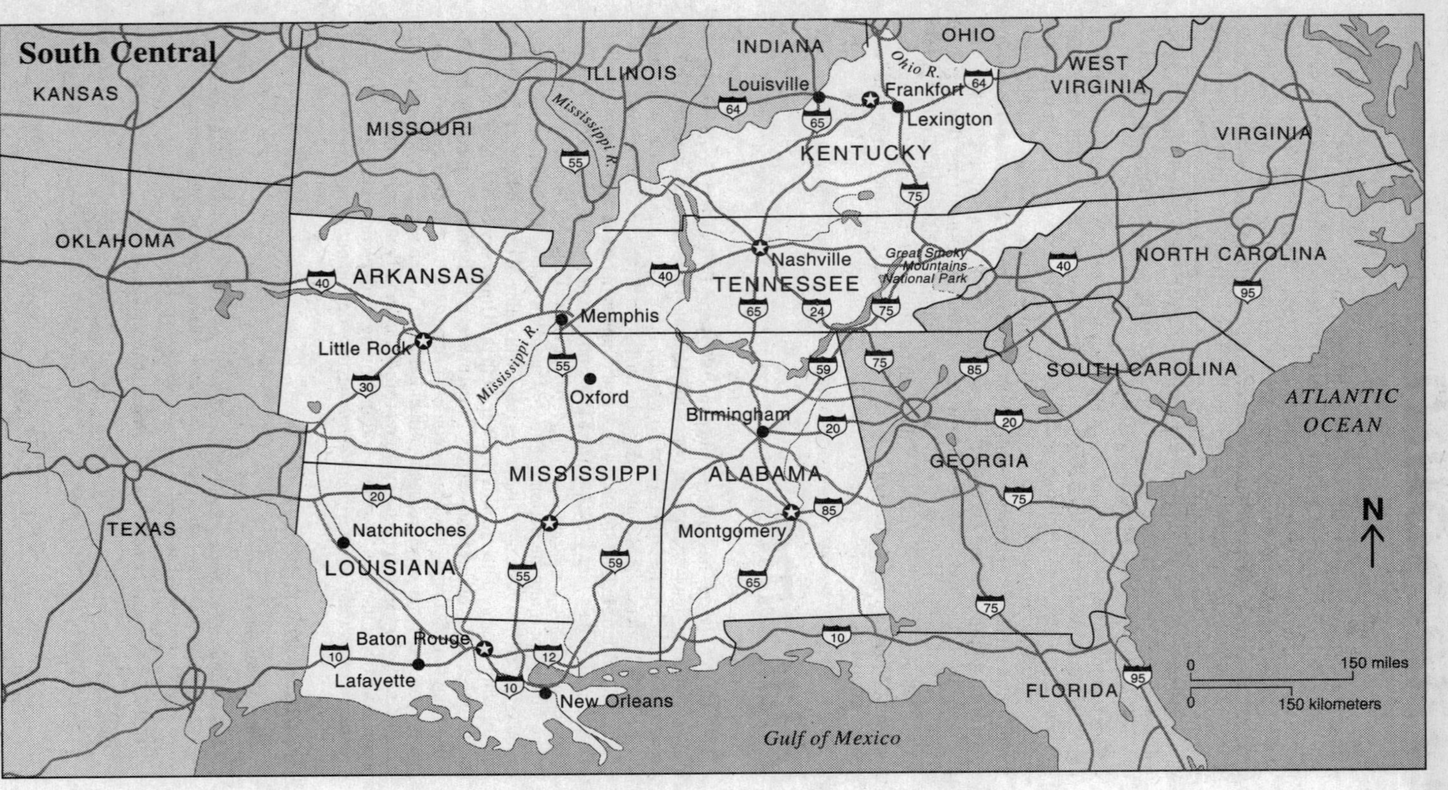
South Central
KANSAS
MISSOURI
ILLINOIS
Mississippi R.
INDIANA
OHIO
Ohio R.
Louisville
Frankfort
Lexington
WEST VIRGINIA
VIRGINIA
KENTUCKY
OKLAHOMA
ARKANSAS
Little Rock
Memphis
Nashville
TENNESSEE
Great Smoky Mountains National Park
NORTH CAROLINA
SOUTH CAROLINA
ATLANTIC OCEAN
Oxford
Birmingham
GEORGIA
MISSISSIPPI
ALABAMA
TEXAS
Natchitoches
Montgomery
LOUISIANA
N
Baton Rouge
Lafayette
New Orleans
FLORIDA
0
150 miles
0
150 kilometers
Gulf of Mexico

Birmingham

This city literally sprung up from the ground. Like its English namesake, Birmingham sits on soil rich in coal, iron ore and limestone—responsible for its lightning transformation into a premier steel industry center. No longer an industrial town, the city's largest employer is now the University of Alabama, home to one of the best cardiology hospitals in the world. Birmingham's hilly terrain provides a landscape for a plenitude of cultural events and chic restaurants. With an urban version of Southern charm and hospitality, the city's residents seem to appreciate and visit their sights as much as unjaded outsiders. This city of a million people has come a long, long way from the days of former police commissioner Eugene "Bull" Connor and his highly publicized racist attacks on nonviolent African-American protesters in 1963.

Practical Information and Orientation

Emergency: 911.

Visitor Information: Birmingham Visitors Center, 1200 University Blvd. (254-1654). Maps, calendars, and coupons for accommodations. Open Mon.-Sat. 8:30am-5pm, Sun. 1-5pm. Another location at the lower level of **Birmingham Municipal Airport** (254-1640), located east of downtown off Airport Hwy. Open daily 8:30am-8pm. **Greater Birmingham Convention and Visitors Bureau** in the **Chamber of Commerce,** 2027 1st Ave N., 3rd floor (252-9825), downtown. Open Mon.-Fri. 8:30am-5pm. For updated information on city events call **Funline,** 939-3866.

Amtrak: 1819 Morris Ave. (324-3033 or 800-872-7245), downtown. To: Montgomery ($12), Atlanta ($31), and Mobile ($54). Open daily 8:30am-4:30pm.

Greyhound: 618 N. 19th St. (252-7171). To: Montgomery ($15), Atlanta ($25), and Mobile ($42). Open 24 hrs.

Public Transport: Metropolitan Area Express (MAX), 252-0101. Runs Mon.-Sat. 7am-6pm. Fare $.80. **Downtown Area Runabout Transit (DART),** 252-0101. Runs Mon.-Fri. 10am-4pm. Fare $.25.

Taxi: Yellow Cab of Birmingham, 252-1131. Base fare $2.95, $1.20 each additional mi.

Help Lines: Crisis Center, 323-7777. **Rape Response,** 328-7273.

Post Office: 351 24th St. N. (521-0209). Open Mon.-Fri. 7:30am-7pm. **ZIP code:** 35203.

Area Code: 205.

The downtown area grid system has "avenues" running east-west and "streets" running north-south. Each numbered avenue has a north and a south. Major cultural and government buildings surround **Linn Park,** located between 19th and 21st St. N. on 7th Ave. N. The **University of Alabama in Birmingham (UAB)** extends along University Blvd. and 8th Ave. S. from 11th to 20th St.

Accommodations and Camping

Passport Inn, 821 20th St. S. (252-8041), 2 blocks from UAB. Large, clean rooms, tasteful decor in a convenient location. Pool. Singles $30. Doubles $32.

Ranch House, 2127 7th Ave. S. (322-0691). Near busy bars and restaurants. Pleasant rooms with cable TV and wood panelling. Check out the cowboy tiling in each bathroom. Local calls $.25 each. Pool. Singles $28. Doubles $32.

Economy Inn, 2224 5th Ave. N. (324-6688). Near some run-down buildings in the middle of downtown. Ample, tidy rooms. Pool, laundry room. Singles $24. Doubles $29.

Oak Mountain State Park (663-3061), 15 mi. south of Birmingham off I-65 in Pelham. Heavily forested area with 85-acre recreational lake. Sites $9.50 for 1-4 people, with electricity $12.

Birmingham South KOA, 1235 Hwy. 33 (664-8832), 8 mi. south of I-459 on I-65 S. in Pelham. Pool, playground, store, showers, laundry. Sites $16, with full hookup $21.

Food

Barbecue remains the local specialty, although more ethnic variations have sprung up downtown. The best places to eat cheaply (and meet young people) are at **Five Points South,** located at the intersection of Highland Ave. and 20th St. S. Food options there range from pesto pizza with sun-dried tomatoes ($2 per slice) at **Cosmo's Pizza,** 2012 Magnolia Ave. (930-9971), to health-conscious vegetarian lunches and groceries at **The Golden Temple,** 1901 11th Ave. S. (933-6333; open Mon.-Fri. 9:30am-5:30pm, Sat. 8:30am-7:30pm, Sun. noon-5:30pm.)

Bogue's, 3028 Clairmont Ave. (254-9780). A short-order diner with true delicious Southern fare (cheese omelette and biscuit $3). Always busy weekend mornings. Open Mon.-Fri. 6am-2pm, Sat.-Sun. 6-11:30am.

Café Bottega, 2240 Highland Ave. S. (939-1000). High-ceilinged and sophisticated, this café serves fresh bread to dip in olive oil and Italian specialties brimming with fresh vegetables and herbs. Marinated pasta with sweet peas and mint $5.25. Open Mon.-Fri. 11am-11pm, Sat. 5-11pm.

Ollie's, 515 University Blvd., near Green Springs Hwy (324-9485). Bible Belt dining in an enormous circular 50s-style building. Pamphlets shout "Is there really a Hell?" while you lustfully consume your beef. BBQ sandwich $2, homemade pie $1.50. Diet plates available. Open Mon.-Sat. 9:30am-8pm.

Sights

Remnants of Birmingham's steel industry are best viewed at the gigantic **Sloss Furnaces National Historic Landmark** (324-1911), adjacent to the 1st Ave. N. viaduct off 32nd St. downtown. Though the blast furnaces closed 20 years ago, they stand as the only preserved example of 20th-century iron-smelting in the world. Ballet and drama performances and music concerts are often held here at night. (Open Tues.-Sat. 10am-4pm, Sun. noon-4pm; free guided tours Sat.-Sun. at 1, 2, and 3pm.) To anthropomorphize the steel industry, Birmingham cast the **Vulcan** (Roman god of the forge) who overwhelms the city skyline as the largest cast-iron statue in the world. Visitors can watch over the city from its observation deck. The Vulcan's glowing torch burns red when a car fatality has occurred that day, green when none occur. (Open daily 8am-11pm. $1, ages 5 and under free.)

Scheduled to open in late 1992, the **Black Heritage Tour** features the dynamic **Birmingham Civil Rights Institute,** corner of 16th St. and 6th Ave. N. (for hours and other info call the Visitors Center; see Practical Information) and documents the Civil Rights Movement since the 1920s. Other significant sights on the tour include the **Sixteenth Street Baptist Church**, 1530 6th Ave. N. (251-9402) at 16th St. N., where four African-American girls died in a September 1963 bombing by white segregationalists after a protest push which culminated in Dr. Martin Luther King's "Letter From a Birmingham Jail." The deaths spurred many protests in nearby **Kelly-Ingram Park,** corner of 6th Ave. and 16th St., where a bronze statue of Dr. Martin Luther King, Jr. sits today, and the **Alabama Sports Hall of Fame,** corner of Civic Center Blvd. and 22nd St. North (323-6665), that honors the careers of outstanding sportspeople like Jesse Owens, Joe Louis, and Birmingham's own Willie Mays. (Open Mon.-Sat. 9am-5pm, Sun 1-5pm.)

A few blocks down from the Hall of Fame blooms the refreshing **Linn Park,** across from the **Birmingham Museum of Art,** 2000 8th Ave. N. (254-2565). The museum displays U.S. paintings and English Wedgewood ceramics, as well as a superb collection of African textiles and sculptures. Free. (Call the Birmingham Visitors Center for hours and info.)

For a breather from the downtown scene, revel in the marvelously sculpted grounds of the **Birmingham Botanical Gardens,** 2612 Lane Park Rd. (879-1227), whose spectacular floral displays, elegant Japanese gardens, and enormous greenhouse vegetate on 68 acres of former Native American grounds. (Open daily dawn-dusk. Free.)

Antebellum **Arlington,** 331 Cotton Ave. (780-5656), southwest of downtown, houses a fine array of Southern decorative arts from the 19th century. Go west on 1st Ave.

N., which becomes Cotton Ave., to reach the stately white Greek Revival building, which also hosts craft fairs throughout the year. (Open Tues.-Sat. 10am-4pm, Sun. 1-4pm. $3, ages 6-18 $2.)

To learn more about the geology of the area, visit the **Red Mountain Museum and Cut,** 1421 22nd St. S. (933-4104). You can wander a walkway above the highway to see different levels of rock formation inside Red Mountain. The museum indoors has various exhibits on the prehistoric inhabitants of Alabama. The **Discovery Place** next door, 1320 22nd St. S (939-1176), invites children of all ages to explore body mechanics, the ins and outs of cities, brainteasers, channels of communication, and much more. (Both sites open Tues.-Fri. 9am-3pm, Sun. 1-4pm; fall and winter Sat. 1-4pm, spring and summer Sat. 10am-4pm. Admission to both sites $2, kids $1.50)

Music lovers lucky or smart enough to visit Birmingham in the middle of June for **City Stages** (251-1272) will hear everything from country to gospel to big name rock groups, with headliners such as James Brown and George Jones. The three-day festival also includes food, crafts, and children's activities. (Weekend pass $10.)

Entertainment and Nightlife

The historic **Alabama Theater,** 1817 3rd Ave. N. (251-0418), shows old movies on occasional weekends throughout the year. Their organ, the "Mighty Wurlitzer," usually entertains the audience before each showing. (Shows Fri.-Sat. at 7pm, Sun. at 2pm. $4, seniors $3, under 12 $2.) Pick up a free copy of *Fun and Stuff* or see the "Kudzu" in the Friday edition of *The Birmingham Post Herald* for listings of all movies, plays, and clubs in the area.

The **Five Points South** (or **Southside** area) has a high concentration of nightclubs. On cool summer nights many people grab outdoor tables in front of their favorite bars or hang out by the fountain. Use caution here, and avoid parking or walking in dark alleys near the square.

For the hippest licks year-round check out **The Nick,** 2514 10th Ave. S. (322-7550). The poster-covered exterior asserts "the Nick...rocks." (Open Mon.-Sat. Live music nightly. Cover $2-5.) For jazz, blues, and even occasional Cajun music, the laid-back **Grundy's Music Room,** 1924 4th Ave. N. (323-3109), actually a basement club, has frequent guest artists. (Open Tues.-Sat. 3pm-until whenever. Call for performance times and cover.) When Grundy's doesn't offer live tunes, you're better off with **The Burly Earl,** 2109 7th Ave. S. (322-5848), specializing in fried finger-foods and local acoustic, blues, and sometimes rock sounds. (Restaurant open Mon.-Thurs. 10am-11pm, bar open until midnight; Fri.-Sat. 10am-1am, bar open until 2am. Live music Wed.-Thurs. 8:30pm-midnight, Fri.-Sat. 9:30pm-2am.)

Mobile

Situated on the Gulf of Mexico, Mobile (mo-BEEL) reflects its checkered past under English, French, and Spanish dominion through its distinctive and diverse architectural styles. Antebellum mansions, Italianate dwellings, Spanish and French historical forts, and Victorian homes line the azalea-edged streets of this, Alabama's oldest major city. Mobile is also awash with museums and gardens that further enhance its color. Site of the first U.S. Mardi Gras, Mobile resembles New Orleans and the Mississippi Coast more than it does the rest of Alabama. Mobile's coastal location proves a nice lagniappe for tourists by offering a moderate climate, fresh seafood, and nearby beautiful white sandy beaches.

Practical Information and Orientation

Emergency: 911.

Visitor Information: Fort Condé Information Center, 150 S. Royal St. (434-7304), in a reconstructed French fort near Government St. Open daily 8am-5pm. **Mobile Convention and Visitors**

Bureau, 1 St. Louis Center #2002 (433-5100; 800-662-6282 outside AL). Open Mon.-Fri. 8am-5pm.

Traveler's Aid: 438-1625. Operated by the Salvation Army; ask for Travelers Services. Lines open Mon.-Fri. 9am-4:30pm.

Amtrak: 11 Government St. (432-4052 or 800-872-7245). The "Gulf Breeze" blows from Mobile to New York via Birmingham ($54 one way); Atlanta ($72 one-way by reservation only); Greenville, S.C. ($113 one way); and Washington, DC.

Greyhound: 201 Government St. (432-9793), at S. Conception downtown. To: Montgomery (4 hr., $27), New Orleans (3 hr., $27), and Birmingham (6 hr., $43). Open 24 hrs.

Public Transport: Mobile Transit Authority (MTA), 344-5656. Major depots are at Bienville Sq., St. Joseph, and Dauphin St. Operates Mon.-Sat. 5am-7pm. Fare $.75.

Taxi: Yellow Cab, 476-7711. Base fare $1.30, $1.20 each additional mi.

Help Lines: Rape Crisis, 473-7273. **Crisis Counseling,** 666-7900. Open 24 hrs.

Post Office: 250 Saint Joseph St. (694-5917). Open Mon.-Fri. 8am-4:30pm, Sat. 8am-noon. **ZIP code:** 36601.

Area Code: 205.

The downtown district fronts the Mobile River. **Dauphin Street** and **Government Boulevard** are the major east-west routes. **Royal Street** and **St. Joseph Street** are the north-south byways. Some of Mobile's major attractions lie outside downtown. The *U.S.S. Alabama* is off the causeway leading out of the city; **Dauphin Island** is 30 mi. south.

Accommodations and Camping

Accommodations are both reasonable and accessible, but stop at the Fort Condé Information Center (see Practical Information) first; they can make reservations for you at a 10-15% discount. The MTA runs a "Government St." bus regularly which reaches the Government St. motels listed below, but they are all within a 15-min. walk of downtown.

Economy Inn, 1119 Government St. (433-8800). Big beds, clean sheets, a pool and dark-panelled walls. Singles $24. Doubles $27.

Motel 6, 4000 Beltline Hwy. (343-8448). Small, dark rooms with tidy furnishings. Free movie channel and local calls. $24 for one person, $6 each additional person.

I-10 Kampground, 400 Theodore Dawes Rd. E. (653-9816), 7½ mi. west on I-10 (exit 13). No public transportation. Pool, kids' playground, laundry, and bath facilities. Sites $13.

Food

Mobile's proximity to the Gulf makes both seafood and Southern cookin' regional specialties. As well-known for its atmosphere as for its seafood, **Wintzels,** 605 Dauphin St., (433-1004) six blocks west of downtown, offers a dozen oysters on the half shell "fried, stewed, and nude" for $5. (Open Mon.-Thurs. and Sat. 11am-9pm, Fri. 11am-9:45pm.) Farther out of the downtown district, **The Lumber Yard Café,** 2617 Dauphin St. (471-1241), serves homemade pizza for $5 and seafood gumbo for $2. Live bands blare weekends, and the big-screen TV entertains during the week. (Open daily 11am-3am.) **Argiro's,** on 1320 Battleship Pkwy. (626-1060), is a quick-stop deli that provides both businesspeople and sailors with cheap hot dogs and sandwiches ($2-5) and Southern specialties such as red beans and rice next to the *U.S.S. Alabama.* (Open Mon.-Tues. and Sat. 8am-3:45pm, Wed.-Fri. 8am-4:45pm.)

Sights and Entertainment

Mobile encompasses four historic districts: **Church Street, DeToni Square, Old Dauphin Way,** and **Oakleigh Garden.** Each offers a unique array of architectural styles. The Information Center (see Practical Information) provides maps for walking or driving tours of these former residences of cotton brokers and river pilots as well as the "shotgun" cottages of their servants. Package tour admission prices are available at the center, as well.

Church St. divides into east and west subdistricts. The homes in the venerable **Church St. East District,** showcase popular U.S. architectural styles of the mid- to late-19th century, including Federal, Greek Revival, Queen Anne, and Victorian. While on Church St., be sure and pass through the **Spanish Plaza,** Hamilton and Government St., which honors Mobile's sibling city—Málaga, Spain—while recalling Spain's early presence in Mobile. Also of interest in this area is the **Christ Episcopal Church,** 115 S. Conception St. (433-1842), opposite the tourist office at Fort Condé. Dedicated in 1842, the church contains beautiful German, Italian, and Tiffany stained glass windows.

In the **DeToni Historical District,** north of downtown, tour the tastefully restored **Richards-DAR House,** 256 North Joachim St. (434-7320), whose red Bohemian stained glass and rococo chandeliers blend beautifully with its antebellum Italianate architecture. On slow days, the staff may invite you in for tea and cookies. (Open Tues.-Sat. 10am-4pm, Sun. 1-4pm. Tours $3, kids $1.) Brick townhouses with wrought-iron balconies fill the rest of the district.

The restored Victorian buildings of the **Old Dauphin Way** are today settings for homes and businesses. Attempts at revitalization, with new restaurants and club opening in the Victorian buildings, will hopefully bring new life to the area that has become rather quiet over the years.

One of the most elegant buildings in Mobile is **Oakleigh,** 350 Oakleigh Place (432-1281) off Government St., with a cantilevered staircase and enormous windows that open onto all the balconies upstairs. Falling away from downtown, take a left on Roper St. Inside, a museum contains furnishings of the early Victorian, Empire, and Regency periods. (Open Mon.-Sat. 10am-4pm, Sun. 2-4pm. Tours every ½ hr.; last tour leaves at 3:30pm. $4, seniors $3, college students with ID $2, ages 6-18 $1; tickets sold next door at the simple **Cox-Deasy House.**) For more information on Oakleigh's heyday and on other periods of Mobile's history, visit the galleries of the **Museums of the City of Mobile,** 355 Government St. (434-7620), which includes **Mobile City Museum** (434-7569) and its exhibits of early 20th-century Mardi Gras queen costumes. Also part of the museum system is the **Carlen House,** Carlen St. off Dauphin St. (470-7768), a 6-room restored Creole cottage with period furnishings. The **Phoenix Fire Museum,** 203 S. Claiborne St., displays several antique fire engines including an 1898 steam-powered fire engine. (All open Tues.-Sat. 10am-5pm, Sun. 1-5pm. Free.)

The fascinating African-American artists' works on display merit a trip to the famous **Fine Arts Museum of the South (FAMOS),** 4850 Museum Dr. (343-2667). (Open Tues.-Sun. 10am-5pm. Free.) The **Exploreum,** 1906 Springhill Ave. (475-MUSE), offers more scientific diversions geared to children with hands-on investigations and experiments. (Open Tues.-Fri. 9am-5pm, Sat.-Sun. 1-5pm; $3, ages 2-17 $2.)

The battleship *U.S.S. Alabama,* permanently moored at **Battleship Park** (433-2703), took part in every major World War II Pacific battle. The park is at the entrance of the Bankhead Tunnel, 2½ mi. east of town on I-10. Berthed along the port side of this intriguing ship is one of the most famous submarines of the war, the *U.S.S. Drum.* (Open daily 8am-sunset. $5, ages 6-11 $2.50. Parking $2.)

Gray Line of Mobile (432-2229) leads interesting one to two-hour sight-seeing tours of the downtown historic areas from the Fort Condé Information Center; see Practical Information. (Tours Mon.-Sat. 10:30am and 2pm, Sun. 2pm. $8, ages 4-14 $4-6.50.)

For nighttime entertainment, stop in at **Trinity's Downtown,** 456 Auditorium Dr. (432-0000), where bands play rock and reggae Wednesday through Saturday nights. (Open Mon.-Wed. 11:30am-midnight, Thurs.-Sat. 11am-2am.) There's more rock and reggae at **G.T. Henry's,** 462 Dauphin St. (432-0300), on a multi-tiered stage, with crawfish boils on Sundays to boot. (Open nightly from about 10pm. Small cover.)

Montgomery

A look into Montgomery's history unveils a concatenation of firsts and beginnings: the first capital of the Confederacy, the first operating electric streetcar in 1886, and the first Wright Brothers' flight school in 1910. Its most significant beginning was in the Dexter Baptist Church where Dr. Martin Luther King, Jr. began his ministry. In late 1955, King went on to lead bus boycotts here that introduced to the nation his nonviolent approach to gaining equal rights for African-Americans. With its nationally acclaimed Alabama Shakespeare Festival and the recently completed Arts Museum, Montgomery lures culture-seekers. Retaining an ambiance of easygoing lifestyles, the capital of Alabama celebrates its rural past alongside a busy, diverse present.

Practical Information and Orientation

Emergency: 911.

Visitor Information: Visitor Information Center, 401 Madison Ave. (262-0013). Open Mon.-Fri. 8:30am-5pm, Sat.-Sun. 9am-4pm. **Chamber of Commerce,** 41 Commerce St. (834-5200). Open Mon.-Fri. 8:30am-5pm.

Traveler's Aid: 265-0568. Operated by Salvation Army. Open 24 hrs.

Greyhound: 210 S. Court St. (264-4518). To: Tuskegee (7 per day, 1 hr., $7), Birmingham (7 per day, 3 hr., $15), Mobile (8 per day, 4 hr., $26), and Atlanta ($28). Open 24 hrs.

Public Transport: Montgomery Area Transit System (MATS), 701 N. McDonough St. (262-7321). Operates throughout the metropolitan area Mon.-Sat. 6am-6pm. Fare $.80, transfers $.10.

Taxi: Yellow Cab, 262-5225. $1.50 first mi., $1 each additional mi.

Help Lines: Council Against Rape, 264-7273. **Help-A-Crisis,** 279-7837.

Post Office: 135 Catoma St. (244-7576). Open Mon.-Fri. 8am-5pm, Sat. 8am-noon. **ZIP code:** 36104.

Area Code: 205.

Downtown Montgomery follows a grid pattern: **Madison Avenue** and **Dexter Avenue** are the major east-west routes; **Perry Street** and **Lawrence Street** run north-south.

Accommodations and Food

Those with a car will find it easy to procure accommodations; I-65 at the Southern Blvd. exit overflows with cheap beds. Two well-maintained budget motels centrally located downtown are the **Capitol Inn,** 205 N. Goldthwaite St. (265-0541) at Heron St., with spacious, clean, and comfortable rooms and a pool (and free continental breakfast), near the bus station on a hill overlooking the city (singles $28, doubles $32) and the venerable, somewhat comfortable **Town Plaza,** 743 Madison Ave. (269-1561), at N. Ripley St. (singles $19, doubles $22). The Plaza, actually closer to the capitol, absolutely prohibits pets. **The Inn South,** 4243 Inn South Ave. (288-7999), has very nicely decorated rooms and a lobby with a grand double staircase and chandelier, but is a 10-min. drive from downtown. (Singles $29. Doubles $31.) For an alternative to these inns, contact **Bed and Breakfast Montgomery,** P.O. Box 1026, Montgomery, AL 36101 (264-0056). **KOA Campground** (288-0728), 1/4 mi. south of Hope Hull exit , four mi. from town, has a pool, laundry, and shower facilities. (Tent sites $11, with water and electricity $16, with A/C add $2.50.)

There is nary an empty seat for the Southern cooking at **The Farmer's Market Cafeteria,** 315 N. McDonough St. Free iced tea comes with every inexpensive meal ($4-5). (Open Mon.-Fri. 5am-2pm.) **Chris's Hot Dogs,** 138 Dexter Ave. (265-6850), with over 70 years under its belt, is an even more established Montgomery institution. This small diner serves gourmet hot dogs (under $2) and thick Brunswick stew ($1.75). (Open Mon.-Thurs. 8:30am-7pm, Fri. 8:30am-8pm, Sat. 10am-7pm.) **Martha's Place** at 458 Sayre St. (263-9135), is a new but soon-to-be-legendary, family-run, down-home restaurant with a daily country-style buffet ($5.50). (Open Mon.-Fri. 11am-3pm and 5-8pm, Sun. 11am-5pm.) At **The China Bowl,** 701 Madison Ave (832-4004), two blocks from the Town Plaza Motel, large portions include a daily special of one entrée, fried rice, egg roll, chicken wing and a fried wonton for $4.20; take-out available. (Open Mon.-Thurs. 11am-9pm, Fri. 11am-9:30pm.)

For a great snack, make your way over to the **Montgomery State Farmers Market,** at the corner of Federal Dr. (U.S. 231) and Coliseum Blvd. (242-5350), and snag a bag of peaches for $.75. (Open spring and summer daily 7am-8pm.)

Sights and Entertainment

Montgomery's newest sight is the **Civil Rights Memorial,** 400 Washington Ave. at Hull St. Maya Lin, the architect who designed the Vietnam Memorial in Washington, DC, also designed this dramatically minimalist tribute to the 40 men, women, and children who died fighting for civil rights. The outdoor monument bears names and dates of significant events on a circular black marble table over which water and flowers of remembrance continuously flow; a wall frames the table with Martin Luther King's words, "...Until Justice rolls down like waters and righteousness like a mighty stream." (Open daily.) The legacy and life of African-American activism and faith can also be seen one block away at the **Dexter Avenue King Memorial Baptist Church,** 454 Dexter Ave. (263-3970), where King preached. At this 112-year-old church, Reverend King and other Civil Rights leaders organized the 1955 Montgomery bus boycott; 10 years later, King would lead a nationwide Civil Rights march past the church to the Montgomery capitol. The basement mural chronicles the King's role in the nation's struggle during the 1960s. (Open Mon.-Fri. 9am-noon and 1-4pm, Sat. 10am-2pm. Free. Tours available.)

Three blocks north is **Old Alabama Town,** 310 N. Hull St. at Madison (263-4355), an artfully maintained historic district of 19th-century buildings. The complex includes a pioneer homestead, an 1892 grocery, a schoolhouse, an early African-American church, and a freed slave's house. (Open Mon.-Sat. 9:30am-3:30pm, last tour at 3:30pm; Sun. 1:30-3:30pm. $5, ages 5-18 $1.50.)

The Confederate flag flies along with the Stars and Bars above the **State Capitol,** closed to the public until late 1992 for restoration. But you can visit the nearby **Alabama State History Museum and State Archives,** 624 Washington Ave. (242-4363). On exhibit are many Native American artifacts along with early military swords and medals. Stop by "Grandma's Attic" where you can try on antique furs and play with antique sewing machines and typewriters in a wooden- frame attic replica. (Open Mon.-Fri. 8am-5pm, Sat.-Sun. 9am-5pm. Free.) Next door to the Archives is the elegant **First White House of the Confederacy,** 644 Washington Ave. (242-1861), which contains many original furnishings from Jefferson Davis's Confederate presidency. (Open Mon.-Fri. 8am-4:30pm, Sat.-Sun. 9am-4:30pm. Free.) Another restored home of interest is the **F. Scott and Zelda Fitzgerald Museum,** 919 Felder Ave. (262-1911), off Carter Hill Rd. Zelda, originally from Montgomery, lived here with Scott from October 1931 to April 1932. The museum contains a few of her paintings and some of his original manuscripts, as well as their strangely monogrammed bath towels. (Open Wed.-Fri. 10am-2pm, Sat.-Sun. 1-5pm.)

Country music fans might want to join the hundreds who make daily pilgrimages to the **Hank Williams Memorial,** located in the Oakwood Cemetery Annex off Upper Wetumpka Rd. Oversize music notes flank the gravestone upon which rests stone cowboy hat and engravings of guitars, cowboy boots, and titles of his most famous hits. Green astro-turf carpets the holy ground. (Open daily 7am-sunset.) For more live entertainment, turn to the renowned **Alabama Shakespeare Festival,** staged at the remarkable $22 million **Wynton M. Blount Cultural Park,** 15 min. southeast of the downtown area. In addition to Shakespeare, Broadway shows and other plays are staged. Nearby, off Woodmere Blvd., is the **Montgomery Museum of Fine Arts,** 1 Museum Dr. (244-5700). This attractive museum houses a substantial collection of 19th- and 20th-century paintings and graphics, as well as ARTWORKS, a hands-on gallery and art studio for children. (Open Tues.-Wed. and Fri-Sat. 10am-5pm, Thurs. 10am-9pm, Sun. noon-5pm. Free.)

Montgomery shuts down fairly early, but if you're in the mood for some blues and beers, try **1048,** 1048 E. Fairview Ave. (834-1048), near Woodley Ave. (Open Mon.-Fri. 4pm-until and Sat. 6pm-until.) For further information on events in the city, call the Chamber of Commerce's 24-hr. **FunPhone** (240-9447).

Near Montgomery: Tuskegee

Late in the 19th century after Reconstruction, Southern states still segregated and disenfranchised "emancipated" African-Americans. Booker T. Washington, a former slave) believed that African-Americans could best combat repression and racism by educating themselves and learning a trade. Therefore, the curriculum at the college Washington founded, **Tuskegee University,** revolved around such practical endeavors as agriculture and carpentry, with students constructing almost all of the campus buildings. Washington raised money for the college by giving lectures on his beliefs regarding social structure across the country. Artist, teacher, and scientist George Washington Carver became head of the Agricultural Department at Tuskegee, where he discovered many practical uses for the peanut, including axle grease and peanut butter.

Today, a more academically oriented Tuskegee covers over 160 acres and a wide range of subjects; the buildings of Washington's original institute also comprise a national historical site. A walking tour of the campus begins at the **Carver Museum,** with the **Visitor Orientation Center** (727-3200) inside. (Both open daily 9am-5pm. Free.) Down the street from the museum, on old Montgomery Rd., is **The Oaks,** a restored version of Washington's home. Free tours from the museum begin on the hour.

To get to Tuskegee, take I-85 toward Atlanta and exit at Rte. 81 south. Turn right at the intersection of Rte. 81 and Old Montgomery Rd. onto Rte. 126. **Greyhound** also runs frequently from Montgomery (1 hr., $7); see Montgomery: Practical Information.

Tuskegee's **ZIP code** is 36083; the **area code** is 205.

Arkansas

Arkansas (AR-ken-saw)—no relation to Kansas (KAN-zis)—merits its moniker "the natural state." Arkansan terrain ranges from flatlands in the south to rolling mountains in the north. Arkansans spend as much time as possible in this varied outdoors. From friendly Little Rock to the old spa town of Hot Springs, mountain music and majestic scenery color this unspoiled natural haven.

Practical Information

Capital: Little Rock.

Arkansas Dept. of Parks and Tourism, 1 Capitol Mall, Little Rock 72201 (501-682-7777 or 800-643-8383). Open Mon.-Fri. 8am-5pm.

Nickname: "Land of Opportunity."

State Bird: Mockingbird.

Time Zone: Central (1 hr. behind Eastern). **Postal Abbreviation:** AR

Sales Tax: 0%.

Hot Springs

Hot Springs is like a good porno film: hot, steamy, and wet. An old-fashioned spa town in a national park established to preserve the natural springs, Hot Springs is just that—143° of *very* purified aqua bubble up from the surrounding oak- and hickory-forested mountains. NASA even used the liquid to protect the Apollo mission moon rocks from bacteria. Native Americans had used the hot springs for centuries before Hernando de Soto "discovered" them in 1541. Since then, the famous and infamous from Franklin D. Roosevelt to Al Capone have come here to enjoy warm baths and peace of mind. Hot Springs had its heyday in the 1920s, when the alleged medicinal properties and healing powers of the springs made it one of the country's most popular resorts. The town has since declined, but throngs of tourists still frequent the spas and national park.

The **Fordyce Bathhouse Visitors Center,** 300 Central Ave. (623-1433), offers information and fascinating tours on the surrounding wilderness areas and on the bathhouse itself, both of which are part of the Hot Springs National Park. (Open daily 9am-5pm.) The **Buckstaff** (623-2308) is the only place you can take a co-ed bath in town (albeit not buck-naked; bathing suits *are* required.) Baths are $11.50, massages $11.75. (Open Mon.-Fri. 7-11:45am and 1:30-3pm, Sat. 7-11:45am.) Down the street is the **Hot Springs Health Spa,** N. 500 Reserve (321-9664; bath $10, massage $10-13; open daily 9am-9pm). The **Arlington** and **Majestic** hotels also have baths open to the public. ($12 bath, $13 massage.)

While there's little chance of drowning in the shallow springs, you may feel asphyxiated by the deluge of commercialism that entices visitors to pet alligators and tour wax museums. To avoid such a fate, escape to **Whittington Park** on Whittington Ave. off Central Ave. and sleep amidst a green oasis of magnolia and oak trees, to be awakened only by the sound of grass growing. When you're not bathing in the springs or hiking in the park, try cruising Lake Hamilton on the **Belle of Hot Springs** (525-4438), with one-hour narrated tours alongside the Ouachita Mountains and Lake Hamilton mansions. (Fare $7, kids $3.25.) In town, the **Mountain Valley Spring Water Company,** 150 Central Ave. (623-6671 or 800-643-1501), offers free samples and tours of its national headquarters. From the **Hot Springs Mountain Observatory Tower** (623-6035), located in the national park (turn off Central Ave. to Rte. 7), you can view the beautiful panorama of the surrounding mountains and lakes. (Open daily May 16-Labor Day 9am-9pm, Nov.-Feb. 9am-5pm, March-Oct. 9am-6pm. $3, kids $1.75.)

Nighttime family entertainment percolates throughout Hot Springs. If you like country, the **Rocky Top Jubilee,** 1312 Central Ave. (623-7504) is for you. Just to keep your interest, they also throw in a smidgen of gospel and loads of comedy. (Shows at 8pm. $7.50, seniors $7, kids $3.75. Reservations recommended.) A short drive out of town is the **Music Mountain Jamboree,** 3300 Albert Pike (767-3841) off U.S. 270 W. Family-style country music shows take place nightly during the summer, and at various times throughout the rest of the year. (Shows at 8pm. $9, kids $4.75. Reservations required.)

Hot Springs has a number of small, inexpensive restaurants. Snack on *beignets* (doughnuts without the hole; 3 for 75¢) and *café au lait* (75¢) at **Café New Orleans,** 210 Central Ave. (624-3200), or try their deliciously filling breakfasts, especially the fruited crepes ($3 for 3). Dinner is also divine, with mouth-watering seafood selections ($5-10). (Open Sun.-Thurs. 7am-9pm, Fri.-Sat. 7am-10pm.) For good ol' country food, try **Maggie's Café,** 362 Central (623-4091), and be sure to have the Mississippi mud pie ($2) for dessert. (Open 9am-9pm.) Also try **Granny's Kitchen,** 322 Central Ave. (624-9201) with sandwiches and veggie plates under $4, and a damn good blackberry cobbler for only $2. (Open daily 7am-8pm.)

For the budget traveler who has a little stashed away in the ol' moneybelt, the **Arlington Resort Hotel and Spa,** at Fountain and Central St. (623-7771 or 800-643-1502), is a lavish, bordering on gaudy, resort of yester-year (Capone used to stay here)—at very reasonable rates. (Singles from $40. Doubles $50. Family rates with 2 double beds from $56.) Walk into a fairy tale at the **Best Motel,** 630 Ouachita (624-5736), which has gingerbread-like cabins, a storybook pool, and relaxing chairs. (Singles $20. Doubles $30.) The **Margrete Motel,** 217 Fountain St., offers an excellent deal with large rooms, each with kitchenettes. (Singles $24-26. Doubles $26-30.) The **Happy Hollow Motel** next door (321-2230) sports older but clean rooms and suites from $30. The motels clustered along Rte. 7 and 88 have similar prices, although rates rise during the tourist season (Feb.-Aug.); camping is far cheaper (see the State Parks below).

Before touring Hot Springs, you should stop by the **visitors center,** downtown at the corner of Central and Reserve St. (321-2277), and pick up their valuable coupon packets for many attractions and restaurants. (Open Mon.-Sat. 9:30am-5pm, Sun. 1-5pm.) Hot Springs becomes especially crowded during the horse racing season at nearby **Oaklawn** racetrack (Feb.-April; $1). Call 1-800-722-3652 for racetrack information. For more information on food, lodging, ranger activities, and current area attractions, call 800-543-2284 or 800-772-2489 or pick up a copy of *Hot Springs Pipeline,* available for free at the visitors center.

Hot Springs's **ZIP code** is 71901; the **area code** is 501.

State Parks Nearby

The 48,000-acre **Lake Ouachita Park** encompasses the largest of three clear, beautiful, artificial lakes near Hot Springs. Travel three mi. west of Hot Springs on U.S. 270, then 12 mi. north on Rte. 227. Numerous islands float offshore promising an escape from civilization in quiet coves and rocky beaches. Fishing abounds, and camping is available from $6 per day (767-9366); fishing boats rent for $10 per day.

By car from Hot Springs you can easily reach **Lake Catherine Park** (844-4176), which covers over 2000 acres of Ouachita Mountain, and stretches along the shores of beautiful Lake Catherine. Campsites start at $12 per day. Take exit 97 off I-30 at Malvern and go 12 mi. north on Rte. 171. (Canoe rentals $3.25 per hr., power boats $18 per ½ day, $25 per day.) **Shore Line Campground,** 5321 Central Ave. (525-1902), just south of town on Lake Hamilton, has full RV hookup, a pool, restrooms, showers, and laundry facilities. ($12 per day, $72 per week.) Call for reservations. Tents and houseboats are permitted.

Little Rock

Once upon a time, a little rock jutting into the Arkansas River served as an important landmark for boats pushing their way upstream. Over time, that rock was overshadowed by the big city that grew up around it. Soon that city became the most important in the state, forgetting in its bustle the namesake pebble. Trouble swept this burgeoning metropolis when in 1957, Little Rock became the focus of a nationwide civil rights controversy. Governor Orval Faubus led a violent segregationist movement, using troops to prevent nine African-American students from enrolling in Central High School; they entered only under National Guard protection. As years passed, this hotbed of racial tension cooled to become the integrated cultural center that it is today. The little rock on the mighty Arkansas river was finally remembered and given a happy green park in which to live. And it lived there happily ever after. The End.

Tourists can visit that legendary "Little Rock" at **Riverfront Park,** along the Arkansas River, a pleasant place for a walk. Pay close attention; the rock has had a hard life and is (oddly enough) *little* and easy to miss. For the best access, cut through the back of the Excelsior Hotel at Markham and Center St. The town celebrates the waterway annually at **Riverfest,** on Memorial Day weekend, with arts and crafts, a number of bands, lots of food, and a firework display the last evening.

One block away from the visitors bureau resides the refined **Old State House,** 300 W. Markham St. (324-9685), which served as the capitol from 1836 until the ceiling collapsed in 1899 while the legislature was in session. The restored building now houses exhibits of the gowns of the first ladies, and provides a good starting point for a downtown tour. (Open Mon.-Sat. 9am-5pm, Sun. 1-5pm. Free.) The functioning **state capitol** (682-5080) at the west end of Capitol St. may look very familiar—it's actually a replica of the U.S. Capitol in Washington, DC. (Perhaps that's why Arkansas Governor Bill Clinton felt comfortable making a Presidential bid in 1992.) Take a free self-guided tour or one of the 45-minute group tours given on the hour. (Open Mon.-Fri. 9am-4pm, Sat. 10am-5pm, Sun. 1-5pm. Call in advance on weekends.) For a look at the history of the townspeople of 19th-century Little Rock, visit the **Arkansas Territorial Restoration,** 214 E. Third St. (371-2348). Tours of four restored buildings include an old grog shop where you can meet Isaac the bartender, and a typical old-fashioned print shop. (Open Mon.-Sat. 9am-5pm, Sun. 1-5pm. 50-min. tours every hr. on the hr. $2, seniors $1, kids 50¢. Free first Sun. of each month.)

On the eastern edge of town lounges **MacArthur Park,** elegant home to several interesting museums such as the **Museum of Science and History** (324-9231). Particularly suited to kids, the museum houses exhibits on Arkansas history, including a walk-through bear cave and an entire room of stuffed birds. (Open Mon.-Sat. 9am-9:30pm, Sun. 1-4:30pm; $1, kids under 12 and seniors 50¢, free on Mondays for self-guided touring.) Next door poses the **Arkansas Art Center** (372-4000) featuring outstanding collections by both the old European masters and contemporary artisans. (Open Mon.-Sat. 10am-5pm, Sun. noon-5pm. Free.) Just a block or so north of the park furbishes the **Decorative Arts Museum,** 7th and Rock St. (372-4000), where innovative silverware and furniture designs demonstrate that art can be functional. Look for the Civil War in the fireplaces. (Tours given Wed. at noon, Sun. at 1:30. Open Mon.-Sat. 10am-5pm, Sun. noon-5pm. Free.) The **War Memorial Park,** northwest of the state capitol off I-30 at Fair Park Blvd. houses the 40-acre **Little Rock Zoo,** 1 Jonesboro Dr. (666-2406), which simulates the animals' natural habitats. (Open daily 9:30am-4:30pm. $2, kids under 12 $1.)

The opening scene of *Gone With the Wind* features the **Old Mill Park,** Lakeshore Dr. at Fairway Ave. (758-2445), in North Little Rock, one of the city's most treasured attractions. The WPA constructed this water-powered grist mill during the Depression. (Open daily. Free.) The opening scene of the TV show "Designing Women" also features a Little Rock location—**The Villa Marre,** 1321 Scott (374-9979), a restored 19th-century house and museum. (Open Sun. 1-5pm, Mon.-Fri. 9am-5pm. $3, seniors $2.)

Archaeologists are uncovering part of Arkansas' past that goes back much farther than the historic homes and parks—all the way to the year 700. More than 1000 years ago, the **Toltec Mounds State Park** (961-9442), 15 mi. east of North Little Rock on Rte. 386, was the political and religious center of the Plum Bayou people. (Open Tues.-Sat. 8am-5pm, Sun. noon-5pm. Guided tours at 9:30am, 11am, 12:30pm and 3:30pm. $2, ages 6-15 $1.)

Many of Little Rock's restaurants and cafés serve up an artsy atmosphere along with good deals. There are a few fast-food joints downtown, but more lie along I-30 closer to the university. **Solar Café,** 1706 W. 3rd (375-4747), across from Capitol, radiates from inside a former gas station. This mellow, laid-back eatery shines with sun-sational lunches for under $4 and dinners under $7, and has nightly live entertainment. (Open Mon.-Fri. 8:30am-9:30pm, Sat. brunch 9am-2pm.) **Hungry's Café,** 1001 W. 7th St. (372-9720), is a popular, lively joint that proves that hillbillies and yuppies know good food. Tasty, filling sandwiches, country chicken, and veggie plates are under $5. Tip your hat to the impressive cap collection on the wall. (Open Mon.-Fri. 6am-2pm, Sat. 7am-12:30pm.) **The Oyster Bar,** 3003 W. Markham St. (666-7100), serves reasonably priced seafood and "Po' Boy" sandwiches ($4-5). It has a big screen TV, pool tables, cheap draft beer, and a decidedly laid-back atmosphere where paper towel rolls take the place of napkins. (Open Mon.-Thurs. 11am-9:30pm, Fri.-Sat. noon-10:30pm. Happy Hour Mon.-Fri. 3-6:30pm.)

Inexpensive accommodations in Little Rock tend to cluster around **I-30** and **University Ave.,** both of which are a good 5 to 10 minute drive from downtown. The few motels in town that cost less and are generally unkempt. The **Little Rock Inn,** 6th and Center St. (376-8301), tenants half of a block downtown and includes a pool, saloon, laundry room and spacious but worn rooms without TV and telephone. ($30 per night for 1-2 people, $65 per week with $20 security deposit.) Other motels collect around the junctions of I-630 and I-430, west of downtown, including the **Mark 4000 Motel,** 4000 W. Markham (664-0950). Don't be fooled by the dingy exterior—recently renovated rooms boast comfortable and attractive decor. (Singles $25, doubles $28.) The **KOA Campground** (758-4598), on Crystal Hill Rd. in North Little Rock, seven mi. from downtown between exit 12 on I-430 and exit 148 on I-48, has a pool. (Sites from $16, with hookups $18.)

Most of Little Rock's streets were "planned" with no apparent pattern in mind. **Broadway** and **Main** are the major north-south arteries. **Markham** and all streets numbered one to 36 run east-west. **Third St.** turns into **W. Markham St.** as it moves west.

The **Arkansas Dept. of Parks and Tourism,** 1 Capitol Mall (800-643-8383 or 682-7777 in-state), in a complex directly behind the capitol building, has any map or brochure that you could possibly need. (Open Mon.-Fri. 8am-5pm.) The **Little Rock Bureau for Conventions and Visitors,** at Markham and Main St. (376-4781 or 800-844-7625), next door to the Excelsior Hotel, also dispenses useful information. (Open Mon.-Fri. 9am-3:30pm; closed for lunch about 11:30am-12:30pm.) For daily Little Rock activities listings, call **Telefun,** 372-3399. The **Amtrak** station is at Markham and Victory St. (372-6841 or 800-872-7245), near downtown. One train runs daily to St. Louis (7 hr.; $70) and Dallas (7 hr.; $77). The **Greyhound** station is at 118 E. Washington St. (372-1861), across the river in North Little Rock. Use the walkway over the bridge to get downtown. Buses lope to St. Louis ($65), New Orleans ($73), and Memphis ($19). Tickets are more expensive weekends, but advance purchases come with variable discounts. **Budget Car and Truck Rental,** 3701 E. Roosevelt St. (375-5521 or 800-527-0700) does its thing for $39 per day, 150 free mi., 20¢ per mi. over 150; $169 per week, 700 free mi.; 20¢ over 700. (Open Mon.-Sat. 6am-midnight, Sun. 7am-10pm.) The **Help Lines** are: **Rape Crisis,** 663-3334 (open 24 hrs.) and **First Call for Help,** 376-4567. In an **emergency,** call 911. The **post office** stamps and sends from 600 W. Capitol at 5th St. (377-6470). (Open Mon.-Fri. 7am-5:15pm.) Little Rock's **ZIP code** is 72201; the **area code** is 501.

Ozark Mountains

The **Ozark Mountains and National Forest** have lorded over the fertile resplendence of northern and central Arkansas for many a moon. Not towering or jagged, they gently ripple over the land. The roads along the range are less docile, twisting and tying a knot of pavement through the mountains. Out of this convoluted landscape emerged indigenous Ozark culture, immune to today's fleeting fashions and bonded by crafts, music, and religion.

Settling the land in northern Arkansas and southern Missouri required self-reliance and stubbornness, but today's traveler should find things a bit tamer than they were a century ago. The Ozarks have become a major resort area for Missouri, Arkansas, and neighboring states; tacky gift shops have sprung up along roadsides like kudzu. The scenery, however, remains outstandingly picturesque, and provides a beautiful background for long hikes. Arkansans love to canoe, fish, and float down the Ozarks' rivers; like-minded travelers should arrive before mid-summer, when the rivers begin to run too low for sport.

Few buses venture into the area, and hitching is *not* recommended. Drivers should follow U.S. 71, or Rte. 7 or 23 for best access and jaw-dropping views. Eureka Springs to Huntsville on Rte. 23 south is a scenic one-hour drive. Also head east or west on U.S. 62 from Eureka Springs for attractive stretches. The **Arkansas Department of Parks and Tourism** (800-643-8383; see Arkansas Practical Information) can help with your trip. If you want to paddle a portion of the **Buffalo National River,** call the ranger station for camping and canoe rental info (449-4311; canoe rental $22 per day, cabin $46 per day), or contact Buffalo Point Concessions, HCR, P.O. Box 388, Yellville 72687 (449-6206). The **Arkansas Bikeways Commission,** 1200 Worthen Bank Bldg., Little Rock 72201, dispenses a bike trail map for the Ozark region. The **Eureka Springs Chamber of Commerce,** (253-8737; 800-643-3546 outside AR) also has helpful vacation-planning material.

Mountain View

Although this petite village (pop. 2439) traces its name to a paper slip picked out of a hat in 1878, the town holds its own, refusing to kowtow to the beautiful surrounding scenery. Deeply rooted ties to early mountain culture help preserve the quaint skills and lifestyles characteristic of central and northern Arkansas. A melisma of mountain music often breezes through here in the several free, impromptu performances which erupt around the town square. Music has long found its home in this region: the dulcimer, a stringed instrument distinguished by a fret that extends the instrument's length, is native to the Ozarks. Mountain View boasts one of the finest dulcimer shops in the world, **McSpadden Dulcimers and Crafts,** P.O. Box 1230 (269-4313), where observers can watch craftspeople fashion this mellow music maker and can even hammer a few strings themselves. (Open Mon.-Fri. 9am-5pm, Sat. 10am-5pm. Free.) The annual **October Beanfest** draws cooks from all over Arkansas, and guarantees free samples from cast-iron pots full of beans. Cold winter nights find the town wrapped around a **community bonfire,** while during March and April, thousands of people from around the world arrive to celebrate spring with parades, square and jig dancing, clogging, and musical tributes. These annual occasions both sustain local traditions and initiate outsiders into the idiosyncrasies of Ozark culture. In the meantime, visitors can revel in the musical charisma of triple Grammy Award winner Jimmy Driftwood, the quintessential Ozark artist. His music emanates from the **Jimmy Driftwood Barn and Folk Museum**. (269-8042; shows are Fri. and Sun., 7:30pm 'til whenever. Free.)

Ozark culture survives most undiluted at the **Ozark Folk Center** (501-269-3851), just minutes north of Mountain View. The center recreates a mountain village and is a living museum of the cabin crafts, music, and lore of the Ozarks. For those who shudder at the steep walk to the center, a tram transports visitors from the central parking lot (free). Among the craftspeople practicing their trades in the **Crafts Forum** are a blacksmith, a basket weaver, a potter, a gunsmith, and a furniture maker. Visitors can taste freshly baked biscuits prepared by a cook in an antique kitchen for free, or for 50¢ dip their own candles in the chandler's shop. A wood carver sculpts faces from dried apples and a local herbalist concocts medicines from a garden beside the cottage. Musicians fiddle, pluck and strum daily at lunchtime and nightly in the auditorium (shows at 7:30pm) while dancers implore the audience to jig and clog along. The activities inspire both respect for the settlers' ingenuity as well as a reverent appreciation and understanding of nature. Seasonal events at the center include the **Arkansas Folk Festival** and the **Mountain and Hammered Dulcimer Championships** in late April, the **Banjo Weekend** in late May, the **Arkansas Old-Time Fiddlers Association State Championship** in late September and the **SPBGMA National Fiddle Championships** in mid-November. The Fiddlers Championships in particular are quite a sight; hundreds of experienced fiddlers, young and old, play the authentic music of the Ozarks. (Open May-Oct. daily 10am-5pm. Crafts area $5.50, ages 6-12 $3.25. Evening musical performances $6, ages 6-12 $4. Combination tickets and family rates are available.)

The areas around Mountain View abound with recreational activities. Fishing on the **White River** is a popular diversion, and licenses can be purchased at the Wal-Mart (425-9299) in Mountain View for around $10. If your legs ache from hiking, climb atop a horse and experience the Ozarks from a saddle for $10 per hour at either **Sylamore Trail Rides,** P.O. Box 210, Mountain View (585-2231; open Tues.-Sun. starting at 8am) or the **OK Trading Post**, Rte. 14 (585-2217), approximately 3½ mi. from the entrance to Blanchard Spring Caverns. Both places offer overnight trips and all-day rides by reservation. If you have your own horse, Sylamore horse trail loop maps are available at the Sylamore Ranger Station.

Daytrips from Mountain View to Buffalo River (about 45 min. northwest) add the option of **canoeing** down the river for about $25 per day. Concessionaires permitted by the National Park Services to rent equipment include **Dodd'd Float Service** (800-423-8731) and **Bennett's Canoe Rental** (449-6431). Such businesses also provide paddles, life jackets, and shuttle services to Take-Out Point. Hunters may purchase licenses at Wal-Mart and should contact the **Buffalo National River Park Services,** P.O. Box 1173, Harrison (741-5443 or 449-4311) for current info on seasons and regulations. For the adventurous hiker, the town of **Rush,** part of the Buffalo National Park River District, slowly decays about 30 mi. northwest of Mountain View off Rte. 14. Now a ghost town, it was formerly a zinc ore mining hub. Rush dates back to the 1880s and still has several buildings and foundations standing. Primitive camping areas with vault toilet, fire grates, and drinking water are available year-round; the town also has river access.

While Mountain View seems refreshingly unfettered by strings of fast-food restaurants (it only has 2), inexpensive food still abounds in local cafés and diners. The **Catfish House,** from Rte. 14 take School Dr. to Senior Dr. (269-3820), runs out of the gym of an old school complex and dishes up some of the best catfish in the area for $5 to $8 as well as nightly hoedowns with banjo and fiddle music, clogging and "Ozark humor." (Open Thurs.-Sat. 11am-9pm, Sun.-Wed. 11am-8pm.) The **Ozark Folk Center Restaurant,** Ozark Folk Center (269-3851) is a nice family-style restaurant that serves sandwiches ($3-4), chicken 'n dumplings ($5), and homemade desserts. All servers dress in period Ozark costumes. (Open daily 7am-8pm.) **Joshua's Mountain View** (269-4136) is a simple diner serving daily lunch specials and several different daily buffets, including a seafood buffet. (Sandwiches $2-3, dinner $6-8. Open Mon.-Sat. 5:30am-9pm, Sun. 5:30am-2pm.)

In spite of its small-town status, Mountain View offers several inexpensive accommodation options to the budget traveler. Sprinkled throughout the area are lodgings such as the **Mountain View Motel,** East Main St. (269-3209), whose rustic but clean rooms come with hot pots of free coffee. (Singles $24. Doubles $33.) The charming bed and country breakfast **Inn at Mountain View,** P.O. Box 812 Washington St. (269-4200 or 800-535-1301), a Victorian home with white trim and flower-lined stone paths, settles elegantly just off the town square. The reasonable price of its plushly decorated rooms and suites (all with private baths) includes a seven-course homemade breakfast. (Rooms/suites $42-88, with 20% discounts in the winter off-season.) Another B&B, the **Commercial Hotel,** P.O. Box 72 (269-4383), also flanks the town square and offers adorable rooms and suites with shared or private baths. (Rooms/suites $33-69.) **The Hearthstone Bakery** (269-3297) next door provides free breakfast for the hotel guests. Other tourists may partake of the bakery's culinary delights too, which include cookies and danishes for under $1, and loaves of homemade bread for $2. Specialty diet breads are also available. Visitors who choose to sleep at the **Ozark Folk Lodge** (269-3871 or 800-264-3655) will enjoy staying in this cottage with simple country furnishings and the convenience to the folk center. ($45 plus $5 each additional person, ages 1-13 free with an adult.)

Because Mountain View lies only 5 to 10 mi. south of the Ozark National Forest, the cheapest way to stay in the area is free: **camping**. Pitching a tent anywhere is free and legal (and usually safe) as long as the campsite does not block any road, path, or thoroughfare. **Blanchard Springs Caverns,** on the southern border of the Ozark Forest (501-757-2291), glow and drip with exquisite cave formations and glassy, cool springs. Two guided trails navigate the caverns (Open daily in summer 9am-6pm. Winter Mon.-Fri. 9am-6pm. Admission $7, ages 6-15, seniors, visitors with disabilities, and those with a Golden Eagle pass $3.50.) Campgrounds around the caverns include **Blanchard Springs Recreation Area** for $7 per site, the **Gunner Pool Recreation Area** for $5 per site, and **Barkshed Recreation Area** for free. For more information about the caverns, camping and the great number of hiking trails through the Ozark Forest, consult the Ozark National Sylamore Ranger District at P.O. Box 1279, Mountain View (757-2211).

The **Chamber of Commerce/tourist information center** is located on Main St. (269-8068; open Mon.-Fri. 8am-4:30pm, Sat. 9am-4pm). **Rental cars** are available at **Lackey Motors Car Rental** (269-3211), at the corner of Main St. and Peabody Ave. ($25 per day plus 25¢ per mi. Open Mon.-Sat. 8am-5:30pm. Check Practical Information, Little Rock for car rental rates from Little Rock to Mountain View.) The number of the **Mental Health and Rape Crisis Hotline** is 800-592-9503. The **Crisis Intervention** number is 800-542-1031. The **Department of Human Services** is at 269-8069. In **emergencies** dial **911.**

Mountain View's **ZIP code** is 72560; the **area code** is 501.

Eureka Springs

In the early 19th century, the Osage spread reports of a wonderful spring with magical healing powers. White settlers flocked to the site and quickly established a small town from which they sold bottles of the miraculous water. Built on piety, holy water and slick marketing, Eureka Springs recently has garnered fame for its **Great Passion Play** (253-9200), a production modeled after Germany's *Oberammergau* Passion Play, which depicts Christ's last days. (Performances April-Oct. Tues.-Wed., Fri.-Sun. 8:30pm. Tickets $8-9, ages 4-11 half-price. For reservations ask at where you're staying, or write P.O. Box 471, Eureka Springs 72632.) The amphitheater is off U.S. 62, just outside of town. **Gray Line Bus Tours** (253-9540) provides transportation to and from the play ($3 per person round-trip). They pick you up and drop you off at your hotel, motel, or campground. The theater is wheelchair-accessible.

The town is filled with tourist-oriented restaurants. Get away from the usual tourist glitz at the **Wagon Wheel,** 84 S. Main St. (253-9934), a country-western bar decorated with antiques. (Open Mon.-Fri. 10am-2am, Sat. 10am-midnight.) Accommodations in Eureka Springs are not difficult to find, as the town has more hotel beds than it does residents, yet prices are impossible to foresee. Daily fluctuations in supply and demand determine the price of a room. They generally drop on Mondays and Thursdays, when Passion Players take a break. For the best deal, call Richard Keller of **Keller's Country Dorm** (253-9100), to make reservations for a dorm bed, breakfast, dinner, and a reserved ticket to the Passion Play, all at $25 per night. This arrangement is particularly suited for church groups. (Open May-Oct.) There are several campgrounds near Eureka Springs, ranging in price from $5 to $10. **Pinehaven Campsites,** on U.S. 62 (253-9052), two mi. east of town, charges $10 per tent and $14 for a full RV hookup.

For extra help in planning your time here, call the **Chamber of Commerce** (800-643-3546 or 253-8737), located on U.S. 62 just north of Rte. 23. (Open May-Oct. daily 9am-5pm; Nov.-April Mon.-Fri. 9am-5pm.)

Eureka Springs's **ZIP code** is 72632; the **area code** is 501.

Georgia

Where else can you find great state roads, restaurants serving pre-sweetened iced tea, TV programs on how to fish and an indigenous population that speaks two languages (English and Suthun)? From the North Georgia mountains to the coastal plains and swamps, Georgia thrives on such alliterative industries as paper products, peanuts, pecans, peaches, poultry, and politicians. President Jimmy Carter's hometown and the only house ever owned by President Franklin D. Roosevelt both stand on red Georgia clay; the state's senior U.S. Senator Sam Nunn is a leader in the Democratic party. Coca-Cola was invented here in 1886; since then, it has gone on to carbonate and caffeinate the rest of the world. As 1996 nears, the leading industry will be tourism when the Olympic Games alight in Atlanta and are shared by coastal Savannah, a city with stately, romantic antebellum homes and colonial city blocks. The state blooms in the spring, glistens in the summer, and and mellows in the autumn, all the while welcoming y'all with peachy Southern hospitality. Stay here long and you'll *never* be able to shake Georgia from your mind.

Practical Information

Capital: Atlanta.

Visitor Information: Department of Industry and Trade, Tourist Division, 230 Peachtree St., Atlanta 30301 (656-3590), across from **Atlanta Convention and Visitors Bureau.** Write for or pick up a comprehensive *Georgia Travel Guide.* Open Mon.-Fri. 8am-5pm. **Department of Natural Resources,** 270 Washington St. S.W., Atlanta 30334 (800-542-7275; 404-656-3530 in GA). **U.S. Forest Service,** 1720 Peachtree Rd. N.W., Atlanta 30367 (347-2385). Info on the Chattahoochee and Oconee National Forests. Open Mon.-Fri. 8am-4pm.

Time Zone: Eastern.

Postal Abbreviation: GA

Sales Tax: 4%.

Atlanta

Atlanta has chutzpah. Not even Union General Sherman's "scorched earth" burning of Atlanta to the ground in 1864 could quench its spirit which—like its seal (the phoenix) and its motto *resurgens*—arose from the ashes to soar today as the largest metropolis in the Southeast and a nationwide economic powerhouse. The city contains the world's largest airport complex, the headquarters of Coca-Cola and CNN, and offices of 400 of the Fortune 500 corporations. Nineteen institutions of higher learning, including Georgia Tech, Morehouse College, Spelman College, and Emory University, call "Hotlanta" home, as does "America's team," the Atlanta Braves.

Not surprisingly, fame and prosperity have diluted Atlanta's Old South flavor. An influx of transplanted Northerners and Californians, the third-largest gay population in the U.S., and a host of ethnic groups contribute to the city's cosmopolitan air. This birthplace of Martin Luther King, Jr. witnessed unrest and activism during the 1960s; deeply impressed by lessons learned in the Civil Rights struggle, Atlanta elected one of the nation's first African-American mayors, Maynard Jackson, in 1974. Sleek and upbeat, Atlantans are already burning with Olympic fever; the city is beseiged by new construction at nearly every turn.

Practical Information and Orientation

Emergency: 911.

Visitor Information: Atlanta Convention and Visitors Bureau, 233 Peachtree St. #200 (659-4270), Peachtree Center, Harris Tower, downtown. Caters more to conventions; stop by to pick up a free copy of *Atlanta and Georgia Visitors' Guide* ($3 at newsstands). Open Mon.-Fri. 9am-5pm. Satellite information centers are at **Peachtree Center Mall** (659-0800), 233 Peachtree St. N.E. (open Mon.-Fri. 10am-6pm, Sat. 10am-5pm), and **Lenox Square Shopping Center** (233-6767), 3393 Peachtree Rd. N.E., in Buckhead (open Mon.-Sat. 10am-9:30pm, Sun. 12:30-5:30pm). Both open Mon.-Fri. 10am-5pm. Also at **Underground Atlanta,** Peachtree St. and Martin Luther King, Jr. Dr. (523-2311). Open Mon.-Sat. 10am-9pm, Sun. noon-6pm.

Traveler's Aid: 81 International Blvd. (527-7400), in the downtown Greyhound terminal. Limited info on accommodations. Open Mon.-Fri. 8am-5pm, Sat. 10am-6pm. After hours, call 522-7370 for assistance.

Hartsfield International Airport: south of the city, bounded by I-75, I-85, and I-285. General info 530-6600; international services and flight info 530-2081. Headquarters of **Delta Airlines** (756-5000 or 800-221-1212). International travelers can get phone assistance in 6 languages at the **Calling Assistance Center,** a computerized telephone system in the international terminal. MARTA (see Public Transport below) is the easiest way to get downtown, with 15-min. rides departing every 8 min., every day from 5am-1am with baggage space available. The **Atlanta Airport Shuttle** (525-2177) runs vans from the airport to midtown, downtown, Emory, and Lenox Sq. ($8-12). **Northside Airport Express** (768-7600) serves Stone Mountain, Marietta, and Dunwoody. Buses run daily 5am-midnight ($15-30).

Amtrak: 1688 Peachtree St. N.W. (872-9815), 3 mi. north of downtown at I-85. Take bus #23 to and from the "Arts Center" MARTA station. To: New Orleans (1 per day; 11 hr.; $95); Washington, DC (1 per day; 14 hr.; $119); Charlotte (1 per day; 5 hr.; $51). Open daily 6:30am-9:30pm.

Greyhound: 81 International Blvd. (522-6300), 1 block from Peachtree Center. MARTA: Peachtree Center. To: New Orleans (7 per day; 9 hr.; $58), Washington, DC (8 per day; 16 hr.; $79), and Chattanooga (8 per day; 2½ hr.; $99). Excellent discounts available with advanced reservations. Open 24 hrs.

Public Transport: Metropolitan Atlanta Rapid Transit Authority (MARTA), 848-4711; schedule info Mon.-Fri. 6am-10pm, Sat.-Sun. 8am-4pm. Combined rail and bus system serves virtually all area attractions and hotels. Operates Mon.-Sat. 5am-1:30am, Sun. 6am-12:30am in most areas. Fare $1.25 in exact change; transfers free. Unlimited weekly pass $11. Pick up a sys-

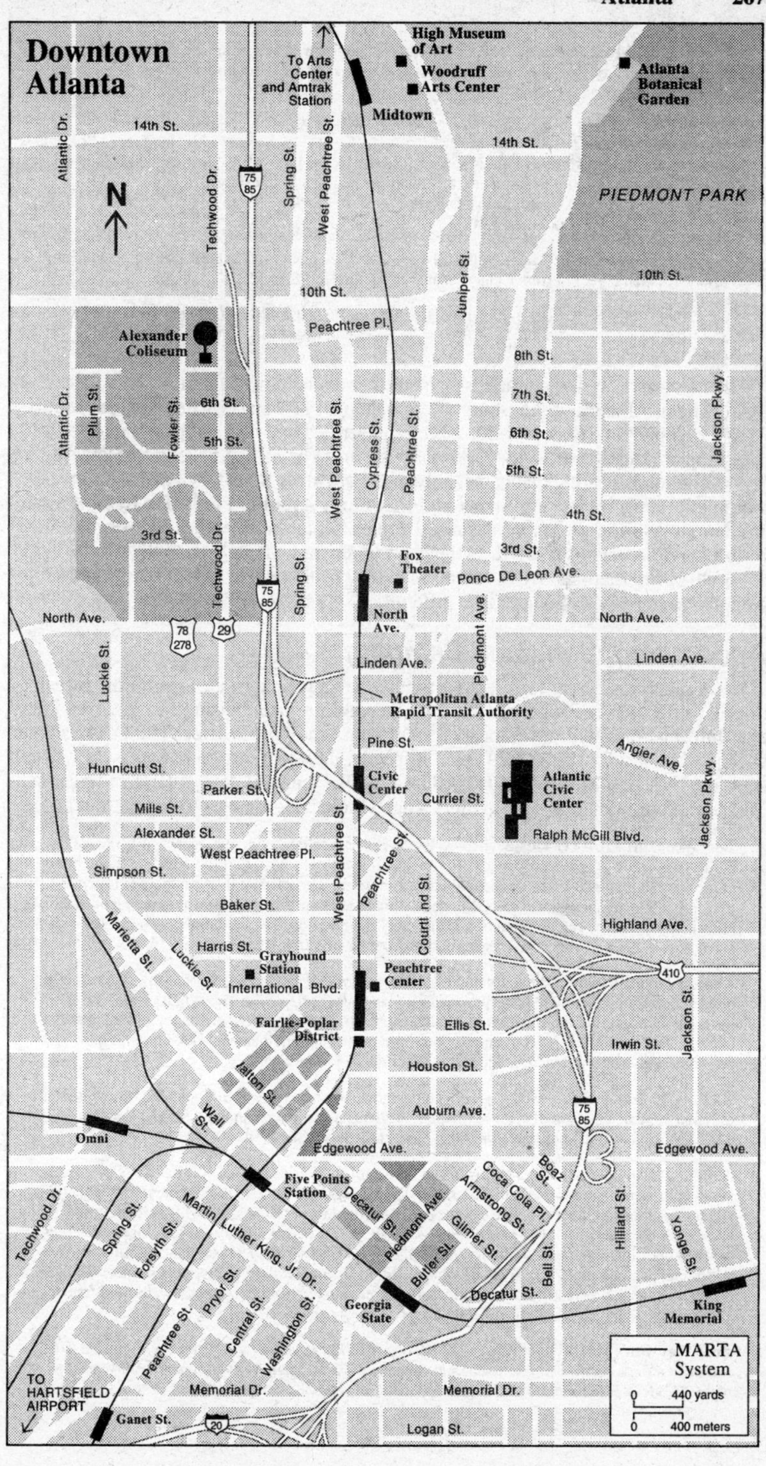
Downtown Atlanta
High Museum of Art
Woodruff Arts Center
To Arts Center and Amtrak Station
Midtown
Atlanta Botanical Garden
14th St.
Atlantic Dr.
Techwood Dr.
Spring St.
West Peachtree St.
PIEDMONT PARK
Juniper St.
10th St.
Peachtree Pl.
Alexander Coliseum
8th St.
7th St.
6th St.
5th St.
4th St.
3rd St.
Plum St.
Fowler St.
Cypress St.
Peachtree St.
Jackson Pkwy.
Fox Theater
Ponce De Leon Ave.
North Ave.
Piedmont Ave.
Linden Ave.
Luckie St.
Metropolitan Atlanta Rapid Transit Authority
Pine St.
Angier Ave.
Hunnicutt St.
Parker St.
Civic Center
Currier St.
Atlantic Civic Center
Mills St.
Alexander St.
Ralph McGill Blvd.
West Peachtree Pl.
Simpson St.
Baker St.
Courtland St.
Highland Ave.
Marietta St.
Harris St.
Greyhound Station
Peachtree Center
International Blvd.
Fairlie-Poplar District
Ellis St.
Irwin St.
Jackson St.
Houston St.
Auburn Ave.
Wall St.
Omni
Edgewood Ave.
Five Points Station
Decatur St.
Coca Cola Pl.
Boaz St.
Armstrong St.
Piedmont Ave.
Gilmer St.
Butler St.
Hilliard St.
Yonge St.
Bell St.
Techwood Dr.
Spring St.
Forsyth St.
Martin Luther King, Jr. Dr.
Pryor St.
Central St.
Washington St.
Georgia State
King Memorial
MARTA System
TO HARTSFIELD AIRPORT
Memorial Dr.
Ganet St.
Logan St.
440 yards
400 meters
75 85
78 278
29
410
20

tem map at the **MARTA Ride Store,** Five Points Station downtown, or at one of the satellite visitors bureaus. If you get confused, just find the nearest MARTA courtesy phone in each rail station.

Taxi: Checker, 351-1111. **London,** 681-2280. Base fare $1.50, $1.20 per mi.

Car Rental: Atlanta Rent-a-Car, 3185 Camp Creek Pkwy. (763-1160), just inside I-285, 3 mi. east of the airport. 9 other locations in the area including one at Cheshire Bridge Rd. and I-85, 1 mi. west of the Liddberg Center Railstop. Rates from $16 per day. 50 free mi., 20¢ each additional mi. Must be 21 with major credit card.

Help Lines: Rape Crisis Counseling, 659-7273. Open 24 hrs. **Gay/Lesbian Center Help Line,** 892-0661. Open daily 6-11pm. Center located at 63 12th St. (876-5372).

Post Office: 3900 Crown Rd. (768-4126). Open Mon.-Fri. 10am-4pm. **ZIP code:** 30321.

Area Code: 404.

Atlanta sprawls and drawls across the northwest quadrant of the state, 150 mi. east of Birmingham, AL and 113 mi. south of Chattanooga, TN. The city lies on north-south I-75 and I-85 and on east-west I-20. It is circumscribed by I-285 ("the perimeter").

Getting around is confusing—*everything* seems to be named Peachtree. However, of the 40-odd roads bearing that name, only one, **Peachtree Street,** is a major north-south thoroughfare, as are **Spring Street** and **Piedmont Avenue. Ponce De León Avenue** and **North Avenue** are major east-west routes. Note that **Gordon St.** is now called **Ralph David Abernathy Blvd.** In the heart of downtown, the area to the west of I-75/85, south of International Blvd. and north of the capitol, where angled streets and shopping plazas run amok, navigation is difficult.

Accommodations and Camping

When planning to stay in Atlanta for more than a few days, check with the **International Youth Travel Program (IYTP).** The convention and visitors bureau (see Practical Information), will try to locate a single for a reasonable price. The IYTP is your cheapest bet besides the YMCA. Unfortunately, these options do not apply to women from the U.S. **Bed and Breakfast Atlanta,** 1801 Piedmont Ave. N.E. (875-0525; call Mon.-Fri. 9am-noon or 2-5pm), offers singles from $45, doubles from $48 to $60.

The Woodruff HI/AYH-Hostel (875-9449) at 223 Ponce de León Ave. Reach it by MARTA: North Ave. station, exit onto Ponce de León, about 3½ blocks east. Part of a B&B in a Victorian home with stained glass windows. Kitchen and showers at no charge. Bike rentals $1. Linens $1. Sleep sack $2. A/C. Free local calls. Luggage storage $1. Free city magazine and map. No alcohol allowed. Free coffee and doughnuts 8-10am. Lockout noon-5pm and midnight-8am but key rentals available at small charge. 3-day max. stay. Members $12.50, nonmembers $14.50.

Atlanta Dream Hostel, 158 Garnett St. (659-3751; MARTA: Garnett St. station), is a recently opened hostel in downtown. If the proprietor's plans materialize, this place will rock with creative décor and a homey, communal living arrangement. Located in a huge former art gallery, it seeks to have 300 beds by the '96 Olympics—but right now it's pretty barren. Lockout 9am-3pm. $14 per night with kitchen, laundry, and shower facilities and free linen.

YMCA, 22 Butler St. (659-8085), between Edgewood and Auburn, 3 blocks from downtown. Men only and usually full of semi-permanent residents. Community shower. Singles $16. Key deposit $5. Hard to find space here, and they don't take reservations.

Motel 6, 4427 Commerce Dr. in East Point exit 2 off the Perimeter Rd. I-285 (762-5201), has a small earth-toned rooms and a pool. $22 for 1 person, $6 for each additional person. 4 other perimeter locations: 3585 Chamblee Tucker Rd. in Chamblee exit 27 (455-8000, singles $24 plus $6 each additional person); 6015 Oakbridge Pkwy. in Norcross exit 37 (446-2311; singles $22 plus $6 each additional person); 4100 Wendell Dr. S.W. exit 14 (696-0757; singles $22 plus $6 each additional person); and 2565 Weseley Chapel Rd. in Decatur exit 36 (288-6911; singles $25 plus $6 each additional person). Each location offers free movie channel, free local calls, and free accommodations for children under 18 staying with their parents.

Best Way Inn, 144 14th St. N.W. (873-4171). A fence separates you from the highway. Tidy rooms in a dark décor. Chinese restaurant. Local calls 30¢. Laundry facilities. Friendly management. Mexican restaurant. Pool. Singles $31. Doubles $36. Key deposit $5.

Red Roof Inn, 1960 Druid Hills exit 31 off I-85 (321-1653), offers rooms with clean, modern décor and pleasant tree-cloistered location. Convenient to downtown. Look carefully for the sign, it's partially hidden by branches. Singles $30. Doubles $39.

KOA South Atlanta, Mt. Olive Rd. in McDonough exit 72 off I-75 (957-2610), offers tent sites with water for $15, add $2 for electricity. Showers, pool, laundry, and fishing pond on the premises. You can also try **KOA West Atlanta,** 2420 Old Alabama Rd. in Austell (941-7485), 3 mi. west of six Flags Amusement Park.

Stone Mountain Family Campground, on U.S. 78 (498-5710), 16 mi. east of town. Exit 30-B off I-285 or subway to Avondale then "Stone Mountain" bus. Part of state park system. Tent sites $12. RV sites $13 with water and electricity and $1 sewer. Reservations not accepted. Entrance fee $5 per car.

Food

You'll have to scrounge to find inexpensive home-style Southern cooking in Atlanta. Some favorite dishes to sample include fried chicken, black-eyed peas, okra, sweet-potato pie, and mustard greens. Dip a hunk of cornbread into "pot likker," water used to cook greens, and enjoy. For a cheap breakfast, you can't beat the Atlanta-based **Krispy Kreme Doughnuts** whose baked delights are a Southern institution. The original company store is at 295 Ponce de León Ave. N.E. (876-7307). Savor Atlanta's many European and ethnic restaurants which, from Russian to Ethiopian, provide a torrent of treats to tantalize tourists' tastebuds. A flock of these foreign flavors fly at **Little Five Points,** at the intersection of Moreland and Euclid Ave. N.E., Atlanta's bohemian "village" of quirky shops, second-hand stores, and cafés run by both true and wanna-be hippies.

Do-it-yourself-ers can procure produce and regionally popular items such as chitlins, pork cracklin', sugar cane, collards, and yams at the **Atlanta Municipal Market,** corner of Butler St. and Edgewood Ave. (659-1665). Serving downtown Atlantans since 1923, this market also houses inexpensive deli stalls such as the **Snack Bar** where the adventurous visitor can munch on a hot pig ear sandwich ($1.25). For a more international arena, shoppers should take the subway to Arondale and then the "Stone Mountain" bus to the **Dekalb County Farmers Market,** 3000 E. Ponce De León Ave. (377-6400), where world-wide specialties run the gustatory gamut from Chinese to Middle Eastern and everything in between. For those who wouldn't mind finding themselves sifting through heaps of fresh fruit and vegetables in the middle of nowhere, head for the 80 acres of **Atlanta's State Farmers Market,** 16 Forest Pkwy. (366-6910), exit 78 off I-75 south. (No MARTA service; open Mon.-Fri. 10am-10pm, Sat.-Sun. 9am-9pm.)

Mary Mac's Tea Room (875-4337), 224 Ponce De León Ave. N.E. Take the "Georgia Tech" bus north. Famous for its amazing home-made cornbread and array of real Southern vegetables. A bit like cafeteria food, but home-cooked and very filling. Order by writing your own ticket. Waiters tend to rush you. Lunches $5-7, dinners $6-10. Students with ID receive 10% discount at dinner. Open Mon.-Fri. 11am-4pm and 5-8pm.

The Varsity, 61 North Ave. N.W. at I-85 (881-1706). Take MARTA to North Ave. station. Order at the world's largest drive-in or brave the local masses to eat inside. Best known for chili dogs ($1-2) and the greasiest onion rings (90¢) in the South. Employees have a language all their own. Eat in one of the giant TV rooms—1 room for each channel and vice-versa. Open Sun.-Thurs. 7am-12:30am, Fri.-Sat. 7am-2am.

Nicola's, 1602 Lavista Rd. N.E. (325-2524), cooks, bakes, and dishes up the most savory and authentic Lebanese cuisine in Atlanta. Try the meza combination platter ($25) that can satisfy 4. Probably the best bet for individuals is to order among the appetizers, forget the silverware, and scoop the flavorful food with the warm pita that comes with the meal. Look for raw kibby, a Lebanese delicacy, on Sat. nights. Open daily 5:30-10:30pm.

Eat Your Vegetables Café, 438 Moreland Ave. N.E. (523-2671), in the Little Five Points area. A friendly corner eatery serving vegetarian entrées $7-8, including a daily macrobiotic dinner special. Chicken and seafood entrées $8-9. Also vegetarian lunches (hummus, soyburgers, and salads) at cheaper prices. Your mother would be proud. Open Mon.-Fri. 11:30am-3pm and 6-10pm, Fri. 'til 10:30pm,. Sat. 11am-3pm and 5:30-10:30pm, Sun. 11am-3pm.

Touch of India, 962 Peachtree St. (876-7777) and 2065 Piedmont Rd (876-7775). 3-course lunch specials $4. Popular with locals. Atmosphere and service worthy of a much more expensive restaurant. Dinners $6-10. Open Mon.-Sat. 11:30am-2:30pm and 5:30-10:30pm.

Sights

Atlanta's sights may seem scattered, but the effort it takes to find them usually pays off. The **Atlanta Preservation Center,** The De Soto, Suite 3 on 156 7th St. N.E. (876-2040), offers seven walking tours of popular areas: Fox Theatre District, West End and the Wren's Nest, Historic Downtown, Miss Daisy's Druid Hills, Inman Park, Underground and Capitol area, and Sweet Auburn—from April through November. The Fox Theater tour is given year-round. All tours last about two hours. ($5, students and seniors $3. Call for exact times and starting points.)

Hopping on MARTA and taking in the sites on your own is the cheapest and most rewarding tour option. An intimate part of southern history can be explored at the **Martin Luther King, Jr. National Historic Site** at the Church, birthplace, burial place, and museum of the youngest man (at 35 years old) ever to be awarded a Nobel Peace Prize. Stop by the **National Park Service Visitors Center,** 522 Auburn Ave. N.E. (331-3920; open daily 9am-5pm), for helpful and informative maps and pamphlets about the **Sweet Auburn District** and the life of King. **Ebenezer Baptist Church,** 407 Auburn Ave. (688-7263), where King was pastor from 1960 to 1968, is now open to the public, as are its Sunday worship services. In the coming year, however, the church will be transmogrified into a visitors center for the National Park Service and a new church for the local congregation will be built across the street. (Open Mon.-Fri. 9am-5:30pm. Call for weekend hours.) The 23½ acre area encompassed by the park also includes the restored Victorian **birthplace of King,** 501 Auburn Ave. N.E. (331-3920; open daily 10am-5pm, hours extended April-Sept; free). King is buried at the **Martin Luther King Center for Nonviolent Social Exchange,** 449 Auburn Ave. N.E. (524-1956), which also holds a collection of King's personal effects and a film about his life. Take bus #3 from Five Points or Edgewood/Candler Park Stations. (Open daily 9am-5pm, later in the summer months. Film admission $1.)

Other fine reflections of Southern history are mounted in the galleries of **Hammonds House,** 503 Peeples St. S.W. (752-8730), which display a fantastic collection of African-American art. Take bus #71 from West End Station South to the corner of Oak and Peeples. (Open Tues.-Fri. 10am-6pm, Sat.-Sun. 1-6pm; ages 16 and older $1.) Also in the **West End**—Atlanta's oldest neighborhood, dating from 1835—hover the **Wren's Nest,** 1050 Ralph D. Abernathy Blvd. (753-5835), home to Joel Chandler Harris who popularized the African folktale trickster Br'er Rabbit through stereotypical slave character Uncle Remus. Take bus #71 from West End station South. (Open Tues.-Sat. 10am-5pm, Sun. 1-5pm. Tours $3, teens and seniors $2, ages 4-12 $1, storytelling is $1 extra.) Visit also the **Herndon Home,** 587 University Place N.W. (581-9813), a 1910 Beaux Arts Classical mansion built by slave-born Alonzo F. Herndon who was a prominent barber before becoming Atlanta's wealthiest African-American in the early 1900s. Herndon amassed his fortune by founding Atlanta Life Insurance Company, the country's largest black insurance company. Take bus #3 from Five Points station to the corner of MLK, Jr. Drive and Maple, walk one block north. (Open Tues.-Sat. 10am-4pm. Free.)

Buckhead shows off one of the most beautiful residences in the Southeast. The Greek Revival **Governor's Mansion,** 391 West Paces Ferry Rd. (261-1776; take bus #40 "West Paces Ferry" from Lenox Station), has elaborate gardens and furniture from the Federal period. (Tours Tues.-Thurs. 10-11:30am. Free.) In the same neighborhood, discover the **Atlanta History Society,** 3101 Andrew Dr. N.W. (261-1837). On the grounds are the **Swan House,** a lavish Anglo-Palladian Revival home, and the **Tullie Smith House,** an antebellum farmhouse. Don't miss the intriguing *"Atlanta Resurgens"* exhibit, in which famous and not-so-famous Atlantans praise the city. A special behind-the-scenes exhibit of the movie *Gone With the Wind* will be on display through July 19, 1993. Look also for the late 1992 opening of the **New Museum of Atlanta History** featuring a Civil War Gallery with one of the finest collections in the country.

(Tours every ½-hr. Open Mon.-Sat. 9am-5:30pm, Sun. noon-5pm. Admission $6, seniors and students $4.50, kids $3.)

In shady **Grant Park,** between Cherokee Ave. and Boulevard, revolves the **Cyclorama,** 800 Cherokee Ave. (758-7625), a massive panoramic painting (42 ft. high and 900 ft. around) that recreates the 1864 Civil War Battle of Atlanta with 3-D features and light and sound effects. (Open June-Sept. daily 9:30am-5:30pm, Oct.-May daily 9:30am-4:30pm. $3.50, students and seniors $3, ages 6-12 $2.) Next door growls **Zoo Atlanta,** 800 Cherokee Ave. (624-5678), whose entertaining animal displays stress conservation and environmental awareness. Among the special exhibits are the Masai Mara, Mzima Springs and the Ford African Rain Forest. Take the Atlanta Express Shuttle during summer months. (Open daily 10am-5pm, 'til 6pm on weekends during Daylight Savings Time. $7, ages 3-11 $4.50, under 3 free.)

North of Grant Park, **Oakland Cemetery,** 248 Oakland Ave. S.E. (577-8163), pushes up daisies with the graves of golfer Bobby Jones and *Gone With the Wind* author Margaret Mitchell. (Open daily sunrise-sunset. Information Center open Mon.-Fri. 9am-5pm. Free. Take bus #3.) True fans of Rhett Butler and Scarlett O'Hara can visit the Margarett Mitchell Room in the **Atlanta Public Library,** 1 Margarett Mitchell (730-1700), to peruse memorabilia such as autographed copies of her famous novel (open Mon and Fri. 9am-6pm, Tues.-Thurs. 9am-8pm, Sat. 10am-6pm, Sun. 2-6pm), or they can drive by the dilapidated three-story house on the corner of 10th and Crescent where Mitchell used to live.

Outside of these historical and culture-preserving sights, however, high-tech "Hotlanta" reigns with multinational business powerhouses situated in business-oriented **Five Points District** downtown. Influential **Turner Broadcasting System** offers an insider's peek with its **Cable News Network (CNN) Studio Tour,** corner of Techwood Dr. and Marietta St. (827-2300), that reveals the day-to-day workings of a 24-hr. cable news station. Witness anchorpeople broadcasting the news live while writers toil in the background. (Open daily 9am-5:30pm, 50-min. tours given on the half-hour with a 10 person min. $5, ages 5-12 and seniors $2.50. Take the subway west rail line to the Omni/Dome/GWCC Station at W1.)

Occasionally the CNN cameras turn a few blocks to the south on the **Georgia State Capitol,** Capitol Hill at Washington St. (656-2844; MARTA: George State.) The gold that gilds the dome was mined nearby in Dahlonega, GA. (Tours Mon.-Fri. on the hr. 10am-2pm except noon. Open Mon.-Fri. 8am-5pm. Free.) Georgia moved into the nation's spotlight when former governor Jimmy Carter became U.S. President. Today the **Carter Presidential Center,** 1 Copenhill (331-3942), north of Little Five Points documents the Carter Administration (1977-1981) through exhibits and films; surrounded by lovely landscaped grounds, the center also houses a Japanese garden and café. Take bus #16 to Cleburne Ave. from Five Points Station. (Open Mon.-Sat. 9am-4:45pm, Sun. noon-4:45pm. Admission $2.50, seniors $1.50, under 16 free.)

Redeveloped **Underground Atlanta** gets down with six subterranean blocks filled with over 120 shops, restaurants, and night spots. Descend the entrance beside the Five Points subway station. In the summer, live musicians often play in and around Underground. (Shops open Mon.-Sat. 10am-9:30pm, Sun. noon-6pm. Bars and restaurants open later.) Take a quantum leap to **Elusive Image,** a gallery of holographic art located in Underground. (Open during regular business hours. Free.) **Atlanta Heritage Row,** 55 Upper Alabama St. in Underground (584-7879), documents the city's past and looks into the future with exhibits and films. (Open Tues.-Sat. 10am-6pm, Sun. 1-6pm. Admission $3, seniors and students over 12 $2.50, kids $2.) Adjacent to the shopping complex is the **World of Coca-Cola Pavilion,** 55 Martin Luther King, Jr. Dr. (676-5151), clearly recognizable with its Times-Square-style neon Coca-Cola sign stretching 26 ft. across. The $15 million facility highlights "the real thing's" humble beginnings in Atlanta with over 1000 artifacts and interactive displays. (Open Mon.-Sat. 10am-9:30pm, Sun. noon-6pm. Admission $2.50, seniors $2, ages 6-12 $1.50.)

North of the city, on the other side of downtown, is **Piedmont Park,** home to the 60-acre **Atlanta Botanical Garden,** Piedmont Ave. at the Prado (876-5858). Stroll through five acres of landscaped gardens, a 15-acre hardwood forest with walking trails, and an exhibition hall. The **Dorothy Chapman Fugua Conservatory** houses hundreds of species of rare tropical plants. Take bus #36 "North Decatur" from the Arts Center subway stop. (Open Tues.-Sat. 9am-8pm during Daylight Savings Time, til 6pm at other times of the year. Admission $4.50, seniors and kids $2.25. Thurs. 1:30-8pm, 6pm during Daylight Savings Time. Free.) Just to the west of the park, the **Woodruff Arts Center,** 1280 Peachtree St. (892-3600; take the subway to Arts Center), houses the **Alliance Theatre** as well as the **High Museum** (892-4444), Richard Meier's award-winning building of glass, steel, and white porcelain. The museum includes European decorative arts, European and American paintings, photography, and a variety of (con)temporary art exhibits. (Open Tues.-Thurs. and Sat. 10am-5pm, Fri. 10am-9pm, Sun. noon-6pm. Admission $4, seniors and students with ID $2, kids $1. Free Thurs. 1-5pm.) The museum branch at **Georgia-Pacific Center** (577-6939), one block south of Peachtree Center Station, is free (open Mon.-Fri. 11am-5pm).

A different mode of culture prances at the **Center for Puppetry Arts,** 1404 Soring St. N.W. (873-3391 or 874-0398), whose museum features Wayland Flower's "Madame," traditional Punch and Judy figures, Asian hand-carved puppets, and some of Jim Henson's original Muppets. Attend one of the center's highly popular productions given at a variety of times throughout the year. Call for current info and reservations. (Museum open Mon.-Sat. 9am-4pm. $3, ages 2-13 $2.)

Entertainment

For sure-fire fun in Atlanta, buy a MARTA pass (see Practical Information above) and pick up one of the city's free publications on music and events. *Creative Loafing, Music Atlanta,* the *Hudspeth Report,* or "Leisure" in the Friday edition of the *Atlanta Journal* will all help you "eat the peach." *Southern Voice* also has complete listings on gay and lesbian news and nightclubs throughout Atlanta. Look for free summer concerts in Atlanta's parks.

The outstanding **Woodruff Arts Center,** 1280 Peachtree St. N.E. (892-3600), houses the Atlanta Symphony and the Alliance Theater Company. For more plays and movies check the Moorish and Egyptian Revival Movie Palace, the **Fox,** 660 Peachtree St. (249-6400), or the **Atlanta Civic Center,** 395 Piedmont St. (523-6275).

Atlanta's nightlife ripens into a frenetic, sweet, and inexpensive fuzziness. Night spots concentrate in Buckhead, Underground Atlanta, Little Five Points, and **Virginia Highlands,** a neighborhood east of downtown with trendy shops and a friendly, hip atmosphere. **Underground Atlanta** has the newest concept in suiting all tastes. A street called **Kenny's Alley** is composed solely of bars—a blues club, a dance emporium, a jazz bar, a country/western place, a New Orleans-style daquiri bar, and an oldies dancing spot. For blues, go to **Blind Willie's,** 828 N. Highland Ave. (873-2583), a dim, usually packed club with Cajun food and occasional big name acts. (Live music 10pm-2am. Open daily at 6pm. Cover Mon.-Fri. $4, Sat.-Sun. $7.) A college-age crowd usually fills Little Five Points heading for **The Point,** 420 Moreland Ave. (577-6468), where you'll always get live music. (Open Mon.-Fri. 4pm-until, Sat. 1pm-3am, Sun. 1pm-4am. Cover $4-5.) Towards downtown, the newly opened **Masquerade,** 695 North Ave. (577-8178), is housed in an original turn-of-the-century mill. The bar has three different levels: heaven, with live hard-core music; purgatory, a more laid-back coffee house; and hell, offering progressive dance music. (Open Wed.-Sun. 9pm-4am. Cover $5-7 or higher, depending on which band is performing. 18 and over.) **The Tower,** 735 Ralph McGill Blvd. (688-5463), is a popular lesbian bar and dance club. (Open Mon.-Thurs. 4:30pm-1am, Fri. 4:30pm-4am, Sat. 4:30pm-3am.) **Backstreet,** 845 Peachtree St. N.E. (873-1986), a hot gay dance spot, stays open almost all night.

A respite from the city is available at **Stone Mountain Park** (498-5600), 16 mi. east on U.S. 78, where a fabulous bas-relief monument to the Confederacy is carved into the world's largest mass of granite. The "Mount Rushmore of the South" features Jefferson Davis, Robert E. Lee, and Stonewall Jackson and measures 90 by 190 ft. Surrounded by a 3200-acre recreational area, the mountain dwarfs the enormous statue. Check out the dazzling laser show on the side of the mountain each summer night at 9:30pm. (Free.) Take bus #120 "Stone Mountain" from the Avondale subway stop; buses leave only Monday through Friday at 4:30 and 7:50pm. (Park gates open daily

6am-midnight; attractions open 10am-9pm in the summer, 10am-5:30pm off-season. Admission $5 per car.)

Six Flags, 7561 Flags Rd. S.W. (948-9290), at I-20 W., is one of the largest (331 acres) theme amusement parks in the nation, and includes several rollercoasters, a free-fall machine, live shows, and white-water rides. On summer weekends, the park is packed to the gills. Take bus #201 ("Six Flags"; $1.25) from Hightower Station. (Open summer Sun.-Thurs. 10am-10pm, Fri.-Sat. 10am-midnight. One-day admission $24, kids under 48 in. $18; be sure to check local grocery stores and soda cans for ticket discounts.)

Brunswick and Environs

Beyond its hostel and the nearby beaches, laid-back Brunswick is of little interest to the traveler except as a relaxing layover between destinations. The **Hostel in the Forest (HI/AYH)** (264-9738, 265-0220, or 638-2623) is located 9 mi. west of Brunswick on U.S. 82, just past a small convenience store. Take I-95 to exit 6 and travel west on U.S. 82 (a.k.a. 84) about 1½ mi. from the interchange until you see the white-lettered wooden sign set back in the trees along the eastbound lane. Make a U-turn ½ mi. farther along at Myer Hill Rd. The hostel itself is of low-impact construction ½ mi. back from the highway; every effort is made to keep the area surrounding the complex of geodesic domes and treehouses as natural as possible. No lock-out, no curfew, and few rules. The low-key managers will shuttle you to the Brunswick Greyhound station for $2. The manager can usually be convinced to use the pickup to make daytrips to Savannah, the Okefenokee Swamp, and the coastal islands. If possible, arrange to stay in one of the two treehouses at the hostel, each complete with a 25-square-ft. picture window and a spacious double bed. Bring insect repellent if you plan to stay in the summertime since mosquitos and yellow biting flies abound. In addition to a peahen named Cleopatra and numerous chickens, the hostel has an extensive patch of blueberry bushes; you can pick and eat as many berries as you wish from late May to mid-June. (HI/AYH members $8.)

Twin Oaks Pit Barbecue, 2618 Norwick St. (265-3131), eight blocks from downtown Brunswick across from the Southern Bell building, features a chicken-and-pork combination ($6). The breaded french fries ($.85) are deep fried and deeeeelicious. (Open Mon.-Sat. 11am-8pm.)

The nearby **Golden Isles,** which include **St. Simon's Island, Jekyll Island,** and **Sea Island,** have miles of white sand beaches. Near the isles, **Cumberland Island National Seashore** is 16 mi. of salt marsh, live-oak forest, and sand dunes laced with a network of trails and disturbed only by a few decaying mansions. Reservations (882-4335) are necessary for overnight visits, but the effort is often rewarded; you can walk all day on the beaches without seeing another person. (Reservations by phone only: call daily 10am-2pm.) Sites are available on a stand-by basis 15 minutes before the twice-daily ferry departures to Cumberland Island. The **ferry** (45 min., $8) leaves from St. Mary's on the mainland at the terminus of Rte. 40, at the Florida border. Daily departures are at 9 and 11:45am, returning at 10:15am and 4:45pm; off-season Thurs.-Mon. only.

The **Greyhound** station, at 1101 Glouster St. (265-2800; open Mon.-Fri. 8am-noon and 1-11pm, Sat. 8am-noon and 3-9pm, Sun. 9-11am and 3-9pm), offers service to Jacksonville (5 per day, 1½ hr., $15) and Savannah (4 per day, 1½ hr., $14).

The **area code** for the region is 912.

Savannah

In February of 1733, General James Oglethorpe and his rag-tag band of 120 colonists founded the state of Georgia at Tamacraw Bluff on the Savannah River. Since then the city has had a stint as the capital of Georgia, housed the first girl scout troop in the U.S., and provided enough inspiration for Eli Whitney, longtime Savannah resident, to invent the cotton gin.

When the price of cotton crashed at the turn of the century, many of the homes and warehouses along River Street fell into disrepair, and the townhouses and mansions that lined Savannah's boulevards became boarding houses or rubble. In the mid-1950s, a group of concerned citizens mobilized to restore the downtown area, preserving the numerous Federalist and English Regency houses as historic monuments. Today four historic forts, broad streets, and trees-hung with Spanish moss enhance the city's classic Southern aura. This beautiful backdrop will serve as the site for the boating and yachting events during the 1996 Olympic Summer Games.

Practical Information and Orientation

Emergency: 911.

Savannah Visitors Center, 301 Martin Luther King, Jr. Blvd. (944-0456), at Liberty St. in a lavish former train station. Excellent free maps and guides. Open Mon.-Fri. 8:30am-5pm, Sat.-Sun. 9am-5pm. The **Savannah History Museum,** in the same building, has photographs, exhibits, and 2 brief films depicting the city's history. Open daily 9am-4pm. Admission $2.75, seniors $2.50, teens $1.25, kids free.

Amtrak: 2611 Seaboard Coastline Dr. (234-2611 or 800-872-7245), 4 mi. outside the city. Taxi fare to city about $6. To Charleston, SC (2 per day; 13/4 hr.; $24) and Washington, DC (7 per day; 11 hr.; $115). Open 24 hrs.

Greyhound: 610 E. Oglethorpe Ave. (232-2135), convenient to downtown. To: Jacksonville (11 per day; 3 hr.; $22), Charleston, SC (3 per day; 2½ hr.; $26), Washington, DC (8 per day; 17 hr.; $109). Open 24 hrs.

Public Transport: Chatham Area Transit (CAT), 233-5767. Buses operate daily 6am-11pm. Fare 75¢, transfers 5¢. **C&H Bus,** 530 Montgomery St. (232-7099). The only public transportation to Tybee Beach. Buses leave from the civic center in summer at 8:15am, 1:30pm, and 3:30pm, returning from the beach at 9:25am, 2:30pm, and 4:30pm. Fare $1.75.

Help Line: Rape Crisis Center, 233-7273.

Post Office: 2 N. Fahm St. (235-4646). Open Mon.-Fri. 8:30am-5pm. **ZIP code:** 31402.

Area Code: 912.

Savannah smiles on the coast of Georgia at the mouth of the **Savannah River,** which runs along the border with South Carolina. Charleston, SC, lies 100 mi. up the coast; Brunswick, GA lies 90 mi. to the south. The city stretches south from bluffs overlooking the river. The restored 2½-sq.-mi. **downtown historic district** is bordered by **East Broad, Martin Luther King, Jr. Blvd., Gaston Street** and the river. This area is best explored on foot. **Tybee Island,** Savannah's beach, is 18 mi. east on U.S. 80 and Rte. 26. Try to visit at the beginning of spring, the busiest and most beautiful season in Savannah.

Accommodations and Camping

Make your first stop in Savannah the visitors center (see Practical Information), where a wide array of coupons offer 15 to 20% discounts on area hotels. The downtown motels cluster near the historic area, visitors center, and Greyhound station. Do not stray south of Gaston St., where the historic district quickly deteriorates into an unsafe and seedy area. For those with cars, Ogeechee Rd. (U.S. 17) has several independently owned budget options.

Quality Inn, 231 W. Boundary St. (232-3200), just west of the Greyhound station. Fairly luxurious rooms with cable TV and in-room movies. Ask about free transportation to the airport and bus station. Singles $45. Doubles $50.

Bed and Breakfast Inn, 117 Gordon St. (238-0518), on Chatham Sq. in the historic district. Pretty little rooms have TV, A/C, and shared bath. Singles $30. Doubles $38. Add $10 on weekends. Reservations required.

Budget Inn, 3702 Ogeechee Rd. (233-3633), a 10-min. drive from the historic district. Take bus #25B ("Towers and Ogeechee"). Comfortable rooms with TV and A/C. Pool. Singles and doubles $28, cheaper with coupons. Suites, family rooms and kitchenettes $40. Reservations recommended; call collect.

Sanddollar Motel, 11 16th St. (786-5362), at Tybee Island 1½ mi. south on Butler Ave. A small, family-run motel practically on the beach. Most rooms rented weekly for $135. Singles may be available for $35 (less on weekdays and in winter). A 4-day stay Sun.-Wed. is $60.

Skidaway Island State Park (356-2523), 13 mi. southeast of downtown off Diamond Causeway. Inaccessible by public transportation. Follow Liberty St. east out of downtown; soon after it becomes Wheaton St., turn right on Waters Ave. and follow it to the Diamond Causeway. Bathrooms and heated showers. Sites $10. Parking $2. Check-in before 10pm.

Richmond Hill State Park, off Rte. 144 (727-2339), ½-hr. drive south of downtown; take exit 15 off I-95. Quieter than Skidaway and usually less crowded. Sites $10. Parking $2. Check-in before 10pm. Registration office open daily 8am-5pm.

Food

In Savannah cheap food is easy to come by. Try the waterfront area for budget meals in a pub-like atmosphere. The early-bird dinner specials at **Corky's,** 407 E. River St. (234-0113), range from $4 to $6. **Kevin Barry's Irish Pub,** 117 W. River St. (233-9626), has live Irish folk music Wednesday to Sunday after 9pm, as well as cheap drinks during happy hour.

Jack's Food World, 30 Barnard St. (223-2552). It doesn't look like much from the outside, but the food is truly good. Sandwiches $3-5, 16-in. pizza $8. Open Mon.-Thurs. 11am-6pm, Fri. 11am-8pm, Sat.-Sun. 7:30am-8pm.

Morrison's Family Dining, 15 Bull St., near Johnson Sq. downtown. Traditional U.S. and Southern cooking, multi-item menu. Full meals $3-5. Whole pies $2. The food is guaranteed—if you don't like it, you don't pay for it. Open Mon.-Fri. 7:30am-8pm, Sat.-Sun. 11am-8pm.

Hard Hearted Hannah's, 318 W. Saint Julian St., in the city market. Live jazz Mon.-Sat. night, and a soft-hearted omelette bar beginning at 10pm Fri.-Sat. Open Mon.-Sat. 4pm-until.

Sights and Events

In addition to restored antebellum houses, the downtown area includes over 20 small parks and gardens. The **Historic Savannah Foundation,** 210 Broughton St. (233-7703; call 233-3597 for reservations; 24-hrs.), offers a variety of guided one- and two-hour tours ($6-10). You can also catch any number of bus and van tours ($7-12) leaving about every 10 to 15 minutes from outside the visitors center (see Practical Information above). Ask inside for details.

The best-known historic houses in Savannah are the **Owens-Thomas House,** 124 Abercorn St. (233-9743), on Oglethorpe Sq., and the **Davenport House,** 324 E. State St. (236-8097), a block away on Columbia Sq. The Owens-Thomas House is one of the best examples of English Regency architecture in the U.S. (Open Feb.-Dec. Sun.-Mon. 2-5pm., Tues.-Sat. 10am-5pm. Last tour at 4:30pm. Admission $4, students $2, kids $1.) The Davenport House typifies the Federalist style and contains an excellent collection of Davenport china. By the 1930s, the house had become a tenement, and the owners planned to raze it for a parking lot. Its salvation in 1955 marked the birth of the Historical Savannah Foundation and the effort to restore the city. There are guided tours of the first floor every 15 minutes; explore the second and third floors at your leisure. (Open Tues.-Sat. 10am-4pm, Sun. 1:30-4pm. Last tour at 4pm. Admission $5.)

Lovers of Thin Mints, Scot-teas, and, of course, Savannahs should make a pilgrimage to the **Juliette Gordon Low Girl Scout National Center,** 142 Bull St. (233-4501), near Wright Square. The association's founder was born here on Halloween of 1860, possibly explaining the Girl Scouts' door-to-door treat-selling technique. The center's "cookie shrine," in one of the most beautiful houses in Savannah, contains an interesting collection of Girl Scout memorabilia. (Open Feb.-Nov. Mon.-Tues. and Thurs.-Sat. 10am-4pm, Sun. 2:30-4:30pm; Dec.-Jan. Mon.-Sat. 10am-4pm. Admission $3, ages under 18 $2.25.) One block down in **Johnson Square,** at the intersection of Bull and E.

Saint Julian St., is the burial obelisk of Revolutionary War hero Nathaniel Green; a plaque contains an epitaph by the Marquis de Lafayette.

For a less conventional view of Savannah's history, arrange to tour the **Negro Heritage Trail,** visiting African-American historic sights from early slave times to the present. Three different tours are available on request from the Savannah branch of the Association for the Study of Afro-American Life and History, King-Tisdell Cottage, Negro Heritage Trail, 514 E. Huntington St., Savannah 31405 (234-8000; open Mon.-Fri. noon-5pm). One day's notice is necessary; admission depends upon the particular tour.

Savannah's four forts once protected the city's port from Spanish, British, and other invaders. The most interesting of these is **Fort Pulaski National Monument** (786-5787), 15 mi. east of Savannah on U.S. 80 and Rte. 26. (Open daily 8:30am-6:30pm. Admission $1 per person, seniors and kids under 15 free.) Fort Pulaski marks the Civil War battle site where walls were first pummeled by rifled cannon, instantly making Pulaski and similar forts obsolete. Built in the early 1800s **Fort Jackson** (232-3945), also along Hwy. 80 and Rte. 26, contains exhibits on the Revolution, the War of 1812, and the Civil War. Together with Fort Pulaski, it makes for a quick detour on a daytrip to Tybee Beach. (Open daily 9am-5pm; July and Aug. 9am-7pm. Admission $2, seniors and students $1.50.)

Special events in Savannah include the **Hidden Garden of the Nogs Tour** (238-0248), on April 20 to 21, when private walled gardens are opened to the public, and the **Tybee Island Beach Bum's Parade** (786-5444), with a beach music festival and other island activities June 18 to 20.

Kentucky

Kentucky's intermediary position between the North and South and between the East and Midwest lends the state more than its share of paradoxes. Although Kentucky is renowned for its bourbon distilleries, most of the counties in the state are dry. Much of the countryside is genuine Appalachia, with problems lingering from mining and 19th-century industrialization; gracious Southern-style mansions rise amidst this crushing penury. With borders on seven different states, Kentucky has more neighbors than any other state, yet 99% of its residents were born in the U.S. and almost 75% were born in-state. Even its signature city, Louisville, has a complex identity—it hosts the aristocratic, eminently Southern Kentucky Derby but is also home to a thriving alternative culture, descendants of the city's labor movement a generation earlier.

Practical Information

Capital: Frankfort.

Tourist Information: Kentucky Department of Travel Development, Capital Plaza Tower, 22nd floor, Frankfort 40601 (502-564-4930 or 800-225-8747). **Department of Parks,** Capital Plaza Tower, Frankfort 40601 (800-255-7275).

Time Zones: Central (1 hr. behind Eastern) and Eastern. **Postal Abbreviation:** KY

Sales Tax: 6%.

Cumberland Gap

Almost completely uncommercialized, **Cumberland Gap National Historical Park** is home to Daniel Boone's **Wilderness Trail,** a natural passage through an 800-ft. break in the Appalachian Mountains. The park surrounds the route that Boone and 30 axe-wielding pioneers blazed along a Shawnee and Cherokee Buffalo trail in 1775.

There are now 50 mi. of hiking trails in the park. As your first stop, head for the **National Park Visitors Center,** 200 yards from Middlesboro, KY, off U.S. 25E (606-248-2817), where rangers will help you plan a trip. The center will also let you know about other programs offered in the park. All walking tours, exhibits, and programs are free. (Open daily Memorial Day-Labor Day 8am-6pm; off-season daily 8am-5pm.) Two popular attractions are **Pinnacle Overlook** and the **Hensley Settlement.** Take a 15-minute drive from the visitors center to the Pinnacle Overlook, from which you can see the gap and the states of Virginia, Kentucky and Tennessee (and Georgia and North Carolina as well, if you have eyes like a peregrine falcon). Every Thursday during the summer from 2 to 4pm, a ranger dressed as a Confederate soldier is stationed at Fort Lyon, on top of the Pinnacle, to tell Civil War stories. Atop Brush Mountain cultivates the Hensley Settlement, an aggregate of 12 farms that worked for 50 years until they were abandoned in the 1940s. The settlers lived in an isolated encampment of rough-hewn chestnut log houses. Since 1965, the park service has restored five of the farmsteads, the schoolhouse, and the cemetery. You can reach the settlement by a 3½-mi. hike from Caylor, 11 mi. from the visitors center on Route 690 N., or in a four-wheel-drive vehicle. Worthwhile three-hour tours depart several times per day ($5, kids $2.50) from the visitors center.

Four **campgrounds** inside the park on the scenic 17-mi. Ridge Trail are accessible by foot only and require permits ($1 per person at the visitors center). Permits are required for backcountry camping as well. Non-hikers can use the **Wilderness Road Campground** on U.S. 58 in Virginia, which offers sites and firewood for $8. (Quiet rules are in effect 10pm-6am.) If camping, there is no real reason to go into **Middlesboro.** A string of unappealing but fairly cheap motels lines U.S. 25E in the city. The **Parkview Motel** (606-248-4516) is clean, very convenient to the park, and offers both the Playboy Channel and a few waterbeds. (Singles $25. Doubles $35. The eager owners will try to keep you there when there are vacancies and may lower the prices.) If you are already in Middlesboro and want to eat, **The Sonic,** directly across from the Parkview Motel, is a 50s-style drive-in diner with burgers ($1.60), malts ($1.25) and roller-skating waitresses. (Open Sun.-Thurs. 9am-11pm, Fri.-Sat. 9am-midnight.) When you tire of commercial Middlesboro, drive over to **Cumberland Gaptown** (pop. 210) in Tennessee and have lunch at the quainte **Ye Olde Tea and Coffee Shoppe** (615-869-4844). (Open Tues.-Sat. 11am-3pm, Wed.-Sat. 6-9:30pm, Sun. noon-5pm.)

Lexington

With Louisville's eyes turned towards Cincinnati, Lexington, Kentucky's second-largest city, has assumed the responsibility of giving the state a focal point. Lexington is rich in Southern heritage, and even recent growth spurts have not changed its atmosphere from *town* to *city,* nor have they divorced it from the rest of the largely rural state. Historic mansions downtown are not too heavily overshadowed by skyscrapers, and a 20-minute drive from any point in the city will set you squarely in bluegrass countryside. Lexington is small enough to retain elements of the country but large enough to accommodate divergent viewpoints and lifestyles. Intellectual life at the University of Kentucky and vestiges of liberal spirit left over from Appalachian labor movements combine to give Lexington a strong alternative culture, a thriving gay and lesbian community, a varied nightlife and generally more heterogeneity and tolerance than you might expect.

Like the rest of Kentucky and almost every 10-year-old girl, Lexington is horse-crazy—the Kentucky Horse Park is heavily advertised, and the shopping complexes and "lite" industries whose presence clutters the outskirts of town still share space with quaint, green, rolling horse farms. The 150-odd farms gracing the Lexington area have nurtured such equine greats as Citation, Lucky Debonair, Majestic Prince, and Whirlaway.

Practical Information and Orientation

Emergency: 911.

Visitor Information: Greater Lexington Convention and Visitors Bureau, Suite 363, 430 W. Vine St. (800-848-1224 or 233-1221), in the civic center. Brochures, maps and bus schedules. Open Mon.-Fri. 8:30am-5pm, Sat. 10am-5pm. Information centers also grace I-75 north and south of Lexington.

Airport: Bluegrass Field, 4000 Versailles Rd. (254-9336). Serves regional airlines/flights; often easier to fly to Louisville's Standiford Field (see Louisville: Practical Information).

Greyhound: 477 New Circle Rd. N.W. (255-4261). Lets passengers off north of Main St. Take Lex-Tran bus #6 downtown. Open daily 6:45am-11:30pm. To: Louisville (1 per day; 1½ hr.; $16); Cincinnati (5 per day; 1½ hr.; $18); Knoxville (4 per day; 3 hr.; $41, $32 if reserved 7 days in advance).

Public Transport: Lex-Tran, 109 W. London Ave. (253-4636). Modest but exuberant system serving the university and city outskirts. Buses leave from the new **Transit Center,** 220 W. Vine St. between Limestone and Quality. Fare 80¢, transfers free. Buses usually operate Mon.-Fri. 6am-6pm, Sat. 9am-6pm; some routes have evening schedules.

Taxi: Lexington Yellow Cab, 231-8294. Base fare $1.90 plus $1.35 per mi.

Transportation for People with Disabilities: WHEELS, 233-3433. 7am-6pm. 24-hr. notice required. After hours call 231-8294, daily.

Help Line: Rape Crisis, 253-2511. Open 24 hrs. **GLSO Gayline,** 231-0335.

Time Zone: Eastern.

Post Office: 1088 Nandino Blvd. (231-6700). Take bus #2. Open Mon.-Fri. 8:30am-5pm, Sat. 9am-1pm. **ZIP code:** 40511. General Delivery is handled through the downtown branch at Barr and Limestone.

Area Code: 606.

New Circle Road highway (Rte. 4/U.S. bypass 60), which is intersected by many roads that connect the downtown district to the surrounding towns, lassoes the city. **High, Vine,** and **Main Streets** are the major east-west routes downtown; **Limestone Street** and **Broadway** the north-south thoroughfares.

Accommodations and Camping

The concentration of horse-related wealth in the Lexington area tends to ride accommodation prices up. The cheapest places gallop out of the city on roads beyond New Circle Rd. If you're having trouble on your own, **Dial-A-Accommodations,** 430. W. Vine St. #363 (233-7299), will locate and reserve a room free of charge in a requested area of town and within a specific price range. (Open Mon.-Fri. 8:30am-5pm.)

Kimball House Motel, 267 S. Limestone St. (252-9565), between downtown and the university. The grungy sign conceals a collection of clean, quaint, quiet rooms, friendly, helpful management, and monkeys in the backyard. Some singles (1st floor, no A/C, shared bath) $20. Ask for them specifically; they often fill by late afternoon. Otherwise, cheapest singles $25. Doubles $28. Key deposit $5. Parking in back.

University of Kentucky, Apartment Housing, 700 Woodland Ave. (257-3721). Full kitchen and private bathroom. Fold-out sleeper. Rooms also available during the school year, space permitting. 14-day max. stay. Singles $21, doubles $26. Call ahead on a weekday. Available June-Aug. Explain that you only want a short stay; longer-term rentals are for U of K affiliates only.

Microtel, 2240 Buena Vista Dr. (299-9600), near I-75 and Winchester Rd. New, light motel rooms. Singles $27, each extra adult $3.

Bryan Station Inn, 273 New Circle Rd. (299-4162). Take bus #4 or Limestone St. north from downtown and turn right onto Rte. 4. Clean, pleasant rooms in the middle of a motel/fast-food strip. No phones. Singles or doubles $28. Rates decrease the longer you stay. Must be 21.

Good, cheap **campgrounds** gallop around Lexington; unfortunately, you'll need a horse or a car to reach them. The **Kentucky Horse Park Campground,** 4089 Ironworks Pike (233-4303), 10 mi. north off I-75, has laundry, showers, tennis, basketball and volleyball courts, swimming pool, more lawn than shade, and a free shuttle to the KY Horse Park and Museum (see Horses and Seasonal Events). (2-week max. stay. Sites $10, with hookup $13.50.)

Food

Lexington specializes in good, down-home cuisine, and the lefty side of town contributes some vegetarian and other self-righteously wholesome options.

Alfalfa Restaurant, 557 S. Limestone St. (253-0014), across from Memorial Hall at the university. Take bus #2A. Fantastic home-cooked international and veg meals. Complete dinners with salad, bread, and entrée under $10. Excellent, filling soups and exotic salads from $2. Live music nightly. Open Tues.-Thurs. 5:30-9pm (in summer until 9:30pm), Fri. 5:30-10pm, Sat. 10am-2pm and 5:30-10pm, Sun. 10am-2pm.

Ramsey's Diner, 49 E. High St. (259-2708). Real classy Southern grease. Vegetarians beware: authenticity means that even the vegetables are cooked with pork parts. Sandwiches under $5, entrées around $8, 4 vegetables for $6. Open Mon.-Sat. 11am-1am, Sun. 11am-11pm.

Everybody's Natural Foods and Deli, 503 Euclid Ave. (255-4162). This pleasant health-food store has a few tables where they serve excellent gazpacho, sandwiches ($2.50-3.50), and a daily lunch special ($3.75). Open Mon.-Fri. 8am-8pm, Sat. 10am-6pm, Sun. noon-5pm.

Central Christian Cafeteria, 205 E. Short St., 1 block north of Main St. (255-3087). Unpretentious country food—greens and cornbread, fried fish, homemade pies. Entrées under $2.50, veggies 70¢. Open Mon.-Fri. 6:30am-2pm.

Sights and Nightlife

To escape the stifling swamp conditions farther south, antebellum plantation owners built beautiful summer retreats in milder Lexington. The most attractive of these stately houses preen only a few blocks northeast of the town center in the **Gratz Park** area near the public library. In addition to their past, the wrap-around porches, wooden minarets, stone foundations, and rose-covered trellises distinguish these estates from the neighborhood's newer homes.

The **Hunt Morgan House,** 201 N. Mill St. (253-0362), hunkers down at the end of the park across from the library. Built in 1814 by John Wesley Hunt, the first millionaire west of the Alleghenies, the house later witnessed the birth of Thomas Hunt Morgan, who won a Nobel Prize in 1933 for proving the existence of the gene, but the house's most colorful inhabitant was Confederate General John Hunt Morgan. Chased by Union troops, the general once rode his horse up the front steps and into the house, leaned down to kiss his mother, and rode out the back door. What a guy. (Tours Tues.-Sat. 10am-4pm, Sun. 2-5pm. $3, ages 6-12 $1, under 6 free.)

Kentucky's loyalties divided sharply in the Civil War. Mary Todd grew up five blocks from the Hunt-Morgan House; she later married Abraham Lincoln. The **Mary Todd Lincoln House** is at 578 W. Main St. (233-9999; open April 1-Dec. 15 Tues.-Sat. 10am-4pm; $4, kids 7-12 $1).

In Victorian Square on the west side of downtown, the **Lexington Children's Museum,** 401 W. Main St. (258-3256), puts kids in a variety of simulated contexts for fun and undercover education. (Open Memorial Day-Labor Day Mon.-Fri. 10am-6pm, Sat. 10am-5pm, Sun. 1-5pm; off-season closed Mon. Kids $1.50, grownups $2.50.) The **Lexington Cemetery,** 833 W. Main St. (255-5522), serves another stage in the life cycle. Henry Clay and John Hunt Morgan are buried here. (Open daily 8am-5pm; free.) At the corner of Sycamore and Richmond Rd., you can admire **Ashland** (266-8581), the 20-acre homestead where statesman Henry Clay lived before he moved to the cemetery. The mansion's carved ash interior came from trees grown on the property. (Open Mon.-Sat. 9:30am-4:30pm, Sun. 1-4:30pm. $4, kids $1.50. Take bus #4A.)

The sprawling **University of Kentucky** (257-7173) gives free campus tours in "Old Blue," an English double-decker bus, at 10am and 2pm weekdays and on Saturday mornings (call 257-3595). The university's specialties include architecture and (surprise!) equine medicine. For updates of U of K's arts calendar, call 257-7173; for more info about campus attractions, call 257-3595.

The enormous and richly stocked **Joseph-Beth Booksellers,** 3199 Nicholasville Rd. (273-2911), holds poetry readings at 7pm on the last Thursday of every month. The volunteer-built and -run **New Morning Coffee House and Community Peace Center,** 504 Euclid Ave. at Woodland (233-1190), a pleasant place to hang out, drink coffee and make peace with the hippie in you and in Lexington, holds occasional musical and other events. (Open Mon.-Wed. 9am-11pm, Thurs. 9am-1am, Fri.-Sat. 7am-1am, Sun. 11am-11pm.)

Lexington's nightlife is pretty good for a town its size. **Breeding's** showcases lively times and music for the breeding set at 509 W. Main St. (255-2822). **The Brewery** is a friendly country-Western bar (both open daily 8am-1am). **Comedy on Broadway,** 144 N. Broadway (259-0013), features stand-up comics most nights. **The Bar,** 224 E. Main St. (255-1551), is a disco popular with gays and lesbians. (Open Sun.-Fri. until 1:30am, Sat. until 3:30am. Cover $3 on weekends.) **The Wrocklage,** 361 W. Shore St. (231-7655), serves up alternative and punkish rock, and **Lynagh's,** in University Plaza at Woodland and Euclid St. (259-9944), is a great neighborhood pub with superlative burgers ($4.35). Meet fraternity-sorority types at **Two Keys Tavern,** 333 S. Limestone (254-5000). *Ace* magazine gives info on stuff to do in the area; *GLSO News,* published monthly and available free at Alfalfa's (see Food), New Morning, Joseph-Beth Booksellers and The Bar, is a key to events in Lexington's substantial gay and lesbian community.

Horses and Seasonal Events

A visit to Lexington is not complete without a close encounter with its quadruped citizenry, and we ain't talkin' wombats. Try **Spendthrift Farm,** 884 Ironworks Pike (299-5271), eight mi. northeast of downtown. (Free tours Feb.-July Mon.-Sat. 10am-noon; Aug.-Jan. Mon.-Sat. 10am-2pm. Take Broadway until it becomes Paris Pike, then turn left onto Ironworks.)

The **Kentucky Horse Park,** 4089 Ironworks Pike, exit 120 (233-4303), 10 mi. north on I-75, is a highly touristified state park with full facilities for equestrians, a museum, two films, and the Man O' War Monument. (Open mid-March-Oct. daily 9am-5pm; times vary the rest of the year. $8, ages 7-12 $4. Horse-drawn vehicle tours included.) The **American Saddle Horse Museum,** on the park grounds (259-2746), continues the celebration of Lexington's favorite animal. (Open Memorial Day-Labor Day daily 9am-6pm; off-season reduced hrs. $2, seniors $1.50, ages 7-12 $1.)

If horse racing is more your style, visit the **Keeneland Race Track,** 4201 Versailles Rd. (254-3412, 800-354-9092), west on U.S. 60. (Races Oct. and April; post time 1pm. $2.) The public can observe morning workouts. (April-Oct. daily 6-10am.) The final prep race for the Kentucky Derby occurs here in April. The **Red Mile Harness Track,** 847 S. Broadway (255-0752; take bus #3 on S. Broadway), has racing from late April to late June and also in late September to early October. (Post time 7:30pm.) The crowds run the gamut from wholesome families to seasoned gamblers. ($3, programs $2; parking free. Seniors free Thurs.) Morning workouts (7:30am-noon) are open to the public during racing season.

In June, the **Festival of the Bluegrass** (846-4995), at the Kentucky Horse Park, attracts thousands. Camping at the festival grounds is free. The **Lexington Junior League Horse Show** (mid-July; 252-1893), the largest outdoor show in the nation, unfolds its pageantry at the Red Mile (see above).

Near Lexington

The Shakers, a 19th-century celibate religious sect, practiced the simple life between Harrodsburg and Lexington, about 25 mi. southwest on U.S. 68, at the **Shaker Village** (734-5411). The 5000-acre farm features 27 restored Shaker buildings. A tour includes demonstrations of everything from apple-butter-making to coopering (barrel-making). (Open daily 9:30am-6pm. $8, $4 for students 12-17, ages 6-11 $2.) Although the last

Shaker to live here died in 1923, you can still eat and sleep in original though somewhat altered Shaker buildings. (Dinner $12-14. Singles $30-55. Doubles $45-65. All rooms have A/C and private bath. Reservations required.) Greyhound bus #350 runs to Harrodsburg, seven mi. from the village (see Lexington: Practical Information). Outside Lexington, in **Richmond,** exit 90 off I-75, is **White Hall** (623-9178), home of the abolitionist (not the boxer) Cassius M. Clay, Senator Henry Clay's cousin. This elegant mansion really consists of two houses, one Georgian and one Italianate. The 45-minute tour covers seven different living levels. (Open April-Labor Day daily 9am-4:30pm; Labor Day-Oct. 31 Wed.-Sun; open briefly in winter for a Christmas celebration. Guided tours only. $3, under 13 $2, under 6 free.) The Richmond pre-packaged tourism experience also includes **Fort Boonesborough** (527-3328), a re-creation of one of Daniel Boone's forts. The park has samples of 18th-century crafts, a small museum, and shows films about the pioneers. (Open April-Aug. daily 9am-5:30pm; Sept.-Oct. Wed.-Sun. 9am-5:30pm. $4, ages 6-12 $2.50, under 6 free. Combination White Hall/Boonesborough tickets available.)

Ten mi. south of Richmond and 30 mi. south of Lexington, where the bluegrass meets the mountains, lies **Berea,** home of tuition-free **Berea College** (986-9341), founded in 1855. Many of the 1500 students, most from Appalachia, pay for their expenses by operating the school's crafts center. Campus tours leave from the corner of **Boone Tavern.** (Tours Mon.-Fri. at 9am, 10am, and 1pm during the school year.) The **Appalachian Museum** (986-9341, ext. 6078), Jackson St. on campus, charts regional history through arts and crafts. (Open Mon.-Sat. 9am-6pm, Sun. 1-6pm.)

Because of the emphasis on craft skills at Berea College, the town concentrates galleries, gift shops and workshops. Of particular interest is **Churchill Weavers,** Lorraine Court (986-3127), north of town off I-75 and U.S. 25, the largest handweaving firm in the country. (Free tours Mon.-Fri. 9am-4pm. Gift shop open Mon.-Sat. 9am-6pm, Sun. noon-6pm. Schedule may change, so call ahead.) The student-run crafts center has two locations: the **Boone Tavern Gift Shop,** in the hotel (986-9341, ext. 5233; open Mon.-Sat. 8am-8pm, Sun. noon-8pm), and the **Log House Sales Room,** on Estill St. (986-9341, ext. 5225; open Mon.-Sat. 8am-6pm, Sun. 1-5pm). During May and early fall, tourists flood the town for the good folk music and food at the **Kentucky Guild of Artists' and Craftsmen's Fair,** in Indian Fort Theater. To reach Berea, take Greyhound bus #360 (3 per day), on the Lexington-Knoxville route, which will leave you at the B&B Grocery, the college, and Boone Tavern (see Lexington: Practical Information).

The **Red River Gorge,** in the northern section of the Daniel Boone National Forest, approximately 50 mi. southeast of Lexington, draws visitors from around the country. A day outing from Lexington will show why song and square dance have immortalized this spacious land of sandstone cliffs and stone arches. **Natural Bridge State Park** (663-2214), two mi. south of Slade, highlights the major attraction of the upper valley. The Red River Gorge highlights the lower valley. Greyhound bus #296 (see Lexington: Practical Information) will get you to Stanton (10 mi. west of Slade) and a **U.S. Forest Service Office** (663-2853). If you're driving, take the Mountain Parkway (south off I-64) straight to Slade, and explore the region bounded by the scenic loop road, Rte. 715. Camp at **Natural Bridge State Resort Park** (800-325-1710). The campground, complete with pool, facilities for disabled people, and organized square dances, hosts the **National Mountain Style Square Dance and Clogging Festival,** a celebration of Appalachian folkdances. (Square dance tickets $1-3. Tent sites $8.50, with hookup $10.50.)

Louisville

Perched on the Ohio River, hovering between the North and the South, Louisville (LOU-uh-vul) has its own way of doing things. An immigrant town imbued with Southern grace and architecture, Louisville's beautiful Victorian neighborhoods surround spewing smokestacks and the enormous meat-packing district of Butchertown. The splayed, laid-back city has riverfront parks and excellent cultural attractions fostered by the University of Louisville. The year's main event is undoubtedly the Kentucky Derby (see below). The nation's most prestigious horse race ends a week-long extravaganza, luring over half a million visitors who pay through the teeth for a week-long carnival, fashion display, and equestrian show, which culminates in a two-minute gallop that you'll miss if you're standing in line for juleps. The $15 million wagered on Derby Day alone proves that Kentuckians are deadly serious about their racing—the winning horse earns studding privileges with hundreds of hot fillies, the winning jockey earns the congratulations of the state and studding privileges with hundreds of short fillies, and the winning owner earns $800,000, enough to make any stable stable.

Practical Information and Orientation

Emergency: 911.

Louisville Convention and Visitors Bureau, 400 S. First St. (584-2121; 800-633-3384 outside Louisville; 800-626-5646 outside KY), at Liberty downtown. The standard goodies, including some bus schedules. Open Mon.-Fri. 8:30am-5pm, Sat.-Sun. 8:30am-4pm. Visitors centers also in Standiford Field airport and in the Galeria Mall at 4th and Liberty St. downtown. **Concert Line,** 540-3210. Information on rock, jazz and country performances.

Traveler's Aid: 584-8186.

Airport: Standiford Field (367-4636), 15 min. south of downtown on I-65. Take bus #2 into the city.

Greyhound: 720 W. Muhammad Ali Blvd. (585-3331), at 7th St. To: Indianapolis (6 per day; 2 hr.; $20-23); Cincinnati (7 per day; 2 hr.; $15.50-20); Chicago (7 per day; 6 hr.; $57, $31 special); Nashville (10 per day; 3 hr.; $23-28); Lexington (2 per day; 2 hr.; $14.50). Storage lockers $1 first day, $3 per additional day (call 561-2870 for locker and storage info). Open 24 hrs.

Public Transport: Transit Authority River City (TARC), 585-1234. Extensive system of thoroughly air-conditioned buses serves most of the metro area; buses run daily, some 4am-1am. Fare 60¢ during peak hours, 35¢ other times. Disabled access. Also runs a trolley on 4th Ave. from River Rd. to Broadway (free). Call for directions.

Taxi: Yellow Cab, 636-5511. Base fare $1.50 plus $1.50 per mi.

Car Rental: Dollar Rent-a-Car, in Standiford Field airport (366-6944). Weekends from $20 per day, weekdays $42. Must be 21 with credit card. Additional $6 per day for ages under 25. Open daily 6am-midnight. **Budget Rent-a-Car,** 4330 Crittenden Dr. (363-4300). From $40 per day. Must be 21 with a major credit card or 25 without one. Open daily 6:30am-9pm.

Help Lines: Rape Hot Line, 581-7273. **Crisis Center,** 589-4313. Both open 24 hrs. **Gay and Lesbian Hotline,** 589-3316. Open Sun.-Thurs. 6-10pm, Fri.-Sat. 6pm-1am.

Time Zone: Eastern.

Post Office: 1420 Gardner Lane (454-1650). Take the Louisville Zoo exit off I-264 and follow Gardner Lane 1 mi. Open Mon.-Fri. 7:30am-7pm, Sat. 7:30am-1pm. **ZIP code:** 40231.

Area Code: 502.

Major highways through the city include I-65 (north-south expressway), I-71, and I-64. The **Henry Watterson Expressway,** also called I-264, is an easily accessible freeway that rings the city. The central downtown area is defined north-south by **Main Street** and **Broadway,** and east-west by **Preston** and **19th Street.**

Aside from theater and riverfront attractions, much activity in Louisville takes place outside the central city, but the fairly extensive bus system goes to all major areas. Call TARC (see above) for help since written schedules are incomplete and sometimes confusing.

Accommodations

Though easy to find, accommodations in Louisville are not particularly cheap. If you want a bed during Derby Week, make a reservation at least six months to a year in advance; be prepared to pay high prices. The visitors center (see Practical Information above) will help after March 13. If you don't choose one of the few affordable downtown options, try one of the many cheap motels that line the roads just outside town.

Kentucky Homes Bed and Breakfast (635-7341) offers stays in private homes from $45. Call at least a few days ahead. **Newburg** (6 mi. away) and **Bardstown** (39 mi. away) are likely spots for budget accommodations.

Collier's Motor Court, 4812 Bardstown Rd. (499-1238), south of I-264. 30 min. from downtown by car, or take bus #17. Inconvenient, but well-maintained and cheap. Singles $29. Doubles $34.

Travelodge, 2nd and Liberty St. (583-2841), downtown behind the visitors center. Big, clean, and oh-so-convenient. Neighborhood Chinese restaurant provides room service. Singles $37. Doubles $42.

Thrifty Dutchman Budget Motel, 3357 Fern Valley Way (968-8124), just off I-65. A hike from downtown. Take bus #18, to Preston and Fern Valley, then walk west (right) 10-15 min. Clean, large rooms. Pool. Singles $31. Doubles $41.

KOA, 900 Marriot Dr., Clarksville, IN (812-282-4474), across the bridge from downtown beside I-65; take the Stansifer Ave. exit. Grocery and playground; mini-golf and a fishing lake at the Sheraton across the street. Sites $15 for 2 people. Each additional person $3, under 18 $2. Kamping kabins (for 2) $26. RV sites $16.50.

Food

If you're so hungry you could eat a horse, never fear. Not only are there plenty of horses around (although a meal of one would probably bust your budget), but Louisville's chefs also whip up a wide variety of cuisines, though prices can be steep. Butchertown and the Churchill Downs area have several cheap delis and pizza places. Bardstown Rd. near Eastern Pkwy. offers budget pizzas and more expensive French cuisine.

The Rudyard Kipling, 422 W. Oak St., just south of downtown (636-1311). Take bus #4. Eclectic menu includes French, Mexican and vegetarian entrées, Kentucky burgoo (a regional stew), and other creative fare ($5-13). Half-jungle, half-colonial tavern rooms. Fun even if you've never kippled before. Weekend nights feature piano music or rock 'n' roll; weeknights range from Celtic to bluegrass or folk music. Free Louisville Songwriters Cooperative acoustic music show each Mon. at 9pm. Open Mon.-Thurs. 11:30am-2pm and 5:30pm-midnight, Fri. 11:30am-around midnight, Sat. 5:30pm-midnight. Call for events calendar. Wheelchair accessible.

Miller's Cafeteria, 429 S. 2nd St., downtown (582-9135). Serve yourself a full breakfast or lunch (entrée, pie, 2 vegetables, and drink) for $3-4. Big, comfortable dining room built in 1826 is barely older than most of the customers. Open Mon.-Fri. 7am-2:30pm, Sun. 10am-2:30pm.

Ditto's, 1114 Bardstown Rd. (581-9129). Large, enthusiastic burgers ($4-5.50), pastas ($5-5.50) and delicious pizzas ($6). Open Mon.-Thurs. 11am-11pm, Fri.-Sat. 11am-midnight, Sun. 9am-10pm.

Smoothie Shop and Deli, 1293 Bardstown Rd. (454-6890). Large, tasty blended-fruit shakes with honey and brewers yeast ($3), named after streets in the area to help you learn your Louisville geography by food association.

Twig and Leaf, 2122 Bardstown Rd. (451-8944). Greasy spoon with cheap breakfasts (1 egg and toast $1.20). Sign advertises "world's best chili"—see Cincinnati, OH, listing to find out what you're getting into.

Ditto's, 1114 Bardstown Rd. (581-9129). Large, enthusiastic burgers ($4-5.50), pastas ($5-5.50) and delicious pizzas ($6). Open Mon.-Thurs. 11am-11pm, Fri.-Sat. 11am-midnight, Sun. 9am-10pm.

In the Neigh-borhood

Even if you miss the Kentucky Derby, try to catch **Churchill Downs,** 700 Central Ave. (636-4400), three mi. south of downtown. Take bus #4 (4th St.) to Central Ave. Bet, watch a race, or just admire the twin spires, colonial columns, gardens, and sheer scale of the track. (Grounds open in racing season daily 10am-4pm. Races April-June Tues.-Fri. 3:30-7:30pm, Sat.-Sun. 1-6pm; Oct.-Nov. Tues.-Sun. 1-6pm. Grandstand seats $1.50, clubhouse $3, reserved clubhouse $5. Parking $2-3.)

The **Kentucky Derby Festival** commences the week before the Derby and climaxes with the prestigious **Run for the Roses** the first Saturday in May. Balloon and steamboat races, music, and all manner of hullabaloo fill the week. Seats for the Derby have a five-year waiting list. You can stand and watch from the grandstand or infield along with 80,000 of your closest friends for $20, but get in line at the Downs early on Derby morning as these tickets aren't available any other way. 120,000 spectators flood the Downs each Derby day.

The **Kentucky Derby Museum** at Churchill Downs (637-1111), offers a slide presentation on a 360° screen, tours of the stadium, profiles of famous stables and trainers (including the African-Americans who dominated racing early on), a simulated horse-race for betting practice, and tips on exactly what makes a horse a "sure thing." (Open daily 9am-5pm. $3.50, seniors $2.50, ages 5-12 $1.50, ages under 5 free.)

The **Louisville Downs,** 4520 Poplar Level Rd. (964-6415), south of I-264, hosts harness racing during most of the year. There are three meets: July to September Monday through Saturday, September through October and December through April Tuesday through Saturday. Post time is 7:30pm; 10 to 12 races leave the gates per night. ($3.50 clubhouse, $2.50 grandstand. Minimum bet $2. Parking $2. Take bus #43 from downtown.)

If you're tired of spectating, go on a trail ride at **Iroquois Riding Stable,** 5216 New Cut Rd. (363-9159; $10 per hr.). Take 3rd St. south to Southern Parkway or ride bus #4 or 6 to Iroquois Park.

Not Just a One-Horse Town

Book, antique, and second-hand shops line **Bardstown Road** north and south of Eastern Pkwy. Between downtown and the university, **Old Louisville** harbors interesting Victorian architecture and a high crime rate. Farther south, in University of Louisville territory, the **J.B. Speed Art Museum,** 2035 S. 3rd St. (636-2893), has an impressive collection of Dutch paintings and tapestries, Renaissance and contemporary art, and a sculpture court. The museum also has a touch-to-see gallery for visually-impaired visitors. (Open Tues.-Sat. 10am-4pm, Sun. 12-5pm. Free. Parking $2. Nominal fee for special exhibitions. Take bus #4.)

The **Riverfront Plaza** (625-3333), a landscape park overlooking the Ohio River, serves as the hub of downtown Louisville. Call any time of year to find what festival or citywide event is taking place, as Louisville hosts many. The **Belle of Louisville** (625-2355), an authentic stern-wheeler, cruises the Ohio, leaving from Riverfront Plaza at the foot of 4th St. (Departs May 27-Sept. 2 Tues.-Sun. at 2pm. Sunset cruises Tues. and Thurs. 7-9pm; nighttime dance cruise Sat. 8:30-11:30pm. Boarding begins 1 hr. before the ship leaves; arrive early especially in July. Fare $7, seniors $6, under 13 $3. Dance cruise $12, no discounts.)

The **Museum of History and Science,** 727 W. Main St. downtown (561-6100), emphasizes hands-on exhibits. Press your face against the window of an Apollo space capsule, then settle back and enjoy the four-story screen at the new IMAX theater. (Open Mon.-Thurs. 9am-5pm, Fri.-Sat. 9am-9pm, Sun. noon-5pm. $4, kids $3; $6/$5 with IMAX tickets.) At the **Louisville Zoo,** 1100 Trevilian Way (459-2181), between Newbury and Poplar Level Rd. across I-264 from Louisville Downs (take bus #18 or 43), the animals are exhibited in neo-natural settings. Ride on an elephant's back or on the tiny train that circles the zoo. (Open Fri.-Tues. 10am-5pm, Wed.-Thurs. 10am-8pm; Sept.-April Tues.-Sun. 10am-4pm. Gate closes 1 hr. before zoo. $4.50, seniors $2.50, kids $2.) The **Kentucky Art and Craft Gallery,** 609 W. Main St. (589-0102), has diverse rotating exhibits by in-state artists. (Open Mon.-Sat. 10am-4pm; free.)

Hillerich and Bradsby Co., 1525 Charleston-New Albany Rd., Jeffersonville, IN (585-5226), six mi. north of Louisville, manufactures the famous "Louisville Slugger" baseball bat. (Go north on I-65 to exit for Rte. 131, then turn east. Tours Mon.-Fri. 8-10am and 1-2pm on the hr. except on national holidays and Good Friday. Free.)

Louisville's newest entertainment complex, the **Kentucky Center for the Arts,** 5 Riverfront Plaza (information and tickets 584-7777 or 800-283-7777), off Main St., hosts major performing arts groups, including the **Louisville Orchestra,** known for its repertoire of 20th-century music. The **Lonesome Pines** series showcases indigenous Kentucky music, including bluegrass. Ticket prices vary as wildly as the music, though student discounts are sometimes offered. The **Actors Theater,** 316 W. Main St. (584-1265), between 3rd and 4th St., a Tony award-winning repertory company, gives performances from September to mid-June at 8pm and some matinees. Call for details. Tickets start at $15, with $7 student rush tickets available 15 minutes before each show. Bring a picnic dinner to **Shakespeare in the Park,** Central Park (634-8237), weekends between June 19 and August 4. (Performances at 8:30pm.) Call the **Louisville Visual Arts Association,** 3005 Upper River Rd. (896-2146), for information on local artists' shows and events.

Tewligans, on Bardstown Rd., has local bands and cheap beer. When it changed owners there was a proposal to reverse its name to Snagilwet, but that didn't catch on. **Uncle Pleasant's,** 2126 S. Preston, one block north of Eastern Pkwy. (634-4804), gets the same bands ($2-5 cover) and sells every kind of beer. The best place in town for dancing is the gay bar **The Connection,** 130 S. Floyd St.

Near Louisville

90% of the nation's bourbon hails from Kentucky, and 60% of that is distilled in Nelson and Bullitt Counties, close to Louisville. At **Jim Beam's American Outpost** (543-9877) in Clermont, 15 mi. west of Bardstown, Booker Noe, Jim Beam's grandson and current "master distiller," narrates a film about bourbon. Don't miss the free lemonade and sampler bourbon candies. From Louisville, take I-65 south to exit 112, then Rte. 245 south for 2½ mi. From Bardstown, take Rte. 245 north. (Open Mon.-Sat. 9am-4:30pm, Sun. 1-4pm. Free.) You can't actually tour Beam's huge distillery, but you can visit the **Maker's Mark Distillery** (865-2099), in Loretto, 19 mi. southeast of Bardstown, for an investigation of 19th-century bourbon production. Take Rte. 49 S. to Rte. 52. E. (Tours March-Dec. Mon.-Sat. every hr. on the ½-hr. 10:30am-3:30pm; Jan.-Feb. Mon.-Fri. only. Free.) Neither site has a license to sell its liquors.

Bardstown proper hosts **The Stephen Foster Story** (800-626-1563 or 348-5971), a mawkish, heavily promoted outdoor musical about America's first major songwriter, the author of "My Old Kentucky Home." (Performances mid-June-Labor Day Tues.-Sun. at 8:30pm, plus Sat. at 3pm. $9, $5 for ages 12 and under).

Now a national historic site, **Abraham Lincoln's birthplace** (358-3874) bulges 45 mi. south of Louisville near Hodgenville on U.S. 31E. From Louisville, take I-65 down to Rte. 61; public transportation does not serve the area. Fifty-six steps representing the 56 years of Lincoln's life lead up to a stone monument sheltering the small log cabin. Only a few of the Lincoln logs that you see are believed to be original. A plodding film describes Lincoln's ties to Kentucky. (Open June-Aug. daily 8am-6:45pm; Labor Day-Oct. and May 8am-5:45pm; Nov.-April 8am-4:45pm. Free.)

Hundreds of enormous caves and narrow passageways wind through **Mammoth Cave National Park** (758-2328), 80 mi. south of Louisville off I-65, west on Rte. 70. Mammoth Cave comprises the world's longest network of cavern corridors—over 325 mi. in length. Devoted spelunkers (ages 16 and over) will want to try the six-hour "Wild Cave Tour" in summer ($25); also available are two-hour, two-mi. historical walking tours ($3.50, seniors and kids $1.75) and 90-minute tours for people with disabilities ($4). Since the caves stay at 54°F year-round, bring a sweater. (**Visitors center** open daily 7:30am-7:30pm; off-season 7:30am-5:30pm.) **Greyhound** serves **Cave City,** just east of I-65 on Rte. 70, but the national park still lies miles away. **Gray Line** (637-6511; ask for the Gray Line) gives tours for groups of more than five people ($30 per person) and bus rides to the caves. Call a few days ahead. (Tours April 10-Labor Day.)

The **area code** for the Mammoth Caves area is 502.

Louisiana

Cross the Mississippi into Louisiana and you'll enter a state markedly different from its Southern neighbors. Here empires, races, and cultures mix in a unique and spicy jambalaya. The battlefields and old forts that liberally pepper the state—some dating back to the original French and Spanish settlers—illustrate the bloody succession of Native American, French, Spanish and American acquisition. The devout Catholicism of early settlers spawned the annual celebrations of Mardi Gras which flavor every February with festivity and parades throughout the state. Louisiana also cooks with Acadians ("Cajuns"), descendants of French Nova Scotians. Exiled by the British in 1755, Cajuns created a culture that contributes the Creole dialect, zydeco music, swampy folklore, and spicy cuisine that enliven the simmering, lazy Southern atmosphere. A final piquant ingredient is Louisiana's African-American culture, best known for its former immersion in voodoo. The cosmopolitan ambience and French tolerance in antebellum southern Louisiana combined to produce a literate black aristocracy found nowhere else in the South at the time. Thomas Jefferson struck quite a bargain when he ordered up the Louisiana Territory from Napoleon in 1803 for a cool $15 million, tip included.

Practical Information

Capital: Baton Rouge.

State Travel Office, P.O. Box 94291, Capitol Station, Baton Rouge 70804 (342-7317 or 800-334-8626). Open daily 8am-4pm. **Office of State Parks,** P.O. Box 1111, Baton Rouge 70821. Open Mon.-Fri. 9am-5pm.

Time Zone: Central (1 hr. behind Eastern). **Postal Abbreviation:** LA

Sales Tax: 4%.

Acadiana

In 1755, the English government expelled French settlers from their homes in Nova Scotia. Migrating down the Atlantic coastline and into the Caribbean, the so-called Acadians received a hostile reception; people in Massachusetts, Georgia, and South Carolina made them indentured servants. The Acadians (Cajuns) soon realized that their only hope for freedom lay in reaching the French territory of Louisiana and settling on the Gulf Coast. Many of the present-day inhabitants of St. Martin, Lafayette, Iberia, and St. Mary parishes descend from these settlers.

Since the 18th century, many factors have threatened Acadian culture with extinction. Louisiana passed laws in the 1920s forcing Acadian schoolchildren to speak English. The oil boom of the past few decades has also endangered the survival of Acadian culture. Oil executives and developers envisioned Lafayette—a center of Acadian life—as the Houston of Louisiana, threatening to flood this small town and its neighbors with mass culture. However, the proud people of southern Louisiana have resisted homogenization. They have made the state officially bilingual and have established a state agency to preserve Acadian French in schools and in the media.

Today "Cajun Country" spans the southern portion of the state, from Houma in the east to the Texas border. Mostly bayou and swampland, this unique natural environment has intertwined with Cajun culture. The music and the cuisine especially symbolize the ruggedness of this traditional, family-centered society. This is the place to try some crawfish or to dance the two-step to a fiddle and an accordion.

Lafayette

The official capital of Acadiana, Lafayette is a perfect place to sample the zydeco music, boiled crawfish, and *pirogues* (carved cypress boats) that characterize Cajun culture. Besides Acadian sites, historical villages, and museums, however, the city has little to offer the tourist. In the late 70s and 80s the town was the center of oil businesses in southern Louisiana, but the drop in crude prices stalled growth.

Full of music, crafts, and food, **Vermilionville,** 1600 Surrey St. (233-4077 or 800-992-2968), is an historic bayou attraction that educates as it entertains. This re-creation of an Acadian settlement invites guests to dance the two-step, ride an Acadian skiff, make a cornhusk doll, and more. (Open Sun.-Thurs. 10am-6pm, Fri.-Sat. 9am-9pm. $8, seniors $6.50, ages 6-18 $5.) A folk-life museum of restored 19th-century homes, **Acadian Village,** 200 Greenleaf Rd. (981-2364), 10 mi. from the tourist center, offers another view of Cajun life. Take U.S. 167 north, turn right on Ridge Rd., left on Mouton, and then follow the signs. (Open daily 10am-5pm. $5, seniors $4, students $2.50.) The **Lafayette Museum,** 1122 Lafayette St. (234-2208), exhibits heirlooms, antiques, and Mardi Gras costumes. (Open Tues.-Sat. 9am-5pm, Sun. 3-5pm. $3, seniors $2, students and kids $1.)

Built on the edge of the Atchafalaya Swamp, Lafayette links up with Baton Rouge via a triumph of modern engineering. The **Atchafalaya Freeway** is a 32-mi. long bridge over the bayous. Get closer to the elements by embarking upon one of the **Atchafalaya Basin Swamp Tours** (228-8567), in the nearby town of Henderson. The captain explains the harvesting of crawfish and the construction of the interstate highway on quavering swamp mud. (Tours given in English and French leave at 10am, 1, 3, and 5pm. Fare $7, kids $4.)

A must-see sight *not* linked with Acadiana flourishes in the yard of St. John's Cathedral, off St. John's. An almost 450-yr. old live tree, **St. John's Cathedral Oak**—one of the largest in the U.S.—shades the entire lawn with its gargantuan spidery limbs that create a spread of 210 ft. The weight of a single limb is estimated at 72 tons. When that bow breaks, boy does that cradle fall. Free. Climb it.

Cajun restaurants with live music and dancing have popped up all over Lafayette, but tend to be expensive. **Mulates,** 325 Mills Ave., Beaux Bridge, calls itself the most famous Cajun restaurant in the world, and the autographs on the door corroborate its claim. Try the house specialty, Catfish Mulate's, to be featured on the EuroDisney-World American Cuisine Restaurant in France. Cajun seafood dinners cost $10-15. (Open Mon.-Thurs. 7am-10pm, Fri.-Sun. 11am-10:30pm. Music noon-2pm and 7:30-10pm.) In downtown Lafayette, visit **Chris' Poboys,** 631 Jefferson St. (234-1696), which (not surprisingly) offers po'boys ($4-5) and seafood platters. (Open Mon.-Fri. 11am-9pm.) **Prejeans,** 3480 U.S. Hwy. 167 North (896-3247) dances in as another Cajun restaurant (dinners $8-12) with savory food and nightly Acadian entertainment at 7pm. Check out the real 14-ft. stuffed alligator by the entrance. (Open Mon.-Thus. 11am-9:30pm, Fri.-Sat. 11am-11pm, Sun. 11am-10pm.)

Several motels are a $3 cab fare from the bus station. The close **Travelodge Oil Center,** 1101 Pinhook Rd. (234-7402) has large, attractive rooms, cable TV, and a pool. (Singles $32. Doubles $38.) The **Super 8,** 2224 N. Evangeline Thruway (232-8826), just off I-10, has ample, plain-looking rooms, a pool, and a stunning view of the highway. (Singles $30. Doubles $32.) Other inexpensive chain motels line Evangeline Thruway, including **La Quinta** (233-5610) and **Motel 6,** (233-2055). Avoid motels on Cameron St.; this area is unsafe. If you have extra cash, treat yourself to bed and breakfast at **T'Frère's House,** 1905 Verot School Rd. (984-9347), which has antique-filled rooms, private baths, Turkish towel robes, large breakfasts, complimentary drinks (mint juleps always on hand) and snacks. (Singles $50. Doubles $65.)

Campgrounds include the lakeside **KOA Lafayette** (235-2739), five mi. west of town on I-10 (exit 97), with a komplete store and a pool. (Sites $14.50, a few small cabins $25.) Closer to town is **Acadiana Park Campground,** 1021 E, Alexander off Louisiana (234-3838) with beautifully shaded grounds, a playground, tennis courts, a football/soccer field, and a nature station offering trail guides and maps (261-8348). (Office open Fri. 3-10pm, Sat. 7-11am and 3-7pm, Sun. 7am-noon and 2-5pm.) Sites from $8.

Pick up a copy of *The Times* (available at restaurants and gas stations all over town or at the **Lafayette Parish Tourist Information** bureau on the median of Evangeline Thruway—open Mon.-Fri. 8:30am-5pm, Sat.-Sun. 9am-5pm) to find out about what's going down this week. Considering its size and location, Lafayette has a surprising variety of after-hours entertainment, including the **Cajun Dance,** a world-class concert hall that regularly brings in acts and concerts of national prominence. Lafayette kicks off spring and fall weekends with **Downtown Alive!,** a series of free concerts featuring everything from new wave to Cajun and zydeco. (All concerts Fri. at 5:30pm. Call 268-

5566 for info.) The **Festival International de Louisiane** (232-8086) in late April blends the music, visual arts, and cuisine of this region into a francophone tribute to the French influence on southwestern Louisiana.

Lafayette stands at Louisiana's major crossroad. I-10 leads east to New Orleans (130 mi.) and west to Lake Charles (76 mi.); U.S. 90 heads south to New Iberia (20 mi.) and the bayou country; U.S. 167 runs north into central Louisiana. Lafayette also provides a railroad stop for **Amtrak's** "Sunset Limited," linking the city with New Orleans (1/day, 3 hr., $27), Houston (3/week, 5 hr., $49), and Los Angeles. The unstaffed station is at 133 E. Grant St., near the bus station; tickets must be purchased in advance through a travel agent. **Greyhound,** 315 Lee Ave. (235-1541), connects Lafayette to New Orleans (7/day, 2½ hr., $21) and Baton Rouge (7/day, 1 hr., $8), as well as to small towns such as New Iberia (2/day, ½ hr., $3). The **Lafayette Bus System,** 400 Dorset (261-8570), runs infrequently and not on Sundays (fare 45¢). You'll need a car to really explore Acadiana and the Gulf Coast bayou country. **Thrifty Rent-a-Car,** 401 E. Pinhook (237-1282), usually has the best deals ($25/day for a compact, 100 free mi. Must be 21 with major credit card).

The **post office** is at 1105 Moss (269-4800; open Mon.-Fri.8am-5:30pm, Sat. 8am-12:30pm). Lafayette's **ZIP code** is 70501; the **area code** is 318.

New Iberia and Southcentral Louisiana

While other plantations made their fortunes off cotton, most plantations in southern Louisiana grew sugarcane. Today most of these stay in private hands, but **Shadows on the Teche,** 317 E. Main St. (369-6446), is open to the public. A Southern aristocrat saved the crumbling mansion, built in 1831, from neglect after the Civil War. (Open daily 9am-4:30pm. $4, kids $2.)

Seven mi. away is **Avery Island,** on Rte. 329 off Rte. 90, actually a salt dome that resembles an island. Avery houses the world-famous **Tabasco Pepper Sauce factory,** where the McIlhenny family has produced the famous condiment for nearly a century. Guided tours include a sample taste. *OOOOOeeeeeee!!!!* (Open Mon.-Fri. 9-11:45am and 1-3:45pm, Sat. 9-11:45am. Free. 50¢ toll to enter the island. Ask about the famed Marsh of the McIlhennys.) Nearby crawls the **Jungle Gardens** (369-6243), 250 acres developed in the 19th century by E. A. McIlhenny that include waterways, a lovely wisteria arch, camellia gardens, Chinese bamboo, alligators, and an 800-year-old statue of the Buddha. The jungle's sanctuary for herons and egrets helped to save the snowy egret from extinction. This elegant bird, once hunted for the long plumes it grows during mating season, now nests in the gardens from February to mid-summer. (Open daily 9am-6pm. $5, kids $3.50.) For a unique look at swamp and bayou wildlife, take an **Airboat Tour** (229-4457) of Lake Fausse Point and the surrounding area. (Tickets $10.)

New Iberia crouches 21 mi. southeast of Lafayette on U.S. 90. **Amtrak** (800-872-7245) serves New Iberia between New Orleans and Lafayette. (One way to New Orleans $26.) **Greyhound** (364-8571) pulls into town at 101 Perry St. Buses head to: Morgan City ($8.50), New Orleans ($18.50), and Lafayette ($3) three times per day.

The **Iberia Parish Tourist Commission** 2690 Center St. at the intersection of Hwy. 14 (365-8246), offers city maps for $1 and free pamphlets. (Open daily 9am-5pm.) The **post office** is at 817 E. Dale St. (364-4568; open daily 8am-4:30pm). The **ZIP code** is 70560; the **area code** is 318.

Wildlife

Much of Acadiana is lush wilderness, subtropical environment of marsh, bottomland hardwoods, and stagnant backwater bayous. You can fish and enjoy the jungle-like terrain about 40 mi. southeast of New Iberia near Bayou Vista. The **Atchafalaya Delta Wildlife Area,** lies at the mouth of the Atchafalaya River in St. Mary Parish. The preserve encompasses bayous, potholes, low and high marsh, and dry ground. Rails, snipes, coot, and gallinules thrive here. Access it by boat launch from Morgan City near the Bayou Boeuf locks. Primitive **campsites** are available in the area.

The center of **Attakapas Wildlife Area,** in southern St. Martin and Iberia Parishes, lies 20 mi. northwest of Morgan City and 10 mi. northeast of Franklin. Flat swampland comprises most of this hauntingly beautiful area, which includes a large amount of raised land used as a refuge by animals during flooding. In Attakapas cypress, tupelo, oak, maple, and hackberry grow on the high ground, and a cornucopia of swamp plants and animals slog about in the wetlands. Squirrel, deer, and rabbit hunting is popular here. The area can be reached by boat; public launches leave from Morgan City on Rte. 70. Watch for signposts. No camping allowed. Bring A LOT of bug repellent.

Baton Rouge

Owing its name to native Indian cultures who, as early as 8000 B.C. delineated their tribal hunting boundaries with a "red stick," Baton Rouge later hosted French explorers and Acadian communities. But until the 1800s, Baton Rouge was little more than a back-woods, (red)-stick-in-the-mud village; at that time, New Orleans was Louisiana's capital. But a group of evangelical North Louisiana politicians was to change all of this. Concerned that the state government was wallowing in a hotbed of debauchery in the "Big Easy," they stuck a provision in the new state constitution mandating that the state capital be at least 60 mi. from New Orleans. Fun-loving legislators responded by drawing a 60-mi. circle on their state map in order to find the nearest legal human settlement that could serve as the capital city. Baton Rouge became the state capital.

Caught between two traditions, Baton Rouge fuses its aggressive Mississippi River industry with a quieter plantation country, yielding a hybrid culture alive with trade, historical museums and homes. Its research university, a progressive music scene and a thriving gay community in Spanish Town attest to a cosmopolitan temperament enriched by eclectic city architecture and a rambunctious and fascinating political history. Baton Rouge served as the home of "Kingfisher" Huey P. Long—a Depression-era populist demagogue who, until his assassination, was considered Franklin D. Roosevelt's biggest political threat. His brother, Uncle Earl, portrayed by Paul Newman in *Blaze,* "governed" the state from a mental asylum for part of his term. Current governor Edwin Edwards, a flamboyant Cajun Democrat, survived two federal indictments and regained the governorship for a third time by defeating Nazi-cum-Republican white supremacist David Duke.

Practical Information

Emergency: 911.

Baton Rouge Convention and Visitors Bureau, 838 North Blvd. (383-1825). Pick up the visitors guide but don't expect too much help from the staff. Open daily 8am-5pm.

Greyhound: 1253 Florida Blvd. (343-4891), at 13th St. A 15-min. walk from downtown. Unsafe area at night. To: New Orleans (11/day, 2 hr., $14) and Lafayette (6/day, 1 hr., $9). Open 24 hrs.

Public Transport: Capital City Transportation, 336-0821. Main terminal at 22nd and Florida Blvd. Buses run Mon.-Sat. approximately 6:30am-6:30pm. Service to LSU decent, otherwise unreliable and/or infrequent. Fare 75¢, transfers 10¢.

Help Lines: Crisis Intervention/Suicide Prevention Center, 924-3900. **Rape Crisis,** 383-7273. Both open 24 hrs.

Post Office: 750 Florida Blvd. (381-0713), off River Rd. Open Mon.-Fri. 8:30am-4:30pm, Sat. 9-11am. **ZIP code:** 70821.

Area Code: 504.

The state capitol sits on the east bank of the river; the city spreads eastward. The heart of downtown, directly south of the capitol, runs until **Government Street. Highland Road** leads south from downtown directly into LSU.

Accommodations, Camping, Food, Nightlife, et al, ad infinitum, ad nauseam, et cetera...

Most budget accommodations snuggle and cuddle outside of town along east-west Florida Blvd., (U.S. 190), or north-south Airline Hwy. (U.S. 61). **Louisiana State University (LSU)** provides cheap accommodations at their on-campus hotel run out of Pleasant Hall (387-0297). Take bus #7 ("University") from North Blvd. behind the Old State Capitol. There is a flat rate of $38 for standard rooms that cover the heads of about four people; for more room try the concierge room ($45) or the suite ($55). **Motel 6,** 9901 Airport Hwy. (924-2130) has small but clean and tidy rooms. (Singles $26, plus $6 per additional person.) The **Alamo Plaza Hotel Courts,** 4243 Florida Blvd. (924-7231), has spacious rooms (some with kitchenettes) in the less safe downtown area. Take bus #6 ("Sherwood Forest") east on Florida Blvd. from the Greyhound station. (Singles $18-22. Doubles $23-26.) The **KOA Campground,** 7628 Vincent Rd. (664-7281), KOs 12 mi. east of Baton Rouge (Denham Springs exit off I-12). Well-maintained sites include clean facilities and pool. (Sites $12.50 for 2 people, with hookup $14.)

The most fun places to eat in Baton Rouge are near LSU on **Highland Road. Louie's Café,** 209 W. State, is a 24-hr. grill that has been lauded in *Rolling Stone;* it's famous for its stir-fried vegetable omelettes served all the time (around $4). Behind Louie's is local favorite **The Bayou,** 124 W. Chimes (346-1765), the site of the bar scene in *sex, lies, and videotape.* You can play free pool from 5 to 8pm and drink select longnecks for 99¢. Downtown, you can't miss the **Frostop Drive-In,** 402 Government, a **giant frothy root beer mug spinning on a post** outside welcomes diners, and a Wurlitzer jukebox entertains them. Try the delicious root beer floats ($1.50) and sandwiches ($1-3). (Open Mon.-Fri. 9:30am-8:30pm, Sat. 10:30am-8:30pm, Sun. 11am-8pm.) For a power breakfast or lunch, join the state lawmakers at the **House of Representatives Dining Hall,** outside the state capitol. Entrées $2-3. (Open daily 7-10:30am and 11am-2pm.) The hippest edition of Baton Rouge nightlife is the **Onegieme Art Bar,** 1109 Highland (393-9335), with art openings and original music ranging from flamenco guitar to experimental rock. (Open Mon.-Sat. 8pm-2am.)

Sights

The most prominent building in Baton Rouge is also the first sight you should visit. In a move reminiscent of Ramses II, Huey Long ordered the unique **Louisiana State Capitol** (342-7317), a magnificent modern skyscraper, built in a mere 14 months between 1931 and 1932. The front lobby alone merits a visit, but visitors should also go to the free 27th-floor observation deck. (Open daily 8am-4:30pm.) One of the most interesting in the U.S., the building attests to the staying power of Long's monumental personality. Look for the bullet holes in a back corridor near the plaque indicating the site of his assassination; the place of his burial is under the statue in front. Right across the lawn fires the **Old Arsenal Museum**, whose smoky smell originates from the powder barrels and other wartime equipment on display. (Open Mon.-Sat. 10am-4pm, Sun. 1-4pm.) You can also tour the great white **Governor's Mansion** by appointment. The **Old State Capitol,** at River Rd. and North Blvd., an eccentric Gothic Revival castle, offers free tours. (Open Tues.-Sat. 9am-4:30pm.) Just south of downtown, the **Beauregard District** boasts typically ornate antebellum homes. Walk down North Blvd. from the Old State Capitol to the visitors center to take in the beauty of this neighborhood.

Just a block away from the Old State Capitol on River Rd. floats the **Riverside Museum** of the Louisiana Arts and Science Center (344-9463). Climb on the old steam engine and train cars parked next door. The museum also has a good collection of sculpture, photographs, and paintings by contemporary Louisiana artists. (Open Tues.-Fri. 10am-3pm, Sat. 10am-4pm, Sun. 1-4pm. $1.50, seniors, students, and kids 75¢.) The museum runs the **Old Governor's Mansion,** the chief executive's residence from 1930-1963, at North Blvd. and St. Charles St. When possible, the mansion houses a planetarium and various art exhibits. (Open Sat. 10am-4pm, Sun. 1-4pm. $1.50, seniors, students and kids 75¢.)

Those who don't have a car to visit outlying plantations (see Plantations under New Orleans) can visit the well-restored **Magnolia Mound Plantation,** 2161 Nicholson Dr. (343-4955), the only plantation on the regular bus line. (Open Tues.-Sat. 10am-4pm, Sun. 1-4pm; last tour at 3:30pm. $3.50, seniors $2.50, students $1.50.) The **LSU Rural Life Museum,** 6200 Burden Lane (765-2437), off Perkins Rd., re-creates everyday rural life in pre-industrial Louisiana. The authentically furnished shops, cabins, and storage houses adjoin meticulously kept rose and azalea-filled gardens. (Open Mon.-Fri. 8:30am-4pm. $3, kids $2. $1 donation for a guide book.)

Tour the harbor in the *Samuel Clemens* steamboat (381-9606), which departs from Florida Blvd. at the river for one-hour cruises. (Tours March-Sept. daily at 10am, noon, and 2pm; Oct.-March Wed.-Sun. at 10am, noon, and 2pm. $5, kids $3.) Open for inspection, the *U.S.S. Kidd* (342-1942), a World War II destroyer, throws militant tantrums on the river just outside the Louisiana Naval War Memorial Museum that features ship models and the Louisiana Military Veterans Hall of Honor. (Open daily 9am-5pm. Ship and museum admission $5, kids $3.50. Ship only $3, kids $2.)

New Orleans (N'awlins)

New Orleans is a country unto itself. Having been ruled by France and Spain and drawing settlers from all over the world to its rich port, the "Crescent City" displays a multicultural heritage in which Spanish courtyards, Victorian verandas, Acadian jambalaya, African-American Gumbo and French beignets mingle, mix and are juxtaposed. Don't try to place the accent of its people—it's a singular combination found nowhere else. Similarly unique to the city, African-American New Orleans jazz fuses traditional African rhythms with popular brass instruments, achieving international notoriety. Architectural styles ranging from old Spanish and French to ultra- and postmodern rub shoulders downtown.

In the 19th century, the red-light district known as "Storyville" flared. Today, New Orleans is still a city that loves to party. Come late February there's no escaping the month-long celebration of Mardi Gras, the apotheosis of the city's already festive atmosphere. Anxious to accrue as much sin as spirit and flesh will allow before Lent, the "city that care forgot" promenades, shuffles, sings, and swigs until midnight of Mardi Gras itself. Afterwards, the soulful melodies of jazz play on, comforting those who have forsaken drunken cavorting for the next 40 long and Lenten days.

Practical Information

Emergency: 911.

Visitor Information: To plan your vacation before you leave home, write or call the **Greater New Orleans Tourist and Convention Commission,** 1520 Sugar Bowl Dr., New Orleans, LA 70112 (566-5011), on the main floor of the Superdome. Open Mon.-Fri. 8:30am-5pm. More convenient and very helpful is the **New Orleans/Louisiana Tourist Center,** 529 St. Ann, Jackson Square (568-5661), in the French Quarter. Free city and walking tour maps. Open daily 10am-6pm. **Tourist Information Service,** 525-5000.

Travelers Aid: 846 Barone St. (525-8726), at the **YMCA**. Assists stranded people by providing temporary shelter, food, and counseling. Open Mon.-Fri. 8am-4pm.

Moisant International Airport (464-0831), 15 mi. west of the city. Served by the major domestic airlines as well as by larger Latin-American carriers. **Louisiana Transit Authority** (737-9611; office open 4am-6pm) runs between the airport and downtown at Elk and Tulane every 30-45 min. for $1.10 in exact change. Pick-up in front of Hertz. Airport limousine to downtown hotels $8, cab $18.

Buses and Trains: Union Passenger Terminal, 1001 Loyola Ave., a 10-min. walk to Canal St. via Elk. Terminus for statewide interstate bus and train systems. Open 24 hrs. **Amtrak,** 528-1610 or 800-872-7245. To Memphis (1/day, 8 hr., $73) and Houston (3/week, 8 hr., $70). **Greyhound** (525-9371). To: Baton Rouge (2 hr., $13.50, $25 round-trip, $9.50/$18 with college ID); Memphis (11 hr., $53, $104 round-trip); Houston (9 hr., $48, $86 round-trip; tickets cheaper if bought a week in advance); and Atlanta ($63, $124 round-trip).

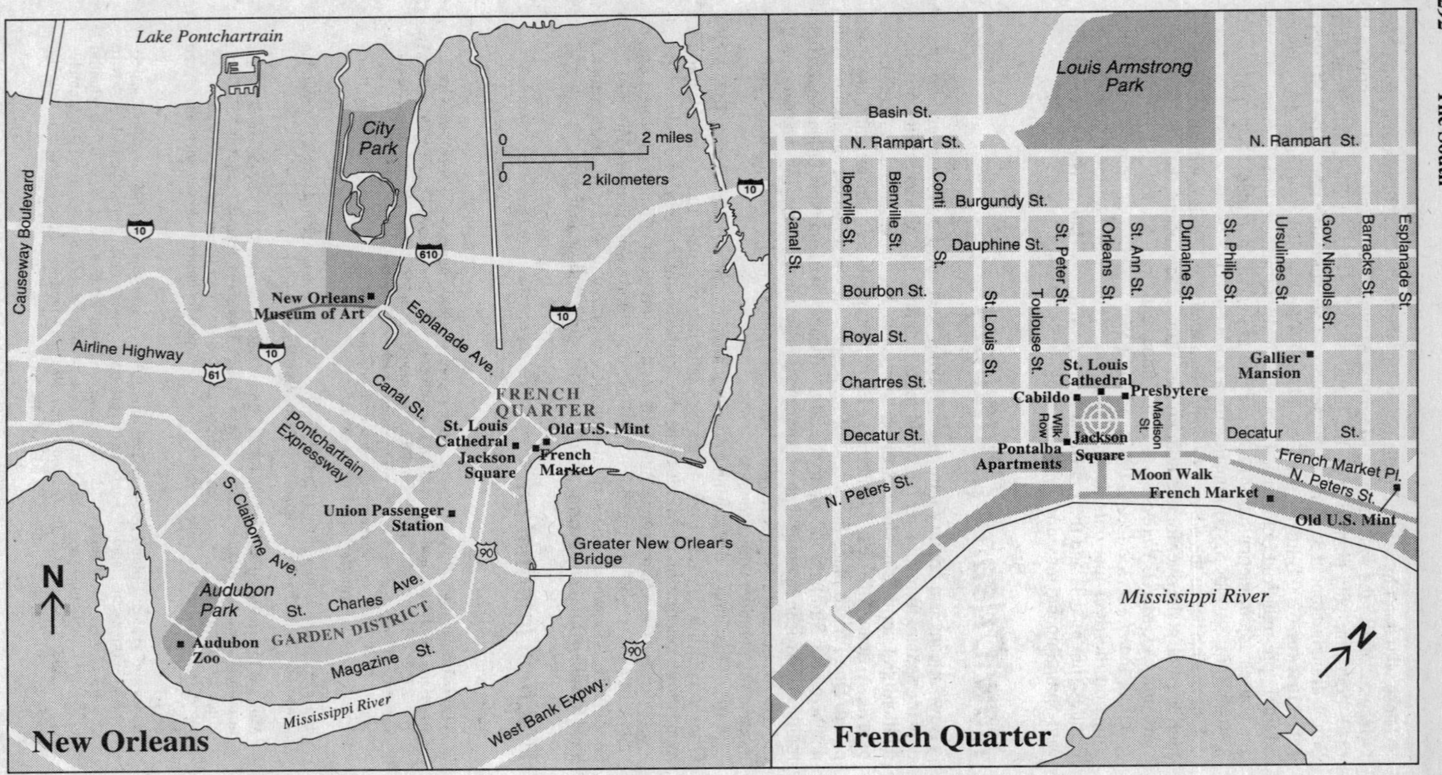
New Orleans
Lake Pontchartrain
City Park
0 2 miles
0 2 kilometers
Causeway Boulevard
10
610
New Orleans Museum of Art
Esplanade Ave.
Airline Highway
61
Canal St.
FRENCH QUARTER
St. Louis Cathedral
Jackson Square
Old U.S. Mint
French Market
Pontchartrain Expressway
S. Claiborne Ave.
Union Passenger Station
90
Greater New Orleans Bridge
N
Audubon Park
St. Charles Ave.
GARDEN DISTRICT
Audubon Zoo
Magazine St.
Mississippi River
West Bank Expwy.
French Quarter
Louis Armstrong Park
Basin St.
N. Rampart St.
N. Rampart St.
Canal St.
Iberville St.
Bienville St.
Conti St.
Burgundy St.
Dauphine St.
Bourbon St.
Royal St.
Chartres St.
Decatur St.
St. Louis St.
Toulouse St.
St. Peter St.
Orleans St.
St. Ann St.
Dumaine St.
St. Philip St.
Ursulines St.
Gov. Nicholls St.
Barracks St.
Esplanade St.
St. Louis Cathedral
Cabildo
Presbytere
Gallier Mansion
Wilk Row
Madison St.
Pontalba Apartments
Jackson Square
Decatur St.
French Market Pl.
N. Peters St.
N. Peters St.
Moon Walk
French Market
Old U.S. Mint
Mississippi River
N

Public Transport: Regional Transit Authority (RTA), Plaza Tower, 101 Dauphin St., 4th floor (569-2700), at Canal St. Bus schedules and transit info. Office open Mon.-Fri. 8:30am-5pm. Phone line provides 24-hr. route information. All buses pass by Canal St., at the edge of the French Quarter. Major buses and streetcars run 24 hrs. Fare $1, transfers 10¢, for disabled and elderly 40¢ and 20¢. 1 and 3-day passes are also available.

Taxi: United Cabs (522-9771). **Checker Yellow Cabs** (943-2411). **Dixie Cabs** (835-CABS). Base fare $1.70, each additional mi. $1.

Car Rental: Budget Car Rental, 1317 Canal (467-2277), and 6 other locations. $40/day, $25 weekends. 100 free mi. Add $5/day if under 25. Open daily 7:30am-5:30pm. Airport branch only closed 1-5am. Must be 21 with credit card or 25 with cash deposit. Reservations suggested.

Bike Rental: Michael's, 618 Frenchman (945-9505), a few blocks west of the Quarter. $3.50/hr., $13/day. Weekly rates. Open Mon.-Sat. 10am-7pm, Sun. 10am-5pm.

Help Lines: Gay Counseling Line, 522-5815. Usually operates 5-11pm. **Crisis Line,** 523-2673.

Post Office: 701 Loyola Ave. (589-1111 or 589-1112), near the Union Passenger Terminal, a 10-min. walk from Canal St. Open Mon.-Fri. 8:30am-4:30pm, Sat. 8:30am-noon. **ZIP code:** 70140.

Area Code: 504.

It's easy to get lost in New Orleans even though it is fairly small. The main streets of the city follow the curve in the river. There are many one-way streets, and drivers must sometimes make U-turns to cross intersections. The major tourist area is the small **French Quarter (Vieux Carré),** bounded by the Mississippi River, **Canal Street, Esplanade Avenue,** and **Rampart Street.** Streets in the French Quarter follow a grid pattern; traveling there on foot is easy. The **Garden District** is west of downtown. Buses to all parts of the city pass by Canal St. at the edge of the Quarter.

Parts of New Orleans are unsafe, particularly the tenement areas directly to the north of the French Quarter and those directly northwest of Lee Circle. Even quaint-looking side streets in the Quarter can be dangerous at night—stick to busy, well-lit thoroughfares. Take a cab back to your lodgings when returning late at night from the Quarter.

Accommodations

Finding inexpensive yet decent accommodations in the French Quarter is as difficult as finding a sober citizen on Mardi Gras. Try one of the few inexpensive **bed and breakfasts** around the Garden District, the best of which are listed below. Dormitory rooms with semi-private baths are available at **Loyola University** (865-3735), from June to August ($20/person).

About the only way to get accommodations for Mardi Gras is to reserve them a year in advance. **Jazzfest** in late April also makes budget rooms scarce. Pay close attention to warnings under individual lodgings regarding the safety of its location; avoid areas where you feel at all uncomfortable, and do not walk around alone at night, anywhere in this city.

Marquette House New Orleans International Hostel (HI/AYH), 2253 Carondelet St. (523-3014), is made up of several smaller houses that congregate around a large, well-lit Victorian home, featuring two dining rooms, a fully equipped kitchen, a locker room (25-50¢ per locker), and a couple of study lounges. Very clean, nice furnishings and bathrooms. Laundry room open 11am-11pm. No alcohol permitted; smoking only in the courtyard; no curfew. $11, nonmembers $14. Private doubles $27-30. Private apartments $39-45. Linens $2.50. Reservations for Mardi Gras must be made far, far in advance—include a self-addressed stamped envelope.

Longpre House (AAIH), 1726 Prytania St. (501-4440), a block off the streetcar route, a 20-min. walk from the Quarter, attracts travelers because of its relaxed atmosphere in a 150-year-old house. Free coffee. Pool. Check-in 8am-10pm. Dorm rooms $10/person, nonmembers $16. Singles $30. Doubles $40-45.

St. Charles Guest House, 1748 Prytania St. (523-6556), in a serene neighborhood near the Garden District and St. Charles streetcar. Backpackers' singles $25-35. Doubles $55. 2 double beds $65, $5 per extra person. Ask about $12.50 student rate for groups of 3 or more. This hostel is not in the best neighborhood; take caution when walking in the area, especially at night. If you feel uncomfortable, pick a different hostel.

Old World Inn, 1330 Prytania St. (566-1330), 1 block from the St. Charles streetcar. Multi-colored carpeting and walls covered with paintings create a slightly tacky but homey atmosphere. Complimentary continental breakfast in the morning. Singles from $30. Doubles from $40.

YMCA, 920 St. Charles Ave. on Lee Circle (586-9622). Drab but sufficient rooms with in a large building complex at the heart of downtown. For men and women. Pay phones in the hall. Guests may use the gym, weightroom, and track. Singles $28. Doubles $34. Linens included.

Hotel LaSalle, 1113 Canal St. (523-5831 or 800-521-9450), 4 blocks east of Bourbon St. downtown. Attractive lobby with coffee around the clock on an antique sideboard. Ample rooms and free movies. Laundry 50-75¢. Singles $28, with bath $42. Doubles $30, with bath $47. Reservations recommended.

Rose Inn, 3522 Tulane Ave. (484-7611), exit gate 232 off I-10, 4 blocks from S. Carrollton. Not in the best of neighborhoods, but perfectly located for drivers, public bus stops in front of inn. Older but spacious rooms. Lone travelers and women may feel uncomfortable. Pool. Extra charge for phone. Singles $25. Doubles $28.

Prytannia Inn, 1415 Prytannia St. (566-1515), includes 3 homes about 5 blocks from each other, each of which offers bright and cheery rooms. Friendly proprietors serve a full gourmet breakfast for $5 from 8-10am, Mon.-Fri., until 10:30am on Sat.-Sun. Each house has a breakfast room, but depending on volume, you may have to walk to your morning meal. Laundry available for an additional charge. Staff speaks French, German, Italian, Spanish, and English. Singles $35-50. Doubles $49-69; rooms may be discounted in off-seasons.

Camping

The several campgrounds near New Orleans are tough to reach via public transportation. Try to enjoy Louisiana's beautiful forests, lakes, and bayous anyway, if only to escape the French Quarter crowds. Bring insect repellent and baking soda (for a poultice); the mosquitos are voracious. Check out the **Golden Pelican passes** available at state parks, which allow you to stay in state campgrounds for $6 per night. ($30 for Louisianians, $50 for others.)

Bayou Segnette State Park, 7777 Westbank Expressway (436-1107). RTA bus transport available. Enchanting park. Cabins on the bayou $50 for up to 8 people. Campsites with water, electricity $12.

KOA West, 219 S. Starrett, River Ridge 70123 (467-1792), off highway I-10. RTA bus transport available. Pool, laundry facilities. Full-hookup sites $26/2 people.

St. Bernard State Park, P.O. Box 534, Violet 70092 (682-2101), 18 mi. southeast of New Orleans. Take I-10 to Rte. 47 south and go left on Rte. 39 through Violet and Poydras. Nearest public transport to New Orleans a ½-mi. hike. Pool. Registration until 10pm. Sites $12.

Parc d'Orleans II, 10910 Chef Menteur Hwy. (242-6176; 800-535-2598 outside LA), 3 mi. east of the junction of I-10 and U.S. 90 (Chef Menteur Hwy.). Near public transport into the city. Pool, showers, and laundry facilities. Sites from $17.

Fontainebleau State Park, P.O. Box 152, Mandeville 70448 (626-8052), southeast of Mandeville on U.S. 190, on the shores of Lake Ponchartrain. Furthest from New Orleans of all the above campgrounds. Sites $9.

Food

You will find more restaurants per capita in New Orleans than in any major city in the world outside of Paris. Acadian refugees, Spaniards, Italians, and African and Native Americans have all contributed to the hot, spicy, Cajun culinary style that—like a good stew—has a bit of everything thrown in. Here, Cajun cult members gather to worship the "holy trinity:" bell peppers, onions, and celery. Jambalaya—a jumble of rice, shrimp oysters, ham or chicken mixed with spices—and the African dish gumbo grace practically every menu in New Orleans. A southern breakfast of grits, eggs, bacon, and corn bread will satisfy even the biggest of eaters. Also sample the regional delights red beans and rice, seafood po'boys (a french-bread sandwich filled with fried oysters and shrimp), and shrimp or crawfish **étouffé**. And you may *not* leave New Orleans without dining on **beignets** and **café au lait** at the 1862 world-famous **Café du Monde** (see below).

Cool off in the summer months and "air condition your tummy" with a snow-blitz sundae from **Hansen's Snow-Blitz Sweet Shop,** 481 Tchoupitoulas St. (891-9788) where if the 50¢- or $1-size cups can't quench your need for a "Hansen's fix," then trash-can-size servings are available for only $200. Always expect a line. (Open Tues.-Fri. and Sun. 3-9pm. Indulge in **Creole pralines** (90¢); some of the best and cheapest bake at **Laura's Candies,** 600 Conti and 155 Royal St. (525-3880; open daily 9am-6pm on Conti; 8am-8pm on Royal). The **French Market,** between Decatur and N. Peters St. on the east side of the French Quarter, sells fresh vegetables. The grocery stores on Decatur St. have the rest of the fixings you'll need for a picnic.

French Quarter

Acme Oyster House, 724 Iberville (522-5973). Slurp fresh oysters shucked before your eyes (6 for $3.75, 12 for $6.50) or sit at the red checkered tables for a good ol' po'boy. Open Mon.-Sat. 11am-10pm, Sun. noon-7pm.

Quarter Scene Restaurant, 900 Dumaine (522-6533). This cornerside café serves delicious salads and seafood and pasta entrees ($6-13). A tasty surprise is the *Dumaine* ($4), a peanut butter and banana sandwich topped with nuts and honey. Open 24 hrs., except Tues. closes at 11:30 pm, and Wed., closes at 8:30 pm.

Croissant d'Or, 617 Ursuline St (524-4663). In a historic building that was the first ice cream parlor in New Orleans. Delicious, reasonably-priced French pastries (75¢-$2) that won't chip your teeth. Courtyard seating available. Open daily 7am-5pm.

Mama Rosa's, 616 N. Rampart (523-5546), on the edge of the French Quarter. The best pizza in New Orleans (10-in. cheese $7.25, with everything, $10.50). Also serves heaping salads and gumbo ($3-5). Open Tues.-Thurs. 10:30am-10:30pm, Fri.-Sun. 10:30am-11:30pm.

Café du Monde, French Market at the intersection of Decatur and St. Ann St. (587-0835). The consummate people-watching paradise since the 1860s. Drink *café au lait* and down perfectly prepared hot *beignets* with powdered sugar (3 for $.75). Open 24 hrs.

Outside the Quarter

Mother's Restaurant, 401 Poydras (523-9656), 4 blocks north of Bourbon St. Yo Mama has been serving up unparalleled crawfish *étouffé* ($7.50) and seafood po'boys ($5-8) to locals for almost half a century. Be daring and try the crawfish or shrimp *étouffé* omelette. Entrées from $4.25. Open Mon.-Sat. 5am-10pm, Sun. 7am-10pm.

Camellia Grill, 626 S. Carrollton Ave. (866-9573). Take the St. Charles streetcar away from the Quarter to the Tulane area. One of the finest diners in America, complete with friendly napkins and cloth servers, or vice-versa. Try the chef's special omelette ($5.50) or partake of the tasty pecan pie. Expect a wait on weekend mornings. Open Sun.-Wed. 8am-1am, Thurs.-Sat. 8am-2am.

Franky and Johnny's, 321 Arabella (899-9146), southwest of downtown towards Tulane off Tchoupitoulas. Good seafood and po'boys served in a fun and lively atmosphere. Try the turtle soup ($2.50-4). Open Mon.-Thurs. 11am-11pm, Fri.-Sat. 11am-midnight, Sun. 11am-10pm.

Bluebird Café, 3625 Prytania St. (895-7166). Delicious healthy sandwiches (around $3) and hearty Southern breakfasts. Open Mon.-Fri. 7am-3pm, Sat.-Sun. 8am-3pm.

Mais Oui, 5908 Magazine Ave. (897-1540). But yes! This is home cooking at its best. Delicious corn bread and gumbo. Entrées run from $5-10. Menu changes daily. Bring your own wine; $1 corkage fee. No credit cards personal checks accepted. AmEx cheques taken in $20 denominations. Open Mon.-Fri. 11:30am-2:45pm and 5:30-8:45pm, Sat. 5:30-8:45pm.

All Natural, 5517 Magazine St. (891-2651). Mostly a take-out health food store with a few tables outside. The food and the customers are very healthy. Probably the only place in the world serving vegetarian Jambalaya ($5 with salad). Open Mon.-Fri. 10am-7pm, Sat. 9am-7pm, Sun. 10am-5pm.

Sights

French Quarter

Allow yourself *at least* a full day (some take a lifetime) in the Quarter. The oldest section of the city, it is famous for its ornate wrought-iron balconies, French, Spanish, and Creole architectures and joyous atmosphere. Known as the **Vieux Carré,** meaning

Old Square, the historic district of New Orleans offers interesting used book and record stores, museums, and shops that pawn off ceramic masks and cheap t-shirts to innocent tourists. Walk through the residential section down **Dumaine Street** to escape the more crowded area near the river. Stop in at a neighborhood bar. Tourists are taken in stride here, and you should feel welcome.

The heart of the Quarter beats at **Jackson Square** in whose center a bronze equestrian statue of General Andrew Jackson, the victor of the Battle of New Orleans. While the square boogies with artists, mimes, musicians, and magicians, the **St. Louis Cathedral** presides at its head. Across the street, the **Jackson Brewery Rivermarket** (586-8021; open Sun.-Thurs. 10am-9pm, Fri.-Sat. 10am-10pm) offers fast food and a modern shopping complex, which, though very nice, doesn't hold a candle to the bundles of flea market paraphernalia, jewelry, and leather goods amassed at the **French Market.** On the eastern side of the market is the **Old U.S. Mint,** 400 Esplanade, which houses interesting collections on the history of New Orleans and Louisiana. The Mint is one of the eight museums that comprise the **Louisiana State Museum,** P.O. Box 2448 (568-6972) three of which—the **Cabildo, Presbytère,** and **1850 House**—are in Jackson Square, and two of which—the Presbytère and the 1850—are open for touring, except the Cabildo. (All open Tues.-Sun. 10am-5pm. $3, students and seniors $1.50, ages 12 and under free.) They contain artifacts, papers, and other changing exhibits on the history of Louisiana and New Orleans.

The rich cultural history of the French Quarter has made it a National Historic Park, and free tours and interpretive programs are given by the **Jean Lafitte National Historic Park,** 916-918 North Peters (589-2636), located in the back section of the French Market at Decatur and St. Phillip St. Because some tours require reservations and fill up quickly, call ahead for specific info.

The Park Service no longer conducts tours of the city cemeteries—these areas have been deemed too unsafe. Ironically, visitors who are interested in touring in the dark graveyards are left with no guide except the **New Orleans Historic Voodoo Museum,** 724 Dumaine St. (523-7685) which offers tour packages including graveyards ($10-28) and haunted plantations ($38) as well as other tours of the Atchafalaya Swamp ($58). (Open daily 10am-dusk.) Be careful here; ghosts may not bother you, but other shady characters might.

Outside the Quarter

The French Quarter is certainly not the only interesting area of New Orleans. In the southernmost corner of the Quarter at the "foot of Canal St." where the riverboats dock, stands the **World Trade Center** where you can take in a blimp's-eye view of New Orleans from 31 flights up ($2, ages 6-12 $1, seniors $1.50; open 9am-5pm daily) and then grab a snack at Riverview Cafeteria on the third floor. (Open 7am-2:30pm.) In this same area ambles the **Riverwalk,** a multi-million dollar conglomeration of overpriced shops overlooking the port. For entertainment and an unbeatable meal, let the **Cookin' Cajun New Orleans Cooking School** store, 116 Riverwalk (586-8832 or 523-6425) prepare a Cajun or Creole meal before your eyes. Call ahead for the menu of the day. ($15 for 2 hrs.) You can take the **Canal Street Ferry** to Algiers Point until about 9pm for a 25-minute view of the Mississippi River. (Free.)

The **Aquarium of the Americas** (861-2537) is across from the World Trade Center, on the river. The aquarium holds over one million gallons of water and reproduces underwater environments of our slimy, scaly friends from North, Central, and South America. Check out the famous piranha, almost banned by the Louisiana Legislature because it might escape into the Mississippi and eat up all the naughty children. ($8, seniors $6.25, kids $4.25. Open daily 9:30am, closing hours vary.)

Relatively new in the downtown area, the **Warehouse Arts District,** on Julia St. between Commerce and Baronne, contains historic architecture and contemporary art galleries housed in revitalized warehouse buildings. Exhibits range from Southern folk art to experimental sculpture. Maps of the area are available in each gallery. Be sure to check out the **Contemporary Arts Center,** 900 Camp St. (523-1216), an old brick building with a modern glass and chrome façade. The exhibits range from cryptic to puzzling, but you will always enjoy the amazing artsy architecture that flourishes within. (Open Wed.-Sun. 11am-5pm. $3, kids, students, seniors $2, ages 1-12 free; everyone free on Thurs.)

Many culturally diverse attractions of New Orleans exist outside downtown. Though the streetcar named "Desire" was derailed long ago, you can take the **St. Charles Streetcar** to the west of the French Quarter to view some of the city's finest buildings, including the elegant, mint-condition 19th-century homes along **St. Charles Avenue.** The old-fashioned train takes you through some of New Orlean's most beautiful neighborhoods at a leisurely pace for a mere $1. Be sure to disembark at the **Garden District,** an opulent neighborhood between Jackson and Louisiana Ave. The legacies of French, Italian, Spanish, and American architecture create an extraordinary combination of magnificent structures, rich colors, ironworks, and, of course, exquisite gardens. Many stand several feet above the ground as protection from the swamp on which New Orleans was built. The wet foundation of the city even troubles the dead—all the city's cemeteries must be elevated to let the deceased rest in dry peaces.

The St. Charles Street Car runs all the way to **Audubon Park,** across from Tulane University. Designed by Frederick Law Olmsted—the same architect who planned New York City's Central Park—Audubon contains lagoons, statues, stables, and the delightful **Audubon Zoo** (861-2537) with its re-created Louisiana swamp harboring alligators and all. A free museum shuttle glides from the Audubon Park entrance (streetcar stop #36) to the zoo. (Zoo open daily 9:30am-4:30pm. $7, seniors and ages 2-12 $3.25.) The steamboat **John Audubon** shuttles four round-trips a day between Canal Street and the zoo (10am-4pm, fare round-trip cruise $10.50, $5.75 kids; one-way cruise $8.50, kids $4.50; package tours include cruise, zoo, and aquarium range from $15-24, kids $8-13). The *Cotton Blossom* (586-8777) sails on five-hour bayou cruises ($14.50, kids $7.25).

You can find quite a bit of nature with a 10-minute drive north of the Quarter, in **City Park,** at the corner of City Park Ave and Marconie Dr. (482-4888), accessible by the Esplanade or City Park bus. This 1500-acre park is one of the five largest city parks in the U.S. In addition to the **Museum of Art** (see Museums below), it contains a botanical garden, golf courses, tennis courts, 800-year-old oak trees, lagoons, and a miniature train.

One of the most unique sights near New Orleans, the coastal wetlands that line Lake Salvador, make up another segment of the **Jean Lafitte National Historical Park** called the **Barataria Unit** (589-2330). Unfortunately, the park can only be reached with a car, but the free park service swamp tours almost warrant renting one. The park is off the West Bank Expressway across the Mississippi River down Barataria Blvd. (Hwy. 45).

A trip to Louisiana is not complete without seeing its mysterious bayous or "sleeping waters." **Riverboat cruises** offer swamp tours and other water journeys. Those with spare time and money may want to jump aboard the **Creole Queen** cruises for (524-0814) an anecdotal, if not royal, history of New Orleans, Cajun, and Creole life during its five-hour cruise ($13, kids $6). **Natchez** (586-8777), New Orleans' only steam boat, also offers river tours and features piped steam Calliope concerts twice daily for $13.50, kids $7. Not to be outdone, the **Gray Line Tours** offers a host of both surf and turf tours to almost any and every site in New Orleans at a wide range of prices. Call 587-0861 for details.

For a different, more serious look at the economic backbone of New Orleans, reserve a free tour at the **Southern Regional Research Center,** 1100 Robert E. Lee Blvd., P.O. Box 19687 (286-4521) where scientists investigate means by which to further improve and cultivate Southern products like cotton. Visitors can see the intricate steps taken in weaving cloth, tanks used for catfish farming analysis, and labs used to flavor-test foods.

Equally fascinating are the tours of the **NASA Michoud Assembly Facility,** 13800 Old Gentilly Rd. (257-3311) that builds Space Shuttle External Tanks. Walk the factory and gape at the 154-ft. long, 28-ft. diameter tanks. Reservations must be made and several restrictions apply; you must be a US citizen to visit the museum.

Museums

Hermann-Grima Historic House, 820 St. Louis St. (525-5661) exemplifies early American architecture and features the only working 1830s Creole kitchen and private stable in the area. Also has period garden and interior restorations. Open Mon.-Sat. 10am-3:30pm. $4, students $3.

Gallier House Museum, 1118-1132 Royal St., French Quarter (523-6722). This elegant restored residence brings alive the taste and lifestyle of mid-19th century New Orleans. Tours every ½ hr., last tour at 3:45pm. Open Mon.-Sat. 10am-4:30pm. $4, seniors and students $3, kids $2.25.

Musée Conti Wax Museum, 917 Conti St. (525-2605). One of the world's finest houses of wax. The voodoo display and haunted dungeon are perennial favorites. Open daily 10am-5:30pm except during Mardi Gras. $5.75, under 17 $3, seniors $4.50.

New Orleans Museum of Art, City Park (488-2631). Take the Esplanade bus from Canal and Rampart. Small collection of local decorative arts, opulent works by the jeweler Fabergé, and a strong collection of French paintings including works by Degas. Guided tours available. Open Tues.-Sun. 10am-5pm. $4, seniors and kids ages 2-17 $2.

Historic New Orleans Collection, 533 Royal St. (523-4662) boasts extensive facilities and offers 2 guided tours ($2 each). The History Tour explores New Orleans' past, while the interesting Williams Residence Tour showcases the eclectic ethnic furnishings of the home of the collection founders, Gen'l and Mrs. L. Kemper Williams. The downstairs gallery displays varying exhibitions and is free. (Open Tues.-Sat. 10am-4:45pm; tours at 10 and 11am, 2 and 3pm.)

K&B Plaza, 1055 St. Charles Ave. on Lee Circle, houses the Virlane Foundation collection of art and sculpture in the hallways and lobbies on six of its seven floors. Among the creative displays of this outstanding contemporary collection, sculpture by Henry Moore, mobiles by Alexander Calder, and a bust by Renoir. Open 24 hrs. Free.

Confederate Museum, 929 Camp St. (523-4522). An extensive collection of Civil War records and artifacts. Located just west of Lee Circle in an ivy-covered stone building. Open Mon.-Sat. 10am-4pm. $3, seniors and students $2, kids $1.

Louisiana Nature and Science Center, 11000 Lake Forest Blvd. (246-5672), in Joe Brown Memorial Park. Hard to reach without a car, but a wonderful escape from the frivolity of the French Quarter. Trail walks, exhibits, planetarium shows, laser shows, and 86 acres of natural wildlife preserve. Open Tues.-Fri. 9am-5pm. ($2, seniors and kids $1), Sat.-Sun. noon-5pm ($3, seniors and kids $2).

Louisiana Children's Museum, 428 Julia St. (523-1357). Invites kids to star on their own news show, shop at a mini-mart, pretend to be a streetcar driver, and much, much more. They'll never know they're learning at the same time. Kids under 12 must be accompanied by an adult. Open Tues.-Sun. 9:30-4:30pm. $3.

Entertainment and Nightlife

On any night of the week, at any time of year, multitudes of people join the constant fête of the French Quarter. After exploring the more traditional jazz, blues, and brass sound of the Quarter, assay the rest of the city for less tourist-oriented bands playing to a more local clientele. Check *Off Beat* for maps of the clubs; try opening *Gambit,* the free weekly entertainment newspaper, or the Friday edition of the *Times-Picayune's* entertainment guide *Lagniappe* to find out who's playing where. There's a large gay community here; check out local newsletters *Impact* and *Ambush* for more information on gay events and nightlife.

Traditional New Orleans jazz, born here at the turn of the century in **Armstrong Park,** can still be enjoyed at tiny, dimly lit, historic **Preservation Hall,** 726 Saint Peter St. (523-8939). This is jazz in its most fundamental and visceral element. If you don't arrive before the doors open, be prepared for a lengthy wait in line, poor visibility and sweaty standing-room only. ($3.) Beverages not sold. Doors open at 8pm; music begins at 8:30pm and goes on until midnight.

Keep your ears open for **Cajun** and **zydeco** bands. Using accordions, washboards, triangles and drums, they perform hot dance tunes (to which locals expertly two-step) and exuberantly sappy waltzes. Their traditional fare is the *fais do-do,* a lengthy, wonderfully sweaty dance. Anyone who thinks couple-dancing went out in the '50s should try one of these; just grab a partner and throw yourself into the rhythm. The locally based **Radiators** do it up real spicy like.

The annual **New Orleans Jazz Festival** (522-4786), held at the fairgrounds in late April, features music played simultaneously on six stages. The entertainment also includes a Cajun food and crafts festival. Though exhilaratingly fun, the festival grows more zoo-like each year. Book a room early.

French Quarter

New Orleans bars stay open late, and few bars adhere to a strict schedule or entrance policy. In general, they open around 11am and close around 3am. Most bars in the area are very expensive, charging $3-5 for drinks. Yet on most blocks, you can find cheap draft beer and "Hurricanes," sweet drinks made of juice and rum; visitors can totter around the streets, get pleasantly soused, and listen to great music without going broke.

The Napoleon House, 500 Chartres St. (524-9752), is one of the world's great watering holes. Located on the ground floor of the Old Girod House, it was built as an exile home for Napoleon in a plan to spirit him away from St. Helena. Food served. Open Mon.-Fri. until 1am, Sat.-Sun. until 2am.

The Absinthe Bar, 400 Bourbon St. (525-8108). Reasonably-priced drinks for the French Quarter, with a blues band sometimes led by Bryan Lee. Has irrigated the likes of Mark Twain, Franklin D. Roosevelt, the Rolling Stones, Humphrey Bogart. Bet you've never heard those four names together in the same sentence! Open Sun.-Thurs. 5:30pm-2am, Fri.-Sat. 5:30pm-3am.

Pat O'Brien's, 718 Saint Peter St. (525-4823). The busiest bar in the French Quarter, bursting with happy (read: drunk) tourists. You can listen to the pianos in one room, mix with local students in another, or lounge beneath huge fans near a fountain in the courtyard. Home of the original Hurricane; purchase your first in a souvenir glass ($6). Open daily. 10:30am-5am.

Bourbon Pub/Parade, 801 Bourbon St. (529-2107). This gay dance bar sponsors a "tea dance" on Sun. with all the beer you can drink for $5. Open 24 hrs. Dancing nightly 9pm-4am.

Old Absinthe House, 240 Bourbon St. (523-3181). The marble absinthe fountain inside has been dry since absinthe was outlawed. The Absinthe Frappe is a re-invention of the infamous drink with anisette or Pernod liqueur ($4.50). Food served. Reputed to be the oldest bar in the U.S. Open daily 10am-2am.

Storyville Jazz Hall, 1104 Decatur St. (525-8199). This large music hall opens onto the street and hosts a variety of bands from Southern metal to cool jazz. Generally a concert hall; call for times and ticket information.

Outside the Quarter

Many great bars frolic outside the French Quarter—those below are grouped according to nearby landmarks.

Snug Harbor, 626 Frenchman St. (949-0696), just east of the Quarter near Decatur. Blues vocalists Charmaine Neville and Amasa Miller sing here regularly, giving 2 shows/night. Ellis Marsalis also performs here. The cover is no bargain ($6-14), but Mon. evening with Ms. Neville is worth it. You can also hear, but not see, the soulful music from the bar in the front room. Food served. Open daily 11am-3am.

Tipitina's, 501 Napoleon Ave. (897-3943 concert line; 895-8477 regular line). This locally renowned establishment attracts the best local bands and even some big names. Favorite bar of late jazz pianist and scholar Professor Longhair; his bust now graces the front hall. Though the prof's pedagogy is no longer, the club books a wide variety of music. Best to call ahead for times and prices. Cover $4-15.

Michaul's, 701 Magazine St. (522-5517), at Girnod. A huge floor for Cajun dancing; they will even teach you how. Open with music Mon.-Thurs. 6-11pm, Fri.-Sat. 6pm-midnight.

Maple Leaf Bar, 8316 Oak St. (866-5323), near Tulane University. The best local dance bar offers zydeco and Cajun music; everyone does the two-step. Poetry readings Sun. at 3pm. The party begins Sun.-Thurs. at 10pm, Fri.-Sat. at 10:30pm. Cover $3-5.

Muddy Water's, 8301 Oak St. (966-7174), near Tulane. Live music every night, mostly blues. Serves food and extracts a small cover. Open Mon.-Thurs. 3pm-4am, Fri.-Sun. noon-6am.

St. Charles Tavern, 1433 St. Charles Ave. (523-9823). Have a blast at this neighborhood gathering spot, frequented by cops and cabbies. Pizza ($3). Open 24 hrs.

Plantations

Called the "Great Showplace of New Orleans," **Longue Vue House and Gardens,** 7 Bamboo Rd. off Metairie Rd. (488-5488) epitomizes the grand Southern estate with lavish furnishings and opulent decor. The sculpted gardens are startlingly beautiful. The Old South is preserved here (in a jar on the second floor). Tours available in English, French, Spanish, Italian, and Japanese. (Open Mon.-Sat. 10am-4:30 pm, Sun. 1-5pm. House and garden $6, students $3;gardens only $3, students $1.) **River Road,** a winding street that follows the Mississippi River, holds several preserved plantations from the 19th century. Pick up a copy of *Great River Road Plantation Parade: A River of Riches* at the New Orleans or Baton Rouge visitors centers for a good map and descriptions of the houses. Free and frequent ferries cross the Mississippi at Plaquemines, White Castle, and between Lutcher and Vacherie. A tour of all the plantations would be quite expensive. Those below are listed in order from New Orleans to Baton Rouge.

San Francisco Plantation House, Rte. 44 (535-2341), 2 mi. north of Reserve, 23 mi. from New Orleans on the north bank of the Mississippi. Beautifully restored plantation built in 1856. Galleried in the old Creole style with the main living room on the 2nd floor. Exterior painted 3 different colors with many colorfully decorated ceilings. (Open daily 10am-4pm. $5.50, kids $2.50.)

Houmas House, River Rd., Burnside (473-7841), just over halfway to Baton Rouge on the northern bank of the Mississippi. Setting for the movie *Hush, Hush, Sweet Charlotte,* starring Bette Davis and Olivia DeHavilland. Built in two sections: the rear constructed in the last quarter of the 18th century; the Greek Revival mansion in front in 1840. Beautiful gardens and furnishings. Open Feb.-Oct. daily 10am-5pm; Nov.-Jan. 10am-4pm. $6.50, ages 13-17 $4.50, ages 6-12 $3.25.

Nottoway, Rte. 405 (545-2730), between Bayou Goula and White Castle, 20 mi. south of Baton Rouge on the southern bank of the Mississippi. Largest plantation home in the South; often called the "White Castle of Louisiana." An incredible 64-room mansion with 22 columns, a large ballroom, and a 3-story stairway. The first choice of David O. Selznick for filming *Gone with the Wind,* but the owners didn't give a damn and simply wouldn't allow it. Open daily 9am-5pm. Admission and 1-hr. guided tour $8, kids $3.

Mississippi

Understandably known as the "Magnolia State," Mississippi grows grass so green around magnolias and oaks so leafy that the flora seems to defy the humid, wilting heat for which the South is so famous. When traveling here, steer off the interstate to explore lush forests, swamps, and countryside. A major passageway for hundreds of years, the Natchez Trace winds gracefully through the shade from Natchez, MS to Nashville, TN, passing through a beautiful national park and many historic landmarks. The park's strictly-enforced 50 mph speed limit encourages travelers to amble at a leisurely pace.

The beauty of this roadway and the Mississippi River contrasts with the many disturbing years of racial conflicts and appalling economic conditions for which the state is notorious. When Vicksburg witnessed a major Civil War battle won by the Union in 1863, the battle for Civil Rights had only just begun—the state would see many more years of turbulent racial strife. Mississippi's culture is strongly influenced by its African-American heritage; the blues, born in Mississippi, derived from African slave songs, and Mississippians Robert Johnson and B.B. King are responsible for popularizing this great art form.

Practical Information

Capital: Jackson.

Visitor Information: Division of Tourism, 1301 Walter Siller Bldg., 550 High St. (359-3414 or 800-647-2290). Open Mon.-Fri. 8am-5pm. **Bureau of Parks and Recreation,** P.O. Box 10600, Jackson 39209.

Time Zone: Central (1 hr. behind Eastern).

Postal Abbreviation: MS

Sales Tax: 6%.

Biloxi and the Mississippi Coast

With a leading seafood canning industry dating back to the 1870s, Biloxi proudly calls itself the "seafood capital of the world" and hosts several annual maritime festival—the most popular being the Shrimp Festival and the blessing of the fleet (a quasi-religious ceremony in June asking the Fisher King for a safe, bountiful shrimp season). Biloxi's resort reputation also goes back to the mid-1800s, when New Orleans families fled to the Mississippi Gulf Coast to escape periodic yellow fever epidemics.

Although the 26-mi. snow-white, sandy **Gulf Islands National Seashore** today sports a few too many souvenir shops, the natural beauty of this—the longest man-made beach in the world—still attracts throngs of sun worshipers and beachcombers. The Spanish moss hanging from the oak trees along the road (actually neither Spanish nor moss, but a relative of the pineapple plant) and old **antebellum mansions** in the **historic district** also merit a glance. Self-guided walking tours of the area are available from the **Visitors Center** (see below). To learn more about Biloxi's fishy past, visit the **Seafood Industry Museum** at Point Cadet Plaza, just off Hwy. 90 at the foot of the Biloxi-Ocean Springs Bridge (435-6320). The museum traces Biloxi's growth from a French colony to its current "Seafood Capital" status. (Open Mon.-Sat. 9am-5pm. $2.50, ages 6-16 and seniors $1.50.) Drop by the **Farmer's Market** stand next door (open Tues.-Thurs.) or try to catch your own shrimp, horsehoe crabs, and other marine life in the "touch tank" at the **J.L. Scott Marine Education Center and Aquarium,** 115 Beach Blvd. (374-5550). The largest public aquarium in the state, the center's cynosure is a 42,000-gallon Gulf of Mexico tank in which sharks, sea turtles, eels and larger residents frolic and feed. (Open Mon.-Sat. 9am-4pm, $3, seniors $2, ages 3-17 $1.50.)

Between Biloxi and **Gulfport** you'll find the garden and grounds of **Beauvoir,** 224 Beach Blvd. at Beauvoir Rd. (388-1313). Jefferson Davis's last home, it is now a shrine in his honor, containing a Confederate Museum, a Davis Family Museum, and a Confederate Veterans Cemetery with the tomb of the Unknown Confederate Soldier. Each October, Beauvoir is the site of a Confederate boot camp simulation, complete with drills. (Open daily 9am-5pm. $4.75, kids $2.50.) Also along the shoreline is the **Biloxi Lighthouse** (435-6293), which legend claims was painted black after President Lincoln's assassination; *actually* the rusty edifice just needed a paint job. Today the South's first cast-metal lighthouse is snowy white and seasonally open for tours. (Open March-Oct. daily 8-10am. Donations accepted.) For a city tour take the **Ole Biloxi Train Tour,** a 1½-hr. ride beginning at the lighthouse; the first tour leaves at 9:30am. (374-8687; tour $6, kids $3.)

Twelve mi. off the Mississippi Coast floats **Ship Island,** far enough out to sea to exempt it from federal bans on liquor and gambling in the 1920s. Crystal blue waters and white sandy beaches are the lures today, as visitors swim, fish and explore. Defending the island is **Fort Massachusetts** (875-0821), which served as both a Confederate and Union command center at different points during the Civil War. (Admission and tour free.) Ship island has had two parts, East and West, since it was sliced in two by Hurricane Camille in 1969. The East is underdeveloped and not accessible by ferry service, although overnight camping is permitted. To get to West Ship Island, where overnight camping is prohibited, take the Skrmetta-family **ferry service** that leaves from Biloxi's **Buena Vista Motel,** Central Beach Blvd. (432-2197). There are two ferries per day, leaving for the island at 9am and noon and returning at 3:45pm and 6:45pm. The trip takes 70 minutes. (Round-trip $12, kids $6.) A different kind of 70-minute cruise is the **Biloxi Shrimping Trip,** Hwy. 90E (374-5718). The *Sailfish* departs from the Biloxi Small Craft Harbor several times a day, giving passengers an opportunity to see what trawling between the Biloxi shore and nearby Deer Island will yield. Call for reservations. (374-5718; $8, kids $4.)

Accommodations with a pretty coastal view will cost you an even prettier penny. Since prices fluctuate according to complex laws which we won't go into, your best bet to find cheap rates is to ask at the Visitors Center or flip through a current copy of *Traveler Discount Guide* distributed there. Sundays through Thursdays are cheaper, as is the off-season which runs from Labor Day to January-February. **Camping** is an inexpensive alternative; rates vary from $10-15 depending on the season. The most convenient site is the **Biloxi Beach Campground,** 3162 W. Beach Blvd. (432-2755), at $10 per site for 2 people plus $2 each additional person. Farther from town are **Martin's Lake and Campground,** 14601 Parker Rd. (875-9157; $12 per site for 2 people plus $2 each additional person), one mi. north of I-10 at exit 50 in Ocean Springs, and the campground at **Gulf Islands National Seashore, Davis Bayou** (875-3962) on Hanley Rd. off U.S. 90 also in Ocean Springs. ($10 per site.)

The **Biloxi Chamber of Commerce,** 1048 Beach Blvd. (374-2717), across from the lighthouse, eagerly offers aid to tourists. (Open Mon.-Fri. 8:30am-5pm.) The **Biloxi Tourist Information Center,** 710 E. Beach Blvd. (374-3105), down the street from the bus station, distributes many helpful brochures. (Open Mon.-Fri. 8am-5pm, Sat. 9am-5pm, Sun. noon-5pm.) For more info contact the **Mississippi Gulf Coast Convention and Visitor's Bureau,** 135 Courthouse Rd. (896-6699 or 800-237-9493), or tune your radio to 1490 AM for beach and tourist info.

Getting into and out of Biloxi is rarely problematic because inter-city buses service the town well. **Greyhound,** 322 Main St. (436-4336; open daily 7am-10pm), offers frequent service to New Orleans (10 per day, 2½ hr., $18.50) and Jackson (2 per day, 4 hr., $25.50). **Coast Area Transit** (896-8080) operates buses (marked "Beach") along the beach on U.S. 90 from Biloxi to Gulfport. (Buses operate Mon.-Sat. every 70 min. Board at any intersection. Fare $.75.)

The **post office** is at 135 Main St. (432-0311), near the bus station. (Open Mon.-Fri. 8:30am-5pm, Sat. 9am-noon.) Biloxi's **ZIP code** is 39530; **area code:** 601.

Jackson

A hybrid of a sunbelt city and sleepy Deep South town, Jackson does its business without the frenetic pace characteristic of most metropoli its size. Sights and stores here keep the shorter hours of a smaller town—the historic and business districts barely flicker with life during working hours; Jackson's commerce never creates the uptight atmosphere of a Northern city. Most of Jackson's action lies outside the downtown. Located directly on the breathtaking Natchez Trace Parkway, Jackson has shaded campsites, cool reservoirs, national forests and Native American burial mounds only minutes away.

Practical Information

Emergency: 911.

Tourist Information Center, 1100 Lakeland Dr. (960-1800), off I-55 Lakeland East exit. Open Mon.-Sun. 8:30am-4:30pm. **Convention and Visitors Bureau,** 921 N. President St. (960-1891), downtown. Open Mon.-Fri. 8:30am-5pm.

Traveler's Aid: 968-3972.

Allen C. Thompson Municipal Airport: East of downtown, off I-20. Cab fare to downtown about $13-14.

Amtrak: 300 W. Capitol St. (355-6350). To Memphis (1 per day; 4 hr.; $45) and New Orleans (1 per day; 4 hr.; $41). Open Mon.-Fri. 7:30am-1pm and 2-7pm, Sat.-Sun. 7:30-10:30am and 4:30-7pm.

Greyhound: 201 S. Jefferson St. (353-6342). Be cautious when walking in the area at night. To: Dallas (6 per day; 10 hr.; $74); Montgomery (2 per day; 7 hr.; $50); Memphis (5 per day; 4½ hr.; $40). Open 24 hrs.

Public Transport: Jackson Transit System (JATRAN) (948-3840), in the Federal Bldg. downtown. Limited service. Bus schedules and maps posted at most bus stops. Buses operate Mon.-Fri. 5am-7pm, Sat. 7am-6pm. Fare 75¢, transfers 10¢.

Help Lines: First Call for Help, 352-4357. Info referral service. **Rape Hotline,** 982-7273.

Taxi: Veterans Cab, 355-8319. Base fare $1.10, $1 per mi.

Post Office: 401 E. South St. (968-0572). Open Mon.-Fri. 7am-7pm, Sat. 8am-noon. **ZIP code:** 39201.

Area Code: 601.

State Street runs north-south through downtown, **High Street** east-west.

Accommodations

There are few motels downtown, but with a car you easily can find inexpensive rooms along I-20 and I-55.

Admiral Benbow Inn, 905 N. State St. (948-4161), downtown. Large, comfortable, clean rooms, pool, remote control TV. Singles and doubles $36-48.

Red Roof Inn, 700 Larson St. (969-5006 or 800-843-7663), by the fairgrounds downtown but not as convenient as Benbow. Utilitarian rooms with free coffee in the morning. Singles $34. Doubles $40-43.

Motel 6, 970 I-20 Frontage Rd. (969-3423). Tidy, small white-walled rooms with spotless bathrooms. Pool. Free local calls. Movie channel. Singles $26. $6 per additional person.

Sun 'n Sand Motel, 401 N. Lamar St. (354-2501), downtown. Large, older-looking rooms in 50s oranges 'n aquas—even a Polynesian room. Cable TV. Lounge/restaurant in motel serving $5 lunch buffet. Singles $30, $5 each additional person.

Food

Jackson eateries specialize in catfish and plate lunch specials, catering to both the young, professional crowd and older regulars. Most establishments are inexpensive and lively. As in any American town, fast-food chains scatter along the east end of High St.

Primo's, 1016 N. State St. (948-4343). A Jackson tradition. Excellent, cheap Southern food; breakfasts with creamy grits and huge omelettes under $4 (breakfast served till 11:30am). Vegetable plates, with country-style dinners $6-8. Open Mon.-Fri. 7am-9pm, Sat.-Sun. 8am-9pm.

The Elite Café, 141 E. Capitol (352-5606). Egalitarian lunch spot with great homemade cornbread, rolls, and veal cutlets. Plate lunch specials with two vegetables and bread under $4.50. Be prepared to wait in line during lunch rush. Open Mon.-Fri. 7am-9:30pm, Sat. 5-9pm.

The Iron Horse Grill, 320 W. Pearl St. (355-8419), at Gallatin. A huge converted smokehouse with a waterfall cascading from the 2nd floor. Checks not accepted. Primarily Tex-Mex ($5-8); steak and seafood entrées more expensive. A pianist accompanies lunch and dinner. Open Mon.-Sat. 11am-10pm.

Sights and Entertainment

The old and the new compete everywhere in Jackson; the city even has two capitol buildings. Built in 1840, the **Old State Capitol** (359-6920), at the intersection of Capitol and State St., houses an excellent, lucid museum of Mississippi's often turbulent history, including artifacts from original Native American settlements and documentaries on the Civil Rights Movement. (Open Mon.-Fri. 8am-5pm, Sat. 9:30am-4:30pm,

Sun. 12:30-4:30pm. Free.) The state legislature's current home is the beautiful **New State Capitol** (359-3114), at Mississippi and Congress St., completed in 1903. A huge restoration project preserved the *beaux arts* grandeur of the building, complete with a gold-leaf-covered eagle perched on the capitol dome. (Guided 45-min. tours Mon.-Fri. at 9, 10, and 11am, and 1:30, 2:30, and 3:30pm. Open Mon.-Fri. 9am-5pm. Free.)

The downtown area maintains several other museums worth a visit. **The Mississippi Museum of Art,** at Pascagoula and Lamar St. (960-1515 or 800-423-4971), has a fabulous collection of Americana and a fun participatory Impression Gallery for kids, including a video sculpture that films visitors and then projects their silhouettes in a spectrum of colors on the wall. (Open Tues.-Sat. 10am-5pm, Sun. noon-5pm. $2, kids $1; students free Tues. and Thurs.) Next door is the **Russell C. Davis Planetarium** (960-1550), considered one of the most stellar worldwide. (Galactic and musical shows Mon.-Fri. at noon, Tues.-Sat. at 8pm; Sat.-Sun. at 4pm. $4, seniors and kids $2.50.)

Look for a terrific family-pleasing presentation of nature and wildlife at the **Mississippi Museum of Natural Science** on Jefferson St. (354-7303), across from the fairground. (Open Tues.-Fri. 8am-5pm, Sat. 9:30am-4:30pm.) Don't miss the Greek Revival **Governor's Mansion** (359-3175), a national historic landmark. The tours every half hour are an enlightening introduction to Mississippian politics. (Open Mon.-Fri. 9:30-11am.) For a more in-depth look at some fine architecture, visit the **Manship House,** 420 E. Fortification (961-4724), a short walk north from the New Capitol. Charles Henry Manship, Jackson's Civil War mayor, built this Gothic Revival "cottage villa," now restored to its 19th-century condition. (Open Tues.-Fri. 9am-4pm, Sat.-Sun. 1-4pm.) Sherman occupied Jackson's oldest house, **The Oaks,** 823 N. Jefferson St. (353-9339), built in 1746, during the siege of the city in 1863. Enjoy a delightful tour by the current loquacious tenant. (Open Tues.-Sat. 10am-4pm, Sun. 1:30-4pm. $2, students $1.)

The **Smith-Robertson Museum and Cultural Center,** 528 Bloom St. (960-1457), directly behind the Sun 'n' Sand Motel, preserves Mississippi's African-American history. This large, expanding museum once housed the state's first black public school, which *Native Son* author Richard Wright attended until the eighth grade. Now it displays folk art, photographs, and excellent exhibits on the Civil Rights Movement, particularly the role of African-American women in Mississippi history. (Open Mon.-Fri. 9am-5pm, Sat.-Sun. 9am-noon. $1, kids 50¢.)

After soaking in the history of life and politics in Jackson, soak up some music and fun at **Hal & Mal's Restaurant and Oyster Bar,** 200 Commerce St. (948-0888), which entertains in a converted warehouse. Everything from reggae to innovative rock bands play Thursday through Saturday nights. (Restaurant open Mon.-Sat. 11am-10pm; bar open until 1am. Cover varies.)

Natchez

Talk about squattin' in high cotton—just before the Civil war, Natchez preened as one of the wealthiest settlements on the Mississippi. Of the thirteen millionaires in Mississippi at the time, eleven built their cotton plantation estates here, as did several other well-to-do farmers. The custom then was to fashion the home on one side of the River and till the soil on the other. Although the cotton-based agricultural economy began to wane, Natchez waxed and matured on the plantation side of Ol' Man River where 40 mansions continue to preside.

Open for public tours, the manorial remnants of the "white gold" days are under the supervision of the efficient **Natchez Pilgrimage Tours,** on the corner of Canal St. and State St., P.O. Box 347 (446-6631 or 800-647-6742). Pick up free tour schedules, maps, miscellaneous pamphlets, and an interesting and informative guidebook about the homes and their histories ($5). (Open Mon.-Fri. 8:30am-5pm, Sat. 10am-noon.) Visitors can marvel at the unbelievable opulence which cotton tycoons were often able to acquire as early as their 13th birthdays.

The largest octagonal house in America, **Longwood,** 140 Lower Woodville Rd. (442-5193), astounds visitors with its creative and elaborate décor and imaginative floor plan designed to be an "Arabian palace." The six-story edifice remains unfinished because the builders, hired from the North, abandoned work at the beginning of the Civil War so that they could fight for the Union. They never returned; their discarded tools and undisturbed crates still lie as they were left. **Stanton Hall,** 401 High St. (442-6282), on the other hand, arose under the direction of local Natchez architects and artisans. Completed in 1857, this mansion regales with almost ostentatious splendor; French mirrors, Italian marble mantels, and specially-cut chandeliers drip with magnificence in this estate. (Tickets for all homes purchased at tour facility $4, ages 6-17 $2. 3-, 4-, and 5-house ticket packages available. Consult facility for specific home hours.)

A different mode of abode can be seen at the **Grand Village of the Natchez Indians,** 400 Jefferson Davis Blvd. (446-6502), where stupendously large burial mounds dominate green, grassy fields. According to historical documentation, when the Great Sun, or chief, of the tribe died, his wife and retainers were strangled and buried also. The house of the chief's successor was supposed to sit atop the mound. In 1729, the Natchez tribe massacred a French garrison at Fort Rosalie but later withered under French retaliation in 1730. (Village open Mon.-Sat. 9am-5pm, Sun. 1:30-5pm. Free.)

Historic **Jefferson College,** off U.S. 61 near Jct. with U.S. 84 East (442-2901), stands six mi. east of Natchez as the first educational institution in the Mississippi Territory. Incorporated in 1802, the peaceful grounds and buildings are rumored to be the site where Aaron Burr, Vice-President under Thomas Jefferson, was hanged. (Grounds open sunrise-sunset, buildings open Mon.-Sat. 9am-5pm, Sun 1-5pm. Free.)

The most economical way to visit Natchez is as a daytrip from either Vicksburg, MS, or Baton Rouge, LA. If you prefer to stay in Natchez, the **Natchez Inn,** 218 John R. Junkin Dr. (442-0221), has attractive, comfortable rooms that are convenient to downtown. (Singles $24. Doubles $32.) **Scottish Inns,** on U.S. 61 (442-9141 or 800-251-1962), advertises rooms for $20 to $30, and **Days Inn,** (800-524-4892), occasionally has specials at $35 for one to four people. Call for current info on possible discounts. If you wish to go for the whole hog and stay in a plantation home, dig deep in your pockets for at least $70—the cheapest rate for a night in one of the homes that doubles as a bed and breakfast. Make B&B reservations through the tour facility (see above).

Satisfying your stomach is somewhat less costly, as inexpensive cafés and diners abound in Natchez. **Nothin' Fancee Delicatessen,** 112 N. Commerce St. (442-6886), has tastee specials and sandwiches for $2 to $3 and a full breakfasts for under $3. At **Fat Mama's Tamales,** 500 S. Canal St. (442-4548), Cajun boudin, chili, and peanut butter pie are served in a log cabin. (Open daily at 5pm.) Several local seafood eateries bake, grill, and broil fresh fish. Try the **Main Street Steamery,** 326 Main St. (445-0608), which prepares absolutely *no* fried foods and has seafood sandwiches, salads, and entrées for $5 to $7. (Open 11am-3pm.)

Make connections to Vicksburg (one way $16) and Baton Rouge (one way $21) at the **Natchez Bus Station,** 103 Lower Woodville Rd. (445-5291). In-town transportation is available at the **Natchez Ford Rental** (445-0076), with rates of $38 per day plus 20¢ per mi. ($250 deposit or major credit card required, must be at least 21 years old.) The **Natchez Bicycling Center,** 334 Main St. (446-7794), will rent you wheels at $7.50 for 1 to 3 hours, $10 for 3 to 5 hours. and $14 for all day. (Must be at least 14 years old. Open Mon.-Fri. 9:30am-6pm, Sat. 10am-4pm.) The **Mental Crisis Intervention Hotline** can be reached at 446-6634. Natchez's **post office** delivers from 214 Canal St. and its **ZIP code** is 39120.

Vicksburg

Started as a mission by Rev. Newit Vick in 1814, Vicksburg holds notoriety for its role in the Civil War. President Abraham Lincoln called this town the "key", and maintained that the war "can never be brought to a close until that key is in our pocket." Its verdant hills and prime Mississippi River location proved extremely strategic for the Confederate forces, though not strategic enough; the "Gibraltar of the South" fell to Union forces on July 4, 1863, after a 47-day siege. The loss of this critical river city augured death for the Confederacy.

Markers of combat sites and prominent memorials riddle the grass-covered 1700-acre **Vicksburg National Military Park** (636-0583 or 800-221-3536 out-of-state) that surrounds the city. If possible, drive to the battlefield, museums, and cemetery east of town on Clay St. at exit 4B off I-20. ($3 per car, $1 per person on bus, seniors and kids free.) The visitors center at the entrance provides maps that detail a brief history as well as prominent sights along the 16-mi. loop. ($3 per car, $1 per person on bus, kids free; tickets are valid for 7 days.) Take a guide with you on a two-hour driving tour ($15) of the military park, or drive the 16-mi. trail yourself. (Open summer daily 8am-8:30pm; visitors center closes at 5pm.)

Within the park, visit the **National Cemetery** and the ***U.S.S. Cairo*** **Museum** (636-2199). The museum's centerpiece is the restored union iron-clad gunboat *U.S.S.Cairo* (KAY-ro), the first vessel sunk by an electronically detonated mine. The museum displays a fascinating array of century-old artifacts preserved for over a century since the ship sank in the Yazoo River. (Open daily 9:30am-6pm; off-season 8am-5pm. Free.) Learn more of the battle at Vicksburg by catching **"Vanishing Glory,"** 717 Clay St. (634-1863), a multi-media theatrical panorama. (Shows daily on the hr. 10am-5pm; $3.50, ages 6-18 $2.) A free tour, either by yourself or guided, of the **U.S. Army Engineer Waterways Experiment Station** explains the role of the Mississippi River in urban and rural development and the functions of locks and dams. The entire floor of one room is a scale model of the dam system of Niagara Falls. (Open daily 7:45am-4:15pm, guided tours at 10am and 2pm. Free.)

The **Old Court House Museum,** 1008 Cherry St. (636-0741), presides over Vicksburg's town center, three mi. from the park's entrance. Many consider it one of the South's finest Civil War museums, with everything from newspapers printed on wallpaper to Jefferson Davis' tie to an interpretation of Klan activities. (Open Mon.-Sat. 8:30am-5pm, Sun. 1:30-5pm. $1.75, seniors $1.25, ages under 18 $1.)

Next door, continuing the martial theme, is **Toys and Soldiers, A Museum,** 1100 Cherry St. (638-1986), where 27,000 toy soldiers from all over the world await you. (Open Mon.-Sat. 9am-4:30pm, Sun. 1:30-4:30pm. Tours $1.50, families $5.) Two blocks away lie the **Museum of Coca-Cola History and Memorabilia** and the **Biedenharn Candy Company,** 1107 Washington St. (638-6514), which first bottled Coca-Cola. Though the two-room museum displays Coke memorabilia from as far back as 1894, the admission fee seems a bit steep for the brief 10 minutes it takes to admire the artifacts. Coke floats and over 100 different Coca-Cola items are sold. (Open Mon.-Sat. 9am-5pm, Sun. 1:30-4:30pm. $1.75, kids $1.25. Disabled access.)

After wandering down the old-fashioned brick pavement of Washington Street, you'll end up near several fine antebellum homes. **Balfour House,** 1002 Crawford St. (638-3690), served as local Union Army headquarters after the capture of Vicksburg. Look down the three-story vertigo-inducing elliptical spiral staircase. (Open daily 9am-5pm. $5, kids $2.) The **Duff Green Mansion,** 1114 First East St. (638-6968), hosted numerous social events before it was converted into a civil hospital during the siege of Vicksburg. (Open daily 9am-5pm. $5, kids $2.) Both homes, like many of the restored Vicksburg estates, double as B&Bs (ask for more information at the visitors center). The **Martha Vick House,** 1300 Grove St. (638-7036), was the home of Martha Vick, an unmarried daughter of Reverend Vick. The restored building contains many elegant French paintings. (Open daily 9am-5pm. $5, ages 12-18 $2.) Slightly farther away, **McRaven,** 1445 Harrison St. (636-1663), is a popular historic home, and was featured in *National Geographic* as a "time capsule of the South." (Open daily 9am-6pm, Sun. 10am-6pm. 1½-hr. guided tours $4.50, ages 12-18 $2, ages 6-11 $1.50.)

While downtown, chow down at the **Burger Village,** 1220 Washington St. (638-0202), home of the happy community of ground chuck on buns and other sandwiches, all under $3. The **New Orleans Café,** 1100 Washington St. (638-8182), serves mouth-watering sandwiches for under $6, delectable Cajun specialties, seafood, and more. (Open Mon.-Thurs. 11am-10pm, Fri.-Sat. 11am-2am.) The café doubles as a bar on weekends and stops serving food at 10pm. Next door is the lively **Other Side Lounge.** (Open Tues.-Sat. 5:30pm-2am.) Across the street is **Miller's Still Lounge,** a real Southern watering hole with live entertainment and popcorn nightly. (Open Sun.-Thurs. 11am-midnight, Fri.-Sat. 11am-2am.) From there (assuming you haven't been drinking) drive south on Washington St. to the **Louisiana Circle,** a secluded overview serving truly breathtaking vistas of the great Mississippi River. For a glimpse of Americana, visit **Holidays Washateria and Lanes** (636-9682), near the park entrance on Rte. 8 across from a KFC. It's a bowling alley, pool room and laundromat, all in one! Ain't *that* America! (Open Sun.-Thurs. 3-10:30pm, Fri.-Sat. 10am-2am.)

Inexpensive accommodations are easily found in Vicksburg, except over the July Fourth weekend, when the military park's war reenactment brings thousands of tourists and inflated hotel rates. Since most hotels are located near the park, don't expect to stay in town, unless you choose to stay at the **Dixiana Motel,** 4033 Washington St. (636-9876) where you pay for a bed and all you get is a bed (and TV, of course.) Note the old-fashioned beauty of the antique bathrooms. (Rooms $17-22.) The **Hillcrest Motel,** 4503 Hwy. 80 E. (638-1491), has a pool and spacious, ground-floor singles for $20, doubles for $24. The **Beachwood Motel,** 4449 Hwy. 80E (636-2271), has no pool but has cable and nicely decorated rooms. (Bed $25, 2 beds $27.) **The Vicksburg Battlefield Kampground,** 4407 I-20 Frontage Rd. (636-9946), has a pool and laundromat. (Sites $10-12 for 2 people.)

For more information about Vicksburg, visit the **Tourist Information Center** (636-9421), across the street from the park. Pick up one of the many pamphlets with discount coupons for area hostels and restaurants, as well as copies of *The Newcomer's Guide* and *Southland Explorer.* (Open daily 8am-5:30pm.) Unfortunately, you'll need a car to see most of Vicksburg: the bus station, the information center, downtown, and the far end of the sprawling military park are at the small city's four extremes. The **Greyhound** station (636-1230) is inconveniently located at 3324 Hall's Ferry Rd., off Frontage Rd.; buses run to Jackson (4 per day; 1 hr.; $9.50). The **Rape and Sexual Assault Service** (638-0031) answers calls all day.

Vicksburg's **ZIP code** is 39180; the **area code** is 601.

North Carolina

North Carolina splits neatly into thirds: the west's down-to-earth mountain culture, the mellow sophistication of the Raleigh/Durham/Chapel Hill Research Triangle in the state's center, and the lonely placidity of the eastern coast and the Outer Banks. Whatever their cultural differences, these three regions share one similarity—an unmatched North Carolinian beauty apparent the moment you cross the state border. Even the occasional urban veneer complements Carolina's fertile resplendence. The streets are unlittered, the buildings well-spaced, the businesses clean, and the universities spacious. North Carolinian mud turtles know how best to enjoy their state: slowly, warmly and quietly.

Practical Information

Capital: Raleigh.

Travel and Tourism Division, 430 N. Salisbury St., Raleigh 27611 (919-733-4171 or 800-847-4862). **Department of Natural Resources and Community Development,** Division of Parks and Recreation, P.O. Box 27287, Raleigh 27611.

Time Zone: Eastern. **Postal Abbreviation:**NC

Sales Tax: 5%.

The Carolina Mountains

The sharp ridges and endless rolling slopes of the southern Appalachian mountain ranges create some of the most spectacular scenery in the East. At one time, North Carolina's verdant highlands provided an exclusive refuge for the country's rich and famous. The Vanderbilts owned a large portion of the nearly 500,000-acre Pisgah National Forest, which they subsequently willed to the U.S. government. Today the Blue Ridge, Great Smoky, Black, Craggy, Pisgah, and Balsam Mountains that comprise the western half of North Carolina beckon budget travelers, not billionaires. Campsites blanket the region, coexisting with elusive but inexpensive youth hostels and ski lodges. Enjoy the area's rugged wilderness while backpacking, canoeing, whitewater rafting, or cross-country skiing. Motorists and cyclists can follow the **Blue Ridge Parkway** to some unforgettable views (see Blue Ridge Parkway, VA).

The Blue Ridge Mountains bifurcate into two areas. The first, northern area is the **High Country**, which includes the territory between the town of Boone and the town of Asheville, 100 mi. to the southwest. The second area comprises the **Great Smoky Mountain National Park** (see Great Smoky Mountain National Park, TN) and **Nantahala National Forest**.

Boone

Named for famous frontiersman Daniel Boone, who built a cabin here in the 1760s on his journey into the western wilderness, the town continues to evoke (and profit from) its pioneer past through shops such as the Mast General Store and the Candy Barrel.

Practical Information

Emergency: 911. National Park Service/Blue Ridge Parkway Emergency, 259-0701 or 800-727-5928.

Visitor Information: Boone Area Chamber of Commerce, 112 W. Howard St. (264-2225), turn from Hwy 321 onto River St., drive behind the university, turn right onto Depot St. then take the first left onto W. Howard St. Info on accommodations and sights. Open Mon.-Fri. 9am-5pm. **North Carolina High Country Host,** 701 Blowing Rock Rd. (264-1299; 800-438-7500). Pick up copies of the North Carolina *High Country Host Area Travel Guide*, an informative and detailed map of the area, and the *Blue Ridge Parkway Directory*, a mile-by-mile description of all services and attractions located on or near the Parkway. Open daily 9am-5pm.

Greyhound: At the AppalCart station on Winkler's Creek Rd. (262-0501), off Rte. 321 at Wendy's. Flag stop in Blowing Rock. One per day to Hickory and most points east, south, and west. To Hickory ($9) and Charlotte (2½ hr., $19). Open Mon.-Fri. 8am-5pm, Sat.- Sun. 10am-4:30pm.

Public Transport: Boone AppalCart, on Winkler's Creek Rd. (264-2278). Local bus and van service; 3 routes. The Red Route links downtown Boone with ASU and the motels and restaurants on Blowing Rock Rd. The Green Route serves Rte. 421. Crosstown route between the campus and the new marketplace. The Red Route operates Mon.-Fri. every hr. 7am-7pm; Green Mon.-Fri. every hr. 7am-6pm; crosstown Mon.-Fri. 7am-11pm, Sat. 8am-6pm. Fare 50¢ in town, charged by zones for the rest of the county.

Post Office: 637 Blowing Rock Rd. (264-3813), and 103 W. King St. (262-1171). Open Mon.-Fri. 9am-5pm, Sat. 9am-noon. Lobby selling stamps until 10pm. **ZIP code:** 28607.

Area Code: 704.

Accommodations, Camping and Food

Catering primarily to wealthy visitors, the area fields more than its share of expensive motels and B&Bs. Scratch the lodging surface, however, and you will also find enough inexpensive motels, hostels and camp sites to answer to one's financial woes.

Blowing Rock Assembly Grounds (HI/AYH), P.O. Box 2530, Blowing Rock (295-7813), near the Blue Ridge Parkway, has clean rooms, communal bathrooms, sports facilities, and a cheap cafeteria, all in a gorgeous setting with access to hiking trails. Ask the bus driver to let you off at Blowing Rock Town Hall or at the Rte. 321 bypass and Sunset Dr., depending on the direction you're traveling—it's about two mi. from both points. Call the hostel for a pick-up, or stay on Rte. 321 and drive down to Goforth Rd. on the left; follow Go along the golf course until you see the "BRAG" signs. Primarily a retreat for religious groups. Check in after 4pm, check out before 1pm. The desk is open from 9am-5pm daily. Package rates available. No laundry facilities. $11, non-members $14

Most inexpensive hotels are concentrated along Blowing Rock Rd. (Hwy 321), or Hwy 105. The red-brick **Red Carpet Inn** (264-2457) has spacious rooms that come with remote TV, a playground, and a pool. Prices may vary with seasonal availability. Some holiday weekends have 2-night minimum stay, e.g. July 4. All credit cards accepted; reservations not required. No laundry facilities. (Singles $34. Doubles $38. Weekend singles and doubles $53.) The **High Country Inn,** Hwy 105 (264-1000) also has a pool, jacuzzi, sauna and exercise room. They even boast a watermill. Standard-sized, comfortable rooms. Check in 4pm, check out 11am (Mid-range prices: Singles $34. Doubles $48. Weekend rates $10 more. Ask about seasonal prices. Breakfast and dinner packages available.)

Boone and **Pisgah National Forest** offer developed and well-equipped **campsites** as well as **primitive camping** options for those who are looking to rough it in the outdoors. Along the Blue Ridge Pkwy., spectacular sites without hookups are available for $8 at the **Julian Price Campground,** mile 297 (963-5911); **Linville Falls,** mile 316 (963-5911); and **Crabtree Meadows,** mile 340 (675-4444); (open May-Oct. only). Cabins in **Roan Mountain State Park** (772-3314) comfortably sleep six and are furnished with linens and cooking utensils. (Sun.-Thurs. $62, Fri.-Sat. $85, weekly $419.) The state park offers pool and tennis facilities and tends to attract smaller crowds than the campgrounds on the parkway. May-Sept. visitors can unwind from a day of hiking at the park's "Summer in the Park" festival featuring cloggers and storytellers. For more info call the **Roan Mtn. Visitors Center** at 772-3314 or 772-3303.

Fast food restaurants deep-fat fry on both sides of Hwy 321. Try the **Daniel Boone Inn** Jct. Hwys 321 and 421 (704-264-8657) for a hefty country sit-down meal served family style, all-you-can-eat. Dinner includes dessert. (Open Mon.-Sun., dinner 11am-9pm, $10; breakfast Sat.-Sun. only, $6.) For an Italian flavor, dine at **Piccadeli's,** 818 Blowing Rock Rd. (704-262-3500). Appetizers from 95¢, with homemade soups and sandwiches $3-5. Italian specialties like spaghetti from $5. (Open Mon.-Sun, 11am-10pm).

Sights and Activities

In an open air amphitheater, **Horn in the West** (264-2120), located near Boone off Rte. 105, presents an outdoor drama of the American Revolution as it was fought in the southern Appalachians. (Shows Tues.-Sun. at 8:30pm. Admission $8-12, children under 13 half-price. Group rates upon request. Reservations recommended.) Adjacent to the theater the **Daniel Boone Native Gardens** celebrate mountain foliage, while the **Hickory Ridge Homestead** documents 18th-century mountain life. **An Appalachian Summer** (262-6084) is a month-long, high-caliber festival of music, art, theater, and dance sponsored by Appalachian State University.

Use Boone as a base from which to explore the mountain towns to the west and south. The community of **Blowing Rock,** 7 mi. south at the entrance to the Blue Ridge Pkwy., is a folk artists' colony. Its namesake overhangs **Johns River Gorge**; chuck a piece of paper (biodegradable, of course) over the edge and the wind will blow it back in your face. AppalCart goes to the Blowing Rock Town Hall from Boone twice daily. Stop by **Parkway Craft Center** mile 294 (295-7938), 2 mi. south of Blowing Rock Village, where members of the Southern Highland Handicraft Guild demonstrate their skills and sell their crafts. The craft center is in the Cone Manor House on the grounds of the **Moses H. Cone Memorial Park,** 3500 acres of shaded walking trails and magnificent views including a picture-postcard view of Bass Lake. Check out the National Park Service desk in the center for a copy of "This Week's Activities." (Open May-Oct. daily 9am-5:30pm.) To see the magnificence of the Moses H. Cone Park from another perspective, take the $15/hr guided horseback ride. Tours leave the **Blowing Rock Stables** from the **L.M. Tate Showgrounds**, "Home of the oldest continuous horse show in America." Get off the Blue Ridge Pkwy. at the Blowing Rock sign, turn left onto Yonahlossee Rd. and look for the "Blowing Rock Stables" sign on the right; call a day in advance for reservations. (295-7847) Open Mon.-Sun,. April-Dec.

Hikers should arm themselves with the invaluable large-scale map *100 Favorite Trails* ($3.50). Consider joining one of the guided expeditions led by the staff of **Edge of the World,** P.O. Box 1137, Banner Elk (898-9550), on Rte. 184 downtown. A complete outdoor equipment and clothing store, the Edge primarily rents equipment and gives regional hiking information. They also lead day-long backpacking, whitewater canoeing, rafting, spelunking and rock climbing trips throughout the High Country for about $65. (Open Mon.-Sat. 9am-6pm, til 10pm in the summer; Sun. 9am-1pm)

Downhill skiers can enjoy the Southeast's largest concentration of alpine resorts. Four converge on the Boone/Blowing Rock/Banner Elk area: **Appalachian Ski Mountain,** P.O. Box 106, Blowing Rock, 28604 (800-322-2373; lift tickets weekends $26, weekdays $18, with full rental $27); **Ski Beech,** P.O. Box 1118, Beech Mountain 28605 (387-2011; lift tickets weekends $26, weekdays $21, with rentals $38 and $28 respectively); **Ski Hawknest,** Town of Seven Devils, 1605 Skyland Dr., Banner Elk (963-6561; lift tickets weekends $20, weekdays $10, with rentals $30 and $16); and **Sugar Mountain,** P.O. Box 369, Banner Elk (898-4521; lift tickets weekends $35, weekdays $25, with rentals $47 and $35). AppalCart (264-2278) runs a daily shuttle in winter to Sugar Mountain and four times per week to Ski Beech. Call the High Country Host (264-1299) for ski reports. It is best to call ahead to the resort for specific prices of ski packages.

Traveled by car, the 5-mi. access road to **Grandfather Mountain** (800-468-7325) reveals an unparalleled view of the entire High Country area. At the top you'll find a private park featuring a mile-high suspension bridge, a nature museum with minerals, bird and plant life indigenous to NC, and a small zoo. ($8, kids $4; children under 4 free.) To hike or camp on Grandfather Mt. you need a permit ($4 per day, $8 per night for camping-available at the Grandfather Mountain Country Store on Rte. 221 or at the entrance to the park). Be sure to pick up a trail map at the entrance to learn which trails are available for overnight use. (Contact the Backcountry Manager, Grandfather Mt., Linville, NC 28646 for more info. Mountain open April-Nov. daily 8am-7pm; Dec.-March 9am-4pm, weather permitting.)

Asheville

Asheville's hazy blue mountains, deep valleys, spectacular waterfalls, and plunging gorges embody classic Appalachian beauty. A drive along the Blue Ridge Parkway best reveals the scenic vistas that surround the city. The Appalachian soil is also fertile for the arts, and boasts a burgeoning local arts and crafts community which hosts numerous festivals throughout the year. The Biltmore Estate, "Versailles of the South," home to George Vanderbilt and his designer-jean family, attracts throngs of gawking tourists.

Practical Information

Emergency: 911

Visitor Information: Chamber of Commerce, 151 Haywood St. (258-3858; 800-257-1300 in NC), off I-240 on the northwest end of downtown. Ask at the desk for the detailed city map, transit route map, and comprehensive sight-seeing guide. Open Mon.-Fri. 8:30am-5:30pm, Sat.-Sun. 9am-5pm.

Greyhound: 2 Tunnel Rd. (253-5353), 2 mi. east of downtown, near the Beaucatcher Tunnel. Bus #13 ("Oteen/Beverly Hills") or 14 ("Haw Creek/Tunnel Rd.") runs to and from downtown every ½-hr. Last bus at 5:50pm. To Charlotte (5 per day, 3 hr., $22), Knoxville (7 per day, 3 hr., $24.50), Atlanta ($44). Open daily 8am-10pm.

Public Transport: Asheville Transit, 360 W. Haywood (253-5691). Service within city limits. All routes converge on Pritchard Park downtown. Buses operate Mon.-Sun. 5:30am-7:30pm, most at ½-hr. intervals. Fare 60¢, transfers 30¢.

Post Office: 33 Coxe Ave. (257-4112), at Patton Ave. Open Mon.-Fri. 8am-5pm, Sat. 9am-noon. **ZIP code:** 28802.

Area Code: 704.

Accommodations and Camping

Asheville's independent motels outdo the budget chains. Many cluster on **Merrimon Avenue,** north of the city (take bus #2), and on **Tunnel Road**. Make reservations early for holidays and for folk and craft festivals. The **American Court Motel,** 85 Merrimon Ave. (253-4427 or 800-233-3582 for reservation desk only), has bright, cozy and well-kept rooms with cable, A/C, pool, and laundromat. (Ask for *Let's Go* discount of 10%. No pets. All credit cards accepted. Singles $36. Doubles $51.) Slightly farther from town (about 1½ mi. out), the **Four Seasons Motor Inn,** 820 Merrimon Ave. (254-5327), breezes in with cheerful rooms and classic walk-in closets. (No laundry facilities. Singles $32. Doubles $38.) The **Downtown Motel,** 65 Merrimon Ave. (253-9841), on Merrimon St. just north of the I-240 expressway, is a 10-minute walk from downtown (or take bus #2), with somewhat dark rooms, big bathrooms and a pool. (Singles $25. Doubles $32 Nov.-April; Singles $30. Doubles $35, April-June) As of June 1992, The Downtown is being renovated, and the on-season prices may rise.

With the Blue Ridge Pkwy., Pisgah National Forest, and the Great Smokies easily accessible by car, you can find a campsite to suit any taste. Close to town is **Bear Creek RV Park and Campground,** 81 S. Bear Creek Rd. (253-0798). Take I-40 exit 47, and look for the sign at the top of the hill. (Pool, laundry, groceries, and game room. Tent sites $16.50. RV sites with hookup $22.) In Pisgah National Forest, the nearest campground is **Powhatan,** off Rte. 191, 12 mi. southwest of Asheville. (All sites along the Pkwy $8. Open May-Sept.)

Food

You'll find greasy links in most major fast-food chains on **Tunnel Road** and **Biltmore Avenue.** The **Western North Carolina Farmers Market** (253-1691), at the intersection of I-240 and Rte. 191, near I-26, hawks fresh produce and crafts. Take bus #16 to I-40, then walk ½-mi. (Open daily 8am-6pm.)

Stone Soup, at Broadway and Walnut St.(252-7687) Also on Wall St. (254-0844), downtown. A cooperative that bakes its own bread and serves nitrate-free sausage. Soup and sandwiches from $2.75. Try the Hungarian Peasant Bread. Packed noon-2pm and for Sun. brunch. Open Mon.-Sat. 7am-4pm, Sun. 9:30am-1:30pm, Thurs.-Sat. 5-9pm.

Malaprops Bookstore/Café, 61 Haywood St. (254-6734), downtown in the basement of the bookstore. Gourmet coffees, bagels, tofu. Sandwiches $3-4. Cerebral readings, great book curriculum, and walking staff. Check out the Malaprops staff art on the walls. Open Mon.-Sat. 9am-8pm, Sun. noon-5pm.

Johnny O's Sandwich Shop, 36 Battery Park Ave. (254-0442). Mom-and-pop grill with a stand-up lunch counter. Everything under $2. Cheeseburger 70¢, hot dogs 75¢. Open daily 6am-2pm.

Sights and Festivals

Elvis's Southern mansion, Graceland, has nothing on the Vanderbilt family's **Biltmore Estate,** 1 North Pack Sq. (255-1700 or 800-543-2961). Take exit 50 off I-40, and go three blocks north. A tour of this true French Renaissance-style castle can take all day if it's crowded; try to arrive early in the morning. The not-so-humble abode was built in the 1890s and is the largest private home in America. The self-guided tour winds through a portion of the 250 rooms, enabling one to view an indoor pool, a bowling alley, rooms lined with Sargent paintings and Dürer prints, and immense rare-book libraries. Tours of the surrounding gardens, designed by Central Park planner Frederick Law Olmsted, and the Biltmore winery (with sour-wine tasting for those over 21) are included in the hefty admission price. (Open daily 9am-6pm; ticket office closes at 5pm. Winery open Mon.-Sat. at 11am, Sun. at 1pm. Admission $21.95, ages 10-16 $16.50, under 9 free. Disabled persons $13. Ticket prices rise $2-3 in November and December in order to defray the cost of Christmas decorations.) Be sure to get your ticket validated—if you decide to return the next day, your visit will be free with a validated ticket. Also, pay a visit to **Biltmore Village,** the quaint shopping district that George Vanderbilt had built right outside the gates of his chateau. It contains craft galleries, antique stores, and a music shop.

Even the most famous of Asheville's visitors have not had the privilege of staying at the Vanderbilt chateau. When passing through this peaceful mountain town, Henry Ford, Thomas Edison, and F. Scott Fitzgerald all stayed in the towering **Grove Park Inn** (Macon St. off Charlotte St. Look for the bright red tile roof peeking through the trees.) Made of stone quarried from the surrounding mountains, the still-operating hotel has many pieces of original early-20th-century furniture and fireplaces so immense you can walk into them. Walk to the right wing of the inn and you will happen upon the **Biltmore Industrial Museum** where looms loom large and homespun handicrafts used on the Biltmore Estate gather dust. Next door is the **Estes-Winn Memorial Museum** which houses about 20 vintage automobiles ranging from a Model T Ford to a 1959 Edsel. Check out the 1922 candy red America La France fire engine. On the way out, peruse the door engraving: "Doing a common thing uncommonly well often brings success." Mr. Vanderbilt must have been pretty darn uncommonly common. (Open Mon.-Sat. 10am-5pm, Sun. 1-5pm for both museums. Free.) Trod on your favorite author at the **Riverside Cemetery,** Birch St. off Montford Ave., north of I-240, where writers Thomas Wolfe and O. Henry are buried. The **Thomas Wolfe Memorial,** 48 Spruce St. (253-8304), between Woodfin and Walnut St., site of the novelist's boyhood home, was a boarding house run by his mother. Wolfe depicted the "Old Kentucky Home" as "Dixieland" in his first novel, *Look Homeward, Angel.* (Open Mon.-Sat. 9am-5pm, Sun. 1-5pm; hours vary in winter. $1, students and kids 50¢.)

Asheville's artistic tradition remains as strong as its literary one; visit the **Folk Art Center** (704-298-7928), east of Asheville at mile 382 on the Blue Ridge Pkwy., north of U.S. 70, to see outstanding work of the **Southern Highland Handicraft Guild**. (Open daily 9am-5pm. Free.) Each year around mid-July the Folk Art Center sponsors a **Guild Fair** (298-7928), at the Asheville Civic Center, off I-240 on Haywood St. Both the Folk Art Center and the chamber of commerce have more info on this weekend of craft demonstrations, dancing, and music.

A well-rounded city, Asheville offers McCormick Field at the intersection of Biltmore Ave. and S. Charlotte St. to baseball enthusiasts. This stadium is home to "the greatest show on dirt" where the farm team for the Houston Astros plays. Scrutinizing observers may catch the next rising baseball star for the Astros. ($3.75, students with ID $3, ages 3-12 $2)

A rare summer day goes by in Asheville when a festival is not taking place. During the last week of July, the downtown **Belle Chere Festival** (253-1009) celebrates "beautiful living" with food and music. An **Appalachian Heritage Fair** (258-6111) occurs at the beginning of August. Also in August, the **Mountain Dance and Folk Festival** (257-1300) at the civic center, now in its 63rd season, sponsors three days of competitive clog and square dancing, mountain traditional and bluegrass music, and individual musicianship. (Tickets $6-8.) The **Swannanoa Chamber Festival** (298-7613) from the first weekend of July through the first weekend of August has weekly chamber music concerts ($11 per performance, $45 for a series ticket).

Outer Banks

England's first attempt to colonize North America took place on the shores of North Carolina in 1587. This ill-fated adventure ended when Sir Walter Raleigh's Roanoke Island settlement inexplicably vanished. Since then, a succession of pirates, patriots, and secessionists have brought adventure to the North Carolina coast. Blackbeard called Ocracoke home in the early 18th century until a savvy serviceman struck down the buccaneer at Pamlico Sound. Most seafarers didn't fare well here; over 600 ships have foundered on the shoals of the Banks' southern shores. Though they were the site of the deaths of countless sailors, the Outer Banks also saw the birth of powered flight—the Wright Brothers flew the first airplane at Kitty Hawk in 1903.

The Outer Banks descend from hellish beach towns southward into heavenly wilderness. Highly developed Bodie Island, on the Outer Banks' northern end, holds the towns of Nags Head, Kitty Hawk, and Kill Devil Hills. In order to get far, far away from the madding crowd, travel south on Rte. 12 through magnificent wildlife preserves and across Hatteras Inlet to Ocracoke island—where you will find the Outer Banks' isolated beaches.

Practical Information and Orientation

Emergency: 911, north of the Oregon Inlet. In **Ocracoke,** 928-4831.

Aycock Brown Visitors Center, off U.S. 158, after the Wright Memorial Bridge, Bodie Island. Info on accommodations and picnic areas plus National Park Service schedules. Record sailfish welcomes visitors in the parking lot. Open Mon.-Thurs. 8:30am-6:30pm, Fri.-Sun. 8:30am-7:30pm; in winter Mon.-Fri. 9am-5pm.

Cape Hatteras National Seashore Information Centers: Bodie Island, Rte. 12 at Bodie Island Lighthouse (441-5711; info and special programs; open daily 9am-6pm; off-season 9am-5pm); Hatteras Island, Rte. 12 at Cape Hatteras (995-4474; camping info, demonstrations, and special programs; open daily 9am-6pm; off-season 9am-5pm); and Ocracoke Island, next to the ferry terminal at the south end of the island (928-4531; info on ferries, camping, lighthouses and wild ponies; open daily 9am-5pm, mid-June to Aug. 9am-6pm).

Ferries: Toll ferries operate to Ocracoke from **Cedar Island,** east of New Bern on U.S. 70 (4-8 per day; 21/4 hr.), and **Swan Quarter,** on the northern side of Pamlico Sound off U.S. 264/Rte. 45 (2½ hr.), both on the mainland. $10 per car (reserve in advance), $l per pedestrian, $2 per biker. (Cedar Island 225-3551, Swan Quarter 926-1111, Ocracoke 928-3841. All open daily 5:30am-8:30pm.) Free ferry across Hatteras Inlet between Hatteras and Ocracoke (operates daily 5am-11pm, 40 min.).

Taxi: Beach Cab, 441-2500. Serves Bodie Island and Manteo.

Car Rental: National, Mile 5½, Beach Rd. (800-328-4567 or 441-4588), Kill Devil Hills. $55 per day. 75 free mi., 30¢ each additional mi. Must be 25 with major credit card. Open daily 9am-5pm.

Bike Rental: Pony Island Motel (928-4411) and the **Slushy Stand** on Rte. 12, both on Ocracoke Island. $2 per hr. Open daily 8am-dusk.

ZIP Codes: Manteo 27954, Nags Head 27959, Ocracoke 27960.

Area Code: 919.

Four narrow islands strung north-to-south along half the length of the North Carolina coast comprise the Outer Banks. **Bodie Island** includes the towns of **Kitty Hawk, Kill Devil Hills,** and **Nags Head,** connecting to Elizabeth, NC, and Norfolk, VA, by U.S. 158. **Roanoke Island** swims between Bodie and the mainland on U.S. 64, and includes the town of **Manteo. Hatteras Island,** connected to Bodie by a bridge, stretches like a great sandy elbow. **Ocracoke Island,** the southernmost, is linked by free ferry to Hatteras Island, and by toll ferry to towns on the mainland. **Cape Hatteras National Seashore** encompasses Hatteras, Ocracoke, and the southern end of Bodie Island. On Bodie Island, U.S. 158 and Rte. 12 run parallel to each other until the beginning of the preserve. After that Rte. 12 (also called Beach Rd.) continues south, stringing Bodie, Hatteras, and Ocracoke together with free bridges and ferries. Addresses on Bodie Island are determined by their distance in miles from the Wright Memorial Bridge.

Nags Head and Ocracoke lie 76 mi. apart, and public transportation is virtually nonexistent. Hitching is fairly common, but may require lengthy waits. (*Let's Go* does not recommend hitchhiking.) The flat terrain makes hiking and biking pleasant, but the Outer Banks' ferocious traffic calls for extra caution.

Accommodations and Camping

Most motels cling to Rte. 12 in the costly town of Nags Head. For budget accommodations, try **Ocracoke.** On all three islands the "in season" usually lasts from mid-June to Labor Day, when rates are much higher. Reserve seven to 10 days ahead for weekday stays and up to a month for weekends. Rangers advise campers to bring extra-long tent spikes because of the loose dirt and tents with extra-fine screens to keep out the flea-sized, biting "no-see-ums." Strong insect repellent is also helpful. Crashing on the beach is illegal.

Nags Head/Kill Devil Hills

Olde London Inn, Mile 12, Beach Rd. (441-7115), Nags Head oceanfront. Oceanfronte location, golfe privileges, and recreationale facilities. Huge picture windows offset drab decor in clean, spacious rooms. More powerful than a silent "e". Cable TV, A/C, refrigerator. Singles or doubles $47; off-season $29.

The Ebbtide, Mile 10½, Beach Rd. (441-4913), Kill Devil Hills. A family place with spruce, wholesome rooms. Cable TV, A/C, sedate pool and hot tub. Offers "inside track" on local activities. Restaurant gives guests 10% discount, even on the 99¢ breakfast special. Singles or doubles $49-57; off-season $29-35.

Nettlewood Motel, Mile 7, Beach Rd. (441-5039), Kill Devil Hills, on both sides of the highway. Imagine that. Private beach access. Don't let the uninviting exterior prevent you from enjoying this clean, comfortable motel. TV, A/C, refrigerator. 4-day min. stay on weekends. Singles or doubles $42; off-season: rooms $27-33. Free day for week-long stays.

Ocracoke

Sand Dollar Motel, off Rte. 12 (928-5571). Head south on Rte. 12, turn right at the Pony Island Inn, right at the Back Porch Restaurant, and left at the Edwards Motel. Accommodating owners make you feel at home in this breezy, quiet, immaculate motel. Singles $38. Doubles $48. Off-season: $37/$45. (Pay in *real* dollars, not sand dollars.)

Beach House, just off Rte. 12 (928-4271), behind the Slushy Stand. B&B with 4 charming, clean, antiques-filled rooms. Rooms $43; spring and fall $35.

Edwards Motel, off Rte. 12 (928-4801), by the Back Porch Restaurant. Fish-cleaning facilities on premises. Bright assortment of accommodations, all with A/C and TV. Rooms with 2 double beds $44, with 2 double beds and 1 single bed $49; efficiencies $58; cottages $75-85. Off-season $37, $42, $53, and $65-70, respectively.

Oscar's House, on the ocean side of Rte. 12 (928-1311), 1 block from Silver Lake harbor. Charming B&B with 4 rooms, shared baths. Memorial Day-June singles $45, doubles $55; July-Labor Day singles $50, doubles $60; off-season: singles $40, doubles $50. Full vegetarian breakfast included.

The five oceanside **campgrounds** on Cape Hatteras National Seashore are all open mid-April to mid-October. **Oregon Inlet** squats on the southern tip of Bodie Island; **Salvo, Cape Point** (in Buxton), and **Frisco** near the elbow of Hatteras Island; and **Ocracoke** in the middle of Ocracoke Island. All have restrooms, cold running water, and grills. All sites (except Ocracoke's) cost $10, and are rented on a first-come, first-served basis. Reserve Ocracoke sites ($12) through **Ticketron Reservation Office,** P.O. Box 2715, San Francisco, CA 94126 (800-452-1111), or stop by the Ocracoke Ticketron terminal. For info, contact Cape Hatteras National Seashore, Rte. 1, P.O. Box 675, Manteo, NC 27954 (473-2111).

Sights and Activities

The **Wright Brothers National Memorial,** Mile 8, U.S. 158 (441-7430), marks the spot in Kill Devil Hills where Orville and Wilbur Wright made the world's first sustained, controlled power flight in 1903. You can see models of their planes, hear a detailed account of the day of the first flight, chat with the flight attendants, and view the dramatic monument the U.S. government dedicated to the brothers in 1932. (Open daily 9am-7pm; winter 9am-5pm. Presentations every hr. 10am-5pm. Admission $1, $3 per car, free with seniors.) In nearby **Jockey's Ridge State Park,** home of the East Coast's largest sand dunes, hang-gliders soar in the wind that Orville and Wilbur first broke.

On **Roanoke Island,** the **Fort Raleigh National Historic Site,** off U.S. 64, offers separately run attractions in one park. In the **Elizabeth Gardens** (473-3234), antique statues and fountains punctuate a beautiful display of flowers, herbs, and trees. (Open daily 9am-8pm; off-season 9am-5pm. Admission $2.50, under 12 free.) Behind door number two lies the theater where *The Lost Colony,* the oldest outdoor drama in the U.S., has been performing since 1937. (473-3414; performed Mon.-Sat. mid-June-late Aug. at 8:30pm; tickets $10, seniors and disabled people $9, ages under 12 $4; bring insect repellent.) **Fort Raleigh** (473-5772) is a reconstructed 1585 battery—basically a pile of dirt. The nearby **visitors center** contains a tiny museum and plays Elizabethan music as part of its losing battle to recall the earliest days of English activity in North America. (Open Mon.-Sat. 9am-8pm, Sun. 9am-6pm.) Lay your hands on a horseshoe crab and make faces at marine monsters in the Shark, Skate, and Ray Gallery at the **North Carolina Aquarium** (473-3493), one mi. west of U.S. 64. A full slate of educational programs keeps things lively. (Open Mon.-Sat. 9am-5pm, Sun. 1-5pm. Donation.)

On **Ocracoke Island,** historical sights give way to the incessant, soothing surf. With the exception of the town of Ocracoke on the southern tip, the island remains an undeveloped national seashore. Speedy walkers or meandering cyclists can cover the same route as **Trolley Tours** (928-4041; $4, seniors $3.50, kids $2.50) in less than an hour. Pick up a walking tour pamphlet at the visitors center (see Practical Information above). Better yet, stroll or swim along the waters that lick the pristine shore. At the **Soundside Snorkel,** park rangers teach visitors to snorkel. Bring tennis shoes and a swimsuit. (Wed. and Fri. at 2:30pm. Equipment rental $1. Make reservations at the Ocracoke Visitors Center from 9am the day before until 2:30pm the day of program.)

Raleigh, Durham, and Chapel Hill

The Research Triangle, a region embracing Raleigh, Durham, and Chapel Hill, contains more PhDs per capita that any other part of the nation. Durham, the former tobacco mecca of the world, is now, ironically, a city devoted to medicine, sprinkled with hospitals and diet clinics. It also houses Duke University, one of the greenest and most prestigious universities in the nation. Chapel Hill, just 20 mi. down the road, holds its own in education as the home of the nation's first public university. Raleigh, the state capital, is an easygoing, historic town.

Practical Information

Emergency: 911.

Raleigh Capitol Area Visitors Center, 301 N. Blount St. (733-3456). Focuses on buildings in the capitol area. Open Mon.-Fri. 8am-5pm, Sat. 9am-5pm, Sun. 1-5pm. **Durham Chamber of Commerce,** People's Security Building, 14th floor. 300 W. Morgan St. (682-2133). *Not* geared to the budget traveler. Complimentary maps and a great view of Durham. Open Mon.-Fri. 8:30am-5pm. **Chapel Hill Chamber of Commerce,** 104 S. Estes Dr. (967-7075). Open Mon.-Fri. 9am-5pm.

Raleigh-Durham Airport: 15 mi. northwest of Raleigh on U.S. 70 (840-2123). Many hotels and rental car agencies provide free airport limousine service (596-2361) if you make reservations with them. Pick up helpful complimentary maps of Raleigh and Durham at the **information counter** on the airport's lower level.

Amtrak: 320 W. Cabarrus, Raleigh (833-7594 or 800-872-7245). To Miami (1 per day, 16 hr., $144) and Washington, DC (2 per day, 6 hr., $45). Open daily 6:30am-8:30pm.

Greyhound: In Raleigh: 314 W. Jones St. (828-2567). To: Durham (8 per day; 40 min.; $6) and Chapel Hill (6 per day; 80 min.; $7). Good north-south coverage of NC. Also to: Greensboro (5 per day; 3 hr.; $15); Richmond (5 per day; 3½ hr.; $38); Charleston (2 per day; 8 hr.; $36 if reservations made 7 days in advance). Open 24 hrs. **In Durham:** 820 Morgan St. (687-4800), 1 block off Chapel Hill St. downtown, 2½ mi. northeast of Duke University. To: Chapel Hill (8 per day; ½ hr.); Charlotte (3 per day; 4 hr.); Winston-Salem (4 per day; 3 hr.). Open daily 7am-11:30pm. **In Chapel Hill:** 311 W. Franklin St. (942-3356), 4 blocks from the UNC campus. Open Mon.-Fri. 9am-4pm, Sat.-Sun. 8am-3:30pm.

Public Transport: Capital Area Transit, Raleigh (828-2567). Operates Mon.-Fri.; fewer buses on Sat. Fare 50¢. **Duke Power Company Transit Service,** Durham (688-4587). Most routes leave from the 1st Federal Building at Main St. on the loop, downtown. Buses operate daily 6am-6pm, some routes until 10:30pm. Fare 50¢, transfers 10¢.

Taxi: Safety Taxi, 832-8800. $1.50 per mi. **Cardinal Cab,** (828-3228). $1.50 per mi., 24-hr. service.

Help Lines: Rape Crisis, 968-4647.

Post Office: Raleigh: 310 New Bern Ave. (831-3661). Open Mon.-Fri. 7am-6pm, Sat. 8am-noon. **ZIP code:** 27611. **Durham:** 323 E. Chapel Hill St. (683-1976). Open Mon.-Fri. 8am-5pm. **ZIP code:** 27701. **Chapel Hill:** Franklin St., at the center of town (967-6297). Open Mon.-Fri. 8:30am-5pm, Sat. 8:30am-noon. **ZIP code:** 27514.

Area Code: 919.

Accommodations and Camping

North Carolina State University HI/AYH Supplementary **Hostel** (515-2908), on central campus, down Allen Dr. in the Metcalf Dorm. Clean dorm-style rooms. Check-in 9am, 7-10pm. $9 for members, $12 for non-members. Linen $2. Open end of May to the beginning of Aug.

YMCA, 1601 Hillsborough St., Raleigh (832-6601), 5 blocks from Greyhound station. Comfortable rooms in a communal atmosphere. Free recreational facilities. Singles $17, with bath $20. Key deposit $2. Call ahead for reservations.

YWCA, 1012 Oberlin Rd., Raleigh (828-3205), ½-mi. east of Cameron Village Shopping Center. Women only. Large, luxurious facility. Hall bath. Free recreational facilities. Singles $15. Must have an informal interview with the director to stay here.

Carolina-Duke Motor Inn, I-85 at Guess Rd., Durham (286-0771). Clean rooms, with duck pics on the walls. Free Movie Channel, swimming pool. Free shuttle to Duke University Medical Center on the main campus. 10% discount for *Let's Go* users, seniors, and AAA cardholders. Singles $27. Doubles $43. $3 for each additional person. The **Wabash Express** (286-0020) next door serves cheap and filling breakfasts (6 pancakes $2.50) Fri.-Sun. and lunches Mon.-Sat.

Friendship Inn, 309 Hillsborough St., Raleigh (833-5771), 3 blocks west of the capitol, 2½ blocks from Greyhound station. Simple, spacious rooms near the heart of downtown. Free local calls, cable TV, and, of course, amiable service. Singles $29. Doubles $33.

Umstead State Park, U.S. 70 (787-3033), 5 mi. northwest of Raleigh. Tent and trailer sites. Large lake for fishing and hiking. Open June-Aug. 8am-9pm; Sept.-May shorter hrs. Sites $7.

Food

The restaurants near the universities are best suited to the budget traveler. In Raleigh, **Hillsborough Street,** across from North Carolina State University, has a wide array of inexpensive restaurants and bakeries staffed, for the most part, by students. The same can be said of **9th Street** in Durham and **Franklin Street** in Chapel Hill.

Ramshead Rath-Skellar, 157-A E. Franklin St., Chapel Hill (942-5158), directly across from the campus. A student hang-out featuring pizza, sandwiches, and hot apple pie Louise. Ship mastheads, German beer steins, and old Italian wine bottles decorate 8 different dining rooms with names such as "Rat Trap Lounge." "Flukey" Hayes, here since 1963, may cook your steak. Full meals $7-8. Open Mon.-Thurs. 11am-2:30pm and 5-9:30pm, Fri.-Sat. 11am-2:30pm and 5-10pm, Sun. 11am-11pm.

The Ninth Street Bakery Shop, 754 9th St., Durham (286-0303). More than a bakery; sandwiches from $2.50. Try the dense bran or blueberry muffins. Live music nightly. Open Mon.-Thurs. 7am-7pm, Fri.-Sat. 7am-11:30pm, Sun. 8am-5pm.

Skylight Exchange, 405½ W. Rosemary St., Chapel Hill (933-5550). A sandwich restaurant with a huge brass espresso machine. Cross-dresses as a used book and record store. Sandwiches $2-3. Live music on weekends. Open Mon.-Thurs. 10am-11pm, Fri.-Sat. 11am-midnight, Sun. 1-11pm.

Side Street, 225 N. Bloodworth St., Raleigh (828-4927), at E. Lane St. 3 blocks from the capitol. A classy place with antique furniture, flower table settings, and huge sandwiches with exotic names. Salads too. All selections under $5. Open Mon.-Fri. 11am-3pm and 5-9pm, Sat. 11am-3pm.

Mariakakis Restaurant and Bakery, 15-501 Bypass, Chapel Hill (942-1453). A heck of a trek from campus, but worth the trip for comfortable chairs, an amazing selection of the world's beers, and free bread with most meals. Spaghetti $3. Large cheese pizza $6. Open Mon.-Sat. 9:30am-9pm.

Two Guys, 2504 Hillsborough St., Raleigh (832-2324), near campus. This college hangout separates real eaters from little girly-men. The best is either the spicy pizza ($6.40) or large spaghetti portions ($4). Open Mon.-Wed. 11am-10pm, Thurs.-Sat. 11am-11pm, Sun. noon-10pm.

Clyde Cooper's Barbeque, 109 E. Davie, Raleigh (832-7614), 1 block east of the Fayetteville Street Mall downtown. If you like BBQ, this is the place to try it NC-style. The local favorites are the baby back ribs ($5) or the barbeque chicken ($3.50). Open Mon.-Sat. 10am-6pm.

Well Spring Grocery, 1002 9th St., Durham (286-2290). A health food grocery with a wide variety of inexpensive fruits, vegetables, and whole grains. Open Mon.-Sat. 9am-8pm, Sun. 10am-7pm.

Sights and Entertainment

While the triangle's main attractions are universities, Raleigh has its share of historical sights. The **capitol building,** in Union Square at Edenton and Salisbury, was built in 1840. (Open Mon.-Fri. 8am-5pm, Sat. 9am-5pm. Tours available for large groups.) Across the street and around the corner at Bicentennial Square is the **Museum of Natural Sciences** (733-7450), which has fossils, gems, and animal exhibits including a live 17-ft. Burmese python named George. (Open Mon.-Sat. 9am-5pm, Sun. 1-5pm. Free.) Just down the way at 109 E. Jones St., the **North Carolina Museum of History** (733-3894) exhibits memorabilia from the state's Roanoke days to the present. (Open Tues.-Sat. 9am-5pm, Sun. 1-6pm. Free.) Pick up a brochure at the visitors center for a self-guided tour of the renovated 19th-century homes of **Historic Oakwood,** where eight North Carolina governors are buried. The **North Carolina Museum of Art,** 2110 Blue Ridge Blvd. (833-1935), off I-40 (Wade Ave. exit), has eight galleries, including works Raphael (the painter, not the Ninja Turtle), Botticelli, Rubens, Monet, Wyeth, and O'Keeffe, as well as some ancient Egyptian artwork. (Tours Tues.-Sun. at 1:30pm. Open Tues.-Sat. 9am-5pm, Fri. 9am-9pm, Sun. noon-5pm. Free.) A tour of **North Carolina State University** on Hillsborough St. (737-3276), includes the **Pulstar Nuclear Reactor.** (Free tours during the semester Mon.-Fri. at noon, leaving from the Bell Tower on Hillsborough St.) Barring a nuclear accident, none of these sights is all that glowing.

For less urban entertainment, visit Chapel Hill where the **University of North Carolina** (962-0331), the oldest state university in the country, sprawls over 729 acres. Astronauts practiced celestial navigation until 1975 at the university's **Morehead Planetarium** (962-1248), which houses one of 12 $2.2 million Zeiss Star projectors. The planetarium puts up six different shows yearly, each involving a combination of films and Zeiss projections. These shows are conceived and produced while you watch. The best part of the planetarium is the staff of friendly UNC students, some of whom are Zeissmeisters; they will give advice to travelers—celestial and otherwise. (Open Sun.-Fri. 12:30-5pm and 6:30-9:30pm, Sat. noon-5pm and 6:30-9:30pm. Admission $3, seniors, students, and kids $2.50.) Over the next year special events will inundate the campus as UNC celebrates its bicentennial. Call the university (962-2296) for info on sporting events and concerts at the Smith Center (a.k.a. the Dean Dome).

In Durham, **Duke University** is the major attraction. The **admissions office,** at 2138 Campus Dr. (684-3214), doubles as a visitors center (open 8am-5pm). The **Duke Chapel** (tours and info 684-2572) is at the center of the university; it has more than a million pieces of stained glass in 77 windows depicting between 800 and 900 figures. The Duke Memorial Organ inside has 5000 pipes; its music may send shivers up the back of your neck—beauty that transcends mathematics. (Open daily during the school year 8am-8pm.)

To the left is the walkway to the **Bryan Center,** Duke's labyrinthine student center, with a gift shop, a café, and a small art gallery; the info desk has brochures on activities, concerts and local buses, as well as free campus maps. Near West Campus on Anderson St. are the **Sarah Duke Gardens** (684-3698), with over 15 acres of landscaped gardens and tiered flower beds. Giant goldfish swim in a small pond near a vined gazebo good for shaded picnics. (Open daily 8am-dusk.) Take the free Duke campus shuttle bus to East Campus, which houses the **Duke Museum of Art** (684-5135), with a small but impressive collection. The six galleries are quiet and uncongested. (Open Tues.-Fri. 9am-5pm, Sat. 11am-2pm, Sun. 2-5pm. Free.) Also take time to enjoy Duke's 7700-acre **forest,** with more than 30 mi. of trails and driveable roads.

On the other side of Durham, up Guess Rd., is the **Duke Homestead,** 2828 Duke Homestead Rd. (477-5498). Washington Duke first started in the tobacco business here, and the beautiful estate is still a small working farm. (Open April-Oct. Mon.-Sat. 9am-5pm, Sun. 1-5pm; Nov.-March Tues.-Sat. 10am-4pm, Sun. 1-4pm.)

At night, students frequent bars along **Franklin Street** in Chapel Hill, and **9th Street** in Durham. Before doing the same, you can catch a **Durham Bulls** (688-8211) baseball game. The Bulls, a class A farm team for the Atlanta Braves, became famous after the movie *Bull Durham* was filmed in their ballpark. (Reserved tickets $6, general admission $3.)

The Research Triangle area always offers something to do, whether it's a concert, guest lecture, exhibit or athletic event. For a complete listing, pick up free copies of both the *Spectator* and *Independent* weekly magazines, available at most restaurants, bookstores, and hotels.

South Carolina

The first state to secede from the Union in 1860, South Carolina takes great pride in its Confederate history, with Civil War monuments dotting virtually every public green or city square. A strange mix of progressive and reactionary, South Carolina houses Harley-riding traditionalists who descend upon the statehouse when legislation is drafted to remove the Confederate flag, while it also prepares for its third reasonably well-attended gay pride parade. The capital, Columbia, is slow-paced with little to ogle—Sherman ruined its future tourist-town potential by burning it to the ground—but Charleston, despite a recent hurricane, still boasts beautiful, stately, antebellum charm. You'll want to do the Charleston for a few days and take in the city's favors and flavors.

Practical Information

Capital: Columbia.

Visitor Information: Department of Parks, Recreation, and Tourism, Edgar A. Brown Bldg., 1205 Pendleton St. #106, Columbia 29201 (734-0122). **U.S. Forest Service,** P.O. Box 970, Columbia 29202 (765-5222).

Time Zone: Eastern.

Postal Abbreviation: SC

Sales Tax: 5%.

Charleston

It seems that natural disasters gravitate to Charleston like tornadoes to trailer parks. In recent years this town has withstood five fires and 10 hurricanes, along with the occasional earthquake. The reconstruction after the most recent unkindness—Hurricane Hugo's rampage in September, 1989—is nearly complete; fresh paint, new storefronts, and tree stumps mix with beautifully refurbished antebellum homes, old churches, and hidden gardens. Dukes, barons, and earls once presided over Charleston's great coastal plantations, leaving in their wake an extensive historic downtown area. The Charleston area also offers visitors the resources of the nearby Atlantic coastal islands. Most noticeably, the people of Charleston are some of the friendliest people you will meet on your journeys in the South. They survive and flourish with a smile.

Practical Information

Emergency: 911.

Visitor Information: New Visitors Center: 81 Mary St. (853-8000), in front of the Municipal Auditorium. Walking tour map (50¢) has historical information and good directions. Catch a showing of the film *Forever Charleston,* which gives an overview of Charleston's past and present. Tickets $3, children $1.50. Open Mon.-Fri. 8:30am-5:30pm, Sat.-Sun. 8:30am-5pm.

Amtrak: 4565 Gaynor Ave. (744-8263), 8 mi. west of downtown. The "Durant Ave." bus will take you from the station to the historic district. Trains to: Richmond (2 per day; 7 hr.; $80); Savannah (2 per day; 2 hr.; $24); and Washington, DC (2 per day; 14 hr.; $104). Open daily 6am-10pm.

Greyhound: 3610 Dorchester Rd. (722-7721), near I-26. Because the downtown bus station is closed, this is the only one available—try to avoid the area at night. To: Myrtle Beach (2 per day; 2 hr.; $18); Savannah (2 per day; 3 hr.; $27); Washington, DC (2 per day; 11 hr.; $69). To get into town, take the **South Carolina Electric and Gas** bus marked "Broad St." or "South Battery" that stops right in front of the station, and get off at the intersection of Meeting and Calhoun St. Pick up the bus marked "Navy Yard 5 Mile Dorchester Rd.," at the same intersection to get back to the station from town. There are two "Navy Yard" buses, so be sure to take the "5 Mile Dorchester Rd." bus outbound; it's the only one that stops in front of the station. Open daily 6am-10pm.

Public Transport: South Carolina Electric and Gas Company (SCE&G) City Bus Service, 2469 Leeds Ave. (747-0922). Operates Mon.-Sat. 5:10am-1am. Fare 50¢. **Downtown Area Shuttle (DASH)** also operates Mon.-Fri. 8am-5pm. Fare 50¢, transfers to other SCE&G buses free.

Car Rental: Thrifty Car Rental (552-7531 or 800-367-2277). $30 per day with 200 free mi., 20¢ each additional mi. Must be 25 with major credit card.

Bike Rental: The Bicycle Shoppe, 283 Meeting St. (722-8168). $3 per hr., $12 per day. Open daily 10am-5:30pm.

Taxi: North Area Taxi, 554-7575. Base fare $1.

Help Lines: Hotline, 744-4357. Open 24 hrs. General counseling and comprehensive information on transient accommodations. **People Against Rape,** 722-7273. Open 24 hrs.

Post Office: 11 Broad St. Open Mon.-Fri. 8am-5pm, Sat. 8am-noon. **ZIP code:** 29401.

Area Code: 803.

Old Charleston is confined to the southernmost point of the mile-wide peninsula below **Calhoun Street. Meeting, King** and **East Bay Streets** are major north-south routes through the city.

Accommodations and Camping

Motel rooms in historic downtown Charleston are expensive. All the cheap motels are far from downtown and not a practical option for those without cars. Investigate the tiny accommodations just across the Ashley River on U.S. 17 South, several of which offer $15 to $20 rooms. Far and away the best budget option in town is the **Rutledge Museum Guest House,** 114 Rutledge Ave. (722-7551), a beautiful historic home with shared rooms and free coffee, tea, hot chocolate, and pastries each morning. ($20 per person; rates lower for extended stays.) The laid-back, friendly manager will not let you set foot in Charleston until she's given you a full orientation. If she can't house you, try **Charleston East Bed and Breakfast,** 1031 Tall Pine Rd. (884-8208), in Mt. Pleasant east of Charleston off U.S. 701. They will try to place you in one of their 16 private homes. (Rooms $20-80. Prior reservations essential—call between 9am-10pm.) **Motel 6,** 2058 Savannah Hwy. (556-5144), four mi. out at 7th Ave., is clean and pleasant but far from downtown and frequently filled. (Singles $25, each additional person $6. Call ahead; fills up quickly in summer months.)

There are several inexpensive campgrounds in the Charleston area, but not a one is near downtown. Eight mi. south on U.S. 17, try **Oak Plantation Campground** (766-5936; sites $9.50). Also look for **Pelican's Cove,** 97 Center St., at Folly Beach (588-2072; sites with full hookup $17).

Food and Nightlife

Most restaurants in the revamped downtown area are also expensive. If you choose to eat out, eat lunch, since most restaurants serve their dinner selections at noonday at discounted prices.

Marina Variety Store/City Marina, Lockwood Blvd. Pleasant view of the Ashley River from an otherwise unremarkable dining room. Good shellfish and great nightly specials under $7. Open Mon.-Sat. 6:30am-3pm and 5-10pm, Sun. 6:30am-3pm.

Henry's, 54 N. Market St. (723-4363), at Anson. A local favorite. Not cheap, but the food is good, especially the grilled shrimp ($8). On weekends, live jazz upstairs starts at 9pm, followed by a late-night breakfast. Open Mon.-Wed. 11:30am-10:30pm, Thurs.-Sun. 11:30am-1am.

T-Bones, 80 N. Market St. (517-2511). Typical steak and seafood in an atypical atmosphere. Live music on Tues. nights is a local favorite. Open daily 11am-midnight.

Hyman's Seafood Company, 215 Meeting St. (723-0233). Kudos to the proprietor, who manages to serve about 15 different kinds of fresh fish daily ($7). If you like shellfish, the snow crabs ($8) are a must. Open daily 11am-11pm.

Before going out in Charleston, pick up a free copy of *Poor Richard's Omnibus,* available at grocery stores and street corners all over town; the *PRO* lists concerts and other events. Locals rarely dance the *Charleston* anymore, and the city's nightlife has suffered accordingly. Most bars and clubs are in the **Market Street** area. **Café 99,** 99 S. Meeting St. (577-4499), has nightly live entertainment, strong drinks ($2-4), and reasonably priced dinners ($4-7). (Open daily 11:30am-2am. No cover.) For the best bands go to **Myskyns Tavern,** 5 Faber St. (577-5595), near Market St., and have a drink ($1-3) at the enormous mahogany bar. Hang out with the locals on Friday and Saturday nights in front of **San Miguel's Mexican Restaurant** off Market St. (723-9745), or sit on the roof at **The Colony House** on East Bay St. and watch the ships sail into the harbor.

Sights and Events

Saturated with ancient homes, historical monuments, churches, galleries and gardens, Charleston gives a tourist something to chew on. A multitude of organized tours allow you to see the city by foot, car, bus, boat, trolley or carriage. Information on these towns can be obtained at the visitors center on Mary Street. **Gray Line Water Tours** (722-1112) gives you your money's worth. Their two-hour boat rides leave daily at 10am, 12:30pm, and 3pm ($9; reservations recommended). The bus tours, however, provide the best overview of the city. **Talk of the Towne** (795-8199) has tours twice a day for two hours and will even pick you up from your hotel. **Trolley Tours** (795-3000) mix the charm and nostalgia of historic Charleston by touring the narrow streets in real trolley cars. 11/4-hr. tours depart from the City Market at "Quarter Hill" every hour and from the visitors reception center on the hour. ($11, ages 12 and under $6.) Before touring, see *Dear Charleston,* an acclaimed documentary on the city's history recounted through the musings of long-time residents (daily every hr. 10am-noon and 2-4pm). The film shows at the **Preservation Society Visitors Center,** 147 King St. (723-4381), and at **Dear Charleston Theater & Gifts,** 52 N. Market St. (577-4743). (Admission at both places $2.50, children $1.) The **Gibbes Gallery,** 135 Meeting St. (722-2706), has a fine collection of portraits by prominent American artists. (Open Sun.-Mon. 1-5pm, Tues.-Sat. 10am-5pm. Admission $2, seniors and students $1, children 50¢.)

The **Nathanial Russell House,** 51 Meeting St. (723-1623), features a magnificent staircase that spirals without support from floor to floor. The house gives an idea of how Charleston's wealthy merchant class lived in the early 19th century. The **Edmonston-Allston House,** 21 E. Battery St. (722-7171), looks out over Charleston Harbor. (Both houses open Mon.-Sat. 10am-5pm, Sun. 2-5pm. Admission to 1 house $4, to both $6. Get tickets to both homes at 52 Meeting St.) Founded in 1773, the **Charleston Museum,** 360 Meeting St. (722-2996; open Mon.-Sat. 9am-5pm, Sun. 1-5pm), maintains a collection of bric-a-brac ranging from natural history specimens to old sheet music. It also offers combination tickets for the museum itself and the three historic homes within easy walking distance: the **Aiken-Rhett Mansion** built in 1817; the 18th-century **Heyward-Washington House,** 87 Church St.; and the **Joseph Manigault House,** 350 Meeting St. (for info on all three tours call 722-2996). The Washington House includes the only 18th-century kitchen open to the public in Charleston. Hope they hide those dirty dishes. (Aiken-Rhett house open daily 10am-5pm. Washington and Manigault homes open Mon.-Sat. 10am-5pm, Sun. 1-5pm. Admission to museum and 3 homes $10, children $5.)

A visit to Charleston just wouldn't be complete without a **boat tour** to **Fort Sumter** (722-1691) in the harbor. The Civil War was touched off when rebel forces in South Carolina, the first state to secede, attacked this Union fortress on April 12, 1861. Over seven million pounds of metal were fired against the fort before those inside finally fled in February 1865. Tours ($8, ages 6-12 $4) leave several times daily from the Municipal Marina, at the foot of Calhoun St. and Lockwood Blvd. **Fort Sumter Tours,** a company that runs the tour boats to the fort, also offers tours to **Patriots' Point,** the world's largest naval and maritime museum. Here you can walk the decks of the retired U.S. aircraft carrier *Yorktown,* or stroke the destroyer *Laffey's* huge fore and aft cannon.

If you are feeling a tad gun-shy, visit the **City Market,** downtown at Meeting St., which vends everything from porcelain sea lions to handwoven sweetgrass baskets in the open air daily from 9:30am to sunset.

Magnolia Gardens, (571-1266), 10 mi. out of town on Hwy. 61 off Rte. 17, is the 300-year-old ancestral home of the Drayton family, and treats visitors to 50 acres of gorgeous gardens with 900 varieties of camelia and 250 varieties of azalea. Get lost in the hedge maze. You'll probably want to skip the manor house, but do consider renting bicycles ($2 per hr.) to explore the neighboring swamp and bird sanctuary. (Open daily 9:30am-5pm. Admission $8, seniors $7, teens $6, kids $4.)

From mid-March to mid-April, the **Festival of Houses** (723-1623) celebrates Charleston's architecture and tradition, as many private homes open their doors to the public. Music, theater, dance and opera converge on the city during **Spoleto Festival U.S.A.** (722-2764) in late May and early June. During **Christmas in Charleston** (723-7641), tours of many private homes and buildings are given, and many motels offer special reduced rates.

Columbia

This quiet, unassuming city sprung up in 1786 when bureaucrats in Charleston decided that their territory needed a right proper capital city. Surveyors found some land near the Congaree River, cleared it, and within two decades, over 1000 people had poured into one of America's first planned cities. President Woodrow Wilson called Columbia home during his boyhood; now thousands of University of South Carolina (USC) students do the same, providing most of the city's excitement and nightlife. In many ways, the pervasive college-town flavor overshadows state politics in this capital city.

Columbia's 18th-century aristocratic elegance has been preserved by the Historic Columbia Foundation in the **Robert Mills House,** 1616 Blanding St., three blocks east of Sumter St. (252-3964; tours Tues.-Sat. 10:15am-3:15pm, Sun. 1-4:15pm; $3, students $1.50). Mills, one of America's first federal architects, designed the Washington Monument and 30 of South Carolina's public buildings. Across the street, at 1615 Blanding, is the **Hampton-Preston Mansion** (252-0935), once used by Union forces as headquarters during the Civil War. (Open Tues.-Sat. 10:15am-3:15pm, Sun. 1-4:15pm. Tours $3, students $1.50, under 6 free.) Stroll through USC's **Horseshoe,** at the junction of College and Sumter St., which holds the university's oldest buildings, dating from the beginning of the 19th century. The **McKissick Museum** (777-7251), at the top of the Horseshoe, offers scientific, folk, and pottery exhibits, as well as selections from the university's extensive collection of Twentieth Century-Fox newsreels. (Open Mon.-Fri. 9am-4pm, Sat. 10am-5pm, Sun. 1-5pm. Free.) Columbia's award-winning **Riverbanks Zoo,** on I-26 at Greystone Blvd. (779-8730), northwest of downtown, is home to more than 2000 animals. See frogs, sharks, cobras and tigers before stopping off at the concessions stand for a sno cone. (Open daily 9am-4pm. Admission $4, seniors $2.50, students $3, ages 3-12 $1.75.)

The new **South Carolina State Museum,** 301 Gervais St. (737-4921) beside the Gervais St. Bridge, is located inside the historic Columbia Mills building. Exhibits include replicas of two denizens of the deep—a great white shark and the first submarine ever to sink an enemy ship. (Open Mon.-Sat. 10am-5pm, Sun. 1-5pm. Admission $3.50, seniors and college students with ID $2.50, ages 6-17 $1.75, under 6 free.)

The **Five Points** business district, at the junction of Harden, Devine, and Blossom St. (from downtown, take the "Veterans Hospital" bus), caters to Columbia's large student population. **Groucho's,** 611 Harden St. (799-5708), in the heart of Five Points, is a Columbia institution and anomaly: a New York-style Jewish deli (large sandwiches $4-6). (Open Mon.-Sat. 11am-4pm, Thurs.-Fri. 11am-9pm.) **Yesterday's Restaurant and Tavern,** 2030 Devine St. (799-0196), serves today's specialties over old newspapers preserved within lacquered tabletops. Enjoy complete dinner specials ($6-8) or vegetarian pies. (Open Mon.-Thurs. 11:30am-midnight, Fri.-Sat. 11:30am-1am, Sun. 11:30am-11pm.) **Kinch's Restaurant,** 1115 Assembly St. (256-3843), across the street from the State House, has an early-bird breakfast special for $2. (Open daily 7am-4pm.) **The Columbia State Farmers Market,** Bluff Rd. (737-3016), across from the USC Football Stadium, is a good place to stock up on fresh produce shipped in from all corners of South Carolina. The university provides most of the city's excitement and nightlife. Try **Club 638,** 638 Harden St. (779-1953), at Five Points for dancing and revelry. Five Points abounds in bars.

The **USC Off-Campus Housing Office** (777-4174), in the "I" building on Devine St. is probably your best budget bet for beauty rest. They can link you up with owners of private homes in the university community who rent rooms, usually on a per-week basis ($40-50 a week). Otherwise, the only budget option downtown is the **Heart of Columbia,** 1011 Assembly St. (799-1140), with a shabby-looking exterior but clean chambers. (Singles $28. Doubles $32-35.) Just west of downtown across the Congaree River, a number of inexpensive motels line Knox Abbot Dr. **Econo-lodge,** 827 Bush River Rd., off exit 108 at I-20 and I-26, has bright rooms, a swimming pool, A/C, and a movie channel. (Singles $25-30. Doubles $28-33.) The **Sesquicentennial State Park** (788-2706) has sites with electricity and water ($11). Take the "State Park" bus from downtown. By car, take I-20 to Two Notch Rd. (Rte. 1) exit, and head northeast four mi.

Emergency is 911. The **Greater Columbia Convention and Visitors Bureau,** 301 Gervais St. (254-0479), is not budget-oriented and caters to larger groups but provides a free street map of the area with all the historical sights marked on it and a free coupon book for discounts at area hotels and restaurants. (Open Mon.-Fri. 8:30am-5pm, Sat. 10am-5pm, Sun. 1-5pm.) The **University of South Carolina Information Desk,** Russell House Student Center, 2nd floor (777-3196), on Green at Sumter St., across from the Horseshoe, provides campus maps, shuttle schedules, advice on nearby budget accommodations, and the low-down on campus life and events. If you get stranded in the area and/or need transportation in a hurry, contact **Traveler's Aid,** 1800 Main St. (733-5450; open Mon.-Fri. 9am-5pm).

Most buses running along the East Coast stop here. The **Congaree River** marks the western edge of the city. **Assembly Street** and **Sumter Street** are downtown's major north-south arteries; **Gervais Street** and **Calhoun Street** cut east-west. **Columbia Metropolitan Airport,** 300 Aviation Way (822-5000), is serviced by **Delta, American, USAir,** and others. **Amtrak,** 903 Gervais St. (252-8246 or 800-872-7245), has trains once per day to Washington, DC (9½ hr.; $87); Miami (12 hr.; $120); and Savannah (2 hr.; $31). The northbound train leaves daily at 5:31am, the southbound at 10:43pm. (Station open Mon.-Sat. 8:30am-4:30pm and 10:30pm-6:30am, Sun. 10:30pm-6:30am.) **Greyhound,** 2015 Gervais St. (779-0650), is near the intersection of Harden and Gervais St., about one mi. east of the capitol. Buses to: Charlotte, NC (5 per day; 2 hr.; $20); Charleston, SC (5 per day; 2½ hr.; $20); Atlanta (6 per day; 4½ hr.; $45). Open 24 hrs. **South Carolina Electric and Gas** (748-3019) operates local buses. Most routes start from the transfer depot at the corner of Assembly and Gervais St.

Fare 50¢. Local **help lines** are **Helpline of the Midlands** (790-4357), **Rape Crisis** (252-8393), and the **AIDS Information Line,** (800-322-2437). The **Richland Memorial Hospital,** 5 Richland Medical Park (765-7561), has emergency services and a walk-in clinic. The **Post Office,** 1601 Assembly St. (733-4647), is open Mon.-Fri. 8:30am-4:30pm. Columbia's **ZIP code** is 29202; the **area code** is 803.

Tennessee

Tennessee, the last state to secede from the Union and the first to rejoin, reveals a landscape noticeably free of the antebellum plantations that seem to blanket every other Southern state. Interestingly enough, industry has been the moving force in this state rather than agriculture—the state leads the South in production of commercial machinery, chemicals, and electronics. Tennessee defies other regional stereotypes. In 1920, it provided the final vote needed to engrave women's suffrage in the Constitution, and Oak Ridge—pivotal in the development of the A-bomb—still houses one of the world's most sophisticated miltary laboratories. Tennessee has added to the culture of the world; country music twangs from Nashville, and the blues wail from their headquarters in Memphis. Both cities offer a veritable treasure trove of modern diversions for the tourist. Balance seems to be the rule in Tennessee—home to the famous original Jack Daniels whiskey distillery as well as the largest Bible producing business in the world. After a spell here, you too'll be singin' "There ain't no place I'd rather be than the grand ol' state of Tennessee."

Practical Information

Capital: Nashville.

Tennessee Dept. of Tourist Development, P.O. Box 23170, Nashville 37202 (741-2158). Open Mon.-Fri. 8am-4:30pm. **Tennessee State Parks Information,** 701 Broadway, Nashville 37203 (742-6667).

Time Zones: Central (Memphis and Nashville; 1 hr. behind Eastern) and Eastern (Chattanooga, Knoxville). **Postal Abbreviation:** TN

Sales Tax: 5.5-8.25%.

Great Smoky Mountain National Park

The largest wilderness area in the eastern U.S., Great Smoky Mountain National Park encompasses a half-million acres of gray-green Appalachian peaks bounded on either side by misty North Carolina and Tennessee valleys. Bears, wild hogs, white-tailed deer, groundhogs, wild turkeys, and more than 1,500 species of flowering plants make their homes here. Whispering conifer forests line the mountain ridges at elevations of over 6,000 ft. Rhododendrons burst into their full glory in June and July, and by mid-October the sloping mountains become a giant crazy-quilt of color, reminiscent of the area's well-preserved crafts tradition.

Start any exploration of the area with a visit to one of the park's three visitors centers. **Sugarlands,** on Newfound Gap Rd., two mi. south of Gatlinburg (436-1200), is next to the park's headquarters. (Open in summer daily 8am-7pm; spring and fall 8am-5pm; winter 8am-4:30pm.) **Cades Cove** (436-1275) is in the park's western valley, 15 mi. southwest of Sugarlands on Little River Rd., seven mi. southwest of Townsend, TN. (Open in summer daily 9:30am-7pm; fall 8:30am-5:30pm; spring 9:30am-5:30pm.) The **Oconaluftee Visitors Center,** four mi. north of Cherokee, NC (497-9147), serves travelers entering the park from the Blue Ridge Parkway and all points south and east (open same hours as Sugarlands). The park's **information line** (615-436-1200; open daily 8:30am-4:30pm) telelinks all three visitors centers. The rangers can answer travel questions, field emergency message calls, and trace lost equipment.

At each visitors center you'll find displays amplifying the park's natural and cultural resources, bulletin boards displaying emergency messages or public information, brochures and films, and comfort stations. Be sure to ask for *The Smokies Guide,* a newspaper offering a comprehensive explanation of the park's changing natural graces. The helpful journal also includes practical information on tours, lectures, and other activities, such as rafting or horseback riding. The standard park service brochure, *Great Smoky Mountains,* provides the best driving map in the region. Hikers should ask the visitors center staff for assistance in locating an appropriately detailed backcountry map. You can also tune your car radio to 1610 AM at various marked points for information.

900 mi. of hiking trails and 170 mi. of road traverse the park. Ask the rangers at the visitors centers to help you devise a trip appropriate to your time and physical ability. Driving and walking routes are clearly charted. To hike off the marked trails, you must ask for a free backcountry camping permit. Otherwise, just choose a route, bring water, and DON'T FEED THE BEARS. Some of the most popular trails are the five mi. to **Rainbow Falls,** the four mi. to **Chimney Tops,** and the 2½ mi. to **Laurel Falls**. For a splendid drive with beautiful scenery, visitors can enjoy **Cades Cove loop,** which lassoes the last vestiges of a mountain community that occupied the area from the 1850s to the 1920s when the GSM national park materialized. What was once a living, breathing settlement today displays splendid grassy, open fields against peaceful mountain backdrop. Deep green contemplative forests enhance the pastoral aura of Cades Cove as do the horses, deer, bears and other roaming animals. The 50¢ tour guide available at the entrance to the 11-mi. loop shares detailed, well-written descriptions of the old churches and homesteads as well as the history. In the summer months, visit **Mingus Mill** located one mi. north of the Oconaluftee visitors center along Newfound Gap Rd. This 1876 Turbine mill boasts 107-year-old wooden tools and machinery which still operate. Visitors can watch corn and wheat being ground. Browse through the book of old photos to see the last miller, John Jones, hard at work. The **Pioneer Farmstead,** next door to the Oconaluftee center, recreates a turn of the century settlement including a blacksmith shop and a corncrib. The 25¢ pamphlets give informative illustrations of the grounds. (Both sights are free.)

Great Smoky Mountains National Park straddles the Tennessee/North Carolina border. On the Tennessee side, the city of **Gatlinburg** just two mi. from Sugarlands, appears and vanishes within the blink of a driver's eye, but is jam-packed enough to keep you occupied for an evening or a day. Touristic hordes occupy its kitschy corners, ranging from a theme park devoted to Dolly Parton (Dollywood) to a wax museum dedicated to President Bush. Also in Gatlinburg, Christus Gardens bills itself as America's #1 religious attraction, and **Ober Gatlinburg** has America's largest cable car. Along "the strip" junky giftstores, boutiques, candy stores, "museums," and restaurants all vie for the attention of fools ready to part with hard earned dough. Two worthwhile attractions are the **Sky Lift** and the **Space Needles** electric elevator ride. Both transport their customers to a spectacular view of the Smokies. Between all these attractions are endless rows of hotels and motor inns. For more guidance, and specific listings of accommodations and campgrounds, stop in at the **Tourist Information Center,** 520 Pkwy. (615-436-4178). (Open May-Oct. Mon.-Sat. 8am-8pm, Sun. 9am-5pm; Nov.-April Mon.-Sat. 8am-6pm, Sun. 9am-5pm.)

On the N.C. side of the Mountains, one mi. from the Oconaluftee Vistors Center is the **Cherokee Indian Reservation,** replete with a guided tour of a re-created 1750-ish Indian village, an outdoor drama about the Cherokee tribe, and an informative museum. Do invest your time and money for a ticket to "Unto these Hills," an outdoor drama that retells the story of the Cherokees and climaxes with a moving re-enactment of the Trail of Tears. (Evening shows Jun-Aug., Mon.-Sat. $8, children 12 and under $5.)

Accommodations, Camping and Food

There are 10 campgrounds in the park, each with tent sites, limited trailer space, water, tables, and comfort stations (no showers or hookups). **Smokemont, Elkmont,** and **Cades Cove** accept reservations; the rest are first-come, first-served. (Sites $11.) For those hauling a trailer or staying at one of the campgrounds near the main roads during the summer, reservations are a must. Obtain them at least eight weeks in advance by writing to Ticketron, P.O. Box 617516, Chicago, IL 60661 (800-452-1111).

Both Cherokee and Gatlinburg have many small motels. The prices vary widely depending on the season and the economy. In general, the cheaper motels are in Cherokee, and the nicer ones are in Gatlinburg, where the best deals are off Main St., especially off street light #6. Check Cherokee and Gatlinburg tourism guides for detailed listing of accommodations and campsites.

Three youth hostels are located in the area around the park. The closest is **Bell's Wa-Floy Retreat (HI/AYH),** 3610 East Pkwy (615-436-5575), 10 mi. east of Gatlinburg on Rte. 321, at mile marker 21. From the center of Gatlinburg catch the east-bound trolley (25¢) to the end of the line. From there, it's a five-mi. walk to Wa-Floy. Located centrally in the Wa-Floy Retreat (which doubles as the Steiner-Bell Center for Physical and Spiritual Rejuvenation), the hostel is no more than a rustic cabin divided into a few apartments with kitchenettes. The shabby interior is clean, though the showers may be unpleasant. If driving, be careful not to hit the ducks and peacocks, which roam the lovely grounds complete with a pool, tennis courts, meditation area, chapel, and bubbling brook. The friendly proprietor, Mrs. Floy Steiner-Bell loves to chat and may welcome you warmly with her poetry. ($10, nonmembers $12, linens $1. Call for reservations at least 1 day ahead. Midnight curfew. Poetry Free.) On the other side of the park, about 35 mi. away on a slow, winding road in North Carolina, you can vegetate after a hike or river ride in the spacious communal living room of Louise Phillip's **Smokeseege Lodge (HI/AYH),** P.O. Box 179, Dillsboro on Rte. 441, 11 mi. south of Cherokee. Contact the **Jackson County Chamber of Commerce** 18 N. Central, Sylva, N.C., (586-2155 or 586-2336), for further info. Walk from the nearest Greyhound stop, nearly three mi. away in Sylva. If you're driving from the Smokies, watch carefully on the right-hand side of Rte. 441 for the small, triangular HI/AYH logo and yellow arrows—the hostel is at the end of a gravel road. This hostel is very isolated, a good distance from the road and any area towns, and operates under a self-help system; women and those traveling alone may feel uneasy going to this hostel. Kitchen facilities are available; no smoking or drinking permitted. (Lockout 9am-5pm. Curfew 11pm. $7. Call ahead. Open April-Oct.)

Further south, near Wesser in the **Nantahala National Forest,** the bustling **Nantahala Outdoor Center (NOC),** U.S. 19 W., P.O. Box 41, Bryson City (704-488-2175), 80 mi. from Gatlinburg and 13 mi. from downtown Bryson City, offers cheap beds. Bunks occupy simple wooden cabins at "base camp" on the far side of the river and fairly large-sized motel rooms with kitchenettes. Showers, kitchen, and laundry facilities included. ($8. Call ahead.) Keep in mind the center is not at all convenient to the GSM park or Gatlinburg. Staying at the NOC is a good idea when planning a whitewater rafting trip. The NOC's rates for 2½-hr. whitewater rafting expeditions are pricey, but you can rent your own raft for a self-designed trip down the Nantahala River. (Sun.-Fri. $14, Sat. $16. 1-person inflatable "duckies" $27 per day. Group rates available. Look out for higher prices on "premium Saturdays," July-Aug.) The NOC also rents canoes and kayaks and offers instruction for the novice. Most trips have minimum age or weight limits; daycare service is available at the center. Trip prices include transportation to the put-in site and all necessary equipment. Don't let *Deliverance* steer you clear. For further information, call (800) 232-7238. Hike on the **Appalachian Trail** to explore some of the old forest service roads. The NOC staff will gladly assist if you need help charting an appropriate daytrip. The NOC also maintains seasonal "outposts" on the **Ocoee, Nolichucky, Chattoga,** and **French Broad Rivers,** all within 100 mi. of its Bryson City headquarters. Although these do not have overnight facilities, a rafting expedition on any of these rivers makes a satisfying daytrip if you have a car. Be sure to look into NOC's 20% discounts during March and April.

After your stomach has settled following a full day of rafting, try **Maxwell's Bakery**, Dillsboro exit off Hwy 74. (586-5046) Relish the heavenly smell of freshly baked bread while munching on a delectable sandwich in this country café. Sandwiches $3-4, biscuits $1, cookies 50¢. Large portions and convenient to GSM. (Open Mon.-Sat. 6am-6pm, Sun. 9am-5pm year-round.)

Memphis

In the southwestern corner of Tennessee, follow the sound of soulful melodies to Memphis, home to the blues and the birthplace of rock 'n' roll. Decades after W.C. Handy published the first blues piece on legendary Beale Street in 1912, Elvis Presley (also a Memphisite) became the "King of Rock 'n' Roll" with the help of his scandalously gyrating pelvis and amazingly versatile voice. Beyond music, Memphis stimulates each of the other four senses, as well. Visitors can feast their eyes on both national and local history in the many museums around town, or focus instead on a live performance given by one of the city's increasingly sophisticated theaters. Their noses and taste buds will be tempted by barbecue, a Memphis specialty. Though travelers' feet may feel sore after trekking to all of these recreations, the feelings of friendliness and genuine geniality evinced by residents are sure to impress even the most jaded tourist.

Practical Information

Emergency: 911.

Visitor Information Center, 340 Beale St. (576-8171), 2 blocks south on 2nd St. and 2 blocks east on Beale from the Greyhound station. Quite helpful, with everything from bus maps to restaurant menus and guides. Open Mon.-Sat. 9am-6pm, Sun. noon-6pm.

Memphis International Airport (922-8000), just south of the southern loop of I-240. Taxi fare to the city $15—negotiate in advance. Public transport to and from the airport only $1.25, but a long and difficult trip for a traveler unfamiliar with the area.

Amtrak: 545 S. Main St. (526-0052 or 800-872-7245), at Calhoun on the southern edge of downtown. *Very* unsafe area even during the day, downright hellish at night. To New Orleans (1 per day; 7½ hr.; $73) Chicago (1 per day; 11 hr.; $92) and Atlanta via New Orleans ($168). Open Mon.-Sat. 8am-12:30pm, 1:30-5pm and 9pm-6am, Sun. 9pm-6am.

Greyhound: 203 Union Ave. (523-7676), at 4th St. downtown. Unsafe area at night, but it beats the Amtrak station. To Nashville ($35) New Orleans ($53) and Atlanta ($63). Open 24 hrs.

Public Transport: Memphis Area Transit Authority (MATA), 61 S. Main St. (274-6282). Extensive bus routes cover most suburbs but buses take their own sweet time and don't run very frequently. The 2 major downtown stops are at Front and Jefferson St. and at 2nd St. and Madison Ave. Operates Mon.-Fri. 6am-7pm, Sat.10am-6pm, Sun. 11am-4pm. Fare 95¢.

Taxi: Yellow Cab, 526-2121. $2.35 first mi., $1.10 each additional mi.

Crisis Line: 247-7477. Open 24 hrs. Also refers to other numbers.

Memphis Activity Hotline: 681-1111.

Time Zone: Central (1 hr. behind Eastern).

Post Office: 555 S. 3rd St. (521-2140), at Calhoun St. Take bus #13. Open Mon.-Fri. 8:30am-5:30pm, Sat. 10am-noon. Front St. Station (576-2013). Open Mon.-Fri. 9am-5pm. **ZIP code:** 38101.

Area Code: 901.

Downtown, named avenues run east-west and numbered ones north-south. **Madison Avenue** bifurcates north and south addresses. Two main thoroughfares, **Poplar** and **Union** Avenues, pierce the heart of the city from the east; 2nd and 3rd Streets arrive from the south.

Accommodations

The accommodations outlook in Memphis is fair to good for those with a car; those without a car will have to take an unreliable bus to reach any reasonably priced lodgings. Downtown establishments are expensive, but cab fare to the hinterlands may make them seem more reasonable. Less expensive but less comfortable motels grace Elvis Presley Blvd. near Graceland. Book ahead if you are coming between August 12 to 16, when Elvis fans from around the universe make a pilgrimage to pay tribute to the

King on the anniversary of his death. The visitor information center has a thorough listing of lodgings. Contact **Bed and Breakfast in Memphis,** P.O. Box 41621, Memphis 38174 (726-5920), for guest rooms in Memphis homes. French- and Spanish-speaking hosts are available. (Singles and doubles $40-60.)

Lowenstein-Long House/Castle Hostelry, 1084 Poplar and 217 N. Waldran (527-7174). Near downtown; take bus #50 from 3rd St. Beautiful accommodations in an elegant Victorian mansion. The hostel is in a small red brick building out back. Key deposit $5. Laundry $2. No breakfast. Kitchens available in the hostel. Lockout 11am-5pm. Singles $10, nonmembers $13, private doubles $30.

Richardson Towers, Central Ave. on Memphis State University campus (678-2290). Nicely furnished, carpeted dorm suites. Each room sleeps 2 people and has its own sink. 2 rooms connected by a semi-private bathroom with a tub, hot shower, toilet. Located in a safe and quiet residential area, convenient to town. MATA bus stops within a short walking distance. Ask to speak with Kendall, the conference housing manager, and laugh at his sardonic wit. Reservations advised. $15 per night, per person, plus $1 for linen.

River Place Inn, 100 North Front St. (526-0583), overlooking the water. Pleasant hotel with very spacious rooms from $44. The visitors information center has a $35 coupon for 1-4 people. No meals or laundry.

Motel 6, 1360 Springbrook Rd. (396-3620), just east of intersection of Elvis and Brooks Rd. near Graceland. There is also a **Motel 6** at I-55 and Brooks Rd. (346-0992). Both have pools and small, clean rooms with movie channels and unlimited local calls. No meals, no laundry, do not pass Go, do not collect $200. Stand-up showers. Singles $24, each additional person $6.

Red Roof Inn, 210 S. Pauline St. off Union Ave. (528-0650 or 800-843-7663). Pleasant rooms convenient to downtown. Free movie channel and unlimited local calls. Checks not accepted. Singles $28. Doubles $34.

Food

When a smoky, spicy smell follows you almost everywhere, you are either extremely paranoid, malodorous, or in Memphis, where barbecue reigns. The city even hosts the World Championship Barbecue Cooking Contest in May. But don't fret if gnawing on ribs isn't your thing—Memphis has plenty of other Southern-style restaurants with down-home favorites like fried chicken, catfish, chitlins, grits and fresh vegetables.

The Rendezvous, Downtown Alley (523-2746), in the alley across from the Peabody Hotel off Union St., between the Ramada and Days Inns. A Memphis legend, serving large portions of ribs ($6.50-10), and cheaper sandwiches ($3-4). Open Tues.-Thurs. 4:30pm-midnight, Fri.-Sat. noon-midnight.

P and H Café, 1532 Madison Ave. (274-9794). The initials aptly stand for Poor and Hungry. This local favorite serves huge burgers, plate lunches, and grill food ($3-5). The waitresses are a Memphis institution—look at the wall murals. Local bands occasionally play Sat. night. Open Mon.-Sat. 11am-3am.

The North End, 346 N. Main St. (526-0319 or 527-3663), downtown. A most happening place with an extensive menu including tamales, wild rice, and creole dishes ($3-8). Delicious vegetarian meals for under $6. Orgasmic hot fudge pie ($2.50). Happy Hour 5-7pm. Live music Wed.-Sun. starts around 10:30pm, with a small cover (around $3). Open 8 days/wk, 11am-3pm. Next door, **Jake's Place** (527-2799) offers a similar menu, but with stir-fry specialties and breakfast.

Spaghetti Warehouse, 40 W. Huling St. (521-0907), off S. Front St. A great, friendly restaurant. Filling plate of pasta, salad, and sourdough bread in a restored trolley car or on a carousel for under $6. Open Mon.-Thurs. 11am-10pm, Fri. 11am-11pm, Sat. noon-11pm, Sun. noon-10pm.

Front St. Delicatessen, 77 S. Front St. (522-8943). Lunchtime streetside deli with almost no room inside. Local yuppie hangout (how *80s!*) Patio dining in sunny weather. Hot lunch specials $2-4. Open Mon.-Fri. 8am-4pm, Sat. 11am-3pm.

Corky's, 5259 Poplar Ave. (685-9744). Very popular with the locals, and justifiably so. The BBQ dinner and ribs are served with baked beans, coleslaw, and homemade bread ($3-9) and are top notch, as are the pies and cobbler. Arrive early or expect a long wait. (Open Mon.-Thurs. 11am-9:30pm, Fri.-Sat. 11am-10:30pm, Sun. noon-9:30pm).

Howard's Donuts, 1776 Union Ave. (725-5595). Wide variety of big, delicious, not-too-greasy donuts, 35-75¢. Assorted muffins, also. Open daily 24 hrs.

Elvissights

Graceland, or rather "GRACE-lin", Elvis Presley's home, is a paradigm of American kitsch that even Paul Simon can love. But any desire to learn about the man, to share his dream, or to feel his music may go unrealized even by those who venture to his monumental home; the complex has been built up to resemble an amusement park that shuffles visitors from one room to another. It seems that the employees adhere to the Elvismotto "Taking Care of Business in a Flash." However, if you're in Memphis, you *have* to go—if only to say that you have seen its mirrored ceilings and carpeted walls. Elvis bought the mansion when he was only 22, and lived there until his death. The King and his family are buried next door in the **Meditation Gardens,** where you can seek the Buddha while reciting a mantra to the tune of "You're So Square". (Admission to amazing Graceland $8, children $5.)

Across the street, you can visit several Elvismuseums, and several more Elvissouvenir shops. (Say hi to Elvis's Uncle Vestor in the **EP LP** store.) The **Elvis Presley Automobile Museum** proves to be the most worthwhile Elvisoption. A huge hall houses a score of Elvismobiles, and an indoor drive-in movie theater shows clips from 31 Elvismovies. ($4.50, seniors $4, kids $3.) *If I Can Dream* is a 20-minute film with performance footage, and the price of viewing it is included with the mansion tour. **Elvis' Airplanes** features—yes, dear reader, yes—the two Elvisplanes: the *Lisa Marie* (named for the Elvisdaughter) and the tiny *Hound Dog II* Jetstar. The cost of visiting these planes is overpriced at $4.25 (seniors $3.80, kids $2.75), but the cost of seeing **Elvis' Tour Bus** is a bargain at $1. The **Elvis Up Close** exhibit, which gives you a glimpse of Elvis's private side by presenting some books he read, some shirts he wore, and his Social Security card. ($1.75, free for Elvis when he finally comes out of hiding and admits he is *not* dead but merely roaming the countryside doing good deeds and spreading the Elvisgospel.)

There are three different combination tickets available: (1) all attractions except the mansion for $10 (seniors $9, kids $7); (2) all attractions except the bus and planes for $13 (seniors $12, kids $8); (3) all the attractions for $16 (seniors $14.50, kids $11). Take Lauderdale/Elvis Presley bus #13 from 3rd and Union. (Open Memorial Day-Labor Day, 8am-7pm, last tour 5pm. 332-3322 or 800-238-2000.)

Non Elvissights

A musical tour of Memphis reaches beyond Graceland's walls, outside the category of solely Elvismusic, and into other locations downtown. Most famous is **Beale Street,** where W.C. Handy invented the blues. After a long period of neglect, the neighborhood has music pouring from almost every door once again. The **W.C. Handy Home and Museum,** 352 Beale (527-2583), exhibits music and photographs. (Open Mon.-Sat. 10am-6pm, Sun. 1-5pm; $2, kids 50¢; call for an appointment.) Earphones that spew blues hits litter the **Memphis Music and Blues Museum** at 97 S. 2nd St. (525-4007) as do photographs and TV footage of actual performances. If you like to sing, listen or watch the blues, this is the place to go. (Open Sun.-Thurs. 11am-6pm, Fri.-Sat. 11am-9pm. $5, ages 1-12 free.) **Center for Southern Folklore,** 152 Beale St. (525-3655), documents various aspects of music history, including a tribute to Memphis's WDIA—the nation's first all-black radio station where notables like B.B. King and Rufus Thomas began their musical careers as disc jockeys. (Open Mon.-Sat. 9am-5:30pm, Sun. 1pm-5:30pm; $2, seniors, students and kids under 12 $1.) The tiny **Sun Studio,** 706 Union Ave. (521-0664), is where Elvis, Jerry Lee Lewis, U2 and Bonnie Raitt first ventilated their vocal chords for producer Sam Phillips. (30-min. tours every hr. on the ½ hr. Open daily 9am-9pm. $4.50, kids $3.)

At the **Mississippi River Museum,** 125 N. Front St. (576-7241), you can experience history firsthand by strolling on the decks of an indoor steamboat, chilling to the blues in the Yellow Dog Café, or spying on a union ironclad gunboat from the lookout of a confederate bluff. Alongside the museum flow 1.2 million gallons of water through an amazing ½-mi.-long concrete sculpture of the river. In the summer, visitors can swim in the enormous pool that doubles as the Gulf of Mexico at the base of the sculpture. Also on **Mud Island** rests the renowned World War II B-17 **Memphis Belle.** Free tours of the Riverwalk and Memphis Belle Pavilion run several times daily. (Open daily May-Labor Day 10am-6pm. Entrance to the Island $1.)

A. Schwab, 163 Beale St. (523-9782), a five-and-dime store run by the same family since 1876, is still offering old-fashioned bargains. A "museum" of relics-never-sold gathers dust on the mezzanine floor, including an array of voodoo potions, elixirs, and powders. Elvis bought some of his flashier ensembles here. (Open Mon.-Sat. 9am-5pm. Free guided tours.) Next door on Beale St., the **Memphis Police Museum** (528-2370) summons visitors to gawk at 150 years of confiscated drugs, homemade weapons, and officer uniforms. (Open 24 hrs. Free.)

The **Lorraine Motel,** site of the assassination of Rev. Dr. Martin Luther King, Jr., today houses the **National Civil Rights Museum,** 450 Mulberry St. (521-9699). A 10-minute movie, candid photographs of lynching victims, and life-size exhibits vividly trace the progress of the Civil Rights Movement. Visitors can see rooms 306 and 307, where King's entourage stayed, preserved in their original condition. (Open Mon.-Sat. 10am-5pm, Sun. 1-5pm; $5, seniors and students with ID $4, children ages 6-12 $3. Free on Mon. 3-5pm.)

The Pink Palace Museum and Planetarium, 3050 Central Ave. (320-6320) details the natural history of the mid-South and expounds upon the development of Memphis. (Open Mon.-Sat. 9am-10pm, Sun. 9am-8pm; Admission $3.) On the corner of Central Ave. and Hollywood mirthfully stands the **Children's Museum** as an wonderfully fun afternoon option for kids. (Open Tues.-Sat. 10am-5pm, Sun. at 1pm; $4, ages 1-12 $3.)

Scheduled to open before 1992, **The Great American Pyramid** (800-627-9726) is not the latest game show but the latest extravaganza in Memphis. You won't be able to miss the 32-story-high, six-acre-wide shining pyramid that will hold the American Music Hall of Fame, the Memphis Music Experience, the College Football Hall of Fame, and a 20,000 seat arena. The whole experience will include daily music shows indoors and in outdoor parks. (Admission will be $25, kids $17.50.)

In the heart of downtown lies the luxurious **Peabody Hotel,** 149 Union St., the social center of Memphis society in the first half of this century. Folklore has it that the Mississippi Delta began in its lobby. Now the hotel keeps ducks in its indoor fountain; every day at 11am and 5pm the management rolls out the red carpet and the ducks waddle to and from the elevator with piano accompaniment. Get there early; sometimes ducks are impatient.

Leaving from 3rd and Beale St. and other spots around the city, the "Showboat" bus (722-7192) runs to the big midtown sights (6:20am-6:15pm, all-day ticket $2). A major sight is the **Victorian Village,** which consists of 18 mansions in various stages of restoration and preservation. The **Mallory-Neeley House,** 652 Adams St. (523-1484), one of the village's two mansions open to the public, went up in the mid-19th century. Most of its original furniture remains intact and there for visitors to see. (Open Tues.-Sat. 10am-4pm, Sun. 1-4pm. $4, seniors and students $3.) For a look at a different lifestyle during the same era, visit the **Magerney House,** 198 Adams St. (526-4464), that once held the clapboard cottage of Eugene Magerney, who helped establish Memphis's first public schools. (Open Tues.-Sat. 10am-4pm. Free. Reservations required.) French Victorian architecture and an extensive antique/textile collection live on in the **Woodruff-Fontaine House,** 680 Adams St. (Open Mon.-Sat. 10am-4pm, Sun. 1-4pm; $4, students $2.) The **Massey House,** 664 Adams St., stands as the oldest home on the block, with a doric-columned portico. (Open Mon.-Fri. noon-1pm. Free.)

Set in attractive Overton Park, the **Memphis Brooks Museum of Art** (722-3500) houses a mid-sized collection of Impressionist painting and 19th-century U.S. art. (Open Tues.-Sat. 10am-5pm, Sun. 11:30am-5pm. $4, seniors, students, and kids $2. Free Fri.) The **Memphis Zoo and Aquarium** (726-4775) squawks next door. (Open daily 9am-4:30pm. $5, seniors and kids $3. Free Mon. after 3:30pm.)

Memphis has almost as many parks as museums, each offering a slightly different natural setting. Brilliant wildflowers in April and a marvelous Heinz of roses (57 varieties) bloom and grow forever at the **Memphis Botanic Garden,** 750 Cherry Rd. in Audubon Park off Park Ave. (685-1566). Open Tues.-Sat. 9am-sunset, Sun. 11am-6pm; $2, children ages 6-17 $1.) Across the street, the **Dixon Garden and Galleries,** Park Ave. (761-2409) flaunts its manicured landscape. (Open Mon.-Sat. 10am-5pm,

Sun. 1pm-5pm; $4, students $3, ages 1-12 $1.) The **Lichterman Nature Center,** 5992 Quince St. off Perkins is a wildscape with virgin forests and wild, wild wildlife. A picnic area is available. (Open Tues.-Sat. 9:30am-5pm, Sun. 1-5pm; $3, students $2, ages 1-3 free).

Entertainment and Nightlife

The visitors center's *Key* magazine, the free *Memphis Flyer,* or the "Playbook" section of the Friday morning *Memphis Commercial Appeal* will give you an idea of what's goin' down 'round town. For more personalized social coordination, go to the **Sun Café,** 706 Union Ave. (521-0664), adjacent to the Sun Studios, for a tall, cool glass of lemonade ($1.75) and a talk with the young waiters and cashiers about what to do. Open June-Aug. daily 9am-9pm, Sept.-May daily 10am-6pm.

The absolutely most happening place is **Beale Street.** Blues waft nightly throughout the street, from **B. B. King's Blues Club,** 147 Beale (527-5464; open daily from noon till the show stops), where the club's namesake still makes appearances, to the **Rum Boogie Café,** 182 Beale (528-0150; open daily 11:30am-2am), to the street performers in the park. For pool, **Peoples** (523-7627) on Beale is open from noon until at least 1am, and charges $7.35 ($8.40 on weekends) for a table.

Off Beale St., the **Antenna Club,** 1588 Madison Ave. (725-9812), showcases hip progressive rock, and the **Babylon Café,** 1783 Union (278-6444), hosts live original alternative music. **Captain Bilbo's,** 263 Wagner Pl. (526-1966), is the place to be for live rock and pop, and the **Daily Planet,** 3439 Park (327-1270), throbulates with R&B.

The majestic **Orpheum Theater,** 89 Beale St. (525-7800), is a dignified movie palace, complete with 15-ft.-high Czechoslovakian chandeliers and an organ. The theater shows classic movies on weekends along with an organ prelude and a cartoon. Call for info on the current summer film series. The **Memphis Chicks,** 800 Home Run Lane (272-1687), near Libertyland, are a big hit with fans of Southern League baseball. ($4, box seats $5.)

Visitors who hit this part of the world at the beginning of the summer may also join the festivities of **Memphis in May** (525-4611), a month long celebration with concerts, art exhibits, food contests and sports events. Book hotel reservations early during this season.

Nashville

Named for long-forgotten Francis Nash, one of only four Revolutionary heroes to have an eponymously named large city (the others being Washington, Wayne and Knox), Nashville has been the capital of Tennessee since 1843. Despite its minor link with America's fight for independence, Nashville is better known for its country music than for its foothold in history. Banjo pickin' and foot stompin' have entrenched themselves securely in Tennessee's central city, providing Nashville with non-stop performances and the Country Music Hall of Fame. Behind this musical harmony resonates "the Wall Street of the South," a slick, choreographed financial hub. The city headquarters the Southern Baptists and higher morality alongside centers of the fine arts and higher learning at Fisk University and Vanderbilt. Nashville is a large, eclectic, unapologetically heterogeneous place. Old Mr. Nash, wherever he lies, must sure be proud.

Practical Information

Emergency: 911.

Visitor Information: Nashville Area Chamber of Commerce, 161 4th Ave. N. (259-4700), between Commerce and Church St. downtown. Ask for the *Hotel/Motel Guide,* the *Nashville Dining & Entertainment Guide,* and a *Calendar of Events.* Information booth in main lobby open Mon.-Fri. 8am-5pm. **Nashville Tourist Information Center,** I-65 at James Robertson Pkwy. exit 85 (259-4747), about ½-mi. east of the state capitol, just over the bridge. Take bus #3 ("Meridian") east on Broadway. Complete maps marked with all the attractions. (Open daily 8am-8pm.) *Spot-*

light on the Arts ($3.50) is available at the **Metro Arts Commission,** 111 4th Ave. S. (862-6720). (Open daily 8am-5:30pm)

Traveler's Aid: 780-9471. (Open Mon.-Fri. 8:30am-4pm.)

Metropolitan Airport: (275-1675) 8 mi. south of downtown. Airport shuttle $8 one way, taxis $15-17, MTA buses 75¢.

Greyhound: 200 8th Ave. S. (256-6141), at Demonbreun St., 2 blocks south of Broadway downtown. Borders on a rough and rowdy neighborhood. To: Memphis (9 per day, 4 hr., $35); Washington, DC (7 per day, 16 hr., $104); Atlanta (7 per day, 7½ hr., $36); Louisville (14 per day; 4 hr.; $25, Fri.-Sat. $41). Discounts for early reservations. Open 24 hrs.

Public Transport: Metropolitan Transit Authority (MTA) (242-4433). Buses operate Mon.-Fri. 5am-midnight, less frequent service Sat.-Sun. Fare 75¢, zone crossing or transfers 10¢. The **Nashville Trolley** (242-4433) runs daily in the downtown area every 10 min. for 75¢.

Taxi: Nashville Cab, 242-7070. 90¢ first mi., $1.50 each additional mi.

Bike Rental: Al's Bike Rentals, 124 2nd Ave. N. (244-3915). Mountain bikes, 10-speeds and beach cruises are $3.50 per hr. to rent.

Car Rental: Alamo Rent A Car, (800-327-9633). At the airport. $30 per day, weekends $20 per day. $6 per day extra for those under 25.

Help Lines: Crisis Line, 256-8526. **Rape Hotline,** 327-1110. **Handicapped Information,** 862-6492. **Gay and Lesbian Switchboard,** 297-0008.

Time Zone: Central (1 hr. behind Eastern).

Post Office: 901 Broadway (255-9447), across from the Park Plaza Hotel and next to Union Station downtown. Open Mon.-Fri. 8am-6pm, Sat. 8am-noon. **ZIP code:** 37202.

Area Code: 615.

The names of Nashville's streets are undeniably fickle. **Broadway,** the main east-west thoroughfare, becomes **West End Avenue** just outside downtown at I-40, and later becomes **Harding Road**. Downtown, numbered avenues run north-south, parallel to the Cumberland River. The curve of **James Robertson Parkway** encloses the north end, becoming **Main Street** on the other side of the river (later **Gallatin Pike**), and **McGavock Street** at the south end. If you ever find it, the area between 2nd and 7th Ave., south of Broadway, is unsafe at night.

Accommodations and Camping

Finding a room in Nashville is not difficult, just expensive. Most cheaper places are within 20 mi. of downtown. Make reservations well in advance, especially for weekend stays. A dense concentration of budget motels line W. Trinity Lane and Brick Church Pike at I-65, north of downtown. Even cheaper hotels inhabit the area around Dickerson Rd. and Murfreesboro, but the neighborhood is seedy at best. **Bed and Breakfast of Middle Tennessee** (297-0883) offers singles for $30, doubles for $50, kitchenettes and free continental breakfast.

Hallmark Inns (800-251-3294) is a local chain; its five inns in the Nashville area provide free continental breakfast and are generally cheaper than national chains. (Singles $20. Doubles $26)

The Cumberland Inn, I-65 North and Trinity Lane (226-1600), has cheerful rooms with bright, modern furnishings, unlimited local calls for $1, laundry facilities, and a free continental breakfast. But no pets, please. (Singles $28. Doubles $32. $4 more on weekends.)

Budget Host Inn, 10 Interestate Dr., exit off of Hwy 65. (244-6050 or 800-234-6779), across from the Tourist Information Center. Has a pool, cable TV, and big rooms. Convenient to downtown. ($25, on weekends up to $40)

Motel 6 three area locations. 311 W. Trinity Lane (227-9696), at exit 87B off I-24/I-65; 323 Cartwright St., Goodlettsville (859-9674), take the Long Hollow Pike west, off I-65, then turn right onto Cartwright; and 95 Wallace Rd. (333-9933), take exit 56 from I-24, go west on Harding Pl. one block, left at Traveler's Inn Lane, and left on Largo. Tidy rooms with dark curtains and free local calls. (Singles $20. $6 per additional person. 18 and under free with parents.)

Interstate Inn, 300 Interstate dr., exit 85 off I-65 (800-444-4401). Look beyond the tacky green and yellow exterior to pleasantly decorated rooms, recently renovated. Family owned and convenient to downtown. Grey Line Tours stops at the inn. Pool, cable TV. (Singles $24-28. Doubles $30-32; higher weekend rates.) You can reach three campgrounds near Opryland USA via public transport from 5th St. For the **Fiddler's Inn North Campground** (885-1440), the **Nashville Travel Park** (889-4225), and the **Two Rivers Campground** (883-8559), take the Briley Pkwy. north to McGavock Pike, and exit west onto Music Valley Dr. (Sites $17-$21 for 2 people with full hookup.) Ten minutes north of Opryland is the **Nashville KOA,** 708 N. Dickerson Rd. (859-0075), I-65 in Goodlettsville, exit 98. (Sites $22 with full hookup.)

Food

In Nashville music even influences the local delicacies. Pick up a Goo-Goo cluster, (peanuts and pecans, chocolate, caramel, and marshmallow) sold at practically any store and you'll bite into the initials of the Grand Ole Opry. Pecan pie is another favorite dessert, perfect after spicy barbecue or fried chicken. Restaurants for collegiate tastes and budgets cram West End Avenue and the 2000 block of Elliston Place, near Vanderbilt. The **farmers market,** north of the capitol between 3rd and 7th Ave., sells fresh fruits and vegetables until sunset.

Loveless Motel Restaurant, 8400 Hwy. 100 (646-9700). Accessible by car only; take 40W from downtown, left at exit 192, then left when you hit Hwy. 100; a 15-20 min. drive. True country-style cooking at its best and most stomach-fillin'. Famous for its preserves, fried chicken, and hickory-smoked ham. For a weighty Southern meal, try the homemade biscuits with red-eye gravy, a special blend of ham drippings and coffee ($3-8). Open Tues.-Sat. 8am-2pm and 5-9pm, Sun. 8am-9pm. Reservations on weekends recommended.

Slice of Life, 1811 Division, next to music studios (329-2526). Yuppie hangout featuring fresh bread and wholesome Tex-Mex. Veggie burritos $6, avocado, tomato and sprouts sandwich $4, carrot and celery juice $2. Try the bakery for giant cookies and muffins, $1. Open Mon.-Fri. 7am-9:30pm, Sat.-Sun. 8am-9:30pm. Favorable location for sighting country musicians.

SATCO, (San Antonio Taco Co.) 208 Commerce St. (259-4413), off Second Ave. Student hangout. Tasty Mexican food that will erect barricades in your arteries before you finish. Enchiladas $2-4, tacos $1-2. Children 10 and under eat free. Open Mon.-Sat. 11am-9pm.

International Market, 2010-B Belmont Blvd.(297-4453) Asian grocery with a large Thai buffet ($4-6). Egg rolls $1. Crowded for lunch. Open Mon.-Sat. 10:30am-9pm.

Rotiers, 2413 Elliston Place (327-9892). Greasy spoon without the grease. Sandwiches and specials ($3-5). Open Mon.-Sat. 9am-10:30pm.

Sights

Music Row, home of Nashville's signature industry, fiddles around Division and Demonbreun St. from 16th to 19th Ave. S., bounded on the south by Grand Ave. (Take bus #3 to 17th Ave. and walk south.) After surviving the mobs outside the **Country Music Hall of Fame,** 4 Music Sq. E. (256-1639) at Division St., you can marvel at Elvis' "solid gold" Cadillac, his 24-kt gold piano, and other coveted country music memorabilia like original handwritten manuscripts of famous country and Western songs. (Open Mon.-Thurs. 9am-5pm, Fri.-Sat. 8am-6pm.) Included in the admission is a tour of RCA's historic **Studio B,** where stars like Dolly Parton and Chet Atkins recorded their first hits. (Open June-Sept. daily 8am-7pm, Sept.-May 9am-5pm. $6.50, ages 6-11 $1.75, under 6 free.) When you want to record your own hit, the **Recording Studio of America,** 1510 Division St. (254-1282), underneath the **Barbara Mandrell Country Museum,** lets you karaoke your own vocals on pre-recorded, high-quality 24-track backgrounds to popular country and pop tunes. Choose a set and make a video, too. (Audio $13, video $20. Open June-Aug. daily 8am-8pm; Sept.-May daily 9am-5pm.) For a taste of southern extravagance, marvel at Webb Pierce's Silver Dollar car (adorned with 150 silver dollars in the upoholstry and a pistol as a hood ornament) at **World Famous Car Collectors' Hall of Fame,** 1534 Demonbreun St. (255-6804). (Open Mon-Thurs. 8am-8pm, Fri.-Sun. 8am-9pm. $5, children ages 6-11 $3.25.)

A 15-minute walk west from Music Row along West End Ave. to **Centennial Park** (entrance on West End Ave.) will soon explain why Nashville calls itself the "Athens of the South." In the park stands a full scale replica of the **Parthenon** (259-6358). Originally built as a temporary exhibit for the Tennessee Centennial in 1897, the Parthenon met with such olympian success that the model was rebuilt to last. A 42-ft. grey-eyed **Athena,** goddess of wisdom with nostrils big enough to snort a watermelon, muses sagely in her intimidating hugeness. This statue is the largest indoor sculpture in the Western Hemisphere. The Nashville Parthenon also houses the Cowan Collection of American Paintings in the basement galleries. Watch Greek theater performed on the steps in mid-July and August. (Open Tues.-Sat. 9am-4:30pm, Sun. 1-5pm. $2.50, kids and seniors $1.25, under 4 free.) The park area also includes the **Upper Room Chapel and Museum,** 1908 Grand St. off 21st Ave. S. (340-7200). The floor to ceiling stained glass window with over 9000 pieces of glass is spectacular. (Open Mon.-Sat. 8am-4:30pm.)

A walk through the downtown area reveals more of Nashville's eclectic architecture. The **Union Station Hotel,** at 1001 Broadway, displays a full stained glass arched ceiling and evokes the glamour of turn-of-the-century railroad travel. The **Ryman Auditorium,** 116 5th Ave. N. (254-1445), off Broadway at 5th, is better known as the "Mother Church of Country Music." In previous incarnations, it has housed a tabernacle and the Grand Ole Opry. (Guided tours daily 8:30am-4:30pm. $2.50, ages 6-12 $1.) Turn up 2nd Ave. from Broadway to study the cast-iron and masonry facades of the handsome commercial buildings from the 1870s and 1880s. Now known as **Market Street,** many of these buildings have been gentrified into restaurants and nightspots.

The **Tennessee State Capitol,** Charlotte Ave. (741-0830) is the comely Greek Revival structure atop the hill next to downtown, offering free guided tours of, among other things, the tomb of James Knox Polk. (Open Mon.-Fri. 9am-4pm, Sat. 10am-5pm, Sun. 1-5pm.) Across the street is the **Tennessee State Museum,** 505 Deaderick (741-2692). (Open Mon.-Sat. 10am-5pm, Sun. 1-5pm. Free.)

If you tire of the downtown area, rest at the **Cheekwood Botanical Gardens and Fine Arts Center,** Forest Park Dr. (356-8000), seven mi. southwest of town. The well-kept, leisurely, Japanese rose and English-style gardens are a welcome change from Nashville glitz. Take bus #3 ("West End/Belle Meade") from downtown to Belle Meade Blvd. and Page Rd. (Open Mon.-Sat. 9am-5pm, Sun. 1-5pm. $4, seniors and college students $2, ages 7-17 $1). Dubbed "The Queen of Tennessee Plantations," the nearby **Belle Meade Mansion,** 5025 Harding Ave. (356-0501) displays Southern antebellum opulence and charm at the site of the nation's first thoroughbred breeding farm. (2 wonderful tours per hr. led by guides in period costumes; last tour at 4pm. Open Mon.-Sat. 9am-5pm, Sun. 1-5pm. $5, ages 13-18 $3.50, 6-12 $2.)

Thirteen mi. east of town is the **Hermitage,** 4580 Rachel's Lane (889-2941); take exit 221 off I-40. Andrew Jackson, the 7th U.S. president and a popular populist, built his beautiful manor house atop 625 gloriously shaded acres. The grounds make an ideal spot for a picnic. Beware the crowded summer months. (Open daily 9am-5pm. $7, seniors $6.50, ages 6-13 $3.50.)

Fisk University's **Van Vechten Gallery,** Corner of Jackson St. and D.B. Todd Blvd. off Jefferson St. (gallery entrance does not face street) (329-8543), exhibits a distinguished collection of U.S. art. The gallery owns a portion of the Alfred Steiglitz Collection, donated to Fisk by Georgia O'Keefe, Steiglitz's widow. Other exhibits feature O'Keefe's work and a range of photography and African art. (Open Tues.-Fri. 10am-5pm, Sat.-Sun. 1-5pm. $3.50, elementary and high school students free.)

A few blocks away down 4th Ave., the city cemetery rests in peace. The distinguished deceased denizens of this pastoral seclusion include Nashville's founder Gen. James Robertson and many notables of Tennessee history. (Free.)

To learn more about one of the South's most lucrative products, visit the **Museum of Tobacco Art and History** 800 Harrison St. off 8th Ave. (271-2349). From the dual-purpose Indian pipe/tomahawk (a slow and a quick way to death) to the giant glass-blown pipes, museum exhibits expound upon the unexpectedly captivating history of tobacco, pipes and cigars. (open Tues.-Sat. 10am-4pm. Free.)

Entertainment

Nashville offers a dazzling array of inexpensive nightspots. Many feature the country tunes for which the town is known, while others cater to jazz, rock, bluegrass, or folk tastes. There are entertainment listings in the *Tennessean* Friday and Sunday, and in the *Nashville Banner* Thursday afternoon. The Nashville *Key,* available at the chamber of commerce, opens many entertainment doors. Comprehensive listings for all live music and events in the area abound in free copies of *Nashville Scene* or *Metro* around town. Muse over these publications plus many more at **Moskós,** 2204-B Elliston Place (327-2658), while stalling at their tasty muncheonette. (Open daily 7am-midnight.) Or stop in at the trendy **Botanical Café,** 124 2nd Ave. N. (244-3915), for listings of events and fresh muffins for $1. (Open Mon.-Thurs. 7am-10pm, Fri. 7am-midnight, Sat. 8am-midnight, Sun. 8am-7pm.)

Opryland USA (889-6611) cross-pollinates between Las Vegas schmaltz and Disneyland purity, or vice versa, with the best in country music thrown in. This amusement park contains all the requisite family attractions, from roller coasters to cotton candy, and it stages a dozen live music shows daily. Sometimes, a soundtrack of piped-in country music cascades through the park. Tune your radio to 580AM for more info. (Open late March-late April and early Oct.-early Nov. Sat.-Sun.; early May-late May and early Sept.-late Sept. Fri.-Sun.; late May-early Sept. daily. $22, 2 days $33. Concert series $5.) The **Grand Ole Opry,** setting for America's longest-running radio show, moved here from the town center in 1976. *The* place to hear country music, the Opry howls every Friday and Saturday night ($12-14). 3pm matinees are added on various days during peak tourist season (April-Oct., $9.75-$12). Reserve tickets from Grand Ole Opry, 2808 Opryland Dr., Nashville 37214 (615-889-3060). General admission tickets can also be purchased at the box office, starting at 9am on Tuesday for weekend shows. Check the Friday morning *Tennessean* for a list of performers.

Many stars got their start at **Tootsie's Orchid Lounge,** 422 Broadway (726-3739), which still has good C&W music and affordable drinks. For years owner Tootsie Bess lent money to struggling musicians until they could get on the Ole Opry. (Open Mon.-Sat. 9:30am-3am, Sun. noon-3am.) The more genteel **Blue Bird Café,** 4104 Hillsboro Rd. (383-1461), in Green Hills, plays blues, folk, soft rock, and a smidgen of jazz. Women traveling solo probably will feel safer in this mellow, clean-cut establishment. Dinner, served until 11pm, consists of salads and sandwiches ($4-6.50). Music begins at 9:30pm. Go west on Broadway, then south on 21st, which becomes Hillsboro Rd. (Open Mon.-Sat. 5:30pm-1am, Sun. 8pm-midnight. Cover $4-5.) The **Station Inn,** 402 12th Ave. S. (255-3307), blues some serious grass. (Open Tues.-Sat. 7pm-until. Music starts at 9pm. Cover $4-6. Free Sun. night jam session.) West of downtown, the **Bluegrass Inn,** 1914 Broadway (244-8877), has beer, chips, and music with a cinderblock-and-cement motif. A good-natured sort of place, the cover (around $3) depends on who's pickin'. (Open Wed.-Thurs. 9pm-midnight, Fri.-Sat. 9pm-1am.)

There's more to entertainment in Nashville than country music; just visit during the first weekend in June for the outdoor **Summer Lights** (259-6374) downtown, when top rock, jazz, reggae, classical, and, of course, country performers all jam simultaneously. (Open Mon.-Thurs. 4pm-12:30am.) For information on **Nashville Symphony** tickets and performances, call Ticketmaster at 741-2787. Rock bands play to a college audience at the **Exit/In,** 2208 Elliston Place (321-4400), near the Vanderbilt campus. (Bands start around 10:30pm. Cover about $4.) In a huge downtown warehouse, **Ace of Clubs,** 114 2nd S. (254-2237), packs 'em in for grand ol' rock 'n' roll. (Open daily. Music around 9pm. Cover $4-7.) **The World's End,** 1709-11 Church St. (329-3480), is a popular gay restaurant and dance club with a huge video screen.

Virginia

Virginians are usually *obviously* Virginians because they'll announce that fact long before you ask them. They're proud of their state. Through the trials and turmoils of its history, "Old Dominion" has retained a deeply-rooted equilibrium and understated confidence. The colonization of British North America began here with the Jamestown colony in 1607. Thirteen years later, the New World's first African slaves set foot on Virginia's shores. Williamsburg burgeoned with the influx of plantation labor and made its fortune on tobacco. Nostalgia for this era swells in Colonial Williamsburg, where guides in costume show tourists around the restored 18th-century capital. Generations later, after continued enslavement of African Americans turned into a political wedge between North and South, secessionists built their capitol in Richmond. Much of the state is rolling farmland, with tobacco still a major crop. But Virginia ain't just whistlin' *Dixie* these days. Charlottesville, Lexington, and Williamsburg are home to some of the finest schools in the nation. The world's most sophisticated military technology docks in Norfolk and checks in with the Pentagon in Arlington. This state with a past also has a future.

Practical Information

Capital: Richmond.

Visitor Information: Virginia Division of Tourism, Bell Tower, Capitol Sq., 101 N. 9th St., Richmond 23219 (800-847-4882 or 786-4484). **Division of State Parks,** 1201 State Office Bldg., Richmond 23219 (226-1981). For the free **Virginia Accommodations Directory,** write to Virginia Travel Council, 7415 Brook Rd., P.O. Box 15067, Richmond 23227.

Time Zone: Eastern.

Postal Abbreviation: VA

Sales Tax: 4.5%.

Charlottesville

This college town in the Blue Ridge foothills proudly bears the stamp of its patron, Thomas Jefferson. The college he founded, the University of Virginia, dominates the town economically, geographically, and culturally, supporting a community of writers such as Peter Taylor and Pulitzer Prize-winning poet Rita Dove—not to mention a community of pubs. Visitors are steered to Monticello, the cleverly constructed classical mansion Jefferson designed. Even C-ville's friendly, hip, and down-to-earth populace seems to embody the third U.S. President's dream of a well-informed, culturally aware citizenry who choose to live close to the land.

Practical Information and Orientation

Emergency: 911. **Campus Police:** dial 4-1766 on a UVA campus phone.

Visitor Information: Chamber of Commerce, 415 E. Market St. (295-3141), within walking distance of Amtrak, Greyhound, and historic downtown. Open Mon.-Fri. 9am-5pm. **Charlottesville/Abermarle Convention and Visitors Bureau,** P.O. Box 161, Rte. 20 near I-64 (977-1783). Take bus #8 ("Piedmont Community College") from 5th and Market St. Same info as Chamber of Commerce: brochures and maps. Combo tickets to Monticello, Michie Tavern, and Ash Lawn-Highland ($16; seniors and kids $14.50). Open daily 9:30am-5:30pm.

University of Virginia Info Center, at the rotunda in the center of campus (924-1019). Some brochures, a university map, and info on tours. Open daily 9am-10pm. Students answer questions in **Newcomb Hall** (no phone). Open daily 9am-10pm. The larger **University Center** (924-7166) is off U.S. 250 west—follow the signs. Transport schedules, entertainment guides, and hints on budget accommodations. Answers phone "Campus Police." Campus maps. Open 24 hrs.

Amtrak: 810 W. Main St. (800-872-7245 or 296-4559), 7 blocks from downtown. To Washington, DC ($22; 3 hrs.; make reservations as far as possible in advance) and New York ($81; 7-8 hrs.).

Greyhound: 310 W. Main St. (295-5131), within 3 blocks of historic downtown. To: Richmond ($11.50; 1½ hrs.), Washington, DC ($20.50; 3 hrs.) Norfolk ($30; 4 hrs.), and Lynchburg ($12.50; 1½ hrs.).

Public Transport: Charlottesville Transit Service (296-7433). Bus service within city limits, including most hotels and UVA campus locations. Maps available at both info centers, Chamber of Commerce, and the UVA student center in Newcomb Hall. Buses operate Mon.-Sat. 6:20am-7pm. Fare 60¢, seniors and disabled 30¢, under 6 free. The more frequent blue **University of Virginia** buses require UVA ID or an expensive long-term pass to board.

Taxi: Yellow Cab, 295-4131. To Monticello $12.

Help Lines: Region 10 Community Services Hotline, 972-1800. **Lesbian and Gay Hotline,** 971-4942. UVA-affiliated.

Post Office: 1155 Seminole Trail (U.S. 29). Open Mon.-Fri. 8am-5:30pm, Sat. 8am-2pm. **ZIP code:** 22906.

Area Code: 804.

Charlottesville streets number east to west, using compass directions; 5th St. N.W. is 10 blocks from (and parallel to) 5th St N.E. Streets running east-west across the numbered streets are neither parallel nor logically named. C-ville has two downtowns: one on the west side near the university called **The Corner,** and **Historic Downtown** about a mile east. The two are connected by **University Avenue,** running east-west, which becomes **Main Street** after the Corner ends at a bridge.

Accommodations and Camping

Budget Inn, 140 Emmet St. (U.S. 29) (293-5141), near the university. 40 comfortable, hotel-quality rooms. TV, A/C, private baths. Senior discounts. Doubles $32-35 (1 bed) or $40-45 (2 beds). Each additional person $5.

Charlottesville KOA Kampground, P.O. Box 144, C-Ville, VA 22901 (296-9881 for info, 336-9881 for reservations). All campsites are shaded. Recreation hall with video games, a pavilion, and a pool (open Mon.-Sat. 10am-8pm). Fishing (not wading or swimming) allowed. Check-in after 1pm, check-out before noon. Sites $16, hook-up $18. Camping season is March 15-Nov. 15.

Food and Nightlife

The Corner neighborhood near UVA has bookstores and countless cheap eats, with good Southern grub in C-ville's unpretentious diners. The town loves jazz, likes rock 'n' roll, and has quite a few pubs. Around the Downtown Mall, ubiquitous posters and the free *Charlottesville Review* can tell you who plays where and when (if not why).

The Hardware Store, 316 Main St. (977-1518), near the middle of the outdoor "mall." Bar atmosphere, but slightly off the beaten track: beers served in glass boots, appetizers in microcosmic basketball courts, and condiments in toolboxes. Collectors will drool over the 1898 building's antique collection. American grille and an eclectic set of entrées, from *ratatouille gratinée* ($5) to *crêpes* both sweet ($1.50-4) and savory ($4-6). Sandwiches ($3-7). Quality desserts. Open Mon. 10am-5pm, Tues.-Thurs. 10am-9pm, Fri.-Sat. 10am-11pm.

Garden Gourmet, 811 West Main St. (295-9991). Northern California circa 1967, with vegetarians, hippies, and "peacenluv." Homemade 7-grain bread, salad dressings, and creative veggie plates. Wooden booths accompany artwork by the owner's family and staff. Nightly folk music. Open Mon.-Fri. 11:30am-2:30pm; Sat. noon-3pm, Mon.-Thurs. 5:30-9pm, Fri.-Sat. 5:30-10pm.

Macado's (MAC-ah-dooz), 1505 University Ave. (971-3558). Great sandwiches (around $4), home-made desserts, and long hours cure the late-night munchies. Pinball machine and candy store. Upstairs is a rockin' bar where Edgar Allen Poe once lived. Listen for the throbulating beat of the tell-tale heart. Open daily 11am-2am.

The Howlin' Pig at Zipper's, 1202 W. Main St. (295-7060). Used to be just a bar, now it's a Southern-style barbecue. Look for the black-and-white checkered tables out front. Pulled pork or pulled chicken sandwich ($3.50). Open daily 5pm-11pm.

The Tavern, 1140 Emmet St. (295-0404). A breakfast Eden; its banana-nut, bacon, or fruit-filled homemade pancakes ($3.50) are enormous. UVA jocks buy their kegs here. Open daily 7am-3pm.

Sights and Entertainment

Most activity on the spacious **University of Virginia** campus clusters around the **Lawn** and down fraternity-lined **Rugby Road.** Jefferson watched the University being built through his telescope at Monticello. You can return the gaze with a glimpse of Monticello from the Lawn, a terraced green carpet which unrolls down the middle of the university. During the year, students study and play here. Professors live in the Lawn's pavilions; Jefferson designed each one in a different architectural style. Lawn tours, led by students, leave on the hour at the Rotunda from 10am to 4pm; self-guided tour maps are provided for those who prefer to find their own way. **The Rotunda** is a target for pranks; students once adorned it with the inevitable cow. The **Old Cabell Building** across the Lawn from the Rotunda houses an auditorium with impressive acoustics. On its wall, a reproduction of Raphael's mural *The School of Athens* echoes Jefferson's vision of student-faculty harmony. The **Bayley Art Museum,** Rugby Rd. (924-3592), features visiting exhibits and a small permanent collection including one of Rodin's castings of *The Kiss.* (Open Tues.-Sat. 1-5pm.)

The **Downtown Mall** is a brick thoroughfare lined with restaurants and shops catering to a diverse crowd. A kiosk near the fountain in the center of the mall has posters on club schedules. At 110 D-Mall, **The Movie Palace** shows current flicks for only $2. Other hip eateries, bars, and specialty stores provide places to treat your nose and tongue.

Jefferson's classical design for his home, **Monticello** (295-8181), derives from the 16th-century Italian architect Andrea Palladio. Jefferson oversaw every stage of design and construction, collecting gadgets for the inside on his travels, including a compass which registers wind direction through a weathervane on the roof. There's nary a non-picturesque spot on Monticello's landscape; from the west lawn, a roundabout floral walk leads to a magnificent hillside view. The garden lets you see **Montalto,** the "high mountain" on which Jefferson wanted to build an observation tower. Tours of Monticello begin every five minutes during the day, but the wait can be as long as 90 minutes during summer Saturdays. Because of the heat and lack of seating areas, come early. (Open daily 8am-5pm; Nov.-Feb. 9am-4:30pm; tickets $7, seniors $6, under 5 $3.)

Minutes away (take a right turn to Rte. 795) is **Ashlawn** (293-9539), the 500-acre former plantation home of one of those presidents who followed Jefferson. More quaint and less imposing than Monticello, Ashlawn has outdoor views to rival its domed neighbor's. The current owner, the College of William and Mary, has turned Ashlawn into a museum honoring its former owner, James Monroe. A colorful, dainty garden lines the pathway to the house, where a docent spews facts about President Monroe. Ashlawn's peacocks stroll the gardens and lawn while making curious noises. (Open daily 9am-6pm; Nov.-Feb. daily 10am-5pm; tour $6, seniors $5.50, under 5 $2.)

In the **Box Gardens** behind Ashlawn, English-language opera highlights the **Summer Festival of the Arts** (box office 293-4500, open Tues.-Sun. 10am-5pm; tickets $14, seniors $13, students $10, plus $1 on Sat.). A 45-minute intermission allows for a picnic supper, which you can order from **Festive Fare** (296-5496) for $8. Ashlawn also hosts **Music at Twilight** (tickets $9, seniors $8, students $6), including New Orleans jazz, Cajun music, blues and swing. Combo tickets for the performance, house tour, and picnic supper are available ($22).

Down the road from Monticello on Rte. 53 is **Michie** (Mick-ee) **Tavern** (977-1234), with an operating grist mill, a general store, and a tour of the 200-year-old establishment (open daily 9am-5pm; $5, seniors $4.50, under 5 $1). Jefferson's daughter supposedly fled the tavern after improperly teaching a waltz to a man in the ballroom. **The Ordinary** (977-1235), located in the tavern, serves up a fixed buffet of fried chicken, beans, cornbread, and other dishes ($9, ages 6-11 $3). Eat outside in good weather. (Open 11:15am-3:30pm.) To see all of the above three sites at a discount price, purchase the President's Pass at the **Thomas Jefferson Visitors Center** on Rte. 20.

Richmond

The former capital of the Confederate States of America, Richmond keeps its face towards its Civil War past, with numerous museums and restored houses showing everything from troop movements to tablecloths belonging to Confederate President Jefferson Davis. But in districts like the sprawling, beautiful Fan and formerly industrial Shockoe Bottom, another Richmond rears a coiffed and powdered head with a relaxed and cultural savvy.

Practical Information and Orientation

Emergency: 911.

Visitor Information: Richmond Visitors Center, 1700 Robin Hood Rd. (358-5511), exit 14 off I-95/64, in a converted train depot. Helpful 6-min. video introduces the city's attractions. Walking tours and quality maps. Open Memorial Day-Labor Day daily 9am-7pm; off-season 9am-5pm. Brochure-only branch office at 301 E. Main St. downtown.

Trains: Amtrak, far away at 7519 Staple Mills Rd. (264-9194 or 800-872-7245). To: Washington, DC ($21; 2 hrs.); Williamsburg ($9; 11/4 hrs.); Virginia Beach ($18; 3 hrs., the last third of the trip is on a shuttle); New York City ($78; 7 hrs.); Baltimore ($28; 3 hrs.) ;and Philadelphia ($45; 43/4 hrs.). Taxi fare to downtown $12. Open 24 hrs.

Buses: Greyhound: 2910 N. Boulevard (353-8903). To get downtown, walk 2 blocks to the visitors center or take GRTC bus #24 north. To: Washington, DC ($18; 2½ hrs.); Charlottesville ($12; 1½ hrs.); Williamsburg ($9; 1 hr.); and Norfolk, VA ($18; 3 hrs.).

Public Transport: Greater Richmond Transit Co., 101 S. Davis St. (358-4782). Maps available in the basement of city hall, 900 E. Broad St., and in the Yellow Pages. Fare 75¢ (exact change required), transfers 10-50¢. Buses serve most of Richmond infrequently, downtown frequently; most leave from Broad St. downtown. Bus #24 goes south to Broad St. and downtown. Free trolleys provide dependable, if limited, service to downtown and Shockoe Slip 10am-4pm daily, with an extended Shockoe Slip schedule from 5pm-midnight.

Help Lines: Traveler's Aid, 648-1767. **Rape Crisis Hotline,** 643-0888. **Gay Hotline,** 353-3626.

Post Office: 10th and Main St. (783-0825). Open Mon.-Fri. 7:30am-5pm. **ZIP code:** 23219.

Area Code: 804.

Creative locals describe Richmond's urban area as a closed ladies' fan placed east to west: the center is the **state capitol,** the short handle to the east is **Court End** and **Shockoe Bottom,** and the long western blade begins downtown and cleverly becomes the **Fan** neighborhood. Streets form a grid, but are illogically named, save for First (west) through 14th (east) St. downtown. Both I-95, leading north to Washington, DC, and I-295 encircle the urban area.

Accommodations and Camping

Budget motels around Richmond cluster along **Williamsburg Rd.,** on the edge of town, and along **Midlothian Turnpike,** south of the James River; public transport (see Practical Information) to these areas is infrequent at best. As usual, the farther away from downtown you stay, the less you have to pay. The visitors center (see Practical Information above) can reserve accommodations, sometimes at substantial ($10-20) discounts.

Massad House Hotel, 11 N. 4th St. (648-2893), 4 blocks from the capitol, nearer town. Shuttles guests via a 1940s elevator to charming rooms with shower and TV. Only inexpensive rooms downtown; in summer call at least a week ahead. Singles $33. Doubles $40.

Executive Inn, 5215 W. Broad St. (288-4011 or 800-542-2801), 3 mi. from center of town; take Bus #6. Offers grand (by motel standards) but slightly faded rooms and a pool. Free breakfast with 2 eggs, toast, juice. Pool and health club. Singles $41. Doubles $45-48.

Motel 6, 5704 Williamsburg Rd., Sandston (222-7600), about 6 mi. east on U.S. 60, across from the airport. Get there by the #7 ("Seven Pines") bus. Sparse but clean rooms. Singles $27. Doubles $33.

The closest **campground, Pocahontas State Park,** 10300 Beach Rd. (796-4255), 10 mi. south on Rte. 10 and Rte. 655, offers showers, biking, boating, lakes, and a huge pool. (Sites $8.50. No hookups. Pool admission $2, ages 3-12 $1.50.) Reserving a site by phone through Ticketron (490-3939) costs an extra $4.50 to $6.

Food and Entertainment

Richmond's good budget restaurants hide among the shade trees and well-kept porches of the gentrified Fan district, formed by the bordering streets Monument Ave., Main St., Laurel St. and Boulevard.

The Commercial Café, 111 N. Robinson St. (353-7110), serves the best barbecue in this barbecue-rich town. Sandwiches start at $5, but real eaters will order the ribs—the "Taster" ($7) is quite filling, and the plates ($9-14) can be shared. (Open daily 5-11pm; in summer Tues.-Sun. 5pm-11pm.)

Texas-Wisconsin Border Café, 1501 W. Main St. (355-2907), features chili, potato pancakes, and *chalupas.* Look for the bar's signs: "Dixie Inn," "Secede," and "Eat Cheese or Die." At night the café secedes to become a popular bar. Lunches $4-6. Dinners $6-10. Open daily 11am-2am.

Piccola's, at the corner of W. Main St. and Harrison (355-3111), orchestrates cheap, delicious and piping-hot pizza, calzones ($3.15), and jumbo sandwiches ($3.25-4.50). Students rave about the cheap and delicious pizza. Open Mon.-Thurs. 11am-midnight, Fri.-Sat. 11am-2am, and Sun. 3pm-midnight.

Helen's Inn, 2527 W. Main St. (354-9659), has inexpensive, standard-fare burgers ($1.49) that have launched a thousand ships and subs ($3-5). Open Mon.-Fri. 11am-6pm, Sat. 11am-5pm.

3rd St. Diner, at the corner of 3rd and Main (788-4750), has prices frozen from days of yore. The $2 meatless breakfast (two eggs, biscuit or toast, and home fries, grits, or Virginia fried apples) is served all day. The waitresses know all the regulars by name. Open Tues.-Sat. 24 hrs., Mon. closed from 2am-7am.

The **Shockoe Slip** district from Main, Canal, and Cary St. between 10th and 14th St. features fancy shops in restored and newly painted warehouses, but few bargains. At the **farmers market,** outdoors at N. 17th and E. Main St., pick up fresh fruit, vegetables, meat, and maybe even a pot swine. Free concerts abound here in the summer; check *Style Weekly,* a free magazine available at the visitors center.

Nightlife crowds Shockoe Slip and sprinkles itself in a less hectic manner throughout the Fan. The **Tobacco Company Club,** 1201 E. Cary St. (782-9555), smokes with top 40 music and no cover charge. (Open Tues.-Sat. 8pm-2am.) **Matt's British Pub and Comedy Club,** at 1045 12th St. (643-5653) next door, lives up to its name with stand-up comedy at 8 and 11pm. (Open Tues.-Sat. 8pm-2am.) **The Metro,** 727 W. Broad St. (649-4952), features local progressive bands most nights. **Flood Zone,** 11 S. 18th St. (643-6006), south of Shockoe Slip, offers a combination of big-name and off-beat comedy acts. (Ticket office open Tues.-Fri. 10am-6pm. Tickets $6-20, depending upon the show.)

Sights

Ever since Patrick Henry declared "Give me liberty or give me death" in Richmond's **St. John's Church,** 2401 E. Broad St. (648-5015), this river city has been quoting, memorializing, and bronzing its historical heroes. On Sundays in summer at 2pm, an actor recreates the famous 1775 speech. You must take a tour to see the church. (Tours given Mon.-Sat. 10am-3:30pm, Sun. 1-3:30pm; admission $2, students $1.) Larger-than-life statues of George Washington and Thomas Jefferson grace the **State Capitol** grounds (786-4344). Jefferson modeled this masterpiece of neo-classical architecture after a Roman temple in France. (Open daily 9am-5pm.) For more sculpture, follow Franklin Ave. from the capitol until it becomes **Monument Avenue,** lined with trees, gracious old houses, and towering statues of Confederate heroes. Robert E. Lee, who survived the Civil War, faces his beloved South; Stonewall Jackson, who didn't, scowls at the Yankees.

The **Court End** district stretches north and east of the capitol to Clay and College Streets and guards Richmond's most distinctive historical sights. The **Confederate Museum,** 1202 E. Clay St. (649-1861), is the world's largest Confederate artifact collection. The main floor leads visitors through the military history of the Civil War; the basement displays guns and flags of the Confederacy; and the top floor houses temporary exhibits on such topics as African-American life in the antebellum South. The museum also runs one-hour tours through the **White House of the Confederacy** next door (ask at the museum desk). Statues of Tragedy, Comedy, and Irony grace the White House's front door; decide for yourself which applies. (Open daily 10am-5pm; tours Mon., Wed., and Fri.-Sat. 10:30am-4:30pm, Tues. and Thurs. 11:30am-4:30pm, Sun. 1:15-4:30pm. Admission to museum or tour $4, students $2.50, under 13 $2.25; for both: $7, $5, $3.50.)

The **Valentine Museum,** 1015 Clay St. (649-0711), enamors visitors with exhibits on local and Southern social and cultural history. Tours through the museum are self-guided, but the admission price includes a tour of the recently renovated **Wickham-Valentine House** next door. (Open Mon.-Sat. 10am-5pm, Sun. noon-5pm. Admission $3.50, seniors $3, students $2.75, ages 7-12 $1.50.) Combination tickets to the Confederate Museum, White House of the Confederacy, Valentine Museum, and **John Marshall House**-all within easy walking distance of each other—are $9, seniors and students $8.50, under 13 $4.

East of the capitol, follow your tell-tale heart to the **Edgar Allan Poe Museum,** 1914 16 E. Main St. (648-5523). Poe memorabilia stuffs the five buildings, including the **Stone House,** the oldest standing structure within the original city boundaries. (Open Tues.-Sat. 10am-4pm, Sun.-Mon. 1:30-4pm. Admission $5, students $3.)

Four blocks from the intersection of Monument Ave. and N. Boulevard stands the Southeast's largest art museum, the **Virginia Museum of Fine Arts,** 2800 Grove Ave. (367-0844). An outstanding art gallery, the museum also holds a gorgeous collection of Fabergé jewelry and Easter eggs made for Russian czars (the largest outside the CIS—the former USSR), a fine showing of U.S. contemporary art (including a Jane Shaw piece), and what might just be the largest collection of horse sculpture and painting in North America. (Open Tues.-Sat. 11am-5pm, Thurs. 11am-8pm in the North Wing Galleries, Sun. 1-5pm. Donation requested.)

The Maggie L. Walker National Historic Site, 110 ½ E. Leigh St. (780-1380), commemorates the life of an ex-slave's gifted daughter. Physically disabled, Walker advocated black women's rights and succeeded as founder and president of a bank. (House tours Wed.-Sun. 9am-5pm. Free.) The first floor of the **Black History Museum and Cultural Center of Virginia,** 00 Clay St. (780-9093), opened in the summer of 1991; the second floor opened in 1992. (Open Mon.-Fri. 9am-4pm, but call first to verify. Free.)

All of the above sites and much, much more can be seen from the **Cultural Link Trolley** (358-5511). Linking 34 of the capitol's most fascinating cultural and historical landmarks, the trolleys run from 10am to 5pm on Saturday and from noon to 5pm on Sunday ($5). All **walking tours** are organized by the Historic Richmond Foundation. There are three main tours: **Old Richmond Today** ($15, kids $12), **Civil War Battlefields** ($20, kids $10; only on Sun.), and the **Civil War City,** (April-Oct. Mon.-Sat.; $18, kids $14). Call 780-0107 for reservations and departure times or 643-7407 for more info.

Two architectural highlights are the opulent,art-deco **Jefferson Hotel,** at Franklin and Adams St. (788-8000), and the **Byrd Theatre,** 2908 W. Cary St. (353-9911), where you can view Hollywood's latest in extraordinary style: marble balconies, enormous stained-glass windows, and a Wurlitzer Organ that rises from the floor to entertain before each show.

Civil War buffs should brave the trip to the city's boundaries to the **Richmond National Battlefield Park,** 3215 E. Broad St. (226-1981). The **Chimborazo Visitors Center,** located in a former Civil War hospital, contains an educational film and exhibits about the Civil War, as well as maps detailing the battlefields and fortifications surrounding the city. (Open daily 9am-5pm. Free.)

Shenandoah National Park

Before 1926, when Congress authorized the establishment of **Shenandoah National Park,** the area held a series of rocky, threadbare farms along the Blue Ridge Mountains. Congress ordered the planning of the park but (in true bureaucratic largesse) offered no monetary incentive. So, to pick up the government's fiscal slack, the state of Virginia appropriated over $1 million, and the citizens donated the rest. Thirteen years later, the farmers and their families had been uprooted and the area was returned to its "natural state." Forests replaced fields, wild deer and bears supplanted cows and pigs, and a two-lane highway was paved over the dirt roads along the ridge.

Today, gawking comes naturally in Shenandoah; on clear days drivers and hikers can look out over miles of unspoiled ridges and treetops. In summer, the cool mountain air offers a respite from Virginia's typical heat and humidity. Go early in June to see mountain laurel blooming in the highlands. In fall, Skyline Drive and its lodges are choked with tourists who come to enjoy the magnificent fall foliage.

Practical Information and Orientation

Emergency (in park): 703-999-2226, or contact the nearest ranger. Collect calls accepted. You must dial the area code.

Park Information: 999-2227 or 999-2229, 999-2266 for 24-hr. recorded message. Mailing address: Superintendent, Shenandoah National Park, Rte. 4, P.O. Box 348, Luray, VA 22835.

Dickey Ridge Visitors Center, Mile 4.6 (635-3566), closest to the north entrance. Daily interpretative programs. Open April-Nov. daily 9am-5pm. **Byrd Visitors Center,** Mile 50 (999-3282, ext. 281), in the center of the park. Movie and museum explain the history of the Blue Ridge Range and its mountain culture. Open daily 9am-5pm; Jan.-Feb. weekends only. Both stations offer changing exhibits on the park, free pamphlets detailing short hikes, daily posted weather updates, and ranger-led nature hikes.

Area Code: 703.

Shenandoah's technicolor mountains—blueish and covered with deciduous flora in summer, smeared with reds, oranges, and yellows in the fall—can be ogled from overlooks along **Skyline Drive,** which runs 105 mi. south from Front Royal to Rockfish Gap. The overlooks provide picnic areas for hikers; map boards also carry data about trail conditions. The drive closes during and after bad weather. Most facilities also hibernate in the winter. (Entrance $5 per vehicle, $2 per hiker, biker, or bus passenger; pass good for 7 days; seniors and disabled persons free.)

Miles along Skyline Dr. are measured north to south, beginning at Front Royal. Hitching is illegal outside the park. **Greyhound** sends buses to Waynesboro, near the park's southern entrance, twice daily from Washington, DC ($35, $65 round-trip), but no bus or train serves Front Royal.

When planning to stay more than a day, purchase the *Park Guide* ($1), a booklet containing all the park regulations, trail lists, and a description of the area's geological history. The *Guide to Skyline Drive* (the *"Blue Bible"* in Ranger parlance—$5.50) provides info on accommodations and activities. The free *Shenandoah Overlook* newspaper reports seasonal and weekly events. All three publications are available at the visitors centers.

Accommodations and Camping

The **Bear's Den HI/AYH,** on Rte. 601 South (554-8708), provides a woodsy stone lodge for travelers with two 10-bed dorm rooms. Drivers should exit from Rte. 7 onto Rte. 601 South and go about a half mi., turn right at the stone-gate entrance, and proceed up the hostel driveway for another half mi. No bus or train service is available. The hostel has a dining room, kitchen, on-site parking, and a laundry room. Ask the friendly staff for activities info. (Check-in 5-9pm. Front gate locked and quiet hrs. begin at 10pm. Check-out by 9:30am. Members $8, nonmembers $11; winter months members $9, nonmembers $10. Camping $4 per person. Reservations recommended; write Bear's Den HI/AYH, Postal Route 1, Box 288, Bluemont, VA 22012.)

The park maintains two lodges, **Skyland** (Mile 42 on Skyline Drive) and **Big Meadows** (Mile 51), with motel-esque rooms in cabin-esque exteriors. Skyland (999-2211 or 800-999-4714), closed December to March, offers brown and green wood-furnished cabins ($38-68, $3 more in Oct.) and slightly more upscale motel rooms. Big Meadows (999-2222 or 800-999-4714), closed November to April, offers similar cabins and motel rooms in a smaller complex. Both locations charge an extra $2 or more Friday to Saturday. Reservations are usually necessary, up to six months in advance for the fall season.

The park service maintains four major campgrounds: **Matthews Arm** (Mile 22); **Big Meadows** (Mile 51); **Lewis Mountain** (Mile 58); and **Loft Mountain** (Mile 80). All have stores, laundry facilities, and showers (no hookups). Heavily wooded and uncluttered by mobile homes, Lewis Mountain makes for the happiest tenters. All sites cost $9 except those reserved at Big Meadows ($11); call a visitors center (see Practical Information above) to check availability.

Back-country camping is free, but you must obtain a permit at a park entrance, visitors center, ranger station, or the **park headquarters** halfway between Thornton Gap and Luray on U.S. 211. Back-country campers must set up 25 yd. from a water supply and out of sight of any trail, road, overlook, cabin or other campsite. Since open fires are prohibited, bring cold food or a stove; boil water or bring your own because some creeks are oozing with microscopic beasties. Illegal camping carries a $50 fine. Hikers on the **Appalachian Trail** can make use of primitive open shelters, three-sided structures with stone fireplaces, which are strewn along the trail at approximately seven-mi. intervals. At full shelters, campers often will move over to make room for a new arrival. These shelters are reserved for hikers with three or more nights in different locations stamped on their camping permits; casual hikers are banned from them. The **Potomac Appalachian Trail Club** maintains six cabins in backcountry areas of the park. You must reserve in advance by writing to the club at 1718 N St. NW, Washington, DC 20036 (202-638-5306), and bring lanterns and food. The cabins contain bunk beds, water, and stoves. (Sun.-Thurs. $3 per person, Fri.-Sat. $14 per group; one member in party must be at least 21.)

Hikes and Activities

The **Appalachian Trail** runs the length of the park. Trail maps and the AMC guide can be obtained at the visitors center (see Practical Information above). The AMC puts out three different topographical maps (each $5) of three different parts of the park. When purchased as a package, the maps come with a trail guide, descriptions, and suggestions for budgeting time ($16). Brochures that cover the popular hikes are available for free. Campers must should avoid lighting fires and use stoves instead and leave *no* litter whatsoever. Overnight hikers should remember the unpredictability of mountain weather. Be sure to get the park service package of brochures and advice before a long hike.

Old Rag Mountain, five mi. from Mile 45, is 3291 ft.—not an intimidating summit—but the 7.2-mi. loop up the mountain is supremely difficult. The hike is steep, involves scrambling over and between granite, and at many points flaunts disappointing "false summits." Bring lots of water, energy food, and gumption. There are plenty of spots to camp around the summit area—avoid the main campground. The **Whiteoak Canyon Trail** beckons from its own parking lot at Mile 42.6. The trail to the canyon is easy; the waterfalls and trout-filled streams below them are spectacular. Visitors centers vend five-day fishing licenses ($6), but hordes of regulations hem in the catch. From Whiteoak Canyon, the **Limberlost** trail slithers into a hemlock forest. At Mile 50.7, **Dark Hollow** Trail takes only 3/4 mi. to reach a gorgeous array of falls—the closest to Skyline Drive in the whole park. The trail descends further (about an hour's walk) to the base of the falls, where water drops 70 ft. over the crumbling stone of an ancient lava flow.

Drivers should enjoy **Mary's Rock Tunnel** (Mile 32), where the road goes straight through almost 700 ft. of solid rock. **Hogback Overlook,** from Mile 20.8 to Mile 21, offers easy hikes and idyllic views of the smooth Shenandoah River and Valley; on a clear day, you can see 11 bends in the river.

Horseback and pony riding from Skyland Lodge competes with driving and hiking. (Reservations taken 1 day in advance at Skyland stables, daily 8:30am-3:30pm; after 3:30pm, reservations taken at the front desk. $14. 30-min. pony rides $16, 2½-hr. ride to White Oak Falls is $32, available daily 9am-3pm.) **Wagon rides** at Big Meadows begin at 9am, with five daily every day except Wednesday ($7, kids $3.50; no reservations). **Canoe and rafting trips** launch daily from **James River Runners,** Rte. 4 in Scottsville, which also provides tubes for trips down the river. Take Rte. 20 south from Charlottesville for 35 minutes, take a right on Rte. 726, go three mi., and make a left onto Rte. 625 to Halton Ferry. ($13-19, depending on the length of the trip. Tubing $11. Group rates available. Reservations recommended. Bring sneakers and sunscreen.)

Outside the park, the **Shenandoah Caverns** (477-3115) tout an iridescent panoply of stalactites and stalagmites, with Rainbow Lake and amusing Capitol Dome among the mimetic underground formations prospering in the year-round 56°F air. Take U.S. 211 to Newmarket, get on I-81 North, go four mi. to the Shenandoah Caverns exit, and follow the signs for the caverns—not the town of the same name. (Accessible to disabled people. $7, ages 8-14 $3.50, under 8 free.) **Skyline Caverns** (635-4545 or 800-635-4599) in Front Royal built a reputation on its anthodites, whose white spikes defy gravity and grow in all directions at the rate of an inch every seven thousand years. The caverns are 15 min. from the junction of Skyline Drive and U.S. 211. ($8, ages 6-12 $4, under 6 free.)

Rafting and canoeing excursions from the **Shenandoah Canoe and Tube Voyagers** leave daily from the Massanutten Resort (433-1109 from 9am-1pm or 433-9457, ask for Keith in the evening.) The voyagers are less than 20 mi. west from the Parkway on Rte. 33,(3-4 hr. trips, tubing $12 per person, canoeing $19 per person). The **Downriver Canoe Co.,** P.O. Box 10, Rte. 1, Box 256-A, Bentonville (703-635-5526), is for the serious canoer. Canoe trips stretch from three mi. to 150-plus mi. From the Skyline Drive Mile 20 follow U.S 211 west for eight mi., then north onto U.S. 340, 14 mi. to Bentonville. Turn right onto Rte. 613 and go one mi. (Prices vary with length of trip. 3-mi. trips $25 per canoe; 40-mi. trips $110 per canoe.)

Take a break from hiking or driving at one of Shenandoah's seven **picnic areas,** located at Dickey Ridge (Mile 5), Elkwallow (Mile 24), Pinnacles (Mile 37), Big Meadows (Mile 51), Lewis Mountain (Mile 58), South River (Mile 63) and Loft Mountain (Mile 80). All have tables, fireplaces, water fountains, and comfort stations. When you forget to pack a picnic basket, swing by the **Panorama Restaurant** (Mile 31.5) for a meal and a view. (Sandwiches $2-3. Dinners $6-14. Open April-Nov. daily 9am-7pm.)

Blue Ridge Parkway

If you don't believe that the best things in life are free, this ride could change your mind. The 469-mi. Blue Ridge Parkway, continuous with Skyline Drive, runs through Virginia and North Carolina, connecting the **Shenandoah** and **Great Smoky Mountains National Parks** (see Tennessee). Administered by the National Park Service, the parkway adjoins hiking trails, campsites, and picnic grounds. Every bit as scenic as Skyline Drive, the Parkway remains much wilder and less crowded. Don't expect to get anywhere fast on this Parkway, however—the speed limit is 45 mph. Also beware of fog during gloomy mornings and afternoons. From Shenandoah National Park, the road winds south through Virginia's **George Washington National Forest** from Waynesboro southwest to Roanoke. The forest offers spacious campgrounds, canoes for rent, and swimming in cold, clear mountain water at **Shenandoah Lake** (Mile 16).

Self-guided nature trails range from the **Mountain Farm Trail** (Mile 5.9), a 20-minute hike to a reconstructed homestead, to the **Hardwood Cove Natural Trail** (Mile 167), a three-hour excursion. Of course, purists tackle the **Appalachian Trail,** which runs the length of the parkway. The Park Service hosts a variety of ranger-led interpretive activities.

Some of the more spectacular sights on and near the parkway include a 215-ft.-high, 90-ft.-long limestone arch called **Natural Bridge,** which now supports an unnatural highway and hosts unnatural nightly audio-visual shows (800-533-1410, 800-336-5727 outside VA; open daily 8am-dusk; shows nightly, times vary with season; admission to bridge and night show $7, seniors $6, kids $3.50). Although this site is beautiful, visitors may chose to purchase a colorful postcard instead rather than paying the admission fee. Thomas Jefferson bought the site from King George III for 20 shillings. George Washington also initialed it; look for the "GW loves Martha" blazon still visible today. At **Mabry Mill** (Mile 176.1) or **Humpback Rocks** (Mile 5.8) you can simulate pioneer life, and at **Crabtree Meadows** (Mile 339), you can purchase local crafts.

The **Blue Ridge Country HI/AYH Hostel,** Rte. 2, P.O. Box 449, Galax 24333 (703-236-4962), rests only 100 ft. from the parkway at Mile 214.5. (3-night max. stay. $10.50, nonmembers $13.50, which includes redeemable $3 stamp for membership. If they know in advance, they'll pick up visitors arriving by bus to Mont Airy, NC or Whytheville, VA. For North Carolina hostels, see Asheville and Boone, NC.) There are nine **campgrounds** along the parkway, each with water and restrooms, located at Miles 61, 86, 120, 167, 238, 297, 316, 339 and 408. The fee is $8, and reservations are not accepted. Contact the parkway for info on backcountry and winter camping. Camping in the backcountry of the George Washington National Forest is free.

The cities and villages along the parkway offer a range of accommodations. You can stay at **The Bear's Den HI/AYH-Hostel,** located 35 mi. north of Shenandoah on the Appalachian Trail in Bluemont. ($8 summer, $9 winter, nonmembers $11, $12. Open year-round except for Christmas/New Year's week.) For a complete listing, pick up a *Blue Ridge Parkway Directory* or the *Virginia Accommodations Directory* at one of the visitors centers. The communities listed have easy access to the parkway and many, such as Asheville and Boone, NC, and Charlottesville, VA, have historic and cultural attractions of their own.

Greyhound provides access to the major towns around the Blue Ridge. Buses run to and from Richmond, Waynesboro, and Lexington; a bus serves Buchanan and Natural Bridge between Roanoke and Lexington once daily. For info, contact the station in Charlottesville (see Charlottesville Practical Information) or Greyhound, 26 Salem Ave. S.W. (703-342-6761; open 24 hrs.), in Roanoke.

For general info on the parkway, call **visitor information** in North Carolina (704-259-0779 or 704-259-0701). For additional details call the park service in Roanoke, VA (703-982-6458), or in Montebello, VA (703-377-2377). Write for info to **Blue Ridge Parkway Headquarters,** 200 BB&T Bldg., Asheville, NC 28801. Ten **visitors centers** line the parkway, and there are also seven stands where you can pick up brochures. Located at entry points where major highways intersect the Blue Ridge, the centers offer various exhibits, programs, and information facilities. Pick up a free copy of the helpful *Milepost* guide.

In an **emergency** call 800-727-5928 anywhere in VA or NC. Be sure to give your location to the nearest mile.

Virginia Beach

Aaah, the beach. Gaze upon glorious miles of unbroken lines of water, sand, and sky; smell the perfume of the tide; listen to the insistent rhythm of the waves. Then turn around and face the boardwalk.

Virginia Beach unabashedly immerses itself in the present. Rows of hotels and motels, ice cream stands, surf shops, and fast-food joints flank the golden coastline, and swarms of cruising college students and servicemen and -women descend upon the beach resort every summer. It's the biggest metropolitan area in Virginia, and it wants you there—with your wallet, of course.

Practical Information and Orientation

Emergency: 911.

Visitor Information; Virginia Beach Visitors Center, 22nd and Parks Ave. (425-7511 or 800-446-8038), across the street from the Center for the Arts. Helps you find budget accommodations and gives info on area sights. Open daily 9am-8pm; Labor Day-Memorial Day daily 9am-5pm. **Amtrak:** The nearest station (245-3589 or 800-872-7245), in Newport News, provides free 45-min. bus service to and from the **Radisson Hotel** at 19th St. and Pavilion Drive in Virginia Beach. You must have a train ticket to get on the bus.

Greyhound, 1017 Laskin Rd. (422-2998), connects with Washington, DC ($36; 6½ hrs.), Norfolk, Williamsburg ($12.50; 2½ hrs.), and Richmond ($21; 3½ hrs.) and with Maryland via the Bridge Tunnel.

Public Transportation: The Virginia Beach Transit/Trolley Information Center (428-3388) provides complete info on area transportation and tours, including trolleys, buses, and ferries. In summer, the Atlantic Avenue Trolley runs from Rudee Inlet to 42nd St. (Memorial Day-Labor Day daily noon-midnight; fare 50¢, seniors and disabled persons 25¢.) Other trolleys run along the boardwalk, the North Seashore, and to Lynnhaven Mall. To Norfolk ($2.50) and Naval Base ($4.50).

Bike Rentals: North End Cyclery, at Laskin Rd. and Arctic Ave. Open 10am-7pm. Bikes $3.50 per hr. or $15 per day. **Moped Rentals, Inc.,** 21st St. and Pacific Ave. Open daily in summer 9am-midnight. Bikes $7 for 1½ hrs., mopeds $22.50 for 1½ hrs.

Post Office: 24th and Atlantic Ave. (428-2821). Open Mon.-Fri. 8-11am and noon-4:30pm. **ZIP code:** 23458.

Area code: 804.

Virginia Beach is confusing to get to, but once you're there, it's easy to navigate. Drivers from the north can take I-64 south from Richmond through the **Bay Bridge Tunnel** into Norfolk, then get on **Rte. 44** (the **Virginia Beach-Norfolk Expressway**), which delivers you straight to 22nd St. and the beach. Virginia Beach's street grid pits east-west numbered streets (from 1st to around 90th) against north-south avenues (Atlantic, Pacific, Arctic and Baltic) parallel to the beach.

Accommodations and Camping

Finding a cheap place to stay in Virginia Beach is easy, especially on Atlantic and Pacific Avenues parallel to the ocean front. **Angie's Guest Cottage-Bed and Breakfast (HI/AYH),** 302 24th St. (428-4690), still ranks as one of the top 10 hostel experiences in the U.S.A. The Yates mother-daughter team welcomes guests with unbelievable warmth; they won't turn anyone away. They'll pick you up from the train station and go out of their way to help guests with job- and house-hunting. If you stay in the guest cottage, breakfast is included. Call for reservations. (Memorial-Labor Day $10.50, non-members $13.50. Off-season $8, non-members $11. Linen $2. Open April-Oct. 1, March and Oct. with reservations.)

Two other lodging options are the **Ocean Palms Motel,** 30th St. and Arctic Ave. (428-8362 or 428-5357; singles $40), and the **Viking Motel,** 2700 Atlantic Ave. (428-7116, 800-828-3063 for reservations), just a block from the beach. (Singles from $45, off-season $25, Doubles $60, off-season $25.) If you're traveling in a group, shop around for "efficiency rate" apartments with cheap weekly rates.

Camping on the beach is illegal, but the number of campgrounds around make it unnecessary. The **Seashore State Park,** about eight mi. north of town on U.S. 60 (481-2131; 490-3939 for reservations), has a desirable location amid sand dunes and cypress trees. The park is very popular, so call two to three weeks ahead (during business hours) for reservations. (Sites $14. Park open 8am-dusk; take the North Seashore Trolley; see Practical Information above.) **KOA,** 1240 General Booth Blvd. (428-1444), runs a quiet campground with free bus service to the beach and boardwalk. (Sites $22, with hook-up $24. Komfortable and kapacious 1-room kamping kabins $38.) **Holiday Travel Park,** 1075 General Booth Blvd. (425-0249), is a mega-campground with 1000 sites, four pools, and miniature golf. (Sites $23, $27 with hook-up.)

Food

Junk-food junkies will love Virginia Beach, thanks to its proliferation of fast-food joints. But the neon glare hides several restaurants with a local flavor. If you *schlepp* to one of the most popular eateries in town, **The Jewish Mother,** 3108 Pacific Ave. (422-5430), you'll be encouraged to enjoy the quiche, omelettes, *crêpes* ($5-9), deli sandwiches ($4-6), and desserts ($2-4). Blythe insists you eat everything on your plate—you look thin! At night, it's a popular live-music bar. (Open daily 9am-3am.) At **The Raven,** 1200 Atlantic Ave. (425-9556), seek surcease of hunger with their well-prepared seafood, steaks, and salad in a tinted-glass greenhouse setting. (Sandwiches and burgers $4-6, dinners $9-15. Open daily 11am-2am.) Prospective picnickers should head for the **Virginia Beach Farmers Market,** 1989 Landstown Rd. (427-4395; open daily 9am-6:30pm; open until dark in winter). At 31st St. (Luskin Rd.) and Baltic Ave., the **Farm Fresh Supermarket** salad bar, stocked with fresh fruit, pastas, and frozen yogurt at $2.39 per lb. is a cheap alternative hostelers love (open 24 hrs.).

Nightlife

In darkness the beach becomes a haunt for lovers, and the boardwalk becomes a haunt for people you may not want haunting you. Singles hover around the bars and clubs between 17th and 23rd St. along Pacific and Atlantic Ave. Locals favor **Chicho's** (422-6011) and the **Edge,** along Atlantic Ave. between 20th and 21st Streets. T-shirts, tight clothes, and tanned skin line the insides of these bars. Young adults of either sex can come here to try to convince people who are already partially unclad to retire someplace where they can be completely unclad. (Chicho's open Mon.-Fri. 5pm-2am, Sat.-Sun. 1pm-2am; no cover. The Edge open daily 4pm-1:30am; no cover.)

Sights

The main sight here is the beach itself, but museum-seekers can start with the **Virginia Marine Science Museum,** 717 General Booth Blvd. (425-3476), which traces marine life from mountain ponds to the Sargasso Sea. The Ocean Drive simulates the porthole view from an underwater research ship. (Open daily 9am-5pm, extended hours in summer. Admission $3.50, seniors and kids $2.75.) Right off the beach at 24th St. in a former life-saving service station (the predecessor to the U.S. Coast Guard) stands the cozy **Life-Saving Museum of Virginia.** Eager and friendly tour guides can tell everything that you wanted to know but were afraid to ask about the origins of the Coast Guard. (Open Mon.-Sat. 10am-5pm, Sun. noon-5pm; Sept.-May. Tues.-Sat. 10am-5pm, Sun. noon-5pm. Admission $2.50, over 60 and military personnel $2, ages 6-18 $1.)

Virginia Beach is biker-friendly, with bike paths along the boardwalk and some of the larger streets. Rent a bike in one of the many stands near the boardwalk (about $5 per hr.) and then ask for the Virginia Beach Bikeway Map at the visitors center (see Practical Information above). If you're feeling athletic, bike south down the coast to **Sandbridge Beach,** where the locals hang out to avoid crowds of tourists; take the bike trail through the Back Bay National Wildlife Refuge. Or bike north to calm, self-descriptive **Seashore State Park. The First Landing Cross,** at Cape Henry in Fort Story, marks the spot where America's first permanent English settlers, the Jamestown colonists, braved the New World's shores on April 26, 1607.

On the way back from Seashore State Park, test your psychic ability at the visitors center of the **Edgar Cayce Association for Research and Enlightenment,** 67th St. and Atlantic Ave. (428-3588), which is dedicated to the development of psychic potential and holistic health. We would tell you to go there, but we already *know* you will. (Open Mon.-Sat. 9am-5:30pm, Sun 1-6pm. June-Aug., Mon.-Sat. 9am-10pm, Sun. 1-10pm.)

Near Virginia Beach: Norfolk

Navy-heavy Norfolk is Virginia Beach's sister city. If you want to see more than one of the tourist sights in Norfolk, buy a "Discover Tidewater" passport for the TRT Trolley at the Virginia Beach Visitors Center or at the blue-and-white info booth at 24th and Atlantic Ave (623-3222). With a one-day passport ($6, seniors, kids, and people with disabilities $3.50) in your hand, you can catch a trolley into Norfolk every half-hour from the dome at 19th St. and Pacific Ave.

The Chrysler Museum, Olney Rd. and Mewbray Arch (622-1211), is Norfolk's jewel, offering an eclectic collection ranging from decorative art to religious icons. Occidental art hangs in chronological order, beginning in the 14th century and ending in the 20th. (Open Tues.-Sat. 10am-4pm, Sun. 1-5pm. Free.) The museum is a stop on the "Discover Tidewater" trolley tour, or take the #20 bus (one-way fare $2.60).

Armchair admirals will love the **Norfolk Naval Base,** the largest naval base anywhere, which keeps Norfolk's economy afloat. The Persian Gulf War, which sent the sailors away, spelled economic disaster for the area. Stroll down the pier to see the massive gray hulks of the battleships. Come early if you want to see the sights; the hours are tricky. The **tour office** at 9809 Hampton Rd. (444-7955) is open daily 8am to 4pm, and a **museum** throws open its doors daily from 9am to 4pm, but be there before 3pm or you'll be turned away. (Ship tours are given Sat. 1-4:30pm.) The "Discover Tidewater" passport includes this tour in its package, or you can purchase a separate Norfolk Naval Base ticket ($4.50, seniors, under 12, and disabled people $2.25). Drivers will need a visitors pass; get one across Hampton Rd. at gate 5.

Williamsburg

At the end of the 17th century, a time when English aristocrats wore brocades and wigs and donned pointed hats, Williamsburg powdered its face as the capital of Virginia. During the Revolutionary War, the state capital moved to Richmond, taking with it much of Williamsburg's grandeur. Then, in 1926, John D. Rockefeller, Jr.'s immense bankroll came to the aid of this distressed city, restoring part of the town as a colonial village and renewing its majesty. The Rockefeller Foundation still runs the restored section, **Colonial Williamsburg,** where fife and drum corps parade and cobblers, bookbinders, blacksmiths and clockmakers go about their tasks using 200-year-old methods. Filled with events, visitors can witness a Punch and Judy show, an evening of 18th-century theater, or a militia review on any given day. Though the fascinating and beautiful ex-capital claims to be a faithfully restored version of its 18th-century self, don't look for dirt roads, open sewers, or African slaves. Williamsburg also prides itself on **William and Mary,** the second-oldest college in the United States. Outside Williamsburg, Virginia's other big tourist sights lie in wait; history buffs should see Yorktown, Jamestown, or one of the restored plantations, while amusement-park aficionados should head to Busch Gardens.

Practical Information and Orientation

Emergency: 911.

Visitor Information: Williamsburg Area Tourism and Conference Bureau, 201 Penniman Rd. (229-6511), about ½-mi. northwest of the transportation center. Free *Visitors Guide to Virginia's Historic Triangle.* Open Mon.-Fri. 8:30am-5pm. **Tourist Visitors Center,** Rte. 132-132y (800-447-8679), 1 mi. northeast of the train station. Tickets and transport to Colonial Williamsburg. Maps and guides upstairs, info on Virginia sights downstairs. Open daily 8am-8pm.

Transportation Center: at the end of N. Boundary St., across from the fire station. **Amtrak** (229-8750 or 800-872-7245). Direct service to: New York ($79; 7 hr.), Washington, DC ($28; 3½ hr.), Philadelphia ($58; 6 hr.), Baltimore ($33; 5 hr.), Richmond ($9; 1½ hr.), and Virginia Beach ($13; 2 hr.). Open Mon.-Tues. and Fri. 7:30am-9pm, Wed.-Thurs. and Sat. 7:30am-3pm, Sun. 1:30-9pm. **Greyhound,** (229-1460). To: Richmond ($9.50), Norfolk ($9.50), and Washington, DC ($20). Ticket office open Mon.-Fri. 8am-6pm, Sat.-Sun. 8am-4pm. **James City County Transit (JCCT),** 220-1621. Service along U.S. 60, from Merchants Sq. in the Historic District, or east past

Busch Gardens. No service to Yorktown or Jamestown. Operates Mon.-Sat. 6:15am-8:30pm. Fare $1, 25¢ per zone change; exact change required.

Williamsburg Limousine Service: 877-0279. Serves as both the local taxi and cheapest guided tour. To Busch Gardens or Carter's Grove $7 round-trip. Guided tours to Jamestown ($19.50), Yorktown ($17.50), or both ($35), with admission price included. Will take you to and from your Williamsburg lodgings. Make reservations for tours at least 24 hrs. in advance, between 9am-1am.

Post Office: 425 N. Boundary St. (229-4668). Open Mon.-Fri. 8am-5pm, Sat. 10am-noon. **ZIP codes:** 23185 (Williamsburg), 23490 (Yorktown), and 23081 (Jamestown).

Area Code: 804.

Travelers should visit in late fall or early spring to avoid the crowds, high temperatures, and humidity of summer. Also be aware that the signs pointing to Colonial Williamsburg do not actually send you there, but to the visitors center. To drive to the restored area proper, take the Lafayette St. exit off the Colonial Pkwy. Parking is surprisingly easy to find.

Accommodations and Camping

The few bargains in the Williamsburg area lie along U.S. 60 west or Rte. 31 south toward Jamestown. From Memorial Day to Labor Day, rooms are scarce and prices higher, so try to call at least two weeks in advance. For a complete listing of accommodations, pick up a free copy of *Visitors Guide to Virginia's Historic Triangle* at the conference bureau, *not* at the visitors center (see Practical Information above).

Sangraal-by-the-Sea Youth Hostel (HI/AYH), Rte. 626 (776-6500), near Urbanna, is the closest hostel, at 30 mi. away. It *does* provide rides to bus or train stations during business hours, but don't expect a daily commute to Williamsburg. ($9, nonmembers $11. Call ahead.) Closer to Williamsburg, **guest houses** are your best bet; some don't require reservations, but all expect you to call ahead, and most expect customers to abstain from rowdiness and behave like houseguests. Five minutes from the historic district is **Mrs. H. J. Carter,** 903 Lafayette St. (229-1117). Dust bunnies wouldn't *dare* hide under the four-poster beds in these large, airy singles and doubles. Prices range from $25 (1 person) to $35 (4 in 2 beds). Mrs. Carter will not let unmarried couples sleep in the same bed. **The Elms,** 708 Richmond Rd. (229-1551), offers elegant, colorful, antique-furnished rooms to one or two visitors for $21. Both houses sleep eight. **Holland's Sleepy Lodge,** 211 Harrison Ave. (229-6321), rents singles for $26.

Hotels close to the historic district, especially chain- or foundation-owned hotels, do not come cheap. The **Lafayette Motel,** 1220 Richmond Rd. (220-4900), a 10-minute walk from William and Mary, has clean, ordinary rooms with colonial-looking façades and a pool. (Singles $31-38. Doubles $55.) **Motel 6,** U.S. 60 W. (565-3433), 2½ mi. from Colonial Williamsburg, offers standard motel fare and a pool. (Singles $30. Doubles $36.) **The Southern Comfort Inn,** 1220 Richmond Rd. (229-8913), a 10-minute walk from William and Mary, has clean rooms with, surprise, surprise, a colonial-looking façade and a pool. (Singles $25-30. Doubles $30-35.)

Several campsites blanket the area. **Anvil Campgrounds,** 5243 Moretown Rd. (565-2300), three mi. west of Colonial Williamsburg Information Center on U.S. 60, offers a swimming pool, bath-house, recreational hall, and store. (Sites $13-15, with hookup $20.) Nearby **Brass Lantern Campsites,** 1782 Jamestown Rd. (229-4320 or 229-9089), charges $10, with full hookup $14.

Food and Nightlife

Although Colonial Williamsburg proper contains several authentic-looking "taverns," few are cheap, and most require reservations and forbid tank-tops. If you decide to eat in the historical district, you will find long lines, but **Chowning's Tavern,** on Duke of Gloucester St., is worth the wait with its stews, sandwiches, and the misleading "Welsh Rabbit" (bread and cheese in beer sauce with ham) from $6. (Open daily 11:30am-3:30pm and 4pm-1am.) From 9pm on at Chowning's the **gambols** take place—costumed waiters serve mixed drinks, sing 18th-century ballads, and teach patrons how to play outdated dice and card games. **The Old Chickahominy House,** 1211 Jamestown Rd. (229-4689), rests over one mi. from the historic district, but make the trip. Share the antique and dried-flowers decor with pewter-haired locals whose ancestors survived "Starvation Winter" in Jamestown. Miss Melinda's "complete luncheon" is Virginia ham served on hot biscuits, fruit salad, a slice of buttermilk pie, and iced tea or coffee ($5). Expect a 20-minute wait for lunch. (Open daily 8:30-10:15am and 11:30am-2:15pm.)

During the summer, few William and Mary students stick around, but their hangouts, inexpensive and comfortable alternatives to fast-food fare, remain. In 50s-style wood and vinyl, **Paul's Deli Restaurant and Pizza,** 761 Scotland St., sells crisp *stromboli* for two ($6-9) and filling subs ($3-5). The "hot Italian" sub makes locals salivate. (Open daily 11am-2am.) Next door, the more upscale **Greenleafe Café** (220-3405) serves sandwiches, salads, and the like ($5-10), throbbing after 9pm on Wednesday (cover $2) with live folk music. (Open daily 11:30am-2am.) Both establishments are just a few blocks up Richmond Rd. from "Confusion Corner" where Colonial Williamsburg ends and W&M begins. For less pomp and more rustic circumstance, pack a picnic from one of the supermarkets clustered around the **Williamsburg Shopping Center,** at the intersection of Richmond Rd. and Lafayette St., or try the fast-food strip along Rte. 60. The rudimentary **farmers market** at Lafayette and North Henry St. sells cheap seafood and vegetables.

Sights

Unless you plan to visit (or apply) to W&M, you've probably come to see the restored gardens and buildings, crafts, tours, and costumed actors in the **Colonial Williamsburg** historic district. The complex claims to recreate 18th-century Virginia, but it may introduce you to the ways of 19th-century robber barons. The Colonial Williamsburg Foundation (CWF) owns everything from the Governor's Palace to the lemonade stands and even most of the houses marked "private home;" most attractions require exorbitantly priced tickets. You'll even need a general admission ticket to enter the historic district, though this technicality is generally not enforced. All tickets entitle you to ride the CWF buses which circle the historic district every few minutes. A **Patriot's Pass** gains admission to all the town's attractions (except the former Rockefeller home, Bassett Hall) for one year, entrance to Carter's Grove, and a guided tour ($26, under 13 $17); a **Royal Governor's Pass** lasts four days and covers all the attractions in the town ($25.50, ages 6-12 $15.25); and a **Basic Ticket** lets you into any 12 attractions except the Governor's Palace and the Decorative Arts Museum ($23, ages 6-12 $13.75). Buy them at the CWF Visitors Center or from booths in town.

"Doing" the historic district without a ticket definitely saves money; for no charge, you can walk the streets, ogle the buildings, browse in the shops, march behind the fife and drum corps, lock yourself in the stockade, and even use the restrooms. Some shops that actually sell goods—notably the Apothecary by the Palace Green—are open to the public. Catch up to a guided **walking tour** moving about Colonial Williamsburg during the day. The poorly named "Other Half" tour relates the experience of Africans and African-Americans. Outdoor events, including a mid-day cannon firing, receive listings in the weekly *Visitor's Companion,* which is given away to ticket-holders—many of whom conveniently discard it where non-ticket-holders can pick it up. A separate pamphlet detailing disabled access in Williamsburg is also available at the Tourist Info Center. Picnickers may find the best spots just outside the historic district on the elegant grounds of the **Abbey Aldrich Rockefeller Museum.** The adjacent unfenced swimming pool is officially open only to guests of CWF's hotels.

Those willing to pay shouldn't miss the **Governor's Palace** on the Palace Green. This mansion housed the appointed governors of the Virginia colony until the last one fled in 1775. Reconstructed colonial sidearms and ceremonial sabers line the reconstructed walls, and the garden includes a hedge maze. (Separate admission; $14.) The **Wallace Decorative Arts Museum** holds excellent collections of English furniture and ceramics. (Open Thurs.-Tues. 9am-5pm, Wed. 9am-5:30pm. Separate admission; $7.50.)

Spreading west from the corner of Richmond and Jamestown Rd. ("Confusion Corner"), the other focal point of Williamsburg, **William and Mary,** is the second-oldest college in the U.S. Chartered in 1693, the college educated Presidents Jefferson, Monroe, and Tyler. The **Sir Christopher Wren Building,** also restored with Rockefeller money, is the oldest classroom building in the country. Nearby, in the historic district, sprawl the shops at **Merchant Square.** Park here and walk straight into Colonial Williamsburg.

Near Williamsburg

Jamestown and **Yorktown** are both important parts of the U.S. colonial story. The National Park System provides free, well-administered visitors guides to both areas. Combination tickets to Yorktown Victory Center and to Jamestown Festival Park are available at either site for $10.25.

At the **Jamestown National Park** you'll see remains of the first permanent English settlement of 1607 and exhibits explaining colonial life. At the visitors center, skip the hokey film and catch a "living history" **walking tour** during which a guide portraying one of the colonists describes the Jamestown way of life. Call ahead (229-1733) for info, since the guides sometimes take the day off. (Site open daily 8:30am-6pm; off-season 9am-5:30pm. Entrance fee $5 per car, $2 per hiker or cyclist.) Also see the nearby **Jamestown Settlement** (229-1607), a museum commemorating the Jamestown settlement, with changing exhibits, a reconstruction of James Fort, a Native American village, and full-scale replicas of the three ships which brought the original settlers to Jamestown in 1607. A "living history" sailor even talks about the voyage. (Open daily 9am-5pm. Admission $7, under 13 $3.50.)

The American Revolution's last significant battle took place at Yorktown. British General Charles Lord Cornwallis and his men seized the town for use as a port in 1781. The colonists and the French soon surrounded and stormed the hold, forcing the British to surrender. Yorktown's **Colonial Park** vividly recreates the battle with an engaging film, fascinating dioramas, and a cool electric map. The park also maintains remnants of the original trenches built by the British. Drivers can take a seven-mi. self-guided tour of the battlefield, or rent a tape cassette and recorder for $2 in the visitors center. (Open daily 8:30am-6pm; last tape rented at 5pm.) The **Yorktown Victory Center** (887-1776), one block from U.S. 17 on Rte. 238, offers a museum filled with items from the Revolutionary War, as well as a film and an intriguing "living history" exhibit. In an encampment in front of the center, a troop of soldiers from the Continental Army of 1772 take a well-deserved break from active combat. Feel free to ask them about tomorrow's march or last week's massacre. (Open daily 9am-5pm. Admission $5.25, under 13 $2.75.)

Without a car, you won't find a cheap way to get to Jamestown or Yorktown; since the "towns" are tourist sights, guided tours provide the only transportation. With **Williamsburg Limousine,** a group of at least four people can see both Jamestown attractions in the morning ($19.50 per person), both Yorktown sights in the afternoon ($17.50 per person), or take the whole day and see both ($35). The unlined **Colonial Parkway** makes a beautiful biking route, but beware of inattentive auto drivers. You can rent a bike for $10 a day plus a $5 deposit at **Bikes Limited,** 759 Scotland Avenue (229-4620). (Open Mon.-Fri. 9am-7pm, Sat. 9am-5pm, Sun. noon-4pm.)

The **James River Plantations,** built near the water to facilitate the planters' commercial and social life, buttressed the slave-holding Virginia aristocracy. **Carter's Grove Plantation,** six mi. east of Williamsburg on U.S. 60, is an example of the early 20th-century "colonial revival" of 18th-century plantations. The last owners doubled the size of the original building but sought to maintain its colonial feel. The Carter's Grove complex also includes reconstructed 18th-century slave quarters and an archaeological dig. The brand-new **Winthrop Rockefeller Archeological Museum,** built unobtrusively into a hillside, provides a fascinating case-study look at archaeology. The exhibits will leave you with more questions than answers about the society of Martin's Hundred, whose settlement at Wolstenholme Town (directly in front of the museum) was attacked by Native Americans in 1622. Williamsburg Limousine (see above) offers daily round-trip tours from Colonial Williamsburg to the plantation ($6), but if you can, bike from South England Street in Colonial Williamsburg along the one-way, seven-mi., wooded Carter's Grove Country Road. (Plantation open daily 9am-5pm, Nov.-Dec. 9am-4pm; museum open daily 9am-5pm; slave quarters open daily 9am-5pm; Country Road open daily 8:30am-4pm, Nov.-Dec. 8:30am-3pm. Plantation admission $8, ages 6-12 $5, free with CWF Patriot's Pass; see Williamsburg: Sights for more info about the Pass.)

When you feel the weight of history, head to one of America's most famous amusement parks, **Busch Gardens: The Old Country,** three mi. east of Williamsburg on U.S. 60 (253-3350). You'll be flung, splashed, throttled, and swooped by the multifarious shows and rides. Each section of the park represents a European nation; trains and sky-cars connect the sections. Questor, a new ride, brings the amusement experience into the video age; the Loch Ness Monster keeps roller-coasting at its most primal. Williamsburg Limousine and local buses serve Busch Gardens (see Practical Information above). (Open daily mid-March-Oct., 10am-midnight. Admission $25. Parking $3.) A free **monorail** from Busch Gardens takes you to the **Anheuser-Busch Brewery** (253-3600), where tourists get two free mugs of Busch beer. Yum! (Accessible from I-64. Open daily 10am-4pm. Free.) You can also cool off at **Water Country, U.S.A.** on Rte. 199 east (229-1000), ¼-mi. east of I-64. The water theme park features a wave tank, water rides, and variety shows. (Open mid-June to mid-Aug. daily 10am-8pm; late Aug.-early Sept. and late May-mid-June 10am-7pm. Admission $16, ages 4-12 $13.95.)

West Virginia

"Hell doesn't scare me—I've been to West Virginia!" the fiery labor organizer Mary Harris Jones once declared. In "Mother" Jones's day, the characterization wasn't far off the mark; the state's rugged wilderness was little more than a giant strip mine for robber barons who laid bare the state's forests, polluted its rivers, and leveled its mountains to extract precious coal. West Virginia mining was once synonymous with the worst excesses of industrial capitalism, and the American labor movement underwent its most violent birth pangs here.

West Virginia formed from the Virginian counties that remained loyal to the Union (whether by choice or by presence of federal troops) during the Civil War. Plundered by Northern industrialists during the postwar era of "free market" capitalism, West Virginia has remained one of America's poorest and most isolated states, largely due to corrupt political machines controlled by unscrupulous profiteers. With the decline of heavy industry in the last 30 years, however, West Virginia has started cashing in on another resource—abundant natural beauty. Thanks to great skiing, hiking, fishing, and the best white-water rafting in the Eastern U.S., tourism has become one of the main sources of employment and revenue. West Virginians remain noticeably attached to traditional ways and despite the tourist onslaught, continue their long-standing penchant for warm hospitality.

Practical Information

Capital: Charleston.

Tourist Information: Travel Development Division, 1900 Washington St., State Capitol Complex, Bldg. 6, #B654, Charleston 25305 (348-2286 or 800-225-5982). **Division of Parks and Recreation,** 1900 Washington St., State Capitol Complex, Bldg. 6, #451, Charleston 25305. **U.S. Forest Service Supervisor's Office,** 200 Sycamore St., Elkins 26241 (636-1800).

Time Zone: Eastern. **Postal Abbreviation:** WV

Area Code: 304.

Sales Tax: 6%.

Harper's Ferry

Ironically, the very event that helped sink Harper's Ferry as a town—the October, 1859 raid on the U.S. armory by radical abolitionist John Brown and his 21-man "army of liberation"—has caused its rebirth as an historic attraction. Before the raid, Harper's Ferry thrived as a military and industrial town because of its prime location at the confluence of the Shenandoah and Potomac Rivers. John Brown, a fiesty and probably psychotic abolitionist who kicked off his career by massacring pro-slavery immigrants in Kansas, raided the town's federal arsenal to gather arms for a planned slave insurrection. Federal troops under then-Col. Robert E. Lee foiled his plans and shot most of the raiders, including Brown's three sons. Brown himself was tried and hanged two months later, inspiring the famous ditty "John Brown's Body." The Harper's Ferry raid convinced many Southerners that the North would stop at nothing to wipe out slavery, and the incident ultimately helped ignite the Civil War. The war, in turn, destroyed the town—retreating troops burned the armory down, and Harper's Ferry endured two years of siege before a series of floods finally KO'd it. Still, Nature may prove more compelling than culture here. The spectacular view from the Harper's Ferry Bluffs above town may be worth more than all the history exhibits combined.

Harper's Ferry National Park has restored many of the town's buildings to their 1850s appearance, when the town flourished with a population of 3200 (today the number is a mere 400). Stop first at the **visitors center** (535-6298) just inside the park entrance off U.S. 340; park rangers will hand you a map of the area, tell you more about the park, and show you a long, remarkably even-handed movie about John Brown. The visitors center also provides free 30-90 min. **tours** guided by park rangers daily 10am-3pm during the summer. Keep your ears open for evening programs throughout the summer. If you drive, park near the visitors center; the shuttle bus running two mi. to and from the restored town runs every 15 min.; you'll get ticketed any closer to town. (Park and visitors center open daily Sept.-May 8:30am-5pm, June-Aug. 8:30am-6pm. $5 per car, $2 per hiker or cyclist.)

The bus from the parking lot stops at **Shenandoah St.** Browse through the renovated blacksmith shop, ready-made clothing store, and general store. Turning left off Shenandoah St. onto High St., you'll find a slew—that's right, a veritable slew—of antique stores, souvenir shops, and the usual tourist-snaring suspects. The **Garden of Food** (535-2202) on High St. serves salads and sandwiches ($3-7) either indoors or outside on the Edenic patio. (Open Mon.-Fri. 11am-6pm, Sat.-Sun. 11am-7pm.) The **Back Street Café** on Potomac St. (725-8019) doubles as a burger joint (burgers and hot dogs $2.25) and a ghoulish guide service; "Ghost Tours" of the town are offered weekend nights (May 1-Nov. 8 Fri.-Sun. 8pm. $2, ages under 11 $1. Reservations recommended in Oct. Café open daily 10am-5pm year-round.) A few three-speed bikes are rented near the café ($3 per hr., $15 per day).

Uphill, stairs on High St. lead to the footpath to **Jefferson Rock;** experience awe and vertigo as you scan the three states (Virginia, Maryland, and guess what the other is) and the two rivers below. Thomas Jefferson declared the view "worth a voyage across the Atlantic." Easy for him to say; he was already here.

Those who prefer nature to history have several options, including hiking and boating. The **Maryland Heights Trail** offers some of the best views in the Blue Ridge Mountains and winds past cliffs worthy of experienced rock climbers; climbers must register at the visitors center. **Appalachian Trail Conference Headquarters** (535-6331) at the corner of Washington and Jackson St., offers catalogues, books, and hiking equipment to members. (Membership $25, students and seniors $18. Write to P.O. Box 807 or call. Open Mon.-Fri. 9am-5pm, Sat.-Sun. 9am-4pm.) Non-climbers can walk along the **Chesapeake & Ohio Canal Towpath.**

If time allows, drive a few mi. north to **Antietam National Battlefield,** in Maryland, where the Civil War's bloodiest battle was fought. On Sept. 17, 1862, 12,410 Union and 10,700 Confederate soldiers died as Robert E. Lee tried and failed to penetrate the line held by General George B. McClellan's Northern army. The pyrrhic Union victory provided President Lincoln the pretext to issue the "Emancipation Proclamation." To get to Antietam from Harper's Ferry, take Rte. 340 for two mi., turn right onto Rte. 230 to Shepardstown, then turn right again onto Rte. 480 to Sharpsburg, MD. Take a left onto Rte. 65 to reach Antietam.

River & Trail Outfitters, 604 Valley Rd., (695-5177), off Rte. 340 at the blinking light, rents canoes, inner tubes, and rafts in addition to organizing guided trips. (Canoes $40 per day; tubes $22.50 per day; raft trips $42 per person.) They also organize cross-country skiing weekends ($199) and daytrips ($60). Call ahead for reservations. **River Riders,** P.O. Box 267, Knoxville, MD 21758 (301-834-8051 or 301-535-2663), organizes two trips daily for rafting (from $60). Reservations are required.

Hikers can try the **Harper's Ferry Hostel (HI/AYH),** 19123 Sandy Hook Rd. off Keep Tryst Rd. in Knoxville, MD (301-834-7652) for cheaper accommodations. (3-day max. stay. Check-in 5pm-9pm only. Members $8 summer/$9 winter; nonmembers $12 summer/$12 winter; camping $4 per person. 50% reservation deposit.) The **Comfort Inn** at Rte. 340 and Union St. (535-6391), a 10-minute walk from town, offers dependable rooms and serves coffee and doughnuts each morning—it also has wheelchair access and non-smoking rooms. (Singles $47. Doubles $54. $4 extra on weekends.)

You can camp along the C&O Canal, where sites lie five mi. apart, or in one of the five Maryland State Park campgrounds lying within 30 mi. of Harper's Ferry. **Greenbrier State Park** (301-791-4767) lies a few mi. north of Boonsboro on Rte. 66 between exits 35 and 42 on I-70. (April-Nov. $12.) Far closer is the commercial **Camp Resort,** Rte. 3, Box 1300 (535-6895), adjacent to the entrance to Harper's Ferry National Park. (2-person sites $21, with water and hookup $21; additional adults $4 per night.)

A natural stop for hikers on the Appalachian Trail, Harper's Ferry also makes a convenient day trip from Washington, DC. The drive to Harper's Ferry from DC takes 1.5 hrs. by car. Take I-270 north to Rte. 340 West. **Amtrak** goes to Harper's Ferry from DC in the afternoon and back to DC in the morning ($13 one way). The closest **Greyhound** bus stations are half-hour drives away in Winchester, VA and Frederick, MD.

Harper's Ferry's **ZIP code** is 25425; the **area code** is 304. Knoxville, MD's **ZIP code** is 21758.

Monongahela National Forest

Mammoth **Monongahela National Forest,** popular with canoers, enshrouds deer, bear, wild turkeys, and spelunkers prowling around below ground in magnificent limestone caverns. Camping is the main attraction here, with 600 mi. of prize hiking trails and over 500 campsites to lure the adventurer. Camp in an established site ($10 or less) or sleep in the backcountry for free. The forest's **Lake Sherwood Area** (536-3660), 25 mi. north on Rte. 92, offers fishing, hunting, swimming, hiking, and boating, as well as several campgrounds that rob from the rich to give to the poor. The campgrounds fill only on major holidays. (2-week max. stay. Sites $6.) A three-hour drive north will bring you to **Blackwater Falls State Park** (800-225-5982), ¼-mi. southwest of Rte. 32. The park's dazzling centerpiece is the most popular waterfall in West Virginia. (Sites $10, $12.50 with electricity. Open April-Oct.) For advice and information on exploring Monongahela, visit the White Sulphur Springs **Forest Service Office,** in the Federal Bldg. (536-2144), at 14 E. Main and Mountain Ave. (Open Mon.-Fri. 8am-4:45pm.) For information on the whole forest, which encompasses much of West Virginia's most scenic mountain country, contact the Supervisor's Office, Monongahela National Forest, 200 Sycamore St., Elkins 26241-3962 (636-1800; open Mon.-Fri. 8am-4:45pm).

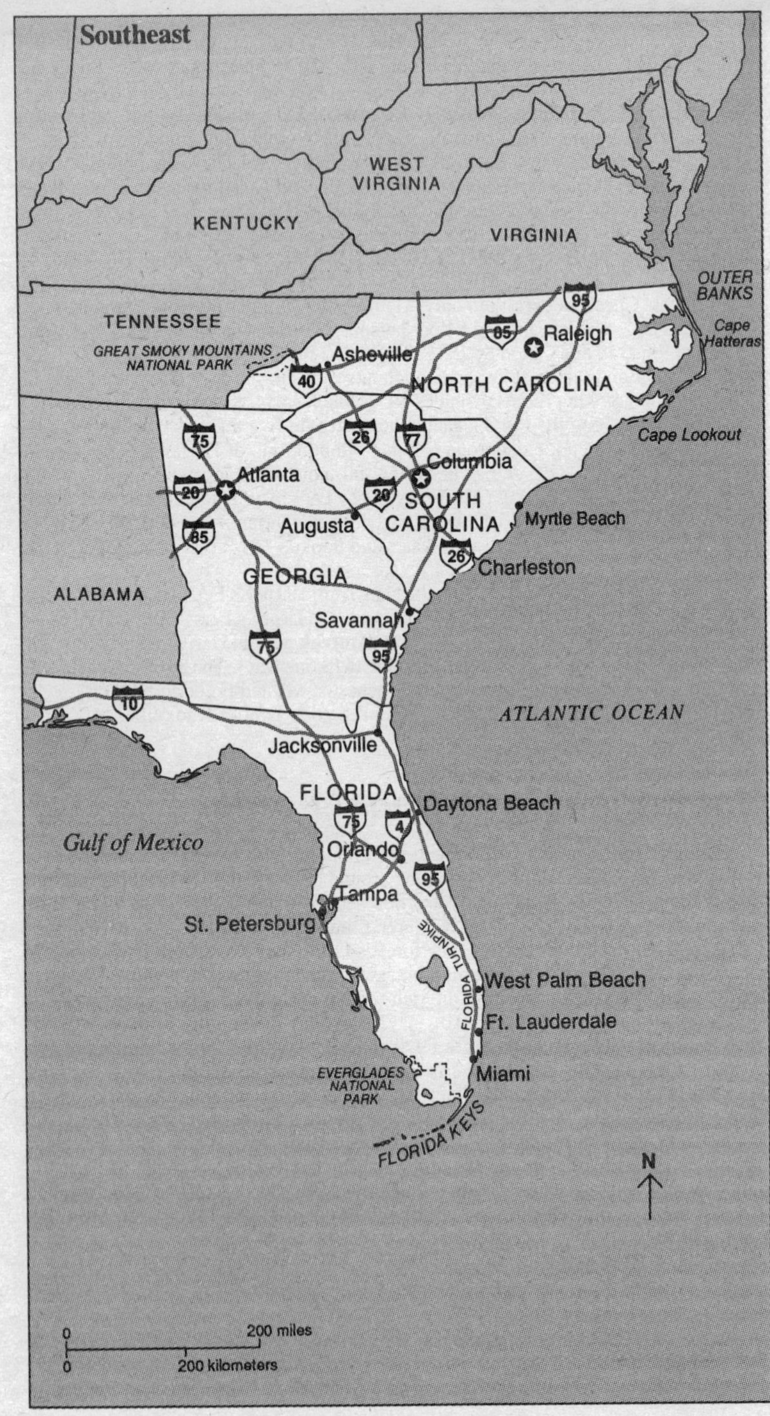
Southeast
WEST VIRGINIA
KENTUCKY
VIRGINIA
OUTER BANKS
TENNESSEE
95
85
Raleigh
Cape Hatteras
GREAT SMOKY MOUNTAINS NATIONAL PARK
Asheville
40
NORTH CAROLINA
75
26
77
Cape Lookout
Columbia
Atlanta
20
20
SOUTH CAROLINA
Myrtle Beach
Augusta
85
26
Charleston
GEORGIA
ALABAMA
Savannah
75
95
10
ATLANTIC OCEAN
Jacksonville
FLORIDA
Daytona Beach
75
4
Gulf of Mexico
Orlando
95
Tampa
St. Petersburg
FLORIDA TURNPIKE
West Palm Beach
Ft. Lauderdale
EVERGLADES NATIONAL PARK
Miami
FLORIDA KEYS
N
0
200 miles
0
200 kilometers

Florida

Ponce de León landed on the Florida coast in 1513, near what would soon be St. Augustine, in search of the elusive Fountain of Youth. Although the multitudes who flock to Florida today aren't desperately seeking fountains, many find their youth restored in the Sunshine State—whether they're dazzled by Orlando's fantasia Disney World or bronzed by the sun on the state's seductive beaches. Droves of senior citizens also migrate to Florida, where they thrive in comfortable retirement communities, leaving one to wonder whether the unpolluted, sun-warmed air isn't just as good as Ponce de León's fabled magical elixir.

But a dark shadow hangs over this land of the winter sun. Anything as attractive as Florida is bound to draw hordes of *people,* the nemesis of natural beauty. Florida's population boom is straining the state's resources; a steady flow of everyone from ultra-rich tycoons to unemployed illegal aliens continually streams across its borders. Commercial strips and tremendous development in some areas have turned pristine beaches into tourist traps. Nevertheless, it is possible to find a deserted strand on this peninsula. Sit yourself down, grease yourself up, and pay homage to the sun.

In August, 1992, Hurricane Andrew, the costliest natural disaster in the U.S. to date, ripped through southern Florida, causing over $20 billion in damage and claiming over 20 lives. The listings in this book were researched before the hurricane. Some tourist facilities may have been disrupted, so call ahead.

Practical Information

Capital: Tallahassee.

Florida Division of Tourism, 126 W. Van Buren St., Tallahassee 32301 (487-1462). **Department of Natural Resources—Division of Recreation and Parks,** 3900 Commonwealth Blvd. #506, Tallahassee 32399-2000 (488-9872).

Time Zones: Eastern and Central (westernmost part of panhandle is 1 hr. behind Eastern). **Postal Abbreviation:** FL

Sales Tax: 6%.

Cocoa Beach/Cape Canaveral

Known primarily for its rocket launches, space shuttle blast-offs, and enormous **NASA** space center complex, the "Space Coast" also has uncrowded golden sand beaches and vast wildlife preserves. Even during spring break the place remains placid because most vacationers and sunbathers are neighborly Florida or Space Coast residents.

The **Kennedy Space Center,** eight mi. north of Cocoa Beach, is the site of all of NASA's flights. The Kennedy Center's **Spaceport USA** (452-2121 for reservations) provides a huge welcoming center for visitors. There are two different two-hour bus tours of the complex. The **red tour** takes you around the space sites, the **blue tour** to the Air Force Station. There are also two IMAX films projected on a 5½-story screen: *The Dream is Alive* is about the space shuttle, and *The Blue Planet* is about environmental issues. Tours depart from Spaceport USA daily from 9:20am to 6pm; $7, ages under 11 $4. Movie tickets $4, ages under 11 $2.) Buy tickets to both immediately upon arrival at the complex to avoid a long line. The center itself is free, as are the five movies in the Galaxy Theater and the half-hour walking tours of the exhibits. The NASA Parkway, site of the visitors center, is accessible only by car via State Rd. 405. From Cocoa Beach, take Rte. A1A north until it turns west into Rte. 528, then follow Rte. 3 north to the Spaceport. With NASA's ambitious launch schedules, you may have a chance to watch the space shuttles Columbia, Atlantis, or Discovery thunder off into the blue skies above the cape. Call 1-900-321-LIFT-OFF for **launch information** ($0.75 per call).

Surrounding the NASA complex, the marshy **Merritt Island Wildlife Refuge** (867-8667) stirs with deer, sea turtles, alligators, and eagles. (Open daily 8am-sunset.) Just north of Merritt Island is **Canaveral National Seashore** (867-2805; open daily 6:30am-sunset), 67,000 acres of undeveloped beach and dunes, home to more than 300 species of birds and mammals. (Take Rte. 406 east off U.S. 1 in Titusville.) Should you feel like shedding your clothes, a nude beach accessible to the public dangles at the northernmost point of the seashore near Turtle Mound.

For a bite to eat, try **Herbie K's Diner,** 2080 N. Atlantic Ave., south of Motel 6. A shiny chrome reproduction of a 50s diner, Herbie K's serves macaroni and cheese, chicken pot pie, "happy haw" (apple sauce), great malteds, and hamburgers ($4-6). (Open weekdays till midnight, Fri. and Sat. 24 hrs.) At the beach, **Motel 6,** 3701 N. Atlantic Ave. (783-3103), has a pool and large, clean rooms with TV and A/C. (Singles $32. Each additional person $6. Reservations required.) If Motel 6 is full, try farther down N. Atlantic Ave. at the **Sunrise Motel** (800-348-0348) where singles are $32 (each additional person $6). If you get stuck in Cocoa or need a place to spend the night between bus connections, walk right behind the Greyhound station to the **Dixie Motel,** 301 Forrest Ave. (632-1600), one block east of U.S. 1. For big clean rooms, a swimming pool, A/C, and friendly service. (Singles $28. Doubles $32.) Or pitch your tent at scenic **Jetty Park Campgrounds,** 400 East Jetty Rd. (783-4001), Cape Canaveral. (Sites $17, with hookup $21. Reservations necessary six months in advance.)

The Cocoa Beach area, 50 mi. east of Orlando, consists of mainland towns Cocoa and Rockledge, oceanfront towns Cocoa Beach and Cape Canaveral, and Merritt Island in between. **Route A1A** runs through Cocoa Beach and Cape Canaveral, and **North Atlantic Avenue** runs parallel to the beach. Inaccessible by bus, Cocoa Beach also lacks local public transport. But Cocoa, eight mi. inland, is serviced by **Greyhound,** 302 Main St. (636-3917), from Orlando ($13). From the bus station, **taxi** fare to Cocoa Beach is about $14 (call 783-8294). A **shuttle** service (784-3831) connects Cocoa Beach with Orlando International Airport, Disney World (round-trip $75 for 1 or 2 people), and the Kennedy Space Center (round-trip only $45, 1 or 2 people). Make reservations one day in advance and ask about special rates for groups of five or more.

The **Cocoa Beach Chamber of Commerce,** main office at 400 Fortenberry Rd., Merritt Island (459-2200; open Mon.-Fri. 8:30am-5pm), has information on special events and can provide suggestions on cheap, temporary housing. For a comprehensive list of restaurants and all kinds of information about the area, ask at the **Broward County Tourist Development Council** (453-0823 or 800-872-1969), at the Kennedy Space Center.

Cocoa Beach's **ZIP code** is 32922; the **area code** is 407.

Fort Lauderdale

Every spring, thousands of pale, lust-crazed college students flock to Fort Lauderdale, the official spring-break party capital. In recent years, open-container laws have been passed, and there have been crack-downs on drunk driving, fake IDs, and indecent exposure. This has caused the spring-break crowds largely to fizzle and head to less restrictive places. When the spring-break hordes finally do leave each year, Fort Lauderdale breathes a huge sigh of relief. In the off-season, tourists less preoccupied with inebriated and anonymous carnal fulfillment and more appreciative of the land and ocean's beauty can peacefully stroll along the wide beach. Broad-sailed boats and luxury yachts frame the seascape as they cruise the coast or anchor at the city's canals and ports.

Practical Information and Orientation

Emergency: 911.

Visitor Information: Chamber of Commerce, 512 NE 3rd Ave. (462-6000), 3 blocks off Federal Hwy. at 5th St. Pick up the helpful *Visitor's Guide.* Open Mon.-Fri. 8am-5pm.

Fort Lauderdale/Hollywood International Airport: 359-1200. 3½ mi. south of downtown on U.S. 1 (Federal Hwy.), at exits 26 and 27 on I-95. **American, Continental, Delta, TWA, Northwest, United,** and **USAir** all serve this airport.

Amtrak: 200 SW 21st Terrace (463-8251 or 800-872-7245), just west of I-95, 1/4-mi. south of Broward Blvd. Take bus #9, 10, or 81 from downtown. Daily service on "The Floridian" to: Miami (2 per day, 1½ hr., $6); Orlando (1 per day, 4 hr., $50); and Jacksonville (2 per day, 6 hr., $75). Open daily 7:15am-6:15pm.

Greyhound: 513 NE 3rd St. (764-6551), 3 blocks north of Broward Blvd. at Federal Hwy., downtown. Unsavory location, especially unfriendly at night. To: Orlando (6 per day, 3 hr., $42); Daytona Beach (9 per day, 3 hr., $35); and Tampa (4 per day, 2½ hr., $49). Open 24 hrs.

Public Transport: Broward County Transit (BCT), 357-8400 (call Mon.-Fri. 8:30am-7pm, Sat. 8am-8pm, Sun. 8:30am-5pm). Extensive regional coverage. Most routes go to the terminal at the corner of 1st St. NW and 1st Ave. N.W., downtown. Operates daily 6am-9pm every ½-hr. on most routes. Fare $.85, seniors $.40, students with ID$. 40, transfers $.10. 7-day passes $8, available at beachfront hotels. Pick up a handy system map at the terminal or at the **Broward County Office Plaza,** 115 S. Andrews Ave., 1 block south of Broward Blvd. **Tri-Rail** (800-874-7245 or 728-8445) connects West Palm Beach, Ft. Lauderdale, and Miami. Trains run Mon.-Sat. 5am-9:30pm. Pick up schedules at the airport or at Tri-Rail stops. Fare $2, students and seniors with ID $1.

Car Rental: Alamo, 2601 S. Federal Hwy. (525-4715 or 800-327-9633). Cheapest cars $18 per day, $70 per week. Unlimited mi., free drop-off in Daytona and Miami. Free shuttle to airport. Must be 21 with credit card or deposit of $50 per day or $200 per week for out-of-state renters through travel agent.

Bike Rentals: International Bicycle Shop, 1900 E. Sunrise Blvd. at N. Federal Hwy. (764-8800). Take bus #10 from downtown or bus #36 from A1A north of Sunrise. $10 per day, $35 per week. $100 deposit. Open Mon.-Fri. 10am-9pm, Sat. 9am-9pm, Sun. 11am-5pm. Must be 18. Avoid the expensive joints on the beach.

Taxi: Yellow Cab (565-5400), $2.20 plus $1.50 per mi.. **Public Service Taxi** (587-9090), $.95 plus $1.50 per mi..

Help Line: Crisis Hotline, 467-6333. Open 24 hrs.

Post Office: 1900 W. Oakland Park Blvd. (527-2028). Open Mon.-Fri. 7:30am-7pm, Sat. 8:30am-2pm. **ZIP code:** 33310.

Area Code: 305.

I-95 runs north-south, connecting W. Palm Beach, Ft. Lauderdale, and Miami. Rte. 84/I-75 (Alligator Alley) slithers 100 mi. west from Ft. Lauderdale across the Everglades to Naples and other small cities on the Gulf Coast of Southern Florida. It is currently under construction; delays are possible, but the road provides a good opportunity to view alligators. Ft. Lauderdale is bigger than it looks. The city extends westward from its 23 mi. of beach to encompass nearly 450 sq. mi. of land area. Most of the maps show distances deceptively; when traveling from the beach to downtown, take a bus. Roads are divided into two categories: streets and boulevards (east-west) and avenues (north-south). All are labeled NW, NE, SW, or SE according to the quadrant. **Broward Boulevard** divides the city east-west, **Andrews Avenue** north-south. The unpleasant downtown centers around the intersection of **Federal Highway** (U.S. 1) and **Las Olas Boulevard,** about 2 mi. west of the oceanfront. Between downtown and the waterfront, yachts fill the ritzy inlets of the **Intracoastal Waterway.** The strip (variously called Rte. A1A, N. Atlantic Blvd., 17th St. Causeway, Ocean Blvd., and Seabreeze Blvd.) runs along the beach for 4 mi. between **Oakland Park Boulevard** to the north and Las Olas Blvd. to the south. Las Olas Blvd. is the pricey shopping street; **Sunrise Boulevard** has most shopping malls. Both degenerate into ugly commercial strips west of downtown.

Accommodations and Camping

Hotel prices vary from slightly unreasonable to absolutely ridiculous, increasing exponentially as you approach prime beachfront and spring break. High season runs from mid-February to early April. Investigate package deals at the slightly worse-for-wear hotels along the strip in Ft. Lauderdale. Many hotels offer off-season deals for under $35.

Small motels crowd each other one or two blocks off the beach area; many offer small kitchenettes. Look along **Birch Rd.,** one block back from Rte. A1A. **The Broward County Hotel and Motel Association** (462-0409) provides a free directory of area hotels. (Open Mon.-Fri. 9am-5pm.) Scan the *Ft. Lauderdale News* and the Broward Section of the *Miami Herald* for occasional listings of local residents who rent rooms to tourists in spring. Call 357-8100 for info on campgrounds in Broward County. Sleeping on the well-patrolled beaches is impossible between 9pm and sunrise.

International Youth Hostel, 3811 Ocean Blvd. (568-1615). Take bus #10 to Coral Ridge. Walk 3 blocks south of Commercial Blvd. on the Strip. Pick up at bus station available. Shuttle service throughout Florida. Rooms with 6 beds, showers, A/C, small kitchens. Pool. Members $12, nonmembers $15. $5 key deposit. One block from beach.

Estoril Apartments, 2648 NE 32nd St. 33306 (563-3840; 800-548-9398 reservations only), 2 blocks west of the Intracoastal Waterway and 1 block north of Oakland Park Blvd. From downtown, take bus #20, 10 55 or 72 to Coral Ridge Shopping Center and walk 2 blocks east on Oakland. Students can probably persuade the proprietors to pick them up from the bus station or airport. A 10-min. walk to the beach. Very clean rooms with A/C, TV, and small kitchenette. Pool and barbecue. Students with *Let's Go* receive 10% discount. Office closes about 11pm. May-Dec.: singles $26; doubles $28. Jan.-April: singles $38; doubles $40. Additional person $6 off-season, $10 in season. Reservations recommended.

Motel 6, 1801 State Rd. 84 (760-7999), 3 blocks east of I-95 and 3 mi. southwest of downtown. Take bus #14 to Rte. 84 and SW 15th Ave. and walk 3 blocks west. Far from the action. Clean, no-frills rooms. May-Sept. singles $31, doubles $38; Oct.-April singles $36, doubles $45.

Budget Inn, 200-300 S. Ocean Blvd., Pompano Beach (942-2030), near the Ft. Lauderdale border on A1A. From downtown, take bus #11 north up A1A. Clean, attractive rooms. May-Dec. singles $29, doubles $33. Jan.-April singles $52, doubles $52.

Easterlin County Park, 1000 NW 38th St., Oakland Park (938-0610), northwest of the intersection of Oakland Park and I-95, less than 4 mi. west of the strip and 3 mi. north of downtown. Take bus #14 from downtown to NW 38th St. or #72 along Oakland Park to Powerline Rd. By car take Oakland Park exit from I-95. 2-week max. stay. Registration open 24 hrs., correct change for the cost of a site recommended after 5pm. Sites with electricity, barbecue pits, and picnic table $17.

Quiet Waters County Park, 6601 N. Powerline Rd. (NW 9th Ave.), Pompano Beach (360-1315), 10 mi. north of Oakland Park Blvd. I-95 exit 37B. Take Hillsboro Blvd. west to Powerline Rd. From downtown, take bus #14. Cramped, commercialized, but friendly. Bizarre 8-person "boatless water skiing" at the end of a cable and other water sports. No electricity. Check-in 2-6pm. 2-night min. stay. Fully equipped campsites (tent, mattresses, cooler, grill, canoe) for up to 6 people, Sun.-Thurs. $17, Fri.-Sat. $25 plus $20 refundable deposit.

Food

The clubs along the strip offer massive quantities of free grub during happy hour: surfboard-sized platters of wieners, chips, and hors d'oeuvres, or all-you-can-eat pizza and buffets. However, these bars have hefty cover charges (from $5) and expect you to buy a drink once you're there (from $2). In addition, these bars are nightclubs, not restaurants, and the quality of their cuisine proves it. In contrast, the restaurants listed below serve "real" food.

La Spada's, 4346 Seagrape Drive (776-7893). Two blocks from the beach, off Commercial Blvd. Best, and biggest, subs in southern Florida. Try the ft.-long Italian sub ($6.50). Open Mon.-Sat. 10am-8pm, Sun. 11am-8pm.

Golden Chopsticks, 4350 N. Federal Hwy. (776-0953). Some of the best Chinese food in town. For a treat, try the steak kew ($13). Most of the uniformly delicious food is more reasonably priced. Open Mon.-Thurs. 11:30am-1am, Fri. 11:30am-3am, Sat. 1pm-3am, Sun.1pm-11pm.

Southport Raw Bar, 1536 Cordova Rd. (525-2526), by the 17th St. Causeway behind the Southport Mall on the Intracoastal Waterway. Take bus #40 from the strip or #30 from downtown. Aggressively marine decor. Spicy conch chowder $2, fried shrimp $4.95. Open Mon.-Sat. 11am-2am, Sun. noon-2am.

Tina's Spaghetti House, 2110 S. Federal Hwy. (522-9943), just north of 17th St. Take bus #1 from downtown. Authentic red-checkered tablecloths, hefty oak furniture, and bibs. Popular with locals since 1951. Lunch specials $4-5. Spaghetti dinner $6-7. Open Mon.-Thurs. 11:30am-10pm, Fri. 11:30am-11pm, Sat. 4-11pm, Sun. 4-10pm.

Sin

Ft. Lauderdale offers all kinds of licit and illicit entertainment by night. Mostly illicit. Planes flying over the beach hawk hedonistic happy hours at local watering holes. Students frequent the night spots on the A1A strip along the beach, with an emphasis on the word "strip." When going out, bring a driver's license or a passport as proof of age; most bars and nightclubs don't accept college IDs. Be warned that this is *not* the place for cappuccino and conversation but for nude jello wrestling and similarly lubricated entertainment.

For those who prefer garbed service, several popular nightspots line N. Atlantic Blvd. next to the beach. **The Candy Store,** 1 N. Atlantic Blvd. (761-1888), was once at the pinnacle of Ft. Lauderdale nightlife. It's still a great hangout for drinking and people-watching; rowdy sailors on leave have been known to liven up the place. Get there for the all-you-can-eat afternoon pizza. (Open Mon.-Fri. 11am-2am, Sat. 11am-3am. Cover $5.) Also try **Banana Joe's on the Beach,** 837 N. Atlantic Blvd. (565-4446), at Sunrise and A1A. (Open Mon.-Fri. 7am-2am, Sat. 7am-3am, Sun. noon-2am. Kitchen open 11:30am-7pm.) For off-the-beach entertainment, Ft. Lauderdale's new hotspot is **Crocco's World Class Sports Bar,** 3339 N. Federal Hwy. (566-2406). Built in an old movie theater, this gargantuan club has lines out the door almost every night. (Open Sun.-Fri 11am-2am, Sat. 11am-3am.) For reggae, try **Mombasa Bay,** 3051 NE 32nd Ave. (561-8220), a new club on the Intracoastal Waterway. Live R&B Thurs., live Reggae Fri.-Mon. (Open Sun.-Fri. 11:30am-2am, Sat. 11:30am-3am. Concerts start at 9:30pm.) If all of this hedonism isn't enough to make you laugh, **The Comic Strip,** 1432 N. Federal Hwy (565-8887), guarantees giggles. (Sun.-Thurs. shows at 9:30pm, Fri. shows at 10pm, Sat. shows at 9pm and 11:15pm. Cover $10, 2-drink minimum. Drinks run $3 or more.)

Sights and Activities

Besides sun and sin, Ft. Lauderdale is pretty low on activities. To see why Ft. Lauderdale is called the "Venice of America," take a tour of its waterways aboard the **Jungle Queen,** located at the **Bahia Mar Yacht Center** on Rte. A1A, 3 blocks south of Las Olas Blvd. (462-5596; 3-hr. tours daily at 10am and 2pm. Fare $7.50, kids $5.) For more intimate acquaintance with the ocean, **Water Sports Unlimited,** 301 Seabreeze Blvd. (467-1316), offers equipment for a variety of water sports. Located on the beach, Water Sports offers wave runners ($35 per ½-hr.), motor boats ($40 per hour, $220 per day), and parasailing trips ($40 per ride).

Atlantis the Water Kingdom, 2700 Stirling Rd. (926-1000), is the third largest water theme park in the U.S. Admission includes unlimited use of the Slidewinder water slides and the Raging Rampage. If rain interrupts your day at Atlantis for 45 consecutive min. or more, you receive a raincheck to return another day. (Open summer Mon.-Thurs. 10am-8pm, Fri.-Sat. 10am-10pm; off-season call for hours. Admission $14, seniors $7, ages 3-11 $11, under 3 free. Head south on I-95, exit at Stirling Rd., and turn left under the overpass.)

The Keys

The coral rock islands, mangrove trees, and relaxed attitude of the residents make the Florida Keys pleasant places to visit and live. With a character quite different from anywhere else in the U.S., these islands off the coast are a nation unto themselves. The Keys are more Caribbean than Floridian, with cool breezes at night, wild tropical rainstorms, and a vertical sun hot enough to roast a turkey. When the sun *does* set, clouds, heat lightning, and the surrounding ocean provide an incredible accompaniment. Approximately six mi. offshore from these islands, a 100-yd. wide chain of barrier reef parallel to the Keys from Key Largo south to Key West. Adored by divers, these reefs harbor some of the ocean's most diverse and colorful marine life as well as hundreds of wrecked ships and legendary lost treasure. Contrary to popular belief, there are very few sharks.

The Keys run southwest into the ocean from the southern tip of Florida, accessible by the **Overseas Highway (U.S. 1). Mile markers** divide the highway into sections and replace street addresses to indicate the location of homes and businesses. They begin with Mile 126 in Florida City and count down to zero on the corner of Whitehead and Fleming St. in Key West.

Greyhound runs three buses per day to Key West from Miami ($30), stopping in Perrine, Homestead (247-2040), Key Largo (451-2908), Marathon (743-3488), Big Pine Key (872-4022), and Key West (296-9072). If there's a particular mile marker where you need to get off, most drivers can be convinced to stop at the side of the road. Biking along U.S. 1 across the swamps between Florida City and Key Largo is impossible because the road lacks shoulders. Bring your bike on the bus.

The **area code** on the Keys is 305.

Key Largo

After traversing the thick swamps and crocodile marshland of Upper Florida Bay, Key Largo opens the door to the islands. Without a car it can be difficult to get around, although everything of importance lies within a 6-mi. range. Largo's **John Pennecamp State Park,** Mile 102.5 (451-1202), 60 mi. from Miami, provides the visitor with a rare though somewhat murky view from glass-bottomed boats of the living reef off the Keys. ($14. 3 trips per day at 9:30am, 12:30pm and 3pm.) Mostly off-shore, the beautiful state park encompasses the largest uninterrupted stretch of the barrier reef in the Keys, the only underwater park in the country, and the only underwater Christ statue in the world. (Admission $3.25 for vehicle operator, each additional person $.50. Camp sites $24, with hookup $26.) The **Coral Reef Company** (451-1621) sails visitors six mi. past mangrove swamps to the reef. (Snorkeling tours daily at 9am, noon, and 3pm. 1½ hrs. of water time and a quickie lesson including gear $22, kids $18.)

The Italian Fisherman, Mile 104 (451-4471), has it all—fine food and a spectacular view of Florida Bay. Formerly an illegal gambling casino, this restaurant was the locale of some scenes from Bogart and Bacall's movie *Key Largo.* (Dinners $7-17. Open daily 11am-11pm.) The seafood and 99-beer selection at **Crack'd Conch,** Mile 105 (451-0732), is superb. Try the "sorry Charlie" tuna fish sandwich ($4.50) or an entire key lime pie ($7.50). (Open Thurs.-Tues. noon-10pm.) With three locations, **Perry's** serves fresh local seafood and charbroiled steaks, at Mile 102 (451-1834); Marathon, Mile 51 (743-3108); and the most famous location at Key West, 3800 N. Roosevelt Blvd (294-8472). (Lunch $4-10, dinner $8-23. Open daily 10:45am-10pm.) They also offer a "you hook 'em, we cook 'em" service for $3.50. Other scenes from *Key Largo* were filmed at the **Caribbean Club,** Mile 104 (451-9970), a friendly local bar. The in-house band Blackwater Sound plays a wide variety of rock for the locals; snapshots of Bogart and Bacall grace the walls. (Open daily 7am-4am.) When you're starring in your own late-night show, call **Island Cab** (743-0077) for a ride home ($3.50 plus $1.50 per mi.).

After the state park's campsites fill up, try crowded but well-run **Kings Kamp Marina,** mile 103.5 (451-0010; sites by the bay $18). Look for the concealed entrance on the northwest (Gulf) side of U.S. 1. The **Hungry Pelican,** mile 99.5 (451-3576), boasts beautiful bougainvillea vines in the trees and friendly managers Phil and Eileen. Stuff your beak full in a clean, cozy trailer or room with a double bed ($40-55).

The **Florida Upper Keys Chamber of Commerce,** Mile 105.5 (451-1414), at Rte. 905, has maps and brochures on local attractions, including scenes from the film *Key*

Largo. (Open Mon.-Fri. 8am-5pm.) The **visitors center,** Mile 103.4 (451-1414 or 800-822-1088), in the pink shopping center, has a Bogart-oriented selection of maps and brochures. (Open daily 9am-6pm.) The dramatic mailroom scene from *Key Largo* was filmed at the **post office,** Mile 100 (451-3155; open Mon.-Fri. 8am-4:30pm). Key Largo's **ZIP code** is 33037; the **area code** is 305.

Key West

This is the end of the road. When searching for a tropical paradise, you can do no better than Key West. The island's pastel clapboard houses, hibiscus and bougainvillea vines, year-round tropical climate, and gin-clear waters make it a beautiful spot to visit in summer or winter.

Key West inhabitants have made their living salvaging wrecked ships, rolling cigars, gathering sponges, writing world-famous novels, fishing for turtles and shrimp, and overcharging tourists for souvenirs. A railroad provided the original access to the island in 1912, built by—you guessed it—that zealous railroad magnate, Henry Flagler. A hurricane not only blew the stuffing out of the railroad but tossed the dirt that Flagler used to fill some of the smaller channels into the ocean. Flagler's legacy to Key West remains with Indian Key Fill, the old railroad bridge running parallel to the highway in some spots, and his cameo scene in *Key Largo.*

Like most of this region, the city of Key West has a relaxed atmosphere, hot sunshine, and spectacular sunsets. Over the years, it has attracted travelers and famous authors like Tennessee Williams, Ernest Hemingway, Elizabeth Bishop, and Robert Frost. Today, an easygoing diversity still attracts a new generation of writers and artists, gay people, recluses, adventurers, and eccentrics.

One note before you off and throw yourself into the Key West sun—the island lies as far south as the Bahamas, and the tropical sun will scald you if you don't take precautions. Especially if you're getting to the farthest key via the Overseas Highway, the sun reflecting off the water is powerful.

Practical Information and Orientation

Emergency: 911.

Visitor Information: Key West Chamber of Commerce, 402 Wall St. (294-2587), in old Mallory Sq. Useful *Guide to the Florida Keys and Key West* available here. Accommodations list of guest houses popular with gay people. Open daily 9am-5pm. **Key West Visitors Bureau,** P.O. Box 866, Key West 33041 (296-3811 or 800-352-5397), produces a detailed guide to accommodations. Open Mon.-Fri. 9am-5pm. **Key West Welcome Center,** 3840 N. Roosevelt Blvd. (296-4444 or 800-284-4482), just north of the intersection of U.S. 1 and Roosevelt Blvd. Arranges accommodations, theater tickets, weddings, and reef trips if you call in advance. Open daily 9am-5pm.

Key West International Airport: on the southeast corner of the island. Serviced by **Eastern** and **Piedmont** airlines. No public bus service.

Greyhound: 615½ Duval St. (296-9072). Obscure location in an alley behind Antonio's restaurant. To Miami, stopping along all the Keys (3 per day, 5 hr., $30). Open Mon.-Fri. 7am-12:30pm and 7-8pm, Sat. 7-11:30am.

Public Transport: Key West Port and Transit Authority, City Hall (292-8159 or 292-8164). One bus ("Old Town") runs clockwise around the island and Stock Island; the other ("Mallory St.") runs counterclockwise. Pick up a clear and helpful free map from the Chamber of Commerce (see above) or any bus driver. Service Mon.-Sat. 6:10am-10:35pm, Sun. 6:40am-6:40pm. Fare $.75, seniors and students $.35. **Handicapped Transportation,** 294-8468.

Taxi: Keys Taxi, 296-6666, $1.40 plus $1.75 per mi.

Car Rental: Alamo, Ramada Inn, 3420 N. Roosevelt Blvd. (294-6675 or 800-327-9633), near the airport. $33 per day, $132 per week. Under 25 $10 per day extra. Must be 21 with major credit card or $50 deposit. It is recommended that foreign travelers pay the deposit through a travel agent. Drop-off in Miami costs a prohibitive $55.

Bike Rental: Key West Hostel, 718 South St. (296-5719). $6 per day, $30 per week. Open daily 8-11am. Credit card and deposit required.

Help Line: 296-4357.

Post Office: 400 Whitehead St. (294-2557), 1 block west of Duval at Eaton. Open Mon.-Fri. 8:30am-5pm. **ZIP code:** 33040.

Area Code: 305.

Just five mi. long and three mi. wide, Key West resides at the southernmost point of the continental U.S. and at the end of Rte. 1, 160 mi. southwest of Miami. Only 90 mi. north of Havana, Cuba, Key West dips farther south than many islands in the Bahamas.

Divided into two sectors, the eastern part of the island, called "Des Moines" or "America" by some, harbors the tract houses, chain motels, shopping malls, and the airport. **Old Town,** the west side of town below White St., is cluttered with beautiful old conch houses. **Duval Street** is the main north-south thoroughfare in Old Town, **Truman Avenue** the major east-west route. Key West is cooler than mainland Florida in summer, and much warmer in winter.

On the way to, and in, the city of Key West, driving is slow; most of the highway is a two-lane road with only an occasional passing lane. Bikers beware: police enforce traffic laws. Use hand signals, stop at signs, and watch for one-way streets.

Accommodations and Camping

Beautiful weather resides year-round in Key West alongside beautiful tourists. As a result, good rooms at the nicer hotels go for up to $400 per day, especially during the winter holidays. There is no "off-season." Key West remains packed virtually year-round, with a lull of sorts from mid-September to mid-December; even then, don't expect to find a room for less than $40.

Try to bed down in **Old Key West;** the beautiful, 19th-century clapboard houses capture the flavor of the Keys. Some of the guest houses in the Old Town offer complimentary breakfasts and some are for gay men exclusively. Do *not* park overnight on the bridges—this is illegal and dangerous.

Key West Hostel, 718 South St. (296-5719), at Sea Shell Motel in Old Key West, 3 blocks east of Duval St. Call for airport or bus station pickup. Even has its own postcards. Rooms with 4-6 beds, shared bath. A/C at night. Famous $1 dinners and $2 breakfasts. Kitchen open until 9pm. No curfew. Office open daily 8am-10pm. Members $12, nonmembers $15 (*not* AYH/HI-affiliated). Key deposit $5. Motel rooms in summer $45, in winter $75. Call ahead to check availability; also call for late arrival.

Eden House, 1015 Fleming St. (296-6868 or 800-533-5397). Bright, clean, friendly hotel, just 5 short blocks from downtown. Rooms with shared bath, some with balconies. Pool, jacuzzi. In-season $70, summer $35.

Caribbean House, 226 Petronia St. (296-1600; 800-736-0179; 800-543-4518), at Thomas St. in Bahama Village. Brand-new, Caribbean-style rooms with cool tile floors, A/C, TV, and ceiling fans. Comfy double beds. Norman, the friendly owner, may be able to place you in the completely furnished Caribbean Cottage (sleeps 5) or an unfurnished low-rent apartment for comfortable summer living. In season: rooms $55, cottage $75. Summer: rooms $40, cottage $55.

Tilton Hilton, 511 Angela St. (294-8697), next to the Greyhound station near downtown. Plain rhyming rooms, as cheap as you'll find. Color TV, A/C. Singles in summer $32, in winter $50.

Boyd's Campground, 6401 Maloney Ave. (294-1465), on Stock Island. Take bus to Maloney Ave. from Stock Island. 12 acres on the ocean. Full facilities, including showers. Primitive sites $21. Water and electricity $5 extra, A/C or heat $5 extra. Waterfront sites $3 extra.

Food

Expensive restaurants line festive Duval Street. Side streets offer lower prices and fewer crowds. Sell your soul and stock up on supplies at **Fausto's Food Palace,** 522 Fleming St. (296-5663), the best darn grocery store in Old Town. (Open Mon.-Sat. 8am-8pm, Sun. 8am-6pm.) Don't leave Key West without having a sliver of (or even a whole) **key lime pie,** although the genuine article with a tangy yellow filling is hard to come by (key limes are not green).

Half-Shell Raw Bar, Land's End Village (294-7496), at the foot of Margaret St. on the waterfront 5 blocks east of Duval. Rowdy and popular with tourists. Great variety of seafood dinners $8-10. Famed for its spring conch chowder ($2.50). Open daily 11am-11pm.

El Cacique, 125 Duval St. (294-4000). Cuban food at reasonable prices. Homey and colorful. Filling lunch and dinner specials, with pork or local fish, black beans, and rice for under $6. Try fried plantains, conch chowder, or bread pudding as side dishes and flan for dessert. Open daily 8am-10pm.

Blue Heaven Fruit Market, 729 Thomas St. (296-8666), 1 block from the Caribbean House. Hemingway used to drink beer and referee boxing matches here when it was a pool hall. Dinners $8-12. Open Mon.-Sat. 3-11pm.

Sights

Biking is a good way to see Key West, but first you might want to take the **Conch Tour Train** (294-5161), a narrated ride through Old Town, leaving from Mallory Sq. This touristy one-and-a-half-hour trip costs $11 (kids $5), but guides provide a fascinating history of the area. (Operates daily 9am-4:30pm.) **Old Town Trolley** (296-6688) runs a similar tour, but you can get on and off throughout the day.

The glass-bottomed boat *Fireball* takes two-hr. cruises to the reefs and back (296-6293; tickets $14, ages 3-12 $7). One of a few cruise specialists, the **Coral Princess Fleet,** 700 Front St. (296-3287), offers snorkeling trips with free instruction for beginners (3 per day, $17; open daily 8:30am-6:30pm).

For many years a mecca for artists and writers, the **Hemingway House,** 907 Whitehead St. (294-1575), off Olivia St., is where "Papa" wrote *For Whom the Bell Tolls* and *A Farewell to Arms.* Tour guides at the houses are rumored to be notoriously awful; grin and bear it, or traipse through the house on your own. About 50 cats (descendants of Hemingway's cats) make their home on the grounds; ask their names from the tour guides and be mildly amused. (House open daily 9am-5pm. Admission $6, kids $1.50.) The **Audubon House,** 205 Whitehead St. (294-2116), built in the early 1800s, houses some fine antiques and a private collection of the works of ornithologist John James Audubon. (Open daily 9:30am-5pm. Admission $5, ages 6-12 $1.)

Down Whitehead St., past Hemingway House, you'll come to the **southernmost point** in the continental U.S. and the adjacent **Southernmost Beach**. A small, conical monument and a few conchshell hawkers mark the spot. The **Monroe County Beach,** off Atlantic Ave., has an old pier allowing access past the weed line. The **Old U.S. Naval Air Station** offers deep water swimming on Truman Beach ($1). **Mel Fisher's Treasure Exhibit,** 200 Greene St. (294-2633), will dazzle you with glorious gold. Fisher discovered the sunken treasures from the shipwrecked Spanish vessel, the *Atocha.* A *National Geographic* film is included in the entrance fee. (Open daily 10am-5pm. Admission $5, kids $1.)

The **San Carlos Institute,** 516 Duval St., built in 1871, is a freshly restored paragon of Cuban architecture that shines with majorca tiles from Spain and houses a research center for Hispanic studies. The **Haitian Art Company,** 600 Frances St. (296-8932), six blocks east of Duval St., is crammed full of vivid Caribbean artworks. (Open daily 10am-6pm.)

Watching a sunset from the **Mallory Square Dock** is always a treat. Magicians, street entertainers, and hawkers of tacky wares work the crowd; swimmers and speedboaters show off; and the crowd always cheers when the sun slips into the Gulf with a blazing red farewell.

Every October, Key West holds a week-long celebration known as **Fantasy Fest,** which culminates in an extravagant parade. The entire population of the area turns out for the event in costumes that stretch the imagination. In April, the **Conch Republic** celebration is highlighted by a bed race, and the January-through-March **Old Island Days** features art exhibits, a conch shell-blowing contest, and the blessing of the shrimp fleet.

Entertainment

The daily *Key West Citizen* (sold in front of the post office) and monthly *Solares Hill* and *The Conch Republic* (available at the Key West Chamber of Commerce—see Practical Information—and in lobbies and waiting rooms) all cover events on the island. Nightlife in Key West revs up at 11pm and runs down very late. Out-of-town goons have been known to heckle gay travelers at the far north end of Duval.

Sloppy Joe's, 201 Duval St., at Greene (294-5717). Reputedly one of "Papa" Hemingway's preferred watering holes; the decor and rowdy tourists would probably now send him packing. Originally located in Havana but moved to "Cayo Hueso" (i.e. Key West) when Castro rose to power. The bar's usual frenzy heightens during the Hemingway Days Festival in mid-July. Reasonable draft prices. R&B day and night. Open daily 9am-4am.

Captain Tony's Saloon, 428 Greene St. (294-1838). The oldest bar in Key West. Tony Tarracino, the owner, usually shows up at 9pm. Open Mon.-Thurs. 10am-1am, Fri.-Sat. 10am-2am, Sun. noon-1am.

Rick's, 208 Duval St. (296-4890). Right across from Sloppy Joe's. Continuous hard rock. *AAAArrrrghhhh.* Open daily 11am-4am.

Miami

Barely a century ago, Ohio's wealthy Julia Tuttle bought herself some Biscayne Bay swampland and decided to build herself a city. Only after convincing ubiquitous Standard Oil magnate Henry Flagler to build a railroad to the place did she manage to instigate the development of a major urban and cultural center. Today Miami is a complicated, international city. Although the rather run-down swampland aesthetic still permeates the area near the beach and the entire city is often ruthlessly hot, the downtown is art-deco cool with stucco and pastel, and the ocean is mere moments away. Many smaller cultures make up this city: Little Havana, a well-established Cuban community; Coconut Grove, with its village-in-the-swampland bohemianism; placid, well-to-do Coral Gables, one of the country's earliest planned cities; and the African-American communities of Liberty City and Overtown.

Practical Information

Emergency: 911.

Visitor Information: Greater Miami Convention and Visitors Bureau, 701 Brickell Ave. (539-3000; 800-283-2707 outside Miami), 27th floor of the Barnett Bank building downtown. Open Mon.-Fri. 8:30am-5pm. **Coconut Grove Chamber of Commerce,** 2820 McFarlane Rd. (444-7270). Mountains of maps and advice. Open Mon.-Fri. 9am-5pm. The **Miami Beach Resort Hotel Association,** 407 Lincoln Rd. #10G (531-3553), can help you find a place on the beach. Open Mon.-Fri. 9am-5pm, Sun. 10am-3pm.

Miami International Airport: 876-7000, 7 mi. northwest of downtown. Bus #20 is the most direct public transportation into downtown (bus #3 is also usable); from there, take bus C or K to South Miami Beach.

Amtrak: 8303 NW 37th Ave. (835-1221 or 800-872-7245), not far from the Northside station of Metrorail. Bus L goes directly to Lincoln Rd. Mall in South Miami Beach. Open daily 7:45am-7:30pm. To: Orlando (1 per day, 5½ hr., $48); Jacksonville (2 per day, 8 hr., $70); and Washington, DC (2 per day, 22 hr., $145).

Greyhound: Miami Beach Station, 7101 Harding Ave. (538-0381 for fare and schedule info). To: Orlando (8-10 per day, 6½ hr., $42); Jacksonville (8-10 per day, 11 hr., $57); and Atlanta (6 per day, 15½ hr., $75). Ticket window open daily 5am-midnight.

Public Transport: Metro Dade Transportation, (638-6700; 6am-11pm for info.) Complex system; buses tend to be quite tardy. The extensive **Metrobus** network converges downtown; most long bus trips transfer in this area. Lettered bus routes A through X serve Miami Beach. After dark, some stops are patrolled by police (indicated with a sign). Service daily 6am-8pm; major routes until 11pm or midnight. Fare $1. Pick up a *Map Manual* at the visitors bureau (see Practical Information) or at information stands at the corner of W. Flagler and NW 1st Ave. and on the Lincoln Rd. Mall in Miami Beach. Both open Mon.-Fri. 8am-5pm. Futuristic **Metrorail** service downtown. Fare $1, rail to bus transfers $.25. The **Metromover** loop downtown, which runs 6:30am-7pm, is linked to the Metrorail stations.The **Tri-Rail** (1-800-874-7245) connects Miami, Ft. Lauderdale, and West Palm Beach. Trains run Mon.-Sat. 5am-9:30pm. Fare $2, students and seniors with ID $1.

Taxis: Yellow Cab, 444-4444 (easy enough). **Metro Taxi,** 888-8888 (eas 5555 (not too hard).

Car Rental: Value Rent-a-Car, 1620 Collins Ave., Miami Beach (532-8257 per week. Drivers under 25 pay $5 additional daily charge. Open daily 8am-6pm credit card or $225 deposit.

Auto Transport Company: Dependable Car Travel, 162 Sunny Isles Blvd. (94 Mon.-Fri. 8:30am-5pm, Sat. 8:30am-noon. Must be 18 with credit card or passport license.

Bike Rental: Miami Beach bicycle Center, 923 W. 39th St., Miami Beach (531-4161 hr., $12 per day, $40 per week, 2-hr. min. Open Mon.-Fri. 9:30am-6pm, Sat. 9:30am-5pm be 18 with credit card or $40 deposit. **Dade Cycle Shop,** 3216 Grand Ave., Coconut Grove 6075). $5 per hr., $15-22 per day. Open daily 9:30am-5:30pm. Must have $10 deposit and driv license or credit card.

Help Lines: Crisis Hotline, 358-4357. **Rape Treatment Center and Hotline,** 1611 NW 12th Ave. (585-7273). **Gay Community Hotline,** 759-3661. **Center for Survival and Independent Living (C-SAIL),** 1310 NW 16th St. (547-5444). Offers info on services for the disabled. All lines open Mon.-Fri. 8am-5pm.

Post Office: 500 NW 2nd Ave. (371-2911). Open Mon.-Fri. 8:30am-5pm, Sat. 8:30am-12:30pm. **ZIP code:** 33101.

Area Code: 305.

Orientation

Three highways criss-cross the Miami area. Just south of downtown, I-95, the most direct route north-south, runs into **U.S. 1,** known as the **Dixie Highway.** U.S. 1 goes as far as the Everglades entrance at Florida City and then all the way out to Key West as the Overseas Highway. **Route 836,** a major east-west artery through town, connects I-95 with the **Florida Turnpike,** passing the airport in between. Take Rte. 836 and the Turnpike to Florida City to avoid the traffic on Rte. 1.

When looking for street addresses, pay careful attention to the systematic street layout; it's *very* easy to confuse North Miami Beach, West Miami, Miami Beach, and Miami addresses. Streets in Miami run east-west, avenues north-south, and numbers into the hundreds refer to both. Miami divides into NE, NW, SE, and SW sections; the dividing lines (downtown) are **Flagler Street** (east-west) and **Miami Avenue** (north-south). Some numbered streets and avenues also have names—i.e., Le Jeune Rd. is SW 42nd Ave., and SW 40th St. is called Bird Rd. Try to get a map with both numbers and names in order to solve this conundrum.

Several four-lane causeways connect Miami to **Miami Beach**. The most useful is **MacArthur Causeway,** which feeds onto 5th St. in Miami Beach. Numbered streets run across the island, with numbers increasing as you go north; the main north-south drag is **Collins Avenue.** In South Miami Beach, **Washington Avenue,** one block to the west, is the main commercial strip, while **Ocean Avenue,** actually on the waterfront, lies one block east. The **Rickenbacker Causeway** is the only connection to Key Biscayne.

Spanish-speakers will have an advantage getting around Miami. The city has a large Spanish-speaking community; the *Miami Herald* now even puts out a Spanish edition. You may even run into problems on buses without speaking Spanish, since many drivers only speak Spanish.

Accommodations and Camping

Finding cheap rooms in Miami should never pose a problem. Several hundred art-deco hotels in South Miami Beach stand at your service. For safety, convenience, and security, stay north of 5th St. A "pullmanette" (in 1940s lingo) is a room with a refrigerator, stove, and sink; getting one and some groceries allows you to save money on food. In South Florida, since any hotel room short of the Fontainebleau Hilton is likely to have two- to three-inch cockroaches ("palmetto bugs"), try not to take them as indi-

of quality; they are actually shy, reticent, even beautiful creatures. In general, the season for Miami Beach runs late December to mid-March.

mping is not allowed in Miami, and the nearest campgrounds are north or west of city. Those who can't bear to put their tents aside for a night or two should head on ne of the nearby national parks.

Miami Beach International Travelers Hostel, 236 9th St. (534-0268), at the intersection with Washington Ave. From the airport, take J bus to 41st and Indian Creek, then transfer to bus C to 9th and Washington. From downtown, take bus C or K or call for directions. Has a relaxed international atmosphere and central location, kitchen, laundry, common room. No curfew. 29 rooms with A/C and private bath. Hostel rooms $12 (max. 4 people). Private rooms $24.

The Clay Hotel (HI/AYH), 1438 Washington Ave. (534-2988). Take bus C or K from downtown. Cheerful chaos reigns in the 7 buildings. Kitchen, laundry facilities, and a useful ride board. Very international crowd. Most rooms have 4 beds; 2 rooms share a bathroom. No curfew. Members $9, winter $10. Nonmembers $12. A/C $1. Hotel singles $21. Doubles $27. Key deposit $5.

Tudor Hotel, 1111 Collins Ave. (534-2934). Beautiful renovations make this one of the nicest hotels in Miami Beach, in all pastels with flamingo murals and deco-period lighting. All rooms have refrigerator, microwave, cable TV, A/C, phone. Singles and doubles $40. Weekly $210.

Kent Hotel, Collins Ave. (531-6771), one block from the beach. Beautifully renovated rooms and friendly staff. TV, A/C, breakfast. Singles or doubles April 15-Dec. 15 $40, Dec. 15-April 15 $60. Ocean view $10 more.

Miami Airways Motel, 5001 36th St. (883-4700). Will pick you up at nearby airport for free. Clean rooms, breakfast, A/C, pool, HBO, but pretty far from the action. Singles $32. Doubles $37.

Larry & Penny Thompson Memorial Campground, 12451 SW 184th St. (232-1049), a long way from anywhere. By car, drive 20-30 min. south along Dixie Hwy. Pretty grounds in a grove of mango trees. Laundry, store, and all facilities, plus artificial lake with swimming beach, beautiful park, and even water slides. For further lake info, call 255-8251. Office open daily 8am-7pm but takes late arrivals. Lake open daily 10am-5pm. Sites $13, with hookup $20. Weekly: sites $81, with hookup $122.

Food

If you eat nothing else in Miami, be sure to try Cuban food. Specialties include *media noche* sandwiches (a sort of Cuban club sandwich on a soft roll, heated and compressed); *mamey,* a bright red ice cream concoction; rich *frijoles negros* (black beans); and *picadillo* (shredded beef and peas in tomato sauce, served with white rice). For Cuban sweets, seek out a *dulcería,* and punctuate your rambles around town with thimble-sized shots of strong, sweet *café cubano* ($.25).

Cheap restaurants are not common in Miami Beach, but an array of fresh bakeries and fruit stands can sustain you with melons, mangoes, papayas, tomatoes, and carrots for under $3 a day.

Irish House, Alton Rd. (534-5667), Miami Beach. A favorite hangout for local journalists, politicos and beach-goers. Noted for its buffalo wings ($5.25) and cheeseburgers ($4.50). Open Mon.-Sat. 11am-2am, Sun. 2am-2am—this place never closes on Sat. night.

La Rumba, 2008 Collins Ave. (538-8998), Miami Beach, between 20th and 21st St. Good, cheap Cuban food and noisy fun. Try their *arroz con pollo* (chicken with yellow rice, $6) with a banana milkshake ($1.75). Open Fri.-Wed. 7:30am-midnight.

Flamingo Restaurant, 1454 Washington Ave. (673-4302), right down the street from the hostel. Friendly service, all in Spanish. Try the *pollo* (chicken) with pinto beans and rice $4.25. Open Mon.-Sat. 9am-7:30pm.

Our Place Natural Foods Eatery, 830 Washington Ave. (674-1322), Miami Beach. All vegetarian fare. New Age books mingle with juices, salads, pita, tofutti, etc. Lunch $3-6, dinner $5-10. Great daily specials with soup ($6). Live folk music on weekends. Open Mon.-Thurs. 11am-9pm, Fri.-Sat 11am-11pm, Sun. 10am-8pm.

King's Ice Cream, 1831 SW 8th St. (643-1842), on Calle Ocho. Tropical fruit *helado* (ice cream, $2) flavors include coconut (served in its own shell), *mamey,* and banana. Also try *churros* (thin Spanish donuts, 10 for $1) or *café cubano* ($.10). Open Mon.-Sat. 10am-11pm, Sun. 2pm-11pm.

Sights

The best sight in Miami is the beach. When you get too burned or dazed and are about to kill an Arab, try the **Seaquarium,** 4400 Rickenbacker Causeway, Virginia Key (361-5703), just minutes from downtown. While not on par with Sea World in Orlando, it has an impressive array of shows, including obligatory dolphins, hungry sharks, and Lolita, the killer whale. The aquarium also displays tropical fish. (Open daily 9:30am-6:00pm; ticket office closes 5pm. Admission $15, kids $11.)

South Miami Beach or **South Beach,** the swath of town between 6th and 23rd St., teems with hundreds of hotels and apartments whose sun-faded pastel façades recall what sun-thirsty northerners of the 1920s thought a tropical paradise should look like. The art-deco palaces constitute the country's largest national historic district and the only one which has preserved 20th-century buildings. A fascinating mixture of people populates the area, including large retired and first-generation Latin communities; knowing Spanish is a big advantage here. **Walking tours** of the historic district are offered every Saturday at 11am ($6). Call 672-2014 to find out the point of departure.

On the waterfront downtown is Miami's newest attraction, the **Bayside** shopping complex, with fancy shops (many beyond the realm of the budget traveler), exotic food booths, and live reggae or *salsa* on Friday and Saturday nights. Near Bayside, visit the **Police Hall of Fame and Museum,** 3801 Biscayne Blvd. (891-1700), and learn more than you ever wanted to know about the police. Watch in your rearview mirror for the police car suspended alongside the building. (Open daily 10am-5:30pm. Admission $3, seniors and kids $1.50.)

Little Havana lies between SW 12th and SW 27th Ave. (Take bus #3, 11, 14, 15, 17, 25, or 37.) The street scenes of **Calle Ocho** (SW 8th St.) lie at the heart of this district; the corresponding section of W. Flagler St. is a center of Cuban business. The changing exhibits at the **Cuban Museum of Arts and Culture,** 1300 SW 12th Ave. (858-8006), reflect the bright colors and rhythms of Cuban art. Take bus #27. (Open Wed.-Sun. 1pm-5pm. Admission by donation.)

An entirely different atmosphere prevails on the bay south of downtown in self-consciously rustic **Coconut Grove** (take bus #1 or Metrorail from downtown). The grove centers around the intersection of Grand Ave. and Main Hwy. Drop into a watering hole like **Señor Frog's,** 3008 Grand Ave. (448-0999), home of bang-up tables and phenomenal *salsa.* (Open Sun.-Thurs. 10:30am-1am, Fri.-Sat. 10:30am-2am.)

On the bayfront between the Grove and downtown stands **Vizcaya,** 3251 S. Miami Ave. (854-6559 and 856-8189; recorded info 579-2813), set in acres of elaborately landscaped grounds. Built in 1916 by International Harvester heir James Deering, the four façades of this 70-room Italianate mansion hide a hodgepodge of European antiques. (Open daily 9:30am-5pm; last admission 4:30pm. Admission $8, ages 6-12 $4. Take bus #1 or Metrorail to Vizcaya.) Across the street from Vizcaya, both the **Museum of Science** and its **Planetarium,** 3280 S. Miami Ave. (854-4247; show info 854-2222), offer laser shows and their ilk. Both congest with kids. (Open daily 10am-6pm, box office closes at 5:30pm. Admission $6, ages 3-12 $4. Planetarium shows $6 extra.)

Entertainment

The art-deco district in South Miami Beach is filled with clubs; Ocean Blvd., on the beach, is crowded with a young, rowdy set nearly every night of the week. Any club will do, just wander down and take your pick. For blues, try the **Peacock Café,** 2977 McFarlane Rd., Coconut Grove (442-8877; open Tues.-Sun. 11:30am-5am). After the money's gone, head for **Friday Night Live,** at **South Point Park,** the very southern tip of Miami Beach, which features free city-sponsored concerts 8-11pm. (Call 673-7730 for info, Mon.-Fri. 8:30am-5pm.) Down Washington Ave. at Española Way, the **Cameo Theater** (call 532-0922 for showtimes and prices), hosts live punk and other rock bands about once per week. For gay nightlife, check out **Uncle Charlie's,** 3673 Bird Ave. (442-8687), just off Dixie Hwy. (cover $3 Mon.-Wed., $4 Thurs.-Sun.).

Performing Arts and Community Education (PACE) (681-1470; open Mon.-Fri. 9am-5pm) offers more than 1000 concerts each year (jazz, rock, soul, dixieland, reggae, *salsa,* and bluegrass), most of which are free. For more info on what's happening in Miami, check *Miami-South Florida Magazine,* or the "Living Today," "Lively Arts," and Friday "Weekend" sections of the *Miami Herald.* Guides to what's happening may be found at all kinds of shops and restaurants in Miami Beach.

Near Miami: Everglades National Park

Near Miami, the **Everglades National Park** teems with exotic life. Visit the park in winter or spring, when heat, humidity, storms, and bugs are at a minimum and when wildlife congregates around the water. *Always* bring mosquito repellent to the Everglades. The park is accessible on the north via the **Tamiami Trail (U.S. 41)** or by the main park road **(Rte. 9336)** out of Florida City. (Entrance to the park $5.) The best way to tour the largely inaccessible park is to take Rte. 9336 40 mi. through the flat grasslands to Flamingo, on Florida Bay, stopping at the various nature trails and pullouts along the way. Stop at the **visitors center,** P.O. Box 279, Homestead 33030 (247-6211), by the park headquarters just outside the entrance, to see a film on the Everglades and to pick up maps and info. (Open daily 8am-5pm.) The visitors center also sponsors a variety of hikes, canoe trips, and amphitheater programs. To get face-to-snout with an alligator, try the **Anhinga Trail,** 2 mi. beyond the entrance. The **Mahogany Hammock** trail boasts the largest living mahogany tree in the U.S. **Pa-hay-okee Overlook** affords a terrific view of the "rivers of grass" for which the Park is named.

There are a number of options for campers in the Everglades. The park **campgrounds** at **Long Pine Key** and **Flamingo** have drinking water, grills, and restrooms. The Flamingo site has showers, but neither site has RV hookups. These sites are free during the summer, and only a small fee is charged in the winter.

The park also has lots of primitive backcountry campsites, accessible by boat, foot, or bicycle. Free permits for backcountry camping are available at ranger stations. Canoe rental ($20 per day) is available at the **Gulf Coast Ranger Station** (800-233-1821), near Everglades City. Airboats are not allowed in the park, but concessionaires offer various boat tours of the Gulf Coast. Check at the Gulf Coast Ranger Station for ticket prices and sailing times.

Within the park the **emergency** number is 305-247-6211. The **Park Headquarters** can be reached at 305-247-7272. If you would like to tune into park info on the radio, turn your dial to AM1610. If you aren't a camper, check with the **Everglades City Chamber of Commerce** at 813-695-3941 for hotel recommendations.

Orlando and Disney World

Though Orlando likes to tout itself as "the world's vacation center" and one of the country's fastest-growing cities, millions annually descend on this central Florida city for just one reason: Disney World, the world's most popular tourist attraction. Walt Disney selected the area south of Orlando as the place for his sequel to California's Disneyland. Disney has since augmented the Magic Kingdom with the Epcot Center and the new Disney-MGM Studios theme park.

A number of parasitic attractions, such as expensive water parks, abound in the area to scavenge the left-overs of Disney tourism. Be warned: of the many ways to blow your dough in this land of illusions, usually you are best off spending your time and money at Disney first. Two exceptions to this rule are Sea World and the spanking new Universal Studios Florida. With fun and exciting exhibits and rides, both are well worth their admission prices.

Practical Information and Orientation

Emergency: 911.

Visitors Information: Orlando-Orange County Visitors and Convention Bureau, 8445 International Dr. (363-5871), several mi. southwest of downtown at the Mercado (Spanish-style mall). Take bus #8 from downtown, and ask the bus driver to drop you off at the Mercado. Maps and info on nearly all of the amusement park attractions in the area. Pick up a free bus system map. Open daily 8am-8pm.

Amtrak: 1400 Sligh Blvd. (843-7611 or 800-872-7245). Three blocks east of I-4. Take S. Orange Ave., turn west on Columbia, then right on Sligh. To: Tampa (2 per day, 2 hr., $17); Jacksonville (2 per day, 3½ hr., $28); and Miami (1 per day, 5½ hr., $50). Open daily 6am-8:30pm.

Greyhound: 300 W. Amelia St. at Hughy Ave. (843-7720 for 24-hr. fare and ticket info), downtown near Sunshine Park 1 block east of I-4. To: Tampa (7 per day, 2½ hr., $16); Jacksonville (8 per day, 3 hr., $30); and Miami (6 per day, 7 hr., $46). Open 24 hrs.

Public Transport: Tri-County Transit, 438 Woods Ave. (841-8240 for info Mon.-Fri. 6:30am-6:30pm, Sat. 7:30am-5pm, Sun. 8am-4pm). Downtown terminal between Central and Pine St., 1 block west of Orange Ave. and 1 block east of I-4. Schedules available at most shopping malls, banks, and at the downtown terminal. Serves the airport (bus #11 at "B" terminal luggage claim), Sea World, and Wet 'n' Wild. Buses operate daily 6am-9pm. Fare $.75, transfers $.10.

Mears Motor Shuttle, 324 W. Gore St. (423-5566). Has a booth at the airport for transportation to most hotels, including the Airport Hostel (see Accommodations below). Cheapest transport besides city bus #11 if you're alone and can't split taxi fare. Also runs from most hotels to Disney ($12.50, $22 round-trip). Open 24 hrs. Call day in advance to reserve seat to Disney.

Taxi: Yellowcab, 422-4455. $2.45 first mi., $1.40 each additional mi.

Car Rental: Alamo, 8200 McCoy Rd. (857-8200 or 800-327-9633), near the airport. $25 per day, $122 per week. Under 25 $10 extra per day. Open 24 hrs. Must have major credit card or a $50 deposit and book through travel agent.

Help Lines: Rape Hotline, 740-5408.

Crisis Information: 648-3028.

Post Office: 46 E. Robinson St. (843-5673), at Magnolia downtown. Open Mon.-Fri. 8am-5pm, Sat. 9am-noon. **ZIP code:** 32801.

Area Code: 407.

Orlando proper lies at the center of hundreds of small lakes and amusement parks. **Lake Eola** reclines at the center of the city, east of I-4 and south of Colonial Dr. Streets divide north-south by **Route 17-92 (Mills Avenue)** and east-west by **Colonial Drive.** I-4, supposedly an east-west expressway, actually runs north-south through the center of town. To reach either downtown youth hostel (see Accommodations) by car, take the Robinson St. exit and turn right. **Disney World** and **Sea World** are 15 to 20 mi. south of downtown on I-4; **Cypress Gardens** is 30 mi. south of Disney off U.S. 27 near Winter Haven. Transportation out to the parks is simple—most hotels offer a shuttle service to Disney, but you can take a city bus or call Mears Motor Shuttle (see above).

Accommodations and Camping

Orlando does not cater to the budget traveler. Prices for hotel rooms rise exponentially as you approach Disney World; plan to stay in a hostel or in downtown Orlando. Reservations are a good idea in December, January, March, April, and on holidays. Or try **Kissimmee,** a few mi. east of Disney World along U.S. 192, which has some of the cheapest places around to camp. One city park and four Orange County parks have campsites ($7, with hookup $10). Contact **Orange County Parks & Recreation Department,** 118 W. Kaley St. (836-4290), and **Orlando Parks Department,** 1206 W. Columbia (246-2283), for more info. (Both open Mon.-Fri. 8am-8pm.)

Orlando International Youth Hostel at Plantation Manor (HI/AYH), 227 N. Eola Dr. (843-8888), at E. Robinson, downtown on the east shore of Lake Eola. Usually full July-Oct., so make reservations. Porch, TV room, kitchen facilities, A/C in most rooms, (negotiable) midnight curfew. Rooms sleep 4-6. Hostel beds $11, nonmembers $13. Private rooms $28. Breakfast $2, linen $2, key deposit $5. The friendly managers will take you to the theme park of your choice for $10 round-trip.

Airport Hostel, 3500 McCoy Rd. (859-3165 or 851-1612), off Daetwiler Rd. behind the La Quinta Motel. Take "Airport" bus #11 from the airport or downtown. Little glamour, but very homey, with tropical fruit trees out back. Kitchen facilities, pool access, no curfew. Check-in by 10pm. 2-night min. $10. Breakfast included.

Young Women's Community Club (HI/AYH), 107 E. Hillcrest St. (425-1076), at Magnolia, 4 blocks from Plantation Manor right behind the Orlando Sentinel. Take bus #10 or 12; staff recommends a taxi. Women aged 16-44 only. Clean, safe, and friendly. Pool. Flexible 3-night max. stay. $12. Linen $2. Good breakfast $2, dinner $4. No reservations.

Sun Motel, 5020 W. Irlo Bronson Memorial Hwy. (396-6666), in Kissimmee. Very reasonable considering proximity to Disney World (4 mi.). Cable TV, phone, pool, A/C. Singles $40-50. Doubles $45-55. Off-season: singles $25, doubles $28.

KOA, U.S. 192 (396-2400; 800-331-1453), down the road from Twin Lakes. Kamping kabins $28-38. Pool, tennis, store (open 7am-11pm). Even in season you're bound to get a site, but arrive early. Free buses twice per day to Disney. Office open 24 hrs. Tent sites with hookup $19. Each additional person $3.50.

Stage Stop Campground, 700 W. Rte. 50 (656-8000), 8 mi. north of Disney in Winter Garden. Take exit 80 off the Florida Turnpike N., then left on Rte. 50. Office open daily 8am-8:30pm. Sites with full hookup $19. Weekly: $112, A/C $1.50 per day.

Food

Lilia's Grilled Delight, 3150 S. Orange Ave. (351-9087), 2 blocks south of Michigan St., 5 min. from the downtown business district. Small, modestly decorated Philippine restaurant—one of the best-kept secrets in town. Don't pass up *lumpia,* a tantalizing combination of sauteed meat, shrimp, vegetables, and peanut butter in a fried dough or the *adobo,* the Philippine national dish. Lunch $3-5, dinner $4-7. Open Mon.-Fri. 11am-2:30pm.

Numero Uno, 2499 S. Orange Ave. (841-3840.) A number one local favorite serving tasty Cuban specialties in a casual setting. Roast pork dinner with rice, plantains, and salad about $8. Open Mon.-Thurs. 11am-3pm, Fri. 11am-3pm and 5-10pm, Sat. 1-10pm.

Deter's Restaurant and Pub, 17 W. Pine St.(839-5975), just up from Orange St. near the Church Street Mall. German-American cuisine in an after-work-let's-have-a-beer-touch-my-monkey atmosphere. Try the amazing chicken in reisling sauce ($10). Live entertainment Fri.-Sat. nights. Open Mon.-Sat. 11am-1am.

Ronnie's Restaurant, 2702 Colonial Plaza, at Bumby St. just past the Colonial Plaza mall (894-2943). Art-deco booths and counters from the 50s. Mix of Jewish, Cuban, and American cuisine. The famous breakfast special (eggs, rolls, juice, coffee, and more) may fill you up for a few days ($4.65). Steak dinner $10, fresh breads, swell pancakes. Open Sun.-Thurs. 7am-11pm, Fri.-Sat. 7am-1am.

China Coast Restaurant, 7500 International Drive (351-9776). Brunch buffet Mon.-Fri. 11am-2pm, Sat.-Sun. 11am-3pm for $4.

Nature's Table, 8001 South Orange Blossom Trail (857-5496). Vegetarian and healthful specialties. Delicious fruit and protein powder shakes ($1-2), yogurt, juice. Excellent, thick sandwiches under $4. Open Mon.-Fri. 9am-5pm.

Entertainment

The **Church Street Station,** 129 W. Church St. (422-2434), downtown between South and Garland St., is a slick, block-long entertainment, shopping, and restaurant complex. Get $.89 beef tacos at **NACO'S,** or the $3 dinner platter at the **Chinese Café**. Listen to free folk and bluegrass music at **Apple Annie's Courtyard.** Boogie down (and enjoy $.05 beers on Wed.) at **Phineas Phogg's Balloon Works** (enphorced 21 age restriction). Or pay $15 to go to the three theme shows. **Rosie O'Grady's** is the most popular show, featuring Dixieland and can-can girls. **Cheyenne Saloon and Opera House** has a country and western show, while rock and roll rules at the **Orchid Garden Ballroom.** For less expensive nightlife, explore **Orange Avenue** downtown. Several good bars and clubs have live music and dancing at very reasonable prices. The **Beach Club Café,** 68 N. Orange Ave. at Washington St. (839-0457), hosts DJ dancing or live reggae nightly.

Disney World

Admit it: you came here to see Disney, the mother of all amusement parks, a sprawling three-park labyrinth of kiddie rides, movie sets, and futuristic world displays. If bigger is better, Disney World certainly wins the prize for best park in the U.S. (824-4321 for info daily 8am-10pm). Like Gaul, Disney World is divided into three parts:

the **Magic Kingdom,** with seven theme regions; the **Epcot Center,** part science fair, part World's Fair; and the newly completed **Disney-MGM Studios,** a pseudo movie and TV studio with Magic Kingdom-style rides. All are located a few mi. from each other in the town of **Lake Buena Vista,** 20 mi. west of Orlando via I-4.

A one-day entrance fee of $35 (ages 3-9 $28) admits you to *one* of the three parks; it also allows you to leave and return to the same park later in the day. A four-day **passport** ($117, ages 3-9 $80) admits you to all three and includes unlimited transportation between attractions on the Disney monorail, boats, buses, and trains. You can opt for a five-day **super-plus pass** ($153, ages 3-9 $122.50), which also admits you to all other Disney attractions. The multi-day passes need not be used on consecutive days, and they are valid forever and ever. Those Disney attractions that charge separate admissions (unless you have a five-day super-plus pass) are: **River Country** ($13.50, ages 3-9 $10) and **Discovery Island** ($8.50, ages 3-9 $5)—for both $15, ages 3-9 $11; **Typhoon Lagoon** ($21, ages 3-9 $15.37); and **Pleasure Island.** ($12—$9 at info center, over 18 only unless with adult). For descriptions, see Other Disney Attractions below.

Gray Line Tours (422-0744) and **Mears Motor Shuttle** offer transport from most hotels to Disney (depart hotel at 9am, depart Disney at 7pm; $11-13 round-trip). Major hotels and some campgrounds provide their own shuttles for guests. **Cyclists** are stopped at the main gate and driven by security guards to the inner entrance where they can stash their bikes free of charge.

Disney World opens its gates 365 days per year, but hours fluctuate according to season. It's busy during the summer when school is out, but "peak times" during Christmas, Thanksgiving, spring break, and the month around Easter also pack in the crowds. More people visit between Christmas and New Year's than at any other time of year. Since the crowd hits the main gates at 10am, arrive before the 9am opening time and seek out your favorite rides or exhibits before noon. During peak period (and perhaps the rest of the year), the Disney parks actually open earlier than the stated time. Begin the day at the rear of a park and work your way to the front. You'll have mondo fun at the distant attractions while lines for those near the entrance are jammed. Persevere through dinner time (5:30-8pm), when a lot of cranky kids head home. Regardless of tactics, you'll often have to wait anywhere from 45 minutes to two hours at big attractions.

Magic Kingdom

Seven "lands" comprise the Magic Kingdom. You enter on **Main Street, USA,** meant to capture the essence of turn-of-the-century hometown U.S. Architects employed "forced perspective" here, building the ground floor of the shops 9/10 of the normal size, while the second and third stories get progressively smaller. Walt describes his vision in the "Walt Disney Movie" at the Hospitality House, to the right as you emerge from under the railroad station. The Main Street Cinema shows some great old silent films. Late afternoons on Main Street turn gruesome when the not-so-impressive "All America Parade" marches through at 3pm; take this chance to ride some of the more crowded attractions. Near the entrance, you'll find a steam train that huffs and puffs its way across the seven different lands.

The **Tomorrowland** area has rides and early-70s exhibits of space travel and possible future lifestyles. Tease the workers who have to wear hideous blue-and-orange polyester jumpsuits. The indoor roller coaster **Space Mountain** proves the high point of this section, if not the high point of the park, and is worth the extensive wait.

The golden-spired Cinderella Castle marks the gateway to **Fantasyland,** where you'll find Dumbo the Elephant and a twirling teacup ride. 20,000 Leagues Under the Sea sinks to new depths of brilliant premise but flawed implementation. The chilly temperatures in **It's A Small World** are the ride's only redeeming feature. Don't ride this until the end of the day. You may never, ever, get the evil tune out of your head, and you may be forced to learn first-hand about those damn unwanted thoughts—it's a small world after all. Catch "Magic Journeys," a plotless 3-D movie with extraordinary effects.

Liberty Square and **Frontierland** devote their resources to U.S. history and a celebration of Mark Twain. History buffs will enjoy the Hall of Presidents, and adventurers should catch the rickety, runaway Big Thunder Mountain Railroad rollercoaster. Haunted Mansion is both spooky and dorky. A steamboat ride or a canoe trip which you help paddle both rest your feet from the seemingly endless trek. Also be sure to stop and watch the entertaining animatronics at the Country Bear Jamboree.

Adventureland is a home away from home for those who feel the White Man's Burden. The Jungle Cruise takes a tongue-in-cheek tour through tropical waterways populated by not-so-authentic-looking wildlife. Pirates of the Caribbean explores caves where animated buccaneers battle, drink, and sing. The Swiss Family Robinson tree house, a replica of the shipwrecked family's home, provides more mental than adrenal excitement.

Epcot Center

In 1966, Walt Disney dreamed up an "Experimental Prototype Community Of Tomorrow" (EPCOT) that would evolve constantly, never be completed, and incorporate new ideas from U.S. technology—functioning as a self-sufficient, futuristic utopia. At present, Epcot splits into **Future World** and **World Showcase.** For smaller crowds, visit the former in the evening and the latter in the morning.

The 180-ft.-high trademark geosphere forms the entrance to Future World and houses the **Spaceship Earth** attraction, where visitors board a "time machine" for a tour through the evolution of communications. The **World of Motion** traces the evolution of transportation, and the **Universe of Energy** traces (in a somewhat outdated fashion, since it glorifies the Alaskan port of Valdez—site of the 1989 Exxon oil spill) the history of energy. The **Wonders of Life** takes its visitors on a tour of the human body (with the help of a simulator) and tells us all where babies come from. **Horizons** lamely presents the lifestyles of the 21st century. **The Land** has a thought-provoking film about people's relationship with the land, and takes visitors on a tour of futurisitic agrarian methods. **The Living Seas** fails to recreate an underwater research station. Finally, the ever-popular **Journey Into Imagination** pavilion features the 3-D "Captain Eo" (starring the moon-walking, sequin-sporting rock star Michael Jackson).

The rest of Epcot is the **World Showcase** series of international pavilions surrounding an artificial lake. An architectural style or monument, as well as typical food, represents each country. People in costumes from past and present perform dances, theatrical skits, and other "cultural" entertainment at each pavilion. Before setting out around the lake, pick up a schedule of daily events at **Epcot Center Information** in Earth Station. Three of the best attractions are the two 360° films made in China and Canada and the 180° film made in France. They all include spectacular landscapes, some national history, and an inside look at the people of the respective countries. **The American Adventure** gives a very enthusiastic and patriotic interpretation of American history. Save your pesos by shopping at your local Pier 1 store rather than the marked-up Mexican marketplace. Norwegian life must be more exciting than the fishing, sailing, and oil exploring shown by the boat ride in the Norway Pavilion. Every summer night at 9pm, Sat. 10pm (off-season Sat. only), Epcot has a magnificent show called **Illuminations,** which features music from the represented nations accompanied by dancing, lights, and fireworks.

The World Showcase pavilions also offer regional cuisine. Make reservations first thing in the morning at the Earth Station World Key Terminal, behind Spaceship Earth. At the **Restaurant Marrakesh** in the Moroccan Pavilion, for example, head chef Lahsen Abrache cooks delicious *brewat* (spicy minced beef fried in pastry) and *bastilla* (sweet and slightly spicy pie). A belly dancer performs in the restaurant every evening. (Lunch $10-15. Dinner $15-20.) The Mexican, French, and Italian pavilions also serve up excellent food at similar prices.

Disney-MGM Studios

Disney-MGM Studios have successfully created a "living movie set." Many of the familiar Disney characters stroll through the park, as do a host of characters dressed as directors, starlets, gossip columnists, and fans. A different has-been movie star leads a parade across Hollywood Boulevard every day. Events such as stunt shows and mini-theatricals take place continually throughout the park.

The Great Movie Ride, inside the Chinese Theater, takes you on a simple but nostalgic trip through old and favorite films; interactive ride varies by your selection of the first or second set of cars. **Superstar Television** projects members of the audience alongside TV stars, and the **Monster Sound Show** requires volunteers to add special effects to a short movie. The biggest attractions at this park are the **Indiana Jones Epic Stunt Spectacular,** in which you watch stuntmen and audience volunteers pull off amazing moves, and the **Star Tours** Star Wars ride, in which you feel the jerk of your space cargo ship dodging laser blasts.

Other Disney Attractions

For those who did not get enough amusement at the three main parks, Disney also offers several other attractions on its grounds with different themes and separate admissions (see Disney World above). The newest is **Typhoon Lagoon,** a 50-acre water park centered around the world's largest wave-making pool. Surf the 7-ft. waves that occasionally appear out of nowhere, or snorkel in a salt water coral reef stocked with tropical fish and harmless sharks. Besides six water slides, the lagoon has a wonderful creek on which you can take a relaxing inner-tube ride, an anomaly at Disney. Built to resemble a swimming hole, **River Country** offers water slides, rope swings, and plenty of room to swim. Both parks fill up early on hot days, and you might get turned away. Across Bay Lake from River Country is **Discovery Island,** a zoological park. Those seeking more (relatively) sinful excitations should head at night to **Pleasure Island,** Disney's attempt to draw students and the thirtysomething set. Those above 21 can roam freely between the theme nightclubs; 18-21-year-olds can enter if they remain with their guardians; under 18 may not enter.

Near Orlando: Sea World, Cypress Gardens, and Universal Studios Florida

One of the country's largest marine parks, **Sea World,** 19 mi. southwest of Orlando off I-4 at Rte. 528 (407-351-3600 for operator; 407-351-0021 for recording), requires about six hours to see everything. Shows feature marine mammals such as whales, dolphins, sea lions, seals, and otters. Though the Seal and Otter Show and the USO water-ski show are enjoyable, the killer whales Baby Shamu and Baby Namu are the big stars. Not only do they share the stage (or pool) with two beautiful white whales and two Orcas, the trainers actually mix it up with the huge creatures and take rides on their snouts. People in the park gravitate towards Shamu Stadium before the show; arrive early to get a seat. After your brow gets sweaty, visit the air-conditioned **Fantasy Theater,** an educational show with live characters in costume. The smallest crowds cling in February and from September to October. Most hotel brochure counters and hostels have coupons for $2-3 off regular admission prices. (Open daily 8:30am-10pm; off-season daily 9am-10pm. Admission $32, under 11 $28. Sky Tower ride $2.50 extra. Guided tours $5.50, kids $4.50. Take bus #8.)

Cypress Gardens (813-324-2111; 407-351-6606 in Orlando), in Winter Haven, is a botanical garden with over 8000 varieties of plants and flowers (open daily 8am-9:30pm; in winter daily 9am-7pm. Admission $17, ages 6-11 $11.50). Take I-4 southwest to Rte. 27 south, then Rte. 540 west. The "Gardens of the World" features plants, flowers, and sculptured mini-gardens depicting the horticultural styles of many countries and periods. Winding walkways and electric boat rides take you through the foliage. The main attraction is a water-ski show performed daily at 10am, noon, 2pm, and 4pm. **Greyhound** stops here once per day on its Tampa-West Palm Beach schedule ($20 from Tampa to Cypress Gardens). Look for coupons at motels and visitors centers.

Universal Studios Florida (363-8000), opened in 1990, is a two-in-one park containing a number of amazing theme rides: **Kongfrontation,** where King Kong will roughouse your cable car; an **E.T.** bike ride; and **Jaws,** a boat trip where you can see the shark used in the movie. Also look for the **Back to the Future** ride, with seven-story high OMNI-MAX surround screens and spectacular special effects.

Since the park serves as a working studio making films, stars abound. Recently, Steve Martin played a dad in *Parenthood* here. Nickelodeon TV programs are in continuous production. Universal also has a number of set blocks that you may have seen before in the movies—displaying Hollywood, Central Park, and Beverly Hills, as well as the infamous Bates Motel from *Psycho.* The park will expand over the next few years, and admission prices will vary as the park swings into full-scale action. Call the studios for info on current ticket prices.

Palm Beach

Palm Beach is the best known of the 23 municipalities that constitute Palm Beach County. Like a moat, the Intracoastal Waterway separates the Mediterranean Fantasyland of Palm Beach from the banal urban problems of its ragged sibling, West Palm. Similar to young Confucius who was shielded from the harsh reality outside his princely poshness, Palm Beach is blinded to the unpleasantness of real life; the city forbids hospitals, funerals parlors and even plumbers from setting up shop on the island. One of the first resort communities in the United States, vital Palm Beach owes some of its original appeal to its hundreds of picturesque coconut palms. It owes these palms, in turn, entirely to *Provincia*, the Spanish brigatine that wrecked on Palm Beach's shores in 1878, spilling its cargo of 20,000 non-native coconuts.

The best way to see the pink stucco mansions of Palm Beach is by bicycle. Pick up a map of established trails at **Palm beach Bicycle Trail Shop,** 223 Sunrise Ave. (659-4583). When they're not sunbathing or golfing, Palm Beach's visitors and residents enjoy shopping. Arguably the most famous shopping street east of Rodeo Drive, **Worth Street** overflows with galleries, designer shops, and Jaguars. Worth St. owes much of its fame to the pretty *faux*-Mediterranean buildings that house its stores. Addison Minzer, the playboy/architect commissioned to renovate Worth St. in the early 1920s, is often credited with introducing stucco pastels to South Florida with his Worth St. designs.

If you find the conspicuous consumption of earlier times more interesting than that of today, you may want to visit **Whitehall,** the Palm Beach home of Florida railroad magnate Henry Flagler, off Coconut Row, across from the Chamber of Commerce (665-2833). Built at the turn of the century, this palatial house contains hundreds of paintings, sculptures, and tapestries, all unlabeled and all decaying in humid, air-condition-less splendor. (Open Tues.-Sat 10am-5pm, Sun. noon-5pm. $5.) If you're looking for the beach in Palm Beach, try **Phipps Ocean Park,** on S. Ocean Blvd. Free. Those in town for the first weekend of May should not to miss **SunFest,** a 2-day bash featuring free concerts by big names in jazz and blues.

Like nearly everything else in the island paradise of Palm Beach or West Palm Beach, hotels are stylish and expensive. There are no hostels in either town, but many of the slightly run-down motels along South Dixie Hwy. offer rooms in the off-season for under $35. The only hotel in Palm Beach itself that even approaches affordability is the **Palm Beach Hotel,** 235 Sunrise Blvd. Palm Beach (659-7665); it is also one of the nicest places around. Take the bus to the corner of Sunrise and County. Very safe, with a friendly staff, 24-hr. check-in, and a pool. Bright clean rooms with double bed April-Dec. $55.; Jan.-March $90. Right across the street from the Palm Coast Shopping Center and its bus stop is **Aqua Motel,** S. Dixie Hwy. (582-7459). The Aqua has a pool, patio, and friendly proprietor. Old, clean, pastel rooms. Jan.-April singles $32, doubles $35; May-Dec. singles $25, doubles $28. Make reservations a week in advance during the season. **Parkview Motor Lodge,** 4710 S. Dixie Hwy. (833-4644), is newer and cleaner than most of the neighboring hotels. Take a northbound bus to the corner of S. Dixie and Murray, walk 1 block north along S. Dixie. Reception 7am-midnight, with 24 hr. security. Continental breakfast included. April-Dec. singles $38, doubles $40; Jan.-March singles $60, doubles $66. **KOA Campground,** off Southern Blvd. West, P.O. Box 16066, W. Palm Beach 33416 (793-9797), 18 mi. from I-95, is the closest campground to Palm Beach. Wooded sites adjacent to Safari Park. Lions may wake campers. ($20 for two with hookup, each additional person $2. Tent sites with electricity $18. Laundry, convenience store, showers, 10pm quiet time. Make reservations a few days ahead in season.)

Palm Beach brims with chic cafés where lunch can cost more than a good bicycle. Travelers staying in Palm Beach proper can buy groceries (especially the fruit—Florida fruit prices are very reasonable) at **Publix Supermarket,** 265 Sunrise Blvd. across from the Palm Beach Hotel. (Open Mon.-Sat. 7am-10pm, Sun. 7am-9pm.) There are also some reasonable restaurants in the area: **Champs-Elysées,** 229 Sunrise Blvd. near County Rd. and Sunrise Blvd. intersection (833-1949). This tiny French-style mom 'n' papa bakery serves breakfast and lunch with an accent. For breakfast, the gigantic fruit-filled croissants ($1.50) are wonderful. "Yesterday's" croissants are a bargain at $2.50 for a bag of five. Also try the quiche ($1.50) and assorted sandwiches with a drink ($4). (Open Mon.-Sat. 7am-5pm.) For style and stucco, skulk into **E.R. Bradley's Saloon,** 111 Bradley Place (833-3520), right across County Rd. from Bradley Park. Funky pink-stuccoed restaurant/bar with loud music, a young clientele, and reasonable prices for Palm Beach. The widely varied menu offers with big portions and very quick service. Snail fanciers will want to try the escargot ($6). Specialties include a steak sauteed with lots of vegetables ($10). The herb-roasted chicken ($12) is especially good, and the salads ($6) are huge. (Open daily 11am-2am.) There's no mamby-pamby stucco at **Ranch's Drug Store and Soda Fountain,** 3800 S. Dixie Hwy., West Palm Beach (833-6451).This is a hard-core drugstore sandwich counter with breakfasts ($2.25-3.75) and sandwiches ($3-3.75). For a taste of the 50s, suck down a malted ($2.25). (Open Mon.-Fri. 7am-7pm, Sat. 7:30am-6pm, Sun. 9am-3pm.)

If you would like to learn more about Palm Beach, contact the **Town of Palm Beach Chamber of Commerce,** 45 Coconut Row (655-3282). Pick up Co-Tran bus maps and pamphlets on attractions in Palm Beach proper. (Open Mon.-Fri. 10am-4pm.) Also try **Discover Palm Beach County, Inc.,** 1555 Palm Beach Lakes Blvd., Suite 204 (471-3995), in the NCNB Building, across from the baseball stadium. They have tons of free maps, visitors guides, and info on events. (Open Mon.-Fri. 8:30am-5pm.)

Amtrak serves Palm Beach county from 201 S. Tamarind Ave., W. Palm Beach (832-6164), in the pink building at the corner of Tamarind and Clematis St. To: Miami (2 per day, $13), Ft. Lauderdale (2 per day, $9), Tampa (1 per day, $37), Orlando (1 per day, $36). (Open daily 8am-5:45pm.) **Greyhound** stops at 100 Banyan Blvd., West Palm Beach (833-0825), at the intersection of Banyan Blvd. and N. Flagler St., on the Intracoastal. To: Orlando (6 per day, $37), Tampa (6 per day, $36), Miami W. Station (10 per day, $13), and Ft. Lauderdale (13 per day, $7). The **Co-Tran Bus System** is the public transportation in the area, covering all of Palm Beach and West Palm Beach with 3 circular bus routes. Fare: $.90. Buses run Mon.-Sat. 7am-9pm. The main office is at Palm Beach International Airport, Building 5-1440 (686-4555). Pick up a route map at the Chamber of Commerce. You can also try the **Tri-Rail System** that connects W. Palm Beach with Miami and Ft. Lauderdale at the Amtrak stop, 201 S. Tamarind Ave. Call 800-874-7245. Trains run Mon.-Sat. 5am-9:30pm. Pick up schedules at the stop in Palm Beach. Fare: $2, all students and seniors with ID $1. The **Yellow Cab Co.** (689-2222) charges $1.25 base fare plus $1.50 per mi. If you'd rather do the driving yourself, try **BEST Car Rental,** 470 S. Congress Ave. (697-1744). Cars go for $17 per day. Must be 21 with major card. No drop-offs except at W. Palm Beach. The **Palm Beach Bicycle Trail Shop** pumps at 223 Sunrise Ave. (659-4583), in the pale pink Palm Beach Building. Bikes for $6 per hr., $15 per ½-day. Pick up bike trail maps here. (Open Mon.-Sat. 9am-7pm, Sun. 10am-5pm.)

In an **emergency,** call 911. The **Rape Crisis and Sexual Abuse** line is at 833-7273, and the **Abuse Registry** is at 800-962-2873.

The **post office** sorts at 95 N. County Rd. (832-0633) and at 355 S. County Rd. (655-4321), both in Palm Beach. Open Mon.-Fri. 8:30am-5pm. The **ZIP code** is 33480.

The **area code** is 407.

Saint Augustine

Spanish adventurer Juan Ponce de León founded St. Augustine in 1565, making it the first European colony in North America and the oldest city in the U.S. Although he never found the legendary Fountain of Youth, de León did live to age 61, twice the expected life span at that time. Much of St. Augustine's original Spanish flavor remains intact, thanks to the town's efforts at preservation. Today in its dotage, the town is fairly quiet; its brick, palm-lined streets see few cars, and during the summer months the heat slows everything and everyone. Yet historic sights, good food, and friendly people make St. Augustine well worth a few rejuvenating days.

Practical Information and Orientation

Emergency: 911.

Visitors Center, 10 Castillo at San Marco Ave. (825-1000). From the Greyhound station, walk north on Ribeira, then right on Orange. Pick up hotel coupons and the free *Chamber of Commerce Map,* a comprehensive city guide. The ½-hr. movie, *St. Augustine Adventure,* cleverly introduces the city (every ½-hr.; free). Open daily 8:30am-5:30pm.

Greyhound: 100 Malaga St. at King St. (829-6401). To Jacksonville (5 per day, 50 min., $6.50) and Daytona Beach (7 per day, 1 hr., $10). Open Mon.-Fri. 8am-5:30pm, Sat. 8am-4pm.

Taxi: Ancient City Taxi, 824-8161. From the bus station to motels on San Marco about $2.

Help Lines: Rape Crisis, 355-7273.

Post Office: King St. at Martin Luther King Ave. (829-8716). Open Mon.-Fri. 8:30am-5pm, Sat. 10am-1pm. **ZIP code:** 32084.

Area Code: 904.

Unfortunately, the city has no public transportation, though most points of interest, such as the bus station, tourist office, budget motels, and tourist district, are within walking distance of one another. Historic St. Augustine, concentrated in the area between the **San Sebastian River** and the **Matanzas Bay** to the east, is easily covered on foot. **King Street,** running along the river, is the major east-west axis and crosses the bay to the beaches. **St. George Street,** also east-west, is closed to vehicular traffic and contains most of the shops and many sights in St. Augustine. **San Marco Avenue** and **Cordova Street** travel north-south. Winter brings a surge of activity to nearby **Vilano, Anastasia,** and **St. Augustine Beaches.**

Accommodations and Camping

Beyond the new, often full, youth hostel, you'll find several clusters of cheap motels in St. Augustine—one is a short walk north of town on San Marco Ave.; another is directly to the east of the historic district, over the Bridge of Lions along Anastasia Blvd.; and a third is near Vilano Beach. Several inns in the historic district offer nice rooms, but rates start at about $49 per night. Those traveling by car should consider the excellent seaside camping facilities at **Anastasia State Park.**

St. Augustine Hostel (HI/AYH), 32 Treasury St. (829-6163), at Charlotte, 6 blocks from the Greyhound station. Large, dormitory-style rooms with shower and fans or A/C. Kitchen available. Singles $10, nonmembers $13. Doubles $20. Guest bike rental $5 per day. Reservation must be made in advance. Open for reservations 8-10am and 5-10pm.

American Inn, 42 San Marco Ave. (829-2292), near the visitors center. Owner won't take your money until you've inspected your room. He also provides transportation to and from the bus station when a car is available. Big, clean singles and doubles $29-36, weekends $38-49. Check visitors center (see Practical Information) for coupons.

Seabreeze Motel, 208 Anastasia Blvd. (829-8122), just over the Bridge of Lions east of the historic district. Clean rooms with A/C, TV. Pool. Good restaurants nearby. Singles $22. Doubles $28.

The St. Francis Inn, 279 Saint George St. (824-6068), at Saint Francis St., 2 doors down from the Oldest House. Built in 1791, it's a charming 10-room inn with a jungle of flowers and a tucked-away pool. Much of its original 18th-century interior has been preserved. Iced tea and juice served all day. Free bike use. Rooms $47-78. Cottage on premises with full kitchen and living room $135 for 4 people, $8 each additional person. Continental breakfast included.

Anastasia State Recreation Area, on Rte. A1A (461-2033), 4 mi. south of the historic district. From town, cross the Bridge of Lions, and bear left just beyond the Alligator Farm. Open daily 8am-sundown. Sites $18, with electricity $21. Make weekend reservations.

Food

The flood of daytime tourists and the abundance of budget eateries make lunch in St. Augustine's historic district a delight. Stroll **Saint George St.** to check the daily specials scrawled on blackboards outside each restaurant; locals prefer those clustered at the southern end of Saint George near King St. Finding a budget dinner in St. Augustine is trickier, since the downtown is deserted after 5pm. However, an expedition along Anastasia Blvd. should unearth good meals for under $6. The seafood-wise will seek out the surf 'n' turf dinners ($15) at **Captain Jack's,** 410 Anastasia Blvd. (829-6846). Those with wheels interested in mass quantities of food should try the all-you-can-eat buffet at the **Quincey Family Steakhouse,** 2 mi. south of town on Rte. A1A at Ponce de León Mall. (Open Sun.-Thurs. 11am-10pm, Fri.-Sat. 11am-11pm.)

St. George Pharmacy and Restaurant, 121 Saint George St. Museum, luncheonette, and bookstore. Cheap sandwiches from $1.20; dinners from $2.50. Try the grilled cheese with a thick chocolate malt ($4). Breakfast special (egg, bacon, grits, toast or biscuit, and jelly) $2. Open Mon.-Fri. 7am-5pm, Sat.-Sun. 7:30am-5pm.

Café Camacho, 11-C Aviles St., at Charlotte St., 1 block from Saint George St. in the historic district. Part vintage clothes shop, part café. Serves delicious fruit shakes, soups, sandwiches, breakfast specials, vegetarian dishes, and an all-you-can-eat lunch bar from 11am-3pm ($5). Open Wed.-Mon. 7:30am-5pm.

El Toro Con Sombrero, 10 Anastasia Blvd., on the left just over the Bridge of Lions from downtown. Look carefully because the sign is hidden by a sign for the adjoining sports bar. If you like Mexican food and 50s music, this is the place. Open daily 7am-1am.

A New Dawn, 110 Anastasia Blvd. A health-conscious grocery store with a sandwich and juice counter. Delicious vegetarian sandwiches; try the tofu salad surprise ($2.55). Fruit shakes and sodas $1-2. Open daily 8am-6pm.

Sights and Entertainment

Saint George St. is the center of the **historic district,** which begins at the Gates of the City near the visitors center and runs south past Cadiz St. and the Oldest Store. Visit **San Agustín Antiguo,** Gallegos House, Saint George St. (825-6830), St. Augustine's authentically restored 18th-century neighborhood, where artisans and villagers in period costumes describe the customs, crafts, and highlights of the Spanish New World. (Open daily 9am-5pm. Admission $5, seniors $4.50, students and ages 6-18 $2.) The oldest masonry fortress in the country, **Castillo de San Marcos,** 1 Castillo Dr. (829-6506), off San Marco Ave., has 14-ft. thick walls built of coquina, the local shellrock. The fort itself resembles a four-pointed star complete with a drawbridge and a murky moat. Inside you'll find a museum, a large courtyard surrounded by guardrooms, livery quarters for the garrison, a jail, a chapel, and the original cannon brought overseas by the Spanish. A cannon-firing ceremony occurs once per day. (Open daily 8:15am-6:30pm; Sept.-May 9am-5pm. Admission $1, over 62 and under 12 free.)

St. Augustine has several old stores and museums. The self-descriptive **Oldest House,** 14 Saint Francis St. (824-2872), has been occupied continuously since its construction in the 1600s. (Open daily 9am-5pm. $5, seniors $4.50, students $2.50.) The **Oldest Store Museum,** 4 Artillery Lane (829-9729), has over 100,000 odds and ends from the 18th and 19th centuries. (Open Mon.-Sat. 9am-5pm, Sun. noon-5pm. Admission $3.) Also in the old part of the city is the coquina **Cathedral of St. Augustine,** begun in 1793. Although several fires destroyed parts of the cathedral, the walls and façade are original.

Six blocks north of the info center is the **Mission of Nombre de Dios,** Ocean St. (824-2809), a moss- and vine-covered mission which held the first Catholic service in the U.S. on September 8, 1565. Soaring over the structure is a 208-ft. steel cross commemorating the city's founding. (Open Mon.-Fri. 8am-8pm, Sat.-Sun. 9am-8pm. Mass Mon.-Fri. at 8:30am, Sat. at 6pm, Sun. at 8am. Admission by donation.) No trip to St. Augustine would be complete without a trek to the **Fountain of Youth,** 155 Magnolia Ave. (829-3168). Go right on Williams St. from San Marco Ave. and continue a few blocks past Nombre de Dios. (Open daily 9am-5pm. Admission $4, seniors $3, ages 6-12 $1.50.) In addition to drinking from the spring that Ponce de León mistakenly thought would give him eternal youth, you can see a statue of the explorer that does not age.

Though oil and water don't usually mix, Henry Flagler, co-founder of Standard Oil and a good friend of the Rockefellers, retired to St. Augustine. He built two hotels in the downtown area that the rich and famous once frequented, making St. Augustine the "Newport of the South." The former Ponce de León Hotel, at King and Cordova St., is now **Flagler College.** In summer the college is deserted, but during the school year students liven the town. In 1947, Chicago publisher and lover of large objets d'art Otto Lightner converted the Alcazar Hotel into the **Lightner Museum** (824-2874), with an impressive collection of cut, blown, and burnished glass. (Open daily 9am-5pm. Admission $4, ages 12-18 $1.)

Visitors can tour St. Augustine by land or by sea. **St. Augustine Sight-Seeing Trains,** 170 San Marcos Ave. (829-6545), offers a variety of city tours (1-8 hr.; open daily 8am-5pm). The one-hour tour ($9, ages 6-12 $4), a good introduction to the city, starts at the front of the visitors center (see Practical Information). **Coleé Sight-Seeing Carriage Tours** (829-2818) begin near the entrance to the fort, take about an hour, and cover the historic area of St. Augustine. ($9, ages 5-11 $4; open daily 8am-10pm.) The **Victory II Scenic Cruise Ships** (824-1806) navigate the emerald Matanzas River. Catch the boat at the City Yacht Pier, one block south of the Bridge of Lions (leaves at 1, 2:45, 4:30, 6:45, and 8:30pm; cruises $7.50, under 12 $3).

On Anastasia Island, at **Anastasia State Park,** you can see Paul Green's *Cross and Sword,* Florida's official state play, telling the story of St. Augustine with the help of a large cast, booming cannon, and swordfights. (Admission $8, ages 6-12 $4; discounts for AAA members and large groups.)

With such a penchant for loudness and liquid, St. Augustine has an impressive array of bars. **Scarlett O'Hara's,** 70 Hypolita St. (824-6535), at Cordova St., is popular with locals. The barbecue chicken sandwiches ($4) are filling and juicy, the drinks hefty and cool. Live entertainment begins at 9pm nightly. (Open daily 11:30am-1am.) Try the **Milltop,** 19½ Saint George St. (829-2329), a tiny bar situated above an old mill in the restored area. Local string musicians play on the tiny stage (daily 11am-midnight). On St. Augustine Beach, **Panama Hattie's** (471-2255) caters to the post-college crowd. Pick up a copy of the *Today Tonight* newspaper, available at most grocery and convenience stores, for a complete listing of current concerts, events, and dinner specials.

Tampa and St. Petersburg

The Gulf Coast communities of Tampa and St. Petersburg have a less raucous style than Florida's Atlantic Coast vacation destinations. The two cities offer quiet beaches, beautiful harbors, and perfect weather year-round unpoisoned by droves of tourists. One of the nation's fastest-growing cities and largest ports, Tampa contains thriving financial, industrial, and artistic communities. Across the bay, St. Petersburg caters to a relaxed, attractive retirement community, with oodles of health-food shops and pharmacies. Meanwhile, the town's beaches beckon with 28 mi. of soft white sand, emerald water, and beautiful sunsets. The high season on the Gulf Coast runs from October to April.

Practical Information and Orientation

Emergency: 911.

Visitor Information: Tampa/Hillsborough Convention and Visitors Association, 111 Madison St. (223-1111 or 800-826-8358). Open Mon.-Fri. 9am-8pm. **St. Petersburg Chamber of Commerce,** 100 2nd Ave. N. (821-4069). Open Mon.-Fri. 9am-5pm.

Traveler's Aid: In Tampa, 273-5936. Open Mon.-Fri. 8:30am-4:30pm. In St. Pete, 823-4891.

Tampa International Airport: (870-8700)) 5 mi. west of downtown. HARTline bus #30 runs between the airport and downtown Tampa. **St. Petersburg Clearwater International Airport** sits right across the bay. **The Limo** (822-3333) offers 24-hr. service from both airports to both cities and the beaches from Ft. De Soto to Clearwater ($10.50). Make reservations 12 hr. in advance.

Amtrak: In Tampa, 601 Nebraska Ave. (221-7600 or 800-872-7245), at Twiggs St., 1 block north of Kennedy. Two trains per day to: Orlando (2 hr., $17); Jacksonville (5 hr., $44); Savannah (8 hr., $75). Open daily 7:30am-8pm. No trains go south of Tampa—no service to St. Pete. In St. Pete, 3601 31st St. N. (522-9475). Amtrak will transport you to Tampa by bus ($5).

Greyhound: In Tampa, 610 E. Polk St. (229-1501 or 229-2112), next to Burger King downtown. To Miami (4 per day, 10 hr., $44) and Orlando (5 per day, 1½ hr., $15.50). In St. Pete, 180 9th St. N., downtown.

Public Transport: In Tampa, **Hillsborough Area Regional Transit (HARTline),** 254-4278. Fare $.85, transfers $.10. To get to St. Pete, take bus #100 express service from downtown to the Gateway Mall ($1.50). In St. Pete, **St. Petersburg Municipal Transit System,** 530-9911. Most routes depart from Williams Park at 1st Ave. N. and 3rd St. N. Ask for directions at the information booth there. Fare $.75, transfers $.10.

Help Lines: In Tampa, **Rape Crisis,** 238-7273. **Gay/Lesbian Crisis Line,** 229-8839. In St. Petersburg, **Rape Crisis,** 531-4664.

ZIP codes: Tampa 33602, St. Pete 33731.

Area Code: 813.

Tampa divides into quarters with **Florida Avenue,** running east-west, and **Kennedy Boulevard,** which becomes **Frank Adams Drive** (Rte. 60), running north-south. Numbered avenues run east-west and numbered streets run north-south. You can reach Tampa on I-75 from the north, or I-4 from the east.

In St. Petersburg, 22 mi. south, **Central Avenue** runs east-west. **34th Street** (U.S. 19) cuts north-south through the city and links up with the new **Sunshine-Skyway Bridge,** which connects St. Pete with the Bradenton-Sarasota area to the south. Avenues run east-west, streets north-south. The St. Pete beachfront is a chain of barrier islands accessible by bridges on the far west side of town, and extends from Clearwater Beach in the north to Pass-a-Grille Beach in the south. Many towns on the islands offer quiet beaches and reasonably priced hotels and restaurants. From north to south, these towns include: **Clearwater Beach, Indian Rocks Beach, Madiera Beach, Treasure Island,** and **St. Petersburg Beach.** The stretch of beach past the Don Cesar Hotel (a pink monstrosity recently declared a historical landmark) in St. Petersburg Beach and Pass-a-Grille Beach has the best sand, a devoted following, and the least pedestrian and motor traffic.

Accommodations and Camping

Inexpensive, convenient lodgings are rare in Tampa, but St. Petersburg has two youth hostels as well as many cheap motels lining 4th St. N. and U.S. 19. Some establishments advertise singles for as little as $16, but these tend to be ancient and dirty. To avoid the worst neighborhoods, stay on the north end of 4th St. and the south end of U.S. 19. Several inexpensive motels also line the St. Pete beach. In Tampa, you can try to contact the Overseas Information Center at the **University of South Florida** (974-3104) for help in finding accommodations. In St. Petersburg, ask around about the **St. Petersburg Youth Hostel,** 326 1st Ave. N (822-4141), which has recently opened its doors to budget travelers on the corner of 1st and 3rd.

Tampa

Motel 6, 333 E. Fowler Ave. (932-4948), near Busch Gardens. From I-275, take the Fowler Ave. exit. On the northern outskirts of Tampa, 30 mi. from the beach. Well-used, small rooms. Singles $22. Each additional person $6.

Holiday Inn, 2708 N. 50th St. (621-2081) From I-4, take Exit #3. Pool, whirlpool, spa, and cable TV. 1-4 people $57.

St. Petersburg

St. Petersburg International Hostel (AAIH), 215 Central Ave. (822-4095), at the Detroit Hotel downtown. Big, clean rooms with 2-4 beds, A/C; some with private bath. Kitchen and laundry facilities. Call for pick-up at Greyhound or Amtrak stations. In the same building, **Club Detroit** offers live music 5 nights per week. Also, **Janus Landing** offers big name concerts with the likes of Depeche Mode. $12.50, nonmembers $15. Weekly: $63, nonmembers $75. Key deposit $5. Private rooms available.

Kentucky Motel, 4246 4th St. N. (526-7373). Large, clean rooms with friendly owners, cable TV, refrigerator in each room, and free postcards. Singles $32. Doubles $36. Dec.-April rooms $10 more.

Grant Motel, 9046 4th St. (576-1369), 4 mi. north of town on U.S. 92. Pool. Clean rooms with A/C; most have a fridge. Singles $28. Doubles $30. Jan. 1-April 15 singles $38, doubles $40.

Windjammer, 10450 Gulf Blvd. (360-4940), on the beach. Large, clean rooms. Laundry, HBO, pool. Doubles $40-42, with kitchen $42-46. High season $50 and $65, respectively. Each additional person $5.

Treasure Island Hotel, 10315 Gulf Blvd. (367-3055). Across the street from beach, big rooms with A/C, fridges and color TV. Pool. Singles $28. Doubles $29. Each additional person $4.

The Trade Winds, 10300 Gulf Blvd. (360-0490). On the beach; nice pool, A/C, color TV. Singles $36. Each additional person $4.

Fort De Soto State Park (866-2662), composed of five islands at the southern end of a long chain of keys and islands, has the best camping. A wildlife sanctuary, the park makes a good daytrip or oceanside picnic spot (2-day min. stay; curfew 10pm; no alcohol; sites $16.50). Disregard the "no vacancy" sign at the toll booth ($.85) by the Pinellas Bayway exit. However, from January to April, you may want to make a reservation in person at the St. Petersburg County Building, 150 5th St. N. #146, or at least call ahead. In Tampa, try the **Busch Travel Park,** 10001 Malcolm McKinley Dr. (971-0008), ¼ mi. north of Busch Gardens, with a pool, store, recreation room, and train service to Busch Gardens and Adventure Island. (Tent sites $9. RV sites $15.)

Food

Prices for food leap high in Tampa, but cheap Cuban and Spanish establishments stretch all over the city. Black bean soup, gazpacho, and Cuban bread usually yield the best bargains. For Cuban food, **Ybor City** definitely has superior prices and atmosphere.

St. Petersburg's cheap, health-conscious restaurants cater to its retired population—they generally close by 8 or 9pm. Those hungry later should try St. Pete Beach or 4th St.

Tampa

JD's, (247-9683) 2029 E. 7th Ave., in Ybor City. Take bus #12. Soups, sandwiches, and Cuban food in a roomy, low-key restaurant. Breakfast $2.50. Lunch $3-5. Open Mon.-Fri. 9am-3pm.

The Loading Dock, 100 Madison St., downtown. Sandwiches $3-5. Try the "flatbed" or the "forklift" for a filling diesel-fueled meal. Open Mon.-Fri. 8am-8pm, Sat. 10:30am-2:30pm.

Cepha's, 1701 E. 4th ave. (247-9022), has cheap Jamaican specialties. Red snapper or curry chicken $4-7. Colorful garden in back and reggae shows throughout the summer. Open Mon.-Wed. 11:30am-10pm, Thurs. 11:30am-1am, Fri.-Sat. 'til 3am.

The Spaghetti Warehouse, 1911 13th St. (248-1720), right in Ybor Square. Lunch or dinner $7. Open Sun.-Thurs. 11am-10pm, Fri.-Sat. noon-11pm.

St. Pete

Crabby Bills, (593-4825) 412 1st St. N., Indian Rocks Beach. Cheap, extensive menu. Ultra-casual atmosphere. Six blue crabs $5.50. Open Mon.-Thurs. 11am-10pm, Fri.-Sat. 11am-11pm. Arrive before 5pm to avoid substantial wait.

Tangelo's Bar and Grille, 226 1st St. NE, St. Pete (894-1695). Try a carb burger ($4.50) or cold gazpacho soup ($2). Open Mon.-Sat. 11am-9pm.

Beach Nutts, 9600 W. Gulf Blvd., Treasure Island. Not much selection, but oh! what an atmosphere. Right on the beach. Live reggae most nights next door. Open 9am-2am.

Russo's Pizza (367-2874), 103-104th Ave. Treasure Island. A local joint connected to an arcade. Try the tasty and filling stromboly ($3.85). Open 11am-midnight.

Sights and Activities

Tampa

Bounded roughly by 22nd Street, Nebraska Avenue, 5th Avenue, and Columbus Drive, **Ybor City** is Tampa's Latin Quarter. The area expanded rapidly after Vincent Martínez Ybor moved his cigar factories here from Key West in 1886. Although cigar manufacturing has since been mechanized, some people still roll cigars by hand and sell them for $1 in **Ybor Square,** 1901 13th St., 247-4497), a 19th-century cigar factory converted into an upscale retail complex. (Open Mon.-Sat. 9:30am-5:30pm, Sun. noon-5:30pm. Free.) **Ybor City State Museum,** 1818 9th Ave. at 21st St. (247-6323), traces the development of Ybor City, Tampa, the cigar industry, and Cuban migration. (Open Tues.-Sat. 9am-noon and 1-5pm. Admission $.50.) The **Three Birds Bookstore and Coffee Room,** 1518 7th Ave. (247-7041), contributes artsily to Ybor City. Sip orange zinger tea or get a slice of black forest cheesecake while you read the latest *Paris Review.* (Open Mon.-Thurs. 11am-6pm, Fri.-Sat. 11am-10pm.) Aside from the square, the Ybor City area has remained relatively unsullied by the rapid urban growth that typifies the rest of Tampa; **East 7th Avenue** still resembles an old neighborhood. Keep an ear out for jazz and a nose out for Cuban cuisine. Be careful not to stray more than two blocks north or south of 7th Ave. since the area can be extremely dangerous, even during the daytime. Bus #5, 12, and 18 run to Ybor City from downtown.

Now part of the University of Tampa, the Moorish **Tampa Bay Hotel,** 401 W. Kennedy Blvd., once epitomized fashionable Florida coast hotels. Teddy Roosevelt trained his Rough Riders in the backyard before the Spanish-American War. The small **Henry B. Plant Museum** (254-1891), in a wing of the University of Tampa building, is an orgy of rococo craftsmanship and architecture; the exhibits themselves, which include Victorian furniture and Wedgewood pottery, pale in comparison. (Guided tours at 1:30pm. Open Tues.-Sat. 10am-4pm. Admission by donation.)

Downtown, the **Tampa Museum of Art,** 601 Doyle Carlton Dr. (223-8130), houses the Joseph Veach Nobre collection of classical and modern works. (Open Tues.-Sat. 10am-5pm, Sun. 1-5pm. Free.) Across from the University of South Florida, north of downtown, the **Museum of Science and Industry,** 4801 E. Fowler Ave. (985-5531), features a simulated hurricane. (Open daily 10am-4:30pm. Admission $4, ages 5-15 $2.) The **Museum of African American Art,** 1308 N. Marion St. (372-2466) is accessible from I-275 and I-4. Features the art history and culture of the classical Barnett-Aden collection. (Open Tues.-Sat. 10am-4:30pm and Sun. 1-4:30pm; $2 donation requested.)

The **waterfront** provides much of Tampa's atmosphere. *"Deo! Deo! Daylight come and me wanna go home."* Banana boats from South and Central America unload and tally their cargo every day at the docks on 139 Twiggs St., near 13th St. and Kennedy Blvd. Every year in February the *Jose Gasparilla,* a fully rigged pirate ship loaded with hundreds of exuberant "pirates," "invades" Tampa and kicks off a month of parades and festivals, such as the **Gasparilla Sidewalk Art Festival.** (Pick up a copy of the visitors guide, for current info on various events and festivals.)

Enjoy everything from bumper cars to corkscrew rollercoasters at Tampa's **Busch Gardens—The Dark Continent,** 3000 Busch Blvd. and NE 40th St. (971-8282). Take

I-275 to Busch Blvd., or take bus #5 from downtown. Not only are people confined to trains, boats, and walkways while giraffes, zebras, ostriches, and antelope roam freely across the park's 60-acre plain, but Busch Gardens has two of only 50 white Bengal tigers in existence. (Open daily 9am-8pm; off-season daily 9:30am-6pm. Admission $29, infants free. Parking $3.) A visit to the **Anheuser-Busch Hospitality House** inside the park provides a sure-fire way to make your afternoon more enjoyable. You must stand in line for each beer, with a three-drink limit.

About ¼ mi. northeast of Busch Gardens at 4545 Bougainvillie Ave. is **Adventure Island** (987-5660), a 19-acre water theme park. (Admission $15. For those under 48 in. $12. Open 10am-5pm with extended hours in summer.)

St. Petersburg

St. Petersburg's main attraction is its coastline. **Pass-a-Grille Beach** may be the nicest, but with parking meters, it exacts a toll. The **Municipal Beach** at Treasure Island, accessible from Rte. 699 via Treasure Island Causeway, offers free parking. When you're too sunburned to spend another day on the sand, head for **Sunken Gardens,** 1825 4th St. N. (896-3187), home of over 7000 varieties of exotic flowers and plants. (Open daily 9am-5:30pm. Admission $7, ages 3-11 $4.)

Well, hello Dalí! The **Salvador Dalí Museum,** 1000 3rd St. S. (823-3767), in Poynter Park on the Bayboro Harbor waterfront, contains the world's largest collection of Dalí works and memorabilia—93 oil paintings, 1300 graphics, and even works from a 14-year-old Dalí. (Tours available. Open Tues.-Sat. 10am-5pm, Sun.-Mon. noon-5pm. Admission $5, seniors and students $3.50, under 9 free.) **Great Explorations,** 1120 4th St. S. (821-8885), is a museum with six areas of exhibits to fondle. Test your strength at the Body Shop, where you can compare your muscles with scores taken from around the country. Admission 4-17 $3.50, 17-65 $4.50, 66 and over $4. (Open Mon.-Sat. 10am-5pm, Sun. 1-5pm.) **The Pier,** at the end of 2nd Ave. NE (821-6164), extends out into Tampa Bay from St. Pete, ending in a five-story inverted pyramid complex that contains a shopping center, aquarium, and restaurant. (Open Mon.-Sat. at 10am, Sun. at 11am.)

The Great Lakes

The Great Lakes are fickle and fierce, changing mood with drastic speed. A day can begin glass-serene and end up as stormy as the North Atlantic, churning with 20-foot swells which can suck 50,000-ton freighters to the bottom. Lake Superior, the largest freshwater lake in the world, has the least populated and most scenic coasts, and dances with the only significant wolf population left in the contiguous United States. Lake Michigan is a sports-lover's paradise, offering deep-water fishing, swimming, sailing, and sugar-fine sand dunes. Lake Erie has suffered the most from industrial pollution, but thanks to vigilant citizens and strict regulations, the shallowest Great Lake is gradually reclaiming its former beauty.

The deep forests and gentle farmlands of the inland regions of the Great Lakes states are not as capricious as their watery neighbors; in Michigan, one virgin stand of pines has remained untouched for over 500 years. Although much of the natural splendor of the Great Lakes region is pristine, the area also bears the scars of industrial boom and rust. In the 19th and early 20th centuries, millions of immigrants came here to search their fortune in the land of the region by farming the rich soil, mining the lodes of iron and copper, and logging the dense forests. Soon, natural resources were exhausted, and the economies of the region had to either change or collapse. Most areas weathered the shift by transporting and manufacturing rather than supplying raw materials. However, in the wake of modernization and adaptation, cities like Cleveland and Detroit were left behind, turning an industrial heartland into an obsolete industrial wasteland.

Today, the Great Lakes region has the strongest draw for the hostel-and-campground crowd, with its multitudinous water and wilderness opportunities in places where the talons of "progress" never reached. But the sophisticated urban traveler should not despair—Minneapolis/St. Paul has all the artsy panache of any coastal metropolis (minus the accompanying angst), and Chicago remains the focal point for Midwestern activity, with world-class music, architecture, and restaurants.

Illinois

Economically, socially and culturally, Illinois divides into two distinct parts: Chicago—the third largest metropolis in the U.S.—and the rest of agricultural Illinois. Back when Abraham Lincoln lived and worked around Springfield, "downstate" Illinois was known as Egypt, for obscure and probably unflattering reasons. This is not to say that downstate Illinois is boring...well, it is, actually, but not necessarily in a bad way. An endearing folksy spirit that is quintessentially Midwestern still exists in many of the semi-industrial and farming communities that pepper the gently rolling hills of Illinois; if you've ever yearned for a land where movies are still only $3.50 and nobody gives up bacon and eggs for oat bran, *this* is the place to be.

Practical Information

Capital: Springfield.

Office of Tourism, 620 E. Adams St., Springfield 62701 (217-782-7500).

Time Zone: Central (1 hr. behind Eastern). **Postal Abbreviation:** IL

Sales Tax: 6.25%.

Great Lakes
0
200 miles
0
200 kilometers
CANADA
Chippewa
National
Forest
Isle Royale
National Park
Lake Superior
N.D.
Duluth
Apostle
Islands WI
MINNESOTA
MICHIGAN
94
35
Lake Huron
S.D.
Minneapolis
St. Paul
WISCONSIN
75
Mississippi River
35
Lake Michigan
Traverse
City MI
90
94
Madison
94
Milwaukee
Detroit
90
94
Ann Arbor
IOWA
Chicago
80
90
Lake Erie
80
PA.
Cleveland
55
65
69
OHIO
ILLINOIS
INDIANA
75
Columbus
71
Springfield
Indianapolis
Cincinnati
70
Columbus
MISSOURI
Bloomington
65
57
KENTUCKY
N

Chicago

The story of Chicago is very much the story of America. A young city, Chicago was incorporated in 1839, and gained preeminence not through aristocratic birthright, but by inventiveness, hustle, gumption and plain ol' hard work. The "City of Big Shoulders" built its muscles hauling lumber and butchering livestock, *not* by pumping itself up in front of a mirror.

Modern America and Chicago were both children of advanced transportation and industrial technology. With the advent of the railroad, Chicago became the gateway to the West by moving larger quantities of natural resources faster than any other city. Always innovative, Chicago traders developed a system of commodity pricing in which grain was first graded and then mixed with grain of a similar quality. The city was the first to develop assembly-line slaughterhouses in which each worker hacked off a chunk of meat and sent the rest on down the line. To transport meat in the summer, Chicago packers developed a method of refrigerating rail cars with ice harvested during the winter.

The "Windy City" is a demographic microcosm of the United States equalled in diversity only by New York City. While most of its ethnic groups have been assimilated, the city is still racially polarized; the South Side and West Side are mostly African-American, while the North Side and suburbs are mostly white, with incoming Asian-Americans. De-industrialization has struck hard. The stockyards and freight depots which made the Armours and the Pullmans rich have been closed for decades.

Yet Chicago refuses to be written off. The city still pulses as the financial hub of the Heartland, its Board of Trade continues to be more inventive than New York's Wall Street, and its cultural variety includes a score of major museums, an impressive collection of public sculpture, one of the world's finest symphonies, excellent small theaters, and the University of Chicago, which has employed more Nobel laureates than any other university in the world.

Practical Information

Emergency: 911.

Visitor Information: Chicago Visitor Information Center, 163 E. Pearson (280-5740 or 800-487-2446), in the Water Tower Pumping Station or at the Chicago Cultural Center, Randolph St. at Michigan Ave. Pick up a copy of the *Chicago Visitors Guide.* Open Mon.-Sat. 9am-5pm. Write to **Chicago Office of Tourism,** 806 N. Michigan Ave., Chicago, 60611. **Illinois Information Center,** 310 S. Michigan Ave. (793-2094 or 800-223-0121), across from the Art Institute. Open Mon.-Fri. 9am-5pm.

Traveler's and Immigrant's Aid: 327 S. LaSalle St. at Jackson St. (435-4500; after hours 222-0265). Open Mon.-Fri. 8:30am-5pm. Other locations at O'Hare Airport (686-7562; open Mon.-Fri. 8am-4:30pm) and Greyhound (435-4537). The main office provides language assistance in Spanish, Polish, Vietnamese and Chinese, legal aid on immigration matters, and information for disabled persons.

Consulates: Australia, 321 N. Clark St. (645-9444); **Canada,** 310 S. Michigan Ave. (616-1870); **France,** N. Michigan Ave. (787-5359); **Germany,** 104 S. Michigan Ave. (263-0850); **Ireland,** 400 N. Michigan Ave. (337-1868); **Israel,** 111 E. Wacker Dr. (565-3300); **Italy,** 500 N. Michigan Ave. (467-1550); **Mexico,** 300 N. Michigan Ave. (726-3942); **U.K.,** 33 N. Dearborn St. (346-1810). Most open Mon.-Fri. 9am-5pm, closed for an hour around lunchtime.

O'Hare International Airport: Off I-90 (686-2200). Inventor of the layover, holding pattern and headache. Depending on traffic, a trip between downtown and O'Hare can take up to 2 hrs. The **Rapid Train** runs between the Airport El station and downtown ($1.50). The ride takes 40 min.-1 hr. **Continental Air Transport** (454-7800) connects the airport to selected downtown and suburban locations including the Marriot Hotel at Michigan and Rush. Runs every 30 min. 6am-11:30pm. Fare $13.75, 60-90 min. **Midway Airport** (767-0500), on the western edge of the South Side, often offers less expensive flights. To get downtown, take CTA bus #54B to Archer, then ride bus #62 to State St. For an extra 20¢, the 99M express runs from Midway downtown 6:30-8:15am and from downtown to Midway during the afternoon rush hour. Continental Air Transport costs $9.50. For **limousine** service to either airport, call **C.W. Limousine Service** (493-2700).

Downtown Chicago
N
0 1/4 Mile
0 1/4 Kilometer
Lincoln Ave.
Lincoln Park
Eugenie St.
North Ave.
N. Larrabee St.
Lake Shore Drive
Gold Coast
Lake Michigan
Division St.
Chicago River
Oak St.
Hancock Building
Chicago Ave.
Old Water Tower
Museum of Contemporary Art
Clark St.
Dearborn St.
State St.
Ontario St.
Ohio St.
Grand Ave.
Kinzie St.
Lake St.
Randolph St.
Washington Blvd.
Madison St.
Monroe St.
Adams St.
Jackson Blvd.
Van Buren St.
Franklin St.
Wells St.
La Salle St.
First National Bank
Wabash Ave.
Michigan Ave.
Chicago Art Institute
Sears Tower
Chicago Harbor
JFK Expressway
Grant Park
Eisenhower Expressway
Congress Parkway
Polk St.
Columbus Dr.
Roosevelt Rd.
Shedd Aquarium
Field Museum Of National History
Adler Planetarium
Bernham Park Yacht Harbor
Ryan Expressway
Jefferson St.
South Branch
Soldier Field

Rides from the South Side, as well as between the two airports (both $9.75). Airport baggage lockers $1 per day.

Amtrak: Union Station (800-872-7245), Canal and Adams St. across the river, west of the Loop. Take the El to State and Adams, then walk west on Adams 7 blocks. Amtrak's main hub may look familiar; it was the backdrop for the final baby-buggy scene of *The Untouchables*. Destinations include: St. Louis ($38), Detroit ($28) and Milwaukee ($16). Station open 24 hrs.; tickets sold daily 7:30am-10pm. Baggage check $1 per day.

Greyhound: 630 W. Harrison St. (781-2900), on corner of Jefferson and Desplaines. Take the El to Linton. The hub of central U.S. Also serves as home base for several smaller companies covering the Midwest. To: Milwaukee ($13), Detroit ($25) and St. Louis ($35). Open 5am-2am.

Public Transport: See Transportation below.

Taxi: Yellow Cab, 829-4222.

Car Rental: Fender Benders Rent-a-Car, 315 W. North Ave. at Orleans (280-8554), 1 block east from the Sedgwick El stop. $25 per day, $125 per week., 100 free mi., 20¢ each additional mi. Car may not leave Illinois. Must be 25 with major credit card. Open Mon.-Fri. 8:30am-6:30pm, Sat. 10am-2pm. **Dollar Rent-a-Car,** at O'Hare and Midway Airports; write P.O. Box 66181, Chicago, IL 60666. $28 per day, $118 per week; age 21-25 $5 surcharge per day. Must be 21 with major credit card.

Auto Transport Company: National U-Drive, 2116 N. Cicero Ave. (889-7737).

American Express: 34 N. Clark St. (263-6617).

Help Lines: Rape Crisis Line, 708-872-7799. 24 hrs. **Gay and Lesbian Hotline,** 871-2273. 24 hrs.

Medical Emergency: Cook County Hospital, 633-6000. Take the Congress A train to the Medical Center Stop.

Medical Walk-in Clinic: MedFirst, 310 N. Michigan Ave. (726-0577). Non-emergency medical care. Open Sun.-Fri. 8am-6pm, Sat. 8am-5pm.

Post Office: 433 W. Van Buren St. (765-3210), 2 blocks from Union Station. Open Mon.-Fri. 7am-5:30pm, Sat. 8am-5:30pm, 24-hr. self-service available. **ZIP code:** 60607.

Area Code: 312 for numbers in Chicago, 708 for numbers outside Chicago's municipal boundaries. All numbers listed here without area code are in the 312 area.

Orientation

Chicago runs north-south along 29 mi. of southwest Lake Michigan lakefront. The city and its suburbs sprawl across the entire northeastern corner of Illinois. Most cross-country road, rail, and airplane trips in the northern U.S. pass through Chicago.

Despite its vast size, Chicago is a neatly organized and comprehensible grid. Street addresses begin at **State Street,** which divides the city into east and west, and **Madison Street,** which cleaves it into north and south. The addresses of streets suffixed N., S., E. or W. increase every "standard block" (1/8 mi.) by 100 in number as the distance from State and Madison increases. This makes it easy to locate any address on a map even if you don't know the nearest cross-street. For example, 3200 N. Clark St. would be on Clark St., four mi. north of Madison, and 1600 W. Division St. would be two mi. west of State. Outside Chicago's municipal boundaries this scheme breaks down, as each suburb maintains its own numbering system.

Chicago is a machine that accepts immigrants and produces Americans. Arriving with little or nothing but a foreign tongue, boatloads of newcomers have found jobs, apartments and a new start here. To ease the transition, many remain in ethnic communities which sustain Old-World traditions in churches, social clubs and local bars. The Chicago immigrant paradigm is a familiar one. Once established, immigrant children move to the suburbs to become middle class, and the neighborhood evaporates. Later, *their* children move back to the city as young professionals, gentrifying worn-out districts and rejoining the churn and bustle of this living city. This cycle continues today, and Chicago's neighborhoods are always in a state of flux. An area that illustrates the first step in this sequence is **Uptown**, whose new name is **New Chinatown;** it centers at Broadway and Argyle and is the center of the Southeast Asian influx into the city. It also has a strong Indian and Arab presence. The areas that were once **Greektown** (Halsted St. at Madison) and **Little Italy** (Taylor St. between Morgan and Racine) have reached middle-age; their residents have begun the exodus to the suburbs. Though it still exists, Greektown is fading; Little Italy is no more. At the end of the story of Chicago neighborhoods lies **Bucktown,** a hot area where young professionals whose parents moved out of their city are moving back. In all, Chicago neighborhoods are neither discrete nor fixed; the city is constantly evolving.

The Chicago River on the north and west, Lake Michigan on the east, and the elevated train enclose the **Loop,** the downtown area and business hub which contains many of America's architectural treasures. Just south of the Loop and southwest of the natural history museum lies **Pilsen,** a center of Chicago's Latino community, and unfortunately *not* a safe place to venture at night. North of the Loop across the river are **Near North,** an area with more office buildings, and the glitzy shopping district known as the **Magnificent Mile:** Michigan Ave. between Grand Ave. and Division St. The north side of Chicago—a broad term subsuming all the territory north of the river—is generally safe during the day, with active commercial streets bounding residential areas. There are over a dozen neighborhoods with fairly ambiguous boundaries; the *Rand McNally Chicago Visitor's Guide and Map* labels them all. The **Gold Coast,** an elite residential area, glitters on North Lake Shore Drive. Further north along the lake sprawls **Lincoln Park,** a 19th-century English-style park which includes a zoo, a conservatory and beaches. South of the Loop, **Chinatown** preserves a sliver of China on Cermak Rd. at Wentworth; there are oodles of noodle restaurants, bakeries and touristy shops. As it is a little dangerous at night, it is wisest to go there for lunch. The city's sizable Polish community has an enclave near **Oak Park. Lakeview** is home to the city's most concentrated gay population, compared by many to equivalent areas in San Francisco. It's a fun area for anyone to visit, with many cheap restaurants and lots of vintage shops selling clothes, eclectic bunches of home furnishings, gewgaws and decorative items. Much farther south, at about 57th St., lies **Hyde Park,** home of the University of Chicago. Although Hyde Park is reasonably safe, especially during the day, avoid neighboring **Near South Side,** one of the country's most dangerous urban ghettos. Parts of the **West Side** are also extremely unsafe. In general, don't go south of Cermak or east of Halsted St. at night.

Transportation

The **Chicago Transit Authority,** part of the **Regional Transit Authority** (836-7000 in the city, 800-972-7000 in the suburbs), runs rapid transit trains, subways and buses. The CTA runs 24 hrs., but late-night service is infrequent and unsafe in some areas, especially the South Side. Some stations do not operate at all at night. Maps are available at many stations, the Water Tower Information Center, and the RTA Office. It is worthwhile to get one of these maps and to spend a few minutes deciphering the system of bus routes and trains. Directions in *Let's Go* are generally given from the downtown area, but obviously there are usually several ways of getting to your destination.

The **elevated rapid transit train** system, called the **El,** bounds the major downtown section of the city, the **Loop.** Downtown some of the routes are underground, but are still referred to as the El. Trains marked "A," "B" or "all stops" may run on the same route, stopping only at stations designated as such. Also, different routes may run along the same tracks in some places. Because of Chicago's grid layout, many bus lines run for several miles along one straight road. Train fare is $1.25, bus fare $1; from 6 to 9am and 3 to 6pm, $1.25; 10 tokens good for one train or bus ride each any time of day cost $9. Remember to get a transfer (25¢) from the driver when you board the bus or enter the El stop, which will get you up to two more rides in the following two hours. A $15 weekly pass (Sun.-Sun.) is available in many supermarkets and at the "Checks Cashed" storefronts with the yellow signs. A $60 monthly pass is available in many supermarkets, including the Jewel and Dominick's chains.

METRA operates a vast commuter rail network with 11 rail lines and four downtown stations snaking far out to the suburbs to the north, west, and south. (For route info call 322-6777 Mon.-Fri. 8am-5pm or 800-972-7000 other times.) Schedules and maps are free at their office at 547 W. Jackson. Fare is based on distance ($1.75-5).

Avoid **driving** in the city as much as possible. Daytrippers can leave the car in one of the suburban subway lots for 24 hrs. ($1). There are a half-dozen such park-and-ride lots; call CTA (see above) for info. Parking downtown costs $6 per day for most lots; most residential areas in the north side have street parking for residents only (look for signs).

Several major highways crisscross the city and urban area. The **Eisenhower (I-290)** cuts west from the Loop. **I-90** pivots around the Eisenhower; to the northwest it's called the **Kennedy,** to the south, the **Dan Ryan.** The **Edens (I-94)** splits off from the Kennedy and heads north to the suburbs. **I-294** rings the city. Some of the highways require tolls.

Accommodations

If you're in the mood for a "nap," Chicago has its share of hotels that charge by the hour. For a full night's sleep at a decent price, stop at one of the three hostels. The family with a car may prefer one of the motels on Lincoln Ave., around 5600 N. Lincoln. The national motel chains have locations off the interstates, about an hour's drive from downtown; they're an inconvenient, expensive ($40 and up) but reliable option if you arrive late at night. **Chicago Bed and Breakfast,** P.O. Box 14088, Chicago, 60614 (951-0085 or 800-484-4056), is a referral service with over 60 rooms of varying prices throughout the city and outlying areas. None have parking, but the majority are near public transit; street parking is occasionally available. (Singles $55-75, doubles $65-85.)

Chicago International Hostel (HI/AYH), 6318 N. Winthrop (262-1011). Take Howard St. northbound train to Loyola Station. Walk south 2 blocks on Sheridan Rd., then east 1 block on Sheridan Rd. (the road zigs) to Winthrop, then ½ block south. Clean rooms that are well worth the 30-min. ride from the Loop by train, 20 min. by #147 express bus. Free parking in the rear. Convenient to several theaters and nightspots. Good place to meet traveling students. Kitchen, laundry room. Rent bikes ($8 per day). Check-in 8-10am, 4-10pm. Lockout midnight, but doors open quickly at 2am to let in late-night carousers. 3-day max. stay enforced only rarely. $12, nonmembers $15. Linen included. Mid-July-mid-Sept. fills up; make reservations 2 weeks in advance.

Arlington House (AAIH), 616 Arlington Pl. (929-5380). Take the El to Fullerton, walk 2 blocks east to Orchard, turn left on Arlington Place; it's on the right. Parking is a hassle. Crowded rooms, most of them in a basement; shares a building with a senior citizens home. Few travelers. Laundry room, kitchenette. No curfew. In a safe, wealthy residential neighborhood. Dorm-style rooms with 10 beds each, $13, nonmembers $16. Singles $25. Doubles $34. Triples $51. Linens $2. Open 8am-12:30am.

International House (HI/AYH), 1414 E. 59th St. (753-2270), Hyde Park, off Lake Shore Dr. Take the Illinois Central Railroad to 59th St. and walk ½ block west. Part of the University of Chicago. Isolated from the rest of the city because the neighborhood can be dangerous at night. 200 comfortable dorm-style rooms; good price if you *need* privacy. Shared bath, cheap cafeteria. $15, nonmembers $27. Open mid-June-Aug., rooms occasionally available during school year. 1 week advance reservations recommended in summer.

Baker Hall, National College of Education, 2808 Sheridan Rd., Evanston, IL 60202 (708-256-5150). 1 hr. from the Loop by train. From station, walk 1 block east on Central St., then 2 blocks north on Ridge St. It's on the left. Take the northbound train from Howard to Central St. Delightful dorm with shared bath and cafeteria. Free parking. Coin-op laundry. No curfew, good neighborhood (of course; my roommate lives there). Singles $25. Doubles $30. Weekly $70 per person. Open July-Aug. Reserve several months in advance.

YMCA and YWCA, 30 W. Chicago Ave. (944-6211). Good security, bare rooms. No free parking, but next to $6-per-day commercial lot. Laundry available. Must be over 18. Singles $25. Doubles $33. Key deposit $5. Students: $75 per week, $270 per month.

Hotel Cass, 640 N. Wabash (787-4030), just north of the Loop. Take subway to Grand St. Convenient location, clean rooms. No parking. Singles $35, doubles $40, $5 extra with TV. A/C $5. Key deposit $5. International students $5 off.

Hotel Wacker, 111 W. Huron (787-1386), Near North Side. Convenient to downtown, no parking. No reservations; often fills on summer weekends. Fill in your own joke here, you lecherous swine, you. 24-hr. check-in. Singles $35. Doubles $40. Weekly: $80-85. Key and linen deposit $5.

Leaning Tower YMCA, 6300 W. Touhy, Niles, IL 60714 (708-647-1122). From Jefferson Park El stop, take bus #85A; 1 hr. from the Loop. Look for a ½-scale replica of the Leaning Tower of Pisa (it's a water tower, not the residence hall itself). Private baths, use of YMCA facilities. Coed. Must be over 21. Singles $28. Doubles $31. Key deposit $5. Off-season $4-5 less. Key deposit $5. Call ahead for summer reservations.

Acres Motel, 5600 N. Lincoln Ave. at Bryn Mawr Ave. (561-7777). Take the #11 bus from State St., about 50 min. from the Loop. Free parking. "The best surprise is no surprise"-style motel rooms. Private bath, 24-hr. check-in. Single or double $40, each extra person $4.50. Near restaurants, supermarkets; within ½ mi. in either direction on Lincoln Ave. there are about a dozen more motels with similar price and quality.

Food

Every nation on the map sends representatives to New York City, and, it seems, cooks to Chicago. You can find every type of cuisine in this cosmopolitan city, but don't go looking for it in the Loop, where high rents prevent immigrant restaurateurs from setting up a stove. On the blocks just south of Wrigley Field, especially on N. Clark St., you can find chow that spans the globe from Ethiopia to Mexico to Mongolia. Those who are dexterous with chopsticks should visit Chinatown at the Cermak El stop or, more conveniently, New Chinatown at Argyle and Sheridan at the Argyle El stop. Most of the original Greeks have left Greektown, on Halsted St. at Monroe, but their restaurants linger. Tourist brochures still call Taylor St. "Little Italy," but most of the Italian-Americans have said *ciao,* and their restaurants, except for three or four fairly expensive joints, have split as well. Chicago's most famous dish is its renowned pizza, which features a thick crust covered with melted cheese, fresh sausage, sautéed onions and peppers, and a spicy sauce made from fresh whole tomatoes. *Chicago* magazine includes an extensive restaurant guide which is cross-indexed by price, cuisine and quality. All of the restaurants listed here can be reached in less than 30 minutes by public transit from the Loop.

Pizza

Pizzeria Uno, 29 E. Ohio (321-1000), and **Due,** 619 N. Wabash (943-2400). Uno is where it all began. In 1943, owner Ike Sewall introduced Chicago-style deep dish pizza, and though the graffiti-stained walls have been painted over and the restaurant is franchised across the nation, the pizza remains damn good. Due sits right up the street, with a terrace and more room than Uno's, but without the attendant legend. Pizzas $5-15. Uno open Mon.-Thurs. 11:30am-11pm, Fri.-Sat. 11:30am-midnight; Due open Mon.-Thurs. 11:30am-1:30am, Fri. 11:30am-2:30am, Sat. noon-2:30am, Sun. noon-11:30pm.

Gino's East, 160 E. Superior (943-1124). Wait 30-40 min. while they make your "pizza de résistance." Graffiti-covered wall. Small pan pizza ($6) easily serves 2. Open Mon.-Thurs. 11am-11pm; Fri.-Sat. 11am-1am, Sun. noon-10pm.

Loop

For a cheaper alternative to most Loop dining, try the surprisingly good fast-food pizza, fish, potato and burger joints in the basement of the State of Illinois Building at Randolph and Clarke St. Entrées run $2.50 to $4.

The Berghoff, 17 W. Adams (427-3170). Moderately priced German and American fare includes terrific strudel and home-brewed beer. German pot roast $7. Open Mon.-Thurs. 11am-9:30pm, Fri.-Sat. 11am-10pm.

Morry's Old Fashioned Deli, 345 W. Dearborn St. (922-2932). Deli favorites sustain Loop-gawkers and the local lunch crowd. Corned beef $4.50. Open Mon.-Fri. 7am-8pm, Sat. 8am-5pm.

Near North

Billy Goat's Tavern, 430 N. Michigan Ave. (222-1525), hidden underground on lower Michigan Ave. Descend through an apparent subway entrance in front of the Tribune building. The gruff service was the inspiration for *Saturday Night Live*'s legendary "Cheezborger, cheezborger—no Coke, Pepsi" greasy spoon. Cheezborgers $2.20. Open Sun.-Fri. 7am-2am, Sat. 7am-3am.

Ed Debevic's, 640 N. Wells (708-945-3242). A gonzo, manic celebration of the 50s diner, complete with waiters who dance on the tables and wisecrack signs on the walls. Burgers, chicken pot pie, and other all-American dishes. Full dinners $5. Packed weekend nights. Open Mon.-Thurs. 11am-midnight, Fri. 11am-1am, Sat. 10am-1am, Sun. 10am-11pm.

Uptown (New Chinatown)

Tokyo Marina, 5058 N. Clark St. (878-2900). Good Japanese food at reasonable prices: steaming bowls of meat, vegetable, and rice for $5.50-7.50, sushi $7-13. Mixed sushi a good intro for novices ($7.50). Open daily 11:30am-11pm.

House of Thailand, 5120 N. Broadway (275-2684). El to Forster. Excellent Thai food at reasonable prices. Lunch special $4. Open Sun., Tues.-Thurs. 5-10pm, Sat. 5-11pm.

Mekong, 4953 N. Broadway (271-0206), at Argyle St. Busy, spotless Vietnamese restaurant. Tasty soups $3.50-4. Open Sun.-Thurs. 10am-10pm, Fri.-Sat. 10am-11pm.

Gin Go Gae, 5433 N. Lincoln Ave. (334-3985). Korean place, popular with locals. *Be bim bob,* steamed rice with marinated beef, spinach, kim-chee and an egg, $7.25. Lunch specials $5.50. Open Thurs.-Tues. 11:30am-10:30pm.

Chinatown

Hong Min, 221 W. Cermak (842-5026). El to Cermak. Attention paid to the food, *not* the furnishings—unlike some Chinese restaurants nearby. Dinner entrées $6-11, excellent seafood. 8 tables. Open daily 10am-2am.

Little Italy

Al's Italian Beef, 1079 W. Taylor St. (226-4017), at Aberdeen near Little Italy. Take a number, please. There are no tables or chairs, so you'll have to eat standing at the long counter. Delicious Italian beef sandwich ($3.60); pass the napkins. Open Mon.-Sat. 9am-1am.

Greektown

The Parthenon, 314 S. Halsted St. in Greektown (726-2407). Enjoy anything from gyros ($6) to *saganaki* (cheese flamed in brandy, $3.25). Try the combination dinner to sample *moussaka,* lamb, *pastitsio* and *dolmades.* Dinners $4.25-13.50. Open daily 11am-1am.

North Side

Café Phoenicia, 2814 N. Halsted St. (549-7088). El to Diversey, then 2 blocks along Diversey to Halsted. A tribute to the Phoenician alphabet and nautical tableaux spice up the walls of this little Lebanese outfit. Outstanding hummus $3, lamb kabob $8. Open Mon.-Thurs. 5-11pm, Fri.-Sat. 5pm-midnight, Sun. 4-10pm. Reservations required weekends.

Marco's Paradise, 3358 N. Sheffield (281-4848), down the street from Wrigley Field. Taste the Mexican standards here after you watch the Cubs play like refried beans. Entrées $6-10. Open Sun.-Thurs. 11am-midnight, Fri.-Sat. 11am-2am. Reservations suggested weekends.

Addis Adeba, 3521 N. Clark, near Wrigley Field (929-9383). Ethiopian cuisine; it's not just food, it's an adventure. No utensils; scoop up dinner with a slap of spongy *injera* bread. Entrées $6-10. Open Mon.-Thurs. 5-10pm, Fri.-Sat. 5-11pm, Sun. 4-10pm.

Café Ba-Ba-Reeba! 2024 N. Halsted (935-5000). *Buena comida.* Hearty Spanish cuisine with subtle spices. Entrées $6-10. Outdoor terrace. Open Tues.-Sat. 11:30am-2:30pm, Mon.-Thurs. 5:30-11pm, Fri. 5:30pm-midnight, Sat. 5pm-midnight, Sun. 5:30-10:30pm.

Sights

New York gets all the press as America's First City, and Chicagoans have always been sensitive about their supposed second-place status. That is why you hear so much about biggest, highest, tallest, oldest. The city is truly massive, and its sights cannot be exhausted in a day, a week or a lifetime. There is always another hole-in-the-wall restaurant, another architectural motif, another museum exhibit to discover. Chicago is a prime walking city, with lakefront, parks, residential neighborhoods and commercial districts all awaiting exploration. Use the public transportation system liberally, though, or you'll spend all your time walking. Avoid touristy and expensive bus tours which zip you past sights. For the price of one of these tours you can buy a pass and ride the city bus for a week.

Museums

Admission to each of Chicago's major museums is free at least one day a week. The "Big Five" allow exploration of everything from ocean to landscape to the stars; a handful of smaller collections represent diverse ethnic groups and professional interests. For more information, pick up the informative pamphlet *Chicago Museums* at the tourist information office (see Practical Information).

Museum of Science and Industry, 5700 S. Lake Shore Dr. (684-1414), housed in the only building left from the 1893 World's Columbian Exposition. In Hyde Park; take the Jeffrey Express, Bus #6 to 57th St. Hands-on exhibits ensure a crowd of grabby kids, overgrown and otherwise. Highlights include the Apollo 8 command module, a German submarine, a life-sized replica of a coal mine, and a new exhibit on learning disabilities. Open Memorial Day-Labor Day daily 9:30am-5:30pm; off-season Mon.-Fri. 9:30am-4pm, Sat.-Sun. 9:30am-5:30pm. $5, ages 5-12 $2, seniors $4; free Thurs. Omni-Max Theatre shows "Ring of Fire;" call for showtimes and prices.

The Oriental Institute, 1155 E. 58th St. (702-9521), take Jeffrey Express, Bus #6, to the University of Chicago campus. Houses an extraordinary collection of ancient Near Eastern art and archeological treasures. You can't miss the massive statue of Tutankhamen. Open Tues. and Thurs.-Sat. 10am-4pm, Wed. 10am-8:30pm, Sun. noon-4pm. Free.

Field Museum of Natural History (922-9410), Roosevelt Rd. at Lake Shore Dr., in Grant Park. Take Bus $146 from State St. Geological, anthropological, botanical, and zoological exhibits. Don't miss the Egyptian mummies, the Native American Halls, the Hall of Gems, and the dinosaur display. Open daily 9am-5pm. Admission $4, seniors and students $2.50, families $13. Free Thurs.

The Adler Planetarium, 1300 S. Lake Shore Dr. (322-0300), in Grant Park. Astronomy exhibits, a sophisticated skyshow, and the recently added $4-million Astro-Center. 5 skyshows per day in summer, less frequently in winter. Open daily 9:30am-5pm, Fri. until 9pm. Exhibits free. Skyshow daily at 11am and hourly 1-4pm. $4, ages 6-17 $2.

The Art Institute of Chicago, Michigan Ave. at Adams St. in Grant Park (443-3500). The city's premier art museum. Finest collection of French Impressionist paintings west of Paris. Also works by El Greco, Chagall, Van Gogh, Picasso and Rembrandt. Call for info on temporary exhibits. Open Mon. and Wed.-Fri. 10:30am-4:30pm, Tues. 10:30am-8pm, Sat. 10am-5pm, Sun. and holidays noon-5pm. Donation of any amount required (you can pay a nickel if you want to). Free Tues.

Shedd Aquarium, 1200 S. Lake Shore Dr. in Grant Park (939-2438). The world's largest indoor aquarium with over 6600 species of fresh and saltwater fish in 206 exhibition tanks, including a Caribbean reef. The Oceanarium features small whales, dolphins, seals and other marine mammals. Parking available. Open March-Oct. daily 9am-6pm; Nov.-Feb. 10am-5pm. Combined admission to Oceanarium and Aquarium $7, students and seniors $5; Thurs. admission $4; Thurs. free to Aquarium, but not Oceanarium. Buy weekend tickets in advance through Hot Tix.

Chicago Historical Society, N. Clark St. at North Ave. (642-4600). A research center for scholars with a good museum open to the public. The Society was founded in 1856, just 19 years after the city was incorporated, like a kid who keeps a diary for future biographers. Permanent exhibits on America in the age of Lincoln, plus changing exhibits. Open Mon.-Sat. 9:30am-4:30pm, Sun. noon-5pm. $3, Mon. free.

DuSable Museum of African-American History, 740 E. 56th Pl. and Cottage Grove (947-0600), Washington Park at the western border of Hyde Park. Take the #6 Jeffrey Express. Illuminating exhibit on everything from ancient African sculpture to the 60s Black Arts movement. Open Mon.-Fri. 9am-5pm, Sat.-Sun. noon-5pm. $2, seniors and students $1, under 13 50¢. Free Thurs.

Terra Museum of American Art, 666 N. Michigan Ave. at Eric St. (664-3939). Excellent collection of American art from colonial times to the present, with a focus on 19th-century American Impressionism. Open Tues. noon-8pm, Wed.-Sat. 10am-5pm, Sun. noon-5pm. $4, seniors $2.50, students with ID $1. Free the first Sunday of each month.

The Museum of Contemporary Art, 237 E. Ontario (280-5161), within walking distance of the Water Tower. Exhibits change often. One gallery devoted to local artists. Open Tues.-Sat. 10am-5pm, Sun. noon-5pm. $4, seniors and students $2. Free Tues.

Museum of Broadcast Communications, in Chicago Cultural Center, Randolph and Morgan, in the Loop (629-6000). Celebrate couch-potato culture with these exhibits on America's favorite pastime: watching the tube. Open Mon.-Sat. 10am-4:30pm, Sun. noon-5pm. Free.

The Loop

After the Great Fire of 1871 left the downtown a pile of ashes, Chicago rebuilt with a Phoenix-like vengeance, in the process creating one of the most concentrated clusters of architectural treasures in the world. From 1870 to 1920, Chicago was at its peak, controlling a hinterland that included most of the Midwest. Partly to establish the city's reputation as more than just an industrial machine, city boosters lavished money on buildings.

The downtown area called the Loop was hemmed in by the Chicago River and the lake, so its buildings had to spread up rather than out. The skyscraper wasn't invented in Chicago, but many architectural historians believe it has received its most sublime expression here. Volunteers trained by the Chicago Architectural Foundation lead excellent **walking tours** of the Loop, starting from the foundation's bookstore/gift shop at 224 S. Michigan Ave. (922-3432). Learn to recognize Louis Sullivan's arch, the Chicago window, and Mies van der Rohe's glass and steel, geometrically rigorous boxes, which refashioned the concept of the skyscraper. Two tours are offered: one of early skyscrapers, one of modern. ($7 for one, $10 for both. Call for tour schedules.) In the **Board of Trade Building** at Jackson and Lasalle (435-3455), cosmopolitan art deco ornament tag teams with a huge monument to Ceres, Greek goddess of grain, standing 609 ft. above street level. Long ago, the city's traders developed the concept of a graded commodity, so that a real-life bag of wheat, once evaluated, could henceforth be treated as an idealized unit of property akin to currency. At the fifth-floor visitors gallery you can watch the frantic trading of Midwestern farm goods at the world's oldest and largest **commodity futures exchange.** (Open Mon.-Fri. 9am-2pm; free.)

In the late 19th century, Sears, Roebuck, along with competitor Montgomery Ward, created the mail-order catalog business, undercutting many small general stores and permanently altering the face of American merchandising. Today, the **Sears Tower**, 233 W. Walker, does more than just serve as an office building; at 1707 ft., it stands as a monument to the insatiable lust of the American consumer. You can view the city from the top of this, the tallest building in the world. (April-Sept. open daily 9am-11pm, Jan.-March 10am-10pm. $6, kids $3.25, seniors $4.50, family $16. Lines can be long.)

The First National Bank Building and Plaza stands about two blocks northeast, at the corner of Clark and Monroe St. The world's largest bank building pulls your eye skyward with its diagonal slope. Marc Chagall's vivid mosaic, *The Four Seasons,* lines the block and sets off a public space often used for concerts and lunchtime entertainment.

State and Madison, the most famous block of "State Street that great street" and the focal point of the Chicago street grid, lies one street over. Louis Sullivan's **Carson Pirie Scott** store building is adorned with exquisite ironwork and the famous extra-large Chicago window (though the grid-like modular construction has been altered by additions). Also visit Sullivan's other masterpiece, the **Auditorium Building,** several blocks south at the corner of Congress and Michigan. Beautiful design and flawless acoustics highlight this Chicago landmark.

Chicago has one of the country's premier collections of outdoor sculpture. Many downtown corners are punctuated by large, abstract designs. The most famous of these is a Picasso at the foot of the **Daley Center Plaza.** Across the street rests Joan Miró's *Chicago,* the sculptor's gift to the city. The **State of Illinois building,** a hypermodern version of a town square designed by Helmut John in 1985, features a sloping atrium, circular floors that expose a full view of hundreds of employees, and eviscerated elevators and escalators.

North Side

Extending north of Diversey Ave., the North Side offers an amalgam of ethnically diverse neighborhoods. Stroll the streets here and you'll find fresh-baked pita bread, vintage clothing stores, elite apartment buildings and humble two-story abodes.

Elaborate tombs and monuments designed by Louis Sullivan and Lorado Taft make **Graceland Cemetery,** east of Clark St. between Irving Park Rd. and Montrose Ave., one of Chicago's most interesting sights and a posthumous status symbol. Famous corpses here include Marshall Field, George Pullman, Daniel Burnham and other Chicago luminaries. The cemetery office at the northeast corner of Clark St. and Irving Park Rd. has guidebooks. (Free.)

Though they finally lost their battle against night baseball in 1988, **Wrigleyville** residents remain, like much of the North Side, fiercely loyal to the Chicago Cubs. Just east of Graceland Cemetery, at the corner of Clark St. and Addison, tiny, ivy-covered **Wrigley Field** is the North Side's most famous institution, well worth a pilgrimage for the serious or simply curious baseball fan. After a game, walk along Clark St. in one of the city's busiest nightlife districts, where restaurants, sportsbars and music clubs abound.

Outdoors

A string of lovely lakefront parks fringes the area between Chicago proper and Lake Michigan. On a sunny afternoon, a cavalcade of sunbathers, dog walkers, roller skaters and skateboard artists ply the shore, yet everyone still has room to stake out a private little piece of paradise. The two major parks, both close to downtown, are Lincoln and Grant, operated by the Recreation Department (294-2200). **Lincoln Park,** which extends over five mi. of lakefront on the north side of town, rolls in the style of the 19th-century English park: winding paths, natural groves of trees and asymmetrical open spaces. The **Lincoln Park Conservatory** encloses fauna from desert to jungle environments under its glass palace (249-4770). Great apes, snow leopards, a rhinoceros and their neighbors call the **Franklin Park Zoo** home (294-4660). (Both zoo and conservatory are free and open daily 9am-5pm.)

Grant Park, covering 14 blocks of lakefront east of Michigan Ave., follows the proper 19th-century French park style: symmetrical, ordered, with squared corners, a fountain in the center, and wide promenades. The **Petrillo Music Shell** hosts many free concerts here during the summer; check the papers.

Colored lights illuminate **Buckingham Fountain** each night at 9pm. The **Field Museum of Natural History,** the **Shedd Aquarium,** and the **Adler Planetarium** beckon museum-hoppers to the southern end of the park (take the #146 bus, it's a 1-mi. walk from the park center), while the **Art Institute** calmly houses its collection on the northern side of the park, east of **Adams St.** Grant Park is also a good place to view the downtown skyline. (For more information see Museums above.)

Lake Michigan lures swimmers to the **Lincoln Park Beach** and the **Oak Street Beach,** on the North Side. Both crowded, popular swimming spots soak in the sun. For a less crowded area, try the smaller, rockier beaches lining the North Shore above Lincoln Park. The beaches are unsafe after dark. Call the Chicago Parks District for further information (294-2200).

Oak Park

Ten mi. west of downtown on the Eisenhower (I-290) sprouts **Oak Park.** Frank Lloyd Wright endowed the community with 25 of his spectacular homes and buildings. Wright pioneered a new type of home, the Prairie House, which sought to integrate the house with the environment, eliminating the discrete break between indoors and out. The **visitors center,** 158 Forest Ave. (708-848-1500), offers maps and guidebooks. (Open daily 10am-5pm.) Don't miss the **Frank Lloyd Wright House and Studio,** 951 Chicago Ave. (708-848-1500), with his beautiful 1898 workplace and original furniture. Two tours are offered: one of the exterior of the homes and one of the interior of the studio. (Tours Mon.-Fri. at 11am, 1pm, and 3pm, Sat.-Sun. every 15 min. 11am-4pm. Mon.-Fri. the exterior tour is self-guided only, with a tape recording. $6 each, $9 combined.) By car, exit north from the Eisenhower on Harlem Ave. and follow markers. By train, take the Lake St./Dan Ryan El to Harlem/Marion stop; it's 20 minutes from downtown. From the station, walk north to Lake St. and east to Forest Ave. to find the visitors center.

Hyde Park

Seven mi. south of the Loop along the lake, the **University of Chicago's** (702-1234) beautiful campus dominates the **Hyde Park** neighborhood. A former retreat for the city's artists and musicians, the park became the first U.S. community to undergo urban renewal in the 50s and is now an island of intellectualism in a sea of dangerous neighborhoods. Don't stray south of Midway Plaisance, west of Cottage Grove, or north of Hyde Park Blvd. Lakeside Burnham Park, to the east of campus, is relatively safe during the day but dangerous at night. On campus, U. Chicago's architecture ranges from knobby, gnarled, twisted Gothic to neo-streamlined high-octane Gothic. Check out Frank Lloyd Wright's famous **Robie House,** at the corner of Woodlawn Ave. and 58th St.; tours ($3 on Sun.) depart daily at noon. Representative of the Prairie school, this large house blends into the surrounding trees; its low horizontal lines now house university offices. From the Loop, take bus #6 ("Jefferson Express") or the Illinois Central Railroad from the Randolph St. Station south to 57th St. The Oriental Institute, Museum of Science and Industry, and DuSable Museum are all in or bordering on Hyde Park (see Museums above).

Near West Side

The **Near West Side,** bounded by the Chicago River to the east and Ogden Ave. to the west, is a fascinating assembly of tiny ethnic enclaves. Farther out, however, looms the West Side, one of the most dismal slums in the U.S. Dangerous neighborhoods lie alongside safe ones, so always be aware of where you stray. **Greektown** might not be as Greek now, but several blocks of authentic restaurants (north of the Eisenhower on Halsted) remain, and still draw people from all over the city.

A few blocks down Halsted (take the #8 Halsted bus), historic **Hull House** stands as a reminder of Chicago's role in turn-of-the-century reform movements. Here, Jane Addams devoted her life to her settlement house, garnering a reputation as a champion of social justice and welfare. The house itself was home to the settlement worker staff, *not* homeless locals, and was the focus of community activities ranging from kindergarten to night-time classes. Hull House has been relocated to 800 S. Halsted, but painstaking restoration, a slide show, and thoughtful exhibits about Near West Side history now make the **Hull House Museum** (413-5353) a fascinating part of a visit to Chicago. (Open Mon.-Fri. 10am-4pm, Sun. noon-5pm. Free.) On Sundays, stop by the **Maxwell Street flea market.** Once the center of immigrant life in Chicago, Maxwell St. is now a fairly seedy neighborhood six days a week. But on Sunday, merchants line the street from Halsted St. for several blocks west with inexpensive food and other merchandise. **Ukrainian Village,** at Chicago and Western, is no longer dominated by ethnic Ukrainians, but now that the Ukraine has regained its independence, you may have even more reason to visit the **Ukrainian National Museum** at 2453 W. Chicago Ave. (276-6565). The **Ukrainian Institute of Modern Art** at 2320 W. Chicago Ave. (227-5522) has free performances and exhibits.

Near North

The city's ritziest district lies above the Loop along the lake, just past the Michigan Ave. Bridge. Overlooking this stretch is the **Tribune Tower,** 435 N. Michigan Ave., a Gothic skyscraper that resulted from a hotly-contested international design competition in the 20s. The building houses Chicago's largest newspaper; quotations exalting the freedom of the press emblazon the inside lobby. Roam the **Merchandise Mart** (entrances on N. Wells and Kinzie; 644-4664), the largest commercial building in the world, 25 stories high and two city blocks long. The first two floors are a mall open to the public; the rest of the building contains showrooms where design professionals converge from around the world to choose home and office furnishings, kitchen products, and everything else that goes into a building, including the "restroom" signs. (Public tours Mon., Wed., and Fri. 10am and 1:30pm. $7, seniors and students $5.50.)

Chicago's **Magnificent Mile,** along Michigan Ave. north of the Chicago River, is a conglomeration of chic shops and galleries. Some of the retail stores here, including the recently opened Banana Republic and Crate and Barrel, were designed by the country's foremost architects. En route you'll pass the **Chicago Water Tower and Pumping Station** (467-7114), at the corner of Michigan and Pearson Ave. Built in 1867, these two structures were among the few to survive the Great Chicago Fire. The pumping station, which supplies water to nearly 400,000 people on the North Side, houses the avoidable multimedia production *Here's Chicago.* Across the street is **Water Tower Place,** a ritzy new vertical shopping mall, worth a browse.

Beautiful old mansions and apartment buildings fill the streets between the Water Tower and Lincoln Park. Known as the **Gold Coast,** the area has long been the elite residential enclave of the city. Early industrialists and city founders made their homes here and, lately, many families have moved back from the suburbs. Lake Michigan and the Oak St. Beach shimmer a few more blocks east.

Urban renewal has made **Lincoln Park,** a neighborhood just west of the park of the same name, a popular choice for upscale residents. Bounded by Armitage to the south and Diversey Ave. to the north, lakeside Lincoln Park is a center for recreation and nightlife, with beautiful harbors and parks and some of the liveliest clubs and restaurants along North Halsted and Lincoln Ave.

If you hear the bells of St. Michael's Church, you're in **Old Town,** a neighborhood where eclectic galleries, shops, and nightspots crowd gentrified streets. Absorb the architectural atmosphere while strolling the W. Menomonee and W. Eugenie St. area. In early June, the **Old Town Art Fair** attracts artists and craftspeople from across the country. Many residents open their restored homes to the public. (Take bus #151 to Lincoln Park and walk south down Clark or Wells St.)

Farther Out

The **Pullman Historic District** on the southeast side was once considered the nation's most perfect community. George Pullman, inventor of the sleeping car, hired British architect Solon S. Beman in 1885 to design a model working town so that his Palace Car Company employees would be "healthier, happier and more productive." Unfortunately, worker resentment over Pullman's power undermined structured bliss in this earliest of planned suburbs. By car, take I-94 to W. 111th St; by train, take the Illinois Central Gulf Railroad to 111th St./Pullman. (Tours leave from the hotel the first Sun. of each month May-Oct. $3.50, seniors $3, students $2.)

In **Wilmette,** the **Baha'i House of Worship,** Shendan Rd. and Linden Ave. (708-256-4400), is an 11-sided Near Eastern-styled dome modeled on the House of Worship in Haifa, Israel. (Open May-Oct. daily 10am-10pm; Oct.-May 10am-5pm.) El to Howard Station, then commuter rail it to Wilmette, Fourth St. and Linden Ave., then walk two blocks east on Linden.

Entertainment

To stay on top of Chicago events, grab a copy of the free weekly *Chicago Reader,* published on Thursday and available in many bars and restaurants. *Chicago* magazine has exhaustive club listings. The Friday edition of the *Chicago Tribune* includes a thick section with full music, theater, and cultural listings.

Theater

Chicago is one of the foremost theater centers of North America. Sure, you can shell out two days of food money for a name-brand New York show blowing through town, but for an authentic local experience visit one of the intimate, smaller theaters that stage home-grown productions. At one point last summer, over 100 shows were running, ranging in respectability from *Macbeth* to *Cannibal Cheerleaders on Crack.* The "Off-Loop" theaters on the North Side specialize in original drama, with tickets in the $15 and under range.

Victory Gardens Theater, 2257 N. Lincoln Ave. (871-3000). Drama by Chicago playwrights. Tickets $20-25.

Center Theatre, 1346 W. Devon Ave. (508-5422). Solid, mainstream work. Tickets $10.

Annoyance Theatre, 3153 N. Broadway (929-6200). Different show each night of the week, original works that play off pop culture; they launched *The Real-Life Brady Bunch.* In the center of an active gay neighborhood.

Bailiwick Repertory in the Theatre building, 1225 W. Belmont Ave. (327-5252). Original works. Tickets from $15.

Live Bait Theatre, 3914 N. Clark St. (871-1212). Shows with titles like *What is this in my coke? Poetic justice.* Tickets $10.

Remains Theatre, 1800 N. Clybourn (335-9800) Innovative, original work. Several members of the company are screen actors returning to the stage. Bring your own brew into the theater. Walk-up tickets available. Tickets $10-20.

Most theater tickets are expensive, although half-price tickets are available on the day of performance at **Hot Tix Booths,** 24 S. State St., downtown. Buy them in person only; show up 15 to 20 minutes before booth opens to get first dibs. (Open Mon. noon-6pm, Tues.-Fri. 10am-6pm, Sat. 10am-5pm. Tickets for Sun. shows on sale Sat.) Phone **Curtain Call** (977-1755) for information on ticket availability, schedules and Hot Tix booths. **Ticket Master** (800-233-3123) supplies tickets for many theaters. Check with theaters to see if they sell half-price student rush tickets 30 minutes before showtime. Two of the Chicago theaters are especially well-known, with prices to match their fame: the **Steppenwolf Theater,** 2540 N. Lincoln Ave. (472-4141), where David Mamet got his start, and the **Goodman Theatre,** 200 S. Columbus Dr. (443-3800), present consistently good original works. (Tickets $20-30.) The big-name presentation houses that host Broadway touring productions are the **Shubert Theater,** 22 W. Monroe St. (977-1700 or 902-1500), and the **Blackstone Theater,** 60 E. Balbo St. (341-8455). The monthly *Chicago* magazine and the weekly *Chicago Reader* both give thumbnail reviews of all major shows, with showtimes and ticket prices.

Comedy

Chicago boasts a giggle of comedy clubs, the most famous being **Second City,** 1616 N. Wells St. (337-3992), with its satirical spoofs of Chicago life and politics. Second City graduated John Candy, Bill Murray and the late John Belushi and Gilda Radner, among others. (Shows Tues.-Thurs. 8:30pm, Fri.-Sat. at 8:30 and 11pm, Sun. at 8pm. Tickets $10-12. Reservations recommended; during the week you can often get in if you show up 1 hr. early.) A free improv session follows the show. **Second City ETC.** (642-8189) offers up yet more comedy next door (same times and prices). The big names drop by and make it up as they go along at **The Improv,** 504 N. Wells (782-6387). (Shows Mon. at 8pm, Sun., Tues., Wed. at 7pm, Thurs. 9:30pm, Fri.-Sat. 6:45pm, 9:30pm, and midnight. Tickets $5-13 depending on day.)

Dance, Classical Music, and Opera

Chicago philanthropists have built the network of high-priced, high-art performance centers you've come to expect in a major metropolis. The **Chicago City Ballet** pirouettes under the direction of Maria Tallchief at the **Auditorium Theater,** 50 E. Congress Parkway (922-2110). From October to May, the **Chicago Symphony Orchestra,** conducted by Sir George Solti, crescendoes at **Orchestra Hall,** 220 S. Michigan Ave. (435-8111). The **Lyric Opera of Chicago** sings from September to February at the **Civic Opera House,** 20 N. Wacker Dr. (332-2244). The **Grant Park Music Festival** is more attractive to the budget traveler. From mid-June to early September, the acclaimed **Grant Park Symphony Orchestra** gives three to four free evening concerts a week at the Grant Park Petrillo Music Shell. (Usually Wed., Fri., Sat., Sun.; schedule varies. Call 819-0614 for details.) *Chicago* magazine has complete listings of music, dance, and opera performances throughout the city.

Seasonal Events

Like Chicago's architecture, the city's summer celebrations are executed on a grand scale. The **Taste of Chicago** festival cooks the week before July Fourth, when over 70 restaurants set up booths with endless samples at Grant Park. Big name bands also come to perform. In early June, the **Blues Festival** celebrates the city's soulful, gritty music; the **Chicago Gospel Festival** hums and hollers in July, and the **Chicago Jazz Festival** swings at the end of August, all at the Grant Park Petrillo Music Shell. Call the Mayor's Office Special Events Hotline (744-3315) for info on all four events.

Chi-town also offers several free summer festivals on the lakeshore, including the **Air and Water Show** in mid-July, when Lake Shore Park, Lake Shore Dr. and Chicago Ave. are the scene of several days of boat races, parades, hang gliding and stunt flying, as well as aerial acrobatics by the Blue Angels precision fliers.

The regionally famous **Ravinia Festival** (312-728-4642), in the northern suburb of Highland Park, runs from late June to late September. The Chicago Symphony Orchestra, ballet troupes, folk and jazz musicians, and comedians perform throughout the festival's 14-week season. (Shows start between 7:30 and 8:30pm. $20-35. $7 rents you a patch of ground for a blanket and picnic.) Round-trip on the train (METRA) costs about $6; the festival runs charter buses for $12. The bus ride is 1½½ hrs. each way.

Sports

The **Cubs** play ball at gorgeous Wrigley Field, at Clark St. and Addison (831-2827), one of the few ballparks in America that has retained the early grace and intimate feel of the game; it's definitely worth a visit, especially for international visitors who haven't seen a baseball game. (Tickets $6-17.) The **White Sox** swing at the South Side at Comiskey Park (924-1000). DA **Bears** play football at Soldier's Field Stadium, McFetridge Dr. and S. Lake Shore Dr. (663-5408). The **Blackhawks** hockey team skates and the **Bulls** basketball team slam-dunks at Chicago Stadium, 1800 W. Madison (Blackhawks 733-5300, Bulls 943-5800). In 1991 and '92, celebrations of the Bulls' championship victories turned into riots which caused millions of dollars in damage. For current sports events, call **Sports Information** (976-1313).

Nightlife

Chicago's frenetic nightlife is a grab bag of music, clubs, bars and more music. "Sweet home Chicago" takes pride in the innumerable blues performers who have played there (a strip of 43rd St. was recently renamed Muddy Waters Drive). For other tastes, jazz, folk, reggae and punk clubs throbulate all over the North Side. Aspiring pick-up artists swing over to Rush and Division, an intersection that has replaced the stockyards as one of the biggest meat markets of the world. To get away from the crowds, head to a little neighborhood spot for a lot of atmosphere. Lincoln Park is full of bars, cafés and bistros, and is dominated by the gay scene, as well as hep singles and young married couples. Bucktown, west of Halsted St. in North Chicago, stays open late with bucking bars and dance clubs.

Blues

B.L.U.E.S. etcetera, 1124 W. Belmont Ave. (525-8989), El to Belmont then 3 blocks west on Belmont. Cover $3.50-12 depending on day. With the aid of a dance floor, it's a more energetic blues bar than its sibling location **B.L.U.E.S.,** 2519 N. Halsted St. (528-1012), El to Fullerton, then westbound Fullerton bus. Cramped, but the music is unbeatable. Music starts at both joints Mon.-Thurs. at 9pm, Fri.-Sun. at 9:30pm. Open Sun.-Fri. 8pm-2am, Sat. 8pm-3am. Cover Sun.-Thurs. $5, Fri.-Sat. $7.

Kingston Mines, 2548 N. Halsted St. (477-4646). Shows 6 nights per week. Watch for the "Blue Monday" jam session. Music starts at 9:30pm. Open Sun.-Fri. until 4am, Sat. until 5am. Cover Sun.-Thurs. $8, Fri.-Sat. $10.

Wise Fools Pub, 2270 N. Lincoln St. (929-1510), El to Fullerton, then go south on Lincoln. Intimate Lincoln Park setting for top blues artists. Mon. night's Big Band Jazz series also great fun. Music 9:30pm-1:30am. Bar open daily 4pm-2am. Cover $4-8 depending on day.

Other Nightlife

Butch McGuires, 20 W. Division St. (337-9080), at Rush St. Originator of the singles bar. Owner estimates that "over 2400 couples have met here and gotten married" since 1961—he's a little fuzzier on divorce statistics. Once on Rush St., check out the other area hang-outs. Drinks $1.75-4.25. Open Sun.-Thurs. 10:30am-2am, Fri. 10am-4am, Sat. 10am-5am.

Cabaret Metro, 3730 N. Clark (549-0203). Cutting-edge concerts from $6 and Wed. night "Rock Against Depression" extravaganzas ($4 for men, women free) entertain a hip, young crowd. Cool dance spot. Open Sun.-Fri. 9:30pm-4am, Sat. 9:30pm-5am. Cover $5-10.

Christopher Street, 3458 N. Halsted (975-9244). Lots of guppies swim in this attractive, upscale fishbowl with 3 bars, a huge dance floor and aquarium wallpaper. Drinks $2-4. Open Sun.-Fri. 4pm-4am, Sat. 4pm-5am. Cover Fri.-Sat. $3 ($1 goes to AIDS research).

Paris, 1122 Montrose (769-0602). El to Addison. A lesbian bar with D.J. and dancing Wed.-Sun. Open Mon.-Fri. 5pm-2am, Sat. 2pm-3am, Sun. 2pm-midnight. No cover.

Jazz Showcase, 636 S. Michigan (427-4300), in the Blackstone Hotel downtown. #1 choice for serious jazz fans. During the jazz festival, big names heat up the elegant surroundings with impromptu jam sessions. No smoking allowed. Music Tues.-Thurs. at 8 and 10pm, Fri.-Sat. at 9 and 11pm, Sun. at 4 and 8pm. Closing time varies; cover around $5.

Wild Hare & Singing Armadillo Frog Sanctuary, 3350 N. Clark (327-0800), El to Addison. Near Wrigley Field. Live Rastafarian bands play nightly to a packed house. Open daily until 2-3am. Cover $3-5.

Sluggers World Class Sports Bar, Inc., 3540 N. Clark (248-0055), near Wrigley Field. El to Addison. If TV monitors tuned to every sporting event imaginable don't turn you on, maybe the game room with ski ball, trampoline hoop and the city's only indoor batting cage will. Drink prices rise 50¢ during Cubs games, but on Wed. nights beer is only 75¢. Open Sun.-Fri. 11am-2am, Sat. 11am-3am.

Tania's, 2659 N. Milwaukee Ave. (235-7120). Exotic dinner and dancing adventure with hot *salsa cumbia* and *merengue* bands. No jeans or sneakers. Live music Wed.-Mon. Open Sun.-Fri. 11am-4pm, Sat. 11am-5am.

Refer to *Chicago* magazine for descriptions of many more clubs, a list of who is playing, current hip spots and old-time favorites. *ChicagoLife* has a more selective, shorter list and will give you a good second opinion.

Springfield

Springfield poet Vachel Lindsay wrote, "In our little town a mourning figure walks, and will not rest." The ghoulish shadow of Abraham Lincoln, who settled in Springfield in 1837 to practice law, still haunts Springfield; the city is completely mobilized to help tourists see Old Abe memorabilia. The state capital's efforts, much like the place and its people, are always tactful but very insistent.

Practical Information and Orientation

Emergency: 911.

Visitor Information: Springfield Convention and Visitors Bureau, 109 N. 7th St. (789-2360 or 800-545-7300). Open Mon.-Fri. 8am-5pm. **Central Illinois Tourism Council,** 631 E. Washington St. (525-7980). **Lincoln Home Visitors Center,** 426 S. 7th (789-2357). Open daily 8:30am-5pm. All locations have very useful brochures on restaurants, hotels, camping, events, recreation, and services for seniors and disabled persons.

Amtrak: 3rd and Washington St. (800-872-7245), near downtown. To Chicago (2-4 per day; 4 hr.; $32) and St. Louis (2-4 per day; 2½ hr.; $20). Free stopovers for those passing through. Lockers 50¢ 1st day, $1 subsequent days. Open daily 6am-9:30pm.

Greyhound: 2351 S. Dirksen Pkwy. (544-8466), on the eastern edge of town. Walk or take a cab ($3 flat rate) to the nearby shopping center, where you can catch the #10 bus into town. To Chicago (Mon.-Thurs. $20.50, Fri.-Sun. $23.50) and St. Louis ($13). Open daily 7:30am-10:30pm. Free stopovers for those passing through. Lockers $1 per day.

Public Transport: Springfield Mass Transit District, 928 S. 9th St. (522-5531). Pick up maps at headquarters or at the tourist office on Adams. All 12 lines serve the downtown area along 5th, 6th or Monroe St., near the Old State Capitol Plaza. Fare 50¢, transfers free. Buses operate Mon.-Sat. 6am-6pm. **Access Illinois Transit Service (AITS),** 522-8594. Buses seniors and people with disabilities. Call 24 hrs. in advance to arrange trip.

Taxi: Lincoln Yellow Cab, 523-4545 or 522-7766.

Post Office: 2105 E. Cook St. (788-7200), at Weir St. Open Mon.-Fri. 7:45am-5:30pm, Sat. 8am-noon. **ZIP code:** 62703.

Area Code: 217.

Numbered streets in Springfield run north-south, but only on the east side of the city. All other streets have names, with **Washington Street** dividing north-south addresses.

Accommodations and Camping

Most inexpensive places congregate in the eastern and southern parts of the city, off I-55 and U.S. 36; bus service from downtown is limited. Downtown rooms cost $10 to $30 more. Make reservations on holiday weekends and during the State Fair in mid-August. Downtown hotels may be booked solid on weekdays when the legislature is in session. Check with the visitors bureau (see Practical Information above) about finding reasonable weekend packages offered by slightly more upscale hotels. All accommodations listed below have color TV and A/C.

The **Dirksen Inn,** 900 N. Dirksen Pkwy. (522-4900; take #3 "Bergen Park" bus to Milton and Elm, then walk a few blocks east), has clean rooms in good condition, with fridgelets. (Singles $24. Doubles $27.) **Motel 6,** 3125 Wide Track Dr. (789-1063), near Dirksen Pkwy. at the intersection of I-90 and State Rte. 29, is, well, Motel 6, this time with a pool. (Singles $23. Doubles $29.) The **Travel Inn,** 500 S. 9th St. (528-4341), near downtown, has a slightly unkempt exterior with clean, fairly large rooms. (Singles $25. Doubles $30.) For a convenient and slightly classier stopover, take a look at the **Mansion View Lodge,** 529 S. 4th St. (544-7411), downtown. Eat your "Special K breakfast" by the pool. (Singles $32-42. Doubles $40-50.) **Mister Lincoln's Campground,** 3045 Stanton Ave. (529-8206), next to the car dealership four mi. southeast of downtown, has a large area for RVs, a field for tents, and showers. Take bus #10 ("Laketown"). (Tent sites $7 per person, with electricity $14, full hookup $16.)

Food

Horseshoe sandwiches gallop to the forefront of Springfield cuisine. Looking more like what ends up *on* horseshoes than horseshoes, these tasty concoctions consist of ham on prairie toast covered by a tangy cheese sauce and french fries. You may end up saying "neigh" to them. In and around the **Vinegar Hill Mall,** at 1st and Cook St., a number of moderately priced restaurants serve horseshoes, barbecued ribs, Mexican and Italian food, and seafood. Plan accordingly because Springfield tends to start shutting down between 3 and 5pm. You can feed your face at the **Feedstore,** 516 E. Adams St., across from the Old State Capitol (528-3355), with a $2.75-4.50 sandwich. No-choice special (sandwich, cup of soup, and beverage specified by the management, no decisions necessary, no substitutions allowed, no spittin', no smokin', no cussin', toilet in the back and have a nice day) $4.25. (Open Mon.-Sat. 11am-3pm.) **Saputo's,** 801 E. Munroe at 8th St. (528-3355), two blocks from Lincoln's home, has been family owned and operated for 40 years. Tasty southern Italian cuisine, red lighting, and red tomato sauce; try the baked lasagna ($4.25). (Open Mon.-Fri. 10:30am-midnight, Sat. 5pm-midnight, Sun. 5-10pm.)

Sights

Springfield markets its tourist attractions zealously. The sights complement each other in order to present a well-rounded view of Mr. Lincoln's world; just let the guides shuffle you from one to the next, or pick up one of the many pamphlets at most museums and, of course, tourist offices for all the necessary info. Pleasing to most budget trekkers, all Lincoln sights are free. The **Lincoln Home Visitors Center,** 426 S. 8th St. at Jackson (523-0222), shows an 18-minute film on "Mr. Lincoln's Springfield." The **Lincoln Home** (492-4150), the only one Abe ever owned, also sits at 8th and Jackson, in a restored 19th-century neighborhood. (10-min. tours every 5-10 min. from the front of the house. Open daily 8:30am-5pm; bad weather may reduce winter hours. Arrive early to avoid the crowds. Free, but you must pick up passes at the Visitors Center; see Practical Information.)

A few blocks northwest, at 6th and Adams right before the Old State Capitol, the **Lincoln-Herndon Law Offices** (782-4836) let visitors experience, barrier-free, the stark, utilitarian "male" world of the office, in contrast to the carefully coordinated décor of Mrs. Lincoln's realm at the Home. (Open for tours only daily 9am-5pm; last tour at 4:15pm. Free.) Around the corner to the left across from the Downtown Mall sleeps the **Old State Capitol** (782-7691), a weathered limestone edifice with a majesty that rivals its Greek models. It was here that, in 1858, Lincoln delivered his stirring and prophetic "House Divided" speech, warning that the nation's contradictory pro-slavery and abolitionist government risked dissolution. A manuscript copy of Lincoln's "Gettysburg Address" is on display. (Tours daily. Open daily 9am-5pm. Free.) The **New State Capitol,** four blocks away at 2nd and Capitol (782-2099), opened in 1877, is a prime example of the Midwestern State Capitol. (Tours Mon.-Fri. 8am-4pm, Sat.-Sun. 9am-3:30pm. Open to public longer.)

Lincolnville, U.S.A. also contains the **Dana-Thomas House,** 301 E. Lawrence Ave. (782-6776), six blocks south of the Old State Capitol. This stunning and well-preserved 1902 home resulted from one of Frank Lloyd Wright's early experiments in design, providing a wonderful example of the Prairie School style. The furniture and fixtures are Wright originals as well. (Budget cuts threaten its accessibility; call for hours. Send a large donation to help keep it open. Tours free when available.) The **Illinois State Museum,** Spring and Edwards St. (782-7386), complements displays on the area's original Native American inhabitants with presentations of contemporary Illinois art. (Open Mon.-Sat. 8:30am-5pm, Sun. noon-5pm. Free.)

In June, the **Thomas Rees Memorial Carillon** in Washington Park hosts the world's only **International Carillon Festival.** Springfield's renowned Fourth of July shebang is called (of course) **Lincolnfest** and more than doubles the town's population with fireworks, patriotism, and, no doubt, the occasional reference to the man himself.

Indiana

The contrast of two popular explanations for Indiana's nickname of "Hoosier" typifies the dichotomy between the state's rural and industrial traditions. The first explanation holds the name to be a corruption of the pioneer's call to visitors at the door, "Who's there?"; the second claims that it spread from Louisville, where labor contractor Samuel Hoosier employed Indiana workers. More than half a century later, visitors still encounter two Indianas: the heavily industrialized northern cities and the slower-paced agricultural southern counties.

Most tourists identify Indiana as either the state of Gary's smokestacks and the Indianapolis 500 or home of rolling hills thick with cornstalks. Most Indiana-types present their state to Easterners (and most Easterners think of Indiana) as a Midwestern Hicksville big on that corn thing. Don't try to choose between the farms and the factories; it is precisely this combination that makes Indiana interesting. Visit the athletic, urban mecca of Indianapolis, but don't miss the rural beauty downstate. The state that produced wholesome TV celebrities David Letterman and Jane Pauley, as well as basketball legend Larry Bird, also features beautiful scenery, especially when the fall foliage around Columbus explodes in a profusion of colors.

Practical Information

Capital: Indianapolis.

Indiana Division of Tourism, 1 N. Capitol #700, Indianapolis 46204 (232-8860; 800-289-6646 in IN). **Division of State Parks,** 402 W. Washington Room: W-298, Indianapolis 46204 (232-4124).

Time Zones: Eastern and Central (1 hr. behind Eastern). During the summer, eastern Indiana does not observe Daylight Savings Time and corresponds to the other half of the state.

Postal Abbreviation: IN

Sales Tax: 5%.

Columbus

In the years following World War II, the Cummins Engine Company brought a boom to Columbus which carried with it a need for better educational facilities. To fill this void, the company established a fund to pay the architectural fees for public buildings, provided that the architect was of world stature. Since then, dozens of schools and other buildings have been hatched under this program, and its example has inspired other private agencies to hire world-class architects for their own building projects. Columbus is now home to 50 public and private buildings that make up the most concentrated collection of contemporary architecture in the world, sharply distinguishing this town of 30,000 from other Midwestern communities.

The helpful **visitors center,** 506 5th St. (372-1954), at Franklin, sells architectural maps ($1, after hours $1.50 from vending machine), and shows a 20-minute film on the city's architecture. (Visitors center open April-Oct. Mon.-Sat. 9am-5pm, Sun. 10am-2pm; Nov.-Dec. Mon.-Sat. 9am-5pm; Jan.-Feb. Wed.-Sat. 9am-5pm; March Mon.-Sat. 9am-5pm.) **Bus tours** ($9.50, $9 seniors, $8.50 AAA members) also leave from the visitors center (Mon.-Fri. 10am, Sat. 10am and 2pm, Sun. 11am during months with Sun. schedule). Upstairs from the visitors center, the **Indianapolis Museum of Art-Columbus** (372-4622) houses rotating exhibits. (Call for hours; free.)

A walking tour of downtown takes about 90 minutes. A block away from the visitors center, well-preserved Victorian homes set off I.M. Pei's **Cleo Rogers Library,** with the concomitant Henry Moore sculpture. Nearby looms the **First Christian Church,** a cube accompanied by a rectangular tower, designed by Eliel Saarinen (father of the architect of the St. Louis Gateway Arch). To the south stands Gunnar Birkerts' **St. Peter's Lutheran Church,** with its spike-like steeple. Of the other specially commissioned buildings, must-sees include: Eero Saarinen's stunning **North Christian Church,** whose futuristic exterior has been copied all over the world; Harry Weese's **Otter Creek Clubhouse,** which sits atop what some consider the nation's finest golf course; and the ultramodern **Commons,** a shopping mall housing a performance center, art gallery, and an indoor playground all designed by Cesar Pelli.

The **Columbus Motel,** 2345 N. National Rd. (379-4467), in the shopping-mall zone north of downtown, has a parking lot, swimming pool, and a memorable street number and is easily reached by any Colum*bus*, but especially #1 or 2. (Singles $31, doubles $38.) **KOA** (342-6229) sets up kamp six mi. south on I-65 at Ogleville. (Primitive sites $12, with hookup and water $15. Each additional person $3, ages 3-18 $1.50, under 3 free.) Restaurants in downtown Columbus are far sparser than architectural attractions. The Commons (see above) has a small shopping-mall food court; head instead across the street to **Zaharako's** (379-9329; known locally as "The Greeks"), 329 Washington St., a soda fountain established in 1900, in whose classy interior one can also ingest inexpensive American sandwiches ($1.25-2.25). (Open Mon.-Sat. 10am-5pm.) **Greyhound** idles at 3555 N. National Rd. (376-3821) and sends two buses daily to Indianapolis ($11), and three to Louisville ($19). (Open Mon.-Fri. 6am-8pm.)

The **ZIP code** for Columbus is 47401; the **area code** is 812.

Indianapolis

On the seam of the Rust Belt and the Corn Belt, Indianapolis focuses more on the former, embracing the decadent, fuel-wasteful but All-American "sport" of automobile racing as its civic symbol. Its midwestern location produces a city that is All-American to the point of being nondescript, but like every good-sized U.S. city, Indianapolis has its points of interest: buildings, museums, ethnic festivals, a local celebrity (one-time meteorologist David Letterman, who was laughed out of town for warning of hail "the size of canned hams"), and, of course, a passion for sports. This reaches its apotheosis each Memorial Day weekend when the Indy 500 fuses exhaust and exhaustion in the largest single-day sporting event in the world.

Practical Information and Orientation

Emergency: 911 or 632-7575.

Visitor Information: Indianapolis City Center, 201 S. Capital St. (237-5200), in the Pan Am Plaza across from the Hoosierdome. Open Mon.-Fri. 10am-5:30pm, Sat. 10am-4pm. Also try 800-233-4639 (800-233-INDY).

Indianapolis International Airport: 7 mi. southwest of downtown near I-465. To get to the city center, take bus #9 ("West Washington").

Amtrak: 350 S. Illinois (263-0550 or 800-872-7245), behind Union Station. In a somewhat deserted but relatively safe area. To Chicago ($28) only. Open Mon.-Fri. 7:15am-3:45pm, Sat. 6:15-10:15am, Sun. 7:15-11:15am.

Greyhound: 127 N. Capital Ave. (635-4501), downtown at E. Ohio St. 1 block from Monument Circle. Fairly safe area. To: Chicago ($39, less if bought in advance), Columbus ($31-37, depending on day), and Louisville ($20-23). Open 24 hrs. **Indiana Trails** operates out of the same station and serves cities within the state.

Public Transport: Metro Bus, 36 N. Delaware St. (635-3344), across from City Council building. Open Mon.-Fri. 7:30am-5:30pm. Fare 75¢, rush hour $1. Transfers 25¢. For disabled service write to P.O. Box 2383, Indianapolis 46206 or call 632-3000.

Taxi: Yellow Cab, 637-5421.

Car Rental: Louie's Rent-a-Bent, 2233 E. Washington St. (632-4429), 2½ mi. east of downtown; take the #8 bus. From $11 per day plus 10¢ per mi.; weekly $99 with unlimited mileage. Car must not leave the state. Check carefully to make sure your car is in good shape. Open Mon.-Fri. 9am-6pm, Sat. 9am-5pm. Required $150 deposit may be paid with credit card. Must be at least 21.

Help Lines: Crisis and Suicide Hotline, 632-7575. **Mayor's Handicapped Hotline,** 236-3620.

Time Zone: Eastern.

Post Office: 125 W. South St. (464-6000), across from Amtrak. Open Mon.-Wed. and Fri. 7am-5:30pm, Thurs. 7am-6pm. **ZIP code:** 46206.

Area Code: 317.

I-465 laps the city and provides access to all points downtown. The center of Indianapolis is located just south of **Monument Circle** at the intersection of **Washington Street** (U.S. 40) and **Meridian Street.** Washington divides the city north-south; Meridian east-west.

Accommodations and Camping

Budget motels in Indianapolis cluster around the I-465 beltway, five mi. from downtown. They are particularly concentrated in the west near the Speedway; buses from downtown to this area cost an extra 25¢. Motels jack up their rates for the Indy 500 in May; make reservations a year in advance.

Fall Creek YMCA, 860 W. 10th St. (634-2478), just north of downtown. Small, clean rooms for both men and women include access to all recreational facilities. Friendly staff. Singles $25, with private bath $34; weekly $63/$73; student weekly rate $50.

Motel 6, I-465 at Exit 16A (293-3220) 3 min. from the Indy Speedway and 8 min. from downtown, or take the #13 bus. Clean, bright rooms; outdoor pool *isn't* in the parking lot. Singles $24. Doubles $30.

Medical Tower Inn, 1633 N. Capitol Ave. (925-9831), in the tall building across from the Methodist Hospital. Pristine, luxurious rooms with décor you wouldn't mind in your own living room. Singles $43. Doubles $53. With student ID $2 less.

Dollar Inn, I-465 at Speedway (248-8500). Take #13 bus. Convenient to the Speedway and Eagle Creek Park. Small, clean rooms. Singles $22. Doubles $27. Key deposit $2.

Kamper Korner, 1951 W. Edgewood Ave. (788-1488), 1 mi. south of I-465 on Rte. 37. No bus access. Open area with no shade. Laundry, grocery, showers, free fishing and swimming. Enforced quiet hours 11pm-7am. Tent sites $16, with water and hookup $17. Limited services Nov. to mid-March.

Food and Nightlife

Indianapolis greets visitors with a variety of restaurants that range from holes-in-the-wall to trendy hotspots decked out in vintage kitsch. Tourists and residents alike head for **Union Station,** 39 Jackson Pl. (267-0700), near the Hoosier Dome four blocks south of Monument Circle. This 13-acre maze of restaurants, shops, dance clubs, bars, and hotels sells every edible substance imaginable in a beautiful, authentically refurbished rail depot. The second-level oval bustles with moderately priced ethnic eateries. Entrées average $2.50-5. (Open Mon.-Thurs. 10am-9pm, Fri.-Sat. 10am-10pm, Sun. 11am-6pm.)

Little Bit of Italy, 5604 Georgetown Rd. (293-6437). If Italian is your thing, you can't lose with the meatball sub or pizza. Lunch or dinner $3-5. Mon.-Wed. 10am-8pm, Thurs.-Sat. 10am-9pm.

Acapulco Joe's, 365 N. Illinois Ave., downtown (637-5160). Their hot 'n' spicy food will make you howl. For the average Joe, they offer peanut butter and jelly sandwiches. 3 tacos $6.50. Mon.-Thurs. 7am-9pm, Fri.-Sat. 7am-10pm.

Iaria's, 317 S. College Ave. (638-7706), about 10 blocks from downtown. A 50s throwback, with shiny vinyl furniture and chrome chairs. Spaghetti and meatballs $6.50. Open Mon.-Thurs. 11am-9:30pm, Fri. 11am-11pm, Sat. noon-11pm.

The City Market, 222 E. Market St., 2 blocks east of Monument Circle. Renovated 19th-century building with produce stands and 15 ethnic markets. Prices reasonable but not rock-bottom. Open Mon.-Sat. 6am-6pm.

Nightlife undulates six mi. north of the downtown area at **Broad Ripple,** at College Ave. and 62nd St., typically swamped with students and yuppies. The area has charming ethnic restaurants and art studios in original frame houses, as well as some artsy bars. You're entering a dimension not only of sight and sound but of...espresso in the **Coffee ZON,** 137 E. Ohio St. downtown (684-0432), which offers excellent coffee concoctions (*latte* $1.75, mocha $2.25) and occasional live folk music. If you like your brew with hops, head for the **Broad Ripple Brew Pub,** 840 E. 65th St. (253-2739).

Sights

"Please touch" is the motto of the **Children's Museum** at 3000 N. Meridian St. (924-5431). Kids help run hands-on exhibits, which include a turn-of-the-century carousel, a huge train collection, petting zoos, and high-tech electronic wizardry. (Open Memorial Day-Labor Day Mon.-Sat. 10am-5pm, Sun. noon-5pm, off-season Tues.-Wed. and Fri.-Sat. 10am-5pm, Thurs. 10am-8pm, Sun. noon-5pm. $4, seniors and ages 2-17 $3.) The **Indianapolis Museum of Art,** 1200 W. 38th (923-1331), houses a large collection of Turner paintings and watercolors as well as Robert Indiana's *LOVE* sculpture. The museum sits among 154 acres of park, beautifully landscaped with gardens and nature trails. (Open Tues.-Wed. and Fri.-Sat. 10am-5pm, Thurs. 10am-8:30pm, Sun. noon-5pm. Free, except special exhibits, which are free only on Thurs.) The **Eiteljorg Museum,** 500 W. Washington St. (636-9378), west of downtown, features Native American and Western art. (Open Tues.-Sat., 10am-5pm, Sun. noon-5pm. $3, seniors $2.50, kids 5-17 and students $1.50.) Stunning African and Egyptian decor graces the **Walker Theatre,** 617 Indiana Ave. (236-2099). Erected in 1927, the theater symbolizes Indianapolis' African-American community, hosting such jazz greats as Louis Armstrong and Dinah Washington. The complex also sponsors plays, dance performances and a week-long black film festival in late October. Even those who don't make one of the shows should go just to see the splendid interior. Upstairs in the ballroom, the **Jazz on the Avenue** series offers live music every Friday night.

The Indianapolis 500: Cars Going Real Fast

The **Indianapolis Motor Speedway,** 4790 W. 16th St. (241-2500), is clearly the quintessential Indianapolis tourist site. Take the Speedway exit off I-465 or bus #25 ("West 16th"). A shrine dedicated to worshipping the automobile, this 1909 behemoth encloses an entire 18-hole golf course. Except in May, you can take a bus ride around the 2½-mi. track for $1. The adjacent **Speedway Museum** (Indy Hall of Fame) houses a collection of Indy race cars and antique autos, as well as racing memorabilia and videotapes highlighting historic Indy moments. (Open daily 9am-5pm. $1, under 16 free.)

The country's passion for the automobile reaches a speeding frenzy during the **500 Festival** when 33 aerodynamic, turbocharged, 2½-mi.-to-the-gallon race cars circle the asphalt track at speeds exceeding 225 mph. Beginning with the "time trials" (the two weekends in mid-May preceding the race), the party culminates with a big blowout on the Sunday of Memorial Day weekend (weather permitting). Book hotel reservations early and buy tickets in advance. For ticket info, call 248-6700 (open daily 9am-5pm). The 500 isn't the only race in town; call for information on other auto events at the **Indianapolis Raceway Park,** 9901 Crawfordsville Rd. (293-7223), near the intersection of I-74 and I-465.

Michigan

Gerald Ford, Malcolm X and Madonna do not make the most likely troika. But all three grew up in Michigan, the Midwest's most post-modern state. Once an economic powerhouse, Detroit's current condition is emblematic of the national crisis of industrial obsolescence. It is a city in pain. Nearby Ann Arbor hosts a vibrant research university, and thrives as a haven for scholars and leftists. But nature is Michigan's best draw, from its 3200 mi. of shimmering Great Lake shoreline to the rugged, solitary forests of the Upper Peninsula. Smoosh together Michigan's unspoilt lakes and woods, its small towns, and the Motor City, and you get a pair of quintessentially American peninsulas.

Practical Information

Capital: Lansing.

Michigan Travel Bureau, 333 S. Capitol Ave., Lansing 48933 (800-543-2937). A recorded listing of the week's events and festivals. **Department of Natural Resources,** Information Services Center, Steven T. Mason Bldg., P.O. Box 30028, Lansing 48909 (517-373-1220). Detailed information on state parks, forests, campsites and other public facilities.

Time Zones: Eastern. The westernmost fifth of the Upper Peninsula is Central (1 hr. behind Eastern). **Postal Abbreviation:** MI

Sales tax: 4%.

Ann Arbor

Home to gargantuan and respected University of Michigan, Ann Arbor is the Midwestern incarnation of the leftist, intellectual college town, a hip mélange of granola, yuppie and Middle America. The Republican Drug War has taken its toll, however; the $5 fine for marijuana use was recently upped to a more noticeable $25.

As tens of thousands of students depart for the summer (and rents plummet), locals and Detroit intelligentsia take over to indulge in a little celebrating of their own. During late July, thousands pack the city to see the **Ann Arbor Summer Art Fair.** Also drawing crowds from late June to mid-July, the **Ann Arbor Summer Festival** assembles numerous dance and theater productions, performances by musicians famous in styles ranging from jazz to country to classical, and free outdoor movies every night at Top of the Park (on top of the Health Service Building on Fletcher St.). Call the visitors bureau (see below) for details on these and other festivals. Also pick up the free monthly entertainment mag, *Current,* which lists whens, wheres and whats.

For information on current classical performances, contact the **University Musical Society** (764-2538; open Mon.-Fri. 10am-6pm) or the **Ann Arbor Symphony Orchestra,** 527 E. Liberty (994-4801). Live jazz can be heard every night in Ann Arbor; for information, call **Eclipse Jazz** (763-0046) or ask around. The **Ann Arbor Civic Theatre,** 1035 S. Main St., performs plays year-round. (Call the visitors bureau for schedule and prices; call 763-8587 to order tickets.)

In the realm of inanimate and non-biological culture, the university proffers a handful of top-notch free museums. The **University of Michigan Art Museum (UMAM),** 525 S. State St. at the corner of University (764-0395), houses a small but choice collection of works from around the world (open Tues.-Fri. 10am-4pm, Sat. 10am-5pm, Sun. 1-5pm; free). Paths crisscross the town and lead through the **Nichols Arboretum,** a university-owned park off Geddes Ave., just east of downtown. The paths also run through the gorgeous **Gallup Park,** 3000 Fuller Rd. (662-9319), on the Huron River, northeast of downtown. Here small, man-made islands connected by arched bridges form ponds for water sports and fishing. (Both parks open daily 6am-10pm.) In the summer, you can rent bikes and canoes at Gallup. (662-9319; bike rental $4 first hr., $1 each additional hr. Canoes $6 first hr., $1 each additional hr., Sat.-Sun. $1 extra. Rental Mon.-Fri. 11am-9pm, Sat.-Sun. 9am-9pm. Must have a $10 cash deposit and driver's license.) On warm afternoons, pastorally inclined students haunt the beautiful **Mathaei Botanical Gardens,** 1800 N. Dixboro Rd. (998-7060). Call the Park and Recreation Department (5th floor of City Hall, N. 5th Ave. and E. Huron St.; 994-2780 or 769-9140) for additional information about Ann Arbor's parks.

Where there are students, there are good budget eats; wander **State St.** and **S. University St**. near the central campus for inexpensive restaurants. Grab some chopsticks at **The Coffee Break,** 1327 S. University St., near Wastenaw St., (761-1327)—not a donut shop but a good Korean restaurant. Try the *be bim bob,* a large bowl of beef, rice, spinach and cabbage, plus soup ($5). (Open Mon.-Sat. 8am-8pm, Sun. 4pm-8pm.) **The Cottage Inn,** 512 E. William St. at Thompson St., serves up the favorite pizza and pasta in town; expect a wait. (Small pizza $7; open Sun.-Thurs. 11am-midnight, Fri.-Sat. 11am-1am.) **Del Río,** 122 W. Washington (761-2530) at Ashley, brings locals together for cheap Mexican food and burgers (burrito $2.25), and jazz on Sunday nights (no cover). Del Río is managed cooperatively by its employees—a vestige of a fast-dying Ann Arbor tradition. (Open Mon.-Fri. 11:30am-2am, Sat. noon-2am, Sun. 5:30pm-2am.) For breakfast, get over easy to **Angelo's,** at Cathedral and Glenn, a U of M tradition since the 1950s. (Open Mon.-Fri. 6am-4pm, Sat. 6am-2pm, Sun. 7am-2pm.) The **Espresso Royale Café,** 324 S. State St., provides ethereal atmosphere, fruit drinks, a large variety of coffees (cappuccino $1.25), and art-covered walls. Drinks are 70¢ to $2; occasionally there's live music. (Open Mon.-Fri. 7am-midnight, Sat.-Sun. 9am-midnight.) Pack a picnic at the **farmers market** that springs up outside the Kerrytown Mall on N. 5th Ave. (Open Sat. and Wed., 7am-3pm.)

Ann Arbor has excellent nightspots that cater to its club-hopping college population. Look for blues, reggae, and rock 'n' roll at **Rick's American Café,** 611 Church St. (996-2747). Voted the best bar in Ann Arbor for the sixth straight year in 1990, Rick's has hosted well-known alternative bands like 10,000 Maniacs. Monday is $1 pitcher night. (Open Mon.-Thurs. and Sat. 7:30pm-2am, Fri. 3pm-2am. Cover $3-6; more for big acts.) The **Bird of Paradise,** 207 E. Ashley St., (662-8310) soars with live jazz every night (cover $0-5), and **The Blind Pig,** 208 S. First St., squeals with alternative rock.

Expensive hotels and motels predominate in Ann Arbor, but it is possible to find reasonable accommodations. Book way ahead if you plan to stay during commencement (early May), during any home-game weekend (in the fall), or during the Summer Art Fair (late July). The **Ann Arbor YMCA,** 350 S. 5th Ave. at William St. (663-0536), in downtown Ann Arbor, sleeps women on separate floors from men. Clean, dorm-style rooms have shared baths with laundry facilities available. Check-in before 10:30pm. (Singles $26, weekly $88.) The **University of Michigan** has rooms available year-round at **Cambridge House,** West Quad, 541 Thompson St. Crash here in air-conditioned, carpeted rooms with cable TV and private bathrooms at the heart of campus. Rate includes parking; check-in daily 7am to midnight; you must have reservations to check-in after midnight. (Singles $44-54. Doubles $52-62.) The U of M sometimes has space in other dorms as well; call 747-2402 for availability.

Commuter Transportation Company and **Kirby Tours** (278-2224 or 800-521-0711 outside MI) run frequent shuttles from the airport (have them drop you off at a hotel for $18; $23 otherwise). Ann Arbor's layout is a well-planned grid. **Main Street** divides the town east-west while **Huron Street** divides it north-south. The central campus of the university lies five to six blocks east of Main St., south of E. Huron St. (about a 5-min. walk from the center of town).

The **Ann Arbor Convention and Visitors Bureau,** 211 E. Huron St. #6 near 5th St. (995-7281), has free guides about area attractions, cultural activities, accommodations and the university. (Open Mon.-Fri. 8:30am-5pm.) **University of Michigan Information** is reached at 763-4636, and has info on Ann Arbor as well as the University (open Tues.-Sat. 7am-2am, Sun.-Mon. 9am-1am). **Amtrak,** 325 Depot St. (994-4906 or 800-872-7245), offers train service to Chicago ($54) and Detroit ($18). (Open daily 7:30am-11:30pm.) **Greyhound,** 116 W. Huron St. (662-5212), at Ashley St. downtown, one block off Main St., offers frequent service to Detroit ($7, students $4) and Chicago ($21). Buy tickets on the bus. The **Ann Arbor Transportation Authority** (973-6500 or 996-0400) runs 25 routes serving Ann Arbor and a few nearby towns. Most buses operate daily 6:45am to 10:15pm. (Fare 60¢, seniors and students 30¢. Office open Mon.-Fri. 8am-5pm.) The 24-hr. **Sexual Assault Crisis Line** is 936-3333. **Emergency** here is 911.

Ann Arbor's **time zone** is Eastern. The **post office** is at 2075 W. Stadium Blvd. (665-1100; open Mon.-Fri. 7:30am-5pm). The **ZIP code** is 48106; the **area code** is 313.

Detroit

An author recently proclaimed Detroit "America's first Third-World city," and indeed, the city has witnessed a quarter-century of hardship. In the 60s, as the country grooved to Motown's beat, the city erupted in some of the era's most violent race riots. Massive white flight to the suburbs has been the norm ever since; the population has more than halved since 1967, turning some neighborhoods into ghost towns. The decline of the auto industry in the late 70s exacerbated problems, and economic disempowerment has engendered frustration, violence, and hopelessness among the city's residents. Today, the bleak cityscape makes for a fascinating if frightening glimpse into America's future. *Robocop* was set here for a good reason.

In spite of this, Detroit survives; the five towers of the Renaissance Center on the Detroit river symbolize hope that the downtown's rejuvenation as a center for business and nightlife can spark a city-wide comeback. But Detroit's rebirth proceeds slowly, and hope for the future is still a cruel fantasy for many of the city's residents.

Practical Information and Orientation

Emergency: 911.

Detroit Convention and Visitors Bureau, on Hart Plaza at 2 E. Jefferson St. (567-1170). Pick up the free *Detroit Visitors Guide.* Open daily 9am-5pm; phone after hours to hear a recorded list of entertainment events. Call 800-338-7648 to mail-order the slick *Metro Detroit Visitor's Guide.*

Traveler's Aid: 211 W. Congress at Shelby, 3rd floor (962-6740). Emergency assistance.

Detroit Metropolitan Airport: 21 mi. west of downtown off I-94 (942-3550). Major carriers: **Northwest** (800-225-2525) and **Delta** (800-221-1212).

Commuter Transportation Company (946-1000) runs shuttles downtown, stopping at major hotels (45 min.; $11 one way; 6am-7pm, 7-11pm by reservation). Make reservations; taxi fare downtown is a steep $25.

Amtrak: 2601 Rose St. (964-5335 or 800-872-7245), at 17th St., 1½ blocks south of Michigan Ave. Not in a good neighborhood, but okay in daytime. To Chicago $28, to New York City $103. Open daily 6:30am-1am. For destinations in Canada, use the station across the river in Canada: **VIA Rail,** 298 Walker Rd., Windsor, Ont. (800-387-1144).

Greyhound: 1001 Howard St., from freeway take Lodge S. exit, turn onto Howard, terminal is on the right (533-0814). To: Chicago ($25, 3-day advance purchase $20); Cleveland ($22/$17.60); Toronto ($41); and New York ($79/$63). Open 24 hrs.; ticket office open daily 6:30am-1am.

Public Transport: Detroit Department of Transportation (DOT), 1301 E. Warren (833-7692). Carefully policed public transport system. Serves the downtown area, with limited service to the suburbs. Many buses now stop service at midnight. Fare $1, transfers 10¢. **People Mover,** Detroit Transportation Corporation, 150 Michigan Ave. (224-2160). Ultramodern elevated tramway facility circles the Central Business District with 13 stops on a 2.7-mi. loop. Worth a ride just for the view. Fare 50¢. **Southeastern Michigan Area Regional Transit (SMART),** 962-5515. Bus service to the suburbs. Fare $1-2.50, transfers 10¢. Pick up a free map of the SMART bus system at their office in the first floor of First National Bank at Woodward and Fort. **Tunnel Bus,** Windsor, Ont. (519-944-4111). Service to Windsor through the tunnel.

Taxi: Checker Cab, 963-7000.

Car Rental: Call-a-Car, 877 E. Eight Mile Rd. (541-2700), in Hazel Park at I-75. No rental for 1 day only. Weekend rate (Fri.-Sun.) $60, 300 mi. free, 20¢ each additional mi. Must be 21 with credit card and insurance. Car must not leave MI.

Help Lines: Crisis Hotline, 224-7000.

Time Zone: Eastern.

Post Office: 1401 W. Fort (226-8301), at 8th St. Open Mon.-Fri. 8am-5:30pm, Sat. 8am-noon. **ZIP Code:** 48200.

Area Code: 313.

Detroit lies on the Detroit River, which connects Lake Erie and Lake St. Clair. Across the river (due south) lies Windsor, Canada (pop. 200,000), reached by a tunnel (just west of the Ren Cen) or the Ambassador Bridge (2 mi. west). Detroit is a tough town—one t-shirt reads "I'm so bad I vacation in Detroit"—but if you stay inside the loop encompassed by the People Mover, you shouldn't have trouble. The suburbs begin at Eight Mile Road. Driving within the Motor City limits is surprisingly mellow; in the suburbs, avoid the roads during rush hour (weekdays 4-6:30pm) at all costs. Parking is plentiful and cheap downtown, from $1 per day.

Metropolitan Detroit's streets form a grid; the major east-west arteries are the **Mile Roads**. **Eight Mile Road** is the northern boundary of the city. Three main surface streets cut diagonally across the grid. **Woodward Avenue** heads northwest from downtown, dividing city and suburbs into "east side" and "west side." **Gratiot Avenue** flares out to the northeast from downtown, and **Grand River Avenue** shoots west. Two main expressways pass through downtown; **I-94** heads west and north; **I-75** scoots north and south.

Accommodations and Camping

Avoid hotels near the bus and train stations. Camping is only an attractive option if you don't mind a 45-minute commute to get into the city.

Park Avenue House, 2305 Park Ave., at Columbia, across from the Fox Theater (961-8310). Some rooms in this once-grand hotel were converted to hostel-style accommodations after the manager's son returned from 2 years of budget traveling. Fresh rooms, new wooden beds. Lounge, store, TV, laundry, parking in guarded lot ($1). Check-in 24 hrs., but preferred if before 11pm. BYO lock for lockers. Bring or rent linen ($1). Beds $12 per night, private rooms for 1 or 2 persons $20. Full apartments $120 per week.

Teahouse of the Golden Dragon Home Hostel (HI/AYH), 8585 Harding Ave. (756-2676), in Centerline, north of 10 Mile and east of Van Dyke (Rte. 53), 9 mi. from downtown. Take SMART bus #510 or 515 to Engleman, then walk 1 block farther and 3 blocks to the right. Safe residential neighborhood. Call ahead so owner will be there to meet you. Colorful rooms filled with Asian chintz, Mickey Mouse paraphernalia, and noisy clocks. Proprietor is all smiles. $5.

Algonac State Park (765-5605) sits on the shore of the Detroit River, 35 mi. from downtown. Take I-94 N., then Rte. 29 N., about 15 mi. Watch the big ships cruise the river at night, carrying cargo to or from Detroit, the fifth largest port in the U.S. (Sites $10.) **Sterling State Park** 2800 State Park Rd., Monroe, MI 48161 (289-2715) splashes at the edge of Lake Erie, 37 mi. south of Detroit, ½-mi. off of I-75 just north of the city of Monroe. Swimming is available. (Open 24 hrs. Sites $10, including electricity.)

Food and Nightlife

Most of the restaurants downtown have fled to the suburbs, leaving the budget traveler with limited dining options. **Greektown,** a block of eateries on Monroe, at the Greektown People Mover stop, has a dozen Greek restaurants and a handful of excellent dessert bakeries, all on one block of Monroe St. at Beaubien. **Trapper's Alley** (963-5445), in Greektown, is a four-story mall of food and retail shops that veer from the usual formula; look for the art gallery on the third floor and the first floor fudge shop with a comedy routine. (Open Mon.-Thurs. 10am-9pm, Fri.-Sat. 10am-midnight, Sun. noon-7pm.) **Mexican Town,** a lively neighborhood south of Tiger Stadium, has a number of terrific restaurants. The **Ren Cen** (local terminology for the Renaissance Center) has generic white-collar mall food with some breakfast places. How do you spell local color? C-O-N-E-Y. **American Coney Islands** and **Lafayette Coney Islands,** 114 and 118 W. Lafayette, just west of Cadillac Square, have the same basic menu of hamburger, fries, and, of course, the Coney: hot dog, chili, mustard and chopped onion ($1.40), invented in Detroit. It's packed at lunch and from 10pm to 4am with the post-bar crowd. (Open 24 hrs.) If your baby has left you, or your momma has done you wrong, the hearty, well-prepared entrées at the **Soup Kitchen Saloon,** 1585 Franklin (259-2643), at Orleans in Rivertown, five blocks east of the Ren Cen, will lift your spirits with steak, chicken, or fish with Cajun leanings ($8-14), or jambalaya (Cajun stew; $11). It's also Detroit's home of the blues (live music Thurs.—Big Band Night—9:30pm-midnight, Fri.-Sat.—blues—9:30pm-2am; cover usually $5, but up to $15 for more prominent acts.)

Sights

The colossal **Henry Ford Museum & Greenfield Village,** 20900 Oakwood Blvd., is off I-94 in nearby Dearborn; take SMART bus #200 or 250 (271-1620 or 271-1976; 24 hrs.). These exhibits alone justify a trip to Detroit. The museum—a 12-acre room—has a comprehensive exhibit on the importance of the automobile in America, with a 1960s Holiday Inn guest room and a 1946 diner rounding off its collection of over 100 cars. The museum is about more than just the auto; it covers the artifacts of industrialization, from 19th-century typewriters and paper copiers to farm machinery and underwater cables. Over 80 historic homes, workplaces, and community buildings from around the country have been moved to **Greenfield Village,** a 240-acre park next to the museum. Visit the workshop of the Wright Brothers or the invention factory where Thomas Edison used systematic research and development methods (98% perspiration, 1% inspiration and 1% dumb luck) to manufacture over 400 inventions. (Museum or Village admission $11.50, ages 5-12 $5.75. Both sights, 2 days, $20, ages 5-12 $10. Open daily 9am-5pm.)

Compact downtown Detroit can be explored easily in one day. The city is in obvious decay—every other storefront is boarded up and the sidewalk is crumbling. The futuristic, gleaming steel and glass **Renaissance Center** provides a shocking contrast to this wasteland. A five-towered complex of office, hotel, and retail space, the Ren Cen encloses a maze of concrete walkways and spiraling stairs, with white-collar workers insulated from the urban blight outside. Ride to the top of the 83-story **Westin Hotel,** the tallest hotel in North America, for a towering view of the city. ($3. For general Ren Cen information call 568-5600; tour information 341-6810; lines open daily 9am-5pm.)

Detroit's Cultural Center at Woodward and Warren St. (take bus #53), clusters public and private cultural institutions such as the **Detroit Institute of Arts (DIA)** (833-7900) and the **Museum of African American History,** which has a continuing exhibit on the technical and social history of the Underground Railroad.

Although Berry Gordy's Motown Record Company has moved to Los Angeles, the **Motown Museum,** 2648 W. Grand Blvd. (867-0991), preserves its memories. Downstairs, shop around the primitive studio in which the Jackson Five, Marvin Gaye, Smokey Robinson and Diana Ross recorded the tunes that made them famous. (Open Mon.-Sat. 10am-5pm, Sun. 2-5pm. $3, under 12 $2.) The museum is east of Rosa Parks Blvd., about one mi. west of the Lodge Freeway (Rte. 10). Take the "Dexter Avenue" bus to the museum from downtown.

Events

Jazz fans jet to Detroit during Labor Day weekend for the four-day **Montreux-Detroit Jazz Festival** at Hart Plaza (259-5400), the U.S. half of the Swiss Montreux International Jazz Festival. The festival is free, dig it? The **Michigan State Fair,** the nation's oldest, gathers bake-offs, art exhibits and the heady whiff of livestock to the Michigan Exposition and State Fairgrounds at Eight Mile Rd. and Woodward (10 days long, end of Aug. to first week of Sept.). Pick up a copy of the weekly arts mag *Metro Times* for complete listings of music, theater, art and freebies. Charge concert or sports tickets at **Ticketmaster,** 645-6666.

Isle Royale National Park

Isle Royale's tourist literature reminds you that "more people visit Yellowstone National Park in one day than visit Isle Royale in the whole year;" this park offers the real backcountry seclusion which sometimes is lacking in the bumper-to-bumper traffic of other parks. Its relative desolation is not due to a lack of appeal but to natural barriers which filter out the Interstate-RV-with-TV and McDelibopper's-meal-style tourists and save the area for serious, quiet nature lovers. Isle Royale (ROY-al, not roy-AL) is, as the name implies, an island. 45 mi. long and 10 mi. wide, it runs parallel to the northwestern coast of Lake Superior. The island itself is a car-, telephone-, and medical service-free wilderness zone, accessible only by boat (or by sea plane for the thick of wallet); visitors to Isle Royale should plan ahead sensibly, hike, and take time to experience it as a living wilderness.

The island was home to quiet-living fisherfolk until it was made a national park in 1940. The inhabitants were allowed to remain on the island until they left or died, at which point their property reverted to the park, a process of eminent domain which is now nearly complete. Howard Sivertson's paintings, with exquisitely sensitive and varied treatments of sky and water, plus the annotations in his book *Once Upon an Isle,* document his childhood in this now-defunct community. Human history on the island has also left points of interest in lighthouses and 1000- to 2000-year-old Native American copper pit mines.

But it is nature which draws people to Isle Royale. Hiking most of the length of the island from Rock Harbor to Windigo on some of the 170 mi. of trails in the park is a two-day perambulation through forests recovered from 19th-century logging, with plenitudes of streams and lakes orders of magnitude smaller than Lake Superior. The **Greenstone Ridge Trail** follows the backbone of the island from Rock Harbor Lodge. **Ojibway Lookout,** on Mt. Franklin, affords a good view of the Canadian shore 15 mi. away. **Monument Rock,** 70 ft. tall, challenges even experienced climbers. **Lookout Louise,** also on the trail, offers one of the most beautiful views in the park. For a superlative time, go to **Ryan Island** in **Siskiwit Lake,** the largest island in the largest lake on the largest island in the largest freshwater lake in the world. Boat and canoe rentals are available at both Rock Harbor and Windigo, and the island's coast provides beautiful and surprising nooks (and crannies!) to explore by water. (Motor rentals $11 half-day, $18.50 full-day. Boat and canoe rentals $9 half-day, $15 full-day.)

There are numerous **campgrounds** scattered around the island; permits, free and available at any ranger station, are required for camping. Some campgrounds have three-sided, screened-in shelters, but they're popular and can't be reserved; bring your own tent just in case. Nights are always cold (mid-40°F in June); bring warm clothes and mosquito repellent. Use a 25-micron filter or boil water for at least two minutes, as it is infested with a nasty tapeworm; iodine tablets and charcoal purification are not sufficient. Wood fires are greatly restricted; bring a camp stove instead. Indoor accommodations are available at Rock Harbor; they tend to be nice but expensive. Housekeeping cottages at **Rock Harbor Lodge,** P.O. Box 405, Houghton (906-337-4993), start at $49 per day.

There are three **ranger stations: Windigo** on the western tip of the island; **Rock Harbor** on the eastern tip of the island; and near **Siskiwit Lake,** on the south shore, midway between Windigo and Rock Harbor. Campers can buy supplies and groceries at Rock Harbor and in limited amounts at Windigo.

Experienced seapersons can navigate to Isle Royale on their own (contact the park headquarters for advice in choosing a route and choosing whether to make the attempt; Lake Superior is big, cold, and treacherous), but the largest share of visitors come on the *Ranger III* (906-482-0984) boat from Houghton, which departs early June to mid-September Tuesday and Friday at 9am (return trip leaves Rock Harbor Wed. and Sat. 9am), and takes 6½ hours. (One way mid-July-late Aug. $43, kids under 12 $20; off-season $35, kids $20. Extra charge to transport a canoe, kayak, outboard motor, or boat under 20 ft. long.) The *Isle Royale Queen III* (operated by Isle Royale Ferry Service, The Dock, Copper Harbor, MI 49918, 906-289-4437; off-season 108 Center St., Hancock MI 49930) makes 4½-hour trips from Copper Harbor, MI, starting at 8am, and return trips the same afternoon. (Mid-May-mid-June and Labor Day-end of Sept. Mon. and Fri.; mid-June-end of June Mon.-Tues. and Thurs.-Sat., July Thurs.-Tues.; Aug.-Labor Day daily. Mid-May-mid-July $30, under 12 $15; mid-July-Sept. $34, kids $17. Extra charge for canoes, kayaks and suchlike; 10% discount for generally pointless same-day round-trips.) Both of these boats land at **Rock Harbor,** near the eastern end of the island, where the most services are available. **Grand Portage, MN,** near the northern end of the Minnesota Superior North Shore, originates two boats to the island, administered by **Sivertson Fishery** in Superior, WI (715-392-5551; $30-40, kids under 12 $15-20).

Despite its closer proximity to the Ontario and Minnesota mainland, the park is officially part of Michigan, and its headquarters are located in **Houghton,** on the Upper Peninsula (mailing address: Isle Royale National Park, Houghton, MI 49931; 906-482-0984).

Lake Michigan Shore

The 350-mi. eastern shore of Lake Michigan stretches south from the Mackinaw Bridge to the Indiana border. It can be reached in less than two hours from downtown Chicago and has been a vacation spot for over a century with its dunes of sugary sand, superb fishing, abundant fruit harvests through October, and deep snow in winter. The region was one of Lake Michigan's shipping centers before the railroad to Chicago was completed, and though the harbors today welcome more pleasure boats than freighters, merchant vessels are still a common sight along the coast.

Many of the region's attractions center around forked **Grand Traverse Bay** and **Traverse City,** the "cherry capital of the world," at the southern tip of the bay. Fishing is best in the **Au Sable** and **Manistee Rivers.** The rich fudge sold in numerous specialty shops, however, seems to have the biggest pull on tourists, whom locals dub "fudgies." The **West Michigan Tourist Association,** 136 E. Fulton, Grand Rapids 49503 (616-456-8557), offers copious free literature on this area. (Open Mon.-Fri. 8:45am-5pm.)

Northern Michigan Shore: Traverse City and Environs

In summer, vacationers head to Traverse City for its sandy beaches and annual **Cherry Festival,** held the first full week in July. The Traverse City area produces 50% of the nation's sweet and tart cherries, and they won't let you forget it—the cherry theme is emblazoned on everything from underwear to overcoats. The surrounding landscape of sparkling blue water, cool forests, and magnificent sand dunes makes this region a Great Lakes paradise, though at times a crowded and expensive one. Grand Traverse Bay is the focal point for swimming, boating, and scuba diving. Free beaches and public access sites dot its shores. Look for the large flock of white swans. The Leeanau Peninsula pokes up between Grand Traverse Bay and Lake Michigan. Explore the coastline on scenic **M-22,** which will channel you to **Leland,** a charming one-time fishing village which now launches the Manitou Island ferries (see below). Five orchards near Traverse City let you pick your own cherries. One of them is **Amon Orchards,** 10 mi. east on U.S. 31 (938-9160), which also bakes cherry products and contends that "cherries aren't just for dessert anymore."

There are many **campgrounds** around Traverse City—in state parks and forests, the **Manistee** and **Huron National Forests,** and various parks run by local townships and counties. The West Michigan Tourist Association's *Carefree Days* gives a comprehensive list of public and private sites. State parks usually charge $7 to $9. As usual, the national forests are the best deal ($4-7). The cheapest beds near downtown Traverse City get made at **Northwestern Michigan Community College,** East Hall, 1701 E. Front St. (922-1406), offers dorms with shared bath. (Singles $20. Doubles $30. Suite with private bath $45. 1-week advance reservation recommended. Open late June-Aug.)

According to legend, the mammoth sand dunes 20 mi. west of Traverse City on M-72 are a sleeping mother bear, waiting for her cubs—the **Manitou Islands**—to finish a swim across the lake. Local legend does *not* explain why the cubs didn't just take the ferry which serves the islands from Leland. (**Manitou Island Transit,** 256-9061. Daily trips to South Manitou, 3 per week to North Manitou, the larger and more wild of the pair. Check-in 9:30am. Round-trip $15, under 12 $10.) Free camping is available on both islands; no cars allowed.

The islands are just a part of the **Sleeping Bear Dunes National Lakeshore** (326-5134), which also includes 25 mi. of lakeshore on the mainland. The dunes are a Godzilla-sized version of the childhood sandpile; mountains of fine sand that rise to a precipitous 400 ft. above Lake Michigan. You can make the gritty climb to the top at the **Dune Climb,** five mi. north of Empire on M-109, or you can hike one of the two trails, 2.8 and 3.5 mi. long. The less adventurous can motor to an overlook along the **Pierce Stocking Scenic Drive,** off M-109 just north of Empire. Call the National Parks service **visitors center** for more info (326-5134). Two rivers which flow through the national lakeshore are suitable for canoeing: the Platte River at the southern end, and the Crystal River on the northern, near Glen Arbor. **Crystal River Canoes** (334-3090) will equip you with a canoe and pick you up at the end of a two-hour paddle ($20). **Riverside Canoes** provides the same service for the same low price on the Platte River.

Sleeping Bear Dunes National Lakeshore has two campgrounds: **DH Day** (334-4634; $8, no showers) in Glen Arbor, and **Platte River** (325-5881; $10, $15 with hook-up, has showers) in Honor. No reservations. For a roof over your head, stay on one of the 12 beds at the **Brookwood Home Hostel,** 538 Thomas Rd. (352-4296), in Frankfort near the Sleeping Bear Dunes, almost 50 mi. south of Traverse City on Rte. 31. ($7. Open mid-June-Sept. 20. Reservations required; call Marjorie Groenwald at 301-544-4514.)

The renowned **Interlochen Center for the Arts** (276-9221) aestheticizes between two lakes 17 mi. south of Traverse City on Rte. 137. Here, the high-powered **National Music Camp** instructs over 2000 young artists and musicians each summer in the visual arts, theater, dance, and music. Faculty and student concerts are free. Renowned performers command a modest $3 to $4 during the **International Arts Festival,** held from late June to mid-August. Recent guest performers have included Tony Bennett, Manhattan Transfer, and the Beach Boys. The **Interlochen Arts Academy** at the center of-

LET'S GO® Travel

1992 CATALOG

When it comes to budget travel we know every trick in the book Discount Air Fares, Eurailpasses, Travel Gear, IDs, and more...

LET'S PACK IT UP

Let's Go Supreme

Innovative hideaway suspension with parallel stay internal frame turns backpack into carry-on suitcase. Includes lumbar support pad, torso and waist adjustment, leather trim, and detachable daypack. Waterproof Cordura nylon, lifetime guarantee, 4400 cu. in Navy, Green or Black.

A $165

Let's Go Backcountry

Full size, slim profile expedition pack designed for the serious trekker. Parallel stay suspension system, deluxe shoulder harness, Velcro height adjustment, side compression straps. Detachable hood converts into a fanny pack. Waterproof Cordura nylon, lifetime guarantee, main compartment and hood 6350 cu. in. extends to 7130 cu.

E $195

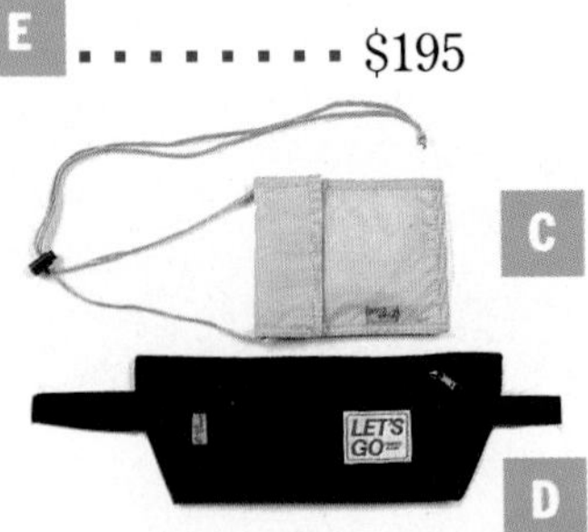

Let's Go Backpack/Suitcase

Hideaway suspension with internal frame turns backpack into carry-on suitcase. Detachable daypack makes it 3 bags in 1. Waterproof Cordura nylon, lifetime guarantee, 3750 cu. in. Navy, Green or Black.

B $119

Undercover NeckPouch

Ripstop nylon with soft Cambrelle back. 3 pockets. 6 1/2 x 5". Lifetime guarantee. Black or Tan.

C $9.95

Undercover WaistPouch

Ripstop nylon with soft Cambrelle back. 2 pockets. 12 x 5" with 30 x 13cm waistband. Lifetime guarantee. Black or Tan.

D $9.95

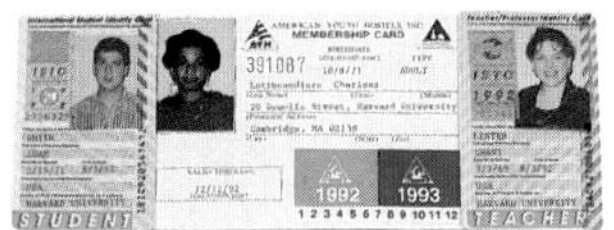

LET'S SEE SOME I.D.

1993 International ID Cards

Provides discounts on accomodations, cultural events, airfares and accident/medical insurance. Valid 9-1-92 to 12-31-93

F1	Teacher (ITIC)	$16.00
F2	Student (ISIC)	$15.00
F3	Youth (IYC)	$15.00

FREE "International Student Travel Guide."

LET'S GO HOSTELING

1993-94 Youth Hostel Card

Required by most international hostels. Must be a U.S. resident.

G1	Adult (ages 18-55)	$25
G2	Youth (under 18)	$10

Sleepsack

Required at all hostels. Washable durable poly/cotton. 18" pillow pocket. Folds into pouch size.

H	$13.95

1992-93 Youth Hostel Guide (IYHG)

Essential information about 3900 hostels in Europe and the Mediterranean.

I	$10.95

Let's Go Travel Guides

Europe; USA; Britain/Ireland; France; Italy; Israel/Egypt; Mexico; California/Hawaii; Spain/Portugal; Pacific Northwest/Alaska; Greece/Turkey; Germany/Austria/Swizerland; NYC; London; Washington D.C.; Rome; Paris.

J1	USA or Europe	$16.95
J2	Country Guide (specify)	$15.95
J3	City Guide (specify)	$10.95

LET'S GO BY TRAIN

Eurail Passes

Convenient way to travel Europe. Save up to 70% over cost of individual tickets. Call for national passes.

First Class

K1	15 days	$460
K2	21 days	$598
K3	1 month	$728
K4	2 months	$998
K5	3 months	$1260

First Class Flexipass

L1	5 days in 15	$298
L2	9 days in 21	$496
L3	14 days in 30	$676

Youth Pass (under 20)

M1	1 month	$508
M2	2 months	$698
M3	5 days in 2 months	$220
M4	10 days in 2 months	$348
M5	15 days in 2 months	$474

LET'S GET STARTED

Please print or type. Incomplete applications will be returned

International Student/Teacher Identity Card (ISIC/ITIC) (ages 12 & up) enclose:

1. Letter from registrar or administration, transcript, or proof of tuition payment. FULL-TIME only.
2. One picture (1 1/2" x 2") signed on the reverse side.

International Youth Card (IYC) (ages 12-25) enclose:

1. Proof of birthdate (copy of passport or birth certificate).
2. One picture (1 1/2" x 2") signed on the reverse side.
3. Passport number
4. Sex: M☐ F☐

Last Name | First Name | Date of Birth

Street | *We do not ship to P.O. Boxes. U.S. addresses only.*

City | State | Zip Code

Phone | Citizenship

School/College | Date Trip Begins

Item Code	Description, Size & Color	Quantity	Unit Price	Total Price

Shipping & Handling

If order totals:	Add
Up to $30.00	$4.00
30.01-100.00	$6.00
Over 100.00	$7.00

Total Merchandise Price	
Shipping & Handling (See box at left)	
For Rush Handling Add $8 for continental U.S., $10 for AK & HI	
MA Residents (Add 5% sales tax on gear & books)	
Total	

Enclose check or money order payable to: Harvard Student Agencies, Inc.

Allow 2-3 weeks for delivery. Rush orders delivered within one week of our receipt.

LET'S GO® Travel

Harvard Student Agencies, Inc., Harvard University, Thayer B, Cambridge, MA 02138

(617) 495-9649 1-800-5LET'S GO (Credit Card Orders Only)

Prices subject to change

fers performances almost every weekend in winter (call 276-6230 for schedule). The 1200-acre wooded grounds are open year-round, and free tours leave the information center Tuesday through Saturday at 10am. Across the road, the huge **Interlochen State Park** (276-9511) has camping facilities. (Primitive sites $5, with hookup $9, plus a $3 vehicle permit; showers $1.) The **park store** (276-7074) rents row boats ($12 per 12 hr., $15 per 24 hrs.; $20 deposit or driver's license required).

Greyhound, 3233 Cass Rd. (946-5180), ties Traverse City to the Upper Peninsula and southern Michigan ($43 to Detroit; open Mon.-Fri. 8am-5pm). **Bay Area Transportation Authority,** at the same address (941-2324), runs buses once per hour on scheduled routes ($1.50 per ride) and can provide personal transportation. (Open Mon.-Fri. 6am-6pm, Sat. 9am-5pm.)

For **visitor information,** contact the **Grand Traverse Convention and Visitors Bureau,** corner of Munson Ave. and Cass, P.O. Box 5119, Traverse City 49685-5119 (947-1120 or 800-872-8377; open Mon.-Fri. 9am-5pm). Ask for the *Traverse City Guide* and *Carefree Days.* For a listing of local events and entertainment, pick up the weekly *Traverse City Record-Eagle Summer Magazine.*

The **post office** is at 202 S. Union St. (946-9616; open Mon.-Fri. 8am-5pm). Traverse City's **ZIP code** is 49684; the **area code** is 616.

Southern Michigan Shore

Manistee beckons tourists with a Victorian shtick. Don't miss the **Firehouse,** built in 1889 and not altered since, or the **A.H. Lyman Store,** 425 River St., where nothing is for sale except postcards: it's an exhibit of a turn-of-the-century store, with goods on the shelves as they were in 1900, including kitchen tools and quack medicines. (Admission $1.)

Further south, **Grand Haven** has perhaps the best beach on Lake Michigan: several miles of fine sugary sand so pure that auto manufacturers use it to make cores and molds for engine parts. A cement "boardwalk" connects the beach to the small downtown; strollers come out for the people-watching and up-close views of ships on the water. Downtown the action centers on Washington St. Catch an almost-first-run flick at the **Grand Theater** (842-4520) for just 99¢.

Moving down the coast, the town of **Holland** was founded in 1847 by Dutch religious dissenters, and remained mostly Dutch until well into the 20th century. Today the town cashes in on its heritage with a wooden shoe factory, Netherlands Museum (392-9084), Veldheer Tulip Gardens (399-1900), and a recreated Dutch Village (396-1475). Explore these places (admission $1-4) or simply wander around downtown to get a sense of how this tightly-knit community has survived.

Grand Rapids is the biggest city in the area, and is the hub of local bus routes. **Greyhound,** in the Grand Rapids Station (456-1709) connects to Detroit, Chicago, Holland and Grand Haven. The cheapest bed in town is at the **YMCA,** 33 Library St. N.E. (458-1141), for $10 a night; no women allowed. Get a more equal-opportunity and architecturally significant night's rest at the **Snow Flake Motel,** 3822 Red Arrow Hwy., St. Joseph, the only motel designed by Frank Lloyd Wright. (Singles $35.) **Camping** is readily available in western Michigan; consult the *Michigan Travel Planner* to find the nearest state park (there are over 20 in the region).

The area's **time zone** is Eastern; the **area code** is 616.

Upper Peninsula

A multimillion-acre forestland bordered by three of the world's largest lakes, Michigan's Upper Peninsula (U.P.) is one of the most scenic and unspoiled stretches of land in the Great Lakes region. One hundred years ago the region was almost completely deforested, its timber destined for houses and fences on the treeless Great Plains and for the fireplaces of voracious Chicago; these trees are only now returning to their former grandeur.

If you want to experience small-town America, *this* is the place; the largest town in the U.P. has a population of 25,000, and the region is a paradise for fishing, camping, hiking, snowmobiling, and getting away from it all. If you're looking for regional cuisine, stick to the Friday night fish-fry: a mess o' perch, walleye or whitefish, available everywhere for about $7 to $8. Try the local ethnic specialty, a meat pie imported by Cornish miners in the 19th century called a pastie (PASS-tee), and you'll taste why they haven't caught on in the rest of the country.

Half a dozen rivers in the U.P. beckon canoers. Those who heed the call of the rapids will be well-served by canoe livery services which outfit would-be explorers with equipment, launch them, and retrieve them at a specified destination. For a brochure listing the businesses along each river, write to **Michigan Recreational Canoeing Association,** P.O. Box 668, Indian River 49749. The area is a great place for campers; it's hard to get more than 15 mi. away from one of the peninsula's 200 **campgrounds,** including those at both national forests. Sleep with your dogs or bring extra blankets; temperatures in these parts can drop to a shivering 40°F even in July. **Welcome centers** operated by the Michigan Department of Transportation guard the U.P. at the five main entry points: **Ironwood, Iron Mountain, Menominee, St. Ignace, Sault Ste. Marie,** and **Marquette.** Their mission: to foist heaps of tourist info on all suspecting travelers. Pick up their handy-dandy *Upper Peninsula Travel Planner.* The **U.S. Forestry Service** has maps and advice to help you plan a trip into the wilderness; visit one of their info centers at most entrances to the national forests and lakeshores, or write to U.S. Forestry Service, Hiawatha National Forest, 2727 N. Lincoln Rd., Escanaba 49829 (786-4062). Contact **Upper Peninsula Travel and Recreation Association,** P.O. Box 400, Iron Mountain 49801 (774-5480) for general info.

Sault Ste. Marie

The water level of Lake Superior is 20 ft. higher than that of Lake Huron, and the first trading vessels to ply the Great Lakes faced a costly and arduous portage between the two. In 1855, entrepreneurs built the first lock at Sault Ste. Marie, and today the city's four locks are the busiest in the world, floating over 10,000 ships annually. For a sailor's-eye-view of the operation, add your bodyweight to some of the 90 million tons of freight the locks handle each year and ride on the **Soo Locks Boat Tours** (632-6301) which leave from two docks (billboards with directions start 100 mi. away). (Mid-May-mid-Oct., $11, kids $7). The U.S. Army Corps of Engineers, which operates the locks, maintains a good **visitors center** with a working model of the locks, a free film, and a free observation deck, at the park near the locks. If you'd like to tour a freighter, head to the waterfront at the end of Johnston St., where the **Valley Camp** (632-3658), a 1917 steam-powered freighter, has been converted into a museum. (Open mid-May-mid-Oct., 10am-6pm, July-Aug. 9am-9pm; $6.)

In Sault Ste. Marie, bed down at **Rest-A-While Motel,** 2014 Riverside Dr., 49783 (632-9490; rooms from $28). On your way west, stay at **Tahquamenon Falls State Park,** 10 mi. east of Paradise (492-3415), on the river near the falls.

Middle Peninsula

The feds keep the trails clean at one of the U.P.'s two huge **national forests,** the **Hiawatha** (786-4062), which blankets central and eastern U.P. If you don't want to get into a pair of rubber waders and slog out into the wilderness, the best place to enjoy the wildlife and outdoors in the U.P. is the **Seney National Wildlife Refuge,** off M-77, 12 mi. north of U.S. 2. This 95,000-acre sanctuary was completely deforested and sold to unsuspecting farmers in the early 20th century. The state later took it over, and during the Depression, the Civilian Conservation Corps (CCC) reconstructed a natural environment here. Most tourists feed the Canada geese in the parking lot at the visitors center and, satisfied with their foray into nature, they leave. More adventurous readers can walk quietly around the ponds on the 1½-mi. walking trail through the forest, where they can view ducks, swans, woodpeckers, and beaver—over 200 different species have been sighted here. There are also 70 mi. of trails open for biking and hiking. The refuge is open during daylight hours and is free. Overnight camping is not allowed. The best time for viewing wildlife is in the early morning and the early evening. In **Shingleton,** 20 mi. west of the refuge, snowshoes are hand-made at the **Iverson Snowshoe Company's** "factory," actually a big garage. Observe the process in action Monday through Friday 8am to 3pm (452-6370).

Drop a penny in and watch it sink all the way down to the bottom of the 45-ft. deep **Big Spring,** on M-149, 10 mi. north of U.S. 2. This pellucid natural spring gushes 10,000 gallons per minute. Hop on the self-propelled raft, haul yourself to the center of the pool, and observe the billows of silt where the water streams in. Greet the two-ft. brown trout which school in the perpetually 49°F pool. ($3.50 per carload, open daily during daylight.) According to folklore, Paul Bunyan, a fictional character who performed such herculean feats as creating a riverbed by dragging his axe, was born in **Manistique**. As you drive through on U.S. 2, you can't miss the 20-ft.-tall painted fiberglass statue of the legend himself. Camp at **Indian Lake State Park** (341-2355), five mi. west of Manistique; take U.S. 2 west, then M-149 north.

You can rent canoes nearby at **Camper's Market** (341-5614; $10 per day, $7 per 6 hrs., $20 deposit).

The scenic beauty and recreational opportunities of the U.P. are concentrated at the **Pictured Rocks National Lakeshore,** which stretches for 40 mi. along Lake Superior between Munising and Grand Marais. The Pictured Rocks have been sculpted by wind, rain, and ice for millenia. The kaleidoscopic beauty of their arches and columns is hard to appreciate from land, but an overlook at **Miner's Castle** off Miner's Castle Rd. from H58, gives a decent perspective of the stone formations. The best way to see the carved cliffs is the **Pictured Rocks Boat Cruise** (387-2379) which leaves from Munising. (June-Oct.; $17, kids $7.) The **Twelvemile Beach** and **Grand Sable Dunes** occupy the other half of the lakeshore. Enjoy the sand and rock beaches, but don't plan to swim unless you have a layer of blubber; Lake Superior is f-f-f-reezing year-round. The **North Country Trail,** which winds from Port Henry, NY to Lake Sakakawea, ND, passes through the lakeshore. You can hike through the lakeshore on the trail and sleep at primitive campsites along the way (free with use permit). The lakeshore is accessible from Munising and Grand Marais; in both towns you can find food, supplies, and lodging. For more info contact the **National Park Service** at P.O. Box 40, Munising 49862 (387-3700), or the **Grand Marais Chamber of Commerce,** P.O. Box 118, Grand Marais 49839 (494-2766). If you prefer to sleep with a roof above your head, the **Voyager Motel,** 312 E. Munising Ave., Munising 49862 (387-2127), is only three blocks from the Pictured Rocks Boat Cruise (from $20).

Keewenaw

Before anybody even suspected that there was gold in California, the copper mines in the Keewenaw Peninsula were making some Boston speculators obscenely wealthy. The curved finger of land in the northwest corner of the U.P. sticks out into Lake Superior, beckoning travelers to tour its copper mines and stretches of wilderness. Between 1847 and 1887, prospectors came to the **Delaware Copper Mine**, 11 mi. south of Copper Harbor on U.S. 41 (289-4688), and extracted eight million pounds of copper form the earth. Now, tourists plunk down coppers to pay for the daily guided tours (June-Oct. 10am-5pm). The **Coppertown U.S.A. Mining Museum,** west of U.S. 41 (337-4364), displays the tools and techniques of digging up the raw material for many a penny. (Open June-Oct. Mon.-Sat. 10am-6pm.) **Estivant Pines,** the largest remaining stand of virgin pines in Michigan, has been preserved near Copper Harbor, three mi. out on Lake Manganese Rd. These trees *average* more than 500 years old.

The Keewenaw Peninsula offers more than memories of metal. Comb the agate beaches, see the Northern Lights, and in winter, ski, snowmobile, or snowshoe over the 250 inches of snow the region receives each year. The **Brockway Mountain Drive** between Eagle Harbor and Copper Harbor rises 1000 ft. above sea level and is one of the most scenic drives in the U.P. With 80 mi. of flash-marked trails, **Porcupine Mountain Wilderness State Park** is one of the best places in the U.P. to hike. The park is on the western side of the U.P., 16 mi. west of Ontonagon off M-107 (885-5275). The **Lake of**

the Clouds glistens high in the mountains of this 58,000-acre preserve. Contact **Ontonagon County Chamber of Commerce,** P.O. Box 266, Ontonagon 49953 (884-4735) for more info.

Copper Harbor functions as the main gateway to **Isle Royale National Park** (See Isle Royale National Park). The *Isle Royale Queen* leaves daily at 8am (4½ hrs.; $30 round-trip, ages under 12 $15, canoes of any age $12.) The *Ranger III* makes two trips per week to Isle Royale from Houghton (6 hrs.; $43, kids $20, canoe $15.) The **Keewenaw Tourism Council** is at 326 Sheldon Ave., Houghton (482-2388 or 800-338-7982).

The region's relative isolation and the distances between its cities make travel on the U.P. problematic. **Greyhound** (632-8643) has just three routes: Sault-Ste. Marie to St. Ignace and points south; St. Ignace to Rapid River, Iron Mountain, and Ironwood along U.S. 2; and Calumet south to Marquette, Rapid River, and on to Green Bay on U.S. 41. (All routes 1 per day.) Car-less travelers should rent in one of the gateway cities: Green Bay from the west or Grand Rapids from the east, or bike the area.

The **area code** for the U.P. is 906.

Minnesota

There are infinite variations on the themes of natural beauty and cultural interest throughout Minnesota. The southern plains are a soothing agricultural adagio; Lake Superior's north shore and inland forests resound with the voices of loons, wolves, woodsfolk and winds; the Twin Cities are flashily dynamic and synthetic; and the Iron Range is of the sort of enigmatic, haunting, but striking timbre that only 20th-century composers could approach. Throughout this symphony are interwoven folk ditties of the ethnic heritages which have colored the region. Add to this the strains of the acclaimed, progressive music of the St. Paul Chamber Orchestra and, of course, the rockin' tunes of natives Bob Dylan, Prince, and Hüsker Dü, and you'll have composed a rhapsody in Minnesota.

Practical Information

Capital: St. Paul.

Minnesota Office of Tourism, 100 Metro Sq., 121 7th Pl. E., St. Paul 55101-2112 (296-5029 or 800-657-3700, in Canada 800-766-8687). Open Mon.-Fri. 8am-5pm.

Time Zone: Central (1 hr. behind Eastern).

Postal Abbreviation: MN

Sales Tax: 6.5%.

Duluth

Duluth is still the largest inland port on the Great Lakes, but the area's population has declined more than a quarter during the past few decades. Many of the area mines are closed, and Duluth has instead become a tourist center of the northern wilderness. Minnesota's "refrigerated city," known for its oh-my-God-it's-soo-fricking-cold weather, is a great place to gear up for fishing, camping or driving excursions into northwestern Minnesota. It retains an honest, raw, unpredictable quality born of its origins, natural surroundings and harsh climate.

The best thing about Duluth is its proximity to majestic **Lake Superior**. Enjoy the Superior coast along Duluth's recently completed **Lakewalk,** a mile-long walkway stretching across the harbor. **Hawk Ridge,** four mi. north of downtown off Skyline Blvd., creates a birdwatcher's paradise. In order to avoid flying over open water, hawks veer in their migration over Duluth; in September and October they fly in flocks past this bluff. **Bayfront Park** hosts the **International Folk Festival** (722-7425) on the first Saturday in August. Call the Park and Recreation Department (723-3337) for more info.

For indoor entertainment, visit **The Depot,** 506 W. Michigan St. (727-8025), in the old Amtrak station, whose several museums include the **Lake Superior Museum of Transportation,** featuring antique locomotives restored to shining splendor by retired railway workers. (Open daily 10am-5pm; Sept. 2-May 27 Mon.-Sat. 10am-5pm, Sun. 1-5pm. Admission $5, seniors $4, families $14, ages 6-17 $2.50.) **Glensheen,** 3300 London Rd. (724-8863), is a 39-room neo-Jacobean mansion; one way to *really* annoy the tour guides is to ask where the double-murder, which apparently occurred in the house during the early 1970s, took place. (Open Feb.-Dec. Thurs.-Tues. 9am-4pm; Jan. Sat.-Sun. 1-3pm; more tours in summer and on weekends. $6, seniors and ages 13-17 $4.50, under 12 $2.50, less in winter. Make reservations for summer visits.)

The restored **Fitger's** brewery, 600 E. Superior St. (722-5624), and the **Canal Park** region south from downtown along **Lake Avenue** have a variety of pleasant eateries. **Sir Benedict's Tavern on the Lake,** 805 E. Superior St. (728-1192), occupies a cottage overlooking the lake, and serves soups and sandwiches ($3-4.50), desserts ($2-3) and a wide variety of beer ($3). Under 21 not admitted. (Live bluegrass Wed., Celtic music every 3rd Thurs. Open Mon.-Tues. and Thurs. 11am-11pm, Wed. 11am-midnight, Fri.-Sat. 11am-12:30am.) The **Blue Note Café,** 357 Canal Park Dr. (727-6549), has sandwiches for $2 to $3 and live music Saturdays from 8 to 10pm. (Open Mon.-Fri. 10am-8pm, Sat. 10am-10pm.)

Duluth **motels**, dependent for their livelihood on the summer migration of North-Shore-bound tourists, raise their prices and are booked early during the warm months; call as far ahead as possible. The **College of St. Scholastica,** 1200 Kenwood Ave. (723-6483), has large, quiet dorm rooms with phones, kitchen access and laundry, available for one- to two-night stays from early June to mid-August for $19. Group rates and week-long apartment rentals are available. Make reservations. Some relatively reasonable motels lie on **London Road,** west of downtown; the **Chalet Motel**, 1801 London Rd. (728-4238 or 800-235-2957), has singles for $29 to 39, doubles for $38 to 57, depending on the season. **Jay Cooke State Park** (384-4610), southwest of Duluth, has 84 campsites in a pretty setting near the dramatic St. Louis River valley. (Open daily 8am-10pm. Sites $10. Vehicle permit $4.) **Spirit Mountain,** 9500 Spirit Mountain Pl. (628-2891), near the ski resort of the same name, is 10 mi. south on I-35, on the top of the hill. (Sites with electricity $13, with electricity and water $15.)

Greyhound, 2212 W. Superior (722-5591, 722-6193 about Twin Cities service), two mi. west of downtown, serves many locations in Minnesota, Wisconsin and Michigan. (To: Calumet, MI: 12½ hr., $93; Minneapolis, MN: 3 per day, 3-4 hr., Mon.-Thurs. $16, Fri.-Sun. $21.) Take #9 "Piedmont" bus from downtown.

The **Convention and Visitors Bureau,** at Endion Station, 100 Lake Place Dr. (722-4011; open Mon.-Fri. 9am-4:45pm), and the **summer visitors center** on the waterfront at Harbor Dr. (722-6024; open daily mid-May-mid-June and Labor Day-mid-Oct. 9am-5pm; mid-June-Labor Day 9am-8pm) have an ample supply of brochures and Duluth maps.

The **post office** is at 2800 W. Michigan St. (723-2590), six blocks west of the Greyhound station. (Open Mon.-Fri. 8am-5pm, Sat. 9am-noon.) Duluth's **ZIP code** is 55806; its **area code** is 218.

Minneapolis and St. Paul

The Twin Cities combine to form an active, dynamic but livable metropolis; they have the culture but not the concomitant problems that make coastal cities so stressful. These twins born of the Mississippi River are more fraternal than identical. Their temperaments are different: The Minneapple (*à la* the Big Apple) is faster-paced and more progressive, while St. Paul is more stately and staid. Many consider Minneapolis as the furthest east of the western cities, and St. Paul, likewise, as the furthest west of the eastern cities; coast-to-coast trekkers can decide for themselves. Both sisters share family traits which include a strong interest in the arts. They have a good, open, cooperative, functional relationship, and seem to have sibling rivalry under control.

Practical Information

Emergency: 911.

Visitor Information: Minneapolis Convention and Visitors Association, 1219 Marquette Ave. (348-4313). Open Mon.-Fri. 8am-5:30pm. Also in the City Center Shopping area, 2nd level skyway, open all hours the mall is open. **St. Paul Convention and Visitors Bureau,** 101 Norwest Center, 55 E. 5th St. (297-6985 or 800-627-6101). Open Mon.-Fri. 8am-5pm. **Cityline,** (645-6060), and **The Connection,** (922-9000). Information on local events, concerts, news, sports, weather and much more.

Twin Cities International Airport: South of the cities, on I-494 in Bloomington (726-8100). **Northwest Airlines** has its headquarters here. Limousines (726-6400) run to downtown and suburban hotels, leaving from the lower level near baggage claim (5am-midnight; $6 to St. Paul, $8 to Minneapolis). Take bus #35 to Minneapolis ($1.10; service available 6-8am and 3-4:45pm). Otherwise, take bus #7 to Washington Ave. in Minneapolis, or transfer at Fort Snelling for bus #9 to downtown St. Paul. Ask for a transfer. Taxis are about $18 to Minneapolis and $15 to St. Paul.

Amtrak: 730 Transfer Rd. (800-872-7245), on the east bank off University Ave. S.E., between the Twin Cities. A nice station, but a fair distance from both downtowns. Take bus #7. Trains to Chicago (8½ hr., $68).

Greyhound: In **Minneapolis,** 29 9th St. at 1st Ave. N. (371-3311), 1 block northwest of Hennepin Ave. Very convenient. 24-hr. security. To: Chicago ($52), New York ($133, $68 with 21-day advance), and Seattle ($126). Open daily 5:45am-2:15am. In **St. Paul,** 7th St. at St. Peter (222-0509), 3 blocks east of the Civic Center in a somewhat unsafe area of town. Open daily 5:45am-8:10pm.

Public Transport: Metropolitan Transit Commission, 560 6th Ave. N. (827-7733). Call for information and directions Mon.-Fri. 6am-11pm, Sat.-Sun. 7am-11pm. Schedules and route maps available at: **Tourism Information Center**, Coffman Student Union, 300 Washington Ave. S.E., University of Minnesota; **Comstock Hall Housing Office**, 210 Delaware St. S.E., University of Minnesota; and the **MTC store**, 719 Marquette, in downtown Minneapolis (Mon.-Fri. 7:30am-5:30pm), which looks like the front of a bus and has bus-like seats inside. Bus service for both cities. Some buses operate 4:30am-12:45am, others shut down earlier. Fare $1.10 peak, 85¢ off-peak, ages under 18 25¢, off-peak express 25¢ extra. #16 bus connects the two downtowns (50 min.); the 94 freeway express is much faster. **University of Minnesota Bus,** 625-9000. Buses run 7am-10pm. Free to campus locations and even into St. Paul, if you are a student. Off-campus routes 35-50¢, 75¢ peak.

Car Rental: Ugly Duckling Rent-A-Car, 6405 Cedar Ave. S. (861-7545), Minneapolis, near the airport. From $20 per day with 100 free mi., weekly from $119. Open Mon.-Fri. 9am-6pm, Sat. 12:30-4pm, or by appointment. Must be 21. Major credit card or a $250-350 deposit required.

Taxi: Yellow Taxi, (824-4444) in Minneapolis. **Yellow Cab,** (222-4433) in St. Paul. Base rate $1.25, $1.20 per mi.

Help Lines: Contact, Twin Cities help line (341-2896); **Crime Victim Center,** 822 S. 3rd St., St. Paul, (340-5400). Open 24 hrs. **Gay-Lesbian Helpline,** 822-8661. **Gay-Lesbian Information Line**: 822-0127.

Post Office: In **Minneapolis,** 1st St. and Marquette Ave. (349-4957), next to the Mississippi River. General Delivery open Mon.-Fri. 8:30am-5pm, Sat. 9am-noon. **ZIP code:** 55401. In **St. Paul,** 180 E. Kellogg Blvd. (293-3011). Same hours. **ZIP code:** 55101.

Area Code: 612.

Minneapolis's layout is straightforward—streets run east-west and avenues run north-south. **Hennepin Avenue** crosses the Mississippi and goes through downtown, curving south toward uptown. Outside of downtown, most avenues are in alphabetical order as you travel west. St. Paul's streets are more confusing to navigate. **Grand Avenue** (east-west) and **Snelling Avenue** (north-south) are major thoroughfares. In both of the cities, **Skywalks** define the downtown areas, where second-story tunnels connect more than 10 square blocks of buildings and transform the area into a giant hamster cage. **University Avenue** connects the Twin Cities.

Accommodations and Camping

While cheap airport hotels abound in the Twin Cities, most are of dubious cleanliness and safety. The convention and visitors bureaus have useful lists of **bed and breakfasts.** The **University of Minnesota Housing Office** (624-2994), in Comstock Hall (see Practical Information), has a list of rooms in different locations around the city that rent on a daily ($8-45) or weekly basis. Write ahead for a copy. The **Oakmere Home Hostel (HI/AYH),** 8212 Oakmere Rd. (944-1210), in Bloomington has beautiful rooms on wooded lakefront property and a friendly proprietor. Singles are $15. It's somewhat remote; the Minneapolis #44a bus comes to the area Monday through Friday three times per day ($1.60).

College of St. Catherine, Caecilian Hall (HI/AYH), 2004 Randolph Ave. (690-6604), St. Paul. Take St. Paul bus #7 or 14, or call for directions. 60 stark but quiet dorm rooms near the river in a nice neighborhood. Shared bath, kitchenette. Singles $12, nonmembers $14. Doubles $25. Triples $30. Max. stay 2 weeks. Open June-mid-Aug.

Kaz's Home Hostel (HI/AYH), 5100 Dupont Ave. S. (822-8286), in South Minneapolis. Call for directions. 1 room with 2 beds. Check-in 5-9pm. Curfew 11pm, checkout 9am. Max. stay 3 nights. Members only, $10. Reservations required.

Evelo's Bed and Breakfast, 2301 Bryant Ave. (374-9656), in South Minneapolis. A 15-min. walk from uptown or take bus #17 from downtown. 3 comfortable rooms with elegant wallpaper and furnishings in a beautiful house filled with Victorian artifacts. Friendly owners. Singles $40. Doubles $50. Reservations required.

Town and Country Campground, 12630 Boone Ave. S. (445-1756), 15 mi. south of downtown Minneapolis. From I-35 W., go west on Rte. 13 to Rte. 101 for ½ mi., then left onto Boone Ave. 60 sites. Well-maintained, with laundry and pool; quiet, but clearly close to an urban area. Sites $12 for 2, with electricity $15, full hookup $17. Each additional person $1.

Minneapolis Northwest I-94 KOA (420-2255), on Rte. 101 west of I-94 exit 213, 15 mi. north of Minneapolis. Noisy kids and all the classic KOA amenities: pool, sauna and showers. Sites $14.50-18. Each additional person $2, $1.50 for kids.

Food

The Twin Cities specialize in casual dining; a gourmet sandwich or salad and a steaming cup of coffee is the favored fare. During the past decade demographics and tastes have changed—many of the Scandinavian smorgasbords have given way to Vietnamese and natural food restaurants. Funky **Uptown** is packed with restaurants and bars to suit every taste. The **Warehouse District,** near downtown Minneapolis, and **Victoria Crossing** (at Victoria and Grand St.) in St. Paul's, have a more upscale flavor. **Dinkytown** and the **West Bank** cater to student appetites.

Minneapolis

The New Riverside Café, 329 Cedar Ave. (333-4814), West Bank. You may find yourself inexplicably drawn to this place; it's the "Biomagnetic Center of the Universe." Take bus #73. Full vegetarian meals served cafeteria-style amidst unframed works by local artists. Nightly live jazz and bluegrass. Sandwiches and Mexican dishes $2-6. Open Mon.-Thurs. 7am-11pm, Fri. 7am-midnight, Sat. 8am-midnight, Sun. 9am-1:30pm. Performances Tues.-Thurs. at 7pm, Fri.-Sat. at 9pm. No cover.

Matin, 2411 Hennepin Ave. (377-2279). Elegant Vietnamese food with French flair. Entrées $3.50-6. Try the *xao cu nang* (tofu or mushrooms sautéed in garlic sauce with rice; $4.75). Open Mon.-Sat. 11:30am-11pm, Sun. 4:30-10:30pm.

Lowry's, 1934 Hennepin Ave. S. (871-0806). Elegant pasta pizza, risotto and polenta ($7-12). Open Mon.-Thurs. 11am-10pm, Fri. 11am-midnight, Sat. 5pm-midnight, Sun. 5-10pm.

It's Greek to Me, 626 Lake St. at Lyndale Ave. (825-9922). Take bus #4 south. Great Greek food that anybody can understand. Gyros $3.50. Dinners $7-12. Open daily 11am-11pm.

Annie's Parlor, 313 14th Ave. S.E. (379-0744) in Dinkytown, 406 Cedar Ave., West Bank (339-6207), and 2916 Hennepin Ave. (825-4455), Uptown. Malts that are a meal in themselves ($3.25) and great hamburgers ($3.25-5). Open Mon.-Thurs. 11am-11pm, Fri.-Sat. 11am-midnight, Sun. noon-11pm.

The Malt Shop, 50th St. at Bryant Ave. in South Minneapolis (824-1352; take bus #4), or Snelling at I-94, St. Paul (take bus #1 or 94). An old-time soda fountain; try a phenomenal phresh phruit malt or shake ($3). Minneapolis shop open Sun.-Thurs. 11am-10:30pm, Fri.-Sat. 11am-11pm, breakfast Sat.-Sun. 8:30-11am. St. Paul shop open Sun.-Thurs. 7:30am-10:30pm, Fri.-Sat. 7:30am-11pm.

The Loring Café, 1624 Harmon Pl. (332-1617), next to Loring Park. Extraordinary pasta and pizza ($8-11) and desserts ($3-5). A great place for dinner, or just for drinks or coffee. A good bar, too, with live music and no cover. Open Sun.-Thurs. 11am-11pm, Fri.-Sat. 11am-2am.

The Black Forest, at 26th and Nicollet (872-0812). Large portions of heavy German food in ersatz German atmosphere. Open Mon.-Sat. 11am-1am, Sun. noon-midnight.

St. Paul

Café Latté, 850 Grand Ave. (224-5687), across the street from Victoria Crossing. Cafeteria-style but elegant, with bi-level seating. Delicious soups, salads ($3.25-4.50), pastries, and espresso. Steaming milk drinks called Hot Moos ($1.65); try the Swedish Hot Moo with cinnamon, cardamon and maple syrup. Lines usually long. Open Mon.-Thurs. 10am-11pm, Fri. 10am-midnight, Sat. 9am-midnight, Sun. 9am-10pm.

Cosetta's, 211 W. 7th St. (222-3476), near downtown. Old-fashioned Italian market with amazing pizza (small $6), pasta ($5) and sandwiches ($3.50). Open Mon-Sat. 11am-10pm, Sun. 11am-8pm.

Cecil's, 651 Cleveland Ave. S. (698-6276). Kosher deli near the College of St. Catherine. Generous sandwiches $5-6. Open 9am-8pm daily.

St. Paul Farmers Market, 5th St. at Wall Market (227-6856), downtown. Fresh produce and baked goods. Get there before 10am on Sat. for the best quality and widest selection. Call to verify location and hours. Open Sat. 6am-1pm and May-Oct. Sun. 8am-1pm.

Mickey's Dining Car, 36 W. 7th St. (222-5633), kitty-corner to the Greyhound station. Small, cheap, and convenient; a great spot for wee-hour munchies runs. Steak and eggs from $4, lunch and dinner from $3. Open 24 hrs.

Sights

Minneapolis

Situated in the middle of the land of 10,000 lakes, Minneapolis boasts a few of its own. Ringed by stately mansions, **Lake of Isles,** off Franklin Ave., about 1½ mi. from downtown, is an excellent place to meet the local population of Canada geese. Bikers, skaters and joggers constantly round **Lake Calhoun,** on the west end of Lake St. south of Lake of Isles, making it a hectic social and recreational hotspot. Rent skates and roller blades at **Rolling Soles,** 1700 W. Lake St. (823-5711; skates $3 per hr., $7.50 per day; blades $5 per hr., $10 per day; open Mon.-Fri. 10am-9pm, Sat.-Sun. 9am-9pm). The **Minneapolis Park and Recreation Board** (348-2226) rents canoes ($4.50 per hr.) at the northeast corner of Lake Calhoun. Situated in a more residential neighborhood, **Lake Harriet** has a tiny paddleboat, a stage with occasional free concerts, and an endless marathon of joggers. The city provides 28 mi. of trails along these lakes for cycling, roller skating, roller blading, jogging or strolling on a sunny afternoon. The circumference of each lake is about three mi. and the paths are well maintained; take bus #28 to all three lakes.

One of the top modern art museums in the country, the **Walker Art Center,** 725 Vineland Place (375-7622), a few blocks from downtown, draws thousands with daring exhibits and an impressive permanent collection, including works by Lichtenstein and Warhol. (Open Tues.-Sat. 10am-8pm, Sun. 11am-5pm. $3, seniors free, ages 12-18 and students with ID $2. Free on Thurs.) Inside is an excellent, not-too-expensive café (sandwiches $1.50-2.50; open Tues.-Sun. 11:30am-3pm), and adjacent is the Guthrie Theater (see Entertainment). Next to the Walker, the **Minneapolis Sculpture Garden** displays dozens of sculptures and a fountain in a "room" of exquisitely landscaped trees and flowers. The **Minneapolis Institute of Arts,** 2400 3rd Ave. S. (870-3131), contains Egyptian, Chinese, American and European art. Take bus #9. (Open Tues.-

Sat. 10am-5pm, Thurs. 10am-9pm, Sun. noon-5pm. Free. Special exhibits $3, students, ages 12-18 and seniors $2; free to all Thurs. 5-9pm.)

St. Anthony Falls and Upper Locks, downtown at one Portland Ave. (333-5336), has a free observation deck that overlooks the Mississippi River. (Open April-Nov. daily 8am-10pm.) Several miles downstream, Minnehaha Park provides a breathtaking view of **Minnehaha Falls,** immortalized in Longfellow's longwinded *Song of Hiawatha.* (Take bus #7 from Hennepin Ave. downtown.)

St. Paul

The capital city of Minnesota boasts some unique architectural sites. west of downtown, Summit Avenue stretches from the Mississippi to the capitol building, displaying the nation's longest continuous stretch of Victorian homes, including the Governor's Mansion and the former homes of American novelist F. Scott Fitzgerald and railroad magnate James J. Hill. Most of these "Grand Old Ladies of Summit Avenue" were built in the 19th century with railroad money. Overlooking the capitol on Summit stands **St. Paul's Cathedral,** 239 Selby Ave. (228-1766), a scaled-down version of St. Peter's in Rome. (Open daily 7:30am-6pm.) Battle school fieldtrips to see the golden horses atop the ornate **state capitol,** at Cedar and Aurora St. (296-3962 or 297-1503; open Mon.-Fri. 9am-5pm, Sat. 10am-4pm, Sun. 1-4pm. Tours on the hour Mon.-Fri. 9am-4pm, Sat. 10am-3pm, Sun 1-3pm.) The nearby **Minnesota Historical Society,** an organization older than the state itself, has just moved to an impressive new building on Kellogg Blvd., where it intends to construct exhibits on (what else?) Minnesota history. The society also recreates life in the fur trapping era at **Fort Snelling,** Rte. 5 and 55 (726-9430). At the site of the original French settlement, this park teems with costumed rôle playing artisans and guides. Housing the **Minnesota Museum of Art** is the historic **Landmark Center,** 75 W. 5th St. (292-3225), a grandly restored 1894 Federal Court building replete with towers and turrets, a collection of pianos, art exhibits, a concert hall and four restored courtrooms. (Open Mon.-Wed. and Fri. 8am-5pm, Thurs. 8am-8pm, Sat. 10am-5pm, Sun. 1-5pm. Free. Tours given Thurs. 11am and Sun. 2pm.) The Minnesota Museum of Art houses other collections in the **Jemne Building** at St. Peter and Kellogg Blvd.

A giant iguana sculpture basks outside the **Science Museum,** 30 E. 10th St. (221-9454), near the intersection of Exchange and Wabasha St. Aside from the mammoth reptile, the museum houses an array of informative exhibits, including an extensive anthropology section. The **McKnight-3M Omnitheater** (221-9400) inside presents a mind-swelling array of gigantic films. (Museum open Mon.-Fri. 9:30am-9pm, Sat. 9am-9pm, Sun. 10am-9pm. Exhibit-only tickets $4.50, seniors and under 13 $3.50; with theater $6.50, seniors and kids $5.50.)

Metro Connections give tours of Minneapolis and St. Paul (333-8687; $15, seniors $13, kids 6-14 $8). Mississippi River paddle boat tours are also available (227-1100; $7.50, seniors $6.50, kids $5).

Entertainment and Events

With more theaters per capita than any U.S. city outside of New York, the Twin Cities' theater scene can't be touched. The brightest star in this constellation is the **Guthrie Theater,** 725 Vineland Place (377-2224), just off Hennepin Ave. in Minneapolis, adjacent to the Walker Art Center. The Guthrie repertory company performs here from June to March. (Box office open Mon.-Sat. 9am-8pm, Sun. 11am-7pm. Tickets $9-38, rush tickets 10 min. before the show $6.)

The **Children's Theater Company,** 3rd Ave. at 24th S. (874-0400), adjacent to the Minneapolis Institute of Art, puts on classics and innovative productions for all ages from September to June. (Box office open Mon.-Sat. 9am-5pm, Sun. noon-4pm except during summer. Tickets $12-20, seniors, students, and kids $9-16. Student rush tickets 15 min. before performance $6.)

In the summer from early July to early August, **Orchestra Hall,** 1111 Nicollet Mall (371-5656), in downtown Minneapolis, hosts the creatively named **Summerfest,** a month-long celebration of Viennese music performed by the **Minnesota Orchestra.**

(Box office open Mon.-Sat. 10am-6pm. Tickets $10-42. Student rush tickets 15 min. before show $4.50.) Don't miss the free coffee concerts and nighttime dance lessons at nearby **Peavey Plaza,** in Nicollet Mall between 11th and 12th St., surrounding a spectacular fountain (no wading allowed).

St. Paul's glass-and-brick, accordion-fronted **Ordway Music Theater,** 345 Washington St. (224-4222), is one of the most beautiful public spaces for music in the country. The **St. Paul Chamber Orchestra,** the **Schubert Club** and the **Minnesota Opera Company** perform here. (Box office open Mon.-Sat. 10am-9pm. Tickets $10-50.) Also notable is the **Theatre de la jeune lune,** (Theater of the young moon), which performs (in English) at the **Loring Playhouse,** 1645 Hennepin Ave. (333-6200; tickets $8-17), and the **Penumbra Theatre Company,** 270 N. Kent St., St. Paul (224-3180), Minnesota's only professional African-American theater company, which performed many of former St. Paul resident August Wilson's early plays.

All of the Twin Cities' many parks feature summertime evening concerts. For information on dates and locations, check at one of the visitors centers. The **Harriet Bandshell** hatches rock, blues, jazz and high school bands and choirs throughout the summer (Take bus #28). Also popular are **Loring Park's** Monday evening events, featuring free local bands, followed by vintage films, on the hill toward the north edge. Take bus #1, 4, 6 or 28 going south.

A giggle of comedy and improvisational clubs make the Twin Cities a downright hilarious place to visit. Dudley Riggs's **Brave New Workshop,** 2605 Hennepin Ave. (332-6620), stages consistently good musical comedy shows in an intimate club. (Box office open Tues.-Sat. 4-10pm. Performances Tues.-Sat. at 8pm. Tickets $12-15.) The **Comedy Gallery** (1219 Main St., S.E., Mpls., and Galtier Plaza, 175 E. 5th St., St. Paul; 331-JOKE (331-5653); tickets $10-12) features individual comedians. For great live music, try the **Uptown Bar and Café,** 3018 Hennepin (823-4719). (Open 8am-1am. Shows at 10:30pm. Weekend cover varies. For band information, call 823-5704.) The **400 Bar,** 4th St. at Cedar Ave. (332-2903), on the West Bank, is a great place, featuring live music nightly on a minuscule stage. (Open daily noon-1am. Occasional $2 cover.) Prince still appears occasionally at his old haunt, **First Avenue and 7th St. Entry** (701 N. First Ave., Mpls.; 338-8388), (Open Mon.-Sat. 8pm-1am. Cover $1-5, for concerts $6-18.) and at **Glam Slam,** 110 N. 5th St., Mpls. (338-3383; open Tues.-Sat. 8pm-1am).

There are several gay and lesbian bars in the Twin Cities, including **The Gay '90s,** Hennepin Ave. at 4th St. (333-7755; open daily 8pm-1am.) Look for *Equal Time* or *Gaze,* free on newspaper stands, for more information on gay and lesbian activities, or call the gay and lesbian information line (see Practical Information).

For general information on the local music scene and other events, pick up the free *City Pages* or *Twin Cities Reader,* or buy *Minneapolis-St. Paul* magazine ($2.50) available throughout the Cities.

In January, the 10-day **St. Paul Winter Carnival,** near the state capitol, cures cabin fever with ice sculptures, ice fishing, parades and skating contests. On the Fourth of July, St. Paul celebrates **Taste of Minnesota** on the Capitol Mall. Following this, the nine-day **Minneapolis Aquatennial** begins, with concerts, parades, art exhibits and kids dripping sno-cones on their shirts. (Call The Connection, 922-9000, for information on all these events.) During late August and early September, spend a day at the **Minnesota State Fair,** one of the largest in the nation, at Snelling and Como. The **Minnesota Zoo** (Rte. 32; 432-9000) houses a wide variety of well-maintained habitats accessible by path or monorail. (Open Mon.-Sat. 10am-6pm, Sun. 10am-8pm; off-season daily 10am-4pm. $6, seniors $4, ages 3-12 $2.50.)

The "Homerdome," also known as the **Hubert H. Humphrey Metrodome,** 501 Chicago Ave. S. (332-0386), in downtown Minneapolis, houses the Twin Cities' baseball and football teams. Professional basketball is played at the **Target Center;** catch the hockey action at the **Met Center** in Bloomington.

Northern Minnesota

Chippewa National Forest Area

The Norway pine forests, interspersed with lovely strands of birch, thicken as you move north into **Chippewa National Forest,** font of the Mississippi River. Camping and canoeing are popular activities, thanks to the hundreds of lakes in the area. Leech, Cass and Winnibigoshish (win-nuh-buh-GAH-shish or simply "Winnie") are the largest, but also the most crowded with speedboats. The national forest shares territory with the **Leech Lake Indian Reservation,** home of 4560 members of the Minnesota Chippewa tribe, the fourth largest tribe in the U.S. The Chippewa migrated from the Atlantic coast, through the Great Lakes, and into this area in the early 1700s, successfully pushing out the local Sioux. In the mid-1800s, the government seized most of the Chippewa's land, setting up reservations like Leech Lake.

Use the town of **Walker** on Leech Lake as a gateway to the Chippewa National Forest. Travelers, especially walkers, can find information on the tourist facilities at the **Leech Lake Area Chamber of Commerce** on Rte. 371 downtown (547-1313 or 800-833-1118; open Mon.-Fri. 8am-5:30pm, Sat. 8:30am-4:30pm, Sun. 10:30am-4:30pm). Material on abundant, cheap outdoor activities is available just east of the Chamber of Commerce at the **forest office** (547-1044; open Mon.-Fri. 7:30am-5pm). **Greyhound** (722-5591), runs from Minneapolis to Walker (5½ hr., $21), stopping at the Lake View Laundromat, just east of the chamber of commerce. The **Deep Portage Conservation Reserve** (682-2325), 10 mi. south of Walker (take Rte. 371, turn left on Woman Lake Rd., turn right at Deep Portage Rd., follow the dirt road), runs a series of naturalist workshops such as bird hikes, morel (an edible mushroom) hunts and discussions of water conservation ($3, Sat. 1:30pm).

The]**Headwaters of the Mississippi** trickle out of **Lake Itasca,** 30 mi. west of Walker on Rte. 200, the only place where mere mortals can wade easily across the Mississippi. The comfortable **Mississippi Headwaters HI/AYH-Hostel** (266-3415), located in a newly-renovated log building, has 33 beds with some four-bed rooms for families. It's open in the winter to facilitate access to the park's excellent cross-country skiing. ($10, nomembers $13, kids $7.) The park itself also has **campgrounds** with showers. (Sites $10, with electricity $12.50. 2-day vehicle permit $4.) The **Itasca State Park Office** (266-3654), through the north entrance and down County Rd. 38, has more information. (Open daily 8am-10pm.)

For those who eventually come to crave the Great *Indoors*, there are alternatives to camping. The **Anchor Inn** (798-2718) bed, boat and breakfast in Spring Lake has B&B-style rooms in the upstairs of a fishing lodge. (Singles $25, $30 for 2 people in one bed, two beds $40; $15 extra with use of motorboat.) The **Dickson Viking Huss** (732-8089) in Park Rapids, south of Itasca, offers rooms for $22 to $43 in a well-kept modern house; the **Dorset Schoolhouse** (732-1377) in nearby Dorset offers elegance and perhaps education; all notices are on small blackboards. (Summer Sun.-Thurs. singles $35, doubles $50, Fri.-Sat. singles $40, doubles $60; fall singles $35, doubles $50; winter-spring singles $30, doubles $40.) In Bemidji, you can stay at **Taber's Log Cabin Court** 2404 Bemidji Ave. (751-5781), a collection of 18 miniature cabins with kitchenettes near the shore of Lake Bemidji ($35-75; open May-Oct.). The motels across from the Greyhound station (see below) are fairly reasonable; try the **Lakeside Motel** 809 Paul Bunyan Dr. N.E. (751-3266). (Singles $26, off-season $24; doubles $40.)

Bemidji, famous for its life-size statue of Paul Bunyan, lumbers northeast of the park. The town has a **Greyhound** station at 902½ Paul Bunyan Dr. (751-7600; open Mon.-Sat. 9am-5pm, Sun. noon-1:30pm; Duluth to Bemidji 3½ hr., $16), but there is no bus from the town to the park. **Bicycles** and **boats** are available from **Itasca Sports Rental** (266-3654) in the park (open early May-early Oct. 7am-9pm, single-speed bikes $2.50 per hr., $15 per day; canoes $3 first hr., $1.50 per hr. thereafter, $12 per day). The area code for northern Minnesota is 218.

The Iron Range

Inland from the North Shore lies the Minnesota **Iron Range,** home to ore boomtowns and hills carved in a man-made parody of the Southwest. Adjacent to the Superior National Forest and Boundary Waters Canoe Area, this region offers natural beauty as well as an interesting perspective on history and technology.

Ely serves as a launching pad both into the BWCAW and the Iron Range. The **International Wolf Center,** 1396 U.S. 169 (365-4695), has informative displays on these creatures. The only significant population of wolves left in the continental U.S. lives in Minnesota. (Open daily 9am-6pm; free.) **Kring's Kabins and Kampgrounds,** 60 West Lakeview Pl., in town (365-6637), has a loft full of bunks for $10 per night each, including linen and shower access.

The **Soudan Underground Mine** (753-2245) in Soudan west of Ely on U.S. 1, was retired in the middle of digging the 27th level, half a mile below the surface. Visitors take a 90-min. tour down the 11°-from-the-vertical mineshaft and are shown the principles and techniques of underground iron mining; unfortunately, the tour shies clear of the **Soudan Underground Research Site,** where an experiment to detect spontaneous conversion of nucleons to energy enjoys the protection of a half-mi.-thick rock roof. (Mine tours $4, ages 5-12 $2.50, plus state park sticker for vehicle. Tours Memorial Day-Labor Day every ½ hr., 9:30am-4pm.) **Chisholm,** farther southwest on U.S. 169, houses **Ironworld U.S.A.** (254-3321 or 800-372-6437), a mining theme park which also contains displays on the area's ethnicity. ($6.25, seniors $5.25, ages 7-17 $4; open Memorial Day-Labor Day daily 10am-7pm.) The **Chisholm KOA** (254-3635) kamps nearby. (Open May-early Oct. Tent sites $12; base rate $12.50, with water and electricity $14.50, with above and sewer $16.)

Hibbing, a few miles south of Chisholm, has made a park out of the open-pit **Hull Rust Mahoning Mine.** (Open mid-May-Sept daily 9am-7pm.) Native son Bob Dylan (né Zimmerman) won't allow the dusty **First Settlers Museum** in the basement of City Hall to show exhibits on him, but the attendants can tell stories about little Bobby Zimmerman and point out where he onced lived. Carfree travelers in particular may wish to pay tribute at the **Greyhound Bus Origin Center,** 23rd St. and 5th Ave. E (263-5814), which features model buses and more bus cartoons than you ever knew existed. Greyhound's puppyhood was spent here as a transport for miners in the Hibbing area. (Open mid-May-mid-Sept. Mon.-Sat. 9am-5pm. $1, ages 6-12 50¢.) **Grand Rapids,** a paper mill town of 7000, houses the **Forest History Center** (327-4482), with informative exhibits in the Interpretive Center and a recreated 1900 logging camp. ($3, ages 6-15 $1. Open mid-May-mid-Oct. daily 10am-5pm; interpretive center and trails also open mid-Oct.-mid-May daily noon-4pm.) Grand Rapids is the hometown of Judy Garland, and celebrates this with its own **Yellow Brick Road,** the world's largest collection of Garland memorabilia (in the **Central School,** 10 5th St. N.W., 326-6431; Open Mon.-Fri. 9:30am-5pm, Sat. 9:30am-4pm, Sun. noon-4pm; $4, ages 6-12 $2), and a **Judy Garland Festival** every June (326-6431).

The **Itascan Motel,** 610 Pokegama Ave. S. (326-3489) has large new rooms with complimentary coffee. (Singles $32.) The **Prairie Lake Campground,** 400 Wabana Rd., 6½ mi. north of Grand Rapids on U.S. 38 (326-8486), has a nice, shady waterfront location. (Tent sites $8, RV with electricity $10, add $1 each for water and sewer.)

The **area code** for the Iron Range is 218.

The Superior North Shore

The North Shore begins with the majestic **Sawtooth Mountains** just north of Duluth and extends 150 wild and woody miles to Canada. This stretch, defined by **Highway 61 (North Shore Drive),** encompasses virtually all of Minnesota's Superior lakeshore and supports bear, moose and the only significant remaining wolf population in the contiguous 48 states. Summer brings a human tide to the area, as flocks of tourists drawn by the cool and breezy weather migrate north to fish, camp, hike and canoe. Bring warm clothes, since even summer temperatures can drop into the low 40s°F at night.

For the car-free or intrepid, the **North Shore Scenic Railroad** (722-1273) offers a scenic train ride ($16.50, kids 3-11 $8.25) from Duluth to **Two Harbors,** which hosts a **folk festival** (834-4898) the first weekend in July. Trains run less often to Lester River and Palmers along the same route. Another option for the carless is the **Superior Hiking Trail,** which is being constructed in loops off U.S. 61 from Duluth to Canada along the Superior coast. For more information write to the **Superior Trail Hiking Association,** P.O. Box 2175, Tofte 55615 (226-3539).

The North Shore teems with state parks, all beautiful, and most with camping facilities. **Gooseberry Falls** (834-3787) offers thundering cataracts and a popular swimming hole. **Split Rock Lighthouse** shines a little way north of the falls. The lighthouse is situated next to an anomalous magnetic location which once fooled compasses and lured ships into the rocky shore. Tour the lighthouse and visit the **History Center** (226-4372) to learn about the shipwrecks caused by the rocks' strange magnetic qualities. (Lighthouse and History Center open daily May 15-Oct. 15 9am-5pm; off-season History Center only, Fri.-Sun. noon-4pm. Admission $3 plus $4 state park sticker.) **Split Rock Lighthouse State Park** (226-3065) has cart-in campsites: borrow a wheelbarrow to move your gear the ½-mi. from the central parking lot. Site #15 even has a split rock of its own. All Minnesota state parks require a $4 daily sticker (or $18 annual permit). Camping is $10 where showers are available, $8 where they are not.

Grand Marais serves as the hub of North Shore activity. The 60-mi. **Gunflint Trail,** now widened into an auto road, begins in Grand Marais and continues northwest into the **Boundary Waters Canoe Area Wilderness (BWCAW).** This unique area includes over two million acres of forests and 1100 lakes. There are no roads, phones, electricity or private dwellings here, and no motorized vehicles are allowed. Permits are required to enter the BWCAW from May to September.

The **Tip of the Arrowhead Tourist Information Center,** Broadway and 1st Ave. (387-2524), has a quiver of information about the area. (Open summer Mon.-Sat. 8am-8pm, Sun. 10am-6pm. Call for winter hrs.) The **National Forest Ranger Station** at the base of the trail, ¼ mi. south of town, offers even more information, and issues BWCAW permits for individual ports of entry into the wilderness. (Open summer daily 6am-6pm.) **Wilderness Waters Outfitters,** just south of Grand Marais on Rte. 61 (387-2525), rents canoes. ($14 per day, $12 per day for more than 3-day trips; $10 deposit. Paddles, life jackets, and car rack included. Open May-Oct. daily 7am-7pm.)

The **South of the Border Café,** (387-1505)—not a Mexican restaurant, the *other* border—is cheap and popular with fishermen. Grand Marais' specialty, the bluefin herring sandwich, costs $2.75. (Open summer daily 4am-2pm, Sept.-mid-May 5am-2pm.) The **Angry Trout Café** (387-1265), right on the dock, serves up a mean fish and chips ($5.75).

Reward yourself at the end of the trail with a stay in the well-kept cabins at **"Spirit of the Land" Island HI/AYH Hostel** (388-2241), on an island in Seagull Lake. The hostel is run by Wilderness Canoe Base, which leads canoe trips and summer island camps for various groups. Call from Grand Marais to arrange a boat pick-up. ($10, nonmembers $13. $2 boat transport. Meals $4-6. Showers $2. Closed Nov. and April.) Though you wouldn't believe it from its elegance, the historic, brightly hand-painted **Naniboujou Lodge,** 15 mi. east of Grand Marais on U.S. 61 (387-2688), has some rooms with shared baths for $32 (double occupancy $39). The **Grand Marais Recreation Area** (387-1712), off Rte. 61 in town, is crowded but offers a great view of Lake Superior, and has a pool. (Office open daily 6am-10pm. Sites $12, with water and electricity $15.50, with full hookup $16.50. Open May-mid-Oct.)

Grand Portage, the furthest town north before the border, runs a ferry to **Isle Royale** (see Michigan). There is a campground adjacent to the marina. ($10; RV hookups $15. Parking at marina $3 per day, $3.50 with trailer.) While waiting for the boat visit the **Witch Tree,** an ancient, sacred cedar growing out of bare rock. (3 free tours per day; sign up at the **Grand Portage Lodge** near the marina.)

Happy Trails runs one bus up the shore per day, leaving the **Duluth Greyhound Station** (722-5591). (Duluth-Grand Marais $17.50.)

The **area code** for the North Shore is 218.

Ohio

Ohio is best known for rust-belt industrial cities like Cincinnati and Cleveland, thought to combine the pollution of the East Coast with the cultural blandness of the Midwest. In reality, these cities have cleaned themselves up, Midwestern blandness is a misrepresentation, and the majority of the state lies outside metropoli in gentle, quintessentially middle-American farmland. Here rolling green wooded hills, verdant river valleys, the Great Lake shore, and enchanting small towns entice you to re-evaluate the mythos of the Midwest.

Oh, and by the way—never, *ever* confuse Ohio with Iowa or Idaho, or the Tri-State Name Council will place you on their widely-distributed blacklist, and residents of all three otherwise friendly states will scorn and publicly humiliate you. Just a warning.

Practical Information

Capital: Columbus.

Tourist Information: State Office of Travel and Tourism, 77 S. High St., P.O. Box 1001, Columbus 43215 (614-466-8844). **Greater Columbus Convention and Visitors Bureau,** 1 Columbus Bldg., 10 W. Broad St. #1300, Columbus 43215 (614-221-6623 or 800-234-2657). Open Mon.-Fri. 8am-5pm.

Time Zone: Eastern.

Postal Abbreviation: OH

Sales Tax: 0%. That's right, nuthin. Go nuts.

Cincinnati

Longfellow called it the "Queen City of the West." In the 1850s, more prosaic folk tagged it "Porkopolis," alluding to its position as the planet's premier pork-packer (say *that* quickly five times!). Winged pigs guarding the entrance of downtown's Sawyer Point Park remind visitors of the divine swine of yore. Today, pigs on the wing no longer snort through the streets, and the frontier has moved on to parts west; the city instead parades an excellent collection of museums, a renowned zoo, a pleasantly designed waterfront, and a blossoming of parks. Hidden in a valley surrounded by seven rolling hills and the Ohio River, insulated Cincinnati seems to live up to Mark Twain's purported claim that, if the world suddenly stopped dead, it would take the city 20 years to notice.

Practical Information and Orientation

Emergency: 911.

Visitor Information: Cincinnati Convention and Visitors Bureau, 300 W. 6th St. (621-2142). Open Mon.-Fri. 8:45am-5pm. Pick up an *Official Visitors Guide.* **Information Booth** in Fountain Sq. Open Mon.-Sat. 8:30am-5:30pm. **Info Line,** 421-4636. Lists plays, opera, cruises and symphonies.

Airport: Greater Cincinnati International Airport, in Independence, KY, 13 mi. south of Cincinnati. The **Jetport Express** (606-283-3702) shuttles passengers downtown ($10).

Amtrak: (921-4172 or 800-872-7245). To Indianapolis ($29) and Chicago ($57). Open Mon.-Fri. 9:30am-5pm, Tues.-Sun. 11pm-6:30am. Avoid the neighborhood north of the station.

Greyhound: 1005 Gilbert Ave. (352-6000), just past the intersection of E. Court and Broadway. To: Indianapolis ($19); Louisville, KY ($15.50); Cleveland ($38). Open daily 7:30am-6:30am.

Public Transport: Queen City Metro, 122 W. Fifth St. (621-4455). Office has bus schedules and information. Telephone information Mon.-Fri. 6:30am-7pm, Sat.-Sun. 8am-5pm. Most buses run out of Government Sq. at 5th and Main St., to outlying communities. Peak fare 65¢, other times 50¢, weekends 35¢, extra 30¢ to get to suburbs.

Taxi: Yellow Cab, 241-2100. Base fare $1.50, $1.20 per mi.

Weather Line: 241-1010.

Help Lines: Rape Crisis Center, 216 E. 9th St. (381-5610), downtown. **Gay/Lesbian Community Switchboard:** 221-7800.

Post Office: 122 W. 5th St. (684-5664), between Walnut and Vine St. Open Mon.-Fri. 8am-5pm, Sat. 8am-1pm. **ZIP code:** 45202.

Area Code: 513; Kentucky suburbs 606.

Fountain Square, E. 5th at Vine St., is the focal point of the downtown business community. Cross streets are numbered and designated East or West, with Vine Street as the divider. **Riverfront Stadium,** the **Serpentine Wall** and the **Riverwalk** are down by the river. The **University of Cincinnati** spreads out from Clifton, north of the city. Overlooking downtown from the east, **Mt. Adams,** adjoining Eden Park, harbors Cincinnati's most active nightlife.

Accommodations and Camping

Cincinnati has many motels, but most cheap places and all the campgrounds are outside the heart of the city. Take a car and make reservations, especially on nights of Reds baseball games and on weekends.

Cincinnati Home Hostel (HI/AYH), 2200 Maplewood Ave. (651-2329), 1½ mi. north of downtown. Take bus #64 to Highland and Earnshaw; walking after dark is iffy, especially coming from the west. A 3-story house with large rooms. Singles $6.

College of Mount St. Joseph, 5701 Delhi Pike (244-4327), about 8 mi. west of downtown off U.S. 50. Take bus #32. Immaculate rooms in a quiet, remote location. Excellent facilities. Cafeteria lunch and dinner $3.50. Singles $15. Doubles $20.

Evendale Motel, 10165 Reading Rd. (563-1570). Take Reading bus (not RR) #43 north to Reading and Columbia, then walk ½ hr. north on Reading. Do not pass Go. Do not collect $200. Dark but clean and cute rooms. Singles and doubles $23.

Camp Shore Campgrounds, Rte. 56 in Aurora, IN (812-438-2135), 30 mi. west of Cincinnati on the Ohio. Tent sites with hookup $12.

Rose Gardens Resort—KOA Campgrounds, I-75 exit 166 (606-428-2000), 30 mi. south of Cincinnati. Award-winning landskaping. Tent sites $16. Cabins $25, including water and electricity. Make reservations.

Food

The city that gave us the first soap opera and the first baseball franchise (the Redlegs) presents as its great culinary contribution **Cincinnati chili.** It's an all-pervasive ritual in local culture, though somehow no other city but Louisville, KY seems to have caught this gastronomical wave. Meat sauce, spaghetti and cheese are the basic ingredients. Chili is cheap. Antacid tablets cost extra.

Camp Washington Chili (541-0061), Hopple and Colerain Ave., 1 block west of I-75 in a somewhat depressed neighborhood. A legendary joint, featured in a song by Lonnie Mack. Chili $2.25-3. Open Mon.-Sat. 24 hrs.

Izzy's, 819 Elm St. (721-4241), also 610 Main St. A Cincinnati institution founded in 1901. Overstuffed sandwiches with potato pancake $3-4.15. Izzy's famous reuben $5. Open Mon.-Fri. 7am-5pm, Sat. 7am-4pm; Main St. restaurant open Mon.-Sat. 7am-9pm.

Graeter's, 41 E. 4th St. (381-0653), downtown, and 10 other locations. Since 1870, Graeter's has dished out fresh ice cream with giant chocolate chips. (Not very) small cone $1.50, $1.60 with chips; larger size 50¢ extra. Open Mon.-Sat. 11am-5:30pm.

Findlay Market, 18th at Elm St., 1½ mi. north of downtown. Produce and picnic items $3-5. Open Wed. 7am-1:30pm, Fri.-Sat. 7am-6pm.

Sights and Events

Downtown Cincinnati orbits around the **Tyler Davidson Fountain,** the ideal spot to people-watch while feigning admiration for this florid 19th-century monstrosity. If you squint your eyes, you can almost see Les Nesman rushing to WKRP to deliver the daily hog report. Check out the expansive gardens and daring design at **Procter and Gamble Plaza,** just east of Fountain Square, or walk along **Fountain Square South,** a shopping and business complex connected by a series of second-floor skywalks. When the visual stimuli exhaust you, prick up your ears for a free concert in front of the fountain. The **Downtown Council,** Carew Tower (579-3191), has more information. (Open Mon.-Fri. 8:30am-5pm.)

Close to Fountain Square, the **Contemporary Arts Center,** 115 E. 5th St., 2nd floor (721-0390), by Walnut, has survived a nationally publicized attack by some Cincinnati citizens on its exhibition of sexually explicit photographs by Robert Mapplethorpe. Rebounding with an enhanced reputation among the national arts community, it continues to change its exhibits frequently, offering evening films, music, and multi-media performances. (Open Mon.-Sat. 10am-6pm, Sun. 1-5pm. Admission $2, seniors and students $1. Mon. free.) The **Taft Museum,** 316 Pike St. (241-0343), also downtown, has a beautiful collection of painted enamels, as well as pieces by Rembrandt and Whistler. (Open Mon.-Sat. 10am-5pm, Sun. 2-5pm. Suggested donation $2, seniors and students $1.)

Cincinnati's answer to Paradise is **Eden Park,** northeast of downtown. Among the park's bounteous fruits is the **Cincinnati Art Museum** (721-5204), with a permanent collection spanning 5000 years, including musical instruments and Middle Eastern artifacts. (Take bus #49 to Eden Park Dr. By car, follow Gilbert Ave. northeast from downtown. Open Tues. and Thurs.-Sat. 10am-5pm, Wed. 10am-9pm, Sun. noon-5pm, closed Mon. $3, seniors $1.50, students $2, under 18 free. Sat. free.) The **Krohn Conservatory** (352-4086), one of the largest public greenhouses in the world, illustrates an indoor Eden. (Open daily 10am-5pm. July-Aug. open Wed. to 9pm. Suggested donation $1.50, seniors and ages under 15 $1.)

One mi. west of downtown, the **Union Terminal,** 1031 Western Ave. (241-7257), near the Ezzard Charles Dr. exit off I-75 (take bus #1), functions more as a museum than as a bus terminal. The building itself is a fine example of art deco architecture and boasts the world's largest permanent half-dome. Cool down in the Ice-Age world of simulated glaciers inside the **Museum of Natural History** (287-7021), or inter yourself in the carefully constructed artificial cavern, featuring a colony of real live bats. On the other side of the dome, stroll about a model of a pre-1860 Cincinnati street at the **Cincinnati Historical Society** (287-7031), or dazzle your senses in the **Omnimax Theater** (shows Mon.-Thurs. hourly 11am-4pm and 7-8pm, Fri. 11am-4pm and 7-9pm, Sat. 11am-5pm and 7-9pm, Sun. 11am-5pm and 7-8pm). (Museums open Mon.-Sat. 9am-5pm, Sun. 11am-6pm; admission to either museum $5, ages 3-12 $3; to both $8/$4; to Omnimax $6/$4; combo ticket $12/$7.)

The **Cincinnati Zoo,** 3400 Vine St. (281-4700), at Forest Ave., can be reached by car (take Dana Ave. off I-75 or I-71), or by bus (#78 or 49 from Vine and 5th St.). The diction wizards at *Newsweek* called it one of the world's "sexiest zoos"; the lush greenery and cageless habitats evidently encourage the zoo's gorillas and famous white Bengal tigers to reproduce enthusiastically. (Open in summer daily 9am-8pm, entrance closes at 6pm; Labor Day-Memorial Day open daily 9am-5pm. Children's Zoo open 10am-7pm. $6, seniors and ages under 12 $3.)

Cincinnati is fanatical about sports. The **Reds** major league baseball team (421-7337) and the **Bengals** NFL football team (621-3550) both play in **Riverfront Stadium.** The **Riverfront Coliseum** (241-1818), a Cincinnati landmark, hosts other sports events and major concerts year-round. In the beginning of July **Summerfair** (800-582-5804), an art extravaganza, is held at **Coney Island,** 6201 Kellogg Ave. (232-8230).

The city basks in its German heritage during **Oktoberfest-Zinzinnati,** held, as Oktoberfests are wont to be, in September (the 3rd weekend, to be precise). More diverse groups celebrate themselves during the **International Folk Festival** two months later. Labor Day's **Riverfest** and mid-October's **Tall Stacks** memorialize the roles of the river and steamboats in Cincinnati's history. For more info on festivals, contact the Convention and Visitors Bureau (see Practical Information).

Entertainment and Nightlife

The cliff-hanging communities that line the steep streets of Mt. Adams also support a vivacious arts and entertainment industry. Perched on its own wooded hill is the **Playhouse in the Park,** 962 Mt. Adams Circle (421-3888), a theater-in-the-round remarkably adaptable to many styles of drama. The regular season runs from mid-September to July, with special summer programs as well. Performances run daily Tuesday through Sunday. (Tickets $15-27.50, 15 min. before the show student and senior rush tickets $9. Accessible to the vision- and hearing-impaired.)

For a drink and a voyage back to the 19th century, try **Arnold's,** 210 E. 8th St. (421-6234), Cincinnati's oldest tavern, between Main St. and Sycamore downtown. After 9pm, Arnold's does that ragtime, traditional jazz, and swing thing while serving sandwiches ($4-5) and dinners ($6-10). (Open Mon.-Sat. 11am-1am.) Check out the antique toys inside or listen to jazz and blues in the courtyard at **Blind Lemon,** 936 Hatch St. (241-3885), at St. Gregory St. in Mt. Adams. (Open Mon.-Fri. 4pm-2:30am, Sat.-Sun. 3pm-2:30am. Music at 9:30pm.) The **City View Tavern,** also in Mt. Adams at 403 Oregon St. (241-8439), off Monastery St., is hard to find but worth the effort. This down-to-earth local favorite proudly displays an article heralding it as one of the best dives in Cincinnati. The deck in back offers a great view of the city's skyline and the Ohio River. Locally brewed draft beer is 90¢. (Open Mon.-Fri. noon-1am, Sat. 1pm-1am, Sun. 2-11pm.)

The University of Cincinnati's **Conservatory of Music** (556-9430) often gives free classical recitals. A tad more upscale, the **Music Hall,** 1243 Elm St. by Ezzard Charles Drive (721-8222), hosts the **Cincinnati Symphony Orchestra** (381-3300) from September to May (tickets $7-45). Other companies performing at the Music Hall are the **Cincinnati Ballet Company** (621-5219; performances Sept.-May; tickets $6-45) and **Cincinnati Opera** (241-2742; limited summer productions). For updates, call **Dial the Arts** (751-2787).

Near Cincinnati

If you can't get to California's Napa or Sonoma Valleys, the next best thing may be **Meiers Wine Cellars,** 6955 Plainfield Pike (891-2900). Take I-71 to exit 12 or I-75 to Galbraith Rd. Free tours of Ohio's oldest and largest winery allow you to observe the entire wine-making operation and taste the fermented fruits of their labor. (Free tours June-Oct. every hr. 10am-3pm; other times of the year by appointment.)

In the town of **Mason,** 24 mi. north of Cincinnati off I-71 at exit #24, the **Kings Island** amusement park (241-5600) cages **The Beast,** the world's second-fastest roller coaster. Admission entitles you to unlimited rides, attractions, and the opportunity to buy expensive food. Lines shrink after dark. (Open May 27-Sept. 2 Sun.-Fri. 10am-10pm, Sat. 10am-11pm. $23, seniors and ages 3-6 $11.50.) Get your hands on (or in) less expensive kids' entertainment at **The Village Puppet Theatre,** 606 Main St., in Covington, just across the river in Kentucky (606-291-5566). (Shows Tues.-Sun., $5, under 12 $4.) Covington is also home to **Mainstrasse Village,** 616 Main St. (606-491-0458),an ersatz German village replete with boutiques and Germania galore.

Cleveland

Abandoned railroad bridges, steel factories, and warehouses lining the Cuyahoga River attest to the fact that Cleveland has always been a tough industrial city, living and dying by the fortunes of Gilded Age magnates like Rockefeller and Hanna. In the 1970s Cleveland became the first major city to default on its loans since the Great Depression and turned into a national joke after the filthy Cuyahoga River caught fire downtown. Now Cleveland is experiencing a major rebirth. Planners have spent billions on downtown construction, waterfront development, and historic renovation; the city's thriving arts community and I.M. Pei's much-anticipated Rock and Roll Hall of Fame have also put it in a different national spotlight. Now only the perennially lackluster Cleveland Indians baseball team (as of August 4, 1992, 15½ games out of first place) can legitimately be called the "Mistake on the Lake."

Practical Information and Orientation

Emergency: 911.

Visitor Information: Cleveland Convention and Visitors Bureau, 3100 Tower City Ctr. (621-4110 or 800-321-1001), in Terminal Tower at Public Square. Free maps and helpful staff. Open Mon.-Fri. 8:30am-5pm.

Cleveland Hopkins International Airport: (265-6030) in Brookpark, 10 mi. west of downtown, but accessible on the RTA airport rapid line, which goes to the Terminal Tower on train #66X ("Red Line") for $1.25.

Amtrak: 200 Cleveland Memorial Shoreway N.E. (696-5115 or 800-872-7245), across from Municipal Stadium, east of City Hall. To New York ($94) and Chicago ($73). Open Mon.-Sat. 10:30am-4:30pm.

Greyhound: 1465 Chester Ave. (781-0520; schedules and fares 781-1400), at E. 14th St. near RTA bus lines and about 7 blocks east of Terminal Tower. To: Chicago ($39), New York City ($92), Pittsburgh ($21) and Cincinnati ($41).

Regional Transit Authority (RTA): 315 Euclid Ave. (566-5074), across the street from Woolworth's. Schedules for city buses and rapid transit lines. Bus lines, connecting with the Rapid stops, provide public transport to most of the metropolitan area. 24-hr. **rideline** (623-0180), accessible from touch-tone phones. Train fare $1.25, bus $1 ("local" service, free transfers—remember to ask), $1.25 express. Office open Mon.-Fri. 7:30am-5:30pm. Phone info Mon.-Sat. 6am-6pm (621-9500). Service daily 4:30am-12:30am.

Taxi: Yellow Cab, 623-1500; 24 hrs. **Americab,** 881-1111.

Help Line: Rape Crisis Line, 391-3912. 24 hrs.

Post Office: 2400 Orange Ave. (443-4199 or 443-4096). Open Mon.-Fri. 8am-7pm. **ZIP code:** 44101.

Area Code: 216.

Terminal Tower in **Public Square** cleaves the city's land into east and west. North-south streets are numbered and given an east-west prefix, e.g.: E. 18th St. is 18 blocks east of the Terminal Tower. To reach Public Square from I-90 or I-71, follow the Ontario Ave./Broadway exit. From I-77, take the 9th St. exit to Euclid Ave., which runs into the Square. From the Amtrak station, follow Lakeside Ave. and turn onto Ontario, which leads to the tower. Almost all of the RTA trains and buses run downtown.

Accommodations and Camping

For cheap lodgings, travelers are better off staying in the suburbs. Hotel taxes are a hefty 10%, not included in the prices listed below. If you know your plans well in advance, try calling **Cleveland Private Lodgings** (249-0400), which places people in homes around the city for as little as $25. All arrangements must be made through the office. Leave two to three weeks for a letter of confirmation. (Open Mon.-Tues. and Thurs.-Fri. 9am-noon and 3-5pm.) **North Point Inn,** 1500 Superior Ave. at E. 17th St. (861-5660), rents about the cheapest room downtown (singles $43, doubles $47).

Stanford House Hostel (HI/AYH), 6093 Stanford Rd. (467-8711), 22 mi. south of Cleveland in Peninsula. Exit 12 off I-80. Take bus #77F to Ridgefield Holiday Inn (the last stop) and call the hostel for a ride. Beautifully restored Greek Revival farmhouse in the Cuyahoga Valley National Recreation Area is on National Register of Historic Places. Excellent facilities; friendly houseparent. All hostelers required to perform task (vacuuming, emptying trash, etc.). Check-in 5-9pm. Flexible curfew 11pm. $10, sheets and pillow $2, sleep sack $1. Reservations only.

Lakewood Manor Motel, 12019 Lake Ave. (226-4800), about 3 mi. west of downtown in Lakewood. Take bus #55CX. Neat and clean. TV, central A/C. Complimentary coffee daily and donuts on weekends. Singles $27. Doubles $32.

Gateway Motel, 29865 Euclid Ave. (943-6777), 10 mi. east of Public Sq. in Wickliffe. Take Euclid Ave. exit off I-90 or bus #28X. Spacious, clean rooms with A/C and color TV. Singles $25. Doubles $30.

Two **campgrounds** are 40 minutes east of downtown, off I-480 in Streetsboro: **Woodside Lake Park,** 2256 Frost Rd. (626-4251; tent sites for 2 $15, with electricity $16; $2 per additional guest, ages 3-17 75¢); and **Valley View Lake Resort,** 8326 Ferguson (626-2041; tent sites $19, water and hookup available).

Food

You'll find Cleveland's culinary treats in tiny neighborhoods surrounding the downtown area. To satiate that lust for hot corned beef, step into one of the bakers' dozens of delis in the city center. Over 100 vendors sell produce, meat, cheese and other groceries at the indoor-outdoor **West Side Market** at W. 25th St. and Lorain Ave. (Open Mon. and Wed. 7am-4pm, Fri.-Sat. 7am-6pm.) For an extensive listing of restaurants, turn to the monthly magazine *Live* ($2).

Tommy's, 1820 Coventry Rd. (321-7757), just up the hill from University Circle. Take bus #9X east to Mayfield and Coventry Rd. Delicious, healthful pita bread sandwiches ($2.50-5.25) and friendly service. Try the Brownie Monster for dessert. Open Mon.-Sat. 7:30am-10pm, Sun. 9am-5pm.

Mama Santa's, 12305 Mayfield Rd. (231-9567), in Little Italy just east of University Circle. Authentic Sicilian food served beneath subdued lighting. Medium pizza $3.25, spaghetti $4.25. Open Mon.-Thurs. 11am-midnight, Fri.-Sat. 11am-1am. There are many other Italian cafés and restaurants nearby on Mayfield St.

Otto Moser's, 2044 E. 4th St. (771-3831), A bar and deli a few steps south of Euclid Ave. Décor right out of *The Untouchables*; the classic Cleveland deli experience. Corned beef $3.50.

Sights and Entertainment

Downtown Cleveland has escaped the blight which has struck other Great Lakes manufacturing cities such as Detroit. Fortune 500 companies are moving *into* town rather than out, and construction proceeds at a furious pace—$5 billion worth of construction projects are currently underway. 1990 witnessed the opening of the long-awaited **Tower City Center** (771-6611), a three-story shopping complex in the Terminal Tower. Although essentially a luxury mall with prices to match, Tower Center is a notable emblem of the tremendous renovation and revitalization of downtown Cleveland.

Seriously, folks, one of the most beautiful things about Cleveland is Lake Erie. **Cleveland Lakefront State Park** (881-8141), two mi. west of downtown and accessible from Lake Ave. or Cleveland Memorial Shoreway, is a mile-long beach with great swimming and picnicking areas. To understand why the city was built here in the first place, you must see the river, and the best way to do this is by boat. Cast off with the **Goodtime Cruise Lines,** at the E. 9th St. Pier, for a two-hr. cruise, a *two-hour cruise* ($8.50).

Playhouse Square Center, 1501 Euclid Ave. (771-4444), a 10-minute walk east of Terminal Tower, is the third-largest performing arts center in the nation. The **Cleveland Opera** (575-0900) and the famous **Cleveland Ballet** (621-2260) perform from September to May nearby at 1375 Euclid Ave. Four mi. east of the city resides **University Circle,** a cluster of 75 cultural institutions. Check with the helpful visitors bureau (see Practical Information above) for details on museums, live music, and drama. The world-class **Cleveland Museum of Art,** 11150 East Blvd. (421-7340), in University Circle, contains a fine collection of 19th-century French and American Impressionist paintings, as well as a version of Rodin's ubiquitous "The Thinker." A beautiful plaza and pensive pond face the museum. (Open Tues. and Thurs.-Fri. 10am-5:45pm, Wed. 10am-9:45pm, Sat. 9am-4:45pm, Sun. 1-5:45pm. Free.) Nearby is the **Cleveland Museum of Natural History,** Wade Oval (231-4600), where you can see the only existing skull of the fearsome Pygmy Tyrant *(Nanatyrannus)*. (Open Mon.-Sat. 10am-5pm, Sun. 1-5pm. $4.25, seniors, students and children $2.25. Free after 3pm Tues. and

Thurs.) The renowned **Cleveland Orchestra,** one of the nation's best, blows, plucks and bows in University Circle at Severance Hall, 11001 Euclid Ave. (231-7300; tix $10-23). During the summer, the orchestra performs at **Blossom Music Center,** 1145 W. Steels Corners Rd., Cuyahoga Falls (920-8040), about 45 minutes south of the city (lawn seating $10). University Circle itself is safe, but some of the nearby neighborhoods can be rough, especially at night. East of University Circle, in a nice neighborhood, is the **Dobama Theatre,** 1846 Coventry Rd., Cleveland Hts. (932-6838). This little-known theater gives terrific, inexpensive ($6-9) performances in an intimate, living-room atmosphere. Peruse the monthly *Live* or the daily *Plain Dealer* for entertainment listings.

A great deal of Cleveland's nightlife is focused in the **Flats,** the former industrial core of the city along both banks of the Cuyahoga River. The northernmost section of the Flats, just west of Public Square, contains several nightclubs and restaurants. On weekend nights, expect large crowds and larger traffic jams. On the east side of the river, from the deck at **Rumrunners,** 1124 Old River Rd. (696-6070), you can watch the sunset across the water through the steel frames of old railroad bridges. Live bands play (Thurs.-Sun.), and draft beer is $1.75. (Open daily 4pm-2am. $3 cover.) **Peabody's Down Under,** 1059 Old River Rd. (241-0792 or 241-2451), draws crowds not for the view but for the variety of local and nationally famous rock bands that play most nights. (Open daily 8pm-2:30am, and sometimes later. Cover $4 to $18 depending on the band.) On the west side of the river are several other clubs, including **Shooters,** 1148 Main Ave. (861-6900), a beautiful bar/restaurant with a great view of the river and Lake Erie. Prices are fairly high (dinners $7-10), but you can capture the flavor of Cleveland nightlife inexpensively by taking your drink to the in-deck pool. (Open Mon.-Sat. 11:30am-1:30am, Sun. 11am-1:30am.)

Within an hour's drive of Cleveland lie the Amish communities of bucolic **Holmes County.** Outsiders can visit the **Amish Farm** (893-2951) in **Berlin,** which offers a film presentation, demonstrations of non-electrical appliances, and a tour of the grounds. (Open April 1-Nov. 1 Mon.-Sat. 10am-6pm. Tours $2.25, children $1. Buggy ride $2.75.) Unserved by public transportation, Berlin lies 70 mi. south of Cleveland on Rte. 39, 17 pastoral mi. west of I-77.

Lake Erie Islands

No man is an island. Conversely, no island is a man. Interestingly enough, one of the Lake Erie Islands (Cawtawba Island) is neither an island *nor* a man—it's really a peninsula separated by 100 yards of marshland. As we go to press, the rest of the Lake Erie Islands are indeed islands and can be visited by men, women, children, and even the occasional farm animal. There are four major American islands and one Canadian island in the Lake Erie Islands region. North Bass Island and Middle Bass Island are closed to the public, except for a winery on Middle Bass. South Bass Island and Kelly's Island are both emphatically open to the public and share a relaxed atmosphere; cars are allowed but scarce, and the best way to get around is by bicycle. Both islands have a tram running between the dock, the sights and the campground ($1). Both islands also have some organized tourism activities, but the most enjoyable activity is just a leisurely bike ride around the islands' perimeter (both islands are about 3 mi. in diameter).

South Bass Island

Two mi. northeast of the South Bass ferry docks the small town of **Put-in Bay**. Here's where you'll find the island's biggest attraction: the bars. The **Round House** (285-4595) in—you guessed it—a round house, attracts sippers and guzzlers with glasses and buckets of beer ($2.25 and $22.50, respectively). The bucket holds 13 glasses and is thus more economical, provided you don't spill any—plus you get to keep the nifty plastic bucket. Just a few steps down Lorain Ave., the **Beer Barrel Saloon** (285-BEER) can probably find you elbow room at its bar, the longest in the world at 405 ft. 10 in. (Glasses $2.50.) Music at both bars starts daily around 2pm, and both are open noon to 1am. Find fun for under-21sters at **Kimberly's Carousel** downtown, one of just 100 carousels with wooden horses left in America (75¢). On the eastern edge of Put-in Bay, **Perry's Victory and International Peace Memorial**, honoring both Commodore Oliver Hazard Perry's 1813 victory over the British in the Battle of Lake Erie and the 100 years of peace between the U.S. and Canada, rises 352 ft. above lake-level, the tallest Doric column in the world. (Elevator ride to the top $1.) In the center of the island, at the corner of Catawba Ave. and Thompson Rd., the **Heineman Winery** ferments a fun time. Tours of the wine-making equipment cost $3 and include a sampling. Their grape juice is made from the same recipe as the wine but not fermented; the heavenly nectar shames the store-bought variety. (Tours daily 11am-5pm hourly; bottle of wine $4.50, of grape juice $2.25). While digging for the wine cellar, they happened upon the **largest geode ever discovered** (you can step inside); a look at this "Crystal Cave" is included in the winery tour.

Rooms on the island start at $55; the **South Bass Island State Park** on the western edge of the island charges $12 per night (showers, no hookup, no reservations). To get a site on weekends arrive before 8:30am on Friday. For more info on this park or the one on Kelly's Island, call the park office in Catawba (419-797-4530).

At the ferry dock, **Island Bike Rental** (285-2016) rents one-speeds ($2 per hr., $6 per day). Pick up a free map of the island a few yards away at **E's Golf Carts** (285-5553; carts $8 per hr., $45 per day). The **Miller Boat Line** (285-2421) ferries passengers and cars to South Bass Island from Catawba Point (June-Sept. 7:30am-7:30pm every ½-hr., less frequently in April, May, Oct. and Nov.; $4 one way, ages 6-11 $1, bike $1.50, car $7). (Exit Rte. 2, follow Rte. 53 north to the end. Park at one of the ferry's free lots; be careful of the ones that charge $5 per day.) **Sonny S. Ferry** runs from Put-in Bay to **Lonz Winery** on Middle Bass Island. ($5 round-trip, winery tours $1.50.) Miller Boat Line also serves Middle Bass from Catawba Point ($4.50 one way).

Kellys Island

Kellys Island is, if possible, even more laid-back than South Bass. The bars are more low-key, the bike paths are closer to the lake, the island is less developed, and wildlife is more plentiful—you will almost certainly see several (dozen) rabbits and perhaps some deer and a blue heron. The island was once a large source of limestone; you can wander around abandoned, water-filled quarries, the best of which is **East Quarry**, in the center of the island, a great place to watch birds in the air and carp in the water. The glaciers that blanketed North America carved deep grooves in that limestone; a small section of the grooves has been preserved on the northern side of the island; to the uninitiated, it looks like a 60-ft. section of dry streambed, but it excites geologists and glacier scientists. Go figure. The **Kellys Island State Park** (419-797-4530), near the "grooves," charges a groovy $12 per night for sites. No reservations; arrive by early afternoon on Friday for weekend spots. (Has showers, toilets, a beach, and allows pets.) The **Neuman Boat Line** (798-5800) serves the island from a dock in Marblehead (open April-late Nov.; $7.80 round-trip, ages 6-11 $4.50, bike $2.50, car $14). **First Place Rentals** (746-2314), right by the ferry dock, rents bikes ($1.50 per hr., $6 per day).

Sandusky, et al.

There are 40 motels and hotels on the mainland in nearby Sandusky; the **Visitors and Convention Bureau** (800-255-3743) has a directory. If you aren't camping, the best place to stay is the **Hotel Lakeside** (798-4461), on the lake in the heart of **Lakeside,** near Marblehead (turn off Rte. 163 at the Mobil Station onto Erie Beach Rd.). Lakeside is one of the few remaining **Chautauqua Villages,** Methodist family resorts founded in the 19th century. Families still come here year after year, drawn by the activities available for children, nightly shows at the **Hoover Auditorium,** and good old-fashioned Christian fellowship. The **Hotel Lakeside** *seems* not to have changed much in 100 years; only electric light and phones have been added. Actually, the rooms have recently been restored to their original charm; only a non-profit institution like this has such a high quality/price ratio (with shared bath from $20, with private bath from $45; reservations usually not required). The restaurant in the hotel has great buffet all-you-can-eat dinners ($5-8). Admission to **Lakeside** grounds includes all lectures, concerts, sport facilities, and other entertainment ($8 per day, plus $1 per day for cars).

Near Sandusky, experience **Cedar Point,** the scenic playground's scenic amusement park (627-2350) off U.S. 6. Take the Ohio Turnpike (I-80) to exit 7 and follow signs north on U.S. 250 to the home of the **Magnum XL200,** the world's largest, fastest, longest and steepest roller coaster. (Open mid-May-mid-Sept. Sun.-Thurs. 10am-10pm, Fri. and Sat. 10am-midnight. Admission $23, seniors $12.50, under 4 ft. $5, under 4 years free. After 5pm, when the lines diminish, the admission drops to $12.50.)

Greyhound, 6513 Milan Rd., Sandusky, on U.S. 250 south of Rte. 2 (625-6907) hurtles to: Cleveland ($9.50-14.50), Detroit ($22), and Chicago ($39). **Taxis** to downtown Sandusky are $8; to Catawba Point $30 to $40. The **area code** for the region is 419.

Wisconsin

The state that calls itself "America's Dairyland" is also one of the nation's most popular playlands, with forests, rivers and lakes to suit the tenacious and the tenderfoot alike. Lake Superior to the north and Lake Michigan to the east give the Wisconsin coast the natural beauty that makes the Great Lakes area famous. The state's appeal comes from more than just nature; Wisconsin residents pick up where the wilderness leaves off.

The French first explored the area in search of lucrative, furry fauna. Later, hearty and bold Norsemen lumbered to the logging and mining camps of this once-rugged frontier. By the time the virgin forests had fallen and the mines had been exhausted, German immigrant farmers came to the fore. Wisconsin celebrates these variegated ethnic roots in its food and drink. Fishboils—feasts fit for Thor—seethe throughout the state in a tradition dating back to the 19th century. Each summer, Milwaukee, the self-proclaimed "City of Fabulous Festivals" explodes in a concatenation of ethnic fêtes, each with indigenous food, music and (of course) lots of beer.

Practical Information

Capital: Madison.

Division of Tourism, 123 W. Washington St., Madison 53707 (266-2161, 266-6797, or 800-372-2737).

Time Zone: Central (1 hr. behind Eastern).

Postal Abbreviation: WI

Sales Tax: 5%.

Apostle Islands

Once a logging area, today 20 of the 22 islands in this glacial archipelago are protected as a national lakeshore. Summer tourists visit the wind- and wave-whipped caves by the thousands, camping on unspoiled sandstone bluffs and hunting for wild blueberries and raspberries.

Bayfield

All Apostle Islands excursions begin in the sleepy mainland town of **Bayfield.** The **Bayfield Chamber of Commerce,** 42 S. Broad St. (779-3335), has helpful information on the area. (Open summer daily 9am-5pm.) The **Apostle Islands National Lakeshore Headquarters Visitors Center,** 410 Washington Ave. (779-3397), dispenses information and free camping permits for the islands. (Open daily 8am-6pm; off-season Mon.-Fri. 8am-4:30pm.) **Trek & Trail** on Rittenhouse Ave. (779-3320) rents sea kayaks ($15-35 ½-day, $25-55 per day) and offers kayak safety instructions.

In early summer, Bayfield's basket overflows with berry pies. **Maggie's,** 257 Manypenny Ave. (779-5641), also has sandwiches and burgers ($3-5). (Open May-Oct. 6am-10pm, Nov.-April 11:30am-10pm. There are numerous campgrounds in the area. The **Dalrymple** park, ¼-mi. north of town on Rte. 13 (779-5712), offers sites under tall pines, right on the Lake, but has no showers. ($7, $8 with electricity.) **Red Cliff,** a Chippewa settlement three mi. north on Rte. 13, offers tourists a campground (779-3743) with more modern conveniences ($10, tents with electricity $11, trailers with electricity $12). Talk to the Native Americans for a different perspective on the area and its offerings. For those who prefer indoor accommodations, the **Frostman Home,** 24 N. 3rd St. (779-3239), has three spotless and comfortable rooms for $25 each. Down the street and around the corner, **Greunke's Inn,** 17 Rittenhouse Ave. (779-5480), has pleasant, old-fashioned rooms from $35.

Bayfield is in the northwest part of Wisconsin on the Lake Superior coast. The nearest **Greyhound** station barks in **Ashland,** at 101 2nd St. (682-4010), 22 mi. southeast of Bayfield. (To Duluth, 2 hr., $7.50.) The **Bay Area Rural Transit (BART)** (682-9664) offers a shuttle to Bayfield. (4 per day, Mon.-Fri., $1.80, seniors/disabled $1.10, students $1.50.)

The Bayfield **post office** is open Monday through Friday from 9am to 12:30pm and from 1:30 to 4:30pm, and on Saturday from 10 to 11am. The **ZIP code** is 54814.

Madeline Island

A few hundred years ago, the Chippewa came to **Madeline Island** from the Atlantic in search of the *megis shell,* a light in the sky that was purported to bring prosperity and health. The **Madeline Island Historical Museum** (747-2415), right off the dock, accompanies the legend with other historical info. (Open late May-Labor Day daily 9am-5pm; Labor Day-early Oct. daily 10am-4pm. $3, seniors $2.70, ages 5-12 $1.25.) The **Indian Burial Ground** one mi. south of La Pointe has meandering dirt paths that lead to the graves of early settlers and christianized Chippewa, including Chief Great Buffalo. Towards the end of the day, head to **Sunset Bay** on the north side of the island. **Madeline Island Tours** (747-2051) offers two two-hour tours of the island each day from late June to Labor Day. ($6.75, ages 6-11 $3.75). From late June to late August they run shorter tours which skip Big Bay State Park (1¼ hr., $5, ages 6-11 $2.75). **Grandpa Tony's** perky red-and-white decor houses tasty sandwiches ($2.50-3.75). (Open summer Mon.-Fri. 8am-9pm, Sat.-Sun. 8am-10pm.) The **Beach Club,** just off the ferry in La Pointe, has a relaxed atmosphere, a view of the lake, superlative shortcake ($3.50), and a superb shrimp basket with fries ($7). (Open summer daily 11:30am-3:30pm and 5:30-9:30pm.)

Madeline Island has two campgrounds. **Big Bay Town Park** is 6½ mi. from La Pointe, right next to beautiful Big Bay Lagoon (sites $9). Across the lagoon, **Big Bay State Park** has sites for $8, plus a daily vehicle permit ($6 and $4 for Wisconsin residents). (Sites can be reserved by mail; $3 reservation fee.) The **Madeline Island Motel** (747-3000) lets clean rooms, each of which are named for a different personality in the Island's history. (July-Labor Day singles $49, doubles $54; May-June and Labor Day-Nov. $41 and $45, Dec.-April all rooms $31.) On Colonel Woods Blvd., **La Pointe Lodgings Motel** (747-5205 or 779-5596) offers spacious rooms with walls of fresh-smelling pine. (Singles $55, off-season $35). Rooms in the area are generally scarce during the summer; call ahead for reservations.

Ferry service to and from Bayfield and **La Pointe,** on Madeline Island, is provided by **Madeline Island Ferry Line** (747-2051; summer ferries daily every ½ hr. 6am-11pm; less frequently March-June and Sept.-Dec.; late June-Labor Day one way $2.75, ages 6-11 $1.75, bikes $1.50, cars $6.25, less off-season.).

Transport on Madeline Island is by foot, car or bicycle. Rent a moped at **Motion to Go,** 102 Lake View Pl. (747-6585), about one block from the ferry. ($8.50-10 per hr., $35-45 per day. Open summer daily 9am-9pm.) Rent fat-tired bikes at **Island Bike Rental** (747-5442), ½ block north of the town dock in La Pointe. ($2.50 per hr., $15 per day. Open daily May 27-early Oct., 10am-5:30pm.)

The **Madeline Island Chamber of Commerce,** Main St. (747-2801), provides helpful information, especially concerning accommodations. (Open summer daily 9am-5pm.) The **La Pointe post office** (747-3712) lies just off the dock on Madeline Island. (Open Mon.-Fri. 9am-4:30pm, Sat. 9:30am-1pm.) The **ZIP code** is 54850.

The Other Apostles

The other islands have subtle charms of their own. The sandstone quarries of Basswood and Hermit Island, as well as the abandoned logging and fishing camps on some of the others, are mute reminders of a more vigorous and animated era. Some of the sea caves on Devils Island are large enough to accommodate a small boat. Museums in their own right, the restored lighthouses on Sand, Raspberry, Michigan, Outer and Devils Islands offer spectacular views of the surrounding country. An easy way to visit all of these sights is on one of three narrated cruises provided by the **Apostle Islands Cruise Service** (779-3925; tickets $19, kids $8). From late June to late August, the cruise service runs other trips ($19) from which passengers can disembark to camp on the islands and then be picked up the next time the cruise schedule brings the boat to that island. At other times, you can charter a **Water Taxi** (779-5153) for a steep price.

Legend has it that the islands were named in the 18th century when a band of pirates called the Twelve Apostles hid out on Oak Island. Today you don't have to hide to stay there, as long as you get a free camper's permit, available at the **National Lakeshore Headquarters Visitors Center,** 410 Washington Ave. in Bayfield (779-3397). The permit allows you to camp on 19 of the 22 islands. The Headquarters will also tell you which islands allow camping only at designated sites and which are more generally open.

The Apostle Islands lazily swim off the northern coast of Wisconsin, and are easily accessible from Bayfield. They are 90 mi. from Duluth, 220 mi. from the Twin Cities, and 465 mi. from Chicago.

The **area code** for Bayfield and the Apostle Islands is 715.

Door County

Door County, a beautiful, 40-mi.-long peninsula stretching north into Lake Michigan, attracts more and more visitors every year—and for good reason. The peninsula (technically an island cut off from the rest of Wisconsin by the Sturgeon Bay Canal) hosts famous fishboils and boasts five state parks, 250 mi. of shoreline, and eight inland lakes. Despite the recent tourist onslaught, the peninsula remains low-key and relaxed; dairy farms and cherry orchards abound, streets often don't have addresses, and businesses close "around sunset." For the time being, Door County swings wide open to visitors, providing stores, restaurants, and parks, while also managing to shut out reckless developers.

Practical Information and Orientation

Emergency: 911

Visitor Information: Door County Chamber of Commerce, 6443 Green Bay Rd. (743-4456), on Rte. 42/57 entering Sturgeon Bay. Free brochures for every village on the peninsula and biking maps (25¢). Mailing address P.O. Box 346, Station A. Open June-Oct. Mon.-Fri. 8am-5pm, Sat. 10am-4pm; off-season Mon.-Fri. 8am-5pm. Each village has its own visitors center. **Triphone,** a free service located outside the Chamber of Commerce, allows you to call any hotel on the peninsula, as well as restaurant, police, weather, and fishing hotlines.

Buses: Greyhound, 800 Cedar, **Green Bay** (414-432-4883). The closest station to Door County, about 50 mi. from Sturgeon Bay. To: Milwaukee ($18.50, students $14), Chicago ($29), and Minneapolis ($39). Open Mon.-Fri. 6:15am-6pm and 8:15-9:30pm, Sat. 6:15am-12:30pm and 4-6pm, Sun. 9am-12:30pm and 4-6pm.

Car Rental: Advantage, 1629 Velp at Military, in Green Bay, 50 mi. from Sturgeon Bay (414-497-2152). 3 mi. from Greyhound station in Green Bay (taxi ride $5-10, no city bus service). $14 per day, $89 per week, 10¢ per mi., extra $5 insurance. Must be 25 years old with credit card. Open daily 8:30am-6pm.

Other Rentals: Nor Door Sport and Cyclery, Fish Creek (868-2275), at the entrance to Peninsula State Park. Mountain bikes $7 per hr., $20 per day; 18- and 21-speeds $5 per hr., $15 per day, $30 for 3 days. **The Boat House,** Fish Creek (868-3745). Mopeds $12.50 for the 1st hr., $7.50 per additional hr. Must have $50 deposit and driver's license. **Kurtz Corral,** 3 mi. east of Carlsville on C.R. "I" (743-6742). Horseback riding on 300 acres. $19 per hr., kids' rides $9; instruction included. Open daily 9am-3pm

Police: 123 S. 5th Ave. (743-4133), in Sturgeon Bay.

Post Office: 359 Louisiana (743-2681), at 4th St. in Sturgeon Bay. Open Mon.-Fri. 8:30am-5pm. **ZIP code:** 54235

Area Code: 414.

The real Door County begins north of **Sturgeon Bay** where Routes 42 and 57 converge and then split again—57 running up the eastern coast of the peninsula, 42 up the western side. The peninsula is 200 mi. northeast of Madison (take U.S. 151 and then Rte. 57 north) and 150 mi. north of Milwaukee (take I-43, then Rte. 42, north). The Peninsula has no land access except Sturgeon Bay. Summer is high season in Door's 12 villages, the biggest of which are **Fish Creek** (rhymes with "fish stick"), **Sister Bay,** and **Ephraim.** There is no public transportation on the peninsula. The eastern side is slower paced and less developed than the western; the peninsula is less developed and more traditional the farther north you go. Wherever in the area you are, dress warmly; temperatures can dip to 40°F at night in July, and strong bay winds make it even cooler.

Accommodations and Camping

Most motels on the peninsula cater to the family-with-boat crowd who have the money to get away from it all for $60 and up per night. Fortunately, motels for $40 and under do exist, but don't expect a concierge. The best deal is cultivated at the **Century Farm Motel,** on Rte. 57, three mi. south of Sister Bay (854-4069); mail address 100 68 Hwy. 57, Sister Bay 54234. The individual cottages have pine walls, showers, and cozy bedspreads and curtains. The friendly owner lives in the log cabin built by his grandfather a century ago. (Cottage for 2 $35, for 5 $45. Pets are allowed for extra $5.) Reserve one week ahead, more for holiday weekends. At the **Liberty Park Lodge** (854-2025), in Sister Bay north of downtown on Rte. 42, you can sit on a huge porch and watch the sun set over the lake. (Lodge rooms $42-56.) The **Chal-A Motel,** 3910 Rte. 42/57 (743-6788), rests three mi. north of the bridge in Sturgeon Bay. Ask the proprietor to display her private collection of several thousand dolls, including the original Barbie. In the same barn her husband shows off his 24 vintage automobiles, ranging from a 1924 Model T to a 1983 DeLorean. (July-Oct. singles $39, doubles $44; Nov.-June singles $19, doubles $24.)

Camping is the way to go in Door County, and four out of the five **state parks** surveyed (all except Whitefish Dunes State Park) have sites. Camping at all state parks in Wisconsin costs $10 per site per night, with an extra $1.75 for electricity. In addition, you must pay the daily admission fee of $6 per vehicle or get an annual admission sticker ($28). **Peninsula State Park,** P.O. Box 218, Fish Creek 54212 (868-3258), by Fish Creek village on Rte. 42, is the largest, with 472 sites. Make reservations *way* ahead of time (i.e. 6 months), or come in person and put your name on the waiting list for one of the 127 sites reserved for walk-ins. Peninsula has showers and flush toilets, 20 mi. of shoreline, a spectacular view from Eagle Tower, and 17 mi. of hiking. **Potawatomi State Park,** 3740 Park Dr., Sturgeon Bay 54235 (746-2890), just outside Sturgeon Bay off Rte. 42/57, has 125 campsites, half of which are open to walk-ins. Write for reservations. **Newport State Park,** a wildlife preserve at the tip of the peninsula, is six or seven mi. from Ellison Bay off Rte. 42, has only 16 sites and does not allow motorized vehicles. To get to **Rock Island State Park,** take the ferry from Gill's Rock to Washington Island (see Sights and Activities below) and another ferry (847-2252; total price $12 round-trip) to Rock Island. (40 sites, open May-Dec.)

The best private campground is **Path of Pines** (868-3332), in Fish Creek, which has scenic sites and a truly hospitable staff. It's one mi. east of the perennially packed Peninsula, on County "F" off Rte. 42. (Sites with water and electricity $15, free showers. $2.50 per additional adult.)

Food and Drink

Many people come to Door County just for **fishboils,** not a trout with blemishes but a Scandinavian tradition dating back to 19th-century lumberjacks. Fifty meals are cooked at a time in a steaming cauldron over a wood fire. To remove the fish oil from the top of the water, the boilmaster throws a can of kerosene into the fire, producing a massive fireball; this causes the cauldron to boil over and signals chowtime. The best fishboils are at: **White Gull Inn,** in Fish Creek (868-3517; $13.50 for all-you-can-eat, May-Oct. Wed. and Fri.-Sun.; Nov.-April Wed. and Sat. at 5:45, 7, and 8:15pm; reservations required); the **Edgewater Restaurant,** in Ephraim (854-4034; $11, June-mid-Oct. Mon.-Sat. at 5:30 and 6:45 pm; reservations best); and **The Viking,** at Ellison Bay (854-2998; $11, mid-May-Nov. 4:30-8pm about every ½-hr.). Cherries are another county tradition, and each fishboil concludes with a big slice of cherry pie.

For groceries, locals shop at **Piggly Wiggly,** on Country Walk Rd. off Rte. 42 at the Amoco station (854-2391), in Sister Bay. **Hy-Line Orchards** (868-3067), on Rte. 42 between Juddville and Egg Harbor, is a huge barn full of produce and a few old Model T's. Try the cherry cider. (Open daily 7am-7pm.)

Al Johnson's Swedish Restaurant, in Sister Bay on Rte. 42 (854-2626), down the hill and 2 blocks past the information center. Excellent Swedish food popular with locals and visitors. Goats keep the sod roof trimmed. Entrées $9-16. Open daily 6am-9pm.

Kirkegaard's Yum-Yum Tree (839-2993) in Bailey's Harbor. Floats $2.25, sundaes $1.85-3.25, cones $1.25, beer brats $1.95, deli sandwiches $2.50-4.50, and plenty of *Fear and Trembling* for dessert. Open mid-May-Oct. daily 10am-10pm.

Bayside Tavern, Fish Creek on Rte. 42 (868-3441). Serves serious burgers ($2.50-4) and a delicious Friday perch fry ($8). Also a hip bar. Beer 90¢. No one under 21. Open daily 11am-2am.

The Fish Creek General Store, Fish Creek (868-3351). The best deal on prepared food on the peninsula. Thick deli sandwiches with chips $2.25. Carry-out only. Open May-Nov. daily 8am-7pm.

Sights and Activities

Door County is best seen by bike; ask for free bike maps at the tourist offices. **Cave Point County Park** offers the most stunning views of the peninsula. The park is on Cave Point Rd. off Rte. 57, just south of Jacksonport. (Open daily 6am-10pm. Free.) Next door is **Whitefish Dunes State Park,** with hikin' a-plenty through a well-kept wildlife preserve. (Open daily 8am-8pm. $6.) Visit the small public beaches along Door's 250-mi. shoreline; one of the nicest is **Lakeside Park** at **Jacksonport.** The beach is wide and sandy, backed by a shady park and playground. (Open daily 6am-10pm. Free.) You can go windsurfing off the public beach at **Ephraim,** in front of the Edgewater Restaurant and Motel. **Windsurf Door County** (854-4071), across from the public beach at South Shore Pier, rents boards ($12 per hr., $30 per ½-day; $100 deposit or major credit card required). **Peninsula State Park,** a few miles south of Ephraim in Fish Creek, has 3763 acres of forested land. (Open daily 6am-11pm. $6 per car, $2 per bike; under 18 free.) Ride a moped or bicycle along the 20 mi. of shoreline road, or mix, mingle, and sunbathe at **Nicolet Beach** in the park. From the immense Eagle Tower one mi. east of the beach, 110 steps up, you can see clear across the lake to Michigan.

Kangaroo Lake, the largest of the eight inland lakes on this thin peninsula, offers warmer swimming and a less intimidating stretch of water than Lake Michigan. Kangaroo Lake Road, south of Bailey's Harbor off Rte. 57, provides lake access; follow the county roads around the lake to find your own secluded swimming spot. The **Ridges Sanctuary,** north of Bailey's Harbor off Hwy. "Q," has an appealing nature trail that leads to an abandoned lighthouse. (Open daily 10am-6pm. Free.) **Newport State Park,**

six mi. east of Ellison Bay on Newport Dr. off Rte. 42, provides more satisfying hiking than Peninsula (no vehicles allowed). Newport has an expansive 3000-ft. swimming beach and 13 mi. of shoreline on Lake Michigan and on inland Europe Lake.

For more scenic seclusion, seek out **Washington Island,** off the tip of the Door Peninsula; ferries run by **Washington Island Ferry Line** (847-2546; round-trip for cars $14, adults $6, kids $3) and Island Clipper (854-2972; round-trip for adults $6, kids $3). Both leave Gills Rock and Northport Pier several times daily.

Near Door County: Green Bay

Most routes to Door County pass through Green Bay (the city, not the body of water), and several attractions here warrant a look. For those interested in American culture, perhaps the most gripping spectacle is the **Oneida Bingo and Casino,** County Route GG, southwest of downtown (414-497-8118). European exploiters stole land from Native Americans with baubles and trinkets; now watch Native Americans take their revenge with numbered grids. A fascinating reversal of history even for non-gamblers. (Free; 18 and over.) If that orange and blue-upholstered Amtrak car seems dated, the **National Railroad Museum**, 2285 S. Broadway, Green Bay (414-435-7245), will seem like ancient history. Pullman cars to modern sleepers, Eisenhower's WWII staff train, and more. (Open May-Oct. daily 9am-5pm; $5.50, kids $2.75.)

Milwaukee

Milwaukee opened for settlement in 1835, and it quickly attracted Irish and German immigrants. Together they gave the city its reputation for *gemütlichkeit*—hospitality. Recent immigrants, including Italians, Poles, and Hispanics, seem to have adopted the city's spirit of generosity as their own. Milwaukee's ethnic communities alternate throwing city-wide parties every weekend during the summer. This self-proclaimed "City of Fabulous Festivals" has top-notch museums, quality arts organizations, baklava, and bagpipes. And beer. Lots of beer.

Practical Information and Orientation

Emergency: 911

Greater Milwaukee Convention and Visitors Bureau, 510 W. Kilbourne (273-7222 to talk to a human, 273-3950 or 800-231-0903 to talk to a machine), downtown. Open Mon.-Fri. 8am-6pm. Also at the airport (open Mon.-Fri. 7am-9:30pm, Sat. 10am-6pm, Sun. 1-9:30pm) and Grand Avenue Mall at 3rd St. (open Mon.-Fri. 10am-8pm, Sat. 10am-6pm, Sun. noon-5pm). Pick up a copy of *Greater Milwaukee Official Visitor's Guide.*

Airport: General Mitchell International Airport, 5300 S. Howell Ave. (747-5300). Take bus #80 from downtown (30-min.).

Amtrak: 433 W. St. Paul Ave. (800-872-7245), at 5th St. 3 blocks from the bus terminal. To Chicago ($14.50). Open Mon.-Fri. 6am-9pm, Sat.-Sun. 7:30am-9pm. Fairly safe during the day, less so at night.

Buses: Greyhound, 606 N. 7th St. (272-8900), off W. Michigan St. downtown. Open daily 5am-11:30pm. To Chicago ($14) and Madison ($9). **Wisconsin Coach,** in the Greyhound terminal (542-8861). Service to southeast Wisconsin. Ticket office open daily 2-3:30am and 6am-11:30pm; station open 24 hrs. **Badger Bus** (276-7490) is across the street. To Madison (6 per day; $8). Stations are not very safe at night.

Public Transport: Milwaukee County Transit System, 1942 N. 17th St. (344-6711). Efficient service in the metro area. Most lines run 4:30am-12:30am. $1, weekly pass $8.50, seniors 50¢ with Medicare card. Pick up free map at the library or the info center at the Grand Ave. Mall.

Car Rental: Payless Car Rental, 4939 S. Howell (482-0300), take bus #80 south to airport. $29 per day with unlimited mileage. $11 collision insurance. Must be 21 with liability insurance and major credit card; ages 21-25 $5 surcharge. Open daily 6am-midnight.

Taxi: City Veteran Taxi, 291-8080. Base rate $1.50, plus $1.25 per mi.

Auto Transport Company: Auto Driveaway Co., 9039 W. National Ave. (962-0008 or 327-5252), in West Alice. Must be 21 with good driving record. $250 deposit refunded at destination; driver pays for gas. Open Mon.-Fri. 9am-5pm, Sat. 9am-noon.

Help Lines: Crisis Intervention Center, 257-7222. Open 24 hrs. **Rape Crisis Line,** 547-4600 or 542-3828. **Gay People's Union Hotline,** 562-7010. Open 7-10pm.

Traveler's Aid: At the airport (747-5245). Open daily 9am-9pm.

American Express: 777 E. Wisconsin Ave. (271-1250).

Post Office: 345 W. St. Paul Ave. (291-2450), south along 4th Ave. from downtown, next to the Amtrak station. Open Mon.-Fri. 7:30am-6pm. **ZIP code:** 53203.

Area Code: 414.

Downtown Milwaukee starts at **Lake Michigan** and runs west to about 10th St. The city is constructed in a grid pattern, with address numbers increasing as you move away from **Second Street** and **Wisconsin Avenue.**

Accommodations and Camping

Sleeping rarely comes cheap in downtown Milwaukee, but there are two attractive hostels nearby, as well as the convenient University of Wisconsin dorms. **Bed and Breakfast of Milwaukee** (571-0780) is a reservation service; the closest B&B is eight mi. south of downtown ($48 for 2 people). Avoid staying downtown at night, as it can be dangerous.

University of Wisconsin at Milwaukee (UWM): Sandburg Halls, 3400 N. Maryland Ave. (229-4065). Take bus #30 north to Hartford St. and look for the tall stone building. Laundry, cafeteria, free local calls available, no kitchen. Convenient to nightlife and east side restaurants. Private singles with shared bath $20. Doubles $27. Open May 31-Aug. 15. 2-day advance reservations required.

Red Barn Hostel (HI/AYH), 6750 W. Loomis Rd. (529-3299), 13 mi. southwest of downtown via Rte. 894, exit Loomis. Take bus #10 or 30 west on Wisconsin Ave., get off at 35th St. and take the #35 south to the Loomis and Ramsey intersection; cross over to the Pick 'n' Save store and walk 3/4 mi. south on Loomis. Dark rooms in an enormous, red barn; bathroom is campground-quality. Full kitchen. The bus ride out is not perfectly safe at night. Check-in after 5:30pm. Members only, $8. Open May-Oct.

Halter Home Hostel (HI/AYH), 2956 N. 77th St. (258-7692), 4 mi. west of downtown. Take bus #57 to 76th and Center St. Dangerous bus ride at night. The closer of the two hostels, but also the smaller: 4 beds in 2 comfortable rooms. Members only, $10.

Hotel Wisconsin, 720 N. 3rd St. (271-4900), across from the Grand Avenue Mall. 250 old but clean rooms at a convenient downtown location with parking. Singles $49, with 2 persons $54, $8 each extra adult. Key deposit $5. For summer weekends, reserve 1 month in advance.

Food

Milwaukee does not cater to dainty eaters—prices are small and portions hearty. **Brady Street** has many Italian restaurants, and the **South Side** is heavily Polish. The **Grand Avenue Mall's** third floor, a huge *Speisegarten* ("meal garden") on Wisconsin Ave. between 2nd and 4th St., cultivates reasonable ethnic and fast-food places. **East Side** eateries are a little more cosmopolitan, and good Mexican food sambas at S. 16th St. and National.

Taquería Jalisco, 1035 S. 16th St. (672-1000) and 2207 E. North Ave. (291-0645), on the East side. Authentic Mexican food, huge portions, at low prices. Burrito $2.50, tacos $1.25. Sit-down or take-out, 24 hrs.

Abu's Jerusalem of the Gold, 1978 N. Farwell (277-0485), at Lafayette on the East Side. A wall-inscribed poem dedicated to Abu, exotic tapestries, and plenty of kitsch adorn this tiny corner restaurant. Try the rosewater lemonade. Plenty of veggie entrées, including falafel sandwich ($2.40). Open Mon.-Thurs. 11:30am-10pm, Fri.-Sat. 11:30am-11pm, Sun. 1-10pm.

Albanese's, 701 E. Keefe Ave. (964-7270), 3 mi. north of downtown, 3 blocks west of Humboldt. Generous portions of homemade Italian food (pasta dishes $5.25-6.25). Open Mon.-Thurs. 5-10pm, Fri.-Sat. 5-11pm, Fri. 11:30-1:30pm.

Three Brothers, 2414 St. Clair St. (481-7530), #15 bus to Conway and walk 4 blocks east. One of the best known of Milwaukee's famed Serbian restaurants, this family-owned business serves dishes such as *burek,* a strudel puff pastry filled with beef or chicken ($10). Open Tues.-Thurs. 5-10pm, Fri.-Sat. 4-11pm, Sun. 4-10pm. Reservations recommended.

Sights

Although many of Milwaukee's breweries have left, the city's name still conjures up thoughts of a cold one. No visit to the city would be complete without a look at the yeast in action. **The Miller Brewery,** 4251 W. State St. (931-2337), offers free one-hour tours with free samples. (3 tours per hr. Mon.-Sat. 10am-3:30pm. Must be 21.) **Pabst Brewing Company,** 915 W. Juneau Ave. (223-3709), offers free tours (Mon.-Fri. 10am-3pm, Sat. 10am-2pm on the hr., Sept.-May closed Sat.). As Dennis Hopper attests in *Blue Velvet,* "Fuck Heineken, Pabst Blue Ribbon!" The micro-brewery **Sprecher Brewing Co.,** 730 W. Oregon St. (272-2337), has a $2 tour on Saturday only.

You've seen the t-shirts and the bikers, now see the factory. **Harley-Davidson Inc.,** 11700 W. Capitol Dr. (342-4680), assembles their engines in Milwaukee. (Tours Mon., Wed. and Fri. 10:30am and 12:30pm, free. Call to confirm times.)

Milwaukee is graced with several excellent museums. The **Milwaukee Public Museum,** 800 W. Wells St. (278-2702), at N. 8th St., allows visitors to walk through exhibits of the streets of Old Milwaukee and a European village, complete with cobblestones and two-story shops. Other exhibits focus on Native American settlements and North American wildlife. (Open daily 9am-5pm. $4.50, kids $2.50.) The lakefront **Milwaukee Art Museum,** in the War Memorial Building, 750 N. Lincoln Memorial Dr., houses Haitian art, 19th-century German art, and U.S. sculpture and paintings, including two of Warhol's soup cans. (Open Mon.-Wed. and Fri.-Sat. 10am-5pm, Thurs. noon-9pm, Sun. noon-5pm. $3, seniors, students, and persons with disabilities people $1.50.) The **Charles Allis Art Museum,** 1801 N. Prospect Ave. (278-8295), at Royall Ave., is an English Tudor mansion with a fine collection of Chinese, Japanese, Korean, Persian, Greek, and Roman artifacts, as well as U.S. and European furniture. (Open Wed. 1-5pm and 7-9pm, Thurs.-Sun. 1-5pm. $2. Take bus #30.) The stone and ivy **Milwaukee County Historical Center,** 910 N. 3rd St. (273-8288), details the early years of the city with many artifacts, photographs, documents, and displays. (Open Mon.-Fri. 9:30am-5pm, Sat. 10am-5pm, Sun. 1-5pm. Free.)

The **Mitchell Park Horticultural Conservatory,** 524 S. Layton Blvd. (649-9800), at 27th St., better known as "The Domes," recreates a desert, a rain forest, and seasonal displays in a series of three seven-story conical glass domes. (Open daily 9am-5pm. $2.50, seniors, kids, and disabled people $1.25. Take bus #27.) Four mi. west, you'll find the **Milwaukee County Zoo,** 10001 W. Bluemound Rd. (771-3040), where zebras and cheetahs eye each other across a moat in the only predator-prey exhibit in the U.S. Also look for the elegant, misunderstood black rhinos and the trumpeter swans. (Open Mon.-Sat. 9am-5pm, Sun. 9am-6pm; shorter hours in winter. $6, under 12 $4. Parking $4. Take bus #10.)

Historic Milwaukee, Inc., P.O. Box 2132 (277-7795), offers tours focusing on ethnic heritage, original settlements, and architecture ($2-3). Ask about Milwaukee's many beautiful churches, including **St. Josaphat's Basilica,** 2336 S. 6th St. (645-5623), a turn-of-the-century landmark with a dome larger than the Taj Mahal's. Make phone arrangements to see the church, since it's usually locked. The Milwaukee County Transit System runs a 45-min.ute trolley tour of downtown that leaves from Grand Ave. at 2nd St. ($2; 11:15am and 12:15pm daily), and four-hour **bus tours** that include a stop at a brewery and the domes. ($10; call 344-6711 for details.)

Events and Entertainment

The Milwaukee lakefront throws a city-wide party or ethnic festival almost every summer weekend. One of the best is the **Summerfest** (273-3378), held over 11 days in late June and early July, fronting a potpourri of renowned musical acts, culinary specialties, and an arts and crafts marketplace. Tykes should enjoy the circus watershow and children's theater. The **Rainbow Summer** (273-7206) is a series of free lunchtime concerts throughout the summer running the spectrum from jazz and bluegrass to country music. Concerts are held weekdays from noon to 1:15pm in the Peck Pavilion at the Performing Arts Center (see below). Milwaukeeans line the streets for **The Great Circus Parade** (273-7877) in mid-July, an authentic re-creation of turn-of-the-century processions, with trained animals, daredevils, costumed performers, and 75 original wagons. (Call their office for information on special weekend packages at local hotels and motels during the parade.) In early August the **Wisconsin State Fair** (372-3770) rolls into the fairgrounds, toting big-name entertainment, 12 stages, exhibits, contests, rides, fireworks, and, of course, a pie-baking contest. ($5, under 11 free.) Pick up a copy of the free weekly entertainment mag, *Downtown Edition*, for the full scoop on festivals. There are ethnic festivals every weekend; the most popular are **Festa Italiana** (223-2180) in mid-July, **Bastille Days** (271-1416) near Bastille Day (July 14), and **German Fest** (464-7328) in late July (tickets $6-7).

For quality arts performances, visit the modern white stone **Performing Art Center (PAC),** 929 N. Water St. (800-472-4458), across the river from Père Marquette Park. The PAC hosts the Milwaukee Symphony Orchestra, First Stage Milwaukee, a Ballet Company, and the Florentine Opera Company. (Tickets $10-46, ½-price student and senior tix available day of show.) For information about events in the Milwaukee area, call **Milwaukee Tix** (271-3335, Mon.-Sat. noon-3pm). They also have ½-price tickets on the day of some shows.

The **Milwaukee Brewers** baseball team plays at County Stadium (933-9000), as do the **Green Bay Packers** for half of their home games. The **Milwaukee Bucks,** the local basketball team, lock horns with opponents at Bradley Center (277-0500); the **Milwaukee Admirals** (277-0550) also skate there.

Nightlife

If you've got the time, Milwaukee has the bars. Downtown gets a little seedy at night; the best nightlife district is on North Ave. on the East side, near the UW campus.

Downtown, come in from the cold to **Safehouse,** 779 N. Front St. (271-2007). Step through a bookcase passage and enter a bizarre world of spy hideouts, James Bond music, and a phone booth with 90 sound effects. A brass plate labeled "International Exports, Ltd." marks the entrance. Draft beer (code name: "liquid gold") costs $1.50, simple dinners $7 to $12. (Open Mon.-Sat. 11:30am-2am, Sun. 5pm-2am. Cover $1-2.) For British-style drinking fun, dip into **John Hawk's Pub,** 607 N. Broadway (964-9729), on the National Register of Historic Places. (Beer $1.75. Open daily 11am-2am, live jazz Fri.-Sat. at 9:30pm.)

On the East Side, North Ave. has a string of campus bars: **Von Trier's,** 2235 N. Farwell (272-1775), at North, is the nicest. Don't miss the ceiling mural of the town of Trier. There are no pitchers—strictly bottled imports (average $3.50 per bottle) in the lavish German interior or on the large outdoor patio. (Open Mon.-Fri. 4pm-2am, Sat.-Sun. 4pm-2:30am.) **Hooligan's,** a block or so south at 2017 North Ave. (273-5230), is smaller, louder, and—as the name might suggest—rowdier. (Open daily 11am-2:30am. Pitchers $5. Live music Sept.-June on Mon. at 9:30pm. Cover $2-4.) For good food and drink and a widely renowned comedy show, try **Kalt's,** 2856 N. Oakland (332-6323) at Locust, where **Comedy Sportz** (962-8888) entertains crowds. (Shows Thurs.-Sun. at 7:30pm, additional show Fri.-Sat. at 10pm. Bar open Sun.-Thurs. 4pm-midnight, Fri.-Sat. 4pm-2am.)

The Great Plains

The Great Plains have been much maligned by big-city critics and freeway travelers who don't take the time to figure out what this region is all about. Over 200 years ago, a newborn country stretched westward onto these prairies. Here was forged the character of America. This is the territory of Paul Bunyan, Buffalo Bill, Laura Ingalls Wilder, and Chief Crazy Horse—the legend, the cowboy, the pioneer farmer, and the native.

Before the Homestead Act of 1862, the Plains were simply a huge, flat barrier to be crossed en route to the fertile valleys of the West Coast. The new law and the new transcontinental railroad began an economic boom that did not bust until the Great Depression of the 1930s, when the emerging "Bread Basket" region became a devastated Dust Bowl. Modern farming techniques have since tamed the soil, and the region now produces most of the nation's grain and livestock; cities such as Des Moines and Dodge City thrive once more on the trading of farm commodities.

The land still rules the Great Plains. Some of the most staggering sights in the region, and the country, are those created without the touch of a human hand—the Badlands and Wind and Jewel Caves of the Dakotas. Others overwhelm the visitor with the combined sheer power of earth and human—Mount Rushmore and the insanely gigantic Crazy Horse National Monument. And in the south the "amber waves of grain" quietly reign as perhaps the greatest of all symbols of the American land.

The great tragedy of the Great Plains is the history of the Native American tribes who were, for a long and painful era, considered obstacles to an "inevitable" process of American expansion. Despite a period of proud resistance in the time of Crazy Horse, Native Americans have been relegated to reservations and historical museums; their heritage and their rights have been sadly ignored. Only recently has the government begun to return the land—or at least some of it—to its first settlers, and only recently has a renaissance of Native pride occurred.

Iowa

Depending on your perspective, the name "Iowa" evokes images of patchwork corn and soybean farmland, of idyllic "fields of dreams," or of Hicksville, U.S.A. To see Iowa's real beauty, exit the freeway and meander along the old country roads. Here, far from the beaten and pummeled concrete path, you can cast your line into one of the state's innumerable fishing streams, bike 52 miles along the Cedar Valley Nature Trail, see the dust-created Loess Hills in the west, or travel back in time at one of the many traditional communities polka-dotting the area.

Practical Information

Capital: Des Moines.

Tourist Information: Iowa Department of Economic Development, 200 E. Grand Ave., Des Moines 50309 (515-281-3100). **Conservation Commission,** Wallace Bldg., Des Moines 50319 (515-281-5145).

Time Zone: Central (1 hr. behind Eastern). **Postal Abbreviation:** IA.

Sales Tax: 4%.

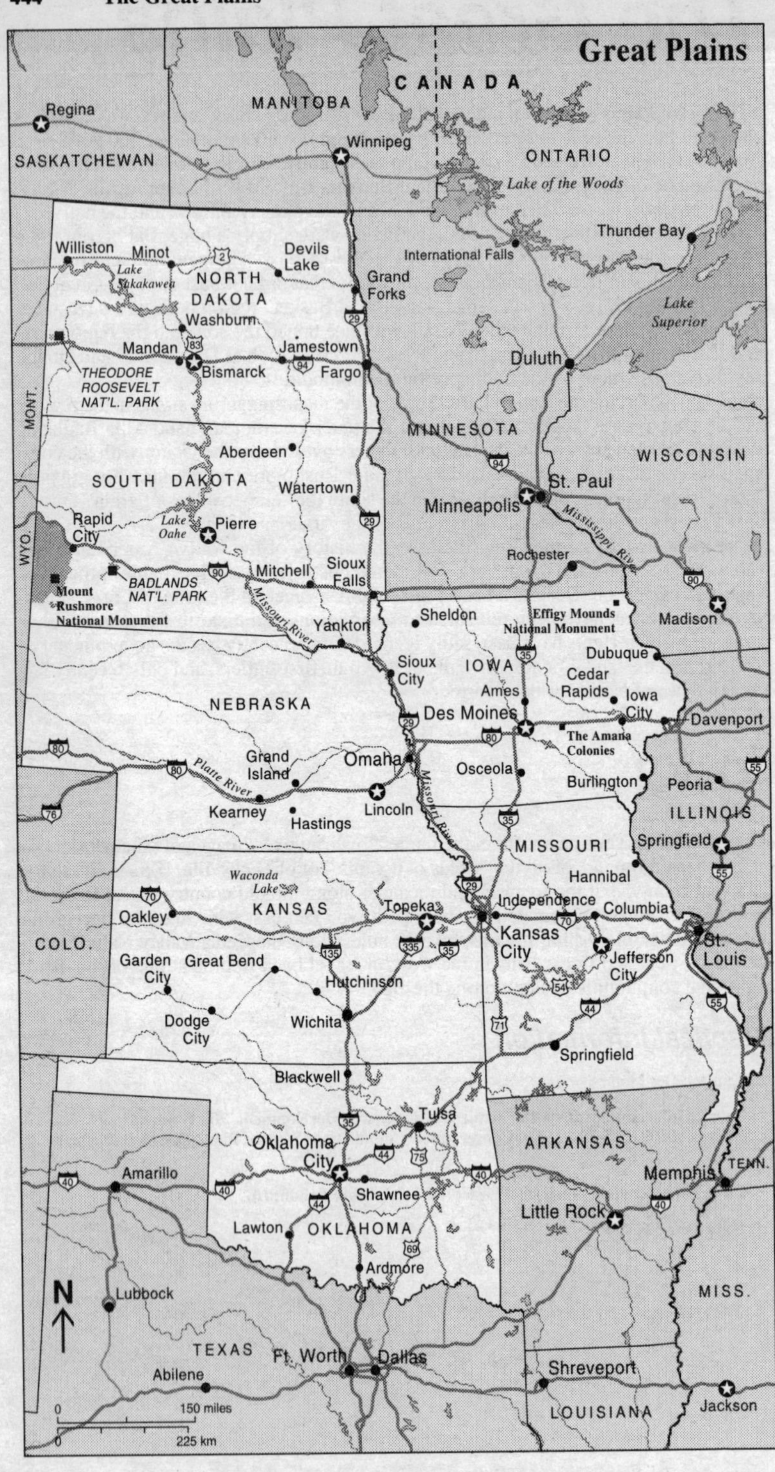
Great Plains
CANADA
MANITOBA
SASKATCHEWAN
ONTARIO
Regina
Winnipeg
Lake of the Woods
Thunder Bay
International Falls
Lake Superior
Williston
Minot
Lake Sakakawea
Devils Lake
NORTH DAKOTA
Grand Forks
Washburn
Mandan
Bismarck
Jamestown
Fargo
Duluth
THEODORE ROOSEVELT NAT'L. PARK
MONT.
MINNESOTA
WISCONSIN
Aberdeen
SOUTH DAKOTA
Watertown
St. Paul
Minneapolis
Mississippi River
Rapid City
Lake Oahe
Pierre
WYO.
Rochester
Mitchell
Sioux Falls
BADLANDS NAT'L. PARK
Mount Rushmore National Monument
Missouri River
Sheldon
Effigy Mounds National Monument
Madison
Yankton
Dubuque
Sioux City
IOWA
Cedar Rapids
Iowa City
Ames
NEBRASKA
Des Moines
Davenport
The Amana Colonies
Grand Island
Omaha
Osceola
Platte River
Burlington
Peoria
Kearney
Hastings
Lincoln
ILLINOIS
MISSOURI
Springfield
Waconda Lake
Hannibal
KANSAS
Topeka
Independence
Columbia
Oakley
Kansas City
St. Louis
COLO.
Garden City
Great Bend
Hutchinson
Jefferson City
Dodge City
Wichita
Springfield
Blackwell
Tulsa
ARKANSAS
Oklahoma City
TENN.
Amarillo
Memphis
Shawnee
Little Rock
Lawton
OKLAHOMA
Ardmore
N
Lubbock
MISS.
TEXAS
Ft. Worth
Dallas
Shreveport
Abilene
Jackson
LOUISIANA
0
150 miles
0
225 km

The Amana Colonies

In 1714, the religious movement known as the Community of True Inspiration was born in Germany. Believers migrated to the U.S. in 1842, alighted briefly in Buffalo, NY, and relocated to Iowa in 1855, where they established the Amana Colonies ("Amana" means "to remain faithful"). They led a communal lifestyle until 1932, when declining religious fervor and economic expediency caused them to embrace free enterprise and create the hugely successful Amana Refrigeration Company. Unlike the Amish, the Inspirationists were never anti-technology; their asceticism lay in such things as ambivalence towards marriage and children, as family ties distanced one's relationship with God. Today it is primarily the church that gives the colonies a sense of cultural and spiritual unity.

In keeping with Old-World village custom, there are no addresses in the colonies, only place names. Anything that isn't on the road leading into town is easily found by following the profusion of signs that point to attractions off the main thoroughfare. **Main Amana** is the largest and most heavily touristified of the seven Amana villages.

The **Museum of Amana History** (622-3567) runs a sentimental, jingoistic but informative slide show; it also has some nifty old toys and an impressive meteorite which fell into a nearby field. (Open April 15-Nov. 15 Mon.-Sat. 10am-5pm, Sun. noon-5pm; $2.50, ages 6-17 $1.) At the **Woolen Mill** (622-3051), visitors can watch the machinery run on weekdays. Buy your famous Amana blankets, sweaters and clothes here. (Open Mon.-Sat. 8am-6pm, Sun. 11am-5pm.) Across the street, watch artisans plane, carve and sand wooden creations in occasional open workshops at the **Amana Furniture and Clock Shop** (622-3291; open Mon.-Sat. 9am-5pm, Sun. noon-5pm, visitors' workshop gallery open Mon.-Fri. 9-11:30am and noon-3pm). Beyond the **Amana Refrigeration Plant**, in **Middle Amana,** tour the **Communal Kitchen Museum** (622-3567), the former site of all local food preparation. (Open May-Oct. daily 9am-5pm. $1.50, kids 75¢.) If your whirlwind tour of museums and gift shops leaves you uncertain of the survival of *any* Amana spirit beyond a commercial one, take some time to gaze at the lotus lilies on **Amana Lily Lake** if you can catch them in bloom.

Numerous restaurants throughout the colonies serve huge portions of heavy food family-style. One of the best deals is the **Colony Inn** in Main Amana (622-6270), which serves up hefty portions of delicious German and American food. Dinners ($10-12) and lunches ($7) are served with cottage cheese, bread, diced ham, sauerkraut, fruit salad and mashed potatoes. Breakfast ($6) is an all-you-can-eat orgy of fruit salad, huge pancakes, fried eggs, thick sausage patties, bacon, and a bowl piled high with hash browns. (Open Mon.-Sat. 7:30am-10:30pm, Sun. 11am-8pm.) Middle Amana's **Hahn's Hearth Oven Bakery** (622-3439) sells the scrumptious products of the colonies' only functional open-hearth oven. (Open April-Oct. Tues.-Sat. 7:30am to sell-out around 4:30pm; Nov.-Dec. and March Wed. and Sat. only.) Sample the Iowa tradition of rhubarb wine at one of the several wineries scattered through the colonies, mostly in Amana.

Most lodging options consist of pricey but personal B&Bs such as **Lucille's Bett und Breakfast** (668-1185), **Loy's Bed and Breakfast** (624-7787) and the **Rettig House Bed and Breakfast** (622-3386). The **Dusk to Dawn Bed and Breakfast** (622-3029) in Middle Amana offers beautiful rooms, a lovely garden with a hot tub, and a great breakfast ($40). Camp at the **Amana Community Park** in Middle Amana (622-3732, sites $2.50 per vehicle, $3.50 with electricity and water, no showers) or at the new **Amana Colonies RV Park** (622-6262), a grassy field right across from the visitors center. (Sites $8, $2 extra each for electricity and water.)

The Amana Colonies lie 10 mi. north of I-80, clustered around the intersection of U.S. 6, Rte. 220 and U.S. 151. From Iowa City, take U.S. 6 west to U.S. 151; from Des Moines, take exit 220 off I-80 east to U.S. 6 and U.S. 151. There is no public transportation to the Colonies. The **Amana Colonies Visitors Center** just west of Amana on Rte. 220 (622-6262), shows promotional films and sometimes runs car caravan tours (2½-3 hr., $7; open Mon.-Wed. 9am-5pm, Thurs.-Sat. 9am-10pm, Sun. 10am-5pm).

Throughout the colonies look for the *Visitors Guide*; it has maps and detailed listings including hours for all establishments, and most info is up to date.

Amana's **ZIP code** is 52203; the **area code** is 319.

Cedar Rapids

The second largest city in Iowa follows the lead of Des Moines with its tidy downtown, excellent museums, relaxed pace, and success in agriculture-related industries. The Czech ethnic flavor which adds spice to this Iowan corndog, however, is all Cedar Rapids' own.

From 1870 to 1910, thousands of Czech immigrants settled in Cedar Rapids. Take bus #7 to 16th Ave. and C St. to visit the **Czech Village,** on 16th Ave. between 1st St. and C St. S.W., where the meat markets and harness shop have a charming Old-World feeling. At the end of the block Czech out the **Czech Museum and Library,** 10 16th Ave. S.W. (362-8500), which houses the largest collection of traditional costumes outside now-dissolved Czechoslovakia. (Open Tues.-Sat. 9:30am-4pm; Dec.-Jan. Sat. 9:30am-4pm. $2.50, ages 8-13 $1.)

Downtown Cedar Rapids is filled with moderately priced restaurants and delis, many of which cater to the lunchbreak market and close early. For fries with everything, try **Fries, BBQ and Grill,** 305 3rd Ave. S.E., (383-3743). Sandwiches and burgers are $3 to $6 (all with fries), BBQ dinners are $6 to $14. (Open Mon.-Sat. 10am-9pm.) In the Czech Village, try the *houskas* (braided raisin bread) or *kolace* (fruit-filled sweet rolls) at family-owned **Sykora's Bakery,** 73 16th Ave. S.W. (364-5271). (Open daily 6am-5pm.) Try more substantial Czech meals at **Konecny's,** 72 16th Ave. S.W. (364-9492), a local favorite. Sandwiches cost $2 to $3, goulash $1.25; fortunate travelers may catch the sausage & sauerkraut special for $3.75. (Open daily 6-10am and 11am-2pm.)

There are plenty of budget motels on 16th Ave. S.W. The **Shady Acres Motel,** 1791 16th Ave. (362-3111), is a row of cottage-like, spotlessly clean rooms near a beautiful wooded area. Rooms have A/C, showers and TV, but no phone. (Singles $20. Doubles $24. Take bus #10 to the K-Mart 5 blocks away.) The **Red Cedar Campground** (398-5190) in the Seminole Valley Park has primitive and electric sites on shady riverbanks ($5).

Cedar Rapids lies at the junction of I-380 and U.S. 30 and 151. The Amana Colonies are 19 mi. southwest. The **Greyhound** station, 145 Transit Way S.E. (364-4167), sends buses to: Des Moines (3 per day, 3 hr., $10.50 Mon.-Thurs., $14 Fri.-Sun.) and Chicago (3 per day, 6½ hr., $27 Mon.-Thurs., $37 Fri.-Sun.). Get around town in **Easyride** buses. (Buses run daily 5:30am-5:30pm; fare 50¢, seniors 25¢, students 30¢, transfers 10¢, reduced fare with receipts from local restaurants.) All routes stop at the **Ground Transportation Center,** 200 4th Ave. S.E. (398-5335), across from the Greyhound station. For taxis, try **Yellow Cab** (365-1444).

The **Cedar Rapids Area Convention and Visitors Bureau,** 119 1st Ave. S.E. (398-5009), has lots of info and helpful brochures. (Open Mon.-Fri. 8am-5pm, Sat. 9am-4pm). Or call the **Visitor Info Line** (398-9660).

The **post office** is at 615 6th Ave. S.E. (399-2911; open Mon.-Fri. 8:30am-5pm, Sat. 9am-noon). Cedar Rapids' **ZIP code** is 52401; the **area code** is 319.

Des Moines

French explorers originally named the Des Moines river the "Rivière des Moingouenas," for a local Native American tribe, but then shortened the name to "Rivière des Moings." Because of its identical pronunciation (mwan), later French settlers called their river and city by a name much more familiar to them: Des Moines (of the monks). Today, Des Moines shows neither Native American nor monastic influence, but rather the imprint of the agricultural state that spawned it. The price of soybeans are as hotly discussed here as stock prices are in New York. The World Pork Expo is a red letter event on the Iowan calendar and the city goes hog-wild for the Iowa State Fair every

August. If Iowa's capital city is a meat market, it's a very cosmopolitan one; it's the third largest insurance center in the world, after London and Hartford. Des Moines also boasts a world-class art museum and hosts events even more highbrow than appearances by humorist/folksinger Dan Hunter (author of *Let's Keep Des Moines a Private Joke*).

Practical Information

Emergency: 911.

Des Moines Convention and Visitors Bureau, 2 Ruan Center, Suite 222 (near the Kaleidoscope and Locust Malls downtown; 286-4960 or 800-451-2625). Open Mon.-Fri. 8:30am-5pm.

Des Moines International Airport: Fleur Dr. at Army Post Rd. (256-5857), about 5 mi. southwest of downtown; take #8 Havens bus.

Greyhound: 1107 Keosauqua Way (243-5211), at 12th St. just northwest of downtown. To: Kansas City (2 per day; 4 hr., $43); St. Louis (3 per day, 10½ hr., $98); Chicago (3 per day, 7-10 hr., $54). Open 24 hrs.

Public Transport: Metropolitan Transit Authority (MTA), 1100 MTA Lane (283-8100), just south of the 9th St. viaduct. Open Mon.-Fri. 8pm-5pm. Pick up maps at the MTA office or at any Dahl's market. Routes converge at 6th and Walnut St. Buses operate Mon.-Fri. 6:20am-6:15pm, Sat. 6:45am-5:50pm. Fare 75¢, transfers 5¢.

Taxi: Capitol Cab, (282-8111). **Yellow Cab,** (243-1111). $1.40 base rate, $1.20 per additional mi. Airport to downtown $8-9.

Car Rental: Budget (287-2612), at the airport. $41 first day, $36 per day thereafter, 100 free mi. per day, 25¢ per additional mi. Open Sun.-Fri. 6am-11:30pm, Sat. 6am-10pm. Must be 21 with major credit card. Under 25 add $5.

Help Lines: Crisis Intervention, 244-1000. **Gay/Lesbian Resource Center,** Information line 277-1454. Open Mon.-Thurs. 4-10pm, Sun. 4-8pm.

Post Office: 1165 2nd Ave. (283-7500), just north of I-235, downtown. Open Mon.-Fri. 8:30am-5:30pm. **ZIP code:** 50318.

Area Code: 515.

Des Moines idles on the northwest side of the confluence of I-35 and I-80. Numbered streets run north-south, named streets east-west. Numbering begins at the **Des Moines River** and increases east or west, starting at **South Union** where the river twists east. **Grand Avenue** divides addresses north-south along the numbered streets. Other east-west thoroughfares are **Locust Street, Park Avenue, Douglas Avenue,** University Avenue, and **Hickman Road.**

Accommodations and Camping

Finding cheap accommodations in Des Moines is usually no problem, though you should make reservations for visits in March (high school sports tournament season) and in August, when the State Fair comes to town. Several cheap motels cluster around I-80 and Merle Hay Rd., five mi. northwest of downtown. Take bus #4 ("Urbandale") or #6 ("West 9th") from downtown.

Econo Lodge, 5626 Douglas Ave. (278-1601), across from Merle Hay Mall. Unaesthetic neighborhood. Bus stop in front. Large, newly furnished rooms with cable TV, free coffee, juice, rolls and newspaper. Spa and sauna available. Reservations recommended on weekends. Singles $36. Doubles $40.

Royal Motel, 3718 Douglas Ave. (274-0459), 1 mi. from Merle Hay Mall. Take bus #6. Eleven clean, comfortable, cottage-like rooms. Singles $27. Doubles $32. $35 for 3.

YMCA, 101 Locust St. (288-2424), at 1st St. downtown on the west bank of the river. Small rooms, convenient downtown location. Lounge, laundry, athletic facilities, including pool. Men only. Key deposit $5. Singles $19.50, $61 per week.

YWCA, 717 Grand Ave. (244-8961), across from the Marriott Hotel downtown. In a fairly safe area. Women only. Clean dorm-style rooms with access to lounge, kitchen, and laundry. Pool Mon. and Wed. evenings, Sat. afternoons. All rooms shared; its main purpose is to provide social services and emergency shelter. $8 per day, $44 per week.

Iowa State Fairgrounds Campgrounds, E. 30th St. at Grand Ave. (262-3111; open mid-May-mid Oct.). At fairtime, enter from Dean St. Take bus #1 or 2 to the Grand Ave. gate. 2000 (yes, *2000*) sites with water and electricity; at fairtime, 2500 additional primitive sites are squeezed in. No fires allowed. $8 per vehicle; fee collected in the morning.

Walnut Woods State Park, S.W. 52 Ave. (285-4502), 4 mi. south of the city on Rte. 5. Secluded campground with horse and hiking trails nearby; not accessible by public transportation. Floods occasionally; if the front gate is locked, it's for a good reason. Primitive sites $5, with electricity $7.

Food

Cheap, clean fast-food places are located on the lower level of the **Locust Mall** downtown on 8th and Locust St. (244-1005). **Kaleidoscope Skywalk** (244-3205), just east of the Locust Hall, at 6th and Walnut St. in the Hub Tower, also has quick eats. Both food courts close at 5:30pm; sup here early. You'll think that you saw it on **Mulberry Street,** but in reality **Court Avenue** (the continuation of Mulberry), two blocks south of Locust around 3rd St., has reasonable Mexican and Italian restaurants in a renovated warehouse. A popular **farmers market** (286-4987) peddles its produce at 4th and Court Ave. every Saturday from 7am to 1pm.

Spaghetti Works, 310 Court Ave. (243-2195). Old-fashioned interior with fire truck for salad bar. Watch for the 50-ft. green, red and blue sea serpent writhing and churning on the wall. Large portions. Spaghetti dinners with salad and garlic bread $3.75-6, lunch versions $3-4. Open daily 11am-2pm and 5-10pm.

A Taste of Thailand, 215 E. Walnut St. (243-9521), east of downtown. Authentic Thai food in American setting, and seventy-one zillion different kinds of beer. Dinners around $7. Mon.-Sat. 11am-2pm and 5-9pm.

Juke Box Saturday Night, 206-208 3rd St. (284-0901). Hot spot for fun and drink. Decorative '57 Chevy motif. Aid your digestion by participating in the frequent hula-hoop, twist and jitterbug contests. Drinks average $2.50. Cocktails Mon.-Fri. 4:30-7pm. Open daily 4:30pm-2am.

Sights

The green (copper) and gold (gold!) domed **state capitol** (281-5591), on E. 9th St. across the river and up Grand Ave., displays Midwesternness at its most self-serious, with solemn paintings glorifying farm equipment and more kinds of marble than a geologist would care to identify. (Tours hourly Mon.-Fri. 9:15am-3:15pm, subject to cancellation when school groups pass through.) Take bus #5 "E. 6th and 9th St.," #1 "Fairgrounds," #2, 4 or 7. Further downhill collects the **Iowa State Historical Museum and Archives,** at Pennsylvania and Grand Ave. (281-5111), a beautiful building with three floors exhibiting Iowa's natural, industrial and social history, including an exhibit describing the subtle pros and cons (ecologically speaking) of cloth vs. disposable diapers. (Open Tues.-Sat. 9am-4:30pm, Sun. noon-4:30pm. Free. Take any bus that goes to the capitol.) Also vaguely related to Iowan government is the grandiose Victorian mansion **Terrace Hill,** 2800 Grand Ave. (281-3604), built in 1869 and currently the gubernatorial mansion. (Tours Feb.-Dec. Tues.-Sat. 10am-1:30pm, Sun. 1-4:30pm every 30 min. Tickets $2, kids 50¢.) The geodesic greenhouse dome of the **Botanical Center,** 909 E. River Dr. (238-4148), next to I-235 and not far from the capitol, encompasses a wide array of exotic flora, and is more comfortable temperature-wise during the cooler months. (Mon.-Thurs. 10am-6pm, Fri. 10am-9pm, Sat.-Sun. 10am-5pm. Admission $1.50 seniors, 25¢ ages 6-18, under 6 free.)

Most cultural sights cluster west of downtown. The **Des Moines Art Center,** 4700 Grand Ave. (277-4405), is acclaimed for its wing of stark white porcelain tile designed by I.M. Pei. Impressive modern works include George Segal's *To all Gates,* with which every wayworn traveler can identify; also Impressionist and other collections. American artists predominate. (Open Tues.-Wed. and Fri.-Sat. 11am-5pm, Thurs. 11am-9pm,

Sun. noon-5pm. $2, seniors and students $1. Free all day Thurs. and until 1pm Fri.-Wed. Take "West Des Moines" bus #1.) Flapper-era cosmetics manufacturer Carl Weeks realized his aristocratic aspirations after he had salvaged enough ceilings, staircases and artifacts from English Tudor mansions to complete **Salisbury House,** 4025 Tonawanda Dr. (279-9711; public tours Mon.-Fri. at 2pm, additional tour June-July 10am or by appointment; $3, kids $1.) **Living History Farms,** 2600 N.W. 111 St., Urbandale (278-2400) at I-35 and Hickman Rd., features reenacted farm life from different periods of Iowa history, as well as a Crop Center where visitors can learn about soil erosion. (May 1-Oct. 25, Mon.-Sat. 9am-5pm, Sun. 11am-6pm).

One way to see Iowa which will convince you once and for all that it isn't completely flat is to participate in **RAGBRAI,** the Des Moines ***Register*'s Annual Great Bicycle Ride Across Iowa.** Contact the *Register* (515-284-8000) for more info.

The **Iowa State Fair,** one of the largest in the nation, captivates Des Moines for 10 days during the middle of August. Come see prize cows (and crafts and cakes and ears of corn) and enjoy rides and shows and more soybean recipes than you ever knew existed. For information contact the 24-hr. info line at the Administration Building, Iowa State Fair Grounds, Des Moines 50306 (262-3111).

Near Des Moines

The **Des Moines Metro Opera** (961-6221) produces three full-scale operas every summer in the Blank Performing Arts Center at Simpson college in **Indianola,** 12 mi. south of Des Moines on U.S. 69. Tickets $22-47. The nearby **National Balloon Museum,** 1601 N. Jefferson, (961-3714) is rumored to derive its hot air from the operatic performers, and sometimes holds balloon regattas. (Mon.-Fri. 9am-noon and 1-4pm, Sat. 10am-4pm, Sun. 1-4pm.) **Pella,** 25 mi. west of Des Moines on Rte. 163, hosts Iowa's most famous festival, **Tulip Time** (628-4311), the second weekend in May. At other times the town maintains a tangible Dutch presence and several excellent Dutch bakeries.

Iowa's "other university town," and home of the Iowa State University of Science and Technology, **Ames** lies 30 mi. north of Des Moines along I-35 (take **Greyhound** bus from Des Moines; 2 per day; $6.40). Stay downtown in the dark-wood paneled **Lincoln Lodge,** 202 E. Lincoln Way (232-4263; singles $24, doubles $28). For Midwestern flavor, stop in at **Hickory Park,** 121 S. 16th St. (232-8940), for sandwiches and burgers ($2-5) or barbecue ($4-12). (Open Sun.-Thurs. 11am-9pm, Fri.-Sat. 11am-10pm.) Or try the "Herbivore," "Prairie," or "Buffalo" pizza (10 in. pie $6.50) at **The Great Plains Sauce and Dough Company,** 129 Main St. (232-4263). (Open Mon.-Fri. 11am-2pm, Mon.-Thurs. 4pm-midnight, Fri. 4:30pm-1am, Sat. 11am-1am, Sun. noon-11pm).

Life in Ames—as its nickname suggests—centers around the ISU campus. Check out the new **Molecular Biology Building,** which features audacious satirical art such as the clown-like "G-Gnomes", by Andrew Leicester. The first weekend in May, the entire campus is taken over by **VEISHA** (VEE-sha), the largest student-run festival in the nation, whose name is an acronym for the seven original colleges of Iowa State University. There are displays, a Saturday-morning parade, and much general revelry. (Call 294-1026 for info.)

Just north of Ames on I-35 the automobile traveler will encounter a sign advertising a **Scenic View,** built in anticipation of a view which never materialized. The lookout provides a clear (if not very scenic) view of a broad valley full of fields, pastures, and the occasional tree, not all that different from most of central Iowa. The roadside stop dates from a plan to dam the **Skunk River** (which flows along the eastern edge of Ames, and which doesn't smell that bad) and create Lake Ames. This plan was stopped by environmentalists concerned for Skunk ecology, but not before some people had bought stilted lakefront houses at lakefront prices and the Scenic View had been constructed.

Ames' **area code** is 515. The **ZIP code** is 50010.

Kansas

If America is a body politic, then Kansas, located in its geographic center, is its left ventricle. Kansas has a heart of golden grain, pumping out a half a gigabushel of wheat each year—more than any other state in the nation. Highway signs in the Sunflower State remind passers-by that, "every Kansas farmer feeds 75 people—and *you*." In heart-rending Civil War times, Kansas was actually given the moniker "Bleeding Kansas" after abolitionists and pro-slavery forces did battle here. Later, temperance advocate Carry Nation used her hatchet in a heartfelt rampage to bring down saloons.

Today, Kansas has considerably fewer palpitations. The state fair, held in Hutchinson during the second and third weeks of September, is more delightful than dizzying: sure, it has heart-stopping ferris wheels and roller-coaster rides but it also features heart-warming quilting contests, bake-offs and hog auctions. Kansas is home to the heart of the world—the Garden of Eden (in Lucas, on the corner of 2nd and Kansas, just off I-70 on Rte. 181), a meticulous re-creation planted in 1907, nearly 20 billion years after the original.

Practical Information

Capital: Topeka.

Visitor Information: Department of Economic Development, 400 W. 8th, 5th floor, Topeka 66603 (296-2009). **Kansas Park and Resources Authority,** 900 Jackson Ave., suite #502N, Topeka 66612 (296-2281).

Time Zone: Central (1 hr. behind Eastern). **Postal Abbreviation:** KS

Sales Tax: 6.25%.

Dodge City

Legends haunt Dodge City, the epitome of cowtowns. At the turn of the century, gunfighters, prostitutes, federal marshals, and other lawless types used the town as a stopover along the Santa Fe trail. Chaos reigned. At one time **Front Street,** the main drag, had one saloon for every 50 citizens. Since most, according to legend, died "with their boots on" in drunken brawls and heated gunfights, their makeshift cemetery became known as Boot Hill. In actuality, fewer people were shot or stabbed in Dodge City during heyday than are killed in acts of violence every week in New York City. Seems the town had more newspapers (at one time, five) than knock-down, drag-out violence; the storytelling competition did much to magnify a few intoxicated incidents.

For a taste of life during Dodge City's wild heyday, saunter on down to the **Boot Hill Village Museum,** a block-long complex replicating the Boot Hill cemetery and Front St. as they looked in the 1870s. Among the buildings is the **Boot Hill Museum** (227-8188), which displays a 1903 Santa Fe locomotive and the restored and furnished **Hardesty House,** a rancher's Gothic Revival home. On summer evenings the **Long Branch Saloon** holds a variety show at 7:30pm, preceded by a campy gunfight. (Open daily 8am-8pm; Sept.-May Mon.-Sat. 9am-5pm, Sun. 1-5pm. Show $3.75. Museum $4.50, seniors and kids $4, families $13; off-season $3, $1, and $13, respectively.)

Diagonally across from Boot Hill is the **Wax Museum,** at 603 5th Ave. (225-7311; open Mon.-Sat. 8:30am-8:30pm, Sun. 1-5pm; $2 adults, $1.25 ages 6-13, free 6 and under). Walk up 5th Ave. to Spruce, and head east; at 4th Ave. and Spruce, on the lawn outside the Chamber of Commerce (227-3119), sits the town memorial sculpture garden, carved by the late dentist O.H. Simpson. Monuments include "Lest We Forget," an enormous, mournful-eyed cow bust honoring the seven million longhorns sent to market from Dodge City during the 1870s and 80s, early evidence that animal rights activism began in the West. Dr. Simpson also sculpted pairs of stone cowboy boots placed toes-up in mock burial form, but most were stolen.

On the corner of 2nd Ave. and Spruce sits what was once Carnegie Library, complete with stained-glass windows and a reading patio out back, and is now the **Carnegie Art Center** (225-6388; open Tues.-Fri. noon-5pm, Sat. 11am-3pm). Walk down 2nd Ave. to Front St. to check out "El Capitan," yet another enormous longhorn cattle statue commemorating the 1870s cattle drives, this one cast in bronze by Jasper d'Ambrosi. The trail of quirky, bovine sympathy art continues at the **Hyplains Dressed Beef Packing Plant** (227-7135), south of Wyatt Earp Blvd., on Trail St. between 2nd and 3rd Ave. Appropriately named Kansas environmental artist Stan Herd painted a wraparound mural depicting Kansas livestock history, from the first horse introduced by Spaniards in the 1500s to the last wild buffalo circa 1890.

Today, longhorn cattle lumber through town only during **Dodge City Days** at the end of July, when the city recalls its past with a rodeo, a beauty pageant, a pancake-eating contest, turtle racing, and a huge festival. Call 225-2244 for rodeo information, or write or call the Dodge City Convention and Visitors Dept. for general info (P.O. Box 1474, Dodge City 67801 (225-8186).

Where's the BEEF?!? Try **Muddy Waters,** 2303 W. Wyatt Earp Blvd. (225-9493), for a ½-lb. burger ($3), or the less blatantly carnivorous giant tostada ($5.75), in a very bar-like atmosphere ($1 draws). (Open Mon.-Sat. 11am-2am. Food served till 11pm.) **Ozzie's** at North and "A" Ave. (227-8255), fries most everything including chicken dinners ($5.25). Take Central north from downtown, and go west on the bypass. (Open Tues.-Fri. 4pm-2am, Sat.-Sun. noon-2am.)

A warning to the car-less: except for the **Western Inn Motel** (225-1381) across from the bus station (rooms $30-40), most motels tucker out about four mi. west along Wyatt Earp Blvd., a busy highway that becomes U.S. 50 outside of town. The **Holiday Motel,** a.k.a. **The Wagonmaster,** 2100 W. Wyatt Earp (227-2169), rounds up cheap, clean, big rooms with HBO, and a nice pool. (Singles $32. Doubles $36. 10% discount for seniors.) The **Econolodge,** 1610 W. Wyatt Earp (225-0231), has lots o' features at moderate rates: free HBO, indoor pool, jacuzzi, sauna, gameroom, dry-cleaning service, laundry facilities, and shuttle service. (Singles $30. Doubles $36.) There are two adequate **campgrounds** close to town: the highly developed **Gunsmoke Campground,** W. Hwy. 50 (227-8247), three mi. west of Front St., which has special breakfasts, chuckwagon dinners, and a pool (tent sites $10 for 2 people, RV sites with hookup $13; each additional person $1.50), and the **Water Sports Campground Recreation,** 500 Cherry St. (225-9003), on a small lake 10 blocks south from Front St. on 2nd Ave. (2-person sites with full hookup $12, A/C $2).

Dodge City barebacks 150 mi. west of Wichita near U.S. 54, north of the Oklahoma panhandle, and 310 mi. east of Colorado Springs on U.S. 50. The center of town and hub of all business activity is, and historically has been, the railway. **Amtrak** (800-872-7245) runs out of the **Santa Fe Station,** a century-old national historic landmark at Central and Wyatt Earp Blvd. Contact a travel agent, since no tickets are sold at the station. One train daily heads eastbound, and one westbound, to Kansas City (7 hr., $82), La Junta, CO (2 hr., $56), and Lamy, NM (8 hr., $89). **Greyhound,** 2425 E. Central. (221-9547), serves Dodge once daily from Wichita ($20.25). (Open Mon.-Sat. 8am-5pm.) There is no public transportation in town. The **post office** meters at 700 Central (227-8618; open Mon.-Fri. 8:15am-4:30pm, Sat. 11am-1pm). Dodge City's **ZIP code** is 67801; the **area code** is 316.

Topeka

Like **Lawrence,** its neighbor 25 mi. to the east, Topeka was founded in 1854 by abolitionist settlers willing to use their votes and bodies to keep Kansas a free state. When Kansas was admitted to the Union as a free state on January 29, 1861, Topeka became its capital with only 200 residents.

Today the **state capitol building** (296-3966), bounded by 10th and 8th Ave. and Jackson and Harrison St., boasts a beautiful dome and murals of John Brown and the settling of the plains. Free tours let you ride the Willy Wonka-esque old glass elevator to the dome. (Tours Mon.-Fri. 9-11am and 1-3pm on the hr., Sat. every 2 hrs. 9am-3pm.) Try the cheap sandwiches downstairs. (Building open daily 8am-6pm.)

One block east of the state capitol, **Pore Richard's Café,** 705 S. Kansas Ave. (233-4276), struggles as the only late-night place in town. Besides burgers and delicious shakes, Dick serves breakfast all day in booths with personal jukeboxes. (Open Mon.-Thurs. 11am-2am, Fri.-Sat. 11am-3am.) Every 10 minutes from 11am to 1:30pm, a 10¢ trolley runs along Kansas Ave.

For a place to stay, take the West 6th bus from downtown to **Motel 6,** 3846 SW Topeka Blvd. (267-1222, 505-891-6161 for reservations; singles $24, doubles $31, $6 per additional person.)

The **Amtrak** station is at 5th and Holiday (357-5362 or 800-872-7245). One train goes west, one east daily to Lawrence (½ hr., $10), Kansas City (1½ hr., $18), and St. Louis (6 hr., $56). **Greyhound** is at 200 S.E. 3rd (233-2301) at Quincy, a few blocks northeast of the capitol. Buses motor to: Kansas City (6 per day, 1½ hr.; $16.50); Lawrence (6 per day, 35 min., $5.65); Denver (3 per day, 11 hr., $18.50); Wichita (4 per day, 3 hr.; $24.50); and Dodge City (1 per day, 8 hr., $44). (Open Mon.-Fri. 7am-10pm.) **Topeka Transit** provides local bus transportation (354-9571; Mon.-Fri. 6am-6pm, fare 75¢, seniors 35¢). Topeka's General Delivery **ZIP code** is 66601; the **area code** is 913.

Wichita

When Coronado came to Wichita's present-day site in 1541 in search of the mythical gold-laden city Quivira, he was so disappointed that he had his guide strangled for misleading him. By the 1870s, however, settlers had taken a permanent shine to Wichita and proudly gave their city such endearing (and alliterative) names as the "Peerless Princess of the Plains." Today one of the largest aircraft manufacturing centers in the U.S., Wichita lures tourists to its worthiness with wellsprings of festivals, attractions, and rumors of gold.

In the **Old Cowtown Historic Village Museum,** 1871 Sim Park Dr. (264-8894), 30 buildings take you through the rough and tumble cattle days of the 1870s. (Open Mon.-Sat. 10am-5pm, Sun. noon-5pm. $3, ages 6-12 $2, under 6 free; AAA discount.) In the **Wichita-Sedgwick County Historical Museum,** 204 S. Main (265-9314), posh antique furniture and heirlooms sit beside historical oddities, such as the hatchet used by crusading prohibitionist Carrie Nation when she demolished the bar of the Carey Hotel. (Open Tues.-Fri. 11am-4pm, Sat.-Sun. 1-5pm. $2, ages 6-16 $1, under 6 free.) Further from the town's center is the **Mid-American Indian Center and Museum,** 650 N. Seneca (262-5221), which showcases traditional and modern works by Native American artists. The late Blackbear Bosin's monolithic sculpture, *Keeper of the Plains,* stands guard over the grounds. (Open Tues.-Sat. 10am-5pm, Sun. 1-5pm. $1.75, ages 6-12 $1, under 6 free.)

The **Wichita State University** campus, at N. Hillside and 17th St., contains an outdoor sculpture collection comprised of 53 works, including pieces by Rodin, Moore, Nevilson, and Hepworth. Get free sculpture maps at the **Edwin A. Ulrich Museum of Art** (689-3664), also on campus. One side of this striking building contains a gigantic glass mosaic mural by Joan Miró. (Open late-Aug. to mid-June Wed. 9:30am-8pm, Thurs.-Fri. 9:30am-5pm, Sat.-Sun. 1-5pm. Free.) Take "East 17th" or "East 13th" bus from Century II.

In Wichita they spell their meals "m-e-a-t;" if you have only one slab of meat in Wichita, go to **Doc's Steakhouse,** 1515 N. Broadway (264-4735), where the most expensive entrée is the 17-oz. T-bone at $8.75. (Open Mon.-Thurs. 11:30am-9:30pm, Fri. 11:30am-11pm, Sat. 4pm-11pm.) The **Old Mill Tasty Shop,** 604 E. Douglas (264-6500), recalls a long-lost Wichita with its old-time soda fountain and spitoons. Sandwiches cost $3.25-5.75, and ice cream treats are 65¢-$3.50. (Open Mon.-Fri. 11am-3pm, Sat. 8am-3pm.) **Dyne Quik,** 1202 N. Broadway (267-5821), is homey and awfurrs catfish with salad, potatoes, bread, and coffee ($3.50) or a 21-piece shrimp dinner ($4.75). (Open Mon.-Sat. 5:30am-2:30pm.)

Wichita presents a Quivira of cheap hotels. Try South Broadway, but be wary of the neighborhood. The **Mark 8 Inn,** 1130 N. Broadway (265-4679), is right on the mark, with clean rooms, huge pillows, in-room movies, and fridges. (Singles $25. Doubles $28.) Closer to downtown and the bus station is the **Royal Lodge,** 320 E. Kellogg (263-8877), with a clean interior and cable TV. (Singles $25, with king-size bed $30. Doubles $34.) Several other cheap, palatable motels line East Kellogg five to eight mi. from downtown. The **Wichita KOA Kampground,** 15520 Maple Ave. (722-1154), has private showers, a laundromat, gameroom, pool, and convenience store. (Office open daily 8am-noon, and 3-9:30pm. Tent sites $12.50 per 2 people, with hookup $16. Adults $3, ages 3-17 $2.)

Wichita sits on I-35, 170 mi. north of Oklahoma City and about 200 mi. southwest of Kansas City. **Main Street** is the major north-south thoroughfare. **Douglas Avenue** lies between numbered east-west streets to the north and named east-west streets to the south. The **Convention and Visitors Bureau,** on 100 S. Main St. (265-2800), has a "Quarterly Calendar" of local events. (Open Mon.-Fri. 8am-5pm.) The **Wichita Fun Phone** (262-7474) lists current festivals, activities, sports, and entertainment.

The closest **Amtrak** station is in Newton, 25 mi. north of Wichita, at 5th and Main St. (283-7533; tickets sold Wed.-Fri. 7:30am-4pm, station open 11:30pm-7am). One train chugs daily to Kansas City (4 hr., $49) and Dodge City (2½ hr., $40). **Greyhound,** 312 S. Broadway (265-7711), two blocks east of Main St. and two blocks south of Douglas Ave., provides bus service to the Newton Amtrak station for $12; schedules vary. Buses also serve: Kansas City (4 per day, 4 hr., $24 Mon.-Thurs., $29 Fri.-Sun.); Denver (1 per day, 12 hr., $75); Dodge City (1 per day, 3 hr., $24); and Dallas (3 per day, 9 hr., $75). (Open daily 3:30am-1:30am.) The **post office** is at 7117 W. Harry (946-4511), at Airport Rd. (Open daily 4-7am, 8:30am-noon, and 2:30-7pm.) Wichita's **ZIP code** is 67276; the **area code** is 316.

Missouri

Missouri's license plates read, rather cryptically, "Show Me State." This is *not* a state that encourages exhibitionists; rather, it is the home of gruff, incredulous farmers who don't believe a damn thing until they see it with their own two eyes. Appropriately enough, it was the birthplace of the quintessential skeptic Mark Twain.

Missouri's troubled entry into the Union and its Civil War-era status as border state were harbingers of a future of perpetual ambiguity. Missouri is smack dab in the middle of the contiguous United States, but a stranger to every region. Ohioans think Missouri is too far west to be Midwest, while Kansans feel it is too far east to be Great Plains. In Minneapolis, at the head of the Mississippi River, they think Missouri, with its river boat jazz and French settlements, is somehow connected to New Orleans; in New Orleans, if they think of Missouri at all it's as that stodgy place up north near Chicago. Missouri resists all attempts at pigeonholing because none applies.

And so it goes—to those in the know, Missouri is a patchwork quilt of a state. In the north, near Iowa, amber waves of grain undulate. Along the Mississippi, towering bluffs inscribed with Native American pictographs evoke western canyonlands. In central-eastern Missouri descendants of German immigrants have created an ersatz Rhine with vintages to match. Towards the Mississippi spelunk the world's largest limestone caves—made famous by erstwhile explorers Tom Sawyer and Becky Thatcher. Further south, rippling into Arkansas, are the ancient and underrated Ozarks. To be sure, Missouri has MO exciting stuff than you'd ever realize. And besides, Missouri loves company.

Practical Information

Capital: Jefferson City.

Missouri Division of Tourism, Department MT-90, P.O. Box 1055, Jefferson City 65102 (751-4133; 869-7110 in St. Louis). **Missouri Department of Natural Resources,** 205 Jefferson St., Jefferson City 65102 (751-3443 or 800-334-6946).

Time Zone: Central (1 hr. behind Eastern). **Postal Abbreviation:** MO

Sales Tax: 4.225%.

Kansas City

Established as a trading post in 1821 by a French fur trader, Kansas City had already become a rollicking river city long before Kansas and Missouri drew state lines. As a result, two Kansas Cities exist: one in Kansas, and one in Missouri. Although no one notices this distinction until tax time, Kansas City, KS is a bit more residential while Kansas City, MO bubbles with nightlife. Kansas City, at the confluence of the two mightiest rivers in the United States, proudly evinces river culture. Clods of frontier history float down from the Great Plains on the Missouri River while hot streams of jazz flow upstream from New Orleans on the Mississippi. A 1920s haven for gamblers, prostitutes, stray cowpokes, and musicians, today's Kansas City remains a tough town. Practical values, hard-nosed business and meat 'n' potatoes continue to shape the concerns of its citizens, and help to create some glaring economic divisions.

Practical Information

Emergency: 911.

Visitors Center, 1100 Main St. #2550 (221-5242 or 800-767-7700), in the City Center Square bldg. downtown. Pick up *A Visitor's Guide to Kansas City.* Open Mon.-Fri. 8:30am-4:30pm. Also at 4010 Blue Ridge Cutoff (861-8800), just off I-70 next to the stadium. **Daily Visitors Information** (691-3800) is a recorded listing of theater activity in the downtown area. **Jazz Hotline,** 931-2888. **Ticketmaster,** 931-3330.

Kansas City International Airport: (243-5237) 18 mi. northwest of Kansas City off I-29.The **KCI Shuttle** (243-5000 or 800-243-6383) has shuttles departing every 30-45 min. that service downtown, Westport, Overland Park, Mission, and Lenexa ($10-15 one-way).

Amtrak: 2200 Main St. (421-3622 or 800-872-7245), directly across from Crown Center. Check bus schedules for correct number bus. To: St. Louis (2 per day, 5½ hr., $40-60) and Chicago (2 per day, 9 hr., $74). Open 24 hrs.

Greyhound: 1101 N. Troost (698-0080 or 221-2885). To: St. Louis (5 per day, 4-5 hr., $30, $25 with 3-day advance); Chicago (7 per day, 11 hr., $56, $48 with 3-day advance); Des Moines (4 per day, 5 hr., $43, $37 with 3-day advance); Omaha (4 per day, 3-4 hr., $44, $37 with 3-day advance); and Lawrence (9 per day, 1 hr., $11, $9.50 with 3-day advance). Open daily 5:30am-12:30am.

Kansas City Area Transportation Authority (Metro): 1350 E. 17th St. (221-0660; open Mon.-Fri. 6am-6pm), at Brooklyn. Excellent downtown coverage. Fare 90¢, plus 10¢ for crossing zones. Free transfers; free return receipt available downtown. Pick up maps and schedules at headquarters, airport gate #62, or buses.

Taxi: Checker Cab, 474-8294. **Yellow Cab,** 471-5000. Fare about $25-30 from airport to downtown; determine fare before trip.

Car Rental: Thrifty Car Rental, 2001 Baltimore (842-8550 or 800-367-2277), 1 block west of 20th and Main St; also at the KCI airport (464-5670). Compact Mon.-Thurs. $30 per day, 150 mi. free, 29¢ per mi. thereafter. Drivers under 25 add $3. Must be 21 with major credit card.

Post Office: 315 W. Pershing Rd. (374-9275), near the train station. Open Mon.-Fri. 8am-6:30pm, Sat. 8am-12:30pm. General Delivery open Mon.-Fri. 8am-5:30pm. **ZIP code:** 64108.

Area Codes: 816 in Missouri, 913 in Kansas.

Quite ironically, almost every sight worth visiting in KC lies south of the Missouri River on the Missouri side of town; KCMO, as it is known, is organized like a grid with numbered streets running east-west and named streets running north-south. **Main Street,** the central artery, divides the city east-west. The KC metropolitan area sprawls across two states, and travel may take a while, particularly without a car. Most sights are *not* located downtown. All listings are for Kansas City, MO, unless otherwise indicated.

Accommodations

Kansas City is a big convention center and can usually accommodate everyone who needs a room. The least expensive lodgings are near the interstate highways, especially those leading from Kansas City to Independence, MO. Downtown, most hotels are either expensive, uninhabitable, or unsafe—sometimes all three. Most on the Kansas side require a car. The Westport area is lively, but prices can be steep.

Travelodge, 3240 Broadway (531-9250), just north of Westport. Bright rooms with phones and cable TV in a lively area near several jazz spots. Worth the extra cost. Security guard at night. Singles $39. Doubles $45.

White Haven Motor Lodge, 8039 Metcalf (649-8200 or 800-752-2892), 4 mi. west of state line, on the Kansas side. Amusing, 1950s-style family motor lodge with cold-war-era prices to match. Wrought-iron fenced-in pool, restaurant, HBO. Free coffee, 5¢ doughnuts in the mornings. Singles $32. Doubles $39. Triples $41. Quads $43.

American Inn (299-2999) at I-70 and 78th St., about 1 mi. from Stephensons' Old Apple Farm Restaurant. Quick service, clean rooms with phones, cable TV, pool, and lounge. No pets, no checks. (Singles from $25, doubles from $29.)

Food

Kansas City rustles up a herd of meaty, juicy barbecue restaurants that serve unusually tangy ribs. For fresh produce year-round, visit the **farmers market,** in the River Quay area, at 5th and Walnut St. Arrive in the morning, especially on Saturday.

Arthur Bryant's, 1727 Brooklyn St. at 17th (231-1123), about 1 mi. east of downtown. Take bus #71 ("Prospect") or #8. A local legend. The meat and sauce are superb, the servings more than generous. Barbecued beef sandwiches ($5.75) thick enough to stuff any living human. Open Mon.-Thurs. 10am-9:30pm, Fri.-Sat. 10am-10pm, Sun. 11am-8pm.

Strouds, 1015 E. 85th St., off Troost (333-2132). Sign proclaims "We choke our own chickens." Don't choke on the incredible fried chicken with cinnamon rolls, biscuits, and honey. Enormous dinners ($7-15) in a weathered wooden hut. Open Mon.-Thurs. 4-10pm, Fri. 11am-11pm, Sat. 2-11pm, Sun. 11am-10pm.

Stephenson's Old Apple Farm Restaurant, 16401 E. U.S. 40, several mi. from downtown (373-5345). The hickory-smoked specialties are worth the trip and the prices. The accompanying side dishes (fruit salad, apple fritters, corn relish) are as noteworthy as the entrées. ($6 lunch, $7-18 dinner, Sunday brunch $11, kids 6-10 $6.) Open Mon.-Fri. 11:30am-10pm, Sat. 11:30am-11pm, Sun. 10am-9pm.

The Pumpernickel Deli, 319 E. 11th St., 4 blocks from downtown (421-5766). Friendly, busy place with simple, no-frills décor. Often sells cheap, fresh veggies outside. Sandwiches $1-2.50, jumbo hoagie tops the menu ($2.65). Sunrise special of bagels, ham, egg, and cheese $1.50. Open Mon.-Fri. 7am-5:30pm.

Gates & Sons Bar-B-Q, 1411 Swope Pkwy. (921-0409). Best ribs in town. Barbecue beef sandwiches ($4) and titanic short-end ribs ($8). Open Sun.-Wed. 11am-midnight, Thurs.-Sat. 11am-2am. Also at 12th and Brooklyn St. (483-3880).

Sights

Located at 45th Terrace and Rockhill, 3 blocks east of Country Club Plaza, the **Nelson-Atkins Museum of Fine Art** (751-1278 or 561-4000) contains one of the best East Asian art collections worldwide. A Chinese temple room, Japanese screens, and a huge bronze Buddha are particularly impressive. A Henry Moore sculpture garden and interior display, plus a small, intriguing collection of 19th- and 20th-century art (including a room devoted to Thomas Hart Benton's works), make this museum a must-see. (Open Tues.-Thurs. 10am-4pm, Fri. 10am-9pm, Sat. 10am-5pm, Sun. 1-5pm. $4, students and kids 6-18 $1.)

A few blocks to the west, the **Country Club Plaza** (known as "the plaza") is the oldest and perhaps most picturesque U.S. shopping center. Built in 1922 by architect J.C. Nichols, the plaza is modeled after buildings in Seville, Spain, replete with fountains, sculptures, hand-painted tiles, and the reliefs of grinning gargoyles. A country club plaza bus runs downtown until 11pm. Just south of the plaza is the luxurious **Mission Hill** district.

Two mi. north of the plaza is **Crown Center,** 2450 Grand Ave. (274-8444), at Pershing. The headquarters of Hallmark Cards, it houses a maze of restaurants and shops alongside a hotel with a five-story indoor waterfall. Inside, the **Hallmark Visitors Center** (274-5672) joyfully illustrates the process and history of greeting card production. (Reservations required for groups of 10 or more. Open Mon.-Fri. 9am-5pm, Sat. 9:30am-4:30pm. Free.) Also in the Crown Center are the **Coterie Children's Theatre** (474-6552) and the **Ice Terrace** (274-8411), KC's only public ice skating rink. (Take bus #40, 56, or 57, or any trolley from downtown; $3.) The Crown Center has free **Concerts in the Park** every Friday evening at 8pm during the summer. Performers have included the Guess Who and the Grateful Dead. Run through a huge fountain designed for exactly that purpose; you can't have more fun on a hot summer night with your clothes on (uh, you *do* have to keep your clothes on). To the west stands the **Liberty Memorial,** 100 W. 26th St. (221-1918), a tribute to those who died in World War I. Pay to ride the elevator to the top for a fantastic view, then visit the free museum. (Open Wed.-Sun. 9:30am-4:30pm. $2, under 12 free.)

Entertainment

Formerly the crossroads of the Santa Fe, Oregon, and California Trails, and an outfitting post for travelers to the West, the restored **Westport** area (931-3586), located near Broadway and Westport Rd. a ½-mi. north of the plaza, is now packed only by nightspots. **Blayney's,** 415 Westport Rd. (561-3747), in a small basement, hosts live bands six nights a week, offering reggae, rock, or jazz. (Open Mon.-Sat. 8pm-3am. Max. cover $2-3 on weekends.)

In the 20s, Kansas City was a jazz hot spot. Count Basie and his "Kansas City Sound" reigned at the River City bars, while Charlie "Yardbird" Parker, spread his wings and soared in the open environment. Stop by the **Grand Emporium,** 3832 Main St. (531-7557), voted best live jazz club in KC for the last six years and recently voted the #1 blues night club in the U.S., to hear live jazz on Friday and Saturday; weekdays feature rock, blues, and reggae bands. (Open Mon.-Sat. 9am-3am.) Find sultry ambience at **Milton's Jazz,** 805 W. 39th St. (753-9476). The late Miltie once sponsored Basie, Parker, and other jazz greats. (Live music Mon.-Sat. 3pm-1:30am. Cover $2.) **City Lights,** 7425 Broadway (444-6969), may not be as nostalgic as Miltie's, but it is dependable and fun with live bands Tuesday to Saturday 9pm to 1am. (Open Mon.-Sat. 4pm-1:30am. Cover $4.) **Kiki's Bon-Ton Maison,** 1515 Westport Rd. (931-9417), features KC's best in-house soul band, the Bon-Ton Soul Accordion Band on Wednesdays 9-11pm and Saturdays at 10:30pm. Kiki's serves up cajun food with zydeco and hosts the annual Crawfish Festival (complete with a "Crawfish Look-Alike Contest") the last weekend in May. (Open Mon.-Thurs. 11am-10pm, Fri. 11am-midnight, Sat. 11am-11pm. Food until 10pm.)

Sports fans will be bowled over by the massive **Harry S. Truman Sports Complex;** even Howard Cosell could not muster enough inscrutable superlatives to describe **Arrowhead Stadium,** 1 Arrowhead Dr. (924-3333), home of the Chiefs football team (924-9400). Next door, the water-fountained, artificial turf-clad wonder of **Royals Stadium,** 1 Royal Way (921-8000), houses the Royals baseball team. The stadium express bus runs from downtown on game days.

St. Louis

Ever since Pierre Laclede founded the first trading post west of the Mississippi, St. Louis has been a second city—second to New Orleans in steamboat commerce, to Chicago in train traffic, to Detroit in automobile production, and to Kansas City in jazz. Yet, if you plan to spend time in the Great Plains, St. Louis should be your first choice. St. Louis is a vibrant cultural center and a pleasure to tour, thanks in large part to renewed interest in preserving historic housing and developing and beautifying neighborhoods.

An important transportation hub when it opened in 1894, St. Louis Union Station encompasses a National Historic Landmark as well as a festive shopping center in the downtown district. Flora and fauna grace the Soulard Historic District in South St. Louis, only recently rescued from urban blight. Farther west lie the charming Central West End and the attractions of Forest Park, the largest urban park in the country. At the Riverfront and Laclede's Landing, riverboats rest along the banks of the muddy and mighty Mississippi. And above it all arches the steel rainbow of the Gateway Arch (like one-half of the McDonald's golden arches or one-fourth of a tetrarch), the manifest symbol of America's destiny of westward conquest, designed by Finnish architect Eero Saarinen. Incidentally, Mark Twain penned his arch humor in Hannibal, north of the city along the river; Samuel Langhorne Clemens even found himself residing here for a time.

Practical Information

Emergency: 911.

Visitor Information: Convention and Visitors Bureau, 10 S. Broadway #1000 (421-1023 or 800-247-9791), at Market St. Open daily 8:30am-5pm. **St. Louis Visitors Center,** 308 Washington Dr. (241-1764). Pick up the *Quickguide,* maps, brochures and friendly advice. Open daily 10:30am-4:30pm. Other visitors information locations at the airport and at Kiener Plaza. (Mon.-Fri. 10am-2:30pm).

Travelers Aid: 809 N. Broadway (241-5820). Open Mon.-Fri. 8:30am-5pm, Sat. 10am-2pm.

Lambert St. Louis International Airport: (426-8000), 12 mi. northwest of the city on I-70. Served by Bi-State "Natural Bridge" bus #4 (runs hourly 5:50am-5:45pm from 9th and Locust St.) and Greyhound (see below).

Amtrak: 550 S. 16th St. (331-3300 or 800-872-7245), at Market St. downtown. To: Chicago ($38); Dallas ($127); New Orleans ($100); Denver ($191); and Kansas City, MO ($38). Open daily 6am-midnight. Additional station in Kirkwood (966-6475), at Argonne Dr. and Kirkwood Rd.

Greyhound: 13th and Cass (231-7800). Bus #30 "Cass" takes less than 10 min. from downtown; a 20-min. walk. To: Kansas City, MO ($38); Chicago (Mon.-Thurs. $25, Fri.-Sun. $31); Indianapolis (Mon.-Thurs. $20, Fri.-Sun. $23); Oklahoma City ($97, $52 with reservations); Memphis ($52/$37.). Airport service. Open 24 hrs. Additional station in Kirkwood at 11001 Manchester (965-4444). Open Mon.-Fri. 8am-midnight.

Public Transport: Bi-State, (231-2345 in St. Louis; 271-2345 in E. St. Louis). Extensive daily service, but buses infrequent during off-peak hours. Reduced service on weekends and holidays. Maps, schedules available at the Bi-State Development Agency, 707 N. 1st St., on Laclede's Landing, or at the reference desk of the public library's main branch, 13th and Olive St. Fare $1, transfers 20¢; seniors, people with disabilities and ages 5-12 50¢, transfers 10¢. Free in the downtown area (bordered by I-40, Broadway, Jefferson, and Cole). The **Levee Line to and** around downtown, offers free service to points of interest between Union Station and the Riverfront. A rail system is under construction, so many lines have been rerouted; ask drivers where to catch a specific route.

Taxi: Yellow Cab, 991-1200. **County Cab,** 991-5300.

Help Lines: Rape Crisis, 531-2003. Open 24 hrs. **Gay and Lesbian Hotline,** 367-0084.

Post Office: 1720 Market St. (436-4458). Open Mon.-Fri. 7am-5pm. Open 24 hrs. **ZIP code:** 63166.

Area Code: 314 (in Missouri); 618 (in Illinois)

The city of St. Louis hugs the Mississippi River in a small crescent. University City, home of Washington University, lies west of downtown. Other suburbs (the "county") fan out in all directions. I-44, I-55, I-64, and I-70 meet in St. Louis. **U.S. 40/I-64** is the main drag running east-west through the entire metropolitan area. Downtown, **Market Street** divides the city north-south. Numbered streets begin at and run parallel to the river, with **1st Street** closest to the river. The city's most dangerous sections include East St. Louis (across the river in Illinois), the Near South Side and some of the North Side.

Accommodations

The motels and universities that offer budget accommodations are generally located several miles from downtown: try **Lindbergh Drive** near the airport or the area north of the junction of I-70 and I-270 in **Bridgeton,** five mi. beyond the airport. Buses cover a broad area but can be slow and cumbersome.

Huckleberry Finn Youth Hostel (HI/AYH), 1904-1906 S. 12th St. (241-0076), 2 blocks north of Russell St. in South St. Louis. From downtown, take bus #73 ("Carondelet"), or walk south on Broadway to Russell and over (30-40 min.); don't walk on Tucker, as the hostel is just past an unsafe neighborhood. Dorm-style accommodations, 4-8 beds per room. Open doors; guard your belongings. Bring your own linen. Office open 7-10am and 6-10pm. $11, nonmembers $14.

Washington University: Eliot or Shepley Halls (889-5050 or 935-4637) at the corner of Big Bend Blvd. and Forsyth. Buses #91 and 93 take 40 min. from downtown. Dorm rooms with A/C, free local calls, laundry, and near Mallinckrodt student center cafeterias. Singles $16. Doubles $28. Reservations recommended. Open May 25-Aug. 20.

Lewis and Clark Hostel (HI/AYH), 1500 S. 5th in St. Charles, MO (946-1000 ext. 119); 6 mi. from Lambert Airport and 1 mi. from Greyhound. Will arrange pick-up from airport and downtown St. Louis. Drivers should take I-70 about 15 mi. west of St. Louis to the 5th St. exit. The hostel is located in Noah's Ark Motor Inn. Look for the big boat. Near the head of the Katy Trail. 24-hr. check-in. $10, nonmembers $13.

Food

Although noted for its German and French heritage, St. Louis's best culinary creations emerge from Italian and American traditions. The young and affluent gravitate to **Laclede's Landing** and the **Central West End.** Downtown on the riverfront, Laclede's Landing (241-5875) has experienced an amazing transformation from industrial wasteland to popular nightspot; the area is closed to minors from midnight to 6am. Bars and dance clubs in this area occupy restored 19th-century buildings; most have no cover charge. Walk north along the river from the Gateway Arch or towards the river along Washington St. The Central West End caters to a slightly older crowd. Just north of Lindell Blvd., for five blocks along Euclid Ave., a slew of restaurants has won the urban professional seal of approval. Take bus #93 ("Lindell") from Broadway and Locust downtown.

Farther west, **Clayton** offers a pleasant setting for window-shopping and dining. Historic **South St. Louis** (the Italian "Hill") and the University City Loop (Delmar Blvd. west of Skinker) offer dozens of restaurants.

Blueberry Hill, 6504 Delmar (727-0880), near Washington University. *The* college hangout. Collection of record covers and antique toys festoons the premises. Plenty of options for the health-conscious. Find your thrill with sandwiches and specials $4-6. Open Mon.-Sat. 11am-2am, Sun. 11am-11pm. No minors after 3pm.

Charlie Gitto's Pasta House, 207 N. 6th St. (436-2828). Tangy Italian food. Hundreds of bottles of beer on the walls. Take one down. Pass it around. Pasta $4.50-10.25. Open 11am-11pm.

The Sunshine Inn, 8½ S. Euclid (367-1413). Vegetarian and other nourishing, imaginative fare, all served with wonderful, chewy, sunflower-seed-and-raisin-filled rolls. Sandwiches $4-6.50, entrées $4-9. Open Tues.-Fri. 11:30am-10pm, Sat. 8am-10pm, Sun. 10am-2:30pm, 5-9pm.

The Old Spaghetti Factory, 727 N. 1st St. (621-0276), on Laclede's laundry. A link in the chain, sure, but here it's an institution. Menus feature the history of the building and the funky artifacts contained therein. "Pasketti dinners" $4.25-6. Open Mon.-Thurs. 5-10pm, Fri. 5-11pm, Sat. 4-11pm, Sun. 3:30-10pm.

Ted Drewe's Frozen Custard, 6726 Chippewa, and 4224 S. Grand (352-7376). The place for the summertime St. Louis experience. Stand in line to order chocolate-chip banana concrete ice cream. Toppings blended, as in a concrete mixer, but the ice cream stays hard enough to stay in an overturned cup. Open March-Dec. Sun.-Thurs. 11am-midnight, Fri.-Sat. 11am-1am.

Sights

It is impossible to miss the **Gateway Arch** (425-4465), on Memorial Dr. by the Mississippi River, even if you try. The arch—the nation's tallest monument at 630 ft.—has become so much the symbol of St. Louis that its image pervades the city. Give in and take advantage of your only chance to ride an elevator whose path is an inverted catenary curve, the shape assumed by a chain hanging freely between two points. (8am-10pm, winter 9am-6pm; $2.50, kids 3-12 50¢). Spend your one- to two-hour wait at the **Museum of Westward Expansion,** under the arch. Don't miss the *Monument to the Dream,* a half-hour documentary chronicling the sculpture's construction. (17 showings per day in summer, $1. Museum hours same as arch's.)

Sightseers can also view St. Louis from the water with **Gateway Riverboat Cruises** (621-4040), leaving from docks on the river right in front of the arch. (Daily summer departures every 45 min. beginning at 10:15am; spring and fall every 1½ hrs. beginning 11am. Cruise $7, kids $3.50.)

North of the arch, on the riverfront, is historic **Laclede's Landing,** the birthplace of St. Louis in 1764. The cobblestone streets of this district are bordered by restaurants, bars and two museums. The **Wax Museum,** 720 N. Second St. (241-1155), features heroes and anti-heroes of all kinds; strangely enough, the recording of ex-oilman George Bush's voice is not consigned to the Chamber of Horrors. ($3.50, ages 6-12 $2.50. Open Mon.-Sat. 10am-10pm, Sun. 11am-8pm.) The **National Video Game and Coin-Op Museum,** 801 N. Second St. (621-2900), charts the development of video games and pinball machines; you'll feel really old when you see Space Invaders, Pac-Man, and Donkey Kong treated as historic artifacts. Admission includes four game tokens. (Open Mon.-Sat. 10am-10pm, Sun. noon-8pm. $3, ages 12 and under $2.) There are other unique museums in St. Louis. **The Dog Museum,** 1721 S. Mason Rd. (821-DOGS or 821-3647), between Manchester and Clayton, depicts the history of the canine. (Open Mon.-Sat. 9am-5pm, Sun. 1-4pm. $3, seniors $1.50, kids $1). The **Dental Health Theatre,** 727 N. 1st St. (241-7391), fills the gaping cavity of American dental museums. (Open Mon.-Fri. 9am-4pm. Free. Call ahead for reservations). Stroll down the lane at the **National Bowling Hall of Fame and Museum,** 111 Stadium Plaza (231-6340), across from Busch Stadium. (Open Mon.-Sat. 9am-7pm, Sun. noon-7pm; Sept.-May Mon.-Sat. 9am-5pm, Sun. noon-5pm. $3, seniors $2, kids under 13 $1.50. Free after 4pm and on Sun.) The **Mercantile Money Museum,** Mercantile Tower, 7th and Washington (425-8199), caters to numismatists and the business school crowd. (Open daily 9am-4pm. Admission, oddly enough, is free.) Travelers should whiz through the **National Museum of Transport,** 3015 Barrett Station Rd. (965-7998), full of trains, planes, ferries and more, which nonetheless seems to remain in one place. (Open daily 9am-5pm, $3, seniors and kids 5-12 $1.50.)

Walk south of downtown down Broadway or 7th St. or take bus #73 ("Carondelet") to **South St. Louis.** The city proclaimed this area a historic district in the early 70s; it once housed German and East European immigrants, great numbers of whom worked in the breweries. Young couples and families are revitalizing South St. Louis but have not displaced an older generation of immigrants. The **Soulard Farmers Market,** 1601 S. 7th St. (622-4180), claims a 200-plus-year tradition, but the produce is *still* fresh. (Open daily 7am-6:30pm.) The end of 12th St. in the historic district features the **Anheuser-Busch Brewery,** 1127 Pestalozzi St. (577-2626), at 13th and Lynch. Take bus #40 ("Broadway") or 73 from downtown. Watch the beer-making process from barley to bottling and meet the famous Clydesdale horses. The 70-minute tour stops in the hospitality room, where guests can sample each beer Anheuser-Busch produces. Don't get too excited about the free brew, bucko--you'll get booted after 15 min. (Summer tours Mon.-Sat. 10am-5pm; off-season 9am-4pm. Pick up tickets at the office. Free.) Between downtown and south St. Louis, the **Eugene Field House and Toy Museum,** 634 S. Broadway (421-4689), blows its own horn. Eugene Field, the author of "Little Boy Blue" and "Wynken, Blynken, and Nod," apparently wrote erotic poems as well, in order to refute claims that he was merely a "children's poet." Eugene's childhood home was saved from conversion into apartments by serving as a house of ill repute in the 1920s before it was preserved as a museum with period furnishings and an abundance of toys, only a few of them Eugene's. (Open Tues.-Sat. 10am-4pm, Sun. noon-4pm. $2, kids 50¢.)

Also in South St. Louis, built on grounds left by botanist Henry Shaw, thrive the internationally acclaimed **Missouri Botanical Gardens,** 4344 Shaw (577-5100), north of Tower Grove Park. From downtown, take bus #99 ("Lafayette") from 4th and Locust St. going west, or take I-44 by car; get off at Shaw and Tower Grove. The gardens display plants and flowers from all over the globe; the Japanese Garden truly soothes the weary budget traveler. (Open Memorial Day-Labor Day daily 9am-8pm; off-season 9am-5pm. $2, seniors $1, under 12 free. Free Sat. mornings and all day Wed.) The second largest of its kind in the U.S., **Laumeier Sculpture Park,** 12580 Rott Rd. (821-1209), cultivates over 50 contemporary works on 96 acres. The park also hosts free outdoor summer jazz concerts on Sunday evenings. (Open daily 8am to ½ hr. past sunset. Gallery open Tues.-Sat. 10am-5pm, Sun. noon-5pm. Free.) The **Magic House,** 516 S. Kirkwood Rd. (822-8900), exposes kids to scientific principles under the aegis of fun. (Call for hours. Free.) About one mi. west of downtown, visit magnificent old **Union Station,** easily accessible by the free and frequent Levee Line bus. At 18th and Market, this modern shopping mall retains the structure of the old railroad station and is a National Historical Landmark.

West of downtown, and worth as much of your time as the rest of St. Louis, is **Forest Park,** home of the 1904 World's Fair and St. Louis Exposition. Take bus #93 ("Lindell") from downtown. The park contains two museums, a zoo, a planetarium, a 12,000-seat amphitheater, a grand canal, countless picnic areas, pathways, and flying golf balls. The **St. Louis Science Center-Forest Park** (289-4444) offers hands-on exhibits and a planetarium projector. (Planetarium $3, kids $2; Discovery Room 50¢.) Marlin Perkins, formerly rugged (now dead) host of the TV show *Wild Kingdom,* turned the **St. Louis Zoo** (781-0900; at the southern edge of the park) into a world-class institution. At the "Living World" exhibit, view computer-generated images of future human evolutionary stages. (Open daily 9am-5pm. Free.) The **Missouri Historical Society** (361-1424), at the corner of Lindell and DeBaliviere on the north side of the park, is filled with U.S. memorabilia including an exhibit devoted to Charles Lindbergh's flight across the Atlantic in the *Spirit of St. Louis.* (Open Tues.-Sun. 9:30am-4:45pm. Free.) Atop **Art Hill,** just to the southwest, stands an equestrian statue of France's Louis IX, the city's namesake and the only Louis of France to achieve sainthood. The king beckons with his raised sword toward the **St. Louis Art Museum** (721-0067), which contains masterpieces of Asian, Renaissance and Impressionist art. (Open Tues. 1:30-8:30pm, Wed.-Sun. 10am-5pm. Free except for special exhibits.) From Forest Park, head north a few blocks to gawk at the residential sections of Central West End, where every house is actually a turn-of-the-century version of a French château or Tudor mansion or baronial estate, all plunked down next to each other.

Near Forest Park, **Washington University** livens things up with a vibrant campus and interesting students. The **Washington University Gallery of Art,** in Steinberg Hall at the corner of Skinker and Lindell (889-5490), has a diverse collection including a Pollack, a couple of Warhols and Conrad Atkinson's *Critical Mats*, which proffers an inviting welcome to "the seductiveness of the end of the world." (Open Mon.-Fri. 10am-5pm, Sat.-Sun. 1-5pm; free.) The **Cathedral of St. Louis,** 4431 Lindell Ave. (533-2824), just north of Forest Park at Newstead, strangely combines Romanesque, Byzantine, Gothic and baroque styles. Gold-flecked mosaics depict episodes from 19th-century church history in Missouri. (Free tour Sun. at 1pm. Open daily 7am-6pm. Take "Lindell" bus #93 from downtown.)

Entertainment

In the early 1900s, showboats carrying ragtime and brassy Dixieland jazz regularly traveled to and from Chicago and New Orleans. St. Louis, a natural stopover, fell head over heels in love with the music and, happily, has never recovered. For purists, the annual **National Ragtime Festival** takes place on a riverboat in mid-June (tickets $19.50). Those with thin wallets can try sitting by the boat and listening to the music from the pavement. Float down the Mississippi while listening to jazz on the *President* (621-4040), a five-story paddleboat. (2½-hr. cruises Wed.-Sun. 10:30am and 7pm, Tues. at 10:30am. $10, kids $5; rates higher at night. Open June-Oct.) For other seasonal events, check *St. Louis Magazine,* published annually, or the comprehensive calendar of events put out by the Convention and Visitors Bureau (see Practical Information).

For year-round musical entertainment, head to Laclede's Landing. Bars and restaurants featuring jazz, blues and reggae fill "the landing." Try **Kennedy's Second Street Co.,** 612 N. Second St. (421-3655), for good, cheap food (burgers $3.25-4.75) and varied bands (shows for all ages 8pm; the 11:15 show is for 21-plus only). (Open Mon.-Sat. 11am-3am, Sun. noon-3am.) Or take your pick of one of the dozens of clubs and bars lining the narrow streets. **The Metropol,** 118 Morgan (621-1160), features funky neo-classical décor and late-night dancing. (Open Mon.-Sat. 9pm-3am.)

Founded in 1880, the **St. Louis Symphony Orchestra** is one of the finest in the country. **Powell Hall,** 718 N. Grand (534-1700), which houses the 101-member orchestra, is acoustically and visually magnificent. (Performances Sept.-May Thurs. 8pm, Fri.-Sat. 8:30pm, Sun. 3pm and 7:30pm. Box office open Mon.-Sat. 9am-5pm and before performances. Tickets $9-40. Take bus #97 to Grand Ave.)

St. Louis offers theater-goers many choices. The outdoor **Municipal Opera** (534-1111), the "Muny," performs hit musicals in Forest Park during the summer. Tickets cost $5-32. Arrive around 6:15pm for 8:15pm shows, and bring a picnic (no bottles). Hot dogs and beer are also sold at moderate prices. Other regular productions are staged by the **St. Louis Black Repertory,** 2240 St. Louis Ave. (534-3807), and the **Repertory Theatre of St. Louis,** 130 Edgar Rd. (968-4925). Call for current show information. Tour the **Fabulous Fox Theatre** (534-1678; $2.50, under 12 $1.50; Tues., Thurs., and Sat. at 10:30am; call for reservations), or pay a little more for Broadway shows, classic films, Las Vegas, country, and rock stars. Renovated and reopened in 1982, the Fox was originally a 1930s movie palace.

St. Louis Cardinals baseball games (421-3060; April-Oct.; tickets $4-12) swing at Busch Stadium, downtown. **Blues** hockey games (781-5300) scat at the Arena. (Sept.-May; tickets $10-21.)

Nebraska

Nebraska has seen more movement than just the sway of its abundant grain fields. From 1840-66, more than 350,000 settlers followed the Platte River along the Mormon and Oregon Trails from Omaha through Scottsbluff. In 1863, the westward flow was given steam power when the Union Pacific Railroad Co.—now based in Omaha—broke ground and lay its tracks here. Although the state was initially characterized by transience rather than settlement (Nebraska achieved statehood in 1867, but the capitol in Lincoln was not constructed until the next century), it has given birth to a number of famous movers and shakers, including Buffalo Bill, Henry Fonda, Gerald Ford, and Malcolm X—to say nothing of ex-late-nite-talk-show-maven-native-son Johnny Carson.

Practical Information

Capital: Lincoln.

Tourist Information: Nebraska Department of Economic Development, P.O. Box 94666, Lincoln 68509 (471-3796). **Nebraska Game and Parks Commission,** 2200 N. 33rd St., Lincoln 68503 (471-0641). Permits for campgrounds and park areas ($10). Open Mon.-Fri. 8am-5pm.

Time Zone: Central (1 hr. behind Eastern) and Mountain (2 hr. behind Eastern). **Postal Abbreviation:** NE

Sales Tax: 5-6.5%.

Omaha

Omaha, just across the Missouri River from Council Bluffs, Iowa, is an old packing house and railroad town. Flanked on the west by corn and cow country, to the south by apple orchards, and tangled with Union Pacific Railroad lines, Omaha is the crossroads for many of America's calories. Omaha's eclectic and impressive architecture exudes the pride that residents take in their heterogeneous city. During the course of history, countless scores of immigrants from Bohemia, freed African slaves, and more recently, Mexican migrant workers have come to Omaha for jobs in the packing houses. Evidence of these ethnic communities appears most prominently on grocery shelves, where corn tortillas with Spanish labels sit alongside bags of Vic's popcorn and Czechoslovakian liver dumplings. Ironically, tracing Native American history in Omaha proves most elusive; its influence surfaces most tangibly in the region's place names.

Practical Information

Emergency: 911.

Nebraska/Omaha Tourist Information Center, 1212 Deer Park Blvd. (595-3990), at I-80 and 13th St. (U.S. 75). Take bus #6 from downtown. Open April-Oct. daily 9am-5pm. **Greater Omaha Convention and Visitors Bureau,** 1819 Farnam St. #1200 (444-4660 and 800-332-1819), in the Omaha-Douglas Civic Center. City bus schedules in the basement, behind the cafeteria area. Open daily 8:30am-4:30pm. **Mayor's Commission on the Handicapped,** 444-5021. Information on transportation, access, and services. Open Mon.-Fri. 8am-4:30pm. Call for appointment. **Events Hotline,** 444-6800.

Amtrak: 1003 S. 9th St. (342-1501 or 800-872-7245). One train per day to: Chicago (9 hr., $97), Denver (9 hr., $100), and Salt Lake City (24 hr., $172). Open Mon.-Fri. 10:30pm-3:30pm, Sat.-Sun. 10:30pm-8am.

Greyhound: 1601 Jackson (341-1900). To: Lincoln (6 per day, 1 hr., $12); Kansas City (4 per day, 4½ hr., $44); Chicago (6 per day, 12 hr., $81); and Denver (4 per day, 10½-12 hr., $89). Open 24 hr.

Public Transport: Metro Area Transit (MAT), 2222 Cuming St. (341-0800). Schedules available at the Park Fair Mall, 16th and Douglas near the Greyhound station. Open Mon.-Fri. 8am-4:30pm. **Buses** have thorough service for downtown, Creighton University area, North Omaha, and 24th St., but don't reach as far as M street and 107th, where several budget hotels are located. Fare 90¢, transfers 5¢. Bus numbers change occasionally; check the schedule.

Taxi: Happy Cab, 339-0110. $1.50 first mile, $1 each additional mi. Fare to airport $7.

Car Rental: Cheepers Rent-a-Car, 7700 L St. (331-8586). $17 per day with 50 free mi., 15¢ per additional mi. Must be 21 and have a major credit card. Open Mon.-Fri. 7:30am-6pm, Sat. 9am-3pm.

Help Lines: Crisis Line, Inc., 341-9111 or 341-9112. **Rape Crisis,** 345-7273. **Gay/Lesbian Crisis Line** (in Lincoln), 475-5710.

Time Zone: Central (1 hr. behind Eastern).

Post Office: 1124 Pacific St. (348-2895). Open Mon.-Fri. 7:30am-5pm, Sat. 7:30am-noon. **ZIP code:** 68108.

Area Code: 402.

Numbered north-south streets begin at the river; named roads run east-west. **Dodge Street** divides the city north-south. When night falls, it's probably makes good sense to avoid 24th St., andto stay within a stone's throw of Creighton University at 25th and California.

Accommodations and Camping

Many budget motels are off the L or 84th St. exits from I-80, 6½ mi. southwest of downtown. Buses #11, 21, and 55 service the area. An 11% Nebraska hotel tax creates higher prices.

Excel Inn, 2211 Douglas St. (345-9565 or 800-386-4400). Ideal for the car-less. Feels safe, despite the slightly frayed neighborhood. (Singles $25, with cable TV and VCR $29; doubles and singles with kitchenettes $34 and up. Stay 4 nights and 3 more nights are free!)

Budgetel Inn, 10760 M St. (592-5200) near 108th. Bus #55 will get you only as close as 108th and Q. Free continental breakfast delivered to room, which already has coffee and coffeemaker. Singles $38, with kingsize bed $44. Doubles $44.

Motel 6, 10708 M St. (331-3161), adjacent to the Budgetel Inn. Outdoor pool, phone, basic brown-bed-and-Bible rooms. Singles $24. Doubles $30.

Super 8, 7111 Spring St. (390-0700 or 800-800-8000), near 72nd and Grover St. Non-smoking rooms, HBO, free local calls, no pets. Restaurants nearby. Singles $33. Doubles $38. Also at 108th and L St. (339-2250).

Bellevue Campground, at Haworth Park (291-3379), on the Missouri River 10 mi. from downtown at Rte. 370. Take the infrequent bus ("Bellevue") from 17th and Dodge to Mission and Franklin, and walk down Mission. Showers, toilets, shelters. Sites with hookup $9. Free water. Open daily 6am-10pm; quiet stragglers sometimes enter after hours.

Food and Nightlife

Once a warehouse district, the **Old Market,** on Howard St. between 10th and 13th, has been converted into cobblestone streets, quaint shops, restaurants, and bars. **Coyote's Bar and Grill,** 1217 Howard St. (345-2047), howls with fun Tex-Mex appetizers like the "holy avocado" ($4), salads, chili, and staggeringly large burgers ($4-5) in hip wood and bevelled glass surroundings. (Open Mon.-Thurs. 11am-11pm, Fri.-Sat. 11am-midnight, Sun. noon-11pm.) **Trini's,** 1020 Howard St. (346-8400), marinates, sautées, and serves profoundly authentic Mexican and vegetarian food in an elegant, candlelit cavern. Try the "big Juan." Dinner $2.50-7. (Open Mon.-Thurs. 11:30am-10pm, Fri.-Sat. 11:30am-11pm, Sun. 1-8pm.) The **Spaghetti Works,** 1100 Howard St. (422-0770), offers spaghetti and unlimited salad bar. (Open for lunch Mon.-Thurs. 11am-2pm, Fri. 11am-3pm, Sat.-Sun. 11:30am-3pm. Dinner Sun.-Thurs. 5-10pm, Fri.-Sat. 5-11pm. Lunch from $3, dinner from $4. No reservations.) The **Bohemian Café,** 1406 S. 13th St. (342-9838), in South Omaha's old Slavic neighborhood, sells meaty fare, accompanied by onions and potatoes, for under $6.50. (Open daily 11am-10pm.) **Joe Tess' Place,** 5424 S. 24th St., at U St. in South Omaha (731-7278; take bus from Farnam and 16th) is renowned for its fresh, fried carp and catfish served with thin-sliced potatoes and rye bread. Entrées $4-8. (Open Mon.-Thurs. 10:30am-10pm, Fri.-Sat. 10:30am-11pm, Sun. 11am-10pm.)

Omaha caters to several universities in the area, so punk and progressive folk all have found a niche. Check the window of the **Antiquarium Bookstore,** 1215 Harney, in the Old Market, for information on shows. For tickets, call Tix-Ticket Clearinghouse at 342-7107. **Sokol Hall,** at 13th and Martha (346-9802), headlines local and national punk and progressive rock bands on Thursdays. (Tickets around $5.) In the Old Market area, head to the **Howard St. Tavern,** 1112 Howard St. (341-0433). The local crowds and good music create a pleasant atmosphere. Live music downstairs ranges nightly from blues to reggae to alternative rock. (Open Mon.-Sat. 3pm-1am, Sun. 7pm-1am. Cover $2-3.50.) **Omaha's Magic Theater,** 1417 Farnam St. (346-1227; call Mon.-Fri. 9am-5:30pm), is devoted to the development of new American musicals. (Evening performances Fri.-Mon. Tickets $10, seniors, students and kids $5.) **The Max,** 1417 Jackson (346-4110), caters to gay men, has five bars, a disco dance floor, DJ, patio, and fountains. (Open daily 4pm-1am. Cover $2 on weekends.) Another gay bar, **The Run,** 1715 Leavenworth (449-8703), is popular for its "after hours" weekends from 1:30-4:30am, when $4 gets you enough coffee, soda, and music to last the night. (Otherwise open daily 2pm-1am. $4 cover.)

Sights

Omaha's **Joslyn Art Museum,** 2200 Dodge St. (342-3300), is a three-story art deco masterpiece with an exterior made of Georgian Pink marble and an interior of over 30 different marble types. It contains an excellent collection of less prominent 19th- and 20th-century European and American art. In the summer, they host "Jazz on the Green" each Thursday from 7 to 9pm. (Open Tues.-Sat. 10am-5pm, Sun. 1-5pm. $2, seniors and ages under 12 $1. Free Sat. 10am-noon.)

The **Western Heritage Museum,** 801 S. 10th St. (444-5071), has historic exhibits, but its main attraction is its architecture. Once the old **Union Pacific Railroad Station** in 1929, the museum glitters with kitsch. (Open May 27-Sept. 2 daily 10am-5pm; off-season Tues.-Sat. 10am-5pm, Sun. 1-5pm. $3, seniors and ages under 12 $2.50.) Housed in the historic Nebraska Telephone Building, the **Great Plains Black Museum,** 2213 Lake St. (345-2212), presents the history of African American migration to the Great Plains in photographs, musical instruments, documents, dolls, and quilts. Especially compelling are the portraits and biographies of the first African American women to settle in Nebraska, as well as the exhibit commemorating the life of Malcolm X, born Malcolm Little in Omaha in 1925. (Open Mon.-Fri. 9am-5pm. Donation $2. Take bus from 19th and Farnam, or from Dodge.)

The **Omaha Children's Museum,** 551 S. 18th St. (342-6164), features hands-on science and art exhibits. (Open June-Aug. Tues.-Sat. 10am-5pm, Sun. 1-5pm; Sept.-May Tues.-Fri. 2:30-5pm, Sat. 10am-5pm, Sun. 1-5pm.) The **Henry Doorly Zoo,** 3701 S. 10th St. (733-8400), at Deer Park Blvd., is home to white Siberian tigers, aquariums, and the largest aviary in North America. (Open April-Oct. Mon.-Fri. 9:30am-5pm, Sat.-Sun. 9:30am-6pm; in winter daily 9:30am-4pm, Mutual Education Building and aquarium only. $6, $4.50 seniors, kids 5-11 $3.)

Near Omaha: Lincoln

In 1867, soon after this fledgling city became the state's capital, settlers in the town of Lancaster renamed their outpost in honor of the recently-deceased President. This hospitable pioneer town is now the seat of the nation's only unicameral (one-house) state legislature. The "Tower on the Plains," the **Nebraska State Capitol Building,** 14th at K St. (471-2311), remarkable for its streamlined exterior and detailed interior, is an appropriate centerpiece for Lincoln, itself an oasis of learning, legislation, and culture on the prairie. Visible from nearly 20 mi. away, it soars far above the city and surrounding farmlands and maintains all the pomp and majesty of an art deco museum. Its floor, reminiscent of a Native American blanket in design, is an incredible mosaic of inlaid Belgian and Italian marble. Each pattern represents some facet of the land and peoples of Nebraska. Take the elevator to the 14th floor for a terrific view of the entire city. (Open daily 9am-5pm. Excellent tours on the hour. Free.)

There's not that much to do in Lincoln, and there aren't that many eateries, either, but there is one place that has it all for you, and is worth visiting. For roller-skating waitresses, foot-long chili cheese dogs ($4.25) and your ultimate diner experience, bop on into the **Rock 'n' Roll Runza** (474-2030) at 210 W. 14th St. (Open Mon.-Wed. 7am-11pm, Thurs.-Fri. 7am-12:30pm, Sat. 8am-12:30pm, Sun. 8am-10pm.) Lincoln has one hostel. The small, ministry-run **Cornerstone Hostel (HI/AYH),** 640 N. 16th St. (476-0355 or 476-0926), is located on the university's downtown campus. The two big rooms with couches, tables, and futons are single-sex. Bring a sleeping bag or blankets and pillow. Showers and full kitchen. Curfew 10pm. ($8 members, $10 nonmembers.) If you are looking to camp, you need a permit. They can be obtained at the Nebraska Game and Parks Commission in Lincoln (see NE Practical Information).

Emergency: 911. **Tourist Offices,** 1221 N St. #320 (476-6300). Open Mon.-Fri. 8am-4:45pm. Open late May-Sept. daily 9am-5pm. **League of Human Dignity,** 1701 P St. (471-7871). Advice and aid, including local transportation for disabled persons. Open Mon.-Fri. 8am-5pm. **Amtrak:** 201 N. 7th St. (476-1295 or 800-872-7245). To: Omaha (1 per day, 1 hr., $13) and Denver (1 per day, 7½ hr., $101). Open daily 7am-11pm. **Greyhound:** 940 P St. (474-1071), close to downtown and city campus. Buses run east-west to Omaha (7 per day, 1 hr., $12) and Chicago (6 per day, 10-12 hr., $81). Open Mon.-Fri. 7:30am-5:30pm, Sat. 8:30am-5:30pm, Sun. 9am-noon. **Post Office:** 700 R St. (473-1695). Open Mon.-Fri. 7:30am-5pm, Sat. 9am-noon. **ZIP code:** 68508. **Area Code:** 402.

O Street is the main east-west drag, splitting the town north-south. Alphabetized streets increase northwards.

North Dakota

Though a state (the 39th) since 1889, North Dakota and most of its windswept terrain remains a mystery to both foreign and domestic travelers. Those who do visit often pass like wildfire through the eastern prairie to the more sensational "badlands," the infertile, pock-marked buttes that dominate the western half of the state. Blessed solitude, however, is the reward for those who savor the tranquil expanses of farmland before moving on to a high time in tourist-filled western towns. But whether in the east or west of North Dakota, locals will extend an eager welcome. People here are about as sparse as snow in June (there are fewer than 10 per square mi.), but they are twice as amiable.

Practical Information

Capital: Bismarck.

Tourism Promotion Division, Liberty Memorial Bldg., Capitol Grounds, Bismarck 58505 (224-2525; 800-437-2077 outside ND). **Parks and Recreation Department,** 1424 W. Century Ave. #202, Bismarck 58502 (224-4887).

Time Zone: Central (1 hr. behind Eastern) and Mountain (2 hrs. behind Eastern). **Postal Abbreviation:** ND

Area Code: 701.

Sales tax: 5-6%.

Bismarck

Bismarck takes every opportunity to flout its 20-story art deco **State Capitol,** at 900 East Blvd. (224-2000). Built during the early 1930s art deco rage, the building showcases the very short history of flamboyant architecture in North Dakota. Walk across the wide green lawn in front of the capitol to reach the **North Dakota Heritage Center** (224-2666) and its sophisticated exhibits on the Plains tribes, buffalo, and the history of white settlement in the region. (Open Mon.-Fri. 8am-5pm, Sat. 9am-5pm, Sun. 11am-5pm. Free.)

Below **Mandan,** on the opposite bank of the Missouri, lies **Fort Lincoln**. General Custer's march towards his fatal encounter with Sitting Bull at Little Bighorn (see Little Big Horn National Monument, MT) began here. The fort is part of the worthwhile **Fort Lincoln State Park** (663-9571), which also features a reconstructed Mandan village on its original site, renovated army blockhouses, and a small collection of artifacts and memorabilia from Native Americans and early settlers. (Park open daily 9am-sunset; Sept.-May Mon.-Fri. 9am-sunset. Museum open daily 9am-9pm; Sept.-May Mon.-Fri. 9am-5pm. $3 vehicle admission fee.)

At the end of July, join lifetime fans and lifers at the **Annual North Dakota Prison Rodeo** (223-5986), held at the penitentiary east of Bismarck. In the first week of August, watch for the **Art Fair,** held on the Capitol Mall lawn. Call ahead (255-3285) for information on the **United Tribes Pow Wow,** held in mid-September, one of the largest gatherings of Native Americans in the nation; the festival includes dancing, singing, food, and crafts of many tribes. To find out more about local entertainment, drop by or call the new **Bismarck Civic Center,** at the terminus of Sweet Ave. E. (222-6487), for a schedule of events. The **Cross Ranch State Park and Nature Trail** has 150 archeological sites in its 575 acres along the Missouri River. Pick up the trail off Rte. 1806, 15 mi. north of Mandan ($3 per vehicle).

The **Highway Motel,** 6319 E. Main St. (223-0506), two mi. east on Rte. 10, rents rooms to local workers by the month but often has space for those staying only a night or two. (Singles $22. Doubles $26.) **Motel 6,** 2433 State St. (255-6878), right off I-94, offers clean, small rooms and a pool. (Singles $29. Doubles $35. Under 18 free.) Your best bet close to town is the **Bismarck Motor Hotel,** 2301 E. Main Ave. (223-2474). (Singles $21. Doubles $29.)

The **Hillcrest Campground** (255-4334), 1½ mi. out of town on E. Main St., provides showers and scenery from April to September. (Sites $9.) The sylvan **General Sibley Park** (222-1844), four mi. south of Bismarck on S. Washington St., merits a visit even if you don't stay the night. Those who do decide to stay should call ahead for reservations, and then set up camp in a glen of huge, shady trees on the banks of the Missouri River. The park has showers. (Sites $6, with full hookup $11.) **Fort Lincoln State Park** (663-9571), five mi. south of Mandan on Rte. 1806, has a quiet campground on the east bank of the Missouri. (Sites $10, with water and electricity $13. Daily pass to park and showers included.)

Bismarck has several local diners that serve tasty, inexpensive meals. The **Little Cottage Café,** 2513 E. Main St. (223-4949), brings in droves of workers at the lunch whistle and families at dinnertime. Fantastic muffins cost $1.25, an 8-oz. sirloin steak $7. (Open daily 6am-10pm.) The **Drumstick Café,** 307 N. 3rd St. (223-8449), serves breakfast all day. The home-baked desserts (fresh strawberry pie $1) and fresh-ground coffee are superb. Sandwiches are $2 to $3.50. (Open Mon.-Sat. 24 hrs.)

Most of Bismarck is lassoed in an oval formed by I-94 and its corollary Business 94, otherwise known as **Main Street.** Bismarck's small downtown shopping district coalesces in the southwest curve of this oval, bounded by Washington St. and 9th St. on the west and east, and Rosser Ave. and Business 94 on the north and south.

The **Bismarck-Mandan Convention and Visitors Bureau** dispenses pamphlets aplenty at 523 N. 4th St. (222-4308). (Open Mon.-Fri. 8am-5pm.) The largely defense-oriented **Bismarck Municipal Airport,** 2½ mi. south of Bismarck, lies near the intersection of University Dr. (Rte. 1804) and Airport Rd. **Greyhound,** 1237 W. Divide (223-6576), three inconvenient mi. west of downtown off I-94 exit 35, provides service to Minneapolis (10 hr.; $56) and Seattle (1½ days; $134). (Open Mon.-Fri. 3:30-5am, 8am-1pm, and 4-9pm, Sat.-Sun. 3:30-5am, 9am-12:30pm, and 6-9pm.) Bismarck's **time zone** is Central (1 hr. behind Eastern), except for Fort Lincoln, which is Mountain (2 hrs. behind Eastern). The **post office** is at 220 E. Rosser Ave. (221-6517; open Mon.-Fri. 8am-5:30pm, Sat. 10am-noon); the **ZIP code** is 58501. Bismarck's **area code** is 701.

Theodore Roosevelt National Memorial Park and Medora

President Theodore Roosevelt appreciated the beauty of the Badlands' red- and brown-hued lunar formations so much that he bought a ranch here. After his mother and his wife died on the same day, he came here seeking "physical and spiritual renewal"; today's visitor can find the same rejuvenation among the quiet canyons and dramatic rocky outcroppings which earned the park the nickname "rough-rider country."

The park is split into southern and northern units, and bisected by the border between Mountain and Central time zones. The entrance to the better-developed **south unit** (time zone: Mountain) is just north of I-94 in the historic frontier town of **Medora.** Restored with tourist dollars in mind, Medora is a place to hold tightly to your purse strings. **Joe Ferris' General Store** (623-4447), is spotless and still inexpensive. (Open daily 8am-8pm.) For more immediate nourishment, stop by the **Badlands Bake Shoppe,** four doors to the left of Ferris, for a midday snack. Large muffins cost $1, and a loaf of Dakota bread—perfect hiking food—is $2.50. (Open May-Sept. daily 8am-4pm.) In pleasant weather, indulge at the **Chuckwagon Restaurant** (623-4820), an outdoor buffet ($9.50, kids $4.25) serving ribs and chicken in the summer. (Open daily 4:30-7pm.) Budget motels are even harder to find than budget food, but the **Dietz Motel,** 401 Broadway (623-4455), offers clean basement rooms at the lowest rates in town. (Singles from $14. Doubles from $16.)

Medora's only sight is the **Museum of the Badlands,** on Main St. (623-4451), which tells all you need to know about the town. (Open Tues.-Sat. 10am-9pm, Sun.-Mon. 10am-7pm. $2, kids $1.) **Greyhound** serves Medora from the Dietz Motel, with three buses daily to Bismarck ($21).

Pay the park entrance fee ($3 per vehicle, $1 per pedestrian) at the **visitors center** (623-4466), on the western edge of town. The center serves as a mini-museum, displaying a few of Teddy's guns, spurs and old letters, and showing a beautiful film of winter Badlands scenes. Copies of *Frontier Fragments,* the park newspaper, with listings of ranger-led talks, walks and demonstrations, are available here. (Open daily 8am-8pm; Sept.-May 8am-4:30pm. Inquire at desk for film times.) A 36-mi. scenic automobile loop ambles through the park, and many hiking trails start from the loop and penetrate into the wilderness. The world's third-largest **petrified forest** lies 14 mi. into the park. **Painted Canyon Overlook,** seven mi. east of Medora, has its own **visitors center** (575-4020; open daily 8am-8pm), picnic tables, and a breathtaking view of the badlands.

The **north unit** of the park (time zone: Central) is 75 mi. from the south unit on U.S. 85. Most of the land is wilderness; very few people visit, and fewer stay overnight. This combination results in virtually unlimited backcountry hiking possibilities. Check in at the ranger station (623-4466 or 842-2333; open daily 8am-4:30pm) for information and a free overnight camping permit. As a compromise between the wilderness and Medora, the park maintains **Squaw Creek Campground,** five mi. west of the north unit entrance. (Sites $8.) For more information on the park, write to Theodore Roosevelt National Memorial Park, Medora, ND 58645.

South Dakota

From the forested granite crags of the Black Hills to the glacial lakes of the northeast, the Coyote State has more to offer than casual passers-by might expect. WALL DRUG. In fact, the state has the highest ratio of sights-to-people in all of the Great Plains. Stunning natural spectacles like the Black Hills, the Badlands, and the Wind and Jewel Caves, as well as colossal man-made attractions such as Mt. Rushmore and the Crazy Horse Monument, have made tourism the state's largest industry after agriculture. WALL DRUG. Cartographically speaking, South Dakota is the most average state in the Union, home to the geographic center of the United States (approximately 35 miles north of Spearfish). Climatically, however, South Dakota is a land of extremes. Temperatures during the year oscillate between Arctic frigidity and Saharan heat. YOU ARE NOW ONLY A FEW PAGES FROM WALL DRUG.

Practical Information

Capital: Pierre.

Division of Tourism, 221 S. Central, in Capitol Lake Plaza, P.O. Box 1000, Pierre 57051 (773-3301 or 800-952-2217; 800-843-1930 outside SD). Open Mon.-Fri. 8am-5pm. **U.S. Forest Service**, Custer 57730 (673-4853). Provides camping stamps for the national forest, Golden Eagle passes for those over 62, and Black Hills National Forest maps ($1). Open Mon.-Fri. 8am-5pm. **Division of Parks and Recreation,** Capitol Bldg., Pierre 57501 (773-3371). Information on state parks and campgrounds. Open Mon.-Fri. 8am-5pm.

Time Zones: Central (1 hr. behind Eastern) and Mountain (2 hrs. behind Eastern). **Postal Abbreviation:** SD **Area Code:** 605

Sales Tax: 4%.

Badlands National Park

Some 60 million years ago, when much of the Great Plains was under water, tectonic shifts thrust up the Rockies and the Black Hills. Mountain streams deposited silt from these nascent highlands into what is now known as the Badlands, fossilizing in layer after pink layer the remains of wildlife that once wandered these flood plains. Erosion has carved spires and steep gullies into the land of this area, creating a landscape that contrasts sharply with the prairies of eastern South Dakota. The Sioux called these arid and treacherous formations "Mako Sica," or "bad land;" Gen. Alfred Sully—the opposition—simply called them "hell with the fires out."

The Badlands still smolder about 50 mi. east of Rapid City on I-90. Highway 240 winds through the wilderness in a 32-mi. detour off I-90 (take exit 131 or 110). There is almost no way to visit the park by highway without being importuned by employees from **Wall Drug,** 510 Main St. (279-2175), in Wall; the store is a towering monument to the success of saturation advertising. After seeing billboards for Wall Drug from as far as 500 mi. away, travelers feel obligated to make a stop in Wall to see what all the ruckus is about, much as they must have done 60 years ago when Wall enticed travelers on the parched Plains by offering free water. The "drug store," itself is quite a disappointment, mostly hawking overpriced souvenirs and other assorted kitsch. (Open daily 6:30am-9pm; Sept.-Nov. and May-Aug. 6am-10pm; Dec.-April Mon.-Sat. 8am-5pm.) All of the other cafés and shops on Main St. are just as overpriced (a chunk of fudge at The Country Store, located in the Wall Drug Mall, costs 71¢). All in all the town is just another brick in the...well, forget it.

From Wall, take Rte. 240, which loops through the park and returns to I-90 30 mi. east of Wall in Cactus Flat. From Rapid City, take Rte. 44 and turn northeast at Scenic, where it leads to Sage Creek and Rte. 240. There are ranger stations at both entrances off I-90, although the western portion of the park is much less developed. **Jack Rabbit Buses** (348-3300) makes two stops daily at Wall from Rapid City ($19). You can probably ask around for a ride into the park from Wall. Entrance to the park costs $1 per person, $5 per carload ($1.50 for a carload of Arikara Sioux).

The **Cedar Pass Visitors Center** (433-5361), five mi. inside the park's eastern entrance, is more convenient than the **White River Visitors Center** (455-2878), 55 mi. southwest, off Rte. 27 in the park's less-visited southern section. Both centers sell trail guides and distribute the *Prairie Preamble*, a free paper detailing park programs. (Cedar Pass open June-Aug. 7am-8pm; Sept.-May hours vary; call for times. White River open May 31-Aug. 31 7am-8pm.) Stock up on gasoline, food, and insect repellent before entering the park. Both of the visitors centers spout potable water. The Badlands experience extreme temperatures in midsummer and winter, but in late spring and fall offer pleasant weather and few insects. Always watch (and listen) for rattlesnakes.

Accommodations, Camping, and Food

Two campgrounds lie within the park. **Cedar Pass Campground,** near the visitors center, has shaded picnic tables and a bathroom with running water, but no showers (sites $8). The **Sage Creek Campground,** 11 mi. from the Pinnacles entrance south of Wall, is free. It is merely an open field with pit toilets, no water, and it does *not* allow fires. What did you expect for nothing?

Try backcountry camping for a more intimate introduction to this austere landscape. Bring at least one gallon of water per person per day and set up camp at least half a mile from a road. Go ahead and share the stars with local wildlife, but don't cozy up to the bison, especially in the spring when nervous mothers become, shall we say, overprotective.

For tenderfoot tourists, the **Cedar Pass Lodge,** P.O. Box 5, Interior 57750 (433-5460), next to the visitors center, has air-conditioned cabins. (Singles with showers $35. Doubles $39. Each additional person $4. Open mid-April-mid-Oct. Try to make reservations; leave a 50% deposit.) Try a buffalo burger ($3) at the lodge's mid-priced restaurant (the only one in the park). (Open June-Aug. daily approximately 7am-8pm.)

Sights and Activities

The park protects large tracts of prairie along with the stark rock formations. The Cedar Pass Visitors Center has an **audio-visual program** on the Badlands, and the park rangers lead **nature hikes,** all of which leave from the Cedar Pass amphitheater. The free hikes (at 6am, 8am and 6pm, 1½ hr.) provide an easy way to appreciate the Badlands—you may find Oligocene fossils right at your feet. In the evening, the amphitheater slide program narrates Badlands history (cover up—the mosquitoes can be ravenous). A one-hour night-prowl or sky-trek (stargazing) follows the program. Check the *Prairie Preamble* for details on daily events.

You can also hike through the Badlands on your own. Pick up a trail guide at one of the visitors centers. If you're planning an overnight hike, be certain to ask for their **backcountry camping** information. Try the short but steep **Saddle Pass Trail** or the less hilly **Castle Trail** (10 mi. round-trip). If you'd rather drive than hike, follow **Loop Road** and pull over at the spectacular overlooks. Highlights of Loop Road are **Robert's Prairie Dog Town** and the **Yellow Mounds Overlook,** where brilliant red and yellow formations relieve the ubiquitous Badland bleached rose. Keep your eyes shucked along Sage Creek Rd. for the park's herd of about 400 bison. Respect the intense midday sun, and at all times be wary of crumbly footholds, prickly cacti, and the occasional rattlesnake. It is easy to lose your bearings in this convoluted territory, so consult with a ranger or tote a map.

Black Hills

The Black Hills, named for the dark hue that distance lends the green pines covering the hills, have long been considered sacred by the Sioux living in the area. The Treaty of 1868 gave the Black Hills and the rest of South Dakota west of the Missouri River to the Sioux, but the U.S. government broke it during the gold rush of 1877-79. In 1980, the Supreme Court awarded the Sioux a "just compensation" of $200 million, which the tribe did not accept; the Sioux want the government to return their land to them, which it has not yet done. Today, white residents dominate the area, which contains a trove of treasures, including Mount Rushmore, Crazy Horse Monument, Custer State Park, Wind Cave National Park, Jewel Cave National Monument, and the Black Hills National Forest.

I-90 skirts the northern border of the Black Hills from Spearfish in the west to Rapid City in the east. The interconnecting road system through the hills is difficult to navigate without a good map; pick up one for free at the Rapid City Chamber of Commerce.

Powder River Lines serves only Deadwood, Lead, and Hot Springs (see Rapid City Practical Information). Rent a car to explore the area thoroughly. Alternatively, take advantage of the excellent and informative **Gray Line** tours (342-4461). Tickets can be purchased at Rapid City motels, hotels, and campgrounds. Make reservations, or call one hour before departure; they will pick you up at your motel. Tour #1 is the most complete Black Hills tour, going to Mt. Rushmore, Black Hills National Forest, Custer State Park, Needles Highway, and the Crazy Horse Monument (mid-May- mid-Oct. daily, 8 hrs., $28). Tour #4 heads to Spearfish for the Black Hills Passion Play, which has been "Praised by Press, Acclaimed by Clergy, Endorsed by Educators," and "Lauded by Laymen" (June-Aug. Sun., Tues., and Thurs., 5 hrs., $19). Tour #5 provides nighttime transportation to Mt. Rushmore, which is illuminated for viewing (June 1-Sept. 2 Sun., Tues. and Thurs. 4½ hrs., $9; buy tickets at any campground or motel).

Hiking in the hills is quite enjoyable—there is little underbrush beneath the conifer canopy. The abandoned mines and strange rock outcroppings may beckon you to explore, but stay on the marked trails. Rainy, cool weather is common as late as May and June. Dress accordingly.

Black Hills National Forest

The Black Hills, like other national forests, adheres to the principle of "multiple use"; mining, logging, ranching, and tourism all take place in close proximity. "Don't miss" attractions like reptile farms and Flintstone Campgrounds lurk around every bend in the Black Hills' narrow, sinuous roads. Visit the forest outside of the peak tourist season (July-mid-Sept.), during which heathen hordes of cars and campers descend on the area in a rush for the modern-day gold of glow-in-the-dark souvenirs.

The most convenient information centers are the **Pactola Ranger District,** 803 Soo San Dr., Rapid City (343-1567; open Mon.-Fri. 8am-5pm), and the **Spearfish Ranger District,** 2041 North Main St., Spearfish (642-4622; open Mon.-Fri. 8am-5pm). The main information office and visitors center at Pactola Reservoir, 17 mi. west of Rapid City on U.S. 385, has forestry exhibits in the summer in addition to the usual tourist literature. You can buy supplies before you head off to the hinterland at small grocery stores in Keystone and Custer, or at the KOA campground five mi. west of Mt. Rushmore on Rte. 244.

Spearfish, located directly off I-90 at the northern end of the Black Hills National Forest, is an excellent access point for the hills. Comfortable accommodations can be found at the **Canyon Gateway Motel** on Route 14A (642-3402) at the edge of the famed **Spearfish Canyon.** (Singles $29. Doubles $38.) Also stop in at the **Valley Café,** 608 Main St. (642-2423), for pleasant conversation and great pancakes (3 enormo-flapjacks for $2) before heading into the woods. If you're feeling vigorous, climb or bike the 5.7 mi. of aspen and pine-lined Rim Rock Trail to an altitude of 6,280 ft. The trailhead is approximately 18 mi. southwest of Spearfish on Highway 14A.

Camping in the national forest is free. To save money the adventurous way, disappear down one of the many dirt roads (make sure it isn't someone's driveway) and set up camp. There are a few rules to follow: you can't park on the side of the road, your campsite must be at least a mile away from any campground or visitors center, and you can't build a campfire. Watch for poison ivy and afternoon thunder showers. The most popular established campgrounds include **Bear Gulch** and **Pactola** (343-4283), on the Pactola Reservoir just south of the junction of Rte. 44 and U.S. 385 (sites $9-11). You must register for sites at the Pactola campground (on 385 South, 1 mi. past the visitors center; turn right at sign for the Black Forest Inn). They fill quickly, so call for reservations up to 10 days in advance. Other favorites include **Sheridan Lake Campground** (574-2873 or 800-283-2267), east of Hill City on U.S. 385 (sites $9-11), which provides picnic tables, pit toilets, water hydrants, and movies and talks on Saturday at 9pm at the Sheridan Amphitheater on the campground. For more information, contact the Pactola or Spearfish Ranger District (see above).

Mt. Rushmore National Monument

South Dakota historian Doane Robinson originally conceived this "shrine of democracy" in 1923 as a memorial for local Western heroes such as Kit Carson. By its completion in 1941, the monument portrayed the 60-ft.-tall faces of George Washington, Thomas Jefferson, Abraham Lincoln, and Theodore Roosevelt. Think about it, these heads have nostrils large enough to snort a human! Millions have stood in awe before the four stony faced patriarchs, designed and sculpted by chiseler extraordinaire (and former KKK-member) Gutzon Borglum. The monument is proof that Americans do take great men for granite.

From Rapid City, take U.S. 16 to Keystone and Rte. 244 up to the mountain. The **visitors center** (574-2523) has multi-media exhibitions as well as braille brochures and wheelchairs. Programs for the disabled are held daily at 9pm. (Visitors center open daily 7am-10pm; Sept. 18-May 14 8am-5pm.) Borglum's Sculptor's Studio, in the visitors center, holds the plaster model of the sculptor's mountain carving, as well as his tools and plans. (Ranger talks held in summer every ½-hr. 9:30am-6:30pm; studio open daily 8am-7pm.) Also in the visitors center is **Mt. Rushmore Memorial Amphitheater,** the location of the evening monument-lighting programs. (May 14-Sept. 4 program at 9pm, monument lit 9:30-10:30pm; Sept. 5-16 program at 8pm, monument lit 8:30-9:30pm; trail lights off at 11pm.) For close accommodations, try the **Hill City-Mt. Rushmore KOA** (574-2525), five mi. west of Mt. Rushmore on Rte. 244. With kabins ($52) kome use of showers, stove, heated pool, laundry facilities, and free shuttle service to Mt. Rushmore. (Office open daily 7am-11pm, Oct.-April 8am-10pm. Kampsites $17 for 2 people, $22 with water and electricity, $24 with full hookup.) For a more remote and scenic sleeping place, try **Kemp's Kamp** (666-4654; kampsites $14, kabins $36, full hookups, showers, laundry facilities, and pool available; ½-mi. west of Keystone off Rte. 16A).

Crazy Horse National Monument

If you thought Mount Rushmore was big, think again. This monument is a wonder-of-the-world-in-progress; an entire mountain is being transformed into a 500-ft.-high memorial sculpture of the great Oglala chief Crazy Horse. When finished, this will relegate the denizens of Rushmore to the status of girly-men. The project began in 1948 and receives no government funding of any kind; the sculptor, Korczak Ziolkowski, believed in the American spirit of free enterprise, and twice refused $10 million in federal funding. Crazy Horse himself was a resolute Native American leader who fought against the U.S. government to regain his people's land, rights, and pride. He was stabbed in the back (literally) by an American soldier in 1877, while at Fort Robinson, NE, under a flag of truce. The Monument, on Rte. 385 14 mi. south of Mt. Rushmore, includes the **Indian Museum of North America** as well as the mountain statue, and will one day become the site of the **University and Medical Training Center for the North American Indian.** (Open daily 6:30am-10pm, Sept.-May 8am-5pm. Admission $5, students $1.75, under 6 free, $10 per carload. Special rates for groups and AAA members. For information or to give a tax-deductible donation, write: Crazy Horse Memorial, Crazy Horse, SD, 57730-9506, or call 673-4681.)

Custer State Park

Peter Norbeck, governor of South Dakota during the late 1910s, loved to hike among the thin, towering rock formations that haunt the area south of Sylvan Lake and Mt. Rushmore. Norbeck not only created Custer State Park to preserve the area's treasures, but spectacular Needles Highway as well, which follows his favorite hiking route. He purposely kept the highway narrow and winding so that newcomers could experience the pleasures of discovery. Watch for mountain goats and bighorn sheep among the rocky spires. For information, contact HC 83, P.O. Box 70, Custer 57730 (255-4515; open Mon.-Fri. 7:30am-5pm). There is a daily entrance fee ($4 per person, $6 per carload). At the entrance, ask for a copy of *Tatanka* (meaning "buffalo"), the informative Custer State Park newspaper. The **Peter Norbeck Welcome Center** (255-4464), on U.S. 16A, one mi. west of the State Game Lodge, is the park's central information center. (Open May-Sept. daily 8am-8pm.) All six **state park campgrounds** charge $8-10 per night and have showers and restrooms. Restaurants and concessions are available at all of the four park lodges—State Game, Blue Bell, Sylvan Lake, and Legion Lake—but you can save money by shopping at the local general stores in Custer, Hermosa, or Keystone.

Sylvan Lake, on Needles Hwy. (Rte. 87), is as lovely as its name, with hiking trails, fishing, horse concessions, paddle boats, and canoes. Horse rides are available at Blue Bell Lodge (255-4531, stable 255-4571; rides $13.50 per hr., under 12 $11.50; $21.50 per 2 hr., under 12 $19.50). Paddle and row boat rentals are available at Legion Lake Lodge (255-4521; boats $3 per person for ½-hr.; $22.50 for 3 people to fish in row boat for 6 hrs.). All lakes and streams permit fishing, with a $6.50 daily license. Five-day nonresident licenses are $14.50. There is a limit of eight trout per day, six times per summer. Summer fishing is the best, especially around the first of the month when officials stock the waters. Rental equipment is available at the four area lodges.

Caves

In the cavern-riddled Black Hills, the subterranean scenery often rivals what lies above-ground. Private concessionaires will attempt to lure you into the holes in their backyards, but the government owns the area's prime real estate. **Wind Cave National Park** (745-4600), adjacent to Custer State Park on Rte. 87,and **Jewel Cave National Monument** (673-2288), 14 mi. west of Custer on U.S. 16A, are in the southern hills. There is no public transportation to the caves.

In the summer, both Wind and Jewel Cave visitors centers offer excursions daily, including short candlelight tours and strenuous but exhilarating spelunking tours, during which tourists crawl on the floor of the cave just like real explorers. Guides provide knee pads, helmets with lanterns, and instruction. Wear well-soled shoes, preferably ankle-high laced boots, and expendable clothing. Bring a sweater on all tours—Jewel Cave remains a constant 47°F, Wind Cave 53°F.

Though discovered in 1881, most of Wind Cave was not explored until 1890 when 17-year-old Alvin McDonald probed its depths. You can still see his name burned on the walls of some of the deeper chambers. The cave lies 12 mi. north of Hot Springs on U.S. 385. Besides several short walks, Wind Cave Park offers four **tours.** The easy **Garden of Eden Tour** gives a quick overview of the cave's interior (6 per day 8:40am-5:30pm; $2, seniors and under 15 $1). The one-hour **Natural Entrance Tour** leaves on the hour, 9am-6pm, and covers ½-mi. of the cave. (Admission $4, ages 6-15 $2.) The more strenuous, 1½-hr. **Fairgrounds Tour** snakes ½ mi. through two levels of the cave (9:40am-4:20pm, admission $5, ages 6-15 $2.50). The four-hour **Spelunking Tour,** limited to 10 people ages 14 and over, leaves at 1pm ($6, reservations required). To make reservations for these tours, contact Wind Cave National Park, Hot Springs 57747 (745-4600; open daily 8am-7pm; Aug. 24-June 4 8am-5pm). **Self-guided tours** begin at the Elk Mountain Campground Amphitheater (see below).

Jewel Cave sprawls underground in one of the largest unexplored labyrinths in the world. Though formed of the same limestone as Wind Cave, the similarities end there. Grayish calcite crystal walls are the highlight of the tours. Guides sponsor three kinds of tours during the summer. The ½-mi. **Scenic Tour** takes you over 700 stairs (every 20 min., 1 hr., admission $4, ages 6-15 $2). Make reservations for the **Spelunking Tour**, limited to 10 people ages 16 and over, and be sure to wear sturdy foot gear (Sun., Tues., Thurs., and Sat., admission $6). Contact Jewel Cave National Monument, Custer 57730 (673-2288; open June 12-Aug. 27 daily 8am-4:30pm).

The **Elk Mountain Campground** offers primitive sites with flush toilets for $7. There are no overnight accommodations at the Jewel Cave Monument, but you can camp at the national forest's facility six mi. east on Rte. 16A.

Lead and Deadwood

Many interesting small towns glitter like gold dust amidst the Black Hills, but Lead and Deadwood are truly 24-carat. During the 1877 gold rush, these towns attained legendary status for their idiosyncratic prospectors and boom-town exploits.

Lead

In **Lead** (LEED), almost everybody works for Homestake, the locally prominent gold-mining corporation. Here, after the hills "panned out" in 1878, hardrock or lode mining began in earnest. Homestake still owns much of the northern Black Hills and continues to operate the largest gold mine in the Western Hemisphere. The **Open Cut,** a yawning chasm where a mountain once stood, is a monument to Homestake's handiwork. You'll see huge vats of tailings, conveyor belts loaded with ore, and contraptions that lower the miners down almost a mile into the belly of the earth. Operations there ceased some time ago—long enough for a Piggly-Wiggly store and many miners to make their homes in its path. The **Lead Civic Association** (584-3110) gives surface tours of the mine. (Tours June-Aug. daily 8am-5pm every hr.; May and Sept.-Oct. Mon.-Fri. 8am-4pm every ½ hr. $3.50, high school students $2.50; check for group rates.) To get a more *in-depth* feeling for the mines, check out the **Black Hills Mining Museum** (584-1605) where you can tour fake mines and try your hand at panning for gold. (323 W. Main St. Open 9am-5pm daily, May 20-Oct. 10; $3.25, students $2.25, under 6 free. Tours every 5 min.)

The **post office** in Lead is at 329 W. Main St. (584-2110; open Mon.-Fri. 8:15am-4:15pm, Sat. 10am-noon); the **ZIP code** is 57754.

Deadwood

Gunslinging hero/outlaws Wild Bill Hickok and Calamity Jane sauntered into **Deadwood** at the height of the Gold Rush. Bill stayed just long enough—two months—to spend eternity here. Legend has it he was shot while playing poker, and since he fell while holding eights and aces, this full house became known as "the dead man's hand." Visit **Mt. Moriah Cemetery** on Boot Hill**,** where Bill and Jane are buried beside each other in a plot overlooking the city (on Rte. 14A, just outside Deadwood; open daily 7am-8pm, admission $1) or take the one-hour **Alkali Iki Bus Tour** (578-3147) of historic Main St., Saloon #10, the Franklin Hotel, and Mt. Moriah Cemetery (10am-5pm; call for meeting place; $4.50, students $2.50).

In 1989 Deadwood voted to reinstate small-stakes gambling to recapture some of the town's less murderous Wild West atmosphere in order to lure tourists. As a result, **Main Street** sometimes resembles a smaller version of Las Vegas or Atlantic City. Parking in the narrow canyon has also grown inconvenient and expensive; check with your motel to see if it can arrange a guaranteed space for your car. Otherwise, take the 50-cent trolley which comes every 15 minutes and passes all the motels.

The **Nugget Café,** 815 W. Main St. (584-3337) in Lead, is almost a museum in its own right, decorated with photos documenting the town's history. Try the nugget burger ($3.75) or the tasty omelettes ($2.75-3.75). (Open Mon.-Sat. 6am-7pm.) Jack McCall, Wild Bill's assassin, was captured at **Goldberg Gaming,** 672 Main St. (578-1515) in Deadwood, where you can down an old-fashioned phosphate for $.50 or a huge "Goldburger" for $1.50-3,50. (Open June-Sept. 2 Mon.-Sat. 6:30am-6pm.) The **#10 Saloon,** 657 Main St. (578-3346), claims to own Wild Bill's "death chair," and has live rock bands every night at 8:30pm (open daily 8am-2am).

There ain't no budget lodging in Lead or Deadwood. Your best bet is to stay at **Wild Bill's Campground** (578-2800), on Rte. 385 about two mi. south of Lead and Deadwood. It's a scenic spot with a swimming pool, showers, hookups, and cozy cabins among the mountain pines, and boasts a free shuttlebus to Deadwood (sites $12.50, $14.50 with water and hookup, cabins $40). Or try the **Jackpot Inn,** ½-mi. south of Rte. 85 on U.S. 385, outside Deadwood and Lead (singles $50, Sept.-May $25 (negotiable), with shower, HBO, phone, and use of hot tub) which is on the trolley route (see above). If you'd rather commute, the **Deadwood Express** (343-5044) comes from Rapid City twice per day (1 hr., $2).

Check in at the **Chamber of Commerce,** 735 Main St., Deadwood (578-1876; open Mon.-Fri. 8:30am-5pm, Sat. 8am-noon). The Deadwood **post office** is in the Deadwood Federal Building (578-1505); the **ZIP code** is 57732.

The **area code** for Lead and Deadwood is 605.

Pierre

Pierre (PEER), South Dakota's capital, sits smack dab in the middle of the state. Situated on the Missouri River, it lies near the **Oahu Dam,** the 2nd-largest rolled-earth dam in the world. Forever a bustlin' cow town, Pierre still serves as a commercial center for farmers and ranchers. The newly restored copper-domed **capitol building** (773-3765; free 40-min. tours depart Mon.-Fri. at 9, 10, 11am and 1, 2, 3pm) is open daily 8am-10pm. Behind the capitol, an unusual fountain dedicated to Korean and Vietnam War veterans spouts flame from a natural gas deposit. In the event of a sudden thermonuclear war, head for the brand-new, bunkerlike **Cultural Heritage Center,** 900 Governors Dr. (773-3458). Built into the side of a hill above the capitol, the museum gives an interesting and detailed history of both the Native American and white inhabitants of South Dakota. (Open Mon.-Fri. 9am-4:30pm, Sat.-Sun. 1-9:30pm. Free.)

Find cheap eats at the **D & E Café,** 115 W. Dakota Ave. (224-7200), where a burger is $.90, and the priciest item on the menu is $4.70. (Open 24 hrs., except Sun.) Grab a kup of koffee at the **Kozy Korner Restaurant,** 217 E. Dakota Ave. (224-9547), a family place with generous dinners for $5-6. (Open daily 5am-10pm.)

Sleep cheap four blocks from the capitol at the **Bel-Aire Motel,** 900 N. Euclid Ave. (224-6240). Rooms are clean, comfortable, and have TV, phone, and bathroom. (Singles $18, doubles $21.) Conveniently located across the street from the bus station, the **Days Inn,** 520 W. Sioux Ave. (224-0411), serves free doughnuts, coffee, and milk every morning and popcorn upon arrival. (Singles $30. Doubles $38.) The popular **Farm Island State Park** (224-5605), three mi. east on Rte. 34, has campsites and showers for $7 ($10 with hookup) and **Griffen Park,** along Oahu Lake at the end of Missouri Ave., serves as a free campsite with bathrooms.

To reach Pierre from I-90, go 30 mi. north on U.S. 83. **Greyhound/Jack Rabbit,** in the Phillips 66 station at 621 W. Sioux Ave. (224-7651), runs buses to Omaha ($86), Rapid City ($44), and Minneapolis ($98). Visit the **Chamber of Commerce,** 108 E. Missouri St. (224-7361 or 800-962-2034; open Mon.-Fri.8am-5pm). Pierre is in the **Central time zone** (1 hr. behind Eastern). The **post office** is at 225 S. Pierre St.(224-2912; open Mon.-Fri. 8am-5:30pm, Sat. 10am-noon). Pierre's **ZIP code** is 57501; the **area code** is 605.

Rapid City

Rapid City's location, approximately 40 mi. east of the Wyoming border, makes it an ideal base from which to explore both the Black Hills and the Badlands. Every summer the area welcomes about 2.2 million tourists, over 40 times the city's permanent population.

Practical Information

Emergency: 911.

Rapid City Chamber of Commerce, Visitors Bureau, 444 Mt. Rushmore Rd. N. (343-1744), in the Civic Center. Visitors Bureau (341-0079) open May 27-Sept. 2 daily 7am-6pm; Chamber of Commerce open year-round Mon.-Fri. 8am-5pm, but times vary; call ahead.

Buses: Milo Barber Transportation Center, 333 6th St. (348-3300), downtown. **Jack Rabbit Lines** runs east from Rapid City. To Pierre (1 per day, 3 hr., $44) and Sioux Falls (2 per day, 8 hr., $75). **Powder River Lines** services Wyoming and Montana. To Billings (5pm, 9 hr., $69) and Cheyenne (5pm, 8½ hr., $88). Both honor the Greyhound Ameripass. Station open Mon.-Fri. 6am-10pm, Sat.-Sun. 6am-12:30pm, 4-5:15pm, and 9:30-10pm.

Public Transport: Milo Barber Transportation Center, 394-6631. City bus transportation available by reservation. Call 24 hrs. in advance. One way trip $1, seniors $.50. Office open Mon.-Fri. 8am-4pm.

Taxi: Rapid Taxi, 348-8080. Base fare $2.20, $1 per mi.

Car Rental: Black Hills Car Rental, 301 Campbell (342-6696). Budget cars $38 per day plus $.16 per mi.; off- season $16 per day, subject to availability. Open Mon.-Fri. 8am-5pm, Sat. 9am-4pm. Must be 21 with major credit card.

Time Zone: Mountain (2 hr. behind Eastern).

Post Office: 500 East Blvd. (394-8600), several blocks east of downtown. Open Mon.-Fri. 8am-5pm, Sat. 9:30am-12:30pm. **ZIP code:** 57701.

Area Code: 605.

Orienting yourself may be difficult at first, since Rapid City sprawls across 27 flat sq. mi., and few of the buildings in town stand taller than four stories. The center of the downtown area is bordered on the east and west by 6th and 9th St., and on the north and south by Omaha and Kansas City St.

Accommodations, Camping, and Food

The **HI/AYH hostel,** 815 Kansas City St. (342-8538), downtown in the YMCA, consists of 14 cots, with no separation between men and women. Access to YMCA facilities (pool, gym, game room) is free, but no bedding or kitchen facilities are available. A cot for the night costs $8 for HI/AYH members.

Rapid City accommodations are considerably more expensive during the summer. Make reservations, since budget motels often fill up weeks in advance. The **Big Sky Motel,** 4080 Tower Rd. (348-3200), looms large on a hill just south of town, affording a spectacular view of the city and the surrounding farmland. (Spotless but phoneless singles $29, doubles $40.) **Motel 6** is less conveniently located northeast of town, off I-90 at exit 59, about a $4 cab trip from downtown. Some rooms have disabled access. There is a pool. Swim. (Singles $36. Doubles $42.) **The Berry Patch Campground,** 1860 E. North St. (341-5588), one mi. east of I-90 off exit 60, has 14 berry nice grass campsites, a gameroom, playground, showers, and swimming. (Tent sites $14 for 2, with hookup $15.50 from end of May-Labor Day. Each additional person $1.50.)

Aunt Jane's, 807 Columbus (341-4529), on the first floor of a Victorian house stuffed with antiques, will sate your appetite. Aunt Jane prepares her own recipes, such as the Rocky Mountain salad sandwich (ham, swiss cheese, and peaches; $3.45). (Open Mon.-Fri. 8am-4:30pm, Sat. 9am-2pm.) **Tally's,** 530 6th St. (342-7621), downtown under the orange awning, serves family-style country meals such as chicken-fried steak for under $5. (Open daily 7am-8pm; Sept. 2-May 27 7am-7pm.) The **Flying T** (342-1905), six mi. south on U.S. 16, next to the Reptile Gardens, serves a chuck wagon meal on a tin plate for $10.50, under 11 $4.75, singing cowboys included. Dinner (7:30pm sharp) and a Western musical show (8:15pm) are offered every night.

Sights and Entertainment

Tourism rears its flashing neon head in Rapid City. If you got dem *walkin' blues,* take the **Rapid City Walking Tour** of the historic and well-preserved downtown area; pick up a guide at the visitors center. The **Sioux Indian Museum** and the **Pioneer Museum** (both 348-0557) cohabitate at 515 West Blvd., between Main and St. Joseph St. in Halley Park. The two museums present interesting but limited exhibits. (Open Mon.-Sat. 9am-5pm, Sun. 1-5pm; Oct.-May Tues.-Sat. 10am-5pm, Sun. 1-5pm. Free.) **The Museum of Geology,** 501 E. St. Joseph St. (394-2467), in the administration building of the School of Mines and Technology, just east of Main St., exhibits the beautiful minerals and textbook fossils of the Badlands. (Open Mon.-Sat. 8am-6pm, Sun. noon-6pm; off-season Mon.-Fri. 8am-5pm, Sat. 9am-2pm, Sun. 1-4pm. Free.) The **Dahl Fine Arts Center,** 7th and Quincy St. (394-4101), houses rotating exhibits of local and Native American art, as well as the enormous "Cyclorama of American History," a circular 200-ft. mural. (Open Mon.-Fri. 9am-9:30pm, Sat. 9am-5pm, Sun. 1-5pm. Free.)

For nightlife, try Main St. between 9th and Mt. Rushmore St. **Filly's Food, Fun, and Firewater** (348-8300), in the Hilton, is a fantastic spot for a quiet drink or a comedy show. (Shows Fri.-Sun. at 8:30pm. Open Mon.-Sat. 11am-2am, Sun. 12:30pm-midnight. Cover $6 for shows, no cover other times.) For boot-stompin', knee-slappin' country-western music and dancing, head to **Boot Hill,** 26 Main St. (343-1931), where live bands perform nightly. (Open Mon.-Sat. 3pm-2am, Sun. 5-11:30pm. Cover Tues.-Sat. $2.)

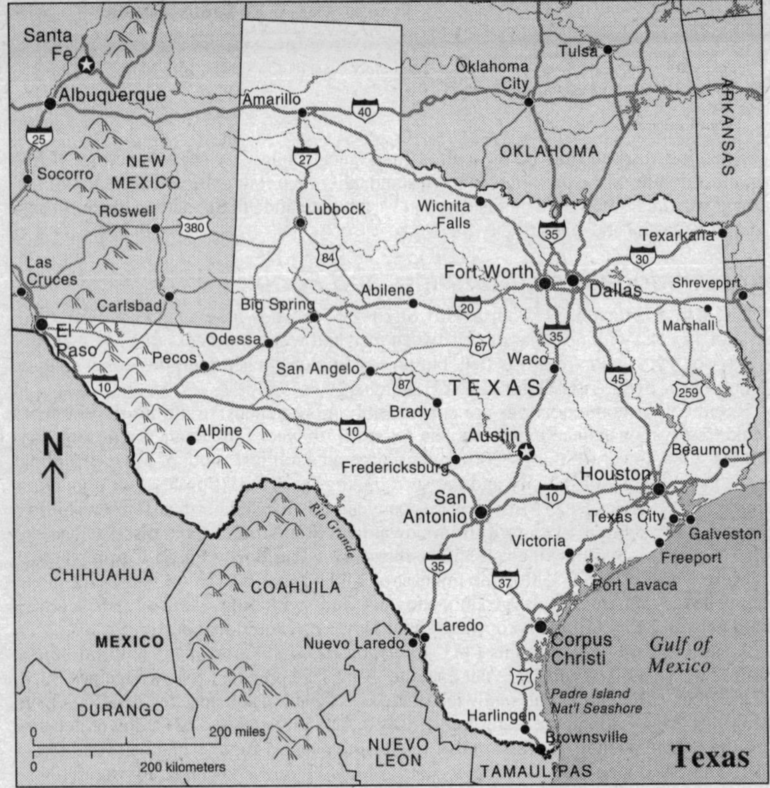

Texas

What most people imagine when they think of Texas—vast desert plains, grazing cattle, oil fields, and dusty towns—can be found only in West Texas. Those who've already seen *The Last Picture Show,* however, will want to see the rest of the state, most of which defies the dry, flat, John Wayne stereotype. The cosmopolitan bustle of Dallas and Houston provides refuge from the wooded hills of East Texas, whose miles of cool pine forests look more Cajun than Texan. The rugged Texas hill country, the state's most picturesque region, rolls to the west of bohemian Austin and European San Antonio. And, just when you thought you'd never see civilization again, El Paso and Juárez rise, phoenix- and Phoenix-like, from the desert, over 500 mi. from any other major city.

Practical Information

Capital: Austin.

Texas Division of Tourism, P.O. Box 12728, Austin 78711 (512-463-8586). **U.S. Forest Service,** P.O. Box 130, Lufkin 75901 (409-831-2246). **State Parks and Recreation Areas,** Austin Headquarters Complex, 4200 Smith School Rd., Austin 78744 (512-463-4630).

Time Zones: Central (1 hr. behind Eastern) and Mountain (2 hr. behind Eastern).

Postal Abbreviation: TX

Sales Tax: 6-8%.

Travel

Car travelers have the run of most of this huge state, but public transport serves areas frequented by tourists. The constellation of major cities in eastern Texas forms a triangle with **Dallas/Ft. Worth** at the apex, **San Antonio** and **Houston/Galveston** defining the lower leg and **Austin** part way along the San Antonio-Dallas line. Each leg measures 200-300 mi. in length. Interstate highways, frequent bus schedules, and Amtrak routes connect the points. **Kerrville Bus Lines,** a Greyhound affiliate, covers the entire region, while **Greyhound** varooms along the edges.

Outside of this triangle, the two areas of greatest interest to visitors are **western Texas** and the **Gulf Coast/Mexican Border** area, accessible by interstates and bus routes. Greyhound has frequent service on I-10 and I-20 into western Texas and convenient service to Corpus Christi and the southern border towns. Another Greyhound affiliate, **TNM&O Coaches,** provides thorough regional coverage in northwestern Texas and southern New Mexico. El Paso/Ciudad Juárez, a major urban area straddling the Mexican border, is a convenient base for exploring western Texas and southern New Mexico.

Regional cuisine, like most of Texan culture, is enriched by the state's Mexican heritage. "Tex-Mex" is a variation of the dishes served across the border: chefs throw jalapeño peppers into chili as casually as a McDonald's crew chief shakes salt on french fries. Mexican pastries and genuine longhorn beef are staples, but also indispensable is chicken-fried steak—originally created to disguise bad meat at roadside dives, today a delicacy. And of course, get some BBQ with plenty of sauce.

Outdoors

Some folks say Texas has only two seasons: summer and January. It's hot in summer. Really hot. The heat is more bearable in the west, where the air is dry; the eastern coastal humidity can be stifling. Winter varies across the state, from warm and mild in the south to potentially severe and blizzardy in the northern panhandle.

Take advantage of the state's wide open space by camping. The stars at night, are big and bright (this is your cue to clap four times) deep in the heart of Texas. Bring a tent and insect repellent to deter squadrons of mosquitos. The state park system has excellent camping at over 60 parks, recreation areas, and historic sites. Some parks charge an admission fee of $2 per car, $.50 per pedestrian or bicyclist. Sites usually cost $4. In the open ranching countryside of western Texas or in the Hill Country, finding sites should present few problems.

Austin

Apart from the grandiosity of the place, Austin (pop. 465,622) doesn't seem like Texas. The city has acquired a reputation as a haven for bohemians and panhandlers alike, due largely to the vast student population (50,000) at the University of Texas (UT). It's an oasis of culture in a rugged and scruffy state and one of the few cities in Texas compact enough to navigate *à pied.* Hints reminding visitors that, yes, they *are* in traditional Texas are usually in the form of typically Southern political antics (for example, when a state legislator threatened to withdraw UT funding over a collegiate football controversy). But more progressive factors outweigh them—for example, the 1990-91 election of Toni Luckett, a black lesbian, to the UT student government.

Practical Information and Orientation

Emergency: 911.

Visitor Information: Austin Convention Center/Visitor Information, 500 E. 1st St. (467-5561). Open Mon.-Fri. 8:30am-5pm, Sat. 9am-5pm, Sun. 1-5pm. **University of Texas Information Center,** 471-3151. **Texas Parks and Wildlife,** 389-4800 or 800-792-1112 in TX. Open Mon.-Fri. 8am-5pm. Call for info on camping outside Austin. Or write to or visit Texas Parks and Wildlife Dept., 4200 Smith School Rd., Austin 78744.

Amtrak: 250 N. Lamar Blvd. (476-5684 or 800-872-7245). To: Dallas (7 per week, 6 hr., $34), San Antonio (7 per week, 3 hr., $15, continues to Houston), and El Paso (4 per week, 10 hr., $122).

Greyhound: 916 E. Koenig (458-5267), several mi. north of downtown off I-35. Easily accessible by public transportation. Buses #15 and 7 to downtown stop across the street. To: San Antonio (11 per day, 2-3 hr., $11); Houston (11 per day, 4 hr., $18); Dallas (11 per day, 5 hr., $20); San Antonio (11 per day, 13 hr., $11), El Paso (5 per day, 14 hr. $80). Open 24 hrs.

Public Transport: Capitol Metro, 504 Congress (474-1200; line open Mon.-Sat. 6am-midnight, Sun. 6am-7pm). Maps and schedules available Mon.-Fri. 7am-6pm, Sat. 9am-1pm, or at the Visitors Information at the Convention Center. Fare $.50, seniors, kids, and disabled $.25. Downtown, the **Armadillo Express** connects major downtown points and runs every 10-15 min. in green trolley cars Mon.-Fri. 6:30am-10pm, Sat. 11am-7pm. Free. The **University of Texas Shuttle Bus** serves the campus area. Map and schedule at the UT Information Center (471-3151) or at any library, including the Main Library, 8th and Guadalupe St. This service is officially only for UT affiliates, but drivers rarely ask for ID.

Airport: Robert Mueller Municipal Airport, 4600 Manor Rd., 5 mi. northeast of downtown (480-9091). Cab fare to downtown runs about $8.

Taxi: Yellow Cab, 472-1111. Base fare $1.25, $1.25 per mi. Airport to downtown $7.50.

Car Rental: Rent-A-Wreck, 6820 Guadalupe (454-8621). $20-22 per day, 100 free mi., $.25 per additional mi. Open Mon.-Fri. 8am-7pm, Sat. 10am-3pm, Sun. 10am-1pm. Ages under 21 pay $5 extra charge. Must have major credit card.

Bike Rental: Bicycle Sports Shop, 1426 Toomey St. At the corner of Jesse and Toomey (477-3472). Mountain bikes $10 per day, $15 on weekends. $100 deposit or credit card required. Open Mon.-Fri. 10am-8pm, Sat. 9am-6pm, Sun. 1-5pm.

Help Lines: Crisis Intervention Hotline, 472-4357. **Austin Rape Crisis Center,** 440-7273.

Time Zone: Central (1 hr. behind Eastern).

Post Office: 300 E. 9th St. at Lavaca. (929-1252). Open Mon.-Fri. 7:30am-6pm, Sat. 8am-noon. **ZIP code:** 78767. **Area Code:** 512.

Highway signs lead to the **capitol area** near Congress Ave. and 11th St., in the center of the city. Dividing the city into east and west addresses, **Congress Avenue** runs about 20 blocks south of the from the **Colorado River** and 12 blocks north to the capitol. Seven blocks north of the capitol starts the main campus of the **University of Texas (UT).** The university splits numbered streets into east and west and includes most tourist spots in this stretch. Austin is a cyclist's paradise, with roller-coaster hills and clearly marked bikeways.

Accommodations and Camping

Cheap accommodations abound in Austin. **I-35,** running north and south of Austin, features a string of inexpensive hotels well outside downtown. Three co-ops run by **College Houses** (476-5678) at UT rent rooms to hostelers, including three meals per day. Those who are interested in staying at these co-ops should call College Houses, not the individual co-ops, to get info. The co-ops, particularly ideal for young travelers, welcome everyone. Patrons have access to all their facilities including a fully-stocked kitchen.

21st St. Co-op, 707 W. 21st St. (476-1857), has large and comfortable but unfurnished rooms and fills rapidly in summer. To get from the bus station to the hostel, take bus #15 to 7th and Congress St., walk down 7th one block to Colorado, and take #3 to 21st and Nueces St. $10 per person, plus $5 for three meals and kitchen access.

Pearl Street Co-op, 2000 Pearl St. (472-2657). 2 blocks west to the end of 21st St. Large, clean, sparsely furnished rooms. Laundry, kitchen, and a beautiful courtyard pool. Open and friendly atmosphere. Rooms, including 3 meals, $13, $18 for two.

Taos Hall, 2612 Guadalupe (474-6905), 6 blocks down Guadalupe, across the UT campus. Same deal as the other co-ops. Latest check-in time 9pm. You're most likely to get a private room here, and when you stay for dinner, the friendly residents will give you a welcoming round of applause. 3 meals and a bed $15.

Goodall Wooten Dorm, 2112 Guadalupe (472-1343). The "Woo" has private rooms with a small fridge, plus access to a TV room and basketball courts. Call ahead. (Singles $20. Doubles $25.)

Austin International Youth Hostel (HI/AYH), 2200 S. Lakeshore Blvd. (444-2294), farther from the center of town but still conveniently located. From the Greyhound station take bus #7 ("Duval") to Lakeshore Blvd. and walk about ½ mi. to the hostel. From I-35 east, exit at Riverside, head east, and turn left at Lakeshore Blvd. About 3 mi. from downtown on Town Lake. Kitchen, A/C; located near a grocery store and a noisy power plant. Members $10, non-members $15. Linen $2. No curfew.

Motel 6, 9420 N. I-35 at the Rundberg exit (339-6161), 12 mi. north of the capitol off N. Lamar and E. Rundberg Lane. Take a bus to Fawnridge and walk four blocks. Clean, air-conditioned rooms. Pool and color TV. ($23, $6 per additional adult.)

Camping is a 15- to 45-minute drive away. The **Austin Capitol KOA** (444-6322), six mi. south of the city along I-35, offers a pool, game room, laundry, grocery, and playground. Some cabins are available. (Sites $18 for 2, cabins $25, $35 for 2.) **Emma Long Metropolitan Park,** 2000 Barton Springs (346-1831), is a large preserve in the bend of the Colorado River. Take I-35 north to the 2222 Junction. Continue on 2222 until Park Rd. The park is 1½ mi. south. Hookup, tent sites, boat ramp, and a concession stand. (Open 8am-10pm. Park entry fee $5. Tent sites $6. Full hookups $10.)

Food

Two main districts compete for Austin's restaurant trade. Along the west side of the UT campus, **Guadalupe Street** ("the drag") has scores of fast-food joints and convenience stores, including the **Party Barn,** replete with drive-through beer. Those who disdain the $3 all-you-can-eat pizza buffets and sub shops that line the drag can eat in the UT Union ($2-5). The second district clusters around **Sixth Street,** south of the capitol. Here the battle for happy hour business rages with unique intensity; three-for-one drink specials and free hors d'oeuvres are common. Although famous for its Texan specialties, Austin seems to offer more cosmopolitan fare to its student population and visitors.

Trudy's Texas Star, 409 W. 30th St. (477-2935). Fine Tex-Mex dinner entrées $7-9, and a fantastic array of margaritas. Famous for *migas,* a corn tortilla soufflé ($4). Open Mon.-Thurs. 7am-midnight, Fri.-Sat. 7am-2am, Sun. 8am-2am.

Sholz Garden, 1607 San Jacinto (477-4171), near the capitol. An Austin landmark recognized by the legislature for "epitomizing the finest traditions of the German heritage of our state." German only in name, though. Great chicken-fried steaks and Tex-Mex meals $5-6. Live country-rock music jazz. Open Mon.-Thurs. 11am-midnight, Fri.-Sat. 11am-2am.

Katz's, 618 6th St. (472-2037). Offers delicious deli-style sandwiches in a high-class setting. Entrées tend to be a bit more expensive but are worth the dough. Great kosher sandwiches. Try homemade blintz with sour cream ($5.50, $3.50 for a half-order). Open 24 hrs.

Quackenbush's, 2120 Guadalupe (472-4477). Café/deli popular with students. Plowman sandwiches $2.50-4. Meet UT students over a cup of espresso ($1). Open daily 7am-9pm.

Amy's, 3403 Guadalupe (458-6895). Just to be cool in Austin and at UT, try your favorite ice cream on a freshly baked belgian waffle cone. $1-2.

Sam's Bar-B-Que, 2000 E. 12th St. Take bus #12 or 6 eastbound. Tiny, dive-like interior thick with locals on weekends. Very popular, but it's in a seedy neighborhood. BBQ plates (with beans and potato salad) $4. Open Mon.-Thurs. 10am-3:30am, Fri.-Sat. 10am-5am, Sun. 10am-3am.

Sights

In 1882, not to be outdone by Washington, DC, Texans built their **state capitol,** Congress Ave. (463-0063), seven ft. higher than the national one. This colossal building with colorful inlaid marble floors has "Texas" inscribed on everything from door hinges to hallway benches. (Open during legislative session 24 hrs.; off-season 6am-11pm. Free tours Mon.-Sat. 8:30am-4:30pm.) The **Tourist Information Center,** (463-8586), in the south foyer, is open daily 8am to 5pm. Across the street from the capitol, at 11th and Colorado St., sleeps the **Governor's Mansion** (463-5516), built in 1856. The bottom level stores the furniture of the past 10 Texas governors. (Free tours Mon.-Fri. every 20 min. 10-11:40am.)

The **University of Texas at Austin,** the wealthiest public university in the country, forms the backbone of cultural life in Austin. With a 50,000 plus student enrollment, UT is the second largest university in the country. There are two **Visitors Information Centers** (471-1420), one in Sid Richardson hall at 2313 Red River and the other in the Nowotny building at the corner of I-35 and Martin Luther King, Jr. Blvd. Campus tours leave from the admissions office, adjacent to the Nowotny building, Mon.-Sat. at 11am and 2pm. Campus highlights include: the **Lyndon B. Johnson Library and Museum,** 2313 Red River St. (482-5279), which houses 35 million historical documents (open daily 9am-5pm; free) and the **Harry Ransom Center,** which houses one of the four extant copies of the Gutenberg Bible. An art museum complex on the western edge of the campus at Guadalupe and 21st St (471-8944), the center also hoards a vast collection of Aleister Crowley's manuscripts and correspondence as well as his personal library, perhaps the most complete Evelyn Waugh collection around, and the complete personal libraries of both Virginia Woolf and James Joyce. (Open Mon.-Sat. 9am-5pm, Sun. 1-5pm. Free.)

The **Laguna Gloria Art Museum,** 3809 W. 35th St. (458-8191), eight mi. from the capitol in a Mediterranean villa-lookalike, is an exemplary blend of art, architecture, and nature in Austin. With rolling, spacious grounds that overlook **Lake Austin,** the Laguna displays 20th-century artwork and hosts **Fiesta Laguna Gloria,** a May arts and crafts festival, as well as inexpensive evening concerts and plays. Take bus #21. (Tours Sun. at 2pm. Open Tues.-Sat. 10am-5pm, Thurs. 10am-9pm, Sun. 1-5pm. $2, seniors and students $1, ages under 16 free. Free Thurs.)

On hot afternoons, many zip to riverside **Zilker Park,** 2201 Barton Springs Rd., just south of the Colorado River. **Barton Springs Pool** (476-9044), in the park, is a popular swimming hole flanked by walnut and pecan trees. The spring-fed pool is 1000 ft. long and 200 ft. wide. Beware: the pool's temperature rarely rises above 60°F. Get away from the crowd and avoid paying by walking upstream (take an inner tube) and swimming at any spot that looks nice. ($1.75, Sat.-Sun. $2, ages 12-18 $.50, under 12 $.25. Swimming is free and at your own risk Nov.-Jan. Open daily 10am-7:30pm.) Zilker Park also has a botanical garden (477-8672), rentable canoes (478-3852), playgrounds, playing fields, and picnic areas. Parking inside the grounds costs $2 but is free on the roads near the entrance. For more fun and sun, drive to the **Windy Point** (266-9459 or 250-1963), a picturesque sandy park on **Lake Travis,** and try your hand (and body) at windsurfing or scubadiving. The park is on Comanche Rd., three mi. west off the 620 intersection.

Entertainment

Austin draws all sorts of musicians from all over the country and has boosted many to lone-stardom. On weekends fans from around the city and nearby towns converge to swing to a wide range of music. Austin's version of Broadway is **Sixth Street,** a stretch of seven blocks east of Congress, dotted with warehouse night clubs, fancy bars, a tatoo workshop, and an Oriental massage parlor. The *Weekly Austin Chronicle*, available at libraries and stores, provides detailed listings of current music performances, shows, and movies.

For great rock 'n' roll, try **Emo's,** 603 Red River, just off 6th St. (477-3667). Local bands rock this former garage on Thursday, Friday, and Saturday nights. On other days try your hand at the pool tables and play tunes of your choice on their jukebox. (Open daily, 3pm-2am. No cover. Happy hour 2-11pm.) The **Chicago House,** 607 Trinity, also off 6th St. (473-2542), plays a different tune on weekends as well as hosting the occasional poetry reading. (Open Mon.-Sat. 5pm-2am, Thurs. 8pm-2am. $7, students and seniors $6.) Stumble safely along 6th St. (the street is closed to traffic after 7pm daily), especially on weeknights when there is neither crowds nor cover charges, to sample the bands from the sidewalk. For raunchy Texas-style rock 'n' roll and cheap beer, try **Joe's Generic Bar.** (No phone, no cover. Open daily 11am-until...) On campus, the **Cactus Café,** 24th and Guadalupe (471-8228), hosts different musicians almost every night. (Hours vary; usually 8am-1am. Cover $2-12.) Next door, the **Texas Tavern** (471-5651) favors country music and fast food. (Hours vary; usually 11:30am-1:45am. Cover $2-5.) Those journeying out to Lake Travis should seek out the **Oasis Cantina De Lago,** 6550 Comanche Trail (266-2441), a restaurant and bar bathed in a gorgeous sunset. (Open Sun.-Thurs. 11am-9pm, Fri.-Sat. 11am-10pm. No cover.)

From early May through late August, the **Zilker Park Hillside Theater,** 2000 Barton Springs Rd. (499-2000), on Rte. 2244, produces free variety shows and concerts under the stars. Shows usually start between 7 and 9pm. The **Austin Symphony Orchestra** sponsors concerts of all kinds in the amphitheater downtown at 1101 Red River Rd. (476-6064), while last year UT's **Performing Arts Center,** 23rd at E. Campus Dr. (471-1444), staged professional productions of *Les Misérables* and *Hair.*

The historic **Paramount Theater,** 713 Congress (472-5470), shows daily double-features ($4; seniors, students, and under 12 $2.50).

Corpus Christi

After you've taken in all of Corpus Christi's sights—in other words, after half an hour—you may begin to wonder what you're doing in the "body of Christ." Look eastward into Corpus Christi Bay and the Gulf of Mexico, and you'll find the same answer as thousands before you. The sun and the sea are the city's religion; its piers and beaches are the temples on which devotees prostrate themselves. The popularity of Galveston and South Padre Island have left Corpus Christi unencumbered by unruly spring-break throngs and have allowed the city to retain its relatively peaceful seaside charm. This charm is augmented by the city's substantial Mexican-American population, most easily visible in the abundance of absolutely superior Tex-Mex restaurants. You may not be enlightened when you leave Corpus Christi, but after a while—about three days—you may feel divinely resurrected.

Practical Information and Orientation

Emergency: 911

Visitor Information: Convention and Visitors Bureau, 1201 N. Shoreline (882-5603), where I-37 meets the water. Piles of pamphlets, bus schedules, and local maps. Open Mon.-Fri. 8:30am-5pm, Sat. 9am-3pm. Info also available at the **Corpus Christi Museum,** 1900 N. Chaparral (883-2862). Open Sat. 10am-5pm, Sun. 1-5pm. The **Information Line** (854-8540) provides info on events, restaurants, clubs, and shopping.

Airport: Corpus Christi International Airport, 1000 International Dr. (289-0171), 15 min. west of downtown, bordered by Rte. 44 (Agnes St.) and Joe Mireur Rd. Cabs to downtown about $7. Served by major airlines.

Greyhound: 702 N. Chaparral (882-2516), at Starr downtown. To: Dallas (4 per day, 8 hr., $45), Houston (12 per day, 5 hr., $30), and Austin (5 per day, 6 hr., $32). Open 24 hrs. Lockers $1.

Public Transport: Regional Transit Authority (The "B"), 289-2600. Pick up route maps and schedules at the main station on the corner of Water and Schatzel St. or at the visitors bureau (see above). Central transfer point is City Hall, downtown. Buses run infrequently Mon.-Sat., until around 8pm. Fare $.50, seniors, disabled, students, and kids $.25. All buses $.10 on Sat. **The Tide,** an old-fashioned trolley, runs along the shoreline and to the aquarium. All $.25.

Taxi: American Cab Co., 949-8850. Base fare $1.35 per mi., $1.25 each additional mi. Major credit cards accepted. Airport-downtown $12.

Car Rental: Thrifty, 1928 N. Padre Island Dr. (289-0041), at Leopard St. $33 per day, 150 free mi. each day, $.20 each additional mi. Weekends $19 per day, 100 free mi. each day. Open Mon.-Fri. 6am-9pm, Sat.-Sun. 8am-9pm. Must be 21 with a major credit card.

Help Lines: 24-Hour Crisis Hotline, 887-9816. **Crisis Services,** 887-9818. **Women's Shelter,** 881-8888. Open 24 hrs.

Post Office: 809 Nueces Bay Blvd. (886-2200). Open Mon.-Fri. 8:30am-5pm, Sat. 8:30am-noon. **ZIP code:** 78469.

Area Code: 512.

The tourist district of Corpus Christi (pop. 225,000) follows **Shoreline Drive,** which borders the Gulf coast. The downtown business district lies one mi. west. Unfortunately, the streets don't quite follow a grid pattern, and the largely one-way roads downtown may frustrate drivers, sending them in circles up and down the bluff. **Agnes Street** and **Leopard Street** are the easiest routes to follow when approaching downtown from the west. Agnes St. goes directly downtown from the airport; Leopard follows a parallel path from most of the cheaper motels. Both streets end within one block of Shoreline Dr.

Accommodations and Food

Cheap accommodations are a scarce commodity in the downtown area. Much of the scenic and convenient shoreline is gilded with posh hotels and expensive motels. Overshadowed by the plethora of expensive lodgings, the **Sand and Sea Budget Inn,** 6013 N. Shoreline Dr. (882-6518), five blocks from the Greyhound station and across the street from the visitors bureau. Rooms have a color TV, plush carpeting, and free local calls. On weekends and holidays, it's a good idea to make your reservations in advance, and expect a busy management. (Singles $24. Doubles $30, with a view of the bay $40.)

For the best motel bargains, drive several mi. south on Leopard St. (served by bus #27) or I-37 (served by #27 Express). (Be sure to check the bus schedule, since they don't run frequently.) Conserve sleep at the **Ecomotel,** 6033 Leopard St. (289-1116). Exit I-37 north at Corn Products Rd., turn left and go to the second light (at Leopard St.), and take another left. By bus, take #27 from downtown right to the motel. Comfortable, generic rooms with cable TV and pool. (Singles $29. Doubles $35.) Campers should head to **Padre Island National Seashore** or **Mustang State Park** (see Padre Island National Seashore below). Also, **Nueces River City Park** (241-1464), north on I-37 (exit 16 at Nueces River), has free tent sites and three-day RV permits.

The mixed population of Corpus Christi and its seaside locale have resulted in a wide range of cuisine. The downtown area transubstantiates into many inexpensive and tasty eating establishments. **Bahía,** 224 Chaparral (884-6555), serves simple but rib-sticking Mexican breakfasts and lunches. The authentic food compensates for the tacky decor. Try *nopalitos* (cactus and egg on a tortilla, $1.25) or a taco and two enchiladas with rice beans, tea, and dessert ($3.75). Live entertainment rocks the *casa* on Friday from 7 to 9pm. (Open Mon.-Thurs. 7am-6pm, Fri. 7am-9pm, Sat. 7am-3pm.) Four blocks west, **Top Hat,** 601 N. Chaparral (887-0117), serves juicy steak and standard U.S. cuisine in a trendy setting. (Entrées $4.25-7.75, all-you-can-eat on Wed. and Thurs. nights $6; open daily 7:30am-10:30pm.) The barbecue specialist in town is **Papaw's Bar-be-cue,** 200 N. Staples, near the city hall (882-0312). A former saloon, the diner has been broilin' and burnin' beef for over 30 years. (Entrées $2.75-5.75.) The restaurant has an impressive collection of piggy banks from the 1930s. (Open Mon.-Fri. 11am-5:30pm.)

Sights

Corpus Christi's most significant sight is the shoreline, which is bordered for miles by wide sidewalks with graduated steps down to the water. Recently built lighthouses along the shoreline make the night view spectacular. The piers are filled with overpriced seaside restaurants, sail and shrimp boats, and hungry seagulls. Feeding these birds will produce a Hitchcockian swarm; wear a hat and prepare to run for your life.

Almost all of the beaches on North Shoreline Dr. are open for swimming; just follow the signs.

The **Texas State Aquarium,** P.O. Box 331307 (881-1200), focuses on marine life in the Gulf of Mexico and the Caribbean Sea. It is located in the **Corpus Christi Beach,** a five-minute walk from downtown. This undersea adventureland is worth the time and money to visit. (Open 9am-6pm. $6, seniors and kids $3.50.) The Tide (see Practical Information) runs between downtown and the aquarium. Just offshore floats the aircraft carrier **U.S.S Lexington,** a World War II relic now open to the public. A new gem in Corpus Christi's treasure chest, the carrier is a world of amazement to the curious visitor. Walk on the runways and check out the machine that destroyed hundreds of enemy aircraft. (Open Mon.-Sat. 9am-5pm, Sun. 11am-5pm. $7, children $3.75. Seniors and active military personnel $5.) For those determined to eke out a little culture after a day in the sun, your only option is on the north end of Shoreline Dr., where the Convention Center houses the **Art Museum of South Texas,** 1902 N. Shoreline (884-3844), whose small but impressive collection includes works by Monet, Matisse, Picasso, Rembrandt, Goya, and Ansel Adams. Wheelchair access. (Open Tues.-Sat. 10am-5pm, Sun. 1-5pm. $1-2, depending on the temporary exhibit.) The **Texas Jazz Festival** (883-4500), jams for its 32nd annual concert under the stars. The three-day performance in early July draws hundreds of musicians and thousand of fans from around the country. (Most performances free.)

Dallas

Denizens of Dallas like to brag about the number of contrasting elements in their city: a little bit of country, a little bit of rock 'n' roll, too many businessmen reeking of Stetson cologne, and a stampede of cowgirls sporting short mini-skirts all tossed in together in a cosmopolitan mishmash of skyscrapers, neon lights and modern shopping malls. The dreams of founding father John Neely Bryan seem to have come true. In 1841 Bryan, an ambitious Tennessee lawyer, built a tiny little loghouse outpost in the hopes that one day it would grow into a bustling metropolis. Grow it did. Dallas rose to prominence in the 1870s when a major north-south railroad crossed a transcontinental east-west line just south of the town. Converging waves of settlers in the 20th century, lured by prospects of black gold, caused the population to swell even further.

The eighth largest city in America, Dallas today is a major business and cultural center. Its reputation as the "City of Dreams" has attracted immigrants from the Far East and Latin America. While the city's legendary preoccupation with commerce is evident, recent massive campaigns for historic preservation have restored many run-down urban areas to their pre-petro glory, and the new Arts District and Deep Ellum have nurtured Texan culture.

Practical Information

Emergency: 911

Dallas Convention and Visitors Bureau, 1201 Elm St., Suite 24 (746-6677). Open Mon.-Fri. 8:30am-5pm. **Union Station Visitors Center,** 400 S. Houston Ave. (746-6603), in a booth in the lobby. Open daily 9am-5pm. **Special Events Info Line,** (746-6679).

Dallas-Ft. Worth International Airport: (214-574-8888), 17 mi. northwest of downtown. Sprawling, chatty conversational computer-run shuttle system makes even the longest layover bearable. **Love Field** (670-6080; take bus #39) has mostly intra-Texas flights. To get downtown from either airport, take the **Super Shuttle,** 729 E. Dallas Rd. (817-329-2001; in terminal, dial 02 on phone at ground transport services). 24-hr. service. DFW airport to downtown $10.50, Love Field to downtown $8.50.

Amtrak: 400 S. Houston Ave. (653-1101 or 800-872-7245), in Union Station, next to Reunion Tower. One train per day to Houston (6 hr., $31) and St. Louis (16 hr., $130).

Greyhound: 205 S. Lamar (655-7000), at Commerce 3 blocks east and 1 block north of Union Station. To: Houston (6 per day, 6 hr., $29); San Antonio (15 per day, 6 hr., $34); El Paso (6 per day, 12½ hr., $85); New Orleans (10 per day, 12½ hr., $75). Open 24 hrs.

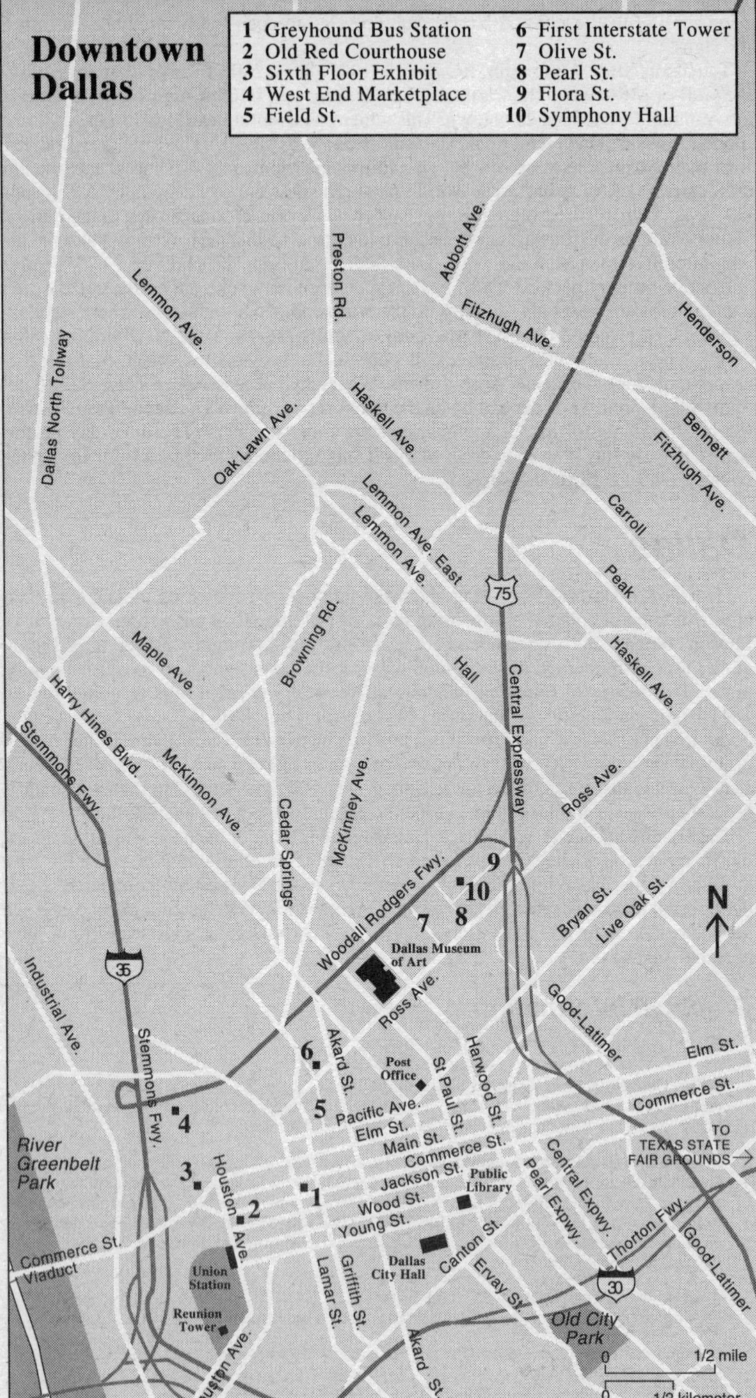
Downtown Dallas
1 Greyhound Bus Station
2 Old Red Courthouse
3 Sixth Floor Exhibit
4 West End Marketplace
5 Field St.
6 First Interstate Tower
7 Olive St.
8 Pearl St.
9 Flora St.
10 Symphony Hall
Abbott Ave.
Preston Rd.
Lemmon Ave.
Fitzhugh Ave.
Henderson
Dallas North Tollway
Haskell Ave.
Oak Lawn Ave.
Bennett
Fitzhugh Ave.
Lemmon Ave. East
Lemmon Ave.
Carroll
Peak
75
Browning Rd.
Maple Ave.
Hall
Haskell Ave.
Central Expressway
Harry Hines Blvd.
Stemmons Fwy.
McKinnon Ave.
McKinney Ave.
Cedar Springs
Ross Ave.
Woodall Rodgers Fwy.
Bryan St.
Live Oak St.
N
Dallas Museum of Art
35
Industrial Ave.
Ross Ave.
Good-Latimer
Stemmons Fwy.
Akard St.
Post Office
St Paul St.
Harwood St.
Elm St.
Commerce St.
Pacific Ave.
Elm St.
Main St.
Commerce St.
TO TEXAS STATE FAIR GROUNDS
River Greenbelt Park
Houston Ave.
Jackson St.
Public Library
Central Expwy.
Pearl Expwy.
Wood St.
Young St.
Thorton Fwy.
Good-Latimer
Commerce St. Viaduct
Union Station
Lamar St.
Griffith St.
Dallas City Hall
Canton St.
Ervay St.
30
Reunion Tower
Old City Park
Houston Ave.
Akard St.
0 1/2 mile
0 1/2 kilometer

Public Transport: Dallas Area Rapid Transit (DART), 601 Pacific Ave. (979-1111). Serves most suburbs; routes radiate from downtown. Service 5am-midnight, to suburbs 5am-8pm. Base fare 75¢. Info desk open Mon.-Fri. 8:30am-4:45pm. Maps available at Main and Akard St. (Mon.-Fri. 8am-5pm), or at Elm and Ervay St. (Mon.-Fri. 7am-6pm). **Hop-a-Bus** (979-1111) is DART's downtown Dallas service, with a park-and-ride system. Three routes (style blue, red, and green) run about every 10 min. Fare 25¢, transfers free. Look for buses with a blue bunny, a red kangaroo, or a green frog. No Hop-A-Bus service on weekends.

Taxi: Yellow Cab Co., 426-6262. $2.70 first mi., $1.20 each additional mi. DFW Airport to downtown $25.

Car Rental: All-State Rent-a-Car, 3206 Live Oak (741-3118). $20 per day with 100 free mi., 16¢ per additional mi. Open Mon.-Sat. 7:30am-6pm. Must be 21 with major credit card.

Bike Rental: Bicycle Exchange, 11716 Ferguson Rd. (270-9269). Rates from $50 per week, $75 for two weeks. Open Mon.-Fri. 9am-7pm, Sat. 9am-5pm. Must have a credit card. Free delivery.

Help Lines: Gay Hotline, 368-6283. Open Sun.-Thurs. 7-11pm, Fri.-Sat. 7:30pm-midnight. **Dallas Gay and Lesbian Community Center,** 2701 Reagan (528-4233), open daily 9am-9pm. **Senior Citizen Call Action Center** 1500 Marilla St. (744-3600) gives info on reduced fares, recreational activities, and health care.

Time Zone: Central (1 hr. behind Eastern).

Post Office: 400 N. Ervay St. (953-3045), on Thanksgiving Sq. downtown. Open Mon.-Fri. 8am-6pm. **ZIP code:** 75201; General Delivery, 75221; **Area Code:** 214.

Be aware that jaywalking is illegal in Dallas and is strictly enforced.

Accommodations and Camping

Cheap accommodations of the non-chain motel type are hard to come by; conventions and big events like the Cotton Bowl (Jan. 1) and the State Fairin Oct. exacerbate the problem. If you can afford it, your most luxurious option undoubtedly is **Bed and Breakfast Texas Style,** 4224 W. Red Bird Ln. (298-5433 or 298-8586). They'll place you at a nice home, usually near town, with friendly residents who are anxious to make y'all as comfortable as possible. Just give them a call when you arrive in town and they'll direct you to your host. Good deal for groups of two. (Singles $45. Doubles from $50.)

The best deal around is the **Delux Inn,** 3111 Stemmons Hwy. (637-0060). Accessible by bus (#49 "Brookhollow"), the inn has beautifully-furnished rooms with balconies, a nice pool, free morning coffee, free local calls, cable and HBO. Fast food restaurants and banks are only blocks away. (Singles $24. Doubles $25.) Major credit cards accepted. **U.S. 75 (Central Expressway), I-635 (LBJ Freeway),** and the suburbs of **Irving** and **Arlington** also have many inexpensive motels. Try **Motel 6** (505-891-6161), with 11 locations in the Dallas area, **Exel Inns** (800-356-8013), or **Red Roof Inns** (800-843-7663) for singles from $23 to 35.

If you have a car and camping gear, and are sleepy, grumpy, dopey, bashful, doc, sneezy, happy or just downright pissy try the **Hi-Ho Campground,** 200 W. Bear Creek Rd. (223-8574), south of town. Take I-35 14½ mi. to exit 412, turn right, and go 2 more mi. (Tent sites $10 for 2 people, with hookup $6.50, $1 per additional person.)

Food

Pick up a copy of the Friday weekend guide of the *Dallas Morning News* for an overview of what's available. The **West End Historic District,** popular with family vacationers, supplies vittles, libations, and entertainment in the heart of downtown. For fast Tex-Mex food and a variety of small shops, explore the **West End Marketplace,** 603 Munger St. (954-4350). The **Farmers Produce Market,** 1010 S. Pearl Expressway (748-2082), between Pearl and Central Expressway near I-30 (open daily sunrise-sunset), can satisfy all of your picnicking fantasies. For gourmet restaurants and low-priced authentic barbecue joints mosey down **Greenville Ave**.

Snuffer's, 3526 Greenville (826-6850). Has the best burgers ($3.50) in town. Nice all-wooden interior with friendly service and fun crowd. Don't miss the fried mushrooms ($3.25). Snuffer's has recently built an adjacent wooden patio. Cash bar. Other dishes range from $5-6. Open daily 11am-2am.

Herrera's Café, 4001 Maple Ave. (528-9644). Take bus #29. Informality doesn't daunt business people who partake of the excellent Tex-Mex dinners. Filling meals $4-6. Bring your own beer, and expect to wait on weekends. Open Mon. and Wed.-Thurs. 10am-9pm, Fri. 10am-10pm, Sat. 9am-10pm, Sun. 9am-9pm.

Bubba's, 6617 Hillcrest Ave. (373-6527). A remodeled, '50s-style diner near the heart of SMU. Serves the best fried chicken and chicken-fried steak dinners in town ($4-5.40). Open daily 6:30am-10pm.

Sonny Bryan's Smokehouse, 302 N. Market St. (744-1610). Located at the threshhold of the historic West End, this landmark is the ultimate Dallas experience. Eat where Queen Elizabeth II of England ate when she was in Dallas. The barbecue combination ($8) comes with your choice of vegetables, relish tray, and Sonny's own barbecue sauce. You don't need to worry about tipping. (Open Mon.-Sat. 11am-midnight, Sun. 11am-4pm.)

Aw Shucks, 3607 Greenville Ave. (821-9449). A casual seafood bar with an unbeatable outdoor patio for slurping raw oysters ($3-7) in the summer. Open Mon.-Thurs. 11am-11pm, Fri.-Sat. 11am-mid., Sun. 11:30am-10pm.

Kuby's, 6601 Snider Plaza near SMU (363-2231) or 3121 Ross Ave., downtown (821-3121). This German deli/market serves cheap breakfasts ($2-4) and sandwiches ($3-5) as well as their own packaged sausages and kraut. Open Mon.-Sat. 6am-6pm, Sun. 9am-3pm; downtown stores open 7am-2pm.

Two Pesos, 1827 Greenville (823-2092). Fast-food style, but "Dos Pesos" is a late-night Dallas tradition. Serves tasty Mex dishes at prices slightly higher than two pesos. ($3-4 for a la carte items and great tacos and fajitas $1-2). Take bus #1 to "Belmont" from downtown and get off at Greenville and Ross. Has downtown locations. Open 24 horas.

Sights

Historically, Dallas has been a static city. Most of historic Dallas remains in present-day downtown. The 1841 log cabin of **John Neely Bryant,** the City's founder, still stands in the heart of Dallas (at Elm and Market St.). A full view of the city's layout can be viewed from 50 stories up, atop **Reunion Tower,** 300 Reunion Blvd. (651-1234). This is a good place to start a walking tour and to get acquainted with the city. (Open Mon.-Fri. 10am-10pm, Sat.-Sun. 9am-midnight; $2, seniors and kids $1.)

On your way out of Reunion Tower, take the underground walkway to the adjoining **Union Station,** 400 S. Houston Ave., and explore one of the city's few grand old buildings. Upon exiting the building, walk north along Houston, and you'll come upon the **West End Historic District,** an impressive example of urban gentrification. Two blocks down and six flights up on Elm is the sixth floor of the former **Texas School Book Depository** from where Lee Harvey Oswald allegedly fired the fatal shot at President John F. Kennedy on November 22, 1963. This floor, now a museum devoted to the Kennedy legacy, traces the dramatic and macabre moments of the assassination in various media. (Open Mon.-Fri. 10am-6pm, Sat. 10am-7pm. Last ticket sold one hour before closing. $4, seniors $3, ages 6-18 $2.) Philip Johnson's illuminating **Memorial to Kennedy** looms nearby, at Market and Main St. At the corner of Houston and Main St. is the old **Dallas County Courthouse,** nicknamed "Old Red" for its unique red sandstone composition. Built in 1892, the romanesque structure is one of Dallas' most revered landmarks.

Continue north on Houston as it curves east and becomes Ross Ave. in the heart of the commercial area of the West End. The streets of red brick warehouses converted to restaurants and bars end in the **West End Marketplace,** 603 Munger Ave., a passel of fast-food eateries, bars, shops, and tourists. (Open Tues.-Thurs. 11am-10pm, Fri.-Sat. and Mon. 11am-midnight, Sun. noon-8pm.) Just east of the West End on the corner of Ross Ave. and Field St. stands Dallas' most impressive skyscraper, **The First Interstate Tower,** a multi-sided prism towering above a glistening water garden.

Walking farther east along Ross Ave. leads you to the new **Arts District,** the centerpiece of which is the **Dallas Museum of Art,** 1717 N. Harwood St. (922-1200). The museum offers Indonesian, impressionist, modern, and U.S. decorative art. The outdoor sculpture garden and art room will delight the children. (Open Tues.-Wed. and Fri.-Sat. 10am-5pm, Thurs. 10am-9pm, Sun. and holidays noon-5pm. Children's room open Wed.-Thurs. and Sat. noon-5pm. Both free.)

Walking south from the museum on St. Paul, toward the downtown area, turn right on Bryan St. and walk one block to **Thanksgiving Square** (969-1977), a tiny park beneath massive towers. While viewing this monument to Thanksgiving in all religions, you too will give thanks for the respite from the busy streets the park's sunken gardens and waterfalls provide. (Open Mon.-Fri. 9am-5pm, Sat.-Sun. and holidays 1-5pm.) Continue south from Thanksgiving Square along Ervay St. to the imposing **Dallas City Hall,** 100 Marilla St. (670-3957), designed by the ubiquitous I.M. "Everywhere" Pei.

About nine blocks south of City Hall on Ervay St. is the **Old City Park,** at Gano St. (421-5141). The park is both the oldest and the most popular recreation area and lunch spot in the city. Open spaces and picnic facilities are scattered among restored buildings, which include a railroad depot and a church. (Park open daily 9am-6pm. Exhibit buildings open Tues.-Sat. 10am-4pm, Sun. 1:30-4:30pm. Tours $4.)

Fair Park, southeast of downtown on 2nd Ave. (670-8400), has been home to the state fair since 1886, although most of the structures there today remain from the 1936 State Fair celebrating the Texas Centennial. The park is home to the Cotton Bowl, numerous museums, and a Texas-sized ferris wheel, all within walking distance of each other. A standout is the **Museum of Natural History** (670-8457), which has a small permanent display on prehistoric life. (Open Mon.-Sat. 9am-5pm. Free.) Other buildings include the **Museum of African-American Life and Culture** (565-9026; open Mon.-Fri. 9am-5pm); the **Aquarium** (670-8441; open daily 10am-4:30pm, 50¢); the **Age of Railroad Steam Museum** (428-0101; open Thurs.-Fri. 10am-3pm, Sat.-Sun. 11am-5pm; $2, under 17 $1); the **Science Place** (428-5555; open daily 9:30am-5:30pm; $5, seniors and ages 7-16 $2); and the **Dallas Garden Center** (428-7476; open Tues.-Sat. 10am-5pm, Sun. 1-5pm).

Nearby **White Rock Lake** is good for walking, biking or rollerblading. On the eastern shore of the lake is the **Dallas Arboretum,** 8525 Garland Rd. (327-8263), a 66-acre botanical heaven on earth with resplendent flowers and trees. It's only a 15-min. bus ride from downtown. To gaze upon Dallas' mansions, drive up the **Swiss Avenue Historic District** or through the streets of **Highland Park,** a town within Dallas whose high-school boasts a million-dollar astroturf football stadium.

Entertainment

Dallas' culture and nightlife exploded out of nowhere in the late 1970s and continue to gush. The free weekly *Dallas Observer* (out Thursdays) will help you to sort your entertainment options. Enjoy free summer theater during July and August at the **Shakespeare in the Park** festival (599-2778), at Samuell-Grand Park just northeast of State Fair Park between Grand Ave. and Samuell Blvd. Two plays are performed annually; each runs about two weeks. The **Music Hall** (565-1116) in Fair Park houses the **Dallas Civic Opera** (443-1043) from November to February (tickets $7-75) and **Dallas Summer Musicals** from June to October. (Performances nightly, $4-37; 565-1116 for info, 787-2000 for tickets, 696-4253 for ½-price tickets on performance days). The **Dallas Symphony Orchestra** (692-0203) now performs at the newly completed **Morton H. Meyerson Symphony Center,** at Pearl and Flora St. in the arts district. The I.M. Pei-designed structure is renowned for its classic acoustics. (Tickets $10-40.)

Downtown nightlife is centered on the oft-visited **West End,** unless you have dem **Deep Ellum** blues. The West End offers **Dallas Alley,** 603 Munger (988-0581), an ensemble of clubs with a single ($4-8) cover charge. The **Outback Pub** (761-9355) and **Dick's Last Resort** (747-0001), both at 101 N. Market, are locally popular bars with no cover, good beer selections, and raucous crowds. (Both open daily 11am-2pm; Dick's closed on Sun.) On weekends and occasionally during the week, various bands perform concerts out on the red brick marketplace.

Deep Ellum, on the east side of downtown, was known as the "Harlem of Dallas" in the 1930s, when it was home to such blues greats as Blind Lemon Jefferson. By the early 1980s, however, the area had become an urban wasteland. A renaissance of sorts began with clandestine late-night parties thrown by artists and musicians in Deep Ellum's empty warehouses. Today, the area has become downright commercialized, but is still enjoyable. **Club Dada,** 2720 Elm (744-3232), former haunt of Edie Brickell, has scaled up with art on the walls, an outdoor patio, and live local acts. (Open daily 8pm-2am; cover $3-5, drinks $2-4.) **Tree's,** 2709 Elm (748-5009), hosts an eclectic range of local and national acts in a vast warehouse with pool tables in the loft. (Open daily 8pm-2am. Cover $2-10, drinks $1.50-4. Min. age 18.)

The areas around SMU and Greenville Ave. rollick with nightlife. **Poor David's Pub,** 1924 Greenville (821-9891), stages live music for an older crowd that leans towards folk and blues. (Open Mon.-Sat. 8pm-2am. No cover charge.) The **Greenville Bar and Grill,** 2821 Greenville, a Dallas classic, is an old-fashioned blues and rhythm bar with cheap beer ($1) and a cheeky attitude. (Open daily 11am-2am. Pianist on Fri. 5-8pm) Popular nightspots conveniently line **Yale Blvd.,** home of SMU's fraternity row. The current bar of choice is the **Green Elephant,** 5612 Yale (750-6625), a pseudo-'60s extravaganza complete with lava lamps and tapestries. (Open daily 10pm-2am.)

Six Flags Over Texas (817-640-8900), 15 mi. from downtown off I-30 in Arlington, is the original link in the nationwide amusement park chain. The name alludes to the six different ruling states that have flown their flags over Texas. This is a thrill-lover's paradise, replete with an vomitous array of rides, restaurants, shops, and entertainment venues. The hefty admission charge itself is enough to induce nausea. ($23, over 55 years or under 4 ft. $17—includes unlimited access to all rides and attractions. Open June-Aug. Sun.-Thurs. 10am-10pm, Fri.-Sat. 10am-midnight; March-May and Sept.-Oct. Sat.-Sun. 10am-8pm. Parking $3.)

Fort Worth

Lost but not forgotten alongside the cosmopolitan pretensions of Dallas, **Fort Worth** is a 30-minute drive west on I-30. You can't say you've visited Dallas if you haven't visited the Fort. If Dallas is the last Eastern city, Fort Worth is undoubtedly the first Western one; a daytrip here is worth your while if only for the **Stockyards District** (817-625-9715), at the corner of N. Main and E. Exchange Ave., which hosts weekly rodeos (Sat. 8pm, April-Sept.) and cattle auctions (Mon. at 10am). The **Tarantula** steam train that connects downtown with the stockyards also takes the rider on a nostalgic journey through the Old West and on a comprehensive tour of downtown. The stockyards hosts such seasonal festivities as the **Chisholm Round-Up.** The Round-Up is a three day jamboree during the second weekend of June commemorating the heroism of cowhands who led the long cattle drive down to Kansas during the Civil War. Also check out the **Armadillo Races** in which grandfather and grandson work together to blow the beast to move. For more info. call 817-625-7005. The district's frontier feeling is accessorized by numerous Western bookstores, restaurants, and saloons. For more on the stockyards, go to the **visitor information center** kiosk (817-624-4741) 130 Exchange Ave. (Open Mon.-Sat. 10am-5pm; Sun. noon-6pm.) A far cry from the rugged stockyards is the **Kimbell Art Museum,** 3333 Camp Bowie Blvd. (817-332-8451), a beautiful building designed by the late Louis Kahn. Inside is a choice selection of pre-20th-century European painting and sculpture, one of the best in the Southwest. (Open Tues.-Sat. 10am-5pm, Sun. 11am-5pm. Free.)

Fort Worth's **area code** is 817.

El Paso

Your map may say Texas, but you'll have hard time believing it—El Paso, along with Mexican sister city Juárez, forms a bi-national metropolis with a heavy emphasis on the Mexican side. Certainly the city's heritage is more Mexican than Texan; Spanish Mexicans first explored the area 400 years ago while fleeing a Pueblo revolt, dubbing the fertile valley "El Paso del Norte" (Passage of the North). Not until the Mexican-American War in 1848 did *gringos* begin to inhabit the area. Some are still bitter about

Mexican losses suffered in the war; graffiti along the Río Grande compares North American imperialism to Iraq's 144-year-long occupation of Kuwait—the U.S. also conquered New Mexico and California 144 years ago. More North Americans arrived in El Paso in 1873, and the line in the sand drawn by the Mexican-American War across Ciudad Juárez became increasingly important; many refugees from the Mexican Revolution of 1909 fled here. In more recent years, immigrants have been used in the region to bust unions and keep wages low on the U.S. side. Hispanic culture defines the flavor of El Paso; if not for the collegiate atmosphere of the University of Texas at El Paso (UTEP) and downtown's high-rise bank buildings, you would think you had accidentally crossed the border along the way—which, by the way, is just about how hard it is to visit Juárez.

Note: To reach Mexico by phone from the U.S., dial (011-52), the city code, and then the phone number. The **city code** for Juárez is 16.

Practical Information

Emergency: 911. **Juárez Police,** 248-35.

Visitor Information: El Paso Tourist Information Center, 5 Civic Center Plaza (544-0062) in downtown across the street from the Greyhound station. Open daily 8:30am-5pm.

Amtrak: 700 San Francisco Ave. (545-2247; 800-872-7245 for reservations), on the western side of the Civic Center, near Greyhound. Office open daily 11am-7pm. Reservations required.

Greyhound: 111 San Francisco Ave. (544-7200), at Santa Fe across from the Civic Center. To: Albuquerque (4 per day, 6 hr. $35); Dallas (8 per day, 13 hr. $53); and San Antonio (4 per day, 11 hr. $81). For info on buses into Mexico, call 533-3837. Office open 24 hrs. Lockers $1.

El Paso-Los Angeles Limousine Service, 72 S. Oregon (530-4061). Offers cheaper service to Albuquerque and Tucson en route to Los Angeles. To: Albuquerque $20, Tucson $25, Los Angeles $25.

Public Transport: Sun City Area Transit (SCAT), 533-3333. Extensive service. All routes begin downtown at San Jacinto Plaza (Main at Mesa). Fewer routes in the northwest. Connects with Juárez system. Maps and schedules posted in the Civic Center Park and at public libraries. Mon.-Fri. 8am-noon and 1-5pm. Most buses stop around 5pm; limited service on Sun. Fare 75¢, seniors 15¢, students with ID 35¢.

Taxi: Yellow Cab, 533-3433. Base fare $1.20, $1.30 per mi.

Car Rental:Dollar-Rent-A-Car, 778-5445. $39 per day with unlimited free mileage. Open 24 hrs. They will deliver. Major credit cards accepted. **Rent-a-Heap,** 4305 Anapro (532-2170). Will deliver. $20 per day, unlimited free mi., 3-day min. rental. Cars must be kept within a 50-mi. radius of El Paso and are not allowed across the border. Must be 18 with a major credit card. Open Mon.-Fri. 9am-5pm, Sat. 9am-noon.

Help Lines: Crisis Hotline, 779-1800. **U.S. Customs Service,** 541-6794. Both open 24 hrs.

Post Office: 219 Mills St. (775-7500), General Delivery at 5300 E. Paisano, at Alameda about 5 mi. from downtown. Both open Mon.-Fri. 8:30am-5pm, Sat. 8:30am-noon. **ZIP code:** 79910.

Area Codes: El Paso, 915. International direct dialing to Ciudad Juárez is 011-52 (country code)-16 (city code)-local number.

The geographical intrusion of the Río Grande and the Franklin Mountains complicates the city's road plan. Split by the Franklins, the city roughly forms a letter "Y," angling northwest to southeast along the river.

Accommodations, Camping, and Food

The cheapest hotel rooms land across the border, but downtown El Paso has several good budget offerings within easy walking distance of downtown. The **Gardner Hotel,** 311 E. Franklin (532-3661), at Stanton, is only six blocks from the Greyhound station and the visitors center. It is also home to the **El Paso International Hostel (HI/AYH).** The hostel has a pool table, laundry, and kitchen in the basement and pay phones in the lobby. (Members only $11.) Nonmembers can buy a membership card for

$18 or stay in the hotel. (Singles with bath $20. Doubles $25. Private room for 4 with TV $43.) Most other downtown motels are either very expensive or very shabby. The **Mesa Inn,** 4151 N. Mesa (532-7911), is a large, luxurious exception to this rule. Rooms are clean and come with cable TV and free local calls. Pool and restaurant. (Singles $25. Doubles $30. Weekends $5 less.)

There are a few small RV campgrounds near downtown but the nicest outdoor lodgings lie miles outside El Paso and are not very accessible by public transportation. The **Hueco Tanks State Park** (857-1135), a 32-mi. hike east of El Paso on U.S. 62/180, is a great place for hiking and rockclimbing but offers meager service. (Shaded site with full hookup $15. Showers and restrooms.)

A great place to experience local culture and eat spicy Mexican food is **The Tap,** 500 San Antonio, at Stanton downtown (532-4456). Loud bar, cheap food. Mexican plate $3.25. Other entrées $2-5. (Open daily 7am-1am.) **Arnold's Mexican Restaurant,** 315 Mills Ave. at Kansas downtown (532-3147), just a few blocks south of the hostel, serves excellent authentic Mexican dishes ($2.50-5. Breakfast special $1.75.) (Open Mon.-Fri. 7am-3pm.) Also downtown, a block from the hostel, is **Big Bun Burger,** 501 Stanton at Franklin (546-9359), which serves your standard diner fare at 1950s prices. Burgers ($1), fountain drinks (60¢), and tacos (70¢). (Open Mon.-Sat. 8am-8pm, Sun. 10am-4pm.)

Sights and Entertainment

The majority of visitors to El Paso are either stopping off on the long drive through the desert or headed across the border for a taste of Mexico. Two pedestrian and motor roads cross the Río Grande: **El Paso**, an overcrowded one-way street, and **Santa Fe**, a parallel road lined with Western wear stores, clothing shops, and decent restaurants. Entry to Mexico is $.25, and the trip back into the U.S. costs $.50. Day trippers, including foreign travelers with a multi-entry visa, need only flash their documents of citizenship in order to pass in and out. A walk across the border is worth your while but try to make it to downtown Juárez and avoid the border area tourist businesses. (For more on Ciudad Juárez, see *Let's Go: Mexico.*)

Volatile downtown El Paso has more to offer than just a cross-border trip. Historic **San Jacinto Plaza** swarms daily with men and women, young and old. Catch the true flavor of local culture and listen to street musicians perform here where Spanish *conquistadores*, Fort Bliss cavalry men, and *señoritas* once rested. South of the square, **El Paso Street** is another place you don't want to miss. Hundreds of locals hurry along the street and dash into stores trying to grab the best bargain. You can buy a pair of Wranglers for as little as $10. To take in a complete picture of the Río Grande Valley, head northeast of downtown on Rim Rd. (which becomes Scenic Dr.) to **Murchison Park,** at the base of the mountains; the park offers a fine view of El Paso, Juárez, and the Sierra Madre.

Strategic timing can make your visit to El Paso more entertaining. The town hosts the **Southwestern Livestock Show & Rodeo** (532-1401) in February, the **World Championship Finals Rodeo** (544-2582) in November, and a **Jazz Festival** (534-6277) in October at the Chamizal Memorial.

Houston

Houston (pop. 3,232,000) arose in the wake of Texas' battle for independence from Mexico when two New York speculators bought 2000 acres of land on Buffalo Bayou in 1906. An energy center since the discovery of nearby oil deposits in 1901, the settlement emerged as a major cotton shipping port with the 1915 completion of the Houston Ship Channel. Not surprisingly, Houston's geographical expansion parallels its history of quick economic growth; in all, the city sprawls over almost 500 square mi. The absence of zoning laws, combined with a recklessly swift building boom in the 70s and early 80s, has resulted in a peculiar architectural mix: a museum, an historic home, a 7-

Eleven, and a mini-mall may share the same city block, while the downtown area showcases an oil-sprouted array of modern skyscrapers.

Practical Information and Orientation

Emergency: 911.

Greater Houston Convention and Visitors Bureau, 3300 Main St. (523-5050), at Stuart. Approximately 1 mi. off I-45. Take any bus serving the southern portion of Main St. (#7, 8, 14, 25, 65, 70, or 78). Open Mon.-Fri. 8:30am-5pm.

Traveler's Aid, 2630 Westbridge (668-0911). Open Mon.-Fri. 8am-5:30pm. Take bus #15 "Hiram Clark" from Main St. The **American Red Cross**, 2701 SW Freeway, (668-0911) is open 24 hrs. and tends to stranded travelers and provides referral information. Both offices are staffed by caring people who will find you a place to stay—as our Southwest researcher Masood Farivar will personally attest!

Houston Intercontinental Airport: 25 mi. north of downtown (230-3000). Get to the city center via the **Airport Express** (523-8888). Buses depart every 30 min. between 7am and midnight (fare $9.75, kids $4.75). **Hobby Airport** is 9 mi. south of downtown, just west of I-45. Take bus #73 to Texas Medical Center and then catch any bus to downtown. **Hobby Airport Limousine Service** (644-8359) leaves for downtown every 30 min. between 7:30am and midnight (fare $5, under 13 free). **Southwest Airlines** (237-1221 or 800-435-9792) has commuter flights to most major Texas cities. Flights from Hobby to San Antonio, Dallas, and Austin (as low as $44).

Amtrak: 902 Washington Ave. (224-1577 or 800-872-7245), in a rough and tumble neighborhood. During the day, catch a bus by walking west on Washington (away from downtown) to its intersection with Houston Ave. At night, call a cab. To: San Antonio (3 per week, 4 hr., $43); New Orleans (3 per week, 9 hr., $70); Dallas (daily, 6 hr., $30); El Paso (3 per week, 16 hr., $132).

Greyhound: 2121 S. Main St. (222-1161), on or near several local bus routes. All late-night arrivals should call a cab—this is an unsafe area. To: San Antonio (7 per day, 4 hr., $27); Dallas (6 per day, 5 hr., $30); El Paso (8 per day, 4 via San Antonio—the shorter route—, 4 via Dallas, $106); Corpus Christi (13 per day, 5 hr., $28); Galveston (6 per day, 1½ hr., $9). Open 24 hrs. Lockers $1.

Public Transport: Metropolitan Transit Authority (METRO Bus System), (658-0854, for route and schedule info call 635-4000). Mon.-Fri. 6am-8pm, Sat.-Sun. 8am-5pm. Buses usually operate 6am-midnight; less frequently on weekends. An all-encompassing system that can take you from NASA (15 mi. southeast of town) to Katy (25 mi. west of town). Get system maps at the Customer Services Center, 912 Dallas St. (658-0854; open Mon.-Fri. 10am-6pm). Individual route maps can also be obtained at Metro headquarters, 500 Jefferson at Smith, 12th floor; the Houston Public Library, 500 McKinney at Bagby (236-1313; open Mon.-Fri. 9am-9pm, Sat. 9am-6pm; Sun. 2-6pm); or at the Metro RideStore at 813 Dallas and 700 Fannin, where packs of 10 tokens ($6.80) are available. Half fare available to students, seniors and people with disabilities with an ID ($2). Fare 85¢. Transfers free.

Taxi: Yellow Cab, 236-1111. Base rate $3.05 plus $1.20 per mi. Be *sure* to ask for a flat rate in advance.

Car Rental: Rent-A-Heap Cheap, 5818 Star Lane (977-7771). Cars from $27 a day with 100 free mi., 25¢ each additional mi. Open Mon.-Fri. 9am-6pm, Sat.-Sun. 9am-5pm. Must be 21 with major credit card or a $350 cash deposit.

Help Lines: Crisis Center Hotline, 228-1505. Open 24 hrs. **Rape Crisis,** 528-7273. Open 24 hrs. **Gay Switchboard of Houston,** 529-3211. Counseling, medical and legal referrals, and entertainment info. Open daily 3pm-midnight.

Time Zone: Central (1 hr. behind Eastern).

Post Office: 401 Franklin St. (224-1474). Open Mon.-Fri. 7am-7pm, Sat 8am-noon. **ZIP code:** 77052.

Area Code: 713.

The flat Texan terrain supports several mini-downtowns. True downtown Houston, a squarish grid of interlocking one-way streets, borders the Buffalo Bayou at the intersection of I-10 and I-45. The city's notorious traffic jams will halt drivers during rush hour, but a car in Houston is almost a must; distances are vast and bus service is spotty and infrequent. Houstonians orient themselves by **The Loop,** (I-610) which lassoes the city center with a radius of six mi. Anything inside The Loop is easily accessible by car or bus. Find rooms on the southern side of the city—near Montrose Ave., the museums, Hermann Park, Rice University, and Perry House—for easy access to several bus lines and points of interest.

Although all of Texas is hot in the summer, Houston's humidity makes it especially stifling; 85°F in Houston can feel worse than 100°F in El Paso.

Accommodations and Camping

It is not a surprise that a city the size of Houston would have plenty of motels. The cheaper motels are concentrated southwest of downtown along the **Katy Freeway** (I-10 west), but for better and more convenient rooms, drive along **South Main Street.** Singles are as low as $20, doubles as low as $24. The rooms may be decent once you get inside, but these parts of town can be quite dangerous at night. (Buses #8 and 9 go down S. Main, and #19, 31, and 39 go out along the Katy Freeway.) Ask around about **The Mayflower/Space City Hostel (HI/AYH)** at 2242 West Bay Area Blvd., Friendswood, TX (996-0323/482-2432) which opened in the late summer of 1992. It is situated between Galveston and Houston and is accessible by bus from downtown Houston, and the perspicacious proprietor offers tours of nearby attractions.

Perry House, Houston International Hostel (HI/AYH), 5302 Crawford (523-1009), at Oakdale. From the Greyhound station, take bus #8 or 9 south to the Southmore St. (Bank of Houston) stop. Walk 5 blocks east to Crawford and one block south to Oakdale. Friendly management, nice rooms, and in a quiet neighborhood near Hermann park. Owners will sometimes offer makeshift city tours; ask about the nighttime version. Rooms and office closed 10am-5pm, but you can always show up during lock-out and hang out in the TV room. Curfew 11pm. Members $10.25, nonmembers $13.25. Linen $1.50.

Houston Youth Hostel, 5530 Hillman #2 (926-3444). Take bus #36 to Lawndale at Dismuke. Farther from downtown than Perry House with fewer beds, but more laid-back. No curfew. Coed dorm room, $7 per bunk. Linen $1.

YMCA, 1600 Louisiana Ave. (659-8501), between Pease and Leeland St. One of the better YMCAs in the Southwest. Men only. Good downtown location and only blocks from the Greyhound station. Separate floor for women. Clean rooms with daily maid service. TV, selected movies upon request, wake-up calls, pool and gym, common baths. Rooms $15, key deposit $5. Another branch at 7903 South Loop (643-4390) is farther from downtown but less expensive. Take Bus #50 at Broadway. $13, plus key deposit $10.

The Roadrunner, 8500 S. Main. (666-4971). One of 2 locations in Houston. Friendly and helpful management. Cable TV, mini pool, free coffee and local calls. Large, well-furnished rooms. Singles $22 ($20 if you ask for a discount). Doubles $28. Beep beep!

Grant Motor Inn, 8200 Main St. (668-8000), near the Astrodome. Clean and safe. Satellite TV, swing-set, and pool. Maid service and continental breakfast. Luxurious rooms near the palm-tree-covered, sand-banked pool that adds a tropical flavor. Singles $31, $34 for two people. Doubles $38, $42 for four people.

Two campgrounds grace the Houston area. Both the **KOA Houston North,** 1620 Peachleaf (442-3700), and the **Houston Campground,** 710 State Hwy. 6 S. (493-2391), are out in the boondocks, inaccessible by METRO Bus. KOA, about 20 mi. north on I-45, has a pool, showers, playground, and 24-hr. security. $18 per site for two people, $1.50 per additional adult. Houston Campground charges $11 per site for two ($3 per additional adult, $1.50 per additional child).

Food

A port town, Houston has witnessed the arrival of many immigrants (today its Indochinese population is the second largest in the nation), and its range of restaurants reflects this diversity. Houston's cuisine mingles Mexican and Vietnamese food, and the state specialty, BBQ. Look for reasonably priced restaurants among the shops and boutiques along **Westheimer St.,** especially near the intersection with Montrose. This area, referred to as "Montrose," is Houston's answer to Greenwich Village. This area is also popular with gay men. Bus #82 follows Westheimer from downtown to well past

The Loop. For great Vietnamese cuisine, go to **Milam St.,** where it intersects Elgin St., just south of downtown.

Hobbit Hole, 1715 S. Shepherd Dr. (528-3418). A reddish, 2-story, dimly-lit diner with a nice backyard patio. A few blocks off Westheimer. Take bus #82 and get off at Shepard Drive intersection. For the herbivorous adventurer. Entrées ($4-8) named after Tolkein characters. Ramble on to Led-Zep-inspired Misty Mountain Strawberry ($3). Open Mon.-Thurs. 11am-11pm, Fri.-Sat. 11am-midnight, Sun. 11:30am-10pm.

On The Border, 4608 Westheimer Rd., near the Galleria (961-4494). Take bus #82 at Louisiana and Pierce. Standard Tex-Mex fare with a twist (mesquite-grilled vegetable platter $6). Try the Tex-Mex combo platter served with rice, beans, soft taco and enchilada ($5.75). Nice bar, loud crowd. Open Sun.-Thurs. 11am-11pm, Fri.-Sat. 11am-midnight.

Van Loc, 3010 Milam St. (528-6441). Yummy Vietnamese and Chinese food (entrées $5-8). The great all-you-can-eat luncheon buffet ($3.65) includes unlimited iced tea. Open Sun.-Thurs. 9:30am-11:30pm, Fri.-Sat. 9:30am-12:30am. Downtown location, 825 Travis, has a similar buffet but charges a bit more. Live music 6-8pm. Same hrs.

New Orleans Po'Boy, 3902 S. Main (524-5778). Serves great sandwiches and burgers. Good place to have breakfast and hear yuppie gossip. Po'boys $2.50-3.50. Open Mon.-Fri. 4:30am-6:30pm, Sat. 4:30am-4:30am.

Good Company, 5109 Kirby Dr. (522-2530). Might be the best BBQ (and the most popular) in Texas, with honky-tonk atmosphere to match. Sandwiches $3, dinner $5-6. Try the Czech sausage ($5). Open Mon.-Sat.11am-10pm, Sun. noon-1pm. Expect a line.

Cadillac Bar, 1802 N. Shepherd Dr. (862-2020), at the Katy Freeway (I-10), northwest of downtown. Take bus #75, change to #26 at Shepherd Dr. and Allen Pkwy. Wild fun and authentic Mexican food. Tacos and enchiladas $5-7; heartier entrées more expensive. Open Mon.-Thurs. 11am-10:30pm, Fri. 11am-midnight, Sat. noon-midnight, Sun. noon-10pm.

Luther's Bar-B-Q, 8777 S. Main St. (432-1107). One of twelve locations in the Houston area. Good Texas barbecue entrées ($3-6) and free refills on iced tea. Open Sun.-Thurs. 11am-10pm, Fri.-Sat. 11am-11pm. Downtown location, 1110 Smith St. (759-0018).

Sights

Amid Houston's sprawling sauna of oil refineries and food chains are a few worthwhile sights. Focus on the **downtown,** the nexus of virtually all the city's bus routes (see Practical Information).

In the southwest corner of the downtown area is **Sam Houston Park,** just west of Bagby St. between Lamar and McKinney St. **Saint John's Lutheran Church,** built in 1891 by German farmers, contains the original pulpit and pews. Catch the one-hour tour to see four buildings in the park. (Tours on the hr. Mon.-Sat. 10am-3pm, Sun. 1-4pm. Tickets $4, students and seniors $2.)

Central downtown is a shopper's subterranean paradise. Hundreds of shops and restaurants line the underground **Houston Tunnel System,** which connects all the major buildings in downtown Houston, extending from the Civic Center to the Tenneco Building and the Hyatt Regency. On hot days, everyone ducks into the air-conditioned passageways via any major building or hotel. To navigate the tunnels, pick up a map at the Houston Public Library, the Pennzoil Place, the Texas Commerce Bank or call Tunnel Walks at 840-9255.

Antique-lovers will want to see the collection of 17th- to 19th-century American decorative art at **Bayou Bend,** Museum of Americana, 1010 Milam (659-3800), in **Memorial Park.** The collection is housed in the palatial mansion of millionaire Ima Hogg (we *swear*), daughter of turn-of-the-century Texas governor Jim "Boss" Hogg. The museum houses some of the more obscure Remington paintings. Open Tues.-Fri. 11am-4pm, Sun. 1-4pm. $2, seniors and students $1.

On Main Street, 3½ mi. south of downtown, lies the beautifully landscaped **Hermann Park,** near all of Houston's major museums. The **Houston Museum of Natural Science** (639-4600) offers a splendid display of gems and minerals, permanent exhibits on petroleum, a hands-on gallery geared toward grabby children, and a planetarium and IMAX theater to boot. (Open Tues.-Sat. 9am-6pm, Sun. 10am-6pm. $7, seniors and kids $5.) The **Houston Zoological Gardens** (525-3300) feature small mammals, alligators, and hippopotami eating spicy hippoplankton food. (Open daily 10am-5pm. $2.50, seniors $2, ages 3-12 50¢.) The **Museum of Fine Arts,** 1001 Bissonet (639-7300), adjoins the north side of Hermann Park. Designed by Mies van der Rohe, the museum boasts a collection of Impressionist and post-Impressionist art, as well as a slew of Remingtons. (Open Tues.-Sat. 10am-5pm, Thurs. 10am-9pm, Sun. 12:15-6pm. $3, seniors and college students $1.50, under 18 free. Free Thurs. 10am-5pm.) Across the street, the **Contemporary Arts Museum,** 5216 Montrose St. (526-0773), has multi-media exhibits. (Open Tues.-Fri. 10am-5pm, Sat.-Sun. noon-5pm. Free.) Also on the park grounds are sports facilities, a zoo, a kiddie train, a Japanese garden and the Miller Outdoor Theater (see Entertainment below). The **University of Houston, Texas Southern University,** and **Rice University** all study in this part of town.

The **Astrodome,** Loop 610 at Kirby Dr. (799-9555), a mammoth indoor arena, is the home of the **Oilers** football team and the **Astros** baseball team. (Tours daily 11am, 1pm, 3pm, and 5pm; off-season 11am, 1pm, and 3pm. $2.75, ages under 7 free. Parking $3). At these prices, you're better off paying admission to a game. Football tickets are hard to get, but seats for the Astros are usually available for as low as $4. (Call 526-1709 for tickets.)

Wander down Space Age memory lane at NASA's **Lyndon B. Johnson Space Center** (483-4321), where models of Gemini, Apollo, Skylab, and the space shuttle are displayed in a free walk-through museum. This NASA is the home of Mission Control, which is still HQ for modern-day Major Toms; when astronauts ask, "Do you read me, Houston?" the folks here answer. (Control center open daily 9am-4pm. Free.) Arrive early to secure a *space* in mission control and allow 3-4 hrs. to orbit the complex. For launch info call 483-8600. Handicap facilities. Cameras allowed. By car, drive 25 mi. south on I-45. The car-less should take the Park and Ride Shuttle #246 from downtown.

Terminus of the gruesomely polluted Houston Ship Channel, the **Port of Houston** leads the nation in foreign trade. Free 90-minute guided harbor tours are offered on the inspection boat *Sam Houston.* (Tours Tues.-Wed. and Fri.-Sat. at 10am and 2:30pm, Thurs. and Sun. at 2:30pm.) Reservations for these deservedly popular tours should be made in advance, but you can join one if the boat doesn't reach its 90-person capacity. Call to make last-minute reservations between 8:30am and noon. To reach the port, drive five mi. east from downtown on Clinton Dr., or take bus #30 "Clinton/Clinton Drive" at Capital and San Jacinto to the Port Authority gate. For more info or reservations, write or call Port of Houston Authority, P.O. Box 2562, Houston 77252 (225-4044; open Mon.-Fri. 8am-5pm).

Head westward along Westheimer to the **Galleria,** an extravagant, Texas-sized shopping mall with an ice-skating rink surrounded by pricey stores. The mall is full of young, pretty people "catacombing"—Texan for cruising. (Rink open Sun.-Fri. noon-5pm and 8-10pm, Sat. noon-10pm. Skate rental $7.) Next door is the **Transco Tower,** 2800 Post Oak Blvd. (439-2000), Houston's latest monument outside of downtown. The view from the top is impressive; just walk in and take an elevator to the 61st floor. Don't miss the 25-ft. **Wall of Water Fountain.** Accessible by bus #82 from downtown or Louisiana and Pierce.

Back toward downtown, just east of Montrose, are two of the city's more highly acclaimed museums. The **Menil Collection,** 1515 Sul Ross (523-5888), is an eclectic collection of African and Asian artifacts and 20th-century European and American paintings and sculpture. Be sure to see Magritte's hilarious *Madame Récamier.* (Open Wed.-Sun. 11am-7pm. Free.) One block away, the **Rothko Chapel,** 3900 Yupon (524-9839), houses some of the artist's paintings. Fans of modern art will delight in Rothko's sanctified simplicity; others will wonder where the actual paintings are. (Open daily 10am-6pm.)

Entertainment

Anyone with cable TV sorely remembers the period-piece *Urban Cowboy,* in which John Travolta proves his love for Debra Winger by riding a mechanical bull. Sexy, wasn't it? Alas, Gilley's has long since closed, but despair not; rip-roaring nightlife is still bullish here.

The **Westheimer** strip offers the largest variety of places for no cover. Rub elbows with venture capitalists and post-punks alike at **The Ale House,** 2425 W. Alabama at Kirby (521-2333). The bi-level bar and beer garden offer over 100 brands of beer served with a British accent. Upstairs you'll find mostly New Wave music and dancing. (Open daily noon-2am.) A similar mix can be encountered at the more exclusive **Cody's Restaurant and Club,** penthouse of 3400 Montrose St. (522-9747). Sit inside or out on the balcony, and listen to live jazz. (Open Tues.-Fri. 4pm-2am, Sat. 6pm-2am. Informal dress.) **Sam's Place,** 5710 Richmond Ave. (781-1605), is your typical spring-break-style Texas hangout. On Sunday afternoons a band plays outdoors (5-10pm), and various booths proffer different beers. An indoor band continues from 7pm to 1am. (Happy Hour Mon.-Fri. 4-8pm and Mon.-Thurs. 11pm-closing. Open Mon.-Sat. 11am-2am, Sun. noon-2am. Clothes required.) **The Red Lion,** 7315 Main St. (795-5000), features cheap beer and nightly entertainment that ranges from bluegrass to heavy metal. (Open Mon.-Fri. 11am-2am, Sat. 4pm-2am, Sun. 4-10pm.)

Houston offers ballet, opera, and symphony at **Jones Hall,** 615 Louisiana Blvd. Tickets for the **Houston Symphony Orchestra** (224-4240) cost $8-30. The season runs from September to May. During July, the symphony gives free concerts Tuesday, Thursday, and Saturday at noon in the Tenneco Building Plaza. The **Houston Grand Opera** (546-0200) produces seven operas each season, with performances from October through May. (Tickets $5-25, 50% student discount ½ hr. before performance.) Call 227-2787 for info on the ballet, opera, or symphony. If you're visiting Houston in the summer, take advantage of the **Miller Outdoor Theater** in Hermann Park (520-3290). The symphony, opera, and ballet companies and various professional theaters stage free concerts here on the hillside most evenings from April to October, and the annual **Shakespeare Festival** struts and frets its hour upon the stage from late July to early August. For an event update call 520-3292. Sneak your Sally into the downtown **Alley Theater,** 615 Texas Ave. (228-8421), which stages Broadway-caliber productions at moderate prices. (Tickets $18-33. Student rush seats 15 min. before curtain $10.) For last-minute, half-price tickets to many of Houston's sporting events, musical and theatrical productions, and nightclubs, take advantage of **Showtix** discount ticket center, located at 11140 Westheimer St. at Wilcrest (785-2787; open Mon.-Fri. 11am-5pm, Sat. 10am-noon).

Near Houston: Galveston Island

Fifty mi. southeast of Houston on I-45, the narrow, sandy island of **Galveston** (pop. 65,000) offers not only a beach resort's requisite t-shirt shops, ice cream stands, and video arcades, but also beautiful vintage homes, oak-lined streets, and even a few deserted beaches. In the 19th century, Galveston was Texas' most prominent port and wealthiest city, earning the nickname "Queen of the Gulf." The advent of the 20th century dealt the city's economy two blows from which it could never recover. In September, 1900, a devastating hurricane struck the island, killing 6,000 people. The survivors were determined to rebuild the decimated city and built a 17-ft. seawall as protection. But the crippled shipping industry could not be protected from the refocus of commerce along the Houston Ship Channel, completed in 1914. Wealthy residents debarked for greener pastures, leaving the former port and their austere mansions behind.

Galveston's streets follow a grid that appears elementary. Lettered streets (A to U) run north-south, numbered streets run east-west, with **Seawall** following the southern coastline. Some confusion may arise from the fact that most streets have two names; Avenue J and Broadway, for example, are the same thoroughfare.

Finding your favorite beach is not difficult in tiny Galveston. Just stroll along the seawall and choose a spot. You can immerse yourself in families, partying teenagers, and high-spirited volleyball games at **Stewart Beach,** near 4th and Seawall. If you prefer a kinder, gentler student crowd, try **Pirates Beach,** about three mi. west of 95th and Seawall. There are two **Beach Pocket Parks** on the west end of the island, just east of Pirates Beach, with bathrooms, showers, playgrounds, and a concession stand (parking

$3). **Apfel Park,** on the far eastern edge of the island, is a quiet, clean beach with a good view of ships entering and leaving the port. (Entry $5.)

You can start your day with a visit to the historic **Strand,** near the northern coastline, between 20th and 25th St., a national landmark with over 50 Victorian buildings; today the preserved district houses a range of cafés, restaurants, gift shops and clothing stores. The **Strand Visitors Center,** 2016 Strand (765-7834; open daily 9:30am-6pm) provides information about island activities and serves as a station for two trolleys. The **Galveston Island Trolley** takes visitors to the seawall area and all the beaches. (Trains leave every 30 min. May-Oct., hourly Oct.-April. Tickets $2, seniors and kids $1.) A narrated tour of the island is given by the **Yellow Rubber Trolley,** running between the Strand and the seawall and to most major attractions and hotels. (Every 30 min., tickets $4, seniors $3.50, kids $3. One ticket good all day.) You can take either trolley at the **Convention and Visitors Bureau,** at 21st St. and Seawall (763-4311 or 800-351-4236; open daily 8:30am-5:30pm.) You can take a two-hour cruise in Galveston harbor aboard the ***Colonel*** (409-763-4900), a Victorian paddlewheel boat. Catch the Colonel at Pier 22, at the far east end of 22nd St.

Seafood is abundant in Galveston, along with traditional Texas barbecue. Plenty of eateries line Seawall and the Strand. For seafood, go to **Benno's on the Beach,** 1200 Seawall (762-4621), and try a big bowl of the shrimp gumbo ($3.75) or one of their crab variations. (Open Sun.-Thurs. 11am-10pm, Fri.-Sat. 11am-11pm.) **El Nopalito,** 614 42nd St. (763-9815) offers cheap Mexican breakfast and lunch. Menu changes daily, but the favorites are always available. Entrées $3.75-5. (Open Tues.-Fri. 6:30am-2pm, Sat.-Sun 6:30am-4pm.) After a day at the beach, indulge yourself with a delectable root-beer malt ($2.30) at **LaKing's Confectionery,** 2323 Strand (762-6100), a large, old-fashioned ice cream and candy parlor. (Open Mon.-Fri. 10am-9pm, Sat. 9am-10pm, Sun. 10am-9pm.)

Money-minded travelers will avoid lodging in Galveston. Accommodation prices fluctuate by season and can rise to exorbitant heights during holidays and weekends. The least expensive option is to make Galveston a daytrip from Houston. RV-equipped families can rest at any of the several parks on the island. The **Bayou Haven Travel Park,** 6310 Heards Lane (744-2837), on Offatts Bayou, is nicely located on a peaceful waterfront. Laundry facilities and showers. (For 4 with full hookup $12, waterfront sites $15, each additional person $2.) From the bus station, go left off 61st St., then ½-mi. to Heards Lane. You can pitch a tent at **Galveston Island State Park,** on 13 Mile Rd. (737-1222), about 10 mi. southwest of the trolley-stop visitors center. (Sites $12.) There are a few cheap motels along Seawall, but many of these are correspondingly shabby. Perhaps the best in the bunch is the **Treasure Isle Inn,** 1002 Seawall, (763-8561) with TV, pool, A/C. (Singles from $29. Doubles from $39; seniors receive a 10% discount.)

Texas Bus Lines, a **Greyhound** affiliate, operates out of the station at 4913 Broadway (765-7731), providing service to Houston (6 per day, 1½ hr., $9). **Emergency** is 911. Galveston's **time zone** is Central (1 hr. behind Eastern). Its main **post office** is at 601 25th St. (763-1527; open Mon.-Fri. 8:30am-5pm, Sat. 9am-noon) Galveston's **ZIP code** is 77550; the **area code** is 409.

Padre Island National Seashore

Bounded on the north by North Padre Island's string of condos and tourists and on the south by the Mansfield ship channel, which separates the national seashore from South Padre Island (a haven for hundreds of thousands of rowdy spring breakers every year), the **Padre Island National Seashore (PINS)** is an untainted gem, with over 60 mi. of perfectly preserved beaches, dunes, and a wildlife refuge. The seashore is an excellent place for windsurfing, swimming, or even surf-fishing—an 850-lb. shark was once caught at the southern, more deserted end of the island.

Hiking and driving are also popular activities at PINS. Those with four-wheel-drive vehicles can make the 60-mi. trek to the **Mansfield Cut,** the most remote and untraveled area of the seashore. Loose sands prevent vehicles without four-wheel drive from venturing far on the beach. Although the seashore has no hiking trails, the **Malaquite** (MAL-a-kee) **Ranger Station** (949-8173), three and a half mi. south of the park entrance, conducts hikes and programs throughout the year. (Call 949-8060 for info on group programs.) They also provide first aid and emergency assistance.

Entry into PINS costs $3. For just a daytrip to the beach, however, venture toward the beautiful and uncrowded **North Beach** (24 mi. from Corpus Christi), which lies just before the $3 checkpoint.

The headquarters for PINS lie, ironically, off the island in nearby Corpus Christi. The **PINS Visitors Center,** 9405 S. Padre Island Dr. (512-937-2621), provides info on weather conditions, safety precautions, and sight-seeing opportunities in nearby **Mustang State Park** and **Port Aransas.** (Visitors Center open Mon.-Sat. 8:30am-4:30pm.) Within the national seashore, the **Malaquite Visitors Center** (512-949-8068), about 14 mi. south of the JFK Causeway turn-off, supplies similar info while also offering exhibits and wildlife guidebooks. (Open June-Aug. daily 9am-6:30pm; Sept.-May daily 9am-4pm.)

Nothing beats camping on the beach at PINS, where crashing waves will lull you to sleep. Bring insect repellent, or you will end up awakening to the slurping noise of thousands of mosquitoes sucking you dry. The **PINS Campground** (949-8173) consists of an asphalt area for RVs, restrooms, and cold-rinse showers (RV sites $5, tent sites $2). Five mi. of beach is devoted to primitive camping, and free camping is permitted wherever vehicle driving is allowed. Near the national seashore is the **Balli County Park,** on Park Rd. 22 (949-8121), three and a half mi. from the JFK Causeway. Running water, electricity, and hot showers are available. (3-day max. stay. Full hookup $10. Key deposit $5.) Those who value creature comforts should head a few mi. farther north to the **Mustang State Park Campground** (749-5246), on Park Rd. 53, six mi. from the JFK Causeway, for electricity, running water, dump stations, restrooms, hot showers, shelters, trailer sites, and picnic tables. Make reservations; there's often a waiting list, especially in winter when the "snowbirds" (northern tourists) arrive. (Entry fee $2. Camping fee $9. Overnight camping on the beach $4.)

Motorists enter the PINS via the JFK Causeway, which runs through the Flour Bluff area of Corpus Christi. PINS is difficult to reach by public transportation. Corpus Christi bus #8 (which makes only 2 trips per day Mon.-Fri.) takes you to the tip of the Padre Isles (get off at Padre Isles Park-n-Ride near the HEB. This bus also stops at the Visitors Center). To reach the national seashore, call the **American Cab Shuttle** (949-8850; fare $1 per mi.). Note that round-trip distance from the bus stop to the Malaquite Visitors Center is over 26 mi. There is no post office on the PINS; mail should be sent **general delivery** to Flour Bluff sub-station, 10139 Security Dr., Corpus Christi (937-3530). (Open Mon.-Fri. 8am-5pm, Sat. 10am-noon.) The **ZIP code** is 78418.

San Antonio

A relaxing ride on a river taxi, a visit to a Catholic mission, a tour of the Spanish Governor's palace—can it be that we're talking about *Texas*? Welcome to San Antonio (pop. 935,933), the best little tour-house in the Lone Star State. Originally a Spanish missionary outpost, the city came under Native American control prior to Mexico's laying claim to it. German settlers later came in waves, influencing even the most mundane details of life—city signs at one time had to be posted in English, Spanish and German. Today, the Hispanic community outnumbers both whites and African-Americans, giving San Antonio the fastest growing population of any of metropolitan city in the state, while the German population has all but disappeared. Spanish architecture dots the landscape, and the city's ethnically diverse population easily supports a double food industry of European cuisine and Tex-Mex.

Practical Information

Emergency: 911.

Visitor Information Center, 317 Alamo Plaza (299-8155), downtown across from the Alamo. Open daily 9am-5:30pm.

San Antonio International Airport (821-3411), north of town. Served by I-410 and U.S. 281. Cabs to downtown $12 50. **Super Van Shuttle** (344-7433) departs for downtown every 15 min. 6am-6:45pm, every 45 min. 6:45pm-midnight. Fare $6, kids $3. By bus, take Rte. #12 at Commerce and Navarro or Market and Alamo.

Amtrak: 1174 E. Commerce St. (223-3226 or 800-872-7245), off the I-37 Montana St. exit. To: Dallas (7 per week, 8 hr., $40); Houston (3 per week, 4 hr., $42); and El Paso (3 per week, 11½ hr., $106).

Greyhound: 500 N. Saint Mary's St. (270-5800; 270-5860 in Spanish). To: Houston (8 per day, 4 hr., $25); Dallas (11 per day, 6 hr., $34; and El Paso (6 per day, 11 hr., $81). Lockers $1. Open 24 hrs.

Public Transport: VIA Metropolitan Transit, 112 Soledad (227-2020), between Commerce and Houston. Buses operate 5am-10pm, but many routes stop at 5pm. Inconvenient service to outlying areas. Fare 40¢ (more with zone changes), express 75¢. Cheap (10¢) and frequent old-fashioned **streetcars** operate downtown Mon.-Fri. 7am-9pm, Sat. 9am-9pm, Sun. 9:30am-6:30pm. Office open daily 6am-8pm. Maps available at VIA office.

Taxi: Yellow Cab, 226-4242. $2.70 for first mi., $1.10 each additional mi.

Car Rental: Chuck's Rent-A-Clunker, 3249 SW Military Dr. (922-9464). $14-26 per day with 100 free mi. Must be 19 with a major credit card or cash deposit. Open Mon.-Fri. 8am-7pm, Sat. 9am-6pm, Sun. 10am-6pm.

Bike Rental: Abel's, 119 Ada (533-9927). Free delivery.

Help Lines: Rape Crisis Center, 349-7273. Open 24 hrs. **Presa Community Service Center,** 532-5295. Referrals and transport for elderly and disabled. Open Mon.-Fri. 8:30am-noon and 1-4pm.

Gay and Lesbian Switchboard, 733-7300 for referral and entertainment info.

Time Zone: Central (1 hr. behind Eastern).

Post Office: 615 E. Houston (227-3399), 1 block from the Alamo. Open Mon.-Fri. 8:30am-5pm. General Delivery: 10410 Perrin-Beitel Rd. (650-1630); really in the boondocks—about 15 mi. northeast of town. **ZIP** code: 78205.

Area Code: 512.

Accommodations and Camping

Since San Antonio is a popular city, downtown hotel managers have no reason to keep prices low to meet the needs of budget travelers. Furthermore, San Antonio's dearth of rivers and lakes makes for few good campsites. But cheap motels are bountiful along Roosevelt Ave., an extension of St. Mary's. This area is only 2 mi. from downtown, is accessible by the VIA bus (see Practical Information), and is near the missions. Inexpensive motels also clutter Broadway between downtown and Breckenridge Park. Drivers should follow I-35 north to find cheaper and often safer accommodations within 15 mi. of town. The best value in public camping is about 30 mi. north of town at Canyon Lake in **Guadalupe River State Park** (512-438-2656; sites $4).

Bullis House Inn San Antonio International Hostel (HI/AYH), 621 Pierce St. (223-9426), 2 mi. northeast of the Alamo, across the street from Fort Sam Houston. From downtown take bus #11 at Market and St. Mary's to Grayson St. and get off at the stop after the Stop & Go store. Friendly hostel in a quiet neighborhood. Pool, kitchen. Lockout 11am-5pm. Curfew 11pm, but night key available ($5 deposit). $13.50, nonmembers $16.50. Private singles from $17, nonmembers from $19. Doubles from $24/$26. Linen $2. Fills rapidly in summer. Large, sparsely furnished rooms $30.

Elmira Motor Inn, 1126 East Elmira (222-9463), about 3 blocks east of St. Mary's, a little over 1 mi. north of downtown. Take bus #8 from downtown and get off at Elmira St. Best deal in town.

Very large and well-furnished rooms. More luxurious than any other at this price. TV, laundry service and free local calls. Caring management. Singles $25. Doubles $27. Key deposit $2.

Navarro Hotel, 116 Navarro St. (224-0255). A bit shabby but deep in the heart of town. A/C, color TV, daily maid service, laundry facilities, and free parking. Refreshments in the lobby. Singles $24. Doubles $36.

El Tejas Motel, 2727 Roosevelt Ave. (533-7123), at E. Southcross, 3 mi. south of downtown near the missions. Take bus #42. Family-run with some waterbeds, color TV, and a pool. Rooms have thin walls. Singles $22. Doubles $28. On weekends $2 more.

San Antonio KOA, 602 Gembler Rd. (224-9296), 6 mi. from downtown. Take bus #24 ("Industrial Park") from the corner of Houston and Alamo downtown. Showers, laundry, A/C, pool, playground, movies, fishing pond. Full hookup $15.75 for two people, $1 for each additional person. Open daily 7:30am-10:30pm. A bit far from downtown but lots of cool shade and a BBQ on the premises.

Traveler's World RV Park, 2617 Roosevelt Ave. (532-8310 or 800-755-8310), 3 mi. south of downtown. Sites are large and have tables and benches. Showers, laundry, pool, spa, playground. Next to golf course and restaurants. Open daily 8am-8pm. Tent sites $10 for 2. RV sites $16 for 2. Each additional person $7.

Food

Explore the area east of S. Alamo and S. Saint Mary's St. for the best Mexican food and BBQ. The **Riverwalk** abounds with expensive cafés and restaurants. Breakfast alone could clean you out, if you don't settle for just a muffin and coffee. **Pig Stand** diners offer decent, cheap food from all over this part of Texas; the branch at 801 S. Presa, off S. Alamo, is open 24 hours. North of town, many East Asian restaurants line Broadway across from Breckenridge. The best fast-food-style Mexican diner is **Casa Cabana,** with many locations across downtown.

Casa Río, 430 E. Commerce (225-6718). Oldest and largest San Antonio restaurant on the river. *Cantando* mariachis, tasty Mexican cuisine, and a bargain to boot. Entrées $4-7. À la carte items $1.50-3. Open Mon.-Sat. 11:30am-10:30pm, Sun. noon-10:30pm. Frozen margaritas $2.25. Ask about dessert on the boat. Large parties should make reservations.

Schilo's, 424 E. Commerce, two blocks from the Alamo (223-6692). Old deli opened by a German Salooner during Prohibition. Offers great sandwiches and hot dogs ($2.50-4). For lunch, try the Kraut Dog ($3) with German potato salad. Open Mon.-Sat. 7am-8:30pm. Major credit cards accepted.

Sulema's Mexican Kitchen, 319 E. Houston (222-9807). A standard Mexican diner serving cheap lunch and breakfast entrées. Lunch plates $4-6 with free iced tea or coffee. Breakfast special. Open Mon.-Sat. 7am-8pm.

Hung Fong Chinese and American Restaurant, 3624 Broadway (822-9211), 2 mi. north of downtown. Take bus #14. The oldest Chinese restaurant in San Antonio. Consistently good and crowded. Big portions. Try the egg rolls and lemon chicken. Meals $3-5. Open Mon.-Thurs. 11am-11pm, Fri. 11am-midnight, Sun. 11:30am-11pm.

Sights

Much of historic San Antonio lies in present-day downtown and surrounding areas. The city may seem diffuse, but almost every major site and park is within a few miles of downtown and accessible by public transportation.

The Missions

The five missions along the San Antonio River once formed the soul of San Antonio; the city still preserves their remains in the **San Antonio Missions National Historical Park.** To reach the missions by car or bike, follow the blue-and-white "Mission Trail" signs beginning on S. Saint Mary's St. downtown. **San Antonio City Tours** (680-8724), in front of the Alamo, provides a two-hour tour of all the missions and the Alamo for $10, while **Tours for Kids,** 15411 Aviole Way (496-6030), offers what you might guess (9am-3pm). Bus #42 stops right in front of Mission San José, within walking distance of Mission Concepción. All of the missions are open daily 9am to 6pm; September to May from 8am to 5pm. For general info on the missions, call 229-5701.

Mission Concepción, 807 Mission Rd. (533-7109), 4 mi. south of the Alamo off E. Mitchell St. The oldest unrestored church in North America (1731). Traces of the once-colorful frescoes are still visible. Active parish sanctuary. Open daily 9am-6pm. Sun. mass 5:50pm.

Mission San José, 6539 San José Blvd. (922-0543). The "Queen of the Missions" (1720), with its own irrigation system, a church with a gorgeous sculpted rose window, and numerous restored buildings. The largest of San Antonio's missions, it provides the best sense of the self-sufficiency of these institutions. Catholic services (including a noon "Mariachi Mass") are held 5 times Sun.

Espada Aqueduct, 10040 Espada Rd, about 4 mi. south of Mission San José. Features a tiny chapel and a functioning mile-long aqueduct, built between 1731 and 1745.

Mission San Juan Capistrano (534-3161) and **Mission San Francisco de la Espada** (627-2064), both off Roosevelt Ave., 10 mi. south of downtown as the swallow flies. Smaller and simpler than the other missions, it is best at evoking the isolation these outposts once knew.

Downtown Tourist District

"Be silent, friend, here heroes died to blaze a trail for other men." Disobeying orders to retreat with their cannons, the defenders of the Alamo, outnumbered 20 to one, held off the Mexican army for 12 days. Then, on the morning of the 13th day, Mexican buglers commenced the infamous *degüello* (throat-cutting). Forty-six days later General Sam Houston's small army defeated the Mexicans at San Jacinto amidst cries of "Remember the Alamo!" Now phalanxes of tourists attack the **Alamo** (225-1391), at the center of Alamo Plaza by the junction of Houston and Alamo St., and sno-cone vendors are the only defenders. A single chapel and barracks preserved by the state are all that remain of the former Spanish mission. If you're looking for a lost bike, be warned that the Alamo does *not* have a basement. (Open Mon.-Sat. 9am-5:30pm, Sun. 10am-5:30pm. Free.) The **Long Barracks Museum and Library,** 315 Alamo Plaza (224-1836), houses Alamo memorabilia. (Open Mon.-Sat. 9am-5:30pm.) Next door, the **Clara Driscoll Theater** shows an historical documentary titled "The Battle of the Alamo." Shows run every 20 min. Mon.-Sat. 9am-5:30pm.

Heading southwest from the Alamo, black signs indicate access points to the **Paseo del Río (Riverwalk),** with shaded stone pathways following a winding canal built in the 1930s by the WPA. Lined with picturesque gardens, shops, and cafés, and connecting most of the major downtown sights, the Riverwalk is well-patrolled, safe, and especially beautiful at night. Ride the entire length of the Riverwalk by taking a boat ($2.50, kids $1) from the front of the Hilton Hotel. The **Alamo Imax Theater** (225-4629), in River Center, shows "The Price of Freedom," a 45-min. docudrama Alamo film, on its six-story screen. (7 shows 10am-7pm. $6, seniors and military $5.50, kids $4.) A few blocks south, a cluster of 27 restored buildings called **La Villita** (299-8610) houses restaurants, crafts shops, and art studios. (Open daily 10am-6pm.)

To take a self-guided tour of the downtown area, hop on an **old-fashioned street car** (10¢; see Practical Information), and spend at least an hour tooting by the sites. The purple-line street car has the more extensive route, stretching from the Alamo to the Spanish Governor's Mansion to La Villita. The streetcar runs 7am-9pm.

Hemisfair Plaza, on S. Alamo (229-8570), the site of the 1968 World's Fair, is another top tourist spot. The city often uses the plaza, surrounded by restaurants, museums, and historic houses, for special events. The **Tower of the Americas,** 200 S. Alamo (299-8615), rises 750 ft. above the dusty plains, dominating the meager skyline. Get a view of the city from the observation deck on top. (Open daily 8am-11pm. $2, seniors $1.25, ages 4-11 $1.) Within the plaza, stroll through the free museums, including the **Institute of Texan Cultures** (226-7651; open Tues.-Sun. 9am-5pm; parking $2), and the **Mexican Cultural Institute** (227-0123), filled entirely with modern Mexican art (open Mon.-Fri. 9am-5pm, Sat. 11am-5pm). On a spot near Hemisfair on Commerce St., across from the San Antonio Convention Center, German Americans erected **St. Joseph's Church** in 1868. Since this beautiful old church stubbornly refused to move, a local department store chain built their establishment around it. Sunday Mass 8am and 11am in English, 9:30am and 12:30pm in Spanish.

Walk west to the **Main Plaza** and **City Hall,** between Commerce and Dolorosa St. at Laredo. Directly behind the City Hall lies the **Spanish Governor's Palace,** 105 Plaza de Armas (225-4629). Built in Colonial Spanish style in 1772, the house has carved doors and an enclosed, shaded patio and garden. (Open Mon.-Sat. 9am-5pm, Sun. 10am-5pm. $1, kids 50¢.)

Market Square, 514 W. Commerce (229-8600), is a center for the sale of both schlocky souvenirs and handmade local crafts. The walkway **El Mercado** continues the block-long retail stretch. At the nearby **Farmers Market,** you can buy produce, Mexican chilis, pastries, candy, and spices. Come late in the day, when prices are lower and vendors more willing to haggle. (Open June-Aug. daily 10am-8pm; Sept.-May daily 10am-6pm.)

San Antonio North and South

Head to **Brackenridge Park,** main entrance 3900 N. Broadway (735-8641), five mi. north of the Alamo, for a day of unusual sight-seeing. From downtown, take bus #8. The 343-acre showground includes a Japanese garden, playgrounds, a miniature train and an aerial tramway. Check out the **San Antonio Zoo,** 3903 N. Saint Mary's St. (734-7183). The zoo is one of the country's largest, housing over 3,500 animals from 800 species housed in their natural settings, including an extensive African mammal exhibit. (Open daily 9:30am-6:30pm; Nov.-March daily 9:30am-5pm. $5, seniors $3.50, ages 3-11 $3.) Nearby **Pioneer Hall,** 3805 N. Broadway (822-9011), contains a splendid collection of artifacts, documents, portraits, cowboy and household accessories related to early Texas history. Three exhibit rooms are separately devoted to the Pioneers, the Texas Rangers and the Trail Drivers. Open Tues.-Sun. 10am-5pm, Oct. Wed.-Sun. 11am-4pm. $1, kids 25¢. Next door, at the **Witte Museum,** (rhymes with city) 3801 Broadway (226-5544), permanent exhibits focus on Texas wildlife while curators mount new shows. (Open Mon., Wed.-Sat. 10am-6pm, Tues. 10am-9pm, Sun. noon-6pm; off-season closes at 5pm. $4, seniors $2, ages 4-11 $1.75. Free Thurs. 3-9pm. Ticket receipt grants you half-price admission to the Museum of Art.) The 38-acre **Botanical Center,** 555 Funston Pl. (821-5115), one mi. east of Brackenridge Park, includes the largest conservatory in the Southwest. (Open Tues.-Sun. 9am-6pm. $2.50.)

The **San Antonio Museum of Art,** 200 W. Jones Ave., just north of the city center, inhabits a restored Lone Star Brewery building. Towers, turrets, and spacious rooms decorated with ornate columns house Texan furniture and pre-Columbian, Native American, Spanish Colonial, and Mexican folk art. (Open Mon. and Wed.-Sat. 10am-5pm, Tues. 10am-9pm, Sun. noon-5pm. $4, seniors $3, ages 6-12 $1.75. Free Tues. 10am-9pm. Free parking.) The former estate of Marion Koogler McNay, the **McNay Art Institute,** 6000 N. New Braunfels (824-5368), displays a collection of mostly post-Impressionist European art. It also has a charming inner courtyard with sculpture fountains and meticulous landscaping. (Open Tues.-Sat. 9am-5pm, Sun. 2-5pm. Free.)

The **Lone Star Brewing Company,** 600 Lone Star Blvd. (226-8301), is about two mi. south of the city. Trigger-happy Albert Friedrich had managed to accumulate a collection of 3,500 animal heads, horns, and antlers when he opened the Buckhorn in 1887. What better place to put them than in his bar? Now you can pity his prey on tours which leave every 30 minutes and provide beer samples. (Open daily 9:30am-5pm. $3.50, seniors $3, ages 6-12 $1.50.) For a day of unusual and thrilling experience, drive 40 mi. to the **Natural Bridge Caverns,** off I-35 N. (651-6101). The Caverns, only discovered in 1960, contain some of the most beautiful, awe-inspiring caves and rock formations in the U.S. Open daily 9am-6pm. Tours $6, seniors $5, kids $3.

Entertainment

Every April, the 10-day **Fiesta San Antonio** ushers in spring with concerts, parades, and plenty of Tex-Mex to commemorate the victory at San Jacinto and honor the heroes at the Alamo. However, San Antonio offers entertainment more often than just once a year. For fun after dark any time, any season, stroll down the Riverwalk. Peruse the Friday *Express* or the weekly *Current* which will guide you to concerts and entertainment. **Floore's Country Store,** 14464 Old Bandera Rd. (695-8827), toward the northwestern outskirts, is an old hangout of scruffy but lovable country music star Willie Nelson. Dancing takes place outside on a large cement platform. (Cover varies.)

Some of the best Mexicali blues in the city play at **Jim Cullen's Landing,** 123 Losoya (222-1234), in the Hyatt downtown. The music inside starts at 9pm and goes until around 2am. A jazz quartet performs on Sunday nights. The riverside café outside opens at 11:30am (cover $3). For rowdy rock 'n' roll beat, stroll along **North Mary's Street** about 15 blocks from downtown. Most clubs are open late into the night.

West Texas

On the far side of the Río Pecos lies a region whose extremely stereotypical Texan character verges on self-parody. This is the stomping ground of Pecos Bill—a mythical cowpoke raised by coyotes whose exploits included lassoing a tornado. The land here was colonized in the days of the Texan Republic, during an era when the "law west of the Pecos" meant a rough mix of vigilante violence and frontier gunslinger machismo. Today, this desolate region does not lack urban attractions (although it *does* lack attractive urban areas). The border city of El Paso, and its Chihuahuan neighbor, Ciudad Juárez beckon way, *wayyyy* out west—700 mi. from the Louisiana border.

Big Bend National Park

Roadrunners, coyotes, wild pigs, mountain lions, and 350 species of birds make their home in Big Bend National Park, a 700,000-acre tract that lies within the great curve of the Río Grande. The spectacular canyons of this river, the vast **Chihuahuan Desert,** and the cool **Chisos Mountains** have all witnessed the 100 million years necessary to mold the park's natural attractions. Although the Chihuahuan Desert covers most of the park, colorful wildflowers and plants abound.

You must get a free **wilderness permit** at the park headquarters to take an overnight hike. The park rangers will suggest hikes and places to visit. Most roads are well-paved, but many of the most scenic places are only accessible by foot or four-wheel-drive vehicle. The **Lost Mine Peaks Trail,** an easy three-hour hike up a peak in the Chisos, leads to an amazing summit view of the desert and the Sierra de Carmen in Mexico. Another easy walk leads up the **Santa Elena Canyon** along the Río Grande. The canyon walls rise up as much as 1000 ft. over the banks of the river. Three companies offer river trips down the 133-mi. stretch of the Río Grande owned by the park. Info on rafting and canoeing is available at the park headquarters (see below).

The only motel-style lodging within the park is the expensive **Chisos Mountain Lodge** (915-477-2291) in the Chisos Basin. This lodge offers four types of service: a new hotel with lots of modern facilities (singles $53, $7 each additional person); an older motel with two-bed rooms (singles $51, $7 each additional person); lodge units equipped with shower and baths but no A/C (singles $45, doubles $53, $7 each additional person); and stone cottages with simple furnishing and facilities and three double beds ($62, $7 each additional person). Reservations are a must, since the lodge is often booked up a year in advance. The lodge also runs a restaurant and coffee shop, where entrées run $5-12. (Open daily 7am-8pm; off-season daily 7am-7:30pm.) The entire complex is located in the **Chisos Basin,** 10 mi. southwest of the park's visitors center. Cheaper motels line 118 and 170 near Terlingua and Lajitas, 21 and 28 mi. respectively from the park headquarters. Designated **campsites** within the park are allotted on a first-come, first-served basis. **Chisos Basin** and **Río Grande Village** have sites with running water ($5), while **Cottonwood** has toilets but no running water ($3). Free primitive sites pop up along the hiking trails, available with a required permit from any ranger station. Because of the relatively high temperatures at the river, you won't have to worry about getting a site at Río Grande Village, though you may have to quarrel with the resident buzzards. The best (and coolest) campsites by far are those in Chisos Basin. Get here early, as the basin sites fill up fast; try to get a campsite near the perimeter.

Groceries are available in Panther Junction, Río Grande Village, and the Chisos Basin at Castolon, but stock up before leaving urban areas for better prices and selections.

Get wet at the park's only public **shower** (75¢ per 5 min.) at the Río Grande Village Store.

The **park headquarters** (915-477-2291) are at Panther Junction, about 20 mi. from the park entrance. (Open daily 8am-6pm. Vehicle pass $5 per week.) For info, write Superintendent, Big Bend National Park 79834. The **Texas National Park Services** (800-452-9292) provides info on the park and will help you plan your excursion. The other **ranger stations** are at Río Grande Village, Persimmon Gap, Chisos Basin (open daily 8am-4pm), and Castolon (open daily 8am-6pm). In case of **emergency,** call 477-2251 until 6pm. Afterwards, call 477-2267 or any of the other numbers listed at each ranger station.

Big Bend may be the most isolated spot you'll ever encounter. The park is only accessible by car via I-118 or I-385. **Rental cars** are only available in Odessa, approximately 222 mi. north of the park entrance. **Amtrak** serves Alpine three times per week.

Guadalupe Mountains National Park

The existence of the Guadalupes in the vast Texas desert land is a miracle; extending from southern New Mexico, the range peaks at nearly 9000 ft., Texas's highest point. The Guadalupes carry with them a legacy of unexplored grandeur. Early westbound pioneers avoided the area, fearful of the climate and the Mescalero Apaches who controlled the range. By the 1800s, when the Apaches had been driven out, only a few homesteaders and *guano* miners inhabited this rugged region. Today the national park encompasses 86,000 acres of desert, canyons, and highlands. With over 70 mi. of trails, the mountains ensure challenging hikes in a mostly desert environment for those willing to journey to this remote part of the state. The passing tourist who hopes to catch only the most established sights should stop to see **El Capitán,** a 2000-ft. limestone cliff, and **Guadalupe Peak,** at 8749 ft. the aforementioned highest point in Texas. Less hurried travelers should hike to **McKittrick Canyon,** with its spring-fed stream and amazing variety of vegetation. Lush maples grow next to desert yuccas, and thorny agaves circle stately pines. Mule deer and whiptail lizards sometimes greet visitors on the trails. **The Bowl,** a stunning high-country forest of Douglas fir and ponderosa pine, is an easy hike.

Most major trails begin at the **Headquarters Visitors Center** (915-828-3215), right off U.S. 62/180 where the bus drops you. The Guadalupe Peak is an easy three- to five-hr. hike, depending on your mountaineering ability, while the McKittrick Canyon and the Bowl can be hiked in a full day. At the headquarters, you can pick up topographical maps, hiking guides, backcountry permits, and other info. (Open June-Aug. daily 7am-6pm; Sept.-May daily 8am-4:30pm. After-hours info is posted on the bulletin board outside.) An alternative trail to the Canyon begins at the **McKittrick Visitors Center,** off U.S. 62/180. Here the Guadalupe Mountains Park Service conducts half- and full-day hikes from June to August, as well as evening programs. The center is staffed during the fall and sporadically throughout the year. Visit the park in the fall for fabulous foliage free of summer heat or spring winds.

Guadalupe National Park's lack of development may be a bonus for backpackers, but it makes daily existence tough. All water in the backcountry is reserved for wildlife—you'll find no food available nearby. Bring water for even the shortest, most casual hike. The **Pine Springs** (915-828-3338), ½-mi. east of the headquarters visitors center, sells ready-made but reasonably priced sandwiches, sodas, and beer. You can get ice cream and hamburgers at **Nickel Creek Café** (915-828-3348), five mi. east or fill up on a pancake and coffee breakfast ($3-6) before visiting McKittrick Canyon, three mi. farther east.

The **Pine Springs Campgrounds** (915-828-3251), just past the headquarters directly on the highway, has water and restrooms but no hookup. No fires allowed. (Sites $6, Golden Age and Golden Access Passport holders receive a 50% discount.) **Dog Canyon Campground** (505-981-2418), just south of the state line into New Mexico at the north end of the park, can be reached only by a 70-mi. drive from Carlsbad, NM, on Rte. 137. Dog Canyon also lacks hookups but provides water and restrooms. There are 10 backcountry campgrounds in the park, almost at every major site. There is no charge for the necessary permit that can be obtained at the headquarters. When convenience takes priority over proximity to the trails, you should use **Carlsbad, NM** as a base. The town, 55 mi. northeast of the park, has several cheap motels, campgrounds, and restaurants.

Guadalupe Park is less than 40 mi. west of Carlsbad Caverns in New Mexico (see Southern New Mexico for more information), 115 mi. east of El Paso, and a 90-mi. drive from Kent. **TNM&O Coaches,** (808-765-6641) an affiliate of **Greyhound,** runs along U.S. 62/180 between Carlsbad, NM and El Paso, passing Carlsbad Caverns National Park and Guadalupe National Park en route. This line makes flag stops at the park three times per day in each direction ($25, $47.50 round-trip). Ask the driver to let you off at the park entrance. The headquarters is 200 yards away. Make sure you know their daily schedule so you can plan your time properly and won't miss the bus. Guadalupe Mountains National Park is in the Mountain time zone (2 hr. behind Eastern).

For further info, write: Guadalupe Mountains National Park, HC60, P.O. Box 400, Salt Flat, TX 79847 (915-828-3251).

Rocky Mountains

These "purple mountain majesties" soar unexpectedly out of the Midwestern plain. Sagebrush, ponderosa, and mountain lupine replace corn and wheat as grasslands yield to open pine forest, and then, at the timberline, the forest gives way to the sharp-edged, snow-capped peaks of the Rocky Mountains. This continental divider stretches from the Canadian border to central Utah, all the while blushing with pristine alpine meadows, forbidding rocky gorges and unpolluted streams. The beauty of the Rockies overwhelms the senses and renders even the most eloquent observer awestruck and respectfully silent.

The states which frame these mountains are appropriately square and spacious. The whole Rocky Mountains area supports less than five percent of the population of the United States, and much of the land belongs to the public, preserved in national parks, forests, and wilderness areas. The stunning Waterton-Glacier International Peace Park straddles Montana's border with Alberta, Canada; Idaho encompasses two impressive back-country regions, as well as acre upon thrilling acre of state and national forest; Wyoming and Colorado are the proud landlords of Yellowstone and Rocky Mountain National Parks. The area boasts stunningly scenic trails for car, foot, or bike—there's a way for everyone to experience the Rockies.

Not surprisingly, most residents of the Mountain states live close to the land; even in Colorado, agriculture is still bigger business than tourism. The people of Denver, the only major metropolis in the region, combine big-city sophistication with an abiding appreciation for the area's rich natural endowment. Most other cities are oil towns, ski villages, university seats, or mining towns—commercial centers are in short supply in the Mountains.

Colorado

Southwestern Colorado's cliff dwellings around Mesa Verde suggest that Native Americans took their architectural inspiration from the state's rivers, with the Gunnison carving Black Canyon and the Colorado chiseling methodically away at the monoliths of Colorado National Monument. Europeans dug a lot faster for more pecuniary purposes—silver and gold attracted many of the state's first white immigrants. Even the U.S. military has dug enormous "intelligence" installations into the mountains around Colorado Springs, constructed to survive a nuclear holocaust. There is something for everybody to dig in Colorado.

Back on the surface, skiers worship Colorado's slopes, giving rise to the omnipresent, oh-so-chic condos of Aspen, Vail, and Crested Butte. As the hub of the state and the entire Rocky Mountain region, Denver provides both an ideal resting place for cross-country travelers and a "culture fix" for people heading to the mountains; Boulder is the crunchy alternative.

Bus transportation readily connects the Denver-Boulder area and most of the north, but driving is the way to see the more remote south. Luckily, finding accommodations proves easier; Colorado contains 23 youth hostels and a majority of the Rockies' B&Bs, and offers camping in 13 national forests and eight national parks.

Practical Information

Capital: Denver.

Colorado Board of Tourism, 1625 Broadway #1700, Denver 80202 (592-5510 or 800-433-2656). Open Mon.-Fri. 8am-5pm. **U.S. Forest Service,** Rocky Mountain Region, 11177 W. 8th Ave., Lakewood 80225 (236-9431). Tour maps free, forest maps $3. Open Mon.-Fri. 7:30am-4:30pm. **Ski Country USA,** 1540 Broadway #1300, Denver 80203 (837-0793, open Mon.-Fri.

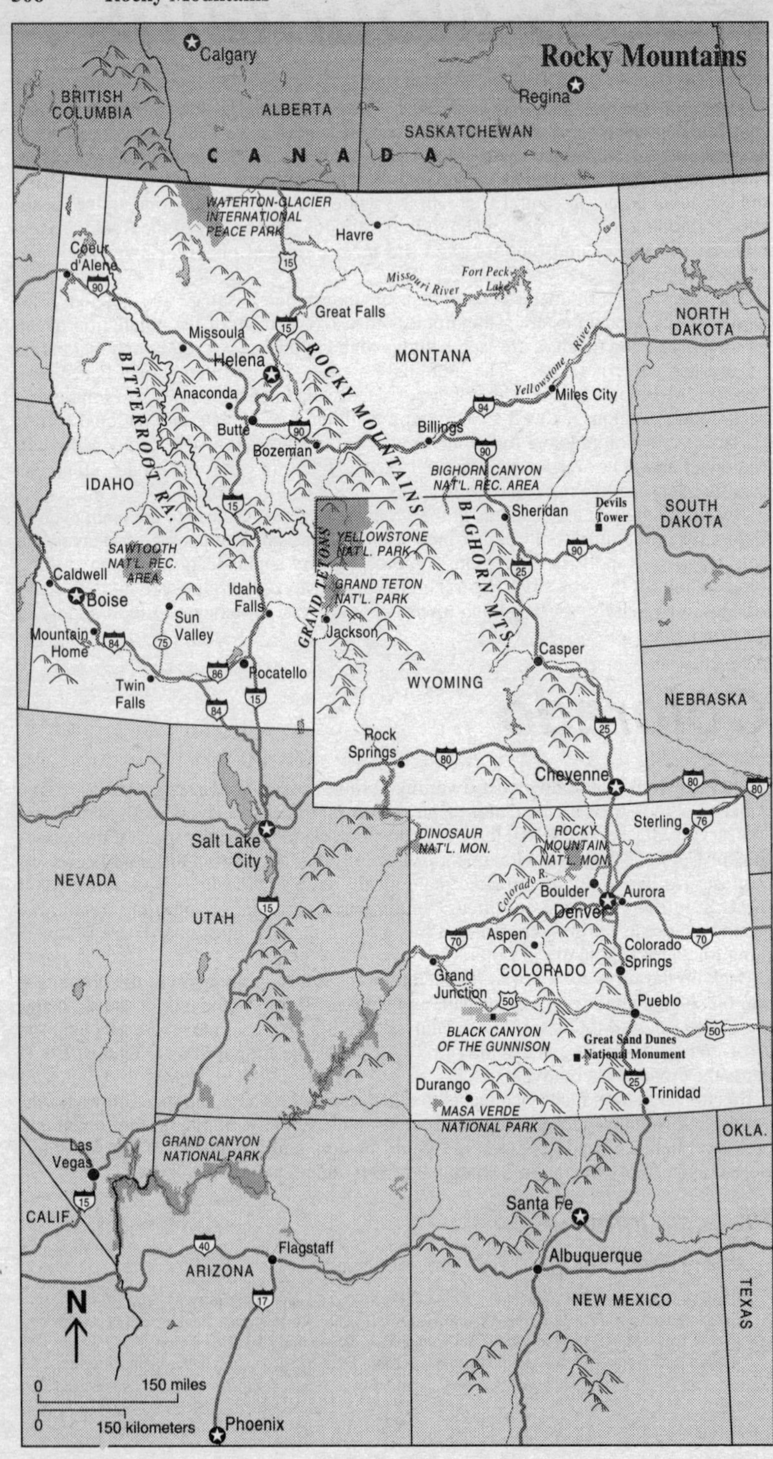
Rocky Mountains
Calgary
BRITISH COLUMBIA
ALBERTA
Regina
SASKATCHEWAN
C A N A D A
WATERTON-GLACIER INTERNATIONAL PEACE PARK
Havre
Coeur d'Alene
Missouri River
Fort Peck Lake
Great Falls
NORTH DAKOTA
Missoula
Helena
ROCKY MOUNTAINS
MONTANA
BITTERROOT RA.
Yellowstone River
Anaconda
Miles City
Butte
Billings
Bozeman
BIGHORN CANYON NAT'L. REC. AREA
IDAHO
Sheridan
Devils Tower
SOUTH DAKOTA
YELLOWSTONE NAT'L. PARK
BIGHORN MTS.
SAWTOOTH NAT'L. REC. AREA
GRAND TETONS
Caldwell
GRAND TETON NAT'L. PARK
Boise
Idaho Falls
Sun Valley
Mountain Home
Jackson
Casper
Pocatello
Twin Falls
WYOMING
NEBRASKA
Rock Springs
Cheyenne
Salt Lake City
DINOSAUR NAT'L. MON.
ROCKY MOUNTAIN NAT'L. MON.
Sterling
NEVADA
Colorado R.
Boulder
Aurora
Denver
UTAH
Aspen
Colorado Springs
Grand Junction
COLORADO
Pueblo
BLACK CANYON OF THE GUNNISON
Great Sand Dunes National Monument
Durango
Trinidad
MASA VERDE NATIONAL PARK
OKLA.
Las Vegas
GRAND CANYON NATIONAL PARK
CALIF.
Santa Fe
Flagstaff
Albuquerque
ARIZONA
NEW MEXICO
TEXAS
N
0 150 miles
0 150 kilometers
Phoenix

8am-5:30pm; recorded message 831-7669). **National Park Service,** 12795 W. Alameda Pkwy., P.O. Box 25287, Denver 80255 (969-2000). Handles some reservations for Rocky Mountain National Park. Open Mon.-Fri. 8:30am-4pm. **Colorado State Parks and Recreation,** 1313 Sherman St. #618, Denver 80203 (866-3437). Guide to state parks and metro area trail guide. Open Mon.-Fri. 8am-5pm.

Hostel Information: HI/AYH, Rocky Mountain Council, 1058 13th St., P.O. Box 2370, Boulder 80306 (303-442-1166).

Bed and Breakfast of Rocky Mountain, 906 S. Pearl, Denver 80209 (800-733-8415). Write for information and a free host list, call for reservations.

Campsite reservation number: 800-365-2267.

Road Conditions: 639-1234 (I-25 and East), 639-1111 (Denver and West).

Time Zone: Mountain (2 hr. behind Eastern). **Postal Abbreviation:** CO

Sales Tax: 3%

Aspen and Glenwood Springs

A world-renowned asylum for dedicated musicians and elite skiers, Aspen looms as the budget traveler's worst nightmare. Aspen was settled first by venturesome miners seeking a Colorado Eldorado. When the veins of silver began drying up in the 1940s, the shanty settlement went into a 20-year decline. But the Aspen of the 1990s shows no traces of its past hardships. A community of high-browed connoisseurs and wine lovers, Aspen has become too exclusive in the minds of many. In this upper-class playground, low-budget living will probably remain as much a thing of the past as the forsaken mining industry.

The hills surrounding town contain four ski areas: **Aspen Mountain, Buttermilk Mountain,** and **Snowmass Ski Area** (925-1220) sell interchangeable lift tickets. ($40, ages over 70 free, kids $20. Daily hours: Aspen Mtn. 9:30am-3:30pm, Buttermilk Mtn. 9am-4pm, Snowmass 8:30am-3:30pm.) **Aspen Highlands** (925-5300) does *not* provide interchangeable tickets ($33, seniors with ID and kids ages 13 and under $15; open daily 9am-4pm). Favorite slopes include **Sheer Rock Face** at Aspen, **Nipple** at Buttermilk, and **Catholic School** at Snowmass. You can enjoy the beauty of the mountains without going into debt paying for lift tickets. In the summer, ride the **Silver Queen Gondola** ($11) to the top of Aspen mountains. Hiking in the Maroon Bells and Elk Mountains is permitted when the snow isn't too deep. Undoubtedly Aspen's most famous event, the **Aspen Music Festival** (800-332-7736) holds sway over the town from late June to August. Free bus transportation goes from Rubey Park downtown to "the Tent," south of town, before and after all concerts. (Concerts June-late Aug. Free concert held almost every day. Tickets $10-3;. Sun. rehearsals $2.)

Budget accommodations don't come easy in Aspen, but surrounding national forests offer inexpensive summer camping, and some reasonably priced skiers' dorms double as guest houses in summer. The largest crowds and highest rates arrive during winter. Consider lodging in **Glenwood Springs,** 70 mi. north of Aspen, where inexpensive accommodations are plentiful (see below). Call the **Aspen Central Reservations Travel** (800-262-7736 or fax (303-925-9008.) **Little Red Ski Haus,** 118 E. Cooper (925-3333), 2 blocks west of downtown. If you plan to stay at least one week, this is the place. Clean, bright, wood-paneled rooms. In winter, dorm bunks $37. Private rooms for 1 or 2 $70. Off-season: dorms $20, private rooms $48. Breakfast included. Wed. night spaghetti dinner $5. Call to ensure vacancies are available. **Aspen International Hostel at the St. Moritz Lodge,** 334 W. Hyman Ave. (925-3320). Dorms, shared baths. Pool, jacuzzi, sauna HBO, party/game room. March 27-April 17 and Nov. 26-Dec. 20 $25; **Alpine Lodge,** 1240 Hwy. 82 E. (925-7351), ½ mi. east of town just beyond Independence Pass. B&B run by sweet family. Luxurious private rooms for 2, $35, $55 in the winter. Two rooms with a bath $50. Huge sunny room downstairs with bunks for groups of 4 $65, winter $68. In summer, shared bath, bedroom for two $40.

Unless six ft. of snow cover the ground, try **camping** in the mountains nearby. Hike well into the forest and camp for free, or use one of the nine **National Forest Campgrounds** within 15 mi. of Aspen. Maroon Creek offers beautiful campgrounds. **Maroon Lake, Silver Bar, Silver Bell,** and **Silver Queen** are on Maroon Creek Rd. just west of Aspen. (3-5 day max. stay. Sites fill well before noon. Open July-early Sept.) Southeast of Aspen on Rte. 82 toward Independence Pass are six campgrounds: **Difficult, Lincoln Gulch, Dispersed Sites, Weller, Lost Man,** and **Portal.** Ironically, Difficult is the only one with water. Some have max. stays and charge reservation fees. Write the **White River Ranger National Forest,** Aspen Ranger District 806 W. Hallam, Aspen, CO 81611 for a current brochure or call 303-925-3445 for updated info. before arriving.

The best eateries in Aspen make their meals on Main St. **The Main Street Bakery,** 201 E. Main St. (925-6446), offers sweets, gourmet soups ($3.50), homemade granola ($3.75), and a reprieve from pretension. (Open Mon.-Sat. 7am-9pm, Sun. 7am-4pm.) Two doors east of the Explore bookstore (see Entertainment and Nightlife below) is the **In and Out House,** 233 E. Main St. (925-6647), a minuscule joint that doles out huge sandwiches on fresh-baked bread ($2-4). (Open Mon.-Fri. 8am-7pm, Sat.-Sun. 8am-4pm.)

The **Visitors Center,** at the Wheeler Opera House, is at 320 E. Hyman Ave. (925-5656). Pick up free *What to Do in Aspen and Snowmass.* (Open daily 8am-7pm; winter 10am-5pm.) **Aspen Chamber and Resort Association,** 425 Rio Grand Pl. (925-1940). Open Mon.-Fri. 8:30am-5:30pm. **Aspen District of the White River National Forest Ranger Station,** 806 W. Hallam at N. 7th St. (925-3445). Info. for hikers and a map of the whole forest ($3). Open July 7-Sept. 2 Mon.-Sat. 8am-5pm; off-season Mon.-Fri. 8am-5pm. **Public Transport: Roaring Fork Transit Agency,** 450 Durant Ave. (925-8484), 1 block from the mall. Service in summer daily 7am-midnight, in winter 7am-1am. Buses to Snowmass, Woody Creek, and other points down valley as far as El Jebel daily 6:15am-12:15am; in winter 6:15am-1am. Five buses per day round-trip to Maroon Bells ($3.50 one way adults, $1.50 children and seniors.). Free shuttles around town. Out-of-town service 50¢-$3.50. **Bike Rental: The Hub,** 315 E. Hyman St. (925-7970). Mountain bikes with helmets $6 per hr., $15 per 4 hr., $20 per 8 hr. Open daily 9am-8pm. Must have credit card or $500 deposit. **Weather Line: 831-7669. Road Conditions:** 920-5454. **Post Office:** 235 Puppy Smith Rd. (925-7523). Open Mon.-Fri. 9am-5pm, Sat. 9am-noon. The **ZIP code** is 81611. The **Area Code** is 303.

In the winter, you must take I-70 west to Glenwood Springs before you can pick up CO Rte. 82 south to Aspen, which adds about 70 mi. to the trip. Once in Aspen, you will have no trouble getting around. CO Rte. 82 forms **Main Street,** to the south of which lies the downtown shopping district, and to the north of which lie opulent villas.

Glenwood Springs

Forty mi. northwest of Aspen on Colorado Rte. 82, **Glenwood Springs** is neither as glitzy nor as overpriced as its larger-than-life neighbor to the south. This tranquil village relies upon the nearby **Glenwood Hot Springs,** 401 N. River Rd. (945-6571), for most of its income. (Open daily 7:30am-10pm. Day pass $5.75, ages 3-12 $3.50.) Ski 10 mi. west of town at **Sunlight,** 10901 County Rd. 117 (945-7491). Ski passes cost $22 per day for hostelers, including access to the hot springs.

Within walking distance of the springs you'll find the **Glenwood Springs Hostel (HI/AYH),** 1021 Grand Ave. (945-8545), a former Victorian home with spacious dorm and communal areas as well as a full kitchen. Ask Gary to play one of his collection of 1100 records. At night, Halka will take you to the local pool hall where you can rack and shoot 'em with the best. Here you can also rent mountain bikes for $9 per day and receive a free ride (by car) from train and bus stations. (Closed 10am-4pm. $10.25. Linen included.) The Victorian home next door is **Aducci's Inn,** 1023 Grand Ave. (945-9341). Private rooms (1-2 persons) in this B&B cost $28 Mon.-Thurs., $38-65 Fri.-Sun. Includes breakfast every morning and wine in the evenings. Hot tub. Call for free pick-up from bus and train stations.

The **Amtrak** station thinks it can at 413 7th St. (872-7245; for reservations 800-872-7245). One train daily goes west to Denver (6 hr., $50) and one east to Salt Lake City (7 hr., $78). (Station open daily 9:30am-4:45pm.) **Greyhound** serves Glenwood Springs from 118 W. 6th Ave. (945-8501). Two buses run daily to Denver (4 hr., $18) and three buses daily to Grand Junction (2 hr., $8). (Open Mon.-Fri. 6:15am-noon and 4-5pm.) For further information on the town, contact the **Glenwood Springs Chamber Resort Association,** 1102 Grand Ave. (945-6589; open Mon.-Fri. 8:30am-5pm, Sat.-Sun. 10am-2pm; self-service info center open 24 hrs.). Call 800-221-0098 for lodging info and reservations.

Boulder

Boulder lends itself to the pursuit of both higher knowledge and better karma. It is home to the central branch of the University of Colorado (CU) and the only accredited Buddhist university in the U.S., the Naropa Institute. Only *here* can you take summer poetry and mantra workshops lead by Beat guru Allen Ginsberg at the Jack Kerouac School of Disembodied Poets. Boulder's universities also attract a range of musical performers, from bands with more of an edge, like the Dead Milkmen, to more traditional folk heroes, such as Tracy Chapman and the Indigo Girls. You often can hear top performers in the Pearl Street cafés, while being refreshed by ceiling fans and iced cappuccino.

Boulder is both an aesthetic and athletic mecca. The nearby Flatiron Mountains, rising up in big charcoal-colored slabs on the western horizon, beckon rock climbers, while an admirable system of paths make Boulder one of the most bike- and pedestrian-friendly areas around. For those motorists seeking a retreat into nature, Boulder is *On the Road* (Colorado Rte. 36) to Rocky Mountain National Park, Estes Park, and Grand Lake.

Practical Information

Emergency: 911.

Boulder Chamber of Commerce/Visitors Service, 2440 Pearl St. (442-1044 or 800-444-0447), at Folsom about 10 blocks from downtown. Take bus #200. Well-equipped, with comprehensive seasonal guides. Open Mon. 9am-5pm, Tues.-Fri. 8:30am-5pm. **University of Colorado Information** (492-6161), 2nd floor of UMC student union. Campus maps. Open Mon.-Thurs. 7am-11pm, Fri.-Sat. 7am-1am, Sun. 11am-11pm. **CU Ride Board,** UMC, Broadway at 16th. Lots of rides, lots of riders—even in the summer.

Public Transport: Boulder Transit Center, 14th and Walnut St. (299-6000). Routes to Denver and Longmont as well as intra-city routes. Buses operate Mon.-Fri. 6am-8pm, Sat.-Sun. 8am-8pm. Fare 50¢, 75¢ Mon.-Fri. 6-9am and 3-6pm. Long-distance: $1.50 to Nederland ("N" bus) and Lyons ("Y" bus); $2 to Golden ("G" bus) and to Boulder Foothills or Denver ("H" bus). Several other lines link up with the Denver system (see Denver Practical Information). Get a bus map ($1) at the terminal.

Taxi: Boulder Yellow Cab, 442-2277. $2 first mi., $1.20 each additional mi.

Car Rental: Budget Rent-a-Car, 1545 28th St. near the Clarion Harvest House (444-9054) ($34 per day; $169 per week). Must be 21 to rent; under 25 years of age, $15 service fee. Open Mon.-Thurs. 7am-6pm, Sat. 8am-4pm, Sun. 9am-4pm.

Bike Rental: University Bicycles, 839 Pearl St. (444-4196), downtown. 12- and 14-speeds and mountain bikes $12 per 3 hr., $16 per day, $20 overnight, with helmet and lock. Open Mon.-Fri. 10am-6pm, Sat. 9am-5pm, Sun. 10am-4pm.

Help Lines: Rape Crisis, 443-7300. Open 24 hrs. **Crisis Line,** 447-1665. Open 24 hrs. **Gays, Lesbians, and Friends of Boulder,** 492-8567.

Post Office: 1905 15th St. (938-1100), at Walnut across from the RTD terminal. Open Mon.-Fri. 8:45am-5:15pm, Sat. 9am-noon. General Delivery 8:45am-5:15pm. **ZIP code:** 80302.

Area Code: 303.

Boulder (pop. 83,300) is a small, manageable city. The most developed part of Boulder lies between **Broadway** (Rte. 93) and **28th Street** (Rte. 36), two busy streets running parallel to each other north-south through the city. **Baseline Road,** which connects the Flatirons with the eastern plains, and **Canyon Boulevard** (Rte. 7), which follows the scenic Boulder Canyon up into the mountains, border the main part of the **University of Colorado** campus (CU). The school's surroundings are known locally as the **"Hill."** The pedestrian-only **Pearl Street Mall,** between 11th and 15th St. centers hip life in Boulder. Most east-west roads have names, while north-south streets have numbers; Broadway is a conspicuous exception.

Accommodations and Camping

After spending your money at the Pearl St. Mall on tofu and yogurt, you may find yourself a little strapped for cash, and without a roof under which to sleep—Boulder doesn't offer many inexpensive places to spend the night. In summer, you can rely on the **Boulder International Youth Hostel (AAIH),** 1107 12th St. about two blocks west of the CU campus and 15 minutes south of the RTD station. (442-9304 7-10am and 5pm-midnight; 442-0522 10am-5pm.) 1107 12th St. serves guests in the summer. 1127 hosts weary travelers in the winter. The wonderfully friendly atmosphere and laid-back management more than make up for the slight scruffiness of these frat-house rooms. Bring or rent sheets, a towel, and a pillow. (Open 7:30-10am and 5pm-midnight. Curfew midnight in private rooms. Private singles $22 per night, $92 per week; doubles $27 per night, $100 per week. Towels and linen $2. Key deposit $5.) Reservations are recommended at the **Chautauqua Association,** 9th St. and Baseline Rd. (442-3282), which offers rooms big enough for two in their lodge ($30 for one person, $34 for two) and quaint, highly popular cottages ($41 per night; 4-night minimum stay). Guests at this cultural institution can take in films for free. Take bus #203. **The Boulder Mountain Lodge,** 91 Four Mile Canyon Rd. (444-0882), is a 2-mi. drive west on Canyon Rd., near creek-side bike and foot trails. One room with bunks holds six people. ($25 for one or two guests, each additional person $12.50) Facilities include phone and TV; hot tub and pool a nice plus. Check-in after 10pm for campsites. Summer rate with RV hookup are $15 per night for up to three people, each additional person $2; $80 per week. Two week maximum stay. Sites without hookup $14 per night, each additional person $2.

You'll have an easy time finding camping spots elsewhere. Info on campsites in **Roosevelt National Forest** is available from the **Forest Service Station** at 2995 Baseline Rd. #16, Boulder 80303 (444-6600; open Mon.-Fri. 8am-5pm, and in the summer, Sat. 8am- 5pm). Maps $2. A site at **Kelly Dahl,** three mi. south of Nederland on Rte. 119, costs $7. **Rainbow Lakes,** six mi. north of Nederland on Rte. 72, thenfive mi. west on Arapahoe Glacier Rd., is free, but no water is available. (Campgrounds open from late May to mid-Sept.) **Peaceful Valley** and **Camp Dick** (north on Rte. 72; $7 per site) have cross-country skiing in the winter and first-come, first-served sites.

Food and Hangouts

The streets on the "Hill" and those along the Pearl St. Mall burst with good eateries, natural foods markets, cafés, and colorful bars. Many more restaurants and bars line Baseline Rd. As one might expect given the peace-love-nature-touchy-feely climate, Boulder has more restaurants for vegetarians than for carnivores.

When the word went out in 1989 that the **Sink,** 1165 13th St. (444-7465), had reopened, throngs of former "Sink Rats" commenced their pilgrimage back to Boulder; the restaurant still awaits the return of its former janitor, Robert Redford, who quit his job and headed out to California back in the late 1950s. (Open Mon.-Sun. 11am-2am. Food served until 10pm.)

Hanna's Kitchen, 1122 Pearl St. Mall (443-0755), at the back of the health food store, **New Age Foods**. Some of the cheapest meals in town, featuring healthful and veggie food. Cafeteria-style restaurant offers a soup and sandwich deal for $1.75. Open Mon.-Fri. 9am-5:30pm, Sat. 9am-4pm. Restaurant open Mon.-Fri. 11:30am-3pm.

The L.A. Diner (for "Last American"), 1955 28th St. (447-1997). Roller skating staff serves green chili in a silver spaceship of a restaurant. 10-oz. sirloin steak, potato, vegetables, soup or salad $10.50 or open-faced turkey sandwich on sourdough bread ($4.95). Open Mon.-Thurs. 6:30am-midnight, Fri. 6:30am-3am, Sat. 8am-3am, Sun. 8am-midnight.

The Walrus Café, 1911 11th St. (443-9902). Universally popular night spot. Alas, Paul McCartney is nowhere to be found. Beer $1.50. Open Mon.-Fri.4pm- 1am, Sat.-Sun. 2pm-1am. Free pool until 6pm daily. Coo coo ka choo.

CU Student Cafeteria, 16th and Broadway, downstairs in the student union (UMC). The large **Alfred Packer Grill** (named after the West's celebrated cannibal) serves burgers ($1.75) and sizeable burritos ($3). Open Mon.-Fri. 7am-7pm, Sat. 10am-4pm, Sun. 11am-4pm.

Harvest Restaurant and Bakery, 1738 Pearl St. (449-6223), at 18th St. inside a little mall. A fine example of mellow, "back-to-nature" Boulder. Very popular among CU students. Try the "Swiss Granola," with frozen yogurt and a pumpkin muffin ($4.50). You can sit at the community table to make friends. Open daily 7am-10pm.

The Trident Bookstore Café, 940 Pearl St. (443-3133). Boulder's "Buddhist" coffeehouse with Naropa professors and CU students translating poems before class. Order a half-price book with a tall iced coffee ($1.15). Open Mon.-Sat. 6:30am-11pm.

Expresso Roma, 110 13th St. (442-5011), on the Hill near the youth hostel. Students head here for jumps of caffeine (85¢) and the almond biscotti (37¢). When the Cabaret Voltaire gets too grating, head for the more peaceful back room. Open daily 7am-midnight.

Sights and Activities

University of Colorado's intellectuals collaborate with wayward poets and back-to-nature granolas to find innovative things to do. Check out the perennially outrageous street scene on the Mall and the Hill and watch the university's kiosks for the scoop on downtown happenings.

The university's **Cultural Events Board** (492-8409) has the latest word on all CU-sponsored activities. The most massive of these undertakings is the annual **Arts Fest** in mid-July. Phone for tickets or stop by the ticket office in the **University Memorial Center** (492-2736; open Mon.-Sat. 10am-6pm). As part of Arts Fest, the **Colorado Shakespeare Festival** (492-8181) takes place from late June to mid-August. (Previews $8, general admission $10.) Concurrently, the **Chautauqua Institute** (442-3282; see Accommodations above) hosts the **Colorado Music Festival** (449-1397; 8am-5pm, on concert days 8am-6pm; performances June 23-Aug. 5; tickets $10-22) The **Boulder Blues Festival** (443-5858; tickets at 444-3601 cost $10-15) is held the second week of July. The Parks and Recreation Department (441-3400; open Mon.-Fri. 8am-5pm) sponsors free performance local parks from May to August; dance, classical and modern music, and children's theater are staples. **The Boulder Center for the Visual Arts,** 1750 13th St. (443-2122), focuses on the finest in contemporary regional art and has more wide-ranging exhibits as well. (Open Tues.-Fri. 11am-5pm, Sat. 9am-3pm, Sun. noon-4pm. Free.)

Boulder Public Library, 1000 Canyon Rd. (441-3100), and CU's **Muenzinger Auditorium,** near Folsom and Colorado Ave. (492-1531), both screen international films. Call for times and price. Museums in Boulder don't quite compare with the vitality and spectacle of Pearl St. and the Hill. When the need to see a more formal exhibit overtakes you, the intimate and impressive **Leanin' Tree Museum,** 6055 Longbow Dr. (530-1442), presents an interesting array of Western art and sculpture. (Open Mon.-Fri. 8am-4:30pm, Sat. 10am-4pm. Free.) The small **Naropa Institute** is located at 2130 Arapahoe Ave. (444-0202). Drop by and drop off at one of their many free meditation sessions with Tibetan monks.

The **Flatiron Mountains,** acting as a backdrop to this bright and vibrant town, offer countless variations on walking, hiking, and biking. Take a stroll or cycle along **Boulder Creek Path,** a beautiful strip of park that lines the creek for 15 mi. Farther back in the mountains lie treacherous, less accessible rocky outcroppings. Trails weave through the 6000-acre **Boulder Mountain Park,** beginning from several sites on the western side of town. **Flagstaff Road** winds its way to the top of the mountains from the far western end of Baseline Rd. The **Boulder Creek Canyon,** accessible from Rte.

119, emits splendid rocky scenery. Nearby **Eldorado Canyon,** as well as the Flatirons themselves, has some of the best **rock climbing** in the world.

Well-attended **running** and **biking** competitions far outnumber any other sports events in the Boulder area. The biggest foot race by far is the 10km Memorial Day challenge known as the "Bolder Boulder," which brings in 30,000 international athletes. The winner takes home $4000. For information on any running event, call the Boulder Roadrunners (499-2061; open daily 9am-6pm).

The **Boulder Brewing Company,** 2880 Wilderness Place (444-8448), offers tours for those who prefer sedentary pleasures to exercise. Yes, they feed you free beer at the end. (25-min. tours Mon.-Fri. at 11am and 2pm and Sat. at 2pm; open Mon.-Fri. 8am-7pm, Sat. 11am-3pm.)

Colorado Springs

The large Victorian houses and wide streets of Colorado Springs' older sections reflect the idle elegance of this long-time resort. Visitors today come for the same reasons that 19th-century travelers did: clean, dry air, and easy access to inspiring mountains—most especially Pikes Peak, which surges 14,110 ft. above sea level. The Ute, frequently traveling across the region in the 1600s on their way over the southern front range of the Rockies, stopped in Colorado and Manitou Springs for their healing mineral waters. However, Colorado Springs bubbles with more than water. Home to the United States Olympic Team (the high altitude builds hemoglobin levels), the Springs churn out champion lugers and synchronized swimmers. While tourists pour millions into the Colorado Springs economy during the summer, the U.S. government pours in even more: North American Air Defense Command Headquarters (NORAD) lurks beneath nearby Cheyenne Mountain.

Practical Information

Emergency: 911.

Colorado Springs Convention and Visitors Bureau, 104 S. Cascade #104, 80903 (635-7506 or 800-368-4748), at Colorado Ave. Check out the *Colorado Springs Pikes Peak Park Region Official Visitors Guide* and the city bus map. Open Mon.-Sat. 8:30am-5pm, Sun. 9am-3pm; Nov.-March Mon.-Fri. 8:30am-5pm. **Manitou Springs Chamber of Commerce,** 354 Manitou Ave., Manitou Springs 80829 (685-5089 or 800-642-2567). Near the trailhead of Pikes Peak. Open summer Mon.-Fri. 8:30am-5pm, Sat.-Sun. 8am-4pm. **Funfone,** 635-1723. Information on current events.

Colorado Springs Airport: 596-0188. Directly east of the downtown area, off Nevada Ave. at the end of Fountain Blvd.

Greyhound: 327 S. Weber St. (635-1505). To: Denver (9 per day, 2 hr., $8); Pueblo (8 per day, 50 min., $4.50); Albuquerque, NM (5 per day, 7-9 hr., $60); Kansas City, MO (3 per day, 16-17 hr., $89). Tickets available daily 5am-midnight. Open daily 5:15am-9pm.

Public Transport: Colorado Springs City Bus Service, 125 E. Kiowa at Nevada (475-9733), 5 blocks from the Greyhound station. Serves the city and Widefield, Manitou Springs, Fort Carson, Garden of the Gods, and Peterson AFB. Service Mon.-Fri. 5:45am-6:15pm, Sat. hours vary. Fare 75¢, seniors and kids 35¢, ages 5 and under free; long trips 15¢ extra. Exact change required.

Tours: Gray Line Tours, 3704 Colorado Ave. (633-11810 or 800-345-8197), at the Garden of the Gods Campgrounds. Trips to the U.S. Air Force Academy and Garden of the Gods ($15, kids $7.50), Pikes Peak ($20, kids $10) and a nighttime tour of the Cave of the Winds and Seven Falls ($25, kids $15). All tours are 4 hr. Office open daily 7am-11pm.

Taxi: Yellow Cab, 634-5000. $3 first mi., $1.35 each additional mi.

Car Rental: Ugly Duckling, 2128 E. Bijou (634-1914). $18 per day, $108 per week. Open Mon.-Fri. 9am-5:30pm, Sat. 9am-5pm. Must drive only in-state and be 21 with major credit card or $200 deposit.

Help Lines: Crisis Emergency Services, 635-7000. Open 24 hrs. **Gay Community Center of Colorado Springs,** 512 W. Colorado Ave. (471-4429). Phones answered Mon.-Fri. 6-9pm, Sat. 3-5pm.

Post Office: 201 Pikes Peak Ave. (570-5336), at Nevada Ave. Open Mon.-Fri. 7:30am-5pm. **ZIP code:** 80903.

Area Code: 719.

Colorado Springs is laid out in a fairly coherent grid of broad, manicured thoroughfares. **Nevada Avenue** is the main north-south strip, known for its many bars and restaurants. **Pikes Peak Avenue** serves as the east-west axis, running parallel to **Colorado Avenue,** which connects with **U.S. 24** on the city's west side. **U.S. 25** from Denver plows through the downtown area. Downtown itself is comprised of the square bounded on the north by **Fillmore Ave**., on the south by Colorado Ave., on the west by **Cascade,** and on the east by **Nevada Ave.** A word of warning: the city's attractions are diffused over a wide area, and city bus service is only available Mon.-Sat. from 5:45am-6:15pm.

Accommodations

Avoid the mostly shabby motels along Nevada Ave. If the youth hostel fails you, head for a nearby campground or the establishments along W. Pikes Peak Ave. For information on B&Bs, contact Bed and Breakfast of Colorado (see Colorado Practical Information).

Garden of the Gods Youth Hostel (HI/AYH), 3704 W. Colorado Ave. (475-9450 or 800-345-8197). 4-bunk shanties. Showers and bathrooms shared with campground. Swimming pool, jacuzzi, laundry. $11; members only. Open April-Oct.

Amarillo Motel, 2801 W. Colorado Ave. (635-8539). Take bus #1 West down Colorado Ave. to 34th St. Ask for rooms in the older National Historic Register section. Bunker-like rooms lack windows, but all have kitchens, TV, and phones. Laundry available. Singles $24. Doubles $28-30. Off-season: from $20. Next to the hotel office is **Leisure's Treasures,** the largest display of military relics in the Rockies. (Open Mon.-Sat. 10am-6pm.) Elden Leisure will show you a silver-hilted Civil War sword that you can buy for $6000, a real bargain for the budget traveler. Look through albums of WWI and WWII snapshots.

Apache Court Motel, 3401 W. Pikes Peak Ave. (471-9440). Take bus #1 west down Colorado Ave. to 34th St., walk 1 block north. Very spiffy pink adobe rooms. Doubles have kitchens. A/C and TV, hot tub. Seasonal rates: May-Sept. 15 singles $31 for one person, $35 for two; doubles $46 for one person, $50 for two; Sept. 6-April singles $25 for one person, $27 for two, doubles $35 for one, $40 for two. No pets. $5 extra for a kitchen in the summer.

Motel 6, 3228 N. Chestnut St. (520-5400), at Fillmore St. just west of I-25 exit 145. Take bus #8 west. TV, pool, A/C. Some rooms with unobstructed view of Pikes Peak. Some rooms with unobstructed view of parking lot. June-Sept. singles $33. Doubles $40. Off-season singles $24, doubles $31.

Camping

Located in the city itself is the four-star **Garden of the Gods Campground,** 3704 W. Colorado Ave. (475-9450 or 800-345-8197). Enjoy flapjack breakfasts Sundays and coffee and doughnuts for a small fee. Large pool and recreation area. (Sites $16.50, with electricity and water $19.50, full hookup $22.) Several popular **Pike National Forest** campgrounds lie in the mountains flanking Pikes Peak, generally open May through September. Some clutter around Rte. 67, five to 10 mi. north of **Woodland Park,** which is 18 mi. northwest of the Springs on U.S. 24. Others fringe U.S. 24 near the town of Lake George. (Sites $6.) You can always camp off the road on national forest property for free if you are at least 100 yards from road or stream.The **Forest Service Office,** 601 S. Weber (636-1602), has maps ($3) of the campgrounds and wilderness areas. (Open Mon.-Fri. 7:30am-4:30pm.) Farther afield, you can camp in the **Eleven Mile State Recreation Area** (748-3401 or 800-678-2267), off a spur road from U.S. 24 near Lake George. (Sites $6. Entrance fee $3. Reserve on weekends, but no reservations accepted after July 4.) Last resorts include the **Woodland Park KOA**

(687-3535), ¼mi. north of U.S. 24 on Rte. 67, three blocks west on Bowman Ave. (sites $16, with water and electricity $19, full hookup $20; call for reservations; open daily 8am-10am and 4pm-8pm) and the **Peak View Campground,** 4954 N. Nevada Ave. (Sites $10; with water and electricity $14; full hook-up $15-16.)

Food

You can get cheap, straightforward fare downtown, or try the stylish restaurants along W. Colorado Ave.

Poor Richard's Restaurant, 324½ North Tejon (632-7721). The local coffeehouse/college hangout. Pizza and veggie food. Open Sun.-Thurs. 11am-10pm, Fri.-Sat. 11am-midnight.

Kennedy's 26th St. Café, 2601 W. Colorado Ave. One of the cheapest eateries in Colorado Springs. Enormous Ranchman's breakfast (2 eggs, ham, and all the flapjacks you can eat) served all day ($4), cheeseburger with large fries ($2-4). Open Mon.-Fri. 6:30am-4pm, Sat. 6:30am-3pm.

Meadow Muffins, 2432 W. Colorado Ave. (633-0583), in a converted warehouse. Bright neon lights, smoke, beer and the "Original burger" ($4.50). Open daily 11am-2am.

Henri's, 2427 W. Colorado Ave. (634-9031). Genuine, excellent Mexican food. Popular with locals for 40 years. Fantastic margaritas. Cheese enchiladas ($2.25), and great free chips. Open Mon.-Sat. 11:30am-10pm, Sun. noon-10pm.

Sights and Entertainment

The town's major attraction looms large on its western horizon; you can see **Pikes Peak** from the town as well as from the quieter expanses of the **Pike National Forest.** You can climb the peak via the 13-mi. **Barr Burro Trail,** and then buy plastic lunch-money purses at the top. The trailhead is in Manitou Springs by the "Manitou Incline" sign. Catch bus #1 to Ruxton. Don't despair if you don't reach the top—explorer Zebulon Pike never reached it either, and they still named the whole mountain after him. Otherwise, pay the fee to drive up the **Pikes Peak Highway** (684-9383), administered by the Colorado Department of Public Works. (Open May-June 10 daily 9am-3pm, June 11-Sept. 2 7am-6:30pm; hours dependent on weather. Admission $4, under 13 $1.) You can also reserve a seat on the **Pikes Peak Cog Railway,** 515 Ruxton Ave. (685-5401; open May-Oct. 8 daily; round-trip $21, seniors $18 ages 5-11 $9, under 5 free if held on lap). At the summit, you'll see Kansas, the Sangre de Cristo Mountains, and the ranges along the Continental Divide. Expect cold weather; even when the temperature is in the 80s in Colorado Springs, the temperature at the acme only reaches the mid-30s; roads often remain icy through the summer.

Pikes Peak is not Colorado Springs' only outdoor attraction. Eat amid the *other* Olympians in **Garden of the Gods City Park** at 1401 Recreation Way (578-6640). Take Hwy. 24 to 30th St. and then north on Gateway Rd. The park, composed of red rock monuments that Native Americans believed were the bodies of their enemies thrown down by gods, contains many secluded picnic and hiking areas. (Free. Visitors center open daily 9am-5pm; off-season 10am-4pm.) The oft-photographed "balanced-rock" is at the park's south entrance. For more strenuous hiking, head for the **Cave of the Winds** (685-5444), 6 mi. west of exit 141 off I-25 on Hwy. 24, with guided tours every 15 minutes of the fantastically contorted caverns, daily from 9am to 9pm in the summer; 10am-5pm daily off-season. Just above Manitou Springs on Rte. 24 lies the **Manitou Cliff Dwellings Museum** (685-5242), U.S. 24 bypass, where you can wander through a pueblo of ancient Anasazi buildings. (Open daily May-Sept. 9am-5pm. Admission $4, ages 7-11 $2, under 6 free.)

Buried in a hollowed-out cave 1800 ft. below Cheyenne Mountain, the **North American Air Defense Command Headquarters (NORAD)** (554-7321) was designed to survive even a direct nuclear hit. A 3-mi.-long tunnel leads to this telecommunication center, which monitors every single plane in the sky. The **Peterson Air Force Base,** on the far east side of the city (take Hwy. 24 east to the Peterson Air Force Base exit) offers a **visitors center** and the **Edward J. Peterson Space Command Museum** (554-4915; open Tues.-Fri. 8:30am-4:30pm, Sat. 9:30am-4:30pm; free).

The **United States Air Force Academy,** a college for future officers, marches 12 mi. north of town on I-25. Its chapel is made of aluminum, steel, and other materials used in airplanes. On weekdays during the school year, uniformed cadets gather at 12:10pm near the chapel for the cadet lunch formation—a big production just to chow down. The **visitors center** (472-2555) has self-guided tour maps, info on the many special events, and a 12-minute movie every ½ hr. (Open daily 9am-5pm.)

The **Pioneers' Museum,** downtown at 215 S. Tejon St. (578-6650), covers the settling of Colorado Springs, including a display on the techniques and instruments of a pioneer doctor. (Open Mon.-Sat. 10am-5pm, Sun. 1-5pm. Free.) Everything you ever wanted to know about mining awaits at the **Western Museum of Mining and Industry,** 025 N. Gate Rd. (488-0880; open Mon.-Sat. 9am-4pm, Sun. noon-4pm; admission $4, students $3.50, ages 12 and under and seniors $3.50; closed Dec.-Feb.). Take exit 156-A off I-25. And all your questions about those famous Olympians will be answered at the **U.S. Olympic Complex,** 750 E. Boulder St. (632-5551; tour hotline 578-4444), which offers informative one-hour tours every ½ hour with a tear-jerking film. Watch Olympic hopefuls practice in the afternoons. (Open Mon.-Sat. 9am-5pm, Sun. 10am-noon.) Take bus #1 east to Farragut.

For information about the arts in Colorado Springs, drop in at the **Colorado Springs Fine Arts Center,** 30 W. Dale (634-5583; open Tues.-Fri. 9am-5pm, Sat. 10am-5pm, Sun. 1-5pm; admission $2.50, students ages 13-21 and seniors $1.50), or call **Colorado College** (389-6606), which stocks the city with cultural events, including the **Summer Festival of the Arts.** Tickets and info available at Worner Campus Center (389-6606) at Cascade and Cache La Poudre St. (Open daily 8am-11pm.)

At night, Colorado College's literati find comfortable reading at **Poor Richard's Espresso Bar,** (577-4291) adjacent to the bookstore (see Food above). The bar occasionally hosts comedy, acoustic performances, and readings. (Open Mon.-Thurs. 7am-midnight, Fri.-Sat. 7am-1:30am.) The **Dublin House,** 1850 Dominion Way at Academy St. (528-1704), is a popular sports bar, with Sunday night blues downstairs. (Open daily 4pm-2am. No cover.)

Near Colorado Springs: Cripple Creek

Former mining towns pepper the area about Colorado Springs, nostalgic reminders of the state's glory days. In order to enliven these God-forsaken towns and bring back the spirit of the Old West, the state introduced small-stakes gambling up on **Cripple Creek** (sung about by The Band), **Central City,** and **Blackhawk.** Hotels and casinos offer poker, blackjack and slot machines with a $5 maximum bet. If fortune fails you in gambling, look for riches at the **Mollie Kathleen Gold Mine** (689-2465), two hours north of Colorado Springs via Rte. 67 in Cripple Creek. Every 10 minutes during the day, miners lead 40-minute tours down a 1,000-ft.-deep shaft. (Open May-Oct. daily 9am-5pm. Tours $8, kids $3.50.) For info. about other activities, try the **Cripple Creek Chamber of Commerce,** P.O. Box 650, Cripple Creek 80813 (689-2169 or 800-526-8777).

In a car (with good suspension), the most exciting way to reach Cripple Creek is via **Phantom Creek Road.** This route splinters off of U.S. 50, 30 mi. southwest of Colorado Springs, and meanders up an ever-narrowing canyon, in which the vertical walls get closer and closer to the road. Finally, near the tourist-haunt mining town of **Victor,** the road reaches a 9000-ft. highland. Cripple Creek still lies six mi. ahead. On the return trip, take the most scenic route over the unpaved **Gold Camp Road** (open only in summer), once described by Teddy Roosevelt as "scenery that bankrupts the English language."

Denver

Gold! Gold! GOLD!!! In 1858 the word went out from the South Platte River Valley: the South Platte and its smaller neighbor, Cherry Creek, harbored glittering, drool-inducing gold for the taking. Within weeks the rumor of riches lured thousands of miners to northern Colorado, and Denver was born, complete with Colorado's first saloon. (Back then, you didn't get in trouble for serving miners.) Most of the mines have since gone out of business, with cycling shops and sporting goods stores now contributing more to Denver's economy than saloons ever did. Colorado's capital is the Rockies' largest and fastest-growing metropolis. Centrally located between Colorado's eastern plains and western ski resorts, Denver today serves as the industrial, commercial, and cultural nexus of the region and has recently gone to the show with the newest major league baseball team, the Colorado Rockies.

A curious mix of transplanted New Yorkers and Chicagoans, rednecked cowpokes, Mexican immigrants, and outdoor enthusiasts comprise Denver's population (1.8 million). After sipping ginseng soda at Bohemian hangouts, explore fine museums, numerous parks, and the nation's first symphony in-the-round; all the while enjoying Denver's splendiferous mountain view.

Practical Information

Emergency: 911

Denver and Colorado Convention and Visitors Bureau, 225 West Colfax Ave. (892-1112 for convention info or 892-1505 for tourist info), near Civic Center Park just south of the capitol. Open Mon.-Fri. 8am-5pm in the winter; Mon.-Sat. 8am-5pm, Sun. 10am-2pm in the summer. Pick up a free copy of the comprehensive *Denver and Colorado Official Visitors Guide.* **Big John's Information Center,** 1055 19th St., at the Greyhound station. Big John, an ex-professional basketball player, offers enthusiastic information on hosteling in Colorado. Open Mon.-Sat. 6:15am-noon. **Stapleton Airport Information Center,** located on B, C, D, E concourses. Open daily 7am-10pm. Brochures available 24 hrs. **16th St. Ticket Bus,** in the 16th St. Mall at Curtis St. Double-decker bus with visitor information, half-price tickets to local theater performances, and RTD bus info. Open Mon.-Fri. 10am-6pm, Sat. 11am-3pm.

Stapleton International Airport (398-3844 or 800-247-2336), in northeast Denver. Easily accessible from downtown. RTD bus lines #28, 32, 38 serve the airport. Cab fare to downtown $8-12. The 9th busiest airport in the world; delays are common. **Ground Transportation Information** on the 1st floor can arrange transport to surrounding areas such as Estes Park and Vail. Open daily 7am-11pm.

Amtrak: Union Station, at 17th St. and Wynkoop (534-2812 or 800-872-7245), in the northwest corner of downtown. One train per day to: Salt Lake City (14 hr., $103); Omaha, NE (9 hr., $102); Chicago, IL (18 hr., $153); Kansas City (12 hr., $130).

Buses: Greyhound, 1055 19th St. (292-6111; 800-531-5332 for Spanish-speaking visitors), downtown. Four per day to: Cheyenne (3 hr., $18); Albuquerque (12 hr., $68); Kansas City (15 hr., $89); Salt Lake City (12 hr., $93). Also comprehensive service within CO. The **Ski Train-Budweiser Eagle Line,** 555 17th St. (296-4754). Leaves from Amtrak Union Station and treks through the Rockies, stopping in Winter Park (Dec.-April only). Departs Denver at 7:15am, Winter Park at 4:15pm; 2 hr.; $25 round-trip.

Public Transport: Regional Transportation District (RTD), 1600 Blake St. (299-6000). Service within Denver and to Longmont, Evergreen, Conifer, Golden, and the suburbs. Many routes shut down by 9pm or earlier. Fare Mon.-Fri. 6-9am and 4-6pm $1, all other times 50¢, over 65 15¢. Free 16th Street Mall Shuttle covers 14 blocks downtown. Over 20 buses per day to Boulder (45 min., $2.50). Call Mon.-Fri. 6am-8pm, Sat.-Sun. 8am-8pm. Bus maps $1.

Gray Line Tours: At the bus station (289-2841). 2½-hr. tours of Denver twice daily in summer, once during the rest of the year. $15, under 12 $10. 3½-hr. "City Tour" ($18). The **Denver Mountain Parks tour** includes many of the sights outside Denver in the nearby Rockies.

Taxi: Zone Cab, 444-8888. **Yellow Cab,** 777-7777. Both $1.20 base fare, $1.20 per mi.

Car Rental: Be wary of renting clunkers in the mountains; check out the car before accepting it. **Rent-a-Heap,** 940 S. Jason St. (698-0345) $15 per day, $95 per week, unlimited free mileage. but you must remain in the metro area. Open Mon.-Fri. 8am-5pm, Sat. 8am-1pm. Must have $50 de-

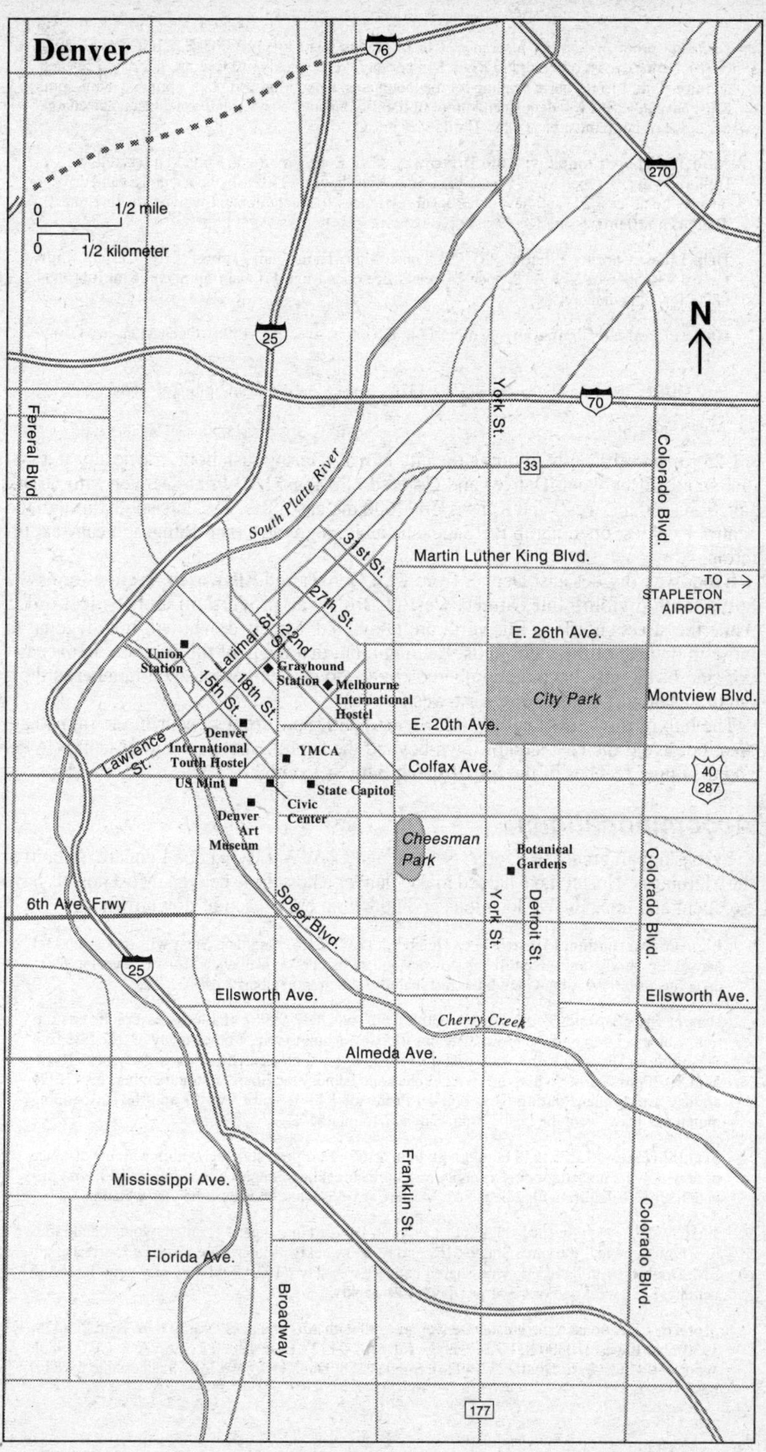

Denver
76
270
0
1/2 mile
0
1/2 kilometer
N
25
70
York St.
Colorado Blvd.
Feral Blvd.
33
South Platte River
31st St.
Martin Luther King Blvd.
TO STAPLETON AIRPORT
27th St.
E. 26th Ave.
Larimar St.
22nd St.
Union Station
Grayhound Station
Melbourne International Hostel
15th St.
18th St.
City Park
Montview Blvd.
E. 20th Ave.
Denver International Touth Hostel
Lawrence St.
YMCA
Colfax Ave.
40
287
US Mint
State Capitol
Civic Center
Denver Art Museum
Cheesman Park
Botanical Gardens
Colorado Blvd.
6th Ave. Frwy
Speer Blvd.
York St.
Detroit St.
25
Ellsworth Ave.
Ellsworth Ave.
Cherry Creek
Almeda Ave.
Franklin St.
Mississippi Ave.
Colorado Blvd.
Florida Ave.
Broadway
177

posit and proof of liability insurance. **Cheap Heaps Rent-a-Car,** 6005 E. Colfax Ave. (393-0028), 8 blocks east of Colorado Blvd. $15 per day, $110 weekly; 30 free mi. per day, 12¢ each additional mi. $15 if you're heading for the mountains. Open Mon.-Fri. 8am-6pm, Sat. 8am-2pm. Must have at least $100 deposit and proof of liability insurance or $7 additional insurance charge per day. For both, must be at least 21 and stay in CO.

Auto Transport Company: Auto Driveaway, 5777 E. Evans Ave. (757-1211); take bus #21 to Hollis and Evans. Open Mon.-Fri. 8:30am-5pm. Must have a $250 cash deposit and a valid drivers license, be at least 21, and have three local references (last requirement waived for foreigners). There is a $10 processing fee.

Help Lines: Contact Lifeline, 237-4537, open Mon.-Thurs. 7am-11pm, Fri. 1pm-11pm. **Rape Crisis,** 430-5656 or 329-9922, open 24 hrs. Office open Mon.-Fri. 9am-5pm; call **Comitus** 343-9890, for immediate crises.

Gay and Lesbian Community Center: 1245 E. Colfax Ave. (837-1598). Open Mon.-Fri. 10am-10pm.

Post Office: 350 16th St., basement (592-1326). Open Mon.-Fri. 8am-5pm. **ZIP code:** 80201.

Area Code: 303.

I-25 runs north-south, dividing the city in half. During rush hour, traffic sits at a virtual standstill between Denver and Colorado Springs. I-70 links Denver with Grand Junction (250 mi. west) and Kansas City (600 mi. east). Rte. 285 cuts south through the central Rockies, opening up the Saguache and Sangre de Cristo Ranges to easy exploration.

Broadway divides east Denver from west Denver and **Ellsworth Avenue** forms the north-south dividing line. Streets west of Broadway progress in alphabetical order, while the streets north of Ellsworth are numbered. Streets downtown run diagonal to those in the rest of the metropolis. Keep in mind that many of the avenues on the eastern side of the city become numbered *streets* downtown. Most even-numbered thoroughfares downtown run only east-west.

The hub of downtown is the **16th Street Mall.** Few crimes occur in the immediate area, but avoid the east side of town beyond the capitol, the west end of Colfax Ave., and the upper reaches of the *Barrio* (25th-34th St.) at night.

Accommodations

Ex-basketball great "Big John" Schrant and ex-WWII flying ace Leonard Schmitt at the Melbourne Hostel have helped make Denver a hosteler's heaven. Most hostels have excellent and inexpensive locations and lie within easy reach of downtown.

Big Al's International Hostel, 1714 Humboldt (837-9313). Tami and Sang will make you feel part of the family here. Beautiful woodwork and stylish decor. Call ahead for free evening pick-up at bus or train station. Great breakfast included. $8, nonmembers $10.

Denver International Youth Hostel, 630 E. 16th Ave. (832-9996), 10 blocks east of the bus station, 4 blocks north of downtown. Take bus #15 to Washington St., 1 block away or take free 16th St. shuttle to Broadway and walk east on 16th Ave. for 6 blocks. Office open daily 8am-10am, 5pm-10:30pm. Dorm-style rooms with kitchen and laundry facilities. $6, nonmembers $7. Call to arrange arrival plans during these hours. "Professor K's" tours of Denver and the surrounding mountains leave from the hostel Mon.-Sat. at 9:15am. ($12.)

Franklin House B&B, 1620 Franklin St. (331-9106). European style inn within walking distance of downtown. Fantastic rooms, friendly hosts, free breakfast. Singles $20. Doubles $30, with private bath $40. Triples with 2 beds $45. MasterCard, Visa, and travelers cheques welcome.

YMCA, 25 E. 16th St. (861-8300) at Lincoln St. Divided into 3 parts for men, women and families. Laundry and TV rooms. Single $16 per day, $66 weekly. With a shared bath $17, private bath $18. Doubles with bath $31, with shared bath $29 per day, $102 weekly. Family suite for 3 $35 per day, $138 weekly. For 4 $41 per day, $149 weekly.

Motel 6, 4 locations in the greater Denver area, all with A/C and pool. North: 6 W. 83rd Pl. (429-1550). Northwest: 10300 S. I-70 Frontage Rd. (467-3172). East: 12020 E. 39th Ave. (371-1980). West: 480 Wadsworth Blvd. (232-4924). Singles $28. Doubles from $33. All accessible by RTD bus.

Melbourne International Hostel (HI/AYH), 607 22nd St. (292-6386), downtown at Welton St. 6 blocks from the 16th St. Mall. Members: dorms $8, private rooms $15, couples $20; for non-members: $9 dorms, $18 private, $20 doubles. Call ahead. Women and lone travelers should be aware that this hostel is not in the best neighborhood.

Camping

Cherry Creek Lake Recreation Area (699-3860 or 800-678-2267). Take I-25 to exit 200, then west on Rte. 225 for about 3 mi. and south on Parker Rd.—follow the signs. Take the "Parker Road" bus. The 102 sites fill only on summer weekends. Sites $7. Entrance fee $4. $6.75 reservation fee. Max. 60 days advance for reservations, 120 days for cabins. Min. 14 days if reserving by check; 3 days for MasterCard or Visa.

Chatfield Reservoir, (791-7275 or 800-470-1144); take Rte. 75 or 85 4 mi. past the center of Littleton to 153 well-developed sites. Sites $7, with electricity $10. Open mid-May to mid-Oct. Make reservations for weekends.

Aspen Meadows Campground, 19 mi. south of Nederland (791-1957). Sites $6. Entrance fee $3. Contact the Metro-Regional office of the Colorado Division of Parks and Recreation. (Open Mon.-Fri. 9am-5pm) for more info on campgrounds.

National Forest Campgrounds are plentiful in the mountains 25 mi. west of Denver near Idaho Springs, Rte. 103 and 40, and in the region around Deckers, 30 mi. southwest of downtown on Rte. 67. Sites marked, but difficult to find. **Painted Rocks Campground,** on Rte. 67, in the Pikes Peak Ranger District (719-636-1602). Sites $7. **Top of the World,** off Pine Junction on Rte. 126 (236-7386). Look down on creation. Free but no water. Most sites open May-Sept. Call ahead or pick up maps at the National Forest's Rocky Mountain Regional Headquarters, 11177 W. 8th Ave., Lakewood (236-9431). Open Mon.-Fri. 8am-5pm.

Food

The *Barrio,* north of the mall between 20th and 30th St., contains some inexpensive—if slightly seedy—bars and Mexican restaurants, while **Sakura Square,** at 19th St. and Larimer, offers several Japanese restaurants surrounding a pleasant rock garden. A young crowd haunts Colfax Ave. in the east, Sheridan, Wadsworth, and Federal Ave. in the west. For those over 21, the cheapest food fries at the Glendale nightclubs around Colorado Ave. and Alameda.

The Market, 1445 Larimer Sq. (534-5140), downtown. Popular for lunch and afternoon iced tea with a young artsy crowd that people-watches from behind salads, pastry, and oversized magazines. Open Mon.-Tues. 6:45am-6pm, Wed.-Thurs. 6:45am-10pm, Fri. 6:45am-midnight, Sat. 8am-midnight, Sun. 8:30am-6pm.

Goldie's Deli, 511 16th St. (623-6007) at the Glenarm on the Mall. Try the self-proclaimed "sandwich from the best deli in Denver." ($3-4.)

Lim's Chinese Kitchen, 1530 Blake St. (893-1158) Lim's specials are very generous and tasty. Sweet and sour pork or chicken with egg roll, fried rice and, of course, a cookie, ($3.75). (Open Mon.-Thurs. 10:30am-9pm.)

The Old Spaghetti Factory, 18th and Lawrence (295-1864), 1 block from Larimer St. Part of a national chain. Located in a gorgeously renovated old tramway building. Large, delicious spaghetti dinner with salad and great bread only $3.25 at lunchtime. Open for lunch Mon.-Fri. 11:30am-2pm, for dinner Mon.-Thurs. 5-10pm, Fri.-Sat. 5-11pm, Sun. 4-10pm. Visa and MasterCard accepted. Don't miss this great deal!

Wynkoop Brewery, at 18th St. and Wynkoop across from Union Station. (297-2700) An American Pub in a renovated warehouse that serves beer on tap, an Alfalfa mead, and a homemade rootbeer. Try one of their favorites ($4.25-6.50) for lunch or dinner and then head downstairs to the **Jazz Works** for a little live entertainment. (Cover $2 weekdays, $5 weekends.) Brewery open Mon.-Sat. 11am-2am, Sun. 11am-midnight. Free brewery tours Sat. 1-5pm.

City Spirit Café, 1434 Blake St. (575-0022), a few blocks from the north end of the 16th St. Mall. Happy, naive urban scenes in mellow pastels painted directly on the walls, doors, and bar. Specialties or tasty sandwiches $5. Live entertainment Fri. and Sat. Open Mon.-Thurs. 11am-1am, Fri.-Sat. 11am-2am.

The Eggshell, 1520 Blake St. (623-7555). Huge breakfast specials $2. Sandwiches $4-5. Open Mon.-Fri. 6:30am-2pm, Sat 7am-2pm., Sun. 7:30am-2pm.

Daddy Bruce's Bar-B-Q, 1629 E. 34th St., at Gilpin. (295-9115) Take bus #38. The sign on the back of the owner's truck says: "God loves you. So does Daddy Bruce." With that welcome, wait until you taste the best barbecue in Denver. Lucky parties may meet 92-year-old Daddy himself. Ribs from $5.25. Open Tues.-Thurs. 11am-midnight, Sun. 4pm-midnight.

Sights

With over 300 crystalline days of sunshine per year, Denver basks in its low-humidity air. **City Park,** one of the loveliest of over 205 tranquil spots throughout the city, lies between 17th and 23rd Ave. from York St. to Colorado Blvd. Nearby, the **Botanical Gardens,** 1005 York St. (331-4100) charges a hefty admission of $4 ($2 for seniors, children under 6 free with a paying adult) for entrance into the outdoor gardens and conservatory. Take bus #20 or #23 to Colorado Ave. (Open daily 9am-4:45pm.) Many people socialize at **Cheesman Park,** four blocks to the south, and enjoy the view of the snow-capped peaks that rise above the Denver skyline. (Take bus #6 or 10.) These parks are terrific for bicycling and strolling during the day, but none is safe after dark. For Denver Parks info, call 698-4900. The **Denver Municipal Band** performs summer concerts at 7:30pm in the parks. Pick up a schedule at the visitors bureau (see Practical Information above). For a wilder park experience from June to September, take I-70 from Golden to Idaho Springs, and then pick up Rte. 103 south over the summit (14,260 ft.) of **Mt. Evans.** Journey to **Red Rocks** (see below) or other parts of Denver's 25,000-acre park system. Check with **Denver Parks and Recreation,** 1805 Bryant Ave. (459-4000) about road conditions in fall and winter. (Open Mon.-Fri. 8am-5pm.)

The **16th Street Mall,** a 14-block pedestrian area in the heart of downtown, is a major tourist destination. The shuttle buses which skirt this strip from 6am to 8pm are the only free convenience you'll find here. **Larimer Square,** between 14th and 15th St., has been restored to Victorian elegance, and now houses expensive souvenir shops, galleries, and restaurants. Larimer's wild **Oktoberfest** also draws large crowds.

An appropriately gilded dome tops the gray Colorado granite of the **capitol building,** on Colfax and Broadway between Grant and 14th St. (866-2604). The lucky 13th step on the west side perches exactly one mi. above sea level; the gallery around the dome gives a great view of the Rocky Mountains. (Free tours from the foyer every hr. on the ½-hr. 9am-3:30pm Mon.-Fri. and from 10am-1pm on Sat. Open Mon.-Fri. 9am-4pm, Sat. 9:30am-2pm.)

A modern reminder of Colorado's old silver mining days, the **U.S. Mint,** 320 W. Colfax (844-3582), issues U.S. coins with a small "D" for Denver embossed beneath the date. Free 20-minute tours, every 20 minutes in summer and every 30 minutes in winter, will lead you past a million-dollar pile of gold bars and expose you to the deafening roar of money-making machines that churn out a total of 20 million shiny coins per day. And, no, they do *not* give free samples. Arrive early in summer, lines often reach around the block. (Open Mon.-Tues., Thurs.-Fri. 8am-3pm, Wed. 9am-3pm.)

Just a few blocks from the U.S. Mint, and right behind Civic Center Park, stands the **Denver Art Museum,** 100 W. 14th Ave. (640-2793). Architect Gio Ponti designed this six-story "vertical" museum in order to accommodate totem poles and period architecture. The museum's collection of Native American art rivals any in the world. The fabulous third floor of pre-Columbian, pre-Christian art of the Americas resembles an archeological excavation site, with temples, huts, and idols. Call for info on special exhibits. (Museum open Tues.-Sat. 10am-5pm, Sun. noon-5pm. Optional admission $3, seniors and students $1.50.) Housed in the Navarre Building, once the brothel for the Brown Palace, the **Museum of Western Art,** 1727 Tremont Place (296-1880), holds a collection of stellar Russell, Benton, O'Keeffe, and Grant Wood paintings and drawings. The **Brown Palace,** across the street at 321 17th St. (297-3111) is a historic grand hotel that once hosted presidents, generals, and movie stars. **The Black American West Museum and Heritage Center,** 91 California St. (292-2566), will show you a side of frontier history left unexplored by John Wayne movies. Come here to learn that 1/3 of all cowboys were African-American, and other details left out of textbooks. (Open Wed.-Fri. 10am-2pm, Sat. 10am-5pm, Sun. 2-5pm. Admission $2, seniors $1.50, ages 12-16 75¢, under 12 50¢.)

The **Natural History Museum,** 2001 Colorado Blvd. (322-7009) in City Park presents amazingly lifelike wildlife sculptures and dioramas. (Open daily 9am-5pm $4, ages 4-12 and seniors $2.) The Natural History Museum complex includes the **Gates Planetarium** with its popular "Laserdrive" show and an **IMAX theater** (370-6300. Call for shows, times and current prices). Combination tickets to the museum, planetarium, and IMAX cost $6.50, seniors and ages 4-12 $4.50. Across the park roars the **Denver Zoo,** at E. 23rd St. and Steele (331-4100), where you can view the live versions of the museum specimens. (Open daily 10am-6pm. $4, seniors and ages 6-15 $2.)

The dramatic **Red Rocks Amphitheater and Park** (693-1234), 12 mi. southwest of Denver on I-70, is carved into red sandstone. As the sun sets over the city, even the most well-known of performers must compete with the natural spectacle behind them. (For tickets call 623-8497 Mon.-Fri. 8am-5pm. Park admission free. Shows $9-25.) West of Denver in nearby Golden is the **Coors Brewery,** 3rd and Ford St. (800-642-6116; 277-2337), the largest brewery in the world founded by brewer Adolf Coors. (Free tours Mon.-Sat. 10am-4pm.)

Entertainment, Nightlife, and Seasonal Events

Denver is a city for the young. College-age singles come out of the woodwork in droves and let loose every evening. Although clubs downtown tend to come and go, some have gained a lasting reputation. One tried and true establishment is **Basins Up,** 1427 Larimer St. (623-2104), where you can wallow in live rock music all evening. (Open Mon.-Sat. 8pm-2am. Cover Fri.-Sat. $5. Music starts at 8:30pm Sat.-Wed. and at 9pm Thurs.-Fri. Must be 21 or over.) The "Hill of the Grasshopper," **El Chapultepec,** 20th and Market St. (295-9126), is a great hole-in-the-wall jazz club. (Open daily 7am-2am. No cover if you can pronounce "Chapultepec" correctly.) The magazine *Westwood* has details on the downtown club scene, and can be found in most restaurants and coffee shops. For a calendar of alternative art and music events, pick up a copy of *ICON* (455-4643) in the foyer of Muddy's Java Café, 2200 Champa St (see Food above) or other coffee and food stops downtown. To locate the happening places in the 'burbs, head for Glendale, where the nocturnal bar-hoppers can show you the best places to enjoy a quiet, intimate evening of slam dancing. At **Bangles,** 4501 E. Virginia (377-2702), live bands blare in the evening, and the afternoon volleyball matches often become jubilant free-for-alls after a few pitchers of beer ($4). (Open daily 8pm-2am. Volleyball games Tues.-Fri. at 5:30pm. Cover $1-5.)

Denver's two most popular festivals are the **Greek Festival** and **A Taste of Colorado.** The Greek festival takes place in June, downtown, featuring good Greek food, music, and dancing. An outdoor *fête,* the Taste is the last weekend in August, during which time food vendors line the streets near the capitol among open-air concerts.

Mountain Resorts Near Denver

Sixty-eight mi. northwest of Denver on U.S. 40, **Winter Park** slaloms among delicious-smelling mountain pines, surrounded by 600 mi. of skiing, hiking, and biking trails. On the town's southern boundary, Olympic cross-country skier Polly runs the **Winter Park Hostel (HI/AYH)** (726-5356), one block from the Greyhound stop and 2 mi. from Amtrak (free shuttle). The hostel features four kitchens, bunks, and three couples' rooms in spotless, cheery trailers. (Nov. to mid-April $11, nonmembers $13; mid-June to Oct. $7.50, nonmembers $9.50. Call for reservations in winter. Open June 15-April 15.) **Le Ski Lab,** 7894 U.S. 40 (726-9841), next door offers discounts on bike and ski rentals for hostelers. (Mountain bikes regularly $9 full day, $6 for ½ day. Skis $6-20. Full-day raft trips on the Colorado River $46 per adult, $39 child.) The Lab also cooks up $35 all-day rafting trips down the Colorado river. (Open daily in summer 9am-6pm; in winter 8am-8pm.) The **Winter Park-Fraser Valley Chamber of Commerce,** 50 Vasquez Rd. (726-4118; from Denver 800-422-0666), provides information about skiing at the Winter Park Mary Jane Ski Area. (Open winter daily 9am-8pm; summer 10am-5pm.) The chamber also serves as the Greyhound depot. (From Denver 2 buses per day, 2 hr., $9.) From December through April, the **Ski Train-Budweiser**

Eagle Line, (296-4754) leaves from Denver's Union Station, 555 17th St. at 7:30am, arriving in Winter Park at 9:30am, and returns to Denver at 4:15pm on weekends only ($25 round-trip).

Those stout of heart and strong of leg should head out to **Frisco,** 55 mi. west of Denver on I-70, for hikes through the Rockies. Along with Breckenridge, Dillon, Copper Mountain, Keystone, and Silverthorne, Frisco hosts numerous sporting events throughout the year. All six towns fall under the jurisdiction of the **Summit County Chamber of Commerce,** 110 Summit Blvd., P.O. Box 214, Frisco, CO 80443 (668-5800), which provides information on current area events. (Open daily 9am-5pm.) The only reasonable accommodations in the county are at the delightful **Alpen Hütte,** 471 Rainbow Dr. in Silverthorne (468-6336). A bed in the sparsely decorated, gleaming bunk rooms costs $12 May 1-mid-Nov.; $18 mid-Nov.-Dec. 19; $23 Dec. 20-Jan. 4; $20 Jan. 5-Jan. 29; $23 March; $19 April.Guest rooms closed 9:30am-3:30pm. Free county-wide shuttle and **Greyhound** stop here. Reservations recommended.

Grand Junction

Grand Junction gets its hyperbolic name from its location at the confluence of the Colorado and Gunnison Rivers and the conjunction-junction of the Río Grande and Denver Railroads. As western Colorado's trade and agricultural center, this unassuming city serves as a fantastic base from which to explore the Gunnison Valley, the Grand Mesa, and the western San Juans. Travelers without a car will be severely limited in this area without a packed wallet. **Avis Rent-A-Car,** on Walker Field (244-9170), rents economy cars for $34 per day, $139 per week with unlimited mileage. You must be at least 25 years of age and have a major credit card.

Within walking distance from the bus or train station is the **Melrose Hotel (HI/AYH),** 337 Colorado Ave. between 3rd and 4th St., an immaculate, well-maintained hotel with oodles of old-fashioned charm. The rooms are spacious with a touch of antique elegance. (Rooms with shared bath $10.50 members, $16 nonmembers. Private bath $15 members, $20 nonmembers. 50¢ extra for linen and towels.) **Lo Master Motel,** 2858 North Ave. (243-3230), has singles as lo as $17, doubles $21. Camping in **Highline State Park** (858-7208), 22 mi. from town and seven mi. north of exit 15 on I-70 with fishing access and restrooms, or **Island Acres State Park** (464-0548), 15 mi. east on the banks of the Colorado River, costs $6 per site plus a $3 day pass to enter the park. A **KOA,** 3238 F Rd. (434-6644), knocks them out in Clifton, just east of Grand Junction off I-70. (Sites $15 for two adults, $3 per additional adult, $2 per additional child, $2.25 for electricity, $2 for sewer.)

Some affordable restaurants conjoin grandly here. **Dos Hombres Restaurant,** 421 Branch Dr. (242-8861), just south of Broadway (Rte. 340) on the southern bank of the Colorado River, serves great Mexican food in a casual, family-style setting. (Combination dinners $3.75-5.75. Open daily 11am-10pm.) During the day, the **B & J Coffee Shop,** 400 Main St. (245-5866), in the back of a downtown dime store, has some charming touches, like Coke in bottles, a soda fountain, and full meals for $4, along with thick, iced cinnamon rolls. (Open Mon.-Sat. 7am-4pm.) For breakfast, go to **Talley's,** Main St. (245-7799), for *huevos rancheros* ($3.75). (Open Mon.-Sat. 7am-4pm, Sun. 8am-2pm.)

Shopping is plentiful along Main St. Browse through **A Haggle Vendors Emporium,** 510 Main St. (245-1404), for a piece of Americana or the Old West. Items are assembled from 40 different vendors, so shop carefully for the best buys. (Open Mon.-Sat. 9:30am-5:30pm.) Also along Main St. between 3rd and 7th St., watch for **Art on the Corner,** an outdoor exhibit of discreetly placed sculptures.

For literature on the area, visit the **Tourist Information Center,** 759 Horizon Dr., Suite F (243-1001; open daily 9am-8pm), or the **Convention and Visitors Bureau** and **Chamber of Commerce,** both at 4th and Grand downtown (244-1480; open Mon.-Fri. 8:30am-5pm).

Grand Junction lies at the prudent juncture of U.S. 50 and U.S. 6 in northwestern Colorado. Denver skis 228 mi. to the east; Salt Lake City slithers 240 mi. to the west.

The **bus station,** 230 S. 5th S. (242-6012), has service to: Denver (4 per day; 7 hr.; $24); Durango (1 per day; $32); Salt Lake City (1 per day; 8 hr.; $37); and Los Angeles (4 per day; $135). (Open Mon.-Fri. 3:30am-6pm and 8:30-9:30pm, Sun. 3:30-8am, 1:30-3:30pm.)

Grand Junction's **post office** is at 241 N. 4th St. (244-3401; open Mon.-Fri. 8:30am-5pm, Sat. 9am-12:45pm). Its **ZIP code** is 81502; its **area code** is 303.

Near Grand Junction: Colorado National Monument

European settlers once dismissed the arid, red, fearsome canyons and striated sandstone of the **Colorado National Monument** as unusable land. If not for the efforts of intrepid trapper and hunter John Otto, who in 1911 helped petition for the land to become a national monument, the area's natural beauty might very well have been dismissed as a stony wasteland. Facilitate your explorations by renting a mountain bike in nearby Grand Junction at **Cycle Center,** 141 N. 7th St. (242-2541). ($8 per half day, $15 per day. Open Mon.-Fri. 9:30am-6pm, Sat. 9:30am-5pm.)

Saddlehorn Campground offers campsites in the monument on a first-come, first-served basis, with picnic tables, grills, and restrooms. (Sites $6; free in winter.) The **Bureau of Land Management** (244-3000; open Mon.-Fri. 7:30am-5pm) maintains three less-developed, free "campgrounds" near **Glade Park** at Mud Springs. Bring your own water. **Little Dolores Fall,** 10½ mi. west of Glade Park, has fishing and swimming. The monument charges an additional admission fee of $3 per vehicle, $1 per cyclist or hiker. Check in at the monument **headquarters and visitors center** (858-3617), near the campground on the Fruita side of the monument. No permit is required. (Open daily 8am-8pm; off-season Mon.-Fri. 8am-4:30pm.)

Grand Mesa

Fifty mi. east of Grand Junction plops Grand Mesa ("Large Table"), the world's largest flat-top mountain. An ancient Native American story tells how an enormous eagle who lived on the rim of Grand Mesa captured a human child in its beak and flew away. The child's vengeful father found the eagle's nest and tossed out the baby eagles, who then became lunch for a serpent sunning at the base of the Mesa. In turn, the mother eagle snatched up the viper, flew to a dizzying height, and tore it to pieces, sending snake segments careening to the earth to make deep impressions in Grand Mesa; this explains the area's many lakes. Stodgy, boring geologists say no such thing. Instead, they claim that some 600 million years ago, a 300-ft.-thick flow of lava covered the area where the mesa now stands. Since then, wind and rain has eroded the surrounding land by over 5000 ft., leaving only the pitted, rocky eagle perch.

Whatever the Mesa's origin, this area, as you would expect, offers numerous outdoor attractions, including fine **backcountry hiking**. Climbers covet the soft-rock climbs here, including the **Monument Spire.** To reach Grand Mesa from Grand Junction, take I-70 eastbound to Plateau Creek, where Rte. 65 cuts off into the long climb through the spruce trees to the top of the mesa. Near the top is the Land's End turn-off leading to the very edge of Grand Mesa, some 12 mi. down a well-maintained dirt road. On a clear day, you can see halfway across Utah.

The mesa not only has an excellent view, but excellent camping as well. The National Forest Service maintains a dozen **campsites** on the mesa; **Carp Lake, Island Lake**, and **Ward Lake** are $7 each, and the rest are free. The district **forest service,** 764 Horizon Dr. in Grand Junction (242-8211), disseminates truckloads of info. (Open Mon.-Fri. 8am-5pm.) You can buy a map of the mesa's trails, campsites, and trout ponds ($2.50) here, or at **Surplus City,** 200 W. Grand Ave. (242-2818; $4; open Mon.-Fri. 8am-8pm, Sat. 8am-7pm, Sun. 9am-6pm). **Vega State Park** (487-3407), 12 mi. east of Colbrain off Rte. 330, also offers camping in the high country. (Park entrance fee $3 per vehicle; campsites $6 per night.)

Great Sand Dunes National Monument

After Colorado's splendid mountains begin to look the same to you, make a path to the unique waves of grainy sand at the northwest edge of the **San Luis Valley.** The 700-ft. dunes lap the base of the **Sangre de Cristo Range,** representing thousands of years of wind-blown accumulation. The progress of the dunes at passes in the range is checked by the shallow but persistent **Medano Creek.** Visitors can wade across the creek from April to mid-July. For a short hike, head out on **Mosca Trail,** a ½-mi. jaunt into the desert sands. Try to avoid the intense afternoon heat.

Rangers preside over daily naturalist activities, hikes, and other programs. Full schedules are available at the **visitors center** (719-378-2312), ½ mi. past the entrance gate, where you can also view a 15-minute film on the dunes, shown every half hour. (Open daily 8am-7pm; Sept. 2-May 27 8am-5pm. Entrance fee for vehicles $3, pedestrians and bikers $1.) For more info contact the Superintendent, Great Sand Dunes National Monument, Mosca 81146 (378-2312).

For those who thirst for more than just the first wave of dunes, the **Oasis** complex (378-2222) on the southern boundary also provides four-wheel-drive tours of the back-country. The three-hour tour takes the rugged Medano Pass Primitive Road into the nether regions of the monument. (2 tours daily; 3 hr.; $14, under 12 $8.)

Pinyon Flats, the monument's campground, fills quickly in summer. Camping here among the prickly pear cacti is on a first-come, first-served basis. Bring mosquito repellent in June. (Sites $8.) If the park's sites are full, you can camp at Oasis. (Sites $9.50 for 2 people, with hookup $14.50. Each additional person $2.50. Showers included.) **Backcountry camping** requires a free permit. For information on nearby National Forest Campgrounds, contact the Río Grande National Forest Service Office, 1803 W. Hwy. 160, Monte Vista, CO 81144 (852-5941). All developed sites are $7 to $8.

Great Sand Dunes National Monument blows 32 mi. northeast of Alamosa and 112 mi. west of Pueblo, on Rte. 150 off U.S. 160. **Greyhound** sends one bus per day out of Denver to Alamosa (5 hr.; $43; see Denver: Practical Information), with a depot at 8480 Stockton St. (589-4948; open Mon.-Fri. 10am-4:30pm, Sat. 3-4:30pm). The country road from Mosca on Rte. 17 is strictly for four-wheel-drive vehicles. In case of an **emergency** within the park, call 911.

Mesa Verde National Park

Fourteen centuries ago, Native American tribes settled and cultivated the desert mesas of southwestern Colorado. In the year 1200 they constructed and settled the cliff dwellings which they mysteriously abandoned in 1275. Navajo tribes arriving in the area in 1450 named the previous inhabitants the Anasazi, or the "ancient ones." Today only five of the 1000 archeological sites are open to touring, because the fragile sandstone wears quickly under human feet. Such caution results in crowding within the park; it is best to arrive early.

Entrance fees to the park are $5 per car, $2 per pedestrian or cyclist. The southern portion of the park divides into the **Chapin Mesa** and the **Wetherill Mesa.** The **Far View Visitors Center** (529-4593) near the north rim offers info on the park. (Open in summer 8am-5pm.) In the winter months, you can obtain park info at the **Colorado Welcome Center/Cortez Chamber of Commerce,** at 928 E. Main St. in Cortez. (800-253-1616 or 565-3414). (Open in the summer daily 8am-6pm; winter 8am-5pm.) On Wetherhill Mesa, tours run only from June to September and leave from Far View Lodge (3-hr. tours $12, under 12 $5; 5-hr. tours $15, under 12 $5). You may take guided tours up ladders and through the passageways of Anasazi dwellings. **Spruce Tree House** is one of the better-preserved ruins. To get an overview of the Anasazi lifestyle, visit the **Chapin Mesa Museum** (529-4475) at the south end of the park. (Open daily 8am-6:30pm.) At the balcony house ruins, ranger-led guided tours leave every ½ hr. from 9am to 6pm daily.

Mesa Verde's only lodging, **Far View Motor Lodge** (529-4421), is extremely expensive, but a few nearby motels can put you up for under $30. Try the **Ute Mountain Motel,** 531 S. Broadway (565-8507) in Cortez, CO. (Singles from $24. Doubles from $34. A few rooms go for $20. Kids under 12 free.) However, your best bet is to stay at the nearby **Durango Hostel** (see Durango). The only camping in Mesa Verde is at **Morfield Campground** (529-4400 or off-season 533-7731), four mi. inside the park, with some beautiful and secluded sites. In summer, come early to beat the crowds. (Sites $8, with full hookup $16. Showers 75¢ for 5 min. Senior discount with Golden Age Pass.) Outside the park, 1/4 mi. east on U.S. 160, is the **Double A Campground and RV Park** (565-3517 or 800-972-6620 for reservations; sites $14, with hookup $18 for two people, each additional person $2.50.) Nice pool and spa; owners supply nightly "country shows" for guests that include guitar and washboard.

The park's main entrance is off U.S. 160, 36 mi. from Durango and 10 mi. from Cortez. **Greyhound** will drop you off on its daily Durango run, but only in the wee hours of the morning. The Durango station is at 275 8th Ave. (259-2755). **Durango Transportation** (259-4818) will take you on a nine-hour tour of the park, from 8:30am to 4:30pm ($27, kids $13.50); bring a lunch. Since sights lie up to 40 mi. apart, a car is helpful. Van transportation is also available at the Far View Lodge (see above) for self-guided tours with 24-hr. notice.

Mesa Verde's **ZIP code** is 81330; nearby Mancos is 81328. The **area code** is 303.

Rocky Mountain National Park

Try to visualize every rustic and rugged Grape Nuts and Coors commercial you have ever seen on television. Cool glacier-fed brooks babble. Deer graze in an alpine meadow. A deep azure lake mirrors the scene, its tranquility disturbed only by a leaping fish. All around, snow-streaked crags pierce a clear summer sky. Hawks describe lazy circles overhead. Ahhh, *this* is Colorado. This is Rocky Mountain National Park. Although purists disparage it for its overpopularity, this remarkable sanctuary makes even the slickest city dweller don a flannel shirt and take in some of the best scenery in the Rockies.

The mountain wilds are made accessible by tourist towns on the park's borders and by **Trail Ridge Rd., (U.S. 34)** the highest continuously paved road in the U.S. The Ute shied away from **Grand Lake,** believing that mists rising from its surface were the spirits of rafters who drowned in a storm. Today, this glacial lake and its town of the same name squat in the west end of Rocky Mountain National Park. Trail Ridge Road runs 45 mi. through the park from the town of **Grand Lake** to the town of **Estes Park**. At the road's peak of over 2 vertical mi., oxygen is rare and an eerie silence prevails among the low vegetation of the tundra.

Practical Information

Emergency: 911. Estes Park police 586-4465; Grand Lake police 627-3322.

Visitor Information: Estes Park Chamber of Commerce, P.O. Box 3050, Estes Park 80517, at 500 Big Thompson Hwy. (586-4431 or 800-443-7837). Slightly east of downtown. Open June-Aug. Mon.-Sat. 8am-8pm, Sun. 9am-6pm; off-season Mon.-Sat. 9am-5pm, Sun. 10am-4pm. **Grand Lake Area Chamber of Commerce,** 14700 Hwy. 74 (800-462-5253), just outside of the park's west entrance. Open daily 9am-5pm; off-season Mon.-Fri. 10am-5pm.

Park Entrance Fees: $5 per vehicle, $2 per biker or pedestrian, under 16 free, and over 61 half price. Valid for 7 days.

Park Visitor and Ranger Stations: Park Headquarters and Visitors Center, on Rte. 36 2.5 mi. west of Estes Park (586-2371), at the Beaver Meadows entrance to the park. Call for park info, or to make sure the Trail Ridge Rd. is open. Headquarters open daily 8am-9pm; 8am-5pm off-season. Visitors center open daily 8am-9pm; off-season Mon.-Fri. 8am-5pm. **Kawuneeche Visitors Center** (627-3471), just outside the park's western entrance, 1.3 mi. north of Grand Lake. Open daily 7am-7pm; off-season (Sept.-May) 8am-5pm. **Moraine Park Visitors Center and Museum** (586-3777), on the Bear Lake Rd. Open summer daily 9am-5pm. Alpine Visitors Center, at the crest of Trail Ridge Rd. (586-4927). Check out the view of the tundra from the back window. Open June 1-July 4 daily 10am-4pm, July 5 to mid-Aug. 9am-5pm.

Public Transport: Estes Park Trolley, (586-8866). Red trolleys operate in the summer daily 9:30am-9pm. Frequent service connects everything you could want to see in Estes Park; guided tour included. $2 round-trip every hour, full day $4. **Charles Limousine** (586-5151 or 800-950-3274), $24 adults, $12 children from Denver bus station or airport to Estes; $15 from Boulder to Estes. (Open daily 6am-9pm.)

Horse Rental: Sombrero Ranch, 1895 Big Thompson Rd. (586-4577), in Estes Park 2 mi. from downtown on Hwy. 34 E., and on Grand Ave. in Grand Lake (627-3514). $15 for 1 hr., $25 for 2. The breakfast ride (at 7am, $25) includes a 2-hr. ride and a huge breakfast. Call ahead. Hostelers get 10% discount; special rates for those staying at the H Bar G Ranch. Both open daily 7am-5:30pm.

Help Lines: Roads and Weather, 586-9561. Hearing Impaired Visitors, 586-8506.

Post Office: Estes Park, 215 W. Riverside (586-8177). Open Mon.-Fri. 9am-5pm, Sat. 10am-12:30pm. **Grand Lake,** 520 Center Dr. (627-3340). Open Mon.-Fri. 8:30am-5pm. **ZIP code:** 80517.

Area Code: 303.

You can reach the National Park most easily from Boulder via Rte. 36 or from Loveland up the Big Thompson Canyon via Rte. 34. Busy during the summer, both routes lead to Estes Park and are easy biking trails. From Denver, take the RTD bus (20 per day, 45 min., $2) to its last stop in Boulder, and transfer (free) to bus #202 or 204 which will drop you off on U.S. 36 W. From there, you'll have to hike 30 miles or hitch a ride in order to get into the park. In Boulder you can find the entrance to U.S. 36 at 28th and Baseline Rd.

Estes Park lies 65 mi. from Denver, 39 mi. from Boulder, and 31 mi. from Loveland. Hitching within the park is prohibited. With a car, "loop" from Boulder by catching U.S. 36 through Estes Park, pick up Trail Ridge Rd. (U.S. 34), go through Rocky Mountain National Park (45 mi.), stop in Grand Lake, and take U.S. 40 to Winter Park and I-70 back to Denver.

Reach the western side of the park from Granby (50 mi. from I-70) via Rte. 40. One of the most scenic entrances, Rte. 7 approaches the park from the southeast out of Lyons or Nederland, accessing the **Wild Basin Trailhead,** the starting point for some glorious hikes. When Trail Ridge Rd. (open May-Oct.) closes, you can drive around the park from Walden and Fort Collins, via Rte. 125 out of Granby and then Rte. 14 to Fort Collins. Or take the more traveled Rte. 40 over spectacular **Berthoud Pass** to I-70, then Rte. 119 and 72 north to the park. Note: when Trail Ridge Rd. is closed, the drive jumps from 48 to 140 mi.

Accommodations

Although Estes Park and Grand Lake have an overabundance of expensive lodges and motels, there are few good deals on indoor beds near the national park, especially in winter when the hostels close down.

Estes Park

H Bar G Ranch Hostel (HI/AYH), 3500 H Bar G Rd.,P.O. Box 1260, 80517 (586-3688). Hillside cabins, horses Blackie and Spot, tennis courts, kitchen, and a spectacular view of the front range. Proprietor Lou drives you to the park entrance or into town every morning at 7:30am, and picks you up again at the Chamber of Commerce. Members only, $7.50. Rent a car for $26 per day. Open late May to mid-Sept. Call ahead.

YMCA of the Rockies, 2515 Tunnel Rd., Estes Park Center 80511 (586-3341), 2 mi. south of the park headquarters on Rte. 66 and 5 mi. from the Chamber of Commerce. Caters largely to clan gatherings and conventions. Extensive facilities on the 1400-acre complex, as well as daily hikes and other events. Four people can get a cabin from $48, kitchen and bath included. Lodge with bunk beds that sleep up to 5 $37. Guest membership $3. Families $5. This large resort has plenty of room for recreation; great for kids.

The Colorado Mountain School, 351 Moraine Ave. (586-5758). Dorm-style accommodations open to travelers unless already booked by mountain-climbing students. Wood bunks with comfortable mattresses and shower $16. Shower only $2. Reservations are recommended at least one week in advance. (Open in summer 8am-5pm daily.)

Grand Lake

Shadowcliff Hostel (HI/AYH), P.O. Box 658, 80447 (627-9220). Near the western entrance to the park. Entering Grand Lake, take the left fork after the visitors center on West Protal Rd.; their sign is 2/3 mi. down the road on the left. Beautiful, hand-built pine lodge on a cliff overlooking the lake. Offers easy access to the trails on the western side of the park and to the lakes of Arapahoe National Recreation Area. Kitchen. Large hall showers. $7.50, nonmembers $9. Private rooms $25-30. Open June 1-Oct. 1.

Sunset Motel, 505 Grand Ave., (627-3318). Friendly owners and gorgeous, cozy singles and doubles will warm your stay in Grand Lake. ($34-36; each additional person, $3).

Camping

Most sites fill up pretty quickly in summer; call ahead or arrive early.

National Park Campgrounds: Moraine Park (5.5 mi. from Estes; open year-round) **Glacier Basin,** (9 mi. from Estes),($9) require reservations in summer. **Aspenglen** 5 mi. west of Estes Park near the Fall River entrance; **Longs Peak,** 11 mi. south of Estes Park and 1 mi. off Hwy. 7; and **Timber Creek,** 10 mi. north of Grand Lake, the only campground on the western side of the park, all operate on a first-come first-served basis for $7. Longs Peak and Timber Creek are open all year; Aspenglen is open May 8- Sept. 30. Three-day limit enforced at Longs Peak, one-week limit elsewhere. Reservations can be made by calling or writing Mistix (P.O. Box 85705, San diego, CA., 92138-5705; 800-365-2267). Make reservations eight weeks in advance for family/individual; 12 weeks advance for groups. In winter, there is no water and no charge.

Spring Lake Handicamp: The park's free backcountry campsite for the disabled (586-4459). Open summer daily 7am-7pm is 7 mi. from Estes Park Headquarters at Sprague Lake Picnic Area. (586-4459 for information; 586-2371, ext. 242 for reservations.)

Backcountry camping: Offices at Park Headquarters (586-2371) and Kawuneeche Visitors Center (627-3471) on the western side of the park at Grand Lake. Open daily 8am-5pm. Get reservations and free permits at these offices or write the **Backcountry office**, Rocky Mountain National Park, Estes Park 80517 (586-0526). No charge for backcountry camping, but many areas are in no-fire zones; you may want to bring along a campstove.

Olive Ridge Campground, 15 mi. south of Estes Park on CO Rte. 7, in Roosevelt National Forest. Call 800-283-2267 for reservations. First-come, first-served sites $8. Contact the **Roosevelt-Arapahoe National Forest Service Headquarters,** 161 2nd St., Estes Park (586-3440). Open June-July daily 8am-noon and 1-5pm; Aug.-May Mon.-Fri. 9am-noon and 1-4pm.

Indian Peaks Wilderness, just south of the park, jointly administered by Roosevelt and Arapahoe National Forests. Permit required for backcountry camping during the summer. On the east slope, contact the Boulder Ranger District, 2915 Baseline Rd. (444-6003; open Mon.-Fri. 8am-5pm). Last chance permits ($4) are available in Nederland at Coast to Coast Hardware (take Hwy. 7 to 72 south; open Mon.-Sat. 9am-9pm). On the west slope, contact the Hot Sulphur Ranger District, 100 U.S. 34, in Granby (887-3331; open May 27-Sept. 2 daily 8am-5pm).

Food

Both cities near the park have several grocery stores where you can stock up on trail snacks. Look out for the "bulk foods" at **Safeway** in Estes—they are ideal. If you are aiming to get away from the kitchen on your vacation, the following establishments offer inexpensive and tasty food so you don't have to cook.

Johnson's Cafe (586-6624), 2 buildings to the right of Safeway, across from the Chamber of Commerce. Must try Milt's waffles (from $2.95) made from scratch and served all day long. Also, homemade "Arizona" hashbrowns, chili, crepes, and luscious pies at a great price. (Open Mon.-Sat. 7am-2:30pm.)

Coffee Bar Cafe 167 E. Elkhorn Ave.(586-3626)Start the day off with the best cup of coffee this side of the Rockies. Friendly, speedy waitresses also serve a variety of well-priced American meals (Charbroiled burger $4.25), including a great selection of items easy on your waistline and your budget. (Open summer 7am-9:30pm).

Boardwalk Pizza, 110 W. Elkhorn Ave. (586-5900); 351 S. St. Vrain Ave., just south of the Holiday Inn (586-5747). New York style pizza and subs ($1.50 per slice, meatball sub $3.95) Tell Larry that you're a Let's Go-er and he'll take good care of you! (Open daily 11am-10pm).

Ed's Cantina 362 E. Elkhorn (586-2919). Best Mexican food in the park area. Combination plate (cheese enchilada, bean burrito, and bean tostada) $5.95. Open daily 7am-10pm.

Pink walls and heart-shaped chairs set the mood for old-fashioned sweetness at the **Humphrey Fountain** in Grand Lake. 1100 Grand Ave. (627-3513) Sundaes (from $2.75), sandwiches, and other goodies only in the summer, 10am-8pm daily.

The Terrace Inn, 813 Grand Ave. in Grand Lake (627-3029). Homemade, homemade, homemade! Breakfast, lunch, dinner, or just a piece of pie, you can be sure it's fresh. Debby's special Italian sauce and huge fluffy pancakes ($3.50) are definite favorites. (Open summer 7am-10pm; call for winter hours.)

Sights and Activities

The star of this park is **Trail Ridge Road**. At its highest point, this 50-mi.-long stretch reaches 12,183 ft. above sea level; much of the road rises above timberline. The round-trip drive takes three hours by car, 12 hours by bicycle. For a closer look at the fragile tundra environment, walk from roadside to the **Forest Canyon Overlook,** or take the half-hour round-trip **Tundra Trail**. **Fall River Road,** a one-way dirt road going from east to west merging with Trail Ridge Rd. at the alpine center, offers even more impressive scenery, but also sharp cliffs and tight cutbacks along the road.

Rangers can help plan a **hike** to suit your interests and abilities. Since the trailheads in the park are already high, just a few hours of hiking will bring you into unbeatable alpine scenery along the Continental Divide. Be aware that the 12,000- to 14,000-ft. altitudes can make your lungs feel as if they're constricted by rubber bands; give your brain enough time to adjust to the reduced oxygen levels before starting up the higher trails. Some easy trails include the 3.6-mi. round-trip from Wild Basin Ranger Station to **Calypso Cascades** and the 2.8-mi. round-trip from the Long Peaks Ranger Station to **Eugenia Mine.** From the nearby **Glacier Gorge Junction** trailhead, take a short hike to **Mills Lake** or up to the **Loch.**

From the town of Grand Lake, a trek into the scenic and remote **North** or **East Inlets** should leave camera-toting tourists behind. Both of these wooded valleys offer excellent trout fishing. The park's gem is prominent **Longs Peak** (14,255 ft.), which dominates the eastern slope. The peak's monumental east face, a 2000-ft. vertical wall known simply as the **Diamond,** is the most challenging rock climbing spot in Colorado.

You can traverse the park on a mountain bike as a fun and challenging alternative to hiking. **Colorado Bicycling Adventures,** 184 E. Elkhorn (586-4241), Estes Park, rents bikes ($5 per hr, $9 for 2 hr., $14 per ½-day, $19 per day; discounts for hostelers; helmets included). Guided mountain bike tours are also offered ($20 for 2 hr., $35 for 4 hr.; open daily 9am-8pm; off-season 10am-5pm). The expertise required for the tight turns and sheer drops of the Horseshoe Park/Estes Park Loop make it the least traveled of the three bike routes in the park.

During the summer, the three major campgrounds have good nightly amphitheater programs that examine the park's ecology. The visitors centers have information on these and on many enjoyable ranger-led interpretive activities, including nature walks, birding expeditions, and artists' forays.

Of the two towns, Grand Lake draws fewer crowds in the summer. Though inaccessible without a car in the winter, the town offers hair-raising snowmobile and cross-country routes. Ask at the visitors center about seasonal events. Camp on the shores of adjacent **Shadow Mountain Lake** and **Lake Granby.**

San Juan Mountain Area

Ask Coloradans about their favorite mountain retreats, and they'll most likely name a peak, lake, stream or town in the San Juan Range of southwestern Colorado. Four national forests—the Uncompahgre (pronounced un-cum-PAH-gray), the Gunnison, the San Juan and the Río Grande—encompass this sprawling range.

Durango is an ideal base camp for forages into these mountains. In particular, the **Weminuche Wilderness,** northeast of Durango, tempts the hardy backpacker with a particularly large expanse of hilly terrain. You can hike for miles where wild, sweeping vistas are the rule. Get maps and info on hiking in the San Juans from **Pine Needle Mountaineering,** Main Mall, Durango 81301 (247-8728; open Mon.-Sat. 9am-9pm, Sun. 11am-4pm; winter Mon.-Sat. 9am-6pm, Sun. 11am-4pm; maps $2.50).

The San Juan area is easily accessible on U.S. 50, traveled by hundreds of thousands of tourists each summer. **Greyhound** and **Rocky Mountain Stages** service the area, but very poorly. Car travel is the best option in this region.

On a happier note, the San Juans are loaded with HI/AYH hostels and campgrounds, making them one of the most economical places to visit in Colorado.

Black Canyon of the Gunnison National Monument

According to the geologist who first mapped this area, "No other canyon in North America combines the depth, narrowness, sheerness, and somber countenance of the Black Canyon." This steely black canyon plunges 2500 ft. to the powerful and sculpting waters of the Gunnison River.

The **North Rim** of the canyon is the more remote, accessible only via a 12-mi. dirt road which leaves Rte. 92 near the Crawford Reservoir east from Delta or west from Blue Mesa. There are seven "overlooks" along the rim, and a self-guiding nature trail starts from the campground. The better-developed, more-populated **South Rim** is reached from U.S. 50, via Rte. 347 just outside of Montrose. The eight-mi. scenic drive along this rim boasts spectacular **Chasm View,** where you can peer 2000 ft. down a sheer vertical drop. Inspired hikers can descend to the bottom of the canyon; the least difficult trail (more like a controlled fall) drops 1800 ft. over a distance of one mi. The hike up is a *tad* more difficult. At certain points you must hoist yourself up on a chain in order to gain ground. Suffice it to say, this hike is *not* to be undertaken lightly. A backcountry permit and advice from a ranger are required before any descent. But don't let this daunt your spirit of adventure—rangers are helpful, and the wild beauty of this canyon climb awaits the brave. For more info, call the **visitors center** at 249-1915. The visitors center also offers 30-minute guided nature walks at 11am and 2pm; meet at the visitors center. Also, free narrated evening programs are given at the park's entrance daily in summer at 8:30pm. (Visitors center open Memorial Day-Labor Day daily 8am-7:30pm, less during the off-season. Park entrance fee $3 per car; if one of the passengers is 62 or over, everyone goes free. Try to pick up elderly hitchers.) A short walk down from the visitors center affords a view startling enough in its steepness to require chest-high rails to protect the vertiginous from falling.

Camp in either rim's beautiful desert **campgrounds.** Each has pit toilets and charcoal grills; the one in the **South Rim** has an amphitheater with summer evening programs at 9pm. Water is available, but use it sparingly. (Sites $6.) Since wood gathering is not allowed, bring your own wood/charcoal or pick up some at the Information/Gift Shop at the turn off to the park on U.S. 50. (Open about May 1-Nov. 15.) Backcountry camping and driftwood fires in the canyon bottom are permitted; beware the abundant poison ivy. Call the National Park Service office at 249-7036 or the **South Rim Visitor Info Center** at 249-1915 for details.

The closest town to the Gunnison National Monument is **Montrose,** with administrative offices for the monument located at 2233 E. Main St. (249-7036; open in summer daily 8am-7:30pm, fewer hours in the off-season). The **Black Canyon Friendship Inn,** 1605 Main St. (U.S. 50) (800-453-4511 or 249-3495), offers all the "extras" for only a little extra cash. Clean cable-and-air-conditioning-equipped rooms, nice pool and extremely friendly and helpful owners. (Singles $32. Doubles $38 and up.) The **Stockman's Café & Bar,** 320 E. Main St. (349-9446), serves hearty Western and Mexican meals (sandwiches $2.75, meal specials $4.25) across the street. (Open Mon.-Tues., Thurs.-Sun. 7am-11pm.) The town's **visitors center** assists at 2490 S. Townsend Ave. (249-1726; open May-Oct. daily 9am-7pm).

A few miles south of Montrose on U.S. 550, the **Ute Indian Museum,** 17253 Chipeta Dr. (249-3098), displays exhibits from the Bear Dance and the bilingual letters of chief Ouray (leader of the Southern Ute tribe). (Open May 27-Sept. 2 Mon.-Sat. 10am-5pm, Sun. 1-5pm. Admission $2, 65 and over and ages 6-16 $1.)

Greyhound serves Montrose, 50 N. Townsend Ave. (249-6673), and Gunnison, 303 Tomichi Ave. in the Changing Hands building (641-0060). Gunnison lies about 55 mi. east of Montrose on U.S. 50. The bus will drop you off at the junction of U.S. 50 and Rte. 347, six mi. from the canyon. **Western Express Taxi** (249-8880) will drive you in from Montrose for about $30.

Montrose's **ZIP code** is 81401. The **area code** for the region is 303.

Durango

As Will Rogers once put it, Durango is "out of the way and glad of it." Despite its increasing popularity as a tourist destination, Durango retains an almost insidiously relaxed small-town atmosphere. Come here to see nearby Mesa Verde and to raft down the Animas River, but don't be surprised if you end up staying longer than you expected. Winter is Durango's busiest season, when nearby **Purgatory Resort** (247-9000), 20 mi. north on U.S. 550, hosts skiers of all levels. (Lift tickets $34, kids $17, one free child per adult.) When the heat is on, trade in your skies for a sled and test out the **Alpine Slide.** (Tickets $3.50, under 6 must ride with an adult. Open summer daily 9:30am-6pm.)

Durango is best known for the **Narrow Gauge Silverton Train,** 479 Main St. (247-2733), which runs along the Animas River Valley to the glistening tourist town of **Silverton.** Old-fashioned locomotives wheeze and cough through the San Juans four times per day, leaving Durango at 7:30am, 8:30am, 9:30am, 10:15am and 4:40pm. The six-hour round-trip stops midway for an additional two hours in Silverton. (Tickets $37, kids $19.) If the prospect of sitting all day doesn't sound that great, consider buying a one-way train ticket and taking a bus back from Silverton along U.S. 550. **Buses** wait at the Silverton train station to service the weary. (1½-hr.; $17.) The train is wheelchair accessible.

To backpack into the scenic **Chicago Basin,** purchase a round-trip ticket to Needleton ($34). To get into the **New York Basin,** you'll need $37 and a ticket to Elk Park. The train will drop you off here on its trip to Silverton. When you decide to leave the high country, return to Needleton and flag the train, but you must have either a return pass or $24 in cash to board. The train chugs through at 4:43pm. For more info on the train and its services for backpackers, contact the Durango and Silverton Narrow Gauge Railroad, 479 Main St., Durango 81301. (Offices open May-Aug. daily 6am-9pm; Aug.-Oct. 7am-7pm; Oct.-May 8am-5pm.)

For river rafting, **Rivers West,** 520 Main St. (259-5077), has good rates. ($10 for a 1-hr. rapids ride, $19 for a two-hr. ride plus lunch. Kids get a 10% discount. Daily 8am-9pm.) **Durango Rivertrippers,** 720 Main St. (259-0289), organizes two-hour rides for $15 and ½-day rides for $23, under 15 $15. (Open daily 9am-9pm.) Biking gear is available from **Hassle Free Sports,** 2615 Main St. (259-3874; bikes $8 per hr., $20 per day; open Mon.-Sat. 8:30am-6pm, Sun. 10:30am-5pm; must have driver's license and major credit card).

The simplest way to ensure a pleasant stay in Durango is to rest up at the **Durango Youth Hostel,** 543 E. 2nd Ave. (247-9905), a quaint old building one block from downtown. David, the host, will help orient you to the area and will admit that he knew Timothy Leary at Princeton if you ask. (Check-in 5-10pm. Check-out 7-10am. Bunks $10.) The **Budget Inn** has clean, spacious rooms and a nice pool and hot tub. (Singles $30, doubles $34.) Less during the off-season. The **Cottonwood Camper Park,** on U.S. 160 (247-1977), 1/3 mi. west of town, has tent sites ($10, with shower $12, with electricity and water $15, full hookup $16).

For fixin's, head to **City Market,** on U.S. 550 one block down 9th St., or at 3130 Main St. (Both open 24 hrs.) Or breakfast with locals at **Carver's Bakery and Brewpub,** 1022 Main Ave. (259-2545), which has good bread and breakfast specials ($2-4.50). (Fri.-Sat. pitchers of beer $5. Open Mon.-Sat. 6:30am-10pm, Sun. 6:30am-2pm.)

The **Durango Diner,** 957 Main St. (247-9889), serves up mongo cheeseburgers ($2.50) and enormous, scrumptious pancakes cooked by a singing chef. (Open Mon.-Sat. 6am-2pm, Sun. 7am-1pm.) Race over to **Pronto,** 150 E. 2nd Ave. (247-1510), for their $4.25 spaghetti dinner or all-you-can-eat specials or mozzarella burger for just $3. **Farquhart's,** 725 Main Ave. (247-9861), serves up delicious burritos for $5.75. Come to this bar at night for the best live music in town; keep an eye open for Walt Richardson and Morningstar. (Free rock 'n' roll Tues.-Sat. and bluegrass Sun.-Mon. Open daily 11am-2am.)

Durango parks at the intersection of U.S. 160 (east to Alamosa, 150 mi.) and U.S. 550 (south to Farmington, NM, 45 mi.). Streets run perpendicular to avenues, but everyone calls Main Avenue "Main Street." **Greyhound,** 275 E. 8th Ave. (259-2755), serves Grand Junction ($29), Denver ($49), and Albuquerque ($34). (Open Mon.-Fri. 7:30am-noon and 3:30-5pm, Sat. 7:30am-noon, Sun. 7:30-10am.)

You can pick up care packages at the **Durango Post Office,** 228 8th St. (247-3434; open Mon.-Fri. 8:30am-5pm, Sat. 9am-noon.) Durango's **ZIP code** is 81301, the **area code** is 303.

Telluride

Site of the first bank Butch Cassidy ever robbed (the San Miguel), Telluride has a history right out of a 1930s black-and-white film. Prize fighter Jack Dempsey used to wash dishes in the Athenian Senate, a popular saloon/brothel that frequently required Dempsey to double as bouncer between plates. Now it simply serves delicious Greek food (see below). The **Sheridan Theatre** (see below) hosted actresses Sarah Bernhardt and Lillian Gish on cross-country theater tours. Vice-President William Jennings Bryan delivered his "Cross of Gold" speech in silver-scooping Telluride from the front balcony of the Sheridan Hotel. More recently, in his autobiography *Speak, Memory,* Vladimir Nabokov relates his pursuit of a particularly rare type of butterfly through Telluride. Not so rare (especially after its devaluation) was the silver that attracted all the less aesthetically inclined hoodlums to Telluride in the first place, beginning in 1875.

Today, music lovers, environmentalists, granolas, downhill skiers and mountain bikers inhabit Telluride, lingering for a weekend or several years. These young nomads, with an insatiable appetite for bluegrass, foreign film, and outdoor sports, lend Telluride the slightly "groovy" and daredevilish atmosphere of a college town. Self-proclaimed atheists can be spied crossing themselves before tipping their planks down "Spiral Stairs" and the "Plunge," two of the Rockies' most gut-wrenching slopes. For more information, contact the **Telluride Ski Resort,** P.O. Box 307, 81435 (728-3856). For a copy of the *Skier Services Brochure*, call 728-4424. A free shuttle connects the mountain village with the rest of the town. Pick up a current schedule at the visitors center (see below).

Neither rockslide nor snowmelt signals the end of the festivities in Telluride. The quality and number of summer arts festivals seem staggering when you consider that only 1500 people call the town home. While get-togethers occur just about every weekend in summer and fall, the most renowned include the **Bluegrass Festival** in late June—last year the likes of James Taylor and the Indigo Girls attracted crowds of 16,000. Although area music stores sell tickets for about $30 per night, people have managed to sneak in. Sssshhh, don't tell. On the weekend of the festivals, you can easily find dishwashing or food-serving jobs in exchange for tickets to the show. Telluride also hosts a **Talking Gourds** poetry fest (late June), a **Composer to Composer** festival (mid-July), and a **Jazz Festival** (early Aug.), among others. You can often hear the music festivals all over town, all day, and deep into the night as you try to sleep. Above all, the **Telluride International Film Festival** (Labor Day weekend), now in its 19th year, draws famous actors and directors from all over the globe. Guests in years past have included Academy Award-winning actor Daniel Day Lewis, Hasty Pudding Award-winning actor Clint Eastwood, and twinly-piqued director David Lynch. The **Visitors Center** is upstairs at **Rose's,** near the entrance to town at the demonic address of 666

West Colorado Ave. (728-6621 or 800-446-3192; Open 24 hrs.) For ticket info and lodging hints for the festivities, call 800-525-3455.

Two blocks from the visitors center lies the **Coonskin Chairlift,** which will haul you up 10,000 ft. for an excellent view of Pikes Peak and the La Sal Mountains. (Open June 11-Sept. 14 Thurs.-Mon. 10am-2pm. $7, seniors and ages 7-12 $4.) Biking, hiking and backpacking opportunities around Telluride are endless; ghost towns and alpine lakes tucked behind stern mountain crags fill the wild terrain. For an enjoyable day hike, trek up the San Miguel River Canyon to **Bridal Veil Falls.** Drive to the end of Rte. 145 and hike the steep, misty dirt road to the spectacular waterfall. **Paragon Ski and Sport,** 213 W. Colorado Ave. (728-4525), has camping supplies, bikes, skis and roller blades. (Open summer Mon.-Thurs. 9am-7pm, Fri.-Sun. 9am-8pm; winter daily 8am-9pm.) Stop at the local sportshop or **Between the Covers** bookstore, 224 W. Colorado Ave. (728-4504), for trail guides and maps. (Open daily 9am-9pm.)

The **Oak Street Inn (HI/AYH),** 134 N. Oak St. (728-3383), offers dorm-style lodging complete with a sauna. Beware, even hostels succumb to Colorado gold fever! Bunk rooms are not available during festivals or the Christmas season. (Members $15, nonmembers $27 for singles with shared bath; doubles $40, $54 for 3 guests, $68 for four. Showers $3.) When Oak Street is out of beds, head for the **New Sheridan Hotel,** 231 W. Colorado (728-4351), where a three-bunk room for two people goes for $39 in the summer, $25 in the spring; $8 for each additional person. You can **camp** in the east end of town in a town-operated facility with water, restrooms, and showers (728-3071). (2-week max. stay. Sites $8, except during the festivals.) If visiting Telluride for a festival, bring a sleeping bag; the cost of a bed on which to sleep—if you can find one—is outrageous. **Sunshine,** four mi. southwest on Rte. 145 toward Cortez, and **Matterhorn,** 10 mi. farther on Rte. 145 (1-800-283-2267), are well-developed national forest campgrounds; the latter can accommodate trailers with hookup. (2-week max. stay. Sites $7.) Accessible by jeep roads, several free primitive campgrounds huddle nearby. During festival times, you can crash just about anywhere in town, and hot showers are mercifully available at the high school ($2 during festivals).

Baked in Telluride, 127 S. Fir St. (728-4775,) has enough rich coffee and delicious pastry, pizza, salad and bagels (42¢) to get you through a festival weekend without sleeping, even if you *are* baked in Telluride. (Open daily 6am-2am in the summer, 10pm in the winter.) The **Athenian Senate,** 123 S. Spruce (728-3018), the only place to feed after dark, serves locally praised Greek and Italian food from $5. (Open daily 11am-2:30am in the summer, daily 5pm-2:30am in the winter.) Delicious Italian fare bakes at **Eddie's Café,** 300 W. Colorado (728-5335) including eight-in. pizzas ($5) and hefty pasta entrées all under $10. (Open Tues.-Sun. 11:30am-10pm.)

You can only get to Telluride by car, on U.S. 550 or Rte. 145. Telluride's **post office** stamps and sorts at 101 E. Colorado Ave. (728-3900; open Mon.-Fri. 9am-5pm, Sat. 10am-noon). The **ZIP code** is 81435; the **area code** is 303.

Idaho

Although most of the U.S. associates Idaho with "Famous Potatoes" (until recently its motto), Idaho ain't just tubers. The wild western scenery north of southern Idaho's potato farms ranges from the 12,000-ft. mountains and rippling estuaries of the Salmon River in the center to the spectacular dense pine forests in the northern panhandle. The U.S. government quietly guards Idaho's most spectacular parts in the Selway-Bitteroot Wilderness and the Idaho Primitive Area, through which rushes the meandering Salmon. The Snake River's serpentine waters have carved out Hell's Canyon, the deepest gorge in North America. Idaho gets mixed reviews literarily: it is the native state of poet-cum-Nazi Ezra Pound and Ernest Hemingway, who expressed his affection for Idaho by killing himself in it.

Practical Information

Capital: Boise.

Idaho Information Line, 800-635-7820. **Boise Convention and Visitors Bureau,** corner of 9th and Idaho, 2nd floor (344-7777). **Parks and Recreation Department,** 7800 Fairview Ave., Boise 83720 (327-7444). Open Mon.-Fri. 8am-5pm.

Idaho Outfitters and Guide Association: P.O. Box 95, Boise 83701 (342-1438). Info on companies leading whitewater, packhorse and backpacking expeditions in the state. Free vacation directories.

Time Zones: Mountain (2 hr. behind Eastern) and Pacific (3 hr. behind Eastern). The dividing line runs east-west at about the middle of the state; if you straddle it, you'll break the bonds of time.
Postal Abbreviation: ID

Area Code: 208.

Sales tax: 5%.

Boise

While not exactly a tourist haven, Idaho's capital contains numerous grassy parks, making this small city both a verdant residential bulwark amid the state's dry southern plateau and a relaxing way station on a cross-country jaunt. Most of the city's sights lie between the capitol and I-84 a few miles south; you can manage pretty well on foot. **Boise Urban Stages** (336-1010) also runs several routes through the city, with maps available from any bus driver and displayed at each stop. (Buses operate Mon.-Fri. 6:45am-6:15pm, Sat. 9am-6pm. Fare 50¢, seniors 25¢.)

The **Boise Tour Train** (342-4796) shows you 75 sites around the city in one hour. Tours start and end in the parking lot of **Julia Davis Park,** departing every 75 minutes. (Tours Mon.-Sat. 10am-3pm, Sun. noon-5pm. Fare \$4.75, seniors \$4.25, ages 3-12 \$2.75.) To learn about Idaho and the Old West at your own pace, walk through the **Historical Museum** (334-2120) in Julia Davis Park. (Open Mon.-Sat. 9am-5pm, Sun. 1-5pm. Free.) Also in the park, the **Boise Art Museum,** 670 Julia Davis Dr. (345-8330), displays international and local works. (Open Tues.-Fri. 10am-5pm, Sat.-Sun. noon-5pm. Admission \$2, students and seniors \$1, under 18 free.) Take a self-guided tour through the country's only **state capitol** to be heated with natural geothermal hot water. (Open Mon.-Fri. 8am-5pm, Sat. 9am-5pm.) The tiny and crowded **Boise Zoo** (384-4260) roars and howls beyond these two buildings. (Open Mon.-Wed. and Fri.-Sun. 10am-5pm, Thurs. 10am-9pm. Admission \$2, seniors and ages 3-12 \$1, under 3 free. Thurs. ½ price.) Taloned avians perch and dive at **World Center for Birds of Prey** (362-3716), six mi. south of I-84 on Cole Rd. Call ahead to arrange a tour. For more back-to-nature fun, try the 22-mi. **Boise River Greenbelt,** a pleasant, tree-lined path ideal for a leisurely walk or picnic.

Bask in the region's cultural history at the **Basque Museum and Cultural Center** (343-2671), at 6th and Grove St. in downtown Boise, where you'll find out about the surprisingly rich Basque heritage in the Great Basin and the Western Rockies. (Open Tues.-Fri. 10am-5pm.)

Food in Boise is more than just potatoes. Look to the downtown area, centered around 6th and Main St., where the Basque specialties of northern Spain lend spice to the region's cuisine. For the unadventurous palate, a good measure of down-home burgers and fries is also available there. Try **Moon's Kitchen,** 815 W. Bannock St. (385-0472), in the rear portion of Criner's Tackle and Cutlery (soup, sandwich, drink special \$5, open Mon.-Sat. 7am-3pm.) You can contemplate the rifles and shotguns mounted behind the counter while enjoying your meal. For nighttime entertainment, head for **Old Boise,** the area between S. 1st and S. 6th St., where the town's bars fire up.

Finding lodging in Boise is harsh; neither the YMCA nor the YWCA provide rooms, and even the cheapest hotels charge more than \$20 per night. The more reasonable places tend to fill quickly, so make reservations. One of the most spacious is the **Capri**

Motel, 2600 Fairview Ave. (344-8617), where air-conditioned rooms come with coffee and queen-sized beds. (Singles and doubles $28.) Farther out of town, the **Boisean,** 1300 S. Capitol Ave. (343-3645 or 800-365-3645), has smaller rooms but a more personable staff. (Singles $31.50. Doubles $35.50.) The **Forest Service Campground** lies three mi. north of town. Contact **Boise National Forest,** 1715 Front St. (334-1516), for a map. (Open Mon.-Fri. 7:30am-4:30pm.) The nearest campground with hookups is **Fiesta Park,** 11101 Fairview Ave. (375-8207). (Sites $15, hookup without water and electricity $17.50, full hookup $18.50.)

Amtrak (800-872-7245) serves Boise from the beautiful Spanish-mission-style **Union Pacific Depot,** 1701 Eastover Terrace (336-5992), easily visible from Capitol Blvd. One train per day goes east to Salt Lake City (7½ hr., $68) and beyond; one goes west to Portland (11 hr., $80) and Seattle (15½ hr., $108). **Greyhound** has I-84 schedules from its terminal at 1212 W. Bannock (343-3681), a few blocks west of downtown. Two buses per day head to Portland (8-10 hr., $50); three to Seattle (11 hr., $94).

Boise's main **post office** is on 770 S. 13th St. (383-4211; open Mon.-Fri. 7:30am-5:30pm, Sat. 10am-2pm). The **ZIP code** is 83707. The **area code** is 208.

Coeur d'Alene

The gaggles of tourists—one may also use the term "pride" or "annoyance" to denote such a group—can do little to mar the rustic beauty of this isolated spot. No matter how many people clutter its beaches, the deep blue water of Lake Coeur d'Alene offers a serene escape from whichever urban jungle you call home. Sandpoint, to the north, is less touristy and equally spectacular.

Practical Information

Emergency: 911.

Visitor Information: Chamber of Commerce, 161 N. 3rd St., at Spruce (664-3194). Open Mon.-Fri. 8am-8pm. **Visitors Center,** corner of First and Sheridan St. Open Mon.-Fri. 9am-5pm, Sat.-Sun. 10am-3pm; no phone. **Toll-free Visitors Info:** 800-232-4068.

Bus Station: 1923½ N. 4th St. (664-3343), 1 mi. north of the lake. **Greyhound** serves Spokane (1 hr., $5.50), Lewiston (1 per day, $26) and Missoula (5 hr., $32). **Empire Lines** connects Coeur d'Alene to Sandpoint at 5th and Cedar St. (1 per day, $8.30). Open Mon.-Sat. 8-10am and 4-8pm, Sun. 8-10am.

Car Rental: Auto Mart Used Car Rental, 120 Anton Ave. (667-4905), 3 blocks north of the bus station. $28 per day, $180 per week; 100 free mi. per day, 25¢ per extra mi. Open Mon.-Sat. 8am-6pm; phone line open 24 hrs. With personal insurance you can rent a car at age 18. Credit card or $100 cash deposit required.

Help Line: Crisis Services, 664-1443. Open 24 hrs.

Time Zone: Pacific (3 hrs. behind Eastern).

Post Office: 111 N. 7th St. (664-8126), 5 blocks east of the Chamber of Commerce. Open Mon.-Fri. 8:30am-5pm. **ZIP code:** 83814.

Area Code: 208.

Accommodations, Camping and Food

Cheap lodgings are hard to find in this booming resort town. You'll have your best luck in the eastern outskirts of the city. In town, the **Star Motel,** 1516 Sherman Ave. (667-5035), has large, furnished rooms with TV, phones and fridges (singles $38, doubles $46; off-season all rooms $25). In Sandpoint, by all means stay at the elegant lakefront **Whitaker House,** 410 Railroad Ave. (263-0816). Rooms cost $32 to $48 and include breakfast. Near Silver Mt., about 35 mi. east of Coeur d'Alene, is a new **Youth Hostel**, 834 W. McKinley Ave., Kellogg, ID (783-4171); it has laundry, TV, VCR and 40 beds. (April-Oct. $10, Nov.-March $12.)

There are five **public campgrounds** within 20 mi. of Coeur d'Alene. The closest is **Robin Hood RV Park,** 703 Lincoln Way (664-2306); it has showers, laundry and hookups, no evil sheriffs, and is within walking distance of downtown. (Sites $12.50.) **Beauty Creek,** a forest service site 10 mi. south along the lake, is the next closest. Camp alongside a lovely stream trickling down the side of a mountain. Drinking water and pit toilets provided. (Sites $6. Open May 5-Oct. 15.) **Honeysuckle Campground,** about 25 mi. to the northeast, has nine sites with drinking water and toilets. (Free. Open May 15-Oct. 15.) **Bell Bay,** on the shores of Lake Coeur d'Alene, off U.S. 95 south, then 14 mi. to Forest Service Rd. 545, offers 26 sites, a boat launch, and good fishing. (Sites $5. Open May 5-Oct. 15.) Call the Fernan Ranger District Office, 2502 E. Sherman Ave. (765-7381), for information on these and other campgrounds. (Open Mon.-Fri. 7:30am-4:30pm, Sat. 8:30am-3pm.) **Farragut State Park** (683-2425), 20 mi. north on U.S. 95, is an extremely popular 4000-acre park dotted with hiking trails and beaches along Lake Pend Oreille (pronounced pon-do-RAY). (Sites $8, with hookup $11. $2 day-use fee for each motor vehicle not camping in the park. Open May 27-Sept. 2.)

There are oysters aplenty in Coeur d'Alene, but if you like your snacks to come without shells, sit at the sidewalk tables at the **Coeur d'Alene Coffee Rosery,** 511 Sherman Ave. Sip their gourmet coffee (free refills) and indulge in hot cinnamon rolls. (Open Mon.-Thurs. 7am-6pm, Fri. 7am-9pm, Sat.-Sun. 8am-6pm.)

Sights and Activities

The lake is Coeur d'Alene's raison d'être. Hike up **Tubbs Hill** to a scenic vantage point, or head for the **Coeur d'Alene Resort** and walk along **the world's longest floating boardwalk** (3300 ft.). You can tour the lake on a **Lake Coeur d'Alene Cruise** (765-4000), which departs from the downtown dock every afternoon between June and September. (Cruises at 1:30, 4 and 6:30pm, returning at 3, 5:30 and 8pm respectively. Fare $9.50, seniors $8.50, ages under 10 $5.50.) Rent a canoe from **Eagle Enterprises** (664-1175) at the city dock to explore the lake yourself ($5 per hr., $15 per half-day, $25 first whole day, $10 per day thereafter). A three-mi. bike or walking path also circles the lake.

Twenty mi. east of town on I-90 is the **Old Mission at Cataldo** (682-3814), now contained in a day-use state park. Built in 1853 by Native Americans, the mission is the oldest extant building in Idaho. (Free tours daily. Open June-July daily 8am-6pm; Aug.-May daily 9am-7pm. Vehicle entry fee $2.) Near Sandpoint, about 50 mi. north of Coeur d'Alene, the **Roosevelt Grove of Ancient Cedars** nurtures trees of up to 12 ft. in diameter.

Continue another 35 mi. east on I-90 through mining country to the town of **Wallace,** where you will find retail shops shaped like mining helmets and the **Wallace Mining Museum,** 509 Bank St. (753-7151), which features turn-of-the-century mining equipment. (Open Mon.-Fri. 8am-7pm, Sat.-Sun. 9am-5pm; off-season Mon.-Sat. 9am-6pm. Admission $1, seniors and kids 50¢.) Next door, take the one-hour **Sierra Silver Mine Tour** (752-5151; leaves from museum) through a recently closed mine. (Tours May-Sept. daily every 20 min. 9am-4pm; July 9am-6pm. Admission $6, seniors and ages under 12 $5.) Mining, mining, mining. Twenty mi. north on Hwy. 95, ride the **world's largest gondola** up Silver Mountain. Mountain bikes can be transported in the gondola. (Call 783-1111 for info on hiking, biking or eating on the mountain; admission $10.50, students and seniors $8.50, kids under 6 free; chairlift rides $2.) "Rise and dine" packages (gondola ride and dinner) available Fri.-Sun. evenings, $26 per person. (Open mid-May-early Oct. Mon.-Thurs. 10am-6pm, Fri.-Sat. 10am-10pm, Sun. 10am-9pm; Oct. weekends only.)

Sawtooth National Recreation Area

Rough mountains pack the 756,000 acres of wilderness in this recreation area. Home to the **Sawtooth** and **White Cloud Mountains** in the north and the **Smokey** and **Boulder** ranges in the south, the **Sawtooth National Recreation Area (SNRA)** is surrounded by four national forests, encompassing the headwaters of five of Idaho's major rivers.

If you have a car, getting to the heart of the SNRA is easy. Don't miss the chance to pause at the **Galena Summit,** 25 mi. north of Ketchum on Rte. 75. The 8701-ft. peak provides an excellent introductory view of the range. If you don't have a car, take the bus to Missoula (250 mi. north on U.S. 93) or Twin Falls (120 mi. south on Rte. 75); from there, rent a car with at least six cylinders or plan for a long beautiful hike.

Places for **hiking**, **boating** and **fishing** in all four of the SNRA's little-known ranges are unbeatable and innumerable. Two mi. northwest of Stanley on Rte. 21, take the three-mi. Iron Creek Rd. which leads to the trailhead of the **Sawtooth Lake Hike.** This 5½-mi. trail is steep but well worn, and not overly difficult if you stop to rest. Bolder hikers who want to survey the White Cloud Range from above should head southeast of Stanley to the **Casino Lakes** trailhead. This trek terminates at **Lookout Mountain,** 3000 ft. higher than far-away Stanley itself. (If you plan to have a campfire or have 9 or more people, you must have a camping permit, available at all ranger stations; plan to stay overnight.) The long and gentle loop around **Yellow Belly, Toxaway** and **Petit Lakes** is recommended for novice hikers or any tourists desiring a leisurely overnight trip. For additional hiking information, consult the detailed topographic maps in Anne Hollingshead and Gloria Moore's *Day Hiking Near Sun Valley,* available at McCoy's Tackle Shop (see above). Stock up on food at the **Mountain Village Grocery Store** (774-3392) before venturing into the mountains.

In the heat of summer, the cold rivers beg for **fishing**, **canoeing** or **whitewater rafting**. **McCoy's Tackle Shop** (774-3377), on Ace of Diamonds St. in Stanley, rents gear and sells a full house of outdoor equipment. (Open daily 8am-9pm.) The **Redfish Lake Lodge Marina** (774-3536) rents paddleboats ($4-5 per ½-hr.), canoes ($5 per hr., $15 per ½-day, $25 per day), and more powerful boats for higher prices. (Open in summer daily 7am-9pm.) **The River Company,** based in Ketchum (726-8890) with an office in Stanley (774-2244), arranges whitewater rafting and float trips. (Ketchum office open daily 8am-6pm. Stanley office open in summer daily 8:30am-6pm, unless a trip is in progress.)

The most inexpensive way to enjoy the SNRA waters is to visit the **hot springs** just east of Stanley. Watch for the rising steam on the roadside, often a sign of hot water. **Sunbeam Hot Springs,** 13 mi. from town, is the best of the batch. Be sure to bring a bucket or cooler to the stone bathhouse; you'll need to add about 20 gallons of cold Salmon River water before you can get into these hot pools. For evening entertainment, try to get in on the regionally famous **Stanley Stomp,** when fiddlers in **Casanova Jack's Rod and Gun Club** (774-9920) keep the foot-stomping going all through the night. (Open Mon.-Sat. noon-2am, Sun. 11am-2pm; live music Wed-Sat.)

In the heart of Stanley, on Ace of Diamonds St., the **Sawtooth Hotel and Café** (774-9947) is a perfect place to stay after a wilderness sojourn. (Singles $21.50, with private bath $36.50. Doubles $24.50, with private bath $40.50.) More scenic is **McGowan's Resort** (774-2290), one mi. down Rte. 75 in Lower Stanley. Hand-built cabins here sit directly on the banks of the Salmon River, house up to four people each, and usually contain kitchenettes. The resort's tackle shop rents kayaks and rafts ($15 per person, per day). They also offer a terrific view of the Sawtooths and unmatched hospitality. ($50; Sept.-early June $35.) Campgrounds line Rte. 75; clusters are at **Redfish Lake** at the base of the Sawtooths and **Alturas Lake** in the Smokies. At Redfish, the pick of the litter is the small campground at the Point, which has its own beach. The two campgrounds on nearby Little Redfish Lake are the best spots for trailers. Other free sites are **Redfish Overflow** just off Rte. 75, and **Decker Flats,** Just north of 4th of July Rd. on Rte. 75. Sites in the SNRA cost $6-18; primitive camping is free anywhere you find it.

Information centers in the SNRA are almost as plentiful as the peaks themselves. Stop by the **Stanley Chamber of Commerce** (774-3411) on Rte. 21 about three-quarters of the way through town. (Open daily 10am-6pm.) Topographical maps ($2.50) and various trail books are available at the **Stanley Ranger Station** (774-3681), three mi. south on Rte. 75 (open June 16-Sept. 6, daily 8am-5pm; off-season Mon.-Fri. 8am-5pm). The **Redfish Visitors Center** (774-3376) lies eight mi. south and two mi. west of Stanley at the **Redfish Lake Lodge.** (Open June 19-Sept. 2 daily 9am-6pm). Whatever you can't find at these three places awaits at **SNRA Headquarters** (726-7672), 53 mi. south of Stanley off Rte. 75. The headquarters building itself is an interesting example of mountain architecture—its roof mimics the peaks of the Sawtooths. (Open daily 8am-5:30pm; off-season Mon.-Fri. 8am-4:30pm.) All the info centers provide maps of the Sawtooths ($2) and free taped auto tours of the impressive Ketchum-Stanley trip on Rte. 75.

The SNRA's **time zone** is Mountain (2 hr. behind Eastern). The **post office** (774-2230) is on Ace of Diamonds St. (open Mon.-Fri. 8am-5pm); the **ZIP code** is 83278.

Near SNRA

Craters of the Moon National Monument

Sixty mi. south of Sun Valley on U.S. 20/26/93, the black lava plateau of **Craters of the Moon National Monument** rises from the surrounding fertile plains. Windswept and remarkably quiet, the stark, twisted lava formations are speckled with sparse, low vegetation. Volcanic eruptions occurred here as recently as 2000 years ago. In 1969, the monument was used for astronaut training.

Park admission is $3 per car, and the bizarre black campsites cost $8. Wood fires are prohibited but charcoal fires are permitted. You can also camp for free in the adjacent **Bureau of Land Management** properties. The park's sites often fill by 4pm on summer nights. Unmarked sites in the monument are free with free backcountry permits, but even with the topographical map ($4), it may be hard to find a comfortable spot: the first explorers couldn't sleep in the lava fields for lack of bearable places to bed down.

The **visitors center** (527-3257), just off U.S. 20/26/93, has displays and videotapes on the process of lava formation, and printed guides for hikes to all points of interest within the park. They also distribute backcountry camping permits and sell the maps mentioned above. Rangers lead evening strolls (giant steps?) and programs at the campground amphitheater (daily mid-June-mid Sept.). (Open daily 8am-6pm; off-season daily 8am-4:30pm.) Explore nearby **lava tubes,** caves formed when a surface layer of lava hardened and the rest of the molten rock drained out, creating a tunnel. If a ranger does not escort you, bring a flashlight. From nearby Arco, Blackfoot, or Pocatello you can connect with **Greyhound**. There is, however, neither public transportation to the national monument nor food available when you get there.

Ketchum and Sun Valley

In 1935, Union Pacific Railroad heir Averill Harriman sent Austrian Count Felix Schaffgotsch to scour the U.S. for a site to develop into a ski resort area rivaling Europe's best. The Count settled on the small mining and sheep-herding town of Ketchum in Idaho's Wood River Valley, which has since become Sun Valley, a ski resort for the American rich and famous. The budget traveler should avoid the Valley and head for the hills, where the surrounding Boulder, Pioneer and Sawtooth Mountains provide endless warm-weather opportunities for camping, hiking, mountain biking, and fishing.

The hills around Ketchum have more natural **hot springs** than any spot in the Rockies except Yellowstone; bathing is free, legal and uncrowded in most of the springs. Like the ghost towns of the surrounding mountains, many springs can be reached only by foot; for maps, inquire at the **Chapter One Bookstore** (726-5425) on Main St. across from Pedro's Market, or **Elephant's Perch,** on Sun Valley Rd. (726-3497). "The

Perch" is also the best source for mountain bike rentals and trail information. (Bikes $12 per ½-day, $18 per day.)

More accessible, non-commercial springs include **Warfield Hot Springs** on Warm Springs Creek, 11 mi. west of Ketchum on Warm Springs Rd., and **Russian John Hot Springs,** eight mi. north of the Sawtooth National Recreation Area headquarters on Rte. 75, 100 yd. west of the highway. For the best information on fishing conditions and licenses, as well as equipment rentals, stop by **Silver Creek Outfitters,** 507 N. Main St. (726-5282; open daily 7am-6pm). The *Mountain Bike Adventure Guide* ($8.50) is also available there.

Though it's a small town, Ketchum has plenty of inexpensive, enjoyable restaurants (check out **Irving's,** the legendary local hot-dog stand), though the same cannot be said for its indoor accommodations. From early June to mid-October, **camping** is the best option for cheap sleep. The **Sawtooth National Forest** surrounds Ketchum—drive or hike along the forest service road and camp for free. The **North Fork** and **Wood River** campgrounds lie seven and 10 mi. north of Ketchum, respectively, and cost $3 per site. Wood River has an amphitheater and flush toilets. You must bring your own water to the three **North Fork Canyon** campgrounds seven mi. north of Ketchum. (Free.) Call the Ketchum Ranger Station for information.

The best time to visit the area is during "slack," (Labor Day-Thanksgiving and April-July 4th), when the tourists magically vanish. For local info, visit the **Sun Valley/ Ketchum Chamber of Commerce,** at 4th and Main St., Ketchum, P.O. Box 2420, Sun Valley 83353 (800-634-3347), where a well-informed, helpful staff shines. (Open daily 9am-5pm.) The **Ketchum Ranger Station,** 206 Sun Valley Rd., Ketchum (622-5371), three blocks east of Rte. 75, is the place to go for information on national forest land around Ketchum, and tapes and maps on the Sawtooth Recreation Area. (Open daily 8am-5pm.)

The **post office** in Ketchum (726-5161) is at 301 1st Ave. (Open Mon.-Fri. 8:30am-5:30pm, Sat. 11am-1pm.) The **ZIP code** is 83340.

Montana

Despite the recent acquisition of large amounts of acreage by such Eastern celebrities as Ted Turner, Tom Brokaw and Liz Claiborne, Montana remains true to its image as Marlboro country. Prairies rise gently from the Great Plains grasslands occupying the eastern two-thirds of the state. The Rocky Mountains punctuate the western third of the state with three million wild and woolly acres of wilderness, national parks, glaciers and grizzlies. *And* it's the only state in the union in which smoking is allowed everywhere.

Practical Information

Capital: Helena.

Montana Promotion Division, Dept. of Commerce, Helena 59620 (444-2654 or 800-541-1447). Write for a free *Montana Travel Planner.* **National Forest Information,** Northern Region, Federal Bldg., 5115 Hwy. 93, Missoula 59801 (329-3511). Gay and lesbian tourists can write to the **Lambda Alliance,** P.O. Box 7611, Missoula, MT 59807, for information on gay community activities in Montana.

Time Zone: Mountain (2 hrs. behind Eastern). **Postal Abbreviation:** MT

Area Code: 406.

Sales Tax: None.

Bozeman

Bozeman keeps on growing in Montana's broad Gallatin River Valley, wedged between the Bridger and Madison Mountains. The valley, originally settled by farmers who sold food to Northern Pacific Railroad employees living in the neighboring town of Elliston, is still chock full of fertile farmlands and still supplies food to a large portion of southern Montana. Bozeman's rapid expansion and the presence of Montana State University elicit a cosmopolitan air, but visitors can still find plenty of Western hospitality in both urban bars and farmhouse kitchens.

Livingston, a small town about 20 mi. east of Bozeman off I-90, is an angler's heaven; the town is near the Yellowstone, Madison and Gardiner rivers, all of which are known for their abundance of trout. The **Yellowstone Angler,** P.O. Box 660, Highway 89S (222-7130), will equip you with fishing gear and outdoor wear, and can answer questions about fishing conditions. (Open daily 7am-7pm.) After a day of flyfishing, cast a line over to **Livingston's Bar and Grill,** 130 N. Main St. (222-7909), where the vast quantities of imported and domestic beer will hook you to the bar. (Open daily 11:30am-10pm.)

In Bozeman, eat cheaply and well at the **Western Café,** 443 E. Main St. (587-0436), which boasts the best chicken fried steak in the West ($7.25). (Open Mon.-Fri. 5am-7:30pm, Sat. 5am-2pm.) In the **Baxter Hotel,** 105 W. Main St. (586-1314), the **Rocky Mountain Pasta Company** serves an Italian spaghetti dinner with bread and salad for $8.50. In the same building, the **Bacchus Pub** provides cocktails, ample soup, and salad plates for Bozeman's intellectual and yuppie crowds. (Both open daily 7am-10pm. Reservations advised.) The **Pickle Barrel,** 809 W. College (587-2411), across from the MSU campus, serves delicious, filling sandwiches on fresh-baked sourdough bread. Even half a sandwich ($4) is hard to finish. (Open daily 11am-11pm; off-season daily 11am-11pm.)

Summer travelers in Bozeman support a number of budget motels. The **Alpine Lodge,** 1017 E. Main St. (586-0356), has fairly clean but rather small rooms. (Singles $14. Doubles $19.) The **Ranch House Motel,** 1201 E. Main St. (587-4278), has larger rooms with free cable TV and A/C. (Singles $24. Doubles $28.) At the **Rainbow Motel,** 510 N. 7th Ave. (587-4201), the friendly owners disburse good travel advice and offer large, pleasant rooms. (Singles $31. Doubles $41.) The **Sacajawea International Backpackers Hostel,** 405 West Olive St. (586-4659), guides latter-day transcontinental trekkers with showers, laundry, full kitchen facilities, and transport to trailheads ($8, kids $5).

Greyhound, and **RimRock Stages** serve Bozeman from 625 N. 7th St. (587-3110). Greyhound runs to Butte (3 per day; $12) and Billings (3 per day; $14). RimRock runs two buses per day to Helena ($16.50) and Missoula ($24). (Open Mon.-Sat. 7:30am-5:30pm and 8:30-10pm, Sun. 12:30-5:30pm and 8:30-10pm.) **Rent-a-Wreck,** 112 N. Tracey St. (587-4551), rents well-worn autos from $29 per day, with 100 free mi., 18¢ each additional mi. You must be 21 with a major credit card. (Mon.-Fri. 8am-6pm, Sat. 8am-5pm, Sun. by appointment.) The **Bozeman Area Chamber of Commerce,** 1205 E. Main St. (586-5421), provides ample information concerning geography and local events. (Open Mon.-Fri. 8am-5pm.)

The Bozeman **post office** is at 32 E. Babcock St. (586-1508; open Mon.-Fri. 9am-5pm). Bozeman's **ZIP code** is 59715; the **area code** is 406.

Little Big Horn National Monument

Little Big Horn National Monument, until recently known as the Custer Battlefield National Monument, marks the site where Sioux and Cheyenne warriors, fighting in 1876 to protect land ceded to them by the Laramie Treaty, wiped out Lt. Col. George Armstrong Custer and five companies from the Seventh Cavalry. Ironically, the monument is located on what is now a Native American reservation, 60 mi. southeast of Billings off I-90. A five-mi. self-guided car tour through the Crow Reservation takes you past the area where Custer made his "last stand." You can also see the park on a 45-min. bus tour ($3). The **visitors center** (638-2622) has a small museum that includes eyewitness 100-year-old drawings depicting the Native American warriors' view of the battle. (Museum and visitors center open daily 8am-8pm; fall 8am-6pm, winter 8am-4:30pm. Free. Battlefield open daily 8am-8pm. Entrance $3 per car, $1 per person.) To get to the monument, your best bet is to **Rent-a-Wreck** (252-0219) in Billings. (From $28 per day, $22.50 in winter. $130-140 per week, with 100 free mi. and 18¢ per additional mi.; open Mon.-Fri. 8am-6pm, Sat. 9am-3pm, Sun. by appt. Must be 21 with credit card and have liability insurance.)

Missoula

People visit Missoula less for the city itself than for the Great Outdoors. Many of the locals, including students of the **University of Montana,** moonlight as nature enthusiasts; you'll be hard-pressed to resist their pastime.

Cycling enthusiasts have put the town on the map with the rigorous **Bikecentennial Route.** The Bikecentennial Organization Headquarters, 150 E. Pine St. (721-1776), provides information about the route. To participate in Missoula's most popular sport, visit the **Braxton Bike Shop,** 2100 South Ave. W. (549-2513), and procure a bike for a day ($12), overnight ($15) or a week ($75). (Open Mon.-Sat. 10am-6pm.) Leave a credit card or a blank check as a deposit.

Ski trips, raft trips, backpacking and day hikes are other popular Missoula diversions. The **University of Montana Recreation Annex,** University Center #164 (243-5172), posts sign-up sheets for all these activities and proves a good source of information on guided hikes (open Mon.-Thurs. 7am-4pm, Fri. 7am-5pm), while the **Department of Recreation** (243-2802) organizes day hikes and overnight trips. (Open Mon.-Fri. 9am-5pm. Fees vary.) The **Rattlesnake Wilderness National Recreation Area** rattles a few miles northwest of town off the Van Buren St. exit from I-90 and makes for a great day of hiking. Wilderness maps ($2.20) are available from the **U.S. Forest Service Information Office,** 340 N. Pattee St. (329-3511; open Mon.-Fri. 7:30am-4pm). The Clark Fork, Blackfoot and Bitterroot Rivers provide gushing opportunities for float trips. For river maps ($1), visit the **Montana State Regional Parks and Wildlife Office,** 3201 Spurgin Rd. (542-5500; open Mon.-Fri. 8am-5pm).

The hottest sight in town is the **Aerial Fire Depot Visitors Center** (329-4934), seven mi. west of town on Broadway (I-90/U.S. 93), where you'll learn to appreciate the courage and folly aerial firefighters need when jumping into flaming, roadless forests. (Open daily 8:30am-5:30pm; Oct.-April by appointment. Free tours every hr. in summer, except noon-1pm.)

Missoula's dining scene offers much more than the West's usual steak and potatoes greasefest. The **Mustard Seed,** the mustard-colored building at 419 W. Front St. (728-7825), serves wonderful midsummer night's dishes from a variety of Asian cuisines. Full dinners (soup, vegetables and a main course) go for $7 to $8. (Open Mon.-Sat. 11am-2:30pm, Sun.-Thurs. 5-9:30pm, Fri.-Sat. 5-10pm.) **Torrey's** restaurant and natural food store, 1916 Brooks St. (721-2510), serves health food at absurdly low prices. Seafood stir-fry costs $3.50; incongruous eight-oz. sirloin steak just $4. (Restaurant open Mon.-Sat. 11:30am-8:30pm; store open Mon.-Sat. 10am-8:30pm.) If you'd rather be happy than healthy, slurp up creamy and refreshing smoothees at **Goldsmith's Premium Ice Cream Shop**, 809 E. Front St. (721-6732), next to the Chamber of Commerce. (Open Mon.-Sat. 7am-11pm, Sun. 8am-11pm.)

Spend the night in Missoula at the **Birchwood Hostel (HI/AYH),** 600 S. Orange St. (728-9799), 13 blocks east of the bus station on Broadway, then eight blocks south on Orange. The spacious, immaculate dormitory room sleeps 22. Admirably clean laundry, kitchen and bike storage facilities are available. ($8 for members and cyclists, $10 otherwise. Open daily 5-10pm. Closed for 2 weeks in late Dec.) The **Canyon Motel,** 1015 E. Broadway (543-4069 or 543-7251), has newly renovated rooms at prices that won't gouge your wallet. (Singles $20-25. Doubles $25-30.) Closer to the bus station, the **Sleepy Inn,** 1427 W. Broadway (549-6484), has soporific singles for $25 and doubles for $30. The **Outpost Campground** (from I-90 take exit 96, go two mi. north on U.S. 93; 549-2016), has showers, laundry and scattered shade from its young trees. (Tent sites $7, full hookups $10; open year-round.)

Traveling within Missoula is easy thanks to reliable city **buses** (721-3333; buses operate Mon.-Fri. 6am-7pm, Sat. 9:30am-6pm; fare 50¢). The **Missoula Chamber of Commerce,** 825 E. Front St. (543-6623), provides bus schedules. (Open daily 9am-7pm.)

The **Greyhound terminal** sprints at 1660 W. Broadway (549-2339). Catch a bus to Bozeman (3 per day, $24) or Spokane (3 per day, $32). **Intermountain Transportation** serves Kalispell (2 per day, $28) and **RimRock Stages** serves Helena (1 per day, $15) and Bozeman (1 per day, $22) from the same terminal. **Rent-a-Wreck,** 2401 W. Broadway (728-3838), offers humble autos ($20 per day, $119 per week; 100 free mi. per day, 26¢ each additional mi.; you must be 21; credit card or $100 cash deposit.)

Missoula's **post office** is at 1100 W. Kent (329-2200), near the intersection of Brooks, Russell and South St. (Open Mon.-Fri. 8am-5pm.) The **ZIP code** is 59801; the **area code** is 406.

Waterton-Glacier International Peace Park

Waterton-Glacier transcends international boundaries to unite two of the most pristine but relatively accessible wilderness areas on the continent. Symbolizing the peace between the United States and Canada, the park provides sanctuary for bighorn sheep, moose and mountain goats—and for tourists weary of the more crowded parks farther south and north.

Technically one park, Waterton-Glacier is, for all practical purposes, two distinct areas: the small Waterton Lakes National Park in Alberta, and the enormous Glacier National Park in Montana. Each park charges its own admission fee ($5 each), and you must go through customs to pass from one to the other. Several **border crossings** pepper the park: **Chief Mountain** (open May 18-May 31 daily 9am-6pm; June 1-Sept. 14 daily 7am-10pm; closed in winter); **Piegan/Carway** (open May 16-Oct. 31 daily 7am-11pm; Nov. 1-May 15 daily 9am-6pm); **Trail Creek** (open June-Oct. daily 9am-5pm); and **Roosville** (open 24 hrs.).

Since snow melt is an unpredictable process, the parks are usually in full operation only from late May to early September. To find the areas of the park, hotels and campsites that will be open when you visit, contact the headquarters of either Waterton or Glacier (888-5441).

Glacier National Park, Montana

Backcountry trips are the best way to appreciate the pristine mountain scenery and the wildlife which make Glacier famous. The **Highline Trail** from Logan Pass is a good day hike and passes through prime bighorn sheep and mountain goat territory. The visitors center's free *Nature with a Naturalist* pamphlet has a hiking map marked with distances and backcountry campsites. All travelers who camp overnight must obtain a free wilderness permit from a visitors center or ranger station 24 hrs. in advance, in person; backcountry camping is allowed only at designated campgrounds. The **Two Medicine** area in the southeast corner of the park is well traveled, while the trek to **Kintla Lake** rewards you with fantastic views of nearby peaks. Before embarking on any hike, familiarize yourself with the precautions necessary to avoid a run-in with a bear. Rangers at any visitors center or ranger station will instruct you on the finer points of noise-making and food storage to keep bears away.

Going-to-the-Sun Rd., the only road traversing the park, may be the most beautiful 50-mi. stretch of road in the world. Even on cloudy days when there's no sun to go to, the constantly changing views of Alpine peaks will have you struggling to keep your eyes on the road. Snow keeps the road closed until late June; check with rangers for exact dates.

Although The Sun is a popular **bike route,** only experienced cyclists with appropriate gearing and legs of titanium should attempt this grueling stint. The sometimes nonexistent shoulder of the road creates a potentially hazardous situation for cyclists: in the summer (June 15-Sept. 2), bike traffic is prohibited from the Apgar turn-off at the west end of Lake McDonald to Sprague Creek Campground, and from Logan Creek to Logan Pass, between 11am and 4pm. The east side of the park has no such restrictions. Bikes are not permitted on any hiking trails.

Boat tours explore all of Glacier's large lakes. At Lake McDonald and Two Medicine Lake, one-hr. tours leave throughout the day. (Tours at Lake McDonald $6, ages 4-12 $3 ; tours at Two Medicine $5.50, ages 4-12 $2.75.) The tours from St. Mary and Many Glacier (75 min.) provide access to Glacier's backcountry. (Tours from St. Mary $7.50, ages 4-12 $4; tours from Many Glacier $7, ages 4-12 $3.50.) The $7 sunset cruise proves a great way to see this quotidian phenomenon, which doesn't commence until about 10pm in the middle of the summer. **Glacier Raft Co.,** in West Glacier (800-332-9995 or 888-5454) hawks full- and half-day trips down the middle fork of the Flathead River, near West Glacier. A full-day trip (lunch included) costs $55; half-day trips ($28, under 13 $17) leave in both the morning and the afternoon. Call for reservations.

Rent **fishing rods** ($3 per day), **canoes** ($5 per hr.), **rowboats** ($5 per hr., $25 per 10 hr.) and **outboards** ($10 per hr., $50 per 10 hr.) at Apgar, Lake McDonald, Many Glacier and Two Medicine. All require a $50 deposit. Fishing is excellent in the park—cutthroat trout, lake trout, and even the rare Arctic Grayling challenge the angler's skill and patience. No permit is required—just be familiar with the fishing regulations of the park, as explained by the pamphlet *Fishing Regulations,* available at all visitors centers.

While in Glacier, don't overlook the interpretive programs offered by the rangers. Inquire at any visitors center for the day's menu of guided hikes, lectures, bird-watching walks, interpretive dances, and children's programs.

Staying indoors within Glacier is absurd and expensive. **Glacier Park, Inc.** handles all lodging within the park and offers only the **Swiftcurrent Motor Inn** for budget travelers. Cabins without bathrooms at the Swiftcurrent are $20, $29 for two bedrooms (each additional person $2; open late June-early Sept.). The Swiftcurrent has a motel, but rooms cost twice as much. Reservations can be made through Glacier Park, Inc. From mid-September to mid-May, contact them at Greyhound Tower Station, 1210, Phoenix, AZ 85077 (602-248-6000); from mid-May to mid-September at East Glacier Park 59434 (406-226-5551, in MT 800-332-9351). Other than the Swiftcurrent, the company operates seven pricier lodges which open and close on a staggered schedule. Agpar opens first, in mid-May, and the other six open in late May or early June.

Excellent, affordable lodging can be found just across the park border in **East Glacier,** which sits on Rte. 2, 30 mi. south of the St. Mary entrance, and about five mi. south of the Two Medicine entrance. East Glacier boasts the **Backpackers Inn,** 29 Dowson Ave. (226-9392), opened in 1991 by Pat and Renée Schur, who saw a need for budget accommodations in the Glacier area. The Inn offers clean beds and hot showers for only $8 per night (bring a sleeping bag or rent one for $1), which includes Pat and Renée's warm hospitality and excellent advice on hikes and activities in the park. There is also a hostel at **Brownies Grocery (HI/AYH),** 1020 Hwy. 49 (226-4426), in East Glacier. It offers comfortable accommodations in its dorm ($10 members, $13 nonmembers) and private rooms (singles $15 members, $18 nonmembers; doubles $20/$23). The **Kalispell/Whitefish Home Hostel (HI/AYH),** 2155 Whitefish Stage Rd., Kalispell, MT 59901, beckons 25 mi. from Glacier's west entrance, between U.S. 93 and U.S. 2 (756-1908). The home has comfortable beds (bring a sleeping bag), kitchen utensils, a stereo, and rents mountain bikes. ($10 members, nonmember rates fluctuate.)

Camping offers a cheaper and more scenic alternative to indoor accommodations. All developed campsites are available on a first-come, first-camped basis ($6-8); the most popular sites fill by noon. However, "Campground Full" signs sometimes stay up for days on end; look carefully for empty sites. All 11 campgrounds accessible by car are easy to find. Just ask for the handout *Auto Campgrounds*, listed in the *Waterton Glacier Guide,* at any visitors center and follow the map distributed as you enter the park. **Sprague Creek** on Lake McDonald has many peaceful sites near the lake, but arrive early to avoid those near the road; there are only 25 sites total. Some sites at Sprague, Apgar and Avalanche remain reserved for bicyclists; towed units are prohibited. Campgrounds without running water in the surrounding national forests usually offer sites for $5. Check at the Apgar or St. Mary visitors centers for up-to-date information on conditions and vacancies at established campgrounds.

Glacier's layout is simple: one road enters through West Glacier on the west side, and three roads enter from the east—at Many Glacier, St. Mary and Two Medicine. West Glacier and St. Mary provide the two main points of entry into the park, connected by **Going-to-the-Sun Road** ("The Sun"), the only road that traverses the park. Fast-paced **U.S. 2** runs between West and East Glacier along 82 mi. of the southern park border. Look for the "Goat Lick" signs off Rte. 2 near **Walton.** Mountain goats often descend to the lick for a salt fix in June and July.

Stop in at the **visitors centers** at **St. Mary,** at the east entrance to the park (732-4424; open daily in early June 8am-5pm, late June-early Sept. 8am-9pm), or at **Apgar,** at the west park entrance (open daily early June 8am-5pm, late June-early Sept. 8am-8pm). A third visitors center graces **Logan Pass** on Going-to-the-Sun Rd. (Open daily mid-June 9am-5pm, late June-early Sept. 9am-6pm.) An **info center** (888-5743) on Alberta is in West Glacier; ask any questions there before hiking. (Open daily 8am-7pm.)

Amtrak (800-872-7245) traces a dramatic route along the southern edge of the park. Daily trains huff and puff to West Glacier from Whitefish ($17), Seattle ($119) and Spokane ($60); Amtrak also runs from Stanley, ND to East Glacier ($101). **Greyhound** can get you to Kalispell or as far as Great Falls, MT, over 100 mi. southeast of East Glacier on U.S. 89. As with most parts of the Rockies, a car is the most convenient mode of transport, particularly within the park. **Rent-a-Wreck** rents used cars from Kalispell, 1194 U.S. 2 E., (755-4555; $35 per day), West Glacier, at the Glacier Highland Motel (888-5427; $49 per day), and East Glacier, at the Sears Motel (226-9293; $49 per day). You must be over 21; major credit card or cash deposit required. One hundred free mi. per day, 25¢ each additional mi.

The Glacier **post office** is at Lake McDonald Lodge, in the park. (Open Mon.-Fri. 9am-3:45pm.) The General Delivery **ZIP code** is 59921. The **area code** rings in at 406.

Waterton Lakes National Park, Alberta

Unlike the whole of Canada, Waterton is only a small fraction of the size of its U.S. neighbor. While a trip north is not essential, a hike in Waterton's backcountry may prove a less crowded alternative during Glacier's peak tourist season (mid-July to Aug.).

The **Waterton Information Office** lies five mi. south of the park entrance. Stop and grab a copy of the annual *Waterton-Glacier Guide* for detailed information on local services and activities. (Open daily 8am-9pm.) The **port of entry to Canada** is open mid-May to May 31 daily 9am-6pm; June 1 to mid-Sept. 7am-10pm. The entrance fee is $5 per day, $10 for 4 consecutive days.

Once you've entered Waterton Lakes, all you can do is go five mi. south to **Waterton Townsite.** Drive the **Akamina Parkway** or the **Red Rock Canyon Road.** Both leave the main road near the Townsite and end at the heads of popular backcountry trails. Those who brought only their high-tops to Waterton should take a boat ride ($9 round-trip) to the **Crypt Lake Hike,** which runs four mi. from Waterton Townsite; you'll feel like a car as you pass through a two-ft.-long tunnel bored through the side of a mountain. Those fleeing the Royal Canadian Mounted Police should choose the **International Hike,** which puts you in Montana some four mi. after leaving the Townsite. To camp overnight you must obtain a free permit from the information center or the park headquarters. A boat tour of Upper Waterton Lake (1½ hr.) leaves from the **Emerald Bay Marina** in the Townsite. (Admission $14, ages under 13 $7.) When you want to get some exercise on the lake, rent a **rowboat** ($6 per hr.) or **canoe** ($8 per hr.) at Cameron Lake. If you want to get some exercise on land, climb **Bear's Hump,** a short but steep trail leading from the visitors center to a spectacular overlook of the entire village. **Pat's** (859-2266) rents mountain bikes and scooters and awards $50 worth of fishing supplies to the person who catches the largest fish in the park. (Bikes $5.50 per hr., $27 per day; scooters $13 per hr., $60 per day.) The Townsite comes out of its winter hibernation to sock summer sun- and sight-seekers with exorbitant prices. Waterton sorely lacks budget restaurants; your best bet in the Townsite is the **Zum Burger Haus** (859-2388), which serves decent if misspelled hamburgers for $4.75 on the pleasant patio. (Open daily 7:30am-10pm.)

The **Prince of Wales Hotel** (236-3400) maintains a civilized perch away from the majestic Waterton Lake at prices which Prince Charles would find to be prohibitive. Instead, pitch your tent at the **Townsite Campground** (859-2224) at the south end of town (sites $12.50, with full hookup $17.50), or **Crandley Campground,** on Red Rock Canyon Rd. (sites $10.50, no showers). To stay indoors, drop by **Dill's General Store,** on Waterton Ave. (859-2345), and ask to sleep in one of the nine rooms of the Stanley Hotel. Rooms will drain $45 from your pocket, and you won't even have a private pot to piss in.

If you find yourself in *really* dire straits, call the **Royal Canadian Mounted Police** (859-2244). The **post office** is on Fountain Ave. at Windflower, Waterton Townsite, Alberta. (Open Mon.-Fri. 8:30am-4:30pm.) The postal code is **T0K 2M0**. Waterton's **area code** is 403.

Wyoming

America's least-populated state, Wyoming is a natural Western wonderland, replete with expansive vistas and inexpensive adventure. It has, from a visitor's standpoint, everything you'd ever want to see in a state in the Mountain Time Zone: seasonal festivals (such as Frontier Days); national parks (Yellowstone and Grand Teton); spectacular mountain ranges (the Bighorns and the Winds); breath-taking panoramas; and, of course, plenty of beer. And cattle. Lots of cattle.

Practical Information

Capital: Cheyenne.

Wyoming Travel Commission, I-25 and College Dr. at Etcheparc Circle, Cheyenne 82002 (777-7777 or 800-225-5996). Write for their free *Wyoming Vacation Guide.* **Wyoming Recreation Commission,** Cheyenne 82002 (777-7695). Information on facilities in Wyoming's 10 state parks. Open Mon.-Fri. 8am-5pm. **Game and Fish Department,** 5400 Bishop Blvd., Cheyenne 82002 (777-4600; license assistant 777-4599). Open Mon.-Fri. 8am-5pm. **Wyoming Recreation Hotline,** 307-777-6503.

Time Zone: Mountain (2 hr. behind Eastern). **Postal Abbreviation:** WY

Sales Tax: 3%.

Bighorn Mountains

The Bighorns erupt from the hilly pastureland of northern Wyoming, a dramatic backdrop to the grazing cattle and sprawling ranch houses at their feet. In the 1860s, violent clashes occurred between the Sioux, defending their traditional hunting grounds, and incoming settlers. Cavalry posts such as **Fort Phil Kearny,** on U.S. 87 between Buffalo and Sheridan, could do little to protect the settlers. The war reached a climax at the **Fetterman Massacre,** in which several hundred Sioux warriors wiped out Lt. Col. Fetterman's patrol. The massacre temporarily forced settlers out of the Bighorns, but within 20 years they were back, forging the Bighorns into permanent cattle country.

For sheer solitude, you can't beat the Bighorns' **Cloud Peak Wilderness.** To get to **Cloud Peak,** a 13,175-ft. summit in the range, most hikers enter at **Painted Rock Creek,** accessible from the town of Tensleep, 70 mi. west of Buffalo on the western slope. (Tensleep was so named because it took the Sioux ten sleeps to travel from there to their main winter camps.) The most convenient access to the wilderness area, though, is from the trailheads near U.S. 16, 25 mi. west of Buffalo. From the **Hunter Corrals** trailhead, move to beautiful **Mistymoon Lake,** an ideal base for forays into the high peaks beyond. You can also enter the wilderness area from U.S. 14 out of Sheridan in the north.

Campgrounds fill the forest, and all sites cost $6 per night. Near the Buffalo entrance, **Lost Cabin Middle Fork** (has water and toilets; 28 mi. southwest of Buffalo on U.S. 16; open mid-May-Nov.; 4-day limit; for reservations call 800-284-2267; altitude 8,200 ft.) and **Crazy Woman** (25 mi. from Buffalo on U.S. 16; open mid-May-Oct.; altitude 7,600 ft.) boast magnificent scenery, as do **Cabin Creek** and **Porcupine** campgrounds near Sheridan. If you choose not to venture into the mountains, you can spend one night only free just off Coffeen St. in Sheridan's grassy **Washington Park.**

Most travelers will want to use either Buffalo or Sheridan as a base town from which to explore the mountains. If you have become jaded by postcard-perfect scenery and are hankerin' after a bit o' frontier history, visit the **Jim Gatchell Museum of the West,** 10 Fort St. (684-9331), or the museum and outdoor exhibits at the former site of **Fort Phil Kearny** (684-7629 on U.S. 87 between Buffalo and Sheridan; open daily 8am-6pm; Oct. 16-May 14 Wed.-Sun. 12-4pm; $2, $1 students). If that doesn't sate you, become an occidental tourist at the historic **Occidental Hotel,** the town hall/ polling place/ hospital since 1880 (10 N. Main St.; open daily 10:30-8pm; free).

The **Mountain View Motel** (684-2881, call for reservations in summer) is by far the most appealing of Buffalo's cheap lodgings. Pine cabins with TV, A/C, and/or heating complement the assiduous service. (Singles $24, doubles $28.) Also try the **Z-Bar Motel** next door (684-5535), with HBO, refrigerator or kitchen, and A/C (singles $30, doubles $34, reservations necessary). Stock up on sandwiches at the **Breadboard,** 57 S. Main St. (684-2318), where an eight-in.-long "Freight Train" (roast beef and turkey with all the toppings) knows it can for $3. (Open Mon.-Sat. 11am-8pm.) Or **Dash Inn**, 610 E. Hart St., (684-7930) for scrumptious fried chicken (2 pieces $3.50). (Open Mon. 11am-2pm, Tues.-Sun. 11am-10pm.)

The **Buffalo Chamber of Commerce** is located at 55 N. Main St. (684-5544 or 800-684-5122), one mi. west of the bus station. (Open Mon.-Sat. 8am-7pm, Sun., 1-5pm; Sept.-June Mon.-Fri. 9am-5pm.) The **U.S. Forest Service Offices,** at 300 Spruce St. (684-7981), will answer your questions about the Buffalo District in the Bighorns and sell you a road and trail map of the area for two greenbacks. (Open Mon.-Fri. 8am-4:30pm.) At **Alabam's,** 421 Fort St. (684-7452), you can buy topographical maps ($2.50) hunting, fishing, and camping supplies, and fishing licenses (1 day $5, 5 days $20). (Open daily 6am-9:30pm; off-season daily 6am-8pm.)

The town of **Sheridan,** 30 mi. to the north of Buffalo, escaped most of the military activity of the 1860s. But Sheridan has its own claim to fame: Buffalo Bill Cody used to sit on the porch of the once luxurious **Sheridan Inn,** at 5th and Broadway, as he interviewed cowboy hopefuls for his *Wild West Show.* The Inn has recently hit hard times, and may soon close. Motels, many with budget rates, line the town's two main drags, Coffeen Ave. and Main St. Try the **Parkway Motel** (674-7259; 2112 S. Coffeen St.), which offers large, cheerfully decorated singles ($22) and doubles ($30).

Sheridan's **U.S. Forest Service Office,** 1969 S. Sheridan Ave. (672-0751), offers maps of the Bighorns ($3), along with numerous pamphlets on how to navigate them safely. The **Sheridan Chamber of Commerce,** 5th St. at I-90 (672-2485), can also provide information on the national forest, as well as other useful tips for lodging and activities in Sheridan. (Open daily 8am-8pm.)

At the junction of I-90 (east to the Black Hills area and north to Billings, MT) and I-25 (south to Casper, Cheyenne, and Denver), **Buffalo** is easy to reach. **Powder River Transportation** serves Buffalo from a terminal at **Big Horn Travel** (684-5246), where twice daily you can catch a bus north to Sheridan ($9) and Billings ($33), or south to Cheyenne ($33). Buffalo, as the crossroads of north-central Wyoming, remains a popular place for hitchhikers to catch rides to the southern cities of Casper and Cheyenne. Getting a lift on the freeway in Sheridan is more difficult. But never fear—**Powder River buses** run from the depot at the **Rancher Motel,** 1552 Coffeen Ave. (674-6188), to: Billings (2 per day, $29); Buffalo (2 per day, $9); and Cheyenne (2 per day, $48). (Station open Mon.-Fri. 8am-5am; Sat. 9am-noon, 4-5:30pm, 9:30-11pm, and 2:30-5:30am; Sun. 10am-noon, 4-5:30pm, 9:30-11pm, 2:30-5:30am.)

The **time zone** for both Sheridan and Buffalo is Mountain (2 hr. behind Eastern). The **ZIP code** for Buffalo is 82834, and for Sheridan 82801. The **area code** for the Bighorns is 307.

Casper and Environs

Built primarily as a stop for the Union Pacific Railroad, Casper has a history characteristic of hundreds of other similar railroad towns. Casperites are proud of their city's raison d'être and their chief claim to fame: nine of the pioneer trails leading west, including the Oregon and Bozeman trails, intersected at a point not far from what is today the city's southern limit. The convergence of those famous paths lives in the minds of those who call Casper by its nicknames, "the Hub," and "the Heart of Big Wyoming."

Casper's pride and joy, **Fort Casper,** 4205 W. 13th St., is a reconstruction of an old army fort on the western side of town. There is an informative **museum** on the site. (Open Mon.-Fri. 9am- 6pm, Sat. 9am-5pm, Sun. 2-5pm. Free.) From Ft. Casper you can hike to **Muddy Mountain** or **Lookout Point** to survey the rugged terrain that hosted some of the last, bloody conflicts between the Native Americans and the white pioneers.

Forty-five mi. northwest of Casper on U.S. 20-26, you can see **Devil's Kitchen** (also called Hell's Half Acre), a 320-acre bowl serving up hundreds of crazy colorful spires and caves. Fifty-five mi. southwest on WY Rte. 220, **Independence Rock** still welcomes travelers to the entrance of a hellish stretch of the voyage across Wyoming. In 1840, Father Peter DeSmet nicknamed it the "Great Registry of the Desert," honoring the godless renegades and Mormon pioneers who etched their name into the rock as they passed by. Explore the abandoned prospecting town on Casper Mountain or follow the **Lee McCune Braile Trail** through Casper Mountain's Skunk Hollow. If you are here at the end of August, check out the week-long **Central Wyoming Fair and Rodeo,** 1700 Fairgrounds Rd. (266-4228), which keeps the town in an extended state of Western hoopla replete with parades, demolition derbies, livestock shows, and, of course, rodeos.

If you are pasing through Casper in the winter, consider surrendering to the snowy slopes nearby mountains have to offer. Eleven mi. south of Casper, Casper Mountain hosts the **Hogadon Ski Area** (266-1600), with 60 acres of downhill, cross country and snowmobile trails and runs rising 8000 feet above sea level. For equipment, stop in at **Mountain Sports,** 543 S. Center St. (266- 1136). Downhill and cross-country skis are available here to adults at $14/day and to children 12 and under $10/day. Children under five can rent skis for $5/day. (Open in the winter Mon.-Sat. 9am-6pm, and Sun. noon-5pm; in summer Mon.-Sat. 9am-6pm.) credit card or cost of equipment in cash required. For information on ski conditions, contact **Community Recreation, Inc.**, (235-8383; open Mon.-Fri. 8am-5pm.)

When you've kicked up enough dust for one day and are "hankerin' for a hunk of cheese," mosey on into the **Cheese Barrel,** 544 S. Center St. (235-5202), for a hearty and affordable breakfast or lunch. Try the pita veghead ($3.85) and be sure to have to at least one order of cheese bread (80¢ for two gooey slices); open Mon.-Sat. 6:30am-2:45pm) **Anthony's,** 241 S. Center St. (234-3071), serves huge portions of Italian food by candlelight (spaghetti $5.50; open Mon.-Sat. 11:30am-2pm and 5pm-10pm, Sun. "off-the-menu" brunch 9am-2pm and dinner 5pm-10pm). Everything about **Honey's Café,** 250 S. Center St., is small—especially the prices. Fill up on anything from biscuits and gravy ($1.50) to a grilled ham and cheese ($1.50) and save those extra bucks to savor the sights of downtown Casper. (Open Mon.-Fri. 7:30am-2:30pm).

If you are lookin' to stay overnight in Casper, check out and check in to the **Traveler Motel,** 500 E. 1st St. (237-9343), which offers spotless rooms near the center of town for only a fist full of dollars. (Singles $16.50. Doubles $20.) For just a few dollars more, guests of **The Royal Inn,** 440 E. A St.(234-3501, or toll-free reservations 800-96ROYAL or 800-967-6925) can enjoy regal treatment. Folks from the inn will pick guests up at the bus station for free and let then choose from a variety of rooms, all with showers and baths, 29 channels of color cable, and direct-dial phones. Friendly owners are eager to please. Outdoor heated pool. Pets allowed. (Singles $19, with fridge and remote control TV $23. Doubles with fridge and remote control TV $30. Extra person charge $5.) Just across the street, **The Virginia Motel,** 830 E. A St. (266-9731), has been renovated in Victorian style but has not been repriced. (Singles $15-18/night and$60/week. Doubles $22/night and $90/week. Key deposit $2).

Campers can bunk down at the **Ft. Casper Campground,** 4205 W. 13th St. (234-3260). (Tents $10. Full hookup $13.50.) **Casper Mountian Park,** (472-0452), 12 mi. south of Casper on Rte. 251, near Ponderosa Park, has $4 sites. **Alcova Lake Campground,** 32 mi. southwest of Casper on Country Rd. 407 off Rte. 220, is a popular recreation area with beaches, boats, and private cabins. (Sites $4.) The **Hell's Half Acre Campground** (472-0018), 45 mi. west on U.S. 20-26, has showers and hookups (full hookup $10.80, $12 for five). The **Natrona County Parks Office,** (265-2643), 182 Casper Mt. Park, provides information about camping in the greater Casper area. (Open Mon.-Fri. 9am-5pm.) The informative **Casper Chamber of Commerce** assists tourists at 500 N. Center St. (234-5311, FAX 265-2643; open Mon.-Fri. 8am-7pm, Sat.-Sun. 10am-7pm; off-season Mon.-Fri. 8am-5pm.) The **Powder River Transportation Services,** 315 N. Wolcott (266-1904; 800-433-2093 outside WY), sends three buses per day to: Buffalo ($20.80). Sheridan ($26), Cheyenne ($30.16); and two per day to Billings ($63.65), Rapid City ($60.50). **Casper Affordable Used Car Rental,** 131 E. 5th St. (237-1733), rents cars for $19.95 per day at 10¢/mi; $125/week at 10¢/mi. after the first 100 mi. (Open Mon.-Fri. 8am-5:30pm. Must be 22 to rent; $100 or credit card deposit required.) Casper's main **post office** is at 150 E. B St. (266-4000; open Mon.-Fri. 7:30am-5:30pm.) The **ZIP code** is 82601; the **area code** is 307.

Cheyenne

What's in a name? Cheyenne, named for the Native American tribe that once roamed the wilderness surrounding the city, has had a nomenclatorial history worthy of note. For a period in the mid-nineteenth century, Cheyenne was considered a prime candidate for the name of the Wyoming Territory. This moniker was struck down in by vigilant Senator Sherman who pointed out that the pronunciation of Cheyenne closely resembled that of the French word *chienne* meaning, shall we say, female dog. Residents of the city were not as bothered by such esoteric linguistic quibbles so they kept the name. By the 1860s the Union Pacific Railroad reached the end of the line in Cheyenne and Wyoming's capital had become known as "Hell on Wheels." The red dust and general diabolism of the Wild West today lays dormant in Cheyenne most of the year, lending it a "Heck on Wheels" ambience. However, come during Frontier Days when throngs of visitors kick up the dust and come creaking through the doors of its few remaining weathered wood saloons and you'll call the place anything but dull.

Practical Information

Emergency: 911.

Visitor Information: Cheyenne Area Convention and Visitors Bureau, 309 W. 16th St. (778-3133; 800-426-5009 outside WY), just west of Capitol Ave. Extensive accommodations and restaurant listings. Open Mon.-Fri. 8am-6pm. **Wyoming Information and Division of Tourism:** I-25 and College drive (777-7777; 800-225-5996 outside WY; open daily 8am-5pm).

Cheyenne Street Trolley: (778-3133) From mid-May through mid-September, a trolley departs from 16th St. and Capitol St. Tours of downtown, Warren Air Force Base, and Old West Museum. Mon.-Sat. 10am-1:30pm, Sun. at 1:30. Purchase tickets at Visitors Bureau on weekdays; Wrangler

Department Store (16th and Capitol) on Sundays and Holidays. Fare: Adults $6; children 12 and under $3, children under 2, free.

The Howdy Wagon, an old chuck wagon next door, is chock-full of brochures. Open summer Sat.-Sun. 10am-3pm.

Cheyenne Street Railway: (778-1401). 2-hr. trolley tours of Cheyenne leaving in summer Mon.-Sat. 10am and 1pm, Sun. at 1pm. Tickets $5, seniors $4.50, children $2.50 from the convention and visitors' bureau. Tours depart from 16th and Capitol Ave.

Greyhound: 1503 Capitol Ave. (634-7744), at 15th St. Three buses daily to: Salt Lake City (9 hrs., $98); Chicago ($147); Laramie ($9); Rock Springs ($33); Denver ($18). **Powder River Transportation**, in the Greyhound terminal (635-1327). Buses south to Rapid City twice daily ($92); north to Casper ($31) and Billings ($109) twice daily. Greyhound passes honored.

Taxi: Yellow Cab, 638-3333. $2.50 for the first mi.;$1.50/mi. thereafter

Help Line: **Rape Crisis**, 637-7233. Open 24 hrs.

Post Office: 2120 Capitol Ave. (772-6580), 6 blocks north of the bus station. Open Mon.-Fri. 8am-5pm, Sat. 8am-noon. General Delivery open Mon.-Sat. from 6:30am. **ZIP code:** 82001.

Area Code: 307.

Cheyenne's downtown area is small and manageable. Central, Capitol, and Carey Avenues form a grid with 16th-19th Streets, which encompasses most of the old sights and accommodations. 16th St. is part of I-80; it intersects I-25/84 on the western edge of town. Denver lies 90 mi. south on I-25.

Accommodations, Camping, and Food

It's not hard to land a cheap room here among the lariats, plains, and pioneers, unless your visit coincides with **Frontier Days**, which is held the last full week of July (see Sights and Entertainment). During this week, beware of the doubling rates.

Many budget motels line **Lincolnway** (U.S. 30), 1 mi. east down 16th St. the **Guest Ranch Motel,** 1100 W. 16th St. (634-2137) is a short hike west from the bus stop. Large, tidy rooms with cable and phones, shower and bath. Leave the pets at home. (Singles with one queen bed $26. Doubles $32.) South of town, on the other side of the Union Pacific Railroad, is the **Lariat Motel,** 600 Central Ave. (635-8439), next to the Los Amigos restaurant. A friendly family welcomes guests to the two-tone blue, cozy motel with cable TV, showers and baths and a few kitchenettes. (Singles $22/night; $60 weekly. Doubles $29 per night; $95 weekly.) Just a few blocks from the bus station, the old **Plains Motel,** 1600 Central Ave. (638-3311) offers very attractive, oversized rooms with marble sinks, HBO and phones in a grand-lobbied, Western setting. In addition to the great rooms and large beds, the motel boasts a 24-hour coffee shop and saloon that are convenient and affordable. (Singles $30. Doubles $37. Extra person charge $5.)

For campers, spots are plentiful (except during Frontier Days) at the **Restway Travel Park,** 4212 Whitney Rd. (634-3811), 1½ mi. east of town. (Sites $12.50 for up to four people, with electricity and water $13.50, full hookup $14.50; prices rise slightly in July. Each pet, kept on a leash $1 per night). You might also try **Curt Gowdy State Park,** 1319 Hynds Lodge Rd., (632-7946) 23 mi. west of Cheyenne on Rte. 210, this year-round park has shade, scenery, fishing, hiking, and an archery range, as well as land for horseback riding—BYO horse. (Sites $4 per night; $25 per week.)

Cheyenne is basically a meat 'n potatoes place, but there are also a few cheap, good ethnic eateries sprinkled around downtown. Here, the price difference between the humble café and posh restaurant can be a mere $4-6. For a taste of some home cookin', float into the **Driftwood Café,** 200 E. 18th St. (634-5304) and try the pies and specials ($4.25 and under) concocted daily in the diner's small kitchen. (Open Mon.-Fri. 7am-4pm.) **Ruthie's Sub Shoppe,** 1651 Carey Ave., (635-4896) a few doors down from the Pioneer Hotel, has the best tuna salad sandewiches around ($2.25), and morning donuts. (Open Mon.-Fri. 6am-5pm, Sat. 7am-3:30pm.) Next door to the Lariat Motel, **Los Amigos,** 620 Central Ave., (638- 8591) serves burritos ($1.95-4.25) and humongous, friendly dinners (from $7.25). You might want to go with a half-order (60% of the price), or swing by for the $4 lunch specials. (Open Mon.-Thurs. 11am-8:30pm, Fri.-Sat. 11am-9pm.) Lunch buffets are available at the **Twin Dragon Chinese Restaurant,** 1809 Carey Ave. (637-6622) weekdays 11am-2pm ($4.75); children under 11, $2.85. Vegetarian egg rolls just $1.80; regular dinners from $5.50. (Open Mon.-Sat. 11am-10pm, Sun. noon-9pm.)

When the urge to guzzle consumes you, **D.T.'s Liquor and Lounge,** 2121 Lincolnway, will help you get the DTs. Look for a pink elephant above the sign; if you are already seeing two, move on. (Open daily 7am-11pm.) The **Cheyenne Club,** 1617 Capitol Ave. (635-7777), is a spacious good-time country nightspot, hosting live bands nightly at 8:30pm. Every Wednesday night from 7:30pm-9pm you can learn to swing your partner for free! You must be 19 to enter and 21 to drink. (Open Mon.-Thurs. and Sat. 8:30pm-2am, Fri. 5pm-2am. Cover $1.)

Sights and Entertainment

If you're within 500 mi. of Cheyenne between July 17 and 26, make every possible effort to attend the **Cheyenne Frontier Days,** nine days of non-stop Western hoopla. The town doubles in size as anyone worth a grain of Western salt comes to see the world's oldest and largest rodeo competition and partake of the free pancake breakfasts (every other day in the parking lot across from the chamber of commerce), parades, and square dances. Most remain inebriated for the better part of the week. Reserve accommodations in advance or camp nearby. For information, contact Cheyenne Frontier Days, P.O. Box 2477, Cheyenne 82003 (800-227-6336; FAX (307) 778-7213; open Mon.-Fri. 8am-5pm).

If you miss Frontier Days, don't despair; Old West entertainment abounds in "The Magic City of the Plains." Throughout June and July the **Cheyenne Gunslingers** perform a mock gunfight at W. 16th and Carey St. (Shows Mon.-Fri. at 6pm, Sat. at noon. Free.) The **Cheyenne Frontier Days Old West Museum** (778-7290), in Frontier Park at 8th and Carey St., is a half-hour walk north down Carey St. The museum chronicles the rodeo's history from 1897 to the present, housing an "Old West" saloon, an extensive collection of Oglala Sioux clothing artifacts, and one of the nation's best Western covered wagon collections. (Open Mon.-Sat. 8am-7pm, Sun. 10am-6pm; off-season daily 9am-5pm. Admission $3, seniors $2, under 12 free, families $6.)

The **Wyoming State Museum,** 2301 Central Ave. (777-7024), presents an especially digestible history of Wyoming's cowboys, sheepherders, and suffragists, along with exhibits on the Oglala, Cheyenne, and Shoshone who preceded them. (Open Mon.-Fri. 8:30am-5pm, Sat. 9am-4pm, Sun. noon-4pm; off-season closed Sun. Free.) The **Wyoming State Capitol Building,** at the base of Capitol Ave. on 24th St. (777-7220), shows off its stained glass windows and yellowed photographs to tour groups trekking through. (Open Mon.-Fri. 8:30am-4:30pm. Summer tours every 15 min.)

This oversized cowtown rolls up the streets at night; except for a few bars, the downtown goes to sleep at 5pm. One delightful exception is the **Old Fashioned Melodrama,** playing at the Old Atlas Theater (638-6543 mornings, 635-0199 aft. and eve.), an old vaudeville house at 211 W. 16th St., between Capitol and Carey Ave. (Shows July-late Aug. Wed.-Sat. 7pm, Fri.-Sat. 9:15pm. Tickets $6.50, under 12 $4. Wed. $1 off.) To find out about beauty pageants and other theatrical events in the Atlas Theatre contact the **Cheyenne Civic Center** 510 W. 20th St. (637-6363; box office open Mon.-Fri. 11am-5:30pm).

Devil's Tower National Monument

We are not alone. 60 million years ago, in northeastern Wyoming, fiery magma forced its way through a layer of sedimentary rocks and cooled without breaking the surface. Centuries of wind, rain and snow eroded the surrounding sandstone, leaving a stunning spire that was named the first National Monument in the U.S. in 1906. If looking at this obelisk of stone inspires you to play with mashed potatoes or gives you an eerie feeling of déjà vu, you will be comforted to know that Devils Tower was the cinematic landing strip for extra-terrestrials in *Close Encounters of the Third Kind.* Giant flying saucers are not the only mode of transportation to the top. More than 1000 people climb it each year; there are more than 80 possible routes to the top. Those interested in making the climb must register with a ranger at the **visitors center** (7am-8pm daily, 3 mi. from entrance) before you set out and when you return. There is also a **nature trail** around the tower and a **campground,** (water, bathrooms, fireplaces, picnic tables, no showers, open May 15-Nov.) but watch out for rattlesnakes. From I-90 take U.S. 14 25 mi. north to Rte. 24.

Grand Teton National Park

When French fur trappers first peered into Wyoming's wilderness from the eastern border of Idaho, they found themselves face to face with three craggy peaks, each topping 12,000 ft. In an attempt to make the rugged landscape seem more trapper-friendly, they dubbed the mutant mountains "Les Trois Tetons," French for "the three tits." When they found that these triple nipples had numerous smaller companions, they named the entire range "Les Grands Tetons." Today the snowy heights of Grand Teton National Park delight modern hikers and cyclists with miles of strenuous trails. The less adventurous will appreciate the rugged appearance of the Tetons; the craggy pinnacles and glistening glaciers possess stunning beauty. Visitors will relish the park's relative lack of crowds in comparison with Yellowstone, its sometimes zoo-like neighbor to the north.

Practical Information

Park Headquarters: Superintendent, Grand Teton National Park, P.O. Drawer 170, Moose 83012 (733-2880). Office at the Moose Visitors Center (see below). Open daily 8am-7pm.

Park Entrance Fees: $10 per car, $4 per pedestrian or bicycle, $5 per family (non-motorized), under 16 (non-motorized) free. Good for 7 days in both the Tetons and Yellowstone.

Visitors Center: Moose, Rockefeller Pkwy. at the southern tip of the park (733-2880). Open June-Aug. daily 8am-7pm; Sept.-May daily 8am-5pm. **Jenny Lake,** next to the Jenny Lake Campground. Open June-Aug. daily 8am-6pm. **Colter Bay,** on Jackson Lake in the northern part of the park (543-2467). Open early June-early Sept. daily 8am-8pm; May and late Sept. daily 8am-5pm. Park information brochures available in Braille, French, German, Japanese, Spanish and Hebrew. Topographical maps ($2.50). Pick up the *Teewinot* newspaper (free) for a complete list of park activities, lodgings and facilities.

Park Information and Road and Weather Conditions: 733-2220; 24-hr. recording.

Bike Rental: Mountain Bike Outfitters, Inc., at Dorman's in Moose (733-3314). Adult mountain bikes $6 per hr., $24 per day, kids $3.50 per hr, $12 per day. Open summer daily 9am-6pm. Credit card or deposit required.

Medical Care: Grand Teton Medical Clinic, Jackson Lake Lodge (543-2514 or 733-8002 after hours), near the Chevron station. Open June-mid-Sept. daily 10am-6pm. In a dire emergency, contact **St. John's Hospital** (733-3636), in Jackson. **Emergency:** 911. Also 733-2880 or 543-2581; **sheriff's office** 733-2331.

Post Office: in **Colter Bay General Store** (733-2811), in **Moose** (733-3336). Open mid-May-mid-Sept. Mon.-Fri. 8am-noon and 1-5pm, Sat. 9am-1pm. **ZIP codes:** Colter Bay 83001, Moose 83012, Moran 83013, Kelly 83011.

Area Code: 307.

The national park occupies most of the space between Jackson to the south and Yellowstone National Park to the north. **Rockefeller Parkway** connects the two parks and is open year-round. The park is directly accessible from all directions except the west, as those lonely French trappers found out centuries ago.

Accommodations

If you want to stay indoors, grit your teeth and pry open your wallet. **The Grand Teton Lodge Co.** has a monopoly on lodging within the park. Make reservations for any Grand Teton Lodge establishment by writing the Reservations Manager, Grand Teton Lodge Co., P.O. Box 240, Moran 83013 (543-2855 or 800-628-9988 outside Wyoming). Accommodations are available late May through early October and are most expensive from late June to early August. Reservations are recommended and can be made up to a year in advance. (See Jackson below for accommodations outside the park.)

Colter Bay Tent Cabins: (543-2855) Cheapest accommodations in the park, but not the place to stay in extremely cold weather. Canvas shelters with wood-burning stoves, table and 4-person bunks. Sleeping bags, wood, cooking utensils and ice chests available for rent. (Office open June-early Sept., daily 7am-10pm, or call Maintenance, 543-2811.) Cabins $19 for 2, each additional person $2.50. Restrooms and showers ($1.50) nearby.

Colter Bay Log Cabins: (543-2855) Quaint, well-maintained log cabins near Jackson Lake. Room with semi-private bath $25, with private bath $47-68. 2-room cabins with bath $68-89. Open mid-May-early Oct.

Flagg Ranch Village: P.O. Box 187, Moran 83013 (733-8761 or 800-443-2311), on the Snake River near the park's northern entrance. Simple, clean cabins for 2 with private bath $58.

Camping

Camping is the way to see the Tetons without emptying your savings account. The park service maintains five campgrounds, all on a first come-first served basis (sites $8). In addition, there are two trailer parks and designated acres of backcountry open to visitors whenever the snow's not too deep. RVs are welcome in all but Jenny Lake, but hookups are unavailable. Information is available at any visitors center (see Practical Information above).

Park Campgrounds: All campgrounds have rest rooms, cold water, fire rings and picnic tables. Large groups can go to Colter Bay and Gros Ventre; all others allow a maximum of 6 people and 2 vehicles per site. **Jenny Lake:** 49 highly coveted sites; arrive early. No RVs. **Signal Mountain:** A few miles south of Colter Bay. 86 spots, usually full by noon. **Colter Bay:** 310 sites, shower, grocery store and laundromat. Usually full by 2pm. **Snake River:** Northern campgrounds, with 60 sites, convenient to Yellowstone. Fills in late afternoon. **Gros Ventre:** On the park's southern border. 360 sites. A good bet if you arrive late. Max. stay in Jenny Lake 7 days, all others 14 days. Reservations required for large groups.

Colter Bay RV Park: 112 sites, electrical hookups. Reserved through Grand Teton Lodge Co. (733-2811 or 543-2855). Grocery store and eateries. Sites May 15-June 7 and Sept.-Oct. 4, $17. June 7-Aug. $21.40. Showers $1.50, towel rental $1.25.

Flagg Ranch Village Camping: Operated by Flagg Ranch Village (543-2861 or 800-443-2311). Grocery and eateries. Sites $15 for 2, $20 with hookup. Make reservations.

For **backcountry camping,** reserve a spot in a camping zone in a mountain canyon or on the shores of a lake by submitting an itinerary to the permit office at **Moose Ranger Station** (733-2880) from January 1 to June 1. Pick up the permit on the morning of the first day of your hike. You can make reservations by mail, but two-thirds of all spots are left open for reservation on a first come-first served basis; you can get a permit up to 24 hrs. before setting out at the Moose, Colter Bay or Jenny Lake Ranger Stations. (Moose and Colter Bay open daily 8am-7pm, Jenny Lake mid-May-late Sept. daily 8am-6pm.) Camping is unrestricted in some off-trail backcountry areas (though you must have a permit). Wood fires are not permitted above 7000 ft. As the weather can be severe, even in the summer, backcountry campers should be experienced before venturing too far from civilization and help.

Food

As in Yellowstone, the best way to eat in the Tetons is to bring your own grub. If this isn't possible, stick to what non-perishables you can pick up at the **Flagg Ranch Grocery Store** (543-2861 or 800-443-2311, open daily 7am-10pm; reduced hours in winter), or **Dornan's Grocery** in Moose (733-2415, open daily 8am-6pm; reduced hours in winter). In Jackson, you can stock up on provisions at **Albertson's** supermarket (733-5950).

Sights and Activities

As the youngest mountain range in North America, the Tetons provide hikers, bikers, climbers, rafters and sightseers with challenges and vistas not found in more weathered ranges. The Grandest Teton rises to 13,700 ft. above sea level, virtually without foothills. While Yellowstone wows visitors with its geysers and mudpots, Grand Teton's geology boasts some of the most scenic mountains in the U.S., if not the world.

Cascade Canyon Trail, one of the least arduous (and therefore most popular and populated) hikes, originates at Jenny Lake. To start, take a boat trip (operated by monopolistic Grand Teton Lodge Co.) across Jenny Lake ($2.75, round-trip $3.50; children $1.25, round-trip $1.75), or hike the two-mi. trail around the lake. Trail guides (25¢) are available at the trailhead, at the west boatdock. ½ mi. from the trail entrance plunges the **Hidden Falls Waterfall;** only the lonely can trek six mi. further to **Lake Solitude.** Another pleasant day hike, popular for its scope of wildlife, is the four-mi. walk from Colter Bay to **Hermitage Point.** The **Amphitheater Lake Trail,** which begins just south of Jenny Lake at the Lupine Meadows parking lot, will take you 4.6 breathtaking miles to one of the park's many glacial lakes. Those who were bighorn sheep in past lives can take the challenge of **Static Peak Divide,** a 15-mi. trail that climbs 4020 ft. from the Death Canyon trailhead (4½ mi. south of Moose Visitors Center) and offers some of the best lookouts in the park. All information centers (see Practical Information above) provide pamphlets about the day hikes and sell the *Teton Trails* guide ($2).

For a leisurely afternoon on Jackson Lake, rent boats at the **Signal Mountain Marina** (543-2831). (Rowboats and canoes $6 per hr. Motorboats $13.50 per hr. Waterski boats and pontoons $26 per hr. Open daily 7am-6pm.) **Colter Bay Marina** has a somewhat smaller variety of boats at similar prices. (Open daily 7am-8pm, rentals stop at 6pm. No per-day rates.) The **Grand Teton Lodge Company** (733-3471 or 543-2811) can also take you on scenic Snake River float trips within the park. (10½-mi. ½-day trip $23.50, under 17 $12.75. 20½-mi. luncheon or supper trips $31, under 17 $20.) **Triangle X Float Trips** (733-5500) can take you on a five-mi. river trip for less ($17, under 13 $12). **Fishing** in the park's lakes, rivers and streams is excellent. Wyoming state fishing licenses ($5) are required and may be purchased at the visitors centers and ranger stations. **Horseback riding** is available through the Grand Teton Lodge Company (1-4 hr. rides, $16-28 per person).

The **American Indian Art Museum** (543-2467), in the Colter Bay Visitors Center, offers an extensive private collection of Native American artwork, artifacts, movies and workshops. (Open June-Sept. daily 8am-7pm; late May and late Sept. daily 8am-5pm. Free.) During July and August you can see Cheyenne, Cherokee, Apache and Sioux dances at Jackson Lake Lodge (Fri. at 8:30pm). At the **Moose** and **Colter Bay Visitors Centers**, June through September, rangers lead a variety of activities aimed at educating visitors about such subjects as the ecology, geology, wildlife and history of the Tetons. Check the *Teewinot* for exact times, as schedules change daily.

In the winter, all hiking trails and the unplowed sections of Teton Park Road are open to cross-country skiers. Pick up the trail map *Winter in the Tetons* or *Teewinot* at the Moose Visitors Center. From January through March, naturalists lead **snowshoe hikes** from Moose Visitors Center (733-2880; snowshoes distributed free). Call for reservations. **Snowmobiling** along the park's well-powdered trails and up into Yellowstone is a noisy but popular winter activity. Grab a map and guide at the Jackson Chamber of Commerce, 10 mi. south of Moose. For a steep fee you can rent snowmobiles at **Signal Mt. Lodge**, **Flagg Ranch Village**, or down in **Jackson**; an additional $5 registration fee is required for all snowmobile use in the park. All campgrounds close during the winter. The Colter Bay parking lot is available for RVs and cars, and backcountry snow camping (only for those who know what they're doing) is allowed with a free permit from Moose. Check with a ranger station for current weather conditions—many early trappers froze to death in the 10-ft. drifts—and avalanche danger.

Jackson

Colorado has Aspen, Idaho has Sun Valley, and Wyoming has Jackson—an expensive refuge for transplanted Eastern "outdoorsy" types. Mixing with tanned, svelte mountain bikers and rock climbers, you'll find busloads of camera-snapping tourists rushing to the Ralph Lauren and J. Crew outlets. If you hang around long enough, you may catch a glimpse of some real cowboys, of the type that established Jackson long before climbing mountains became fashionable.

Practical Information

Emergency: 911.

Visitor Information: Jackson Hole Area Chamber of Commerce, 32 N. Cache St. (733-3316), in a modern wooden split-level with grass on the roof. A crucial information stop. Open mid-June-mid-Sept. daily 8am-8pm; off-season daily 8am-5pm. **Bridger-Teton National Forest Headquarters,** 340 N. Cache St. (739-5500), 2 blocks south of the chamber of commerce. Maps $2-4. Open Mon.-Sat. 8am-4:30pm, off-season Mon.-Fri. 8am-4:30pm.

Buses: Grand Teton Lodge Co. (733-2811) runs a shuttle twice daily in summer to Jackson Lake Lodge ($14).

Bus Tours: Grayline Tours, 330 N. Glenwood St. (733-4325), in front of Dirty Jack's Theatre. Full-day tours of Grand Teton National Park and Yellowstone National Park lower loop ($40). Call for reservations. **Wild West Jeep Tours,** P.O. Box 7506, Jackson 83001 (733-9036). In summer only, half-day tours of the Tetons and other areas ($29, seniors $26, under 12 $15). Call for reservations.

Car Rental: Rent-A-Wreck, 1050 U.S. 89 (733-5014). $29 per day, $128 per week; 150 free mi., 20¢ each additional mi. Must be 21 with credit card or a $300 cash deposit. Must stay within 500 mi. of Jackson. Open daily 8am-5pm.

Ski and Bike Rental: Hoback Sports, 40 S. Millward (733-5335). 10-speeds 2 hrs. $7, $16 per day, mountain bikes 2 hrs. $10, $20 per day; lower rates for longer rentals. Skis, boots and poles $13 per ½-day, $16 per day. Open peak summer 9am-8pm, peak winter 7:30am-9pm, off-season daily 9am-7pm. Must have credit card. **Skinny Skis,** 65 W. Deloney St. (733-6094). Skis $9 per day, $17 for mountaineering, rollerblades $8 per ½-day, $12 per day, camping equipment also available. Major credit card or deposit for value of equipment. Open daily 9am-9pm.

Weather Line, 733-1731. 24-hr. recording.

Help Lines: Rape Crisis Line, 733-5162. **Road Information,** 733-9966, outside WY 800-442-7850.

Post Office: 220 W. Pearl St. (733-3650), 2 blocks east of Cache St. Open Mon.-Fri. 8:30am-5pm. **ZIP code:** 83001.

Area Code: 307.

Although most services in Jackson are prohibitively expensive, the town makes an ideal base for trips into the Tetons, 10 mi. north, or the Wind River Range, 70 mi. southeast. U.S. 191, the usual southern entry to town, ties Jackson to I-80 at Rock Springs (180 mi. south). This road continues north into Grand Teton Park and eventually reaches Yellowstone, 70 mi. to the north. The streets of Jackson are centered around **Town Square,** a small park on Broadway and Cache St.

Accommodations, Camping and Food

Jackson's constant influx of tourists ensures that if you don't book ahead, rooms will be small and expensive at best and non-existent at worst. Fortunately you can sleep affordably in one of two local hostels. **The Bunkhouse,** in the basement of the Anvil Motel, 215 N. Cache St. (733-3668), has a lounge, kitchenette, laundromat, ski storage and, as the name implies, one large but quiet sleeping room with comfortable bunks. ($20. Linens $2.) **The Hostel X (HI/AYH),** P.O. Box 546, Teton Village 83025 (733-3415), near the ski slopes, 12 mi. northwest of Jackson, is a budgetary oasis among the wallet-parching condos and lodges of Teton Village, and a favorite of skiers because of its location. It also has a game room, TV room, ski waxing room, and movies nightly in winter. Accommodations range from dorm-style rooms ($15 members, $25 for two members) to private suites ($34 for 2 people, $44 for 3 or 4; nonmembers may *only* take private rooms). All are clean and well maintained. If you prefer to stay in a Jackson motel, the **Lazy X Motel,** 325 N. Cache St. (733-3673), offers lovely rooms with lazy teddy bears during the summer. (Singles $55, doubles $60, off-peak $36/$40.) You can always fall back on **Motel 6,** 1370 W. Broadway (733-1620), even though their rates rise steadily as the peak season approaches. (Singles from $36. Each additional person $6.)

While it doesn't offer amazing scenery, Jackson's RV/tent campground, the **Wagon Wheel Village** (733-4588), doesn't charge an arm and a leg either. Call for reservations. (Sites from $16.50.) Cheaper sites and more pleasant surroundings are available in the **Bridger-Teton National Forest** surrounding Jackson. Drive toward Alpine Junction on U.S. 26/89 to find spots. Check the map at the chamber of commerce for a complete list of campgrounds. (Sites $4-6, no showers.)

The Bunnery, 130 N. Cache St. (733-5474), in the "Hole-in-the-Wall" mall, has the best breakfast in town—two eggs, peaches, cottage cheese, toast $3.25. Sandwiches $4-6. (Open daily 7am-9:30pm.) Chow down on barbecued chicken and spare ribs ($7) at **Bubba's** 515 W. Broadway (733-2288). No reservations. (Open daily 7am-9pm.) On weekdays, a mixture of Western barbecue and Mexican delicacies is set out at **Pedro's,** 139 N. Cache St. (733-9015) for the $3 all-you-can-eat buffet. (Open summer daily 11am-9:30pm.) For a cheap, light meal, away from the cache on Cache St., head to **Pearl St. Bagels,** 145 Pearl St. (733-1218), where myriad bagel sandwiches are under $3 each. (Open Mon.-Fri. 6:30am-6pm, Sat.-Sun. 7:30am-3pm.) Another good option for cheap, quality food and excellent coffee is **Shade's Café,** 82 S. King St. (733-2015; open daily 7:30am-6pm).

Nightlife and Activities

Western saddles serve as bar stools at the **Million Dollar Cowboy Bar,** 25 N. Cache St. (733-2207), Town Square. This Jackson institution is mostly for tourists, but attracts some rodeoers and local cowboys. (Open Mon.-Sat. 10am-2am, Sun. noon-10pm. Live music Mon.-Sat. 9pm-2am. Cover $2-6 after 8pm.) The **Mangy Moose,** Teton Village (733-4913), is a great place for live moosic, food, and general rambunctiousness. (Dinner daily 5:30-10:30pm, bar open 10pm-2am. 21 and over.)

Cultural activities in Jackson fall into two camps—the rowdy foot-stomping Western celebrations and the more formal, sedate presentations of music and art. Every summer evening except Sunday, the Town Square hosts a kitschy episode of the 37-year-old **Longest-Running Shoot-Out in the World.** For $2.50 on Friday evenings at 6:30pm, you can join in at the **Teton Twirlers Square Dance,** in the fair building on the rodeo grounds (733-5269 or 543-2825). Each June, the town celebrates the opening of the **Jackson Hole Rodeo** (733-2805; open June-Aug. Wed. and Sat. 8pm; tickets $6:50, ages 4-12 $4.50, under 4 free). The prestigious **Grand Teton Music Festival** (733-1128) blows and bows in Teton Village from mid-July through August. (Performances weeknights at 8pm, Sat.-Sun. 8:30pm; student tickets $3-5. Fri. and Sat. symphony at 8:30pm; student tickets $9. Reserve in advance.) On Memorial Day, the town bursts its britches as tourists, locals and nearby Native American tribes pour in for the dances and parades of **Old West Days.** Throughout September, the **Jackson Hole Fall Arts**

Festival attracts painters, dancers, actors and musicians to Jackson's four main theaters.

Between May 15 and Labor Day over 100,000 city slickers and backwoods folk go white-water rafting out of Jackson. **Mad River Boat Trips,** 1060 S. Hwy. 89 (U.S. 89), 25 mi. from Jackson (733-6203 or 800-458-7238), offers the cheapest white-water and scenic raft trips ($19 for 2 hrs.). **Long Eagle Expeditions** (377-1090) gives you a meal on your eight-mi. raft trip (Breakfast and lunch trips $17.50 per person; afternoon and evening dinner trips $24 per person). Cheaper thrills include a lift 10,452 ft. up Rendez-Vous Mountain on the **Jackson Hole Aerial Tram** (733-2292; $14, seniors $12, teens $7, ages 6-12 $2). In winter, the **Jackson Hole Ski Resort** (733-2292) at Teton Village offers some of the steepest, most challenging skiing in the country.

The Wildlife Museum (733-4909), in Grand Teton Plaza on Broadway, exhibits the trophies of local hunters in extremely realistic settings. (Open May-Oct. daily 9am-6pm. Admission $2, families $5, ages 6-12 $1, under 6 free.)

Yellowstone National Park

Had legendary mountain man John Colter been religious, he probably would have compared his 1807 trek into the Yellowstone area with a descent into the nether regions. In any case, his graphic descriptions of boiling, sulfuric pits, spouting geysers and smelly mudpots inspired a half-century of popular stories about "Colter's Hell." In 1870 the first official survey party, the Washburn Expedition, reached the area. As they crested a ridge, the explorers were greeted by a fountain of boiling water and steam spurting 130 ft. into the air. Members of the expedition watched it erupt nine times and named it "Old Faithful" before leaving the Upper Geyser Basin. One year later, President Grant declared Yellowstone a national park, the world's first.

Visitors in Grant's time might have encountered a handful of other adventurers amidst Yellowstone's 3472 square mi. Today's visitors will find the park cluttered with the cars, RVs and the detritus of some 50,000-odd tourists. The park's main attractions are huge, tranquil Yellowstone Lake, the 2100-ft.-deep Yellowstone River Canyon, and the world's largest collection of reeking, sputtering geysers, mudpots, hot springs, and fumaroles (steam-spewing holes in the ground). In the backcountry, you can escape the madding crowd and observe the park's abundant bear, elk, moose, bison, and bighorn sheep.

In 1988 Yellowstone was ravaged by a blaze that charred almost half the park. Crowds in Yellowstone doubled in 1989 in an extraordinary example of rubberneck tourism, with people pouring in to see "what really happened." While the effects of the fire are still visible throughout much of the park, crowds have returned to their normal large size. The toasted forests do make for interesting, if somewhat bleak, viewing; rangers have erected exhibits throughout the park to better explain the fire's effects.

Practical Information

Emergency: 911.

Park Information and Headquarters: Superintendent, Mammoth Hot Springs, Yellowstone National Park 82190 (344-7381). The switchboard serves all visitors centers (each one has its own extension, listed below) and park service phones. General information, campground availability, and emergencies. Headquarters open off-season Mon.-Fri. 8am-5pm. **Park Admission:** $10 for non-commercial vehicles, $4 for pedestrians and bikers. Good for 1 week and also valid at Grand Teton National Park.

Visitors Centers and Ranger Stations: Most regions in this vast park have their own center/station. The district rangers have a good deal of autonomy in making regulations for hiking and camping, so check in at each area. All visitors centers have guides for the disabled and give backcountry permits, or have a partner ranger station that does. Each visitors center's display focuses on the attributes of its region of the park. **Mammoth Hot Springs** (ext. 2357): natural and human history. Open June 8-Sept. 7 daily 8am-7pm; Sept.-May daily 9am-5pm. **Grant Village** (ext. 6602): wilderness. Open mid-June-late Aug. daily 8am-6pm, late May-mid June and late Aug.-Labor Day 9am-5pm. **Old Faithful/Madison** (ext. 6001): geysers. Open early June-mid Aug.

8am-8pm, mid-April-early June 9am-6pm, call for hrs. after late Aug. **Fishing Bridge** (ext. 6150): wildlife and Yellowstone Lake. Open daily 8am-6pm; off-season daily 9am-5pm. **Canyon** (ext. 6205): natural history and history of canyon area. Open mid-June-late Aug. 8am-6pm, late Aug.-Labor Day and late May-mid-June 9am-5pm. **Norris** (ext. 7733): park museum. Open mid-May-early June daily 9am-5pm, early June-Oct. 8am-9pm. **Tower/Roosevelt Ranger Station** (344-7746): special temporary exhibits. Open daily 8am-5pm. *Discover Yellowstone,* the park's activities guide, has a thorough listing of tours and programs at each center.

Radio Information: Tune to 1610AM for service information and radical interpretive meta-discourse within the park.

West Yellowstone Chamber of Commerce: 100 Yellowstone Ave., West Yellowstone, MT 59758 (406-646-7701). Located 2 blocks west of the park entrance. Open daily at 8am; call for closing time.

Greyhound: 127 Yellowstone Ave., W. Yellowstone, MT (406-646-7666). To: Bozeman, (1 per day, 2 hr., $12); Salt Lake City, (1 per day, 9 hr., $68). Open summer only, daily 8am-6:30pm.

TW Services, Inc. (344-7311). Monopolizes concessions within the park. 9-hr. bus tours of the lower portion of the park leave daily from all lodges ($24, ages under 12 $12). Similar tours of the northern region leave Gardiner, MT and the lodges at Mammoth Lake and Fishing Bridge ($15-22, depending on where you start and end). Individual legs of this extensive network of tour loops can get you as far as the Grand Tetons or Jackson, but the system is inefficient and costs much more than it's worth. (West Yellowstone to Old Faithful, 3 per day: $7, children $3.80; does *not* include park entrance fee.)

Gray Line Tours: 211 W. Yellowstone Ave, West Yellowstone, MT (406-646-9374). Offers full-day tours from West Yellowstone around the lower loop ($30, under 12 $15), upper loop ($30, under 12 $15), and Grand Tetons and Jackson ($40, under 12 $20). Open daily 8am-5pm.

Car Rental: Big Sky Car Rental, 429 Yellowstone Ave., (646-9564 or 800-426-7669). $30 per day, 100 free mi., 25¢ each additional mi. Must be 21 with a credit card, $100 deposit, or passport.

Bike Rental: Yellowstone Bicycles, 132 Madison Ave., West Yellowstone, MT (406-646-7815). 10-speeds $16.50 per day, mountain bikes $10.50 per ½-day, $3.50 per hr. Open daily 9am-9pm.

Horse Rental: Mammoth Hot Springs Hotel, late May-mid-Sept. **Roosevelt Lodge,** mid-June-Sept. 2. **Canyon Lodge,** June 4-Sept. 2. $11.50 per hr., $22 for 2 hrs. Call TW Services (394-7901) for more information.

Medical Facilities: Lake, Clinic, Pharmacy and **Hospital** at Lake Hotel (242-7241). Clinic open late May-mid-Sept. daily 8:30am-8:30pm. Hospital Emergency Room open May-Sept. 24 hrs. **Old Faithful Clinic,** at Old Faithful Inn (545-7325). Open mid-May-mid-Oct. daily 8:30am-5pm. **Mammoth Hot Springs Family Clinic** (344-7965) open year-round Mon.-Fri. 8:30am-5pm.

Post Offices: Old Faithful Station (545-7572), in the park behind the visitors center. Open Mon.-Fri. 8:30-11am and 1-5pm. **ZIP code:** 82190. Also at **West Yellowstone, MT,** 7 Madison Ave. (646-7704). Open Mon.-Fri. 8:30am-5pm. **ZIP code:** 59758.

Area Codes: 307 (in the park), 406 (in West Yellowstone and Gardiner). Unless otherwise listed, phone numbers have a 307 area code.

The bulk of Yellowstone National Park lies in the northwest corner of Wyoming with slivers slicing into Montana and Idaho. **West Yellowstone, MT,** at the park's western entrance, and **Gardiner, MT,** at the northern entrance, are the most built-up and expensive towns along the edge of the park. The southern entry to the park is through Grand Teton National Park. The northeast entrance to the park leads to U.S. 212, a gorgeous stretch of road known as **Beartooth Highway**, which climbs to **Beartooth Pass** at 11,000 ft. and descends to **Red Lodge,** a former mining town. (Road open summer only because of heavy snowfall; ask at the chamber of commerce for exact dates.)

Yellowstone's extensive system of roads circulates its millions of visitors. Side roads branch off to park entrances and some of the lesser-known sights. It's unwise to bike or walk around the deserted roads at night since you may risk startling large wild animals. Approaching any wild beast at any time is illegal and extremely unsafe, and those who don't remain at least 100 ft. from bison, bear, or moose risk being mauled, gored to death, or made the victim of a *Far Side* cartoon. One unwise tourist tried to take a picture of his three-year-old son astride a buffalo; father and son were both killed when the buffalo objected to being photographed.

The park's high season extends from about June 15 to September 15. If you visit during this period expect large crowds, clogged roads and motels, and campsites filled to capacity. A better option is to visit in either late spring or early fall, when it is still fairly warm and the Winnebagos and the tame animals they transport are safely home.

Accommodations

Cabin-seekers will find many options within the park. Standard hotel and motel rooms for the nature-weary also abound, but if you plan to keep your budget in line, stick to the towns near the park's entry-points.

In The Park

TW Services (344-7311) controls all of the accommodations within the park, and uses a special set of classifications for budget cabins: "Roughrider" means no bath, no facilities; "Western Frontier" means with bath, somewhat furnished. All cabins or rooms should be reserved well in advance of the June to September tourist season.

Old Faithful Inn and Lodge, near the west Yellowstone entrance. Offers pleasant Roughrider cabins ($19) and Western Frontier cabins ($31). Well-appointed hotel rooms from $35, with private bath $56.

Roosevelt Lodge, in the northwest corner. A favorite campsite of Roughrider Teddy Roosevelt. Provides the cheapest and most scenic indoor accommodations around. Rustic shelters $19, each with a wood-burning stove (bring your own bedding and towel). Also Roughrider cabins ($22—bring your own towel) and more spacious "family" cabins with toilet ($35).

Mammoth Hot Springs, 18 mi. west of Roosevelt area, near the north entrance. Unremarkable budget cabins $24. Frontier cabins from $49.

Lake Yellowstone Hotel and Cabins, near the south entrance. Overpriced, but with a nice view of the lake. Frontier cabins identical to Old Faithful's ($39) and Western cabins with a little more space ($72).

Canyon Village. Less authentic and more expensive than Roosevelt Lodge's cabins, but slightly closer to the popular Old Faithful area. Roughrider cabins $43, Frontier cabins $72.

West Yellowstone, MT

West Yellowstone International Hostel, at the Madison Hotel and Motel, 139 Yellowstone Ave. (406-646-7745). Friendly manager presides over old but clean, wood-adorned hotel. Singles $22, with bath $30. Doubles with bath $38. Rooms $2 cheaper in the spring. Hostelers stay in more crowded rooms for $14, no bedding, no kitchen. Open May 27-mid-Oct.

Alpine Motel, 120 Madison (406-646-7544). Plastic but clean rooms with cable TV and A/C. Singles $35. Doubles $43. $3 less in off-season.

Traveler's Lodge, 225 Yellowstone Ave. (406-646-9561). Comfortable, large rooms; ask for one away from the hot tub. Singles $44, off-season $29. Doubles $46, off-season $35. $5 discount if you rent a car from them (see Practical Information above).

Ho-Hum Motel, 126 Canyon Rd. (646-7746). Small, dark, ho-hum, but clean rooms. Singles $28. Doubles $36.

Gardiner, MT

Located about 90 minutes northeast of West Yellowstone, Gardiner served as the original entrance to the park and is considerably smaller and less tacky than its neighbor.

The Town Motel, Lounge, and Gift Shop (848-7322), on Park St., across from the park's northern entrance. Pleasant, wood-paneled, carpeted rooms. Phones and baths but no showers. Singles $28. Doubles $32.

Wilson's Yellowstone River Motel (406-848-7303), E. Park St., ½-block east of U.S. 89. Large, well-decorated rooms overseen by friendly manager. Singles $45. Doubles $45-49. Off-season singles $35, doubles $39.

Hillcrest Cottages (848-7353), on U.S. 89 near where it crosses the Yellowstone River. Small but clean singles $28. Doubles $36. $6 each additional adult, $3 each additional kid under 12. 7 nights for the price of 6.

Camping

All developed campsites are available on a first-come first-served basis except for the **Bridge Bay Campground,** which reserves sites up to eight weeks in advance through Mistix (800-365-2267). During summer months, most campgrounds fill by 2pm. All regular sites cost $6-8, $10 if reserved. Arrive very early, especially on weekends and holidays. If all sites are full, try the free campgrounds outside the park in the surrounding National Forest land. Bring a stove or plan to search for or buy firewood. Except for **Mammoth Campground,** all camping areas close for the winter.

Two of the most beautiful and tranquil areas are **Slough Creek Campground,** 10 mi. northeast of Tower Junction (open late May-Oct.), and **Pebble Creek Campground,** 15 mi. farther down the same road (open mid-June-early Sept.). Both relatively uncrowded spots have good fishing. You can also try **Canyon Village. Fishing Bridge Campgrounds** (344-7311) is for non-tenting travelers only (RV hookup $18; open late May-early Sept.). The popular and scenic campgrounds at **Norris** (open May-Sept.) and **Madison** (May-Oct.) fill early (by 1pm), while others, such as **Canyon** and **Pebble Creek,** sometimes have sites until 6pm. **Bridge Bay** (open late May-mid-Sept.), **Indian Creek** (open June-Sept.) and **Mammoth** (open year-round) campgrounds are treeless and non-scenic. You'd be better off camping in the **Gallatin National Forest** to the northwest. Good sites line U.S. 20, 287, 191 and 89. Call the Park Headquarters (344-7381) for information on any of Yellowstone's campgrounds.

More than 95% (almost two million acres) of the park is backcountry. To venture overnight into the wilds of Yellowstone, you must obtain a free **wilderness permit** from a ranger station or visitors center. It is always best to consult a ranger before any hike. Be sure you understand the most recent instructions regarding the closure of campgrounds and trails due to bears and other wildlife. Other backcountry regulations include: sanitation rules, pet and firearms restrictions, campfire permits, and firewood rules. The more popular areas fill up in high season, but you can reserve a permit up to 48 hours in advance.

The campgrounds at Grant, Village Lake, Fishing Bridge, and Canyon all have coin-operated laundries and pay showers ($1 plus 25¢ for towel or soap). The lodges at Mammoth and Old Faithful have no laundry facilities but will let you use their showers for $1.50.

To discourage bears, all campers should keep clean camps and store food in a locked car or suspended 10 ft. above ground and four ft. horizontally from a post or tree trunk.

Food

Be very choosy when buying food in the park, as the restaurants, snack bars, and cafeterias are quite expensive. If possible, stick to the **general stores** at each lodging location (open daily 7:30am-10pm). Harvest from the vast amounts of inexpensive food at **Food Farm** corner of Park and 2nd St., Gardiner, MT (406-848-7524), or lasso some chow at the **Food Round-Up Grocery Store,** 107 Dunraven St., W. Yellowstone, MT (406-646-7501).

Sights and Activities

TW Services, for unbelievable amounts of money, will sell you tours, horseback rides, and chuckwagon dinners until the cows come home. But given enough time, your eyes and feet will do an even better job than TW's tours, and won't bankrupt you. Hiking to the main attractions is much easier if you make reservations at the cabins closest to the sights you most want to see.

The **geysers** that made Yellowstone famous are clustered on the western side of the park, near the West Yellowstone entrance. Geysers are holes in the earth's crust into which water slowly trickles, then turns to steam; when the pressure reaches a certain point, the steam bursts out to the surface. The duration of the explosion depends on how much water has leaked into the hole and how hot the steam is. **Old Faithful,** while neither the largest, the highest, nor the most regular geyser, is certainly the most popular; it gushes in the **Upper Geyser Basin,** 16 mi. south of **Madison Junction** where the entry road splits north-south. Since its discovery in 1870, the granddaddy of geysers has consistently erupted with a whoosh of spray and steam (5000-8000 gallons worth) every 45 to 70 minutes. Avoiding crowds here in summer is nearly impossible unless you come for the blasts at dusk or dawn. Enjoy other geysers as well as elk in the surrounding **Firehole Valley.** Swimming in any hot springs or geysers is prohibited, but you can swim in the **Firehole River,** three-quarters of the way up Firehole Canyon Drive (turn south just after Madison Jct.), or in the **Boiling River,** 2½ mi. north of Mammoth, which is not really hot enough to cook pasta. Still, do not swim alone, and beware of strong currents.

From Old Faithful, take the easy 1½-mi. walk to **Morning Glory Pool,** a park favorite, or head eight mi. north to the **Lower Geyser Basin,** where examples of all four types of geothermic activity (geysers, mudpots, hot springs and fumaroles) steam, bubble and spray together in a cacophonous symphony. The regular star here is **Echinus,** which erupts about every hour from a large basin of water. If you are lucky enough to witness it, the biggest show on earth is put on by **Steamboat,** the largest geyser in the world. Eruptions can last 20 minutes and top 400 ft. The last such enormous eruption occurred on Oct. 2, 1991; they tend to occur about once a year. Don't hold your breath waiting for another one, but you might get lucky.

Whether you're waiting for geysers to erupt or watching them shoot skyward, don't go too close, as the crust of earth around a geyser is only two ft. deep, and the Surgeon General has determined that falling into a boiling sulfuric pit *could* be hazardous to your health. Pets are not allowed in the basin.

Mammoth Hot Springs has famous hot springs terraces, built of multicolored striated limestone deposits which enlarge six in. every year. Wildlife is quite abundant in the northern part of the park, both along the road from Mammoth to Roosevelt—perhaps on the road itself—and past Roosevelt in the Lamar Valley.

The pride of the western area of the park is the **Grand Canyon of the Yellowstone,** carved through glacial deposits and amber, volcanic bedrock. For the best views, hike or drive to the 308-ft. Lower Falls at Artist Point, on the southern rim, or head for Lookout Point on the northern rim. All along the canyon's 19-mi. rim, keep an eye out for the rare bighorn sheep, and at dawn or dusk the bear-viewing management area (at the intersection of the northern rim and Tower roads) should be loaded with opportunities to use your binoculars.

Yellowstone Lake, 16 mi. south of the Canyon's rim at the southeastern corner of the park, contains tons o' trout; after procuring a free Yellowstone fishing permit, catch a few and have the chef fry them for you in the Yellowstone Hotel Dining Room. Most other lakes and streams allow catch-and-release fishing only. The aptly yellow **Lake Yellowstone Hotel,** originally built in 1891 and renovated in 1989, merits a visit, although its room rates place it well out of the range of budget travelers. The bright, airy lobby with large windows provides a magnificent view of the lake. Walks around the main body of the lake, as well as those that take you around one of the lake's three fingers, are scenic and serene rather than strenuous. Nearby **Mud Volcano,** close to Yellowstone Lake, features boiling sulfuric earth and the **Dragon's Mouth,** a vociferous steaming hole that early explorers reportedly heard all the way from the lake. You'll smell it that far away for sure.

Although most of the spectacular sights in the park are accessible by car, a hiking trip through the backcountry will remove you from the masses. The multilayered petrified forest of **Specimen Ridge** and the geyser basins at **Shoshone** and **Heart Lakes** are only accessible by well-kept trails. **Cascade Corner,** in the southwest, is a lovely area accessible by trails from Belcher. Over 1000 mi. of trails crisscross the park, but many are poorly marked. If you plan to hike, pick up a topographical trail map ($2.50) at any visitors center and ask a ranger to describe all forks in the trail and the wording of trail markings. Even after annoying the ranger, allow yourself extra time (at least 1 hr. per day) in case you lose the trail.

Winter

Yellowstone can be as blanketed with snow during winter as it is blanketed with tourists and bothersome bears during the summer. Native animals can still be seen clustered around the sparse vegetation, while the traveling well-wrapped humans convert the park into snowboarding city. Cross-country skiing, ranger-sponsored snowshoe tours, and evening programs with hot chocolate and noisy snowmobile excursions are all available at off-season rates. Contact Park Headquarters (344-7381), **Snowmobile Touring** (545-7249), or the visitors centers at Mammoth Hot Springs, Old Faithful (mid-Dec.-mid-March) and West Yellowstone (mid-Dec.-mid-March).

Plowed roads make winter bus service available to West Yellowstone and Flagg Ranch on the western and southern borders; the Mammoth-Tower-Cooke City park road is kept open and accessible from Bozeman via Gardiner. All other roads are used by snowmobilers and the snowcoach only. The **snowcoach,** a heated, enclosed tank-like vehicle, run by TW Services, provides transportation from the south gate at Flagg Ranch, the west gate at West Yellowstone, and the north gate at Mammoth to bring travelers to the Old Faithful Lodge. With a permit (free from any visitors center), you may use the undeveloped backcountry sites. But exercise caution: people do get snowed in. You can find heated restrooms at Madison and Mammoth campgrounds. Food is available at Old Faithful and the **Canyon Snack Shop,** snowmobile fuel at Old Faithful, Mammoth and Canyon. The **Three Bears Hotel,** 217 W. Yellowstone Ave. (406-646-7353), rents snowmobiles ($72 per day, $79 for 2 people). Porridge prices are unavailable as we go to press.

The Southwest

Every fall, enormous flocks of Winnebagos migrate from the cold northern lands of the Northwest and Canada to the sun-baked lands of the Southwest. These "snowbirds" come in search of warmer weather and an arid clime, but the states of the Southwest have much more to offer than sun-tan-perfect weather. Here clusters some of the world's most awe-inspiring scenery, including the Grand Canyon and Carlsbad Caverns, as well as a rich history of cultural intermingling unmatched in the rest of the U.S.

The Anasazi of the 10th and 11th centuries were the first to discover that the arid lands of the Southwest—with proper management—could support an advanced agrarian civilization. With the addition of a little water, the desert in areas like Chaco Canyon bloomed like a freeze-dried Eden. The Navajo, Apache, and Pueblo nations later migrated into the region, sharing the land with the Hopi tribe, descendents of the Anasazi. Spanish conquest came early in the 17th century, bringing European and *mestizo* colonists to modern-day Texas and New Mexico. Mexican independence in 1821 was followed by Anglo-American conquest of the region. The Texan War of Independence in 1836 began as a revolt by Mexican and U.S. settlers against Santa Anna's dictatorship, and culminated in the Mexican-American War. Santa Fe, Nuevo Mexico, became the first foreign capital ever to fall to the U.S. In 1853, Mexico's defeated governement agreed to sell a tract of land south of the Gila River that today forms a large part of Arizona and New Mexico.

The legacy of this bloody history is evident everywhere in the Southwest. Here live the largest Hispanic and Native American populations in the country; many Spanish and tribal place-names remain, as do several of the historical sites in the region. But much of the land retains the tranquility of nature unsullied by human hands. The austere, lonely beauty of the desert stretches for hundreds of miles, and the water- and wind-scored landscape stands in silent testimony to millenia of incessant battles waged by erosion. The cliffs of the Guadalupe Mountains, the gorges of the Colorado and Río Grande, the redstone arches and twisted spires of southern Utah and northern Arizona all await exploration and meditation. For information on safety precautions in the desert, see Desert Survival in the Health Section of the General Introduction to this book.

Arizona

Arizona's identity draws on multiple climes and cultures. Though much of the state is the arid desert most people envision it to be, it is neither homogeneous nor barren: Tucson and much of southern Arizona offer greener pastures, the northern regions pine forests and plains. The Arizona-Sonora Desert Museum, in the Saguaro cactus forest west of Tucson, illustrates the sheer variety that even desert flora and fauna can attain.

The human beings who inhabit Arizona are similarly diverse, as are their methods of coping with the demanding climate. The land was first settled by the Hopi, Navajo, and the Yavapai; their communities were sometimes built in vast canyons, which offered protection from the elements and from rivals, while herds and agriculture were maintained on the mesas above. Today, about one-fourth of Arizona is designated as Native American reservations. The modern metropolis of Phoenix and the surrounding cities provides a marked contrast to this way of life: here people have chosen to adjust the elements themselves rather than adjust *to* them. One air-conditioned shopping mall includes an ice-skating rink; swimming pools are as common as household appliances.

But Arizona's varied ecosystem and population are nowhere near as astounding as is the majestic power of the land itself. Within these state lines lie the Painted Desert, Monument Valley, Oak Creek Canyon, the Petrified Forest, Sunset Crater, and, of course, the breathtaking natural wonder of the Grand Canyon.

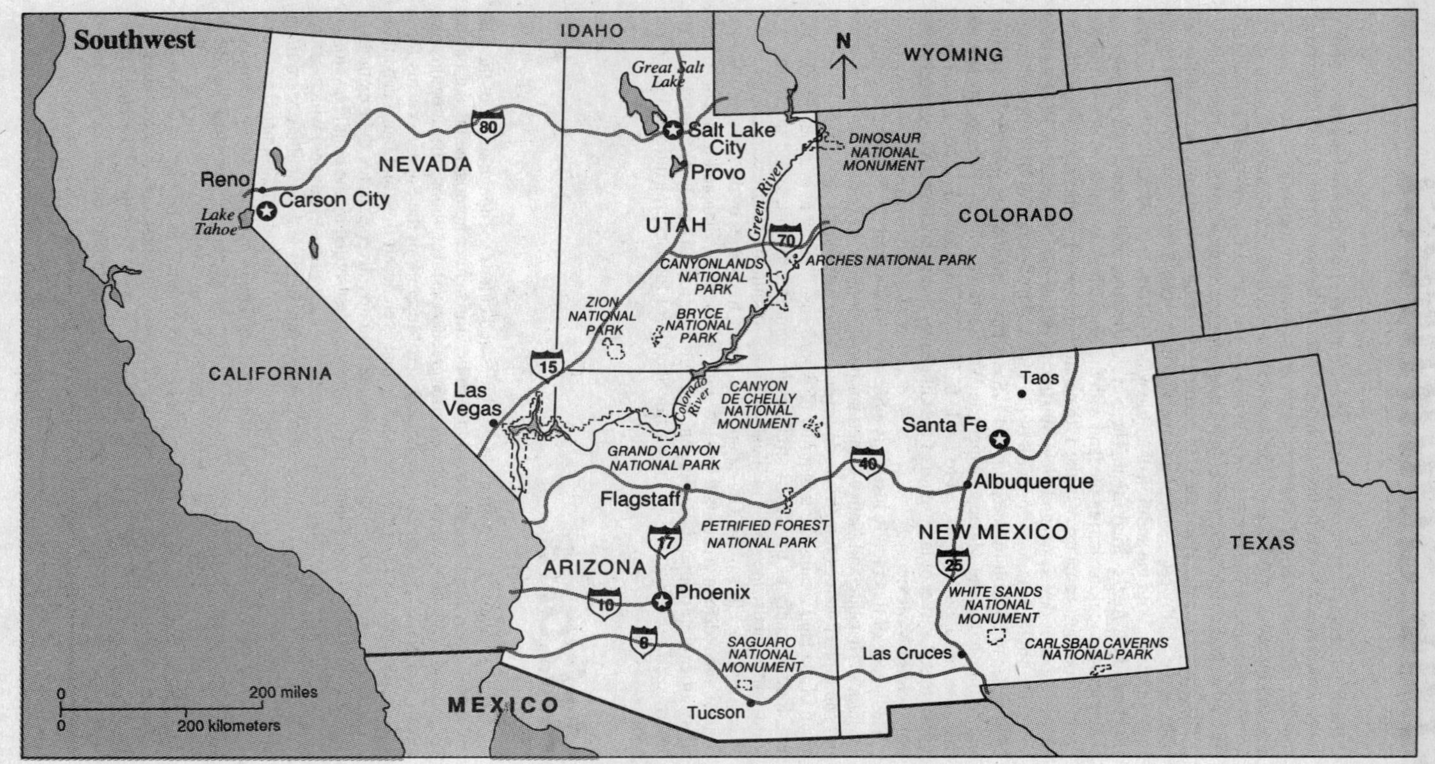
Southwest
N
IDAHO
WYOMING
COLORADO
NEVADA
UTAH
ARIZONA
NEW MEXICO
TEXAS
CALIFORNIA
MEXICO
Reno
Carson City
Lake Tahoe
Las Vegas
Great Salt Lake
Salt Lake City
Provo
DINOSAUR NATIONAL MONUMENT
ARCHES NATIONAL PARK
CANYONLANDS NATIONAL PARK
BRYCE NATIONAL PARK
ZION NATIONAL PARK
Green River
Colorado River
CANYON DE CHELLY NATIONAL MONUMENT
GRAND CANYON NATIONAL PARK
PETRIFIED FOREST NATIONAL PARK
SAGUARO NATIONAL MONUMENT
Flagstaff
Phoenix
Tucson
Taos
Santa Fe
Albuquerque
Las Cruces
WHITE SANDS NATIONAL MONUMENT
CARLSBAD CAVERNS NATIONAL PARK
80
15
70
17
10
8
40
25
0
200 miles
200 kilometers

Practical Information

Capital: Phoenix.

Arizona Office of Tourism, 3507 N. Central Ave. #506, Phoenix 85012 (602-542-8687). **Arizona State Parks,** 1688 W. Adams St., Phoenix 85007.

Time Zone: Mountain (2 hrs. behind Eastern). Arizona (with the exception of the reservations) does not follow Daylight Savings Time; in summer it is one hr. behind the rest of the Mountain Time Zone. **Postal Abbreviation:** AZ

Sales Tax: 5-5½%.

Flagstaff

For over a century, Flagstaff has been a symbol of Western expansion and exploration. Early pioneers celebrated their settlement by flying the American flag on Independence Day in 1876, thus naming their outpost. Today this sprawling, dusty town offers more than appears at first glance. If your schedule allows, consider Flagstaff as more than just a point of entry to the Grand Canyon. Some of the most spectacular natural treasures of northern Arizona lie in the immediate vicinity of the town. A hike in the nearby San Francisco mountains or a slide at the rocky creeks will leave an indelible memory.

Practical Information and Orientation

Emergency: 911. **Police/Medical Assistance,** 774-1414.

Visitor Information: Flagstaff Chamber of Commerce, 101 W. Rte. 66 (800-842-7293 or 774-9541), across from the Amtrak station. Free city map, national forest map $2. The friendly folks here will help you plan your trip anywhere in Arizona. Open Mon.-Sat. 8am-9pm, Sun. and holidays 8am-5pm. **Special Events Hotline,** 779-3733; 24-hr. recorded message.

Tours: Blue Goose Backpacker Tours and Travels, 774-6731 or in Arizona 800-332-1944. Full-day guided tours and trips to: the Grand Canyon ($22); Sedona and Oak Creek ($15); and Walnut Canyon, Wupatki, Indian ruins and Sunset Crater ($17). All tours run daily mid-March-mid-Oct. Leave from Motel DuBeau International Hostel at 19 W. Phoenix Ave. (See Accommodations below.) **Gray Line/Nava-Hopi,** 774-5003; 800-892-8687 outside AZ. One-day sightseeing tours to: the Grand Canyon ($32); Monument Valley and the Navajo Reservation and Monument ($74); the Hopi Reservation and Painted Desert ($58); and the Museum of N. Arizona, Sunset Crater, Wupatki, and Walnut Canyon (May-Oct.; $32). Kids under 13 ride ½-price on all tours. All tours except Grand Canyon run early April-mid-Nov. Grand Canyon runs year-round. Reservations required. Purchase tickets at the Amtrak and Greyhound stations.

Amtrak: 1 E. Santa Fe Ave. (774-8679 or 800-872-7245). 1 train per day to Los Angeles (11 hr.; $85) and Albuquerque (6 hr.; $80). 1 connecting shuttle bus to the Grand Canyon ($12). Open daily 5:45-10am, 11am-2pm, 2:30-6pm, and 7-10:30pm.

Buses: Greyhound, 399 S. Malpais Lane (774-4573), across from NAU campus, 5 blocks southwest of the train station on U.S. 89A. To: Phoenix (5/day; $21); Albuquerque (6/day; $74); Los Angeles (5/day; $112); and Las Vegas via Kingman, AZ (3/day; $51). Terminal open 24 hrs. **Gray Line/Nava-Hopi,** 774-5003; 800-892-8687 outside AZ. Shuttle buses to the Grand Canyon (2/day; $25 round-trip, $13 with Greyhound Ameripass). First leaves Flagstaff at 8:20am, last one at 5:30pm.

Public Transport: Pine County Transit, 2323 N. Walgreen St. (779-6624 or 779-6635). 3 routes covering most of town. Fare 75¢; seniors, disabled persons, and kids 60¢. Runs once per hr. In summer a free trolley runs to the mall Mon.-Sat.

Camping Equipment Rental: Peace Surplus, 14 W. Santa Fe Ave. (779-4521), 1 block from the hostel. Daily rental of dome tents ($5-8), packs ($5), stoves ($3), plus a good stock of cheap outdoor gear. Credit card or cash deposit required. Open Mon.-Fri. 8:30am-9pm, Sat. 8:30am-7pm, Sun. 9am-6pm.

Bike Rental: Cosmic Cycles, 113 S. San Francisco St. (779-1092), downtown. Mountain bikes $20/day. City bikes with wide tires $10/day. Open Mon.-Fri. 9am-6pm, Sun. 11am-4pm.

Taxi: Dream Taxi, (774-2934). Open 24 hrs.; airport to downtown $9.50.

Car Rental: Budget Rent-A-Car, 100 N. Humphreys St. (774-2763), within walking distance of the hostels. Guarantees the lowest rates in the competitive Flagstaff car rental market. Economy cars from $27/day, with 100 free mi., 19¢ each additional mi. $129 weekly, 1050 free mi. Open daily 7am-9pm. Must be 21 or older with a major credit card or at least $200 cash deposit. Ask for Tom about *Let's Go* discount rates.

Post Office: 104 N. Agassiz (524-2440). Open Mon.-Fri. 9am-3pm. **ZIP code:** 86001. General Delivery at 2400 Postal Blvd., 86001-9999.

Area Code: 602.

Flagstaff is easily accessible by U.S. 89A from the north and the south. Downtown lies at the intersection of **Beaver Street** and **Route 66**. Within ½-mi. of this spot are both bus stations, the three youth hostels, the chamber of commerce, and several inexpensive restaurants. Other commercial establishments lie on **South Sitgreaves Street** (U.S. 89A), near the NAU campus.

Because Flagstaff is a mountain town, it stays cooler than much of the rest of the state and receives frequent afternoon thundershowers. You can walk around most of downtown, but to get anywhere worth seeing, rent a car or take a tour bus.

Accommodations and Camping

When buzzing swarms of tourists descend upon Flagstaff in the summer, accommodation prices shoot up. However, the town is blessed with three rival youth hostels, all of which offer good services in order to lure *Let's Go*-toting budget travelers. For cheap motels cruise historic Rte. 66. Camping in **Coconino National Forest** surrounding the city is a pleasant and inexpensive alternative.

Motel Du Beau, 19 W. Phoenix (774-6731 or 800-332-1944), just behind the train station. A registered National Landmark hotel, built in 1929, which once hosted L.A. film stars and Chicago gangsters. Now a top-rated hostel in the Southwest, offering superlative service to hostelers. Free ride to and from airport, bus and train stations. Free breakfast and coffee all day. Kitchen, library, nightly videos, gift and necessities shop. No charge to borrow bikes. 4 campsites. $11. Open 6am-midnight.

Downtowner Independent Youth Hostel, 19 S. San Francisco (774-8461). Flexible management will send a Mercedes to shuttle between hostel and bus stations. Decent rooms with wooden floors and comfortable beds. Kitchen, lounge, free bikes and free coffee. Private rooms $16/person, more crowded $11. Bunks $9. Linen included. Open mid-May to mid-Aug. Open 7am-9:30pm.

The Weatherford Hotel (HI/AYH), 23 N. Leroux (774-2731). Friendly management and convenient location. Dorm rooms, baths in rooms and halls, kitchen, and a cozy common area; ride board in lobby. Curfew midnight. $10. Required sleepsheet $1. Private singles $22. Doubles $24. Open daily 7am-10am, noon-1pm, and 5-10pm. Guests enjoy ½ off the cover price at **Charly's,** downstairs, which has live music.

KOA, 5803 N. Hwy. 89 (526-9926), 6 mi. northeast of Flagstaff. Municipal bus routes stop near this beautiful campground. Showers, restrooms and free nightly movies. Sites $19 for 2 people. Each additional person $3.

You'll probably need a car to reach the **public campgrounds** that ring the city. Campgrounds at higher elevations close during the winter; many are small and fill up quickly during the summer, particularly on weekends when Phoenicians flock to the mountains. If you stake out your site by 3pm you shouldn't encounter problems. National forest sites are usually $2 to $3 per night. Pick up a **Coconino National Forest** map ($2) in Flagstaff at the Chamber of Commerce (see Practical Information above). **Lake View,** 13 mi. southeast on Forest Hwy. 3 (U.S. 89A), has 30 sites ($7). **Bonito,** two mi. east at Forest Rd. 545, off U.S. 89, has 44 sites at Sunset Crater ($7). All have running water and flush toilets. Those (and only those) who can live without amenities can camp for free on any national forest land outside the designated campsites, unless you see signs to the contrary. For more info, call the Coconino Forest Service (556-7400; Mon.-Fri. 7:30am-4:30pm; 24-hr. **emergency** 526-0600).

Food and Entertainment

To suit every European taste, Flagstaff offers an odd blend of cafés and diners. Downtown eateries serve great sandwiches for as low as $4, but to get a real meal in a real restaurant be prepared to foot a fat bill.

Macy's, 14 S. Beaver St. (774-2243), behind Motel DuBeau. This tourist and college student hangout serves fresh pasta ($3.25-5.25), plus a wide variety of vegetarian entrées, pastries, and espresso-based drinks. Open daily 7am-8pm; food served until 7pm.

Café Espresso, 16 N. San Francisco, near the Weatherford. Fine danishes ($1.50), plus various sandwiches and coffees ($1). The artsy staff makes a point of serving healthy food and keeping the lights low. Open daily 7am-9pm.

Alpine Pizza, 7 Leroux St. (779-4109) and 2400 E. Santa Fe Ave. (779-4138). A popular spot for beer, pool, and (oh, yeah) pizza. Excellent, huge *calzones* ($4.75) and *strombolis* ($5.50). Alpine with whole wheat crusts and a variety of toppings. Open Mon.-Thurs. 11am-11pm, Fri.-Sat. 11am-2am, Sun. 2-11pm. Must be 21 Tues. and Thurs. after 3pm.

Main St. Bar and Grill, 4 S. San Francisco (774-1519), across from the Downtowner. When the vegetarian meals and non-alcoholic drinks of the cafés get too healthy, try the delicious barbecued red meat ($2-11), the Buttery Texas Toast, and the calorie-laden but excellent selection of beers. Live music Fri.-Sat. at 8pm. No cover. Open Mon.-Sat. 11am-midnight, Sun. noon-10pm.

While there isn't much to see within Flagstaff proper, the one or two nights you spend here could be full of lively entertainment. Party animals with a taste for the wild West will enjoy the **Museum Club,** 3404 E. Rte. 66 (526-9434). Known locally as the **Zoo**, it rocks with live country-western and cowboys and cowgirls. The cover charge is $3 but you can call **Dream VIP Taxi** (774-2934) for your free round-trip ride. Below the Weatherford HI/AYH, **Charley's,** 23 N. Leroux (779-1919) plays great blues on weekends. HI/AYH hostelers pay half the cover.

Near Flagstaff

Because most of Flagstaff's legions of tourists are Grand Canyon-bound, they miss the many other (uncrowded) natural wonders surrounding the city. Seventeen mi. north on U.S. 89 lies **Sunset Crater National Monument** (556-7042). This volcanic crater erupted in 1065, and formed cinder cones and lava beds; oxidized iron in the cinder gives the pre-nuclear crater its dramatic dusky color. (**Visitors center** open daily 8am-5pm; in winter may close due to snow. $3 per car or $1 per person.) A half-mi. self-guided tour wanders through the plain's surreal lava formations, 1½ mi. east of the visitors center. All interpretive materials along the trail are also available in Spanish, Dutch, French, and German. Guided tours of the lava tubes begin daily at noon and 3pm; aspiring spelunkers can rent a hard hat and light from the visitors center, don a coat, and explore as far as they dare.

Eighteen mi. north and several hundred feet down from Sunset Crater on a scenic loop road rests **Wupatki National Monument.** The ancestors of the Hopi moved here over a thousand years ago when they found the black-and-red soil ideal for agriculture. However, 300 years later, droughts and over-farming precipitated the abandonment of the pueblos. Some of the Southwest's most scenic ruins, these stone houses perched on the sides of *arroyos* in view of Monument Valley and the San Francisco Peaks just for your vacation pleasure. Five major abandoned pueblos stretch along a 14-mi. park road from U.S. 89 to the visitors center. The largest and most accessible, **Wupatki Ruin,** rises three stories high. Below the ruin, you can see one of Arizona's two stone ballcourts, the sites of ancient games employing a rubber ball and a stone hoop in a circular court. Get info at the **Wupatki Ruin Visitors Center** (774-7000; open daily 7am-7pm, off-season 8am-5pm). When visiting Wupatki or Sunset Crater you can camp at the park's **Bonito Campground,** just across from the Sunset Crater Visitors Center. (Running water, no hookups. Sites $6. Overflow campers can pitch their tents for free in the National Forest.)

In the 13th century, the Sinagua people built more than 300 rooms under hanging ledges in the walls of a 400-ft.-deep canyon. The remaining structures form the **Walnut Canyon National Monument,** seven mi. east of Flagstaff off I-40. From a glassed-in observation deck in the visitors center you can survey the whole canyon; a stunning variety of plants sprout out of its striated grey walls. A trail snakes down from the visitors center past 25 cliff dwellings; markers along the trail describe aspects of Sinagua life and identify the plants they used for food, dyes, medicine and hunting. Rangers lead hikes down a rugged trail to the original Ranger Cabin and many remote cliff dwellings. These strenuous two-and-a-half-hour hikes leave daily from the visitors center at 10am. Hiking boots and long pants are required. A walk along the main trail takes about 45 minutes. (Monument open daily 7am-6pm; Labor Day-Memorial Day 8am-5pm. Admission $1 per person.)

The **San Francisco Peaks** are the huge, snow-capped mountains visible to the north of Flagstaff. **Humphrey's Peak**—the highest point in Arizona at 12,670 ft.—is sacred to the Hopi, who believe that the Kachina spirits live there. Nearby **Mt. Agassiz** has the area's best skiing. The **Fairfield Snow Bowl** operates four lifts from mid-December through mid-April; its 32 trails receive an average of 8½ ft. of powder each winter. Lift tickets cost $28 on weekdays, $26 on weekends. Call the **Fairfield Resort** switchboard (779-1951; 24 hrs.) for information on ski conditions, transportation, and accommodations.

During the summer, the peaks are perfect for hiking. You can see the North Rim of the Grand Canyon, the Painted Desert, and countless square miles of Arizona and Utah from the top of Humphrey's Peak when the air is clear. Those not up to the hike should take the **chairlift** (20-30 min.) up the mountain (779-1951; runs weekends and holidays 10am-4pm; $7, seniors $5, ages 6-12 $3.50). The vista from the top of the lift proves almost as stunning. Picnic facilities and a cafeteria are open from May to October. Since the mountains occupy national forest land, camping is free, but no organized campsites are available. To reach the peaks, take U.S. 180 about seven mi. north to the Fairfield Snow Bowl turnoff. **Gray Line/Nava-Hopi** offers a tour of the Museum of Northern Arizona, Walnut Canyon, Sunset Crater, and Wupatki National Monument (see Flagstaff: Practical Information), but no other public transportation is available to these sights, or, during the summer, to the San Francisco Peaks.

From Flagstaff to Phoenix

The main thoroughfare between the two cities is **I-17.** Route **U.S. 89A** traces a more circuitous path between Flagstaff and Phoenix, but it makes up for the longer travel time with more awesome scenery—the 27-mi. segment from Flagstaff to Sedona affords a spectacular view of the green shady mountains of the **Oak Creek Canyon.** Once in Sedona, if you have four wheels, take **Schnebley Hill Road,** a 13-mi. dirt road that winds through the rugged backcountry with the speed of a tortoise and the charm of a snake. A few miles south of Flagstaff, U.S. 89A descends into Oak Creek Canyon, a trout-stocked creek bordered by trees and reddish canyon cliffs. You can pull over to swim or fish at several points along the route; look for **Slide Rock,** an algae-covered natural water chute. National forest **campsites** are scattered along 12 mi. of Oak Creek Canyon on the highway. Arrive early; sites fill quickly. Most of the campgrounds are open from April to October. Call the forest service (282-4119) for info. **Manzanita** has a three-day limit, and **Cave Spring** and **Pine Flat** have seven-day limits. All have running water and toilets. (Sites $8.)

Twenty-seven mi. south of Flagstaff, the walls of Oak Creek Canyon open up to reveal the striking red rock formations surrounding **Sedona,** the setting for many western movies. The town itself is an incongruous blend of wealthy retirees and organic trend-followers. For info on backcountry camping, contact the **Oak Creek Canyon Chamber of Commerce** at 602-282-7722.

Twenty mi. southwest of Sedona (take U.S. 89A to Rte. 279 and continue through the town of Cottonwood) lies **Tuzigoot National Monument,** which consists of a dramatic Sinaguan ruin overlooking the Verde Valley. (Open daily 8am-7pm. Entrance fee $3/vehicle.)

From Sedona, Rte. 179 leads south to I-17. An amazing five-story cliff dwelling sits 10 mi. south back on I-17. **Montezuma Castle National Monument** (567-3322) is a 20-room adobe abode. The dwellings were constructed around the year 1100, when overpopulation in the Flagstaff area forced the Sinagua south into the Verde Valley along Beaver Creek. Visitors can view the "castle" from a path below. (Path open daily 7am-7pm, visitors center open daily 8am-6pm. $3 per car.) Eleven mi. away is **Montezuma Well National Monument,** a beautiful lake formed by the collapse of an underground cavern which served as a source of water for the Sinagua who lived here. (Open daily 7am-7pm. Free.)

If you're familiar with the stereotypes about so-called "New Agers" but have never met or seen them in action, have we got the place for you. From Montezuma Castle, follow I-17; from the turnoff at Cordes Junction, 28 mi. south, a three-mi. dirt road leads to **Arcosanti.** When completed around the turn of the century, Arcosanti will be a self-sufficient community embodying Italian architect Paolo Soleri's concept of "arcology," somewhat mysteriously defined as "architecture and ecology working together as one integral process." Budgetarians will appreciate the architect's vision of a city where personal cars are obsolete. The complete city, with its subterranean parks, will surprise even the most imaginative Legoland architect. (Tours daily every hr. 10am-4pm. Open to the public daily 9am-5pm. $4 donation.) For more info, contact Arcosanti, HC 74, P.O. Box 4136, Mayer 86333 (632-7135). **Arizona Central** buses (see Phoenix: Practical Information) can drop you off in **Cordez Junction,** 1½ mi. away from Arcosanti, but no tours go there.

Grand Canyon

Here's the story of a lovely canyon—227 mi. long, 13 mi. wide, and over one mi. deep—big enough to accommodate the countless pilgrims (such as the Bradys) that travel to this tourist magnet. One day, long before Bobby and Cindy's time, the Colorado River met this mountain range and decided to disobey the usual laws governing the flow of rivers and cut *through* the mountains instead of going around them. Greg knew that it was much more than a hunch that the river would someday form a canyon in the soft limestone, sandstone, and shale, exposing countless families of strata. The result, as Martha might add impetuously, is how the Canyon became a glimpse into millions of years of geological evolution. Of course, as Mike points out, the mind-boggling size is reason enough to visit the Grand Canyon, but a short trip will not allow you to appreciate the canyon's unbelievable sublimity. Alice just leers, pining for Sam.

That's the way this became the **Grand Canyon National Park,** which consists of three areas: the **South Rim,** including Grand Canyon Village; the **North Rim;** and the canyon gorge itself. The slightly lower, slightly more accessible South Rim draws 10 times more visitors than the higher, more heavily forested North Rim.

The 13-mi. distance that traverses the canyon equals a two-day adventure for sturdy hikers, while the 214 mi. of road prove a good five-hour drive for those who would rather explore from above. Despite commercial exploitation, the Grand Canyon is still untamed; every year several careless hikers take what locals morbidly refer to as "the 12-second tour;" please remember to observe all safety precautions and the rules of common sense; drinking and climbing don't mix.

South Rim

In summer, everything on two legs or four wheels converges from miles around on this side of the Grand Canyon. If you plan to visit during this mobfest, make reservations for lodging or campsites, and mules if you want them—and prepare to battle crowds. During the winter there are fewer tourists; however, the weather is brisk and many of the canyon's hotels and facilities are closed.

Practical Information and Orientation

Emergency: 911.

Park Headquarters: 638-7888. Open daily 8am-5pm. Information on programs 24 hrs.

Tourist Center: 638-2626. Further information about tours, taxis, trips, etc. Ask for their *Trip Planner.*

Lodging Reservations: Reservations Dept., Grand Canyon National Park Lodges, Grand Canyon 86023 (638-2401).

Nava-Hopi Bus Lines: 774-5003. Leaves Flagstaff Greyhound station for Grand Canyon daily at 8:20am and 3:15pm; departs from Bright Angel Lodge at Grand Canyon for Flagstaff daily 10:20am and 5:30pm. $12.50 each way, children $6.50; $2 entrance fee for Canyon not included.

Transportation Information Desk: In **Bright Angel Lodge** (638-2631). Reservations for mule rides, bus tours, Phantom Ranch, and taxi. Open daily 6am-6pm.

Equipment Rental: Babbit's General Store, in Mather Center Grand Canyon Village (638-2262 or 638-2234), near Yavapai Lodge. Rents comfortable hiking boots ($7 for the first day), sleeping bags ($7-8), tents ($15), and camping gear. Open daily 8am-8pm.

Post Office: next to Babbit's (638-2512). Open Mon.-Fri. 9am-4:30pm, Sat. 11am-1pm. Lobby open Mon.-Sat. 5am-10pm. **ZIP code:** 86023.

Area Code: 602.

From Las Vegas, the fastest route to the Canyon is U.S. 93 south to I-40 east, and then Rte. 64 north. From Flagstaff, I-40 east to U.S. 89 north is the most scenic; from there, Rte. 64 north takes you to the Desert View entrance in the eastern part of the park. The **entrance fee** to the Grand Canyon is $10 per car and $4 for travelers using other modes of transportation—even bus passengers must pay. Upon arriving in the South Rim, grab a copy of *The Guide*, a small but comprehensive reference guide available at the entrance gate and the visitors center (free).

The National Park Service operates two free **shuttle buses.** The **West Rim Loop** runs between West Rim Junction and Hermit's Rest, with stops at all the scenic vistas along the way (operates Memorial Day-Labor Day every 15 min. 7:30am-sunset). The **Village Loop** covers Bright Angel Lodge, West Rim Junction, the visitors center, Grand Canyon Village, and Yavapai Point (operates year-round every 15 min. 6:30am-9:30pm).

Thanks to the efforts of the park service, much of the South Rim is wheelchair-accessible; pick up the free pamphlet *Accessibility Guide* at the visitors center. Pets are allowed in the park, provided they are on a leash. Pets may not go below the rim. There is a **kennel** on the South Rim; call 638-2631, ext. 6549.

Accommodations and Camping

Compared with the six million years it took the Colorado River to cut the Grand Canyon, the six months it takes to get a room on the South Rim is a blink of an eye. Since the youth hostel closed in 1990, it is now nearly impossible to sleep indoors anywhere near the South Rim without reservations or a wad of cash; if you arrive unprepared, check at the visitors center (see Practical Information above) for vacancies.

Most accommodations on the South Rim other than those listed below are very expensive. The campsites listed usually fill by 10am in summer. Campground overflow usually winds up in the **Kaibab National Forest,** adjacent to the park along the southern border, where you can pull off a dirt road and camp for free. Sleeping in cars is *not* permitted within the park, but is allowed in the Kaibab Forest. The Nava-Hopi bus pauses at Bright Angel Lodge, where you can check your luggage for 50¢ per day. Reservations for **Bright Angel Lodge, Maswik Lodge, Trailer Village,** and more expensive rooms can be made through Grand Canyon National Park Lodges, P.O. Box 699, Grand Canyon, AZ 86023 (602-638-2401). All rooms should be reserved six months in advance for the summer, six weeks for the winter.

Bright Angel Lodge, Grand Canyon Village. Scout-style rustic cabins with plumbing but no heat. Very convenient to Bright Angel Trail and both shuttle buses. Singles $32-53, depending on how much plumbing you want. Each additional person $9.

Maswik Lodge, Grand Canyon Village. Small, clean cabins with shower $45 (singles or doubles). Each additional person $7. Reservations required.

Mather Campground, Grand Canyon Village, half-mi. from the visitors center. Shady, relatively isolated sites without hookups $10. Make reservations through Ticketron outlets 8 weeks in advance.

Trailer Village, next to Mather Campground. Clearly designed with the RV in mind. Campsites resemble driveways and lack seclusion. Sites with hookup $15 for 2 people. Each additional person 50¢.

Desert View Campsite, 25 mi. east of Grand Canyon Village. No hookups. Sites $8. Open May 15-Oct. 30. No reservations accepted; arrive early.

Ten-X Campground in the Kaibab National Forest, (638-2443), 10 mi. south of Grand Canyon Village on Rte. 64. Chemical toilets, water. Sites $10. Open April-Nov. No reservations, no hookups.

Phantom Ranch, on the canyon floor, a 4-hr. hike down the Kaibab Trail. Reservations required 6 months in advance for the April-Oct. season, but check at the Bright Angel Transportation Desk (see above) for last-minute cancellations. The ranch has a snack bar and serves expensive meals; bring your own food to conserve money. Don't show up without reservations made well in advance—they'll send you back up the trail, on foot. Dorm beds $20. Cabins for 1 or 2 people $53, each additional person $11.

Food

Fast food has not sunk its greasy talons into the rim of the Canyon. While you might find meals for fast-food prices, uniformly bland cuisine is harder to locate. **Babbit's General Store** (638-2262), in Maswik Lodge, is more than just a restaurant—it's a supermarket, in fact, its a superdupermarket. Stock up on trail mix, water, and gear. (Open daily 8am-8pm; deli open 8am-7pm.) **The Maswik Cafeteria,** also in Maswik Lodge, has a variety of inexpensive options grill-made and served in a swish cafeteria atmosphere. (Open daily 6am-10pm.) **Bright Angel Restaurant,** in Bright Angel Lodge (638-6389), has hot sandwiches from $4 to $6. (Open daily 6:30am-10pm.) The soda fountain at Bright Angel Lodge offers 16 flavors of ice cream (one scoop $1) to hikers emerging from the Bright Angel Trail. (Open daily 11am-9pm.)

Activities

At your first glimpse of the canyon, you will realize that the best way to see it is to hike down into it, an enterprise that is much harder than it looks. Much sorrow has come to the plaid-clad, would-be hiker armed with a telephoto lens and an unopened can of Diet Coke—park rangers average over three rescues per day in this National Park with the highest fatality rate in the country. Even the young at heart must remember that what seems to be an easy hike downhill can become a nightmarish 100° incline on the return journey. Heat exhaustion, the second greatest threat after slipping, is marked by a monstrous headache and termination of sweating. You *must* take two quarts of water along; it's absolutely necessary. A list of hiking safety tips can be found in the *Grand Canyon Guide,* available at the entrance gate and the visitors center, and should be read thoroughly, underlined, and annotated before hitting the trail. Overestimating your limits is a common mistake, and parents should think twice about bringing children more than a mile down the trails—kids have long memories and might exact revenge when they get bigger.

The two most accessible trails into the Canyon are the **Bright Angel Trail,** which begins at the Bright Angel Lodge, and **South Kaibab Trail,** originating at Yaki Point. Bright Angel is outfitted to accommodate the average tourist, with rest houses stationed strategically 1.5 mi. and three mi. from the rim. **Indian Gardens,** 4.5 mi. down, offers the tired hiker restrooms, picnic tables, and blessed shade; all three rest stops usually have water in the summer. Kaibab is trickier, steeper, and lacks shade or water, but it rewards the intrepid with a better view of the canyon's hypnotic contours. Consult the *Guide* for a more detailed description of these trails, and remember that hiking back up is much, *much* more arduous and takes twice as long as the hike down.

If you've made arrangements to spend the night on the canyon floor, the best route is to hike down the **Kaibab Trail** (3-4 hr., depending on conditions) and back up the Bright Angel (7-8 hr.) the following day. The hikes down Bright Angel Trail to Indian Gardens and **Plateau Point,** six mi. out, where you can look down 1360 ft. to the river, make excellent daytrips. But start early (around 7am) to avoid the worst heat. One local rule: if you meet a mule train, stand quietly by the side of the trail and obey the wrangler's instructions so as not to spook the animals. Backcountry permits are required for any overnight stay.

If you're not up to descending into the canyon, follow the **Rim Trail** east to Grandeur Point and the **Yavapai Geological Museum,** or west to **Hermit's Rest,** using the shuttles as desired. There are no fences or railings between you and certain death—watch your footing. The Eastern Rim Trail swarms at dusk with sunset-watchers, and the Yavapai Museum at the end of the trail has a sweeping view of the canyon during the day from a glassed-in observation deck. The Western Rim Trail leads to several incredible vistas, notably **Hopi Point,** a favorite for sunsets, and the **Abyss,** where the canyon wall drops almost vertically to the Tonto Plateau 3000 ft. below. To watch a sunset, show up at your chosen spot 45 minutes beforehand and watch the earth-tones and pastels melt into darkness.

The park service rangers present a variety of free informative talks and hikes. Listings of each day's events are available at the visitors center or in the *Grand Canyon Guide* (10¢), available everywhere in the village. A free presentation, at 8:30pm in the summer and 7:30pm in the winter, highlights some aspect of the Grand Canyon in **Mather Amphitheater,** behind the visitors center. The younger set will be kept busy with the *Grand Canyon Young Adventurer,* a magazine full of stories of the canyon and a variety of puzzles for children ages 5 to 12. By finishing all the games inside, the kids can become Junior Rangers, an early civil-service position which just might lead to the presidency.

In addition to the freebies offered by the National Park Service, a variety of **commercial tours** cover the South Rim. Prices for tours by helicopter, airplane, inflatable raft, and mule soar beyond the reach of most budget travelers. You can book plane and chopper tours at **Tusayan,** seven mi. south of the Grand Canyon Village. Of the three bus tours, the Sunset and West Rim tours cover places mostly accessible by free shuttle buses. You may decide to take the tour to **West Desert View** (4 hr.; 2 per day in summer, 1 per day in winter; tickets $17, children $8.50), which provides the only non-automobile access to Desert View—26 mi. east of the village—as well as to the Painted Desert to the east. Contact the Bright Angel Transportation Desk (638-2401) for information on all commercial tours.

North Rim

If you are coming from Utah or Nevada, or if you simply want a more solitary Grand Canyon experience, consider the North Rim. Here the canyon experience is a bit wilder, a bit cooler, and much more serene—with a view equally groovy as that from the South Rim. Unfortunately, because it is less frequented, it's tough to get to the North Rim by public transportation. The only rim-to-rim transportation available is from **Transcanyon,** P.O. Box 348, Grand Canyon, AZ 86023 (638-2820), from late May to mid-October ($50, $85 round-trip. Departs South Rim 1:30pm, arrives at North Rim at 6pm. Call for reservations.) Canyon visitors are wary of those on foot, making hitching a non-option. From the South Rim, the North Rim is a 200-plus-mi., stunningly scenic drive away. Take Rte. 64 east to U.S. 89 north, which runs into Alt. 89; off Alt. 89, take Rte. 67 south to the edge. Between the first snows at the end of October and May 15, Rte. 67 is closed to traffic. Then, only a snowmobile can get you to the North Rim. The **National Park Service Information** desk is in the lobby of **Grand Canyon Lodge** (638-2611), and is open 24 hrs. The lodge dangles at the very end of Rte. 67. In an **emergency** call 911.

Accommodations, Camping, and Food

Since camping within the confines of the Grand Canyon National Park is limited to designated campgrounds, only a lucky minority of North Rim visitors get to spend the night "right there." If you can't get in-park lodgings, visit the **Kaibab National Forest,** which runs from north of Jacob Lake to the park entrance. Camp in an established site, or pull off the main road onto any forest road and camp for free. Campsite reservations can be made through MISTIX (800-365-2267). If you don't have reservations, mark your territory by 10am.

Canyonlands International Youth Hostel, 143 E. South, Kanab, UT 84741 (801-644-5554), 1½ hrs. north of the Grand Canyon on U.S. 89, an equal distance south of Bryce Canyon. Errol fixes you up with a private room and bath, plus a do-it-yourself breakfast, all for the amazingly low price of $9. Office open daily 8-10am and 5-10pm. Reservations recommended.

Grand Canyon Lodge, on the edge of the rim. Call TW Recreational Services, 801-586-7686. Doubles from $50. Front desk open 24 hrs. Open in summer daily 8am-7pm, off-season Mon.-Fri. 8am-5pm.

Jacob's Lake Inn, 44 mi. north of the North Rim at Jacob Lake (643-7232). Cabins $48 for 2, $59 for 4, $65 for 6. Pricier motel units. Also offers 50 campsites at $10 per vehicle. Half the sites available first-come, first-served; others can be reserved through MISTIX (800-283-2267; $7 fee). Has dining room and coffee shop.

North Rim Campground, on Rte. 67 near the rim. You really cannot see into the canyon from the pine-covered site, but you know it's there. Near food store; has laundry facilities, recreation room and showers. Sites $10. Reserve by calling MISTIX, 800-365-2267.

Kaibab National Forest Sites: DeMotte Park Campground, 5 mi. north of the park entrance. 25 sites ($7). First-come, first-served. Open camping also permitted in the National Forest surrounding the Grand Canyon.

Both of the eating options on the North Rim are placed strategically at the **Grand Canyon Lodge.** The restaurant slaps together dinners for $4.50 to $12 and breakfast for $3.50. A skimpy sandwich at the "buffeteria" costs about $2.50. North Rim hostelers are better off eating in Kanab or stopping at the Jacob Lake Inn for snacks and great shakes.

Activities

A half-mi. paved trail takes you from the Grand Canyon Lodge to **Bright Angel Point,** which commands a seraphic view of the Canyon. **Point Imperial,** an 11-mi. drive from the lodge, overlooks Marble Canyon and the Painted Desert.

The North Rim offers nature walks and evening programs, both at the North Rim Campground and at Grand Canyon Lodge (see Accommodations). Check at the info desk or campground bulletin boards for schedules. Half-day mule trips ($30) descend into the canyon from Grand Canyon Lodge (638-2292; open daily 7am-8pm). If you'd prefer to tour the Canyon wetly, pick up a *Grand Canyon River Trip Operators* brochure and select among the 20 companies which offer trips.

On warm evenings, the Grand Canyon Lodge fills with an eclectic group of international travelers, U.S. families, and rugged adventurers. Some frequent the **Lodge Saloon** for drinks, jukebox disco, and the enthusiasm of a young crowd. Others look to the warm air rising from the canyon, a full moon, and the occasional shooting stars for their intoxication at day's end.

Northeastern Arizona

Canyon de Chelly National Monument

While not matching the Grand Canyon's awesome dimensions, Canyon de Chelly more than makes up in beauty what it lacks in size. In the aptly-named Beautiful Valley, the canyon's 30- to 1000-ft. sandstone cliffs tower over the sandy, fertile valley created by the Chelly River. The oldest ruins in the eroded walls of the Canyon date back to the Anasazi civilization of the 12th century. By the 1800s, the Navajo sought refuge here during hostilities with European Americans. In what was to become a sickening pattern, dozens of Native American women and children were shot by the Spanish in 1805; the sight of the executions is now called Massacre Cave. Kit Carson starved the Navajo out of the Canyon in the 1860s. Today, Navajo farmers once again inhabit the canyon, cultivating the lush soil and living in traditional Navajo dwellings, *hogans.*

The land constituting Canyon de Chelly National Monument is owned by the Navajo Nation and is administered by the National Park Service. All but one of the park trails are closed to public travel unless hikers are escorted by Navajo representatives. Although the park service offers free short tours into the canyon, the only way to get far into the canyon or close to the Anasazi ruins is to hire a Navajo guide. Check with the **visitors center** (674-5436), two mi. east of Chinle on Navajo Rte. 64, off U.S. 191, which houses a small museum. The staff can arrange for guides and tours at any time of day, although guides usually arrive at the visitors center at about 9am. Guides generally charge $7 per hour to walk or drive into the canyon. Advance reservations are helpful, but you can try dropping in. (Open daily 8am-6pm; off-season 8am-5pm.) To drive into the canyon with a guide, you must provide your own four-wheel-drive vehicle. Horseback tours can be arranged through **Justin's Horse Rental,** on South Rim Dr. (674-5678), at the mouth of the canyon. (Open daily approximately 8am-6pm. Horses "rented" at $7/hr.; mandatory guide "hired" at $7/hr. If you have a philosophical bent, notice that the horse's time is worth as much as the human guide's, and consider the social implications—or at least give a generous tip.) **Twin Trail Tours** (674-3466) also rents horses. For complete service listings, pick up a copy of *Canyon Overlook.*

Seven mi. from the visitors center, the one-mi. trail to **White House Ruin,** off South Canyon Rd., winds down a 400-ft. face, past a Navajo farm and traditional hogan, through an orchard, and across the stream wash. The only one you can walk without a guide, this trail is best in the spring when you can hike in the canyon heat with the cool stream swirling about your ankles. Take one of the paved **Rim Drives** (North Rim 44 mi., South Rim 36 mi.), which skirt the edge of the 300- to 700-ft. cliffs. The South Rim is the more dramatic. Try to make it all the way to the **Spider Rock Overlook,** 20 mi. from the visitors center, a narrow sandstone monolith that towers hundreds of feet above the canyon floor. Native American lore has it that the whitish rock at the top of Spider Rock contains bleached bones of victims of one of the *kachina* spirits, Spider Woman, or her husband Peter Parker. A written guide to the White House Ruins and the North or South Rim Drives costs 50¢ at the visitors center.

Camp for free in the park's **Cottonwood Campground,** a half-mi. from the visitors center. This giant campground in a pretty cottonwood grove rumbles at night with the din of a hungry army, and stray dogs tend to wander the site. Don't expect to find any budget accommodations in nearby Chinle or anywhere else in Navajo territory. Farmington, NM, and Cortez, CO, are the closest major cities with cheap lodging.

It's impossible to take an ugly approach to the park. The most common route is from Chambers, 75 mi. south of the park, at the intersection of I-40 and U.S. 191. The other approach is from the north, where U.S. 191 leaves U.S. 160 in Colorado near Four Corners, 50 mi. from the monument. Public transportation is not available.

Monument Valley and Navajo National Monument

You may have seen the red rock towers of **Monument Valley Navajo Tribal Park** (801-727-3287) in one of numerous westerns filmed here. Rather ironically, the 1000-ft. monoliths helped boost "injun"-killer John Wayne to heights of movie slaughter. The best and cheapest way to see the valley is via the Park's looping 17-mi. **Valley Drive.** This dirt road winds in and out of the most dramatic monuments, including the famous paired **Mittens** and the slender **Totem Pole.** The gaping ditches, large rocks, and mudholes on this road will do horrible things to your car: drive at your own risk, and hold your breath. Much of the valley can be reached only in a sturdy four-wheel-drive vehicle or by a long hike. In winter, snow laces the rocky towers, and almost all the tourists flee. Inquire about snow and road conditions at the Flagstaff Chamber of

PLACE
STAMP
HERE

HOSTELLING INTERNATIONAL

American Youth Hostels
Membership Services Department
P.O. Box 37613
Washington, D.C. 20013-7613

Commerce (800-842-7293). (Admission $3, seniors and kids $2. No National Park passes honored.)

The park entrance is 24 mi. north on U.S. 163 from the town of Kayenta and the intersection with U.S. 160. (Park open May-Sept. daily 7am-8pm; off-season 8am-5pm. Admission $2.50, seniors and kids 6-12 $1.)

Twenty mi. past Kayenta on U.S. 160, Rte. 564 takes you nine mi. to **Navajo National Monument.** This stunning site consists of three Anasazi cliff-dwellings, including **Keet Seel,** the best-preserved site in the Southwest. Inscription House has closed, and entrance into Keet Seel and **Betatakin,** a 135-room complex, is limited to 25 people per day in ranger-led groups. (Tours daily at 9am, noon, and 2pm; try to make reservations at least two months in advance. Write Navajo National Monument, Tanalea 86044.) For $50, Navajo guides will put you on a horse, lead you down the eight-mi. trail, and leave you with a ranger to explore the 400-year-old ruins left by the Anasazi. Allow a full day for the ride and the strenuous hike. Rangers also lead five-mi. hikes. You can hike on your own, but you must obtain a permit. The **visitors center** (672-2366) has a craft shop as well as pottery and artifacts displays. (Open daily 8am-6pm; off-season 8am-5pm.)

The Navajo maintain a small campground with water and restrooms next to the Monument Valley Tribal Park Visitors Center. (Sites $10.) The site at the National Monument has no showers or hookups, but it's free and has the added advantage of nightly ranger talks. If you need hookups, stop at **KOA** (801-727-3280), in Monument Valley, UT, four mi. west of Monument Valley Park off U.S. 163. (Sites $14 for 2 people, each additional person $2.)

Navajo and Hopi Reservations

Seeing *Dances With Wolves* can't substitute for the moving experience of visiting a reservation and actually trying to understand the lifestyles and hardships of Native Americans. The Navajo and their neighbors the Hopi, also enclosed by the Navajo Reservation, have lived in this region for centuries. Despite U.S. citizenship, most don't really consider themselves part of a national "melting pot." They, and not the U.S. government, have sovereignty over this large but agriculturally unproductive land. Most of this reservation is closed off to the public.

"Navajo" is actually a European name for these proud, stoic people, who call themselves "Dinee." Reservation politics are lively but obscure, written up only in the *Navajo Times* or in regional sections of Denver, Albuquerque, or Phoenix newspapers. In addition to the town and tribal government, Window Rock features the geological formation that gives the town its name. For a taste of the Dinee's unusual language and even some Native American ritual songs, tune to 660AM, from Window Rock, "The Voice of the Navajo."

The reservations have no central visitors centers. For information on the Hopis visit the **Hopi Cultural Center** (734-2401), on Rte. 264 in the community of **Second Mesa,** which delineates the world of the tribe whose ancestors, the Anasazi, lived here centuries before the Navajo and their cousins the Apache arrived. The center consists of a museum of pottery, photography, and handicrafts, along with four gift shops, a motel, and a restaurant (see below).

Inquire at the cultural center or at the Flagstaff Chamber of Commerce for the dates and sites of the **Hopi village dances.** Announced only a few days in advance, these religious ceremonies last from sunrise to sundown. The dances are highly formal occasions; tourists may come to watch, but should not wear shorts, tank tops, or other casual wear. Photography is strictly forbidden. (see below). Several tribal parks have their own small information booths. Pick up the excellent *Visitors Guide to the Navajo Nation* ($3), which includes a detailed map. Hotels charge exorbitant rates, so plan on camping at the national monuments or Navajo campgrounds, some of which also charge guests. The hotel at the Hopi Cultural Center (734-2401) is expensive but decent and requires reservations two weeks to a month in advance. (Singles $50. Doubles $55.) The restaurant is surprisingly reasonable. (Open daily 6:30am-9pm.) Alternatively, you can make your visit a day trip from Flagstaff or Gallup.

The "border towns" of **Gallup,** NM, and **Flagstaff** (see above) provide good entry points to the reservations; you can rent cars in one of these towns. Frequent **Greyhound** routes along I-40 serve both. No public transportation goes into or runs within the reservations, with the notable exception of the **Navajo Transit Authority** (729-5457) in Fort Defiance, six mi. north of Window Rock. One bus per day leaves Tuba City, at 6am and travels along Rte. 264 through the Hopi mesa towns (flag stops) to Window Rock, arriving at 9:50am. (Leaves Window Rock heading west at 3:10pm, arriving at 7:50pm. $13.) I-40, and U.S. highways 89, 160, and 191, form an imperfect circle through the reservation, with Rte. 264 cutting through to the Hopi reservation and through Window Rock.

Petrified Forest National Park and Meteor Crater

Don't expect to see a forest here; that's the *last* thing the Petrified Forest Resembles. Color postcards may make it appear impressive, but the park consists of 60,000 acres of monotonous Arizona desert sparsely dotted with tree logs that turned into rock some 225 million years ago. Petrification involves an unlikely set of circumstances: logs must fall into a swamp, be cut off from air and water rapidly, then have each cell replaced by crystal—all in all, about as likely as seeing Tipper Gore at a Mötley Crüe concert. The park is 107 mi. from Flagstaff on I-40. The sunset view at its **Painted Desert,** (named for the magnificent multicolored bands of rock inlaid with quartz and amethyst crystals that scatter across the desert floor) is spectacular—creating a sparkling kaleidoscope of color. Other than this view, the park is not really worth the transportation hassle.

Entrances are off I-40 to the north and U.S. 180 to the south (entrance fee $5/vehicle). The **Painted Desert Visitors Center,** near the north entrance, shows a film explaining petrification every half hour. A 27-mi. park road connects the two entrances, winding past piles of petrified logs and Native American ruins. Stop to look at oddly-named **Newspaper Rock,** covered not with newsprint but Native American petroglyphs; the headlines are a bit out-of-date but still cool to see. At **Blue Mesa,** a hiking trail winds through the desert. **Long Logs Crystal** and **Jasper Forest** contain some of the most exquisite fragments of petrified wood. Picking up fragments of petrified wood in the park is illegal and traditionally unlucky (a result of ancient curses cast by capitalist shamans); if the demons don't getcha then the district attorney will. Those who *must* take a piece home should buy one at a store along I-40, since the storekeepers are immune to both curses. To camp overnight, make arrangements at the visitors center in the **Rainbow Forest Museum,** at the park's southern entrance (524-6228; open in summer daily 6:30am-7:30pm, in spring and fall 7:30am-6:30pm, in winter 8am-5pm). Public transport does not feed the Petrified Forest; several bus lines do stop in Holbrook, on I-40, 27 mi. away.

Between Flagstaff and the Petrified Forest off I-40 is the privately-owned **Meteor Crater** (602-774-8350), located 35 mi. east of Flagstaff off the Meteor Crater Rd. exit. This meteor crater, the world's largest, was originally believed to be just another ancient volcanic cone. However, geologic tests in the crater and on rock fragments from the surrounding desert proved the hypothesis, once scoffed at, that about 50,000 years ago a huge nickel-iron meteorite plummeted through the atmosphere and onto the desert to create the 570-ft. deep pothole. The site was used to train the Apollo astronauts in the 1960s. (Open daily 9am-7pm. Admission $5.)

Phoenix

Forget genetics—Phoenix is a product of its environment. Rising out of the aptly-named Valley of the Sun, it is a winter haven for frostbitten tourists and sun-loving students. During these balmy months, golf, spring-training baseball, and the Fiesta Bowl flourish. Phoenix's beautiful weather and proximity to the natural sights of the area make it an excellent point of entry to the Southwest. However, weather only goes so far. The city's urban sprawl and relative dearth of cultural activities also makes it a good place to leave after intercepting a few rays.

During the summer, the city crawls into its air-conditioned shell. Visitors at this time should be certain to carry a bottle of water with them if they plan on walking for *any* length of time. Although summer highs almost always top 100°F (37°C), the abundance and sophistication of cooling systems (some of them outdoors) make occasional jaunts outside tolerable. In addition, the drier air and lower prices of the summer make the asphalt-melting weather slightly more bearable.

Practical Information and Orientation

Emergency: 911.

Visitor Information: Phoenix and Valley of the Sun Convention and Visitors Center, 400 E. Van Buren St. (254-6500) at 1 Arizona Center. Ask for a Valley Pass to save up to 50% at the more expensive resorts, hotels and attractions. Open Mon.-Fri. 8am-5pm. Convenient branch offices downtown on 2nd St. at Adams (open Mon.-Fri. 8am-4:30pm), and in Terminals 2 and 3 at Sky Harbor Airport (open Mon.-Fri. 9am-9pm, Sat.-Sun. 9am-5pm). **Weekly Events Hotline,** 252-5588. 24-hr. recorded information.

Amtrak: 401 W. Harrison (253-0121 or 800-872-7245), 2 blocks south of Jefferson St. at 4th Ave. NOT safe at night. 3 per week to Los Angeles (8½ hr.; $82) and El Paso (9 hr.; $82). Station open Sun.-Wed. 5:45am-11:30pm, Thurs. and Sat. 3-9:30pm.

Greyhound: 5th and Washington St. (248-4040). To: Flagstaff (5 per day; 2½ hr.; $19), Tucson (10 per day; 2½ hr.; $10), and Los Angeles (11 per day; 7 hr.; $32). Open 24 hrs. Lockers $1.

Public Transport: Phoenix Transit, 235-5000. Most lines run to and from the **City Bus Terminal,** Central and Washington. Most routes operate Mon.-Fri. 5am-9:30pm, severely reduced service on Sat. Fares 85¢, disabled persons, seniors, and kids 40¢. To Mesa 85¢. 10-ride pass $7.50, all-day $2.50, disabled persons and seniors half-price. Pick up free time tables, maps of the bus system, and bus passes at the terminal. Buses running along Central Ave., Washington St., and Jefferson St. downtown cost only 25¢ within a limited zone Mon.-Fri. 9am-3pm. City bus #13 runs between the **Sky Harbor International Airport,** only minutes southeast of downtown. **DASH,** (253-5000) a free shuttle bus, runs every ½-hr. between the airport and downtown. Mon.-Fri. 6:30am-6pm. After hours or on weekends, call a cab ($8). **Dial-A-Ride** (271-4545) takes passengers anywhere in Phoenix only on Sun. and holidays 6:30am-6:30pm. Fare $1.50 plus 60¢ for each additional zone; seniors, disabled people, and under 12 60¢ plus 30¢ per zone. Call 258-9977 for weekday service in specified areas only. Some buses and Dial-a-Ride vans have wheelchair lifts; call for details.

Car Rental: Rent-a-Wreck, 2422 E. Washington St. (254-1000). Economy cars from $18 a day; unlimited mileage; 150-mi. radius. Open Mon.-Fri. 7am-6:30pm, Sat.-Sun. 9am-5pm. Must be 21 with credit card or cash deposit. **Admirals,** 427 N. 44th St. (275-6992). $20/day with unlimited mileage within state and 200 mi. out-of-state. 30¢ each additional mi. Open Mon.-Fri. 8am-5pm, Sat.-Sun. 9am-4pm. Must be 21 with credit card and Arizona driver's license.

Auto Transport Company: Auto Driveaway, 3530 E. Indian School Rd. (952-0339). First tank of gas free. Open Mon.-Fri. 9am-4:30pm, Sun. 9am-5pm. Must be 21 with $200 deposit.

Taxi: Ace Taxi, 254-1999. $2.25 base fare, 90¢/mi. **Yellow Cab,** 252-5252. $2.05 base fare, $1.30/mi.

Help Lines: Center Against Sexual Assault, 241-9010. Open 24 hrs. **Gay and Lesbian Hotline,** 234-2752. **Community Switchboard,** 234-2752.

Post Office: 522 N. Central (223-3658), downtown. General Delivery at 4949 E. Van Buren St. Open Mon.-Fri. 8:30am-5:30pm. **ZIP code:** 85026.

Area Code: 602.

The **city bus terminal** at Central Ave. and Washington St. idles in the heart of downtown Phoenix. **Central Avenue** runs north-south; "avenues" are numbered west from Central and "streets" are numbered east. **Washington Street** divides streets north-south.

Accommodations and Camping

Summer is the best season for the budget traveler to visit Phoenix. Almost all motels near downtown have vacancies and slash their rates by up to 70%. In the winter, however, when temperatures and vacancy signs go down, prices go up; be sure to make reservations if possible. Those without reservations should cruise the 25-mi. row of motels on the occasionally decrepit and slightly dangerous East and West **Van Buren Street** or on **Main Street** (Apache Trail) in Tempe and Mesa. The strip is full of 50s ranch-style motels with names like "Kon-Tiki" and "Deserama," as well as the requisite modern chains. In the summer almost all lower their rates and offer gimmicks, making accommodations very cheap. **Bed and Breakfast in Arizona,** P.O. Box 8628, Scottsdale 85252 (995-2831), can help visitors find accommodations in homes in Phoenix and throughout Arizona. (Preferred 2-night min. stay. Singles from $25. Doubles $35. Reservations recommended.)

Metcalf House (HI/AYH), 1026 N. 9th St. (254-9803), a few blocks northeast of downtown. From the city bus terminal, take bus #7 down 7th St. to Roosevelt St., then walk 2 blocks east to 9th St. and turn left—the hostel is ½ block north. About a 20-min. walk from downtown. Dorm-style rooms, wooden bunks, and common showers. Kitchen, porch and common room, laundry. Sleepsack required. Check-in 7-9:30am and 5-11pm. $9, nonmembers $12. Linen $1. Bike rental $3/day.

Airport Central Inn, 2247 E. Van Buren St. (244-9341 or 800-492-2904). Nice, large rooms and a pool. In summer, singles from $20, doubles from $25. Winter rates jump significantly.

Budget Lodge Motels, 402 W. Van Buren St. (254-7247), near downtown. Large, clean, rooms with A/C, TV, and free local calls, plus a small pool in the parking lot. Singles $20, doubles $27, weekly $100 in summer, but prices vary by season. Reserve a few weeks ahead in winter.

KOA, 2550 W. Louise (869-8189), 3 mi. north of Bell Rd. on I-17 at Black Canyon City. Showers, pool, spa, laundry, playground. AAA discount. Sites $15 for 2 people, $18 with hookup. Each additional adult $2.

Food

Rarely will you find several restaurants together amid Phoenix's sprawl. Downtown is fed mainly by small coffeeshops, most of which close on weekends. An exception to this rule is **The Mercado,** a faux-Mexican mall on E. Van Buren between 5th and 7th St., which contains several inexpensive eateries, most open on weekends. For more variety, drive down McDowell St.

Bill Johnson's Big Apple, 3757 E. Van Buren (275-2107), 1 of 4 locations. A down-south delight with sawdust on the floor. Sandwiches ($4-6), hearty soups ($2-3). Open Mon.-Thurs. 6am-11pm, Fri.-Sat. 6am-1am.

Tacos de Juárez, 1017 N. 7th St. at Roosevelt (258-1744), near the hostel. Standard Mexican fare at rock-bottom prices. Specializes in tacos. À la carte items all under $3. Open Sun.-Tues. 11am-8pm, Wed. 11am-3pm, Thurs.-Sat. 11am-9pm.

The Matador, 125 E. Adams St. (254-7563), downtown. Standard Mexican dinners $5-8. The deep-fried ice cream is a novelty. Live music Fri. and Sat. nights. Open daily 6am-11pm. Lounge open until 1am.

The Purple Cow Deli, 200 N. Central (253-0861), in the San Carlos Hotel; also in the Park Central Mall. I've never met a purple cow, I never hope to meet one; but I can tell you anyhow, I'd rather eat than be one. Great sandwiches ($4) and frozen yogurt. Kosher food available. Open Mon.-Fri. 7am-4pm.

Sights

If you're a connoisseur of the arts, stick around downtown for Phoenix's many museums and beautiful buildings. The **Heard Museum,** 22 E. Monte Vista (252-8848), one block east of Central Ave., near the hostel, has outstanding collections of Navajo handicrafts and promotes the work of contemporary Native American artists and craftspeople, many of whom give free demonstrations. The museum also sponsors occasional lectures and Native American dances. Educate and prepare yourself for the journey among the Southwest's omnipresent Native American artifact vendors. (Guided tours daily. Open Mon.-Sat. 10am-5pm, Sun. noon-5pm. Admission $4, seniors $3, students and kids $1, Native Americans free.) The **Phoenix Art Museum,** 1625 N. Central Ave. (257-1222), three blocks south, has excellent exhibits of European, modern, and U.S. folk art. (Open Tues. and Thurs.-Sat. 10am-5pm, Wed. 10am-9pm, Sun. 1-5pm. Admission $3, seniors $2.50, students $1.50. Free Wed.) With a Valley Pass from the visitors bureau (see Practical Information above) you'll get half-price admission to both the Heard and the Art Museum.

The **Desert Botanical Gardens,** 1201 E. Galvin Way (941-1225), in Papago Park, five mi. east of the downtown area, grows a beautiful and colorful collection of cacti and other desert plants. Visit in the morning or late afternoon to avoid the midday heat. (Open daily 8am-sunset. Admission $4, seniors $3.50, kids 5-12 $1. Take bus #3 east to Papago Park.)

South of Phoenix across the dry Salt River lies Tempe's **Arizona State University (ASU)** and its exuberant college atmosphere. Cafés and art galleries abound in this area. The **Gammage Memorial Auditorium** (965-3434), at Mill Ave. and Apache Trail, is one of the last major buildings designed by omnipresent Frank Lloyd Wright. Painted in pink and beige to match the surrounding desert, the eccentric edifice's coloration is sure to either astound or nauseate you. (20-min. tours daily in winter. Take bus #60, or #22 on weekends.)

Entertainment

Phoenix is the progressive rock and country capital of the Southwest, with an active (though awfully fashion-conscious) nightclub scene. **Phoenix Live** at Arizona Center, 455 N. 3rd St. (252-2112), quakes the complex with four bars and clubs. For the hefty $5 cover you'll have access to the entire building. On Friday and Saturday **LTL Ditty's** plays piano and encourages sing-alongs and wild fans. New Music bands with names like Feedhog and Dead Hot Workshop blister the paint on the dark walls of the **Sun Club,** 1001 E. 8th St. (968-5802), in Tempe. (Music nightly at 8 or 9pm. Cover from $3.) **Char's Has the Blues,** 4631 N. 7th Ave. (230-0205), is self-explanatory. Dozens of junior John Lee Hookers rip it up nightly. (Music nightly at 9pm. Cover from $4.) Headbangers find their black leather, big guitar Eldorado in the bottom of the **Mäson Jar,** 2303 E. Indian School (956-6271). (*Heavy* jams nightly at 9 or 10pm. Cover from $3.) The free *New Times Weekly* (271-0040), on local magazine racks, lists club schedules. Pick up a copy of the *Cultural Calendar of Events,* a concise guide covering three months of area entertainment activities.

Near Phoenix

The drive along the **Apache Trail** to Tonto National Monument makes a great daytrip from Phoenix. Take U.S. 60-89 to Apache Junction, about 30 mi. east of Phoenix, then turn right onto Rte. 88, which follows the Apache Trail through the **Superstition Mountains.** Three mi. after Canyon Lake, the first of three artificial lakes along the trail, lies the good-humored town of **Tortilla Flat,** a way station for hot and dusty travelers. Five mi. east of Tortilla Flat begins a spectacular stretch of scenery. A dangerous dirt road winds its way through 22 mi. of mountains and canyons to **Roosevelt Dam,** an enormous arc of masonry wedged between two huge red cliffs. Four mi. beyond the dam is the turn-off for **Tonto National Monument** (467-2241), where preserved dwellings of the Saledo tribe are tucked into sheltered caves in the cliffs. A one-hour self-guided hike up the mountainside, through the apartments and back, affords a lovely view of Roosevelt Lake. (Monument open daily 8am-5pm. Admission $3/car or $1/person.)

Tucson and Southwestern Arizona

Immortalized in song by Little Feat ("I've been from Tucson to Tucumcari, Tehachapi to Tonopah") as a western outpost for those willin' to be movin', Tucson at first glance appears indeed to be little more than a glorified truck stop. Dig deeper, though, and you'll find a lot more here than I-10. Settled by the Hohokam and Pima, the region witnessed the arrival of the Spanish in 1776, who built a collection of forts and missions in this dry valley. What gives modern Tucson most of its zip and zing is the University of Arizona (UA). If modern Tucson gets you down, head to the outskirts of town and cavort with the cacti at Saguaro National Monument.

Practical Information and Orientation

Emergency: 911.

Metropolitan Tucson Convention and Visitors Bureau, 130 S. Scott Ave. (624-1817). Ask for a city bus map, the *Official Visitor's Guide* and the Arizona campground directory. Open Mon.-Fri. 8:30am-5pm, Sat.-Sun. 9am-4pm.

Tucson International Airport: 573-8000. On Valencia Rd., south of downtown. Bus #25 runs once per hr. to the Laos Transit Center, where bus #16 goes downtown. Last bus daily at 7:17pm. **Arizona Stagecoach** (889-1000) has a booth at the airport and will take you downtown for about $10.25 plus tip. Open 24 hrs.

Amtrak: 400 E. Toole at 5th Ave. (623-4442 or 800-872-7245), in a large red-roofed building, next to Greyhound station. Open Sun.-Wed. 7:45am-8:30pm, Thurs. 1:15-8:30pm, Sat. 7:45am-3pm. 3 trains per week to: Phoenix ($26), Los Angeles ($97), and El Paso, TX ($71).

Greyhound: 2 S. 4th Ave. (792-0972), downtown between Congress St. and Broadway. To: Phoenix (11/day; 2 hr.; $10); Los Angeles (7/day; 10 hr.; $52); Albuquerque (6/day; $103); and El Paso (7/day; $47). Open 24 hrs. Lockers $1.

Sun-Tran: (792-9222). Buses leave from the Ronstadt terminal in downtown at Congress and 6th. Approximate times of operation are Mon.-Fri. 5:30am-10pm, Sat.-Sun. 8am-7pm. Fare 60¢, students 18 and under 40¢, seniors 25¢. The "4th Avenue Trolley" (an eco-friendly, natural-gas burning, trolley-shaped van) runs from downtown, along 4th Ave., and to the university for 25¢. Racks containing maps and schedules are at the Congress Hotel, the university visitors center, and the terminal booth. The *Rider's Information Guide* is particularly helpful.

Car Rental: Care Free (790-2655). For the car free. $16/day with 100 free mi. per day; within Tucson only. Open Mon.-Fri. 9am-5pm, Sat. 9am-3pm. Must be 21 with major credit card.

Bike Rental: The Bike Shack, 835 Park Ave. (624-3663), across from UA campus. $15/day. Open Mon.-Thurs. 9:30am-6pm, Fri. 10am-5pm, Sat. 10am-5pm, Sun. noon-4pm.

Helplines: Rape Crisis, 623-7273. **Traveler's Aid of Tucson,** 622-8900. Referrals and crisis intervention.

Post Office: 141 S. 6th St. (620-5157). Open Mon.-Fri. 8:30am-5pm, Sat. 9am-noon. General Delivery at 1501 Cherry Bell (620-5157). **ZIP code:** 85726.

Area Code: 602.

Tucson's downtown area is just east of I-10, around the intersection of Broadway (running east-west) and Stone Ave., and includes the train and bus terminals. The **University of Arizona** studies one mi. northeast of downtown at the intersection of Park and Speedway Blvd.

Although surrounded by mountains, Tucson is flat as an armadillo on I-10, making most major streets (the downtown area a notable exception) perfectly straight. Streets are marked north, south, east or west relative to Stone Ave. and Broadway. Avenues run north-south, streets east-west; because some of each are numbered, intersections such as "6th and 6th" are possible—and probable.

Accommodations and Camping

When summer arrives, Tucson opens its arms to budget travelers. For motel bargains, browse through the stack of accommodation leaflets at the visitors center (see Practical Information above). The motel row lies along **South Freeway,** the frontage road along I-10 just north of the junction with I-19. The historic **Hotel Congress,** 311 E. Congress (622-8848), is conveniently located across the Greyhound and the Amtrak stations. The hotel doubles as an AAIH hostel, offering bunk beds in a clean room. Prices are higher in winter and for a renovated room. A café, a bar, and a club swing downstairs. (Hostel $11, nonmembers $12. Singles $32. Doubles $36. Students receive 20% discount on all hotel rooms.) **The Tucson Desert Inn,** I-10 Fwy. and Congress (624-8151, 800-722-8458 outside AZ), has the largest pool in Arizona. Large, clean rooms have good furnishings and plenty of sun. (Singles $22. Doubles $32. Seniors receive 10% discount. Light breakfast included.) **Old Pueblo Homestays Bed and Breakfast,** P.O. Box 13603, Tucson 85732 (790-2399 or 800-333-9776; open daily 8am-8pm), arranges overnight stays in private homes. (Singles from $30. Doubles $40. Reservations usually required 2 weeks in advance for winter.)

The best place to camp is the **Mount Lemmon Recreation Area** in the **Coronado National Forest,** that offers unofficial, but legal camping in the wilderness. Campgrounds and picnic areas are two minutes to two hours outside Tucson via the Catalina Hwy. The best unofficial camping in the forest is in Sabino Canyon, on the northeastern outskirts of Tucson. **Rose Canyon,** at 7000 ft., is heavily wooded, comfortably cool, and has a small lake. Sites at the higher elevations fill quickly on summer weekends. (Sites $5 at Rose and Spencer Canyons; General Hitchcock Campground free, but no water available.) For more info, contact the **National Forest Service,** 300 W. Congress Ave. (670-6483), at Granada, seven blocks west of Greyhound. (Open Mon.-Fri. 7:45am-4:30pm.) Among the commercial campgrounds near Tucson, try **Cactus Country RV Park** (574-3000), 10 mi. southeast of Tucson on I-10 off the Houghton Rd. exit. It has showers, restrooms, and a pool. (Sites $12 for 1 or 2 people, with full hookup $16.50. Each additional person $2.)

Food

The downtown business district and the area farther east around the University feature—would you believe it?—excellent Tex-Mex cuisine. Those homesick for institutional food can help themselves at any of the eateries at UA's student union.

Big Ray's Barbeque, 356 E. Grant Rd. (624-RIBS). Welcome to the real deal. Big Ray's not only has some of the most friendly service in town, but the BBQ sandwiches ($2.50-4) and homemade sauce are...well, they're just damn good. Open Mon.-Thurs. 11am-9pm, Fri.-Sat. 11am-10pm, Sun. 1-8pm.

El Charro, 311 N. Court Ave. (622-5465), 4 blocks north of the Civic Center. The oldest Mexican restaurant in Tucson. Flavorful but not fiery sun-dried *carne seca* in various forms (enchilada $4.75). Chips, HOT salsa, and a pitcher of water (to douse the fire in your mouth) free with every order. Open Sun.-Thurs. 11am-9pm, Fri.-Sat. 11am-10pm.

El Minuto, 354 S. Main Ave. (882-4145), just south of the community center. Colorful atmosphere and impeccable quality. Voted Tucson's best restaurant in 1988. Usually packed with locals. Open daily 11am-2:30am.

Bentley's House of Coffee and Tea, 121 E. Congress Ave. (798-1715), in downtown. Sophisticated folk hang out in this bookstore-café. A wide variety of desserts and non-alcoholic drinks, plus enormous french toast with fruit and coffee ($3.75). Open Mon.-Tues. 7:30am-10pm, Wed.-Thurs. 8am-10pm, Fri.-Sat. 8am-midnight.

Entertainment

In Tucson, musical tastes are as varied as Arizona's climate. While UA students rock and roll on Speedway Blvd., more subdued folks do the two-step in several country music clubs on North Oracle. Pick up a copy of *Tucson Weekly* at any restaurant for current entertainment listings.

Berkey's, 5769 E. Speedway (722-0103). A smoke-filled blues and rock club. Open daily noon-1am. Live music Tues.-Sun. at 9pm. Cover Fri.-Sat. $2.

Mudbuggs, 136 N. Park Ave. (882-9844). DJs during the week, live rock (including "Rainer & Das Combo") on weekends. Good stuff. Open Tues.-Sat. 8pm-2am. Cover $2-4.

Hotel Congress Historic Tap Room, 311 E. Congress (622-8848). Frozen in its 1938 incarnation. Eclectic—perhaps even weird—crowd, but very friendly. Open daily 11am-1am. Across the hall, a DJ plays "Mod/New-Age/Alternative" dance music Thurs.-Sat. at **Club Congress.** Occasional live music. Drink specials $1.25. Club opens 9pm.

Wild Wild West, 4385 W. Ina Rd. (744-7744), not accessible by public transportation. The most authentic manifestation of the Old West saloon with continuous country-western music and the largest dance floor in Arizona. An acre of dancin' and romancin'. *Don't* come in shorts. Buffet ($2) 5-8pm. $3 cover Fri.-Sat. Open daily 4pm-1am.

Sights

Most of Tucson's attractions lie some distance outside of town and are accessible by car or tour bus only. The city itself offers few diversions. The downtown is not "historic" by East Coast or European standards; few buildings date from before the Civil War. Tucson lays a better claim to being "artsy," with galleries and the **Tucson Museum of Art,** 140 N. Main Ave. (624-2333), downtown, whose impressive collection focuses on the pre-Columbian. (Open Tues.-Sat. 10am-4pm, Sun. noon-4pm. Admission $2, seniors and students $1. Free Tues.-Fri. at 11am and 2pm.)

The **University of Arizona,** whose "mall" sits where E. 3rd St. should be, parades another main concentration of in-town attractions. The mall itself is lovely, less for the architecture than for the varied—and elaborately irrigated—vegetation. The **UA Visitors Center,** at Cherry and the Mall (621-5130), stocks maps, event calendars, and info on current museum exhibits; the helpful staff answers questions both about the university and Tucson in general. (Open Mon.-Fri. 8am-5pm, Sat. 9am-2pm.) Across the Mall, the **Flandrau Planetarium** (621-7827) has a museum and a public telescope in addition to planetarium shows. (Eccentric hours for museum and shows; call ahead. Museum free; shows $3.75, seniors, students, and kids $3.) Across from Park Ave. from the west end of campus, **University Blvd.** jams with shops catering to student needs—with clothing, records, and photocopies. **The Wild Cat Den,** 9111 E. University Blvd., prices its fully flavored sodas as low as 15¢, perhaps out of pure philanthropy. (Open Mon.-Fri. 7:30am-9pm, Sat. 9am-7pm, Sun. 10am-6pm.)

A vibrant local event, the **mariachi mass,** thrills at **St. Augustine Church,** 192 S. Stone Ave., downtown. The singing and dancing, which are not intended as tourist attractions, take place in Tucson's old white Spanish cathedral. (Sun. 8am mass in Spanish.) The **Tucson Parks and Recreation Department** (791-4873) sponsors free concerts periodically throughout the summer. Call for info or check the Thursday evening *Citizen.*

Near Tucson

The natural and man-made attractions which surround Tucson are the city's saving grace for tourists. To the north, a **tram** whisks visitors from the visitors center through **Sabino Canyon** (749-2861), where cliffs and waterfalls make an ideal spot for picnics and day hikes. (Tram daily every ½ hr. 9am-4:30pm.) From Tucson, take I-10 and turn at exit 270. **Sabino Canyon Tours** (749-2861) runs a shuttle bus ($5) daily.

If you've ever wondered where to find those tall, gangly cacti you always see in Westerns and on the Arizona license plate, go to the **Saguaro National Monument** (296-8576), a park devoted to preserving the Saguaro cacti, which can live up to 200 years and grow over 40 ft. tall. Tucson divides this monument into two parts. To the west of the city, the **Tucson Mountain Unit,** on N. Kinney Rd. at Rte. 9 (883-6366), has limited hiking trails for day use only and an auto loop. (Visitors center open daily 8am-5pm. Park open 24 hrs. Free.) Just south of this unit is the **Arizona-Sonora Desert Museum,** 2021 N. Kinney Rd. (883-2702), a naturalist's dream, which gives an up-close look at the flora and fauna of the Sonoran desert, including an excellent walk-though aviary, an underwater look at otters, and a beaver the size of a small cow. Take at least two hours to see the museum; the best time to visit is the cool morning hours when the animals have not begun their afternoon siesta. (Open winter daily 8:30am-5pm; summer 7:30am-6pm. Admission $6, ages 6-12 $1.) The way to and from the Tucson Mountain Unit and the Desert Museum goes through **Gates Pass,** whose vistas make it a favorite spot for watching sunrises and sunsets. To the east of the city, the **Rincon Mountain Unit** (296-8576), on the Old Spanish Trail east of Tucson, offers the same services as the Tucson Unit as well as overnight hikes. (Visitors center open daily 8am-5pm. Admission $3/vehicle.)

Pima's **Titan II Missile Museum,** La Canada Dr. (791-2929), in Green Valley, 25 mi. south of Tucson, is a chilling monument built around a deactivated missile silo. (Open Wed.-Sun. 9am-5pm; Nov.-April daily 9am-5pm. Admission $5, seniors and active military $4, ages 10-17 $3. Reservations advised.) The Southwest is the desert graveyard for many an outmoded aircraft; low humidity and sparse rainfall combine to preserve the relics. Over 20,000 warplanes, from WWII fighters to Vietnam War jets, are parked in ominous, silent rows on the **Davis-Monthan Air Force Base** (750-4570), 15 mi. southeast of Tucson. Take the Houghton exit off I-10, then travel west on Irvington to Wilmont. (Free tours Mon. and Wed. at 9am. Call ahead for reservations.) You can also view the two-mi. long graveyard through the airfield fence.

Just next to the Desert Museum lies **Old Tucson,** a movie set attempting to convey the feel of the Old West. Since 1939, over 200 motion pictures were filmed here. More authentic is the small desert town of **Tombstone,** 70 mi. southeast of Tucson. This aptly named mining town will live forever in Western lore as the sight of the legendary **Shootout at the O.K. Corral** between the Earp brothers and the Clanton gang, as well as the home of such renowned Western figures as Wyatt Earp, Bat Masterson, and Doc Holiday. The **O.K. Corral,** on Allen St. (457-3456) next to City Park, is open to visitors and doubles as a general tourist info center. (Open daily 8:30am-5pm. Admission $1. Tickets $3—includes a movie screening and a copy of the *Epitaph.*) Tombstone's sheriffs and outlaws, very few of whom died of natural causes, were laid to rot in the **Boothill Cemetery** northeast of downtown. Try to catch the mock gunfights staged every Sunday at 2pm alternately between the O.K. Corral and the town streets. Come prepared to open your wallet; "the town too tough to die" touts an almost irresistible assortment of kitschy curios in several shops. For more info on Tombstone's sights, contact the O.K. Corral or the **Tombstone Tourism Association,** on the corner of 4th and Allen St. (457-2211; open Mon.-Fri. 9am-5pm, Sat.-Sun. 10am-5pm)

Nevada

Nevada once walked the straight and narrow. Explored by Spanish missionaries and settled by Mormons, the Nevada Territory's arid land and searing climate seemed a perfect place for ascetics to strive for moral uplift. But the discovery of gold in 1850 and silver in 1859 won the state over permanently to the worship of filthy lucre. When the precious metal boom-bust ferris wheel finally stalled during the Great Depression, Nevadans responded by shirking the last vestiges of traditional virtue, and gambling and marriage-licensing became the state industries. In a final break with the rest of the country, Silver Staters legalized prostitution—except in Reno and Las Vegas—and began paying Wayne Newton enormous amounts of cash for his concerts. Nevada's unique convergence of vice and chance have combined to make the state the tackiest in the Union.

But a different Nevada exists outside the gambling towns. The forested slopes of Lake Tahoe, shared with California, offer serenity in little resorts a far cry away from the casinos of the south shore. The rest of a mostly expansive and bone-dry Nevada is countryside, where the true West lingers in its barren glory.

Practical Information

Capital: Carson City.

Visitor Information: Carson City Visitors Authority, 1900 South Carson St. Suite #200, Carson City 89701 (883-7442). **Nevada Division of State Parks,** Nye Bldg., 201 S. Fall, Carson City 89701 (885-4384). Open Mon.-Fri. 8am-5pm.

Time Zone: Pacific (3 hrs. behind Eastern).

Postal Abbreviation: NV

Area Code: 702.

Sales Tax: 5.75-6%.

Las Vegas

Only in Vegas could there be a major museum devoted to Liberace. Forget Hollywood images of Las Vegas glamour—the city is basically nothing but an adult Disneyland in the desert, an arena for mild, middle-age debauchery. Vegas simply trades in Mickie and Minnie for overbright neon marquees, monolithic hotels/casinos, besequined showgirls, and Kwik-wedding chapels. But for all its laughable garishness, the city takes itself very seriously—employees literally wear poker faces and fail to see anything amusing about a nightmarishly overdecorated casino lobby.

The thing Las Vegas is most serious about is money. The city makes *its* cash by taking *yours* away. The casinos here rake in a substantial share of the $150 billion annually spent at American gaming tables and slot machines. Serious dough. Hey, *sure* there's more to do here than gamble. You can call a private stripper in more easily than you can dial a pizza. Or you can gamble. You can go hiking in the hellishly hot desert. Or you can gamble. You can take in a stage show featuring aging, alcoholic crooners. Or you can gamble. You can...well, you get the picture.

The wise traveller (i.e., one who believes more in the laws of probability than that little voice inside which says, "I just know I'll be lucky *this* time!") will take Las Vegas for what its worth. Scarf down inexpensive buffets, tip back cheap drinks, keep a tight rein on the wallet, and simply enjoy the bizarre and free spectacle of decadent Las Vegas itself.

Practical Information and Orientation

Emergency: 911.

Visitor Information: Las Vegas Convention and Visitors Authority, 3150 Paradise Rd. (892-7575), at the Convention Center, 4 blocks from the Strip, by the Hilton. Up-to-date info on hotel bargains and buffets. Open daily 8am-5pm.

Tours: Gray Line Tours, 1550 S. Industrial Rd. (384-1234). Bus tours: Hoover Dam/Lake Mead Express (4½ hr.; $18); the Grand Canyon (2 days; $104; March 1-Oct. 31 Mon., Wed. and Fri. 7am).; Mini City Tours (1 per day; ½-day; $17.50). **Ray and Ross Tours,** 300 W. Owens St. (646-4661 or 800-338-8111). Bus tours to Hoover Dam (6 hr.; $17) and Hoover Dam/Lake Mead (7 hr.; $24).

Airport: McCarran International Airport: 798-5410, at the southeast end of the Strip. Main terminal on Paradise Rd. Within walking distance of the University of Nevada campus and the southern casinos. Buses and taxis to downtown.

Amtrak: 1 N. Main St. (386-6896; fares and schedules 800-872-7245), in the Union Plaza Hotel. To: Los Angeles ($66), San Francisco ($116), and Salt Lake City ($86). Ticket office open daily 6am-3am; terminal open 24 hrs.

Greyhound: 200 Main St. (382-2640), at Carson Ave. downtown. To: L.A. ($40), Reno ($51), Salt Lake City ($45), and Denver ($85). **Las Vegas-Tonopah-Reno Lines** provides service to Phoenix ($30). Ticket office open daily 6am-3am; terminal open 24 hrs.

Public Transportation: Las Vegas Transit: 384-3540. Common transfer point at 200 Casino Center downtown. Trolley shuttle runs downtown along Fremont St. (Fare 50¢, seniors and under 12 25¢.) Most buses run 5:30am-9pm. Strip buses (#6) every 15 min. 7am-midnight, every ½ hr. midnight-3am, every hr. 3-7am. Fare $1.25, ages 6-17 40¢, seniors and disabled persons 10 rides for $4.60, transfers 15¢.

Taxi: Checker Cab, 873-2000. $3.60 first mi., $1.40 each additional mi.

Car Rental: Showcase Rent-a-Car, 5201 Swenson St. (387-6717). From $23 per day with unlimited mi. Must be 17; ages under 25 pay a surcharge. Open daily 8am-8pm. Look for coupons in the visitor guides for good rental deals. **Fairway Rent-A-Car,** 3469 Industrial (736-1786 or 800-634-3476), near the airport. $19 per day. 100 free mi. per day, 35¢ each additional mi. Must be 21; car for local use only. Open daily 8am-9pm.

Help Lines: Crisis Line, 876-4357. **Gambler's Anonymous,** 385-7732. Both open 24 hrs.

Post Office: 301 E. Stewart (385-8944), behind Lady Luck. Open Mon.-Fri. 9am-5pm. General delivery open Mon.-Fri. 10am-3pm. **ZIP code:** 89114.

Area Code: 702.

Gambler's specials number among the cheapest and most popular ways to reach Las Vegas. These bus tours leave early in the morning and return at night or the next day; ask in L.A., San Francisco, or San Diego tourist offices. You can also call casinos for info. Prices include everything except food and gambling, and although you are expected to stay with your group, "getting lost" shouldn't be a problem.

Vegas has two major casino areas. The **downtown** area, around Fremont and 2nd St., is foot-friendly; casinos cluster close together, and some of the sidewalks are even carpeted (man, oh man). The other main area, known as the **Strip,** is a collection of mammoth casinos on both sides of intimidatingly busy **Las Vegas Blvd. South.** Stay downtown during the day, unless you have a car or like long, hot, unshaded stretches of sidewalk. Except for the neighborhoods just north and west of downtown, Vegas is generally, and especially on the Strip, a safe place for late-night strolling. Security guards and lights reproduce in amoeba-like fashion, and there is almost always pedestrian traffic.

Accommodations and Camping

You can easily find cheap food and lodging in Vegas. Watch the travel and entertainment sections of local newspapers for ever-changing specials. Prices rise on weekends and holidays, but with over 67,000 hotel rooms, you can probably find some place to rest that slot-machine arm.

Las Vegas Independent Hostel, 1208 Las Vegas Blvd. S. (385-9955). Spartan, airy rooms with foam mattresses. Free do-it-yourself breakfast. Ride board in kitchen. Check-out 7-11am. Tours to Zion, Bryce, and the Grand Canyon ($100). Office open daily 7am-11pm, Nov.-March 8-10am and 5-11pm. Shared room and bath $9, private room and shared bath $20. Winter rates lower. Key deposit $5.

Las Vegas International Hostel (HI/AYH), 1236 Las Vegas Blvd. S. (382-8119). Small kitchen. Rooms in separate cabins, private showers. Lots of common areas, even grass. Office open daily 7-10am and 4-10pm. $8, nonmembers $11.

High Hat Regency, 1300 Las Vegas Blvd. S., next to the International Hostel (382-8080). TV, phones, pool, laundry, free airport pickup with 2-night stay. $24 for up to 2 people, $12 for each additional person. Discount for students.

Aztec Inn, 2200 Las Vegas Blvd. S. (385-4566). Pool, phone, A/C. Singles and doubles $25 with second night free, except on weekends and holidays.

El Cortez, 600 E. Fremont (385-5200; 800-634-6703 for reservations). TV, A/C. Singles and doubles $23, 2 double beds $28.

Ambassador East, 916 E. Fremont (384-8281). Pool, phone, TV and A/C. Stark and a bit loud but satisfactory. Singles $16, doubles $20. Restaurant open 6am-8pm.

You'll need a car to reach any of the noncommercial campsites around Vegas. Twenty mi. west of the city on Rte. 159 rolls **Red Rock Canyon** (363-1921), where you can see an earthquake fault-line and other geological marvels. Camp here for free, but only in **Oak Creek Park.** Twenty-five mi. east, **Lake Mead National Park** (293-4041) has several campgrounds. Fifty-five mi. northeast via I-15 and Rte. 169, **Valley of Fire State Park** has campsites and spectacular sandstone formations.

Food

Astonishingly cheap prime rib dinners, all-you-can-eat buffets, and champagne brunches beckon high- and low-rollers alike into the casinos. In most cafeterias, buffet food is served nonstop from 11am to 10pm. Expect the "all-you-can-stomach" quality that results from leaving food on a warming table for three hours. Cruise the Strip or roam downtown for advertised specials. The Convention Center (see Practical Information above) keeps a reasonably up-to-date list of buffets, the best of which may be the one at **Circus Circus,** 500 Circus Circus Dr. (794-3767); pay $5, grab a 16-in. plate, and eat everything in sight, including the chips, *ha ha* (4:30-11pm). Not as crowded as the bigger casinos, **El Rancho,** 2755 Las Vegas Blvd. S. (796-2222), serves a brunch buffet on weekends ($3.25; Sat.-Sun. 8am-3pm). The **Hacienda,** 3950 Las Vegas Blvd. S. (739-8911), lies a cut above comparably priced buffets, with a champagne brunch and 12 entrées at lunch (breakfast Mon.-Fri. 7-11am, $4; lunch 11:30am-3pm, $5). **Caesar's Palace,** 3570 Las Vegas Blvd. S. (731-7731), is considerably more expensive than most; yet its comfortable chairs, friendly service, and especially appetizing display of fresh foodstuffs make it *the* place for a gastronomic orgy. Go for breakfast to get the most for your money. (Breakfast Mon.-Fri. 8:30-11am, $6.25. Lunch 11:30am-2:30pm, $7.75.)

Like inexpensive food, liquid meals come easy, operating on the same principle: casino operators figure that a tourist drawn in by cheap drinks will stay to spend tons more playing the slots or losing at cards. Drinks in most casinos cost 75¢ to $1, but are free to those who look like they're playing. Look for 50¢ shrimp cocktail specials and offers of free champagne at casino entrances. Look like you're gambling; acting skills will stretch your wallet, but don't forget to tip that cocktail waitress in the interesting get-up.

Casino-Hopping and Nightlife

Casinos and their restaurants, nightclubs, and even wedding chapels stay open 24 hrs. You'll almost never see clocks or windows in a casino—the owners are afraid that players might realize it's past midnight, turn into pumpkins, and neglect to lose a nickel more. You'll quickly discern which games are suited for novices and which require more expertise, from penny slots in laundromats to baccarat games in which the stakes can soar into the tens of thousands of dollars. Hotels and most casinos give first-timers "funbooks," with alluring gambling coupons that can stretch your puny $5 into $50 worth of wagering. But always remember: *in the long run, chances are you're going to lose money.* Don't bring more than you're prepared to lose cheerfully. Keep your wallet in your front pocket, and beware of the thieves who prowl casinos to nab big winnings from unwary jubilants. You can get an escort from the casino security, or leave your winnings with the cashier, to be picked up later. Seniors, favorite targets of thieves, should be especially careful. Those under 21 may or may not be able to get into the casino, depending on how lucky, or perhaps unlucky, they are.

For best results, put on your favorite loud outfit, bust out the cigar and pinky rings, and begin. The atmosphere, décor, and clientele differ from casino to casino, so gambol as you gamble. **Caesar's Palace,** 3570 Las Vegas Blvd. (731-7110), has taken the "theme" aspect of Vegas to the extreme; whereas other casinos have miniature, mechanized horse racing, Caesar's has chariot racing. Next door, the **Mirage,** 3400 Las Vegas Blvd. S. (791-7111), includes among its attractions Siberian white tigers and a "volcano" that erupts in fountains and flames every quarter hour from 8pm to 1am, barring bad weather. **Circus Circus,** 2880 Las Vegas Blvd. S. (734-0410), attempts to cultivate a (dysfunctional) family atmosphere, embodied by the huge clown on its marquee. While parents run to the card tables and slot machines downstairs, their children can spend 50¢ tokens upstairs on the souped-up carnival midway and enjoy the titanic, futuristic video game arcade. Two stories above the casino floor, tightrope-walkers, fire-eaters, and rather impressive acrobats perform from 11am to midnight. The **Excalibur,** 3850 Las Vegas Blvd. S. (597-7777), has a medieval England theme that may make you nostalgic for the Black Plague.

Aside from gambling, every major casino has nightly shows, some featuring free performances by live bands. Caesar's Palace houses multi-storied **OMNIMAX** theaters (731-7900) with domed screens and daily shows every hour on the hour from 11am to midnight. Extra bucks will buy you a seat at a made-in-the-U.S.A. phenomenon—the Vegas spectacular. The overdone but stunning twice-nightly productions feature marvels such as waterfalls, explosions, fireworks, and casts of thousands (including animals). You can also see Broadway plays and musicals, ice revues, and individual entertainers in concert. Some "production shows" are topless; most are tasteless. To see a show by the musical stars who haunt the city, such as Diana Ross or archetypal Vegasite Wayne Newton, you may have to fork over $35 or more. Far more reasonable are the many "revues" featuring imitations of (generally deceased) performers. In Vegas you can't turn around without bumping into an aspiring Elvis clone, or perhaps the real Elvis, pursuing anonymity in the brilliant disguise of an Elvis impersonator.

Pick up a copy of *Las Vegas Today,* which has plenty of discount coupons, show info, and up-to-date special events listings, or *What's On,* distributed by the Visitors Authority (see Practical Information above). Also good are *Entertainment Today* and *Vegas Visitor. The Games People Play,* distributed by the Golden Nugget Hotel, explains how each casino game is played. Many casinos also offer gambling classes for novices.

Nightlife in Vegas gets rolling around midnight and keeps going until everyone drops. The casino lounge at the **Las Vegas Hilton,** 3000 Paradise Rd. (732-5111), has a disco every night (no cover, 1-drink min.). A popular disco, **Gipsy,** 4605 Paradise Rd. (731-1919), southeast of the Strip, may look deserted at 11pm, but by 1am the medium-sized dance floor packs in a gay, lesbian, and heterosexual crowd. **Carrow's,** 1290 E. Flamingo Rd. (796-1314), has three outdoor patios, plus plenty of people and plants. During happy hour (4-7pm), the filling hors d'oeuvres are free.

Fans of klassical music and kitsch will be delighted by the **Liberace Museum,** 1775 E. Tropicana Ave. (798-5555), devoted to the flamboyant late "Mr. Showmanship." There's fur, velvet and rhinestone in combinations that boggle the rational mind. Though $6.50 might be a bit much for the privilege of sharing the experience, the proceeds go to the Liberace Foundation for the Performing and Creative Arts. (Open Mon.-Sat. 10am-5pm, Sun. 1-5pm. $5, seniors $4.50, ages 6-12 $2.)

Reno

The chance for quick money lures most tourists to Reno, the so-called "biggest little city in the world." The **Reno Arch,** on Virginia at Commercial, emblazoned with this light-bulbed city slogan, gained 1600 bulbs a few years ago. Outnumbered only by pawnshops and wedding chapels, casinos spill anxious crowds onto sidewalks and flower beds beneath their neon glow.

Each casino claims fame and uniqueness for its "loosest slots" or accountant-certified "highest paybacks," but **Harrah's** currently holds the world jackpot record (over $10 million, made in June, 1992). Most venues have live music in the evenings, the most famous of which, **Bally's,** 2500 E. 2nd St. (789-2285), hosts aging vocalists like Sinatra and Liza Minnelli. Check details in the weekly freebie *Showtime.* A free **shuttle** runs every 40 minutes from El Dorado on Plaza St. to Bally's and every half-hour between Bally's and the airport (6:15am-11:45pm). Before you "stack 'em or rack 'em" (your chips, that is), you might try the **Behind the Scenes** gaming tour, which takes you to the other side of the one-way mirrors, and teaches you the rudiments of the games—the only time you'll be given chips for nothing (well, almost nothing—$5-tours leave at 12:30pm daily from the visitors center, 135 N. Sierra, 348-7788).

Tying and untying the knot has become a Reno industry, and ceremonies are available 24 hours a day ($20-100) at any **wedding chapel** near you (call 800-MARRY-US. No joke.) Those seeking less permanent love affairs should head 10 mi. east on Rte. 80 to the **New Mustang Ranch** (342-0176), the most famous legal brothel in America, serving 200,000 "clients" annually. Those who seek other car-nal knowledge can check out the **William F. Harrah Automobile Museum,** 10 S. Lake St. (333-9300), displaying over 500 antique cars, including models made of gold, *papier mâché,* and leather. (Open daily 9:30am-5:30pm. $8, seniors $7, kids $3, under 6 free.)

The casino buffets in Reno make an average dinner in a diner seem expensive; to bring gamblers in, or to prevent them wandering out in search of food, hotels provide a range of all-you-can-eat places. The dining room may resemble the *Starship Enterprise,* but **Fitzgerald's** buffet is filling and good for breakfast (7:30-11am, $3), lunch (11am-4pm, $3.50), or dinner (4-10pm, $5). **Circus Circus,** 500 N. Sierra, offers enormous quantities on plastic plates. Breakfast (6-11:30am, $3), brunch (noon-4pm, $3.50), dinner (4:30-11pm, $4.50). Be aware that price directly reflects quality, so have your Tums ready and remember locals eat at only *some* of the buffets. Drinks are also cheap (beer nominally priced $.75 or free) at hotel bars, or in the casino served by sadly stereotypical, scantily-clad women. But beware: no matter how drunk you are, you are still held responsible for your gambling debts.

For peaceful eating, outside the bustle of smoke-filled casinos, Reno has a varied selection of inexpensive restaurants, specializing in Basque cuisine. **Louis' Basque Corner,** 301 E. 4th St., at Evans, three blocks east of Virginia, is a local institution. A hefty $14 will buy you a terrific full-course family-style meal, including wine. (Open Mon.-Sat. 11am-2:30am, Sun. 4-11pm.) The **Santa Fe Hotel,** 235 Lake St., offers Basque dinners ($13) in a classic dining room with a 1950s atmosphere and jukebox. (Open 12:30-1:30pm and 6:30-9pm.) **The Blue Heron,** 1091 S. Virginia (786-4110), is a haven for vegetarians. Delicious carrot cake ($2). (Open Mon.-Fri. 11am-9:30pm, Sat. noon-9pm.)

The **Chute No. 1,** 1099 S. Virginia St. (323-7825), provides the best floor to dance on (open 24 hrs.), but **Ron's Piano Bar** at 145 Hillcrest St. (829-7667), farther south on Virginia St., proves a quieter place for beer and conversation. (Open daily 11am-3am.) **Harrah's,** at Virginia and Commercial (800-648-3773), offers musical groups for a younger crowd. Gay and lesbian travelers should be aware that public displays of affection are actively ticketed and can even lead to arrests in Nevada. Even so, Reno has a fairly large community and 10 gay bars that complement its other nightlife.

Reno is blessed with a battery of inner-city hotels, though most are hardly savory. For the cheapest accommodations, head to the southwestern part of town. The **Windsor Hotel,** 214 West St. (323-6171), 1½ blocks from the Greyhound station toward Virginia St., has wonderfully clean hall showers and rooms, but no A/C—just fans. (Singles $19, with bath $23; Fri.-Sat. $26, with bath $28. Doubles $27; Fri.-Sat. $31.) **El Cortez,** 239 W. 2nd St. (322-9161), one block east of the Greyhound station, features pleasant management and great bargains. Ask for a private bath. The cheapest singles don't have A/C. (Singles and doubles $27, triples $37; off-season: $24, $33. Add $3 on weekends and holidays.) **Motel 6** has three locations in Reno, all with pools, and all about 1½ mi. from the downtown casinos: 866 N. Wells (786-9852), north of I-80 off Well Ave. exit; 1901 S. Virginia (827-0255), near Virginia Lake; 1400 Stardust St. (747-7390), north of I-80 off Keystone Ave. exit, then west on Stardust. At all three locations, ages under 18 stay free with an adult. (Singles $31, $7 each additional adult.) **Boca Basin,** just over the California line, 23 mi. west on I-80, is a safe bet for campers heading on towards San Francisco or Sacramento. (2-week max. stay. No hookups. Free.)

Scan West Coast big-city newspapers for **gambler's specials** on bus and plane fare excursion tickets. Some include rebates and casino credits. Although the city sprawls for miles, most of the major casinos are clustered downtown along **Virginia** and **Sierra Streets,** between 2nd and 4th St. The adjacent city of **Sparks** also has several casinos along I-80. The bus station and all the hotels listed are downtown or within a 10-minute walk. Downtown Reno is compact, and its wide streets and well-lit 24-hour activity are heavily patrolled.

The **Reno/Tahoe Visitors Center,** 135 N. Sierra (348-7788), has a friendly staff and the usual deluge of maps and brochures. Pick up the excellent *Reno/Tahoe Travel Planner.* The weekly *Showtime* lists current events and performers. (Open Mon.-Fri. 9am-5pm, Sat. 9am-2pm.) Adjacent to the chamber, **Ticket Station** sells tickets for shows (348-7403). **Cannon International Airport** is at 2001 East Plumb Lane and Terminal Way, on I-580 three mi. southeast of downtown (328-6400). Take bus #24 on Lake Ave. near 2nd St. Most major hotels have free shuttles for their guests; taxi fare downtown is around $8. The **Amtrak** station, on E. Commercial Row and Lake St. (329-8638 or 800-872-7245), offers one train per day to San Francisco ($59), Salt Lake City ($108), and Chicago ($219). (Open daily 8:45am-noon and 2-4:45pm.) **Greyhound,** on 155 Stevenson St. (322-2970), a half block from W. 2nd St., runs to San Francisco (14 per day, $43), Salt Lake City (4 per day, $67), and Los Angeles (10 per day, $55-60). **Gray Line Tours,** 2570 Tacchino St. (329-1147; outside NV 800-822-6009), offers bus tours to Virginia City (Mon.-Fri., 5 hr., $16) and Lake Tahoe/Virginia City (daily at 9am, 8½ hr., $35). **Reno Citifare** at 4th and Center St. (348-7433; open 24 hrs.) provides local bus service. (Fare $.75, students $.50, seniors and people with disabilities $.35.) Most routes operate from 5am to 7pm, some 24 hrs. **Lloyd's International Rent-a-Car,** 2515 Mill St. (348-4777 or 800-654-7037), rents at $25 per day, $145 per week. You must be 21 and have a credit card.

Reno's **post office** lounges at 50 S. Virginia St. (786-5523; open Mon.-Fri. 9am-5pm; general delivery Mon.-Fri. 10am-3pm). The **ZIP code** is 89501. The **area code** is 702.

New Mexico

Native Americans lived within beautiful present-day New Mexico for millennia before Spanish explorers burst onto the scene in the 16th century—an invasion which provoked years of hostilities between the two cultures. The Pueblo revolt of 1680 drove the Spaniards out, only to lose the region again 10 years later. By the 1800s, Native Americans and Hispanics had devised a more peaceful cohabitation, but President James K. Polk's "Manifest Destiny" facilitated the American acquisition of the territory during the 1848 Mexican War. Navajo and Pueblo tribes now attempt to preserve their heritage in the face of tremendous poverty. In the cities, descendants of Spanish and Mexican Americans have incorporated elements of Native American cultures into their own. The latest invasion has been slightly more benign; thousands of New Age devotees have made a pilgrimage here seeking the heightened spirituality in Native American religions and the sublime beauty of New Mexico.

Practical Information

Capital: Santa Fe.

Tourist Information: New Mexico Dept. of Tourism, 491 Old Santa Fe Trail, Santa Fe 87501 (827-0291 or 800-545-2040; open Mon.-Fri. 8am-5pm). **Park and Recreation Division,** Villagra Bldg., P.O. Box 1147, Santa Fe 87504 (827-7465). **U.S. Forest Service,** 517 Gold Ave. SW, Albuquerque 87102 (842-3292).

Time Zone: Mountain (2 hr. behind Eastern). **Postal Abbreviation:** NM

Sales Tax: 5-6.75%.

Albuquerque

Don't forget to make that left turn at Albuquerque, Doc. While Santa Fe and Taos are more artsy and laid-back, Albuquerque's youthful flavor (the average age here is 29) and size (pop. 493,000) lend it a cosmopolitan air. Approximately one-third of New Mexico's population thrives amidst the energy of the state's only "real" city. Against the dramatic backdrop of the Sandía Mountains, Albuquerque sprawls across a desert plateau. Although the town's Spanish past gave rise to touristy Old Town, the roadside architecture lining Route 66 and the city's high-tech industry speak to Albuquerque's modern image; the adobe campus of the University of New Mexico accentuates the town's bright-eyed vigor.

Practical Information and Orientation

Emergency: 911.

Albuquerque Convention and Visitors Bureau: 121 Tijeras N.E. 87102 (243-3696 or 800-284-2282). Free maps and the useful *Albuquerque Visitors Guide*. Open Mon.-Fri. 8am-5pm. After hours, call for recorded events info. **Old Town Visitors Center,** 305 Romero St. at N. Plaza (243-3215). Open Mon.-Sat. 10am-5pm, Sun. 11am-5pm. They also have an information booth at the airport. (Open Mon.-Sun. 9:30am-8pm.)

Albuquerque International Airport: 2200 Sunport Blvd. S.E. (842-4366), south of downtown. Take bus #50 from Yale and Central downtown Mon.-Sat. 6:47am-6:05pm. Cab fare to downtown $6.

Amtrak, 314 1st St. S.W. (842-9650 or 800-872-7245). Open daily 9:30am-5:45pm. 1 train per day to Los Angeles (13 hr., $88); Kansas City (17 hr., $149); Lamy—Santa Fe— (1 hr., $22); Flagstaff (5 hr., $80). Reservations required.

Buses: 300 2nd St. S.W., 3 blocks south of Central Ave. **Greyhound** (243-4435) and **TNM&O Coaches** go to: Santa Fe (5 per day, 1.5 hr., $10.50); Flagstaff (5 per day, 6 hr., $51) Oklahoma City (6 per day, $84); Denver (5 per day, $68); Phoenix (5 per day, $40); and Los Angeles (6 per day, $69).

Public Transport: Sun-Tran Transit, 601 Yale Blvd. S.E. (843-9200 for schedule info, Mon.-Sat. 7am-5pm). Most buses run Mon.-Sat. 6am-6pm. Pick up system maps at the transit office or the main library. Fare $.75, ages 5-18 and seniors $.25.

Taxi: Albuquerque Cab Co., 883-4888. Fare $2.90 the first mi., $1.40 each additional mi.

Car Rental: Rent-a-Wreck, 501 Yale Blvd. S.E. (242-9556 or 800-247-9556). Cars with A/C from $22 per day. 150 free mi., $.15 each additional mi. Open Mon.-Sat. 8:30am-5:30pm, Sun. 10am-5pm. Must be 21 with credit card.

Bike Rental: The Wilderness Center, 4900 Lomas Blvd. N.E. (268-6767). Mountain bikes $18 per day, $40 per weekend, $50 per week. Open Mon.-Fri. 10am-7pm, Sat. 10am-6pm, Sun. noon-5pm.

Help Lines: Rape Crisis Center, 1025 Hermosa S.E. 87108 (266-7711). (Center open Mon.-Fri. 8am-noon and 1-5pm; hotline open 24 hrs.) **Gay and Lesbian Information Line,** 266-8041. Open daily 7am-10pm.

Post Office: 1135 Broadway N.E. (247-2725). Open Mon.-Fri. 8am-6pm. **ZIP code:** 87101.

Area Code: 505.

Central Avenue and the **Santa Fe railroad tracks** create four quadrants used in city addresses: Northeast Heights (N.E.), Southeast Heights (S.E.), North Valley (N.W.), and South Valley (S.W.). The all-adobe campus of the **University of New Mexico (UNM)** stretches scenically along Central Ave. N.E. from University Ave. to Carlisle St.

Accommodations and Camping

Along Central Ave., even near downtown, there are tons of cheap motels, but too many of them are too cheap to avoid the temptation of running at low maintenance. Hostelers usually head to the average, but well-located **Albuquerque International Hostel (AAIH),** 1012 W. Central Ave. (243-6101), at 10th St., clean dorm-style rooms, clean common room and even clean bathrooms. No curfew but required morning chores. (Office open daily 7:30-11am and 4-11pm. Check-out 11am. $8, nonmembers $10. Key deposit $5. Linen $1. Included kitchen fee of $1 includes plenty of food and coffee.) Most of Central Ave.'s cheap motels lie east of downtown around the university. The **De Anza Motor Lodge,** 4301 Central Ave. N.E. (255-1654), has bland décor but well-kept rooms, free Movie Channel, and continental breakfast to boot. (Singles $19-23. Doubles $24-30.)

Named for the Spanish adventurer who burned some 250 Native Americans shortly after his arrival in 1540, **Coronado State Park Campground** (867-5589), one mi. west of Bernalillo on Rte. 44, about 20 mi. north of Albuquerque on I-25, offers unique camping. Adobe shelters on the sites provide respite from the heat. The Sandía Mountains are haunting, especially beneath a full moon. Sites have toilets, showers, and drinking water. (2-week max. stay. Open daily 7am-10pm. Sites $7, with hookup $11. No reservations.) The nearby **Albuquerque West Campground,** 5739 Ouray Rd. N.W. (831-1912), has a swimming pool. Take I-40 west from downtown to the Coors Blvd. N. exit, or bus #15 from downtown. (Tent sites $13 per 2 people, each additional person $2.) Camping equipment and canoes ($35 per day) can be rented from the friendly folks at **Mountains & Rivers,** 2320 Central Ave. S.E. (268-4876), across from the university. (Deposit required; reservations recommended. Open Mon.-Fri. 9:30am-6:30pm, Sat. 9am-5pm.)

Food and Nightlife

Downtown Albuquerque offers a myriad of excellent New Mexican restaurants. The best is the **M and J Sanitary Tortilla Factory,** 403 2nd St. S.W. (242-4890), at Lead St. in the hot pink and blue building. Free jug of water and chips with salsa. Crowds materialize at lunchtime. Entrées $4-6. (Open Mon.-Sat. 9am-4pm.)

Tasty, inexpensive food eateries border the University of New Mexico, which stretches along Central Ave. N.E. **Nunzio's Pizza,** 107 Cornell Dr. S.E. (262-1555), has great, inexpensive pizza at $1.50 per huge slice. (Open Sun.-Thurs. 11am-10pm, Fri.-Sat. 11am-11pm.) "Feed your Body with Love, Light, and high VIBRATIONAL Food," advises **Twenty Carrots,** 2110 Central Ave. S.E. (242-1320). Wheatgrass smoothies ($2.25) and bulk organic food are, apparently, sufficiently vibratory. (Open Mon.-Sat. 10am-6:30pm.) The homemade ice cream (one scoop $1.10) and pastries at the nearby **Hippo Ice Cream,** 120 Harvard Dr. S.E. (266-1997), could turn you into one. (Open Mon.-Thurs. 7:30am-10:30pm, Fri.-Sat. 7:30am-11:30pm, Sun. 9am-9pm.)

You can also dig in your spurs at **Caravan East,** 7605 Central Ave. N.E.(265-7877). (Continuous live music every night 4:30pm-2am. Cover weekends only $3.) Less rurally-inclined music lovers can hear rock, blues, and reggae bands over cheap beer ($1.50) at **El Ray,** 622 Central Ave. S.W. (242-9300), a spacious old theater transformed into a bar and nightclub. (Open 8am-2am. Music daily at 8:30pm. Cover $3.)

Sights

Old Town, on the western end of downtown, consists of Albuquerque's Spanish plaza surrounded by restaurants and Native American art galleries. Located at the northeast corner of the intersection of Central Ave. and Rio Grande Blvd., one mi. south of I-40, Old Town provides the best place to hang out and watch tourists.

The **National Atomic Museum,** 20358 Wyoming Blvd., Kirkland Air Force Base (845-6670), tells the story of the development of the atomic bombs "Little Boy" and "Fat Man," and of the obliteration of Hiroshima and Nagasaki. *Ten Seconds that Shook the World,* an 3600-second-long documentary on the development of the atomic bomb, is shown four times daily at 10:30 and 11:30am, 2 and 3:30pm. Access is controlled; ask at the Visitor Control Gate on Wyoming Blvd. for a visitors museum pass. Be prepared to show *several* forms of ID. The Air Force base is several mi. southeast of downtown, just east of I-25. (Museum open daily 9am-5pm. Free.)

For a different feel, the **Indian Pueblo Cultural Center,** 2401 12th St. N.W. (843-7270), just north of I-40, provides a sensitive introduction to the nearby Pueblo reservations. The cafeteria serves authentic Pueblo food (fry-bread $1.75; open 7:30am-3:30pm) and hosts colorful Pueblo dance performances on weekends year-round at 11am and 2pm. (Open daily 9am-5:30pm. Admission $2.50, seniors $1.50, students $1. Take bus #36 from downtown.)

Near Albuquerque

Located at the edge of suburbia on Albuquerque's west side, **Indian Petroglyphs National Park** (897-8814) includes a trail leading through lava rocks written on by Native Americans. Take the Coors exit on I-40 north to Atrisco Rd. to reach this free attraction, or take bus #15 to Coors and transfer to bus #93. (Open daily 9am-6pm; off-season 8am-5pm. Parking $1, weekends and holidays $2.)

On the east side of the city, the **Sandía Crest** rises 10,678 ft., providing a pleasant escape from Albuquerque's heat and noise. The Sandía, Spanish for "watermelon," peaks are *not* named for their taste but rather for the color they turn at sunset. The peaks are a short drive from Albuquerque. Take Tramway Rd. from either I-25 or I-40 to the **Sandía Peak Aerial Tramway** (298-8518), a thrilling ride to the top of Sandía Crest, which allows you to ascend the west face of Sandía Peak and gaze out over Albuquerque, the Río Grande Valley, and western New Mexico. The ascent is most striking at sunset. (Operates daily 9am-10pm; Sept. 2-May 25 Mon.-Tues, Thurs. and Sun. 9am-9pm, Wed. 5-9pm, Fri.-Sat. 9am-10pm. Fare $11, seniors and students $8.50. 9-11am rates $8.50 and $7, respectively. Departs every 20-30 min., lasts 1½ hrs.)

A trip through the **Sandía Ski Area** makes for a beautiful 58-mi., day-long driving loop. Take I-40 east up Tijeras Canyon 17 mi. and turn north onto Rte. 44, which winds through lovely piñon pine, oak, ponderosa pine, and spruce forests. Rte. 44 descends 18 mi. to Bernalillo, through a gorgeous canyon. A seven-mi. toll-road (Rte. 536) leads to the summit of **Sandía Crest,** and a dazzling ridge hike covers the 1½ mi. separating the crest and **Sandía Peak.** Rangers offer guided hikes on Saturdays in both summer and winter. Make reservations for the challenging winter snowshoe hikes (242-9052). In the summer, hiking and mountain-biking trails are open to the public during specific hours; call for complete hours, prices, and costs for lifts up the mountain to the trails.

Also, see the entry on **Riverbend Hot Springs,** a terrific HI/AYH hostel, in the Southern New Mexico section. The hostel is not extremely close to Albuquerque, but it is so nice that many travelers use it as a base of exploration for much of the state.

Gila Cliff Dwellings National Monument

While most of the civilized world flocks to the Grand Canyon or Yellowstone, the discerning tourist always searches for that rare place with great hiking and profound scenery devoid of family tenderfoots. The Gila Cliff Dwellings (505-536-9461) are just the place. Accessible only by a 44-mi. drive on State Hwy. 15 from Silver City in the southwest part of the state, the drive to the park winds up and down mountains to the canyon of the Gila River; deer cavort along the scenic drive. As if the drive weren't enough, at the end of the trail are the Gila Cliff Dwellings, named not for their creators (Pueblos), but the river which flows nearby. Built over 700 years ago, the remarkably well-preserved dwellings have been protected from erosion by overhanging caves. The one mi. round-trip hike to the dwellings moves quickly and provides plenty of photograph opportunities. The surrounding **Gila National Forest** beckons with excellent hiking and backcountry camping; for maps or info head to the **visitors center,** at the end of Hwy. 15, one mi. from the dwellings, or write to the district ranger at Rte. 11, Box 100, Silver City 88601. Camping throughout the national forest is free. (Visitors center open daily 8am-5pm; cliff dwellings daily 8am-6pm, off-season 8am-5pm.)

When you tire of camping, **Silver City** provides a nice, more urban stop. The city grew in the late 1800s as (surprise, surprise) a mining town; several large open pits still surround the city. Silver City was also home to fabled outlaw and Emilio Estevez lookalike Billy the Kid. The nearby ghost town of **Piños Allos** was less fortunate than Silver City; the town's only modern residents are deer and birds. In Silver City, stay at the excellent **Carter House (AYH),** 101 North Cooper St. (505-388-5485). Owners Lucy and Jim Nolan make it a point of pride to ensure your stay is enjoyable. The hostel has separate dorm-style rooms, a kitchen, and laundry facilities; upstairs is a B&B. Check-in is officially 5-9pm; if you're going to be later than 9pm, call ahead. ($13, nonmembers $15. B&B doubles from $50.)

Santa Fe

Santa Fe is more of a *mood* than a city. Coming to New Mexico's capital and visiting its museums and historic town plaza will tell you much less about the town than will a casual *paseo* down Camon Road, the local artists' turf. Santa Fe's multi-cultural population and its laws demanding all downtown buildings be in 17th-century adobe-style (and painted in one of 23 approved shades of brown) provide the perfect backdrop for the city's laid-back *zeitgeist.* This legendary spirit has attracted scores of artists to work and live amongst the city's earth-toned beauty and its mountainous backdrop. In the summer, when the town is besieged by tourists, the locals can adopt an attitude, but most visitors will only encounter a wealth of beauty and enlightenment.

Practical Information and Orientation

Emergency: 911.

Visitor Information: Chamber of Commerce, 510 N. Guadalupe (983-7317 or 800-777-2489). Open Mon.-Fri. 8am-5pm.

Gray Line Tours: 983-6565. Free pickup from downtown hotels. Tours Mon.-Sat. to: Taos and Taos Pueblo (at 9am, $50); Bandelier, Los Alamos, and San Ildefonso (at 1pm, $35); around Santa Fe (at 9:30am and 1pm, 3 hr., $15). Also operates the Roadrunner, a sight-seeing trolley around Old Santa Fe leaving from the La Fonda Hotel on the plaza downtown (5 per day; 1.5 hr.; $6, ages under 12 $3).

Greyhound: 858 St. Michael's Dr. (471-0008). To: Denver (via Raton, NM; 5 per day; $55); Taos (2 per day, 1.5 hr., $15); Albuquerque (5 per day, 1.5 hr., $10.50).

Public Transport: Shuttlejack, 982-4311 or 800-452-2665. Runs from the Albuquerque ($20) and Santa Fe airports; also goes to the opera ($6 round-trip).

Taxi: Village Cab Co, 982-9990. Coupons for a 45% discount on taxi fare available free from the public library, behind the Palace of the Governors, and at the hostel. Open 24 hrs.

New Age Referral Service: 474-0066. Info clearinghouse for holistic healing services and alternative modes of thought.

Post Office: in the Montoya Office Bldg. S. Federal Pl., (988-6351), next to the Federal Courthouse. Open Mon.-Fri. 8am-5:30pm, Sat. 9am-noon. **ZIP code:** 87501.

Area Code: 505.

Except for a cluster of museums southeast of the city center, most restaurants and important sights in Santa Fe cluster within a few blocks of the downtown plaza and inside the loop formed by the circular **Paseo de Peralta. Santa Fe Detours** (983-6565) offers 2½-hour walking tour and open-air bus tour of the city (daily at 9:30am and 1:30pm, $15) that leave from the La Fonda Hotel, on the corner of the plaza. Because the narrow streets make driving troublesome, park your car and pad the pavement. You'll find brown adobe parking lots behind Santa Fe Village, near Sena Plaza, and one block east of the Federal Courthouse near the plaza. Parking is available at two-hour meters on some streets.

Accommodations and Camping

Hotels become swamped with requests as early as May for **Fiesta de Santa Fe** week in early September and **Indian Market** the third week of August; make reservations if you're coming then or plan on sleeping in the street. At other times, look around the **Cerrillos Road** area for the best prices. At many of the less expensive adobe motels, bargaining is acceptable. The beautiful adobe **Santa Fe Hostel (AAIH),** 1412 Cerrillos Rd. (988-1153), one mi. from the adobe bus station, and two mi. from the adobe plaza, has a kitchen, library, and very large dorm-style adobe beds. ($9, nonmembers $12. Linen $2. $1 kitchen fee includes lots of free adobe. B&B rooms $25-30.)

To camp around Santa Fe, you'll need a car. Several miles out of town, **Santa Fe National Forest** (988-6940) has numerous campsites as well as free backcountry camping in the beautiful Sangre de Cristo Mountains. **New Mexico Parks and Recreation** (827-7465, 800-283-2267 for site reservation) operates the following free campgrounds on Rte. 475 northeast of Santa Fe from May through October (sites with hook-up $4-6): **Black Canyon** (8 mi. away); **Big Tesuque** (12 mi.); and **Aspen Basin** (15 mi.).

Food

About the only thing Santa Fe doesn't do with adobe is eat it. Instead, spicy Mexican food served on blue corn tortillas is the staple. The few vegetarian restaurants here are expensive, catering to an upscale crowd. The better restaurants near the plaza dish up their chilis to a mixture of government employees, well-heeled tourists, and local artistic types. Because many serve only breakfast and lunch, you also should look for inexpensive meals along **Cerrillos Road** and **St. Michael's Drive** south of downtown. One little-known fact: the **Woolworth's** on the plaza actually serves a mean bowl of chili ($2.75).

San Francisco Street Bar & Grill, 114 W. San Francisco St. (982-2044), 1 block from the plaza. Excellent sandwiches and the best pasta salad ($6) in town. Open daily 11am-11pm.

Tomasita's Santa Fe Station, 500 S. Guadalupe (983-5721), near downtown. Locals and tourists line up for their blue corn tortillas and fiery green chili dishes ($4.50-5). Indoor and outdoor seating. Open Mon.-Sat. 11am-10pm.

Josie's, 225 E. Marcy St. (983-5311), in a converted house. Pronounce the "J" in the name like an "H." Family-run for 26 years. Incredible Mexican-style lunches and multifarious mouthwatering desserts worth the 20-min. wait. Specials $4-6. Open Mon.-Fri. 11am-4pm.

The Burrito Company, 111 Washington Ave. (982-4453). Excellent Mexican food at reasonable prices. Burrito plates $2-4.25. Open Mon.-Sat. 7:30am-7pm, Sun. 11am-5pm.

Tortilla Flats, 3139 Cerrillos Rd. (471-8685). Frighteningly bland family atmosphere belies the Mexican masterpieces ($4-8). Breakfasts ($3-7), *huevos rancheros* ($4.75). Open daily 7am-10pm; winter Sun.-Thurs. 7am-9pm, Fri.-Sat. 7am-10pm.

Upper Crust Pizza, 329 Old Santa Fe Trail (983-4140). Practically the only downtown restaurant open in the evening. Thick, chewy 10-incher with whole-wheat crust ($5.25). Open Mon.-Sat. 11am-10pm, Sun. noon-10pm.

Sights

Since 1609, **Plaza de Santa Fe** has held religious ceremonies, military gatherings, markets, cockfights, and public punishments. The city also provided a pit-stop on two important trails: the **Santa Fe Trail** from Independence, MO and **El Camino Real** from Mexico City. The plaza is a good starting point for exploring the city's museums, sanctuaries, and galleries.

Since the following four museums are commonly owned, their hours are identical and a two-day pass bought at one admits you to all. (Open March-Dec. daily 10am-5pm; Jan.-Feb. Tues.-Sun. 10am-5pm. $3.50, under 16 free. Two-day passes $6, kids $2.50.) The **Palace of the Governors** (827-6483), the oldest public building in the U.S., on the north side of the plaza, was the seat of seven successive governments after its construction in 1610. The *haciendas* palace is now a museum with exhibits on Native American, Southwestern, and New Mexican history. To buy Native American crafts or jewelry, check out the displays spread out in front of the Governor's Palace each day by artists from the surrounding pueblos. Their wares are often cheaper and of better quality than those found in the "Indian Crafts" stores around town.

Across Lincoln St., on the northwest corner of the plaza, lies the **Museum of Fine Arts** (827-4455), a large, undulating, adobe building with thick, cool walls illuminated by sudden shafts of sunlight. Exhibits include works by major Southwestern artists, including Georgia O'Keeffe and Edward Weston, and an amazing collection of 20th-century Native American art.

Two other museums lie southeast of town on **Camiro Lejo,** just off Old Santa Fe Trail. The **Museum of International Folk Art,** 705 Camiro Lejo (827-8350), two mi.

south of the plaza, houses the Girard Collection of over 100,000 works of folk art from around the world. Amazingly vibrant but unbelievably jumbled, the collection is incomprehensible without the gallery guide handout. In the nearby **Museum of American Indian Arts and Culture,** photographs and artifacts unveil a multifaceted Native American tradition.

About five blocks southeast of the Plaza lies the **San Miguel Mission,** on the corner of DeVargas and the Old Santa Fe Trail. Built in 1710, the adobe mission is the oldest functioning church in the U.S. Inside, glass windows at the altar look down upon the original "altar" built by Native Americans. (Open Mon.-Sat. 9am-4:30pm, Sun. 1-4:30pm. Free.) Just down DeVargas St. is the adobe **Oldest House** in the U.S. (983-3883), dating from 1200 AD. Built by the Pueblos, the house contains the remains of a certain Spaniard named Hidalgo, who allegedly bought some love potion from a woman who resided here. Apparently he started kissing everything in sight and was beheaded several days later. (Open Mon.-Sat. Love Potion 9am-5pm. Free.)

Entertainment and Events

With numerous musical and theatrical productions, arts and crafts shows, and Native American ceremonies, Santa Fe offers rich entertainment year-round. Fairs, rodeos, and tennis tournaments complement the world-famous musicians who often play in Santa Fe's clubs and the active theater scene. For info, check *Pasatiempo* magazine, a supplement to the Friday issue of the *Santa Fe New Mexican.*

Don Diego De Vargas's peaceful reconquest of New Mexico in 1692 marked the end of the 12-year Pueblo Rebellion, now celebrated in the traditional three-day **Fiesta de Santa Fe** (988-7575). Held in early September, the celebration reaches its height with the burning of the 40-ft. *papier-mâché* **Zozobra** (Old Man Gloom). Festivities include street dancing, processions, and political satires. Most events are free. The *New Mexican* publishes a guide and schedule for the fiesta's events.

The **Santa Fe Chamber Music Festival** (983-2075) celebrates the works of great baroque, classical, and 20th-century composers. Tickets are not readily available. (Performances July to mid-Aug. Sun.-Mon. and Thurs.-Fri. in the St. Francis Auditorium of the Museum of Fine Arts. Tickets from $6-30.) The **Santa Fe Opera,** P.O. Box 2408, Santa Fe 87504-2408 (982-3855), seven mi. north of Santa Fe on Rte. 84, performs in the open, so bring a blanket. The downtown box office is in the gift and news shop of the El Dorado Hotel, 309 W. San Francisco St. (988-4455; open for ticket purchasing Mon.-Sat. 10am-1pm and 2-4pm). Standing-room only tickets can be purchased for $6. (Performances July-Aug. All shows begin at 9pm.) **Shuttlejack** (982-4311; see Practical Information) runs a bus from downtown Santa Fe to the opera before each performance.

In August, the nation's largest and most impressive **Indian Market** floods the plaza. Native American tribes from all over the U.S. participate in dancing as well as over 500 exhibits of fine arts and crafts. The **Southwestern Association on Indian Affairs** (983-5220) has more info.

At night, **Chez What?,** 213 W. Alameda (982-0099; cover $2-6), is a unique bistro and nightclub offering reggae, blues, jazz, and funk. Chez it again, Cham. More subdued revelers relax at the **El Farol,** 808 Canyon Rd. (983-9912), which features excellent up-and-coming rock and R&B musicians.

Near Santa Fe

Pecos National Monument, located in the hill country 25 mi. southeast of Santa Fe on I-25 and Rte. 63, features ruins of a pueblo and Spanish mission church. The small monument includes an easy one-mi. hike through various archeological sites. Especially notable are Pecos's renovated *kivas*—underground ceremonial chambers used in Pueblo rituals—built after the Rebellion of 1680. Off-limits at other ruins, these *kivas* are open to the public. (Open daily sunrise-sunset. $1.) The monument's **visitors center** has a small but informative museum and a 10-min. introductory film shown every half hour. (Open daily 8am-6pm; Sept. 2-May 27 8am-5pm. Free.) **Greyhound** sends early-morning and late-evening buses daily from Santa Fe to the town of Pecos, two mi. north of the monument (see Santa Fe: Practical Information). Use the campsites, or simply pitch a tent in the backcountry of in the **Santa Fe National Forest,** six mi. north on Rte. 63 (see Santa Fe: Accommodations above).

Bandelier National Monument, 40 mi. northwest of Santa Fe (take U.S. 285 to Rte. 4), features some of the most amazing pueblo and cliff dwellings in the state (accessible by 50 mi. of hiking trails), as well as 50 sq. mi. of dramatic mesas and tumbling canyons. The most accessible of these is **Frijoles Canyon,** site of the **visitors center** (672-3861; open daily 8am-6pm, winter 9am-5:30pm). A five-mi. hike from the parking lot to the Río Grande descends 600 ft. to the mouth of the canyon, past two waterfalls and fascinating mountain scenery. The **Stone Lions Shrine** (12-mi., 8-hr. roundtrip from the visitors center), sacred to the Anasazi, features two stone statues of crouching mountain lions. The trail also leads past the unexcavated Yapashi Pueblo. A two-day, 20-mi. hike leads from the visitors center past the stone lions to **Painted Cave,** decorated with over 50 Anasazi pictographs, and to the Río Grande. Both hikes are quite strenuous. Free permits are required for backcountry hiking and camping; pick up a topographical map ($6) of the monument lands at the visitors center. A less taxing self-guided one-hour tour takes you through a pueblo and past some cliff dwellings near the visitors center. You can camp at **Juniper Campground,** 1/4 mi. off Rte. 4 at the entrance to the monument. (Sites $6.) Park rangers conduct evening campfire programs at 8:45pm. (Park entrance fee $5 per vehicle.)

Los Alamos, 10 mi. north of Bandelier on NM Loop 4, stands in stark contrast to nearby towns such as Santa Fe, Taos, or Española. The U.S. government selected Los Alamos, a small mountain village at the outset of World War II, as the site of a top-secret nuclear weapons development program; today, nuclear research continues at the **Los Alamos Scientific Laboratory.** The facility perches eerily atop several mesas connected by highway bridges over deep gorges, supporting a community with more Ph.D.s per capita than any other city in the U.S. The public may visit the **Bradbury Museum of Science,** Diamond Dr., for exhibits on the Manhattan Project, the strategic nuclear balance, and the technical processes of nuclear weapons testing and verification. (Open Tues.-Fri. 9am-5pm, Sat.-Mon. 1-5pm. Free.) The **Los Alamos County Historical Museum,** 1921 Juniper St. off Central (662-6272), details life in the 1940s, when Los Alamos was a government-created "secret city." (Open in summer Mon.-Sat. 9:30am-4:30pm, Sun. 1-4pm; in winter Mon.-Sat. 10am-4pm, Sun. 1-4pm.)

Southern New Mexico

Carlsbad Caverns National Park

Imagine the surprise of the first Europeans wandering through southeastern New Mexico when tens of thousands of bats began swarming from out of nowhere at dusk. The legendary bat population of Carlsbad Caverns (a staggering 250,000) is responsible not only for its discovery at the turn of the century, when curious frontiersmen tracked the bats to their home, but also for its exploration. Miners first began mapping the cave in search of bat *guano,* an excellent fertilizer found in 100-ft. deposits in the cave. By 1923, the caverns had been designated a national park, and herds of tourists began flocking to this desolate region. The caverns are one of the world's largest and oldest cave systems. Beneath the surface rests a world of unusual creation that would make even the most jaded spelunker stand in awe. Gaping visitors can only whisper their appreciation. The unusual rock formations (with odd but descriptive names such as the Temple of the Sun and the King's Palace), the dripping waterfalls, and the enormity of this natural museum are absolutely breathtaking. There are 75 caves in the park, but only two are regularly open to the public.

Today, the **Carlsbad Visitors Center** (505-785-2232 or 885-8884; for a 24- hr. recording, call 785-2107) has replaced dung-mining with a restaurant, gift shop, a nursery, and a kennel. For $.50 you can rent a small radio that transmits a guided tour. (Open May 27-Sept. 2 daily 8am-7pm; off-season daily 8am-5:30pm.) There are two ways to see the caverns. Those with strong knees and solid shoes can take the "blue tour," traveling by foot down a steep (but paved) three-mi. descent. If you can handle it, you must take this tour—it winds dramatically from the natural entrance 750 ft. downwards, giving the best sense of the depth and extent of the caverns. The "red tour" follows an easier, shorter route, descending from the visitors center by elevator. Most of the trail is wheelchair-accessible. There are no guided tours, but explanatory plaques are posted along the paths, and small radios which transmit a guided tour are available both at the visitors center and down in the Big Room. Almost all visitors return to the surface by elevator, the last of which leaves a half-hour before the visitors center closes. Tourists should give thanks for the elevators; your 1920s counterparts either had to walk back up or ride in a bucket otherwise reserved for bat *guano*. ("Red tours" June-Aug. 8:30am-5pm; Sept.-May 8:30am-3:30pm; "blue tours" June-Aug. 8:30am-3:30pm; Sept.-May 8:30am-2pm. Tours cost $5, over 62 and ages 6-15 $3.)

Plan your visit to the caves for the late afternoon so as not to miss the magnificent nightly **bat flights**. An army of hungry bats pour out of the cave at the incredible rate of 6000 per minute. (Daily just before sunset from May to Oct.) A ranger talk precedes this amazing ritual. (Free *guano* samples.) The pre-dawn return can also be viewed. Talk to a ranger for details.

For a rugged and genuine caving experience, visit the undeveloped **Slaughter Canyon Cave** (formerly **New Cave**). Two-hour, 1¼-mi. flashlight tours traverse difficult and slippery terrain; there are no paved trails or handrails. Even getting to the cave takes some energy, or better yet, a car; the parking lot is 23 mi. down a dirt road off U.S. 62/180 south (there is no transportation from the visitors center or from White's City), and the cave entrance is still a steep, strenuous half-mi. from the lot. Call 785-2232 at least two days in advance for reservations; the park limits the number of persons allowed inside each day. Bring a flashlight. (Tours May 27-Sept. 2 daily 9am-12:30pm; in off-season weekends only. Adults $6, ages 6-15 $3. With Golden Age and Golden Access Passports $3.) Backcountry hiking is allowed in the Carlsbad Caverns National Park. Trails range up to 60 mi., and hikers are advised to talk to ranger.

Since no camping is allowed in the park, the closest source of accommodations is **White's City,** a tiny, rather tacky town on U.S. 62/80 which serves as the access point to the caverns and is the only viable option for an overnight stay in the caverns area. Much of the town's business is owned by capitalist Jack White; although motels are criminally expensive, there are some reasonable places to bed down for the night. The **Carlsbad Caverns International Hostel** (785-2291) has spacious six-bed rooms that include a kitchen, TV, pool, and spa. Modern conveniences such as A/C, stove, and TV may not be functional; to stay over night, bring insect repellent and plan on eating out. Membership required. ($10. Open 24 hrs.) The **Shady Park Entrance Campground** (785-2291; ask to be connected), is just outside the park entrance. The campground provides water, showers, restrooms, and pool. (Full hookups $15.) For cheap motel rooms, drive 20 mi. north to Carlsbad's **Motel 6,** 3824 National Parks Hwy. (885-0011). In summer, make reservations. (Singles $27. Doubles $33.) Several more inexpensive motels lie farther down the road. Additional campsites are available at nearby **Guadalupe Mountains National Park** (see West Texas).

White's City is 20 mi. southeast of Carlsbad, and seven mi. from the caverns along steep, winding mountain roads. Because flash floods occasionally close roads, call ahead. From Las Cruces on I-25, take U.S. 82 east to Alamogordo, crossing the Sacramento Mountains; then take U.S. 285 south to Carlsbad, a trip of 213 mi. in all. From El Paso, TX, also on I-25, take U.S. 62/180 east 150 mi., passing Guadalupe Mountains National Park, which is 35 mi. southwest of White's City. **Greyhound,** in cooperation with **TNM&O Coaches** (887-1108), runs three buses a day from El Paso ($25, $47.50 round-trip) or Carlsbad ($5.75 round-trip) to White's City. Two of these routes use White's City only as a flag stop. From White's City, you can take the overpriced **Carlsbad Cavern Coaches** to the visitors center ($15 round-trip for 1-3 people); buy tickets in the White's City Gift Shop where Greyhound drops you off. The **post office,** located just next to the Best Western Visitors Center, is open Mon.-Fri. 8am-noon and 1-5pm. **ZIP code:** 88268-0218. The **area code** is 505.

Truth or Consequences

The important thing about T or C for the average traveler isn't *what* it is so much as *where* it is. Smack dab in the middle of Billy the Kid country, T or C provides a launching pad for exploring the diverse attractions of this "wild West" area. T or C draws budget travelers with the **Riverbend Hot Springs Hostel,** 100 Austin St. (505-894-6183). Located on the banks of the Río Grande, with hot outdoor mineral baths, Apache tepee sleep quarters ($7 per night), nearby Turtleback Mountain, and sportsperson's paradise Elephant Butte Lake—a stay at Riverbend is a fulfilling vacation all by itself. Riverbend also has more traditional hostel sleeping accommodations ($9.50), as well as private apartments. Ask Sylvia, the hostel's friendly and concerned proprietor, for directions to area attractions: Geronimo Springs Museum, Bosque del Apache Wildlife Refuge, "Reach for the Stars" Space Center, Monticello Box Canyon, and the Mescalero Apache Reservation. She also has discounts for local movies, museums, bowling, food, and bike rentals.

Taos

Lodged between the Sangre de Cristo mountains and the canyon gouged by the Río Grande, Taos first attracted Native American tribes; still-vital pueblos are scattered throughout the valley. Spanish missionaries came later in a vain attempt to convert the indigenous populace to Christianity. The 20th century saw the town invaded by dozens of artists, such as Georgia O'Keeffe and Ernest Blumenschein, captivated by Taos's untainted beauty. Aspiring artists still flock to the city, accompanied by athletes anxious to ski or hike the nearby mountains or brave the whitewaters of the Río Grande. Taos rocks the haos.

Practical Information

Emergency: Police, 758-2216. **Ambulance,** 911.

Visitor Information: Chamber of Commerce, Paseo del Pueblo Sur (Rte. 68) (758-3873 or 800-732-8267), just south of McDonald's. Open daily 9am-5pm, Sat.-Sun. 9am-5pm. **Information booth** (no phone) in the center of the plaza. Hours vary according to number of volunteers available. Pick up maps and tourist literature from either.

Taos Municipal Airport: 758-4995, northwest of town off Hwy. 64.

Greyhound: Paseo del Pueblo Sur (Rte. 68) (758-1144), about 1 mi. south of Taos at Rte. 68 and 64 East. To: Albuquerque (2 per day, $20) and Denver (2 per day, $50). Open Mon.-Fri. 9am-1pm and 3-7pm, Sat.-Sun. and holidays 9-11am and 5-7pm.

Public Transport: Pride of Taos Trolley, 758-8340. Serves several hotels and motels as well as the town plaza and Taos Pueblo. Schedules available in the plaza, the chamber of commerce, and most lodgings. Operates daily 7:30am-6pm. Variable fare depending on destination.

Taxi: Faust's Transportation, 758-3410 or 800-345-3738. Operates daily 7am-10pm. If you sell your soul, he'll take you to hell.

Help Line: Rape Crisis, 758-2910. Open 24 hrs.

Post Office: 318 Paseo Del Pueblo Norte (Rte. 68) (758-2081), ¼ mi. north of the plaza. Open Mon.-Fri. 8:30am-5pm. **ZIP code:** 87571.

Area Code: 505.

Drivers should park on **Placitas Road,** one block west of the plaza, or at the Park-and-Ride lots along Rte. 68 at Safeway and Fox Photo.

Accommodations and Camping

The **Plum Tree Hostel (HI/AYH),** on Rte. 68, 15 mi. south of Taos in Pilar (758-4696 or 800-678-7586), hunkers down next to the Río Grande. Though angling more for the B&B crowd (hot-tub and massage $40), the manager still organizes river rafting and fine arts workshops in summer and leads free hikes into the surrounding mountains every Monday when enough guests are interested. Because the hostel is a flag stop on the Greyhound and airport shuttle routes between Santa Fe and Taos, getting in and out of town isn't a problem. (Office open daily 7:30am-10pm. $8, nonmembers $11. Linen $2.) Named for its proximity to Taos Ski Valley, the **Abominable Snowmansion Hostel (HI/AYH)** (776-8298) has been spotted in **Arroyo Seco,** a tiny town 10 mi. northeast of Taos on Rte. 150. The friendly, young hosts keep an exotic menagerie including a llama and a parrot. Guests may sleep in dorm rooms, bunk houses, or even a teepee. (Office open daily 8-10am and 4-9pm. Flexible 11pm curfew. $8.50, nonmembers $10.50; in winter $18.50 and $28. Breakfast included.) Hotel rooms are expensive in Taos. The cheapest rooms rent at the **Taos Motel** (758-2524 or 800-323-6009), on Rte. 68, three mi. south of the plaza. (Singles $25-39. Doubles $28-41.)

Camping around Taos is easy for those with a car. Up in the mountains on wooded Rte. 64, 20 mi. east of Taos, the **Kit Carson National Forest** operates three campgrounds. Two are free but have no hookups or running water; look for campers and tents and pull off the road at a designated site. **La Sombra,** also on this road, has running water. (Sites $5.) An additional six free campgrounds line the road to Taos Ski Valley. No permit is required for backcountry camping in the national forest. For more info, including maps of area campgrounds, contact the **forest service office** (758-6200; open Mon.-Fri. 8am-4:30pm). On Rte. 64 west of town, next to the awesome **Río Grande Gorge Bridge** (758-8851), is a campground operated by the Bureau of Land Management. (Sites with water and porta-potty $7. Porta-visitors center open daily 7:45am-4:30pm.)

Food

The **Apple Tree Restaurant,** 123 Bent St. (758-1900), two blocks north of the plaza, serves up some of the best New Mexican and vegetarian food in the state. Dinner ($10-18) includes a huge entrée (swimming in melted cheese and liberally garnished with chilis), homemade bread, and soup or salad. (Open Mon.-Sat. 11:30am-3pm and 5:30-9pm, Sun. 10am-3pm and 5:30-9pm.) **Michael's Kitchen,** 304 N. Pueblo Rd. (758-4178), makes mainstream munchies such as donuts, sandwiches ($4.50), and great apple pie ($1.25). (Open daily 7am-8:30pm.) Local sheriff's deputies and late night snackers frequent the **El Pueblo Café** (758-2053), located on N. Pueblo, on the east side of the road about a half-mi. north of the plaza. The café serves standard Tex-Mex fare ($4-6) and cheap breakfasts ($3.25-5.25). (Open Sun.-Thurs. 6am-midnight, Fri.-Sat. 6am-3am.) In the rear of **Amigo's Natural Foods,** 326 Pueblo Rd. (758-8493), across from Jack Donner's, sits a small but holistic deli serving such politically and nutritionally correct dishes as a not-so-spicy tofu on polygranulated bread ($3.25). (Open Mon.-Sat. 9am-7pm, Sun. 11am-5pm.) For other cheap eats, check out the pizza and fast-food places on the strip south of the plaza.

Sights and Activities

The spectacle of the Taos area has inspired artists since the days when the Pueblo exclusively inhabited this land. Many "early" Taos paintings hang at the **Harwood Foundation's Museum,** 238 Ledoux St. (758-9826), off Placitas Rd. (Open Mon.-Fri. noon-5pm, Sat. 10am-4pm. Free.) The plaza features other galleries with works by notable locals such as R.C. Gorman, as do **Kit Carson Road, Ledoux Street,** and **El Prado,** a village just north of Taos. Taos' galleries range from high-quality operations of international renown to upscale curio shops. In early October of each year, the **Taos Arts Festival** celebrates local art.

Taos artists love rendering the **Mission of St. Francis of Assisi,** Ranchos De Taos plaza (758-2754), patron saint of New Mexico. The mission has a "miraculous" painting that changes into a shadowy figure of Christ when the lights go out. (Open Mon.-Sat. 9am-4pm.) Exhibits of Native American art, including a collection of beautiful black-on-black pottery, grace the **Millicent Rogers Museum** (758-2462), north of El Prado St., four mi. north of Taos off Rte. 522. (Open daily 9am-5pm; Nov.-April Tues.-Sun. 9am-4pm. $3, seniors $2, kids $1, families $6.)

Remarkable for its five-story adobes, pink and white mission church, and striking silhouette, the vibrant community of **Taos Pueblo** (758-9593) unfortunately charges visitors dearly to look around. Much of the pueblo also remains off-limits to visitors; if this is the only one you will see, make the trip—otherwise, skip it. (Open daily 9am-5pm. $5 per car, $2 per pedestrian. Camera permit $5, sketch permit $10, painting permit $15.) Feast days highlight beautiful tribal dances; **San Gerónimo's Feast Days** (Sept. 29-30) also feature a fair and races. Contact the **tribal office** (758-9593) for schedules of dances and other info. The less-visited **Picuris Pueblo** lies 20 mi. south of Taos on Rte. 75, near Peñasco. Smaller and somewhat friendlier to visitors, Picuris is best known for its sparkling pottery, molded from mica and clay.

The state's premier ski resort, **Taos Ski Valley,** about five mi. north of town on Rte. 150, has powder conditions on bowl sections and "short but steep" downhill runs rivaling Colorado's. Reserve a room well in advance if you plan to come during the winter holiday season. (Lift tickets $35, equipment rental $10 per day. For info and ski conditions, call the Taos Valley Resort Association at 776-2233 or 800-776-1111.) In summer, the ski-valley area offers great hikes.

After a day of strenuous sight-seeing, soak your weary bones in one of the natural **hot springs** near Taos. One of the most accessible bubbles nine mi. north on Hwy. 522 near Arroyo Hondo; turn left onto a dirt road immediately after you cross the river. Following the dirt road for about three mi., turn left when it forks just after crossing the Río Grande—the hot spring is just off the road at the first switchback. Though not very private, the spring's dramatic location part way up the Río Grande Gorge more than compensates. Located 10 mi. west of Taos, the **U.S. 64 Bridge** over the Río Grande Gorge is the nation's second-highest span, affording a spectacular view of the canyon and a New Mexico sunset.

Western New Mexico

West of Albuquerque lies a vast land of forests, lava beds, and desert mesas populated by Native Americans and boomtown coal and uranium miners. Though difficult to explore without a car, the region can prove very rewarding for the dedicated adventurer.

Sun-scorched and water-poor, **Chaco Canyon** seems an improbable setting for the first great flowering of the Anasazi. At a time when most farmers relied on risky dry farming, Chacoans created an oasis of irrigated fields. They also constructed sturdy five-story rock apartment buildings while Europeans still lived in squalid wooden hovels. By the 11th century, the canyon residents had set up a major trade network with dozens of small satellite towns in the surrounding desert. Around 1150 AD, however, the whole system collapsed; with no food and little water, the Chacoans simply abandoned the canyon for greener pastures.

Only the ruins remain, but these are the best-preserved sites in the Southwest. **Pueblo Bonito,** the canyon's largest town, demonstrates the skill of Anasazi masons. Among many other structures, one four-story wall still stands. Nearby **Chetro Ketl** houses one of the canyon's largest great *kivas*, used in Chacoan religious rituals. Bring water, since even the visitors center occasionally runs dry.

The **visitors center** (988-6727 or 786-7014; 24 hrs.), at the eastern end of the canyon, houses an excellent museum that includes exhibits on Anasazi art and architecture, as well as a description of the sophisticated economic network by which the Chacoan Anasazi traded with smaller Anasazi tribes of modern Colorado and northern Mexico. (Museum open daily 8am-6pm; Sept. 2-May 27 daily 8am-5pm. Entrance fee $1 per person or $3 per carload.) **Camping** in Chaco costs $5; arrive by 3pm since space is limited to 46 sites. Registration is required. You can also make Chaco a daytrip from **Gallup,** where cheap accommodations are plentiful.

Chaco Canyon, a 160-mi., 3.5-hour drive northwest from Albuquerque, lies 90 mi. south of Durango, CO. When the first official archeologist left for the canyon at the turn of the century, it took him almost a year to get here from Washington, DC. Today's visitor faces unpaved **Rte. 57,** which reaches the park from paved Rte. 44 (turn off at the tiny town of **Nageezi**) on the north (29 mi.), and from I-40 on the south (about 60 mi., 20 mi. of it unpaved). **Greyhound's** I-40 run from Albuquerque to Gallup serves **Thoreau,** at the intersection of Rte. 57, five times per day (see Albuquerque:Practical Information).

Just west of the Continental Divide on Rte. 53, four mi. southeast of the Navajo town of **Ramah,** sits **Inscription Rock** (505-783-4226), where Native Americans, Spanish *conquistadores,* and later European pioneers made their mark while traveling through the scenic valley. Today, self-guided trails allow access to the rock as well as to ruins farther into the park. (Open daily 8am-6:30pm.) The **visitors center** (open daily 8am-7pm; in winter 8am-5pm) includes a small museum as well as several dire warnings against emulating the graffiti artists of old and marking the rocks. For those unable to resist the urge to inscribe, an alternate boulder is provided.

White Sands National Monument

Do you remember walking in the sand? Located on Hwy. 70, 15 mi. southeast of Alamogordo and 52 mi. northeast of Las Cruces, White Sands (505-479-6124) is the world's largest gypsum sand dune, composed of 300 square mi. of beach without ocean. Located in the Tularosa Basin between the Sacramento and San Andres mountains, the dunes were formed when rainwater dissolved gypsum in a nearby mountain and then collected in the basin's Lake Lucero. As the desert weather evaporated the lake, the gypsum crystals were left behind and eventually formed the continually growing sand dunes. Walking, rolling, or hiking through the dunes can provide hours of mindless fun; the brilliant white sand is especially awe-inspiring at sunset. Tragically, the basin is also home to a missile test range, as well as the **Trinity Site,** where the first atomic bomb was exploded in July 1945. Although a visit today won't make your hair fall out, the road to the park is subject to closures, usually no more than two hours, while missiles are tested; call ahead to make sure, and run like hell if you see a mushroom cloud. (Visitors Center open Memorial Day-Labor Day 8am-7pm, off-season 8am-4:30pm; dunes drive open 7am-10pm, off-season 7am-sunset. $3 per vehicle. Handicapped-accessible.) The park has a nice backcountry **campsite;** pick up maps at the visitors center. If you're not camping, make nearby **Alamogordo** your base. The city is home to several motels and restaurants, including ol' faithful, **Motel 6,** Panorama Dr. (505-434-5470), off Hwy. 70, with clean, sparse rooms, TV, a pool (one pool, not a pool in each room, silly), and a view. (Singles $21. Doubles $27.)

Oklahoma

Between 1831 and 1835, President Andrew Jackson ordered the forced relocation of "The Five Civilized Tribes" from Florida and Georgia to the designated Oklahoma Indian Territory. Tens of thousands of Native Americans died of hunger and disease on the brutal, tragic march that came to be known as the "Trail of Tears." The survivors rebuilt their decimated tribes in Oklahoma, only to be moved again in 1889 to make way for whites rushing to stake claims on newly-opened settlement lands. Those who slipped in and claimed plots before the first official land run were called "sooners"—what Oklahomans have been dubbed ever since. Ironically, when the territory was admitted to the union in 1907, it did so with a Choctaw name; Oklahoma means "land of the red man" and despite the serious mistreatment of the Native Americans, many street names carry Indian names, and cultural life seems to center around Native American heritage and experiences. There are reenactments and interpretations of the Trail of Tears in Tulsa and Oklahoma, and the world's largest collection of American art in Tulsa features 250,000 Native American artifacts.

Practical Information

Capital: Oklahoma City.

Oklahoma Tourism and Recreation Department, 500 Will Rogers Building, Oklahoma City 73105 (521-2409 or 800-652-6552 out of state), in the capitol complex.

Time Zone: Central (1 hr. behind Eastern). **Postal Abbreviation:** OK

Sales Tax: 0%.

Oklahoma City

At noon on April 22, 1889, a gunshot sent settlers scrambling into Oklahoma Territory to claim land. By sundown, Oklahoma City, set strategically on the tracks of the Santa Fe Railroad, had a population of over 10,000 homesteaders. The city became state capital in 1910. The 1928 discovery of oil modernized the city; elegant homes rose with the oil derricks. As the wells dried up and the oil business slumped, Oklahoma City fell on hard times. The **OKC National Stockyards** still thrive with activity, and the **National Cowboy Hall of Fame** pays homage to the city's rugged past.

Orientation and Practical Information

Emergency: 911.

Chamber of Commerce Tourist Information, 4 Santa Fe Plaza (278-8912), at the corner of Gaylord. Open Mon.-Fri. 8am-4:30pm.

Traveler's Aid: 417 N.W. 5th (232-5507), at Main. Open Mon.-Fri. 8am-5pm.

Will Rogers Memorial Airport, 681-5311, southwest of downtown. **Airport Limousine, Inc.,** 3805 S. Meridian (685-2638), has van service to downtown ($9).

Greyhound: 427 W. Sheridan Ave. (235-6425), at Walker. In a rough part of town. Take city bus #5, 6, 11, or 12. To: Tulsa (8 per day, 2 hr., $13); Dallas (4 per day, 5 hr., $29); and Kansas City (6 per day, 10 hr., $57). Open 24 hrs.

Public Transport: Oklahoma Metro Area Transit, 300 E. California Blvd. (235-7433). Bus service Mon.-Sat. 6am-7pm. All routes radiate from the station at Reno and Gaylord, where maps are available for 50¢. Route numbers vary depending on the direction of travel. Fare 75¢, seniors and kids 35¢.

Taxi: Yellow Cab, 232-6161. $2.50 first mi., $1.45 each additional mi. Airport to downtown fare $12.50.

Car Rental: Rent-a-Wreck, 2930 N.W. 39th Expressway (946-9288). Used cars $27 per day with unlimited free mileage within the state, 125 free miles out of state, 24¢ each additional mi. Open Mon.-Fri. 8am-6pm, Sat. 8am-noon. Must be 21 with major credit card. The state of Oklahoma does *not* honor the International Driver's License.

Bike Rental: Miller's Bicycle Distribution, 215 W. Boyd. (321-8296). Ten-speeds and mountain bikes $3 per day, if rented for more than three days. Open Mon.-Sat. 9am-6pm. Major credit card or $75 cash deposit required ($250 deposit for mountain bikes).

Help Lines: Contact, 848-2273 or 840-9396 for referrals and crisis intervention. **Rape Crisis,** 943-7273. **Gays Anonymous,** 672-3733. **Oasis Community Center** 525-2437 provides a weekly meeting place for gays and lesbians. All open 24 hrs.

Post Office: 320 S.W. 5th St. (278-6300). Open Mon.-Fri. 8:30am-5:30pm, Sat. 9am-noon. **ZIP code:** 73125.

Area Code: 405.

Main Street divides the town east-west. Traveling by car is the best way to go; almost all of the city's attractions are outside the city center, but are accessible by the all-encompassing Metro Transit.

Accommodations, Camping, and Food

The **YMCA,** 125 N.W. 5th St. (232-6101), has rooms for men only. Shared bath. Pool, gym, TV lounge. (Singles $12. Key deposit $5.) Nearby, the **Kirkpatrick Hotel,** 620 N. Robinson Ave., (236-4033) offers the cheapest motel-type rooms only 3 blocks from downtown. The aging building has nice clean rooms in a youthful neighborhood. Laundry service. (Singles $12. Doubles $15.) The **Travel Inn,** 501 N.W. 5th Ave. (235-7455) beats it all. Unmatched in price and service an easy 5 blocks from the Greyhound station, the Inn has large well-furnished rooms. A/C, heat, free local calls, cable and HBO. (Singles $23. Doubles $33.) The **Brass Lantern Inn,** 700 N.W. 9th St. (232-0505) proffers clean, quiet, comfortable and amply lit rooms. From downtown, take bus #8,11, or 38 and get off at St. Anthony's hospital—it's across the street. (Singles $25. Doubles $28.) I-35 near Oklahoma City is lined with inexpensive hotels that offer singles for under $25.

Oklahoma City has two readily accessible campgrounds. **RCA,** 12115 Northeast Expy. (478-0278), next to Frontier City Amusement Park 10 mi. north of the city on I-35, has a pool, laundry room, and showers and lots of fast-food restaurants nearby. (Tent sites for two $9, RV sites with hookup $16. Open 8am-10pm.) The nearest state-run campground lies on Lake Thunderbird about 30 mi. south of OKC at **Little River State Park** (360-3572 or 364-7634). Take I-40 East to the Choctaw Rd. exit, then south until the road ends, and make a left. Simply set up a tent, and a collector will come around for your money. (Tent sites $4, $5 in area with gate attendant; showers included. Seniors, and people with disabilities pay ½-price. Open 8am-5pm.)

Since Oklahoma City contains the largest feeder cattle market in the U.S., beef tops most menus. Founded in 1926, the **Cattlemen's Café,** 1309 S. Agnew (236-0416), is a classic diner a block away from the stockyards. Try the chopped sirloin dinner ($7) or the navy bean soup with cornbread ($1.50). (Open Sun.-Thurs. 6am-10pm, Fri.-Sat. 6am-midnight.) **Sweeney's Deli,** 900 N. Broadway (232-2510), serves up tasty dishes in a friendly atmosphere; play pool or watch the big-screen TV. The restaurant received the 1988 "good country cooking" award. Sandwiches $3-4, burgers $2.20, hot plates $4. (Open daily 11am-11pm.) **Pump's Bar and Grill,** 5700 N. Western (840-4369), is a renovated gas station serving innovative fuel, like "Oklahoma crepes" (chicken, cream cheese, and jack cheese enchiladas topped with sour cream), burgers, and sandwiches ($3.50-7). (Open Sun.-Thurs. 11am-11pm, Fri.-Sat. 11am-midnight.) Downtown, the **Century Center Plaza,** 100 Main St., oozes with cheap lunch spots. (Open Mon.-Sat. 11am-3pm.)

Sights and Entertainment

The **Oklahoma City Stockyards,** 2500 Exchange Ave. (235-8675), are the busiest in the world. Cattle auctions, held here Monday through Wednesday, begin at 7 or 8am and sometimes last into the night. Monday and Tuesday are the busiest days; Monday morning is the best time to visit. An auctioneer fires bids in a rapid monotone as cowhands chase the cattle through a maze of gates and passages into the auction building. Visitors enter free of charge via a calfwalk over the pens, leading from the parking lot east of the auction house. Take bus #12 from the bus terminal to Agnon and exchange.

The plight of Native Americans along the "Trail of Tears" is commemorated by James Earle Fraser's *The End of the Trail.* Ironically, his sculpture of a man slumped over an exhausted pony is on display at the **National Cowboy Hall of Fame and Western Heritage Center,** 1700 N.E. 63rd St. (478-2250). The Hall contains such pistol-packin' frontiersmen as Barry "Buck" Goldwater and Ronald "Brawny Ronny" Reagan. Along with Frederic Remington sculptures and cowboy memorabilia, you'll find John Wayne's collection of Pueblo kachina dolls (and you thought *real* men didn't play with dolls!) Every summer, the museum showcases 150 works of the National Academy of Western Art. Take bus #22 from downtown. (Open May 27-Sept. 2 daily 8:30am-6pm; off-season daily 9am-5pm. $5, seniors $4, ages 6-12 $2.) The **State Capitol,** 2300 N. Lincoln Blvd. (521-3356), is the world's only capitol building surrounded by working oil wells. Completed in 1917, the Greco-Roman structure was inadvertantly but appropriately built atop a large reserve of crude oil. (Open daily 8am-7pm. Guided tours 8am-3pm. Free.)

The **Kirkpatrick Center Museum Complex,** 2100 N.E. 52nd St. (427-5461) is a sort of educational amusement park. It looks like a mall but it's actually a pastiche of eight separate colorful and entertaining museums. Highlights are the **Air and Space Museum** and the **International Photography Hall of Fame.** Take bus #22. (Open May 27-Sept. 2 Mon.-Sat. 9am-6pm, Sun. noon-6pm; off-season Mon.-Fri. 9:30am-5pm, Sat. 9am-6pm, Sun. noon-6pm. Admission to all 8 museums $6, seniors and ages 3-12 $3.50.)

Nightlife in Oklahoma City is as rare as the elusive jackelope. For ideas, pick up a copy of the *Oklahoma Gazette.* City slickers beware: the **First National Bar,** 4315 N. Western (525-9400), ain't no sushi place. Live bands, pool tables and a raucous crowd make this bar a local favorite. (Open Mon.-Sat. 10am-2am.) The **Oklahoma Opry,** 404 W. Commerce (632-8322), is home to a posse of country music stars. (Regular performances Sat. at 8pm; tickets $6, seniors $5, kids $2.) The **Black Liberated Arts Center,** 1901 N. Ellison (528-4666), provides plays and musical events at the Classen Theater from October to May. (Office open Mon.-Fri. 10am-4pm.)

Near Oklahoma City

Prudent travelers will skip OKC's nightlife, wake up early and drive to **Anadarko,** a short 60-mi. drive through the Great Plains. Anadarko is home to **Indian City USA** (405-247-5661), a museum which has reconstructed villages of seven Native American tribes. During the summer, each tour begins with a performance of Native American dances by prize-winning dancers. Talk to the dancers or one of the guides; the conversation will tell more about the tragedy of Native Americans than any Oscar-winning Kevin Costner movie ever can. Drive south from Oklahoma City on I-44 40 mi. to exit #83, take a right on 9 West, go about 20 mi. to Anadarko, take a left on 8 South, and go two mi. to the museum entrance. (Open daily 9am-6pm, 9am-5pm during off-season. $7, kids $4.)

For those in search of a home where the buffalo roam and the deer and the antelope play, check out the **Wichita Mountain Wildlife Refuge** (405-429-3222), an hour south of Anadarko. Created in 1905 by Teddy Roosevelt, the National Park is home to 625 buffalo, thousands of deer and Texas longhorns, and various other wildlife, all of which cavort freely in the park. **Mount Scott** is only 2464 ft. high, but because it rises over a plain, it offers a stupendous vista those who drive or hike to the top. Camping is permitted in certain areas of the park; stop at a refuge office for maps. Take exit #49 off I-44. (Open daily; some areas close at dusk.)

Tulsa

First settled by Creeks arriving from the "Trail of Tears," Tulsa's location on the banks of the Arkansas River made it a logical trading outpost for Europeans and Native Americans. The advent of railroads and the discovery of huge oil deposits catapulted the city into an oil capital by the 1920s. The city's varied heritage is visible today in its art deco skyscrapers, French villas, and Georgian mansions, as well as its Native American community, the second largest among U.S. metropolitan areas.

Practical Information

Emergency: 911.

Convention and Visitors Division, Metropolitan Tulsa Chamber of Commerce, 616 S. Boston (585-1201 or 800-558-3311).

Greyhound: 317 S. Detroit (584-4427). To: Oklahoma City (8 per day, 2 hr., $13); St. Louis (9 per day, 7½-9½ hr., $69); Kansas City (4 per day, 6-8 hr., $55); Dallas (5 per day; 7 hr.; $44). Lockers $1. Open 24 hrs.

Public Transport: Metropolitan Tulsa Transit Authority, 510 S. Rockford (582-2100). Buses run Mon.-Sat. 6am-5pm. Fare 60¢, transfers 5¢, seniors and disabled (disabled card available at bus offices) 30¢, ages 5-18 50¢, under 5 free with adult. Maps and schedules are available at the main office (open Mon.-Fri. 8am-4:45pm), the chamber of commerce, and most libraries and restaurants, but are not always reliable.

Taxi: Yellow Cab, 582-6161.

Bike Rental: River Trail Sports Center, 3949 Riverside Dr. (743-5898), at 41st St. Five-speeds $4 per hr., $12 per day. Rollerblades $5 per hr., $10 per day. Open Mon.-Sat. 10am-8pm, Sun. 11am-6pm. Must have driver's license or cash deposit.

Help Lines: 583-4357, for information, referral, crisis intervention. Open 24 hrs. **Gay Information Line,** 743-4297. Open daily 8am-10pm.

Post Office: 333 W. 4th St. (599-6800). Open Mon.-Fri. 8:30am-5pm. **ZIP code:** 74101.

Area Code: 918.

Tulsa is divided into blocks of one square mile. Downtown lies at the intersection of **Main Street** and **Admiral Boulevard.** All "North" addresses are north of Admiral; all "South" addresses are south of Admiral. Numbered streets lie along the north and south of Admiral in increasing order. Named streets stretch north to south in alphabetical order. Those named after western cities are on the west side of Main St.; after eastern cities on the east side of it. (Note: not all north-south streets are city-named.) Every time the alphabetical order reaches the end, the cycle begins again. If possible, navigate by car. Outside of downtown, sidewalks are scarce and bus routes limited.

Accommodations and Camping

Most cheap accommodations in Tulsa are outside of city center. An exception is the **YMCA,** 515 S. Denver (583-6201), for men only. Ask for a room on the third floor. Guests have access to a TV lounge, pool and gym; the office is open 24 hrs. (Singles $11; key deposit $10.) The cheapest downtown motel is the **Darby Lane Inn,** 416 W. 6th St. (584-4461). Clean, spacious rooms have cable TV. (Singles $36. Doubles $42. Suites with two queen-size beds and kitchen $40. Call for reservations.) Budget motels are plentiful along I-44 and I-244. To reach the **Gateway Motor Inn,** 5600 W. Skelly Dr. (446-6611), take bus #17 and get off at Rensor's Grocery. Clean rooms replete with large beds, HBO, and cable. (Singles $19. Doubles $24.) The **Roadway Motel,** 4724 S. Yale (496-9300), just south of I-44, is notable for its central location. From downtown take bus #15, get off at 49th and Yale, and walk two blocks north. (Singles $25. Doubles $30.)

The **KOA Kampground,** 193 East Ave. (266-4227), ½ mi. west of the Will Rogers Turnpike Gate off I-44, has a pool, laundry room, showers, and game room. (Sites $14, with hookup $15.) **Keystone State Park** (865-4991) offers three campgrounds along the shores of Lake Keystone, 20 mi. west of Tulsa on the Cimarron Turnpike (U.S. 64). The wooded park offers hiking, swimming, boating, and excellent catfish and bass fishing. (Sites $10, with hookup $14. Tent camping $4.) Four-person cabins with fireplaces and kitchenettes are also available for $43; call 800-522-8565 for reservations.

Food

Nelson's Buffeteria, 514 S. Boston (584-9969), takes you on a sentimental journey through Tulsa's past while you eat. Operating since 1929 and now run by Nelson Jr., this old-style diner's walls are blanketed with Mid-American memorabilia. Try a blue plate special (two scrambled eggs, hash browns, toast and jam, $2) or the famous chicken-fried steak ($4.50). Remember to ask for extra gravy. (Open Mon.-Fri. 6am-2:30pm.) Only three blocks from the YMCA is the **Little Ancient Denver Grill,** 112 S. Denver (582-3790). Frequented by rough-hewn locals, this family-run eating house offers a wide-variey of local treats at reasonable prices. Lunch specials ($4) include a salad, freshly baked rolls, and a choice of vegetable. (Open Mon.-Sat. 6am-8pm, Sun. 8am-4pm.) **Casa Bonita,** 2120 S. Sheridan Rd. (836-6464), offers large Mexican feasts ($5-7) and all-you-can-eat dinners ($8) in a highly entertaining atmosphere. The dining areas range in décor from rustic candle-lit caves to south-of-the-border villages. (Open Sun.-Thurs. 11am-9:30pm, Fri.-Sat. 11am-10pm). Route 66 (between Main and Lewis) welcomes hungry budget travelers. Many low-priced restaurants are open on weekends. Inconspicuous but unrivaled among them is the **Route 66 Diner,** 2639 E. 11th St. (592-6666). Run by a couple with old Tulsa blood and a long culinary tradition, the diner is a great bargain for lunch ($3-6). Meatloaf ($4), the are-you-sure-you're-*that*-hungry double burger ($5.50)—daily special ($4.75). Menu varies but will never leave you hungry. Many downtown restaurants close at 3pm weekdays and 1pm Saturdays.

Sights and Entertainment

Perched atop an Osage foothill two mi. northwest of downtown, the **Thomas Gilcrease Museum,** 1400 Gilcrease Museum Rd. (582-3122), houses one of the world's largest collections of American art. Designed as an anthropological study of North America from pre-history to the present, the museum contains 250,000 Native American artifacts and more than 10,000 paintings and sculptures by artists such as Remington and Russell. Take bus #7 ("Gilcrease") from downtown. (Open Mon.-Sat. 9am-5pm, Sun. 1-5pm. Donation requested. Disabled accessible.) The **Philbrook Art Center,** 2727 S. Rockford Rd. (749-7941), in the former Renaissance villa of an oil baron, houses a collection of Native American pottery and artifacts alongside Renaissance paintings and sculptures. Picnic by the lovely pond on the grounds. Take bus #16 ("S. Peoria") from downtown. (Open Tues.-Sat. 10am-5pm, Thurs. 10am-8pm, Sun. 1-5pm. $3, seniors and students $1.50, ages 12 and under free.) The **Fenster Museum of Jewish Art,** 1223 E. 17th Pl. (582-3732), housed in B'nai Emunah Synagogue, contains an impressive if oddly located collection of Judaica dating from 2000 BC to the present. (Open Tues.-Fri. 10am-4pm, Sun. 1-4pm.)

The most frequented tourist attraction in Tulsa, **Oral Roberts University,** 7777 S. Lewis (495-6161), was founded in 1964 when Oral had a dream in which God commanded him to "Build Me a university." The heavenly edict inspired a divine design so radiant it puts any secular campus to shame. Walking onto the campus is like entering the twilight zone. The ultra-modern, gold-mirrored architecture rising out of an Oklahoma plain, the 80-ft.-high praying hands sculpture guarding the campus, and the hordes of believers flocking to visit make this eerie and kitschy experience a must. The **Prayer Tower** (495-6807) takes visitors through an exhibition honoring the university's founder. You might remember this as Oral's retreat when, a few years back, he threatened to have God "take him home" if he didn't get a giant wad of cash from his followers. Choirs sing in the background, spotlights illuminate mementos from the Roberts' childhood, and doors open and close automatically as if by divine command. Oral Roberts' City of Faith Hospital, commissioned by a 900-ft.-tall Jesus, is now leased to a cancer research center. The **ORU Healing Outreach** (496-7700) hosts a "Journey Through the Bible" tour, where Old Testament scenes are re-created in life-like, three-dimensional exhibits. (Open Mon.-Sat. 10:30am-4:30pm, Sun. 1-5pm. Tours every 15-20 min. Free.) The rest of the non-drinkin', non-smokin', and non-dancin' campus is (alas! alack!) closed to the public. The university is about six miles south of downtown Tulsa between Lewis and Harvard Ave. Take bus #9 ("S. Lewis"). (Prayer Tower and visitors center open Mon.-Sat. 10:30am-4:30pm, Sunday 1-4:30pm.)

During the oil boom years of the 1920s, art deco architecture was all the rage in Tulsa. The best example of this style is the **Boston Avenue United Methodist Church,**

1301 S. Boston (583-5181). Built in 1929, the house of worship is vaguely suggestive of the witch's palace in *The Wizard of Oz.* Climb the 14-story tower to the pea-green worship room with a skyline view of Tulsa. (Tours given Mon.-Fri. 9am-4pm, Sun. 12:15pm. Free)

Rodgers and Hammerstein's *Oklahoma!* continues its run under the stars at the **Discoveryland Amphitheater** (245-0242, for tickets 800-338-6552), 10 mi. west of Tulsa on 41st St., accessible only by car. It features what is now the state song and commemorates the suffering of the Okie farmers in the 19th century. (Shows June-Aug., Mon.-Sat. at 8pm. Mon.-Thurs. $12, seniors $11, under 12 $7) Arrive early for the pre-show barbecue, starting at 5:30pm. ($7, seniors $6.50, kids $5.) A short western review precedes the show. A most moving commemoration of Native American heritage is the **Trail of Tears Drama,** a show reenacting the Cherokees' tragic march, performed in Tahlequah, 66 mi. east of Tulsa on Rte. 51. (Performances June-Sept. 2 Mon.-Sat. at 8pm. For tickets, call 456-6007, or write P.O. Box 515, Tahlequah, OK 74465; reservations recommended. $9, under 13 $4.50.) For more cultural enlightenment, the **Tulsa Philharmonic** (747-7445) and **Tulsa Opera** (582-4035) perform year-round. The **Tulsa Ballet** (585-2573) has been acclaimed one of America's finest regional troupes. These performances take place at the **Performing Arts Center** at the corner of 3rd St. and Cincinnati. (596-7111.)

Exercisers should rent a bike and ride down beautiful **Riverside Drive,** on the east bank of the Arkansas River. The neighborhood west of Riverside between 21st and 50th Streets is full of nice homes and is an excellent place for a walk or a bike ride. Nature-lovers should visit the **NW Park and Rose Garden,** at Peoria and 23rd. (749-6401). This 46-acre wooded park features beautiful flowers including Azeleas, Irises, and spring bulbs. (Open daily 6am-9pm.)

At night, head to the bars along 15th St. east of Peoria, or in the 30s along S. Peoria. Down at the **Sunset Grill,** 3410 S. Peoria (744-5550), nightly rowdy rock bands accompany free popcorn and a free midnight buffet. (Open daily 8pm-2am; must be 21; no cover.) Keep up to date on Tulsa's nightlife with a free copy of *Urban Tulsa,* available at newsstands, bookstores, and the chamber of commerce, or by calling 585-2787.

The best times to visit Tulsa are during annual special events like the **International Mayfest** (582-6435) in mid-May. This outdoor food, arts, and performance festival takes place in downtown Tulsa over a ten-day period. The mid-August **Pow-Wow** (835-8699), held at Mohawk Park just northwest of the airport, attracts Native Americans from dozens of different tribes. The three-day festival includes a trade fair, arts and crafts exhibits, and nightly dancing contests which visitors may attend. Admission is $5 per car.

Utah

Once home to dinosaurs, Utah now beckons bipedal mammals to its variegated landscape, which ranges from a vast lake of salt water to a multitude of bizarre rock formations. Southern Utah is an otherworldly amalgam of redstone canyons, deep river gorges, arches, spires and columns carved out of the terrain by erosion. Northeastern and central Utah feature the Uinta Mountains and National Forests, dotted with lakes and speckled with aspens and ponderosa pine.

Driven westward by religious persecution, members of the Church of Jesus Christ of Latter Day Saints began settling Utah in 1848; today Mormons make up over 80% of the state population. Mormon culture is characterized by intensely family-oriented values, abstinence from alcohol and caffeine, and a history of polygamy. Mormon culture is ubiquitous in the state, making a trip to Utah a journey outside the "mainstream" U.S—unless, like the skiers who flock to Park City and Alta, you only come for the snow.

Practical Information

Capital: Salt Lake City.

Visitor Information: Utah Travel Council, Council Hall/Capitol Hill, 300 N. State St., Salt Lake City 84114 (538-1030), across the street from the capitol building. Information on national and state parks, campgrounds, and accommodations. Open summer Mon.-Fri. 8am-5pm. Pick up a free copy of the *Utah Travel Guide,* with a complete listing of motels, national parks, and campgrounds. **Utah Parks and Recreation,** 1636 W. North Temple, Salt Lake City 86116 (538-7220). Open Mon.-Fri. 8am-5pm.

Time Zone: Mountain (2 hrs. behind Eastern).

Postal Abbreviation: UT

Area Code: 801.

Sales Tax: 6.25%.

Arches National Park

In Arches National Park, nature has experimented with modern sculpture for eons. Three hundred million years ago, a constantly moving primordial sea deposited an uneven, unstable salt bed on the Colorado Plateau. The sea evaporated, but periodic washes, along with the tireless winds, deposited layer after layer of debris upon the new salt crust. This detritus compacted into extremely heavy rock, and the salt twisted and crumbled under the weight. Through buckling and caving below and erosion above, the sandstone layers were shaped into fantastic spires, pinnacles, and, of course, arches. Arches National Park has more than 200 arches; because of their nearly perfect form, explorers first thought the huge arches were the works of some lost civilization.

The park **visitors center,** 27 mi. on U.S. 191 south of I-70, 3½ mi. north of Moab, provides $3 self-guided car tours. (Open daily 8am-7pm; off-season daily 8am-4:30pm.) For additional information, contact the Superintendent, Arches National Park, P.O. Box 907, Moab 84532 (259-8161). An **entrance pass** ($3 per carload) remains valid for seven days; pedestrians and bikers pay only $1. Water is available in the park.

Plenty of scenic wonders embellish the 25-mi. road between the visitors center and Devil's Garden. No matter how short your stay, be sure to see the **Windows** section at **Panorama Point,** about halfway along the road. Cyclists will enjoy this ride in spring or fall, but the steep inclines make the trip almost unbearable in the summer heat. **Rim Cyclery,** 94 W. 100 North (259-5333), offers rimming bikes for $20 per day, including helmet and water bottle. (Open daily 9am-6pm.) At the end of the paved road by the campground, **Devil's Garden** boasts an astounding 64 arches. A challenging hike from the **Landscape Arch** leads across harrowing exposures to the secluded **Double O Arch.** The climax of your visit should be **Delicate Arch,** the symbol of the monument. Take the Delicate Arch turn-off from the main road, two mi. down a graded unpaved road (impassible after rainstorms). Once you reach Wolfe Ranch, go down a 1½-mi. foot trail to the free-standing Delicate Arch. Beyond, you can get a glimpse of the Colorado River gorge and the La Sal Mountains. If you're lucky, you may come across petroglyphs on the stone walls left by the Anasazi and Ute who wandered the area from 1000 to 100 years ago.

Of course, arches aren't the only natural wonders here. Two of the most popular trails, the mile-long **Park Avenue** and the moderately strenuous two-mi. **Fiery Furnace Trail,** lead downward into the canyon bottoms, providing views of the cliffs and monoliths above. Only experienced hikers should attempt the Fiery Furnace Trail alone; a ranger leads group tours into this labyrinth at both 9am and 5pm daily.

The park's only campground, **Devil's Garden,** has 53 sites; get there early since sites are often snatched up by noon. The campground is 18 mi. from the visitors center and has running water April through October. (No wood-gathering allowed. 2-week max. stay. Sites $3. Make reservations through the Superintendent, Arches National Park,

P.O. Box 907, Moab, UT 84532; 801-259-8161.) **Dead Horse Point State Park** ($3), perched on the rim of the Colorado Gorge south of Arches and 14 mi. south of U.S. 191, is accessible from Rte. 313. The campground has modern restrooms, water, electric hookups, and covered picnic tables. (Sites $8. Open April-Oct.) Winter camping is allowed on Dead Horse Point itself. For more information, contact the Park Superintendent, Dead Horse Point State Park, P.O. Box 609, Moab 84532 (259-6511).

Backcountry camping in Arches National Park is a free adventure. Register at the National Park Service office in Moab (2 blocks west of the Ramada Inn on Main St.) first, and pick up a USGS map to avoid getting lost. Bring plenty of water, and avoid hiking on summer afternoons. In the summer, escape the heat, crowds, and biting gnats at the **Manti-la-Sal National Forest**. Campgrounds here are about 4000 ft. higher up and about 20 to 25 mi. southeast of Moab off U.S. 191. All cost $6 to $8, except **Oowah,** which is free. Three mi. down a dirt road is **Oowah Lake,** a rainbow trout heaven, at least from an angler's point of view (fishing permit $5 per day). For more information on the forest, contact the Manti-la-Sal National Forest Service office in Moab, 125 W. 200 South (259-7155; open Mon.-Fri. 8am-4:30pm).

The entrance to the Arches National Park is a paved road that winds for 25 mi. into its interior. This road is accessible from U.S. 191 at the junction five mi. north of Moab. The park is 230 mi. from Salt Lake City. There is no public transportation to Arches, but buses run along I-70, stopping in Crescent Junction.

Bryce Canyon National Park

The fragile, slender spires of pink and red limestone that rise gracefully out of Bryce's canyons often seem more like an surrealist painting than the result of whimsical wind and water currents. Beautiful as they may be, these barren canyons etched by millenia of erosion made life extremely difficult for both the Paiute natives and the white settlers who had to navigate the area. Ebenezer Bryce, the first white man to glimpse the canyon, called it "one hell of a place to lose a cow."

The park's **visitors center** (801-834-5322) is the place to begin any tour. Pick up a copy of the free Bryce Canyon *HooDoo,* which lists all park services, events, suggested hikes, and sight-seeing drives. (Open daily 8am-8pm; off-season daily 8am-4:30pm.)

Many designated hikes let you explore Bryce without guessing. The most popular scenery is concentrated within two mi. of the visitors center. Three spectacular lookouts—**Sunrise Point, Sunset Point,** and **Inspiration Point**—invigorate even the weariest traveler. Sunrises here are particularly rewarding. The section between Sunrise and Sunset Points is wheelchair-accessible. The three-mi. loop of the **Navajo** and **Queen's Garden** trails wind you into the canyon itself. If you are up to the challenge, branch off onto the **Peek-A-Boo Trail,** a four-mi. round-trip. Escape the crowds by conquering the **Trail to the Hat Shop,** a strenuous 3.8-mi. journey along an extremely steep descent. And if you think climbing *down* is tough...

If you don't want to hike, drive the 15 mi. from the visitors center to **Rainbow Point** and stop at the various lookouts along the way. Or take the **1938 Limousine Tour** that departs from Bryce Lodge. If you prefer organic transportation, arrange a horseback tour through **Bryce-Zion-Grand Trail Rides,** Box 58, Tropic, UT 84776 (801-834-5219 in summer, 801-679-8665 off-season).

Bryce has two campgrounds planted among the tall ponderosa pines: **North Campground** and **Sunset Campground.** Both have toilets, picnic tables, and drinking water. (Sites at both $6.) Sunrise Point (834-5361), west of both campgrounds, has public showers and a small grocery store. (Open from May 1 8am-8pm. Showers $1.25 per 10 min., available 8am-10pm.) **Backcountry camping** at designated sites is a lovely way to get intimate with the canyon's changing moods and wildlife. A free permit is required and available at the **Nature's Center** by **Sunrise Point.** Of the six **Dixie National Forest** campgrounds, most about an hour away just off Rte. 14, the best are **TE-AH Campground, Spruces Campground,** and **Navajo Lake Campground.** All except Navaho have toilets; all have running water, swimming, boating and fishing. (All

$6 per night; no showers.) The nearest forest service office is in **Panguitch,** 225 E. Center St. (676-8815; open Mon.-Fri. 8am-4:30pm).

Memorial Day through Labor Day, **Ruby's Inn Rodeo** (834-5341) pits human against beast every night except Sunday at 7:30pm (admission $5, kids $3). Another popular annual event, the **Fiddler's Association Contest,** tunes up in early July.

Bryce Canyon lies five hours south of Salt Lake City and 45 minutes east of Cedar City on U.S. 89 in southwestern Utah. From U.S. 89 at Bryce Junction (7 mi. south of Panguitch), turn east on Rte. 12 and drive 17 mi. to the park entrance (entrance fee $5 per car, $2 per pedestrian). There is no public transportation within the park or from Cedar City; this is *not* the place to get stranded.

Bryce has a **post office** at Ruby's Inn (open Mon.-Fri. 8:15am-2:15pm, Sat. 8:15am-12:15pm). The **ZIP code** is 84764. The 24-hr. park **emergency** number is 801-676-2411. You can call collect.

Near Bryce

To hike into the desert environment of the ominously named **Phipps Death Hollow Outstanding Natural Area,** part of a network of sandstone canyons just north of Escalante, contact the **Bureau of Land Management,** Escalante Ranger District, Escalante 84726 (826-4291), on Rte. 12, about one mi. west of town. (Open Mon.-Fri. 7:45am-4:30pm, Sat. 8am-noon; off-season Mon.-Fri. 8am-4:30pm.) Fifteen mi. east of Escalante on Rte. 12 is the popular **Calf Creek** camping grounds, with a great hike near a cascading waterfall. (Sites $5, including drinking water and fresh toilets.) Boulder has the **Anasazi Museum** off Rte. 12 (335-7308), which displays a reconstructed Anasazi village dating from about the year 1100. (Open daily 8am-6pm.) The Anasazi ("ancient ones") disappeared almost completely around 1250. The style of basket-weaving among present-day Hopis indicates a connection to the Anasazi, whom anthropologists think left the area to assimilate with other tribes during a 23-year drought around 1150. If you don't mind dodging cows and driving on dirt roads, head out three mi. to **Lower Bowns Reservoir Lake** (826-4221; no drinking water, pit toilets).

Wandering out of Bryce in the opposite direction, on Rte. 14 to Cedar City, you'll come across the refreshing and surprisingly green **Cedar Breaks National Monument** ($3 per car, $1 per pedestrian). The rim of this giant amphitheater is a lofty 10,350 ft. above sea level; 2000 ft. of flowered slopes separate the rim from the chiseled depths (disabled access). At **Point Supreme** you'll find a 30-site **campground** (sites $5) and the **visitors center** (586-9451; open summer Mon.-Thurs. 8am-6pm, Fri.-Sat. 8am-7pm). For more information, contact the Superintendent, Cedar Breaks National Monument, P.O. Box 749, Cedar City 84720.

Cedar City's **Iron Mission State Park,** 585 N. Main St. (586-9290), has an amazing horse-drawn vehicle collection which merits a visit. (Open daily 9am-7pm; off-season daily 9am-5pm. $1, under 6 free.) The **Economy Motel,** 443 S. Main St. (586-4461), has very basic rooms; try to get one with a book-sized window. (Singles $30. Doubles $35.) For more information, contact the **Cedar City Visitors Center,** 100 E. Center St. (586-4484; open Mon.-Fri. 8am-5pm).

Canyonlands National Park

The grooved and gnarled landscape of Utah is largely indebted to the constant chiseling of the Green and Colorado Rivers. It is at Canyonlands National Park that these two arch-landscapers combine forces. The merging rivers here have gouged out rifts and gorges that sink into the desert's crust with a dizzying declivity. Harsh desert prevails in the rest of the park, producing a unique desert environment. Largely neglected by the family-with-a-Winnebago tourist throngs, this area is a diamond in the rough.

Outside the park, there are two visitors centers. Monticello's **Interagency Visitors Center,** 32 S. 1st E. (587-3235), sells area maps ($3-6). (Open Mon.-Fri. 8am-4:30pm) In **Moab** (see below), the **Park Service** resides at 125 W. 200 S. (259-7164) and has the same business hours. Both can provide information in German and Italian.

The park contains three distinct areas. The visitors center for **Needles** (259-2652) lies in the park's southeast corner. To get there, take Rte. 211 west from U.S. 191, about 40 mi. south of Moab. There is neither gas nor water available within the park. (Open daily 8am-4:30pm.) Farther north, the **Island in the Sky** visitors center sits deep within the "Y" formed by the two rivers (259-4351; open daily 8am-6pm). Take Rte. 313 west from U.S. 191 about 10 mi. north of Moab. The most remote district of the park is the rugged **Maze** area (visitors center 259-2652; open daily 8am-4:30pm), to the west of the canyons, accessible only by four-wheel drive. Once you've entered a section of the park, you're committed to it—unless you're flying a helicopter, transferring from one area to another involves retracing your steps and re-entering the park, a tedious trip lasting from several hours to a full day.

Each visitors center has a booklet of possible hikes (including photos), so you can pick your own. Hiking options from the Needles area are probably the best, though Island in the Sky offers some spectacular views. Cyclists should check at the visitors centers for lists of trails. If hiking in desert heat doesn't appeal to you, you can rent jeeps and mountain bikes in Moab, or take a one-hr. airplane flight from **Red Tail Aviation** (259-7421) that can cost as little as $45 per person for a group of four.

There are no food services in the park. Just outside the boundary in the Needles district, however, the **Needles Outpost** houses a limited, expensive grocery store and gas pumps. Hauling groceries, water, and first-aid supplies in from Moab or Monticello is the best budget alternative.

Each region has its own official **campground.** In the Needles district, **Squaw Flat** is situated in a sandy plain surrounded by giant sandstone towers, 35 mi. west of U.S. 191 on Rte. 211. Avoid this area in June, when insects swarm. Bring fuel and water, although the latter is usually available from April through September. A $7 fee is charged year-round. **Willow Flat Campground,** in the Island in the Sky unit, sits high atop the mesa, on Rte. 313, 41 mi. west off U.S. 191. You must bring your own water; sites are free. Willow Flat and Squaw Flat both have picnic tables, grills, and pit toilets; they operate on a first-come, first-served basis. The campground at the **Maze Overlook** has no amenities at all. Dead Horse Point State Park (adjacent to Island in the Sky) and Manti-la-Sal National Forest (adjacent to the Needles) provide alternative campsites. (See Arches National Park for information on these campgrounds.) Before **backcountry camping,** get a free permit from the visitors center in the proper district and take along plenty of water (at least 1 gallon per person per day). Summer temperatures regularly climb to over 100°F.

Moab

Dubbed "the mountain bike capital of the Known Universe," Moab's tongue-in-cheek sobriquet nevertheless evokes its dual populace—the hippie, Birkenstocked group whose universe is forever groovy, and the die-hard athletes who've hardly let the snow melt from their ski boots before they go white-water rafting or mountain biking. With its proximity to Arches and Canyonlands, and its youthful, "crunchy" character, the booming town of Moab provides a great base for exploring the region, either by car, mountain bike, or raft on the Green River.

Adrift Adventures, 378 North Main (259-8594 or 800-874-4483), will show you the territory via raft, jeep, jet boat, mountain bike or horseback. Any way you choose will cost a pretty penny, but a ½-day rafting trip does the least damage at $26, ages 7 to 17 $22.

In summer Moab fills up fast, especially on weekends; call ahead to guarantee your reservations. The manager of the **Lazy Lizard International Hostel,** 1213 S. U.S. 191 (259-6057), goes out of the way to be helpful and will route your trip through Arches or elsewhere. The kitchen, VCR, laundry, and hot tub are at your beck and call. (Bunks $6. Singles $15. Doubles $20.) **The Prospector Lodge,** 186 N. 1st West (259-5145), one block west of Main Street, offers cool, comfy rooms across the street from the local hippie co-op. (Singles $23. Doubles $26.) All motels will charge a little less in the off-season.

Private campgrounds speckle the area surrounding Moab. The **Holiday Haven Mobile Home and RV Park,** 400 West (259-5834), charges $12 per site, $11 with water, $14 with electricity and water, and $16 with full hookup. The **Canyonland Campark,** 555 S. Main St. (259-6848), asks $11.50 per site, $15 for electricity and water, $17 for a full hookup, and $2 per extra person, and has a pool. The **Moab KOA,** four mi. south on U.S. 191 (259-6682), charges $12 for a tent site, $16 with electricity and water, $16.25 for full hookup, and $18.25 for full hookup with A/C. It has a pool, TV room, laundry facilities, rec center, snack bar, mini golf, and a playground. Fun for the whole family!

Moab bakes 50 mi. southeast of I-70 on U.S. 191, 15 mi. south of Arches. There is no public transportation to Moab, although buses will stop along I-70, in Crescent Junction.

The **Moab Visitors Center,** 805 N. Main St. (259-8825 or 800-635-6622), can provide information on lodging and dining in Moab. (Open Mon.-Sat. 8am-5pm, Sun.10am-7pm.) The **Post Office** is at 39 S. Main St. (644-2760; open Mon.-Fri. 8:30am-4pm, Sat. 9am-noon); the **ZIP code** is 84532.

Salt Lake City

In a little town outside of Rochester, NY, in 1830, 15-year-old Joseph Smith had a vision commanding him to start a new religion: the Church of Jesus Christ of Latter Day Saints. Known as Mormons because of the *Book of Mormon,* which Smith is said to have translated from ancient tablets, his followers fled westward from persecution, stopping for periods in Ohio, Illinois, Missouri and Nebraska until finally settling in Salt Lake City in 1847. Situated in mountainous, desert terrain near an inland salt lake, Salt Lake City bears a peculiar resemblance to the better-known Christian Holy Land. The city is graced with the spiritual centers of the Church of Latter Day Saints, including the gargantuan Mormon Temple and the Mormon Tabernacle Choir, as well as most of the cultural and intellectual institutions of Utah.

Practical Information and Orientation

Emergency: 911.

Visitor Information: Salt Lake Valley Convention and Visitors Bureau, 180 S. West Temple (521-2868 or 800-831-4332), 2 blocks south of Temple Sq. Open Mon.-Fri. 8am-7pm, Sat. 9am-4pm, Sun. 10am-4pm; off-season Mon.-Fri. 8am-5:30pm, Sat. 9am-6pm, Sun. 10am-4pm. Has a very handy phone system that allows you to call local motels and attractions for free. Other **visitors centers** at: Crossroads Mall, 50 S. Main St.; ZCMI Mall, 36 S. State St. (321-8745; open Mon.-Fri. 7:30am-9pm, Sat. 8am-6pm); and terminal 2 at the airport. The free *Salt Lake Visitors Guide* details a good self-guided tour.

Tours: Gray Line, 553 W. 100 South (521-7060). 2½-hr. tours of the city focusing on Mormon historical sites. Departures in summer daily at 9am and 2pm. Fare $14, kids $7. A tour of the Great Salt Lake copper mine is also offered daily at 2pm ($22).

Salt Lake City International Airport: 776 N. Terminal Dr. (539-2205), 4 mi. west of Temple Sq. UTA buses provide the best means of transport to and from the airport. Bus #50 serves the terminal directly. **Delta/Western Airlines** flies here from Los Angeles, San Francisco, and Denver.

Amtrak: 325 S. Rio Grande (364-8562 or 800-872-7245). Trains once daily to: Denver (13½ hr.; $103); Las Vegas (8 hr.; $86); Los Angeles (15 hr.; $136); and San Francisco (17 hr.; $140). Ticket office open Mon.-Sat. 4am-9:30am, 10am-12:30pm and 5:15pm-1am; Sun. 5:15pm-1am.

Greyhound: 160 W. South Temple (355-4684), 1 block west of Temple Sq. To: Cheyenne (3 per day; 9 hr.; $61); Las Vegas (2 per day; 10 hr.; $46); San Francisco (3 per day; 15 hr.; $81); Boise (3 per day; 7 hr.; $46); Denver (4 per day; 12 hr.; $60). Ticket counter open daily 5am-10pm. Terminal open 24 hrs.

Public Transport: Utah Transit Authority, 600 S. 700 West (287-4636 until 7pm). Frequent service to the University of Utah campus; buses to Ogden (#70/72 express), suburbs, airport, and east to the mountain canyons. Buses every ½ hr. or more 6:30am-11pm. To Provo 5:30am-10pm; fare

60¢, seniors 30¢ under 5 free. Maps available from libraries or the visitors bureau (see above). Information desk at ZCMI Mall, 36 S. State St.

Taxi: City Cab, 363-5014. **Ute Cab,** 359-7788. **Yellow Cab,** 521-2100. 95¢ base fare, $1.40 per mi., about $12 from the airport to Temple Sq.

Car Rentals: Payless Car Rental, 1974 W. North Temple (596-2596). $23 per day with 200 free mi., or $110 per week with 1200 free mi.; 12¢ each additional mi. Open Sun.-Fri. 6am-10pm, Sat. 8am-6pm. Must be 21 with a major credit card. If you drive outside UT with one of their cars you will be charged by the mi.

Bike Rental: Wasatch Touring, 702 E. 100 South (359-9361). 21-speed mountain bikes $15 per day. Open Mon.-Sat. 9am-7pm.

Help Lines: Rape Crisis, 467-7273. 24-hr. hotline.

Post Office: 230 W. 200 South (530-5902), 1 block west of the visitors bureau. Open Mon.-Fri. 8am-5:30pm, Sat. 9am-2pm. **ZIP code:** 84101.

Area Code: 801.

Salt Lake's grid system makes navigation quite simple. Brigham Young, the city's founder, designated **Temple Square,** in the heart of today's downtown, as the center. Street names indicate how many blocks east, west, north or south they lie from Temple Square. **Main Street,** running north-south, and **Temple Street,** running east-west, are the "0" points. Smaller streets and streets that do not fit the grid pattern often have non-numerical names. Occasionally, a numbered street reaches a dead end, only to resume a few blocks farther on.

The city's main points of interest lie within the relatively small area bounded by the railroad tracks around 400 West, the **University of Utah** at 1300 East, the **State Capitol** at 300 North, and **Liberty Park** at 900 South. Liberty Park can be dangerous at night—watch your back. The downtown is equipped with audible traffic lights for the convenience of blind pedestrians. A "cuckoo" is a green light for east-west travel while "chirps" indicate a green light for north-south travel.

Accommodations and Camping

The Avenues (HI/AYH), 107 F St. (363-8137), 5 blocks east of Temple Sq. Bright rooms with 4 bunks each or private singles and doubles. Popular with British and German students. Blankets and linens provided. Kitchen and laundry available. Check-in 8am-10pm. Dorm rooms with shared bath $10, nonmembers $14-25. Singles with private bath $20. Doubles $30. Hostel closed 11am-5:30pm daily.

Kendell Motel, 667 N. 300 West (355-0293), 10 blocks northwest of Temple Sq. Enough room for you and your entourage. Well-kept rooms with kitchens, color TV, and A/C $25. Huge dorm-style rooms with kitchen and nice bath for $15 per person. More hostel accommodations are under construction.

Dean's Motor Lodge, 1821 S. Main (486-7495). Basic rooms with A/C and heat, color TV with HBO. Check out the cute lobby. Singles start at $27. Doubles start at $28.

Motel 6, 3 locations: 176 W. 600 South (531-1252); 1990 W. North Temple (364-1053), 2½ mi. from the airport (take bus #50); and 496 N. Catalpa (561-0058), just off I-15 with white cockatoo in office. All fill quickly. Singles $32. Doubles $39. Catalpa and downtown locations $3 more.

Camping is available outside the city. The **Wasatch National Forest** (524-5030) skirts Salt Lake City on the east, proffering many established sites. The terrain by the city is quite steep, making the best sites those on the far side of the mountains. Three of the closest campgrounds lie near I-215, which fronts the mountain off of I-80. Between Miles 11 and 18 out of Salt Lake City on I-80, there are four campgrounds with more than 100 sites altogether (no hookups). Go early on weekends to ensure a space (sites $5; take "Fort Douglas" bus #4). The **Utah Travel Council** (538-1030) has detailed information on all campsites in the area, including the three near the ski areas off Rte. 152 and 210 to the south of Salt Lake. The **state parks** around Salt Lake also offer camping, though no sites on the lake itself. **East Canyon State Park,** 30 mi. from Pioneer State Park in Salt Lake, near the junction of Rte. 65 and 66, has sites by East Canyon Reservoir—a good place to go boating and fishing. (Open April-late Nov.) State parks normally charge $3 for day use and $5 for sites. For more information, contact **Utah Parks and Recreation** (see Utah: Practical Information above). If you need a hookup, the **KOA,** 1400 W. North Temple (355-1192; sites $15, with water and electricity $18, full hookup $20) and other private campgrounds are your only options.

Food

Affordable food abounds in Salt Lake City, but is rarer downtown. Fill up on **scones,** adopted from the British and made into a Utah specialty. Otherwise stick to ethnic food downtown or the cheap, slightly greasy eateries on the outer fringe.

La Frontera, 3784 West 3500 S. (967-9905), west of downtown but worth the trip. Live music and delicious cheese enchiladas ($2). Open Sun.-Thurs. 10am-10pm, Fri.-Sat. 10am-11pm. Another location at 1736 West 4th St. (532-3158). No credit cards accepted.

Bill and Nada's Café, 479 S. 6th St right by Trolley Sq. (354-6984). One of Salt Lake's most revered cafés. Patsy Cline on the jukebox and paper placemats with U.S. presidents on the tables. Two eggs, hash browns, toast $3. Roast leg of lamb, salad, soup, vegetable and potatoes $5.25. Open 24 hrs.

Río Grande Café, 270 Rio Grande (364-3302), in the Rio Grande Railroad depot, 4 blocks west of the Temple by Amtrak and the Historical Society. Take bus #16 or 17. Stylish, fun Mexican restaurant with neon-and-glass décor. Open for lunch Mon.-Sat. 11:30am-2:30pm and for dinner Mon.-Thurs. 5-10pm, Fri-Sat. 5-11pm, Sun. 5-10pm.

Union Cafeteria (581-7256), at the university. Serves the cheapest grub in town—choose from a café, a sweet shop, or a deli. Chat with students over breakfast ($1-2), lunch, or dinner ($2-3). Open Mon.-Fri. 7am-6:30pm, Sat. 8am-8pm, Sun. 10:30am-8pm.

Salt Lake Roasting Company, 249 E. 400 South (363-7572). Classical or jazz music amidst burlap bags of coffee beans. Caters to the twentysomething set. Coffee (80¢) and pastries; quiche ($3); soup ($1.50). Open Mon.-Sat. 6:45am-midnight.

The Sconecutter, 2040 S. State St. (485-9981). The Elvis of sconemakers. Your favorite flavor of fluffy but stuffing scone only $1. Try the cinnamon and butter. Restaurant open Sun.-Thurs. 7am-midnight, Fri.-Sat. 7am-3am. Drive-through open 24 hrs.

Café Rude, 961 S. State St. (595-6660), belches out breakfast all day long ($2.50-4.50) and creative veggie meals for lunch and dinner (around $5).

Mormon Sights

Salt Lake City is the world headquarters of the **Church of Jesus Christ of Latter Day Saints** whose followers hold both the *Book of Mormon* and the *Bible* to be the word of God. The highest Mormon authority and the largest Mormon temple reside here.

Temple Square (240-2534) is the symbolic center of the Mormon religion. Feel free to wander around the flowery and pleasant 10-acre square, but the sacred temple is off-limits to non-Mormons. Alighting on the highest of the building's three towers, a golden statue of the angel Moroni watches over the city. The square has two **Visitors Centers** (north and south), each of which stocks information and armies of smiling guides. A 45-minute **Historical Tour** leaves from the flagpole every 10 minutes. Also, a **Book of Mormon Tour** and a **Purpose of Temple Tour** leave alternately every 30 minutes and explain the religious meaning behind Temple Square. (Visitors centers open daily 8am-10pm; off-season daily 9am-9pm.)

Visitors on any tour in Temple Square will visit the **Mormon Tabernacle,** the earthbound UFO that houses the famed Choir. Built in 1867, the structure is so acoustically sensitive that a pin dropped at one end can be heard 175 ft. away at the other end. Rehearsals on Thursday evening (8pm) and Sunday morning broadcasts from the tabernacle are open to the public (arrive by 8:45am). Though supremely impressive, the Choir can't match the size and sound of the 11,623-pipe organ that accompanies it. (Recitals Mon.-Sat. at noon; summer Sun. 2pm as well.) **Assembly Hall,** next door, also hosts various concerts almost every summer evening.

Around the perimeter of Temple Sq. stand several other buildings commemorating Mormon history in Utah. The **Genealogical Library,** 35 N. West Temple (240-3702), provides the resources for Mormons and others to research their lineage, in accordance with Mormon belief that ancestors must be baptized by proxy to seal them into an eternal family. If you've ever wanted to research your roots, this may be the place to do it; the library houses the largest collection of genealogical documents in the world. An orientation film is available. (Open Mon. 7:30am-6pm, Tues.-Fri. 7:30am-10pm, Sat. 7:30am-5pm. Free.)

The **Museum of Church History and Art,** 45 N. West Temple (240-3310), houses Mormon memorabilia from 1820 to the present. (Open Mon.-Fri. 8am-4:45pm. Call a week in advance to make reservations for a tour. Free.) Once the official residence of Brigham Young while he served as governor of the Territory and president of the Church, the **Beehive House,** N. Temple at State St. (240-2671), two blocks east of Temple Sq., gives half-hour guided tours every 10 to 15 minutes (Open June 1-Aug. 31 Mon.-Fri. 9:30am-6:30pm, Sat. 9:30am-4:30pm, Sun. 10am-1pm. Closes 1pm on all holidays. Free.)

The city of Salt Lake encompasses the **Pioneer Trail State Park,** 2601 Sunnyside Ave. (584-8391), in Emigration Canyon on the eastern end of town. Take bus #4 or follow 8th South St. until it becomes Sunnyside Ave., then take Monument Rd. The **"This is the Place" Monument** commemorates Brigham Young's decision to settle in Salt Lake; a **visitors center** will tell you all about the Mormons' long march through Ohio, Illinois, and Nebraska. Tour **Brigham Young's forest farmhouse** (open daily 11am-5pm), where the dynamic leader held court with his numerous wives. (Park grounds open in summer daily 8am-8pm, but visit 9am-7:30pm for the best reception. Parking fee $1.50 adults and $1 ages 6-15.)

Secular Sights and Activities

The grey-domed **capitol** lies behind the spires of Temple Square. Tours (521-2822) are offered daily from 9am to 3:30pm. For more info, contact the **Council Hall Visitors Center** (538-1030), across from the main entrance. (Open daily 8am-5pm.) While in the capitol area, hike up City Creek Canyon to **Memory Grove,** savoring the shade as you gaze out over the city, or stroll down to the **Church of Jesus Christ of Latter Day Saints Office Building,** 50 E. North Temple, and take the elevator to the 26th-floor observation deck from which you can see the Great Salt Lake to the west, and the Wasatch Mountain Range to the east. (Open April-Oct. Mon.-Sat. 9am-5pm; Oct.-April Mon.-Fri. 9am-5pm.) Also on capitol hill is the **Hansen Planetarium,** 15 S. State St. (538-2098). Even if you don't pay for a show, enjoy the fabulous free exhibits. (Open daily 10am-8pm.) Head for the **Children's Museum,** 840 N. 300 West (328-3383), to pilot a 727 jet or implant a Jarvik artificial heart in a life-sized "patient." (Open Mon. 9:30am-9pm, Tues.-Sat. 9:30am-5pm, Sun. noon-5pm. $3, ages 2-14 $2.50. Take bus #61.) You also can walk through the University of Utah campus to the **Utah Museum of Natural History,** 215 South and 1350 East (581-4303), which catalogues the variety of flora and fauna that has lived on the Salt Lake plain. (Open Mon.-Sat. 9:30am-5:30pm, Sun. noon-5pm. $2, ages under 14 $1, students free.) Next door is the yard-sale-like collection at the **Utah Museum of Fine Arts** (581-7332; open Mon.-Fri. 10am-5pm, Sat.-Sun. 2-5pm; free). For information on university happenings contact the **Information Desk** in the U. of Utah Park Administration Building (581-6515; open Mon.-Fri. 8am-8pm), or the **Olpin Student Center** (581-5888; open Mon.-Sat. 8am-9pm).

Next to the Amtrak station, the **Utah State Historical Society,** 300 Rio Grande (533-5755), hosts an interesting series of exhibits, including pre-Mormon photographs and quilts. (Open Mon.-Fri. 8am-5pm, Sat. 10am-2pm. Free.)

The **Utah Symphony Orchestra** (533-6407) performs in **Symphony Hall,** Salt Palace Center, 100 S. West Temple, one of the most spectacular auditoriums in the country. (Free tours Tues. and Fri. at 1, 1:30, 2 and 2:30pm. Concert tickets $12-18, student rush $5.) Dance and opera performances occur at the neighboring **Salt Lake Art Center** (328-4201; open Mon.-Sat. 10am-5pm; donation).

Alcohol and Nightlife

The Mormon Church's prohibitions against alcohol consumption among its members have led to a number of state restrictions. Utah law requires that all liquor sales be made through state-licensed stores; don't be surprised if you can't get more than a beer at most restaurants or bars. The drinking age of 21 is well-enforced. (State liquor stores open Mon.-Sat. 11am-7pm. There are6 within3 mi. of downtown Salt Lake City.) A number of hotels and restaurants have licenses to sell mini-bottles and splits of wine, but consumers must make drinks themselves. Public bars serve only beer. Only private clubs requiring membership fees are allowed to serve mixed drinks. Some clubs have two-week trial memberships for $5; others will give a free, temporary membership to visitors in town for a night or two.

Despite the alcohol restrictions, there are several fun downtown bars and clubs, which collegians keep fairly crowded. The **Dead Goat Saloon,** 165 S. West Temple (328-4628), attracts Anglo-Saxon tourists as well as locals. (Open Mon.-Fri. 11:30am-1am, Sat. 6pm-1am, Sun. 7pm-1am. Beer served until 1am. No BYOB. Cover $3, Fri.-Sun. $5.) Head over to the **X Wife's Place,** 465 S. 700 East (532-2353), to shoot stick with the boys. (Open Mon.-Fri. 4pm-1am, Sat. 5pm-1am. Beer served. No cover.)

Club DV8, 115 S. West Temple (539-8400), deviates from the straight and narrow. Friday is college night. (Open Thurs.-Sat. 9pm-1am. ½-price drafts from 9-10pm. Thurs. is modern music night. Cover $1.) **The Zephyr,** 79 W. 300 South (355-2582), blows with live rock and reggae nightly. (Open daily 7pm-2am; off-season daily 7pm-1am. Cover $5-10.) **Junior's Tavern,** 202 E. 500 South (322-0318), is the favorite local watering hole for jazz and blues aficionados. (Open daily noon-1am. Music starts at 9pm. Cover varies.)

Near Salt Lake City

The **Great Salt Lake,** a remnant of primordial Lake Bonneville, is a bowl of salt water in which only blue-green algae and brine shrimp can survive. The salt content varies from 5 to 15% and provides such buoyancy that it is almost impossible for the human body to sink; only the Dead Sea has a higher salt content. Unfortunately, flooding sometimes closes the state parks and beaches on the lakeshore, but you can still try **Saltair Beach,** 17 mi. to the west, or head north 40 minutes to fresh-water **Willard Bay.** Bus #37 ("Magna") will take you within only four mi. of the lake. Be warned that the aroma around the lake ain't rosy. Contact the visitors center (see Practical Information above) or the state parks (538-7220) for current information on access to the lake, as it is fairly difficult to reach without a car.

In the summer, escape the heat with a drive or hike to the cool breezes and icy streams of the nearby mountains. One of the prettiest roads over the Wasatch Range is **Route 210.** Heading east from Sandy, 12 mi. southeast of the city, this road goes up **Little Cottonwood Canyon** to the Alta ski resort. The **Lone Peak Wilderness Area** stretches away southward from the road, around which the range's highest peaks (over 11,000 ft.) tower. **City Creek, Millcreek,** and **Big Cottonwood** also make good spots for a picnic or hike.

Of the seven **ski resorts** within 40 minutes of downtown Salt Lake, **Snowbird** (521-6040; lift tickets $34) and **Park City** (649-8111; lift tickets $32) are two of the classiest. For a more affordable alternative, try the nearby **Alta** (742-3333; lift tickets $22). The **Alta Peruvian Lodge** (328-8589) is a great place to pass the night. (Bunks $12.50.) **UTA** (see Practical Information above) runs buses from Salt Lake City to the resorts in winter, with pick-ups at downtown motels. You can rent equipment from **Breeze Ski Rentals** (800-525-0314), at Snowbird and Park City ($15; 10% discount if reserved over 2 weeks in advance; lower rates for rentals over 3 days). Call or write the Utah Travel Council (see Utah: Practical Information above). Ask for the free *Ski Utah* for listings of ski packages and lodgings. The **Utah Handicapped Skiers Association,** P.O. Box 108, Roy 84067 (649-3991), provides information, specialized equipment, and instruction for disabled skiers. (Open Mon.-Fri. 9am-5pm.)

Some resorts offer summer attractions as well. You can rent mountain bikes at **Snowbird** (see above) for $16 per day or $9 per half-day. Snowbird's **aerial tram** climbs to

11,000 ft., offering a spectacular view of the Wasatch Mountains and the Salt Lake Valley below. (Open daily 11am-8pm. $6, seniors and under 16 $3.50.) During the summer, **Park City** offers a comparable **gondola ride**. (Open Fri.-Mon. noon-6pm. $5, under 12 $4.) Their **alpine slide** provides the fastest transport down the mountain. (Open daily 10am-10pm. $3.75, seniors and kids $2.75. Take I-80 east 30 mi. from Salt Lake.)

Northeastern Utah

In this little-known region where Utah, Colorado, and Wyoming meet, you'll find a microcosm of the entire history and landscape of the west. The Drive Through the Ages, on U.S. 191 from the Wyoming border to Vernal, twists and turns through a billion years of the Earth's history in just a couple hundred mi. The giant lizards that once lumbered through the long-vanished marshes are now neatly exhibited at Dinosaur National Monument; nearby, the spiny points of the snow-capped Uinta Mountains protrude from the desert plateau.

In addition to U.S. 191, many other roads (U.S. 40, Rte. 150, Rte. 414, and Rte. 530) break away from mind-numbing I-80 and facilitate exploration of the region. **Greyhound** sends its beasts of burden down I-80 four times per day as well as past the Uintas and Dinosaur Monument on the south, along U.S. 40. Even the most remote parts of the area are within a half-day's drive of Salt Lake City.

Dinosaur National Monument

Dinosaur National Monument is more than just a heap of bones. The Green and Yampa Rivers have here created vast, colorful gorges and canyons, and the harsh terrain evokes eerie visions of its reptilian past. Pick, pick, pick up, up, up the monument visitors guide *Echoes* for more detailed information.

The park **entrance fee** is $5 per car, $2 for bikers, pedestrians, and those in tour buses. The more interesting western side lies along Rte. 149 off U.S. 40 just outside of **Jensen,** 30 mi. east of Vernal. Seven mi. from the intersection with U.S. 40 is the **Dinosaur Quarry Visitors Center** (789-2115; open 8am-7pm), accessible from the road by free shuttle bus or a fairly strenuous half-mi. walk (cars prohibited in summer). A hill inside the center has been partially excavated to reveal the hulking remains of dinosaurs. (Center open daily 8am-4:30pm, with extended summer hours. You can drive your car in after closing.) Winter finds the park lonely, cold, and fossilized with neither shuttle service nor the possibility of self-guided tours. A few miles farther along Rte. 149 you'll find the shady **Green River Campground** with flush toilets, drinking water, and tent and RV sites. (Open late spring-early fall. Sites $6.) There are also several free primitive campsites in and around the park; call the visitors center for info. Past the campgrounds on Rte. 149, just beyond the end of the road, you can see one of the best examples of the monument's many Native American petroglyphs.

The eastern side of the park is accessible only from U.S. 40, outside **Dinosaur, CO.** The 25-mi. road (closed in winter) to majestic **Harper's Corner,** at the junction of the Green and Yampa River gorges, begins two mi. east of Dinosaur. From the road's terminus, a two-mi. round-trip nature hike leaves for the corner itself. It's worth the sweat; the view is one of the most spectacular in all of Utah.

A rugged 13 mi. east of Harper's Corner is the **Echo Campground,** the perfect location for a crystalline evening under the stars. Watch for signs near Harper's Corner leading to a dirt road that snakes its way past cattle and sheep into the valley below. (Free.) The **Dinosaur National Monument Headquarters,** on U.S. 40 in Dinosaur, CO (303-374-2216), at the intersection with the park road, provides orientation for exploring the canyonlands of the park and information on nearby river rafting. (Open June-Aug. daily 8am-4:30pm; Sept.-May Mon.-Fri. 8am-4:30pm.) For more information on this side of the park, write to the Monument Superintendent, P.O. Box 210, Dinosaur, CO 81610. Also, along U.S. 40, on the border between Utah and Colorado, is the **Colorado Welcome Center,** 101 Stegosaurus Rd., which offers information on various seasonal activities in Colorado. (Open May 1-Nov. 8am-6pm daily.)

The **Terrace Motel,** 301 Brontosaurus Blvd. (303-374-2241), has clean, beautiful rooms in mobile home units. (Singles $24-25. Doubles $32.) The **Park Motel,** 105 E. Brontosaurus Blvd. (303-374-2267), offers three beds for $28 or a family unit (5 people) for $43. (Closed during the winter.)

Greyhound makes a daily run both east and west along U.S. 40, fortunately *not* fueled by Fred and Barney's feet. (2 per day July-Aug.) Buses stop in Vernal and Dinosaur en route from Denver and Salt Lake City. Jensen is a flag stop, as is the monument headquarters, two mi. west of Dinosaur. The **Vernal depot** is at 38 E. Main St. (789-0404; open Mon.-Fri. 10am-1pm and 4:30-5:30pm, Sat. 11am-noon and 4:30-5:30pm). From Salt Lake City to: Vernal (3½ hr.; $33) and Dinosaur, CO (4 hr.; $42; there is no depot in Dinosaur—if you would like the bus to stop there, you must call ahead and arrange a time).

Dinosaur, CO's **post office** is at 198 Stegosaurus Dr. (303-374-2353; open Mon.-Fri. 8:30am-12:30pm and 1-5pm). The **ZIP code** is 81610.

Zion National Park

Some 13 million years ago, the cliffs and canyons of Zion made up the sea floor. That sea has been reduced to the lone, powerful Virgin River, which today carves fingers through the Navajo sandstone. Cut into the Kolob Terrace, the walls of Zion now tower 2400 ft. above the river. In the 1860s, Mormon settlers came to this area and enthusiastically proclaimed they had found the promised land. But Brigham Young thought otherwise and declared to his followers that the place was awfully nice, but "not Zion." The name "not Zion" stuck for years until a new wave of entranced explorers dropped the "not," giving the park its present name.

The main visitors center in the park, **Zion Canyons Visitors Center** (722-3256), takes up the southeast corner of the park, a half mi. off Rte. 9, which connects I-15 and U.S. 89 along the southern border of the park. It has an introductory slide program and a small but interesting museum. The **Kolob Canyons Visitors Center** (586-9548) lies in the northwest corner of the park, off I-15. (Both open daily 8am-5pm; off-season daily 8am-4:30pm.) The **park entrance** fee is $5 per car, $2 per pedestrian. Carry water wherever you go in the park. For **emergency assistance,** call 772-3256 during the day, 772-3322 after hours.

Even if you wisely plan to visit **Kolob Canyon's** backcountry, be sure to make the pilgrimage to **Zion Canyon.** Drive along the seven-mi. dead-end road that follows the floor of the canyon, take the bus-tram (summer only; $5, kids $2.50), or the upper canyon tour (summer only; $2.75, kids $1.75). You'll ride through the giant formations of **Sentinel, Mountain of the Sun,** and the overwhelming symbol of Zion, the **Great White Throne.** Short hikes to the base of the cliffs may be made by wheelchair as well as on foot. A challenging trail takes you to **Observation Point,** where steep switchbacks let you explore an impossibly gouged canyon. Another difficult trail (5 mi.) ascends to **Angel's Landing,** a monolith that offers a heart-stopping path along the ridge and an amazing view of the canyon. A great two-mi. hike runs to the Upper Emerald Pool, passing the less spectacular lower and middle pools on the way. For fun without the sweat, rent an inner tube ($3) from the shop across from the Canyon Supermarket, and float down the **Virgin River** near the campgrounds at the southern entrance.

If you don't plan to spend the night under the stars, spend it **Under the Eaves,** 980 Zion Park Blvd., in Springdale (772-3457). Make reservations early, for these gorgeous rooms, featuring four-poster beds and stained glass windows go quickly. Perfect for couples and small families; pluses include a quaint hot tub and a full breakfast. (Rooms from $35 for 2 people, $10 per additional person.)

Forty mi. south of Zion in the town of **Kanab** is the **Canyonlands International Youth Hostel,** 143 E. 100th S. (801-644-5554). The hostel offers roomy bunks, and manager Errol offers free coffee and friendly conversation. Feels like home. (Room with private bath and breakfast $9.)

The park maintains two campgrounds at the south gate, **South Campground** and **Watchman Campground.** Bathrooms and drinking water available. (Sites $7; 2-week max. stay. Always open.) **Zion Canyon Campground** (772-3237) has a supermarket, showers and laundry facilities for the weary, hungry and filthy. (Sites $12 for 2 people, full hookup $14. Extra adult $2, kids ages 4-15 50¢. Open 8am-9pm.) The visitors center rangers present campfire programs nightly at 9pm. Conveniences include a grocery store (772-3402; open 8am-8pm) and coin-op laundry just outside the south entrance, about a 10-minute walk from the campgrounds. The park's only other campground is a primitive area at **Lava Point,** accessible from a hiking trail in the midsection of the park or from the gravel road that turns off Rte. 9 in **Virgin.** You must obtain a free permit from a visitors center for **backcountry camping,** but don't camp within the canyon. Check the backcountry shuttle board in the Zion Canyon Visitors Center for rides into and out of the canyon's rough. Observation Point provides one of the only canyon rim spots where you can pitch a tent. Many backpackers spend a few nights on the 27-mi. **West Rim Trail** (too long for a day's hike) or in the Kolob Canyons, where crowds never converge. Zion Campground doesn't take reservations and often fills on holiday and summer weekends; if you don't get in, try one of the six campgrounds in Dixie National Forest (see Bryce Canyon).

Zion National Park can be reached from I-15, via Rte. 17 (Toqueville exit) or from U.S. 89, via Rte. 9 (at Mount Carmel Junction). The main entrance to the park is in **Springdale,** on Rte. 9, which bounds the park to the south along the Virgin River.

Greyhound runs along I-15, to the west of the park; ask to be let off, since the park is not a scheduled stop. In St. George (43 mi. southwest of the park on I-15), the bus station is located on 70 W. St. George Blvd. (673-2933), next to the Travelodge. Buses run to: Salt Lake City (2 per day; 6 hr.; $52) and Provo (5 hr.; $42.50); Los Angeles (6 per day; 15 hr., $92) and Las Vegas (2 hr.; $29).

The Pacific Northwest

The drive of "manifest destiny" brought 19th-century pioneers to the Pacific Northwest, some of the most beautiful and awe-inspiring territory in the United States. Lush rainforests, snow-capped peaks, and the deepest lake on the continent all reside in this corner of the country. Oregon's Dunes, Washington's Cascade Mountains, miles and miles of the Pacific Crest Trail, and a long, stormy coast inhabited by sea lions and giant redwoods draw the rugged individualist and the novelty-seeking city-slicker alike.

Settled like jewels amidst the wet and wild lands of the Pacific Northwest, the cities of this region sparkle with all the urban flair of their Northeastern counterparts. But unlike New York, Washington, DC, or Boston, the cosmopolitan communities of Seattle and Portland have spectacular mountain ranges in their backyards. The Northwestern traveler can hike the Cascade Range by day and club-hop by night, ride Seattle's monorail or a raft down southern Oregon's wild river rapids.

The Northwest coastal region remains cool and misty year-round. The fertile central valleys enjoy a mild climate, with warm summers and rainy winters. The Cascade Range keeps moisture and cool air from dripping into eastern Washington and Oregon, where the arid climate resembles that of the Rocky Mountain states.

For info on national parks in the region, contact the Pacific Northwest Regional Office, National Park Service, 2001 6th Ave., Seattle, WA 98121 (206-442-0170). The national forest system manages huge expanses of land, including the West Coast's least spoiled natural landscapes—the designated wilderness areas. Reach the Pacific Northwest Region at U.S. Forest Service, P.O. Box 3723, Portland, OR 97212. For more comprehensive coverage of the Pacific Northwest than can be provided here, please consult *Let's Go: Pacific Northwest, Western Canada, & Alaska.*

Oregon

Although their shoreline, inland forests, and parks share all the lush drama of those in California, Oregon residents for years disdained the gaggles of tourists that overran their southern neighbor. The 1980s brought hard times for Oregonians, however, and with them a reconsideration of this once-widespread xenophobia. Bumper stickers that read "Don't Californicate Oregon" disappeared, and cities that once thrived as mining and forestry centers were resurrected as tourist havens.

But travelers are nothing new to the Beaver State. Lewis and Clark rented canoes and slipped quietly down the Columbia River to the sea; later, waves of settlers surged westward towards the coastal terminus of the Oregon Trail. Most present-day explorers seek Oregon's unadulterated wilderness, including 11,000-ft. mountains, sun-scorched deserts, and windy capes overlooking the stormy Pacific. The state park system preserves Oregon's natural landmarks and beautiful vistas; modern Oregon sees its future in tourism as well as its past. For a more in-depth look at Oregon, see *Let's Go: Pacific Northwest, Western Canada and Alaska.*

Practical Information

Capital: Salem.

State Tourist Office, 775 Summer St. N.E., Salem 97310 (800-547-7842). **Oregon State Parks,** 525 Trade St. S.E., Salem 97310 (378-6305). **Department of Fish and Wildlife,** P.O. Box 59, Portland 97207 (229-5403). **Oregon American Youth Hostel Travel Center,** 311 E. 11th Ave.,

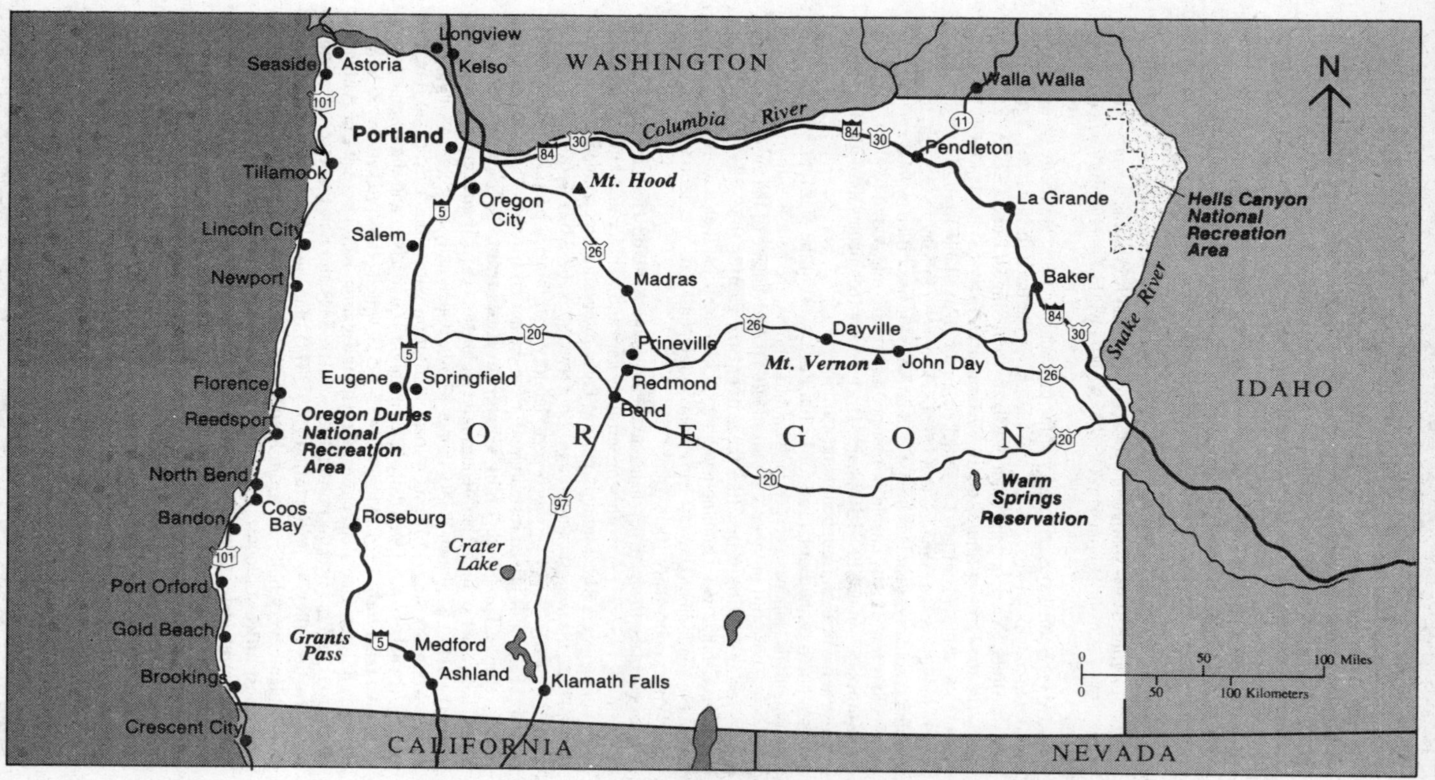
WASHINGTON
IDAHO
NEVADA
CALIFORNIA
OREGON
N
Hells Canyon National Recreation Area
Snake River
Columbia River
Walla Walla
Longview
Kelso
Seaside
Astoria
Portland
Tillamook
Oregon City
Salem
Lincoln City
Newport
Mt. Hood
Madras
Pendleton
La Grande
Baker
Prineville
Redmond
Bend
Dayville
Mt. Vernon
John Day
Florence
Reedsport
Eugene
Springfield
Oregon Dunes National Recreation Area
North Bend
Coos Bay
Bandon
Roseburg
Crater Lake
Warm Springs Reservation
Port Orford
Gold Beach
Grants Pass
Medford
Ashland
Klamath Falls
Brookings
Crescent City
101
5
84
30
11
26
20
97
0 50 100 Miles
0 50 100 Kilometers

Eugene 97402 (683-3685). **U.S. Forest Service, Pacific Northwest Regional Office,** 319 S.W. Pine St., P.O. Box 3623, Portland 97208 (326-2877).

Time Zone: Pacific (3 hrs. behind Eastern) and Mountain (2 hrs. behind Eastern). **Postal Abbreviation:** OR

Sales Tax: 0%.

Ashland

Before their expropriation by the guardians of highbrow culture, Shakespeare's plays were popular entertainment for rough-hewn 19th-century Americans. Ashland's informal, rural setting as the southernmost Oregon town on I-5 returns the plays to this lost stage each year from February to October with its world-famous **Shakespeare Festival.**

Due to the tremendous popularity of the productions, reservations are recommended one to two months in advance for plays at one of the three theaters: the **Agnus Bowmer,** the **Black Swan,** and the outdoor **Elizabethan Stage.** (Tickets $7.50-22; for more info, write the **Oregon Shakespeare Festival,** P.O. Box 158, Ashland, OR 97520, or call 503-482-2111.) Half-price rush tickets are often available from March to May, an hour before every performance that is not sold out. From May to October, almost everything is sold out; your best option is to arrive at the box office by 9am and wait until the precious few, if any, unsold or returned tickets are released at 9:30am. The **backstage tours** ($7, under 12 $3.50), guided by actors or technicians, provide a wonderful glimpse at the festival from behind the curtain.

When bored of the Bard, head for **Lithia Park,** west of the plaza off Main St. With its hiking trails, Japanese garden, and babbling brook, the park is sure to relax and refresh you. Those full of vigor and vim should take advantage of the variety of companies offering **rafting trips,** like the **Adventure Center** (488-2819), which also organizes fishing, rock climbing and horseback riding trips. It also rents bikes, jet skis and hot air balloons. (Day raft trips from $40. Open Mon.-Sat. 8am-8pm, Sun. 8am-6pm. Winter hours daily 10am-5pm.)

The best place to sleep, perchance to dream, is the **Ashland Hostel (HI/AYH),** 150 N. Main St. (482-9217), with wonderful owners and laundry and kitchen facilities. ($10, nonmembers $12. Midnight curfew. Early reservations recommended.) **Jackson Hot Springs,** the nearest campground, 2253 Hwy. 99 N. (482-3776), off exit 19 from I-5, is equipped with hot showers, pool, laundry, and mineral baths. (Sites $10, with hookup $13.) High-priced restaurants for the theater crowd abound, but so do cheap grocery stores. The **North Light Vegetarian Restaurant,** 36 S. Second St. (482-9463), is another crunchy bet, featuring bean burritos ($3.25) and an all-you-can-eat buffet (breakfast $5, lunch $6.50, dinner $7.50). (Open daily 8am-9pm.) **Geppetto's,** 345 E. Main St. (482-1138), is a local institution with a fantastic pesto omelette ($6.50). (Lunches $4-6. Open daily 8am-midnight.) Grab a beer and shoot some pool at **O'Ryan's Irish Pub,** 137 E. Main St. (482-2951), which offers pitchers for $5 to 8.50. (Open daily 11am-2am.) The closest **Greyhound** station, in Medford at 212 Bartlett St. (779-2103), offers buses to Portland (8 per day, $31) and San Francisco (2 per day, $54). **Rogue Valley Transportation** (779-2877) runs the #10 bus between Medford and Ashland every half-hour from Monday to Saturday from 5am to 7:30pm. Ashland's **post office** soliloquizes at 120 N. 1st St. (482-3986). The **ZIP code** is 97520. Ashland's **area code** is 503.

Crater Lake National Park and Klamath Falls

Mirror-blue Crater Lake, Oregon's only national park, was regarded as sacred by Indian shamans who forbade their people to view it. The placid surface of the lake rests at an frigid and translumined 6000 feet above sea level. Iceless in winter and flawlessly circular, it plunges to a depth of 2000 ft., making it the nation's deepest lake.

The tiny **visitors center** (524-2211), on the lake shore at **Rim Village,** distributes books and maps on hiking and camping. (Open daily 8am-7pm.) The **Rim Drive,** open only in summer, circumscribes the lake on a 33-mi. route high above the lake. Points along the drive offer views and trailheads for hiking. Among the most spectacular are **Discovery Point Trail** (1.3 mi. one way, from which the first pioneer saw the lake in 1853), **Watchman Lookout** (.8 mi. one way), and **Garfield Peak Trail** (1.7 mi. one way). The hike up **Mt. Scott,** the park's highest (9000 ft.), begins from the drive near the lake's eastern edge. Although steep, the 2½-mi. trail to the top gives persevering hikers a unique overhead view of the lake. Also steep, **Cleetwood Trail,** a one-mi. switchback, provides the only trail that leads down to the water's edge. From here a boat tours the lake (fare $10, under 11 $5.50; July-Sept., check with the lodge (594-2511) for times). Picnics and fishing are allowed, as is swimming, providing you can withstand the frigid 50°F temperature. Park rangers lead free walking tours daily in the summer and periodically in winter (on snowshoes). (Call the visitors center at Rim Village for schedules.) If pressed for time, walk the easy 100 yd. from the visitors center down to the **Sinnott Memorial Overlook** for the area's best and most accessible view. Rangers give short lectures on the area's history and geology at Rim Village.

Eating inexpensively in the Crater Lake area is difficult. Buying food—for instance, at the **Old Fort Store** (381-2345; open daily 8am-9pm) in **Fort Klamath—**and cooking it yourself is the best option. The cafeteria-style **Llao Rock Café** in Rim Village has deli sandwiches for $4.25. (Open daily.) The **Klamath Grill,** 717 Main St. (882-1427), has breakfast and lunch fare; try the Dutch Babies (an old family pancake recipe, $3.75). (Open Mon.-Fri. 6am-2:30pm, Sat. 7am-2pm.) In **Klamath Falls,** try **McPherson's Old Town Pizza,** 722 Main St., for some of the tastiest and cheapest food in the area. (Small pizzas from $3. Open daily 11am-10pm.)

Inexpensive campsites dot U.S. 97 to the north, and Klamath Falls also sports several affordable ones. Some of the best (free) sites are National Forest Service primitive campgrounds on the **Rogue River** off Rte. 62. (Pit toilets, fire pits, no water—-fetch it from the river.) There are *no* campsites on the lake itself. Those who wish to camp within the parks have only two options: the small **Lost Creek Campground** (594-2111), with 16 sites for tents only, water and pit toilets (sites $5, open mid-July-Sept.), and the **Mazama Campground** (594-2111) with 200 sites. (Toilets, pay laundry and showers, and plenty of RVs but no hookups. Sites $10.) The Rim Village visitors center has **backcountry camping** permits. In Klamath Falls, try the **Fort Klamath Lodge Motel** (381-2234), on Rte. 62, six mi. from the Park. The closest motel to the lake, it offers cozy rooms with knotted-pine walls, a friendly manager, and TV. (Singles $28. Doubles $33.) The **Value 20 Motel,** 124 N. 2nd St. (882-7741), has rooms equipped with kitchenettes, TV, and A/C, and allows pets. (Singles $27, doubles $32.)

Route 62 cuts through Crater Lake National Park's southwest corner and then heads southwest to **Medford** or southeast to **Klamath Falls.** To get to the park from Portland, take I-5 to Eugene, then Rte. 58 east to U.S. 97 south. Travel south on 97 for 18 mi. and then head west on Rte. 138. Klamath Falls lies 24 mi. south of the Rte. 62/U.S. 97 intersection, and is on Rte. 66, 39, and 140. Call ahead for road conditions during winter (594-2211). (Park admission charged only in summer. $5 per car, $3 for hikers and bikers. Seniors free.)

Oregon Coast

The so-called "Pacific" hurls itself at the Oregon Coast with a decidedly unpacific abandon, creating impressive explosions of spray. Only the most daring swim in this ice-cold surf; most are satisfied by the matchless views and huge stretches of unspoiled beach and leave the ocean for the seals, sea lions and water fowl which cavort and frolic off shore.

Possessively bear-hugging the coastline, **U.S. 101,** the renowned coastal highway, edges by in a concatenation of high-perched viewpoints. From A to B (Astoria in the north to Brookings in the south), it laces together the resorts and historic fishing villages clustered around the mouths of rivers feeding into the Pacific. Still, it appears most beautiful between the coastal towns, where hundreds of miles of state and national parks allow direct access to the beach. Whenever the highway leaves the coast, look for a beach loop road; these quieter ways afford some of the finest scenery on the western seaboard.

Drive or bike for the best coastal encounter. When searching for a site to pull in for the night, look to the small villages, as they tend to be the most interesting (and often the cheapest) places to stay. From north to south, **Nehalem, Wheeler, Depoe Bay, Winchester Bay, Charleston, Bandon,** and **Port Orford** all offer an escape from the larger and more commercialized towns of **Seaside, Tillamook, Lincoln City, Newport,** and **Coos Bay.** The state park system is both extensive and excellent along the coast, featuring 17 major campgrounds with electricity and showers. Bikers should write the Oregon Dept. of Transportation, Salem 97310 or virtually any visitors center on the coast for the free *Oregon Coast Bike Route Map;* it provides invaluable info on campsites, hostels, bike repair facilities, temperatures, wind speed, etc.

For those without a car or bike, transportation is a bit tricky. **Greyhound** has only two coastal routes from Portland per day; one of these takes place under cover of the night. Local public transport hooks Astoria to Cannon Beach, but south of Cannon Beach intercity transportation is virtually nonexistent. Gasoline and grocery prices en route to the coast cost about 20% more than in inland cities. Motorists may want to fuel up on both gas and food before reaching the coast-bound highways.

Reedsport and the Dunes

For 50 mi. between Florence and Coos Bay, the beach widens to form the **Oregon Dunes Recreational Area.** At their most spectacular the dunes rise to 500 ft. (as high as a 50-story building). Created by glaciation 15,000 years ago, they reached their maximum development 9000 years later, and today are reshaped continually by strong coastal winds. Hiking trails snake through the dunes and around the surrounding lakes to isolated places where all you can see is bare sand and sky. Other areas roar with dune buggies traversing the Saharan terrain. Campgrounds fill early with beer-swilling dune-buggy fanatics, especially on weekends. The local **National Recreation Area (NRA)** headquarters will provide trail maps and camping info, and will give any visitor a report on just how many decibels a dune-buggy engine can produce. (The answer: too many.) (855 U.S. 101, Reedsport, south of Umpqua Bridge, 271-3611. Open Memorial Day-mid-June daily 8am-4:30pm, mid-June-Labor Day daily 9:30am-6pm, off-season daily 10am-4pm.)

Oregon Dune Tours, Wildwood Dr., 10 mi. south of Reedsport, off U.S. 101 (759-4777), takes passengers on 30-minute ($25) or one-hour ($45) adventures through the dunes. But if you really want to rock and roll, shell out $30 for an hour ($25 for 2nd hr., $20 for 3rd) on your own dune buggy; **Dunes Odyssey,** on U.S. 101 in Winchester Bay (271-4011), and **Spinreel Park,** Wildwood Dr., 10 mi. south on U.S. 101 (759-3313; open daily 9am-6pm), both offer rentals. The best access to the dunes is at **Eel Creek Campground,** 11 mi. south of Reedsport. Leave your car in the parking lot of the day-use area and hike a short and easy distance through scrubby pines and grasses until the dunes tower above you. Watch out; many travelers get lost wandering between the sandy rises. The ocean dips another two mi. to the west.

Inside **Umpqua Lighthouse State Park,** six mi. south of Reedsport, the Douglas County Park Department operates the **coastal visitors center** (271-4631), in the old Coast Guard administration building. The center has small exhibits on the shipping and timber industries at the turn of the century. (Open May-Sept. Wed.-Sat. 10am-5pm, Sun. 1-5pm. Free.)

Restaurateurs of **Winchester Bay** (3 mi. south of Reedsport) pride themselves on their seafood, especially their salmon. The **Seven Seas Café,** Dock A, Winchester Bay, sails at the end of Broadway at 4th St. This small diner, crowded with marine memorabilia and navigational charts, is the place where old salts crowd to swap fish stories. (Fish and chips $4, all-you-can-eat fish fry Fri.-Sat. $5. Open daily 6am-8pm.) The **Seafood Grotto and Restaurant,** 8th St. and Broadway, Winchester Bay, serves unexpectedly excellent seafood around a large Victorian dollhouse. Lunches go for $4-7 and a large salmon steak costs $13. (Open daily 11am-9pm.) **Sugar Shack Bakery and Restaurant,** 145 N. 3rd (Rte. 38), Reedsport (271-3514), offers indulgently saccharine baked goods. Great chili "with trimmings" (i.e. a biscuit and sliced orange cake) ($1.25). Two mi. up the road, just past the **Elk Viewing Area,** you'll find the best places to observe the majestic Roosevelt Elk.

Whether you prefer motels or campsites, head to peaceful Winchester Bay. The **Harbor View Motel,** on Beach Blvd. (271-3352), across from the waterfront, may look a little shabby, but harbors clean rooms with color TV and some kitchenettes. (Singles $24. Doubles $29. Mid-Sept.-April singles $21; doubles $25.) You may want to blow dough in the **Winchester Bay Motel,** at the end of Broadway at 4th St. past Dock A (271-4871), after weeks of grungy camping. (Color TV, free continental breakfast. Singles $45. Doubles $58. Labor Day-Memorial Day singles $32; doubles $40.) The rather small rooms in the **Fir Grove Motel,** 2178 Winchester Dr. (U.S. 101), Reedsport (271-4848), come with color TV, free coffee and a pool. (1-2 person room $40, off-season $32.)

The National Forest Service's pamphlet *Campgrounds in the Siuslaw National Forest* covers **campgrounds** in the dunes. The sites closest to Reedsport lie in Winchester Bay. The campgrounds that allow dune-buggy access—Spinreel, Lagoon, Waxmyrtle, Driftwood II, Horsfall and Bluebill—are generally loud and rowdy. The **Surfwood Campground,** a half-mi. north of Winchester Bay on U.S. 101 (271-4020), serves up all the luxuries of home—including a laundromat, heated pool, grocery store, sauna, tennis court and hot showers. (Sites $9, full hookup $12. Call at least a week in advance in the summer.) The county's **Windy Cove Campground** (271-5634), adjacent to Salmon Harbor in Winchester Bay, offers drinking water, hot showers, flush toilets and beach access. (Sites $8.50, full hookup $10.50.) Serenity for campers with a tent and a car can be found off Hwy. 48, just north of Umpqua River Bridge, at **Noel Ranch** (8 mi.) or almost anywhere you drive along **Smith River** (free).

Reedsport's **post office** licks and affixes at 301 Fir St. (271-2521; open Mon.-Fri. 8:30am-5pm). The **ZIP code** is 97467. The **area code** is 503.

Portland

Portland has grown up out of the wilderness of America's western coastland like a quiet child in a chaotic household. Its modest "human scale" 200-ft. city blocks, humble building height restrictions, and noticeably large number of parks seem to acquiesce to the splendor of the surrounding wilderness. The mighty Columbia River rushes past to the north, while the Willamette River cuts through the city's heart. Mt. Hood, and more distantly, Mt. St. Helens, which covered the city in volcanic ash in 1980, tower just beyond the city limits. But the humility of this gentle metropolis will win a visitor's heart. If you can decline the invitation of the Oregon countryside, you will find that polite young Portland has much to offer.

Prize-winning urban efforts have made the city pleasantly navigable; it also boasts such historic urban self-assurances as the first enclosed mall in the U.S. (Lloyd Center, built in 1956) and the first office building with sealed windows and mechanical climate control (the Commonwealth Building). City and state funding for public art has been secured through a 1% tax on new building construction. The result is a growing family of outdoor sculpture pieces and an equally healthy number of animate artistic endeavors in music and theater. Outdoor jazz concerts flourish around the city, and Portland's symphony orchestra, the oldest in the U.S., recently cut its first CD. There are tons of improvisational theaters, and the recently constructed Center for the Performing Arts lures actors north from the Shakespeare festival in Ashland. Even Portland's mayor has taken inspiration from the city's thriving arts community—he sashayed into office shortly after posing as a flasher revealing himself to a sidewalk sculpture for an "Expose Yourself to Art" poster.

Practical Information and Orientation

Emergency: 911.

Portland/Oregon Visitors Association, 26 S.W. Salmon St. (is it one-way, uphill?) (275-9750 or 222-2223), at Front St. Free *Portland Book* contains maps, general info, and historical trivia. Open Mon.-Fri. 9am-5pm, Sat. 9am-3pm. Detailed city road maps are free at **Hertz,** 1009 S.W. 6th at Salmon (249-5727).

Portland International Airport: north of the city on the banks of the Columbia. Served by I-205. To get downtown, take Tri-Met bus #12, which will arrive on S.W. 5th Ave. (Fare 90¢.) **Raz Tranz** (recorded info 246-4676) provides an airport shuttle ($6) that leaves every 30 min. and takes 35 min. to reach major downtown hotels and the Greyhound station.

Amtrak: 800 N.W. 6th Ave. (800-872-7245), at Hoyt St. To Seattle (3 per day; $26) and Eugene (1 per day; $24). Open daily 7:30am-9:45pm.

Buses: Greyhound, 550 N.W. 6th St. (243-2323). Buses almost every hr. to Seattle ($19 one way; 243-2313 for schedule) and to Eugene ($16 one way; 222-3361 for schedule). Ticket window open daily 5:30am-12:30am. **Green Tortoise,** 205 S.E. Grand Ave. (225-0310), at Ash St. To Seattle (Tues., Thurs., Sat., Sun. at 4pm; $15) and San Francisco (Sun., Tues., Thurs., Fri. at noon; $49).

Public Transport: Tri-Met, Customer Service Center, #1 Pioneer Courthouse Sq., 701 S.W. 6th Ave. (233-3511). Open Mon.-Fri. 7:30am-5:30pm. Seven regional service routes, each with its own color totem. Buses with black and white totems cross color-coded boundaries, and crux at the downtown **mall,** which boasts covered bus stops and information centers. Fare 90¢-$1.20. All rides free within **fareless square**, bounded by the Willamette River, N.W. Hoyt St., and I-405. Service generally 7am-midnight, reduced Sat.-Sun. Tri-Met's splendiferous light rail system **MAX** only serves 1 line (running between downtown and the city of Gresham), but uses the same fare system as the buses.

Taxi: Broadway Cab, 227-1234. **New Rose City Cab Co.,** 282-7707. Both charge $2 for the first mi., $1.50 each additional mi. From Airport $21-24.

Car Rental: Practical Rent-a-Car, 1315 N.E. Sandy (224-8110). $30 per day, 100 free mi., 15¢ each additional mi.

Help Lines: Crisis Line, 223-6161. Open 24 hrs. **Senior Citizens Crisis Line,** 223-6161. **Gay and Lesbian Services,** 223-8299. **Women's Crisis Line,** 235-5333.

Local Events Hotline: 233-3333. Recording.

Time Zone: Pacific (3 hrs. behind Eastern).

Post Office: 715 N.W. Hoyt St. (294-2300). Open Mon.-Fri. 8:30am-5pm, Sat. 9am-1pm. **ZIP code:** 97208.

Area Code: 503.

Portland sits just south of the Columbia River about 75 mi. inland from the Oregon coast. The city blazes 637 mi. north of San Francisco and 172 mi. south of Seattle. The primary east-west highway, I-84 (U.S. 30), follows the route of the Oregon Trail through the gorgeous Columbia River Gorge. West of Portland, U.S. 30 follows the Columbia downstream to Astoria. I-405 curves around the west side of the business district to link I-5 with U.S. 30.

Portland can be divided into five districts. **Burnside Street** divides the city into north and south, while east and west are separated by the Willamette River. **Williams**

Avenue slices off a corner of the northeast sector, simply called "North." The **Southwest district** is the city's hub, encompassing the downtown area, historical Old Town in the northern end, and a slice of the ritzy West Hills. The very core of the hub lies at the downtown mall area between S.W. 5th and 6th Ave. Car traffic is prohibited here; don't mess with the transit system's turf. The **Northwest district** contains the southern end of Old Town, an industrial area to the north, and a residential area, culminating in the posh Northwestern hills area to the west. Most students enrolled in Portland's several colleges and universities live in the Northwest. The **Southeast district** keeps a somewhat less well-to-do residential neighborhood, but its main drag, **Hawthorne Boulevard,** is lined with the city's best ethnic restaurants, cafés, and funky theaters. Anomalous amidst its surroundings, **Laurelhurst Park** is a collection of posh houses around E. Burnside St. and S.E. 39th St. The **North** and **Northeast** districts are chiefly residential, punctuated by a few quiet, small parks.

Accommodations and Camping

With Portland's increasing gentrification, finding cheap lodgings has become more challenging. **Northwest Bed and Breakfast,** 610 S.W. Broadway, Portland 97205 (243-7616), extensively lists member homes in the Portland area and throughout the Northwest. You must become a member ($25 per yr.) to use their lists and reservation services. They promise singles from $30 to $55 and doubles from $50 to $80.

The remaining cheap downtown hotels are generally unsafe; the hostel and—for women—the **YWCA** undoubtedly provides the best options. **Barbur Ave**. also hosts a comely and accessible strip of motels.

Portland International Hostel (HI/AYH), 3031 S.E. Hawthorne Blvd. (236-3380), at 31st Ave. Take bus #5. Cheerful, clean, and crowded. Sleep inside or on the porch. Kitchen; laundromat across the street. Reasonably priced van trips to Mt. St. Helens or the Columbia River Gorge and Mt. Hood offered frequently. Open daily 7:30-10am, 5pm-midnight. $10, nonmembers $13. Reserve in summer.

YWCA, 1111 S.W. 10th St. (223-6281). Women only. Close to major sights and clean. Small rooms. Shared double $16. Singles $24, with semi-private bath $26. Hostel-style bunk bed $6.

Bel D'air Motel, 8355 N. Interstate Ave. (289-4800); take the Lumbard W. exit off I-5, or bus #5 from S.W. 6th Ave. Pretentious in name but not in décor. Very small; call 1 week in advance for reservations. Singles $28. Doubles $33.

Midtown Motel, 1415 N.E. Sandy Blvd. (234-0316). Take bus #12 from 6th Ave. Standard rooms with TV and A/C. Singles from $22, doubles from $25.

Aladdin Motor Inn, 8905 S.W. 30th (246-8241 or 800-292-4466), at Barbur Blvd. about 10 min. from downtown by bus #12 from S.W. 5th Ave. Clean, comfortable. A/C, kitchens available. Singles $30. Doubles $35.

Mel's Motor Inn, 5205 N. Interstate Ave. (285-2556). Take exit 303 off I-5, or bus #5 from 6th Ave. No aspirations to elegance but clean and comfortable with A/C, refrigerators, and HBO. No comedic diner attached. Singles $28. Doubles $32.

Ainsworth State Park, 37 mi. east of Portland on I-84, along the Columbia River Gorge. Hot showers, flush toilets, hiking trails. Sites with full hookup $13.

Milo McIver State Park, 25 mi. southwest of Portland, off Oregon Rte. 211, 5 mi. west of the town of Estacada. Fish, boat, and bicycle along the nearby Clackamas River. Hot showers, flush toilets. Sites with electricity $12.

Food

Although Portland's restaurants reflect the health-conscious attitude of the people, juicy carnivorous meals are as plentiful as broccoli tofu bacchanals, and ethnic eateries abound.

Macheesmo Mouse, 723 S.W. Salmon St. Also at 811 N.W. 23rd St. (274-0500) and 3553 S.E. Hawthorne Blvd. (232-6588; 5 blocks from the HI/AYH hostel). Fast and healthy Mexican food—the mice are in the name only. The $3.25 veggie burrito stands out. Open Mon.-Sat. 11am-9pm, Sun. noon-8pm.

Hamburger Mary's, 840 S.W. Park St. at Taylor. Take bus #5 or 15; 2 blocks up from 6th St. A carnivore's carnival near the museums and theaters, with a relaxed atmosphere and eclectic décor: floor lamps hang upside down from the ceiling. Burgers with everything and fries $5. Excellent vegetarian fare. Open daily 7am-2am.

The Original Pancake House, 8600 S.W. Barbur Blvd. Take yellow rose bus #12, 41, or 43 to Barbur Transit Center. The Northwest's place for pancakes ($4.75-6). Hr.-long lines on Sat. and Sun. morning. Open Wed.-Sun. 7am-3pm.

Escape from New York Pizza, 913 S.W. Alder St. Also at 622 N.W. 23rd St. Fred Astaire gazes down from the wall upon what is arguably the best 'za in town. Hefty cheese slice $1.25. Large cheese pie $8.75. Open Mon.-Thurs. 11:30am-9pm, Fri.-Sat. 11:30am-11pm.

Dan and Louie's Oyster Bar, 208 S.W. Ankeny St. (227-5906). Legendary since 1907, Dan and Louie's has its own Oyster Bay in Newport, OR. Lunch specials are particularly cheap. Try the shrimp and oyster fry ($10) or 4 "shuck-'em-yourself" oysters ($3). Open Sun.-Thurs. 11am-10pm, Fri.-Sat. 11am-midnight.

Western Culinary Institute Chef's Corner, 1235 S.W. Jefferson (242-2433). The proving grounds for the cooking school's great adventures. All lunch creations under $6. Try the gourmet hashbrowns at the **Breakfast Café** (open 7am-3pm). Restaurant open Mon. 8am-2:30pm, Tues.-Fri. 8am-6pm.

Chang's Mongolian Grill, 1 S.W. 3rd St. at Burnside. Also at 2700 N.W. 185th and 1600 N.E. 122nd. All-you-can-eat lunches ($5.50) and dinners ($8.50). Select your meal from a buffet (fresh vegetables, meats, and fish), mix your own sauce to taste, and then watch your chef make a wild show of cooking it on a grill the size of a Volkswagen. Rice and hot and sour soup included. Open daily 11:30am-2:30pm and 5-10pm.

Rose's Deli, 315 N.W. 23rd Ave. (227-5181), at Everett St. Take bus #15 ("red salmon"). Also at 12329 N.E. Glisan (254-6545) and Beaverton Town Sq. (643-4287). Rose butters the city's best bagels in a bustling atmosphere. Great matzoh-ball soup ($2.50), cheese blintzes, and a pastry case that could fill you up by osmosis. Open Sun.-Thurs. 8am-11pm, Fri.-Sat. 8am-midnight.

Saigon Kitchen, 3594 S.E. Division (236-2312). Take bus #5 ("brown beaver"). Thai cuisine; superb spring rolls. Dinners $5.25-9. Open Mon.-Fri. 11am-10pm, Sat. noon-10pm, Sun. 5-10pm.

Hawthorne St. Café, 3354 S.E. Hawthorne (232-4982). Take bus #5 (brown beaver). Great neighborhood place to sit, eat breakfast, and read the newspaper. Muffins 85¢. Open Mon.-Fri. 7am-2:30pm, Sat.-Sun. 7:30am-3pm.

Sights

The most difficult thing about sightseeing in Portland is choosing from the vast array of attractions that the city offers. Since some of the best things to do in Portland are outside, visit in late spring and early summer when the city blooms after the wet winter weather. This also proves the best season in which to appreciate Portland's **fountains,** all of which seem to have long, intricate histories. The best include the 20 bronze drinking fountains located on street corners throughout Portland, donated by Simon Benson, a wealthy Prohibition-era Portlander, ostensibly to ease the thirst of loggers.

Almost all the major sights are grouped downtown in the southwest district. Portland's downtown area centers on the **mall,** running north-south between 5th and 6th Ave. and closed to all traffic except city buses. **Pioneer Courthouse,** the elder of downtown landmarks, stands at 5th Ave. and Morrison St. The monument now houses the U.S. Ninth Circuit Court of Appeals, overlooking **Pioneer Courthouse Square,** 701 S.W. 6th Ave. (223-1613), opened in 1983. 48,000 citizens financed construction of the square by purchasing personalized bricks; the live jazz, folk, and ethnic music of the summer **Peanut Butter and Jam Sessions,** held Tuesdays and Thursdays from noon to 1pm, seem to draw all 48,000 back to visit their gift to the city.

Michael Graves' postmodern **Portland Building** (823-4000), the most controversial building in the downtown area, struts its stuff on the mall. This amazing agglomeration of pastel tile and concrete has received both star-reaching praise and condemnation as an overgrown jukebox, and even once had a full-sized inflatable King Kong placed on its roof. Make sure to check out the inside as well, which looks like something out of *Blade Runner.*

West of the mall extend the **South Park Blocks,** a series of shady, rose-laden enclosures running down the middle of Park Ave. A number of museums open onto the parks, including the **Portland Art Museum,** 1219 S.W. Park Ave. (226-2811), at Jefferson St. Dote on the museum's especially fine exhibit of Pacific Northwest Native American art, including masks, textiles and sacred objects, or the interspersed international exhibits and local artists' works. (Open Tues.-Wed. and Fri.-Sat. 11am-5pm, Sun. 1-5pm. Admission $4, seniors and students $2, under 12 $1. Seniors free Thurs.) The **Northwest Film and Video Center** (221-1156), in the same building, screens classics and off-beat flicks. Half-price tickets are available on the day of all non-sold-out shows for those who show up in person with cash at PDX-TIX, 921 S.W. Morrison (241-4903).

A century ago, rowdy sailors fresh off their ocean-going trawlers rollicked around **Old Town,** to the north of the mall. Now, large-scale refurbished store fronts, new "old" brick, and a bevy of recently-owned shops and restaurants cater to the upper crust. A popular people-watching vantage point, the **Skidmore Fountain,** at S.W. First Ave. and S.W. Ankeny St., marks the entrance to the quarter. Had the city accepted resident draftsman Henry Weinhard's offer to run draft beer through the fountain, it would have been a truly cordial watering hole indeed. Old Town marks the start of **Tom McCall Waterfront Park,** an enormous expanse of grass and flowers along the river that offers little shade but is an excellent place to picnic, fish, and stroll.

From March until Christmas, the area under the Burnside Bridge turns into the **Saturday Market** (222-6072), 108 W. Burnside St. On Saturdays from 10am to 5pm and Sundays from 11am to 4:30pm, the area is clogged with street musicians, artists, craftspeople, chefs, and produce sellers.

Portland's finest galleries are centered downtown. On the first Thursday of every month all the galleries stay open 'til 9pm and fill with local enthusiasts (an event, predictably enough, called **"First Thursday"**). On the edge of the Northwest district is **Powell's Book Store,** 1005 W. Burnside St. (228-4651), a cavernous establishment with more volumes than any other bookstore in the U.S. (almost 500,000). If you tend to dawdle in bookstores, beware—or bring a sleeping bag and several meals. Powell's also features frequent poetry and fiction readings in the afternoons and an extensive travel section on Portland and the Northwest. (Open Mon.-Sat. 9am-11pm, Sun. 9am-9pm.)

Less than two mi. west of downtown, in the mowed **West Hills,** looping trails for day hiking, running, and picnic-laden expeditions crisscross **Washington Park.** The **Hoyt Arboretum InfoCenter,** 4000 S.W. Fairview Blvd. (228-8732 or 823-3655), at the crest of the hill above the other gardens, hands out trail maps to the arboretum, which features towering conifers and "200 acres of trails." (Free nature walks April-Nov. Sat.-Sun. at 2pm; visitors center open daily 9am-3pm.) The five-acre **Japanese Garden** (223-4070) holds a formal arrangement of idyllic ponds and bridges. Cherry blossoms ornament the park in summer, thanks to Portland's sibling city of Sapporo, Japan. (Open April-May and Sept. daily 10am-6pm, June-Aug. 9am-8pm, Oct.-March 10am-4pm. Daily tours April-Oct. at 10:45am and 2:30pm. Admission $4.50, seniors and students with ID $2.50.) Roses galore and spectacular views of the city await a few steps away at the **International Rose Test Garden,** 400 S.W. Kingston St. (248-4302).

Next to the Hoyt Arboretum stands Portland's favorite tourist-attracting triad: the **Washington Park Zoo,** 4001 S.W. Canyon Rd. (226-1561 for a person; 226-7627 for a tape; open daily 9:30am-7pm, gates close at 6pm; winter hours daily 9:30am-4pm; admission $5, seniors $3.50, kids $3, Tues. 3-7pm free); the **World Forestry Center,** 4033 S.W. Canyon Rd. (228-1367; open daily 9am-5pm; admission $3, seniors and kids $2); and the **Oregon Museum of Science and Industry,** (better known as **OMSI;** 4015 S.W. Canyon Rd., 222-2828; open Sat.-Thurs. 9am-7pm, Fri. 9am-9pm; admission $5.25, seniors and under 17 $3.50). "Zoo Bus" #63 connects many points in the park with the downtown mall. A miniature **choo-choo** connects the Washington Park Rose Gardens to the zoo (fare $2.50, seniors and students $1.75). Beginning in late June, the zoo sponsors **Your Zoo and All That Jazz,** a nine-week series of open-air jazz concerts (Wed. 6:30-8:30pm), free with regular zoo admission. Bring a picnic dinner. **Zoograss Concerts** features a 10-week series of bluegrass concerts (Thurs. 6:30-

8:30pm; $5 each without zoo admission). The World Forestry Center specializes in exhibits of Northwestern forestry and logging. OMSI will occupy children and adults with do-it-yourself science, computer, and medical exhibits. Within OMSI, the **Kendall Planetarium** (228-7827) gives daily astronomy shows ($1.50) and rocks in the evening to "laser fantasy" performances (schedule of shows 242-0723; admission $5.50, seniors and kids $4). The new **Vietnam Memorial** rests a few steps up the hill. From Washington Park, you have easy access to sprawling **Forest Park,** jampacked with hiking trails and picnic areas affording spectacular views of Portland.

The funky clientele in the cafés, theaters, and restaurants on Hawthorne Blvd. are artists and students from "politically correct" **Reed College,** S.E. 28th and Woodstock, a small liberal arts school founded in 1909. Reed sponsors numerous cultural events. In 1968, it somewhat incongruously became the first undergraduate college to open its own nuclear reactor. Tours of the campus leave Eliot Hall twice per day during the school year. (Call 771-7511 for hrs.)

Farther southeast sleeps **Mt. Tabor Park,** one of two city parks in the world on the site of an extinct volcano. More of a molehill than a mountain, the park serves as the Southeast's lone hill. Take bus #15 from downtown, or drive down Hawthorne to S.E. 60th Ave.

Entertainment

Portland is no longer the hard-drinking, carousing port town of yore; ships still unload sea-weary sailors daily, but their favorite waterfront pubs have evolved into upscale bistros and nightclubs that cater to everyone from the casual college student to the hard-core rocker. Current listings abound in the Friday edition of the *Oregonian* and a number of free handouts: *Willamette Week* (catering to students), the *Main Event, Clinton St. Quarterly, Just Out* (catering to gay and lesbian interests), the *Portland Guide,* and the *Downtowner* (catering to the yuppwardly mobile). They are all available in restaurants downtown and in boxes on street corners.

Portland has its share of good, formally presented concerts, but why bother with admission fees? You'll find the most exciting talent playing for free in various public facilities around the city. Call the **Park Bureau** (796-5193) for information. Most of Portland's countless movie theaters have half-price days or matinee shows; consult the *Oregonian* for info.

The **Oregon Symphony Orchestra** (228-1353) plays in the Arlene Schnitzer Concert Hall, on the corner of S.W. Broadway and S.W. Main St. (Tickets $15-28. "Symphony Sunday" afternoon concerts $8. Performances Sept.-April.) **Chamber Music Northwest** performs summer concerts at Reed College Commons, 3203 S.E. Woodstock Ave. (223-3202). (Classical music Mon., Thurs., and Sat. at 8pm. Admission $16, under 15 $9.) Ten minutes before any non-sold-out concerts, students with ID can get tickets for $7.

Portland's many fine theaters produce everything from off-Broadway shows to experimental drama. At **Portland Civic Theatre,** 1530 S.W. Yamhill St. (226-4026), the mainstage often presents musical comedy, while the smaller theater-in-the-round puts on less traditional shows. (Tickets $12-20.) **Oregon Shakespeare Festival/Portland,** at the Intermediate Theatre of PCPA, corner of S.W. Broadway and S.W. Main St. (274-6588), has a five-play season running from November to February. **New Rose Theatre,** 904 S.W. Main St. in the Park Blocks (222-2487), offers an even mix of classical and contemporary shows. (Tickets $15-18.)

The best clubs in Portland are the hardest to find—neighborhood taverns and pubs often sneak away on backroads. **Produce Row Café,** 204 S.E. Oak St. (232-8355), has 21 beers on tap ($1.50-2.50), 72 bottled domestic and imported beers, and a lovely outdoor beer garden. (Open Mon.-Fri. 11am-1am, Sat. noon-1am, Sun. 2pm-midnight.) The **Mission Theater and Pub,** 1624 N.W. Glisan St. (223-4031), serves excellent home-brewed ales as well as delicious and unusual sandwiches. Relax in the balcony of this old moviehouse with a pitcher of Ruby, a fragrant raspberry ale ($1.50 glass, $7 pitcher). (Open daily 5pm-1am.) **Key Largo,** 31 N.W. 1st Ave. (223-9919), has an airy, tropical atmosphere. Dance to rock, R&B, or jazz on the patio. (Cover $2-8. Open

Mon.-Fri. 11am-2:30am, Sat.-Sun. noon-2:30am.) The mostly gay clientele at **Embers,** 110 N.W. Broadway (222-3082), dances until 4am. The **Bridgeport Brew Pub,** 1313 N.W. Marshall (241-7179), packs 'em in with a much-acclaimed home-brew and great pizza.

Washington

Washington has two personalities, clearly split by the Cascade Range. The western ridge of the range blocks Pacific moisture heading east and hurls it back toward the ocean, bathing the Olympic Peninsula in 135 inches of rain a year. Always drawn to moisture, most inhabitants cluster with the seafood around Puget Sound. But don't pity comparatively arid eastern Washington; 10 fewer feet of water per annum isn't the end of the world, especially with the miracles of modern refrigeration and irrigation. Residents use their time in the sun savoring fresh fruit and enjoying the rolling countryside without jostling for space.

Washington is a textbook of terrain; deserts, volcanoes, pristine Pacific Ocean beaches, and the world's only non-tropical rain forest all await exploring readers. Mount Rainier has fantastic hiking, while the Cascades keep perfect conditions for nearly any winter activity. Indoors in Seattle, look to the arts; the *New York Times* has been known to lament that there is more good theater in Seattle than on Broadway (a backhanded compliment, but a compliment nonetheless). Best of all, Washington is a compact state by West Coast standards—everything remains less than a daytrip away. For the inside scoop on Washington state, see *Let's Go: Pacific Northwest, Western Canada and Alaska.*

Practical Information

Capital: Olympia.

State Tourist Office, Tourism Development Division, 101 General Administration Bldg., Olympia 98504-0613 (206-586-2088 or 206-586-2102; 800-544-1800 for vacation planning guide). Open Mon.-Fri. 9am-5pm. **Washington State Parks and Recreation Commission,** 7150 Clearwater Lane, Olympia 98504 (206-753-5755; May-Aug. in WA 800-562-0990). **Forest Service/National Park Service Outdoor Recreation Information,** 915 2nd Ave. #442, Seattle 98174 (206-553-0170). Open Mon.-Fri. 8am-5pm.

Time Zone: Pacific (3 hrs. behind Eastern). **Postal Abbreviation:** WA

Sales tax: 6.5%.

Cascade Range

Northwestern Native Americans are said to have called the Cascades "the home of the Gods." Although a relatively young mountain range, the Cascades have long been the Northwest's most tangible reminder of nature's eternal supremacy over mankind. The mountains refuse to slumber; they are noisy and cantankerous. Crashing waterfalls, rumbling volcanoes, and falling ice characterize the Cascades' boisterous reign. These huge mountains are stretching their peaks the length of a human fingernail each year, and their steep grade draws rock climbers the world over to cling to the peaks' icy cuticles.

The tallest, white-domed peaks of Baker, Rainier and St. Helens understandably attract the most attention and have, for the most part, been made accessible by four major roads which offer good trailheads and impressive scenery for those on the air-conditioned side of the car window. **U.S. 12** through White Pass goes nearest Mt. Rainier National Park; **Interstate 90** sends four lanes past the major ski resorts of Snoqualmie Pass; scenic **U.S. 2** leaves Everett for Stevens Pass and descends along the Wenatchee River, a favorite of white-water rafters; and **Rte. 20,** the **North Cascades Highway,**

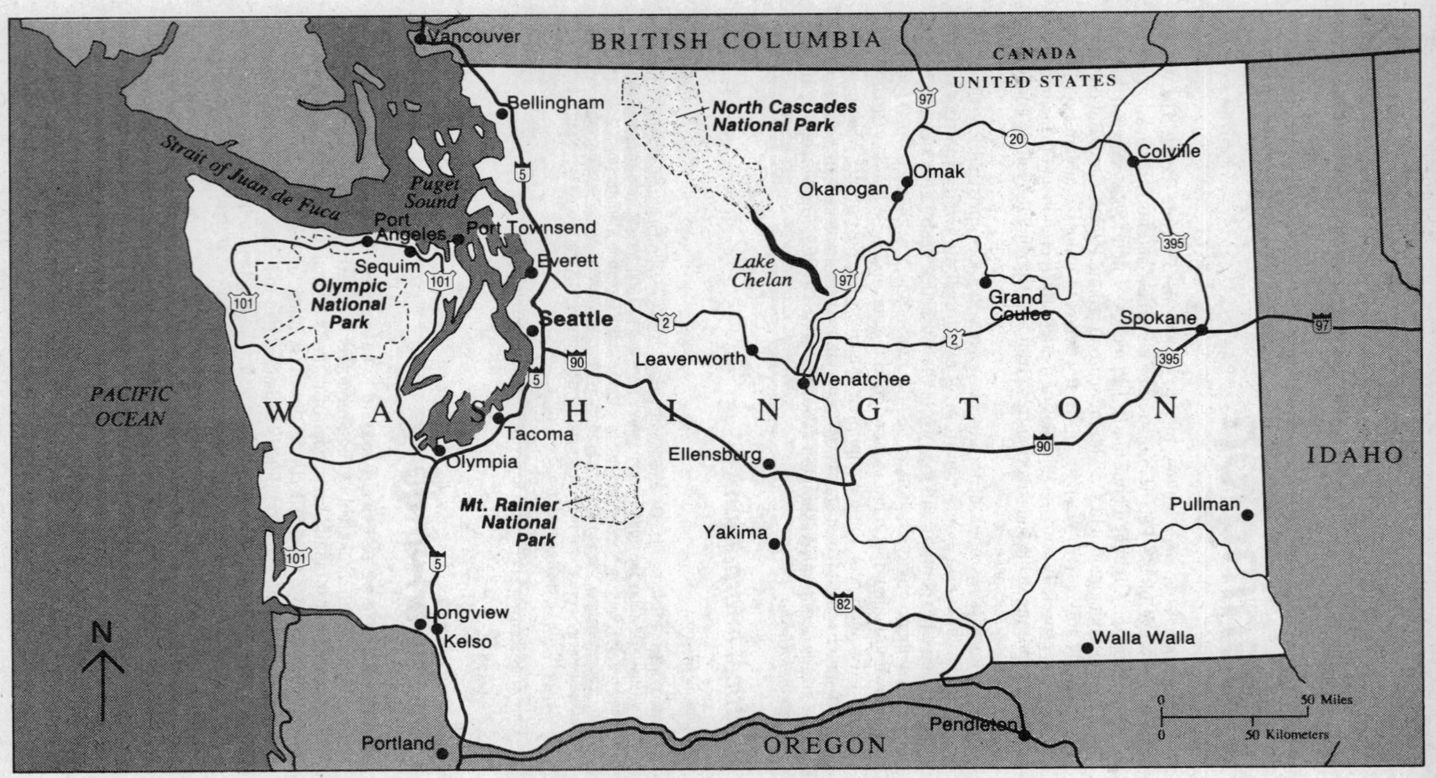
BRITISH COLUMBIA
CANADA
UNITED STATES
IDAHO
WASHINGTON
OREGON
PACIFIC OCEAN
Strait of Juan de Fuca
Puget Sound
North Cascades National Park
Olympic National Park
Mt. Rainier National Park
Lake Chelan
Vancouver
Bellingham
Port Townsend
Port Angeles
Sequim
Everett
Seattle
Tacoma
Olympia
Longview
Kelso
Portland
Leavenworth
Wenatchee
Ellensburg
Yakima
Okanogan
Omak
Grand Coulee
Colville
Spokane
Pullman
Walla Walla
Pendleton
5
90
2
97
20
395
82
101
0 50 Miles
0 50 Kilometers
N

provides access to North Cascades National Park from April to November, weather permitting. These last two roads are often traveled in sequence as the **Cascade Loop.**

Greyhound travels the routes over Stevens and Snoqualmie Passes to and from Seattle, while **Amtrak** cuts between Ellensburg and Puget Sound. Locals warn against thumbing across Rte. 20, where a few hapless hitchers have vanished over the last several years. The mountains are most accessible in the clear months of July, August, and September; many high mountain passes are snowed in the rest of the year. For general info on the Cascades contact the **National Park/National Forest Information Service,** 915 2nd Ave., Seattle 98174 (206-553-0170).

Mount Rainier National Park

Rising two mi. above the surrounding foothills, Mt. Rainier presides regally over the Cascade Range at 14,411 ft.; residents of Washington refer to it simply as "The Mountain." Rainier is partly responsible for western Washington's wet weputation: warm ocean air condenses when it reaches Rainier and falls on the mountain-side as rain or snow. Clouds mask it over 200 days each year. When the sun *does* shine, you may understand why Native Americans called Mt. Rainier "Tahoma" (Mountain of God).

Nearly 75 glaciers etch the slopes and conspire with sharp ridges and steep gullies to make mountain inhospitable to climbers. Despite (or perhaps because of) the danger of the ascent, nearly 3000 adventure-seekers clamber to the summit each year. Those who do not feel the need to scale Rainier can find countless places to ponder and play skirting the mount. With over 305 mi. of trails, solitude is just a hike away.

Admission to the park costs $5 per car or $2 per hiker; the gates stay open 24 hrs. For **visitor information** stop in at the **Longmire Hiker Information Center** (open Sun.-Thurs. 8am-6pm, Fri. 8am-7pm, Sat. 7am-7pm); **Paradise Visitors Center** (open mid-June-mid-Sept. daily 9am-7pm; off-season hours vary); **Ohanapecosh Visitors Center** (same hours as Paradise); **Sunrise Visitors Center,** (same hours as Paradise); or **White River Hiker Information Center** (open summer only Mon.-Thurs. 8am-4:30pm, Fri. 8am-9pm, Sat.-Sun. 7am-7pm). All centers can be contacted c/o Superintendent, Mt. Rainier National Park, Ashford, WA 98304, or through the park central operator (569-2211). Any activity on Rainier should begin in one of these centers. Each has displays, a wealth of literature on everything from hiking to natural history, postings on trail and road conditions, and extremely helpful rangers. Naturalist-guided trips, talks, campfire programs, and slide presentations take place at the visitors centers and vehicle campgrounds throughout the park. Check at a visitors center or pick up a copy of the free activity and program guide, *Tahoma,* for details.

A car tour provides a good intro to the park. All major roads offer scenic views of the mountain and have numerous roadside pull-offs for camera-clicking and gawking. The roads to Paradise and Sunrise prove especially picturesque. **Stevens Canyon Road** connects the southeast corner of the National Park with Paradise, Longmire, and the Nisqually entrance and affords truly spectacular vistas of Rainier and the rugged Tatoosh Range with the accessible roadside attractions of **Box Canyon** and **Grove of the Patriarchs** along the way.

Several less-developed roads provide access to more isolated regions. These roads often adjoin trailheads that crisscross the park or lead to the summit. Cross-country hiking and camping outside designated campsites are permissible through most regions of the park, but overnight backpacking trips *always* require a permit. The **Hiker Centers** at Longmire, White River, and Carbon River have info on day and backcountry hikes through the park and dispense the requisite permits for camping. (See below for hours.)

A segment of the **Pacific Crest Trail (PCT)** crosses through the southeast corner of the park. The U.S. Forest Service maintains the PCT for both hikers and horse riders. Primitive campsites and shelters line the trail; camping requires no permit, although you should contact the nearest **ranger station**—try **Naches** (509-965-8005) and **Packwood** (206-494-5515)—for info on site and trail conditions. The trail, overlooking the sometimes snow-covered peaks of the Cascades, snakes through delightful scenery where wildlife abounds.

Hardcore campers will be positively thrilled by the **Wonderland Trail,** a 95-mi. loop around the entire mountain. Because it includes some brutal ascents and descents, rangers recommend that even experts plan on covering only seven to 10 mi. per day. Rangers can provide info on weather and trail conditions, and can even help with food caches at stations along the trail. Specific dangers along Wonderland include snow-blocked passes in June, muddy trails in July, and early snowstorms in September. (Solution? Go in August.) Expert climbers can discuss options for reaching the summit with rangers. Novices can sign up for a summit climb with **Rainier Mountaineering, Inc. (RMI),** headquartered in their Guide House in Paradise. RMI is also the only organization in the park that rents equipment. For more information, contact RMI (569-2227; Oct.-May contact 535 Dock St. #209, Tacoma, WA 98402; 206-627-6242).

Less ambitious, ranger-led **interpretive hikes** feature themes ranging from local wildflowers to area history. Each visitors center conducts its own hikes, each with a different schedule. The hikes, lasting anywhere from 20 minutes to all day, especially suit families with young children. These free hikes complement evening campfire programs, also conducted by each visitors center.

Llama Wilderness Pack Trips, Tatoosh Motel, Packwood (491-LAMA; 491-7213) offers a llunch with the llamas in the park for $25 per person (4-5 hrs.). They also llease their llamas for pack trips and have guided trips of their own.

The towns of **Packwood** and

Ashford have a few motels near the park. The **Hotel Packwood** (494-5431) and the **Gateway Inn Motel,** Ashford (569-2506) are both reasonable. **Camping** at the auto campsite costs $5 to $8 between mid-June and late September. Subject to certain restrictions, alpine and cross-country camping require free permits. Pick up a copy of the *Wilderness Trip Planner* at any ranger station or hiker center before you set off. Alpine and cross-country permits are strictly controlled to prevent environmental damage, but auto camping permits are easy to procure. Each campground has its own personality. Go to **Ohanapecosh** for the gorgeous and serene high ceiling of old growth trees, **Cougar Rock** for the strictly maintained quiet hours, and **White River** and **Sunshine Point** for the views. Open on a first-come, first-camped basis, they fill up only on the busiest summer weekends. Only Sunshine Point, however, remains open throughout the year. With a permit, cross-country hikers can use any of the free, well-established **trailside camps** scattered throughout the park's backcountry. Most camps have toilet facilities and a nearby water source; some have shelters. Fires are prohibited and party numbers are limited. Mountain and glacier climbers must always register in person at ranger stations to get permits.

To reach Mt. Rainier from the west, drive south on I-5 to Tacoma, then go east on Rte. 512, south on Rte. 7, and east on Rte. 706. This scenic road meanders through the town of Ashford and into the park by the Nisqually entrance. Rte. 706 is the only access road kept open throughout the year; snow usually closes all other park roads from November through May. The city of **Yakima** provides the eastern gateway to the park. Take I-82 from the center of town to U.S. 12 heading west. At the junction of the Naches and Tieton Rivers, go either left on U.S. 12 or continue straight up Rte. 410. U.S. 12 runs past Rimrock Lake, over White Pass to Rte. 123, where a right turn leads to the Stevens Canyon entrance to Rainier.

Mount Saint Helens

On the morning of May 18, 1980, Mt. St. Helens erupted violently, shaking the entire state of Washington out of bed. In the three days that followed, a hole two mi. long and one mi. wide opened in the mountain. Ash from the crater blackened the sky for hundreds of miles and blanketed the streets of nearby towns with inches of soot. Debris from the volcano flooded Spirit Lake, choked rivers with mud, and sent house-sized boulders tumbling down the mountainside. The blast leveled entire forests, leaving a stubble of trunks on the hills and millions of trees pointing arrow-like away from the crater.

Once the jewel of the Cascades, **Mt. St. Helens National Monument** (now administered by the National Forest Service) is slowly but steadily recovering from that explosion. Thirteen years later, the devastated grey landscape is brightened by signs of returning life—saplings press past their fallen brethren, insects flourish near newly formed waterfalls, and many small rodents scurry between burrows. Nature's power of destruction, it seems, is matched only by her power of regeneration.

Start any trip to the mountain at the **Mount St. Helens National Volcanic Monument Visitors Center** (274-6644 or 274-4038 for 24-hr. recording), on Rte. 504, five mi. east of Castle Rock (exit 49 off of I-5). Interpretive talks and displays recount the mountain's eruption and subsequent regeneration and are augmented by a 20-minute film, a 10-minute slide show, and many hands-on activities. The center also provides camping and mountain access information. (Open April-Sept. 9am-6pm, off-season 9am-5pm.) If time permits, plan to spend the whole day in the monument and visit either the **Pine Creek Information Center** in the south or the **Woods Creek Information Center** in the north. While not as large as the main center near Castle Rock, these two are each within one mi. of excellent viewpoints and offer displays, maps, and brochures on the area. Pick up free copies of the *Volcano Review* and the *Tourist Guide to Volcano Country,* sources of local information, at any of these centers. (Open approximately May-Oct. 9am-5pm, depending on funding and environmental conditions.) These centers are also the places to head in case of an **emergency** in the park. From the north get on U.S. 12 and turn south on Forest Road 25 at the town of Randle towards Woods Creek. From the south, take Rte. 503, which becomes Forest Road 90 at Yale; follow 90 to Pine Creek.

All drivers should fill up their gas tanks before starting the journey, as fuel is not sold within the monument. Drivers of trailers or RVs should avoid Road 26, which turns off to the east from Road 25; it's a one-lane road which is often steep and very curvy. Both Road 25 and Road 26 intersect road 99; at the junction of Roads 25 and 99, **Wakepish Sno-Park** serves as a trailer drop during the summer, and guests may find their trip along Road 99 to **Windy Ridge** without the additional weight of a trailer. The newly paved, two-lane Road 99 leads visitors along 17 mi. of curves, clouds of ash, and precipices, past Spirit Lake, to a point just 3.5 mi. from the crater. Without stops it takes nearly an hour to travel out and back, but the numerous interpretive talks and walks, and the spectacular views along the way are definitely worth exploring. Check with one of the visitors centers or the free newsletters for times and meeting places of these interpretive activities. Continue 25 mi. south on Road 25, 12 mi. west on Road 90, then two mi. north on Road 83 to **Ape Cave,** a broken 2.5-mi.-long lava tube formed in an ancient eruption, which is now open for visitors to explore. Be sure to wear a jacket and sturdy shoes; you can rent a lantern for $3. Interpreters lead cave walks daily; check at the center there for times.

Something new to look for is the **Coldwater Ridge Visitor Services Center,** scheduled to open in May of 1993. Rte. 504, under construction as we go to press, will access the area, opening up spectacular western view of the crater, dome, Toutle River Valley, and new lakes formed by the 1980 eruption. The Coldwater Center plans include interpretive exhibits, trails, picnic and restaurant facilities, and a boat launch. A shuttle bus will run from the lake to Johnson Ridge, allowing direct views into the crater. Check with one of the other centers to see if construction is progressing on schedule.

For those who want an early start touring the mountain, there are two primitive **campgrounds** relatively near the scene of the explosion. **Iron Creek Campground,** just south of the Woods Creek Information Center on Forest Road 25, has 98 sites ($8 each, call 800-283-2267 for reservations), and **Swift Campground,** just west of the Pine Creek Information Center on Forest Road 90, has 93 sites ($6 each, no reservations). Just west of Swift Campground on Yale Reservoir lie **Beaver Bay** and **Cougar Campgrounds,** both of which have flush toilets and showers and are run by Pacific Power & Light. (Sites $6; for reservations call 503-464-5035.) The **Gifford Pinchot National Forest Headquarters,** 6926 E. Fourth Plain Blvd., P.O. Box 894, Vancouver, WA (696-7500), also has camping and hiking info. For 24-hr. recorded info on current **volcanic activity,** call 696-7848.

Gray Line, 400 N.W. Broadway, Portland, OR (503-226-6755; 800-426-7532) runs buses from Seattle to Mt. St. Helens. (Round-trip $26, under 13 $14.)

Mount St. Helens' **area code** is 206.

North Cascades

A favorite stomping ground for deer, mountain goats and bears, the North Cascades—an aggregation of dramatic peaks in the northern part of the state—remain one of the last great expanses of untouched land in the continental U.S. **Route 20,** a.k.a. the **North Cascades Hwy.,** provides the major access to the area, as well as astounding views awaiting each twist in the road. Use the information below to follow the road eastward from Burlington (exit 230 on I-5) along the Skagit River to the Skagit Dams (whose hydroelectric energy powers Seattle), then across the Cascade Crest at Rainy Pass (4860 ft.) and Washington Pass (5477 ft.), finally descending to the Methow River and the dry Okanogan rangeland of eastern Washington. **Route 9** branches off of Rte. 20 and leads north through the rich farmland of **Skagit Valley,** travels through inspiring forested countryside, an offers roundabout access to **Mt. Baker** via forks at the Nooksack River and Rte. 542. Mt. Baker (10,778 ft.) has been belching since 1975, and in winter jets of steam often snort from its dome.

Concrete to Marblemount

You would only have to sneeze three times in succession to miss the town of **Concrete** and its two neighbors, Rockport and Marblemount—and you may want to do so. The road off Rte. 20 from Concrete to Mt. Baker runs past the lakes created by the Upper and Lower Baker Dams. Concrete facts are available from the surprisingly large **Concrete Chamber of Commerce** (853-8400), in the old depot, tucked between Main St. and Rte. 20—follow the railroad tracks upon entering town. (Open Mon.-Fri. 8am-4pm, Sat. 10am-4pm.) If you drive through Concrete at lunchtime, stop at the **Mount Baker Café,** 119 E. Main St. (853-8200; open Mon.-Thurs. 6am-9pm, Fri.-Sat. 6am-10pm, Sun. 8am-4pm).

Neighboring **Rockport** borders **Rockport State Park** which features magnificent Douglas firs, a trail that accommodates wheelchairs, and 62 campsites that rank among the largest in the state ($8, with full hookup $12). The surrounding **Mt. Baker National Forest** permits free camping closer to the high peaks.

Marblemount is the next town east and the nearest one to the **Cascade Pass:** from Rte. 20 take Cascade River Rd. across the Skagit River; 22 mi. up the road you'll find the trailhead for a nine-mi. hike to the pass. Replenish your energy in Marblemount at the **Mountain Song Restaurant,** 5860 Rte. 20 (873-2461), which serves hearty and healthy meals—try the pasta special ($9.25). (Open daily 8am-9pm.) Pitch your tent at the free sites in the **Cascade Islands Campground,** on the south side of the Cascade River (ask for directions in town). Bring heavy-duty insect repellent. **The Barrett House Hostel** (*not* HI/AYH; 873-2021), offers warm beds in a building that looks like the Bates Motel ($7.50 each).

Newhalem to Washington Pass

Newhalem is the next major town on Rte. 20, and the first town in the **Ross Lake National Recreation Area,** a buffer zone between the highway and North Cascade National Park. A small grocery store and hiking trails to the dams and lakes nearby are the highlights of the town. Info emanates from the **visitors center,** on Rte. 20. (Open late June-early Sept. Thurs.-Mon. 8am-4pm.) At other times, stop at the **general store** (open Mon.-Fri. 9:30am-7pm; 206-386-4489).

Plugged up by Ross Dam, the artificial expanse of **Ross Lake** penetrates into the mountains as far as the Canadian border. Fifteen **campgrounds** gird the lake, some accessible by boat only, others by trail. The trail along Big Beaver Creek, a few miles north of Rte. 20, leads from Ross Lake into the Picket Range and eventually to Mt. Baker and the **Northern Unit** of North Cascades National Park. The **Sourdough Mountain** and **Desolation Peak** lookout towers near Ross Lake have eagle's-eye views of the range.

Diablo Lake fumes directly to the west of Ross Lake, the foot of Ross Dam acting as its eastern shore and the top of the Diablo Dam stopping it up on the west. The town of **Diablo Lake,** on the northeastern shore, is the main trailhead for hikes into the southern portion of the North Cascades National Park. The **Thunder Creek Trail** traverses

Park Creek Pass to the Stehekin River Rd. in **Lake Chelan National Recreation Area.** Diablo Lake has a boathouse and a lodge that sells groceries and gas.

Thirty mi. farther on Rte. 20, the **Pacific Coast Trail** traverses **Rainy Pass** (alt. 4860 ft.) on one of the most scenic and challenging legs of its 2500-mi. Canada-to-Mexico span. The trail leads up to **Pasayten Wilderness** in the north and down to **Glacier Peak** (10,541 ft.), which dominates the central portion of the range. Glacier Peak can also be approached from the secondary roads extending northward from the Lake Wenatchee area near Coles Corner on U.S. 2, or from Rte. 530 to Darrington. **Washington Pass,** at Mile 163 of Rte. 20, has short, wheelchair-accessible trails leading to a flabbergasting view of the **Early Winters Creek's Copper Basin.**

Winthrop and Twisp

Despite its Harvardian namesake, the town of **Winthrop** (25 mi. east of Rainy Pass as the crow flies, farther as Rte. 20 runs) was actually founded by a Yalie and is now imbued with a kitschy wild-West theme. *Yee-haw!* While in Winthrop, mark time at the **Shafer Museum,** 285 Castle Ave. (996-2712), up the hill overlooking town, one block west of Riverside Ave. The museum features all sorts of peculiar pioneer paraphernalia in a log cabin built in 1897. (Open daily 10am-5pm. Free.) You can rent real horses at the **Rocking Horse Ranch** (996-2768), nine mi. north of Winthrop on the North Cascade Hwy. ($10 per hr.), and mountain bikes at **The Virginian Hotel** just east of town on Rte. 20 ($5 for the 1st hr., then $3.50 per hr., full day $25).

The great billows of hickory-scented smoke draw customers to the **Riverside Rib Co. Bar B-Q,** 207 Riverside (996-2001), which serves tasty ribs in a converted prairie schooner; satisfying vegetarian dinners ($8) are also available. (Open Mon.-Fri. 11am-9pm.) Across the street chats the **Winthrop Information Station** (996-2125), on the corner of Rte. 20 and Riverside. (Open Memorial Day-Labor Day daily 9am-5pm.) The **Winthrop Ranger Station,** 24 W. Chewuch Rd., P.O. Box 579 (996-2266), up a marked road west of town, has info on camping in the surrounding National Forest. (Open Mon.-Fri. 7:45am-5pm, Sat. 8:30am-5pm.)

North of Winthrop, the **Early Winters Visitors Center,** outside Mazama, stocks info about the **Pasayten Wilderness,** an area whose relatively gentle terrain and mild climate endear it to hikers and equestrians (996-2534; open in summer daily 9am-5pm, in winter weekends only). **Early Winters** has 15 simple campsites ($6) 14 mi. west of Winthrop on Rte. 20, and **Klipchuk,** one mi. farther west, has 39 better developed sites ($6). Cool off at **Pearrygin Lake State Park** beach. From Riverside west of town, take Pearrygin Lake Rd. for four mi. Sites ($6) by the lake have flush toilets and pay showers. Arrive early, since the campground fills up by early afternoon.

Leave Winthrop's prohibitively expensive hotel scene and travel nine mi. south of Winthrop on Rte. 20 to stay in **Twisp,** the town that should have been a breakfast cereal, which offers low prices and few tourists. **The Sportsman Motel,** 1010 E. Rte. 20 (997-2911), tries to hide its tasteful rooms and kitchens behind a gruff, barracks-like exterior. (Singles $28, doubles $33; Nov. 1-May 1 $23/$28.) The **Twisp Ranger Station,** 502 Glover St. (997-2131), has an extremely helpful staff ready to load you down with trail and campground guides. (Open Mon.-Sat. 7:45am-4:30pm; closed on Sat. in winter.) The **Methow Valley Tourist Information Office,** at the corner of Rte. 20 and 3rd St., slings area brochures. (Open Mon.-Fri. 8am-noon and 1-5pm.)

The **Methow Valley Farmers Market** sells produce from 9am to noon on Saturdays (April-Oct.) in front of the community center. Join local workers and their families at **Rosey's Branding Iron,** 123 Glover St. (997-3576), where the wonderfully droll staff serves all-you-can-keep-down soup and salad for $5, as well as really cheap specials (under $3), and special menus for dieters, seniors and kids. (Open daily 5am-9pm.)

Five mi. east of Twisp stands a training station for **Smoke Jumpers,** folks who get their kicks by parachuting into the middle of blazing forest fires for strategic firefighting. Occasionally they give tours or have training sessions for public viewing. Call the base (997-2031) for details.

Practical Information

Greyhound stops in Burlington once per day, and **Empire Lines** (affiliated with Greyhound), serves Okanogan, Pateros, and Chelan on the eastern slope. No public transportation lines run within the park boundaries or along the North Cascades Highway. Avoid hitching in this area. Information on **North Cascades National Park** (surrounding Rte. 20 and the Ross Lake Recreation Area between Marblemount and Ross Dam) is available at 2105 Rte. 20, Sedro Wooley 98284 (206-856-5700; open Sun.-Thurs. 8am-4:30pm, Fri.-Sat. 8am-6pm). The info office for the **Okanogan National Forest** (surrounding Rte. 20 east of Ross Dam) is at 1240 2nd Ave. S., P.O. Box 950, Okanogan 98840 (509-422-2704); for **Wenatchee National Forest** (south of Okanogan National Forest and north of U.S. 2) it's at 301 Yakima St., P.O. Box 811, Wenatchee 98801 (509-662-4335). For **snow avalanche info** on all these jurisdictions call 206-526-6677.

Olympic Peninsula and Olympic National Park

In the fishing villages and logging towns of the Olympic Peninsula, locals joke about having webbed feet and using Rustoleum instead of suntan oil. The Olympic Mountains wring the area's heavy rainfall (up to 200 in. per year on Mt. Olympus) from the moist Pacific. While this torrent supports bona fide rain forests in the western peninsula's river valleys, towns such as Sequim in the range's rain shadow are some of the driest in all of Washington, with as little as 17 in. of rain in a typical year. The peninsula's geography matches its extremes of climate. The beaches along the Pacific strip are a hiker's paradise—isolated, windy and wildly sublime. The glaciated peaks of the Olympic range offer spectacular alpine scenery. In the north, seaports afford access to both the park and to the azure Strait of Juan De Fuca. In the east, fjord-like Hood Canal threatens to pull your eyes off the road with its jaw-dropping beauty. Because it compresses such variety into a relatively small area, the Olympic Peninsula attracts those seeking accessible wilderness and outdoor recreation. Be certain to bring rain gear; the area is damp even in the summer. U.S. 101 circumnavigates the peninsula, stringing together scattered towns and sights around the nape of the mountains. The numerous secondary roads spurring from 101 were designed with exploration in mind, although some are steep and gravel-covered, making bicycling into the heart of the park difficult.

Lodged among the august Olympic mountains, **Olympic National Park** sprawls over 900,000 acres of green velvet rainforest, jagged snow-covered peaks and dense evergreen forest. This enormous region in the heart of the peninsula affords limited access even to four-wheeled traffic. No scenic loops or roads cross the park, and only a handful of secondary roads make efforts to penetrate the interior. The roads that do exist serve mainly as trailheads for over 600 mi. of hiking trails. Come prepared for rain; a parka, good boots and a waterproof tent are essential.

Never drink untreated water in the park. A nasty microscopic parasite living in the water causes severe diarrhea, gas and abdominal cramps. Bring your own water supply, boil local water for five minutes before drinking it, or, in emergencies, purify your water with tablets you can buy at the visitors center. Dogs aren't allowed in the backcountry and must be restrained at all times within the park. **Fishing** within park boundaries is allowed without a permit, but you must obtain a state game department punch card for salmon and steelhead trout at local outfitting or hardware stores, or at the game department in Olympia. The **Elwha River** is best for trout. The more popular entrances of the park, such as the Hoh, Heart O' the Hills and Elwaha, charge a $3 entrance fee per car ($1 for hikers/bikers), good for seven days. The park service runs **interpretive programs** such as guided forest walks, tidal pool walks and campfire programs from its various ranger stations (all free). For a full schedule of events everywhere in the park, obtain a copy of the park newspaper, available at ranger stations and the visitors centers.

Campsites on the peninsula are numerous and are managed by a confusing patchwork of local, state and federal institutions. **Olympic National Park** maintains a number of campgrounds within the park (sites $6). Numerous **state parks** between the eastern boundary of the park and Hood Canal charge $5 to $8 per night, with an occasional site for tenters at only $3 to $4 per night. The **National Forest** and the park services welcome **backcountry camping** (free everywhere), but a permit—available at any ranger station or trailhead—is required for areas within the park. Camping on the beaches in the west is especially easy, although you should pack a tide table and a supply of fresh water and make certain to know and obey local restrictions.

Eastern Peninsula and Hood Canal

The long ribbon of the **Hood Canal** dangles down from Puget Sound, neatly separating the Kitsap Peninsula from its parent Olympic Peninsula. The canal's structure invites comparison with Scandinavia's famous fjords—the same narrow, steeply banked waterway, the same jagged peaks as backdrops, the same little towns tucked in the crevices of the coastline. U.S. 101 hugs the western shore of the canal from Potlatch State Park on its southern tip to Quilcene in the north. The **Eastern Rim** of Olympic National Park is accessible by several roads which leave from U.S. 101. Several car-accessible campgrounds lure hikers who use them as trailheads to the interior of the park. **Staircase Campground** (877-5569), 16 mi. northwest of Hoodsport at the head of Lake Cushman, has 59 sites and a ranger station with interpretive programs on weekends. (Open year-round. Sites $6.) **Dosewallips** (doh-see-WALL-ups), on a road that leaves U.S. 101 three mi. north of Brinnon, offers free but less developed sites. (Open June-Sept.)

The **Olympic National Forest** rims the eastern edge of the National Park. Much of the forest is more developed and more accessible than the park and gives those with limited time or appetites for the outdoors a taste of the peninsula's wildlife. Stop by one of the forest's **ranger stations** along the canal to pick up info on camping and trails in the forest. The two stations are in **Hoodsport,** P.O. Box 68 (877-5552; open daily Memorial Day-Labor Day 8am-4:30pm, off-season Mon.-Fri. 8am-4:30pm), and **Quilcene,** U.S. 101 S. (765-3368; open daily, same hours as Hoodsport). Adjacent to the Hoodsport Ranger Station stands a **post office** (877-5552; open Mon.-Fri. 8am-12:30pm and 1:30-5pm, Sat. 8:30-11:30am; **ZIP Code:** 98548). Many of the forest service **campgrounds** cost only $4, including **Hamma Hamma,** on Forest Service Rd. 25, seven mi. northwest of Eldon; **Lena Creek,** two mi. beyond Hamma Hamma; **Elkhorn,** on Forest Service Rd. 2610, 11 mi. northwest of Brinnon; and **Collins,** on Forest Service Rd. 2515, eight mi. west of Brinnon. All have drinking water, as well as hiking, good fishing and gorgeous scenery. Unfortunately, many of these require travel along gravel roads, tough for bicyclists.

Lake Cushman State Park (877-5491), seven mi. west of Hoodsport on Lake Cushman Rd., stretches by a beautiful lake with good beaches. Many use it as a base camp for extended backpacking trips into the forest. It has 70 tent sites ($8) and 30 more with full hookup ($12), as well as flush toilets and pay showers (25¢ for 6 min.). Clinging to a quiet cove just north of Eldon, **Mike's Beach Resort and Hostel,** N. 38470 U.S. 101 (877-5324), lacks a kitchen, and too many bunks crowd its tiny rooms, but it does have a small grocery store. Check-in from 7am to 10pm. ($5, nonmembers $7.50. Open April 15-Nov. 1.) The **Hungry Bear Café** in Eldon is inhabited by scores of taxidermic bears (but please don't feed the animals; they're already stuffed). Burgers are $2.75, fries $1.50. (Open Mon.-Fri. 9am-7pm, Sat. 8am-8pm, Sun. 8am-7pm.)

Northern Peninsula

Bleak lumber and fishing villages dominate the northern coast of the Olympic Peninsula. An exception to this dreary rule is Port Townsend—at one time expected to become a San Francisco of the north. In anticipation of its glorious future, beautiful Victorian homes were built atop its strategic and steep bluff overlooking both the Strait of Juan de Fuca and Puget Sound. With the coming of the railroad, Seattle supplanted

Port Townsend's status as nexus of the Northwest. In spite of this, the town retains a defiantly cosmopolitan mien. Bookstores and art galleries line its streets. It is one of the few places west of Seattle where espresso stands outnumber live bait shops. While there, stay at the **Fort Worden Youth Hostel (HI/AYH)** (385-0655), in Fort Worden State Park, two mi. from downtown. The hostel is situated amidst barracks used as the set of *An Officer And a Gentleman.* ($8.50, nonmembers $11.50. Closed from Dec. 21-Jan. 31.) A nearby campground (385-4730; also on the grounds of the state park) offers sites for $12 a night. The **Port Townsend Chamber of Commerce** (385-2722) assists at 2436 Sims Way, Port Townsend 98368.

Never confuse Port Townsend with grim Port Angeles. The former is the civilized frontal lobe of the peninsula, the latter is its smelly armpit. However, even armpits have a function. Use Port Angeles as a supply base and a jumping off point for points within the park. Stop at the **Olympic Visitors Center,** 3002 Mt. Angeles Rd. off Race St., Port Angeles (452-0330), for a map of the locations of other ranger stations and answers to all your questions about camping, backcountry hiking, and fishing in the park. (Open daily 8am-6pm; off-season reduced hours.) The visitors center also guards the entrance to the very steeply graded Hurricane Ridge Road, leading to (you guessed it) **Hurricane Ridge**. Here roam deer, bears and other tundra-dwellers amidst verdant rolling alpine meadows dropping off into blue and white oblivion. With a backdrop of stunning glacier-capped peaks, the scenery looks as though it has been lifted directly from *The Sound of Music.* A visitors center at the peak helps travelers appreciate the delicate beauty of a tundra ecosystem.

Camping in the park's Northern Rim is abundant. **Heart o' the Hills** (452-2713) and **Elwha Valley** (452-9191) campgrounds both have interpretive programs and ranger stations, as does **Fairholm Campground** (928-3380), 30 mi. west of Port Angeles at the western tip of Lake Crescent. (Sites $6.) The **Lake Crescent** station (928-3380) has an interpretive program but no camping. (**Information booth** open July-Aug. daily 11am-4pm.) A roving naturalist is on duty in the afternoons at **Soleduck Hotsprings Campground** (327-3534), southeast of Lake Crescent, 13 mi. off U.S. 101, adjoining the hot springs resort. (Sites $6.)

Western Peninsula

The western portion of the Olympic Peninsula contains some of the wildest and most isolated terrain to be found west of the Cascades. Here fall buckets upon buckets of rain—more than in any other area of the contiguous United States. This deluge supports unimaginably lush vegetation and a boisterous timber industry.

Down Hoh River Rd., 19 mi. from its junction with U.S. 101, the park service's **Hoh Rain Forest Campground and Visitors Center** (374-6925) explain the effects of over 200 in. of rain a year on the vegetation. The center is wheelchair-accessible, as are some of the trails leading from the center into the only non-tropical rain forest in the world. (Sites $6; visitors center open summer daily 9am-4:30pm.) For shelter from the area's incessant rain, seek out the **Rain Forest Home Hostel** (374-2270) between mileposts 169 and 170 on U.S. 101. Jim and Kay will gladly acquaint you with sites in the region. (Jim is a dead ringer for Paul Simon—the singer not the senator.) Their fireplace is a particularly cozy place to chat on a cold, wet night. (Check-in 5-10pm daily. $8.) After U.S. 101 rejoins the coast, the park's boundaries extend southwest to edge the banks of the **Queets River.** The unpaved road here leads to free campsites at the top. (Open June-Sept.) The park and forest services share the land surrounding **Quinault Lake** and **Quinault River.** The park service land is accessible by foot only. The forest service operates a day-use beach and an info center in the **Quinault Ranger Station,** South Shore Rd. (288-2444; open daily 9am-5pm; winter Mon.-Fri. 9am-5pm).

Over 57 mi. of pristine coastline await visitors on the western section of the park, which edges the Pacific coast from the Quinalt Reservation in the south to the Makah Reservation at its northern border. **Mora** (374-5460) and **Kalaloch** (KLAY-lok; 962-2283) have campgrounds (sites $6) and ranger stations. The Kalaloch Center, including lodge, general store and gas station, stays more scenic with 177 sites near the ocean.

Better yet, find a beach access path, hike a few miles and camp amid roaring surf and piled driftwood—out of sight and sound of any other human. Be sure to bring fresh water and rain gear. Also, make certain to bring tide tables to prevent being trapped in a cove with the tide cutting off your exits.

San Juan Islands

The San Juan Islands are an (as yet) untainted treasure. Bald eagles circle above haggard hillsides and family farms. Pods of killer whales spout offshore, and the sun shines perpetually. To travelers approaching from summer resorts infested with vacationers, the islands seem blissfully quiet. Even in mid-summer, you can drive the back roads and pass another car only about once an hour. For this reason, islanders don't begrudge admission to their towns and campsites. Although tension has built between the locals and Seattleites who are buying up huge chunks of the islands, well-behaved tourists and their dollars are still very welcome on the San Juans.

An excellent guide to the area is *The San Juan Islands Afoot and Afloat* by Marge Mueller ($10), available at book and outfitting stores on the islands and in Seattle. *Islands Sounder,* the local paper, annually publishes *The San Juans Beckon* to provide up-to-date info on island recreation. You can pick it up free on the ferries and in island stores.

Washington State Ferries serve the islands daily from **Anacortes** on the mainland. To reach Anacortes, take I-5 north from Seattle to Mt. Vernon. From there, Rte. 20 heads west; the way to the ferry is well-marked. Buses to Anacortes depart Seattle from the **Greyhound depot** at 8th Ave. and Stewart St. once a day ($13.25 one way). Call 624-5077 for exact times.

Ferries depart Anacortes about nine times daily, on a route that stops at **Lopez, Shaw, Orcas**, and **San Juan Island**. One ferry per day continues to **Sidney, BC,** just north of Victoria on Vancouver Island. Not every ferry services all the islands, so check a schedule or call 206-464-6400 or 800-843-3779. During the summer, two additional ferries per day travel directly to San Juan Island, and one additional ferry makes it to Sidney, BC. The ferry revises its system seasonally.

Buy tickets in Anacortes. You pay only on westbound trips to or between the islands; no charge is levied on eastbound traffic. A money-saving tip: travel directly to the westernmost island on your itinerary and then make your way back to the mainland island by island (that is, if you ever want to go back). It is possible to purchase one way tickets to or from Sidney. Foot passengers travel in either direction between the islands for free. Fares from Anacortes to San Juan Island are $4.65 for pedestrians, $2.35 for seniors and ages 5-11 ($1 surcharge in summer), $6.25 for bikes, and $9.50 for motorcycles; cars cost $19, $16 in winter. Fares to the other islands en route generally run a few dollars cheaper. Inter-island fares average $2.25 for bikes and motorcycles, $7.75 for cars. The one way fare to Sidney, BC costs $6 for pedestrians, $8.55 for bikes, $13 for motorcycles, and $31.25 for cars in summer ($26 in winter). Some car spaces are available from the islands to Sidney; make reservations. Call Washington State Ferries (206-464-6400; in WA 800-542-0810) before noon on the day before your trip to ensure a space. On peak traveling days, arrive with your vehicle at least one hour prior to scheduled departure. The ferry authorities accept only cash and in-state checks as payment. You may park your vehicle for free at the Anacortes parking lot on the corner of 30th and T St. A free, reliable shuttle then whisks you four mi. to the terminal.

San Juan Island

Although the ferry makes its last stop in San Juan, it is the most frequently visited island, home to the largest town in the group, **Friday Harbor.** Since the ferry docks right in town, the island proves the easiest to explore on foot.

To begin a loop of the island, head south out of Friday Harbor on Argyle Rd., which merges into Cattle Point Rd., on the way to **American Camp** (378-2902). The camp dates to the infamous Pig War of 1859, when the U.S. and England remained at loggerheads over possession of the islands. An interpretive shelter near the entrance to the park explains the history of the war; a self-guided historic trail leads from the shelter through the buildings.

Returning north on **Cattle Point Rd.,** consider taking the gravel False Bay Rd. to the west. The road leads to **False Bay,** home to a large number of nesting bald eagles. Farther north on False Bay Rd., you'll run into **Bailer Hill Road,** which turns into West Side Rd. when it reaches Haro Straight. (You can also reach Bailer Hill Rd. by taking Cattle Point Rd. to Little Rd.) Along the road, sloping hills blanketed with wildflowers rise to one side, while rocky shores crash on the other. **San Juan County Park** on Smallpox Bay provides a convenient opportunity to park your bike or car and examine this scenery more closely.

English Camp, the second half of San Juan National Historical Park, rests on West Valley Rd. amid the forest surrounding Garrison Bay. From West Side Rd., take Mitchell Bay Rd. east to West Valley Rd. Here, four preserved original buildings, including the barracks, now function as an **interpretive center,** which does, English-style, the same thing the American one does. (Park open year-round; buildings open Memorial Day-Labor Day daily 8am-4:30pm. Free.)

Friday Harbor loses much of its charm when the tourists arrive in full force, but remains quite appealing in the winter. Take the time to poke around the galleries, craft shops, and bookstores. The **Whale Museum,** 62 1st St. (378-4710), will teach you everything you ever wanted to know about the giant cetaceans, starring skeletons, sculptures and info on new research. The museum even has a **whale hotline** (800-562-8832) for you to report sightings and strandings. (Open daily 10am-5pm; winter 11am-4pm. Admission $3, seniors and students $2.50, kids under 12 $1.50.) **The Inn at Friday Harbor,** 410 Spring St. (378-4351), sends a double-decker bus around the island via English Camp and Lime Kiln Park (for whalewatching) daily at 1pm ($10). If you're eager to fish or clam, pick up a copy of the Department of Fisheries pamphlet, *Salmon, Shellfish, Marine Fish Sport Fishing Guide,* for details on regulations and limits. The guide is available free at **Friday Harbor Hardware and Marine,** 270 Spring St. (378-4622), where you can also get fishing licenses. (Open Mon.-Sat. 8am-6pm, Sun. 10am-4pm.) Check with the **red tide hotline** (800-562-5632) if you'll be gathering shellfish; the nasty bacteria can wreak horrors on your intestines.

The local hostel recently closed, but **San Juan County Park,** 380 Westside Rd. (378-2992), 10 mi. west of Friday Harbor on Smallpox and Andrews Bays, provides a public alternative. (Cold water, flush toilets, no hookups. Bikers and hikers $5; cars, campers, and trailers $12.) **Lakedale Campgrounds,** 2627 Roche Harbor Rd. (378-2350), four mi. from Friday Harbor, has fishing ($4, no permit required), canoe rental ($4.50 per hr., $18 per day), swimming (free, $1.50 for noncampers, under 12 $1) and showers ($1). (Bikers and hikers $4.50, July-Aug. $5.50, camping for 1-2 persons $12.50/$15, each additional person $3/$3.50, RV and trailers $15/$18; open April 1-Oct. 15.) The parks and shoreline drives beg you to pack a picnic lunch and leave Friday Harbor behind. Stock up on bread and cheese at **King's Market** (378-4505), 160 Spring St. (Open daily 8am-10pm.)

The **National Park Service Information Center,** 1st and Spring, P.O. Box 429 (378-2240), will answer questions about the British and American camps. (Open Mon.-Fri. 8am-4:30pm, Sat.-Sun. 9am-4:30pm; winter Mon.-Fri. 8am-4:30pm.) The **post office** stamps at Blair and Reed St. (378-4511; open Mon.-Fri. 8:30am-4:30pm); the **ZIP code** is 98250. San Juan Island's **area code** is 206.

Orcas Island

With a breathtaking state park and a funky youth hostel, Orcas has the best tourist facilities of all the islands. The 2409-ft. peak of **Mt. Constitution** offers a view of the San Juans, Olympics and Vancouver Island. The best way to see the island is by bike; you can rent one at **Wildlife Cycle,** A St. and North Beach Rd. in Eastsound (376-4708), for $5 per hr., $20 per day. (Open Mon.-Sat. 10:30am-5:30pm.) Because Orcas is shaped like a horseshoe, getting around is a bit of a chore. The ferry lands on the southwest tip. Travel nine mi. northeast up the horseshoe to reach **Eastsound,** the island's main town. Stop in one of the shops at the landing to get a free map.

Trippers on Orcas Island don't need to travel with a destination in mind. At least half the fun is getting there—pick a side road, follow it to where it leads, select a particularly moving vista, and meditate on llife, llove, and llamas. Follow Horseshoe Hwy. straight into what is unquestionably Orcas's greatest attraction. **Moran State Park**, Star Rte. Box 22, Eastsound 98245 (376-2326), has over 21 mi. of hiking trails, ranging in difficulty from a one-hr. jaunt around Mountain Lake to a day-long constitutional up the south face of Mt. Constitution. Stock up on chow at **Templin's General Store** in the middle of Eastsound (376-2101; open Mon.-Sat. 8am-8pm, Sun. 10am-6pm) or at the **Farmers' Market** in front of the museum, every Saturday at 10am.

The aforementioned funky hostel is called the **Doe Bay Village Resort,** Star Rte. 86, Olga 98279 (376-2291), off Horseshoe Hwy., on St. Lawrence Rd., eight mi. out of Moran State Park. It's on a secluded bay, has kitchen facilities, a health-food store, and plenty of grounds and hiking trails on which to wander. The crowning attraction is the steam sauna and mineral bath, available to hostelers at $3 per day (nonlodgers $5, bathing suits optional). ($9.50, nonmembers $12.50, camping $8.50, cottages from $32.50. Imaginative and flexible work-trade program. Reservations recommended.) If the hostel's full (it only has nine beds), camp at **Moran State Park;** it has 151 sites, 12 of which remain open year-round. The park has no backcountry camping, but the best of island fun is all there: swimming, fishing, boating and hiking. (Has showers and restrooms. Sites $8, hiker/biker sites $4. Reservations recommended; $5 fee; park open daily 6:30am-dusk; Sept.-March 8am-dusk.)

The Orca Island **post office** is on A St., in Eastsound Market Place (376-4121; open Mon.-Fri. 9am-4:30pm). The General Delivery **ZIP code** is 98245. The **area code** is 206.

Whidbey Island

Now the longest island in the contiguous U.S. (since Long Island built a bridge and became a peninsula), telephone-receiver-shaped Whidbey Island sits in the rain shadow of the Olympic Mountains. Clouds, wrung dry by the time they pass over Whidbey, 40 mi. due north of Seattle, release a mere 20 in. of rain per year and a luxurious ration of sunshine. This leaves visitors free to enjoy rocky beaches bound by bluffs blooming with wild roses and crawling with blackberry brambles; also look out for loganberries and penncove mussels, Whidbey's biggest "exports." Whidbey also swims in smoked salmon; every town (and every milepost along the highway) has its share of salmon shacks. In Langley, **Mike's Place,** 215 1st St. (321-6575), serves the best clam chowder on the island ($2.25). The all-you-can-eat specials also come highly recommended. (Lunch $4-6, dinner under $10. Open Sat.-Thurs. 8am-9pm, Fri. 7am-9pm.) Inexpensive motels are few and far between on Whidbey; those that do exist are frequently in need of repairs. The **Tyee Motel and Café,** 405 S. Main St., Coupeville (678-6616), offers clean, straightforward rooms with showers. Check-in at the lounge (open 11:30am-2am) if the café is closed. (Café open Mon.-Sat. 6:30am-8:30pm. Singles $33, doubles $37.) Four state park campgrounds service the island, each with sites for $8. **Fort Ebey State Park,** on N. Fort Ebey Rd., north of Fort Casey and just west of Coupeville (678-4636), is the island's newest campground; miles of hiking trails and easy access to a pebbly beach make it the island's best. (50 sites for cars and RVs, 3 for hikers and bikers, $3.)

To reach Whidbey from the north, take exit 189 off I-5 and head west toward Anacortes. Stay on Rte. 20 when it heads south through the stunning Deception Pass State Park (signs will direct you); otherwise you will end up in Anacortes. **Evergreen Trailways** runs a bus to Whidbey from Seattle. You can reach Whidbey Island by ferry from Port Townsend on the Olympic Peninsula. Call Washington State Ferries at 800-843-3779.

The **post office** in Langley registers at 115 2nd St. (321-4113), **ZIP code** 98260; in Coupeville at 201 N.W. Coveland (678-5353), **ZIP code** 98239; in Oak Harbor at 7035 70th N.W. (675-6621), **ZIP code** 98277. The **area code** for Whidbey is 206.

Seattle

The skyscrapers of downtown Seattle have risen to compete with the Olympic peaks that ring the city's eastern skyline. Although it is expanding at an alarming rate, Seattle has integrated its diverse populace into a cohesive and successful modern city. Everyone paws through the fresh greens and sea creatures at Pike Place Market, nearly everyone wears Birkenstocks, and even the police ride mountain bikes. In relative size, the repertory theater community ranks second only to that of New York, and the Seattle Repertory Theater recently won the Tony Award for best Regional Theater. Residents of Seattle will tell tourists to bring raincoats, galoshes, gondolas and arks to dissuade them from invading. Actually, Seattle catches less precipitation a year than quite a few major cities. Clouds are another story. The register of a clear day in Seattle is whether "the mountain is out;" referring to the great ice cream scoop on the skyline—Mt. Rainier—one of the most spectacular hikes in the Northwest only two hours away. Sporting Seattleites will just do it even in the drizzle, and a blossoming entertainment industry makes indoor excursions just as rewarding.

Practical Information

Emergency: 911

Visitor Information: Seattle-King County Visitors Bureau, 666 Stewart St. (461-5840), on the Galleria level of the Convention Center. Entrance at Union and 7th. Well-stocked with maps, brochures, newspapers, and transit schedules. Open Mon.-Fri. 8:30am-5pm, Sat.-Sun 10am-4pm. Weekend hours only in summer. From 5-7:30pm, call the airport branch at 433-5218.

Seattle Parks and Recreation Department, 5201 Green Lake Way N. (684-4075). Open Mon.-Fri. 8am-6pm. **National Park Service, Pacific Northwest Region,** 915 2nd Ave., Room 442, Mon.-Fri. 8am-4:30pm (553-4830).

Traveler's Aid: 909 4th Ave. #630 (461-3888), at Marion in the YMCA. Free services to stranded travelers with lost wallets, companions or marbles. Open Mon.-Fri. 8:30am-9pm, Sat. 9am-1pm, Sun. 1-5pm.

Seattle-Tacoma International Airport (Sea-Tac), on Federal Way (433-5217), south of Seattle proper. **Sea-Tac Visitors Information Center** (433-5218), in the central baggage claim area across from carousel 10. Open daily 9:30am-7:30pm. International visitors should contact **Operation Welcome** (433-5367), at the Information Center, where staff members answer questions on customs, immigration, and foreign language services in just about every possible language. Take Metro **buses** #174 and 194 to downtown; they run daily every ½-hour from 6am-1am. ($1.50 peak, $1 off-peak; under 18 $1/75¢.) Taxi fare to Seattle costs about $22.

Amtrak: King St. Station, 3rd and Jackson St. (800-872-7245). Trains to: Portland (3 per day, $24), Tacoma ($8), and San Francisco ($157). Station open daily 6am-10pm; ticket office 6am-5:30pm.

Buses: Greyhound, 8th Ave. and Stewart St. (624-3456). To: Sea-Tac Airport (2 per day, $3.50 round-trip); Vancouver, BC ($22); and Portland (8 per day, $19). Open daily 5am-9pm and midnight-1:30am. **Green Tortoise,** 324-7433 or 800-227-4766. Leaves from 9th and Stewart, Tues., Thurs.-Fri. and Sun. at 8am to: Portland (4 hr., $15); Berkeley, CA (24 hr., $69); and San Francisco (24 hr., $69). Reservations required 5 days in advance. See Getting Around by Bus in the General Introduction for more info.

Metro Transit: Customer Assistance Office, 821 2nd Ave. (553-3000; TDD service 684-1739), in the Exchange Bldg. downtown. Open Mon.-Fri. 8am-5pm. Buses run 6am-1am. Within the city limits fare 75¢, during weekday peak hours $1; beyond city limits $1/$1.50. Weekend all-day pass $1.50. Ride free 4am-9pm from Jackson St. to Battery St. and between 6th Ave. and the waterfront. Transfers valid for 2 hrs. and for Waterfront Streetcars as well. Discounts for seniors and ages 5-17.

Ferries: Washington State Ferries, Colman Dock, Pier 52 (464-2000, ext. 4; in WA 800-542-0810 or 800-542-7052). Service to Bremerton (on Kitsap Peninsula) and Winslow (on Bainbridge Island). Ferries leave frequently daily 6am-2am. Summer fares from $3.30, car and driver $6.65, winter $5.55.

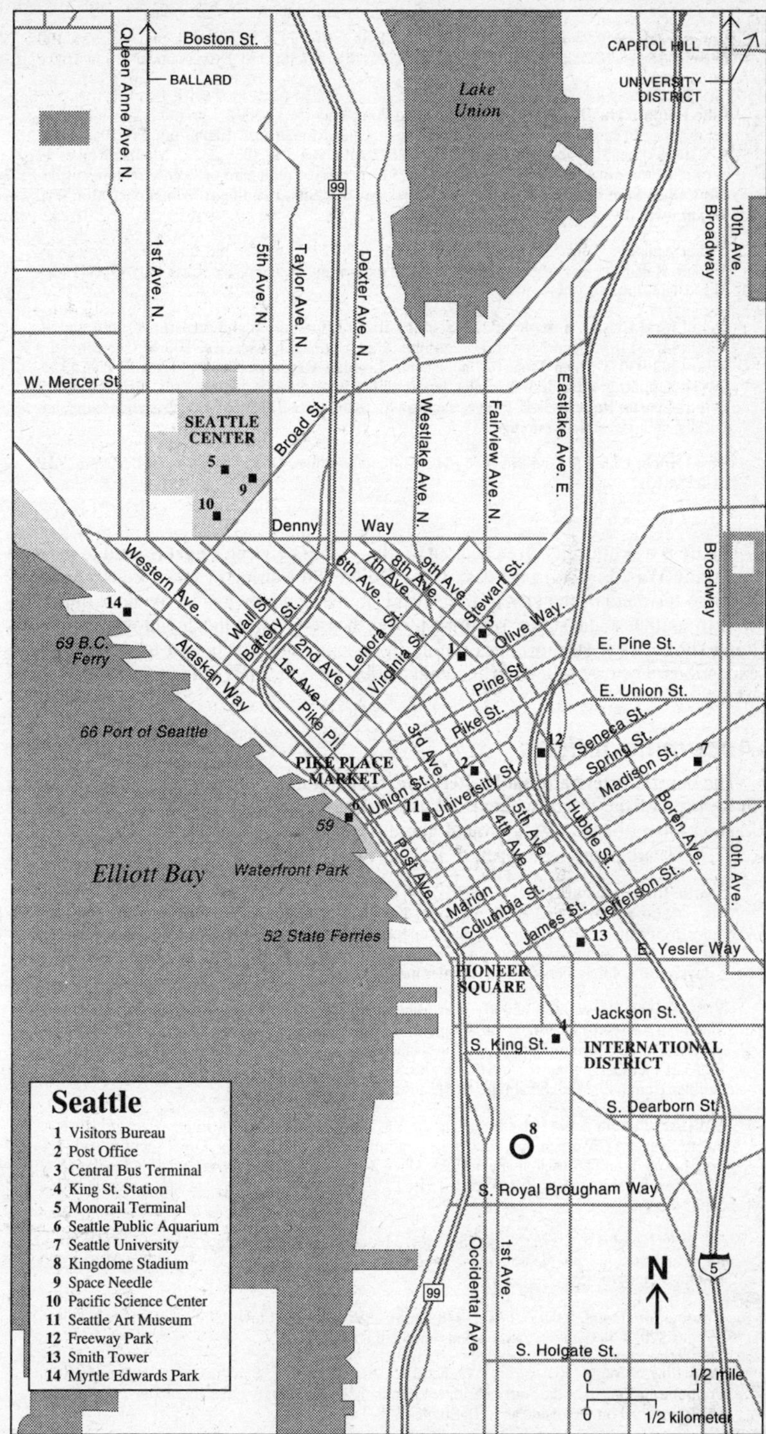

Boston St.
BALLARD
Queen Anne Ave. N.
1st Ave. N.
5th Ave. N.
Taylor Ave. N.
Dexter Ave. N.
Lake Union
CAPITOL HILL
UNIVERSITY DISTRICT
Broadway
10th Ave.
W. Mercer St.
SEATTLE CENTER
Broad St.
Westlake Ave. N.
Fairview Ave. N.
Eastlake Ave. E.
Denny Way
Western Ave.
Wall St.
Battery St.
6th Ave.
7th Ave.
8th Ave.
9th Ave.
Stewart St.
Olive Way
69 B.C. Ferry
Alaskan Way
2nd Ave.
1st Ave.
Lenora St.
Virginia St.
E. Pine St.
Pine St.
E. Union St.
Pike St.
Pike Pl.
66 Port of Seattle
3rd Ave.
Seneca St.
Spring St.
Madison St.
PIKE PLACE MARKET
Union St.
University St.
Boren Ave.
59
Post Ave.
4th Ave.
5th Ave.
Hubble St.
Elliott Bay
Waterfront Park
Marion
Columbia St.
James St.
Jefferson St.
52 State Ferries
E. Yesler Way
PIONEER SQUARE
Jackson St.
S. King St.
INTERNATIONAL DISTRICT
S. Dearborn St.
S. Royal Brougham Way
Occidental Ave.
1st Ave.
S. Holgate St.
N
0
1/2 mile
1/2 kilometer
Seattle
1 Visitors Bureau
2 Post Office
3 Central Bus Terminal
4 King St. Station
5 Monorail Terminal
6 Seattle Public Aquarium
7 Seattle University
8 Kingdome Stadium
9 Space Needle
10 Pacific Science Center
11 Seattle Art Museum
12 Freeway Park
13 Smith Tower
14 Myrtle Edwards Park

Car Rental: A-19.95-Rent-A-Car, 804 N. 145th St. (364-1995). $20 per day, under 21 $25. 100 free mi., 15¢ each additional mi. Free delivery. Must have credit card. Drivers under 21 must have auto insurance.

Bike Rental: The Bicycle Center, 4529 Sand Point Way (523-8300). 2 hr. min., $3 per hr., $15 per day. Credit card or license required as deposit. Open Mon.-Thurs. 10am-7pm, Fri. 10am-8pm, Sat. 10am-6pm, Sun. noon-5pm. **Alki Bikes,** 2622 Alki Ave. S.W. (938-3322). Mountain bikes $9 per hr., $20 per day; touring bikes $7 per hr., $17 per day. Credit card or license required as deposit. Open Mon.-Thurs. noon-7pm, Fri. 10am-8pm, Sat.-Sun. 10am-6pm. Winter open Mon.-Fri. 3-7pm.

Ticket Agency: Ticket/Ticket, 401 Broadway E. (324-2744) on the 2nd floor on the Broadway Market. Half-price day-of-show tickets to local theater, music and dance. Cash only. Open Tues.-Sun. 10am-7pm.

Help Lines: Crisis Clinic, 461-3222. **Senior Citizen Information and Assistance,** 1601 2nd St. #800 (448-3110). Open Mon.-Fri. 9am-5pm. **Gay Counseling Service,** 200 W. Mercer, suite #300 (282-9307). Open Mon.-Fri. noon-9pm. **Lesbian Resource Center,** 1208 E. Pine (322-3953). Support groups, drop-in center, lending library, workshops, job referrals. Open Mon.-Fri. 2-7pm. **Seattle Rape Relief:** 1905 S. Jackson St., #102 (632-7273). 24-hr. crisis counseling, advocacy, and prevention training.

Post Office: Union St. and 3rd Ave. (442-6340), downtown. Open Mon.-Fri. 8am-5:30pm. **ZIP code:** 98101.

Area Code: 206.

Seattle is a skinny city stretched out north to south between **Puget Sound** to the west and **Lake Washington** to the east. **Lake Union** and a string of locks, canals and bays separate the head of the city from its heart. In the downtown area, avenues run northwest to southeast and streets southwest to northeast. Outside the downtown area everything simplifies vastly: avenues run north to south and streets east to west, with few exceptions. The city splits into quadrants: 1000 1st Ave. N.W. is a far cry from 1000 1st Ave. S.

Accommodations

The **Seattle International Hostel** is the best option for those staying downtown. For those tired of the urban scene, the **Vashon Island Hostel** is Ideal (see Near Seattle: Vashon Island below). Ask around about the hostel that the folks at Green Tortoise (324-7433) are planning to open in 1993 at 1210 Pine St.

Seattle International Hostel (HI/AYH), 84 Union St. (622-5443), at Western Ave. downtown. Take Metro bus #174 or 194 from airport. 125 beds, common kitchen, antiseptic facilities and modern amenities. View of the bay makes up for loud traffic. Sleep sacks required. Offers discount tickets for Aquarium and Omnidome. Open daily 7am-midnight, curfew 2am, max. summer stay 5 days. $13, nonmembers $16. In summer members only.

YMCA, 909 4th Ave. (382-5000), near Madison St. Must be 17. Good location, tight security. Small but well-kept rooms, worse dorm bunks; bring bedding. TV lounge on each floor, laundry facilities, use of swimming pool and fitness facilities, free local calls. Men and women welcome. HI/AYH members: bunk room $17, singles $27, doubles $33. Nonmembers, singles from $38, doubles from $42. Weekly: singles $151, doubles $173.

YWCA, 1118 5th Ave. (461-4888), near the YMCA. Shared kitchen facilities. Take any 4th Ave. bus to Seneca St. Women only; under 18 require advance arrangement. Great security and location, but an older facility than the YMCA. Open 24 hrs. Singles $31, with bath $36. Doubles $42/$48. Weekly: singles $186/$216. Key deposit $2. Additional charge for health center use. Max. stay 2 weeks.

St. Regis Hotel, 116 Stewart St. (448-6366), 2 blocks from the Pike Place Market. Neighborhood not as safe as some, but pleasant management. No visitors after 10pm. Singles $26, with bath $33. Doubles $33/$39. Key deposit $1.

Commodore Hotel, 2013 2nd Ave. (448-8868), at Virginia downtown. Not as well-kept but clean. Singles $29, with bath $37, with 2 beds and bath $45.

Park Plaza Motel, 4401 Aurora Ave. N. (632-2101). Take bus #6 to 46th Ave. or #5 to 43rd and Fremont. Just north of the Aurora bridge. Friendly and surprisingly quiet. The external orange decor is matched on the inside as well. Singles $28. Doubles $40.

The College Inn, 4000 University Way N.E. (633-4441). European-style B&B in the University District. Breakfast served in a lovely refinished attic; ask for quieter rooms facing 40th. All rooms have shared shower and bath, but a cozy breakfast is included. Singles from $41. Doubles from $56.

Food and Bars

As the principal marketplace for Washington's famous fruit-pickin' and fish-catchin' industries, Seattle is practically pelted with salmon and apples. You will be hard-pressed to dodge the catch of the day. But Seattle restauranteurs also seem inclined to stick their heads in ovens—bakeries proliferate, and few Seattleites seem to move in the morning without an *espresso Americano* fill-up. The best options for fish, produce, and baked goods can be culled from the various vendors at the **Pike Place Market,** created in 1907, when angry Seattle citizens demanded an alternative to the middle merchant. The fury at the Sound continues today, as crazy fishmongers and produce sellers yell at customers and at each other, while street performers do their thing—meanwhile tourists gawk and wonder what the hell they've wandered into. (Market open Mon.-Sat. 6:30am-6pm, Sun. 6:30-5pm.)

Soundview Café, on the mezzanine level in the Main Arcade (623-5700). This wholesome self-serve sandwich-and-salad bar offers fresh food, a spectacular view of the Sound, and occasional poetry readings. Get a View Special (eggs and potatoes) for $2.70, try the West African nut stew ($2.15), or bring a brown-bag lunch; the café offers public seating. Open Mon.-Thurs. 7am-5pm, Fri.-Sat. 7am-7pm, Sun. 9am-3pm.

Three Girls Bakery, corner of Post and Pike Pl. (622-1045). Order to go or sit in the café. The display alone will make you drool. Mammoth apple fritters for 95¢. Open Mon.-Sat. 7am-6pm.

Fran-Glor's Creole Café, 547 1st Ave. S. (682-1578), near the viaduct. Genuine gumbo with crabmeat, sausage, and who knows what else. The bric-a-brac and the jazz are classic New Orleans. Lunches from $4.50. Open Tues.-Sat. noon-9pm.

Phnom Penh Noodle Soup House, 414 Maynard Ave. S. (682-5690). Excellent Cambodian cuisine at a *Phnom*enal price. Head to the upstairs dining room for a good view of the park and a spicy, steaming bowl of #1, the Phnom Penh noodle special ($3.70). Open Mon.-Tues. and Thurs.-Sun. 8:30am-6pm.

Hamburger Mary's, 401 Broadway E. (325-6565), in the ritzy Broadway Market. Rockin' and racin' with the Broadway Ave. step, this branch of Portland's famous H.M. is a hot-spot for the gay community. Nightly specials offer less bloody options than the obvious fare. (Hamburgers around $5, entrées under $12.) Open Mon.-Fri. 10am-2am, Sat.-Sun. 9am-2am.

The Cause Célèbre, 524 E. 15th Ave. (323-1888), at Mercer St., at one end of Capitol Hill. The special province of Seattle's well-fed left. Stay away if you don't like feminist music or discussions on the struggle for Chinese succession. Extensive vegetarian selection. Great Sun. brunch ($3-5), lunch $3.75-6. Open Mon.-Fri. 9am-3pm, Sat. 9am-9pm, Sun. 9am-3pm.

Kokeb Restaurant, 926 12th Ave. (322-0485). Behind Seattle University at the far south end of Capitol Hill, near the First Hill neighborhood. An intriguing and tasty Ethiopian restaurant offering hot and spicy stews served on *injera,* a soft bread. Watch Ethiopian movies while you eat. Entrées $7-11. Open Mon.-Fri. 10:30am-2pm lunch, dinner 5-10pm, Sat. 5pm-2am.

Asia Deli, 4235 University Way N.E. No corned beef here—this atypical deli offers quick service and generous portions of delicious Vietnamese and Thai food (mostly of the noodle persuasion). Try the sautéed chicken and onions ($3.45), and don't forget the banana with tapioca in coconut milk (90¢), a superb palate cleanser. Open Mon.-Sat. 11am-9pm, Sun. noon-8pm.

One of the joys of living in Seattle is the abundance of community taverns dedicated to providing a relaxed environment for dancing and spending time with friends. In Washington taverns serve only beer and wine; a fully licensed bar or cocktail lounge must adjoin a restaurant. You must be 21 to enter bars and taverns. The Northwest produces a variety of local beers (none bottled): Grant's, Imperial Russian Stout, India Pale Ale, Red Hook, Ballard Bitter, and Black Hook, and also Yakima Cider.

The best spot to go for guaranteed good beer, live music and big crowds is **Pioneer Square.** Most of the bars around the square participate in a joint cover ($10) that will let you wander from bar to bar and sample the bands you like. **Central Tavern** (622-0209) and **The Spoon Café** (343-5208) rock consistently, while **Larry's** (624-5208) and **New Orleans** (622-2563) feature great jazz and blues nightly. The **J and M Café,** also in the center of Pioneer Square, has no music—only the classic bar hum. All Pioneer Square clubs shut down around 2am on Fri. and Sat. nights, and around midnight during the week. Another option in the Square is to catch an evening of live stand-up comedy in one of Seattle's many comedy clubs such as Pioneer Square's **Swannie's Comedy Underground,** 222 Main St. (628-0303). (Acts daily at 9 and 11pm. Tickets around $5.)

Most of the theaters that screen non-Hollywood films are on Capitol Hill and in the University District. Before 6pm, most matinees are $4; after 6pm, $6.50. $20 buys admission to any five films at the **Metro,** the **Neptune,** the **Egyptian** and **Seven Gables.** The Egyptian, at 801 E. Pine St. at Harvard (323-4978), is best known for hosting the **Seattle Film Festival,** held in May. The **Harvard Exit,** 807 E. Roy (323-8986), is a converted residence; the lobby was once someone's living room. Arrive early for complimentary cheese and crackers over a game of chess, checkers or backgammon.

Sights and Activities

If you have only a day to spare in Seattle, despair not. The best way to take in the city and its fantastic skyline is from any one of the **ferries** that leave the waterfront at frequent intervals (see Practical Information above). The finest view of Seattle, however, is an exclusively female privilege; the athletic club on the top floor of the **Columbia Tower,** the tallest building west of Houston (big, black and Freudian at 201 5th Ave.) has floor-to-ceiling windows in the ladies' room that look out over the entire city. Views from the main desk and the men's room are also worth the snide looks from the club staff, so don't be disheartened if you're of the non-Sacagawean gender. You can get a closer look at most of the city sights in one energetic day—most are within walking distance from each other, within Metro's free zone. You can easily explore Pike Place, waterfront, Pioneer Square and the International District in one excursion. Or skip the downtown thing altogether and take a rowboat out onto Lake Union, bike along Lake Washington, or hike through Discovery Park.

At the south end of Pike Place Market (see Food) begins the **Pike Place Hillclimb,** a set of staircases leading down past chic shops and ethnic restaurants to Alaskan Way and the **waterfront.** (An elevator is also available.)

The waterfront docks once accepted shiploads of gold coming in from the 1897 Klondike gold rush. Now, on a pier full of shops and restaurants, the credit card is standard currency. On Pier 59 at the base of the hillclimb, the **Seattle Aquarium** (386-4320) explains the history of marine life in Puget Sound and the effects of tidal action. (Open late May-early Sept. daily 10am-7pm; Labor Day-Memorial Day 10am-5pm. Admission $6, seniors and ages 6-18 $3.50, ages 3-5 $1.) The new **Seattle Art Museum** hangs at 100 Univ. Ave. (654-3100). It boasts the design of Philadelphia architect Robert Venturi, and houses a variety of genres. Until February 7, 1993, the Paley Collection of impressionists and post-impressionists will be on exhibition. From March 11 to May 9, Art of the American Frontier visits. Call for info on films and lectures. (Free guided tours Tues.-Sat. 2pm, Sun. 1pm, Thurs. 7pm. Museum open Tues.-Sat. 10am-5pm, Thurs. 10am-9pm, Sun. noon-5pm. $5, seniors and students $3. Free on the first Tues. of each month.)

Four blocks inland from Pier 70 you'll find **Seattle Center,** a 74-acre, pedestrians-only park originally constructed for the 1962 World's Fair. Sightseers still visit each day. Take the monorail from Pine St. and 5th Ave. downtown. (Fare 60¢, seniors and children 25¢.) The **Pacific Science Center** (443-2001), within the park, houses a laserium and IMAX theater. (Science Center open daily 10am-6pm; Labor Day-June Mon.-Fri. 10am-5pm, Sat.-Sun. 10am-6pm. Admission $5, seniors and ages 6-13 $4, ages 2-5 $3. Laser shows $1 extra.) The **Space Needle** (443-2100), a.k.a. the world's tackiest monument, has an observation tower and restaurant. On clear days, you can see a lot of **stuff.** (Admission $5.50, ages 5-12 $3.) After working up an appetite in the Center's amusement park, head next door to the **Center House,** home to dozens of shops and restaurants serving everything from Mongolian to Mexican. (Open summer daily 11am-9pm; spring 11am-7pm; fall and winter Sun.-Thurs. 11am-6pm, Fri.-Sat.

11am-9pm.) The Center has an **information desk** (625-4234) on the court level in the Center House which can inform you of events. (Open daily 1-4pm.)

Pier 57 holds Seattle's new maritime museum, **The Water Link** (624-4975). Wallow in the city's waterfront history or probe the geological mysteries of the ocean floor. (Open May 17-Sept. 30 Tues.-Sun. noon-6pm. Admission $1.)

Two blocks from the waterfront bustles historic **Pioneer Square,** where 19th-century warehouses and office buildings were restored in a spasm of prosperity during the 70s. The *Complete Browser's Guide to Pioneer Square,* available in area bookstores, provides a short history and walking tour.

When Seattle nearly burned to the ground in 1889, an ordinance was passed to raise the city 35 ft. At first, shops below the elevated streets remained open for business and were moored to the upper city by an elaborate network of stairs. In 1907 the city moved upstairs permanently, and the underground city was sealed off. The vast **Bill Speidel's Underground Tours** (682-4646) does exactly what its name suggests. Speidel spearheaded the movement to save Pioneer Square from the apocalypse of renewal. The tours are informative and irreverent glimpses at Seattle's beginnings; just ignore the rats that infest the tunnels. Tours (1½ hr.) leave from Doc Maynard's Pub at 610 1st Ave. (March-Sept. 6-8 per day 10am-6pm. Make reservations. Admission $4.75, seniors and students $3.50, ages 6-12 $2.75.)

Once back above ground, learn about eating boots at the **Klondike Gold Rush National Historic Park,** 117 S. Main St. (442-7220). The "interpretive center" depicts the lives and fortunes of the miners. The first Sunday of every month at 3pm, the park screens Charlie Chaplin's 1925 classic, *The Gold Rush.* (Open daily 9am-5pm. Free.)

Three blocks east of Pioneer Square, up Jackson on King St., is Seattle's **International District.** Though sometimes still called Chinatown by Seattleites, this area has peoples from all over Asia. Behold the **Tsutakawa Sculpture** at the corner of S. Jackson and Maynard St. and the gigantic dragon mural in **Hing Hay Park** at S. King and Maynard St. Peep in or duck into the **Wing Luke Memorial Museum,** 414 8th St. (623-5124). This tiny museum houses a permanent exhibit on the different Asian groups that have settled in Seattle as well as temporary exhibits by local Asian artists, such as sculptor George Tsutakawa. There are occasional free demonstrations of traditional crafts. (Open Tues.-Fri. 11am-4:30pm, Sat.-Sun. noon-4pm. $2.50, students and seniors $1.50, ages 5-12 75¢. Thursdays free.)

Capitol Hill inspires extreme reactions from both its residents and neighbors. The district's leftist and gay communities set the tone for its nightspots (see Entertainment), while the retail outlets include a large number of collectives and radical bookstores. Saunter down Broadway or its cross-streets to window-shop, or walk a few blocks east and north for a stroll down the hill's lovely residential streets, lined with beautiful Victorian homes. Bus #10 runs along 15th St. and #7 along Broadway.

With 35,000 students, the **University of Washington** is the state's cultural and educational center of gravity. The **"U district"** swarms with bookstores, shops, taverns and restaurants. Stop by the friendly and helpful **visitors information center,** 4014 University Way N.E. (543-9198), to pick up a map of the campus and to obtain university info. (Open Mon.-Fri. 8am-5pm.)

On campus, visit the **Thomas Burke Memorial Washington State Museum,** 45th St. and 17th Ave. N.E. (543-5590), in the northwest corner of the grounds. The museum houses artifacts of the Pacific Northwest Native American tribes. The scrimshaw display will remain sketched in your memory. (Open daily 10am-5pm, Thurs. 10am-8pm, donation requested: $2.50, students and seniors $1.50.) The **Henry Art Gallery,** 15th Ave. and 41st St. N.E. (543-2256), houses a collection of 18th- to 20th-century European and American art. (Open Tues.-Wed. and Fri.-Sun. 10am-5pm, Thurs. 10am-9pm. Admission $3, students and seniors $1.50.) The **UW Arts Ticket Office,** 4001 University Way N.E., has info and tickets for all events. (Open Mon.-Fri. 10:30am-6pm.) To reach the U district, take buses #71-74 from downtown, #7 or 43 from Capitol Hill.

Waterways and Parks

A string of attractions stud the waterways linking Lake Washington and Puget Sound. Houseboats and sailboats fill **Lake Union.** Here, the **Center for Wooden Boats,** 1010 Valley St. (382-2628), maintains a moored flotilla of new and restored small craft for rental. (Sailboats $10-15 per hr., rowboats $8-12 per hr. Open daily 11am-6pm.) **Kelly's Landing,** 1401 Boat St. N.E. (547-9909), below the UW campus, rents canoes for outings on Lake Union. (Sailboats $10-20 per hr., 12 hr. minimum. Hours determined by weather; usually open Mon.-Fri. 10am-dusk.) Tour the houseboat moorings along Lake Union's shores or go through the Montlake Cut to Lake Washington.

Mock and ridicule trout and salmon as they flop and flounder up 21 concrete steps at the **Fish Ladder** (783-7059) on the south side of the locks. Take bus #43 from the U District or #17 from downtown. On the northwestern shore of the city lies the **Golden Gardens Park** in Loyal Heights, between 80th and 95th N.W., with a frigid beach. Several expensive restaurants line the piers to the south; the unobstructed views of the Olympics almost make their uniformly excellent seafood worth the price on salmon chanted evening.

Directly north of Lake Union, "Beautiful People" run, roller skate, and skateboard around **Green Lake.** Take bus #16 from downtown. The lake also draws windsurfers, but woe to those who lose balance. Whoever named Green Lake wasn't kidding; even a quick dunk results in gobs of green algae lodged in every pore and follicle. Next door grows Woodland Park and the **Woodland Park Zoo,** 5500 Phinney Ave. N. (684-4034), best reached from Rte. 99 or N. 50th St. Take bus #5 from downtown. The park looks shaggy, but the zoo is one of only three in the U.S. to receive the Humane Society's highest standard of approval. (Open daily 10am-6pm; winter daily 8:30am-4pm. Admission $5, ages 6-17, disabled persons and seniors $2.75, ages 3-5 50¢.)

Entertainment

The **Seattle Opera** (443-4700) performs in the Opera House in the Seattle Center throughout the winter. In 1993, this imaginative and expert company will put on *Pelleas et Melisande* and *The Merry Widow,* among other works. Rush tickets are sometimes available 15 minutes before curtain-time (from $8). Write to the Seattle Opera, P.O. Box 9248, Seattle 98109. Seattle also boasts the second-largest number of professional theater companies within one city in the U.S., and hosts an exciting array of first-run plays (many eventually move on to New York) and alternative works, particularly in the many talented semi-professional groups. The **Seattle Repertory Theater,** which won the 1990 Tony award for Regional Excellence, plays at 155 Mercer (443-2222), in the wonderful Bagley Wright Theater in Seattle Center. Their winter season combines contemporary, original, and classic productions. Recent Broadway hits that got their start at the Rep. include *The Heidi Chronicles, Fences* and *I'm Not Rappaport.* 1993 will include *Julius Caesar* and *the Piano Lesson.*(Tickets $11-26.)

During summertime lunch hours downtown, city-sponsored free entertainment of the **"Out to Lunch"** series (623-0340) brings everything from reggae to folk dancing to the parks and squares of Seattle.

Near Seattle: Vashon Island

The **Vashon Island Youth Hostel**, 12119 S.W. Cove Rd. (463-2592), sometimes called "Seattle B," is really the only place to stay, and is in itself the best reason to come to the island. The manager has never turned a hosteler away, so there isn't much need to worry. It's a wonderful retreat from civilization with all the comforts of home: free pancakes for breakfast, free use of old bikes (at your own risk), free campfire wood, free volleyball games in the afternoon, and a manager/mother. The hostel accommodates 14 in bunk rooms but those are for the weak of heart; sleep in the huge tepees she has set up under the stars. When all beds are full, you can pitch a tent. Tents or beds $8, $11 nonmembers. Open year-round, winter rates available on request. To get to the hostel, jump on the bus you see at the ferry terminal, and ride it until it gets to

Thriftway market; call at the pay phone inside the market marked with an HI/AYH sticker (free). Judy will come pick you up if the hour is reasonable.

The Seattle **ferry** is passengers-only, departs from Pier 50, and takes 25 min. It runs Monday through Friday from 6am to midnight with nine departures, Saturday from 9:30am to 11:30pm, with six departures.

California

California is the most populous and dynamic state in the U.S., and its diversity and size make it practically a nation unto itself. Indeed, its citizens often come across as blithely ignorant of the existence of the 49 other states to the north, east, and west. Californians have an understated pride, which comes across not as the boastfulness of Texans, the snobbery of New Yorkers, or the insecurity of Floridians, but rather as the quiet confidence of a people who firmly believe that they have found the best *lebensraum* on the planet. For nearly two centuries men and women have come to the Far West, fleeing hard times or simply seeking a change of pace. From Twain's 49ers to Steinbeck's Okies, from John Muir to Jack Kerouac to Thomas Pynchon's Oedipa Maas, the voyager to the American West follows a path that is well-worn by footsteps that are many and varied.

Don't come to the Golden State looking for America. You won't find it. You will find a culture and lifestyle that is peculiarly Californian, from sprawling Los Angeles, with its many suburbs in search of a city, to compact San Francisco, which combines the cultural flair of the East Coast with the laid-back, liberal attitudes of the Left Coast. The small towns and countryside in the hinterland of the two megalopoli have characters of their own, from the quiet beach settlements on the coast, to the agri-business centers of the Central Valley, to the boom-and-bust towns of the Sierra Nevada. You will find low, sweltering deserts and cool alpine ski country. You will find towering redwoods and drifting sands. And in the end, you will perhaps understand how Californians exhibit vestiges of provincialism in the age of the global village—with a whole world right in their backyard, why look any farther? For more information on California, consult *Let's Go: California and Hawaii.*

Practical Information

Capital: Sacramento.

California Office of Tourism, 801 K St. #1600, Sacramento 95814. Call 800-862-2543 ext. A1003 to have a package of tourism materials sent to you. **National Park Information,** 415-556-0560.

Time Zone: Pacific (3 hr. behind Eastern). **Postal Abbreviation:** CA

Sales Tax: 7.5%.

Central Coast

Although the popular image of the California dream is dominated by San Francisco and Los Angeles, it is the stretch of coast between these two cities that embodies everything that is uniquely Californian: rolling surf replete with surfers, sandy white beaches filled with tall palms, self-actuating New Agers, and dramatic cliffs topped with towering redwoods.

San Simeon anchors the southern end of Big Sur, a 90-mi. strip of sparsely inhabited coastline where the **Pacific Coast Highway** (Rte. 1), inches motorists right to the edge of jutting cliffs overhanging the ocean. Winding its way through this stunning wilderness, Rte. 1 reaches north to the Monterey Peninsula, where golf courses and the shopping mall lifestyle of Carmel announce a return to civilization. Just above Monterey, 79 mi. south of San Francisco, Santa Cruz fuses Southern Californian surfer culture with San Francisco's off-beat quirkiness.

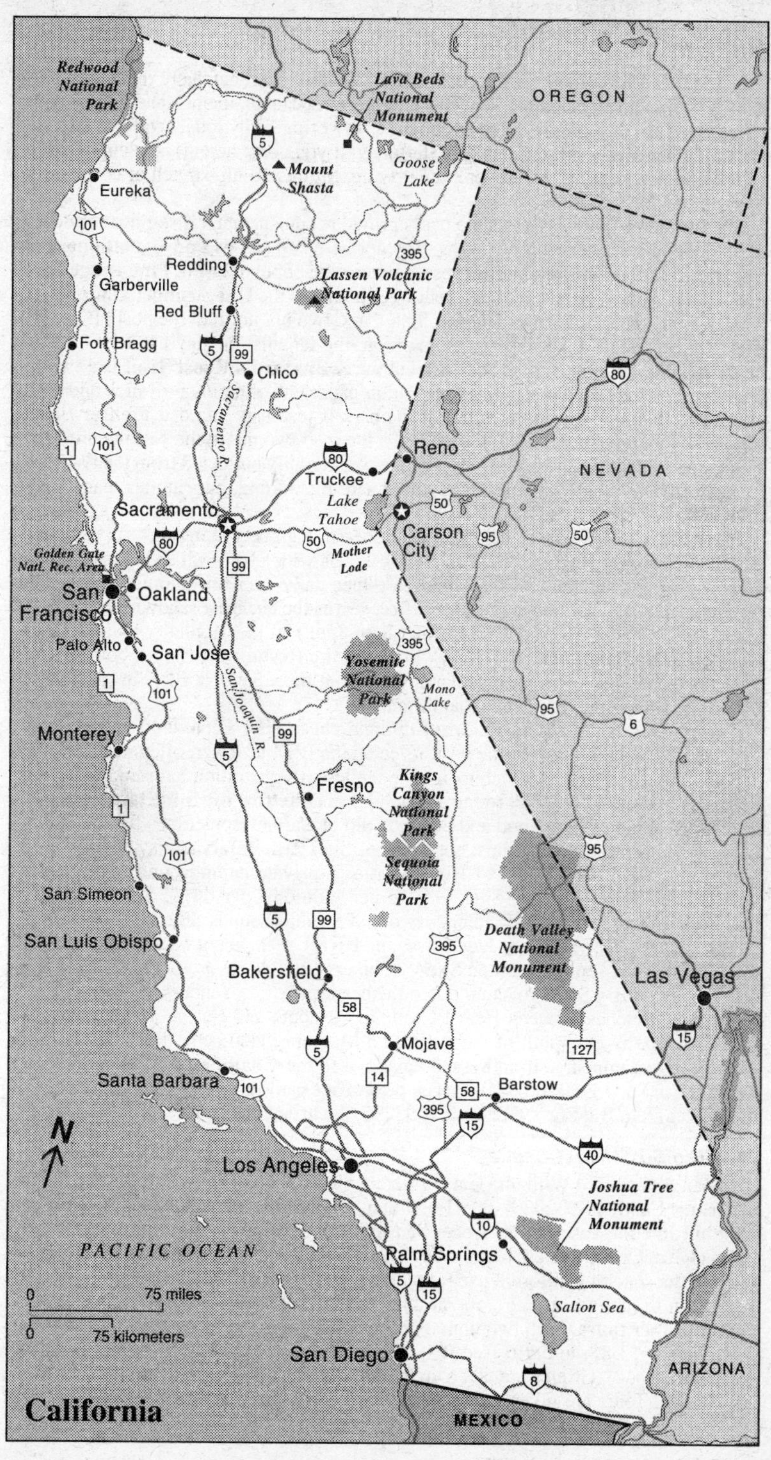
Redwood National Park
Lava Beds National Monument
OREGON
Mount Shasta
Goose Lake
Eureka
Redding
Garberville
Lassen Volcanic National Park
Red Bluff
Fort Bragg
Chico
Sacramento R.
Reno
NEVADA
Truckee
Lake Tahoe
Carson City
Sacramento
Golden Gate Natl. Rec. Area
Mother Lode
San Francisco
Oakland
Palo Alto
San Jose
San Joaquin R.
Yosemite National Park
Mono Lake
Monterey
Fresno
Kings Canyon National Park
Sequoia National Park
San Simeon
San Luis Obispo
Death Valley National Monument
Bakersfield
Las Vegas
Mojave
Santa Barbara
Barstow
N
Los Angeles
Joshua Tree National Monument
PACIFIC OCEAN
Palm Springs
0 75 miles
0 75 kilometers
Salton Sea
San Diego
ARIZONA
MEXICO
California

Big Sur

In 1542 Cabrillo sailed off the cost of Big Sur and wrote that "here there are mountains which seem to reach the heavens, and the sun beats on them." The imposing geography of the region—rugged mountains, towering redwoods, frothing surf and glistening beaches—still defines Big Sur today. If you come here, it is to enjoy nature, be it by hiking, boating, fishing or even driving, for this 90-mi. stretch of coast has no golf, no bowling, no movies.

Big Sur area wilderness and state parks provide exquisite natural settings for dozens of outdoor activities especially hiking. The northern end of **Los Padres National Forest,** known as the **Ventana Wilderness,** contains the popular 24-mi. **Pine Ridge Trail.** Pick up a map ($.50) and a required (but free) permit at the **USFS ranger station** (667-2423), .5 mi. south of Pfeiffer Big Sur State Park, two mi. north of the post office. **Pfeiffer Big Sur State Park** has six trails of varying lengths; the day use fee is $6, and maps are available for $.50 at the park entrance. **Buzzard's Roost Trail** is a two mi. jaunt through the redwoods with a spectacular panorama of mountain valley and ocean at the end. Just one mi. to the south of the park is jealously guarded **Pfeiffer Beach,** reached by an unmarked, narrow road. Take the road two mi. to the parking area, then follow the footpath to the beach. The small cove, partially protected from the Pacific by a huge offshore rock formation, is reported safe for wading, but riptides make swimming risky.

The Fernwood Motel (see below) includes a bar, a grocery store, a cheap gas pump, and the **Fernwood Burger Bar,** Rte. 1 (667-2422), with a bar. Fish and chips or chicken cost $5-6.50; hamburgers start at $3.25 (Open daily 11:30am-midnight.) The **Center Deli,** right beside the Big Sur post office, serves the cheapest sandwiches ($2.80-5) in the area. (Open daily 8am-9pm; winter 8am-8pm.) At the Monterey-Salinas Transit bus stop, **Café Amphora** (667-2660), in **Nepenthe Restaurant,** serves coffee and liquor on an outdoor patio spectacularly situated at the edge of a Big Sur cliff. (Open Mon.-Fri. 10am-4pm, Sat.-Sun. 10am-5pm.)

Campgrounds are abundant, beautiful, and cheap. The **Fernwood Motel,** Rte. 1 (667-2422), two mi. north of the post office on the Big Sur River, offers friendly management, 65 campsites, and cabins for the tentless. (Registration 8am-midnight. Sites $19, with hookup $21. Motel rooms from $45.) The **Pfeiffer Big Sur State Park** (667-2315), just south of Fernwood and 26 mi. south of Carmel, sometimes fills all 218 developed campsites. (No hookups; hot showers. Sites $16. Reservations 800-444-7275.) **Limekiln** (667-2403), south of Big Sur, runs a private campground with grocery, showers, and beach access. (Sites $15, $5 per additional person. $5 reservation fee.) **Los Padres National Forest** includes two USFS campgrounds: **Plaskett Creek** (667-2315), south of Limekiln near Jade Cove, and **Kirk Creek,** about five mi. north of Jade Cove. (Toilets and running water. Sites $8, hikers $10. No reservations.) The cheapest way to stay on Big Sur is to camp out in the beautifully free Ventana wilderness.

Big Sur stretches between Hearst Castle in the south and Carmel in the north, two groovy hours by car south of the cultivated Monterey Peninsula. For a guide to the area, send a stamped, self-addressed envelope to the **Chamber of Commerce,** P.O. Box 87, Big Sur 93920 (667-2100). The **post office** mails on Rte. 1 (667-2305), next to the Center Deli. Big Sur's **ZIP code** is 93290; the **area code** is 408.

Near Big Sur: Hearst Castle

In San Simeon did William Hearst a stately pleasure dome decree. Popularly known as **Hearst Castle** (927-2020), the Hearst San Simeon Historic Monument perches high on a hill five mi. east of Rte. 1 near San Simeon. Satirized as Charles Foster Kane's "Xanadu" in Orson Welles' *Citizen Kane,* the castle lives up to every adjective ever applied to the state of California itself: opulent, plastic, beautiful, fake, dazzling. It is the American dream/nightmare gone architectural; a must-experience. Visitors have a choice of four **tours,** each two hours. You can take all four in one day, but each costs $14 (ages 6-12 $8, under 6 free if well-behaved—otherwise they meet the fate of Kane's Rosebud). Groups are taken up the hill in buses, shepherded around, then taken back down. Tours are given at least once per hour October through March from 8am until 3pm (except tour #4, which runs April-Nov. only), later and more frequently according to demand in summer. To see the Castle in summer, make MISTIX reservations (800-444-7275), since tours sell out quickly. The gates to the visitors center open in summer at 6am, in winter at 7am; tickets go on sale daily at 8am.

Monterey

In the 1940s, John Steinbeck's Monterey docked as a coastal town geared to sardine fishing and canning. When Steinbeck revisited his beloved Cannery Row around 1960, he scornfully wrote that the area had transmogrified into a tourist trap. Where packing plants once stood, espresso bars and fudge shops now rule. But residents do treat with dignity some of the area's history—both as a canning town and former capital of Spanish and Mexican Alta California—visitors should forgive Monterey its crasser side.

The **Monterey Bay Aquarium,** 866 Cannery Row (648-4888), pumps in raw, unfiltered seawater, making the tanks an almost exact duplicate of the environment in the bay—right down to the dozens of species of algae and the simulated waves. In addition to staples such as enormous octopi and docile starfish, the aquarium contains 30-ft. kelps, diving birds, and a clever exhibit that allows otters to be seen from both above and below the water's surface. The aquarium is sardined with tourists mornings and holidays, but after 3pm things ebb. (Open daily 10am-6pm. Admission $10.50, seniors and students $7.75, ages 3-12 $4.75.)

On the waterfront, southeast of the aquarium, lies Steinbeck's **Cannery Row.** Once lined with languishing sardine-packing plants, this one-mi. street has been transformed into a strip of glitzy mini-malls, bars, and discos. To make your visit more endurable, visit one of the **wine tasting** rooms for a free sample of California's Lethe. The **Great Cannery Row Mural,** stretching 400 ft. of Cannery Row's 700 blocks, impressively depicts Monterey in the 1930s.

At the south end of the row floats yet another **Fisherman's Wharf,** built in 1846. The fishermen have left, and the wharf now lures tourists with expensive restaurants and shops vending seashells and Steinbeck novels. The best thing about the wharf, and maybe even all of Monterey, is the smoked salmon sandwiches ($5.50) sold by local vendors, made with fresh sourdough bread, cream cheese, and plenty of the local salmon (smoked right on the pier).

Monterey State Historic Park envelopes six **historic adobe buildings** headquarted at the **Cooper-Molera Complex,** 525 Polk St. (649-7118). Two of the park's buildings are museums near Fisherman's Wharf. In 1846, Commodore John Sloat raised the Stars and Stripes over the **Customs House,** claiming California for the U.S. Today, goods typical of the days when Monterey was the busiest port in Mexican Alta California clutter the place. Next door, the **Pacific House** has a less impressive display of costumes and artifacts. (Both open daily 10am-5pm; winter 10am-4pm. Customs House free. Pacific House $2, ages 6-17 $1.) Farther from the water, the park's other four adobe houses, including the **Robert Louis Stevenson House** and the oddly-landscaped **Casa Soberanes,** are accessible only by tours, given six times daily, five in the winter. (Admission $2 per house, kids $1; all six $5, kids $2.) For the hardcore history buff, there is a 1.5 hr. **House and Garden Tour** of 10 buildings and five gardens (departs park headquarters Tues., Thurs., and Fri. at 2pm; $3, kids $1.25). Or buy *The Path of History,* a walking tour book, at the headquarters ($2). In the same neighborhood as the adobes lies the **Monterey Peninsula Museum of Art,** 559 Pacific St. (372-5477), with a downstairs exhibit of European and American monochrome works from across the centuries, an upstairs collection of Western art including works by Charlie Russell, and another gallery for temporary shows. (Open Tues.-Sat. 10am-4pm, Sun. 1-4pm. Suggested donation $2.)

The huge annual **Monterey Jazz Festival** (373-3366), held during the third week in September, comprises five concerts over three days. Season tickets ($80-90) sell out by the end of May. The **Blues Festival** (394-2652) wails in late June. From late June to early August, **Monterey Bay's Theatrefest** hams it up between the Customs House and the Pacific House. Every Saturday and Sunday from 11am-6pm, tourists are beguiled by hours of free afternoon theater.

Seafood. The whales may be gone and the sardines with them, but the unpolluted Monterey Bay still teems with squid, crab, rockcod, red snapper, and salmon. No matter how you like it, Monterey has some delicious seafood for your dining pleasure. The **Casa de Gutierrez,** 590 Calle Principal (375-0095), an 1841 structure now serving as a Mexican restaurant, offers dinner served on weathered wooden tables on the patio out back. HUGE portions of traditional fare for all tastes and appetites. Try the full-fledged buffet for $9, or a couple of tacos for $3. (Open Mon.-Thurs. 11am-9pm, Fri.-Sun. 10am-10pm.) Also try the **Tutto Buono Gastronomic Specialties,** 2400 Del Monte Ave. (373-5800). Incredibly low prices for fruits, nuts and veggies. Plums for $.10. Open daily 8am-6pm. Aside from the snacks on the wharf, seafood dinners usually run high; however, many restaurants offer money-saving early-bird specials between 4 and 6:30pm. You also don't have to eat at a specifically fish-oriented joint; Thai and Japanese places access the same fresh catch.

The rates at Monterey's hotels and motels vary by day, month, and proximity to events such as the Jazz Festival. The visitors bureau's free *Monterey Peninsula Hotel and Motel Guide* (see below) has prices for all area accommodations. Generally, hotels along **Fremont Street** in Monterey and **Lighthouse Avenue** in nearby Pacific Grove are the most reasonable. The **Monterey Peninsula Youth Hostel (HI/AYH)** (649-0375) has no fixed location, but for the past few summers has bunked and debunked in the gym of the Monterey High School on Larkin St. The hostel lacks a kitchen and mattresses lie directly on the floor, but the friendly staff tries to make up for its deficiencies by providing cheap food (full meals under $9) and lots of info. To reach the high school, take Pacific away from the water, make a right Madison and a left on Larkin St. (Lockout 9am-6pm. Curfew 11pm. Open mid-June to mid-Aug.) The **Paramount Motel,** 3298 Del Monte Blvd. (384-8674) in Marina, eight mi. north of Monterey, is clean and well-run. This motel, (and its furnishings) date back to the 1950s. The **Del Monte Beach Inn,** 1110 Del Monte (649-4410), is smack-dab in the middle of downtown, on the beach. This Victorian-style *pensione* offers pleasant rooms and a hearty breakfast for $45-55. (Shared bath.) Mention *Let's Go* on a weekday, and you will save $10. **Veteran's Memorial Park Campground,** Via Del Rey, (646-3865), 1.5 mi. from the town center, has a beautiful view of the bay. Take Skyline Dr. off the section of Rte. 68 called W.R. Holman Hwy. Form downtown, take Pacific St. south., turn right on Jefferson, and follow the signs, or take bus #3. Hot showers. First-come, first-camped. Arrive before 3pm in the summer and on weekends in the winter. Sites $12, hikers $3. The **Laguna Seca Recreational Area,** Hwy. 68 (422-6138), is a lovely park with oak-strewn verdant hills overlooking valleys and a race track. Sites $15, with hookup $20. Showers, restrooms, barbecue pits, tables and sump station.

Monterey, 115 mi. south of San Francisco, shares the Monterey Peninsula with Pacific Grove to the west, Ft. Ord and Salinas to the east, and **Carmel-by-the-Sea,** an oversized shopping mall, to the south. Just south of Carmel on Rte. 1 is the **Point Lobos Reserve** (624-4909), a state-run, 1276-acre wildlife sanctuary, popular with skin-divers, dayhikers, and naturalists. On weekends a line of cars frequently waits to get in by 8am; park outside the tollbooth and walk or bike in for free. (Open daily 9am-7pm; winter 9am-5pm. Admission $3 per car. Map $.50. No dogs allowed.)

The **Monterey Peninsula Chamber of Commerce,** 380 Alvarado St. (648-5350), sits on Monterey's main commercial street. Get advance info by writing to P.O. Box 1770, Monterey 93942. (Open Mon.-Fri. 8:30am-5pm.) **Greyhound,** 351 Del Monte Ave. (373-4735), goes to L.A. (4 per day, $50) and San Francisco (4 per day, $13). The **post office** sorts at 565 Hartnell (372-5803; open Mon.-Fri. 9am-5pm). Monterey's **ZIP code** is 93940; the **area code** is 408.

Santa Cruz

Santa Cruz sports an uncalculated hipness that other coastal towns can only envy. Far removed from the staid lifestyle of the mission Father Junípero Serra founded here in 1791, Santa Cruz is the epitome of California cool; the town's beaches and bookstores even lure visitors from San Francisco, 75 mi. to the north. Restaurants offer everything from avocado sandwiches to industrial coffee, and the town is accepting enough to embrace surfers and a thriving lesbian community.

The epicenter of the 1989 earthquake was only 10 mi. away from this mellow town, and it caused serious damage. The temblor destroyed the pleasant Pacific Garden Mall and forced many shops to relocate temporarily to "pavilions" (i.e., tents). While some of the shops are still in the pavilions, Santa Cruz has recovered from the quake quickly with the help of a state-wide tax increase.

A three-block arcade of ice cream, caramel apples, games, rides, and tacos, the **Boardwalk** (426-7433) dominates Santa Cruz's beach area. The classiest rides are two grizzled warhorses: the 1929 **Giant Dipper,** one of the largest wooden roller coasters in the country (rides $2.25), and the 1911 **Looff Carousel,** accompanied by an 1894 organ ($1.35). (Unlimited rides $16. Boardwalk open May 27-Sept. 2 daily; weekends the rest of the year. Call for hours.)

Broad **Santa Cruz beach** generally jams with high school students from San Jose during summer weekends. When seeking solitude, try the banks of the San Lorenzo River immediately east of the boardwalk. Nude sunbathers should flop on over to the **Red White and Blue Beach;** take Rte. 1 north to just before Davenport and look for the line of cars to your right. Women should not go alone. ($7 per car.) Those who prefer tan lines should try the **Bonny Doon Beach,** 11 mi. north of Santa Cruz on Bonny Doon Rd. off Rte. 1, a free but somewhat untamed surfer hangout.

A pleasant 10-minute walk along the beach to the southwest will take you to two madcap and mayhem-filled Santa Cruz museums. The first is the unintentionally amusing **Shroud of Turin Museum,** 544 W. Cliff Dr. (423-7658), at St. Joseph's shrine. Earnest curators shepherd you through many exhibits, including one of only two replicas of Jesus' alleged burial shroud, "casting doubt" on recent carbon-14 tests that suggest the shroud isn't old enough to have graced anyone's corpse in Biblical times. The Geraldo Rivera video is particularly telling. (Open Sat.-Sun. noon-5pm. Call to visit weekdays.) Just south lies Lighthouse Point, home to the **Santa Cruz Surfing Museum** (429-3429). The cheerful, one-room museum features vintage boards and surfing videos which show little sign of the tragedy that inspired its creation; the lighthouse and gallery were given in memory of a surfer who drowned in a 1965 accident. (Open Wed.-Mon. noon-5pm. Donation of $1.) You can still watch people challenge the sea right below the museum's cliff. The stretch of Pacific along the eastern side of the point offers famous **Steamer Lane,** a hotspot for local surfers for over 100 years.

The 2000-acre **University of California at Santa Cruz (UCSC)** hangs out five mi. northwest of downtown. Take bus #1 or ride your bike along a scenic path to the campus. B-movie actor and political dabbler Ronald Reagan's attempt to make it a "riot-proof campus" (without a central point where radicals could spark a crowd) resulted in beautiful, sprawling grounds. University buildings appear intermittently, like startled wildlife, amid spectacular rolling hills and redwood groves. The school itself remains more Berkeley than Berkeley; extracurricular leftist politics supplement a curriculum offering such unique programs as the "History of Consciousness." Guided tours start from the **visitors center** at the base of campus. You need a parking permit when driving on weekdays. (Permits and maps available at the **police station,** 429-2231.) The UCSC **Arboretum** is one of the finest in the state. (Open daily 9am-5pm. Free.) Directly south of UCSC, the **Natural Bridges State Beach** (423-4609), at the end of W. Cliff Dr., offers a nice beach, tidepools, and tours twice daily during Monarch butterfly season from October to February. **Welcome Back Monarch Day** flutters on October 9 of each year, but it's best to visit from November to December, when thousands of the little buggers swarm along the shore. (Open daily 8am-sunset. Parking $3 per day.)

Whale-watching season is late January to April; boats depart from the Santa Cruz Municipal Wharf (425-1234). A different kind of mammal is on view during the **National Nude Weekend** in mid-July, held yearly at the **Lupin Naturalist Club** (393-2250); admission is free, but reservations are required. (You may, of course, you already have reservations about this type of thing.) August brings the **Cabrillo Music Festival** (662-2701), an eclectic celebration of classical music from Beethoven to the Kronos Quartet.

Santa Cruz innkeepers metamorphose winter bargains into summer wallet-drainers. The **Santa Cruz HI/AYH Hostel,** 511 Broadway (423-8304), is 10 minute walk from the beach and a mall. From the bus depot, turn left on Laurel, veer left over the bridge, and you're on Broadway. Reservations are essential during summer; send half of the fee to P.O. Box 1241, Santa Cruz 95601. ($12, members only.) Also try the **Harbor Inn,** 645 7th Ave. (479-9731 or 476-6424), near the harbor and a few blocks north of Eaton St. A small and beautiful hotel well off the main drag. One queen bed per room (1 or 2 people). Rooms $30, with bath $45. Weekends $45, with bath $70. A bargain during the week—rooms even come with coupons for a free breakfast at the **Yacht Harbor Café,** two blocks south on 7th St. RV sites with a full hookup in back for $18. A 10-minute walk north of the Boardwalk is **Inn California,** 370 Ocean St. (458-9220), at Broadway. Cross the bridge east from Boardwalk, take Edge Cliff Dr. north until it intersects Ocean St., and take Ocean north. A touch more tasteful that the average budget motel. Telephone, A/C, color TC, and pretty quilts. Coin-operated laundry room. (Budget rooms—1 double bed—are $20 Sept.10-June 9, $30 June 10-Aug. 1, and $40 Aug. 2-Sept. 10; with a $10 added on Fri. and Sat. nights and $5 added if two people are staying together. It's another $500 to hire an accountant to figure out the complex room rates for you. No reservations; show up between 11am-2pm to ensure getting a room.)

Reservations for **state campgrounds** can be made by calling 800-444-7275 at least two weeks in advance. The **New Brighton State Beach** (688-3241), four mi. south of Santa Cruz off Rte. 1 near Capitola, offers 112 lovely campsites on a high bluff overlooking the beach. (1-week max. stay. No hookups. Sites $16, $14 in winter. Reservations highly recommended. Take SCMDT "Aptos" bus #54.) The **Henry Cowell Redwoods State Park,** off Rte. 9 (335-9145), communes three mi. south of Felton. Take Graham Hill Rd., or SCMDT buses #30, 34, or 35. (1-week max. stay. Sites $16, $14 in the winter.) **Big Basin Redwoods State Park,** north of Boulder Creek (338-6132), merits the 45-min. trip from downtown. Take Rte. 9 north to Rte. 236 north, or on weekends take the #35 bus to Big Basin. This spectacular park has 188 sites surrounded by dark red trees. **Mountain bikes** are available for rental (338-7313), and **horseback tours** can be arranged. (Showers. 15-day max. stay. Sites $16, tent cabins $32. Backpackers $3 at special backcountry campsites. Security parking $4 per night. Reservations recommended May-Oct. Open year-round.)

For a city on the California coast, Santa Cruz sports and amazing number of restaurants in the budget range. For the fast-food junkie, there's a normal spread of chain burger joints, but much better food (served just as fast) is available at **Food Pavilion,** at the Pacific Mall Food Court, at Lincoln and Cedar. If it's a sit-down meal you want, there's lovingly hand-rolled pita bread, steaming curry, or any of a dozen other mouth-watering options at **Royal Taj,** 270 Soquel Ave., (427-2400). Exquisite and exotic Indian dishes in a comfortable setting. (Open daily 11am-10pm.)**Zoccoli's Delicatessen,** 1334 Pacific Ave. (423-1711), has great food at great prices. The lunch special of lasagna, salad, garlic bread, salami and cheese slices, and an Italian cookie goes for $4.44. (Open Mon.-Sat. 9am-5:30pm.) **The Crêpe Place,** 1134 (429-6994), just north of the Water St. intersection, is a casual but classy restaurant putting Santa Cruz's former courthouse to good use. Try "the Whole Thing": chocolate, bananas, walnuts, and ice cream in a crêpe ($3.50). (Open Mon.-Thurs. 11am-midnight, Fri. 11am-1am, Sat. 9am-1am, Sun. 9am-midnight.) **The Whole Earth,** at UCSC's Redwood Tower Building (426-8255), is simply amazing for a university food service—$4 buys a full meal and a view of the stunning redwoods. (Open during the term Mon.-Fri. 7:30am-8pm, Sat.-Sun. 9am-6pm; in summer Mon.-Fri. 7:30am-4pm.)

Santa Cruz fashions itself a classy operation, and most bars frown on backpacks and sleeping bags. Carding is stringent. The restored ballroom at the boardwalk makes a lovely spot for a drink in the evening, and the boardwalk bandstand also offers free Friday night concerts. The **Kuumbwa Jazz Center,** 320-322 E. Cedar St. (427-2227), has regionally renowned jazz, and welcomes music lovers under 21. (Tickets $5-14. Most shows at 8pm.) **The Catalyst,** 1011 Pacific Garden Mall (423-7117), is a 700-seat concert hall which draws second-string national acts and college favorites with local bands. A boisterous, beachy bar. Serves pizza ($2) and sandwiches ($4-5). Open daily

9am-2am. Shows 9:15pm. **Blue Lagoon,** 923 Pacific Ave. (423-7117), a relaxed gay bar, swims with a giant aquarium in back, taped music, videos, and dancing. (No cover. Drinks about $1.50. Open daily 4pm-2am.)

Santa Cruz lies about one hour south of San Francisco on the northern lip of Monterey Bay, along U.S. 101 and Rte. 1, two roads which some find conducive to hitchhiking. **Greyhound/Peerless Stages,** 425 Front St. (423-1800), cruzes to San Francisco (3 per day, $9.50) and L.A. (4 per day, $49). (Open Mon.-Fri. 7:49am-11am and 2-7:49pm; call for weekends hours.) **Santa Cruz Metropolitan District Transit (SCMDT),** 920 Pacific Ave. (425-8600 or 688-8993), serves the city and environs. Pick up a free copy of *Headways* here for route info. (Open Mon.-Fri. 8am-5pm.) **Surf City Rentals,** 46 Front St. (423-9050), rents bikes for $6 per hour, $18 per half day. (Open daily 9am-6pm.) The **Santa Cruz Conference and Visitor's Council** santas at 701 Front St. (425-1234 or 800-833-3494). The **post office** dates at 850 Front St. (426-5200; open Mon.-Fri. 9am-5pm). Santa Cruz's **ZIP code** is 95060; the **area code** is 408.

The Desert

Mystics, misanthropes, and mescaline users have long shared a fascination with the desert's vast spaces and austere scenery. California's desert region has worked its spell on generations of passersby, from the Native Americans of yore to city slickers of today who are disenchanted with smoggy L.A. The fascination stems partly from the desert's seasonal metamorphoses from a pleasantly warm refuge in winter to a technicolored floral landscape in spring to a blistering wasteland in summer. Considering that only six inches of rain drip onto the parched sand each year, the desert supports an astonishing array of plant and animal life.

Southern California's desert is on the fringe of the North American Desert, a 500,000-sq.-mi. territory stretching east into Arizona and New Mexico, northeast into Nevada and Utah, and south into Mexico. The California portion claims desert parks, shabby towns around Death Valley, unlikely resorts such as Palm Springs, and dozens of highway settlements serving as pit stops for those speeding to points beyond.

Orientation

The desert divides into two major regions. The **Sonoran,** or **Low Desert,** occupies southeastern California from the Mexican border north to Needles and west to the Borrego Desert; the **Mojave,** or **High Desert,** spans the southcentral part of the state, bounded by the Sonoran Desert to the south, San Bernardino and the San Joaquin Valley to the west, the Sierra Nevada to the north, and Death Valley to the east.

The **Low Desert** is flat, dry, and barren. Sparse vegetation makes shade-providing plants a necessary but scarce commodity, and one that relies on an even rarer one—water. Humans and animals thrive in the oases in this area, the largest supporting the super-resort of **Palm Springs**. Despite the arid climate, water from the Colorado River irrigates the Imperial and Coachella Valleys. Other points of interest are **Anza-Borrego Desert State Park** and the **Salton Sea**.

By contrast, the High Desert consists of foothills and plains nestled within mountain ranges approaching 5000 ft., making it cooler (by about 10°F in summer) and wetter. Although few resorts have sprung up, **Joshua Tree National Monument** remains a popular destination for campers. **Barstow,** the central city of the High Desert, often functions as a rest station on the way to Las Vegas or the Sierras.

Death Valley marks the eastern boundary of the Mojave but might best be considered a region unto itself, containing both high and low desert areas. Major highways cross the desert east-west: I-8 hugs the California-Mexico border, I-10 goes through Indio on its way to Los Angeles, and I-40 crosses Needles to Barstow, where it joins I-15, which runs from Las Vegas and other points east to L.A.

For special health and safety precautions in the desert, see Desert Durvival in the Health section of the General Introduction to this book.

Barstow

Barstow is an adequate place to prepare for forays into the desert. Once a booming mining town, this desert oasis (pop. 60,000) now thrives on business from local military bases, tourists, and truckers. Stop in at the **California Desert Information Center,** 831 Barstow Rd. (256-8313), for free maps and information on hiking, camping, exploring, and nearby ghost towns, such as the commercialized **Calico Ghost Town,** Ghost Town Rd. (254-2122), 10 mi. northeast of town on I-15.

What Barstow lacks in charm (and it truly lacks) is made up for by its abundant supply of inexpensive motels and eateries. To prevent a Big Mac attack in this fast-food town, head for the **Barstow Station McDonald's,** on E. Main St. Constructed from old locomotive cars, this Mickey D's serves more burgers per annum than any other U.S. outfit.

All Star Inns, 150 N. Yucca Ave. (256-1752), relatively close to Greyhound and Amtrak stations, offers standard, clean chain-motel rooms with cable TV, free local calls, and a pool. (Singles $20. Doubles $24.) The **Economy Motel,** 1590 Coolwater Lane (256-1737) off I-40, has singles for $22 and doubles for $32. The **Calico KOA,** I-15 and Ghost Town Rd. (254-2311), is overpopulated with Ghost Town devotees. (Sites for 2 $15, with electricity $19, full hookup $21. Each additional person $2.50.)

Barstow, the western terminus of I-40, orders drinks midway between Los Angeles and Las Vegas on I-15. At the **Amtrak** station, N. 1st St. (800-872-7245), you can get on or off a train—that's all. Two trains per day go to L.A. ($33) and San Diego ($53); one per day ventures to Las Vegas ($44). **Greyhound,** 120 S. 1st St. (256-8757), at W. Main St., goes 13 times a day to L.A. ($18) and Las Vegas ($30). (Open daily 8am-6pm.)

Death Valley

Dante, Blake, and Sartre would have been inspired. Nowhere on and few places beneath this planet can touch the daily summer temperatures here. The *average* high temperature in July is 116°F, with a nighttime low of 88°. Ground temperatures hover near an egg-frying 200°. Much of the landscape resembles *Viking* photographs of the surface of Mars, with its reddish crags and canyons, immobile and stark. The strangeness of the landscape lends to it a certain beauty. The earth-hues of the sands and rocks change hourly in the variable sunlight. The elevation ranges from 11,049-ft. Telescope Peak to Badwater, the lowest point in the hemisphere at 282 ft. below sea level. The region features pure white salt flats on the valley floor, impassable mountain slopes, and huge, shifting sand dunes. Nature appears to have focused all of its extremes and varieties here at a single location.

The region sustains a surprisingly intricate web of Dantean life. Casual tourists and naturalists alike may observe a tremendous variety of desert dwellers, such as the great horned owl, roadrunner, coyote, kit fox, gecko, chuckwalla, and raven.

Late November through February are the coolest months (40-70° in the valley, freezing temperatures and snow in the mountains) and also the wettest period, with infrequent but violent rainstorms that can flood the canyons. Desert wildflowers bloom in March and April, accompanied by moderate temperatures and tempestuous winds that can whip sand and dust into an obscuring mess for hours or even days. Over 50,000 people vie for Death Valley's facilities and sights during the **'49ers Encampment Festival,** held the last week of October and the first two weeks of November. Other times that bring traffic jams include three-day winter holiday weekends, Thanksgiving, Christmas through New Year's Day, and Easter.

Practical Information and Orientation

Emergency: 911.

Visitor Information: Furnace Creek Visitors Center (786-2331), on Rte. 190 in the east-central section of the valley. Simple and informative museum. Slide shows every half hr., nightly lecture. Office open daily 8am-5pm. Center open daily 8am-5pm; Nov.-Easter 8am-8pm. For info by mail, write the Superintendent, Death Valley National Monument, Death Valley 92328.

Ranger Stations: Grapevine, junction of Rte. 190 and 267 near Scotty's Castle; **Stove Pipe Wells** on Rte. 190; **Wildrose,** Rte. 178, 20 mi. south of Emigrant via Emigrant Canyon Dr.; and **Shoshone,** outside the southeast border of the valley at the junction of Rte. 178 and 127. Weather report, weekly naturalist program, and park info posted at each station. **Emergency** help too. All open year-round.

Gasoline: Fill up outside Death Valley at **Olancha, Shoshone**, or **Beatty,** NV. Otherwise, you'll pay about 20¢ more per gallon at the stations across from the Furnace Creek Visitors Center, in Stove Pipe Wells Village, and at Scotty's Castle (all Chevron). Don't play chicken with the fuel gauge—Death Valley takes no prisoners. **Propane gas** available at the Furnace Creek Chevron; **white gas** at the Furnace Creek Ranch and Stove Pipe Wells Village stores; **diesel fuel** is pumped in Las Vegas, Pahrump, and Beatty, NV, and in Lone Pine, Olancha, Ridgecrest, Stateline, and Trona, CA.

Road Service: Furnace Creek Garage (AAA), 786-2232. Open daily 8am-4pm.

Groceries and Supplies: Furnace Creek Ranch Store. Expensive but well-stocked. Open daily 7am-9pm. **Stove Pipe Wells Village Store.** Same price range. Open daily 7am-8pm. Both sell charcoal and firewood. Ice available at the Furnace Creek Chevron and the Stove Pipe Wells Village Store.

Post Office: Furnace Creek Ranch (786-2223). Open Mon.-Fri. 8:30am-5pm. **ZIP code:** 92328.

Area Code: 619.

Death Valley spans over two million isolated acres (1.5 times the size of Delaware). However, visitors from the south can reach it with a small detour on the road to Sierra Nevada's eastern slope; those from the north will find it reasonably convenient on the way to Las Vegas.

There is no regularly scheduled public transportation into Death Valley; only charter buses make the run. Bus tours within Death Valley are monopolized by **Fred Harvey's Death Valley Tours,** the same organization that runs Grand Canyon tours. Excursions begin at Furnace Creek Ranch, which also handles reservations (786-2345, ext. 61; $15-25, children $8-13, small discount for seniors).

The best way to get into and around Death Valley is by car. The nearest agencies rent in Las Vegas, Barstow, and Bishop. Be sure to rent a reliable car: this is emphatically *not* the place to cut corners; it's worth the money not to get stuck with an overheated car in the middle of Death Valley. Each vehicle is charged a $5 entrance fee (bicyclists and pedestrians $2); paying this fee grants you entrance to the park for seven days.

Of the 13 monument entrances, most visitors choose Rte. 190 from the east. The road is well-maintained, the pass less steep, and more convenient to the visitors center. However, since most of the major sights adjoin the north/south road, a daytripper at the helm of a trusty vehicle should enter from the southeast (Rte. 178 west from Rte. 127 at Shoshone) or the north (direct to Scotty's Castle via NV Rte. 267 from U.S. 95) in order to see more of the monument. Unskilled mountain drivers probably should *not* attempt to enter via the smaller roads Titus Canyon or Emigrant Canyon Dr., since no guard rails prevent cars from falling from the canyon's cliffs.

Eighteen-wheelers have replaced 18-mule teams, but transportation around Death Valley still takes stubborn determination. Radiator water (*not* for drinking) is available at critical points on Rte. 178 and 190 and NV Rte. 374, but not on any unpaved roads. Obey the signs that advise "four-wheel-drive only." Those who do bound along the backcountry trails by four-wheel-drive should carry chains, extra tires, gas, oil, water (both to drink and for that radiator), and spare parts; also leave an itinerary with the visitors center. Be sure to check which roads are closed—especially in summer. Never drive on wet backcountry roads.

Death Valley has **hiking** trails to challenge the mountain lover, desert rat, or backcountry camper. Ask a ranger for advice (see Sights below). Backpackers and dayhikers alike should inform the visitors center of their route, and take appropriate topographic maps. During the summer the National Park Service recommends that valley-floor hikers spend several days prior to the hike getting acclimated to the heat and low humidity, plan a route along roads where assistance is readily available, and outfit a hiking party of at least two people with another person following in a vehicle to monitor the hikers' progress. Wearing thick socks and carrying salve to treat feet parched by the nearly 200°F earth also makes good sense.

Check the weather forecasts before setting out—all roads and trails can disappear during a winter rainstorm. The dryness of the area, plus the lack of any root and soil system to retain moisture, transforms canyon and valley floors into riverbeds for deadly torrents during heavy rains. For other important tips, see Desert Survival, under Health in the General Introduction to this book.

Accommodations

Fred Harvey's Amfac Consortium retains its vise-like grip on the trendy, resort-style, incredibly overpriced facilities in Death Valley. Look for cheaper accommodations in the towns near Death Valley: **Olancha** (west), **Shoshone** (southwest), **Tecopa** (south), and **Beatty, NV** (northwest).

The National Park Service maintains nine **campgrounds,** none of which accepts reservations. Call the visitors center to check availability and prepare for a battle if you come during peak periods (see below). Park Service campgrounds include **Mesquite Springs** ($5), **Stove Pipe Wells** ($4), **Emigrant** (free), **Furnace Creek** ($8), **Sunset** ($4), **Texas Springs** ($5), and **Wildrose** (free), but camping fees are not pursued with vigor in the summer. All campsites have toilets; all except Thorndike and Mahogany Flat have water. Be warned that water availability is not always reliable, especially in the winter. All except Sunset and Stove Pipe Wells have tables. Open fires are prohibited at Stove Pipe Wells, Sunset, and Emigrant; bring a stove. Fires are permitted at Thorndike and Mahogany Flat, though both lack places in which to build them; collecting wood, alive or dead, is prohibited everywhere in the monument. **Backcountry camping** is free and legal, as long as you check in at the visitors center and pitch tents at least one mi. from main roads and five mi. from any established campsite.

Sights

The **visitors center and museum** (see Practical Information above) offers info on tours, hikes, and special programs. The nearby museums are amusing as well. If you're interested in astronomy, speak to one of the rangers; some set up telescopes at Zabriskie Point and offer spontaneous shows. In **wildflower season** (Feb.-mid-April), tours are lead to some of the best places for viewing the display. **Hells Gate** and **Jubilee Pass** are especially beautiful, **Hidden Valley** even more so, though it is accessible only by a difficult, seven-mi. four-wheel-drive route from Teakettle Junction (itself 25 mi. south of Ubehebe Crater). Both the **Harmony Borax Works** and the **Borax Museum** are a short drive from the visitors center.

Artist's Drive is a one-way loop off Rte. 178, beginning 10 mi. south of the visitors center. The road twists and winds through rock and dirt canyons on the way to **Artist's Palette,** a rainbow of green, yellow, and red mineral deposits in the hillside. Several miles south you'll find **Devil's Golf Course,** a huge plane of spiny salt crust left from the evaporation of ancient Lake Manly. Amble across the gigantic links; the salt underfoot sounds like crunching snow.

Zabriskie Point is a marvelous place from which to view Death Valley's corrugated badlands, particularly at sunrise. The trip up to **Dante's View,** 15 mi. by paved road south off Rte. 190 (take the turn-off beyond Twenty Mule Team Canyon exit), will reward you with views of Badwater, Furnace Creek Ranch, the Panamint Range, and, on a clear day, the Sierra Nevadas. Faintly visible on the valley floor are ruts from 20-mule-team wagons. Snows are common here in mid-winter, as are low temperatures anytime but mid-summer.

Joshua Tree National Monument

The low, scorching Sonoran Desert and the higher, cooler Mojave Desert mingle here, precipitating more than a half-million acres of extraordinarily jumbled scenery. The monument stars the Joshua Tree, a member of the lily family whose erratic limbs sometimes reach as high as 50 ft. The Mormons who came through here in the 19th century thought the crooked branches resembled the arms of the prophet Joshua leading them to the promised land. Spare forests of gangly Joshuas extend for miles in the high central and eastern portions of the monument, punctuated by great piles of quartz monzonite boulders, some over 100 ft. high. This bizarre landscape emerged over millenia as shoots of hot magma pushed to the surface and erosion wore away the supporting sandstone. Together, the two forces have created fantastic textures, shapes, and rock albums. Alongside the natural environment appear vestiges of human existence: ancient rock pictographs, dams built in the 19th century in order to catch the meager rainfall for livestock, and the ruins of gold mines that operated as late as the 1940s.

Over 80% of the monument is designated wilderness area; for those experienced in backcountry desert hiking and camping, Joshua Tree provides some truly remote territory. Hikers should go to one of the visitors centers for the rules and advice on use of isolated areas of the monument, and to pick up a topographic map ($2.50). The wilderness lacks water except for the occasional flash flood; even these evaporate rapidly. Carry at least a gallon of water per person per day—two during the summer months. You must register at roadside boxes before setting out (see maps) to let the monument staff know your location, and to prevent your car from being towed from a roadside parking lot.

Less hardy desert fans can enjoy Joshua Tree for a day or a weekend in relative comfort. The most popular time, as with other desert parks, is **wildflower season** (mid-March to mid-May), when the floor of the desert explodes in yucca, verbena, cottonwood, mesquite, and dozens of other floral variations. Summer is the hottest and slowest season. Bear in mind that no off-road driving is permitted.

A drive along the winding road from **Twentynine Palms** to the town of **Joshua Tree** (34 mi.) passes by the **Wonderland of Rocks,** a spectacular concentration of rock formations. The slightly longer drive between Twentynine Palms and I-10 through the monument offers a sampling of high and low desert landscapes. Along the way on both of these tours, explore as many of the side roads as time allows. Signs indicate whether turnoffs are paved, dirt, or only suitable for four-wheel-drive vehicles. One site not to miss, **Key's View,** off the park road just west of Ryan Campground, offers a stupendous vista. You can see as far as Palm Springs and the Salton Sea on a clear day. Also of note are the **palm oases** (Twentynine Palms, Forty-nine Palms, Cottonwood Spring, Lost Palms) and the **Cholla Cactus Garden** off Pinto Basin Rd.

A number of **hiking trails** lead to the most interesting features of Joshua Tree: oases, mine ruins, and fine vantage points. Short trails run near picnic areas and campsites. Visitors center brochures describe these trails, which range from a mere 200 yd. (the Cholla Cactus Garden) to 35 mi. (a section of the California Riding and Hiking Trail). The degree of difficulty varies almost as widely; the staff at the visitors center can help you choose. Plan on at least one hour per mi. on even relatively easy trails.

Campgrounds in the monument accept no reservations, except for group sites at **Cottonwood, Sheep Pass,** and **Indian Cove,** for which Ticketron handles mandatory reservations. Sites are also available at **White Tank** (closed in summer), **Belle, Black Rock Canyon, Hidden Valley, Ryan,** and **Jumbo Rocks.** All campsites have tables, fireplaces, and pit toilets; all are free except Cottonwood ($8) and Black Rock Canyon ($10), which have the only available water. You must bring your own firewood. If your trip to Joshua Tree is an educational endeavor contributing to a degree, you can secure a fee waiver at one of the group sites; write to the monument on your best official stationery and explain your "bona fide educational/study group" purposes. **Backcountry camping** is unlimited. Pitch your tent more than 500 ft. from a trail, one mi. from a road. (14-day max. stay Oct.-May; 30 days max. in summer. Entrance fee $2 per person or $5 per vehicle, good for a one-week stay at any state park.)

Joshua Tree National Monument occupies a vast area northeast of Palm Springs, about 160 mi. (3-3½ hr. by car) from west L.A. From I-10, the best approaches are via Rte. 62 from the west, leading to the towns of Joshua Tree and **Twentynine Palms** on the northern side of the monument, and via an unnumbered road that exits the interstate about 25 mi. east of Indio. **Desert Stage Lines** (367-3581), based in Palm Springs, stops in Twentynine Palms.

The monument's main **visitors center** offers displays, lectures, and maps at 74485 National Monument Dr., (367-7511), Twentynine Palms 92277, ¼-mi. off Rte. 62.

(Open daily 8am-5pm.) Another visitors center sits at the southern gateway approximately seven mi. north of I-10 (exit 4 mi. west of the town of Chiriaco Summit); an information kiosk adjoins the west entrance on Park Blvd., several mi. southeast of the town of Joshua Tree.

Palm Springs

Former Mayor Sonny Bono having led by example from next to his swimming pool, Palm Springs continues to be a playground for the nouveau-riche. The beautiful San Jacinto Mountains grind to a halt only blocks from **Palm Canyon Drive,** the city's main drag. The smog that nowadays begrimes L.A. creeps through Gorgonio Pass in the mountains only rarely, and then only with diminished potency. The resulting clear, dry air makes even the summer heat bearable. Medicinal waters bubbling from the town's hot springs have preserved not only the health of the area's opulent residents, but also the town's resort status. And cheap thrills are available for the budget-minded, not the least of which is the vantage of jaw-dropping opulence.

Rising over 5000 ft., the **Palm Springs Aerial Tramway** works its dramatic way up the side of Mt. San Jacinto to an observation deck that affords excellent views of L.A.'s distant smog. Stairs from the deck lead to a 360° viewing platform, usually covered by snow drifts. The base station is located on Tramway Dr., which intersects Rte. 111 just north of Palm Springs. (Tram operates at least every ½ hr. Mon.-Fri. from 10am, Sat.-Sun. from 8am. Last car 9pm; Nov.-April 7:30pm. Round-trip tram $15, seniors $12, ages under 12 $10. Ride and dine service $4 extra.)

The Desert Museum, 101 Museum Dr. (325-7186), behind the Desert Fashion Plaza on Palm Canyon Dr., boasts a collection of Native American art, desert dioramas, and live animals. The gorgeously posh museum also sponsors curator-led field trips ($3) into the nearby canyons, leaving every Friday at 9am; some involve up to 9 mi. of hiking. (Open late Sept.-early June Tues.-Sun. 10am-4pm. Admission $4, seniors $3, under 17 $2, kids with adult free. Free first Tues. of each month.) The four **Indian Canyons** (325-5673) are oases containing a wide variety of desert life and remnants of the Native American communities that once lived there. A permit ($10) is needed to gain entrance to Taquitz, one of the four canyons, available at the front gate at the end of S. Palm Canyon Dr. (Open daily Sept.-July 7, 8am-5pm. $3.25, students and military $2.50, seniors $2, kids 6-12 75¢.)

The **Living Desert Reserve** in Palm Desert, 47900 Portola Ave. (346-5694), 1½ mi. south of Rte. 111, display re-creations of various desert environments, from Saharan to Sonoran, along with rare desert fauna such as Arabian oryces and desert unicorns. (Open Sept. to mid-June daily 9am-5pm. Admission $6, seniors $5.25, kids $3. Disabled access.) Bizarre **Moorten's Desertland Botanical Gardens,** 1701 S. Palm Canyon Dr. (327-6555), is a botanist's heaven: ocotillo, yucca, prickly pear, and beavertail cactus you can see, smell, and (ouch!) touch.

Of course, most visitors to Palm Springs have no intention of studying the desert or taking in high culture. Palm Springs means sunning, with no activity more demanding than drinking a gallon of iced tea each day to keep from dehydrating or swimming in the Olympic-sized pool at **Palm Springs Leisure Center**, on Ramon Rd. just east of Sunrise Way (323-8278; open summer daily 11am-5pm, Tues. and Thurs. 7:30-9:30pm; off-season daily 11am-5pm; admission $3, ages 3-13 $2). For complete info about other recreactional activies (including tennis, golf and hot-air ballooning), call the Leisure Center at 323-8272. **Oasis Water Park** (825-7873), off Rte. 111 on Gene Autry Trail, is awash with a wave pool and seven water slides, including the seven-story-tall near-free-fall Scorpion. (Admission $16, ages 4-11 $11, under 4 free.)

Palm Springs' cheapest lodgings are at nearby state parks and national forest campgrounds. If you need a room with a roof, put your money on either **Motel 6** location: 595 E. Palm Canyon Dr. (325-6129; $32 for up to four guests) or the more convenient 660 S. Palm Canyon Dr. (327-4700; $36 for up to four guests). Both locations have a big pool and A/C, and both fill quickly, sometimes up to six months in advance in winter. Some on-the-spot rooms are available as no-shows are frequent.

For those who want to picnic—an excellent idea, given the surroundings—chain supermarkets abound in Palm Springs. **Ralph's,** 1555 S. Palm Canyon Dr. (323-8446), and **Vons,** in the Palm Springs Mall on Tahquitz-McCallum (322-2192), are both reliably low-priced. Cool Mexican mists pour out onto the sidewalk, inviting you to dine on the **Terazza,** 222 S. Palm Canyon Dr. (325-2794). Enjoy the *quesadilla special* with mushrooms and bacon ($6) as you watch the nightly entertainment. (Open Mon.-Sat. 11am-10pm, Sun. 10am-10pm.)

Palm Springs lies off I-10, 120 mi. east of L.A., just beyond a low pass that marks the edge of the Colorado Desert. The **Chamber of Commerce** is at 190 W. Amado (325-1577). Ask for a map ($1) and a free copy of *The Desert Guide.* (Open Mon.-Fri. 8am-5pm, Sat. 10am-2pm.) **Amtrak,** on Jackson St. in Indio, 25 mi. southeast of Palm Springs (connect to Greyhound in Indio) sends three trains per week to and from L.A. ($29) with frequent stops along the way. **Greyhound,** 311 N. Indian Ave. (325-2053) is much more convenient (5 per day, $18). **Desert Stage Lines** (367-3581) serves Twentynine Palms and Joshua Tree National Monument (3 buses per day, $9), with Friday service to L.A. ($20) and San Diego ($23.50). **Sun Bus** (343-3451) is the local bus system, serving all Coachella Valley cities (50¢, plus 25¢ per zone and 25¢ per transfer). Rent a car at **Rent-a-Wreck,** 67501 Rte. 111 (324-1766), for $20 per day, or $120 per week; 700 free mi., 19¢ each additional mi. (must be 21 with major credit card). **Desert Cab** is at 325-2868.

The Palm Springs **post office** disburses, among other things, commemorative mugs from 333 E. Amado Rd. (325-9631; open Mon.-Fri. 8:30am-5pm). Palm Springs' **ZIP code** is 92262; the **area code** is 619.

Los Angeles

Los Angeles is perhaps the most American of cities. It embodies much of what is wrong with the U.S., yet millions of people would never live anywhere else. Here, substance lost to style long ago. However, the gilded body of Los Angeles is flaking and peeling—beyond the mammoth billboards of the Sunset Strip lies a laundry list of urban woes that are eating away at the soul of the city.

Most of the issues confronting Los Angeles as the sprawling megalopolis hurtles toward the 21st century arise from the tension between the demands of excess and the limitations of reality. The city's freeways are overcrowded to the point that rush hour has ceased to be a meaningful concept. Too late—Los Angeles has embarked upon construction of a light-rail system that will cost billions and will not be completed until well into the next century. Environmental apocalypse looms in the thick smog that Los Angelenos breathe and the scarce water they pour into their swimming pools, depleting natural resources in the rest of the state.

But perhaps the most telling demonstration of reality asserting itself through layers of L.A. fantasy were the riots in April of 1992. The acquittal of four white police officers who were accused of beating African-American L.A. resident Rodney King galvanized days of bloody protests ending in millions of dollars in property damage and hundreds of arrests. Some thought that the video recording of the incident would assure the officers' conviction; others did not believe that the poverty and frustration in South Central L.A. was so serious. Both views were mistaken, and those tragic days in the spring frighteningly blurred the line between the good and the bad guys.

Despite it all, L.A. keeps growing, proving that if you build (and water) it, they will come. A drive into the far reaches of the L.A. Basin, to Simi Valley, to San Bernardino, and even up Route 14 toward Lancaster and Palmdale and the Mojave Desert reveals the wooden skeletons of new tract houses and the creeping tendrils of outer suburbia. Even Bakersfield, over 100 mi. to the northwest, plans to build a light-rail connection to L.A. and anticipates the day when it forms just another of the proverbial "suburbs in search of a city."

In the meantime, tensions between conceptions and realities in L.A. reach the emblematic. There are traffic jams at 1am on the Harbor Freeway while film crews stage yet another Hollywood car chase. Actor Mickey Rourke blames the April riots on Afri-

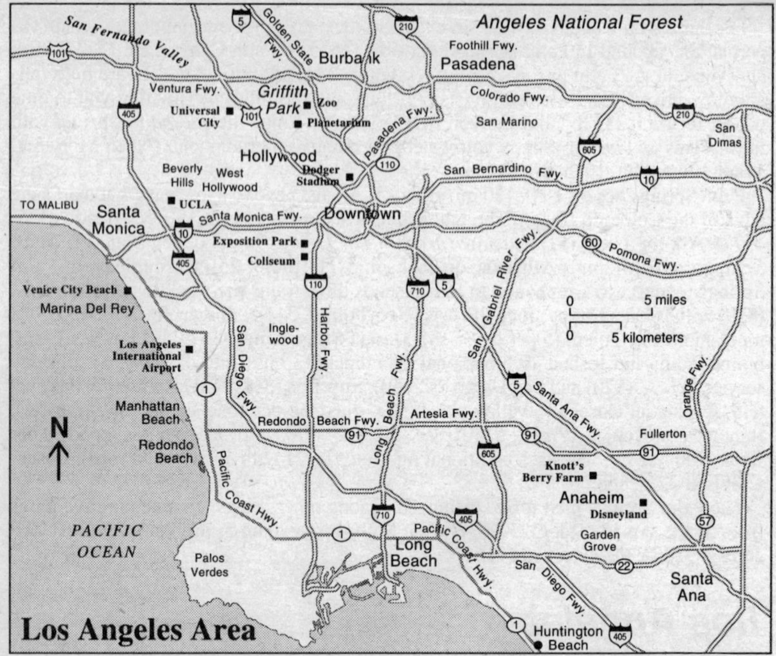

can-American filmmakers. A West L.A. swimsuit store dresses its saleswomen in bikinis and high heels. The glitterati assemble at courtside for Laker games. Nowhere else in the country do Americans wrestle so fiercely with America.

Practical Information

Emergency: 911.

Los Angeles Convention and Visitors Bureau, 685 S. Figueroa St. 90015 (213-689-8822), between Wilshire and 7th St. in the Financial District. Hundreds of brochures. Staff speaks Spanish, Filipino, Japanese, French, and German. Good maps for downtown streets, sights, and buses. Publishes *Datelines* and *Artsline,* quarterly guides to Southern California events. *Los Angeles Visitors Guide* and *Lodging Guide* are both free and available by mail (3 weeks delivery time). Second location in Hollywood at 6541 Hollywood Blvd. (213-461-4213). Open Mon.-Fri. 8am-5pm, Sat. 8:30am-5pm. **Los Angeles Council HI/AYH,** 1434 2nd St., Santa Monica (310-393-3413). Guidebooks, low-cost flights, rail passes, and ISIC cards. Open Tues.-Sat. 10am-5pm. **Sierra Club:** 3550 W. 6th St., #321 (213-387-4287). Hiking, biking, and backpacking info. Open Mon.-Fri. 10am-6pm.

National Park Service: 30401 Agoura Rd., Agoura Hills (818-597-9192 for local parks Info Center; 818-597-1036 for other offices), in the San Fernando Valley. Info on the Santa Monica Mtns. and other parks. Open Mon.-Sat. 8am-5pm.

American Express: 901 W. 7th St. (213-627-4800). Open Mon.-Fri. 8am-6pm. Locations in Beverly Hills (at the Beverly Center), Pasadena, Torrance, and Costa Mesa. Open Sat. 10am-6pm at 8493 W. 3rd St. (213-659-1682).

Western Union, 800-988-4726. Call for locations and info about receiving cash.

Los Angeles County Parks and Recreation: 433 S. Vermont (213-738-2961). Has helpful specifics for bicyclists. Open Mon.-Fri. 8am-5pm.

Amtrak: Union Station, 800 N. Alameda (213-624-0171), downtown. To: San Francisco (1 per day, 11 hr., $74) and San Diego (8 per day, 3 hr., $24) with stops in San Juan Capistrano, San Clemente, Oceanside, and Del Mar.

Greyhound: 208 E. 6th St. (620-1200), downtown terminal. To: San Diego (20 per day, 2½-3½ hr., $11); Tijuana (16 per day; 3½-4½ hr.; $17, round-trip $26); Santa Barbara (11 per day; 2-3½ hr.; $13, round- trip $22); and San Francisco (14 per day, 8½-12½ hr., $40). Occasional special deals for advance purchases. (See also Greyhound listings in Hollywood, Santa Monica, and Pasadena below.)

RTD Bus Information Line: 213-626-4455. Customer Service Center at 5301 Wilshire Blvd. (213-972-6235; open Mon.-Fri. 8am-4:15pm).

Taxi: Checker Cab (213-482-3456), **Independent** (213-385-8294), **United Independent** (213-653-5050), **Celebrity Red Top** (213-934-6700). Cabbies don't cruise the streets for fares—you'll need to call.

Car Rentals: Avon Rent-A-Car, 8459 Sunset Blvd. (213-654-5533). $15 and up per day with unlimited mileage, from $101.70 per week. Collision and damage waiver (CDW) $9 and up per day. Must be 18 with a major credit card; drivers 18-22 face a steep $15 per day surcharge, $5 per day for those 22-25. Open Mon.-Fri. 7:30am-9:30pm. **Penny Rent-A-Car,** 12425 Victory Blvd., N. Hollywood (818-786-1733). $15-17 with 75 free mi., $.15 per mi. after that. $98-111 per week with 500 free mi. CDW $8 per day. Must be 21 with major credit card or an international driver's license. Open Mon.-Fri. 7:30am-6pm, Sat. 9am-4pm. **Ugly Duckling,** 920 S. La Brea (213-933-0522). $19 per day with 100 free mi., $110 per week. CDW $8 per day, $50 per week. Must be 21 with major credit card. Open Mon.-Sat. 9am-6pm.

Automobile transport services: Dependable Car Travel Service, Inc., 18730 Wilshire Blvd., #414, Beverly Hills (310-659-2922). Must be 18. References from L.A. or destination. Most cars to the northeast, especially N.Y., but also to Florida and Chicago. $150 refundable deposit. Call 1-2 days ahead to reserve. Open Mon.-Fri. 8:30am-5:30pm. **Auto Driveaway,** 3407 W. 6th St. (213-666-6100). Must be 21 with references in L.A. and destination. Foreign travelers need passport, visa, and an international driver's license rather than references. Photo and either cash deposit ($250), traveler's checks, or money order required. Call a week before departure. Open Mon.-Fri. 9am-5pm.

Green Tortoise (310-392-1990; 415-285-2441 in San Francisco), the northbound "hostel on wheels," leaves L.A. every Sun. night with stops in Venice, Hollywood, and downtown. Arrives in San Francisco ($32) on Mon. morning, Eugene and Portland, OR ($72) on Tues. afternoon, and Seattle ($80) on Tues. night. Call for reservations and exact departure location and times. (See Getting There in the General Introduction for more info on tours.)

Ticketron: 310-642-4242 for nearest location. Open Mon.-Sun. 9am-6pm.

Weather: 213-554-1212 for excessively detailed report.

Highway Conditions: 213-636-7231. Helps you to avoid freeway jams.

Help Lines: National Gay Advocates Hotline, 800-526-5050. **Rape Crisis,** 310-392-8381. 24-hr. hotline. **Battered Women's Assistance:** 818-887-6589. 24-hr. hotline.

Ambulance: Los Angeles City Ambulance Emergency Service: 213-483-6721.

Police: 213-626-5273.

Post Office: Main office at Florence Station, 7001 S. Central Ave. (213-586-1723). Info on rates and schedules, 213-586-1467. General Delivery, 900 N. Alameda (213-617-4543), at 9th St. General Delivery **ZIP Code:** 90055.

Area Codes: Southern half of Los Angeles County (including Westwood and parts of Beverly Hills, Long Beach, Malibu, the Pacific Coast Highway, Santa Monica, UCLA, Venice, and parts of West Hollywood) **310;** northern half (including parts of Beverly Hills, Downtown, Hollywood, parts of West Hollywood, and Wilshire District and Hancock Park) **213;** north of Hollywood (including Pasadena and San Marino) **818.**

Hollywood

Emergency: 911. Police: 1358 N. Wilcox (485-4302)

Visitor Information: The Janes House, 6541 Hollywood Blvd. (461-4213), in Janes House Sq. Provides L.A. visitor guides. Open Mon.-Sat. 9am-5pm. **Hollywood Chamber of Commerce,** 6255 W. Sunset Blvd., #911 (469-8311).

Greyhound: 1409 N. Vine St. (466-6381), 1 block south of Sunset Blvd. To: Santa Barbara (5 per day, $13); San Diego (14 per day, $11); San Francisco (9 per day, $42). Terminal open daily 7:30am-11pm.

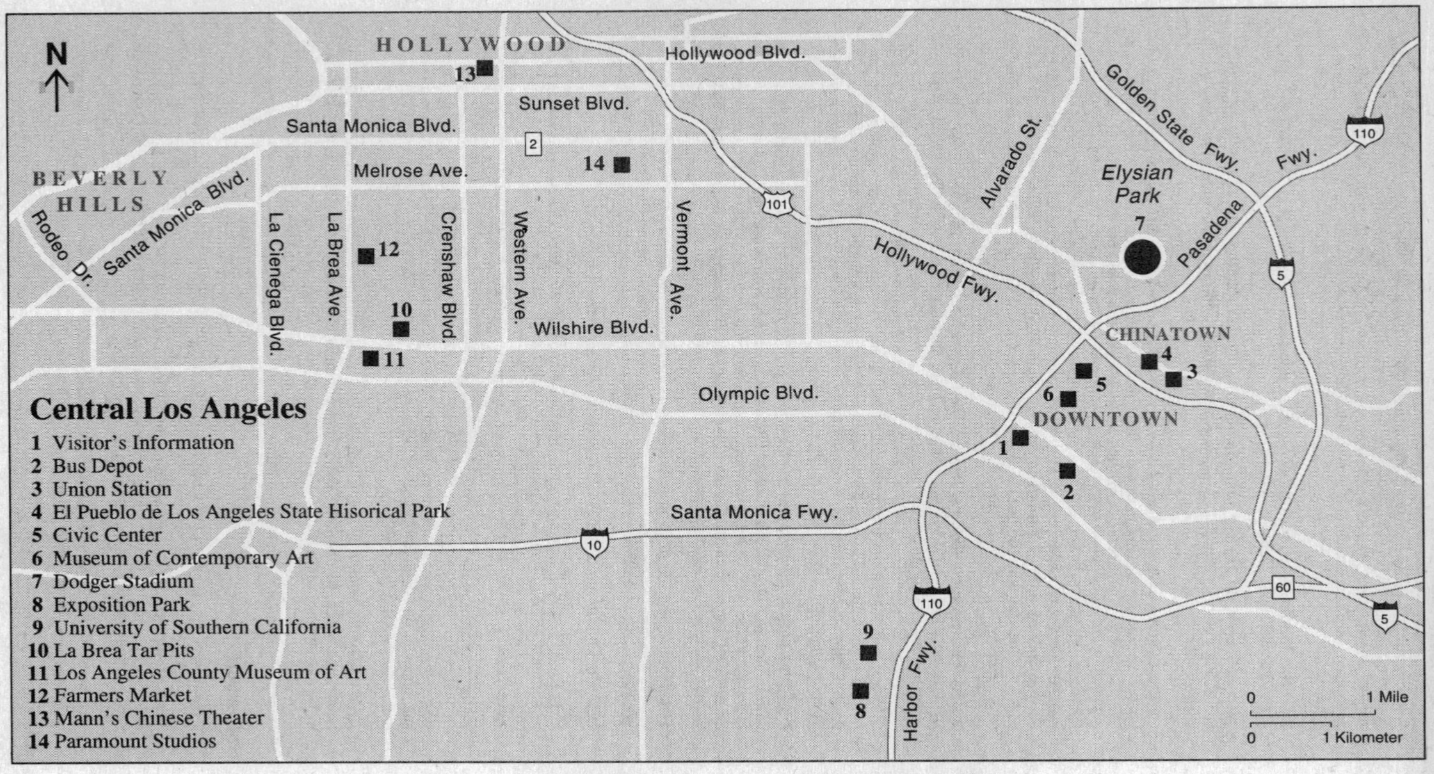
N
HOLLYWOOD
Hollywood Blvd.
Sunset Blvd.
Santa Monica Blvd.
Melrose Ave.
BEVERLY HILLS
Santa Monica Blvd.
Rodeo Dr.
La Cienega Blvd.
La Brea Ave.
Crenshaw Blvd.
Western Ave.
Vermont Ave.
Wilshire Blvd.
Olympic Blvd.
Santa Monica Fwy.
Hollywood Fwy.
Alvarado St.
Golden State Fwy.
Pasadena Fwy.
Elysian Park
CHINATOWN
DOWNTOWN
Harbor Fwy.
2
101
10
110
5
60
0 1 Mile
0 1 Kilometer
Central Los Angeles
1 Visitor's Information
2 Bus Depot
3 Union Station
4 El Pueblo de Los Angeles State Hisorical Park
5 Civic Center
6 Museum of Contemporary Art
7 Dodger Stadium
8 Exposition Park
9 University of Southern California
10 La Brea Tar Pits
11 Los Angeles County Museum of Art
12 Farmers Market
13 Mann's Chinese Theater
14 Paramount Studios

Public Transportation: RTD Customer Service Center, 6249 Hollywood Blvd. (972-6000). Free info, maps, timetables, and passes. Open Mon.-Fri. 10am-6pm. **Important buses:** #1 along Hollywood Blvd., #2 and 3 along Sunset Blvd., #4 along Santa Monica Blvd., #10 along Melrose.

Post Office: 1615 Wilcox Ave. (464-2194). Open Mon.-Fri. 8am-5pm, Sat. 8am-1pm. General Delivery **ZIP Code:** 90028

Area Code: 213.

Santa Monica

Police: 1685 Main St. (395-9931).

Visitor Information: 1400 Ocean Ave. (393-7593), down in Palisades Park. Local maps, brochures, and info on attractions and events. Open daily 10am-5pm; in winter 10am-4pm.

Public Transportation: Santa Monica Municipal (Big Blue) Bus Lines, 1660 7th St. (451-5445), at Olympic. Open Mon.-Fri. 8am-5pm. Faster and cheaper than the RTD, this local bus service costs $.50; transfers to RTD routes $.25. Buses #1 and 2 continue through to Hollywood. Bus #10 provides express service from downtown Santa Monica to downtown LA.

Greyhound: 1433 5th St. (395-1708), between Broadway and Santa Monica Blvd. To: Santa Barbara (3 per day, 2½ hr., $13); San Diego (3 per day, 4½ hr., $20); San Francisco (2 per day, 11 hr., $50). Open Mon.-Fri. 8:30am-5:30pm.

Surfboard Rental: Natural Progression Surfboards, 22935½ W. Pacific Hwy., Malibu (456-6302). Boards $20 per day, plus $5 insurance. Wetsuits $8. Also sailboard rental ($50 per day, plus $5 insurance), and windsurfing lessons. Open daily 9am-6pm.

Post Office: 5th and Arizona (576-2626). Open Mon.-Fri. 9am-5pm, Sat. 9am-1pm.

Area Code: 310.

Pasadena

Emergency: 911. Police: 207 N. Garfield Ave. (405-4501).

Convention and Visitors Bureau, 171 S. Los Robles Ave. (795-9311), across from the Hilton Hotel. Open Mon.-Fri. 9am-5pm, Sat. 10am-4pm.

Greyhound: 645 E. Walnut (792-5116). To: Santa Barbara (3 per day, 2½ hr., $13); San Diego (3 per day, 4 hr., $14); San Francisco (2 per day, 11 hr., $53). Open Mon.-Fri. 8:30am-5:30pm, Sat. 8:30am-3pm, Sun. 9am-3pm.

Post Office: 600 N. Lincoln (304-7122), at Orange. Open Mon. and Fri. 8am-6pm; Tues.-Thurs. 8am-5pm; Sat. 9am-2pm. General Delivery **ZIP Code:** 91109.

Area Code: 818.

Orientation

Getting There

Los Angeles sprawls along the coast of Southern California, 127 mi. north of San Diego and 403 mi. south of San Francisco. You can still be "in" L.A. even when you're 50 mi. from downtown. Greater L.A. encompasses the urbanized areas of Orange, Riverside, San Bernardino, and Ventura counties.

By Car

General approaches to Greater L.A. are I-5 from the south, California Highway 1, U.S. 101, or I-5 from the north, and I-10 or I-15 from the east. The city itself is crisscrossed by over a dozen freeways. Driving into L.A. can be unnerving if you are not familiar with the gauntlet of ramps, exits, and four-story-high directional signs. Plan your route carefully so you won't be forced to cut across 10 lanes of traffic to exit. (See Getting Around below.)

By Train and Bus

Amtrak pulls into **Union Station,** 800 N. Alameda (213-624-0171), at the northwestern edge of the heart of downtown Los Angeles. Once the end of the line for westbound rail passengers from all over the U.S., this gloriously designed Spanish colonial-revival building has recently been renovated. Buses travel out of the station to Pasadena and Longbeach; info about their schedules can be obtained at the station.

Visitors arriving by **Greyhound** will disembark at 208 E. 6th St. (213-620-1200), at Los Angeles St. downtown, in a rough neighborhood; continuing on to other area stations is far safer than disembarking in downtown, especially if you are arriving after dusk. Greyhound also stops in Hollywood, Santa Monica, Pasadena, and other parts of the metropolitan area (see Practical Information). If you must get off, RTD buses #320 and 20 stop at 7th and Hill St., two blocks southwest of the downtown station, and carry passengers westward along Wilshire Blvd. Bus #1 stops at 5th and Broadway, four blocks to the west and one block north, and travels westward along Hollywood Blvd.

By Plane

Los Angeles International Airport (LAX) (310-646-5252) is divided into two levels, the upper serving departures and the lower, arrivals. Nine contiguous terminals are arranged in a large horseshoe, with Terminal 2 serving international carriers. The airport complex is located in Westchester, about 15 mi. southwest of downtown, 10 mi. southeast of Santa Monica, and onemi. east of the coast.

Many car rental agencies run shuttle buses directly from the airport terminals to their lots. All Rapid Transit District (RTD) service to and from the airport stops at the **transfer terminal** at Vicksburg Ave. and 96th St. To get downtown, take bus #439 (Mon.-Fri. rush hr. only) or #42 (daily 5:30am-11:15pm, from downtown daily 5:45am-12:10am) from the transfer terminal. To and from UCLA, take express #560; Long Beach, #232; West Hollywood and Beverly Hills, #220. From West Hollywood to Hollywood, take bus #1 (along Hollywood Blvd.), 2 (along Sunset Blvd.), or 4 (along Santa Monica Blvd.).

Metered cabs are costly: $1.95 plus $1.60 per mi. Checker Cab (213-482-3456) fare from the airport to downtown is about $24, to Hollywood $28, and to Disneyland a goofy $85.

The best option is to take one of the many **shuttle vans** which offer door-to-door service from the terminal to different parts of L.A. for a flat rate. Vans are cheaper than cabs; several people with the same destination can share the fare. The vans pick up outside of baggage claim areas where dispatchers will call the company of your choice. For specific info regarding RTD buses, cabs, and shuttles, ask at the kiosks located on the sidewalks directly in front of the terminals. Some hostels will pay shuttle fares; call ahead to inquire.

Getting Around

Before you even think about navigating Los Angeles's 6500 mi. of streets and 40,000 intersections, get yourself a good map; centerless and amorphous Los Angeles defies human comprehension otherwise. The best investment for a stay of longer than a week is the *Thomas Guide Los Angeles County Street Guide and Directory* ($14).

Los Angeles is a city of distinctive boulevards; its shopping areas and business centers are distributed along these broad (and hardened) arteries. Streets throughout L.A. are designated east, west, north, and south from First and Main St. at the center of downtown. East-west thoroughfares are the most prominent; use them to get your bearings. Beginning with the northernmost, they are Melrose Ave. and Beverly, Wilshire, Olympic, Pico, Venice, and Washington Blvd. Melrose is filled with boutiques, galleries, and trendy night spots; Wilshire is studded with large department stores and office buildings; Olympic is residential and the least congested. The important north-south streets of this huge grid, from downtown westward, are Vermont, Normandie, and Western Ave.; Vine St.; Highland, La Brea, and Fairfax Ave.; and La Cienega and Robertson Blvd.

The area west of downtown is known as the **Wilshire District** after its main boulevard. Wilshire is a continuous wall of tall buildings (called the "Miracle Mile") with bungalows and duplexes huddled in the skyscrapers' shadows. **Hancock Park,** a green park and affluent residential area, covers the northeast portion of the district, on the 5900 block, and harbors the Los Angeles County Museum of Art and the George C. Page Fossil Museum.

Sunset Boulevard runs from the ocean to downtown piercing beach communities, famous nightclubs, sleazy motels, and elegant Silver Lake. Farther north is **Hollywood Boulevard,** just beneath the Hollywood Hills, where split-level buildings perched precariously on hillsides house screenwriters, actors, and producers.

Once the sun sets, those on and off well-lit main drags should exercise caution, and not walk alone *anywhere.* Hollywood and the downtown area, east of Western Ave., are considered particularly crime-ridden. Gang- and drug-related crimes have increasingly threatened public safety. Whether walking, riding, or driving, always know where you are and where you are going.

Public Transportation

Nowhere in America is the great god of automobile held in greater reverance than in L.A. In the 1930s and 1940s, General Motors, Firestone, and Standard Oil conspired to buy up the street car companies and run them into the ground, later ripping up all the rails. In 1949, G.M. was convicted in federal court of criminal conspiracy—but it didn't bring back the trolleys or make public transportation any easier.

Although most Angelenos will insist that a car is necessary to live in or visit their city, the **Southern California Rapid Transit District (RTD)** does work—sort of. With over 200 routes and several independent municipal transit systems buttressing RTD, you may need an extra day just to study timetables. Using the RTD to sightsee in L.A. can be frustrating simply because attractions tend to be spread out. Those determined to see *everything* in L.A. should get a car, or at least base themselves centrally, make daytrips, and carry plenty of change for the bus.

To familiarize yourself with the RTD, write for a **Riders Kit** from RTD, Los Angeles 90001 (this address is sufficient), or stop by one of 10 **customer service centers.** The three downtown locations are**: ARCO Plaza,** 505 S. Flower St., Level B (open Mon.-Fri. 7:30am-3:30pm); **419 S. Main St.** (open Mon.-Fri. 8am-4:30pm); and **1016 S. Main St.** (open Mon.-Sat. 10am-6pm). RTD prints route maps for the different sections of the city, as well as a brochure called *RTD Self-Guide Tours,* which details how to reach the most important sights from downtown. For transit info anywhere in the L.A. area, call 800-2-LA-RIDE (252-7433; lines open daily 5:30am-11:30pm).

Bus service is best downtown and along the major thoroughfares west of downtown. (There is 24-hr. service, for instance, on Wilshire Blvd.) The downtown **DASH shuttle** is only $.25 and serves Chinatown, Union Station, Olvera Street, City Hall, Little Tokyo, the Music Center, ARCO Plaza, and more. DASH also operates a shuttle on Sunset Blvd. in Hollywood, as well as shuttles in Pacific Palisades, Fairfax (running from Farmer's Market to 3rd and LaBrea), Venice Beach, and Watts. (Downtown DASH operates Mon.-Fri. 6:30am-6:30pm, Sat. 10am-5pm; other DASH shuttles run about the same hours but not on Sat.) For schedule info call 800-253-7433. Those with hearing impairments can call 800-252-9040. Bus service is dismal on the periphery of the city, and two-hour journeys are not unusual.

RTD's **basic fare** is $1.10, disabled passengers $.55. Additional charges for express buses, buses taking the freeway, sports events, services, etc., can raise the fare to as much as $3. Exact change is *required.* Transfers are $.25, whether you're changing from one RTD line to another or from RTD to another transit authority, such as Santa Monica Municipal Bus Lines, Culver City Municipal Bus Lines, Long Beach Transit, or Orange County Transit District. If you plan to use the buses extensively over a long visit, buy a **bus pass.** Unlimited use for a month costs $42, $25 for college students, $18 for students under 18, and $10 for seniors and the disabled.Roughly 90% of RTD's lines, designated by the appropriate symbol, are **wheelchair accessible.** For more info call 800-622-7828 (open daily 6am-midnight). If you don't want to spend tedious hours on an RTD bus to get from one end of the basin to the other, consider paying more to take **Greyhound** (213-620-1200) to such places as Long Beach, Anaheim, and Glendale.

Gray Line Tours, 6541 Hollywood Blvd., Hollywood (213-856-5900), is a more expensive but easier way to reach distant attractions. Costs include transportation and admission: Disneyland $57, Magic Mountain $52, Universal Studios $46, San Diego Zoo $46, and Sea World $48. Tours leave from the Gray Line office for 200 different locations in summertime. Some larger hostels offer reasonably priced bus trips to area beaches and attractions. Call to inquire.

In a desperate, expensive, last-ditch effort to alleviate the traffic congestion that threatens to choke the city, L.A. has finally started building a subway. The first leg of L.A.'s 300-mi. **Metro Rail Plan,** the **Blue Line,** presently runs from 7th St. in Downtown to Long Beach (call 213-626-4455 for info). The **Red Line,** which will run through downtown and out to the San Fernando Valley, is scheduled to open in late 1993. Also in the works are lines to LAX and Pasadena. For information on construction progress call 213-620-RAIL.

Freeways

The freeway is perhaps the most enduring of L.A.'s images. When uncongested, these 10- and 12-lane concrete roadways offer speed and convenience; the trip from downtown to Santa Monica can take as little as 20 minutes. More often, they brim with autos spewing noxious fumes, and movement over the hot concrete is slow.

Perhaps to help them "get in touch with their freeway," Californians refer to the highways by names rather than by numbers. These names are little more than hints of a freeway's route, at best harmless, and at worst misleading.

I-405, the **San Diego Freeway.** Roughly parallel to the Pacific Coast Highway (Rte. 1), but approximately 10 mi. inland, it links the San Fernando Valley with Westwood, Beverly Hills, LAX, and Long Beach. This freeway runs north-south, and meets I-5 in the San Fernando Valley and Orange County.

I-10, the **Santa Monica Freeway,** west of downtown. The main commuter link to the western portions of the city: Century City, Westwood, Santa Monica, and Brentwood. Called the **San Bernardino Freeway** east of downtown.

I-5, the **Golden State Freeway,** pierces the heart of central California parallel to I-405 and Rte. 1. It comes to within 15 mi. of the coast as it moves through the L.A. Basin. Called the **Santa Ana Freeway** south of downtown, it serves Anaheim and Orange County.

I-110, called the **Pasadena Freeway** north of downtown (it starts in Pasadena) or the **Harbor Freeway** south of downtown where it runs by USC, Exposition Park, and Watts on its way to San Pedro, is the world's oldest freeway.

U.S. 101, the **Ventura Freeway** from Ventura to North Hollywood, runs inland from Ventura along the outer rim of the Santa Monica Mountains in the San Fernando Valley, serving Thousand Oaks, Woodland Hills, Encino, Van Nuys, Sherman Oaks, Studio City, and North Hollywood. In North Hollywood it veers over the Santa Monica Mountains toward Hollywood, Silver Lake, and downtown, becoming the **Hollywood Freeway.**

I-105, the **Glen Anderson Freeway,** is scheduled to open in mid-1993. It will run east from LAX and the San Diego Fwy. to the San Gabriel Riverbed.

Bicycles

The best bike routes are along beaches. The most popular route is the **South Bay Bicycle Path.** It runs from Santa Monica to Torrance (19 mi.), winding over the sandy beaches of the South Bay before heading south all the way to San Diego. For maps and advice, write to any **AAA** office. Their local headquarters is at 2601 S. Figueroa (213-741-3111), near Adams, where you can talk to helpful and friendly **Norty Stewart,** "the Source" for bicycling information in Southern California.

Renting a bike has become increasingly expensive. Most shops are found near the piers of the various beaches and are especially concentrated on Washington Blvd. near the Venice/Marina Del Rey beach. Those planning extended stays should look into purchasing a used bike; check the classifieds or the weekly *Recycler.*

Walking and Hitchhiking: Not

The band Missing Persons was bang-on when it sang "Nobody walks in L.A." L.A. pedestrians are a lonely breed. The largely deserted streets of commercial centers will seem eerie to the first-time visitor. Unless you're running in the L.A. Marathon, moving from one part of the city to another on foot is a ludicrous idea—distances are just too great. Nevertheless, some colorful areas such as Melrose, Westwood, and Hollywood are best explored by foot. Venice Beach is a most enjoyable place to walk. Here, you'll be in the company of the thousands of Venetian beach-goers, and Venice's sights and shopping areas are all relatively close to one another. You may also wish to call **Walking Tours of Los Angeles** for tours of El Pueblo de Los Angeles State Historic Park (213-628-1274), City Hall (213-485-4423), or the Music Center (213-972-7483). The **Los Angeles Conservancy** (213-623-8687) offers nine different walking tours of the downtown area. Tours cost $5; advance reservations required.

D*o not* hitchhike. It is neither safe nor legal on freeways and many streets.

Accommodations

Warning: If you arrive at LAX, do not accept an offer of free transportation to an unknown hostel. Hostels that are operating illegally often find business by meeting international flights to seek out backpackers. Stricter policing of hostels by the city should reduce such encounters, but do not compromise your safety. *Let's Go* only lists legitimate hostels, all of which provide transportation assistance or are accessible by public transportation.

Many inexpensive lodgings in Los Angeles bear a frightening resemblance to the House of Usher. Dozens of flophouses around the Greyhound station charge between $10 and $20 nightly, but those unnerved by skid-row street life should look elsewhere. Tolerable lodgings fall roughly into four categories: hostels, run-down but safe hotels, residential hotels offering weekly rates (which can save a bundle), and budget motels well off the beaten track. Unless you're set on a specific place, reservations are only necessary for July and August. The useful and comprehensive (though a bit upscale) *L.A. Lodging Guide* is available at the L.A. Visitors Center (see Practical Information). **Youth hostel passes** may be obtained from UCLA's Expo Center (310-825-0831).

Los Angeles has no **campgrounds** convenient to public transport. Even motorists face at least a 40-minute commute from campsites to downtown. The only safe place to camp in L.A. County that is even vaguely nearby is **Leo Carrillo State Beach,** on PCH (Rte. 1), 28 mi. northwest of Santa Monica at the Ventura County line (818-706-1310). The north part of the beach lays out 134 sites on the sand at $9 per night. Inland are developed sites with coin showers for $16 a night. Make reservations through MISTIX. Sites are first-come, first-served.

Downtown

Though busy and relatively safe by day, the downtown area metamorphoses when the workday ends. Never venture here alone after dark, especially in the area between Broadway and Main. When renting, don't be afraid to haggle, especially off-season. (The following phone numbers are all **area code 213.**)

Royal Host Olympic Motel, 901 W. Olympic Blvd., (626-6255). The ritziest of the budget hotels—beautiful rooms, with bathtubs, balconies, telephone, radio, and color cable TV. Some rooms have kitchens. Singles $36. Doubles $43, with kitchenettes $45-50. Students can get a double for as low as $34.

Hotel Stillwell, 828 S. Grand St. (627-1151). Recently refurbished, this ultra-clean hotel is the most sensible downtown. Rooms bright and pleasantly decorated. Indian restaurant and American grill in hotel, Mexican restaurant next door. A/C, color TV.Singles $35. Doubles $45.

Park Plaza Hotel, 607 S. Park View St. (384-5281), on the west corner of 6th St. across from MacArthur Park. Built in 1927, this eerily grandiose art deco monument has a 3-story marble-floored lobby and a monumental staircase. The Plaza once entertained Bing Crosby and Eleanor Roosevelt, but now caters mainly to semi-permanent residents, especially students from the Otis Art Institute next door. Olympic size pool. A/C, color TV. Ignore the more expensive rooms; the older ones are quite pleasant. Singles $35. Doubles $40. Suite $60. Make reservations at least a week in advance.

Motel de Ville, 1123 W. 7th St. (213-624-8474). 2 blocks west of the Hilton. Multilingual staff (Japanese, Chinese, English) welcomes international travelers. Heated pool, free HBO. Singles $35. Doubles $37.

Orchid Hotel, 819 S. Flower St. (624-5855). Central downtown location and cleanliness make up for the cramped rooms. A/C, color TV. Singles $30. Doubles $35. Weekly: singles $152; doubles $183. Reservations recommended.

Budget Inn, 1710 W. 7th St. (483-3470). Location across the Harbor Fwy. from downtown could be more convenient. Rooms are fairly antiseptic. Color TV, swimming pool. One or two people $35; up to four people $45. Weekly $150, $200 respectively.

Hollywood

Jam-packed with activities and blessed with excellent bus service to other areas of L.A., Hollywood is a convenient tourist base. **Hollywood Blvd.,** east of the main strip, is lined with budget motels, as is **Sunset Blvd.** Despite its charms, the area gets creepy at night; side streets can be dangerous. (The following phone numbers are all **area code 213.**)

Hollywood International Guest House and Hostel, 6561 Franklin Ave. (850-6287). Located 2 blocks north of Hollywood Blvd. on the corner of Whitley and Franklin. Look for street number; no sign. Beautiful house with full kitchen, living room, and carpeted rooms for 2-4 people. Linen included. No curfew. Check-in 9am-8pm. $10 per night. Call for a ride.

Banana Bungalow Hollywood, 2775 Cahuenga Blvd. (851-1129) in W. Hollywood, just past Hollywood Bowl in Highland. Airport pick-up and shuttles to area attractions. Nightly movies and weekend parties. Mostly mixed-sex rooms for six with decent bathrooms. Linen and breakfast included. $14. International passport required. Double rooms $42 per night; no passport required.

Hollywood Wilshire YMCA Hotel and Hostel, 1553 Hudson Ave. (467-4161). By far the best budget lodging in Hollywood. Located 1½ blocks south of Hollywood Blvd., the hostel rooms are clean and light, with no phones, TV, or A/C. They do, however, come with use of gym and pool. Pay phone on each floor. Must be over 18. Visitors allowed 7-10pm. Singles $29. Doubles $39. No reservations. Kitchen, laundry, and lounge. 7-day max. stay. Hostel rate $8 per night.

Folks Tel International Hostel, 8775 Sunset Blvd. (310-657-3889) in W. Hollywood. Look for Beverly Sundet Hotel sign. Rooms and bathrooms are visibly old, but pool, airport pick-up, and meals compensate. $15, passport required. Private rooms $54, no passport required.

Hollywood Downtowner Motel, 5601 Hollywood Blvd. (464-7191). Pleasant rooms, swimming pool, helpful management, A/C, telephone, TV. Full kitchen units $2-3 extra (min. 4-night stay for kitchenette rooms). Singles $38. Doubles $40-46. Cheaper rates in winter. Free parking.

Beverly Hills, Westside, Wilshire District

The Westside is an attractive part of town, but room rates are generally ugly. Call the **UCLA Off-Campus Housing Office** (310-825-4491), 100 Sproul Hall, and see if they can find you students who have a spare room (through their "roommate share board").

Century City-Westwood Motel, 10604 Santa Monica Blvd. (310-475-4422). Attractive rooms with fridges, color TV, A/C. Even the bathrooms sparkle. On the southern part of "Little Santa Monica," the smaller road that parallels the divided boulevard. Singles $45, additional person $5; 4-person max.

Bevonshire Lodge Motel, 7575 Beverly Blvd. (213-936-6154), near Farmers Market and Beverly Center. A popular choice for families. A/C, color TV. Singles $39. Doubles $43.

Crest Motel, 7701 Beverly Blvd. (213-931-8108), near Hollywood and Beverly Hills. An agreeable place, although some bathrooms would make Mr. Clean cringe. Pool, color TV, and A/C. Singles $36. Doubles $38. Key deposit $5.

Wilshire Orange Hotel, 6060 W. 8th St. (213-931-9533), in West L.A. near Wilshire Blvd. and Fairfax Ave. Buses #20, 21, 22, and 308 serve Wilshire Blvd. from downtown. In a residential neighborhood near many major sights. Most rooms have fridges, color TV; all but two have private or semi-private bath. Weekly housekeeping. 2-day min. stay. Singles $45. Doubles $48. Weekly: singles $145; doubles $225.

Santa Monica and Venice

The hostels at Venice Beach are budget havens—they're just about the cheapest way to stay and the most enjoyable way to play in L.A. You may miss the Sunset Strip (and L.A. traffic), but you'll find dazzling beaches, funky architecture, and a mellow, eccentric sun-worshipping community. The city center is serviced by Santa Monica's Big Blue Bus (see Practical Information). The hostels are a popular destination for foreign students. (The following phone numbersare all **area code 310.**)

Santa Monica International HI/AYH Hostel, 1436 2nd St., Santa Monica (393-9913). Still a gem among beach area's many hostels. Boasts a colossal kitchen, copious common rooms, and a casual, California-cool clientele. Curfew 2am. $13.50 per night, HI/AYH members only. $2 rental for bedsheets.

Share-Tel International Hostel, 20 Brooks Ave., Venice (392-0325). ½-block off the boardwalk. Student ID or passport required. Family-style atmosphere; pleasant rooms with kitchen facilities and bathroom fit 4-12 people each. Kitchen, continental breakfast, safe, linen service, no curfew. $15 per person, $100 per week.

Centerpoint Backpackers, 11 S. Venice Blvd. Shared suite accommodations for 6 include wooden bunks, linen, and full kitchen. $14 per night. Area tours and outings with spunky staff. No curfew or age restrictions. Children welcome. Call about airport pick-up.

Venice Beach Hostel, 701 Washington St. (306-5180), above Celebrity Cleaners. Relaxed and homey, with a large lounge, cable TV, and sunroof (bathing suits optional). Popular with international travelers. Near bars and nightclubs. Free transportation from LAX. $12 per night, $70 per week. Double rooms $15 per person. Open 24 hrs.

Jim's at The Beach, 17 Brooks Ave., Venice (396-5138), across the street from Share-Tel. Passport required. 6 beds per room max. Clean, bright rooms, kitchen. No curfew. $15 per night, $90 per week. Linen included.

Venice Beach Cotel, 25 Windward Ave., Venice (399-7649), on the boardwalk between Zephyr Court and 17th Ave. Located close to beaches; shuttle from LAX. To stay in the hostel part you must show your passport. A lively hostel full of young international travelers. 3-6 people share each tidy, functional room. No food allowed. Bar and social area lively from 7pm-1am. No curfew. $12 per person, with bath $15. Private rooms with and without ocean view $33-49.50.

Marina Hostel, 2915 Yale Ave., Marina Del Rey (301-3983), 3 blocks west from Lincoln Blvd. Near Venice in a quiet residential neighborhood. Privately owned, friendly household with lockers, linen, laundry, and a kitchen with microwave. Some bunks, some floor mattresses. Living room with cable TV. $12 per guest.

Airport Interclub Hostel, 2221 Lincoln Blvd., Venice (305-0250), near Venice Blvd. Passport required. Festive after-hours common-room with many nationalities bumping elbows. Surfer murals on the walls. Rooms sleep 6, or you can sleep in the 30-bed dorm. Mixed-sex accommodations. No lockout during summer, otherwise 11am-4pm. Curfew 4am. If you're out later than *that*, you're probably not coming back that night anyhow. Linen. Laundry room. $14 per person plus $5 deposit. Open 24 hrs.

Cadillac Hotel, 401 Ocean Front Walk, Venice (399-8876). A beautiful art deco landmark. Airport shuttle service, limited parking. Boardwalk and beach just outside. Private sundeck. No curfew. Shared accommodations $18 per night, private ocean-view rooms $49 and up.

Food

The range of culinary options in L.A. is directly proportionate to its ethnic diversity: Jewish and Eastern European food center in the Fairfax area; Mexican in East L.A.; Japanese, Chinese, Vietnamese, and Thai around Little Tokyo and Chinatown; seafood along the coast; and Hawaiian, Indian, and Ethiopian scattered throughout.

One of the few foods truly indigenous to the area—and perhaps the one that best epitomizes L.A. culture—is fast food. Birthplace of the Big Mac, **McDonald's** got its start in Southern Cal in the 50s, and Los Angelenos seem to have spent the intervening years trying to improve upon the recipe; burger joints deep-fat-fry on nearly every corner. To study the phenomenon, try **In 'n' Out Burger** (various locations, call 818-287-4377), a family-owned chain that has steadfastly refused to franchise its stores or expand beyond the L.A. area. The edible rewards of this stubbornness are evidenced by In 'n' Out's burgers and fries, arguably the best in the business.

The best way to enjoy the natural foods that made California famous is to find a health-food store or co-op that sells organic and small-farm produce. Prices are lower than those in the enormous public markets, and the quality generally superior, although the markets offer greater variety. The **Farmer's Market,** 6333 W. 3rd St. (213-933-9211), at Fairfax in the Wilshire District, has over 160 produce stalls, meat vendors, small restaurants, and sidewalk cafés. The market has become a tourist attraction, so bargains have become an endangered species. (Open Mon.-Sat. 9am-7pm, Sun. 10am-6pm; Oct.-May Mon.-Sat. 9am-6:30pm, Sun. 10am-5pm.) A less touristy, less expensive source of produce is the **Grand Central Public Market,** 317 S. Broadway (624-2378), a large baby-blue building downtown. The main market in the Hispanic shopping district, Grand Central has more than 50 stands selling produce, clothing, housewares, costume jewelry, vitamins, and fast food. (Open Mon.-Sat. 9am-6pm, Sunday 10am-6pm.)

Nearby cafés keep the same hours as the markets. The most famous is **Vickman's** at 1228 E. 8th St. (213-622-3852; open Mon.-Fri. 3am-3pm, Sat. 3am-1pm, Sun. 7am-1pm). For listings on late night cafés, restaurants, and combination club/restaurants see Entertainment.

Downtown

The following are all in **area code** 213.

Philippe's, The Original, 1001 N. Alameda (628-3781), 2 blocks north of Union Station. The sheer variety of food combined with sizeable portions and low prices make this an exemplary locale for mid-day victuals. Philippe's claims to have originated the French-dipped sandwich; varieties include beef, pork, ham, turkey, or lamb ($3-4). Macaroni salad $.85 and a glass of iced tea $.40. Top it off with a large slice of pie ($1.80) with a $.10 cup of java, and you've got a colossal lunch at this L.A. institution. Open daily 6am-10pm.

The Pantry, 877 S. Figueroa St. (972-9279). Open since the 20s. You may have to share a table with a complete stranger, and the waiter is as likely to insult you as to talk your ear off, but the patrons like it that way. The restaurant seats only 84 but serves 3000 meals a day. The owners recently opened a deli/bakery next door (roast beef sandwich $4.25). Be prepared to wait for enormous breakfast specials ($6), especially on weekends. Sunday brunch at the Pantry is an L.A. tradition. Open 24 hrs.

La Luz Del Dia, 1 W. Olvera St. (628-7495). This authentic and inexpensive Mexican restaurant is hidden amidst the many tourist-trap Mexican joints along historic Olvera St. Tortillas are still made on the premises, and the salsa is *picante*. Combo plates ($4). Open Tues.-Sun. 11am-10pm.

Gorky's, 536 E. 8th St. (627-4060). On the southeast edge of downtown. One-of-a-kind restaurant, serving Socialist Realist Russian cuisine (i.e. cafeteria-style) in an avant-garde setting. Entertaining entrées from $5.50. Brewery on premises; live music Wed.-Sun. at 8:30pm. Open 24 hrs.

Café China, 1123 W. 7th St. Filling combination plate ($4.50) like spicy shrimp or almond chicken served with soup, egg roll, and rice all day. Open Mon.-Fri. 9am-8:30pm, Sat. 9am-2am.

Sushi Bukyu, 318 E. 2nd St. (617-2280), in Little Tokyo. The best Japanese food for your money in Little Tokyo. À la carte menu $2.50-7.50. Full dinner $8-10. Open Thurs.-Tues. 11:30am-midnight.

Hollywood and West Hollywood

Hollywood is famed for its outrageously priced celebrity hangouts and less well-known for the best budget dining in L.A., with its scores of good ethnic restaurants.

Seafood Bay, 3916 Sunset Blvd. (213-664-3902), at Sanborn in Silver Lake, east of Hollywood. This modest eatery in a quiet residential area skimps on decor to support a wide variety of seafood at great prices. "Light meals" such as fettucine with clam sauce are plenty filling and run around $6. The fish is fantastic, and the accompaniment—sourdough garlic bread, pungent rice pilaf, heaps of sautéed mushrooms—receive the same loving attention. Open Mon.-Thurs. 11:30am-10pm, Fri.-Sat. 11:30am-10:30pm, Sun. 4-10pm.

Lucy's El Adobe Café, 5536 Melrose Ave. (213-462-9421), 1 block east of Gower St. This tiny family-run restaurant is a favorite among downtown politicos and Paramount executives from across the street. Former-governor-*cum*-presidential-candidate Jerry Brown and rock-star-*cum*-big-band-belter Linda Ronstadt allegedly met here. Some of the best Mexican food in town. As you munch on your tostada ($6), glance at the celebrity photos adorning the walls. Full dinners (entrée, soup or salad, rice, and beans) $8-10. Open Mon.-Sat. 11:30am-11pm.

Ara's, 4953 Hollywood Blvd. (213-660-3739). Authentic and tantalizing Armenian restaurant. Various kebabs ($7) include pita bread, rice pilaf, and curried vegetables. Open Mon.-Sat. noon-8:30pm.

Sammy's Thai BBQ, 8281 Santa Monica Blvd. (213-654-7952) in W. Hollywood. A friendly place with even chummier prices. Teriyaki beef dinner with rice and salad $3.75. Twelve BBQ shrimp for a zippy $5.75. Open Sun.-Thurs. 11am-10pm, Fri.-Sat. 11am-11pm.

Boardner's Restaurant, 1652 N. Cherokee Ave. (213-462-9621). Boardner's has been serving Americana at nearly the same prices ($3-8) since WW II. Open daily 11am-10pm, drinks 'til 2am.

Pink's Famous Chili Dogs, 711 La Brea Ave. (213-931-4223). The chili dogs are good and cheap ($2) and that's why Pink's has been around since 1939, every minute, every hour, every day. Open 24 hrs.

Beverly Hills, Westside, Wilshire District

Beverly Hills and the Wilshire District offer some of the finest dining in the country; don't expect any bargains, however. La Brea Ave. and Pico Blvd. both offer a wide variety of restaurants. The following are in **area code** 310.

Ed Debeure's, 134 N. La Cienoga Blvd. (659-1952), in Beverly Hills. Far and away the most mirthful of the phony 50s diners ("famous since 1984"). Fun burgers like Hoppin' John's Atomic Burger with jalapeño and jack cheese ($5.25). Hamburgers $4.55-5.55. Full bar. Open Sun.-Thurs. 11:30am-11pm, Fri.-Sat. 11:30am-1am.

Trattoria Angeli, 11651 Santa Monica Blvd. (213-478-1191). Rustic and comfortable. Order a large *agua* with your spicy Pizza Puttanesca ($7.25) with olives, capers, and red hot peppers. Open Sun-Thurs. 11:30am-9:30pm, Fri.-Sat. noon-11pm.

El Nopal, 10426 National Blvd. (559-4732), in West L.A., between Motor and Overland, just south of the Santa Monica Fwy. Known as "home of the pregnant burrito." This famed burrito *embarasado* ($5.50), stuffed with chicken and avocado, will make your tummy look like it has a bun in the oven. Smaller burritos $2-3. Tasty tacos and tangy salsa ($1.75). Take-out available. Open Mon.-Sat. 11am-10pm, Sun. 11am-9pm.

Tommy's Original Hamburgers, 2575 W. Beverly Blvd. (389-9060), Wilshire District. Ignore the multitude of Tommy's knock-offs and head to the winner of the sloppiest chili dog contest (the paper towel dispensers every 2 ft. along the counters aren't just there for looks). Chili dog $1.25, chili burger $1.75, double cheeseburger $3. Open 24 hrs.

Westwood

Westwood is filled with chic and convenient eateries perfect before a movie or while shopping, and you'll find everything from falafel to *gelato* in corner shops. The following are all in **area code 310.**

Sak's Teriyaki, 1121 Glendon Ave. (208-2002), in Westwood. Excellent, low-priced Japanese plates including chicken and beef teriyaki ($3.70-5). Popular with students. Happy hour special ($2.50) 3-6pm. Open Mon.-Thurs. 11am-10pm, Fri.-Sat. 11am-11pm, Sun. 11am-9pm.

Tacos Tacos, 1084 Glendon Ave. (208-2038), Westwood Village. Trendy "Southwestern café" with blue corn chicken tacos ($1.75). Try the *horchata* (cinnamon-flavored rice water, $1.25). Open Sun.-Wed. 11am-10:30pm, Thurs.-Sat. 11am-12:30pm.

Fatburger, 10955 Kenross (310-208-7365). Order a Double King chili-cheese-egg-burger, roll up your sleeves, and open wide. Fat 'n' juicy burgers from $2.50. Open Sun.-Thurs. 10am-3am, Fri.-Sat. 10am-4am.

Earth, Wind, and Flour, 1776 Westwood Blvd. (310-470-2499). A place to kick back and admire rustic wood panelling. $13 gets you a large pizza that stuffs four. Open Mon.-Thurs. 11:30am-11pm, Fri.-Sat. 11:30am-midnight, Sun. 4-11pm.

Santa Monica and Venice

Unfortunately, most of Santa Monica's eateries are overpriced, and most of Venice's eateries are overgreased. The new **EATZ Café** in Santa Monica Place offers 17 different types of mall food to choose from, a number of which are tasty and reasonably priced. The following are all in **area code** 310.

Tijuana Restaurant, 11785 W. Olympic Blvd. (473-9293), in West L.A. The menu here looks like a Tijuana jai alai program, but the food is first-rate. A woman stands in the entryway of the dining room hand-making the tortillas for dinner. If you're feeling adventurous, try the *nopalitas,* young cactus served on a tortilla ($2.75). Mexican seafood entrées and combo plates run $7-9. Dinner special from $6. Open Sun.-Thurs. 11am-10pm, Fri.-Sat. 11am-11pm.

Humphrey Yogart Café, 11677 San Vicente Blvd. (207-2206), in Brentwood. Come here for dessert, schweetheart. Start with vanilla frozen yogurt (sweet or tart) and blend in whatever bizarre ingredient combination you wish. A medium with 2 ingredients is $2.60. Humphrey's also serves sandwiches, soups, and salads. Always crowded. Open Sun. 11am-10:30pm, Mon.-Thurs. 9am-11:30pm, Fri. 9am-10:30pm, Sat. 10am-11:30pm.

Tito's Tacos, 11222 Washington Place (391-5780), in Culver City at Sepulveda, 1 block north of Washington Blvd., virtually *beneath* the San Diego Fwy. The name should have been Tito's Burritos, since the burrito, with its huge hunks of shredded beef, is the star attraction. At a measly $2.10, it's also the most expensive menu item. You can order to go. Plenty of parking. Open daily 9am-11:30pm.

Benita's Frites, 1437 3rd St. Promenade (458-2889), in Santa Monica. French fries served the Belgian way, in a paper cone with *andoulause* sauce (red and green bell peppers, mayonnaise, tomato, and garlic), chili, or peanut curry satay on top ($2-2.80, toppings $.30-45.) Open Sun. noon-8pm, Mon. 11:30am-4pm., Tues.-Thurs. 11:30am-10pm, Fri.-Sat. 11:30am-10:30pm.

San Fernando Valley

The entirety of Ventura Blvd. is chock full of restaurants. Lunch in Studio City is your best chance to catch sight of the stars, but *don't ask for autographs.* One notable stop is **Chili John's,** 2018 W. Burbank Blvd. (818-846-3611), in Burbank. The chili recipe hasn't changed since 1900 (the price has—a bowl is $4.25). As your mouth burns, check out the mountain landscape on the wall; it took the former owner/chef/artist over 20 years of in-between-customer moments to paint. Take-out. (Open Sept.-June Tues.-Fri. 11am-7pm, Sat. 11am-4pm.)

Pasadena

Fair Oaks Ave. and Colorado Blvd., in the Old Town section of Pasadena, are punctuated with cafés and Mexican restaurants. The two notable ones that follow are in **area code 818.**

Los Tacos, 1 W. California Blvd. (795-9291). Enter around the corner of Fair Oaks Blvd. Fast-food Mexican-style. Soft tacos with choice of filling ($1.15). Combo plates ($4.69). A popular weekend stop for local teeny-boppers. Open Sun.-Mon. 9am-10pm, Tues.-Thurs. 9am-1am, Fri.-Sat. 9am-2am.

Dora's Sandwich Shop, 725 E. Green (795-3881). From the outside, a tiny lean-to, with inside décor no more inspiring. Undaunted crowds flow through at lunchtime for made-to-order sandwiches of every conceivable variety ($2-4). Open Mon.-Fri. 6am-6pm.

Sights

Downtown

A downtown area is the theoretical epicenter for Los Angeles' splintered communities. Various ethnic neighborhoods, white-collar workplaces, and a substantial homeless population coexist here by a cruel joke of geography. This uneasy convergence is no longer openly explosive, but visitors should be cautious. The average sightseer will not likely encounter the widely publicized racial tensions but may face dangers engendered by the extreme poverty in this area. Keep valuables at home, and leave nothing in your car that you want to see again. Pay to park in a secured lot and walk in groups even during the day. The downtown area alone is larger than most cities. The financial district is a jungle of glass and steel, where gigantic corporate offices of such companies as ARCO, Bank of America, Wells Fargo, and AT&T crowd the busy downtown center (an area bounded roughly by 3rd and 6th St., Figueroa St., and Grand Ave.). The brand new I.M. Pei-designed **First Interstate World Center,** 633 W. 5th St. (955-8151), dominates a skyline made famous by the TV show *L.A. Law.* At 73 stories and 1017 ft., it is the tallest building west of the Mississippi River.

The **Oviatt Building** at 617 S. Olive St. is the downtown area's art deco masterpiece. The **Times Mirror Building** at 220 W. 1st, with the exception of the 1970s addition, is a classic example of Cal Moderne. Five cylindrical fingers of the **Westin Bonaventure Hotel,** 404 S. Figueroa St. snatch the smog. The **Civic Center,** a solid wall of bureaucratic architecture bounded by the Hollywood Fwy. (U.S. 101), Grand, First and San Pedro St., runs east from the Music Center. It ends at **City Hall,** 200 N. Spring St. Another of the best-known buildings in the Southland, the hall was cast as the home of the *Daily Planet* in the *Superman* TV series and has an **observation deck** on the 27th floor.

Farther north lies the historic birthplace of Los Angeles. In the place where the original city center once stood, **El Pueblo de Los Angeles State Historic Park** (680-2525; open Mon.-Fri. 10am-8pm) preserves a number of buildings from the Spanish and Mexican eras. Start out at the **docent center,** 130 Paseo de la Plaza (628-1274). The center offers free walking tours (Tues.-Sat. 10am-1pm on the hour, but call to check first, as tours are sometimes cancelled, 628-1274) and a free bus tour of L.A. (1st and 3rd Wed. of each month; make reservations as early as possible.) The **Old Plaza,** with its century-old Moreton Bay fig trees and huge bandstand, sprawls at the center of the pueblo. Tours start here and wind their way past the **Avila Adobe** (1818), 10 E. Olvera St., the oldest house in the city (the original adobe has been replaced with concrete in order to meet earthquake regulations), followed by **Pico House,** 500 N. Main St., once L.A.'s most luxurious hotel. Farther down, at 535 N. Main St., the **Plaza Church,** established in 1818, almost melts away from the street with its soft, rose adobe façade. Most tours also include the catacombs that formerly held gambling and opium dens. The **visitors center** is located in the **Sepulveda House** (1887), 622 N. Main St. (628-1274; open Mon.-Fri. 9am-4pm.) For interested visitors, they screen *Pueblo of Promise,* an 18-minute history of L.A. **Olvera Street,** one of L.A.'s original roads, has miraculously survived; it is now called Tijuana North by the locals, and one tawdry stand after another sells schlocky Mexican handicrafts. Here L.A.'s large Chicano community celebrates Mexican Independence Day on **Cinco de Mayo.** In December, the **Los Posados** celebration includes a candlelight procession commemorating Mary's search for budget lodgings in which to give birth to Jesus (Dec. 16-24; 625-5045). Across Alameda St. from El Pueblo is the grand old **Union Station,** undergoing renovations in 1992.

Bustling **Chinatown** lies north of this area, roughly bordered by Yale, Spring, Ord, and Bernard St. From downtown, take the DASH shuttle. (See Getting Around, Public Transportation.) This once vice-ridden neighborhood taught Roman Polanski's Jake Giddis (played by Mr. L.A. himself, Jack Nicholson) just what a tough ol' world it is out there. **Little Tokyo,** yet another of downtown L.A.'s ethnic neighborhoods, is centered on 2nd and San Pedro St. on the eastern edge of downtown. The **New Otani Hotel,** 120 S. Los Angeles St., one block south of the Civic Center between 1st and 2nd, rents its lavish Meiji-style rooms for up to $700 per night. For slightly less, you can have a drink in the elegant rooftop garden. The **Japanese Village Plaza** (213-620-8861), in the 300 block of E. 2nd St., is the center of the district and is a florid fusion of American shopping mall and Japanese design. The **Japanese American Cultural and Community Center,** 244 S. San Pedro St. (628-2725), was designed by Buckminster Fuller and Isamu Noguchi, who crafted the monumental sculpture for the courtyard. (Administrative offices open Mon.-Fri. 9am-5pm.)

Broadway south of First St. is predominantly Mexican-American. All billboards and store signs are in Spanish, and the **Grand Central Public Market** (see Food) takes center stage. One of many Spanish-language cinemas housed in old movie palaces is the **Million Dollar Theater,** 307 S. Broadway (239-0939). Peek into the baroque auditorium and inspect the stars in the sidewalk out front, each bearing the name of a Chicano celebrity, a *rambla de fama* to complement Hollywood's. Across the street, the **Bradbury Building,** 304 S. Broadway, stands as a relic of L.A.'s Victorian past. Uninspiring from the street, this exquisite 1893 office building is mostly lobby. Its ornate staircases and elevators (wrought in iron, wood, and marble) often are bathed in sunlight, which pours in through the glass roof. Film crews regularly shoot period scenes here. (Open Mon.-Sat. 10am-5pm. Self-guided tour $1.)

Perhaps the best reason to spend time downtown is to see L.A.'s cultural attractions. Undoubtedly the most striking, chic, and caffeinated museum in the area is the **Museum of Contemporary Art (MOCA),** showcasing art from 1940 to the present. The main museum is located at California Plaza, 250 S. Grand Ave. (626-6222), and is a sleek and geometric architectural marvel. Its collection focuses on Abstract Expressionism, and includes works by Pollock, Calder, Miró, and Giacometti. Its interior is spacious, illuminated by the pyramidal skylights in the ceiling. The second MOCA facility is the **Temporary Contemporary,** 152 N. Central Ave., in Little Tokyo. This location has been closed until the spring of 1994 to accommodate construction. (MOCA admission $4, seniors and students with ID $2, under 12 free. Everyone free Thurs. 5-8pm. Wheelchair accessible.) Across from City Hall East, between the Santa Ana Fwy. and Temple in the L.A. Mall, is the **L.A. Children's Museum,** 310 N. Main St. (687-8800), where many of the exhibits are hands-on. Children are invited to fill performance spaces with giggling costumed improv or to hit the arts and crafts tables with their sights set on the MOCA. (Open Wed.-Thurs. 2-4pm, Sat.-Sun. 10am-5pm. Admission $4, under 2 free.)

Perhaps the most peculiar and best-hidden of the downtown museums is the **Museum of Neon Art (MONA),** 704 Traction Ave. (617-1580), in the artists' neighborhood to the east of Little Tokyo. Exhibits range from neon artwork to other types of electric and kinetic sculpture. Pick up a MONA t-shirt, depicting a neon sculpture of the *Mona Lisa.* Traction Ave. runs east of Alameda St., between 2nd and 3rd St. (Open Tues.-Sat. 11am-5pm. Admission $3, seniors and students $1.75, under 17 free.) Los Angeles' **Museum of African-American Art,** the first of its kind in the American West, anchors pieces in historical context in a way that both disturbs and inspires. (Open Wed.-Sat. 11am-6pm, Sun. noon-5pm. Free.)

Exposition Park

Among the most notable sights near downtown is **Exposition Park,** a dying area kicked into life for the 1932 and 1984 Olympics. The park, southwest of downtown just off the Harbor Fwy., is bounded by Exposition Blvd., Figueroa St., Vermont Ave., and Santa Barbara Ave. From downtown, take bus #40 or 42 (both from 1st and Broadway) to the park's southern edge. From Hollywood, take #204 down Vermont.

The park is dominated by several major museums, including the **California Museum of Science and Industry,** 700 State Dr. (744-7400). Enter at the corner of Figueroa and Exposition next to the United DC-8 parked out front. Many of the exhibits are either corporate or governmental propaganda; those left to the MSI's own devices are rather amateurish. IBM and Bell Telephone sponsor mathematics and communications, while McDonald's is inexplicably allowed to handle a display on nutrition. One exhibit re-creates an earthquake—complete with a shaking floor and mock news report. The museum also includes the **Kinsey Hall of Health,** which has an exhibit on AIDS and uses interactive computer displays to educate visitors about their bodies and the effects of diet, alcohol, and drug use. The **Hall of Economics and Finance** does its best to enliven what even its practitioners call "the dismal science." The **Aerospace Building,** as big as a hangar, exhibits $8 million worth of aircraft, including the *Gemini 11* space capsule. New for 1993 are exhibits on Antarctica. (Open daily 10am-5pm. Free. Parking $2, bring quarters.) The museum also runs an **IMAX Theater** (744-2014), which projects films onto a five-story-tall screen and bombards viewers with six-channel surround sound. Films are an hour long, covering such subjects as space flight and the great outdoors. (Showings daily every hr. 10am-9pm. Admission $5.50, over 55, students, and ages 4-17 $4. Call ahead for show info.)

In the same complex, separate from the MSI, is the **California Afro-American Museum,** 600 State Dr. (744-7432), with a permanent sculpture collection, and a research library focused on Afro-American contributions to science, humanities and sports. (Open daily 10am-5pm. Free. Research library open Mon.-Fri. 10am-5pm.)

The park's other major museum is the **Los Angeles County Natural History Museum,** 900 Exposition Blvd. (744-3466). Exhibits here cover American history from 1472-1914, pre-Columbian cultures, North American and African mammals, and dinosaurs. The **E. Hadley Stuart, Jr. Hall of Gems and Minerals** showcases a dazzling array of precious rocks. (Open Tues.-Sun. 10am-5pm. Admission $5, seniors and students $2.50, ages 5-12 $1, under 5 free.)

Exposition Park also includes the galactic **Los Angeles Memorial Coliseum,** 2601 S. Figueroa St., home of the Los Angeles Raiders and the USC Trojans football teams, and the **Sports Arena,** home of the Los Angeles Clippers basketball team and a common venue for rock concerts.

The **University of Southern California (USC)** campus is opposite Exposition Park on Exposition Blvd. The campus is wide, beautiful, and generally safe during the day. Note the blue paw prints left on Tommy Trojan by raiding arch-rival UCLA Bruins. The **Fisher Gallery,** 823 Exposition Blvd. (743-2799), includes the Armand Hammer collection of 18th- and 19th-century Dutch paintings. (Open early Sept.-early May Tues.-Sat. noon-5pm. Free.)

To the south and east of the USC campus seethes **Watts,** a neighborhood made notorious by riots in 1965 and 1992. From the center of what is formally known as the Watts District rise the **Watts Towers,** 1765 E. 107th St. (569-8181), a remarkably impressive work of folk art. Watts resident Simon Rodia singlehandedly built the towers over a period of 33 years. These delicate towers of glistening fretwork, decorated with mosaics of broken glass, ceramic tile, and sea shells, are an inspiring testament to the power of one man's extraordinary vision and tireless dedication. Although the towers are a good seven-mi. drive from Exposition Park and are in a dangerous part of town, they are worth the trip. (By bus, take RTD #55 from Main St. downtown and get off at Compton Ave. and 108th St. The towers are one block to the east.) For a guided tour of the towers, which are undergoing restoration, call the Watts Towers Arts Center at 569-8181. The center is located at 1727 E. 107th St., right next to the towers, and is open Tues.-Sat. 9am-5pm. (From downtown take the Metro Blue Line and get off at 103 St. Station. Walk on 104th east to Beach, and then south to the corner of 106th and 107th.) The towers are open for exploration Sat.-Sun. from 10am-4pm. During the week the towers undergo restoration, and appointments must be made in advance. Next door, at 1727 E. 107th St. is the **Watts Tower Arts Center** (569-8181), which houses a permanent exhibit of folk instruments, as well as a changing gallery (open Tues.-Sat. 9am-4pm).

Hollywood Park, 1050 S. Prairie Ave. (419-1500), sponsors thoroughbred racing between April and July, and in November and December. The lovely track is landscaped with lagoons and tropical trees, and the facility is complete with restaurants and a children's play area. (Racing held Wed.-Sun. Post time 1:30pm. Admission $3, ages under 18 free.) At the corner of Manchester and Prairie Ave. is the **Great Western Forum** (673-1300), home of Wayne Gretzky's **Los Angeles Kings** hockey team as well as the **Los Angeles Lakers** basketball team, perhaps the most popular of L.A.'s many sports franchises.

Wilshire District and Hancock Park

Wilshire Boulevard, especially the "Miracle Mile" between Highland and Fairfax Ave., played a starring role in Los Angeles' westward suburban expansion. On what was then the end of the boulevard, the Bullocks Corporation gambled on attracting shoppers from downtown and in 1929 erected the massive, bronze-colored **Bullocks Wilshire** at 3050 Wilshire Blvd., near Vermont Ave., now called the **I. Magnin BW Wilshire.** Tours of this art deco landmark are offered by docents of the Los Angeles Conservancy (call 623-2489 to arrange one). The nearby residential neighborhoods and their 20s architecture are worth exploring in a car but potentially unsafe on foot. The streets south of Wilshire opposite Hancock Park are lined with Spanish-style bungalows and the occasional modernist manse.

A few miles further down Wilshire, in **Hancock Park,** an acrid smell pervades the vicinity of the **La Brea Tar Pits,** one of the world's most popular hangouts for fossilized early mammals. Most of the one million bones recovered from the pits between 1913 and 1915 have found new homes in the **George C. Page Museum of La Brea Discoveries,** 5801 Wilshire Blvd. at Curson and Wilshire (for a fossilized recording 936-2230, for a live person 857-6311). Wilshire buses stop right in front of the museum to make finding a fossil more facile. The museum includes reconstructed Ice Age animals and murals of L.A. Ice Age life, a laboratory where paleontologists work behind plate-glass windows, and a display where you can feel what it's like to be struck in tar. Archeological digging continues in Pit 91 behind the adjacent county art museum. (Open Tues.-Sun. 10am-5pm. Admission $4, seniors and students $2, kids $.75. Free 2nd Tues. of each month. Tours of the museum are offered to the public Wed.-Sun. at 2:00pm. Tours of the grounds at 1pm.)

The **Los Angeles County Museum of Art (LACMA),** 5905 Wilshire Blvd. (857-6000), at the west end of Hancock Park, has a distinguished, comprehensive collection that should rebut any who argue that L.A.'s only culture is in its yogurt. Opened in 1965, the LACMA is the largest museum in the West and still growing. Five major buildings cluster around the **Times Mirror Central Court:** a Japanese pavilion, the Ahmanson Building (the museum's original building and home to most of its non-modern permanent collection), the Hammer Building (named for Arman, not M.C.), the Bing Center, and the Robert O. Anderson Building, a spectacular 1986 addition to the museum, with its façade of salmon-colored sandstone and glass. The museum offers a variety of tours and free talks daily. For schedules, check the info desk in the Central Court or contact the Docent Council at 857-6108. (Open Tues.-Fri. 10am-5pm, Sat.-Sun. 10am-6pm. Admission $5, seniors and students $3.50, ages 6-17 $1. Free 2nd Tues. of each month.)

Further down the street, at its temporary home in the May Company Building, the **Craft and Folk Art Museum,** 6067 Wilshire Blvd. (938-7197), displays a changing sample of folk art and contemporary crafts in a third floor gallery. (Free. Open Tues.-Sat. 10am-5pm, Sun. 11am-5pm.)

Similar to Jerusalem's famous Yad VaShem Holocaust Memorial is the **Martyrs Memorial and Museum of the Holocaust** (852-1234, ext. 3200), located in the Jewish Community Building, 6505 Wilshire Blvd., just east of Beverly Hills. Horrifying photographs and prisoners' personal items are displayed next to paintings and drawings made in the ghettos and death camps. The museum is on the 12th floor; sign in at the security desk. (Open Mon.-Thurs. 8:30am-5pm, Fri. 8:30am-3:30pm, Sun. 10am-5pm. Free.)

Hollywood

Today's visitors won't see a trace of the sunny farm community that first lured movie men to Hollywood's groves. In the early days of silent movies, independent producers and directors, many of them Jewish, sought to escape the tight control and restrictions of the conservative anti-Semitic Movie Trust based in New York. They began shooting films in the empty groves of Hollywood both to avoid the Trust's surveillance and to take advantage of the steady sunlight and infrequent rain (indoor lighting techniques had not been refined at the time). By the early 1920s, all the major studios had moved from the East Coast to this then-obscure suburb. Hollywood quickly became synonymous with the celluloid image. Home to the great stars (Garbo, Gable, Crawford) and the great studios (MGM, Paramount, Warner Bros., 20th Century Fox), Hollywood became an important arbiter of American mores and interpreter of the American Dream. Hollywood today has lost much of its glitter. The major studios have moved over the mountains into the San Fernando Valley, where they have more space to weave their ever-more-elaborate fantasies, and blockbusters are increasingly shot elsewhere in the U.S. or overseas. Hollywood Boulevard and other thoroughfares, once glittering and glamorous, are now rated XXX. At night, prostitutes peddle with their wears; pretty women work Hollywood and Sunset Blvd., while boys ply their trade on Santa Monica Boulevard (also known as S&M Blvd.). Hollywood is still a fascinating place, but a far cry from the Emerald City it was once thought to be. At 106, the *grand dame* shows her age and lives on memories of her more glorious past.

The **Hollywood sign**—those 50-ft.-high, slightly erratic letters perched on Mt. Cahuenga north of Hollywood—stands with New York's Statue of Liberty and Paris's Eiffel Tower as a universally recognized symbol of its city. The original 1923 sign, which read HOLLYWOODLAND, was an advertisement for a new subdivision in the Hollywood Hills (a caretaker lived behind one of the Ls). Over the years, people came to regard it as a civic monument. The city, which by 1978 had acquired the sign, reconstructed the crumbling letters, leaving off the last syllable. The sign has been a target of pranksters who have made it read everything from "HOLLYWEED" to "OLLYWOOD," after gap-toothed errand boy Lt. Col. Oliver North. For a closer look at the site, follow Beachwood Dr. up into the hills (bus #208; off Franklin Ave. between Vine St. and Western Ave.). Drive along the narrow twisting streets of the Hollywood Hills for glimpses of bizarre homes of the Rich and Famous, or detour to **Forest Lawn Memorial Park,** 6300 Forest Lawn Dr. (818-984-1711), on the other side of the hills. The park is a museum of early American history, with a mosaic mural and a collection of statues. (Open daily 9am-5pm. Free.)

Hollywood Boulevard itself, lined with souvenir shops, porno houses, clubs, and theaters, is busy day and night. The façade of **Mann's Chinese Theater** (formerly Grauman's), 6925 Hollywood Blvd. (464-8111), between Highland and La Brea, is an odd tropical interpretation of a Chinese temple and Hollywood hype at its finest. Tourists always crowd the courtyard, worshiping cement impressions of various parts of the stars' anatomies and trademark possessions (Al Jolson's knees, Trigger's hooves, R2D2's wheels, Jimmy Durante's nose, George Burns' cigar, etc.) If you want to stroll among stars, have a look at the **Walk of Fame** along Hollywood Blvd. and Vine St. More than 2500 bronze-inlaid stars are embedded in the sidewalk, inscribed with names—some familiar, some forgotten—and feet. Across the street and two blocks east is another unique theater, the **UA Egyptian,** 6712 Hollywood Blvd. (467-6167), inspired in 1922 by the then-newly-discovered tomb of King Tut.

Two blocks east of Mann's is the **Hollywood Wax Museum,** 6767 Hollywood Blvd. (462-8860), where you'll meet almost 200 figures from Jesus to Cher. (Open Sun.-Thurs. 10am-midnight, Fri.-Sat. 10am-2am. Admission $7.50, kids $5, seniors $6.50.) Other Hollywood Blvd. attractions include the original **Frederick's of Hollywood,** 6608 Hollywood Blvd. (466-8506), a purple and pink bastion of tasteful teddies and licorice lingerie, which now houses its own **museum of lingerie** in the back of the store. (Open Mon.-Thurs. 10am-8pm, Fri. 10am-9pm, Sat. 10am-6pm, Sun. noon-5pm. Free.) A few blocks away, you'll find the **Max Factor Museum**. Free admission makes it worth traipsing thorugh this shrine to artificial beauty. Soak up the aura of Judy Garland and Rita Hayworth, who paid homage to Max's museum on its opening.

Down the street, **Larry Edmund's Cinema and Theater Bookshop,** 6658 Hollywood Blvd. (463-3273), sells Ken Schessler's *This Is Hollywood: Guide to Hollywood Murders, Suicides, Graves, Etc.*, a guide to nondescript places made famous by the fact that stars courted, married, fooled around, were discovered, made movies, or committed suicide there. (Open Mon.-Sat. 10am-6pm.)

Hollywood Fantasy Tours, 1651 N. Highland (469-8184), two blocks south of Hollywood Blvd., offers two-hour tours of Tinseltown in double-decker buses with knowledgeable but corny tour guides. (Tours of Beverly Hills and other areas also. Call for info.) The **Hollywood Studio Museum,** 2100 N. Highland Ave. (874-2276), across from the Hollywood Bowl, provides a refreshingly un-hyped-up look at the history of early Hollywood film-making. Back in 1913, when it was a barn, famed director Cecil B. DeMille rented this building as a studio and shot Hollywood's first feature film, *The Straw Man,* there. Antique cameras, costumes, props, and other memorabilia clutter the museum along with vintage film clips. (Open Sat. and Sun. 10am-4pm. Admission $3.50, seniors and students $2.50, kids $1.50. Ample free parking.)

Music is another industry greasing Hollywood's cash-register runners. The pre-eminent monument of the modern record industry is the 1954 **Capitol Records Tower,** 1750 Vine St., just north of Hollywood Blvd. The building looks like a stack of records, American architectural kitsch-literalism at its most Californian. More esoteric music and associated paraphernalia can be found at **The Rock Shop,** 6666 Hollywood Blvd. (466-7276), which carries records and tapes, CDs, posters, t-shirts, thousands of buttons, handkerchiefs, tour and promotional merchandise, World War II artifacts, and leather and metal accessories. Isn't that special? Hollywood stars prove less elusive when they are six feet under, and the **Hollywood Cemetery,** at 6000 Santa Monica Blvd. (469-1181), between Vine St. and Western Ave., is the permanent home of the remains of Rudolph Valentino, Douglas Fairbanks, Sr., and other Hollywood notables. (Open daily 8am-5pm.)

The **Hollyhock House,** 4808 Hollywood Blvd. (662-7272), commands a 360° view of Los Angeles and the mountains. Completed in 1922 for eccentric oil heiress Aline Barnsdall, the house remains one of Frank Lloyd Wright's most important works. It is the first building by this pre-eminent modern American architect to reflect the influence of pre-Columbian Mayan temples. The name of the house derives from Barnsdall's favorite flower, which she had Wright reproduce (grudgingly) in abstract all over the house. (Tours Tues.-Thurs. on the hour from 10am-1pm; Sat. and all but the last Sun. each month noon-3pm. Admission $1.50, seniors $1, under 13 free. Buy tickets at the Municipal Art Gallery.) Call to arrange foreign language tours of Hollyhock House (485-4581). About three mi. northeast of downtown is **Elysian Park;** with 525 acres of greenery, the park is divine for picnicking. The park largely surrounds and embraces the area of Chavez Ravine, home of **Dodger Stadium** (224-1400) and the Los Angeles Dodgers baseball team. Tickets, which cost from $5 to $10 (all seats have good views of the field), are a hot commodity when the Dodgers are playing well. Purchase in advance if possible, or get a lesson in supply and demand from scalpers outside. Once in the ballpark, grab yourself a Dodger Dog, one of the best dogs in the majors, although a 1991 brouhaha over a change in the wieners' preparation left a bad taste in the mouths of many fans. Sprawling over 4500 acres of hilly terrain is **Griffith Park.** The L.A. Zoo, the Greek Theater, Griffith Observatory and Planetarium, Travel Town, a bird sanctuary, tennis courts, two golf courses, campgrounds, and various hiking trails blanket the dry hills and mountains. This formidable recreational region stretches from the hills above Hollywood north to the intersection of the Ventura and Golden State Freeways. Pick up a map at any of the entrance points. A full day in the Park might include the zoo in the morning, the rest of the park during the afternoon, and the Greek Theater or the planetarium's laser show in the evening. For info, stop by the **visitors center and ranger headquarters,** 4730 Crystal Spring Dr. (665-5188; open daily 7am-5pm).

If you enjoy seeing stars of the celestial variety, head for the park's **Observatory and Planetarium** (664-1181, for a recording 664-1191). The white stucco and copper domes of this Art Deco structure are visible from around the park. You also might remember it from the climactic last scene of the James Dean film, *Rebel Without a Cause.* The exhibits in the Hall of Science are good but no different from other planetarium displays. One of the most interesting is a seismograph that runs continually. Stomp *really* hard to produce an earthquake of your own. A 12-in. telescope opens the sky to the public every clear night from dusk-9:45pm; in winter Tues.-Sun. 7-10pm. (Call the sky report at 663-8171 for more info.) The planetarium also presents popular **Laserium** light shows (818-997-3624), psychedelic symphonies of colored lasers and music. (Observatory open daily 12:30pm-10pm; winter hours Tues.-Sun. 2-10pm. Free. Hour-long planetarium show Mon.-Fri. at 3 and 7:30pm, Sat.-Sun. also at 4:30pm; in winter Tues.-Fri. 3 and 8pm, Sat.-Sun. also at 4:30pm. Admission $3.50, seniors and under 12 $2. Laser shows Sun., Tues.-Thurs. at 6pm and 8:30pm; Fri.-Sat. also at 9:45pm. Admission $6, kids $5.)

A large **bird sanctuary** at the bottom of the observatory hill serves its function well, but if you crave the sight of land-bound animals, you might go to the **L.A. Zoo,** 5333 Zoo Dr., (666-4090) at the park's northern end. The zoo's 113 acres accommodate 2000 crazy critters, and the facility is consistently ranked among the nation's 10 best. Camel rides for children. (Open daily 10am-6pm; in winter 10am-5pm. Admission $6, seniors $5, ages 2-12 $2.75, under 2 free. Ticket office closes 1 hr. before zoo.)

On the southern side of the park, below the observatory, the 4500-seat **Greek Theater** (665-5857) hosts a number of concerts in its outdoor amphitheater virtually year-round. Check ads in the *Sunday L.A. Times* "Calendar" section for coming attractions. Those with a hankerin' to relive those wild, wild days of yore will enjoy the recently opened **Gene Autry Western Heritage Museum,** 4700 Zoo Dr. (667-2000), also located within Griffith Park at the junction of Golden State (I-5) and Ventura Fwy (Rte. 134). The museum's collection covers both fact and fiction of the Old West, with exhibits on pioneer life and on the history of western films. The Hollywood section includes costumes donated by Robert Redford, Gary Cooper, and Clint Eastwood. Firearms owned by George Custer, Wyatt Earp, Billy the Kid, and Teddy Roosevelt are on display in the historical exhibit. (Open Tues.-Sun. 10am-5pm. Admission $6, seniors and students $4.50, kids $2.50.) To get to the Observatory and Greek Theater, take bus #203 from Hollywood. To reach the Zoo and Travel Town, take bus #97 from downtown. There is no bus service between the northern and southern parts of Griffith Park.

West Hollywood

Once considered a no-man's-land between Beverly Hills and Hollywood, West Hollywood was incorporated in 1985 and was one of the first cities in the country to be governed by openly gay officials. There's always a lot going on here, and a list of each week's events can be found in the *L.A. Weekly.*

In the years before incorporation, lax zoning and other liberal laws gave rise to the voluptuous **Sunset Strip,** nurturing bands such as The Doors and Guns 'n' Roses. These days, most of the music on this stretch is heavy metal and hard rock, and weekend nights draw tremendous crowds and traffic jams. Restaurants and comedy clubs flourish here as well.

Melrose Avenue, south of West Hollywood, is lined with swish restaurants, ultra-trendy boutiques, and art galleries. Punk clothing pits like **Retail Slut** and functional novelty shops like **Condom Mania** outfit clubbies for the evening. The choicest stretch is between La Brea and Fairfax, but the entire three-mi. distance between Highland and Doheny is packed with frumpy people-watchers and the stylized creatures who keep them busy. At the corner of Beverly and San Vicente Blvd. is the Los Angeles **Hard Rock Café** (310-276-7605). A pistachio-green '57 Chevy juts out of the roof, unsuccessfully attempting to escape the trendy crowds within. Indiana Jones's leather jacket, one of Pete Townshend's guitars, a six-ft.-tall martini glass, license plates, and college banners adorn the interior. Expect to tarry for a table every night of the week—over an hour on weekends. (Open Sun.-Thurs. 11:30am-midnight, Fri.-Sat. 11:30am-1am.)

North of the Beverly Center, at Melrose and San Vicente, is the **Pacific Design Center,** 8687 Melrose Ave. (310-657-0800), a huge blue-and-green glass complex with a wavey profile (nicknamed **The Blue Whale**). The building, completed in 1976, seems destined for architectural history texts. In addition to some design showrooms, the PDC houses a public plaza with a 350-seat amphitheater, used to stage free summer concerts. Call or inquire at the info desk in the entryway for details about such events. West Hollywood's **Gay Pride Weekend Celebration** (in late June) is usually held at the PDC plaza.

Beverly Hills

Though smack dab in the middle of Greater Los Angeles, Beverly Hills remains an exclusive enclave of wealth. Beverly Hills seceded from L.A. in 1914 and has remained in every way distinct from the city ever since. Consider this: the Beverly Hills Post Office (Zip Code: 90210, of course) has *valet parking.* Even the homeless are well-dressed (otherwise they'd be gently escorted to the city's edge by Beverly Hills' remarkably efficient police force). The heart of the city rests in the **Golden Triangle,** a wedge formed by Wilshire and Santa Monica Blvd. centering on **Rodeo Drive,** known for its many opulent clothing boutiques and jewelry shops. You might feel underdressed simply window-shopping. Across the way is the venerable **Beverly Wilshire Hotel** (310-275-5200), whose old and new wings are connected by El Camino Real, a cobbled street with Louis XIV gates. Inside, hall mirrors reflect the glitter of crystal chandeliers and marble floors. Beverly Hills' new **Civic Center,** completed in September 1990, includes the Beverly Hills Fire Department, Police Station, and library. It took nine years and $120 million to build. Designed by Charles Moore, the Civic Center's Post-Modern pastiche of Spanish baroque, art deco, and Art Moderne is stunningly constructed (even the library's parking structure is something to see). The **Beverly Hills Library** (444 N. Rexford Dr.; 213-228-2220) is a case study in the city's overriding priorities—the interior is adorned with marble imported from Thailand, but contains a paltry collection of books.

Those who may be considering hopping on a stargazing **tour bus,** be forewarned: the only people visible on the streets are gardeners, and many of them don't even know whom they're working for. Since you'll never know the difference, some tours feel free to make things up as they go along. A better alternative is the **Beverly Hills Trolley,** (310-275-2791) which can be picked up at Dayton and Rodeo and runs to Sunset and back every half hour ($1; open Tues.-Sat. 10am-6:15pm). Celebrity-hungry visitors with cars should have plenty of time and pride to spare before buying a streetcorner "Star Map." Hawkers may imply these are accurate and up-to-date, both of which are questionable claims.

Just outside of Beverly Hills, the **Beit HaShoa Museum of Tolerance,** 9786 W. Pico Blvd. on the corner of Roxbury (310-553-9036) opened in April of 1992. Previously known as the **Simon Wiesenthal Center,** the museum received $5 million from former Governor Deukmeijian to build a new, larger structure on the condition that the museum include displays on the Armenian and Native American genocides. The new museum's high-tech wizardry is designed to help visitors explore their own prejudices, with displays on the Holocaust, anti-semitism and prejudice in the U.S., and the U.S. Civil Rights movement. (Hours and prices have not been determined, but are likely to be: Mon.-Thurs. 9am-5pm, Fri. 9am-3pm, Sun. 11am-4pm. $5 with student and senior discounts.)

Westwood and UCLA

Welcome to Scooterville! The gargantuan **University of California at Los Angeles** campus (covering over 400 acres in the foothills of the Santa Monica Mountains, bounded by Sunset, Hilgard, Le Conte, and Gayley) and the dearth of parking spaces make both UCLA and Westwood look like motorbike versions of Disneyland's *Autopia.* The school is directly north of Westwood Village and west of Beverly Hills. To reach the campus by car, take the San Diego Fwy. (I-405) north to the Wilshire Blvd./ Westwood exit, heading east into Westwood. Take Westwood Blvd. north off Wilshire, heading straight through the center of the village and directly into the campus. By bus, take RTD route #20, 21 (the best, since it goes directly to the campus), 22, 320, or 322 along Wilshire Blvd. to Westwood. Exit at Wilshire and Gayley and walk north to Gayley and Weyburn Ave., where you can pick up a free UCLA Campus Express shuttle to the center of campus. Drivers can find free parking behind the Federal Building and, on Friday and Saturday nights, avoid the 10-minute walk into the village by riding the 10-cent **RTD Shuttle** (Fri. 6:30pm-1:30am, Sat. 11am-1:30am). Those who wish to park on campus may do so by paying $4 at one of the campus info kiosks; you will receive a day permit allowing you to park in the student garages.

The best place to start a tour of UCLA is at the **Visitors Center,** 10945 Le Conte Ave., #147 (206-8147), located in the Ueberroth Olympic Office Building. Free 90-minute walking tours of the campus depart from the visitors center at 10:30am and 1:30pm Monday to Friday. Campus maps are also available at the info kiosks located at each of the streets leading into the campus.

Royce Hall, situated in the Quadrangle, is the architectural pride and joy of the UCLA Campus, and **Powell Library,** at the campus's south end, is the main undergraduate library and reflects an Islamic influence in its architectural design. At the northernmost reach of the campus, the **Dickson Art Center** (825-1462) houses the Wight Art Gallery, home to the Grunwald Center for the Graphic Arts, as well as frequent internationally recognized exhibitions. (Open Sept.-June Tues. 11am-8pm, Wed.-Fri. 11am-5pm, Sat. and Sun. 1-5pm. Free.) The **Murphy Sculpture Garden,** containing over 70 pieces scattered over five acres, lies directly in front of the Art Center. The collection includes works by Rodin, Matisse, and Miró. Another heralded piece of outdoor artwork is UCLA's **Inverted Fountain,** located between Knudsen Hall and Schoenberg Hall, directly south of Dickson Plaza. Water spouts from the fountain's perimeter and rushes down into a gaping hole in the middle. The **Botanical Gardens** (825-3620), in the southeast corner of the campus, encompass a subtropical canyon where brook-side redwoods and palms mingle (open year-round Mon.-Fri. 8am-5pm, Sat.-Sun. 8am-4pm). There is also a surreally serene **Japanese Garden.** (Open Tues. 10am-1pm, Wed. noon-3pm, by appointment only. Reservations should be made a couple of weeks in advance. Call the visitors center at 825-4574 or 825-4338 to arrange for a tour.)

Ackerman Union, 308 Westwood Plaza (825-7711), stands southwest of the Quadrangle, at the bottom of the hill and is the campus info bank. A calendar lists the month's lengthy line-up of movies (first-runs often free), lectures, and campus activities. The Expo Center, on level B, has travel info and a complete **rideboard.** Next door you'll find a bowling alley and enough fast-food joints to satisfy a sumo wrestling team. (Open Mon.-Fri. 8:30am-6pm, Sat. 10am-5pm, Sun. noon-5pm.) The ground floor is swallowed by the **Associated Students Students' Store** (825-0611), the largest on-campus store in the U.S. (Open Mon.-Thurs. 7:45am-7:30pm, Fri. 7:45am-6pm, Sat. 10am-5pm, Sun. noon-5pm.)

Westwood Village, just south of the campus, with its myriad movie theaters, trendy boutiques, and upscale bistros, is geared more toward the residents of L.A.'s Westside than collegians. Like most college neighborhoods, however, Westwood hums on Friday and Saturday nights when everyone (high schoolers, collegians, tourists, gang members, and police) show up to do their thing.

Hidden off the main drag at 1218 Glendon Ave. is the **Westwood Memorial Cemetery.** Flowers, teddybears, even sprouting Chia Pets are left by family and friends who make pilgrimages to the graves of Marilyn Monroe, Natalie Wood, and young Heather O'Rourke.

At 14523 Sunset, hike around **Will Rogers State Historical Park** (454-8212) and take in the panoramic views of the city and the distant Pacific. You can visit the famous horseman's home and eat a picnic brunch while watching polo matches on the grounds on Saturday afternoons (2-5pm) and Sunday mornings (10am-noon). Follow Chautauqua Blvd. inland from PCH to Sunset Blvd., or take bus #2 along Sunset Blvd. (Park open daily 8am-7pm; Rogers's house open daily 10am-5pm.)

Santa Monica

To a resident of turn-of-the-century L.A., a trip to the beach resort of Santa Monica meant a long ride over poor-quality roads. The Red Car electric train shortened the trip considerably, and today it takes about half an hour (with no traffic) on Big Blue express bus #10 or on the Santa Monica Freeway (I-10) from downtown. No longer far away, SaMo is still pretty far out, with an extremely liberal city council and the former Mr. Jane Fonda (Tom Hayden, one of the Chicago Seven) as one of its assemblymen. Its beach is the closest to L.A. proper, and thus crowded and dirty. Still, the magical lure of sun, surf, and sand causes nightmarish summer traffic jams on I-10 and I-405 (beaches to the north and south are much prettier and cleaner). The colorful **Santa Monica Pier** is still a nostalgic and popular, if a bit sleazy, spot. The gem of the pier is the magnificent turn-of the-century carousel, which was featured in *The Sting*. **Palisades Park,** on the bluff overlooking the pier, provides a shaded home for numerous homeless people. With the creation of the **Third Street Promenade** in 1989, and the recent remodeling of its upscale neighbor, **Santa Monica Place** (see Shopping), Santa Monica has recently become one of L.A.'s major walking, movie-seeing, and yuppie mating areas. The Promenade sports some cool cafés, a couple of L.A.'s better bookshops, overpriced bars and restaurants, and a number of fine, fresh street artists (not to mention some water-spouting, ivy-lined, mesh dinosaur sculptures). **Main Street** attracts attention with its vintage collectible and apparel shops and browser-friendly galleries.

Venice

The most unique part of a unique city, Venice is Los Angeles' saving grace for budget travelers. A perennial favorite among foreigners, Venice is wacky on weekdays, wild on weekends. A typical Sunday includes trapeze artists, spontaneous rollerblade dancing competitions, and your run-of-the-mill clowns, jugglers, comedians, glass-eaters, hemp advocates, bikini-clad skaters, fortune tellers, and choirs of gaping Los Angelenos. With everyone crowding the beachfront, trying either to see or be seen, life in Venice is, as one hostel brochure aptly puts it, "spontaneous theater."

Venice's story begins just after the turn of the century, when Abbot Kinney dug a series of canals throughout the town and filled them with water, intending to bring the romance and refinement of Venice, Italy, to Southern California. But the water became dirty and oily, and instead of attracting society's upper crust, developed a crust of its own. Venice became home to gamblers, bootleggers, and other assorted rogues. The canals eventually were forgotten and, for the most part, filled in and buried. Skateboarders use some of the others. For a sense of the Venice that Kinney envisioned, head for the traffic circle at Main St. and Windward Ave., three blocks inland from the beach pavilion. This was once a circular canal, the hub of the whole network. The post office on the circle's west side has a small mural inside that sums up Venice's cluttered history in an appropriately jumbled way—with oil derricks seemingly perched on Kinney's shoulders. Back outside on Main St., walk down Windward to its intersection with Pacific Ave. Columns and tiled awnings are all that remain of the grandiose hotels that once housed vacationers from Los Angeles. Health-food shops and vintage clothing stores lie behind the colonnades where sedans once discharged high-styled passengers. One of the sole surviving canals is at Strong's Dr., off Washington St. Ducks are its liveliest inhabitants.

Venice finally came into its own in the 70s, when the Sexual Revolution spawned a swinging beach community. Although the revolution may have been quelled, Venice's peculiar beach renaissance lives on, a testament to the ongoing allure of the credo, "Do your own thing." Ocean Front Walk, Venice's main beach front drag, is a drastic demographic departure from Santa Monica's Promenade. Street people converge on shaded clusters of benches, healthy-types play paddle tennis, and bodybuilders of both sexes pump iron in skimpy outfits at the original **Muscle Beach** (1800 Ocean Front Walk, closest to 18th and Pacific Ave.). This is where the roller-skating craze began, and this is probably where it will breathe its last. Even the police wear shorts while slapping nude sunbathers (hopefully not too hard) with $55 fines. New Wave types, cyclists, joggers, groovy elders (such as the "skateboard grandma"), and bards in Birkenstocks make up the balance of this funky playground population. Venders of jewelry, snacks, and beach bric-a-brac overwhelm the boardwalk and are sights themselves. Collect your wits and take in the crowds from a distance at one of the many cafés or juice bars. If your feet don't move you through the crowds fast enough, rent rollerblades or a bike. The cheapest rental place is **Sports and Stuff,** on Washington. (Rollerblades $4 per hour, $8 per day; bikes $2.50 per hour, $5 per day. Open daily 9am-6pm.)

Venice's **street murals** are another free show. Don't miss the brilliant, graffiti-disfigured homage to Botticelli's *Birth of Venus* on the beach pavilion at the end of Windward Ave.: an angelically beautiful woman, wearing short-shorts, a Band-aid top, and rollerskates, boogies out of her seashell. The side wall of a Japanese restaurant on Windward is covered with a perfect imitation of a Japanese Hokusai print of a turbulent sea. Large insect sculptures loom in the rafters of many of the city's posh restaurants. To look at paintings indoors, you might want to stop by **L.A. Louver,** 77 Market St. and 55 N. Venice Blvd. (822-4955), a gallery showing the work of some hip L.A. artists (open Tues.-Sat. noon-5pm).

To get to Venice from downtown L.A., take bus #33 or 333 (or 436 during rush hour). From downtown Santa Monica, take Santa Monica bus #1 or 2.

The Pacific Coast Highway

From Santa Monica, where it temporarily merges with I-10, the **Pacific Coast Highway (PCH)** (Rte. 1) runs northward along the spectacular California coast. Several of L.A. county's best beaches line the PCH between Santa Monica and the Ventura County line.

Heading north from Santa Monica, the first major attraction is the **J. Paul Getty Museum,** 17985 PCH (458-2003), set back on a cliff above the ocean. Getty, an oil magnate, built this mansion as a re-creation of the 1st-century Villa dei Papiri in Herculaneum, with a beautiful main peristyle garden, a reflecting pool, and bush-lined paths. Due to the museum's operating agreement with its residential neighbors, access to the museum is more difficult than it could be. The parking lot is small, and reservations are needed, a day in advance most of the time, weeks in advance in summer. You are not permitted to park outside the museum unless you do so at the county lot. Bicyclists and motorcyclists are admitted without reservations. Take RTD #434 (which you can board at Sunset and PCH in Malibu or Ocean and Colorado in Santa Monica) to the museum and mind that you ask for a free **museum pass** from the bus driver. The museum gate is ½ mi. from the bus stop, so be prepared to walk. (Open Tues.-Sun. 10am-5pm. Free.)

The celebrity colony of **Malibu** stretches along the low-20000 blocks of PCH. With their multi-million-dollar homes and celebrity neighbors, Malibu residents can afford to be hostile to nonlocals, especially to those from the Valley. The beach lies along the 23200 block of the PCH. You can walk onto the beach via the **Zonker Harris** access way at 22700 PCH, named after the quintessential Californian of Garry Trudeau's comic strip, *Doonesbury.* **Corral State Beach,** an uncrowded, windsurfing, swimming, and scuba-diving beach, lies on the 26000 block of PCH, followed by **Point Dume State Beach,** which is small and generally uncrowded.

North of Point Dume, along the 30000 block of PCH, lies **Zuma,** L.A. County's northernmost, largest, and most popular county-owned sandbox, with lifeguards, restrooms, and a $5 parking fee. Stations eight to 12 belong to solitude-seekers. The Valley high-schoolers have staked out six and seven, which are the most crowded and lively parts. Zuma three, four, and five are frequented by families who keep things slightly more sedate. If you don't want to bring food, pick something up at **Trancas Market** (PCH and Trancas Canyon, around Station 12). Evade the beach stands unless you're willing to pay $2.75 for an indigestible hamburger or hot dog.

Visitors with cars should not miss **Mulholland Drive,** nature's answer to the roller coaster (south of Big Sur). Twisting and turning for 15 spectacular mi. along the crest of the Santa Monica Mountains, Mulholland stretches from PCH, near the Ventura County line, east to the Hollywood Fwy. and San Fernando Valley. Whoever's driving will have a hard time concentrating—numerous points along the way, especially between Coldwater Canyon and the San Diego Fwy., offer compelling views of the entire Los Angeles basin. Avoid Mulholland on late weekend nights, when the road is fraught with drag-racing teenagers and parked cars on Lover's Lane. Racers use both lanes, and four headlights coming at you at 70 mph can be an even more arresting sight than all the panoramic lights of what Aldous Huxley called "the city of dreadful joy." Find respite from PCH among the waterfalls and gardens of the **Self-Rehabilitation Fellowship Lake Shrine,** 17190 Sunset Blvd. (310-454-4114).

San Fernando Valley

North of L.A. proper, beyond the Santa Monica Mountains, lies the spiritual center of the American suburbia, a seemingly infinite series of bedroom communities with tree-lined streets, cookie-cutter homes, lawns, and shopping malls. A third of L.A.'s population resides here. The portion of the Valley incorporated into the City of Los Angeles alone covers 140 million acres. The area was settled after city engineer William Mulholland first brought water to the valley in 1913. Standing on a hillside overlooking the basin, Mulholland watched the first torrents pour out of the Los Angeles Aqueduct, and proclaimed "There it is; take it!" The city rushed to obey.

Ventura Boulevard is the main commercial thoroughfare. The sprawling valley viewed from the foothills at night, particularly from Mulholland Drive, is just, well, ya' know, bitchin'. Among the valley's worthwhile sights is the **Mission San Fernando Ray De España.** The mission was founded in 1797 by Padre Fermin Lasuen, but no structures remain from this period. The old **Iglesia** was razed by the 1971 earthquake, and the **Convento** has been covered with stucco, making the cemetery and the park across the street the most intriguing part of the mission. Once you've made the trek to the valley, consider driving another hour out of your way to Simi Valley, home to the jury which absolved the LAPD of using unnecessary force on Rodney King. In a striking coincidence, Simi Valley is also home to the **Ronald Reagan Presidential Library,** 40 Presidential Dr. (805-522-8444), off the 23 Fwy. (Open Mon.-Sat. 10am-5pm, Sun. noon-5pm. $2, seniors $1, under 15 free.)

Pasadena

Pasadena, a city-sized suburb 10 mi. northeast of downtown Los Angeles, offers some respite from the frazzling pace of greater L.A. Pasadena is placid, with pleasant tree-lined streets and outstanding cultural facilities. You can get there along the Pasadena Fwy. (Rte. 110 North), where drivers are required to merge almost instantaneously with 55-mph traffic from a dead stop.

In the gorge that forms the city's western boundary stands Pasadena's most famous landmark, the **Rose Bowl,** 991 Rosemont Blvd. (818-793-7193, Rose Bowl Event Information Line 577-3106). Home to the college football bowl game of the same name, the annual confrontation between the champions of the Big Ten and Pac 10 conferences, the Rose Bowl is also regular-season home to the UCLA Bruins football team. The New Year's Day Rose Bowl game follows the **Tournament of Roses Parade,** (818-449-4100) which runs along Colorado Blvd. through downtown Pasadena. Thousands line the Pasadena streets (having staked out choice viewing spots days in advance) to watch the flower-covered floats go by. To reach the Rose Bowl, take the Pasadena Fwy. to its end and follow the signs of Arroyo Pkwy.

At the western end of the downtown area (also called Old Pasadena) lies Pasadena's answer to LACMA and the Getty Museum, the **Norton Simon Museum of Art,** 411 W. Colorado Blvd. (449-3730), at Orange Grove Blvd. The collection includes numerous Rodin and Brancusi bronzes, and masterpieces by Rembrandt, Raphael, and Picasso. The ancient Southeast Asian art collection is one of the world's best. Simon's eclectic, slightly idiosyncratic tastes, as well as the well-written descriptions of the works, make this museum more interesting than similar assemblages elsewhere. (Open Thurs.-Sun. noon-6pm. Admission $4, seniors and students $2, under 12 free. Wheelchair accessible.) From downtown L.A. take bus #483 from Olive St., anywhere between Venice Blvd. and First St., to Colorado Blvd. and Fair Oaks Ave. in Pasadena. The museum is four blocks west. Some of the world's greatest scientific minds do their work at the West Coast rival of the Massachusetts Institute of Technology, the **California Institute of Technology,** 1201 E. California Blvd. (356-6811), about 2½ mi. southeast of downtown. The campus is lush, filled with bush- and olive-tree-lined brick paths. The buildings incorporate a mishmash of Spanish, Italian Renaissance, and modern styles. Cal Tech, founded in 1891 as Throop University, has amassed a faculty which includes several Nobel laureates (Albert Einstein once taught here) and a technogeek student body which prides itself both on its high I.Q. and its elaborate and ingenious practical jokes. These range from the mundane (unscrewing all the chairs in a lecture hall and bolting them in backwards) to the audacious (altering the Rose Bowl scoreboard during the big game with the aid of computers).

A half-mile to the south of Cal Tech lies the **Huntington Library, Art Gallery, and Botanical Gardens,** 1151 Oxford Rd., San Marino 91108 (405-2100, ticket info 405-2273). Despite the ban on picnics and sunbathing, families and tourists still flock here on Sundays to stroll around the grounds and visit the library and galleries. The stunning botanical gardens nurture 207 acres of plants, many of them rare. The library houses one of the world's most important collections of rare books and English and American manuscripts, including Benjamin Franklin's handwritten autobiography and the obligatory Gutenberg Bible. The art gallery also is known for its 18th- and 19th-century British paintings. Sentimental favorites on exhibit include Thomas Gainsborough's *Blue Boy* and its companion piece, Sir Thomas Lawrence's *Pinkie.* (Open Tues.-Sun. 1am-4:30pm; free, but donation expected.) The museum sits between Huntington Dr. and California Blvd. in San Marino, just south of Pasadena. From downtown L.A., bus #79 leaves from Olive St., and takes you straight to the library (a 40- to 45-min. trip).

Near Pasadena

Recent remodeling and a spate of innovative exhibits may earn the **Southwest Museum,** 234 Museum Dr. (213-221-2163), the attention it deserves. L.A. offers no better resource to those interested in the history and culture of the Southwest. The museum, housed in a palatial Hispano-Moorish home on a hill, sports a collection of artifacts among the best in the nation, including contemporary Native American art. Take bus #83 along Broadway to Museum Dr. and trek up the hill. Drivers should take the Pasadena Fwy. (I-110) to Ave. 43 and follow the signs. (Open Tues.-Sun. 11am-5pm. Admission $4, seniors and students $2, ages 7-18 $1. Library open Wed.-Sat. 11am-5pm.)

If you don't find any celebrities on the street, you can find many in their graves at the renowned **Forest Lawn** cemetery, 1712 Glendale Ave., Glendale (241-4151). Analyzed by Jessica Mitford as the showy emblem of the "American Way of Death," its grounds include reproductions of many of Michelangelo's works, the "largest religious painting on earth" (the famous 195-ft. version of the *Crucifixion* a stained-glass *Last Supper,* and innumerable other works of "art." Stop at the entrance for a map of the cemetery's sights, and pick up a guide to the paintings and sculpture at the administration building nearby. (Open daily 8am-5pm.) From downtown, take bus #90 or 91 and disembark just after the bus leaves San Fernando Rd. to turn onto Glendale Ave. Forest Lawn is easily approached from this side of paradise via the Golden State Fwy. or Glendale Fwy. (Rte. 2).

Entertainment

"Vast wasteland" mythology to the contrary, L.A.'s cultural scene is in fact active and diverse. If you're staying in Hollywood or have a car, you can spend all your time in L.A. enjoying a Vampire-like revelry.

Film and Television Studios

All of the major TV studios offer free tickets to show tapings. Some are available on a first-come, first-served basis from the Visitors Information Center of the Greater L.A. Visitor and Convention Bureau or by mail. Some networks won't send tickets to out-of-state addresses, but they will send a guest card or letter that can be redeemed for tickets. Be sure to enclose a self-addressed, stamped envelope. Write: Tickets, Capital City/**ABC Inc.,** 4151 Prospect, Hollywood 90027 (557-7777); **CBS Tickets,** 7800 Beverly Blvd., Los Angeles 90036 (310-840-3537); **NBC-TV,** 3000 W. Alameda Ave., Burbank 91523 (818-840-3537); or **FOX Tickets,** 100 Universal City Plaza, Bldg. 153, Universal City 91608 (818-506-0067). Tickets also are available to shows produced by **Paramount Television,** 780 N. Gower St., Hollywood 90038 (213-956-5575). Tickets don't guarantee admittance; arrive a couple of hours early, as seating is also first-come, first-seated. Min. age for many studios is 16.

Universal Studios, Universal City (818-508-9600). Hollywood Fwy. to Lankershim. Take bus #424 to Lankershim Blvd. For a hefty fee, the studio will take you for a ride; visit the Bates Motel and other sets, watch Conan the Barbarian flex his pecs, be attacked by Jaws, get caught in a flash flood, experience an 8.3 earthquake, and witness a variety of special effects and other demonstrations of movie-making magic. No reservations are accepted. Arrive early to secure a ticket. Allow 2.5 hr. for the tour and at least an hr. for wandering. Tours in Spanish Sat. and Sun. Open summer and holidays 8am-10pm (last tram leaves at 5pm); Sept.-June 9am-6:30pm. Admission $25, ages 3-11 and over 65 $19. Parking $4.

NBC Television Studios Tour, 3000 W. Alameda Ave. (818-840-3572), at Olive Ave. in Burbank, 2 mi. from Universal. Hollywood Fwy. north, exit east on Barham Blvd., which becomes Olive Ave. Take bus #420 from Hill St. downtown. The tour is cancelled but may reopen in 1993. Call for info.

Warner Bros. VIP Tour, 4000 Warner Blvd., Burbank (818-954-1744). Personalized, unstaged tours (max. 12 people) through the Warner Bros. studios. These are technical, 2-hr. treks which chronicle the detailed reality of the movie-making art. No children under 10. Tours Mon.-Fri. 10am and 2pm, additional tours in summer. $22 per person. Reservations required in advance.

Cinema

In the technicolored heaven of Los Angeles, movie theaters smother the city like smog. Foreign films play consistently at the six **Laemmle Theaters** in Beverly Hills, West L.A., Santa Monica, Pasadena, Encino, and downtown.

A unique movie-going treat is the **Mitsubishi IMAX Theater,** at the California Museum of Science and Industry (213-744-2014; see Exposition Park Sights). Movies are shown on a 54-by-70-ft. screen. The films, of the entertainment-documentary variety, surround the viewer with brilliant sights and sounds. (Admission $5, seniors and under 12 $5.50.)

For film screening info, dial 777-FILM.

Cineplex Odeon Universal City Cinemas, atop the hill at Universal Studios (818-508-0588). Take the Universal Center Dr. exit off the Hollywood Fwy. (U.S. 101). Opened in 1987 as the world's largest cinema complex. The 18 wide-screen theaters, 2 *Parisienne* cafés, and opulent decoration put all others to shame. Hooray for Hollywood.

Mann's Chinese, 6925 Hollywood Blvd. (213-464-8111). Hollywood hype to the hilt. For more details, see Hollywood Sights.

Beverly Cineplex (310-652-7760), atop the Beverly Center, on Beverly Dr. at La Cienaga. Unlike most first-run cinemas in California, the Cineplex screens movies in auditoriums hardly bigger than your living room. But it shows 14 of them every night, a combination of recent hits and artsy discoveries.

Village Theatre, 961 Broxton (310-208-5576), in Westwood. No multiplex nonsense here. One auditorium, one big screen, one great THX sound system, a balcony, and Art-Deco design. Watch the back rows and balcony for late-arriving celebrities.

Comedy

The talent may be imported from New York and other parts of the country, but that doesn't change the fact that L.A.'s comedy clubs are the best in the world (unless you happen to chance upon an amateur night, which is generally a painful experience for all involved). Some clubs are open only a few nights weekly. Call ahead to check age restrictions. Cover charges are cheaper during the week, with fewer crowds but just as much fun.

Comedy Store, 8433 Sunset Blvd. in Hollywood (213-656-6225). The shopping mall of comedy clubs, with 3 different rooms, each featuring a different type of comedy. (Each room charges its own cover.) Go to the Main Room for the big-name stuff and the most expensive cover charges (around $14). The Original Room features mid-range comics for $7-10. The Belly Room has the real grab-bag material, often for no cover charge. Over 21 only; 2-drink min.

The Improvisation, 8162 Melrose Ave. (213-651-2583). Offers L.A.'s best talent, including, on occasion, Robin Williams or Robert Klein. Their restaurant serves Italian fare. Open nightly, check *L.A. Weekly* for times. Cover $8-10, 2-drink minimum. Reservations recommended.

Improvisation in Santa Monica, 321 Santa Monica Blvd. (310-394-8664). The beach version of its Hollywood cousin is more laid-back, and brand new. Tex-Mex food in the restaurant, cover $5-10, 2-drink minimum. A 3rd Improvisation is located in Irvine, and a 4th in the Valley.

The Comedy Act Theater, 3339 W. 43rd St. (310-677-4101). A comedy club targeted at an African-American audience, often featuring such nationally known comedians as Robert Townsend and Marsha Warfield. Open Thurs.-Sat. 8:30pm on. Cover $10.

Theater and Classical Music

Los Angeles is blessed with one of the most active theater circuits on the West Coast. About 115 Equity Waiver theaters (under 100 seats) offer a dizzying choice for theatergoers, who can also take in small productions in museums, art galleries, universities, parks, and even garages. During the summer hiatus, TV stars frequently return here to revel in the "legitimate theatre." Mainstream theater merits the high prices for shows that are either Broadway-bound or beginning their national tour after a New York run. The *L.A. Weekly* has comprehensive listings of L.A. theaters both big and small.

Concerts

The commonly used concert venues range from small to massive. The **Wiltern Theater** (213-381-5005) has presented artists such as Suzanne Vega and The Church. The **Hollywood Palladium** (213-466-4311) is of comparable size. Mid-size acts head for the **Universal Amphitheater** (818-890-9421) and the **Greek Theater** (310-410-1062). Capacious indoor sports arenas, such as the **Sports Arena** (213-748-6131) or the **Forum** (310-419-3182), double as concert halls for large shows. Few performers dare to play at the over 100,000-seat **L.A. Coliseum.** Only U2, Bruce Springsteen, the Rolling Stones, Guns 'n' Roses and the Pope have attempted this feat in recent years.

Bars

L.A. isn't known for its bar scene, but bars do exist, and generally serve a slightly older and more subdued crowd than do the clubs. Bars on Santa Monica Promenade are presently some of the most popular in L.A.

Molly Malone's, 575 S. Fairfax (213-935-1579). Not your typical Irish pub—showcases some of L.A.'s big up-and-coming bands. Cover varies. Open 10am-1:30pm.

Stratton's, 1037 Broxton Ave. (310-208-0488). Hot spot with UCLA students. Open daily 11am-2am.

Al's Bar, 305 S. Hewitt St. (625-9703), in downtown. One of L.A. nightlife's best-hidden secrets. Wide range of nightly entertainment: traditional rock 'n' roll, poetry, experimental bands, performance art and more. Call for info. Open daily 1pm-2:30am.

Clubs

The club scene *is* L.A.'s nightlife. With the highest number of bands per capita in the world, most clubs are able to book top-notch bands night after sweaty night. The distinction between music clubs and dance clubs is nominal in L.A. Coupons in *L.A. Weekly* can save you a bundle, and many are also handed out in reams inside the clubs. To enter the club scene it's best to be 21; the next best option is to look it. Nevertheless, if you're over 18, you'll still find a space to dance. For more extensive listings of gay men's and women's bars contact the Gay and Lesbian Community Services Center (see Practical Information).

Blak and Bloo, 7574 Sunset Blvd. in Hollywood (213-876-1120). Artistic, funky people. Funk, industrial, and alternative music. Maybe the only place on Sunset without serious attitude problems. Pool room, 2 bars, 2 dance rooms. Open Tues.-Sun.Cover varies. 21 and over.

Kingston 12, 814 Broadway (451-4423), Santa Monica. L.A.'s only full-time reggae club presents both local and foreign acts. Dreadlocks and fragrant smoke flow freely. Dance floor, 2 bars. Open Wed.-Sun. 8:30pm-2am. Cover varies. Must be 21. Jamaican food.

Club Lingerie, 6507 Sunset Blvd., Hollywood (466-8557). The favored music club of all kinds of people. Rock, reggae, ska, and funk. They've got it. 2 full bars. Must be 21.

Roxbury, 8225 W. Sunset (213-656-1750). L.A. pretension at its fullest. Contends with Vertigo in downtown as the most hotsy-totsy place in the city (you probably won't get in, but it might be fun trying). Jazz room downstairs, huge bar and dancing upstairs. VIP room only admits the wealthy, famous, and startlingly beautiful. Open Tues.-Sat. 7pm-2am.

Whisky A Go-Go, 8901 Sunset Blvd. (310-652-4202). Another venerable spot on the Strip. Like the Roxy, part of L.A.'s music history. The Whisky played host to many progressive bands in the late 70s and early 80s, and was a major part of the punk explosion. Mostly metal nowadays. Full bar, cover varies. No age restrictions.

Roxy, 9009 Sunset Blvd. (310-276-2222). One of the best known of L.A.'s Sunset Strip clubs, the Roxy is filled with record-company types and rockers waiting to be discovered. Many big acts at the height of their popularity play here. Cover varies. No age restrictions.

Gazzarri's, 9039 Sunset Blvd. (310-273-6606). An enormously popular heavy metal club on the Sunset Strip. Don't go if you're disturbed by hordes of long-haired crazies sharing your space. Cover $6-10. No age restrictions.

Rage, 8911 Santa Monica Blvd., W. Hollywood (310-652-7055). Dance and R&B sounds for a mainly gay crowd.

Blowfish, 301 Santan Monica Pier (310-969-2515), Santa Monica. Outdoor patio opens onto the beach where revelers can find respite from acid, jazz, and funk inside. Full bar, cover $6. Nightly from 10pm-2am. Must be 21.

The Palms, 8572 Santa Monica Blvd. (310-652-6188), W. Hollywood's oldest women's bar. Top 40 dancing every night. Full bar. Low cover, if any. 21 and over.

Peanuts, 7969 Santa Moncia Blvd. (213-654-0280). Management varies nightly, and generally offers some of the hottest clubs in L.A. Mostly over 18.

Amusement Parks

For information on **Disneyland** and **Knott's Berry Farm,** see Orange County.

Six Flags Magic Mountain, 26101 Magic Mountain Pkwy. (818-367-5965), in Valencia, a 40-min. drive up I-5 from L.A. Not for novices, Magic Mountain has the hairiest roller-coaster in Southern California (even hairier than Disneyland's Space Mountain). Highlights of the park are The Revolution, a smooth metal coaster with a vertical 360° loop; Colossus, the world's largest wooden roller coaster; Free Fall, a simulated no-parachute fall out of the sky; Ninja, a coaster whose cars are suspended on a rail from above and are allowed to swing back and forth as they turn; the park's newest coaster, Flashback, with an electrifying hairpin drop; the Viper, which is said to approach the limits of what coaster builders can do with G-forces without *really* hurting people. For roller-coaster-o-phobes, there's also a crafts fair area and a children's playland with a Bugs Bunny theme. The truth is, however, that few people over 48 in. tall come to Magic Mountain for the crafts fair or for the love of Bugs Bunny. This becomes especially apparent when you encounter the lines for Colossus on a hot summer afternoon. Open Memorial Day to mid-September, and Christmas and Easter weeks Mon.-Fri. 10am-6pm, Sat. 10am-midnight, Sun. 10am-10pm; mid-September to Memorial Day (save Christmas and Easter holiday weeks) weekends only. Admission $22, seniors $16, children under 48 in. tall $14. Parking $4.

Raging Waters Park, 111 Raging Waters Dr. (714-592-6453 for recorded message, 714-599-1251 for directions), in San Dimas. (Yes, this *is* where Bill and Ted are from.) Near the intersection of the San Bernardino and Foothill Fwy. (I-10 and 210). Beat the heat with 44 acres and 5 million gallons of slides, pools, whitewater rafts, inner-tubes, fake waves, and a fake island (don't fret, they recycle). A cool but costly alternative to the beach. Hurl yourself over the 7-story water-slide "Drop Out" if you dare, or slide through a tropical rain forest. Open Mon.-Fri. 10am-6pm., Sat.-Sun. 10am-7pm. Admission $17, 42"-48" $9, under 2 free.

Seasonal Events

Grunion runs throughout spring and summer. A voyeuristic pleasure: slippery, silver fish squirm onto the beaches (especially San Pedro) to mate. The fish can be caught by hand, but a license is required, oddly, for those over 16, from the Fish and Game Department (310-590-5132) for $10.50, valid until Dec. 31 each year. 1-day license $5.50. Fishing prohibited April-May. Free programs on the Grunion run given at the Cabrillo Marine Museum, San Pedro (310-548-7562).

UCLA Mardi Gras, mid-May, at the athletic field (310-825-8001). Billed as the world's largest collegiate activity (a terrifying thought). Features food, games, and entertainment. (Admission $3, children $1.) Proceeds benefit charity.

Gay Pride Week, late June (213-656-6553). The lesbian and gay community of L.A. comes out in full force. Art, politics, dances, and a big parade all center on the Pacific Design Center, 8687 Melrose Ave., Hollywood. Tickets $16.

Renaissance Pleasure Faire, every weekend from late April-mid-June in the city of Devore (714-880-6211). From L.A., take the I-10 east to I-15 north, and look for signs as you approach the city. Decked out in their best Elizabethan finery, San Bernardino teenagers are versed in Shakespearean vocab before working at the Faire. Food, games, and music. Open 9am-6pm. Admission $14.50, seniors (over 62) $11.50, children $8.

Northern California

Napa Valley and Wine Country

Transplanted Europeans recognized the Dionysian virtues of this area when California was still a part of Mexico. Prohibition, however, turned the vineyards into fig plantations; only in the last 20 years have local vintners resurrected Bacchus. Today, the wine-tasting carnival lasts from sunup to sundown, dominating the life of small towns in Napa, Sonoma, Dry Creek, Alexander, and Russian River Valleys. **Napa Valley** holds the best-known U.S. vineyards. For more info contact the **Napa Visitors Center,** 1310 Town Center, on 1st St. (226-7455).

Sonoma offers slightly less-crowded wineries than Napa, as well as more exciting local history. The Sonoma Mission, General Vallejo's home, and Jack London's Beauty Ranch may interest the wine-sodden traveler. Farther north, the **Russian River** flows lazily between small towns and smaller wineries.

Although wine country's heavyweights offer well-organized tours, head to the smaller wineries of Sonoma Valley or Oregon to discuss vintages with the growers themselves. The vineyards listed below are some of the valley's larger operations. Napa is home to the wine country's heavyweights; vineyards there include national names such as Inglenook, Christian Brothers, and Mondavi. The large vineyards are better for neophytes since their tours are well-organized, and there's no pressure to say anything intelligent at the tastings. To reach the smaller places, pick up a list of vineyards from the Napa visitors center or look for signs along the roadside. Visitors unfamiliar with U.S. drinking laws should be forewarned: you must be 21 years old to purchase or drink alcohol—and this also goes for tastings at wineries. Also, the vineyards in Napa do not allow picnicking.

Robert Mondavi Winery, 7801 St. Helena Hwy. (963-9611), in Oakville. Spirited tours through marvelous catacombs and past towering stacks of oaken barrels with mellowing wine. The best free tour and tasting for the novice. Open daily 9am-5pm; May-Sept. 10am-4:30pm. Reservations required. Tours (every 15 min.) fill fast in summer; call before 10am.

Domaine Chandon, California Dr. (944-2280), next to the Veteran's Home in Yountville. One of the finest tours in the valley; available in French by prior arrangement. Owned by Moët-Chandon of France (makers of *Dom Perignon*), and, not surprisingly, most capable of divulging the secrets of the making of sparkling wine. Champagne tastings $3-4 per glass at the restaurant attached to the winery. Open daily 11am-6pm; Nov.-April Wed.-Sun. 11am-6pm.

Hanns Kornell Champagne Cellars, 1091 Larkmead Lane (963-2334), 4 mi. north of St. Helena. A 1-room testing area with excellent dry champagne (try the *Sehr Trocken*). Entertaining, informative tours until 3:45pm. Open daily 10am-4pm.

Clos Du Val Wine Company Ltd., 5330 Silverado Trail (252-6711), in Napa. Outdoor picnic area with whimsical drawings by Ronald Searle. Tours by appointment at 10am and 2pm. Tasting room open all day. Open daily 10am-5pm.

Newlan, 5225 Solano Ave. (257-2399). A small premium winery, with the best in *Pinot Noir* and dessert wines. Tastings daily 10am-5pm, by appointment.

Budget motels amid the valleys are scarce and inaccessible to those without cars. For the valley's best deal ssslip into the wooden cabins at the **Triple S Ranch,** 4600 Mountain Home Ranch Rd. (942-6730), in Calistoga. Take Rte. 29 north to Calistoga; turn left on Petrified Forest Rd., and then right on Mountain Home Ranch Rd. Reservations recommended, especially weekends. (Singles $35. Doubles $45, $5 off second night. Open April-Jan. 1.) **Silverado Motel,** 500 Silverado Trail (253-0892), in Napa near Second Ave., dry, balanced, precocious (but never busy) rooms with kitchenette and cable TV. Recently refurbished, it has more personality than its motel-chain competitors. **Napa Valley Budget Inn** (formerly Motel 6), nestles at 3380 Solano Ave. (257-6111). From Rte. 29, take the Redwood Rd. exit, and turn left immediately onto Solano. Rooms with TV and A/C, plus a small pool. Usually full by 6pm in summer. (Singles $36. Each additional adult $6.) Campers can camp at the **Bothe-Napa Valley State Park,** 3601 St. Helena Hwy. (942-4575; 800-444-7275 for reservations), north of St. Helena on Rte. 29. (Open daily 8am-sunset; Oct.-April 9am-5pm. Sites with hot showers $14. Reservations recommended.)

Napa and its neighboring communities support numerous delis where you can pick up inexpensive picnic supplies. The **Jefferson Food Mart** (224-7112), 1704 Jefferson, is open daily 7am to 11pm. **Villa Corona Panadería-Tortellería,** 3614 Bel Aire Plaza (257-8685), behind the Citibank Bldg., is a tiny restaurant on an alley, with a *piñata*ed ceiling. Impressive selection of Mexican beers, drinks, and spices. Mexican pastries made on premises cost $1 to $2. (Open 9am-8:30pm daily in summer, 9am-7:30pm winter.) If you're looking to prepare a picnic, **Guigini's,** 1227 Main St. (963-3421), in St. Helena, is the best place to slap one together. It is an unpretentious, friendly grocery store with sandwiches for $3. (Open daily 9am-5pm.) Should you tire of the Valley's delicate slices of brie on baguette, try **Taylor's Refresher,** Rte. 29 across from Sunny St. Helena Winery (963-3486), a burger stand with vegetarian and traditional burgers ($2.25) and an array of Mexican dishes. (Outdoor seating only.)

Route 29 runs through the middle of the Valley with the main town of **Napa** at its southern end and **Calistoga** to the north. The best way to see the area is by bicycle; the valley is dead level and no more than 30 mi. long. The **Silverado Trail,** parallel to Rte. 29, is a more scenic and less crowded route than the highway. If you're planning a weekend trip from San Francisco, the 60-mi. trip may take up to 1½ hours on Saturday mornings or Sunday afternoons. If at all possible, try to visit the Valley on weekdays and avoid the bus tours with plastic glasses and frantic wine-pouring in over-crowded tasting rooms. Rent a bike at **Napa Valley Cyclery,** 4080 Byway E. (255-3377; $6 per hr., $20 per day, $70 per week. Open Mon.-Sat. 9am-6pm, Sun. 10am-5pm. Major credit card required). **Greyhound** stops in Vallejo (643-7661); one bus per day lopes through the Valley. It stops in Napa at 9:30am in front of the Napa State Hospital, 2100 Napa-Vallejo Hwy., and also makes stops in Yountville, St. Helena, and Calistoga.

Napa's **post office** does its thing at 1625 Trancas St. (255-1621; open Mon.-Fri. 8:30am-5pm). The **ZIP code** is 94558; the **area code** is 707.

Redwood National Park

Northern California's pride and joy, Redwood National Park (464-6101) flaunts an astonishing variety of flora and fauna in addition to the burly 500-year-old trees themselves. The region's fishing is famous, and the variegated terrain is ideal for hikers and backpackers. The park begins just south of the Oregon border and extends 50 mi. south, hugging the coast for about 40 mi., and encompassing three state parks. The lack of public transport within the park demands perseverance, however. Beaches line the coastal trail that marches most of the length of the park; the heavy rains, created by moisture off the Pacific, foster a lush environment of elk, bear, birds, and marine life. Day use of state parks costs $5 per car; hikers and bikers are charged $5, as well.

The park divides naturally into five segments—Orick, Prairie Creek, Klamath, Crescent City, and Hiouchi—stacked from south to north along Rte. 101, each with its own ranger station (except Klamath). Although the terrain varies widely, the imposing *Sequoia sempervirens* are ubiquitous. **Orick,** the southernmost section of the park, has a **ranger station** about one mi. south on U.S. 101 and onemi. south of the Shoreline Deli (the Greyhound stop). This area's main attraction is the **tall trees grove,** an 8½-mi. hike from the ranger station. In peak season, a shuttle bus ($7 donation requested of each person) runs twice per day from the station to the tall trees trail, and once a day from May 23 to June 13. From there, you can hike 1.3 mi. to the tallest known tree in the world (367.8 ft.). Be sure to leave extra time, since the strenuous return hike is mostly uphill; the round-trip can take about five hours. Backpackers may camp anywhere along the way after obtaining a permit at the ranger station. Orick itself (pop. 400) is a sleepy but friendly town brimming over with souvenir stores selling expensive "burl" (tacky, expensive wood carvings).

The **Prairie Creek** area, equipped with state park campgrounds, is perfect for hikers. Starting at the **Prairie Creek Visitors Center** on U.S. 101 (488-2171), the 10-mi. **James Irvine Trail** winds through magnificent redwoods, around clear and cold creeks, through **Fern Canyon** (famed for its 50-ft. fern walls and crystalline creek), and by a stretch of the Pacific Ocean. The **Revelation** and **Redwood Access Trails** were designed for physically challenged people. The bookstore at the visitors center sells an excellent, if expensive, book entitled *Hip Pocket Guide to Humboldt Coast* that details virtually all the trails in this area. To the north, the **Klamath** area comprises a thin stretch of park land connecting Prairie Creek with Del Norte State Park. Klamath River, the main attraction here besides the rugged coastline, lures salmon. (Fishing permit required.) The **Klamath Overlook,** where Requa Rd. meets the Coastal Trail is an excellent whale- and sea lion-watching site, but 25 mi. south of the Prairie Creek Redwood State Park on Hwy. 101 at **Patrick's Point** makes an ever better one; the view from this promontory is fantastic as it is closer to migratory routes.

Crescent City, the largest metropolis north of Eureka and south of the Oregon border calls itself the city where "the Redwoods meet the sea." It really did meet the sea when, in 1964, the great tsunami caused by seismic activity brought 500 mph winds that leveled the city. Today the rebuilt city serves as an outstanding location from which to explore the National Park *and* a maximum-security prison. The well-supplied **Visitors Center** at 1001 Front St. (464-3174) is surprisingly large for such a depressing town (open Mon.-Fri. 9am-5pm, and Sat.-Sun. 10am-6pm in the summer). Seven mi. south of the city lies the **Del Norte Coast Redwoods State Park's Mill Creek Campground,** an extension of the Redwood Forest. The park's magnificent ocean views—along with picnic areas, hiking trails, and nearby fishing—lure enough campers to keep the sites full during peak season. (Tent sites $14, day-use fee $5.) The **Hiouchi** region sits in the northern part of the park inland along Rte. 199 and offers several excellent trails. The **Stout Grove Trail,** an easy half-mi. walk, boasts the park's stoutest redwood, 18 ft. in diameter. The path is also accessible to the disabled; call 458-3310 for arrangements. **Kayak** trips on the Smith River leave from the **ranger station** on U.S. 199 (458-3134).

In Orick, buy some grub at the **Orick Market** (488-3225). Or dine on elk steak ($16), buffalo steak ($15), wild boar roast ($15), and other dainties at **Rolf's Park Cafe** (488-3841), two mi. north of Orick off U.S. 101's Fern Canyon exit, just after the turn-off to Davison Rd. In Crescent City, try the inexpensive seafood at **Harbor View Grotto,** 115 Citizens Dock Rd. (464-3815; open daily 11am-10pm) or the Mexican cuisine at **Los Compadres,** Hwy. 101 South (464-7871; open daily 11am-9pm, 11am-8pm in the winter). Don't leave the area without trying **salmon jerky,** a Native American specialty widely distributed locally.

If you're not camping, the **Redwood Youth Hostel (HI/AYH),** 14480 U.S. 101, in Klamath 95548 (482-8265), is a great deal. Overlooking the ocean and housed in the historic De Martin House, the Redwood features modern amenities—kitchen, dining room, laundry facilities, two sundecks, and wheelchair access. Reservations are recommended for summer and weekend stays; they must be made by mail three weeks in advance. ($9, under 18 with parent $4.50. Family rooms available by reservation. Linen $1. Check-in 4:30-9:30pm. Curfew 11pm. Closed 9:30am-4:30pm.) In Orick, one- or two-person rooms at the **Park Woods Motel,** 121440 Rte. 101 (488-5175), go for $35; two-bedroom units with kitchens are only $40. Crescent City is absolutely *not* the place to stay; it's as overpriced as national security.

Campsites are numerous, ranging from the well equipped (flush toilets and free hot showers; sites $12, hikers $2) to the primitive (outhouses at best; free). Peak season begins in the third week of June and concludes in early September. Try to visit from mid-April to mid-June or September to mid-October, when the park's summer crowds and fogs dissipate. Call MISTIX (800-444-7275) for reservations (highly recommended in the peak season).

Greyhound, 1125 Northcrest Dr. (464-2807) in Crescent City, supposedly stops at three places within the park: Shoreline Deli (488-5761), 1 mi. south of Orick on U.S. 101; Paul's Cannery in Klamath on U.S. 101; and the Redwood Hostel. Capricious bus drivers may ignore you. Call the Greyhound station directly preceding your stop to alert the driver of your presence. **AAA Emergency Road Service** is located in **Crescent City AAA,** 1000 Northcrest Dr.(464-5626); open Mon.-Fri. 8am-5pm. **Dial-A-Ride** (464-9314) operates in the immediate Crescent City area. Rides are all the same price, regardless of distance. (Open Mon.-Fri. 7am-11pm, Sat. 7am-7pm.) $1, seniors and youths $.75.) The Crescent City **post office** hunkers at 751 2nd St. (464-2151; open Mon.-Fri. 8:30am-5pm.) The **ZIP code** is 95531. The **area code** for the park region is 707.

Sacramento

The indistinctive capital of a very distinctive state, Sacramento is so average that it is often used by market researchers to test brands of soap. But Sacramento has been the capital since 1854—just long enough to accumulate a few interesting sights. A hobo-hangout in the 1960s, **Old Sacramento** has undergone restoration, now attracting cash-besotted tourists with upmarket shops. A pleasant atmosphere pervades a number of historic structures, among them the **B.F. Hastings** building at the corner of 2nd and J St. Dating from 1852, the building houses Wells Fargo's offices, a museum, and the reconstructed chambers of the California Supreme Court. Pick up a self-guided walking tour at the **Old Sacramento Visitors Center,** or join a tour beginning at the center (1104 Front St., 442-7644).

Before overdosing on souvenir stores and cutesy-pie potpourri gift shops, try the excellent historical museums in Old Sacramento's northern end. The **California State Railroad Museum,** 125 I St. (448-4466), at 2nd St., will delight even those who don't know the difference between a cowcatcher and a caboose. The museum houses a fascinating collection of historical locomotives in its enormous exhibition space. The same ticket admits you to the **Central Pacific Depot and Passenger Station,** at First and J St., a reconstruction of a station that once stood here. (Both open daily 10am-5pm. Admission $5, ages 6-17 $2, under 6 free.)

The **Sacramento History Museum,** 101 I St. (264-7057), at Front St., housed in the reconstructed 1854 City Hall, presents scintillating exhibits on California history in a two-story glass-and-chrome extravaganza, with interactive videos. (Open daily 10am-5pm. Guided tours upon request. $3, ages 6-17 $1.50, under 6 free.)

Gallery-hoppers should enjoy the elegant **Crocker Art Museum,** 216 O St. (264-5423), at 3rd St., housed in a restored Victorian building, with mainly 19th-century European and American oil paintings. One large gallery showcases photography, another contemporary works by California artists. (Open Tues.-Sun. 10am-5pm, Thurs. 10am-9pm. Admission $2.50, seniors and ages 7-18 $1, under 7 free. Tours available.)

Two modern twin towers very nearly replaced the **State Capitol,** at 10th St. and Capitol Mall (324-0333), in Capitol Park, when the old and abused structure began to crumble under the rule of ex-B-movie-actor Ronald Reagan in the 1970s. But California taxpayers forked over $68 million, and the building was finally restored in 1982 to its glorious 1906 finery, replete with pink and green décor, oak staircases, gilt, and flattering oil paintings of forgotten governors. The "Restoration" tour covers the chambers; the "Historic" delves into the recreated office spaces, decorated as they were decades ago. (Both hr.-long tours daily on the hr. 9am-4pm. Free.) Another tour explores the gardens, including the elaborate **Vietnam Memorial,** daily at 10am. (Capitol open daily 9am-5pm, fall and winter Sat.-Sun. 10am-5pm. For info, self-guided walking tour brochures, and an excellent free 10-min. film, go to Room B-27 in the basement.)

Before the arrival of a certain Ronald Reagan, who demanded more spacious surroundings, the **Old Governor's Mansion,** 16th and H St. (324-0539), fit the bill. This 15-room Victorian masterpiece (circa 1877) housed 13 of California's governors. The building practically bursts with gables and attics, displaying the architectural subtlety of a three-tiered wedding cake. (Open daily 10am-5pm. half-hr. tours on the hour. Last tour at 4pm. Admission $2, age 6-17 $1, under 6 free.)

Across town at 27th and L St. stands **Sutter's Fort** (324-0539), a reconstruction of the 1839 military settlement that launched Sacramento. All supplies had to be dragged overland from the river to build the settlement, which now contains the **State Indian Museum** (324-0971). Rangers fire the fort's cannon at 11am and 2pm. (Both open daily 10am-5pm. Admission to each $2, under 18 $1.)

Though perhaps a bit disheartened by the dominance of compact discs, vintage vinyl collectors will still enjoy a trip to the original **Tower Records,** at the corner of Landpark Dr. and Broadway (444-3000). Tower Records began in 1941 when an ambitious teenager, Russ Solomon, started selling records in the back of his dad's drugstore; he now owns a national chain of stores. The store's overwhelmingly large selection and late hours are replicated in the adjacent Tower Books, Drugs, Theater, Tobacco, *ad nauseum.* (Record store open daily 9am-midnight.)

The kid in you (or with you) will enjoy the **Sacramento Zoo** (264-5885), at 3930 W. Land Park Dr. (Open daily 9am-4pm; admission $3.50, ages 3-12 $2, under 3 free. 50¢ more on weekends.) Another kids' place is the **Visionarium,** 2901 K St. (443-7476), on the 2nd level of the Sutter square galleria, an aggressively interactive children's museum billed as "Kids on Kampus." (Open Mon.-Sat. 10am-6pm, Sun. noon-5pm. $2.50, ages 3-18 $2, under 3 free.)

Downtown Sacramento supports a bunch of breakfast and lunch spots; unfortunately, many close by early afternoon when the government does. Old Sacramento is the place to go for ice cream, light snacks, and classier wining and dining. But the best meals appear in the blocks between 19th St. and 22nd St., concentrated around Capitol St. **Zelda's Original Gourmet Pizza** (447-1400), 1415 21st St., although distant from the town's center, has awesome deep-dish pizza (medium $8). Their Vegetarian Supreme is indeed both ($13). (Open Mon.-Thurs. 11:30am-2pm and 5-10pm, Fri. 11:30am-2pm and 5-11:30pm, Sat. 5-11:30pm, Sun. 5-9pm.) In Old Sacramento, **Annabelle's,** 200 J

St. (448-6239), boasts an all-you-can-eat lunch buffet ($3.75) which includes pasta, lasagna, pizza, and salad bar. (Open daily 11:30am-8pm.)

Sacramento's supply of motel rooms wanes when one of the city's frequent large conventions is in progress; all but the sleaziest dives are fully booked by midweek. Try to reserve a month in advance. The cheapest places lie near the Greyhound station across from Capitol Park but provide questionable cleanliness and security. Several motels east of Capitol Park, along 15th and 16th St., also average $30 for singles. For even cheaper rates go to West Sacramento, a 20- to 30-minute walk along W. Capitol Ave. from Old Sacramento. Jibboom St., one mi. from Old Sacramento, also has a lot of cheap motels. Call the **West Sacramento Motel & Hotel Association** (372-5378) or the **West Sacramento Chamber of Commerce** (372-5378; open Mon.-Fri. 8am-5pm). Yolo buses #40, 41, or 42 go to West Sacramento from the L St. terminal. The quality of rooms even ranges within some of the motels; see your room before paying.

With nine comfortable beds, the **Gold Rush Home Hostel (HI/AYH),** 1421 Tiverton Ave. (421-5954), on the outskirts of town near Florin Rd. and I-5, is like visiting your favorite relatives, except they charge you. Very comfortable. (Lockout 9am-6pm. $8, nonmembers $10. Reservations required; no walk-ins.) Primarily apartments for the elderly, **Capitol Park Hotel** (441-5361), 1125 9th St., at L St., two blocks from Greyhound, rents some well-worn rooms nightly. The ancient hotel, with a fabulous downtown location, keeps cool with large windows. (Singles $28. Doubles $35, plus $5 key deposit.) The **Americana Lodge** (444-3980), 818 15th St., the nicest in the range, features a small pool, A/C, and HBO. (Local calls 25¢, check-out 11am. Singles from $37. Doubles $42. Confirm reservations with advance payment.)

The small, congenial **Sacramento Convention and Visitors Bureau** (264-6711), 1421 K St., between 14th and 15th St., presents a tidy stand of brochures on the corner table. Find there the only accommodations guide in town, the free *Sacramento*. (Open Mon.-Fri. 8am-5pm.) The **Old Sacramento Visitors Center** (264-7777; holidays and weekends 442-7644), 1104 Front St., also has a modest handful of brochures. (Open daily 9am-5pm.)

Amtrak (800-872-7245), at 5th and I St., has a huge terminal (open daily 5:15am-11:15pm). Daily trains roll to Reno ($52), Chicago ($205), L.A. ($75), Seattle ($144), and San Francisco ($16). Reservations must be made months in advance for all eastbound and most westbound trains in order to get discounts. The **Greyhound** station (444-6800), idles at 715 L St., between 7th and 8th St. in a relatively safe if unpleasant neighborhood. Buses run to Reno (gambler's round-trip special, 3-day max. stay,.$19), L.A. ($39), and San Francisco ($8). (Open 24 hrs.) **Sacramento Regional Transit Bus** (321-2877) offers service in downtown Sacramento. ($1 including 1 transfer, all-day pass $3, $1.25 express buses run Mon.-Fri. 6:30-9am and 3:30-6pm.) An 18.3-mi. **light rail transit** line connects the central business district with the eastern regions of the city. (Trains run every 15 min. 4:30am-1:30am. Fare $1.25.) The **Yolo Bus Commuter Lines** (371-2877) connect downtown with Old Sacramento, West Sacramento, Davis, and Woodland. (Fare $1, 50¢ surcharge on express buses #43, 44, 45.)

Block numbers in Sacramento correspond to the lettered cross-streets, so 200 3rd St. intersects B St., 1700 C St. is on 17th St., 300 3rd St. intersects C, and so on. The Capitol and endless state government buildings occupy the rectilinear downtown area. The **Broadway** area, home of the original Tower Records, lies beyond Z St. The 40 avenues north of Broadway, known as the "fabulous forty," contain the mansions of Sacramento's industrial barons; one housed Ronald Reagan during his term as governor. **West Sacramento** lies, strangely enough, west of downtown, on the other side of the river. With well-marked lanes, the city is a good biker's town. Rent at the **American River Bike Shop,** 9203 Folsom Blvd. (363-6271; $3 per hour, $15 per day).

The **post office** governs at 2000 Royal Oak Dr. (921-4339; on weekends, holidays, and after 5pm, call 921-4564; open Mon.-Fri. 8:30am-5pm). **General Delivery** mail can be picked up at Metro Station, 801 I St. (442-0764), at 8th. (Open Mon.-Fri. 8am-5:30pm.) The General Delivery **ZIP code** is 95814. The **area code** is 916.

Orange County

Orange County, Los Angeles' neighbor to the south, was part of Los Angeles County until 1861, when "O.C." seceded over a tax dispute. The two have become sibling rivals. Orange County's population is less ethnically diverse and economically challenged than that of trouble-plagued Los Angeles. Many O.C. residents live in "planned communities," neighborhoods designed by strict codes governing exactly where schools, shopping centers and gas stations must be placed. Drive through inland Orange County and you'll be plagued by the eerie feeling that you are under a giant developer's model-community bubble. If regimented living isn't to your taste, head for the coast, where Orange County's fine surf and string of clean, uncrowded beaches have produced the truest approximation of stereotypical Southern California beach life.

Practical Information

Emergency: 911.

Anaheim Area Visitors and Convention Bureau, 800 W. Katella Ave., Anaheim 92802 (999-8999). In the Anaheim Convention Center. Free brochures. Open Mon.-Fri. 8:30am-5pm.

Airport: John Wayne Orange County, Campus Dr. (755-6500). Flights to and from many major U.S. cities.

Amtrak, 5 stops: 120 E. Santa Fe Ave. (992-0530), in Fullerton, at Harbor Blvd.; 1000 E. Santa Ana (547-8389), in Santa Ana; Santa Fe Depot (661-8835), in San Juan Capistrano; 2150 E. Katella (385-1448), in Anaheim by Anaheim Stadium; unstaffed stop in San Clemente, off I-5, by the municipal pier.

Greyhound, terminals at 2080 S. Harbor (635-5060), in Anaheim, 3 blocks south of Disney (open Mon.-Thurs. 7am-7:30pm, Fri.-Sun. 7am-9:30pm); 1000 E. Santa Ana Blvd. (542-2215), in Santa Ana (open daily 7am-8pm); and 510 Avenida de la Estrella (492-1187), in San Clemente (open Mon.-Thurs. 7:45am-6:30pm, Fri. 7:45am-8pm).

Orange County Transit District (OCTD): 11222 Acacia Parkway (636-7433), in Garden Grove. Thorough service, useful for getting from Santa Ana and Fullerton Amtrak stations to Disneyland, or for beach-hopping along the coast. Long Beach, in L.A. County, serves as the terminus for several OCTD lines. Bus #1 travels the coast from Long Beach down to San Clemente, with service twice per hour from early morning until around 8pm. Schedules available in many public places. Fare $1, transfers $.05. Most buses accept dollar bills but will not provide change. Transfers free. Info center open Mon.-Fri. 6am-7pm; Sat.-Sun. 8am-5pm.

Local RTD Information: 800-2-LA-RIDE (252-7433). Lines open daily 5:30am-midnight. RTD buses run from L.A. to Disneyland and Knott's Berry Farm.

Help lines: Rape Crisis Hotline, 831-9110. 24-hr. service of the Orange County Sexual Assault Network.

Police: 425 S. Harbor Blvd. (999-1900), in Anaheim.

Post Office: 701 N. Loara (520-2609), in Anaheim. One block east of Euclid, 1 block north of Anaheim Plaza. Open Mon.-Fri. 8:30am-5pm. General Delivery **ZIP Code**: 92803.

Area Code: 310; 213 in Seal Beach; 714 in southern Orange County.

Accommodations and Camping

Its proximity to Disneyland and the other amusement parks grants **Anaheim** a thriving tourist trade. Because it's fairly remote from L.A.'s other sights, the Magic Kingdom is the only reason to stay here. Start by contacting the Anaheim Visitors Center, a travel industry dating service, which matches people with rooms they can afford. The road to Disneyland along Harbor Blvd. is lined with economy motels.

The county coast is the other big attraction, and bargain rates can be found at motels scattered along Pacific Coast Hwy. and Newport Beach's Newport Blvd.

Fullerton Hacienda Hostel (HI/AYH), 1700 N. Harbor Blvd. (738-3721), in Fullerton, about a 15-min. drive north of Disneyland. OCTD bus #43 runs up and down Harbor Blvd. to Disneyland, and the hostel managers can arrange car rentals for groups. A large, comfortable house with a porch swing, set back from the road on a quiet hill hopping with rabbits. This convenient house is a favorite among hostelers. New kitchen, weekly BBQs, common bathrooms, spiffy singles and mixed-sex accomodations. 3-day max. stay. Open daily 7:30-9:30am and 4-11pm. Members $13.20, nonmembers $16.20. Linen $1.

Huntington Beach Colonial Inn Youth Hostel, 421 8th St. (536-3315), in Huntington Beach, 4 blocks inland at Pecan. In a large yellow Victorian house shaded by huge palm trees. Nine 2-person rooms, 3 more accommodate 4-5 people. Common showers, bathroom, large kitchen. Reading/TV room. Check-in 7am-11pm. Curfew 11pm. Late night key rental $1 ($20 deposit). $11 per night. Must have picture ID.

Mesa Motel, N. Newport Blvd. (646-3893). A ½-mi. to the beach. Small swimming pool, TV, and typical motel rooms. Singles $30. Doubles $35.

Motel 6, 2 Anaheim locations: 921 S. Beach Blvd. (220-2866), and 7450 Katella Ave. (891-0717), both within a 10-min. drive of Disneyland. The excitement of the nearby amusement park permeates the motels osmotically; both have pools filled with couples and their hyperactive, Mickey Mouse-eared children. *Not* the place to stay if you're seeking peace and quiet. Rooms $32 for 1-4 people on S. Beach Blvd; $24 for singles, $30 for doubles on Katella Ave.

State beaches in Orange County with campgrounds are listed below from north to south. Reservations are required for all sites except the Echo Arch Area in San Onofre, made through MISTIX (800-444-7275) a maximum of 56 days in advance.

Bolsa Chica, Rte. 1 (848-1566), 3 mi. west of Huntington Beach. Self-contained vehicles (read: RVs) only. 7-day maximum. $14 per vehicle, $12 for senior citizens.

Doheny, Rte. 1 (496-6771), at the south end of Dana Point. Beachside location turns this place into a zoo as suburban families howl out. TVs, lounge furniture, play pens, and more. Beachfront sites $21, otherwise $16.

San Clemente, I-5 (492-3156). 157 sites, 85 developed. Sites $16. Tricky Dick Nixon sees you.

San Onofre, I-5 (492-0802), 3 mi. south of San Clemente. 221 campsites along an abandoned stretch of PCH; about 90 suitable for tents. The **Echo Arch Area** has 34 more primitive hike-in sites between the bluffs and the beach. The San Mateo Campground is a brand new park with 140 sites and hot showers. These three areas are the most secluded, and the site of the most partying (still fairly calm). All three are within mutating distance of the nuclear power plant. Sites $16.

Sights and Food

Among the architectural attractions in Orange County not blessed by Walt Disney is the **Crystal Cathedral,** 12141 Lewis St., Garden Grove. Opinions are split on this shining all-glass structure completed in 1980 by Phillip Johnson and John Burgee; some find it inspiring, others call it garish. It's from the pulpit of this church that Dr. Robert Schuller preaches his weekly TV show, "Hour of Power." With 7000 people moving in and out every Sunday, the Cathedral is also a model of efficiency. Free daily guided tours Mon-Sat. 9am-3:30pm, Sun. noon-3:30pm.

Inland Orange County is graced with a number of attractions, the newest of which is a tribute to everyone's favorite president—the tan, rested, and ready Richard Nixon. At **The Richard Nixon Library and Birthplace,** 18001 Yorba Linda Blvd., Yorba Linda (993-3393), you can "enjoy the first lady's garden" and engage in a video conversation with Dick himself. ($3.95, seniors $2, open daily 8:30am-5pm).

Despite inland fun, recreation for residents and visitors revolves primarily around the ocean. Visitors should not be lulled off guard by swishing coastal waters. Pedestrians should take extreme care in the cities, and vacationers should not be tempted to crash on the wide beaches. Transients make unsafe what is already illegal.

Huntington Beach (area code 714 for all subsequent beaches) served as a port of entry for the surfing craze, which transformed California coast life after being imported from Hawaii by Duke Kahanamoku in the early 1900s. Still popular, the sport culminates each year in the **surfing championships** (536-5486) held in late July. The newly remodeld pier provides a perfect vantage point for oglers.

Newport Beach and the surrounding cities inland are the jewels of Orange County, with stunning multi-million-dollar homes lining Newport Harbor, the largest leisure craft harbor in the world. The beach itself displays few signs of ostentatious wealth; it is crowded with young, frequently rowdy, hedonists in neon-colored bikinis and trunks. The area around Newport Pier is a haven for families; the streets from 30th to 56th give way to teenagers and college students sunning, surfing, and playing volleyball. The boardwalk is always a scene in the summer, with beach house renters partying wildly on their porches.

The sands of Newport Beach run south onto the **Balboa Peninsula,** separated from the mainland by Newport Bay. The peninsula is only two to four blocks wide and can be reached from PCH by Balboa Blvd. The Victorian **Balboa Pavilion,** once a sounding board for Big Band great Benny Goodman, is now a hub for harbor tours and winter whale-watching. At the end of the peninsula, **The Wedge,** seasonally pounded by waves up to 20 ft. tall, is a bodysurfing mecca. Bodysurfers (ostensibly furloughed from mental institutions) risk a watery grave for this monster ride. Melt into the crowds on Newport Beach and the Balboa Peninsula by hopping on a bicycle or strapping on a pair of rollerblades. Expensive **rental shops** cluster around the Newport Beach pier and at the end of the peninsula, letting bikes ($4-5 per hr., $18-20 per day), skates ($3-6 per hr., $15-18 per day), and boogie boards ($6-7 per day).

North of Newport Beach is **Costa Mesa,** home of the new and dazzling **Orange County Performing Arts Center,** 600 Town Center Dr. (556-2121), on Bristol St. off I-405. The opulent, 3000-seat structure was constructed in 1986 at a cost of $70 million and has enlivened Orange County arts by hosting the American Ballet Theatre and the Kirov Ballet, among other troupes.

More tourists than swallows return every year to **Mission San Juan Capistrano** (493-1424), one half-hour south of Anaheim on I-5; take Ortega Hwy. to Camino Capistrano. This "jewel of the missions" offers a peek at California's origins as a Spanish colony. Established in 1776 as one of 21 California missions of the Catholic church, it is somewhat run-down today due to an 1812 earthquake. Father Junípero Serra, the mission's founder, officiated from inside the beautiful **Serra Chapel,** the oldest building in the state (1777). The chapel is dark and womby, warmed by a 17th-century Spanish cherrywood altar and Native American designs painted on walls and ceiling. It's still used by the Catholic Church, so enter quietly and inhale the scent of candles lit by worshipers. (Open daily 8:30am-7pm; Oct. 1-May 14 8:30am-5pm. Admission $3, ages 3-11 $1.) The mission is perhaps best known as a home to the thousands of swallows who return here from their annual winter migration to nest in mid-March. They are scheduled to return to Capistrano on St. Joseph's Day, March 19, but the birds aren't all that religious, and have a tendency to show up whenever you're not around. The swallows leave in mid-October. The best time to see the birds is when they feed in the early morning or early evening.

The **San Onofre Nuclear Power Plant** provides residents with energy and an eerie breast-like blight on their State Beach landscape. Nevertheless, the beach is a prime surfing area where dozens of wave-riders test the breakers at any given time. The southern end of the beach is frequented by nudists (drive down as far as you can go on I-5, and walk left on the trail for ¼ to½ mi.; beach contains both a gay and a straight area). Be forewarned: nude bathing is illegal, since it shatters an American myth that people don't have genitalia. For info on the coast farther south, see Near San Diego.

Disneyland

The stunningly animated *Beauty and the Beast* and the long-anticipated EuroDisney are among the recent additions to the ever-evolving Disney Empire, but Walt's original themepark has not been left to stagnate amidst the Mouse's global expansion. Opened in 1955 through the vision of Walt Disney, the "happiest place on earth" has delighted even the most hardened cynics. Soviet premier Nikita Kruschev was livid when jingoist Walt barred him from the park at the height of the Cold War.

All this otherworldliness gets disturbing at times, especially with crowds of 75,000 per day jamming the park in search of artificial happiness. Admission to the gleaming fantasy world is gained through the **Unlimited Use Passport** (one day $29, ages 3-11 $23). The park is open daily in summer from 8am-1am. In the off-season, the park ordinarily closes at 6pm on weeknights, 9pm weekends, though hours vary, especially around major holidays; call 714-999-4000 for more information.

Getting There

The park is located at one of the most famous addresses in the world: 1313 Harbor Blvd., in Anaheim in Orange County, bounded by Katella Ave., Harbor Blvd., Ball Rd., and West St. From L.A., take **bus #460** from 6th and Flower St. downtown, about 1½ hours to the Disneyland Hotel. (Service to the hotel from 4:53am, back to L.A. until 1:20am.) From the hotel, take the free shuttle to Disneyland's portals. Also served by Airport Service, OCTD, Long Beach Transit, and Gray Line (see Public Transportation for prices). If you're driving, take the Santa Ana Fwy. to the Katella Ave. exit. Be forewarned, however: while parking in the morning should be painless, leaving in the evening often will not be. In addition, when the park closes early, Disneygoers must contend with L.A.'s maddening rush-hour freeway autopia from hell.

In the Park

Visitors enter the Magic Kingdom by way of **Main Street, U.S.A.,** a collection of shops, arcades, and even a movie theater designed to recreate Walt's maudlin turn-of-the-century childhood memories. Main Street, a broad avenue leading to a replica of Sleeping Beauty's castle at the center of the park, includes a bank, an info booth, lockers, and a first aid station. The **Main Street Electrical Parade** makes its way each summer night at 8:45 and 11pm (with the earlier parade followed by fireworks). Floats and even humans are adorned with thousands of multi-colored lights, making for a potentially shocking nighttime display. This is one of Disneyland's most popular events and people begin lining the sidewalks on Main Street by 7pm. The new **Fantasmic!** laser show projects fiery villains and whirling heroes into the night sky.

Four "lands" branch off Main Street. **Tomorrowland,** to your immediate right at the top of Main Street, contains the park's best thrill rides, **Space Mountain** and the George Lucas-produced **Star Tours.** Moving counter-clockwise around the park, next is **Fantasyland,** with the **Matterhorn** rollercoaster, some excellent kids' rides, and the ever-popular **It's A Small World** (a hint: unless you want the cute, but annoying, theme song running through your head for the rest of the day, you may want to save this one for last). Next is **Frontierland,** with the **Thunder Mountain Railroad** coaster and **Tom Sawyer Island.** Last, but not least, is **Adventureland,** with the **Jungle Cruise** and the **Swiss Family Robinson Treehouse.** In addition, tucked between Frontierland and Adventureland are two more areas that aren't official "lands." One is **New Orleans Square,** with **Pirates of the Caribbean,** the **Haunted Mansion,** and some excellent dining. The other is **Critter Country,** with Disneyland's latest super-attraction, **Splash Mountain,** a log ride that climaxes in a wet, five-story drop.

Food services in the park range from sit-down establishments to fast-food eateries such as the **Lunch Pad**. Save much time and money by packing a picnic lunch and eating a big breakfast before you leave home. Food in the park is mediocre and generally overpriced. If you're looking for a martini, you'll be left high and dry: alcohol doesn't exist in the Magic Kingdom.

Fall months and weekdays are generally less crowded than summer days and weekends. Arrive shortly before the park opens to beat ticket queues. Lines for the most popular attractions are shorter just after opening and late at night; try midday and you'll see why some call it "Disneyline."

Knott Just Disneyland

For more amusing rides and replicas, head to **Knott's Berry Farm,** 8039 Beach Blvd. (714-220-5200 for a recording), at La Palma Ave. in Buena Park, just five mi. northeast of Disneyland. Take the Santa Ana Fwy. south, exit west on La Palma Ave. Bus #460 stops here on its way to Disneyland. An actual berry farm in its early days, Knott's now cultivates a county-fair atmosphere with a recreated ghost town, Fiesta Village, Roaring Twenties Park, rides, and a replica of Independence Hall. The insane rollercoaster Montezuma's Revenge takes you through a backwards loop. The Sky Tower plunges you 20 stories in a free fall parachute jump. The kingdom of the Dinosaurs feature three pre-history thrill rides. The Chicken Dinner Restaurant has been serving tender, inexpensive chicken dinners since 1934. (Open Sun.-Fri. 10am-midnight, Sat. 10am-1am; in winter Mon.-Fri. 10am-6pm, Sat. 10am-10pm, Sun. 10am-7pm. Admission $23, seniors 60 and over $15, ages 3-11 $10.)

Not Knotts

Wild Rivers Waterpark, 8800 Irvine Center Dr., Laguna Hills (714-768-9453), in Orange County, has over 40 water-slide rides, two wave pools, and picnic areas. (Open May-Sept. daily 10am-8pm, Sat.-Sun. 11am-5pm in winter. Admission $16, ages 3-9 $12.)

San Diego

Centuries after its founding on hills of chaparral, San Diego manages to maintain clean air and sandy beaches, a sense of culture and history, and even lush greenery in the face of population growth and droughts. A solid Navy industry cushions the economy; local architecture is pleasant, not gaudy; and rain and cold winters are virtually unknown. But even "America's Finest City" is challenged with very Californian problems of water shortages and immigration surpluses.

San Diego has ample tourist attractions—a world-famous zoo, Sea World, and Old Town—but your most enjoyable destination might simply be a patch of sand at one of the superb beaches. For relief from beach bumming, retreat to the nearby mountains and deserts, or head for Mexico, almost next door. You'll find San Diego a nice place to visit, and don't be surprised if you (too) want to live there.

Practical Information

Emergency: 911.

Visitor Information Center, 11 Horton Plaza (236-1212), downtown at 1st Ave. and F St. They have whatever you need under the counter. Open Mon.-Sat. 8:30am-5:30pm, Sun. 11am-5pm. **Old Town and State Park Information,** 4002 Wallace Ave. (237-6770), in Old Town Square next to Burguesa. Take the Taylor St. exit off I-8, or bus #5. Historical brochures on the Old Town ($2). Open daily 10am-5pm. **National Parks Information,** 226-6311. Recorded info. **Arts/Entertainment Hotline,** 234-2787. Recorded calendar of performances, exhibitions, and other events.

San Diego Council American Youth Hostels: 1031 India St. 92101 (239-2644), 335 W. Beech St. Student travel info, including full lists of hostels. Bike accessories, travel gear, and guides. Sponsors domestic and European trips. Open Mon.-Fri. 10:30am-5:30pm, Sat. 10am-5pm.

Traveler's Aid: Airport, 231-7361. One station in each terminal. Directions for lost travelers. Open daily 9am-10pm. **Downtown office,** 1765 4th Ave. and Elm St. #201 (232-7991). Open Mon.-Fri. 8:30am-4:30pm.

San Diego International Airport (Lindbergh Field): at the northwestern edge of downtown, across from Harbor Island. Divided into east and west terminals. San Diego Transit "30th and Adams" bus #2 goes downtown ($1.25). Buses run Mon.-Fri. 5am-11:30pm, Sat.-Sun. 6am-midnight.

Amtrak: Santa Fe Depot, 1050 Kettner Blvd. (239-9021, for schedules and info 800-872-7245), at Broadway. To L.A. (8 per day Mon.-Fri. 5:15am-9:15pm; $24, round-trip $31). Info. on bus, trolley, car, and boat transportation available at the station. Ticket office open daily 4:45am-9:15pm.

Greyhound: 120 W. Broadway (239-9171), at 1st Ave. To L.A. (12 per day Mon.-Thurs. 5:30am-midnight; $16, round-trip $25).

Taxi: Yellow Cab, 234-6161. Cab fare from airport to downtown around $7.

Car Rental: Rent-A-Wreck, 3309 Midway Dr. (224-8235) $19.95 per day, $119/week; 100 free mi. per day, 16¢ each additional mi.; 125 mi. radius restriction; cannot drive in Mexico. $2 charge for drivers under 25. Must be 21 with credit card or $200 minimum cash deposit. (Open Mon.-Fri. 8am-5pm, Sat. 8am-3pm, Sun. 10am-3pm.) **Aztec Rent-A-Car,** 2401 Pacific Hwy. (232-6117). $24 per day, 150 free mi., 25¢ each additional mi. $125 per week with 1000 free mi. Cars may venture south of the border as far as Ensenada with purchase of Mexican insurance ($16 per day). Open Mon.-Fri. 7am-8pm, Sat.-Sun. 8am-5pm. Must be 21 with major credit card.

Driveaway Companies: A-I Automovers, 3650 Clairmont Dr., Suite 5-C (274-0224), has offices nationwide. **Driveaway Service,** 3585 Adams Ave. in Normal Heights (280-5454); must be over 21 with $250 deposit. **Auto Driveway Co.,** 4672 Park Blvd. (295-8060) Open Mon.-Fri. 8am-5pm.

Bike Rental: Bike San Diego, at the corner of 1st and Harbor Dr. (232-4700) Bikes $6 per hr., or $22 per day. Open Mon.-Fri. 8am-6pm, Sat.-Sun. 7am-6pm. (233-7696), 520 5th Ave., in the Gaslamp Quarter. Bikes $4 per hr., $30 per day. $90 per week. Open daily 9am-6pm. **La Jolla Cyclery,** 7443 Girard (459-3141), in La Jolla. Limited rental bikes $4 per hr., $16 per day with a 2-hr. min. Tandems $6 per hr., $20 per day. Open Tues.-Fri. 10am-6pm, Sat. 9am-5pm.

Help Lines: Crisis Hotline, 800-479-3339 or 236-3339. Open 24 hrs. **Rape Crisis Hotline,** 233-3088. Open 24 hrs. **Lesbian and Gay Men's Center,** 3780 5th Ave. (692-2077). Open Mon.-Fri. 9am-5pm.

Senior Citizen's Services: 202 C St. (236-6905), in the City Hall Bldg. Provides ID cards so that seniors can take advantage of senior discounts. Plans daytrips and sponsors "nutrition sites" (meals) at 8 locations. Open Mon.-Fri. 8am-5pm.

Community Service Center for the Disabled: 1295 University Ave. (293-3500), Hillcrest. Attendant referral, wheelchair repair and sales, emergency housing, motel/hotel accessibility referral, and **TDD Line** services for the deaf (293-7757). Open Mon.-Fri. 9am-5pm.

Post Office: 2535 Midway Dr. (547-0477), between downtown and Mission Beach. General Delivery. Open Mon.-Fri. 7am-1am, Sat. 8am-4pm. General Delivery **ZIP code:** 92138. Take bus #6, 9, or 35.

Area Code: 619.

Orientation

A group of skyscrapers in the blocks between Broadway and I-5 makes up downtown San Diego. Streets running parallel to the bay (north-south) on the western end of downtown have proper names until they hit Horton Plaza in the east, then they become consecutively numbered avenues. Going east-west are lettered streets; "A" St. is the farthest north, L the farthest south. In their midst, Broadway replaces D St. and runs directly east from the bay. North of A, Ash St. begins a string of alphabetized streets named after plants that continues north all the way to Walnut (*you* try to find a plant that starts with X!) Other alphabetical schemes crop up throughout the metro area, the most impressive is Point Loma's literary references that run from "Addison" to "Zola."

On the northeastern corner of downtown, **Balboa Park,** larger than the city center, is bounded by 6th Ave. on the west, I-5 and Russ Blvd. on the south, 28th St. on the east, and Upas St. on the north. To the north and east of Balboa Park are the main residential areas. **Hillcrest,** San Diego's most cosmopolitan district and a center for the gay community, lies at the park's northwestern corner, around the intersection of 5th and University Ave.; **University Heights** and **North Park** sit along the major east-west thoroughfares of University Ave., El Cajon Blvd., and Adams Ave.

San Diegan custom is to wait obediently for the walk signal, no matter how clear the coast. Jaywalking is illegal (tickets are given occasionally). The 17-mi. bay, west of downtown, is formed by Coronado Peninsula (jutting northward from Imperial Beach) and Point Loma (dangling down from Ocean Beach). North of Ocean Beach lie Mission Beach (with neighboring Mission Bay), Pacific Beach, and La Jolla.

Getting Around

Buses reach most areas of the city. The **public transport systems** (San Diego Transit, North County Transit, DART, FAST, and Dial-A-Ride) cover the area from Oceanside in the north to Tijuana in Mexico, and inland to Escondido, Julian, and other towns. Call for public transit information (233-3004; daily 5:30am-10pm) or stop by the **Transit Store,** 449 Broadway (234-1060), at 5th Ave. (open daily 8:30am-5:30pm). Pick up the *Transit Rider's Guide,* which lists routes to popular destinations. Fares vary: $1.25 for North County Transit routes and local routes, $1.50-1.75 for express routes, and $2.25-2.50 for commuter routes. Transfers within San Diego are free; North County transfers cost 25¢. Exact change is required; most city buses accept dollar bills. About 60% of the buses are wheelchair accessible. Visitors age 60 and over with ID receive discounts. Bike racks equip buses on some routes, especially those to the beaches. When you frequent buses, save money by using **Day Tripper** passes, which allow unlimited magical mystery tours on buses, trolleys, and even the Bay Ferry (1 day $4, 4 days $12). These and the various monthly passes are available at the Transit Store. Most urban routes originate, terminate, or pass through downtown.

The wheelchair-accessible **San Diego Trolley** runs on two lines from a starting point near the Santa Fe Depot on C St., at Kettner. One heads east for **El Cajon.** The other, popularly known as the "TJ Trolley," heads 16 mi. south to **San Ysidro** at the Mexican border (5am-6pm every 7 min., 6-10pm every 15 min., 10pm-1am every 30 min.). From the border, cabs to the Tijuana Cultural Center or shopping district cost less than $5. The trolley also provides access to local buses in National City, Chula Vista, and Imperial Beach. (Fare 50¢-$2.25 depending on distance, over 60 and disabled passengers 50¢. Transfers free.) You're on the honor system; purchase a ticket from machines at the stations and board the trolley. Don't try to fool the system—inspectors regularly check for tickets and fines are high.

Accommodations

Lodging rates skyrocket in response to the number of tourists during the summer, particularly on weekends. Reservations can save you time and disappointment; weekly rates can save you money. Consider camping outside San Diego (see Camping). If not, staying downtown will give you access to bus routes that will take you most places.

El Cajon Blvd., a large commercial strip devoted primarily to selling cars, has many inexpensive, bland hotels east of downtown. Bus #15 offers a lackluster tour of the entire boulevard. Try the **Lamplighter Inn Motel,** 6474 El Cajon Blvd. (582-3088 or 800-225-9610; singles $42, doubles $48) or **Aztec Motel,** 6050 El Cajon Blvd. (582-1414 or 800-225-9610; singles $34, doubles $36).

Downtown

Hostel on Broadway, 500 W. Broadway (232-1133), near train and bus stations. Renovated facility features primarily 2-person rooms, communal bathrooms and access to common room. Color TV with cable available in some rooms. Security guard, cameras and friendly management make this an ideal place to crash downtown. Check-out 9:30am. ($10 for HI/AYH members, $13 for non-members.) Linen included.

La Pensione on Second, 1546 2nd Ave., downtown (236-9292). Close to I-5. Pretty rooms with microwave, fridge, and cable TV. Attractive courtyard. New European-style building with 24-hr. deli. Singles $29-39. Doubles $34-49. Weekly: singles $125-165; doubles $155-180.

Jim's San Diego, 1425 C St., south of the park at City College trolley (235-8341). Clean, hostel-type rooms. Management caters to international travelers; passport and $20 deposit required. Kitchen and laundry. $15. Weekly $90. Breakfast and Sunday BBQ included.

YWCA Women's Hostel, 1012 C St. at 10th Ave. (239-0355). Women only. Friendly. Check-out 11am. Dorm beds for ages 18-34 or older $10.25. Linen $1. Hall bath. Nonmembers singles $19; doubles $32. Key deposit $5.

Mission Hills, Hillcrest, Mission Valley

Hillcrest Inn, 3754 5th Ave., Hillcrest (293-7078). All rooms have microwave and refrigerator. Singles $39, doubles $44.

Old Town Budget Inn, 4444 Pacific Hwy. near Old Town (260-8024; for reservations 800-225-9610). Simple and reasonable. Ask for rooms in the old building. Singles from $34. Doubles from $37. Without A/C $2 less. Microwave and refrigerator $5 more.

South of Downtown and the Beaches

Imperial Beach International Hostel (HI/AYH), 170 Palm Ave. (423-8039). Take bus #901 from the Amtrak station or take the trolley on C St. to Palm St. Station (35 min.). Transfer to bus #933 westward-bound (every hr. on the ½-hr.). In a converted firehouse 2 blocks from the the beach, 5 mi. from Mexico. Quiet and fairly remote, with a well-equipped kitchen and a large common area with a TV. Bunkbeds for 36 (more if people share). Open 8-10am and 5:30-12pm. Check-in 5:30-10pm. Curfew midnight. Members $10, nonmembers $13. Key deposit $2. Make reservations by phone or by sending one night's payment.

Elliot International Hostel (HI/AYH), 3790 Udall St., Point Loma (223-4778). Take bus #35 from downtown; get off at first stop on Voltaire and walk across the street. By car, take I-5 to Sea World exit, then left to Sunset Cliffs Blvd. Take left on Voltaire, right on Warden and look for hostel sign painted on building. Airy 2-story building 1.5 mi. from Ocean Beach. Wooden bunk beds for 60, common room, kitchen. Check-out 10am. Office open 7-10am, 4pm-midnight. Lockout 11am-4pm. Curfew 2am. Members $12, nonmembers $15. 3 night max. stay, reserve 48 hr. in advance.

Camping

All state **campgrounds** are open to bikers for $2 nightly; state law requires that no cyclist be turned away due to overcrowding. Only Campland on the Bay lies within city limits. For info on state park camping, call the helpful people at San Elijo Beach (753-5091). MISTIX (800-444-7275) can handle reservations. Most parks fill in summer; make weekend reservations eight weeks in advance.

Campland on the Bay, 2211 Pacific Beach Dr. (274-6260). Take I-5 to Grand Ave. exit and follow the signs, or take bus #30 and get off on Grand at the sign on the left. Expensive and crowded because it's the only central place to pitch a tent or plug in an RV. Cheapest sites in "dirt area" where there is nothing to block the wind coming off the water. Sites $23-41; winter $20-38.

South Carlsbad Beach State Park, Rte. 21 (729-8947), near Leucadia, in north San Diego County. 225 sites, half for tents. On cliffs over the sea. Sites $21, winter $16. Reservations necessary in summer.

San Elijo Beach State Park, Rte. 21, south of Cardiff-by-the-Sea (753-5091). 271 sites (150 for tents) similar to South Carlsbad to the north. Good landscaping gives the illusion of seclusion. Hiker/biker campsites. Sites $21, $16 in winter. Make reservations in summer.

Food

The birthplace of the genre, San Diego has hundreds of fast-food joints, but the lunchtime business crowd has nurtured a multitude of slightly less fattening, but still cheap, restaurants. Pick up fresh breads and high-quality fruits and vegetables at the **Farmers Market,** 1 Horton Plaza, Downtown (696-7766), open daily 8am-8pm. Or visit one of Ocean Beach's organic grocery stores on Voltaire Ave. For a wide selection of cheap meals downtown, the food court on the top floor of **Horton Plaza** metes out more than the standard 31 flavors of junk food.

Anthony's Fishette, 555 Harbor Ln., at the foot of Market St. on the bay, (232-2933). Ocean eats, a good bay view, and bargain prices. This is where the locals dine on fried scallop ($5.50), shrimp ($6) and trout ($7) dinners. Cheaper lunch prices. Open Sun.-Thurs. 11am-7pm.

El Indio, 3695 India St., in India St. Colony. Lines all day long, but speedy service and high quality eats. Large portions; combination plates from $3. Buy a bag of fresh corn tortillas (12 for 55¢) or their "fantabulous" tortilla chips. Open daily Mon.-Thurs. 7am-9pm, Fri.-Sat. 7am-10pm.

Kansas City Barbeque, 610 W. Market St., south of Broadway near the bay (231-9680). Enjoy decent BBQ in the bar where the lip synching scenes from *Top Gun* were shot. Dinners with 2 side orders around $8. One-sided sandwiches $4.50 (served only after 10pm). Open daily 11am-2am.

Filippi's Pizza Grotto, 1747 India St., on a block of Italian restaurants. Other locations—all family-owned—around town. Subs big enough to threaten the Pacific fleet ($3.25-4.25). Try the homemade sausage. Open Sun.-Fri. 11am-10:45pm, Sat. 11am-11:45pm.

Corvette Diner Bar and Grill, 3946 5th Ave. (542-1001). A fun '50s-style joint packed with cases of Bazooka. Roast turkey and chicken pot pie dinners around $6.50. The soda jerk will smooth you a peppermint shake for $2.95. (Open Sun.-Thurs. 7am-11pm. Fri.-Sat. 8am-midnight.

The Big Kitchen, 3003 Grape St. in Golden Hill (234-5789). Try the huge waffles ($2.75) or pancakes ($3) served on dishes that Whoopi Goldberg used to wash. Open Mon.-Fri. 6am-2pm, Sat.-Sun. 7am-3pm.

Ichiban, 1449 University Ave. (299-7203). Sushi and other Japanese dishes around $4. Open Mon.-Sat. 11am-2:30pm and 5:30-9pm, Sun. 4-8:30pm.

John's Waffle Shop, 7906 Girard Ave., La Jolla (454-7371). Basic golden waffles ($3), all the way up to whole grain banana nut waffles ($5.75). Breakfast and sandwiches average $4.50. Open Mon.-Sat. 7am-3pm, Sun. 8am-3pm.

Sights

In contrast to the rest of Southern California, where pre-fab houses and planned communities resemble a package of instant, dehydrated city, San Diego's buildings form a tangible record of the city's history. The oldest buildings are the early 19th-century adobes of **Old Town.** Just up Juan St. from Old Town, **Heritage Park** displays old Victorian homes, carefully trimmed gingerbread houses. Extending south from Broadway to the railroad tracks and bounded by 4th and 6th Ave. on the west and east, the **Gaslamp Quarter** houses a notable concentration of pre-1910 commercial buildings now resurrected as upscale shops and restaurants. Well-preserved houses and apartment buildings from 1910 to the 1950s, in styles ranging from Mission Revival to zigzag Moderne, are found on almost every block. For more relaxing pleasures, head toward the beaches, San Diego's biggest draw. Surfers catch tubular waves, sun-worshippers catch rays, and everybody gets caught up in sun-stimulated serenity. Or heatstroke.

Downtown

The **Embarcadero,** (a fancy Spanish name for a dock) sits at the foot of Broadway on the west side of downtown. **San Diego Harbor Excursion** (234-4111) offers cruises past the Navy ships and under the Coronado Bridge. (7 per day 1 hr., $10; 5 per day 2 hr., $15. Those over 55 and ages 3-11, half-price on all cruises. Whale watching in winter twice daily.) Harbor Excursion also sells tickets for the ferry departing for Coronado (every hr. 9am-10pm, returning on the ½-hr. 9:30am-10:30pm, with one additional trip each way Fri.-Sat. evenings; $2). The ferry lands at the Olde Ferry Landing in Coronado on 1st and Orange St., a 10-block trolley ride from the Hotel del Coronado.

Past the Gaslamp Quarter, the **Coronado Bridge** stretches westward from Barrio Logan to the Coronado Peninsula. High enough to allow the Navy's biggest ships to pass underneath, the sleek, sky-blue arc executes a near-90° turn over the waters of San Diego Bay before touching down in Coronado. (Bridge toll $1. Bus #901 and other routes also cross.) When it was built in 1969, the bridge's eastern end cut a swath through San Diego's largest Chicano community. In response to the threatening division, the community created **Chicano Park** beneath the bridge, taking spiritual possession of the land by painting splendid murals on the piers. The murals, visible from I-5, are heroic in scale and theme, drawing on Hispanic-American, Spanish, Mayan, and Aztec imagery. Take bus #11 or the San Ysidro trolley to Barrio Logan station.

Horton Plaza, at Broadway and 4th Ave., centers San Diego's redevelopment. This pastel-colored, multi-faceted, glass and steel shopping center encompasses seven city blocks; its complex architecture, top-floor views of the city and occasional live entertainment set it apart from the average mall. (3-hr. parking free with validation at one of the shops.) Another noteworthy example of local architecture is the domed **Santa Fe Depot,** Kettner Blvd., a Mission Revival building whose grand arches welcomed visitors to the 1915 exposition. Standing just three blocks west of Horton Plaza, the building now serves as the San Diego Amtrak depot.

Balboa Park

Balboa Park was established in 1868, when San Diego was a small town. The population is now over a million, but the 1000-plus acre park remains relatively unmaimed by city expansion, drawing huge crowds with its concerts, theater, Spanish architecture, entertainers, lush vegetation, and a zoo. Bus #7 runs through the park and near the museum and zoo entrances. Drivers should take Laurel St. east from downtown to one of the parks many parking lots.

With over 100 acres of exquisitely designed habitats, the **San Diego Zoo** (231-1515) is one of the finest in the world, with flora as exciting as the fauna. They have recently moved to a system of "bioclimactic" areas, in which animals and plants are grouped together by habitat rather than by taxonomy. The stunning **Tiger River** and **Sun Bear Forest** are among the first of these areas to be completed. The newly competed **Gorilla Tropics** enclosure houses lowland gorillas and plant species imported from Africa. In addition to the usual elephants and zebras, the zoo houses such unusual creatures as Malay tapirs and everybody's favorite eucalyptus-chomper, the koala. Arrive as early as possible, sit on the left, and take the 40-minute open-air **double-decker bus tour,** which covers 70% of the park and avoids long lines ($3, ages 3-15 $2.50). The **children's zoo** squawks up a barnyard storm (free with admission). The **"skyfari" aerial tram** will make you feel like you're suspended over a box of animal crackers, allowing you to spit on a rhinocerous without getting killed. Most of the zoo is wheelchair-accessible (wheelchairs can be rented), but steep hills make assistance necessary. (Main zoo entrance open daily July-Labor Day 9am-5pm, must exit by 7pm; Labor Day-Memorial Day 9am-4pm, exit by 6pm. $12, ages 3-15 $4. Group rates available. Free on Founder's Day, Oct. 1.)

Balboa Park has the greatest concentration of museums in the U.S. outside of Washington DC. The park focuses at **Plaza de Panama,** on El Prado St., where the Panama-Pacific International Exposition took place in 1915 and 1916. Designed by Bertram Goodhue in the florid Spanish colonial style, many of the buildings were intended as temporary structures, but their elaborate ornamentation and colorfully tiled roofs make them too beautiful to demolish.

Before exploring El Prado on your own, stop in the House of Hospitality's **information center** (239-0512) which sells simple maps (60¢), more elaborate guides ($1.50), and the **Passport to Balboa Park** ($10). The passport contains six coupons to gain entrance to the park's museums. (Passports also available at participating museums. Open daily 9:30am-4pm.) The western axis of the plaza stars Goodhue's California State Building, now the **Museum of Man** (239-2001). The museum recaps millions of years of human evolution with permanent exhibits on primates, the Mayan, Hopi, and other Native American societies. Behind the museum, the **Old Globe Theater** (239-2255), the oldest pro theater in California, plays Shakespeare and others nightly (Tues.-Sun., weekend matinees). The **Lowell Davies Outdoor Theater** across the street also draws top name performers. (Ticket prices at both performance spaces range from $17-30.) The **Spreckels Organ Pavilion** (236-5471 for info) at the south end of the Plaza de Panama opposite the Museum of Art, resounds with free concerts. Ranging from ancient Asian to contemporary Cal, the **San Diego Museum of Art** (232-7931), across the plaza, gathers an eclectic range of art. Nearby is the outdoor **Sculpture Court and Garden** (236-1725), with a typically rounded and sensuous Henry Moore presiding over other large abstract blocks. Farther east along the plaza is the **Botanical Building** (236-5717), a wooden Quonset structure accented by tall palms threatening to burst through the slats of the roof. The scent of jasmine and the gentle play of fountains make this an oasis within an oasis.

Next door, the **Casa de Balboa,** a recent reconstruction of the 1915 Electricity Building, contains several museums: **The Museum of Photographic Arts** (239-5262) that features works of Southwestern masters, **San Diego Hall of Champions,** (234-2544) a slick museum with an astroturf carpet and the square footage of a baseball diamond, and the **San Diego Model Railroad Museum** (696-0199), that with its elaborate train sets, gives some idea of what Santa's basement would look like if he had a 10-year-old son.

From the end of El Prado St., which is closed to cars, a left onto Village Place St. will take you to **Spanish Village,** a crafts center offering free demonstrations and exhibits for browsers and buyers alike. At the other end of Village Place lies the **Natural History Museum** (232-3821), with exhibits on paleontology and ecology.

South of the Natural History Museum is the **Reuben H. Fleet Space Theater and Science Center** (238-1168), where two Omnimax projectors, 153 speakers, and a hemispheric planetarium whisk viewers inside the human body, up to the stars with the space shuttle, or 20,000 leagues under the sea. The world's largest motion pictures play here about 10 times per day. At 9 and 11pm every night lasers dance on the ceiling of the **Laserium** to the tune of Pink Floyd's "The Wall." Tickets to the space theater also valid for the **Science Center,** where visitors can play with a cloud chamber, telegraph, light-mixing booth, and other gadgets.

Elaborate singing puppets grace the **Marie Hitchcock Puppet Theatre,** where the city's Puppet Guild performs on summer and holiday weekends. (Shows Fri. 10am, 11:30am; Sat.-Sun 11am,1pm, 2:30pm. $1.50, children $1.)

Old Town, Mission Valley, and Mission Hills

The high prices and ubiquitous gift shops of **Sea World** (226-3901) won't let you forget it's a commercial venture; this is no San Diego Zoo. Though its famous animal shows range from educational to exploitative, once inside you shouldn't miss seeing five-ton killer whales jump high above water. Sea World also encompasses several impressive, well-lit state-of-the-art aquaria, and open pools where you can touch and feed various wet critters. (Open daily 9am-dusk, ticket sales end 2 hr. before closing time; mid-June through Labor Day the park remains open until 11pm and adds special shows. $24, ages 3-11 $18.)

The site of the original settlement of San Diego, **Old Town** remained the center of San Diego until the late 19th century. Take bus #4 or 5 from downtown. The Spanish *Presidio,* or military post, started here in 1769. Before becoming a museum, Old Town held the county courthouse, the town gallows, and a busy commercial district. Now the partially enclosed pedestrian mall is an overcrowded, overpriced tourist trap. The state park people offer free walking tours Fri.-Sun. at 2pm, starting at the Casa de Machado y Silvas (237-6770). To appreciate Old Town's buildings on your own, pickup the indispensable visitors center's walking tour ($2). **La Panadería** serves coffee and Mexican pastries (75¢).

Mission Basilica San Diego de Alcalá (281-8449) was moved in 1774 to its present location in the hills north of the Presidio, in order to be closer to the Native American villages. Take I-8 east to Mission Gorge Rd. and follow the signs, or take bus #43. The mission has a chapel, a garden courtyard, a small museum of artifacts, and a reconstruction of the living quarters of would-be-saint-cum-mission-builder Junípero Serra.

Entertainment

San Diego is not renowned for its nightlife, but a certain amount of spelunking could turn up some action. Scores of free publications highlight local happenings. The *Around San Diego* monthly previews nightlife, visual and performing arts. It is available at street venders throughout the city. *E Ticket* runs down movies, concerts and dinner theatres. Also try the **What's Happening Hotline** (560-4094) for sports info. **Arts Tix,** 121 Broadway (238-3810), at 1st Ave., offers half-price tickets to shows on the day of the performance.

Gorgeous weather and strong community spirit make San Diego an ideal place for local festivals, many of them annual affairs of over 30 years' standing. The visitors bureau (see Practical Information above) publishes a thorough yearly events brochure. A 24-hour **Events Hot Line** (696-8700) lists the latest performances and activites in downtown San Diego.

Club Diego's, 860 Garnet Ave. (272-1241), Pacific Beach. The young come here en masse for the big dance floor and flood of videos. No dress code, but trendoids get decked out for the evening. Happy Hour Mon.-Fri. 3-6pm. Cover Sun.-Thurs. $3, Fri.-Sat. $5. Open Mon.-Sat. 11am-1:30am, Sun. 10am-10pm.

Confetti's, 5373 Mission Center Rd. (291-8635). A singles saturnalia. Lots of confetti and lots of comparison shopping. Drinks $1.75-3.75. Happy Hour (5-8pm) includes free buffet. Cover Mon.-Wed. $2, Thurs. and Sun. $3, Fri.-Sat. $5. No cover before 8pm. Open Mon.-Fri. 5pm-2am, Sat. 7pm-2am, Sun. 9pm-2am.

The Comedy Store, 916 Pearl St. (454-9176), in La Jolla. Drinks $3. Potluck night Mon.-Tues. at 8pm with local comics. Well-known comedians other evenings. Shows Wed.-Thurs. and Sun. at 8pm ($7), Fri.-Sat. at 8 and 10:30pm ($9-12). Wed.-Thurs. 2-for-1 admission with any college ID. Two-drink minimum enhances performances. Must be 21.

Near San Diego

With 70 mi. of beaches, Sun Diego even has a place for man's best friend at Dog Beach and a resting ground for the wasted and indisposed at Garbage Beach. Sun worshippers freckle the coast from Imperial Beach in the south to La Jolla in the north; it may take a little ingenuity to find room to bask. Chic places like Mission Beach and La Jolla will likely be as packed as funky Ocean Beach come prime sunning time on summer weekends.

The **Hotel del Coronado,** Orange Ave. (435-6611), on the Coronado Peninsula, was built in 1888 as a remote resort. Take the Coronado Bridge from I-5 (toll $2) or bus #910 from downtown. Or take a ferry from San Diego Harbor. Excursions $2. (Every hr. on the hr. See Waterfront Sights.) One of the great hotels of the world, the "Del" has hosted 12 presidents. The 1959 classic *Some Like It Hot* showcased its white verandas and red circular towers. Wander onto the white, seaweed-free beach in back; it's seldom crowded, even on weekends.

Mission Beach and **Pacific Beach** are more respectable wave-wise than **Ocean Beach,** (codename O.B.). On San Jose Place, in one of the wind-beaten shacks, screams **Keith's Klothing Kastle.** The proprietor, Keith Nolan, sells his collection of silk Hawaiian shirts from the '40s and '50s at $100 apiece; the San Diego Museum of Art even featured some a few years ago. He also sells vintage Ocean Pacific and Hang Ten beachwear, at more conscionable prices. Hours, like Keith, are unpredictable—open most afternoons and evenings.

Situated on a small rocky promontory, **La Jolla** (pronounced la-HOY-a) was, in the 30s and 40s, the hideaway of wealthy Easterners who built luxurious houses and gardens atop bluffs overlooking the ocean. Jags, Mercedes, and BMWs purr along Girard Ave. and Prospect St. past boutiques and financial institutions. At the summit of this runway sits the **San Diego Museum of Contemporary Art,** 700 Prospect St. (454-3541), a collection of pop, minimalist, conceptualist, and Californian artwork in galleries overlooking the Pacific. Exhibits change frequently so call ahead for more info. (Open Tues. and Thurs.-Sun. 10am-5pm, Wed. 10am-9pm. Admission $4, seniors and students $2, under 12 50¢. Free Wed. 5-9pm.) Pick up a copy of the *South Coast Gallery Guide* from a sidewalk box for details on other galleries. La Jolla also claims some of the finest beaches in the city. Grassy knolls run right down to the sea at **La Jolla Cove,** and surfers especially dig the waves at **Tourmaline Beach** and **Windansea Beach.** At **Black's Beach,** people run, sun, and play volleyball in the nude. It is a public beach, not *officially* a nude beach, but you wouldn't know it from the color of most beachcombers' buns. Take I-5 to Genesee Ave., go west and turn left on N. Torrey Pines Rd. until you reach the **Torrey Pines Glider Port** (where clothed hang gliders leap off the cliffs).

Take bus #30 or 34 to La Jolla from downtown San Diego; both the Veteran's Hospital here and the University Towne Centre are transfer points for North County buses.

The University of California at San Diego (UCSD; operator 452-2230, info 534-8273) rests above La Jolla, surrounded on three sides by Torrey Pines Rd., La Jolla Village Dr., and I-5. Despite the thousands of eucalyptus trees and varied architecture, the campus falls somewhere between bland and really bland. Buses #30 and 34 will get you to the campus, but once there a car or bike is invaluable in going from one of the five colleges to the next. An info pavilion on Gilman Dr., just north of La Jolla Village Dr., has campus maps (open daily 7am-8:30pm).

San Francisco

San Francisco—a city whose name evokes images of cable cars, LSD, gay liberation, and Rice-A-Roni—began its life in 1776 as the Spanish mission of *San Francisco de Asis*. In 1848, just two years after the United States took possession of California, gold was discovered in dem dar hills up the Sacramento River delta. "Frisco's" 800 or so residents looked around and realized that not *only* did they live just a short river trip

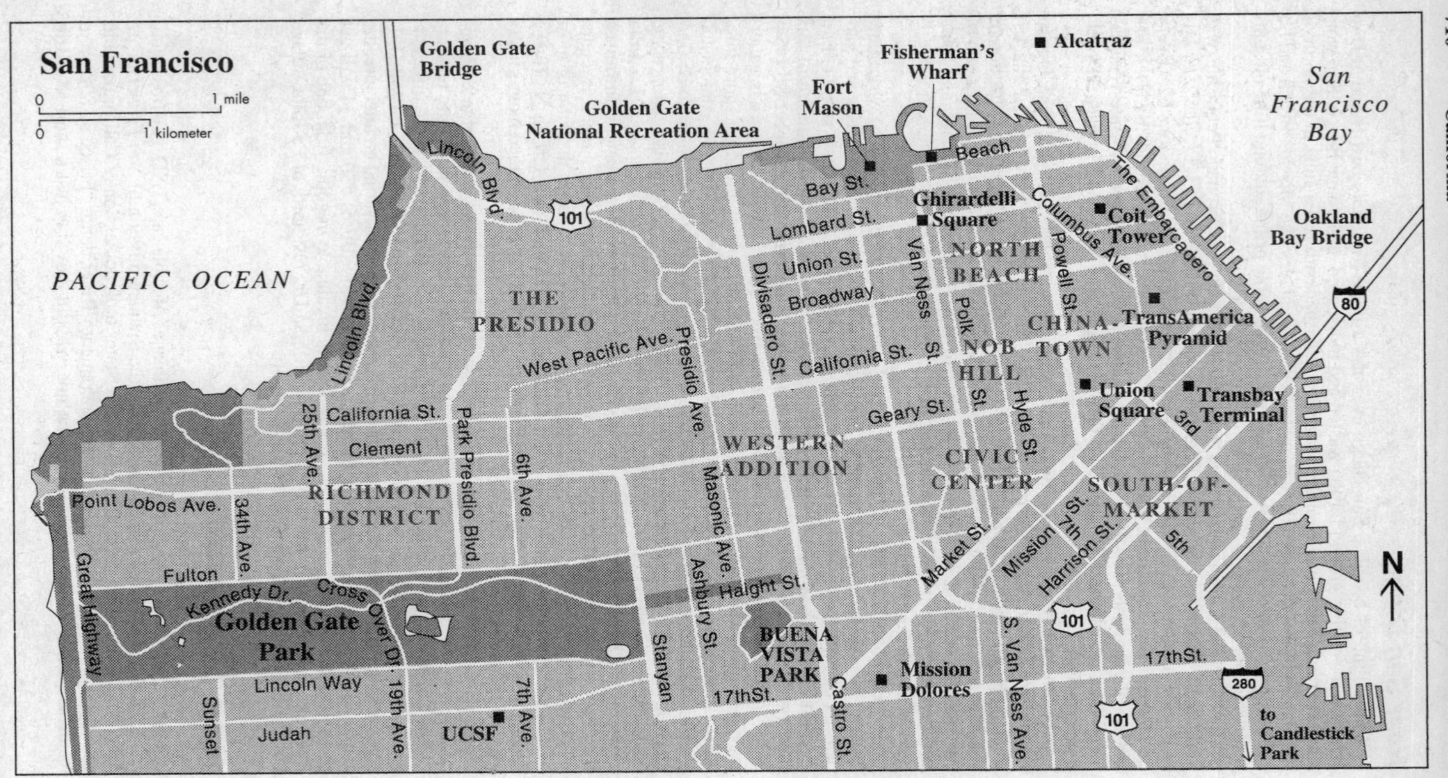
San Francisco
0 1 mile
0 1 kilometer
Golden Gate Bridge
Golden Gate National Recreation Area
Fort Mason
Fisherman's Wharf
Alcatraz
San Francisco Bay
Oakland Bay Bridge
80
PACIFIC OCEAN
Lincoln Blvd.
101
THE PRESIDIO
West Pacific Ave.
Presidio Ave.
Bay St.
Beach
Lombard St.
Ghirardelli Square
Union St.
Broadway
Divisadero St.
Van Ness St.
NORTH BEACH
Polk St.
Powell St.
Columbus Ave.
Coit Tower
The Embarcadero
CHINA-TOWN
TransAmerica Pyramid
California St.
NOB HILL
Hyde St.
Union Square
Transbay Terminal
3rd
Geary St.
WESTERN ADDITION
CIVIC CENTER
SOUTH-OF-MARKET
25th Ave.
California St.
Clement
Park Presidio Blvd.
6th Ave.
RICHMOND DISTRICT
Point Lobos Ave.
34th Ave.
Masonic Ave.
Market St.
Mission St.
7th St.
Harrison St.
5th
N
Great Highway
Fulton
Kennedy Dr.
Cross Over Dr.
Golden Gate Park
Ashbury St.
Haight St.
101
BUENA VISTA PARK
Stanyan
17thSt.
Castro St.
Mission Dolores
S. Van Ness Ave.
17thSt.
280
101
to Candlestick Park
Lincoln Way
19th Ave.
Sunset
Judah
UCSF
7th Ave.

from the gold fields, but they were also sitting on one of the greatest natural ports in the world. That year, 10,000 people passed through the Golden Gate, and a city was born.

The city's history, like its geology, has moved in abrupt fits and starts. The city dug itself out of the massive earthquake of 1906 shaken but not stirred—though it didn't completely recover until the 1930s, when the openings of the Oakland and Golden Gate Bridges ended its isolation from the rest of the Bay Area. Moving to San Fran has often meant joining the cultural vanguard—the Beat Generation arrived here in the 1950s, and the 60s saw Haight-Ashbury blossom into the hippie capital of the universe. In the 70s, the gay population emerged as one of the most powerful and visible groups in the city; the 80s once again saw San Francisco leading the nation, this time teaching the United States to fight AIDS, not people with AIDS. But the land continues to buck San Francisco's progress—the city's latest tragedy came when the biggest quake since 1906 killed 62 people, knocked out the Bay Bridge, and cracked Candlestick Park during a World Series game on October 17, 1989.

San Francisco is a mélange of diverse neighborhoods; the average San Franciscan thinks in terms of the Mission District, Chinatown, and Nob Hill rather than of the city as a whole. Subdivisions follow no discernible logic: a few blocks will take you from ritzy Pacific Heights to the impoverished Western Addition; the crime-ridden Tenderloin abuts the steel-and-glass wonders in the Financial District. Quaint small-scale streets, turreted houses, and extensive parks afford a European air.

Practical Information

Emergency: 911.

Visitor Information Center, Hallidie Plaza (391-2000), at Market and Powell St. beneath street level. Free street maps, events calendars, and the helpful *San Francisco Book.* Open Mon.-Fri. 9am-5:30pm, Sat. 9am-3pm, Sun. 10am-2pm. 24-hr. event and info recordings in English (391-2001), French (391-2003), German (391-2004), Japanese (391-2101), and Spanish (391-2122).

Budget Travel: Center for International Educational Exchange (CIEE), 312 Sutter St. (421-3473), between Stockton St. and Grant Ave. downtown. Student flight, discount, and lodgings information. ISICs. Open Mon.-Tues., Thurs.-Fri. 9am-5pm, Wed. 10am-5pm.

Sierra Club Store, 730 Polk St. (923-5600), just north of the Civic Center. Tremendous resource for those planning wilderness trips. They prefer and encourage visitors to join the club. Open Mon.-Sat. 10am-5:30pm.

San Francisco International Airport (SFO) (761-0800), inconveniently placed on a small nub of land in San Francisco Bay about 15 mi. south of the city center on U.S. 101. **San Mateo County Transit (samTrans)** (800-660-4287) runs 2 buses from SFO to downtown San Francisco. You can only bring carry-on luggage onto the 35-min. express (#7F) (every ½-hr. 5:30am-1am; $1.25, under 17 75¢, seniors 60¢). On the #7B bus you can carry all the luggage you want (every half hr. 5am-12:13am; 1 hr.; $1.75, seniors and under 17 60¢). **Airporter** shuttles (495-8404) run from all 3 terminals to major hotels and a downtown terminal at 301 Ellis St. (every 20 min. 5:45am-10:50pm; $6). **Taxis** downtown from SFO cost about $25. **Lorrie's Travel and Tour** (334-9000), on the upper level at the west end of all 3 terminals, provides door-to-door van service to and from the airport. Make reservations only for service to the airport. (Vans run daily 4:30am-11:30pm. $9, seniors $8 ages 2-12 $6, under 2 free.) **Franciscus Adventures** (821-0903) runs a small bus between San Francisco and SFO ($8, $7 per person for groups of 5 or more). Traffic to the airport can be thick; give yourself some time.

Trains: Amtrak, 425 Mission St. (for ticket info 800-872-7245), First floor of Transbay Terminal. Just a boarding area for the free shuttle bus to the actual train station in Oakland on 16th St. (982-8512). Shuttle trip takes 30 min. Open daily 6:45am-10:45pm. **CalTrain,** 4th and Townsend St. (800-660-4287), 6 blocks south of Market St., is a regional commuter train running to Palo Alto ($3, seniors and those with disabilities $1.50) and San Jose ($3.50, seniors and those with disabilities). The depot is at 4th and Townsend St. and is served by MUNI buses #15, 30, 32, and 42.

Buses: Greyhound, at the Transbay Terminal, 425 Mission St. (558-6789), between Fremont and First St. downtown. A regional transport hub. Second floor info center has maps and displays. Open daily 5am-12:35am. First St. and Natoma, behind the Transbay Terminal, is the pickup point for **Green Tortoise** (285-2441), the transportation company/hostel on wheels, which runs trips to L.A. (Fri. night; $30) and Seattle (Mon., Wed., and Fri.-Sat.; $69). Also to New York and Boston (both 14 days; $400, including food). Make reservations in advance.

Gray Line Tours: (558-9400). 3.5-hr. bus tours of the city $23.50, ages 5-11 $11.75, plus a variety of other tours departing from Union Square, or the Transbay Terminal for night tours. Reservations required.

Public Transport: San Francisco Municipal Railway (MUNI) (673-6864) operates buses, cable cars, and a combined subway/trolley system. Fares for both buses and trolleys is 85¢, ages 5-17 25¢, seniors and disabled passengers 15¢. Exact coins required. Ask for a free transfer, valid in any direction for several hrs., when boarding. MUNI's *San Francisco Street and Transit Map,* available at most bookstores ($1.50), not only contains info on MUNI service, but is also a complete street index and good general street map.

Taxi: Luxor Cabs, 282-4141. **DeSoto Cab Co.,** 673-1414. $1.70 initial charge, $1.80 each additional mi. Both open 24 hrs.

Car Rental: Rent-A-Wreck, 555 Ellis St. (776-8700), between Hyde and Leavenworth St. Used, mid-sized cars $29 per day with 100 free mi., $159 per week with 700 free mi. 20¢ each additional mi. Under 25 $10 extra. Open Mon.-Fri. 8am-6pm, Sat. 9am-4pm, Sun. 9am-1pm. Must be 21 with major credit card. **Bob Leech's Auto Rental,** 435 S. Airport Blvd. (583-3844), south San Francisco. New Toyotas $20 per day with 150 free mi., 10¢ each additional mi. Travelers coming into SFO should call for a ride to the shop. Open Mon.-Fri. 8am-9pm, Sat.-Sun. 9am-5pm. Must be 23 with major credit card.

Auto Driveaway Company, 330 Townsend (777-3740). Open Mon.-Fri. 9am-5pm. Must be 21 with valid license and references. $360 cash deposit. **A-1 Auto,** 1300 Old Bayshore Rd., Burlingame (342-9611). Call 10 days in advance. Must be 21 with major credit card. Cash deposit $200-300. Open Mon.-Fri. 9am-5pm.

Bike Rental: Lincoln Cyclery, 772 Stanyan St. (221-2415), on the east edge of Golden Gate Park. Mountain bikes $5 per hr., $20 per day, plus $15 deposit. Driver's license or major credit card required. Open Mon. and Wed.-Sat. 9am-5pm, Sun. 11:30am-5pm. **Presidio Bicycle Shop,** 5335 Geary (752-2453), between 17th and 18th Ave. 10-speed or mountain bike $25 per day. Open Mon.-Sat. 10am-6pm, Sun. 11am-4pm.

Help Lines: Rape Crisis Center, 647-7273. **Helpline,** 772-4357. **Gay Switchboard and Counseling Services,** 841-6224. Helpful staff has info on gay community events, local clubs, etc. Open Mon.-Fri. 10am-10pm, Sat. noon-4pm, Sun. 6-9pm.

Post Office: 7th and Mission St. (621-6838), opposite the Greyhound station. Open Mon.-Fri. 9am-5pm, Sat. 9am-1:30pm. **Rincon Annex,** 99 Mission St. Open Mon.-Fri. 7am-6pm, Sat. 9am-2pm. **ZIP code:** 94101.

Area Code: 415 for San Francisco and Peninsula.

Getting There

The **San Francisco International Hostel** and **San Francisco State University** (469-1842, in the student union; open Mon.-Fri. 7am-10pm, Sat. 10am-4pm) have ride boards; these are often the best way to rides in the area.

Getting Around

The hilly city of San Francisco, surrounded by water on three sides, is an amalgam of distinct neighborhoods organized along a few central arteries. Each neighborhood is compact enough to explore comfortably on foot. San Francisco once radiated outward from its docks, on the northeast edge of the peninsula just inside the lip of the bay. Many of San Francisco's attractions still cluster here, within a wedge formed by **Van Ness Avenue** (U.S. 101) running north-south, **Market Street** running northeast-southwest, and the **Embarcadero** (waterfront road) curving along the coast. Streets radiating north from Market and west from Market and the Embarcadero are numbered from these thoroughfares, although you should keep in mind that parallel streets do not bear the same block numbers.

At the north end of this wedge wafts **Fisherman's Wharf,** an area frequented mainly by tourists, and **North Beach,** a district shared by Italian-Americans, artists, and professionals, and in former times by the Beats. The focal point of North Beach is **Telegraph Hill,** topped by **Coit Tower** and fringed counterclockwise from the northwest to the southeast by **Columbus Ave.** Across Columbus begin the **Nob Hill** and **Russian Hill** areas, resting places of the city's old money. This fan-shaped area is confined by

Columbus along its northeast side, Van Ness along the west, and (roughly) Geary and Bush St. on the south. The core downtown area centers on **Union Square** and then, beyond Jones St., the **Civic Center,** an impressive collection of municipal buildings including City Hall, the Opera House, and Davies Symphony Hall.

Also within this wedge is the **Tenderloin,** often unsafe at night, where drugs and homelessness fester amidst sprouting high-rises. The Tenderloin is roughly bounded by Larkin St. to the west and to the east by Taylor St. extending from Market St. north to Geary. Some of the area's seediness, however, seeps across Market to the area near the Greyhound station (6th and 7th St.).

South-of-Market-Area (SoMa) is home to much of the city's nightlife. SoMa extends inland from the bay to 10th St., at which point the Latino **Mission District** begins and spreads south. The **Castro** area, center of the gay community, adjoins the Mission District at 17th and also extends south, centered upon Castro St.

West of Van Ness Ave., the city extends all the way to the ocean side of the peninsula. At the top of Van Ness, the commercially developed **Marina** area embraces a yacht harbor, Fort Mason, and the youth hostel. Fisherman's Wharf lies immediately east. Above the marina rise the wealthy hills of **Pacific Heights. Japantown** is located within the Western Addition. North of **Golden State Park** nods San Francisco's token suburb within the city, the **Richmond District.**

Bay Area Rapid Transit (BART) (778-2278) operates comfortable trains along four lines connecting San Francisco with the East Bay, including Oakland, Berkeley, Concord, and Fremont. One-way fares range from 80¢ to $3. A special excursion deal for $2.60 is designed for tours of the system: you must begin and end at the same station, and your trip must not take more than three hours. (Trains run Mon.-Sat. 6am-midnight, Sun. 9am-midnight.) Maps and schedules are available at the visitor info center and all BART stations (see Practical Information). BART stations and trains are wheelchair accessible.

Within San Francisco itself, **cable cars** are a great way to get around—noisy and slow (9.5mph), but indescribably hip. They run promptly and frequently and cover the entire city. Of the three cable lines, the California St. one is by far the least crowded; it runs from the Financial District up Nob Hill. (Fare $2, ages 5-17 75¢, seniors 15¢, under 5 free. Unlimited transfers allowed within a given 3-hr. period. Cars run daily 7am-1am.)

In San Francisco, cars are not necessary. Furthermore, parking spots are scarce and very expensive. However, driving is definitely the best way to explore the outer reaches of the Bay Area. In the city, contending with the hills is the first task; those in a standard-shift car will need to develop a very fast clutch foot, since all the hills have stop signs at the crests. The street signs admonishing you to "PREVENT RUNAWAYS" refer not to wayward youths but to cars parked improperly on hills. When parking facing uphill, turn the wheels toward the center of the street and put the car in first gear; when facing downhill, turn the wheels toward the curb; and *always* park in gear with the brake set. When renting, get an automatic. And remember, in San Francisco cable cars have the right of way.

Accommodations

Unlike most cities, San Francisco has a wide selection of conveniently located, relatively satisfying budget accommodations. But don't expect miracles for these prices. Note that a rapacious 11% bed tax is *not* included in the prices given below. Most hotels listed here are in areas such as the Tenderloin, the Mission District, Union Square, and downtown, where caution is advised both on the streets and within the buildings, particularly at night.

Downtown

The Hostel at Union Square (HI/AYH), (formerly SF Summer Hostel), 312 Mason, at O'Farrell (788-5604). Rooms in this brand new hostel are clean, spacious and comfortable. Kitchen, dining room, 2 common rooms. No curfew, but host emphasizes security. $14 per night for a shared room of 2-3 people. Open 24 hrs.

Olympic Hotel, 140 Mason St. (982-5010) at Ellis St., a few blocks from Union. Caters mostly to Japanese students and Europeans. Comfortable, with ugly wallpaper. Tends to fill during summer. Singles and doubles $30, with bath $40.

Pensione International, 875 Post St. (775-3344), east of Hyde St., 4.5 blocks west of Union Sq. Very nice rooms with interesting art. Singles $40, with bath $55. Doubles $50, with bath $75. Breakfast included.

Adelaide Inn, 35 Isadora Duncan (441-2261), off Taylor near Post St., 2 blocks west of Union Sq. Warm hosts and jumbled paintings. Does not answer door after 11pm. Steep stairs, no elevator. All rooms with bright outside exposure. Kitchenette and microwave available. Hall baths. Singles $38. Twin bed or doubles $46. Triples $52. Continental breakfast included. Reservations required.

The Ansonia, 711 Post St. (673-2670), 3 blocks west of Union Sq. in a nice area between Jones and Leavenworth St. Pretty nice rooms with firm mattresses. Laundry facilities. Breakfast and dinner included Mon.-Sat. Singles $38, with shared bath $44, with private bath $55. Doubles $50/$55/$65. Weekly: singles $220/$270/$300; doubles $300, with bath $380. Student rates for stays of a month or longer if you ask nicely.

Sheehan Hotel, 620 Sutter St. (775-6500 or 800-848-1529), at Mason St. near Union Sq. Excellent location near public transport and trendy art galleries. Busy, elegant lobby is something of a scene on warm summer evenings. Many international students. Worn, very English rooms; doubles have tea settings. Cable TV, pool, phone, exercise room. Economy singles $45, with bath $60. Economy doubles $55, with bath $75. Additional people $10. Under 12 free with parents. Continental breakfast included.

Pacific Bay Inn, 520 Jones St. (673-0234 or 800-445-2631, within CA 800-343-0880), 3 blocks west of Union Sq. Entirely renovated rooms that are modern, clean, and simple with TV, phone, and bath. Pleasant rooms with TV. Singles and doubles $50; $249 weekly.

Chinatown

YMCA Chinatown, 855 Sacramento St. (982-4412), between Stockton St. and Grant Ave. Near the city center. Men over 18 only. Friendly young staff, pool, and gym. Spartan rooms. Registration Mon.-Fri. 6:30am-10pm, Sat. 9am-5pm, Sun. 9am-1pm. No curfew. Singles $24. Doubles $37. 7th day free. Reserve 2 weeks in advance.

Sam Wong Hotel, 615 Broadway (781-6836), between Grant Ave. And Stockton St. Popular for location. Rooms are slightly run-down, but they're clean and feel secure. Singles with toilet $24, with bath $29. Add $2 for double occupancy. Triples with bath $40.

Grant Plaza, 465 Grant Ave. (434-3883 or 800-472-6899; in CA 800-472-6805), at Pine St. near the Chinatown gate. Excellent location. Recently renovated like a chain motel, but more colorful. Rooms with bath, phones, and color TV. Check-in after 2:30pm. Singles $39. Doubles $49. Twin beds $49. Reservations recommended 2-3 weeks in advance.

South of Market

The Interclub Globe Hostel, (formerly International Network Hostel), 10 Hallam Pl. (431-0540), just off Folsom St.. Hostel requires that its guests be international travelers, including Americans (show off your passport-full of international stamps). Clean, convenient, and newly renovated. 4-5 beds per room with chairs and tables. No kitchen, but sundeck and laundry room are good places to meet international students. Serves continental breakfast and dinner. $15. Key deposit $5. Free parking. No curfew. Open 24 hrs.

European Guest House, 761 Minna St. (861-6634), between 8th and 9th St., in a quiet but run-down neighborhood. Free-wheeling, relaxed, improvised, friendly; people sleep on sofas, mats, cushions. Co-ed rooms. TV room, laundry, kitchen, small info board. Check-in 7am-3am. No curfew. Bed in huge, hot dorm $12. Bunks in 6-bed room $14.

Marina

San Francisco International Hostel (HI/AYH), Bldg. 240, Fort Mason (771-7277). Entrance at Bay and Franklin St., 1 block west of Van Ness Ave. at the northern end of the peninsula. From Transbay Terminal, take MUNI bus #42 to Northpoint and Van Ness, then walk up the hill to Bay St.; follow signs to hostel. One of the largest HI/AYH-affiliated hostels in the nation, with about 160 beds. Clean, well-run, and efficient. Chore-a-day rule enforced. Extensive lounges, large kitchen, spic-and-span food-storage areas, and pay lockers for valuables. Good ride board. Frequented by students, families, and seniors. Crowded in summer. Arrive around 7am or send a night's fee 3 weeks ahead to reserve a place. 5-day max. stay. Check-in 7am-2pm and 3pm-midnight. Lockout 11am-3pm. Members and nonmembers $13.

Near the Civic Center

YMCA Hotel, 220 Golden Gate Ave. (885-0460), at Leavenworth St., 1 block north of Market St. Men and women. One of the city's largest lodgings. Spartan rooms. Has the only indoor track in the city. Double locks on all doors. Pool and gym. No curfew. Hostel beds for members only, $16. Singles $30. Doubles $43. Breakfast included. $5 key deposit.

Sutter/Larkin Hotel, 1048 Larkin (474-6820). Take Bus #19 from the Civic Center. Clean and well-maintained. Extremely accommodating manager. Check-in after 10am. Singles with shared bath $20. Doubles $25. Weekly: singles $90, with bath $110, doubles $105.

Hotel Essex, 684 Ellis St. (474-4664; outside CA 800-453-7739), between Hyde and Larkin St., north of Civic Center. Very friendly. Popular with German travelers. Free coffee. The recently renovated rooms are clean and comfortable with private bath, color TV, and phones. Check-out noon. Singles $49. Doubles $59. Weekly: singles $120-150. Rates slightly higher in summer.

Mission District

International Guest House, 2976 23rd St. (641-1411), at Harrison St. Away from the most touristy areas, but 24th St. fairly busy. Ideal for young travelers. Strict foreign-travelers-only rule. 2 full kitchens for 28 guests. Common room, TV, stereo, fireplace. 5-day min., no max. stay. No curfew. Bunks $13 for each of the first 10 nights, $11 thereafter. No reservations.

El Capitán, 2361 Mission St. (695-1597), north of 20th St. Rooms clean, in this converted movie theater of the 1950s. Two locked gates. Singles $20. Doubles $22.

Haight-Ashbury

The Red Victorian Bed and Breakfast Inn, 1665 Haight St. (864-1978), 2 blocks east of Golden Gate Park. 3 mi. from downtown, but close to buses and the "N" trolley. More of a state of mind than a hotel. Individually decorated rooms honor butterflies, the nearby Golden Gate Park, and the 1960s. Even the 4 hall baths, shared by some rooms, have their own names and motifs. If canopied and teddy-bear-festooned beds aren't enough to soothe your mind, try the meditation room, the therapeutic massage ($60 per hr.), or a talk with the hotel cat. Downstairs, a newly opened global family network center promotes planetary consciousness with a café, market, and computers. A non-smoking, angst-free environment. Stop by for a tour. Check-in 3-6pm. Check-out 11am. Summer rates $65-135 depending on room size, weekends $5 more; winter $55-120. Extra futon $15. Singles deduct $5, extra persons add $15. Breakfast of fresh bread, pastry, and requisite granola included. Complimentary tea, coffee, popcorn, and cheese in the evenings. Make reservations for summer months. 2-night stay usually required on weekends. Weekly rates available.

Food

The pizzas that emerge from the wood ovens of the Bay Area range from North Beach Neapolitan to trendy goat cheese and *pancetta.* Sourdough is a city hallmark, and San Franciscans are as serious about their coffee as they are about the wines of Napa Valley. The city has been recently invigorated by immigrants from all over Asia and Latin America, and this is well reflected in the variety of cuisine. Head to **Chinatown** for awesome food and the **Mission District** for inexpensive gastronomic diversity; elsewhere, cheap eats are few and far between. The **Haight** has a fabulous selection of bakeries, and Columbus Ave. in **North Beach** lures visitors to café after café.

Chinatown

House of Nanking, 919 Kearny St. (421-1429). Great food, pleasant atmosphere. Very very popular with workers who walk all the way from the Financial District on their lunch hours. *Mu-shui* vegetables ($5), onion cakes ($1.75). Anything made with Tsing-Tao beer is bound to be good. Open Mon.-Sat. 11am-10pm, Sun. 4pm-10pm.

Sam Wo, 813 Washington (982-0596). The late hours, cheap food, and BYOB policy make this restaurant a favorite among students from all over the Bay. Patrons walk through the kitchen to get to their seats. Most dishes $2-5. Open Mon.-Sat. 11am-3am, Sun. 12:30-9:30pm.

Dol Ho, 808 Pacific Ave. (392-2828). Perfect for afternoon tea and *dim sum.* Four *har gow* (steamed shrimp), sweet doughy sesame balls, or pork buns each $1.60. Open daily 8am-4pm.

Yuet Lee, 1300 Stockton at Broadway (982-6020). Not an outstanding atmosphere, but the seafood makes up for it. Seasonal exotic specialties such as sautéed pork stomach with boneless duck feet. Open Mon.-Sun. 11am-3am.

North Beach

Tommaso's, 1042 Kearny St., between Pacific and Broadway. For a break from *nouvelle pizza* try some of the very best traditional Italian pizza this side of the Tiber. The super deluxe, piled high with mushrooms, peppers, ham, and Italian sausage sates 2 ($13.50). Francis Ford Coppola has been known to occasionally toss pizza dough in front of the huge wood-burning ovens. Long wait worth it. Open Tues.-Sat. 5-10:45pm, Sun. 4-9:45pm.

Bohemian Cigar Store, 566 Columbus Ave., corner of Union Sq. Excellent espresso ($1) and agreeable Italian food. Try their Italian sandwiches (around $5). Open daily 10am-midnight.

Caffe Trieste, 609 Vallejo St. (392-6739), at Grant. Only a few beatniks now; sip coffee and remember the exciting Eisenhower years when Ginsberg and Ferlinghetti hung out here. Loud live music Sat. 1-4pm. Otherwise settle for a tune from the opera jukebox. Coffees $2.25. Open Sun.-Thurs. 7am-11:30pm, Fri.-Sat. 7am-12:30am.

Gira Poli, 659 Union St. (434-4472). Like Col. Sanders, the owners have founded a restaurant on the basis of a single chicken recipe, but theirs is Palermo roasted, not Kentucky Fried; seasoned with rosemary, lemon, and olive oil. Order a half-chicken to go ($10), and picnic at Washington Square.

Marina and Pacific Heights

Bepple's Pies, 1934 Union St. A tad bit expensive, but perfect pies. Fruit pie slices $3. Another 95¢ for a solid slab of excellent vanilla ice cream. Whole pies $11. Meat pies $6. Open Sun.-Thurs. 8am-midnight, Fri.-Sat. 8am-2am.

Jackson Fillmore, 2506 Fillmore St. Usually a long wait at this popular and hip *trattoria,* with great southern Italian cuisine and a lively atmosphere. Put your name down and browse the Fillmore scene while you wait. Large portions; you can maybe sneak out for less than $10 per person. Eat lots of tasty breadsticks to fill up. Open Mon.-Thurs. 5:30pm-10:30pm, Fri. 5:30-11pm, Sat. 1:30-11pm, Sun. 1:30-10:30pm.

Mai's Vietnamese, 1838 Union St. Sidewalk dining on Union St. The crab claws get good marks ($6.75) as does the vegetarian imperial roll ($5). Clear, flavorful crabmeat soup $4. A romantic spot on warm summer city nights. Open daily 11am-10pm.

Mission District and Castro Street

Café Macondo, 3159 16th St. (863-6517). Central-American food and coffee in a homey, artfully-designed café—you'll feel like you've discovered some wonderful museum. A great place to read a book while sipping cappuccino ($1.50) and munching sandwiches ($2.50-3.25). Open Mon.-Thurs. 11am-10pm, Fri.-Sun. 11am-11pm.

New Dawn, 3174 16th St. at Guerrero (553-8888). Absolutely anything is considered art at this hip restaurant, from the dolly parts and eggbeaters hanging on the walls to the eardrum-melting music to the chef's magenta mohawk. The menu, mainly breakfast food and burgers, is written around the room on mirrors. Enormous servings. Vegetable home fries ($5.25), burgers ($4.25). Open Mon.-Fri. 8am-3pm, Sat.-Sun. 8am-4:30pm.

La Cumbre, 515 Valencia St. The top. Ample superlative burrito ($2.50, planet-sized $4). Open Mon.-Sat. 11am-10pm, Sun. noon-9pm.

Taquería San Jose, 2830 Mission St., at 24th. Don't be put off by the fast-food-style menu; real care goes into the cooking. Soft tacos with your choice of meat—from magnificent pork to brains or tongue $1.60, 5 for $3.50. Free chips and guacamole. Open daily 8am-1am, Fri.-Sat. 8am-4am.

Manora, 3226 Mission. Attractive Thai restaurant with delicious cuisine at reasonable prices. Especially light with its sauces—food not smothered in peanut. The red beef curry ($5.75) gets good reviews. Most dishes under $8. Open daily 5-10pm, Tues.-Fri. also 11:30am-2:30pm.

Haight-Ashbury and Richmond

Cha Cha Cha, 1805 Haight St. Love children join hands with yuppies here. Trendy, but best Latin restaurant in the Haight. Be prepared to wait up to 2 hrs. Try the *tapas.* Entrées $5-8. Open Mon.-Thurs. 11:30am-3pm and 5-11:30pm, Fri. 11:30am-3pm and 5:30pm-midnight, Sat. noon-3pm and 5:30pm-midnight, Sun. noon-3pm and 5-11pm.

Ganges, 755 Frederick St. Not exactly in the Haight, but close enough. Veggie Indian food draws health-conscious students from the nearby medical school. Traditional Indian seating in back. Dinners $7.50-11.50. Open Tues.-Sat. 5-10pm.

Beau Seventh Heaven, 1448 Haight St. (626-4448). French-Russian bakery with an eclectic selection of pastries. Open daily 7am-10:30pm.

Tassajara Bread Bakery, 1000 Cole St. at Parnassus, 5 blocks south of Haight St. One of the best bakeries in the city. A branch at Fort Mason, but the purist will want to make the pilgrimage to Haight-Ashbury for the original. Pastries are delicious, but small. Open Mon.-Sat. 7am-7pm, Sat. 8am-2pm.

Sights

Mark Twain called San Francisco "the liveliest, heartiest community on our continent," and any resident will tell you that this city is not made of landmarks or "sights," but by neighborhoods. Whether defined by ethnicity, tax brackets, topography, or simply a groovy spirit, these communities keep the city vibrant for visitors and residents alike. Off-beat bookstores, Japanese folk festivals, cosmopolitan Union Street, America's most vibrant gay community, Strawberry Hill in Golden Gate Park, the Club Fugazi in North Beach, Haight-Ashbury's tie-dyed crunch...all conspire to steal even the most stolid visitor's heart.

Downtown

Union Square is the center of San Francisco. Now an established shopping area, the square has a rich and somewhat checkered history. During the Civil War, at a large public meeting here, citizens decided whether San Francisco should secede. The square became the rallying ground of the Unionists, who bore placards reading "The Union, the whole Union, and nothing but the Union."

Even when the Barbary Coast (now the Financial District) stayed down and dirty, Union Square stayed cheaper. **Morton Alley,** in particular, offered off-brand alternatives to the high-priced prostitutes and stiff drinks of the coast; the prices were low, but the action sizzled. At the turn of the century, murders averaged one per week on Morton Alley, and prostitutes with shirts unbuttoned waved to their favorite customers from second-story windows. After the 1906 earthquake and fire destroyed most of the flophouses, a group of right proper capitalists moved in and renamed the area **Maiden Lane** in hopes of changing the street's image. The switch worked. Today Maiden Lane, extending two blocks from Union Square's eastern side, boasts smart shops and classy boutiques. Traces of the old street live on, however, in words like "hoodlum," "shanghaied," and "Mickey Finn," all added to the national vocabulary by the people who frequented the area.

The best free ride in town is on the outside elevators of the St. Francis Hotel. As you glide up the building, the entire Bay Area stretches out before you. The "elevator tours" offer an unparalleled view of Coit Tower and the Golden Gate Bridge. The Powell St. cable cars also grant an excellent view of the square.

Financial District

North of Market and east of Kearny, snug against the bay, beats the West's financial heart, or at least one of its ventricles. Try to catch **Montgomery St.,** the Wall Street of the West, before the workday ends. After 7:30pm, the heart stops, to be resuscitated the next morning. At the foot of Market St. is **Justin Herman Plaza** with its famous geodesic **Vallaincourt Fountain,** through which you can walk as water flows above you.

San Francisco's most distinctive structure, dwarfing the surrounding buildings, is the 853-ft. **TransAmerica Pyramid,** at Montgomery St. between Clay and Washington St. Designed mainly to show off the talents of its architects, the building's pyramidal shape and subterranean concrete "anchor" base make it one of the city's most stable, earthquake-resistant buildings. A free observation deck faces north on the 27th floor. (Open Mon.-Fri. 9am-4pm.) Diagonally across from the pyramid is the **Old TransAmerica Building,** 701 Montgomery St., at Washington St., the opulent showpiece of the corporation and a gem of older commercial architecture. Among the best of banking mini-museums in the area, the **Wells Fargo Museum,** 420 Montgomery St. (396-2619), at California St., contains an impressive display of Gold Rush exhibits, including gold nuggets and a 19th-century stagecoach. The affable guide possesses the sort of quiet yet fathomless expertise usually found only in National Park Service rangers.

(Open Mon.-Fri. 9am-5pm.) Nearby, the **Chinese Historical Society,** 650 Commercial St. (391-1188), tells the history of the Chinese in California. Gawk at the 1909 parade dragon head and a queue once worn in loyalty to the Manchu Emperor. (Open Wed.-Sun. noon-4pm.)

Chinatown

The largest Chinese community outside of Asia, Chinatown also stays the most densely populated of San Francisco's neighborhoods. Chinatown was founded in the 1880s when bigotry fueled by unemployment engendered a racist outbreak against the "Yellow Peril." To protect themselves, Chinese residents banded together in a small section of the downtown area. As the city grew, speculators tried but failed to take over the increasingly valuable land—especially after the 1906 earthquake leveled the area. Yet Chinatown remains almost exclusively Chinese. **Grant Avenue,** of Rodgers and Hammerstein fame, remains the most picturesque part of Chinatown. From the monumental **Chinatown Café,** which straddles Grant at Bush St., and for a few blocks north, Grant cultivates a forest of Chinese banners, signs, and architecture. The less famous streets, such as Jackson, Stockton, and Pacific, give a better feel for this neighborhood where Chinese-newspaper vendors eat their morning noodles out of thermoses. You can watch cookies being shaped by hand at the **Golden Gate Cookie Company,** 56 Ross Alley (781-3956), between Washington and Jackson St. just west of Grant Ave. The **Chinese Culture Center,** 750 Kearny St., 3rd floor (986-1822), houses exhibits of Chinese-American art and sponsors Heritage and Culinary walking tours of Chinatown. (For schedules and reservations call Tues.-Sat. 9am-5pm.)

Late January and early February feature the ear-shattering **Chinese New Year** celebrations.

North Beach

As one walks north along Stockton St. or Columbus Ave., supermarkets displaying ginseng give way to those selling provolone. Lying north of Broadway and east of Columbus, North Beach splits personalities between the bohemian Beats who made it their home—Kerouac, Ginsberg, Ferlinghetti—and the residents of a traditional Italian neighborhood. North Beach bohemianism flourished in the 1950s when the artists and brawlers nicknamed the Beats (short for "beatitude" according to Kerouac) first moved in. Drawn to the area by the low rents and cheap bars, the group came to national attention when Ferlinghetti's **City Lights Bookstore** (see Entertainment below) published Ginsberg's anguished and ecstatic dream poem *Howl.* The Beats have left. Through the middle of North Beach runs Broadway, the neon netherworld of pornography purveyors. North Beach is most fun to visit at night as the after-dinner, after-show crowd flocks to the area's numerous cafés for cappuccino.

Between Stockton and Powell lies **Washington Square,** a lush lawn edged by trees. Across Filbert to the north of the square the **Church of St. Peter and St. Paul** beckons tired sight-seers to an island of quiet in its dark, wooden nave. Mrs. Lillie Hitchcock Coit's famous gift to the city, **Coit Tower** (274-0203) looms a few blocks east on Telegraph Hill, the steep mound from which a semaphore signalled the arrival of ships in Gold Rush days. An elevator will take you to the top of the fire-nozzle-shaped Tower for a spectacular 360° view. (Open June-Sept. daily 10am-5pm; Oct.-May daily 9am-4pm. Elevator fare $3, seniors $2, ages 6-12 $1, under 6 free. Last tickets sold a half-hr. before closing.) Parking is limited; leave your car on Washington St. and walk up the **Filbert Steps,** which rise from the Embarcadero to the eastern base of the tower. The short walk allows excellent views, passing by many gorgeous art deco buildings. The **Tattoo Art Museum,** 841 Columbus at Lombard (775-4991), displays a fantastic collection of tattoo memorabilia.

Fisherman's Wharf

Continuing northward, toward the water, one leaves San Francisco proper and enters tourist limbo. "Fisherman's Wharf" maintains 4/5-mi. of porcelain figurines and t-shirt shops. Crowded, very expensive, and quite bland, the wharf manages to provide something to offend almost anyone. The area basically consists of a strip of boutiques flanked by shopping malls on each end; on the west end sits **Ghirardelli Square** (GEAR-a-deli), 900 N. Point St. (Information booth, 775-5500; open daily 10am-9pm.) The only remains of Ghirardelli's chocolate factory now lie in the back of the overpriced **Chocolate Factory,** a soda fountain (open daily 10am-midnight). Pricey boutiques now fill the rest of the old factory's red brick buildings, and local musicians and magicians wow the masses. To escape from this chocolate morass, take one of the **tour boats** or ferries from the wharf. The **Blue & Gold Fleet** (781-7877) and the **Red & White Fleet** (546-2896) take you on technicolor voyages. Blue & Gold's 15-minute tour floats under both the Golden Gate and Bay Bridges, and past the San Francisco Skyline and the Marin Hills, Angel, Alcatraz, and Treasure Islands ($14, seniors and ages 5-18 $7, military and under 5 free). Red & White at Pier 41 offers 45-minute journeys under the Golden Gate Bridge and past Alcatraz ($15, over 55 and ages 12-18 $11, 5-11 $8) while another 45-minute tour circumnavigates Alcatraz, narrated by a former guard. (Summer only. $7.50, seniors $7, ages 5-11 $4.) Red & White boats also discharge passengers at Alcatraz (see below). For a really pleasant escape, try one of the **sailboat charters** that line the wharf. The *Ruby* (861-2165) sails at lunchtime (with sandwiches) daily from May to October, departing from the China Basin building at 12:30pm and returning by 2pm, but call as the schedule often changes (tickets $25, under 10 $12.50). The *Ruby* also takes a three-hour tour—*a three hour tour*—in the bay on Friday and Saturday at 6pm. Reservations are required for sailboat charters. Bring a heavy sweater in summer and a jacket in winter.

A former federal prison, designed to hold those who had made too much trouble within other jails, **Alcatraz** made life for prisoners extremely harsh. Security was tight—of the 23 prisoners who attempted to escape, all were recaptured or killed, save the five "presumed drowned." The prison closed in 1962. Once on Alcatraz, you can wander by yourself or take an audiotape-guided 35-minute tour. Ask about the Native American civil rights takeover in the late 60s. (Departures from Pier 41 in summer every half-hr. 9:15am-4:15pm, in winter 9:45am-2:45pm. Fare $5.50, seniors $4.60, ages 5-11 $3. Tape tours $3 extra.) Reserve tickets in advance through Ticketron (392-7469) for $1 extra or suffer long lines and risk not getting a ride.

Nob Hill and Russian Hill

Until the earthquake and fire of 1906, railroad magnates occupied the mansions of Nob Hill. Today, Nob Hill remains one of the nation's most prestigious addresses. Fine buildings line the streets with a certain settled wealth. Sitting atop a hill and peering down upon the working masses can prove a pleasant afternoon diversion. Nearby Russian Hill is named after Russian sailors who died during an expedition in the early 1800s and were buried on the southeast crest.

The notorious **Lombard Street Curves,** on Lombard between Hyde and Leavenworth St. at the top of Russian Hill, afford a fantastic view of the city and harbor—if you can keep your eyes open down this terrifying plunge. Devising transportation capable of navigating the city's steep streets inspired the vehicles celebrated at the **Cable Car Museum,** at the corner of Washington and Mason St. (474-1887). The building also houses the cable-winding terminus for the picturesque cable cars, the working center of the system. (Open daily 10am-6pm; Nov.-March 10am-5pm. Free.)

Grace Cathedral, 1051 Taylor St. (776-6611), crowns Nob Hill. The castings for its portals imitate Ghiberti's on the Baptistry in Florence so exactly that they were used to restore the originals. Inside, modern murals mix San Franciscan and national historic events with scenes from the lives of the saints. Grace is still in use as a house of worship.

Marina, Pacific Heights, Presidio Heights

The Marina, Pacific Heights, and the adjoining Presidio Heights are some of the most sought-after residential addresses in San Francisco. Centered about Union and Sacramento St., Pacific Heights boasts the greatest number of Victorian buildings in the city. The 1906 earthquake and fire left the Heights area west of Van Ness Ave. unscathed. In 1989, the Heights area was not as lucky and sustained serious damage. Victorian restoration has become a full-fledged enterprise; consultants try to determine the original form of fretwork, friezes, fans, columns, corbels, cartouches, rosettes, rococo plaster, and so on. The **Octagon House,** 2645 Gough St. (885-9796), and **Haas-Lilienthal House,** 2007 Franklin St. (441-3004), allow the public a look inside. Rather sedate free tours of the impeccably preserved Octagon House are given on the first Sunday and second and fourth Thursdays of each month between 1 and 4pm. The Haas-Lilienthal House has more regular hours (open Wed. noon-3:15pm, Sun. 11am-4pm; admission $4, seniors and under 18 $2).

For those who prefer shopping to architecture, however, **Union Street** is your salvation. Between Scott and Webster St., Union St. is chock-full of upscale shops, bars, restaurants, and bakeries.

Down from Pacific Heights toward the bay sits the **Marina** district. **Marina Green** by the water seethes with joggers and walkers and is well-known for spectacularly flown two-line kites. To the west lies the **Palace of Fine Arts,** on Baker St. between Jefferson and Bay St. The strange, domed structure and two curving colonnades are reconstructed remnants of the 1915 Panama Pacific Exposition, which commemorated the opening of the Panama Canal and symbolized San Francisco's completed recovery from the great earthquake. The domed building houses the **Exploratorium** (561-0360), whose hundreds of interactive exhibits may teach even poets a thing or two about the sciences. (Open Tues.-Sun. 10am-5pm, Wed. 10am-9:30pm. Admission $8, students and seniors $6, ages 6-17 $14. Free the first Wed. of every month.) Inside sits the **Tactile Dome** (561-0362), a pitch-dark maze of tunnels, slides, nooks, and crannies designed to help refine your sense of touch—a wonderful place to bring kids and anyone not afraid of the dark or claustrophobic. (Admission $7. Reservations required for a month in advance. Plenty of free parking.) A short walk from the Exploratorium's main entrance, along the Bay, is the **Wave Organ.** Designed by local artists, the organ is activated by the motion of the waves, and beckons you to sit and meditate to the sound of the water's natural ebb and *om.*

Civic Center

You have two reasons to see the **Civic Center:** the architecture and museums by day and performing arts at night. The **San Francisco Museum of Modern Art,** Van Ness Ave. (252-4000), at McAllister St. in the Veterans Bldg., displays a collection of 20th-century European and U.S. works. Exhibits scheduled for 1992 include Klee and Pollock. (Open Tues.-Wed. and Fri. 10am-5pm, Thurs. 10am-9pm, Sat.-Sun. 11am-5pm. Admission $4, seniors and students $2, under 13 free. Tues. seniors and students free. Thurs. 5-9pm, seniors and students $1.)

In the evening, **Louise M. Davies Symphony Hall,** 201 Van Ness Ave. at Grove St. (431-5400), rings with the sounds of the San Francisco Symphony (box office open 9:30am-5:30pm). Next door, the **War Memorial Opera House,** 301 Van Ness Ave. (864-3330), hosts the San Francisco Opera Company and the San Francisco Ballet. The Civic Center has two other theaters: the **Orpheum,** 1192 Market St. (474-3800), tends to draw flashy shows, while the smaller **Herbst Auditorium,** 401 Van Ness Ave. (392-4400), at McAllister St., hosts string quartets, solo singers, and ensembles. Tours of the symphony hall, opera house, and Herbst Auditorium leave on the hour and half-hour from the Grove St. entrance of the Davies Hall. (Tours ½-hr., Mon. 10am-2:30pm. Admission $3, seniors and students $2. For more info, call 552-8338.) The **San Francisco Women Artists Gallery,** 370 Hayes St. (552-7392) exhibits women's photographs, paintings, prints, and crafts. (Open Tues.-Wed. and Fri.-Sat. 11am-6pm, Thurs. 11am-8pm.)

Mission District and Castro Street

Castro Street and the Mission District enjoy the city's best weather, often basking in sunlight while fog blankets nearby Twin Peaks. Two thriving cultures make their home in this area: the gay community around **Castro St.** and the Hispanic community to the east. Although the scene has mellowed considerably from the wild days of the 70s, Castro St. still remains a proud and assertive emblem of gay liberation. In the Hispanic **Mission District,** the colorful murals along 24th St. reflect the rich cultural influences here of Latin America.

The best way to see Castro St. is to wander, peering into shops or stepping into bars. Two popular hangouts are **Café Flor,** 2298 Market St. (621-8579), and **Café San Marco,** 2367 Market St. (861-3846).

Down the street, **The Names Project,** 2362 Market St. (863-1966), sounds a powerful and somber note. This organization has accumulated over 12,000 panels for an AIDS memorial quilt, each three ft. by six ft. section bearing the name and memory of a person who died of AIDS. In addition to housing the project's administration, the building contains a workshop where friends and relatives of those who have died of AIDS can create panels; several of these beautiful and poignant panels are on display. (Open Mon.-Fri. 10am-10pm, Sat.-Sun. noon-8pm.)

At 16th and Dolores St. lies the old heart of San Francisco, **Mission Dolores.** The building, the oldest in the city, turned 201 last year. Father Junípero Serra founded it 1776, and named it in honor of St. Francis of Assisi. However, the Mission sat close to a marsh known as *Laguna de Nuestra Señora de los Dolores* (Lagoon of Our Lady of Sorrows) and, despite Serra's wishes, it gradually became known as *Misión de los Dolores.* Exotic bougainvillea, poppies, and birds of paradise bloom in the cemetery, which was featured in Alfred Hitchcock's *Vertigo.* (Admission $1. Open daily 9am-4:30pm, Nov.-April 9am-4pm.)

Like the Castro, the Mission is best seen by strolling. The **Mission Cultural Center,** 2868 Mission St., between 24th and 25th, (821-1155) includes a graphics workshop, a theater, and often stunning art exhibits, as well as other cultural events throughout the year. (Open Tues.-Fri. 1-6pm, Sat. 11am-4pm. Free.)

Haight-Ashbury

The 60s live on in Haight-Ashbury, though more self-consciously than 20 years ago. The Haight willfully clings to an era that many seek to forget. Originally a quiet lower-middle-class neighborhood, the Haight's large Victorian houses—perfect for communal living—and the district's proximity to the University of San Francisco drew a large hippie population in the mid- and late-1960s. LSD flooded the neighborhood, since consciousness-opening was not yet a felony. The hippie scene reached its apogee in 1966-67, when Big Brother and the Holding Company, Jefferson Airplane, and the Appreciative Corpses all lived or played in the neighborhood. During 1967's "Summer of Love," young people from across the country converged on the grassy Panhandle of Golden Gate Park for the celebrated "be-ins." Despite recent gentrification, Haight-Ashbury remains cheap and exciting. Many of the bars and restaurants are remnants of a past era, with faded auras, games in the back rooms, and live-in regulars.

Check out the eclectic shops down Haight St. **Aardvark's Odd Ark,** 1501 Haight St. (621-3141), at Ashbury, has an immense selection of used new wave jackets, good music in the background, and prices that will take you back. (Open Sat.-Mon. 11am-9pm, Wed. 11am-7pm, Thurs. 11am-9pm, Fri. 11am-8pm.) Another used clothing store, **Wasteland,** 1660 Haight St. (863-3150), is worth checking out if only for its great facade and window displays. (Open Mon.-Fri. 11am-6pm, Sat. 11am-7pm, Sun. noon-6pm.) The **Global Family Networking Center,** 1665 Haight St. (864-1978), contains a café, market, and global awareness. The rooms at the **Red Vic,** upstairs, could be a museum but for the lack of velvet rope and "Do Not Touch" signs (see Accommodations above). Resembling a dense green mountain in the middle of the Haight, **Buena Vista Park** has a predictably bad reputation. Enter at your own risk, and once inside be prepared for those doing their own thing.

MUNI buses #6, 7, 16x, 43, 66, 71, and 73 all serve the area, while Metro line N runs along Carl St., four blocks south (see Practical Info above).

Golden Gate Park

No visit to San Francisco is complete without a picnic in Golden Gate Park. Frederick Law Olmsted, designer of New York's Central Park, said it couldn't be done when San Francisco's 19th-century leaders asked him to build a park to rival Paris's Bois de Boulogne. But engineer William Hammond Hall and Scottish gardener John McLaren proved him wrong. Hall designed the 1000-acre park—gardens and all—when the land on the city's western side was still shifting sand dunes, and then constructed a mammoth breakwater along the oceanfront to protect the seedling trees and bushes from the sea's burning spray.

The major north-south route through the park is named Park Presidio By-Pass Drive in the north and Cross Over Drive in the south. The **Panhandle,** a thin strip of land bordered by Fell and Oak Street on the north and south respectively, is the oldest part of the park; originally the "carriage entrance," it contains the oldest trees in the park, surrounded by the intriguing Haight-Ashbury. **Park headquarters,** home of info and maps, advises at Fell and Stanyan St. (556-2920), in McLaren Lodge on the eastern edge of the park. (Open Mon.-Fri. 8am-5pm.)

Three museums invigorate the park, all in one large complex on the eastern side between South and John F. Kennedy Dr., where 9th Ave. meets the park.

California Academy of Sciences (221-5100; 750-7145 for a recording; 750-7138 for Laserium), the West Coast's oldest institution of its kind, contains several smaller museums (admission to all $6). The **Steinhart Aquarium** (221-5100) is more lively than the natural history exhibits. The engaging alligator and crocodile pool pales in comparison with the unique Fish Roundabout, a large tank shaped like a doughnut where the fish swim around the visitors. The "Far Side of Science" gallery shows dozens of Gary Larson's best cartoons about nature and scientists. The academy also includes the **Morrison Planetarium** with its shows about white dwarves and black holes. (Additional charge of $2.50, seniors and students $1.25. Schedule changes; call 750-7141.) The **Laserium** (750-7138) orients its argon laser show to such robust themes as the Summer of '69 and Pink Floyd's *Dark Side of the Moon.* The synesthetic spectacle may be too intense for children under 6. (Tickets $6, 5pm matinee $5, seniors and ages 6-12 $4. Academy open daily 10am-7pm; Sept. 2-July 3 10am-5pm. Admission $4, $3 with MUNI Fast Pass or transfer, seniors and ages 12-17 $2, 6-11 $1, under 6 free. Free first Wed. each month until 8:45pm.)

M. H. de Young Museum (750-3600) takes visitors through a 21-room survey of U.S. painting, from the colonial period to the early 20th century, including several works by John Singer Sargent. Mixed in with the survey are some sculptures and pieces of furniture, which include Shaker chairs and a redwood and maple bed made in San Francisco in 1885. Also noteworthy is the museum's glass collection.

Asian Art Museum (668-8921), occupies the west wing of the building, boasting a collection of rare jade and fine porcelain plus bronze works over 3000 years old. Most pieces were donated by Avery Brundage in 1966 in a gift that inaugurated the museum. (Both museums open Wed.-Sun. 10am-5pm. Admission $4, $3 with MUNI Fast Pass or transfer, seniors and ages 12-17 $2, under 12 free.

One admission fee covers the de Young, Asian, and Palace of the Legion of Honor (see Richmond) museums for one day; save your receipt. (All free first Wed. each month and 10am-noon on the first Sat.)

Despite its sandy past, the soil of Golden Gate Park appears rich enough today to rival the black earth of the Midwest. Flowers blossom everywhere, particularly in spring and summer. The **Conservatory of Flowers** (386-3150), the oldest building in the park, was allegedly constructed in Ireland and shipped from Dublin via Cape Horn. The delicate and luminescent structure, modeled after Palm House in London's Kew Gardens, houses brilliant displays of tropical plants. (Open daily 9am-6pm; Nov.-March 9am-5pm. Admission $1.50, seniors and ages 6-12 $1, under 6 free.) The **Strybing Arboretum,** on Lincoln Way at 9th Ave. (661-1316), southwest of the academy, shows 5000 varieties of plants. Walk through the Garden of Fragrance for the vision-impaired, with labels in Braille and plants chosen especially for their texture and scent. (Tours daily at 1:30pm and at 10:30am Thurs.-Sun. Open Mon.-Fri. 9am-4:30pm, Sat.-Sun. 10am-5pm. Free.) Near the Music Concourse on a path off South Dr., the **Shakespeare Garden** contains almost every flower and plant ever mentioned by the herbalist of Avon. Plaques with the relevant quotations are hung on the back wall; a map helps you find your favorite hyacinths, cowslips, and gillyvors. (Open daily 9am-dusk; winter Tues.-Sun. 9am-dusk. Free.)

A relic of the 1894 California Midwinter Exposition, the **Japanese Tea Garden** is a serene, if overpriced, collection of dark wooden buildings, small pools, graceful footbridges, carefully pruned trees and plants, and tons of tourists. Buy some tea and cookies for $1 and watch the giant goldfish swim placidly in the central pond. (Open daily 9am-6:30pm; Oct.-April 8:30am-5:30pm. Admission $2, seniors and ages 6-12 $1, under 6 free. Free first and last half-hr. of operation, and all national holidays.)

At the extreme northwestern corner, the **Dutch Windmill** turns and turns again. Rounding out the days of old is the **Carousel** (c. 1912), accompanied by a $50,000 Gebruder band organ. (Open daily 10am-4pm; Oct.-May Wed.-Sun. 10am-4pm. Tickets $1, ages 6-12 25¢, under 6 free.)

Herd of **buffalo**? A dozen of the shaggy beasts roam a spacious paddock at the western end of John F. Kennedy Dr., near 39th Ave.

To get to the park, hop on bus #5 or 21. On Sundays traffic is banned from park roads, and bicycles and roller skates come out in full force. Bike rental shops are plentiful: skates, though harder to come by, are also available. Numerous MUNI buses cover the streets that surround Golden Gate Park and the north-south Park Presidio By-Pass/Cross Over Dr. (see Practical Info above).

Richmond District

The **Golden Gate Bridge,** the rust-colored symbol of the West's bounding confidence, sways above the entrance to San Francisco Bay. Built in 1937 under the directions of chief engineer Joseph Strauss, the bridge exudes almost indescribable beauty from any angle on or around it.

Lincoln Park, the Richmond district's biggest attraction, grows at the northwest extreme of the city. To get there, follow Clement St. west to 34th Ave., or Geary Blvd. to Point Lobos Ave., or take MUNI bus #1 or 38 to the edge of the Park. The **California Palace of the Legion of Honor** (750-3659), modeled after the Colonnade Hôtel de Salm in Paris, houses San Francisco's major collection of European art. The gallery's particularly strong French collection includes one of the best Rodin inventories in the country, both in plaster and bronze. Downstairs you'll find portions of the **Achenbach Foundation's** extensive graphic arts holdings. (Open Wed.-Sun. 10am-5pm. Admission $4, $3 with MUNI pass or transfer, seniors and ages 12-17 $2, under 12 free. Price includes same-day admission to the de Young and Asian Art Museums in Golden Gate Park. Free first Wed. and Sat. of each month 10am-noon.) Take the **Land's End Path,** running northwest of the cliff edge, for a romantic view of the Golden Gate Bridge.

Entertainment

San Francisco abounds with free publications listing the events in the Bay Area, distributed in record stores, bookshops, and street-corner distribution boxes. The two that natives rely on most are the *San Francisco Bay Guardian* and the *East Bay Express.* For a more detailed listing of Berkeley theater and the Oakland jazz scene, try the *Express.* For listings of the visual and performing arts, listen to the monthly *CenterVoice* (398-1854). The **Entertainment Hotline** is 391-2001 or 391-2002. The *Bay Times* (626-8121), the gay and lesbian paper, also appears monthly. The weekly *Advocate,* whose own pink pages are another thing entirely, offers a large amount of information on San Francisco's gay community.

Gay and Lesbian Clubs

While less visible than in recent years, gay nightlife in San Francisco still flourishes. Most popular bars thrive in the city's two traditionally gay areas—the **Castro** (around the intersection of Castro St. and Market St.) and **Polk St.** (for several blocks north of Geary St.).

The Stud, 399 9th St. (863-6623). A classic club with great dance music. Funk on Mon. No cover on weekdays. Open daily.

The Kennel Club, 628 Divisadero (931-1914). Hosts both "The Box" and "The Q Club". The former offers stupendous dancing and is popular among straights as well. Open Thurs. and Sat. 9pm-2am. "The Q Club", open on Thurs., has dancing for women.

Amelia's, 647 Valencia (552-7788). Dance bar for lesbians. No cover. Open Wed.-Sat. 4pm-2am.

Café San Marco, 2367 Market St. (861-3846). Popular gay bar. Open Mon.-Fri. 2pm-2am, Sat.-Sun. noon-2am.

Other Clubs

The Paradise Lounge, 1501 Folsom St. (861-6906). 3 stages, 2 floors, 5 bars, and up to 5 live bands a night. Pool tables upstairs. Open daily 3pm-2am.

DNA Lounge, 375 11th St. (626-1409), at the corner of Hanson. The best night for dancing is Wed. Cover rarely exceeds $10. Open 'til 3:30am.

The I-Beam, 1748 Haight St. (668-6006), Haight-Ashbury. Specializes in post-Branca bands and DJs playing high-tech rock. Décor includes shooting light beams and 2 screens full o' clips from cartoons, golden oldies, and Japanese monster flicks. Often free student night Wed. or Thurs. Sun. features a gay tea dance starting at 5pm. Open daily from 9pm. Cover $5-10.

Kimballs', 300 Grove St. (861-5555), at Franklin St. Great jazz musicians scare off the New Age/fusion frauds at this popular club/restaurant. Shows Wed.-Thurs. at 9pm, Sat.-Sun. at 11pm. Cover usually $8-12.

Club DV8, 540 Howard St. (777-1419). 3 floors of sheer dance mania. For the best dancing, stick to the third floor "osmosis." Open until 4am.

Perry's, 1944 Union St. (922-9022). A famous pick-up junction. Lackadaisical by day, hopping at night. Open daily 9am-2am.

Nicki's BBQ, 547 Haight (863-2276), on Lower Haight. D.J. nightly. Mon. features great country music. No cover. Open 11:30am-1:30pm.

San Francisco Bay Area

Berkeley

Almost 30 years ago Mario Salvo climbed onto a police car and launched the free speech movement that would give Berkeley its lingering reputation for political activism. Today, Berkeley is still a national symbol of political activism and social iconoclasm, and Telegraph Avenue, the Champs-Elysées of the 60s, remains the home of street-corner soothsayers, funky bookstores, aging hippies, countless cafés, and itinerant street musicians. Even as today's trends turn to climbing corporate ladders rather than digging ditches in undeveloped countries, the Berkeley City Council eagerly considers an initiative to curb "excess profits" in real estate. The site of the country's best public university, Berkeley is as renowned for its streetpeople and chefs as for its political cadres and academics.

Practical Information and Orientation

Visitor Information: Chamber of Commerce (549-7000), 1834 University Ave. at Martin Luther King, Jr. Dr. Open Mon.-Fri. 9am-noon and 1-4pm. **Council on International Educational Exchange (CIEE) Travel Center** (848-8604), 2486 Channing Way at Telegraph Ave. Open Mon.-Tues. and Thurs.-Fri. 9am-5pm, Wed. 10am-5pm. **Recorded Event Calendar,** 676-2222. **U.C. Berkeley Switchboard** (642-6000), 1901 8th St. Info on community events. Irregular hours.

Public Transport: Bay Area Rapid Transit (BART), 465-2278. Berkeley Station at Shattuck Ave. and Center St., close to the west edge of the university. **Transportation Info: Berkeley TRIP,** 644-7665. Info on public transport, biking, and carpooling. Mostly local transport, but not confined to daily commuting. The free university **Humphrey-Go-BART shuttle** (642-5149) connects the BART station with the central and eastern portions of campus. During the school year, the shuttle leaves the station every 10-12 min. Mon.-Fri. 7am-7pm—does not operate on university holidays. **Alameda County Transit (AC Transit),** 839-2882. Buses leave from Transbay Terminal for Berkeley every 30 min. from 5:50am-midnight ($2.50, ages over 64 and between 5-16 $1.25, $2). Within town, AC Transit City buses run approx. every 20 min. $1.10, seniors and people with disabilities 40¢, ages 5-16 $1. Sometimes the buses reach Berkeley faster than BART does.

Ride Boards: Berkeley Ride Board, ASUC building near the bookstore, on the 1st floor. Or call 642-5259.

Help Lines: Rape Hotline, 845-7273. Open 24 hrs. **Suicide Prevention,** 849-2212 or 889-1333. Open 24 hrs.

Post Office: 2000 Allston Way (649-3100). Open Mon.-Fri. 8:30am-5pm, Sat. 10am-2pm. **ZIP code:** 94704.

Area Code: 510.

You can reach Berkeley by crossing the bay on **BART** ($1.85); both the university and Telegraph Ave. are a five-minute walk from the station. The UC-Berkeley campus stretches into the hills, but most buildings reside in the westernmost section near BART.

Lined with bookstores and cafés, **Telegraph Avenue,** which runs south from the student union, is the town's spiritual center. The downtown area, around the BART station, contains what few businesses Berkeley will allow. The public library and central post office shelve and sort there. The **Gourmet Ghetto** encompasses the area along Shattuck Ave. and Walnut St. between Virginia and Rose St. West of campus and by the bay lies the **Fourth St. Center,** home to great eating and window shopping. To the northwest of campus, **Solano Avenue** offers countless ethnic restaurants (the best Chinese food in the city), bookstores, and movie theaters as well as more shopping.

Accommodations

The town has no good hostels, and clean, cheap motels are few. Most of the city's hotels are flophouses. You might try renting a fraternity room for the night: check the classified ads in the *Daily Californian* for possibilities. The **Bed and Breakfast Network** (540-5123) coordinates 15 B&Bs in the East Bay, some of which start around $30.

YMCA, 2001 Allston Way (848-6800), at Milvia St. Men over 17 only. No membership needed. Pool and basic fitness facilities included. Registration 8am-noon. Check-out 11:30am-noon. 14-day max. stay. Small rooms $22. Medium rooms $23. Key deposit $2.

University of California Housing Office (642-5925), 2700 Hearst Ave., in Stern Hall at the northern end of campus. Fairly spacious, clean rooms with large windows and phones available in summer to university visitors (loosely defined). Singles $34. Doubles $44. Open daily 7am-11pm. Call ahead.

California Hotel, 1461 University Ave. (848-3840), 2 blocks from the North Berkeley BART station. Singles and doubles $32, 2 beds $40. Key deposit $1.

Food

Berkeley supports several exceptional restaurants, many of them budget-busters. The area Northwest of campus around the famous Chez Panisse (where California Cuisine is said to have originated), is now called "Gourmet Ghetto" because of the abundance of voluptuous ingredients hawked there. The free Berkeley monthly *Bayfood* (652-6115) devotes articles, ads, and recipes to cooking and dining.

Plearn Thai Cuisine, 2050 University Ave. (841-2148), between Shattuck and Milvia. Elegant décor. One of the Bay Area's best. Busy at peak hours. Lunch entrées $4.25, dinner entrées $5-8.50. Try the *gai-young* chicken ($6.75). Open daily 11:30am-10pm.

Panini, 2115 Allston Way (849-0405), in the Trumpet Vine Court. The best gourmet bargain around. Discuss Sanskrit grammar in the courtyard while consuming exotic sandwiches that change daily—all are delicious ($3.75-5.50.) Open Mon.-Fri. 7:30am-4pm, Sat. 10am-4pm.

Smokey Joe's, 1620 Shattuck (548-4616), "where the elite meet to eat no meat"—a vegetarian diner noted for its breakfasts. Lunch $3.25-4.25, omelette $4.50. Open Mon.-Thurs. 7:30am-3pm, Fri. 7:30am-9pm, Sat. 8am-9pm, Sun. 8am-3pm.

Noah's New York Bagels, 3170 College Ave. (654-0944). One of the few kosher restaurants in the area, this popular place gets really packed at lunch, but service is quick and friendly. Choose from an enormous selection of bagels and flavored cream cheeses, like lox, walnut raisin, or vegetables and herbs. Plain bagels 50¢, with cream cheese $1.25. Open Mon.-Fri. 7am-6:30pm, Sat. 7:30am-6pm, Sun. 7:30am-5pm.

Café Intermezzo (849-4592), Telegraph at Haste. The enormous helpings of salad, served with fresh bread, distinguish this café from the multitudes of others along Telegraph. A combination sandwich and salad ($4.25) is enough to keep you chewing all the live-long day. Open Mon.-Fri. 10:30am-9pm.

Mario's La Fiesta, 2444 Telegraph Ave. (848-2588), at Haste St. Great Mexican food and a bopping atmosphere. Large chicken *flauta* combination plates, with rice, beans, guacamole, and chips $7.20. Open daily 10:30am-10:30pm.

The Cheese Board Collective, 1504 Shattuck Ave. (549-3183). A pillar of the Gourmet Ghetto. Add a few hundred cheeses to the excellent French bread for a great picnic. Very generous with samples. 10% discount for customers over 60, 15% for ages over 70, and so on. Open Tues.-Fri. 10am-6pm, Sat. 10am-5pm.

Blondie's Pizza, 2340 Telegraph Ave. (548-1129). A Berkeley institution. The 'za is pretty good too. Dagwood-sized slices, $1.25. Daily special, $1.75. Open Mon.-Thurs. 10:30am-1am, Fri.-Sat. 10:30am-2am, Sun. noon-midnight.

Long Life Vegi House, 2129 University Ave. (845-6072). Tasty and innovative Chinese cooking. No red meat served. Vegetarian plates $3.65, seafood plates $4.15. Chinese brunch served Sat. and Sun. 11:30am-3pm. Open daily 11:30am-9:30pm.

Peet's Coffee Bar, 2124 Vine St. (841-0564), at Walnut, northwest of campus.Where everybody buys their beans. You can get a cup of toe-curling brew (cream a must) for 60-90¢ if you bring your own mug. Open Mon.-Sat. 8am-6pm, Sun. 10am-6pm.

Sights

Pass through Sather Gate into **Sproul Plaza** and enter the university's intellectual Arcadia of gracious buildings, grass-covered hills, and sparkling streams. The **information center** (642-4636), in the student union building at Telegraph and Bancroft, has maps and booklets for self-guided tours. (Open Mon.-Fri. 8am-6pm, Sat. 10am-6pm.) Guided tours start at the **visitors center** (642-5215), room 101, University Hall, Oxford St. and University Ave. The Berkeley campus swallows 160 acres, bounded on the south by Bancroft Way, on the west by Oxford St., by Hearst Ave. to the north, and by extensive parkland to the east. The school has an enrollment of over 30,000 and more than 1000 full professors (with all those cafés nearby, it's not surprising!) Imposing **Bancroft Library,** with nearly seven million volumes, is among the nation's largest. Located in the center of campus, the library contains exhibits ranging from California arcana to folio editions of Shakespeare's plays. You can see the tattered bronze plaque left by Sir Francis Drake in the 16th century, vainly claiming California for England. (Open Mon.-Fri. 9am-5pm, Sat. 1-5pm. Free.)

The most dramatic on-campus attraction is **Sather Tower,** the 1914 monument to Berkeley benefactor Jane K. Sather. The 500-ton steel frame is designed to withstand large earthquakes. (Open daily 10am-4:15pm. Admission 50¢.)

The **University Art Museum,** 2626 Bancroft Way (642-1124; 24-hr. events hotline 642-0808), holds a diverse permanent collection. Innovative directors have put together a number of memorable shows over the years on everything from Cubism to the interaction of U.S. painting and popular 50s culture. (Open Wed.-Sun. 11am-5pm. Admission $5, seniors and ages 6-17 $4. Thurs. 11am-noon free.)

The **Lawrence Hall of Science** (642-5132) stands above the northeast corner of the campus in a concrete octagon. Take bus #8 from the Berkeley BART. Exhibits stress learning science through hands-on use of everyday objects. (Open Mon.-Fri. 10am-4:30pm, Sat.-Sun. 10am-5pm. Admission $3.50; seniors, students, and ages 7-18 $2.50; under 7 free.)

Outside of campus stand more museums and noteworthy architecture. The **Judah Magnes Museum,** 2911 Russell St. (849-2710), displays one of the West Coast's leading collections of Judaica. (Open Sun.-Fri. 10am-4pm.) The **Julia Morgan Theater** (845-8542), 2640 College Ave., is housed in a beautiful former church designed by its namesake and constructed of dark redwood and Douglas fir.

People's Park, on Haste St. one block off Telegraph Ave., is an unofficial museum of sorts, featuring a mural that depicts the 60s struggle between the city and local activists over whether to develop it commercially. During that struggle, then-governor Ronald Reagan sent in state police to break a blockade, resulting in the death of a student. In 1989, a rally was held to protest the university's renewed threats to convert the park; some demonstrators began turning over cars, looting stores, and setting fires. Last year the city constructed restrooms and volleyball courts, and increased security around the park, but these remain somewhat desolate while the forces of law and order coexist uneasily with the homeless habituated to the site. It is still relatively unsafe.

Relax and enjoy the **Takara Sake Tasting Room** (540-8250), 708 Addison St. at 4th St. You can request a sample of several varieties, all made with California rice. A narrated slide presentation on *sake* brewing is shown on request. (Open daily noon-6pm.)

A short drive or BART ride (to the Lake Merritt stop) into Oakland will take you to the **Oakland Museum,** 1000 Oak St. (834-2413); a well-designed complex of three galleries devoted to California's artistic, historical, and natural heritage. The top floor houses the **Gallery of California Art,** where everything from traditional 19th-century portraits to contemporary works using car doors finds a wall. The gallery also has some splendid Currier cartoons about the Gold Rush. One floor down, the fantastic **Cowell Hall of California History** takes visitors through California's boom-like social and economic history, using artifacts, costumes, and even vehicles. On the lowest level, the **Hall of California Ecology** uses state-of-the-art fish-simulation technology in its new Aquatic California gallery. (Open Wed.-Sat. 10am-5pm, Sun. noon-7pm. Tours Wed.-Sat. at 2pm. Free. Small fee for special exhibits.)

Entertainment

Hang out with procrastinating students at the **student union** (642-5215). The ticket office, arcade, bowling alleys, and pool tables are all run from a central desk. (Open Mon.-Fri. 8am-6pm, Sat. 10am-6pm; off-season Mon.-Fri. 8am-10pm, Sat. 10am-6pm.) Next door the **Bear's Lair** (843-0373), a student pub, sells pitchers of Bud for $4. (Open Sat.-Wed. 11am-6pm, live music Thurs. and Fri., academic year Mon.-Thurs. noon-midnight, Fri. 11am-8pm.) **CAL Performance,** 101 Zellerbach Hall (642-7477), is a university-wide concert and lecture organizer, with info on all the rock, classical, and jazz concerts, lectures, and movies on campus. Ask about non-paying ushering jobs, a good way to see shows for free. Big concerts usually are held in the **Greek Theater** (642-5550), a frequent site for Grateful Dead shows, or Zellerbach Hall. (Open Mon.-Fri. 10am-5:30pm, Sat. noon-4pm.)

U.C. Theater (843-6267), 2036 University Ave., west of Shattuck Ave. Standard reruns, *film noir* series, studio classics; nicely-matched double features. Schedules available throughout Berkeley or at the theater. Creative film festivals. Admission $3.50 before 6pm, $5 after 6pm, seniors and children $3.50.

Larry Blake's Downstairs (848-0886), 2367 Telegraph, at Durant Ave., through the upstairs dining room and down a flight. An excellent drinking and meeting spot. Sawdust on the floor and live jazz. Drinks from $2. Cover $3-6. Restaurant open Mon.-Sat. 11:30am-2am, Sun. 4pm-2am. Bar open until 1am.

Starry Plough, 3101 Shattuck Ave. (841-2082). Pub with Irish bands and Anchor Steam on tap. Posters espouse the pro-Irish, anti-nuclear, and U.S.-out-of-Nicaragua points of view. Mon. nights they offer Irish dance lessons at 7pm and traditional Irish music 9pm Tues. and Wed. Other nights, California bands play live. Nights with bands $3-6 cover. Open Mon.-Sat. 11am-2am, Sun. 4pm-2am.

Triple Rock Brewery, 1920 Shattuck Ave. (843-2739). Micro-brewery producing 3 delicious regular beers (2 pale ales and 1 porter) and occasional specials. A bargain at $2.25 per pint. Old beer logos grace the walls. Roof garden, too. After 7pm, you can only stand in the crowded barroom. Open daily 11am-midnight.

Marin County

The undeveloped, fog-shrouded hills just west of the Golden Gate Bridge comprise the **Marin Headlands,** part of the **Golden Gate National Recreation Area** which sprawls across the Bay Area. The view from the Headlands back over the bridge to San Francisco is arguably the most spectacular vista in the Bay Area. You should consider hiking the one-mi. trail that leads from the parking area down to the sheltered (and usually deserted) beach at **Kirby Cove.** You can get to the Headlands (and the viewpoints) easily by car; simply take the Alexander Ave. exit off U.S. 101 and take your first left. You'll go through an underpass and up a hill on your right. San Francisco Municipal

Railway (MUNI) bus #76 will transport those without autos (see San Francisco: Practical Information).

About five mi. west along the Panoramic Hwy. off U.S. 101 stands **Muir Woods National Monument,** a congregation of primeval coastal redwoods. A loop road takes you through the most outstanding area. (Open daily 8am-sunset.) The **visitors center** (388-2595), near the entrance, keeps the same hours as the monument. West of Muir Woods lies **Muir Beach,** which offers a tremendous view of San Francisco from the surrounding hills.

North of Muir Woods lies the isolated, largely undiscovered, and utterly beautiful **Mount Tamalpais State Park.** The heavily forested park has a number of challenging trails that lead to the top of "Mount Tam," the highest peak in the county, and to a natural stone amphitheater. **Stinson Beach,** also in the port, is a local favorite for sunbathing. **Park headquarters** is at 810 Panoramic Hwy. (388-2070). The park opens a half-hour before sunrise and closes a half-hour before sunset.

Encompassing 100 mi. of coastline along most of the western side of Marin, the **Point Reyes National Seashore** audaciously juts into the Pacific from the eastern end of the submerged Pacific Plate. Here the infamous San Andreas Fault grinds to an end. The remote position of the point brings heavy fog and strong winds, unique flora and fauna, and crowds of tourists to gawk at it all. For bus info call **Golden Gate Transit** (332-6600; see San Francisco: Practical Information).

Limantour Beach, at the end of Limantour Rd. west of the seashore headquarters, and **McClures Beach,** at the extreme north of the seashore near the end of Pierce Point Rd., are two of the nicest area beaches. Both have high, grassy dunes and long stretches of sandy beach. In summer a free shuttle bus runs to Limantour Beach from the seashore headquarters. Strong ocean currents along the point make swimming tantamount to suicide. To reach the dramatic **Point Reyes Lighthouse** at the very tip of the point, follow Sir Francis Drake Blvd. to its end and then head right along the long stairway to Sea Lion overlook. From December to February, gray whales occasionally can be spotted off the coast from the overlook.

Marin, to its credit, has managed to avoid the cheap motel blight that can ruin otherwise lovely areas. The **Golden Gate Youth Hostel (HI/AYH)** (331-2777), a few miles south of Sausalito, sits among rolling hills, close to a waterbird sanctuary, and houses 66 beds in an spacious building that is part of deserted Fort Barry.(Laundry, game room, kitchen. Check-in 7:30-9:30am and 4:30-11pm. Curfew 11pm. Members and nonmembers $9. Linen $1. Reservations best in summer.) By car from San Francisco, take the Alexander Ave. exit off U.S. 101; take the second Sausalito exit if going toward San Francisco. Follow the signs into the Golden Gate National Recreation Area, then follow the hostel signs through the park (about 3 mi.). **Golden Gate Transit buses** (see below) #10, 20, 30, and 50 stop at Alexander Ave. From there, you will have to go it on your own. A taxi from San Francisco costs about $12.

Twenty-five mi. north, the spectacularly situated **Point Reyes Hostel (HI/AYH),** Limantour Rd. (663-881), opens nightly for groups and individuals. You're more likely to get a late-notice room here than in the Golden Gate Hostel, although reservations are advised on weekends, and must be received by mail, with a deposit. Hiking, wildlife, birdwatching, and Limantour Beach are all within walking distance, but the hostel itself is a six-mi. trek into the park. Bring food to cook in the well-equipped kitchen since the nearest market hawks its wares eight mi. away. (Registration 4:30-9:30pm. $9. Linen $1.) By car take the Seashore exit west from Rte. 1. Take Beer Valley Road to Linatour Rd., and follow until you see a hostel sign. For public transportation info, contact **Golden Gate Transit** or call the hostel (two buses per day to the hostel).

The campground closest to Sausalito hunkers down in **Samuel Taylor State Park** (488-9897), on Sir Francis Drake Blvd., 15 mi. west of San Rafael (itself 10 mi. north of Sausalito on U.S. 101). The park's 60 sites ($14) with hot showers (25¢ for 15 min.) stay open year-round. A hiker/biker camp costs $3 per person with a seven-day maximum stay. Reservations needed a week in advance from April 1 to Oct. 31 (800-444-7275 or 619-452-1950). Four campgrounds (accessible only by foot) line the national seashore in the south, inner-cape portion of Pt. Reyes. All are fairly primitive, with pit toilets, firepits, and tap water; all require permits from the **Point Reyes National Sea-**

shore Headquarters, Bear Valley Rd. (663-1092; open Mon.-Fri. 9am-5pm, Sat.-Sun. 8am-5pm). All camps command exquisite views of the ocean and surrounding hills.

The **Sausalito Chamber of Commerce,** 333 Caledonia St. (332-0505), is open Monday through Friday from 9am to 5pm. **Point Reyes National Seashore Headquarters,** on Bear Valley Rd. (663-1092), a half-mi. west of Olema, offers wilderness permits, maps, and campsite reservations. (Open Mon.-Fri. 9am-5pm, Sat.-Sun. 8:30am-4:30pm.) Marin has little public transportation. **Golden Gate Transit** (453-2100; 332-6600 in San Francisco) provides daily bus service between San Francisco and Marin County via the Golden Gate Bridge, as well as local service within the county. Buses #10, 20, 30, and 50 run from the Transbay Terminal at First and Mission St. in San Francisco ($2). The **Golden Gate Ferry** (453-2100, in San Francisco 332-6600) serves Sausalito, departing from the ferry building at the end of Market St. for a 25-minute crossing (Mon.-Fri. 7am-8:25pm, Sat.-Sun. 10:45am-6:55pm). The one-way fare to Sausalito is $3.75, $3 for seniors and persons with disabilities. Boats return from Sausalito roughly one hour later than departures.

The **area code** for Marin County is 415.

Sierra Nevada

Sierra Nevada is the highest, steepest, and most physically stunning mountain range in the contiguous United States. The heart-stopping sheerness of Yosemite's rock walls, the craggy alpine scenery of Kings Canyon and Sequoia National Parks, and the abrupt drop from the eastern slope into Owens Valley conspire to inspire drivers, hikers, and climbers alike. An enormous hunk of granite created by plate tectonics and shaped by erosion, the Sierra Nevada (Spanish for "snowy mountains") stretches 450 mi. north from the Mojave Desert to Lake Almanor. At 14,495 ft., Mt. Whitney surmounts all other points in the U.S. outside Alaska.

The **Sequoia National Forest** encompasses the southern tip of the Sierras and embraces popular recreational areas and isolated wilderness. **Forest headquarters** sit in Porterville, 900 W. Grand Ave. (209-784-1500), 15 mi. east of Rte. 99 between Fresno and Bakersfield. The **Sierra National Forest** fills the area between Yosemite, Sequoia, and Kings Canyon. The forest is not exactly "undiscovered"—droves of Californians jam the busier spots at lower elevations, and even the wilderness areas can be overpopulated in summer. The main **information office** counsels at the Federal Bldg., 1130 O St. #3017, Fresno (209-487-5155; 209-487-5456 for 24-hr. recorded info). Pick up an excellent map ($2.10) of the forests here or in Porterville, or order one from the Three Forest Interpretive Association (3FIA), 13098 E. Wire Grass Lane, Clovis, CA 93612.

Overnight temperatures can dip into the 20s°F year-round. Normally, only U.S. 50 and I-80 are kept open during the snow season. Exact dates vary from year to year, so check with a ranger station on local road and weather conditions from October through April. During all times of the year bring sunscreen—the ultra-violet rays at this high elevation are harsh.

Kings Canyon and Sequoia National Park

If your impression of national parks has been formed by touristy Grand Canyon- and Yosemite-like parks, you'll love the twin parks of Kings Canyon and Sequoia that can go sight-for-jaw-dropping-sight with those more famous national parks. The terrain of these two parks has been alternately tortured and healed by ambivalent nature; cool waters numb scars left by glaciers, a snowy gauze bandages mountains that have broke the skin of the earth and thrust themselves heavenward. Meadow life buzzes, blooms, and breeds in expanses that were once cleared by fire. Uncertain Sequoia saplings cower beside that stumps and felled remains of their ancestors, suggesting that even the blight left by humans may someday be erased. Kings Canyon and Sequoia offer visitors a chance to tailor their level of immersion in the wilderness.

Glacier-covered **Kings Canyon** displays a stunning array of imposing cliffs and sparkling waterfalls. Home to the deepest canyon walls in the country, turn-outs along the roads offer breathtaking vistas into gaping near-vertical declivities. In **Sequoia,** the Sierra Crest lifts itself to its greatest heights. Several 14,000-ft. peaks scrape the clouds along the park's eastern border, including **Mt. Whitney,** the tallest mountain in the contiguous U.S. (14,495 ft.). Both parks contain impressive groves of massive sequoia trees in addition to a large and cantankerous bear population. Visitors like to cluster around the largest sequoias, which tower near the entrances to the parks; the vast stretches of backcountry remain relatively empty. Developed areas like **Grant Cove** and **Giant Forest** offer interpretive trails, lodging amenities, and paved vehicle access. In contrast, the backcountry at **Road's End** in Kings Canyon or along the **High Sierra Trail** across Sequoia offer little but the guidance of cumulative footsteps of the trail trekers before you. The "summer season" usually runs from Memorial Day through Labor Day, "snow season" from November through March.

Seasonal changes are definitive and exaggerated in this area of the Sierras. Peak foliage on dogwood, aspen, and oak is between October and November as the parks settle into a winter freeze, leaving trails and many roads impassable. Spring brings opportunities for skiing, late storms, low fogs, and flooding meltwater. Be prepared for marked temperature drops at night in these high elevations.

Sequoia Guest Services, Inc., P.O. Box 789, Three Rivers 93271 (561-3314), has a monopoly on indoor accommodations and food in the parks. Their rustic **cabins** cluster in a little village in Sequoia's Giant Forest, as well as at Grant Grove. (Cabins available May-Oct., $31 per person, $3.50 each additional person up to 8.) Most park service **campgrounds** open from mid-May to October (2-week limit year-round). For info about campgrounds, contact a ranger station or call 565-3351 for a recording. Kings Canyon offers sites for $8 at **Sunset, Azalea,** and **Crystal Springs,** all within spitting distance of Grant Grove Village, and at **Sheep Creek, Sentinel, Canyon View,** and **Moraine,** at the Kings River near Cedar Grove. Sequoia has sites without hookups at **Lodgepole** (900-370-5566), four mi. northeast of Giant Forest Village in the heart of Sequoia National Park. (Sites $8-10; free in winter.) Reserve up to eight weeks in advance through Ticketron (800-452-1111) from mid-May to mid-September. Other options are **Atwell Mill** and **Cold Springs,** about 20 mi. along the Mineral King Rd., in the Mineral King area. (Sites $8 for tents only.)

The two parks are accessible to vehicles from the west only. You can reach trailheads into the John Muir Wilderness and Inyo National Forest on the eastern side from spur roads off U.S. 395, but *no* roads traverse the Sierras here. From **Fresno** follow **Rte. 180** through the foothills; a 60-mi. sojourn takes you to the entrance of the Grant Grove section of Kings Canyon. Rte. 180 ends 30 mi. later in the Cedar Grove, an island of park land enveloped within Sequoia National Forest. The road into this region closes in winter. From **Visalia,** take **Rte. 198** to Sequoia National Park. **Generals Highway** (Rte. 198) connects the Ash Mountain entrance to Sequoia with the **Giant Forest,** and continues to Grant Grove in Kings Canyon.

In summer (June-Nov.), the treacherous road to **Mineral King** opens up the southern parts of Sequoia. From Visalia, take Rte. 198; the turnoff to Mineral King is three mi. past Three Rivers, and the **Lookout Point Ranger Station** lies 10 mi. along the Mineral King Rd. Take a break from driving here: Atwell Springs Campground and the nearby town of Silver City are 10 mi. (but 45 min.) farther along. **Cold Springs Campground, Mineral King Ranger Station,** and several **trailheads** lie near the end of Mineral King Rd. in a valley framed by 12,000-ft. peaks. The route to Mineral King includes stunning scenery—that is, if you can tear your eyes away from the tortuous road while making 698 turns between Rte. 198 and the Mineral King complex. Allow two hours for the trip from Three Rivers.

Roads can't touch the northern two-thirds of Kings Canyon and the eastern two-thirds of Sequoia; here the backpacker and packhorse have free rein. Check at a ranger station or visitors center for more detailed info. Bicycles are not permitted on hiking trails or in back country. A car is indispensable. Seqouia/Kings Canyon does operate two **bus tours** around Giant Forest and Kings Canyon. These are pricey, however, and leave little time to savor and explore the sites. Inquire at the visitors center in either park.

Kings Canyon's **Grant Grove Visitors Center,** two mi. east of the Big Stump Entrance by Rte. 180 (335-2856), has books, maps, exhibits, nightly campfire programs and daily hikes. (Open daily 8am-6pm; winter 8am-5pm.) Sequoia's **Ash Mountain Visitors Center,** Three Rivers 93271 (565-3134), on Rte. 198 out of Visalia, has info on both parks; the **Lodgepole Visitors Center** on Generals Hwy. four mi. east of the Giant Forest, (565-3341, ext. 631), climbs in the heart of Sequoia, near the big trees and the tourists.

Lake Tahoe

The tectonic upheaval that propelled the Sierras to their grand height left a basin which became the setting for Lake Tahoe, North America's third-deepest lake. Located 118 mi. northeast of Sacramento and 35 mi. southwest of Reno, NV, Tahoe's cerulean waters, surrounded by evergreens and peaks, form a glorious mountain oasis. These waters are never warmer than 39°F; however inviting they may seem, don't plan on doing much backstroking here. Native Americans who used to live around Lake Tahoe buried their dead by pushing them, fully garbed, off the side of their canoes into the Lake. The lake's frigid temperatures kept the bodies perfectly preserved, suspended in the water. Convection currents in the lake occasionally bring these bodies to the surface. Who knows, you might bump into Fredo Corleone.

Californian vapidity meets Nevadan avarice along the lake, as the two states split the area's southern shores into two parts—**South Lake Tahoe,** a nature-lover's dream, in California, and **Stateline,** a gambling resort, in Nevada. California's **North Lake Tahoe** is a dynamic town rich with campsites.

To see the lake in style, board a boat. The glass bottoms of the *Tahoe Queen* (541-3664) leave from Ski Run Blvd. for tours of Emerald Bay (3 per day, $12.50), and the *M.S. Dixie* (588-3508) leaves Zephyr Cove on I-80 (702-588-3833), four mi. north of the casino on U.S. 50 (5 per day, $10-32). Several marinas rent out fishing boats, and you can get paddle boats for under $10 per hour. Or share the cost with several people, and rent a motorboat and waterskis ($52 per hr.), or a jet-ski ($45 per hr.), at Zephyr Cove. Rent a wet suit or you may as well prepare to hypotherm.

Incline Village, just into Nevada north of Tahoe, holds the famed **Ponderosa Ranch** (702-831-0691) of *Bonanza* fame, located in the village on Tahoe Blvd. Try the "Haywagon Breakfast" for a scenic buffet and hayride (daily at 8am). (Open April-Oct. daily 9am-6pm. Admission $7.50, ages 5-11 $6 under 5 free.) Both the **Forest Service Fire Lookout** and the **Mount Rose Scenic Overlook** (Rte. 431 from Incline to Reno) afford beautiful views of the lake. The **Heavenly Mountain chairlift** (541-1330) will carry you up 2000 ft. for a bird's-eye view. (Open Mon.-Sat. 10am-10pm, Sun. 9am-10pm.)

For those who prefer to earn their views with boot leather, the U.S. Forest Service (573-2674) produces a series of leaflets and can advise on many different trails. The western side of Tahoe offers the **Tahoe State Recreation Area** (583-3074), **Sugar Pine Point Park** (525-7982), and the **D.L. Bliss** and **Emerald Bay State Parks** (both 525-7277). Magnificent **Emerald Bay** contains Tahoe's only island. A quarter mi. off U.S. 50 at Emerald Bay sits **Vikingsholm** (541-3030), a Scandinavian-style castle built in the 1920s. (Open for tours June-Sept. daily 10am-4pm. Admission $1, kids $.50.) The ultimate hike, along the 150-mi. **Tahoe Rim Trail,** loops around the entire lake and takes about 15 days (call 577-0676 for info).

Winter draws tourists to Lake Tahoe with nine cross-country areas, 16 ski resorts, and snowmobile routes. **Squaw Valley** (800-545-4350), home of the 1960 Winter Olympics; **Alpine Meadows** (800-824-6348); and **Diamond Peak** own the biggest reputations, but the smaller, less crowded **Homewood** (525-7256) draws rave reviews.

Stateline offers Nevada's usual assortment of cheap casino buffets. Restaurants in California include: **Red Hut Waffles,** 2723 U.S. 50 (541-9024), with great breakfasts (open 6am-2pm); **The Siam Restaurant,** 2180 U.S. 50 (544-0370), with large, spicy entrées from $4 (open Mon.-Tues. and Thurs.-Sun. 10am-9:45pm); and **Cantina Los Tres Hombres,** Rte. 89 at 10th St. (544-1233), a Margaritaville with free chips and salsa (open 11:30am-10:30pm).

The strip off U.S. 50 on the California side of the state line supports the bulk of Tahoe's 200 motels. Others line the quieter Park Ave. Many other motels have been razed to make room for luxury hotels, and the remaining inexpensive lodgings are booked solid on weekends year-round. The cheapest deals cluster near Stateline on **U.S. 50.** The standard-issue **Motel 6,** 2375 Lake Tahoe Blvd., 95731 (542-1400), fills quickly, especially on weekends. It has a pool and TV. (Singles $33. Each additional adult $6. Make reservations far in advance.) At the clean, comfortable **Midway Motel,** 3876 U.S. 50 (544-4397), bargain gently for weekday rates. (Double bed $22, weekends $65. 2 double beds $33, weekends $75.) You also can hit the **Jack Pot Inn,** 3908 U.S. 50 (541-5587), one mi. south of the casinos. (Singles $20. Doubles $22. Fri.-Sat. rooms from $35.)

The forest service at the visitors bureau provides up-to-date info on the 30-plus campgrounds around Lake Tahoe. Make reservations for state park campgrounds by calling MISTIX at 800-283-2267. Free campgrounds include **Bayview** (544-6420; max. stay 1 night, open June-Sept.), and **Emerald Bay State Park,** Rte. 89 (541-3030), 10 mi. west of town. Emerald has lovely scenery, with an oft-photographed tree-rimmed cove. Peaceful. Hot showers. Sites $14. Open June-Labor Day. **Nevada Beach,** U.S. 50 and Country Rd. (573-2600),2 mi. north of South Lake Tahoe, has a quaint sandy beach. (Sites $10, $12 Sept.-May.)

The **Visitors Bureau and Chamber of Commerce,** 3066 U.S. 50 (541-5255) at San Francisco Ave., has gallons of helpful brochures, maps, and free copies of *101 Things to Do in Lake Tahoe* and *Handbook for the Handicapped.* (Open Mon.-Fri. 8:30am-5pm, Sat.-Sun. 9am-4pm.) The **U.S. Forest Service,** 870 Emerald Bay Rd., S. Lake Tahoe (541-6564), supervises campgrounds and publishes the free, informative *Lake of the Sky Journal.* (Open Mon.-Fri. 8am-4:30pm.) **Greyhound,** 1099 Park Ave. (544-2241), on the state line, has service to San Francisco (5 per day, $31) and Sacramento (5 per day, $18). **Showboat Lines** sends buses from Reno Airport daily 8:30am-5pm (8 per day, $13.50). **Tahoe Area Regional Transport** (581-6365) connects to the western and northern shores from Tahoma to Incline Village. (12 buses daily 6:10am-6pm. Fare $1, unlimited travel day pass $2.50.) **South Tahoe Area Ground Express** (573-2080) STAGEs 24-hr. bus service around town, and daily seven-hr. jaunts to the beach (1 per ½-hr.; fare $1.25, under 8 free). For those traveling without luggage, the major hotels all offer free shuttle service along U.S. 50 to and from their casinos. **Harvey's** (702-588-2411) runs a bus daily from 8am to 2am. **Budget** (541-5777), at the airport, rents from $35 per day, with surcharges for drivers under 25. Rent bikes at **Anderson's Bicycle Rental,** 645 Emerald Bay Rd. (541-0500), convenient to the west shore bike trail. (Full day $20, half-day $15. Open daily 8:30am-6:30pm. License required for deposit.) Mopeds are available from **Country Moped,** 800 Emerald Bay Rd. at Rte. 89 South and 10th St. (544-3500; $10 first hr., less for additional hours; helmets available).

The **post office** registers at 1085 Park Ave. (544-6162), next to the Greyhound station. (Open Mon.-Fri. 8:30am-5pm.) Lake Tahoe's **ZIP code** is 95729; the **area code** is 916 in California, 702 in Nevada.

Mammoth Lakes

Home to one of the most popular ski resorts in California, the town of Mammoth Lakes is a year-round playground, subject to unpredictable weather, including the occasional snow in June. The intriguing geological oddity **Devil's Postpile National Monument** was formed when lava flows oozed through Mammoth Pass thousands of years ago and then cooled to form perfect hexagonal columns 40 to 60 ft. high. Ancient glaciers exposed and polished the basalt posts to create the mammoth jewels that glitter today. A pleasant three-mi. walk away is **Rainbow Falls,** where the middle fork of the San Joaquin River drops 140 ft. past dark cliffs into a glistening green pool. From U.S. 395, the monument and its bubbly hot springs can be reached by a 14-mi. drive past Minaret Summit on Rte. 203. Three mi. south of Mammoth Junction on U.S. 395 bubbles **Hot Creek,** open to bathers. Ask locals about late-night skinny-dips. (Open sunrise to sunset.) None of the more than 100 lakes near town is called "Mammoth Lake."

Lake Mary is the largest, popular with boaters and fishers; **Twin Lakes** is the closest, three mi. from the village on Rte. 203; swimming is allowed only at **Horseshoe Lake,** the trailhead for **Mammoth Pass Trail.**

Adventurous travelers can enjoy hot-air balloons, snowmobiles, mountain bike paths, and dogsled trails. **Mammoth Adventure Connection** (800-228-4947) helps you evaluate your options. With 132 downhill runs, over 26 lifts, and oodles of nordic trails, Mammoth is also a skier's paradise. Lift tickets may be bought for several days at a time ($27 per day, $108 for 5 days). They can be purchased at the **Main Lodge** (934-2571) at the base of the mountain on Minaret Road (open Mon.-Fri. 8am-3pm, Sat.-Sun. 7:30am-3pm) or at **Warming Hut II** (934-0771) at the end of Canyon and Lakeview Blvd. (open Mon.-Fri. 8am-5pm, Sat.-Sun. 7:30am-5pm). A free shuttle bus transports skiers between lifts, town and the Main Lodge.

Chow on chili ($5.50) at the **Brewhouse Grill,** 170 Mountain Blvd. (934-8134; open Tues.-Sat. 11:30am-whenever, Sun. 5-10:30pm). **Blondie's Kitchen** (934-4048) at the Sierra Center Mall on Old Mammoth Rd. serves mammoth breakfast specials ($3.25) including all-you-can-eat pancakes ($4). (Open daily 6:30am-1:30pm.)

Call the Mammoth Ranger District (934-25050) for info on nearly 20 Inyo Forest public **campgrounds** in the area. (Sites $7-9). Otherwise, the **ULLR Lodge** (934-2454), on Minaret Rd. just south of Main St., is the best deal in town. (Winter dorm rooms $16. Singles $37, $41 on weekends. Doubles $40, $46 on weekends. Cheaper in summer.) **Asgard Chalet,** 19 Davidson Rd. (716-962-6773), is excellent for groups. Dormitory and 7-18 person lodging units available. Small room sleeps 1-3 ($12-15 per person in the summer, $19 in winter). Lower unit sleeps seven ($115, weekends $125.)

Mammoth Lakes is located on U.S. 395 about 160 mi. south of Reno and 40 mi. southeast of the eastern entrance to Yosemite. Rte. 203 runs through the town as Main St., then veers off to the right as Minaret Summit Rd. The **Visitors Center and Chamber of Commerce** (934-2712) spiels inside Village Center Mall West. (Open Sat.-Thurs. 8am-5pm, Fri. 8am-8pm.) The **Mammoth National Forest Visitors Center** (934-2505) is east off U.S. 395. (Open daily 6am-5pm, Oct.-June 8am-4:30pm.) **Greyhound** (872-2721) stops in front of the Main St. McDonalds and goes once a day to Reno (1am) and L.A. (12:30pm). No office, no phone. Board here, and buy ticket at next station. The **post office** (934-2205) is across from the visitors center. (Open Mon.-Fri. 8:30am-5pm.) The **ZIP code** is 93546; the **area code** is 619.

Yosemite National Park

Three years ago the worst forest fire in the park's 100-year history destroyed more than 22,000 acres in one horrific week. Although this represented only 2% of the park, the destruction is highly visible along Tioga and Big Oak Flat Rd. Father Time, Mother Nature, and Uncle Sam are healing the park's wounds—no fire could staunch the flow of tourists flooding the park every year for a glimpse of its stunning waterfalls, rushing rivers, alpine meadows, and granite cliffs. Underneath the dark tombstones of charred trees, fresh, pale green growth and stunning wildflowers are visible.

Purists bemoan Yosemite's snack shops, delis, photo galleries, and grocery stores as casual visitors counter that the valley's unique splendor belongs to *everyone,* not just to hardcore backpackers. Fortunately, the embattled valley occupies only a handful of the nearly 1200 square mi. encompassed by this national park. Yosemite graciously manages to accommodate all its suitors; whether backpackers or hotel guests, visitors to this region are invariably uplifted by their stay. One can never come too often or stay long enough, for the park has infinite offerings. Experience the park's dramatic beauty, and you'll understand why Muir remarked, "No description of heaven seems half so fine."

Practical Information

Visitor Information: General Park Information, 372-0265; 372-0200 for 24-hr. recorded info. Advice about accommodations, activities, and weather conditions. TTY users call 372-4726. Open Mon.-Fri. 8am-5pm. **Yosemite Valley Visitors Center,** Yosemite Village (372-4461, ext. 333). Open daily 8am-8pm. Sign language interpreters available daily 2-5pm. **Tuolumne Meadows Visitors Center,** Tioga Rd. (372-0263), 55 mi. from Yosemite Village. Headquarters of high-country activity, with trail info, maps, and special programs. Open summer daily 8am-8pm. **Big Oak Flat Information Station,** Rte. 120 W. (379-2445), in the Crane Flat/Tuolumne Sequoia Grove Area. Open summer daily 7:30am-6pm. **Wawona Ranger Station,** Rte. 141 (375-6391), at the southern entrance near the Mariposa Grove. Open Mon.-Fri. 8am-5pm, Sat.-Sun. 7am-5pm. **Backcountry Office,** P.O. Box 577, Yosemite National Park 95389 (372-0308; 372-0307 for 24-hr. recorded info), next to Yosemite Valley Visitors Center. Backcountry and trail info. Open daily 7:30am-7:30pm. Free map of the park and informative free *Yosemite Guide* available at visitors centers. Information folders and maps available in French, German, Japanese, and Spanish. Wilderness permits available at all centers.

Yosemite Park and Curry Co. Room Reservations: 5410 E. Home, Fresno 93727 (252-4848; TTY users 255-8345). Except for campgrounds, YP&C has a monopoly on all the facilities of what has become a full-fledged resort within the park. Contact for info and reservations.

Tour Information: Yosemite Lodge Tour Desk (372-1240), in Yosemite Lodge lobby. Open daily 7:30am-8pm, or contact any other lodge in the park.

Bus Tours: Yosemite Via, 300 Grogan Ave., Merced 95340 (384-1315 or 722-0366). 2 trips daily from the Merced Greyhound station to Yosemite ($15; seniors discount). **Yosemite Gray Line (YGL),** P.O. Box 2472, Merced 95344 (383-1563). Picks up morning passengers from Merced's San Fran train, takes them to Yosemite, and returns them in time for the trip back ($15). Also runs to and from Fresno ($19). **Yosemite Transportation System (YTS),** (372-1240) connects the park with Greyhound in Lee Vining ($32.50). Reservations required; runs July-Labor Day. Be aware that Greyhound does not sell tickets in Lee Vicinity—be prepared when you board the bus. **Green Tortoise** (415-285-2441) based in San Francisco. 2- or 3-day trips. Buses leave San Francisco at 9pm. "Sleep-aboard" bus arrives at popular sites before the crowds. 2-day trip $79, 3-day trip $99, food $8 per day. Reservations required.

Equipment Rental: Yosemite Mountaineering School, Rte. 120 at Tuolumne Meadows (372-1335; Sept.-May 372-1244). Sleeping bags $5 per day, backpacks $4 per day, snowshoes $6 per day. License or credit card required.

Bike Rentals: at **Yosemite Lodge** (372-1208) and **Curry Village** (372-1200). $4.50 per hr., $16 per day. Both open daily 8am-6pm.

Post Offices: Yosemite Village, next to the visitors center. Open Mon.-Fri. 8:30am-5pm; Sept.-May Mon.-Fri. 8:30am-12:30pm and 1:30-5pm. **Curry Village,** near Registration Office. Open June-Sept. Mon.-Fri. 9am-3pm. **Yosemite Lodge,** open Mon.-Fri. 9am-4pm. General Delivery **ZIP code:** 95389.

Area Code: 209.

Accommodations and Food

Those who prefer some kind of roof over their heads must call 252-4848 for reservations and info. Clean, sparsely furnished cabins are available at **Yosemite Lodge** (singles or doubles $40-50, with bath $53.75). Southeast of Yosemite Village, **Curry Village** offers noisy but clean cabins ($41, with bath $55). **Housekeeping Camp** has canvas and concrete units that accommodate up to six people. Bring your own utensils, warm clothes, and industrial-strength bug repellent ($34 for 1-4 people). **Tuolumne Meadows,** on Tioga Rd. in the northeast corner of the park, has canvas-sided tent cabins (2 people $34; each additional person $5, kids $2.50.) **White Wolf,** west of Tuolumne Meadows on Tioga Rd., has similar cabins ($34) and cabins with bath ($55).

Most of the park's **campgrounds** are crowded with trailers and RVs. In Yosemite Valley's drive-in campgrounds, reservations are required from April to November and can be made through Ticketron (900-370-5566) up to eight weeks ahead. Sleeping in cars is emphatically prohibited. With the exception of major holidays, you should be able to camp in one of the first-come, first-served campgrounds provided you arrive at a reasonable hour. **Backcountry camping** (for general info 372-0307) is prohibited in the valley (you'll get slapped with a stiff fine if caught), but it's unrestricted along the high-country trails with a free wilderness permit. Reserve specific sites by mail February through May (write Backcountry Office, P.O. Box 577, Yosemite National Park 95389), or take your chances with the remaining 50% quota held on 24-hr. notice at the Yosemite Valley Visitors Center, the Wawona Ranger Station, or Big Oak Flat Station. To receive a permit, you must show a planned itinerary (though you needn't follow it exactly). Most hikers stay at the undeveloped mountain campgrounds in the high country for the company and for the **bear lockers,** used for storing food (not bears). These campgrounds often have chemical toilets.

Restaurants in Yosemite are expensive and dull. Buy your own groceries and supplies from the **Yosemite Lodge Store** or the **Village Store** (open daily 8am-10pm; Oct.-May 8am-9pm).

Orientation and Sights

Yosemite can be reached by taking Rte. 140 from Merced, Rte. 41 north from Fresno, and Rte. 120 east from Sonoma and west from Lee Vining. **Park admission** costs $2 on foot, $5 for a seven-day vehicle pass. The best bargain in Yosemite is the free **shuttle bus system.** Comfortable but often crowded, the buses have knowledgeable drivers and great viewing windows. They operate throughout the valley daily at 10-minute intervals from 7:30am to 10pm. Drivers planning to visit the high-country in spring or fall should have snow tires, also sometimes required in early and late summer. Of the five major approaches to the park, the easiest route is **Rte. 140** into Yosemite Valley. The eastern entrance, **Tioga Pass,** closes during snow season. The road to Mirror Lake and Happy Isles is forbidden to private auto traffic; free shuttle buses serve the road during the summer. In winter, snow closes the road to Glacier Point and sections of Tioga Road. **Biking** is an excellent way to see the Valley. For info on and reservations for **horseback trips,** call 372-1248.

Yosemite National Park divides into several areas. **Yosemite Valley** is the most spectacular and consequently receives the most traffic. Bus tours operate throughout the valley, as well as up to **Glacier Point** and the giant sequoias in the **Mariposa Grove.** Day-hikers often venture up the falls' trails and into **Little Yosemite Valley.** For a moderate hike with varying landscapes, water of all speeds, and an optional ridge or two, head toward **Lake Merced** from Glacier Point and then down toward the **Clark Range.** Weekday hiking almost guarantees privacy. The two main backcountry trailhead areas, **Tuolumne Meadows** and **Happy Isles Nature Center,** are served by bus (372-1240) after July 1; ask to be let off at the trailhead. Buy both a topographical and a trail route map from a visitors center, namely the *Guide to Yosemite High Sierra Trails* ($2.50). A map of valley trails is also available ($.50). Acquire a wilderness permit from the Backcountry office, the Tuolumne Permit Kiosk (both open daily 7:30am-7:30pm), Big Oak Flat Station (open daily 7am-6pm), or the Wawona Ranger Station (open daily 8am-5pm).

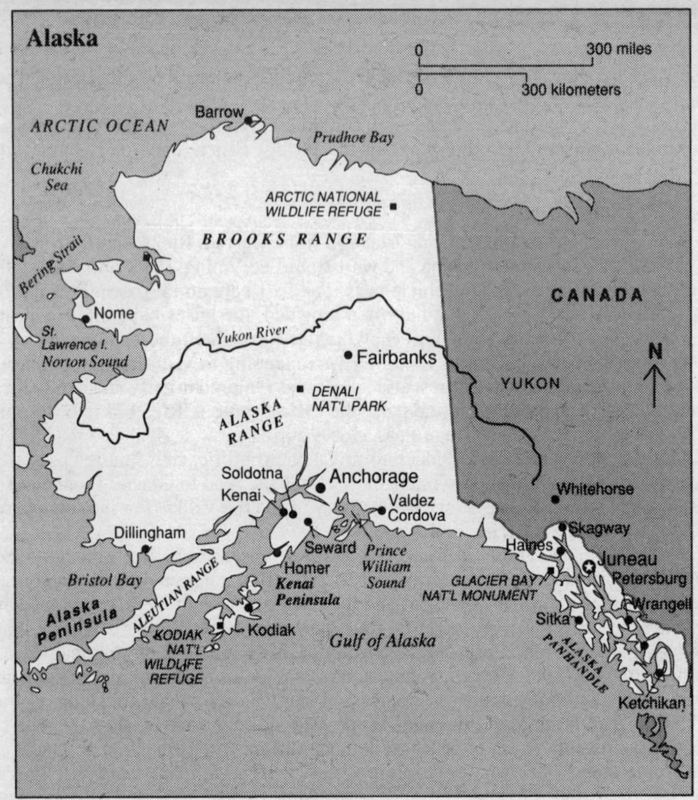

Alaska

In a country given to hyperbole, Alaska is the ultimate land of extremes. By far the largest of the 50 states, it comprises fully one-fifth of America's land mass. It has the highest mountain in North America (20,320-ft.-tall Mt. McKinley/Denali), the largest American National Park (13 million acre Wrangell-St. Elias National Park), the hugest carnivore in North America (the Kodiak brown bear), and the greatest collection of bald eagles in the world. At the height of summer, Alaska becomes the "Land of the Midnight Sun," where you can start a pickup game of softball at 2am; in the depths of winter it is land of the noonday moon, where shimmering curtains of spectral color known as the *aurora borealis,* or "Northern Lights," dance like smoke in the darkened midday sky.

Alaska's history, like the state itself, is larger than life. The first humans to colonize North America crossed the Bering Strait into Alaska via a now-sunken land bridge. Russian-sponsored Danish navigator Vitus Bering was the first European visitor to arrive, bringing in his wake a wave of Russian fur traders who exhausted the fur supply within a century. Worldwide esteem for Alaska was at its nadir in 1867, when Secretary of State James Seward negotiated the United States' acquisition of the territory from Russia for a trifling $7,200,000 (about 2¢ per acre). The senator became the laughingstock of the nation—the purchase was called "Seward's Folly,"—but within 20 years Alaska showed its worth by revealing a mother lode of gold ore. In 1968, long after the gold rush had slowed to a trickle, the state's fortunes rebounded yet again, with the discovery of "black gold" (oil) on the shore of the Arctic Ocean. By 1981, $7,200,000 worth of crude oil flowed from the Arctic oil field every four-and-a-half hours. Recently, the state witnessed the second largest oil spill ever; in 1989, the Exxon *Valdez* ran aground in Prince William Sound, coating much of the surrounding coastline with 11 million gallons of thick, gooey crude and strangling the life from countless fish , waterfowl and sea mammals. For more information on Alaska, consult *Let's Go: Pacific Northwest, Western Canada and Alaska.*

Practical Information

Visitor Information: Alaska Division of Tourism, 337 Willoughby St., (465-2010); P.O. Box 11081, Juneau 99811. Open Mon.-Fri. 8am-5pm. **Alaskan Public Lands Information Center,** Old Federal Building, Anchorage 99510 (271-2737). Tips for traversing any and all wilderness areas. Branch office in Fairbanks. Open daily 9am-7pm. **Alaska State Division of Parks,** Old Federal Building, Anchorage 99510 (762-2617). Open Mon.-Fri. 8am-4:30pm. **United States Forest Service,** 101 Egan Dr., Juneau 99802 (586-8751). General info regarding national parks and reserves. Open Mon.-Fri. 8am-5pm. **National Park Service,** Parks and Forests Information Center, W. 4th Ave., Anchorage 99503 (271-2737). Info on how to reserve wilderness cabins. Open Mon.-Fri. 9am-7pm. **State Department of Fish and Game,** P.O. Box 3-2000, Juneau 99802. Info on hunting and fishing regulations. **U.S. Fish and Wildlife Service,** 1011 E. Tudor Rd., Anchorage 99504 (786-3486).

Employment Information: Alaska Employment Service, 2030 Sea Level Dr., Suite 220 (225-3831), in Ketchikan. Ask for their guide *How to Find Work in the Alaskan Salmon Fisheries.* Open Mon.-Fri. 8am-4:30pm.

Time Zones: Alaska (4 hrs. behind Eastern); Aleutian-Hawaii (5 hrs. behind Eastern). **Postal Abbreviation:** AK

Area Code: 907.

Sales Tax: 0%.

Climate

No single temperate zone covers the whole state; Prudhoe Bay differs from Ketchikan in climate as much as Minneapolis does from Atlanta. Fairbanks, Tok, and the Bush frequently enjoy 95°F hot spells, receiving less than eight in. of precipitation annually. The Interior freezes with 50° temperatures in winter. Farther south, the climate is milder and rainier. Cordova rusts with 167 in. of precipitation annually. Anchorage and other coastal towns in the southcentral are blessed with the Japanese Current, which has a moderating effect on the climate. Average temperatures for Anchorage range from 13°F in January to 57°F in July.

Travelers should prepare for wet, wind and cold year-round. In summer, those staying below the Arctic Circle probably won't need anything heavier than a light parka or jacket and sweater. If you make forays into the "Bush" (Alaskans' term for the wilderness), be absolutely certain to bring waterproof boots and sturdy raingear. Wool and polypropylene are staples for socks, underwear, pants, shirts and hats. The warmest coats and snowsuits are hollofil, not down-filled, garments.

Winter travelers should always expect the unexpected. The National Park Service advises that visitors learn to recognize the symptoms of hypothermia (see Health in the General Introduction to this book); also carry extra dry clothing, blankets and food. Read Jack London's "To Build a Fire"—if you're a North American high school graduate, you probably already have—to learn what a bummer freezing to death can be. For more information about hiking and camping in Alaska, consult *Adventuring in Alaska,* published by the Sierra Club.

Travel

Driving in Alaska is not for the faint of heart. Roads reach only a quarter of the state's area, and many of the major ones remain in deplorable condition. Dust and flying rocks are a major hazard in the summer, as are miserable 10- to 30-mi. patches of gravel. "Frost heaves" from melting and contracting permafrost cause dips and surreal "twists" in the road. Radiators and headlights should be protected from flying rocks with wire screens, and a fully functioning spare tire and a good set of shocks are essential. Winter can actually offer a smoother ride. Active snow crews keep roads as clear as possible, and the packed surface and thinned traffic permit easier driving without summer's mechanical troubles. At the same time, the danger of avalanches and ice is cause for major concern. Check the road conditions before traveling; in Anchorage call 243-7675 (winter only), or tune in to local radio stations. Both winter and summer travelers are advised to let a friend or relative know of their position along the highway several times in the course of a trip. Drivers also should take into account the cost of gas, which varies significantly from station to station. Anyone venturing onto Alaska's roads should own a copy of *The Milepost,* published by the **Alaska Northwest Publishing Company,** 130 2nd Ave. S., Edmond 98020 (907-563-1141; open Mon.-Fri. 8:30am-4:30pm). Each volume ($19) packs in information about Alaskan and Canadian communities as well as up-to-date ferry schedules and maps of the highways and roads. *Let's Go* does not recommend hitchhiking as a means of transportation. The information below is not intended to do so.

Many people **hitchhike** instead of depending on buses in Alaska. In fact, state law prohibits moving vehicles from *not* picking up stranded motorists, as the extreme climate can be life-endangering. However, hitchhiking backpackers may only legally thumb on the on- and off-ramps of major highways, *not* on the highways themselves. Beware of being stranded on lightly traveled stretches of road. A wait of a day or two is not unusual on certain stretches of the Alaska Hwy. Luckily, Alaskans are generally friendly and cooperative, and many rides last at least a day. Women, of course, are always safer traveling in pairs or with a man.

The **Alaska Marine Highway** consists of several ferry systems. The **southeast** network runs from Bellingham up the coast to Skagway and stops in Juneau, Ketchikan, Haines, and other towns. The **southcentral** network serves Kodiak Island, Seward, Homer, and the Prince William Sound. Practically none of southeast Alaska (the Panhandle) is accessible by road; most of the area can be reached only by plane or on the Marine Highway. The whale- and bald eagle-filled three-day trip from Bellingham to Skagway ($236, ages 6-12 near ½-price, under 6 free) features free showers and cafés, historical and ecological lectures, and a heated top-deck solarium where cabinless passengers can sleep (bring a sleeping bag!). Cabins are expensive ($196 extra) and unnecessary—nearly everyone sleeps in the solarium. The **southwest** ferries are more expensive and less plush, and they ride the open sea, which your alimentary canal will really appreciate.

The Aleutian Islands

Defining the fiery boundary of two tectonic plates, the string of snow-capped volcanoes and volcanic remnants that comprises the Aleutian Islands stretches like an icy tendril more than 1000 mi. into the stormy North "Pacific." These lava-scarred cones and verdant but treeless islands are some of the most remote locations on earth. The few habitated settlements which attempt to exist—hardy Aleut villages, small military installations and some larger towns consecrated to deep-sea fishing—are whipped by some of the world's worst weather. Yet in the summer, hundreds of dedicated tourists flock here, both to explore the tempestuous natural beauty of the volcanic wilderness and to view the millions of migratory seabirds who call the islands home in the summer; some species nest nowhere else in the world.

A quick glance at a map will show you that there are only two ways to see the Aleutians, both of which are expensive. A round-trip flight from **Kodiak** to **Dutch Harbor** costs around $1000 and takes about four hours; the same trip on the **Alaska Marine Highway** (see Travel in the introduction above) costs $400 and takes about five days. Obviously, the latter choice is far and away the better one, since the point of traveling in the Aleutians is not so much to get where you're going as to enjoy the unique panoramas while you're getting there. If you choose the ferry, remember that the trip only occurs seven times a year between May and September; it is best to go in July, when the weather is at its mildest. Be sure to make reservations a few weeks in advance. If you like volcanoes, forbidding cliff-faced islands, exotic seabirds, and if you *really* like Dramamine (they don't call the *M/V Tustumena* the "Vomit Comet" for nothing), then this is a once-in-a-lifetime trip that is well worth the investment. For info on the area, contact the **Dept. of Parks, Culture, and Recreation,** in the Community Center Building at 5th and Broadway in downtown Unalaska (581-1297; open Mon.-Fri. 8am-5pm). Alaska Marine Highway docks at "City Dock," about 1½ mi. from Dutch Harbor and 2½ mi. from Unalaska. (Call 800-642-0066 or 581-1254.) The **ZIP code** for **Unalaska** is 99685, for **Dutch Harbor**, 99692. The **area code** is 907.

Anchorage

Only 80 years ago, Anchorage was merely a shack in the wilderness. In 1914, however, the Alaska Railroad decided to move its headquarters here, beginning a steady flow of trains, pioneers, and oil, and transforming it into the state's commercial center. Today 250,000 people—half of the state's population—live here. Perhaps the most remarkable fact about Anchorage is that *everything*, from the glass and steel of its buildings to the diapers and bottles for its babies, arrives here the same way its people do—it all must travel 1500 mi., either by tortuous drive, by expensive plane, or by barge or container ship across one of the roughest seas in the world. The city has an aroma of prefabrication—writer John McPhee called it "condensed, instant Albuquerque." "Los Anchorage," as some rural residents prefer to call it, is as close to "big city" as Alaska gets.

Practical Information and Orientation

Emergency: 911.

Visitor Information: Log Cabin Visitor Information Center, W. 4th Ave. at F St. (274-3531). Open May-Sept. daily 7:30am-7pm; off-season 8:30am-6pm. Grab their free bus line map. The **All About Anchorage Line** (276-3200) runs a recorded listing of each day's events. Smaller visitor information outlets are located in the airport near the baggage claim in the domestic terminal, in the overseas terminal in the central atrium, and in the first level of the Valley River Mall.

Alaska Public Lands Information Center, Old Federal Bldg. (271-2737), 4th Ave. between F and G. An astoundingly rational conglomeration of 8 state and federal offices (including the **National Park Service, U.S. Forest Service, Division of State Parks,** and **U.S. Fish and Wildlife Service**) under 1 roof provides the latest information on the entire state. Open daily 9am-6pm.

Alaska Employment Center, 3301 Eagle St. (269-4800). P.O. Box 107224. Open Mon.-Fri. 8am-noon and 1-4:30pm. Take bus #60 or 3.

Planes: Alaska International Airport, a few miles southwest of downtown off International Airport Rd. (266-2525). Nearly every airport in Alaska can be reached from Anchorage, either directly or through a connecting flight in Fairbanks. **Dynair Charter Service** runs downtown ($6), to and from all major hotels every hr. on the ½-hr. from 5:30am-2:30am. Call ahead for pickup. **People Mover** has 3 buses per day for $1.

Trains: Alaska Railroad: 411 W. 1st Ave. (265-2494 or 800-544-0552). To Denali ($85), Fairbanks ($115), and Seward ($40). For more info write to Passenger Service, P.O. Box 107500, Anchorage 99510. Office open daily 6am-10:30pm; may close if no trains are arriving.

Buses: Alaskan Express, P.O. Box 100479, Anchorage 99510 (277-5581). 2 buses per week in summer through Whitehorse, YT to Anchorage, Skagway and Haines. You must pay for overnight accommodations. (One way $187; lodging $50 or tent it.) **Caribou Express,** daily to Fairbanks ($75 one way; 278-5776). **Homer and Seward Bus Lines**(278-0800), to the Kenai Peninsula ($30) and Seward ($35). Several enterprising van owners run small operations from Haines to Anchorage, synchronized with the ferry. Fares as low as $120, but service is often unreliable.

Public Transit: People Mover Bus, in the Transit Center on 6th St. between G and H, 1 block from the hostel (343-6543). Most buses run from here to all points in the Anchorage Bowl 6am-9 or 10pm. Restricted schedule on weekends. Cash fare $1, tokens 90¢, daypass $2.50. Office open Mon.-Fri. 8am-5pm.

Big Boats: Alaska Marine Highway: 333 W. 4th St. (272-4482), in the Post Office Mall. No terminal, but ferry tickets and reservations. Open Mon.-Fri. 8am-4:30pm.

Taxi: Yellow Cab, 272-2422. **Checker Cab,** 276-1234. $1 pickup, $1.50 per mi.

Car Rental: Payless Rent-A-Car (243-3616). $28 per day with unlimited mileage. **Allstar Rent-A-Car** (561-0350). $34 per day. Both located at the airport.

Road Conditions: 243-7675. Winter only.

Time Zone: Alaska (4 hrs. behind Eastern).

Post Office: W. 4th Ave. and C St. (277-6568), on the lower level in the mall. Open Mon.-Fri. 10am-5:30pm, Sat. 10am-4pm. **ZIP code:** 99510.

Area Code: 907.

The downtown streets are an ordered grid—your map will resemble a waffle. Don't eat it. Numbered avenues run east-west, with addresses designated East or West from **A Street.** North-south streets have letters alphabetically west of A Street, and names alphabetically east of A St. The rest of Anchorage oozes out along the major highways. The **University of Alaska, Anchorage** campus lies on 36th Ave. off Northern Lights Blvd.

Accommodations and Camping

Several bed and breakfast referral agencies operate out of Anchorage. Try **Alaska Private Lodgings,** 1236 W. 10th Ave., Anchorage 99511 (258-1717), or **Stay With a Friend,** 3605 Arctic Blvd., Anchorage 99503 (278-8800). Both can refer you to singles from $50 and doubles from $60.

There are several free campgrounds outside the city limits; for info contact the **Alaska Division of Parks,** 3601 C St., 10th Floor, Pouch 7-001 Anchorage 99510, or the **Anchorage Parks and Recreation Dept.,** 2525 Campbell St. #404 (271-2500).

Anchorage Youth Hostel (HI/AYH), 700 H St. (276-3635), 1 block south of the Transit Center downtown. Excellent location. Clean rooms (some for families) with common areas, kitchens, showers, and laundry. Local grocery stores drop off boxes and boxes of day-old fruit, pasta and assorted canned goods on Mondays. Lockout noon-5pm. Midnight curfew. $12, nonmembers $15. Frequently stuffed to the gills in summer; make reservations. 4-day max. stay in summer.

Qupquqiag Bed and Breakfast, 3801 Spenard near the intersection with Minnesota (562-5681). 5 min. from the airport. Surprisingly plush rooms with hall bathroom and continental breakfast. Singles $18-20, doubles $20-25.

Inlet Inn, 6th and H (277-5541), kitty-corner from the hostel. Has rooms with sink and hall bath for $40 for 1 or 2 people. Also has prettier, pricier rooms with cable TV.

Midtown Hotel, 604 W. 20th St. (258-7778), off Arctic Blvd. (bus #9). Rooms are simple but spotlessly clean. Shared bath, free continental breakfast and free soup and sandwiches in the lobby for lunch. Singles $40, doubles $45.

Centennial Park, 8300 Glenn Hwy. (333-9711), north of town off Muldoon Rd.; look for the park sign. Take bus #3 or 75 from downtown. Facilities for tents and RVs. Showers, dumpsters, fireplaces, pay phones, and water. 7-day max. stay. Check-in before 6pm in summer. Sites $12, seniors $10.

Lions' Camper Park, 5800 Boniface Pkwy. (333-9711), south of the Glenn Hwy. in Russian Jack Springs Park across from the Municipal Greenhouse. Take bus #12 or 45 to the Boniface Mall and walk 4 blocks. Connected to the city's bike trail system. 10 primitive campsites with water station, fire rings, and showers. Self-contained vehicles only. 14-day max. stay. Open daily 10am-10pm. Sites $12. Open May-Sept. Overflow for Centennial; check there first.

Food

By virtue of its size and largely imported population, Anchorage wears a culinary coat of many colors. Within blocks of each other stand greasy spoons, Chinese restaurants, and classy hotel-top French *maisons*. You will also find huge portions of Alaskan sourdough and seafood—halibut, salmon, clams, crab and snapper. The city's finer restaurants line the hills overlooking Cook Inlet and the Alaska Range. The closest major grocery store to downtown is the **Carrs** at 13th and Gamble (277-2609; take bus #11), about 1.5 mi. from the hostel. (Open 24 hrs.)

Tito's Gyros, (279-8961), on 4th St. next to McDonald's. Pizza by the slice ($2), a rarity in Alaska. Juicy gyro sandwich ($5.50), and the best ice cream downtown. Open Mon.-Sat. 10am-10pm, Sun. 11am-8pm.

Wings and Things, 529 I St. (277-9464), at 5th. Unbelievably delicious BBQ chicken wings. Decorated with wing memorabilia and inspirational poetry. Ten wings, celery, and sauce $6. Open daily 10am-9pm.

Cyrano's Book Store and Café (274-1173), on D between 4th and 5th. Come here to ghost-write love letters. Classical music, a current *Wall Street Journal,* tall glass of lemonade, and an excellent bowl of chicken gumbo ($6). Sandwiches $4.25-5.75. Live folk music possible at any time.

Simon and Seafort's Salon and Grill, 420 L St. (274-3502). Simon says, down a few beers and a bowl of great clam chowder ($4). Prices are steep (dinner $13-30), but the incredible view of Cook Inlet and delectable seafood and pasta continue to draw hordes. Open for lunch Mon.-Sat. 11:15am-2:15pm, for dinner Mon.-Thurs. 4:30-10:30pm, Fri.-Sat. 4:30-11pm, Sun. 4:30-10pm. Salon open daily 11:15am-midnight. Make reservations.

Legal Pizza, 1034 W. 4th Ave. (274-0686). Home to *the* Anchorage lunch buffet (Mon.-Fri. 11:30am-3pm). What every hungry backpacker dreams about: all-you-can-eat pizza, salad bar, soup, and drinks—a steal at $6. Live folk music nightly after 8pm. Open Mon.-Thurs. 11am-3pm and 5-11pm, Fri. 11am-3pm and 5pm-1am, Sat. 5pm-1am.

Sights and Entertainment

Mount Susitna, known to locals as the "Sleeping Lady," watches over Anchorage from Cook Inlet. For a fabulous view of Susitna, as well as the rest of the mountains that form a magnificent backdrop for Anchorage's ever-growing skyline (on a clear day you can see **Mount McKinley/Denali**), drive out to **Worzenof Point** at the end of Northern Lights Blvd. On the way you'll pass **Earthquake Park,** once a fashionable neighborhood, now a memorial to the disastrous effects of the Good Friday earthquake in 1964, a day Alaskans refer to as "Black Friday." Registering at 9.2 on the current Richter scale, this was the strongest earthquake ever recorded in North America.

The visitors center (see Practical Information) can set you up with a four-hour self-guided walking tour of downtown. **Gray Line Tours** (274-6454) offers a 3½-hour tour of Anchorage City (daily at 8am and 3pm; $21).

The **Anchorage Museum of History and Art,** 121 W. 7th Ave. (343-4326), at A St., features permanent exhibits of Alaska Native artifacts and art, as well as an Alaska wilderness film series (3 times daily; open daily 9am-6pm. Admission $4.) To see honest-to-goodness Alaskan wildlife in the comfort of urbania, visit the **Alaska Zoo,** Mile 2 on O'Malley Rd. (346-2133; open daily 10am-6pm; admission $5, seniors $4, ages 13-18 $3, ages 3-12 $2, under 3 free). For some heavy-duty culture, watch Anabell the Elephant at work (summer Fri.-Sun. 12:30pm and 3:30pm); her proboscan paintings are on sale in the gift shop.

The **Visual Arts Center,** 5th and G St. (274-9641), showcases the best of Alaskan artists; their biannual solstice show is truly bizarre. (Gallery open Mon.-Sat. 10am-6pm. Admission $2.) The **Imaginarium,** 725 5th Ave. (276-3179), a hands-on "science-discovery center," recreates Arctic marine environments, glacier formation, and other scientific oddities of the north. (Open Mon.-Sat. 7am-6pm, Sun. noon-5pm. Admission $4, under 12 $3.)

If you want to shop where the air literally reeks of authenticity, head to the close confines of the nonprofit gift shop at the **Alaska Native Medical Center** at 3rd and Gampbell (257-1150). Because many Native Americans pay for medical services with their own arts and handicrafts, the Alaska State Museum in Juneau sent its buyers here last year to outfit its exhibitions. Walrus bone *ulus* (knives; $17-60), fur moccasins, Eskimo parkas, and dolls highlight the selection. (Open Mon.-Fri. 10am-2pm.) Craftworks from Alaska's bush country, similar to those on display at the Museum of History and Art, are sold at the **Alaska Native Arts and Crafts Showroom,** 333 W. 4th Ave. (272-3008; open Mon.-Sat. 10am-6pm).

A strong candidate for #1 coolest entertainment attraction in the city, the **Fourth Avenue Theater,** 630 W. 4th Ave., has been newly restored to its original 1940s décor. Wander in, grab some of the reasonably priced grub in the lobby cafeteria (big $4 sandwiches and salads), then sit back at your dinner table in the balcony and watch free films on their big silver screen. On your way out, stop in at the gift shop downstairs.

Anchorageans of all types and incomes party at **Chilkoot Charlie's,** 2435 Spenard Rd. (272-1010; take bus #7 or 60), at Fireweed. The six bars have a rocking dance floor and a quiet, "share-my-space" lounge. Ask about the nightly drink specials; otherwise you'll end up paying an outrageous amount to subsidize those who do. Less crowded and more interesting is **Mr. Whitekey's Fly-by-Night Club,** 3300 Spenard Rd. (279-SPAM), a "sleazy bar serving everything from the world's finest champagnes to a damn fine plate of Spam." The Monty Pythonesque house special gives you anything with Spam at half-price when you order champagne (free with Dom Perignon). Try Spam nachos or Spam and cream cheese on a bagel ($3-7). Nightly entertainment ranges from rock to jazz to blues to singing Vikings. The anti-tourist tourist attraction, the *Whale Fat Follies,* plays nightly at 8pm. (Open daily 4pm-2:30am.)

Denali National Park

Established in 1917 to protect its abundant wildlife, Denali National Park's namesake is Denali itself, "The Great One" in Athabascan. Anglicized as **Mt. McKinley,** Denali towers as the tallest mountain in North America and the greatest vertical relief in the world from base to summit. At 20,320 ft. above sea level and 18,000 ft. above the surrounding meadows, Denali is so big that it makes its own weather; it is only visible about 20% of the summer. Missing the mountain doesn't ruin a Denali trip—the park's tundra, taiga, wildlife, and lesser mountains are more subtle but equally worthwhile attractions.

If you land in Denali unprepared, you'll probably be at a loss; camp sites and park buses should be reserved 14 to 21 days in advance, and backcountry permits *must* be reserved in person. Make reservations at the Anchorage or Fairbanks park offices (in Fairbanks at 250 Cushman St., Suite 1A; 451-7352; for Anchorage office, see Anchorage Practical Information). Only two to twelve hikers can camp in each of the park's 43 zones, so select a few different areas in the park in case your first choice is booked.

Denali Park has no trails. *No trails.* Just an 88-mi. bus access road. Get on a park **shuttle bus** (free with $3 park entrance fee) and ask the driver to stop at the quadrant (for backcountry camping) or campground you've reserved. If, like most visitors, you're not familiar with the park, you have two options. One is camping the first night at the no-reservations-required **Morino Campground** ($3 per night), centrally located at Mile 1.9 on the Denali Park Rd. near the Denali Park Hotel, with showers ($2) and a post office. The next day, take a shuttle bus into the park and survey your camping prospects. Go back to Morino that evening, and make reservations at the visitors center for your handpicked sites. You may have to wait another day or two to get your first choices, so bring sufficient food—the nearby **convenience store** has necessary supplies, but is predictably pricey.

The second option is to make reservations based on the very general overview of the park provided here. The first third of the park is varying degrees of taiga forest and tundra which is hellish to hike—imagine walking on old wet mattresses with bushes growing out of them. The last third or so of the park is infested with mosquitoes in July and gnat-sized, biting "no-see-ums" in August. *Ergo,* prime hiking and camping spots are in the middle third of the park. Especially good locations are **Toklat**, **Marmot Rock,** and **Polychrome Pass.** You'll want to take the 10-hour round-trip bus ride to Wonder Lake Campground for your best chance at a glimpse of Denali *sans* clouds, but if you're planning to camp there, reserve the last bus out to the campground and the first bus back in the morning, and bring protective netted head gear (available in the convenience store).

There are six **campgrounds** within the park. All have water and some form of toilet facilities (sites $15). The **Denali Hostel,** P.O. Box 801 Denali Park 99755 (683-1295), is 9.2 mi. north of the park entrance, to the left on Otto Lake Rd.; it's the second house on the right. They offer bunks, showers, kitchen facilities and morning shuttles into and out of the park ($22.)

The park is accessible by **Alaska Railroad** (see Anchorage Practical Information) or by car from the George Parks Highway, 237 mi. north of Anchorage. For bus travel into Denali, try **Caribou Express** (278-5776), with daily departures to Fairbanks (3pm; $35), and Anchorage (10:55am; $54). **Moon Bay Express** (274-6454), runs daily from Denali to Anchorage at 3pm ($35). All visitors must check in and pay the $3 entrance fee at the **Visitor Access Center** (683-1266, 24-hr. **emergency** number 683-9100), less than one mi. from Rte. 3. The park's **shuttle buses** depart from the VAC.

Somewhat Near Denali: Talkeetna

A small speck of a town on the George Parks Hwy. 120 mi. south of Denali, **Talkeetna** is the fly-off point for mountain climbers to Mt. McKinley/Denali. It has the state's best road overlook of the mountain, and is known as an unusual enclave of bush pilots and climbers from around the world. Every year in the beginning of August Talkeetna also sponsors the best three-day bluegrass and rock and roll music festival in Alaska, the **Alaska Music Festival**. Beards, dogs, children and tie-dye abound. Free, of course. By the way, Talkeetna also has a **Moose Dropping Festival** on the second Saturday of July, which culminates with the infamous "Gilded Moose Dropping Toss," always a big crowd-pleaser.

Fairbanks

At the end of the 19th century, thousands of immigrants flocked to America's cities in search of streets "paved with gold." Felix Pedro, an Italian miner, did his peers one better by heading to the largely unexplored Alaskan Interior and, on July 22, 1902, unearthing a shiny fortune on the banks of the Chena River. Within a year of his discovery, thousands of treasure hunters had followed his lead and flocked to the Interior. The city is today—as it was at the century's start—largely a service and supply center for the surrounding Bush. Oil from the Trans-Alaska Pipeline now pumps money into the city, but it retains the rough-and-ready character of the gold boom-town it once was.

Perched on a hill overlooking the Fairbanks cityscape stands the **University of Alaska-Fairbanks.** The **University of Alaska Museum,** 907 Yukon Dr. (474-7505), on West Ridge Hill, 1½ mi. back from the corner of College Rd. and University Ave., presents an eclectic jumble of exhibits on subjects ranging from the formation of coal to Russian Orthodox vestments to native baskets; the most popular one is a video of the *aurora borealis.* (Open daily 9am-7pm; May and Sept. 9am-5pm; Oct.-April noon-5pm. Admission $4, seniors and students $3, families $12.50.) There's no fee to view the **Trans-Alaska Pipeline,** one of the technological wonders of the modern world, on the Steese Hwy. heading out of Fairbanks. The pipeline was elevated to protect the tundra's delicate ecological system; thermal coolers keep the tundra super-cooled so the 108° oil won't melt the permafrost and sink into the ground. The best time to visit Fairbanks is in mid-July, when the city sparkles with **Golden Days,** a celebration of Felix Pedro's much-celebrated discovery. Watch out for the traveling jail; if you haven't purchased the silly-looking button commemorating the event, you may be taken prisoner and forced to pay a steep price to spring yourself. (Most stores and businesses in town sell the buttons.) The adventurous traveler might as well stay on board the paddywagon for a free ride through Fairbanks. For details, contact the **Fairbanks Chamber of Commerce,** 709 2nd Ave., 99701 (452-1105).

The Whole Earth, in College Corner Mall (479-2052), below Gulliver's Used Books, has the whole world of health-food eating—grocery, deli, and restaurant—in its hand. A Natchester Sandwich (beans, cheese, Greek peppers, and spices in a spread on a whole-wheat roll) is $3.25, a No Bull Burger $4. (Store and seating open Mon.-Fri. 10am-7pm, Sat. 10am-6pm, Sun. noon-5pm. Hot food served Mon.-Sat. 11am-3pm.) The live rock-and-roll scene is a scream at the **Howling Dog Saloon,** 11½ mi. down Steese Hwy. (457-8780), where everybody and their eye doctors hang out. Volleyball and horseshoe games go on until 4am or so, just like the band. (Open Tues.-Fri. 5pm-5am, Sat.-Sun. noon-5am.) After the Howling Dog, head for highway fast food like you've never experienced it at **(The Inimitable) Denny's Farthest North,** on Airport Way near Wilbur. OK, it's Denny's, but it's Denny's *Farthest North;* how can you pass this 24-hour legend up? Veggie cheese melts are $5; breakfast is $4.35 to $6.80.

The **Fairbanks Youth Hostel (HI/AYH),** P.O. Box 72196, 99707 (456-4159), has been migrating around town for a number of years, shepherded by the constantly mellow Paul Schultz. Call up and Paul will find you a place to crash for $6.25, nonmembers $10.25. He also has a wealth of information about the area and is always willing to direct hostelers toward adventure. There's no curfew, no lockout, and free showers. The **John Alfonsi Sr. Memorial Campground** (474-7355) is somewhat off the beaten path (take Geist off University, then turn right at Fairbanks onto the University of Alaska campus, then look for Alatna Dr.), but it's also one of the cheapest campgrounds in urban Alaska and has toilets, free showers, and water at the Woods Center on the UAF campus. (Non-UAF people $4.50 per day, $15 per week.)

The Fairbanks **airport** is located five mi. from downtown on Airport Way (George Parks Hwy.). The **Alaska Railroad** chugs next to the *Daily News-Miner* building, at 280 N. Cushman (456-4155). Trains leave for Anchorage ($115) and Denali National Park ($45). Ages 2 to 11 travel half-price. (Depot open daily 7am-4pm and 7-10pm.) The **Caribou Express bus** departs daily in summer to Denali ($35) and Anchorage ($75); the **Denali Express** (800-327-7621) also has daily runs to Denali ($25).

Fairbanks lies 508 mi. north of Kodiak Island and 358 mi. away from Anchorage via the **George Parks Highway.** For **road conditions,** call 456-7623.

The **Convention and Visitors Bureau Log Cabin** is at 550 First Ave. (456-5774); pick up their free walking art tour pamphlet *Visitors Guide*, listing tourist offices, transportation services, maps, annual events, activities, and shops, or take a one-hour walking tour of the city with one of their knowledgeable guides. (Open daily 8am-8pm; Oct.-April Mon.-Fri. 8am-5pm.) The **Alaska Public Lands Information Center (APLIC),** at 3rd and Cushman St. (451-7352), welcomes requests for info about hiking; write to 250 Cushman St. #1A. (Open daily 8:30am-9pm; in winter Tues.-Sat. 10am-6pm. Come after 5pm to avoid busloads of tourists.)

In case of **emergency,** call 911.

The Kenai Peninsula and Kodiak Island

The Kenai (KEEN-eye) Peninsula mirrors Alaska in miniature. Like parts of Alaska's interior, Kenai's interior is flat; like the state itself, mountains ring the peninsula. Kenai stands on all three legs of Alaska's economy: oil, tourism, and fishing. The Russian influence on the Panhandle can be seen in the town of Kenai, the first Russian settlement in Alaska, and the urban sprawl of Anchorage and Fairbanks mimics road-side towns like Soldotna.

The Peninsula is the place Alaskans, especially those from Anchorage and Fairbanks, go for vacation. Take a hint from the Native Alaskans: find an isolated campsite and fish. (All state-run tent sites $16, 1-day fishing license $10.) Every town can set you up cheaply with the requisite permits and gear. Stay in **USFS Campgrounds,** located every eight or 10 mi. on **Seward** and **Sterling Highways.** There are also great spots in between—ask the locals. For more info on hiking, hunting, fishing, camping and other recreational opportunities, as well as regulations, contact the following: **Kenai Fjords National Park** (see Seward); **Kenai National Wildlife Refuge** (see Soldotna); **Chugach National Forest,** 201 E. 9th Ave. #206, Anchorage 99501 (261-2500); **State of Alaska, Division of Parks and Outdoor Recreations,** P.O. Box 1247, Soldotna 99669 (262-5581); and **State of Alaska, Department of Fish & Game,** P.O. Box 3150, Soldotna 99669 (262-9368). If you're unclear about which of these offices to contact, check out the **Alaska Public Lands Information Center** (see Anchorage: Practical Information) for a referral.

The Kenai Peninsula is serviced by the Seward and Sterling Highways, as well as by the **Alaska Marine Highway,** which runs between Homer, Seward, and Whittier and extends out to Kodiak Island and Prince William Sound. To reach the peninsula from Anchorage, simply take any of the buses that run onto the New Seward Hwy. (such as the #2 or 9) as far south as possible and hitch. Hitching is common, and those who hitch find it as safe as it ever gets.

Kenai

Kenai, the second-oldest non-Native settlement in Alaska, is the largest and fastest-growing city on the peninsula. Named for the Kenaitze who first settled here, the spot later attracted Russians seeking sea otters and Captain Cook in his quest for a northwest passage. In the 1950s the area's most valuable resource—"black gold" (oil)—was discovered offshore, forever quickening the pulse of life in Kenai and Alaska. Vestiges of each era are scattered throughout town—Native American artifacts, a Russian Orthodox church, and oil rigs coexist here.

The **Kenai River** wriggles with fish; pink, king, red, and silver salmon glide through during the summer, as well as steelhead and dolly varden. Numerous **fishing charters** run the river, usually charging $100 to $125 for a half-day of halibut or salmon fishing, or $150 for both (contact the Kenai Visitors Center for more info). **Fishing licenses** are available at any sporting goods store. (1-day $10, 3-day $15, 14-day $30, annual $50.)

Those tired of oversexed seafood and maniacal sportspeople encased in rubber bodysuits should wander over to the **Kenai National Wildlife Refuge Visitors Center** (262-7021), off Funny River Rd. at the top of Ski Hill Rd., a great source of info on this 197-million-acre refuge for moose, Dall sheep and other wild animals. Scratch and sniff woolly patches of fur, or pick up a phone to talk to a loon or a wolf. (Open Mon.-Fri. 8am-4:30pm, Sat.-Sun. 1-5pm.) On Overland and Mission St. in Kenai is the **Holy Assumption Russian Orthodox Church,** the oldest building in Kenai and the oldest standing church in Alaska (1896). This national historic landmark contains a 200-year-old Bible. Call the rectory (283-4122) for a tour.

Recreational opportunities in the Kenai area abound. Check with the Forest Service for canoeing and hiking opportunities. The **Captain Cook State Recreation Area,** 30 mi. north of the city at the end of Kenai Spur Rd., offers swimming, canoe landing points on the Swanson River, superb fishing, and free camping. Contact the Kenai Chamber of Commerce for rules and regulations. The **Kenai National Wildlife Refuge** has dozens of one- to four-day canoe routes. For free maps, contact the Refuge Manager, Kenai National Wildlife Refuge, P.O. Box 2139, Soldotna (262-7021).

For a quick fix, hit **Little Ski-Mo's Burger-n-Brew** on Kenai Spur Hwy. across from the visitors center (283-4463). It has a stunning array of burgers; try a Polynesian ($6.50) or a Russian Patty Melt ($5.25). And like the man says: a burger-n-brew is $5 all day, every day. Nostalgic international travelers and polyglots should stop in the **Black Forest Restaurant**, 44278 Sterling Hwy. (262-5111), as the owners are fluent in English, French, German and Filipino. They also speak the international language of the budget diner: 1/2-lb. cheeseburgers are $5.25, 12-in. sub sandwiches $4.75-5.50. (Open daily 11am-9pm.) **Carr's Quality Center** (283-7829), in the Kenai Mall on Kenai Spur Rd., is one of the most gigantic grocery stores you are likely to encounter, with every type of food imaginable. (Open 24 hrs.)

To save money, head for the Kenai city **campground** on Forest Dr. off Kenai Spur Rd. (283-2855), where you can spend three happy days camping for free.(Near the beach not far from the center of town; has water and pit toilets.) Hard-sided campers can head for the **Overland RV Park,** P.O. Box 326, next to the visitors center on the highway (283-4227; sites $12, full hookup $16).

Kenai, on the western Kenai Peninsula, preens 148 mi. from Anchorage and 81 mi. north of Homer. It can be reached via **Kalifornsky Beach Rd.,** which joins Sterling Hwy. from Anchorage just south of Soldotna, or **Kenai Spur Rd.,** which runs north through the Nikishka area. (Mile markers on Kalifornsky start at Kenai, while mile markers on the Kenai Spur Rd. start at Soldotna.) Both roads boast superb views of the peninsula's lakes and snow-capped peaks. Kenai's **Visitor and Cultural Center,**

11471 Kenai Spur Hwy. (283-1991), was built for the town's 1991 bicentennial and has one room filled with stuffed native wildlife, another filled with Native artifacts, a small theater showing films on the area, and, of course, plenty of pamphlets. (Open Mon.-Fri. 9am-5pm, extended summer hours.) Kenai's **ZIP code** is 99611; its **area code** is 907.

Seward

The best thing about Seward is its proximity to **Kenai Fjords National Park.** Much of this park consists of a coastal-mountain system supporting an abundance of wildlife. The best way to see this area is on a boat; pick up the list of charters at the Park Service visitors center or from companies along the boardwalk next to the harbormaster's office. Most run $80 to $100 per day, $50 to $65 per half-day. For more information, contact **Kenai Fjord National Park Tours** (224-8068), **Kenai Coastal Tours** (224-7114), **Mariah Charters** (243-1238), **Kenai Fjord Tours** (224-8030), or **Quest Charters** (224-3025; open in summer daily 6am-10pm).

Seward also offers good day hikes. Every Fourth of July locals run (or walk) up nearby **Mt. Marathon,** which affords a great view of the city and ocean. The trail begins at the end of Lowell St. People also flock to Seward for the mid-January **Seward Polar Bear Jump** and three days of accompanying festivities. **Exit Glacier,** billed as Alaska's most accessible glacier, chills nine mi. west on the road that starts at Mile 3.7 of the Seward Hwy.

Fishing is heavenly in the Seward area. Salmon and halibut thrive in the bay, and grayling frolic right outside of town. Some people just fish off the docks. For a less luck-oriented approach, try a fishing charter with **Mariah** or **Quest** (see above), available for both halibut and salmon throughout the summer. Prices run from $90 to $100, with all gear provided. The **Silver Salmon Derby** opens on the second Saturday in August and closes eight days later. Prizes run up to $10,000.

Downtown Seward has seafood restaurants, hamburger joints, and pizza parlors aplenty. Pick up groceries at the **Eagle Quality Center,** Mile 2 of the Seward Hwy. **Don's Kitchen,** at 4th Ave. and Washington St., serves up the biggest Alaskan breakfast ever—two eggs, two bacon strips, two sausage links, toast, hash browns, biscuit with gravy, and coffee ($5.75). (Open Mon.-Sat. 5am-9pm, Sun. 5am-7pm.) The **Breeze Inn,** Small Boat Harbor, is not your average hotel restaurant. Breeze in for the huge all-you-can-eat buffet ($8). (Open daily 6am-10pm.) Look for the local catch at **Seward Salmon Bake and Bar-B-Q** near the municipal boat harbor, across from the National Park Center. It serves great salmon ($12) and by far the best barbecue in Alaska ($6-8). (Open daily 11am-9pm.)

Seward's three municipal campgrounds are typical: no showers, pleasant view, grassy sites. The best, the **Municipal Waterfront Campground,** stretches along Ballaine Blvd. (Tent sites $5.) The nearest full-hookup RV park is **Kenai Fjords** on 4th Ave. (224-8779; sites $13.) Lodging ain't cheap here. Try the **Van Gilder,** at 308 Adams St. (224-3079), which offers clean, frontier-style rooms. (Singles and doubles without private bath $50, with bath $85. Make reservations.) The **Snow River International Home Hostel,** at Mile 16 of the Seward Hwy., has no phone; just follow the signs, or call the central number in Anchorage (276-3635) for info. It has shower, laundry and kitchen facilities. ($10, $12 nonmembers.)

Seward bobsleds on the southeast side of the Kenai Peninsula, in Resurrection Bay. It connects to Anchorage due north on the 127-mi.-long Seward Hwy., the only nationally designated "Scenic Byway" in Alaska. **Visitor Information** (224-3094), in the streetcar on 3rd and Jefferson, offers a self-guided walking tour booklet (yawn). (Open summer daily 11am-5pm.) The **Seward Ranger Station (USFS),** 334 4th Ave. at Jefferson, has info on local hikes and trails (224-3374; open Mon.-Fri. 8am-5pm), while the **National Park Visitors Center,** 1212 4th Ave. (224-3874), near the harbor, has info and maps of the Kenai Fjords and western Prince William Sound. (Open summer daily 8am-7pm, shorter winter hours.)

Neither rain, nor snow, nor dark of night will keep Seward's **post office** from delivering mail from its location at 5th and Madison. (Open Mon.-Fri. 9:30am-4:30pm, Sat. 10am-2pm.) The **ZIP code** is 99664; the **area code** is 907.

Kodiak Island

Kodiak was the first capital of Russian Alaska, before Alexander Baranov moved the Russian-American Company headquarters to Sitka. It was here that the Russians committed their worst atrocities, importing Aleut slaves and using them to hunt the area's sea otters to near-extinction. The area also has been subject to the capricious whims of mother nature; in 1912, Mt. Katmai erupted, covering the island with 18 inches of ash and decimating the area's wildlife; in 1964 the biggest earthquake ever recorded in North America shook the area and created a tidal wave that destroyed much of downtown Kodiak, including 158 homes.

The island's man-made attraction is the Baranov Museum, 101 Marine Way (486-5920), the oldest Russian structure in Alaska, and the oldest wooden structure on the U.S. West Coast. (Open Mon.-Fri. 10am-4pm, Sat.-Sun. noon-4pm. $1, under 12 free.) The natural attractions are to be found in **Kodiak National Wildlife Refuge,** a two-million-acre reserve on the western half of the island. An estimated 2600 Kodiak bears live on the island and are usually seen in July and August fishing in streams. Though the bears usually avoid contact with humans, be careful. Kodiaks are the largest and most powerful carnivores in North America, and can easily kill humans with one paw tied behind their back. Because of the relatively small number of Kodiaks in existence, hunters are permitted to kill only one bear apiece every four years. The cheapest way to access the Refuge is by **float plane,** in a group. There are almost a dozen air charter companies in town; a standard drop-off and pickup is around $700. Tenting in the Refuge is not recommended because of the bears; there are 10 cabins available ($10 per night, 7 night max. stay), but you must make reservations and then hope that you're one of the lucky few selected in the lottery held every three months. For info contact the **Kodiak National Wildlife Refuge Managers,** 1390 Buskin River Rd., Kodiak 99615 (487-2600).

Kodiak growls 100 mi. off the Kenai Peninsula. To get to Kodiak, take the Alaska Marine Highway, which sails from Homer ($46), Seward ($52), Whittier ($118), and Valdez or Cordova ($96). (Runs May-Sept. 1-3 times per week, less often in winter). For info on the area, contact the **Visitor Information Center,** at Center St. and Marine Way (486-4070), or the **Chamber of Commerce,** P.O. Box 1485, Kodiak 99615 (486-5557), in the same building.

Southeastern Alaska (The Panhandle)

The Panhandle flings 500 mi. from the Gulf of Alaska to Prince Rupert, BC. The Tlingit (pronounced KLING-kit) and Haida (pronounced HI-duh) tribes have left a deep mark on this loose network of islands, inlets and deep saltwater fjords surrounded by deep valleys and rugged mountains. Temperate rain forest conditions, 60-odd major glaciers, and 15,000 bald eagles distinguish the Panhandle.

While the Interior and the Southcentral regions of Alaska have experienced extensive urban sprawl (by Alaskan standards), the communities of Southeastern Alaska cling to the coast. Gold Rush days haunt such towns as Juneau; others like Sitka hearken back to the era of the Russian occupation.

The Alaska Marine Highway system provides the cheapest, most exciting way to explore the area. The state-run ferries connect Bellingham, WA, Sitka, Juneau and Haines, as well as some smaller Native American and fishing communities. You can avoid the high price of accommodations in smaller communities by planning your ferry trip at night and sleeping on the deck.

Haines and the Northern Panhandle

Haines is by far the most strikingly beautiful city on the Southeast coast, with high bluffs overlooking a turquoise bay, granite mountain, and an abundance of superb hiking trails. Walt Disney productions capitalized on this beauty by filming its adaptation of Jack London's *White Fang* here. The movie set still sits on the edge of town. **Chilkat State Park,** a 19-mi. drive up the highway, protects the area's true star attraction: the convergence of over 3000 bald eagles (more than double the town's population) in the park's "Council Grounds" from November to January each year. In the fall, **Alaska Nature Tours** leads you to the eagles for a three-hour tour, a *three-hour tour* ($45). For more information, write P.O. Box 491 (766-2876). The people with Nature Tours are experts at observing and photographing bears, moose and sea lions. The **S.E. Alaska State Fair** lights up the fairgrounds in mid-August. The **Alaska Bald Eagle Music Festival** runs concurrently.

Those wishing to avoid restaurant fare can hit **Howser's Supermarket** on Main St. (766-2040). The store has a great deli counter, a salad bar with a large pasta selection ($3 per lb.), and chicken dinners ($4). (Open Mon.-Sat. 9am-8pm, Sun. 10am-7pm.) The **Chilkat Bakery and Restaurant,** on 5th Ave. near Main, is a family-style restaurant serving healthy portions and the *best* baked goods. (Bread loaves $1.70, sandwiches $3.50 to $5.25, all-you-can eat soup and salad bar $8.) The **Port Chilkoot Potlatch** at the Tribal House of Ft. Seward (766-2000) is a tourist trap, but the all-you-can-eat salmon bake and BBQ with all the trimmings ($19) is unbeatable. Reservations are recommended.

Backpacking campers can stay at the beautiful mountain location of **Portage Cove Wayside,** 3/4 mi. outside of town on Beach Rd. (Pit toilets, water. Sites $6.) For indoor accommodations, the **Hotel Halsingland,** Box 1589, Haines 99827 (766-2000 or 800-542-6363), is Haines's luxury address. (Singles from $30, with bath $70.) Less luxurious is the **Bear Creek Camp & Hostel (HI/AYH),** Box 1158, Haines 99827 (766-2259), on Small Tract Rd. almost three mi. outside of town. From downtown, follow 3rd Ave. out Mud Bay Rd. to Small Tract Rd.; call ahead for ferry pickup. (Kitchen, laundry, showers. No curfew. $10, nonmembers $12. Cabins $30. Tent sites $3.25.)

"Haines" was originally called "Deishu," or "End of the Trail," in Tlingit. Today Haines still marks the end (or the beginning) of the **Haines Hwy.,** the main passage into Southeast Alaska from the Yukon; the 40-mi. stretch through the **Chilkat Range** has views guaranteed to blow you through the back of your Winnebago. The **Alaska Marine Highway** can take you up to Haines from the opposite direction ($18 from Juneau, vehicle up to 15 ft. long $39); for more info see Travel in the Alaska introduction. The **Alaska Marine Highway Terminal,** 5 Mile Lutake Rd. (766-2111), is four mi. (a $5 cab ride) from downtown, or a quick hitchhike connection. *(Let's Go* does not recommend hitchhiking.) Both the U.S. and Canada have **customs offices** at Mile 42 Haines Hwy. (767-5511 and 767-5540; open daily 7am-11pm.)

Catch the most excellent **Ranger Bill Zack** at the **State Park Information Office,** 259 Main St. (766-2292), for in-depth trail suggestions and information. Your best chances of finding him are Tuesday through Saturday, from 8 to 8:30am and from 4 to 4:30pm. The town maintains a **visitors information center,** 2nd Ave. near Willard St. (766-2234 or 800-458-3579), with info on accommodations and nearby parks. Pick up the *Haines is for Hikers* pamphlet. (Open mid-May-mid-Sept. Mon.-Sat. 8am-8pm, Sun. 10am-6pm, winter shorter hours.)

Gentlemen prefer Haines' **post office** at the corner of 2nd Ave. and Haines Hwy. (726-2930; open Mon.-Fri. 8am-5:30pm, Sat. 1-3pm). General Delivery **ZIP code** is 99827; the **area code** is 907.

Juneau

Compressed into a tiny strip of land at the base of noble Mt. Juneau, Alaska's capital city is the only one in the nation inaccessible by highway. This "Little San Francisco" mixes and matches with a mélange of Victorian mansions, log cabins, Russian Orthodox churches, "Federal" style *quonset* huts, and simple frame houses all set on nearly vertiginous streets leading down to the wharf/tourist mecca.

Its architectural styles only hint at the richness of Juneau's history. Tlingit Chief Kowee led Joe Juneau and Richard Harris up Gold Creek to the "mother lode" of gold in October, 1880. By the next summer, boatloads of prospectors found themselves at work in the already claimed mines. Twenty-five years later Juneau superseded Sitka as capital of the territory of Alaska. Mining ended in Juneau in 1941, but by then fishing, lumber and the government had already supplanted gold's economic niche. Today, Juneau thrives on government (which from the point of view of Alaska's many libertarians means "organized crime") and tourism.

Practical Information and Orientation

Emergency: 911.

Visitor Information: Davis Log Cabin, 134 3rd St. (586-2284), at Seward St. Open Mon.-Fri. 8:30am-5pm, Sat.-Sun. 10am-5pm; Oct.-May Mon.-Fri. 8:30am-5pm. **Marine Park Kiosk,** Marine Way at Ferry Way, right by the cruise ship unloading dock. Open May-Sept. daily 9am-6pm. **U.S. Forest and National Park Services,** 101 Egan Dr. (586-8751), in Centennial Hall. Makes reservations for USFS cabins in Tongass Forest. Write for application packet. Open daily 8am-5pm.

Juneau International Airport: 9 mi. north of town on Glacier Hwy. **Alaska Air,** in the Baranov Hotel, S. Franklin at 2nd St. (789-0600 or 800-426-0333). To Anchorage and Sitka.

Public Transport: Capital Transit (789-6901). Runs from downtown to Douglas, the airport, and Mendenhall Glacier; daily 7am-3pm ($1). **Eagle Express Line** (789-5720) runs vans from major hotels to the airport in time for all flights ($6).

Alaska Marine Highway: P.O. Box R, Juneau 99811 (465-3941 or 800-642-0066). Ferries dock at the Auke Bay terminal at Mile 13.8 Glacier Hwy. To: Bellingham, WA ($216, car and driver $457), and Sitka ($24, car and driver $50).

Taxis: Capital Cab, 586-2772. **Taku Taxi,** 586-2121. Both conduct city tours (½ hr.; $25) and run to Mendenhall (1 hr. round-trip at Glacier; $46).

Car Rental: Rent-a-Wreck, 9099 Glacier Hwy., next to the airport (789-4111). $30 per day, 100 free mi., 15¢ each additional mi.

Post Office: 709 W. 9th St. (586-7138). Open Mon. 8:30am-5pm, Tues.-Fri. 9:30am-5pm. General Delivery **ZIP code:** 99801.

Area Code: 907.

Juneau stands on the Gastineau Channel opposite Douglas Island. **Glacier Highway** connects downtown, the airport, the residential area of the Mendenhall Valley, and the ferry terminal.

Accommodations and Camping

For those not interested in Juneau's wonderful hostel, the **Alaska Bed and Breakfast Association,** P.O. Box 3/6500, #169 Juneau 99802 (586-2959), will provide information on rooms in local homes year-round. Most Juneau B&Bs lie uphill, beyond 6th St., offering singles from $45 and doubles from $55. Reservations are recommended.

Juneau International Hostel (HI/AYH), 614 Harris St. (586-9559), at 6th. Clean and friendly, with houseparents jammin' on guitars. 24 bunk beds. Showers (50¢ per 5 min.), laundry (wash $1.25, dry 75¢), kitchen facilities and common area. Curfew 11pm. $8, nonmembers $11. Make reservations by May for July and Aug.

Alaskan Hotel, 167 Franklin St. (586-1000 or 800-327-9347), in the center of downtown. Handsome hotel built with dark wood has been restored to its 1913 Victorian decor. Singles $40, with bath $55. Doubles $50, with bath $65. Hot tubs noon-4pm $10.50, after 4pm $21. If you're gonna splurge, this is the one.

Driftwood Lodge, 435 Willoughby Ave. (586-2280), near the Federal Building. Courtesy van will whisk you to and from the airport and daily at 7pm out to Mendenhall Glacier. Singles $55, doubles $68, 2-bedroom suite $95 (sleeps up to 4, $7 each extra person).

Campgrounds: Run by the forest service (see Practical Information above). 14-day max. stay. **Mendenhall Lake Campground,** Montana Creek Rd. Take Glacier Hwy. north 9 mi. to Mendenhall Loop Rd.; continue 3½ mi. and take the right fork. If asked, bus driver will let you off within 2 mi. of camp (7am-10:30pm only). Cool view of glacier with trails to take you closer. 61 sites. Fireplaces, water, pit toilets. Sites $5. **Auke Village Campground,** 15 mi. from Juneau on Glacier Hwy. 11 sites. Fireplaces, water, pit toilets. Sites $5.

Food

Travelers on a shoestring should head to the **Foodland Supermarket,** 631 Willoughby Ave., near the Federal Bldg. (Open Mon.-Sat. 9am-7pm, Sun. 9am-8pm.) Pay a bit more for health food at **Rainbow Foods,** 2nd and Seward St. (586-6476; open Mon.-Fri. 10am-7pm, Sat. 10am-6pm, Sun. noon-6pm). Seafood lovers should haunt **Merchants Wharf,** next to Marine Park. **Taku Smokeries,** 230 S. Franklin St. (463-3474) has the best lox this side of Zabar's ($12 per lb.). Always packed with tourists and locals, **Armadillo Tex-Mex Café,** 431 Franklin St., has heaping platefuls of T. Terry's nachos ($5.50). (Open Mon.-Sat. 11am-10pm, Sun. 4am-10pm.) **Thane Ore House Salmon Bake,** 4400 Thane Rd. (586-3442), is a few miles out of town, but "Mr. Ore" will pick you up at your hotel. All-you-can-eat salmon, ribs, and fixings are $16.

Sights

Juneau's greatest attraction is undoubtedly the **Mendenhall Glacier,** about 10 mi. north of downtown. The glacier, oozing down from the 1500-sq.-mi. Juneau Ice Field to the east, glowers over the valley where most downtown workers reside. At the glacier **visitors center,** rangers explain *everything* you could possibly want to know about the glacier—like, for example, why the ice is blue. (Open daily 9am-6:30pm.) The rangers give good ecology walks daily at 10:30am. The best view of the glacier without a helicopter is from the 3½-mi. **West Glacier Trail.** To reach the glacier, take the local public bus down Glacier Hwy. and up Mendenhall Loop Rd. until it connects with Glacier Spur Rd. From here it's less than a half-hour walk to the visitors center. **Eagle Express** runs excellent tours (see Practical Information), but you can better explore this hulk on your own.

In Juneau itself, the **Alaska State Museum,** 395 Whittier St. (495-2910), provides a good introduction to the history and ecology of "The Great Land" and its four main Native American cultures: Tlingit, Athabaskan, Eskimo, and Aleut. It also houses the "First White Man" totem pole, on which the artist carved the likeness of Abraham Lincoln. (Open May 15-Sept. 15 Mon.-Fri. 9am-6pm, Sat.-Sun. 10am-6pm; off-season Tues.-Sat. 10am-4pm. $2, students free.)

The unimpressive **state capitol** building, on 4th and Main, offers summer tours daily from 9am to 5pm. Your time is better spent wandering uphill to **St. Nicholas Russian Orthodox Church** on 5th St. between North Franklin and Gold St. Built in 1894, the church is the oldest of its kind in southeastern Alaska. Services are conducted in English, Slavonic (old Russian) and Tlingit. (Open to the public; $1 donation requested.)

If you're looking for the best view of the Juneau area and you've got a day to kill, go to the end of 6th St. and head up the trail to the summit of **Mt. Roberts** (3576 ft.), a steep but worthwhile four-mi. climb. Though no longer active in Juneau, the mines on Mt. Bob are active tourist sights and frequently host salmon bakes. The **Alaska-Juneau Mine** was the largest in its heyday. **Last Chance Basin,** at the end of Basin Rd., now holds Gold Creek's mining museum.

Juneau stalks as one of the best hiking centers in southeast Alaska. In addition to the ascent of Mt. Roberts, one popular daytrek is along the first section of the **Perseverance Trail,** which leads past the ruins of the historic **Silverbowl Basin Mine** behind Mt. Roberts. For more details on this as well as several other area hikes, drop by the state museum bookstore, the Park Service Center, or any local bookstore to pick up *Juneau Trails,* published by the Alaska Natural History Association ($2.50). The rangers will provide copies of particular maps in this book at the Park Service Center. (See U.S. Forest and National Park Services under Practical Information.)

During winter the slopes of the **Eaglecrest Ski Area,** on Douglas Island (contact 155 S. Seward St., Juneau 99801, 586-5284 or 586-5330), offers decent alpine descents ($22 per day, kids under 12 $10, under 18 $15). In summer, the Eaglecrest "Alpine Summer" self-guided nature trail soaks in the mountain scenery of untouched Douglas Island.

At night, tourists head to the **Red Dog Saloon,** 278 S. Franklin (463-3777), where grey-hair and cats-eye glasses types mingle with student backpackers over the sawdust on the floor. The Red Dog may not be authentic, but who cares—it's still fun. It also has live music on weekends. (Open daily 11:30am-12:30am.) Locals hang out farther uptown; the **Triangle Club,** 251 Front St. (586-3140), attracts a hard-drinking set, while young people and the cruise ship crowd congregate at the **Penthouse,** on the fourth floor of the Senate Bldg. (Open 8pm-whenever.) The **Lady Lou Revue** (586-3686), a revival of Gold Rush days, plays multiple shows daily at the **Perseverance Theatre** in Merchants' Wharf, 2 Marine Way. (Admission $14, kids $7.)

Sitka

Russian explorer Vitus Bering made the first European landfall here in 1741, beginning decades of bloody fighting between Russian settlers and Tlingits. After defeating the Native Americans, the Russians established "New Archangel" as the capital in 1804. This settlement remained Russia's "Paris of the Pacific" for the next 63 years; visitors came here for the lure of money from sea otter pelts and the trappings of glittering society life. After the U.S. purchased Alaska in 1867 (the transaction was officiated in Sitka), the city ruled as the territory's capital from 1884 until 1906.

The beautiful, onion-domed **Saint Michael's Cathedral** shows much of the city's earlier colonial influence. Decimated by fire in 1966 but rebuilt in accordance with the original, this Russian Orthodox Church still displays precious icons and vestments. (Open Mon.-Sat. 11am-3pm and when cruise ships are in. $1 donation required.) The park service recently restored the **Russian Bishop's House,** two blocks further down Lincoln, to duplicate its 1842 appearance when built for its first resident, Bishop Ivan Veniaminov. Unlike at St. Mike's, you can even photograph the beautiful gold and silver icons. (Tours every ½-hr. Open daily 8:30am-4:30pm.) Historic **Castle Hill,** site of Baranov's Castle and Tlingit forts, offers an incredible view of **Mt. Edgecumbe,** an inactive volcano known as the "Mt. Fuji of Alaska."

Stroll down the manicured trails of the **Sitka National Historic Park** (Totem Park, as locals call it), at the end of Lincoln St. (747-6281), one mi. east of St. Michael's. The trails pass by many restored totems en route to the side of **Tlingit Fort,** where hammer-wielding chieftain Katlian almost held off the Russians in the battle for Alaska in 1804. The park **visitors center** offers audio-visual presentations and the opportunity to watch native artists in action in the Native American Cultural Center. (Open daily 8am-5pm.)

The Sitka area offers excellent **hiking** opportunities—make sure to pick up the free booklet *Sitka Trails* at the **USFS information booth,** in front of the Centennial Bldg. at Lincoln St. Several outstanding trails include the **Indian River Trail,** an easy 5.5-mi. trek up the valley to the base of **Indian River Falls,** and the three-mi. uphill trail to the top of **Gavan Hill. The Sitka Music Festival** in June draws world-renowned musicians. (Tickets $12 at the Centennial Bldg.)

Stock up on grub at the **Market Center Grocery** at Biorka and Baranov St., uphill from the Bishop's House (open daily 24 hrs.), or closer to the hostel at **Lakeside Grocery,** 705 Halibut Pt. Rd. (Open Mon.-Sat. 9am-9pm, Sun. 11am-7pm.) Fresh seafood is available from fishmongers along the docks or at **Alaskan Harvest,** a new store run by Sitka Sound Seafood on Katlian St. (Open Mon.-Sat. 9am-5pm.) **The Bayview Restaurant,** upstairs in the Bayview Trading Company at 407 Lincoln St. (747-5440), cooks up everything from *piroshki,* a Russian delicacy (with salad and cup o' borscht, $7) to a Mousetrap sandwich (grilled cheese, $3.75). It also has a great view of the harbor. (Open Mon.-Sat. 6am-7:30pm.) **Staton's Steak House,** 228 Harbor Dr., across from the Centennial Bldg. (747-3396), offers lunch specials like halibut and french fries ($7.50). (Open Mon.-Sat. 11am-2pm and 5-10pm.)

Sitka has 11 **bed and breakfasts** from $40 per person. The **Chamber of Commerce,** Centennial Bldg., 330 Harbor Dr. (747-3225; open Mon.-Sat. 8am-5pm), has a complete list. The small **Sitka Youth Hostel (HI/AYH),** 303 Kimsham St., Box 2645 (747-8356), has reasonably comfortable army cots in the United Methodist Church on Edgecumbe and Kimsham St. Find the McDonald's, one mi. out of town on Halibut Pt. Rd. and walk 100 ft. up Peterson St. to Kimsham. (Kitchen facilities, free local calls. Will store packs during the day. Lockout 10am-6pm. Curfew 11pm. $5, nonmembers $8.) The **Sitka Hotel,** 118 Lincoln (747-3288), has cheap, clean, quiet rooms with tacky decor. (Singles $49, with bath $54. Doubles $54/$59. Key deposit $5. Senior discounts available.) The **Sheldon Jackson College** also rents rooms nightly from its campus housing at the east end of Lincoln St. (747-2518). Dormitory rooms have bedding, shared bath and no curfew. Register in Sweetland Hall. (Summer only; singles $30, doubles $50.) The USFS runs the **Starrigaven Creek Campground,** at the end of Halibut Pt. Rd., one mi. from the ferry terminal, eight mi. from town. (Water, pit toilets. 14-day max. stay. Sites $5.)

For transportation from the ferry terminal to the Centennial Bldg., look for the **Sitka Tour Buses**. They're cheap ($2.50; tours $8), and will also pick you up at the HI/AYH Hostel if you're heading to the ferry terminal.

Sitka sits on the western side of Baranov Island, 95 mi. southwest of Juneau. The O'Connell Bridge connects downtown to Japonski Island and the airport. Sitka's **post office,** 1207 Sawmill Creek Rd. (747-3381), is a fair lick from downtown. (Open Mon.-Fri. 8:30am-5pm.) The **ZIP code** is 99835; the **area code** is 907.

Hawaii

No alien land in all the world has any deep, strong charm for me but that one, no other land could so longingly and beseechingly haunt me, sleeping and waking, through half a lifetime, as that one has done. Other things leave me, but it abides; other things change, but it remains the same....In my nostrils still lives the breath of flowers that perished twenty years ago.

—Mark Twain

Mark Twain's effusive recollections of his 1889 trip to what were then called the Sandwich Islands foreshadow the exotic image that Hawaii conjures today. Dribbled across the ocean blue of the Pacific—2400 miles off mainland America—the state is both physically and psychologically removed from the other United States. 162 islands comprise the Hawaiian chain, though only seven are inhabited.

Hawaii is one of the most ethnically diverse regions in the world. A community with no racial majority, the state serves as a home to a multitude of cultures. Polynesian pioneers traveled in double-hulled canoes across thousands of miles of unbroken ocean as early as the 6th century AD and developed a high degree of civilization on the islands. By the time Captain Cook arrived in 1778, a rigidly hierarchical society and advanced irrigation techniques allowed the native Hawaiians to support a population estimated at 800,000—at a standard of living higher than most of Western Europe at that time. King Kamehameha I, with the aid of Western weapons, united the islands in a single kingdom early in the 19th century. But Western diseases decimated the Hawaiian population; 100 years after Cook's arrival, only 50,000 native Hawaiians remained. An expanding sugar (and later pineapple) industry supplanted the whaling and sandalwood trades following the arrival of Calvinist missionaries from Boston in 1820. American plantation owners brought in Chinese, Japanese, and Filipino laborers. Hawaiian commerce developed uneventfully until the Japanese attack on Pearl Harbor on December 7, 1941. The valiant service of the *nisei* Japanese during World War II was a large factor in mitigating racial prejudice on the islands. In 1959, Hawaii became the 50th state.

Hawaiians have combined their different ethnic heritages into a single "local" culture. Visitors of an artistic bent will find in Hawaii a rich heritage of native handicrafts like woodcarvings and *lei*-making, as well as a vibrant contemporary art community focusing on Hawaii's natural beauty—often with an ecological slant—and on ancient and modern Hawaiian culture.

When in Hawaii, first enjoy the weather and the islands' natural environs. With a little effort you can escape the islands' commercialism and get a true taste of Hawaii's unique flavor. Witness lava ooze out of Kilauea and drift down to the sea, investigate off-shore aquatic life with a snorkel, amble along the beach and into caves. Tourist-tailored traps will draw you of course, and you might well heed their call. All the while, attune your sixth sense to the mysteries of the islands. For the best take on Hawaii, see *Let's Go: California and Hawaii.*

Practical Information

Visitor Information: Hawaii Visitors Bureau, 2270 Kalakaua Ave., 5th floor, Honolulu 96815 (923-1811). Open Mon.-Fri. 8am-4:30pm. The ultimate source. The other islands staff offices at major towns, as listed in the appropriate sections. **Department of Land and Natural Resources,** 1151 Punchbowl St., Honolulu 96813 (548-7455). Open Mon.-Fri. 8am-4pm. Information and permits for camping in state parks and trail maps.

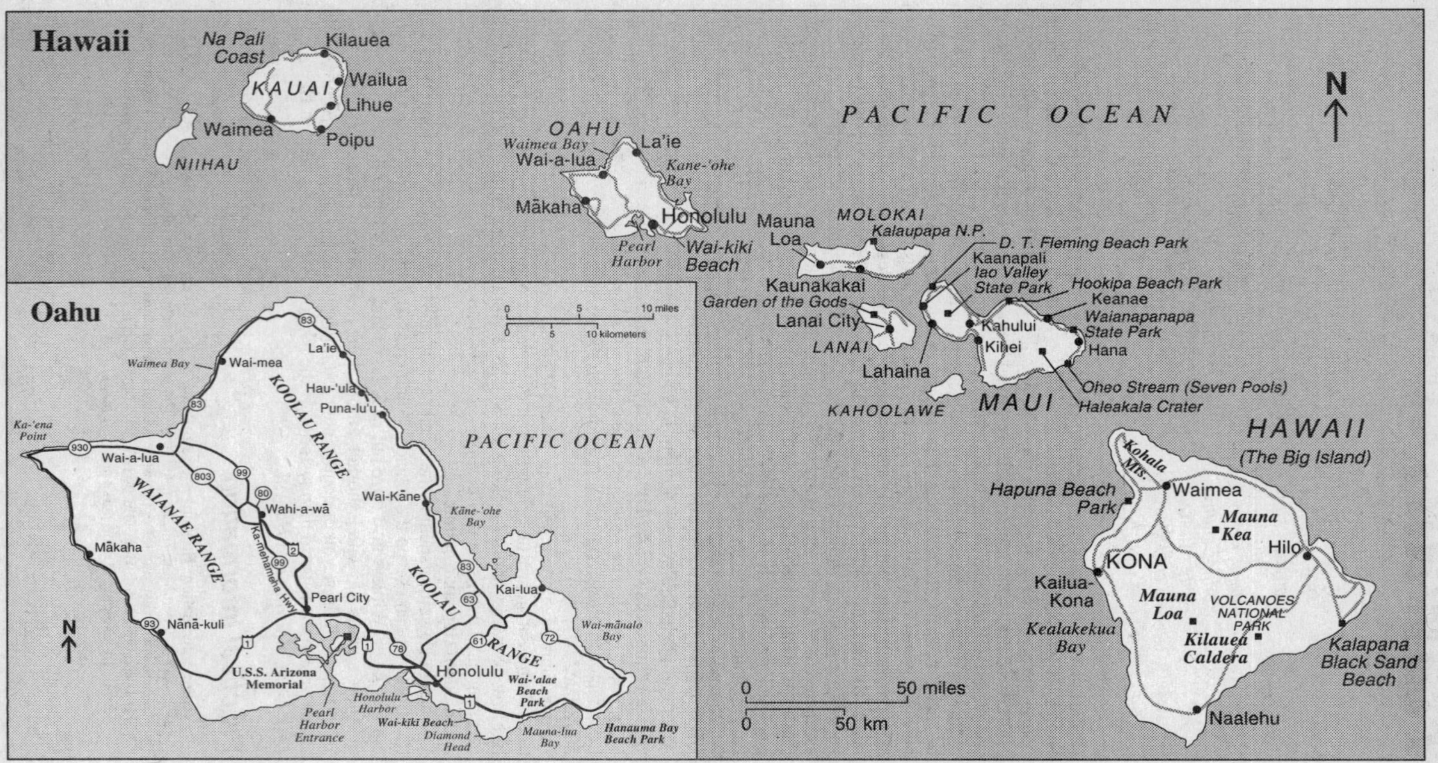

Hawaii
Na Pali Coast
Kilauea
KAUAI
Wailua
Lihue
Waimea
Poipu
NIIHAU
PACIFIC OCEAN
N
OAHU
Waimea Bay
La'ie
Wai-a-lua
Kane-'ohe Bay
Mākaha
Honolulu
Pearl Harbor
Wai-kiki Beach
Mauna Loa
MOLOKAI
Kalaupapa N.P.
D. T. Fleming Beach Park
Kaanapali
Iao Valley State Park
Hookipa Beach Park
Keanae
Waianapanapa State Park
Kaunakakai
Garden of the Gods
Lanai City
LANAI
Kahului
Kihei
Hana
Lahaina
Oheo Stream (Seven Pools)
KAHOOLAWE
MAUI
Haleakala Crater
HAWAII
(The Big Island)
Kohala Mts.
Hapuna Beach Park
Waimea
Mauna Kea
Hilo
KONA
Kailua-Kona
Mauna Loa
VOLCANOES NATIONAL PARK
Kealakekua Bay
Kilauea Caldera
Kalapana Black Sand Beach
Naalehu
0 50 miles
0 50 km
Oahu
0 5 10 miles
0 5 10 kilometers
Waimea Bay
Wai-mea
La'ie
KOOLAU RANGE
Hau-'ula
Puna-lu'u
Ka-'ena Point
Wai-a-lua
PACIFIC OCEAN
WAIANAE RANGE
Wahi-a-wā
Wai-Kāne
Kāne-'ohe Bay
Ka-mehameha Hwy
Mākaha
KOOLAU
Kai-lua
Pearl City
N
Nānā-kuli
Wai-mānalo Bay
RANGE
U.S.S. Arizona Memorial
Honolulu
Wai-'alae Beach Park
Honolulu Harbor
Pearl Harbor Entrance
Wai-kiki Beach
Diamond Head
Mauna-lua Bay
Hanauma Bay Beach Park

National Park Service, Prince Kuhio Federal Bldg., #6305, 300 Ala Moana Blvd., Honolulu 96850 (541-2693). Permits are given at individual park headquarters. Open Mon.-Fri. 7:30am-4pm.

Capital: Honolulu.

Time Zone: Hawaii (3 hr. behind Pacific in spring and summer; 2 hr. otherwise). 11-13 hr. of daylight year-round.

Postal Abbreviation: HI

Area Code: 808.

State Bird: Nene, a rare clawed goose.You might be turned away at the airport if you do not know this.

General Excise Tax: 4%. **Sales Tax:** 4%.

Getting There: 1/10 of the Fun

Reaching paradise isn't as expensive as you might think. While prices increase in winter (Feb.-April), reasonable fares can be found even then. Investigate the *L.A. Times* or the *New York Times* Sunday "Travel" section for discount packages, which usually include airfare from major mainland cities, accommodations, and a bevy of fringe benefits. Be sure to learn the nitty-gritty details: tour packages often list sights without including admission fees, and rates listed are almost always per person rate based on double occupancy. An individual traveling alone usually ends up paying more.

From Los Angeles and San Francisco, many major carriers fly round-trip for $300 and up. If all you need is a plane ticket, look for special advance purchase fares or bulk rates from cut-rate travel agencies. **Cheap Tickets** (808-947-3717 or 800-234-4522 from the mainland) in Honolulu, for instance, offers fares substantially below normal rates.

Getting Around

Island Hopping

When deciding which islands to visit, think carefully about what you would like to do. Each island offers its own atmosphere and range of activities. **Oahu** is heavily populated and revolves around tourism, making it the most accessible island, but leaving few unexplored, and therefore unexploited, places. The **Big Island (Hawaii)** has lots of open space and the added attraction of Volcanoes National Park, where you can see the goddess Pele spit hot lava from the bowels of the earth into the boiling ocean. **Maui's** strong winds have made it one of the premier windsurfing destinations of the world and with the windsurfers comes a hopping nightlife. The major inter-island carriers, **Hawaiian Airlines** (537-5100), **Aloha Airlines** (836-1111), and **Aloha Island Air** (833-3219) can jet you quickly from Honolulu to any of the islands for around $65, $45 for the first and last flights of the day. Travel agents, such as **Pali Tour and Travel, Inc.,** 1300 Pali Hwy., Suite 1304 (533-3608), in Honolulu, sell Hawaiian Air inter-island coupon books that are extremely convenient for island-hopping (6 flights $305). For cheap, individual tickets ($44 each) on Aloha and Hawaiian airlines, try the **Hotel Exchange** on 1946 Ala Moana Blvd. (808-942-8544). Also consider Hawaiian's unlimited inter-island flights with a 5-, 7- or 14-day pass. (Consult a travel agent for details.) Check the miscellaneous section of the classified ads in the *Star-Bulletin* or *Advertiser* for individuals selling these coupons at cut-rate prices. Most carriers offer the same fare to each island they serve.

Aloha and Hawaiian often coordinate with resorts and/or car rental agencies to create economical **package tours.** Ask a local travel or reservations agent about deals best suited to your needs, and keep an eye out for advertisements in pamphlets and newspapers.

Many companies offer one-day airplane and helicopter cruises of the islands (kind of like on *Magnum, P.I.*). Consult a travel agent about current deals and specials or look in the Sunday paper travel section.

On the Islands

While the **bus** system is fairly reliable and extensive on Oahu, it is patchy on the Big Island and local transit is nonexistent on the other islands (see individual island listings). You will probably want to rent your own set of wheels for a sojourn on any island other than Oahu.

Car rental agencies fill major island airports and tourist areas in towns. If you have not booked a rental through an airline or other package deal, check local weekly and monthly travel guides for specials and ask about weekly rates. Because car rental agencies are not state-regulated, a day's use of an automatic, air-conditioned compact car can range from $12 to $40. Hawaii is a no-fault insurance state, so insurance coverage is *optional,* but most companies will not honor your individual coverage, even if you already own a car. **Budget** is one of the few agencies that will rent to those aged 18 to 20, but only to those with a major credit card, and it will add hefty surcharge atop the regular price. For those over 21 but still under 25, your best bet for a new car might be **Tropical Rent-A-Car.** Waiting to start your car rental search until arrival at an airport is a sure way to be stuck with the most expensive rates. Whenever possible, do your research before you get there and make reservations at least 24 hours in advance.

Bicycle and **moped rentals,** available in most tourist centers, are an enjoyable way to see Hawaii in an easy-going, close-up manner. The congestion in Honolulu may be too much for two wheels; mopeds and bikes are more useful on the other side of Oahu, or on the neighbor islands. Inter-island airlines charge about $20 to bring your bike with you on the flight. Mainland airlines charge about $15.

Hawaii (The Big Island)

Pele, Polynesian goddess of the volcanoes, is believed to reside on Hawaii, the southeasternmost island in the Hawaiian chain. Hawaii possesses the archipelago's only two active volcanoes—Mauna Loa, the still-active Long Mountain (13,677 ft.), and Kilauea (4000 ft.), home of the hyperactive Halemaumau Crater. Kilauea is currently in its 49th phase of eruption without showing any signs of relenting; Pele, no doubt, is inexhaustible.

The Big Island is twice the size of all the other islands combined, but is home to scarcely a tenth of the state's population. But Hawaii certainly holds its own. The island's pastures support Hawaii's varied post-sugar economy and as well as experiments with many alternative energy sources; 13,000 ft. up Mauna Kea, Hawaii boasts the premier observatory in the world. The towns of Hilo and Kailua-Kona, on opposite sides of the island, are the main arrival points for tourists. The rest of the island is considered "country" by residents. The northwestern corner is the Kohala Peninsula, former sugar land and the northern border of the island's gigantic cattle range. The southern land mass is Kau, where the first Polynesian immigrants settled. You'll need a car to get to the countryside, but keep a careful eye on the fuel gauge, as distances between gas stations can be great. Coastal highways circle both volcanoes. In Volcanoes National Park, both the old Saddle Road (Rte. 200) and the Chain of Craters Road in Kilauea Crater permit closer views of the volcanoes. The Big Island does have a rudimentary bus system, and you should find most of the island's sights accessible.

Practical Information

Visitor Information: Hawaii Visitors Bureau (Hilo), 250 Keawe St. (961-5797). Bus schedules, brochures, island guides, and maps (all free). Open Mon.-Fri. 8am-noon and 1-4pm. **Wailoa Center,** P.O. Box 936, Hilo 96720 (961-7360), on the *makai* (seaward) side of the State Building. Helpful in planning itineraries. Open Mon.-Fri. 8am-4:30pm. **Volcanoes National Park Visitors Center (Volcanoes),** Volcano, Hawaii 96785 (967-7311), on Rte. 11, 13 mi. from Hilo. Offers trail maps, free ranger-guided hikes, and important safety information. Open daily 8am-5pm. **Hawaii Visitors Bureau (Kona),** 75-5719 W. Alii Dr. (329-7787), across from the Kona Inn Shopping Center. Bus schedules, brochures, maps, and accommodations information. Open Mon.-Fri. 8am-noon and 1-4pm.

Buses: Hele-on-Bus, 25 Aupuni St. (935-8241). Information on bus schedules. Operates Mon.-Sat. 6:30am-6pm. Fare ranges from $.75 to $6. Luggage and backpacks $1. Runs between Kona and Hilo ($5.25) once per day, making a convenient circuit of the island ($5.25).

Taxi: Ace Taxi, 935-8303. **ABC Taxi,** 935-0755. Airport-city runs about $10.

Car Rentals: All national and state chains are located at Hilo airport. Make reservations several days in advance or take advantage of fly/drive deals for cheaper rates. **Tropical Rent-A-Car,** 800-367-5100. Rents to those 21 and over for $17 a day for 3 days. They charge a $5 surcharge to those under 21. **VIP Rentals** 74-5588 Pawai Pl. Lends out their cars for $13 a day, with a 3-day min. *Must* be over 21. **Budget,** 935-7293, rents to those 18-25 for a $20 per day surcharge.

Bikes and Mopeds: DJS, 75-5663A Palani Rd. in Kona (529-1700), across from the King Kamehameha Hotel. Scooters $25 for 8 hrs; cruisers $15 per day. **Hawaiian Pedals,** Kona Inn Shopping Village has 21-speed mountain bikes for $20 a day, $63 a week. Open daily 9am-5pm.

Water Equipment Rentals: Nautilus Dive Center, 382 Kamehameha Ave., Hilo (935-6939). Mask/snorkel $3 per day. Also offers beginner and certified dive charters, $55. Open Mon.-Sat. 9am-4pm. **Island Divers,** Kona Market Village (329-9188), in the back. Masks, fins, and snorkels $6 per day, prescription masks $9. Boogie boards $9 per day. Charters, introductory dives, and scuba rentals are also available at affordable rates. Open daily 8am-8pm.

Crisis/Help Line: 969-9111.

Area Code: 808.

Hilo

After Honolulu, Hilo is the largest city in the state, a sleepy version of its bigger cousin. The center of the Hawaiian orchid and anthurium industry, the city is primarily residential; Hilo works best as a base from which to visit the island's attractions. The city averages nearly 125 in. of rain per year; keep this in mind when you start those "three-hour tours"—Gilligan didn't. If the weather gets too rough for you, just head for the sunny Kona-Kohala coast (a 2-hr. drive away).

To get the most out of Hilo, start your sightseeing early in the day. Rte. 11 will take you directly from the Hilo airport to the national park, but it's more rewarding to explore the town first by morning light. The **Liliuokalani Garden** (an elaborate Japanese-style garden named after one of the royal princesses) affords a great view of Mauna Kea before the clouds roll in. Hilo is the orchid capital of the world. **Orchids of Hawaii,** 2801 Kilauea Ave. (959-3581), immediately past the first one-lane bridge, features beautiful *leis* and an exotic variety of orchids and anthuriums. (Open Mon.-Fri. 7:30am-4:30pm.) The **Hilo Tropical Gardens,** 1477 Kalanianaole Ave. (935-4957 or 935-1146) are a lush botanical experience, perfect for an afternoon stroll. (Open Mon.-Fri. 9am-4:30pm.)

Near Hilo, recent lava flows have covered the once-glistening shores of **Kaimu Black Sand Beach** and various parts of the highway as well, making **Rte. 11** the only way to round South Point from Hilo. **Lava Tree State Park,** which blooms year-round with lava casts of trees formed during the 1790 eruption, is still accessible. From Hilo, take Rte. 11 south to Keau, turn onto Rte. 130 to Pahoa, and then take Pahoa-Pohoiki Rd. (Rte. 132). Continue around the loop on Rte. 132 past the **Kapoho Lighthouse** and the gardens nearby. Here a 1960 lava flow covered Kapoho Village; only trees and the lighthouse remain.

The hotels clustered on Banyan Dr. by the bay are quiet and often empty. Try **Arnott's Lodge,** 98 Apapane Rd. (969-7097). By car, from Airport Rd, turn right at the first traffic light, turn right again at the next light (next to Dairy Queen) onto Kalanianaele St., go 1½ mi. and make a left onto Keokea. Apapane Rd. is on the right about 50 yd. down. Arnott's is totally renovated and scrupulously clean. Laundry, TV and cooking facilities, and the beaches are within walking distance. (Bunks $15. Private singles $25. Suites for 5 $80. Students receive a 20% discount.) The **Country Club Hotel,** centrally located at 121 Banyan Dr. (935-7171), has good, scenic rooms with *lanais* (porches), A/C, TV, and phones. (Singles and doubles $39, with kitchenette $50.) **Dolphin Bay Hotel,** 333 Iliahi St., Hilo 96720 (935-1466), in the Puueo section of town, boasts cool, tropical gardens, fans, TV, and kitchens. (Singles from $39. Doubles from $49. Pre-payment required; make deposit 10 days prior to stay.) Campers can try the **Onekahakaha Beach Park** and **Kealoha Beach Park** (both 961-8311), within three mi. of Hilo, but be forewarned: they are known as local tough-guy hangouts. (Tent camping, bathrooms, and shower facilities. $1 permit required; see Practical Information.)

You'll find macadamia nut bread, cookies, cakes and pies galore to accompany cups of steaming Kona coffee grown on the island. Free samples of the nuts are given out at the **Hawaiian Holiday Macadamia Nut Company** in Haina, off Rte. 19 near Honokaa. For more substantial fare, head to downtown Hilo which is loaded with fast-food joints, cheap restaurants, sushi counters, and *okazu-ya*. **Reuben's Mexican Food,** 336 Kamehameha Hwy. (961-2552), has authentic Mexican food (entrées $7-9) served on colorful tablecloths, and a wide selection of beers and margaritas. (Open Mon.-Fri. 11am-9pm, Sat. noon-9pm.) **Bear Coffee,** 106 Keawe St. (935-0708) has a great décor and serves superb kona coffee and espresso. The locals swear by it. (Open Mon.-Fri. 7am-4pm, Sat. 7am-7pm.) **Ken's Pancake House,** 1730 Kamehameha Ave. (935-8711), is the Hawaiian IHOP you always dreamed about, serving macadamia nut, coconut, and fresh banana pancakes ($4) with a variety of syrups. Burgers, hot dogs, *et al.* are also served, giving you an alternative that banana-happy Gilligan never had. (Open 24 hrs.)

Hilo rests at the mouth of the Wailuku River. Its airport, **General Lyman Field,** is accessed by inter-island service and flights from the mainland. Travelers should stop and talk to the folks at the airport's visitor information booth. For General Delivery, go to the airport **post office** (935-6685) on the Airport Access Rd., (obviously) near the airport. The **ZIP Code** is 96720.

The Volcano Area

The volcanoes of the Big Island are unique in their size, frequency of eruption, and accessibility. Resting above the geological hot spot that fashioned each of the Hawaiian islands in turn, the two mountains in **Volcanoes National Park** continue to heave and grow, adding acres of new land each year. **Kilauea Caldera,** with its steaming vents, sulfur fumes, and periodic eruptions, is the star of the park, although the less active **Mauna Loa** and its dormant northern neighbor, **Mauna Kea,** are in some respects more amazing. Each towers nearly 14,000 ft. above sea level and drops some 16,000 ft. to the ocean floor. Mauna Loa is the largest volcano in the world, while Mauna Kea, when measured from its base on the ocean floor, is the tallest mountain on earth. (Park entrance $5, good for 7 days.)

The 11-mi. scenic drive around the Kilauea Caldera on **Crater Rim Drive** is a good way to see the volcano by car. The road is accessible via Rte. 11 from the east and west or via the Chain of Craters Rd. from the south. Well-marked trails and lookouts dot the way, so stop frequently to explore. You might also take the easy hike along the vista-filled **Crater Rim Trail,** which traverses *ohia* and giant fern forests, *aa* (rough) and *pahoehoe* (smooth) lava flows, and smoldering steam and sulfur vents. Take a beautiful walk through the **Thurston Lava Tube,** formed by lava that cooled around a hot core which continued to move, leaving the inside of the flow hollow. The nearby **Jaggar Museum** explains the rolling geological background with a pictorial history of the volcano; other displays focus on Hawaiian legends. (Open daily 8:30am-5pm. Free.)

The four-mi. **Kilauea Iki Trail** starts at the Kilauea Iki overlook on Crater Rim Rd. It leads around the north rim of Kilauea Iki, through a forest of tree ferns, down the wall of the little crater, past the vent of the 1959 eruption, over steaming lava, and back to Crater Rim Rd., passing *ohelo* bushes laden with red berries. According to legend, you must offer berries to Pele before eating any, or you'll incur her wrath. I'd do it if I were you. The 3½-mi. **Mauna Iki Trail** begins nine mi. southwest of park headquarters on Rte. 11 and leads to ashen footprints left in 1790. From here you can hike down into the coastal area.

An unpaved road leads to Mauna Kea's summit from **Rte. 200 (Saddle Rd.).** The terrain is stark, but the views of the earth below and the stars above are transcendent.

The notion of altitude sickness at 13,796 ft., however, may deter you from making the trek.

When seeking shelter for the night, consider the **Holo Holo Inn,** Kalani Honua Rd., Volcano Village (967-7950). Hostel-like accommodations inside a private home. ($15; call in advance for good directions.) Call the **Volcano House,** P.O. Box 53, Hawaii Volcanoes National Park, 96718 (967-7321) for their the **Namakanipaio** cabins, located 3 mi. behind the Volcano House in an *ohia* forest. (Check-in after 3pm. 4-person cabins $25. Linen and some blankets provided.) **Morse Volcano B&B,** P.O. Box 100, Volcano, 96785 (967-7216), in Volcano Village just outside the park, is a historic missionary-style home with roomy common areas. (Singles $30, with bath $40. Doubles $50, with bath $60.) **Volcanoes National Park** (967-7311) offers free campsites at **Kipukanene, Namakanipaio** (near Kilauea Crater), and **Kamoamoa** (on the coast), each with shelters and fireplaces, but no wood. (Reservations are not accepted. 7-day maximum.)

Kona

Occupying the western side of Hawaii, Kona claims a disproportionate share of the Big Island's white sand beaches, resorts, and realtors. It is also home to the town of **Kailua** (officially hyphenated as Kailua-Kona), a booming resort center with shops, nightlife, and perfect weather. The calm, deep waters along this coast of the Big Island offer splendid snorkeling, scuba diving, and big game fishing.

Kailua-Kona itself is small enough to see in a short walk, and most of what's worth seeing is what's worth lying down on. **Magic Sands** (also called "Disappearing Sands") at the Kona Magic Sands Hotel, 77-6452 Alii Dr. (329-9177), is a good place to park your towel and wade. Or travel up Rte. 19 to prime **Hapuna Beach** and **Spencer Beach Parks,** 35 mi. north, where you can rent sailboards at make-shift stands.

Staying overnight in Kailua-Kona can be expensive, since its hotels cater to the affluent traveler; neighboring towns provide cheaper lodgings. The **Kona Hotel,** Holualoa (324-1155), on Rte. 18 southeast of Kona, enjoys clean, comfortable surroundings and friendly management. Make sure to reserve well in advance, as this fabulous find fills up frighteningly fast. (Singles $15. Doubles $23.) The **Manago Hotel,** P.O. Box 145, Captain Cook, 96704 (323-2642), is austere but comfy and clean, with a generally older clientele. (Singles from $22. Doubles from $25.)

The **Ocean View Inn,** 75-5683 Alii Dr. (329-9998), serves good, diverse food. (Breakfast $4, lunch $4-7, dinner $7-10. Open Tues.-Sun. 6:30am-2:45pm and 5:15-9pm.) **Stan's,** 75-5646 Palani Rd. (329-2455), in the Kona Seaside, is a good bet for breakfast (all-you-can-eat hotcakes $4.25) and complete dinners ($8). (Open daily 7-9:30am and 5:30-8pm.) **Betty's Chinese Kitchen,** Palani Rd., in the KTA Shopping Center, has large portions and a daily plate ($3-4). (Open Mon.-Sat. 10am-8:30pm.) For nightlife, try the **Jolly Roger Restaurant,** 75-5776 Alii Dr. (329-1344), with live music and no cover, or **Kona Surf,** 78-128 Ehukai St. (322-3411), where the avuncular Jerry Garcia, has played, among others.

The door to Kailua-Kona is opened by **Keahole Airport,** nine mi. (15 min.) north of town. **Taxi** rides into town are about $16, plus $.30 per parcel. Kailua-Kona is a small settlement and can be toured in one day without a car. The city is split by two streets running parallel to the ocean: **Alii Drive,** nearest the ocean, and **Kuakini Highway,** one block *mauka* (inland). Kona's **post office** erupts at Palani Rd. (329-1927). Open Mon.-Fri. 9am-4pm, Sat. 9am-noon. The **ZIP code** is 96740.

Kohala

Once home to several sugar mills, much of **Kohala** (the Big Island's northwest coast) offers beachside camping and good biking roads on the Kona side, one of the world's largest ranches, the beautiful Waipio Valley, and tourist-free splendor. As Kohala is inaccessible by bus, some people hitch a ride from Waimea.

From the Kona Coast beyond Hapuna Beach, head up the mountain on Rte. 19 toward **Kamuela.** Founded in 1847 by a Boston missionary, the **Parker Ranch** spans 225,000 acres and is home to 40-50,000 head of Hereford cattle; the ranch annually produces enough beef for 40 million Quarter-Pounders. The **Visitors Center and Museum** (885-7655) has cool audio-visual presentations on the Ranch and its *paniolos*—Hawaiian cowboys. (Open daily 9:30am-4:30pm. Admission $4, ages 4-11 $2.) Hop along down Rte. 24 to the edge of the lush **Waipio Valley,** eight mi. away, for one of the most striking panoramas anywhere in the islands. The 2000-ft. gorge, the islands' largest, is the most abysmal in a series of breathtaking canyons between Waipio and Pololu. Bountiful flora and fauna made Waipio (the islands' largest gorge) the center of ancient Hawaiian civilization. The adventurous should consider the nine-mi. hike between the **Waipio Valley Lookout** and **Waimanu Bay. Waimanu Valley** holds ancient Hawaiian ruins, and the scenery can't be beat.

Campsites are plentiful in Kohala; try the **Hapuna Beach State Park,** off Rte. 19 (882-7995), three mi. south of Kawaihae. The park is great for swimming, volleyball, sunning, relaxing, and people-watching. Reserve well in advance. (A-frame shelters only; no tent camping. $7.)

Maui

Long before college athletes proclaimed "We're Number One," Maui's warlike chieftains proudly announced their island's supremacy over the archipelago with the words *Maui No Ka Oi.* As a tourist destination, Maui is rapidly re-claiming that vaunted position over the other Hawaiian islands. Named for the demi-god Maui, who, according to legend, pulled the islands up from the sea-bottom with fish hooks. "The Valley Island," as it is known, features an astounding variety of attractions for its size. You can visit clapboard cane towns, concrete condos, sunny beaches, a sometimes-snowcapped volcano, and a rain forest without even leaving the island. Once you've been "Mauied," you'll never want to get divorced.

Practical Information and Orientation

Emergency: 911

Hawaii Visitors Bureau, the original moving tourist center. Call for location in Ka ului (871-8691). Friendly assistance with itinerary planning, activities, and accommodations, but they won't make reservations. Information on Molokai and Lanai. Open Mon.-Fri. 8am-4:30pm. **Haleakala National Park** (572-7749) provides recorded information on weather conditions, daily ranger-guided hikes and special activities. For information on camping and cabins, call 572-9177. **Department of Parks and Recreation,** War Memorial Gym, 1580 Kaahumanu Ave. (243-7389), between Kahului and Wailuku. Information and permits ($3) for county parks. Open Mon.-Fri. 8-11am and noon-4:15pm. **Division of State Parks,** 54 High St. (243-5354), in Wailuku. Maui and Molokai state parks information. Open Mon.-Fri. 8-11am and noon-4:15pm.

Tours: GrayLine Maui, (877-5507 or 834-1033 from Honolulu, 800-367-2420 from the mainland) offers frequent tours. To: Iao Valley/Lahaina ($18), and Hana ($75 for a 10-hr. extravaganza including lunch). Call the Honolulu office for more info and to make reservations.

Kahului Airport, on the isthmus's northern coast. Regular flights from the mainland and other islands. Planes also fly into **Kaanapali** and **Hana. TransHawaiian** (877-7308), offers hourly service between Kahului Airport and the major Kahaina-Kaanapali hotels ($13). Runs daily 7am-8pm.

Boats: Ferries are the ideal mode of transport to Molokai and Lanai. The **Maui Princess** (661-8397) runs daily from Lahaina, Maui to Kaunakakai, Molokai at 7am, and from Molokai to Maui at 3:55pm. The crossing takes about 13/4 hr. and costs $25 one way. **Expeditions** (661-3756) sails to Lanai 4 times a day for $25.

Taxi: Kaanapali Taxi (661-5285). Airport to Kahului/Wailuku $9.

Car Rental: Word of Mouth, Dairy Rd. (877-2436), near Kahului Airport. $15 per day for a used car, $17 with A/C; $85 per week, $95 with A/C. Must be 25. **VIP,** Haleakala Hwy. (877-2054), neat the Kahului Airport. 3-day special on used cars ($13 the 1st day, $15 for the next 2; or $80 a week.) **Maui Discount,** (871-6147), $18 a day for 3 days. 21 and over only. The national chains all have desks or courtesy phones at the airport.

Bicycle, Mopeds and Scooters: A&B Moped and Scooter Rentals, 3481 Lower Honoapilani Rd. (669-0027), near Kaanapali. $15 per day for Beachcruiser bikes, $60 per week. Open daily 9am-5pm.

Water Equipment Rentals: Maui Dive Shop, Azeka Pl. (879-3388), Kihei, and Wakea Ave. (661-5388), Kahalui. Complimentary scuba lessons with equipment rental, and free 1-hr. introductory snorkeling lessons. Mask $3, snorkel $1.50, boogie board $8, wetsuit $6. Open Mon.-Fri. 8am-9pm, Sat. 8am-6pm. **Hunt Hawaii,** 120 Hana Hwy., (579-8129), Paia. Surf, boogie, and sailboards for rent or sale. Biggest surfboard rental fleet on Maui. Surfboards $15 for 2 hrs., $20 per day. Windsurfers $35 per day, $135 per week. Surf or sailboard lessons $60 per 2½ hr. Open daily 9am-6pm. **Hawaiian Reef Divers,** 129 Lahainalua Rd. (667-7647 or 667-6002), Lahaina. Good deals, friendly advice, and an excellent beach map. Snorkel set $2, boogie boards $3 per day. Boat trips with snorkeling or scuba offered. Open daily 8am-6pm.

Help Lines: Gay and Bisexual Information, 572-1884 (serves Maui, Molokai, Lanai). 24 hrs.

Post Office: Lahaina, Baldwin Ave. Open Mon.-Fri. 8:15am-4:15pm. **ZIP Code:** 96761. **Paia,** Baldwin Ave. Open Mon.-Fri. 8am-4:30pm, Sat. 10:30am-12:30pm. **ZIP Code:** 96779. **Wailuku,** next to State Office Building, on High St. Open Mon.-Fri. 8:30am-4:30pm, Sat. 9-11am. **ZIP Code:** 96793. **Kihei,** 1254 S. Kihei Rd., in Azeka Market Place. Open Mon.-Fri. 9am-4:30pm, Sat. 9-11am. **ZIP Code:** 96753.

Maui consists of two mountains joined at an isthmus. The highways follow the shape of the island in a broken figure-eight pattern. To the west lie **Kahului** and **Wailuku,** business and residential communities offering less expensive food and supplies than the resort towns. From Kahului, Rte. 30 will lead you clockwise around the smaller western loop of the figure eight to hot and dry **Lahaina,** the former whaling village, and **Kaanapali,** the major resort area.

Most roads are well marked but poorly lit. Heed the warnings "road recommended for four-wheel-drive vehicles only;" a passing rainstorm can quickly drain your funds, since most rental car contracts stipulate that dirt road driving is at the driver's risk.

Accommodations and Camping

There is a rise in the number of vacation rentals and B&Bs on Maui, many catering to windsurfers and offering space to store equipment. Some go for as little as $20 a night. Hostels are another way to sidestep tourist traps, but book them a month in advance. In East Maui camping is the watchword. Campsites and hostels provide an economical alternative to Maui's resort hotels. The Wailuku hostels cater to windsurfer and other aquatically inclined mammals (though dolphins are rare). During the winter season—especially during windsurfing events— these hostels are packed to the gills, so book reservations at least a month in advance.

Northshore Inn, 2080 Vineyard St. (242-8999), Wailuku. Clean shared bathrooms, comfy common room with TV, microwave, fridge, laundry, coffee; periodic barbecues. Bunks $15. Singles $33. Doubles $43.

Banana Bungalow Hotel and International Hostel, 310 North Market St., Wailuku (244-5090). Wonderfully clean hostel accommodations. Lots of international travelers and windsurfers. Free airport pick-up. Day trips to various places on the island. Laundry. Bunks $13. Singles with double bed $29. Doubles $39.

Maui Palms Hotel, 170 Kaahumanu Ave. (877-0071), Kahului. Unpretentious hotel by the sea. TV. Singles $47. Doubles $50. Triples $65.

Nani Kai Hale, 73 N. Kihei Rd. (879-9120, 800-367-6032 from the mainland), Kihei. Condominium on a sandy beach. Doubles with bath $32.50, 3-day minimum; Dec. 16-April 15 $42.50, 7-day min. stay. Reserve ahead by phone.

Wailana Sands, 25 Wailana (879-2026 or 879-3661), off the 500 block of S. Kihei Rd. in Kihei. In a quiet cul-de-sac. Full kitchen, small pool. 4-day min. stay. 2-person studio $40. Reserve a month in advance.

Pioneer Inn, 658 Wharf St. (836-1411), Lahaina. One of Hawaii's 2 oldest hotels, this popular meeting spot is directly in front of the boat harbor, next to the famous giant banyan tree. The lively **Old Whaler's Saloon** spouts liquor long into the night. Pool. Ask for a room with a view of the harbor. Singles and doubles $30, with bath $35; in Mauka building $70. Call months in advance for reservations, especially for Dec.-March.

Renting a car and **camping** on the island may be the best and cheapest way to ebulliate in Maui's natural magnificence. The county maintains **H.A. Baldwin Park** in Paia about five mi. east of the Kahului Airport. (Tent and permit required. 3-day max. stay. Sites $3, ages under 18 $.50.) For more information, contact the Department of Parks and Recreation (see Practical Information above).

The state maintains two parks for camping with a five-night maximum stay. Required permits can be obtained free at the Department of Parks and Recreation. **Waianapanapa State Wayside** in Hana, about 52 mi. east of Kahului Airport, has the best state camping facilities on the island. Sites include restrooms, picnic tables, barbecue grills, and outdoor showers. (Cabin singles $10, $5 per person in groups of 6 or more. Reservations necessary for cabins, not for camping.)

Maui's two federal parks require no permit. **Hosmer Grove,** 7000 ft. up Haleakala's slope, is a small campground with drinking water, toilet, grills, and firewood. On a weekend night, however, you'll have to squeeze your tent in with a crowbar. Groups are limited to 15 people and a three-night stay. **Oheo** is at sea level, about 67 mi. from Kahului Airport, 1/4 mi. south of **Oheo Stream** near the Seven Pools. (No drinking water and firewood. 3-day max. stay.)

Camping at the **national campsites** within the Haleakala Crater requires a permit and a hike to the site. Permits are available from the **Haleakala National Park Headquarters,** P.O. Box 369, Makawao, Maui 96768 (572-9306).

Food

Locals claim that it is possible to live on Maui without spending a penny on food. The waters around the coast teem with fish and the trees drip breadfruit, mango, coconut, pine nuts, papaya, and guava. The ground bears its share of delicacies as well, including pineapple and the sweet Kula onion, world famous and sold for up to $6 per pound at the local market. *Guri guri,* a locally made pineapple or strawberry sherbet, has lured generations of islanders to its main supply source **Tasaka Guri Guri,** in Kahului's Maui Mall (871-4512; open daily Hawaiian time—whenever). If you would like to bite into some fresh, juicy Hawaiian fruit, tutti-frutti on down to **Paradise Fruit,** 2439 Kihei Rd., at the back of Rainbow Mall; they have truly paradisiacal fruit and goodies. (Open daily 6am-10pm.) The cheapest places to eat are away from the resorts.

Tasty Crust, Mill St., Wailuku (244-0845). A bare-bones backpacker diner serving beverages in paper cups and hearty food at unbeatable prices. Fill up on dinosaur-sized hot cakes ($.85, served all day). Open daily 5:30-11:15am and 5pm-9pm. Closed Mon. evenings.

Azeka's, S. Kihei Rd. (879-0078), in Azeka Marketplace, Kihei. In the same building as Azeka's Market, this window-service snack shop sells inexpensive box lunches ($4.50). Hamburgers and sandwiches start at $1.50. Open Mon.-Fri. 9:30am-4pm, Sat.-Sun. 9:30am-5pm.

The Bakery, 991 Limahana Place (667-9062), near the railroad depot in Lahaina. It's hard to find, but have faith; breads and pastries await your arrival. Good pizza, too. Made-to-order sandwiches ($4.50). Open daily 6am-3:30pm.

Paia Fish Market, 2A Baldwin Ave. (579-8030), in Paia. Elegant but casual, with woody net-filled interior. Freshest fish around. Dinner specials $12-17. Open daily 11am-9:30pm.

Mana Foods, 49 Baldwin Ave. (579-8078), in Paia. Full-service health food grocery store and deli. Try the Maui Ginger Blast drink to wash down your tofu on wheat (all natural, no preservatives). Open daily 8am-8pm.

Komada's Market, Macawao (572-7261). Neighboring islanders make special trips here to buy their cream puffs ($.80). If you leave without trying them, you will probably die. Open Mon.-Sat. 6:30am-2pm.

Casanova's Italian Restaurant and Deli, 1188 Makawao Ave. (572-0220), in Makawao. In addition to serving moderately priced Italian cuisine, Casanova's is one of Makawao's central night spots, with a front *lanai* convenient for drinking and chatting. Local bands some nights. Deli open daily 8:30am-9pm. Restaurant Mon.-Sat. 5:30-9:30pm, closed Sun.

Sights and Activities

Haleakala Crater, the "House of the Sun," dominates the eastern end of the island from its perch 10,000 ft. above the sea. According to Polynesian legend, the demigod Maui ascended Haleakala to slow the sun's trip across the sky so that his mother would have more time to dry her *tapa* cloth. When the sun arose at the end of the sky, Maui lassoed him by his genitals, and the sun mincingly agreed to cruise across the sky more slowly. The House of the Sun is still a spectacular place for watching the sun rise. **Haleakala National Park** is open 24 hours (Admission $3 per car.) Be sure to stop at the **park headquarters** (572-9306) about one mi. from the Rte. 378 entrance. **Haleakala Visitors Center** (572-9172), near the summit, has exhibits on the geology, archeology, and ecology of the region. (Free ranger talks are given at 9:30, 10:30, and 11:30am. Open daily 6:30am-4pm.) The **Puuulaula Center,** at Haleakala's summit, offers shelter to those who forgot a sweater or jacket. (Open 24 hrs.) An 12-mi. descent into the crater via **Sliding Sands Trail** and out again via **Halemauu Trail** is well worth the trip; your feet may feel like lead the next day, but that's only because they will have taken you light years, not just 12 mi. The silence of this journey is as vast as the crater itself. Heed the park's advice about sturdy walking shoes, water, and sun screen, however. **Kaluuokaoo Pit** is one of several exposed lava tubes in the crater. Early Hawaiians threw the umbilical cords of their newborns into the pit to safeguard the sacred coils from the valley's evil rodents. Drive farther south on Rte. 37 to **Tedeschi Winery** (878-6058), and taste their "Maui Blanc" pineapple wine (free). (Open daily 9am-5pm. Tours given on the ½hr. until 2:30pm.)

Missing the **Hana Coast** would be like visiting China without seeing the Great Wall. The northern route (**Hana Hwy. 360**) through **Paia** and **Keanae** redefines beauty with each twist and turn. This road has the dubious honor of being the most pitted road west of NYC—but behind each curve reveals yet another breathtaking valley. Visit **Blue Pond** for a secluded swim in a waterfall-fed pond at the end of Ulaino Rd., past the Kakano Gardens. Cross the river and walk along the beach. And don't miss **Oheo**, known to tourists as Seven Sacred Pools, 10 mi. south of **Hana.** Make sure you start out from Paia with a full tank of gas, and don't go if the road is wet. It's a long way down. Paia's **Hookipa Beach Park** is an international windsurfing mecca.

In central Maui, be sure to step into the unspoiled **Iao Valley,** on the southern slope of Puu Kukui. The valley is especially beautiful in the moonlight. **Iao Valley State Park,** at the end of Rte. 32, includes the **Iao Needle,** a 1200-ft. basalt spire (open daily 7am-7pm). Tour buses arrive by 10am, and clouds by 2pm; both leave by 6pm. The name is onomatopoeic, the cry of an unfortunate god who sat on this pointed peak. Really.

The **Hale Kii** ("House of Images") served as a place of worship throughout the 18th century until destroyed by natural erosion in 1819. Reconstructed in 1958, the *heiau* is now a temple of love. High-school love bunnies make the pilgrimage uphill on Thursday evenings for the island's most idyllic views. Follow Main St. (Rte. 32) to the traffic light at Rte. 330. Make a left, pass the macadamia nut grove, and turn right on Rte. 340. Continue to Kuhio Place, and follow the nerve-racking route to the right. The **Vineyard Tavern,** 2171 Vineyard (242-9938), is close to the hostels and a good nighttime hangout. It's a dim, dusty bar and grill with a shuttleboard table and a hefty dose of charm. Last call 1:30am.

Lahaina, an old whaling port in west Maui, was the capital of the islands during the time of Kamehameha the Great. It's a sunny, dry town that infects visitors with drowsy calm. When Mark Twain visited, he planned to stay one week and work; he stayed a month and never lifted a pen. The enormous tree in Lahaina's town square is a 114-year-old East Indian banyan tree, rivaling Kauai's for the title of the islands' largest. The island's only remaining **steam locomotive** still carries tourists, if not sugar, between Lahaina and Kaanapali. (One way $5, round-trip $8, under 12 half-price.) A new **OMNI Theater,** 824 Front St. (661-8314), Lahaina, presents Hawaii's history on the big, big screen with *Hawaii: Island of the Gods!* (Daily every hr. 10am-10pm; admission $6, under 12 $4; $1 discount coupons available at nearby tourist centers.) The best snorkeling on the island is at the **14-mile marker** near Olowalu. Fish eat out of your hand in **Honolua Bay.** Those seeking more strenuous exercise should try their hand (shoulder and back, too) at windsurfing.

For nightlife, gravitate toward West Maui which hosts the island's hottest dance scene. **Spats,** in the Hyatt Regency Maui (667-7474), rocks until 2am with two bars, two dance floors, a dress code and no cover. **The Wunderbar,** 89 Hwy. (579-8808), brings back memories of *Deutschland.* A fine selection of German beer. (Open daily 7:30am-10pm.)

Oahu

By the time missionaries arrived in 1820, Oahu, and its principle city Honolulu, had become the economic and cultural center of Hawaii. Oahu's preeminence increased in ensuing decades as Honolulu's commercial traffic expanded and the U.S. Navy acquired exclusive rights to the neighboring inlet at infamous Pearl Harbor.

Oahu can be roughly divided into four sections: **Honolulu,** the **Windward Coast,** the **North Shore,** and the **Leeward Coast.** The slopes of two extinct volcanic mountain ridges (to which the island owes its existence), **Waianae** in the east and **Koolau** in the west, make up the bulk of Oahu's 600 square mi. The narrow inlets of **Pearl Harbor** push in from the sea at the southern end of the valley between the two ridges. Honolulu spreads along 6 mi. of oceanfront southeast of Pearl Harbor, hemmed in by the Koolau Range. **Waikiki Beach** tans near Diamond Head, the island's southernmost extremity; the downtown area clusters three mi. west. With the exception of the Leeward Coast and Kaena Point, well-maintained highways circle the rest of the coast and pierce the central valley.

Honolulu

As the cultural, commercial and political focal point of modern Hawaii, the city of Honolulu is a schizophrenic mix of high-rise buildings and white sand beaches, business suits and bikinis. Trade winds keep Honolulu free of stagnant pollution, and the pleasant climate brightens this prosperous urban environment. Waikiki, the world's quintessential vacation destination, is a great place to people-watch and enjoy the sun, if you can find space to spread your towel.

Honolulu's temperate weather influences the lifestyle of its residents. Even in rush hour, motorists retain an amazingly friendly disposition toward fellow drivers. In the office, informal dress (Hawaiian shirts are *de rigeur*) is the rule. At night, the city vibrates with transient revelers, to whom residents pander by peddling everything from party cruises to the odd sexual favor. Neither is likely to be a bargain, but hell, you're on vacation.

Practical Information and Orientation

Emergency: 911

Hawaii Visitors Bureau, 2270 Kalakaua Ave., 7th Floor, Honolulu 96815 (923-1811). Information on Oahu and the rest of the state. Pick up the *Accommodation Guide,* the *Restaurant Guide,* a map of points of interest, and a walking tour of downtown Honolulu. All are free. Most brochures, including the *Accommodation Guide* and the *Restaurant Guide*, contain info for travelers with disabilities. Also publishes the *Aloha Guide to Accessibility* for persons with mobility impairments. Open Mon.-Fri. 8am-4:30pm. **Information centers** located in both the overseas and inter-island air terminals and at the Ala Moana Shopping Center. **Department of Parks and Recreation,** 650 S. King, Honolulu 96817 (587-0300), disperses information and permits for county parks. Open Mon.-Fri. 7:45am-4pm. Permits available no earlier than 2 weeks in advance. **Department of State Parks,** 1151 Punchbowl St., Honolulu 96813 (548-7455). Information, trail maps, and permits for camping in state parks. Open Mon.-Fri. 8am-4pm.

Public Transport: 848-5555. Buses traverse the entire island, but call to avoid getting stuck somewhere remote. Free Honolulu/Waikiki route maps available at tourist pamphlet stands throughout Waikiki. Fare $.60. The way to go on Oahu.

Taxi: Sida, 439 Kalewa St. (836-0011). All cabs charge $.25 per 1/7 mi. Base rates about $1.75. Airport to Waikiki $19.

Car Rental: Try **Tropical Rent A Car,** airport (957-0800). $19 per day, $5 surcharge for those between 21 and 25. Another local company, **Discover Rent A Car,** 1920 Ala Moana Blvd. (949-4767), offers rented cars for $13 the first day, and $17 the next 2 with a 3-day min. **Alamo** rents to those 21 and over with major credit card. **Budget** rents to those 18-25 for $20 extra. All major agencies are on the island.

Moped and Bike Rentals: Mopeds get great mileage and are an exciting way to see the island. **Aloha Funway Rentals,** 1778 Ala Moana (942-9696) and 2976 Koapakapaka St. (834-1016), near the airport. Mopeds $16 per half day, $20 per day, $75 per week; bikes $13.50 per day. Open daily 8am-5pm. **Inter-Island Rentals,** 353 Royal Hawaiian Ave. (946-0013). Must be 18 with cash or credit card deposit and valid driver's license. Mopeds $25 per day, $100 per week. Bikes $15 per day. Open daily 8am-5:30pm.

Water Equipment Rentals: Ohana Rentals, near the breakers at Queen's Beach, rents boogie boards and fins ($15 per day). Open daily 8am-6pm. **Star Beachboys,** Kuhio Beach, to the left of the pavilion. Canoe rides $7, surfboard lessons $25 per hr., boogie boards $5 per hr. **Snorkel Bob's,** 702 Kapahulu Ave. (735-7944) is *the* place for snorkel equipment rentals. Decent equipment is $15 per week—$30 per week gets you higher quality equipment.

Gay Information Services: Gay and Lesbian Community Center, 1820 University Ave., 2nd floor (951-7000). See also the Practical Information section of Hawaii.

Help Lines: Information and Referral Service 275-2000. **Gay and Lesbian Information Services 24-hr. Hotline,** 926-1000 Provides info about services and community events on Oahu.

Post Office: Main Office, 3600 Aolele Ave. (423-3990). Near the airport. Open daily 8am-4:30pm. **ZIP Code:** 96813.

The **H-1 Freeway** stretches the length of Honolulu. Downtown Honolulu is about six blocks long and four blocks wide, wedged between Honolulu Harbor and Punchbowl Street. In Waikiki, **Ala Wai Boulevard, Kuhio Avenue,** and **Kalakaua Avenue** run parallel to the ocean and are the main routes of transit. Bike and running abound in the city.

Accommodations

Finding a reasonably priced room in Honolulu is a surmountable challenge. Check for housing specials in the *Honolulu Advertiser,* available on most street corners for $.35, for good deals. B&Bs are also viable lodging alternatives. See the General Introduction to this book for more info on B&Bs.

Polynesian Hostel, 212 Hawaiian Colony Bldg., 1946 Ala Moana Blvd. (949-3382). From the airport, take the Airport Motorcoach direct. Co-ed dorm rooms, each with kitchen, cable TV, and A/C. To deter islanders from taking advantage of cheap rates, Tina asks her guests to present passport during check-in. Laundry. Staff on call 24 hrs. Check-in and check-out 10am. Bunks $15, per week $100. Hostel not licensed as of June 1992.

Honolulu International Hostel (HI/AYH), 2323A Seaview Ave., (946-0591), 1½ mi. north of Waikiki, near University of Hawaii at Manoa. By car, take University Ave. exit off H-1. By bus, take #6 from Ala Moana Shopping Center, to Metcalf and University Ave. (near Burger King). Common area, rec room with TV and free movies. Beds guaranteed for 3 nights; if you want to stay longer in Honolulu, the management can usually arrange to move you to the Hale Aloha Hostel. Lights out at 11pm; rooms are locked from noon-4:30pm. Members $10, nonmembers $13. Sheet sack rental $1. Reservations recommended year-round.

Hale Aloha Hostel (HI/AYH), 2417 Prince Edward St. (926-8313), in Waikiki, 2 blocks from the beach. Members only. Beds guaranteed for 3 nights. Open daily 8am-noon and 5-9pm. Lights out at 11pm, but no curfew. Dorm bunks $11.50 per night, nonmembers $14.50. Studio doubles for $26. Reservations required.

Royal Grove Hotel, 151 Uluniu Ave. (923-7691). Clean, simple, carpeted rooms close to Waikiki Beach. Single or double room with bath, TV, and fridge $38; with kitchenette $43.

Big Surf, 1690 Ala Moana Blvd. (946-6525), near Ala Moana Canal. Sparse and slightly gloomy, but the gate is always locked and only guests have keys. Suites for up to 4 people with twin beds and a sofabed, full kitchen, color TV. Sept. 15-Dec. 15 and Feb. 15-June 15 $45; $65 other times. Studios with patio for one or two people, $35 low season, $39 high and $42 with TV.

YMCA, 401 Atkinson Dr. (941-3344), across from Ala Moana Shopping Center downtown. Men over 18 only, caters to a lot of semi-permanent residents. Check in or out at noon. Singles $29, with bath $36. Doubles $35, with bath $50.

Camping on Oahu is less convenient than on the other islands. Campgrounds are located in rural areas, and native Hawaiians often consider the campgrounds *their* domain, especially on Oahu's western shore. Four state parks and 13 county parks allow camping. For free required **permits** contact the Department of Parks and Recreation (see Practical Information). In Honolulu, tent camping is allowed at two state parks, **Sand Island** and **Keaiwa Heiau State Recreation Area** (5-day max. stay). Apply at the Division of Land and Natural Resources (see Practical Information). Sand Island, outside of Honolulu Harbor, offers flat camping. Take Sand Island Access Rd. from Nimitz Hwy. (Rte. 92). Keaiwa Heiau State Recreation Area, at the end of Aiea Heights Dr. (488-6626), has forest sites a short hike from the ruins of the *heiau hoosola* ("temple of healing").

Food

Eating in Honolulu can be an international dining experience. There's no reason to eat in Waikiki—if you're trapped there try the **Waikiki Shopping Plaza.** The neighborhoods surrounding Waikiki support many inexpensive restaurants that avoid the corny tourist ambience. A variety of ethnic restaurants, including Hawaiian, Japanese, Thai, and French, are located between the 500 and 1000 blocks of **Kapahulu Avenue** and in the surrounding area. Catch bus #2 going up Kapahulu Ave. from the Diamond Head area of Waikiki.

Travelers to Waikiki will be deluged with ads and flyers recommending *luaus.* These Brady Bunch-style feasts replete with Polynesian dancing rake in the tourist bucks and are often pretty cheesy, but some can be fun and belly-filling (and a few are even reasonably priced). The **Queen Kapiolani,** 150 Kapahulu Ave. (922-1941), offers a $11 unlimited *luau* luncheon buffet with entertainment (Mon.-Weds. and Fri.-Sat. 11am-2pm.)

Ono Hawaiian Food, 726 Kapahulu Ave., Waikiki (737-2275), next to the Ala Wai golf course. Family-style restaurant that lives up to its name *(ono* means good). Try the *poi* or *opihi* (limpets) if you're adventurous. Go early. The lines often extend out the front door. *Kalua* plate $5.75. Combination plate $7.75. Open Mon.-Sat. 11am-7:30pm.

Rainbow Drive-In, 3308 Kanaina Ave. (737-0177). Probably the best plate lunches around. Heaps and heaps of tasty local food. Plate lunches come on a bed of rice and macaroni salad. Try the mixed plate of Hawaiian-style barbecued pig, boneless chicken and *mahi mahi* for $4.35. Open 8am-9pm.

Leonard's Bakery, 933 Kapahulu Ave. (737-5591). A fabulous bakery, this Hawaiian institution has served hot *malasadas* (a Portuguese dessert) for years. Leonard's *malasadas* are, quite simply, the best on this planet ($.65); you'll forget that you were ever on a diet. Virtually a landmark. Open daily 6am-10pm.

Patti's Kitchen, Makai Market, Ala Moana Shopping Center (946-7214), also in the Windward Mall in Kaneohe. Build your own buffet-style Chinese plate lunches ($5-6). Also has a counter selling *dim sum.* An incredible bargain; apparently Elizabeth Taylor has eaten here, and when you see the portions you won't be surprised. Open Mon.-Sat. 9:30am-9pm, Sun. 10am-5pm.

Ruffage Natural Foods, 2443 Kuhio Ave. (922-2042). Serves up great vegetarian classics to go: tuna and avocado sandwich with sprouts and tomato ($5), large container of veggie-chili with brown rice ($3.25). Stop in for sushi at the sushi bar. Open Mon.-Sat. 8:30am-7pm, Sun. 10am-6pm. Sushi bar open daily from 5:30-10pm.

Sights and Activities

The one-hour loop on the #14 bus cuts across a sampling of Honolulu's diverse neighborhoods. Waikiki is, of course, centered on Waikiki Beach; Kaimuke and Kapahula are small, close-knit communities; Moliliili's lifeblood is the university; and downtown pulses the shipping and business district, alongside Chinatown.

In the 1950s, the image of a 3/4-mi. crescent of white sand beach set against the profile of Diamond Head lured platoons of vacationers and honeymooners, eager to spend their post-war boom bucks, to wonderful Waikiki. Today, more savvy visitors spend time on the less crowded isles. Nevertheless, despite its glitzy façade, Waikiki remains fascinating. **Waikiki Beach,** actually comprised of several smaller beaches, is lined with shops and hotels of all varieties and is generally crammed with tourists. Furthest to the east is the **Sans Souci Beach,** with no showers or public restrooms. The **Queen's Surf Beach,** closer to downtown, attracts swimmers and roller skaters. The area to the left of the snack bar is a popular tanning spot for gay travelers. At the far end of the beach, **Fort de Russy Beach Park** features the liveliest games of two-player beach volleyball this side of Orange County, CA.

When you want a break from sun and surf, hike the one mi. into the **Diamond Head Crater.** To get there, take bus #58 from Waikiki. Bring a flashlight to guide you through the pitch-dark section of the tunnel. The view of Waikiki is spectacular. If the gods do not favor your excursion to Diamond Head try visiting the **Damien Museum,** 330 Ohua St. (behind the St. Augustine Church; 923-2690), for a peek at the dark side of Hawaii's past. With original documents and a one-hour video, the museum displays the history of Father Damien's Molokai leper colony. (Open Mon.-Fri. 9am-3pm, Sat. 9am-noon. Free.) For the animal inside you, the **Honolulu Zoo,** 151 Kapahulu Ave. (971-7175), across from Kapiolani Park, is located on the east end of Waikiki. Call for a recorded schedule of events. ($4, under 13 free. Open daily 8:30am-4pm.)

Across the street is the **Waikiki Shell,** home to the **Kodak Hula Show** (833-1661), which is Waikiki at its photogenic tackiest. This production packages *hula* dancing and palm tree climbing into bite-size tourist portions. You may have discombobulating Brady Bunch flashbacks, but it *is* a laugh. (Shows Tues.-Thurs. at 10am. Free.) For more authentic dancing performances, contact the **Hawaii Visitor's Bureau** (923-1811) and ask about any upcoming performances or competitions among the **hula halau** (schools).

Several cultural and historic attractions are found around downtown. The **Iolani Palace,** at King and Richard St. (522-0832), was first the residence of King Kalakaua and his sister Queen Liliuokalani and later served as the nerve center in the TV show *Hawaii Five-0.* The deposed Liliuokalani spent nine months here as a prisoner. The fabulous palace displays sumptuously carved *koa* furniture and elegant European décor. (Tours Weds.-Sat. every 15 min. 9am-2:15pm. 45-min. tours by reservation only at the barracks in the palace grounds. Tours $4, ages 5-12 $1, under 5 not admitted.) Nearby, the **Honolulu Academy of Arts,** 900 S. Beretania St. (538-1006), houses one of the finest collections of Asian art in the U.S. The 30 galleries and six garden courts also display 17th-century samurai armor, African art, and temporary exhibits. (Open Tues.-Sat. 10am-4:30pm, Sun. 1-5pm. Tours Tues.-Weds. and Fri.-Sat. at 11am, Thurs. at 2pm, and Sun. at 1pm. Free.) The **Bishop Museum,** 1525 Bernice St. (848-4129), in Kalihi, houses a well-respected, albeit disorganized, collection of artifacts from the Indo-Pacific region. It is the best Hawaiiana museum in the world, and deserves a good portion of your day. Their **planetarium** features a show entitled "Journey by Starlight" (daily at 11am and 2pm, Fri.-Sat. at 8pm) which projects the history of Polynesian celestial navigation. Take bus #2 from ("School St.") from Waikiki. (Open daily 9am-2:30pm; call 848-4106 for further information. Museum open Mon.-Sat. 9am-5pm. $5, ages 6-16 $2.50.)

Fifty-two years ago on December 7th, a stunned nation listened to the reports of the Japanese obliteration of the U.S. Pacific Fleet in **Pearl Harbor.** The **U.S.S. Arizona National Memorial** (422-2771) is an austere, three-part structure built over the sunken aircraft carrier hull in which over a thousand servicemen perished. Count on long lines. (Free tours 7:45am-3pm. Launches out to the hull every 15 min. No children under six years of age or under 45 inches tall are admitted on the launch. The **Visitors Center** is open Tues.-Sun. 7am-5pm. Take bus #20 from Waikiki or the #50, 51, or 52 from Ala Moana, or the $2 shuttle (839-0911) from major Waikiki hotels.)

One of the best dayhikes on the island begins *mauka* at the end of Manoa Rd. and trails through one mi. of lush tropical greenery to **Manoa Falls**. Once there you can take a cold, fresh-water dip in the pool under the falls. Take bus #5 from Waikiki to the end of Manoa Rd. Disembark to catch the bird shows in **Paradise Park,** 3737 Manoa Rd. (988-0200), a natural Hawaiian rainforest sheltering hundreds of tropical birds, some of which perform their own musical compositions daily. (Open daily 9:30am-5pm. Call for shows. Admission $15, ages 8-13 $10, 3-7 $8.)

Parallel to the Manoa Valley, the **Pali Highway** (Rte. 61) winds its way through **Nuuanu Valley** and over into Kailua, on the windward side of the island. On the way, stop at the **Pali Lookout.** Here, Kamehameha the Great consolidated his kingdom by defeating Oahu's soldiers and driving them over this cliff. Although this observation point is always packed with tourists, the view overlooking the windward side is undoubtedly one of the finest in all of the islands. Hang onto your hat—the wind can gust hard.

Entertainment

Bars, restaurants, and theaters abound in Waikiki, making nightlife about as wild as your feet, liver, and wallet can take. The University of Hawaii's **Hemenway Theatre** (948-8111), in the Physical Sciences Building, shows second-run films for $3.50. Don't miss the Honolulu Zoo's "wildest show in town" summer series of Wednesday night entertainment (923-7723). Admission is free starting at 4:30pm, and performances begin at 6pm.

Pink Cadillac, 478 Ena (942-5282). One of the few dancing options for the 18-21 crowd, featuring cutting-edge progressive music. Open 9pm-1:45am. Under 21 cover $15; 21 and over $5, Thurs.-Sat. $6.

Anna Bananas, 2440 S. Beretania (946-5190), near the university. On Tues. and Sat. nights skank to the Pagan Barbies. The crowd is generally local bikers and surfers with a liberal sprinkling of college students. Don't miss the exceedingly tastefully decorated bathrooms. Steinlager on draft $2.25. Open until 2am.

Hula's Bar and Leis, 2103 Kuhio Ave. (923-0669), at Kalaamoku. Popular gay bar. Dark and intimate. No cover. Open daily 10am-2am.

Moose McGillycuddy's Pub & Café, 1035 University Ave. (944-5525), near the university (also at 310 Lewers St., 923-0751, near the hostels). Get loose with the moose. Student domain serving huge sandwiches for lunch and dinner. Pub happy hour offers draft beer and magaritas. Must be 21 for the disco after 9pm Tues. and Sat. only. No cover. Happy hour 4-8pm. Open Mon.-Sat. 11:30am-2am, Sun. 10am-2am.

The Wave, 1877 Kalakaua Ave. (941-0424), on the edge of Waikiki. A fine locale for loud music and dancing. Mixed crowd. Open daily 9pm-4am.

The Other Side of the Island

Everything on Oahu outside Honolulu is considered "the other side." Concrete and glass quickly transmogrify into pineapple and sugarcane fields sprinkled with small outlying communities. A tour of the island can be done in five hours, but it's best to leave yourself at least a day. Start on the Windward Coast and work your way around the perimeter. To reach the southern **Windward Coast,** take bus #55 from Ala Moana. To see the **North Shore,** hop on bus #52 at Ala Moana. Both buses run every hour daily from 7am until 6pm.

Miles of beaches and rural towns span the 40-mi. stretch of the Windward Coast, running from **Laie** in the north to **Mokapu Point** in the south. This is one of the most scenic drives on the island, and good snorkeling abounds. From Waikiki, take **Kalanianaole Highway** (Rte. 72) east to **Koko Head Crater.** Some of the most colorful fish and best snorkeling in the Pacific reside in **Hanauma Bay.** A 10-minute walk to the left of the bay brings you to the less well-known **Toilet Bowl**—you supply the joke about the name. Climb in when it's full and get flushed up and down as waves fill and empty the chamber through natural lava plumbing. One mi. farther, similar plumbing drives the **Halona Blow Hole** to release its spray. **Secret Beach,** to the right of Halona Blow Hole, was the site of Burt Lancaster and Deborah Kerr's famous "kiss in the sand" in *From Here to Eternity.* If you want your life to imitate art (or Burt), be our guest.

Sandy Beach, just beyond Halona, is a prime spot for bodysurfing and boogieboarding, the center of the summer surf circuit, and a year-round hangout for locals. **Makapuu Beach,** 41-095 Kalanianaole Hwy., is another prime place to bodysurf, but when the lifeguards put up red flags, stay out of the water. For novices, the best bodysurfing can be found at **Sherwoods** and, on weekends, at **Bellows Air Force Base.** Both are on Kalanianaole on the road to Kailua. Be warned, however, that neither of these parks provides lifeguards. Kalanianaole ends by intersecting **Kailua Road.** Follow this road toward **Kailua Town** and **Kailua Beach Park.** This is prime sailboarding territory. The sandy beach and strong, steady onshore winds are perfect for learning waterstarts. **Windsurfing Hawaii** (261-6067) rents beginner boards in the parking lot for $30 per day (harness $5 extra) and shortboards for $40 per day. They also have boogie boards ($10 per day), wave skis ($25 per day) and two-person kayaks ($35 per day). Sailboarding lessons run $35 per person for a three-hour group clinic. If you can bear the airborne grit, this is a great place to swim.

Dig the **Valley of the Temples,** 47-200 Kahekili Hwy., a burial ground matching the Punchbowl for beauty. The serene **Byodo-In Temple,** with tropical gardens and a three-ton brass bell, can be found on the grounds. (Open daily sunrise to sunset. Admission to the valley $2 per person.) Right around the bend from **Punaluu** is the entrance to **Sacred Falls Park.** The falls and the pool underneath make the two-mi. hike from the parking lot worthwhile. Farther up the coast, the city of **Laie** is home to the **Polynesian Cultural Center,** 55-370 Kamehameha Hwy. (293-3333), a carefully recreated village representing the indigenous cultures of New Zealand, Samoa, Tonga, Fiji, Hawaii, Tahiti, and the Marquesas. (Open Mon.-Sat. noon-6:30pm for daytime activities. Dinner served 4:30-7pm, followed by an evening spectacle 7:30-9pm. $25, with dinner and show $40.)

Fruit vendors and drive-in restaurants with plate lunches and shaved ice speckle the Windward Coast. **Kaaawa Country Kitchen and Grocery,** 51-480 Kamehameha Hwy. (237-8485), Kaaawa, across from Swana Beach Park, has kept the locals of Kaaawa satisfied for more than 30 years. (Open Mon.-Fri. 6am-2:30pm, Sat.-Sun. 6am-3:30pm.) **Bueno Nalo,** 41-865 Kalanianaole Hwy. (259-7186), in Waimanalo, serves flavorful Mexican meals ($6.25-7.75). (Open Tues.-Fri. 5-9pm, Sat.-Sun. 3-9pm.) The budget traveler's best lodging bet is the **Backpacker's Vacation Inn and Plantation Villas,** 59-788 Kamahameha Hwy. (638-7838), 1/4-mi. north of Waimea Bay, with a young and rowdy crowd, weekend BBQs, and free snorkeling equipment. (Bunks $14-16, doubles $35-45. 3-night min. stay.) However, the buses provide reliable enough transportation to make it a day trip. Your best camping option is **Malaekahana State Recreation Area** (293-1736), north of Laie, ranger-patrolled for safety. At low tide, wade across the water to **Mokuauia Island,** a bird refuge and great picnic spot. Bear in mind that escalating tension between locals and tourists may make some beach parks unsafe. Those on the Windward Coast are probably your best choice.

Home to the sugar cane fields and surfers, the **North Shore** and Central Oahu are different worlds from Honolulu (and most other parts of the world). The pace is slow and peaceful in the summer, with beautiful sunsets and plenty of empty beaches. Things heat up in the winter when the surfer crowd descends to shred the infamous waves along **Sunset Beach** and the **Banzai Pipeline,** and the North Shore hops with surfing competitions and their concomitant bikini contests.

The action on the North Shore centers on **Haleiwa,** the surfers' Graceland. Haleiwa once was a plantation town, but now is enlivened by surf shops and art galleries. **Hawaii Surf and Sail,** 66-214 Kamehameha Hwy. (637-5373), rents all kinds of watersport equipment and gives surfing and sailboarding lessons ($30 per 2-hr. lesson). To the North of Haleiwa is **Waimea Beach Park,** where locals jump off a high rock formation into the sea daily at 11am, 12:30, 2, 2:45, and 3:30pm.

On the way home, take a poke around the **Dole Pineapple Pavilion,** 64-1550 Kamehameha Hwy. (621-8468). Displays offer the visitor a crash course on the ins and outs of pineapple breeding. Inside you can buy classy pineapple memorabilia, from t-shirts to the puzzling Dole Whip. Be sure to drink some of the free pineapple juice flowing from the plastic pineapple in the corner. Also drop by the **Coffee Gallery,** 66-250 Kam. Hwy. (637-5571), and try their vegetarian chili ($1.75-$2.95) or a thirst-quenching ice coffee ($1). (Open Mon.-Fri. 6am-9pm, Sat.-Sun. 7am-9pm.)

When you get hungry, park at the **Country Drive-In,** 66-200 Kam. Hwy. (637-9122), in Haleiwa, which offers 20 varieties of plate lunches ($4-5), *shaka min,* and yummy smoothies. (Open 7am-6pm.) **The Sugar Bar and Restaurant,** 67-069 Kealohanui (637-6989), is a classic dive, with bikers, surfers, locals, and occasional area bands, and without a cover. Open 11pm-2am.

LET'S GO: CANADA

Canada is the second largest country in the world (after Russia), but one of the most sparsely populated. Ten provinces and two territories sprawl over more than 9,000,000 square km of land, spanning seven time zones. But numbers don't tell Canada's story, geography does. Framed by the rugged Atlantic coastline to the east and the Rockies to the west, Canada spreads north from fertile farmland and urbanized lakeshores to barren, frozen tundra.

The name Canada derives from the Huron-Iroquois world "kanata," meaning "village" or "community." However, the Canadian community is anything but unified. Periodically, ethnic, linguistic and cultural tensions flare into actual conflict. The division between Canada's two dominant cultures—the French and the English—is so strong that Canadian society has been described as "two solitudes." Although the grounds of the conflict shift from linguistic to philosophical, from religious to economic, it persists. Recently, the collapse of the Meech Lake Accord—which would have given French-speaking regions such as Québec Province increased autonomy—has strengthened *québécois* separatist movements.

Another persistent schism is that which divides the dominant Euro-colonist cultures and the aboriginal tribes. Treatment of Native Americans in Canada historically has not been much better than in the United States. A recent headline-grabbing conflict involved *québécois* Mohawks, who spent weeks under police siege after they armed themselves to prevent sacred burial grounds from being converted into a golf course.

The division between West and East also tears at the Canadian fabric. French monarchists and English tories settled the Eastern provinces; their intellectual descendants in the politically dominant provinces of Ontario and Québec are comfortable with Canada's active federal government. But the Western provinces probably have more in common with America's libertarian West—from which came many of their settlers—than with the rest of Canada; here, opposition parties led by anti-government politicos such as Preston Manning are growing in popularity.

Finally, the blurring between the United States and Canada must be mentioned. (Although our book is called *Let's Go: USA* while including most of Canada as well, we do *not* think the Canadian provinces are part of the U.S.) The U.S./Canadian border is the largest—and perhaps the most irrelevant—undefended border in the world. Canadian nationalists have become concerned that the ubiquity of American culture and mass communication in the provinces threatens the survival of indigenous attributes; steps have been taken to protect genuine Canadian media and cultural products from Americanization. At the same time, recent approval of a free trade pact between the United States and Canada has further eroded the distinctions between the two national identities.

Holidays

Canadians celebrate both national and provincial holidays. All government offices and most businesses close on national holidays, except on Easter Monday and Remembrance Day. Check local newspapers for a list of what is and isn't open. For a list of the major national holidays in 1993, see When to Go in the General Introduction to this book.

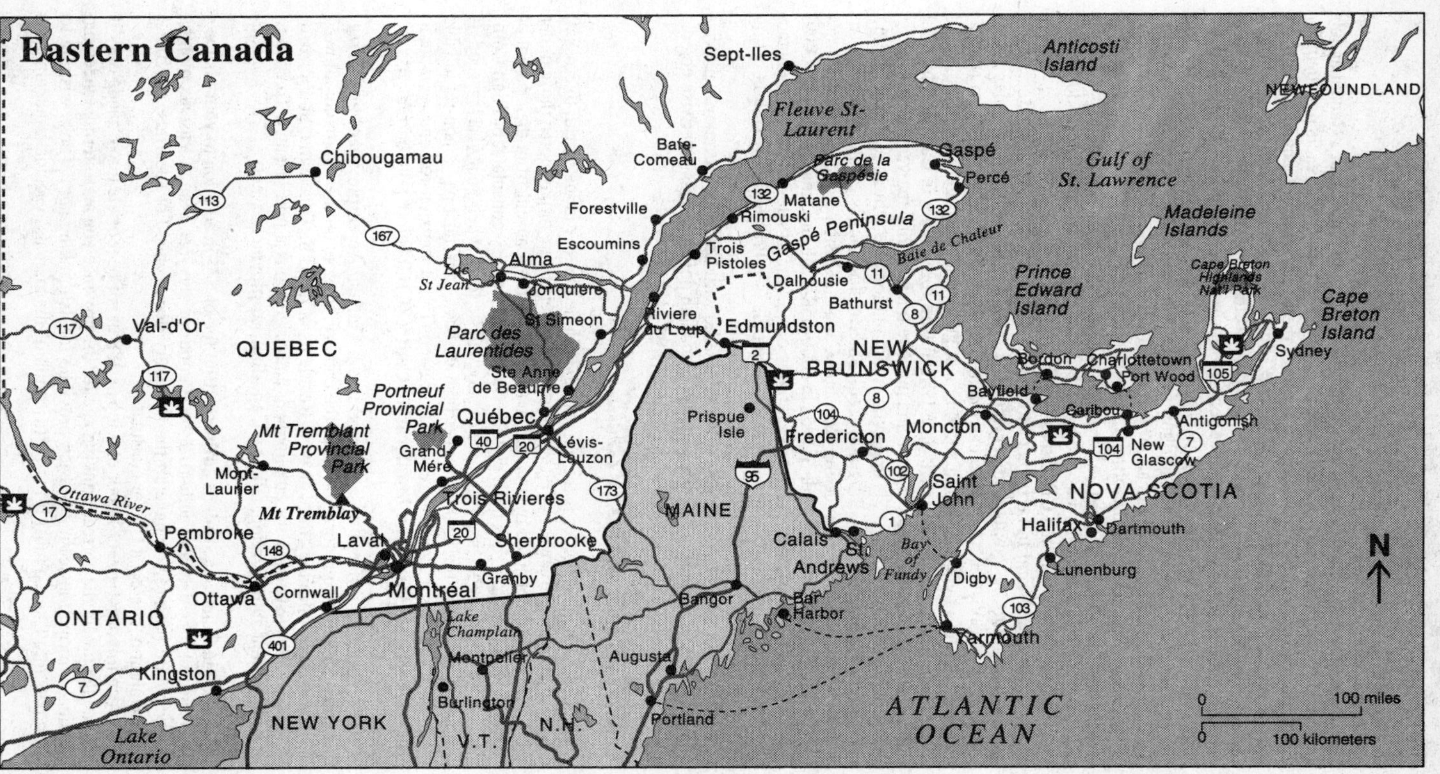
Eastern Canada
QUEBEC
ONTARIO
NEW YORK
MAINE
NEW BRUNSWICK
NOVA SCOTIA
NEWFOUNDLAND
V.T.
N.H.
Anticosti Island
Gulf of St. Lawrence
Madeleine Islands
Cape Breton Island
Cape Breton Highlands Nat'l Park
Prince Edward Island
Fleuve St-Laurent
Gaspé Peninsula
Parc de la Gaspésie
Baie de Chaleur
Bay of Fundy
ATLANTIC OCEAN
Lake Ontario
Lake Champlain
Ottawa River
Lac St Jean
Parc des Laurentides
Portneuf Provincial Park
Mt Tremblant Provincial Park
Mt Tremblay
Chibougamau
Val-d'Or
Mont-Laurier
Pembroke
Ottawa
Kingston
Cornwall
Laval
Montréal
Grand Mére
Trois Rivieres
Sherbrooke
Granby
Québec
Ste Anne de Beaupre
Lévis-Lauzon
St Simeon
Jonquière
Alma
Escoumins
Forestville
Baie-Comeau
Sept-Iles
Riviere du Loup
Trois Pistoles
Rimouski
Matane
Gaspé
Percé
Edmundston
Dalhousie
Bathurst
Fredericton
Moncton
Saint John
St Andrews
Calais
Bar Harbor
Bangor
Prispue Isle
Augusta
Portland
Burlington
Montpelier
Bayfield
Bordon
Charlottetown
Port Wood
Caribou
New Glascow
Antigonish
Sydney
Halifax
Dartmouth
Lunenburg
Digby
Yarmouth
117
113
167
17
7
148
401
40
20
173
132
2
95
104
11
8
102
1
103
105
N
0
100 miles
0
100 kilometers

Money

If you will be traveling between the U.S. and Canada, remember that a Canadian dollar and a U.S. dollar are identical in name only, and you will have to exchange them for the other country's currency when you go over the border. Many Canadian shops, as well as vending machines and parking meters, accept U.S. coins at face value (which is a small loss for you). Some stores will even convert the price of your purchase for you, but these tend to be located in more expensive tourist centers or border towns, and are under no legal obligation to offer you a fair exchange. Banks provide a reasonable exchange rate, but often charge a handling fee and shave off several percentage points; ATM **Cirrus** and **Plus** networks allow you to draw Canadian currency from American or British bank accounts at the official exchange rate. Exchange houses have the best rates and hours, with most open on weekends when banks close. During the past several years, the Canadian dollar has been worth 20 to 25% less than the U.S. dollar; the exchange rate hovers around CDN$6 to US$5.

Prices in general tend to be higher in Canada than in the U.S., as are taxes; you'll quickly notice the 7% **goods and services tax (GST)** and a comparable **sales tax** in some provinces. Visitors to Canada can claim a rebate of the GST they pay on accommodations of less than one month and on most goods they buy and take home, so be sure to save your receipts and pick up a GST rebate form while in Canada. The total claim must be at least CDN$7 of GST and must be made within one year of the date on which you purchased the goods and/or accommodations for which you are claiming your rebate. A brochure detailing numerous other restrictions is available from local tourist info booths or by contacting Revenue Canada, Customs and Excise Visitor's Rebate Program, Ottawa, Canada K1A 1J5 (800-668-4748 in Canada, 613-991-3346 outside Canada). Some provinces offer refunds of provincial sales tax as well; contact the Provincial Tourist Information Centres for details (see Practical Information listing of each province).

Symbols for dollars ($) and cents (¢) are the same with Canadian currency—all prices in the Canada section of this book are for Canadian dollars unless otherwise noted.

Customs and Visas

The U.S./Canadian border is the longest undefended border in the world; to cross it, U.S. visitors need only proof of citizenship (a birth certificate or passport); those under age 18 and unaccompanied by an adult must have written consent from their parent or guardian. Non-U.S. citizens must call the Canadian Embassy consulate, or High Commission, for a **visitor's visa.** Your time of stay will be fixed when your visa is issued. If you ask to remain in the country longer than 90 days, you must pay a non-refundable fee of $50, whether or not your request is granted. To get an extension once you are in Canada, apply at a **Canadian Immigration Centre (CIC)** before your current visa expires.

You will need a different visa for working in Canada. An **employment authorization** must be obtained before you enter the country; visitors ordinarily are not allowed to change status once they have arrived. Residents of the U.S., Greenland, St. Pierre, or Miquelon only may apply for employment authorization at a port of entry. To acquire an employment authorization, talk to a **Canadian Employment Centre (CEC)** or consulate.

To study in Canada, a **student authorization fee** of $75 in addition to your visitor's visa is necessary. A student authorization is good for one year. Plan at least six months in advance to be sure you have all the necessary documents. For specifics on official documentation, contact a CIC or consulate.

You can import 40 oz. of liquor or wine or 288 oz. of beer or ale into Canada only if you can document the correct drinking age for the province you are entering (check the Practical Information section of each province for its drinking age). Those wishing to bring pets into Canada must bring certification of the animals' vaccination against rabies. Drivers entering Canada should fill their gas tank before crossing the border; gas prices in Canada are about double that of the United States. Likewise, smokers should be aware that tobacco products are heavily taxed in Canada.

Visitors who spend at least 48 hours in Canada may take back to the U.S. up to US$400 worth of goods duty-free, including up to 100 non-Cuban cigars, one carton of cigarettes, and 32 oz. of liquor. U.S. residents who stay in Canada for fewer than 48 hours may return with US$25 worth of duty-free merchandise (40 oz. of alcohol, no tobacco). For information on bringing goods back into Canada after a trip in the U.S., see the Customs section in the General Introduction to this book, under Additional Information for International Visitors.

Getting There and Getting Around

Canada's border with the U.S.—its only international border—is easily accessible from Boston, New York City, Detroit, Chicago, Minneapolis/St. Paul, Seattle, and Alaska. Canada's highway system makes driving easy, even in remote areas of the country, although gas is twice as expensive as in the U.S. Because of excellent public transportation both within urban centers and throughout the country, even budget travelers can manage without a car. Canada has two official languages—English and French—but communication should not pose a problem if you speak only English, and Canadians are generally hospitable to visitors from all over the world.

By Train

VIA Rail handles all of Canada's passenger rail service. VIA Rail's routes are as scenic as Amtrak's and its fares are often more affordable. If you're traveling in the Québec City-Windsor corridor or in Atlantic Canada on any day but Fri. or Sun., a minimum five-day advance purchase will lower your fare by 40%; buy your ticket at least seven days in advance to get the same discount in those two regions for travel in the off-season (not near Christmas or in the summer). People over 60 and full-time students receive an automatic 10% discount. In the corridor, New Brunswick, and Nova Scotia, students receive a 50% discount with a minimum five-day advance purchase. Book well ahead—seats are snapped up quickly.

If you'll be traveling by train a great deal or across the rest of Canada as well, you may save money with the **Canrailpass,** which allows unlimited travel and unlimited stops for 30 days. Passes cost CDN$470 (US$377), tax included. (CDN$427 and US$343 for youths under age 24.) A number of discounts apply on full-fare tickets: children ages 2-11 accompanied by an adult (half-fare); students and senior citizens (10% discount); passengers with disabilities and their companions together are charged a single fare. For more information, call 800-561-7860.

Amtrak (800-426-8725) links with VIA Rail in Toronto and Montréal. For more info, contact VIA Rail Canada, P.O. Box 8116, Montréal, PQ H3C 3N3 (in Montréal 871-1331, in Québec City 692-3940, elsewhere in Québec 800-361-5390; in Toronto 366-8411, in Ottawa 238-8289, elsewhere in Ontario 800-361-1235; in western Canada 800-561-8630. In the U.S., contact a travel agent.)

By Bus, Car, and Bicycle

The major inter-provincial bus carriers are **Gray Coach, Greyhound, Voyageur,** and **Charterways.** Greyhound makes the most convenient links between the Canadian and U.S. bus networks. The **Trans-Canada Highway,** the world's longest national highway, stretches 8000 mi. from St. John's, Newfoundland to Victoria, British Columbia. In Canada, **automobile insurance** with coverage of CDN$200,000 is *mandatory.* If you are involved in a car accident and you don't have insurance, the stiff fine you will incur will not improve the experience. U.S. motorists are advised to carry the **Canadian Non-Resident Inter-Provincial Motor Vehicle Liability Card,** which is proof of coverage, available only through U.S. insurers. Drivers entering Canada from the U.S. also must carry a vehicle registration certificate. If the car is borrowed, have on hand a letter of permission from the owner; if rented, keep a copy of the rental contract for use when crossing the border. Radar detectors are illegal in Canada. British Columbia, Ontario, and Québec law requires that auto passengers wear seatbelts.

A valid **driver's license** from any country (including the U.S.) is good in Canada for varying amounts of time, depending on the region. Although international bridges, tunnels, and ferries charge a fee, highways are toll-free. Along the Trans-Canada Hwy., some toll-free ferries are part of the highway system and operate during daylight hours. In summer, cross early in the morning or late in the afternoon to avoid long waits.

If you plan to rent a car in Canada, investigate the discount **White-Corp** rate, offered to Hostelling International-Canada members over 21. In addition, agencies dealing in late-model automobiles rent cars throughout Canada for significantly less than their U.S. counterparts. You can contact one of the numerous **auto-transport agencies;** if you are 21, have a valid driver's license, and agree to travel at least 400 mi. per day on a reasonably direct route to the destination, you could have use of a car for the price of the gasoline. **Drive-rider matching agencies** may also cheapen your travel.

Rocky Mountain Cycle Tours, Box 1978, Canmore, AB T0L 0M0 (403-678-6770 or 800-641-2463), organizes bicycle tours in Alberta and British Columbia.

Student Travel

Air Canada (800-776-3000) offers a 51% discount for Canadians ages 12 to 21 flying standby in Canada. The **Canadian Federation of Student Services** sponsors a number of student travel assistance organizations. The **Studentsaver National Student Discount Program** provides 10 to 25% discounts on food, clothing, books, and other goods at some Canadian retail stores, with the **International Student Identity Card (ISIC),** available at most travel agencies. A list of outlets that give discounts, details on the program, and a great deal more advice for student and budget travelers is available at **Travel CUTS** (Canadian Universities Travel Service, Ltd.). A fully licensed national travel agency, CUTS will help you plan trips within Canada or to other countries. The federation also publishes *Canadian Student Traveler,* available free at Canadian universities.

Headquarters for CFS Services and Travel CUTS are at 187 College St., Toronto, Ont. M5T 1P7 (416-979-2406). Other Travel CUTS locations (all open regular business hours) include:

Montréal: McGill University Student Union, 3480 rue McTavish, Montréal, Québec H3A 1X9 (514-849-9201).

Toronto: 74 Gerrard St. E., Toronto, Ont. M5B 1G6 (416-977-0441).

Vancouver: Student Union Building, University of British Columbia, Vancouver, BC V6T 1W5 (604-822-6890). Downtown location at 501-602 W. Hastings (604-681-9136).

Victoria: Student Union Building, University of Victoria, Victoria, BC V8W 3P3 (604-721-6916).

Accommodations

The price of Canadian hotels, combined with the lack of budget motel chains, may force budget travelers toward the wilderness. Almost every city has homes that take travelers into their **Bed and Breakfasts** for $25 to $60. A similar but more structured lodging option is the **farm vacation.** Nightly rates begin at $25 for singles and $35 for doubles, although some require a minimum duration of one week (average rate about $250 per person). The family-oriented farm vacation system integrates guests into the daily life of farm families in the Maritimes (New Brunswick, Nova Scotia, and Prince Edward Island), Québec, and Ontario. Guests eat with the family and are encouraged to help with the chores. For travelers who prefer urban lodgings, the network of **YMCAs** and **YWCAs** in the larger cities offers clean and affordable rooms, generally in downtown areas. In summer, other budget choices include **university dorms,** open for travelers early to mid-May and closing mid- to late August.

Hostelling International-Canada (HI-C), formerly the **Canadian Hostelling Association (CHA),** was founded in 1933, and maintains over 70 hostels nationwide. Graded "basic," "simple," "standard," or "superior," hostels ($8-15 per night) have kitchens, laundries, and often meal service. Open to members and nonmembers, most hostels allow a maximum stay of three nights. For hostels in busy locations, reservations are recommended. In addition, hostelers must have a sleeping bag or "sleep-sheet"—two sheets sewn together; rentals are usually available for $1. HI-C generally upholds the same rules and rates as Hostelling International/American Youth Hostels (HI-AYH) (see the General Introduction to this book under Accommodations).

Members of HI-C receive a discount of approximately $1 to $4 on room rates and the opportunity to take advantage of concessions at many local businesses. Furthermore, HI-C membership includes membership in Hostelling International (formerly IYHF), which allows for discounts at hostels around the world. Likewise, HI memberships and non-expired IYHF memberships purchased in any country are valid in Canada. Memberships are valid for one calendar year from the date purchased. Annual membership costs $25, $12 for ages under 18. For information, write Hostelling International-Canada, 1600 James Naismith Dr., Gloucester, Ont. K1B 5N4 (613-748-5638).

Canada's **national** and **provincial parks** entice travelers with vast expanses of excellent **campgrounds.** National parks sprinkle Canada: 12 in western Canada, six in the central provinces, seven in the Atlantic Provinces, and four in the Yukon and Northwest Territories (all free). Both provincial and national parks prohibit campfires on the beach, and no camping is allowed in picnic parks.

For topographical and geographical maps, write to the **Canada Map Office,** 615 Booth St., Ottawa, Ont. K1A 0E9 (613-952-7000). For info on National Parks and Forests write to **Canadian Parks Service,** 220 4th Ave. S.E., #522, Calgary AB T2P 3HB (403-292-4401). The Winnipeg office of the Canadian Parks Service distributes *Parks West,* a book about all the national parks of Western Canada.

Telephones and Mail

The Canadian telephone system is essentially the same as that in the U.S., with seven-digit phone numbers, three-digit area codes, cheaper long-distance (LD) rates in the evening or on weekends, and 25¢ local calls (See Additional Information for International Visitors in the General Introduction to this book). Calls to the U.S. can be made as if the border did not exist.

Canada Post requires a 40¢ Canadian postage stamp for all domestic first-class mail. Letters or postcards sent to the U.S. cost 46¢; items mailed to Europe weighing less than 20g cost 80¢. Add a 7% tax on postage. Postal prices increase yearly; expect to pay a bit more in 1993. When sending mail to destinations within Canada, be sure to note the six-character **postal code** (of numbers and letters, e.g. A1B 2C3). The postal codes listed in the Practical Information sections are for **General Delivery** only, unless otherwise specified (for more information on General Delivery, see Keeping in Touch in the General Introduction to the book).

Measurements

Canadians use the metric system (as do all but two nations in the world). For residents of those anachronistic nations, simple conversions are as follows:

Distance: 1 centimeter (cm)=.394 inches (in.); 1 meter (m) = 3.281 feet (ft.) = 1.094 yards (yds.); 1 kilometer (km) = .621 miles (mi.).

Volume: 1 liter (l) = .2642 gallons (gal.).

Mass or Weight: 1 gram (g)= .0353 ounces (oz.); 1 kilogram (kg) = 2.2046 pounds (lbs.).

Alberta

The icy peaks and turquoise lakes of Banff and Jasper National Parks sparkle as Alberta's most sought-after landscapes. Alberta has much more—more farmlands, wheat fields and oil rigs, that is. Calgary transcended its just-another-prairie-town status when it hosted the XV Winter Olympics, and is perennially host to the wild and woolly Stampede. For a more detailed look at Alberta, see *Let's Go: Pacific Northwest, Western Canada and Alaska.*

Practical Information

Emergency: 911.

Capital: Edmonton.

Alberta Tourism, 10155 102nd St., Edmonton T5J 4L6 (800-661-8888, in AB 800-222-6501). **Provincial Parks Information,** Standard Life Centre #1660, 10405 Jasper Ave., Edmonton T5J 3N4 (427-9429). Information on Alberta's provincial parks. **Canadian Parks Service,** Box 2989, Station M, Calgary T2P 3H8 (292-4440). Information on the province's national parks (Waterton Lakes, Jasper, Banff and Wood Buffalo). **Alberta Wilderness Association,** P.O. Box 6398, Station D, Calgary T2P 2E1. Information on off-highway adventures.

Time Zone: Mountain (2 hr. behind Eastern). **Postal Abbreviation:** AB

Area Code: 403.

Banff National Park

Banff is Canada's best-known and best-loved preserve of natural beauty, offering 2543 square mi. (6600 square km) of peaks and canyons, white-foaming rapids and placid turquoise lakes, dense forests and open meadows. In summer, the overpriced, colorless townsite is overrun with visitors who prefer to admire nature "from a distance;" purists take refuge in the still-unsullied backcountry.

Practical Information and Orientation

Banff Information Centre, 224 Banff Ave. Includes **Chamber of Commerce** (762-8421) and **Canadian Parks Service** (762-4256). Open daily 8am-10pm; Oct.-May 10am-6pm. **Lake Louise Information Centre** (522-3833). Open mid-May-mid-June daily 10am-6pm; mid-June-Aug. 8am-10pm; Sept.-Oct. 10am-6pm. **Park Headquarters,** Superintendent, Banff National Park, P.O. Box 900, Banff T0L 0C0 (762-1500).

Greyhound: operates out of the Brewster terminal. To: Lake Louise (5 per day; $6.50) and Calgary (5 per day; $14.75). The Lake Louise buses continue to Vancouver ($89).

Brewster Transportation: 100 Gopher St. (762-6767), near the train depot. Specializes in tours of the area, but runs 1 express daily to Jasper ($36). Depot open daily 7:30am-midnight.

Taxis: Legion Taxi, 762-3353.

Car Rental: Banff Used Car Rentals, corner of Wolf and Lynx (726-3352). $34 per day. 150km free, 10¢ each additional km. Must be 18 with credit card. **Avis,** 209 Bear St. (762-3222). $44 per day. 100km free, 19¢ each additional km. HI-C member discount gives 50 extra km free. Must be 21 with major credit card.

Bike Rentals: Bactrax Rentals, 339 Banff Ave. (762-8177). Mountain bikes $3.50 per hr., $15 per day. Less for HI-C members. Open daily 8am-8pm.

Post Office: 204 Buffalo St. at Bear St. (762-2586). Open Mon.-Fri. 9am-5:30pm. **Postal Code:** T0L 0C0.

Area Code: 403.

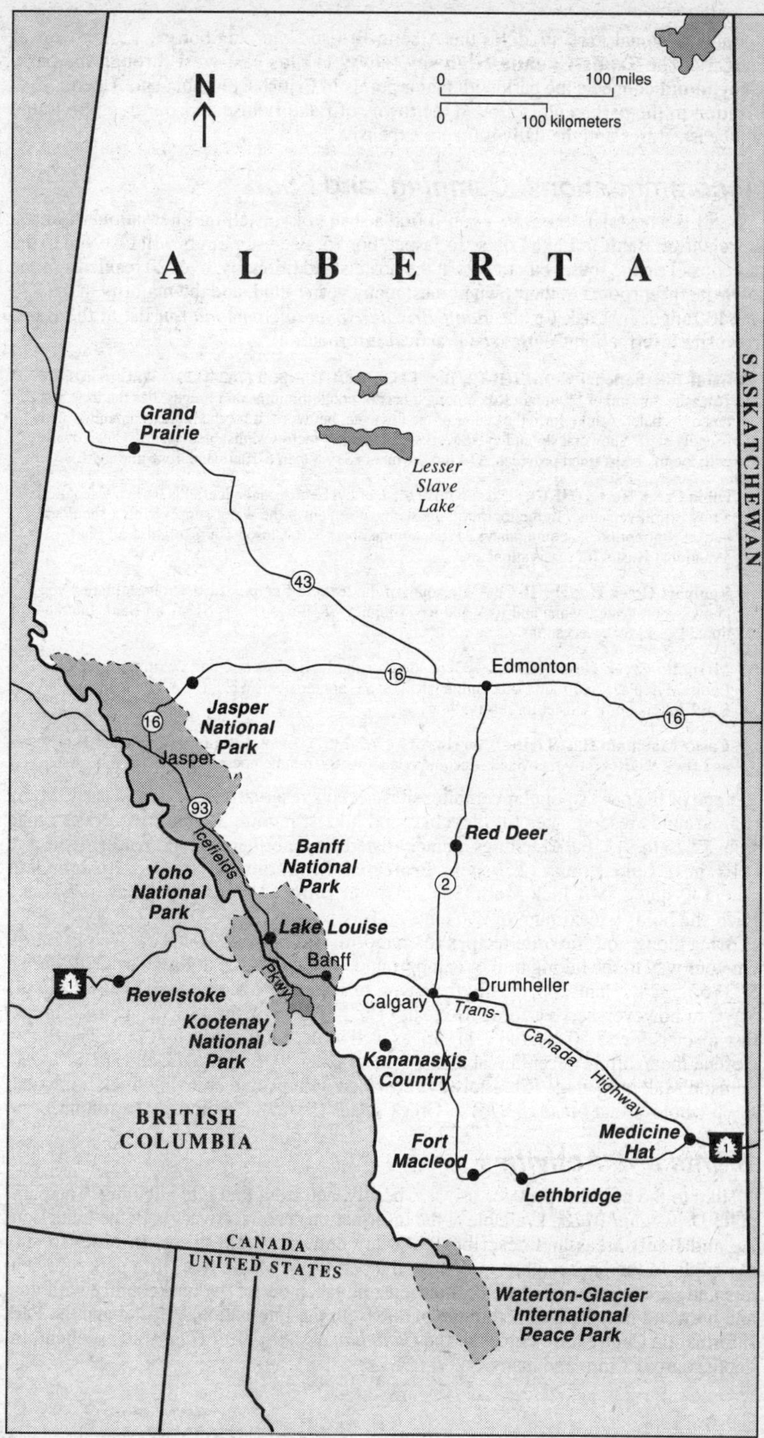
N
0
100 miles
0
100 kilometers
A L B E R T A
SASKATCHEWAN
Grand Prairie
Lesser Slave Lake
43
Edmonton
16
16
16
Jasper National Park
Jasper
93
Icefields
Red Deer
2
Banff National Park
Yoho National Park
Lake Louise
Banff
Pkwy
1
Revelstoke
Kootenay National Park
Calgary
Drumheller
Trans-Canada Highway
Kananaskis Country
BRITISH COLUMBIA
Fort Macleod
Medicine Hat
1
Lethbridge
CANADA
UNITED STATES
Waterton-Glacier International Peace Park

Banff National Park straddles the Alberta-British Columbia border, 120km west of Calgary. The **Trans-Canada Highway** (Hwy. 1) runs east-west through the park. **Greyhound** connects the park with major points in British Columbia and Alberta. Civilization in the park centers around the towns of Lake Louise and Banff, 55km to the southeast. Buses and the daily train are expensive.

Accommodations, Camping, and Food

Banff is a hostelers' heaven—you'll find a string of Hostelling International-Canada hostels from Banff to Lake Louise to Jasper. For $5, Brewster Tours will take you to the next hostel on the route; buy tickets at the hostels. Additionally, over 20 residents of the townsite offer rooms in their own homes; many year-round, and the majority in the $20 to $40 range. Just ask for the *Banff Private Home Accommodation* list at the Banff Townsite Information Centre (see Practical Information).

Banff International Hostel (HI-C), Box 1358, Banff T0L 0C0 (762-4122), 3km from Banff Townsite on Tunnel Mountain Rd., among a nest of condominiums and lodges, has the look and feel of a chalet. A hike from the center of the townsite, but worth it for the modern amenities and friendly staff. Showers, ski and cycle workshop, laundry facilities, disabled access. Clean quads with 2 bunk beds; linen provided. $14, nonmembers $19. Open 6-10am and 4pm-midnight.

Hilda Creek Hostel (HI-C), 8.5km south of the Icefield Centre on the Icefields Parkway, features a tiny primitive sauna. In the morning, guests must replenish the water supply with a shoulder-bucket contraption. Accommodates 21. $8, nonmembers $13. Closed Thurs. night. Call Banff International Hostel for reservations.

Rampart Creek Hostel (HI-C), 34km south of the Icefield Centre. The usual hostel fare—you know, wood-heated sauna and rock and ice-climbing. $8, nonmembers $13. Call Banff International Hostel for reservations.

Mosquito Creek Hostel (HI-C), 103km south of the Icefield Centre and 26km north of Lake Louise. Fireplace and sauna. Accommodates 38. $8, nonmembers $13. Closed Tues. night. Call Banff International Hostel for reservations.

Castle Mountain Hostel (HI-C), on Hwy. 1A (762-2367), 1.5km east of the junction of Hwy. 1 and Hwy. 93. Recently renovated. Accommodates 36. $9, nonmembers $14. Closed Wed. night.

None of the park's popular camping sites accepts reservations, so arrive early. Many campgrounds reserve sites for bicyclists and hikers; inquire at the office. Rates range from $7.25 to $13. Park facilities include (listed from north to south): **Waterfowl Lake** (116 sites), **Lake Louise** (221 sites), **Protection Mountain** (89 sites), **Johnston Canyon** (140 sites), **Two Jack Main** (381 sites) and **Tunnel Mountain Village** (622 sites). Each site holds a maximum of two tents and six people.

Bring along your favorite recipes for campfire cooking and you'll eat well in Banff. On your way to the hiking trail or campground, make a pitstop at **Safeway,** 318 Marten St. (762-5378), Banff, open daily from 8am to 10pm. The International Hostel and the YWCA, however, serve affordable meals. The hostel's cafeteria serves up great breakfast specials for $3.50 (served 7-11am), as well as decent dinners (5-10pm). The **Spray Café** at the Y offers decent breakfast specials ($2.25-5). **Laggan's Deli** (522-3574), in Samson Mall on Village Rd., is always crowded with people enjoying thick sandwiches on whole-wheat bread ($3.75) or Greek salads ($1.75). (Open daily 6am-8pm.)

Sights and Activities

Hike to the **backcountry** for privacy, beauty, and trout that bite anything. The pamphlet *Drives and Walks,* available at the information centers, covers both the Lake Louise and Banff areas and describes both day and overnight hikes. In order to stay overnight in the backcountry, you'll need a permit, available free from park info centers and park warden offices. All litter must be taken out of the backcountry with you, and no wood may be chopped in the parks. Both the International Hostel and the Park Information Centre have copies of the *Canadian Rockies Trail Guide,* an excellent, in-depth source of info and maps.

Two easy but rewarding trails within walking distance of the Banff townsite are **Fenland** and **Tunnel Mountain.** Fenland winds 2km through an area creeping with beaver, muskrat and waterfowl. (Follow Mount Norquay Rd. out of Banff and look for signs either at the bridge just before the picnic area or across the railroad tracks on the left side of the road.) The summit of Tunnel Mountain provides a spectacular view of Bow Valley and Mt. Rundle. (Follow Wolf St. east from Banff Ave. and turn right on St. Julien Rd. to reach the head of the 2.4km trail.)

About 25km out of Banff toward Lake Louise along the Bow Valley Parkway, **Johnston Canyon** offers a moderately taxing but popular half-day hike. The 1.1km to the Canyon's lower falls and the 2.7km to the upper falls consist mostly of a catwalk along the edge of the canyon. Don't stop here, though; if you proceed along the more rugged trail for another 3.1km, you'll see seven blue-green, cold-water springs known as the **Inkpots.** Your car will find **Tunnel Mountain Drive** and **Vermillion Lakes Drive** two particularly scenic places to cough gas fumes into Banff's clear air.

When Banff was established in 1885 to drum up business for the newly-built Canadian Pacific Railway, it was called Hot Springs Reserve, featuring **Cave and Basin Hot Springs**. In 1914, a resort went up at the springs. The refurbished resort, now called the **Cave and Basin Centennial Centre** (762-4900), screens documentaries and stages exhibits. Relax in the hot springs pool, watched over by lifeguards in unflattering pre-WWI bathing costumes, or explore the original cave. The center lies southwest of the city on Cave and Basin Rd. (Center open early June-Sept. daily 10am-7pm; Oct.-early June 10am-5pm. Pool open early June-Sept. only. Admission to pool $3, ages 3-16 $2.) If you find Cave and Basin's 32°C (90°F) water too cool, try the **Upper Hot Springs pool,** a 40°C (104°F) cauldron up the hill on Mountain Ave. (Cooler in spring during snow run-off. Open Mon.-Thurs. 12:30pm-9pm, Fri.-Sun. 8:30am-11pm. Admission $3, under 12 $2.) Bathing suit rental at either spring ($1.50), towel rental ($1) and locker rental (25¢) available.

The **Sulphur Mountain Gondola** (762-5438), located next to the Upper Hot Springs pool, affords a good view of Banff Townsite, and offers a $4.25 "early bird" breakfast special. (Open summer and Nov. 15-Dec. 15 daily 9am-8pm. $8.50, under 12 $3.75.) **Brewster Tours** (762-6767) offers an extensive array of bus tours with knowledgeable and entertaining guides. If you have no car, these tours may be the only way to see some of the main attractions, such as the spiral railroad tunnel bored into a mountain. (The trains are so long, you can see them entering and exiting the mountain at the same time.) If you were planning to take the regular Brewster bus from Banff to Jasper ($36), you may want to spend $25 more to see the sights in between. (One way $60, round-trip $83. Tickets can be purchased at the bus depot.)

Fishing is legal virtually anywhere you find water, but you must have a national parks fishing permit, available at the info center ($5 for a 7-day permit, $10 for an annual one). Those who prefer more vigorous water sports can raft the white waters of Kootenay River; **Kootenay River Runners** offer half- and full-day ($69) trips, as well as a more boisterous full-day trip on the Kicking Horse River ($69). Tickets are available at **Tickets** (762-5385), on the corner of Caribou St. and Banff Ave. A particularly good deal is offered through the Banff International Hostel—rafting on the Kicking Horse River (transportation included) for $40. A stop in a pub is promised afterwards.

The hilly road leading to Lake Minnewanka provides **cyclists** with an exhilarating trip, as do many other small paths throughout the park. Bicycling is also allowed on most trails in the Banff Townsite areas. Remember, however, to dismount your bike and stand to the downhill side if a horse approaches. Also be forewarned that bears are more likely to be surprised by a quick and quiet bicycle than by tromping hikers. Since **horseback riding** rates are almost identical throughout the park, pick your favorite location. Banff's bartenders contend that "the real wildlife in Banff is at the bars," but it's their job to say those kinds of things. Banff Avenue is lined with establishments where you can dance, cruise and drink 'til you barff.

North American filmmakers often use the crystal waters of **Lake Louise,** framed by snow-capped peaks, as a backdrop for "Swiss" alpine scenes. Rent a canoe from **Château Lake Louise Boat House** (522-3511) for $20 per hour; you can also rent binoculars to scan the hills for wildlife. Several hiking trails begin at the lake. The **Friendly**

Giant Sightseeing Lift (522-3555), which runs up Mt. Whitehorn across the Trans-Canada Hwy. from Lake Louise, provides another chance to ooh and aah at the landscape. (Open mid-June-late Sept. daily 9am-6pm. Fare $8, ages 5-11 $4. "One-way hiker's special" $5.50.)

Calgary

Calgary was founded in 1875 as the summer outpost of the Northwest Mounted Police. The discovery of oil in 1947 transformed this cowtown into a wealthy, cosmopolitan city, and in 1988 Calgary hosted the Winter Olympics. The oil may be crude, but the city is refined. Skyscrapers overshadow oil derricks, businesspeople scurry about, and a modern transport system threads soundlessly through immaculate downtown streets. But Calgary hasn't forgotten its frontier roots; when the Stampede yahoos into town in July, cowboy hats, Wranglers and Western accents are *de rigueur.*

Practical Information

Convention and Visitors Bureau, 237 8th Ave. S.E., Suite 200 (263-8510). Will help locate accommodations, especially around Stampede time in July. Open daily 8am-5pm. Three **Information centres** are scattered throughout the city, including one on the ground floor of Calgary Tower (open daily 8:30am-5pm) and one at the airport on the arrivals level (292-8477; open daily 7am-10pm). **Travel Alberta,** 455 6th St. S.W. (297-5038; in AB 800-222-6501), on the main floor. Open Mon.-Fri. 8:15am-4:30pm. **Trans-Canada Highway Office,** 6220 16th Ave. N.E. Open daily 8am-9pm; Sept.-June 10am-5pm. **Visitor Information Phone Line,** 262-2766.

Calgary International Airport: (292-8477), is about 5km northwest of the city center. Bus #57 provides sporadic service to the city. The **Airporter Bus** (291-3848) offers frequent and friendly service for $7.50. **Brewster Tours** (221-8242) operates a 12:30pm bus and a 5:45pm bus to Banff ($25) and a 12:30pm bus to Jasper ($47).

Greyhound: 877 Greyhoundway S.W. (265-9111 or 800-661-8747). Frequent service to Edmonton ($26) and Banff ($14.50). Free shuttle bus from C-train at 7th Ave. and 10th St. to bus depot runs every hr. 6:30am-7:30pm with additional buses at 9am, 6pm and 9pm. 10% senior discount.

Public Transport: Calgary Transit, 206 7th Ave. SW. Bus schedules, passes and maps. Open Mon.-Fri. 8:30am-5pm. Buses and streetcars (C-Trains). Buses run all over the city; C-Trains cover less territory, but they're free in the downtown area (along 7th Ave. S.; between 10th St. SW and City Hall). Fare $1.50, ages 6-14 90¢, under 6 free; exact change required. Day pass $4.50, kids $3. Book of 10 tickets $12, kids $8.50. **Information line** (276-7801) open Mon.-Fri. 6am-11pm, Sat.-Sun. 8:30am-9:30pm.

Taxi: Checker Cab, 272-1111. **Associated Cab,** 299-1111.

Car Rental: Rent-a-Wreck, 2339 Macleod Trail (287-9703). From $26 per day with 120 free mi. $14 per day surcharge for under 25. Open Mon.-Fri. 8am-7pm, Sat.-Sun. 9am-5pm. **Dollar** (221-1888 airport, 269-3777 downtown) rents from $37 per day with unlimited mi. Weekend special for $33 per day. Must be 23 with major credit card.

Bike Rental: Global Sports Rental, 7218 Macleod Trail S.W. (252-2055). $15-20 per day. **Abominable Sports,** 1217 11th Ave. S.W. (245-2812). Mountain bikes $25 per day.

Police: 316 7th Ave. S.E. (266-1234).

Post Office: 220 4th Ave. S.E. (292-5512). Label mail General Delivery, Station M, Calgary, AB T2P 2G8. Open Mon.-Fri. 8am-5:45pm. **Postal Code:** T2P 180.

Area Code: 403.

Accommodations

Calgary International Hostel (HI), 520 7th Ave. S.E. (269-8239). Conveniently located several blocks south of downtown with access to C-Train and public buses. Complete with snack bar, meeting rooms, cooking and barbecue facilities, laundry and a cycle workshop. Disabled access. Lockout 10am-4:30pm. Front desk closes at midnight. $12, nonmembers $16.

University of Calgary, 3330 24th Ave. (220-3203), in the N.W. quadrant of the city. A little out of the way, but very accessible via bus #9 or the C-Train. Olympian-sized rooms for competitive prices. Cafeteria and a pub on campus. Rooms available May-Aug. Room rental office, in the Kananaskis Hall, open 24 hrs. Singles $29, doubles $38. Student rate: singles $21, doubles $32. More lavish suites with private bathrooms are available in Olympus Hall or Norquay Hall for approximately $30; book through Kananaskis Hall.

YWCA, 320 5th Ave. S.E. (263-1550). As luxurious as a Y can be, in a fine quiet neighborhood. A range of rooms. The tradeoff for security is a somewhat lifeless lodging—men can't even visit. Cafeteria. Dorm beds $15. Singles $25, with bath $30. 10% senior discount.

St. Louis Hotel, 430 8th Ave. S.E. (262-6341), above the St. Louis Tavern. The few grim-looking long-term residents generally keep to themselves. Friendly management. Singles $18, with TV and bath $24.50. Doubles with bath and TV $30.

Sights

Ride to the top of the **Calgary Tower,** 101 9th Ave. S.W. (266-7171), for a spectacular view of the Rockies on clear days. ($3.75, kids $1.75.) The **Glenbow Museum,** 130 9th Ave. S.E. (264-8300), is just across the street. The proximate placement of such unrelated objects as 19th-century firearms, abstract paintings, and mineral samples endows the museum with the feel of a world's-most-expensive garage sale. (Open Tues.-Sun. 10am-6pm. Admission $3, seniors $1, students and kids $2, under 12 free. Free Sat.)

Five blocks west on 8th Ave. are the **Devonian Gardens.** Located on the fourth floor of the Toronto Dominion Sq. (at 3rd St. S.W.), this 2.5-acre indoor park contains fountains, waterfalls, bridges and over 20,000 plants, representing 138 different species. Budget travelers can reserve the Gardens for themselves for a mere $695 an hour. (Open daily 9am-9pm. Free.) A few blocks to the northwest, the **Energeum,** 640 5th Ave. S.W. (297-4293), in the lobby of the Energy Resources Building, is Calgary's paean to fossil fuel. A film in the upstairs theater effectively recreates the mania of Alberta's first oil find. In an interactive display, you can run a gloved hand through a pile of the oozing glop. (Open Sun.-Fri. 10:30am-4:30pm; Sept.-May Mon.-Fri. 10:30am-4:30pm. Free.)

Farther west, about 4.3 light-years from Alpha Centauri, warps the **Alberta Science Centre and Centennial Planetarium,** 11 St. and 7th Ave. S.W. (221-3700). Weekend laser shows feature music from the Rolling Stones and (of course) Pink Floyd. (Open daily 10am-9pm, closed Mon. and Wed. in winter. Admission to Planetarium and Science Centre $8, seniors $7, kids $4; Science Centre only $5, seniors $4, kids $3.50.)

The **Calgary Zoo** on **St. George's Island** is accessible by the river walkway to the east. The new Canadian Wilds exhibit brings the sights, sounds and yes, the smells of the Canadian wilderness to the heart of the city. A pamphlet available at the gate lists feeding times. The zoo also features a **prehistoric park,** which takes you back in time some 65 million years, a **botanical garden** and a **children's zoo**—a zoo *for* children, not of them. (Open daily at 9am; closing time seasonally adjusted. For more info, call Zooline, 232-9300. Admission $7.50, seniors $4.75, kids $3.75. Tues. $5, seniors free.)

The Stampede

Even people who find rodeo grotesque still have trouble saying "Calgary" without letting a quick "Stampede" slip out. Indeed, Calgarians take great pride in their "Greatest Outdoor Show on Earth." Every year around Stampede time, local merchants whip up free pancake breakfasts and paint every ground-level window downtown with cartoon cowboy figures offering hokily misspelled greetings ("Welcum, y'all"). Capped by ten-gallons, locals command tour groups to yell "Yahoo" in the least likely of circumstances. Simply put, at Stampede time the entire city of Calgary goes nuts.

And why not? Any event that draws millions from across the world deserves hoopla. Take the short trip out to **Stampede Park,** just southeast of downtown, to get a glimpse of steer wrestling, bull riding, wild cow milking, and the famous chuckwagon races. The Stampede also features a **midway,** where you can perch yourself atop the wild, thrashing back of a roller coaster.

Take the C-Train from downtown to the Stampede stop. In 1993, the Stampede will run July 3 through 12. For official info and ticket order forms, write Calgary Exhibition and Stampede, Box 1860, Station M, Calgary T2P 2L8, (800-661-1260). In Calgary, visit **Stampede Headquarters,** 1410 Olympic Way, or call 261-0101. Tickets prices range from $15 to $38, depending on the event and seats; ask about rush tickets ($7.50, youth $6.75, seniors and kids $3.50).

Jasper National Park

The completion of the Icefields Parkway in 1940 paved the way for everyone to appreciate Jasper's astounding beauty. In contrast to its glitzy southern counterpart Banff, Jasper's landscape reflects its inhabitants' tranquility. Even the townsite, a cluster of buildings dropped amid 10,000 square km of virgin wilderness, remains serene. Jasperites gladly share their territory with wildlife and pride themselves on the vast network of trails that penetrate into some of the Rockies' most captivating scenery.

Practical Information and Orientation

Emergency: 852-4848.

Park Information Centre, 500 Connaught Dr. (852-6176). Trail maps and info on the park. Open daily 8am-8pm; early Sept.-late Oct. daily 9am-5pm; late Dec.-mid-May daily 9am-5pm; mid-May-mid-June daily 8am-5pm. **Alberta Tourism,** 632 Connaught Dr. (in AB 800-222-6501, outside AB 800-661-8888). Open Victoria Day-Labor Day daily 8am-8pm. **Jasper Chamber of Commerce,** 634 Connaught Dr. (852-3858). Open Mon.-Fri. 9am-5pm. **Park Headquarters,** Superintendent, Jasper National Park, 632 Patricia St., Box 10, Jasper T0E 1E0 (852-6161).

VIA Rail: 314 Connaught Dr. (852-3168). 3 per week each to: Vancouver ($115); Edmonton ($67); and Winnipeg ($185). 10% off for seniors and students with ID. 50% off for kids.

Greyhound: In the VIA station (852-3926). To: Edmonton ($40), and Vancouver ($82).

Brewster Transportation and Tours: Also in the VIA station (852-3332). To Banff (full-day tour $60; daily 41/4-hr. express $36) and Calgary (1 per day; 8 hr.; $47).

Taxis: Jasper Taxi, 852-3146.

Car Rental: Tilden Car Rental, in the bus depot (852-4792). $44 per day with 100 free km. Must be 21 with credit card. $2500 insurance deductible for drivers under 25.

Bike Rental: Home Hardware, 623 Patricia Ave. (852-5555). Mountain bikes $4-5 per hr., $15-18 per day. Open Mon.-Fri. 8am-9pm, Sat. 9am-9pm, Sun. 11am-5pm. **Whistlers Mountain Hostel** (see below) rents mountains bikes for $13 per day, $17 nonmembers.

Post Office: 502 Patricia St. (852-3041), across Patricia St. from the townsite green. Open July-Aug. Mon.-Fri. 9am-5pm. **Postal Code:** T0E 1E0.

Area Code: 403.

All of the above addresses are in **Jasper Townsite,** which sits near the middle of the park, 362km southwest of Edmonton and 287km north of Banff. **Highway 16** conducts travelers through the park north of the townsite, while the **Icefields Parkway** (Hwy. 93) connects to Banff National Park in the south. Buses run to the townsite daily from Edmonton, Calgary and Vancouver. Trains arrive from Edmonton and Vancouver. Renting a bike is the most practical option for short jaunts within the park.

Accommodations, Camping, and Food

Ask for the *Approved Accommodations List* at the Park Information Center if you wish to sleep cheaply in a Jasper B&B (singles $15-35, doubles $25-45, quads $40-55). If you prefer mingling with the youthful and un*approved* set, head to a hostel (listed below from north to south). Reservations, as well as information on closing days and on the winter "key system," channel through the Edmonton-based **Northern Alberta Hostel Association** (439-3089).

Maligne Canyon Hostel (HI-C), on Maligne Canyon Rd. (852-3584), 11km east of the townsite. An ideal place for viewing wildlife; the knowledgeable manager is happy to give guided hikes or to discuss with you the fowl and fauna with whom he has shared his last 8 years. Accommodates 24. $8, nonmembers $12. Closed Wed. in winter.

Whistlers Mountain Hostel (HI-C), on Sky Tram Rd. (852-3215), 7km south of the townsite. Closest to the townsite and the park's most modern (and crowded) hostel. A hike from town, mostly uphill. Accommodates 50. $12, nonmembers $16.

Mount Edith Cavell Hostel (HI-C), on Edith Cavell Rd. off Hwy. 93A. Road closes in winter, but the hostel welcomes anyone willing to ski or snowmobile the 11km from Hwy. 93A. Really. Accommodates 32. $8, nonmembers $12. Open mid-June-early Oct. Closed Thurs.

Athabasca Falls Hostel (HI-C) (852-5959), on Hwy. 93, 30km south of Jasper Townsite near the namesake falls; 6 gumball machines in the rec room. Accommodates 40. $8, nonmembers $12. Closed Tues. in winter.

Beauty Creek Hostel (HI-C), on Hwy. 93, 78km south of Jasper Townsite. Beautifully situated next to a brook. Accommodates 24. Accessible through the "key system" in winter(groups only). $8, nonmembers $12. Open May-mid-Sept. Closed Wed.

For campground updates, tune in to **1450 AM** on your radio near Jasper Townsite. The park maintains sites at 10 campgrounds, including (north to south): **Pocahontas** (140 sites), **Snaring River** (56 sites), **Whistlers** (781 sites), **Wapiti** (366 sites), **Wabasso** (238 sites), **Columbia Icefield** (33 sites) and **Wilcox Creek** (46 sites). Rates range from $7.25 to $17.50.

For cheap eats, stock up at a local market or bulk foods store and head for the backcountry. For around-the-clock grocery supplies, stop at **Wink's Food Store,** 617 Patricia St. (852-4223). **Nutter's,** 622 Patricia St. (852-5844), offers grains, nuts, dried fruits and (if you're sick of healthful food) candy, all in bulk form. They also sell deli meats, canned goods and fresh-ground coffee. (Open Mon.-Sat. 9am-10pm, Sun. 10am-9pm.) For a sit-down meal, the Egyptian food at **Roony's,** 618 Connaught Dr. (852-5830), will make your mouth light up like a slot machine and pay off in silver dollars. Try the *kofta,* spicy ground beef with parsley and onions on toasted bread ($7). Burgers are also cheap ($3.25-3.75). (Open daily noon-2am; 2pm-2am in winter.)

Sights and Activities

An extensive trail network connects most parts of Jasper, with many paths starting at the townsite. Info centers distribute free copies of *Day Hikes in Jasper National Park* and a summary of the longer hikes.

Mt. Edith Cavell, named after a WWI hero, often thunders with the sound of avalanches off the Angel Glacier. Take the ½km loop trail or the eight km return **Path of the Glacier.** Mt. Edith Cavell rears 30km south of the townsite on Mt. Edith Cavell Rd. **Maligne Lake,** the largest glacier-fed lake in the Canadian Rockies, is located 50km southeast of the townsite at the end of Maligne Lake Rd. One special feature of Jasper National Park is **Medicine Lake,** 30km east of Jasper Townsite. Water flows into the lake with no visible outlet. The trick? The water seeps out through a series of underground caves and emerges in such areas as **Maligne Canyon,** which drops over 46m (11km east of the townsite on Maligne Canyon Rd.). Don't try to imitate the local squirrels, who like to leap this narrow gorge; your jump will send you flying into the great beyond. For $34, you can have **Fun on a Bike** (852-4242), peddling 20km downhill from Medicine Lake to Maligne Canyon.

Horseshoe Lake, 30km south of town and five km north of Athabasca Falls, is a splendid location for **cliff diving,** but only try it in July and August, and remember—drinking and diving don't mix. A more common but equally adventurous water activity is rafting. **Whitewater Rafting (Jasper) Ltd.** (852-7238) runs several rafting trips from $35 to $45; register at the Esso station. After dipping in Jasper's glacier-fed waters, revive your numbed body at the 102°F, odorless **Miette Hot Springs,** north off Hwy. 16 along the eponymously named road. (Open mid-June-Labor Day 8:30am-10:30pm. Admission $2, kids $1.25.)

Joining the Banff tradition, Jasper has a **gondola** of its own. Rising 2½km up the side of Whistlers Mountain, the Jasper Tramway will make you jasp with excitement with its majestic views of the park, as well as an opportunity to spend money at its gift shops and restaurant. (Open mid-April-Sept. 8am-9:30pm; Sept.-mid-Oct. 9am-4:30pm. Fare $9.65, under 12 $4.85. Call 852-3093 for more info.) A trail starting from the Whistlers Mountain Hostel also leads up the slope, but it's a steep 10km; you may want to take the tram ride down ($5).

British Columbia

Larger than California, Oregon, and Washington combined, British Columbia (BC) attracts enough visitors year-round to make tourism the province's second largest industry (after timber). The million flowers of Victoria and the million people of Vancouver draw city slickers, while the graceful lakes of the nearby Okanagan Valley lure those intent on escaping civilization.

BC, Canada's westernmost province, covers over 350,000 square mi. and borders on four U.S. states and three other Canadian provinces. The difficulty of road travel throughout the province varies with the immensely diverse terrain. When taking your own vehicle, be sure to avoid potential hassles by obtaining a Canadian non-resident interprovince motor vehicle liability card from your insurance company before leaving; border police may turn you away if you aren't properly insured. In the south, roads are plentiful and well paved; farther north, the asphalt (and the towns) seem to have been blown away by the Arctic winds. For a sharper look into British Columbia, see *Let's Go: Pacific Northwest, Western Canada and Alaska.*

Practical Information

Capital: Victoria.

Ministry of Tourism and Provincial Secretary, Parliament Bldg., Victoria V8V 1X4 (604-387-1642). Write for the accommodations guide, which lists prices and services for virtually every hotel, motel and campground in the province. In the U.S., write **Tourism BC,** P.O. Box C-34971, Seattle, WA 98124. Branches also available in **San Francisco,** 100 Bush St. #400, San Francisco, CA 94104 (415-981-4780) and **Irvine,** 2600 Michelson Dr. #1050, Irvine, CA 92715 (714-852-1054). **Canadian Parks Service,** Senior Communications Officer, 220 4th Ave. S.E., P.O. Box 2989, Station M, Calgary, AB T2P 3H8, or call **BC Parks** at 604-387-5002.

Time Zone: Pacific (3 hrs. behind Eastern) and Mountain (2 hrs. behind Eastern). **Postal Abbreviation:** BC

Alcohol: Drinking age 19.

Vancouver

Canada's third largest city comes as a pleasant surprise to the jaded, metropolis-hopping traveler. Tune out the language, and Vancouver could be a North American Switzerland, with immaculate and efficient public transport and spotless sidewalks; even the seedy areas can be safe. Mayor Gordon Campbell has promised that his city will "not become like a city in the United States." With nature walks among 1000-year-old virgin timber stands, wind-surfing, and the most technologically advanced movie theater in the world all downtown, Vancouver is keeping that promise.

Practical Information and Orientation

Police: Main and Powell St. (665-3321). **Emergency:** 911.

Travel Infocentre, 1055 Dunsmuir (683-2000), near Burrard in the West End. Buy the larger-scale street map ($2). Open daily 8am-6pm.

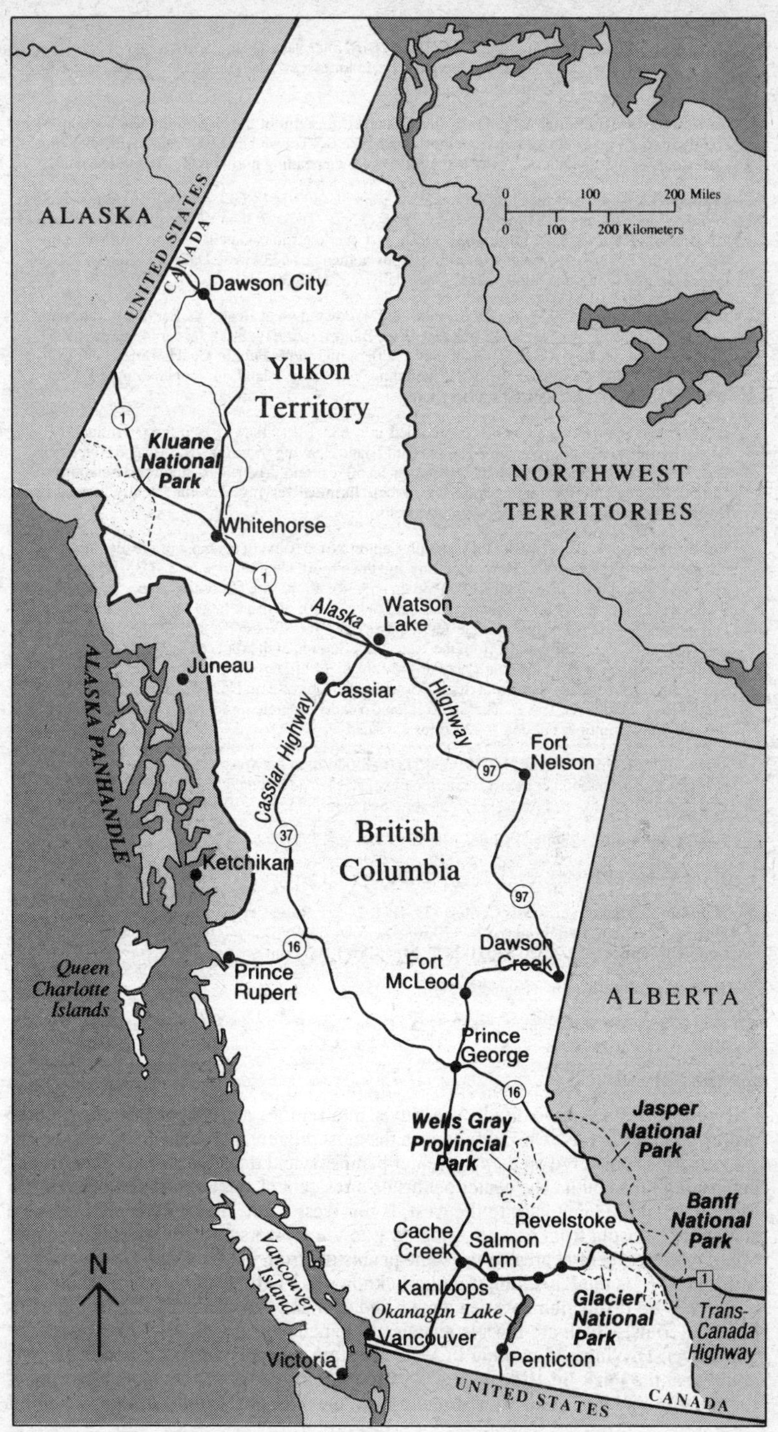
ALASKA
UNITED STATES
CANADA
Dawson City
Yukon
Territory
1
Kluane
National
Park
Whitehorse
NORTHWEST
TERRITORIES
0 100 200 Miles
0 100 200 Kilometers
1
Alaska
Watson
Lake
Highway
Juneau
Cassiar
ALASKA PANHANDLE
Cassiar Highway
Fort
Nelson
97
37
British
Columbia
Ketchikan
97
16
Dawson
Creek
Queen
Charlotte
Islands
Prince
Rupert
Fort
McLeod
ALBERTA
Prince
George
16
Jasper
National
Park
Wells Gray
Provincial
Park
Banff
National
Park
Revelstoke
Cache
Creek
Salmon
Arm
N
Vancouver
Island
Kamloops
1
Okanagan Lake
Glacier
National
Park
Trans-
Canada
Highway
Vancouver
Victoria
Penticton
UNITED STATES
CANADA

Gray Line Tours: 900 W. Georgia St. (681-8687), in Hotel Vancouver. Expensive but worthwhile city tours with a number of package options. Basic tours leave daily and last 3½ hrs. (fare $30, seniors $27, kids $17). Reservations required.

Vancouver International Airport: on Sea Island 11km south of the city center. Connections to major cities. To reach downtown from the airport, take BC Transit bus #100 to Granville and 70th Ave.; transfer there to bus #20, which arrives downtown heading north on the Granville Mall.

Trains: VIA Rail Canada, 1150 Station St. at Main St. (800-561-8630 or 669-3050). 3 per week to Jasper ($116) and Edmonton ($161). Open Thurs.-Tues. 7:30am-9:30pm, Wed. 7:30am-2:30pm. **BC Rail,** 1311 W. 1st St. (631-3500), just over the Lions Gate Bridge in North Vancouver. Take the SeaBus downtown to North Vancouver, then bus #239 west. Daily to: Whistler ($14), Prince George ($75), and points north. Open daily 6:30am-8:30pm.

Buses: Greyhound, 150 Dunsmuir St. (662-3222), downtown at Beatty St. Service to the south and across Canada. To: Calgary (7 per day; $90); Banff (6 per day; $85); Jasper (4 per day; $83); and Seattle (4 per day; US$25). Open daily 5:30am-midnight. **Pacific Coach Lines,** 150 Dunsmuir (662-3222). Serves southern BC including Vancouver Island, in cooperation with Greyhound. To Victoria ($21, including ferry fare).

BC Ferries: (general info 669-1211; recorded info 685-1021; Tsawwassen ferry terminal 943-9331). Ferries to Victoria, Nanaimo and the Gulf Islands leaving from Tsawwassen and Horseshoe Bay. Mainland to Vancouver Island (passenger $5.50, car and driver $26, motorcycle and driver $15.50, bicycle and rider $8, ages 5-11 ½-price). Terminal serving Victoria actually located in Swartz Bay, north of Victoria. (See Victoria below.)

Public Transport: BC Transit (Information Centre: 261-5100) covers most of the city and suburbs, including Tsawwassen, Horseshoe Bay and the airport. Central zone fare $1.35, seniors and ages 5-11 70¢. 2-zone peak-hour (6:30-9:30am and 3-6:30pm) fare $2, seniors and ages 5-11 $1; 3-zone peak-hour travel $2.75, seniors and ages 5-11 $1.40; off-peak fares same as 1-zone price. Day-passes $4, transfers free. Single fares, passes and transfers are good for the SeaBus and SkyTrain also. The **SeaBus** runs from the Waterfront Station, at the foot of Granville St. in downtown Vancouver, to the Lonsdale Quay at the foot of Lonsdale Ave. in North Vancouver. The **SkyTrain** runs from the Waterfront Station Southeast to Scott Rd. in New Westminster. Schedules available at Vancouver Travel. The SkyTrain and SeaBus operate on an honor system; cheating the system is tempting, but don't—the fines are steep.

Car Rental: Rent-A-Wreck, 180 W. Georgia (688-0001), in the West End, and 340 W. 4th Ave. at Manitoba. From $45 per day; 150km free plus 15¢ each additional km. Must be 19 with credit card. Both locations open Mon.-Fri. 7am-7pm, Sat. 9am-5pm, Sun. 10am-3pm.

Road Conditions: 525-4997, 24 hrs.

Taxis: Yellow Cab, (681-3311), 24 hrs. $2.10 plus $1.21 per km.

Help Lines: Vancouver Crisis Center, 733-4111. 24 hrs. **Rape Crisis Center,** 255-6344. 24 hrs. **Gay and Lesbian Switchboard,** 1-1170 Bute St. (684-6869). Daily 7-10pm. **Seniors Information and Support,** 531-2320 or 531-2425. Mon.-Fri. 10am-4pm.

Time Zone: Pacific (3 hrs. behind Eastern).

Post Office: 349 W. Georgia St. (662-5725). Open Mon.-Fri. 8am-5:30pm. **Postal Code:** V6B 3P7.

Area Code: 604.

Rivers, inlets and bays divide Vancouver into regions and neighborhoods, and the profusion of waterways can confuse even the most diligent map-reader. Most of the city's attractions converge on the city-center peninsula and the larger rhino-snout-shaped peninsula to the south. The center peninsula's residential area, bounded by downtown to the east and Stanley Park to the west, is the **West End.** The western portion of the southern peninsula from around Alma Ave. to the University of BC campus is **Point Grey,** while the central area on the same peninsula, from the Granville Bridge roughly to Alma Ave., is the **Kitsilano,** (familiarly known as **"Kits"**).

There is no distinction between streets and avenues in Vancouver, except the numbered arterials, which are always *avenues* in Vancouver proper, and *streets* in North Vancouver. Driving and parking in Vancouver are a serious hassle; consider leaving your car at the **Park 'n' Ride** in New Westminster instead of paying outrageous prices for underground lots. (Exit Hwy. 1 and follow signs for the Pattullo Bridge; watch for

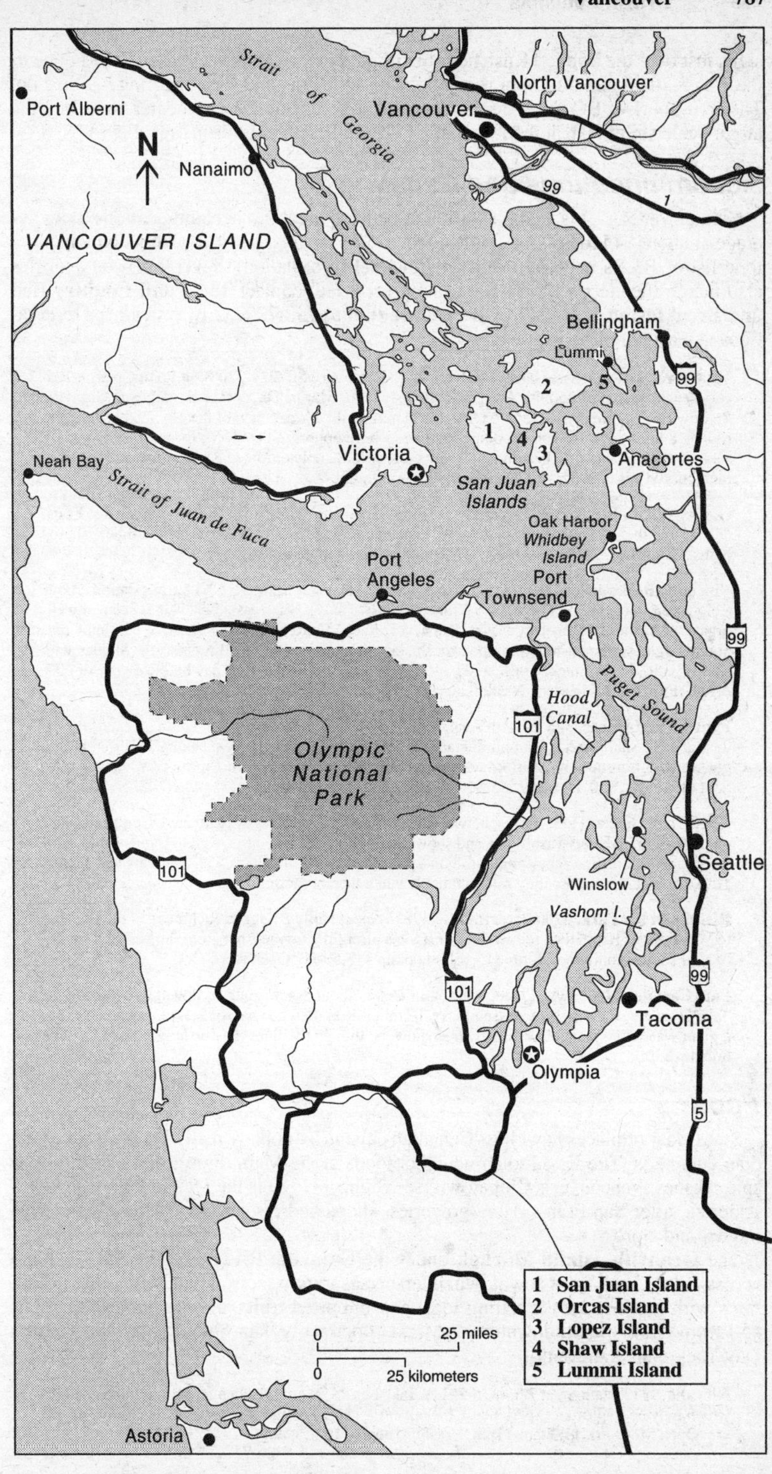
Strait of Georgia
Port Alberni
Nanaimo
N
North Vancouver
Vancouver
99
1
VANCOUVER ISLAND
Bellingham
Lummi
2
5
99
1
4
3
Victoria
Anacortes
Neah Bay
Strait of Juan de Fuca
San Juan Islands
Oak Harbor
Whidbey Island
Port Angeles
Port Townsend
99
Hood Canal
Puget Sound
101
Olympic National Park
Seattle
101
Winslow
Vashom I.
99
101
Tacoma
Olympia
5
1 San Juan Island
2 Orcas Island
3 Lopez Island
4 Shaw Island
5 Lummi Island
0
25 miles
0
25 kilometers
Astoria

signs just over the bridge.) Rush hour begins at dawn and ends at sunset. Take notice of the 7 to 9:30am and 3 to 6pm restrictions on left turns and street parking—police do. The free Tourism BC maps don't cover the area outside the city center well; buy the larger-scale street map at the Infocentre ($2; see Practical Information above).

Accommodations and Camping

Greater Vancouver is a rabbit warren of bed and breakfast accommodations; rates average at about $45 to $60 for singles, $55 to $75 for doubles. The visitors bureau has a long list of B&Bs in Vancouver (see Practical Information). Several private agencies also match travelers with B&Bs, usually for a fee; contact **Town and Country Bed and Breakfast** at 731-5942 or **Best Canadian** at 738-7207. Always call for reservations at least two days in advance.

Vancouver International Hostel (HI-C), 1515 Discovery St. (224-3208), in Point Grey on Jericho Beach. Turn north off 4th Ave., following signs for Marine Dr., or take bus #4 from Granville St. downtown. Comely location on beach and park, with a great view of the city. 285 beds, dorm rooms, 8 family rooms, good cooking facilities, chore opportunities (work for your lodging), TV room, cafeteria, laundry. In summer, 3-day max. stay. Strictly enforced 2am curfew. $12.50, nonmembers $18. Linen $1.50. Check-in 7:30am-midnight.

Globetrotter's Inn, 170 W. Esplanade in North Vancouver (988-5141). Take the SeaBus to Lonsdale Quay, then walk 1 block east to W. Esplanade and Chesterfield. Kitchen facilities, shared baths. Singles $13. Private singles $27. Doubles $33, with bath $38.

Vincent's Backpackers Hostel, 927 Main (682-2441), right next to the VIA train station, above a big green store called "The Source." Take "Main St." bus #3 or "Fraser" #8. Not as clean or well-organized as the HI-C hostel (above). Kitchen, fridge, TV, stereo, and the music of barking Greyhound engines. Check-in before noon for the best shot at a bed. Shared rooms $10. Singles with shared bath $20. Doubles with shared bath $25. Weekly rates available; pay before 10am for 20% off all rates. Office open 8am-midnight.

Paul's Guest House, 345 W. 14th Ave. (872-4753), at Alberta. Take bus #15. In a beautiful residential area. Shared baths, complimentary full breakfast. Paul boasts of speaking 11 different languages; trip him up with your knowledge of !Kung. Check-in before 11pm. Tidy, cozy singles $35, off-season $30. Doubles $45/$40. Call ahead for reservations.

YMCA, 955 Burrard (681-0221), between Smithe and Nelson. Newly renovated. Concerned staff on duty 24 hrs. Shared washrooms and showers. Pool, gym, ball courts, weight rooms (free). Cafeteria open Mon.-Fri. 7am-4pm, Sat. 8am-2pm. Singles $31. Doubles $52. Students and seniors 10% off. Weekly and monthly rates available when there's room.

Richmond RV Park, 6200 River Rd. (270-7878), near Holly Bridge in Richmond. Take Hwy. 99 to Westminster Hwy., then follow the signs. Sites offer little privacy, but great showers and friendly staff soothe your woes. Sites $15, with hookup $18.50-20. Open April-Oct.

ParkCanada, 4799 Hwy. 17 (943-5811), in Delta, about 30km south of downtown Vancouver. Take Hwy. 99 south to Tsawwassen Ferry Terminal Rd., then go east for 2½km. Located next to a giant waterslide park; flush toilets, free showers, though the lines may be long. Sites $12, with hookup $20.

Food

Steer clear of places hawking "Canadian cuisine"—nobody really knows what Canadian cuisine is. The East Indian neighborhoods along Main, Fraser and 49th St. offer spicy dishes. Vancouver's Chinatown (see Sights below) is the second largest in North America, after San Fran's. Here groceries, shops and restaurants cluster around East Pender and Gore St.

The **Granville Island Market,** under the Granville Bridge, off W. 4th Ave. and across False Creek from downtown, intersperses trendy shops, art galleries, and restaurants with produce stands selling local and imported fruits and vegetables. Take bus #50 from Granville St. downtown. (Market open daily 9am-6pm, Labor Day-Victoria Day Tues.-Sun. 9am-6pm.)

Nirvana, 2313 Main St. at 7th, (876-2911). Take bus #8, 3, or 9. Authentic, savory Indian cuisine which may be a spiritual experience. Chicken curry ($6.50), vegetable *biryani* ($8). Come as you are. Open Mon.-Fri. 11:30am-11pm, Sat.-Sun. noon-11pm.

Slice of Gourmet, 1152 Denman near Stanley Park (689-1112). Pizza like you never thought of it before. Try the peppery potato or BBQ Salmon pizzas, $3 per filling slice. Open Sun.-Thurs. 11:30am-11:30pm, Fri.-Sat. 11:30am-midnight.

The Green Door, 111 E. Pender (685-4194), in central Chinatown. Follow the alley off Columbia St. to find the hidden entrance. This wildly green establishment plays a prominent role in the annals of Vancouver hippie lore. Huge servings of slightly greasy Chinese seafood ($6-7). BYOB. Open Thurs.-Tues. noon-10pm; Oct.-May Wed.-Mon. noon-10pm.

The Naam, 2724 W. 4th Ave. (783-7151), in the Kits area. Take bus #4 or 7 from Granville. Vancouver's oldest natural-foods restaurant has great people-watching. Tofu-nut-beet burgers ($5), spinach enchiladas ($8.25), and salad bar ($1.25 per 100g). Live music nightly 7-10pm. Open 24 hrs.

Nuff-Nice-Ness, 1861 Commercial Dr. (255-4211). Hudson's home for Jamaican cuisine. Vegetable and meat patties ($2). Jerk chicken with salad and rice ($7.50). Open Tues. 12:30-8pm, Wed.-Sat. 11am-8pm, Sun. 1-6pm.

Sights

The remaining landmark of the Expo '86 World's Fair is a 17-story, metallic, geodesic sphere which houses **Science World,** 1455 Quebec St. (687-7832), at Terminal Ave. Science World features hands-on exhibits for kids and the **Omnimax Theatre** (875-6664), the largest, most technologically advanced theater in the world. (Call for show times. Admission to both $11, youth and seniors $7; to Science World only $7, youth and seniors $4.50; to Omnimax alone after 4pm $9.) The second expo site is the Canada Pavilion, now called **Canada Place,** about ½km away. You can reach it by SkyTrain from the main Expo site. Visitors who make this four-minute journey can view Canadian arts and crafts as well as films in the **CN IMAX Theatre** (682-4629). Ranging in price ($6.25-9.25, youth and seniors $5.25-8.25), the images on the flat, five-story screen may not be as stunning as those on domed IMAX screens, but they have incredible clarity with no peripheral distortion. So there. (Open daily noon-9pm.)

Newly renovated, the **Lookout!** 555 W. Hastings St. (649-0421), offers fantastic 360° views of the city and surrounding areas. Though expensive, your ticket lasts all day; you can leave and come back for the romantic night skyline. (Open daily 8:30am-10:30pm. Admission $5.35, seniors and students $3.75.) The **Vancouver Art Gallery,** 750 Hornby St. (682-5621), in Robson Sq., has a small but well-presented collection of classical, contemporary, and Canadian art and photography. Tag along with one of the free tours for large groups. (Open Mon.-Wed. and Fri.-Sat. 10am-5pm, Thurs. 10am-9pm, Sun. noon-5pm. Admission $4.25, seniors and students $2.50. Donation requested Thurs. 5-9pm.)

Gastown, named for "Gassy Jack" Deighton, the con man who opened Vancouver's first saloon, is a tourist snare disguised as a restored turn-of-the-century neighborhood. Listen for the continent's only steam-powered clock on the corner of Cambie and Water St.—it whistles every 15 minutes. Gastown is a fair walk from downtown or a short ride on bus #22 along Burrard St. to Carrall St. Just east, **Chinatown** also lies within walking distance of downtown, but you can take bus #22 on Burrard St. northbound to Pender St. at Carrall St. and return by bus #22 westbound along Pender St. Vancouver's Chinatown spreads out along Pender St. and both sides of Main St., replete with restaurants and shops. The area is rundown and somewhat unsafe. Gray Line Tours (see Practical Information) provides a safer but costlier way to see Chinatown.

One of the city's most alluring sites is **Stanley Park,** on the westernmost end of the city-center peninsula (take bus #19). Surrounded by a **seawall promenade,** this thickly wooded park is crisscrossed with cycling and hiking trails and is a testament to far-sighted urban planning. Within the park's boundaries lie various restaurants, tennis courts, the **Malkin Bowl** (an outdoor theater), and equipped beaches. Nature walks leave May to September on Tuesdays at 10am, from July to August at 7pm. (May, June, and Sept. morning walks leave from the Lost Lagoon bus loop, all other times from Lumberman's Arch Water Park.) Rent practically new bikes at **Bayshore,** 745 Denman St. (688-2453), for $5.50 per hour, $20 per 12 hours, $25 per day. (Open May-Sept. daily 9am-9pm.) Cavort alongside beluga whales at the **Vancouver Aquarium** (682-

1118), on the eastern side of the park, not far from the park's entrance. (Open daily 10am-5:30pm. Admission $8.50, seniors and ages 13-18 $7.25, under 12 $5.25.) Visit Stanley Park's small, crowded, but free **zoo** next door, if only to see the monkeys taunt nearby polar bears. (Open daily 10am-5pm.)

Follow the western side of the seawall south to **Sunset Beach Park** (738-8535), a strip of grass and beach that extends south all the way to the Burrard Bridge. All of Vancouver's beaches have lifeguards from Victoria Day to Labor Day daily from 11:30am to 9pm. At the southern end of Sunset Beach splashes the **Aquatic Centre,** 1050 Beach Ave. (665-3424), a public facility with a 50m indoor saltwater pool, sauna, gymnasium, and diving tank. (Open Mon.-Thurs. 7am-10pm, Sat. 8am-9pm, Sun. 11am-9pm. Pool open Mon.-Thurs. at 7am. Gym use $3.20; pool use $2.85.)

Vancouverites frequent Kitsilano Beach, known to locals as **"Kits,"** on the other side of English Bay from Sunset Beach. Its heated saltwater outdoor pool (731-0011; open summer only) has changing rooms, lockers and a snack bar. (Pool open June-Sept. Mon.-Fri. 9am-8:30pm, Sat.-Sun. 10am-8:30pm. Admission $2.85, seniors $1.40, kids $1.80.)

Jericho Beach, to the west, tends to be used less heavily than Kits Beach. Jericho begins a border of beaches and park lands that lines Point Grey and the **University of British Columbia (UBC).** At the University, visit the terrific **Museum of Anthropology,** 6393 N.W. Marine Dr. (822-3825 for recording, 822-5087 for operator), where a dramatic glass and concrete building houses totems and other massive sculptures crafted by Native Americans. (Open Tues. 11am-9pm, Wed.-Sun. 11am-5pm. Admission $5, seniors and students $2.50, under 16 free. Tues. after 5pm free.)

Scramble down the cliffs to the southwest of the UBC campus to **Wreck Beach,** an unofficial, unsanctioned, unlifeguarded beach for the unclothed. Any UBC student can point you toward one of the semi-hidden access paths.

Entertainment and Events

To keep abreast of the entertainment scene, pick up a copy of the weekly *Georgia Straight* or the monthly *AF Magazine,* both free at magazine stands and record stores. The 25¢ *West Ender* lists entertainment in that lively neighborhood, while free *Angles* serves the city's growing gay community.

The Fringe Café, 3124 West Broadway (738-6977). One of the hottest bars in town, with a mixed student and professional crowd. Open Sun.-Thurs. noon-midnight, Fri.-Sat. noon-2am.

Graceland, 1250 Richards St. (688-2548). Warehouse space beating to house music on Fri. and Sat. nights. Wed. night reggae fiesta. Open Mon.-Fri. 9pm-2am, Sat. 8:30pm-2am, Sun. 8pm-2am.

Celebrities, 1022 Davie St. (689-3180). Very big, very hot, very popular with the gay community. Sun. night techno-music, Mon. classic disco. Open Mon.-Sat. 9pm-2am, Sun. 9pm-midnight.

The **Robson Square Conference Centre,** 800 Robson St. (661-7373), sponsors events almost daily during the summer and weekly the rest of the year, either on the plaza at the square or in the center itself. Their concerts, theater productions, exhibits, lectures, symposia and films are all free or low-cost. Pick up the center's brochure *What's Happening at Robson Square* from the visitors bureau or stores in the square.

The **Arts Club Theatre,** Granville Island (687-1644), hosts big-name theater and musical productions, while the **Theatre in the Park** program (687-0174) in Stanley Park's Malkin Bowl, has a summer season of musical comedy. The annual **Vancouver Shakespeare Festival** (734-0194), from June to August in Vanier Park, often needs volunteer ushers and program-sellers, who get to watch the shows for free.

Vancouver's universities have dance cards filled with cultural activities. At Simon Fraser University, the **SFU Centre for the Arts** (291-3514) offers both student and guest-professional theater, primarily from September to May. For UBC activities, call 822-3131 or pick up a free copy of *Ubissey.* UBC's film series (228-3698) screens high-quality movies Thursday and Friday nights for $2.50.

Seasonal Events

Attend one of Vancouver's annual fairs, festivals or celebrations to confirm rumors of the city's cosmopolitan nature. The famed **Vancouver Folk Music Festival** takes place in mid-July in Jericho park, when North America's best big- and little-name performers give concerts and workshops for three days. You can purchase tickets à la carte, or for the whole weekend (with a discount before June 1). For more details, contact the festival at 3271 Main St., Vancouver V6V 3M6 (879-2931). The annual **Du Maurier International Jazz Festival** (682-0706) in late June features over 500 performers and bands. The 10-day festival is totally red, hot and blue. Write 435 W. Hastings, Vancouver V6V 1L4 for details.

Vancouver celebrates its love affair with the sea several times a year. The Maritime Museum in Vanier Park hosts the annual **Captain Vancouver Day** (737-2211) in mid-June to commemorate the exploration of Canada's west coast by Captain George Vancouver. In mid-July, the **Vancouver Sea Festival** (684-3378) schedules four days of parades, concerts, sporting events, fireworks and salmon BBQs. All events take place in English Bay and are free, although the salmon isn't. The headline attraction is the notorious **Nanaimo to Vancouver Bathtub Race,** a journey across the rough waters of the Strait of Georgia.

Near Vancouver

Huff and puff along on the **Royal Hudson Steam Locomotive,** operated by BC Rail (688-7246). After a two-hour ride along the coast from Vancouver to Squamish (the gateway to Garibaldi Provincial Park), passengers are set loose for 90 minutes to browse in town before they head back. (Excursions June-Sept. 20 Wed.-Sun.; Fare $27, seniors and ages 12-18 $22.50, kids 5-11 $16.50.) The train departs from the BC Rail terminal, 1311 W. First St., across the Lions Gate Bridge in North Vancouver. Reservations are required.

To the east, the town of **Deep Cove** maintains the briny atmosphere of a fishing village. Sea otters and seals gather on the pleasant Indian Arm beaches. Take bus #210 from Pender to the Phibbs Exchange on the north side of Second Narrows Bridge; from there, take bus #211 or 212. **Cates Park,** at the end of Dollarton Hwy. on the way to Deep Cove, has popular swimming and scuba waters, and makes for a good bicycle daytrip out of Vancouver. Bus #211 also leads to beautiful **Mount Seymour Provincial Park.** Trails leave from Mt. Seymour Rd., and a paved road winds the eight km to the top. One hundred campsites ($7) are available, and the skiing is superb.

For a less vigorous hike that still offers fantastic views of the city, head for **Lynn Canyon Park.** The suspension bridge here is free and uncrowded, unlike its more publicized look-alike in **Capilano Canyon.** Take bus #228 from the North Vancouver Seabus terminal and walk the ½km to the bridge.

Grouse Mountain is the ski resort closest to downtown Vancouver and has the crowds to prove it. Take bus #246 from the North Vancouver SeaBus terminal; at Edgemont Village transfer to bus #232, then the "supersky ride." The aerial tramway runs from 9am to 10pm ($14, students $9). The slopes are lit until 10:30pm. On sunny days, helicopter tours leave from the top of the mountain, starting at $30 per person. For more info contact Grouse Mountain Resorts, 6400 Nancy Greene Way, North Vancouver V7R 4K9 (984-0661; ski report 986-6292). Ski rental is available for $21 a day, no deposit required. Adult lift tickets are $28.

The **Reifel Bird Sanctuary** on **Westham Island,** 16km south of Vancouver, is just northwest of the Tsawwassen ferry terminal. Bus #601 from Vancouver will take you to the town of **Ladner,** 1½km east of the sanctuary; 230 species of birds live in the 850 acres of marshlands, and spotting towers are set up for long-term birdwatching. (Open daily 9am-4pm.) For info contact the **BC Waterfowl Society** at 946-6980.

Fifty km north of Vancouver (on the way to Whistler) is the **BC Museum of Mining** in **Britannia Beach** (688-8735 or 896-2233). An electric mine train pumps passengers through an old copper artery into the mountain that poured out the most metal in the British Empire: 1.3 billion pounds. (Open mid-May-June Wed.-Sun. 10am-5pm; July-

Labor Day daily 10am-5pm; Sept.-mid-Oct. Wed.-Sun. 10am-5pm. Admission $7, seniors $5, students $4, kids under 5 free, families $22; $1 off if you book beforehand.)

Golden Ears Provincial Park is 50km east of the town of **Haney.** Turn north on 224th St. and follow it four km until it ends, then turn right and proceed for eight km. The roads are not well-marked, but all roads lead to Golden Ears. Inside the park, the **Cultus Lake Campground** operates 346 tentsites ($10 per site). Ask whether the name comes from that of the fabled *Cultosaurus erectus.* The park itself has a myriad of hiking trails, including some short ones leading to waterfalls.

A classic trip farther outside Vancouver is the two-hour drive up Rte. 99 to the town of **Whistler** and nearby **Garibaldi Provincial Park.** Follow Rte. 99 north from Horseshoe Bay, or take local **Maverick Coach Lines** (255-1171). **BC Rail** (see Practical Information above) also serves Whistler from Vancouver; their run stops directly behind the local youth hostel. Check the ride board at the HI-C hostel in Vancouver, since people frequently trek between the two. Whistler Mountain has top skiing, with the highest accessible vertical drop in North America (1 mi.). Slopes for the beginner and intermediate are also available. For more info contact Whistler Resort Association, Whistler V0N 1B0 (932-4222). The park also offers some fine wilderness hiking but vehicle access is out of the question. On the western shore of Alta Lake in Whistler the **Whistler Youth Hostel (HI-C)** (932-5492), has 35 beds, laundry, and extensive kitchen facilities, and is one of the best hostels in the Pacific Northwest. Call for directions. ($12.50, nonmembers $17.50.) In cahoots with Vincent's in Vancouver, a **Backpackers Hostel,** 2124 Lake Placid Rd. (932-1177), lies near the train station. With nice but cramped rooms ($12, $15 in winter), the hostel also has a kitchen, TV, and VCR.

Victoria

The sun may have set on the British empire years ago, but like an aging, eccentric Redcoat, Victoria still dresses up and marches to the beat of a bygone era. Set within the rough-hewn logging and fishing towns of Vancouver Island, this jeweled capital city of British Columbia evinces enough reserve and propriety to chill even the Windsors. On warm summer days, residents sip their tea on the lawns of Tudor-style homes in the suburbs, while downtown, horse-drawn carriages clatter through the streets. Victoria is eminently worthy of its namesake.

Practical Information and Orientation

Emergency: Police/Fire 911.

Tourism Victoria, 812 Wharf St., Victoria V8W IT3 (382-2127), in the Inner Harbor. Enough pamphlets to have decimated a forest. Open daily 9am-9pm; in winter 9am-5pm.

Buses: Pacific Coach Lines and **Island Coach Lines,** 700 Douglas St. at Belleville (385-4411), both located in the same building. Service to most island cities. To Vancouver (8 per day; $21) and Seattle (1 per day; $29). Lockers $2 for 24 hrs.

Ferries: BC Ferry, 656-0757 or 386-3431. Service to Vancouver or the mainland (20 per day; $5.50 per person, $2.50 per bike, $20 per car). **Washington State Ferries,** 381-1551. To the San Juans (passengers $6, seniors and ages 5-11 $4, car and driver $31). Take bus #70 to ferry.

Public Transport: Victoria Regional Transit, 382-6161. Daily service throughout the city. Single-zone travel $1.25, multi-zone (to Sidney and the Butchart Gardens) $1.75. Daily passes for unlimited single-zone travel available at visitors center and at 7-11 stores ($4, seniors and under 12 $3).

Car Rental: Sigmar Rent-A-Car, 752 Caledonia Ave. (388-6686). $19-24 per day plus 10¢ per km. Must be 21 with a major credit card. Open Mon.-Sat. 8am-5pm.

Taxi: Victoria Taxi, 383-7111. 24 hrs., $2.25 plus $1.25 per km.

Bike Rental: Harbour Scooter, 843 Douglas St. (384-2133). Mountain bikes $5 per hr., $15 per day. Includes lock and helmet. Open daily 9am-6pm.

Help Lines: Crisis Line, 386-6323.

Time Zone: Pacific (3 hr. behind Eastern).

Post Office: Victoria CRO, 714 Yates (363-8887). Open Mon.-Fri. 8:30am-5pm. **Postal Code:** V8W 1L0.

Area Code: 604.

Ferries and buses connect Victoria, on Vancouver Island's southern tip, to many cities in British Columbia and Washington. The city of Victoria enfolds the Inner Harbor; **Government Street** and **Douglas Street** are the main north-south thoroughfares and are where most of the tourist attractions can be found.

Accommodations and Camping

Note that there is a 17% tax (8% provincial sales tax, 7% goods and services tax, and 2% tourism tax) applied to rooms costing more than $20 per night. Campgrounds are exempt.

Victoria Youth Hostel (HI-C), 516 Yates St. (385-4511), at Wharf St. Big, modern, clean. Kitchen, laundry. $12.50, nonmembers $17.50. Open daily 7:30am-midnight.

Salvation Army Men's Hostel, 525 Johnson St. (384-3396), at Wharf St., around the corner from the youth hostel. Men only. Immaculate and well-run. Dorms $10. Private rooms $19. Meals $1.50-3.25.

YWCA, 880 Courtney St. (386-7511), at Quadra near downtown. Women only. Private rooms with shared bath. Check-in 11am-6pm. Check-out 6-11am. Singles $31. Doubles $46.

Battery Guest House, 670 Battery St. (385-4632), 1 block in from the ocean between Douglas and Government St. Dutch spoken in this spacious B&B; non-smokers only. Singles from $35, doubles from $55.

McDonald Park Campground (655-9020), 30km north of downtown on Hwy. 17, but first-class. No showers. Sites $9.50. Reservations recommended.

Fort Victoria Camping, 127 Burnett (479-8112), 7km northwest of downtown off the Trans-Canada Hwy. Free showers, laundromat. Sites $15, with hookup $18. RV only.

Food and Bars

Victoria's predilection for the old ways surfaces in its culinary customs. Victorians actually do take tea—some only on occasion, others every day. Other foods exist, of course, but to indulge in the trimmed-lawn romanticism of the city you should partake of the ceremony at least once—and don't ask for lemon, it's *just not done.* To masticate more filling substances, head into **Chinatown,** west of Fisgard and Government St. Create your own culinary delight by picking up the day's catch at **Fisherman's Wharf** between Superior and St. Lawrence.

Eugene's, 1280 Broad St. Wonderful variety of Greek foods; try the *rizogalo* or the *bougatsa* for breakfast ($2). Dinners $5-7.50. Open Mon.-Fri. 8am-8pm, Sat. 10am-8pm.

Old Victoria Fish and Chips, 1316 Broad St. (380-9994). Classic English-style fish and chips joint. 1 piece of each $3.75. Open Mon.-Sat. 11am-7pm, Sun. noon-7pm.

James Bay Tearoom, 332 Menzies St. at Superior (598-1413). Portraits of the Royal family and their tree, which dates back to the year 900, set the scene for a regal afternoon tea ($6). Open Mon.-Sat. 7am-9pm, Sun. 8am-9pm.

Goodies, 1005 Broad St., 2nd floor (382-2124), between Broughton and Fort. Make your own omelette ($4.45 plus 65¢ per ingredient), or choose from a list of sandwiches like the "Natural High" (mushroom and avocado, $5). Open daily 7am-9pm.

Rising Star Bakery, 1320 Broad St. (384-2534). The locals know about this celestial gem. Giant cheese croissant $1. Open Mon.-Sat. 7:30am-5:30pm, Sun. 8:30am-2:30pm.

Spinnakers, 308 Catherine (386-2739), across the Johnson St. bridge. Great local bar that brews 38 beers on the premises. Live music. No cover. Open daily 11am-11pm.

Rumors, 1325 Government St. (385-0566). Bar with gay and lesbian clientele. Open Mon.-Sat. 9pm-3am.

Sights and Activities

Most sights cluster together, except for the elegant residential neighborhoods and the parks and beaches, which are better accessed by car or bus. The first stop for every visitor should be the **Royal British Columbian Museum,** 675 Belleville St. (387-3014 for a recording, 387-3701 for a living, breathing person). Arguably the best museum in Canada, it chronicles the geological and cultural histories of the province and showcases detailed exhibits on logging, mining and fishing. The extensive exhibits of Native American art, culture and history include full-scale replicas of various forms of shelter used centuries ago. The gallery of Haida totem art is particularly moving; "Open Ocean" provides a wonderfully tongue-in-cheek recreation of the first desert in a bathysphere. (Open daily 9:30am-7pm; Oct.-April daily 10am-5:30pm. 2-day admission $5, seniors, disabled persons and students with ID or HI-C card $3, ages 6-18 $2. Free after 5:45pm and on Mon. Oct.-April.) Behind the museum, **Thunderbird Park** displays a striking bevy of totems and longhouses, backed by the intricate towers of the Empress Hotel.

Across the street from the museum stand the imposing **Parliament Buildings,** 501 Belleville St. (387-3046), home of the provincial government since 1898. Almost 50 *taels* (an anachronistic British measure equalling slightly more than an ounce) of gold grace the 10-story dome and Renaissance-inspired vestibule. (Free tours leave the steps every 20 min. in summer, every hr. in winter, daily 9am-5pm.)

On Wharf St., the **Emily Carr Gallery,** 1107 Wharf St. (387-3080), features original work of this turn-of-the-century BC artist who synthesized British landscape conventions and Native American style. The collection includes many of her paintings of totems, conscious attempts to preserve what she saw as "art treasures of a passing race." Free films on Carr's life and work show at 2:30pm. (Open Tues.-Sun. 10am-5:30pm. $2, seniors $1.)

South of the Inner Harbor, **Beacon Hill Park** (take bus #5) surveys the Strait of Juan de Fuca splendiferously. One mi. east of the Inner Harbor, **Craigdarroch Castle,** 1050 Joan Crescent (592-5323), embodies Victoria's wealth. Take bus #10, 11 or 14. The house was built in 1890 by Robert Dunsmuir, a BC coal and railroad tycoon, in order to tempt his wife away from their native Scotland. It's quite a temptation. (Open daily 9am-7pm, in winter 10am-4:30pm. Admission $5, students $4.)

The **Art Gallery of Greater Victoria,** 1040 Moss (384-4101), shifts one block back towards the Inner Harbor on Fort St. Save for a wooden Shinto shrine, the gallery has no permanent collection, instead culling temporary exhibits from local and international sources. (Open Mon.-Sat. 10am-5pm, Thurs. 10am-9pm, Sun. 1-5pm. Admission $4, students and seniors $2. Thurs. free after 5pm.)

Almost worth the exorbitant entrance fee are the stunning **Butchart Gardens,** 800 Benvennto, 22km north of Victoria (652-4422 Mon.-Fri. 9am-5pm; 652-5256 for recording). Jennie Butchart began the rose, Japanese and Italian gardens in 1904 in an attempt to reclaim the wasteland that was her husband's quarry and cement plant. From mid-May to September, the whole area is lit at dusk, and the gardens, still administered by the Butchart family, host variety shows and cartoons; Saturday nights in July and August, the skies shimmer with fireworks displays. Take bus #75. (Gardens open daily at 9am; closing depends on the season. Summer admission $9.50, ages 13-17 $5, ages 5-12 $1; prices vary at other times depending on how many flowers are in bloom. Re-admission within 24 hrs. only $1.) Motorists should consider an approach to Butchart Gardens via the **Scenic Marine Drive,** following the coastline along Dalls and other roads for a spectacular 45 minutes.

Entertainment

You can get an exhaustive listing of jazz, blues, rock, folk and country in the free weekly *Monday Magazine* (inexplicably released every Wednesday), available around the city. The **Victoria Symphony Society,** 846 Broughton St. (385-6515), performs regularly under conductor Peter McCoppin, and the **University of Victoria Auditorium,** Finnerty Rd. (721-8480), stages a variety of student productions. The **Pacific Opera** performs at the McPherson Playhouse, 3 Centennial Sq. (386-6121), at the corner of Pandora and Government St; during the summer, they undertake a popular musical comedy series.

The **Folkfest** in late June to early July celebrates Canada's birthday (July 1) and the country's "unity in diversity" with performances by a politically correct and culturally diverse array of musicians (call 388-5322 for info). The **JazzFest,** sponsored by the Victoria Jazz Society (388-4423 or 386-2441), also runs in late June. Pick up a free copy of *Victoria Today* from the Infocenter (see Practical Information) for a detailed listing of festivals in the area.

New Brunswick/ Nouveau-Brunswick

Two cultures dominate New Brunswick today. The Acadians, French pioneers who originally landed and settled in Nova Scotia in the 17th century, migrated to the northern and eastern coasts and established the farming and fishing nation of *l'Acadie,* or Acadia. When the British took control of the area in 1755, they expelled many of these farmers who then drifted all the way down the Mississippi to the Gulf of Mexico to found Acadiana amidst their compatriots in Louisiana. The southern region of New Brunswick was settled by the United Empire Loyalists, British subjects who fled in the wake of the American Revolution. Although over a third of the province's population is French-speaking, it is rare to encounter someone in the larger cities who doesn't speak English.

New Brunswick clearly prides itself on its natural attractions above all else. The tremendous Bay of Fundy gives rise to many of them, as well as to 30-foot tides, the world's highest. Other oddities include the Reversing Falls in St. John and Moncton's Magnetic Hill. Museums and cultural products may take a back seat here, but that's a tolerable loss for a province best seen when seats are left behind.

Practical Information

Capital: Fredericton.

Department of Economic Development and Tourism: P.O. Box 12345, Fredericton, NB E3B 5C3. Distributes free publications including the *Official Highway Map, Outdoor Adventure Guide, Craft Directory, Fish and Hunt Guide,* and *Travel Guide* (with accommodation and campground directory and prices). For more info, contact the **Tourist Information Centres** located at most points of entry into NB (800-561-0123 from Canada and U.S.A.).

Time Zone: Atlantic (1 hr. ahead of Eastern). **Postal Abbreviation:** NB

Area Code: 506.

Provincial sales tax: 11%.

Fundy National Park

Fundy is characteristically New Brunswickian in that its main attractions are its natural wonders. Here oscillate the world's largest tides. The size of the bay is such that it resonates at the same frequency as the tides—about once every twelve hours. The effect is similar to that of water sloshing around in a giant bathtub. In the park, you can hike through the wooded trails or slog out more than one km onto the ocean floor at low tide. The park occupies a territory along the Bay of Fundy, about an hour's drive from Moncton or Sussex. Rte. 114 is the only major access road to and through the park, running northwest to the Trans-Canada Highway, and east along the shore to Moncton.

About 120km of park trails are open year-round. Each trail, along with complete description, is detailed in *Salt and Fir*, available at park entrance stations. Only a handful are open to mountain bikes. Look for such highlights as waterfalls, ocean views and wild animals. Deer are still fairly common though declining in numbers, and raccoons are thick as thieves around the campsites. Catching a glimpse of a moose or a peregrine falcon will require considerably more patience.

Most recreational facilities open only in the summer season (mid-May-early Oct.), including interpretive programs, boat rentals, the nine-hole golf course, lawn bowling, a heated salt-water swimming pool, tennis courts, campgrounds and restaurants. The daily interpretive activities are free, friendly and always fun. Try a **Beach Walk,** during which the guide takes you down to the beach during low tide to examine ocean-bottom critters, the **Evening Program** held in the Amphitheatre, or guided **nature walks** which are never cancelled due to inclement weather. Activities are organized for kids (ages 6-12), and **campfire programs** are held weekly. Virtually all facilities are wheelchair-accessible. Many seniors visit the park in September and October to avoid the crush of vacationers and to catch the fall foliage. Those seeking quiet, pristine nature would be wise to visit in the chillier off-season.

National Park **fishing permits** ($4 per day, $6 per week, $13 per annum) are available at all information and campground kiosks. Brook trout open season runs from May 18 to September 15. Salmon angling was banned in 1991 due to low fish populations. Fishing in general is rather poor throughout the park.

Fundy weather can be unpleasant for the unprepared. Evenings are often chilly, even when days are warm. It's best to always bring a wool sweater or jacket, as well as a can of insect repellent for the warm, muggy days. **Weather** forecasts are available from the info centers by calling 887-2000.

The park operates four **campgrounds** totalling over 600 sites; getting a site is seldom a problem, although landing one at your campground of choice may be a little more difficult. Reservations are *not* accepted; all sites are first-come, first-grab. **Headquarters Campground** is in highest demand, often commanding a two-day wait in summer, because of its three-way hookups and proximity to facilities. When the campground is full, put your name on the waiting list, and sleep somewhere else for the night. Return the next day at noon when names from the list admitted for that night are read. Showers and washrooms available. (Open mid-May-mid-Oct. Sites $10, with hookup $15.50; $30 for 4 nights, with hookup $47; $50 per week, with hookup $78.) **Chignecto North Campground,** off Rte. 114, five km inland from the headquarters, is the other campground with electrical hookups. The forest and distance between campsites affords more privacy. Ten sites here offer three-way hookup, 42 offer electricity and water, 56 offer electricity only, and 212 have no hookup at all. Since the sites with three- and two-way hookup will be new for 1993, prices have not yet been determined. (Open mid-June-mid-Sept. Sites $7.75, with electricity $11; $23 for 4 nights, with electricity $33; $39 per week, with electricity $55.) **Point Wolfe Campground,** scenically located along the coast west of Headquarters, stays cooler and more insect-free than the inland campgrounds. (Open late-June-early Sept. Sites $7.75, $23 for 4 nights, $39 per week.) The **Wolfe Lake Campground** offers primitive sites near the northwest park entrance. About a minute's walk from the lake; no showers or washrooms. (Open mid-May-early Oct. Sites $6, $18 for 4 nights, $30 per week.) Wilderness camping is also available, and those sites are located in some of the most scenic areas of the park, especially at **Goose River** along the coast. The campsites are open year-round, are free, and all have fireplaces, wood, and an outhouse. Reservations are accepted only during the summer, and should be made one or two weeks in advance (call 887-2000).

For those wishing a roof over their heads, the new **Fundy National Park Hostel** is near Devil's Half Acre in the general vicinity of the park headquarters buildings (887-2216). It has a full kitchen and showers, although both are located in separate buildings from the bunkrooms. ($8.50, nonmembers $10; open June-early Sept.) Other accommodations can be found in Alma, by the park's eastern entrance, as well as grocery stores, postal services, banks and laundry facilities. For a cheap, home-cooked meal, try the **Harbor View** on Main St. (887-2450). The breakfast special is two eggs, toast, bacon and coffee ($2.75); after lunch or dinner (or for breakfast, if you want) try the fantastic strawberry shortcake ($1.50). (Open June-Aug. daily 7am-10pm; off season daily 7:30am-8pm.)

Park Headquarters, P.O. Box 40, Alma, NB, E0A 1B0 (887-2000), is made up of a group of buildings in the southeastern corner of the Park facing the Bay, across the Upper Salmon River from the town of Alma. The area includes the administration building, the assembly building, an amphitheater, and the **Alma Beach Information Center,** which sits at the east entrance (open mid-May-mid-June daily 10am-5pm, and mid-June-Sept. daily 9am-9pm). **Wolfe Lake Information,** the park's other visitors center, lurks at the northwest entrance, off Rte. 114 (open mid-June-Sept. daily 9am-9pm). In the off-season, contact Park Headquarters (open Mon.-Fri. 8:15am-4:30pm). The 24-hour **Park Emergency Number** is 882-2281. No public transport serves Fundy, and the nearest bus depots are in Moncton and Sussex. The park extracts a car entrance fee of $5 per day and $10 for four days from mid-June to Labor Day, but is free year-round for bicyclists and walkers. The free and invaluable park newspaper *Salt and Fir,* available at the park entrance stations, includes a map of all hiking trails and campgrounds as well as details on all of the interpretive programs and activities.

A worthwhile excursion from Fundy National Park is **The Rocks Provincial Park,** located at Hopewell Cape, off Rte. 114, 45km east of Alma and 34km south of Moncton. The Rocks are 50-ft.-high sandstone formations with trees on top. At high tide, they look like little islands off the coast. The best time to view the Rocks is during low tide, when they look like gigantic flowerpots rising from the ground. Then tourists are free to explore the Rocks on foot. Call the nearby craft shop (734-2975) or Tourism New Brunswick for tide info.

Moncton

Moncton is the unofficial capital city of the province's Acadian population. Its demographics accurately reflect New Brunswick's cultural schizophrenia; the francophone one-third and anglophone two-thirds of Moncton's population coexist without tension. English predominates except around the campus of the Université de Moncton, Canada's only French-language university outside of Québec. The city's inexpensive B&Bs and restaurants and its central location to the Fundy and Kouchibouguac National Parks, the Rocks Provincial Park, the town of Shediac on the coast, and to Halifax farther east in Nova Scotia make it an excellent base for exploring the region.

Practical Information

Tourist Information Centres have summer locations at Lutz Mountain on Trans-Canada Highway (Rte. 2) (853-3540; open mid-May-Oct. daily 9am-7pm), and on 575 Main St. (855-7690; open mid-May-Aug. daily 9am-7pm). **City Hall's Convention and Visitor Services** handles tourists Sept.-mid-May Mon.-Fri. 9am-5pm and distributes the *Moncton Information* booklet which covers everything down to tide schedules.

Bus: SMT, 961 Main St. at Bonaccord St. downtown (859-5060), runs to Halifax (5 hr., $33) and to St. John (2 hr., $19). Open 7:30am-8:30pm.

Car rental: Econo, 1510 Mountain Rd. (858-9100), rents for $23 per day, with 200km free, 10¢ per km thereafter. Must be 25 with major credit card. Open Mon.-Fri. 8:30am-5:30pm, Sat. 9am-1pm.

Weather: 851-6610, in French 851-6191.

Help line: Greater Moncton Crisis Line, (857-9780), a United Way agency. Lines open daily 4pm-8am.

Post Office: 281 St. George St. near Highfield St. (851-7081). Open Mon.-Fri. 8am-5:30pm. **Postal code:** E1C 8K4.

Area Code: 506.

Accommodations, Camping, and Food

Lodging in Moncton is scarce, often seasonal. The dozen or so B&Bs in the area offer the best prices, as well as clean, comfortable rooms. Motels line up along the Trans-Canada Highway, preying on those who drive through the area to experience Magnetic Hill.

The **Université de Moncton** (858-4014) in the LaFrance building—the tallest on campus—provides spacious but Spartan dorm rooms, with sofas that double as beds, as well as sinks and desks. Laundry facilities are available. From Queen St. downtown, follow Archibald St. all the way out (10 min. drive). (Open May-Aug. Singles $20, students $18. Doubles $30/$25.) The **YWCA** (855-4349) on 35 Highfield St. one block from Main St. also provides good-sized, clean rooms for women only ($15). You must check in by midnight. In July and August, it doubles as a hostel, renting bunks for $6 (bring a sleeping bag or sheets; all guests have access to lounges with TV and VCR). It's the best place for the money by far.

The area does have a campground, **Camper's City,** located on Trans-Canada Highway at Mapleton, only five km north of downtown (384-7867). The campground has 193 sites, with showers, toilets, pool, grocery, and laundry. Mostly RVs. ($15, with hookup $17.50. Office open daily 7:30am-11pm.)

Pubs are generally the cheapest place for a meal, short of fast food. **Alibi's Pub,** 841 Main St. (848-5090), serves inexpensive daily specials ($2-5) and cheap draughts, provided you can prove you're there. (Open Mon.-Sat. 10am-2am.) **Fancy Pokket,** 589 Main St. (858-7898), is an elegant Lebanese restaurant, carrying a wide variety of pita pokkets ($4-5) and brochettes ($7.25-8.25). (Open Mon.-Wed. and Sat. 11am-9pm, Thurs.-Fri. 11am-10pm.)

Sights

Moncton is deservedly proud of its two natural wonders, the Tidal Bore and Magnetic Hill. Both are more impressive in person than on paper. The **Tidal Bore,** best viewed from Tidal Bore Park near the corner of Main St. and King St., is yet another product of the Bay of Fundy tides. Twice a day the incoming tide surges up the Petitcodiac River, a muddy river bottom along whose banks Moncton is situated, sometimes with birds surfing on the Bore, and within an hour fills up to its 25-ft.-high banks. Then the flow of water reverses direction, and a mighty river starts flooding back into Chignecto Bay. It's best to arrive 15 minutes before posted Tidal Bore times (consult the city guide) in case it hits early. Spring and fall are the best seasons to catch the phenomenon at full force, as well as at a full or new moon.

Magnetic Hill on Mountain Rd. just off Trans-Canada Hwy. (Rte. 2) northwest of central Moncton, is a phenomenon notorious among Canucks. You drive your car down to the bottom of the hill, put it in neutral, and feel your car inexplicably rolling back up to the top of the hill. (Feel free to supply your own explanation.) Best of all, it's never closed; you can try it as many times as you like; and it's always free (although the commercialized complex of theme parks built next to and upon the fame of Magnetic Hill is not).

Near Moncton

The Acadian town of **Shediac,** 30km north of Moncton on Rte. 15, stakes its claim as the Lobster Capital of the World by holding their annual **Shediac Lobster Festival** in mid-July. More important to sun worshipers is the popular **Parlee Beach Provincial Park** (533-3363) in Shediac Bay near the warm salt waters of the Northumberland Strait. For more info about scheduled events, write to **Town of Shediac Information,** P.O. Box 969, Shediac E0A 3G0 (533-8800; open May-Aug. daily 9am-9pm).

Kouchibouguac, the "other" National Park in New Brunswick, suffers no inferiority complex from being the less popular sibling. In sharp contrast to Fundy National Park's rugged forests and high tides along the Loyalist coast, Kouchibouguac (meaning "river of the long tides" in Micmac) proudly emphasizes its warm lagoon waters, salt marshes, peat bogs and white sandy beaches along the Acadian coast. Swim or sunbathe along the 25km stretch of barrier islands and sand dunes. Canoe waterways that were once the highways for the Micmacs. You can rent canoes and bikes at **Ryans Rental Center** (876-2571) in the park between the South Kouchibouguac Campground and Kellys Beach. The park operates two campgrounds in the summer (sites $8, $11 with shower), neither with hookups. Several nearby commercial campgrounds just outside of the park are available for off-season campers. Kouchibouguac National Park charges a vehicle permit fee of $4 per day, $9 per four days, or $25 per year. The **Park Information Centre** is located at the Park Entrance on Rte. 117 just off Rte. 11, 90km north of Moncton. (Open mid-May-mid-June daily 9am-5pm, mid-June-early Sept. daily 9am-8pm, early Sept.-mid-Oct. Fri.-Sun. 9am-4:30pm. Park administration (876-2443) open year-round Mon.-Fri. 8:15am-4:30pm.)

A stone's throw from the Nova Scotia border is the **Fort Beauséjour National Historic Park,** located on a hill off the Trans-Canada Highway (Rte. 2) in Aulac, 40km southeast of Moncton (536-0720). One of the numerous forts built by the French and captured by the English, Fort Beauséjour (renamed Fort Cumberland under the Union Jack) is not much more than foundations and rubble these days. Some trinkets of the soldiers, including coins, weapons and handiwork (check out the ship-in-a-bottle crafted by a French prisoner), have been excavated by archaeologists and put on display at the museum. The real reason to visit the site, though, is the panoramic view from the Fort on a clear day. Looking southward to the Cumberland Basin of the Chigneto Bay and northward toward the Tantramar River Valley, one is immediately struck by the aesthetic and strategic importance of this location, on a narrow strip of land connecting Nova Scotia to the rest of the continent. (Site always open. Reception and museum open June-mid-Oct. daily 9am-5pm. Free.)

Saint John

The city of Saint John was founded literally overnight on May 18, 1783, by a band of about 10,000 American colonists (known as the United Empire Loyalists) loyal to the British crown. Saint John's long Loyalist tradition is apparent in its architecture, festivals and institutions; the walkways of King and Queen Squares in central Saint John (never abbreviated so as to prevent confusion with St. John's, Newfoundland) were laid out to resemble the Union Jack. The city rose to prominence in the 19th century as a major commercial and shipbuilding port. Today, Saint John is the largest city in New Brunswick (pop. 124,000), and in terms of land area, is also the largest city in Canada, covering more than 124 square mi. Saint John's location on the Bay of Fundy ensures cool summers and mild winters, albeit foggy and wet; locals joke that Saint John is where you go to get your car, and yourself, washed for free.

Practical Information and Orientation

Emergency: 911.

Visitor Information: Saint John Visitor and Convention Bureau (658-2990), on the 11th floor of City Hall at the foot of King St., operates year-round. Open Mon.-Fri. 8:30am-4:30pm. **The Little Red Schoolhouse** (658-2555) and the **City Centre** offer info in Loyalist Plaza by the Market Slip uptown. Open mid-May-mid-June and mid-Sept.-mid-Oct. daily 9am-7pm, mid-June-mid-Sept. daily 9am-9pm. Other **Tourist Information Centres** are located at Reversing Falls (658-2937; open mid-May-mid-June and mid-Sept.-mid-Oct. daily 9am-6pm, mid-June-mid-Sept. daily 8am-9pm) and at Highway 1 West in the Island View Heights district of Saint John West (658-2940; open mid-May-mid-June and mid-Sept.-mid-Oct. daily 9am-6pm, mid-June-mid-Sept. daily 9am-9pm).

Train: VIA Rail (642-2916), 125 Station St. next to Rte. 1 north of Market Square. To Halifax ($49, 5 days in advance, not on Fri. or Sun. $44, students $29, 5-day advance $25). Station open Tues., Fri., and Sun. 7:30am-1pm, Mon., Thurs., and Sat. 4-9pm.

Bus: SMT, 300 Union St. (648-3555) provides service to Montréal (2 per day, 14 hr., $80), Moncton (3 per day, 2 hr., $19), and Halifax (2 per day, $50). Station open daily 7:30am-9pm.

Saint John Transit (658-4700), runs daily 6am-12:30am with frequent service through King Square. $1, under 14 75¢. Also gives 3-hr. guided tour of historic Saint John leaving from Loyalist Plaza and Reversing Falls June 15-Sept. 30. Tour fare $13.50, ages 6-14 $5. Office open 5am-12:30am.

Ferry: Marine Atlantic, at the Ferry Terminal on the Lancaster St. extension in West Saint John, near the mouth of Saint John Harbor (636-4048 or 800-341-7981 from the continental U.S.), crosses to Digby, Nova Scotia (1-3 per day, 2½ hr.; June-Sept. $15, off-season $20, seniors $15/$11, ages 5-12 $10/$7.50, bike $10/$7.50, car $60/$50). To get to the ferry, take the Saint John Transit East-West bus, then walk 10 min.

Taxi: ABC, 635-1555; **Diamond,** 648-8888. Both open 24 hrs.

Car Rental: Downey Ford, 10 Crown St. (632-6000); 20 per day, with 100km free. Ages 21-24 must have major credit card. No charge for insurance, but the deductible is a hefty $1500. This is the time to check whether your credit card covers rental insurance. All cars are automatics. (Open Mon.-Fri. 7am-6pm, Sat. 8am-5pm, Sun. 9am-5pm.)

Weather: 636-4991. **Dial-a-Tide:** 636-4429.

Post Office: Main, 125 Rothesay Ave. (636-4754). Open Mon.-Fri. 7:30am-5:15pm. **Postal Code:** E2L 2B0. More convenient, uptown branch with full services in **Lawton Drug Store** (634-1422) inside the Brunswick Square Mall on the corner of King and Germain St. Open Mon.-Wed. 9am-5:30pm, Thurs.-Fri. 9am-9pm, Sat. 10am-5:30pm. **Postal Code:** E2L 4W3.

Area Code: 506.

Saint John is divided from West Saint John by the Fort Latour Harbor Bridge (toll 25¢), on Hwy. 1. Saint John's busy downtown (Saint John Centre) is bounded by Union St. to the north, Princess St. to the south, King Square on the east and Market Square and the harbor on the west.

Accommodations and Camping

Finding lodging for under $35 per night is difficult, especially in summer. A number of nearly identical motels cover the 1100 to 1300 blocks of Manawagonish Rd. in West Saint John (take the Gault bus), usually charging $35 to 40 for a single.

Saint John YM/YWCA (HI-C), 19-25 Hazen Ave. (634-7720), 2 blocks north of Market Square. Drab, bare, but clean rooms. Access to YMCA recreational facilities. Reservations recommended in the summer. $19, nonmembers and nonstudents $21. Open daily 5:30am-11pm.

Tartan B&B, 968 Manawagonish Rd. (672-2592). No frills, but clean and well-decorated. Stay here in off-season; with the full breakfast included, it's a better deal. Shared baths. (Open mid-May-mid-Oct.; singles $30, doubles $35, room with 2 single beds $40. Off-season $25, $30, $35, respectively.)

Hillside Motel, 1131 Manawagonish Rd. (672-1273). Standard clean motel room with TV and private bath. Haggle with the owner over the room price, which ranges around $35 for singles, $40 for doubles, Sept.-April $25, $30.

Rockwood Park Campground, at the southern end of Rockwood Park, off Hwy. 1, 2km north of uptown in a semi-wooded area (652-4050). Sites $11, with electric hookup $14; 2 days $19/$26; weekly $47/$70. Take University bus to Park entrance, then walk 5 min. Open mid-May-Sept.

Food and Entertainment

Reggie's Restaurant, 26 Germain St. (657-6270), provides fresh, homestyle cooking of basic North American fare. Reggie's uses famous smoked meat from Ben's Deli in Montréal. Two eggs, sausage, homefries, toast and coffee is $3.25. (Open June-Oct. daily 6am-9pm; off-season Mon.-Wed. 6am-6pm, Thurs.-Fri. 6am-7pm, Sat. 6am-5pm, Sun. 7am-3pm.) For cheap, fresh produce and seafood, your best bet is the **City Market,** between King and Brunswick Squares. The oldest building of its kind in Canada, City Market is opened and closed by the ringing of the 83-year-old Market Bell. It is also your best source for **dulse,** or sun-dried seaweed picked in the Bay of Fundy's waters, a local specialty not found outside New Brunswick. (Market open Mon.-Thurs. and Sat. 8:30am-5pm, Fri. 8:30am-9pm.) At **Slocum and Ferris** (652-2260) in the market, you can sample everything from Argentinian *empanadas* to Ukrainian *pierogis* to Indian *samosas*, and wash it down with a glass of fantastic PEI peach juice. In 1993 the best time to be in Saint John will be July 18 through 24, when the unique **Loyalist Days** festival (634-8123) celebrates the long-ago arrival of Loyalists, complete with re-enactment, costumes and street parade. The **Festival By the Sea** (632-0086), August 6 through 15 1993, brings in a number of stage and musical productions and is the city's second largest celebration.

Sights

Saint John's main attraction is **Reversing Falls,** but before you start imagining 100-ft. walls of gravity-defying water, read on. The "falls" are actually beneath the surface of the water; what patient spectators will see is the flow of water at the nexus of the St. John River and Saint John Harbor slowly halting and changing direction due to the powerful Bay of Fundy tides. Most amazing may be the number of people amazed by the phenomenon. (24 hr. Free.) You can learn more about the phenomenon by watching the 15-minute film offered at the **Reversing Falls Tourist Information Centre** (658-2937), located at the west end of the Rte. 100 bridge crossing the river, but unfortunately the film does not show the Big Event. (Center open daily mid-June-mid-Sept. 8am-9pm; mid-May-mid-June and mid-Sept.-mid-Oct. daily 9am-6pm. Film admission $1.25; screenings every hr. on the hr. To reach the viewpoint and tourist center, take the East-West bus.)

Moosehead Breweries (635-7020), at 49 Main St. in West Saint John, offers free one-hour tours of the factory twice daily, mid-June through August, leaving from the Country Store. Since tours are limited to 20 people, make reservations one or two days ahead. (The tours, of course, include samples.)

Three thematic **walking tours** are provided by the city, each lasting about two hours. **The Loyalist Trail** traces the places frequented by the Loyalist founders; the **Victorian Stroll** takes you past some of the old homes in Saint John; and **Prince William's Walk** details commerce in the port city. All of the walking tours heavily emphasize history, architecture and nostalgia. The walking tour brochures can be picked up at any tourist info center. The **Trinity Church,** 115 Charlotte St. (693-8558) on the Loyalist Trail tour, displays some amazing stained-glass windows, as well as the Royal Coat of Arms of the House of Hanover, stolen (residents here say "rescued") from the walls of the old Boston Council Chamber by fleeing Loyalists during the American Revolution. (Church open Mon.-Fri. 8am-4pm.)

Fort Howe Lookout affords a fine view of the city and her harbor. The landmark bristles with cannon, originally erected to protect the harbor from American privateers. Shooting still occurs here—though predominantly with tripod-mounted cameras rather than with the huge, now-defunct guns. To visit the Lookout, walk a few blocks in from the north end of the harbor and up the hill; look for the wooden blockhouse atop the hill. (24 hr. Free.)

Nova Scotia

French colonists known as Acadians began sharing the Annapolis Valley and Cape Breton's shores with the indigenous Micmac Indians around 1605. The next wave of colonists added 50,000 Highland Scots in the 1800s. A strong Scottish identity has been preserved in Pictou and Antigonish Counties, where Scots primarily settled. Subsequent immigration of the English, Irish and Northern Europeans also has been added to the original population of Micmacs.

The early settlers had extremely strong trading ties with Massachusetts to the south. However, when the rebellious American colonies declared their sovereignty from the British throne, Nova Scotia declined the opportunity to become the 14th colony in the emerging United States, demonstrating what some called independence and others called truckling, largely depending on the latitude of the speaker. Instead, the area served as a refuge for fleeing Loyalists—those who supported the British monarchy.

Fearing an American takeover, Nova Scotia joined three other provinces in 1867 to form the Confederation of Canada.

Four distinct geographies dominate the province: the rugged Atlantic coast, the agriculturally lush Annapolis Valley, the calm coast of the Northumberland Strait, and the magnificent highlands and lakes of Cape Breton Island.

Practical Information

Capitol: Halifax

Visitor Information: Nova Scotia Department of Tourism and Culture, Historic Properties, P.O. Box 130, Halifax, Nova Scotia B3J 2M7. A dozen provincial info centers providing free comprehensive maps and the *Nova Scotia Travel Guide/Outdoors Guide* are scattered throughout Nova Scotia. Call 800-565-0000 (from Canada) or 800-341-6096 (from the continental U.S.) to make reservations with participating hostelries.

Time Zone: Atlantic (1 hr. ahead of Eastern time). **Postal abbreviation:** NS

Area Code: 902.

Provincial Sales Tax: 10%.

Annapolis Valley

Green and fertile, the Annapolis Valley stretches along the **Bay of Fundy** between **Yarmouth** and the **Minas Basin.** Its calm, sunny weather draws harried city-folk seeking a relaxed lifestyle. The Annapolis River Valley runs slightly inland, but parallel to the coast flanked by the imaginatively named North and South Mountains, on either side. Charming towns scatter along the length of the Valley connected by scenic Rte. 1. In spring, orchards covered with aromatic pink apple blossoms perfume the Valley.

French Acadian farmers settled this serene valley in the 17th century. Their expulsion from the Valley by the British in 1755 was commemorated by Henry Wadsworth Longfellow's tragic epic poem "Evangeline", and although Longfellow himself never actually visited his "forest primeval" the appellation "Land of Evangeline" has nevertheless stuck. Rushing from sight to sight is not the most satisfying method of exploring the Valley. Take it slowly and without worries; bicycling is an ideal means of transport.

Digby, home of the famous Digby scallops, harbors one of the world's largest scallop fleets as well as the annual August **Scallop Days** festival. About 104km up the coast from Yarmouth, Digby is connected by the **Marine Atlantic Ferry** (245-2116, 800-341-7981 from the continental U.S.), to Saint John, New Brunswick, which lies across the Bay of Fundy. (1-2 trips daily, 2-3 daily in summer. Fare June-Sept. $20, seniors $15, ages 5-12 $10, car $60; off-season $16, seniors $11.25, age 5-12 $7.50, car $50.)

Brier Island, the home of Joshua Slocum (the first person to sail around the world solo) prickles at the top of Digby Neck, a 90-minute drive south from Digby on Rte. 217. The island's surrounding waters apparently provide a very attractive habitat for whales; sightings have been so numerous that **Brier Island Whale and Seabird Cruises** (839-2995) in **Westport** guarantees whale sightings or you go again free. The guides are scientific researchers from the **Brier Island Ocean Study** or from local universities. (Voyages made only when weather permits. Fare $33, ages 6-12 $16. Reserve at least 1 week in advance.)

Founded by French explorer Samuel de Champlain in 1605, the **Habitation Port-Royal** was the earliest permanent European settlement in North America north of Florida. It served as the capitol of French Acadia for nearly a century until its capitulation to the British in 1710, who renamed it Annapolis Royal in honor of Queen Anne. The original town later fell into ruin but has been restored faithfully in the form of the **National Historic Park** (532-2898) across the Annapolis Basin, 12km from modern-day Annapolis Royal. The restoration affords a rare glimpse of the wooden palisades and stone chimneys typical in early French fur-trading posts. To get to the Habitation, turn off Rte. 1 at the Granville Ferry and go on about 10km. (Open May 15-Oct. 15 daily

9am-6pm. Free.) **Kejimkujik National Park** (682-2772), Rte. 8, about 60km inland from Annapolis Royal and 160km west of Halifax, lies relatively close by. Called Keji (KEJ-ee), the park is remote, densely wooded, and liberally peppered with small lakes and unspoiled waterways best explored by canoe. Fees are charged for bringing vehicles into the park ($5 for 1 day, $10 for 4 days). The park also has a **campground** with hot showers ($10.50, no hookup).

For a less historical park experience, seek out the **Upper Clements Theme Park,** on Rte. 1 six km west of Annapolis Royal (532-7557 or 800-565-7275 from the continental U.S.), a new amusement park. Yes, there are roller coasters, water rides and a mini-golf course, but you'll also find petting farms, artisans and craftspeople plying their trade, and storytellers. (Open late June-Aug. daily 10am-7pm, Sept.-late June Sat.-Sun. 10am-7pm. Park admission free, but pass for attractions $10, after 3pm $5.50. Tickets for rides also sold individually.) Of note to engineers and "tidophiles" is the **Annapolis Tidal Generating Station,** just off Rte. 1 (532-5454), the first attempt to generate electrical energy by harnessing the powerful Bay of Fundy tides. (Open daily 9am-5:30pm, July-Aug. daily 9am-8pm. Free.)

Wolfville, 50 to 60 km north of Annapolis Royal, attracts students from all over Canada to Acadia University, with its serene Valley campus. Wolfville was renamed in the 1800s at the urging of Judge de Wolf, whose daughter was ashamed of saying she was from the town of Mud Creek. The most panoramic view in the Valley is from **The Lookoff,** Rte. 358, 20km north of Rte. 1, perched on a mountain top within view of four counties.

Grand Pré, or Great Meadow, stands at the eastern head of Annapolis Valley, 100km northwest of Halifax. The highlight is the **Grand Pré National Historic Site** (542-3631), a memorial of the deportation of the Acadians in 1755. After refusing to take oaths of allegiance, the Acadians of Grand Pré were imprisoned in the Stone Church before their deportation from the British colonies. They were the first of 6000 Acadians to be deported that year. Deported Acadians resettled further south on the continent, establishing communities in modern-day Louisiana (where they became known as Cajuns, a bastardization of "Acadians"). (Grounds always open. Buildings open mid-May-mid-Oct. Free.) Canada's best wines ferment in the Annapolis Valley; the **Grand Pré Estate Vineyard** (542-1470) gives daily tours of their grounds. (Three guided tours per day. Open May-Sept. daily 9am-5pm. Free.)

The port of **Yarmouth,** 339km from Halifax, is on the southwestern tip of Nova Scotia, a major ferry terminal with ships departing across the **Bay of Fundy** to Maine. **Marine Atlantic Ferry** (742-6800 or 800-341-7981 from continental U.S.) provides service to Bar Harbor (1 per day in summer, otherwise 3 per week; 6-7 hr.; fare June-Sept. $45, seniors $34, ages 5-12 $22.50, car $75; off-season $30, seniors $22.50, ages 5-12 $15, car $55). **Prince of Fundy Cruises** (742-6460, 800-565-7900 in Maritimes), sails from Yarmouth's port to Portland, ME. (Departs only May 2-Oct. 20 at 10am, but still doesn't sail many days, so call ahead; 11 hr.; May 2-June 20 and Sept. 19-Oct. 20 $50, age 5-14 $25; June 21-Sept. 17 $70, ages 5-14 $35.) Renting a car upon arrival in Yarmouth is a very popular idea, so reserve ahead. **Avis,** 44 Starr's Rd. (742-3323), and **Budget,** 509 Main St. (742-9500), are the only rental agencies.

Atlantic Coast

The deep, dazzling blue of the Gulf Stream waters perpetually crash onto the rocky Atlantic Coast, sending up flumes of white ocean spray. The basis of the coastal economy is the ocean, so piers, fishing boats and lobster traps are commonplace sights. Stiff ocean breezes and thick morning fog further enhance the breath-taking scenery. Frequent lighthouses blip along **Lighthouse Route,** a driving trail winding down the coastline.

One place where you will find a lighthouse, and a beautiful one at that, is **Peggy's Cove,** off of Rte. 333, 43km southwest of Halifax. No public transportation serves Peggy's Cove, but most tour bus companies offer packages which include the village. These buses, coupled with the throngs of cars that arrive in the summer, make a mockery of the cove's proclaimed population of 60. It's definitely wise to arrive either early in the morning or in the off-season, so you won't be inundated by two seas—one of water and one of people. Despite the crush of visitors, Peggy's Cove itself remains remarkably uncommercialized. The famous lighthouse, which sits in the midst of a massive, smooth field of granite at the top of the road leading into the cove, houses a tiny **post office** boasting its own cancellation stamp. (Open Mon.-Sat. 9am-5pm, Sun. 10am-4pm.)

Head south down either Rte. 103 or the more scenic Rte. 3 for about 50km to the small town of **Mahone Bay** (from Rte 103 take exit 10), whose **tourist office** (624-6151) provides a wealth of information on the area's attractions, accommodations, campgrounds, and beaches. (Open mid- to end of May and Sept.-mid-Oct. daily 10am-6pm, June-Aug. daily 9am-7:30pm.) For five days at the end of July, Mahone Bay hosts the **Wooden Boat Festival,** a celebration of the region's ship-building heritage, which includes a parade of a number of the old-style schooners.

The fishing and shipbuilding center **Lunenburg,** 11km east of Mahone Bay on Rte. 3, built the schooner Bluenose in 1921, which because it remained undefeated in international races earned a place on the back of Canada's dime and on the new Nova Scotia license plate. The **Fisheries Museum of the Atlantic,** on the harborfront (634-4794), brings the fishing industry to life with three stories of aquariums, fresh fish exhibits, a display on Prohibition-era rum-running vessels, and countless exhibits on the local fishing and fish-processing industries. Don't miss the chance to go aboard and explore the schooner and trawler docked at the museum. (Open May 15-Oct. 15 daily, 9:30am-5:30pm. Admission $2.25, kids 6-12 50¢, family $5.50.)

The **Ovens Natural Park** (776-4621), a 16km trip from Lunenburg, west on Rte. 3 and then south and east on Rte. 332, is home to a spectacular set of natural caves as well as the region's best campground. You can hike into the caves, but for non-campers there's a $2.50 fee. The Ovens has two sets of **campsites,** both of which have fairly secluded sites overlooking the ocean. (Open mid-May-mid-Oct., tent sites $14, with hookup $16. Showers, grocery store, small restaurant available. Make reservations for July-Aug. 3-4 weeks ahead.)

Rte. 332 continues along the shore and into the town of **East LaHave.** There, a **ferry** runs across the LaHave river and into **LaHave,** a great and incredibly cheap way to move along the coast without a lot of extra driving (daily, on the ½-hr., 6am-midnight; 50¢ fare including car). About 1000 ft. from the ferry dock on the left is the **LaHave Marine Hostel (HI-C)** (688-2908), upstairs from the **LaHave Bakery.** The hostel has nine bunks, a cozy living room with a wood-burning stove, a giant set of moose antlers, and a mean-spirited red-crested bird resembling, but smaller than, a parrot. If the owner takes it out of its floor-to-ceiling cage, you might want to step aside, as its wings aren't clipped and it has a fetish for swooping. (Open June-Oct., $8, nonmembers $10.) The bakery downstairs offers fresh breads so exquisite you'll be preaching "flour" power even if you missed the 60s. Try an amazing cinnamon-orange-raisin scone (80¢) or a cheese-bread biscuit (50¢). (Open daily 9am-5:30pm.) **Crescent Beach,** a one-km stretch of hard-packed white sand, is just a 10-minute drive south down Rte. 331 from LaHave. You can drive a car down onto the beach, but be sure the tide isn't coming in.

Cape Breton Island

> *"I have travelled around the globe. I have seen the Canadian and American Rockies, the Andes and the Alps, and the Highlands of Scotland; but for simple beauty, Cape Breton out rivals them all."*
>
> *—Alexander Graham Bell*

Bell backed up his words by building Beinn Bhreagh, the estate where he spent the waning years of his life, in Cape Breton. Breathtaking coastline, loch-like finger-lakes, steep, dropping cliffs and rolling green hills characterize Cape Breton, which has been called Scotland's missing west coast.

Cape Breton Island, the northeastern portion of Nova Scotia, connects to the mainland by the **Trans-Canada Hwy.** across the **Canso Causeway** lying 280km from Halifax and 270km from the New Brunswick border. **Port Hastings** is the first town you'll encounter in Cape Breton, and it supports a **Tourism Nova Scotia** center (625-1717), on the right-hand side of the road after crossing the causeway. At the center, pick up the booklet *Vacation Planner to National Parks & Historic Sites on Cape Breton Island.* (Open May 15-June and Sept.-Oct. 15 9am-5pm, July-Aug. 9am-9pm.) Public transport serves only the major cities, bypassing Cape Breton's renowned scenery. The **Bras d'Or Lake,** an 80km-long inland sea, roughly divides Cape Breton into two halves. The larger northern section includes the scenic **Cape Breton Highlands** and the **Cabot Trail.** The industrial southern section has been developed with revenues dug from steel and coal mining. **Sydney** and **Glace Bay,** Cape Breton's two largest cities, are depressed industrial centers.

The **Cabot Trail,** named after English explorer John Cabot who supposedly landed in the Highlands in 1497, is the most scenic marine drive in Canada—the Canadian answer to California's Rte. 1. The 300km-long loop of the Trail winds precipitously around the perimeter of the northern tip of Cape Breton. A photographer's dream, the Cabot Trail takes 7 to 10 hours to enjoy (allowing for a lunch break, stops at overlooks, and slow traffic). Lodging is expensive along the Trail, generally between $40 and $50 for a double (except the **Keltic Lodge** in Ingonish Beach, where it can range up to $240). There is one hostel on the island, the **Glenmore International Hostel,** in Twin Rock Valley west of Wycocomagh (258-3622; call for directions). Although dilapidated and miles from nowhere, it's the only reasonably priced way to put a roof over your head within 100 mi. (Full kitchen, linen and sheets provided; $7, nonmembers $10). Very few B&Bs line the Cabot Trail. However, **campgrounds** abound both on the Trail and within **Cape Breton Highlands National Park.** To prevent morbid thoughts about plunging off the edge, you should drive the trail clockwise, shying away from the sheer cliffs. Bicyclists, too, should go clockwise, to take full advantage of the predominantly westerly winds. For info on **bike rentals,** contact the non-profit **Les Amis Du Plein Air,** P.O. Box 472, Cheticamp B0E 1H0 (224-3814).

The stretch of land extending across the northern tip of Cape Breton and wedged within the northern loop of the Cabot Trail belongs to the **Cape Breton Highlands National Park,** 950 sq. km of highlands and ocean wilderness. One **park info center** is located along the Cabot Trail in **Cheticamp,** five km south of the southwest park entrance (224-2306), and the other at the southeast entrance in **Ingonish Beach** (285-2535). (Both centers open mid-May-late June and early Sept.-late Oct. 9am-5pm, late June-early Sept. 8am-9pm; mid-Oct.-mid-May Mon.-Fri. 8am-4:30pm for phone inquiries only.) The park provides six **campgrounds** within its boundaries. (First-come, first-served basis; weekdays yield the best selection. Sites $8-10, with fireplace $11, with hookup $15; if pay for 3 days, you can camp for 4. Park motor vehicle admission $5 per day, $10 per 4 days. Open mid-May-mid-Oct.)

On the southern loop of the Cabot Trail, the resort village of **Baddeck** lies on the shore of Lake Bras d'Or. **The Alexander Graham Bell National Historic Site,** Chebucto St. (Rte. 205) in the east end of Baddeck (295-2069), provides a spectacular view of the lake from its roof gardens. Inside the building is an insidiously fascinating museum dedicated to the life and inventions of Bell. More than just the inventor of the telephone, Bell was a fountain of ideas, spewing forth such creations (some useful, some not) as medical tools, hydrofoils and airplanes. Bell's humanitarian spirit also inspired his toils to allay problems of the deaf and sailors lost at sea. (Open July-Sept. daily 9am-9pm, Oct.-June 9am-5pm. Free.)

Not all of Cape Breton is scenic. Innumerable immigrants once migrated to the grimy, industrial city of **Glace Bay** for hazardous jobs in the Sydney coalfields. Although coal mining has now ceased, the **Miners' Museum,** Birkley St. off of South St. east of downtown (849-4522), preserves its memory with exhibits on the techniques of coal mining and the plight of organized labor, as well as a reconstructed miners' village and films on life as a coal miner. The real highlight of the museum, though, is the 1/4-

mi. tour of an underground coal mine, guided by experienced miners who paint a bleak, unromanticized picture of the hard days' toil. Watching tourists knocking their heads on the five-ft.-high ceiling supports (safety hat and cape provided) is almost as much fun as navigating the dim, dank, narrow passages of coal. (Open June-Aug. daily 10am-6pm, Sept.-May 9am-4pm. Admission $5, without tour $2.75; kids $3, without tour $1.75.)

At North Sydney, 430km northeast of Halifax, **ferries** depart daily for **Newfoundland.** The terminal sits at the end of the Trans-Canada Hwy. (Rte. 105). **Marine Atlantic Ferry** (794-5700 or 800-341-7981 from continental U.S.) leaves for Port-aux-Basques, Newfoundland. (1-3 per day; 5-7 hr.; $16, seniors $12, ages 5-12 $8, cars $50) and Argentia, Newfoundland. (2 per week; 14 hr.; $45, seniors $34, kids $22.50, cars $100). **Argentia** lies 50km away from **St. John's,** the capital of Newfoundland, while Port-aux-Basques is closer to the spectacular fjords and gorges of **Gros Morne National Park** (458-2417). For more information on Newfoundland, contact the **Newfoundland Department of Tourism,** Box 2016, St. John's, Nfld. A1C 5R8 (800-563-6353).

Sydney, 140km northeast of the Canso Causeway, is the commercial center of Cape Breton, a good base for lodging and accommodations. **Delta,** 501 Esplanade near the Sydney River (562-1155), rents economy cars for $22 per day, 100km free, 12¢ per km thereafter. You must be 21 with a major credit card; if under 25 expect an extra $13 per day insurance charge. Make reservations early in summer. (Open Mon.-Fri. 7:30am-6pm, Sat. 8am-1pm.) You can find lodging at **Paul's Hotel,** 10 Pitt St. (562-5747). (June-Sept. singles $28, doubles $35; off-season $26, doubles $32; shared bath.)

The **Fortress of Louisbourg** (LOO-iss-burg; in French Loo-ee-BOORG) was the King of France's most ambitious military project in the Colonies, his "New World Gibraltar"—the launching pad from which France would regain the Americas. A small band of New Englanders laid siege to and quickly captured Louisbourg in 1745. A treaty soon returned it to France, but then the British took the fortress back again in 1758, with even greater ease. The $25 million rebuilding of Louisbourg, the largest historic reconstruction in North America, resulted in **Fortress of Louisbourg National Historic Park,** 37km southeast of Sydney on Rte. 22 (733-2280), far more successful as a tourist attraction than it ever was as a military outpost. Every attempt has been made to recreate the atmosphere of 1744. Speaking French will help you get past the gate sentries, who don't take kindly to intruders wearing red coats. Most of the buildings feature either period rooms, staffed by costumed actors doing their 1744 thing or historical museums depicting life in the fortress. The scope is startling, the recreation, well, almost convincing. The **Hôtel de la Marine** within the fortress prepares full-course meals ($8.50) from authentic 1744 French recipes—lots of fun, but be forewarned that the 18th century had no Cordon Bleu chefs. No red meat is served on Fridays and Saturdays—it was outlawed as a religious observance. Peek at the kitchen, if you can skirt the actors. The 80% whole wheat/20% rye bread from the **King's Bakery** ($2.50) looks like a cannonball and is almost as hard. From the visitors center, where tickets are purchased and cars parked, a shuttle bus takes you to the fortress gates. The fort offers two to four guided walking tours daily, in English and French. (Open June and Sept. 9am-5pm, July-Aug. 9am-6pm. May and Oct. daily 9:30am-5pm. Admission $6.50, ages 5-16 $3.25, seniors free, family $16.) The modern town of **Louisburg** also has 10 **B&Bs** (singles $30-35, doubles $35-40). Contact **Louisbourg Tourist Bureau** (733-2720), off Rte. 22 near the fortress, for info and reservations. (Open mid-May-mid-Oct. daily 9am-7pm.)

Halifax

The Halifax Citadel was erected in 1749 as a British garrison to counter the French Fortress of Louisbourg on the northeastern shoulder of Cape Breton Island. Both fortresses still stand today, completely renovated and refurbished. Although the Halifax Citadel was never captured or even attacked in the days of the colonial empires, it is now engaged in a rather fierce battle with its Cape Breton cousin for the most sizeable portion of the tourist trade. From its perch on a hill overlooking one of the world's finest natural harbors, the Citadel has seen the surrounding city grow to become the largest in Atlantic Canada. Metropolitan Halifax, population 280,000, claims a third of the province's population, and the area is a national center of medical research. With an active nightlife and quality museums and cultural attractions, the city merits a visit on its own; it is all the more attractive as a base for travel throughout the province's beautiful, pacific, and un-self-conscious areas up and down the coast.

Halifax's placid history is marred by one event: the Halifax Explosion of 1917. Miscommunication between a Belgian relief ship and a French ship carrying picric acid and 400,000 tons of TNT resulted in a starboard-to-starboard collision in Halifax Harbor, hurling sparks into the picric acid. One hour later, Halifax felt the brunt of the largest human-made explosion before the atomic bomb. Approximately 11,000 people were killed or injured, north Halifax was razed, and windows were shattered as far as 50 mi. away.

Practical Information and Orientation

Emergency: 4105

Visitor Information: Halifax Tourist Information, City Hall, on the corner of Duke and Barrington (421-8736). Open June Sat.-Wed. 9am-6:30pm, Thurs.-Fri. 9am-7pm; July-Aug. Sat.-Wed. 8:30am-6:30pm, Thurs.-Fri. 8:30am-7:30pm; Sept.-May Mon.-Fri. 9am-5pm. Another branch on the corner of Sackville and S. Park, across from the Public Garden (421-2772). Open mid-June-Labor Day, same hours. **Tourism Nova Scotia** has locations on the downtown harbor boardwalk, Historic Properties (424-4247; open early June-Labor Day Mon.-Fri. 8:30am-8pm, Sat.-Sun. 9am-8pm; off-season Mon.-Fri. 8:30am-4:30pm), just off Rte. 102 near the airport exit (873-3608; open May 15-Oct. 15 daily 9am-5pm), and an info counter inside Halifax International Airport (426-1223; open daily 7:30am-11:30pm).

Consulates: U.S. Consulate General, Scotia Sq., Cogswell Tower, Suite 910 (429-2480). Open Mon.-Fri. 8:30am-4:50pm with 24-hr. emergency message service at the same phone number. **U.K. Consulate,** 1459 Hollis St. (422-0130; after hours, 434-3758). Open Mon.-Fri. 9am-5pm.

Halifax International Airport, 40km from the city on Rte. 102. The **Aerocoach City Shuttle** (468-1258) runs between the airport and downtown, 7:30am-11pm (14 per day; $12.50, round-trip $20, under 10 free with adult). **Share-a-cab** (429-4444) runs service to the airport 5am-9pm. Phone 3 hrs. ahead of pick-up time. Fare $18 from anywhere in Halifax.

VIA Rail: 1161 Hollis St. on the corner of South, in the South End near the harbor (429-8421). Service to Montréal $126, with 7-day advance purchase $76, students $113, with 5-day advance purchase $63. Open daily 9am-5:30pm.

Buses: Acadian Lines and **MacKenzie Bus Line** share the same terminal, 6040 Almon St. (454-9321), near Robie St. To get downtown from the bus terminal, take bus #7 or #80 on Robie St., or any of the 6 buses running on Gottingen St. 1 block east of the station. MacKenzie runs service along the Atlantic coast to Lunenberg (2 per day; 2 hr.; $10) and to Yarmouth (1 per day; 6 hr.; $26). Acadian covers most of the remainder of Nova Scotia, with connections to the rest of Canada: Annapolis Royal (2 per day; 5 hr.; $22), Charlottetown (2 per day; 81/3 hr.; $41). Senior discount 25%. Station open daily 7am-11pm.

Metro Transit (421-6600; info line open Mon.-Fri. 7:30am-10pm, Sat.-Sun. 8am-10pm.) Efficient and thorough. Pick up route map and schedules at any info center. Fare $1.15, seniors and ages 5-15 65¢. Buses run daily roughly 7am-midnight.

Dartmouth-Halifax Ferry: On the harborfront (464-2336). 15-min. harbor crossings depart both terminals every 15-30 min. Mon.-Fri. 6:30am-midnight; every 30 min. Sat. 6:30am-midnight and Sun. noon-6pm. Fare 75¢, kids 5-12 50¢. Call 464-2217 for parking info.

Taxi: Aircab (456-0373), open daily 24 hrs.; **Share-a-Cab** (429-5555), no credit cards accepted.

Car Rental: Rent-a-Wreck, 2823 Robie St. at Almon St. (454-2121). $30 per day, 200km free, 12¢ per extra km. Insurance $9 per day, ages 21-25 $11. Must be 21 with credit card. Open Mon.-Sat. 8am-5pm.

Cabana Tours, 3227 Kempt Rd. at Stairs (455-8111), offers daily tours of Halifax (2½ hr.; $15), Peggy's Cove (4 hr.; $22), and Annapolis Valley (8 hr.; $47; Mon., Wed., and Sat. only). Reservations required. **Velo Bicycle Club** conducts free bicycle tours of Halifax and throughout the province. Contact Mark Beaver (home 455-2878, work 423-4438).

Outdoor Equipment Rental: The Trail Shop, 6210 Quinpool Rd. (423-8736), offers complete selection. Bicycles $13 first day, then $10 per day. Weekend rental (Fri.-Mon.) $25. Deposit $75. Kayaks $17 first day, then $12 per day; weekend rental $30; deposit $50. Open Mon.-Wed. 10am-6pm, Thurs.-Fri. 10am-9pm, Sat. 9am-5pm.

Student Travel Agency: Travel CUTS, Dalhousie University Student Union Building 1st floor (494-2054). Open Mon.-Fri. 9am-4:30pm. **Rideboard** posted near Travel CUTS, near the cafeteria.

Help Lines: Sexual Assault: 425-0122, 24 hrs.; **Crisis Centre:** 421-1188, 24 hrs.; **Youth Help:** 420-8336, daily 6-10pm; at other times calls forwarded to the Crisis Centre.

Post Office: Station "A," 6175 Almon St. between Robie and Windsor St. in the North End (426-8988). Open Mon.-Fri. 8am-5:15pm.

General Delivery Postal Code: B3K 5M9

Area Code: 902.

Barrington is the major north-south street. **Sackville Street,** approaching the Citadel and the Public Garden, runs east-west, parallel to **Spring Garden Road,** Halifax's shopping thoroughfare. Flanking downtown are the **North End,** considered unsavory by locals, and the **South End,** mostly quiet and arboreal on the ocean. Downtown traffic is bearable, but parking difficult. If you visit in the winter, do *not* park on the street; it's prohibited in case snow plows are needed. Heed this warning even if it is sunny and warm; if you park for any length of time you will be towed.

Accommodations

Summer accommodations are tight in Halifax. Universities provide clean dorm rooms which are often swamped by conventions; book in advance. All accept major credit cards. If the dorms let you down, try contacting **Hostelling International-Canada,** 5516 Spring Garden Rd. (425-5450; open Mon.-Fri. 9am-5pm). Another, more luxurious option is the **Halifax Metro Bed and Breakfast** (434-7283), which has at least 25 homes at its command. (Singles from $30, doubles from $40.)

Halifax International Youth Hostel (HI-C), 2445 Brunswick St., 1 block from MacDonald Bridge in the North End (422-3863). Newly renovated, with casual atmosphere, great lounge. Kitchen and laundry. No curfew. Check in 8:30-10:30am and 4:30-11pm. $11.45, nonmembers $13.75.

Technical University of Nova Scotia, M. M. O'Brien Bldg., 5217 Morris St. at Barrington (420-7780). Heart of downtown. Usually has a vacancy. Free laundry. Check-in daily 8am-midnight. Singles $23. Doubles $38. Students: singles $20, doubles $34.Open May-Aug.

Dalhousie University (494-3401, after 8pm 494-2108), Howe Hall on Coburg Rd. at LaMarchant, 3km southwest of downtown. Usually packed, so arrive early. Laundry, access to Dal recreation facilities extra. Singles $33 (breakfast included), students $19 ($4.50 extra for breakfast). Under 11 free. Open May 8-Aug. 24, 24 hrs. Make July-Aug. reservations 1 week in advance.

Saint Mary's University, 923 Robie St. in the Loyola building (420-5591), 2km from downtown in the South End. Look for the big tower on campus. Serene neighborhood near Point Pleasant Park. Standard dorm rooms on an active campus. Singles $25. Doubles $37, students: $17.50, $33. Under 12 free. Open May 15-Aug. 15, 24 hrs.

Metro Halifax YMCA, 1565 S. Park St. (423-9622), across from Public Gardens/Citadel. Men only. Bright, active place with café. Use of rec facilities $3.50. Singles $31, doubles $42. Reception 24 hrs.

YWCA Halifax, 1239 Barrington St. (423-6162), downtown. Laundry, exercise facilities. Meals available. Singles $31, weekly $132. Doubles $47, weekly $198. $5 key deposit.

Gerrard Hotel, 1234 Barrington St. between South and Morris St. (423-8614). Subdued. Kitchen and parking. Must check in Mon.-Fri. 8am-6pm, Sat. 10am-4pm. Singles $30. Doubles $45. $5 per additional person.

Food and Entertainment

Downtown pubs provide cheap grub and vitality. Over 40 pubs are crammed into a few competitive city blocks, inciting draught wars and wonderfully low prices; at night, $1 draughts are common. Try the local mussels (about $3), served on generous platters. Pubs are generally open from 11am to midnight or 2am, although kitchens close a few hours earlier. Separate food and drink servers take your orders and collect payment; tip is requested upon delivery of your order at the table.

Granite Brewery, 1222 Barrington St. (423-5660). The best pub food in town and its own microbrewery, which produces three labels; the Old Peculiar is particularly good ($2.20 for 9 oz. glass). Try some with the shrimp and sausage jambalaya ($8). Open daily 11:30am-12:30am.

Lawrence of Oregano, 1726 Argyle St. (422-6907). Called Larry O's by the regulars; you can grill your own bread at the eat-in bread-and-salad bar ($3.75). Satisfying Italian and seafood dishes around $5, daily specials $2-4. Open daily 11am-2am.

Hungry Hungarian, 5215 Blowers St. (423-4364). Try the *pierogis* with tomato sauce ($2.75) or the seafood crêpes ($10). Open Mon.-Thurs. noon-9pm, Fri.-Sat. noon-10pm, Sun. noon-9pm. Closed Mon.-Fri. 2:30-5pm in summer.

J.J. Rossy's, 1883 Granville St. in Barrington Place (422-4411). The city's largest tavern. All-you-can-eat lunch specials $4. 12-oz. steak and fries $3.50. The catch: you have to buy a drink (sodas $1.60, beer $3). Tremendously cheap specials attract crowds of college students. Open daily 11am-2am, except Sun. noon-2am.

Different bars and pubs tend to be the favorite hangouts of students from different local universities. One exception to this is the **Seahorse Pub,** 1665 Argyle St. (423-7200), in a dark, heavily carved basement room, which attracts a varied and loud clientele. (Open Mon.-Wed. 11:30am-12:30am, Thurs.-Sat. 11:30am-1am, Sun. 3-11pm.) **Peddler's Pub,** in Barrington Place on Granville St. (423-5033), is huge and always packed; good pub food includes wings ($3.75-4) and steamed mussels ($3.25). (Open daily 11am-11pm.) **The Split Crow,** 1855 Granville St. at Duke (423-5093), has good live music on the weekends. (Open Mon.-Thurs. 11am-midnight, Fri.-Sat. 11am-1am.)

For a taste of fermented malt and hops much closer to its source, visit **Moosehead Breweries,** 656 Windmill Rd., Dartmouth (468-7040). Free tours and samples are given from mid-June to August. Take the Dartmouth-Halifax ferry across the Harbor. After downing a few at the Breweries, experience a buzz of a different type by turning on and tuning in to the **National Film Board of Canada,** 1571 Argyle St. (426-6001), which shows free screenings of international films Friday evenings at 8pm.

Sights

The star-shaped **Halifax Citadel National Historic Park** (426-5080) in the heart of Halifax, with noonday cannon firings and the old **Town Clock** at the foot of Citadel Hill, has become a well-ensconced Halifax tradition. A walk along the walls affords a fine view of the city and harbor. Small exhibits and a one-hour film hide behind the fortifications. (Open June 15-Labor Day daily 9am-6pm, Labor Day-June 15 daily 9am-5pm. Admission $2, kids $1, seniors free. Free June 15-Labor Day.)

The **Halifax Public Gardens,** across from the Citadel near the intersection of South Park and Sackville St., provide a relaxing spot for a lunch break. Overfed loons on the pond, Roman statues, a Victorian bandstand, gaslamps and exquisite horticulture are very properly British in style. From July to September, concerts are given Sundays at 2pm. (Gates open daily 8am-sunset.)

Point Pleasant Park, a car-free, wooded tract of land encompassing the southern tip of Halifax, boasts ownership of the **Prince of Wales Martello Tower,** an odd fort built by the British in 1797 that started leaking within 15 years of its construction. Perhaps Halifax's motive for preserving the structure is to subtly chortle at British engineering. To reach the park, take bus #9 from downtown Barrington St. Much farther south, overlooking the mouth of Halifax Harbor, is another example of British architecture, the **York Redoubt.** Built to defend British holdings against the French, this fort apparently has survived *sans* drainage problems; it was used until World War II. The tower commands a gorgeous view of the harbor. To get to the fort, take bus #15 to Purcell's Cove.

The **Historic Properties** district, downtown on lower Water St. (429-0530), holds reconstructed early-19th-century architecture. The charming stone-and-wood façades, however, are only sheep's clothing disguising wolfishly overpriced boutiques and restaurants of tourist-trap commercialism. The real items of interest here are the summer docking of the *Bluenose II* (hint: look at a Canadian dime) and the annual **International Town Crier's Championship** in late July. *Oye! Oye! Oye!*

Province House, on the corner of Granville and George St., can be a show in itself during parliament. Inside the small, Georgian brownstone, the Assembly Speaker and Sergeant-at-Arms don elegant top hats and black cloaks for sporadically lively debate.

Museums in Halifax don't stack up to the competition within Nova Scotia. However, die-hard museum-goers might enjoy the **Maritime Museum of the Atlantic,** 1675 Lower Water St. (424-7490), which has an interesting display on the Halifax Explosion. (Open Mon., Wed.-Sat. 9am-5:30pm, Tues. 9:30am-8pm, Sun. 1-5:30pm. Closed Mon. mid-Oct.-mid-May. Free.) The **Nova Scotia Museum,** 1747 Summer St. behind Citadel Hill (429-7353), offers exhibits on the natural history, geology, and native cultures of the province. (Open June-Oct. 15 Mon.-Tues. and Thurs.-Sat. 9:30am 5:30pm, Wed. 9:30am-8pm, Sun. 1-5:30pm. Off-season reduced hours. Free.)

Festival 93 (421-2900) celebrates Halifax's birthday for 10 days in late July and early August. The highlight is the **Natal Day** parade and fireworks. The **Buskerfest** (425-4329), held for a week in mid-August, showcases street performers from around the world in the streets. Also in Halifax is the **Nova Scotia International Tattoo** (422-1343), presented by the Province of Nova Scotia and the Canadian Maritime armed forces. In the first week of July, the festival is kicked off by a street parade of international musicians, bicyclists, dancers, acrobats, gymnasts, and military display groups. At noon, the Metro area spawns lots of free entertainment. Later a two-hour show, featuring the 1800 performers, is held in the Halifax Metro Centre. (Tickets for the show $16, seniors and kids $8. Call 451-1221 to purchase them.)

Ontario

First claimed by French explorer Samuel de Champlain in 1613, Ontario soon became the bastion of English influence within Canada. The British tentatively asserted control with a takeover of New France in 1763 at the end of the French and Indian War. Twenty years later, a flood of Loyalist emigrés from the newly-forged United States streamed into the province, fortifying the province's British character. To this day Ontario remains the standard bearer of English cultural hegemony within Eastern Canada, home to an ersatz Stratford and eminently Victorian Niagara-on-the-Lake.

Aside from being the most English, Ontario is also the most Americanized of the provinces. In the south you'll find world-class Toronto—American in that it is multicultural, enormous (3 million plus, by *far* the largest city in sparse Canada), and vibrant; un-American, perhaps, in that it is clean and safe as well. Surrounding this sprawling megalopolis are yuppified suburbs, the occasional beer-soaked college town, and farms. Head further north, and the layers of cottage country and ski resorts will yield to true Canadian wilderness; land of national parks and beautiful lakes.

Practical Information

Capital: Toronto.

Ontario Ministry of Tourism and Recreation, 77 Bloor St. W., 9th floor, Toronto M7A 2R9 (800-268-3735 or 800-668-2746; open daily 8am-6pm, Mon.-Fri. off-season). Free brochures, guides, maps, and info on upcoming special events.

Alcohol: Legal drinking age 19.

Time Zone: Eastern. **Postal Abbreviation:** Ont.

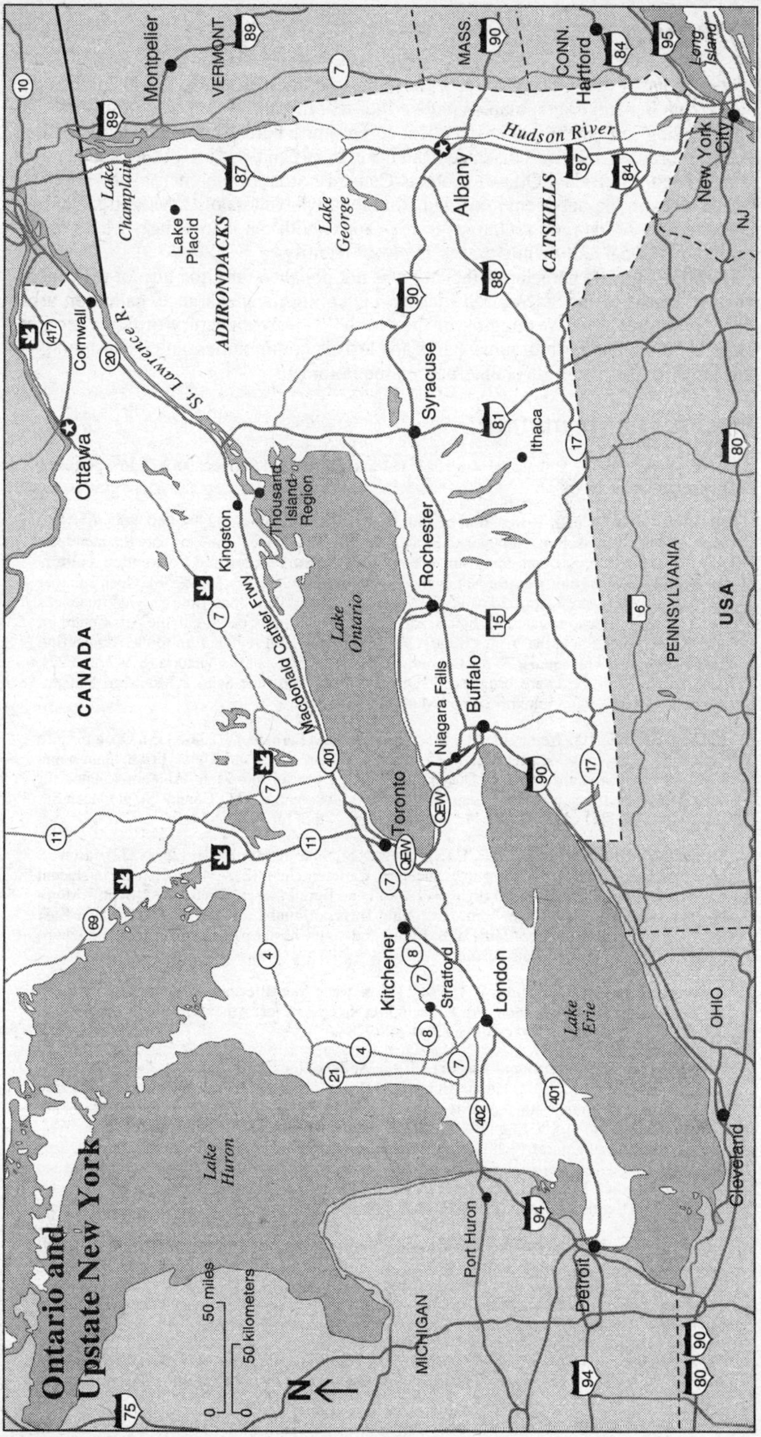
Ontario and Upstate New York
50 miles
50 kilometers
N
CANADA
USA
Ottawa
Cornwall
Kingston
Thousand Island Region
St. Lawrence R.
ADIRONDACKS
Lake Placid
Lake Champlain
Montpelier
VERMONT
MASS.
CONN.
Hartford
Long Island
New York City
NJ
Hudson River
Albany
CATSKILLS
Lake George
Syracuse
Ithaca
Rochester
Lake Ontario
Macdonald Cartier Fwy
Buffalo
Niagara Falls
Toronto
Kitchener
Stratford
London
Lake Erie
Lake Huron
Port Huron
Detroit
Cleveland
MICHIGAN
OHIO
PENNSYLVANIA
10
89
7
87
90
84
95
88
81
417
20
17
80
15
6
401
QEW
11
69
4
8
21
402
94
75

Ottawa

Legend has it that Queen Victoria chose this capital of Canada by closing her eyes and poking her finger at a map. Whatever her real method, the choice of this once-remote logging settlement was an excellent compromise between French and English interests; moreover, the site's distance from the ever-expanding U.S. border added much-needed security. Today, Ottawa protects Canada not from the encroachments of the U.S.A. or from the harsh environs, but from the divisiveness of Canada itself: each of the provinces sends representatives to the capital with the increasingly tricky task of forging a national unity while preserving local identity.

The rough-hewn character of the city was not polished until the turn of the century, when Prime Minister Sir Wilfred Laurier, lamenting its appearance, called on urban planners to create a "Washington of the North." Nearly a century of cultivation has borne fruit in Ottawa's museums, parks and artistic communities, and its cosmopolitan flair today rivals that of its counterpart on the Potomac.

Practical Information

Emergency: (Police, Ambulance, Fire) 911. **Ontario Provincial Police:** 800-267-2677. **Ottawa Police:** infoline: 230-6211.

National Capital Commission Information Center, 14 Metcalfe St. (239-5000, 800-465-1867 across Canada), at Wellington opposite Parliament Buildings. Open summer daily 8:30am-9pm; Sept. 3-May 5 Mon.-Sat. 9am-5pm, Sun. 10am-4pm. **Ottawa Tourism and Convention Authority Visitor Information Centre,** National Arts Centre, 65 Elgin St. (237-5158). Open summer daily 9am-9pm; Sept. 3-April 30 Mon.-Sat. 9am-5pm, Sun. 10am-4pm. Both provide free maps and a visitors guide to restaurants, hotels, and sights. Free 30-min. parking in the Arts Centre lot with ticket validation at the Visitor Centre. For info on the Hull region, turn to the **Association Touristique de l'Outaouais,** 25 rue Laurier, Hull, on the corner of rue Victoria (819-778-2222). Also has info on the entire province of Québec. Open mid-June-Sept. 2 Mon.-Fri. 8:30am-8:30pm, Sat.-Sun. 9am-5pm; off-season Mon.-Fri. 9am-5pm.

Embassies: U.S., 100 Wellington St., directly across from Parliament (238-5335). Open for info Mon.-Fri. 10am-4pm. Visa services at 85 Albert St., Mon.-Tues. and Thurs.-Fri. 8:30am-noon. **U.K.,** 80 Elgin St. at the corner of Queen (237-1530). Open for info Mon.-Fri. 8am-4:30pm; for visas Mon.-Fri. 10am-1pm, for passports 10am-4pm. **Australia,** 50 O'Connor St. at Queen St., suite 710 (236-0841). Open Mon.-Fri. 9am-noon and 2-4pm for visas and info.

Student Travel Agencies: Travel CUTS, 1 Stewart St, Suite #203 at Waller (238-8222), just west of Nicholas or on the 1st level of the Unicentre, Carleton Univ. (238-5493). Experts in student travel: youth hostel cards, cheap flights, VIA Rail and Eurail passes. Open June 1-Sept. 1 Mon.-Fri. 9am-5pm, off-season 9am-4pm. **Hostelling International-Canada (HI-C), Ontario East Region,** 18 Byward Market (230-1200). Eurail and youth hostel passes, travel info and equipment. Open Mon.-Sat. 9:30am-5:30pm.

American Express: 220 Laurier W. (563-0231), between Metcalfe and O'Connor in the heart of the business district. Open Mon.-Fri. 8:30am-5pm. In case of lost Amex Traveler's Checks, call 800-221-7282, in case of lost cards call 800-268-9284.

Airport: Ottawa International Airport, 20 min. south of the city off Bronson Ave. (998-3151). Take bus #96 from Le Breton station, Albert St. at Booth, or Slater St. for regular fare. Tourist info available daily 8:30am-9:30pm in arrival area. Express airport **Pars Transport** buses (523-8880) from Lord Elgin Hotel, 100 Elgin Blvd. at Slater, and 10 other hotels including the Delta, the Westin and the Château Laurier. Pick-up from 14 other hotels can be arranged by phone. Fare $8, ages 7-12 $5, under 7 free. Daily every ½-hr. 6:30am-8:40pm, plus 1 at 5am. Call for later pick-up and schedule specifics. Service from airport too. **Air Canada** (237-1380) has student standby rates for those under 21 with ID. **Delta** (236-0431) has youth fares for ages 12-21 on transatlantic flights.

VIA Rail Station: 200 Tremblay Rd. (244-8289 for reservations or recorded departure info), off Alta Vista Rd. To: Montréal (4 per day; 2 hr.; $30, student $27); Toronto (5 per day; 4 hr.; $65/$59). To Quebec City, must travel via Montréal ($59/$53). (AMTRAK 800-426-8725.) 40% discount for reservations 5 days in advance for students while tickets last, for adults traveling Sat. or Mon.-Thurs. Ticket office open Mon.-Sat. 6am-9pm, Sun. 7am-9pm.

Voyageur Bus: 265 Catherine St. (238-5900), between Kent and Lyon. Service throughout Canada. To: Montréal (18 per day, 21/3 hr., $22), Toronto (7-8 per day, 4½ hr., $44), Québec City (14 per day, 6 hr., $53). For service to the U.S. must first go to Montréal or Toronto; connections made through Greyhound. Open daily 5:30am-midnight. Tickets can be purchased at station only.

Public Transport: OC Transport, 1500 St. Laurent (741-4390). Excellent bus system. Buses congregate on either side of Rideau Centre; Mackenzie Bridge and the corner of Nicholas and Rideau. Fare $1.30, rush hour (6-8:30am and 3-5:30pm) $2, express routes (green buses) rates $2.60. Seniors $1.30 at all times. **Minipass** for a day of unlimited travel after 9am $2, plus 70¢ additional during peak hrs., under 6 free.

Taxi: Blue Line Taxi, 238-1111. **A-1,** 746-1616. Rates fixed by law ($1.90 plus distance and waiting). 24 hrs.

Car Rental: Hertz, 30 York St. in Byward Market (238-7681). $27 per day with 200km free, 10¢ per additional km. Insurance $12 per day. Must be 21 with credit card. (Open Mon. 7am-7pm, Tues.-Wed. 7:30am-7pm, Thurs.-Fri. 7:30am-8pm, Sat.-Sun. 8am-6pm.) **Budget,** 443 Somerset W. at Kent (232-1526). $43 per day; usually offer specials for less. 200km free, 10¢ each additional km. Insurance $12 per day. Must be 21 with credit card. (Open Mon.-Fri. 7am-7pm, Sat.-Sun. 8am-6pm.) **Tilden,** 226 Queen St. at Bank (232-3536), and **Myers,** 1200 Baseline St. (225-8006) also serve Ottawa/Hull. Amex will cover insurance for members. Most companies run summer specials.

Rider/Driver Matching Agency: Allostop, 246 Maisonneuve at Verdun St., Hull (778-8877). To: Toronto ($22), Québec City ($29), Montréal ($14), New York ($50) and Boston ($42). Membership ($6 per yr.) required. Open Mon.-Wed. 9am-5pm, Thurs.-Fri. 9am-7pm, Sat.-Sun. 10am-5pm.

Bike Rental: Rent-A-Bike-Location Velo, 1 Rideau St. (233-0268), behind the Château Laurier Hotel. $4-8 per hr., $12-25 per day. Family deals. Escorted tours for a price. Maps, locks free. Tandems available. Open mid-May-mid-Oct. daily 9am-7pm. Credit card required.

Alcohol: Legal ages 19 (Ottawa) and 18 (Hull). Bars stay open in Ottawa until 1am, in Hull until 3am.

Help Line: Gayline-Telegai, 238-1717. Info on local bars, special events and meetings, as well as counseling. Open Mon.-Fri. 7:30-10:30pm, Sat.-Sun. 6-9pm. **Ottawa Distress Centre,** 238-3311, English-speaking. **Tel-Aide,** 741-6433, French-speaking. **Rape Crisis Centre,** 729-8889. All 3 lines 24 hrs.

Post Office: Postal Station "B," 359 Sparks St. at Elgin St. (992-4779). Open Mon.-Fri. 8am-6pm. **Postal Code:** K1P 5A0.

Area Code: 613 (Ottawa); 819 (Hull).

The **Rideau Canal** divides Ottawa into eastern and western sections. West of the canal, Parliament buildings and government offices line **Wellington Street,** one of the main east-west arteries. **Laurier** is the only other east-west street which permits traffic in both directions on both sides of the canal. East of the canal, Wellington St. becomes Rideau St., surrounded by a fashionable new shopping district. To the north of Rideau St. lies the **Byward Market,** a recently renovated shopping area and the focus of Ottawa's nightlife. **Bank Street,** which traverses the entire western side of the city and services the other, older shopping area, is the primary north-south street. **Elgin Street,** the other major north-south artery on the western side, stretches from the **Queensway (Hwy. 417)** to the War Memorial in the heart of the city in front of **Parliament Hill.** The canal itself is a major access route: in winter, thousands of Ottawans skate to work on the world's longest skating rink; in summer, power boats breeze by. Bike paths and pedestrian walkways border the canals, allowing a pleasant alternative to car or bus transit. Parking is painful downtown; meters cost 25¢ for 10 minutes with a one-hour limit. Residential neighborhoods east of the canal have one-hour and three-hour limits and the police ticket less often than on main streets. OC Transpo runs a **Park-n-Ride** system, with one lot to the east and one to the west of downtown. (For info: 741-3490.)

Across the Ottawa River lies **Hull,** Québec, most notable for its proximity to Gatineau Provincial Park and the many bars and discos that rock nightly until 3am. Hull is accessible by several bridges and the blue Hull buses from downtown Ottawa.

Accommodations and Camping

Clean, inexpensive rooms and campsites are not difficult to find in Ottawa, except during May and early June, when gaggles of young students make a pilgrimage to the capital and pack budget lodgings solid. The area also boasts a number of B&Bs for those who can afford the extra expense. An extensive listing can be found in the *Ottawa Visitor Guide,* available at the National Capital Commission Info Center (see above); the guide also lists two referral services. The **Olde Bytown Bed & Breakfast,** 459 Laurier E., K1N 6R4 (235-1442), in one of Ottawa's wealthiest neighborhoods, is a 20-minute walk from downtown; Renée Galioto rents 16 airy rooms in two old Ottawa houses. Full breakfast; free pick up at train or bus station or airport. Equipped for those in wheelchairs and the blind. Especially welcoming to graduate students and summer interns for longer stays. Reservations recommended. Parking available. (Singles from $35. Doubles from $60.)

Nicholas Gaol International Hostel (HI-C), 75 Nicholas St. K1N 7B9 (235-2595), near Daly St. in downtown Ottawa. Take bus #4 from the inter-city bus terminal, bus #95 west from the train station, or exit at Nicholas St. from the Queensway (Hwy. 417). The site of Canada's last hanging, this trippy hostel now "incarcerates" travelers in the former Carleton County Jail. 4-8 prisoners per cell. Hot communal showers, kitchen, laundry, and large, comfortable lounges. The wardens serve a good, fresh breakfast ($3) in the **Hard-Lock Café** in the exercise yard out back—a great place to mingle with international visitors. Canoe and skate rental. All-day access; doors locked 2am-7am, make your escape some other time. Entrance free; you pay to leave—in cold cash, not hard time. Peak season $15, nonmembers $20. Rates slightly higher for Canadian non-members; non-peak rates lower.

University of Ottawa Residences, 100 University St. (564-5400), in the center of campus. Take bus #1,7 or 11 on Bank St. to the Rideau Centre from the bus station and walk up Nicholas to the U of O campus, bus #95 west from the train station or the easy walk from downtown. Clean dorm rooms. Shared hall showers. Free local phone in hall. Check-in 4:30pm but they'll store your luggage until then. Linen, towels free. Access to university student center (with bank machines). Continental breakfast $2. Singles $34. Doubles $44. Students with ID: $18/$31. Open early May-late Aug.

YM/YWCA, 180 Argyle St. at O'Connor (237-1320). Close to the bus station; walk left on Bank and right on Argyle. Nice-sized rooms in a modern high-rise. Phones in every room. Kitchen with microwave available until midnight. Guests can use gym facilities. Singles with shared bath $38, with private bath $44. Doubles $47. Under 12 with adult free. Weekly and group rates available. Payment must be made in advance. Cafeteria (breakfast $2.75) open Mon.-Fri. 7am-7pm, Sat.-Sun. 8am-2:30pm.

Centre Town Guest House Ltd., 502 Kent St. (233-0681), just north of the bus station, a 10- to 15-min. walk from downtown. Impeccably clean rooms in a friendly, comfortable house. Free breakfast (eggs, cereal, bacon, toast) in a cozy dining room. Singles $30. Doubles $35. 2 twin beds $40. Monthly rates from $300. Reservations recommended.

Camp Le Breton, in a field at the corner of Fleet and Booth (943-0467). Urban tent-only camping within sight of Parliament, a 15-min. walk from downtown. More of a football field tailored with trees than a campsite. Washrooms, showers. Parking, playground. 5-day max. stay. Check-in 24 hrs. Sites $6.50 per person, seniors $3.25, under 12 free. Reservations unnecessary—they'll squeeze you in.

Gatineau Park, northwest of Hull (reservations 456-3494; info 827-2020). Map available at visitors center. Three rustic campgrounds within 45 min. of Ottawa: **Lac Philippe Campground,** with facilities for family camping, trailers, and campers; **Lac Taylor Campground,** with 34 "semi-wilderness" sites; and **Lac la Pêche,** with 36 campsites accessible only by canoe. (Canoeing equipment $7 per hr., $15 per ½-day, $23 per day, $38 overnight. Mountain bikes, paddleboats available; same rates.) All campgrounds off Hwy. 366 northwest of Hull—watch for signs. From Ottawa, take the Cartier-MacDonald Bridge, follow Hwy. 5 north to Scott Rd., turn right onto Hwy. 105 and follow it to 366. To reach La Pêche continue on 366 to Eardley Rd. on your left. Camping permits for Taylor and Philippe available at the entrance to the campground. Pay for a site at La Pêche on Eardley Rd. June 14-Sept. 2 all sites $14, seniors $7; Sept. 3-Oct. 8 and May 15-June 13 $11, $5.50; off-season (some sites open at Lac Philippe) $3.

Food and Nightlife

Look for restaurant/bars in Ottawa serving dirt-cheap food to lure you into their dens of high-priced beer. **Fathers and Sons** (see listing below) has 15¢ wings on Monday and Saturday. **Tramps,** 53 William St. (238-5523; open daily 11am-1am), serves 20¢ chicken wings Monday through Thursday, and 20¢ shrimp Friday and Saturday. If it's cheap beer, and not cheap food that you want, head to **Grand Central,** 141 George St. (233-1435; recorded music info 233-1216), where the 99¢ draft is the cheapest in the Byward Market area. (Bands nightly, $1 cover Thurs.-Sat. after 8pm. Jazz on Sun. Open daily 11am-1am.) During the day, fresh fruit, vegetable, and flower stands cluster at **Byward Market** on Byward between York and Rideau. (Open daily 8am-6pm.)

The International Cheese and Deli, 40 Byward St. (234-0783). Deli and middle eastern sandwiches to go. Vegetable *samosa* $1.25. Turkey and cheese $4, falafel on pita $2.25. Open Sat.-Thurs. 8am-6pm, Fri. 8am-8pm.

Grenville's, 315 Somerset W. at O'Connor (235-0369). Although a bit off the budget track, fabulous food in an elegant, uncrowded setting make Grenville's worth the money. In summer eat on the patio and watch the Somerset street strollers go by. Menu changes monthly. (Dinner $11-15, Tues.-Sat. 5:30-10pm. Lunch, $7-10, Tues.-Fri. 11:30am-2:30pm. Parking next door.)

Dunn's Delicatessen and Restaurant, 126-128 George St. at Dalhousie (235-3866). Quality deli with friendly service. Sandwiches $3-4. Breakfast special (2 eggs, bacon, toast, coffee) $1.75, served Mon.-Fri. 6-10am. Evening special (smoked meat, fries, pickle and soft drink) $4, served daily 4pm-midnight. Open daily 24 hrs.

Sunset Grill, 47 Byward St. at Parent St. (594-9497). Sit on the huge outdoor terrace and lay into the oh-my-God-it's-so-big "sunset beach club sandwich" ($8). The less ambitious appetite can tackle the "good friends, good times taco dip" ($8). Open Mon.-Sat. 11am-1am, Sun. 11am-11pm.

Father and Sons, 112 Osgoode St. (233-6066), at the eastern edge of the U of O campus. Student favorite for tavern-style food with some Lebanese dishes thrown in. Try the falafel platter ($6.15) or a triple decker sandwich ($6-6.50). Drink-encouraging specials daily 8-11pm: Mon. and Fri. wings 15¢, Thurs. shooters $2.50. Open daily 8am-1am, kitchen until midnight.

Boko Bakery, 87 George St. in the Byward Market Mall (230-1417), is a local favorite. The Boko's menu displays a very British blurb from the management which promises to maintain the "olde-fashioned" methods of baking fresh breads. Breakfast (7:30-11am) special: 2 eggs, bacon or ham, croissant or toast, and coffee ($3). Sandwiches with salad $3.75-5.

The dedicated nightlifer should descend into Hull, where most establishments grind and gnash until 3am every day of the week and the legal drinking age is 18. In Ottawa, the Byward Market area contains most of the action. Ottawa clubs close at 1am (many at 11pm on Sun.) but most, in an effort to keep people from going to Hull, offer free admission. **Stoney Monday's,** 62 York St. (236-5548), just west of William, is a trendy bar for people in their early to mid-20s. **Chateau Lafayette,** 42 York St. (233-3403), the oldest tavern in Ottawa, lures the budgeteer with $1.40 draft beer and $2.90 pints. The regulars are hard-core beer drinkers who hold their mugs with both hands, pound a beer, slam the mug down on the bar, and say "Mr. Keeper, I'll hava 'nuther." The management steadfastly refuses to serve hard liquor, upholding the noble tavern tradition. For a taste of life, the universe, and a bit of everything, head to **Zaphod Beeblebrox,** 27 York in Byward Market, (562-1010), a popular alternative club with live bands Tuesday and Thursday through Saturday nights. Be advised of one small hitch: the cover is usually hiked up to $5 on nights with bands; whatever you do, stay away from that Ol' Janx Spirit. (Open noon-1am daily.) Over 20 popular nightspots populate the **Promenade du Portage** in Hull, just west of Place Portage, the huge government office complex. **Le Coquetier,** 147, promenade du Portage (771-6560), is one of the more peaceful places on the promenade to treat a friend to a "brewski" (open daily 11:30am-3am).

Sights

Although overshadowed by Toronto's size and Montréal's cosmopolitan color, Ottawa's status as capital of Canada is shored up by its cultural attractions. Since the national museums and political action are packed in tightly, most sights can be reached on foot. **Parliament Hill,** on Wellington St. at Metcalfe, towers over downtown as the city's focal point, while its Gothic architecture sets it apart. Roast a marshmallow over the **Centennial Flame** at the south gate, lit in 1967 to mark the 100th anniversary of the Dominion of Canada's inaugural session of Parliament. The central parliament structure, **Centre Block,** contains the House of Commons, the Senate and the Library of Parliament and is where reigning "blockhead" Prime Minister Brian Mulroney can occasionally be spotted. The Library was the only part of the original (1859-66) structure to survive the 1916 fire. On display behind the library is the original bell from Centre Block, which crashed to the ground after chiming midnight on the night of the fire. Free, worthwhile tours in English and French depart every 10 minutes from the Infotent. (During the summer make same-day reservations at the Infotent. Group reservations year-round 996-0896. Public Information 992-4793. Open mid-May-early Sept. Mon.-Fri. 9am-8:30pm, Sat.-Sun. 9am-5:30pm; off-season daily 9am-4:30pm. Last tour each day begins ½ hr. before closing time.) Watch Canada's Prime Minister and his government squirm on the verbal hot seat during the official **Question Period** in the House of Commons chamber (call 992-4793 for info on days and times; free). Far less lively or politically meaningful, the sessions of the **Senate of Canada** (992-4791) also welcome spectators. See (while you can) the body of "sober second thought," on which some Canadians are ready to lock the doors and throw away the gavel. After the tour, climb the 293-ft. **Peace Tower** to get a stunning view of the Ottawa valley. The white marble **Memorial Chamber** honors Canadian war dead. Those interested in trying to make a number of statuesque soldiers giggle should attend the **Changing of the Guard,** on the broad lawns in front of Centre Block (June 22-Aug. 25 daily at 10am). At dusk, Centre Block and lawns transform into the set for *Sound and Light,* which relates the history of the Parliament Buildings and the development of the nation (early May-early June Wed.-Sat.; early June-early Sept. daily. May-July 9:30 and 10:30pm; Aug.-Sept. 9 also at 10pm). Catch the carillon concerts that chime year-round most weekdays (12:30-12:45pm, in July also 8-9pm and Aug. 7:30-8:30pm). A five-minute walk west along Wellington St. is the **Supreme Court of Canada** (995-4330), where nine justices preside. Worthwhile 30-minute tours of the Federal Court and the Supreme Court, both housed in this building, are offered. (Open summer daily 9am-5pm; off-season Mon.-Fri. 9am-5pm. Free.) One block south of Wellington, Sparks St. greets one of North America's first pedestrian malls, hailed as an innovative experiment in 1960. The **Sparks Street Mall** recently received a $5-million facelift, rejuvenating many of Ottawa's banks and upscale retail stores. The **Rideau Centre,** south of Rideau St. at Sussex Dr., is the city's primary shopping mall as well as one of the main OC Transport stations. The sidewalks in front of Rideau Street's numerous stores are enclosed by glass, making them bearable during the cold winter months.

East of the Parliament Buildings at the junction of Sparks, Wellington, and Elgin stands **Confederation Square,** its enormous **National War Memorial** dedicated by King George VI in 1939. The towering structure symbolizes the triumph of peace over war, an ironic message on the eve of WWII.

Nepean Point, several blocks northwest of Rideau Centre and the Byward Market by the Alexandra Bridge, provides a panoramic view of the capital. An open-air theater, the **Astrolabe,** was constructed on Nepean Point in 1967 and is one of the sites of **Cultures Canada** (239-5000), not a disease convention but a festival of song and dance from July to Labor Day.

Parks and Museums

Ottawa boasts a multitude of parks and recreational areas: green spaces, walkways, and bike paths surrounding the canal. Find your thrill on **Major Hill's Park,** the city's oldest park, behind the Château Laurier Hotel on the banks of the Ottawa. Half a league onward within it stands a relic from the Crimean War, the **Noon Day Gun,** which fires Monday through Friday at noon. **Dow's Lake** (232-1001), accessible by means of the Queen Elizabeth Parkway, is an artificial lake on the Rideau Canal, 15 minutes south of Ottawa. Pedal boats, canoes, and bikes are available at the Dow's Lake Pavilion, just off Queen Elizabeth Parkway.

The Governor-General, the Queen's representative in Canada, opens the grounds of **Rideau Hall,** his official residence, to the public. Tours leave from the main gate at One Sussex Dr. (Call 998-7113, 998-7114 or 800-465-6890 for tour info; free.) At nearby **24 Sussex Drive** you'll find the official residence of the Prime Minister. Gawk from afar or use a scope; you can't get any closer to the building than the main gates.

Ottawa headquarters many of Canada's huge national museums. **The National Gallery** (990-1985), in a spectacular glass-towered building at 380 Sussex Dr., adjacent to Nepean Point, contains the world's most comprehensive collection of Canadian art, as well as outstanding European, American and Asian works. The building's exterior is a postmodern parody of the facing neo-Gothic buttresses of the Library of Parliament. (Open May-Labor Day Sat.-Tues. 10am-6pm, Wed.-Fri. 10am-8pm; Labor Day-April 30 Tues.-Sun. 10am-5pm, Thurs. 10am-8pm. Public tours daily at 11am and 2pm. Admission $5, seniors and students $3, under 16 free.) The gallery is wheelchair-accessible and free on Thursday, as are most of Ottawa's public museums and galleries. The **Canadian Museum of Contemporary Photography,** 1 Rideau Canal between the Chateau Laurier and the Ottawa Locks (990-8257), opened its doors for the first time in 1992. The museum allows a glimpse of life in modern Canada which might not otherwise be seen. (Open daily 11am-6pm except Wed. 4-8pm. $2.50, students and seniors $1.50. Free Thurs.) A spaceship-like structure across the river in Hull houses the **Canadian Museum of Civilization** at 100 Laurier St. (776-7000). Admire the architecture but be wary of overly ambitious exhibits that attempt perspective on 1000 years of Canadian history. Don't miss breathtaking films screened in **Ciné Plus,** the first in the world capable of projecting both Imax and Omnimax. (Open April-June 30 daily 9am-5pm, Thurs. 9am-8pm; July 1-Sept. 2 daily 9am-6pm, Thurs. 9am-8pm; winter Tues.-Sun. 9am-5pm, Thurs. 9am-8pm. Museum $4.50, seniors and students $3, under 15 free; Thurs. free. Ciné Plus $7, seniors and students $5, under 5 free.) The **Canadian Museum of Nature,** at McLeod St. at Metcalfe (996-3102), explores the natural world, from dinosaur skeletons to minerals, through multi-media displays. Be sure to check out the Discovery Den. (Open May 1-Labor Day Sun.-Mon. and Thurs. 9:30am-8pm, Tues.-Wed. and Fri.-Sat. 9:30am-5pm; winter daily 10am-5pm, Thurs. 10am-8pm. Admission $4, students $3, ages 6-16 and seniors $2, under 6 free; Thurs. ½ price 10am-5pm, free 5-8pm.)

Canadian history buffs could easily lose themselves in the **National Library Archives,** 395 Wellington St. at Bay St. (995-5138), which houses oodles of Canadian publications, old maps, photographs and letters, as well as historical exhibits. (Library open Mon.-Fri. 8:30am-4:45pm and will provide group tours for those with professional interest only. Exhibit area open daily 9am-9pm.) Anyone who enjoys an occasional guffaw at the government's expense (and who doesn't?) will double up with laughter at the new **Canadian Museum of Caricature,** 136 Patrick St. at Sussex (995-3145). (Open Sat.-Tues. 10am-6pm, Wed.-Fri. 10am-8pm. Free.) Walk to the elegant **Laurier House,** 335 Laurier Ave. E. (692-2581), from which Liberal Prime Minister William Lyon Mackenzie King governed Canada for most of his lengthy tenure. Admire at your leisure the antiques accumulated by King, as well as the crystal ball he used to consult his long-dead mother on matters of national importance. (Open April-Sept. Tues.-Sat. 9am-5pm, Sun. 2-5pm; Oct.-March Tues.-Sat. 10am-5pm, Sun. 2-5pm. Free.)

Further out of town, the **National Museum of Science and Technology,** 1867 St. Laurent Blvd. at Smyth (991-3044), lets visitors explore the developing world of mech, tech and transport with touchy-feely exhibits. The museum entrance is on Lancaster, 200m east of St. Laurent. (Open daily 9am-5pm, Thurs. 9am-9pm; Labor Day-April closed Mon.; $4.25, students and seniors $3.50, ages 6-15 $1.50, under 6 free. Free Thurs. 5-9pm.) The **National Aviation Museum** (993-2010), at the Rockcliffe Airport off St. Laurent Blvd. north of Montréal St., illustrates the history of flying, and displays more than 100 aircraft. (Open daily 9am-5pm, Thurs. 9am-9pm; admission $4.25, students and seniors $3.50, ages 6-15 $1.50; free on Thurs. after 5pm.)

Entertainment

The **National Arts Centre,** 53 Elgin St. at Albert St. (tickets 755-1111; info 996-5051), home of an excellent small orchestra and theater company, frequently hosts international entertainers. **Odyssey Theatre** (232-8407) holds open-air comedy at **Strathcona Park,** at the intersection of Laurier Ave. and Range Rd. well east of the canal, on the Rideau River. (Shows late July-mid-Aug. Admission $10, students and seniors $8, under 12 $6.) In summer on Parliament Hill, roving acting troupes sporadically present historical vignettes (late June-Aug. Wed.-Sun. 10:45am-3:30pm is the general time frame). Don't be surprised if you're suddenly entangled in a wild political rally or an emotional legal case—you've merely stumbled through a dimension of time and mind into one of these intriguing skits.

Ottawans seem to have a celebration for just about everything, even the bitter Canadian cold. During early February, **Winterlude** (239-5263) lines the Rideau Canal with a number of ice sculptures which illustrate how it feels to be an Ottawan in the winter—frozen. In mid-May the **Tulip Festival** (562-1980) explodes around Dow's Lake in a colorful kaleidoscope of more than 100,000 blooming tulips. Labor Day weekend the politicians over on Parliament Hill farm out some of their bombast to the **Hot Air Balloon Festival** (243-2330), which sends aloft hundreds of beautiful balloons from Canada, the U.S., and Europe.

Stratford

'Tis no mischance that Stratford lieth upon Avon River and runneth over with Falstaff St., Portia Blvd., and gentlemanly Verona Park. As the fates fain would have it, ere the town's mill-based economy collapsed in 1953 Stratford-born scribe Tom Patterson foundeth the **Stratford Shakespeare Festival.** Yea, the inaugural season, staged in a tent, saw Sir Alec Guinness perform the title role in *Richard III*. Today, the town and the festival are inextricably entwined. The Festival runs from late April, when previews begin, through early November. Several brilliant blasts from Shakespeare's canon form the vanguard of the season's program; musicals, comedies, and Canadian plays complete the revue. In high season there are six different shows per day. A matinee at 2pm and evening performance at 8pm run at each of the three theaters: the crown-shaped **Festival Theatre,** the **Avon Theatre,** once a vaudeville house, and the intimate **Tom Patterson Theatre.** Alas, tickets are expensive, you know the problem well. Complete info about casts, performances and other aspects of the Festival can be obtained by phone (273-1600; free from Toronto at 416-363-4471; free from Detroit at 313-964-4668) or by writing the Stratford Festival, P.O. Box 520, Stratford, Ont. N5A 6V2. Ticket prices vary from $27.50 to $47.50 depending on show, day of week, and location. Some rush tickets are reserved for every performance and are sold at 9am on the morning of the show at the Festival Theatre Box Office ($23.50-28.50). Student and senior tickets are available for some shows in May, September, and October ($11.50-13.50). Between shows, you may (Ophelia-like) fain jump in the Avon River or cast bread to the swans. Also, you may (un-Ophelia-like) rent bicycles and canoes nearby. Spend time browsing through bookstores, art galleries and taking in local daily events, ranging from a farmer's market to free jazz concerts.

Stratford's cuisine runs the gullet from $2 hot dogs to $50 French meals. The info booth (see below) publishes a guide to 50 local restaurants and has all of their menus. Budget travelers' best bet for accommodations is the **Stratford General Hospital Residence,** 130 Youngs St. (271-5084), a 15-minute walk from the bus station. Space is usually available; large groups should call ahead. (Singles $28.) The info booth also has an album of photos, prices and info on over 60 B&Bs. The **Festival Accommodations Bureau** (273-1600) can book you into local B&Bs ($40-100) and hotels. Their office is also the only way to access Stratford guest homes, providing you with a room and possibly a continental breakfast in a private home whose owner wishes only to cater to Festival patrons. Be warned that the homes are not necessarily within walking distance of the theaters. (Single bed $28. Double bed $31. Twin beds $33.)

You can get to Stratford by **train** on **VIA RAIL** (273-3234 or 800-361-1235 for reservations); depot at the station on Shakespeare St. (To: Toronto, $22; buy 5 days ahead for 40% off; Ottawa: $77; Chicago: $85, via Amtrak.) **Chaco Trails** (271-7870), owned by Greyhound, operates buses to surrounding cities, among them Kitchener, Toronto (4 per day, 3hrs. $22), and (in a roundabout way) Niagara Falls.

The **Tourism Stratford Information Booth,** 30 York St. on the river (273-3352 or 800 561-7926; open 8:30am-4:30pm), has extensive info on Stratford, the surrounding area, and much of Ontario. Call ahead and they will send you a 75-page visitor's guide, with a season calendar, accommodations, food, shopping, and maps of town. Stop in to choose from a wide array of brochures. (Open Sun.-Mon. 9am-5pm, Tues.-Sat. 9am-8pm.)

Stratford's **post office** is at 75 Waterloo St. (271-1282). (Open Mon.-Fri. 8am-5:30pm.) The **postal code** is N5A 7M3, the **area code** is 519.

Toronto

The United Nations dubbed Toronto the world's most multi-cultural city in 1988. And in the late 70s, when the perceived threat of *québecois* nationalism caused a number of companies to move their head offices from Montréal to Toronto, the city donned the crown as Canada's financial capital. Today, the Toronto Stock Exchange handles over 70% of the country's stock trade.

Toronto is as big-city as Canada gets. With that, comes the obligatory superlatives: biggest "free-standing" structure (the CN tower), biggest retractable roof (the SkyDome) Most important to the visitor, however, is the diversity of cultures which Toronto manages to squeeze into its variegated ethnic neighborhoods—comparable only to New York and Chicago in this respect. What it *doesn't* come with are many of the urban problems that plague these American Metropoli to the south.

Torontonians maintain an efficient and safe public transportation system, promote recycling virtually everywhere, and keep the city impeccably clean and safe. Two film crews learned this the hard way. One crew, after dirtying a Toronto street to make it look more like a typical "American" avenue, went on a coffee break and returned a short time later only to find their set spotless again, swept by the ever-vigilant city maintenance department. Another, filming an attack scene, was twice interrupted by Toronto residents hopping out of their cars to "rescue" the actress.

Practical Information

Emergency: 911.

Travel Information Center in Eaton Centre, corner of Dundes and Yonge, shares a kiosk with Five Star Tickets. Open Mon.-Sat. 9am-7pm, Sun. 9:30am-6pm. Temporary booth at the **Royal Ontario Museum,** Queen's Park Crescent. **Metropolitan Toronto Convention and Visitor's Association,** 207 Queen's Quay Terminal at Harborfront, 5th floor, P.O. Box 126, M5J 1A7. Infoline 368-9821 in Toronto; 387-3058 or 800-363-1990 in Canada and the continental U.S. Open Mon.-Fri. 9am-5pm. It has pamphlets, including the *Metropolitan Toronto Visitor's Guide,* but is primarily administrative.

Student Travel Agency: Travel CUTS, 187 College St. (979-2406), just west of University Ave. Subway: Queen's Park. Smaller office at 74 Gerrard St. E. (977-0441). Subway: College. Open Mon.-Fri. 9am-5pm, Sat. 10am-4pm. **Ontario Travel,** (800-668-2746). Enter Eatons at Dundas and Yonge, go down 2 flights, exit store; it's on the right. Info and brochures on all of Ontario. Open Mon.-Fri. 10am-9pm, Sat. 9:30am-6pm, Sun. 1-5pm. **YHA Travel/Hostelling International-Canada,** 219 Church St. (862-0226), 2 doors down from the hostel. Subway: Dundas. Excellent for advice. Open Mon.-Fri. 8am-7pm, Sat. until 6pm.

Traveler's Aid Society: each terminal at Pearson Airport, and Union Station (366-7788). Mon.-Fri. 9am-9pm.

Canada Customs: (973-8022). Location at Pearson Airport (676-3643; open daily 7:30am-11pm).

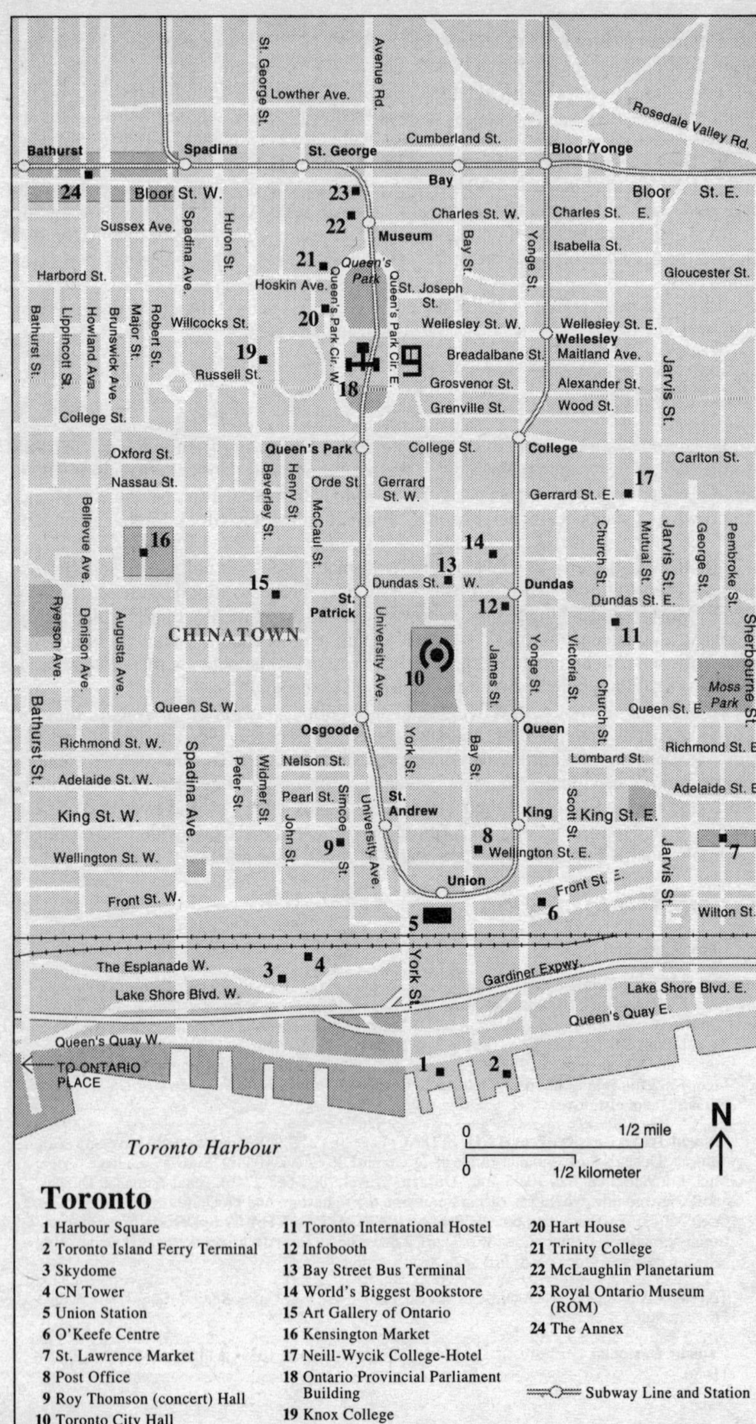
Bathurst
Spadina
St. George
Bloor/Yonge
Bay
Museum
Wellesley
Queen's Park
College
St. Patrick
Dundas
Osgoode
Queen
St. Andrew
King
Union
St. George St.
Avenue Rd.
Lowther Ave.
Cumberland St.
Rosedale Valley Rd.
Bloor St. W.
Bloor St. E.
Sussex Ave.
Spadina Ave.
Huron St.
Charles St. W.
Charles St. E.
Isabella St.
Bay St.
Yonge St.
Harbord St.
Hoskin Ave.
Queen's Park
Queen's Park Cir. W.
Queen's Park Cir. E.
St. Joseph St.
Gloucester St.
Bathurst St.
Lippincott St.
Howland Ave.
Brunswick Ave.
Major St.
Robert St.
Willcocks St.
Wellesley St. W.
Wellesley St. E.
Breadalbane St.
Maitland Ave.
Russell St.
Grosvenor St.
Alexander St.
Grenville St.
Wood St.
Jarvis St.
College St.
Oxford St.
Carlton St.
Nassau St.
Beverley St.
Henry St.
Orde St.
Gerrard St. W.
Gerrard St. E.
Bellevue Ave.
McCaul St.
Church St.
Mutual St.
George St.
Pembroke St.
Dundas St. W.
Dundas St. E.
CHINATOWN
Ryerson Ave.
Denison Ave.
Augusta Ave.
University Ave.
James St.
Victoria St.
Sherbourne St.
Moss Park
Queen St. W.
Queen St. E.
Richmond St. W.
Richmond St. E.
York St.
Lombard St.
Adelaide St. W.
Adelaide St. E.
Peter St.
Widmer St.
Nelson St.
Pearl St.
Simcoe St.
John St.
King St. W.
King St. E.
Scott St.
Wellington St. W.
Wellington St. E.
Front St. W.
Front St.
Wilton St.
The Esplanade W.
Gardiner Expwy.
Lake Shore Blvd. W.
Lake Shore Blvd. E.
Queen's Quay W.
Queen's Quay E.
TO ONTARIO PLACE
Toronto Harbour
0 1/2 mile
0 1/2 kilometer
N
Toronto
1 Harbour Square
2 Toronto Island Ferry Terminal
3 Skydome
4 CN Tower
5 Union Station
6 O'Keefe Centre
7 St. Lawrence Market
8 Post Office
9 Roy Thomson (concert) Hall
10 Toronto City Hall
11 Toronto International Hostel
12 Infobooth
13 Bay Street Bus Terminal
14 World's Biggest Bookstore
15 Art Gallery of Ontario
16 Kensington Market
17 Neill-Wycik College-Hotel
18 Ontario Provincial Parliament Building
19 Knox College
20 Hart House
21 Trinity College
22 McLaughlin Planetarium
23 Royal Ontario Museum (ROM)
24 The Annex
Subway Line and Station

Consulates: U.S., 360 University Ave. (595-0228, 595-1700 for visa info). Subway: St. Patrick. Open Mon.-Fri. 8:30am-2pm for consular services. **Australia,** 175 Bloor St. E., suite #314-6 (323-1155). Subway: Bloor St. Open Mon.-Fri. 9am-1pm and 2-5pm for info; 9am-1pm for visas. **U.K.,** 777 Bay St. #1910 (593-1267). Subway: College. Open Mon.-Fri. 9:30am-3:30pm, 9am-4:50pm for telephone info. **Germany,** 77 Admiral Rd. (925-2813). Subway: St. George. Open Mon.-Fri. 9am-noon.

Currency Exchange: Toronto Currency Exchange, 391 Yonge St. and 780 Yonge St. Gives the best rates around, and doesn't charge a service fee. Both open daily 9am-6pm; 313 Yonge St. (598-3769) at Dundas. Open daily 9am-9pm. **Royal Bank of Canada** has exchange centers at Pearson Airport (676-3220). Open daily 6am-11pm.

American Express: 50 Bloor St. W. (967-3411; 800-221-7282 for lost or stolen traveler's checks). Subway: Bloor-Yonge. Open Mon.-Wed. and Sat. 10am-6pm, Thurs.-Fri. 10am-7pm.

Pearson International Airport: (247-7678) about 20km west of Toronto via Hwy. 427, 401, or 409. Take Bus #58 west from Lawrence W. subway. **Gray Coach Airport Express** (351-3311) runs buses each day directly to downtown hotels every 20 min. 5:05am-10:45pm. Last bus from downtown at 11:10pm. $11, round-trip $18.50. Buses also serve the Yorkdale ($6.50), York Mills ($7.50), and Islington ($6) subway stations every 40 min. 6:20am-12:10am. **Air Canada,** 925-2311 or 800-422-6232. To: Montréal ($205); Calgary ($572); New York City ($179); and Vancouver ($683). All flights 50% less for "student standby;" max. age 24. 50% off round-trip fare if you book 21 days in advance. 10% discount for seniors age 60 and over and their traveling companions. **Toronto Island Airport:** on Hanlan's Point, 10-min. free ferry from foot of Bathurst St. (868-6942). **Air Ontario** flies from here to Newark, Montréal, Ottawa, and Windsor; fares the same as from Pearson Airport (see above).

Trains: Union Station, 61 Front St. at Bay (366-8411). Subway: Union. **VIA Rail** (366-8411) To: Montréal (6 per day, $72); Windsor (4 per day; $55); Vancouver (3 per week; $404). Seniors, students 10% discount. 40% off tickets purchased at least 5 days in advance, seniors and students 50%. **Amtrak** (800-426-8725) to New York City (1 per day, 12 hrs. $116) and Chicago (1 per day, 11 hr., $109). Seniors 10% discount on all fares. Students and seniors 40% off tickets purchased at least 5 days in advance; same deal for adults Mon.-Thurs. and Sat. Ticket office open Mon.-Sat. 7am-9pm, Sun. 8am-9pm.

Buses: Voyageur (393-7911) and **Greyhound** (367-8747), 610 Bay St., just north of Dundas. Subway: St. Patrick or Dundas. Service to: Calgary, Montréal (5 per day, 7 hr., $54), Vancouver ($187), New York City (US$60). Rates vary. Call for special deals. No student discounts. Ticket office open daily 5:30am-1am.

Public Transport: Toronto Transit Commission (TTC) (393-4636). Network includes 2 subway lines and numerous bus and streetcar routes. Free pocket maps at all stations. Some routes 24 hrs. New policy requires buses running after dark to stop anywhere along the route at a female passenger's request. Free transfers among subway, buses, and streetcars, but only within stations. Fare $2, 5 tokens $6.50, seniors 50% off with ID (10 for $6.50 or $1 fare), under 12 50¢, 8 for $2.50. Unlimited travel day pass, good for subway, bus and streetcar, $5. Monthly pass $69.50.

Toronto Island Ferry Service (392-8193, 392-8194 for recording). Numerous ferries to Centre Island, Wards Island and Hanlans Point leave daily from Bay St. Ferry Dock at the foot of Bay St. Service approximately every ½-hr., 8am-11:45pm. Fare $2.75 round-trip; seniors, students, ages 15-19 $1.50, under 15 $1.

Taxi: Co-op Cabs, 364-7111. $2.20 plus distance and waiting.

Car Rental: Wrecks for Rent, 77 Nassau St. (585-7782). Subway: Spadina or Bathurst. $25 per day; first 200km free, 12¢ each additional km. Insurance $9.50 if over 25 with credit card, $15 without. Surcharge for ages 21-25. Open Mon.-Fri. 8am-6pm, Sat. 9am-4pm. **Hertz** (800-263-0600), **Tilden** (922-2000), **Budget** (673-3322), **Thrifty** (800-367-2277), and **Discount** (961-8006) also serve Toronto.

Auto Transport Company: Toronto Driveaway, 5803 Yonge St. (225-7754 or 225-7759), just north of the Finch subway stop, north of Hwy. 401. In summer, pay gas plus $50-100 to transport someone's car to western Canada or Florida. No fee in winter; they'll contribute gas money. **Allostop,** 663 Yonge St., Suite 301 (323-0874), at Bloor. Matches riders with drivers. To: Ottawa ($22); Montréal ($26); Québec City ($41); and New York ($40). Open Wed. 9am-5pm, Thurs.-Fri. 9am-7pm, Sat.-Sun. 10am-5pm.

Bike Rental: Brown's Sports and Cycle Bike Rental, 2447 Bloor St. W. (763-4176). $14 per day, $32 per weekend, $42 per week. $100 deposit or credit card required. Open Mon.-Wed. 9:30am-6pm, Thurs.-Fri. 9:30am-8pm, Sat. 9:30am-5pm.

Help Lines: Rape Crisis, 597-8808. **Services for the Disabled,** Ontario Travel, 314-0944. **Toronto Area Gays (TAG),** 964-6600. Open Mon.-Fri. 7-10pm. **Distress Centre,** 367-2277.

Post Office: Toronto Dominion Centre (973-3120), at King and Bay St. General Delivery at Postal Station K, 2384 Yonge St. (483-1334). Subway: Eglington. Open Mon.-Fri. 8am-5:45pm. **Postal Code:** M4P 2E0.

Area Code: 416.

Orientation

The city maps available at tourism booths are inadequate for getting around. At any drugstore or postcard shack, buy the indispensable *Downtown and Metro Toronto Visitor's Map Guide* in the yellowish-orange cover ($1.50). If you plan to venture outside the downtown area, also purchase the plan of metropolitan Toronto published by Allmaps ($2). The pocket *Ride Guide*, free at all TTC stations and tourism info booths (see Practical Information), clearly conveys the subway and bus routes for the metro area; it only shows major streets, but is vital for getting around once you know where you are and where you're going.

There is no one spot downtown that can be called the heart of the action. Instead, there are many decentralized neighborhoods; each has its own distinctive character. Zoning regulations require that Toronto developers include housing and retail space in commercial construction; this has kept downtown from becoming a barren canyon of glass boxes at night, since people actually live there.

The city streets lie in a grid pattern, running north-south or east-west. The addresses on north-south streets increase as you head north, away from Lake Ontario. **Yonge Street** is the main artery. East-west streets have the suffix East or West depending on which side of Yonge they are. Numbering for both sides starts at Yonge and increases as you move in either direction. Heading west from Yonge St., the main streets are **Bay Street, University Avenue, Spadina Avenue,** and **Bathurst.** Major east-west routes are **Queen Street, Dundas, College,** and **Bloor.**

Traffic is heavy in Toronto—avoid rush hour. Parking on the street is hard to find and usually limited to one hour, except on Sundays when street parking is free and abundant. Parking in garages is easy to find during the week: pay outrageous $4 per hour rates or a reasonable daily fee ($7-10). Avoid lots in the financial district which charge up to $35 per day. Street parking is free at night, but your car must be gone by 7am. Day parking is free at outlying subway stations, the best bet for inbound day-trippers. From the west, get off Queen Elizabeth Way at the Kipling Ave. or Islington Ave. exit, head north two mi. and park at Kipling or Islington subway. From the east, exit Rte. 401 at McCowan Rd. and go south ½ mi. The ride into the city takes about 30 minutes from these stops. Parking overnight at the subway stations is prohibited.

Getting Around

There are many neighborhoods worth exploring. **Chinatown** is on Dundas St. W. between University Ave. and Spadina Ave. **Kensington Market** is found on Kensington Ave., Augusta Ave., and the western half of Baldwin St.—a largely Portuguese neighborhood with many good restaurants, vintage clothing shops, and an outdoor bazaar of produce, luggage, spices, nuts, clothing, and shoes. The **University of Toronto** campus occupies about 200 acres in the middle of downtown. The law-school cult-flick *The Paper Chase* was filmed here because the campus looked more Ivy-League than Harvard, where the movie was set. **Queen Street West,** from University Ave. to Bathurst St., is a fun mix of shopping from upscale uptight boutiques to reasonable used book stores, restaurants, and cafés. Listen to street musicians or visit the store devoted exclusively to condoms. **The Annex** on Bloor St. W. starts at the Spadina subway and goes west. Excellent budget restaurants of many ethnic groups center here (see Food) as do some nightclubs. This is the best place to come at night when you're not sure exactly what you're hungry for. **Harborfront** is on Queen's Quay W. from York St. to Bathurst, on the lake. Take the street car from Union subway. A paradigm for what a city can do with its waterfront with a little money and a lot of TLC: music, food, ferry rides, dance companies and art all dock here. Call 973-3000 for info. There are three main **Toronto Islands,** all accessible by ferry (see Practical Info above). The islands offer beaches, bike rental, and an amusement park for the tykes. To get to the former resort community of **Beaches,** named for nearby Kew Beach, take bus #501 east to the end of the line from the Queen subway stop. The area has a two mi. boardwalk with stores and restaurants.

Corso Italia is on St. Clair W. at Dufferin St.; take the subway to St. Clair W. (*not* to St. Clair) and bus #512 west. **Little India** is on Gerrard St. E. at Coxwell. Subway: Coxwell; bus #22 south to 2nd Gerrard stop. **Greek Village** (better known as "**the Danforth**") is on Danforth Ave., at Pope Ave.; subway: Pope. These three ethnic enclaves are similar in form. Street signs are bilingual, and most businesses cater to locals, not tourists. All three take about 30-45 minutes by public transit from downtown, not worth the ride if you're coming just for the food, but okay if you want to explore specialty food shops.

Accommodations and Camping

Budget travelers in Toronto face several attractive choices, including a good youth hostel, dorms at U. of Toronto, and B&Bs. Avoid the cheap hotels concentrated around Jarvis and Gerrard St. For relatively inexpensive accommodations in a private home, reserve ahead through **Toronto Bed and Breakfast,** P.O. Box 269, 253 College St., M5T 1R5 (961-3676 or 588-8800, fax.: 537-0233), for 20 homes, all with subway access. (Singles from $41. Doubles from $51. Call Mon.-Fri. 9am-noon or 2-7pm.) **Metropolitan Bed and Breakfast,** Ste. 269 #615, Mount Pleasant Rd. M45 3C5 (964-2566), offers a similar service for 30 homes in the Toronto area. (Singles from $40, doubles from $50. Parking included. Call 8am-noon or 3-8pm.) Camping alternatives are uninspiring and far-removed from the city center.

Toronto International Hostel (HI), 223 Church St. (368-1848 or 368-0207); walk east on Dundas and turn right onto Church. 5 min. from Eaton Centre. Subway: Dundas. 150 beds, no TV. Huge lounge, excellent kitchen, laundry facilities, ping-pong table and oodles of tourist info. Daily organized activities run the gamut from dart tournaments to bar-hopping. Memberships sold. Check-out 10am for semi-private rooms. Quiet hours midnight-7am. Dorm (4-14 beds) $16, nonmembers $21. Cramped semi-private rooms $18 and $23. $5 key deposit. 10% discount for members at nearby **Passport Café,** 217 Church. Breakfast ($3.25) served until 10am Mon.-Fri., noon Sat.-Sun. Open daily 8am-1am, Sun. opens at 9am.

Knox College, 59 St. George St. (978-2793). Subway: Queen's Park; walk west on College and right on St. George. Huge rooms with wood floors around an idyllic courtyard. Common rooms, baths on each floor. Great location in the heart of U of T's campus. Singles $25. Call for reservations Mon.-Fri. 9am-4pm. Open June-Aug.

Trinity College and St. Hilda's College Residences, 6 Hoskin Ave., bursar's office for check-in (978-2523), on Queen's Park Crescent on U of T campus. Subway: Museum. Clean, large dorm rooms with desks; some have good views. Shared bath and kitchenette. TV lounge, laundry. Singles $37, students $30. Doubles $68, students $42. Key deposit $15. Reservations recommended. Office hours Mon.-Fri. 9am-4pm.

Karabanow Guest House and Tourist Home, 9 Spadina Rd. (phone and fax. 923-4004), at Bloor St. 6 blocks west of Yonge. Subway: Spadina. Good location. Small and intimate. 20 rooms with desks (mostly doubles) in a mixture of old-fashioned and renovated modern styles. TV, free parking. Check-in 9am-9pm, later by arrangement; check-out 11am. No curfew. Singles $40. Doubles $50. $10 key deposit. Oct.-April rooms $10 less. Reservations recommended.

Neill-Wycik (WHY-zeek) **College Hotel,** 96 Gerrard St. E. (977-2320). From College subway stop, walk 1 block east on Carleton to Church St., turn right, walk to Gerrard and make a left. Rooms impeccably clean, some with beautiful views of the city. Kitchen on every floor, but no utensils. Check-in after 1pm (locked storage room provided). Check-out 11am. Singles (including simple breakfast) $37-39, mini-twin $41-43, doubles $42.50-44.50. Family room $47-49. 10% discount for 7-night stay if you pay up front; 20% standby discount for students and seniors after 8pm. Will cancel reservations after 6:30pm unless arrangements made. Open early May-late Aug.

YWCA Woodlawn Residence, 80 Woodlawn Ave. E. (923-8454). Subway: Summerhill. Walk uphill on Yonge and turn right on Woodlawn. For women only. Clean, comfortable rooms with sinks in wealthy, safe neighborhood. TV lounge. Laundry. Cafeteria serves free breakfast Mon.-Fri. 7:30-10:30am, Sat.-Sun. 8:30-11am. Check-in 2:30pm (locked storage provided). Check-out noon. Quiet hours 11pm-7am. Singles $41. Doubles $55. $2 key deposit. No parking. Reservations recommended.

Indian Line Tourist Campground, 7625 Finch Ave. W. (678-1233), at Darcel Ave. Follow Hwy. 427 north to Finch and go west. Showers, laundry. Close to Pearson Airport. Sites $13.50, with hookup $17. Open May 10-early Oct.

Food

A burst of immigration from around the world has made Toronto a mecca for good ethnic food rivalled in North America only by New York City. 5000 restaurants squeeze into metro Toronto; you could eat at a different place every night for the next 15 years. Best bets are Bloor St. W. and the area bordered by College St., University Ave., Queen St. W., and Bathurst St. For fresh produce, go to Kensington Market (see Getting Around, above) or the St. Lawrence Market at King St. E. and Sherbourne, six blocks east of the King subway stop. The budget traveler staying in town for more than a few days will want *Toronto Dinners for $7.95 or Less,* by PBG Productions, a pocket guide to 100 restaurants. ($6, available at **World's Largest Bookstore,** Edward and College St. Subway: Dundas; they also stock other books listed here.) "L.L.B.O" posted on the window of a restaurant means that it has a liquor license.

Chinese: Real Peking Restaurant, 355 College St., at Augusta Ave. (920-7952). See directions for Saigon Palace. The effort many Chinese restaurants put into decorations goes instead into the food. Understanding server explains the menu. Entrées $6.50-8.50.

Deli: Shopsy's, 33 Yonge St. at Front St., 1 block from Union Station (365-3333). *The* definitive Toronto deli. About 300 seats, quick service. Sandwiches $4.25, take-out $5.50.

Euro-Lite: Hart House, cafeteria inside Hart House residential college on U of T campus. Subway: Museum. The best lunch deal in the city. Dine on gourmet cuisine in the vaulted dining hall or in the Gothic courtyard of Hart House. Cold entrees such as poached filet of salmon with watercress dressing, $3.75. Hot entrees $4.15. Salads 25¢ per oz., bread 20¢, fresh fruit 65¢. Open lunch only, 11:30am-2pm.

Greek: Mr. Greek, 568 Danforth Ave. at Carlow (461-5470); subway: Pope. Shish kabobs, salads, steak, chicken, Greek music and wine. Family atmosphere, fast service. Open Sun.-Thurs. 11am-1am, Fri.-Sat. until 3am.

Health: Renaissance Café, 509 Bloor St. W. (968-6639). Subway: Spadina. Fun for tofu-lovers and other hip health eccentrics. Moon burger (tofu, spices and *tahini* sauce) $7. Lite bites (noon-4pm) $5. Luncheon specials $6. Open daily noon-midnight.

Hungarian: Country Style Hungarian Restaurant, 450 Bloor St. W. Hearty stews, soups, casseroles. Entrees come in small and large portions; better terms would be "more than enough" and "way more than enough." Entrées $3-8. Open daily 11am-10pm.

Mexican: Viva, 459 Bloor St. W. at Major St. (922-8482). Latin music, colorful Latin-American costumes on walls. Seafood, chicken, vegetables, beef, pork or sausage in corn or flour tortillas, $5. BBQ plates with corn meal, sticky rice, and vegetable $7. Open daily 11:30am-1am.

Persian/Afghan: Ariana, 255 College St., at Spadina Ave. (599-2618). Same directions as Saigon Palace, below. Chicken, beef or lamb kabob, $4-6. Good falafel plate: 3 balls of fried chick peas with parsley, onion, and spices; with salad and pita, $4.

Thai/Lao: Vanipha, 193 Augusta Ave., across from playground (340-0491). Curry, poultry, meat, vegetarian—the standard range of Thai food. Menu has good English explanations of dishes titled in Thai. Entrées $8-9. Open Tues.-Sun. noon-11pm.

Vietnamese: Saigon Palace, Spadina Ave. at College St. Subway: Queen's Park; walk west on College St. 6 blocks, or take bus #506 west from subway. Popular with locals. Great spring rolls. Variety of beef, chicken, or vegetable dishes over rice or noodles, $7. Open daily 9am-10pm, Fri.-Sat. until 11pm.

Sights

Exploring the **ethnic neighborhoods** on foot is one of the most enjoyable (and cheapest) activities in Toronto. Life takes place on the streets here: watch locals haggling at outdoor produce markets, teenagers courting, and old men chatting on the corner, all in a foreign tongue. For a more organized expedition, join one of the 10 free **walking tours** operated by the **Royal Ontario Museum** (Wed. and Sun. in summer; 586-5514). Study the varied architecture of the downtown financial district on a $10 **Toronto Architecture Tour.** Modern architecture aficionados should also visit **City Hall** at the corner of Queen and Bay St. between the Osgoode and Queen subway stops (392-9111), with its curved twin towers and a rotunda which was considered quite avant-garde when completed in 1965 (now the garde has passed). (922-7606; open Tues.-Sun.) The **University of Toronto** has free guided tours of the campus (978-5000). The Ontario government legislates in the **Provincial Parliament Buildings,** at Queen's Park in the city center. Subway: Queen's Park. Free guided tours daily every ½-hour, 9am-3:30pm. Free visitors gallery passes available at info desk in main lobby at 1:30pm. (Building open 8:30am-6:30pm, chambers close 4:30pm. Parliament in session Oct.-Dec. and March-June, Mon.-Thurs. 1:30-6pm, and Thurs. 10am-noon.) At 553m, the **CN Tower** (360-8500; subway: Union, and follow the skywalk) does not quite pierce the ozone layer, but the ride to the top, at a towering $11, will poke a big hole in your wallet and may split your eardrums. (Ages 13-16 $5.35, 5-12 $4.25, under 5 $2.25. Open Mon.-Sat. 9am-1am, Sun. 10am-10pm.) Another classic tourist attraction is the 98-room **Casa Loma,** Davenport Rd. at 1 Austin Terrace (923-1172), near Spadina a few blocks north of the Dupont subway stop. Although the outside of the only real turreted castle in North America belongs in a fairy tale, the inside's dusty old exhibits can be skipped. (Open daily 10am-4pm. Admission $8, seniors and ages 5-16 $4.50, under 5 free with parent.) The **Royal Ontario Museum**, 100 Queen's Park, subway: Museum (586-5551), is a royal success. It has artifacts from ancient civilizations (Greek, Chinese, Egyptian), a floor of life sciences (kids will love the stuffed animals and live bugs), plus more imaginative displays such as "Caravans and Clipper Ships—the story of trade" and a self-conscious one that shows how museum experts study new specimens. (Open in summer daily 10am-6pm, Tues. and Thurs. until 8pm; closed Mon. in winter. Admission $6, seniors and kids $3.25. Free Tues. after 4:30pm. Admission covers entry to the **George M. Gardiner Museum of Ceramic Art** across the street.) Attached to the ROM, the **McLaughlin Planetarium** (586-5736) lets the stars shine in mid-afternoon and has laser shows at night, accompanied by (you guessed it) Pink Floyd, Led Zeppelin, or Guns 'n Roses. (Admission $5, seniors and kids $2.50. Astronomy shows Tues.-Sun. 3pm and 7:30pm; laser shows Wed.-Sun. 8:45pm, Fri.-Sat. also 10:15pm.) The **Art Gallery of Ontario (AGO),** 317 Dundas St. W., subway: St. Patrick (979-6648), three blocks west of University Ave. in the heart of Chinatown, houses an enormous collection of Western art spanning from the Renaissance to the 1980s, with a particular concentration of Canadian artists. (Open mid-May to early Sept. daily 10:30am-5:30pm, Wed. 10:30am-9pm. Admission $4.50, seniors and students $2.50, under 12 free, families $9. Free Wed. 5-9pm. Seniors free Fri.) Toronto also has a range of smaller museums dedicated to subjects such as textiles, sugar, hockey, the Holocaust, marine history, and medicine. Budget travelers who have spent all day on their feet may enjoy the **Bata Shoe Museum,** (924-7463), 131 Bloor St. W., 2nd floor, two blocks from the Museum subway stop. A fascinating collection of footwear from many cultures and ages: the moon boot worn by Buzz Aldrin, boots with nasty spikes on the soles, used to crush chestnuts, two-inch slippers once worn by Chinese women with bound feet. (Open Tues.-Sun. 11am-6pm. Admission $3, students and seniors $1, families $6.) From April to September, the Toronto Blue Jays (info. 341-1111) swing for the hotel in the four-year-old **Sky Dome**; subway: Union and follow the signs. The dome is more of an entertainment center than a ballpark; it lacks the charm and chutzpah of a Fenway Park or Wrigley Field, but boasts a retractable roof, a 348-room hotel (some of its windows face the field), and retail outlets and offices. All games sell out, but before the game the box office usually has some obstructed view seats. (Tickets $4-17.50.) Scalpers sell tickets for far beyond face value; wait until the game starts and you can get tickets from them at face value. To get a behind-the-scenes look at the Sky Dome, take the tour (341-3663; daily 10am-5pm on the hr.; admission $8, seniors and under 16 $5.50). In the fall the **Toronto Argonauts** (CFL) play football at the Dome (595-1131 for info; 872-5000 to buy tickets; tickets from $11.) For info on concerts and other Sky Dome events, call 341-3663. Hockey fans should head for **Maple Leaf Gardens,** at Carlton and Church St., subway: College, (977-1641) to see the knuckle-crackin', puck-smackin' **Maple Leafs**. **Biking and hiking trails** wriggle through metropolitan Toronto. For a map of the trails, write the **Metro Parks and Property Department,** 365 Bay St., 8th floor, Toronto M5H 2V1. Serious hikers might want *Great Country Walks Around Toronto* by Elliot Katz ($4). For a relaxing afternoon, go to **High Park** (392-1111) for the free summer Shakespeare festival, the fishing pond, or the sports facilities. Subway: High Park. **Toronto Islands Park,** a four-mi. strip of connected islands just opposite the downtown area (15-min. ferry trip; 392-8193 for ferry info), is a popular "vacationland," with a boardwalk, bathing beaches, canoe and bike rentals, a Frisbee golf course, and a children's farm and amusement park. Ferries leave from the Bay Street Ferry Dock at the foot of Bay St. (see Practical Information above). Further out from the city are **Canada's Wonderland** (832-2205), Canada's answer to Disneyland, the **Ontario Science Center** (429-0193), and the **Metro Toronto Zoo** (392-5200). All three are about one hour from downtown and accessible by public transportation. For info on offbeat recreation near the metro area, check out *52 Weekend Activities for the Toronto Adventurer,* by Sue Lebrecht ($13). For info on everything else there is to do in Toronto, buy *The Toronto Guide,* by Margaret and Rod MacKenzie ($17), eh?

Entertainment

Nightlife

Many of Toronto's clubs and pubs remain closed on Sundays because of antiquated liquor laws. Some of the more formal clubs uphold dress codes and the city still shuts down at 1am. To mingle with students try **The Brunswick House, Lee's Palace** (see below), and the **All-Star Eatery,** 277 Victoria (977-7619), at Dundas one block east of the Dundas subway stop. The most interesting new clubs are on trendy **Queen Street West.** The gay scene centers around Wellesley and Church, although there's also some gay activity on Queen and Yonge St. *Now* magazine, published every Thursday, is the city's comprehensive entertainment guide, available in restaurants and record stores all over Toronto. *Eye* magazine, also published on Thursday and free, has similar info. *Where Toronto,* a monthly available free at tourism booths, gives a good arts and entertainment run-down. *Toronto Life* is an excellent magazine that highlights Toronto happenings.

Bamboo, 312 Queen St. W. (593-5771), 3 blocks west of the Osgoode subway stop. Popular with students. Live reggae, jazz, rock, and funk daily. Great dancing. Patio upstairs. Open Mon.-Sat. noon-1am. Hefty cover varies from band to band.

Brunswick House, 481 Bloor St. W. (964-2242), at Brunswick between the Bathurst and Spadina subway stops. Rowdy dive reeling with students. Beer $2.95. Upstairs is **Albert's Hall,** famous for its blues. Open Mon.-Fri. 11:30am-1am, Sat. noon-1am.

George's Spaghetti House, 290 Dundas St. E. at Sherbourne St. (923-9887). Subway: Dundas; take the streetcar east to Sherbourne. The city's best jazz club attracts the nation's top ensembles. Dinner entrees from $8.50. Restaurant open Mon.-Thurs. 11am-11pm, Fri. 11am-midnight, Sat. 5pm-midnight. Jazz Mon.-Sat. 6pm-1am. Cover Tues.-Thurs. $4, Fri.-Sat. $5; none on Mon. No cover at bar.

Lee's Palace, 529 Bloor St. W. (532-7383), just east of the Bathurst subway stop. Amazing crazy creature art depicting rock 'n roll frenzy. Live music nightly. Pick up a calendar of bands. Dancing upstairs Thurs.-Sat. starting 10pm. Cover $2-5. Open daily noon-1am.

Second City, in The Old Firehall, 110 Lombard St. at Jarvis (863-1111), 2 blocks east and 2 short blocks south of Queen's Park subway stop. One of North America's wackiest and most creative comedy clubs. Spawned comics Dan Akroyd, John Candy, Gilda Radner, Dave Thomas, Rick Moranis and Martin Short; a hit TV show (SCTV); and the legendary "Great White North." Dinner and theater $28-33. Theater without dinner $12.50-17, students $8 and dinner discount. Free improv. sessions (Mon.-Thurs. at 10:15pm)—students welcome. Shows Mon.-Thurs. at 6 and 8:30pm, Fri. at 8 and 11pm, Sat. 8:30 and 11pm. Reservations required.

Festivals and Cultural Events

The city offers a few first-class freebies. **Ontario Place,** 955 Lakeshore Blvd. W. (314-9811; 314-9980 recording), features top-notch cheap entertainment in summer—the Toronto Symphony, National Ballet of Canada, Ontario Place Pops, and top pop artists perform here free with admission to the park. (Park open mid-May-early Sept. daily 10am-1am. Admission $7.50, seniors and kids $2.) Kids should love the slides and water games of **Children's Village** (waterslide, bumper boats $2.15 each; 5 attractions for $10). Spectacular IMAX movies can be seen at the **Six-Storey Cinesphere** (admission $4, seniors and kids $2. Call for screening schedule). On five evenings in early July, watch the **International Fireworks Competition** blaze in the Toronto skies. From mid-August through Labor Day, the **Canadian National Exhibition (CNE)** brings a country carnival atmosphere to Ontario Place. Enjoy superb performances of Shakespeare by **Canadian Stage** (367-8243) amid the greenery of High Park, Bloor St. W. at Parkside Dr. (Subway: High Park.) Bring something to sit on or wedge yourself on the 45° slope to the stage. ($5 donation requested. Call for performance schedules.) Now in its sixth year, the **du Maurier Ltd. Downtown Jazz Festival's** (363-5200) mix of old and new talents mesmerizes the city in late June. Budget travelers will appreciate the abundance of free, outdoor concerts at lunchtime and in the early evening.

Roy Thomson Hall, 60 Simcoe St. at King St. W. (872-4255), is the home of the Toronto Symphony Orchestra. Tickets are expensive ($10-$75), but rush tickets ($8-10) go on sale at the box office the day of the concert (at 11am for concerts Mon.-Fri., 1pm Sat.) Or order by phone (592-4828; Mon.-Fri. 10am-6pm, Sat. noon-5pm; office opens 2 hrs. before Sun. performance). Ask about discounts and seniors rates. The same office serves **Massey Hall,** 178 Victoria St. near Eaton Centre (subway: Dundas), a great hall for rock and folk concerts and musicals. The opera and ballet companies perform at **O'Keefe Centre,** 1 Front St. E. at Yonge (393-7474; tickets from $30). Rush tickets (for the last row of orchestra seats) on sale at 11am ($9 ballet, $12 opera). Seniors and students can line up one hour before performances for the best unsold seats ($10.75). (Box office open daily 11am-6pm or until 1 hr. after curtain.) Next door, **St. Lawrence Centre,** 27 Front St. E. (366-7723), presents excellent classic and Canadian drama and chamber music recitals in two different theaters. Special student and senior tickets may be available depending on the company performing. (Box office open Mon.-Sat. 10am-8pm.)

You can beat the high cost of culture by seeking out standby or student discount options. **Five Star Tickets** (596-8211) sells half-price tickets for theater, music, dance, and opera on the day of performance: their booth at Dundas and Yonge in front of Eaton Centre opens at noon, so arrive before 11:45am for first dibs. (Subway: Dundas. Open Mon.-Sat. noon-7:30pm, Sun. 11am-3pm.) **Ticketmaster** (870-8000) will supply you with tickets to many events, among them the **Player's International** tennis tournament (665-9777) in late July (early round tickets $6-10).

"Near" Toronto: Algonquin Provincial Park

The wilder Canada of endless rushing rivers and shimmering lakes awaits in Algonquin Provincial Park, about 300km north of Toronto. Experience Algonquin through one of two venues: the Hwy. 60 Corridor, where tents and trailers crowd the roadside; or the park interior, the "essence of Algonquin." You can rent gear for a backcountry adventure at several outfitting stores around and inside the park. Try **Algonquin Outfitters,** RR#1-Oxtongue Lake, Dwight P0A 1H0 (705-635-2243), just off Hwy. 60 about 10km west of the park's west gate. They have two other locations in the park. To enter the park, you'll need an Interior Camping Permit ($3.25 per person each night), available at the main gate or from any outfitter.

Prince Edward Island

Prince Edward Island, more commonly called "P.E.I." (not to be confused with the architect) or simply "the Island," is the smallest and most densely populated province in Canada. Referred to as "a million-acre farm," the Island is blanketed with soil that is brick-red from its high iron-oxide content. In addition to agriculture, tourism is the mainstay of the Island economy. Prince Edward Island radiates an array of arresting hues in the spring and summer. The Island's red soil complements the green crops and shrubbery, azure skies and turquoise waters, and purple roadside lupin. Even some stretches of the endless beaches on the north and south coasts are layered with red sand. The relaxing countryside and slow pace of life are what attract "outsiders" from all over Canada.

A P.E.I. city is an oxymoron; always small, towns on the Island seem to exist more for visitors than for residents and consist mainly of restaurants and attractive shopping areas. The largest "city" on the Island is Charlottetown, the provincial capital, with a whopping 15,000 residents. Effusively hospitable, the Island's population is 17% Acadian French and 80% British. Ancestral residents named the Island's three counties Kings, Queens and Prince.

Public transportation is nearly non-existent on the Island, although SMT and island Transit (see Practical Information below) connect Charlottetown with the mainland. Fortunately, distances are minuscule—driving from Charlottetown on the south coast to the beaches on the north coast requires less than 20 minutes. The network of highways, actually country roads, is superb for bikers. You never have to worry about getting lost; just keep going and you'll eventually hit a major road, most of which are well-marked. Three scenic drives cover the Island for those who simply want to unhurry themselves and breathe deeply the saliferous country air.

Practical Information and Orientation

Emergency: 911.

Capital: Charlottetown.

Time Zone: Atlantic (1 hr. ahead of Eastern time). **Postal Abbreviation:** P.E.I.

Area code: 902.

Provincial Sales Tax: 10%

Visitor Information: P.E.I. Visitor Services Centre, P.O. Box 940, C1A 7M5 (368-4444). With summer locations in Borden, Cavendish, Pooles Corner, Portage, Summerside, Souris and Wood Islands. Hours vary widely. The **P.E.I. Visitor Information Centre,** on the corner of University Ave. and Summer St. in the plaza next to Papa Joe's Restaurant (368-4444), distributes the *P.E.I. Visitor's Guide* (with map). Open daily 9am-5pm, mid-May-Sept. 8am-10pm. The **Charlottetown Visitors Bureau,** 199 Queen St. inside City Hall (566-5548), distributes free maps of Charlottetown. Open Mon.-Sat. 8am-8pm, Sun. 10am-6pm. **Dial-the-Island,** toll-free info line, 800-565-7421 from the Maritimes, 800-565-0267 from the North American continent. The number in the Maritimes also books reservations.

Tours: Abegweit Tours, 157 Nassau St. (894-9966), offers sightseeing tours on a London double-decker bus. Tours include Charlottetown (7 per day; 1 hr.; $5, kids under 11 $1), the North Shore including Green Gables (1 per day; 7 hr.; $25, kids $12), and the South Shore (1 per day; 5 hr.; $25, kids $12). To reach Abegweit Tours, catch buses at Confederation Centre (corner of Grafton and Queen St.) or at Charlottetown Hotel. Tours run June-Sept.

Buses: SMT, 330 University Ave. (566-9744), provides service to Moncton (2 per day; 4-5 hr.; $26.50) and to Halifax (1 per day; 8 hr.; $40), via **Acadian Lines** connections in Amherst, Nova Scotia. Station open Mon.-Fri. 7am-5:30pm and 9:30-10pm, Sat. 7am-1pm and 9:30-10pm, Sun. 7-8am, 11:30am-1pm, 4:30-5:30pm, 9:30-10pm. **Island Transit:** 308 Queen St. (892-6167). Mon.-Sat. makes one round-trip to Tignish along Rte. 2 ($15.50) and services Summerside (1 per day; 1 hr.; $7.15), Surrey (1 per day; $9.50) and New Glasgow, Nova Scotia (1 per day; $24). Buses run late May-mid-Oct. Station open Mon.-Sat. 8am-5pm, and at 7:45am Sun. for New Glasgow bus.

Beach Shuttles: Sherwood Beach Shuttle (566-3243) picks up at P.E.I. Visitor Information Centre (see above) and drops off in Cavendish (5 per day; $7, round-trip $12).

Ferries: Marine Atlantic, in Borden, 56km west of Charlottetown on Trans-Canada Hwy. (Rte. 1) (855-2030 or 800-341-7981 from continental U.S.), makes runs to Cape Tormentine, New Brunswick (12-18 per day; 1 hr.; round-trip $6.50, seniors $5, ages 5-12 $3.25, cars $17). **Northumberland Ferries,** in Wood Islands 61km east of Charlottetown on Trans-Canada Hwy. (Rte. 1) (962-2016; for traffic info call 800-565-0201 from P.E.I. and Nova Scotia, otherwise 566-3838), goes to Caribou, Nova Scotia (12-19 per day; 1½ hr.; round-trip $8.50, seniors $6, ages 5-12 $4, cars $25.50). For both ferries, fares are only round-trip and only collected leaving P.E.I. Thus, it is cheaper to leave from Borden than from Wood Islands, no matter how you come over.

Taxi: City Cab, 892-6567. No credit cards accepted. **Star Cab** (892-6581) does accept credit cards. Both open daily 24 hrs.

Car Rental: Rent-a-Wreck, 114 St. Peter's Rd. (894-7039). $27 per day, with 200km free, 12¢ per km thereafter, damage waiver $9 per day, ages 21-25 $10.50. Must be 21 with credit card or $200 deposit. Open Mon.-Fri. 7am-10pm, Sat.-Sun. 8am-10pm. **Hillside Autohost,** 207 Mt. Edward Rd. (894-7037), rents for $25 per day, 200km free, 15¢ per extra km; insurance $9 per day; must be 21 with major credit card. Open Mon.-Fri. 7:30am-5pm, Sat.-Sun. 9am-4pm.

Bike Rental: MacQueens, 430 Queen St. (368-2453), rents road and mountain bikes, $20 per day, $75 per week, helmets $5 per day. Must have credit card for deposit. Open Mon.-Fri. 8:30am-6pm, Sat. 8:30am-5pm.

Charlottetown Police: 566-5548. **Royal Canadian Mounted Police:** 566-7100.

Help lines: Crisis Centre, 566-8999. 24 hrs.

Post Office: 135 Kent St. (566-7070). Open Mon.-Fri. 8am-5:15pm.

General Delivery Postal Code: C1A 7N1.

Queen St. and **University Ave.** are Charlottetown's main thoroughfares, straddling **Confederation Centre** along the west and east, respectively. The most popular beaches lie on the north shore in the middle of the province, opposite but not far from Charlottetown. Hamlets (villages, not Danish princes) and fishing villages dot the Island landscape of **Kings County** on the east, as well as **Prince County** on the west. Acadian communities thrive on the south shore of Prince County. **Rte. 1** follows the southern shore, from ferry terminal to ferry terminal, passing through Charlottetown.

Accommodations

Almost a hundred **bed& breakfasts** and **country inns** litter every nook and cranny of the province, many are open year-round. Rates generally bounce around $25 for singles and $35 for doubles. **P.E.I. Tourism** (see Practical Information) distributes info about available B&Bs and will make reservations for you. In addition, 26 farms participate in a provincial **Farm Vacation** program, in which tourists spend some time with a farming family.

P.E.I. has one hostel, the **Charlottetown International Hostel (HI-C),** situated at 153 Mt. Edward Rd. (894-9696), across the yard from University of P.E.I., one long block east of University Ave. in a big, green barn with curious acoustics. The sociable staff attracts many international guests. (Laundry. Bike rentals $5. Blanket rental $1. Curfew midnight. Check-in 7-10am and 4pm-midnight Max. stay 3 nights. $10.70, nonmembers $14. Open June-Labor Day.) The **University of Prince Edward Island,** 550 University Ave. (566-0442), in Blanchard Hall in the southwestern end of campus overlooking Belvedere St., offers fully serviced and furnished two-bedroom apartments with kitchen, living room and hall laundry room—a great value for four people. (Check-in 8:30am-10pm. $50 plus tax for up to 4 people, extra cot $5. Weekly and monthly rates also available. Open May 20-Aug.) The University also runs a B&B in **Marion Hall,** with a full all-you-can-eat breakfast i:.cluded. ($22 per person, open July-Aug.)

Prince Edward Island National Park (672-2211 or 963-2391) operates three campgrounds (sites $8.75-13.50, serviced $19), and 14 of the 30 provincial parks offer camping. Additionally, there are over 30 other private campgrounds scattered throughout the Island, ensuring that there will always be a campsite available. (Campgrounds are open at different dates, but one is always open mid-June-Sept.)

Food

Lobster suppers, sumptuous feasts originally thrown by churches and community centers, have become deeply ingrained in Island tradition. The "run-of-the-mill" lobster suppers supplement their crustacean guest of honor with a host of all-you-can-eat goodies such as clam chowder, salad bars and desserts. The delicious suppers are quite expensive ($18-26, depending on the size of lobster), so fast all day before the feast. Fresh seafood, including the world famous **Malpeque oysters,** can be found for sale along the shores of the Island, especially in North Rustico on the north shore. See the back of the *P.E.I. Visitor's Guide* (see Practical Information) for a listing of fresh seafood outlets.

Fisherman's Wharf, Rte. 6 in North Rustico (963-2669), is the most famous lobster-supper house, featuring the world's largest lobster pound (holding tank, as in "dog pound") in a restaurant and a 60-ft.-long buffet bar. All-you-can-eat dinner, including lobster, mussels, chowder, salads and desserts $20. Seating capacity 500. Open mid-May-mid-Oct. 4-10pm.

Bonnie Brae Restaurant, Rte. 1 in Cornwall, 11km west of Charlottetown (566-2241). The lobster smorgasbord ($32) promises all-you-can-eat lobster and more than 60 side-dishes. Open mid-June-Labor Day 4-9pm.

Cedar's Eatery, 81 University Ave. (892-7377). A local favorite serving Lebanese and Canadian cuisine. Try their sizeable lunch specials ($5). Open Mon.-Thurs. 11am-midnight, Fri.-Sat. 11am-1am, Sun. 4-10:30pm.

Peake's Quay (PEEKS KEY), Great George St. below Lower Water St. (368-1330), on the Charlottetown waterfront overlooking the Marina. Seafood sandwich and salad $5-9. Scallops $7.50. Supper entrées $13-19. Open daily 11am-2am.

Sights

Prince Edward Island National Park (672-2211 or 963-2391), a coastal strip of 32 square km, embraces some of Canada's finest beaches, over a fifth of P.E.I.'s northern coast. It is the most popular Canadian national park east of Banff (see Alberta). Along with the beaches, heap-big sand dunes and salt marshes rumple the park's terrain. The park is home to many of the Island's 300-odd species of birds, including the endangered **piping plover;** birdwatchers might want to pick up the *Field Check List of Birds* (free) from any National or Provincial Park office. Campgrounds, programs and services in the park operate from mid-June to Labor Day, with **Cavendish campground** staying open until late September. At the entrance kiosks, receive a copy of the park guide *Blue Heron.* (Vehicle permits $5 per day, $10 per 4 days.)

The National Park also runs **Green Gables House** (672-2211), located off Rte. 6 in Cavendish near Rte. 13. Popularized by Lucy Maud Montgomery's novel, *Anne of Green Gables,* this house is the mecca for adoring readers. Interestingly, Montgomery's series of books about the freckle-faced orphan of Cavendish have a cult-following among Japanese schoolgirls, many of whom drag their families here to pay homage. The House and Haunted Woods are certain to be recognized by fans but will appear to be just a nice little estate for the uninitiated. Green Gables can get very crowded between late July and September, so it's best to arrive in the early morning or the evening. Tours available in English and French. (Open mid-June-Labor Day daily 9am-8pm, May-mid-June and Labor Day-Oct. daily 9am-5pm. Free.)

Woodleigh, just off Rte. 234 in Burlington (836-3401), midway between Cavendish and Summerside, will satisfy the monarchist in you. It contains miniature but still sizeable replicas of British architectural icons such as the St. Paul Cathedral, Tower of London, and Lord Nelson's statue in Trafalgar Square—all available for exploration. Yes, the Crown Jewels are inside the Tower. The craftsmanship is striking, but the cuteness of the whole concept can rankle after a while. (Open June and Sept. 9am-5pm, July-Aug. 9am-8pm. Admission $6, seniors $5.50, kids $3.25, preschoolers free.)

Charlottetown prides itself on being the "Cradle of Confederation." The brownstone **Province House,** on the corner of Great George and Richmond St. (566-7626), was where delegates from the British North American colonies met to discuss the union which would become, in 1867, the Dominion of Canada. Chambers of historical importance are open for viewing, as are exhibits and the modern-day legislative chambers. (Open Oct.-May Mon.-Fri. 9am-5pm, June and Sept. daily 9am-5pm, July-Labor Day daily 9am-8pm. Free.) Adjoining the Province House is the **Confederation Centre for the Arts,** located on the corner of Queen and Grafton St. (628-1864), a modern performing-arts complex with theaters, displays, a library and an art gallery. Free hour-long guided tours of the Centre are conducted July through August. (Open July-Aug. daily 9am-8pm, Sept.-June Mon.-Sat. 9am-5pm, Sun. 2-5pm.) Every summer, the musical production of **Anne of Green Gables** warbles in Mackenzie Theatre located inside Confederation Centre, as part of the Charlottetown Festival. (Performances mid-June-early Sept. Mon.-Sat. at 8pm. Tickets $19-30. For ticket info, call 566-1267 or 800-565-1267 in the Maritimes.)

Québec

Home to 90% of Canada's French-origin citizenry, Québec continues to fight for political and legal recognition of its separate cultural identity. All of the signs here are in French only, flouting a Supreme Court ruling. Canada's 1990 failure to ratify the Meech Lake Accord, which would have awarded recognition of Québec as a "distinct society," has reopened debate over the possibility of secession, formerly rejected in a 1980 referendum. Many now share the attitude of former Premier René Lévesque, who quipped, "If you can't sleep together, you might as well have separate beds." (*Très français.*) For all their pillowfighting, and despite the constantly looming threat of another referendum, the two bedmates seem reluctant to tamper with a healthy trading relationship. In Québec's struggle to retain a French-Canadian identity in a North American sea of English, the provincial motto *Je me souviens* might promise a prosperous future as well as a remembered past.

Practical Information

Capital: Québec City.

Tourisme Québec, c.p. 20,000, Québec G1K 7X2 (800-363-7777; 514-873-2015 in Montréal).

Postal abbreviation: QU

Time Zone: Eastern.

Alcohol: Legal drinking age 18.

Transportation Information

Excellent train and bus networks cover the entire province. The one **bus line** in Québec, **Voyageur,** offers service within the province and to Ontario's larger cities. Besides its regular fares, Voyageur offers a **Tour Pass** ($149) in summer for 10 days of unlimited travel. Call for dates (Montréal 514-842-2281, Québec City 418-524-4692). **VIA Rail** of Canada provides the main railroad for passenger and tourist service, with frequent runs between major urban centers. (For info on train travel on VIA Rail, see Train Travel in the Canada General Introduction, above.) **Traveling by car** in Québec can be expensive, since gas is heavily taxed. You'll pay about 57 to 61¢ per liter (about $2.50 a gallon). Québec requires that you have enough liability coverage to meet the insurance requirement of your home state or country. For more info, call the **Régie de l'assurance automobile du Québec** (Québec Automobile Insurance Board), 425, blvd. de Maisonneuve O., Bureau 900, Montréal H3A 3G5 (514-288-6015). If you receive bodily harm in an accident, call 873-7620 in Montréal, 643-7620 in Québec City, and 800-361-7620 elsewhere in the province. Note that turning right on red is illegal, as is carrying a radar detector in your car, even if it is turned off. The speed limit on highways is 100km/hr (about 62 mph). A pamphlet describing in full the differences between Canadian and U.S. traffic laws is available at Infotouriste (see Montréal Practical Information below). Another brochure explaining Québec's insurance laws is also available.

Popular provincial activities include fishing, canoeing, hunting, and skiing. A shimmering summer and fabulous fall beckon people to bike, camp, windsurf, and waterski. Fishers and hunters must obtain a Québec permit. Contact the **Ministère du Loisir, de la Chasse et de la Pêche** (Ministry of Leisure, Hunting and Fishing), Direction des Communications, 150, blvd. St.-Cyrille E., Québec G1R 4Y3 (418-890-5349).

Accommodation Information

For general assistance in locating accommodations, try the following organizations.

Bed and Breakfast: Vacances-Familles, 1291, blvd. Charest Ouest, Québec G1N 2C9 (418-682-5464; in Montréal 514-282-9580). $40 yearly membership in club provides discounts between 10 and 15% on lodging throughout the province.

Camping: Association des terrains du camping du Québec, 2001 rue de la metropole, Bureau 70 Longuevil, Québec J4G 1S9 (514-651-7396) and **Fédération québecoise du camping et de carvaning,** 4545 ave. Pierre-de-Coubertin c.p. 1000, succursale "M", Montréal H1V 3R2 (514-252-3003) can send you complete lists.

Farm Vacations: Fédération des Agricotours du Québec, at the address listed above for the *Fédération québecoise* under Camping (514-252-3138). Write a week in advance.

Hostels: Regroupement Tourisme Jeunesse (HI), again at the Fédération address (514-252-3117).

Montréal

In the 17th century the city of Montréal struggled with Iroquois tribes for control over the area's lucrative fur trade, and erected walls circling the settlement as a defensive measure. Today the remnants of those ramparts do no more than delineate the boundaries of Vieux Montréal (Old Montréal), and the most serious conflict Montréalers endure is a good bit of polyglottal bickering amongst themselves. As one of the world's largest bilingual cities, Montréal has had to work through a number of disputes between its Anglo- and Francophone inhabitants. The current French hegemony—all students learn French in Québec schools and all city signs read only in French—seems at the same time oppressive to English speakers and vital to those clinging to their Continental culture. For visitors, however, this tension imparts a dynamic, romantic atmosphere to this city on the St. Lawrence where cultures and tongues simultaneously mingle and chafe.

Practical Information

Emergency: 911.

Visitors Information: Infotouriste, 1001, rue du Square-Dorchester (873-2015; outside Montréal 800-363-7777), on Dorchester Sq. between rue Peel and rue Metcalfe. Métro: Peel. Free city maps and guides, and extensive food and housing listings. Avoid the currency exchange office, which will surreptitiously charge you $1.50 on all transactions. Go instead to one of the many close—and free—currency exchange shops downtown. Open June-Labor Day daily 8:30am-7:30pm; off-season daily 9am-6pm. Branch offices in **Old Montréal,** 174, rue Notre-Dame est. at Place Jacques-Cartier, and at **Dorval International Airport** and **Mirabel International Airport.** All are open the same hours and seasons as the main branch.

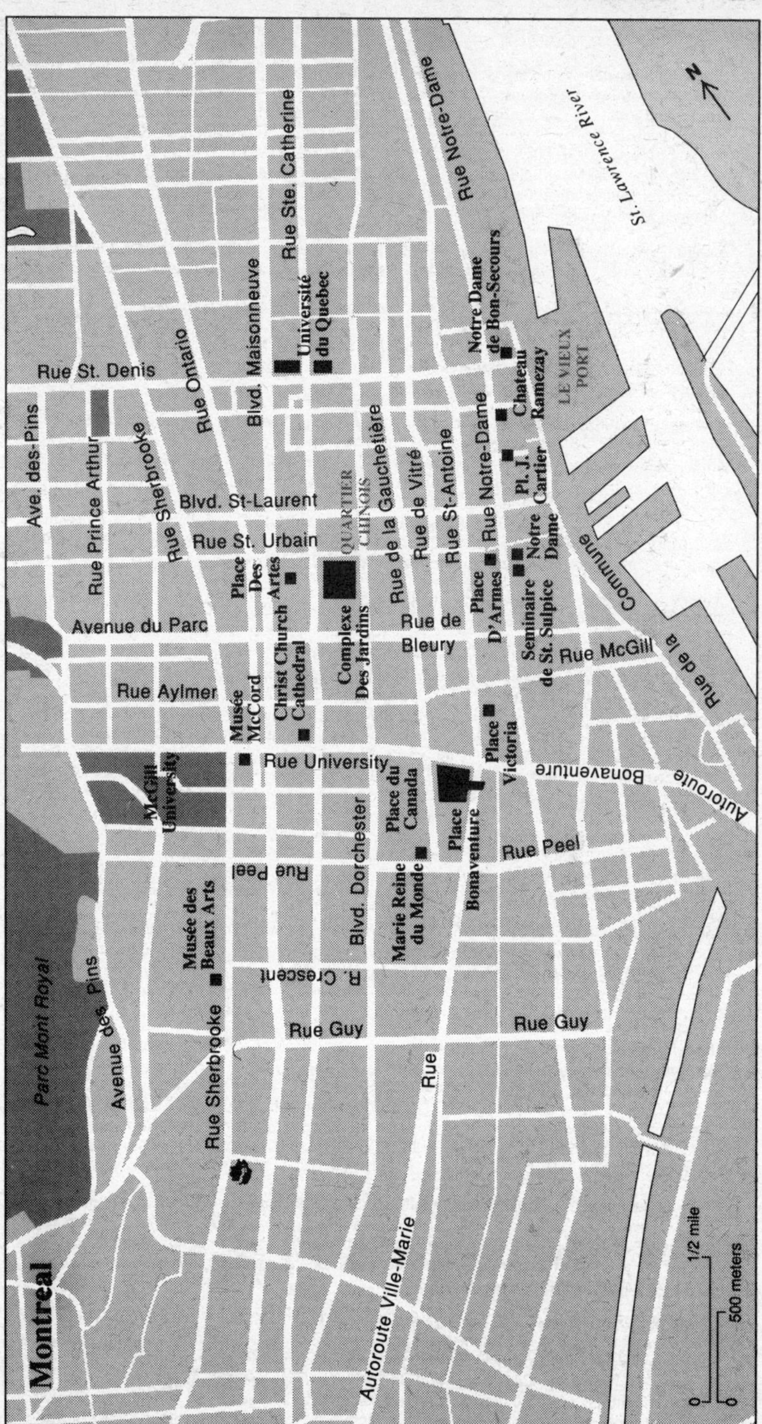
Montreal
Parc Mont Royal
Avenue des Pins
Rue Sherbrooke
Musée des Beaux Arts
McGill University
Rue Peel
R. Crescent
Rue Guy
Blvd. Dorchester
Marie Reine du Monde
Place Bonaventure
Place du Canada
Rue University
Musée McCord
Christ Church Cathedral
Rue Aylmer
Avenue du Parc
Rue Prince Arthur
Ave. des-Pins
Rue St. Denis
Rue Ontario
Blvd. Maisonneuve
Rue Ste. Catherine
Université du Quebec
Blvd. St-Laurent
Rue St. Urbain
Place Des Arts
Complexe Des Jardins
QUARTIER CHINOIS
Rue de la Gauchetière
Rue de Vitré
Rue St-Antoine
Rue de Bleury
Rue Notre-Dame
Place D'Armes
Place Victoria
Seminaire de St. Sulpice
Notre Dame
Pl. J. Cartier
Chateau Ramezay
Notre Dame de Bon-Secours
LE VIEUX PORT
Rue McGill
Rue de la Commune
Autoroute Bonaventure
Rue Peel
Rue Guy
Rue
Autoroute Ville-Marie
St. Lawrence River
N
0 1/2 mile
0 500 meters

Tourisme Jeunesse (youth tourist info), **Boutique Temps Libre,** 3063 rue St. Denis (252-3117). Métro: Sherbrooke. Free maps; youth hostel info available. Travel gear and helpful suggestions from friendly staff. A non-profit organization that inspects and ranks all 16 officially recognized youth hostels in Québec. Open Mon.-Wed. 10am-6pm, Thurs.-Fri. 10am-8pm, Sat. 10am-5pm. Mailing address: c.p. 1000, Succursale "M," Montréal P.Q., H1V 3R2. **Travel CUTS,** a student travel agency at the McGill Student Union, 3480, rue McTavish (849-9201). Métro: McGill. They specialize in budget travel for college students. (See Canada General Introduction: Student Travel.) Open Mon.-Fri. 9am-5pm.

Language: The population of Montréal is 65% French-speaking. Many citizens are bilingual. If you know French, speak it; you're less likely to be dismissed as an English-speaking Canadian.

Consulates: U.S., 1155, rue St.-Alexander (398-9695). Open Mon.-Fri 8:30am-1pm for passports; for visas Mon.-Fri. 8:30am-noon. **U.K.,** 1155, rue de l'Université, suite 901 (866-5863). Open for info Mon.-Fri. 9am-5pm. For consular help, open Mon.-Fri. 9am-12:30pm and 2-4:30pm. **Germany,** 3455, Mountain (286-1820). Open for info Mon.-Fri. 9am-4pm, for visas and passports Mon.-Fri. 9am-noon.

Currency Exchange: Bank of America Canada, 1230, rue Peel (393-1855). Métro: Peel. Open Mon.-Fri. 8:30am-5:30pm, Sat. 9am-5pm. **Thomas Cook,** 625, blvd. René-Lévesque ouest (397-4029). Métro: Square-Victoria. Open Mon.-Sat. 9am-5pm. Dorval Airport location (636-3582) open daily 6am-11:30pm. **National Commercial-Foreign Currency,** 1250, rue Peel (879-1300). Métro: Peel. Another office at 390, rue St.-Jacques (844-3401). Métro: Square-Victoria. Open Mon.-Fri. 8am-5pm, Sat. 8am-3pm. Although many cafés will take U.S. dollars, you'll get a better deal from a currency exchange store. The locations listed here exchange for free, but many don't—be sure to ask. Most **bank machines** are on the PLUS system.

American Express: 1141, blvd. de Maisonneuve ouest at Stanley (284-3300). Métro: Peel. Open Mon.-Fri. 9am-5:30pm.

Airports: Dorval (info service: 633-3105), 20-30 min. from downtown by car. From the Lionel Groulx Métro stop, take bus #211 to Dorval Shopping Center, then transfer to bus #204 (total fare $1.60). **Connoisseur Grayline** (934-1222) runs bus service daily to Dorval from the Queen Elizabeth Hotel at the corner of René-Lévesque and Mansfield. Other regular stops include the Château Champlain, the Sheraton Center, and the Voyageur Terminal. (Buses run every ½-hr., 5:20-6:30am, every 20 min. 7:20am-11:30pm. $8.50 one way, $16 round-trip; under age 5 free.) **Mirabel International Airport** (476-3040), 45 min. from downtown by car, handles all flights from outside North America. **Aeroplus** (476-1100) buses make a loop between Mirabel, the Voyageur station, and the city's main train station at 5, rue de la Gauchetière O. (daily 3-9am every 2 hrs., 10am-noon and 8pm-midnight every hr., noon-8pm every ½-hr.; $11.75.)

Trains: Central Station, 935, rue de la Gauchetière under the Queen Elizabeth Hotel. Métro: Bonaventure. Served by **VIA Rail** (871-1331) and **Amtrak** (800-426-8725). Direct service to: Québec City (3 per day; 3 hr.; $36, students $32; booked at least 5 days in advance $22/$18); Toronto (6 per day; 5 hr.; $72, student $65; 5 days in advance $43/36); Ottawa (4 per day, 2 hr., $30, student $27; 5 days in advance $18/15); Vancouver (3 per week, $444, student $400); Amtrak service to New York City (2 per day, 10 hr., US$67). Inconvenient connections to Boston (4 per day, 15 hr., US$97, change trains in New London). VIA ticket counters open daily 6am-9pm. Amtrak ticket counters open daily 7:30am-7:30pm.

Buses: Terminus Voyageur, 505, blvd. de Maisonneuve est (842-2281). Métro: Berri-UQAM. Voyageur offers 10-consecutive-day unlimited tour passes for $160 May-Oct., which will take you all over Québec and Ontario. Toronto (6 per day, 6½ hr., $54); Ottawa (17 per day, 21/3 hr., $24). The Ottawa Bus also leaves from **Dépanneur Beau-soir,** 2875 Blvd. St. Charles, (on the West Island). **Greyhound** serves New York City (5 per day, 83/4 hr., $100). **Vermont Transit** serves Boston (2 per day, 8½ hr., $82); Burlington, VT (2 per day, 3 hr., $19); and Québec (16 per day, 3 hr., $32)

Public Transport: STCUM Métro and Bus, (288-6287). A safe and efficient network, with Métro subway service. The four Métro lines and most buses operate daily 5:30am-12:30am; some have night schedules as well. Get network maps at the tourist office, or at any Métro station toll booth. Take a transfer ticket from the bus driver; it's good as a subway ticket. Fare for trains or bus $1.60, under 18 85¢, 6 tickets $6.50.

Car Rental: Beau Bazou, 295, rue de la Montagne (939-2330). Métro: Lucien l'Allier. $29 per day. 100km free plus 10¢ each additional km; insurance included. Open Mon.-Fri. 9am-9pm, Sat. 10am-5pm. Must be 25 with credit card; car must stay in Québec. Reserve in advance. **Via Route,** 1255 rue MacKay at Ste.-Catherine (871-1166; collect calls accepted). $27 per day; 200km free, 12¢ each additional km. Insurance for over age 25 $10 per day; ages 21-24 $13. Must be 21 with credit card. Open Mon.-Fri. 8am-7pm, Sat. 8am-5pm, Sun. 9am-5pm. **Avis** (800-879-2847), **Budget** (800-268-8900), and **Hertz** (800-263-0678) also serve Montréal.

Driver/Rider Service: Allo Stop, 4317, rue St.-Denis (985-3032). Will match you with a driver (a portion of the fee goes to the driver, who must be a member as well) heading for Québec City ($15), Ottawa ($10), Toronto ($26), Sherbrooke ($9), New York City ($50), or Boston ($42). Fees for Vancouver vary; riders and drivers fix their own fees for rides over 1000 mi. Membership ($6) required. Open Mon.-Wed. 9am-5pm, Thurs.-Fri. 9am-7pm, Sat. 10am-5pm, Sun. 10am-7pm.

Canadian Automobile Association (CAA), 1180, rue Drummond at blvd. René-Lévesque (info 861-7111; emergencies 861-1313). Métro: Bonaventure. Affiliated with American Automobile Association (AAA). Members have access to tourist info and emergency road service. Open Mon.-Fri. 8:30am-5pm.

Bike Rental: Cycle Peel, 6665, St.-Jacques (486-1148). Take bus #90 West from Vendome Métro stop. Peel out on a mountain bike or 10-speed; first day $22, $6 per additional day. Open Mon.-Wed. 9:30am-6pm, Thurs.-Fri. 9:30am-9pm, Sat. 9:30am-5pm, Sun. 9am-4pm. Credit card or $200 cash deposit required.

Ticket Agencies: Ticketmaster (514-790-2222) Open Mon.-Sat. 9am-9pm, Sun. noon-6pm. Also try **Admission Ticket Network,** (514-522-1245 or 800-361-4595). Credit card number required.

Help Lines: Tel-aide, 935-1101. Open 24 hrs. **Sexual Assault,** 723-4000. **Suicide-Action,** 522-5777.

Pharmacy: Pharmaprix, 5122, chemin de la Côte des Neiges (738-8464), Métro: Côte des Neiges). Open 24 hrs.

Post Office: Succursale "A," 1025, St.-Jacques (283-2567). Open Mon.-Fri. 8am-5:45pm. **Postal code:** H3C IT1.

Area Code: 514.

Two major streets divide the city, making it convenient for orientation. The **boulevard St.-Laurent** (also called "The Main") runs north-south, splitting the city and streets east-west. The Main also serves as the unofficial French/English divider: English **McGill University** lies to the west while St.-Denis, the **French student quarter** (also called the *"Quartier Latin")* is slightly east. According to the city maps, **Rue Sherbrooke** runs east-west almost the entire length of Montréal. Parking is often difficult in the city, particularly in winter when snowbanks narrow the streets and slow traffic. Take the **Métro** instead.

Accommodations and Camping

The **Québec Tourist Office** is the best resource for info about hostels, hotels, and *chambres touristiques* (rooms in private homes or small guest houses). B&B singles cost $25 to $40, doubles $35 to $75. The most extensive B&B network is **Bed & Breakfast à Montréal,** P.O. Box 595, Snowdon H3X 3T8 (738-9410), which recommends that you reserve by mail ($15 per night deposit upon confirmation). (Singles from $35. Doubles from $55. Open daily 9am-7pm; leave a message on the answering machine if the owners are out.) The **Downtown Bed and Breakfast Network,** 3458, ave. Laval, Montréal H2X 3C8 (289-9749), at Sherbrooke, lists about 80 homes downtown. (Singles $25-40. Doubles $35-55. Open spring and summer daily 8:30am-9pm; fall and winter 8:30am-7pm.) For cheaper B&B listings check with the **Marbel Guest House,** 3507, blvd. Décarie, H4A 3J4. Métro: Vendôme (486-0232; singles $25 without breakfast, $35 with; doubles $35/$45). Make reservations by sending a check for the first night as deposit. Virtually all B&Bs have bilingual hosts.

Montréal Youth Hostel (HI), 3541, rue Aylmer, Montréal H2X 2B9 (843-3317), in the McGill campus area, 10 min. walk from downtown. Métro: McGill. Recent renovations and a great location make this a clean, comfortable and extremely enjoyable place to stay. Carpeted rooms with 4-16 beds, huge kitchen and refrigerator, laundry facilities. Activities include free tours of the city; noticeboard listing downtown nightspots and their covers, extensive ride board. Breakfast special (pastry, yogurt, and OJ or coffee) $2.25. Linen $1, sleeping bags allowed. Open 24 hrs., no curfew. Max. stay 10 days. $14, Canadian nonmembers $16, non-Canadian nonmembers $19.35. Reservations by credit card accepted with 24-hr. notice. Overflow and groups housed at 267, ave. Rachel, a 15-min. walk away. Métro: Mont-Royal, then walk south on Berri and west on Rachel (843-8890). Right near the *Quartier Latin.* Older and bigger (150 beds) than the main hostel, with airy rooms and a big living room (smoking permitted here only). Big kitchen and fun-loving management. Prices, curfew, checkout same as above. Guided tours. Open daily, summer months only.

Collège Français, 5155, de Gaspé, Montréal H2T 2A1 (495-2581 or 270-9260 after 5pm and on holidays). Métro: Laurier, then walk west and north to corner of Fairmount. Rooms year-round. Clean, comfortable, and well-located. Access to gym. Young clientele. Prices vary from $9.50-$15.50 depending on the number of beds in the room (2-10) and whether the showers are in the room or down the hall. Free parking. Breakfast in summer $3. Open daily 8am-2am. More beds inconveniently located at 1391, rue Beauregard Longueuil (Métro: Longueuil, then take Bus 71 up Tascherau and Ségin), open June-Aug.

McGill University, Bishop Mountain Hall, 3935, rue de l'Université, H3A 2B4 (398-6367). Métro: McGill. Follow Université through campus, up the hill until it ends. Ideally located singles. Kitchenettes and pay phones on each floor. Common room with TV, laundry. Ask for Gardner building, where the views are best. Desk open Mon.-Fri. 7am-11pm, Sat.-Sun. 8am-10pm; a guard will check you in late at night. $24, non-students $32.50. $43 per 2 nights. Weekly $110. Continental breakfast served Mon.-Fri. 7:30-9:30am ($2.75). Open May 15-Aug. 15. Reservations by mail (one-night deposit) needed for July and Aug.

Université de Montréal, Residences, 2350, Edouard-Montpetit H2X 2B9 off Côte-des-Neiges (343-6531). Métro: Edouard-Montpetit. Located on the edge of a beautiful campus; try East Tower for great views. Singles $31, $21 for students, alumni and conferees (weekly $90). Open May 6-Aug. 19. Laundry, mailbox. Phone and sink in each room. Desk open 24 hrs. Cafeteria open Mon.-Fri. 7am-2pm.

YWCA, 1355, rue René-Lévesque ouest (866-9941). Métro: Lucien l'Allier. Women only. Clean, safe rooms in the heart of downtown. Newly-renovated. Access to Y facilities. Kitchen, TV on every floor. Doors lock at 10pm but the desk will buzz you in all night. Singles $35, with shared bathroom $46, with private bath $50. Doubles $53, with semi-private bath $62. Meals available in **Biotrain Café** downstairs (open daily 8am-7:30pm; sandwiches $3.25). Linen changed daily. $5 deposit. Reservations accepted.

YMCA, 1450, rue Stanley (849-8393), downtown. Métro: Peel. 331 rooms. Singles (men-only): $30, with sink $33. Doubles $48. Triples $57. Quads $66. Extra cot in any room $9. Students and seniors $2 off. Cafeteria open Mon.-Fri. 8am-8pm, Sat.-Sun. 8am-3pm. Access to Y facilities. TV and phone in every room. Usually fills up June-Aug. No reservations.

Many of the least expensive *maisons touristiques* (tourist homes) and hotels are around rue St.-Denis, which ranges from quaint to seedy. The area flaunts lively nightclubs, a number of enjoyable cafés and bistros, and abuts Vieux Montréal. Before choosing a place to stay, pick up a **Tourist Guide** at the Tourist Office; it maps the location of hundreds of accommodations.

Maison André Tourist Rooms, 3511, rue Université (849-4092). Métro: McGill. Mrs. Zanko will rent you a room in her old, well-located house (singles $25-35, doubles $38-45, $10 per extra person in room) and spin great yarns, but only if you don't smoke. Nice-sized and clean rooms with German-style decor. Reservations recommended.

Hotel Le Breton, 1609, rue St. Hubert (524-7273). Around the corner from bus station. Métro: Berri-UQAM. Prides itself on international clientele. Lobby and some rooms recently renovated. Looks like the Huxtables' neighborhood from the *Cosby Show.* All 12 rooms have TV and A/C. Singles $30-52. Doubles $42-58. Fills up quickly—make reservations.

Hotel Louisburg, 1649, rue St. Hubert (598-8544). Métro: Berri-UQAM. Newly-renovated, has new furniture. Clean rooms with TV. June-Sept. singles $30-45, doubles $35-54; Oct.-May $35-55, $40-59. Connected with the slightly more upscale **Hotel Jay**, 1655, rue St. Hubert.

Those with a car and time can camp at **Camping Parc Paul Sauvé** (479-8365), 45 minutes from downtown. Take 20 west to 13 north to 640 west and follow the signs to the park. There are 873 beautiful sites on the **Lac des Deux Montagnes.** (Sites $15, with hookup 19.) For private sites, try **KOA Montréal-South,** 130, blvd. Monette, St.-Phillipe J0L 2K0 (659-8626), a 15-minute drive from the city. Follow Rte. 15 south, take exit 38, turn left at the stop sign, and go straight about one mi. (1.6km)—it's on your left. (Sites $16, with hookup $20.50.) If these don't wet your camping whistle try **Camping Pointe-des-Cascades,** 2 chemin du Canal, Pte. des Cascades (455-9953). Take 40 west, exit 41 at Ste. Anne de Bellevue, junction 20, direction west to Dorion. In Dorion, follow "Théâtre des Cascades" signs. (Sites $12, with hookup $17.)

Food

French-Canadian cuisine is unique but generally expensive. When on a tight budget, look for *tourtière,* a traditional meat pie with vegetables and a thick crust, or *québecois crêpes,* stuffed with everything from scrambled eggs to asparagus with *béchamel.* Wash it down with *cidre* (hard cider). Other Montréal specialties include French bread (the best on the continent), smoked meat, Matane salmon, Gaspé shrimp, lobster from the Maydalen Islands, and *poutine,* a gooey concoction of French fries *(frites),* cheese curds, and gravy, which you can find everywhere—even McDonald's.

Montréal's ethnic restaurants offer a variety of cuisine ranging from curry to *pierogis* at reasonable prices. Look for Greek *souvlaki* or Vietnamese asparagus and crab soup. A small **Chinatown** orients itself along rue de la Gauchetière, near old Montréal's Place d'Armes. A Jewish neighborhood complete with Hebrew neon signs, delis, and bagel bakeries lies north of downtown around blvd. St.-Laurent. Don't miss the best bagels in town (30-50¢)—baked before your eyes in brick ovens—at **La Maison de Original Fairmount Bagel,** 74, rue Fairmount ouest (272-0667), Métro: Laurier, or the **Bagel Bakery,** 263, rue St.-Viateur ouest (276-8044), Métro: Place-des-Arts, both open 24 hrs.

For a quick sampling of Montréal's international cuisine, stop by **Le Faubourg,** 1616, rue Ste.-Catherine ouest at rue Guy (939-3663). Métro: Guy. The food here is diverse (crêpes, falafel, Szechuan) and fresh, despite the fast-food atmosphere. Markets here sell seafood, meats, bread, and produce. Before you leave Le Faubourg, stop by **Monsieur Félix and Mr. Norton Cookies** (939-3207). Aside from summing up the French-English duality in Montréal, they make the richest cookies in town. (Open Mon.-Thurs. 9am-10pm, Fri-Sat. 9-midnight.) Look for other locations around the city.)

The drinking age in Montréal is 18. You can save money by buying your own wine at a *dépanneur* or at the **SAQ** (Sociéte des alcools du Québec) and bringing it to unlicensed restaurants, concentrated on the blvd. St.-Laurent, north of Sherbrooke, and on the pedestrian precincts of rue Prince Arthur and rue Duluth. When preparing your own grub, look for produce at the **Atwater Market** (Métro: Lionel-Groulx); the **Marché Maisonneuve,** 4375, rue Ontario est, Métro: Pie-IX; or the **Marché Jean-Talon** (Métro: Jean Talon). (For info on any call 872-2491; all open Mon.-Wed. 7am-6pm, Thurs.-Fri. 7am-9pm, Sat.-Sun. 7am-5pm.)

Rue St.-Denis, the main thoroughfare in the French student quarter, has many small restaurants and cafés, most of which cater to student pocketbooks. **Da Giovanni,** 572, Ste.-Catherine est, Métro: Berri, serves generous portions of fine Italian food; don't be put off by the lines or the diner atmosphere. The sauce and noodles cook up right in the window. (842-8851; open Sun.-Wed. 7am-1am, Thurs. 7am-2am, Fri. 7am-3am.)

You'll be charged 15% tax for meals totaling more than $3.25. All restaurants are required by law to post their menus outside, so shop around. For more info, consult the free *Restaurant Guide,* published by the Greater Montréal Convention and Tourism Bureau (844-5400) which lists more than 130 restaurants by type of cuisine and is available at the tourist office.

Café Santropol, 3990, Duluth at St.-Urbain (842-3110). Métro: Sherbrooke, then walk north on St.-Denis and west on Duluth. Student hangout which likes to see itself as a bit weird: the menu greets you with a friendly "Bienvenue à la planète Santropol!" Huge veggie sandwiches served with piles of fruit ($6.50-8). Chicken also available for carnivores. Open Mon.-Thurs. 11:30am-midnight, Fri. 11:30-2am, Sat. noon-2am, Sun. noon-midnight.

Terasse Lafayette, 250, rue Villeneuve ouest at rue Jeanne Mance (288-3915), west of the Mont-Royal Métro. Pizzas, pastas, souvlaki and salad $6-10; gyro plate $8.50. One of the better Greek restaurants, with a huge outdoor terrace. BYOB. 10% discount on orders for pick-up. Open daily 11am-1am. Free delivery.

Etoile des Indes, 1806, Ste.-Catherine ouest near St.-Matthieu (923-8330). Métro: Guy. Split-level dining room with tapestries covering the walls. The best Indian fare in town. Dinner entrees $7-17. The brave should try their bang-up *bangalore phal* dishes. Open Mon.-Fri. 11am-2:30pm and 5-11pm, Sat. noon-3pm and 5-11pm, Sun. 5-11pm.

Le Mazurka, 64 Prince Arthur (844-3539). Métro: Sherbrooke; cross St.-Denis and dance through the park; Prince-Arthur is on the other side. Classy décor belies great prices and fine Polish fare. *Pierogis* (Polish ravioli) with soup, $4.50. Specials abound, especially Mon.-Thurs. after 9pm; it gets crowded. Dine on the terrace. Open daily 11:30-1am.

Schwartz's Deli, 3895, St.-Laurent, near Napoléon (842-4813). Métro: Sherbrooke. Arguably the best smoked meat in town piled on thick (sandwiches $3.40, larger meat plates $7-8.50). Often jam-packed, always fun; you'll get your food in 5 min. Open Mon.-Thurs. and Sun. 9am-1am, Fri. 9am-2am, Sat. 9am-3am.

Wilensky's, 34, rue Fairmount ouest (271-0247). Métro: Laurier. A great place for quick lunch in the heart of the old Jewish neighborhood. Or pull out a book from Moe Wilensky's shelf, note the sign advising "We always put mustard on it," and linger. Hot dogs $1.50, sandwiches $1.75-2.35. Open Mon.-Fri. 9am-4pm.

The Peel Pub, 1107, rue Ste.-Catherine (844-6769). Métro: Peel. Other location: 1106, de Maisonneuve (845-9002). At the main branch, students and suits sit side by side in a raucous, rollicking pub. TV screens and live bands nightly. 99¢ spaghetti every day; daily $5 specials ranging from lasagna and salad to *tourtière*. Ste. Catherine: happy hour pitchers $5, 3-7pm; open Mon.-Sat. 6:30am-midnight; de Maisonneuve: open Mon.-Fri. 11am-3am, Sat.-Sun. 4:30pm-3am, Mon.-Thurs. nights $1 shooters.

McGill Student Union, 3480, rue McTavish, 5 min. from HI hostel. Métro: McGill. Cheap cafeteria food with surprisingly friendly service. Grill, pizza, salad bar, frozen yogurt. Breakfast special (toast, hash browns, and coffee) $2. Sandwiches ($2-3) and burgers ($1.75) for lunch. Beer to boot. Open May-Aug. Mon.-Thurs. 8am-3pm, Fri. 8am-2:30pm; also open during academic year. Check out the pool tables at **Gert's Pub** downstairs, open in summer Thurs.-Fri. 4pm-midnight.

Sights

An island city, Montréal has matured from a riverside settlement of French colonists into a major metropolis. The city's ethnic pockets and architectural diversity can captivate you for days on end. Museums, Vieux-Montréal (Old Montreal), and the new downtown may be fascinating but don't forget that the island's greatest asset is the amount of hustle and bustle crammed into such a small area. Wander aimlessly and often—and *not* through the high-priced shops and boutiques that the tourist office touts. Many attractions between Mont-Royal and the St. Laurent River are free: from parks (Mont-Royal and Lafontaine) and universities (McGill, Montréal, Concordia, Québec at Montréal) to ethnic neighborhoods.

Walk or bike down **boulevard St.-Laurent** north of Sherbrooke. Originally settled by Jewish immigrants, this area now functions as a sort of multi-cultural welcome wagon, home to Greek, Slavic, Latin American, and Portuguese immigrants. **Rue St.-Denis,** abode of the French language elite around the turn of the century, still serves as the mainline of Montréal's **Latin Quarter** (Métro: Berri-UQAM). Jazz fiends command the street the first week of July during the **14th Montréal International Jazz Festival** (525-7732 HQ; info 871-1881) with over 200 outdoor shows. Headliners play many other concerts indoors. **Carré St.-Louis,** or Saint Louis Square, (Métro: Sherbrooke), with its fountain and sculptures, **rue Prince-Arthur,** (Métro: Sherbrooke) packed with street performers in the summer, and **Le Village,** a gay village in Montréal from rue St.-Denis est to Papineau along rue Ste.-Catherine est, are also worth visiting.

The **McGill University** campus (main gate at the corner of McGill and Sherbrooke St.; Métro: McGill) stretches up Mont-Royal and boasts Victorian buildings and pleasant spots of green grass in the midst of downtown. More than any other sight in Montréal, the university illustrates the impact of British tradition in the city. The campus also contains the site of the 16th-century Native-American village of Hochelaga and the **Redpath Museum of Natural Science** (398-4086), with rare fossils and two genuine Egyptian mummies. (Open June-Labor Day Mon.-Thurs. 9am-5pm; Oct.-May Mon.-Sat. 9am-5pm, Sun. 1-5pm. Free.) Guided tours of the campus are available Mon.-Fri. with 24-hr. notice (398-6555).

The Underground City

Montréal residents aren't speaking cryptically of a sub-culture or a hideout for dissidents when they rave about their Underground City. They mean *under the ground:*

29km of tunnels link Métro stops and form a subterranean village of climate-controlled restaurants and shops. The ever-expanding network now connects railway stations, a bus terminal, restaurants, banks, cinemas, theaters, hotels, two universities, two department stores, 1200 businesses, 1250 housing units, and 1400 boutiques. Rather frighteningly hailed by the city as "the prototype of the city of the future," these burrows give the word "suburban" a whole new meaning. Enter the city from any Métro stop or start your adventure at the **Place Bonaventure,** 901 rue de la Gauchetière ouest (397-2205; Métro: Bonaventure), Canada's largest commercial building. The **Viaduc** shopping center inside contains a diverse mélange of shops, each selling products of a different country. The tourist office supplies city guides that include treasure maps of the tunnels and underground attractions. (Shops open Mon.-Fri. 9:30am-6pm, Sat.-Sun. 9:30am-5pm.) Poke your head above ground long enough to see **Place Ville-Marie** (Métro: Bonaventure), a 1960s office-shopping complex. Revolutionary when first built, the structure triggered Montréal's architectural renaissance. **Cathédrale Marie Reine du Monde** (Mary, Queen of the World Cathedral), corner of René-Lévesque and Mansfield (Métro: Bonaventure; 866-1661) is a scaled-down replica of St. Peter's in Rome. (Open Mon.-Fri. 7:30am-7:15pm, Sat.-Sun. 8:30am-7:15pm.)

Parks and Museums

The finest of Montréal's parks, **Parc du Mont-Royal,** Centre de la Montagne (844-4928), Métro: Mont-Royal, swirls in a vast green expanse up the mountain from which the city took its name. Visitors from New York may recognize the green hand of Frederick Law Olmsted, the architect who planned Central Park (and half the U.S.). From rue Peel, hardy hikers can take a foot path and stairs to the top. The lookouts on Camillien-Houde Parkway and the Mountain Chalet both offer phenomenal views of Montréal. In 1643, De Maisonneuve, founder of Montréal, promised to climb Mont-Royal bearing a cross if the flood waters of the St.-Laurent would recede. The existing 30-ft. cross (which, it's safe to assume, is not the same one) commemorates this climb. When illuminated at night, you can see the cross for miles. In winter, *montréalais* congregate on "the Mountain" to ice-skate, toboggan, and cross-country ski. In summer, Mont-Royal welcomes joggers, cyclists, picnickers and amblers. (Officially open 6am-midnight.) **Parc Lafontaine,** bordered by Sherbrooke, Rachel, Papineau and Parc Lafontaine St., Métro: Sherbrooke, has picnic facilities, an outdoor puppet theater, seven public tennis courts (hourly fee), ice-skating in the winter, and an international festival of public theater in June.

Musée des beaux-arts de Montréal (Fine Arts Museum), 80, Sherbrooke ouest (285-1600; Métro: Guy), houses a small permanent collection that touches upon all major historical periods and includes Canadian and Inuit work. (Open Mon.-Sat. 11am-6pm; Wed. and Sat. closes at 9pm. Admission $10, seniors and students $5, under 12 $2; prices and hours vary depending on the exhibit.) It also hosts visiting exhibits. **Musée d'art contemporain** (Museum of Contemporary Art), 185 Ste.-Catherine Ouest at Jeanne-Mance (847-6226), Métro: Place-des-Arts, has the latest by *québecois* artists, as well as textile, photography, and avant-garde exhibits. (Open Tues.-Sun. 11am-6pm. Admission $4.75, seniors $3.75, students $2.75, under 12 free.)

The newly renovated and expanded **McCord Museum of Canadian History,** 690 Sherbrooke O (398-7100; Métro: McGill), saves and studies a collection of textiles, costumes, paintings, prints and 700,000 pictures spanning 133 years in their photographic archives (archives by appointment only; contact Nora Hague). (Open Tues., Wed. and Fri. 10am-6pm, Thurs. 10am-5pm, Sat.-Sun. 10am-5pm. Admission $5, students $2, seniors $3.) Opened in May 1989, the **Centre Canadien d'Architecture,** 1920 Baile St. (939-7000; Métro: Guy), houses one of the most important collections of architectural prints, drawings, photographs and books in the world. (Open Tues., Wed. and Fri. 11am-6pm, Thurs. 11am-8pm, Sat.-Sun. 11am-5pm. Admission $5, students and seniors $3, free for kids.) **Olympic Park,** 4545, ave. Pierre-de-Coubertin (252-4737; Métro: Pie-IX or Viau), hosted the 1976 Summer Olympic Games. Its daring architecture includes the world's tallest inclined tower and a stadium with one of the world's only fully retractable roofs. Despite this, games *still* get rained out because the roof cannot be put in place with crowds in the building (really smart, guys). (Guided tours daily at 12:40 and 3:40pm; more often May-Sept. Admission $7, seniors $6, ages 5-17 $5.50, under 5 free.) Take the *funiculaire* to the top of the tower for a panoramic view of Montréal. (Leaves daily every 10 min., 10am-11pm; off-season 10am-6pm. Fare same as for tour of the park. For combined tour and *funiculaire* $12, seniors $10, ages 5-17 $8.) The most recent addition to the attractions at the Olympic Park is the **Biodôme,** (872-3034). Housed in the building which was once the Olympic Vélodrome, the Biodôme is a "living museum" in which four complete ecosystems have been reconstructed: the Tropical Forest, the Laurentian Forest, the Saint-Laurent marine ecosystem, and the Polar World. The goal is environmental awareness and conservation; the management stresses repeatedly that the Biodôme is *not* a zoo, rather a means for people to connect themselves with the natural world. (Open late June-Labor Day daily 9am-8pm, off-season daily 9am-6pm. Admission $8.50, seniors $6, $4.25 ages 6-17. Special packages available for viewing the Gardens and Biodôme together.) In the summer a train will take you across the park to the **Jardin Botanique** (Botanical Gardens), 4101, Sherbrooke E. (872-1400; Métro: Pie-IX), one of the most important gardens in the world. The Japanese and Chinese areas opened only recently, and house the largest bonsai and penjing collection outside of Asia. (Gardens open 8am-sunset; greenhouses 9am-6pm. Admission $7, seniors and ages 6-17 $4.75, under 6 free. 30% less mid-Oct.-mid-May.)

Vieux Montréal

Montréal's first French settlement dug itself in at Vieux-Montréal (Old Montréal), on the stretch of riverbank between rue McGill, Notre-Dame, and Berri. The fortified walls that once protected the quarter have crumbled, but the beautiful 17th- and 18th-century mansions of politicos and merchants retain their full splendor. (Métro: Place d'Armes.)

The 19th-century church **Notre-Dame-de-Montréal,** 116 Notre-Dame Ouest (849-1070), towers above the Place d'Armes and the memorial to De Maisonneuve. A historic center for the city's Catholic population, the neo-Gothic church once hosted separatist rallies, and, more recently, a tradition-breaking ecumenical gathering; it seats 4000, and is one of the largest and most magnificent churches in North America. Concerts are held here throughout the year. After suffering major fire damage, the **Wedding Chapel** behind the altar re-opened in 1982 replete with an enormous bronze altar. (Open June 24-Labor Day, daily 7am-8pm; off-season daily 7am-6pm. Guided tours offered.)

From Notre-Dame walk next door to the **Sulpician Seminary,** Montréal's oldest remaining building (built in 1685) and still a functioning seminary. The clock over the façade is the oldest public timepiece in North America and has overseen the passage of over nine billion seconds since it was built in 1700. A stroll down rue Saint-Sulpice will bring you to **rue de la Commune** on the banks of the St. Lawrence River. Here the city's old docks compete with the new. Proceed east along rue de la Commune to **rue Bonsecours.** At the corner of Bonsecours and the busy rue St.-Paul stands the 18th-century **Notre-Dame-de-Bonsecours** (845-9991), founded on the port as a sailor's refuge by Marguerite Bourgeoys, leader of the first congregation of non-cloistered nuns. Sailors thankful for their safe pilgrimages presented the nuns and priests with the wooden boat-shaped ceiling lamps in the chapel. The church also has a museum in the basement and a bell tower with a nice view of Vieux Montréal and the St. Lawrence River. (Chapel open May-Nov. daily 9:30am-5pm; Dec.-April 10am-5pm. Tower and museum open May-Nov. Tues.-Sat. 9am-4:30pm, Sun. 11:30am-4:30pm; Dec.-April Tues.-Fri. 10:30am-4:30pm, Sat. 10am-4:30pm, Sun. 11:30am-4:30pm. Admission $2, under 12 50¢.)

Opening onto rue St.-Paul is **Place Jacques Cartier,** site of Montréal's oldest market. Here the modern European character of Montréal is most evident; cafés line the square and in summer street artists strut their stuff. Visit the grand **Château Ramezay,** 280, Notre-Dame est (861-3708), Métro: Champ-de-Mars, built in 1705 to house the French viceroy, and its museum of *québecois,* British, and American 18th-century artifacts. (Open Tues.-Sun. 10am-4:30pm. Admission $2, seniors and students $1.) Meanwhile, in the square of Place Vauquelin, metes the Vieux Palais de Justice, built in

1856; across from it stands City Hall. **Rue St.-Jacques** in the Old City, established in 1687, is Montréal's answer to Wall Street.

There are many good reasons to venture out to **Ile Ste.-Hélène,** an island in the St. Lawrence River, just off the coast of Vieux Montréal. The best is **La Ronde** (872-6222), Montréal's popular amusement park: it's best to go in the afternoon and buy an unlimited pass. From late May to mid-June on Wednesday and Saturday, stick around La Ronde until 10pm to watch the **International Benson & Hedges Fireworks Competition** (872-8714). (Park open daily June-Sept. Sun.-Thurs. 11am-11pm, Fri.-Sat. 11am-midnight. Admission $19.50, under 12 $8.50.) To cool off after your frolics, slide over to **Aqua-Parc** (872-7326) and splash the day away. (Open mid-June-late Aug. daily 10am-5pm. Admission $15.25, under 12 $8.50; after 3pm $10.25, $6.25.) **Le Vieux Fort** (The Old Fort, also known as the **David M. Stewart Museum;** 861-6701), was built in the 1820s to defend Canada's inland waterways. Now primarily a military museum, the fort displays artifacts and costumes detailing Canadian colonial history. Three military parades take place daily from late June to the end of August. (Museum open May-Aug. Wed.-Mon. 10am-6pm; off-season Wed.-Mon. 10am-5pm. Admission $5, seniors, students, and kids $3, under 6 free.) Take the Métro under the St. Lawrence to the Ile Ste.-Hélène stop.

Whether swollen with spring run-off or frozen over during the winter, the **St. Lawrence River** can be one of Montréal's most thrilling attractions. The whirlpools and 15-ft. waves of the **Lachine Rapids** once precluded river travel. No longer—now St. Lawrence and Montréal harbor cruises depart from Victoria Pier (842-3871) in Vieux Montréal (mid-May-mid-Oct., 4 per day, 2 hr., fare $18.75). Tours of the Lachine Rapids (284-9607) leave five times per day (May-Sept. 10am-6pm; ½-hr. cruise $45, seniors $40, ages 13-18 $35, ages 6-12 $25).

Explore the **West Island,** formerly the summer residence for affluent city dwellers, by bike (along the Lachine Canal and the Lakeshore Rd.) or by bus (#211 from Lionel Groulx). Walk along the boardwalk in Ste. Anne de Bellevue and watch the River locks in action. The local crowd rocks Ste. Anne's at night, at one of the many *brasseries,* or the renowned **Annie's** and **Quai Sera.**

Nightlife and Entertainment

Should you choose to ignore the massive neon lights flashing "films érotiques" and "Château du sexe," you can find blander nightlife in Québec's largest city—either in **brasseries** (with food as well as beer, wine, and music) or in **pubs** (with more hanging out and less eating). Downstairs at 1107, rue Ste.-Catherine ouest, for example, is **Peel Pub** (844-6769; see listing in Food, above), providing live rock bands and good, cheap food nightly. Here waiters rush about with three pitchers of beer in each hand to keep up with the mötley crue of Montréal's university students; this pub has another location on De Maisonneuve as well.

For slightly older and more subdued drinking buddies, search the side streets of rue Ste.-Catherine ouest. Try the English strongholds around **rue Crescent** and **rue Bishop** (Métro: Guy), where bar-hopping is a must. **Déjà-Vu,** 1224, Bishop near Ste. Catherine (866-0512), has live bands each night. (Open daily 3pm-3am; happy hour 3-10pm. No cover.) Set aside Thursday for a night at **D.J.'s Pub,** 1443, Crescent (287-9354), when $12 gets you 12 mixed drinks. (Open 11:30am-3am.) **Déjà-Vu,** 1224, Bishop near Ste. Catherine (866-0512), has live bands each night. **Christopher's,** 1446, Crescent (847-0275) is the other major hotspot. (Open daily 11:30am-3am.) French nightlife parleys in the open air cafés on **rue St.-Denis** (Métro: UQAM). Stop in for live jazz at **Le Grand Café,** 1720, rue St.-Denis (849-6955; open daily 11am-3:30am; evening cover $5-10). While in the Latin Quarter, scout out energetic **rue Prince Arthur,** which vacuum-packs Greek, Polish, and Italian restaurants into its tiny volume. Here maître-d's stand in front of their restaurants and attempt to court you toward their cuisine. Street performers and colorful wall murals further enliven this ethnic neighborhood. The accent changes slightly at **avenue Duluth,** where Portuguese and Vietnamese establishments prevail. Vieux Montréal, too, is best seen at night. Street performers, artists, and *chansonniers* in various *brasseries* set the tone for lively summer evenings of clapping, stomping, and singing along; the real fun goes down on St.-Paul, in the *brasseries* near the corner of St.-Vincent.

The city bubbles with a wide variety of theatrical groups: the **Théâtre du Nouveau Monde,** 84, Ste.-Catherine ouest (861-0563), and the **Théâtre du Rideau Vert,** 4664, St.-Denis (844-1793), stage *québecois* works (all productions in French). For English language plays, try the **Centaur Theatre,** 453, rue St.-François-Xavier (288-3161), Métro: Place-d'Armes, whose season runs mainly October through June. The city's exciting **Place des Arts,** 260 de Maisonneuve Ouest (842-2112 for tickets), houses the **Opéra de Montréal,** the **Montréal Symphony Orchestra** (842-3402), and **Les Grands Ballets Canadiens. The National Theatre School of Canada,** 5030, rue St. Denis (842-7954), stages excellent student productions during the academic year. **Théâtre Saint-Denis,** 1594, St.-Denis (849-4211), hosts traveling productions like *Cats* and *Les Misérables.* Check the *Calendar of Events* (available at the tourist office and reprinted in daily newspapers), or call **Ticketmaster** (790-2222) for tickets and further info.

Montréalais are rabid sports fans, and there's opportunity aplenty for like-minded visitors to foam at the mouth. During the second weekend in June, the **Circuit Gilles-Villeneuve** on the Ile Notre-Dame hosts the annual **Molson Grand Prix**, a Formula 1 race (392-0000), and this August, as in every other August, **Tennis Canada** will host the world's best tennis players at Jarry Park (Métro: De Castelau). This year men compete in the **Player's Challenge,** August 1 to 17. (Call 273-1515 for info and tickets.) Football fans are not forgotten: the **Montreal Machine** (WLAF football team) join the **Expos** in Olympic Stadium (see address in Sights above; for Expos info call 253-3434; for tickets in either town call 522-1245 in Montréal, 800-361-4595 outside).

Montréalais don't just watch: their one-day **Tour de l'île** is the largest participatory cycling event in the world, with a 40,000-member fan club attending. (Call 847-8687 to see how you can attend too.) A trip to Montréal between October and April is incomplete without attending a **Montréal Canadiens** hockey game: **the Montréal Forum,** 2312, Ste. Catherine O (Métro: Atwater), is the shrine to hockey and **Les Habitants** (nickname for the Canadiens) are its acolytes. Games are usually sold out, so call for tickets as early as possible. (For more info, call 932-2582.)

Québec

Québec is Canada's oldest city, and its citizens gleefully steep themselves in their history; fully staffed, admission-charging, tour-giving historic sites rear their heads everywhere you look. Built on the rocky heights of Cape Diamond, where the St. Lawrence River narrows and joins the St. Charles River in northeast Canada, the city has been called the "Gibraltar of America" because of the stone escarpments and military fortifications protecting the port. Despite British control of the area, the French have shaped Québec with their heritage and language. At least 95% French-speaking, Québec City offers traditional French-Canadian cuisine, music, and ambience. Visitors who speak French should do so, but Anglophones will squeak by. Steeping themselves so gleefully in their cultural history, it is surely cause for wonder—and for pleasure—that the Québecois and their city can retain such vitality, energy, and *joie de vivre*. The best times to sample this are during the summer arts festival in mid-July and February's winter carnival, a raucous French-Canadian Mardi Gras.

Practical Information and Orientation

Emergency: Police, 691-6911 (city); 623-6262 (provincial). **Info-santé:** 648-2626, a 24-hr. service providing info by qualified nurses.

Centre d'information de l'office du tourisme et des congrés de la communauté urbaine de Québec, 60, rue d'Auteuil (692-2471), in the Old City. Visit here for accommodation listings, brochures, free maps (look for the one with a black cover, on the wall with the brochures), and friendly bilingual advice. Free local calls. Open June-Labor Day daily 8:30am-8pm; April, May, Sept., Oct. Mon.-Fri. 8:30am-5:30pm; off-season Mon.-Fri. 8:30am-5pm. **Ste.-Foy Centre d'informa-**

tion de l'office du tourisme et des congrés de la communauté urbaine de Québec, 3005, blvd. Laurier, Ste.-Foy (651-2882), is just down Laurier from Ste. Foy bus station, at rue Lavigerie, 4 mi. (2.5km) southwest of the Old City. Same services as the Centre in the Old City, without traffic and parking hassle. Open June-Labor Day daily 8:30am-8pm; Sept. 3-Oct. 14 daily 8:30am-6pm; Oct. 15-April 15 daily 9am-5pm; April 16-June daily 8:30am-6pm. **Maison du tourisme de Québec** 12, rue Ste.-Anne (the office has no phone; call 514-873-2015 or 800-363-7777 to contact the main office in Montréal, which dispenses the same info), deals specifically with provincial tourism, distributing accommodation listings for the entire province and free road and city maps. Some bus tours and Budget (see Car Rental below) also have desks here. Open June 10-Labor Day 8:30am-7:30pm; off-season 9am-6pm.

Youth Tourist Information: Boutique Temps-Libre of Regroupement tourisme jeunesse 2700 Blvd. Laurier, Ste.-Foy (651-7108), in the Place Laurier. Sells maps, travel guides and equipment, ISICs and HI-C memberships, and health insurance. Can also make reservations at any hostel in Québec province, or you can do it yourself by calling 800-461-8585 with a credit card. (Open Mon.-Wed. 9:30am-5:30pm, Thurs.-Fri. 9:30am-9pm, Sat. 9:30am-5pm.) Smaller boutique with fewer services at 19, Ste.-Ursule (694-0755) in the Centre de Séjour (see Accommodations and Camping below). Open same hours as main boutique.

U.S. Consulate: 2 Terrasse Dufferin (692-2095). Issues tourist visas Mon., Wed., and Fri. 9-11am. Open for American citizens Tues. and Thurs. 9-11am and 2-4pm; Mon., Wed., and Fri. 2-4pm.

Airlines: Air Canada (692-0770 or 800-361-7413) and **Inter-Canadian** (692-1031). Special deals available for youths under 24 (with ID) willing to go standby. The airport is way, way out of town with no quick method, if any, to get there by public transport. By car, turn right onto Rte. de l'aéroport and then take either Blvd. Wilfred-Hamel or, beyond it, Autoroute 440 to get into the city. **Maple Leaf Sightseeing Tours** (649-9226) runs a shuttle service between the airport and the city's major hotels. Shuttles run daily 8am-8pm, about 8 times per day. ($7.50, under 13 $3.75.)

Trains: VIA Rail Canada, 450, rue de la Gare du Palais in Québec City (524-6452); 3255, chemin de la Gare in Ste.-Foy (658-8792); 5995, St.-Laurent Hwy. 20 Lévis (833-8056). Call 800-361-5390 anywhere in Canada or the U.S. for reservations and info. To Montréal (3 per day; 3 hr.; $36, students $32; $22 for adults if booked in advance and not traveling on Fri., Sun., or a holiday; $18 for students if booked at least 5 days in advance).

Buses: Voyageur Bus, 225, blvd. Charest est (524-4692). Open daily 5:30am-1am. Outlying stations at 2700, ave. Laurier, in Ste.-Foy (651-7015; open daily 6am-1am), and 63, rte. Trans-Canada ouest (Rte. 132), in Lévis (837-5805; open Mon.-Sat. 6:30am-11pm, Sun. 8am-11pm). To Montréal (every hr. 6am-9pm and 11pm, 3 hr., $34) and Ste.-Anne-de-Beaupré (2 per day, $5). Connections to U.S. cities via Montréal or Sherbrooke.

Public Transport: Commission de transport de la Communauté Urbaine de Québec (CTCUQ), 270, rue des Rocailles (627-2511 for route and schedule info; open Mon.-Fri. 7am-9:30pm; for lost objects, call 622-7412). Buses operate daily 5:30am-12:30am although individual routes vary. Fare $1.75, seniors $1.20.

Taxis: Coop Taxis Québec, 525-5191. **Driver/Rider Service: Allo-Stop,** 467, rue St. Jean (522-0056) will match you with a driver heading for Montréal ($15), or Ottawa ($29). Must be a member ($6 per yr.). Open Mon.-Wed. 9am-5pm, Thurs.-Fri. 9am-7pm, Sat. 10am-5pm, Sun. 10am-7pm.

Car Rental: Budget, 29 côte du Palais (692-3660), is open Mon.-Wed. 7am-5:30pm; Thurs.-Fri. 7am-8pm; Sat.-Sun. 8am-5pm. **Hertz,** across the road at 44 côte du Palais (694-1224), is open July-mid-Sept. Mon.-Fri. 7:30am-8pm; Sat. 8am-6pm, Sun. 8am-8pm; off-season Mon.-Fri. 7:30am-7:30pm, Sat. 8am-6pm. Check the yellow pages for full listings; prices start at $33 per day.

Moped and Bike Rental: Location Petit Champlain, 94, rue Petit-Champlain (692-2817). Bikes $5 per hr., $25 per day; mopeds $20 per hr., $5 each additional hr., $40 per day (insurance included). Strollers for rent, too ($20 per day). Guided walking tours of Petit Champlain, Place Royale, and le Vieux Port also offered. Open daily 9am-midnight, mid-Nov.-mid-April daily 9am-6pm.

Help Lines: Tel Aide, 683-2153. Open Sun.-Thurs. noon-midnight, Fri.-Sat. noon-2am. **Violscours** (sexual assault line), 692-2252. **Centre de prévention de suicide,** 525-4588.

Canada Post: 3, rue Buade (648-4686). Open Mon.-Fri. 8am-5:45pm. **Postal Code:** G1R 2J0. Another location at 300 rue St.-Paul (648-3340). **Postal code:** G1K 3W0.

Area Code: 418.

Québec's main thoroughfares, both in the Old City (*Vieux Québec*) and outside it, all tend to run parallel to each other in a roughly east-west direction. Within the **Old City, St. Louis, Ste. Anne,** and **St. Jean** are the main streets. Most streets in the Old City are one way, the major exception being rue d'Atteuil, just inside the walls, which is the best bet for parking during the busy times of day. Outside the walls of the Old City, both St. James and St. Louis continue (St. Louis becomes **Grand-Allée**). **Ste. Cyrille,** the other major street outside the walls, runs between them. Rue Saint-Vallier Est separates *la Basse-ville* (Lower Town) from *la Haute-ville* (Upper Town).

Accommodations and Camping

Québec City now has two B&B referral services. Contact Denise or Raymond Blancher at **B&B Bonjour Québec,** 3765, blvd. Monaco, Québec G1P 3J3 (527-1465) for lodgings throughout the city, city maps, and descriptions of houses. (Singles $35-45. Doubles $45-60; call Mon.-Fri. 9am-5pm.) **Gîte Québec** offers similar services. Contact Thérèse Tellier, 3729, ave. Le Corbusier, Ste.-Foy, Québec G1W 4R8 (651-1860). (Singles $30-40. Doubles $60-75; call 8am-1pm or after 6pm.) Hosts are usually bilingual, and the B&B services inspect the houses for cleanliness and convenience of location.

You can obtain a list of nearby campgrounds from the Maison du Tourisme de Québec (see Practical Information), or by writing Tourisme Québec, C.P. 20,000 Québec, Québec G1K 7X2 (800-363-7777, June-Aug. daily 9am-7pm, off-season daily 9am-5pm).

Centre international de séjour HI-C, 19, Ste.-Ursule (694-0755), between rue St.-Jean and Dauphine. Follow Côte d'Abraham uphill from the bus station until it joins Avenue Dufferin. Turn left on Jean, pass through the walls, and walk uphill, to your right, on Ste.-Ursule. If you're driving, follow St. Louis into the Old City, and take the second left past the walls onto Ste.-Ursule. The rooms are cramped, but a friendly staff, youthful clientele, and fabulous location should make it your first choice. Laundry machines, microwave, TV, pool and ping-pong tables, living room. No kitchen, but cafeteria in basement; breakfast served 7:30-10am ($3.50). Check-out 10am, new check-ins starting at 11am. Doors lock at 11pm, but front desk will let you in if you flash your key. Singles $32. One bed in a 2-bed room $16, in a 4-to 8-person room $14, in an 8- to 16-person room $11; nonmembers pay $3 more, kids under 9 free; ages 9-12 ½-price. HI-C memberships sold. Usually full July-Aug.; make reservations or arrive early.

Auberge de la Paix, 31, rue Couillard (694-0735). Has neither the activity nor the facilities of the Centre; stay here when the Centre's full. Both offer great access to the restaurants and bars on rue St.-Jean. Rooms a bit smaller and mattresses a bit better than the Centre; 56 beds; 2-8 beds per room, most have 3-4. Curfew 2am. $14. Breakfast of toast, cereal, coffee and juice included (8-10am). Kitchen open all day. Linen $1.50. Make reservations July-Aug.

Campus de l'université Laval, Pavillion Parent (656-2921), Ste.-Foy. 15-20 min. bus ride from the city on bus #11 or #8. Modern building with dorm rooms. Rooms clean and big enough, but stay in Vieux Québec if possible. Singles with sink and desk $26, students $20. Doubles $35/24. Cafeteria breakfast $3. Pay fee for access to sports facilities on a campus full of activity. Reserve in advance for stays during festivals or holidays. Open mid-May-early Aug.

Montmartre Canadien, 1675, chemin St.-Louis, Sillery (681-7357), on the outskirts of the city, in the Maison du Pelerin; a small white house behind the main building at 1671. Take bus #25. Clean house in a religious sanctuary overlooking the St. Lawrence River. Relaxed, almost ascetic, setting—don't expect to meet tons of exciting new people here. Mostly used by groups. Run by Assumptionist monks. Common showers. Dorm-style singles $15. Doubles $26. Triples $36. Bed in 7-person dormitory $11; groups of 20 or more, $13. Breakfast (eggs, cereal, bacon, and pancakes) $3.50. Reserve 2-3 weeks in advance.

Manoir La Salle, 18, rue Ste.-Ursule (647-9361), opposite the youth hostel. Clean private rooms fill up quickly, especially in the summer. Cat haters beware: felines stalk the halls. Singles $25-40. Doubles $40, with shower $45, a few dollars less in the winter.

Maison Demers, 68 rue Ste.-Ursule GIR 4E6 (692-2487), up the road from the youth hostel. Clean, comfortable rooms with TV in the Demers home; all rooms have a sink, some have a private bath. Singles $30-32. Doubles with shower $45-60, 2-bed, 4-person room $70. Breakfast of coffee and fresh croissants included. Parking available. Reservations recommended.

Camping Canadien, Ancienne-Lorette (872-7801). Sites $15, with hookup $17.50. Showers, laundry. Open May 15-Oct. 15. Take Autoroute #73 out of the city to Blvd. Wilfred-Hamel. Follow signs for the campground after passing Autoroute #40.

Municipal de Beauport, Beauport (666-2228). Take Autoroute 40 east, exit #321 at rue Labelle onto 369, turn left, and follow signs marked "camping." Ask tourism about buses to Beauport and enjoy this campground overlooking the Montmorency Falls. Showers, laundry. 128 sites. $12, with hookup $16; weekly $70 and $100, respectively. Open June-early Sept.

Food and Nightlife

In general, rue Buade, St.-Jean, and Cartier, as well as the **Place Royale** and **Petit Champlain** areas offer the widest selection of food and drink. Also check out the **Grand Allée;** it's a mile-long strip of nothing but restaurants on both sides, with patios along the sidewalk. Food tends to be cheaper outside the walls of the old city. One of the most filling yet inexpensive meals is a *croque monsieur,* a large, open-faced sandwich with ham and melted cheese (about $5), usually served with salad. Be sure to try *québecois* French onion soup, loaded with onions, slathered with melted cheese, and generally served with bats of French bread. Also try *aux pois* (pea soup) and *tourtière,* a thick meat pie. Other specialties include the French crêpe, stuffed differently for either main course or dessert, and the French-Canadian "sugar pie," made with brown sugar and butter. For basic grilled meals, eat at the clean and cheap cafeteria in the basement of the **Centre internationale de séjour** (see Accommodations and Camping above). Remember that some of these restaurants do *not* have non-smoking sections.

For those doing their own cooking, **J.A. Moisan,** 685, rue St. Jean (522-8268) sells groceries in an old country-style store. Open Mon.-Sun. 9am-10pm. **Dépanneurs** are Québec's answer and challenge to the corner store. Besides milk, bread, and snack food, they'll also sell you booze. **Dépanneur Proprio,** down Ste.-Ursule from the Centre is open Tuesday through Saturday, 24 hours.

Casse Crêpe Breton, 1136, rue St.-Jean (692-0438). Great, inexpensive crêpes with friendly service in a casual atmosphere. Breakfast special (2 eggs, bacon, toast, and coffee) $3.25. Lunch specials (11am-2pm) an even better bargain. Have a crêpe for a meal ($3-5) and then one filled with fruit for dessert ($2.25-3). Sandwiches, salads, and soups also available. Open daily 7:30am-1am.

Café Mediterranée, 64, St. Cyrille O (648-1849 lunchtime; 648-0768 dinner). Take the #25 bus or walk for about 10 min. outside the walls. Elegant surroundings for a Mediterranean buffet. Enjoy vegetable platters, *couscous,* spicy chicken dishes—or all 3: the ideal, filling lunch. Soup, dessert, coffee, and as much as you want for a main meal for $7.50 (lunch), $19.95 (dinner). Open Mon.-Fri. 11:30am-2pm, Thurs.-Sun. 6-11pm. The buffet depletes quickly, so arrive early. Reservations recommended.

Les Couventines, 1124, rue St.-Jean (692-4850). Buckwheat crêpes in a quiet, elegant dining room. Great spot for serious conversation. Try a crêpe with almonds and raspberry sauce ($5), or a "Guillaume Tell" with apples and cheese ($6.25). Open Tues.-Sat. 11am-3pm and 5-11pm; Sun. 10am-11pm.

La Fleur de Lotus, 38, Côte de la Fabrique (692-4286), across from the Hôtel de Ville. Cheerful and unpretentious. Thai, Cambodian, Vietnamese, and Japanese dishes $2.75-14. Open Mon.-Wed. 11:30am-10:30pm, Thurs.-Fri. 11:30am—11pm, Sat. 5-11pm, Sun. 5-10:30pm.

Restaurant Liban, 23, rue d'Auteuil, off rue St.-Jean (694-1888). Great café for lunch or a late-night bite. Tabouli and hummus plates $3.25, both with pita bread. Excellent falafel ($4) and a fantastic variety of baklava. The owner parks his big Caddy in front of the store (a no-parking zone) and leans against it, smiling, while he watches his customers eat. Open for coffee at 10am, for meals 11am-4am.

Mille-Feuille, 32, rue Ste.-Angèle (692-2147). Vegetarian meals ($5-$7) served in a chic restaurant with an outdoor terrace to match. Try *tourtière* or vegetable quiche ($4). Open Mon. 9am-10pm, Tues. and Sun. 9am-11pm, Wed.-Sat. 9am-11:30pm.

Le Piazzetta, 707, rue St.-Jean (529-7489), and 1191, rue Cartier (649-8896). Eat spicy square pizza at the marble lunch counter to the buzz of lively discussion. Or sit at a table and linger over piccolos (small, 1-person pizza; $3.75-$5.25). Open Mon.-Wed. 11:30am-midnight, Thurs.-Sat. noon-2am, Sun. noon-midnight.

Café Ste-Julie, 865, rue des Zouaves off St.-Jean (647-9368). No frills lunch-counter joint with specials scrawled on the walls—breakfast (2 eggs, bacon, coffee, toast, beans) $3.25; lunch (2 cheeseburgers, fries, and a soft drink) $5. Open Mon.-Fri. 7am-9pm, Sat. 8am-9pm, Sun. 9am-9pm.

La Vieille Maison du Spaghetti, 625, Grand Allée est or 40, rue Marché Champlain. Both in the Petit-Champlain quarter near Place Royale. Great, fresh Italian food in a perfect setting—red tablecloths and wine glasses at each table. Spaghetti with tangy sauces, a skimpy salad bar, bread, and tea or coffee $6.55-8.75. Pizza $7.25-9.50. Open Mon.-Wed. 11am-9pm, Thurs.-Sun. 11am-11:30pm.

Numerous boisterous nightspots line rue St.-Jean. Duck into any of these establishments and linger over a glass of wine or listen to some *québecois* folk music. Most don't have cover charges and close around 3am. **L'Apropos,** 598, rue St.-Jean (529-1242), frequently has live music. (Open daily noon-3am.) At the **B-52,** 58, Côte du Palais, locals get bombed and play pool. (Half-price drinks daily noon-8pm.) Try the **Pub Saint-Alexandre,** 1091, rue St.-Jean (694-0015), for standard pub food and a wide selection of beer. In summer, musicians, magicians, and other performers take their act to the street. The many bars along Grand Allée and Ste. Cyrille are also good places to go hunting.

Sights

Confined within walls built by the English, *le vieux Québec* (old Québec City) holds most of the city's historic attractions. Though monuments are clearly marked and explained, you'll get more out of the town with the tourist office's *Greater Québec Area Tourist Guide* which contains a walking tour of the Old City. (Available from all three tourist offices listed in Practical Information above.) It takes one or two days to explore Old Québec on foot, but you'll learn more than on the many guided bus tours. Take the time to hang out with the corpses in **Saint Matthew's Cemetery,** 755, rue St. Jean, and to stumble past monuments such as the one commemorating the first patent issued in Canada.

Begin your walking tour of Québec City by climbing uphill to the top of **Cap Diamant** (Cape Diamond), just south of the **Citadelle.** From here take Promenade des Gouverneurs downhill to **Terrasse Dufferin.** Built in 1838 by Lord Durham, this popular promenade offers excellent views of the St. Lawrence River, the Côte de Beaupré (the "Avenue Royale" Highway), and Ile d'Orléans across the Channel. The promenade passes the landing spot of the European settlers, marked by the **Samuel de Champlain Monument,** where Champlain built Fort St.-Louis in 1620, securing the new French settlement. A *funiculaire* (cable car; 692-1132; operates June-Labor Day daily 7:30am-11pm; 90¢, under 6 free) connects Upper Town with the Lower Town and Place Royale.

At the bottom of the promenade, towering above the *terrasse* next to rue St.-Louis, you'll find **le Château Frontenac,** built on the ruins of two previous *châteaux.* The immense, baroque Frontenac was built in 1893 by the Canadian Pacific Company and has developed into a world-renowned luxury hotel. Named for Comte Frontenac, governor of *Nouvelle-France,* the château was the site of two historic meetings between Churchill and Roosevelt during WWII. Although budget travelers must forego staying here, the hoi polloi can still enter the grand hall and browse in its small shopping mall.

Near Château Frontenac, between rue St.-Louis and rue Ste. Anne, lies the **Place d'Armes.** The *calèches* (horse-drawn buggies) that congregate here in summer provide atmosphere, especially strong scents in muggy weather; carriage tours cost $50. Also on rue Buade, right next to Place d'Armes, is the **Notre-Dame Basilica** (692-2533). The clock and outer walls date back to 1647; the rest of the church has been rebuilt twice (most recently after a fire in 1922). (Open daily 6am-6pm. Tours in multiple languages, May 1-Oct. 15 daily 9am-11:30am and 1-4:30pm.) An ornate gold altar and a sky painted on the ceiling help worshippers reach their God (free, but in mysterious ways). Notre-Dame, with its odd mix of architectural styles, contrasts sharply with the adjacent **Seminary of Québec,** founded in 1663, which stands as an excellent example of 17th-century *québecois* architecture. At first a Jesuit boot camp, the seminary became the *Université de Laval* in 1852. The *Université* has since moved to its present site in Ste. Foy. The **Musée du Séminaire,** 9, rue de l'Université (642-2843), lurks nearby. (Open June-Sept. daily 10:30am-5:30pm; Oct.-May Tues.-Sun. 10am-5pm. Admission $3, seniors $2, students $1.50, under 17 $1.)

The **Musée du Fort,** 10, rue Ste.-Anne (692-2175), presents a sound-and-light show that narrates (in French and English) the history of Québec City and the series of six battles fought to control it. (Open daily 10am-6pm. Admission $4.25, seniors and students $2.75.)

The **Post Office,** 3, rue Buade, now called **The Louis St. Laurent Building** (after Canada's second French Canadian Prime Minister) was built in the late 1890's and towers over a statue of Monseigneur de Laval, the first bishop of Québec. Across the Côte de la Montagne, a lookout park provides an impressive view of the St. Lawrence River. A statue of Georges-Etienne Cartier, one of the key French-Canadian Fathers of Confederation, presides over the park.

Walk along rue St.-Louis to see its 17th- and 18th-century homes.The surrender of Québec to the British occurred in 1759 at **Maison Kent,** 25, rue St.-Louis, built in 1648. The Québec government now uses and operates the house. At the end of rue St.-Louis is **Porte St.-Louis,** one of the oldest entrances to the fortified city.

Walk down Côte de la Montagne and negotiate the *casse-cou* staircase ("breakneck"—but the stairs don't live up to the name), or take the *funiculaire* down to the oldest section of Québec. Either way leads to **rue Petit-Champlain,** the oldest road in North America. Many of the old buildings that line the street have been restored or renovated and now house coy craft shops, boutiques, cafés, and restaurants. The **Café-Théâtre Le Petit Champlain,** 68, rue Petit-Champlain (692-2631), presents *québecois* music, singing, and theater.

From the bottom of the *funiculaire* you can also take rue Sous-le-Fort and then turn left to reach **Place Royale,** built in 1608, where you'll find the small but beautiful **l'Eglise Notre-Dame-des-Victoires** (692-1650), the oldest church in Canada, dating from the glorious year of 1688. (Open May 1-Oct. 15 Mon.-Sat. 9am-4:30pm, closed on Sat. if a wedding is being held, Sun. 7:30am-4:30pm; Oct. 16-May Tues.-Sat. 9am-noon, Sun. 7:30am-1pm. Free.) The houses surrounding the square have undergone restoration to late 18th-century styles. Considered one of the birthplaces of French civilization in North America, the Place Royale now provides one of the best spots in the city to see outdoor summer theater and concerts. Also along the river stands the recently opened, ambitiously named **Musée de la Civilisation,** 85, rue Dalhousie (643-2158). A celebration of Québec's culture of past, present, and future, this thematic museum targets French-speaking Canadians, though English tours and exhibit notes are available. One permanent exhibit looks at communications, tingling the senses with giant phone booths, satellites, videos, and recreated moon landings. (Open late June-early Sept. daily 10am-7pm; off-season Tues.-Sun. 10am-5pm, Wed. 10am-9pm. Admission $4.75, seniors $3.75, students $2.75, under 16 free. Free Tues.)

The **boardwalk** on the shore of the St. Lawrence River provides access to Québec's active marina. The "lock" still maintains the safety of the boats docked in the city's Bassin Louise.

Outside the Walls

From the old city, the **promenade des Gouverneurs** leads to the **Plains of Abraham** (otherwise known as the Parc des Champs-de-Bataille) and the **Citadelle** (648-3563). Hike or bike through the Plains of Abraham, site of the September, 1759 battle between General James Wolfe's British troops and General de Montcalm's French forces. Both leaders died during the decisive 15-minute confrontation, won by the British. A beautiful park, the Plains have since served as drill fields and the Royal Québec Golf Course. A **tourist reception center** (648-4071) at 390, ave. des Berniéres, offers maps and pamphlets about the park (open daily 10am-5:45pm, except Wed. 10am-9:45pm). A magnificent complex, the **Citadel** is the largest fortification still guarded by troops in North America, home to the Royal 22 Regiment (the Van-Douze in English parlance, from the French *vingt-deuxième).* Visitors can witness **the changing of the guard** (10am daily mid-May-Labor Day) and the **beating of the retreat** (July-

Aug. Tues., Thurs., Sat.-Sun. 7pm). Tours are given every 55 minutes. (Citadel open daily mid-June-Labor Day 9am-7pm; May-mid-June and Sept. daily 9am-5pm; March, Oct. and April Mon.-Fri. 9am-4pm; Nov. Mon-Fri. 9am-noon; Dec.-Feb. open by reservation only. Admission $4, ages 7-17 $1.50, disabled persons and ages under 7 free.)

At the far end of the Plains of Abraham you'll find the newly transformed **Musée du Québec,** 1, ave. Wolfe-Montcalm, parc des Champs-de-Bataille (643-2150), which contains a collection of *québecois* paintings, sculptures, decorative arts, and prints. The Gérard Morisset pavilion, which greets you with the unlikely troika of Jacques Cartier, Neptune, and Gutenberg, houses a portion of the Musée's permanent collection, while the renovated old "prison of the plains," the Baillarce Pavilion, displays temporary exhibits. (Open June-Labor Day Thurs.-Sun. 10am-5:45pm, Wed. 10am-9:45pm; off-season Tues., Thurs.-Sun. 10am-5:45pm, Wed. 10am-9:45pm. Admission $4.75, seniors $3.75, students $2.75, disabled persons with companions $3, under 16 free. Free admission Wed.) At the corner of la Grande Allée and rue Georges VI, right outside Porte St.-Louis, stands **l'Assemblée Nationale** (643-7239). Built in the style of French King Louis XIII's era and completed in 1886, the hall merits a visit. You can view debates from the visitors gallery; Anglophones and Francophobes have recourse to simultaneous translation earphones. (Free 30-min. tours June 24-Labor Day daily 9am-4:30pm; off-season Mon.-Fri. 9am-4:30pm. Call ahead to ensure space is available.)

Locals follow the **Nordiques,** Québec's atrocious hockey team, with near-religious fanaticism; they play from October through April in the Coliseum (For info, call 529-8441; for tickets, Nordtel 523-3333). The raucous **Winter Carnival** (626-3716) parties February 4 through 14, 1993. Québec's **Summer Festival** (692-4540), July 8 through 18, 1993 boasts a number of free outdoor concerts. The **Plein Art** (694-0260) exhibition of arts and crafts takes over the Pigeonnier on Grande-Allée in early August. **Les nuits Bleue** (849-7080), Québec's rapidly growing jazz festival, bebops the city for two weeks in late June. But the most festive day is June 24, **la Fête nationale du Québec** (Saint-Jean-Baptiste Day), a celebration of the *québécois* culture.

Near Québec City

Québec City's public transport system leaves St. Lawrence's **Ile-d'Orléans** untouched. The island's proximity to Québec (about 10km or 6 mi. downstream), however, makes an ideal short side trip by car or bicycle; take Autoroute Montmorency (440 est), and cross over at the only bridge leading to the island (Pont de l'Ile). A tour of the island covers 64km. Originally called *Ile de Bacchus* because of the plethora of wild grapes fermenting here, the Ile-d'Orléans still remains a sparsely populated retreat of several small villages, with strawberries as its main crop. The **Manoir Mauvide-Genest,** 1451, chemin Royal (829-2630), dates from 1734. A private museum inside has a collection of crafts as well as traditional French and Anglo-Saxon furniture. (Open June-Aug. Mon.-Tues. 10am-5pm, Wed.-Sun. 10am-8pm; Labor Day-mid-Oct. Sat.-Sun. 10am-5pm. Admission $3, ages 10-18 $1.50.)

Exiting Ile-d'Orléans, turn right (east) onto Rte. 138 (blvd. Ste.-Anne) to view the splendid **Chute Montmorency** (Montmorency Falls), which are substantially taller than Niagara Falls. In winter the falls freeze completely and look, well, very frozen. About 20km (13 mi.) along 138 lies **Ste.-Anne-de-Beaupré** (Voyageur buses link it to Québec City, $4.28). This small town's entire *raison d'être* seems to be the famous **Basilique Ste.-Anne-de Beaupré,** 10018, ave. Royale (827-3781). Since 1658, this double-spired basilica containing a Miraculous Statue and the alleged forearm bone of Saint Anne (the mother of the Virgin Mary) reportedly has pulled off miraculous cures. Every year more than one million pious pilgrims trek here in the hopes that their prayers, gallstones and mortgages will divinely be spirited away. (Open daily 8:30am-9:30pm.) Ask the tourist office about bike rentals in this scenic area. Go to Ste.-Anne in the winter months (Nov.-April) for some of the best skiing in the Province. (Lift tickets $36 per day or $97 for 3 consecutive days.) Contact **Parc du Mont Ste.-Anne,** P.O. Box 400, Beaupré, G0A IE0 (827-4561), which has a 625m/2050ft. vertical drop and night skiing to boot. Ask the tourist office on rue d'Auteuil for a copy of *Ski Greater Québec Area.*

The Yukon

Although the Yukon and Northern British Columbia were the first regions of North America to be settled some 20,000 years ago, today they remain largely untouched and inaccessible. With an average of only one person per 15 square km, the loneliness of the area is overwhelming—as is its sheer physical beauty, a reward for those willing to put up with nasty weather and poor road conditions. Native Americans recognized the majesty of this land when they dubbed the Yukon River "Yuchoo," or Big River. For a more detailed description of the Yukon, see *Let's Go: Pacific Northwest, Western Canada and Alaska.*

Kluane National Park

On July 16, 1741—St. Elias Day—Captain Vitus Bering, on the deck of a sealer one month out of Russia, sighted the mountains of what is now the southwest Yukon. One hundred and fifty years later, the St. Elias mountains presented a formidable obstacle to the few prospectors who attempted the grueling "Glacier Route" from Disenchantment Bay, Alaska, to the Klondike Gold Fields. It wasn't until the completion of the Alaska Highway in 1942 that the region was opened to significant settlement.

The St. Elias Mountains are made up of two ranges: the **Kluane Range** (kloo-AH-nee), whose crenelated, snow-veined peaks rise from the Alaska Highway at the eastern park boundary, and the **Icefield Range,** Canada's highest and most massive mountains. This vast frozen wasteland contains the largest accumulation of nonpolar ice in the world. Kluane Park is Canadian wilderness at its most unspoiled, at its most rugged, at its most beautiful.

The 4km **Dezdeash River Loop** begins at the Haines Junction Visitor Reception Centre (see below) and offers prime wildlife viewing mornings and evenings. Back-country camping is free, but must be registered with the reception center. Stay outdoors and fall victim to bloodthirsty mosquitoes; head for shelter and fall victim to exorbitant hotel rates (solution: get some bug spray, bite the bullet and pitch a tent). If you're allergic to bug spray, try the **Kathleen Lake Lodge,** Mile 142 Haines Rd., about 25km south of Haines Junction (634-2319), and stay two to a cabin with private bath-tubs but no shower. The restaurant is a bit spendy, but the watchdog is free. (Single $36, double $44.) If you're a stoic, hit the **Pine Lake Campground,** about 7km east of Haines Junction on the Alaska Hwy. (634-2345). It has 40 sites, seven of which are tent only, with pit toilets, hand-pumped cold water, nearby hiking, and a boat launch. (Sites $8.) Kluane National Park is located in the southwest corner of the Yukon Territory. Haines Junction is at the park's eastern boundary, 158km west of Whitehorse on the Alaska Hwy. Catch a bus from **Alaska Direct** (800-288-1305), which runs thrice weekly to Anchorage (US$125), Fairbanks (US$100), Haines (US$50), and White-horse (US$20).

The **Haines Junction Visitor Centre,** on Logan St., includes the **Canadian Park Service** (634-2251) and **Tourism Yukon** (634-2345). Pick up their brochures and schedule of guided hikes and "campfire talks." (Open mid-May-mid-Sept. 8:30am-9pm.) In a **medical emergency,** call 634-2213; in case of **fire,** 634-2222; the **police** station is at the junction of Haines Rd. and the Alaska Hwy. (635-5555; if no answer, call 1-667-5555). The **postal code** is Y0B 1L0; the **area code** is 403

Dawson City

There are strange things done in the midnight sun
by the men who moil for gold.
—*R. Service,* "The Cremation of Sam McGee"

Gold. Gold! GOLD! Men have killed and died for it, nations have warred over it, and empires have crumbled for the lack of it. But of all the insanity ever inspired by a lust for the dust, the creation of Dawson City must surely be ranked among the most amazing. For a glorious year from July 1898 to July 1899, Dawson City, on the doorstep of the Arctic Circle and a thousand miles from any established settlement, was the largest Canadian city west of Toronto and every bit as cosmopolitan as Seattle or San Francisco. Its 30,000-plus residents, with names like Swiftwater Bill, Skookum Jim, Arizona Charlie Meadows and The Evaporated Kid, had each somehow dragged, pushed, sledded or otherwise gotten 1000 lb. of provisions over some of the most rugged terrain on earth—all driven by the desire to be rich beyond the wildest dreams of avarice.

The towns along the various routes into the Klondike were named in memory of the 70,000 or so who never made it; Hell's Mountain, Destruction City and Death Gulch are monuments to the forgotten thousands who failed. You didn't need to find gold to "succeed" in Dawson, you merely had to survive.

When the torrent of gold slowed to a trickle in 1900, the city didn't prove as hardy as its inhabitants and quickly devolved into a ghost town. It wasn't until the early 1960s that the Canadian federal government, recognizing the historical importance of Dawson, began to restore the Arctic El Dorado to its former glory. The work has been slow, but the results have been worthwhile. There is no tacky Hollywood à la Yukon show biz here but rather a faithful re-creation of one of the greatest gold rushes that ever was. More than three-quarters of a century after her moment in the Midnight Sun, Dawson City is once again the jewel of the Yukon.

Perhaps to compensate for the cost of everything else, Dawson City sponsors a wide variety of free tours and attractions. Free **walking tours** leave from the center five times daily and from the Commissioner's Residence twice daily. The guides are extremely well-informed, and these tours are the best way to appreciate Dawson City.

Make time to catch the **Robert Service Readings,** in front of the very cabin on 8th Ave. at Hanson where the Bard of the Yukon penned such immortal ballads as "The Cremation of Sam McGee" and "The Shooting of Dan McGrew." There are two presentations daily at 10am and 3pm. Just down the street is the relocated **Jack London Cabin.** The life and times of the great Yukon author are recounted with interpretive readings daily at 1pm. The **Dawson City Museum,** on 5th St., south of Church (993-5007), concisely elaborates on the history of the region with exhibits ranging from the mastodons of millenia gone by to modern mining machinery. The museum also holds temporary shows by local artists. (Open daily 10am-6pm; admission $3.25, students and seniors $2.25; tours given by request.) The Park Service also maintains a National Historical Sight at **Bear Creek,** 13km south of town on the Klondike Hwy. The mining operations here were halted all at once in 1966, leaving behind tools, machinery, and the eerie feeling of an entire community deserted overnight.

There aren't many gastronomic options around, but for the most part prices are reasonable, especially when compared to Thanksgiving Day in 1899, when one turkey fetched over $100. **Klondike Kate's** (993-6527), by Klondike Kate's Motel (no affiliation), has a veggie sandwich ($5), and the K.K. Breakfast Special ($4) is the best am deal in town. (Open mid-May-mid-Sept. daily 7am-11pm.)

The hostel and the campground on the west side of town are the cheapest lodging options. **Dawson City River Hostel,** on the first left as you come off the ferry, has brand-new bunks in brand-new log cabins; each hosteller is *guaranteed* a minimum (minimum!) of 4.6 square meters of being-space. It also has ingenious homemade aluminum urinals, a magnificent, wood-heated "prospector's bath" and shower siphoned from the creek above. The cozy lounge has a wood stove and a hilltop view of the Yukon river and the city beyond. All this and friendly management...this is the hostel to end all hostels. ($12.50, nonmembers $15. Tent sites $6 per person.) If you choose to pass up this golden hostelling opportunity, try the **Westminster Hotel,** at 3rd and Queen (993-5463), the oldest operating hotel in the Yukon (est. 1898). The façade has been restored to its original splendor, but the rooms inside need a little work. Check the cracks in the floors and walls for gold dust. (Singles $45. Doubles $55. Shared bath.)

To reach Dawson City, take the Klondike Hwy. 533km north from Whitehorse, or follow the Top of the World Hwy. about 100km east of the Alaskan border. Dawson can easily be covered by foot in only a few hours. Dawson City's **Visitor Reception Centre,** on Front and King St. (993-5566), has historic slide shows and movies. (Open mid-May-mid-Sept. daily 9am-9pm, late Sept. 9am-8pm.) **Tourist radio** (96.1 FM) broadcasts weather, road conditions and seasonal events. In case of a **medical emergency,** call 993-2222. The **police station** is on Front St., north of Craig St., in the south end of town (993-5555; if no answer, 1-667-5355). The **post office** is on 5th Ave. and Princess St. (993-5342). (Open Mon.-Fri. 8:30am-5:30pm, Sat. 8:30am-12:30pm.) The **postal code** is Y0B 1G0. The **area code** is 403. Yes.

INDEX

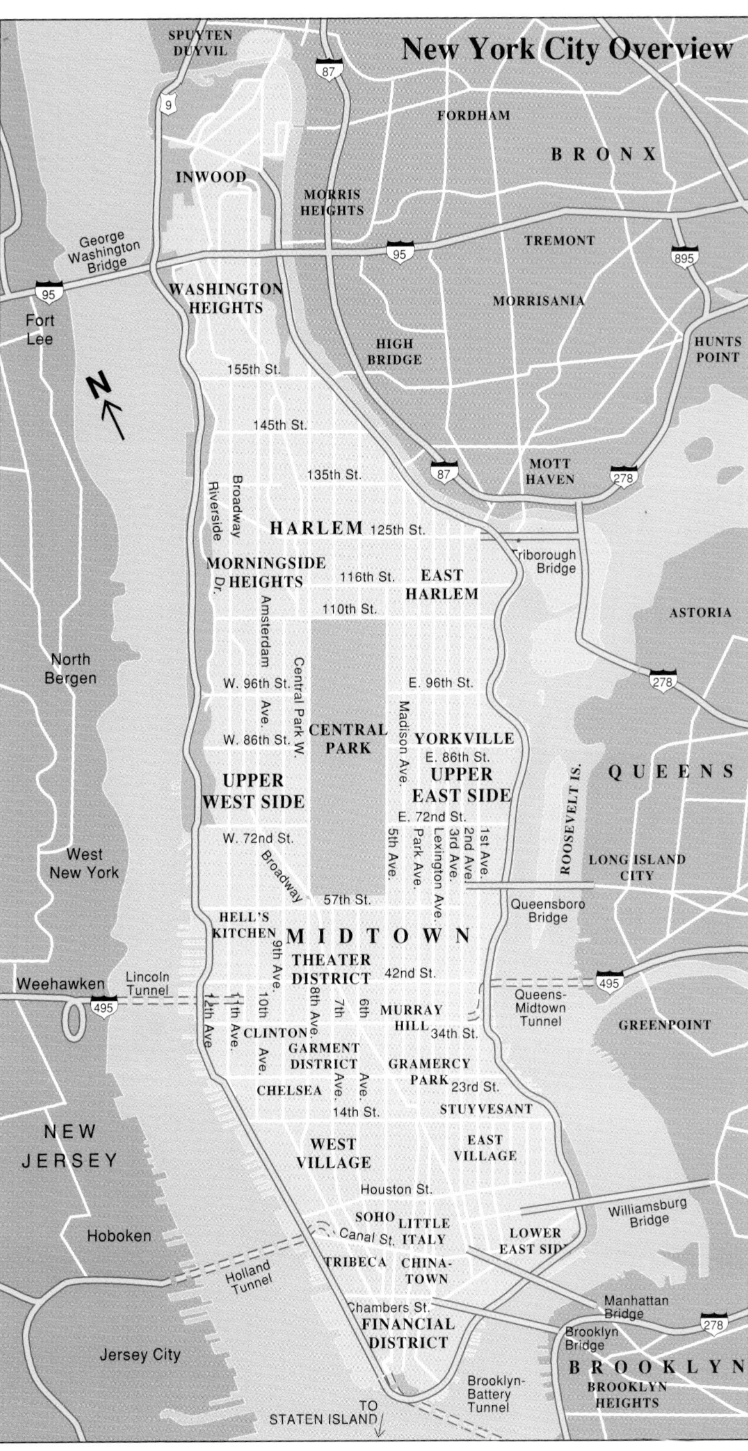

New York City Overview
SPUYTEN DUYVIL
FORDHAM
BRONX
INWOOD
MORRIS HEIGHTS
TREMONT
George Washington Bridge
WASHINGTON HEIGHTS
MORRISANIA
Fort Lee
HIGH BRIDGE
HUNTS POINT
155th St.
145th St.
135th St.
MOTT HAVEN
Riverside Dr.
Broadway
HARLEM
125th St.
Triborough Bridge
MORNINGSIDE HEIGHTS
116th St.
EAST HARLEM
110th St.
ASTORIA
Amsterdam Ave.
North Bergen
W. 96th St.
Central Park W.
E. 96th St.
Madison Ave.
CENTRAL PARK
YORKVILLE
W. 86th St.
E. 86th St.
UPPER WEST SIDE
UPPER EAST SIDE
ROOSEVELT IS.
QUEENS
E. 72nd St.
W. 72nd St.
5th Ave.
Park Ave.
Lexington Ave.
3rd Ave.
2nd Ave.
1st Ave.
West New York
Broadway
LONG ISLAND CITY
57th St.
Queensboro Bridge
HELL'S KITCHEN
MIDTOWN
9th Ave.
THEATER DISTRICT
42nd St.
Weehawken
Lincoln Tunnel
Queens-Midtown Tunnel
12th Ave.
11th Ave.
10th Ave.
8th Ave.
7th Ave.
6th Ave.
MURRAY HILL
34th St.
GREENPOINT
CLINTON
GARMENT DISTRICT
GRAMERCY PARK
CHELSEA
23rd St.
14th St.
STUYVESANT
NEW JERSEY
WEST VILLAGE
EAST VILLAGE
Houston St.
Williamsburg Bridge
SOHO
LITTLE ITALY
Canal St.
Hoboken
LOWER EAST SIDE
TRIBECA
CHINA-TOWN
Holland Tunnel
Chambers St.
Manhattan Bridge
FINANCIAL DISTRICT
Brooklyn Bridge
Jersey City
BROOKLYN
Brooklyn-Battery Tunnel
BROOKLYN HEIGHTS
TO STATEN ISLAND

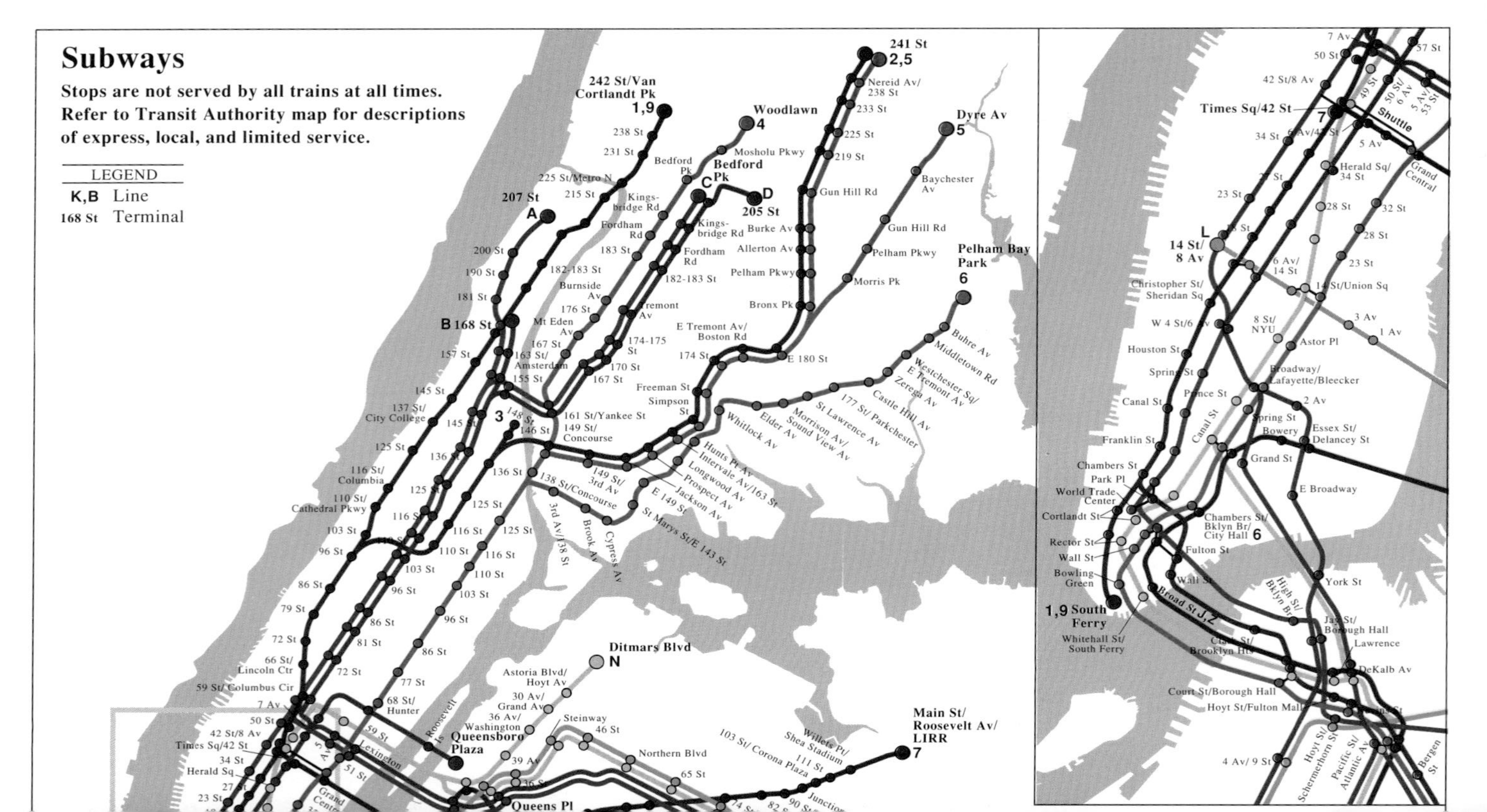

Subways
Stops are not served by all trains at all times.
Refer to Transit Authority map for descriptions
of express, local, and limited service.
LEGEND
K,B Line
168 St Terminal
242 St/Van Cortlandt Pk
1,9
238 St
231 St
225 St/Metro N
215 St
207 St
A
200 St
190 St
181 St
B 168 St
157 St
145 St
137 St/ City College
125 St
116 St/ Columbia
110 St/ Cathedral Pkwy
103 St
96 St
86 St
79 St
72 St
66 St/ Lincoln Ctr
59 St/ Columbus Cir
Woodlawn
4
Mosholu Pkwy
Bedford Pk
Bedford Pk
C
D
205 St
Kings- bridge Rd
Fordham Rd
183 St
182-183 St
Burnside Av
176 St
Mt Eden Av
167 St
163 St/ Amsterdam
155 St
3
148 St
146 St
161 St/Yankee St
149 St/ Concourse
Tremont Av
174-175 St
170 St
167 St
E Tremont Av/ Boston Rd
174 St
Freeman St
Simpson St
241 St
2,5
Nereid Av/ 238 St
233 St
225 St
219 St
Gun Hill Rd
Burke Av
Allerton Av
Pelham Pkwy
Bronx Pk
E 180 St
Dyre Av
5
Baychester Av
Gun Hill Rd
Pelham Pkwy
Morris Pk
Pelham Bay Park
6
Buhre Av
Middletown Rd
Westchester Sq/ E Tremont Av
Zerega Av
Castle Hill Av
177 St/ Parkchester
St Lawrence Av
Morrison Av/ Sound View Av
Elder Av
Whitlock Av
Hunts Pt Av
Intervale Av/163 St
Longwood Av
Prospect Av
Jackson Av
E 149 St
St Marys St/E 143 St
Cypress Av
Brook Av
3rd Av/138 St
138 St/Concourse
149 St/ 3rd Av
136 St
125 St
116 St
110 St
103 St
96 St
86 St
81 St
77 St
72 St
68 St/ Hunter
Ditmars Blvd
N
Astoria Blvd/ Hoyt Av
30 Av/ Grand Av
36 Av/ Washington
Steinway
46 St
Northern Blvd
65 St
39 Av
Queensboro Plaza
Roosevelt Is
Queens Pl
Main St/ Roosevelt Av/ LIRR
7
Willets Pt/ Shea Stadium
111 St
103 St/ Corona Plaza
59 St
Lexington
51 St
7 Av
50 St
42 St/8 Av
Times Sq/42 St
34 St
Herald Sq
23 St
57 St
49 St
50 St/ 6 Av
5 Av/ 53 St
Shuttle
5 Av
Grand Central
Herald Sq/ 34 St
6 Av/42 St
28 St
32 St
14 St/ 8 Av
L
23 St
14 St/Union Sq
3 Av
1 Av
6 Av/ 14 St
Christopher St/ Sheridan Sq
W 4 St/6 Av
8 St/ NYU
Astor Pl
Houston St
Broadway/ Lafayette/Bleecker
2 Av
Canal St
Prince St
Spring St
Bowery
Essex St/ Delancey St
Grand St
Franklin St
Chambers St
Park Pl
World Trade Center
Cortlandt St
Rector St
Wall St
Bowling Green
1,9 South Ferry
Whitehall St/ South Ferry
Chambers St/ Bklyn Br/ City Hall
6
Fulton St
E Broadway
York St
Broad St J,Z
High St/ Bklyn Br
Clark St/ Brooklyn Hts
Jay St/ Borough Hall
Lawrence
DeKalb Av
Court St/Borough Hall
Hoyt St/Fulton Mall
4 Av/ 9 St
Hoyt St/ Schermerhorn St
Pacific St/ Atlantic Av
Bergen St

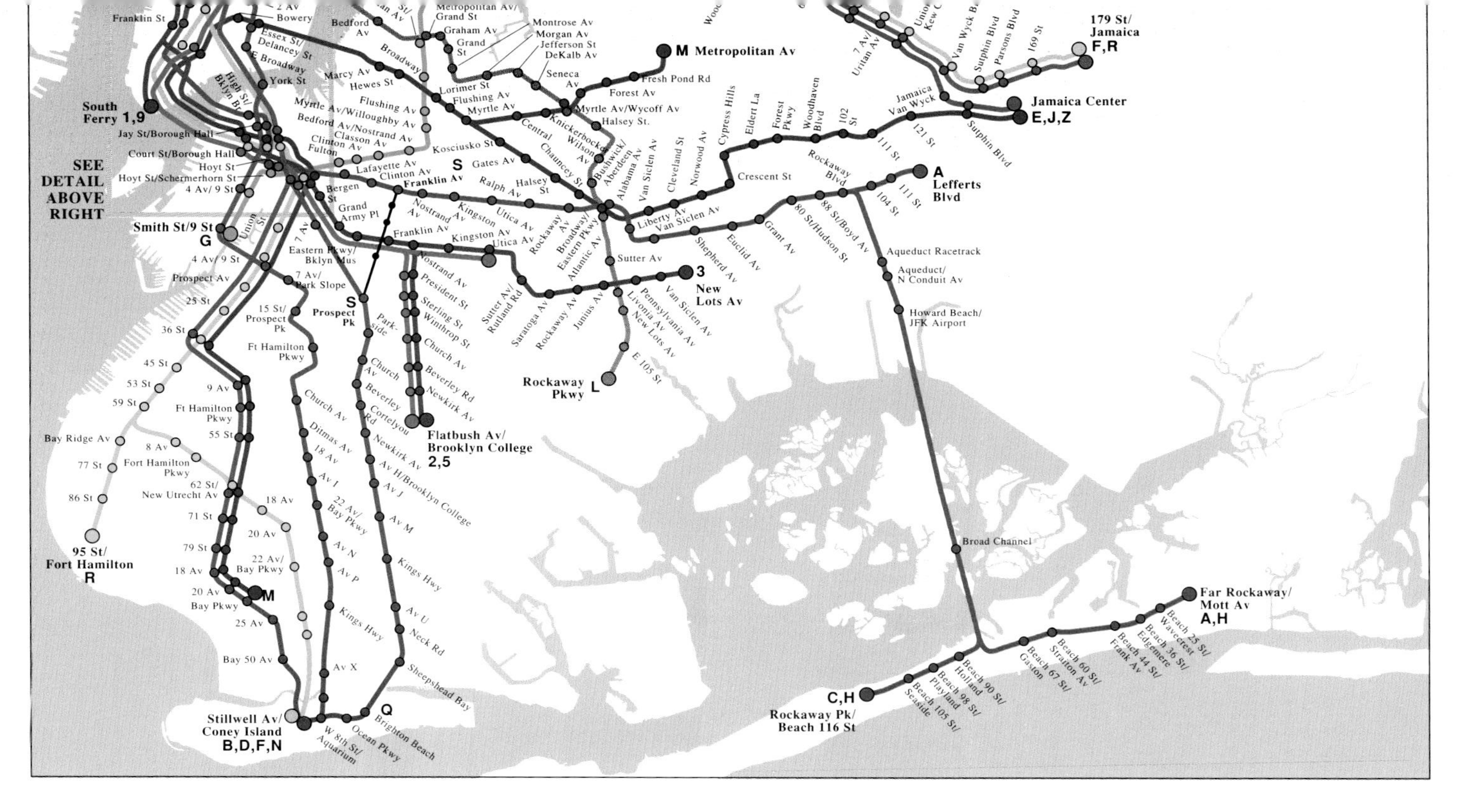

SEE
DETAIL
ABOVE
RIGHT
South
Ferry 1,9
Franklin St
Bowery
Essex St/
Delancey St
E Broadway
York St
High St/
Bklyn Br
Jay St/Borough Hall
Court St/Borough Hall
Hoyt St
Hoyt St/Schermerhorn St
4 Av/ 9 St
Smith St/9 St
G
Union
St
4 Av/ 9 St
Prospect Av
25 St
36 St
45 St
53 St
59 St
Bay Ridge Av
77 St
86 St
95 St/
Fort Hamilton
R
9 Av
Ft Hamilton
Pkwy
55 St
8 Av
Fort Hamilton
Pkwy
62 St/
New Utrecht Av
71 St
79 St
18 Av
20 Av
Bay Pkwy
M
25 Av
Bay 50 Av
18 Av
20 Av
22 Av/
Bay Pkwy
Stillwell Av/
Coney Island
B,D,F,N
W 8th St/
Aquarium
Ocean Pkwy
Brighton Beach
Q
Sheepshead Bay
Neck Rd
Av U
Kings Hwy
Av M
Av J
Av H/Brooklyn College
Newkirk Av
Cortelyou
Rd
Beverley
Rd
Church
Av
Park-
side
Prospect
Pk
S
7 Av/
Park Slope
Eastern Pkwy/
Bklyn Mus
7 Av
15 St/
Prospect
Pk
Ft Hamilton
Pkwy
Church Av
Ditmas Av
18 Av
Av I
22 Av/
Bay Pkwy
Av N
Av P
Kings Hwy
Av X
Bedford
Av
Marcy Av
Hewes St
Broadway
Flushing Av
Myrtle Av/Willoughby Av
Bedford Av/Nostrand Av
Classon Av
Clinton Av
Fulton
Lafayette Av
Clinton Av
Franklin Av
Bergen
St
Grand
Army Pl
S
Nostrand
Av
Kingston
Av
Utica Av
Franklin Av
Kingston Av
Utica Av
Nostrand Av
President St
Sterling St
Winthrop St
Church Av
Beverley Rd
Newkirk Av
Flatbush Av/
Brooklyn College
2,5
Metropolitan Av/
Grand St
Graham Av
Grand
St
Lorimer St
Flushing Av
Myrtle Av
Kosciusko St
Gates Av
Ralph Av
Halsey
St
Montrose Av
Morgan Av
Jefferson St
DeKalb Av
Seneca
Av
Myrtle Av/Wycoff Av
Halsey St.
Forest Av
Fresh Pond Rd
M Metropolitan Av
Central
Knickerbocker
Wilson
Av
Chauncey St
Bushwick/
Aberdeen
Alabama Av
Van Siclen Av
Cleveland St
Norwood Av
Cypress Hills
Elderts La
Forest
Pkwy
Woodhaven
Blvd
102
St
111 St
121 St
Jamaica
Van Wyck
Sutphin Blvd
Jamaica Center
E,J,Z
7 Av/
Uritan Av
Van Wyck Bl
Sutphin Blvd
Parsons Blvd
169 St
179 St/
Jamaica
F,R
Rockaway
Av
Broadway/
Eastern Pkwy
Atlantic Av
Sutter Av/
Rutland Rd
Saratoga Av
Rockaway Av
Junius Av
Sutter Av
Livonia Av
New Lots Av
E 105 St
Rockaway
Pkwy
L
Pennsylvania Av
Van Siclen Av
3
New
Lots Av
Liberty Av
Van Siclen Av
Shepherd Av
Euclid Av
Grant Av
Crescent St
80 St/Hudson St
88 St/Boyd Av
Rockaway
Blvd
104 St
111 St
A
Lefferts
Blvd
Aqueduct Racetrack
Aqueduct/
N Conduit Av
Howard Beach/
JFK Airport
Broad Channel
C,H
Rockaway Pk/
Beach 116 St
Beach 105 St/
Seaside
Beach 98 St/
Playland
Beach 90 St/
Holland
Beach 67 St/
Gaston
Beach 60 St/
Straiton Av
Beach 44 St/
Frank Av
Beach 36 St/
Edgemere
Beach 25 St/
Wavecrest
Far Rockaway/
Mott Av
A,H

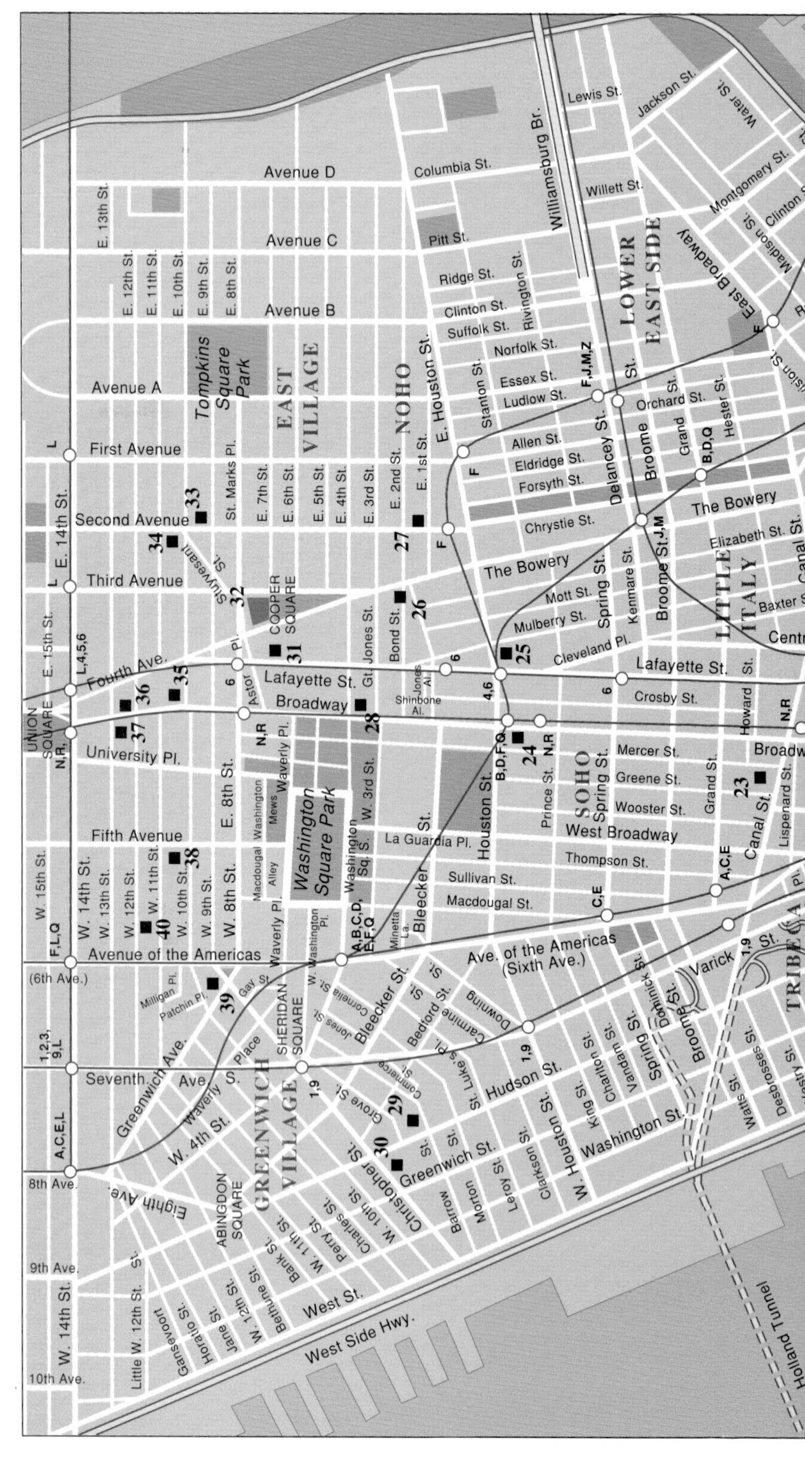

Avenue D
Avenue C
Avenue B
Avenue A
First Avenue
Second Avenue
Third Avenue
Fourth Ave.
University Pl.
Fifth Avenue
Avenue of the Americas
(6th Ave.)
Seventh Ave. S.
8th Ave.
9th Ave.
10th Ave.
E. 13th St.
E. 12th St.
E. 11th St.
E. 10th St.
E. 9th St.
E. 8th St.
E. 14th St.
E. 15th St.
St. Marks Pl.
E. 7th St.
E. 6th St.
E. 5th St.
E. 4th St.
E. 3rd St.
E. 2nd St.
E. 1st St.
E. Houston St.
Tompkins Square Park
EAST VILLAGE
NOHO
COOPER SQUARE
Stuyvesant St.
Astor Pl.
Lafayette St.
Broadway
Gt. Jones St.
Bond St.
Jones Al.
Shinbone Al.
UNION SQUARE
Columbia St.
Pitt St.
Ridge St.
Clinton St.
Suffolk St.
Norfolk St.
Essex St.
Ludlow St.
Stanton St.
Rivington St.
Allen St.
Eldridge St.
Forsyth St.
Chrystie St.
Williamsburg Br.
Lewis St.
Willett St.
Jackson St.
Water St.
Montgomery St.
Clinton St.
Madison St.
East Broadway
Division St.
Delancey St.
Broome St.
Grand St.
Orchard St.
Hester St.
LOWER EAST SIDE
The Bowery
Elizabeth St.
Canal St.
Baxter St.
Centre
Mott St.
Mulberry St.
Spring St.
Kenmare St.
Cleveland Pl.
Crosby St.
Howard St.
LITTLE ITALY
Mercer St.
Greene St.
Wooster St.
West Broadway
Thompson St.
Sullivan St.
Macdougal St.
Prince St.
Houston St.
SOHO
Lispenard St.
La Guardia Pl.
Bleecker St.
Minetta La.
W. 3rd St.
Washington Sq. S.
Washington Square Park
Washington Mews
Waverly Pl.
Macdougal Alley
W. Washington Pl.
E. 8th St.
W. 8th St.
W. 9th St.
W. 10th St.
W. 11th St.
W. 12th St.
W. 13th St.
W. 14th St.
W. 15th St.
Milligan Pl.
Patchin Pl.
Gay St.
Waverly Place
Greenwich Ave.
W. 4th St.
SHERIDAN SQUARE
GREENWICH VILLAGE
Cornelia St.
Jones St.
Bleecker St.
Bedford St.
Downing
Carmine St.
Ave. of the Americas (Sixth Ave.)
Commerce St.
St. Luke's Pl.
Grove St.
Christopher St.
Hudson St.
Greenwich St.
Barrow St.
Morton St.
Leroy St.
Clarkson St.
W. Houston St.
King St.
Charlton St.
Vandam St.
Spring St.
Dominick St.
Broome St.
Varick St.
Washington St.
Watts St.
Desbrosses St.
Vesty St.
TRIBECA
Holland Tunnel
West St.
West Side Hwy.
ABINGDON SQUARE
Eighth Ave.
W. 14th St.
Little W. 12th St.
Gansevoort St.
Horatio St.
Jane St.
W. 12th St.
Bethune St.
Bank St.
W. 11th St.
Perry St.
Charles St.
W. 10th St.
L
L,4,5,6
N,R
F,L,Q
1,2,3,9,L
A,C,E,L
6
4,6
B,D,F,Q
N,R
A,B,C,D,E,F,Q
1,9
C,E
A,C,E
F
F,J,M,Z
J,M
B,D,Q
23
24
25
26
27
28
29
30
31
32
33
34
35
36
37
38
39
40

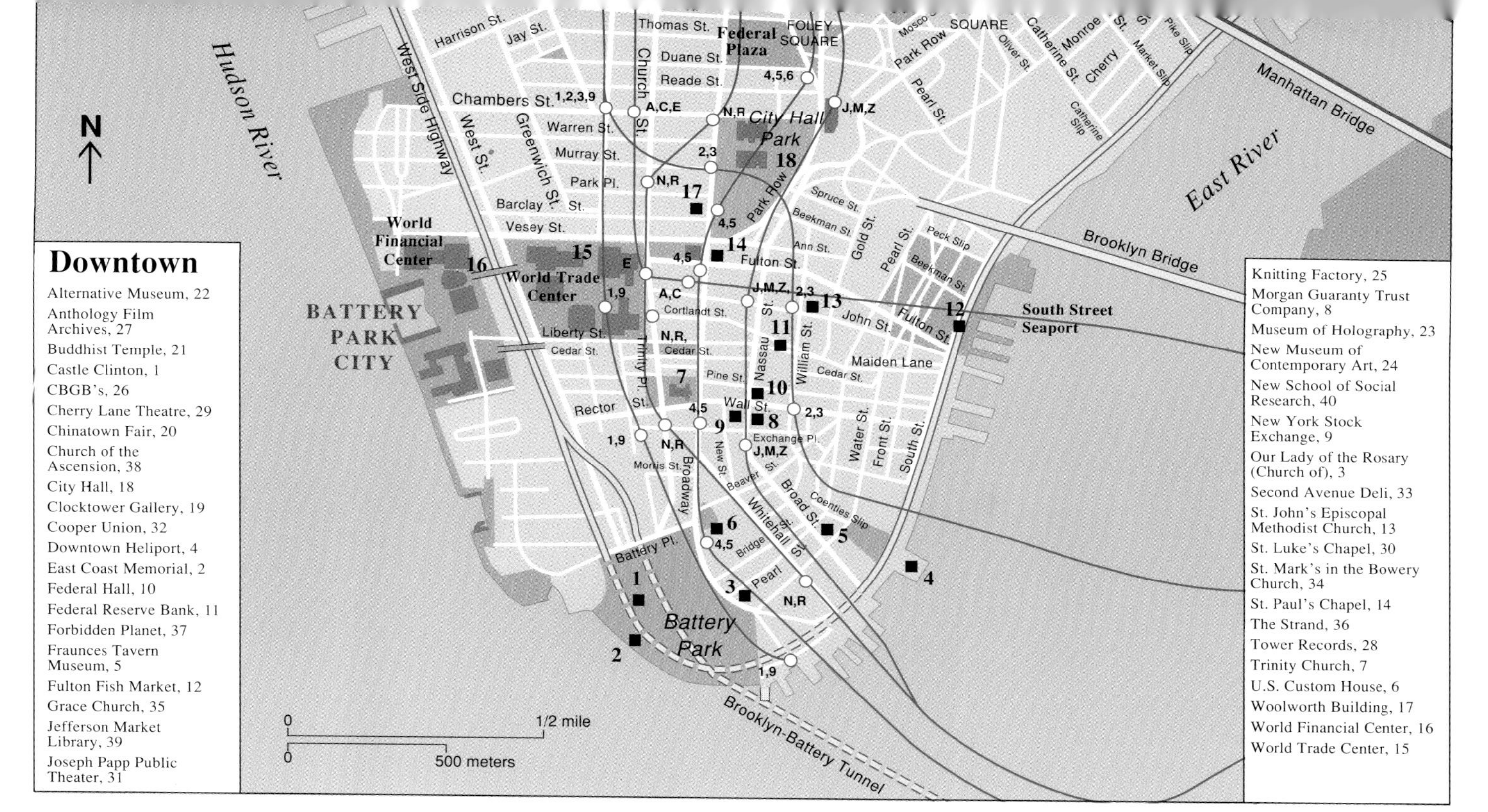

Downtown

Alternative Museum, 22
Anthology Film Archives, 27
Buddhist Temple, 21
Castle Clinton, 1
CBGB's, 26
Cherry Lane Theatre, 29
Chinatown Fair, 20
Church of the Ascension, 38
City Hall, 18
Clocktower Gallery, 19
Cooper Union, 32
Downtown Heliport, 4
East Coast Memorial, 2
Federal Hall, 10
Federal Reserve Bank, 11
Forbidden Planet, 37
Fraunces Tavern Museum, 5
Fulton Fish Market, 12
Grace Church, 35
Jefferson Market Library, 39
Joseph Papp Public Theater, 31
Knitting Factory, 25
Morgan Guaranty Trust Company, 8
Museum of Holography, 23
New Museum of Contemporary Art, 24
New School of Social Research, 40
New York Stock Exchange, 9
Our Lady of the Rosary (Church of), 3
Second Avenue Deli, 33
St. John's Episcopal Methodist Church, 13
St. Luke's Chapel, 30
St. Mark's in the Bowery Church, 34
St. Paul's Chapel, 14
The Strand, 36
Tower Records, 28
Trinity Church, 7
U.S. Custom House, 6
Woolworth Building, 17
World Financial Center, 16
World Trade Center, 15

Queensboro Bridge
First Ave.
Second Ave.
Thirrd Ave.
Lexington Ave.
Park Ave.
Madison Ave.
Fifth Ave.
Seventh Ave.
Eighth Ave.
Ninth Ave.
Tenth Ave.
Eleventh Ave.
Twelfth Ave.
West Side Highway
Dyer Ave.
Broadway
Central Park S.
W. 60th St.
W. 59th St.
W. 58th St.
W. 57th St.
W. 56th St.
W. 55th St.
W. 54th St.
W. 53rd St.
W. 52nd St.
W. 51st St.
W. 50th St.
W. 49th St.
W. 48th St.
W. 47th St.
W. 46th St.
W. 45th St.
W. 44th St.
W. 43rd St.
W. 42nd St.
W. 41st St.
W. 40th St.
W. 39th St.
W. 38th St.
W. 37th St.
W. 36th St.
W. 35th St.
W. 34th St.
W. 33rd St.
E. 60th St.
E. 59th St.
E. 58th St.
E. 57th St.
E. 56th St.
E. 55th St.
E. 54th St.
E. 53rd St.
E. 52nd St.
E. 51st St.
E. 50th St.
E. 49th St.
E. 48th St.
E. 47th St.
E. 46th St.
E. 45th St.
E. 44th St.
E. 43rd St.
E. 42nd St.
E. 41st St.
E. 40th St.
E. 39th St.
E. 38th St.
E. 37th St.
E. 36th St.
E. 35th St.
E. 34th St.
E. 33rd St.
E. 32nd St.
Visitors Center
New York
Cultural Center
Carnegie Hall
Museum of Modern Art
Citicorp Center
Rockefeller Center
Grand Central Terminal
Bryant Park
Public Library
TURTLE BAY
United Nations Headquarters
Queens-Midtown Tunnel
MURRAY HILL
GARMENT DISTRICT
HELL'S KITCHEN
Javits Convention Center
Lincoln Tunnel
Port Authority Bus Terminal
General Post Office
Madison Square Garden
A,B,C,D,
1,2,3,9
N,R
B,Q
4,5,6
B,D,E
E,F
6
C,E
1,2,3,9
B,D,F,Q
1,2,3,
N,R,9
A,C,E
7
B,D,F,
Q,7
4,5,6,S
1,2,3,9
1
2
3
4
5
6
7
8
9
10
11
12
16
27
28
29
30
31
32
33
34
35
36
37
38
39
40
41
42
43
44
45
46
47
48
49
50
51
52
53
54
55
56
57
58
59
60
61
62
63
64
65

EMPLOYMENT LAW

AUSTRALIA
Law Book Co.
Sydney

CANADA and USA
Carswell
Toronto

HONG KONG
Sweet & Maxwell Asia

NEW ZEALAND
Brookers
Wellington

SINGAPORE and MALAYSIA
Thomson Information (S.E. Asia)
Singapore